TWO THOUSAND NOTABLE AMERICANS

TWO THOUSAND
NOTABLE AMERICANS

First Edition

published by:
the **American Biographical Institute**
main offices
205 West Martin Street, Post Office Box 226
Raleigh, North Carolina 27602 USA
ISBN Prefix: 934544

Library of Congress Catalog Card Number 81-71697

International Standard Book Number 0-934544-23-9

Printed and bound in the United States of America by
BookCrafters, Inc.
Chelsea, Michigan

Table of Contents

Preface	vii
ABI Biographical Titles	viii
Delineative Information	ix
Biographies	1
Appendix I Honorary Editorial Advisory Board The American Biographical Institute	xi
Appendix II Roster of Fellow Members The American Biographical Institute	xxi
Appendix III National Board of Advisors The American Biographical Institute	xxxi
Appendix IV Roster of Life and Annual Members The American Biographical Institute Research Association	xxxix

Preface

TWO THOUSAND NOTABLE AMERICANS, First Edition, is a select edition. Its birth came from an earlier ABI series *NOTABLE AMERICANS* which accumulated three popular editions. Compilation of the new First Edition is confined to a select two thousand of some of the most notable individuals of America.

This series is dedicated to enriching the Institute's current reference collections by providing a channel of biographical documentation for permanence in future historical research. ABI editions are authoritative guides for historians, genealogists, reporters, academicians, students and general researchers. *TWO THOUSAND NOTABLE AMERICANS* enhances this purpose as well as provides selectivity of a limited number.

The biographical facts collected within this edition are current, comprehensive and relevant to today's endeavors of leadership. In keeping with the strict editorial standards maintained for sixteen years, inclusion is based on merit without regard for ethnic, cultural, financial or religious backgrounds. Purchase prerequisites for inclusion or listing fees are totally against Institute policies.

I express thanks to all persons and organizations who assisted in efforts to compile the First Edition of *TWO THOUSAND NOTABLE AMERICANS.* I also offer appreciation to colleagues and advisors throughout America who have contributed unceasing nominations, ideas and opinions for this publication.

J. S. Thomson
Editor in Chief
Chairman, The Governing Board of Editors
The American Biographical Institute

ABI Biographical Titles

The Directory of Distinguished Americans
International Youth in Achievement
The Registry of American Achievement
Community Leaders of America
Notable Americans
Two Thousand Notable Americans
Personalities of America
Personalities of the South
Personalities of the West and Midwest
Five Thousand Personalities of the World
The Book of Honor
International Book of Honor

Delineative Information

Individual biographical entries are arranged according to standard alphabetical practice and information for publication is consistently and uniformly presented in categorical order.

Editors of the Institute make all attempts to edit accurately the information furnished by each biographee. In the rare event of an error by the publisher, the sole responsibility of the publisher will be to correct such in the subsequent edition of the publication.

Editorial evaluation is the ultimate determinant of publication selection. Admission in this series is based on the value of achievement or recognized outreach of endeavor.

All submissions and files at the Institute are maintained in confidence and adequate security.

Due to the variance in quality of submitted photographs, it is possible for some not to reproduce or print well. Thus, their appearance will not measure up to publication standards. In such cases these unsuitable photographs would not be included.

Nomination sources for *ABI* publications are received from personal recommendations of the Institute's National Board of Advisors, National Educational Advisory Board, Governing Board of Editors, Media Research Department and Board of Directors. Recommendations are filed by nationwide universities and colleges; national, state and local professional organizations; service and civic organizations; businesses; and individuals. Mailing lists have never been bought or sold. Neither nominees or nominators are placed under any financial obligation. Nominees are contacted for their personal submissions of biographical materials and it is these credentials that are editorially reviewed by the Governing Board of Editors upon receipt. Inclusion in an *ABI* publication series is based on merit.

THE AMERICAN BIOGRAPHICAL INSTITUTE is a reference publisher documenting biographical facts for research. **ABI** reference sourcebooks are used by and provide authoritative guides for business consultants, researchers, reporters, scholars, biographers, librarians, prospective employers, interviewers, students, historians, genealogists. Career, civic, personal, and other applicable areas are formated for total and individualized coverage. The multiple publication series themselves are regional, national and international in geographical scope. Since establishment in 1967, it has been the aim of the **Institute** to publish factual, permanent profiles of accomplished, active and dedicated individuals who make substantial contributions to international, national, state and regional levels. There is no discrimination as to the level of contribution, but only in the effort and involvement in achieving worthwhile endeavors. **Main Offices of Publisher:** 205 West Martin Street, Post Office Box 226, Raleigh, North Carolina 27602 USA. **Library Distribution Agent:** *BIBLIO* Distribution Centre (Worldwide), 81 Adams Drive, Post Office Box 327, Totowa, New Jersey 07511. **References:** *THE DIRECTORY OF DIRECTORIES*, National Library of Congress, Copyright Office. **ISBN Prefix:** 934544.

THE AMERICAN BIOGRAPHICAL INSTITUTE RESEARCH ASSOCIATION (ABIRA) is a more generalized research division as compared with the professionally-oriented *ABIPRD. ABIRA* was established in 1979 to further extend biographical research and expand the objectives of the *Institute*, provide a framework for individuals of varied backgrounds to join together to share knowledge and interests, and offer incentive for dedication and stimulation. All members of the *ABIRA* are chosen by the Executive Council based on individual merit and they comprise an alliance of more than six hundred members. They are drawn from all regions of the North American Continent and are involved in a search for social, intellectual, and cultural enrichment in general. Backgrounds are varied with wide-ranging educations, outstanding professional careers, and extensive involvement in public affairs on community, state, regional and/or national levels. Benefits include group assemblies, media coverage, biographical research, consultation, advertising, association magazines/publications, awards. Forward all communications to: Chairman, ABIRA, The American Biographical Institute, 205 West Martin Street, Post Office Box 226, Raleigh, North Carolina 27602 USA. Reference: *Gale Encyclopedia of Associations.*

TWO THOUSAND NOTABLE AMERICANS

Aakre, S Maureen

Sociologist, Executive Director, Educator. Personal: Born December 30, 1945; Daughter of Bernard and Marjorie Aakre; Partner-in-Life, Glenn E. Williams. Education: B.S. magna cum laude 1973, M.A. 1978, both from Northern Arizona University. Career: Owner, Aakre Consultants; Director, Human Resources Department, Calista Corporation; Incorporator and Executive Director, Women in Crisis Counseling and Assistance; Coodinator, Adult Learning Center, Fairbanks Native Association; Sociology/Psychology Instructor, Anchorage Community College and Tanana Valley Community College. Organizational Memberships: American Sociological Association; Pacific Sociological Association; Alaska Adult Education Association (secretary 1977-78); Fairbanks Jaycees (director 1978); Business and Professional Women, 1981 to present. Community Activities: Alaska Network on Domestic Violence and Sexual Assault (steering committee, chairman on policies and procedures, past chairman of training); Abused Women's Aid in Crisis (member 1979-80, president of the board 1980, chairman of finance committee 1979, Fairbanks Police Department orals board 1978-79); National Organization of Women (Fairbanks task force coordinator 1977). Religion: Matriarchal and Goddess Centered, Convenor. Honors and Awards: Outstanding Young Woman of the Year, Alaska, 1977; Phi Kappa Phi; Certified Police Instructor, Alaska Police Standards Council, 1978 to present; Listed in *The World Who's Who of Women, Who's Who of Women.* Address: 585 Dowling Road, Anchorage, Alaska 99502.

Abbott, John David

Clergyman, Church Administrator. Personal: Born September 29, 1922; Son of John Wesley and Mary Mabel Boggs Abbott (both deceased); Married Gladys Irene Kirkendall; Father of John David, Kenneth Wayne. Education: Th.B., United Wesleyan College, 1943; D.D. (honorary), Houghton College, 1969. Career: Pastor, The Wesleyan Church, 1943-53; District Superintendent 1953-60, General Secretary of Sunday Schools and Youth 1960-62, General Secretary-Treasurer 1962-66, Pilgrim Holiness Church; General Superintendent, The Wesleyan Church, 1966 to present. Organizational Memberships: Christian Holiness Association (vice president 1968-70 and 1972-74, recording secretary 1970-72, president 1976-78); World Methodist Council (executive committee 1971 to present, first vice president of American section 1977-80, secretary of American section 1980 to present); Wesleyan World Fellowship (vice president 1976 to present). Religion: General Commission on Chaplains and Armed Forces Personnel (executive committee 1977-80); *Sunday School Advance* (editor 1960); *Pilgrim Youth News* (editor 1960-62); Eastern Pilgrim College (board of directors 1956-61); The Wesleyan Church (board of pensions 1960-80). Honors and Awards: Delta Epsilon Chi Honor Society; Alumni Achievement Award, Eastern Pilgrim College, 1968. Address: 1413 Glendale Drive, Marion, Indiana 46952.

Abbott, Mary Ellen

School Principal. Personal: Born January 12, 1932; Daughter of Alvah M. Hoffheiser; Married David Carson Abbott. Education: B.S., Towson State University, 1952; Masters Degree, University of Maryland, 1965; Undertook post-graduate studies at Johns Hopkins University 1966-70 and Loyola College 1971-78. Career: Currently Principal, Chatsworth School; Formerly a Public School Teacher, Regular and Special Education; Assistant Principal, Chatsworth School. Organizational Memberships: National Association of Elementary School Principals; Maryland Elementary School Principals; Teachers Association of Baltimore County; Association for Children with Learning Disabilities; Council for Exceptional Children; Council for Basic Education; Amateur Radio Association. Community Activities: Amateur Radio Organization (supporter); Active in Learning Disabilities Days. Religion: Member Maryland Line Methodist Church. Published Works: Contributed Articles on Teaching Methods to Professional Journals. Address: 1342 Martin Drive, Baltimore, Maryland 21229.

Abel, Theodora Mead

Clinical Psychologist. Personal: Born September 9, 1899; Daughter of Mr. and Mrs. Robert G. Mead (both deceased); Married Theodore Abel; Mother of Peter, Caroline, Zita. Education: B.A., Vassar College, 1921; M.A. 1924, Ph.D. 1925, Columbia University; Diploma in Psychology, University of Paris, 1923. Career: Clinical Psychologist, Individual, Marital and Family Psychotherapy; Formerly Psychology Instructor, Sarah Lawrence College, University of Illinois, Long Island University; Several Research Projects funded by the National Research Council, Laura Spellman Fund, Office of Naval Research, Keith Fund. Organizational Memberships: American Psychological Association (fellow); American Orthopsychiatric Association (former vice president); American Psychopathological Association (past vice president); New York Society of Clinical Psychology (past president); American Board of Professional Psychology (diplomate in clinical psychology); Others. Community Activities: School Board, Palisades, New York (former president, trustee); Workshops at Home and Abroad; Donations to United Way, Various Funds for Animals, Environmental Preservation. Religion: Unitarian. Published Works: Author of One Book; Co-Author of Three Books; 85 Articles in Scientific Journals or Chapters in Books. Honors and Awards: Psychologist of the Year, New York Society of Clinical Psychologists, 1972; Phi Beta Kappa; Sigma Xi; Sigma Delta Epsilon. Address: 4200 Sunningdale N.E., Albuquerque, New Mexico 87110.

Abernathy, Bobby Franklin

Independent Petroleum Exploration. Personal: Born June 25, 1933, in Athens, Texas; Son of George R. and Mary Lou Jernigan Abernathy (both deceased); Married Donna Childers, February 28, 1963; Father of Julie Ann, Scott Franklin. Education: B.S.P.E., University of Texas-Austin, 1955; Post-Graduate Study, University of Western Ontario. Career: Director, Calnev Pipe Line Company; Senior Vice President of Exploration and Product Director, Champlin Petroleum Company, Fort Worth, 1976-81; Vice President, American Quasar Petroleum Company, Fort Worth, 1973-76; Executive Vice President, Director, Quasar Petroleum Ltd., Calgary, Alberta, Canada, 1972-73; Various Engineering Positions, Amoco Production Company, United States and Canada, 1955.

Organizational Memberships: American Petroleum Institute; Independent Petroleum Association of America (vice president, Texas-Central area); New Mexico Oil and Gas Association; International Oil Scouts Association; Texas Mid-Continent Oil and Gas Association; Texas Independent Producers and Royalty Owners Association; West Central Texas Oil and Gas Association; Natural Gas Society of North Texas; International Association of Drilling Contractors. Community Activities: West Texas Chamber of Commerce; Former Republican Precinct Chairman, Tarrant County; Tarrant County Republican Committee; Fort Worth Political Action Committee (founder, first chairman); Shady Oaks Country Club; Fort Worth Petroleum Club. Religion: Methodist. Honors and Awards: Cedrick K. Ferguson Medal, Society of Petroleum Engineers, 1965. Address: 2005 Mount Royal Terrace, Fort Worth, Texas 76107.

Abrams, Rosalie S

Legislator. Personal: Born in Baltimore, Maryland; Daughter of Isaac and Dora Rodbell Silber; Married William Abrams; Mother of Elizabeth Joan. Education: R.N., Sinai Hospital School of Nursing; B.S. suma cum laude 1963, M.A. 1969, The Johns Hopkins University. Military: Served in the United States Navy Nurse Corps, World War II. Career: Senator, State of Maryland, 1970 to present; Senate Majority Leader, 1979 to present; Served on Budget and Taxation Committee, Legislative Policy Committee, Spending Affordability Committee, Environment and Health Subcommittee, Special Joint Committee on Mental Health Laws, Others; Elected to House of Delegates, 1966-70; Nursing Supervisor, Sinai Hospital; Public Health Nursing, Baltimore City; Business Manager, Silber's Bakery, Inc.; Realtor, Baltimore, Maryland, 1980 to present. Organizational Memberships: Democratic Party of Maryland (chairman 1979 to present); Democratic National Stragegy Council, 1981 to present; Humane Practices of Maryland (chairman 1978 to present); National Conference of State Legislatures (state federal committee on human resources). Honors and Awards: Most Distinguished Woman in Government, Maryland Chapter of the National Organization for Women; Award for Legislative Excellence, Maryland Council of Jewish National Fund; Award for Distinguished Service, Baltimore Area Council on Alcoholism; Award for Legislative Excellence, Maryland Nurses Association; Award of Distinction, *Baltimore News-American;* Achievement Award, American Academy of Comprehensive Health Planning; Hilda Katz Blaustein Distinguished Women-in-Community Service Award, American Jewish Committee; Margaret Sanger Award, Planned Parenthood of Maryland; Leader in Lifesaving Award, Safety First Club of Maryland; Honored by the Maryland Public Health Association; Honorary Membership, Pi Chapter, Sigma Theta Tau, National Honor Society of Nursing; Listed in *Who's Who; Who's Who in the East; Who's Who in American Jewry; Who's Who in Politics; Biography of Women in Politics; Who's Who Internationally; Who's Who of American Women; Anglo-American Who's Who; International Yearbook and Statesmen's Who's Who.* Address: 6205 Wirt Avenue, Baltimore, Maryland 21215.

Abramson, Katherine Holman

Retired. Personal: Born in Weimar, Texas; Daughter of Jesse Burette and Addie Alston DeGraffenried Holman; Married Dillon Abramson (deceased), November 23, 1942. Education: B.S. in History and English, State University of Texas-San Marcos; M.S.L.S., Our Lady of the Lake University. Career: Retired Librarian, University and Medical, Los Angeles, California; Previously Librarian, Woodbury College; Medical Librarian, Harriman Jones Hospital; Served as Director of Music and Drama, Public Schools and Hospitals; Former History and Music Teacher, Public Schools. Organizational Memberships: American Association of University Women. Community Activities: Council of Presidents; Federated Clubs; Chamber of Commerce; Five Writer's Clubs; Others. Religion: Presbyterian. Address: 503 W. King's Highway, San Antonio, Texas 78212.

Abse, David Wilfred

Psychiatrist and Psychoanalyst. Personal: Born March 15, 1915; Son of Rudolph and Kate Abse; Married Elizabeth S. Smith; Father of Edward, Nathan. Education: B.Sc. 1935, M.D. 1948, University of Wales; D.P.M., University of London, 1950. Military: Served in the Royal Army Medical Corps, 1942-47, achieving the rank of Major. Career: Psychiatrist and Psychoanalyst, Neurology and Internal Medicine; Clinical Psychologist. Organizational Memberships: Royal College of Psychiatrists (fellow); British Psychological Society (fellow); American Psychiatric Association (fellow); Virginia Psychoanalytic Society (president 1976-78); Neuropsychiatric Society of North Carolina (president 1958-59); University Press of Virginia (president, board of directors, 1970). Published Works: *Speech and Reason; Hysteria and Related Mental Disorders; Clinical Notes on Group Analytic Psychotherapy; Marital and Sexual Counseling in Medical Practice.* Address: 1852 Winston Road, Charlottesville, Virginia 22903.

Abu-Lughod, Janet Louise

Professor of Sociology, Urban Affairs and Public Policy. Personal: Born August 3, 1928; Married Ibrahim Ali Abu-Lughod; Mother of Lila, Mariam, Deena, Jawad. Education: B.A. 1947, M.A. 1950, University of Chicago; Ph.D., University of Massachusetts, 1966. Career: Director of Research, American Society of Planning Officials, 1950-52; Sociologist Consultant, American Council to Improve Our Neighborhoods, 1953-58; Assistant Professor of Sociology, American University in Cairo, 1958-60; Associate Professor of Sociology, Northwestern University, 1967-71; Professor of Sociology, Urban Affairs and Public Policy, Northwestern University, 1971 to present. Organizational Memberships: American Sociological Association (committee on world sociology, 1976 to present); International Sociological Association; Social Science History Association (board member, 1972-74); International Network of Network Analysis. Community Activities: Chicago Council on Foreign Relations (board member, 1974-76). Honors and Awards: Phi Beta Kappa, University of Chicago, 1949; Associate Scholar, Radcliffe Institute for Independent Study (now Bunting Institute), 1963-64; Ford Faculty Fellow, 1971-72; Fellow, National Endowment for the Humanities, 1977-78; Guggenheim Fellow, 1976-77. Address: Department of Sociology, Northwestern University, Evanston, Illinois 60201.

Abu-Yousef, Monzer M

Assistant Professor of Radiology. Personal: Born February 5, 1946; Son of Mohammad Musa Abu-Yousef; Married Farida El-Ezaby; Father of Ramy, Dina. Education: M.B., Ch.B., Cairo University Medical School, 1970; Certified, American Board of Radiology, 1976. Career: Intern, Cairo University Hospital, 1970-71; Assistant Surgeon, Mahassed Hospital, Jerusalem, 1971-72; Radiology Resident 1972-76, Associate 1976-80, Assistant Professor 1980 to present, Department of Radiology, Iowa University Hospital. Organizational Memberships: American College of Radiology; Radiological Society of North America; Iowa Radiological Society; Johnson County Medical Society; Iowa Medical Society; American Medical Association: American Institute of Ultrasound in Medicine; American Roentgen Ray Society. Honors and Awards: M.B., Ch.B. Degree with Honors; Certificate of Merit, "Case of the Season" Winner, Seminars in Roentgenology; Honorable Mention, Radiological Society of North America; Certificate of Appreciation, American Roentgen Ray Society. Address: 386 Koser Avenue, Iowa City, Iowa 52240.

TWO THOUSAND NOTABLE AMERICANS

Ackerman, Helen Ruth Penner

Independent Practitioner, Psychological Consultant. Personal: Born March 5, 1939, in New York City, New York; Married Ross S. Ackerman, Mother of Eric, Ruth. Education: B.A., Hofstra University, 1960; M.A., George Washington University, 1962; Ed.D., University of Maryland, 1967. Career: High School Instructor, Army Education Center, Bad Kissingen, Germany, 1961-63; Lecturer in Psychology, University of Maryland European Campus, Schweinfurt and Bad Kissingen, Germany, 1962-63; Psychologist, Crownsville State Hospital, Maryland, 1963-65; Research Psychologist, Johns Hopkins University, 1965; Assistant Professor of Psychology, Anne Arundel Community College, 1968; School Psychologist, Baltimore County Board of Education, 1966-68, and The Mills School, Fort Lauderdale, Florida, 1968-69; Consultant, Hospital Management and Planning Associates, Miami, Florida, 1968-75; Independent Practitioner, Fort Lauderdale, 1975 to present; Maryland Psychological Consultant, 1979-80; Psychological Consultant, Broward County School System, 1980-81. Organizational Memberships: American Psychological Association; Florida Association of School Psychologists; Southeastern Psychological Association; Canadian Psychological Association; Maryland Psychological Association; New Hampshire Psychological Association. Community Activities: Anne Arundel County Police Community Relations Council (planning director, 1967-68); Plantation American Association of University Women (first vice president, 1974-75); Florida Mental Health Association (legislative representative, 1981); Red Cross Volunteer, Bad Kissingen, Germany and Annapolis, Maryland, 1961-66; Plantation Golf Estates Civic Association (chairperson, 1968-69); Psi Chi, George Washington University; Plantation Chamber of Commerce; Plantation Education Committee, 1978-79, 1980-81; Voices of Interested Parents; Peters Elementary School Parent-Teacher Association (corresponding secretary, volunteer chairperson); West Broward Symphony Guild (by-laws chairperson, 1978-79); Mental Health Association of Broward County (board of directors, 1978-80); Broward County Psychological Association (ethics committee, second vice president, 1978-79); Gables Academy (advisory board member, 1979-81). Religion: Plantation Jewish Congregation; Founder's Group First Vice President, Editor of Bulletin *Life* 1974-1976-1977, Non-Salaried Pre-School Director 1975-77. Published Works: Number of Articles including "Taking the Guesswork out of Studying for Undergraduate Psychology Courses", *Directory of Teaching Innovations in Psychology;* "Children of All Ages Need TV Supervision", *Today's Child;* "Kids and TV Sometimes Don't Mix", *Miami Herald;* Author *American-Jewish Holiday Fun for the Public School.* Honors and Awards: University of Maryland Fellowship, 1964-65; Second Place Winner, Florida Osteopathic Medical Association Logo Contest, 1976; Listed in *Who's Who of American Women, The World Who's Who of Women, Personalities of the South, Who's Who Among Students in American Universities and Colleges.* Address: 5921 Almond Terrace, Plantation, Florida 33317.

Adams, Louis William

Minister, Pastoral Care Center Director. Personal: Born December 29, 1929; Married Dolores Ann Reid; Father of Wendy Kaye. Education: B.A., Texas Christian University, 1954; M.Div., Austin Presbyterian Theological Seminary, 1966; Th.M. 1973, D.Min. 1975, Texas Christian University. Military: Served in the United States Air Force as Staff Sergeant 1947-51, and as Captain 1955-63; Served in the Texas Army National Guard, 1979-80, and the Texas Air National Guard, 1980 to present. Career: Chaplain and Associate Executive Secretary, Synod of Texas, Presbyterian Church in the United States, 1966-73; Supply Pastor, First Presbyterian Church, Cumby, Texas, 1974-75; Supply Pastor, Union Hill Community Presbyterian Church, Joshua, Texas, 1977-79; Counselor, Northeast Pastoral Care and Counseling Center, 1974-79; Director, Azle Pastoral Counseling Center, Azle, Texas, 1976-79; Director, Pastoral Care and Training Center, Texas Christian University, Fort Worth, Texas. Organizational Memberships: American Protestant Correctional Chaplains Association (board of directors, 1969-72; college of fellows, 1974 to present); American Association of Pastoral Counselors (diplomate; regional memberships committee, 1978 to present); American Association of Marriage and Family Therapists (clinical member); Texas Corrections Association (board of directors, 1971 and 1972); American Correctional Association. Community Activities: Civil Air Patrol (chaplain, 6th group, 1973 to present); Texas Christian University-Fort Worth Week Committee, 1980-81. Religion: Ordained, June 26, 1966, Presbyterian Church of the United States; Minister in Good Standing, P.C.U.S. and U.P.C.U.S.A.; Member, Grace Union Presbytery; Chairman, Synod of Texas Task Force on Hunger and Poverty, 1970-72. Honors and Awards: Graduated Summa Cum Laude, 1954; Pi Sigma Alpha; Alpha Chi, 1953-54; Theta Phi. Address: 910 Largo, DCBE, Granbury, Texas 76048.

Adams, Marianne Kathryn

Consultant in Administrative Management. Personal: Born January 10, 1924; Daughter of Harold J. and Marion Adams. Education: B.A. 1945, M.A. 1946, New York State College for Teachers (now State University of New York-Albany). Military: Volunteer, Air Defense Command. Career: Consultant in Administrative Management; Former Public Administrator, Management Analyst, Program Coordinator, Personnel Administrator. Organizational Memberships: International Personnel Management Association (director, capital district chapter); American Society for Public Administration (director, capital district chapter, 1972-74); New York State Academy of Health Administration (vice president, 1975-77; task force member, 1974-80); American Academy of Health Administration; American Public Health Association; New York State Public Health Association (secretary of health administration section); Business and Professional Women of Albany, 1965-81; National Association of Female Executives; Cornell Club of New York (associate member, 1977-80); American Association of University Women (member 1980 to present, treasurer 1981 to present, Rancho Bernardo Branch). Community Activities: Bundles for Britain (volunteer, 1944); Air Defense Command Filter Center, 1943-45, 1953-54; United Way Budget Panel, 1960-62; Mohawk-Hudson Council of Girl Scouts (secretary, employed personnel committee, 1961-62); Employees Federated Fund, New York State Department of Civil Service (treasurer, 1961; chairman, 1962); State University of New York-Albany Alumni Association (board of directors, 1974-77); Alumni House Fundraiser, 1973; Albany Symphony Orchestra Vanguard (member/campaign worker, 1968-80); Saratoga Performing Arts Center (member/campaign worker, 1970-80); United Way; New York State Department of Social Services (vice chairman, 1964); New York State Department of Health (vice chairman, 1975, 1976); San Diego Symphony Orchestra Association (member/campaign worker, 1981 to present); Recreation Council of Rancho Bernardo, 1981 to present; Rancho Bernardo Center for Continuing Education, 1981 to present; Salk Institute (contributor, 1975 to present); San Diego Zoological Society, 1980 to present. Religion: Trinity United Methodist Church, Albany, Member, Secretary of the Administrative Board, 1973-75; Rancho Bernardo Community Church, 1981 to present. Honors and Awards: New York State Merit Suggestion Award, 1962; 25 Year and 30 Year New York State Service Awards; Letter of Commendation, Secretary of the Department of Health, Education and Welfare, 1976; Certificate of Outstanding Contribution, State University of New York-Albany Alumni Association Board of Directors, 1978; Citation from the Governor of New York, 1980. Address: 12417 Lomica Drive, San Diego, California 92128.

Adams, William Richard

Research and Instruction in Zoo Archeology. Personal: Born February 21, 1923; Son of William B. and Mildred Adams; Married Connie Christie; Father of W. H., James E., Margaret E., Richard B., Scott C., Teresa M. Education: A.B. 1944, M.A. 1949, Indiana

University. Career: Research and Teaching in Zoo Archeology; Former Bank President, Zoo Archeologist. Organizational Memberships: American Bankers Association; Indiana Bankers Association; National Association of Bank Auditors and Controllers; National Association of Bank Women; American Anthropological Association; Society of American Archeology; S.O.P.A.; Indiana Association of Science; Indiana Historical Society. Community Activities: Monroe County Auxiliary Police; Monroe County Merit Board. Religion: First Methodist Church of Bloomington, Board of Trustees. Honors and Awards: Indiana Gearworks Arctic Expedition, 1957; Monroe County Auxiliary Police Award, 1979. Address: 215 W. Chester Drive, Ellettsville, Indiana 47429.

Addington, William Hubert

Rancher, Businessman and Politician. Personal: Born March 8, 1924, in Elkhart, Kansas, U.S.A. Education: A.B., University of Kansas, 1948. Military: Served with U.S.A.A.F., 1943-48. Career: Former Granary Executive, operating grain elevators in Kansas, Texas and New Mexico; Operated ranches in Texas, Wyoming, New Mexico and Nevada; Owned and operated one of the largest ranches in the United States, the Nevada Ranch, with 387,000 acres; Director of East Side National Bank of Wichita, Kansas, 1960-63; President of Haskell County Grain Company, Inc., 1956-61. Community Activities: For many years has been involved in a campaign to clean up government by exposing dishonest and corrupt politicians and government employees; Has filed 35 Impeachment Memorials with the U.S. House of Representatives, including charges against 2 former presidents, 1 attorney-general, 3 U.S. senators, 1 member of the House, 10 I.R.S. officials, 4 F.B.I. agents (including the director), and 2 U.S. district attorneys; Republican Candidate for Governor of Kansas, 1960; Member of Kansas House of Representatives, 1958-61; State Highway Commissioner of Kansas, 1955-57. Honors and Awards: Listed in *Men of Achievement, Book of Honor, International Who's Who of Intellectuals, Who's Who in Finance and Industry, Community Leaders and Noteworthy Americans, Notable Americans, Personalities of the South, Personalities of America, International Who's Who in Community Service, Dictionary of International Biography, Men and Women of Distinction, American Registry Series, The Directory of Distinguished Americans.* Address: 3418 Henry Drive, Fort Worth, Texas 76118.

Adix, Shauna McLatchy

Center Director, Assistant Professor. Personal: Born June 13, 1932; Daughter of Charlotte McLatchy; Married Vern Adix; Mother of David Matthew, Alison. Education: B.A., University of Utah, 1953; M.A., Ohio University, 1958; Ph.D., University of Utah, 1976. Career: Director, Women's Resource Center, and Assistant Professor, Graduate School of Social Work, University of Utah; Director, HERS/West; Former Executive Vice President, et al inc.; Counselor, Division of Continuing Education, University of Utah; Director, Girl's Camp; Coordinator, Project on Aging. Organizational Memberships: National Association for Women Deans, Administrators and Counselors; National Women's Studies Association; American Association of Higher Education; Council on Social Work Education. Community Activities: Community Crisis Center (board of directors); Ririe-Woodbury Dance Company (board of directors); Mortar Board, Inc. (national president, 1970-73); University of Utah Alumni Association (vice president, 1967-69); Consortium for Utah Women in Higher Education (executive director, 1973-76). Honors and Awards: Susa Young Gates Award for Service to Women of Utah. Address: 1532 Michigan Avenue, Salt Lake City, Utah 84105.

Adler, David Leo

Pathologist, Laboratory Director. Personal: Born September 5, 1913; Father of David, Philip, Douglas. Education: A.B. 1934, M.D. 1938, Indiana University. Military: Served as a Major in the Medical Corps, 1941-46. Career: Laboratory Director, Bartholomew County Hospital, Johnson County Hospital. Organizational Memberships: Indiana Association of Pathologists (president); Indiana State Board of Health (president); Bartholomew County Medical Society (president). Community Activities: American Red Cross (director, 1955-70); Indiana Hospital Licensing Council, 1954-58. Honors and Awards: Governor's Citation for Meritorious Service, 1958; Citation for Service, American Red Cross, 1970. Address: 4224 N. Riverside Drive, Columbus, Indiana 47201.

Adler, Freda

Professor of Criminal Justice. Personal: Born November 21, 1934. Education: B.A. 1956, M.A. 1968, Ph.D. 1971, University of Pennsylvania. Career: Teaching Fellow, University of Pennsylvania, 1967-68; Research Assistant 1968-69, Instructor in Psychiatry, Research Coordinator, Addiction Science Center, Temple University, 1971-72; Research Director, Section on Drug and Alcohol Abuse, Assistant Professor of Psychiatry, Medical College of Pennsylvania, 1972-74; Associate Professor of Criminal Justice 1974-79, Professor of Criminal Justice 1979 to present, Rutgers University. Organizational Memberships: American Society of Criminology; American Sociological Association; International Association of Penal Law. Honors and Awards: Herbert Block Award, American Society of Criminology, 1972; Beccaria Medal in Gold, German Criminological Society, 1979; Chi Omega Award, University of Pennsylvania, 1956. Address: 30 Waterside Plaza, Apt. 37J, New York, New York 10010.

Adler, Joyce Sparer

Author, Literary Critic. Personal: Born December 2, 1915; Mother of Laura Lambie. Education: M.A., Brooklyn College of the City University of New York, 1951. Career: Author, Literary Critic; Former University Teacher of English. Organizational Memberships: Vermont Academy of Arts and Sciences (secretary, 1981 to present); Modern Language Association of America, 1963 to present; Commonwealth Literature Association, 1968 to present. Community Activities: Vermont Council on the Arts; Bennington Museum; Putnam Memorial Hospital; Referee for Articles for Publications of the Modern Language Association of America. Published Works: *War in Melville's Imagination, Language and Man, Attitudes Toward Race in Guyanese Literature*; ; Articles in *P.M.L.A.*, *Journal of Commonwealth Literature*, Others. Honors and Awards: Second Place National Award, *English Journal*, 1953. Address: R.D. 2, North Bennington, Vermont 05257.

Adler, Lee

Artist, Author, Professor of Marketing, Marketing Executive. Personal: Born May 22, 1926, in New York City; Son of Isidore and Anne Blasser Adler; Married Florence Blumenkrantz, December 28, 1948; Father of Derek Jonathan Tristan. Education: B.A., Syracuse University, 1948; M.B.A., New York University, 1960. Career: Research Account Executive, Amos Parrish & Company, New York City, 1954-56; with Interpublic, Inc., 1958-68; Client Service Director, Marplan, 1958-63; Marketing Development, McCann-Erickson, Inc., New York City, 1963-64; Vice President, Research and Planning, Pritchard, Wood, Inc., New York City,

1964-65; Vice President, Marketing Services, McCann-I.T.S.M., Inc., New York City, 1966-67; Director of Research, Market Planning Corporation, New York City, 1967-68; President, Flouton, Adler & Associates, New York City, 1969-70; Director, Marketing Research, R.C.A. Corporation, New York City, 1970-74; Professor of Marketing, Fairleigh Dickinson University, 1974 to present; Guest Lecturer, Columbia University, Emory University, New York University, University of Connecticut, St. John's University; One-Man Shows, including Ruth White Gallery (New York City) 1968, Salpeter Gallery (New York City) 1967, New York City Community College 1967, New York University 1972, New Bertha Schaefer Gallery (New York City) 1973-75, Hagley Museum (Wilmington, Delaware) 1974, Mickelson Gallery (Washington) 1975, Norton Gallery (St. Louis) 1974, Fairleigh Dickinson University 1975, John Leech Gallery (Auckland, New Zealand) 1975, Poster Place (Dallas) 1975, Canterbury Society of Arts (Christ Church, New Zealand) 1975, Numerous others in the United States and Abroad; Represented in many Permanent Collections, including Whitney Museum of American Art, Metropolitan Museum of Art, British Museum, Art Institute of Chicago, Corcoran Gallery (Washington), Fogg Art Museum, Harvard University, Museum of Contemporary Art (Sao Paulo, Brazil), Brooklyn Museum, Finch College Museum, Seattle Art Museum, Others. Organizational Memberships: American Marketing Association (vice president, 1970-71; director, 1968-70; chairman, attitude research committee, 1963-65); American Association of Public Opinion Research; American Sociological Association; New York University Graduate School of Business Administration Alumni Association (director, 1964-67). Community Activities: Brooklyn Heights Association (board of governors, vice president, chairman of the research committee); Marketing Communication Research Center (trustee). Published Works: Author, Editor, *Attitude Research at Sea; Plotting Marketing Strategy; Attitude Research on the Rocks;* Numerous Articles Published; Contributing Author to *Modern Marketing Strategy; Handbook on Modern Marketing,* Others. Honors and Awards: Burndy Corporation Award, 1969; Grumbacher Award, 1968; Winner, Childe Hassam Fund Competition, 1969. Addres: 168 Clinton Street, Brooklyn, New York 11201.

Adomian, George

Professor of Mathematics, Mathematics Center Director. Personal: Son of Haig (deceased) and Rose Adomian; Married Corinne Hodgson; Father of Haig, Deane, Laura, Aram. Education: B.S.E.E., M.S.E.E., University of Michigan; Ph.D., University of California-Los Angeles, 1963. Military: Served in the United States Navy, achieving the rank of Lieutenant s.g. Career: David C. Barrow Professor of Mathematics, Director of Center for Applied Mathematics, University of Georgia; Former Professor of Mathematics and Engineering, Pennsylvania State University; Senior Scientist, Hughes Aircraft Company. Organizational Memberships: American Mathematical Society; American Physical Society; Society of Industrial and Applied Mathematics; Institute of Electrical and Electronics Engineering. Community Activities: Consultant to Government and Industry; Naval Studies Board (committee member); National Academy of Sciences (consultant); National Defense Panels. Honors and Awards: Invited Speaker, Numerous International Conferences; Distinguished Professorship, David C. Barrow Chair of Mathematics. Address: 155 Clyde Road, Athens, Georgia 30605.

Adrounie, V Harry

Environmental Administrator. Personal: Born April 29, 1915; Son of H. A. (deceased) and Dorothy Adrounie; Father of Harry Michael, Vee Patrick. Education: B.S. 1940, B.A. 1959, St. Ambrose College; Command and Staff College Air University, United States Air Force, Maxwell Air Force Base, Alabama, 1956-57; Additional Studies. Military: Served in the United States Army and the United States Air Force 27 Years; Achieved the Rank of Lieutenant Colonel. Career: Environmental Specialist, School of Public Health, University of Hawaii, 1978-80; Director, Division of Environmental Protection, Chester County, Pennsylvania, Department of Health, 1970; Director, Environmental Health, Berrien County, Michigan, 1975; Past Deputy Commander, First Aeromedical Evacuation Group T.A.C.; Technical Director, Large Organization Selling Services to Hospitals and Other Medical Care Facilities Throughout the United States, 1968-70; Deputy Commander, World Wide United States Air Force Medical Unit, 1966-68; Acting Chairman and Visiting Associate Professor, Department of Environmental Health, American University, Beirut, Lebanon, 1963-66; Commander, Detachments 10 and 11, First Aeromedical Transport Group, 1961-63; Enviromental Health Specialist, U.S. Air Force Surgeon General and U.S. Air Force Environmental Health Representative to National Academy of Sciences and U.S. Interdepartment Committee on Nutrition for National Defense, Consultant U.S. Public Health Service Mobilization, 1957-61; Environmental Health Specialist Medical Division and Biological and Chemical Warfare Specialist in Special Weapons Division, Office of the Inspector General Headquarters, U.S. Air Force, 1953-56; Chief of Planning and Reporting Branch, Field Test and Meterology Division, Fort Detrick, Maryland, 1951-52; Preventive Medicine Officer, U.S. Army I Corps, Japan, 1947-50; Commander, 20th Medical Laboratory, Fort Lewis, Washington, 1946-47; Calhoun County Health Department Bacteriologist TB Research, 1946; Base Medical Inspector, Lincoln Air Force Base, Nebraska, 1943-46; Only Air Force Medical Service Corps Officer Qualified as Medical Administrative Staff Officer, Staff Biomedical Science and Biological Environmental Engineer; Consultant, Ministry of Health, Indonesia, 1978-80. Organizational Memberships: American Public Health Association (fellow); Royal Society of Health (fellow); American Association for the Advancement of Science (fellow); National Environmental Health Association (life member, board of directors, president); International Health Society (charter member, board of governors); New York Academy of Science; American Association of University Professors; American Management Association; Association of Military Surgeons of the United States; North Carolina Public Health Association; Institute of Sanitation Management; Chester County Water Resources Authority (chairman, board of directors); Pennsylvania Environmental Health Association (board of directors); Legal and Public Relations Committee, Pennsylvania Health Council and Environmental Health Review and Study Committee of the Regional Comprehensive Health Planning Council (board of directors); Sanitarians Regional Board of Pennsylvania (chairman); National Association of Sanitarians (president, 1961-62); American Academy of Sanitarians (founder, diplomate); Chester County Board of Health (member); Michigan Association of Local Environmental Health Administrators (founder, first president); American Board of Industrial Hygiene (diplomate); Pennsylvania Public Health Association, Section on Environment (chairman); Certified by the American Academy of Sanitarians, American Board of Industrial Hygiene in Comprehensive Practice of Industrial Hygiene; Registered Sanitarian in the States of California, Pennsylvania, Michigan, Nevada, North Carolina, Others; Number of Other Professional Activities and Offices. Community Activities: Chester County Solid Waste Management Plan (coordinator, 1973-75); Barry County, Michigan, Solid Waste Planning Committee (chairman, 1980 to present); Western Michigan University Citizen Center for Science (policy council, 1981 to present); National Rifle Association of America (life member, certified rifle marksmanship instructor); American Museum of Natural History (associate member); National Geographic Society; Elks; American Legion; United States Air Force Association; Number of Other Civic Activities. Honors and Awards: Walter S. Mangold Award, 1963; Alumnus of the Year, Hastings High School, Michigan, 1961; Received Oak Leaf Cluster to Air Force Commendation Medal; Legion of Merit, Only Serviceman Appointed as University Department Chairman, American University, Beirut; United States Air Force Commendation Medal (last 2 positions responsible for world wide operations of United Staes Air Force); Commendation for Responsibilty for Southern Half of Japan, 1947-50; Listed in *American Men of Science, Who's Who in the South and Southwest, Personalities of the West and Midwest, Notable Americans, Community Leaders and Noteworthy Americans, Personalities of America, Who's Who in Health Care, Who's Who in Technology Today, Who's Who in the East, Dictionary of International Biography*. Address: 1905 N. Broadway, Hastings, Michigan 49058.

Aebischer, Delmer W

Music Consultant. Personal: Born December 10, 1933; Son of Harold and Alma Aebischer; Married JoAnn Johnston; Father of Kathy, Linda, Beth. Education: B.S. 1957, M.S. 1959, Ed.D. 1967; Studies undertaken at Seattle Pacific College, University of Oregon, University of California-Berkeley. Career: Music Consultant, Oregon Department of Education, 1969 to present; Former Head of the Music Department, Trevecca Nazarene College; Principal Trombonist, University of Oregon Symphonic Band, Eugene-University Symphony, 440th Army Band; Tenor, Seattle Pacific College A Capella Choir; Trombone Soloist, A Capella Choir. Organizational Memberships: Oregon Alliance for Arts Education (executive secretary). Community Activities: Youth Work. Religion: Choir Director and Minister of Music, Sunday School Teacher, Church Board Member. Published Works: Six Times Yearly, Column in *Oregon Music Educator*; "How to Win Funds and Influence People", *Music Educators Journal*, February 1971; "Oregon Calls the Tune", Oregon Association for Supervision and Curriculum Development; *Music Education Guide*; Number of Professional Pamphlets. Honors and Awards: John Hay Fellow, University of California, 1963-64; Selected to Participate with 57 Other Arts Educators from the United States to Study the Arts and Education Systems in Romania, Fall 1975; Listed in *International Who's Who in Music and Musicians Directory*. Address: 3945 Kendall Avenue, Salem, Oregon 97302.

Affeldt, Harley Paul

Dean of Engineering Technologies. Personal: March 31, 1926; Son of Mrs. H. A. Affeldt; Married Virginia F. Affeldt; Father of James Kent. Education: B.S. 1950, M.Ed. 1958, Virginia Polytechnic Institute and State University; Ed.D., Nova University, 1981. Military: Served in the United States Air Force, 1944-46, achieving the rank of Sergeant. Career: Dean of Engineering Technologies, Forsyth Technical Institute; President, Forsyth Technical Institute, 1971-81; Director, Richmond Technical Center and Director of Vocational and Adult Education, Richmond Public Schools, 1966-71; Director, Student Personnel, Forsyth Technical Institute, 1960-66; Coordinator, Industrial Cooperative Training, Portsmouth, Virginia, Public Schools, 1958-60; Apprentice Instructor, N.A.S., Norfolk, Virginia, 1952-55. Organizational Memberships: American Vocational Association (life member); North Carolina Vocational Association; A.T.E.A.; North Carolina Adult Education Association; American Society of Engineering Education. Community Activities: Goodwill Industries Rehabilitation Center (board of directors, 1972-80; chairman, 1979); Winston-Salem Industries for the Blind (member, 1972-81; chairman, 1979); Winston-Salem Hospice, 1979 to present; Winston-Salem Employment and Training Advisory Council, 1971 to present; Winston-Salem Jobs Committee, 1979-81; Wesley Foundation, Wake Forest University, 1974-77; Phi Delta Kappa, 1980 to present; Straford Rotary, 1979 to present; Shrine; United Way (division chairman, 1978). Religion: Trinity United Methodist Church, Administrative Board and Trustees. Address: 301 Pineridge Drive, Winston-Salem, North Carolina 27104.

Afield, Walter Edward

Psychiatric Institute Director. Personal: Born December 28, 1935; Married Nancy Browning; Father of Waller Edward III, Neva Browning. Education: A.B., University of Pennsylvania, 1956; M.D., Johns Hopkins University, 1960; Intern, Grady Memorial Hospital; Resident and Fellow in Psychiatry, Harvard University, 1961-67. Military: Served in the United States Air Force, 1964-66, achieving the rank of Captain. Career: Professor of Child Psychiatry, Johns Hopkins University, 1967-70; Professor and Chairman, University of South Florida College of Medicine, Department of Psychiatry, 1970-74; Director, Tampa Bay Neuropsychiatric Institute, 1970 to present; Numerous Consultantships throughout the United States. Community Activities: Rotary Club; Harvard Club; Sky Club (New York); Florida Lyric Opera (president). Religion: Catholic. Address: 4619 Bay to Bay Blvd., Tampa, Florida 33609.

Agostino, Nellie Agnes

Educator. Personal: Born November 2, 1927, in Hartford, Connecticut; Daughter of Paul and Lucy (deceased) Agostino. Education: B.A., St. Joseph College, 1949; M.A.Ed. 1952, M.A. Latin Literature 1966, Trinity College. Career: Substitute Teacher, Hartford High Schools, 1949-51; Instructor, Chairman of the Foreign Language Department, East Hartford High School, 1951 to present (also Student-Faculty Basketball Program Chairman, Coordinator of Advanced Placement and Cooperative Programs, Chairman of the Graduating Committee, Member of the Discipline Committee, Chairman of Faculty Social Committee); Chairman, Language Section for the Evaluating Committee, New England Secondary School Team, Dorchester High School. Organizational Memberships: Delta Kappa Gamma (publicity secretary); East Hartford Education Association (secretary); Junior Classical League (state chairman); Connecticut Language Teachers Association (secretary); Classical Association of America; Classical Association of New England; Connecticut, East Hartford, Education Associations;American, Connecticut (vice president), Associations of Italian Teachers; Trinity Alumni Association. Community Activities: Town Language Articulation Committee (chairman); St. Joseph Alumni Association (president, publicity chairman); Latin State Contest (local chairman of arrangements); East Hartford High School Parent-Teacher Association (program chairman, treasurer); Active in the Ann Uccello for Mayor Campaign, First Congressional District Republican Party; Hartford Council of Catholic Women; Italian Historical Society (co-adviser student section La Voce). Religion: Church of St. Timothy, Reader, Member of the Liturgy Committee, Building Fund; C.Y.O. Instructor, St. Mary's East Hartford. Honors and Awards: Listed in *Who's Who of American Women, World Who's Who of Women, Notable Americans, International Who's Who in Community Service, Who's Who in the East, Personalities of America, Dictionary of International Biography, International Who's Who of Intellectuals, American Catholic Who's Who, Men and Women of Distinction, Community Leaders and Noteworthy Americans*. Address: 228 King Philip Drive, West Hartford, Connecticut 06117.

Ahmed, S Basheer

Executive. Personal: Born in 1934; Son of M. Hussain and Aminabi Ahmed; Married Alice Pearce; Father of Ivy. Education: M.A., Osmania University, 1957; M.S. 1963, Ph.D. 1966, Texas A&M University. Career: President, Princeton Economic Research, Inc.; Previously Professor of Economics, Western Kentucky University; Professor of Business Administration, Western Kentucky University; Consultant to Oak Ridge National Laboratory; Assistant Professor of Quantitative Methods, Ohio University; Assistant Professor of Economics, Tennessee Tech University. Organizational Memberships: Systems, Man and Cybernetics Society (president 1980-81); American Association for the Advancement of Science (fellow); American Nuclear Society. Community Activities: Princeton Rotary Club. Honors and Awards: Award of Achievement, Oak Ridge National Laboratory, 1978; Honorary Citizen of Tennessee. Address: 410 Blue Spring Road, Princeton, New Jersey 08540.

Ahner, David Hurley

Osteopathic Physician (Speciality in Psychiatry). Personal: Born April 29, 1943; Son of Hurley Thomas Ahner (deceased), Elizabeth Show Gade; Married Conchita Uy de Leon. Education: B.A., University of Delaware, Newark, Delaware, 1965; D.O., Philadelphia College of Osteopathic Medicine, Philadelphia, Pennsylvania, 1970; Internships, Tri-County Hospital, Springfield, Pennsylvania, 1970-71, and Albert Einstein Medical Center, Philadelphia, Pennsylvania, 1971-72; Residency in Psychiatry, The Institute of the Pennsylvania Hospital, Philadelphia, Pennsylvania, 1972-75. Career: Community Services for Human Growth, Inc., Paoli, Pennsylvania, 1981 to present; Crozer-Chester Medical Center, Upland, Chester, Pennsylvania: By Laws Committee 1981 to present, Chairman of Utilization and Admissions Committee 1979-81, Department of Psychiatry 1975 to present, Medical Director, Comprehensive Alcoholism Program, Community Mental Health Center 1975-81; Fair Acres Farm, Glen Riddle-Lima, Pennsylvania, 1976 to present; The Fairmount Institute, Philadelphia, Pennsylvania, 1980 to present; Metropolitan Hospital, Springfield, Pennsylvania, 1976 to present; Riddle Memorial Hospital, Media, Pennsylvania, 1977 to present; Sacred Heart General Hospital, Chester, Pennsylvania, 1977 to present; Taylor Hospital, Ridley Park, Pennsylvania, 1976 to present. Organizational Memberships: American Psychiatric Association; Pennsylvania Psychiatric Society; Philadelphia Psychiatric Society; American Osteopathic Association; American College of Neuropsychiatrists; Pennsylvania Osteopathic Medical Association; Philadelphia County Osteopathic Medical Society; American College of Utilization Review Physicians; American Medical Society on Alcoholism; National Council on Alcoholism. Honors and Awards: The Chapel of Four Chaplains Legion of Honor, 1979; Listed in *Biographical Roll of Honor, Book of Honor, Community Leaders of America, International Register of Profiles, Outstanding Young Men of America, Personalities of America, Personalities of the East, Who's Who in the East.* Home Address: 1139 Dorset Drive, West Chester, Pennsylvania 19380. Business Address: Media Medical and Professional Building, 280 North Providence Road, Media, Pennsylvania 19063.

David H Ahner

Aitken, Molly Bennett-Marks

Corporation Executive. Personal: Born July 25, 1944; Married Gerard James Aitken III; Mother of Bridget Marks, Sean Marks, Frederick Marks, Jacqueline Marks, Gerard James Aitken IV, Mary Hannah Aitken. Education: Attended Nevada Southern University, New York University. Career: Board of Directors, Marks Polarized Corporation; Vice President, Thora Energy Corporation; President, The World Energy Foundation; Past Contributing Editor, *North Shore Club Life* and Numerous Horseman Publications, including *Horsemen's Yankee Pedlar* and *Chronicle of the Horse;* Interviewer/Moderator, KLAS Television Channel 8, Las Vegas. Community Activities: North Shore Auxiliary United Cerebral Palsy (president, 1973); First Annual Association for the Help of Retarded Children Horse Show (manager, 1973); American Horseshows Association (life member); Screen Actors Guild; Century Horse Show to Benefit the United States Equestrian Team (manager, 1974-77). Religion: Catholic. Honors and Awards: Papal Certificate from the Vatican, 1964; Certificate of Merit, United Cerebral Palsy, 1973; Numerous Awards for Horsemanship. Address: Green Gables Farm, Athol, Massachusetts 01331.

Akers, Charles David

Attorney. Personal: Born January 6, 1948; Son of Mr. and Mrs. J. I. Akers. Education: B.A., Vanderbilt University, 1970; J.D., Vanderbilt Law School, 1973. Military: Served with the United States Army Military Intelligence, Commissioned a Lieutenant in 1970; Currently serving with the Individual Ready Reserve. Career: Attorney. Organizational Memberships: American Bar Association; Tennessee Bar Association. Community Activities: Nashville Area Junior Chamber of Commerce; Descendents of the Fort Nashboro Pioneers; Tennessee Progressive Network; American Civil Liberties Union; Planned Parenthood. Religion: First Unitarian-Universalist Church of Nashville. Honors and Awards: Mensa; Listed in *Outstanding Young Men of America, Who's Who in the South and Southwest, Who's Who in Finance and Industry.* Address: 4502 Harpeth Hills Drive, Nashville, Tennessee 37215.

Alala, Joseph Basil

Lawyer. Personal: Born April 29, 1933; Son of Wahada T. Alala; Married Nell Powers; Father of Sheron J., Tracy Marie, J. B. III. Education: B.S.B.A., University of North Carolina, 1957; J.D. cum laude, University of North Carolina Law School, 1959. Military: Served in the United States Army, Infantry, Military Police, 24th Division. Career: Lawyer, Managing Partner, Garland & Alala, P.A.; Associate, Garland and Eck, Attorneys, 1962; Certified Public Accountant, Arthur Anderson and Company, 1959-62. Organizational Memberships: American Judicature Society; American Bar Association; American Association of Attorney-Certified Public Accountants, Inc.; North Carolina Bar Association (committee on taxation); Gaston County Bar Association; American Institute of Certified Public Accountants; North Carolina Association of Certified Public Accountants; National Association of Accountants. Community Activities: Gastonia Chapter of Rotary International (director); Junior Chamber of Commerce (past president, director); Grand Knights of Malta; Gaston Country Club (past member of the board of directors, president); Salvation Army Boy's Club (board of directors); Chamber of Commerce (past director); Independence National Bank (board of directors); Garrison Community Foundation (board of directors); Young Men's Christian Association (past director, president); Piedmont Council of Boy Scouts of America (executive board); Belmont Abbey College (board of advisors); Greater Gastonia Citizens Commission (board of directors). Religion: St. Michael's Catholic Church, Past Member of the Board of Trustees, Chairman of Finance Committee. Published Works: Author of *Family Tax Planning;* Co-Author of "Professional Corporations" Courses for North Carolina Association of Certified Public Accountants. Honors and Awards: Board of Editors, *North Carolina Law Review;* Continuing Legal Education Award, North Carolina Bar Association; Key Lecturer Award, C.P.E. of North Carolina Association of Certified Public Accountants; Listed in *Who's Who in the South and Southwest, Outstanding Young Men of America, Outstanding Personalities of the South, Dictionary of International Biography, The American Catholic Who's Who, Who's Who in Finance and Industry.* Address: 1216 South Street, Gastonia, North Carolina 28052.

Molly B M Aitken

Aland, Merrel Kent

Hospital Administrator. Personal: Born January 2, 1943; Son of Ernie and Phyllis Zoppi; Married Sharon Chadwick; Father of Terri Lyn, Trevor, Troy, Timothy. Education: B.S., Brigham Young University, 1968; M.P.H., University of California, 1970. Military: Served as a Commissioned Officer, United States Public Health Service, 1970-73. Career: Administrator, Kane County Hospital; Formerly, Director of Personnel and Purchasing, Supervisor of Communication Center and Responsible for Laundry, House Keeping and Respiratory Therapy, American Fork Hopital; Manager of Residential Sales, Lauritzen and Associates; Director, Office of Program Development; Director, Utah Cost Improvement Project. Organizational Memberships: American Hospital Association; Salt Lake Board of Realtors (associate). Community Activities: American Kennel Club; Licensed Life and Health Care Insurance Associate; Granite Community Zoning Committee. Religion: South German Mission, Latter Day Saints Church, 1962-64. Published

Works: Co-Author "Hospitals in Utah Reduce Costs, Improve Use of Facilities". Honors and Awards: Outstanding Work Performance, Utah State Division of Health, 1974; Commendation for Work Performance at Winslow, Arizona Hospital, 1973; Certificate and Cash Award, Assistant Surgeon General, United States Public Health Service, for superior work performance, 1971; Traineeship to attend University of California, 1968-70; Listed in *Outstanding Young Men of America, Who's Who in the West, Who's Who in Health Care.* Address: 376 North Vermillion, Kanab, Utah 84741.

Albert, Janyce Louise

Vice President and Director of Personnel. Personal: Born July 27, 1932, Daughter of Howard and Glenola Blessing (deceased); Widow; Mother of John Richard, James Howard. Education: Attended Ohio Wesleyan University, 1949-51; B.A.B.A., Michigan State University, 1953; M.S., Iowa State University, 1980. Career: Vice President and Director of Personnel, Republic Bancorporation, 1981 to present; Job Evaluation Analyst, Phillips Petroleum Company; Other Former Positions include Personnel Analyst, Engineering Administration Manager, Professional Engineering Recruiter, Training and Education Manager, Training Officer, Personnel Officer, Assistant Personnel Manager, Volunteer Coordinator, Newspaper Correspondent, Perceptual Testing. Organizational Memberships: American Society for Personnel Administration; American Society for Training and Development, 1974-78. Community Activities: 300th Anniversary of Tenafly, New Jersey (publicity chairman, 1968); United Way of Ames, Iowa (board member, 1976-77); Ames Society for the Arts (volunteer, 1975-77); Philbrook Art Center, Tulsa, Oklahoma (volunteer); Mary Greeley Hospital Auxiliary, Ames, Iowa, 1971-74; P.E.O., Ames and Cedar Rapids, Iowa and Bartlesville, Oklahoma; Desk and Derrick, Bartlesville; Women in Energy, Bartlesville. Religion: Presbyterian Church, Board of Deacons; Ames, Iowa, 1974-77. Honors and Awards: President's Scholar, Michigan State University, 1952-53; Outstanding Student Scholarship, 1949-53; Phi Kappa Phi; Listed in *Who's Who in the Midwest, Personalities of the West and Midwest.* Address: 6623 S. 93rd E. Avenue, Tulsa, Oklahoma 74133.

Albert, Lois Eldora Wilson

Archeologist. Personal: Born June 2, 1938, in Alva, Oklahoma; Daughter of Clinton L. and Daisy M. Wilson; Married Abbott H. Albert. Education: B.S., Northwestern State College, 1960; M.S., Oklahoma State University, 1963; Further Study, Oklahoma City University, Central State University; M.A., University of Oklahoma, 1974. Career: Co-Principal Investigator, Red River Survey Project, 1980 to present; Oklahoma Archeological Survey, University of Oklahoma - Archeologist II 1981 to present, Research Assistant 1979-81, Acting Director 1978-79, Research Assistant I 1976-78, Secretary I 1975-76; Co-Principal Investigator, Spiro Mounds Project, Phase I, 1979; Project Director, Prehistoric People of Oklahoma Film Series Planning Project, 1979; Editor, *Studies in Oklahoma's Past,* 1978-79; Clerk-Typist, Oklahoma Highway Department, 1975; Archeological Assistant, Oklahoma River Basin Survey, University of Oklahoma, 1973; Archaeological Assistant to Dr. Robert Bell, Department of Anthropology, University of Oklahoma, 1971; Research Assistant, Department of Microbiology, University of Oklahoma Health Sciences Center, 1966-70, 1974; Research Assistant, Cancer Section, Oklahoma Medical Research Foundation, 1964-66. Organizational Memberships: American Chemical Society; Sigma Xi; American Association of Stratigraphic Palynologists; Society of American Archeology; Oklahoma Anthropological Society; Oklahoma Academy of Science; Arizona Archaeological and Historical Society; Society for Archeological Sciences; American Association for the Advancement of Science. Honors and Awards: Phi Sigma; Listed in *Who's Who in American Colleges and Universities, Outstanding Young Women in America, Who's Who in the South and Southwest.* Address: 1610 N. Peters, Norman, Oklahoma 73069.

Donald A Alberts

Alberts, Donald Allan

Oil Spill Consultant. Personal: Born March 29, 1932 in Cleveland, Ohio; Son of Milton Charles and Ruth Louise Graves Alberts; Married Shirley Ethel Tripp, March 25, 1952; Father of Donald, Beverly Ann, Keith, Dawn. Education: B.A.B.A., Bowling Green University, 1968; L.L.D., LaSalle University, 1971. Military: Served with the United States Coast Guard, 1949-73. Career: Executive Vice President, All Point Associates, Inc., Oil Spill Consultants, 1979 to present; Texaco Inc., Senior Environmental Specialist 1978-79, with the company 1973-79. Organizational Memberships: International Association of Pollution Control; American Standards and Testing Association; American Petroleum Institute. Religion: Roman Catholic. Address: Route 1 Box 3309, Monroeville, Ohio 44847.

Albott, William leRoy

Clinical and Research Psychologist. Personal: Born July 6, 1942; Son of W. L. Albott; Married Carolyn Ramirez; Father of Sophia, Andreana. Education: Associate B.A., Journalism, Garden City Junior College, 1961; B.A., Psychology and Speech Pathology, Fort Hays State University, 1965; M.S., Psychology, Fort Hays State University, 1965; Ph.D., Clinical Psychology, Ohio University, 1971. Career: Clinical Psychologist and Research Psychologist; Formerly a Clinical and Consulting Psychologist; Faculty, Menninger School of Psychiatry; Adjunct Faculty, Washburn University, Wichita State University, Others. Organizational Memberships: American Psychological Association; Kansas Psychological Association (president, 1981-82; board of governors, 1980-81; chairman, continuing education committee, 1979-81); Society for Clinical and Experimental Hypnosis; International Society of Hypnosis; American Association for the Advancement of Science. Community Activities: Central Plains Comprehensive Drug Rehabilitation Center, Inc. (board of directors, 1973-75); Volunteer Work for Community Groups. Religion: Unitarian. Honors and Awards: Sigma Xi, 1973; First Place Honors, National Psi Chi Dissertation Proposal Competition, 1970; Published in Professional Journals; Listed in *Who's Who in the Midwest.* Address: 1607 Boswell, Topeka, Kansas 66604.

Aldan, Daisy

Writer, Lecturer, Publisher, Poet. Personal: Born September 16, 1923; Daughter of Louis Firfer (deceased), Esther Edelheit (deceased). Education: B.A., M.A., Ph.D., Honorary L.L.D. Career: Free-Lance Poet; Workshop Lecturer; Small Press Publisher; Former Actress (began as child actress, age of 10 years, on "Let's Pretend"), Teacher. Organizational Memberships: International P.E.N.; Poetry Society of America (executive board); *New York Quarterly* (advisory board); French University of New York (faculte de lettres); World Congress of Poets; New York State Small Press Association, C.O.S.M.E.P. Published Works: Poems and Essays in Periodicals in United States and Abroad; Poetry Books *The Destruction of Cathedrals, The Masks Are Becoming Faces, Seven: Seven, Breakthrough, Or Learn to Walk on Water, Stones, Verses For The Zodiac, Love Poems of Daisy Aldan, Between High Tides, The Art and Craft of Poetry;* Prose *A Golden Story, "Poetry and Consciousness", Contemporary Poetry And The Evolution of Consciousness;* Translations; Editor of Anthologies, Magazines. Honors and Awards: National Endowment of the Arts Grant to

Publish Novella *A Golden Story*, 1980; The Dewitt American Lyric Poetry Award; First Prize for Poetry, Rochester Festival of the Arts; National Endowment for the Arts Poetry Prize; National Endowment for the Arts Poetry Award; Chosen by W.B.A.I. as International Woman Artist; Hunter College Hall of Fame; Listed in *International Who's Who in Literature, Dictionary of International Biography*, All *Who's Who* Publications. Address: 103-26 68th Road, Forest Hills, New York 11375.

Alderman, Louis Cleveland Jr

College President. Personal: Born August 12, 1924; Married Anne Whipple; Father of Amelia Anne, Louis C. III, Fielding D., Jonathan A. Education: A.A., South Georgia College, 1942; A.B., Emory University, 1946; M.S., University of Georgia, 1949; Ed.D., Auburn University, 1959. Military: Served in the United States Army during World War II, Asiatic-Pacific Theatre. Career: President, Middle Georgia College; Former Instructor in Biology, University of Georgia-Rome Center; Director and Instructor in Biology, University of Georgia-Savannah Center; Director and Assistant Professor of Biology, University of Georgia-Rome Center; Director, University of Georgia-Columbus Center; Director, Henderson College, University of Kentucky. Organizational Memberships: Georgia Association of Junior Colleges (past president); Georgia Education Association; National Education Association; Association of Higher Education; Georgia Association of Colleges; Southern Association of Junior College (vice president, 1981-82). Community Activities: Rotary International (past district governor, district 692; college of governors, district 692; scholarship committee; conference chairman, 1981); Cochran Rotary Club (past president); Rotary Student Loan Fund (board of trustees); Georgia Historical Society; Sons of the American Revolution, Middle Georgia Chapter (organizing president); Order of Kentucky Colonels; Cochran-Bleckley Chamber of Commerce (board of directors); Bleckley County Hospital Authority; Georgia State Society, National Society of the Sons of the American Revolution (board of managers, vice president); President's Academy, A.A.C.J.C. Religion: First Baptist Church, Cochran, Georgia, Board of Deacons (past chairman), Building and Finance Committee, Teacher of Men's Bible Class. Honors and Awards: Graduate Research Assistantship, United States Public Health Service, 1948-49; Good Citizenship Award, Civitan Club, 1955; Special Award, Rotary Club, 1969; Fellowship Fund for the Advancement of Education, Ford Foundation, Auburn University, 1958-59; Kendall Award, National Society Sons of the American Revolution, 1980; Paul Harris Fellow, Rotary International, 1981; Listed in *Community Leaders of America, Creative and Succesful Personalities of the World*. Address: Old Chester Road, Cochran, Georgia 31014.

Minnis A Alderman

Alderman, Minnis Amelia

Educator, Counselor, Psychologist, Executive. Personal: Born October 14, 1928; Daughter of Louis Cleveland and Minnis Amelia Wooten Alderman. Education: A.B., Georgia State College for Women, 1949; M.A., Murray State University, 1960; Undertaking courses toward Ph.D. in Clinical Psychology. Career: Music Teacher, Grades 1-12, Lake County School District, Umatilla, Florida, 1949-50; Band, Orchestra, Chorus Director, Music Instrumental Instructor, Fulton County School District, Campbell High School, Fairburn, Georgia, 1950-54; English, Speech Instructor, Drama Director, Band, Orchestra, Chorus Director, Private Vocal and Instrumental Instructor, Elko County High School District, Wells High School, Wells, Nevada, 1954-59; English, Social Studies Instructor, Christian County School District, Sinking Fork School, Hopkinsville, Kentucky, 1960; Counselor, White Pine School District, White Pine High School, Ely, Nevada, 1960-68; Test Supervisor, Educational Testing Service, American College Testing Program, University of Nevada, 1960-68; Guidance, Counselor-Education, Psychology Instructor, Murray State University, Kentucky, Summers of 1961, 1962, and University of Nevada Extension, 1963-67; Owner, Minisizer, 1969-71; Owner, Knit Knook Shop, 1969 to present; Owner, Mini-Mineo, 1969 to present; Psychologist, Nevada Personnel, Ely Mental Health Center, 1969-75, and Nevada Job Service, 1975-76; Director, Retired Senior Volunteer Program, 1973-74; Originator: White Pine Senior Citizens Nutrition Program, January 1974; White Pine Senior Citizens Center, January 1974; White Pine Rehabilitation Center, June 1972; Creative Crafters, Associates, June 1976; Owner, Gift Gamut, 1977 to present. Organizational Memberships: Delta Kappa Gamma; Alpha Chi State (parliamentarian, 1971-73; president, 1969-71; first vice president, 1967-69; program chairman, 1965-69); Beta Chapter, Alpha Chi (parliamentarian, 1974-78; president, 1968-72; first vice president, 1966-68; second vice president, 1964-66); American Association of University Women (state handbook publisher, 1972-75; Nevada state division area advisor, 1969-73; implementation chairman in education, 1967-69; area representative in education, 1967-69; White Pine branch president, 1965-66; Wells branch president, 1957-58); Counselors on Alcoholism, Addictions and Related Dependencies, 1974; National Federation of Business and Professional Women's Clubs, Nevada Federation (president, 1972-73; president elect, 1971-72; first vice president, 1970-71; second vice president, 1969-70; recording secretary, 1968-70; civic participation chairman, 1967-68; district director, 1968-70; assistant district director, 1967-68), Ely Club (parliamentarian, 1973-78; president, 1966-68, 1974-76; first vice president, 1965-66; second vice president, 1964-65); Marquis Who's Who Board, 1969 to present; Mensa, 1965 to present (test administrator, 1966 to present); The International Platform Association, 1967 to present; White Pine Knife and Fork Club International (president, 1970-71; first vice president, 1969-70; second vice president, 1968-69; secretary-treasurer, 1979 to present); American Personnel and Guidance Association (state membership chairman, 1953-65, 1967-68); National Association of Women Deans and Counselors, 1966 to present; White Pine Community Concert Association (board of directors, 1965 to present; president, 1967-68; second vice president, 1966-67); American Federation of Women's Clubs (state status of women chairman 1974-76; state chairman C.A.R.E., 1972-74; district president, 1970-74; Ely women's club president, 1969-70); National Federation of Independent Business (district chairman, 1971 to present); National Association of Female Executives, 1972 to present; National Organization for Women, 1973 to present; Common Cause, 1974 to present; White Pine Mental Health Association (president of board, 1961-65; 1979 to present; editor, 1975 to present); National Education Association (life member); United Daughters of the Confederacy, 1946 to present; Daughters of the American Revolution, 1967 to present; Creative Crafters, Associates, 1976 to present (board of directors, 1976 to present; chairman of the board, 1976 to present); Home Economics Advisory Board, University of Nevada Extenstion Service, 1977-80. Community Activities: White Pine Chapter American Red Cross (board of directors, 1978 to present); Nevada Association of Highway Safety Leaders (board of directors, 1977 to present); Governor's Commission on Highway Safety, 1979 to present; Methodist Conference Council on Status and Role of Women, 1981 to present. Religion: Member, Ely Methodist Church, 1960 to present; Choir Director, 1960 to present; Council on Ministries: Worship, 1970 to present; Lay Speaker, 1967 to present; Lay Lead to Regional Conference, 1976. Honors and Awards: Woman of the Year, Radio School of the Air Contest, 1940; Woman of the Year, Ely Business and Professional Women's Club, 1964; Listed in *Who's Who of American Women, Who's Who in the West, National Social Directory, Who's Who in the World*; Other Biographical Reference Books. Address: 945 Ave. H, East Ely, Nevada 90315.

Mary H Aldridge

Aldridge, Mary Hennen

Educator. Personal: Born January 11, 1919; Divorced mother of Cecily Joan Ward. Education: B.S., University of Georgia, 1939; M.A., Duke University, 1941; Ph.D., Georgetown University, 1954. Career: Professor 1962 to present and Chairman of Chemistry Department 1979 to present, American University, Washington, D.C.; Associate Professor 1955-62, Assistant Professor of Chemistry 1947-55, University of Maryland at College Park; Chemist, E.I. du Pont de Nemours and Company, Buffalo, New York, 1941-47. Organizational Memberships: American University Senate (member, 1963-72 and 1980-83, executive secretary, 1970-72); A.U.

Faculty Relations Committee (member, 1966-69, chairman, 1969); A.U. Graduate Studies Committee, 1979-80; A.U. Interdisciplinary Committee (chairman, 1980-81); A.U. Committee on Facilities and Service (chairman, 1981-82); Chemical Society of Washington (chairman of organic topical group, 1962-63, board of managers, 1962-77, secretary, 1967-68, councilor, 1967-77, president, 1970); American Chemical Society (chairman, national committee for women's activities, 1962, member joint-board council committee on chemistry and public affairs, 1971-74, board of trustees for insurance affairs, 1977-82, chairman of public affairs symposia at national meeting, 1974); Washington Academy of Sciences (general chairman of science achievement award, 1972-74, chairman of teaching of science panel for scientific achievement awards, 1960-71, secretary, 1974-75, treasurer, 1976-77, president, 1978-79, chairman of physical science achievement awards, 1980, 1981 and 1982); Washington Chromatography Discussion Group (organization chairman of 4-day course in theory and practice of gas, liquid and thin layer chromatography sponsored by Department of Chemistry at American University, 1966-74, president, 1974-75, board of governors, 1966 to present). Honors and Awards: Received Professional Service Award, Alpha Chi Sigma, 1977. Address: 2930 45th Street Northwest, Washington, D.C. 20016.

Aldridge, Victor E Jr

Lawyer. Personal: Born January 31, 1919; Son of Victor E., Sr., and Cleta B. Aldridge; Married Sandra Anderson; Father of Mary Victoria Turner, Victor E. III. Education: A.B. 1941, J.D. with distinction 1943, Indiana University. Military: Served in the United States Army Reserve Judge Advocates Corps, 1942-72, achieving the rank of Lieutenant Colonel (retired). Career: Lawyer. Organizational Memberships: Terre Haute Bar Association (president, 1959-60); Sixth District Bar Association (president, 1955-56); Indiana State Bar Association. Community Activities: Young Men's Christian Association (board of directors; president, 1965-67); United Fund of Terre Haute (board of directors, 1965-67); Indiana University Club of Terre Haute (board of directors; president, 1950-51); Young Democrats Club of Vigo County (treasurer, 1947-50); Shriner; Scottish Rite; Benevelent and Protective Order of Elks; Sigma Alpha Epsilon; Phi Delta Phi. Religion: United Methodist. Honors and Awards: Order of the Coif, Scholastic Legal Honorary Society, 1943; Pi Sigma Alpha, Government Scholastic Honorary Society, 1940; Bronze Star Medal, 1944; Purple Heart Medal, 1944. Address: 2929 Winthrop Road, Terre Haute, Indiana 47802.

Aldunate, Armand Joseph

Real Estate Investor, Financier, Economist, Writer, Poet. Personal: Born October 30, 1930; Son of Guillermo Aldunate (deceased). Education: Bachelor of Arts and Letters, University of Chile, 1949; Master of Public Social Sciences 1956, Doctor in Jurisprudence 1957, Central University, Quito, Ecuador; Lawyer, Supreme Court Republic of Ecuador and Chile, 1957. Career: English Professor, State Technical University, Santiago, Chile, 1954; Assistant Professor of Economics, Criminal Law, Philosophy of Law, History of Law, University of Chile, 1950-56; Internal Revenue Service, Ministry of Finances, Santiago, Chile; Founder, Lawyer's Club; Reformer, Chilean Bar Association, 1958; Head Organizer, Private Law Firm, Specialization in Corporations and International Law; Real Estate Investor; Financier; Economist; Writer; Poet. Organizational Memberships: Chilean Statesmen Law Professors (created InterAmerican Development Bank, helped create Asia, African Development Banks); Creator of Latin American Total Integration Policy (helped create new world economic order); Pioneer of Taxpayers Movement; National Taxpayers Committee for Better Education, Coalition for Fair Taxes and Public Services (organizer, head); National Taxpayers Association Against Rent Control; National Tenants Association Against Rent Control. Community Activities: National Committee for Civil Rights in Education. Religion: Catholic; Private Meeting with Pope Pius XII, 1952; Organizer, California Catholic Literary Artistic Association, 1970. Published Works: Author Famous Latin Essay on Latin American Total Integration. Honors and Awards: Direct Descendant of Bishop Aldunate, Vice President Assembly (junta) Proclaimed Independence from Spain, 1910; Conservative Party Special Medal of Merit, Santiago, Chile, 1955; Special Guest, City of Montreal, Canada, and Presidents of Major Universities and Institutions of the United States and Canada to Diffuse Ideas About Latin American Integration and Common Market, 1967-69; Listed in *Who's Who in America*. Address: P.O. Box 24842, W. Los Angeles, California 90024.

Alexander, Andrew Lamar

Governor of Tennessee. Personal: Born July 3, 1940, Blount County, Tennessee; Son of Andy and Flo Alexander; Married Leslee Kathryn (Honey) Buhler, January 4, 1969; Father of Drew, Leslee, Kathryn, Will. Education: B.A., Vanderbilt University; J.D., New York University, 1965. Career: Accepted to Tennessee State Bar, 1965; Associate, Firm of Fowler, Rountree, Fowler and Robertson, Knoxville, Tennessee, 1965; Former Law Clerk, United States Court of Appeals for the 5th Circuit, New Orleans; Campaign Coordinator, Howard Baker's United States Senate Race, 1966; Legislative Assistant to United States Senator Howard Baker, 1967-69; Executive Assistant to Counselor in Charge of Congressional Relations at the White House, 1969-70; Manager, Gubernatorial Campaign of Winfield Dunn, Tennessee, 1970; Partner, Firm of Dearborn and Ewing, Nashville, 1971-78; Political Commentator, Television Station, Nashville, 1975-77; Special Counsel to Senate Majority Leader Howard Baker, 1977; Governor, State of Tennessee, 1979 to present. Organizational Memberships: Tennessee Citizens for Revenue Sharing (founder, co-chairman, 1971); Tennessee Council on Crime and Delinquency (founder, first chairman, 1973); American Bar Association; Phi Beta Kappa; Appalachian Regional Commission (co-chairman, 1980-81); President's Advisory Committee on Intergovernmental Relations (vice-chairman); President's Task Force on Federalism; National Governor's Association Committee on Executive Management and Fiscal Affairs (chairman). Religion: Presbyterian. Address: Office of the Governor, State Capitol Building, Nashville, Tennessee 37219.

Alexander, Mary E

Environmental Health Scientist. Personal: Born November 16, 1947; Daughter of Theron and Marie Alexander. Education: B.A., 1969; M.P.H., 1975; J.D. Candidate, 1982. Career: Toxicology Research, Medical Research; Research and Consulting in Environmental and Occupational Safety and Health for Industry and Government; President, Alexander Associates. Organizational Memberships: American Industrial Hygiene Association (national member, northern California section, board of directors, 1979-81); Environmental Law Society, University of Santa Clara School of Law (treasurer, 1977-79; vice president). Community Activities: Affirmative Action Committee, Stanford Research Institute, 1975-78. Religion: Presbyterian. Honors and Awards: National Honor Society, 1964; N.I.O.S.H. Scholarship in Industrial Hygiene; Dean's List, Santa Clara University School of Law. Address: 270 Aldrin Dr., Ambler, Pennsylvania 19002.

Allen, Arcola Jeanne

Consultant. Personal: Born May 8, 1939; Daughter of Monroe and Rosie Pickett; Married Robert I. Allen; Mother of Robert Jr.,

Michael, Brian, John, Mark and Jeffrey. Education: Graduate, Thornton Township High School, 1951; A.A., San Jose State University, 1952; R.N., O'Connor School of Nursing, 1955; B.S.N., University of California, 1963; C.R.N.A., Wichita Clinical School of Anesthesia, 1972; Attended Wichita State University, 1976; B.A., Columbia College, 1977; Currently enrolled in Masters of Nursing Administration Program, expected degree date 1982. Career: Director, Wichita Clinical School of Anesthesia; Clinical Institute, Didactic Instructor Anesthesia; Charge Nurse Urology; Charge Nurse Surgery, Night Shift; Staff Surgery Heart Team; Insurance Executive; Anesthesia Educational Consultant; Owner-Chief CPO Jenn Arc EMT. Organizational Memberships: American Association of Nursing Administrators; Kansas Association of Nursing Administrators (membership chairman 1977); American Nurses Association; National Association Female Executives; American Asociation Executive and Professional Women; National Association Life Underwriters; International Platform Association; Toastmistress International (membership chairman, 1981). Community Activities: Les Fleurs, 1968-72 (secretary-treasurer); Progressive Women of Wichita (secretary, 1974-1981); Jack & Jill of America (Wichita chapter, president, 1981, vice-president, 1977); Les Jeune Amies (secretary, 1968); Committee for Exploring the Feasibility of Implementing an Academic Program in Anesthesia for Nurses, 1979; Wichita State University Committee for Establishing and Implementing a Graduate Program in Anesthesia, 1981; St. Francis Hospital, In-Service Education for Registered Nurses, 1977-79; Honors and Awards: Listed in *Who's Who of American Women* 12th edition, *Who's Who in the World of Women*, 6th edition; Nominated for *Community Leaders of America*, 1982, *Personalities of the West & Midwest*, 1982, *The Book of Honor*, 1982, *International Registry of Profiles*, 1982. Address: 305 Wind Rows Lake Drive, Goddard, Kansas 67052.

Allen, Belle

Executive. Personal: Born August 1; Daughter of Isaac and Clara Allen (both deceased). Education: Attended the University of Chicago. Career: Chairman of the Board and President, William Karp Consulting Company, Inc.; President, Belle Allen Communications; Vice President and Treasurer, Cultural Arts Surveys, Inc., Chicago; 3-Panel Member, Governor's Grievance Panel for the State of Illinois Employees, 1979 to present; Federal Reserve System Nominee to the Consumer Advisory Council of the Board of Governors, 1979; Illinois Coalition on the Employment of Women, Member of the Advisory Governing Board, 1980 to present; Illinois Commission on Technological Progress, Special Assistant 1965-67; Special Program Consultant, The City Club of Chicago Civic Assembly, 1962-65. Organizational Memberships: Chicago Area Association for Affirmative Action Compliance (member 1980 to present, board of directors 1981 to present); Society of Personnel Administrators, 1979 to present; Women's Equity Action League, 1975 to present; Chicago Press Club (member 1967 to present, chairperson women's activities 1969-71); Publicity Club of Chicago (member 1958 to present, chairperson inter-city relations committee 1960-61, employment committee; program committee, admissions committee, education committee, membership committee, entertainment committee); The Fashion Group (member 1969 to present, chairperson "A Retrospective View of a Historical Decade, 1960-70" 1970, regional council 1981 to present, editor *Bulletin* 1981 to present); Industrial Relations Research Associates (member 1958-62 and 1981 to present, director personnel placement 1960-61); National Association of Inter-Group Relations Officials (member 1958-62, national conference program committee 1959); Welfare Public Relations Forum, 1958-62. Community Activities: Illinois State Chamber of Commerce, 1961-74 (community relations committee, alternate for the labor relations committee); Chicago Association of Commerce and Industry, 1961-63 (merit employment committee, public relations committee); Field Museum of Natural History, 1966-74; Chicago Historical Society, 1962-64; Regional Ballet Ensemble of Chicago, 1961-62 (board of directors, executive committee, chairperson public affairs committee); Society for the Chicago Strings, Chicago Symphony Orchestra Members, 1963-64 (board of directors); United Cerebral Palsy Association of Chicago, Women's Division, 1954-58 (founding member, board of directors); Adlai E. Stevenson Campaign Staff, 1952, 1956; John F. Kennedy Campaign Staff, 1960; Press Conference Staff for Eleanor Roosevelt, 1960; Democratic Federation of Illinois (president 1958-61); Independent Democratic Coalition, 1968-69; Citizens for Political Change (founding member and board of directors 1969); City Council Aldermanic election, 42nd Ward, Campaign Manager, 1969. Published Works: Editor and Contributor to more than 65 articles and papers in professional and business publications and journals, speeches, hearing materials, commission reports, manuals, and a book (*Operations Research on the Management of Mental Health Systems*). Honors and Awards: Reference Source, American Bicentennial Research Institute Library of Human Resources, 1973; Special Communications Program, The White House, 1961; Distinguished Service Award, Publicity Club of Chicago, 1968; Citation for Outstanding Service, United Cerebral Palsy Association of Chicago, 1954; Listed in *Who's Who of American Women, The World Who's Who of Women, Who's Who in the Midwest, Who's Who in Finance and Industry; Foremost Women in Communication, Two Thousand Women of Achievement, International Who's Who in Community Service, Who's Who in Public Relations, Directory of International Biography, Women's Organizations and Leaders, Directory of Public Affairs, Notable Americans, Personalities of America, Personalities of the West and Midwest, Community Leaders and Noteworthy Americans, Men and Women of Distinction, Contemporary Personages, Contemporary Personalities.* Address: 900 North Michigan Avenue, Chicago, Illinois 60611.

Allen, Benjamin H

Center Director. Personal: Born April 7, 1931; Son of Nancy J. Hagy; Married Martha Payne; Father of Martha Jean and Mary Joan, John Charles. Education: B.A., Wofford College, 1956; M.A. 1957, Ph.D. 1962, Peabody College. Military: Served in the United States Navy, Submarine Service, 1949-53. Career: Director, Southwestern Virginia Training Center, Hillsville, Virginia, 1974 to present; Director, Programs and Services, Sunland Regional Center, Fort Myers, Florida, 1970-74; Program Consultant/Project Director, Manpower Utilization Project, 1970; Director, Division of Mental Retardation, Alabama Department of Mental Health, 1969-70; Associate Professor, Department of Special Education, University of Georgia, 1968-69; Assistant/Associate Professor, Department of Special Education, Florida State University, 1965-68; Associate Professor of Psychology, East Carolina College, 1963-65; Psychological Consultant, Board of Health, Wilmington, North Carolina, 1961-63; School Psychologist, Nashville, Tennessee, 1959-61. Organizational Memberships: American Association of Mental Deficiency (past president, state chapter; chairperson, region IX); American Psychological Association; Association for Retarded Citizens; Health Systems Agency; National Association of Superintendents of Public Residential Facilities for the Mentally Retarded (board of directors); Council for Exceptional Children. Community Activities: Lion's Club (president, 1980); Mental Health Technology Committee of Wytheville Community College; Tice Elementary School Parent-Teacher Association, Fort Myers, Florida (president, 1973). Religion: Presbyterian Church, Elder. Honors and Awards: National Institute of Mental Health Grant, 1956-58; Health, Education and Welfare S.W.E.A.T. Program, 1966-69; Phi Beta Kappa, Wofford College, 1956; A.B. magna cum laude, 1956; Pi Gamma Mu Social Science Recognition, 1956. Address: P.O. Box 9, Hillsville, Virginia 24343.

Allen, Frank Carroll

Banker. Personal: Born November 10, 1913, Hazlehurst, Mississippi; Son of Walter Scott and May Ellis Allen; Married Clara Marnee Alford, June 23, 1937; Father of Marnee Louise, Susan Carroll, Elizabeth Jane. Education: A.A. with high honors, Copiah-Lincoln Junior College, 1933; Attended American Institute of Banking, 1935, 1936, 1937, 1947, 1949. Military: Served in the United States Army, 1942-46, achieving the rank of First Lieutenant. Career: Georgetown Bank, Mississippi, Bookkeeper, Teller 1933-34, Cashier,

Director 1937-41; Bookkeeper, Deposit Guaranty Bank and Trust Company, Jackson, Mississippi, 1934-37; Bank Examiner, Mississippi, 1942-46; Cashier, Director, Brookhaven Bank and Trust Company, Mississippi, 1947-49; President, Director, Lawrence County Bank, Monticello, Mississippi, 1949-65; President, Monticello Bank, Branch Deposit Guaranty National Bank, 1966-78; Chairman, Advisory Board, Monticello/Newhebron Bank Branches, 1966 to present; Advisory Board, Deposit Guaranty National Bank, Jackson, 1966 to present; Commissioner of Banking and Consumer Finance, State of Mississippi, February-July 1980. Organizational Memberships: American Bankers Association (chairman, Mississippi district 7 on United States savings bonds, 1952 to present); Mississippi Bankers Association (chairman, bank management committee, 1948-49; group vice president, 1948-49); Insurance and Realty Underwriters (chairman of the board, 1971-75; director, 1961-76); Mississippi Economic Council (board of directors, 1950-53); Monticello Planning Board (commissioner, 1964-74); Southwest Mississippi Development Association (board of directors, 1960-72). Community Activities: Monticello Manufacturing Company (chairman, scholarship board, 1960-72); Andrew Jackson Council, Boy Scouts of America (executive board, 1975 to present); Monticello Chamber of Commerce (president, 1951-53, 1960-61; director, 1951-81); Newcomen Society of North America; Lion's Club (president, 1954-55). Address: P.O. Box 297, Monticello, Mississippi 39654.

Allen, Gary Irving

Coordinator. Personal: Born April 7, 1942; Son of Ralph W. Allen; Married Elaine Irene Allen; Father of Michelle Irene, Elisa Joy, Scott Jeremy. Education: B.S., Electrical Engineering, Cornell University, 1965; Ph.D., Physiology, State University of New York at Buffalo, 1969. Career: Neurophysiologist; Assistant Professor (1971-76), Director (1975-76), Laboratory of Neurobiology, Department of Physiology, School of Medicine, State University of New York at Buffalo; Lecturer/Visiting Scholar, Department of Physiology and Anatomy, University of California at Berkeley, 1976-79; Adjunct Assistant Professor, Department of Physiology, New York Medical Center; Coordinator, Christian Embassy, United Nations. Organizational Memberships: American Physiological Society; Society for Neuroscience; International Brain Research Organization. Community Activities: Asia Society; America-Nepal Society; American Scientific Affiliation; Asia Christian Medical Congress, Philippines (speaker, 1978, 1979, 1981); Medical Lecturer, United States, Canada, Germany, Singapore; Christian Conference Speaker, United States, India, Korea, Singapore; Christian Lecturer, Indonesia, Japan, Thailand. Address: 965 Knollwood Road, White Plains, New York 10603.

Allen, James Curtis

Manufacturing Company Executive. Personal: Born June 7, 1922, in Winston, Missouri; Son of Vernon, (deceased), and Carrie Belle Palmer Allen; Married Juanita G. Kennedy on December 4, 1944; Father of Daryl Curtis, Karen Ann, Marti Lu, James C., Randall George. Education: Graduate of Chillicothe Business College, 1941. Military: Served with United States Naval Reserve, 1942-1945. Career: Accountant, National Bellas Hess, Kansas City, Missouri, 1946-48; Secretary-Treasurer, EFCO Corporation, Monett, Missouri, 1963-66; Controller, Lawn Boy Division, Outboard Marine Corporation, Lamar, Missouri, 1948-63; Co-Owner and Secretary-Treasurer, Thorpe Manufacturing Company, 1966 to present. Community Activities: Community Betterment (chairman, 1968-1969); United Fund (president, 1971); Barton County State Bank (director); Sowemco Council Boy Scouts (chairman, 1964-66); Arrowhead Council Boy Scouts (chairman, 1972, executive board of Missouri-Kansas area council; vice president B.S.A.; Big Three Council chairman, 1981 to present); Lamar School Board, 1969-71; Lamar Park Board (current member); Lamar Rotary Club (president 1973 to present); Monett Kiwanis Club (president); Mason; Shriner. Religion: Methodist -Treasurer, Chairman of the Board, Superintendent, Chairman of the Finance Committee, Educational Committee, Trustee, Served on Conference Boards of Education and Audit. Honors and Awards: Distinguished Service Award, Kiwanis, 1965; Leadership Award, Missouri Community Betterment, 1970; Golden Sun, Order of the Arrow, BSA; Outstanding Leadership, Missouri Municipal League, 1971; Man of Year, Rotary Club, 1977; Boss of Year, A.B.W.A.; F.F.A. Honorary Farmer Award, 1979. Address: 400 West First, Lamar, Missouri 64759.

Gary T Allen

Allen, Karen S

Associate Chief of Staff for Education, Clinical Assistant Professor. Personal: Born March 12, 1943, Columbus, Georgia; Daughter of Col. and Mrs. William A. Drowns; Married R. Michael Allen; Mother of Brandwyd Michele. Education: B.S. 1965, M.S. 1967, University of Idaho; Ph.D., University of Maryland, 1973; A.P.A. Approved Clinical Psychology Internship, Walter Reed Army Hospital, 1974. Military: Served in the United States Army Medical Service Corps, 1973-76, achieving the rank of Captain. Career: Associate Chief of Staff for Education, Dallas Veterans Administration Medical Center, 1982 to present; Clinical Assistant Professor of Psychology, Southwestern Medical School, Dallas, Texas, 1982 to present; Clinical Assistant Professor, Allied School of Health, Dallas, Texas, 1982 to present; Clinical Assistant Professor, Louisiana State University Medical School, Department of Psychiatry, 1981-82; Assistant Professor, Coordinator of Clinical Behavioral Neurology, Louisiana State University Medical School, Department of Psychiatry, 1980-81; Assistant Professor, Louisiana State University Medical School, Department of Family Medicine, 1979-80; Assistant Professor, Texas Tech Medical School, R. E. Thomason General Hospital, Psychiatry, 1977-78; Chief, Psychology Service, Department of Psychiatry and Neurology, Fort Hood, Texas, 1974-76; Psychologist, Great Oaks Center, Silver Spring, Maryland, 1971-73. Organizational Memberships: American Psychological Association; Texas Psychological Association; Bell County Psychological Association, 1975-76; Consultant to Private Professional Group in Areas of Development Psychology, Special Education and Behavior Modification Techniques, 1970; Kappa Alpha Theta. Published Works: Co-Author *Mental Status Interview; Behavior Modification in Health Care: The ABC's of Operant Conditioning; Basic Cerebral Neurology*; Author *Statistics Workbook for Medical Students*; Films and Trigger Tapes; Original Soundtrack with Music and Lyrics "Flowers Bloom Forever"; Original Music and Lyrics for "Time Has Gone to Sleep"; Others. Honors and Awards: Psychology Graduate Assistantship, 1965; Army National Defense Service Medal, 1973; Listed in *Who's Who in the South and Southwest, Who's Who of American Women, Personalities of America, Cambridge International Biography, International Platform Association, World Who's Who of Women*. Address: V.A. Medical Center, 4500 South Lancaster, Dallas, Texas 75216.

Allen, Virginia R

Associate Professor. Personal: Born February 21, 1946; Daughter of Henry and Ruth Allen. Education: B.S. with high distinction, Indiana University, 1967; Registration Examination with honors, 1967; M.H.E., Medical College of Georgia, 1977; Doctoral Student, University of Georgia, 1980 to present. Career: Medical College of Georgia, Department of Occupational Therapy, Associate Professor 1981 to present, Assistant Professor 1977-81, Instructor 1973-77, Appointed to Graduate School Faculty 1979, Awarded Tenure 1981; Georgia War Veterans Nursing Home, Chief Occupational Therapist 1973-75, Consultant 1975 to present; Gracewood State School and Hospital, Consultant 1974-76; South Carolina Vocational Rehabilitation Comprehensive Center, Consultant 1978 to present; St. Joseph's Home Health Care, Back-Up Therapist 1977-80; Medical College of Georgia Family Practice Department, Occupational Therapy Liaison 1976 to present, Family Practice Interdisciplinary Team Project 1977-78; Institute of Rehabilitation

Technology, Atlanta, M.C.G. Liaison 1981 to present; Other Short Term Consultations. Organizational Memberships: World Federation of Occupational Therapy; Alpha Eta (member, 1976 to present; M.C.G. chapter executive board, 1977-78); American Coalition of Citizens with Disabilities; American Association for the Advancement of Science (film reviewer for *Science Books and Films*); American Occupational Therapy Association (member, 1965 to present; public information and recruitment committee, 1967-69; organized summer experience program orientation for Ohio, 1968; student representative to 1966 annual business meeting, American Journal of Occupational Therapy Book Reviewer, 1974 to present; alternate representative, 1979-82; representative, 1982-85; recognitions committee member, 1981 to present); American Society of Allied Health Professions (book reviewer, 1977 to present; member, 1980 to present); National Spinal Cord Injury Association (member, 1970 to present; allied health professions advisory committee, 1972 to 1981; board of directors, 1978-84; executive committee, 1979-81; chairman, nominating committee, 1979-80; chairman, by-laws and policies committee, 1980-82; conference planning committee, 1976, 1980, 1981); Rehabilitation Engineering Society of North America; Society for Behavioral Kinesiology (nominating committee, 1978-81); Able-Disabled (Group of Augusta); Biofeedback Society of Georgia, 1979-81; Georgia Society of Allied Health Professions; Georgia Occupational Therapy Association (state practice chairman, 1974-76; state vice president, 1976, 1978; district practice chairman, 1974-77; district nominating committee, 1974, 1975; nominating committee chairman, 1977; executive board, 1974 to present). Community Activities: United Cerebral Palsy of the Central Savannah River Area (workshop committee, 1980 to present). Published Works: Professional Articles including "The Role of the Educator in the Community" and "The Role of Occupational Therapy in the Rehabilitation of the Cord Injured"; Co-Author *How to Get Help if You Are Paralyzed;* Number of Book and Film Reviews. Honors and Awards: Honorable Mention, Greater Cleveland Hospital Association Achievements Contest, 1971; Alpha Eta; Roster of Fellows, American Occupational Therapy Association, 1977; Distinguished Faculty Member, 1980, Medical College of Georgia; Sounds of Science Project, "Role Model for Science Careers", 1981; Local Awards for Photography, Gardening, Flower Arranging, China Painting; National Awards for Ballroom Dancing; T. J. Nujent Award of Merit for Service, National Spinal Cord Injury Association, 1981; Listed in *Community Leaders and Noteworthy Americans, Dictionary of International Biography, International Who's Who in Community Service, Men and Women of Distinction, Notable Americans, Outstanding Young Women of America, Who's Who of American Women, World Who's Who of Women, Personalities of America, Personalities of the South, Who's Who in the South and Southwest.* Address: O.T. Department, Medical College of Georgia, Augusta, Georgia 30912.

Allen, William Thomas

Regional Director, Group Claims. Personal: Born June 4, 1935; Son of Rohma Allen; Married Jan Allen; Father of Tami Lynette, William Lawrence. Education: B.S., University of Iowa, 1957; M.S., LaVerne College, 1977; Graduate, Command and General Staff College, 1973; Industrial College of the Armed Forces, 1975; Graduate, International Claims Association, 1968; Graduate, Life Office Managment Association, 1966. Military: Served in the United States Army, 1957-58, achieving the rank of Lieutenant; Colonel with the United States Army Reserve, 1958 to present. Career: Regional Director of Group Claims. Organizational Memberships: Los Angeles Life and Accident Claims Association (president, 1972); H.I.A.A. California State Council; F.L.M.I. Society of Southern California. Community Activities: Reserve Officers Association (chapter president, 1972); 63rd Infantry Division Association (president, 1972); H.S.A. of Los Angeles County, Inc. (vice president, 1978 to present); Comp. Los Angeles (director, 1975-76). Honors and Awards: Civic Award, City of Redondo Beach, 1978; Distinguished Military Graduate, 1957; Honor Graduate, Command and General Staff College, 1973; F.L.M.I., 1966; Meritorious Service Medal, United States Army Reserve; Parachute Badge, United States Army. Address: 21031 Ventura Blvd., Woodland Hills, California 91364.

Alls, Willard Jess Jr

Pharmacist. Personal: Born September 6, 1938, Paducah, Kentucky; Son of Willard Sr., and Catherine (deceased) Alls ; Married Martha Jean Harding; Father of Joe Mark. Career: Pharmacist, REVCO Drug, Murray, Kentucky; Owner, The Bookmark, Murray. Organizational Memberships: Kentucky Society of Hospital Pharmacists (president, 1966-67); Kentucky Pharmacists Association (member of several committees); First District Pharmaceutical Association; American Pharmaceutical Association; American Society of Hospital Pharmacists; Phi Delta Chi Alumni Association. Community Activities: Jackson Purchase Area Health Education Services (board of directors, 1977-80); Calloway County Council on Drug Education (chairman, 1970-75); Murray Colt Baseball League (board of directors, 1978-80; coach for five years); Mid-South Youth Camp, Henderson, Tennessee (board of directors, 1978-80); Board of Development Council of Freed-Hardeman College; Murray-Calloway County Hospital (director, poison control center, 1970-80); Murray Middle School Parent-Teacher Association (president, 1974-75); Murray-Calloway County Hospital (chairman disaster committee, 1974-80); Guest Lecturer, Classes at Murray State University, Murray City Schools and Calloway County Schools. Religion: University Church of Christ, Deacon, Youth Development Committee, Personal Evangelism Committee. Published Works: *What the Christian Should Know About Drug Abuse; What the Christian Should Know About Alcohol; Christianity and Tobacco;* Writer for Christian Publications *World Evangelist, Gospel Advocate,* Others. Honors and Awards: Distinguished Service Award, Murray Kiwanis Club, 1971; Outstanding Young Man, Murray Jaycees, 1972; Distinguished Service Award, Calloway County Drug Council, 1972-73; Special Vocational Award, Kentukcy State Vocational School, 1976; Duke of Paducah Honor, 1976; Distinguished Kentuckian Award, University of Kentucky College of Pharmacy, 1981; American Druggist Magazine Award, 1971; Personal Letter of Commendation from Former U.S. President Richard Nixon; Personal Letter of Commendation from Former Kentucky Governor, Louis B. Nunn; Listed in *Outstanding Young Men of America, Personalities of the South, Notable Americans of the Bicentennial Era, Profiles of Freedom-A Cross Section of Proud Bicentennial Americans, Community Leaders and Noteworthy Americans, Men of Achievement, Who's Who in the South and Southwest, Personalities of America, Directory of Distinguished Americans, International Who's Who of Intellectuals, Directory of International Biography.* Address: 1610 Keenland, Murray, Kentucky 42071.

Almond, Gerald Edwin

Hospital Administrator. Personal: Born May 13, 1932; Son of Mrs. P. C. Almond; Married Shirley A. Miller; Father of Kenneth, Celia, Carla. Education: Degree in Accounting and Business Administration; Fellow, American College of Hospital Administrators. Military: Served in the United States Air Force, achieving the rank of Staff Sergeant. Career: President, Memorial Hospital, Chester, Illinois; Executive Director, Wabash County Hospital, Wabash, Indiana, 1966-72; Administrator, Doctors/Northwest Hospital, Des Moines, Iowa, 1964-66; Administrator, Riverside Community Hospital, Waupaca, Wisconsin, 1961-64. Organizational Memberships: American Hospital Association (delegate to Washington, D.C., 1961 to present); Illinois Hospital Association (trustee at large, 1981 to present; council on research and development, 1980 to present; council on shared services, 1979 to present; chairman, council on patient expectations, 1977-80; council on government relations, 1974-77; council on small and rural hospitals, 1978 to present); Illinois Hospital Association Region IV (president, 1975). Community Activities: Rotary Club of Chester (past president); Baptist Children's Home (past board member). Religion: Baptist, Sunday School Teacher, Deacon, Trustee, Choir Director. Honors and Awards: Chairman, Committee on Credentialing, Illinois Hospital Association; Local Dean, Southern Illinois

University Rural Allied Health, 1976-78; Listed in *Who's Who in the Midwest, Personalities of the West and Midwest*. Address: 1718 Swanwick Street, Chester, Illinois 62233.

Alt, Hansi

Educator. Personal: Married Fred Alt (deceased). Education: Teacher's degree, Piano and Composition, Vienna Conservatory; Undertook post graduate studies in theory and composition. Career: Teacher, Piano and Theory, Private Schools and Music Schools in New York City; Teacher, Los Angeles Conservatory; Composer of Educational Piano Pieces. Organizational Memberships: National Guild of Piano Teachers (judge); Mu Phi Epsilon; Music Teachers Association; Friday Morning Music Club. Published Works: Approximately 35 educational piano pieces; Author, 6 music books; Various serious compositions for piano, violin, flute, and voice. Honors and Awards: "March" for piano received Honorable Mention, Composition Contest of California Music Teachers Association; "The Parade" piano solo on "Best of the Year" list, *Piano Quarterly*; "My Car", "Best of the Year" list; Various piano pieces listed by the National Guild of Piano Teachers, included in the California Certificate of Merit Syllabus, recommended by the National Federation of Music Clubs, or recommended by the Music Educators National Conference, Southern California School Music Teachers Association; Honorable Mention, Composers Press Composition Contest; Cash Award, Outstanding Educational Composer, A.S.C.A.P. and National Federation of Music Clubs; Listed in *Who's Who of American Women, Who's Who of Women International*. Address: 5200 Carlton Street, Washington, D.C. 20016.

Altchuler, Steven Ira

Nutritional Physiologist. Personal: Born August 1, 1951; Son of Murray and Lyn Altchuler. Education: S.B., 1973, Ph.D., 1979, both from Massachusetts Institute of Technology. Career: Teaching Assistant, 1975-77, and Research Assistant, 1977-78, Massachusetts Institute of Technology; Nutritional Physiologist, National Aeronautical and Space Administration/Lyndon B. Johnson Space Center, 1978 to present; Reviewer, science books and films, 1980 to present; Adjunct Assistant Professor of Nutrition, Department of Human Development and Consumer Sciences, University of Houston, Central Campus, 1980 to present; Reviewer, *Journal of Nutrition Education*. Organizational Memberships: Aerospace Medical Association; American Association for the Advancement of Science; American College of Nutrition (affiliate fellow); American Institute of Nutrition; American Statistical Association; Houston Area Calcium Metabolism Society (founding member); National Association of Emergency Medical Technicians/Paramedics; New York Academy of Science; Nutrition Today Society (charter member); Sigma Xi; Texas Association of Emergency Medical Technicians. Community Activities: Alpha Phi Omega, Alpha Chi Chapter, 1971-75; American Red Cross (instructor, captain, shelter manager, 1969 to present); American Heart Association (instructor, trainer, board of directors, 1974 to present); Boy Scouts of America, 1969-74; Clear Lake Emergency Medical Corps (paramedic, training officer, 1979 to present); Experiment in International Living, 1969-74; Forest Band Civil Defense (director, 1979 to present). Published Works: Technical Articles and Presentations. Honors and Awards: Rensselaer Polytechnic Institute Award, 1969; Grumman Aerospace Corporation Scholar, 1969; Number of Red Cross Service Awards, 1969 to present; Frederick Gardiner Fassett, Jr., Award, 1973; Vicks Fellow, 1977; Outstanding Young Man of America, 1981. Address: 535 N.A.S.A. Road One #403A, Webster, Texas 77598.

Altenhaus, Amy L

Chief Psychologist, Program Director. Personal: Born July 7, 1950; Daughter of Julian and Corrinne Altenhaus. Education: B.A. with honors, University of Wisconsin-Madison, 1972; M.S. 1977, Ph.D. 1978, Rutgers University. Career: Chief Psychologist, Director of Pregnant Adolescent Program; Private Practice; Staff of Outpatient Department, Freehold Area Hospital; Consultant, The Mt. Sinai Medical School, New York City; Former Staff Psychologist and Director of Rutgers Hotline. Organizational Memberships: American Psychological Association (chairperson, task force on clinical psychology and competent female behavior); New Jersey Psychological Association; Monmouth-Ocean Psychological Association; Pi Lambda Theta. Community Activities: Academic Review, New York City (advisory board); March of Dimes of Monmouth County (advisory board); New Jersey Network on Adolescent Pregnancy (advisory board); Monmouth Adolescent Programs and Services Network. Honors and Awards: Diplomate, American Academy of Behavioral Medicine. Address: 89 E. Main Street, Freehold, New Jersey 07728.

Alter, Estelle

Psychiatric Social Work Supervisor. Personal: Mother of Kenneth, Karen, Stuart. Education: B.A., Brooklyn College, 1966; M.S.W., Yeshiva University, Wurzweiler School, 1976; Doctoral Candidate, Columbia University. Career: Psychiatric Social Work Supervisor, Manhattan Psychiatric Center; Producer, Host, Cable Television Program on Psychiatrically Oriented Problems; Lecturer on Jewish Subjects; Speakers Bureau, Greater New York Conference for Soviet Jewry. Organizational Memberships: National Association of Social Workers; New York Academy of Science; Association of Orthodox Jewish Scientists. Community Activities: B'nai B'rith (vice president of programming, 1978-80); United Jewish Appeal (chairman, single professionals division, 1981); Hillel School Parent-Teacher Association (president, 1975); Mizrachi Women (vice president, 1965-70). Religion: Congregation Shaaray Tefila, Vice President of Programming. Honors and Awards: Kappa Delta Pi; High School Valedictorian; Listed in *Who's Who of American Women*. Address: 20 West 64 Street, New York, New York 10023.

Alter, Joanne Hammerman

Elected Official. Personal: Born July 3, 1927; Daughter of Sol and Celia Hammerman; Married James M. Alter; Mother of Jennifer, Jonathan, Elizabeth, Harrison. Education: B.A cum laude, Mt. Holyoke College, 1949. Career: Elected Commissioner, Metropolitan Sanitary District of Greater Chicago, 1972, Re-elected 1978; Former Assistant Foreign Student Program Director, Institute of International Education; Radio/Interview Shows, Producing and Conducting, Radio Station WIND Call for Action (co-founder). Community Activities: Democratic National Committee (committee woman, 1980 to present); Candidate, Democratic Primary, Lieutenant Governor of Illinois, 1976; Illinois Democratic Woman's Caucus (founder and co-convenor, 1971); Council of Governments of Cook County (board representative, 1978 to present); Illinois Department of Local Government Affairs (advisory council, 1973-76); International Women's Year Conference (Illinois delegate, 1977); Illinois International Women's Year Committee, 1977; United Nations World Conference, International Women's Year, Mexico (Illinois delegate, 1975); United Nations Day (Illinois state chairman, 1975); Mount Holyoke College (board of trustees); Art Institute of Chicago (woman's board); Young Women's Christian Association of Metropolitan Chicago (board of directors, 1980-82); Bright New City, University of Chicago (board of directors); Augustana Hospital (board of directors); Mount Holyoke College (art advisory committee); International Visitors Center (co-founder; advisory council); Contemporary Art Workshop (board of directors). Honors and Awards: Young Women's Christian

Association Leadership Award, Metropolitan Community Leadership, 1975; Audubon Society Award, Protector of the Environment, Political Service, 1979. Address: 568 Hawthorne Place, Chicago, Illinois 60657.

Alvarino de Leira, Angeles

Biologist-Oceanographer, Planktologist. Personal: Born October 3, 1916; Daughter of Dr. Antonio Alvarino-Grimaldos and D[a] Carmen Gonzalez Diaz-Saavedra de Alvarino (deceased); Married Sir Eugenio Leira-Manso; Mother of Angeles Leira-Alvarino. Education: Ph.D., summa cum laude, University of Madrid, 1967; Biologist-Oceanographer, Spanish Institute of Oceanography, 1952; Certificate, Doctorate University, Madrid, 1951; M.N.S., honors, University of Madrid, 1941; Bachelor of Sciences and Letters, summa cum laude, University Santiago de Compostela, 1933. Career: Fishery Research Biologist, N.O.A.A., N.M.F.S., Southwest Fisheries Center, La Jolla, California, 1970 to present; Associate Professor, San Diego State University, 1978 to present (honorary appointment); Biologist, Scripps Institute of Oceanography, University of California, La Jolla, 1958-69; Biologist-Oceanographer, Spanish Institute of Oceanography, 1950-57; Fishery Research Biologist, Department of Commerce, Madrid, Spain, 1948-52; Histologist, Spanish Superior Council of Scientific Research, 1948-52; Professor, College El Ferrol, Spain, 1941-48. Organizational Memberships: Latin-American Association of Researchers on Marine Science (delegate to the U.S., life member 1975 to present); Oceanography Research Latin-American Countries (coordinator 1977-79); University National Autonomous Mexico (visiting professor 1976 to present); Adviser on Research for Universities in the United States and Abroad. Community Activities: Southwest Fisheries Center (women program coordinator 1974-76, Hispanic program manager 1980 to present). Published Works: Author of 70+ Scientific Papers. Honors and Awards: Discoverer of 14 New Species; British Council Fellow, 1953-54; Fulbright Fellow, 1956-57; N.S.F., U.S. Office of Naval Research, California Coorperative Oceanic Fisheries Investigations Grants; Life Member, Latin-American Association, for advise and dedication to students and researchers in the projects and works on various subjects of oceanic research. Address: 7535 Cabrillo Avenue, La Jolla, California 92037.

Ambrose, John Augustine

Educator, Biochemical Geneticist, Analytical Bio-organic Chemist, Nutritional Biochemist. Personal: Born February 15, 1923; Son of Abraham and Josephine Ambrose (both deceased); Married Edith Louise Brockman; Father of Dianne Louise. Education: Attended Marquette University, 1944-45; B.A., Johns Hopkins University, 1948; M.S., Marquette University, 1951; United States Public Health Service Fellow, Indiana, 1958-60; Fellow, Ph.D., University of Miami (Florida), 1965. Career: Research Chemist, Oregon State University, 1951-52; Research Biochemist, Chicago Medical School, 1952-54; Medical School, Johns Hopkins University, 1954-57; Center for Disease Control, United States Public Health Service (1964 to present): Research Chemist, Metabolic Disorders Laboratory 1964-65, Chief of Mental Retardation Laboratory 1965-67, Chemical Disorders Laboratory 1967-70, Chief of Biochemical Genetics and Metabolic Disorders Laboratory 1970-72, Chief of Pediatric and Genetic Chemistry Laboratory 1972-73, Chief of Genetic Chemistry Laboratory 1973-74, Research Chemist, Metabolic Laboratory 1974-75, Research Chemist, Nutritional Biochemistry Branch, 1975 to present; Consultant, State Health Department, Mental Retardation Activities, Chemical Genetics; Director, National and State Health Department Multistate Fluorometric and Mental Retardation Workshops; Research. Awards and Honors: Sigma Xi; Phi Kappa Phi; F.A.I.C., Fellow, American Public Health Association; International Platform Association; Fellow, I.B.A.; F.N.A.C.B.; A.C.S.; New York Academy of Science; N.A.R.C.; Moose Legion; Sigma Phi Epsilon; Listed in *American Men of Science, Who's Who in the South and Southwest, Community Leaders of America, Dictionary of International Biography, Two Thousand Men of Achievement, Personalities of the South, International Who's Who in Community Service, International Register of Profiles, Outstanding Atlantans,* Others. Address: 3352 Old Chamblee-Tucker Road #3, Chamblee, Georgia 30340.

John Ambrose

Ames, John Dawes

Investment Banker. Personal: Born May 7, 1904; Son of Mr. and Mrs. Knowlton L. Ames (both deceased); Married Constance H. Ames; Father of John Jr., William, Knowlton. Education: Princeton, Class of 1928. Military: Served in the United States Army during World War II, achieving the rank of Lieutenant Colonel. Career: Investment Banker, 1951-82; Publisher, *Chicago Journal of Commerce,* 1933-50. Community Activities: United States Golf Association (president, 1958-59). Religion: Episcopal, Church of the Holy Spirit. Honors and Awards: Bronze Star, 1944. Address: 600 Washington Road, Lake Forest, Illinois 60045.

Ames, Richard Galyon

Epidemiologist-Demographer. Personal: Born: June 2, 1935; Son of Mrs. L. M. Ames; Married Sue Ann Ames; Father of Andrea. Education: B.A., George Washington University, 1958; M.A., American University, 1962; Ph.D., University of North Carolina, 1970; M.P.H., University of California, Berkeley, 1980. Career: Epidemiologist/Demographer, National Institute for Occupational Safety and Health, 1980 to present (on assignment from California State University-Hayward); Associate Professor, Sociology, West Virginia University, 1981 to present; Assistant Professor, Sociology, Syracuse University, 1967-69; Instructor, University of Southern California, 1965-67; Associate Professor, California State University-Hayward, 1969 to present. Organizational Memberships: American Thoracic Society; American Public Health Association; Epidemiological Research Association; American Sociological Association. Community Activities: Hayward South Rotary (executive committee, 1980); Alameda County Family Planning Forum, 1979. Honors and Awards: Listed in *Dictionary of International Biography, Men of Achievement, International Who's Who in Community Service, Who's Who in California.* Address: 673 Nueva Drive, Morgantown, West Virginia 26505.

Amir-Moez, Ali Reza

Professor. Personal: Born April 7, 1919, in Teheran, Iran; Son of Mohammad and Fatemeh Amir-Moez. Education: B.A., University of Teheran, 1941; M.A., 1951, and Ph.D., 1955, both from the University of California, Los Angeles. Military: Served as a Second Lieutenant in the Persian Army. Career: Instructor, Assistant Professor, Associate Professor, Professor: University of California-Santa Barbara, University of Idaho, Queens College, University of City of New York, Purdue University, University of Florida, Clarkson College of Technology, Texas Tech University. Organizational Memberships: American Mathematical Society; Mathematical Association of America; Sigma Xi; Pi Mu Epsilon; Kappa Mu Epsilon; Texas Academy of Science; New York Academy of Science. Religion: Universal Theist. Published Works: Author Books: *Elements of Linear Spaces,* 1962; *Extreme Properties of Linear Transformations and Geometry in a Unitary Space,* 1971; *Classes Residues et Figure anec Ficelli,* 1968; Plays: "Kaleeleh and Demneh", "Three Persian Tales"; Over 150 papers, articles and books. Honors and Awards: The Medal of Pro Mundi Beneficio, Academia Brasileira de Ciencos Humanas, 1975. Address: Math Department, Texas Tech University, Lubbock, Texas 79409.

Amos, Marvin C

Airline Executive. Personal: Born July 29, 1924, Seymour, Indiana; Son of Mary Eva Amos; Married Anne Addison; Father of Patrick M., Joanne L., Judy M., Mark A. Education: B.A., Hanover College. Military: Served in the United States Army, 1943-46. Career: Senior Vice President, Personnel and Corporate Administration, Eastern Air Lines, Inc.; Former Director, Industrial Relations, Curtiss-Wright Corporation; Has also been associated with General Electric Company, R.C.A., Goodyear Engineering Company. Organizational Memberships: Gamma Sigma Pi. Community Activities: Hanover College (board of trustees, executive committee, chairman of buildings and grounds committee); Governor Graham's Advisory Council on Productivity in the State of Florida (chairman of subcommittee #2, 1980); Working Group for Business Roundtable Task Force on National Planning and Employment Policy (Eastern Air Lines representative). Religion: Roman Catholic. Honors and Awards: Awarded Battlefield Commission, 1945. Address: 7745 S.W. 138 Terrace, Miami, Florida 33158.

Anand, Suresh C

Physician, Executive. Personal: Born September 13, 1931; Son of Dr. and Mrs. Sat-Chit-Anand (both deceased); Married Wiltrud Blum; Father of Miriam, Michael. Education: M.B., B.S., University of Lucknow, India, 1954; M.Sc., University of Colorado, 1962; Diplomate, American Board of Allergy and Immunology, 1975, Recertified, 1980. Career: Medical Officer, U.P. India, 1954-57; National Jewish Hospital, Denver, Colorado: Fellow in Pulmonary Disease, 1957-58; Resident in Chest Medicine, 1958-60; Chief Resident, Allergy and Asthma, 1960-62; Mt. Sinai Hospital, Toronto, Ontario, Canada: Internship, 1962-63; Resident in Medicine, 1963-64; Chief Resident in Medicine, 1964-65; Research Associate, Department of Allergy and Asthma, National Jewish Hospital, 1966-69; Demonstrator in Clinical Technique, 1963-64, and Fellow in Medicine, 1964-65, University of Toronto; Clinical Instructor in Medicine, University of Colorado Medical Center, 1967-69; President, Allergy Associates and Laboratory, Ltd.; Staff Member: Phoenix Baptist Hospital, John C. Lincoln Hospital, Good Samaritan Hospital, Doctor's Hosptial, Memorial Hospital, St. Lukes Hospital, St. Joseph's Hospital, Scottsdale Memorial Hospital, Mesa Lutheran Hospital, Desert Samaritan Hospital, Maryvale Hospital, Tempe Community Hospital. Organizational Memberships: Interasma Association; World Medical Association; American Medical Association; Arizona Medical Association (chairman, scientific assembly committee, 1980-81); Maricopa County Medical Society; Arizona Allergy Society; Arizona Thoracic Society; Western Society of Allergy and Immunology; New York Academy of Sciences; National Geographical Society; Smithsonian Institute. Community Activities: Carmelbask Hospital Citizens' Advisory Board, 1972-80; Scottsdale Sertoma Club, 1972-76; Sertoma International (life member). Honors and Awards: Physicians Recognition Award, American Medical Association, 1972, 1975, 1978, 1980; Fellow: American College of Physicians, American College of Chest Physicians, American College of Allergists, American Academy of Allergy, American Association of Allergy and Clinical Immunology; Listed in *Who's Who in the West*. Address: 2200 W. Bethany Home Rd., Phoenix, Arizona 85015 and 2034 E. Soutern Ave., Tempe, Arizona 85283.

Stephen Anderl

Andelson, Robert Vernon

Professor of Philosophy. Personal: Born February 19, 1931; Son of Abraham and Ada Markson Andelson (both deceased); Married Bonny Johnson. Education: A.A., Los Angeles City College, 1950; A.B. equivalent, University of Chicago, 1952; A.M. 1954, Ph.D. 1960, University of Southern California. Career: Educator, Arlington College 1954-58, Northland College 1962-63, Northwestern State University (Louisiana) 1963-65, Auburn University (1965 to present): Professor of Philosophy 1973 to present, Graduate School Faculty 1969 to present; Executive Director, Henry George School of Social Science, 1959-62. Organizational Memberships: Alabama Philosophical Society (president, 1968-69, 1978-79); American Association of University Professors (president, Auburn chapter, 1975-76). Community Activities: Republican National Convention (assistant sergeant-at-arms, 1952); Henry George School of Social Science (academic advisory council, 1970 to present). Published Works: Editorial Board Member, *The Personalist*, 1975-80; Editorial Board Member, *The American Journal of Economics and Sociology*, 1969 to present; Author/Editor Two Books and Numerous Scholarly Articles. Religion: Ordained to Ministry of the Congregational Christian Church, 1959 to present. Honors and Awards: George Washington Honor Medal, Freedoms Foundation, 1970, 1972; Research Awards, Foundation for Social Research, 1959, and Relm Foundation, 1967; Subject of Collection at the Archive of Contemporary History, University of Wyoming; Listed in *Who's Who in America*. Address: 534 Cary Drive, Auburn, Alabama 36830.

Anderl, Stephen

Roman Catholic Priest. Personal: Born July 13, 1910, in Chippewa Falls, Wisconsin; Son of Henry A. Anderl (deceased); Katherine Schneider (deceased). Education: Graduate, McDonell Memorial High School, Chippewa Falls, Wisconsin, 1928; B.A., magna cum laude, St. John's University, 1932; M.Div., St. John's University, 1974. Military: Served as a Civilian Chaplain, Fort McCoy, during World War II. Career: Curate, Sts. Peter and Paul Parish, Wisconsin Rapids, Wisconsin, 1936-37, and Holy Trinity Parish, La Crosse, Wisconsin, 1937-40; Instructor, Vice-Principal, Guidance Counselor, Aquinas High School, La Crosse, 1937-49; Pastor, Sacred Heart Parish, Spring Valley, Wisconsin, 1949-52, St. Michael's Parish, Hewitt, Wisconsin, 1952-53, and St. Mary's Parish, Durand, Wisconsin, 1953 to present; Dean, Durand Deanery, Diocesan Board of Education, 1953 to present. Organizational Memberships: Catholic Society Agency (executive board); Diocesan Personnel Board; Religious Censor Librorum (vicar general); Committee for Continued Education of the Clergy; Committee for the Elderly. Community Activities: Boy Scouts and Girl Scouts (diocesan chaplain); Diocesan Catholic Committee on Scouting (vice chairman); Council Catholic Committee on Scouting (chaplain); National Catholic Committee on Scouting; National Catholic Committee on Scouting; Chippewa Valley Council Boy Scouts of America (executive board); Silver Waters Girl Scout Council (board of directors); West Central Wisconsin Community Action Agency (founder, executive board); Diocesan Sodality and C.Y.O. (executive secretary); Governor's Commission on Children and Youth; State Committee on Mental Health and Retardation; XII World Jamboree of Boy Scouts (chaplain, 1967); 7th and 8th National Jamborees of Boy Scouts of America (chaplain, 1969-73); Pope John XXIII General Assembly Fourth Degree Knights of Columbus (faithful friar); Knights of Columbus Council 12422 (chaplain); American Academy of Religion; Wisconsin Geneological Society; Wisconsin Academy of Arts, Sciences and Letters; American Numismatic Society; Collectors of Religion on Stamps. Published Works: *Technique of the Catholic Action Cell*, 1943; *Adult Christians*, 1955; *Religious and Catholic Action*, 1947; *Thy Will Be Done*, 1946; *Parish of the Assumption*, 1960. Honors and Awards: Domestic Prelate by Pope John XXIII, St. George Award, 1970; Silver Beaver, Boy Scouts of America, 1968; Citation for Outstanding Service to the Poor, West Cap, 1972; American Honorarium, 1968; Fellow, Internatioal Institute of Community Service; Honorary Fellow, Anglo-American Academy; Listed in *Who's Who in the Midwest, American Catholic Who's Who, Who's Who in Religion, 2000 Men of Achievement, Personalities of the West and Midwest, Blue Book, National Social Directory, Notable Americans of the Bicentennial Era, National Register of Notable Americans, Dictionary of International Biography, Hereditary Register of the U.S.A., Wisconsin Men of Achievement, Men and Women of Achievement, Book of Honor, International Who's Who of Intellectuals, International Register of Profiles, Creative and Successful Personalities, International Who's Who in Community Service, Verlag für Industrie und Kultur, International Who's Who of Intellectuals.* Address: 911 W. Prospect Street, Durand, Wisconsin 54736.

Anderson, Claire Ann

Sales Representative. Personal: Born July 31, 1940; Daughter of Mr. and Mrs. A. G. Saegert; Married Bill J. Anderson; Mother of Dana Elaine Norman Baysden, Toni Denise Norman. Education: Graduate Pflugerville High School, 1958. Career: Legal Secretary (5 years); Sales Representative, Knickerbocker Toy Co. (15 years in toy industry). Organizational Memberships: Southwestern Toy and Hobby Association, 1967 to present. Community Activities: American Society of Professional and Executive Women, 1980-81; National Association of Female Executives, Inc., 1979-81; Eastern Star, Chapter #710, Conroe, Texas, 1979-81. Religion: Park Place Lutheran Church, Houston, Texas, 1962-80; Grace Lutheran Church, Conroe, Texas, 1979-81. Honors and Awards: Sales Achievement Awards from Mattel, Inc., including High Achievers Award and a Trip to Spain, 1965 and Leisure Dynamics #1 Region Award, 1979; Listed in *Who's Who of American Women*, 1981-82. Address: 3140 White Oake Valley, Conroe, Texas 77302.

Claire A Anderson

Anderson, Clara B

Special Needs Teacher. Personal: Born July 25, 1918; Daughter of Clarence and Zenobia Strong (deceased); Widow; Mother of Orville H., LaVern H. Education: R.N., Homer Phillips Hospital School of Nursing; A.B., West Virginia State College, 1944; M.S., The University of Chicago, 1948; Teaching Certificate, Michigan State University, 1961. Career: Assistant Director of Nursing Services, Tuskegee Institute, 1944-47; Instructor, Florida A&M University, 1948-53; Instructor, Mississippi Valley College, 1953-55; Assistant Director of Nursing Education, St. Lawrence Hospital School of Nursing, 1955-57; Director, In-service, Sparrow Hospital, Lansing, Michigan, 1958; Clinical Instructor, Sparrow Hospital, 1959; Teacher of Hospitalized Children, Lansing School District, 1960-78; Homebound Teacher, Lansing School Distrcit, 1978-81; Special Need Teacher, Mathematics, Otto Junior High School. Organizational Memberships: Capitol Area District Nurses Association (president, 1958-60); Michigan Nurses Association (secretary, 1958-61); Lansing Schools Education Association (treasurer, 1977 to present); Alpha Psi Chapter, Sigma Theta Tau (treasurer); Michigan Education Association (life member); American Nurses Association; National Education Association; Michigan Association of the Physically Impaired; Council of Exceptional Children. Community Activities: Lincoln Community Center (first vice president, 1968-70); Alpha Kappa Alpha (life member; president, Basileus alumni chapter); Lansing Visiting Nurses Association (board member, 1968-70); March of Dimes (chairperson, patient services, 1970 to present); Jean Granger Pre-Natal Clinic (board member, 1971 to present); Ingham County Lung Association (treasurer, 1957-60); Lansing Sickle Cell Disease Foundation (secretary, 1971 to present); National Association for the Advancement of Colored People. Religion: Ruling Elder, Westminster Presbyterian Church, 1976 to present; Chairperson, Community Outreach, 1977 to present. Honors and Awards: Lansing Human Relations Award, 1959; Outstanding Alumni, Homer G. Phillips Hospital School of Nursing, 1962. Address: 3000 Forest Road, Lansing, Michigan 48910.

Anderson, Eva K

Psychologist, College Professor. Personal: Born June 17, 1935; Daughter of Dr. and Mrs. Gustav Samak; Married William F. Anderson; Mother of Adam. Education: A.B., Cornell University, 1957; M.A. 1959, Ph.D. 1965, Syracuse University. Career: Psychologist; Assistant Professor, Salisbury State College; Formerly an Adjunct Professor of Psychology and Special Education, Syracuse University; Consulting Psychologist, Child and Family Service; Department of Social Services; Association for Retarded Children, Syracuse, New York; Consulting Psychologist, Vocational Rehabilitation in New York, Maryland; Social Security Administration (Disability), Maryland, Virginia. Organizational Memberships: American Psychological Association; Maryland Psychological Association; Council of Exceptional Children; American Association of University Professors. Community Activities: Maryland State Department of Education (special education consortium); Appointed by Maryland State Commissioner of Education to Satellite Committee, Institutions of Higher Education; Head Start Health Advisory Committee of Wicomico and Worcester Counties, Maryland. Address: 104 Aberdeen Road, Salisbury, Maryland 21801.

Anderson, Fletcher Clark

Associate Professor of Music, Chairman of Fine Arts. Personal: Born December 7, 1939; Son of Fletcher and Alla Anderson; Married Virginia Fullerton; Father of Fletcher Charles, Nathaniel Joseph, James Patrick. Education: B.M.E., A.B., Birmingham-Southern College, 1962; M.S., University of Illinois, 1967; Ed.D., University of Georgia, 1978. Career: Wesleyan College (Macon, Georgia), Associate Professor of Music and Chairman of Fine Arts, President of the Faculty 1980-82, Chairman of the Music Department 1979-82; Former Assistant Professor of Music, Edinboro, Pennsylvania; Choral Director, Elizabethtown High School, Elizabethtown, Kentucky; Elementary Music Coordinator, Atlanta, Georgia. Organizational Memberships: Georgia Music Educators Association (research chairman, 1977-79; state student chairman, 1979-80; college division chairman, 1980-81); M.E.N.C.; A.G.O.; College Music Society. Religion: Director of Music, Centenary United Methodist Church, 1979 to present; Director of Music, First United Methodist Church, Burnesville, Georgia, 1971-74; Worship Committee, South Georgia Conference of United Methodist Church, 1980-81. Honors and Awards: Pi Kappa Lambda. Address: 367 Wesleyan Drive, Macon, Georgia 31210.

Frances S Anderson

Anderson, Frances Swem

Retired Nuclear Medical Technologist. Personal: Born November 27, 1913; Daughter of Frank and Carrie S. Swem (both deceased); Married Clarence A. F. Anderson; Mother of Robert Curtis, Clarelyn Christine Schmelling, Stanley Herbert. Education: Attended Muskegon School of Business; Certificate Course, Muskegon Community College, 1964. Career: Hackley Hospital, Muskegon, Michigan, X-Ray File Clerk and Film Librarian 1957-59, Radioisotope Technologist and Secretary 1959-65; Nuclear Medical Technologist, Butler Memorial Hospital, Muskegon Heights, 1966-70; Senior Nuclear Medical Technologist, Mercy Hospital, Muskegon, 1970-79; Retired, 1979. Organizational Memberships: American Registry of Radiologic Technologists; Certified Nuclear Medical Technologists; American Society Radiologic Technologists, 1964-80; Society of Nuclear Medicine, 1971-80; Society of Nuclear Medical Technologists (charter member). Community Activities: Parent-Teacher Association (mother-teacher singers, 1941-48; treasurer 1944-48); Civic A Capella Choir, Muskegon, 1932-39; Civic Opera Association, Muskegon, 1950-51; Jackson Hill Reunion (co-chairman, 1982); International Platform Association, 1971 to present. Religion: Muskegon Evangelical Covenant Church, Member 1953 to present, Choir 1953-79, Secretary 1963-69, Sunday School Teacher 1954-75, Sunday School Superintendant 1975-78, Sunday School Treasurer 1981 to present, Church Secretary 1982. Honors and Awards: Frances Anderson Day, proclaimed by peers and department co-workers, Mercy Hospital, 1979. Address: 5757 E. Sternberg Road, Fruitport, Michigan 49415.

Anderson, Gordon Wood

Research Physicist, Electronic Engineer. Personal: Born March 8, 1936; Son of Gordon Hilmer and Avis Elizabeth Hillman Anderson; Married Gillian Anne Bunshaft. Education: B.E.E., Cornell University, 1959; M.S. 1961, Ph.D. 1969, University of Illinois at Urbana-Champaign. Career: Research Physicist, Naval Research Laboratory, Washington, D.C., 1971 to present; Consultant, Planning and Human Systems, Inc., 1978-79; National Research Council Research Associate, Naval Research Laboratory, 1969-70; Ford Foundation Fellow, Research Assistant, Teaching Assistant, University of Illinois at Urbana-Champaign, 1959-69; Physics Teacher, Tougaloo College, 1965. Organizational Memberships: American Physical Society; Institute of Electrical and Electronics Engineers; American Association for the Advancement of Science; Foundation for Science and the Handicapped; Federation of American Scientists; Union of Concerned Scientists. Community Activities: Epilepsy Foundation of America (board of directors, 1979 to present; Washington area chapter president 1976-78, executive committee 1974 to present, founding member of the board of directors 1972-73, 1974 to present); Colonial Singers and Players, Inc. (secretary-treasurer; founding member of the board of directors, 1974 to present); District of Columbia Services for Independent Living, Inc. (founding member of the board of directors, 1981 to present); Cornell Club of Washington; University of Illinois Alumni Association; Capitol Hill Restoration Society; American Civil Liberties Union; Amnesty International; National Organization of Women; Alpine Club of Canada; Oesterreichischer Alpenverein; Sierra Club; Wilderness Society; Friends of the Earth; Environmental Defense Fund; Alpha Delta Phi. Religion: St. Mark's Episcopal Church, Convener 1980, Member 1979-81, Seminarian Lay Training Committee. Honors and Awards: Life Fellow, American Biographical Institute Research Association; Sigma Xi; Tau Beta Pi; Eta Kappa Nu; Ford Foundation Fellowship; National Science Foundation Grant to N.A.T.O. Surface Physics School; National Research Council Post-Doctoral Research Associate, 1969-70; Sloan Foundation National Scholarship; Cornell National Scholarship; William College Book Award; Red Key, Sphinx Head Undergraduate Honor Societies; Author, Papers in Field; Patent; Listed in *Who's Who in the East, American Men and Women of Science, Resource Directory of Handicapped Scientists, Directory of Distinguished Americans, Personalities of the East, Personalities of America, Community Leaders of America, Who's Who in Technology Today*. Address: 1320 North Carolina Avenue, N.E., Washington, D.C. 20002.

Anderson, James William

Ordained Minister. Personal: Born July 16, 1930; Son of William John Wylly Anderson (deceased); Married Carroll Wombacher; Father of James Carroll, Mark Christian. Education: B.S., Tulane University, 1952; B.D, Austin Presbyterian Theological Seminary, 1955; Attended Duke University Graduate School of Religion, 1958-61; Th.D., New Orleans Baptist Theological Seminary, 1976. Career: Pastor, Benton and Rocky Mount Presbyterian Churches, Louisiana, 1955-58; Pastor, Pittsboro Presbyterian Church, North Carolina, 1958-61; Pastor, Lockhart and Mount Tabor Presbyterian Churches, South Carolina, 1961-67; Teacher, Presbyterian College, Clinton, South Carolina, 1963-64; Pastor, Albany Presbyterian Church, Louisiana, 1968-74; Pastor, First Presbyterian Church, Ponchatoula, Louisiana, 1967 to present. Organizational Memberships: Presbyterian Historical Society; American Church Historical Society; Medieval Historical Society; Presbyterian Historical Society of the Southwest. Community Activities: Big Brother/Big Sister Program (board member, 1978-81); Youth Service Bureau of Tangipahoa Parish (board member, 1980 to present); Boy Scouts of America (executive board of Istrouma area council, 1978-80; chairman, Chappepeela district, 1978-80); District 684 of Rotary International (health, humanity and hunger program, 1978 to present); Ponchatoula Rotary Club (president, 1977-78; treasurer, 1978 to present). Religion: Chairman, Executive Committee and Council, Presbytery of South Louisiana, 1981; Chairman, Division of Care for Churches, 1979-80. Honors and Awards: Silver Beaver Award, Boy Scouts of America, 1981; Presidential and Lily Scholarships, Duke University, 1958-60; Tulane Presidential Scholarships, 1950-52; Aaron Hartmann Medal in Psychology, Tulane University, 1952. Address: P.O. Box 326, Ponchatoula, Louisiana 70454.

James W Anderson

Anderson, Margaret Tayler

Director of Career Counseling Service. Personal: Born May 1, 1918; Daughter of George L. and Tressie Huntington Tayler (both deceased); Married James Kress Anderson; Mother of Bret D., Blythe A. Knapp, Beth Lynn, Burke Stuart. Education: A.B. 1939, M.A. 1940, Willamette University; M.A. 1967, Professional Diploma 1970, Columbia University. Career: Director of Career Counseling Service, Rockland County Guidance Center; Associate Faculty, Empire State College, 1982 to present; Former Realtor, Vocalist, Adult Educator. Organizational Memberships: New York State Department of Education (member task force on counseling adults, 1982); National Association of Women Deans, Administrators and Counselors; American Personnel and Guidance Association; Rockland County Board of Realtors (president, 1967); National Association of Women in Junior and Community Colleges (northeast regional coordinator, 1974-77); Professional Women's Caucus (national president, 1973; vice president for programs, 1974); Cornell University Conference "Women in Mid-Life Crisis" (conference paper, 1976); National Adult Education Conference, Boston (conference paper, 1976). Community Activities: Rockland State Hospital (board of visitors); Candidate for County Clerk, Rockland County, 1961; Board Member of Day Care Centers and Rockland County Day Care Council; Rockland County Manpower Council, 1974 to present; Task Force for Adult Learner Project, Channel 13, 1977; New York State Education Department of Adult Education Systems Task Force, 1979. Honors and Awards: Business and Professional Women Award, 1967; Woman of the Year, American Association of University Women, 1979; Listed in *Who's Who of American Women, Who's Who in New York State*. Address: Route 9W, Box 257, Palisades, New York 10964.

Anderson, Mary Elizabeth

Government Official. Personal: Daughter of Mary E. Webber Anderson. Education: B.S., Virginia Union University; Post-Graduate Study undertaken at American University, Chicago College of Commerce, United States Department of Agriculture Graduate School; Executive Management Training, United States Department of Education. Career: Education Program Specialist, United States Department of Education; Former Counselor, Special Assistant, Virginia Union University; Representative, Women's National Advisory Council; High School Teacher; Fiscal Officer, Health, Education and Welfare Adult Education. Organizational Memberships: Women's National Advisory Council, 1976; American Association of School Administrators; Virginia Teachers Association. Community Activities: National Association for the Advancement of Colored People (life member; executive board of directors, Washington, D.C. chapter, 1975-77); National Alliance of Black School Educators (affiliate); D.C. Women's Political Caucus; Friends of Frederick Douglass Museum of African Art; Alpha Kappa Alpha; D.C. Citizens for Better Education. Religion: Church of the Redeemer, Presbyterian, Choir Member 1974 to present; Choir Member for Concert Tours, Virginia Union University. Published Works: Author, *Sex Equality in Education*; Co-Author, *History of United States Office of Education and Field Services*. Honors and Awards: Special Citation, United States Civil Service Commission, 1973; Scholarship to Virginia Union University; Distinguished Service Award, National Association for the Advancement of Colored People, 1976; Listed in *Who's Who Among Black Americans, Who's Who of Intellectuals, World Who's Who Among Women*. Address: 5300 Lansing Drive, Camp Springs, Maryland 20748.

Anderson, Ruth I

Professor of Business Administration. Personal: Born April 17, 1919. Education: B.S., Grove City College; M.C.S., E.D., Indiana University. Career: Instructor, United States Naval Training School, Bloomington, Indiana, 1943-44; Professor and Head, Department of Business Education and Secretarial Administration, Texas Christian University, 1946-53; Professor, School of Business, North Texas State University, 1953 to present; Visiting Summer Professor, University of Oregon, University of Colorado, New York University, University of Tennessee, Indiana University, Others. Organizational Memberships: Texas Business Education Association (past vice president); National Business Education Association (state membership chairman); Delta Pi Epsilon (national executive secretary, 1957-60; national president, 1964-65); Institute of Certifying Secretaries (chairman of education committee and research committee; associate dean and dean, 1953-59); National Association of Business Teacher Education (board member and program chairman, 1964-65); N.O.M.A. (national research committee, 1961); Mountain-Plains Convention, M.-P.B.E.A. (program chairman, 1963); Leadership Training Conference, 1964; Council for Business and Economic Education (3-year terms ending 1971); National Board for M.-P.B.E.A. and N.B.E.A., 1970-73. Community Activities: Denton County Heart Association (board of directors, 1962-63); Denton Business and Professional Women's Club (president, 1962-64); Fairhaven, Home for Senior Citizens (board of directors, 1957-70); City of Denton Board of Adjustments, 1969-75; Altrusa Club (president, 1973-74). Published Works: *Teaching Business Subjects; Complete College Typewriting; Secretarial Careers; 130 Basic Typewriting Jobs; Word Finder;* Over 85 Articles in Professional Business Education Publications and Yearbooks. Honors and Awards: Pi Gamma Mu; Pi Kappa Delta; Delta Pi Epsilon; Beta Gamma Sigma; Honorary Member, Pi Omega Pi, National Secretaries Association, Phi Chi Theta; Business Teacher of the Year, Fort Worth, 1955; Woman of the Year 1969, District Winner 1971, Business and Professional Women, Denton; Mountain-Plains Leadership Award, 1970; Distinguished Alumni Award, Grove City College, 1970; State Business Education Teacher of the Year, Texas, 1972; John Robert Gregg Award, 1972; Distinguished Teaching Award, North Texas State University Alumni Association, 1972; Piper Professor, Minnie L. Stephens Foundation, 1973; Special Recognition Award, Honors Day, North Texas State University, 1977; Listed in *Who's Who in American Education, Who's Who in the South and Southwest, Who's Who in Texas, Who's Who of American Women, Contemporary Authors, Directory of Prominent Women in Communications, Directory of British and American Writers, Community Leaders of America, Outstanding Educators of America, Who's Who in the World of Women.* Address: 810 Stanley, Denton, Texas 76201.

Anderson, Thomas Jefferson

Legislator. Personal: Born November 21, 1919; Married Margaret Anderson; Father of Laurel B. Moore, Eugene Thomas, Craig Jeffrey. Education: Ford Motor Co. Engineering School, 1946-48; U.S. Marine Corps Institute, 1946-51; U.S. Marine Corps Electronic Schools, 1950-51; U.S. Army Electronic Schools, 1943-45. Military: Served with the United States Army, achieving the rank of Technical Sergeant, 1943-46; Served with the United States Marine Corps Reserve, achieving the rank of Master Sergeant, 1946-51, active 1950-51. Career: Quality Analysis Engineer; Engineering Coordinator; Technical Writer, Ford Motor Company; Legislator, State of Michigan, 1965 to present. Organizational Memberships: Mayor, City of Southgate, Michigan, 1958-61; City Council (president, 1963-64); Ecorse Township (supervisor, 1953-58); Intergovernmental Science, Engineering and Technology Advisory Panel, 1975-81; National Conference of State Legislators (chairmanships, 1970 to present). Religion: Protestant. Honors and Awards: U.S. Environmental Protection Agency Awards in Environmental Activities; State, Federal and Organizational Awards: Audubon Society Awards; Michigan United Conservation Clubs and Soil Conservation Service Awards. Address: 13726 Sycamore, Southgate, Michigan 48195.

Wendell B Anderson

Anderson, Wendell Bernhard

Poet, Writer. Personal: Born January 10, 1920; Son of Gustav B. and Ebba Reed Anderson (both deceased); Married Emily Ferry. Education: Attended the University of Oregon, Reed College; B.A., Franklin Pierce College, 1969. Career: Writer, Poet; Former Teacher, Creative Writing, Hampshire Country School, Rindge, New Hampshire; Family Services Caseworker, New Hampshire Department of Public Welfare, 1969-73; Social Worker, New Mexico Department of Social Services, Child Welfare, 1973-75; Operator, Harwood Foundation Library Bookmobile Program, University of New Mexico, 1949-51; Served with 5 National Forests as Fire Control Aide; Clerk-Patrolman, United States Fish and Wildlife Service; United States Park Service Fire Control Aide, Bandelier National Monument, 1955. Organizational Memberships: Otero County Board for Alcoholism and Alcohol Abuse (board member, 1973-74); New Mexico Social Service Agency; Rio Grande Writers Association. Published Works: Collections of Poetry, *The Heart Must Be Half Eagle; Hawk's Hunger; Yes or No; Endangered Island; Season of the Crow; Rocky Mountain Vigil.* Honors and Awards: Ye Taborde Inn Writers Honorary, University of Oregon, 1940-42; Peter B. Allen Student Award for Excellence in English, Franklin Pierce College, 1969; Honors for Thesis for B.A. in English, 1969; Poems have been Anthologized. Address: 1002 La Quinta Street, Las Cruces, New Mexico 88005.

Andreoli, Kathleen Gainor

Director of Academic Affairs, Special Assistant to the President. Personal: Born September 22, 1935, Albany, New York; Daughter of Dr. and Mrs. John E. Gainor; Married Thomas E. Andreoli; Mother of Paula, Thomas, Karen. Education: B.S.N., Georgetown University School of Nursing, 1957; M.S.N., Vanderbilt University School of Nursing, 1959; D.S.N., University of Alabama School of Nursing, 1979. Career: The University of Texas Health Science Center at Houston: Special Assistant to the President and Director of Academic Affairs 1981 to present, Acting Dean of the School of Allied Health Sciences 1980-81, Special Assistant to the President for Educational Affairs 1979; University of Alabama Medical Center: Professor of Nursing 1979, Associate Professor of the Department of Public Health 1978, Associate Professor of Nursing 1977, Associate Director of the Family Nurse Practitioner Program 1976-77, Associate Professor of the School of Public and Allied Health 1973, Associate Professor of Nursing 1972, Assistant Professor of Nursing 1971, Clinical Associate Professor of Cardiovascular Nursing 1970, Educational Director of the Physician Assistant Program 1970-75; Duke University Medical Center Department of Medicine: Instructor-Coronary Care Unit Nursing Inservice Education 1965-70, Educational Coordinator of the Physician Assistant Program 1965-70; Instructor, Bon Secours Hospital School of Nursing, Baltimore, Maryland, 1962-64; Instructor, Duke University School of Nursing, 1960-61; Instructor, Georgetown University School of Nursing, 1959-60; Instructor, St. Thomas Hospital School of Nursing, Nashville, Tennessee, 1958-59; Staff Nurse, Albany Hospital Medical Center, Albany, New York, 1957. Organizational Memberships: Institute of Medicine of the National Academy of Sciences; American Academy of Nursing (fellow); American Nurses Association; National League of Nursing; American Association of Critical Care Nurses; American Heart Association Council on Cardiovascular Nursing; The Council of Family Nurse Practitioners and Clinicians; Alabama Academy of Science; Association of Physician's Assistant Programs (vice president, 1975-76); Sigma Theta Tau; Alpha Eta; Phi Kappa Phi; Texas State Forum, American Council on Education National Identification Program for Women in Higher Education Administration; Cancer Prevention and Control Advisory Committee, The University of Texas System Cancer Center. Published Works: Editorial Board, *Health News*, HEALTHFAX, Inc., New York, 1980 to present; Editorial Board, Texas

Health Letter, The University of Texas Health Science Center at Houston, 1980 to present; Co-Author *Comprehensive Cardiac Care;* Number of Professional Articles and Book Reviews. Honors and Awards: North Carolina Heart Association Founder's Award, 1970; Outstanding Service to Heart and Lung, *The Journal of Total Care*, 1972; Listed In *Outstanding Young Women of America, Who's Who in America, American Men and Women of Science, Who's Who of American Women, Who's Who in Health Care, Distinguished Leaders in Health Care* (inaugural edition), *The World Who's Who of Women in Education*. Address: 1604 Bissonnet, Houston, Texas 77005.

Andrews, Frank Meredith

Research Scientist, Professor. Personal: Born April 2, 1935. Education: B.A, Dartmouth College, 1957; Further Studies at the University of Sydney (Australia) and the New School for Social Research; Ph.D., University of Michigan, 1962. Career: Institute for Social Research, University of Michigan: Assistant Study Director 1959-61, Study Director 1962-68, Senior Study Director 1968-71, Program Director 1971 to present; Department of Psychology, University of Michigan: Lecturer 1963-67, Assistant Professor 1967-71, Associate Professor 1971-76, Professor 1976 to present; Professor, Population Planning Program, School of Public Health, University of Michigan, 1979 to present; Study Director, Russell Sage Foundation, 1959. Organizational Memberships: American Psychological Association; American Sociological Association; Society for International Development; American Statistical Association; International Sociological Association; Society for Social Studies of Science. Published Works: Books and Monographs include *A Study of Company-Sponsored Foundations; Creativity and the Scientist; Barriades de Lima: Dwellers' Attitudes Toward Public and Private Services; Comparative Studies of Life Quality;* Number of Articles and Chapters in Edited Books. Honors and Awards: B.A. magna cum laude with distinction in major; Rotary Foundation International Fellow, 1958; University of Michigan Rackham Fellow, 1961-62; Visiting Fellowship, Australian National University, 1974-75 (not used); Phi Beta Kappa; Sigma Xi; Listed in *American Men and Women of Science, Who's Who in America, International Authors and Writers Who's Who, Contemporary Authors*.

Anguiano, Lupe

Executive. Education: M.A., Antioch University, 1978. Career: President, Lupe Anguiano and Associates, 1982 to present; Founder, President and Chief Executive Officer, National Women's Employment and Education, Inc., 1977-81; Southwest Regional Director, Southwest Regional Office for the Spanish Speaking, National Council of Catholic Bishops, 1973-77; United States Department of Health, Education and Welfare: Program Chief Officer of Social and Rehabilitation Services 1973, Chief California Region Office for Civil Rights in Higher Education 1972, Women's Action Program Task Force 1970-71, Civil Rights Specialist; Southwest Regional Director, National Association for the Advancement of Colored People, Legal Defense and Education Fund, 1969; Appointed by President Lyndon B. Johnson to the Mexican-American Unit, United States Office of Education; 1967; Supervisor, Los Angeles Federation of Neighborhood Centers, United Way, 1965-66; Religious Teacher, Our Lady of Victory Missionary Sisters, 1949-65. Organizational Memberships: Appointed by Governor William Clements to the Advisory Council for Technical-Vocational Education in Texas; United States Department of Labor (monitoring committee); Association of General Contractors (Texas highway-heavy branch manpower advisory committee); National Association for Female Executives; National Chicana Foundation (founding member, founder board). Community Activities: International Women's Year National Conference (delegate for Texas, 1978); National Women's Political Caucus (founding member, advisory council); Greater San Antonio Chamber of Commerce (steering commitee, small business council). Published Works: Wrote and Published Six Handbooks "N.W.E.E. Model Program", 1981; Editor and Publisher, *Women and Employment*, 1978-80; *Report of the Women's Action Program*, 1972; Others. Honors and Awards: Liberty Bell Award, San Antonio Young Lawyers Association, 1982; Citation for Distinguished Service, Greater San Antonio Chamber of Commerce Small Business Council, 1980; Vista Award, 1980; Women of the 80's, *MS.* Magazine, 1980; Headliner Award, Women in Communications in San Antonio, 1978; Women of the Year, Texas Women's Political Caucus, 1978; Outstanding American Women of Mexican Descent, University of Texas, 1975; Outstanding Woman of the Year, 1972; California Delegate to the White House on Status of Mexican-Americans in the United States, 1967; Listed in *Who's Who in American Women, American Catholic Who's Who*. Address: 531 Marquette Avenue, San Antonio, Texas 78228.

Anjard, Ronald P Sr

Quality Control Manager. Personal: Born July 31, 1935; Son of Florence M. Anjard; Married Marie Sampler; Father of Ronald P. Jr., Michael P., John R., Michele M. Education: A.S., 1973; B.A. Humanities, 1979; B.S.B.A., 1978; B.S.M.E., 1957; M.S.I.A., 1963; P.D.E., 1979; Ph.D. Education, 1980; Ph.D. Metallurgical Engineering, 1981. Military: Served as a Captain in the United States Army. Career: Quality Control Manager, Johnson Matthey Inc., Electronic Materials Division, AVX Materials; President, A. G. Technology; Senior Engineer, General Motors, Delco Electronics Division; University of Phoenix, National University, Ball State University, Industrial Vocational Technical College; Anjard Enterprises and Imports. Organizational Memberships: A.S.T.M. (subcommittee national chairman); I.S.H.M. (midwest regional manager, industrial president); Indiana Trustees Association (5th district coordinator). Community Activities: Elected County Councilman, Ho County, Indiana, 1980; Elected Township Trustee, Ho County, Indiana, 1970-75; Member of Three State Committees; Sigma Xi; Numerous Local Leadership Positions; Heart Association (president); Lafayette Diocesan Pastoral Council (president); Greater Kokoma Association of Churches (president). Honors and Awards: General Motors Award; Young Republican National Hard Charger; Fellow, Truman Library; Author of Over 600 Publications. Address: 10942 Montego, San Diego, California 92124.

Antell, Morton F

Physician. Personal: Born May 17, 1937; Son of Ray Antell; Married Marilyn Engel; Father of Craig, Debra, Diane. Education: B.A., New York University, 1959; B.S., Columbia University, 1963; D.O., Chicago College of Osteopathy, 1969; Intern, Interboro General Hospital, 1970; Board Certified Family Practice. Career: Medical Administration, Brooklyn Community Health Center; Staff Member, Hillcrest Hospital, Deepdale Hospital, Parkway Hospital, Terrace Heights Hosipital; Former Pharmacist. Organizational Memberships: Kings County Health Care Review Organization, 1981; Queens County Health Care Review Organization, 1981; New York State A.O.A. (finance and budget committee); New York City A.O.A.; National A.O.A. Community Activities: United States Senatorial Business Advisory Board, Washington, D.C., 1980. Honors and Awards: New York State Regents Scholar, 1955; Listed in *Who's Who in the East, Men of Achievement, Personalities of America*. Address: 3384 Jason Court, Bellmore, New York 11710.

Anthony, Perry

Executive. Personal: Born July 8, 1940; Son of Frederick and Marjorie Anthony; Married Alyce Anderson; Father of Victoria Lynn,

Theordore Perry. Education: B.A., Grove City College, 1963; Undertook Post-Graduate Studies, Newark State University, 1964-65. Career: Vice President, Household Goods Division, Allied Van Lines, Inc.; Former Manager, National Distribution, Westinghouse Appliance Division; Manager of Marketing Communications, Westinghouse Electric Corporation. Organizational Memberships: American Movers Conference Representative to the American Trucking Association's Energy Committee; National Traffic Club; Household Carriers Bureau. Community Activities: Chamber of Commerce. Address: 1111 Ridgewood Avenue, Omaha, Nebraska 68124.

Antoun, M Lawreace

Nun, College President. Personal: Born December 30, 1927; Daughter of George K. and Freda Habib Antoun. Education: B.S., Villa Maria College, 1954; M.S. 1959, Ph.D. (A.B.D.) 1965, University of Notre Dame. Career: Entered the Sisters of Saint Joseph, 1947; Villa Maria College: Instructor of Chemistry 1955-61, Assistant Professor of Chemistry 1965-66, President 1966 to present. Organizational Memberships: National Fuel Gas (board of directors audit committee); Pennsylvania Post-Secondary Education Planning Commission/1203 Commission (chairperson); Pennsylvania State Board of Education (chairperson of council of higher education and of advisory committee). Community Activities: Commission for Independent Colleges and Universities (executive board); Commonwealth Judicial Council; Cornell University (advisory board, human ecology); Erie Conference on Community Development (board of directors); Hamot Medical Center (board of corporators); King's College (board of trustees, student affairs); McMannis Education Trust Fund (chairperson, advisory council); Middle States Association, Commission of Higher Education (planning consultant); Saint Vincent Health Center (board of corporators). Religion: Catholic. Honors and Awards: Atomic Energy Commission Grant for Research in Chemistry; Honorary Doctorate, Gannon University; Award for Distinguished Service, Pennsylvania Association of Adult Education; Listed in *International Who's Who of Women; The World's Who's Who of Women, Outstanding Educators of America, Who's Who in Religion, Who's Who of American Women, Community Leaders and Noteworthy Americans, Contemporary Personalities.* Address: Villa Maria College, 2551 West Lake Road, Erie, Pennsylvania 16505.

Clara T Appell

Appell, Clara Taubman

Family Therapist, Executive, Consultant. Personal: Born July 31, 1921; Daughter of Max and Yetta Schuber Taubman (both deceased); Married Morey L. Appell (deceased); Mother of Laurie, Randy Johnson, Glenn, Jodie, Jonathan. Education: B.S. 1942, M.A. 1946, Ohio State University; Ed.D., Columbia University, 1959; Undertook Post-Doctoral Studies, Academic-Clinical Program, Ackerman Institute for Family Therapy, 1971-73. Career: Consultant on Human Development; Private Practice in Family Therapy; President, Morey L. Appell Human Relations Foundation; Lecturer, University of Connecticut, 1982 to present; Adjunct Professor, Queens College, City University of New York, 1975-79; Title XX Project Associate, University of Connecticut-Stamford, 1978-79; Consultant, Butterick Publications, Risp Series of Filmstrips, 1979-80; Co-Director of Family Life Center, New York Society of Ethical Culture, 1972-73; Coordinator of Child Development and Family Life Education, Greenwich Health Association, 1969-71; Consultant, Connecticut State Department of Education, 1968-69; Director, Home Care Training and Child Development Family Specialist, Bank State College, 1967-68; Professor of Child Development and Family Relations and Head Start Coordinator, University of Wisconsin-Stout, 1966-67; Associate Professor of Child Development and Family Life and Co-Director of Family Life Institute, Indiana State University, 1964-66; Child Guidance League Parent Educator, Brooklyn, New York, 1954-61; Brooklyn College, City University of New York, 1954-61; Home Economics Teacher, Long Island City High School, 1947-48; Educational Director, Day Care Center, Colony House, Brooklyn, 1946-47; High School Teacher, 1943-46. Organizational Memberships: American Association for Marriage and Family Therapy (programs chairperson, Connecticut division, 1978); American Association of Sex Educators, Counselors and Therapists; American Orthopsychiatric Association (fellow); American Home Economics Association; American Psychological Association; Forum for Death Education and Counseling; International Council of Psychologists; Groves Conference on Marriage and Family; National Council on Family Relations; Tri-State Council on Family Relations (treasurer, 1958-59); Society for Research in Child Development. Community Activities: Morey L. Appell Human Relations Foundation (founder and president, 1978 to present); Hospice of Stamford, Inc. (volunteer consultant, 1981-82); Connecticut Media and Communications Task Force for White House Conference on Families, 1979-80; Mothering Center, Inc., Cos Cob, Connecticut (board member, 1979 to present); Stamford Family Life Workshops, Inc. (board member, 1979-80); Public Service Radio Program Hostess/Moderator, "Family Talk", WGCH-AM, Greenwich, Connecticut, 1974-80; Connecticut Association of Marriage and Family Counselors, Court Judicial Department, Family Conciliation Courts (chairperson, state conference, divorce collaboration); Groves Conference (program committee, 1978); National Family Life Education Workshop (planning committee, 1971); Indiana State University Auspices Radio & TV Series, Co-Host "Family Talk", 1964-66; Talks, Seminars, Workshops to Professionals and Community Groups, 1953 to present; Child Study Association of America (book committee, 1950-61); Community Newspaper Column Co-Author, "Living with Our Children", 1951-53. Religion: Speaker at Numerous Religiously Sponsored Meetings of Church Groups, Jewish Groups, Young Women's Christian Association; Member of Mental Health Professionals, Sponsored by Jewish Family Service of Stamford, Connecticut. Honors and Awards: Fellow, International Council of Sex Education and Parenthood, 1981; Certificate of Appreciation, Gateway Dental Hygienists, 1980; Greenwich Kiwanis Certificate of Appreciation, 1975; Ohio State University Diamond Anniversary Award Recipient in Home Economics, 1971; Omicron Nu; Delta Kappa Pi; Pi Lambda Theta; Graduate Fellowship, Ohio State University, 1945-46; Listed in *Who's Who of American Women.* Address: 145 Old Church Road, Greenwich, Connecticut 06830.

Mahmoud Z Arafat

Arafat, Mahmoud Zaky

Civil Engineer. Personal: Born February 20, 1935, in Cairo, Egypt; Son of Zaky Ibrahim Arafat (deceased) and Fahima Ahmed Gad; Married Helen So-Ching; Father of Tarek. Education: B.S., distinction, Ein-Shams University, Cairo, 1957; Ph.D., Scientific Research Institute of Concrete and Reinforced Concrete, Moscow, U.S.S.R., 1965; Undertook postgraduate studies at the Urban Institute of the University of Paris, 1970-71. Career: Assistant Professor, School of Civil Engineering, Ein-Shams University, 1966-69; Associate Professor of Engineering, Pratt Institute, Brooklyn, New York, 1979-80; Consultant and Research Engineer internationally, 1960 to present; Building Official, City of Jersey City; Supervising Principal Engineer, City of Jersey City, New Jersey, present; Licensed Professional Engineer in New York, New Jersey, France, Egypt. Organizational Memberships: American Society of Civil Engineers; American Concrete Institute; Prestressed Concrete Institute; Prestressed Concrete Institute Committee on Precast Prestressed Concrete Storage Tanks (chairman). Honors and Awards: Listed in *Dictionary of International Biography, Who's Who in the Arab World, Directory of Distinguished Americans, Book of Honor, Who's Who in Finance and Industry*, Others. Address: 51 A Sherman Place, Jersey City, New Jersey 07307.

Aranda, Juan M

Physician. Personal: Born February 3, 1942; Son of Juan M. and Eva Aranda; Married Carmen Amador; Father of Juan, Robert,

Mary, Elizabeth, David. Education: B.S., University of Puerto Rico; M.D., 1967, Internship, 1968, Residency in Internal Medicine, 1971, all at the University of Puerto Rico School of Medicine; Cardiology Fellowship, University of Miami School of Medicine, 1974. Military: Served with the United States Army Medical Corps in the rank of Major, 1971-73. Career: Chief, Department of Medicine, Beach Army Hospital, Fort Walters, Texas, 1972-73; Assistant Chief, Cardiac Catheterization Laboratory, Veterans Administration Hospital, 1974-76; Assistant Professor of Medicine, University of Miami School of Medicine, 1974-77; Adjunct Associate Professor of Medicine, University of Miami School of Medicine, 1977 to present; Associate Professor of Medicine, University of Puerto Rico School of Medicine, 1977 to present; Chief Cardiology Service, Veterans Administration Hospital, San Juan, Puerto Rico, 1977 to present. Organizational Memberships: American Federation of Clinical Research, 1978; Southern Society of Clinical Investigation, 1978; Puerto Rico Society of Cardiology (president, 1981). Honors and Awards: United States Army Commendation Medal, 1973; Harry Botwick Memorial Award for Superior Performance as a Cardiology Fellow, 1973; Bulletin of the Puerto Rican Medical Association, (editorial board 1977-1978, editor 1977-82), Revista Latina de Cardiologia, 1978; Fellow, American College of Cardiology, 1979; Fellow, International College of Angiology, 1978. Service Award, Veterans Administration Hospital, 1980. Address: Palmasola Street H-A-7, Guaynabo, Puerto Rico.

Arango, Abelardo de Jesus

General and Vascular Surgeon. Personal: Born July 6, 1944; Son of Dr. Abelardo and Julia Arango (both deceased); Married Janet Rossi; Father of Julia, Jannette, Abelardo, David Anthony. Education: M.D., cum laude, University of Antioquia, Medellin, Colombia; N.I.H. Research Fellow in Liver Diseases, University of Miami, 1968; Fellow in Surgery, University of Texas Southwestern, Medical School of Dallas, 1974; American Board of Surgery, 1974; Fellow, American College of Surgeons, 1977; Fellow, American College of Gastroenterology, 1980; Fellow, American Society of Abdominal Surgeons, 1981. Career: Chief Surgical Resident, Jackson Memorial Hospital, University of Miami School of Medicine, 1972-73; Clinical Instructor, Department of Surgery, University of Miami School of Medicine, 1973-74; Visiting Assistant Professor, University of Texas Southwestern Medical School, 1973-74; Assistant Professor of Surgery, Department of Surgery, University of Miami School of Medicine, 1975-80; Clinical Assistant Professor, Department of Surgery, University of Miami School of Medicine, 1981 to present. Organizational Memberships: Dade County Medical Society; Florida Medical Association; American Medical Association; Southern Medical Association; American Gastroenterology Association; New York Academy of Science; American Trauma Society; Florida Association of General Surgery; Dade-Monroe Professional Standards Review Organization. Religion: Catholic. Honors and Awards: Manuel Uribe Award, University of Antioquia, 1967. Address: 17203 S.W. 79th Place, Miami, Florida 33157.

David Arant

Arant, David Eugene

Professor. Personal: Born April 17, 1935; Father of Brenda Luyben, Bradford Arant. Education: B.S., Accounting, Pepperdine University, 1957; M.S., Business Education, University of Southern California, 1960; Candidate for Ph.D., International College, Westwood, California, 1981. Career: Treasurer, Veteran Escrow Company, Inc.; Professor of Accounting, Los Angeles Metropolitan College of Business; Exchange Specialist, Thom Major and Associates; Professor of Management, Harbor College, 16 years; Film Representative, Los Angeles Harbor College, 12 years; Faculty President, Los Angeles Metropolitan College, 1963; Owner, Dave Arant Realty; Owner, "Synthicomp" (computer development company). Organizational Memberships: Delta Pi Epsilon; California Association of Realtors; Alpha Gamma Sigma; Pi Gamma Mu. Community Activities: National Association of Realtors; Torrance-Lomita-Carson Board of Realtors. Honors and Awards: V.A. Film Grant, 1973; Cited for Innovation in Educational Methodology, 1975; Gold Card Holder, National Exchangers Association, 1981; Contribution Citation to Research and Development Programs of Real Estate Counseling Principles, Advanced Education and the Professionalization of the Real Estate Business, Research Institute of Counselists, 1981; Listed in *Who's Who in the West, International Who's Who of Intellectuals, Community Leaders of America.* Address: 1890 Peninsula Verde Dr., Lomita, California 90717.

Arauz, Carlos Gaspar

Government Official. Personal: Born January 6, 1949; Son of A. A. Arauz; Married Ana Isabel Alvarez; Father of Barbara Ann. Education: B.S, Loyola University at Los Angeles, 1970; M.S., Georgia Institute of Technology, 1975. Career: Government Official, City of Miami; Industrial Psychology Consultant; Director of Personnel. Organizational Memberships: International Personnel Management Association (president, southern region, 1981-82); Florida Public Personnel Association (state chairman, 1978-79); American Society for Public Administration; American Society for Personnel Administration. Community Activities: New World Bicultural Generation Inc. (board of directors); Leadership Miami Alumni Association; Partners for Youth; Committee to Aid the Cuban Refugees that Arrived in the Freedom Flotilla. Religion: Roman Catholic. Honors and Awards: Young Personnel Professional Award, International Personnel Management Association, Metro Atlanta Chapter, 1975; Citation for Work with Cuban Refugees, City of Miami, 1980; Listed in *Who's Who in the South and Southwest.* Address: 9820 S.W. 120 Street, Miami, Florida 33176.

Carlos J Arboleya

Arboleya, Carlos J

Banking Executive. Personal: Born February 1, 1929; Son of Fermin Arboleya, (deceased); Ana Quiros; Married Marta Quintana, on August 29, 1954, in San Cristobal, Pinar del Rio, Cuba; Father of Carlos Jr. Education: Graduate, Stuyvesant High School, New York; Undertook Courses in Commercial and Administrative Law, Accounting and Commercial Science, Havana University, Cuba. Career: Teacher: Bankers Institute, Havana; American Institute of Banking, Miami, Florida; Bank Administration Institute, Miami; Duquesne University, School of Business Administration, Pittsburgh, Pennsylvania; University of Miami, School of Business Administration, Miami; University of Southern California, School of Business Administration; Lecturer in Banking and Finance, Americanism vs. Communism, Scouting, Youth Work, Cuban Influx to the Miami Area, Free Enterprise System, Investing in America, Businessman's Role in the Community, Enthusiasm - "The Magic in Man"; Office Boy - Manager of the Trust and Fiduciary Department, Main Havana Branch, First National City Bank of New York, Havana, Cuba, 1946-57; Assistant Manager, The Trust Company of Cuba, Havana, 1957-59; Comptroller's Division Chief Auditor, Banco Continental Cubano, Havana, 1959-60; Clerk - Office Manager and Comptroller, Allure Shoe Corporation, Miami, 1960-62; Operations Officer, Personnel Director, Cashier, Vice President, Secretary to the Board of Directors, Boulevard National Bank, Miami, 1962-66; Executive Vice President and Cashier, President and Director, President and Vice Chairman of the Board, Fidelity National Bank of South Miami, 1966-73; Co-Owner, President, Organizer, Director, Chairman of the Board, The Flagler Bank, Miami, 1973-75; President and Director, Barnett Bank at Westchester, Miami, 1975-76; President and Director, Barnett Bank at Midway, Miami, 1975-76; Chairman of the Board, Barnett Bank BankAmericard Center, Miami, 1975-76; President and Chief Operating Officer and Director, Consolidated Barnett Banks of Miami (8 Offices), 1977 to present; Chairman of the Board and Chief Executive Officer, Barnett Bank BankAmericard Center, 1977 to present; President, Barnett Leasing Company, 1977 to present. Organizational Memberships: Banker's Club, Havana, Cuba (director, sports commissioner); City Bank Club, Havana (past president and director); National Amateur Athletic Association; Quivican Amateur Athletic Union; American Institute of Banking (board of governors, vice president); National Association for Bank Audit Control (director); Bank Administration Institute (past president and director); InterAmerican Association of Businessmen (director); Bankers Advisory Board of the Latin Chamber of Commerce (past president and director); Dade County Bankers Association (director); Small Business Administration (district advisory council); National Advisory Council for Economic Opportunity; Invest in America National Council (board of governors); American Arbitration Association (director); Florida Bankers Association (economic development committee, board member). Community Activities: Children's Rehabilitation Center Committee, Havana; Baseball Little League, Havana; Cuban Olympic Committee (director); National Softball Association (director); Havana University Honor Athletes Association (director); Junior Achievement (advisor); Sts. Peter and Paul Youth Center (manager); Tamiami Kiwanis Club; Young Men's Christian Association International Jose Marti (director); March of Dimes (director); Dade County Association for Retarded Children (director); Leukemia Society of America (trustee); Latin Chamber of Commerce (economic advisor); Citizens Advisory Planning Committee; State of Florida Latin American Affairs Committee (director); International Affairs Action Committee (director); Bi-Racial Commission of Dade County; United Fund (co-chairman, Latin-American division); National Health Agencies (director); Heart Association of Greater Miami (director); Heart Sunday Drive Fund (director); Catholic Committee on Scouting (chairman, Archdiocese of Miami); Speak Up for America Program (director); Third Century U.S.A. Committee (director); Keep Florida Beautiful (director); Boy Scouts of America (assistant council commissioner, council advancement chairman, council executive board); American Red Cross (director); Museum of Science (director); Ballet Concerto of Miami (director); Catholic Committee on Scouting (national executive board, director); Duquesne University, School of Business Administration (board of advisors). Religion: Catholic. Honors and Awards: Certificate of Merit, American Heart Association, 1965; Distinguished Service to Youth Award, Young Men's Christian Association, 1968; Distinguished Service Award, Bank Administration Institute, 1968; Banker of the Year, 1978; Knighted to the Order of St. John of Jerusalem, Knights of Hospitalier, Knights of Malta, 1979; Listed in *Florida Lives, Who's Who in Florida, National Society Directory, Personalities of the South, Who's Who in the South and Southwest, Who's Who in Banking, Who's Who in Industry and Finance, Community Leaders of America, Two Thousand Men of Achievement, Prominent Cuban Families, Who's Who in Commerce and Industry, International Who's Who in Community Service.* Address: 1941 S.W. 23 St., Miami, Florida 33145.

Arbuckle, Wendell S

Professor Emeritus, Dairy and Food Consultant. Personal: Born March 11, 1911; Son of Charles E. and Julia Barton Arbuckle (both deceased); Married; Father of J. Gordon, Wendy Ellen Wood. Education: B.S.A., Purdue University, 1933; A.M., 1937 and Ph.D., 1940, University of Missouri. Career: Earlham Farms, Richmond, Indiana, 1933-36; University of Missouri, Columbia, 1936-41; Texas A&M, College Station, 1941-46; North Carolina State University, 1946-49; University of Maryland, College Park, 1949-72; Professor Emeritus, 1972 to present; Consultant, Dairy and Food Industry, 1972 to present. Organizational Memberships: Institute of Food Technology, 1957 to present; American Dairy Science Association, 1936 to present; Maryland-District of Columbia Dairy Technology Society, 1949 to present (president); Sigma Xi; Dairy Shrine. Community Activities: Boy Scouts of America; Kiwanis; Scientist Cliffs Association; Pachaderms. Religion: Methodist. Honors and Awards: Distinguished Service Award, Dairy Technology Society of Maryland and District of Columbia, 1972; Honorary Life Member, Dairy Technology Society of Maryland and District of Columbia, 1978; Emeritus Professor, Dairy Science, University of Maryland, 1972; Maryland Dairy Shrine Hall of Fame, 1975; Life Member, American Dairy Science Association, 1972; Outstanding Alumnus, Scottsburg, Indiana, High School, 1980. Address: 4602 Harvard Road, College Park, Maryland 20740.

W S Arbuckle

Archer, Lloyd Daniel

Director of Media, Assistant Professor. Personal: Son of Dallas L. and Wilma C. Archer; Married Carol Sue Archer; Father of Elisa Carol. Education: B.S., M.S., Indiana University. Career: Director of Media and Assistant Professor, Fort Valley State College. Address: 224 Kinsbury Circle, Warner Robins, Georgia 31093.

Archer, Violet Balestreri

Retired Composer, Pianist, Adjudicator, Professor of Music. Personal: Born April 24, 1913; Daughter of Cesar Balestreri and Beatrice Azzi Archer (both deceased). Education: Teachers Licentiate in Piano 1934; B.Mus. 1936, McGill University; Associate Diploma, Royal Canadian College of Organists, 1938; B.Mus. 1948, M.Mus. 1949, Yale University; Honorary D.Mus., McGill University, 1971. Career: Music Instructor, McGill University, 1943-47; Music Instructor, University of Alberta, Summers 1948, 1949; Resident Composer, North Texas State University, 1950-53; Visiting Professor of Music, Cornell University, Summer 1952; Assistant Professor of Music, University of Oklahoma, 1953-61; University of Alberta: Associate Professor of Music 1962-70, Professor of Music 1970-78, Chairman of the Division of Theory and Composition 1962-78, Professor Emerita 1978 to present; Resident Composer, Banff School of Fine Arts, Summers 1978, 1979. Organizational Memberships: Sigma Alpha Iota (honorary member); Pi Kappa Lambda; Canadian Music Center; American Music Center; Canadian League of Composers (selection committee, 1974-76; council member, 1975-77); Canadian Federation of Music Teachers; Alberta Registered Music Teachers' Association; Music Educator's Association; Canadaian Folk Music Society (executive committee representing Alberta, 1964-67); Canadian Music Library Association; International Music Library Association; International Folk Music Council; Canadian Association of University Schools of Music (theory and composition committee, 1965-70); Royal Canadian College of Organists Association; College Music Society; Edmonton Chamber Music Society; Edmonton Musicians Association Local 390 A.F. of M.; P.R.O. Canada Ltd.; Unione Della Legion D'oro (learned society of Rome, Italy); American Association of University Composers; Canadian Federation of University Women; Canadian Music Competition (board member, second vice president); The Society of Music Theory; Alberta Composers Association (first vice president; founder); American Women Composers, Inc. (associate member); Frau und Music, Interationaler Arbeitskreis (composer member); Canadian Music Centre, Prairie Region (counsel member); Latitude 53, Society of Artists (board member); Okanagan Music Festival for Composers (executive committee); Alberta Registered Music Teachers Association (honorary life member); Canadian Federation of Music Teachers Association (honorary life member); Association of Canadian Women Composers (composer member). Published Compositions: "Three Scenes for Piano", "Sonatina #2 for Piano", "Twenty-Third Psalm for Medium Voice and Piano", Minute Music for Small Hands", "Ten Folk Songs for Four Hands", "O Lord Thou Hast Searched Me and Known Me", "I Will Lift Up Mine Eyes", "A La Claire Fontaine", "Proud Horses", Many, Many Others. Honors and Awards: Composition Trophy, Quebec Music Festival, 1937; Four Scholarships for Composition, McGill University, 1940-44; Grants for Study Abroad, Quebec Government, 1947, 1948; Bradley Keeler Memorial Scholarship, Yale University, 1947; Charles Ditson Fellowship, Yale University, 1948; Woods Chandler Prize for Composition, Yale University, 1949; Bursary for Study Abroad, Ladies Morning Musical Club, Montreal, 1949; Fellowship to MacDowell Colony, MacDowell Club of Oklahoma City, 1956; Canada Council Senior Fellowship, 1958-59; Citation for Distinguished Service in the Field of Music, Yale School of Music, 1968; Merit Award, Government of Alberta, 1970; Honorary Degree of Music, McGill University, 1971; Creative and Performance Award, City of Edmonton, 1972; Certificate of Appreciation for Significant Contributions in the Field of "Women in the Arts", City of Edmonton, 1976; Guest Lecturer and Composer, "Women in Music", School of Music, University of Oklahoma, 1976; Queen's Jubilee Silver Medal for Long and Distinguished Service in the Field of Music, 1978; Life Academic Member, The Accademia Tiberina, Rome, Italy, 1979; Award for Outstanding Success in the Concert Music Field, Performing Rights Organization of Canada, Ltd., 1981; Listed in *Who's Who in the World, The Book of Honor, Who's Who in Alberta, International Who's Who in Community Service, International Register of Profiles, World's Who's Who in Music, International Who's Who in Music and Musician's Directory, Men and Women of Distinction, The New Groves Dictionary of Music and Musicians, Larousse de la Musique, Living Music of the Americas, The Oklahoma Almanac, The American Women's Who's Who, The Canadian Who's Who, Two Thousand Women of Achievement, Who's Who in the West, The Blue Book, Dictionary of International Biography, Who's Who in America, Compositeurs Contemporains Canadiens,* Others. Address: 10805 85th Avenue, Edmonton, Alberta, Canada T6E 2L2.

Armstrong, Anne L

Executive. Personal: Born December 27, 1927; Daughter of Armant and Olive (Martindale) Legendre; Married Tobin Armstrong; Mother of John Barclay, Katharine A., Sarita S., Tobin Jr. and James L. (twins). Education: Graduate, Foxcroft High School, Middleburg, Virginia, 1945; B.A., Vassar College, 1949. Career: Counsellor to the President, Cabinet rank to Presidents Nixon and Ford, 1973-74; U.S. Ambassador to Great Britain, 1976-77; Board of Directors: Boise Cascade, First City Bancorporation of Texas, General Foods, General Motors, Halliburton. Organizational Memberships: Center for Strategic and International Studies, Georgetown University (chairman of advisory board, vice chairman of executive board, 1977 to present); Smithsonian Institution (citizen regent, board of regents, 1978 to present); Southern Methodist University (board of trustees, 1977 to present); John F. Kennedy School of Government, Harvard University (visiting committee, 1978 to present); Bob Hope U.S.O. Center Campaign (co-chairman, 1979 to present); President's Foreign Intelligence Advisory Board (chairman 1981 to present). Religion: Episcopalian. Honors and Awards: Honorary Doctor of Laws Degree: Bristol University, England (1976), Washington & Lee University (1976), Williams College (1977), St. Mary's University (1978), Tulane University (1978); Republican Woman of the Year Award, 1979; Texan of the Year, 1981; Gold Medal, National Institute of Social Sciences for Distinguished Service to Humanity, 1977. Address: Armstrong Ranch, Armstrong, Texas 78338.

Arnaboldi, Joseph Paul

Retired Veterinarian. Personal: Born December 2, 1920, Union City, New Jersey; Married Mary Louise Shoemaker, August 24, 1944; Father of Allan Charles, Sally-Jo Ann, Loren Joseph. Education: D.V.M., Cornell University Veterinary College of New York, 1943. Military: Served in the United Staes Army Veterinary Corps, 5th Service Command and 14th Air Force, 1943-46, achieving the rank of Captain. Career: Veterinarian, General Practice in Port Jefferson, New York, 1946-81, Owner Port Jeff Animal Hospital; Retired 1981; Protestant Minister, A.M.E. Church, Ordained 1966; Associate Minister, Setauket Bethel A.M.E. Church, Setauket, New York, 1966 to present; Interim Pastor, First Baptist Church, Port Jefferson, 1975; Long Island Council of Churches WALK Radio Ministry, 1975-77. Organizational Memberships: Long Island Veterinary Medical Association (president, 1952); American Society of Composers, Authors, and Publishers. Community Activities: Port Jefferson Rotary Club (president, 1959-62); Rotary International District 725 (governor, 1970-71); Northern Brookhaven Toastmasters Club (founder, charter president, 1959; area governor district 46, Toastmasters International); Setauket Parent Teacher Association (past president); Noble Grand of Port Jefferson, International Order of Odd Fellows; First Park Commissioner of Incorporated Village of Port Jefferson. Honors and Awards: Able Toastmasters Certificate; Toastmasters International Hall of Fame; Life Member, Northern Brookhaven Toastmasters Club; Rotary International Paul Harris Fellow. Address: P.O. Box 3, Port Jefferson, New York 11777.

Leo Arsen

Arnold, Sheila

Legislator. Personal: Born January 15, 1929; Married George Longan Arnold; Mother of Michael, Peter, (stepsons) Drew, George, Joe. Education: Undertook Several College Courses. Career: Wyoming State Legislature, 1978 to present; Former Secretary, Researcher, Homemaker. Organizational Memberships: State Land Use Advisory Committee (member; secretary, 1975-79); Legislative Mines, Minerals and Industrial Development Committee; Highways and Transportation Committee. Community Activities: Laramie Area Chamber of Commerce (president, 1982; former member of executive board; former chairman, legislative action committee); League of Women Voters (state land use chairman, 1974); University of Wyoming Faculty Women's Club (past president); Jane Jefferson Democratic Women's Club (past president); Laramie Women's Club; Albany County Democratic Central Committee (past vice-chairman); Democratic State Committeewoman, 1977-79. Honors and Awards: Top Hand Award, Laramie Area Chamber of Commerce, 1977. Address: 1058 Alta Vista Drive, Laramie, Wyoming 82070.

Arsen, Leo

Insurance Executive. Personal: Born March 22, 1933; Married to Barbara; Father of Steve, Stephanie, John, Aron. Military: Served with United States Air Force, 1951-55. Career: Vice President of Union Bankers Insurance, Dallas, Texas; Former Vice President of National Bankers Life. Organizational Memberships: Texas Association of Life Underwriters; National Association of Life Underwriters; National Association of Health Underwriters; Meeting Planners International. Community Activities: Member City Council of Frisco, Texas, 1978 to present; Mayor pro-tem, City of Frisco, 1981 to present; Y.M.C.A. Coach, 1966-70. Honors and Awards: Athletic Scholarship, University of Southern California, 1951; Received 5 Battle Stars for service in the Korean Conflict; Member of World-wide U.S. Air Force Track and Field Team, 1954. Address: 600 Humingbird, Frisco, Texas 75034.

Artemel, Engin M

Director of Planning and Community Development. Personal: Born July 31, 1938; Son of Belkis Artemel; Married Janice Finch; Father of Suzan, Deniz, Sibel. Education: A.A., Santa Ana College; B.S. Architecture, B.S.C.E., M.Arch., University of Kansas. Military: Served in the Navy, 1970-72, achieving the rank of Lieutenant. Career: Director of Planning and Community Development, City of Alexandria, Virginia; Former United Nations Consultant, Professor of Urban Planning. Organizational Memberships: American Institute of Certified Planners; American Society of Public Administrators; Partners for Livable Spaces. Community Activities: Rotary Club International; Environmental Quality Advisory Council, Fairfax County, Virginia; United Way (executive committee). Religion: Moslem. Honors and Awards: Excellence in Design Award, American Institute of Architects National Capital Area Chapter; Award, National Capital Area Chapter, American Planning Association. Address: 33 West Myrtle Street, Alexandria, Virginia 22301.

Artman, Paul Compton Jr

Broadcasting Executive. Personal: Born July 21, 1951; Son of Mr. and Mrs. Paul Artman; Married Barbara Deaton; Father of Paul Compton III, Catherine Clare. Education: B.S.E. 1973, M.Ed. 1975, Delta State University. Career: Broadcasting Executive; Former Teacher. Organizational Memberships: National Association of Broadcasters. Community Activities: Chamber of Commerce; National Right to Life Committee (board of directors); National Right to Life Political Action Committee (board of directors); Mississippi Right to Life (president); Delta Children's Museum (board of directors); Greenville (Mississippi) United Way (board of directors); Kappa Alpha (alumnus advisor); Local Keep America Beautiful Program (board of directors); Knights of Columbus (grand knight, president). Religion: St. Joseph's Catholic Church, Parish Council, Commissioned as Lay Minister. Honors and Awards: Kappa Alpha Order's Court of Honor; Knight of the Year, Knights of Columbus, 1980-81; Listed in Several Biographical Directories. Address: 729 Shattuck Street, Greenville, Mississippi 38701.

Ashbridge, G Harry

Business Executive. Personal: Born December 22, 1929; Son of Harry and Laura Ashbridge; Married Donna D Ashbridge; Father of Stephen, Susan, Brian, (Stepson) Casey Franklin. Military: Served with the United States Naval Reserve, 1949-53, and the United States Army, 1953-55. Career: Development Engineer, Burroughs Corporation; Manager, Product Planning, Bryant Computer Products, Ampex Computer Co. and General Electric; Vice President, Product Planning, Telex Computer; Vice President, Business Ventures, Control Data Corporation. Organizational Memberships: Institute of Electrical and Electronic Engineers. Community Activities: Christian Literature Evangelism (treasurer); Triangle Fraternity; Tulsa Metro Chamber of Commerce. Honors and Awards: American Legion Award, 1945; Alfred G. Hill Scholarship, 1948; United States Naval Scholarship, 1949; Rotary Scholarship, 1949; Addy Award; Author and Patentee. Address: 8501 W. 133 St., Apple Valley, Minnesota 55124.

Ashby, Eugene Christopher

Regents' Professor. Personal: Born October 25, 1930; Son of Mrs. A. Ashby; Married Carolyn Bruce; Father of Eugene C. Jr., Stephen Richard, Terrance Charles, Marie Elise, Julie Suzanne, Angela Dianne, Rachel Kathleen. Education: B.S., Loyola University of the South, 1951; M.S., Auburn University, 1953; Ph.D., University of Notre Dame, 1956. Military: Served with the United States Army Reserve, 1947-51, achieving the rank of Staff Sergeant. Career: Research Associate, Ethyl Corporation, Baton Rouge, Louisiana, 1956-63; Regents' Professor of Chemistry, Georgia Institute of Technology, 1963 to present. Organizational Memberships: American Chemical Society; Sigma Xi; Editorial Advisory Board: *Journal of Organic Chemistry, Organometallics;* International Conference on Organometallic Chemistry (chairman, international advisory board, 1981-83). Community Activities: Assistance to Offenders; Youth Counselling. Religion: Catholic; Sunday School Teacher, 1965 to present. Published Works: Over 200 publications in leading chemical journals. Honors and Awards: Lavoisier Medal, French Chemical Society, 1971; Research Award, Sigma Xi, 1968, 1975. Address: 2516 Flair Knoll Dr., Atlanta, Georgia 30345.

Ashley, Leonard R(aymond) N(elligan)

Professor. Personal: Born December 5, 1928; Son of Leonard Seville and Sarah Anne Constance Nelligan Ashley (both deceased). Education: B.A., first class honors, 1949, and M.A., 1950, both from McGill University; A.M., 1953, and Ph.D., 1956, both from Princeton University. Military: Served as a Flying Officer with the Royal Canadian Air Force, 1956-58. Career: Faculty Member, University of Utah, 1953-56; Assistant to the Air Historian, Royal Canadian Air Force, 1956-58; Faculty Member, University of Rochester, 1958-61; Faculty Member, The New School for Social Research, 1962-72; Faculty Member, Brooklyn College, City University of New York, 1961 to present (full professor since 1972). Organizational Memberships: The American Name Society (president 1979); The International Linguistic Association (section secretary 1980-81, 1981-82); Comparative Literature Section, Northeast Modern Language Association (secretary, 1981-82); Others. Community Activities: McGill Graduates Society, New York (past president); Brooklyn College Chapter, The American Association of University Professors (past president); City University of New York Council of the American Association of University Professors (past secretary-treasurer). Published Works: Poetry in more than 60 periodicals and anthologies; Articles and Reviews in many scholarly journals; Articles and Columns in popular press; Author of books, textbooks, editions; Contributor to encyclopedia and reference books. Honors and Awards: The Shakespeare Gold Medal, 1949; Various Research Grants and Awards. Address: 1901 Avenue H, Brooklyn, New York 11230.

Askew, Reubin O'Donovan

Attorney. Personal: Born September 11, 1928; Son of Leo and Alberta O'Donovan Askew; Married Donna Lou Harper; Father of Angela A. Cook, Kevin O'Donovan. Education: B.S., Florida State University, 1951; L.L.B., University of Florida, 1956; Post-Graduate Studies, University of Denver; Honorary Degrees, Florida Southern College 1972, University of Notre Dame 1973, University of Miami 1975, University of West Florida 1978, Barry University 1979, Rollins College 1972, Eckerd College 1973, Stetson University 1973, Bethune-Cookman College 1975, St. Leo College 1975. Military: Served in the United States Army, 1946-48, and in the United States Air Force, 1951-53. Career: Assistant County Solicitor, Escambia County, Florida, 1956-58; Partner, Levin, Askew, Warfield, Graff and Magie, 1958-70; Member, Florida House of Representatives, 1958-62; Florida Senate 1962-70, President, Pro-Tem, 1969-70; Governor of Florida, 1971-79; Partner, Greenberg, Traurig, Askew, Hoffman, Lipoff, Quentel, and Wolff, P.A., 1979; United States Trade Representative, Washington, 1979-80; Partner, Greenberg, Traurig, Askew, Hoffman, Lipoff, Quentel and Wolff, P.A., 1981. Organizational Memberships: American Bar Association; Florida Bar Association; Dade County Bar Association; American Association of Museums; American Judicature Society; Delta Tau Delta; Omicron Delta Kappa; Phi Alpha Delta; Education Commission of States (chairman, 1973); Southern Governors Association (chairman, 1974); National Democratic Governors Conference (chairman, 1976); National Governors Association (chairman, 1977); Southern Growth Policies Board (chairman, 1977); Presidential Advisory Board on Ambassadorial Appointment (chairman, 1977-79); Select Commission on Immigration and Refugee Policy (chairman). Community Activities: Children's Home Society; Democratic National Convention (keynote address, Miami, 1972); Center for Fine Arts, Miami (board of trustees, 1979 to present); Kennedy School of Government, Harvard (visiting fellow, 1979); Yale University (Chubb fellow); City of Hope (national board of directors); Rotary Club; Florida Council of 100; American Legion; Scottish Rite; York Rite; Shrine; Knights of Red Cross of Constantine; Knight Commander Court of Honour Scottish Rite. Religion: Presbyterian Church, Elder. Honors and Awards: One of Outstanding Members of Florida House of Representatives and Florida Senate, 1959, 1965, 1966, 1967; Profiles in Courage Award, J. F. Kennedy Chapter, B'nai B'rith of Washington, 1971; Special Conservation Award, National Wildlife Federation, 1972; General William Booth Award, Salvation Army, 1973; John F. Kennedy Award, National Council of Jewish Women, 1973; Herbert H. Lehman Ethics Medal, Jewish Theological Seminary of America, 1973; Alumnus of the Year, University of Florida Law Review, 1973; Florida Engineering Society

Protector of the Environment Award, 1973; Leonard L. Abess Human Relations Award, Anti-Defamation League, 1974; Theodore Roosevelt Award, International Platform Association, 1975; Herbert Harley Award, American Judicature Society, 1975; Collier County Conservancy Silver Medal, 1978; Cumberland Order Jurisprudence, Cumberland Law School, 1978; Florida Society of Newspaper Editors Award, 1978; F. Malcolm Cunningham Achievement Award, Florida Chapter, National Bar Association, 1978; Leadership Honor Award, American Institute of Planners, 1978; Medal of Honor, Florida Bar Foundation, 1979; Champion of Higher Independent Education in Florida Award, 1979; Distinguished Community Service Award, Brandeis University, 1979; Order of the Coif, 1980; Common Cause, Ethics in Government Award, 1980, Council on Foreign Relations. Address: 1401 Brickell Avenue, PH-1, Miami, Florida 33131.

Aspey, Wayne P

Professor. Personal: Born March 26, 1946; Son of Evelyn Aspey; Married Lynn M. H. Aspey; Father of Ryan Arnold, Chantelle Erin. Education: A.B., cum laude with special honors in psychology, Ohio University, 1968; Undertook coursework and research, University of Georgia Marine Institute, 1969; A.M., Dartmouth College, 1970; Undertook further coursework and research, Marine Biological Laboratory, Woods Hole, Massachusetts, 1972; Ph.D., Ohio University, 1974; Postdoctoral Research Fellow, The Marine Biomedical Institute, The University of Texas Medical Branch, Galveston, 1974-78. Career: Instructor, Department of Marine Biology, Moody College of Texas Agricultural and Mechanical University, Galveston; Professor, Ohio State University. Organizational Memberships: International Society for Research of Aggression (fellow 1980 to present); Association for Chemoreception Sciences, 1980 to present; Ohio Academy of Science, 1980; National Association of Biology Teachers, 1978 to present; Cambridge Entomological Club, Harvard University, 1976 to present; Texas Academy of Science, 1975-76; American Institute of Biological Sciences, 1974-81; British Arachnological Society, 1973 to present; American Arachnological Society, 1972 to present; Sigma Xi, 1971 to present; American Society of Zoologists, 1971 to present (division of invertebrate zoology, division of ecology); American Association of University Professors, 1970 to present; American Association for the Advancement of Science, 1969 to present; International Society for Development Psychobiology, 1968-77; Animal Behavior Society, 1968 to present (chairperson of the education committee 1980-83, editor of "Graduate Programs in Animal Behavior" 1981-82, judge of the Allee Competition for best student paper in animal behavior 1979). Community Activities: The Ohio State University, University-wide Service: Learning Resources Advisory Council, 1980-81; Policy Advisory Council, O.S.U. Child Care Program, 1980-81; Contributor, Committee on Institutional Cooperation, 16th Edition, Technological Advances in Education, 1981; Lecture, Tour and Demonstration of BioLearning Center Facilities, O.S.U. Mother's Alumni Association, 1981; Alumni Weekends, 1980; The Ohio State University, College of Biological Sciences: 7th Annual Biosciences Colloquium Co-Organizer, "Behavioral Energetics: Vertebrate Costs of Survival", with Dr. Sheldon I. Lustick, 1980; "Showcase Faculty Lecturer", Parent Orientation Program, University College, 1980; College ad hoc Committee to Recommend Microscopes, 1979; Organizer of "Audio-Tutorial Hands-on Mini Lesson in Biology", Parent Orientation Program, University College, 1979; The Ohio State University, Department of Zoology: Graduate Program Brochure, 1981; Search Committee for Bioacoustician, 1979; Texas A&M, Moody College: Convocation Committee, Awards Chairperson, 1977-78; Faculty Advisor, Wrestling Team, 1977-78; Non-majors Biology Consulting Panel, Random House; Manuscript Referee: *Behaviour, Animal Behaviour, Behavioral Biology, Journal of Experimental Marine Biology & Ecology;* Grant Reviewer: N.S.F. Psychobiology Program, N.S.F. Neurobiology Program, N.S.F. Ecology Program, N.S.F. Population Biology & Physiological Ecology Program, Research Corporation; Symposium Proposal Reviewer, New York Academy of Sciences; Book Reviewer, *A.A.A.S. Science Books & Films,* Zoology/Marine Science; American Cancer Society (public education committee, university & college subcommittee); Columbus Zoological Gardens; Northwest Swim Club; Dartmouth Club of Central Ohio. Published Works: Reviews including *How Animals Behave, How Wild Animals Fight, Animal Ecology in Tropical Africa, How Animals Communicate,* and *A Bat is Born;* Books *Humanistic Biology* and *Behavioral Energetics;* Number of Journal Articles, Symposium Proceedings and Book Chapters. Honors and Awards: Third Place Winner, Scientific Photography, Color Division, The University of Texas Medical Branch Student Photography Contest, 1976; Honorable Mention, Undergraduate of the Year, Phi Epsilon Pi 64th National Convention, Bahamas, 1968; Honors College Graduate with Special Honors in Psychology, 1968; Psi Chi, 1968; Phi Beta Kappa, 1968; Blue Key, 1967; Pi Gamma Mu, 1967; Listed in *Dictionary of International Biography, Dictionary of Distinguished Americans, Men of Achievement, Personalities of the West and Midwest, Who's Who in the Midwest, Outstanding Young Men of America, American Men & Women of Science, Who's Who Among Students in American Universities and Colleges.* Address: 3051 Kilcullen Drive, Columbus, Ohio 43220.

Atkins, Marylin Elnora

Assistant Attorney General. Personal: Born July 19, 1946; Daughter of Clyde J. (deceased) and Billie Alice Bowman; Married Thomas Lee Atkins; Mother of Elizabeth, Catherine. Education: B.A., Saginaw Valley State College, 1973; J.D., University of Detroit, 1980. Career: Assistant Attorney General, 1981; Attorney, Legislative Service Bureau, Lansing, Michigan, 1980-81; Attorney, Appeals and Interpretation Standards, M.E.S.C., Detroit, 1980; Assistant to the Director, Labor Relations Division, M.E.S.C., Detroit, 1976-80; Claims Adjudicator, Detroit and Saginaw, 1973-76. Organizational Memberships: Various Bar Associations. Religion: Roman Catholic. Honors and Awards: Outstanding Alumnus of Year, Saginaw Valley State College, 1981. Address: 4695 Kingswood Drive, Okemos, Michigan 48864.

Atkins, Thomas Lee

Roman Catholic Priest, Training Specialist. Personal: Born December 4, 1921; Son of Samuel Merritt III (deceased) and Alphonsine Atkins; Married Marylin E. Bowman; Father of Elizabeth, Catherine. Education: B.A., University of Notre Dame, 1943; Graduate Studies, Catholic University; Ordained Priest, 1951. Military: Served in the United States Naval Reserve, 1943-46, Lieutenant (j.g.). Career: Training Specialist, Personnel, 1974-81; Employment Counselor, 1967-74; Catholic Parish Priest/Pastor, 1951-66; Catholic Chaplain, Veterans Hospital, Saginaw, Michigan, 1954-58; Catholic Chaplain, United States Naval Reserve Training Center, Bay City, Michigan, 1958-64. Organizational Memberships: Amvets Post #60 (provost marshall); International Association of Personnel in Employment Security, Michigan Chapter. Community Activities: Lansing Masters Swimming Club; Saginaw Valley Indian Association (president, 1981-82); Social Workers Roundtable of Bay City (president, 1969-74); Michigan Retired Officers Association; Sebewaing Hospital Corporation (president, 1960-61); Bishop's Representative for Civil Defense, 1956-66; Republican. Religion: Roman Catholic Priest. Honors and Awards: Honor Man, Recruit Training Command, 1943; WXYZ Radio-TV Good Citizen, 1981. Address: 4695 Kinsgwood Drive, Okemos, Michigan 48864.

Atkins, William Thomas

Executive. Personal: Born June 18, 1948; Son of J. W. and Rebecca Atkins; Married Yanick Bouchereau; Father of Natalie Elizabeth.

Education: B.S.C.E., Washington State University, 1970. Career: Vice President, Mittelhauser Corporation; Former Senior Process Engineer, C. F. Braun and Company; Process Engineer, Texaco Inc. Organizational Memberships: Water Pollution Control Federation. Community Activities: Young Men's Christian Association (president; board of directors, 1974); Community Action Corps (executive committee, 1972-73); Jaycees (vice president, director, secretary, 1970-74). Religion: Methodist. Honors and Awards: National Aeronautical and Space Administration Certificate of Recognition, 1980. Address: 26066 Ramjit Court, El Toro, California 92630.

Atkinson, Elizabeth Ann

Educator. Personal: Born December 3, 1946; Daughter of Mr. and Mrs. K. Lee Atkinson. Education: B.S.Ed. 1968, M.Ed. 1970, Ed.S. 1974, Ed.D. 1982, University of Georgia. Career: Educator, Secondary and Post-Secondary Level; Former Director of Admissions, DeVry Institute of Technology (a Bell and Howell School); Consultant, National Leisure Enterprises (Atlanta) and Elberton Foods, Inc. (Elberton). Organizational Memberships: American Vocational Association; Georgia Vocational Association; National Business Education Association; American Management Association; National Association of Educators; Georgia Business Education Association; Delta Pi Epsilon (historian, 1971). Community Activities: Muscular Dystrophy Association (president, 1976-77); March of Dimes (president, 1972-73); Optimist Club (co-chairman, Halloween haunted house, 1978-81); Speaker for Business and Civic Groups; Chairman of Charity Drive for Two High School Students Injured in Automobile Accident, 1980. Religion: Baptist, Youth Coordinator, 1972-73). Honors and Awards: Phi Kappa Phi; Delta Pi Epsilon; Kappa Delta Pi; Most Outstanding Business Education Teacher of the Year, Administrative Management Society, 1971; Certificate of Achievement, United Life Insurance Company; Listed in *Who's Who of American Women, Personalities of America.* Address: 23 Chestnut Street, Box 424, Elberton, Georgia 30635.

Atkinson, Evelyn Rorex

Architect. Personal: Born December 29, 1931; Married Atmar L. Atkinson; Mother of Charles Michael, Linda Carol Allen. Education: Attended West Texas State College, 1949-50; B.Arch, Texas Tech College, 1965. Career: Architect. Organizational Memberships: American Institute of Architects; Texas Society of Architects; Lubbock Chapter, American Institute of Architects. Community Activities: Lubbock Cultural Affairs Council (board of directors, 1971-76). Honors and Awards: Outstanding Graduating Student in Architecture, Texas Tech College; Merit Award, Porter Exchange Building, Southwestern Bell Telephone Company. Address: 3201 29th, Lubbock, Texas 79410.

Augustine, Norman Ralph

Aerospace Executive. Personal: Born July 27, 1935; Son of Ralph and Freda Augustine; Married Margareta E. Engman; Father of Gregory E., Rene I. Education: B.S.E. 1957, M.S.E. 1959, Princeton University; Undertook Post-Graduate Courses, Columbia University, University of California-Los Angeles, University of Southern California. Career: Engineer; Government Official. Organizational Memberships: American Institute of Aeronautics and Astronautics (vice president, board member, 1977 to present); American Helicopter Society (board of directors, 1974-79). Community Activities: Under Secretary of the Army, 1975-77; Assistant Secretary of the Army, 1973-75; Assistant Director of Defense and Engineering, Office of Director of Defense, 1965-70; Association of the United States Army (president, 1981 to present); Boy Scouts of America (national committee chairman); Defense Science Board (chairman, 1980 to present); Young Men's Christian Association (fund raiser); Advisory Boards to American University, Princeton University, Florida State University. Religion: Presbyterian. Honors and Awards: Phi Beta Kappa; Sigma Xi; Tau Beta Pi; Department of Defense Meritorious Service Medal; Department of Defense Distinguished Service Medal; Department of Army Distinguished Service Medal; Fellow, American Institute of Aeronautics and Astronautics; Fellow, American Astronautical Society. Address: 1329 Merrie Ridge, McLean, Virginia 22101.

Austen, William Gerald

Surgeon. Personal: Born January 20, 1930; Son of Mrs. Bertyl Arnstein; Married Patricia Ramsdell; Father of Karl R., W. Gerald Jr., Christopher M., Elizabeth P. Education: B.S., Massachusetts Institute of Technology, 1951; M.D., Harvard University Medical School, 1955. Military: Served with the United States Public Health Service Commissioned Corps, 1961-62, as a Surgeon. Career: Edward D. Churchill Professor of Surgery 1974 to present, Professor of Surgery 1966-74, Associate Professor of Surgery 1965-66, Associate in Surgery 1963-65, Teaching Fellow in Surgery 1960-61, Harvard Medical School; Chief of Surgical Services 1969 to present, Visiting Surgeon 1966-69, Chief Surgeon, Cardiovascular Research Unit 1963-69, Massachusetts General Hospital, Surgeon, Clinic of Surgery, National Heart Institute, Bethesda, Maryland, 1961-62; Visiting Professorships, University of Leyden (Holland), University of North Carolina, University of Miami, University of Texas at San Antonio, University of Vermont, Ohio State University, Brown University, University of Illinois, University of Chicago, University of Pittsburgh, University of Texas at Galveston, University of California at San Diego, Loyola University, Mount Sinai University, University of Wisconsin at Milwaukee, Ohio State University, University of Texas Health Science Center, Yale University, Case Western Reserve University, University of Pennsylvania, University of Athens; Sample Lecturer, Yale University; Sir James Wattie Visiting Professor, New Zealand. Editorial Board Member, Circulation, 1972-76, *The New England Journal of Medicine* 1972-75, *The Annals of Thoracic Surgery* 1970-80; *Review of Surgery* 1970-72, *Annals of Surgery* 1972 to present, *Current Surgery* 1972 to present, *American Heart Journal* 1980 to present, *Journal of Thoracic and Cardiovascular Surgery* 1981 to present, *Current Concepts in Cardiovascular Disease* 1981 to present. Organizational Memberships: American Heart Association (president, 1977-78); New England Cardiovascular Society (president, 1972-73); Massachusetts Heart Association (president, 1972-74); Association for Academic Surgery (president, 1970); The Society of University Surgeons (president, 1972-73); American Medical Association; New England Surgical Society; American Surgical Association; American College of Cardiology; Boston Surgical Society; Society of Thoracic Surgeons; American College of Surgeons; New York Academy of Sciences; Societe Internationale de Chirurgie; Massachusetts Medical Society; Society for Vascular Surgery; Pan Medical Association; American Academy of Arts and Sciences; Society of Clinical Surgery; Allen O. Whipple Surgical Society; American Trauma Society; Italian Research Society; Canadian Cardiovascular Society; Institute of Medicine of the National Academy of Sciences; American Association for Thoracic Surgery; American Heart Association; American Society for Clinical Investigation; Association for Academic Surgery; Halsted Society; International Cardiovascular Society; James IV Association of Surgeons, Inc.; Pan-Pacific Surgical Association; Society for Surgical of the Alimentary Tract; Society of Surgical Chairman; The Society of University Surgeons; Surgical Biology Club II. Honors and Awards: Honorary Member, Panhellenic Surgical Society, Canadian Cardiovascular Society, Dutch Cardiology Society; Fellow, American Academy of Arts and Sciences; Markle Scholar in Academic Medicine, Outstanding Young Men Award, Boston, 1965; Affiliate, Royal Society of Medicine; Secretary, The American Surgical Association; Honorary Doctor of Humanities, University of Akron; Gold Heart Award, American Heart Association; Paul

Dudley White Cardiac Medal, Massachusetts Heart Association; Louis Mark Memorial Lecturer Award, American College of Chest Physicians; Honorary Doctor of Science, University of Athens, Greece; Life Member of the Corporation, Massachusetts Institute of Technology; Listed in *National Register of Prominent Americans and International Notables.* Address: 163 Wellesley Street, Weston, Massachusetts 02193.

Austin, Michael Herschel

Attorney at Law. Personal: Born November 7, 1896; Son of Michael G. and Willie C. Austin (both deceased); Married Inez Austin. Education: L.L.B., University of Mississippi, 1922; Attended Akron University, 1919; L.L.B., Ohio State University, 1923; J.D., 1970. Military: Served in the Coast Artillery during World War I. Career: Rural School Teacher, Mississippi; Partner in Law Firm Pfeiffer and Austin, 1927-30; Attorney for Farmers Home Administration, 1963-70; Attorney for Franklin County, Ohio, 1965-69; Law Practice in Columbus, Ohio, 1924 to present. Organizational Memberships: Big Four Veterans Council (president, 1956-57); Columbus Lawyers Club (secretary, 1931-32); American, Ohio and Columbus Bar Associations; American Judicature Society; Columbus Real Estate Board. Community Activities: Chamber of Commerce; Ohio State University Alumni Association; American Legion (post commander, 1953-54; district commander, 1955-56; state treasurer, 1958-59); International Platform Association; Truman Library Association (fellow); Mason. Honors and Awards: Cross of Honor, United Daughters of the Confederacy, 1944; Executive and Professional Hall of Fame, 1966; Wisdom Award, 1970; Title of Senior Council for 50 Years of Practice, Columbus Bar Association, 1972 and Ohio State Bar, 1974; Outstanding Legionnaire, 1967; 50 Year Banquet, American Legion of Ohio; Golden Service Certificate, Ohio State University Alumni Association; Listed in *Who's Who in Ohio, Who's Who in the Midwest, World Who's Who in Commerce and Industry, Dictionary of International Biography, Who's Who in the World.* Address: 47 Richards Road, Columbus, Ohio 43214.

Arthur W Avery

Avery, Arthur William

Laboratory Director. Personal: Born June 11, 1949; Son of Arthur Wolcott and Merylyn Meeks Avery. Education: B.A., cum laude, 1971, M.S., 1973, Ph.D., 1975, all from Pennsylvania State University. Career: Graduate and Groves Fellow, Pennsylvania State University, 1975; Assistant Professor of Family Studies, Texas Tech University, 1975-77; Director, Graduate Program in Human Development and Family Studies, Texas Tech University, 1977-79; Director, Human Development Laboratory, University of Arizona, 1979 to present. Organizational Memberships: American Psychological Association, Division 27 (program committee, continuing education committee); American Association for Marriage and Family Therapy (directors of clinical training committee); National Council on Family Relations (chairperson, national meeting site selection committee); Groves Conference on Marriage and Family (national planning committee); Approved Site Training Reviewer, Commission on Accreditation in Marriage and Family Therapy Education, Accrediting Agency, U.S. Department of Health and Human Services. Honors and Awards: Phi Beta Kappa; Psi Chi; Alpha Kappa Delta; Associate Editor, *Family Relations: Journal of Applied Family and Child Studies;* National Institute of Health Grant; Certified/Licensed Psychologist, Arizona, Texas; Listed in *Who's Who in the West, Community Leaders of America.* Address: 444 W. Orange Grove #915, Tucson, Arizona 85704.

Aya, Roderick Honeyman

Tax Consultant. Personal: Born September 17, 1916; Son of Alfred Anthony Aya and Grace Myrtle Honeyman (both deceased); Married Helen Marjorie Riddle; Father of Roderick Riddle, Deborah Germaine Reynolds, Ronald Honeyman. Education: Attended the University of Oregon, 1935-36; International Accountants Society, 1937-39; La Salle Extension University, 1940-42; Walton School of Commerce, 1942; University of California Extension, 1945. Career: Chief Statistician, Hotel Employers Association of San Francisco, 1939-42; Various Tax Assignments, Pacific Telephone and Telegraph, San Francisco, 1942-65; Tax Executive, American Telephone and Telegraph, New York, 1965-79; Retired, 1979; Public Accountant, 1940 to present; Music Teacher, 1959 to present; Vice President, Treasurer, Director, Snell Memorial Foundation, 1957-80; Vice President, Treasurer, Director, Snell Research Associates, 1974-79; Trustee, Snell Memorial Foundation, (U.K.), Ltd., 1975 to present. Organizational Memberships: National Society of Public Accountants, 1942 to present; American Statistical Association, 1939-44; Music Educators National Conference, 1959-66; California Music Teachers Association, 1959-65; New York Music Teachers Association, 1965-67; American Musicological Society, 1960-67; Society for Ethnomusicology, 1960-67; Telephone Pioneers of America; St. Andrews Society; U.S. Naval Institute; The Anglo-American Academy (honorary fellow). Community Activities: San Francisco Junior Chamber of Commerce (industrial committee, 1939-45); Boy Scouts of America (Marin council, California; committeeman, 1959-60; committee chairman, 1959-61); Marin County, California, Sheriff's Reserve, 1963-65; Committee on Juvenile Control, Tiburon, California, Law Enforcement Liaison, 1964-65; Guest Lecturer on Taxes, Westchester County, New York, Adult Education Program; American National Standards Institute (secretary, committee on protective headgear, 1967-80); American Society for Testing and Materials; U.S. Senatorial Business Advisory Board (chairman's committee, 1980 to present); Republican Presidential Task Force, 1981 to present; Stuart Highlanders Pipe Band of San Francisco (director, past president); Little League; Corinthian Yacht Club, Tiburon, California; Sports Car Club of America (San Francisco regional director, 1957-59; regional treasurer, 1957-58; chief safety inspector, 1955-56; membership committee, 1956). Published Works: Author *The Legacy of Pete Snell, Determination of Corporate Earnings and Profits for Federal Income Tax Purposes,* Volumes I and II, 1966. Honors and Awards: Wisdom Award of Honor, Wisdom Society, 1970; President's Medal of Merit, 1981. Address: Maid of Barra, P. O. Box 148, Rowayton, Connecticut 06853-0148.

Janet Ayres

Ayers, James Wilber

Yard Worker. Personal: Born April 1, 1928; Son of Jay W. and Thelma Harbin Ayers (both deceased). Education: Graduate, Etowah High School, 1947. Career: Self-Employed Yard Worker. Organizational Memberships: Attalla's Lions Club (honorary member); International Platform Association; National Space Institute. Community Activities: National Society of Published Poets. Religion: Presbyterian. Published Works: Two Songs Published on Religious Albums; Co-Author *Tears,* a Christian How-To Book. Honors and Awards: Etowah Count Author, Gadsden Public Library, 1969; Holder of State Record of Letters to Editors of Newspapers; Fifty Dollar Warbond, Clover Publishing Company, 1976. Address: 609 First Street, Attalla, Alabama 35954.

Ayres, Janet Sprang

Director of Administration. Personal: Born September 24, 1948; Daughter of Francis and Virginia Sprang; Married John Parker Ayres; Mother of Barret Parker. Education: B.S.Ed., Kansas State University, 1970. Career: Director of Administration, The Master Teacher, Inc., Educational Publishing Firm; Associate Director, Alumni Association, Kansas State University, 1970-77.

Organizational Memberships: Council for the Advancement and Support of Education (national board of trustees, 1976-78). Community Activities: United Way of Riley County, Inc. (board of directors, 1974-80; president, 1979-80); Memorial Hospital (board of directors, 1977 to present; committee chairperson, 1980); KSAC Radio Community Advisory Board, 1979 to present (vice chairman); University for Man State Outreach Board, 1977 to present; Mortar Board, Inc. (national officer, 1976-79); Manhattan Arts Council (board of directors, 1974-79; vice president, 1977-79); Business and Professional Women (state board of directors, 1976-77); Manhattan Chamber of Commerce (committee chairman, 1978 to present); American Association of University Women; Phi Kappa Phi; Mobile Art Gallery (board of advisors, 1979 to present); Kansas State University (union governing board, 1972-77); Kansas State University Department of Health, Physical Education and Recreation (advisory board, 1971-77). Religion: First United Methodist Church; Order of Eastern Star. Honors and Awards: Kansas Young Careerist, 1975; Kansas Federation of Business and Professional Women; Outstanding Young Manhattanite, Manhattan Jaycees, 1979; Chapter Citation Award, Mortar Board, Inc., 1976; Woman of the Year, Business and Professional Women, Inc., 1976; Kansas Dairy Princess, American Dairy Association of Kansas, 1969; Outstanding Senior Selection, Kansas State University Royal Purple, 1970. Address: 1309 Givens Road, Manhattan, Kansas 66502.

Bachman, Albert Lorence III

Director of Laboratory Services. Personal: Born December 16, 1948; Son of Albert L. Jr., and Ethel R. Bachman; Married Mary Bienemann; Father of Marie Elizabeth. Education: Attended Forbes Trail Technical School, 1967; B.A., Hope College, 1972. Career: Director of Laboratory Services, Chemist, W. E. Long Company; Former Chemical Technician, Mellon Institute. Organizational Memberships: American Chemical Society; American Society of Bakery Engineers; Institute of Food Technologists; American Association of Cereal Chemists (local secretary-treasurer, 1979-80; vice chairman, 1980-81; chairman, 1981-82). Community Activities: Kiwanis Club of Western Springs (committee chairman, 1976; club director, 1976; secretary, 1981); Kiwanis Club of Oak Park (secretary, 1980); American Red Cross, West Cook Region (village representative, 1976 to present; secretary, 1978-79); Lyons Township District 74 Republican Party (assistant precinct captain, 1975-77). Honors and Awards: Listed in *Who's Who in the Midwest*. Address: 4932 Woodland Avenue, Western Springs, Illinois 60558.

Badalamente, Marie Ann

Assistant Professor, Director of Neuromuscular Research. Personal: Born July 17, 1949; Daughter of Elizabeth Badalamente. Education: B.A. 1971, M.S. 1973, Long Island University; Ph.D., Fordham University, 1977. Career: Assistant Professor, Department of Orthopaedics and Director of Neuromuscular Research, State University of New York-Stony Brook; Assistant Professor, Director of Electron Microscopy, Department of Anatomy and Cell Biology, State University of New York Downstate Medical Center, 1978-79; Assistant Professor, Department of Biology, C. W. Post Center, Long Island University, 1975-78. Organizational Memberships: New York Academy of Sciences; Electron Microscopy Society of America; New York Society of Electron Microscopy; Sigma Xi; Scientific Research Society; American Association for the Advancement of Science; Orthopaedic Research Society. Honors and Awards: Easter Seals Research Foundation Grantee, 1981-84; Muscular Dystrophy Association Grantee, 1979-81; National Institute of Health Research Associate, Fordham University (while Ph.D. candidate), 1976-78. Address: 109 St. Marks Place, Roslyn Heights, New York 11577.

Badeaux, Laura McQuaig

Assistant Professor. Personal: Born December 14, 1946; Daughter of Neil McQuaig, Jr.; Married Lloyd (Chip) Badeaux; Mother of Kelly and Shelly. Education: B.S., Louisiana State University, 1968; M.B.A., Nicholls State University, 1971; Ph.D., Louisiana State University, 1981. Career: Welfare Visitor, Lafourche Parish Department of Public Welfare, 1969-71; Telephone Salesman, Sears Roebuck, 1970; Instructor, Business Communications, Louisiana State University, 1972-77; Assistant Professor, Management and Economics, Nicholls State University, 1977 to present. Organizational Memberships: Academy of Management; American Business Women's Association; American Business Communication Association; Beta Gamma Sigma; Alpha Lambda Delta; Alpha Beta Chi. Community Activities: United States Jaycettes (national leadership training team, 1981); Louisiana Jaycee Jaynes (past president; state chairman, leadership training, 1975-78; leadership advisor, 1979; president, 1975; executive vice president, 1974; jewelry chairman, 1973; speak-up chairman, 1972); Louisiana Federation of Woman's Club (junior board of directors; educational and leadership chairman, 1978-80; third district corresponding secretary, 1978-80; state convention speaker on leadership, 1979; third district director of juniors, 1976-78; chairman, district nominating committee, 1976; district vice president, 1980-82); Louisiana Federation of Music Clubs (state executive committee, 1978-80; state publications chairman, 1979-80; state convention co-chairman, 1979; state convention em-cee, 1979); Thibodaux Jaycee Jaynes (board member, 1972-78; press secretary, 1978; president, 1976; membership chairman, 1974; vice president, 1973; secretary, 1972; editor, club newsletter, 3 years); Bayou Junior Woman's Club (charter chairman, 1975; president, 1975, 1976-78; community improvement chairmanships); Interorganizational Council of Thibodaux (charter chairman, 1978; president, 1979-80, 1980-81; press secretary, 1981-83); Delta Zeta (charter committee for Nicholls State chapter, 1969; rush advisor, 1979; chapter advisor, 1972-76); Thibodaux City Panhellenic (charter chairman, 1976; chairman, Panhellenic Tea, 1975-77; Delta Zeta Delta delegate, 1975-77); Thibodaux Music Club (president, 1977-78; vice president, 1976-77; corresponding secretary, 1975-76; membership chairman, 1974-75; music and arts in the schools committee, 1975-76, 1976-77); Red Cross (fund raising chairman); WYES Auction Go Getter (fund raiser); Bayou Chapter, Daughters of the American Revolution (historian, 1978-80; chairman, junior membership, 1976-78, 1978-80); Krewe of Thalia (carnival crew choreographer); Thibodaux Playhouse (leading roles in "Sunday in New York", "Charlie's Aunt"; publicity chairman, 1972-74); Acadienne Business and Professional Woman's Club (legislative chairman, 1975); Nicholls State University Woman's Faculty (banquet committee, 1978). Religion: St. Joseph Catholic Church. Honors and Awards: In Top Four, Outstanding Young Women of Louisiana, 1977; Outstanding Young Woman of Thibodaux, 1977; President, Outstanding Club in District 3 for Louisiana Federation of Woman's Club, 1977; First Runner-Up, Outstanding Young Woman of Thibodaux, 1976; Bayou Junior Woman's Club Enthusiasm Award, 1976; Thibodaux's Outstanding New Jayne, 1973; Thibodaux Jayne Spirit Award, 1976; Outstanding Delta Zeta Alumna in Louisiana and Mississippi, 1976; Honored for Outstanding Local Service to Delta Zeta, 1972-76; Outstanding State Chairman, Louisiana Jaynes, 1972; Outstanding Speaker in Louisiana Competition, Louisiana Jaynes, 1972; Outstanding Delta Zeta Collegiate Woman in Louisiana, 1968; One of Six Outstanding Delta Zeta Collegiates in Nation, 1967; Scholarship for Outstanding Student in College of Business, 1965; Outstanding Freshman Woman, Louisiana State University, 1965; Life Member, Louisiana Jaynes, 1981; Listed in *Who's Who in Outstanding Young Women in America, Community Leaders and Noteworthy Americans, Who's Who in American Colleges*. Address: 113 Half Oak, Thibodaux, Louisiana 70301.

Bae, Kun Chae

Executive. Personal: Born July 10, 1934; Son of Kil Moon Bae; Married Myoung Hwa Baeck; Father of Donald, Kevin, Scott, Stefanie. Education: B.A. Millikin University, 1960. Career: Plant Manager; Company President. Organizational Memberships: Chicago Drug and Chemical Association; National Pharmaceutical Alliance; Korean Association of Chicago (board of directors). Community Activities: U.S. Senatorial Business Advisory Board, 1981. Religion: Presbyterian. Honors and Awards: The Best

Minority Business Man of the Year, Chicago Economic Development Corporation. Address: 6846 N. Lorel, Skokie, Illinois 60077.

Baer, Norbert S

Professor, Editor. Personal: Born June 6, 1938; Married; Father of Two Children. Education: B.S., Brooklyn College, 1958; M.S., University of Wisconsin, 1962; Ph.D., New York University, 1969. Career: Physicist, The Warner & Swasey Company, Control Instrument Division, 1962-63; Queensborough Community College, Department of Physical Science, Department of Chemistry, 1967-69: Assistant Professor (1968), Lecturer (1967); New York University, Institute of Fine Arts, Conservation Center, 1969 to present: Professor (1978), Associate Professor (1975), Assistant Professor (1970), Instructor (1969); Co-Chairman (1975); Time Incorporated, Book Division, Science Library: Researcher (1963-65), Consultant (1970-71); *Studies in Conservation*: Assistant Editor (1971-73), Associate Editor (1974-76), Editorial Advisor (1977 to present); *Restaurator*, Associate Editor, 1975 to present; U.S. Executive Editor, Series "Conservation in the Arts, Archaeology and Architecture", Butterworths, 1979 to present. Organizational Memberships: American Association for the Advancement of Science; American Chemical Society; American Institute of Chemists (fellow); American Institute for Conservation (fellow); Coblentz Society; Instrument Society of America (member, senior grade); International Metallographic Society (member, senior grade); International Institute for Conservation (fellow); New York Academy of Science; Sigma Xi; U.S. Steering Committee, N.A.T.O./C.C.M.S. Monuments Preservation Pilot Study, 1978 to present; Institute of Fine Arts Directorial Search Committee, 1978-79; International Foundation for Art Research (advisory council 1976-77); American Institute for Conservation (committee on accreditation and standards 1977-80, board of examiners for paper conservation 1976-79, board of directors 1973-76); Conservation Analytical Laboratory, Smithsonian Institution (chairman of the ad hoc visiting committee 1977-78); National Endowment for the Arts (conservation panel 1976-77); National Conservation Advisory Council (library and archives committee 1975-79, chairman of the education and training committee 1972-79, executive committee 1972-79); Scholarly Catalogue of the Robert Lehman Collection (executive board chairman 1978-79); National Archives and Records Service (chairman of the advisory committee of preservation 1980 to present); Others. Published Works: Author/Co-Author Numerous Articles and Reports, including "James B. Duke House: A Case Study in Architectural Conservation", "The Evaluation of Adhesives for Use in Book and Paper Conservation", and "The Properties of Commercial Fixatives for Use in the Preservation of Works of Art". Honors and Awards: Listed in *Who's Who in America, Who's Who in American Art, American Men and Women of Science*. Address: 194 Ascan Avenue, Forest Hills, New York 11374.

Henry R Baerg

Baerg, Henry Ralph

Pastor. Personal: Born August 12, 1918; Son of John J. and Margaret Baerg (both deceased); Married Justina Anne Wiebe; Father of Donald Milton, Eleanor Ruth, Samuel Ron, Charity Anne, Paul Henry, David John. Education: Diploma, Coaldale Bible Institute, Alberta, Canada, 1938; Diploma, Prairie Bible Institute, Alberta, 1940; Attended Menn. Brethren Bible College, Winnipeg, Canada, 1946, 1947; B.A. 1949, B.D. 1951, Tabor College, Hillsboro, Kansas; M.A., Wichita University, 1953; Attended Central Baptist Seminary 1955, University of Kansas-Lawrence 1959, University of Manitoba 1960-61; Ph.D. Candidate, University of North Dakota, 1965-74. Career: Pastor, Kingwood Bible Church, Salem, Oregon, 1979 to present; Pastor, First Baptist Church, Durham, Kansas, 1948-53; Pastor, Henderson Menn. Brethren Church, Nebraska, 1953-56; Professor, Menn. Brethren Bible College, 1956-62; Pastor, Portage Avenue Menn. Brethren Church, Winnipeg, 1962-69; President, Winkler Bible Institute, Winkler, Manitoba, Canada, 1969-78. Organizational Memberships: Chairman and Member, Various Denominational Committees and Boards; Director of Camp Arnes, Manitoba; Canadian Bible Society (second vice president). Religion: Founder and Treasurer, Kansas State Sunday School Association, 1951, 1952; Speaker, Youth for Christ, Hyderabad, India, Crusade, 1973; Secretary, Greater Salem Evangelical Pastor's Association, Salem, Oregon, 1980, 1981. Honors and Awards: Graduated with high honors, Tabor College, 1949. Address: 1150 Alpine Drive, N.W., Salem, Oregon 97304.

Bagby, Joseph Rigsby

Author, Investor. Personal: Born August 23, 1935; Son of Mrs. P. R. Bagby; Married Martha Lane Green; Father of Meredith Elaine. Education: B.A., University of Miami, 1959. Military: Served in the United States Army, 82nd Airborne Division, 1959-61, achieving the Rank of Private First Class. Career: Author; Investor; Director and Manager of Real Estate Development, Burger King Corporation; Vice-President, Jack Thomas Realty; General Real Estate, Oscar Dooly Associates. Organizational Memberships: National Association of Corporate Real Estate Executives (founder, chairman, president, 1974 to present). Published Works: *Real Estate Financing Desk Book; The Real Estate Dictionary; The Complete Book of Real Estate.* Honors and Awards: Certificate of Achievement, United States Army, 1961; Iron Arrow (highest honor attained by men), University of Miami; Sigma Chi Chapter Balfour Award, 1959. Address: 125 Brazilian Avenue, Palm Beach, Florida 33408.

William W Bagby

Bagby, William Woodrow

Minister. Personal: Born November 11, 1912; Son of Frank E. Bagby, Lucy O'Shellie Stokes (both deceased); Married Mary Elizabeth Alexander; Father of Mary Elizabeth Shoemaker. Education: A.B., Millsaps College, 1943; M.Div. cum laude, Columbia Theological Seminary, 1946; Graduate Study undertaken at the University of Southern Mississippi, 1963-64. Career: Engineering Draftsman, Mississippi State Highway Department, 1936-43; Pastor, Sandersville Group of Presbyterian Churches, Mississippi, 1946-66; Pastor, First Presbyterian Church, Tuskegee, Alabama, 1966 to present; Board Member, The Presbyterian Home for Children, Talladega, Alabama; Member of Nominating Committee and Many Other Committees, Presbytery of John Knox. Organizational Memberships: Jones County Ministerial Association, 1948-66; Synod of Mid-South, Presbyterian Church of the United States (staff coordinating committee, 1972-77); Stated Clerks Association (second vice-president); Meridian and South Mississippi Presbytery (premanent clerk, 1948-66); East Alabama Presbytery (permanent clerk, 1968-72; stated clerk, 1972-77); Commissioner to General Assembly, Presbyterian Church of the United States, 1949, 1960, 1971, 1981. Community Activities: American Red Cross, Laurel, Mississippi (board of directors, 1958-64); Pine Burr Area, Choctow Council, Boy Scouts of America, 1960-66; Lion's Club, Sandersville, Mississippi (charter member, 1962-66). Religion: Presbyterian; Minister to Sick and Sorrowing, Ordained 1946. Honors and Awards: Rural Minister of the Year, *The Progressive Farmer* Magazine and Candler School of Theology, Emory University, 1963; Town and Country Award, Town and Country Department of PCUS, 1961; Rural Minister Award, Mississippi State University, 1963. Address: P.O. Box 127, Tuskegee, Alabama 36083.

Bagnall, Janice Ann

Executive. Personal: Born March 8, 1943; Daughter of Mr. and Mrs. Thomas Bagnall. Education: Diploma, The Bryn Mawr Hospital

School of Nursing; B.S.N., M.S.N., University of Pennsylvania. Career: Assistant Vice President; Staff Nurse; Clinical Instructor; Assistant Director, Nursing Service; Associate Director, Nursing Service; Director, Nursing Service. Organizational Memberships: American Nurses Association; National League of Nursing; Bryn Mawr Hospital School of Nursing Alumni Association (president, 1972-74); Sigma Theta Tau (corresponding secretary, 1972-76); Pennsylvania Society for Nursing Service Administrators (executive committee, 1981 to present). Community Activities: Hospital Association (the nursing management simulation model advisory committee); Community Nursing Bureau of Philadelphia (board member, 1980 to present); Roxboro High School Honor Society. Religion: Wissahickon Baptist Church. Honors and Awards: Scholarship Award, 1961; Award of Highest Average First Year 1962, Highest Average Second Year 1963, 2nd Highest Average Third Year 1964, Bryn Mawr Hospital School of Nursing, 1962. Address: 112 Osborn Street, Philadelphia, Pennsylvania 19128.

Bailey, Bernadine Freeman

Free-Lance Writer. Personal: Born November 12, 1901; Daughter of Dr. and Mrs. T. O. Freeman (both deceased); Married John Hays Bailey (deceased). Education: B.A., Wellesley College, 1922; M.A., University of Chicago, 1924; Certificate of Studies, Sorbonne, Paris, 1956. Career: Editor, Laidlaw Brothers; Quarrie Corporation (*World Book Encyclopedia*); Publicity for National Parent Teachers Association. Organizational Memberships: Illinois Women's Press Association (president, 1941-45); Midland Authors; Society of London Press Club; Chicago Press Club. Community Activities: Green Pastures Health Retreat (benefactor). Published Works: Author of 104 published books, including *Abe Lincoln's Other Mother; American Shrines in England; Bells, Bells, Bells; Wonderland of Bears; Austria and Switzerland;* Juvenile Fiction: *Paris, I Love You; Maureen Marshall, Private Eye; Carol Carson, Books Across the Border;* Author of several hundred articles in a variety of publications, including *New York Times, Chicago Tribune, Christian Science Monitor, Travel Magazine, Ford Times, San Francisco Chronicle, Readers Digest, News Digest International* (Australia). Honors and Awards: Award for *Paris, I Love You*, Societe des Arts, Science et Lettres, Paris, 1962; Listed in *Who's Who in the Midwest, Who's Who of American Women, International Authors and Writers Who's Who, World Who's Who of Women, Foremost Women in Communications, 2000 Women of Achievement, Dictionary of International Biography, Contemporary Authors.* Address: 1516 Wabash Ave., Mattoon, Illinois 61938.

Bernadine F Bailey

Bailey, Exine Margaret Anderson

Professor, Professional Singer, Administrator. Personal: Born January 4, 1922; Daughter of Dr. J. L. Anderson (deceased). Education: B.S., University of Minnesota, 1944; M.A., Columbia University, 1945; Professional Diploma, Columbia University, 1951. Career: Professor, School of Music, University of Oregon-Eugene; Professional Singer; Administrator. Organizational Memberships: American Association of University Professors; Music Teachers National Association (national voice chairman, 1973-75, 1981-83); High Schol Voice Auditions (national chairman, 1970-74); Oregon Music Teachers Association (state president); National Association Teachers of Singing (northwest college chairman; lieutenant governor, northwest region, 1968-72; national voice education committee, 1971 to present). Community Activities: Lobbyist for Oregon State Board of Higher Education, 1977; Judge for Various Community Competitions and Performances. Honors and Awards: Metropolitan Opera Association Scholarship, 1945; New York City Teacher's Award, Singer of the Year, 1945; Honorable Mention, Music Federation of New York City, 1950. Address: 17 Westbrook Way, Eugene, Oregon 97405.

Bailey, Robert Clifton

Statistician. Personal: Born March 29, 1941; Son of Mr. and Mrs. J. Edward Bailey; Married Susan G. Goodman; Father of Linda, Alice. Education: B.S., Randolph-Macon College, 1962; M.S., Iowa State University, 1964; Ph.D., Emory University, 1972. Career: Statistician; Former Biometrician, Educator, Physicist. Organizational Memberships: American Statistical Association (Atlanta chapter treasurer, 1970-71; secretary, 1971-72; vice president, 1972-73; chairman, committee of representatives, 1978-81); American Association for the Advancement of Science; Biometric Society; Philosophical Society of Washington; Washington Academy of Sciences; Institute for Mathematics Statistics. Honors and Awards: Phi Beta Kappa; Sigma Xi (associate, 1964; member, 1972); Freshman Physics Award, 1960; N.I.H. Fellow in Biometry, 1964-67; N.I.H. Special Fellowship, 1970-71. Address: 6507 Divine Street, McLean, Virginia 22101.

Bair, Mary Helen

Program Director. Personal: Born November 1, 1929; Daughter of Mr. and Mrs. O. D. Griffin; Married Charles E. Bair; Mother of Michael Wayne. Education: Graduate, Idabel High School, Oklahoma, 1946; Graduate, B.M.I. Business College, 1948; Attended numerous seminars and workshops on radio; Graduate, Dale Carnegie Course, 1949. Career: Radio Station KFRO: Secretary to Manager, 1948-62; Program Director, 1962 to present; Holds 3rd Class Radio License; 30-minute "Christmas Shopping with Mary Helen" Show, Thanksgiving until Christmas Eve, 1952 to present. Organizational Memberships: Texas Press Women, District 9 (president, 1972-73; membership chairman, 1974-75; nominating committee chairman, 1974-75; treasurer, 1976-78; vice president, 1978-80; state sites chairman, 1974-75; state resolutions chairman, 1977-79); National Federation of Press Women, 1968 to present; Texas Press Women, Inc., 1968 to present; Epsilon Sigma Alpha, Theta Lambda Chapter (chapter president, 6 times; vice president, 5 times; secretary, 1 time; treasurer, 1979-81; district vice president, 1956-57; district president, 1957-58; district PPAC chairman, 1970-71; district co-ordinator, 1974-75; district chaplain, 1977-78). Community Activities: Muscular Dystrophy Association of America (charter member, first treasurer, northeast Texas chapter); American Cancer Society (director, Gregg-North chapter, 1976-82; public information committee); Gregg County Association for Retarded Citizens (team captain on membership drive, 1977-78; membership advisory committee, 1978-79); Longview Woman's Forum, 1977 to present; Young Men's Christian Association (team member on membership drive, 1979-81); Longview Public Schools (public information advisory council, 1979-80); Pine Tree Independent School District (communications advisory board, 1980-81); Longview Chamber of Commerce (information and public relations committee, 1980-81, 1981-82). Religion: St. Andrew Presbyterian Church; Deacon, 1968-71; Elder, Member of the Session, 1972. Honors and Awards: Texas Press Women, Inc: Woman of Achievement Award, 1977; Annual Communications Award, First Place in Radio Feature and Radio News, 1981; A.B.I.R.A. Life Fellow; Listed in *Who's Who of American Women, The World Who's Who of Women, Community Leaders of America, Personalities of America.* Address: 1105 W. Garfield, Longview, Texas 75603.

Baird, Clyde Ray

University Administrator. Personal: Born January 31, 1921; Son of Clyde and Elva Baird; Married Ann A. Anderson; Father of Catherine Ann. Education: A.B. Southwestern College, Kansas, 1942; M.A., Teacher's College, Columbia University, 1947; Ed.D.,

University of Oklahoma, 1956. Military: Served in the United States Air Force. Career: Pittsburg State University- Vice President for Administration 1979 to present, Executive Vice President 1968-79, Professor 1958, Associate Professor 1957, Director of Admissions/Registrar 1953-68, Counselor/Guidance Bureau 1947-53; Consultant/Examiner, North Central Association. Organizational Memberships: American Association of Collegiate Registrars and Admissions Officers (chairman); Kansas Association of Collegiate Registrars and Admissions Officers (president); American Psychological Association; Rotary International. Community Activities: Pittsburg Area Chamber of Commerce. Religion: First United Methodist Church, Board of Trustees, Administrative Board. Honors and Awards: Omicron Delta Kappa. Address: Rural Route 5, Box 345, Pittsburgh, Kansas 66762.

Bairstow, Frances

Professor, Arbitrator. Personal: Born February 19, 1920; Married David Bairstow; Mother of Dale Owen, David Anthony. Education: B.S., University of Wisconsin, 1942; Undertook Graduate Studies, University of Louisville, Oxford University (England), McGill University (Montreal). Career: Professor and Arbitrator, McGill University; Former Government Research Economist, Corporation Research Economist. Organizational Memberships: National Academy of Arbitrators (program chairman; governing board, 1977-78); Industrial Relations Research Association (executive board, 1966-69); McGill University Association of University Teachers (president, 1977-78). Community Activities: Canadian Government National Inquiry Commission on Wider-Based Bargaining (chairman, 1978). Honors and Awards: Fulbright Scholar, Oxford University, 1953-54. Address: 3450 Redpath Street, Montreal, Quebec, Canada W3G 2G3.

Frances Bairstow

Bajzer, William Xavier

Research Specialist. Personal: Born June 17, 1940; Son of Edward and Theresa Bajzer; Married Elizabeth Ann Mocnik; Father of Christopher, Cheryl Ann, Michael and Susan. Education: B.S., Case Institute of Technology, 1963; M.S., 1966 and Ph.D., 1968, Ohio State University. Career: Dow Corning: Senior Research Specialist (1976-81), Section Manager (1975-76), Development Manager (1973-75), R & D Supervisor (1971-73), Research Chemist (1969-71), Chemist (1963-65), Process Engineering Section Manager (1981 to present). Organizational Memberships: American Chemical Society, 1962 to present; New York Academy of Sciences, 1970 to present; Sigma Xi, 1971 to present. Community Activities: Boy Scouts of America (committee chairman, 1971-74); Parent Teacher Association (president, vice president, treasurer); School Carnival (chairman, 1974-76). Religion: Lay Minister, 1972 to present; Parish Education Committee, 1977. Honors and Awards: Veasey Award in Physical Chemistry, 1962. Address: 4201 McKeith Road, Midland, Michigan 48640.

Baker, Betty Louise

Educator. Personal: Born October 17, 1937; Daughter of Russell J. and Lucille J. Baker. Education: B.Ed., 1961, M.A., 1964, both from Chicago Teachers College; Ph.D., Northwestern University, 1971. Career: Mathematics Teacher and Department Chairperson. Organizational Memberships: National Council Teachers of Mathematics; Illinois Council Teachers of Mathematics; Mathematics Association of America; Chicago Teachers Union; Phi Delta Kappa; Kappa Delta Pi. Community Activities: Hubbard High School Parent Teacher Student Association (president, 1979-81; vice president, 1981 to present). Religion: Lutheran; Church Organist, 1963 to present; Sunday School Teacher, 1954 to present. Honors and Awards: University Fellowship, Northwestern University, 1969-70; Outstanding Senior, Chicago Teachers College, 1961; Book of Recognition, 1981. Address: 3214 W. 85th Street, Chicago, Illinois 60652.

Baker, Bruce Nelson

Professor of Managment, Management Consultant. Personal: Born December 9, 1930; Son of Mrs. Elvera Baker; Married Mary Kathryn Shaw; Father of Sara Susan, Ashlee Anne, Andrea Lynne, Melanie Marie, James Winslow. Education: A.B., Princeton University, 1953; M.B.A., Stanford University, 1955; D.P.A., The George Washington University, 1972. Military: Served in the United States Navy, 1956-57. Career: Professor of Management; Management Consultant; Former Associate Professor, Boston College; Lecturer/Professor, University of Southern California; Senior Consultant, Management Systems Corporation; Management Systems Supervisor, Philco-Ford Corporation; Operations Planning Analyst, Senior Manufacturing Engineer, Lockheed Missiles and Space Company. Organizational Memberships: Academy of Management; American Society for Public Administration; Project Management Institute (editorial board, 1973-78); World Future Society (vice president, Boston-Cambridge chapter, 1973); International Management Systems Association. Community Activities: United Nations Food and Agriculture Organization (headquarters consultant, Rome, Italy, 1980 to present); United States Environmental Protection Agency, Water Quality Division Headquarters and Regional Offices (consultant, 1979 to present); Consulting Work and Seminars Presented to Over 25 Federal Agencies, State Agencies and Municipalities, 1962 to present. Honors and Awards: $100,000 N.A.S.A. Grant to Investigate Success and Failure Patterns in Project Management, 1972-74. Address: 1200 Washington Avenue, Oshkosh, Wisconsin 54901.

Baker, Deanna

Travel Agent. Personal: Born January 20, 1937; Daughter of Edna Alice Bolin; Married Marion K. Baker; Mother of G. Michael, Brenda Diane Baker-Brooks, Douglas R., Kimberly Ann. Education: A.A., Harper College. Career: Owner/Manager, Travel Agency. Organizational Memberships: American Business Women's Association; American Society of Travel Agents. Community Activities: Foster Parents Association; International Exchange Student Association; Girl Scouts; Boy Scouts. Religion: First Southern Baptist Church, Sunday School Teacher, Women's Missionary Union President, Children's Church Coordinator. Honors and Awards: Military Wife of the Year, 1970; Listed in *Who's Who in Industry and Finance*. Address: 4342 Scorpio Road, Lompoc, California 93436.

Baker, Frank Hamon

Animal Scientist, International Stockmen's School Director. Personal: Born May 2, 1923; Son of Dewitt and Maude Baker (both deceased); Married Melonee Gray; Father of Rilda, Necia, Twila, Dayna. Education: B.S., 1947, M.S., 1951, Ph.D., 1954, all from Oklahoma State University. Military: Served with the United States Army, 1943-45. Career: Oklahoma Extension Agent, 1947-48; Veterans Agriculture Teacher, 1948-50; Graduate Student, 1950-53; Animal Scientist, Kansas State University, 1953-55; Animal Scientist, University of Kentucky, 1955-58; Extension Animal Scientist, Oklahoma State University, 1958-62; Coordinator Extension

Animal Science, U.S. Department of Agriculture, Washington, D.C., 1962-66; Chairman, Animal Science Department, University of Nebraska, 1966-74; Dean of Agriculture, Oklahoma State University, 1974-79; Director, International Stockmen's School, Winrock Morrilton, Arkansas, 1981 to present. Organizational Memberships: American Society of Animal Science (vice president, 1973; president, 1974); Council for Agricultural Science and Technology (president elect, 1978; president, 1979); National Beef Improvement Federation (executive secretary 1968-74); American Meat Science Association; American Society for the Advancement of Science. Community Activities: 4-H Club; Block and Bridle Club; Agriculture Student Association (president, 1946); Alpha Zeta; Blue Key; Phi Kappa Phi; Farm House Fraternity; Sigma Xi; Gamma Sigma Delta; Epsilon Sigma Phi; Omicron Delta Kappa; American Legion; Kiwanis; Advisory Committee to U.S. Secretary of Agriculture, 1972-76; National Beef Records Committee (chairman, 1963-65); American Polled Hereford Association (advisory committees); American Hereford Association; American Angus Association; National Cattlemen's Association; Great Plains Range & Livestock Committee (chairman, 1971-73); North Central Research Advisory Committee (chairman, 1972-73); U.S.A.I.D. and Agriculture Agencies of Turkey, Colombia, Ecuador, Botswana (consultant). Religion: Methodist. Honors and Awards: American Society of Animal Science: Fellow, 1977 and Animal Industry Service Award, 1981; Oklahoma Farmers Union Service Award, 1980; Hall of Merit, American Polled Hereford Association, 1974; Agriculture Achievement Award, Knights of AKSARBEN, 1974; Oklahoma State University Animal Science Alumni Hall of Fame, 1968; American Association for the Advancement of Science Fellow; U.S. Department of Agriculture: Special Merit, 1966 and Outstanding Service Award, 1965; Distillers Feed Research Council Distinguished Nutritionist, 1964; Beef Improvement Federation Service Award, 1974; Future Farmers of America Honorary Farmer Award, 1976; National 4-H Award, 1941; Purple Heart, 1945. Address: Winrock International, Rt. 3, Morrilton, Arkansas 72110.

Baker, John Stevenson

Author. Personal: Born June 18, 1931; Son of Everette B. (deceased) and Ione M. Baker. Education: B.A., cum laude, Pomona College, 1953; M.D., University of California School of Medicine, Berkeley and San Francisco, 1957. Career: 48 poems, including "A Lake for Those Who Died of Syphilis", "Os", "Stahr", "The Sun's a Bug" (published in *Tenth Assembling*, 1980); "Solomon's Seal", "Recall", "The Sprocket of a Metaphor"; Also poems published under the name Michael Dyregrov: "Nuthatch", "Rose-breasted Grosbeak", "Ermine", "Owl Pillow"; Author of a fictional diary "The Diary of Sesso-Vesucci", *Trace*, Autumn 1963; Short Story, "Mister Carcoleotes", *The Human Voice Quarterly*, May 1965; Number of Articles in Professional Journals, including, "Electroencephalograms during hypoxia in healthy men" in *Archives of Neurology*, December 1961 and "Patterns of the electroencephalogram during tilt, hypoxia and hypercapnia: response characteristics for normal aging subjects" in *Neurology*, April 1963. Honors and Awards: First Prize, Jennings English Prize, Pomona College, 1950; Distinguished Service Award, Minnesota State Horticultural Society, 1976; Certificate of Appreciation, United States National Arboretum, Washington D.C., 1978. Address: P.O. Box 16007, Minneapolis, Minnesota 55416.

Baker, Kerry A

Senior Manufacturing Engineer. Personal: Born September 21, 1949; Son of Austin C. and Betty Baker. Education: B.I.E., Georgia Institute of Technology, 1971; M.B.A., Georgia State University, 1973. Military: Served in the United States Army, 1973-77, achieving the rank of Captain. Career: Senior Project Engineer, Plough, Inc. Organizational Memberships: American Institute of Industrial Engineers (senior member); American Management Association; American Institute of Plant Engineers; Society of American Military Engineers; Society for the Advancement of Management. Community Activities: Alpha Phi Omega (life member); International Platform Association; American Defense Preparedness Association (life member); 32° Mason; Sigma Phi Epsilon. Honors and Awards: Pi Delta Epsilon; Scabbard and Blade; Order of St. Barbara; Army Commendation Medal, 1977; Listed in *Who's Who in Greek Fraternities, Who's Who in the South and Southwest, Who's Who in Technology Today, Dictionary of International Biography, Personalities of America*. Address: 3548 Evening Light Drive, Bartlett, Tennessee 38134.

Lillian Baker

Baker, Lillian

Author, Editor, Lecturer. Personal: Born December 12, 1921, in New York; Married Roscoe Albert Baker; Mother of Wanda Georgia, George Riley. Education: Attended the University of California-Los Angeles, El Camino College; Certificate of Completion, Famous Writer's School. Career: Author, Editor, Lecturer; Journalist. Organizational Memberships: National League of American Pen Women; National Writers Club. Community Activities: National Trust for Historic Preservation (founding member, 1970); The National Historical Society. Published Works: *Collector's Encyclopedia of Hatpins and Hatpin Holders; 100 Years of Collectible Jewelry; Art Nouveau & Art Deco Jewelry; The Concentration Camp Conspiracy: A Second Pearl Harbor*. Honors and Awards: Certificate for newspaper column, Freedoms Foundation at Valley Forge, 1971; The National Writers Club Article Contest Awardee, 1977; International Poetry Contest Award, Clover Publishing Company, 1969; Gardena Valley Friends of the Library Award, 1968; Certificate of Recognition, International Toastmistress, 1964; Ladies Auxiliary, Veterans of Foreign Wars Award for Services Performed, 1974-75; Listed in *Who's Who in America*. Address: 15237 Chanera Avenue, Gardena, California 90249.

Baker, Robert Hart

Music Director. Personal: Born March 19, 1954, Bronxville, New York; Son of Jeanne Baker. Education: A.B. cum laude, Harvard College, 1974; M.Mus. 1976, M.M.A. 1978, Yale School of Music. Career: Music Director, Asheville Symphony Orchestra; Formerly with the Youth Symphony Orchestra of New York at Carnegie Hall; Connecticut Philharmonic Orchestra; Bach Society Orchestra, Cambridge, Massachusetts; Putnam (New York) Symphony Orchestra. Organizational Memberships: American Symphony Orchestra League Conductor's Guild; American Society of Composers, Authors and Publishers; American Verdi Institute; International Double Reed Society. Community Activities: Guest Conductor, Rhode Island Philharmonic, St. Louis Philharmonic, Spoleto (Italy) Festival Orchestra, York (Pennsylvania) Philharmonic, Connecticut Music Educators Association Orchestra; Guest Speaker, Kiwanis International, Civitan International, National Association of American Pen Women. Honors and Awards: American Society of Composers, Authors and Publishers Award for Modern Music Programming, 1981; Yale School of Music Alumni Association Award, 1978; National Federation of Music Clubs Composition Award, 1976; McCord Book Prize at Harvard, 1974; Jellinek Gold Medal for Composition, New York City, 1971. Address: 129 Evelyn Place, Asheville, North Carolina 28801.

Baker, T Lindsay

Curator of Science and Technology. Personal: Born April 22, 1947. Education: B.A. 1969, M.A. 1972, Ph.D 1977, Texas Tech

University. Career: Curator of Science and Technology, Panhandle-Plains Historical Museum; Program Manager and Lecturer, History of Engineering Program, Texas Tech University, 1971-75, 1977-79; Fulbright Lecturer, Technical University of Wroclaw, Poland, 1975-77; Passenger Service Attendant, Atchison, Topeka and Santa Fe Railway Company, 1967-70. Organizational Memberships: American Historical Association; American Association of Museums; American Association for State and Local History; National Trust for Historic Preservation; Western History Association; Polish American Historical Association; International Molinological Society; Texas State Historical Association. Community Activities: Boy Scouts of America (volunteer leader, 1966-70); Polish American Congress of Texas (board member, 1977-81). Published Works: *Water for the Southwest: Historical Survey and Guide to Historic Sites; The Early History of Panna Maria, Texas; The First Polish Americans: Silesian Settlements in Texas; A Field Guide to American Windmills; The Polish Texans.* Honors and Awards: Eagle Scout, 1962; Fulbright Lecturer, 1975-77; Research Scholarships, Kosciuszko Foundation, 1973-74, 1977; Coral H. Tullis Award, Texas State Historical Association, and Elizabeth Broocks Bates Award, Daughters of the Republic of Texas, for *The First Polish Americans*, as Best Book on Texas in 1979. Address: P.O. Box 7, W. T. Station, Canyon, Texas 79016.

Baker, William Duncan

Liaison Engineer. Personal: Born September 27, 1950; Married Katherine Ann; Father of Gray Duncan, Ryan Patrick, Brandon Dale. Education: B.S., Texas A&M University, 1971. Career: Liaison Engineer, Bell Company, 1977 to present, 1975-76; Safety Engineer, United States Government, 1976-77; Boeing Company -System Safety Engineer 1974-75 and 1971-72, Programming Analyst 1972-74. Organizational Memberships: Experimental Aircraft Association; National Society of Professional Engineers; Texas Society of Professional Engineers; Alpha Phi Omega; Sigma Gamma Tau; Tau Beta Pi. Honors and Awards: Listed in *International Youth in Achievement, Personalities of America, Personalities of the South, Community Leaders of America, Who's Who in the South and Southwest, Who's Who in Technology Today, Dictionary of International Biography, Directory of Distinguished Americans, International Register of Profiles, Book of Honor.* Address: 3612 Thurman, Amarillo, Texas 79109.

Baker, William Oliver

Retired Chairman of the Board. Personal: Born July 15, 1915, in Chestertown, Maryland; Son of Harold M. and Helen Stokes Baker (both deceased); Married Frances Burrill in 1941; Father of Joseph, Wendy (deceased). Education: B.A., Washington College, 1935; Ph.D., Princeton University, 1938; Recipient of 21 honorary degrees. Career: Bell Laboratories, 1939-80: In Charge of Polymer Research & Development, 1948-51; Assistant Director of Chemical & Metallurgical Research, 1951-54; Director of Research, Physical Sciences, 1954-55; Vice President of Research, 1955-73; President, 1973-79; Chairman of the Board, 1979-80. Organizational Memberships: Director: Summitt and Elizabeth Trust Company 1958 to present, Babcock and Wilcox Company 1962-78, Mead Johnson & Company 1966-68, Annual Reviews Incorporated 1969 to present, Council on Library Resources 1970 to present, Bell Telephone Laboratories Incorporated 1973-80, Clinical Scholars Program of the Robert Wood Johnson Foundation 1973-76, Sandia Corporation 1973-80, The Third Century 1974-76, American Bell International Incorporated 1975-79, Western Electric Company Incorporated 1975-80, Harry Frank Guggenheim Foundation 1976 to present, Western Electric International Incorporated 1978 to present, Johnson and Johnson; Trustee: Rockefeller University 1960 to present (vice chairman 1970-80, chairman 1980 to present), Urban Studies Incorporated 1960-78, Aerospace Corporation 1961-76, Princeton University 1964 to present, The Andrew W. Mellon Foundation 1965 to present (chairman 1975 to present, Old Dominion Foundation 1965, Avalon Foundation 1967), Carnegie-Mellon University 1967 to present, The Fund for New Jersey 1974 to present, General Motors Cancer Research Foundation 1978 to present, The Charles Babbage Institute 1978 to present, The Newark Museum 1979 to present; American Chemical Society, 1938 to present (carbon committee, third carbon conference, 1958; councilor, North Jersey section; committee advisory to the chemical corps, 1961-63; committee on national defense, 1963-69; committee on chemistry and public affairs, 1965-77; consultant, 1978-79; education steering committee, 1969-80); Industrial Research Institute, 1955-80 (director, 1960-63; membership committee, 1961-62; advisory editorial board of *Research Management*, 1962-63); Directors of Industrial Research, 1956 to present; Cosmos Club, 1959 to present; American Society for Testing and Materials (administrative committee on research, 1959-60); National Academy of Sciences, 1961 to present (council, 1969-72); Scientific Research Society of America (board of governors, 1961-67; R.E.S.A. Proctor Award committee, 1962, 1963, 1964; R.E.S.A. nominating committee, 1965); American Physical Society (fellow, 1962 to present); American Philosophical Society, 1963 to present; American Academy of Arts and Sciences, 1965 to present; American Institute of Chemists (fellow, 1968 to present); Institute of Medicine, 1972 to present (council, 1973-75; finance committee, 1976-79); The Chemist's Club (honorary member, 1974 to present); National Academy of Engineering, 1975 to present; The Franklin Institute (fellow, 1977 to present). Published Works: *Listen to Leaders in Engineering, Science and Society: A Symposium, Perspectives in Polymer Science*, numerous others books in the professional realm; approximately 100 research papers. Honors and Awards: 1 of top 10 Scientists in U.S. Industry, 1954; A.I.C. Honor Scroll, 1962; Perkin Medal, 1963; Priestley Medal, 1966; Edgar Marburg Award, 1967; A.S.T.M. Award to Executives, 1967; Industrial Research Institute Medal, 1970; Frederik Philips Award, 1972; Industrial Research Man of the Year Award, 1973; Proctor Prize, 1973; James Madison Medal, Princeton University, 1975; Gold Medal, American Institute of Chemists, 1975; Mellon Institute Award, 1975; Award for Distinguished Contributions to Research Administration, Society of Research Administrators, 1976; American Chemical Society Parsons Award, 1976; Franklin Institute Delmer S. Fahrney Medal, 1977; J. Willard Gibbs Medal, American Chemical Society, 1978; von Hippel Award, Materials Research Society, 1978; New Jersey Science/Technology Medal, 1980; Madison Marshall Award, 1980; Vannevar Bush Award, 1981; Jefferson Medal, 1981; Sarnoff Award, A.F.C.E.A., 1981; Holder of 13 patents. Address: Spring Valley Road, Morristown, New Jersey 07060.

Balasa, Richard Wayne

Associate Pathologist, Director of Clinical Biochemistry. Personal: Born February 11, 1946, Chicago, Illinois. Education: B.A. cum laude, Yale University, 1968; M.D., St. Louis University School of Medicine, 1973; Research Fellow, Department of Pathology, Rush-Presbyterian-St. Luke's Medical Center, Chicago, 1968-69; Acting Intern, Department of Pathology, Peter Bent Brigham Hosptial, Boston, 1972-73; Resident in Anatomic Pathology, Laboratory of Pathology, National Cancer Institute, National Institutes of Health, Bethesda, Maryland, 1973-75; Fellow in Surgical Pathology, Department of Laboratory Medicine and Pathology, University of Minnesota Medical School, 1975-76; Resident in Laboratory Medicine, University of Minnesota Medical School, 1976-77; Fellow in Chemical Pathology, University of Minnesota Medical School, 1977-78. Military: Served in the United States Public Health Service as Senior Assistant Surgeon, 1973-75. Career: Associate Professor, Department of Pathology, University of Illinois College of Medicine; Director of Clinical Biochemistry, Lutheran General Hospital. Organizational Memberships: American Medical Association; American Society of Clinical Pathologists; College of American Pathologists; Medical Licensure, Illinois, California; Certifications, National Board of Medical Examiners, American Board of Pathology. Published Works: Co-Author "The Brenner Tumor: A Clinicopathologic Review". Address: Apt. 103, 5451 N.E. River Road, Chicago, Illinois 60646.

Balducci, Carolyn

Writer, Lecturer. Personal: Born February 13, 1946; Daughter of Mrs. Ernest J. Feleppa; Married; Mother of One Daughter. Education: B.A., Manhattanville College; Various Courses in Creative Writing and Film. Career: Writer for Visual Media and Children's Books; Lecturer; Former Editor. Organizational Memberships: Author's Guild; University of Michigan Children's Literature Council; Director of American Writers of Fiction; Society of Children's Book Writers. Community Activities: Michigan Council for the Arts Writers in the Schools Program. Published Works: *Is There Life After Graduation, Henry Birnbaum?; Earwax; A Self-Made Woman: The Biography of Nobel Prize Winner Grazia Deledda.* Honors and Awards: *Mademoiselle* Magazine Guest Editor, 1966; Ohio Public Program in the Humanities Grants, 1975, 1977; Notable Book Award, American Library Association, 1971; Book of the Year Award, Child Study, 1976. Address: 624 Fifth Street, Ann Arbor, Michigan 48103.

Baldwin, Jack Lyell

Extension Entomologist. Personal: Born February 14, 1949; Son of Mr. and Mrs. James E. Frierson; Married Anne Frierson; Father of Belinda Marie, Priscilla Michelle, Kimberly Leigh. Education: B.S. 1971, M.S. 1972, Texas A&M University; Ph.D., Oklahoma State University, 1980. Career: Extension Entomologist, Louisiana State University; Field Biologist, Agricultural Chemicals Division, I.C.I. America, Inc., 1974-76. Organizational Memberships: American Registry of Professional Entomologists; Entomological Society of America; Louisiana Entomology Society; Southwestern Entomological Society. Honors and Awards: Distinguished Graduate, Texas A&M University, 1971; Silver Caduceus Society of Korea; Listed in *Who's Who in the South and Southwest.* Address: 17212 Gaines Mill Avenue, Baton Rouge, Louisiana 70816.

Baldwin, Ruth W

Professor. Personal: Born January 3, 1915, Chicago, Illinois; Daughter of John J. and Lucille Hayes Workman; Married Gary Martin Baldwin, September 2, 1939; Mother of John Workman, Gary Martin Jr., Thomas Michael, Robert Hayes. Education: B.S, University of Maryland, 1942; M.D., University of Maryland School of Medicine, 1943; Intern, West Baltimore General Hospital, 1943-44; New Lutheran Hospital, Assistant Residency in Medicine 1944-45, Residency in Medicine 1945-46; Assistant Residency in Pediatrics, University Hospital, 1946-49; Post-Doctoral Fellowship, Harvard Medical School, 1950; Board Qualified, Fellow, American Academy of Pediatrics, 1952. Career: University of Maryland School of Medicine - Director of Seizure Unit and Assistant in Pediatrics 1950-54, Director of Seizure Unit and Assistant Professor in Pediatrics 1954-63, Director of Clinic for the Exceptional Child 1963 to present, Associate Professor in Pediatrics 1964-76, Professor in Pediatrics 1976 to present; Organizational Memberships: State of Maryland Motor Vehicle Administration (chairman, medical advisory board); Council for Developmental Disabilities (chairman, 1971-73); Executive Coalition for the Handicapped (chairman); American Academy of Pediatrics (chairman, handicapped and mental health committee, Maryland chapter); Consultant in Epilepsy, Maryland State Department of Health and Mental Hygiene; Rosewood Center, Henryton Center, Holly Center, Provident Hospital, Kernan's Hospital, Peninsula General Hospital; Angel's Haven (board of directors); Epilepsy Association of Maryland, Inc. (board of directors, medical advisory board); Medical Advisory Board, Baltimore County Parents and Friends of the Retarded, Maryland Eastern Shore Epilepsy Association, Baltimore Association for Mentally Retarded Citizens, Inc., Association for Children with Specific Learning Disabilities, Frederick County Association for Epilepsy, Maryland State Society for Autistic Children; American Automobile Association for Medicine; Trauma Society; American Academy of Pediatrics; Maryland Chapter, American Academy of Pediatrics; Maryland State Chirurgical Faculty; American Medical Association; Eastern Association of Electroencephalographers; American League Against Epilepsy; National Rehabilitation Association; American Academy of Neurology (associate member); Baltimore Neurological Association; American Medical Womens Association Maryland Chapter, A.W.A. Published Works: Number of Articles in Professional Journals and Books. Honors and Awards: Baltimore Association of Retarded Children, 1952; Maryland State Traffic Safety Commission, 1966; Frederick Epilepsy Association, 1970; Governor's Citation for Work with Epilepsy, Work in Traffic Safety, Governor's Task Force on the Alcoholic Driver; Epilepsy Association of Maryland; Epilepsy Advocates; Listed in *Two Thousand Women of Achievement.* Address: 324 Gun Road, Relay, Maryland 21227.

Louis A Ball

Balkema, Charles R

Executive. Personal: Born July 10, 1933; Son of Mr. and Mrs. Jack H. Balkema; Married Louise K. Kleis; Father of Charles R. Jr., Curtis B., Christopher L., Cara L., Jennifer L., Jamison B. Education: Attended the University of Michigan. Military: Served in the United States Air Force, 1953-57, achieving the rank of Staff Sergeant. Career: President and Chief Executive Officer, Haviland Enterprises, Inc.; Vice Chairman of the Board, Haviland Products, Haviland Agricultural and Wheaton Chemical; Haviland Products Company, Executive Vice President, Vice President, Director of Marketing; Manager of Packaging Coatings Division, Guardsman Chemical Coatings. Organizational Memberships: National Association of Chemical Distributors (president, 1980 to present; executive vice president, 1978-79; treasurer, 1974-78). Community Activities: Economic Development Corporation for Grand Rapids (past director, 1978-80); Ottawa Hills Elementary School (past president, 1969); Ottawa Hills Neighborhood Association (president, 1974-78); Grand Rapids Neighborhood Alliance (co-chairman, 1975); City High School (parents advisory board, 1977-78); Grand Rapids Public Schools (board member, world affairs council, 1979-80); World Affairs Council of Western Michigan (board member, 1970-75); Kent Intermediate School Board (president, 1980 to present). Religion: East Congregational Church, Board of Deacons 1972-74, Church Choir 1965-76. Honors and Awards: Airman of the Month, United States Air Force, 1956; Listed in *Who's Who in Finance and Industry, Who's Who in the Midwest.* Address: 157 Alexander Road, S.E., Grand Rapids, Michigan 49506.

Ball, Louis Alvin

Corporate Secretary, Systems and Procedure Manager. Personal: Born October 25, 1921, in Kansas City, Missouri; Son of George Rhodam and Frances Beals Ball (both deceased); Married Norma Jane Laudenberger. Education: B.A., Kansas State University, 1947. Career: Assistant Purchasing Agent, Ford Motor Company, Kansas City Branch, 1942-46; Farm Bureau Mutual Insurance Company: Underwriting Department, 1947-56; Claims Underwriting Manager, 1956-75; Systems and Procedures Manager; Assistant Secretary, 1975-81; Corporate Secretary, 1981 to present. Organizational Memberships: National Association of Independent Insurers; The Conference of Casualty Companies (general chairman of methods seminar, 1979); Association for Systems Management (general chairman, annual conference, 1982; has held every elective office of Kansas City chapter, including president, 1969-70 and division director, 1972-78). Community Activities: Manhattan Country Club (past vice president, former member of board of directors); Manhattan Sunflower Lions Club (past board member). Religion: First Presbyterian Church; Former member Board of Trustees and Board of Deacons. Honors and Awards: Association for Systems Management: International Merit Award, International

Achievement Award, Kansas City Chapter Merit Award, Past President Award, Diamond Merit Award, Distinguished Service Award; Listed in *Personalities of the West and Midwest, Book of Honor, Who's Who in the Midwest.* Address: 1101 Pioneer Lane, Manhattan, Kansas 66502.

Ballance, Charlotte Ann

Accountant, Corporate Treasurer, Farmer. Personal: Born April 28, 1944; Daughter of T. S. and F. J. Ballance. Education: Attended Illinois State University; B.A., McKendree College, 1969; M.A.Ed., Murray State University, 1973. Career: Former Elementary School Teacher; Currently an Accountant; Corporate Treasurer and Board of Directors; Farmer. Organizational Memberships: American Business Women's Association (various committee chairmanships, 1970-81); National Education Association; American Association of University Women (co-chairman of antique show, 1980). Community Activities: Beta Sigma Phi (volunteer, telethon for Easter Seals, 1980). Religion: Teacher Training Course, Bethel Bible Series, 1979-81. Honors and Awards: Kappa Delta Pi, Murray State University, 1973. Address: P. O. Box 11, Decatur, Illinois 62525.

Glenn G Balmer

Balmer, Glenn Graves

Highway Research Engineer. Personal: Born December 24, 1914; Son of Mr. and Mrs. Clarence A. Balmer (both deceased); Married Mary Faith Neely; Father of Darrell Gene, Glenn Bruce. Education: A.B., Fort Hays State College; M.S., State University of Iowa; Attended the summer session at University of Michigan; A.A.F. Technical Training Center, Commissioned; Undertook Night Courses, University of Colorado and Northwestern University; Attended Graduate School, U.S. Department of the Agriculture. Military: Served with the United States Air Force Reserves, achieving the rank of Lieutenant Colonel. Career: Graduate Assistant, State University of Iowa; Teacher, Estherville Junior College, Estherville, Iowa; Weather Officer, United States Air Force, Pacific Ocean Areas; Physicist, Bureau of Reclamation, Denver, Colorado; Senior Development Engineer, Portland Cement Association, Skokie, Illinois; Highway Research Engineer, Federal Highway Administration, U.S. Department of Transportation, Washington D.C. Organizational Memberships: American Society for Testing and Materials (committees D4, first vice chairman of E17, F9); American Concrete Institute; Transportation Research Board; National Safety Council (committee on winter driving hazards); American Psychological Association (accident research committee). Religion: Assembly of God; Board of Deacons, Bible Teacher. Honors and Awards: Sigma Xi; Delta Epsilon; Air Medal; Asiatic Pacific Campaign Medal; American Defense Medal; World War II Victory Medal; Reclamation Technical Club; Listed in *Two Thousand Men of Achievement, Who's Who in the United States, International Who's Who in Community Service, Dictionary of International Biography, Who's Who in the Midwest, Who's Who in the South and Southwest, Who's Who in the East, Who's Who in Maryland.* Address: 11128 Hunt Club Drive, Potomac, Maryland 20854.

Balthaser, Linda Irene

University Administration. Personal: Born February 25, 1939; Daughter of Mr. and Mrs. Earl Showalter; Married Kenneth James Balthaser. Education: B.S. magna cum laude, Indiana Central University, 1961; M.S., Indiana University, 1962. Career: Assistant to the Dean of Arts and Letters, Indiana University-Purdue University, Fort Wayne, 1970 to present; Founding Co-Director, I.P.F.W. Weekend College, 1979-80; Acquisitions Assistant, I.P.F.W. Library, 1969-70; Secretary, Administrative Secretary, The President's Office, Indiana University-Bloomington, 1962-63; Teacher of Business Education, Southpost High School, Indianapolis, 1962-63. Organizational Memberships: Delta Pi Epsilon; American Association of University Administrators; International Platform Association. Community Activities: Associated Churches of Fort Wayne and Allen County (board member, 1980); Fort Wayne-Allen County Historical Society; Embassy Theatre Foundation; A.R.C.H.; Fort Wayne Museum of Art; Philharmonic Women's Committee, Historic Fort Wayne; Fort Wayne Zoological Society; Friends of I.P.F.W.; University Women's Club (president, 1969-69; various offices and committee responsibilities); Civic Theatre; Fort Wayne Philharmonic Society; Fine Arts Foundation; League of Women Voters; United Way. Religion: Messiah Lutheran Church, Daily Practitioner of Christian Principles. Honors and Awards: High School Valedictorian, 1957; Four-Year Academic Scholarship, Indiana Conference North, Evangelical United Brethren Church, 1957-61; Phi Alpha Epsilon; Epsilon Sigma Alpha; Delta Pi Epsilon; Mensa; Listed in *Who's Who in American Colleges and Universities, Outstanding Young Women of America, Who's Who of American Women.* Address: 2917 Hazelwood Avenue, Fort Wayne, Indiana 46805.

Carroll A Baltimore

Baltimore, Carroll Arthur

Pastor, Evangelist. Personal: Born May 14, 1943; Son of Helen V. Baltimore; Married Shirley F. Baltimore; Father of Gregory Lamont, Vanessa Louisa, Carroll Arthur Jr. Education: Attended Washington Baptist Theological Seminary, 1967-70; A.A., Luther Rice College, 1977; B.I.S., George Mason University, 1978; Th.M., 1980, Th.D., 1980, Honorary D.D., 1981, all from the International Bible Institute and Seminary; Attended Hampton Ministers Institute, 1980 & 1981. Military: Served with the United States Army, 1962-65, achieving the rank of E-4. Career: Former Mail Carrier; Pastor and Evangelist: Chestnut Grove Baptist Church, Brightwood, Virginia, 1969-72; Shiloh Baptist Church, Woodville, Virginia, 1970-72; Mount Pleasant Baptist Church, Alexandria, Virginia, 1972 to present. Organizational Memberships: Lott Carey Foreign Mission Convention (executive board, 1974 to present); Northern Virginia Baptist Association (executive board, 1973 to present; auditor board, 1978-79; educational board, 1976-81; scholarship committee, 1979; Baptist Center board, 1973-76); Mount Vernon Baptist Association (ordination commission, 1975-78; ministries commission, 1979 to present); Committee for Pastoral Awareness, 1976-77; National Black Pastors Conference of the World, 1980-81; Alexandria Ministers Conference (vice president, 1981); Southern Christian Leadership Conference, 1981; Southern Baptist Conventions, Inc. Community Activities: National Drug Abuse Foundation (board of directors, 1980); Masonic Lodge #292, Falls Church, Virginia (king tyree, 1977-81); Consortium for Continuing Higher Education in Northern Virginia (citizens advisory committee, 1978 to present); Virginia Governors Conference on Library and Informational Services (delegate, 1979); Bethany House, Inc., for Battered and Abused Women and Men (board of directors, 1979 to present); Social Center Inc. (board of directors, 1980-81); Steering Committee for President Carter's Election, 1976; National Association for the Advancement of Colored People; Fairfax Hospital Association Bronze Member, 1978-81; George Mason University Alumni Association, 1978-81; International Bible Institute and Seminary Alumni Association, 1981. Religion: Radio Ministry, WUST, Washington, D.C., 1979 to present; Three Week Crusade in India, 1979, 1982; Prison Ministry, 1979 to present; Tape Ministry, 1979-81; Recorded Album "If God's Not Home, Nobody's Home", 1980; *Evangelistic Outreach Journal*, 1980-81; Virginia Conference on Evangelism 1978-81; Baptist General Convention of Virginia, Commission on Evangelism, 1980-81; Speaker for the Virginia General Convention, State Evangelism Conference, 1980. Honors and Awards: Certificate of Contribution, Baptist Ministers Conference of Washington, D.C. and Vicinity for Outstanding Leadership to His Congregation in Acquiring a New and More Suitable Building and Facilities for Worship and the Christian Church, 1980; Recognition for Outstanding Support and Participation, George Mason University, Division of Continuing

Education, 1980; Certificates of Special Recognition of Excellence in Th.D., Certificate of Honor, International Bible Institute and Seminary, 1980; Certificate of Distinction, Man of Troas, Lott Carey Foreign Mission Convention, 1973-81; Meritorious Achievement in Religious Studies, History and Economics, Luther Rice College, 1975; Certificate for Volunteer Services, District of Columbia Department of Human Resources, 1980; Certificate of Appreciation, Outstanding Religious Sevices Rendered to Residents of Lorton Prison, 1980; Certificate of Recognition for Outstanding Achievement in Leading the Mount Vernon Baptist Association in Baptisms Reported, 1978-79; Letter of Recognition for Being Nominated to Receive the Fairfax County Human Rights Award, 1981; Listed in *Book of Honor, Personalities of the South.* Address: 12826 Kettering Drive, Herndon, Virginia 22070.

Bandy, Irene Gesa

Executive Director for Administration. Personal: Born August 30, 1940; Daughter of Mrs. Gesa Wolff; Mother of Nicholas Ernest Bandy. Education: B.S.Ed., Ohio University, 1962; M.A., Eastern Kentucky University, 1967; Ph.D., Ohio State University, 1979. Career: Teacher, Biology and General Science, 1962-64; Teacher, English, 1964-65; Guidance Supervisor, 1967-68; Guidance Counselor, 1968-73; Ohio Department of Education: Consultant, Division of Guidance & Testing, 1973-77; Assistant Director, Division of Guidance & Testing, 1977-79; Executive Director for Administration, 1979 to present. Organizational Memberships: American Personnel & Guidance Association (board of directors 1979-82); Buckeye Association for School Administrators; Phi Delta Kappa (president, 1981-82, Ohio State University chapter); Others. Honors and Awards: "You Done Good" Award, Ohio Personnel and Guidance Association, 1979-80. Address: 1922 Queensbridge Dr., Worthington, Ohio 43085.

Banik, Sambhu N

Administrator. Personal: Born November 7, 1935; Son of Padma and Dakambini Banik; Married Promila Roy; Father of Sharmila, Kakoli. Education: I.Sc., Vidyasagar College, 1954; B.Sc. 1956, M.Sc. 1958, Calcutta University; Ph.D., University of Bristol, England, 1964; Postdoctoral Fellowship, Norwich Hospital, Connecticut. Career: Chief, South Community Mental Health Center, Washington, D.C.; Chief, Mental Health Divisions, Glenn Dale Hospital and D.C. Village; Assistant Chief, Director of Training and Research, Glenn Dale Hospital and D.C. Village; Director, Psychological Services, University Hospital, Saskatoon, Canada; Assistant Professor, University of Saskatchewan, Saskatoon, Canada; Staff Psychologist, Des Moines Child Guidance Center, Des Moines, Iowa; Tutor, University of Bristol, England; Visiting Professor of Psychology and Special Education, Bowie State College, Bowie, Maryland. Organizational Memberships: Saskatchewan Psychological Society (president, 1969-70); American Psychological Association; American Group Psychotherapy Association; D.C. Psychological Association; World Federation for Mental Health; Pan American Medical Association; International Association of Forensic Psychology. Community Activities: Durgapur General Merchants Association (founder, president, 1958-60); Yoga Demonstration to Raise Money for Youngsters with Problems, Bristol, 1962-64; Prabashi (founder, president, 1974-78); India Cultural Coordinating Committee (president, 1979-81); Association of Indians in America (president, 1979-81); Sanskriti (executive committee, 1977-78); Nutana Rotary Club, 1969-71; Asian Pacific Cultural Heritage Council (secretary, 1981 to present); Talks and Seminars to Various Community Groups and Organizations on Number of Topics. Religion: Indian House of Worship, 1979-80. Honors and Awards: Awards in Yoga Demonstration, 1954-56; Trophy in Cooking Competition, Canadian Chef de Cuisine, 1970; Award from D.C. Psychologists Association, 1977; Award from Government of the D.C. for Outstanding Service, 1977, 1978, 1979; Listed in *Who is Who in Sakatchewan, Community Leaders of America, American Men and Women of Science, Men of Achievement, Who's Who in the East, Noteworthy Americans, International Who's Who in Community Service, Personalities of the South, Who's Who in America, International Who's Who of Intellectuals, Anglo-American Who's Who.* Address: 8606 Bradmoor Drive, Bethesda, Maryland 20034.

Harry Barba

Baranov, Andrey I

Botanist. Personal: Born October 17, 1917; Son of Ippolit G. and Varvara M. Baranov (both deceased); Married Nina M. Shcherbakov; Father of Elena. Education: First Class Diploma (LL.B. equivalent), Harbin Law School, 1938; M.S., Northeastern University, 1973. Career: Botanist, Harvard University Herbaria; Bibliography Researcher, World Life Research Institute, 1967-69; Herbarium Assistant, Arnold Arboretum, Harvard University, 1963-67; Research Fellow, Academia Sinica (Institute of Forestry and Soil Science), 1950-58; Research Fellow, Harbin Regional Museum, 1946-50. Organizational Memberships: New England Botanical Club (council member, 1974); American Fern Society; Botanical Society of America; International Association for Plant Taxonomy; Sigma Xi (associate member). Honors and Awards: Board of Advisors, Institute for Traditional Medicine and Preventive Health Care, 1979 to present; Commemorative Award, American Biographical Institute, 1982. Address: 18 Locke Street #2, Cambridge, Massachusetts 02140.

Baras, Carol Rose

Corporation Executive, Lecturer, Public Relations Director, Writer. Personal: Born October 1, 1930; Married Bill Baras; Mother of Gary Rose, Frank Rose, Linda Rose. Education: Attended San Diego State University; University of California Extension Courses; Specialized Education, University of London. Career: Corporation Executive; Lecturer; Public Relations Director; Professional Writer, "The Story Lady of San Diego"; Chief Financial Officer. Organizational Memberships: National Academy of Television Arts and Sciences; Media Club of San Diego. Community Activities: City Club of San Diego; We Can Organization; Big Sisters, 1979-80; Veterans Hospital, La Jolla (volunteer, weekly alcoholic treatment program, 1973-80); In-Depth Hypnotic Counseling for All Local Law Enforcement Agencies Regressing Witnesses to Violent Crimes to Recall Data to Further Acquire Information for Investigation Regarding Suspect (volunteer, 1974 to present); Semi-Annual Program for Law Students Preparing to Take the California Bar Exam, Stressing Relaxation Techniques, Habit Conditioning and Postitive Mental Control (conductor, 1976 to present); KIDS, Hotline for Children Ages 4 to 12, Promoting Building Self Reliance and Confidence (administrator, director, 1978 to present). Honors and Awards: Commendations from San Diego Police Department 1977-80, San Diego Sheriffs Department 1977-81, Escondido Police Department 1979-81, Department of Motor Vehicles 1980; Featured Guest, "Good Morning America", 1980; Featured Guest, "The Today Show", 1980; Featured on ABC News, CBS News, NBC News, Every Major Radio Station Nationwide, 1980; Featured on "Hour Magazine" and Cable Network News, 1981. Address: P.O. Box 3189, San Diego, California 92103.

Barba, Harry

Publisher, Writer, Educator. Personal: Born June 17, 1922; Son of Michael and Sarah Barba (both deceased); Married Marian Barba; Father of Gregory. Education: A.B., Bates College, 1944; M.A., Harvard University, 1951; M.F.A. 1960, Ph.D. 1963, University of Iowa; Further Studies undertaken at the City College of New York, New York University, Columbia University. Career: Instructor,

English and Writing, Wilkes College, Pennsylvania, 1947; Instructor in Literature and Writing, University of Connecticut-Hartford, 1947-49; English Teacher, Seward Park High School, 1955-59; Graduate Assistant, Part-time Instructor, University of Iowa, 1959-63; Fulbright Visiting Professor, American Specialist, Damascus University, 1963-64; Assistant/Associate Professor, Literature and Writing, Skidmore College, 1964-68; Professor of English, Director of Writing (creative and expository, first in United States), Marshall University, 1968-70; Distinguished Visiting Lecturer, Contemporary Literature and Consultant to the Writing Committee, State University of New York-Albany, 1977-78; Writer, Publisher. Organizational Memberships: Modern Language Association; College English Association; Conference on College Composition and Communication; Harvard Graduate Research Society; Harvard Club of Northeastern New York; Harvard Club of Eastern New York (board of directors, 1976-81; conference director, 1976-81); Authors Guild, Inc.; Authors League of America, Inc.; P.E.N.; Associated Writing Programs. Published Works: Books *For the Grape Season*, (first novel, 1960); *One of a Kind (The Many Faces and Voices of America)*, (first major collection of short stories and novellas); Short Works Appear in International Literary and Art Magazines. Honors and Awards: President, Spofford Club, Bates, 1943-44; Yaddo Residence Fellowship, 1950; Simon & Schuster Option Contract for a First Novel, 1953; MacMillan Option Contract for a Novel, 1958 (published 1960); University of Iowa Graduate Fellowship, 1963-64; Fulbright Post-Doctoral Fellowship 1961-62, Renewed 1962; Skidmore Summer Research Grants, 1965-68; Title I-HEA 1965, State of West Virginia and Marshall University 1969-70, Secured and Disbursed $100,000 for the Development of Writing Arts in West Virginia (Directed Year-Long Writers and Educators Conference out of Marshall University, 1968-70); C.A.P.S. Semi-Finalist, 1975; Poets and Writers Sponsored Reader Workshopper and Lecturer, 1975 to present; Listed in *Directory of American Scholars, Who's Who in the East, Contemporary Authors, Dictionary of International Biography, Civic Leaders, Community Leaders International, Writing Directory, Who's Who Among World's Authors and Writers.* Address: 47 Hyde Blvd., Ballston Spa, New York 12020.

Barcus, Nancy B

News Coordinator. Personal: Born November 9, 1937; Daughter of Doris Bidwell; Married Dr. James E. Barcus; Mother of Heidi, Hans. Education: A.B., University of Kentucky, 1961; M.A., State University of New York at Geneseo, 1970. Career: Assistant Professor of English, Houghton College, Houghton, New York, 1964-80; Editor, *Today* Magazine, Trinity College, Deerfield, Illinois, 1980; Freelance Author, 1970 to present; Science and Research News Coordinator, Baylor University, 1980 to present. Organizational Memberships: Modern Language Association; Women in Communications; Texas Press Women. Community Activities: Initiated Radio Interviews of Nationally Known Experts on Local Commercial Radio, KRZI; Conducted Workshops in Free-Lance Writing in Philadelphia and New York; Allegany County Council of Adoptive Parents (co-chairperson 1974-77); Danforth Foundation Associate (convening values clarification sessions for college students); Teacher, Suzuki Violin Method for Small Children in Community. Religion: Southern Baptist; Discussion Leader for Campus Groups, 1975 to present; Regular Writer for Religious Magazine, 1970 to present; Speaker on Christianity and Personal Lifestyle, 1975 to present. Honors and Awards: Phi Beta Kapa, 1961; Danforth Foundation Associate, 1966-80; Rated in Top 10% for Teaching Effectiveness on Middle States Evaluation Survey at Houghton College; Stanley Foundation Lecturer, 1981; Listed in *World Who's Who of Women, Outstanding Educators of America.* Address: 8217 Gatecrest Drive, Waco, Texas 76710.

Bardis, Panos D

Professor. Personal: Born September 24, 1924, in Lefcohorion, Arcadia, Greece; Son of Kali D. Bardis; Married Donna Jean Bardis; Father of Byron Galen, Jason Dante. Education: Attended Panteios Supreme School, Athens, Greece; B.A., magna cum laude, Bethany College; M.A., Notre Dame University; Ph.D., Purdue University. Career: Professor of Sociology and Editor, *International Social Science Review,* The University of Toledo; Editorships: *College Journal of Education, Darshana International, Indian Journal of Social Research, Indian Psychological Bulletin, International Journal of Contemporary Sociology, International Journal of Sociology of the Family, International Review of History and Political Science, International Review of Modern Sociology, International Review of Sociology, Journal of Education, Journal of Political and Military Sociology, Journal of Sociological Studies, Review of Social Sciences,* Numerous Others in the Field of Sociology and Social Sciences. Organizational Memberships: Alpha Kappa Delta, 1954 to present; American Association for the Advancement of Science (fellow 1960 to present); American Association of University Professors, 1955 to present; American Sociological Association (fellow 1953 to present, membership committee 1966-71); Conference Internationale de Sociologie de la Religion, 1969 to present; Council of Social Science Journal Editors, 1979 to present; Democritos, 1973 to present; Free Press International (editorial advisor 1980 to present); Group for the Study of Sociolinguistics, 1967 to present; Groves Conference (Ernest Groves memorial fund committee 1977 to present); Institut International de Sociologie (fellow 1969 to present; chairman, membership committee 1970 to present; coordinator for the U.S. 1974 to present); Institute for Mediterranean Affairs (advisory council 1968 to present); Institute for the Study of Plural Societies, University of Pretoria, South Africa (honorary associate 1974 to present); Intercontinental Biographical Association (fellow 1976 to present); International Association of Family Sociology, 1976 to present; International Institute of Arts and Letters (life fellow 1966 to present); International Personnel Research (honorary advisor 1971 to present); International Scientific Commission on the Family, 1969 to present; International Sociological Association, 1970 to present (research committee on social change, 1972 to present; research committee on family sociology 1974 to present); Kappa Delta Pi, 1975 to present; KRIKOS, 1975 to present (advisory council for academic affairs 1977 to present); Marquis Biographical Library Society (advisory member 1973 to present); Marriage Museum, New York City (board of trustees 1969 to present); Modern Greek Society, 1973 to present; National Academy of Economics and Political Science (board of directors 1959 to present); National Association on Standard Medical Vocabulary (consultant 1963 to present); National Council on Family Relations, 1953 to present; National Society of Literature and the Arts, 1975 to present; National Society of Published Poets, 1976 to present; National Writers Club (professional member 1963 to present); New York Academy of Sciences, 1963 to present; News World Communications (advisory board 1980 to present); North Central Sociological Association, 1972 to present; Ohio Council on Family Relations, 1959 to present; Ohio Society of Poets, 1976 to present; Ohio Valley Sociological Society, 1953-72; Phi Kappa Phi (life member 1972 to present); Pi Gamma Mu, 1959 to present; Professors' World Peace Academy (founding member 1979 to present); Sigma Xi, 1979 to present; Smithsonian Institution (associate 1977 to present); World Academy of Scholars (fellow 1976 to present); World Poetry Society Intercontinental, 1980 to present. Honors and Awards: Winner of Seminario de Investigacion Historica y Arqueologica Award, Museo de Historia, Barcelona, Spain, 1967; Listed in *American Hellenic Who's Who, Who's Who in Business and the Professions, American Men and Women of Science, American Men of Science, American Registry Series, Authors and Writers Who's Who, Biographical Encyclopedia of the United States, Book of Honor, Community Leaders and Noteworthy Americans, Contemporary Authors, Contemporary Notables, Creative and Successful Personalities of the World, Dictionary of International Biography, Directory of Distinguished Americans, Ellenicon Who's Who, International Authors and Writers Who's Who, International Biographical Association Yearbook and Biographical Directory, International Directory of Sex Research and Related Fields, International Directory of Sociology, International Portrait Gallery, International Scholars Directory, International Who's Who in Community Service, International Who's Who in Education, International Who's Who in Sociology, Men of Achievement, Who's Who in America, Who's Who in American Education, Who's Who in the Midwest, Who's Who in the World, World Who's Who in Science,* number of other biographical listings. Address: 2533 Orkney, Ottawa Hills, Toledo Ohio 43606.

Barfield, Virginia Grant

Executive Director. Personal: Born January 2, 1918; Daughter of J. D. and Ina M. Grant (both deceased); Married William H. Barfield. Education: B.S., Murray College; Undertook graduate studies at the University of Georgia, University of North Carolina, University of Missouri. Career: Manager, Bookkeeper, 1950-65; Executive Director, Enrichment Services Program Inc., 1965 to present. Organizational Memberships: Kentucky Education Association; Georgia Education Association; Georgia Gerontology Society (secretary, 1971-72; treasurer, 1972-73); Georgia Planning Association (member of the board, 1972-77); Georgia Rehabilitation Association (member of the board, 1969-74); Georgia Planning Council (vice president, 1969-73; charter member; impetus of coordination of planning in the state department and office of economic opportunity); National C.A.A. Executive Directors Association. Community Activities: Muscogee County Education Association; Title I Emergency Assistance Program for Muscogee County (board member 1970-73); Muscogee County School District Policy Advisory Board; Mayor's Committee on Employment of the Handicapped; Federal Executive Association (president, 1971; vice president, 1970); Muscogee Day Care Board, 1972-73; Lower Chattahoochee Area Planning and Development Commission, 1964-65; Muscogee County Senior Citizens (board of directors, 1970-76); Lower Chattahoochee Valley Area Manpower Council; Richland Planning Commission (chairperson, 1960-65); Assisted in Development of: Gas System, Mobile Home Industry, Industrial Park, Water Works and Sewerage Disposal; Georgia Community Action Agencies Association; Georgia's Committee on Children and Youth; Committee on Welfare Reform; Girl's Camp (counselor); Scout Work; Garden Club; Red Cross Drive (head); Southeastern Association Community Action Agencies (member of the board, 1970-77; secretary, 1971-72; vice president, 1975-76); National Association of Community Development (third vice president); National Net Work Legislative Forum (chairperson); National Rehabilitation Association; National Council on Aging; National Council for the Transportation of the Disadvantaged; C.S.A. Transition Team; Westville Historical Handicrafts Inc. (secretary-treasurer, 1969-70); Stewart County Historical Association (charter member); Board of Directors of Westville, 1968-77; Health Society of America. Honors and Awards: Urban Service Award by Sargent Shriver, 1957; Office of Economic Opportunity Service Award, Columbus Opportunity, 1967; Office of Economic Opportunity Service Award, Lower Chattahoochee C.A.A., 1967; Rural Service Award, Sargent Shriver, 1968; T.A.P. Committee Organizational Award; Citizenship Award, Joint Action in Community Service, 1975; National Civil Service League, 1972; Georgia Rehabilitation Association, 1972; N.A.C.D., 1975; Community Services Administration, 1976; Listed in *Who's Who Child Development Professionals, International Who's Who in Community Service.* Address: 215 E. Broad St., Richland, Georgia 31825.

Barfield, Vivian Miller

Vivian M Barfield

Athletic Consultant. Personal: Born December 19, 1930; Mother of Nancy Ann, Walter Lowry. Education: B.S. 1966, M.Ed. 1969, University of Houston; Ph.D., University of New Mexico, 1972; Post-Doctoral Study, Iliff School of Theology, 1974; Management Institute, National Association of Collegiate Directors of Athletics, Dartmouth Management Institute. Career: Physical Education and Health Specialist, Houston Independent School District, Crockett Elementary School, 1966-67; Seventh and Eighth Grade Health and Physical Education Teacher, Pasadena Independent School District, Jackson Junior High School, 1967-69; Mathematics and English Teacher, National Education Association Job Corps Conservation Center, Colbran, Colorado, June-July 1969; Substitute Teacher, Albuquerque Public School System, 1969-72; Coordinator of Physical Education Department, 1972-73; Colorado Women's College, Assistant Professor 1972-75, Director of Sports and Recreation 1973-75, Director of Summer Session 1973-75; Assistant Director of Athletics, University of Massachusetts-Amherst, 1975-76; Director, Department of Women's Intercollegiate Athletics, University of Minnesota, 1976-81; Visiting Professor, Women in Sport, Athletic Administration, Adelphi University, Summers 1976, 1977, 1979; Athletic Consultant. Organizational Memberships: American Alliance for Health, Physical Education and Recreation; National Association of Collegiate Directors of Athletics; American Association of University Women; National Association for Physical Education in Higher Education; International Committee on Comparative Physical Education and Sport. Community Activities: Zonta International; National Organization of Women; Women's Equity Action League; The Women's Club of Minneapolis; Minnesota Women's Political Caucus; Minneapolis Aquatennial Association (board of directors, assistant vice president for community relations); Gamma Phi Beta (Kappa chapter house corporation board); Minnesota Explorer Olympics, Boy Scouts of America (chairperson, 1979); Minneapolis Girl Scout Council (board of directors, 1980-82); Minneapolis Young Women's Christian Association (board of directors, 1980-83); Minnesota Coalition of Organizations for Sex Equity in Education. Religion: Westminster Presbyterian Church, Deacon, Chairperson of Mission Program Committee, Chairperson of Solicitation Committee for Stewardship Drive, Solicitor Capitol Fund Drive. Honors and Awards: Elizabeth Lee Closs Award, University of Houston, 1966; Project Interchange, National Education Association, 1969; Special Training Institute on Problems of School Desegregation, Texas Southern University, 1967; Lloyd Shaw American Dance Scholarship, 1971; Young Women's Christian Association Outstanding Leader Award in Sport, 1981; Omicron Delta Kappa; Listed in *Personalities of the West and Midwest, International Who's Who in Community Service, Community Leaders and Noteworthy Americans, Dictionary of International Biography, The World Who's Who of Women, Notable Americans, Book of Honor, Who's Who of American Women, Personalities of America.* Address: 2605 40th Avenue South, Minneapolis, Minnesota 55406.

Barker, Judy

Executive. Personal: Born February 5, 1941, in Burlington, North Carolina; Married David P. Barker; Mother of two daughters and one son. Career: Director, Corporate Social Responsibility; Executive Director, Borden Foundation, Inc. (Member of the Conference Board and Contributions Council). Organizational Memberships: Philanthropic Advisory Services (corporate advisory committee); Council of Better Business Bureaus, Inc.; New York Contributions Advisory Group; Association of Black Foundation Executives, Inc. (board of directors); Women and Foundations, Inc.; Independent Sector (board of trustees). Community Activities: Citizens' Scholarship Foundation of America (board of directors); Council on Foundations (committee on corporate philanthropy); United Negro College Fund (contributions advisory board); National Urban League (advisory board). Honors and Awards: National Community Service Award, United Negro College Fund, 1980; City of New York and Young Women's Christian Association Award to Women Achievers, 1981; Listed in *Who's Who of American Women, Who's Who in America.* Address: Borden Foundation Inc., 180 East Broad Street, Columbus, Ohio 43215.

Barkin, Jamie Stephen

Gastroenterologist. Personal: Born June 1, 1943; Son of Mazie Barkin; Married Faith Block. Education: Graduated magna cum laude, University of Miami (Florida), 1965; M.D., University of Miami School of Medicine, 1970; Jackson Memorial Hospital, Veterans Administration Hospital - Intern 1970-71, Junior Residency Medicine 1971-72, Senior Residency Medicine 1972-73, Junior Fellow Gastroenterology 1973-74, Senior Fellow Gastroenterology, 1974-75. Military: Served in the United States Army Reserve 324th General Hospital, achieving the rank of Major. Career: Assistant Professor, Department of Medicine, University of Miami School of Medicine, 1975-80; Associate Professor, Department of Medicine, University of Miami School of Medicine, 1980 to present; Assistant

Professor, Department of Oncology, University of Miami School of Medicine, 1978 to present; Active Attending Staff, Jackson Memorial Hospital 1975 to present, Veterans Administration Hospital 1975 to present, National Children's Cardiac Hospital; Gastrointestinal Tract Study Group, National Cancer Institute, 1975 to present (chairman, 1981). Organizational Memberships: American College of Gastroenterology (board of trustees, 1980-83; awards and protocol committee, 1978-79; program committee, 1978-79, 1979-81; fellow); American Society for Gastrointestinal Endoscopy (constitution and by-laws, 1980-81, 1981-82; scientific program committee, 1981-82); Alpha Omega Alpha; American Society of Internal Medicine; American College of Physicians; American Medical Association; American Gastroenterological Association; Southern Medical Association; American Pancreatic Society; Florida Society of Gastrointestinal Endoscopy (vice president, 1978; president, 1979-81; councillor, 1981-82); American Federation for Clinical Research; Bockus International Society of Gastroenterology; American Association for the History of Medicine, Inc. Honors and Awards: Best Fellow, University of Miami, 1974; Veterans Administration Performance Award, Special Advancement for Performance, 1977; Fellow, American College of Physicians, 1973; Honorable Mention, "Percutaneous Transhepatic Insertion of a Permanent Internal Prosthesis in the Biliary Tree: A Non-Surgical Method for the Relief of Obstructive Jaundice", Radiological Societv of North America, 1978. Address: 171 S.E. 21st Road, Miami, Florida 33129.

Barkley, Owen Herbert

Photographer. Personal: Born August 9, 1922; Son of Kirk D. and Mabel E. Barkley (both deceased); Married Karen Ann Gray; Father of Matthew Scott, Russell Dean, Jeffrey Wade. Education: Graduate, Climax High School, 1940; Graduate, United States Navy School of Photography, 1943; Graduate, National Camera Repair School, 1972. Military: Served as Chief Photographer in the United States Navy, 1943-64. Career: Professional Photographer; Co-Owner, K&O Photography, Inc. Organizational Memberships: Professional Photographers of America, 1974 to present; Society of Photographic Technologists. Community Activities: Boy Scouts of America, 1958-64 (committeeman, cubmaster, scout master, assistant district commissioner); Mason Temple Board (president 1974); Climax (Michigan) Village Council (trustee 1975-76); Village of Climax (president 1976 to present); 4-H Leader, Kalamazoo County, Michigan, 1977 to present. Honors and Awards: Photographic works exhibited at professional photographers exhibition, 1975 and 1979; Listed in *Who's Who in the Midwest, Community Leaders and Noteworthy Americans, International Who's Who in Community Leaders, Men of Achievement, Dictionary of International Biography,* Others. Address: 126 North Main Street, Climax, Michigan 49034.

Barlow, Herman Jr

University Executive. Personal: Born October 8, 1949, in Houston, Texas; Son of H. Barlow, Sr.; Widower; Father of Meredith Arden. Education: B.A., Houston Baptist Univerity, 1972; M.Ed., University of Houston, 1974; D.Phil., Cambridge University, 1977. Career: Admissions Counsellor, Houston Baptist College, 1972; Houston Baptist University: Acting Dean of Admissions 1973-74, Dean of Admissions 1974-78, Vice President for Development 1978 to present. Organizational Memberships: Council for the Advancement and Support of Education; Southwest Society of Fund Raisers; American Academy of Political and Social Sciences; American Academy of Arts and Sciences; American Association for Higher Education; National Association of College Admissions Counselors; American Association of Collegiate Registrars and Admissions Officers; Texas Personnel and Guidance Association; Houston Personnel and Guidance Association. Community Activities: Symphony North of Houston (music director); American Symphony Orchestra League; Texas Orchestra Directors Association; American Choral Directors Association; Texas Choral Directors Association; Fellowship of United Methodist Musicians; Music Educators National Conference; Texas Music Educators Association; Houston Choral Society; Phi Mu Alpha Sinfonia Fraternity. Religion: Westbury United Methodist Church (director of music). Honors and Awards: Kappa Alpha Order, Council of Honor; Omicron Delta Kappa, National Honor Society; Distinguished Alumnus Award, Houston Baptist University, 1974; International Platform Association; Listed in *International Who's Who in Music, Dictionary of International Biography, International Register of Profiles, International Who's Who in Community Service, International Who's Who of Intellectuals, Outstanding Young Men of America, Notable Americans, Personalities of the South, Community Leaders and Noteworthy Americans, Men of Achievement, Personalities of America, Book of Honor, Men and Women of Distinction, The American Cultural Arts Registry, The American Educational Registry, Who's Who in the South and Southwest, Two Thousand Notable Americans.* Address: 2819 Nottingham, Houston, Texas 77005.

Jamie Barkin

Barnes, Charles M

College President. Personal: Born October 15, 1917, in Baltimore, Maryland; Son of Charles M. and Florence M. Boyle Barnes; Married Nellie E. Dorsey on July 6, 1940, in Oak Park, Illinois; Father of Roger Clifford. Education: Attended Roosevelt College, Chicago, 1938-40; B.S. Education, 1950 and M.S., 1950, Kansas State College, Pittsburgh; Attended University of Kansas, Summers 1951 and 1952; Attended University of Colorado, Summers 1953 and 1954; Fellowship, Community College Leadership Program, Michigan State University, 1961. Military: Served with the United States Army in the European Theatre of Operations, (Scotland, England, Belgium, France, Germany), 1943-46, achieving the rank of Sergeant. Career: Instructor at Ottawa Senior High School, 1950-51, and at Fort Scott Junior College, 1951-53; Assistant Dean, Fort Scott (Kansas) Junior College, 1953-56; Executive Dean, Pratt (Kansas) Junior College 1956-59, Executive Dean, Dodge City (Kansas) College, 1959-65; President, Dodge City Community College, 1965 to the present. Organizational Memberships: Kappa Delta Pi, National Education Fraternity, 1950; Phi Alpha Theta, National History Fraternity, 1950; National Education Association, 1950; Kansas State Teachers Association, 1950; Kansas History Teachers Association, 1950 (member of the executive council, 1951); Kansas Public Junior College Association (secretary, 1956-58, vice-president, 1958-61, president, 1961-63); Council of North Central Junior Colleges (president, 1965-66); Kansas Association of Colleges and Universities (president, 1966-67), Kansas-Nebraska Educational Consortium (vice-president, 1967-69, president, 1969-70, treasurer, 1970 to present); Commission on Institutions of Higher Education, North Central Association of Colleges and Schools (consultant-examiner, 1966 to present, member council on research and service, 1972-78); AACJC Program with Developing Institutions (coordinator, 1968-70); Plains Consortium, Title III Program with Developing Institutions (coordinator, 1970-73); Board of Directors, North Central Association of Colleges and Schools, 1975-77; Board of Directors, Kansas Association of Community Colleges, 1974-76. Community Activities: President, Rotary Club (president, 1963-64). Religion: Methodist. Published Works: Articles in *Kansas Teacher* and *Junior College Journal.* Honors and Awards: Danforth Foundation Leave Grant, 1971; Recipient of the First Annual Clyde U. Phillips Award for Outstanding Alumnus in Education, Pittsburg State University, Pittsburg, Kansas, 1975; Recipient of an Award of Merit for Outstanding Contributions to Community Colleges, Kansas Association of Community Colleges, 1978. Address: 2514 Thompson, Dodge City, Kansas 67801.

Barnes, James J

Professor. Education: B.A., Amherst College, 1954; B.A., New College, Oxford University, 1956; Ph.D., Harvard University, 1960;

D.H.L., College of Wooster, 1976. Career: Instructor in History, Amherst College, 1959-62; Wabash College, Assistant Professor of History 1962-67, Associate Professor of History 1967-76, Professor of History 1976 to present, Department Chairman and Hadley Professor of History 1979 to present. Organizational Memberships: American Historical Association; Conference on British Studies; Southern Historical Association; Research Society for Victorian Periodicals; Society for Values in Higher Education; American Rhodes Scholars; Society for Historians of American Foreign Relations; United States Chess Federation; Bibliographical Society; National Book League; Dominions Fellowship Trust. Community Activities: Crawfordsville Community Action Council, 1966-69; Crawfordsville Community Day Care Survey, 1966-67; St. John's Episcopal Church Vestry, 1966-69; Indiana Advisory Committee to State Rehabilitation Services for the Blind, 1979-81; Ouiatenon, Crawfordsville Literary Society, 1980 to present. Honors and Awards: B.A. magna cum laude, Amherst College; Phi Beta Kappa; Rhodes Scholarship, Oxford University; Woodrow Wilson Fellowship, Harvard University; Kent Fellowship, 1958; Great Lakes Colleges Association Teaching Fellowship, 1975; Great Lakes Colleges Association Teaching Consultant, 1976; Fulbright Scholarship, 1978; Research Grants, Amherst College 1960-61, Social Science Research Council 1962, 1970, Wabash College 1962 to present, American Council of Learned Societies 1964-65, 1980, American Philosophical Society 1964, 1968, 1976. Published Works: *Free Trade in Books: A Study of the London Book Trade since 1800*, 1964; *Authors, Publishers and Politicians: the Quest for an Anglo-American Copyright Agreement, 1815-54*, 1974; *Hitler's Mein Kampf in Britain and America, 1930-39*, 1980 (co-authored with Patience P. Barnes); Number of Other Articles and Book Reviews, Papers and Presentations. Address: 7 Locust Hill, Crawfordsville, Indiana 47933.

Barnes, Jim Weaver

Associate Professor, Editor. Personal: Born December 22, 1933; Son of Bessie V. Barnes; Married Carolyn Louise Turpin; Father of Bret Alan, Blake Anthony. Education: B.A, Southeastern Oklahoma State University, 1964; M.A. 1966, Ph.D. 1972, University of Arkansas. Military: Served in the Oklahoma National Guard, 1949-50. Career: Editor, *The Chariton Review*; Associate Professor of Comparative Literature, Northeast Missouri State University; Formerly, Instructor of English, Northeastern Oklahoma State University; Lumberjack, Giustina Brothers Lumber Company, Eugene, Oregon. Organizational Memberships: Modern Language Association of America (delegate-at-large for ethnic studies, 1974-76); Coordinating Council of Literary Magazines, 1975 to present. Community Activities: Missouri Art Council, 1981, 1982; Coordinating Council of Literary Magazines (grants committee, 1981). Published Works: Author of Four Books of Poetry, including *The American Book of the Dead*. Honors and Awards: National Endowment for the Arts Creative Writing Fellowship in Poetry, 1978; Translation Award, The Translation Center, Columbia University, for translation of *Summons and Signs: Poems by Dagmar Nick*, 1980. Address: 918 Pine Street, Macon, Missouri 63552.

Barnes, Melver Raymond

Scientific Researcher. Personal: Born November 15, 1917; Son of Oscar Lester, and Sarah Albertine Rowe Barnes (both deceased). Education: B.A. Chemistry, University of North Carolina-Chapel Hill, 1947; Further study in chemistry, mathematics and physics at the University of North Carolina- Chapel Hill; M.D., McCoy College, Baltimore; Further study: University of Utah, Brigham Young University, University of California-Los Angeles. Military: Served with the United States Army, March 1942 to October 1945. Career: Private Scientific Researcher; Retired Chemist; Research Chemist, United States Civil Service, Department of the Army, 1951-70; Chemist, North Carolina State Highway and Public Works Commission, Raleigh, North Carolina, 1949-51; Chemist, Pittsburgh Laboratories, Greensboro, North Carolina, 1948-49. Organizational Memberships: American Chemical Society; American Physical Society; American Association for the Advancement of Science; New York Academy of Sciences. Address: Route 1, Box 424, Linwood, North Carolina 27299.

Barnes, Roy Eugene

Senator, Attorney at Law. Personal: Born March 11, 1948; Son of W. C. and Agnes Barnes; Married Marie Dobbs; Father of Harlan, Allison, Alyssa. Education: A.B., University of Georgia, 1969; J.D. cum laude, University of Georgia Law School, 1972. Served in the United States Army, achieving the rank of Captain; Served in the United States Army Reserve, Control Group Reinforcement. Career: Attorney at Law; Former Assistant District Attorney, Cobb Judicial Circuit Court. Organizational Memberships: Cobb County Bar Association; Association of Trial Lawyers of America; American Bar Association; Georgia Trial Lawyers Association; State Bar of Georgia. Community Activities: Senator, 33rd District, State of Georgia, 1974 to present; South Cobb Improvement Association (president); South Cobb Cancer Society (board of directors); South Cobb Jaycees; Marietta Kiwanis Club; Cobb County Chamber of Commerce; Heart Fund Drive (chairman of special gifts); Latham Lodge #12; Gridiron Secret Society. Religion: First Methodist Church, Marietta, Georgia, Administrative Board, Sunday School Teacher. Honors and Awards: Law School Student Bar President and Board of Governors; Blue Key; Phi Kappa Phi; Outstanding Senior, University of Georgia Law School; 1 of 5 Outstanding Young Men in Georgia, Georgia Jaycees, 1976; Listed in *Who's Who Among American Colleges and Universities*. Address: 4841 Brookwood Drive, Mableton, Georgia 30059.

Barnes, Symiria Peters

Educator and Professional Singer. Personal: Born July 10; Daughter of Matilda J. Peters; Married Luther Rree Barnes; Mother of Stanford Orrin, Cedrick, Audwin. Education: B.Mus., Jackson State University, 1959; Further study at American Conservatory of Music, 1971-73; M.A.S., Roosevelt University, 1982. Career: Soloist, Edgewater Presbyterian Church, 3 years; Soloist, United Church of Rogers Park, 2 years; Understudy Soloist and Member, Chicago Symphony Chorus, 10 years. Community Activities: Lung Association; Crusade of Mercy; Cub Scouts (den mother); Girl Scouts of America (troop leader); Cancer Research; Religious Organizations. Religion: Substitute Soloist, Christian Science Church of Chicago. Published Works: Selected by Deputy Superintendent of Chicago Public School System to formulate a handbook for teachers on curriculum in the area of music for grades kindergarten through eight. Honors and Awards: Soprano of opera and oratorio including performance in Aida Premiere Performance with Opera/South, Jackson, Mississippi, 1971; Debut in concert, Wigmore Hall, London, England; Recitalist, Young Artist Series, Chicago, 1973; Winner annual commencement solo audition, American Conservatory of Music, Chicago, 1972; Recipient, Music Scholarship Award, American League of Pen Women, 1972; Listed in *Who's Who of American Women, Who's Who in the Midwest, The World Who's Who of Women, Personalities of America, Personalities of the Midwest*. Address: 8004 S. Kimbark Ave., Chicago, Illinois 60609.

Barnett, Camille Cates

City Management. Personal: Born April 29, 1949; Daughter of Mr. and Mrs. George T. Cates; Married Jim Barnett. Education: B.A.,

Lawrence University of Wisconsin, 1971; M.P.A. 1973, Ph.D. 1977, University of Southern California. Career: Research Assistant, International City Management Association and Center for Government Studies, 1970-71; Administrative Assistant, Sunnyvale, California, 1973-75; Assistant to City Manager, Sunnyvale, 1975-77; Assistant to City Manager, Dallas, Texas, 1977-80; Assistant City Manager, Dallas, 1980 to present. Organizational Memberships: International City Management Association (endowment committee); Texas Management Association (professional development committee); American Society of Public Administrators. Community Activities: Goodwill Industries (board of directors, executive committee); Southern Methodist University, Cox School of Business (associate board member, women in management advisory board); North Central Texas Council of Governments (environmental resources advisory committee); Chamber of Commerce International Committee. Honors and Awards: Outstanding Woman in Government, Sanger Harris Lifestyle Award, 1978; Honored by the Dallas County National Organization of Women for Special Contributions to the City of Dallas, 1977; Listed in *Who's Who in American Women, Outstanding Young Women in America.* Address: 2551 Sweetbriar, Dallas, Texas 75228.

Barney, Michael C

Senior Research Microbiologist. Personal: Born September 27, 1946; Son of Fredrick C. (deceased) and Dorothy E. Barney; Married Jill A. Guenther. Education: Attended University of Illinois and Parsons College; B.S., 1970 and M.S., 1972, University of Wisconsin; Undertook five years of postgraduate work at the Medical College of Wisconsin. Career: Biology and Bacteriology Instructor, University of Wisconsin; Research Chemist, Kimberly Clark Corporation; Senior Research Microbiologist, Miller Brewing Company. Organizational Memberships: American Society for Microbiology; Society for Industrial Microbiology; American Society of Brewing Chemists (chairman of the committee for microbiological controls, 1976-79); Miller Management Club (president, 1980-81). Religion: Presbyterian. Published Works: Articles published in scientific journals. Honors and Awards: National Honor Society, 1963-64; Scholarship to the University of Wisconsin, 1971; Registered Microbiologist, National Registry of the American Academy of Microbiology; Invited to participate in seminars at universities. Address: 2325 N. 83rd Street, Wauwatosa, Wisconsin 53213.

Barrett, Bernard M Jr

Physician, Plastic and Reconstructive Surgeon. Personal: Born May 3, 1944, Pensacola, Florida; Son of Dr. and Mrs. Bernard M. Barrett Sr., Married Julia May Prokop, November 25, 1972; Father of Beverly Frances, Julie Blaine, Audrey Blake, Bernard Joseph. Education: B.S., Tulane University, 1965; M.D., University of Miami School of Medicine, 1969; Intern, The Methodist Hospital and Ben Taub Hospital, Houston, 1969-70; General Surgery Residency, Baylor College of Medicine, 1970-71; Plastic Surgery Residency, University of Miami Affiliated Hospitals, 1973-75; Fellowship in Plastic Surgery, Clinica Ivo Pitanguy, Rio de Janeiro, Brazil, 1973. Military: Served as Lieutenant Commander in the United States Navy, Honorably Discharged 1974. Career: Clinical Associate in Plastic Surgery, University of Texas Medical School, 1976 to present; Baylor College of Medicine, Clinical Assistant Professor in Plastic Surgery 1980, Clinical Instructor 1977; Attending Physician, Junior League Clinic, Texas Children's Hospital, Houston, 1977 to present; Instructor in Surgical Emergencies, Harris County Community College, Houston, 1977 to present; Plastic Surgery Coordinator for Junior Medical Students, University of Miami School of Medicine, 1975; Instructor in Surgical Emergencies, Los Angeles County Paramedics, 1972-73; Instructor in Surgery, Baylor College of Medicine, 1970-71. Organizational Memberships: Plastic and Reconstructive Surgeons, P.A. (president, chairman of the board); American Society of Plastic and Reconstructive Surgeons; American College of Surgeons; American Physicians Insurance Exchange (director, 1976 to present); Doctors Center Hospital, Houston (director, 1978 to present); University of Miami School of Medicine National Alumni Association (director, 1975-77); A.P.I. Life Insurance Company (director, 1979 to present); D. Ralph Millard Plastic Surgical Society (historian; past vice president, secretary, treasurer); Denton A. Cooley Cardiovascular Surgical Society; Michael E. DeBakey International Cardiovascular Society; Royal Society of Medicine, London; Texas Society of Plastic Surgery; Texas Medical Association; Harris County Medical Society; Houston Society of Plastic Surgery; Houston Academy of Medicine. Community Activities: Southwestern Bank, Houston (director); The Houstonian; University Club, Houston; Honorary Deputy Sheriff, Harris County; Miss Woodlands Pageant (judge); Houston Oilers Football Team (consulting physician, 1978 to present); Royal Biscayne Racquet Club; The Commodore Club, Key Biscayne, Florida; Ontario Motor Speedway (attending physician, 1972-73). Published Works; Number of Professional Articles; Textbook, *Patient Care in Plastic Surgery.* Honors and Awards: Outstanding Surgical Intern, The Methodist Hospital, 1969-70; Surgical Exchange Scholarship to Royal College of Surgeons, England, 1968; Certificate of Appreciation, City of Miami, 1967. Address: 7000 Fannin Street, Suite 2150, Houston, Texas 77030.

Barrett, Melanie Taylor

Management. Personal: Born September 22, 1943; Daughter of Gail R. and Lois E. Taylor; Mother of Michael Gail, Eric Edward. Education: Studies in Business Administration and Journalism, Walla-Walla Community College; Studies in Gerontology, Spokane Falls Community College; Public Administration Studies, City College, Seattle. Career: Management, Social Services National Association; Chief Administrator, Social Services Agency. Organizational Memberships: Washington Association C.A.A. (quad chair, 1978-80; chairman of personnel committee, executive board, 1979-80); National Association C.A.A.; Washington Association of Social Welfare; American Society of Association Executives. Community Activities: Washington State Governors Commission of Prison Reform; Fair Housing, Mason County; Mason County Planning Task Force; Washington State Pioneers Association; Veterans of Foreign Wars Auxiliary; Mason County Independent Mothers Association; National Council on Aging. Religion: Member, Garden Grove Community Church, Garden Grove, California. Address: 8941 Footed Ridge Road, Columbia, Maryland 21045.

Barrins, Phyllis Caroline

Marriage and Family Counselor, Hypnotherapist. Personal: Born April 9, 1921; Daughter of Frank A. and Catherine M. Willy; Married Edward F. Barrins (deceased); Mother of Edward, Mary Roberts, Barbara O'Shea, Patricia Schipper, James, Gerard, Janine Perry. Education: Diploma, St. Mary Mercy Hospital School of Nursing, 1942; B.A. 1971, M.A. 1972, B.A. 1973, Ph.D. 1973, all from Eastern Nebraska Christian College. Career: Marriage and Family Counselor/Hypnotherapist; Registered Nurse; Former Police Officer, Free-Lance Writer. Organizational Memberships: American Sociological Association; American Association of Suicidology; American Association of University Professors; Association of Christian Marriage Counselors; Association of Women in Psychology; Federation of American Scientists; International Association of Applied Psychology. Published Works: Author, *Manual for Hypnotherapy; What It's Really Like To Be a Free-Lance Writer; Sick Call!;* Editor and Co-Author, *Hypnosis, New Tool in Nursing Practice;* Pamphlets Authored, "Visiting Patients: Hints On What To Say and Do" and "On Curbing of Drug Use"; Number of Articles, Children's Stories and Verse. Address: 2023 East Adams Street, Tucson, Arizona 85719.

Barshay, Marshall E

Physician. Personal: Born November 10, 1938; Son of Murray Barshay; Married Patricia Gross; Father of Adam Dale, Brigitte Alana, Devin Elan. Education: B.A., Brooklyn College, 1959; M.D., State University of New York at Buffalo School of Medicine, 1963. Military: Served in the United States Army, 1964-66, achieving the rank of Captain. Career: Physician; Assistant Clinical Professor of Medicine, University of California-Los Angeles, 1979 to present. Organizational Memberships: American College of Physicians (fellow); American Medical Association; California Medical Association; Los Angeles County Medical Association; American Society of Nephrology; American Geriatric Society; American Society of Clinical Hypnosis; Los Angeles County Society of Clinical Hypnosis; Nutrition Today Society. Community Activities: Santa Monica Hospital (chairman, patient care committee, 1979). Religion: Jewish; Member University Synagogue, 1977 to present. Honors and Awards: Finished 2nd 3 consecutive years, *New York Daily Mirror* 50 Meter Free-Style Event, 1955-57; Captain, Brooklyn College Swimming Team, 1958-59. Address: 12321 20th Helena Drive, Los Angeles, California 90049.

Elizabeth Bartlett

Bartlett, Elizabeth

Poet. Personal: Born in New York City; Daughter of Lewis and Charlotte Rosefield Winters; Married Paul Bartlett, April 19, 1943; Mother of Steven. Education: B.S., Teacher's College, 1931; Post-Graduate Study, Columbia University, 1938-40. Career: Poet; Instructor, University of California-Santa Barbara, San Jose State University, Southern Methodist University, San Diego State University; Director, Creative Writers Association, New School for Social Research, 1954-55; Poetry Editor *ETC: Review of General Semantics*, 1963-76. Organizational Memberships: Poetry Society of America; International Women's Writing Guild (honorary). Published Works: *Poems of Yes and No; Behold This Dreamer; Poetry Concerto; It Takes Practice to Die; Twelve-Tone Poems; Threads; Selected Poems; The House of Sleep; Dialogue of Dust; In Search of Identity; Address in Time; A Zodiac of Poems; Memory is No Stranger*. Honors and Awards: Grantee, National Institute of Arts and Letters, P.E.N.; Poetry Award, National Endowment of the Arts, 1969; Fellowships, Huntington Hartford Foundation, Montalvo Association, Yaddo, MacDowell Colony, Dorland Mountain Colony. Address: 2875 Cowley Way, San Diego, California 92110.

Bartley, Vanessa DeSaussure

Assistant to the Vice President for Development. Personal: Born August 6, 1958; Daughter of Solomon and Mary J. Bartley. Education: B.A.-B.S., Bennett College, 1979; M.S.W., Tulane University, 1980. Military: Served in the United States Army Reserve as a Medical Social Worker, attaining the rank of Second Lieutenant. Career: Assistant to the Vice President for Development, Johnson C. Smith University; Former Positions include Acting Southeast Regional Youth Field Director, National Association for the Advancement of Colored People, Atlanta, Georgia; Part-time Instructor, Atlanta Junior College. Organizational Memberships: National Federation of Thanatology; Forum for Death Education and Counseling, Inc.; National Association of Social Workers; National Association of Educators. Community Activities: Delta Sigma Theta; Big Brothers/Big Sisters of America. Religion: Seventh Day Adventist. Honors and Awards: Listed in *Personalities of the South*. Address: 1004 N. McAlway Road, Charlotte, North Carolina 28211.

Nelda A Barton

Barton, Nelda Ann Lambert

Republican National Committeewoman. Personal: Born May 12, 1929, in Providence, Kentucky; Daughter of Eulis Grant, and Rubie Lois West Lambert; Married Harold Bryan Barton (deceased) on May 11, 1953; Mother of William Grant (deceased), Barbara Lynn, Harold Bryan Jr, Steven Lambert, Suzanne. Education: Graduate of Providence High School, 1947; Attended Western Kentucky University, 1947-49; Graduate of Norton Memorial Infirmary School of Medical Technology, 1950. Career: Long Term Care Consultant; Licensed Nursing Home Administrator, Kentucky Board; Registered Medical Technologist, A.S.C.P.; President, Barton and Associates, Inc. (Hillcrest Nursing Home), Corbin; President, Hazard Nursing Home, Inc., Hazard, Kentucky; Partner, Harold B. Barton, M.D. Memorial Nursing Home, Williamsburg, Kentucky; President, Corbin Nursing Home, Inc., (Mountain Laurel Manor), Corbin, Kentucky; President, Health Systems, Inc., Corbin. Community Activities: Republican National Committeewoman for Kentucky, 1968 to present; Republican National Committee (member of the executive committee, 1976 to present); 1981 Presidential Inaugural Coordinator for Kentucky; Corbin Republican Women's Club (president, 1968); Whitley County Republican Party (chairwoman, 1968-72, campaign chairwoman, 1968-72); 5th District Kentucky Federation of Republican Women (governor, 1968-70, 2nd vice president, 1968-70, member of the executive committee, 1963 to present, chairman of state convention, 1970); Republican Party of Kentucky (advisory committee, 1974 to present); 5th District Lincoln Club Advisory Committee, 1970 to present; Kentucky Candidate Search Committee (co-chairman, 1974-75); American Medical Political Action Committee; Kentucky Educational Medical Political Action Committee; Kentucky Association Nursing Home Political Action Committee; Kentucky Federation College Republican Advisory Committee, 1981; Kentucky Federal Advisory Committee, 1981; Western Kentucky University Beta Omega Chi (president, 1948-49); Fair Housing Task Force, City of Corbin, 1980 to present; Corbin Deposit Bank Board (director, 1980 to present); Kentucky Peer Review Organization (long term care advisory committee, 1978 to present); Cumberland College Associate Degree Nursing (advisory committee, 1973 to present); Number offices previously held in other political and civic organizations. Religion: First Christian Church; Christian Women's Fellowship #2; Stewardship, Property, Education, Chairman Youth Fellowship, Circle Chairman, Others. Honors and Awards: Valedictorian, Providence High School, 1947; Academic Scholarship to Western Kentucky University, 1947-49; P.T.A. Life Membership, 1964; Kentucky Republican Woman of the Year, Kentucky Federation of Republican Women, 1968-69; Bluegrass Council Boy Scout Thank You Award, 1974; Kentucky Colonel, 1968; Indiana Sagamore of the Wabash, 1973; The Dwight David Eisenhower Award, 1970; Mayor of Corbin Proclaimed "Nelda Barton Day", October 22, 1973; Recognition Award, Joint Republican Leadership of the US Congress, 1979; Listed in *Who's Who in the Southeast, Who's Who in America, World Who's Who of Women, Directory of Distinguished Americans, Book of Honor*. Address: 1311 Seventh Street Road, Corbin, Kentucky 40701.

Richard Barton

Barton, Richard

Financial Consultant. Personal: Born September 23, 1941; Son of Frederick Barton and Elizabeth L. Benson; Father of Richard Jr., Nicole Lynn. Education: Graduate, Findlay College, 1965; Undertook graduate studies at Morgan State University, 1967-68; Further studies from North American Institute, Alexander Hamilton Institute, International Business Machines Corporation, Merrill Lynch Inc., Investors Diversified Services Inc. Career: Accounts Executive, Merrill Lynch, Inc.; Vice President of Marketing, Hartford *Inquirer* Newspaper Group; Barton & Sharp Associates, Inc.: Personal Financial Planning, Business Financial Management, Security Investments, Computer Consultant Services. Community Activities: Waverly Opportunities Workshop (advisor and member of the advisory board, career development program); Urban Leauge of Greater Hartford (member economic development and employment committee); National Association for the Advancement of Colored People (board member). Religion: Hopewell Baptist Church, 1976 to present. Honors and Awards: Outstanding Sales Award, International Business Machines, 1973-74; Waverly's Opportunity Workshop Award, 1971-76; Listed in *Who's Who in the East*, 1982. Address: 127 Mansfield Street, Hartford, Connecticut 06112.

Bashore, Irene Saras

Humanist. Personal: Daughter of Mrs. Eva Saras. Education: B.A. Pepperdine University; M.A., California State University at Fullerton, 1977. Career: Author, Playwright, Editor, Publisher, Teacher, Professor and Producer. Organizational Memberships: American Theatre Association (regional chairman for region VIII); Member of numerous professional associations and affiliations. Community Activities: Involved in various civic organizations and projects. Address: P.O. Box 4040, Fullerton, California 92634.

Catherine A Baska

Baska, Catherine Ann

Social Worker. Personal: Born October 29, 1933; Daughter of Joseph Aloysius and Mary Stanley Baska (both deceased). Education: A.A., Donnelly College, 1953; B.A., Mount Saint Scholastica College, 1955; M.S.W., St. Louis University, 1957. Career: School Social Worker, 1959 to present; Caseworker, Department of Children, Catholic Charities, St. Louis, Missouri, 1957-59. Organizational Memberships: Illinois Association of School Social Workers; National Association of Social Workers; Academy of Certified Social Workers; Mental Health Association; International Council on Social Welfare. Religion: Parishoner, St. Francis Xavier Church, St. Louis Cathedral. Honors and Awards: Certificate of Recognition, Youth Department, Baptist General State Convention of Illinois, 1974; Honorary Doctorate, Benedictine College, Atchison, Kansas, 1975; Board of Governors, Benedictine College, 1980. Address: Grand Towers East, 3520 Laclede Avenue, St. Louis, Missouri 63103.

Bassi, Sukh D

Microbiologist, Adjunct Professor. Personal: Born February 11, 1941; Son of Mr. and Mrs. Telu Ram Bassi; Married; Father of Neal, Nathan, Sean. Education: B.S., Knox College, 1965; M.S. 1967, Ph.D. 1970, St. Louis University. Career: Technical Director, Midwest Solvents Co., Inc.; Adjunct Professor of Biology. Organizational Memberships: American Association for the Advancement of Science; The Society of Sigma Xi; American Association of Cereal Chemists; American Chemical Society. Community Activities: Rotary International (president, Atchison Club, 1979); Boy Scouts of America (chairman of Sunflower District, 1979-80; chairman Kanza scout camp, 1981 to present). Honors and Awards: Queen's Scout, England, 1959; Outstanding Educator of America, 1975; Listed in *Outstanding Young Men of America, Who's Who in the Midwest*. Address: R.R. #3, Box 159B, Atchison, Kansas 66002.

Suk H Bassi

Bast, Rose Ann

Associate Professor, Department Chairperson, Member of Catholic Order. Personal: Born September 10, 1934; Daughter of Mr. and Mrs. Lester Bast. Education: B.S., Notre Dame College, 1960; M.S. 1963, Ph.D. 1966, University of Oklahoma. Career: Associate Professor, Chairperson, Department of Biology, Mount Mary College; Formerly Chairperson, Biology Department, Notre Dame College; Graduate Teaching Assistant, University of Oklahoma, 1961-64; Secondary Teacher, Sacred Heart High School, New Orleans, Louisiana, 1958-61; Elementary Teacher, Iowa and Illinois, 1954-57. Organizational Memberships: Sigma Xi; Phi Sigma Society (secretary, University of Oklahoma chapter, 1965); American Association for the Advancement of Science; Theta Alpha Chapter, Beta Beta Beta (advisor, 1977 to present); Wisconsin Society of Science Teachers; Institute of Society, Ethics and Life Sciences (associate member); New York Academy of Sciences. Community Activities: Wisconsin School Evaluation Consortium (evaluator, two secondary schools, 1979-80, 1980-81); Southeastern Wisconsin Science Fair (judge); International Science and Engineering Fair, Milwaukee (judge); Curricular Development Committee (member, 1977-80; secretary 1978-79; chairperson, 1979-80); Teacher Education Committee, 1980 to present; Mount Mary College Library Building Campaign (class coordinator for parents phase, 1978). Religion: Member, School Sisters of Notre Dame, 1954 to present. Honors and Awards: High School Valedictorian, 1952; B.S. cum laude, 1960; Listed in *World Who's Who of Women in Education* and Others. Address: 2900 N. Menomonee River Parkway, Milwaukee, Wisconsin 53222.

Bastedo, Ralph Walter

Public Opinion Statistician. Personal: Born February 18, 1953; Son of Walter Jr., and Barbara Catherine Manning Bastedo. Education: A.B. with honors, Princeton University, 1975; M.A. with honors, University of California-Berkeley, 1976; Doctorate with honors, Berkeley and State University of New York-Stony Brook, 1982. Career: Public Opinion Statistician; Editor, *Harbour Chronicle* (weekly newspaper); Editor, *Wopowog* (monthly bulletin of the Stony Brook Village Civic Association); Previously a University Professor, Laboratory Researcher, Newspaper Reporter, Survey Researcher, Campaign Pollster. Organizational Memberships: World Association for Public Opinion Research; American Political Science Association. Community Activities: Pollster and Campaign Advisor, Long Island Citizens for Kennedy. Religion: Teacher of Religious Education, Unitarian Fellowship of the Three Villages. Published Works: Co-Author, *Paranormal Borderlands of Science;* Reviser, *Three Village Guidebook*. Honors and Awards: 11 Scholarships; Honors from Princeton, Berkeley, Stony Brook. Address: 10 Blinker Road, Stony Brook, Long Island, New York 11790.

Rose A Bast

Batch, Donald L

Professor, Dean. Personal: Born July 9, 1938; Married Mary E. Batch; Father of Lynn Ann Smart, Karyn Dee. Education: B.S., Illinois College, 1960; M.S., University of Illinois-Urbana, 1962; Studies at the Marine Biological Laboratory of Duke University, Summer 1962; Ph.D., University of Illinois-Urbana, 1965; Water Pollution Control Technical Training Program, 1969; Workshop in Environmental Studies, Argonne National Laboratory, 1970; Varian Aerograph Chromatography Training Course, 1971; Workshop in Thin Layer Chromatography and Electrophoresis, 1972; Titration and Specific Ion Measurement Workshop, 1979. Career: Professor and Dean, College of Natural and Mathematical Sciences, Eastern Kentucky University. Organizational Memberships: Phi Beta Kappa; Phi Sigma Society; Sigma Xi (Eastern Kentucky University Club: secretary-treasurer, 1969-71; vice president, 1971-72; president, 1972-73); North American Benthological Society (executive coordinating committee, 1970-73; chairman, site and nomination committee, 1971-72); Kentucky Academy of Science (secretary, 1970-71; vice president, 1971-72; president-elect, 1972-73; president, 1973-74; committee on rare and endangered species, 1980-81); Kentucky Conservation Council; American

Conference of Academic Deans; National Wildlife Federation; Council of Colleges of Arts and Sciences. Religion: First United Methodist Church, Richmond, Administrative Board 1967-81, Vice Chairman 1969, Chairman 1970-71. Address: 129 Westwood Drive, Richmond, Kentucky 40475.

Batcheller, Joseph Ann

Investor. Personal: Born December 11, 1932; Daughter of Mr. and Mrs. Osmer S. Deming; Married David Springsteen Batcheller; Mother of Elizabeth St. Clair, Osmer Deming, John Alden. Career: Seminole Oil Company, Miami, Florida, Secretary 1957, President/Director 1961 to present; Secretary, Director, Blue Grass Plant Foods, Inc., Cynthiana, Kentucky, 1958; Chairman of the Board, Superior Plant Foods, Inc., Lakeland, Florida, 1958; Vice President, Director, Pensacola Petroleum Company, Inc., 1961 to present; Vice President, Director, Top Power Stations, Inc., Miami, 1961 to present; Chairman of the Board, Blue Water Mobile Home Subdivision, Inc., Tavernier, Florida, 1967 to present; President, Blue Water Mobile Home Sales, Inc., 1970. Community Activities: Miami Heart Institute (board of directors, 1970 to present; vice president auxiliary, 1970 to present; trustee, 1973 to present; vice president, 1975 to present); Convent of Sacred Heart (advisory board, 1973 to present); The Debutant Committee of Miami (co-chairman, 1977); Florence Crittenton Society (board of directors, 1970 to present); Young Patronesses of Opera; Symphony Club; Beaux Arts; Daughters of the American Revolution; English Speaking Union (vice president, Miami branch, 1975 to present); Pi Beta Phi. Religion: Episcopal. Honors and Awards: Miami Heart Institute Donor Award 1970, Humanitarian Award 1973, Silver Medallion for Distinguished Service 1978, Builders Silver Shovel Award 1979; Commander, The Military and Hospitaller Order of Saint Lazarus of Jerusalem, 1981. Address: 4595 Sabal Palm Road, Miami, Florida 33137.

Battin, R Ray

Clinical Neuropsychologist, Audiologist, Speech Pathologist. Personal: Born May 29, 1925; Married Tom C. Battin. Education: Attended Kent State University, University of California-Los Angeles; B.A., University of Denver, 1948; M.S., University of Michigan, 1950; Ph.D., University of Florida, 1959; Undertook Post-Doctoral Work, University of Iowa, University of Miami Medical School, University of Utah. Military: Served in the United States Women's Army Corp, 1945-46, achieving the rank of private first class. Career: Clinical Neuropsychologist, Audiologist, Speech Pathologist, Director, The Battin Clinic; Former Clinical Instructor, The University of Denver, The University of Texas Medical Branch, The University of Houston. Organizational Memberships: American Speech and Hearing Association (has served on numerous committees in 25 year period); American Academy of Private Practice in Speech Pathology and Audiology (treasurer, 1965-67; president, 1967-69; board of directors, 1964-74, 1976 to present); American Psychological Association; Texas Psychological Association; Harris County Association; I.A.L.P.; Academy of Aphasia; Cleft Palate Association; Biofeedback Society; Others. Community Activities: Governor's Committee, 1979 to present; Juvenile Court Volunteers (board of directors, 1979 to present); Houston School for Deaf Children (volunteer director, 1960-61); Talk-Show Host, Call-in Radio Program, KTRH. Religion: Emerson Unitarian Church; Religion Education Committee, First Unitation Church, Houston, 1963-66. Honors and Awards: First Prize, Scientific Exhibit, Texas Medical Association, 1964; Second Prize, Scientific Exhibit, American Speech and Hearing Association, 1961, 1971; Gold Medal, Educational Exhibit, American Academy of Pediatrics, 1969; Fellow, American Speech and Hearing Association; Fellow, World Academy, Inc. Address: 3837 Meadow Lake Lane, Houston, Texas 77027.

Charles J Baum

Bauer, Edward Alphonse

Electrical Contractor. Personal: Born August 6, 1942; Son of Michael Frank and Olive Ann (Lardy) Bauer; Married Carol Ann Lobb on July 8, 1967; Father of Steven James, Gwen Marie, John Edward. Education: Graduate, Cathedral High School, 1960; Junior Accountant, Drews Business College, 1961; Electrical Degree, Dunwoody Industrial Institute, 1967; A.A., Mechanical Engineering Technology, St. Cloud State University, 1969. Military: Retired from the United States Naval Reserve. Career: Vice President, JAB, Inc., Importers of North Sea Imports; Electrician; President, Bauer Inc., Electrical Contractor. Organizational Memberships: Minnesota Electrical Association (director). Boy Scouts of America (scoutmaster, troop 20, Waite Park, Minnesota); Fire Chief, City of Waite Park; Waite Park Boosters Rifle Club (vice president, 1972); Loyal Order of Moose; Waite Park American Legion. Religion: Roman Catholic; President of the Parish Council, St. Joseph's Church. Honors and Awards: United States Naval Reserve: National Defense Medal, Naval Meritorious Service Medal, Naval Expeditionary Medal, Armed Forces Reserve Service Medal. Address: 149 Seventh Avenue North, Box 358, Waite Park, Minnesota 56387.

Baum, Charles James

Pastor Emeritus. Personal: Born January 2, 1908, in Charleston, South Carolina; Son of John and Mary Beatrice Croghan Baum (both deceased). Education: Graduate, St. Charles College, Catonsville, Maryland, 1928; B.A. 1930, M.A. 1932, S.T.B. 1933, St. Mary's University, Baltimore; D.D., Southeastern University, 1977. Career: Pastor Emeritus, St. Mary's Church, Greenville, South Carolina, 1973 to present; Board of Consultors, Diocesan Pastoral Council, Diocesan Ecumenical Commission of the Diocese of Charleston (which embraces all of the state of South Carolina); Pastor, St. Mary's Church, Greenville, South Carolina, 1952-73; Dean, Greenville Deanery, 1952-73; Pastor, Church of St. Paul the Apostle, Spartanburg, South Carolina, 1945-52; First Pastor, St. Louis Church, Dillon, South Carolina, 1943-45; First Resident Chaplain, St. Eugene Hospital, Dillon, 1943-45; Associate Pastor, St. Peter's Church, Columbia, South Carolina, 1940-43; Chaplain, Newman Club, University of South Carolina, 1940-43; Associate Pastor, St. Joseph's Church and the Anderson Missions, 1935-40; Pastor, Cathedral of St. John the Baptist and St. Joseph's Church, Charleston, 1934-35; Faculty, Bishop England High School, Charleston, 1934-35; Chaplain, C. C. C. Camps, 1934-35; Ordained Priest, 1934. Community Activities: Catholic Chaplain - Greenville Sertoma Club, Andrew Gwynn Council of the Knights of Columbus, Greenville County Mental Health Association (former board member), Greenville General Hospital (advisory council, 1979-81). Religion: Appointed a Domestic Prelate with the title Right Reverend Monsignor by Pope John XXIII, 1959, a life-time honor. Honors and Awards: Plaque from the City of Greenville, "In Official Recognition and Appreciation", 1973. Address: 7 South Memminger Street, Greenville, South Carolina 29601.

Baumol, William Jack

Professor. Personal: Born February 26, 1922, in New York City, New York; Married Hilda; Father of Ellen Frances, Daniel Aaron. Education: B.S.S., College of the City of New York, 1942; Ph.D., University of London, 1949. Career: Junior Economist, United States Department of Agriculture, 1942-43, 1946; Assistant Lecturer, London School of Economics, 1947-49; Professor, Department of Economics, Princeton University, 1954 to present (with school since 1949); Professor of Economics, New York University, 1971;

(Joint Appointment, Princeton University and New York University, 1971). Organizational Memberships: American Economic Association (past president); Eastern Economic Association (past president); Association of Environmental and Resource Economists (past president); Resources for the Future, Inc. (research advisory board); Committee on Economic Development (research advisory board); Econometric Society (fellow); Economic Policy Council, State of New Jersey (former chairman and member); Committee on Economic Status of the Profession (former chairman); American Association of University Professors (former vice president); Central New Jersey Chapter, American Statistical Society (past president); Social Science Research Council (former member, board of directors); Various Consulting Activities with Government Agencies and Private Industry. Published Works; *Economic Dynamics; Welfare Economics and the Theory of the State; Economic Processes and Policies; Business Behavior, Value and Growth; The Stock Market and Economic Efficiency; Performing Arts, The Economic Dilemma; Economics: Principles and Policy;* Others. Honors and Awards: Guggenheim Fellow, 1957-58; Honorary L.L.D., Trustee Emeritus, Rider College, 1965; Ford Faculty Fellowship, 1965-66; Honorary Fellow, London School of Economics, 1970; Elected to the American Academy of Arts and Sciences, 1971; Honorary Doctorate, Stockholm School of Economics, 1971; Honorary Doctor of Humane Letters, Knox College, 1973; Honorary Doctorate, University of Basel; John R. Commons Award, Omicron Delta Epsilon, 1975; Townsend Harris Medal, Alumni Association of the City College of New York, 1975; Elected Member, American Philosophical Society, 1977. Address: 61 Jefferson Road, Princeton, New Jersey 08540.

Bauwens, Eleanor E

Associate Dean. Personal: Born December 13, 1931; Daughter of Mr. and Mrs. R. W. King; Married Maurice J. Bauwens; Mother of Paul Joseph. Education: Diploma, St. Mary's Hospital School of Nursing, 1952; B.S.N, with high distinction 1966, M.A. 1970, The University of Arizona; Undertook Graduate Study in Nursing, The University of Arizona, 1972-73; Ph.D., The University of Arizona, 1974. Career: Associate Dean, College of Nursing, University of Arizona; Former Associate Professor, Research Assistant, University of Arizona; Office Nurse; Industrial Nurse. Organizational Memberships: American Academy of Nursing (fellow, 1979 to present); American Anthropological Association (fellow, 1975 to present); Society for Applied Anthropology (fellow, 1978 to present); Sigma Theta Tau (past president, Beta Mu chapter); Phi Kappa Phi; National Research Awards Review Committee; Arizona Nurses Association (council on practice, 1978-80); Editoral Board Reviewer, *Image*, 1978 to present; Council on Nursing and Anthropology (president-elect, 1981 to present); Sigma Xi; University of Arizona Undergraduate Council (chairman, 1981-82); Council on Nursing and Anthropology (president-elect, 1981 to present). Community Activities: Pima County Home Health Advisory Committee (chairman, 1979 to present); Speaker, Seminars and Conferences; WISE Center (panel member); Conducted Community Swine Flu Immunization Clinics, Wellness Subcommittee, Health Systems Agency Southeastern Arizona. Published Works: 24 Publications including 2 Books. Honors and Awards: Certificate of Honors, University of Arizona, 1966; Nurse Scientist Pre-Doctoral Fellowship, United States Public Health Service, 1967-72; Publishing Grant, C. V. Mosby Company, 1980; 6 Funded Research Projects; Western Writers Regional Conference Committee, Sigma Theta Tau; Listed in *Who's Who in Health Care, Who's Who of American Women, World Who's Who of Women, Who's Who in America, International Gold Award Book*. Address: University of Arizona College of Nursing, Tucson, Arizona 85721.

Baxter, George William Jr

Professor of Psychology. Personal: Born October 8, 1925; Married Jane F.; Father of George William III, Elizabeth Lynne. Education: B.S., Emory University, 1946; M.Div., Yale Divinity School, 1951; M.A. 1968, Ph.D. 1969, George Peabody College. Military; Served in the United States Navy, 1943-45. Career: Professor of Psychology, King College, Bristol, Tennessee, 1969 to present; Registar and Assistant Academic Dean, Florida Southern College, 1960-66. Organizational Memberships: American Psychological Association; American Association of Higher Education; Society for Psychological Study of Social Issues; Phi Delta Kappa; Southeastern Psychological Association; Society for Scientific Study of Religion. Community Activities: Offender Aid and Restoration, Bristol, Virginia (chairman, board of directors, 1977-80); Television Awareness Training. Religion: State Street United Methodist Church, Bristol, Virginia, Lay Leader, 1982-83; Chairman of Administrative Board 1981; Chairman of Council on Ministries, 1978-79; Sunday School Teacher; Finance Committee. Honors and Awards: Phi Beta Kappa; M.Div. cum laude; Listed in *Who's Who in the South and Southwest*. Address: Florida Avenue, Bristol, Tennessee 37620.

Maria E Baylor

Bayazeed, Abdo Fares

Petroleum Engineer. Personal: Born August 20, 1924 in Damascus, Syria; Father of Fares, David, Raina, Jason (deceased), Nadia. Education: Graduate of Wentworth Military Academy Junior College; B.S. Petroleum Engineering, University of Oklahoma, 1955. Career: Petroleum Engineer, Sinclair Oil and Gas Company, Tulsa, Oklahoma, 1955-60; Petroleum Engineer, Layton Oil Company, Independence, Kansas, 1960-62; Petroleum Engineer, Department of Energy, Bartlesville Energy Research Center, Bartlesville, Oklahoma, 1962 to present. Organizational Memberships; Society of Petroleum Engineers of A.I.M.E.; Oklahoma Chapter of Society of Petroleum Engioneers (advisory committee, 1967; board of directors, 1968-71; chairman of education committee). Community Activities: Science Fair, Bartlesville, Chairman of Arrangements and Registration 1967, Judge 1968; Bartlesville Y.M.C.A.; Junior Hi-Y Club (youth committee, 1969-70; advisor, 1969-70). Published Works: Author/Co-Author Number of Technical Papers. Honors and Awards: Award of Honor, Wentworth Military Academy, 1950; Listed in *Who's Who in the South and Southwest, Personalities of the South, Book of Honor, Community Leaders and Noteworthy Americans, Notable Americans, Personalities of America, American Register of Profiles, Who's Who in Technology Today, Who's Who in America, Dictionary of International Biography, Men of Achievement, Men and Women of Distinction, International Who's Who of Intellectuals, International Register of Profiles, International Who's Who in Community Service*. Address: 312 S.W. Sante Fe 40, Bartlesville, Oklahoma 74003.

Baylor, Maria Elizabeth

Senior Equal Opportunity Specialist. Personal: Born July 26, 1928; Daughter of Clarence and Nettie M. (Brooks) Baylor (both deceased). Education: B.A., Howard University, 1950; Undertook graduate studies in English, Howard University, 1955-56. Career: Federal Women's Program Coordinator; Deputy Chief, Public Programs Division, Senior Equal Opportunity Specialist. Organizational Memberships: American Association of University Women; Business and Professional Women's League. Community Activities: Notary Public for the U.S. Government, 1962 to present; Howard University Alumni Club (recording secretary, 1959-60; vice president, 1960-64); Howard University Women's Club (corresponding secretary, 1958-60; vice president, 1966-68; archivist, 1972-75). Religion: Baptist. Honors and Awards: Miss Alma Mater, Howard University, 1966; Annual Achievement Award, Sigma Gamma Rho, 1972; Secretary's Award for Meritorious Achievement, Department of Transportation, 1975. Address: 621 Otis Place, N.W., Washington D.C. 20010.

Bayne, Barbara S

Professor of English. Personal: Born November 5, 1939; Daughter of Mr. and Mrs. William E. Sanchivies; Mother of Erich Wayne Grissom, Beverlyn Yvelle Grissom. Education: A.B., Albany State College, 1959; M.A., North Carolina Central University, 1963; Ph.D., Indiana University of Pennsylvania, 1983. Career: Instructor, Florida A&M University; Instructor, Shaw University; Assistant Professor, Winston-Salem University; Presently, Professor of English, Essex County College, Newark, New Jersey. Organizational Memberships: Delta Sigma Theta; Sigma Rho Sigma; Albany State Alumni Association. Community Activities: Implemented Program in English, North Baptist School of Religion, 1978; Donation Given to Leaguers, Organization Designed to Assist Students in Need of Financial Assistance; American Association of University Women; Implemented Course "Women in Literature", Essex County College. Religion: Monclair Unity Church, Soloist, Speaker at Women's Day Programs. Honors and Awards: Humanities Award for Literature, Essex County College; Educator Award, National Council of Negro Women, 1967; Listed in *Who's Who in American Colleges and Universities, Outstanding Educators of America; Who's Who in the East, Directory of Distinguished Americans.* Address: 76 Elliot Place, East Orange, New Jersey 07018.

Beale, Everett Minot

Symphonic Musician. Personal: Born July 7, 1939; Son of Minot A. and June T. Beale (deceased); Married Eva Piscitelli; Father of Dawn and Tania. Education: B.M., New England Conservatory of Music. Career: Timpanist, Boston Pops Esplanade Orchestra, 1965 to present; Principal Percussionist Boston Ballet Orchestra, 1965 to present; Associate member, Boston Symphony Orchestra, 1965 to present; Principal Percussionist, Boston Pops Tour Orchestra with Arthur Fiedler, 1960-61; Head, Percussion Department, Dartmouth College, Hanover, New Hampshire, 1963-68; Head, Percussion Department, University of Lowell, Lowell, Massachusetts, 1968 to present; Freelance Percussionist with Foremost Orchestras and Choral Groups in Boston Area; Number of Recordings with the Boston Pops and the Boston Symphony. Organizational Memberships: Phi Mu Alpha Sinfonia Fraternity; Percussive Arts Society; North American Radio Archives. Published Works: *Playing and Teaching of Percussion Instruments;* Article, "Arthur Fiedler, A Recollection", in the *Lowell Sun*, Lowell, Massachusetts. Honors and Awards: John Philip Sousa Band Award, 1958; Appointed by Arthur Fiedler to be a member of the World Symphony Orchestra, 1971; Listed in *International Who's Who in Music, Who's Who in the East, Book of Honor, Notable Americans, Personalities of America; International Book of Honor.* Address: 104 Redgate Road, Tyngsborough, Massachusetts 01879.

Everett Beale

Beaman, Margarine

Personal: Born in Hilda, Mason County, Texas; Daughter of Mr. and Mrs. Ryland Geistweidt; Married Robert W. Beaman, 1974; Mother of stepsons Richard and Ronald. Education: Attended Texas Luthern College; Certificate of Distinction, University of Michigan. Career: Auditing Office, Driskell Hotel, Austin, Texas; Part-Time employment at Nixon-Clay Commercial College Night School, Bond's Television Sales and Service, Bohn's Travel Agency, Austin Radio and Television Association; Texas Legislature Sessions, 1969 and 1971; Mt. Vernon Motor Hotel; Office Manager, Monroe the Calculator Company; Director, Nixon-Clay Commerical College, Nixon-Clay Technical College, Nixon-Clay Vocational School; Co-Owner and Vice President, Beaman Metal Company; Owner, Accounting and Consulting Business; Advisory Committee, Texas Guaranteed Student Loans, 1980-81; Governors Sub-Committee, International Year of the Disabled Person, 1980-81. Organizational Memberships: Hotel-Motel Greeters International (past national secretary, past national treasurer, past regional secretary, treasurer and director, past president, secretary and treasurer of local chapter); Hotel-Motel Sales Association (past director); Hotel-Motel Accountants Association (past secretary and vice president); Southern Association of Colleges and School Accreditation Team (C.O.E.I. team); Credit Women of Austin (past secretary); Consumer Credit Executives of Austin (past director); T.L.C. Executive Student Association (past secretary and treasurer); Business and Professional Women of Austin (past president); Capital City Business and Professional Women's Clubs (president, two years; secretary, two years; treasurer, two years; young careerist chairman); District #6 Business and Professional Women's Club; Texas Federation of Business and Professional Women's Clubs (past membership chairman, state recording secretary, 1981-82); Capitol District Federation of Women's Clubs (past second vice president; first vice president, 1981-82); Austin Junior Woman's Federation (past president, past committee chairman, corresponding secretary 1981-82, service project chairman 1980-82); Zonta Austin Chapter (public relations chairman, 1981-82); National Federation of the Blind (associate member, 1981-82); Texas Association of Private Schools (past vice president; secretary and treasurer, 1979-82; newsletter editor, 1981-82). Community Activities: Austin Ethnic History Association; Texas Heritage Association; Volunteer Worker: Old Bakery Emporium, Travis County Adult Probation, Cancer Drive, Heart Fund, United Way, M.D. Anderson Cancer Research Hospital, Battered Women's Center, Austin State Hospital, Travis School, Girls Town U.S.A., Braille Signs for the Blind. Religion: Lutheran. Honors and Awards: Outstanding Volunteer Service, Travis County Adult Probation; Governor's Award, Outstanding and Significant Personal Service as a Texas Volunteer; Award for Outstanding Contribution, Texas Association of Private Schools; Certificate of Appreciation, State of Texas; Executive Pin, Governor's Committee on Employment of the Handicapped; Nominee, Austin's Most Worthy Citizen, 1981; Woman of the Year, Austin Business and Professional Women, 1965; Mayor's Award for Outstanding Contributions, 1981; Certified Consumer Credit Executive, 1966; Outstanding District President, State Federation of Business and Professional Women's Clubs, 1980; Listed in *Who's Who of American Women, Directory of Distingished Americans, American Personalities.* Address: 1406 Wilshire Blvd., Austin, Texas 78722.

Beatty, William Andrew

Pastor. Personal: Born August 27, 1937; Son of Mr. and Mrs. Dwight Beatty; Married Clara Ann Gillis; Father of Stephen Andrew, Deborah Ann, Brenda Ann. Education: B.A., Westminster College, 1959; M.Div., Fuller Theological Seminary, 1963; D.Min., San Francisco Theological Seminary, 1977. Career: Senior Pastor, Covenant Presbyterian Church; Senior Pastor, Second Presbyterian Church, Duluth, Minnesota; Youth Director, Westminster Presbyterian Church, Temple City, California; Youth Director, Trinity Presbyterian Church, Santa Ana, California. Organizational Memberships: Skyline Manor (board of directors, 1970-81); Omaha World Impact (president of the board of advisors, 1976-81); Duluth Presbytery (vice moderator, 1966-67, chairman of the evangelism committee, 1966-68); Omaha Presbytery (chairman of the public relations committee, 1970-73); Missouri River Valley Presbytery (chairman of the interpretation & support committee, 1979-82); Synod of Lakes and Prairies (support department, 1973-78, chairman of the communications committee, 1975-78); National General Assembly Property Committee, 1978 to present; National General Assembly Support Agency, 1978 to present; Support Agency of the United Presbyterian Church (executive committee, 1980 to present). Honors and Awards: Listed in *Who's Who in Religion*, 1st edition 1976-77; *Who's Who in Religion*, 2nd edition, 1977-78; *Dictionary of International Biography*, 13th edition; *Men of Achievement*, 4th edition; *Notable Americans*, 3rd edition, 1976-77; *Community Leaders and Noteworthy Americans*, 10th edition; *Men of Achievement International*, 6th edition; *Men and Women of Achievement*, 1979; *Personalities of the West and Midwest*, 1977-78. Address: 7943 Manderson Street, Omaha, Nebraska 68134.

Beck, Frances Patricia

Writer, Director, Producer. Personal: Born in Philadelphia, Pennsylvania; Married John Roger Beck; Mother of 1 son and 1 daughter. Education: Degree in Psychology, Columbia University, 1959; Degree in Drama/Speech, American Academy of Dramatic Arts, 1962; Ph.D., Bryn Mawr College, Pennsylvania, 1980; PhD 1981. Career: President, Fran Beck Enterprises, 1966 to present; Writer/Producer, Manhattan Cable TV, 1973 to present; Director of a number of commercials, documentaries, travelogues; Writer, Director, Producer of Plays; Actress in Theatre; Producer of Talk Shows. Organizational Memberships: Society of Stage Directors & Choreographers (secretary); Actors Liberation (president); Screen Actors Guild (counsel). Published Works: Contributor to several journals. Honors and Awards: George Foster Peabody Award; International Golden Eagle Award. Address: 319 E. 24 Street, New York City, New York 10010.

Becker, Gail L

Marketing Communications Consultant. Personal: Born May 14, 1943; Daughter of Mrs. Max Becker. Education: B.S., Drexel University. Career: Marketing Communications Consultant, Gail Becker Associates, Inc.; Former Dietitian. Organizational Memberships: American Dietetics Association; American Home Economics Associaton; Home Economics in Business; American Women in Radio and Television; Women in Communications; Society of Consumer Affairs Professionals; American Medical Writers Association; Institute of Food Technologists. Honors and Awards: Listed in *Who's Who Among Students in Colleges and Universities, Outstanding Young Women in America, Who's Who of American Women.* Address: 2357 Linwood Avenue, Fort Lee, New Jersey 07024.

Francis Beck

Becker, Johanna Lucille

Professor, Member of Catholic Order. Personal: Born December 17, 1921; Daughter of Mr. and Mrs. A. J. Becker. Education: B.F.A., University of Colorado, 1943; M.A., The Ohio State University, 1945; M.A. 1967, Ph.D. 1974, The University of Michigan. Career: College of St. Benedict - Professor of Art and Asian Studies 1950 to present, Chairman of the Department of Asian Studies 1972-77, Academic Dean 1957-61; Professor in Art, St. John's University, 1952-60; Chairman, Art Department, Maryville College, St. Louis; Instructor, Illinois State University. Organizational Memberships: World Affairs Council (board of directors, 1972 to present); Association for Asian Studies; Oriental Ceramic Society (London); Asiatic Society of Japan (Tokyo); American Association of University Women; The Japan Society; Midwest Art History Society; Global Education Associates. Community Activities: Newman Federation (national secretary, 1943; vice president, 1944; national president, 1945); International Congress on Religion, Architecture and Art (seminar leader, 1967); American Association of University Women (corporate representative, 1977 to present); 2 International Symposium on Japanese Ceramics, Seattle Art Museum, 1972. Religion: Joined the Benedictine Sisters, St. Joseph, Minnesota, 1950. Published Works: *New Catholic Encyclopedia* Entry "Sacred Vestments"; *Encyclopedia of Japan* Entry "Karatsu Ceramics"; *Karatsu Ceramics of Japan: Origins, Fabrication and Types;* Entries included in *Keramos; Museum of Art Bulletin; Journal of Asiatic Society of Japan.* Honors and Awards: Phi Beta Kappa; Mortar Board; Delta Phi Delta; Fulbright Scholar in India, 1963; Hill Foundation Award, Study in India and Japan, 1960; C. L. Freer Fellow, 1967; Schmitt Fellow, 1967; American Association of University Women Fellow, 1969; Horace H. Kackham Fellow, 1969; Northwest Foundation Grant, Study in Japan and Southeast Asia, 1975; Tri-College East Asia Studies Grant, Study in China, 1980. Address: Convent of St. Benedict, St. Joseph, Minnesota 56374.

Becker-Theye, Betty

College Dean. Personal: Born October 10, 1935; Daughter of Mrs. R. B. Friend; Married Larry Theye; Mother of David Becker. Education: B.A., Washburn University, 1963; M.S., Emporia State University, 1967; Ph.D., State University of New York-Binghamton, 1979. Career: Kearney State College, Dean of the School of Fine Arts and Humanities, Former Professor and Chairman of the Department of Foreign Languages. Organizational Memberships: American Translators Association; Modern Language Association; American Comparative Literature Association; International Comparative Literature Association; International Comparative Literature Association; Association of Teachers of French; American Association of University Professors (chapter president, 1971; state conference treasurer, 1970). Community Activities: Nebraska State Advisory Council on the Teaching of Foreign Languages, 1980 to present; National Association for the Advancement of Colored People (Topeka branch and Kansas conference board member, 1962-67). Honors and Awards: Alpha Omicron Phi Recognition Award, 1970; Chevalier de l'Ordre, Les Amis de la Courtoise francaise, 1981; Outstanding Educator, 1975. Address: 4103 Avenue E, Kearney, Nebraska 68847.

Marion P Behrman

Beebe, Mary Livingstone

Visual Arts Center Director. Personal: Born November 5, 1940; Daughter of Mr. and Mrs. Robert L. Beebe. Education: B.A., Bryn Mawr College, 1962; Undertook Further Study at the Sorbonne, University of Paris, L'Ecole du Louvre, Paris, France, 1962-63. Career: Executive Director, Portland Center for the Visual Arts, 1973 to present; Director of Public Relations, Assistant Director, Sally Judd Gallery, The Catlin Gabel School, 1971-73; Secretary of the Theatre Arts Department, Assistant Producer of the American Theatre Company, Manager of the Coaster Theater, Producer of the American Theater Company, Portland State University, 1969-71; Sally Judd Gallery, 1969; Boutique Co-Owner, Portland, 1967-69; Secretary, Curatorial Assistant, Fogg Art Museum, Harvard University, 1966-67; Assistant to the Registrar and Secretary, Museum of Fine Arts, Boston, 1965-66; Museum Apprentice, Portland Art Museum, 1962-64. Organizational Memberships: Western Association of Art Museums (board of directors, vice president, 1978 to present); National Research Center of the Arts, Inc. (project consultant, 1978-79); Henry Gallery, University of Washington-Seattle (board of directors, 1977-80). Community Activities: Portland Development Commission (art steering committee, 1977-78); Portland Transit Mall (art selection jury, 1977). Honors and Awards: Juror, Roaring Fork Valley Annual, Aspen, Colorado, 1981; Consultant, Outdoors Across America Exhibition, 1981; Juror, Second Biennial Juried Exhibition for Idaho Artists, 1981; Juror, Honolulu Academy of Arts, Artists of Hawaii, 1980; Visiting Artist, University of Colorado-Boulder, 1980; National Endowment for the Arts Fellowship for Independent Travel, $10,000 Award, 1979-80; Others. Address: 2737 S.W. Fern, Portland, Oregon 97201.

Behrmann, Marion Polly

Special Education Consultant, Author. Personal: Born November 24, 1925; Daughter of Marjory R. Piper; Married John W. Behrmann; Father of James Piper, Charles Robert, Judith B. Richardson, Roland A. Education: B.S.Ed., B.S. Recreational

Leadership, University of Massachusetts; Undertook Education Courses, Boston University, 1946; Studies in Learning Disabilities, Reading Research Institute, 1965-66; Psychology Courses, Clark University, 1973-74; Special Education Courses, Boston College, 1974-75; Special Education Courses, Lesley College, 1977. Career: Kindergarten Director, Teacher, Reading Tutor for Emotionally Disturbed, Mentally Retarded, Physically Handicapped, Tutor and Home Teacher, Substitute Teacher, Camp Director, 1948-65; Supervisor, Learning Disabilities for Reading Research Institute, 1966; Master Teacher, American International College, Summer Institute for Learning Disabilities, 1968-69; Remedial Reading and Learning Disabilities, Framingham, 1966-71; Teacher/Diagnostician, Liberty Council of Schools, 1970-71; Master Teacher, Framingham State College, Summer Institute for Learning Disabilities, 1971; Coordinator, Learning Disabilities, Framingham Middle Schools, 1971-73; Teacher, Clark University, 1973; Special Educator, Resource Center, Wellesley, Massachusetts, 1973 to present; Instructor, League of Women Voters Paraprofessionals, 1974. Lecturer/Consultant, Harvard University, Boston College, Boston University, Clark University, University of Massachusetts, Lesley College, Assumption College, Boston State College, Tufts University, American International College, Mount Holyoke College, Framingham State College, and for over 200 School Systems in Massachusetts Communities, Association for Children with Learning Disabilities Conferences throughout the United States and Canada, Massachusetts Teachers Association Conferences, Others, 1967 to present; Conductor of Workshops, Demonstrations and College Courses, 1966 to present; Television Demonstrations and Radio Programs, 1968 to present. Organizational Memberships: Massachusetts Association for Children with Learning Disabilities (co-founder Framingham chapter; advisory board member, 1973-79; board of directors, 1968-72); Massachusetts Council for Exceptional Children (treasurer, 1974-75); Selected Participant in H.E.W. Conference on Technology for Children, 1972. Community Activities: Cub Scout Leader; Girl Scout Leader; Framingham Square Dance (co-founder); Local Republican Leader. Religion: Sunday School Teacher, Choir Member. Published Works: Author *Why Is It Always Me?; Number and Letter Dice; Activities for Developing Auditory Perception; Activities for Developing Visual Perception; How-to-Make-it Cards;* Co-Author *Parents As Playmates; How Many Spoons Make a Family?; EXCEL I - Experience for Children in Learning; EXCEL II;* Co-Department Editor, *Day Care Magazine, Highlights, Parents.* Honors and Awards: Massachusetts Mother of the Year, 1979; Massachusetts Association for Children with Learning Disabilities Award for Outstanding Contribution to the Field of Learning Disabilities, 1970; Phi Kappa Phi; Listed in *Who's Who in Learning Disabilties, Who's Who in American Colleges, Who's Who in Outdoor Education, Who's Who of American Women, Who's Who of International Women, Who's Who in Education.* Address: 115 Lake Road, Framingham, Massachusetts 01701.

Mildred L Belden

Beineke, Lowell Wayne

Professor of Mathematics. Personal: Born November 20, 1939; Son of Elmer H. Beineke; Married Judith Rowena Wooldridge; Father of Jennifer Elaine, Philip Lennox. Education: B.S. Purdue University, 1961; M.A. 1962, Ph.D. 1965, University of Michigan; Further Studies at University College, London. Career: Professor of Mathematics, Indiana University-Purdue University; Temporary or Part-Time Positions were held at Oxford University, The Open University, University of Michigan, Indiana University, Kutztown State College; Fulbright Teaching Exchange, Polytechnic of North London. Organizational Memberships: Sigma Xi; American Mathematical Society; American Association of University Professors; Indiana Regional Mathematics Consortium. Community Activities: Democratic Party; Common Cause; Embassy Foundation; Fort Wayne Fine Arts Foundation; WIPU-FM; Purdue Alumni Association; University of Michigan Fort Wayne Club (board of directors, 1978-80; secretary, 1979-80); Glenwood Park Community Association (director, 1979-80). Published Works: Author/Editor 2 Books; Author 50 Mathematics Papers; Editorial Board, *Journal of Graph Theory.* Religion: Plymouth Congregational Church; Benev Board 1972-73, Chairman of the Education Board 1974-78; Delegate to the Indiana-Kentucky Conference of the United Church of Christ, 1976, 1979. Honors and Awards: Outstanding Teacher Award, A.M.O.C.O., 1979; N.S.F. Fellowships, 1961-65; Westinghouse Scholar, 1958-61; Bell Aircraft Scholar, 1957-58; Sigma Xi, 1964; Phi Kappa Phi; Phi Eta Sigma; Pi Mu Epsilon; Delta Rho Kappa. Address: 4520 Bradwood Terrace, Fort Wayne, Indiana 46815.

Belden, Mildred Lillian

Retired. Personal: Born in 1903; Daughter of Ora Josiah Belden. Education: A.A., Kidd Key College, 1922; B.A., Austin College, 1934. Career: Retired; Former Teacher, Sherman Public Schools; Supervisor, Eighth Service Command, Dallas; Secretary, Veterans Administration, Dallas; Secretary, Office of the Inspector General, Department of Agriculture, Temple, Texas. Organizational Memberships: Business and Professional Women's Association (treasurer, 1966-69); American Association of University Women (vice president, 1966-70, 1977-78; historian, 1977-79); National Association of Retired Federal Employees (program chairman, Lake Texoma chapter 1290, 1974-75; secretary, 1978-82). Community Activities: Service to Military Families and Veterans, American Red Cross, Sherman-Denison Chapter (chairman, 1975-81); Volunteer Work, San Rayburn Memorial Veterans Center, Bonham, Texas, 1975-81; Sherman Historical Society (assistant secretary, 1978-82). Religion: Trinity Presbyterian Church, Sherman, Texas; Treasurer of Business Women's Circle, 1976-77; Treasurer of Women's Association, 1978-79. Honors and Awards: American Association of University Women, Woman of Achievement Award, 1975. Address: 504 North Woods, Sherman, Texas 75090.

Deanne Bell

Bell, Deanne

Librarian. Personal: Born August 31, 1937, in McCook, Nebraska; Daughter of L. G. Bell and Pauline Smollock. Education: Attended University of Idaho; Silver Wings Recipient, Southwest Airline School, Los Angeles, California, 1957; Certificate, American Institute of Banking, Los Angeles, 1958; A.A., Western Oklahoma State College, 1977; Degree in library science, Oscar Rose College, 1979; Attended American Institute of Foreign Study. Career: Held various positions with Bank of America, Los Angeles and First Security Bank of Nampa, Idaho, 5 years; Photographer's model, 1955-70; Freelance clothing model, House of Nine, Los Angeles; Airline stewardess, Southwest Airlines, Los Angeles, 1956-57; Medical secretary, Horton Nursing Home, Nampa, Idaho, 1959-60; Worked in Accounting Department, Tandy Homes, Inc., Tulsa, Oklahoma, 1960-63; Medical secretary, Tulsa, 1963-64; Owner and operator, Dee's Department Store, Hollis, Oklahoma, 1966-68; Legal secretary, Myers and Cummings Attorneys, Hollis, 1970-73; Head Librarian, Hollis Public Library, 1977 to present. Organizational Memberships: University of Tulsa Law Wives (secretary); National and Oklahoma Associations of Legal Secretaries; American, Oklahoma and Southwestern Library Association. Community Activities: Harmon County History Association (chairman); Notary Public, State of Oklahoma; Oklahoma Arts and Humanities Council; Oklahoma Image Program; Beta Sigma Phi (treasurer); National Girl Scout Council; Garden Club. Published Works: *Planning the Route* (history book of Harmon County, Oklahoma); Page Editor, Western Oklahoma State College student paper, 1977. Honors and Awards: Received first place prize for watercolor painting, "Early Snow", 1979; Named "Miss Nampa", 1955; Contestant in "Miss Idaho" pageant, 1955; Commissioned as Honoray Colonel by Governor of Oklahoma; Made Dean's List and Honor Roll, 1975-79; Named an All-American Senior, 1956; Attended Idaho Girls' State, 1955; Listed in *Who's Who in American Colleges and Universities, National Register of Outstanding Women in America, International Register of Profiles, Community Leaders and Noteworthy Americans, Dictionary of International Biography, The World Who's Who of Women, Book of Honor, Personalities of the South, Who's Who in Library and Information Services, Directory of Distinguished*

Americans, International Who's Who of Intellectuals. Address: Box 384, Hollis, Oklahoma 73550.

Bell, Donna

Retail Executive, Employment Development Specialist. Personal: Born September 21, 1932; Daughter of H. A. Steil; Married Larry Bell; Mother of Barbara, Charles, Sandra, Michael. Education: Attended California State University, 1977-80; Currently attending Lincoln Law School, Sacramento. Career: Traveling Lecturer, Stanley Home Products Company, Topeka, Kansas, 1958-62; Design for Learning System for Women, Nebraska, 1970-74; Administrative Secretary, McBell Industries, Oshkosh, Nebraska, 1971; Owner of a Restaurant, Oshkosh, 1972-74; Owner, Tahoe Gift Shop, Sacramento, 1974 to present; California Employment Development Specialist, 1981 to present. Organizational Memberships: National Association of Female Executives (charter member). Community Activities: Guiding Star Council of Girl Scouts (district chairman, president, board of directors, 1964-73); Affirmative Action National Task Force, 1973-74; Garden County Federation of Women's Clubs (president, 1972; district chairman, music contests, 1972-74); Garden County Young Mother's Council (coordinator, 1974); California Commission on the Status of Women, 1975. Religion: Lutheran, Church School Teacher, 1963-74; Adult Choir Director, 1973-74. Address: 2613 Warrego Way, Sacramento, California 95826.

Bell, Esther Bernice

Occupational Therapist. Personal: Born June 1, 1930; Daughter of Mrs. Esther M. Bell. Education: B.S., University of California-Los Angeles, 1951; Certificate in Occupational Therapy, University of Southern California, 1954; M.A., Texas Women's University, 1971. Career: Occupational Therapist. Organizational Memberships: American Occupational Therapy Association (secretary, 1978-83; representative, 1971-77; nominating committee chairman, 1977; recognition committee chairman, 1975); Texas Occupational Therapy Association (committee on practice representative, 1968-71; representative, 1971-77; vice president, 1976-80; recognition committee chairman, 1968, 1971). Community Activities: St. Philips College Occupational Therapy Curriculum (advisory council, 1973-76); Texas Woman's University Self Study Committee, 1980; Texas Woman's University Clinical Council (chairman, 1968-78); Health Systems Agency (allied health professions committee, 1978 to present); Sierra Club; Texas Republican Party; Texas Rehabilitation Association; Beta Sigma Phi. Religion: Episcopal Church, Vestry 1979-81, Adult Education Leader 1980-81. Honors and Awards: Texas Occupational Therapist of the Year, 1971; Fellow, American Occupational Therapy Association, 1980. Address: 203 McClure, Gonzales, Texas 78629.

Bell, Louise Matheson

Louise M Bell

Retired Photographer. Personal: Born January 21, 1919, in Washington, Georgia; Daughter of Thomas Harold and Lillie Hudson Matheson; Married James Bruce Bell; Mother of Dr. Harold Bruce Bell, Dr. James Milton Bell. Education: Winona School of Photography. Career: Photographer (retired). Community Activities: Friends of the South Carolina Museum (charter member); Historic Pendleton Foundation; South Carolina Heritage Trust (advisory committee); Governor's Beautification and Community Improvement Committee (Oconee County chairman 1977); South Carolina Appalachian Council of Governments (bicentennial task force, leisure resources committee, historic preservation committee vice chairman); Seneca Centennial and Historical Commission (chairman 1972-75); Oconee County Lunney Museum (chairman, board of trustees 1970-78); Oconee County Celebration of the South Carolina Tri-centennial Celebration (co-ordinator); Oconee County Historical Society (charter member, treasurer); Foothills Antique Club (co-founder 1966, president, vice president, secretary); Oconee County Planning and Development Board (charter member); Seneca Council of Clubs (president, vice president); Blue Ridge Garden Club (charter member, president, vice president); Seneca Planning and Zoning Commission; Seneca Band Booster Club (co-founder, secretary); United Daughters of the Confederacy (vice president); Clemson Area Continuing Education Series (instructor 1978-79); Seneca Woman's Club (charter member, historian, board of directors 1981-82). Religion: Baptist. Honors and Awards: Woman of the Year, Blue Ridge Garden Club; Outstanding Service to City of Seneca, 1973; South Carolina Travel Award as Chairman of "The Most Outstanding Nonrecurring Event in South Carolina in 1973"; South Carolina Revolution Bicentennial Commission and Governor's Award for "Patriotic Service to State and Country", 1976; Listed in *Dictionary of International Biography, International Who's Who in Community Service, World Who's Who of Women, Personalities of the South, Notable Americans, Community Leaders and Noteworthy Americans, Americans of the Bicentennial Era, Directory of Distinguished Americans.* Address: 110 South Second Street, Box 595, Seneca, South Carolina 29678.

Bell, Lucy Butler

Professor, Department Chairperson. Personal: Born September 23, 1947; Daughter of William H. and Mattie Raybon Butler. Education: B.A., Fisk University; M.A., George Peabody Teachers College; Undertook further coursework at the State University of New York-Buffalo, University of Florida-Gainesville, Florida Atlantic University. Career: Professor, Chairman, Department of Behavioral Science. Organizational Memberships: F.A.C.C.; A.A.W.J.C.; S.E.P.A.-Heads of Department of Psychology. Community Activities: Atlantic Properties and Development, Inc. (board of trustees); Atlantic Enterprises (president); Equal Access/Equal Opportunity Monitoring Committee (task force on international education); Florida Association of Community Colleges (teacher education task force); Credit Union (board of directors); Florida State Course Numbering Systems/Psychology Discipline; Youth Counselor. Religion: Methodist A.M.E. Church. Honors and Awards: Human Behavior Certification, Institute of Financial Education; Woman Entrepreneur Workshop, Center for Small Business; Nomination, Professional Development Project for Community College Women Administrators; Florida State Department of Education National Identification Program for the Advancement of Women in Higher Education; Board of Advisors, Outstanding Young Women in America; Certification Workshop for Personalized Systems of Instruction, Georgetown University; National Center for Human Potential Seminars and Services, Basic and Advanced Human Potential Seminar, Success Groups for Underachievers; Professional Seminar, Assertiveness Training. Address: 1241 Cadillac Drive, Daytona Beach, Florida 32017.

Bellamy, Terry Leon

Administrator. Personal: Born June 26, 1955; Son of Mr. and Mrs. Alston Bellamy; Father of Justin Randolph. Education: B.A. Political Science, North Carolina A&T University; Further Studies at the University of North Carolina, Institute of Government; M.C.R.P., Iowa State University, 1981. Career: Acting Director of Department of Urban Studies, Former Research Coordinator/Instructor, Johnson C. Smith University. Organizational Memberships: Urban Affairs Association; American Planner Association; Student Organization Urban Planner. Community Activities: Housing and Development Committee of Mecklenburg County; Transit Mall Advisory Board, City of Charlotte; Biddleville-Five Points Housing Corporation (secretary); Biddleville-Five

Points Community Organization (technical advisor); Urban Life Associates; Urban Studies Advisory Board; Citizens League; Omega Psi Phi; Scholar of the Year, 1975, 1980, 1981; Academic-Athletic Award, North Carolina A&T State University, 1974. Address: 2001 Monterey Street, Charlotte, North Carolina 28216.

Bellows, Virginia Louise

Telephone Company Executive. Personal: Born July 25, 1951; Daughter of Ray F. and Abbie V. Bellows; Married Michael F. Ross. Education: B.S. Chemistry 1972, M.B.A. Finance 1979, University of Miami, Florida. Career: District Staff Manager, American Telephone and Telegraph, 1982 to present; Southern Bell Telephone Company, Staff Manager, Atlanta 1979-82, Engineer, Miami 1972-79. Organizational Memberships: Acanthus of Florida, Inc. (president); National Association of Female Executives; National Association M.B.A. Executives; Society of Professional and Executive Women. Community Activities: Arts and Sciences Alumni Association, University of Miami (director, 1979). Honors and Awards: Listed in *Who's Who of American Women, Who's Who in the South and Southwest.* Address: 6036 Millstone Run, Stone Mountain, Georgia 30087.

Bellugi, Ursula

Adjunct Professor and Laboratory Director. Personal: Born February 21, 1931; Daughter of Dr. and Mrs. Max Herzberger; Married Edward S. Klima; Mother of David and Robin. Education: B.A., Antioch College, 1952; Ed.D., Harvard University, 1967. Career: Visiting Lecturer (1968), Assistant Professor and Research Fellow (1967-68), Senior Research Assistant (1964-67), all at Harvard University; Visiting Assistant Professor, Department of Psychology, Rockefeller University, 1969; Research Associate, The Salk Institute for Biological Studies, 1968-69; Adjunct Associate Professor, Department of Psychology, University of California-San Diego, 1970-76; The Salk Institute for Biological Studies: Director, Laboratory for Language and Cognitive Studies (1970 to present), Associate Research Professor (1974-81), Research Professor (1981 to present); Adjunct Professor, Department of Psychology, University of California-San Diego, 1977 to present. Organizational Memberships: Linguistics Society of America (technical committee on language and cognitive development); American Psychological Association; International Linguistic Association; International Association for the Study of Child Language; American Association of Applied Linguistics; Psychonomic Society, Society for Research in Child Development; Program in Cognitive Science (associate); Center for Human Information Processing (associate); Center for Research in Language Acquisition (advisory board); Communicative Disorders Panel, National Institute of Neurological and Communicative Disorders and Stroke (advisory board); Department of Health, Education and Welfare (national advisory committee on education of the deaf); Editorial Board: *Journal of Child Language, Journal of Applied Linguistics, Journal of Speech and Hearing Disorders, Sign Language Studies, American Annals of the Deaf, International Journal of Human Communication, Classics in Psycholinguistics, Contemporary Psychology*; Salk Institute: Seminar Committee (chairman), Committee on Biology and Language (chairman). Published Works: *Signed and Spoken Language: Biological Constraints on Linguistic Form, The Signs of Language, The Acquisition of Language;* Numerous chapters and articles for professional publications. Honors and Awards: Dan Cloud Award, 1979; Association of American Publishers Professional and Scholarly Publishing Division Award for "Most Outstanding Book in Behavioral Sciences" (*The Signs of Language*), 1979. Address: 6649 Michaeljohn Drive, La Jolla, California 92037.

Belting, Natalia Maree

Associate Professor, Author. Personal: Born July 11, 1915; Daughter of Paul E. Belting, Anna Maree Hanselman (both deceased). Education: B.S. 1936, M.A. 1937, Ph.D. 1940, University of Illinois. Career: Associate Professor, Department of History, University of Illinois; Author of 20+ Children's Books; Former Proofreader, Reporter, *Urbana Evening Courier*. Organizational Memberships: Society for Historical Archives; Society of the History of the Early Republic; Southwestern American Indian Society; American Society for Ethnohistory; Author's Guild. Community Activities: Champaign County Bicentennial Commission; Committee on Student Organizations, University of Illinois; Champaign County Historical Society (board of governors); Consultant on Illinois Indian Sites; Numerous Program Committees in Local and State Societies. Honors and Awards: Nominee for 2nd Annual Governor's Award in the Humanities, 1979; Illinois Author of the Year, Association of Teachers of English, 1979; Achievement Award in Community Service, The Arts, Communication and Education, 1st Annual Leader Luncheon, Young Men's Christian Association, 1980; Compatriot of Education, 1976, Kappa Delta Pi; 2 Nominations for Caldecott Award; 1 Nomination for the Newberry Award for Children's Books; Citation for Public Service, Illinois General Assembly, 1979, 1980. Address: R.R. 2, Box 19, The Big Woods, Urbana, Illinois 61801.

Bely, Jeanette Lobach

Professor of Education. Personal: Born January 15, 1916; Widow; Mother of Jeanette Linaida, Leona B. Keeler. Education: B.B.A., St. John's University, 1938; M.A., Teacher's College, Columbia University, 1939; Ph.D., St. John's University, 1961. Career: Professor of Education, The Bernard M. Baruch College of the City of New York, 1954 to present; Temporary Lecturer, Hunter College, 1954; Teacher-in-Charge, Miller Schools, Inc., 1941-48; Instructor, Lamb's Business Training School, 1940. Organizational Memberships: International Society for Business Education; Administrative Management Society; Business Education Association of Metropolitan New York (president, 1975-76; executive committee, 1963 to present); National Business Education Association; Eastern Business Education Association; Business Teachers Association of New York State; Eastern Business Teachers Association; Association of Pitman Teachers (president, 1972-73, 1973-74; chairman, awards committee, 1969-72; chairman, public relations committee, 1963-64). Religion: Sisterhood of the Holy Virgin, 1977; Membership of R.O.C. of The Holy Trinity, 1956 to present; Choir, 1934-45. Published Works: Author *Pitman Secretarial Shorthand for Colleges; Instructor's Handbook and Supplementary Diction, Pitman Secretarial Shorthand for Colleges;* Editor-in-Chief, *Review for C.P.A. Exams*, 1977; Editorial Review Board for McGraw-Hill/Trafalgar House Publishers, 1978. Honors and Awards: Delta Pi Epsilon; Merit Award of Administrative Management Society, 1969; Meritorious Service Award, National Business Education Association, 1978; Annual Fellowship, International Biographical Association, 1979; International Passport, I.B.A., 1979; Invited to have biography and geneology listed in *Burke's Peerage, Ltd.;* Listed in *Leaders in Education, Who's Who of American Women, Dictionary of International Biography, Contemporary Authors, World's Who's Who of Women, World Who's Who of Women in Education, Community Leaders and Noteworthy Americans, International Who's Who of Women, Anglo-American Who's Who, Men and Women of Distinction, Book of Honor, International Who's Who of Intellectuals, Directory of Distinguished Americans, Personalities of America, Community Leaders of America.* Address: 1024 East 93 Street, Brooklyn, New York 11236.

Benenson, Esther Siev

Nursing Home Executive. Personal: Married to Dr. William Benenson; Mother of Michael J., Sharon B. Sydney, Amy, Blanche. Education: A.A.S., Queens College, 1957; B.S., 1972, M.S., 1974, both from Hunter College; Ed.D in Gerontology, Teachers College, Columbia University, 1981. Career: Assistant Administrator, Flushing Manor Nursing Home, 1953-56; Executive Director, Flushing Manor Nursing Home and Flushing Manor Care Center, 1960 to present. Organizational Memberships: American Public Health Association; Gerontological Society; Community Activities: New York State Board of Examiners for Licensing Nursing Home Administrators, 1970-74; New York State Health Planning Commission Advisory Council, 1974; Honors and Awards: Fellow, Royal Society of Health; Fellow, American Academy of Medical Administrators; Fellow, American College of Nursing Home Administrators. Address: 36-21 Parsons Blvd., Flushing, New York 11354.

Benham, Jack E

Executive. Personal: Son of Edward H. and Mary A. Stanton Benham; Married June Gridley, February 14, 1950 (deceased); Father of Cynthia Ann. Education: Attended the University of Cincinnati College of Liberal Arts, University of Cincinnati College of Engineering, United States Armed Forces Institute, Dale Carnegie Institute, Alexander Hamilton Institute, Famous Writer's School. Military: Served in the United States Naval Reserve, achieving the rank of Yeoman 3rd Class, Discharged in 1945; Served in the Ohio State Guard, Medical Corp, achieving the Rank of Sergeant. Career: Draftsman, Kettering Laboratories of Applied Physiology, 1943; Pilot Plant, Proctor and Gamble Corporation, 1943; Laboratory Technician, Hilton-Davis Chemical Corporation, 1944; Laboratory Technician, Engineering Co-Op, Ault and Wiborg, 1944; Paint Technician, Interchemical Corporation, 1945-46; Laboratory Director, Paint Chemist, Southern Manufacturing Company, 1947; Technical Director, Sun and Sea Paint and Varnish Company, 1950-54; Technical Director, Bruning Paint Company, 1954-56; Vice President, Stockholder, Southseas Chemical Corporation, 1956; Vice President, Stockholder, Graphic Arts Screen Process, Inc., 1956; Technical Director, Bruning Paint Company, 1956-64; Stockholder, Boca Raton Office Supply, 1959-61; Vice President, Sales Manager, Stockholder, Palmer Supplies Company of Florida, 1964-71; President, Sales Manager, Chairman of the Board, Majority Stockholder, J. B. International Marketing Corporation, 1971; Vice President, Stockholder, Billie Rose Dinner Theatre, 1969-71; President, Vice President of Southeast Sales Division, J. B. International Marketing Corporation, 1971-82; Board Member, E-Bond Epoxies, Inc., 1971-82; Board Member, Hercules Polymers, Inc., 1978-82; Board Member, Sunburst Paints, Ltd., Nassau, Bahamas, 1978-82; President, J. B. Sales & Consulting, 1982 to present; Technical Director, Commercial Coatings Corporation, 1982 to present. Organizational Memberships: National Association of Chemical Distributors (founder, past national president); Southern Society for Paint Technology (founder; former chairman, Miami section); United Nations Day, U.N.A.-U.S.A. (former vice chairman); American Security Council (national advisory board); American Institute of Chemist (fellow); New York Academy of Sciences; American Chemical Society; International Platform Association. Community Activities: Boca Raton Elks Lodge 2166 (founder, member-at-large); Masonic Lodge 576, Norwood, Ohio; Florida Atlantic University (founder '64 committee); Boca Raton Jaycees (life member); Jaycee's International (senator #17672); United States Senatorial Club. Published Works: Author *Beings, Boundaries and Beauty; Macaronical, Metaphorical, Montage;* Article "Young Men at Work", *All Florida Magazine*, 1957; Game of Three Dimensional Chess; Cookbook. Honors and Awards: Salesman of the Year, Southern Society of Paint Technology, 1966; Listed in *American Men of Science, Who's Who in Commerce and Industry, Who's Who in the South and Southwest.* Address: 558 N.W. 9th Court, Boca Raton, Florida 33432.

Bennett, Bobbie Jean

Assistant Deputy Commissioner. Personal: Born July 13, 1944; Daughter of W. C. and Maude Holcombe; Mother of Terri L. Education: B.B.A., magna cum laude, Georgia State University, 1973. Career: Assistant Deputy Commissioner, Georgia State Merit System. Organizational Memberships: National Association of Deferred Compensation Administrators (secretary, 1981-82); International Personnel Management Association; Georgia Fiscal Management Association (vice president, 1977-78); Georgia Personnel Management Association (secretary, 1975-77); Beta Gamma Sigma (member, 1973-82). Religion: Atlanta First Baptist Church. Honors and Awards: Outstanding Scholarship Award, Mortar Board Honor Society, 1973; Phi Kappa Phi; Dean's Key, 1972. Address: 2072 Malabar Drive, N.E., Atlanta, Georgia 30345.

Bennett, Ivan Stanley

Senior Counselor. Personal: Born January 27, 1949; Son of Ivan F. and Audrey P. Bennett; Married Susan E. Bennett; Father of Jonathan Lee, Jason Charles, Joseph Wesley. Education: A.B., Thomas More College, 1972; M.Ed., Xavier University, 1974. Career: Senior Counselor, Holmes High School, Covington, Kentucky; Former Manager, Job Preparation School (for school dropouts); Director of Admissions-Release, Northern Kentucky State Vocational Technical School; Junior Counselor, Holmes High School. Organizational Memberships: Northern Kentucky Personnel and Guidance Association (president, 1975-76); Kentucky Personnel and Guidance Association (president, 1980-81); American Personnel and Guidance Association (government relations committee, 1977-79); American Personnel and Guidance Association (board of directors, 1981-84). Community Activities: Covington Teacher Advisory Committee, 1973-75; Covington Child Welfare Citizens Committee (secretary, chairperson, 1973-75); Law Enforcement Assistance Administration (sponsored alternative school program advisory committee, chairperson, 1975-76); American College Testing (advisory council for Kentucky, 1980 to present; subcommittee on career exploration programs in Kentucky schools, 1981 to present); Kentucky Council on Higher Education (pre-college curriculum committee); Northern Kentucky Advisory and Resource Council for Teenage Parents, 1975-78; Juvenile Delinquency Task Force; Kentucky Advisory Commission on Criminal Justice Standards and Goals, 1975-77; Regional Council on Substance Abuse, 1976-77. Religion: Lutheran. Honors and Awards: Certificates of Appreciation, Northern Kentucky Personnel and Guidance Association, Kentucky Personnel and Guidance Association, American Personnel and Guidance Association; Awards, Southern Region Branch Assembly, American Personnel and Guidance Association, National Vocational Guidance Association. Address: 2502 Belleview Road, Burlington, Kentucky 41005.

Bennett, Ronald Thomas

Photojournalist. Personal: Born November 6, 1944; Son of E. Al and Donna Mae Bennett; Father of Ronald T. Jr., Gardina W. Education: Attended Multnomah College, 1963-64, and Portland State University, 1964-67. Military: Served in the United States Air Force Reserve, 1972. Career: Senior United Press International White House Photographer, Staff Photojournalist, Photo Editor, 1971 to present; Coverage of Presidents Kennedy, Johnson, Nixon, Ford, Carter, Reagan, 1963 to present; Photo Editor, Staff Photojournalist, United Press International News Pictures, Los Angeles, 1968-71; Staff Photojournalist, *Oregon Journal*, 1965-68. Organizational Memberships: Los Angeles Press Photographers (board of directors); California Press Photographers Association; White House News Photographers Association (board of directors); United States Senate Press Photographers (standing committee,

1980 to present). Honors and Awards: Pulitzer Prize Nomination for Photographs of Senator Robert F. Kennedy Assassination, 1968; Gold Medal, Spot News, World Press Photo, The Hague, 1969; First Place, Spot News, Outstanding Achievement in News Photography, National Headliner, 1969; First Place, Spot News and Sports, California Press Photographers Association Gold Seal Competition, 1969; 8 Ball, Spot News, Greater Los Angeles Press Club, 1969; Picture of the Year for Feature, National Press Photographers, 1970-75; Award for Feature, Forest Lawn Photographers Competition and Exhibition; United Press International Certificates of Merit for Spot News, Sports and Features; First Place in Features Category, National Press Photographers, Outboard Marine Contest; Pulitzer Prize Nominations for Photojournalism, 1968, 1976, 1977, 1978; Photo Exhibition, Library of Congress, 1972-82; First in Presidential, Award for Presidential and Sports Features, Award for Personality Photography, White House News Photographers Association, 1976-82; Award for Outstanding Syndicate Photography, National Headliners, 1978; Listed in *Who's Who in the World; Who's Who in America.* Address: 7203 Early Street, Annandale, Virginia 22003.

Bennie, William Andrew

Professor. Personal: Born October 9, 1921; Son of Andrew R. Bennie; Married Betty Jean Burks; Father of James Andrew, Carol Ann. Education: B.S. 1943, M.S. 1949, Indiana State University; Ed.D., Indiana University, 1955. Military: Served as a Technician 3rd Grade in the United States Army, 1943-46. Career: High School Teacher, Bloomfield, Indiana, 1946-69; Associate Professor, Director of Student Teacher, Miami (Ohio) University, 1949-61; Professor, Director of Student Teaching, University of Texas, 1961-73; Chairman, Department of Curriculum and Instruction, University of Texas, 1973-78; Professor, University of Texas-Austin, 1978 to present. Organizational Memberships: Association of Teacher Educators; National Society for Study of Education; Association for School, College and University Staffing; Phi Kappa Phi; Phi Delta Kappa; Association for Student Teaching (executive committee, 1967-70; delegate assembly, 1979-82). Religion: Presbyterian Church, Elder. Published Works: Author, *Supervising Clinical Experiences in the Classroom; Cooperation for Better Student Teaching;* Over 30 Articles in Professional Journals. Honors and Awards: Distinguished Member, Association of Teacher Educators; Ben E. Coody Distinguished Service Award, Texas Association of Teacher Educators; Appointed to the Council for Professional Development by the American Home Economics Association. Address: 7205 Waterline Road, Austin, Texas 78731.

Benoit, Paul S

Computer Specialist. Personal: Born December 20, 1938; Son of Saul (deceased) and Lena Ancelet Benoit; Married Jane Alice Morrison. Education: B.S., Southwestern University, 1960; Post-Graduate Study, University of Houston, 1961. Military: Served in the United States Navy, 1962-65, achieving the rank of Lieutenant. Career: Accountant, Pan American Petroleum Corporation, Houston, 1960-62; Senior Data Processing Technician, Tulsa, 1965-67; Lead Programmer, Supervisor of Systems and Planning, Manager of Systems Procedures and Data Processing, Singer Corporation, Silver Springs, Maryland, 1967-74; Senior Finance Systems Analyst, Timesharing Administrator, Computer Specialist, G.A.O., Washington, D.C., 1974 to present. Organizational Memberships: Association for Systems Management (charter president, Patuxent chapter, 1972-73; chairman of the by-laws committee 1972-73, chairman of the awards committee 1972-73, Chesapeake Division Council; president, Patuxent chapter, 1973-74; council vice chairman, chairman of the awards committee, Chesapeake division council, 1973-74; chairman of the nominating committee, Patuxent chapter, 1975-76; arrangement coordinator, annual conference, 1977; chairman, awards committee, Chesapeake division council, 1979; president 1980-81, secretary 1982-83, Patuxent chapter). Honors and Awards: Systems Man of the Year, Association for Systems Management, Patuxent Chapter, 1972-73; Certificate of Recognition, American Production and Inventory Control Society, 1973 Metro D.C. Chapter; Service Award, Association for Systems Management, Patuxent Chapter, 1973-74; Merit Award, Association for Systems Management's International Distinguished Service Award Program, 1976; Systems Man of the Year, Association for Systems Management, Patuxent Chapter, 1976-77; Certificate of Appreciation, Association for Systems Management International Organization; Certificate of Appreciation, Association for Systems Management, Patuxent Chapter, 1979; G.A.O. Certificate of Merit with Cash Award for Best Professional Article or Publication, *Journal of Systems Management,* 1979; Achievement Award, Association for Systems Management's International Distinguished Service Award Program, 1981; Certificate of Appreciation, Association for Systems Management, Patuxent Chapter, 1981. Address: 12007 Aspenwood Lane, Laurel, Maryland 20708.

Benscoter, Ruth Arlene

Public Health Educator. Personal: Born June 22, 1920; Daughter of Mrs. Lulu Hess Nagle; Married Henry Franklin Benscoter; Mother of Francine B. Livaditis. Education: R.N., Lucy Webb Hayes School of Nursing, 1941; B.S.Ed., Bloomsburg State College, 1963. Military: Served in the United States Army Nurses Corp, 1943-46, achieving the rank of 1st Lieutenant. Career: Public Health Educator, Pennsylvania Department of Health, 1965 to present; Public Health Nurse, Pennsylvania Department of Health, 1947-51; Staff Nurse, Sibley Memorial Hospital, Washington, D.C., 1941-43. Community Activities: Pennsylvania Public Health Association (continuing education committee, 1981); Nescopeck Parent Teacher Association (president, 1951); Columbia County Area Parent Teacher Association (president, 1952); Rural Health Corporation of Luzerne County (project consultant); Welfare Planning Council of Luzerne County (health planning associate); Pennsylvania Department of Health Emergency Preparedness (primary team member, 1980-81). Honors and Awards: Certificate of Appreciation, Office of Emergency Preparedness, for Outstanding Service to the President's Disaster Assistance Program in Tropical Storm Agnes. Address: 728 E. 4th Street, Nescopeck, Pennsylvania 18635.

Benson, Betty Jones

Assistant Superintendent, Curriculum Director. Personal: Born January 11, 1928, in Statham, Georgia; Daughter of George C. and Bertha Mobley Jones (both deceased); Married George T. Benson; Mother of George Steven, Elizabeth Gayle, James Claude, Robert Benjamin. Education: Associate Degree, Abraham Baldwin College; B.S., North Georgia College, 1958; M.A., 1968, Education Specialist, 1970, both from the University of Georgia. Career: Curriculum Director, Forsyth County Board of Education; Formerly a Teacher in Hall and Forsyth Counties, Assistant Curriculum Director in Forsyth County, Lecturer to North Georgia Curriculum Classes. Organizational Memberships: Georgia Association of Curriculum and Instructional Supervision (president, vice president, program chairman); Georgia Future Teacher Advisor Association (president); Ninth District Association of Curriculum and Instructional Supervision (president); Georgia Association of Supervision and Curriculum Development (secretary); Georgia Association of Educational Leaders (board of directors); Delta Kappa Gamma; Association for Childhood Education International; Head-Start Directors Association; Forsyth County Historical Association; Cumming/Forsyth County Business and Professional Women's Club. Community Activities: Alpine Center for Disturbed Children (juvenile court committee, community action committee, dental clinic committee, mental health committee, exceptional children committee); North Georgia Dean's Grant Advisory Board (North Georgia College right-to-read advisory committee, Georgia textbook committee, Georgia school finance study advisory committee, state textbook selection committee); Forsyth County Board of Education Representative to the Department of Family and Children Services, Georgia Mental Retardation Center, School for the Blind, School for the Deaf and Crippled Children; Boy Scouts of America (advisor); Lake Lanier Island Authority of Georgia. Religion: First Baptist Church of Cumming; Sunday School Teaching Staff; Long Range Planning Committee; Kitchen and Social Hall Committee; Expansion Committee. Honors and Awards: Forsyth County Star Teacher; Georgia Association of Educator's Outstanding Service Award; Boy Scout Service Award; Johnnye V. Cox Distinguished Supervisor Award; Rotary Award, Service for All Seasons; Listed in *Outstanding Teachers in Exceptional Children, Who's Who Biographical Records - School District Officials, Dictionary of International Biography, Personalities of the South, Community Leaders and Noteworthy Americans, World Who's Who of Women, Notable Americans, Men and Women of Distinction, International Who's Who of Intellectuals, International Who's Who in Community Service, Who's Who in the South and Southwest.* Address: Route 1, Box 12, Cumming, Georgia 30130.

Benson, George Stuart

Executive. Personal: Born September 26, 1898, Dewey County, Oklahoma; Son of Mr. and Mrs. S. F. Benson (both deceased); Married Sally E. Benson (deceased); Father of Lois McEuen, Ruth Crowder. Education: B.S., Oklahoma A.&M. University, 1924; B.A., Harding University, 1925; M.A., University of Chicago, 1931; LL.D., Harding University, 1932; LL.D., Knox College, 1948; LL.D., Waynesburg College, 1960; LL.D., Oklahoma Christian College, 1968; LL.D., Freed-Hardeman College, 1981. Career: President, and Executive Director, The National Education Program, 1936 to present; Chairman, Board of Zambia Christian College (Africa), 1966 to present; Chancellor, Alabama Christian College, 1975 to present; Chancellor, Oklahoma Christian College, 1956-67; Owner and Director, Camp Tahkodah (boy's summer camp), 1942-64; President, Harding University, 1936-65; President, Canton Bible School, 1930-36; Professor of English, National Sun Yat Sen University, 1929-30; Missionary, Canton, China, 1925-36; Principal, Harding Academy, 1924-25; Teacher, Oklahoma Public School, 1918-21; Founder, Canton Bible School (1930) and Canton English College (1932), both in Canton, China; Conducted Radio Program "Land of the Free" on 300 Stations, 1945-53; Radio Program "Behind the News" on 120 Stations, 1955 to present; Weekly Column "Looking Ahead" in 2000 Newspapers; Monthly Newsletter to 50,000 Readers. Organizational Memberships: Pi Kappa Delta. Community Activities: Kiwanis Club (honorary); Civitan Club (honorary); Searcy Chamber of Commerce; American Security Council. Religion: College Church of Christ, (Searcy, Arkansas), Elder. Honors and Awards: Freedom Foundation Award; National Recognition Award, Freedom Foundation at Valley Forge, 1974; Arkansan of the Year, 1953-54; Oklahoma Hall of Fame, 1972; Outstanding Alumnus, Oklahoma State University, 1976; Distinguished Alumnus, Harding University, 1963; Christian Leadership Award, 1968; Oklahoma State University Hall of Fame, 1976; Wisdom Award of Honor, Wisdom Society; Horatio Alger Award, 1981; Man of the Year in Education, *Christian Voice*, 1981; Listed in *Personalities of the South, Who's Who in America, National Register of Prominent Americans and International Notables.* Address: Harding University, Box 760, Searcy, Arkansas 72143.

George S Benson

Bent, Margaret Bassington

Professor. Personal: Born December 23, 1940, in Great Britain; Married Ian Bent (divorced); 2nd Marriage to Paul Brainard; Mother of Catherine, Stephen. Education: Organ Scholar, Music Exhibitioner, B.A. 1962, B.Mus. 1963, M.A. 1965, Ph.D. 1969, Cambridge University, England. Career: Part-Time Supervision for Cambridge Tripos and B.Mus., 1963-71; Musicianship Classes and History Lectures, Guildhall School of Music and Royal Academy of Music, London, 1965-71; Undergraduate and Graduate Tutorials and Lectures, London University, King's College, 1965-75; London University, Goldsmith's College, Lecturer 1972-74, Senior Lecturer 1974-75; Brandeis University, Ziskind Visiting Professor 1975-76, Professor 1976-81; Professor, Princeton University, 1981 to present. Organizational Memberships: Early English Church Music Committee, 1974-75; American Musicological Society (council member, 1977-79; board of directors, 1979-80); Renaissance Society of America (council representative of music, 1979-81); Advisor to A-R Editions for Medieval/Early Renaissance Series, 1978 to present; *Early Music History*, Cambridge University Press (editorial board, 1980 to present); Medieval Academy; International Musicological Society; *Pomerium Musices* (advisory board, 1980 to present). Honors and Awards: State Studentship, Great Britain, 1962-64; William Barclay Squire Prize, Cambridge University, 1963; Eggar Memorial Essay Prize, Society of Women Musicians, 1965; Fulbright Travel Award to United States, 1975; Travel Grant for 3-Week Italian Visit, British Academy, 1974; Sachar Travel Grants, Brandeis University, 1976, 1979; Grant to Direct Summer Seminar for College Teachers, Brandeis University, National Endowment for the Humanities, 1979, 1981; Dent Medal for Distinguished Contribution to Musicology, Royal Musical Association in Conjunction with the International Musicological Society, 1979; Number of Professional Publications. Address: Department of Music, Woolworth Center for Musical Studies, Princeton University, Princeton, New Jersey 08544.

Bentley, Kenton E

Program Manager, Director. Personal: Born June 1, 1927; Son of Marion Isabell Norris; Married Elizabeth Jule Montrose. Education: B.S., University of Michigan, 1950; Ph.D., University of New Mexico, 1959. Military: Served in the United States Navy, 1945-46. Career: Director, Science and Applications, and Program Manager, E.P.A. Environmental Programs, Lockheed-E.M.S.C.O.; Former Director of Iran Earth Resources Programs, Lockheed; Head, Electrochemistry Group, Hughes Aircraft; Task Leader/Scientist, Jet Propulsion Laboratory, California Institute of Technology; Research Scientist, Lockheed California Company; Assistant Professor of Chemistry, American University, Beirut, Lebanon; Visiting Professor of Chemistry, Highlands University, New Mexico; Los Alamos Research Fellow, University of New Mexico. Organizational Memberships: American Chemical Society (analytical division); American Association for the Advancement of Science (life member); American Association of University Professors (inactive); A.I.A.A.; N.M.A.; Sigma Xi (life member); Alpha Chi Sigma. Published Works: Co-Author "Pyrolysis Studies: Controlled Thermal Degradation of Mesoporphyrin", "A Gas Chromatography-Mass Spectrometer System for Space Exploration", "Oxygen Detection" (U.S. Patent), "Spectrophotemetric Investigation of Vanadium (II), Vanadium (III), and Vanadium (IV) in Various Media", "Apparatus for Oxygen-Sensitive Volumetric Solutions". Honors and Awards: Los Alamos Research Fellow, University of New Mexico, 1954-56; Rockefeller Foundation Grant, American University of Beirut, 1960. Address: 15811 Dunmoor Drive, Houston, Texas 77059.

Berbary, Maurice Shehadeh

Physician, Military Officer, Hospital Administrator, Educator. Personal: Born January 14, 1923 in Beirut, Lebanon; Son of Shehadeh M. and Marie K. Berbary; Married Bruennhild Hepp; Father of Geoffrey Maurice, Laura Marie. Education: B.A., American University, Beirut, 1943; M.D., University of Texas, 1948; M.A. Hospital Administration, Baylor University, 1970; Diploma, Army Command and General Staff College, Carlisle, Pennsylvania, 1969. Military: Served in the United States Army, 1952-68, advancing through the grades to Colonel. Career: Intern, Parkland Memorial Hospital, Dallas, 1948-49; Resident in Obstetrics and Gynecology,

General Surgery and Urology, Parkland Memorial Hospital, 1949-53; Resident in Obstetrics and Gynecology, Walter Reed Army Hospital, Washington, 1955-57; Fellow in Obstetric and Gynecological Pathology, Armed Forces Institute, Pathology, Washington, 1959-60; Practice, Clinical Medicine in Obstetrics and Gynecology, 1953 to present; Chief, Department of Obstetrics and Gynecology, Womack Army Hospital, Fort Bragg, North Carolina, 1960-62; Division Surgeon, First Infantry Division, Fort Riley, Kansas, 1963-64; Division Surgeon, Third Armored Division, Germany, 1964-65; Corps Surgeon, V. Corps, Germany, 1965-67; Corps Surgeon, 24th Army Corps, South Vietnam Theatre of Operation, 1970; Commander, Hospital Administrator, United States Army Hospital, Teheran, Iran, 1954-55; Commander, Hospital Group Complex, Vietnam, 1969-70; Command Surgeon, United States Armed Forces Command and United States Army South, United States Canal Zone, Panama, 1970-73; Commander, Fifth General Hospital, United States Army, Stuttgart, West Germany, 1973-77; Commander, Munson Army Hospital, Fort Leavenworth, Kansas, 1977 to present; Clinical Staff Officer, Department of Obstetrics and Gynecology, William Beaumont Army Medical Center, Fort Bliss, El Paso, Texas; Assistant Professor, Department of Obstetrics and Gynecology, Kansas University Medical School, Kansas City, 1980 to present; Visiting Lecturer, Obstetrics and Gynecology Pathology, Duke University Medical Center, Durham, North Carolina, 1960-62; Clinical Instructor, Obstetrics and Gynecology, University of Kansas Medical Center, Kansas City, 1963-64; Instructor, Fifth Army N.C.O. Academy, Fort Riley, Kansas, 1963-64. Organizational Memberships: American College of Surgeons (fellow); American College of Obstetricians and Gynecologists (fellow); American College of Hospital Administrators; New York Academy of Sciences; International Platform Association; American Medical Association; Dallas County Medical Association; Texas State Medical Association; Association of Military Surgeons; Society of Army Flight Surgeons. Honors and Awards: Decorated Legion of Merit with Two Oak Leaf Clusters; Bronze Star Medal; Army Commendation Medal. Address: 6299 Martel Avenue, Dallas, Texas 75214.

Berg, M Majella

College President. Personal: Born July 7, 1916; Daughter of Gustov Peter and Mary Josephine Berg (both deceased). Education: B.A., Marymount College, 1938; M.A., Fordham University, 1948; D.H.L. (honorary), Georgetown University, 1970. Career: President, Marymount College of Virginia, 1960 to present; Registrar, Marymount College, Tarrytown, New York, 1958-60; Registrar, Marymount College of Virginia, 1957-58; Professor of Classics and Registrar, Marymount College, Manhattan, New York, 1948-57; Registrar, Marymount School, New York City, 1943-48. Organizational Memberships: American Association of Junior Colleges (commission on instruction), (now renamed the American Association of Community and Junior Colleges); *Junior College Journal* (editorial board); Foundation of Independent Junior Colleges of Virginia (secretary-treasurer, executive committee, 1966-67, 1973), (now Virginia College Fund); Council of Independent College in Virginia (vice president, 1972-73; secretary of the executive committee, 1974). Community Activities: State Council of Higher Education in Virginia (committee of the private college advisory committee); Arlington Citizen Participation Council (executive committee); Arlington Chorus (executive committee); Arlington Committee of 100; League of Women Voters; American Association of University Women; Arlington Health and Welfare Council's Day Care Committee, 1967-69; Arlington Chamber of Commerce; Virginia State Chamber of Commerce (membership committee, 1967-68; education committee, 1969, 1971); Appointed to the Advisory Committee on Staff Development for Two-Year Colleges, Catholic University of America, 1972; Northern Virginia Education Television Association (appointed to the board of directors, 1972); Arlington School Board and Arlington Education Association (chairman of arbitration panel, 1967); Arlington Committee for the Organization of Northern Virginia Technical Institute (now Northern Virginia Community College); Arlington Hall for the Arlington Committee. Religion: Diocese of Arlington's Evangelization Commission, 1979 to present; Bishop's Pastoral Council, 1979 to present; Executive Committee Sister Council, 1978 to present. Honors and Awards: Listed in *Who's Who in American Education, Who's Who of American Women, Leaders in Education, Presidents and Deans of American Colleges, Who's Who International, Personalities of the South, Contemporary Authors, Dictionary of International Biography, Men of Achievement, Who's Who inthe South and Southwest, World Who's Who of Women, American Catholic Who's Who, Who's Who Among Authors and Journalists.* Address: Marymount College of Virginia, 2807 N. Glebe Road, Arlington, Virginia 22207.

Berg, Siegfried K

Electronics Engineer, Radio Broadcaster. Personal: Born May 4, 1922; Son of Adolph and Ida Berg (both deceased); Married Waltraud Rybak. Education: "Behring - School", Hohenstein, Germany, 1939; Professional Merchant, Board of Trade and Industry and Chamber of Commerce, Allenstein, Germany, 1941. Career: Electronics Engineer, G.T.E. Automatic Electric; Former Owner of "Deutscher Rundfunk Chicago" (German Radio Broadcast, Chicago); Owner of Orbit Printing and Advertising Service. Organizational Memberships: Institute of Electrical and Electronics Engineers; American Radio Relay League; National Space Institute. Community Activities: Rheinischer Verein, Chicago; Schlaraffia Chicago (president, 1974 to present); International Platform Association. Honors and Awards: Certified Manufacturing Technologist, Life Certification, Society of Manufacturing Engineers; Listed in *Year Book of German Actors, Blue Book of American Photographers, Who's Who in Finance and Industry, Personalities of the West and Midwest, Who's Who in the World.* Address: 2124 W. Giddings Street, Chicago, Illinois 60625.

Berger, Steven Barry

Research Physicist. Personal: Born December 29, 1946; Son of Bernard and Sylvia Berger. Education: B.S. 1967, Ph.D. 1973, Massachusetts Institute of Technology. Career: Research Physicist, Naval Research Laboratory; Former Instructor, Department of Electrical Engineering, George Washington University; Technical Staff, MITRE Corporation; Technical Staff, TRW; Assistant Editor, *American Journal of Physics;* Technical Staff, ITEK Corporation. Organizational Memberships: American Physical Society; Institute of Electrical and Electronics Engineering (treasurer, northern Virginia chapter, Control Systems Society); Sigma Xi. Community Activities: Cousteau Society; Sierra Club; Friends of the National Zoo; Friends of the National Symphony Orchestra; Smithsonian Associates; Common Cause. Honors and Awards: National Science Foundation Graduate Fellowship, 1972; Sloan Foundation Graduate Fellowship, 1973; Fight-for-Sight, Inc. Post-doctoral Fellowship, 1974-76; Listed in *American Men and Women of Science, Who's Who in the South and Southwest.* Address: 134 Roberts Lane, Apt. 201, Alexandria, Virginia 22314.

Bergeron, Jimmie Leon

Physician. Personal: Born November 1, 1932; Son of Albert R. and Louise M. Bergeron; Married Lynn Ann Peters; Father of James Delbert, Michelle Ann. Education: B.S.M.E., B.S.I.E., University of Washington-Seattle, 1955; Studies in Biology and Chemistry, University of Florida, 1963; M.D., Emory University Medical School, 1968; Intern, Emory-Veterans Administration Hospitals, Atlanta, Georgia; Resident in Internal Medicine, Baylor College of Medicine; Fellowship in Nephrology, Baylor College of Medicine. Military: Served in the United States Army, 1955-57, achieving the rank of 1st Lieutenant. Career: Physician; Former Engineer. Organizational Memberships: Texas Medical Association; Harris County Medical Association; Psi Upsilon. Community Activities:

Houston Northwest Hospital (chairman, utilization review committee; chairman, pharmacy and therapeutics committee; intensive care unit committee; chairman, patient care committee). Religion: Hosanna Lutheran Church. Address: 1023 Maranon Lane, Houston, Texas 77090.

Bergin, Kay V

District Manager. Personal: Born November 29, 1921; Married Francis X. Bergin; Mother of Sandy. Education: B.S., Central Connecticut State College, 1943; M.A.L.S., Wesleyan University, 1957. Career: District Manager, Neighborhood Reinvestment Corporation; Former Deputy Banking Commissioner, State of Connecticut; Executive Director, Permanent Commission on the Status of Women, Connecticut; Associate Professor, Mattatuck Community College. Organizational Memberships: Women in Housing and Finance (board member); Connecticut Housing Investment Fund (board member, 1976-78); Hartford Neighborhood Housing Service (board member, 1976-78). Community Activities: Connecticut Marketing Authority (appointed to board by governor); National Women's Conference, Houston (delegate representing Connecticut, 1977); Connecticut Women's Legal and Education Fund (board member, 1975-78). Religion: St. John's Church, Vestry and Finance Committee. Honors and Awards: Distinguished Women, State of Connecticut, 1976; Business and Professional Women's Award, Outstanding Woman in Connecticut, 1976. Address: 25 Steuben Street, Waterbury, Connecticut 06708.

Bergner, Jane Cohen

Attorney. Personal: Born April 6, 1943; Married Alfred P. Bergner; Mother of Justin Laurence, Lauren Jill. Education: A.B., Vassar College, 1964; L.L.B., Columbia Law School, 1967. Career: Trial Attorney, Tax Division, U.S. Department of Justice, Review Section 1967-69, Court of Claims Section 1969-74; Arnold and Porter, 1974-76; Rogouin, Huge and Lenzner, 1976 to present. Organizational Memberships: Admitted to District of Columbia Bar, U.S. Court of Claims, Tax Court of the United States, U.S. Court of Appeals, District of Columbia Circuit Court, U.S. District Court for the District of Columbia; Member of the American Bar Association (chairman, Subcommittee on Continuing Legal Education, Section of Taxation). Community Activities: Jewish Social Service Agency (legal counsel, board of directors, committee on court procedure, executive committee, budget and priorities committee); United Jewish Appeal Federation (member, former trainee, young leadership division); Service Guild of Washington; Hadassah (life member); American Friends of Hebrew University (lawyers division); National Women's Committee of Brandeis University (life member, former officer, board member of D.C. chapter). Religion: Temple Sinai, Deputy Comptroller, Board of Directors, Executive Committee of Board, Officer in Charge of Religious School Committee. Published Works: Author "Not For Men Only: Why Women Need a Will", *Women's Work*, May-June 1977. Honors and Awards: Harlan Fiske Stone Honor Moot Court Competition Semi-Finalist; Winner, New York State Regents College Scholarship; New York State Scholar Incentive Award for College and Law School; Semi-Finalist, National Merit Scholarhip. Address: 1730 Rhode Island Avenue, N.W., Washington, D.C. 20036.

Bergsten, C Fred

Institute Director. Personal: Born April 23, 1941; Son of Dr. and Mrs. Carl A. Bergsten; Married Virginia Lee Wood; Father of Mark David. Education: B.A., Central Methodist College, 1961; M.A., 1962, M.A.L.D., 1963, and Ph.D, 1969, all from the Fletcher School of Law and Diplomacy. Career: International Economist, Department of State, 1963-67; Visiting Fellow, Council on Foreign Relations, 1968; Assistant for International Economic Affairs to the Assistant to the President, National Security Affairs, 1969-71; Senior Fellow, Brookings Institution, 1972-76; Assistant Secretary of the Treasury for International Affairs, 1977-81; Senior Associate, Carnegie Endowment for International Peace, 1981; Director, Institute for International Economics. Organizational Memberships: American Economic Association; Council on Foreign Relations. Community Activities: Atlantic Institute (board of governors, 1973-76); Center for Law and Social Policy (board of advisors, 1972-76); Consumers Union (board of directors, 1976); Overseas Development Council (board of directors, 1974-76); Overseas Private Investment Corporation (board of directors, 1977-81); U.S.-Israel Binational Industrial Research and Development Foundation, 1977-81; U.S.-Saudi Arabia Joint Economic Commission (U.S. coordinator, 1977-81); Worldwatch (board of directors, 1975-76). Published Works: *The World Economy in the 1980s*, 1981; *The International Economic Policy of the United States*, 1980; *American Multinationals and American Interests*, 1978; *Managing International Economic Interdependence*, 1977; *The Dilemmas of the Dollar*, 1976; *World Politics and International Economics*, 1975; *Toward a New World Trade Policy*, 1975; *Toward a New International Economic Order*, 1975; *The Future of the International Economic Policy*, 1973; *Leading Issues in International Economic Policy*, 1973; *Approaches to Greater Flexibility of Exchange Rates*, 1970. Honors and Awards: Exceptional Service Award, Department of Treasury, 1980; Distinguished Alumnus Award, Central Methodist College, 1975; *Time's* "200 Young American Leaders", 1974; Meritorious Honor Award, Department of State, 1965. Address: 4106 Sleepy Hollow Road, Annandale, Virginia 22003.

Berke, Robert J

Association Executive. Personal: Born August 4, 1920; Married Beverly L. Netschert; Father of Deborah, David. Education: B.A., Queens College, 1941; Certificate, Industrial College of the Armed Forces, 1956. Military: Served in the United States Air Force, 1942-45, achieving the rank of Staff Sergeant, Combat Intelligence. Career: Associate Executive; Former Editor, Newspaper and Magazines. Community Activities: Alumni Association of Queens College, Inc. (past president and trustee); Community Planning Board, Queens (chairman, 1967-70); Community School Board 26, Queens (vice chairman, 1965-70); Flushing Community Forum (chairman, 1968). Religion: Congregational Church of Flushing, Chairman of the Board of Deacons, 1967-72. Address: 341 Manor Road, Douglaston, New York 11363.

Berkey, Barry Robert

Physician, Author. Personal: Born September 28, 1935; Son of Saul M. and Esther Berkey; Married Velma Levin; Father of Kent, Richard, Lori. Education: Attended Washington and Jefferson College, 1953-57. Military: Served in the United States Army Medical Corps, 1965-67, achieving the rank of Captain. Career: Private Psychiatric Practice, 1968 to present; Consultant, Northern Virginia Mental Health Institute, 1966-67; Chief, Mental Hygiene Consultation Branch, Fort Lee, Virginia, United States Army, 1965-67. Organizational Memberships: American Psychiatric Association; American Group Psychotherapy Association; American Orthopsychiatric Association; Washington Psychiatric Society; Fairfax County Medical Society; Medical Society of Virginia; Northern Virginia Chapter, Washington Psychiatric Society (executive committee, 1971-72, 1982-83; *The Group* news, honors and awards editor 1971-73, reporter 1970-71); Phi Delta Epsilon. Community Activities: Consultant, B'nai B'rith Career and Counseling

Consultation Centers of Greater Washington 1973-80, The Pastoral Counseling and Consultation Centers of Greater Washington 1970-73, Group Health Association, Washington, D.C. (panel member psychiatrist, 1968-82), Gulf Science & Technology Company 1979 to present, National Career & Counselling Services 1982 to present. Honors and Awards: Phi Beta Kappa; Graduated from Washington and Jefferson College magna cum laude; Phi Sigma; Delta Phi Alpha; Chi Epsilon Mu. Address: 5031 Prestwick Drive, Fairfax, Virginia 22030.

Berlage, Gai Ingham

Assistant Professor, Department Chairperson. Personal: Born February 9, 1943; Daughter of Paul (deceased) and Grace Artz Ingham; Married Jan Coxe Berlage; Mother of Cari Coxe, Jan Ingham. Education: B.A., Smith College, 1965; M.A., Southern Methodist University, 1968; Ph.D., New York University, 1979. Career: Assistant Professor of Sociology (1974 to present) and Chairperson, Department of Sociology (1981 to present), Iona College, New Rochelle, New York; Research Consultant, Health Studies Institute, New Rochelle, 1980 to present; Instructor of Sociology, Iona College, 1971-74; Teacher, Summer Session Courses, Norwalk Community College, Connecticut, 1971-77; Teacher Summer Session Courses, Southeastern College, Durant, Oklahoma, 1968; Mathematics Teacher, Piner Junior High School, Sherman, Texas, 1968-69; 5th Grade Science and Language Arts Teacher, Ridgefield Public School, Ridgefield, Connecticut, 1966-67; High School Mathematics Teacher, Nelson High School, Lovingston, Virginia, 1965-66. Organizational Memberships: American Sociological Association; Westchester Chapter, National Council on Crime and Delinquency; National Council on Crime and Delinquency; New York State Sociological Association; Population Reference Bureau; North American Youth Sport Institute. Community Activities: Wilton Task Force Committee for the Outreach Program (chairperson, 1981 to present); Wilton Commission on Aging and Social Services (commissioner, 1980 to present); Wilton Association for Gifted Education (advisor, 1981-82; president, 1980-81). Published Works: "Father's Career Aspirations for Sons in Competitive Ice Hockey Programs", "Research Modules in Introductory Sociology", "Is Mom a Vanishing Species?", "Anything Goes: Crime as a By-Product of Individual Problems of Adjustment to Mass Society". Honors and Awards: Iona College - Grant for Research and Writing 1981, Computer Monitored Learning Grant 1980-81, Funding for Faculty Enrichment 1981, Dissertation Fellow 1975; National Science Foundation Traineeship Award, 1967-68; Listed in *World Who's Who of Women, Who's Who in the East, Personalities of America, International Who's Who of Intellectuals.* Address: Sociology Department, Iona College, New Rochelle, New York 10801.

Berlin, Jerome C

Attorney. Personal: Born August 23, 1942; Son of Benjamin and Muriel Weintraub Berlin; Married Gwen Tischler; Father of Bret Jason, Sharon Nicole, Ashley Lauren. Education: B.S.B.A. 1964, J.D. 1968, University of Florida. Career: Partner in Law Firm, Schwartz and Nash, P.A.; Former Certified Public Accountant, Peat, Marwick, Mitchell & Company; Real Estate Developer. Community Activities: A.D.L. (vice chairman, regional board, 1978 to present); Dade County Zoning Appeals Board (chairman, 1970-73); Juvenile Diabetes Foundation (director); University of Miami Project Newborn (executive board); Variety Children's Hospital (planning committee); Temple Beth Am (board of directors). Address: 5425 S.W. 92 Street, Miami, Florida 33156.

Ariane R Berman

Berman, Ariane R

Artist. Personal: Born March 27, 1937; Daughter of Max and Riva Berman (both deceased); Married Mario La Rossa. Education: B.F.A., Hunter College, 1959; M.F.A., Yale University School of Art, 1962. Career: Selected One-Man Shows including Kornblee Gallery (New York), Westenhook Gallery (Massachusetts), Ward-Nasse Gallery (New York), Philadelphia Art Alliance, Silvermine Guild of Artists (Connecticut), Galleria d'Arte Helioart (Rome, Italy), Fontana Gallery (Pennsylvania), Wustum Museum of Fine Arts (Racine, Wisconsin), Public Museum (Oshkosh, Wisconsin), Eileen Kuhlik Gallery (New York), Galleria San Sebastiannello (Rome, Itlay), Graphic Art Gallery (Tel Aviv); Selected Invitational Group Shows and Exhibitions including The Butler Institute of American Art: 36th Annual Exhibit, Allentown Art Museum (Pennsylvania), U.S.I.A. Traveling Print Exhibition to Europe, Philaelphia Art Alliance: 6 Printmakers, Boston Printmakers, Mt. Holyoke College National Print Show, Sarah Lawrence College Gallery (New York), Silvermine National Print Exhibitions, American Color Print Society: Philadelphia Art Alliance, National Exhibition of Small Paintings: Purdue Univeristy, Exhibition of Contemporary American Paintings (Palm Beach, Florida), Cite Internationale de L'Universite de Paris, Fairleigh Dickinson University, New York University, William Penn Museum; Numerous Museum and Private Collections; Corporate Collections, Hearst Corporation. Organizational Memberships: League of Present Day Artists; New York Society of Women Artists (corresponding secretary, 1980-81); Silvermine Guild of Artists (invited member); Philadelphia Art Alliance (artist member); American Color Print Society; National Association of Women Artists; Yonkers Art Association; Hudson River Museum Artists Equity; Pen and Brush Club. Published Works: Cover Illustration for Brochure, National Council of Women of the United States, Inc., 1981 Year of the Handicapped. Honors and Awards: D. L. Latham Award, Pen & Brush Inc.; Award for Excellence, Sheffield Artists League; Purdue University Purchase Award; Yale Printing Prize; Artist Member, Philadelphia Art Alliance; Catherine Lorillard Wolfe Gold Medal; Stella Drabkin Gold Medal and A.C.P.S. Purchase Prize; Hall of Fame, Hunter College Alumni Association; Work Featured in Course "Women in Art", Washington State University, 1975 to present; Listed in *Who's Who in the World, Who's Who in America, Who's Who in American Art.* Address: 161 W. 54th Street, New York, New York 10019.

Berman, Muriel Mallin

Executive. Personal: Married Philip I. Berman; Mother of Nancy, Nina, Steven. Education: Honorary Doctor of Fine Arts, Cedar Crest College, 1972; Honorary Degree, Wilson College, 1969; Doctor's Degree, Pennsylvania College of Optometry; Honorary Fellow, Hebrew University, 1975; Licensed to Practice Optometry in Pennsylvania and New Jersey; Attended University of Pittsburgh, Carnegie Tech University; Studies in Music Appreciation and Art History, University of Pittsburgh Graduate School; Studies in Comparative Religion and History, Cedar Crest College; Studies in Philosophy, Muhlenberg College. Career: Underwriting Member, Lloyd's of London, 1974 to present; Vice Chairman, Vice President, Assistant Secretary, Board Member, Hess's Inc.; Secretary, Board Member, Fleetways, Inc.; Secretary-Treasurer, Board Member, Philip and Muriel Berman Foundation; Secretary, D. F. Bast, Inc., and Fleet-Power, Inc.; Producer and Moderator, Television Program "Guest Spot". Community Activities: United Nations We Believe; League of Women Voters; Young Women's Christian Association; Wellesley Club, New York; Lehigh County Historical Society; Keneseth Israel Sisterhood (past vice president, state budget chairman); Art Collector's Club of America; American Federation of Art; Friends of Whitney Museum; Archives of American Art, Detroit and New York; Museum of Primitive Art, New York; Allentown Art Museum; Reading Art Museum; Jewish Museum, New York; Skirball Museum, Los Angeles; Pennsylvania Academy of Fine Arts, Philadelphia (patron for life); Metropolitan Opera Guild; Philadelphia Museum of Art (associate); University Museum, Philadelphia; Kemmerer Museum, Bethlehem; Historic Bethlehem; Lehigh Art Alliance;

Philadelphia Art Alliance; Metropolitan Museum, New York; Neuberger Museum, New York; Board of Trustees: Pennsylvania Ballet, Jewish Publication Society (treasurer; chairman, endowment fund), United Fund of Lehigh Valley, Smithsonian Art Council (national council member), Women's Club (fine arts chairman), Foreign Policy Association of Lehigh County, Lehigh Valley Education Television (chairman, program committee, Channel 39), Lehigh County Community College Foundation, Hadassah National Board, Pennsylvania Council on Women 1968-79, Allentown Art Museum Auxiliary (art appreciation director), Allentown Symphony (vice chairman; former treasurer of Symphony Ball), Heart Association of Pennsylvania (board of directors), Dieruff High School Art Advisory Committee, Baum Art School, Bonds for Israel, Young Audiences; United Nations International Women's Year Conference, Mexico City (United States State Department delegate by presidential appointment, 1975); National Commission on the Observance of Women's Year (arts and humanities committee, 1975); United States Center for International Women's Year (advisory committee); United Nations Activities: National Board U.N.A.-U.S.A. (elected 1977), N.G.O. delegate to U.N.I.C.E.F. and Executive Board, N.G.O. Representative to the U.S. Mission of United Nations for Hadassah, E.C.O.S.O.C. Mission in Geneva with Husband, N.G.O. Delegate to the Executive Board Meeting of U.N.I.C.E.F. in Santiago, Chile (1970), N.G.O. U.N.I.C.E.F. Board on Latin America and Africa, Other Meetings; Pennsylvania Commission for Women (commissioner); Pennsylvania Public Commission for Humanities (commissioner); Pennsylvania Council on the Arts, 1972-78; Art in the U.S. Embassies Program; Muhlenberg College (art selection committee with the National Endowment for the Arts); "Carnegie-Berman" College "Art Slide Library Exchange" (founder, donor); Berman Circulation Traveling Art Exhibitions; Hadassah-Israel Art Show (chairman); Democratic National Convention (official delegate 1972, 1976; platform committee); Bucks County Collectors Art Show (honorary chairman); Girl Scouts Great Valley Council "Brownies Create Art" Exhibit (chairman); Lehigh County Community College (chairman of the board, trustee, founding board member); Kutztown State College (trustee; vice chairman of the board, 1960-66); Cedar Crest College (advisory council); Conference for Women Trustees, College and University Governing Boards; Aspen Institute of Humanistic Studies. Honors and Awards: Woman of Valor, Bonds for Israel; Henrietta Szold Award, Allentown Chapter, Hadassah; Outstanding Woman Award, Allentown Young Women's Christian Association, 1973; Myrtle Wreath Award, Pennsylvania Region of Hadassah; Listed in *Who's Who in American Art, Who's Who of American Women, Who's Who in the East, Royal Blue Book, National Social Directory, The Israel Honorarium.* Address: "20 Hundred", Nottingham Road, Allentown, Pennsylvania 18103.

Bermello, Guillermo R

Executive Vice President. Personal: Born April 16, 1918; Son of Claudio and Amparo Bermello (both deceased); Married Martha Guardia; Father of Willy A. Education: Graduate, University of Havana: Certified Public Accountant, 1951; Doctor of Commercial Science, 1959; Doctor of Law, 1959. Career: Certified Public Accountant, Havana, Cuba; Justice of the Supreme Court of Accounts, Havana; Executive Vice President of a Publishing Corporation. Organizational Memberships: American Accounting Association. Community Activities: United Way of Dade County (director, 1977-78); Metropolitan Dade County Art Institute (founder, 1979); League Against Cancer (director, 1978-80); Cuban Museum of Arts and Culture (trustee, 1980-81); Greater Miami Opera Association (benefactor, 1981). Religion: Catholic. Honors and Awards: Commendation, City of Miami, 1976; Latin Chamber of Commerce, 1976; Kiwanis of Little Havana, 1978-79. Address: 726 Santander Ave., Coral Gables, Florida 33134.

Bernal, Jesus (Jesse) R

Bilingual Education Director. Personal: Born December 7, 1953; Son of Jose and San Juana Bernal. Education: Graduate, Pearsall Public Schools, 1972; B.A., St. Mary's University of San Antonio, 1976; M.A., The University of Texas-San Antonio, 1977; Undertaking studies toward Ph.D., The University of Texas-Austin, 1978 to present. Career: Library Assistant, Resource Person, Children's Reading Tutor, Frio County Public Library, 1975; Coordinator of Manpower Summer Youth Employment Program, Community Council of South Central Texas, 1976; Library Assistant, St. Mary's University Academic Library, 1973-76; Technical Staff Assistant II, The University of Texas at San Antonio, 1976-78; Accounting Instructor, North East Independent School District Adult and Continuing Education Program, 1978; School Librarian and Media Coordinator, K-6 Elementary School, South San Antonio Independent School District, Antonio Olivares Elementary, 1978; Bilingual Education Director, Pearsall Independent School District, 1978 to present. Organizational Memberships: Phi Delta Kappa; National Education Association; Texas State Teachers Association (state and district XX convention delegate, 1979-80, 1980-81; state board of the Texas educators political action committee for senatorial district #21); Pearsall Educators Association (public relations committee chairman, elections committee chairman, newsletter editor, administration faculty representative); Delta Epsilon Sigma (life member); Mexican American Hispanic Caucus/Texas State Teachers Association; Parent Teachers Association: Pearsall, Texas, National (chairman Pearsall P.T.A. publicity committee); Association for Supervision and Curriculum Development; National Association for Bilingual Education; Texas Association for Bilingual Education; San Antonio Area Association for Bilingual Education; Texas Business Education Association; Delta Pi Epsilon; American Society for Personnel Administration. Community Activities: League of United Latin American Citizens, Council #312. Religion: Catholic Church Parish Councilman; Church Lector; Extraordinary Lay Minister, 1978 to present. Honors and Awards: National Hispanic Scholar, 1977, 1978; Pearsall Educators Association Special Friend Award, 1979-80; Henderson Foundation Fund Scholarship, University of Texas-Austin, Summers of 1980 and 1981; Pearsall Educators Association Scholarship, 1979-80; University of Texas-San Antonio State Scholarship, 1976-78; Graduated with magna cum laude highest honors, St. Mary's University, 1976; Delta Epsilon Sigma; Phi Delta Kappa; Delta Pi Epsilon; Ranked First on the Candidacy Qualifying Examination for the M.A. degree in Education, University of Texas-San Antonio, 1977; Listed in *Dictionary of International Biography, Dictionary of Distinguished Americans, Personalities of America, Personalities of the South, Book of Honor, Who's Who in the South and Southwest, Outstanding Young Men of America, Community Leaders of America, Who's Who Among Students in American Universities and Colleges, Hispanic Who's Who in America, International Youth in Achievement.* Address: 515 S. Bernal St., Pearsall, Texas 78061.

Berry, Eddye Vivian

Professional Singer, Associate Professor. Personal: Born May 2, 1947; Daughter of Edward and Vivian Pierce; Mother of Lisa Michelle. Education: B.Mus. 1969, M.Mus. 1973, University of Colorado-Boulder. Career: Professional Operatic Singer; Associate Professor of Music, Miami University (Ohio); Former Assistant Professor of Music, San Jose State University. Organizational Memberships: Sigma Alpha Iota; American Guild of Musical Artists; Pi Kappa Lambda; National Association of Teachers of Singing; National Opera Association. Honors and Awards: National Finalist, Florence Bruce Award, San Francisco Opera Auditions, 1976; National Finalist, Met Audition, 1970; Third Place Winner, New York Oratorio Society, Carnegie Hall, 1981; Outstanding Young Woman of Ohio, 1980. Address: 715 West Chestnut Street #8, Oxford, Ohio 45056.

Berry, Michael Alden

Physician. Personal: Born June 2, 1946; Son of Charles A. Berry; Married Frankie; Father of Jennifer Alice, Michael David. Education: B.S., Texas Christian University, 1968; M.D., University of Texas Southwestern Medical School, 1971; M.S., O.S.U., 1977. Military: Served in the United States Air Force, 1970-76, achieving the rank of Major. Career: Physician, N.A.S.A. Flight Surgeon. Organizational Memberships: Aerospace Medical Association (education committee, 1979 to present; scientific program committee, 1979 to present; award committee, 1980 to present; president's reception committee, 1979-81); International Academy of Aviation and Space Medicine; American College of Preventive Medicine (fellow; scientific program chairman, 1981); American College of Emergency Physicians; Texas Medical Association; Harris County Medical Society; Society of N.A.S.A. Flight Surgeons; Society of Air Force Flight Surgeons. Community Activities: Clear Lake Unit, American Heart Association (board of directors, 1978; vice president for campaign, 1979; president, 1981). Honors and Awards: Julian Ward Award of the Aerospace Medical Association, 1978; N.A.S.A. Exceptional Service Award, 1980; Fellow, Aerospace Medical Association, 1981. Address: 220 Bayou View, Seabrook, Texas 77586.

Berry, Rose A

Professor of Education. Personal: Married Robert Newton Berry; Mother of Charles W. Education: B.S.Ed., University of Central Arkansas; M.S., Ed.D., University of Arkansas-Fayetteville. Career: Professor of Education, Chairperson of the Department of Elementary and Early Childhood Education 1945-80, Graduate Program Coordinator, University of Arkansas-Little Rock. Organizational Memberships: Student Branch of the Association for Childhood Education, University of Arkansas-Little Rock (founder, organizer, advisor); Student National Education Association, University of Arkansas-Little Rock (advisor, 1961-76); Altrusa Club (chairman, Altrusa Information); American Association of Elementary-Kindergarten-Nursery Education; American Association of University Women (liaison representative for University of Arkansas-Little Rock; chairman; education projects, 1967-68); American Business Women's Association (chairman, education committee, 1967); Arkansas Advocates for Children and Families (education task force, 1979 to present); Arkansas Association on Children under Six (nominee for president-elect, 1977); Arkansas Association of Colleges for Teacher Education (nominations, 1977; institutional representative, 1976 to present; board member, 1978-81); Arkansas Education Association (president, primary section for childhood education, 1960-61; kindergarten committee, 1977 to present); Arkansas Elementary Education Council, 1973 to present; Arkansas Library Association; Arkansas Educational Research and Development Council (charter member, 1973 to present); Arkansas Middle School Association (charter member, 1973; secretary, 1974-75; vice president, 1976-77; president-elect, 1976-77); Association for Childhood Education International (state president, 1962-64; committee on professional affairs, 1965-66; editorial board, 1965-68; contributor to childhood education publication, 1968; study conference planning committee, 1968-71, 1978-81; state representative, 1964-68; state headquarters building chairman, 1964-68; state student branch coordinator, 1971 to present; vice president representing early adolescence 1970-73, committee 1974-77; committee on literature, 1974-79; nominating committee chairman 1976-77, member 1977-78; teacher education committee, 1979-81); A.A.C.T.E. (institutional representative); Central Arkansas Reading Council (president, 1973-74; vice president, 1972-73; executive board, 1974-75; historian, 1976-77); Charlie Mae Simon Book Award Committee, 1971 to present; Children's Literature Association, 1976 to present; Delta Kappa Gamma (president Gamma chapter, 1956-58; state publicity chairman, 1960-64, 1972-74; second vice president, 1980-83; international professional affairs committee, 1965-66; chairperson, international research committee, 1972-74); International Reading Association; Kappa Delta Pi (member, 1954 to present; Nu Chi chapter, secretary 1976-77, vice president 1982-83); Kappa Kappa Iota (state secretary, 1964-65; chairman, national committee on ethics, 1966); National Association for Education of Young Children; National Council of Teachers of English; Arkansas Council for Teachers of English (advisory board); National Council on Social Studies (committee on early childhood education, 1977-81); National Education Association; Phi Mu (vice president, 1967); Pulaski County Mental Health Association, 1965-76; Southern Association on Children Under Six; University of Arkansas at Little Rock Education Association (president, 1979-80); Volunteers in Public Schools (executive board, 1975 to present); Women's National Book Association. Honors and Awards: State D.K.G. Scholarship for Graduate Study, 1960; Annie Webb Blanton, D.K.G. International Scholarship Award, 1965; Teacher of the Year, Federation of Women's Clubs, 1969; Outstanding Woman Educator in Arkansas, Business and Professional Women's Club, 1969; J. L. Milton Children's Book Award, 1972; First Outstanding Teaching Award, Donaghey Foundation, 1974; Arkansas Woman of the Year, Arkansas Democrat, 1975; Donaghey Foundation Grant for Travel Abroad, 1977; Kappa Kappa Iota National Scholarship, 1978; Innovative Teaching Grant, "Dial-A-Story", 1979-80; Listed in *American Educational Registry, Book of Honor, Community Leaders of America, Community Leaders and Noteworthy Americans, The Compendium, Contemporary Personages, Dictionary of International Biography, Directory of Distinguished Americans, International Scholars Directors, International Register of Profiles, International Who's Who in Community Service, International Who's Who in Education, International Who's Who of Intellectuals, Leaders in Education, Men and Women of Distinction, National Gold Book: Distinguished Women in the United States, National Register of Prominent Americans, National Society Directory, Notable Americans, Outstanding Educators of America, Who's Who in America, Who's Who in American Education, Who's Who of American Women, Who's Who of Women in Education, Who's Who in the South and Southwest, World Who's Who of Women, World Who's Who of Women in Education,* Others. Address: 146 Ridge Road, Little Rock, Arkansas 72207.

Rose A Berry

Berthold, Jeanne Saylor

Personal: Born June 4, 1924, Kansas City, Missouri. Education: Graduate, Highland School of Nursing, 1945; B.S. 1953, M.S. 1955, Ph.D. 1961, Universtiy of California-Berkeley; Clinical Specialization and Teaching in Psychiatric Nursing; Further Courses in the Field of Nursing. Career: Public Health Staff Nurse, Visiting Nurse Association, Los Angeles, 1945-46; School Nurse, Board of Education, Los Angeles, 1946-47; Staff Assistant, Sonoma County Hospital, Santa Rosa, 1947-51; Psychiatric Nurse, Langley Porter Neuro-Psychiatric Institute, San Francisco, 1955-61; Instructor, Lecturer, School of Nursing, University of California Medical Center, San Francisco, 1955-61; Assistant Professor 1961-63, Associate Professor 1963-64, Professor 1964-71, Francis Payne Bolton School of Nursing, Case Western Reserve University; Co-Principal Investigator, Sensory Deprivation and Effective Nursing, Intervention, U.S. Public Health Service, 1962-64; Chairperson, Research Group, F. P. B. School of Nursing, 1964-67; Principal Investigator, Concept Attainment and Nurses Preferences, U.S.P.H.S., 1966-71; Program Staff, Faculty Research Development, U.S.P.H.S., 1962-66; Co-Principal Investigator and Program Coordinator 1962-64, Principal Investigator 1964-71, Nurse Scientist Training, U.S.P.H.S.; Program Director, Development of Nursing Education Technology, U.S.P.H.S., 1966-71; Adjoint Professor, University of Colorado School of Nursing, Denver, 1971-73; Principal Investigator and Program Director, Western Interstate Commission for Higher Education, Regional Program for Nursing Research and Development, Department of Health, Education and Welfare, 1971-73; Professor, University of Southern California, School of Medicine, Department of Community and Family Medicine, 1973 to present; Director of Nursing Research 1973-75, Director of Nursing Research and Education 1975 to present, Rancho Los Amigos Hospital, Downey; Adjunct Professor, California State University-Long Beach, 1977 to present. Organizational Memberships: American Psychological Association; American Association of University Professors; American Educational Research Association; National Council of Measurement in Education; New York Academy of Sciences; American Association for the

Advancement of Science; Center for the Study of Democratic Institutions; Center on Evaluation, Development and Research, Phi Delta Kappa; Institute of Society, Ethics and the Life Sciences, The Hastings Center; American Congress of Rehabilitation Medicine; Rancho Professional Staff Association (allied professional staff member); Association of Rehabilitation Nurses; California League for Nursing; California State Board of Nurse Examiners (workshop planning committee, 1956); California Mental Health Association (volunteer advisory committee, representative of California League for Nursing, 1957-59); California State Nurses Association; Pi Lambda Theta; National League for Nursing; American Nurses Foundation (board of trustees, 1965-71; president and member board of trustees, 1969-71); American Nurses Association (standing committee on research and studies, vice chairperson 1967-68, chairperson 1968-70; chairperson, commission on nursing research, 1970-75; ex-officio member, council on nurse researchers executive committee, 1970-75; resource person, committee on interrelationships, 1972-75); *American Journal of Nursing* (editorial board, chairperson 1972-73); American Nurses Association Research Conference (chairperson, advisory committee, 1969-73); American Congress of Rehabilitation Medicine (awards committee, 1976-77; coulter lecture subcommittee 1977-78; scientific exhibits subcommittee, 1978-79; program committee, 1979 to present); Rehab Resources (president, 1979-80); Rehabilitation Nursing Institute (research committee, chairperson, 1979-81). Community Activities: Highland Alumnae Association; California Alumni Association; Rancho Professional Staff Association (research committee, 1973 to present); Rancho Los Amigos (nursing executive committee, 1975 to present); Los Angeles County-University of Southern California Nursing Educational Resources Committee, 1975 to present; Los Angeles County, San Gabriel Valley Region School/Clinical Affiliation Committee, 1976 to present; Los Angeles County Administration Study (advisory committee, 1976 to present); Los Angeles County Productivity Program (advisory committee, 1977 to present); Rancho Professional Staff Association (education committee, 1978 to presaent). Honors and Awards: National League for Nursing Fellowship; Pi Lambda Theta; Sigma Theta Tau, Alpha Mu Chapter; Listed in *Who's Who of American Women, American Men of Science, American Men and Women of Science, Who's Who in American Education, International Scholars Directory, Who's Who in the Midwest, 2000 Women of Achievement, Dictionary of International Biography, World Who's Who of Women, Who's Who in America, Who's Who in the World,* Others. Address: 10330 Downey Ave. #8, Downey, California 90242.

Best, Mary Sue

Free-Lance Writer and Editor. Personal: Born December 18, 1930; Married David B. H. Best; Mother of Melanie Sue. Education: B.A., Millsaps College, 1952; M.A., University of Mississippi, 1954. Career: Free-Lance Writer and Editor; Former College Professor and High School Teacher. Organizational Memberships: National League of American Pen Women; National Society of Arts and Letters; Contemporary Club; Fortnightly Literary Club. Community Activities: Writer's Committee for Senator Richard G. Lugar; People with a Purpose (adjunct to board of directors); Fund Drive for Local New Child Abuse and Neglect Center, The Family Support Center, Inc.; Other Fund-Raising Memberships. Religion: Chairman, Religion and Arts Committee; Director, Easter Pageant; Media and Public Relations Work for Church. Honors and Awards: Nine Awards for Writing, The Mississippi Arts Festival, The Mississippi Arts Commission, Mississippians for Educational Television. Address: 5402 Washington Blvd., Indianapolis, Indiana 46220.

Mary L Betts

Bestor, Charles L

Professor and Department Head. Personal: Born December 21, 1924; Son of Arthur Eugene and Jeannette Lemon Bestor (both deceased); Married Ann Elder; Father of Charles Elder, Geoffrey Grant, Phillip Russell, Leslie Ann, Wendy Lynn, Jennifer Lee. Education: Attended Yale University, 1943-44; B.A., Swarthmore College, 1946; B.S., Juilliard School of Music, 1951; M.Mus., University of Illinois, 1952; D.M.A., University of Colorado, 1974. Served in the United States Navy, 1941-46, achieving the rank of Lieutenant. Career: Professor, Head, Department of Music and Dance, University of Massachusetts-Amherst, 1977 to present; Head, Department of Music, University of Utah, 1975-77; Chairman, Department of Music, University of Alabama, 1971-73; Dean, College of Music, Willamette University, 1967-71; Assistant Professor, University of Colorado, 1959-64; Assistant Dean, Juilliard School of Music, 1951-59. Organizational Memberships: National Association of Schools of Music (graduate commission, 1975-79); College Music Society (national council, 1974-78); National Association of Composers (national council, 1978 to present); Snowbird Arts Foundation (national board, 1977 to present). Community Activities: Leroy J. Robertson Foundation (board member, 1977 to present); Special Consultant to the Joint Commission on Reorganization of Higher Education, Massachusetts, 1979-80; Springfield Junior Symphony (board member, 1977 to present); Massachusetts Council on Arts and Humanities (music panel, 1980 to present). Honors and Awards: Phi Beta Kappa; Pi Kappa Lambda; Theta Alpha Phi; O.D.K. National Service Honorary; National Patron; Phi Beta. Address: 19 Birchcroff Lane, Amherst, Massachusetts 01002.

Bettis, Dorothy Dillard

Educator. Personal: Born February 13, 1931, Mobile, Alabama; Daughter of James Patrick and Inez Leslie Holt Dillard; Mother of Victor Lomant Lett. Education: B.S., Alabama State University, 1956; Undertook Post-Graduate Studies (N.D.E.A. Fellowship), University of Kansas, 1966; M.S., Purdue University, 1968; A.A., University of Southern Alabama, 1976; Certified in Elementary Education Supervision, Library Science; Specialist in Educational Media. Career: Learning Center Teacher, Mobile County Public Schools, 1956 to present. Organizational Memberships: National Education Association; Alabama Education Association; American Library Association; Educators Study, Mobile County Teachers. Community Activities: Missouri Federation of Women; National Congress of Colored Women; Delta Sigma Theta; Orginial Las Amigas Club; Nabers Drive Civic Club. Religion: Methodist. Honors and Awards: 4 Human Relations Awards; Teacher of the Year, Ed A. Palmer School, 1966. Address: 1861 Nabers Drive, Mobile, Alabama 36617.

Betts, Clifford Allen

Civil Engineer. Personal: Born September 12, 1889; Son of Albert Allen and Lila Jane Malkin Betts (both deceased); Married Edna Cantril (deceased); Father of Allen Walker, Edith, Marjorie Seiser. Education: Ph.B., Sheffield Scientific School, Yale University, 1911; C.E., University of Wisconsin, 1913. Career: Civil Engineer, 70 years; Cartographer, Columbia River; Chief Engineer for Lumber for Production of Aircraft, World War I; Engineer, Six Mile Moffat Tunnel, Colorado and 520 Foot Owyhee Dam, Oregon; Engineer for U.S. Forest Service, 27 years. Religion: Episcopalian. Honors and Awards: District of Columbia Council of Engineers and Architects Honor; Thomas Fitch Rowland Prize, American Society of Civil Engineers, 1932; Listed in *Notable Americans.* Address: 2510 South Ivanhoe Place, Denver Colorado 80222.

Betts, Mary Lester

Broadcast Management. Personal: Born September 6, 1926. Education: Graduate, Athens High School. Career: Broadcast

Management. Organizational Memberships: National Association Broadcasters; Georgia Association Broadcasters; American Women in Radio and Television (president, Atlanta chapter, 1968; southern area trustee educational foundation, 1969-71). Community Activities: Athens Young Women's Christian Organization (board of directors, 1977-81); Mayor's Advisory Committee on Tourism and Conventions, 1976-82; Kelly Workshop (board of directors, 1981 to present); Georgia District Pilot International (governor, 1977-78; governor elect, 1976-77; second lieutenant governor, 1972-73); Pilot International (extension leader, 1976-77; public relations leader, 1975-76); Pilot Club of Athens (president, 1970-71); Entre Nous Club (president, 1981-82). Religion: Baptist. Honors and Awards: Athens Woman of the Year, 1963; Georgia Association of Broadcasters Award of Excellence, 1969; Athens Pilot of the Year, 1972; Golden Mike Award, University of Georgia College Students in Broadcasting, 1972. Address: P.O. Box 5723, Athens, Georgia 30604.

Bevill, Tom

Congressman. Personal: Born March 27, 1921; Married Lou Betts; Father of Susan, Donald, Patricia. Education: B.S, University of Alabama, 1943; L.L.B., University of Alabama School of Law, 1948. Military: Served in the United States Army, 1943-46, achieving the rank of Captain; Served in the United States Army Reserves, 1943-66, attaining the rank of Lieutenant Colonel. Career: Congressman, 90th Congress, Re-Elected to 91st, 92nd, 93rd, 94th, 96th, 97th Congresses; Former Lawyer. Organizational Memberships: Walker County Bar Association; Alabama Bar Association; American Bar Association. Religion: Baptist. Honors and Awards, L.L.D. (honorary), University of Alabama, 1981. Address: 3827 North Military Road, Arlington, Virginia 22207.

Bevins, Karl Alten

Musician, Teacher. Personal: Born May 30, 1915; Son of Daniel James Bevins (deceased); Married Blanche Albert; Father of Jean. Education: B.S.E.E., Georgia Institute of Technology, 1939; Fellowship and Certificate in Traffic Engineering, Bureau of Highway Traffic, Yale University, 1941; Studied Clarinet and Other Woodwinds under Carl T. Rundquist, Hymie Voxman, Clarence Warmelin, H. Charles Stumph, Michiel Fusco, Frank Chase; Studied Piano under Mrs. Henry Shields, Charles Beaton; Studied Harmony, Arranging and Conducting at the University of Iowa Summer School, 1930, 1931, 1932. Career: Assistant Engineer, Office of the Transportation Engineer, Georgia Power Company, 1940; Traffic Engineer, Georgia Power Company, 1941-49; City Traffic Engineer, Atlanta, Georgia, 1949-78; Solo Clarinet, Band of Atlanta, 1958-74; First Clarinet, Municipal Theatre of the Stars, 1954 to present; Principal Clarinet, Atlanta Symphony Orchestra, 1945-66; Principal Clarinet, Altanta Pops Orchestra, 1945 to present; Principal Clarinet, Atlanta Philharmonic Orchestra, 1935, 1936; First Clarinet, University of Iowa Summer Symphony Orchestra, 1931, 1932; Instructor in Clarinet, Music Department, Georgia State University, 1964 to present; Private Lessons, 1933 to present; Assistant in Instrumental Music Department, Public Schools, Washington, Iowa, 1933-34; Assistant Director, Hq. Band, Georgia State Guard, 1941-46; Student Conductor, Georgia Tech Band, 1936-39; Assistant Director, Washington, Iowa, Municipal Band, 1934. Organizational Memberships; Registered Professional Engineer, State of Georgia; Institute of Traffic Engineers (president, southern section, 1955; director, district 5, 1955-56); Georgia Society of Professional Engineers; Georgia Engineering Society; American Institute of Electrical Engineers; Kappa Kappa Psi, Iota Chapter (president, 1938); Atlanta Music Clu (vice president, young artists division, 1946-47); Atlanta Federation of Musicians (executive board, 1954 to present; president, 1967 to present). Community Activities: Kiwanis Club of Northside Atlanta; City of Atlanta Traffic Commision (chairman, 1949-54); Southern Safety Conference (chairman, traffic engineering section, 1952-53); Joint Atlanta-Fulton County Bond Committee on Streets and Highways, 1957-62; Georgia Motor Club (president, 1971-72); A.A.A. (national director, 1973-75). Honors and Awards: One of Atlanta's 100 Leaders of Tomorrow, Atlanta Chamber of Commerce and *Time* Magazine, 1953; Good Government Award, Junior Chamber of Commerce, 1962; Award for Outstanding Service, Georgia Society of Professional Engineers, 1966; Herman J. Hoose Distinguished Service Award, 1978; First Place, Clarinet Solo, Iowa High School Music Festival, 1933; 2nd Place, Clarinet Solo, National High School Music Festival, Evanston, Illinois, 1933. Address: 110 Laurel Forest Circle N.E., Atlanta, Georgia 30342.

Bhattacharyya, Ashim Kumar

Associate Professor. Personal: Born July 9, 1936; Son of Mr. and Mrs. V. N. Bhattacharya; Married Bani Chatterjee; Father of Rupa, Gopa. Education: B.S. honors, Presidency College, Calcutta, India, 1957; M.S. 1959, Ph.D. 1965, University of Calcutta. Career: Associate Professor of Pathology and Physiology, Louisiana State University Medical Center; Formerly, Assistant Professor of Pathology and Physiology, Louisiana State University Medical Center; Research Scientist, Clinical Research Center, University of Iowa; Associate Research Scientist, Clinical Research Center, University of Iowa; Post-Doctoral Research Fellow, University of Iowa and University of Minnesota; Lecturer, Krishnath College, Berhampore, West Bengal, India; Demonstrator, Christian Medical College, Ludhiana, Punjab, India. Organizational Memberships: American Physiological Society; American Heart Association; International Athers. Society; American Society of Clinical Nutrition; American Institute of Nutrition; Sigma Xi; American Oil Chemists Society; American Association for the Advancement of Science; American Federation of Clinical Research; Society of Experimental Biological Medicine; New York Academy of Science. Community Activities: American Heart Association (delegate representing council on arteriosclerosis to the annual delegate assembly, 1976, 1977); India Students Association, University of Iowa (past president, 1968). Honors and Awards: Elected Fellow, Council on Arteriosclerosis, American Heart Association, 1972; Listed in *American Men and Women of Science, Who's Who in the South and Southwest, Personalities of the South, Dictionary of International Biography, Directory of Distinguished Americans, Personalities of America.* Address: 1156 Elmeer Avenue, Metairie, Louisiana 70005.

Bick, Rodger L

Physician. Personal: Born May 21, 1942; Son of Jack A. Bick; Married Marcella Meuller; Father of Michelle. Education: Attended University of California-Berkeley, 1963-66; M.D., University of California-Irvine School of Medicine, 1970; Residency, Internal Medicine, University of California-Los Angeles, 1970-73; Fellowship, Hematology-Oncology, 1972-74. Career: Physician, Hematology, Hemostasis, Oncology; Kern County General Hospital, Bakersfield, California: Director Hemostasis/Thrombosis Research Laboratory (1973-74), Chief of Hematology/Medical Oncology (1973-74), Director of Medical Education (1973-74); Cancer Committee, St. John's Hospital, Santa Monica; Santa Monica Hospital: Research Committee, Tumor Board, Cancer Committee; Consultant, Nigeria Hematology Center, Lagos, Nigeria; Founding Director, Oncology Unit, Santa Monica Hospital; Director, National Hemostasis Thrombosis Seminars & Workshops, Commission on Continuing Medical Education, American Society of Clinical Pathologists; Medical Staff: University of California-Los Angeles Center for the Health Sciences, Santa Monica Hospital and Medical Center, St. John's Hospital and Medical Center, Greater Bakersfield Memorial Hospital, Mercy Hospital; Attending Physician, Wadsworth Veterans Hospital, Los Angeles; Chairman: Cancer Committee and Tumor Board, San Joaquin Community Hospital; Founding Director, Oncology Unit, San Joaquin Community Hospital; Adjunct Associate Professor of Medicine/Physiology, Specialized Center for Thrombosis Research, Wayne State University School of Medicine, Adjunct Clinical

Faculty, Wesley Medical Center and University of Kansas Medical School, Clinical Investigator: U.C.B. Pharmaceuticals, Brussels, Belgium and American National Red Cross; Co-Investigator, A.T.-III Project, Bureau of Biologics, Food and Drug Administration; Consultant, Council for Tobacco Research; Clinical Instructor in Medicine, Department of Medicine, School of Medicine, University of California-Los Angeles Center for the Health Sciences; Associate Professor of Allied Health Professions, California State University-Bakersfield; Private Practice, San Joaquin Hematology Oncology Medical Group, 1977 to present. Organizational Memberships: International Society of Haematology; American College of Angiology (fellow); International College of Angiology (fellow); American Association for the Study of Neoplastic Diseases; American Association for Clinical Research; American Society of Mammalogists; Nigerian Haematology Society; California College Honor Society; International Association for the Study of Lung Cancer (founding member); Federation of American Societists; American Geriatrics Society (founding fellow); American Society Hematology; Internatioanl Society on Thrombosis, Hemostasis; Thrombosis Council, American Heart Association; American Society Clinical Pathology; Association of Clincial Scientists; New York Academy of Science; American College of Physicians; American Association for the Advancement of Science. Community Activities: California Heart Association (peer review committee for grants). Published Works: *Modern Concepts and Evaluations of Hemostasis and Thrombosis*, 1975; *Difficult Diagnosis Problems in Hemostasis and Thrombosis*, 1976; *Current Concepts of Hemostatis and Thrombosis: Clinical and Laboratory Evaluation*, 1976; *Recent Concepts and Developments in Evaluating Disorders of Hemostasis and Thrombosis*, 1976; Number of Textbook Chapters, Professional Articles and Abstracts. Honors and Awards: Award for Outstanding Medical Research, University of California-Irvine School of Medicine, 1968, 1969; Vincent P. Carroll Award, University of California-Irvine School of Medicine; Listed in *Who's Who in the West, American Men and Women of Science*. Address: 2727 Eye Street, Bakersfield, California 93301.

Biemer, Linda Briggs

University Professor. Personal: Born May 24, 1942; Daughter of Horace and Jane Hill; Married Robert R. Biemer; Mother of Chance Briggs, Robert G. Erich, Kathryn. Education: A.B., Elmira College, 1963; M.S.Ed., State University of New York, 1967; Ph.D., Syracuse University, 1979. Career: Professor, Graduate School of Education, State University of New York-Binghamton, 1973-76, 1978 to present; Professor, Hartwick College, 1976-77; Professor, Syracuse University, 1972-73; Professor, State University, Cortland, New York, 1968-72; Public School Social Studies Teacher, 1963-68. Organizational Memberships: *Social Science Record* (co-editor); New York State Council for the Social Studies (executive committee, board of directors); National Council for the Social Studies (sexism and social justice committee); New York State Historical Association; Others. Community Activities: Cortland County League of Women Voters (board of directors, 1972-81; vice president, 1974-76, 1979-81); Cortland County Democratic Party (committeewoman, 1974 to present); Cortland County Legislature's Advisory Committee of Consumer Affairs; Cortland Junior High School Parent Teacher Association (president, 1973-74); Campus School Parent Teacher Association (president, 1972-73); Frequent Speaker on Women's Rights, Women and Law. Honors and Awards: Cortland County's Outstanding Young Educator, 1967; First Runer-Up, New York's Outstanding Young Educator, 1967; Black Studies Teacher Fellowship, Syracuse University, 1972; Special Education Teacher Fellowship, 1973; Kempel Fellowship for Women Historians, 1974-75. Address: 1 Melvin Avenue, Cortland, New York 13045.

Biferie, Daniel Anthony Jr

Gallery Director and Instructor. Personal: Born December 17, 1950; Son of Mr. and Mrs. Dan Biferie; Married Kathryn Louise. Education: A.S. with honors, Daytona Beach Community College, 1971; B.F.A. summa cum laude 1972, M.F.A. 1974, Ohio University. Military: Served in the United States Air Force Reserve, 1968-71, achieving the rank of Sergeant. Career: Director, Gallery of Fine Arts, 1978 to present, and Instructor, Photography Department, 1975 to present, Daytona Beach Community College; Exhibition Photographer, 1972 to present; Free-lance Photographer, Mt. Vernon, Ohio, 1974-75; Teaching Assistant, Ohio University, 1973-74; Slide Library Photographer, Ohio University, 1972-73; Aerial Photography Lab Technician, Rader and Associates, Miami, Florida, 1969-72; 301st Squadron Photographer, United States Air Force Reserve, 1968-71; One-Man Exhibits include University of Central Florida, Photoworks (Richmond, Virginia), "A Few People" (Brevard Art Museum, Melbourne, Florida), Images Gallery (New Orleans), McSwain Gallery (Greenville, South Carolina), Museum of Arts and History (Port Huron, Michigan), Sheldon Memorial Art Gallery (Lincoln, Nebraska), The Darkroom (Chicago, Illinois), Middle Tennessee State University; Selected Exhibits include "Southern Exposures" Traveling Exhibition, Gallery of Fine Arts, Daytona Beach, Florida, 1981; "Architectural Forms in Photography", Gallery of Fine Arts, Daytona Beach, 1981; "Florida Images", Gulf Coast Art Center, Bellair, 1980; "Eight Distinguished American Photographers" Invitational Exhibition, Creative Art Gallery, Winter Park, Florida, 1980; Florida State Capitol, Daytona Beach Community College Invitational Exhibition, 1980; "Landscapes in Photography", Gallery of Fine Arts, Daytona Beach, 1980; Permanent Collections, Loch Haven Art Center (Orlando, Florida), DeLand Museum, Middle Tennessee State University, Numerous Private and Individual Collections. Organizational Memberships: Society for Photographic Education (president, southeast region; regional representative); Florida Art Museums Directors Association; Daytona Beach Community College Photographic Society (founder and president, 1979-81); Florida Association of Community Colleges. Community Activities: DeLand Museum; Loch Haven Art Center; Daytona Beach Museum of Arts and Sciences; Juror for Numerous Art Exhibitions and Shows; Lecturer for Colleges, Universities and Art Organizations; Curator of Numerous Travelling Exhibits. Honors and Awards: President's Faculty Service Award, Daytona Beach Community College, 1981; Halifax Area Cultural Arts Award, 1979; Photographs Exhibited Nationally, 1972 to present; Art Work in Numerous Public and Private Collections; Listed in *Outstanding Young Men of America, Who's Who Among Students in Ameridan Colleges and Universities, Who's Who Among Students in American Community Colleges, Who's Who in the South and Southwest, Personalities of the South, Directory of Distinguished Americans, International Dictionary of Biographies*, Others. Address: 22 Virginia Avenue, DeLand, Florida 32720.

Bilbow, James Robert

Police Officer. Personal: Born February 2, 1923; Son of James Michael and Jane Marie Barrett Bilbow; Married Blanche. Education: Associate in Aeronautical Engineering, Pennsylvania Institute of Technology, 1956; University of California Extension Course in Space Technology, 1960-61; Professional Certificate in Law Enforcement Science 1975, Certificate in Narcotics Investigation 1976, Certificate in Arson Investigation 1977, Certificate in Police Management 1980, Certificate in Organized Crime 1980, all from the American Police Academy. Military: Served in the United States Marine Corps, 1942-51, attaining the rank of Platoon Sergeant; Presently a Major in the United States Marine Corps Reserve. Career: Delaware County Park Police Department - Administrative Officer, Officer in Charge Tactical Unit, State Certified Police Firearms Instructor, State Certified Crime Prevention Officer, Criminal Investigator; Former Program Manager and Project Engineer, Field of Aviation Survival Equipment and Open Sea Rescue Equipment, Department of the Navy, Naval Air Engineering Center, Philadelphia. Organizational Memberships: Delaware County Police Officers Legal Rights Fund (president, 1977 to present); Delaware County Lodge #27 Fraternal Order of Police (board member, 1976 to present); American Law Enforcement Officers Association (national vice president, publications, 1977-79); Delaware County Hero Scholarship Fund (board member, 1978 to present; chairman, hero scholarship day, 1977 to present); American Police Hall of

Fame (national advisory board, 1978 to present); American Police Academy (charter member); American Pistol Team (charter member); Police Marksman Association (life member); United States Association of Firearms Instructors and Coaches (life member); International Association of Law Enforcement Firearms Instructors (charter member); Delaware County Police Chiefs Association (associate member); National Association of Police Chiefs (charter member); Pennsylvania Crime Prevention Officers Association. Community Activities: American Security Council (national advisory council); National Republican Committee (life member); Brigadier General Jos. Knowlan Chapter, Marine Corps Reserve Officers Association (board of directors, 1970 to present); United States Reserve Officers Association (life member); Marine Corps Aviation Association; Military Order of World Wars; Marine Corps League (vice commandant, 1978-79). Honors and Awards: Good Samaritan 1974, Silver Star for Bravery 1975, American Federation of Police; Certificate of Commendation, National Police Officers Association, 1975, 1976; Commendation 1976, Honor Award 1976, American Federation of Police Officers; Hero Scholarship, Executive Board, Hero Scholarship Fund of Delaware County, 1979; Nominated for J. Edgar Hoover Award for Outstanding Law Enforcement Officer, 1981; George Washington Honor Medal, Freedom Foundation of Valley Forge, 1972, 1977. Address: 628 N. Lemon Street, Media, Pennsylvania 19063.

Billig, Robert Milton

Psychiatric Social Worker. Personal: Born May 21; Son of Benjamin and Pearl Billig. Education: B.A., McKendree College, 1966; M.S., Fort Hays, Kansas, State College, 1969; M.S.W., Marywood College School of Social Work, 1974. Career: Psychiatric Social Worker: Staten Island Developmental Center, Brooklyn Developmental Center, Manhattan Psychiatric Center, Bellevue Psychiatric Hospital. Organizational Memberships: National Association of Social Workers. Honors and Awards: Certified Social Worker, 1975; Academy of Certified Social Workers, 1977; Listed in *Who's Who in the East, Personalities of America, Personalities of the East, Community Leaders of America.* Address: 10 Park Terrace East, New York, New York 10034.

Binder, Robert Thomas

University Professor. Personal: Born May 25, 1919; Married Betty Corbiere; Father of Bob. Education: Attended the University of Illinois, Purdue University, Heidelberg University (Germany), University of Maryland, University of Hawaii; B.S., M.S., East Texas State University; University of Texas-Austin (A.B.D.). Military: Served in the United States Army, 1940-46, 1950-67, retired from the Corps of Engineers with the rank of Lieutenant Colonel. Career: Professor, Department of Journalism and Graphic Arts, East Texas State University. Organizational Memberships: Public Relations Society of America (accredited public relations practitioner); Texas Public Relations Association (twice director); Texas Public Relations Foundation (life member; charter member, board of trustees); Public Relations Association of America, North Texas Chapter; Texas Association of College Teachers; Association of Educators of Journalism; Academy of Advertising; Specialty Advertising Association International (very important professor); Phi Delta Kappa (executive committee, East Texas State University chapter); Society of Professional Journalists, Sigma Delta Chi (member Dallas Chapter); National Council of College Publications Advisers. Community Activities: Commerce Lions Club (president, 1975-76); Lions Clubs International (district governor, 1979-80); Commerce Chamber of Commerce (president, 1980); Texas Lions Camp for Crippled Children (board of directors, 1979-80; life member); Julien C. Hyer Youth Camp (past member, board of directors); Lefthanders International; Retired Officers Association; American Legion; Commerce Lodge 439, A.F.&A.M. of Texas; Knights Templar; Hello Temple, Nobles of the Mystic Shrine; 102nd Infantry Division Association; East Texas Shrine Club; Past District Governors of Texas Lions; Sheriffs Association of Texas; American Philatelic Society; Texas Philatelic Society; American Topical Association; Military Order of World Wars; East Texas State University Blue and Gold Society; East Texas State University Quarterback Club. Honors and Awards: 100% District Governor, 100% President, Lions Clubs International; Numerous Other Lions Clubs Awards; Chamber of Commerce President's Award; Commerce Humane Association Award; Accredited Public Relations Society of America. Address: 2601 Campbell Street, Commerce, Texas 75428.

R T Binder

Bird, Agnes Thornton

Attorney. Personal: Born September 15, 1921; Daughter of Judge and Mrs E. G. Thornton; Married Frank B. Bird; Mother of Patricia Anne. Education: B.S., Texas Woman's University, 1943; M.A. 1959, Ph.D. 1967, J.D. 1974, University of Tennessee. Career: Partner, Law Firm, Bird, Navratil and Bird; Instructor of Political Science, University of Tennessee, 1966-68, 1974; Assistant Professor of Political Science, Maryville College, 1968-71. Organizational Memberships: Political Science Association (board member of women's caucus, 1970-72); American Bar Association; Tennessee Bar Association; Blount County Bar Association; American Trial Lawyers Association; Tennessee Trial Lawyers Association. Community Activities: Tennessee Commission on the Status of Women (chairman, 1977-79); Tennessee Advisory Committee to the United States Civil Rights Commission (vice-chairman, 1968); Tennessee Human Rights Commission, 1965-68; National Association of Commissions on Women (board member, 1977-78); American Association of University Women (chairman, national topic committee, 1970-72); Tennessee Democratic Executive Committee (vice chairman, 1976-81); Democratic National Committee, 1976-81; National Federation of Democratic Women (parliamentarian, 1974 to present); Tennessee Federation of Democratic Women (president, 1964-65). Religion: Unitarian-Universalist Church. Honors and Awards: Delegate on the Prominent American Women's Tour of People's Republic of China, 1979; Distinguished Alumna Award, Texas Woman's University, 1980. Address: Cold Springs Road, Maryville, Tennessee 37801-0647.

Birkimer, Donald Leo

Technical Director. Personal: Born September 6, 1941; Son of Edgar Earl and Virginia Eileen Birkimer; Married Edith Marie Lowe; Father of Mark Austin, Thomas Edgar, Julie Lee. Education: B.S.C.E., Ohio University, 1963; M.S. 1965, Ph.D. 1968, University of Cincinnati; P.M.D., Harvard Graduate School of Business Administration, 1973; Federal Executive Institute Program for Senior Managers in Government, Harvard Graduate School of Business Administration/Kennedy School of Government, 1976. Career: Technical Director, Naval Civil Engineering Laboratory; Technical Director, United States Coast Guard R&D Center; Assistant Director, Naval Surface Weapons Center; Acting Chief, Construction Materials Branch, United States Army Construction Engineering Research Laboratory; Research Structural Engineer, Battelle Memorial Institute; Research Civil Engineer, United States Army Corps of Engineers; Civil Engineer, Wright-Patterson Air Force Base. Organizational Memberships: American Association for the Advancement of Science; American Management Association; The Institute of Management Sciences; American Society for Testing Materials; National Society of Professional Engineers. Community Activities: Rotary; Benevolent Protective Order of the Elks. Honors and Awards: WASON Medal, American Concrete Institute, 1973; Registered Professional Engineer, Chi Epsilon Honorary Fraternity, 1967; Coast Guard Meritorious Unit Commendation Award, 1976. Address: 1291 Seybolt Avenue, Camarillo, California 93010.

Birsner, Eleanor Patricia

Consultant, Writer. Personal: Born April 12, 1928; Daughter of Helen D. Balsley; Mother of Peggy Lynn, Jane Ellen Compton. Education: B.A., University of Illinois, 1948; M.A., Texas Women's University, 1957; Graduate Studies, University of Illinois, University of Houston. Career: Author/Editor, Consultant, Birsner Associates, 1979 to present; Senior Language Arts Editor 1975-79, Product Manager for Language Arts Products and Systems 1973-75, Consultant/Salesperson for Houston Branch 1970-73, McGraw-Hill, Inc.; President and General Manager, Birsner Educational Services of Texas, Inc., 1962-70; Salesperson, Reagan Audio-Visuals, 1959-62; Teacher, 1948-59. Organizational Memberships: International Platform Association; International Customer Service Association. Published Works: Author *Solving Problems Creatively*, *Listen to Communicate*, *Basic Skills in Customer Service*, *Managing the Customer Service Function*, *Customer Service in the Service Industries*, Number of Instructor Manuals and Course Books; Co-Author with Dr. Ronald D. Balsley, *A Practical Guide to Customer Service Management and Operation*, *The Competitive Edge*, *How to Improve Customer Service*. Honors and Awards: Listed in *Who's Who of American Women*, *Who's Who in the East*, *Dictionary of International Biography*, *Men and Women of Distinction*. Address: 436 Teaneck Road, Ridgefield Park, New Jersey 07660.

Eleanor P Birsner

Bishop, Eliza H

Research Writer, Businesswoman. Personal: Born June 18, 1920; Daughter of William Penn and Carey Ann Bishop (both deceased). Education: B.A., University of Mary Hardin-Baylor, 1941. Career: Owner, Writer, E. B. Promotions; Former Newspaper Editor, *Crockett Democrat*; Reporter, Feature Writer, News Correspondent, *Belton Journal*, *Temple Telegram*, *Houston Post*, *Houston Chronicle*; Newswriter for Radio Station KNET (Palestine), KIVY (Crockett); Medical Assistant for E.E.N.T. Medical Doctor; Author/Editor, *Houston County History*, 1980. Organizational Memberships: Women in Communication; National Federation of Press Women (life member); Texas Press Women (past president, 1977-78; life member); Houston County Historical Commission (chairman, 1970-78, 1981-82); Historical and Cultural Activities Center, Inc. (president/agent, 1978 to present). Community Activities: City Secretary for Crockett, Texas, 1960-61; Deputy District Clerk, 1947-72; Charter Commission for City of Crockett, 1955; Planning and Zoning Commissioner; Delinquent Tax Clerk for Houston County, 1945-47; First Aid Instructor, 1941-45. Religion: All Saints Episcopal Church of Crockett, Former Clerk of Vestry. Honors and Awards: Pilots Woman of Year, 1972; First Lady of Mu Sigma, Beta Sigma Phi, 1973; Woman of Achievement, Texas Press Women, 1977; Best Texas Historical Commission Chairman, 1972, 1973, 1976, 1978; Texan Award for Historical Preservation, 1980; Houston County Heroine for the Texas Heritage Project, 1981. Address: 629 North Fourth Street, Crockett, Texas 75835.

Bisquerra, Jose

Physician. Personal: Born May 12, 1927, in Palma de Mallorca, Spain; Son of Jose and Dolores Bisquerra (both deceased); Married Amalia Riaza; Father of Maria Jose, Jose Miguel. Education: B.A., B.S., La Salle, University of Barcelona, Spain, 1948; M.S., M.D., University of Seville School of Medicine, 1955; Ph.D., University of Seville, Spain, 1956. Career: Professor of Obstetrics-Gynecology, Exploratory Maneuvers and Differential Diagnosis of Abdominal Pathology and Surgery, 1955; Professor, Pharmacology Department, University of Seville School of Medicine, 1955; Professor, Internal Medicine, University of Seville School of Medicine, 1955; Approved American Medical Association Rotating Internship, Memorial Hospital, Charleston, West Virginia, 1957; Approved American Medical Association General Practice Residency, Memorial Hospital, Charleston, 1958; Medical Director and Surgeon, Reynolds Metals Company General Hospital, Guyana, South America, 1960; Staff Physician, Obstetrics and Gynecology, Wilmington Medical Center, Wilmington General Hospital, Wilmington, Delaware, 1963; Staff Physician, Hospital for the Mentally Retarded, Georgetown, Delaware, 1964; Clinical Director, Hospital for the Mentally Retarded, Georgetown, Delaware, 1965; Resident in Psychiatry, Five-year Program, University of Missouri, School of Medicine at Kansas City General Hospital and Medical Center, 1966; Fellowship in Child Psychiatry, University of Missouri School of Medicine at Kansas City General Hospital and Medical Center, 1970; Fellow in Child Psychiatry, Institute of Living, Hartford, Connecticut, 1971; Chief, Child and Adolescent Psychiatry, Scott and White Clinic and Hospital, 1972; Private Practice, Adult and Child Psychiatry, Bisquerra Clinic, Temple Professional Plaza, Texas, 1978-81; Veterans Administration Medical Center, Shreveport, Louisiana, 1981 to present. Organizational Memberships: American Medical Association; Texas Medical Association; American Psychiatric Association, Texas District Branch; American Academy of Child Psychiatry; Texas Society of Child Psychiatry; Houston Chapter, American Society for Adolescent Psychiatry; Helen Scott Saulsbury Day Care Center (board of directors); Missouri Psychiatric Association (president-elect, 1967-68); St. Joseph State Hospital (secretary of medical staff by election, 1969-70); American Association of Psychiatric Services for Children; Bell County Medical Society; American Association of Foreign Graduates (charter member). Honors and Awards: American Medical Association Recognition Award, 1969-81; St. Joseph State Hospital Outstanding Physician of the Year Award, 1971; Recognition Award, State of Missouri Division of Mental Health, 1971; Recognition Award, Western Missouri Mental Health Center, 1971; University of Missouri School of Medicine, Department of Psychiatry Recognition Award, 1971; Medal of Honor, Outstanding Humanitarian Service, Georgetown, Guyana, South America, 1962; Medal of Honor, Kwakwani, Guyana, South America, 1962; Gold Medal, Guyana Miners Union, 1962; Gold Medal, "We The People", Guyana, 1962; Member of and Advisor to the United Nations, Public Health, Guyana, 1960-63; Miguel de Cervantes International Award, Madrid, 1947. Address: 220 Norcross, Bossier City, Louisiana 71111.

Jose Bisquerra

Bissell, Steven Lewis

Entertainment and Advertising Agent. Personal: Born January 30, 1949; Son of Lewis Austin (deceased) and Berniece M. Helmer Bissell; Married Julie Marie Axford, May 1, 1982. Education: Bachelor of General Studies, University of Iowa, 1982. Career: Entertainment and Advertising Agency Press Agent and Cable Television Programmer; Executive Associate, Collegiate Associations Council, University of Iowa; Director and Founder, Campus Cablevision, University of Iowa. Organizational Memberships: American Film Institute. Community Activities: Iowa City Jaycees (director, 1978-79); Public Relations Student Society of America, University of Iowa; Iowa City Muscular Dystrophy Association (chairman, Jerry Lewis Labor Day Telethon Committee, 1977; director, 1978); Nominated by Governor Robert Ray of Iowa and Appointed by President Ronald Reagan to Selective Service Local Board 19, 1982; Character of "Bubee the Clown" Appeared on Iowa City United Way Telethon, May 9, 1981; University of Iowa Video Advisory Committee, 1978-81. Religion: Roman Catholic; Sang Bass and Played Percussion for St. Wenceslaus Folk Choir, 1977-80. Honors and Awards: "Bubee the Clown" was 1st Runner-Up to U.S. Senator Dick Clark for "Human of the Year" Award, *The Daily Planet*, 1979; Spoke Award, United States Jaycees, 1977; Hancher-Finkbine Fellow, University of Iowa, 1978 to present; United States Jaycees Presidential Citation for "Make America Aware" Program, 1978; First Timers Award, Jaycees, 1978; Spark Plug Award, 1978. Address: 634 Westgate Villa, Suite 55, Iowa City, Iowa 52240.

Bittner, Jennie Kathryn

Senior High School Counselor. Personal: Born April 17, 1930; Daughter of August F. E. Bittner (deceased), Kathryn S. Gavorchik. Education: B.S.Ed., California State Teachers College; M.A.Ed., West Virginia University; Also attended the University of Pittsburgh. Career: Senior High School Counselor; Former Teacher of Mathematics; Research Medicine Laboratory Technician. Organizational Memberships: Pennsylvania School Counselors Association; Pennsylvania Personnel and Guidance Association; Pennsylvania Association of Women Deans and Counselors. Community Activities: Fort Gaddis Chapter Daughter of the American Revolution (good citizen committee, national defense committee, program committee, public relations committee, constitution week committee, United States bicentennial committee, scholarships and loans committee, schools committee; page at national conference, 1958; secretary, 1959-62; registrar, 1979-83; vice regent, 1962-65; regent, 1965-68, 1971-74); Elizabeth Van Metre Chapter, Colonial Dames of XVII Century (2nd vice president, 1976-78; custodian of flags, national defense committee, Pocahontas projects committee, scholarships committee, program committee); Pennsylvania State Society Colonial Dames XVII Century (president); Uniontown Branch, American Association of University Women (first vice president); Pennsylvania Junior Academy of Science (assistant director, region 8, 1970-73); Soroptimist International of Fayette County (corresponding secretary, 1972-74; recording secretary, 1977-78; chairman, international goodwill and understanding, education and leadership, training awards program, classification and venture/youth activities committees); Veterans of Foreign Wars Ladies Auxiliary, Post 47. Religion: Presbyterian. Honors and Awards: General Electric Guidance Fellowship, Syracuse University, 1961; Listed in *Outstanding Educators of America, Hereditary Register of the United States of America, Who's Who of American Women, World Who's Who of Women, Personalities of America.* Address: 44 Barton Mill Road, Uniontown, Pennsylvania 15401.

Bivins, Brack Allen

Academic Surgery. Personal: Born November 28, 1943; Son of Mr. and Mrs. B. A. Bivins; Married Brenda Kingston; Father of Brack David, Berkley Kingston. Education: B.S., Western Kentucky University, 1966; M.D., University of Kentucky College of Medicine, 1970. Military: Served in the Kentucky Army National Guard, 1970-81, attaining the rank of Lieutenant Colonel. Career: Academic Surgery, Head of Division of Trauma Surgery, Henry Ford Hospital, Detroit, Michigan. Organizational Memberships: Central Surgical Society; Society of Surgery Alimentary Tract; Association of Academic Surgery; American Society of Parenteral and Enteral Nutrition. Community Activities: Equestrian Events, Inc. (board of directors, 1979 to present). Honors and Awards: Alpha Omega Alpha; American Cancer Society Clinical Fellow, 1972-73; Frederick A. Coller Society Travelling Fellow, 1976; American Society of Hospital Pharmacy Research and Education Award, 1976; Parenteral Drug Association Research Award, 1976; Listed in *Who's Who in Kentucky, Who's Who in the Southeastern United States.* Address: Division of Trauma Surgery, Department of Surgery, Henry Ford Hospital, Detroit, Michigan.

Jennie K Bittner

Black, Asa Calvin Jr

Scientist, Educator. Personal: Born January 2, 1943; Son of Josephine E. Garrott; Married Cynthia Woods. Education: B.A. 1965, Ph.D. 1974, Vanderbilt University; Post-Doctoral Fellow, Department of Anatomy, University of Iowa, 1973-75. Career: Scientist/Educator, Department of Anatomy, University of Iowa. Organizational Memberships: American Association for the Advancement of Science; American Society for Neurochemistry; Alpha Chi Sigma; American Association of Anatomists; Anatomical Society of Great Britain and Ireland; New York Academy of Science; Craniofacial Biology Group; International Association for Dental Research; International Society for Neurochemistry; Iowa Academy of Science; Iowa Heart Association; Research Society of Alcoholism; Society for Neuroscience; Southern Society of Anatomists; Sigma Xi; Society for the Study of Reproduction. Honors and Awards: National Merit Scholarship Finalist, 1961; Full Scholarship, Vanderbilt University, 1961-65; National Institutes of Health Pre-Doctoral Fellow, 1971-72; National Institutes of Health Post-Doctoral Fellow, 1974-75. Address: 537 Terrace Road, Iowa City, Iowa 52240.

Black, David L

Association Executive. Personal: Born April 3, 1934; Son of Wilma Black; Married Susana Soler de Black; Father of Roger David. Education: B.A., Baylor University, 1954; Undertook Post-Graduate Studies at the University of Texas-Austin and Trinity University. Career: Deputy Director, Science/Technology, Organization of American States; Former Director, Special Programs and Assistant to the President, Southwest Research Institute, San Antonio. Organizational Memberships: American Society for Metals (chairman, Latin American relations committee); American Association for the Advancement of Science. Community Activities: Planned Parenthood Association (board member); Community Guidance Center, San Antonio (board member); Friends of McNay (board member); San Antonio Chamber Music Society (president). Religion: Christ Episcopal Church, San Antonio. Honors and Awards: Centennial Award, American Society of Mechanical Engineers, 1980. Address: 2911 45th Street, N.W., Washington, D.C. 20016.

Black, Larry K

Administrator, Professor. Personal: Born September 4, 1923; Son of James and Ina A. Black (both deceased); Married Eythe I. Shoop. Education: B.A. 1961, M.A. 1967, Arizona State University; Ph.D., Hamilton College, 1974. Military: Served in the United States Air Force, 1942-61, retired with the rank of Captain. Career: Teacher, 1961-67; Consultant, 1967-74; Administrator, Cartwright School District #83 and Professor, Glendale Community College, 1970 to present. Organizational Memberships: Cartwright Education Association (past presdient); Phi Kappa Delta; Arizona School Administrators; Arizona Education Association. Community Activities: Phoenix Maryale Rotary (past president); Masons; Shrine; American Federation of Police; Odd Fellows; Hump Pilots Association; American Police Hall of Fame. Religion: Central Methodist Church. Honors and Awards: Air Force Air Medal, Distinguished Flying Cross, Presidential Citation; Listed in *Who's Who in Administration, Who's Who in the West, Men and Women of Distinction, Community Leaders of America.* Address: 2252 N. 55th Avenue, Phoenix, Arizona 85035.

Blackall, Willard Thomas

Mechanical Engineer. Personal: Born March 5, 1934; Son of Willard T. and Mae Hansen Blackall; Married; Father of Troy, Sheri, Ron, John, Veronica, Kelly, Shannon. Education: Attended Centennary College, 1958-59; A.B., Louisiana State University, 1960; B.S.M.E. 1979, B.S.B.A 1979, Columbia Pacific University; Kellog Fellow, Pennsylvania State University, 1972-73. Military: Served in the United States Naval Reserve, 1952-60. Career: Area Foreman, Betty Engineering Company, 1965-69; Project Superintendent,

United Association of Plumbers and Stm. Filters, Williamsport, Pennsylvania, 1969-73; Project Manager, Louis N. Picciano Sr. Corporation, Endicott, New York, 1973-79; Consulting Engineer, Thunder Projects, Johnson City, New York, 1979-80; Facilities Planning Engineer, E. I. duPont, Towanda, Pennsylvania, 1980 to present. Community Activities: Towanda Area School Board (president, 1979-81); Lions Club (3rd vice president, 1981-82); Bradford County Vocational Technical Board (vice chairman, 1976-80); Bradford County Extension Long Range Planning (advisory board, 1973-75); Bradford County Republican Committee; Presidential Appointment, United States Selective Service Board, Bradford County, 1981 to present; Parents and Educators Committee on Education (past vice president and chairman); Masonic Bodies - Scottish Rite 32°, Shriners (past master, Evergreen Lodge); Benevolent and Protective Order of the Elks; Miscellaneous Fund Raisers for County and Local Agencies; Boro Council, Towanda Education Board (advisory committee, 1980-81). Religion: Towanda First Presbyterian Church; Vice Chairman and Chairman, Stewardship Committee, 1981-82. Honors and Awards: Bicentennial Award, Pennsylvania School Boards, 1976; Outstanding Citizenship Award, Pennsylvania State Legislature, 1975; American Patriot Award, 1976; Listed in *Who's Who in the East, Men of Achievement, Personalities of America.* Address: Route 1 Box 187, Monroeton, Pennsylvania 18832.

Blackwell, F Oris

Professor of Environmental Health. Personal: Born February 27, 1925; Son of Floyd W. and Mary Noel Blackwell (both deceased); Married Eleanor L. Edwards; Father of Susan, Betsy, Mary Ruth, Stephen. Education: B.S., Washington State University, 1950; M.S., University of Massachusetts, 1954; M.P.H. 1965, D.P.H. 1969, University of California-Berkeley School of Public Health. Military: Served in the United States Navy, 1943-46, 1950-52. Career: Professor and Chairman, Department of Environmental Health Science, Eastern Kentucky University; Formerly, Professor of Environmental Health, East Carolina University; Associate Professor of Community Medicine, University of Vermont; Associate Professor of Environmental Science, Rutgers University; Assistant Professor and Acting Chairman, Department of Environmental Health, American University of Beirut; Environmental Health Advisor, Government of Pakistan; Sanitarian, Benton-Franklin District Health Department, Pasco, Washington. Organizational Memberships: National Environmental Health Association (president, 1975-76); American Academy of Sanitarians (founder, diplomate; board of directors, 174-78); American Public Health Association (sanitation section council, 1980); International Health Society, Inc. Community Activities: Human Relations Council, East Brunswick, New Jersey (president, 1970); N.I.H. (public health review committee, 1971-73); Red Oak Church Boy Scout Troop 228, Greenville, North Carolina (scoutmaster, 1975-76); Mayor's Committee on Environment, Greenville, 1981. Religion: Religious Society of Friends (Quaker). Honors and Awards: Harry R. H. Nicholas Award for Excellence, New Jersey Association of Sanitarians, 1970; Certificate of Merit, National Environmental Health Association, 1970; Certificate of Appreciation, Virginia Environmental Health Association, 1979. Address: 905 Vickers Village, Richmond, Kentucky 40475.

F Oris Blackwell

Blais, Bernard Raymond

Ophthalmologist. Personal: Born September 19, 1931; Married Claire Aileen; Father of Stephanie Aileen, Kristine Frances. Education: B.S. cum laude, Chemistry, St. Michael's College, Winooski Park, Vermont, 1953; M.D., College of Medicine, University of Vermont and State Agriculture College, Burlington, 1958; Internship, Naval Hospital, Portsmouth, Virginia, 1959; Residency, Ophthalmology, Naval Hospital, Philadelphia, Pennsylvania, 1964; Fellowship, Ophthalmic Pathology, Armed Forces Institute of Pathology, 1968. Military: Service as Captain in the United States Navy. Career: Ophthalmologist, United States Navy. Organizational Memberships: American Medical Association; Society of Military Ophthalmologists (treasurer); American Association of Ophthalmology; Joint Commission on Allied Health Personnel in Ophthalmology (vice president); Association for Research in Vision and Ophthalmology; Association of Military Surgeons of the United States; Society of Medical Consultants to the Armed Forces; American College of Surgeons (fellow). Community Activities: Civitan International, Inc. Religion: Holy Name Society. Honors and Awards: Navy Commendation Medal, 1977; Navy Unit Citation Medal, 1968; National Defense Medal with Bronze Star for Vietnam; National Defense Medal. Address: 15017 Emory Lane, Rockville, Maryland 20853.

Blakely, Martha Cross

Pianist, Teacher. Personal: Born January 30, 1952; Son of Judge Charles B. Jr. and Eleanor Phillips Cross; Married Richard Vance Blakely. Education: B.Mus. 1974, M.Mus. (in progress), University of Cincinnati College Conservatory of Music. Career: Pianist; Teacher of Piano. Organizational Memberships: Washington, D.C. Music Teachers Association (corresponding secretary, 1979-80); Music Teachers National Association; Virginia Music Teachers Association; Mu Phi Epsilon (executive board, Washington, D.C. alumnae chapter, 1976-80); National Guild of Piano Teachers. Community Activities: Piano Recital, Barker Hall, Washington, D.C., 1979; Piano Soloist, Alexandria Showcase Concert, Sponsored by the Performing Arts Council, Alexandria, Virginia, 1978; Piano Recital, Fairfax County Library Recital Series, 1978. Honors and Awards: University Graduate Scholarship in Piano, University of Cincinnati College Conservatory of Music, 1980; Listed in *Personalities of the Midwest.* Address: 320 Kemp Lane, Chesapeake, Virginia 23325.

Blakely, William H Jr

Corporate Manager. Personal: Born February 12, 1927, in Warren, Ohio; Married Marcelle Wallace; Father of Twins. Education: B.S. with honors, North Carolina A&T University; Undertook Graduate Studies, Rutgers University. Military: Served in the United States Army Transporation Corps, 1946-48. Career: Athletic Director, Club Director, Senior Divisional Supervisor, Acting Executive Director, Director of Community Organization, University Settlement, New York City, 1952-62; Evening Director, Lillian Wald Recreation Rooms Settlement, 1963-64; Director, Urban League Skills Bank, 1964-67 (first in country); Industrial Relations Representative, Engelhard Industries, 1967-73; Corporate Manager, Employee Relations, Engelhard Minerals and Chemicals Corporation, 1973-81; Corporate Manager, Employee Relations, Phibro Corporation, 1981 to present. Organizational Memberships: Sigma Rho Sigma (president, 1950-52); Omega Psi Phi. Community Activities: North Carolina A&T State University (chancellor's council); Chamber of Commerce (regional urban affairs committee); E.D.G.E.S. (executive committee); Businessmen in Newark, New Jersey (community affairs group); Kessler Institute for Rehabilitation (board of trustees); United Negro College Fund (New Jersey state corporations committee); Urban League of Essex County (past president; board of directors); West Kenney Junior High School Scholarship Fund (vice president); Leaguers Inc. (president of board of directors); Grand Street Boys Association; Commissioner of Juries, Essex County (first black), 1968-75. Honors and Awards: Outstanding Athlete in his Graduating Class, Alumni Chapter; Honors from the United Community Corporation, Union County Urban League, A&T State University Alumni Association, Field Orientation Center for the Underprivileged Spanish, Leaguers; Frontiersmen of America Achievement Award, 1974; Black Achievers in Industry Award, 1975; Made a Member of Century Club, Young Men's Christian Association, 1972; A&T State University Alumni Award, 1978; North Carolina A&T State University Athletic Hall of Fame, 1978; Project Pride Award,

1979; F.O.C.U.S. Award; New Community Corporation Awards, Groundbreaking Ceremony for "New Community Gardens"; Essex County Urban League Guild's Humanitarian Award, 1980; Brotherhood Award, New Jersey State National Conference of Christians and Jews, 1981; Larrie Stalk's Civic Association Award, 1981; Listed in *Who's Who in American Colleges and Universities, Who's Who Among Black Americans, Who's Who in Finance and Industry, Men of Achievement, Community Leaders and Noteworthy Americans, International Who's Who of Intellectuals, Book of Honor.* Address: 6 North Cobane Lane, West Orange, New Jersey 07052.

Blanchard, Danny

College Professor. Personal: Born April 11, 1949; Son of Louise Blanchard; Married Deborah Hamilton; Father of Lashanice. Education: B.A., Oakwood College, 1971; M.A., Loma Linda University, 1973; Ed.S. 1976, Ph.D. 1980, Vanderbilt University. Military: United States Army Personnel. Career: College Professor; Former Psychologist, Probation Department, Riverside, California. Organizational Memberships: American Personnel and Guidance Association; A.P.A. Community Activities: Huntsville Human Relations Counsel; Huntsville Rural Senior Services (president, board); Oakwood College Alumni Association (vice president). Religion: Seventh Day Adventist, Church School Teacher. Honors and Awards: United States Army Letter of Commendation, 1978. Address: 11007 Rockcliff Drive, Huntsville, Alabama 45801.

Bland-Schricker, Laurel LeMieux

Executive and Author. Personal: Born February 23, 1926, in Spokane, Washington; Daughter of Alfred T. and Bernice K. Lawrence LeMieux; Married Frank H. Schricker in Alaska in 1976; Mother of Laurel K. Bland Eisinger, Daniel M. Bland. Education: A.A., Anchorage Community College, 1966; B.Ed., cum laude, 1968, M.A., 1969, both from University of Alaska; Undertook postgraduate studies at the University of Alaska and the Hebrew University in Israel; Ph.D., University of New Mexico, 1974. Career: Pioneer in the Initiation and Development of Supportive Strategies for Cultural Heritage Documentation and Preservation by and for the Northern Eskimos of Alaska; Known for Landmark Studies Related to the Special Learning Skills of the American Indian and Eskimo Children; Alaska Legal Sevices Liaison, 2nd Judicial District, 1967-68; Consultant to State and Federal Government Agencies, local cities and communities, American Indian Organizations, Alaska Native Villages and Organizations, 1964 to present; Director-Special Historical & Cultural Inventory of Seward Peninsula, Alaska, 1968 to present; Associate Professor, University of Alaska, 1974; Faculty, Alaska Methodist University, 1969-73; Professor, Sheldon Jackson College, Sitka, Alaska, 1975; President and Director, Human Environmental Resources Services, 1969 to present. Organizational Memberships: Arctic Institute of North America; Society of Intercultural Education; Alaska Historical Society; National Indian Education Association; Society for Indian & Northern Education. Community Activities: Sheldon Jackson College Adjunct Faculty (lifetime professor-crosscultural education, 1975); Inducted into the Yakutat Tlinget Indian Tribe, 1975; University of Alaska (fellowship, 1968-69); Brookings Institute Alaska Seminar (legislative appointee, 1969); Named into Kaweramuit Eskimo Community, 1972. Published Works: *People of Kauwerak*, with William Oquilluk; *Northern Eskimo of Alaska; Alaska Native Population & Manpower*, volumes 1, 2 & 3; *Manpower Needs to Construct the Transalaska Pipeline;* Contributor of articles of general interest to various journals; Most of her scholarly articles are on file with the United States Office of Education E.R.I.C./C.R.E.S.S. National Repository. Honors and Awards: Listed in *Who's Who of American Women, Who's Who in the West, Men and Women of Distinction, Personalities of the West and Midwest, Directory of Distinguished Americans, Community Leaders of America, The World Who's Who of Women.* Address: 1921 West 17th, Kennewick, Washington 99336.

Laurel L Bland-Schricker

Blank, Marion Sue

Professor, Consultant. Personal: Born December 20, 1933, in New York City, New York; Married Martin Blank; Mother of Donna, Jonathan, Ari. Education: B.A. 1955, M.S.Ed. 1956, City College of New York; Ph.D., Cambridge University, 1961. Career: Professor, Department of Psychiatry, College of Medicine and Dentistry of New Jersey, Rutgers Medical School, 1973 to present; Consultant, National Advisory Committee of the Frank Porter Graham Child Development Center, Chapel Hill, North Carolina, 1980 to present; Consultant, Maternal and Child Health Committee, National Institute of Child Health and Human Development, 1980 to present; Consultant, Committee on Developmental Pediatrics, William T. Grant Foundation, 1978 to present; Lecturer, Department of Psychiatry, College of Physicians and Surgeons, Columbia University, 1980; Professor of Psychology, Graduate Faculty, Rutgers University, and Director, Reading Disabilities Research Institute, Rutgers Medical School, 1979; Visiting Professor, Thomas Coram Research Unit, University of London, 1974-75; Consultant, Vrije Universiteit, Amsterdam, Holland, 1973-76; Consultant, Hamilton College of Education, Hamilton, Lanarkshire, Scotland, 1973-74; Visiting Research Fellow, The Open University, Milton Keynes, England, 1975; Associate Professor, Department of Psychiatry, Albert Einstein College of Medicine, 1970-73; Visiting Professor, John Dewey School of Education, Hebrew University, 1970; Consultant, "Sesame Street", 1968; Assistant Professor 1965-70, Instructor 1962-65, Department of Psychiatry, Albert Einstein College of Medicine; Visiting Professor, Hebrew University, Jerusalem, 1966; Pre-Doctoral Research Fellow, Department of Psychiatry, Albert Einstein College of Medicine, New York, Instructor, Graduate Psychology Faculty, Yeshiva University, 1960-61; Clinical Psychologist, Child Psychiatric Clinic, Cambridge, England, 1958; Psychologist, Vocational Advisory Service, New York, 1957; Remedial Reading Clinician, Brooklyn College Community Counseling Center, Brooklyn, 1956-57; Teaching Assistant, University of California-Berkeley, 1956; Fellow, Department of Education, City College of New York, 1955-56. Organizational Memberships: American Psychological Association; Eastern Psychological Association; Society for Research in Child Development; Orton Society; American Educational Research Association; Editor, *Modern Approaches to Learning Disabilities*, Swets Publishing, Holland, 1977 to present; Editoral Board, Behavioral and Brain Sciences, 1976 to present; Editorial Board, *Child Development*, 1967 to present; Guest Editor, *Development Psychology, Journal of Experimental Child Psychology, Journal of Educational Psychology, Journal of Applied Psycholinguistics*, 1967 to present; Editorial Board, *Applied Psycholinguistics*, 1980 to present; Editorial Board, *Topics in Learning and Learning Disabilities*, 1981 to present. Published Works: Author *Teaching in the Preschool: A Dialogue Approach;* Co-Author *The Language of Learning: The Preschool Years, Preschool Language Assessment Instrument: The Language of Learning in Practice;* Number of Chapters in Professional Publications, Journal Articles, Book Reviews. Honors and Awards: Award of Commendation, New Jersey Speech and Hearing Association, 1979; Elwyn Morey Memorial Lecturer, Monash University, Clayton, Australia, 1979; United States Public Health Service Career Development Award, 1965-73; Pre-Doctoral Fellowship, Albert Einstein College of Medicine, 1960-61; United States Public Health Pre-Doctoral Fellowship, 1959; Pinsent-Darwin Fellowship, Cambridge University, England, 1957-59; New York State Scholarship, 1954-55. Address: 171 Van Nostrand Avenue, Englewood, New Jersey 07631.

Blankenship, Douglas P

Executive. Personal: Born November 13, 1944; Son of H. and B. Blankenship; Married Amelia A. Education: B.A., Eastern Kentucky

University, 1964; M.A. Administration 1966, M.A. Transportation 1967, University of Kentucky, 1966; Post-Graduate Studies, University of California-Los Angeles; Ph.D., Ohio State University, 1969. Military: R.O.T.C., 1961-64. Career: President, Pacific Coast Development Company, 1977 to present; Vice President, National Research Corporation, 1976-77; Transportation Researcher, Orange County Transit District, 1973-76; Senior Transportation Research, General Motors, 1967-71; Associate Researcher, University of Kentucky, 1966-67; High School Instructor, Pike County School System, 1964-66. Organizational Memberships: American Marketing Association; American Institute of Planners; American Society of Planning Officials; Association of American Geographers; Southern California Marketing Association; Mensa; National Academy of Sciences (transporation research board); Urban and Regional Information Systems Association; Los Angeles Geographical Society; *Mass Transit; Graphic Arts Monthly; Journal of Transporation.* Community Activities: System Task Force for Transit; Citizen Advisory Committee; Modeling Task Force; Civic Petitions in Kentucky; Democratic Party; Impact Task Force; University of Kentucky Alumni Association (vice president, Southern California chapter). Published Works: "The Soviet Union - Expansion at Any Cost", "Theories of World Power and Control", "Multivariate Analysis of Power -A Ten Nation Study", "Human Freedom and Existentialism", Others. Honors and Awards: Creativity Recognition Award, 1972; Enoch Grehan Journalism Award, 1964; Electronic Musical Award, 1969; Mensa Membership Award, 1969; Outstanding Recognition in Strategic and Guerrilla War Gaming, 1968; Developed a Stereo Tape Injection System, 1968; Developed an Audio-File, Computerized Parts Number Identification System with Horizontal Master Computerized Progrm for Inventory Volume Control and Card Selection, 1968; Kappa Iota Epsilon; Omicron Alpha Kappa; Kentucky Colonel, 1977; Listed in *Who's Who in the West, Outstanding Young Men of America, Men of Achievement, Creative and Noteworthy Americans, Who's Who in Government, Community Leaders and Noteworthy Americans, Creative and Successful Personalities, Notable Americans.* Address: 448 S. Alexandria Avenue, Los Angeles, California 90020.

Blanton, Fred

Attorney. Personal: Born July 2, 1919, in Muscle Shoals, Alabama; Married Mercer P. McAvoy. Education: A.B. cum laude, Birmingham-Southern College, 1939; LL.B. 1942, J.D. 1970, University of Virginia Law School; Cook Fellowship, University of Michigan Law School, 1951; LL.M., University of Alabama Law School, 1979. Military: Served in the United States Naval Reserve, attaining the rank of Commander. Career: Private Law Practice, Birmingham, Alabama, 1946-48; Instructor, Birmingham-Southern College, 1947-48; Professor of Law, Dickinson School of Law, 1948-49; Visiting Professor of Law, University of Alabama Law School, Summer 1949; Assistant Professor of Law, University of Virginia Law School, 1949-51; Associated with Martin & Blakey, Lawyers, Birmingham, 1951-54; Private General Law Practice, Birmingham, 1954 to present. Organizational Memberships: Admitted to Supreme Court of the United States, United States Court of Appeals for the District of Columbia Circuit, United States Court of Appeals for the Fifth Circuit, United States Court of Claims, United States Tax Court, United States District Courts - Northern, Middle and Southern Districts of Alabama, Courts-Martial under the Uniform Code of Military Justice; Alabama State Bar Association (committee on code revision, 1975-76; advisory committee on continuing legal education, 1979-81); American Society of E.E.G. Technologists (general counsel until 1980). Community Activities: Jefferson County Republican Executive Committee; General Gorgas Post #1, American Legion; Kelly Ingram Post #668, Veterans of Foreign Wars. Religion: Episcopal Church of the Advent. Published Works: "The Federal Tort Claims Act in Action", "Two More Years of the Federal Tort Claims Act", "Special Damage as an Element in Defamation Actions in Alabama", "Juvenile Courts and the Constitutional Rights of Minors", Others. Address: P.O. Box 569, Fultondale, Alabama 35068.

Alfred J Blasco

Blasco, Alfred Joseph

Business and Finance Consultant; Bank Executive. Personal: Born October 9, 1904, in Kansas City, Missouri; Son of Joseph and Mary Bevacqua Blasco; Married Kathryn Oleno, June 29, 1926; Father of Barbara Blasco Mehrer, Phyllis Blasco O'Connor. Education: Attended Kansas City School of Accountancy, 1921-25 and American Institute of Banking, 1926-30; Ph.D. (honorary), Avila College, 1969. Career: Office Boy to Assistant Controller, Commerce Trust Company, Kansas City, 1921-35; Interstate Securities Company, Kansas City: Controller (1935-45), Vice President (1945-53), President (1953 to present), Chairman of the Board (1961-68); I.S.C. Finance Corporation: Senior Vice President (1968-69), Honorary Chairman of the Board (1970-77), President (1979 to present); Chairman of the Board, Red Bridge Bank, 1966-72; Chairman of the Board, Mark Plaza State Bank, Overland Park, Kansas, 1973-77; Special Lecturer, Consumer Credit, Columbia University, New York City, 1956, and University of Kansas-Lawrence, 1963-64. Organizational Memberships: American Industrial Bankers Association (president, 1956-57); American Institute Banking (chapter president, 1932-33); Bank Auditors and Controllers Association; Finance Executives Institute (chapter president, 1928-29); National Association of Accountants. Community Activities: Fair Public Accomodations Committee, Kansas City, 1964-68; Catholic Community Library (president, 1955-56); Ward Committeeman, Kansas City, 1972-76; Baptist Memorial Hospital (president honorary board of directors, 1970-74); St. Anthony's Home (chairman of board of directors, 1965-69); Avila College (chairman of board of trustees, 1969 to present); Kansas City Chamber of Commerce; Rotary Club; Society of St. Vincent de Paul (president, 1959-67); Hillcrest County Club; Serra Club (president, 1959-60). Published Works: Contributor of articles to professional journals. Honors and Awards: Equestrian Order Holy Sepulchre of Jerusalem: Papal Knight (1957), Knight Commander (1964), Knight Grand Cross (1966), Lieutenant Northern Lieutenancy U.S. (1970-77), Vice Governor-General (1977 to present); Business Man of Year, State of Missouri, 1957; Man of Year, City of Hope, 1973; Recipient Community Service Award, Rockne Club Notre Dame, 1959; Brotherhood Award, N.C.C.J., 1979; Wisdom Aawrd of Honor, 1979; Listed in *Who's Who in America.* Address: 8080 Ward Parkway, Kansas City, Missouri 64114.

Blazer, Dan German II

Psychiatrist. Personal: Born February 23, 1944; Son of Mrs. Dan G. Blazer; Married Sherrill Walls; Father of Dan German III, Natasha Leigh. Education: B.A., Vanderbilt University, 1965; Work toward M.A., Harding Graduate School of Religion, 1966; M.D., Tennessee College of Medicine, 1969; M.P.H., University of North Carolina, 1979; Ph.D., University of North Carolina-Chapel Hill, 1980. Career: Psychiatrist, Duke University Medical Center; Former Director, Christian Mobile Clinic, United Republic of Cameroon. Organizational Memberships: Gerontological Society; Christian Medical Society; American Psychiatric Society; American Psychosomatics Society; Southern Medical Association; Southern Psychiatric Association; American Geriatrics Society; American Association for the Advancement of Science; North Carolina Neuropsychiatric Association; American Public Health Association; Society for Epidemiologic Research. Community Activities: African Christian Hospitals Association (board of directors). Religion: Brooks Avenue Church of Christ (Raleigh, North Carolina), Deacon 1979 to present; Missionary, United Republic of Cameroon, 1970-72. Honors and Awards: National Research Award, Public Health Service; Senior Fellow, Duke University Center for the Study of Aging and Human Development; Research Science Development Award, National Institute of Mental Health; Diplomate, American Board of Psychiatry and Neurology; Delta Omega; Sigma Xi; American College of Psychiatrists; Listed in *Who's Who in the South and Southwest.* Address: 408 Farmington Woods Drive, Cary, North Carolina 27511.

Blend, Henrietta B

Instructional Supervisor. Personal: Born March 10, 1924; Daughter of Max and Sarah Boronstein (both deceased); Married Jake Blend; Mother of Stanley Louis, Stuart Marvin, Sharon Renee Blend Schomburg, Susan Michelle Blend Willis. Education: B.Ed. 1961, M.Ed. 1963, University of Houston; Ed.D., Pacific Western University, 1981; Graduate Study, Texas Southern University, Sam Houston State University, University of New Hampshire, University of Colorado, University of Houston. Career: Instructional Specialist; Former Classroom Teacher, Principal, Editor of *Voice of the Village* Newspaper. Organizational Memberships: Houston Teachers Association (past president); Texas Classroom Teachers Association (past president); Texas State Teachers Association (human relations committee); National Council on Accreditation of Teacher Education (evaluation board); National Education Association (secretary); Texas Education Agency (board of examiners; aerospace aviation education council). Community Activities: United Fund (budget panel); Park Commissioner, Town of the Village; University of Houston Alumni Board; Civil Air Patrol. Religion: Congregation Beth Israel, Houston, Sisterhood Member. Honors and Awards: Franklin Award; Linz Award; Everts Award; Faculty Wives Scholarship. Address: 10419 Greenwillow Drive, Houston, Texas 77035.

Blevins, Dallas Ray

Associate Professor of Finance. Personal: Born December 22, 1938; Son of Virgil James and Mary Birtha Blevins; Married Lois Eunice Stalvey; Father of Deborah Lynn, Teresa Lee, Jennifer Kay. Education: Bachelor of General Education, University of Omaha, 1965; M.B.A., University of South Florida, 1968; D.B.A., Florida State University, 1976. Military: Served in the United States Air Force, 1958-69, advancing from Aviation Cadet to Captain. Career: Assistant/Associate Professor of Finance, University of Montevallo, 1982 to present; Assistant Professor of Finance, University of North Florida, 1979-82; Assistant Professor of Finance, University of Alabama-Birmingham, 1976-79; Assistant Professor of Finance, Valdosta State College, 1970-74. Community Activities: Birmingham Regional Hospital Council (member two finance committees, 1978-79); North Florida Regional Health Systems Agency (board of directors, 1979 to present); American Society of Military Comptrollers (advisor to education committee, 1980 to present). Religion: Active as a Preacher and Teacher, Various Congregations of the Church of Christ. Honors and Awards: Academic Scholarship to Eastern New Mexico University for Excellence in High School Mathematics; Commendation for High Grade Point, University of Utah 1962, University of South Florida 1969; Outstanding Contributions Award, Squadron Officers School of the Air University, 1965; Officially Classified Among the Top Five Percent of All Air Force Fighter Pilots, One of Five Outstanding Young Men Selected by the Valdosta, Georgia, Junior Chamber of Commerce, 1971; Ayres Fellow to the Stonier Graduate School of Banking, 1981; Certificate of Outstanding Service to the American Society of Military Comptrollers, 1981; Certified Cost Analyst, 1982. Address: 124 Oak Street, Montevallo, Alabama 35115.

Blicksilver, Edith Helen

Associate Professor of English. Personal: Born January 6, 1926, in New York City, New York; Daughter of Simon and Fanny Stettner (both deceased); Married Jack Blicksilver, June 27, 1948; Mother of Paul, Diane, Robert. Education: B.A., Queens College, 1947; M.A., Smith College, 1948. Career: Lecturer in History and English, Smith College, Northampton, Massachusetts, 1947-48; Professor of English, Southern State Teachers College, Springfield, South Dakota, 1953-54; Instructor of English, Northeastern University, Boston, 1962-63; Associate Professor of English, Georgia Institute of Technology, 1961-62, 1963 to present. Organizational Memberships: Multi-Ethnic Literary Society of the United States (secretary); College English Association (president, Georgia-South Carolina regional branch); American Association of University Women (corporate representative from Georgia Institute of Technology); Modern Language Association of America. Published Works: Author *The Ethnic American Woman: Problems, Protests, Lifestyle.* Honors and Awards: Grantee, Georgia Institute of Technology and the American Association of University Women; Winner, Best Non-Fiction Book Award of Year, Dixie Council of Authors and Journalists. Address; 1800 Timothy Drive, N.E., Atlanta, Georgia 30329.

Arlene D Blum

Blum, Arlene Diane

Instructor. Personal: Born March 1, 1945, in Davenport, Iowa. Education: B.A., Reed College, 1966; Undertook further study at Massachusetts Institute of Technology, 1966-67; Ph.D., University of California at Berkeley, 1971. Career: NSF Predoctoral Fellow, Massachusetts Institute of Technology, 1966-67; NIH Predoctoral Fellow, Department of Chemistry, University of California-Berkeley, 1968-71; NIH Postdoctoral Fellow, Stanford University Medical Center, 1973-76; Acting Assistant Professor, Department of Human Biology, Stanford University, 1975; Assistant Professor of Chemistry, Wellesley College, 1977; Consultant, Health and Safety Office of the Oil, Chemical and Atomic Workers Union ("Study of Reproductive Risk to Male Workers Exposed to Halogenated Chemicals"); Associate Specialist II, University of California-Berkeley, Department of Biochemistry; Instructor, "Cancer: Current Views on Cause and Prevention", University of California-Berkeley; Participant in many expeditions, including U.S.S.R. (Pamirs, Peak Lenin, to 22,000 feet), Nepal (Mt. Everest, to 24,500 feet), and Nepal, (Annapurna, first all-woman expedition, first American ascent, first ascent by a woman). Organizational Memberships: American Alpine Club (V.W.A.C.O. memorial fund committee); Rendez-vous Haute Montagne; American Women's Himalayan Expeditions (president, co-founder); Society of Women Geographers. Published Works: Mountain photographs published in *National Geographic, Viva,* New York *Times,* Washington *Post,* others; Variety of articles on her expeditions, including "First Climbs" (*Viva,* 1978) and "Two African Volcanoes" (*Summit,* July 1972); Co-Author of scientific articles including "Flame Retardant Additives as Possible Cancer Hazards" (*Science,* 1977) and "Temperature Jump NMR Study of Intermediates in Refolding of Ribonuclease" (*Biophysical Journal,* 1975); Senior Thesis, "Analysis of Fumarole Emanations from Mt. Hood, Oregon". Address: 3367 Dwight Way, Berkeley, California 94704.

Blumstein, James Franklin

Professor. Personal: Born April 24, 1945; Son of David and Rita Blumstein; Married Andree Kahn. Education: B.A., Yale College, 1966; M.A., Yale University, 1970; L.L.B., Yale Law School, 1970. Career: Professor of Law, Vanderbilt Law School, Nashville, Tennessee. Organizational Memberships: American Bar Association; Tennessee Bar Association; Association of American Law Schools (executive council of the section on local government law); Association for Public Policy Analysis and Management. Community Activities: Mayor's Commission on Crime, 1981; President's Commission for the Study of Ethical Problems in Medicine and Biomedical and Behavioral Research (consultant, 1981); Sixth Circuit Judicial Conference (program speaker, 1981); National Center for Health Care Technology Conference on Coronary Artery Bypass Surgery (program speaker, 1981); Health Economics Task Force, Middle Tennessee Health Systems Agency, 1980. Religion: Chairman, Community Relations Committee, Jewish Federation of Nashville and Middle Tennessee, 1980 to present; Board of Directors, Jewish Federation of Nashville and Middle Tennessee, 1980 to present. Honors and Awards: Listed in *Outstanding Young Men of the Year, Who's Who in American Law,*

International Who's Who in Education, International Who's Who of Intellectuals, Community Leaders of America, Directory of Distinguished Americans. Address: 2113 Hampton Ave., Nashville, Tennessee 37215.

Bocan, Carol Ann

Executive. Personal: Born November 5, 1937; Daughter of Ann Bocan. Education: B.S., Mercyhurst College, 1959; M.Ed., Pennsylvania State University, 1967; Ph.D., Florida State University, 1973. Career: President, Pinehedge Media Productions, Conneautville, Pennsylvania; Professor, Department Head, Utah State University, 1979-82; Associate Professor, Acting Chairman, Winthrop College, 1976-79; Assistant Professor, Area Coordinator, Northern Illinois University, 1971-76; Graduate Assistant, Florida State University, 1969-70; Instructor, Mercyhurst College, 1967-69; Color Consultant, Gold and Heidt, Architectural Firm, Summer 1968; Audio-Visual Director for School System and Science Teacher, Conneaut Valley Joint School District, Pennsylvania, 1966-67; Department Chairman, Home Economics Teacher, Azalea Junior High School, St. Petersburg, Florida, 1963-66; Television Producer and Talent and Home Economics Educator, Florida Power Corporation, 1961-63; Home Economics Teacher, H. B. Plant High School, Tampa, Florida, 1959-61. Organizational Memberships: American Vocational Association; Utah Vocational Association; South Carolina Vocational Association; American Home Economics Association (vice president for program development, 1980-82; chairman, program emphasis committee, 1980-82; board of directors and committee on committees, 1980-82; undergraduate commission committee, 1977-79; national program committee for state president's unit workshop and meeting, 1975-76); South Carolina Home Economics Association (state advisory, student member section, 1977-78; chairman, student education fund, 1977-78; delegate, American Home Economics Association convention, 1973-76); Illinois Home Economics Association (president, 1975-76; president-elect, 1974-75; executive board, 1973-74; state advisor, college student chapters, 1973-74; delegate, American Home Economics Association convention, 1973-76); Home Economics Education Association International Platform Association; American Council on Consumer Interests; North Central Evaluation Team, Arlington Heights High School, Illinois District 214, 1976; National Council on Family Relations (co-chairperson, program committee of the education section, 1974 annual meeting); American Association of University Women (state corporate representative, 1981-82; vice president in charge of membership, Logan Branch, 1980-81; education committee, Rock Hill Branch, 1977-78; executive board, DeKalb Branch, 1973-74); Business and Professional Women (educational chairman, Logan Branch, 1981-82). Published Works: Co-Author, Numerous Articles in Professional Journals. Honors and Awards: Phi Delta Kappa; Kappa Omicron Phi; Phi Lambda Theta; Certificate of Recognition for Contribution to the Promotion of Occupational and Career Education, State of Illinois and Nation, 1975; Special Recognition Given for Contribution to Mercyhurst and Erie Community, 1969; Salute from *Seventeen* Magazine, 1960; Listed in *Who's Who of American Women, World Who's Who of Women in Education.* Address: 521 Linesville Road, Conneautville, Pennsylvania 16406.

Boeder, Elizabeth W

Marketing/Promotion Consultant, Photographer. Personal: Born October 14, 1945; Daughter of Ethel O. Wegner. Education: B.S., Northwestern University, Medill School of Journalism, 1967; Practical Public Relations Course, Publicity Club of Chicago; Organizational Planning and Development, American Telephone and Telegraph. Career: Account Executive, Public Relations Director, Copy/Contact Coordinator, Beardsley and Company, William R. Biggs Associates, Hilltop Advertising, 8 years; Vice President, Audio Visual Film Productions, 2½ years; Supervision and Coordination of Public Relations and Publicity Programs, American Telephone and Telegraph, Borgess Hospital, 3 years; Publications Management, Illinois Pharmaceutical Association, Bank Public Relations Association, 3 years; Research Assistant, Marquis Who's Who; Positions with Association of College Admissions Counselors, Northwestern University, Kewaunee Enterprise/Enterprise Printing Company. Organizational Memberships: Women in Communications Theta Sigma Phi (professional membership, 1970; chairman, special publicity, 1970; outstate member, Chicago chapter, 1970-80); International Council of Industrial Editors, 1966-68; Professional and Executives Club of Kalamazoo (co-founder, 1978); Medical Society Executives of Greater Chicago, 1967-68; Industrial Editors Association of Chicago (vice president, 1970; editor, *Intercom*, 1970; treasurer, 1969; membership chairman, 1968; arrangement committee, annual institute committee, 1967; chairman, special events, 1967); Michigan Advertising Roundtable (advisor, program committee, 1977; board of directors, 1977-78; member, 1977-81); Industrial Marketers of West Michigan (treasurer, 1976-78; board of directors, 1978-79). Community Activities: Portage Economic Development Corporation (director, 1980 to present); Young Women's Christian Association of Kalamazoo (advisor, public relations and promotion committee, 1979-81); Distributive Education Clubs of America (professional advisor and judge, state and local competitions, 1976-82); "High on Kalamazoo" Air Show (advisor, promotion, Kalamazoo County Chamber of Commerce, 1981); Advisor, Betty Ongley for Mayor Committee, 1977; Betty Ongley for County Commissioner, 1980 Campaign; Promotion/Publicity Director, Tom Lonze for 47th District Representative, 1982 Campaign; Editor, Portage 2000 Committee Report, 1982 to present; Kalamazoo County Visitors and Convention Bureau (advisor to advertising and promotion committee, 1976-78). Honors and Awards: Recipient of Five Addy Awards 1977, Two Addy Awards 1976; Listed in *American Biographical Registry, Directory of Distinguished Americans, Who's Who of American Women.* Address: 3527 Scots Pine Way, Kalamazoo, Michigan 49002.

Gail Boger

Boger, Gail Parsons

Professor Emeritus. Personal: Daughter of Byron Tennyson and Bula Taylor Green (both deceased); Married Alva Bradley Parsons; 2nd marriage to Clarence O. Boger; Mother of Donald Alva Parsons, Robert Bradley Parsons, Gail Marie Parsons Michael, Helen Jean Parsons Czuba (all from first marriage); Donald C. Boger, Maxine Boger Rideout, Sandra Boger Plummer (stepchildren). Education: B.S., 1950, M.S., 1959, both from Indiana University; Ph.D., University of Utah, 1969; Undertook further studies at Ohio Northern University, Ohio State University, Purdue University, Universidad International (Santendar, Spain), Fresno State College; Dupont Fellow, Harvard University, 1957; Atomic Energy Commission Fellowship, Duke University, 1960; N.S.F. Fellowship, Indiana University, 1961, 1963. Career: Instructor, Fresno State Junior College, 1948-54; Assistant Professor, Purdue Extension, Michigan City, Indiana, 1955-58; Teacher, Junior-Senior High School, Michigan City, 1954-59; Instructor, Indiana University, Bloomington, 1959-64; Professor, Department of Education, Ohio Northern University, 1964-80; Professor Emeritus, Ohio Northern University. Organizational Memberships: American Association Supervision and Curriculum Development; National Association for Education of Gifted (secretary-treasurer, vice president); Kappa Delta Pi; Kappa Sigma Pi; American Association of University Professors; Ohio Education Association; National Education Association; Indiana State Teachers Association; Ohio Association of Gifted Children; National Association for the Advancement of Science; Ohio Academy of Science; Indiana Academy of Science. Community Activities: Northern Indiana Science Fair Program (director, 1955-59); Gifted Children's Study Club (founder, president, 1956-59); Children's International Summer Villages Inc. (founder of 3 of 10 chapters in U.S., 1958-70, national board of trustees, chairman of national research committee, chairman of international research committee, delegate to first village in Denmark, dedicatory address to first village in Africa); 1 of 150 Liberal Arts School Professors chosen to participate in "Business Tomorrow" Conference, Princeton University, 1974; National Association for Creative Children and Adults (national board member). Religion: Episcopal. Honors and Awards: Honored at Indiana University, 1965, at dedication of the Children's

International Summer Villages, Indiana, for having founded more villages than any person in U.S. or other country; Listed in publications of the American Biographical Institute and *Who's Who of Women of The World.* Address: 1703 Wonderlick Rd., Lima, Ohio 45805.

Boghosian, Paula Johanna

Principal Historic Environment Consultant, Architectural Historian and Preservation Planner. Personal: Born February 14, 1934; Daughter of Cecil G. Sorgatz; Married; Mother of Gregory, Michael. Education: B.A., University of California-Berkeley, 1959; Graduate Studies in Education, Junior High School Teaching Credential, Secondary Teaching Credential, California State University, Sacramento, 1961-62; Attended the Attingham School, Royal Oaks Foundation, Great Britain, 1981. Career: Architectural Design and Drafting, Franklin Design Service, Safeway Stores, 1955; Junior High School Instructor, Art and English, Sacramento City Unified School District, 1962; Graphics and Free-lance Commercial Art, 1971-77; Lectures, Historic Architecture and Preservation, University of California Extension, California State University-Sacramento Extension, National Trust for Historic Preservation, 1974-81; Administrator, National Register of Historic Places, California State Historical Landmarks Programs, State of California Office of Historical Preservation, 1976. Organizational Memberships: American Association of University Women (national board of directors, cultural interests representative, 1973-76; education foundation, 1973-76); National Trust for Historic Preservation; Society of Architectural Historians; California Historical Society. Community Activities: Sacramento County Grand Jury (chairman, education committee, 1968); Sacramento City Preservation Board (chairman, 1975-78); Sacramento Heritage, Inc. (chairman, 1975-78); Cityscape, Inc. (grants officer, 1980-82); Kingsley Art Club (board of directors, 1976-79); KVIE (art auction chairperson, 1972). Published Works: Author *Vanishing Victorians.* Honors and Awards: Historic Preservation Citation Award, Sacramento County Historical Society, 1971; Rosalie Stern Award, $500, University of California Alumni Association, 1972; Woman of the Year, California Council, Women's Architectural League, 1973; Listed in *Women's Organizations and Leaders Directory, Who's Who of American Women.* Address: 417 33rd Street, Sacramento, California 95816.

Judy A Boling

Bohning, Elizabeth E

Professor. Personal: Born June 26, 1915; Married William H. Bohning; Mother of Barbara B. Young, Margaret B. Anderson. Education: B.A., Wellesley College, 1936; M.A. 1938, Ph.D. 1943, Bryn Mawr College. Career: Chairman 1971-78, Professor, Department of Language and Literature, University of Delaware. Organizational Memberships: Delaware Humanities Council (vice chairman, 1980-82); Middle States Association of Schools and Colleges (trustee, 1974-80); Delta Phi Alpha (president, 1972); Middle States Association of Modern Language Teachers (president, 1964); American Association of Teachers of German (national contest chairman, 1960-68; national executive council, 1965; chapter president, 1974-75); Phi Kappa Phi (chapter president, 1981-82); Phi Beta Kappa. Community Activities: Delaware Council on International Visitors (president); Delaware Humanities Forum (chairman, project review committee, 1980-82; executive committee, 1980-83); Alpha Chi Omega; Delaware Wellesley Club; Delaware Bryn Mawr Club. Religion: St. Thomas Church. Honors and Awards: Lindback Award for Excellence in Teaching; Phi Beta Kappa; Pi Beta Phi; Goethe Institute and American Association of Teachers of German Certificate of Merit, 1982. Address: Box 574, Newark, Delaware 19711.

Bolen, William Harold

Professor, Administrator, Author, Consultant. Personal: Born February 24, 1943; Son of Harold Jean and Lucy Jane Huggins Bolen; Married Sheron Lee Smith; Father of William H. Jr., Charles Henry. Education: B.S., Georgia Southern College, 1964; M.B.A., 1966, and Ph.D., 1972, both from University of Arkansas. Career: Georgia Southern College: Professor of Marketing (1979 to present), Head of Department of Marketing/Office Administration (1973 to present), Graduate Faculty (1973 to present), Associate Professor (1973-79), Assistant Professor (1966-73). Organizational Memberships: American Marketing Association; American Collegiate Retailing Association; Southern Marketing Association; American Academy of Advertising; Southwest Marketing Association; Georgia Association of Marketing Educators; Pi Sigma Epsilon; Delta Sigma Pi; Others. Community Activities: Statesboro-Bulloch County Chamber of Commerce (retail/service task force 1978-80, college relations task force 1979-80); Economic Outlook Conference Speaker, Georgia Southern and Chamber of Commerce, 1980, 1981; Judge, Various Speaking Contests for Civic Clubs; Speaker on various topics to local organizations. Published Works: *Advertising,* 1981; *Contemporary Retailing,* 1978, 1982; articles on retailing subjects (chain store, department store, discount store, franchise, mail-order house, retailing, supermarket), *World Book;* numerous other publications. Honors and Awards: Very Important Professor, Specialty Advertising Association, 1979; Kiplinger Fellow, Direct Mail/Marketing Association, 1978; Free Enterprise Fellow, Georgia Chamber of Commerce, 1975; Certified Advertising Specialist, Specialty Advertising Association & Case Western Reserve, 1968; Beta Gamma Sigma, 1966; Listed in 12 biographical reference publications. Address: Country Club Estates, Statesboro, Georgia 30458.

Clifton J Bolner

Boling, Judy Atwood

Volunteer Civic Worker. Personal: Born June 19, 1921; Daughter of Frances A. Holdeman; Married Jack L. Boling; Mother of Joseph Edward, Jean Ann Boling Stabile, James Michael, John Charles. Education: A.A., San Antonio Junior College, 1940; Continuing college courses in psychology, anthropology, adult education and management. Career: Trainer, Girl Scouts, 1956 to present; Consultant for Girl Scout Badge Handbook; Staff Member, Girl Scout National Event. Community Activities: Winema Council Girl Scouts (president 1971-73, member 1971-73 and 1979 to present); National Council Delegate, 1966, 1972, 1981; American Red Cross, 1941-46, 1957-65; Jap-American, Franco-American, Anglo-American (liaison person); Fukuoka Women's Club (president); Rogue Craftsmen Board (secretary, vice president, 1972 to present); Rogue Valley Opera Association (board member, secretary, 1978 to present); Community Concert (board member 1979 to present); Public Speaker in schools, clubs, home extension annual meet, colleges, television, 1955 to present; Civil Defense Aircraft Spotter, 1956. Religion: Sunday School Teacher, 1951-57; Administrator, 1953-55; Choir member and Choir Director, 1951-52. Honors and Awards: Thanks Badge, Girl Scouts, U.S.A. 1957, 1960, 1973; Thanks Badge, Girl Scouts, Japan, 1959; Red Cross Recognition; United States Air Force Certificate of Appreciation, 1959; Honors from the City of Hagi, Japan and the City of Fukuoka, Japan, 1959; National Citation, International Book Project, 1975, 1979; Nominated Woman of the Year; Phi Theta Kappa; Listed in *Who's Who of American Women.* Address: 3016 Jumpoff Joe Creek Rd., Grants Pass, Oregon 97526.

Bolner, Clifton Joseph

Manufacturing Company Executive. Personal: Born July 30, 1928, in San Antonio, Texas; Son of Joe and Josephine Grandjean

Bolner; Married Rosalie Richter on January 20, 1949; Father of Tim, Mike, Deb, Cindy, Bev, Chris, Mary. Education: B.S., Distinguished Military Graduate, Texas Agriculture and Mechanical University, 1928. Military: First Lieutenant with the United States Air Force, 1950-52. Career: Partner, Bolner's Grocery & Meat Market, San Antonio, Texas, 1949-55; President, Bolner's Fiesta Products, Inc., San Antonio, 1955 to present. Organizational Memberships: Retail Division, Produce Marketing Association (member of the board, 1979 to present); American Spice Trade Association (membership committee, 1978-81); Community Activities: Catholic Family and Children's Services, San Antonio (president, 1968-69); San Antonio Archdiocese (chairman of the finance committee, 1978-79); NCCJ (chairman annual awards dinner, 1974); San Antonio Symphony Society (board of directors, 1973 to present); San Antonio Music Association, 1973 to present; Opera Superman, 1975 to present; San Antonio Muscular Dystrophy Association, 1975 to present; Incarnate Word College (member of the development board, 1974 to present); San Antonio Representative to NCCJ, 1978 to present; San Antonio Right to Life Committee (member of the board, 1980 to present); United Nations Annual Dinner Committee, 1980 to present; Exchange National Bank, San Antonio (founding board member, 1980 to present); St. Peter's Children's Home (advisory board, 1980 to present); Oblate Association; Association of Holy Family Guilds; San Antonio Serra Vocation Club, Italian-American Young Men's Club; St. Paul's Men's Club; Society of Mary Association. Religion: Roman Catholic, Our Lady of Grace Parish, Lector; Charter Member, Committee to bring back voluntary school prayer. Honors and Awards: Distinguished Alumni Award, Central High School, 1979; Archbishop Furey Outstanding Award Medal, 1969. Address: 110 W. Lynwood Street, San Antonio, Texas 78212.

Bolton, Robert Harvey

Bank Executive. Personal: Born June 19, 1908; Married Elizabeth McLundie; Father of Robert H. Jr., Elizabeth Hassinger (Mrs. Robert), Mary Jennings (Mrs. James Jr.). Education: Attended Culver Military Academy, Indiana, 1926; B.S., Wharton School of Finance and Commerce, University of Pennsylvania, 1930. Military: Served in the United States Navy, 1944-46, attaining the rank of Lieutenant. Career: Rapides Bank and Trust Company - Assistant Cashier 1932, Cashier 1936, Vice President 1943, Executive Vice President 1947, Director 1948, President 1956 to present. Organizational Memberships: Louisiana Bankers Association (president, 1950; legislative committee, 1950 to present; federal affairs committee, 1971 to present; executive management committee, 1981 to present); Louisiana Mortgage Bankers Association (president, 1952; legislative committee, 1952 to present); Federal Reserve Bank of Atlanta, New Orleans Branch (director, 1978-81); Mortgage Bankers Association (legislative committee, 1975 to present); American Bankers Association (past president, state bank division, 1955; executive council, 1953-70); Robert Morris Associates (life member; director, 1943-45); Conference of State Bank Supervisors (state representative, 1958-71). Community Activities: Industrial Development Board of Rapides Parish (president, 1975 to present); Industrial Development Board of Central Louisiana (director, 1974 to present); Central Cities Development Corporation (director, 1976 to present); Alexandria-Pineville Chamber of Commerce (president, 1965); Chamber of Commerce (chairman, aviation committee, 1965 to present); Rapides General Hospital (board of trustees, 1961-63; president, 1964-69); Alexandria Service League (finance committee, 1972-74); Louisiana State University Foundation, 1972-80; President's Club, Louisiana College; Loyola University, New Orleans (visiting committee); Attakapas Council Boy Scouts of America (council finance steering committee, 1972-81); Alexandria Rotary Club (president, 1942); United States Chamber of Commerce (finance committee, 1964-71); Rapides United Givers (board of directors, 1969-80); Council for a Better Louisiana (board of directors, 1968 to present); Mason (worshipful master, 1936); Kisatchie-Delta Regional Planning and Development District (loan review panel, 1980 to present); Rapides Parish Citizens for Coliseum Committee, 1980 to present. Religion: Emmanuel Baptist Church, Deacon 1934 to present. Honors and Awards: Distinguished Service Award as Outstanding Young Man, Rapides Parish, Junior Chamber of Commerce, 1943; Paul Harris Fellow, Rotary Club Foundation. Address: 3200 Parkway Drive, Alexandria, Louisiana 71301.

Bomberger, Audrey Shelley

Education Director. Personal: Born June 12, 1942; Daughter of Mr. and Mrs. Allen A. Shelley (both deceased); Married Edward K. Bomberger; Mother of Beth-Ann, Gary Allen. Education: R.N., Reading School of Nursing, 1963; B.S.Ed., Millersville State Teachers College, 1975; M.S.Ed., Temple University, 1979. Military: Serves as a Major in the United States Army Nurse Corps (Reserve Component), 1977 to present. Career: Education Director, 6 years; Charge Nurse, Coronary Care Unit, 3 years; Staff Nurse, Medical Surgical Psychiatry, 10 years. Organizational Memberships: American Nurses Association; National League for Nurses; Nevada Nurses Association (board of directors, 1980 to present); American Hospital Association; American Society of Health Education and Training (national nomination committee, 1979); National Critical Care Institute of Education. Community Activities: American Cancer Society; American Heart Association (public education committee); American Red Cross; Historical Association of Pennsylvania, 1972-76; United States Reserve Officers Association. Religion: Lutheran. Honors and Awards: Red Cross Pin for Volunteer Nursing Hours; Scholarship for Academic Achievement, 1962; Scholarship for Clinical Excellence, 1961; Unit Citation Award for Education Activities Instituted for Corpsmen, 1979; National Award for Education, American Hospital Association, 1981; Listed in *Who's Who of Women in America*. Address: 1590 Zolezzi Lane, Reno, Nevada 89511.

Bondurant, Byron Lee

Professor. Personal: Born November 11, 1925; Son of Joyce Koneta Bondurant; Married Lovetta May Alexander; Father of Connie Jane Jaycox, Richard Thayne, Cindy Lynn Gardino. Education: B.A.E., Ohio State University, 1949; M.S.C.E., University of Connecticut, 1953; Further Studies at Case Institute of Technology, Renesslaer Polytechnic Institute, University of Delaware, University of Maryland. Military: Served in the United States Navy R.O.T.C., 1943-45. Career: Professor of Agricultural Engineering, Ohio State University, 1964 to present; Fulbright Professor of Agricultural Engineering, University of Nairobi, Kenya, 1979-80; Project Manager, U.N.D.P./F.A.O. and Group Leader, M.U.C.I.A./O.S.U. on Strengthening Agricultural Research, Somalia, 1976-78; Advisor to the Dean, Dean, College of Agricultural Engineering, Punjab Agricultural University, India, 1965-67, 1968, 1969-71, 1972; Visiting Professor of Agricultural Engineering, University of Nairobi, Kenya, 1974; Professor and Head, Department of Agricultural Engineering, University of Maine, 1954-64; Consultant, Harvard University, Nigeria, 1964; Consultant, United States State Department, Sierra Leone, 1962; Associate Professor of Agricultural Engineering and Extenion Agricultural Engineer, University of Delaware, 1953-54; Instructor and Extension Agricultural Engineer, University of Connecticut, 1950-53; District Agricultural Engineer, Cornell University, 1949-50. Organizational Memberships: American Society of Agricultural Engineers (director, international department, 1980-82; senior life member; chairman, Acadia section, 1961; vice chairman, North Atlantic section, 1954; secretary-treasurer, Tri-State region and Ohio sections, 1973-74); American Society for Engineer Education (chairman, agricultural engineering division, 1963); *Technos* (associate editor); American Association for the Advancement of Science (fellow, life member); New York Academy of Science. Community Activities: Society for International Development (life member); Registered Fallout Shelter Analyst; Registered Professional Engineer; Registered Land Surveyor; Civil Defense (deputy director, Orono, Maine, 1962-64); Orono Parent-Teacher Association (chairman, 1963; vice chairman, 1962). Religion: Nazarene Church. Honors and Awards: Tau Beta Pi; Sigma Pi Sigma; Sigma Xi; Gamma Sigma Delta; Epsilon Sigma Phi; Listed in *Who's Who in America, Who's Who in the United States, Who's Who in Consulting, Who's Who in the Midwest, Who's Who in Engineering, American Men of Science, Men of Achievement, Notable Americans.* Address: 265 Franklin Street, Dublin, Ohio 43017.

Bonner, J William

Minister. Personal: Born September 23, 1905; Son of John Wesley Bonner (deceased); Married Ovah Boggs; Father of Ernestine O'Ella, June Lenore, John Wallace. Education: A.B., Elementary Education; A.B., Secondary Education; Undertook graduate work at West Virginia University. Career: Public School Teacher, 1924-44; Minister, American Baptist Churches in the United States. Organizational Memberships: Alderson-Broaddus College (trustee); West Virginia Baptist Convention (board of directors, president); Ministerial Association (president); County Council of Churches (president); Baptist Historical Society. Community Activities: American Red Cross (board of directors); Family Society (board of directors); American Baptist Historical Society (board of directors); Classroom Teachers Association (president); Regional Protestant Commission on Boy Scouting (president). Honors and Awards: Silver Beaver and Silver Antelope Awards, Boy Scouts of America; D.D. degree, Alderson-Broaddus College; Man of the Year, Woodmen of the World; Listed in *Who's Who in American Religion.* Address: 709 Maryland Ave., Fairmont, West Virginia 26554.

J William Bonner

Bonner, Jack W III

Psychiatrist, Medical Director. Personal: Born July 30, 1940, in Corpus Christi, Texas; Son of Mr. and Mrs. Jack W. Bonner Jr.; Married Myra L. Taylor; Father of Jack W. IV, Katherine Lynn, Shelley Bliss. Education: A.A., Del Mar College, 1960; B.A., University of Texas-Austin, 1961; M.D., University of Texas Southwestern Medical School, 1965; Intern, University of Arkansas Medical Center, 1966; Resident in Psychiatry, Duke University Medical Center, 1969. Military: Served as Flight Surgeon, Wing Psychiatrist, in the United States Air Force, 1969-71, attaining the rank of Major. Career: Medical Director, Highland Hospital, Asheville, North Carolina, 1975 to present; Consulting Staff, Memorial Mission Hospital of Western North Carolina, Inc., 1980 to present; Consulting Staff, St. Joseph Hospital, Asheville, 1980 to present; Teaching Staff, Bexar County Hospital, San Antonio, Texas, 1970-71; Consultant in Psychiatry, Austin State Hospital, Texas, 1969; Consultant in Psychiatry, Asheville Veterans Administration Hospital, 1974-78; Clinical Associate Professor of Psychiatry, University of Texas Medical School at San Antonio, 1970-71; Associate in Psychiatry 1971, Assistant Professor of Psychiatry 1972-80, Associate Clinical Professor of Psychiatry 1982 to present, Staff Psychiatrist 1971-72, Director of Outpatient Services 1972-75, Medical Director 1975-81, Duke University Medical Center, Highland Hospital Division, Asheville; The Highland Foundation, President 1980 to present, Chairman of the Board of Directors 1980 to present. Organizational Memberships: Texas State Board of Medical Examiners (diplomate, 1965); National Board of Medical Examiners (diplomate, 1966); American Board of Psychiatry and Neurology (diplomate, 1971); American Psychiatric Association (assembly of district branches, deputy representative 1978-82, representative 1982 to present, nominating committee 1980 to present); American Group Psychotherapy Association; American Medical Association; Buncombe County Medical Society (long-range planning committee, 1976-77; chairman, physician and his/her family committee, 1977; delegate to North Carolina Medical Society, 1978-80; board of directors, 1979-80, 1982 to present; chairman, medical-legal committee, 1979-80; alternate delegate, North Carolina Medical Society, 1981; president-elect, 1982; president, 1983); Medical Society of the State of North Carolina (Blue Shield committee, 1978 to present; chairman, biofeedback ad hoc subcommittee, 1979-80; house of delegates 1978-80; house of delegates alternate, 1981 to present); North Carolina Neuropsychiatric Association (continuing education committee, 1972; chairman, arrangements committee, annual meeting, 1975; area conference chairman, 1975-77; nominating committee, 1977; membership committee, 1977-80; insurance committee, 1978 to present; deputy representative to assembly of district branches, 1978 to present; president-elect, 1981-82; president, 1982 to present); Southern Psychiatric Association (fellow; program committee, 1979 to present); American Association for the Advancement of Science; American College of Psychiatrists (fellow; program committee, 1979-82); Southern Medical Association (section on neurology, neurosurgery and psychiatry, secretary 1977-80, chairman-elect 1980-81, chairman 1982-82); American Society for Adolescent Psychiatry; Central Neuropsychiatric Hospital Association (councillor, 1981-82; president-elect, 1982 to present); National Association of Private Psychiatric Hospitals (nominating committee, 1977; legislative representative, 1977-80; teaching hospitals committee, 1979 to present); *Southern Medical Journal* (editorial reviewer, 1978 to present). Community Activities: Western North Carolina Medical Peer Review Foundation, Inc. (board of directors, 1975-78); National Anorexic Aid Society, Inc. (national anorexia advisory council, 1978 to present); Task Force on Service Delivery, Governor's Conference on Mental Health (co-chairman, institutional care subcommittee, 1979); Governor's Task Force on Mental Health, 1979-80. Published Works: Co-Author Book *The Psychology of Discipline;* Co-Author Several Professional Articles. Honors and Awards: Phi Theta Kappa. Address: 27 Windsor Road, Asheville, North Carolina 28804.

Booker, Reginald Alvis

Research Chemist. Personal: Born January 5, 1953; Son of Dorothy B. Smith. Education: B.S., Tuskegee Institute, 1974; M.S. 1976, Ph.D. 1978, University of Illinois. Career: Research Chemist; Former Research Assistant, Teaching Assistant, Organizational Memberships: Sigma Xi; American Chemical Society; National Organization for the Professional Advancement of Black Chemists and Chemical Engineers. Honors and Awards: Analytical Chemistry Award, 1974; Beta Kappa Chi; Alpha Kappa Mu; Sophomore Chemistry Award, 1972; I. A. Derbigny Award, 1974; Phi Beta Sigma Scholastic Award, 1973; Clarence T. Mason Science Award, 1974; Listed in *Who's Who in American Colleges and Universities, Outstanding Young Men of America, Who's Who in the East.* Address: P.O. Box 183, Rockland, Delaware 19732.

Reginald Booker

Boone, Dora Elma (Judy)

Association Executive. Personal: Born February 9, 1906; Son of Mr. and Mrs. William Lee Pardue (both deceased); Widow; Mother of Daniel Lee. Education: Attended Concord State College; Holder of Teachers Certificate. Career: President, National Shut-In's Day Association; West Virginia Reporter, Logan East Junior High School Band, 1962; Reporter, Logan Senior High School Band, 1963. Community Activities: Woman's Society of Christian Service (board of stewards); Order of the Eastern Star; National/American Association of Retired Persons; League of Women Voters; Logan Woman's Club; Organized First Bear Dean in West Virginia, 1980; Collects Teddy Bears for Hospitals and Nursing Homes. Religion: Nighbert Memorial Church - Organized Youth Group "Pepper Uppers", Member of Sub Group IV, Play Director, President of the Willing Workers Class. Honors and Awards: Certificate of Appreciation, West Virginia Rehabilitation Association, 1976; First May Queen, Elkhorn High School, 1924; West Virginia Governor's Distinguished Award, Governor John D. Rockefeller IV, 1979; Named Mrs. Bearine of West Virginia, 1979; Made Member of International Biographical Association, Cambridge, England, 1979; Award from West Virginia Secretary of State A. James Manchin, 1979; Distinguished Golden Mountaineer Award, Governor John D. Rockefeller IV, 1983; Certificate of Recognition for Contributions to the Community, 1981; Senior Citizen of West Virginia Award, 1981; Distinguished Volunteer Award for

Services of Volunteering, 1982; Certificate of Appreciation for Services to the Handicapped, 1982. Address: 711½ Stratton Street, Logan, West Virginia 25601.

Booth, Jean Young

Speech-Language Pathologist. Personal: Born January 27, 1942; Daughter of Dr. Marion A. and Charlotte B. Young; Mother of Christopher Lee, Virginia Elizabeth, Mary Catherine. Education: Attended Louisiana State University, Baton Rouge, 1960-61, and University of Southern Mississippi, 1963; B.S., University of Mississippi for Women, 1964; Attended Louisiana State University Medical Center, 1976-78; M.C.D., Louisiana State University, Shreveport, 1977. Career: Speech-Language Pathologist. Organizational Memberships: American Speech-Language-Hearing Association; Louisiana Speech-Language-Hearing Association; Shreveport-Bossier Speech-Language-Hearing Association; International Association of Logopedics & Phoniatrics; National Education Association, 1977-79; Louisiana Education Association, 1977-79. Community Activities: Boy Scouts of America (den leader); Muscular Dystrophy (volunteer); American Cancer Society (volunteer). Religion: Member St. Paul's Episcopal Church; Guild of St. Bridget, 1980 to present. Honors and Awards: Annual Associate, American Biographical Research Association; Listed in *Who's Who in the South and Southwest, Personalities of the South, Personalities of America, Directory of Distinguished Americans, International Who's Who of Intellectuals, Book of Honor.* Address: 3533 LaNell, Bossier City, Louisiana 71112.

Borgman, Mary Frances

Professor. Personal: Born September 1, 1943; Daughter of Mr. and Mrs. J. W. Borgman. Education: B.S.N., Duquesne University School of Nursing, 1965; M.Ed., Duquesne University School of Education, 1968; Ed.D., West Virginia University College of Human Resources and Education, 1979. Career: Nurse Educator, Department of Physical Medicine and Rehabilitation, St. Francis General Hospital, Pittsburgh, Pennsylvania; Operating Room Instructor, Presbyterian Hospital School of Nursing, Pittsburgh, Pennsylvania; Staff Nurse; Presbyterian University Hospital; Professor of Nursing, West Virginia University School of Nursing. Organizational Memberships: West Virginia University (university senate 1978-81, senate on policy rules and regulations 1979-81); West Virginia University School of Nursing (executive committee 1979-81, curriculum committee 1979 to present, honors day committee 1980-81, chairperson senior academic unit 1979-81); American Nurses Association, 1965 to present; West Virginia Nurses Association, District #5, 1970 to present; National League for Nursing, 1970 to present; West Virginia League for Nursing, 1970 to present; Sigma Theta Tau, Alpha Rho Chapter (counselor 1980-82, chairman eligibility committee 1980-82, project committee 1980-82); American Rehabilitation Nurses; American Association of University Professors. Community Activities: American Heart Association (national assembly planning committee 1977-79, Willa affiliate - chairman nursing committee 1973-79). Religion: Roman Catholic: Honors and Awards: West Virginia University Outstanding Teacher, 1977; West Virginia University Senator, 1977-81; Editorial Board, *Weather Vane,* 1979 to present; Editorial Board, *Journal of Nursing Education,* 1981 to present; Listed in *Who's Who of American Women, International Who's Who in Education.* Address: 329 East Main Street, Kingwood, West Virginia 26537.

Jean Y Booth

Borthick, Mavis Ary

Special Education Consultant, Counselor. Personal: Born November 21, 1914; Daughter of Elbert (deceased) and Eugenia Harder Ary; Married Joseph William Borthick (deceased); Mother of Joary B. Hampton, Alice Faye. Education: B.S., Middle Tennessee State University, 1939; M.A., Peabody-Vanderbilt University, 1956; Ed.S., University of Tennessee-Nashville, 1970; Advanced Graduate Study, Austin Peay State University, Tennessee State University, University of Wisconsin; Continuing Education, University of Iowa, 1980. Career: Counselor, Greenbrier Elementary School, Greenbrier, Tennessee; Special Education Consultant; Former Positions include Teacher, Perry County Schools; High School Teacher, Marshall County Schools, Robertson County Schools; Reading Specialist, Robertson County Schools; Consultant and Contact Person, National Rural Career Guidance Communication Network. Organizational Memberships: National Education Association; Tennessee Education Association (chairperson guidance section, 1979); M.T.E.A.; R.C.E.A.; American Personnel and Guidance Association; American School Counselors Association; Tennessee Personnel and Guidance Association; T.S.C.A. (president, 1977-78; vice president 1974-77; newsletter editor, 1979 to present); R.C.S.C.A. (president, 1976 to present). Community Activities: Establised Irrevocable Trust Fund in Memory of Husband, J. W. Borthick, Awarded Yearly to Graduating Senior of the Adams-Cedar Hill Community; Robertson County Senior Citizens (secretary of advisory board, 1981 to present; grantee committee, 1979); Tennessee Mental Health Association (chairperson, Robertson County chapter, 1978); Task Force Committee for Guidance in Elementary Schools of Tennessee; Heart Fund (chairperson, 1979); Business and Professional Women of Springfield. Religion: Springfield Baptist Church, Sunday School Secretary 1969-71, Sunday School Teacher for Youth 1965-67; Red River Baptist Church, Sunday School Teacher 1947-52. Published Works: Contributor to Idea Exchange Column; *Elementary School Guidance and Counseling;* One of Seven Counselors to Develop Handbook for Educators to Use in Schools, *Guidance for the Elementary School: Counselor Techniques.* Honors and Awards: Grant for Career Education Workshop, 1970; Chosen as Director of Elementary Guidance Workshop, American Personnel and Guidance Association, New Orleans, 1974; Presenter, American Personnel and Guidance Association Group Guidance Techniques, New York 1975, Chicago 1976, Dallas 1977; Director for Personnel in Guidance for Elementary Schools in Tennessee, 1973, 1976; Woman of the Year, Springfield Business and Professional Women, 1978; Outstanding Educator, Robertson County, 1977; Certificate for Outstanding Work from the President of Field Enterprises Inc., 1970. Address: 613 Crestview Drive, Springfield, Tennessee 37172.

Bortolotti, Norma May

Executive. Personal: Born April 8, 1931; Daughter of Isidoro and Michelina Cominoli Bortolotti. Education: Duchesne College, 1950-54; Undertook postgraduate studies, Creighton University, 1957, 1958, 1977, 1978; Dickinson Secretarial School, 1958; Council Bluffs Adult & Continuing Education, 1981. Career: Accountant, 1954-70; Director, 7301 Corporation, 1964-69; Vice President, Universal Terrazzo & Tile, 1947-77; Vice President, NND Investment Company and NND Investment Corporation. Community Activities: Children's Memorial Hospital (volunteer worker, 1950-54); Fraternal Order of Police; Omaha Police Lodge #1. Religion: Member E de M Catholic Society Scared Heart, Omaha, 1950 to present. Honors and Awards: Outstanding Service Award, Republican Party, 1975; Honor Guard to Our Lady, Marian Year. Address: 9904 Florence Heights Blvd, Omaha, Nebraska 68112.

Borum, Elizabeth Ann

Psychologist. Personal: Born May 4, 1930; Daughter of John Allen and Helen Eliza Borum (both deceased). Education: B.A. with honors 1951, M.A. 1953, University of California-Berkeley. Career: Psychologist, Probation Department, Contra Costa County;

Former Research Psychometrist, Institute of Medical Sciences, San Francisco; Graduate Research Psychologist, Institute of Human Development, Berkeley; Chief Psychometrist and Vocational Counselor, Vocational Service Center, Young Men's Christian Association, City of New York; Research Psychologist, Institute of Child Welfare, Berkeley Center. Organizational Memberships: Northern California Council Psychological Association (secretary, 1978-81; treasurer, Bay Area council, 1976-78); Contra Costa County Psychological Association (president, 1975-76); Counseling Cabinet of the Young Men's Christian Association of the City of New York (secretary, 1957); California State Psychological Association; Western Psychological Association; American Psychological Association; Correctional Psychological Association; American Academy of Political and Social Science; American Association for the Advancement of Science. Community Activities: People-to-People (president, East Bay chapter, 1976 to present); United Nations/U.S.A. (treasurer, Alameda County chapter, 1975 to present); Berkeley Mayor's Bicentennial Committee, 1975-76; Berkeley Business and Professional Women's Club (past president, 1967-68); N.G.O. Advisory Committee to San Francisco Mayor's Committee on the 25th Anniversary of the United Nations; U.N.I.C.E.F. (volunteer); World Federalists Association; Oakland Museum Association; Oakland Symphony Guild; International Platform Association. Religion: West Coast Council for Ethical Culture (chairman, 1965-67); San Francisco Ethical Forum (chairman, pro-tem, 1966-67); Bay Area Fellowship for Ethical Culture (president, 1960-64, 1966-67). Honors and Awards: Fremont Poetry Award, 1946; Anchor Poetry Award, 1972; Meritorious Service Award, U.N.I.C.E.F. Activities, Bay Valley District Business and Professional Women's Clubs, 1973; Woman of Achievement, Business and Professional Women's Club of Berkeley, 1980-81; Listed in *Who's Who in Community Service.* Address: 1830 Lakeshore #304, Oakland, California 94606.

Boucher, Frederick Carlyle

Attorney at Law, State Senator. Personal: Born August 1, 1946. Education: B.A., Roanoke College, 1968; J.D., University of Virginia School of Law, 1971. Career: Attorney at Law; United States District Court for the Southern District of New York; Bar Association of the Commonwealth of Virginia; United States Court of Appeals for the Second Circuit; United States District Court for the Western District of Virginia; United States Court of Appeals for the Fourth Circuit; Association of the Bar of the City of New York; American Bar Association; Virginia State Bar; Virginia Bar Association; American Judicature Society. Community Service: Senator, State of Virginia, 1975 to present; Virginia State Crime Commission, 1979 to present; Virginia Coal and Energy Commission (member, 1979 to present; chairman of the oil and gas subcommittee, 1980 to present); Governor's Overall Advisory Council on the Needs of Handicapped Pesons, 1976-79; Virginia Senate Democratic Caucus Policy Committee (chairman, 1980 to present); Virginia Commission on Interstate Cooperation, 1980 to present; Committee on Law and Justice of the National Conference of State Legislatures, 1980 to present; Client Centered Legal Services of Southwest Virginia, Inc. (board of directors, 1977 to present); Southwest Virginia Legal Services, Inc. (board of directors, 1981 to present). Honors and Awards: Outstanding Young Businessman of the Year, Abingdon, Virginia, Jaycees, 1975. Address: 188 East Main Street, Abingdon, Virginia 24210.

Harisios Boudouias

Boudoulas, Harisios

Professor of Medicine, Cardiology. Personal: Born November 3, 1935, in Velvendo-Kozani, Greece; Son of Konstantinos and Sophia Boudoulas; Married Olga Paspatis; Father of Sophia, Konstantinos. Education: M.D., University of Salonica, 1959; Doctorate Diploma, Faculty of Medicine, University of Salonica, Greece, 1967; Board of Internal Medicine, Greece, 1967; Board of Cardiology, Greece, 1967; Diploma of Educational Council Foreign Medical Graduates, U.S.A., 1970; Permanent License to Practice Medicine in Ohio 1975; Michigan Permanent License, 1980. Career: Resident in Internal Medicine, Red Cross Hospital, Athens, Greece, 1960-61; Resident in Cardiology, Cardiac Clinc of 424 Military Hospital, Salonica, Greece, 1961; Resident in Internal Medicine, First Medical Clinic, University of Salonica, 1962-64; Resident in Cardiology, First Medical Clinic, University of Salonica, Greece, 1964-66; Attending Physician, Renal Unit, First Medical Clinic, University of Salonica, 1966-67; Attending Physician, Coronary Care Unit, First Medical Clinic, University of Salonica, 1967-69; Lecturer in Medicine, First Medical Unit, University of Salonica, 1969-70; Postdoctoral Fellow and Instructor, Ohio State University College of Medicine, Division of Cardiology, 1970-73; Senior Lecturer in Medicine, Head of Coronary Care Unit, First Medical Clinic, University of Salonica, 1973-75; Postdoctoral Fellow, Division of Cardiology, Department of Medicine, Ohio State University College of Medicine, 1975; Assistant Professor of Medicine, Division of Cardiology, Department of Medicine, Ohio State University College of Medicine, 1975-78; Director, Cardiovascular Non-Invasive Research Laboratories, Division of Cardiology, Ohio State University Hospitals, 1978-80; Associate Professor of Medicine, Division of Cardiology, Ohio State University Hospitals, 1978-80; Professor of Medicine, Division of Cardiology, Wayne State University, 1980 to present; Director, Clinical Cardiovascular Research, Division of Cardiology, Wayne State University, 1980 to present; Chief, Cardiovascular Center, Veterans Administration Medical Center, 1980 to present. Organizational Memberships: Medical Association of Salonica, Greece; Greek Society of Biochemistry; Royal Society of Medicine (affiliate member); Greek Renal Association; European Dialysis and Transplant Association; American Heart Association; American College of Cardiology (fellow); Greek Heart Association; Greek Committee against Hypertension; American Federation of Clinical Research; Council on Clinical Cardiology (fellow); American College of Angiology (fellow); American College of Physicians (fellow); Central Society for Clinical Research; American College of Clinical Pharmacology (fellow). Published Works: Author/Co-Author, numerous professional articles and abstracts. Honors and Awards: Listed in *Who's Who in the Midwest, International Who's Who of Intellectuals, Personalities of the West and Midwest, Men of Achievement, Dictionary of International Biography, Book of Honor, Who's Who in America.* Address: 22825 Highbank Dr., Birmingham, Michigan 48010.

Geoffrey Bourne Jr

Bourgeois, David Richard

Manager. Personal: Born October 8, 1938; Son of Joseph and Inez Bourgeois; Married Marsha C. Wing; Father of Derek S. Education: B.S.E.E., Northeastern University, 1977. Military: Served in the United States Navy, 1958-62. Career: Manager, Honeywell; Former Senior Computer Design Engineer. Community Activities: Youth Basketball (coach and director); Youth Baseball (coach); Youth Hockey (commissioner). Honors and Awards: Technical Excellence Award, Honeywell, 1981. Address: 6 Currier Drive, Framingham, Massachusetts 01701.

Bourne, Geoffrey

Vice Chancellor. Personal: Born November 17, 1909; Married Maria Nelly Golarz; Father of Peter, Merfyn. Education: B.Sc., 1930, M.Sc., 1932, D.Sc., 1935, all from the University of Western Australia; D.Phil., University of Oxford. Military: Served as advisor on medical and biological problems for special forces in S.E. Asia (rank of Major); Nutrition advisor to the British Military Administration of Malaya (rank of Lieutenant Colonel). Career: Vice Chancellor, St. Georges University School of Medicine, Grenada, West Indies, 1978 to present; Director, Yerkes Primate Research Center, Emory University, 1962-78; Professor and Chairman of Anatomy, Emory University, 1957-62; Reader in Histology, University of London, 1947-57; Demonstrator in

Physiology, University of Oxford, 1938-47; Biochemist, Commonwealth of Australia Advisory Council on Nutrition, 1936-38; Biologist, Australian Institute of Anatomy, 1934-36. Organizational Memberships: Royal Society of Medicine (fellow); Zoological Society of London (fellow); Royal Institute of Biology (fellow); American Institute of Nutrition; British Nutrition Society (secretary, 1947-57); British Society Research in Aging (secretary, 1950-57); International Primatological Society (secretary general, 1970-75); Aerospace Medical Society; International Academy of Astronautics. Community Activities: Atlanta Zoological Society (founder and first president, 1967); Atlanta Humane Society; Workers Education Association, Oxford, England (lecturer); Oxford University Extra Mural Delegacy. Honors and Awards: Dr. Geoffrey Bourne Day proclaimed by Mayor of City of Miami Beach, May 24, 1981; Distinguished Lecturer, Medical College of Georgia, 1968; Beit Memorial Fellow for Medical Research, 1938-41; Mackenzie Mackinnon Research Fellow, Royal College of Surgeons of England and Royal College of Physicians of London, 1941-43. Home Address: 849 Lullwater Parkway, Atlanta, Georgia 30307. Business Address: St. Georges University School of Medicine, Grenada, West Indies.

Bova, Ben

Author, Lecturer, Executive. Personal: Born in Philadelphia, Pennsylvania. Education: Degree in Journalism, Temple University. Career: Editorial Director, Vice-President, *Omni;* Lecturer to Business, Educational and Industrial Audiences; Has Appeared on Numerous Radio and Television Interviews; Former Manager of Marketing, Avco Everett Research Laboratory; Technical Editor, Project "Vanguard"; Editor, *Analog;* Has also been a Newspaper Reporter, an Aerospace Industry Executive, and a Motion Picture and Television Consultant; National Space Institute (charter member); Science Fiction Writers of America (charter member); International Association for the Advancement of Science; American Associaton for the Advancement of Science; International Free Space Society (honorary chairman). Community Activities: Explorers Club; P.E.N. International. Published Works: Books of Fiction include *Gremlins, Go Home!; The Starcrossed; City of Darkness; The Multiple Man; Colony; Maxwell's Demons; Kinsman; The Exiles Trilogy; Voyagers;* Books of Non-Fiction include *The Amazing Laser; The New Astronomies; Starflight and Other Improbabilities; The Weather Changes Man; Through Eyes of Wonder; The Seeds of Tomorrow; The High Road;* Anthologies include *The Many Worlds of Science Fiction; Analog Annual; Analog Yearbook; Best of Omni Science Fiction; Analog Science Fact Reader.* Honors and Awards: Hugo Award for Best Professional Editor 6 times; Distinguished Alumnus, Temple University, 1981; Listed in Who's Who in the East, International Author's Who's Who, Contemporary Authors, Who's Who in Science Fiction.

Bowden, Charles Malcolm

Research Physicist. Personal: Born December 31, 1933; Son of Charles Edward and Emma Hoover Bowden (both deceased); Married Lou Marguerite Tolbert; Father of Melissa Gail, Steven Mark, David Malcolm. Education: B.S., University of Richmond, 1956; M.S., University of Virginia, 1959; Ph.D., Clemson University, 1967. Career: Research Physicist. Organizational Memberships: American Physical Society; Sigma Xi; Sigma Pi Sigma; New York Academy of Sciences; American Association for the Advancement of Science. Religion: University Baptist Church - Deacon 1979 to present, Vice Chairman of the Deacon Council 1980, Chairman of the Pastor Search Committee 1981 to present, Adult Bible Study Teacher 1972 to present, Young Adult Bible Study Teacher and Leader 1978 to present. Honors and Awards: N.A.S.A. Fellow, 1965-67; Oak Ridge National Laboratory Graduate Fellowship, Summer 1965; Paul A. Siple Scientist Achievement Award, West Point, 1978; United States Army Missile Research and Development Command Science and Engineering Award, 1980; Scientific Achievement Award, United States Army Science Conference, West Point, 1980; Outstanding Performance Award, 1980. Address: 716 Versailles Drive, Huntsville, Alabama 35803.

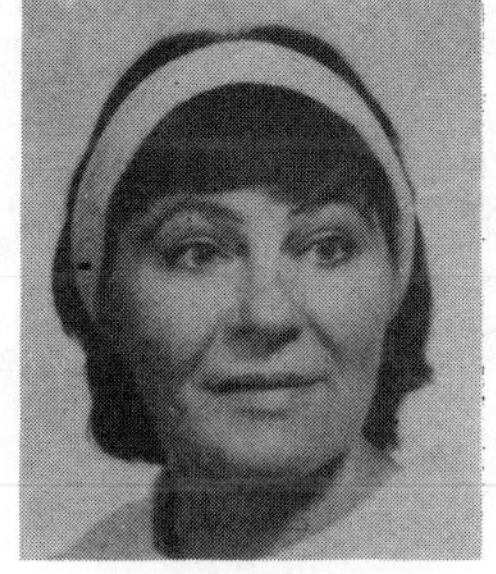

Edith H Boxill

Bowers, Janette Lawhon

Adult and Continuing Education Director. Personal: Born November 13, 1933; Daughter of Mr. and Mrs. Tot Lawhon; Married Richard E. Bowers; Mother of Connie, Clay, Cole, Casey, Kelly, George. Education: B.S., Sam Houston State University, 1954; M.A., Sul Ross State University, 1970. Career: Director, Division of Adult and Continuing Education, Sul Ross State University; Former Public School Teacher and College Instructor. Organizational Memberships: Texas Association for Community Service and Continuing Education (president, 1980; secretary, 1979; board member, 1978). Community Activities: Alpine Independent School District (board of trustees, 1974-82); Sunshine House (chairman of the advisory board, 1976 to present); Pilot International (governor of Texas district, 1981-82); Delta Kappa Gamma, Beta Iota Chapter; American Legion Auxiliary (girls state chairman, 1975 to present); American Cancer Society (president, 1981; board member 15 years; state board, Texas division); Alpine Chamber of Commerce; Alpine Buck Boosters; Alpine Band Boosters; Daughters of the Republic of Texas; United Daughters of the Confederacy (charter member); Sul Ross Women's Organization; American Association of Retired Persons (honorary member, chapter 2100); Senior Citizen's Club of Alpine. Religion: Presbyterian. Outstanding Volunteer in Texas, 1977; Finalists of National Volunteer Activist Award, 1977; Outstanding Citizen of Alpine, 1976; Outstanding Woman of Alpine, 1981; Listed in *World Who's Who of Women, World Who's Who in Community Service, Personalities of the South, Men and Women of Distinction, Notable Americans, Who's Who of American Women, Community Leaders of America, Directory of Distinguished Americans, Outstanding Young Women of America, Personalities of America.* Address: Drawer 1440, Alpine, Texas 79830.

Boxill, Edith Hillman

Assistant Professor, Music Therapist, Consultant, Lecturer. Personal: Daughter of Maurice and Lillian Hillman (both deceased); Married Roger Evan Boxill; Mother of Paul R. Epstein, Emily H. Duby. Education: B.A., Boston University; M.A., New York University; Certification, Dalcroze School of Music. Career: Assistant Professor of Music Therapy, New York University; Head of Music Therapy, Manhattan Developmental Center, New York; Clinical Supervisor, Music Therapy, Interns, 1977 to present; Music Instructor, Composer, Performer, 1954-71; Lecturer, Music Therapy Department, New York University, 1976-78; Music Teacher, Little Red School House and Elisabeth Irwin High School, New York City, 1957-60; Faculty, Mills College of Education, New York City, 1954-57. Organizational Memberships: American Association for Music Therapy (board of directors; chairperson, State Affairs task force); American Association on Mental Deficiency (chairperson, Creative Arts Therapies); American Society of Composers, Authors and Publishers; National Society for Autistic Children; Association of Musicians of Greater New York. Community Activities: New York State Coalition of Creative Arts Therapies (chairperson for music therapy); Arts for the Handicapped (official observer, Very Special Arts Festival, national committee); United Nations Conference of the International Year of Disabled Persons (presenter). Published Works: Author, "Developing Communications with the Autistic Child through Music Therapy", "A Continuum of Awareness: Music Therapy with the Developmentally Handicapped", "Music Therapy: A Primary Treatment Modality for the Developmentally Disabled"; Co-Author, "Essential Competencies for the Practice of Music Therapy"; Work in Progress on Music Therapy with the Mentally Retarded; Producer of Videotape "Music Therapy with the Multiply Handicapped". Honors and Awards: Invited to Author *Handbook on Music Therapy with the Mentally Retarded and Developmentally Disabled;*

Certified Music Therapist; Composer, Arranger, Producer, Record Album, (Folkways) "Music Therapy with the Developmentally Handicapped"; Listed in *Who's Who in the East, Directory of Outstanding Americans, World Who's Who of Women*. Address: 375 Riverside Drive, New York, New York 10025.

Boyce, Ronald Reed

Professor, Administrator, Author. Personal: Born January 7, 1931; Son of Reed S. and Martha Fern Boyce; Married Norma Rae Loraas; Father of Renaye, Susan. Education: B.S., 1946 and M.S., 1957, both from the University of Utah; Ph.D., University of Washington, 1961. Military: Served with the United States Army, Adjutant General's Corp, 1953-54. Career: Director of the School of Social and Behavioral Sciences, Professor of Urbanology, Seattle Pacific University; Professor, Administrator, Author. Organizational Memberships: Association of Washington Geographers (president, 1977-78); Association of American Geographers (chairman, geography and Bible speciality section, 1981-82); Regional Science Association (chairman, west lakes division, 1962); American Institute of Planners; Sigma Xi. Community Activities: Seattle Chamber of Commerce (chairman, open space and farmlands committee, 1979-80); Union Gospel Mission (executive committee, 1977 to present); Property Owners of Washington (vice president, 1980 to present); City Councilman, Woodway, 1969-74; Seattle-Beersheva, Israel Sister City Committee (vice president, 1977 to present); Allied Arts Orchestra (president, 1975, 1978); University of Washington Faculty Club (president); Various Projects: Downtown Development Association of Seattle, Washington Commission for the Humanities Projects, Others. Religion: Interim Pastor, Bellewood Evangelical Presbyterian Church, 1980; Ruling Elder, Calvin Presbyterian Church; President, Vice President, and Chaplain, Lynnwood Camp, Gideons International, 1971 to present. Published Works: *Geographic Perspectives on Global Problems*, 1982; *Geography as Spatial Interaction*, 1980; *The Bases of Economic Geography*, 1974, 1978; *Towns and Cities*, 1970; *Regional Development and the Wabash Basin*, 1964; Co-Author, *Studies of the Central Business District and Urban Freeway Development*, 1959. Honors and Awards: Quadrennial Award, Congress of South African Geographers, 1981; American Council on Education Fellow, 1978-79; Weter Faculty Award for Meritorious Scholarship, Seattle Pacific, 1976; S & H Lecturer, Highlands University, 1965; Outstanding Teacher Award, Geography Department, University of Washington, 1973; National Scholar, National Council of Social Sciences, 1969. Address: 23606 112th Place West, Edmonds, Washington 98020.

Boyd, Hugh Robert

Consultant. Personal: Born July 21, 1913; Father of James, John, Hugh. Education: Attended Michigan State University, 1930-32; B.S., Central Michigan University, 1936; M.S., Wayne State University, 1940; Attended Massachusetts Institute of Technology, 1946-47. Career: Research Manager; Research Engineer; Professor; Consultant. Organizational Memberships: Industrial Research Institute (chairman, seminar on mid-management training; chairman, rules committee); Boston Research Director's Club (past chairman); Institute of Electrical and Electronics Engineers (senior member; past chairman admissions committee). Community Activities: School Committees (committee member and chairman, 1958-73); Massachusetts Association of School Committees (member and chairman: finance committee, executive committee, curriculum committee, nominating committee, pensions committee, 1960-73); Massachusetts Advisory Council on Vocational-Technical Education, 1971-80 (member and past chairman); National School Board Association (delegate, nominating committee, chairman of three convention panels, 1969-73); Boston Research Director's Club, 1953 to present (member and past chairman); Stoneham Chapter of American Red Cross (director and chairman, 1954-58); Little League (director, 1946-48); Musket District Boy Scouts (director and vice chairman, 1968-72); Robinhood School Building Committee, 1958-62; Stoneham Boys Club (director, 1968-71). Honors and Awards: B.S. and M.S. with High Honors; Phi Delta Kappa; New York Academy of Science. Address: 44 Lincoln St., Stoneham, Massachusetts 02190.

Boyd, Louis Jefferson

Sponsored Programs Coordinator. Personal: Born March 14, 1928; Son of Bernice B. and Ethel Turnbow Boyd; Married Rebecca Charlotte Conner; Father of Beverly Gallagher (Mrs. Timothy), Beda Smith (Mrs. Steven), Garth Winston, Bettina Mize (Mrs. Gerald). Education: B.S. 1950, M.S. 1951, University of Kentucky; Ph.D., University of Illinois, 1956. Military: Served in the United States Army, 1946-47, attaining the rank of Staff Sergeant. Career: Coordinator of Sponsored Programs, College of Agriculture, University of Georgia, 1979 to present; Chairman, Animal Science Division and Head, Animal and Dairy Science Department, University of Georgia, 1972-79; Professor of Dairy Science, Michigan State University, 1963-72; Associate Professor of Dairy Science, University of Tennessee, 1956-63; Extension Specialist, University of Kentucky, 1951-53. Organizational Memberships: American Dairy Science Association (board of directors, 1973-76); American Society of Animal Science (board of directors, 1981 to present); Council for Agricultural Science and Technology (board of directors, 1980 to present; chairman, national concerns committee, 1980 to present). Community Activities: Coble Dairy Products Cooperative, Inc. (board of directors, 1976 to present); University Federal Employees Credit Union, University of Georgia (board of directors, 1981 to present); Farm House Fraternity (national director, 1960-64). Religion: Central Presbyterian Church, Athens, Georgia, Elder 1973-76, 1979 to present; United Presbyterian Church, Okemos, Michigan, Elder 1964-68; Presbyterian Center, University of Tennessee, Board of Directors 1959-62. Honors and Awards: Visiting Professor, Institute for Research on Animal Diseases, Compton, England, 1970-71; Outstanding Extension Specialist, Michigan State University, 1971. Address: 106 St. James Court, Athens, Georgia 30606.

Boyd, Ruth Joyce

Teacher of the Visually Impaired. Personal: Born March 12, 1934; Daughter of Charles and Isabelle Dickerson; Mother of Carolyn Rene, Teresa Lynn. Education: B.S., Ball State University, 1966; M.A., Ohio State University, 1974. Career: Dental Assistant, 1952-57; Secretary, H. L. Parsons, Inc., 1957-63; Teacher of the Visually Impaired, 1963 to present. Organizational Memberships: Delta Kappa Gamma (president, 1982-84; vice president, 1980-81); Council for Exceptional Children (past president); Phi Lambda Theta; Akron Association of Early Childhood; Akron Education Association. Community Activities: Representative for Major City Project, 1975; Low Incident State Management Board (representative, 1974); Summit County Blind Society Adult School (director, 1975). Religion: Woodland Methodist Church, Administrative Board 1982. Honors and Awards: Daughters of the American Revolution County Award, 1952; Commercial Award, 1952; Queen DeMolay Ball, 1952; Akron Teacher of the Year, 1976; Nominated for Ohio Teacher of the Year, 1976. Address: 55 Waldorf Drive, Akron, Ohio 44313.

Boyer-Blohm, Alta E

Preservationist. Personal: Born October 18, 1914; Daughter of Lewis Tunison and Edith Lott Essom, (both deceased); Married Charles H. Boyer, (deceased); Second marriage to Charles A. Blohm; Mother of Charles Chapin Boyer, Elizabeth Ann Boyer

Stewart. Education: B.A., William Smith College; M.L.S., State University of New York; Undertook further study at Syracuse University; Certified by Medical Library Association. Career: Medical Librarian, 1957-78; Chief of Library Services, Willard Psychiatric Center; Consultant, Archival Materials, Pennsylvania Hospital, Philadelphia, Pennsylvania, 1980 to present; Trustee, Finger Lakes Library System, 1978 to present. Organizational Memberships: William Smith College Alumnae Council, 1968-72; Medical Library Association (executive committee, board member 1972-75); New York Library Association (executive council 1969-71); Lodi Historical Society (president 1977-79); Seneca County A.R.C. (executive committee); Twentieth Century Club (president 1980 to present). Community Activities: Seneca County Health Services Committee, 1981 to present; New York State Department of Mental Hygiene (commissioners committee 1968-70). Published Works: Numerous bibliographies published for use of Department of Mental Hygiene. Address: 8678 Watkins Glen Rd., Lodi, New York 14860.

Boylan, Hunter Reed

College Administrator and Professor. Personal: Born April 3, 1945; Son of Mrs. B. E. Davis; Father of Heather Marie. Education: B.A., Miami University; M.Ed., Temple University; Ph.D., Bowling Green State University. Military: Served in the United States Air Force, 1967, attaining the rank of Lieutenant. Career: Professor, Director, Kellogg Institute. Organizational Memberships: A.C.P.A. (member, 1969-81; vice chairman commission XVI, 1976-78; chairman, commission XVI task force; newsletter editor, commission XVI); American Personnel and Guidance Association, 1969-81; American Association of Higher Education, 1975-77; National Association for Remedial/Developmental Studies (research chairman). Published Works: Editorial Board, *Journal of Developmental and Remedial Education, Journal of Personalized Instruction;* Author in Developmental Education. Religion: Presbyterian. Honors and Awards: Office of Education Grantee, 1975-76; Fund for the Improvement of Post-Secondary Education Grantee, 198-81; National Association for Remedial/Developmental Student Service Award, 1980; Outstanding Advisor Award, Temple University, 1968. Address: Route 1 Box 421, Blowing Rock, North Carolina 28605.

Boynton, William Lewis

Coordinator. Personal: Born May 31, 1928, in Kalamazoo, Michigan; Son of James (deceased) and Rita Boynton; Married Kei Ouchi, October 8, 1953. Education: Various Military and Technical Institutes and Seminars. Military: Served in the United States Army, 1948-74, Retired Non-Commissioned Officer. Career: Assistant Manager, Speigel J&R, Kalamazoo, 1947-48; Faculty Member, Western Michigan University, 1955-58; Rockwell/Collins Divisions - Materiel Coordinator 1974-78, Supervisor 1978-81, Coordinator 1981 to present. Organizational Memberships: National Management Association. Community Activities: Advisor to Business/Economic Development Committee, California State Legislature, 1979 to present; Orange County Vector Control District (board of trustees, 1980 to present); Smithsonian Institute; National Geographic Society Non-Commissioned Officers Association (life member); Association of the United States Army; Air Force Association; American Security Council; Japanese-American Citizen League. Religion: Roman Catholic. Honors and Awards: Bronze Star, 1970; Meritorious Service Award, United States Army, 1974; United States Army Commendations, 1967, 1969, 1972; Presidential Unit Citation, 1970; Presidential Citation, Korea, 1952; Good Conduct Medal, 1951-74; Numerous Letters of Commendation and Appreciation; Listed in *Who's Who in Finance and Industry, Who's Who in the West and Midwest, Who's Who in the World; Dictionary of International Biography, Who's Who in Orange County, California, Personalities of America, International Book of Honor, Who's Who in the West, Directory of Distinguished Americans.* Address: 5314 W. Lucky Way, Santa Ana, California 92704.

Ernest C Bradley

Bracewell, Thomas Frederick

Psychotherapist. Personal: Born August 19, 1944; Son of Mrs. Francis P. Bracewell; Father of Paul Wesley, Jeremy Sean. Education: A.A., Wallace Community College; B.S., Psychology and Journalism, Troy State University; M.Th., Candler School of Theology, Emory University; M.S., Ph.D., George Washington University. Military: United States Army Reserve, Special Forces Airborne, Captain. Career: Psychotherapist; Military Intelligence, United States Army Special Forces; Sports/New Anchorman, WDHN-TV, WTVY-TV, WJHG-TV; Minister, United Methodist Church, Alabama, Western Florida, Virginia Conference. Organizational Memberships: American Federation of Radio and Television Artists; Association of the United States Army; Reserve Officers Association; American Personnel and Guidance Association. Community Activities: Jaycees; Benevolent Protective Order of the Elks; Olympia Country Club; Young Americans for Freedom; Republican Presidential Task Force, 1981-82; United States Senatorial Club; National Republican Senatorial Committee; Republican National Committee; Alabama Republican Party; Boy Scouts of America (sponsor); Armed Forces Chaplains Association; Special Forces Association; 51st Scottish Highland Regiment Argyles (honorary member). Religion: Minister, United Methodist Church, 1963-79; Communicate, The Episcopal Church, 1979 to present. Honors and Awards: Alumni of the Year, Enterprise Junior College, 1973; ARCOM, 1967; Air Medal with "V" Device, 1967; Silver Star, 1967; Listed in *Who's Who in American Colleges and Universities, Outstanding Young Men in America, Who's Who in the South and Southwest, Personalities of the South.* Address: P.O. Box 1942, Dothan, Alabama 36301.

Bradley, Ernest Cerel

Alcoholism Counselor. Personal: Born September 4, 1915, in Chestnut, Louisiana; Son of Henry and Rosa Bradley (both deceased); Married Carrie Lee Bradley; Father of Ernest C. Jr., Theodore R., Jennette B., Bobby W. Education: Attended Southern University; B.S., Franklin University, 1974. Military: Served with the United States Army for 30 years (1941-71), achieving the rank of Sergeant Major. Career: United States Army, 1941-71; Retired Sergeant Major, II Field Force Vietnam, 1971; Special Problems Consultant, Alcoholism Division, Ohio Department of Health, 1971-78; Certified Alcoholism Counselor, Volunteers of America, 1979 to present. Community Activities: United Supreme Council, Ancient Accepted Scottish Rite of Freemasonry, Southern Jurisdiction, Prince Hall Affiliation; Prince Hall Military Consistory #304, Ancient Accepted Scottish Rite, Frankfurt, Germany; Thomas A. Simms Jr. Lodge #170, Free & Accepted Masons (P.H.A.) (past master); Multi-Gallon Blood Donor, Central Ohio Red Cross Blood Program; National Federation for the Blind of Ohio (vendors chapter); The Columbus Urban League; Ohio Defense Corps Officers Association, Inc.; Veterans of Foreign Wars, Post #3764; The Association for the Study of Afro-American Life and History (life member, treasurer); Military Order of the Purple Heart (life member); National Association for the Advancement of Colored People; Franklin University Alumni Association (board of directors); Salvation Army and Men's Social Center (council member); Volunteers of America (council member); Notary Public; First Air Calvary Division Association (life member); Columbus Area Leadership Program Alumni Association; Young Men's Christian Association; Public Employees Retirees, Inc.; The Ohio Association for Alcoholism Programs; The American Legion, Post #690; The Phylaxis Society; Franklinton Kiwanis Club; Rutgers University Alcoholism Alumni Association; Urban Minority Alcoholism Outreach Program; National Black Alcoholism Council, Ohio Chapter (board of directors). Religion: Baptist; Chairman of Deacon Board, Adult Sunday School Teacher, Member of Senior Choir, New Zion Baptist Church. Published Works: Autobiography *The Soldier Samaritan.* Honors and Awards: George Washington Gold Medal of Honor,

1958; The Satin Flag, presented by Mayor Huang Chi-suie of Taipei Municipal Government, 1960; The Mayor's Medal of Columbus, Ohio, 1978; Received 34 personal decorations during his military career (more than any other retiring enlisted man); Listed in *Who's Who in the West and Midwest*. Address: 468 Oakwood Avenue, Columbus, Ohio 43205.

Bradley, Ramona Kaiser

Museum Director/Curator, Lecturer. Personal: Born August 9, 1909; Daughter of Oliver B. and Grace Edwards Kaiser (both deceased); Married Judson M. Bradley. Education: Attended Schuster-Martin School of Drama, 1933-35. Career: Director/Curator, Sherman (Indian) Museum, Riverside, California; Lecturer; Former Legal Secretary. Organizational Memberships: Ohio Delphian Society (corresponding secretary, 1938-39); Omega Upsilon (editor *Footlights*, 1949-50); National League of American Pen Women (branch president, treasurer). Community Activities: American Indians Committee (national advisor); Daughters of the American Revolution, 1965-68; Children of the American Revolution (senior national chairman, 1966-68); Riverside Library Board (trustee, 1966-74); Riverside Cultural Heritage Board, 1974-80. Religion: Chairman, World Day of Prayer, Church Women United, 1981. Honors and Awards: Appreciation, Sherman Indian High School, 1976-78; Citation from the Officials and Mayor of the City of Riverside for Community Servcie; Citation from the Riverside Board of Supervisors, 1980; Honored by the Ohio Society and Mariemont Chapter, Daughters of the American Revolution, First Restoration Chairman, Waldschmidt House, Historic D.A.R. Shrine, Dennison, Ohio, 1981. Address: 9130 Andrew Street, Riverside, California 92503.

Bradshaw, Lawrence James

Artist and Educator. Personal: Born September 21, 1945; Son of Lawrence and Pauline Bradshaw. Education: B.F.A., 1967, M.A., 1971, Pittsburg State University; M.F.A., Ohio University, 1973. Career: Associate Professor of Art, University of Nebraska at Omaha; Art Student Forum Faculty Advisor, 1974-76 and 1981; Faculty Advocate, Center for the Improvement of Instruction, 1976-80; Logo Consultant, Performing Artists of Omaha, 1977; Gallery Director, University Galleries, 1974-76; Co-editor, University of Nebraska at Omaha Art Department Education Program, Nebraska State Board of Certification (given highest rating), 1975; Assistant Gallery Director, Whitesitt Gallery, Pittsburg State University, 1970-71; Instructor, Akron Art Institute, summer of 1973; Advertising Manager, J.C. Penney Company, Pittsburg, Kansas, 1970-71; Worked in Production Department, Writers' Service, Hollywood, California, 1969-70; Worked in Script Department, C.B.S.-T.V., Hollywood, California, 1967-69; Art Exhibitions include showings at Joslyn Art Museum, Rental and Sales Center Gallery (Omaha), 1981, Porter Fine Arts Center (Wesleyan College, Macon, Georgia), 1980, Alabama School of Fine Arts Gallery (Birmingham), University of South Carolina at Beaufort, Chattahoochee Valley Art Association Art Center (LaGrange, Georgia), Living Arts and Sciences Center (Lexington, Kentucky), Art Guild of Burlington (Iowa), University of Wyoming Art Museum (Laramie), the Rochester Art Center (Rochester, Minnesota), North Carolina Museum of Art, 1980-81, Mendenhall Student Center at East Carolina University (Greenville, North Carolina); Participated in numerous juried and invitational shows throughout the U.S.; Art Juror; Panel member and presenter at numerous workshops and conferences; Commission work includes logo for Douglas County Office of Children and Youth, 1978, poster for Associated Artists of Omaha Exhibition, 1977, 20 illustrations of waterfowl for publicity for Henry Doorly Zoo (Omaha), 1975, stationery designs for Riverfront Forum (1975) and University Gallery (1974). Organizational Memberships: Joslyn Art Museum, 1973-81; Mid-America and National College Art Associations, 1973-81; National Crafts Council, 1979; International Platform Association, 1980-81; Kappa Pi art fraternity (vice president, 1966); Omicron Delta Kappa leadership fraternity (treasurer, 1966). Community Activities: Donated art work to various benefits for local organizations, 1973-80; Organized and directed first Annual Summer City Scholarship Program Exhibition, Akron Art Institute (Akron, Ohio), 1973; University Arts Representative, Omaha Metropolitan Area Planning Agency, 1975; U.S. Friendship Force Ambassador to Costa Rica, 1979. Religion: Attends Roman Catholic Church (received Eagle of the Cross Award from Catholic Youth Organization Convention, 1963, president of church youth society). Published Works: Provided illustrations, cover designs and other artwork for several books and catalogs. Honors and Awards: Academic of Italy with Gold Medal, Accademia Italia delle Arti e del Lavoro, 1980; Fine Arts Merit recipient for general achievement, University of Nebraska at Omaha, 1974, 1975 and 1979; Elected to Blue Key Scholastic Society, Ohio University, 1973; Graduate Assistantship in Art, Pittsburg State University, 1970-71; Received William Parrott Scholarships, Pittsburg State University, 1964-67; Received Bertha A. Spencer Kappa Pi Scholarships, Pittsburg State University, 1965-67; Juror's Award, Kansas 5th National Small Drawing, Sculpture and Print Exhibition, Fort Hays State University, 1980; Best of Show, 3rd Biennial Print, Drawing and Painting Exhibition, College of St. Mary, Omaha, 1978; Sioux City Art Center Purchase Award, 40th Annual Fall Show, 1978; Received numerous other recognitions for artwork, including 2 University of Nebraska at Omaha grants; Biographical listings in many reference sources, including *International Dictionary of Contemporary Artists, American Artists of Renown, Who's Who in American Art*. Address: 5607 Howard, Omaha, Nebraska 68106.

Lawrence J Bradshaw

Brady, Winifred B

Assistant Director. Personal: Born November 28, 1933; Widow. Education: B.S., Rider College, 1954; M.B.A., Temple University, 1962. Career: Assistant Director, New Jersey Employment Service; Former Director, Personnel and Training, Department of Labor and Industry, New Jersey State Government. Organizational Memberships: American Society for Personnel Administration (national secretary, 1980-82; parliamentarian, 1979-82; former regional vice president, district director and chapter president); International Personnel Management Association; International Association of Personnel in Employment Security. Community Activities: Young Women's Christian Association of Burlington County (board of directors, 1980-83; chairman, personnel committee); Burlington County Commission on Women (chairman); Soroptimists International of Trenton; National Federation of Business and Professional Women (past state president; has held all principal state, district and chapter offices). Honors and Awards: 1 of 20 Selected by A.S.P.A. to travel to the People's Republic of China, 1979; United States Civil Service Commission, Career Education Program Fellow; Woman of the Year, New Jersey Business and Professional Women's Federation, 1978. Address: Bordentown, New Jersey.

Branch, Raymond L

Adult Care Home Administrator. Personal: Born August 3, 1928; Son of Augustus Branch, Irene Gilmore; Married Idaline Clark; Father of Joan Roberts, Pamela Gilyard, Pamela Whitaker, Bonnie Marshall. Education: B.S., Wichita State University, 1980. Military: Served in the United States Air Force, 1947-74, attaining the rank of Master Sergeant. Career: Adult Care Home Administrator. Organizational Memberships: Kansas Health Care Association. Community Activities: Wichita State University Alumni Association. Honors and Awards: Meritorious Service Medal, 1974; Bronze Star Medal, 1969; First Oak Leaf Cluster, Air Force Commendation Medal, 1972; Air Force Commendation Medal, 1968. Address: 615 E. Maywood, Wichita, Kansas 67216.

Brannon, Russell H

Professor, Chief of Party. Personal: Born August 25, 1931; Son of Dr. L. H. Brannon; Father of Shaun R., Paula L., Scot A. Education: B.S., Oklahoma State University, 1954; M.A., George Washington University, 1958; M.S. 1965, Ph.D. 1967, University of Wisconsin. Military: Served in the United States Chemical Corps, 1954-56, attaining the rank of First Lieutenant. Career: Professor of Agricultural Economics and Chief of Party, University of Kentucky/U.S.A.I.D. Program in Indonesia, 1981 to present; Professor of Agricultural Economics, University of Kentucky, 1974-81; Professor of Agricultural Economics and Chief of Party, University of Kentucky/U.S.A.I.D. Program in Thailand, 1971-74; Assistant to Associate Professor, University of Kentucky, 1967-71; Ford Foundation Research Associate, Uruguay and Argentina, 1965-67; Agricultural Advisor, U.S. Agency for International Development, Thailand, 1958-63. Organizational Memberships: American Agricultural Economic Association; Southern Agricultural Economic Association; International Association of Agricultural Economists; Gamma Sigma Delta; Phi Eta Sigma. Published Works: Author or Editor of Four Books and Numerous Monographs/Articles on International Agricultural Development. Honors and Awards: American Council Travel Award, International Agricultural Economic Meetings, U.S.S.R., 1969. Address: 3307 Roxburg Drive East, Lexington, Kentucky 40503.

Leo Branovan

Branovan, Leo

Professor Emeritus. Personal: Born April 17, 1895; Married Pearl Lhevine; Father of Rosalind B. Turner. Education: B.S., University of Wisconsin, 1924; M.S., University of Chicago, 1927; Additional part-time post-graduate study in Applied Mathematics, Columbia University, while involved as Consulting Mathematician in New York City, 1935-38. Career: Engineer, General Electric Co., Fort Wayne, Indiana, 1924-26; Instructor and Consultant in Mathematics, University of Minnesota, 1927-31; Consultant in Mathematics, J.P. Goode Co., Chicago, Illinois, 1932-34; Consulting Mathematician, New York City, 1935-38; Instructor and Consultant in Mathematics, Brooklyn Polytechnic Institute, 1939-44; Instructor-Professor of Mathematics, Marquette University, 1944-70; Professor Emeritus, Marquette University, 1970 to present. Organizational Memberships: American Mathematical Society; American Society for Engineering Education; American Association for the Advancement of Science; American Association of University Professors; Wisconsin Academy of Arts, Letters and Science; Number of Foreign Mathematical Associations. Community Activities: Marquette University (president's honor council, 1979 to present). Published Works: Author of an extensive research paper entitled "Umbilics on hyperellipsoids in four dimensions". Honors and Awards: Certificate of Recognition, Marquette University; Pi Mu Epsilon, 1946 to present; Fellow, International Biographical Association, 1977 to present; International Biographical Association Passport and Certificate of Fellowship; Initiated into Quarter Century Club, Marquette University, 1969; Life Membership, Milwaukee Central Young Men's Christian Association, 1974. Address: 3201 N. 48th St., Milwaukee, Wisconsin 53216.

Brasfield, Carolyn Allen

Executive Secretary. Personal: Born October 13, 1923, in Spartanburg, South Carolina; Daughter of Edward L. and Lucille Bonner Allen (both deceased); Married Otis E. Brasfield, on March 5, 1944, at Orlando, Florida; Mother of Otis E. Jr. Education: Graduate, Miami Senior High School, 1941; Associate Degree, Harrison's Business College, 1943; Completed courses at Savings & Loan Institute, 1962-66. Career: Home Savings Association, Odessa, Texas: Receptionist (1962-67), Assistant Secretary (1967-70), Senior Savings Officer and Assistant Vice President (1970-78); Executive Secretary, Financial Advisor, Meister Industries, Inc., 1978 to present. Community Activities: Civic Music Association; The Globe of the Great Southwest; Parent Teacher Association, 1952-58; Boy Scouts of America; Band Boosters Club; DeMolay Mothers' Circle; Nathaniel Davis Chapter, Daughters of the American Revolution, 1959 to present (regent, 1975-77; delegate to continental congress, 1974); General Matthew Duncan Ector Chapter, United Daughters of the Confederacy (charter and organizing member, 1958; president, 1961-62, 1977-80); Magna Charta Dames; Permian Basin Genealogical Society; Order of Eastern Star. Religion: Baptist. Honors and Awards: President's Citation, Odessa Chamber of Commerce, 1977 & 1978; Listed in *Texas Women of Distinction, Who's Who of American Women, Who's Who in Finance and Industry, Personalities of America, The World Who's Who of Women, Personalities of the South.* Address: 3103 North Hancock Avenue, Odessa, Texas 79762.

Carolyn A Brasfield

Braswell, Vernon Shirley (Pete)

Associate Professor. Personal: Born June 10, 1919, in Virginia; Son of Thomas Hilliard and Lottie Beatrice Braswell (both deceased); Married First Wife Laveta Ann Durham Johnson, November 21, 1942 (deceased); Second Wife Judith Anne Gualt Anderson, March 16, 1972; Third Wife Nancy Yvonne Walton, March 8, 1980; Father of Donald Lee. Education: Attended Randolph Macon College, Virginia, 1939-41; B.A., Central State University, Oklahoma, 1964; M.A., University of Oklahoma, 1965; Additional Studies at the University of Texas-Austin, 1978-80; Various Service Schools. Military: Served in the United States Army, 1941-61, attaining rank of Major, Artillery. Career: History Department, Del Mar College, Instructor 1965-70, Assistant Professor 1970-76, Associate Professor 1976 to present. Organizational Memberships: American Historical Association (life member); Retired Officers Association (life member); Reserve Officers Association; Del Mar Education Association; Southwestern Social Studies Association; Texas Junior College Teachers Association. Community Activities: International Lions Club (past member); Ancient Free and Accepted Masons; Scottish Rite of Free Masonry; Ancient Order Nobles Mystic Shrine; John J. Harris #397, National Sojourners (member in perpetuity; past president); Heroes of '76 (past commander); 32° Mason; Al Amin Temple A.A.O.N.M.S. (editor, *Salaam*, monthly magazine); Corpus Christi Youth Football League (coach, 3 years); Actor in Local Theatre Group; Candidate in the 1974 Local School Board Election; Sponsor, Youth Clubs. Religion: Christian Church. Published Works: Book Reviews and Articles in Historical Publications. Honors and Awards: Holder, Distinguished Presidential Unit Badge; Distinguished Philippine Presidential Unit Badge; Bronze Star; Purple Heart; Army Commendation Medal; Master Parachute Badge; Glider Badge; Other U.S. Army Ribbons and Medals; Listed in *International Register of Profiles, International Men and Women of Distinction, Personalities of the South, Notable Americans.* Address: 5902 S. Alameda, Corpus Christi, Texas 78412.

Bray, Charlena H

Executive Director. Personal: Born April 11, 1945; Married Paul Bray (deceased). Education: B.A., Miles College, 1965; M.A., University of Alabama, 1971; Advanced Certificate in Guidance and Counseling, University of Alabama-Birmingham, 1977; Ph.D. Candidate, University of Alabama. Career: Executive Director, Alabama Center for Higher Education; Interim Director, Program Chairman, Alabama Center for Higher Education, 1972-80; Secondary Mathematics Teacher, Jefferson County Public School System, 1965-72. Organizational Memberships: American Association for Higher Education; American Personnel and Guidance Association; Council for Interinstitutional Leadership. Community Activities: Cooper Green Hospital (10 year appointment to the board of trustees by the Jefferson County Commission, chairman of the personnel committee, executive committee); Alabama

Committee on the Humanities (board member); Birmingham Area Manpower Consortium (secretary, planning and advisory council); Council for Interinstitutional Leadership (board of directors); Volunteer and Information Center of Birmingham (board member). Religion: Union Baptist Church - Secretary, Associate Director of Church School. Honors and Awards: Xi Chapter, Kappa Delta Pi; Region IV Special Programs Award, 1976; Boquechitto Community Day Care Award, 1978; Award, Miles College Student Government Association, 1976; Rho Nu Tau Soror of the Year, 1976; Loundes County Health Services Association Award, 1978; Award, Birmingham Veterans Administration Hospital, 1977; Award, Volunteer and Information Center, 1978; Listed in *Who's Who in the South and Southwest*, *Outstanding Young Women of America*. Address: 3101 Lorna Road, Unit 424, Birmingham, Alabama 35216.

Breen, James L

Physician. Personal: Born September 5, 1926, in Chicago, Illinois; Son of John J. and Lucrece B. Breen; Married Doris; Father of Michael, Nash, Ann, Laura, Barbara, Beth. Education: Attended Johns Hopkins University, 1945-46; B.S., Northwestern University, 1948; M.D., Northwestern University Medical School, 1952; Intern, Walter Reed Army Hospital, 1952-53; Diploma, Medical Field Service School, Fort Sam Houston, Texas, 1954; Resident in Obstetrics and Gynecology, Walter Reed Army Hospital, 1954-57; Gynecologic Oncology, Walter Reed Army Hospital, 1957-58; Fellowship, Obstetric, Gynecologic and Breast Pathology, The Armed Forces Institute of Pathology, 1960-61; Additional Training, Gynecological Surgery, The University of Vienna, Austria, 1959; Radiophysics and Radiobiology, The Karolinski Institute, Stockholm, Sweden, 1960. Military: Served in the United States Army Reserve, 1952-53; Assistant Chief, Walter Reed Army Hospital; Assistant Chief and Acting Chief, Second General Hospital, Landstuhl, Germany, 1958-60; Honorable Discharge from the United States Marine Corps, 1961, attaining the rank of Major; Consultant, Armed Forces, Washington, D.C., 1965 to present. Career: Associate Professor, Department of Obstetrics and Gynecology, New Jersey College of Medicine and Dentistry, 1961-69; Director, Department of Obstetrics and Gynecology, Newark City Hospital (Martland Hospital), 1963-69; Director, Department of Obstetrics and Gynecology, Saint Barnabas Medical Center, Livingston, New Jersey, 1969 to present; Clinical Professor of Obstetrics and Gynecology, Jefferson Medical Center, Philadelphia, 1975 to present; Consultant, The Surgeon General's Office, Washington, D.C., 1965 to present; Consultant, Monmouth Medical Center, Long Branch, New Jersey, 1963 to present; Consultant, St. Elizabeth's Hospital, Elizabeth, New Jersey, 1963 to present; Consultant, Rahway Hospital, Rahway, New Jersey, 1965 to present; Consultant, Orange Memorial Hospital Center, Orange, New Jersey, 1965 to present; Consultant, John F. Kennedy Community Hospital, Edison, New Jersey, 1976 to present; Consultant, Margaret Hague Maternity Hospital, Jersey City, 1969 to present; Consultant, Elizabeth General Hospital, Elizabeth, New Jersey, 1972 to present; Consultant, Newton Memorial Hospital, Newton, New Jersey, 1975 to present; Practice Limited to Consultative Oncologic and Gynecologic Surgery. Organizational Memberships: American Medical Association; Association of Military Surgeons of the United States; Vienna Medical Society (life member); New York Academy of Sciences; American Board of Obstetricians and Gynecologists (diplomate); Academy of Medicine of New Jersey (fellow; secretary, ob-gyn section, 1965; chairman, ob-gyn section, 1965; board of trustees, 1966-69; chairman, education committee, 1967-69; board of trustees, 1969-73)); Essex County Medical Association; Association of Medical Writers; Association of Professors of Gynecology and Obstetrics; International Academy of Pathology (fellow); American Society of Cytology; American College of Obstetricians and Gynecologists (program committee, 1965-69; chairman, nurses postgraduate education, 1969-70; chairman, membership committee, 1968-70; section chairman, 1971-73; national committee, continuing education, 1971-74; national committee, audiovisual, 1974-76; national chairperson, syllabus committee, 1975-76; program committee, district I, II and III meeting, 1974-76; vice-chairman, district III, 1974-77; chairman, district III, 1977-80; national vice-chairman, learning resources commission, 1977-80; national task force chairman, 1977-81); Society of Colposcopists and Colpomicroscopists (founding fellow); International College of Surgeons (fellow, regent); New Jersey Hospital Association; American Society of Cytology (certified cytologist); Pan-American Cancer Cytology Society; American Society of Clinical Pathologists (associate member); International Society for the Study of Vulvar Disease; New Jersey Oncology Society; Radium Society; New York Metropolitan Breast Cancer Group; Society of Vaginal Surgeons; American Board of Obstetricians and Gynecologists; New Jersey Medical Society (secretary, ob-gyn section, 1965; chairman, ob-gyn section, 1966; chairman, education committee, 1967-70; board of trustees, 1967-70); American College of Surgeons (audiovisual committee, 1973-75; committee on medical motion pictures, 1972-78, 1978-81; liaison officer for cancer, state of New Jersey, 1973 to present; membership committee, 1979); American Cancer Society (head of task force to conquer uterine cancer for the state of New Jersey, 1973-75; national blue ribbon panel, "Cigarette Smoking and Its Effects on Pregnancy", 1977). Honors and Awards: Golden Apple Award, Student, American Medical Association, 1967; Award for Meritorious Service, American Medical Association, 1966; Consultant, Society of Medical Consultants to the Armed Forces, 1965; Fellow, New York Obstetrical Society, 1964; Fellow, New Jersey Obstetrical and Gynecological Society, 1963; Mid-Eastern Travel Club, 1963. Address: 9 Kermit Road, Maplewood, New Jersey 07040.

Arnold Brekke

Breen, J William

General Manager. Personal: Born August 4, 1945; Son of Joseph J. Breen; Married Linda Jean Miller; Father of Tara Leigh, William Ryan. Education: B.A., B.Ch.E., University of Delaware, 1968; M.B.A., Wharton School of Business, 1971. Military: Served in the United States Army Reserve, 1968-74. Career: Westvaco Corporation - General Manager of Oleochemicals Department 1979 to present, General Marketing Manager 1978, Marketing Manager of Carbon Department 1976, Operations Manager of Custom Chemicals Department 1975, District Sales Manager 1974, Product Manager 1973, Marketing Associate 1971. Organizational Memberships: American Institute of Chemical Engineering; Pulp Chemicals Association; Soap and Detergent Association (steering committee, fatty acid division) Honors and Awards: Award of Special Recognition for Teaching Excellence, Wharton School of Business, 1970-71; Best Article of the Year, *The Wharton Journal*, 1970-71. Address: 6 Beachwood East, Isle of Palms, South Carolina 29451.

Brekke, Arnold

Counselor, Consultant, Scientist. Personal: Born July 31, 1910. Education: Attended Commercial College; B.S., with highest distinction, University of Minnesota, 1942; Undertook graduate studies: University of Minnesota, University of Chicago, Stanford University; Ph.D., University of Minnesota, 1952. Military: Served with the United States Air Force during World War II as a Meteorologist; Served with the United States Army during World War II in Military Intelligence G2. Career: Professor and Scientist, Counselor, Advisor, Administrator, University of Minnesota, University of California, University of Maryland (chairman of European Department of Economics), Michigan State University, Normandale College; Creator/Producer, Proprietor, Brekke Knowledge-Resource-Production Enterprises, and Inventor, 1924 to present; Honorary Appointment to the Editorial Advisory Board of the American Biographical Institute. Organizational Memberships: The Explorers Club (fellow); International Platform Association; International Biographical Centre (fellow); The Planetary Society; Anglo-American Academy (honorary fellow); National Space Institute; New Directions; Success Leaders Speakers Service; International Peace Research Association; The Society for General and Liberal Studies (founder, first president): American Economic Association; Other Relevant Scientific and

Educational Professional Organizations. Published Works: Articles and Outlined Articles, Produced and Published by Brekke Knowledge-Resource Creation-Production Enterprises include "Elements of a Decision Making Theory of Price Establishment, Including Inflation", "A (The) Theoretical System of Achieving Permanent Universal World Peace - An Outline Presentation", "Some Essential Attributes (Constituents) of an Optimally Knowledgeably Functioning International Relations Policy for the United States", many others; Book *Readings in the Social Sciences;* Member of Content Selection and Editorial Committees for *The Development of Agricultural Policy (Towards a Multiscientific Model for Optimally Producing an Optimum Society); Ideology and Capitalistic Stability and Growth: Revised Edition.* Honors and Awards: Alpha Zeta; Gamma Sigma Delta; The Court of Honor, 1942; Valedictorian, University of Minnesota, 1942; Awarded every scholarship prize and honor for which he was eligible, University of Minnesota, 1939-42; Dean's Citation proclaiming him "all-time valedictorian", University of Minnesota, 1942; Honoris Causa, Knight Chevalier, International Order of Michael the Archangel; Honorary Member, American Police Hall of Fame; Honorary Fellow, Harry S. Truman Research Institute; Accepted invitation from International Biographical Center and cooperatively from the Library of Congress to write Autobiography to be deposited and permanently stored in these institutions; Listed in various biographical reference books. Address: 1085 Montreal Ave., #1804, St. Paul, Minnesota 55116.

Charlotte M Brett

Brereton, Maritza Beato

Psychometrist/Psychotherapist. Personal: Born October 9, 1949, Havana, Cuba; Daughter of Dr. and Mrs. Jorge Beato; Married Thomas F. Brereton; Mother of Alejandro Jorge, David Rafael. Education: B.A., University of Texas-San Antonio, 1976; M.A., St. Mary's University, 1981. Career: Psychometrist/Psychotherapist in Private Practice; Advocacy Counselor for the Handicapped, Goodwill Rehabilitation Service, 1980-81. Organizational Memberships: Bexar County Psychological Association; American Rehabilitation Association; American Personnel and Guidance Association; American Orthopsychiatric Association. Community Activities: Mayor's Committee on Employment of the Handicapped; League of Women Voters of San Antonio (board member); San Antonio Literacy Council, Inc. (board member); Republican National Hispanic Assembly of San Antonio (secretary); Texas Delegation of the National Association of Cuban-American Women of the U.S.A., Inc. (president, founder); Mayor's Commission on the Status of Women (associate member); San Antonio Citizens Concerned with the Handicapped; San Antonio Association for Retarded Citizens; San Antonio Mental Health Association; San Antonio Arts Council; San Antonio Museum Association; San Antonio Area Association for Bilingual Education; Friends in Human Potential. Honors and Awards: Psi Chi; Alpha Mu Gamma; Listed in *Minority American Women: A Biographical Directory, Personalities of America, Directory of Distinguished Americans, American Registry Series.* Address: 111 Lindell, San Antonio, Texas, 78212.

Brett, Charlotte Mae

Educator. Personal: Born November 30, 1904, in Dickinson County, Iowa. Education: B.A., University of Northern Iowa, 1933; M.A., Columbia University Teachers College, 1946; Undertook graduate courses at several midwestern universities. Career: Educator, public schools of Iowa, South Dakota, Michigan, and Illinois, 41 years, including appointments as 1st and 2nd Grade Teacher, Blue Island, Illinois, 1944-70; Resource Person, Class in Iowa history and genealogy; Teacher, Iowa Lakes Community College, 1978-79; Speaker on various phases of genealogy for business and social groups, 1976-79. Community Activities: Lydia Alden Chapter, Daughters of the American Revolution (regent 1974-76); Lakes Chapter, Daughters of the American Colonists (regent 1978-80); Iowa Daughters of the American Colonists (state chaplain 1980-82); Iowa State Dames of the Court of Honor (corresponding secretary 1974-78, historian 1978-80); Huguenot Society; First Families of Ohio; Iowa Lakes Genealogical Society (organizing chairman and librarian). Published Works: Author, *Northwest Iowains Share Their Memories.* Honors and Awards: Certificate of Appreciation, Parker Historical Society of Clay County; Life membership, pin and certificate, Illinois Parent Teacher Association; Listed in *Book of Honor.* Address: 218 East 4th Street, Apt. 4A, Spencer, Iowa 51301.

Brewster, Ethel Craig

Retired City Treasurer. Personal: Born July 30, 1889; Daughter of Benjamin Kellar and Anna Bell Young Heisler, (both deceased); Widow. Career: City Treasurer, 32 years; Former Deputy County Clerk, Deputy City Treasurer, Deputy Circuit Clerk, Circuit Clerk (appointed by governor), Others. Organizational Memberships: Quota Club (president, 1955-57, 1957-59, 1969-71, 1973-75 and historian, 1979-81); Step County Humane Society (president, 1952-1981). Community Activities: American Business Women's Association (chairman education committee 1981); Republican Women's Club (parliamentarian and historian 1979-81); Step County Nursing Center (volunteer 1956-81); Donations to all worthy organizations on the local, national and international levels. Religion: First Lutheran Church; Dorcas Circle Recorder, 1979-81. Honors and Awards: Plaque from Dalton Adding Machine Company Touch Operator 1922, March of Dimes 1960-63, American Business Womens Association for being Woman of the Year; Quota Club for being Honorary Member 1969, Step County Nursing Home Service 1973, International Quota Club for Outstanding Achievement 1974; Listed in *Notable Americans of the Bicentennial Era, Community Leaders and Noteworthy Americans, International Who's Who of Community Leaders, Book of Honor, World Who's Who of Women, Community Leaders and Noteworthy Americans.* Address: 725 West Galena Ave., Freeport, Illinois 61032.

K A Brick

Brick, Katherine Adams

Pilot, Safety Counselor. Personal: Born August 8, 1910; Married Frank Reeve Brick, Jr.; Mother of R. Canivet Brick Macario. Education: Graduate Sargent College; B.S., Boston University; M.A., New York University; Undertook graduate work at Columbia University. Military: Active in Civil Air Patrol, Bendix Square; Entered Women's Airforce Service Pilots and graduate Advanced Ferry Command Pilot, 1943. Career: Institutor, Co-Chairman, "Colt for Kim and Women of Korea"; Federal Aviation Administration Safety Counselor, 1972 to present; Co-piloted Queen Air to Australia; Holds current pilot license. Organizatonal Memberships: Ninety-Nines, International Women Pilots (international president, 1950-51); Federal Aviation Administration Advisory Committee, 1968-71; National Pilots Association (secretary of board, 6 years); Aviation/Space Writers Association, 1946 to present; P-47 Thunderbolt Pilots Association (secretary of board, 8 years). Community Activities: Powder Puff Derby (chairman, executive director, 13 years; board of directors, 25 years); Institutor/Chairman for votive model of Amelia Earhart's Lockheed Vega to hang in Protestant Chapel, John F. Kennedy International Airport, New York, 1976. Published Works: *Thirty Sky Blue Years, Powder Puff Derby Album, Powder Puff Derby Commemmorative Update.* Honors and Awards: Special Award, Sargent College Alumni, Boston University; Federal Aviation Administration's Certificate of Commendation; Amelia Earhart Medals, Ninety-Nines, 1949, 1960, 1976; Paul Tissandier Diploma, Federation Aeronautique Internationale, 1973; Aviation Hall of Fame of New Jersey, 1978; National Pioneer Women's Award 1981, OX 5 Aviation Pioneers; Winner, Nolder Derby New York-Miami; Listed in *Notable Americans of the Bicentennial Era, Who's Who of American Women, Who's Who in the East, World Who's Who of Women, International Biographical Dictionary.* Address: 622 Golden Road, Fallbrook, California 92028.

Bridges, Julian Curtis

Professor and Department Head. Personal: Born April 3, 1931; Son of Mrs. B. M. Bridges; Married Charlotte Martin; Father of Rebecca Ann, Deborah Lea, Esther Marelyn. Education: A.B., University of Florida, 1952; B.D. 1956, Th.D. 1961, Southwestern Baptist Theological Seminary; M.A. 1969, Ph.D. 1973, University of Florida. Career: Professor of Sociology and Head, Department of Sociology/Social Work, Hardin-Simmons University; Former Director, University Student Center, National Autonomous University of Mexico. Organizational Memberships: National Council on Family Relations; Texas Council on Family Relations (executive board); Population Association of America; Southwestern Sociological Association. Community Activities: Community Relations Committee of the City of Abilene, 1974-78; Community Development Committee of the City of Abilene (member 1974-76; chairman, 1975-76); Citizens for Better Government (nominating committee for new members of the city council, 1974-76). Religion: Pastor, Spanish-English Speaking Congregations, 1954-57. Published Works: Author *Into Aztec Land; Sociology: A Pragmatic Approach;* Numerous Articles in Professional Journals. Honors and Awards: Phi Kappa Phi; Lily Foundation Teaching Fellow, Southwestern Baptist Theological Seminary, 1957-58; Alpha Kappa Delta; National Defense Education Act Title VI Fellow, University of Florida, 1969-70; Fellow, Institute of Latin American Studies, The University of Texas-Austin, 1975; Listed in *Outstanding Educators of America, Who's Who in Texas, Who's Who in the South and Southwest, American Men and Women in Science*. Address: 1526 N. Pioneer Drive, Abilene, Texas 79603.

Briggs, Hilton Marshall

Retired, University President Emeritus. Personal: Born January 9, 1913; Married Lillian D. Briggs; Father of Dinus M., Janice S. Education: B.S., Iowa State University, 1933; M.S., North Dakota State University, 1935; Ph.D., Cornell University, 1938. Career: Oklahoma State University - Assistant Professor 1936-41, Associate Professor 1941-45, Associate Director of Experimental Station and Associate Dean of Agriculture 1949-50; University of Wyoming - Dean of Agriculture and Director of Agriculture Experiment Station 1950-58; South Dakota State University - President 1958-75, Distinguished Professor of Agriculture 1975 to present, Director of Foreign Program 1977-78, President Emeritus 1975 to present. Organizational Memberships: American Society of Animal Science (secretary, 1947-50; vice president, 1951; president, 1952); National Research Council Committee on Animal Nutrition, 1951-57; Commission of Colleges and Universities North Central Association, 1969-73. Community Activities: Continental Dorset Club (executive committee, 1943-48; president, 1948); American Southdown Breeders Association (director, 1970-76; director for life, 1976 to present); United States Chamber of Commerce; Rotary Club (local president, 1979). Religion: Methodist. Honors and Awards: Fellow, American Society of Animal Science, 1974; Fellow, American Association for the Advancement of Science, 1962; Alpha Zeta; Gamma Sigma Delta; Phi Kappa Phi; Sigma Xi; Builder of Man Award, Farm House Fraternity, 1960; National 4-H Club Alumni Award, 1959; Exceptional Service Award, United States Air Force, 1975; Decoration for Distinguished Civilian Service, Department of Army, 1974 Outstanding Citizen of South Dakota, 1975; Portrait to Saddle and Sirloin Gallery, 1978. Address: 1734 Garden Square, Brookings, South Dakota 57006.

Julian Bridges

Brigman, Constance Morgan

Broadcasting Executive. Personal: Born July 9, 1952, in Winston-Salem, North Carolina; Daughter of Otis Caston and Carol Penrose Brigman. Education: A.A., Stephens College, 1972; B.A., University of Missouri-Kansas City, 1974. Career: Disc Jockey, Station KCUR-FM, Kansas City, 1974; with Quastler Advertising, Fairway, Kansas, 1975; Account Executive, KAYQ-AM (Kansas City) 1976-77, KBEQ-FM (Kansas City) 1977-78, KMBC-TV (Kansas City) 1978-80; National Sales Representative, Metro Television Sales (Metromedia), Chicago, 1980 to present. Organizational Memberships: American Women in Radio and Television (chapter affirmative action chairman, 1979); Broadcast Advertising Club, Chicago; Alpha Epsilon Rho. Community Activities: Member of Republican Party. Religion: Presbyterian. Address: Wrigley Bldg., 410 N. Michigan Avenue, Chicago, Illinois 60611.

Britt, George Gittion Jr

Board Chairman and Certified Management Consultant. Personal: Born May 19, 1949; Son of George Sr., and Mary Britt. Education: B.A., Cheyney State College; Also attended the University of Miami, University of Chicago, Temple University, Pennsylvania State University, Georgetown University, University of Southern California. Career: Board Chairman and Certified Management Consultant; Former Positions include Chairman, West Philadelphia Community Development Program; Chairman, Cobbs Creek Development Association; Executive Director, United Minority Enterprise Associates. Organizational Memberships: National Association of Puerto Rican Youth (chairman); International Economic Development Forum (chairman). Community Activities: American Society for Public Administration; International City Management Association; Chicago Historical Society; North Philadelphia Committee for Total Development; Pennsylvania Education Association; National Education Association; Council on Municipal Performance; National Association of Counties. Religion: Baptist, Pastor Aids. Honors and Awards: Honorary Citizen of Texas, Minnesota, West Virginia, Minneapolis, Alabama, Arkansas, Kentucky; Award from Edison High School. Address: 906 S. 60th Street, Philadelphia, Pennsylvania 19143.

Britton, Michael Linn

Army Chaplain. Personal: Born September 27, 1956; Son of Mr. and Mrs. M. Robert Britton; Married to Cassandra Lynne; Father of Mandy Lynne. Education: Graduate, Terre Haute North Vigo High School, 1974; B.A., cum laude, Johnson Bible College, 1978; M.Div., The Graduate Seminary of Phillips University, 1982; Attended Mansfield College, Oxford University, 1980-81; Officer Basic Course (C-20), Chaplain Center, U.S. Army, 1981. Military: Serving with United States Army as Chaplain, 2nd Lieutenant, 1980 to present. Career: Ordained, June, 1976; Evangelist, 1981; Youth Director; Promotion Person of Christian Children's Home of Ohio, 1975; Participates in Christian singing with his wife; Former Minister, Madison Park Christian Church, Quincy, Illinois; Former Minister, First Christian Church, Lebanon, Tennessee; Former Editor and Associate Producer of T.V. show, *By the Way*. Organizational Memberships: Johnson Bible College Alumni Association; Ministerial Alliance of Covington, Oklahoma; National Ministers Alliance. Community Activities: Special Olympics volunteer; Chairperson, St. Jude Research Hospital Bike-a-thon in Covington, Oklahoma, 1981; World Vision supporter; Member of student senate, Phillips Universtiy, 1980; Student Council (secretary of graduate seminary of Phillips University, 1981-82). Honors and Awards: Marksmanship Award, 1972; Associate Member, A.B.I.R.A., 1981; Y.M.C.A. volunteer awards, 1974 and 1979; Listed in *Personalities of the South, Community Leaders of America, Book of Honor, National Dean's List*. Address: Box 15, Covington, Oklahoma 73730.

Britton, Morrene Hughes

Professional Farmer. Personal: Born June 24, 1941; Daughter of Morrison and Irene Hughes (both deceased); Married to Robert Lynn; Mother of Alison. Education: Salutatorian, Fayette High School, 1959; Attended Carleton College, 1959-60; B.S., cum laude, University of Missouri, 1963; Attended Wilson Flight Training Center, 1966. Career: President and General Manager, Hughes Farms, Inc.; Flight Instructor for Enlow Flying Service (Boonville, Missouri) and Wilson Flight Training Center (Kansas City, Kansas), 1965-70; Co-Manager of Hughes Farms (became Hughes Farms, Inc. in 1971), 1963-65 and 1971. Organizational Memberships: National Federation of Independent Businesses, 1973 to present; American Bonanza Society, 1975 to present; American Farm Bureau Association, 1973 to present. Community Activities: L.T.S. Club (federated club); Volunteer work with bloodmobile, senior citizens and scholarship programs, 1977 to present; National Family Union, 1969 to present; Missouri Extension Service Panel, currently conducting an opinion survey of most important issues affecting the Mid-Missouri area during the coming decade. Religion: Member of First Christian Church, Fayette, Missouri, 1949 to present (member, board of directors). Honors and Awards: John Philip Sousa Music Award; D.A.R. Good Citizen Award, 1959; Member of Gamma Sigma Delta, honorary society of agriculture, 1963. Address: Route 3, Fayette, Missouri 65248.

Brodhead, Quita

Artist. Personal: Mother of Edith Good, Truxtun E., Charles S. W. Education: Attended the Pennsylvania Academy of Fine Arts; Grande Chaumier, Julienne's (Paris); Alexander Archipenko; Arthur Carles; Continuing Private Criticisms. Career: Painter. Organizational Memberships: Artists Equity (charter member); Museum of Modern Art, New York; Philadelphia Art Alliance; Philadelphia Art Museum Institute of Contemporary Art; Veterans Adminstration Center for Creative Arts (fellow); Pennsylvania Academy of Fine Arts (fellowship). Honors and Awards: Gold Medal Award, 1950; Caroline Gibbons Granger Memorial Prize, 1955; Ohio College of Fine Arts 2nd Prize, 1951; Honorary Mention, Wilmington Society of Fine Arts, Chester County Art Association; 8 One-Woman Shows in New York City; 8 One-Woman Shows in Philadelphia; One-Woman Show in Pittsburgh, Pennsylvania, and in Rome, Italy. Address: 311 Atlee Road, Wayne, Pennsylvania 19087.

Brodkey, Robert Stanley

Professor of Chemical Engineering. Personal: Born September 14, 1928; Son of Harold R. Brodkey; Married Carolyn E. Patch; Father of Philip A. Education: A.A., San Francisco City College, 1948; B.S., M.S., University of California, 1950; Ph.D., University of Wisconsin, 1952. Career: Professor of Chemical Engineering; Former Research Chemical Engineer, Esso Research and Engineering Company. Organizational Memberships: American Institute of Chemical Engineers; American Chemical Society; Sigma Xi; Phi Lambda Upsilon; American Institute of Physics; Society of Rheology; American Association for the Advancement of Science. Honors and Awards: Visiting Professor Award, Japan Society for the Promotion of Science, 1978; Alexander von Humboldt Senior U.S. Scientist Award, 1975; Expository Lecture, G.A.M.M. Conference, Goettingen, 1975; Senior Fellowship in Science, N.A.T.O., 1972; Sigma Xi; Highest Honors from the University of California; Phi Lambda Upsilon; Outstanding Paper of Year, Canadian Society of Chemical Engineers; Alpha Gamma Sigma. Address: 246 North Delta Drive, Columbus, Ohio 43214.

Rachel B F Bromberg

Bromberg, Rachel Berezow Frank

Poet, Artist. Personal: Born July 24, 1917; Married Benjamin Bromberg. Education: B.A., New York University, 1940; M.A., University of Wisconsin, 1942; Ph.D., Bryn Mawr College, 1944; Post-Doctoral Scholar, City College of New York, Johns Hopkins University. Career: Poet, Artist. Organizational Memberships: Modern Language Association. Community Activities: General Organization (vice president); The Ruby Seal (founder, president); American Association of University Professors. Honors and Awards: Gold Medal Award, Accademia Italia delle Arti e del Lavoro; Gold Medal and Certificate, Accademia Italia, 1980; Listed in *Dictionary of Contemporary European Artists.* Address: 137-57 228th Street, Laurelton, New York 11413.

Bronson, Shirley Gerene

Financial Manager, Feminist Consultant. Personal: Born October 15, 1936; Daughter of Dee Lawrence (deceased) and Velma Geneva Smith Green; Married Bobby Ed, September 29, 1953; Mother of Richard Ed, David Dee, Daniel Lee, Robert Edward. Education: B.A. cum laude 1975, M.B.A. with distinction 1977, Golden Gate University. Career: Air Force Flight Test Center, Edwards, California - Federal Women's Program Manager 1973-74, Assistant to Comptroller 1974-76, Records Management Officer 1976-77; Program/Budget Analyst 1977 to present, Federal Women's Program Manager 1979 to present, Air Force Space Division, Los Angeles; Contract Teacher, Pacific Christian College, 1977 to present; Former Data Processing Manager, Navy C.O.M.S.U.B.P.A.C., Hawaii; Page Aircraft, Data Processing Division, Hawaii; Western Electric, Nashville, Tennessee. Organizational Memberships: National Association of Female Executives; American Society of Military Comptrollers, Los Angeles Chapter; Federally Employed Women, Inc.; Los Angeles Federal Executive Board (federal women's program committee); Air Force Association, Los Angeles Chapter. Community Activities: Beta Sigma Phi (Gamma Alpha Tau Chapter, historian, librarian, 1970-72; Lancaster City Council, vice president 1972-73, parliamentarian/recording secretary 1972-74; Sigma Omicron Chapter, president 1973-74); Antelope Valley Chapter, Federally Employed Women, Inc. (president, 1976, 1977); Southern California Chapter, Icelandic/American Club (vice president, 1976, 1977). Religion: Protestant. Published Works: "Space Division is Number One Federal Women's Program". Honors and Awards: Certificate of Merit, Air Force Systems Command, 1972; Outstanding Performance Awards, 1971, 1972, 1975, 1976; Sustained Superior Performance Award, Department of Air Force, 1971, 1976; Department of Air Force Certificate of Appreciation, 1976; Air Force Flight Test Center Federal Women's Program Special Recognition Award, 1976; Special Achievement Award, 1971, 1976; Air Force System Command Federal Women's Program Manager of Year, 1979; Department of Air Force Federal Women's Program Manager of Year, Distinguished Equal Employment Opportunity Award, 1980; Los Angeles Federal Executive Board, Distinguished Public Service Award, 1981; Listed in *Who's Who of American Women, Who's Who in the West, Personalities of America, Directory of Distinguished Americans, World Who's Who of Women, Personalities of the West and Midwest.* Address; 8640 Gulana Avenue, #J-1012, Playa Del Ray, California 90291.

Brookeman, Valerie Ann Bain

Professor, Consultant. Personal: Born August 2, 1943, in Dundee, Scotland; Daughter of John T. and Anne N. Bain; Married James Robert Brookeman; Mother of Hamish John Harry, Katharine Anne Rose. Education: B.S. with first class honors 1965, Ph.D. 1968, St. Andrews University, Scotland. Career: Tutor and Laboratory Demonstrator, Physics Department, University of St. Andrews,

Scotland, 1965-68; University of Florida College of Medicine - Instructor in Radiation Physics 1968-70, Assistant Professor of Radiation Physics 1970-72, Associate Professor of Radiation Physics 1972-79, Professor of Radiation Physics 1979 to present, Courtesy Appointment to the Department of Nuclear Engineering Sciences 1972 to present, Student Vocational Advisor for Radiology Department 1972 to present, Graduate Faculty to Teacher Graduate Level Courses and Direct Masters Theses 1972 to present, Graduate Faculty to Direct Doctoral Dissertations 1974 to present; Senior Physicist, Department of Nuclear Medicine, Guy's Hospital, London, 1978-80; Consultant, Veterans Administration Hospital, Gainesville, Florida, 1971 to present; Reviewer, *Physics in Medicine and Biology*, 1979 to present. Organizational Memberships: Society of Nuclear Medicine (board of trustees, 1981 to present; board of governors, instrumentation council, 1980 to present; special committee on quality control, 1976 to present; government relations committee 1977-79); American Association of Physicists in Medicine (nuclear medicine committee, science council, 1979 to present); American Association for the Advancement of Science; Sigma Xi; Institute of Electronic and Electric Engineering Nuclear Society; Technical Electronic Product Radiation Safety Standards Committee of the Food and Drug Administration, 1979 to present; National Institutes of Health (diagnostic research advisory group, National Cancer Institute, 1978 to present); Association for Women Faculty, University of Florida (president-elect, 1981 to present). Published Works: Most recent publications include "Performance Characteristics of Seven-Pinhole Tomography", "Comparison of Seven-Pinhole Computed Tomograms and Planar Scintigrams in Thallium-201 Myocardial Imaging", "Computers and Quality Control in Nuclear Medicine". Honors and Awards: Science Research Council Scholarship for Post-Graduate Studies for Ph.D., 1965; Neil Arnott Prize for Best Performance in Final Honors Degree Examinations, 1965; Listed in *Who's Who in American Men and Women of Science, Who's Who of American Women, World Who's Who of Women, Personalities of America, Personalities of the South*. Address: 2056 N.W. 20th Lane, Gainesville, Florida 32605.

John G Brosky

Brookins, Douglas G

Professor. Personal: Born September 27, 1936; Son of Rex and Ellyn Brookins; Married Barbara H. Flashman; Father of Laura Beth, Rachel Sarah. Education: A.B., University of California-Berkeley, 1958; Ph.D., Massachusetts Institute of Technology, 1963. Career: Professor of Geology, University of New Mexico; Formerly - Physicist, AVCO Corporation; Visiting Staff Scientist, Los Alamos National Laboratory; Assistant/Associate Professor of Geology, Kansas State University; Part-Time Geologist, U.S.G.S., Kansas Geological Survey, Maine Geological Survey, Connecticut Geological Natural History Survey. Organizational Memberships: Geological Society of America (fellow); American Institute of Chemistry (fellow); Explorers Club (fellow); American Association for the Advancement of Science; A.A.P.G.; Geochemical Society; I.A.G.C.; American Association of University Professors; Society of Economical Geology; S.E.P.M.; New Mexico Geological Society; New York Academy of Science; A.G.U.; I.A.G.O.D.; S.E.G.; Mineral Society of America. Community Activities: U.S.D.O.E. (program revision committee, low level waste management); Congregation Albert (board of trustees, 1974-80); Jewish Community Council, Albuquerque (board of trustees, 1973-78); Temple Albert Men's Club, B'nai B'rith (finance section, 1972-73). Religion: Religious School Chairman, 1975-80). Honors and Awards: Phi Beta Kappa (president, Alpha of Kansas State University); Sigma Xi; Outstanding Researcher/Teacher, Kansas State University, 1970. Address: 3410 Groman Court, N.E., Albuquerque, New Mexico 87110.

Brooks, Jan Leeman

Consultant. Personal: Born February 7, 1942; Daughter of Walter Edward and Vivolene Rushing Leeman. Education: B.A., David Lipscomb College, 1964; M.S.W., University of Alabama, 1974. Career: Assistant Professor of Social Work, University of Alabama; Director, Social Work Services, The Retreat Mental Health Hospital; Consultant, Clinical Program, Law School, The University of Alabama. Organizational Memberships: Council on Social Work Education, 1978 to present; National Association of Social Workers, 1979 to present (president, Alabama chapter, 1980-82). Community Activities: State Department of Pensions and Security Advisory Council on Social Services, 1980-83 (appointed by commissioner to governor's cabinet); Tuscaloosa Mental Health Association, 1978 to present; National Wildlife Federation; Alabama Conservancy; Sierra Club; Wilderness Society. Honors and Awards: Alabama's Outstanding Young Woman, 1978; One of Ten Outstanding Young Women in America, 1978; Listed in *Men and Women of Distinction, World Who's Who of Women, Who's Who in the South and Southwest, Who's Who in Community Service, Directory of Distinguished Americans, Personalities of America*. Address: P. O. Box 313, University, Alabama 35486.

Brosky, John G

Superior Court Judge. Personal: Born August 4, 1920; Married to Rose F.; Father of John C., David J., Carol A. Education: B.A., 1942, LL.B., 1949, J.D., 1968, University of Pittsburgh. Military: Retired from United States Air Force with rank of Brigadier General, 1980; Retired from Air National Guard with rank of Major General, 1980; Served in World War II as Captain, Artillery, South Pacific, 1942-46. Career: Judge, Superior Court of State of Pennsylvania; Judge of Common Pleas, Court of Allegheny County, 1961-80; Former Administrative Judge, Family Division, Common Pleas Court; Judge of County Court of Allegheny County, 1956-61; Former Assistant County Solicitor for Allegheny County. Organizational Memberships: Allegheny County Bar Association; Pennsylvania Bar Association; American Judicature Society; American Bar Association; Pennsylvania Association on Probation, Parole and Correction; Pennsylvania Joint State Government Commission Task Force on Military Laws (legislative advisory drafting subcommittee, 1972); Juvenile Court Judges Commission, 1973-79; Conference of Conciliation Courts, 1975; National Council of Juvenile Court Judges, 1970; Association of Trial Lawyers of America; Pennsylvania College of the Judiciary (faculty member); Pennsylvania Joint Family Law Council. Community Activities: Air Force Association (national president, past state president, national director); Member, Boys' Club of Western Pennsylvania; Board of Directors, Cruiser Olympia Association, Inc., 1980; Past Director, Health and Welfare Association; Past President, Information and Volunteer Services of Allegheny County; Past Director, American Cancer Society; Member, Press Club of Pittsburgh; Member, Historical Society of Western Pennsylvania; Member, Borough and Township Police Association; Past President, Greater Pittsburgh Guild for the Blind. Religion: Director of Holy Family Institute, Pennsylvania (member of holy name society, serra club, Catholic War Veterans). Honors and Awards: Received Certificate of Commendation, Masonic S.I.R. Knights of Pittsburgh Commandery, 1980; Distinguished Service Award, Pennsylvania National Guard Association, 1980; Pennsylvania Distinguished Service Medal; Legion of Merit, U.S.A.F.; Man of the Year, American Legion, 1978; State Humanitarian Award, Domestic Relations Association of Pennsylvania, 1978; Jimmy Doolittle Fellow Award, Aerospace Education Foundation, 1975; General Ira Eaker Fellowship Award, 1981; Presidential Citation, Air Force Association, 1970; Distinguished Citation, Military Order of World Wars; Patriotic Civilian Service Award, Army Air Defense Command, 1965; Cited for outstanding Americanism programs by resolution adopted by Pennsylvania House of Representatives, 1965; Man of the Year in the field of Law, Pittsburgh Jaycees, 1960. Address: 29 Greenview Drive, Carnegie, Pennsylvania 15106.

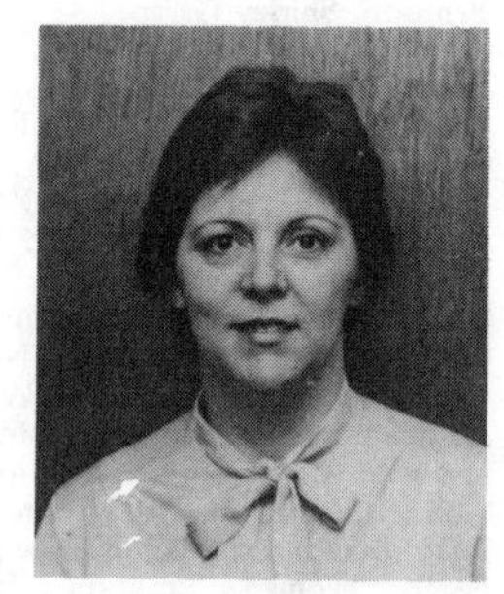
Brenda A Brothers

Brothers, Brenda Alice

Air Traffic Control Specialist. Personal: Born February 2, 1950; Daughter of William and Beverly Michaud; Married Leslie E.

Brothers; Mother of Timothy, Thomas. Education: Attended Sheppard Technical Training Center, August-November 1968; New York State Regents Diploma, Massena Central Schools, 1968; Air Traffic Control Specialist, Federal Aviation Academy, 1977. Military: Served with the United States Air Force, 1968-69; Served with the United States Army Reserve, 1975-76. Career: Air Traffic Control Specialist. Organizational Memberships: National Management Association, 1970-71. Community Activities: Student Guides, 1964-68; United Way, 1975-76; Seaway Credit Union Collector, 1971-76; Veteran's of Foreign Wars Drum and Bugle Corps, 1960-64; Federal Women's Program (coordinator, 1974-76); Cub Scout Den Leader, 1979-80; Marriae Encounter, 1980 to present. Religion: Elected Member, St. Raymond's Church Council, 1982. Honors and Awards: Leadership Award 1968; Special Achievement Award, 1978; Listed in *Who's Who of American Women.* Address: Star Route, Massena, New York 13662.

Arlene S Brotman

Brotman, Arlene Sandra

Social Worker, Psychotherapist. Personal: Born June 7, 1948; Daughter of Sam and Sylvia Brotman. Education: B.A., magna cum laude, State University of New York at Albany, 1970; N.D.E.A. Fellowship for Critical Languages, Indiana University, Summer 1969; M.A., University of Pennsylvania, 1971; M.S.W., Adelphi University, 1977. Career: New York State Certified French Teacher; New York State Certified Russian Teacher; New York State Certified Attendance Teacher; New York State Certified Social Worker, Psychotherapist and Scriptwriter; Social Worker, Oceanside Public Schools, New York; Psychotherapist, Rockville Consultation Center, New York; Scriptwriter, Creative Eye, Inc. (New York). Organizational Memberships: Academy of Certified Social Workers, National Association of Social Workers; New York State School Social Workers Association; Adelphi University Alumni Association (director at large, 1979-81); Adelphi University School of Social Work Alumni Association (executive board, 1979-81). Honors and Awards: Dean's List, 1966-70; Mu Lambda Alpha, State University of New York at Albany, 1969 to present; National Slavic Honor Society, 1971 to present; American Biographical Institute Research Association; Listed in *Who's Who of American Women, Personalities of America, The World Who's Who of Women.* Address: 55 Windsor Ave., Rockville Centre, New York 11570.

Brott, Walter Howard

Cardiothoracic Surgeon. Personal: Born September 5, 1933; Son of Viola H. Brott; Married Marie Helen; Father of Cheryl, Michelle, Kevin. Education: B.A., Yale University, 1955; M.D., University of Kansas School of Medicine, 1959; Diplomat, American Board of Surgery, William Beaumont Medical Center; Diplomat, American Board of Thoracic Surgery, Fitzsimons Army Medical Center. Military: Served in the United States Army, 1959-82, achieving the rank of Colonel. Career: Chief Cardiothoracic Surgeon, Walter Reed Army Medical Center; Former Professor of Surgery, U.S.U.H.S. Medical School. Organizational Memberships: Society of Thoracic Surgeons; American Association for Thoracic Surgery; American College of Surgeons (graduate education committee, 1977-78; executive council, District of Columbia chapter, 1976-78); Association of Military Surgeons; Association of Army Cardiology; Association of Medical Consultants to the Armed Forces. Community Activities: Chief Consultant in Surgery to the Surgeon General, 1976-77; Consultant Panel to C.A.H.E.A. Board of the American Medical Association, 1981 to present; Corcoran Gallery Association, 1978-80; Civic Work with Caritas Cantho and Vietnam Pediatric Hospital Development, 1969-70. Religion: Lutheran. Honors and Awards: Alpha Omega Alpha; Victor Wilson Scholar, Yale University, 1951-55; Legion of Merit, 1970, 1982; Bronze Star, 1970; Meritorious Service Medal, 1976; Cross of Gallantry, 1969; Public Civic Action Award, Vietnam, 1970; Certificate of Achievement from the Surgeon General for Professional Ability, 1978. Address: 3701 Maloney Road, Knoxville, Tennessee 37920.

Johnie M Browder

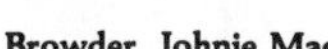

Browder, Johnie Mae

Principal. Personal: Born October 2, 1919; Daughter of Thad J. (deceased) and Irene Gomillian; Married Ralph J. Browder; Mother of Ralph T., Tempie Leah Mutschler. Education: B.S., Troy State University, 1949; M.Ed., Auburn University, 1956; A.A. Certificate in Guidance, 1965. Career: Principal, W. O. Parmer Elementary School, 1971-82; Supervisor of Guidance and Evaluation, Title I Program, Butler County, 1966-71; Teacher, Covington County, 1946-49; Guidance Director, McKenzie High School, 1949-66. Organizational Memberships: Butler County Education Association (former president, vice president, secretary, treasurer); Delta Kappa Gamma (president, 1962-64). Community Activities: International Platform Association; Kappa Delta Pi. Religion: New Home Baptist Church, Treasurer, Sunday School Teacher for 32 years. Honors and Awards: High School Medal for Oratory, 1937; Kappa Delta Pi; Listed in *Personalities of the South and Southwest, Who's Who, International Biographies.* Address: Route 1, McKenzie, Alabama 36456.

Brown, Ellen Mabel

Museum Director, Lecturer. Personal: Born January 19, 1914; Daughter of R. O. and Jessie Fry Edwards (both deceased); Married Charles Wesley Brown; Mother of Jean Martin (Mrs. Richard), Martha Allender (Mrs. John). Education: Attended the University of Wyoming, Black Hills State College, Eastern Wyoming College. Career: Director and Lecturer, Anna Miller Museum; Former Editor/Publisher *Bits and Pieces;* School Librarian, Public Information Officer, Free-lance Writer, Photographer, Lecturer; Author of Numerous Historical Works. Organizational Memberships: Wyoming State Historical Society (president, 1979); Weston County Historical Society (has held all offices); Society of Wyoming Press Women (secretary, historian); Wyoming Writers; Western Writers; Delta Kappa Gamma; Wyoming Education Association; Colorado, Wyoming Museum Associations; American Association for State and Local History; Buffalo Bill Historical Center (patron). Community Activities: Newcastle Chamber of Commerce; American Cancer Society (public service chairman, 1979 to present; education chairman, 1980 to present; crusade chairman, 1980-81); 4-H Leader, 1948-62; American Mothers Committee, 1954-62; Girl Scouts of America (consultant, 1964 to present); Wyoming American Bicentennial Commission, 1972-77; Wyoming Diamond Jubilee Committee, 1965; Governor's Consulting Committee on Historical Sites and Markers, 1979-80; Case Western History Library, Black Hills State College (field historian, 1976 to present). Religion: Methodist. Honors and Awards: State and National Historical and Press Awards, 1962-81; Wyoming Woman of the Year, 1976; Beta Sigma Phi First Lady, 1976; Mother of the Year, 1959; Outstanding 4-H Leader, 1954, 1959; Distinguished Service to Future Farmers, 1972; Honorary Future Farmer of America, 1973; Chamber of Commerce Community Service Award, 1979; Chamber of Commerce Distinguished Service Award, 1980; Jaycee Community Service Award, 1978, Others. Address: Box 746, Newcastle, Wyoming 82701.

John Y Brown Jr

Brown, John Young Jr

Governor of Kentucky. Personal: Born December 28, 1933; Son of John Young, Sr. and Dorothy Inman Brown (deceased); Married

Phyllis George; Father of John Young III, Eleanor Farris, Sandra Bennett, Lincoln Tyler George Brown. Education: Graduate, LaFayette High School, 1952; B.A., 1957, and LL.B., 1960, both from the University of Kentucky. Military: Served with the United States Army Reserve, 1959-65. Career: Chief Executive Officer, Kentucky Fried Chicken; Former Owner, Buffalo Braves and Boston Celtics; Governor, Commonwealth of Kentucky. Organizational Memberships: National Governor's Association (chairman task force on small business 1980); Democratic Governor's Conference (vice-chairman, August 1981); Appalachian Regional Commission (states' co-chairman 1982); Southern States Energy Board (chairman October 1981 to October 1982). Community Activities: John F. Kennedy Presidential Campaign (vice chairman for the state of Kentucky 1960); Democratic National Committee (young leadership council chairman); National Democratic Party (honorary treasurer 1972); Democratic National Telethon (chairman 1972, 1973, 1974); Governor's Economic Development Commission (chairman 1975-77); Honors and Awards: Outstanding Young Man of America, National Junior Chamber of Commerce, 1965; Outstanding Civic Leader of America, Junior Chamber of Commerce, 1967; Louisville's Outstanding Young Man, Louisville Junior Chamber of Commerce, 1969; Outstanding American Award, Lion's Club International, 1974; Youngest person named to the University of Kentucky Hall of Fame; American Academy of Achievement Award, 1980; *Encyclopaedia Britannica;* Award for Achievement in Life, 1980; Honorary Doctor of Law Degree, University of Kentucky, 1981. Address: Cave Hill Place, Lexington, Kentucky 40511.

Brown, June Gibbs

Inspector General. Personal: Born October 5, 1933; Daughter of Tom and Lorna Gibbs; Married Ray L. Brown; Mother of Ellen Rosenthal, Linda Gibbs, Sheryl Brown, Gregory Brown, Victor Janezic, Carol Janezic. Education: B.B.A. summa cum laude, 1971; M.B.A., Cleveland State University, 1972; J.D., University of Denver College of Law, 1978. Career: Inspector General, National Aeronautics and Space Administration, Presidential Appointment with Senate Confirmation, 1981 to present; Former Positions include: Inspector General, Department of the Interior, Presidential Appointment with Senate Confirmation, 1979-81; Manager of Financial Systems Design, Department of the Interior; Director of Internal Audit, Navy Finance Center; Staff Accountant, Frank T. Cicirelli C.P.A., Ohio; Real Estate Broker/Office Manager, Northeast Realty, Ohio; Real Estate Salesman, Lester's Real Estate and Richmond Realty, Ohio. Organizational Memberships: Association of Government Accountants (national executive committee, 1977-80, 1981 to present; financial management standards board, 1981-82); equal opportunity for minorities and women in government committee, 2 years; vice chairman, national ethics board, 2 years); American Institute of Certified Public Accountants; American Accountants Association; Association of Federal Investigators; Beta Alpha Psi (honorary membership). Honors and Awards: Financial Management Improvement Award, Joint Financial Management Improvement Program, 1980; Outstanding Service Award, National Association of Minority Certified Public Accounting Firms, 1980; Outstanding Achievement Award, Association of Government Accountants, Denver, 1979; Outstanding Contribution to Financial Management Award, Federal Executive Board, Denver Region, 1977; Career Service Award for Managerial Excellence, Federal Executive Board, Chicago Region, 1974; Outstanding Achievement Award, United States Navy, 1973; Service Awards, Association of Government Accountants, 1973, 1976; Woman of the Year, Bureau of Land Management, Department of the Interior, 1975. Address: N.A.S.A./Code W, 400 Maryland Avenue, S.W., Washington, D.C. 20546.

Brown, Kenny Don

Chemist, Chemical Engineer. Personal: Born November 25, 1953; Son of Don and Barbara Brown; Married Joan C. Bish; Father of Caryn E., Kathryn A, Jaclyn D. Education: B.A., Math, and B.A., Chemistry, 1977; B.S., Chemical Engineering, 1982. Career: Chemist; Chemical Engineer; Part time College Chemistry Teacher. Organizational Memberships: American Chemical Society; American Institute of Chemists; American Institute of Chemical Engineering; American Association for the Advancement of Science; Sigma Xi. Community Activities: Boy Scout Merit Badge Counselor. Published Works: Author of Numerous Technical and Professional Articles. Honors and Awards: Certified Professional Chemist; Certified Chemical Engineer; Listed in *Directory of Distinguished Americans, Community Leaders of America, Book of Honor, International Book of Honor, Men of Achievement.* Address: 7339 Starlawn, Perrysburg, Ohio 43551.

Brown, Louis Daniel

Attorney at Law. Personal: Born August 31, 1908, San Francisco, California; Son of Louis Thomas and Ella Rose Kelly Brown (both deceased); Married Felice Stamper, September 9, 1932; Father of Lawrence Louis, Ronald Stamper, Carol Felice. Education: A.A., University of San Francisco; B.A., Stanford University; Undertook post-graduate studies at the University of California, Hastings Law School; LL.B., J.D., Southwestern University. Career: Attorney, Counsellor at Law, 1972 to present; President, Romer, O'Connor and Company, Inc., 1939-72; Partner, Romer, Brown, Attorneys, 1944-68; Partner, Romer, Brown, Miller Murphy, 1968-72. Organizational Memberships: California State Bar Association; Los Angeles County Bar Association; American Bar Association; American Judicature Society; Los Angeles Lawyers Club; United States Supreme Court; United States Court of Claims; Department of Justice - Immigration. Community Activities: Alumni Association (past president, Los Angeles chapter); Stanford University Alumni Association (life member); Southwestern University Alumni Association; University of California Hastings Law School Alumni Association; Borrego Springs Chamber of Commerce; International Lions Club (past president, zone chairman); Elks Club; La Quinta Dessert Club; Boy Scouts of America; University of San Francisco Law Society; Stanford University Law Society; Southwestern University Law Society. Published Works: Author of Articles on the Legal Aspects of Credit for Publications of the National Association of the Credit Petroleum Association; Articles for the Lions Club Bulletin; Articles for the Consumer Credit Association. Honors and Awards: Certificate of Appreciation, State Guard of California Medical Corps; Judge Pro-tem, Los Angeles Municipal Court; Listed in *Men of Achievement, Who's Who in the West, Who's Who in California, Martindale Hubbell Law Dictionary, Who's Who in the Western States, Dictionary of International Biography, International Who's Who in Community Service.* Address: 3850 Dublin Street, Los Angeles, California 90008.

Brown, Robert Wade

Executive, Instructor. Personal: Born June 2, 1933, in Dallas, Texas; Married Mozell Rawson, July 2, 1954; Father of Robert Lemoyne, Cathy Gail, Candy Jill, Cindy Rene. Education: B.A., M.S., North Texas State University. Career: Instructor of Chemistry, North Texas State University, 1951-55; Process Analyst "A", Temco Aircraft, 1955-56; Manager of Industrial Research Division, Chemical Engineer Group Supervisor, Research Chemist, The Western Company, 1956-59; Instructor of Mathematics, Odessa Junior College, 1958-59; Instructor, A.P.I. School of Petroleum Technology, 1956-63; Instructor, Massey Realty College, 1973 to present; President and Chairman of the Board, B.P.R. Construction and Engineering, Inc., 1964-70; President, Owner, Robert W. Brown and Associates, 1970 to present; President, Chairman of the Board, Brown Foundation Repair and Consulting, Inc., 1973 to present; President, Chairman of the Board, Webb Properties, Inc., 1968 to present; President, Chairman of the Board,

Brown Oil Production, 1978 to present; President, Chairman of the Board, Brown Publications, 1979 to present; President, Board of Directors, Texas Supply Center, 1980 to present. Organizational Memberships: Alpha Chi Sigma; American Society of Civil Engineers; Society of Petroleum Engineers. Community Activities: Texas Tech Dads Association (trustee, 1973-79); National Home Improvement Council of Dallas (chairman of the board of directors, 1976-78; director, 1976-79); Mean Green, Inc. (chairman, board of directors, 1980 to present); Mean Green Eagle Club (director, 1981 to present). Published Works: Contributor of Articles to Many Professional Journals; Holder of U.S. Patents; Author of Book *Residential Foundations: Design, Behavior, and Repair.* Honors and Awards: Certificate of Meritorious Service, School of Petroleum Technology; Certificate of Proficiency, Oil Well Cementing, The Western Company; Certificate of Completion, Sales Analysts Institute; Listed in *Who's Who in America, World Who's Who in Commerce and Industry, National Social Directory, Royal Blue Book, Community Leaders of America, National Registry of Prominent Americans, Men of Achievement, Notable Americans, Personalities of the South, World Who's Who in Finance and Industry, Dictionary of International Biography, Men and Women of Distinction, Who's Who in Technology Today, Directory of Distinguished Americans, International Who's Who in Community Service, Book of Honor, Community Leaders and Noteworthy Americans, Personalities of America, Who's Who in the South and Southwest, International Who's Who of Intellectuals, America's Patriots of the 1980's.* Address: 6102 Meadowcreek, Dallas, Texas 75240.

Brown, (Robert) Wendell

Wendell Brown

Lawyer. Personal: Born February 26, 1902, in Minneapolis, Minnesota; Son of Robert and Jane Amanda Anderson Brown (both deceased); Married Barbara Ann Fisher, October 20, 1934; Father of Barbara Ann Travis (Mrs. Neil); Mary Alice Fletcher (Mrs. Al). Education: A.B., University of Hawaii, 1924; J.D., University of Michigan Law School, 1926. Career: Admitted to Michigan Bar, 1926; Supreme Court of Michigan, United States Supreme Court, 6th United Circuit Court of Appeals, United States District Court, Eastern and Western Districts of Michigan, United States Board of Immigration Appeals, United States Tax Court; Lawyer, Firm of Routier, Nichols and Fildew, Detroit, 1926; Nichols and Fildew, 1927-28; Frank C. Sibley, 1929; Ferguson and Ferguson, 1929-31; Assistant Attorney General, Michigan, 1931-32; Legal Department, Union Guardian Trust Company, Detroit, 1933-34; Individual Law Practice, Detroit 1934-81, Farmington Hills, Michigan 1981 to present. Organizational Memberships: American Bar Association; Detroit Bar Association (director, 1939-49; treasurer, 1942-44; secretary, 1944-46; second vice president, 1947-48; first vice president, 1947-48; president, 1948-49; chairman or member of various committees, 1935-52, 1977-82); Oakland County Bar Association; State Bar of Michigan (chairman or member of various committees, 1935-72). Community Activities: Wayne County Graft Grand Jury (legal advisor, 1939-40); Wayne County (assistant prosecuting attorney of civil matters, 1940); Special Assistant City Attorney to Investigate Police Department, Highland Park, Michigan, 1951-52; Chairman, Citizens Committee to form Oakland County Community College, 1962-63; Farmington School Board (president, 1952-56); Oakland County Republican County Convention (chairman, 1952); Farmington Township, Oakland County (trustee, 1957-61); Oakland County Lincoln Republican Club (president, 1958); Friends of Detroit Library (treasurer, board of directors, 1943-44); Farmington Friends of the Library, Inc. (board of directors, 1952-58; president, 1956-57); Helped Organize Two Other Friends of the Library Societies; Farmington Historical Society (honorary member, 1966); St. Anthony's Guild, Franciscan Friars, 1975. Religion: Presbyterian, Elder; 30 Years of Board Activities; One of Original Incorporators, Franklin Community Church (Methodist), Franklin, Michigan. Honors and Awards: Listed in *Who's Who in the World, Who's Who in the Midwest, Who's Important in Law, Who's Who in America, Who's Who in American Law, Who's Who in the World, International Who's Who of Intellectuals, Dictionary of International Biography, International Register of Profiles, International Book of Honor, Men of Achievement, Men and Women of Distinction, Personalities of America.* Address: 29921 Ardmore Street, Farmington Hills, Michigan 48018.

Brown, Sandra M

Investor. Personal: Born October 7, 1938; Daughter of Edgar P. Senne; Married Kenneth A. Martin; Mother of Kenneth S., Christopher S. Education: B.A., with distinction, Mount Holyoke, 1960; M.Ed., Springfield College, 1961; Ph.D., University of Connecticut, 1964. Career: President, East Thirty-Eighth Street Capital Corporation; President, Sandra Brown Advertising; Publisher, *The Executive Woman*, first national newsletter for women in business; Radio Personality, NBC News and Information Service, 1976; Producer and Host, weekly show on "Women in Business", WPIX Television, 1975. Community Activities: Department of Health, Education, and Welfare (appointed to the Committee on the Rights and Responsbilities of Women 1975); Women's Forum (New York chapter); Past Member Education Press Association, International Reading Association, Women Business Owners; First Woman in the United States to form a Small Business Investment Corporation licensed by the Small Business Administration. Published Works: American Express Credit Handbook for Women, 1975. Honors and Awards: Award for Excellence, Educational Press Association, 1967; Award for Service to the American Arbitration Association, 1978; Award for Inspiration to Youth, Junior Achievement, 1976. Address: Tinker Hill Road, Putnam Valley, New York.

Brown, Thomas Cartwright

Executive. Personal: Born January 18, 1913; Father of Two Daughters. Education: B.S., University of Missouri, 1934; Rector Scholar, DePauw University, 1931-32; Naval Training School, Harvard University, 1943; Studies in Spanish and French, The Language Center, Indianapolis, 1960, 1962, 1964; Speed Reading and Comprehension Courses, Indianapolis Reading Institute, 1965; M.A., Ball State University, 1972; Instituto Tecnologico y de Estudios Superiores de Monterrey, Summer Sessin, 1972; Doctoral Fellow, Ball State University. Military: Served in the United States Navy, 1943-46, attaining the rank of Lieutenant. Career: President, Owner, Intercor, Inc., 1964 to present; Teacher, United States Navy's Program Afloat for College Education, 1978-79, 1980; Partner, Mid-America International, 1960-64; Consultant in Charge of Manufacturing, Purchasing and Coast Analysis, Ransburg Electro-Coating Corporation, 1957-60; Director of Research and Process Engineering, Chief Inspector, Quality Control and Sales, Sheller Manufacturing Corporation, 1935-57. Community Activities: Board of Trustees, Pennville, Indiana, 1971-75; Regional VI Planning and Development Commission (first vice chairman, 1973; chairman, 1974; executive committee); Indiana Association of Regional Councils (representative from region VI, 1975). Honors and Awards: Listed in *Who's Who in the Midwest, Who's Who in Finance and Industry, Who's Who in Indiana, Indiana Lives, Dictionary of International Biography, National Register of Prominent Americans and International Notables, Personalities of the West and Midwest, Community Leaders and Noteworthy Americans, Who's Who in America.* Address: 145 S. Union Street, Pennville, Indiana 47369.

Wayne Brown

Brown, Wayne

Executive Director. Personal: Married Bonnie Baker; Father of Four. Education: B.S., Union University, 1961; M.S. 1963, Ph.D. 1970, University of Florida; Involvement in Academic Workshops. Career: Executive Director, Tennessee Higher Education Commission, 1975 to present; Union University - Vice President for Academic Affairs 1972-75, Academic Dean 1968-72, Director of Men's Dorm 1963-65, Acting Dean of Men 1963-64. Organizational Memberships: State Higher Education Executive Officers (federal relations committee, member 1976 to present, chairman 1978-79; executive comittee, 1978 to present); Southern Regional Education Board (development study committee, 1976-77; member, 1979 to present); Southern Association of Colleges and Schools (member and chairman of institutional accrediting teams, 1970-75; advisory committee for state coordinating agencies, member 1977 to present, chairman 1977-78); Tennessee State Assistance Corporation (vice chairman of board, 1975 to present); Tennessee State Board of Education (ex officio member); University of Tennessee (board of trustees, ex officio member, 1975 to present); American Council on Education (panelist, 1979); National Identification Program for the Advancement of Women in Higher Education Administration; Southeastern Section, American Physical Society; American Astronomical Society; American Association of Physics Teachers; American Physical Society; Sigma Xi; Kappa Mu Epsilon; Alpha Psi Omega; Sigma Pi Sigma; Alpha Chi; Alpha Tau Omega. Community Activities: Candidate for Democratic Nominination to the United States Congress, 1974; Nashville Rotary Club (program committee, district 676 education awards committee, 1975-77); Southwest Tennessee Development District (committee on aging, 1972-75); Jackson Rotary Club (board of directors, 1973-74); South Madison County Jaycees, 1972-73; Speaker at Civic Clubs, Schools, Churches, 1968 to present. Religion: Brentwood Baptist Church, Southern Baptist Sunday School Board - Member 1976 to present, executive committee 1976 to present, finance committee 1976 to present. Published Works: Five Radio Astronomy Papers, 1963-70; Six Higher Education Papers and Works, 1970 to present. Address: 1219 Twin Springs Drive, Brentwood, Tennessee 37207.

Browne, Joseph Peter

University Library Director. Personal: Born June 12, 1929; Son of Mr. and Mrs. George Browne, (both deceased). Education: A.B., University of Notre Dame, 1951; S.T.L., 1957, and S.T.D., 1961, both from the Pontificium Athenaeum Angelicum (Rome); M.S.L.S., Catholic University of America, 1965. Career: Assistant Pastor, Holy Cross Parish, South Bend, Indiana, 1955-56; Professor, Moral Theology, Holy Cross College, Washington, D.C., 1959-64; Head, Department of Library Science, University of Portland, 1964-70; Dean, College of Arts and Sciences, University of Portland, 1970-73; Director, Graduate School of Library Science, Our Lady of the Lake College, San Antonio, Texas, 1973-75; Director, University of Portland Library, 1975 to present. Organizational Memberships: Oregon Library Association (president 1967-68); Catholic Library Association (president 1971-73); Interstate Library Planning Council (chairman 1977-79); American Library Association; Pacific Northwest Library Association; Catholic Theological Society of America. Community Activities: University of Portland (academic senate, member 1968-73, chairman 1968-70; board of regents 1969-70, 1977-81); Columbia Interstate Library Board (vice chairman 1977-78); Greater Oregon Chapter of the Committee to Combat Huntington's Disease (president 1979 to present); University of Portland *Review* (manuscript editor 1975 to present); Knight of Columbus (member 1947 to present, state chaplain Washington, D.C. 1963-64 and Oregon 1969-73). Religion: Senate of Priests, Archdiocese of Portland, 1967-69, 1978-80; Moderator, Provincial Chapter, Indiana Province, Congregation of Holy Corss, 1973, 1976, 1979; Ordained Priest, June 4, 1955; Professed in Congregation of Holy Cross, August 16, 1948. Honors and Awards: N.D.E.A. Summer Institute Fellowship, 1968; Beta Phi Mu, 1965; Culligan Award, University of Portland, 1979; Oregon Knight of the Year (Knights of Columbus), 1973. Address: 5410 N. Strong Street #8, Portland, Oregon 97203.

Brownell, Daphne M

Genealogy Record Searcher. Personal: Born July 17, 1918; Daughter of Hugh N. Brownell and Flora M. Akin (deceased); Mother of Richard S. Education: B.A., 1940, M.A., 1954, both from John B. Stetson University; M.S.L.S., Catholic University of America, 1959. Career: Certified Genealogy Record Searcher; Circulation & Reference Librarian, Immaculata Junior College, Washington D.C.; Media Specialist for Montgomery County, Maryland School System; Librarian, Florida Military School; Reference Librarian, Dupont-Ball Library, Stetson Univerasity. Organizational Memberships: American Library Association (life member); American Association of University Women, DeLand Chapter; National League of American Pen Women Inc., DeLand Branch; DeLand Public Library Board (trustee). Community Activities: Federation of Womens' Clubs (life member); Volusia County (Florida) Historical Commission; Colonel Arthur Erwin Chapter, Daughters of the American Revolution (chairman of genealogy records, historian, vice-regent, regent); Colonial Dames of XVII Century, Mound of Surruque Chapter, New Smyrna Beach, Florida; Friends of the Library, DeLand (board member); Connecticut Society of Genealogists Inc.; Dutchess County Historical Society, Poughkeepsie, New York; Freer-Low Family Association, Huguenot Historical Society; New England Historic Genealogical Society; Stukely Westcott Family Association; Florida State Genealogical Society. Honors and Awards: Listed in *Hereditary Register of the U.S.A.*, *Personalities of the South*, *Notable Americans*, *Dictionary of International Biography*. Address: 720 South Hill Avenue, DeLand, Florida 32720.

Bruhn, John Glyndon

Dean. Personal: Born April 27, 1934, in Norfolk, Nebraska; Son of Margaret C. Bruhn. Education: B.A., 1956, and M.A., 1958, both from the University of Nebraska; Ph.D., Yale University, 1961. Military: Served on Reserve Duty with the United States Army Reserve, 1957-63. Career: Researcher, Nebraska Psychiatric Institute, University of Nebraska School of Medicine, 1958; Researcher, Connecticut Department of Mental Health, New Haven County Jail Project on Psychiatric, Legal and Sociological Problems of Juvenile Offenders, 1958-59; Instructor in Sociology, Southern Connecticut College, New Haven, Connecticut, 1960-61; Resident Freshman Counselor, Yale University, New Haven, 1960-61; Research Sociologist, Department of Psychological Medicine, University of Edinburgh, Scotland (Fulbright Fellow), 1961-62; Instructor in Medical Sociology (1962-63), Assistant Professor (1963-64), Department of Psychiatry and Behavioral Sciences, University of Oklahoma Medical Center, Oklahoma City; Instructor in Sociology, Oklahoma City University, 1963; Assistant Professor of Preventive Medicine and Public Health, University of Oklahoma Medical Center and Research Sociologist, National Heart Institute Grant on Coronary Heart Disease, Department of Medicine, University of Oklahoma Medical Center, 1964-67; Clinical Investigator, Oklahoma Medical Research Foundation, 1965-67; Associate Professor of Sociology in Medicine, Department of Medicine, University of Oklahoma Medical Center, 1967-72; Associate Professor of Sociology, University of Oklahoma-Norman, 1967-72; Associate Professor of Human Ecology, School of Health, University of Oklahoma Medical Center, 1967-69; Associate Professor of Preventive Medicine and Public Health, University of Oklahoma Medical Center, 1969-72; Associate Dean for Community Affairs, University of Texas Medical Branch, Galveston, 1972-81; Professor of Preventive Medicine and Community Health, University of Texas Medical Branch, 1972 to present; Professor of Human Ecology, University of Texas School of Public Health, Houston, 1975 to present; Acting Dean, School of Allied Health Sciences, University of Texas Medical Branch, Galveston, 1979 (fall semester), 1980-81; Dean, School of Allied Health Sciences and Special Assistant to the President for Community Affairs, University of Texas Medical Branch, Galveston, 1981 to present. Organizational Memberships: American Sociological Association; American Public Health Association (fellow); American Heart Association (fellow); Royal Society of Health (fellow); American Association for the Advancement of Science; Association of American Medical Colleges; American Psychosomatic Society; American Association of University Professors; Association of Teachers of Preventive Medicine; New York Academy of Science; Southwestern Sociological Association; Alpha Kappa Delta; Sigma Xi; Texas Academy of Physician Assistants (board of advisors 1981 to present); The Foundation of Thanatology (board of advisors 1979 to present). Community Activities: St. Vincent's House (board member 1974-75); William Temple Community House (board member 1974-78); Galveston County Cultural Arts Council (board member 1974-75); Galveston Alternative School Program (board member 1976-77); Goals for Galveston (health and human resources task force chairman 1974-75); United Way of Galveston (board of trustees 1975-76, executive committee 1977-78, vice president for agency operations 1978); Galveston County Coordinated Community Clinics (board member 1977-80, vice chairman 1978-80); Health Systems Agency, Houston (chairman of the technical advisory committee on health promotion 1978, member health promotion advisory council 1979-80); Galveston County Cancer Society (board member 1979-80); Galveston County Heart Association (board member 1980); Friends of the Rosenberg Library (board member 1980-81). Published Works: Editorial Board, 1979 to present, and Associate Editor, 1980 to present, *Health Values: Achieving High Level Wellness.* Honors and Awards: Fulbright Fellow, 1961-62; Commonwealth Fund, Yale University Fellow, 1958-60; Career Development Award, National Heart Institute, 1968-69; Danforth Foundation Associate, 1978 to present; Grants received as Principal Investigator: National Heart Institute, National Fund for Medical Education, Texas Regional Medical Program, The Danforth Foundation, The Robert Wood Johnson Foundation, The Charles Stewart Mott Foundation, The National Institute on Child Health and Human Development, and The Moody Foundation. Address: 7521 Beluche, Galveston, Texas 77550.

Bruner, Nancy Louise

National Starch Sales Coordinator. Personal: February 18, 1943; Daughter of Gilbert A. and Ruth E. Kinzey; Married James Christian Bruner. Education: Graduate, Corrine Shover Modeling and Finishing School; B.A., Coe College. Career: National Starch Sales Coordinator, Cargill, Inc. Organizational Memberships: American Business Women's Association (national president, 1981-82; national first vice president, 1980-81; district vice president, 1979-80; north central regional meeting chairman, 1981; past president of the Five Star Chapter and Triangle '64 Chapter); National Association of Female Executives; Professional Women's Network; International Toastmistress Club. Community Activities: Member, Cedar Rapids Riverfront Improvement Commission, 1982-85; 1981 Iowa Governor's Conference; Cedar Rapids Community Service Campaign (former group captain and company coodinator); United Nations Association of the U.S.A. (Linn County Chapter board of directors, 1980; Iowa's board of directors, 1981); Past Affiliation with Mercy Hospital Auxiliary, Servicemen's Wives Club; Past Teacher of Ballroom Dancing to Junior High School Boys and Girls; Past Blue Bird Leader and Assistant Leader of Campfire Girls. Religion: St. Patrick's Roman Catholic Church; National Catholic Society of Foresters. Honors and Awards: One of 1975-76 Top Ten Women in the Nation, American Business Women's Association; Merit Award, Triangle '64 Chapter, American Business Women's Association, 1969; Listed in *Personalities of the West and Midwest, Community Leaders and Noteworthy Americans, Book of Honor, Outstanding Young Women of America, Iowa Women at Work.* Address: 2838 Sue Lane N.W., Cedar Rapids, Iowa 52405.

Bryan, Jacob Franklin III

Chairman of the Board and Chief Executive Officer. Personal: Born February 26, 1908; Son of Jacob F. II and Olive Julia Gibson Bryan (both deceased); Married Josephine Christian Hendley; Father of J. F. IV, Carter B., Kendall G. Education: Graduate of Florida Business University; Completed equivalent of college degree by private tutor, 1932. Career: Chairman of the Board of Directors and Chief Executive Officer of Independent Insurance Group Inc. and the Following Subsidiaries: Independent Life and Accident Insurance Company, Herald Life Insurance Company, Independent Real Estate Management Corporation and Independent Investment Advisory Services Inc., 1957 to present. Organizational Memberships: American Council of Life Insurance (vice president, 1977); American Life Insurance Association (vice president for Florida, 1974); Royal Horticultural Society of London, England (fellow); National Orchid Society (past vice president); Orchid Society of Jacksonville (past president); American Camellia Society (former member of the board of directors); Jacksonville Association of Life Underwriters; Housing and Urban Development (contact committee, 1970 to present); National Association of Manufacturers (public affairs committee, educational committee); Life Insurers Conference (resolutions committee, 1966 to present; past board member); Life Underwriter Training Council, Washington D.C. (board of directors, board of trustees 1974-76); Board Memberships include Florida First National Bank of Jacksonville and National Banks of Florida, Inc.; Florida Federal Savings and Loan Association (advisory board). Community Activities: Florida Yacht Club; Timuquana Country Club; River Club; Seminole Club; Ye Mystic Revellers; Florida Society Sons of the American Revolution; Jacksonville Chapter Sons of the American Revolution (past president); Kirby-Smith Camp, Sons of Confederate Veterans; The Order of the Stars and Bars; Florida Historical Society; Jacksonville Historical Society; National Trust for Historic Preservation; Historic Saint Augustine Preservation (board vice chairman, 1969-74); English-Speaking Union (past president and member of the board of directors); American Bicentennial Commission of Jacksonville, Florida (commissioner, April 1973; finance committee, November 1973); Huxford Genealogical Society, Inc.; Newcomen Society of North America (vice-chairman, Florida committee, 1982 to present); Jacksonville Genealogical Society; Northeast Florida Heart Association (board of directors, 1964-75; president, 1968-69; president elect, 1967-68; vice president, 1966-67); Florida Heart Association (board of directors, 1968-70; honorary chairman heart campaign, 1970; state chairman, heart fund drive, 1970; community program committee, 1968-69; fund raising advisory campaign, 1968-69; long term planning and policy committee, 1968-69); American Cancer Society (Florida division: board of directors and executive committee, 1978 to present; past vice president; honorary life member; member of legacy and memorial committee of Duval County unit: member 1939 to present; past president, 1951-53; honorary life member; board of directors, 1977-80); Junior Achievement (board of directors, 1963 to present); March of Dimes (board of directors, 1964 to present); Girls Clubs of Jacksonville, Inc. (board member, 1972-74); Jacksonville Museum of Arts and Sciences (formerly Children's Museum) (board of directors, 1964-74; advisory committee, 1974-81; honorary trustee, honorary board of trustees, 1981; honorary life member); Child Guidance Clinic (board of directors, 1954 to present); Children's Home Society of Florida (board of directors, 1961 to present); Jacksonville Symphony Association; Community Planning Council of Jacksonville Area, Inc. (board of directors, 1968 to present); Cathedral Foundation of Jacksonville (board of directors, 1963-72); Jacksonville Area Chamber of Commerce (board of governors); Committee of 100. Religion: Episcopal. Published Works: *The First Fifty Years of Independent Life.* Honors and Awards: Boss of the Year, Arlington Junior Chamber of Commerce, 1960; Man of the Year, Florida State Association of Life Underwriters, 1960; Boss of the Year; American Business Women's Association, 1965; Special Award of Appreciation, Florida Cancer Society, 1959; Ted Arnold Award for Outstanding Service and Civic Accomplishments, Jacksonville Junior Chamber of Commerce; Top Management Award in Commerce and Industry, Sales and Marketing Executives Club, 1968; Elected to be Jean Ribault at 400th Celebration; Honorary Life Member, Alpha Kappa Psi; Trail Blazers Award, Jacksonville Association of Life Underwriters, 1969; Chief of Jacksonville Fire Division, 1976; Listed in *World Who's Who in Finance and Industry, Men of Achievement, Dictionary of International Biography, The National Society Directory, Community Leaders and Noteworthy Americans, Who's Who in Insurance, Personalities of the South, Who's Who in the South and Southwest, The Hereditary Register of the U.S.A., Who's Who in the United States, Notable Americans of the Bicentennial Era, The National Encyclopedia of American Biography, International Who's Who in Community Service, Book of Honor.* Address: 4255 Yacht Club Road, Jacksonville, Florida 32210.

Bryant, Donald Wayne

College President. Personal: Born April 24, 1941; Son of George and Lucy Bryant; Father of Tiffany Lynn, Tyler Wayne. Education:

A.A., Presbyterian Junior College, 1961; B.A., Wake Forest University, 1963; M.A., University of Georgia, 1965; Ed.D., North Carolina State University, 1971. Career: President, Carteret Technical College; Former Instructor, Wilson Technical Institute, Wilson, North Carolina; Chairman, Business Department, Martin Community College, Williamston, North Carolina; Dean of Instruction, Sampson Technical College, Clinton, North Carolina; Adjunct Professor, Pepperdine University, Malibu, California. Organizational Memberships: North Carolina Education Association (secretary, local chapter, 1968-69); North Carolina State University (community college advisory committee, 1975-76); North Carolina Association of Public Community College Presidents (chairman, finance committee, 1976-77; executive committee, 1978-79, 1979-80; chairman, nomination committee, 1978-79; chairman, summer conference committee, 1978-79; co-chairman, summer conference committee, 1980-81); Carteret County Community Action Council (board of directors, 1979 to present); A.A.C.J.C. (President's Academy, 1975 to present). Community Activities: Carteret County Marine Science Council, 1973-74; Bogue Banks Lions Club (vice president, 1974-75; president, 1975-76); Morehead City Lions Club (board of directors, 1980-81; president, 1981-82); Carteret County Humane Society. Religion: First Presbyterian Church, Morehead City, North Carolina, Deacon, 1976-77. Honors and Awards: Special Award for most total club merchandise sales, Bogue Banks Lions Club, 1976-77; Selected for President's Academy Forum, Vail, Colorado, 1980-81; Listed in *Who's Who in the South and Southwest*. Address: Route 2, Box 287A, Morehead City, North Carolina 28557.

Bryant, Marie Alene

Council President Emeritus. Personal: Born December 9, 1900; Daughter of David & Amy Bollinger (both deceased); Married Homer L. Bryant (deceased). Education: Graduate, Mound Valley High School, 1919; B.S., Pittsburg (Kansas) State Teachers College, 1922; M.A., Columbia University, 1927. Career: Radio Safety Education Broadcast Producer-Director, 1949-81; Teacher, Speech and Music, Parsons High School, Mound Valley High School and Coffeyville High School (Kansas), 1920-26; Teacher, Hunter College, Jamaica Teachers College, 1927-41; Office Assistant to Ophthalmologist, 1947-49; President, now President Emeritus, Coffeyville Safety Council. Organizational Memberships: National Federation of Business and Professional Women's Clubs Inc. (president, 1955-56; safety chairman, 1955 to present); Coffeyville Safety Council (president, 1951-64; president emeritus); Kansas Citizens Safety Council (board member); Kansas Women for Highway Safety (charter member); American Association of University Women; Kansas and National Federation of Press Women Inc.; General Federation of Women's Clubs (safety chairman, 26 years); Wisconsin Association of Women Highway Safety Leaders; Montgomery County Extension Homemakers Unit (community improvement chairman). Community Activities: Organized County Heart Fund, 1956; Directed 10 continuous yearly safety queen projects, 1962-72; Vehicle Safety Check, 1954-73; Featured Speaker: Governor's Safety Conference (1963-69), Official Opening Ceremony for State Highway 166 in Kansas (1962); 4-H Safety Exhibits, 1951-71; Kansas City Philharmonic Orchestra (women's committee, 1945-46); White House Conference on Highway Safety, 1954; American Medical Association Women's Auxiliary, 1953. Religion: Presbyterian. Published Works: Author first course study for Radio Speech, New York City High Schools. Honors and Awards: Gold Medallion Award, American Heart Association, 1958; Woman of the Year, Kansas, 1966; Citation Award, National Safety Council; Grant by Shell Oil, 1959; $250 Bond, National Safety Council, 1961; Allstate Safety Crusade Award 1961; Paul Harris Fellow, Rotary Foundation of Rotary International; Olin Highway Safety Award for "The Most Outstanding Lady in Safety Work in Kansas", 1971; Kansas Press Women Awards, 1966, 1968. Address: 803 West Ninth, P.O. Box 844, Coffeyville, Kansas 67337.

Bryant, Sylvia Leigh

Editor-Publisher, Poet, Freelance Writer. Personal: Born May 8, 1947, in Lynchburg, Virginia; Daughter of Mrs. and Mrs. Hundley Bryant. Education: D.Lit., World University, 1981. Career: Editor-Publisher, The Anthology Society. Organizational Memberships: International Academy of Poets (fellow); International Biographical Association (fellow); Anglo-American Academy (honorary fellow); American Biographical Institute (associate member); United Poets Laureate International; Dr. Stella Woodall Poetry Society International; World Poetry Society; Centro Studi E Scambi Internazionali-Accademia Leonardo da Vinci; National Trust for Historic Preservation; International Platform Association; Smithsonian Institution (national associate member). Religion: Baptist. Published Works: Poetry can be found in *Adventures in Poetry Anthology, The Poet, Adventures in Poetry Magazine, Modern Images, Hoosier Challenger, Animal World*, Many Others. Honors and Awards: International Poet Laureate, United Poets Laureate International, 1979; Certificate of Merit, International Biographical Centre, 1980; Certificate of Appreciation, American Biographical Institute, 1980; Certificate of Merit, Accademia Leonardo da Vinci, 1980; Certificate of Proclamation, American Biographical Institute, 1980; Distinguished Service Citation, World Poetry Society, 1981; Honorary Certificate of Recognition, American Biographical Institute (for editorial advisory board), 1981; Gold Medal, Accademia Leornardo da Vinci, 1980; Poet Laureate Program, State of Virginia, 1981; Listed in *Who's Who in Poetry, International Register of Profiles, American Cultural Arts Registry, Personalities of the South, Community Leaders and Noteworthy Americans, Men and Women of Distinction, Community Leaders of America, Album of International Poets of Achievement, Personalities of America, World Who's Who of Women, Book of Honor, Directory of Distinguished Americans, International Who's Who in Poetry, International Authors and Writers Who's Who, Directory of International Biography, Anglo-American Who's Who, International Who's Who of Intellectuals, Personalities of America*. Address: Route 5 Box 498A, Madison Heights, Virginia 24572.

Buchele, Wesley Fisher

Professor of Agricultural Engineering. Personal: Born March 18, 1920, in Cedar Vale, Kansas; Married Mary Jagger, June 12, 1945; Father of Rodney, Beth, Sheron, Steven. Education: B.S., Kansas State University, 1943; M.S., University of Arkansas, 1951; Ph.D., Iowa State University, 1954. Military: Served in the United States Army, Artillery, Infantry, Ordnance, 1943-46; Major (Retired), United States Army Reserve. Career: Professor, Department of Agricultural Engineering, Iowa State University, 1963 to present; Vice President, Frederick Instrument Company; Vice President, Agricultural Consultants Associates; Research Engineer, I.I.T.A., Ibadan, Nigeria, 1979; Visiting Scientist, C.S.I.R.O., Melbourne, Australia, 1979; Visiting Professor and Division Head, University of Ghana, 1968-69; Associate Professor, Michigan State University, 1956-63; Assistant Professor, Iowa State University, 1954-56; Assistant Professor, University of Arkansas, 1948-51; Junior Engineer, John Deere Waterloo Tractor Works, 1946-48. Organizational Memberships: A.S.A.E. (fellow); A.S.A.; International Society of Terrain-Vehicle Systems; Toastmasters; Osborn Club; S.A.E.; N.I.A.E. (fellow); Sigma Xi; Gamma Sigma Delta; Phi Lambda Tau; Alpha Epsilon. Community Activities: City of Ames, Energy Committee, 1974-75; Living History Farms (chairman, energy committee, 1977 to present). Religion: Collegiate United Methodist Church, Ames, Iowa. Honors and Awards: A.S.A.E. Outstanding Paper Award, 1959, 1961, 1979; Listed in *Who's Who in Engineering, American Men of Science, Who's Who in the Midwest, Leaders in American Science, Dictionary of Literature Biography, Notable Americans of 1976-77, Community Leaders and Noteworthy Americans, Men of Achievement*. Address: 239 Parkridge Circle, Ames, Iowa 50010.

Buckley, William Frank Jr

Author, Editor, Lecturer, Television Host. Personal: Born November 24, 1925; Son of William Frank and Aloise Steiner Buckley;

Married Patricia Taylor; Father of Christopher. Education: B.A., Yale University, 1950. Military: Served in the United States Army, 1944-46, attaining the rank of 2nd Lieutenant. Career: Host of Television Program "Firing Line"; Author *God and Man at Yale*, *McCarthy and His Enemies* (co-authored with L. Brent Bozell), *Up From Liberalism*, *Rumbles Left and Right*, *The Unmaking of a Mayor*, *The Jeweler's Eye*, *The Governor Listeth*, *Cruising Speed*, *Inveighing We Will Go*, *Four Reforms*, *United Nations Journal*, *Executive Eve*, *Saving the Queen*, *Airborne*, *Stained Glass*, *A Hymnal: The Controversial Arts*, *Who's On First*, *Marco Polo If You Can*; Editor *The Committee and Its Critics* 1962, *Odyssey of a Friend* 1970, *American Conservative Thought in the Twentieth Century* 1970. Organizational Memberships: Council on Foreign Relations. Community Activities: Candidate for Mayor of New York City, 1965; United States Information Agency (advisory committee, 1969-72); United States Delegation to 28th General Assembly of the United Nations (public member, 1973). Honors and Awards: Best Columnist of the Year Award, 1967 University of Southern California Distinguished Achievement Award in Journalism, 1968; Television Emmy for Outstanding Program Achievement, 1969; Cleveland Amory (*TV Guide*) Award for Best Interviewer/Interviewee on Television, 1974; Fellow, Society of Professional Journalists, Sigma Delta Chi, 1976; Bellarmine Medal, 1977; Young Republican National Federation Americanism Award, 1979; American Friends of Haifa University Carmel Award for Journalism Excellence, 1980; American Book Award for Best Mystery for *Stained Glass*, 1980; New York University Creative Leadership Award, 1981; Honorary L.H.D., Seton Hall University 1966, Niagara University 1967, Mount Saint Mary's College 1969; Honorary LL.D., St. Peter's College 1969, Syracuse University 1969, Ursinus College 1969, Lehigh University 1970, Lafayette College 1972, St. Anselm's College 1973, St. Bonaventure University 1974, University of Notre Dame 1978, New York Law School 1981; Honorary Litt.D., St. Vincent College 1971, Fairleigh Dickinson University 1973, Alfred University 1974, College of William and Mary 1981; Honorary D.Sc.O., Curry College, 1970; Froman Distinguished Professor, Russell Sage College, 1973. Address: National Review, 150 E. 35th Street, New York, New York 10016.

Budzinsky, Armin Alexander

Investment Banker. Personal: Born November 25, 1942; Son of Alexander W. Budzinsky, Gisella M. Budzinsky (deceased); Married Pamela Plimmer; Father of Andrea. Education: B.A., John Carroll University, 1964; M.A., Rutgers University, 1969; M.B.A., University of Chicago Graduate School of Business, 1974. Career: Investment Banker; Former College Teacher. Organizational Memberships: Oil Investment Institute; Industry Advisory Committee to North American Securities Administration; Alumni Association Board of Directors of Graduate School of Business, University of Chicago. Honors and Awards: Fulbright Fellowship, N.D.E.A. Fellowship, 1964-67. Address: 4510 Shetland Lane, Houston, Texas 77207.

Buehring, Mary Ellen

Certified Legal Assistant, Administrator. Personal: Born May 8, 1936; Daughter of Fred A. and Madeline H. Rost; Married Charles A. Buehring; Mother of Charles Henry (Chad), Christopher Alan. Education: Graduate with honors, Orange Business College, 1954; South Texas Law School, 1955-57; Raines Reporting School, 1965-67; B.S. with honors, Rollins College, 1980. Career: Certified Legal Assistant; Owner/Administrator, Florida Institute for Legal Assistants. Organizational Memberships: Florida Legal Assistants, Inc. (president, 1980-81; vice president, 1979-80; incorporator and member of the board of directors 1976-79; standards committee, 1977-80); National Association of Legal Assistants (second vice president, 1978-79; secretary, 1977-78; public relations director, permanent historian, curriculum committee and resolutions committees, 1975-77; lawyer/legal assistant referral special committee, 1977); Orange County Association of Legal Secretaries (president, 1967; governor, 1968; past president's committee, 1967-81); Valencia Community College (advisory board, legal assistant and legal secretary programs, 1970-81); Seminole Junior College (advisory board, business department, 1970-81); University of Central Florida (advisory board, legal assistant program); Speaker, The Florida Bar Seminars Statewide. Honors and Awards: One of first three women in world to attain Certified Legal Assistant, Certified Professional Secretary and Professional Legal Secretary certifications by national examination. Address: 1051 Black Acre Trail, Casselberry, Florida 32708.

Bunting, John J

Physician. Personal: Born November 7, 1913; Father of Beverly, J. J. Jr., W. D. Education: B.S., Lafayette College, 1934; M.D., University of Maryland, School of Medicine, 1938; Internship, University Hospital, Baltimore, Maryland, 1938-40; Residency, University Hospital, Baltimore, 1940; Residency, Boston Floating Hospital, Boston, Massachusetts, 1940; Residency, Pollak Hospital for Chest Diseases, Jersey City, New Jersey, 1940-41; Undertook further courses at the Post Graduate School of Medicine, University of Pennsylvania, 1941-42; Undertook graduate study at the School of Tropical Medicine, Washington, D.C., 1944. Career: Instructor, Department of Medicine, University Hospital, Baltimore, 1938-40; Instructor, Department of Medicine, Boston Floating Hospital, Boston, 1940; Instructor, Diseases of the Chest, Jersey City Medical Center, 1940-41; Assistant Clinical Professor, Baylor University, Houston, Texas, 1949-65; Associate Clinical Professor of Medicine, Baylor University, 1965-76; Assistant Clinical Professor of Medicine, Ben Taub Clinic, Houston, 1948-63; Associate Clinical Professor of Medicine, Ben Taub Clinic, 1963 to present; Clinical Associate Professor of Medicine, University of Texas Medical School at Houston, 1972 to present; Consulting Staff Member, Memorial Hospital, 1946 to present; Consulting Staff Member, Hermann Hospital, 1947 to present; Visiting Staff Member, Jefferson Davis Hospital, 1947 to present; Courtesy Staff Member, Methodist Hospital, 1948 to present; Visiting Staff Member, Ben Taub Hospital, 1948 to present; Associate Staff Member, St. Luke's Hospital, 1956 to present; Courtesy Staff Member, St. Anthony Center, 1967 to present; Courtesy Staff Member, Diagnostic Center Hospital, 1970 to present; Courtesy Staff Member, Medical Center Del Oro Hospital, 1975 to present; Private Practive of Internal Medicine, Houston, Texas, 1947 to present. Organizational Memberships: American Board of Internal Medicine (diplomate, 1947); American College of Chest Physicians (fellow); American College of Physicians (fellow); American College of Angiology (fellow); Royal Society of Health (fellow); Texas Association of Disability Examiners, State Chapter of the National Association of Disability Examiners; American Geriatrics Society (fellow); Pan American Medical Association (diplomate); American Heart Association; Texas Heart Association; American Cancer Society; American Diabetes Association; Texas Diabetes Association; American Association for the Advancement of Science; American Thoracic Society; American Society of Tropical Medicine and Hygiene; New York Academy of Sciences; Gerontological Society; Texas Academy of Internal Medicine; Southern Medical Association; Texas Society of Internal Medicine; American Society of Internal Medicine; Houston Academy of Medicine; Harris County Medical Society; Texas Medical Association; Ninth District Medical Association; Post-Graduate Medical Assembly, Houston (chairman, publicity and membership, 1960-70); University of Texas/Hermann Hospital (chairman, medical records committee, 1976 & 1977); Post-Graduate Medical Assembly of South Texas (president, 1970); *Bulletin of the Harris County Medical Society* (editorial committee, 1965-75). Published Works: Author of Numerous Scientific Articles. Honors and Awards: Wisdom Hall of Fame; Wisdom Award of Honor for the Advancement of Knowledge, Learning and Research in Education, Wisdom Society, 1971; Physician's Recognition Award in Continuing Education, American Medical Association. Address: 6307 Rice Avenue, Bellaire, Texas 77401.

Burgos-Sasscer, Ruth

College Dean and Director. Personal: Born September 5, 1931; Daughter of Maria Berly; Married Donald S. Sasscer; Mother of Four Children. Education: B.A., Maryville College, 1953; M.A., Columbia University, 1956; Graduate Studies, Iowa State University, Interamerican University (San German, Puerto Rico). Career: Aguadilla Regional College, University of Puerto Rico, Dean and Director 1981-, Director of Non-Traditional Programs, Administration of Regional Colleges 1976-81, Professor of Humanities 1976-81, Director of Department of Humanities and Social Sciences 1972-76; Instructor, Department of Education, Interamerican University, San German, 1971-72; Others. Organizational Memberships: American Association of University Women; Altrusa International, Aguadilla Chapter; Community College Association for Instruction and Technology; National Association of Bilingual Education. Community Activities: National Conference of Puerto Rican Women; League of Women Voters of Puerto Rico; Aguadilla Art Museum Board; Women in Crisis, Inc.; Commission for Women's Affairs, Office of the Governor of Puerto Rico; National Conference of Puerto Rican Women, Inc.; Academic Senate of Regional College, University of Puerto Rico University Board. Religion: Third United Presbyterian Church of Aguadilla. Honors and Awards: Award, Aguadilla Chapter, Altrusa International, Inc., 1979; Award, Aguadilla Regional College, University of Puerto Rico, 1981; Listed in *Who's Who Among Students in American Universities, Who's Who of American Women, Minority American Women: A Biographical Directory.* Address: D-18, Calle 1, Jdns. Borinquen, Aguadilla, Puerto Rico 00603.

Burke, Margaret Elizabeth

Search Firm Executive. Personal: Born January 18, 1946. Education: B.S., San Francisco State University, 1975. Career: President, Burke and Associates, Inc. (an executive search firm specializing in recruiting women and minorities), 1979 to present; Founder, President, Focus Personnel Service, San Francisco, 1976-79; Personnel Generalist, Van Water and Rogers, San Francisco, 1972-74; Administrative Assistant and Personnel Policy Writer, Loomis Armored Car Service, San Francisco, 1970-72; Personnel Administration, Norton Company, Boston, Massachusetts, 1967-68; Installment Loan Analyst, Valley Bank and Trust, Springfield, Massachusetts, 1965-67. Organizational Memberships: San Francisco National Organization of Women (jobs chairman); Equal Rights Amendment (fundraising chairman, 1976-77); Bay Area Executive Women's Forum (president 1980-81, charter member); San Francisco Big Sisters; Bay Area Professional Women's Network; Embarcadero Women's Forum; Northern California Industrial Relations Council; Personnel Management Association of Aztlan; Peninsula Professioal Women's Network. Address: 84 Surrey Street, San Francisco, California 94131.

Burman, Ceara Sue

Language Consultant, Executive. Personal: Born April 23, 1941; Daughter of Woodrow W. and Garnet W. Withrow; Married Lanny R. Burman. Education: B.A., Heidelberg College, 1963; M.A., University of Toledo, 1969; Graduate Studies, Bowling Green State University, University of Dayton, Utah State University. Career: Owner, Administrator, International Language Services; President, International Information Specialists, Inc., 1981-82; Instructor, Owens Technical College, 1981 to present; Bilingual Consultant, 1978-81; Coordinator, E.S.L., 1977-78; High School Teacher, 1962-76; Area Representative, Youth for Understanding, 1969-75. Organizational Memberships: The Executive Network (counselor; board of directors; president, 1981); The National Association of Female Executives; Toledo Area International Trade Association; American Translators Association. Community Activities: Information and Referral Program (operating board). Address: 2346 Cedarwood Drive, Maumee, Ohio 43537.

Van T Burnette

Burner, Victor Joseph

Physician, Surgeon. Personal: Born December 3, 1937; Son of Carroll and Rose Burner. Education: B.A. 1961, M.D. 1965, Yale University; Stanford Surgical Internship, 1965-66; Residency, Harvard-Massachusetts General Hospital. Military: Served in the United States Army Medical Corps. Career: Physician, Surgeon. Organizational Memberships: Yale Alumni Association; Stanford Alumni Association. Community Activities: Southern California Conservatory of Music (trustee). Religion: Mormon Missionary, England, Ireland, Wales, 1958-60; Unitarian-Humanist. Published Works: *David and Jonathan; The Burner Family in Europe and America; Plasminogen.* Address: 827 Foothill, La Canada, Los Angeles City, California 91011.

Burnette, Van Tyle

Veterinarian. Personal: Born June 24, 1924; Married Jimmie N. Galloway; Father of Vanessa Lynn. Education: Georgia Military College, 1948-50; D.V.M., Auburn University, 1951; B.S., University of Florida, 1956. Military: Served with the United States Marine Corps, 1943-46, achieving the rank of Captain; Served with the National Guard, 1946-50, achieving the rank of Staff Sergeant; Served as Captain in the United States Army Reserve, 1950-60. Career: Associate Veterinarian, Cape Fear Animal Hospital & County Health Department Food Inspector, Fayetteville, North Carolina, 1957-58; Veterinarian, Havendale Animal Clinic, 1958 to present; Federal Veterinary Medical Officer, U.S. Department of Agriculture, 1970-71. Organizational Memberships: American Veterinary Medical Association; U.S. Animal Health Association; American Society of Animal Science; American Association for the Advancement of Science; Academy of Veterinary Allergy; American Veterinary Radiology Society; American Association of Feline Biological Sciences; New York Academy of Sciences; World Small Animal Veterinary Medical Association. Community Activities: Boy Scouts of America (scoutmaster, cubmaster, council executive board, 35 years); Lions Club (secretary, treasurer, vice president, president, board member, 15 years); Boys Club (first aid and marksmanship instructor); American Red Cross (first aid instructor); Jaycees (youth committee, little league coach); United Givers (team captain); Chamber of Commerce (youth committee); Salvation Army (board of directors); Audubon Society (veterinarian for birds and animals); Civil Air Patrol (finance officer & instructor); American Legion (Americanism and youth committee); Honor Guard (vice commander, captain of drug and bugle corps); Coast Guard Auxiliary (first aid & safe board instructor); Amvets (adjutant). Honors and Awards: Distinguished Service Award, American Legion, 1947; Meritorious Service Award, American Legion, 1958; Distinguished Service Award, Lions Club, 1965; Silver Beaver, Boy Scouts of America, 1968; Distinguished Scouter Award, Boy Scouts, 1969; Award of Merit, Boy Scouts, 1975; Distinguished Service Award, Youth Services, 1978-79; Volunteer of the Year, Boys Club, 1971; Distinguished Service Award, Boy Scouts, 1980; Listed in *International Who's Who in Community Service*, 1973. Address: 1619 Pearce Rd., Winter Haven, Florida 33880.

Burns, Maretta Jo

Accountant. Personal: Born November 7, 1941; Daughter of Joseph Wallis and Mary Vesta Shepard Burns. Education: B.B.A.,

Baylor University, 1962; Undertook graduate courses, Denver University, 1971-72. Career: Accounting. Organizational Memberships: Beta Gamma Sigma; Phi Gamma Nu; Beta Alpha Psi. Religion: Choir Member, 1976-80. Honors and Awards: $300 cash award for specific work assignment, 1976; Letters of Commendation, 1964, 1979, 1980; Listed in *Who's Who of American Women, Personalities of the West and Midwest, The World Who's Who of Women*. Address: 3784 S. Quince St., Denver, Colorado 80237.

Burns, Sally Joe

General Manager. Personal: Born January 17, 1925; Daughter of Mrs. Frank Gipe; Married Leonard Odell Burns; Mother of Jim, Alton Jay. Education: Graduate Moody High School; Graduate, Droughans Business School. Career: Previously General Manager, Eastern Hills Country Club, Garland, Texas; Currently General Manager, Lakewood County Club. Organizational Memberships: Club Managers Association of America (regional director, 1976; north Texas region board of directors, president, 1978; Texas chapter: treasurer, 1980, secretary, 1976, 1981; vice president, Texas Lone Star State, 1982); Community Activities: Altrusa Club (president); Soroptimist International; Democratic Party (precinct chairman); Parent Teacher Association (president, 4 times); Volunteer for Jerry Lewis Telethon. Religion: Baptist. Honors and Awards: Altrusa Woman of the Year, 1971; Honorary Deputy Sheriff; Outstanding Club Manager for State of Texas, 1975; Best Club Manager in Dallas, Texas, 1980; Outstanding Award for Service to Community, 1981; Honorary Life Membership, Parent Teacher Association; Listed in *Personalities of the South, Personalities of America, Who's Who, International Who's Who of Intellectuals*. Address: 111 Donna Dr., Mabank, Texas 75147.

Sandra K Burns

Burns, Sandra Kaye

Attorney. Personal: Born August 9, 1949; Daughter of Clyde and Bert Burns; Married John R. E. Terrell; Mother of Scott W. B. Terrell. Education: B.S., University of Houston, 1970; M.A. 1972, Ph.D. 1975, University of Texas-Austin; J.D., St. Mary's University School of Law, 1978. Career: Attorney (private practice); Contracted to Republic Energy Inc., 1981; Visiting Lecturer, Department of Management, College of Business Administration, Texas A&M University, 1981; Visiting Lecturer, Department of Educational Administration, College of Education, Texas A&M University, 1981; Legal Consultant, International Law Firm of Colombotti and Associates, Aberdeen, Scotland, 1980; Committee Clerk-Counsel, Senate State Affairs Committee, Texas Senate, 66th Session, 1979; Instructional Development Assistant, Office of Educational Resources, Division of Instructional Development, University of Texas Health Science Center, 1976-77; Professor, Departments of Child Development/Family Life and Home Economics Teacher Education, College of Nutrition, Textiles and Human Development, Texas Woman's University, 1974-75; Other Former Positions. Organizational Memberships: American Bar Association; State Bar of Texas; Phi Delta Kappa. Community Activities: Grassroots Level Involvement, Democratic Party; Volunteer Consulting and Speaking to Schools, Education Groups, Non-Profit Organizations. Honors and Awards: Listed in *Who's Who in American Law, International Book of Honor, Directory of Distinguished Americans, World Who's Who of Women, International Register of Profiles, International Who's Who of Intellectuals, Biographical Roll of Honor*. Address: P.O. Box 10082, College Station, Texas 77840.

Bursey, Johnnie Beatrice

Educator. Personal: Born February 15, 1943 in Homer, Louisiana; Daughter of John Benjamin and Maggie Mae Flucas Bursey. Education: B.S. Business Education, Grambling State University, 1964; M.S. Business Education, Indiana University, 1969; Postgraduate Studies at Louisiana Technical University 1974, University of Santa Clara 1974, Southern University 1974. Career: Chairman, Business Department, Mansfield DeSoto High School, Louisiana, 1964-69; Assistant Professor of Office Administration 1969 to present, Cooperative Education Coordinator of Business Division, Director of Cooperative Education 1976-80, Southern University, Shreveport-Bossier Campus. Organizational Memberships: American Federation of Teachers; Louisiana Federation of Teachers; Indiana Alumni Association; Grambling Alumni Association; Delta Sigma Theta. Community Activities: Democrat; David Raines Community Council, David Raines Community Center (secretary, 1972-73; receptionist, 1971-72); Campaign Assistant to Representative Alphonse Jackson, 1974-75; Shire House (volunteer assistant to satellite program on drug abuse, 1973-74); Louisiana Bank and Trust Company (relief office assistant, 1978); Volunteer Campaign Assistant, Buddy Roemer 1978 and June Phillips 1979; General Motors (community advisory committee, 1978-79); Queensborough in Action (secretary, 1980); Campaign Assistant to City Councilman, Attorney Hilry Huckaby, in His Bid for City Judge, 1982; Shreveport Civic Opera Association. Religion: Baptist. Honors and Awards: Listed in *Who's Who in the South and Southwest, World Who's Who of Women, Outstanding Young Women of America*. Address: 3441 Sunset Drive, Shreveport, Louisiana 71109.

Cleland P Burton

Burstein, Stephen D

Neurosurgeon. Personal: Born April 10, 1934; Son of Moe and Anna Burstein; Married Ronnie Sue Burstein; Father of Alissa Aimee. Education: B.A., University of Michigan, 1954; M.D., State University of New York, Downstate Medical Center, 1958; M.S., University of Minnesota, 1965. Military: Served in the United States Medical Corps, 1959-61, achieving the rank of Lieutenant; Battalion Surgeon 3rd Marine Division, Okinawa. Career: Neurosurgeon. Organizational Memberships: Nassau County Medical Society (peer review committee); Medical Society of the State of New York (interspecialty committee, neurosurgery); New York State Neurosurgical Society (peer review subcommittee, president; South Nassau Community Hospital (president, medical staff). Community Activities: Long Island Hearing and Speech Society (first vice president, board of directors). Honors and Awards: Team Physician, United States Deaf Olympic Team, 1970; Neurosurgical Travel Award, Mayo Foundation, 1966; Alpha Omega Alpha; Sigma Xi. Address: 19 Bridle Path, Roslyn, New York 11576.

Burton, Cleland Patricia

Historical Abstractor and Writer. Personal: Born July 15, 1918; Daughter of Fred and Fern McCloy Burton (both deceased); Married Robert Waller Bragg III (deceased); Mother of Melissa Bragg Brown. Education: Graduate, Plymouth High School, Plymouth, Michigan, 1937; Attended Fairfax Hall, 1937-39; Further Studies at the University of Michigan, 1939-40. Career: Abstractor, 1947-59; Owner and Manager, Burton Farms for Registered Shetlands, 1960-66; Title Examiner, Palm Beach County, Florida, 1967-69; Historical Abstractor, 1966 to present. Organizational Memberships: Detroit Historical Society; West Virginia Press Women; West Virginia Historical Society; Order of Kentucky Colonels; National Trust for Historical Preservation. Community Activites: Mason County Bicentennial Commission (volunteer historical consultant, 1974-77); Review Board of Point Pleasant, West Virginia. Honors and Awards: Freedoms Foundation at Valley Forge Award for Radio Series "200 Years Ago Today on Virginia's Frontier", 1975; Freedoms Award for Mason County Bicentennial Commission for "Bicentennial Commemoration of the First Battle of the American

Revolution", 1975; Top National Award, National Society of Daughters of the American Revolution for Colonel Charles Lewis Chapter of the Daughters of the American Revolution, also for "Bicentennial Commemoration of the First Battle of the American Revolution", 1975; Certificate, National Society of Daughters of the American Revolution, 1976; Martha Washington Award, George Wasington Cleek Chapter of National Society of the Sons of the American Revolution, 1977; Kentucky Colonel, 1979; Certificate of Appreciation, City of Point Pleasant, West Virginia, 1981. Address: P.O. Box 1774, Bolar, Virginia 24414.

Burton, William Joseph

Program Manager, Professional Engineer. Personal: Born March 22, 1931; Son of Emory Goss and Olivia Copeland Burton. Education: B.S.M.E. 1957, M.S.M.E. 1964, University of South Carolina; Ph.D., Texas A&M University, 1970. Military: Served in the United States Army Military Police Corps, 1951-53, achieving the rank of Corporal. Career: Program Manager, Ocean Engineering, Department of the Navy, 1979 to present; Projects Manager, Tennessee Valley Authority, 1974-79; Assistant Professor, Mechanical and Aerospace Engineering, University of Tennessee, 1970-74; Assistant Professor, Ocean Engineering, Texas A&M University, 1970; Senior Project Engineer, General Motors Corporation, 1964-67; Dynamics Engineer Senior, Lockheed-Georgia Company, 1957-62. Organizational Memberships: American Society of Mechanical Engineers (program chairman and secretary, ocean engineering division, 1982 & 1983); Society of Naval Architects and Marine Engineers; National Society of Professional Engineers; International Platform Association. Community Activities: Exchange Club (board member, chairman of the hospitality committee 1975-76, host at quarter horse show 1976); University South Caroliniana Society (life member); Combined Federal Campaign (division coordinator 1981); South Carolina Historical Society; National Board of Advisors, American Biographical Institute, 1982. Religion: Baptist, Choir Member 1949-51, Program Leader of Training Union 1958-62. Honors and Awards: Tau Beta Pi; Pi Tau Sigma; Sigma Xi; Fellow, International Biographical Association; Order of the Engineer; Fellow, American Biographical Institute; Citation for Outstanding Service to Combined Federal Campaign; Listed in *Notable Americans, Men of Achievement, Book of Honor.* Address: Route 1 Box 753, Iva, South Carolina 29655.

William J Burton

Bush, Martin H

Vice President of Academic Resource Development. Education: B.A. 1958, M.A. 1959, State University of New York-Albany; Ph.D., Syracuse University, 1966. Military: Served in the United States Army, 1953-54 (Military Intelligence, Counter Intelligence Corps, Order of Battle Specialist). Career: Vice President for Academic Resource Development, Wichita State University, 1974 to present; Director, Edwin A. Ulrich Museum of Art, Wichita State University, 1974 to present; Art Consultant, Fourth Financial Corporation in Cooperation with Skidmore, Owings and Merril, 1974 to present; Assistant Vice President for Academic Resource Development, Wichita State University, 1970-74; Associate Professor, History Department, Wichita State University, 1970 to present; Assistant Dean for Academic Resources, Syracuse University, 1965-70; Instructor, History Department, Syracuse University, 1963-65; Consultant, New York State Education Department, 1962-63; Senior Historian (acting), New York State Education Department, 1961-62. Organizational Memberships: Mid-America Arts Alliance (director, 1973-76); University Press of Kansas (vice chairman, 1972-73); Kansas Committee for the Humanities (vice chairman, 1971-74). Community Activities: Kansas Public Television Service (vice chairman, 1973-79); Wichita Festivals, Inc. (director, 1972-74). Published Works: Books include *Robert Goodnough; Ernest Trova; Duane Hanson; Doris Caesar; Revolutionary Enigma; Ben Shahn: The Passion of Sacco and Vanzetti;* Contributions to Books and Magazines, Art Catalogues, Brochures. Honors and Awards: Phi Kappa Phi; Recognition Award, Alumni Association, Wichita State University, 1982; Resolution of Commendation and Appreciation in Recognition of Outstanding Service, Wichita State University, 1980; Outstanding Educator, Kansas Art Education Association, 1979; Wichitan of Year, *The Wichita Sun,* 1976; Legion of Honor, Government of Luxembourg, 1969; George S. Patton Medal, Government of Luxembourg, 1969; *Ben Shahn: The Passion of Sacco and Vanzetti* selected by *American Scholar* Magazine as One of the Best Books Published by a University Press in 1968; New York State Regents War Service Scholarship, 1959-63; Syracuse University Fellowships, 1961-62; Listed in *American Art Directory, Community Leaders and Noteworthy Americans, Contemporary Authors, Dictionary of International Biography, Directory of American Scholars, International Authors and Writers Who's Who, International Directory of the Arts, International Who's Who in Community Service, International Who's Who of Intellectuals, Men and Women of Distinction, Men of Achievement, Notable Americans of the Bicentennial Era, Personalities of America, Personalities of the West and Midwest, The Anglo-American Who's Who, Who's Who in America, Who's Who in American Art, Who's Who in the Midwest, Who's Who in Wichita, The Writer's Directory.* Address: Academic Resource Development, Wichita State University, Wichita, Kansas 67208.

Busha, Charles H

Author and Researcher. Personal: Born December 14, 1931; Son of Rosa Anna Busha. Education: B.A., Furman University, 1958; M.L.S., Rutgers, The State University of New Jersey, 1962; Ph.D., Indiana University, 1971; Commissioned, U.S. Army Field Artillery Officer Candidate School, Ft. Sill, Oklahoma, 1952. Military: Served with the United States Army, achieving the rank of 2nd Lieutenant, 1951-54; Served in the Korean Conflict with the 61st Artillery Battalion, 1st Cavalry Division. Career: Head of Technical Services and Reference Librarian, Greenville County Library, South Carolina, 1958-63; Reference Consultant, South Carolina State Library, Columbia, 1963-67; Fellow, Graduate Library School, Indiana University, 1967-70. Organizational Memberships: South Carolina Library Association (chairman of publications committee, 1963); Southeastern Library Association. Community Activities: Liberty Arts Council, 1976 to present (president 1978-79); Friends of the Sarlin Community Library, Liberty, South Carolina, 1976 to present (program chairperson 1980-81); Friends of the Tampa (Florida) Public Library, 1973-76 (president, 1975-76); Pickens County Historical Association, 1980 to present (curator); Pickens County Council on Aging, Inc. (board member 1981). Religion: Unitarian-Universalist. Published Works: *Freedom versus Suppression and Censorship* (1972), *Research Methods in Librarianship, Techniques and Interpretation* (1980) with Stephen P. Harter; Editor of *An Intellectual Freedom Primer* (1977); Editor of *A Library Science Research Reader and Bibliographic Guide* (1981). Honors and Awards: Beta Phi Mu, 1972 to present (president, Indiana University chapter 1973). Address: Summit Drive, Route 2, Box 496, Liberty, South Carolina 29657.

Charles H Busha

Butler, Edward Franklyn

Attorney at Law. Personal: Born July 1, 1937; Son of Arlene L. Butler; Father of Edward Franklyn II (Rhett), Jeffry Darrell. Education: B.A., University of Mississippi, 1958; J.D., Vanderbilt University School of Law, 1961. Military: Received an Honorable Discharge from the United States Air Force Reserve, 1962; Presently Serving as a Commander in the United States Naval Reserve. Career: Licensed to Practice Law in Tennessee and All Federal Courts, 1961; Admitted to Practice, United States Court of Appeals for the District of Columbia, 1978; Licensed to Practice Law in Texas, 1973; Private Practice as General Practitioner, Memphis, Tennessee, 1974 to present; Senior Vice President, Secretary, General Counsel, Safety First Fire Control Company, 1974 to present;

Secretary, General Counsel, Board of Directors, Hibbard, O'Connor & Weeks, Inc. (a nation-wide securities broker/dealer/underwriter), Houston, Texas, 1971-74; Partner, Butler and McDowell, Attorneys, 1967-71; Partner, Cobb and Butler, Attorneys, 1963-67; Associate Attorney, Erie S. Henrich, Attorney, 1963; Associate Attorney, Nelson, Norvell, Wilson and Thomason, Attorneys, 1961-63; Associate Director, Vanderbilt University Development Foundation, 1961. Organizational Memberships: American Bar Association (member, 1961 to present; corporation, banking and business law section; probate and real estate law section; litigation section; committee on litigation involving securities and subcommittee on litigation with S.E.C. and N.A.S.D.); Tennessee Bar Association (member, 1961 to present; legal aid and lawyer referral committee; corporation and banking section; securities law section; general practice section); Memphis and Shelby County Bar Association (member, 1961 to present; board of directors, 1979 to present; sponsor of committee on judicial selections; former sponsor, committee on moral fitness for admission to bar; former member, discipline and ethics committee; former secretary and director, junior bar conference; lawyer referral service panel); American Association of Trial Lawyers; Tennessee Association of Trial Lawyers; Memphis Trial Lawyers Association (member, 1963 to present; vice president, 1970-71; secretary, 1969-70; board of directors, 1966-71, 1976-77); Tennessee Criminal Defense Attorney's Association; Texas Bar Association (former member, executive council, military law section); Memphis Area Legal Services Association (board of directors, 1978 to present; chairman, bench and bar relations committee; co-chairman, by-laws committee). Community Activities: Opera Memphis (board of directors, 1978 to present); West Tennessee Sportsman Association (board of directors, 1979 to present); American Heart Association, Memphis Chapter (board of directors, 1979 to present; executive committee, 1978-79; general counsel, 1977 to present; cardiovascular pulmonary resusitation committee, 1977 to present; lawyers chairman, fund raising drive, 1963, 1976; delegate, Tennessee Heart Association annual meeting, 1978); Mid-America Ski Association (president, 1978 to present); Memphis Opera Guild; Chickasaw Council, Boy Scouts of America (former assistant scoutmaster, advancement chairman, troop committee, Troop 34; member, troop committee, Troop 240; former district committee member, served as chairman of special gifts section, sustaining membership in enrollment drive; advancement chairman, N.E. district committee; Eastern district merit badge counselor); United States Navy League (former member board of directors, Memphis chapter); Memphis Area Chamber of Commerce (military affairs committee; former deputy chairman for Navy affairs, Houston, Chamber of Commerce military affairs committee); Reserve Officers Association. Religion: Grace St. Lukes Episcopal Church - Usher, Former Member Budget Committee, Former Member Committee on Scouting. Honors and Awards: Invited to Speak at the American Bar Association Meeting on Litigation Involving Securities Transactions, 1977; Speaker, Greater Aspen Medical-Legal Seminar, 1977; Co-Chairman, Moderator and Speaker, Memphis and Shelby County Continuing Legal Education Seminar, 1978; Invited to Testify as Expert at Arkansas Securities Division on Hearing on Revising Arkansas Securities Law, 1971; Special Attorney, Memphis Municipal Bond Dealers Association, 1971; Special Judge, General Sessions Court of Shelby County (Tennessee), Memphis and Shelby County Juvenile Court, City of Memphis Municipal Court, City of Memphis Traffic Court, Probate Court of Shelby County; Key to City of Memphis, 1973; Congressional Community Service Award, Congress of United States, 1978; Listed in *Who's Who in American Law, Who's Who in the South and Southwest, Who's Who in the United States, Men of Achievement, Dictionary of International Biography, Notable Americans, Personalities of the South, Book of Honor, Community Leaders and Noteworthy Americans.* Address: 59 N. White Station Road, Memphis, Tennessee 38117.

Butler, Manley Caldwell

Lawyer, United States Representative. Personal: Born June 2, 1925; Son of W. W. S. (deceased) and Mrs. W. W. S. Butler; Married June Nolde; Father of Manley C. Jr., Henry, Jimmy, Marshall. Education: A.B., University of Richmond, 1948; LL.B., University of Virginia School of Law, 1950; Honorary LL.D., Washington and Lee University, 1978. Military: Served in the United States Naval Reserve, attaining the rank of Ensign. Career: Law Practice, Firm of Eggleston, Holton, Butler and Glenn, Roanoke, Virginia, 1950-72; Elected to Congress, 1972. Community Activities: Virginia House of Delegates, 1962-72; Minority Leader, 1966-72; Chairman, Joint Republican Caucus, 1964-66. Religion: Member and Former Vestryman, St. John's Episcopal Church. Address: 845 Orchard Road, S.W., Roanoke, Virginia 24014.

Butler, Pamela Stone

Senior Quality Analyst. Personal: Born May 3, 1947; Daughter of Ervin and Betty Stone; Married Royce E. Butler; Mother of Royce Lynn, Vincent Alexander, Katrina D'Ann. Education: A.S., Amarillo Junior College; Currently Attending Wayland Baptist University, Plainview, Texas. Career: Clerk, Amarillo Hardware Company, 1967; Secretary, American Quarter Horse, Amarillo, 1968; Mason & Hanger Company (1968 to present): Engineering Assistant, 1974-77, Quality Analyst, 1977-79, Senior Quality Analyst, 1980 to present. Organizational Memberships: American Society for Quality Control (secretary); Community Activities: American Defense Preparedness Association; Order of Eastern Star; Brownie Troop Volunteer, 1980-81; Elks Foundation for Crippled Children (donator). Religion: Baptist. Honors and Awards: Listed in *Who's Who in the South and Southwest*, 1978-79. Address: 3609 Atkinsen, Amarillo, Texas 79109.

Butler, William Gilbert Jr

Obstetrician-Gynecologist. Personal: Born October 1, 1928, Laurinburg, North Carolina; Son of Mr. and Mrs. William G. Butler; Married Winifred Thompson; Father of Ann, William G. III, Robert W. Education: B.A., University of North Carolina, 1949; M.D., Duke University, 1953; Intern, Duke University Medical Center; Residency in Obstetrics-Gynecology, Duke University Medical Center, 1953-59; Resident-Instructor, Duke University Medical Center, 1958-59. Military: Served in the United States Air Force Medical Corp, 1955-57; Served as Chief of Obstetricians-Gynecologists, 7520th U.S.A.F. Hospital, London, England. Career: Physician, Florence Clinic, 1959 to present (past president, former chairman of the executive committee). Organizational Memberships: Florence Clinic Development Company (president); American Board of Obstetricians-Gynecologists (diplomat, certified 1964, recertified 1979); American College of Obstetricians-Gynecologists (fellow); American College of Surgeons (fellow); Southeastern Association of Obstetrics and Gynecology (executive committee, board of directors); Bayard Carter Society of Obstetricians-Gynecologists (executive committee, board of directors, past vice president, president 1981); Alabama Association of Obstetricians-Gynecologists (president, 1969-70; executive committee, 1971 to present); Interspecialty Council Medical Association of Alabama (representative, 1970 to present); Lauderdale County Medical Society (past president, board censors); Lauderdale County Health Department (past chairman); American Society for the Study of Fertility (fellow); American Medical Association; Alabama Medical Association; Lauderdale County Medical Society; American College of Obstetricians-Gynecologists (advisory council, 1972-78; section chairman, 1975-78); England Hypnosis Society; Medical Staff of E.C.M. Hospital (vice president, 1981; president, 1982). Community Activities: Metropolitan Young Men's Christian Association of Northwest Alabama (past president, board of directors, executive committee, board of trustees); Florence Rotary Club (past president); University of North Alabama Sportsmans Club (board of directors); Northwest Alabama Chapter, American Cancer Society (vice president, 1974-75; president, 1977-78; board member, 1978 to present; advisory committee, Alabama Chapter); Lauderdale County Chapter, American Red Cross (board of directors); Lauderdale County United Way (executive board); Boy Scouts & Explorer Scouts (district committee; founder,

Medical Explorer Post); Muscle Shoals Mental Health Association (board of directors, past member); Colonial Manor Hospital (founder; chief, obstetrics & gynecology; vice president; board of directors). Religion: First Presbyterian Church, Ruling Elder, Moderator Pro-tem; Past Vice Chairman, Board of Directors. Honors and Awards: Muscle Shoals Citizen of the Year, 1980. Address: 1708 Monticello Road, Florence, Alabama 35630.

Butts, Priscilla A

Lecturer, Project Director, Student. Personal: Born February 5, 1949; Daughter of James (deceased) and Eva W. Butts. Education: B.S.N., cum laude, Dillard University, 1970; M.S.N., University of Pennsylvania, 1972; Ph.D. Candidate, New York University. Career: Lecturer, University of Pennsylvania Graduate Program; Project Director, Cancer Detection Community Program, Misericordia Hospital, Philadelphia. Organizational Memberships: American Nurses Association; International Childbirth Education Association; Sigma Theta Tau (regional representative); National League for Nursing; Nurses Association of the American College of Obstetrics and Gynacology; American Society for Psychoprophylaxis in Obstetrics (Lamaze); American Academy of Political Science. Community Activities: United Negro College Fund (representaive). Religion: Baptist. Published Works: Co-Author of Grant to Develop a Community Cancer Detection Program in West Philadelphia. Honors and Awards: Sigma Theta Tau; Ethnic/Racial Minority Fellowship for Doctoral Study, American Nurses Association, 1981-82; Rita Miller Scholarship, 1967; Alpha Kappa Alpha Scholarship, 1968; Alpha Kappa Mu; Listed in *Who's Who of American Women, World Who's Who of Women, Who's Who Among Students in American Colleges and Universities, Personalities of America.* Address: 4701 Pine Street, Philadelphia, Pennsylvania 19143.

Buyama, Edward T Jr

General, Electrical, Mechanical Contractor. Personal: Born February 1, 1933; Son of Edward T. and Gloria Buyama; Married Sandra Kay Mandeville; Father of Jeannie Sue, Carol Lynn, Helen Kay, Patricia Ann, Susan Edwina. Education: 2-year Equivalency, Furman University, 1952. Military: Served in the United States Air Force, 1950-53. Career: General, Electrical, Mechanical Engineer; Former Mechanical Inspector, Dade County, Florida. Organizational Memberships: American Society of Heating, Refrigerating, Air Conditioning Engineers; Refrigeration Service Engineers Society (past president); State Electrical Masters Association (immediate past president); Associated Builders and Contractors (political action committee); Florida Roofing, Sheetmetal and Air Conditioning Contractors Association (governmental affairs committee). Community Activities: Building Official of Hialeah Gardens, Florida, 1980-81; Boys Club of America (North West Boys Club Gym, New Building, 1981); Ronald McDonald House of Miami (board of directors, 1980). Religion: Miami Shores Baptist Church. Address: 11611 West Biscayne Canal Road, Miami, Florida 33161.

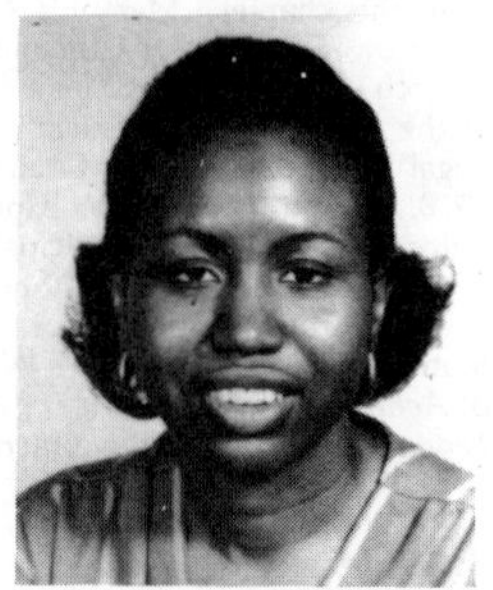

Priscilla A Butts

Byerly, Joan Banta (Mrs Joseph S Byerly)

Public Relations and Financial Consultant. Personal: Born August 19, 1926, in San Saba, Texas; Daughter of Jesse J. and V. Marie Fry Banta; Married Riley C. Harkey, August 12, 1942 (divorced March 1962); Second marriage to Joseph S. Byerly, June 3, 1964; Mother of John R, Bruce W. Education: High School Graduate; Attended University of Texas and University of Nevada. Career: Former Farmer, Contributor of a Column to Local Newspaper, Radio Program; Freelance Photographer; Secretary-Manager, Sparks Chamber of Commerce 1964-65; Owner Jan O'Hara Enterprises; Society Editor Carson City, Nevada, *Appeal*, 1966-67; Staff Photographer, Advertising and Reporting, Sparks *Tribune*; Associate Director, National Conference of Christians and Jews, Reno, Nevada; Correspondent, O & A Marketing News, La Canada, California. Organizational Memberships: American Pen Women; Reno Branch Writers and Artists; Texas Press Women; National Federation Press Women; Reno Executive Club; Reno Press Club. Community Activities: Republican Party; American Red Cross Fund Drive; Heart Fund; Cancer Fund; Parent Teacher Association (former vice president, life member Texas); Band Parents Club (past president); Boy Scouts America; Civil Air Patrol (warrant officer, public relations staff Nevada wing, 1963-66). Honors and Awards: Award for outstanding work with Reno Air Races, 1964; Red Ribbon Award, Civil Air Patrol; Asked to become "Goodwill Ambassador to Indonesia"; Outstanding Awards from Chamber of Commerce, Red Cross, Polio, Cancer, Heart Funds. Address: 1945 4th Street, Apt. 37, Sparks, Nevada 89431.

Byington, Frederick D

Director. Personal: Born May 2, 1930. Career: Director in Private School Setting; Pioneer in Special Education for Language Problems and Gifted Students; Conference Speaker on Secondary and Special Education; Consultant, Gifted Program, Philadelphia School District. Community Activities: Lions Club; Young Men's Christian Association; Boy Scouts of America. Honors and Awards: Phi Delta Kappa; Alpha Phi Omega; Alpha Tau Omega. Address: 1420 Locust, 14I, Philadelphia, Pennsylvania 19102.

Cabrera, Fernando J

Psychiatrist, Executive, Consultant. Personal: Born November 25, 1928, in San Juan, Puerto Rico; Son of Rafael Cabrera Torres and Delores de la Rosa Llorente (both deceased); Married Maria de Jesus Delgado; Father of Fernando, Jose Luis, Maria de Jesus (Maruja). Education: Graduate of Central High School, Santurce, Puerto Rico; B.S. with Honors, Instituto Politecnico de San German, 1950; M.D., Universidad Central de Madrid, Spain, 1955; Rotating Internship, Rio Piedras Municipal Hospital, Rio Piedras, Puerto Rico, 1955-56; Residency, Psychiatry, Hato Rey Psychiatric Hospital, Inc., Hato Rey, Puerto Rico 1956-58, Spring Grove State Hospital, Baltimore, Maryland 1958-61; Postgraduate Study, Psychiatry, Alcoholism; Licensed to Practice, Puerto Rico; Board Diplomate, Psychiatry, American Board of Psychiatry and Neurology, 1962. Career: Hato Rey Psychiatric Hospital, Inc., Chief, Admission Service 1961-66, Assistant Director 1962-66, Director 1966-70, Executive Director 1970 to present, President, Board of Directors, 1970 to present; Consultant Psychiatrist, Workmen Compensation Board, 1962-68, 1979-81; Consultant Psychiatrist, Puerto Rico Retirement Board, 1962-70; Consultant, United States District Federal Court, 1977 to present; Special Consultant, Puerto Rico Senate, Puerto Rico House of Representatives, Judiciary Committee, New Penal Code, 1967-73; Guest Lecturer, Department of Psychiatry, University of Ottawa, 1981; Associate Professor, Clinical Psychiatry, Caribe Medical School, 1977 to present; Licensed Health Service Administrator, 1976 to present. Organizational Memberships: American Board of Psychiatry and Neurology; American Psychiatric Association; American Society of Group Psychotherapy and Psychodrama; National Council on Alcoholism; Maryland Psychiatric Association; Baltimore Area Council on Alcoholism; Puerto Rico Medical Association; American Medical Association; Physical Facilities of Health and Welfare; Puerto Rico Advisory Board on Alcoholism; Puerto Rico Advisory Board on Mental Health; Association of Physicians Graduated in Spain; Pan American Medical Association; Interamerican Council of Psychiatry; Department of Drug Addiction; Puerto Rico Institute of Psychiatry; American Academy of Medical Directors; Puerto Rico District Branch, American Psychiatric Association; New York Academy of Sciences; Department of Public Works and Transportation of Puerto Rico; Department of Health of Puerto Rico; National Police and Firefighter Association of the United States of America; International Platform Association; Puerto Rico Psychiatric Society; National Association of Private Psychiatric Hospitals; International Academy of Criminology; American Police Conference; American Law Enforcement Officers Association; American Security Council National Advisory Board; Woodrow Wilson Foundation; Puerto Rico Association of Hospital Administrators; American Academy of Psychiatry and the Law; Committee for Seminar Drug Addiction and Controlled Substances. Published Works: Numerous Papers, including "Bill of Rights for Patients", "The Magnitude of Alcoholism in Puerto Rico". Honors and Awards: Specialist in Industrial and Occupational Medicine, One of Its Founders in Puerto Rico, 1971; Exchange Clubs Awards for Distinguished Services, 1964, 1965, 1966; Cuban Medical Association in Exile, 1971; Civic Leader, 1972; Section of Psychiatry, Neurology and Neurosurgery, Puerto Rico Medical Association, Dr. Mario Julia Award 1975, Awards, Special Recognition Activity 1968 (also from Hato Rey Psychiatric Hospital, Inc.), Presidential Award 1979, Physician of the Decade, Eastern District 1979; Puerto Rico Chapter, National Association of Social Workers; Sixteen Different Awards for Meritorious and Distinguished Services, Puerto Rico Medical Association; Knights of Malta, Grand Cross, Her. Order, Grand Marshall, International Order; Distinguished Service Award, Alpha Beta Chi, 1971; Award, Mexican Government, 1975; Award, Puerto Rico Association of Graduates of Spanish Universities, 1972, 1974, 1977; Award, American Research Institute for the Practice of Specialized Medicine, 1973; Award, American Legion Post 140, 1971; Physician Recognition Award, American Medical Association, 1977-80, 1980-83; Pro-Mental Health National Association Award, 1977; Award, Meritorious Services in Continuous Medical Education, Harvard University, 1978; Lions Club District 51-E, 1978; Award for Meritorious Services in Mental Health, Governor of the Commonwealth of Puerto Rico, 1978; Certified Continued Medical Education, American Psychiatric Association, 1980-83; Listed in *American Psychiatric Directory, American Medical Association Directory, Directory of Medical Specialties Board Certified and Award, Directory of International Biography, Notable Americans of the Bicentennial Era, American Academy Medical Dictionary, Who's Who in the South and Southwest, United States Medical Directory, International Who's Who of Intellectuals, Book of Honor.* Address: 28 Diamante Street S.E., Golden Gates, Caparra Heights, Guaynabo, Puerto Rico 00920.

Pastora S J Cafferty

Cafferty, Pastora San Juan

Research Associate, Educator, Public Policy Worker. Education: B.A., St. Barnard College, Cullman, Alabama, 1962; M.A. 1966, Ph.D. 1971, American Literary and Cultural History, George Washington University, Washington, D.C. Career: Research Associate, National Opinion Research Center, Chicago, 1980 to present; University of Chicago, School of Social Service Administration, Associate Professor 1977 to present, Assistant Professor 1971-77, Associate Professor, Committee on Public Policy Studies 1976 to present, Director, Task Force to Develop Nationally Distributed 30- and 60-Second Public Service Announcements Dealing with Problems of Desegregated School Districts, Produced in Conjunction with WTTW Public Television Station, Chicago, 1974-75; Co-Host, *Oiga, Amigo*, Public Service Weekly Half-Hour Telecast on WLS/ABC Station, Chicagotive Vice President & Manager, Black Diamond Savings and Loan Association, Norton, Virginia, 1973; Manager, R. E. Wright Realty Company, Johnson City, Tennessee, 1974-78. Organizational Memberships: American Savings & Loan Institute (president, upper east Tennessee chapter, 1970-72). Community Activities: Johnson City Chamber of Commerce, 1966-72; United Fund Worker, Johnson City, Tennessee, 1969-72. Religion: Church of God, Anderson, Indiana, Fund-Raising Committee, Appalachian District, 1957-58); East Tennessee General Assembly of Church of God, Secretary, Treasurer, 1963-73, Treasurer, 1974-81; East Tennessee Kingdom Builders of Church of God, Treasurer 1967-73; Tennessee Ministerial Assembly of Church of God, Ordained Minister 1980; Tennessee State Ministerial Executive Committee, 1970-72; First Church of God, Elizabethton, Tennessee, Interim Pastor, 1968, 1971, 1974; First Church of God, Norton, Virginia, Finance Committee, 1973; East Tennessee Campmeeting Association of Church of God, Treasurer, 1974-81. Honors and Awards: Daughters of the American Revolution Award in American History, 1933; American Savings & Loan Institute Award, 1972; Listed in *Who's Who in Religion, Personalities of the South, Men of Achievement, Who's Who in Community Service.* Address: Route 1, Box 398, Elizabethton, Tennessee 37643.

Caldwell, Stratton Franklin

Educator, Author, Poet. Personal: Born August 25, 1926; Son of Dr. and Mrs. K. S. Caldwell (both deceased); Married Sharee

Deanna Ockerman; Father of Scott Raymond, Karole Elizabeth, Shannon Sharee. Education: B.S. Education, Physical Education 1951, Ph.D. Physical Education 1966, University of Southern California; M.S. Physical Education, University of Oregon, 1953. Military: Served in the United States Navy, 1944-46, attaining the rank of Pharmacist's Mate Third Class. Career: University of California-Los Angeles, Department of Physical Education, Teaching Assistant 1953-54, Associate in Physical Education 1957-65; Director of Physical Education, Regina Young Men's Christian Association, Saskatchewan, Canada, 1954-56; Teacher, Physical Education, Biology, Social Studies, Health Education, Athletic Director, Queen Elizabeth Junior-Senior High School, Calgary, Alberta, Canada, 1956-57; San Fernando Valley State College, Northridge, California, Department of Physical Education, Assistant Professor of Physical Education 1965-68, Associate Professor of Physical Education 1968-71; Visiting Professor of Physical Education, Department of Physical Education (Women's), University of California-Santa Barbara, Spring Quarter, 1969; Professor, Department of Physical Education, California State University-Northridge, 1971 to present. Organizational Memberships: American Association for Health, Physical Education and Recreation (fellow; member, physical education council, southwest district, 1969-71; forum member, 1970-71); American Association for the Advancement of Tension Control (charter member); American College of Sports Medicine (fellow); Association of Transpersonal Psychology; California Association for Health, Physical Education and Recreation (chairman, history and policies committee, 1962-64; president, Los Angeles college and university unit, 1969-70; vice president, physical education, 1970-71); Canadian Association for Health, Physical Eduation and Recreation (fellow; vice president, physical education, southern Saskatchewan branch, 1954-55); International Committee on Comparative Physical Education (charter member); National Association for Physical Education in Higher Education (charter member); Southern Saskatchewan Amateur Volleyball Association (president, 1965-55; Regina representative, prairie provinces, 1955-56); Amateur Athletic Union of Canada (gymnastics chairman, Saskatchewan branch, 1954-55); *CAHPER* (California) *Journal* (member, editorial board, 1970-71); *The Physical Educator* (U.S.A.) (member, editorial board, 1972-74); *Canadian Journal of Health, Physical Education and Recreation* (member, editorial board, 1973-75); American Alliance for Health, Physical Education, Recreation and Dance (member, centennial commission, 1978 to present). Religion: Christian. Published Works: Numerous Books, including *Golf* (with Cecil Hollingsworth and Joan Martin), *Basic Health Science A, B, C, D, E, F,* Teacher's Edition (special contributor, physical education); *Humanizing Physical Education: Methods for the Secondary School Movement Program* (with Rosalind Cassidy); Entries in *Biographical Dictionary of American Educators;* Numerous Newspaper Articles, including "Rosalind Cassidy: The Whole Person", "Why Exercise?", "How to Get the Best from Your Athletes"; Numerous Periodical Articles, including "The Human Potential Movement: Body/Non-Verbal/Movement Approaches to Human Growth", "Humanistic Physical Education: Tomorrow's Challenge", "And Those Who Can't...Teach"; Proceedings, Reports, Guides, including "Oral History: New Horizon for Physical Education and Sport Historians", *Western Society for Physical Education of College Women, Annual Conference Report,* "On the Future as History in Physical Education"; Poetry, including "Requiem: An Apologetic to Carl Sandburg", "No Lady Madonna", "Just Over the Shoulder", "In Morning Softness". Honors and Awards: Fellow, American Association for Health, Physical Education and Recreation 1962, American College of Sports Medicina 1965, Canadian Association for Health, Physical Education and Recreation 1971, Institute for the Advancement of Teaching and Learning, California State University-Northridge 1977, International Biographical Association 1978, American Biographical Institute 1979, International Academy of Poets 1980. Address: 80 North Kanan Road, Agoura, California 91301.

Callan, James R

James R Callan

Researcher. Personal: Son of Mr. and Mrs. Ruskin Callan; Married Earlene Shewmaker; Father of James P., Kelley, Kristi, Diane. Education: Graduate, Jesuit High School, Dallas, Texas; B.A., St. Mary's University; M.A., University of Oklahoma, 1967; Undertook studies toward Ph.D. Career: Consultant, Aerospace Research Laboratory; Researcher, Schlumberger Research Center, 1970 to present (began working on V.L.S.I. design techniques, 1981); Co-founder, C. Systems, Ltd. (advertising-research firm). Organizational Memberships: Institute of Electrical and Electronic Engineers; Mathematical Association of America; Association for Computing Machinery; Institute of Electrical and Electronic Engineers Computer Group. Community Activities: Volunteer work with teenagers; Oak Cliff Civic Theatre, Dallas, Texas (president, 2 years); Town Tennis Tournaments (director, 4 years). Honors and Awards: Received three grants from the National Science Foundation; Fellowship, National Aeronautics and Space Administration; Grant, Data Processing Management Association. Address: 332 North Salem Road, Ridgefield, Connecticut 06877.

Callan, T Earlene

Executive, Advertising Research Firm. Personal: Born November 6, 1938; Daughter of Aubrey and Buena Shewmaker; Married James Ruskin Callan; Mother of Diane Bailey, Jamie, Kelly, Kristi. Education: B.A. Mathematics, Harding College, Searcy, Arkansas; Postgraduate Work, University of Oklahoma; Professional Courses, Data Processing, International Business Machines. Career: President, C Systems, Ltd., Advertising Research Firm; Teacher of Mathematics; Systems Analyst, Data Processing; Programmer, Researcher, Time and Motion Studies. Organizational Memberships: Data Processing Management Association (treasurer). Community Activities: Camp Fire Leader; Fund Raiser, Various Charities. Honors and Awards: Listed in *Who's Who of American Women, World Who's Who of Women.* Address: 332 North Salem Road, Ridgefield, Connecticut 06877.

Calvery, Thomas Cleaton

Bailbondsman, Custom Framer. Personal: Born March 22, 1940; Son of Mrs. J. E. Calvery; Married Faye Potts; Father of Thomas Cleaton Jr., Elizabeth Ashley. Education: Graduate, Corinth High School, 1959; Attended Northeast Mississippi Junior College, 1961-63. Military: Served with the Mississippi Army National Guard, 1957-67, achieving the rank of Staff Sergeant (E-6). Career: Cost Accounting; Production Control Supervisor; Fireman; Owner and Operator of a Hobby Shop; Bailbondsman; Custom Framer. Organizational Memberships: Professional Picture Framers Association, 1977-79. Community Activities: Boy Scouts of America (scoutmaster, 1965-71); Alcorn County Election Commissioner, 1977 to present; Mississippi Lion Sight Foundation (trustee, 1968-79); Lions Club (zone chairman, 1968-72; deputy governor, 1972-76; cabinet secretary, 1976-77); Mississippi Election Commissioners Association (board of directors, 1981 to present). Religion: Baptist. Honors and Awards: Lion of the Year, 1971. Address: 401 Sharp Street, Corinth, Mississippi 38834.

Camacho, Luis Garcia

Orthodontist. Personal: Born April 30, 1927; Son of Dr. Felix M. Camacho (deceased); Married Cynthia Louise Jose; Father of Luis W., Selina M., Anthony R., Charles, Liza, Richard G., Keven F. Education: B.S. 1953, D.D.S. School of Dentistry 1957, Marquette University; M.S., Orthodontics, St. Louis University Graduate School, 1966. Career: Exclusive Practice of Orthodontics, present. Organizational Memberships: American Association of Orthodontists American Dental Association; Guam Dental Society (president, 1972); Education and Research Foundation in Orthodontics, St. Louis University; Pacific Coast Society of Orthodontists;

Delta Sigma Delta Dental Fraternity (life member). Community Activities: Catholic Medical Center (assistant director, dental staff, 1957-64); Government of Guam (vice chairman, commission of licensure in the healing arts, 1979-81); University of Tampa, Florida (vice president, Newman club, 1949-50); Donations to Church-Related Fund Drives and All Civic Activities, present; Bank of Guam (director, 1974-81; chairman, nominating committee, 1979-81; member, audit committee, 1981); Pacific International Corporation (board of directors, 1975-81); Pacific Financial Corporation (vice president, 1977-81); Camacho, Inc. (president, 1975-81); Honors and Awards: Member, Option Committee, Bank of Guam, 1979-82; Listed in *Community Leaders of America, International Who's Who of Intellectuals, Who's Who in the West, International Who's Who in Community Service.* Address: P.O. Box 2164, Agana, Guam 96910.

Cameron, Dorothy S

Educator. Personal: Born January 12, 1927; Daughter of William O. Simmons (deceased) and Ola N. Simmons; Married Archie N. Cameron; Mother of Toni Cameron-Vincent, Andre Cameron. Education: B.S., North Carolina Agricutural & Technical State University, 1948; M.Ed. 1964, Ed.D. 1980, University of North Carolina-Greensboro. Career: Assistant Professor of Business Education and Administrative Services; Secretary, North Carolina Agricultural Extension Service. Organizational Memberships: Alpha Kappa Mu National Honor Society; National Business Education Association; North Carolina Business Education Association; Southern Business Education Association; American Association of University Professors (past member); Delta Pi Epsilon (member, Zeta chapter); Pi Omega Pi; National Collegiate Association of Secretaries. Community Activities: Washington School Parent-Teacher Association (planning committee, 1967-68; chaperone, tour to Morehead Planetarium); Dudley High School Parent-Teacher Association (planning committee, 1967-68); North Carolina Agricultural & Technical State University Alumni Association; University of North Carolina-Greensboro Alumni Association; Greensboro Civic Ballet Auxiliary (committee on communication and social activities, 1967-68); Brown Summit High School (consultant, career day); Booker T. Washington High School, Reidsville, North Carolina (consultant, career day); Pearson Street Young Women's Christian Association (membership, collection, 1968-69); Bluford School (membership, collection, 1968-69; consultant, self-study committee on school's philosophy, 1969-70); Guilford Technical Institute (special study tour on vocational educational opportunities, 1969-70); Lincoln Parent-Teacher Association (chairman, hospitality committee, orientation activities, 1970-71; executive committee, 1971-72, 1972-73); Family Service Traveler's Aid Association of Greensboro, Inc. (collegiate and community affairs conference); Lincoln Junior High School Parent-Teacher Association (hospitality committee, orientation activities, 1970-71); Chamber of Commerce Citizen's Tour of City to Study Water and Sewer Facilities Prior to Voting for Bond Issues, 1970-71; Eastern Music Festival Auxiliary (committee on communication, 1972-73; membership committee, 1974-75; board member, 1974-75); Lincoln Junior High School Open House (executive committee, hospitality committee, 1973-74); National Honor Society Induction Service, 1974-75. Religion: Providence Baptist Church, member 1972 to present, Committee Member, General Greene Council, Boy Scouts of America 1972-73, Committee on Banquet Preparation 1973-74, Introduced Speaker, Missionary Circle No. 1 Anniversary Program 1972-73, Committee Member, Investitude Service, Girl Scouts of America 1974-75; St. James Presbyterian Church, Greensboro, North Carolina, Guest Speaker, Installation of Garden Council Officers, 1970-71; St. Stephen United Church of Christ, Member 1939-72, Sunday School Teacher, Usher, Choir Member, Secretary, Girl Scout Council Member. Published Works: Professional Articles, Proceedings, Proposals, including "Word Processing: An Innovative Concept at North Carolina Agricultural & Technical State University", " A New School Emerges", "Critical Issues in Vocational and Technical Education and Implications for Progress for Teacher Preparation in the Small College and University". Honors and Awards: North Carolina Agricultural & Technical State University, Alpha Kappa Mu National Honor Society 1946, Editor-in-Chief, *The Register*, Student Publication 1947, Pacesetters Award, University Foundation, Inc. 1967, Piedmont University Center Faculty Study Grant 1968, Summer Study Grant 1970, Pi Omega Pi 1974; Delta Pi Epsilon National Honor Society for Business Educators, University of North Carolina-Greensboro, 1966; Grant to Participate in Tri-Faculty Workshop, Texas Southern, Houston, 1970; Award to Study, Certificate, Data Processing Systems Designs for Users Department Managers, International Business Machines Center, New York City, 1971; Grant to Participate in Instructional Media Laboratory Workshop, University of Wisconsin-Milwaukee, 1971; A.I.D.P. Faculty Study Grant, Summer Session, 1975, 1977; W. K. Kellogg, Fellow 1976-77, Fellowship Certificate 1979; Board of Governors' Faculty Doctoral Study Assignment Award for Academic Year, 1979-80; Listed in *Dictionary of International Biography, Two Thousand Women of Achievement, Who's Who of American Women, World's Who's Who of Education, International Who's Who in Education, Community Leaders and Noteworthy Americans.* Address: 1002 Julian Street, Greensboro, North Carolina 27406.

Rondo Cameron

Cameron, Rondo

Educator. Personal: Born February 20, 1925; Son of Burr S. and Annie Mae Cameron (both deceased); Married Claydean Zumbrunnen; Father of Alan, Cindia. Education: A.B. magna cum laude, Economics/Mathematics 1948, A.M. Economics/History 1949, Yale University; Ph.D., Economics/Sociology, University of Chicago, 1952. Military: Served in the United States Navy, Naval Aviation, 1942-46, attaining the rank of Lieutenant (j.g.). Career: Instructor in Economics, Yale University, 1951-52; University of Wisconsin, Assistant Professor of Economics and History 1952-56, Associate Professor of Economics and History 1957-61, Professor of Economics and History 1961-69, Founder, Director, Graduate Program in Economic History, 1960-69; Visiting Professor of Economics, University of Chicago, 1956-57; Special Field Staff, Rockefeller Foundation, Santiago, Chile, 1965-67. Organizational Memberships: Economic History Association (president, 1974-75); International Association of Economic History (member, executive committee, 1973 to present); *Journal of Economic History* (editor, 1975-81); Cliometric Society (charter member); American Historical Association; American Economic Association; Society for French Historical Studies. Community Activities: Albert Schweitzer Fellowship, New York (member, board of directors, 1973 to present); Fulbright American Graduate Student Program (member, national screening committee, 1980, 1981); National Endowment for the Humanities (consultant-panelist); National Science Foundation (consultant-panelist); Atlanta Committee on Foreign Relations (member, speakers council, 1977 to present); Phi Beta Kappa Associates (lecturer, 1977-81); National Convocation of Kenan Professors (member, program planning committee, 1982). Honors and Awards: Phi Beta Kappa, Yale University, 1948; Fulbright Scholarship, France, 1950-51; Social Science Research Council Awards, 1953, 1956, 1960, 1962; Guggenheim Fellowships, 1954-56, 1970-71; Fellow, Center for Advanced Studies in the Behavioral Sciences, 1958-59; Fellow, Woodrow Wilson International Center for Scholars, 1974-75); Fulbright Visiting Research Professor, University of Glasgow, Scotland, 1962-63; Rockefeller Foundation Grants for Research, 1961-65, 1980-81. Address: 1088 Clifton Road, Northeast, Atlanta, Georgia 30307.

Camp, Louise Phifer

Personal: Born March 22, 1912, in Winston-Salem, North Carolina; Daughter of Charles and Louisa Williams Phifer; Married George William Wise (deceased), June 7, 1934; Second marriage to Wofford Benjamin Camp, January 18, 1956; Mother of Wofford B. Camp Jr., Donald M. Camp, Addie Louise Segars, George William Wise, Sarah Cory. Education: B.A., B.Mus., Limestone College, Gaffney, South Carolina, 1933; Undertook post-graduate work in music, Converse College, Spartanburg, South Carolina, 1933-34;

Studied voice in New York City with Metropolitan Opera coaches, summers 1932-34. Career: Minister of Music, Baptist Evangelistic Meetings in North Carolina, South Carolina and Georgia, summers 1929-34; Taught Voice, Limestone College, summer 1932; Organized and Directed Numerous Choral Groups, North Carolina, South Carolina and Georgia, 1935-55; Soloist, St. John's Methodist Church, Augusta, Georgia, 1953-55, and Presbyterian Church, Trenton, South Carolina, 1934-55; Farmer, Edgefield County, South Carolina, 1945-77; Director, Bank of Trenton, 1945-78; Co-Founder, Trenton Development Corporation, 1950; Secretary, W. B. Camp & Sons, Inc., 1956 to present. Organizational Memberships: National Association Bank Women; Farm Bureau. Community Activities: Pro America, Bakersfield, California (president, 1958-59); Kern County (California) Music Association (director, 1957-59); Symphony Associates, Kern County (president, 1972-73); Louise Phifer Camp Foundation, Limestone College (co-founder, 1957); Kern County Free Enterprise Association (co-founder and director, 1960); Freedoms Foundation at Valley Forge (organizer and president, women's division, Kern County chapter, 1969); Freedoms Foundation at Valley Forge (trustee, 1974 to present); South Carolina Foundation of Independent Colleges, Inc. (trustee, 1973 to present); Limestone College (chairman, board of trustees, 1973 to present); John and Beverly Stauffer Foundation (director, 1973 to present); Religious Heritage of America (vice chairman, 1980 to present; treasurer, 1976-80); American Association of University Women; Daughters of the American Revolution; United Daughters of the Confederacy; P.E.O. (past president, local chapter I.W.); Bakersfield Women's Club; Bakersfield Garden Club; Philharmonic Association, Bakersfield; Gospel Music Association (director, 1978 to present); Gospel Music Hall of Fame (national campaign chairman, research library & museum, 1978-81). Religion: Presbyterian. Honors and Awards: Outstanding Cotton Grower of South Carolina, South Carolina Agricultural Extension Service, 1954; Outstanding Alumna Award, Limestone College, 1956; Award, Freedoms Foundation at Valley Forge, 1973; Honorary Degree (Doctor of Humanities), Limestone College, 1977; Order of Knights Hospitallers of St. John, Knights of Malta, 1979. Address: 701 Oleander Ave., Bakersfield, California 93304.

Camp, N Harry Jr

Clinical Psychologist and Research Clinician. Personal: Born March 28, 1918. Education: B.A., 1940, M.A., 1941, both from the University of Chicago; D.Ed., University of California-Los Angeles, 1948; Undertook postgraduate studies to the equivalent of a Ph.D. in Clinical Psychology, Johns Hopkins University, 1950-54, Loyola University, 1950-54, and University of Florida, 1960-65. Military: Served as an Ensign in the United States Navy, 1940-45. Career: High School Principal, 1940-42; Teaching Assistant, University of California-Los Angeles, 1946-48; Director of Clinical Services, Baltimore County, Maryland, 1953-55; Assistant Professor, Brooklyn College, 1948-49; Professor of Education and Psychology, Bucknell University, 1949-53; Director of Clinical Services and Guidance, Brevard (Florida) City Schools, 1955-57; Director of Psychiatric Clinic, School for Boys, State of Florida, 1953-55; Board of Directors, Atlantus Academy (School for Learning Disabilities); Board of Directors, Vanguard School, Miami, Florida (School for Learning Disabilities); Guest Professor, Pennsylvania State College, 1950-55; Guest Professor, University of Miami, Florida, 1965 to present; Clinical Psychologist in Private Practice; Research Clinician, Parkway Hospital, Miami, Florida. Organizational Memberships: Florida Psychological Association; Dade County Psychological Association; American Personnel and Guidance Association; American Psychological Association; Coral Gables Reading Disabilities Association; American Society for Children with Learning Disabilities; Better Opportunity for Children with Learning Disabilities; Florida Association of Children with Learning Disabilities. Community Activities: Speaker: Miami Mental Health Society, Coral Gables Reading Association, Parental Groups and Teacher Groups. Religion: Member Kendall Methodist Church. Honors and Awards: Board of Directors: Atlantus Academy, 1978 to present, Vanguard School, 1971 to present; Listed in *Who's Who in the Southwest*, 1970 to present. Address: 7520 S.W. 105th Terrace, Miami, Florida 33156.

Caroline K Campbell

Campbell, Caroline Krause

Executive. Personal: Born May 5, 1926; Daughter of Mr. and Mrs. Charles J. Krause Sr.; Married Richard E. Campbell, Sr. (deceased); Mother of Richard E. Jr., Don Michael, Scott Gary, Jonathan Miles, Candace Kay. Education: Graduate, Weslaco High School, Weslaco, Texas, 1945; Attended the University of New Mexico, 1951-65; Diploma, Alexander Hamilton Institute, 1969. Career: Various Secretarial Positions; Survey Researcher, Winoma Research Company; Drug Store President. Organizational Memberships: New Mexico Pharmaceutical Company; National Association of Retail Druggists; National Federation of Independent Businesses. Community Activities: Chamber of Commerce (congressional and state legislative committees; chairman, subcommittee on human resources, 1981); International Platform Association; Republican National Committee (sustaining member); Albuquerque Symphony Women's Association; Elks Club; Albuquerque Rose Society. Honors and Awards: Listed in *Who's Who of American Women, The World Who's Who of Women, Personalities of America, Directory of Distinguished Americans, Who's Who in the West*. Address: 8252 Menaul Blvd., N.E., Albuquerque, New Mexico 87110.

Campbell, David

Executive. Personal: Born May 2, 1930, in Oklahoma City, Oklahoma; Son of LaVada (Ray) Henager and Lois Raymond Campbell; Married Janet Newland, March 1, 1958; Father of Carl David. Education: B.S. Geology, University of Tulsa, Oklahoma, 1953; M.S. Geology, University of Oklahoma, Norman, Oklahoma, 1957. Military: Served in the United States Naval Reserve from 1949-53 and in the United States Army from 1953-55. Career: Petroleum Geologist, Lone Star Producing Company, 1957-65; Tenneco Oil Company, Exploration Project Geologist, Denver, Colorado and Oklahoma City 1965-71, District Exploration Geologist, Oklahoma City 1971-73, Division Geological Consultant, Mid-Continent Division, Oklahoma City, 1973-77; Exploration Manager, Mid-Continent Division, Leede Exploration, Oklahoma City 1977-80; President, Earth Hawk Exploration, Oklahoma City, 1980 to present. Organizational Memberships: American Association of Petroleum Geologists (member, 1956 to present; information committee, 1968 national AAPG-SEPM Convention; field trips chairman, 1978 national AAPG-SEPM Convention; house of delegates, member 1980-83, national chairman 1981-82; member, executive committee, 1981-82); Oklahoma City Geological Society (member, 1957 to present; public relations chairman, speakers bureau, 1963-64; chairman, stratigraphic code committee, 1967-68; presidential appointee, executive board, 1968-69; school volunteer program, Oklahoma City public schools, 1969-70; advertising manager, *Shale Shaker*, 1969-70, 1970-71); representative, AAPG house of delegates, 1980-83); American Petroleum Institute; Oklahoma Independent Petroleum Association; Oklahoma City Geological Discussion Group (president, 1975-76); Tulsa Geological Society; Independent Petroleum Association of America; Sigma Xi; New York Academy of Sciences; American Association for the Advancement of Science. Community Activities: Boy Scouts of America (last frontier council, 1960-73; education chairman, eagle district, 1963-67; assistant scoutmaster, Wiley Post district, 1971-73); Oklahoma County Representative, Cherokee Nation, 1976-78; Cherokee National Historical Society (board of directors; heritage council); Oklahoma Historical Society; Thomas Gilcrease Museum Association; Museum of the Cherokee Indian Association; United States Chamber of Commerce; Oklahoma City Chamber of Commerce. Published Works: Three Articles (with Janet Campbell), "The MacIntosh Family Among the Cherokees", "Cherokee Participation in the Political Impact of the North American Indian", "The Wolf Clan", Each Published in *Journal of Cherokee Studies*. Honors and Awards: Petroleum Heritage Certificate of Recognition, Oklahoma-Kansas Oil & Gas Association, 1982; Listed in *Who's Who in the South and Southwest, Who's Who in Finance and Industry, Who's Who in the World, The Oklahoma Petroleum Industry* by Kenny A. Franks. Address: 6109 Woodbridge Road, Oklahoma City, Oklahoma 73132.

Campbell-Goymer, Nancy Ruth

Educator. Personal: Born July 1, 1949; Daughter of Mr. and Mrs. T. C. Campbell; Married George Goymer. Education: B.A. magna cum laude, Psychology, Florida State University, 1971; M.A. 1972, Ph.D. Psychology 1982, University of Alabama; Clinical Psychology Internship, Psychiatry Department, Medical School, University of North Carolina-Chapel Hill, 1976-77. Career: College Professor, Psychology; Master's Level Psychologist, 1974-75; Psychometrist, 1975-76; Psychological Assistant II, 1973-74. Organizational Memberships: American Psychological Association; Southeastern Psychological Association; Alabama Psychological Association. Community Activities: Child Abuse Task Force, Jefferson County, Alabama, 1979 to present; Western Mental Health Center, Ensley, Alabama (visiting professor, summer 1979); Tuscaloosa Community Crisis Center, Alabama (volunteer counselor, trainer, 1971-72); Pregnancy Counseling & Rape Relief Center, Tuscaloosa, Alabama (volunteer counselor, 1975-76). Religion: Darlington Methodist Church. Published Works: Research Articles Published in *Psychological Reports, Perceptual & Motor Skills, Journal of Verbal Learning & Verbal Behavior.* Honors and Awards: Phi Beta Kappa; Phi Kappa Phi; Psi Chi; Alpha Lambda Delta; National Merit Scholar, 1967-71; N.D.E.A. Fellowship, 1971-72; Honors Program, 1967-69; Martin S. Wallach Award for Outstanding Clinical Psychology Intern, 1977; Outstanding Young Woman of Alabama, 1979; Danforth Associate, 1980 to present; Listed in *Outstanding Young Women of America, Who's Who of American Women.* Address: Box A-37, Birmingham-Southern College, Birmingham, Alabama 35254.

Barbara E M Cannon

Campion, Edmund John

Educator. Personal: Born August 28, 1949; Son of Catherine C. Campion; Married Mary Ellen Gallagher. Education: B.A., Fordham University, 1971; Ph.D., Yale University, 1976. Career: Assistant Professor of French, Department of Romance Languages, University of Tennessee-Knoxville. Organizational Memberships: Modern Language Association: Medieval Association of the Midwest; American Association of University Professors; Society for French Studies. Community Activities: American Association of Teachers of French (Tennessee chairperson, national French contest, 1977 to present); Alliance Française (secretary, Knoxville chapter, 1979 to present). Religion: Roman Catholic. Honors and Awards: Travel Grant from Government of Quebec to Attend Professional Conference in Quebec, Summer 1980; French Government Fellowship, Study at University of Toulouse, 1969-70. Address: 721 Walker Springs Road, Apartment B-3, Knoxville, Tennessee 37923.

Cannon, Barbara E M

Higher Education Administrator. Personal: Born January 17, 1936. Education: B.A. 1957, M.A. 1965, San Francisco State University; French Pedagogy, University of Paris (Sorbonne), 1966-67; M.A. 1975, Ed.D. 1977, Stanford University; Administrative Credential, University of California-Berkeley, 1973; M.A. 1975, Ed.D. 1977, Stanford University. Career: Assistant Dean, College of Alameda; Research Associate/Project Coordinator, Instructional Strategies, Stanford University, 1977-78; Research Assistant, Center for Educational Research 1974-75; Administrative Assistant to National Director, Teacher Corps, United States Office of Education, 1975-76; Teacher, Staff Development Associate and Administrator, Berkeley Public Schools, 1958-74. Organizational Memberships: Black Aces, Cultural and Educational Society (president, founder, 1971); Pi Lambda Theta; Phi Delta Kappa; Association of California Community College Administrators. Community Activities: Berkeley Public Schools (coordinator, educational workshops for staff development, 1972, 1974; coordinator, cadre in organization development, 1973-74; team leader, intergroup education project, human relations project, 1968, 1969, 1970, 1971); Portland, Oregon Public Schools (educational consultant, 1973); Far West Educational Laboratory (educational consultant, 1978); United States Office of Education (educational consultant, teacher corps, 1978); Phillips Temple Methodist Church, Berkeley, California (choir director, organist, 1957-62). Honors and Awards: Presser Foundation Scholarship, 1956; Outstanding Senior Award, Mu Phi Epsilon Chapter 1957, Senior Recital, Piano and Flute 1957, San Francisco State University; Governmental Fellowship, University of Ghana, Summer 1969; Sabbatical Year, University of Paris (Sorbonne), 1966-67; Sabbatical Year, Stanford University, 1974-75. Address: 2101 Shoreline Drive #458, Alameda, California 94501.

Davita L Cannon

Cannon, Davita Louise

Public Relations Consultant. Personal: Born March 17, 1949; Daughter of Mrs. Bernice Cannon. Education: Commercial Diploma, Bayonne High School, 1966; B.S., St. Peter's College, 1973; Graduate study in finance and small business, New York University Graduate School of Business, 1979 to present. Career: Public Relations Consultant, Marketing Specialist, 1981 to present; New Jersey Afro-American Press Correspondent, 1980; Freelance Executive Secretary, Office Force, 1978-81; Dictation Secretary, J. M. Fields, 1978; Secretary, J. C. Penney Company, Inc., 1972-77; Senior Transcriptionist, Chemical Bank, 1968-71; N.C.R. Operator, First Jersey National Bank, 1967-68; Production Typist, Bankers Trust Co., 1966-67. Organizational Memberships: American Society of Business and Professional Women, 1980 to present; Bergen-Greenville Development Corporation, 1975-78. Community Activities: Pavonia Girl Scout Council of Hudson County (chairperson of nominating committee, 1980-81; member, 1977-79); National Association for the Advancement of Colored People (secretary, Bayonne branch, 1977 to present); Bayonne Youth Center (board of directors, 1974 to present; past first vice president, recording secretary and corresponding secretary, implemented career forum, basic business skills seminar and talent show); Tau Gamma Delta, Eta Omega Chapter (editor in chief, 1981 to present; public relations chairman, chairman of ways and means committee and parliamentarian, 1980-81); National Women's Commission of Operation Push, Chicago, Illinois, 1977-79; Action for Sickle Cell Anemia, 1981 to present; Coalition of 100 Black Women, 1979 to present; Black Bicentennial Committee of 1976 (co-chairman, editorial committee; member of committee that designed float for memorial day parade); Push National Conventions (delegate, 1974-77); National Association for the Advancement of Colored People (chairman of state coalition, 1978-79); Youth Liaison-Operation Breadbasket, Jersey City, 1971-72; Clara Dean Civic Association (public relations chairman, 1980 to present); Tau Gamma Delta, Psi Chapter (guest speaker for black history program, 1981); William O. Perkins to State Assembly (campaign worker during reelection campaign, 1977); Economic Task Force, New Jersey State Conference of the National Association for the Advancement of Colored People. Religion: African Methodist Episcopal. Honors and Awards: Citation from Bayonne National Association for the Advancement of Colored People, 1977; Community Service Award, Bayonne National Association for the Advancement of Colored People, 1991; Public Relations Award, Clara Dean Civic Association, 1981; Distinguished Service Award, Pavonia Girl Scout Council, 1981; Listed in *Personalities of America, Directory of Distinguished Americans.* Address: 528 Avenue A, Bayonne, New Jersey 07002.

Cannon, William John

Psychologist, Educator. Personal: Born September 16, 1908; Son of Harold and Elsie Cannon (both deceased); Married Lois Lowery; Father of Ruth Gelford, Malcolm Lowry, Dr. Beverley Ludders, Dr. Barbara Willy, Warren Lowry, Susan Bonner, Shelley Freda. Education: Min. Stanborough, 1931; F.L.C.T.H., London, 1946; M.A. 1954, B.D. 1956, Andrews University; Ph.D. Psychology, American University, 1958. Military: Served as England Liaison Officer in World War II. Career: Psychologist, Chairman, Department of Psychology, Staff Member, Various Hospitals, present; Minister, Evangelist. Organizational Memberships: A.P.A.; M.P.A.; E.P.A.; A.P.P. Community Activities: Agricultural Service; Community Service. Religion: Minister, Evangelist, England, 1931-50; Member, Washington, D.C. City Church, Seventh-Day Adventist, 1952-55; Church Elder; Church Leader (present). Honors and Awards: Award of Merit, D.C. Psych., 1977; Listed in *International Who's Who in Community Service, International Biography, National Register of Prominent Americans, Honor's Registry, Who's Who in the East, Community Leaders of America, Personalities of the South, World Who's Who*. Address: 1705 Ritchie Road, Forestville, Maryland 20028.

Capecelatro, Ann J

Doctor of Optometry. Personal: Born January 11, 1925; Daughter of Gennard and Frances Capecelatro (both deceased); Married Joseph V. Levenduski; Mother of David Joseph, Kathryn Frances. Education: Weylister Junior College; University of Bridgeport; Pennsylvania College of Optometry, 1946. Organizational Memberships: American Optometric Association; Connecticut Optometric Society; New Haven County Optometric Society; Graduate Club Association; University of New Haven (board of governors); Cheshire Academy (board of trustees). Community Activities: Connecticut State Board of Examiners in Optometry (commissioner, 1976; secretary, 1980 to present). Religion: Roman Catholic, Member Various Church-Related Clubs. Honors and Awards: Graduate Club Citation for Esteem. Address: 451 Prudden Lane, Orange, Connecticut 06477.

Dario T Cappucci Jr

Cappucci, Dario Ted Jr

Public Health Veterinarian and Scientist. Personal: Born August 19, 1941; Son of Dario and Julie Cappucci. Education: B.S., 1963, D.V.M., 1965, M.S., 1966, all from the University of California, Davis; Ph.D., University of California, San Francisco, 1976; M.P.H., Loma Linda University, 1977; A.S., State University of New York at Albany, 1977. Military: Commissioned Officers Corps of the United States Public Health Services, 1966-68. Career: Public Health Veterinarian; Scientist. Organizational Memberships: American Veterinary Medical Association; American Society of Animal Science; American Association for the Advancement of Science; Conference of Public Health Veterinarians; American Public Health Association; American Institute of Biological Sciences; Wildlife Disease Association; New York and California Academy of Sciences; California Veterinary Medical Association; National Association of Federal Veterinarians. Community Activities: California Veterinary Medical Association (committee member, public health committee, 1970-72); Bureau of Veterinary Medicine/Food and Drug Administration (deputy chairperson, EEO/Affirmative Action, 1979 to present; chairperson, continuing education committee, 1979 to present); Rockville Chapter of the National Association of Federal Veterinarians (president 1981 to present). Religion: Roman Catholic. Honors and Awards: State of California Merit Award presented by Governor Ronald Reagan, 1972. Address: 5600 Fishers Lane, Room 7B-20, Rockville, Maryland 20857.

Carden, Dana Harmon

Accountant (retired), Ordained Minister. Personal: Born March 17, 1915; Son of Mr. and Mrs. Richard P. Carden; Married Dorothy Leonard. Education: Graduate of Elizabethton High School, 1933; Diploma, Higher Accounting, International Correspondence School, Scranton, Pennsylvania, 1954; Diploma, Finance, Banking, American Savings & Loan Institute, Chicago, Illinois, 1970. Military: Served in the United States Navy, 7th Fleet, in the Southwest Pacific War Zone from 1944-46, attaining the rank of Sh. 3/C. Career: Textile Supervisor, North American Rayon Corporation, Elizabethton, Tennessee, 1933-51; Assistant Vice President & Controller, First Federal Savings and Loan Association, Johnson City, Tennessee, 1954-72; Executive Vice President & Manager, Black Diamond Savings and Loan Association, Norton, Virginia, 1973; Manager, R. E. Wright Realty Company, Johnson City, Tennessee, 1974-78. Organizational Memberships: American Savings & Loan Institute (president, upper east Tennessee chapter, 1970-72). Community Activities: Johnson City Chamber of Commerce, 1966-72; United Fund Worker, Johnson City, Tennessee, 1969-72. Religion: Church of God, Anderson, Indiana, Fund-Raising Committee, Appalachian District, 1957-58); East Tennessee General Assembly of Church of God, Secretary, Treasurer, 1963-73, Treasurer, 1974-81; East Tennessee Kingdom Builders of Church of God, Treasurer 1967-73; Tennessee Ministerial Assembly of Church of God, Ordained Minister 1980; Tennessee State Ministerial Executive Committee, 1970-72; First Church of God, Elizabethton, Tennessee, Interim Pastor, 1968, 1971, 1974; First Church of God, Norton, Virginia, Finance Committee, 1973; East Tennessee Campmeeting Association of Church of God, Treasurer, 1974-81. Honors and Awards: Daughters of the American Revolution Award in American History, 1933; American Savings & Loan Institute Award, 1972; Listed in *Who's Who in Religion, Personalities of the South, Men of Achievement, Who's Who in Community Service*. Address: Route 1, Box 398, Elizabethton, Tennessee 37643.

Dave Carden

Carlson, James Gordon

Educator. Personal: Born January 24, 1908; Son of James August and Mabel Johns Carlson (both deceased); Married Elizabeth Shirley; Father of Shirley Johns Bowen, Bette Walker Schrader, James Marvin. Education: Bachelor of Liberal Arts 1930, Ph.D. 1935, University of Pennsylvania. Career: Assistant in Zoology, University of Pennsylvania, Philadelphia, 1929-30; Bryn Mawr College, Bryn Mawr, Pennsylvania, Demonstrator in Biology 1930-31, Instructor in Biology 1931-35; University of Alabama-Tuscaloosa, Instructor in Zoology 1935-39, Assistant Professor of Zoology 1939-45, Associate Professor of Zoology 1945-46; Instructor in Cytology, Mountain Lake Biological Station, University of Virginia, 1936; Guest Investigator, Carnegie Institute of Washington, Cold Spring Harbor, Summers 1937, 1938, 1940; Rockefeller Fellow in the Natural Sciences, Genetics Laboratory, University of Missouri, 1940-41; United States Public Health Service, Associate Biologist Summer 1943, Biologist Summers 1945, 1946, Special Consultant in Biology 1943-46, 1947-48, Special Fellow, University of Heidelberg, Germany 1964-65; Senior Biologist, National Institute of Health, Bethesda, Maryland, 1946-47; Consultant in Biology, Biology Division, Oak Ridge National Laboratory, Oak Ridge, Tennessee, 1947-78; University of Tennessee-Knoxville, Head, Department of Zoology & Entymology 1947-67, Professor of Zoology 1947-48, Director, Institute of Radiation Biology 1955-75, Alumni Distinguished Service Professor 1962-78, Professor Emeritus of Zoology 1978 to present. Organizational Memberships: American Association for the Advancement of Science (fellow; vice president, 1955); American Institute of Biological Sciences; American Society for Cell Biology; Association of Southeastern Biologists; Radiation Research Society (member, board of editors, *Radiation Research*, 1972-74); Tennessee Academy of Science (president, 1961); National Research Council (committee on fellowships in biology and agriculture, 1950-52; evaluation panel for National Science Foundation, predoctoral fellowships and postdoctoral associateships 1962, cooperative graduate fellowships and summer fellowships for graduate teaching assistants 1963-65, summer fellowships for graduate teaching assistants 1966). Published Works: Many Contributions to Scientific Books and Journals in the Fields of Descriptive and Experimental Cytology, and Particularly the Effects of Utraviolet and Ionizing Radiations on Chromosomes and Cell Division. Honors and Awards: Pennsylvania State Scholarship, 1925-29; Pennsylvania Senatorial Scholarship, 1926-29; Alpha Epsilon Delta; Phi Beta Kappa; Phi Sigma; Sigma Xi; Ph Kappa Phi. Address: 2134 Island Home Boulevard, Knoxville, Tennessee 37920.

Carlton, Fran Stewart

State Representative. Personal: Born January 19, 1936; Daughter of D. J. and Delma Stewart; Married Ernest E. Carlton; Mother of Lynne, Julie. Education: A.A., University of Florida, 1956; B.A., Stetson University, 1958. Career: Member, Florida House of Representatives; Host of "The Fran Carlton Show", a nationally syndicated television show. Organizational Memberships: University of Florida Alumni Association (president); National Conference of State Legislatures; National Recreation and Park Association (Florida representative, southern district). Community Activities: Citizens Against Pornography (board of directors); University of Central Florida Dick Pope Sr. Institute of Tourism Studies (advisory board); Preventive Health Strategy to the President's Council on Physical Fitness and Sports (advisory council); Senior Citizens Advisory Board of Sea World; Community Mental Health (board of directors); Epilepsy Association of Central Florida (board of directors); Occupational Placement Specialists and Career Education Advisory Board. Religion: Guest on 700 Club and PTL Club; Featured in *Guideposts* and *Christian Living* Magazines. Honors and Awards: Outstanding Legislator of the Year, Orlando Area Tourist Trade Association (1979), Orange County Classroom Teachers Association (1977), Florida Parent Teachers Association (1980); Distinguished Alumni Award, 1974; Honor Award, President's Council on Physical Fitness and Sports, 1979; Distinguished Service Award, Florida Association of Health, Physical Education and Recreation, 1977. Address: 1250 Henry Balch Drive, Orlando, Florida 32810.

Carmichael, Virgil Wesly

Mining-Engineer, Coal Company Executive. Personal: Born April 26, 1919, in Pickering, Missouri; Son of Ava Abraham and Rosevelt Murphy Carmichael; Married Colleen Fern Wadsworth, October 29, 1951; Father of Bonnie Rae Galbraith, Peggy Ellen Hiner, Jacki Ann Freiberg. Education: B.S. Geology 1951, M.S. Geological Engineering 1956, University of Idaho; Ph.D. Geological Engineering and Management, Columbia Pacific University, 1980. Military: Served in the United States Naval Reserve from 1944-46, attaining the rank of Petty Officer 2nd Class. Career: Assistant Geologist, Day Mines, Wallace, Idaho, 1950; Mining Engineer, Chief Mining Engineer, De Anza Engineering Company, Troy, Idaho and Sante Fe, 1950-52; Highway Engineering Assistant, New Mexico Highway Department, Sante Fe, 1952-53; Assistant Engineer, University of Idaho, 1953-56; Minerals Analyst, Idaho Bureau of Mines, Moscow, 1953-56; Mining Engineer, Northern Pacific Railway Company, St. Paul, 1956-67; North American Coal Corporation, Cleveland, Geologist 1967-69, Assistant Vice President of Engineering 1969-74, Vice President, Head, Exploration Department, 1974 to present; Assistant Chief of Distribution, Civil Defense Emergency Management Fuel Resources for North Dakota, 1968 to present; Registered Geologist, Idaho, California; Land Surveyor, New Mexico, Minnesota, North Dakota, Idaho; Professional Engineer, Idaho, New Mexico, Utah, Minnesota, North Dakota. Organizational Memberships: Northern Great Plains Resource Council, 1964-67; Association of Professional Geological Scientists (past president, local chapter); Rocky Mountain Coal Mining Institution (vice president); North Dakota Geological Society; American Institution of Mining Engineers (president, local section, 1979-80); American Institute of Professional Geologists (president, local section, 1970); American Mining Congress (board of governors, western division, 1973 to present); International Platform Association. Community Activities: Volunteer Fireman, Cottage Grove, Minnesota, 1958-67; Bismarck Kiwanis Club (1967 to present; president, present); Bismarck-Mandan Orchestral Association (board of directors, executive board, 1979 to present; chairman, fund drive, 1980-81); Masonic Organizations (Blue lodge, officer, program organizer, consistory; member, El Zagal shrine); Elks; Republican Party; Regents Club, University of Idaho, 1974 to present. Religion: Protestant. Honors and Awards: Sigma Xi National Scientific Honorary, 1956; Member 1954 to present, Award 'A' for Scientific Writing 1957, Sigma Gamma Epsilon Earth Science Honorary; Featured in Bismarck *Tribune*, 1981; People-to-People Trip to China, 1981, 1982. Address: 1013 North Anderson Street, Bismarck, North Dakota 58501.

Virgil W Carmichael

Carpenter, Charles Whitney II

Educator. Personal: Born January 2, 1918, in New York City, New York; Son of Mr. and Mrs. George W. Carpenter (both deceased); Married Dorothy A. Byford. Education: General Diploma 1937, Postgraduate Degree 1938, Culver Military Academy, Indiana; A.B. German, Cornell University, Ithaca, New York, 1943; M.A. German Literature, University of Southern California, Los Angeles, 1952; National Defense Course Diploma, Industrial College of the Armed Forces, Fort Leslie J. McNair, Washington, D.C., 1961; Ph.D. Germanic Philology, New York University Graduate School of Arts and Sciences, New York City, 1968; M.S.Ed. Educational Administration, Bucknell University, Lewisburg, Pennsylvania, 1973; Ed.D. Candidate Adult & Higher Education, Columbia Teachers' College, New York City, present. Military: Served in the United States Army from 1939, when commissioned 2nd Lieutenant, O.R.C. 303rd Cavalry Regiment, until Honorable Discharge in 1942. Career: Lecturer, German & French, Wagner College, Staten Island, New York, 1954-55; Teaching Assistant, German, Princeton University, New Jersey, 1955-56; Instructor, German, University Heights College, New York University, Bronx, New York, 1956-59; Assistant Professor, French & German, Bronx Community College, New York, 1959-62; Part-Time Evening Instructor, General Language, Adelphi College, Garden City, New York, 1961-62; Instructor, German, University of Vermont, Burlington, 1962-63; Instructor, Graduate and Undergraduate German, University of Hawaii, Honolulu, 1963-65; Assistant Professor, German, Buena Vista College, Storm Lake, Iowa, 1965-66; Bloomsburg State College, Pennsylvania, Graduate and Undergraduate German, Associate Professor 1966-69, Full Professor with Tenure 1969 to present. Organizational Memberships: American Association of Teachers of German; American Association of University Professors; American Institute of Management; American Ordnance Association (life member); Germanic Institute, University of London; Goethe Society of the City of New York; Goethe Society of New England; Holland Society, New York; Linguistic Circle of New York; Linguistic Society of America; Modern Language Association; National Education Association (life member); Intercontinental Biographical Association (life fellow). Community Activities: Cornell Alumni Athletic Association; Friends of the Princeton Library; Military Order of World Wars; National Rifle Association (life member); Order of Lafayette (life member); Orders & Medals Society of America; St. Nicholas Society (life member, New York City chapter); Schlaraffia, German-Speaking Oratorical Society (member, New York chapter); Pilgrim Society of America; Princeton Graduate Alumni Association (life member); Society for the Libraries, New York University; Society of Colonial Wars (life member); Sons of the American Revolution; Sons of the Revolution (life member); Squadron "A" Ex-Members Association, New York City; Staten Island Historical Society (life member); Staten Island Institute of Arts & Sciences; United Hunts Racing Association; Racquet & Tennis Club, New York City; Princeton Club, New York City; Regency Whist Club, New York City; St. Anthony Club, New York City; Nassau Club, Princeton, New Jersey; Delta Psi (alpha chapter, Columbia University); Assistant Coach of Crew, University of Southern California, 1950-51. Religion: Episcopal. Published Works: Plot Summaries, Recommendations Pro/Con, Translated Publications of Various German Modern Novels for St. Martin's Press, New York City; Critic and Reader, German Textbooks, Scott, Foresman & Co., Chicago,

Illinois; Doctoral Dissertation, *The Systematic Exploitation of the Verbal Calque in German*, 1974; M.S.Ed. Thesis, *The Position of the Graduate School Dean in American Colleges and Universities*, currently under Review for Publication. Honors and Awards: Delta Phi Alpha National Academic Honor Society in German (Beta Eta chapter, University of Southern California, 1951); University Honors Scholar, University of New York, 1969; Phi Delta Kappa National Education Honor Society; Phi Kappa Phi National General College Honor Society (president, Bloomsburg State College chapter, 1978-79); Special Faculty Award, Bronx Community College Student Council, 1962; Japanese Red Cross, Silver Order of Merit, Golden Medal of Special Membership, 1963; Golden Order of Merit; Fellow of President's Council, American Institute of Management, 1965; Freshman Crew Numerals, 2 Varsity Crew Letters, Cornell Crew Club, Poker Club, Pershing Rifles Honorary Military Drill Fraternity, 2nd Class Gunner, Alpha Phi Omega National Service Fraternity; Listed in *National Register of Prominent Americans, The Blue Book: Leaders of English-Speaking World, New York Social Register, National Social Register, Directory of International Biogrpahy, International Directory of Scholars, Who's Who in the East, Community Leaders and Noteworthy Americans, Two Thousand Men of Achievement, Directory of Educational Specialties, Hereditary Register of the United States of America, Southwest Blue Book (Los Angeles)*. Address: 144 West 4th Street, Bloomsburg, Pennsylvania 17815.

Carpenter, Donald Blodgett

Real Property Appraiser. Personal: Born August 20, 1916; Son of Professor and Mrs. F. Donald Carpenter (both deceased); Married Lee Burker; Father of Edward G. McGough, John D. McGough, Andrew J. McGough, Dorothy J. McGough, James J. McGough. Education: Graduate of Burlington High School, Vermont, 1934; Summer Session, Journalism 1933-37, Ph.B. Social Sciences 1938, University of Vermont; Studies in Education and Psychology, Sonoma State University, 1968-69. Military: Served in the United States Army Reserve Officer Training Corps, 1934-36; Served with the United States Navy, 1942-46, Commissioned Ensign 1942, Unit Commanding Officer 1967-68, Honorably Retired as Lieutenant Commander 1968. Career: Newspaper Reporter, *Burlington Daily News*, Vermont, 1938-39; Guide Chair Operator, American Express Company, New York World's Fair, 1939; Underwriter, General Exchange Insurance Corporation, Newark, New Jersey, 1939-40; Joseph Dixon Crucible Company, Jersey City, New Jersey, Sales Correspondent 1940-41, Assistant Office Manager/Priorities Specialist 1941-42, San Francisco, California, Sales Representative 1946-52; Field Supervisor, The Traveler's Insurance Company, San Francisco, 1952-58; General Agent, General American Life Insurance Company, San Francisco, 1958-59; Western Supervisor, Provident Life & Accident Insurance Company, San Francisco, 1959-60; Brokerage Supervisor, Aetna Life Insurance Company, San Francisco, 1960-61; Maintenance Consultant, J. I. Holcomb Manufacturing Company, Mill Valley, California, 1961-68; Education Service Representative, Marquis Who's Who, Inc., Mill Valley, 1963-68; Sales Representative, Mendocino, California, Edutec 1965-68, Onox, Inc. 1965-68, Maxwell Library Service 1965-68; Teacher/Coach, Mendocino Junior/Senior High School, 1968; Real Property Appraiser, County of Mendocino, 1968 to present. Organizational Memberships: Association of Government Appraisers (associate appraiser, 1974; scholarship council, 1980-81; public relations committee, 1981); National Association of Review Appraisers (member, 1980 to present; certified review appraiser; senior member); Institute of Valuers (member, 1981 to present; senior certified valuer; senior member). Community Activities: American Legion, 1945 to present; Past Commanders Club of California (post commander, 1973 to present); University of Vermont (northern California alumni club, 1964); Catamount Club (founding president, 1964); Reserve Officers Association of the United States (life member since 1946; chapter president, 1954, 1956, state vice president, 1958-61); Mendocino County Employees Association (member, 1968 to present; director, 1981); Mendocino Cardinals Booster Club (life member since 1968; charter club president, 1971); Rotary International (member, 1969 to present; club president, 1975-76; district governor, area representative, 1977-78; district educational awards committee, 1978-81; district group study exchange committee, 1981 to present); "Citizens for Sewers" Committee (co-chairman, 1971-72); Community Calendar Committee (chairman, 1972 to present); American Diabetes Association, 1973 to present; Oceanic Society (charter member, 1974 to present); Mendocino County Safety Council, 1981; Mendocino County Suggestions Award Committee, 1981; National Association for Uniformed Services (life member); Naval Reserve Association (life member); Retired Officers Association (life member). Religion: Congregationalist. Honors and Awards: Kappa Sigma International Fraternity Scholarship-Leadership Award, 1937-38; SECNAV Commendation with Ribbon, 1946; Commendation, Commandant, 12th Naval District,1968; Community Sportsman of the Year Award, 1971; American Legion State Outstanding Community Service Activities Citation, 1972; District Governor Awards 1974, 1976, Paul Harris Fellow 1979 to present, Rotary International; International Biographical Association Life Fellowship, 1980 to present. Address: Box 87, Mendocino, California 95460.

Donald B Carpenter

Carpenter, Norma R

Retired Journalist. Personal: Born December 27, 1910; Daughter of Melissa Rowe; Married Jarrott Brogdon, (deceased); Second marriage to Maurice C. Carpenter; Mother of Jennie L. Brogdon, Jarrott A. Brogdon, Linda J. Sands and Paul Carpenter, Joanne Judkins (stepchildren). Education: B.A., University of Maryland, 1931; Undertook a course in journalism, 1945. Career: Correspondent, *The Prince George's Post*, Hyattsville, Maryland, *The Hyattsville Independent* and *The Evening Capital*, Annapolis, Maryland; Executive Secretary, The Heart Association of Prince George's County, Hyattsville, Maryland. Community Activities: Heart Association (volunteer campaign manager, Prince George's County 1954); Cancer, United Way and Mental Health (volunteer); Federated Women's Club (district president 1956, state chairman, adult education, 1956, 1957 & 1958); Southern Maryland United Democratic Women's Clubs (secretary and vice chairman, 1977-81). Religion: Methodist; United Methodist Women; Administrative Board (vice president); Church Librarian; Editor Church Newspaper. Honors and Awards: Plaque for Meritorious Service, American Heart Association, 1963; Four Honorary Special Memberships, United Methodist Women, 1940, 1960, 1973, 1979. Address: 3704 Tanglewood Lane, Davidsonville, Maryland 21051.

Carpenter, Robert Hunt

Veterinarian, Educator. Personal: Born March 22, 1948, in Kenedy, Texas; Son of William H. Carpenter, Sr.; Married Betsy Doylene Owens; Father of Robert Owens, Erin Elizabeth. Education: B.S. Veterinary Sciences 1970, D.V.M. 1971, M.S. Laboratory Animal Medicine/Experimental Surgery, 1972, Texas A&M University; Military Training, 1972-76, Veterinary Officers Basic Course (Sheppard Air Force Base, Texas), Squadron Officers School, Command and Staff College (Gunter Air Force Base, Alabama), Medical Aspects of Advanced Warfare, Global Medicine Course, U.S.A.F.S.A.M. (Brooks Air Force Base, Texas), Faculty Development Course, Academy Health Care Sciences (Fort Sam Houston, Texas). Military: Served in the United States Air Force Veterinary Corps, 1972-76; Chief of Surgery, Military Working Dog Center, Lackland Air Force Base, Texas, 1972-73; Base Veterinarian, Brooks Air Force Base, Texas, Base Veterinarian 1973-74, Chief, Disaster Medicine Section, Disaster Medicine/Survival Training Branch, United States Air Force School of Aerospace Medicine 1974-76; Special Consultant to United States Air Force Surgeon General, Medical Aspects of Special Weapons Employment and Biohazardous Accidents, 1974-76. Career: University of Texas System Cancer Center Veterinary Resources Division of the Science Park, Bastrop, Texas, Assistant Veterinarian, Assistant Professor of Veterinary Medicine and Surgery 1979 to present, Assitant Veterinarian 1977-79, M. D. Anderson Hospital & Tumor

Institute, Houston, Texas, Assistant Veterinarian 1976-77; Veterinary Practitioner, Part-Time Staff, Emergency Animal Clinic, San Antonio, Texas, Veterinary Relief Work, Various San Antonio, Texas Area Practices, 1974-76; Texas A&M University, College of Veterinary Medicine, Department of Veterinary Public Health, Adjunct Professor 1981 to present, Graduate Assistant 1971-72, with Additional Training, M. D. Anderson Hospital & Tumor Institute, Baylor College of Medicine, Houston, Texas; Guest Lecturer, U.S.A.F.S.A.M. Courses, Domestic Animal Diseases, Aerospace Medicine, Aerospace Nursing, Global Medicine, 1974-76; Course Supervisor, Emergency Medicine, Medical Disaster Preparedness Operations, 1974-76; Instructor, Disaster Medicine, Brooks Air Force Base, Texas, 1974-76; Principal Investigator, Core Grant C.A. 16672, "Science Park Research Animal Housing and Carcinogen Containment Facility"; Principal Investigator, U.S.A.F./S.C.E.E.E. 82-67, "Large Animal Model of Radiofrequency Radiation Effects on Pregnancy". Organizational Memberships: American Veterinary Medical Association, 1971 to present; Texas Veterinary Medical Association, 1971 to present; American Association for Laboratory Animal Science (member, 1972 to present; member, Texas branch, 1976 to present); Capitol Area Veterinary Medical Association, 1977 to present. Community Activities: Masonic Lodge. Published Works: Numerous Articles in Professional Journals, including "Estrus and Pregnancy Rates Following Synchronization with Cronolone Intravaginal Sponge or Norgestomat Ear Implant in Cycling Ewes" (with J. C. Spitzer), "What is Your Diagnosis?: Chronic Oesophagostomiasis" (with R. H. Hansen, J. F. and M. J. Murphy). Honors and Awards: Listed in *Who's Who in the Southwest U.S.A., Personalities of the South, Dictionary of International Biography, Distinguished Leaders in Health Care, Personalities of America, Men of Achievement, Notable Americans.* Address: 1303 Pecan Street, Bastrop, Texas 78602.

Carr, Maxine McCormack

Educator. Personal: Born July 10, 1916; Daughter of Rennie and Maude Wyatt McCormack (both deceased). Education: Anesthesia Degree, University of Minnesota, 1947; Science Degree, Modesto Junior College, 1971; Attended California State College, Stanislaus 1972-73, University of California at San Francisco, Berkeley, Davis 1976-78; B.A. Anthropolgy/Archeology 1982, California State College, Stanislaus. Military: Served in the United States Navy Nurse Corps from 1944-46 and from 1951-52, attaining the rank of Lieutenant-Commander; Retired in 1964 after twenty years Active and Reserve Duty. Career: Nursing, Asbury Hospital, Salina, Kansas, 1943; United States Navy, Nursing, Personnel, Administration & Leadership, 1944-46; Laboratory & X-Ray Technician; Nurse Anesthetist; Staff Nurse, Head Nurse, Special Care Units; Director of Nursing Administration and Hospital Administration; Operating Room Instructor and Supervisor; Coordinator of Nursing Staff, Rees-Stealy Medical Clinic, San Diego, California, 1953-60; Coordinator of Nursing Staff and Anesthesia, Gould Medical Group, Modesto, California, 1960-67. Organizational Memberships: American Nurses Association; American Association of Nurse Anesthetists (state, regional, national officeholder, 1948-67); Mobile Intensive Care Nurses, 1974-77; Paramedics, 1974-77; International Association of Vocational Nurses; American Association of Respiratory Technicians; Western Hospital Association. Community Activities: American Business Women's Association (officeholder, committees chairman, president 1980-81, Modesto chapter); Lambda Alpha Honorary Anthropological Society (charter president, California State College, Stanilaus's charter chapter, 1982); Soroptimist International, Ceres, California; American Red Cross; American Cancer Society; 4-H Clubs of America; American Legion (post #63, Norton, Kansas); Women International Bowling Congress. Religion: Methodist. Honors and Awards: Many Championship Honors, 4-H Club Work; Highest Honors in Athletics for High School Girls; Woman of the Year 1964, Boss of the Year 1976, American Business Women's Association; Soroptimist of the Year, 1977. Address: P.O. Box 3693, Modesto, California 95352.

Maxine M Carr

Carrabba, Michael Paul

Executive. Personal: Born January 31, 1945; Son of Paul G. and Margie L. Carrabba; Married Carol Frances Young. Education: Attended Miami-Dade Community College. Military: Served in the United States Marine Corps from 1962-66, attining the rank of Sergeant. Career: Business Consulting Executive; Advertising Agency Executive; Aircraft Components Company Executive, present. Organizational Memberships: Professional Aviation Maintenance Association (1981 national convention chairman); National Pilots Association; Air Transportaiton Conference; National Business Aircraft Association; American Helicopter Society; Helicopter Association International; Aviation Maintenance Foundation. Address: 10175 Southwest 53rd Street, Cooper City, Florida 33328.

Carroll, Howard William

Atorney at Law. Personal: Born July 28, 1942; Son of Barney Carroll, (deceased), and Lyla Price Carroll; Married his wife Eda on December 1, 1973; Father of Jacqueline, Barbara. Education: B.S.B.A., Roosevelt University, 1964; Undertook graduate studies at Loyola University Urban Planning Institute, 1964-65; J.D., De Paul University Colege of Law, 1967. Career: Attorney at Law; State Representative, Illinois, 13th District, 1971-72; State Senator, Illinois, 15th District, 1973 to present. Organizational Memberships: Illinois State Bar Association; Chicago Bar Association; American Bar Association; Decalogue Society. Community Activities: State of Israel Bonds (co-chairman of the board of governors, member of the cabinet, chairman of the 1981 inaugural banquet); Society of the Little Flower, Carmelite Order (chairman of the men's board 1978-79); Jewish National Fund (vice president); March of Dimes (vice chairman 1979); Anti-Defamation League of B'Nai B'rith (chairman 1978-79); Jewish United Fund Planning Committee for the Metropolitan Area; Jewish Welfare Fund of Metropolitan Chicago (budget committee); Jewish United Fund (chairman of special gifts, government agencies division); Chicago Association for Retarded Children (board of directors); Zionist Organization of Chicago (member of the board); Bernard Horwich J.C.C. (board of directors); Ner Tamid Congregation of North Town (board of directors); B'nai B'rith Council of Greater Chicago (executive committee); Budlong Woods B'nai B'rith (board of directors); West Rogers Park B'nai B'rith (board of directors); Composit Lodge AF & AM; Scottish Rites; Medinah Temple; Rogers Park-Northtown Mental Health Council; Servite Seminary (board of law advisors); Merton Davis Foundation for the Crippling Diseases of Children (former vice-chairman); Illinois State Senate Appropriations I Committee (chairman 1977 to present); State of Illinois Judicial Advisory Council (chairman); State of Illinois Legislative Information Systems Commission (chairman); Illinois State Senate Revenue Committee (former chairman); Democratic State Platform Committee, 1974 to present; Young Democratic Clubs of America (former vice president and general counsel); Atlantic Alliance of Young Political Leaders (executive board 1970-73); Democratic National Committee (youth advisory board); Young Democrats of Illinois (former alternate national committeeman); Democratic National Convention (treasurer of youth activities and director of concessions of the 1968 host committee, executive staff); Holder of various offices in Young Democrats on 2 wards, city, county, state and national levels. Religion: Jewish. Honors and Awards: Israel Medal of Honor, 1981; Mogan David Adom Award, 1980; Macabean Award of the Zionist Organization of Chicago, 1978; Distinguished Service Award, State of Israel Bonds, 1978; Yeshivas Brisk Special Award, 1978; Suburban Publishers' Right to Know Award, 1975-77; Skokie Youth Baseball Award, 1977-80; Society of Fellows Award, De Paul University; Bar Association Award, 1977; Man of the Year, Jewish National Fund, B'nai B'rith Council of Greater Chicago, City-wide Tribute, 1974; Honoree, B'nai B'rith Anti-Defamation League Dinner, 1975; Distinguished Service Award, State of Israel Bonds, 1974; Honoree, State of Israel Bonds, Budlong Woods Lodge, B'nai B'rith, 1971; Portage Park Kiwanis Club Certificate of Appreciation; PHIL-AM Lions Club Certificate of Appreciation; District 2, Board of Education Certificate of Recognition; District 24, Board of Education Certificate of Recognition; St. Timothy's Sponsors' Award; Edgebrook-Sauganash Little League Sponsors' Award; Dunham Park Sponsors' Award; Decalogue

Society of Lawyers Certificate of Recognition; Illinois Bar Association Legislator's Award; U.S. Jaycees Distinguished Service Award, 1976; North River Commission President's Award for Development of North Park Village; North River Commission President's Award for Strong Assistance to the Lawrence Avenue Developers; Hollywood, North Park Improvement Association President's Award, 1978; Senator of the Year Award, Illinois Chiropractic Association; Outstanding Legislator's Award, Illinois Equal Rights Amendment; Outstanding Legislator's Award, Illinois Credit Union League, 1977-80; Golden Legislator's Award for Preservation and Protection of our Environment, Illinois League of Conservation; Legislative Lecturer Award, Illinois State Medical Society; Special Award, Northern Illinois University College of Law. Address: 2929 W. Albion, Chicago, Illinois 60645.

Carroll, Lillian Rebecca

Volunteer Tutor (retired). Personal: Born October 4, 1912; Daughter of Richard Dunstan and Alice Cotton Fletcher; Married Richard Parker Carroll. Education: Graduate of Nashua High School; R.N. Certificate, Massachusetts General Hospital, 1935; B.S. Health Education 1965, M.S. Education 1967, School of Education, Boston University; Continuing Education, Over 23 Credits, A.E.V.H. Certificate (A.A.), 1972; Attended Florida State University, 1969-73; Teachers Certificate, State of Florida, 1968-88. Career: Head, Surgical & Staff R.N., Baker Memorial Hospital, Boston, Massachusetts, 1935-38; Stewardess, American Airlines, 1938-42; Supervisor of Stewardesses, Assistant Public Relations Director, Lecturer, Northeast Airlines, 1942-48; Founder, Director, Instructor, Standards Training Course, Ward School of Airline Training, 1949-52; Instructor, Airline Standards Training Course 1952-64, Hygiene Instructor 1955-62, Head Clinic R.N. 1963-67, Mount Ida Junior College, Newton Center, Massachusetts; Florida School for the Deaf & Blind, 1968-80, Co-Founder, Instructor, Cooperative Vocational Guidance Course. Organizational Memberships: Pi Lambda Theta (member at large, 1964 to present); International Platform Association (life member); National KIWI Club (chairman, chapter formation, four years; founder, BOS chapter; held all offices; member at large, present); National Biennial Convention Chairman, 1966; A.E.V.H. (national chapter member; southeast chapter member); Florida Council of the Blind; Florida Vocational Association; Association of Classroom Teachers; National Rehabilitation Association. Community Activities: Girl Scouts of America (troop consultant, service team, St. Augustine neighborhood, thirteen years; coordinator, four troops, department for the blind, twelve years; board of directors, Gateway council, 1975-82); Florida Board of Education (coordinator, department of the blind, placement services, follow-up studies, 1974-80); St. Augustine High School (coordinator, pilot program for the visually impaired, 1977-80, continued at present by the campus division of blind services); St. Johns County Committee on Drug Abuse (representative, blind department, 1971-74). Religion: Episcopalian (confirmation, 1929; regular attendance except when airline stewardess). Honors and Awards: Noyes Medal, Nashua High School, 1929; Five-Year Gold Stewardess Wings & Hat Insignia, American Airlines, 1942 (donated to San Diego Aerospace Museum); Silver Plate Award, Gateway Girl Scout Council, 1978; Scholarships, Massachusetts General Hospital 1932, Boston University Trustee 1964, Florida State Department of Education 19698, 1970, 1971; U.S.O.E. Summer Training Grant, Florida State University, 1970; Selected as Alternate Recipient, General Electric Summer Guidance Fellowship, School of Education, University of Southern California, 1971-75. Address: 7 Surf Drive, St. Augustine, Florida 32084.

Lillian R Carroll

Carson, David Loeser

Consultant and Director. Personal: Born January 13, 1932; Son of Charles Lukens and Linda Loeser Carson; Married Louise Hoover; Father of Kathryn Louise, David L. Jr., Daviel Hoover. Education: A.B., Franklin and Marshall College, 1954; M.A., Oklahoma State University, 1964; Ph.D., University of Delaware, 1973. Military: Served with the United States Air Force, achieving the rank of Lieutenant Colonel, 1955-76. Career: Director, Graduate Studies in Technical Communication, Rensselaer Polytechnic Institute; Consultant in Industry, Academics and Government; Former Employment includes: Radio and Television Announcer; High School Teacher; Truck Driver; Fighter Pilot; Test Pilot; Operations Officer, Combat Commander, Tactical Fighters; Director of Humanities; Director of Technical Communication; Director of Social Actions; Director of Advanced and Professional Education. Organizational Memberships: National Council for Programs in Technical and Scientific Communication (president 1980-81); Association of Teachers of Technical Writing (president 1982-83); National Council Teachers of English (board of directors, permanent chairman of committee on scientific and technical communication); Society for Technical Communication (research and liaison committees); American Business Communication Association (liaison committee); Technical Writing Institute for Teachers (director); American Society for the Advancement of Science; S.C.C.A. Community Activities: Daedalians; Sigma Tau Chi (executive director of the board); Capital District Council for the Disabled (board of directors); International Platform Association; Little League; Viet Nam War Veterans; Disabled American Veterans; Variety of fund raising campaigns for charities. Religion: President, Westminster Fellowship, 1952. Honors and Awards: Poetry Prize, 1963, Fiction Prize, 1964, both from Oklahoma State University; Air Force Academy Scholarships, 1962-64 and 1965-67; Distinguished Flying Cross with one oak leaf cluster; Air Medal with nine oak leaf clusters; Meritorius Service Medal with one oak leaf cluster; Presidential Unit Citation with three oak leaf clusters; Cross of Gallantry; Combat Crew Medal; Korean Service Medal; Viet Nam Service Medal; Expert Marksman Medal; Top Interceptor Pilot Award 30th Air Division, 1958; Air Force Award for Best Social Actions Program, 1973; Membership in Daedalians, 1971; Membership in Sigma Tau Chi, 1980. Address: 9 Shepherd Drive, Troy, New York 12180.

Carson, William Edwards

Nuclear and Electrical Engineer. Personal: Born July 31, 1930, in Danville, Virginia; Son of J. E. and Elinor Carson; Father of Kathryn C. Reed, William E. Jr., John E. Education: B.S.E.E. 1952, M.S. in Nuclear Engineering 1959, both from Virginia Polytechnic Institute. Career: Test Engineer (aircraft simulators), E.R.C.O. Division, A.C.F. Industries Inc., Riverdale, Maryland, 1952-53; Field Engineer, E.R.C.O. Division, A.C.F. Industries, Inc., Texas, Florida, North Carolina, 1953-56; Nuclear, Electrical, Instrumentation, Propositions Engineer, Babcock & Wilcox Company, Lynchburg, Virginia, 1957-71; Senior Electrical Engineer, Burns and Roe, Inc., Oradell, New Jersey, 1971; Staff Engineer, Southern Nuclear Engineering, Inc., Dunedin, Florida, 1971-73; Principal Engineer and Project Manager, N.U.S. Corporation, Clearwater, Florida, 1973-81; Senior Professional Staff, Southern Science Applications, Inc., Dunedin, Florida, 1981 to present. Organizational Memberships: Sigma Xi; American Nuclear Society; Institute of Electrical and Electronics Engineers (senior member). Community Activities: Young Republican Federation of Virginia (chairman, 1965-67); Lynchburg Young Republicans Club (president, 1962-64); Young Republicans, 6th Congressional District of Virginia (chairman, 1964-65); Lynchburg City Republican Committee, 1962-68 (vice chairman, 1967-68; publicity chairman, 1962-67); Sertoma. Religion: United Methodist. Published Works: Contributor of technical articles to several publications. Honors and Awards: Life Fellow, American Biographical Institute Research Association; Listed in *Dictionary of International Biography, Personalities of America, Men of Achievement, Book of Honor, Personalities of the South, Community Leaders and Noteworthy Americans, Men and Women of Distinction, International Who's Who of Intellectuals, Who's Who in the South and Southwest, Contemporary Personalities.* Address: 2625 Morningside Drive, Clearwater, Florida 33519.

William E Carson

Carter, Charlotte Hope Radsliff

Educator. Personal: Born May 19, 1916; Mother of Margaret Gargola, David W., Loran E. Education: B.A., Cornell College, Mount Vernon, Iowa, 1937; M.A. 1964, Ph.D. 1972, Northern Illinois University, Dekalb, Illinois; Teaching Certificates, State of Illinois, 1956 to present; Christian Education Leadership Certificate, Chicago, 1959. Career: Joliet Junior College, English Instructor 1976 to present, Rhetoric Instructor, Summer/Evening Division 1975; Visiting Assistant Professor of English, Fisk University, 1975-76; Associate Professor of English, Union College, 1972-74; Instructor, Northland College, 1966-69; Research Assistant, Marquis Who's Who, Inc., 1966; Teacher, Joliet Public Schools, 1956-66; Joliet Junior College, Teacher (Adult Education), Supervisor (Student Publications) 1954-56, Senior Clerk to Dean, Office of Education 1954-56; Secretary, Reader, Consolidated Press Clipping Bureau, Chicago, 1950-54; Claims and Employment Interviewer, Illinois State Employment Service, Unemployment Compensation Division, United States Employment Service, 1939-42; Copy Writer, Louis G. Cowan, Public Relations, 1937-39; Cornell College, News Writer 1936-37, Student Editor, *The Cornellian* Newspaper 1935-36. Organizational Memberships: Modern Language Association of America; American Dialect Society; American Association of University Professors (member, 1966-79; committee worker, Union College, 2 years, chairman, 1 year); Kentucky Council of Teachers of English (college conference, 1972-74); American Association of University Women (board member, education, Union College, 1978-79); Phi Beta Kappa (founding member, secretary, Union College chapter; co-editor, bibliography of faculty publications, 1972-74); Illinois Education Association (past member); Joliet Teachers Association (past member); Sigma Tau Delta (Northern Illinois University chapter; Union College chapter, 1963-64); Phi Beta Kappa, Delta Chapter of Iowa; National Mortar Board (Cornell Torch Society, 1937). Community Activities: Fisk University (special committee on communications, division of humanities and fine arts, 1975-76; chairman, ethics and amenities committee, English Department, 1975-76); Union College (general assembly programs, religious life committee, 1973-74; secretary, English Department, 1972-74; faculty sponsor, Canterbury fellowship, 1972-74; student advisor, 1973-74); Northland College (chairman, honors program, division of humanities, 1969; chairman, English Department honors committee, 1967-69; chairman, faculty research committee, 1968-69; teacher education committee, 1968-69; secretary, library committee, 1967-68; student advisor, 1966-69; curriculum committee, freshman humanities course, art, English, music, 1969). Religion: Secretary, Messiah Lutheran Church, Joliet, Illinois, 1977-80; Christ Episcopal Church, Church Soprano 1946-50, 1976-81, 1974-75, 1976 to present; Licensed Lay Reader, Diocese of Lexington, Kentucky 1972-74, Diocese of Chicago 1982 to present; Writer, Sunday School Weekly Bible Lesson Materials, David C. Cook Publishing Company, Elgin, Illinois, 1954. Published Works: Prose Fiction, "Stag Dance"; Essay, "Letter on Picasso and Jolas", Pamphlet, *What is World Service?*; Booklet, *Your College*; Editorial, "Who's Gonna Pay?"; *Collected Sonnets*; Numerous Articles in Professional Journals, including "African and Related Place Names and Proper Names in Chaucer's *Canterbury Tales*, Poems and Other Works," "The Linguistic and Literary Art of *Pearl*, a Middle English Poem in the Northwest Midland Dialect", "The Homiletic Writings of Dr. Samuel Johnson: Attribution and Dating From Biographical and Religious Sources"; Numerous Poems, including "Swimming Pool", "Moby Dick", "Two Sonnets: Concerning Angels, Concerning Devils". Honors and Awards: Poetry Prize, Xi Delta Chapter, Sigma Tau Delta, Northern Illinois University, 1962; 2nd Prize, Book of Verse, Midwestern Writers' Conference Contest, Chicago, Illinois, 1949; 1st Prize, The League to Support Poetry, New York, 1941; English Prize, Best Poetry Contribution to *The Husk*, 1936-37; 1st Place, Tie, Senior English Comprehensive Examination 1937, 1st Prize, Poem, Creative Writing Contest for Midwest High Schools 1933, Cornell College; 1st Prize Editorial, Iowa State College Press Association, 1936; 3rd Prize, *Forum and Century Magazine* National Inter-Collegiate Poetry Contest, 1934; 2nd Prize, Author's Tournament 1932; 2nd Prize, Extemporaneous Writing Contest 1932, High School; Listed in *Personalities of the South, Book of Honor.* Address: 1607 North Raynor Avenue, Crest Hill, Joliet, Illinois 60435.

Charlotte H R Carter

Carter, Gladys Stone

Doll Collector. Personal: Born January 30, 1907; Daughter of Reed Lewis and Nannie Bassett Stone (both deceased); Married Leonard Clyde Carter (deceased); Mother of Barbara C. Stone, Leonard Clyde Jr. Education: Third Year High School. Career: Homemaker; Doll Collector. Community Activities: Donated Land for Community Center; Donated $50,000 to Bridgewater College; Donations to Ferrum College. Religion: Sunday School Teacher. Honors and Awards: League of 100 Paperweight, Presidents Club of Bridgewater College, 1981; United Campaign Award for Outstanding Citizenship, C.B.N. 700 Club, 1968; Listed in *Community Leaders and Noteworthy Americans, The World Who's Who of Women, Notable Americans, Book of Honor.* Address: Route 4 Box 7, Bassett, Virginia 24055.

Carter, James Byars

Physician. Personal: Born July 15, 1934; Son of A. B. Carter and Naomi Carter Todd (both deceased); Married Jean Foxhall; Father of Greg, Adam, John, Kathy. Education: B.A., University of Texas, 1956; M.D., University of Texas Medical Branch, 1959; M.S., University of Minnesota, 1966. Military: Served in the United States Air Force as Flight Surgeon, 1959-63, attaining the rank of Captain. Career: Internist, Capital Medical Clinic, 1966-71; Allergist, Allergy Associates, P. A., 1973 to present. Organizational Memberships: American Academy of Allergy (fellow, 1974 to present); American College of Allergists (fellow, 1974 to present); American College of Physicians (fellow, 1972 to present); American College of Chest Physicians (fellow, 1973 to present); American Association of Allergists (fellow, 1974). Community Activities: American Lung Association (board member, 1968-70); Brackenridge Hospital, Austin, Texas (consultant, allergy clinic, 1973 to present); Boy Scouts of America (scoutmaster, troop 399, Austin, Texas, 1975-81). Religion: Episcopal Church of Good Shepherd (member, board of Christian education; lay reader; vestry member, 1981 to present). Honors and Awards: Alpha Epsilon Premed Honor Society, 1954; Alpha Omega Alpha Medical Honor Society, 1958; Mead Johnson Postgraduate Scholar, American College of Physicians, 1965-66. Address: 2802 Northwood Road, Austin, Texas 78703.

Gladys Carter

Carter, James Earl Jr

Former President of the United States. Personal: Born October 1, 1924, in Archery, Georgia; Son of James Earl and Lillian Gordy Carter; Married Rosalynn Smith, July 7, 1946; Father of John William, James Earl III, Donnel Jeffrey, Amy Lynn. Education: Attended Georgia Southwestern College 1941-42, Georgia Institute of Technology 1942-43, Postgraduate Union College 1952-53; B.S., United States Naval Academy, 1946, Class of 1947; LL.D., Morehouse College, Morris Brown College, 1972; U.D., University of Notre Dame, 1977; U.D., Emory University, 1979. Military: Served in the United States Navy from 1946-53. Career: Peanut Farmer, Warehouseman, Plains, Georgia, 1953-77; Member, Georgia Senate, 1963-67; Governor of Georgia, 1971-75; President of the United States, 1977-81. Organizational Memberships: Democratic National Committee (chairman, congressional campaign committee, 1974); Candidate, Democratic Nomination, President of the United States, 1976. Community Activities: Sumter County, Georgia, School Board (member, 1955-62; chairman, 1960-62); Americus and Sumter County Hospital Authority, 1956-70; Georgia Crop Improvement Association (director, 1957-63; president, 1961); Sumter County Library Board, 1961; Plains Development Corporation (president, 1963); West Central Georgia Area Planning and Development Commission (chairman, 1964); Georgia Planning Association (president, 1968); March of Dimes (state chairman, 1968-70); Lions Club (district governor, 1968-69). Religion:

Baptist. Published Works: *Why Not The Best?*, 1975; *A Government As Good As Its People*, 1977; *Keeping the Faith*, 1982. Honors and Awards: Honorary D.Ed. Georgia Institute of Technology, 1979; Honorary Ph.D., Weizmann Institute of Science, 1980. Address: 1 Woodland Drive, Plains, Georgia 31780.

Carter, Joseph L Jr

Executive. Personal: Born December 3, 1939; Son of Judge and Mrs. Joseph L. Carter. Education: B.S. Business Administation, Bucknell University. Career: Department of Energy, Chief, HQ ADP and Communication Services (present), Assistant to Director; Chief, HQ Telecommunications, United States Energy Research and Development Administration; Chief, HQ Computer Center, United States Atomic Energy Commission; Manager, Comptroller's Computer Center, State of Maryland; Systems Analyst, International Business Machines Corporation. Address: #C-1401, 12000 Old Georgetown Road, Rockville, Maryland 20852.

Carter, Lillie Mae Bland

Educator, Author, Poet. Personal: Born December 16, 1919, in Bowling Green, Kentucky; Daughter of John and Maude Bland; Married Leon Carter, Jr.; Mother of Three Children. Education: Graduate of High School; B.S. 1941, M.A. 1968, Tennessee State University. Career: Secretary; Clerk; First Grade Teacher, Gunckel School, Toledo, Ohio, eleven years; Teacher, First and Second Grades, Remedial Reading, Team Leader, Resource Teacher, Martin L. King Elementary School, Toledo, Ohio. Organizational Memberships: Delta Kappa Gamma; Alpha Kappa Alpha; Phi Delta Kappa. Community Activities: National Association for the Advancement of Colored People; Afro-American Heritage Club; University of Tennessee (delegate, family life conference, Notre Dame University; delegate, national council for interracial justice, Washington, D.C., 1963; delegate, Ohio's first conference on civil rights, Johns Hopkins University). Religion: Gift-Bearer, Lecturer, St. Patrick's Cathedral Church; Literature, Toledo Council of Churches, 1978; Provided Poems for *Sunday Bulletin* and *Christ the King*, San Diego. Published Works: Author of Poetry Published in the following, *Toledo Blade, Negro History Bulletins, Negro Journal of Religion, Hap, Delta Kappa Gamma Educational Society Bulletin, Ivy Leaf, Sphinx, St. Patrick's Catholic Church Bulletins, The Bronze Raven, T.S.U. Faculty Journal*, Toledo Area Council of Churches' Anthology *A Sheaf of Poetry*, Verse Writers Guild of Ohio's Bicentennial Collection *Fruit of the Song, Kentucky in American Letters* (Volume 3, 1976), *World's Greatest Contemporary Poets;* Collection of papers housed at Western Kentucky University, Kentucky Museum & Library, some at Eastern Kentucky University in John Wilson Townsend Room, Ohioana Library, and Capital University; Author of Books, *Black Thoughts, Doing It Our Way, Our Majestic Mountain, The Grass that Grew in the Trees*, and Poetry *At Christmas;* Author, Several Books of Unpublished Poetry. Honors and Awards: Included in *The Fascinating Story of Black Kentuckians: Their History and Tradition*, by Alice Dunnigan; Recipient, Libby Scholarship, National Science Scholarship; Only Woman Speaker, A.R.C. Leadership Conference, Findley College, 1973; Citation, Creative Workshop, Toledo, 1973; Editorial Yearbook Writer, *Ohioana*, 1976; Inter-Greek Council Achievement in Literature, 1975; Small Booklet of Poems, *Whispering Leaves*, Placed by late Langston Hughes in Schumburg Collection, Center for Black Culture, New York Public Library, and in James Weldon Johnson Memorial Collection, Yale University; Recipient, Martin Luther King Award for Helping to Perpetuate the Dreams of Dr. King, 1981; Listed in *Book of Honor, Directory of Distinguished Americans, International Who's Who of Intellectuals, Personalities of the South, Who's Who Among Black Americans, World Who's Who of Women, Black American Writers*. Address: 645 Woodland Avenue, Toledo, Ohio 43602.

Carter, Marion Elizabeth

Professor. Personal: Born in Washington, District of Columbia. Education: Graduate, Dunbar High School (valedictorian); B.A., Wellesley College; M.A., Howard University; M.A., Middlebury College; M.S., Georgetown University; Ph.D., Catholic University of America; Ph.D., Georgetown University; Cultural Doctorate in Philosophy of Linguistics, World University (Tuscon, Arizona); Additional certificates and diplomas received from summer studies from: the University of Havana (Cuba), Interamerican University (Mexico), the University of Fribourg (Switzerland), the University of Madrid (Spain), and from a year of study at the University of Haiti and the University of La Laguna (Spain). Career: Spanish Teacher via television for public schools, Washington, D.C.; Instructor of Teachers, Petersburg (Virginia) National Defense Education Act Institute; Representative, District of Columbia Teachers College at sessions of the National Association for Foreign Student Affairs; Teacher, English as a Second Language, American Language Institute of Georgetown University; Fulbright Lecturer of English as a Second Language, University of La Laguna, 1967-68; Professor of Foreign Language and Linguistics, Gordon College, appointed 1970. Community Activities: Preservation of Le Droit Park, Section of Washington. Published Works: *Haitian Normal School Methodology and its Applications to Primary and Secondary Education, The Role of the Symbol in French Romantic Poetry;* Poetry published in *The National Anthology of Poetry;* Book Reviews in *Hispania* and *The Modern Language Journal, Escollos Linguisticos, Acentos Literarios Americanos* and *Error Analysis in the Free Compositions of Spanish Speakers*. Honors and Awards: Listed in *Directory of American Scholars, Who's Who in American Education, Community Leaders of America, International Register of Profiles, International Who's Who of Intellectuals, World Who's Who of Women, Book of Honor*. Address: 402 You Street N.W., Washington, D.C. 20001.

Carter, Mary Eddie

Administrator, Agricultural Research. Personal: Born March 14, 1925; Daughter of Mary Esther Stewart. Education: B.A., LaGrange College, Georgia, 1946; M.S., University of Florida-Gainesville, 1949; Ph.D., University of Edinburgh, Scotland, 1956. Career: United States Department of Agriculture, Associate Administrator, Agricultural Research Service, Washington, D.C. (present), Director, Southern Regional Research Center, A.R.S., New Orleans, Louisiana. Organizational Memberships: American Chemical Society; American Association of Textile Chemists; Fiber Society; Sigma Xi; Cereal Chemists Association; Federal Executive League. Community Activities: Combined Federal Campaign, Greater New Orleans Area (chairman, 1980). Honors and Awards: Herty Award, Georgia Section, American Chemical Society, 1979. Address: 4419 Cambria Avenue, Garrett Park, Maryland 20766.

Carter, Virginia Nell

Executive. Personal: Born August 26, 1930; Daughter of Mrs. Effie Gaddie; Married Paul David Carter; Mother of Kay Elaine, David C. Education: Graduate of Whitesboro High School, Texas, 1947; Certified Fire & Casualty Insurance Agent, Grayson County College; Certified Life Underwriter, Dale Carnegie Graduate. Career: Loan Officer, Local Bank; Owner, Operator, Various Insurance Agencies for Many Years; President, Manager, Howe Insurance Agency, Inc. Community Activities: Parent-Teacher Association (district vice president, district #2; speeches; teacher, various courses; past president, Washington School, Wakefield

School, P.T.S.A.); Former City Council President; Business and Professional Women's Clubs (local unit president; parliamentarian; speeches; teacher, various courses; president, past district directors); Texas Sherman Art League (past district director; past president, state nominating committee); Sherman Chamber of Commerce (board of directors; president's club; membership committee; speeches; committees; president's delegate); Muscular Dystrophy Telethon, Four Years; Boy's Clubs of America (board of directors). Religion: Travis Street Church of Christ, Sunday School Teacher, 4th, 5th Grades; Ladies' Classes and Seminars. Honors and Awards: Life Membership, Texas Parent-Teacher Association; Life Membership, National Parent-Teacher Association; Merit Awards, Outstanding Member Awards, Chamber of Commerce; Woman of the Year, Business and Professional Women, 2 Years; Nominee, Mrs. Texas Business and Professional Women's Clubs Woman of the Year. Address: 1119 South Crockett Street, Sherman, Texas 75090.

Carter, William Bailey

Advertising Executive. Personal: Born September 30, 1951, in Shreveport, Louisiana; Son of Mrs. E. L. Carter; Married Catherine Murrell; Father of William Stinson. Education: Graduate of Benton High School, Shreveport, 1969; B.A. Public Relations, Northwestern State University of Louisiana, 1973. Career: Founder, President, Chairman of the Board, Carter Advertising, Inc., 1977 to present; Account Executive, Clenn Mason and Associates Advertising, 1976-77; Account Executive, Director of Public Relations, Jack Hodges, III Communications, Inc., 1973-76; Instructor in Advertising, Centenary College of Louisiana, 1978 to present. Organizational Memberships: American Marketing Association; Business/Professional Advertising Association; Southwest Association of Advertising Agencies; Shreveport Advertising Federation, 1976-80. Community Activities: Caddo Association for Retarded Citizens (board of directors, 1977-80); The University Club. Honors and Awards: Listed in *Outstanding Young Men of America, Who's Who in Advertising, Who's Who in the Southwest*. Address: 521 Atkins Avenue, Shreveport, Louisiana 71104.

Cary, William Sterling

Conference Minister. Personal: Born August 10, 1927; Son of Sadie W. Cary; Married Marie B. Phillips; Father of Yvonne Eileen, W. Sterling Jr., Denise Marie, Patricia Ann. Education: Graduate of Plainsfield High School, 1945; B.A., Morehouse College, Atlanta, Georgia, 1949; M.Div., Union Theological Seminary, New York, 1973. Career: Pastorates, Butler Memorial Presbyterian Church, Youngstown, Ohio 1953-55, Interdenominational Church of the Open Door, Brooklyn, New York 1955-58, Grace Congregational Church, New York City 1958-68; United Church of Christ, Area Minister, Metro and Suffolk Associations of New York Conference 1968-75, Conference Minister, Illinois Conference 1975 to present. Organizational Memberships: National Council of Churches in America (president, 1972-75; vice president, 1975-79); Council of the United Church of Christ Conference Executives (chairperson, 1981). Community Activities: President Gerald Ford's 17-Member Task Force on Vietnamese Refugee Relocation, 1975-76); National Association for the Advancement of Colored People; The Urban League. Religion: United Church of Christ (representative, consultation on church union, 1977; council on ecumenism, 1977). Honors and Awards: Honorary Doctor of Divinity, Morehouse College (Atlanta, Georgia) 1973, Elmhurst College (Illinois) 1973; Honorary Doctor of Laws, Bishop College, Dallas, Texas, 1973; Honorary Doctor of Humanities, Allen University, Columbia, South Carolina, 1975. Address: 206 LeMoyne Parkway, Oak Park, Illinois 60302.

William S Cary

Case, Delvyn Caedren Jr

Physician. Personal: Born January 15, 1945; Son of Mr. and Mrs. Delvyn C. Case; Married Carole A.; Father of Delvyn Caedren III, Wendy Nadia, Keith William. Education: A.B. cum laude, Brown University, 1967; M.D., Jefferson Medical College, 1971; Internship, Residency, Fellowship, Cornell University, 1972-76. Career: Assitant Director, Division of Hematology, Department of Medicine, Maine Medical Center; Clinical Assistant Professor of Medicine, University of Vermont School of Medicine; Hematology Consultant, Ventrex Corporation; Physician, Hematology and Oncology, present. Organizational Memberships: Foundation for Blood Research (board of directors); American Society of Hematology; American Society of Clinical Oncology; American Association for Cancer Research. Honors and Awards: Meller Award, 2nd Prize, Sloan-Kettering Memorial Cancer Center, 1976; New York Academy of Sciences; Sigma Xi; Listed in *Who's Who in New York, Who's Who in the East, International Who's Who*. Address: 18 Ole Musket Road, Cumberland Foreside, Maine 04110.

Caseman, Austin Bert

Educator. Personal: Born February 13, 1922; Married Susan Louise Burleson; Father of Cathy Caseman-Dahljelm. Education: B.S. Civil Engineering 1947, M.S. Civil Engineering 1948, Utah State University; Sc.D. Civil Engineering 1961, Massachusetts Institute of Technology. Military: Served in the United States Army, Infantry, from 1943-46, attaining the rank of 1st Lieutenant. Career: Instructor, Assistant Professor of Civil Engineering, Washington State University; Professor of Civil Engineering, Georgia Tech, present. Organizational Memberships: American Society of Civil Engineers; American Concrete Institute (president, Atlanta chapter, 1967); Sigma Xi; Chi Epsilon; Sigma Tau; Phi Kappa Phi. Religion: Church of the Latter Day Saints (Mormon). Honors and Awards: Science Faculty Fellowship, National Science Foundation, 1957; Outstanding Faculty Award, American Society of Civil Engineers, Awarded by A.S.C.E. Student Chapter, Georgia Tech, 1968. Address: 2136 Kodiak Drive, Northeast, Atlanta, Georgia 30345.

Caskey, Jefferson Dixon

Professor. Personal: Born July 31, 1922; Son of Mrs. John L. Caskey; Married Louise Huffaker; Father of Nora Constance Caskey Huff, Gretchen Louise Caskey. Education: A.B., Erskine College, 1948; M.S.L.S., Syracuse University, 1953; M.A., 1966, and Ed.D., 1972, University of Houston; Diploma, The Institute of Children's Literature, 1977. Military: Served with the United States Navy, 1945-48. Career: English Teacher, South Carolina Public Schools, 1948-52; Catalog Librarian, Auburn University, 1953-54; Associate Librarian and Assistant Professor of Library Science, Shepherd College, 1954-56; Head Librarian and Associate Professor of Library Science, Pfeiffer College, 1956-60; Head Librarian and Associate Professor of Library Science, Little Rock University, 1960-63; Head Librarian and Associate Professor, Houston Baptist University, 1963-70; Associate Professor and Director of Library Science Program, Texas Arts & Industries University, 1970-74; Professor of Library Science, Western Kentucky University, 1974 to present. Organizational Memberships: Friends of the Library, Houston Baptist University (organizer), 1969-70; National Council of Teachers of English, 1970 to present; Kentucky Library Association, 1974 to present; Kentucky School Media Association, 1974 to present; American Association of University Professors, 1976-80; American Library Association, 1976-79. Community Activities: Pianist, Mexican Baptist Church, Kingsville, Texas, 1973; Host, Baraca Sunday School Class, First Baptist Church, Bowling Green, Kentucky, 1977 to present. Religion: Member, First Baptist Church, Bowling Green, Kentucky 1974 to present. Published Works:

Contributing Editor, *Back Home in Kentucky*, 1979 to present; Contributor to children's and church related periodicals; Author *Samuel Taylor Coleridge*, 1977; Writer of reviews for professional and general publications. Honors and Awards: Listed in *Who's Who in Library Service, Who's Who in the South and Southwest, Who's Who in America, Men of Achievement, A Directory of Librarians in the United States and Canada.* Address: 1016 Meadowwood, Bowling Green, Kentucky 42101.

Castle, William Graves Jr

Investor. Personal: Born January 6, 1940; Son of William Graves Sr., and Marguerite Wheeler Castle; Married Linda Morris; Father of William Graves III, Kevin. Education: Studied at Texas Agricultural and Mechanical University, 1958-59, and Louisiana State University, 1959-62; B.S., American Institute of Banking, 1964. Career: Senior Credit Analyst, Bank of the Southwest, Houston, Texas; Oil, Gas and Real Estate Investments. Organizational Memberships: Young Men's Business Club; American Association of Petroleum Landman; Certified Professional Landman; Louisiana Association of Independent Producers and Royalty Owners; Society for the Advancement of Management. Community Activities: Boy's Club of Greater Lake Charles (trustee); Lake Charles Planning and Zoning Commission, 1967-71; Louisiana Expressway Authority, 1973; Notary Public, appointed 1976; Natural Resources Study Commission, 1977. Religion: Methodist. Honors and Awards: Listed in *Who's Who in the South and Southwest, Community Leaders of America.* Address: #7 Little Drive, Lake Charles, Louisiana 70605.

Catalfo, Alfred Jr

Attorney at Law. Personal: Born January 31, 1920; Son of Alfred Catalfo, Sr. (deceased) and Vincenzia Amato Catalfo; Married Caroline Joanne Mosca (deceased April 30, 1968); Father of Alfred T., Carol Joanne, Gina Marie. Education: Graduate of Ecole St. Joseph, Rollinsford, New Hampshire 1936, Berwick Academy 1940; B.A. History, University of New Hampshire, 1945; LL.B., Boston University School of Law, 1947; M.A. History, University of New Hampshire, 1952; School for Prosecuting Attorneys, Northwestern University School of Law, Chicago; Attended Harvard University, University of Alabama, Graduate School of Suffolk University School of Law; American Law Institute, 1959. Military: Served in the United States Navy Air Corps in World War II from 1942-44 as Pilot; Served in the United States Naval Reserve, attaining the rank of Lieutenant Colonel, New Hampshire Governor's Military Staff under Governors John King and Hugh Gallen. Career: Admitted to New Hampshire Bar 1947, United States Supreme Court Bar 1970, United States District Court Bar, United States Board of Appeals Bar; Individual Law Practice, Dover, New Hampshire, 1948 to present; County Attorney, Strafford County, Dover, New Hampshire, 1949-50, 1955-56; Past Employee, Labor Organizer, Pacific Mills, Marx Toy Company, Dover, New Hampshire. Organizational Memberships: United States Department of Justice (board of immigration appeals, 1953 to present); Strafford County Bar Association (member, 1947 to present; vice president, 1966-69; president, 1968-69); New Hampshire Bar Association, 1947 to present; American Bar Association, 1948 to present; Interstate Commerce Commission; Phi Delta Phi International Legal Fraternity; American Trial Lawyers Association; Massachusetts Trial Lawyers Association; National Association of Criminal Defense Lawyers; American Judicature Society. Community Activities: Bellamy State Park (past supervisor); Disabled American Veterans (judge advocate 1950-56, 1957-68, 1972 to present, commander 1956-57, New Hampshire department; chapter commander, 1953-54; chairman, state department conventions, 1957, 1960, 1963, 1970); Young Democrats (president, Dover chapter, 1953-55; first vice chairman, New Hampshire chapter, 1954-56); Dover City Democrat Committee (chairman, ward III, 1958-68); Strafford County Democrat Committee, 1948-75; New Hampshire Democratic State Committee (vice chairman, 1954-56; chairman, 1956-58; chairman, special activities, 1958-60; executive committee, 1960-70); Candidate as Delegate for Adlai Stevenson, 1956; Democratic National Convention (attended 1956, 1976; delegate, 1960); Elected Pledge Delegate to Senator John F. Kennedy for President, 1960; Democratic Nominee, State Senate, 21st District, 1960; Democratic State Convention (chairman, 1958; convention director, 1960); Boutin for Governor Executive Committee, 1960; Democratic Nominee for United States Senator, 1962; Committee to Elect Jimmy Carter for President, 1976; 1972 Committee to Re-Elect Thomas McIntyre for United States Senator; Legal Advisor, Recount for United States Senator John Durkin, 1974; Football Coach, Berwick Academy 1944, Mission Catholic High School, Roxbury, Massachusetts 1945-46; American Legion (member, post #8, Dover; member, 40-8; chairman, state department convention, 1967, 1977); Dover Lions Club; Fraternal Order of Eagles; B.P.O. Elks; Knights of Columbus (council 307, Dover; grand knight, 1975-77; 4th degree); Sons of Italy; Berwick Academy Alumni Association (president, 1974-76); Loyal Order of Moose; Lebanese Club; Navy League of America; Improved Order of Red Men; New Hampshire Historical Society; Dover Historical Society (Northam colonist); Rollinsford Historical Society; University of Alabama (class president, 1940-41); Dover Catholic School Committee (vice chairman, 1969-71); Dover Board of Adjustment, Five Years. Published Works: Author, *Laws of Divorces, Marriages, and Separations in New Hampshire*; First Complete *History of the Town of Rollinsford, 1923-1973*. Honors and Awards: Recipient of Four Keys to Cities, Dover, Somersworth, Concord, Manchester; Four National Plaques, Disabled American Veterans; Two Distinguished Service Plaques, American Legion; Listed in *Who's Who Among Students in American Universities and Colleges, Who's Who in American Law, Who's Who in the East.* Address: 20 Arch Street, Dover, New Hampshire 03820.

Saffet C Catovic

Caton, Hardy Morris

Executive. Personal: Born July 27, 1937; Son of Walter A. (deceased) and Evelyn Caton; Married Sarah Irene Mathis; Father of Jay Lynn, Gregory Glen, Melissa Jane. Education: B.S.M.E., Texas A.&M. University, 1960; Studies in Business Administration, Baylor University, 1966. Military: Served in the United States Army, attaining the rank of 2nd Lieutenant. Career: Group Vice President (Aerospace Group) 1979 to present, Vice President and General Manager (Applied Technology Systems Organization) 1977-79, Vice President and General Manager (Applied Technology Division Sciences and Systems) 1975-77, Engineer/Scientist, Department Director 1967-75, Tracor Inc.; Chairman of the Board, Tracor M.B.A., 1980 to present; Director, Flight Systems Inc., 1981 to present; Chairman of the Board, Tracor Aviation Inc., 1981 to present; President, Tracor Radcon Inc., 1975-80; Senior Test Engineer, Rocketdyn Solid Rocket Division, North American Aviation, McGregor, Texas, 1962-67; Development Test Engineer, Mason and Hangar, Silas Mason Company, Amarillo, Texas, 1961-62. Organizational Memberships: Institute of Environmental Sciences; Society of Logistic Engineers; Association of Old Crows; Wild Goose Association; American Defense Preparedness Association; Air Force Association; Armed Forces Communications and Electronics Association; International Omega Association; Electronics Industries Association (board of directors, 1980). Community Activities: Bergstrom/Austin Community Council; Texas Association for Minorities in Engineering (chairman, Austin Chapter, 1979-80). Address: 8422 Adirondack Trail, Austin, Texas 78759.

Catovic, Saffet Catani

Scientist, Educator. Personal: Born April 21, 1924, in Bilece, Yugoslavia; Son of Abid and Dervisa Cerimagic Catovic; Married Sarah

Cameron Kerr, on December 22, 1961; Father of Saffet Abid, Saffiya Dervisa, Suada Semra, Saliha Sarah, Surayya Hava, Sami Ismet. Education: B.S., Zagreb University, 1950; M.S., University of New Hampshire, 1961; Ph.D., Rutgers University, 1964. Career: Fellow in Entomology and Phytopathology, Zagreb University, 1951-52; Research and Extension Pathologist/Entomologist, Plant Quarantine Inspector, Sarajevo and Siaak, Yugoslavia, 1952-57; Research Entomologist, Institute for Plant Protection, Ankara, Turkey, 1957-58; Research Fellow, Botany Department, University of New Hampshire, 1958-61; Research Fellow, Plant Biology Department, Rutgers University, 1961-64; Assistant Professor 1964-69, Associate Professor 1969-74, Professor 1974 to present, Fairleigh Dickinson University Department of Biological Sciences. Organizational Memberships: American Association for the Advancement of Science; New York Academy of Sciences; New Jersey Academy of Sciences; Mycological Society of America; International Mycological Society; Medical Mycological Society of New York; Sigma Xi Scientific Research Society; Metropolitan Association of College and University Biologists; American Association of University Professors; New Jersey Society of Parasitologists; Smithsonian Associates; New York Botanical Gardens; American Museum of Natural History; National Audubon Society; Yugoslavian Association for Plant Protection; Phytopathological Association of America (past member, Northeast Division). Address: 114 Copley Avenue, Teaneck, New Jersey 07666.

Catovic, Sarah Catani

Educator. Personal: Born October 26, 1937; Daughter of Alexander and Jane Eva Kerr (both deceased); Married Saffet Catani Catovic; Mother of Saffet Abid, Saffiya Dervise, Suada Semra, Saliha Sarah, Surayya Hava, Sami Ismet. Education: B.S. 1959, M.S. 1961, University of New Hampshire; Ph., Rutgers University, 1968. Career: Stet Rutgers University, Teaching Assistant 1959-60; Research Fellow 1960-61; Research Assistant 1961-62, Teaching Assistant 1962-64; Fairleigh Dickinson University, Biology Department, Lecturer 1964-65, Instructor 1965-68, Assistant Professor 1968-73, Associate Professor 1973-77, Professor 1977 to present. Organizational Memberships: New York Academy of Sciences; American Society of Parasitologists; New Jersey Sóciety of Parasitologists; Sigma Xi Scientific Research Society; Metropolitan Association of College and University Biologists; American Association of University Professors. Address: 114 Copley Avenue, Teaneck, New Jersey 07666.

Sarah C Catovic

Cavanagh, Marguerite Evelyn

Registered Nurse, Supervisor (retired). Personal: Born October 3, 1930; Daughter of Edward Winckler (deceased) and Pearl M. Winckler; Married Donald J. Cavanagh; Mother of Michael William, Diane Eilee, Patricia Marie, Gordon John. Education: R.N., St. Lukes Hospital School of Nursing, 1951; Postgraduate Study, Hemodialysis, University of Iowa Hospitals, 1970. Career: Head Nurse, Urology and Surgical, St. Lukes Hospital, Davenport, Iowa, Part-Time Supervisor; Instructor, Urology Update, Scott Community College. Organizational Memberships: St. Lukes Hospital Alumnae (president, 1965-68); American Urological Association Allied; American Association of Nephrology Nurses and Technicians, 1970-75; Iowa Nurses Association (sixth district, president, 1978 to present, board of directors, 1970-76, chairperson, membership committee, 1968-70). Community Activities: Iowa Health Planning System (planning committee); National Kidney Foundation of Iowa (secretary, 1973-74); board of directors, 1974 to present; Iowa chapter, vice president 1977-78, board of directors, 1975 to present). Honors and Awards: Nurse of the Year, Sixth District, Iowa Nurses Association, 1977; Listed in *Who's Who of American Women, Book of Honor, World Who's Who of Women, Men and Women of Distinction, Personalities of the West and Midwest, International Who's Who in Community Service, Community Leaders and Noteworthy Americans.* Address: 2441 Arlington Avenue, Davenport, Iowa 52803.

Cave, Mac Donald

Educator. Personal: Born May 14, 1939; Daughter of E. J. and Adeline M. Cave; Mother of Eric MacDonald, Heidi Lee. Education: B.A., Susquehanna University, Selinsgrove, Pennsylvania, 1961; M.S. 1963, Ph.D. 1965, University of Illinois. Career: Professor of Anatomy 1979 to present, Associate Professor of Anatomy 1972-79, University of Arkansas Medical School; Assistant Professor of Anatomy, University of Pittsburgh, 1967-72; Instructor in Anatomy, University of Illinois, 1964-65. Organizational Memberships: American Association of Anatomists; American Association for the Advancement of Science; American Society for Cell Biology; Sigma Xi; Pi Gamma Mu. Honors and Awards: Swedish Exchange Fellow, American Cancer Society, 1966; United States Public Health Service Postdoctoral Fellow, Max Planck Institute, Tubingen, West Germany, 1966-67. Address: 11143 Bainbridge, Little Rock, Arkansas 72212.

Mac D Cave

Cellini, William Quirino Jr

Electrical Engineer, Operations Research Analyst. Personal: Born March 12, 1951, in Ardmore, Pennsylvania; Son of Mr. and Mrs. Quirino Cellini. Education: B.S.E.E., Drexel University, Philadelphia, Pennsylvania, 1974; M.B.A., University of Pittsburgh, 1975; M.S.E.E. Candidate, George Washington University, Washington, D.C., 1977-81. Military: Attended Army Engineer Officers Basic School, Fort Belvoir, Virginia; Army Reserved Commissioned Officer, Drexel University, 1974; Served with the rank of Second Lieutenant in the United States Army Reserve, 1975-76. Career: Electrical Engineer/Operations Research Analyst, Systems Engineering Division, Systems and Applied Sciences Corporation, Riverdale, Maryland, 1982 to present; Electrical Engineer/Operations Research Analyst, J. J. Henry Company, Inc., Arlington, Virginia, 1982; Systems Analyst, Harry Diamond Laboratories, Adelphi, Maryland, 1981-82; Electrical Engineer, Gauthier, Alvarado and Associates, Falls Church, Virginia, 1981; Research Analyst, Energy Systems, Presearch Inc., Arlington, Virginia, 1980-81; Associate, Solar Electric Power Systems, P.R.C. Energy Analysis Company, McLean, Virginia, 1979-80; Systems Analyst/Electrical Engineer, Advanced Marine Enterprises, Arlington, Virginia, 1977-79. Organizational Memberships: Institute of Electrical and Electronics Engineers; National Society of Professional Engineers; American Management Association; Pennsylvania Society of Professional Engineers; American Society for Engineering Education; Society of American Military Engineers; Association of M.B.A. Executives; Association of the United States Army. Community Activities: Friends of the Kennedy Center; Smithsonian Institution; Friends of the National Zoo; National Italian American Foundation; Pennsylvania Newman Alumni Association; Crystal Plaza Social Club (co-president, 1978-79); Alpha Phi Omega, National Service Fraternity (life member, Kansas City, Missouri); United States Olympic Society and Disabled American Veterans (contributor). Religion: Catholic, Arlington Diocese; Parish Representative, Coordinator, Catholic Young Adults Club, 1980, Prime Time Single Catholics; Catholic Alumni Clubs International, Washington, D.C. Published Works: Four Professional Publications, Private Consultants for the Federal Government. Honors and Awards: Listed in *Who's Who in the South and Southwest, Science and Technology, International Who's Who of Intellectuals.* Address: 2111 Jefferson Davis Highway, 1012-S, Arlington, Virginia 22202.

Chagall, David

Author, Publisher, Magazine Writer, Research Executive. Personal: Born November 20, 1930; Son of Harry and Ida Coopersmith Chagall (both deceased); Married Juneau Joan Alsin; Education: Graduate of Central High School, Philadelphia, Pennsylvania, 1948; B.A. Social Sciences, English, Pennsylvania State University, 1952; Graduate Study, The Sorbonne, University of Paris, 1953-54. Career: Writer, Publisher, and Research Executive; Editor; Educator; Social Scientist; Investigative Reporter; Author, Magazine Writer, Research Executive (present). Organizational Memberships: Academy of Political and Social Science; Academy of Political Science; Judicature Society; Authors Guild; Mark Twain Society. Community Activities: National Advisory Board, Congressman Robert K. Dornan, California; Republican National Committee; Simon Wiesanthal Foundation (contributing member). Religion: Deist: Member, Millenium House. Honors and Awards: Carnegie Award, 1964; University of Wisconsin Poetry Prize, 1971; Nominee, National Book Award, 1972; Nominee, Pulitzer Prize in Letters, 1973; Distinguished Health Journalism Award, 1978; Penney-Missouri Journalism Award, 1980. Address: P.O. Box 85, Agoura Hills, California 91301.

Chalmers, David B

Petroleum Executive. Personal: Born November 17, 1924; Son of Mrs. Dorritt Bay Chalmers; Father of David B., Jr. Education: B.A., 1947, and attended Truck School of Business, Dartmouth College; Attended Harvard Business School Advanced Management Program (49th A.M.P.), 1966. Military: Served with United States Marine Corps with rank of Lieutenant, 1943-45; Served with rank of 1st Lieutenant during the Korean War, 1949-50. Career: President, Coral Petroleum, Inc., Houston, Texas; President, Canadian Occidental Petroleum, Ltd. (formerly Jefferson Lake Petrochemicals of Canada, Ltd.), 1969-73; President and Chief Executive Officer, Petrogas Processing Ltd., 1969-73; Officer (chairman, based on rotation), Cansulex, Limited, 1968-73; Vice President, Occidental Petroleum Corporation, 1967-68; Held various managerial positions, including Vice President of Tenneco Oil Company, Houston, Texas, 1955-67; Involved in all phases of company business with Bay Petroleum Company, Denver, Colorado, 1951-55. Organizational Memberships: Independent Petroleum Association of America; National Petroleum Refiners Association; American Petroleum Institute; American Petroleum Refiners Association; Texas Independent Petroleum and Royalty Owners Association. Honors and Awards: Elected to 25 year club of Petroleum Industry, 1976. Address: 5600 San Felipe, No. 4, Houston, Texas 77056.

Chambers, Janice Elaine

Educator. Personal: Born September 2, 1947; Daughter of Mr. and Mrs. Giles Weston Johnson (both deceased); Married Howard Wayne Chambers. Education: B.S. Biology, University of San Francisco, 1969; Ph.D. Animal Physiology, Mississippi State University, 1973. Career: Mississippi State University, Department of Biological Sciences, Assistant Professor, (present), Research Zoologist. Organizational Memberships: American Chemical Society; American Physiological Society; Society of Toxicology; Society of Environmental Toxicology and Chemistry; American College of Toxicology; Sigma Xi (Mississippi State University Chapter president 1981, president-elect 1980, secretary 1978); Mississippi Academy of Sciences; Phi Kappa Phi. Community Activities: Starville Area Business and Professional Women's Club (first vice-president, 1979-80; committee activities; volunteer activities). Honors and Awards: Sigma Xi Research Award, 1980; Outstanding Young Woman of the Year, 1980; Three Outstanding Young Women of Mississippi, 1978; Listed in *Who's Who in the South and Southwest, Outstanding Young Women of America.* Address: Route 5, Box 3, Starkville, Mississippi 39759.

George E Chappell

Chambers, Lois I

Insurance Executive. Personal: Born November 24, 1935; Daughter of Edward J. Morrison; Married Frederick G. Chambers; Mother of Peter E. Mscichowski. Education: Graduate, Vancouver High School. Career: Insurance Executive. Organizational Memberships: Insurance Women of Southwest Washington, Affiliated with National Association of Insurance Women (corresponding secretary; board member; president-elect; president). Community Activities: Soroptimist International of Vancouver (delegate; treasurer; president-elect; president, two terms); City of Vancouver (central city task force, 1976; black grant task force, 1978-80, 1980-82); Clark Community College (chairman, advisory committee, 1978 to present). Honors and Awards: Insurance Woman of the Year, Insurance Woman of Southwest Washington, 1978-79; Soroptimist of the Year, Soroptimist International of Vancouver, 1979. Address: 8770 Southwest Umatilla, Talatin, Oregon 97062.

Chang, William

Real Estate Broker, Executive, Engineer. Personal: Born 1926, Shanghai, China; Son of Chi-Pan Chang; Married Margaret; Father of Mark, Kris. Education: B.S. Aeronautical Engineering, University of Detroit, 1953; M.S. Aeronautical Engineering, University of Wichita, Kansas, 1957; Attended Massachusetts Institute of Technology, 1958; Ph.D. Applied Mathematics, Polytechnical Institute of Brooklyn, 1959; Company Courses, Computer Programming, Report Writing; Broker, Lumbleau Real Estate School of California; Federal Aviation Agency Licensed Private Pilot, 1955. Career: Technical Staff Member, Space Division, Rockwell International; Technical Developer, Hughes Aircraft Corporation; Technical Developer, Lockheed Aircraft Corporation; Program Developer, Republic Aviation; Beech Aircraft; Cessna Aircraft; President, Chairman, All American Investment Corporation; Partner, President, Argonaut Products Corporation; Partner, Developer, Skycruisers Ltd.; Partner, Jewelry Wholesales, Dora's Jade; Owner, Retail Store, Things; Partner, Organizer, Hsueh Brothers Movie Productions, Taiwan; Owner, Operator, Partner, Apartment, Motel; Real Estate Broker. Organizational Memberships: Engineering Student Council, 1951; American Institute of Aeronautics and Astronautics, 1955-59; Honorary Mechanical Engineering Fraternity, 1951-53; Aircraft Owners and Pilots Association, 1955-71; Secretary, Chinese Engineer and Scientists Association of Southern California (chairman, special programs); U. S. Department of Commerce (advisor, International Trade); Far East National Bank (advisory board). Community Activities: Organization of Chinese-Americans, Los Angeles (president, 1980-82); United Chinese-Americans League (president, 1979-80); Southern California Chinese Businessman's Association (vice president, 1980-81); Civil Air Patrol (pilot, 1955-58); Asian-American Republican National Association (secretary-general, 1982); Chinese American National Nurses Association (director); South Bay Chinese Culture Association (treasurer); Lion's International; 1st Asian-American Achiever's Awards Banquet (chairman); Sponsor, Refugees from Camp Pendleton, California to Los Angeles Area (assist hundreds to find jobs, shelter); Help Boat People to Settle in Los Angeles Area. Address: 1612 Via Barcelona, Palos Verdes Estates, California 90274.

Chappell, George Edward

General Manager, Private Counselor, Freelance Writer. Personal: Born February 22, 1931; Son of Frank Major and Blanche Anna

Ormsbee Chappell. Education: B.S., West Virginia Wesleyan College, 1957; M.Ed., North Adams State College, 1968; Attended Civil Air Patrol National Staff College, Air University, Maxwell Air Force Base, 1969; Commissioned Captain; Certificate as Scout Executive, 200th National Training School, Boy Scouts of America Schiff Scout Reservation, 1957; National Camping School, Boy Scouts of America, Schiff Scout Reservation, 1958; Camp Management School, Boy Scouts of America, 1961; Certificate in Criminal Law & Police Procedure, University of Massachusetts Extension, 1964; Certificate of Training in Search and Rescue, Eastern Rescue Coordination Center, Robbins Air Force Base, 1970; Additional Studies at Antioch College Graduate Center, American International College, Boston College, Berkshire Community College. Military: Served with United States Air Force during the Korean War, 1951-53. Career: Part Time Night Supervisor, Berkshire Learning Center, Pittsfield, Massachusetts, 1981; General Manager, Owner, Berkshire Glad Hands, Bee A Badger Novelty Badges and Related Items Manufacturing and Distribution; Private Counselor, Freelance Writer & Researcher, Lanesborough, Massachusetts, 1978 to present; Foster Care Social Worker, Emergency Care Help Organization, Pittsfield, 1977; Vocational Evaluator, Goodwill Industries, Pittsfield, 1975-76; Social Studies Teacher (Guidance Practicum), Pittsfield Public Schools, 1966-74; District Scout Executive, Berkshire Council, Boy Scouts of America (in Pittsfield) and of Housatonic Council (in Derby, Connecticut), 1957-65. Organizational Memberships: Crosby Junior High School Aerospace Club (founder, 1967); National Speleological Society (former vice president of Berkshire Hills Grotto); National Association of Social Workers; National Foster Parents Association; Boy Scouts of America (has held every office including assistant patrol leader, den chief, dispatch bearer for the office of war information, explorer advisor 1943-61, and professional scout executive 1957-65); National Aerospace Education Association; National Geographic Society; Western Massachusetts Regional Social Studies Council; Massachusetts Teachers Association; C.A.P. Aerospace Education Association; Massachusetts Council for Social Studies. Community Activities: Member, Board of Directors, Derby (Connecticut) Kiwanis Club, 1961-62; Ward Chairman, Ansonia (Connecticut) Community Chest, 1961; Co-Founder, Tamarack Flying Club (Pittsfield), 1970; Founder, Washington Mountain Cycle Club (Pittsfield, Massachusetts), 1947; Pittsfield Composite Squadron Civil Air Patrol (past deputy commander); Harriman Squadron Civil Air Patrol, North Adams, Massachusetts (training officer, captain); C.A.P. National Staff College Alumni Association; North Adams College Alumni Association; West Virginia Wesleyan College Alumni Association; Youth Orator & Preceptor, William T. Pethabridge Chapter of Demolay; Past Member, Demolay International Council. Religion: Unitarian. Published Works: Contributor to *Scouting, Nature, West Virginia Conservation, Intermountain Express* (of Hillsdale, New York), *Berkshire Week Magazine* and several newspapers. Honors and Awards: Recipient, General Eisenhower War Service Medal for extraordinary patriotic achievement, Boy Scouts of America, 1945; Represented United States Air Force Civil Air Patrol in Netherlands Antilles during International Air Cadet Exchange, 1971; Certificate of Merit, American Biographical Institute, for Outstanding Professional and Public Service; American Biographical Institute Fellow; Certified as Radio Operator and Observer by U.S.A.F. National Headquarter Civil Air Patrol; Certified Guidance Director, Guidance Counselor, Secondary School Teacher of Social Studies, Special Subjects Teacher, Boy Scout Executive; Listed in *Personalities of America, Community Leaders of America, The Directory of Distinguished Americans, Who's Who in the East, International Who's Who of Intellectuals, International Book of Honor, Book of Honor, Men of Achievement; Personalities of the East.* Address: 514 South Main Street, Lanesborough, Massachusetts 01237.

Wai S Char

Char, Wai Sinn

Dentist. Personal: Born June 14, 1902, in Honolulu, Hawaii; Son of Man Hoon and Yun Kun Wong (both deceased); Married Bertha Kam Yuk, August 13, 1931; Father of David Kingman, John Kinson, Douglas King Chee, Cynthia Moonyeen, Claudia Moontoy. Education: Attended McKinley High School; Graduate of Omaha Central High School, 1922; D.D.S., Creighton Dental College, 1926. Military: Served in a Civilian Defense capacity in 1941. Career: Hunan-Yale Hospital, Changsha, China, Head of Dental Department, Lecturer, Senior Medical Class, Dentistry, 1926-27; Dentist in Charge, Shanghai Chinese Red Cross Hospital, Margaret-Williamson Hospital, 1928-30; Dental Board Member, Shanghai, 1928-30; Associate Work with Dr. C. Jackson, Shanghai, 1927-30; Dental Staff, Strong-Carter Dental Clinic, Palama Settlement, 1930-44; Private Practice, Honolulu, 1934-79; Board Director, Woodrose Condominium, 1971-72; Columnist, *Hawaii Weekly Journal*, 1950-61; Contributor, *Honolulu Star-Bulletin, Honolulu Advertiser*. Organizational Memberships: Association of Honolulu Artists (president, 1970); Hawaii Dental Association (life member); American Dental Association (life member); Honolulu County Dental Society (life member, 1972 to present; founder, women's auxiliary, 1951); China Dental Examiners Board, 1927-28; American Professional Practice Association, 1972 to present; American Academy of Dentistry; University of Hawaii (charter member, 35 years); Kuakini Hospital and Home (life member). Community Activities: Chinese Junior Chamber of Commerce (founder, 1953); The Char's Association of Hawaii (originator, 1953); Creighton Alumni Club (founder, Hawaii chapter, 1939; secretary-treasurer, 1963-70; president, 1941-45, 1947); Honolulu County Dental Society Bowling League (president, 1949-62); Chinese Bowling League (director); Grocery Bowling League; "Pop" Stagbar's Grand-dads Bowling Club (chairman, welfare and social committee, 23 years; historian; first executive vice-president, 1982 to present); Kibitzers Bowling Club; A.A.R.P.; Golden Age Club (program chairman, January 1982); Chamber of Commerce of Hawaii (American Way committee; public health, municipal affairs, education, legislation, governmental affairs, planning, quarter committees); Ket Fui Kon Association (Chinese Mason Society); See Dai Doo; United Chinese Society (president, 1946 to present); Chinese University Club; American Chinese Club (charter member); Chinese Chamber of Commerce; Chinese Amateur-Athletic Association (first president, 1919); Hawaii State Association of Parliamentarians (corresponding secretary, 1972; president, 1974); American Automobile Club; Chinese Bowling Club (director); American Association of Retired Persons; Imu (charter director, 1950-53); Nuuanu Young Men's Christian Association (sustaining member, over 20 years); Hawaii Chinese History Center; International Platform Association, 1974 to present; National Trust for Historic Preservation; Hawaii Chapter of Arthritis Foundation; Center on National Labor Policy; Writer, Proclamations for then-Governors Burns and Ariyoshi, "Week for Art Appreciation"; "Week for Parliamentary Law"; Republican Club, 46 Years; Bishop Museum (charter member); Hawaii Tourist Bureau (charter member); Downtown Improvement Association; Volunteer Dentist, Benjamin Parker School 1934-35, Kikapa School 1934-35; Chinese Jaycees (founder). Religion: United Church of Christ, Member over 66 Years, Chairman of Standing, Executive, Campaign and Building Committees 1951-52, Helped Raise $33,000 to Build Chapel, Obtained Pledges of $10,000 for New Classroom and Administrative Building; Volunteer Dentist, Kaukakapili Church Dental Clinic, 1978. Honors and Awards: Certificate of Honor, Chinese Jaycees, 1970; Resolution Citing 34 Years of Active Participation as Life Member, Chamber of Commerce of Hawaii, 1974; Honorary Plaque, Service to Creighton University; Certificate of Recognition, National Republican Congressional Committee; Certificate of Appreciation, Travel Club; Letter of Commendation from President Richard M. Nixon, 1974; Letter of Commendation from Senator Hiram Fong, 1934; Listed in *Men of Achievement, Men and Women of Distinction, Notable Americans of the East and West, Personalities of America, Book of Honor.* Address: "The Woodrose", 780 Amana Street, Honolulu, Hawaii 96804.

James Charlesworth

Charlesworth, James Hamilton

Associate Professor and Center Director. Personal: Born May 30, 1940; Son of Jean Charlesworth; Married Jerrie Lynn Pittard; Father of Rachel Michelle, Eve Marie, James Hamilton, Jr. Education: A.B., Ohio Wesleyan, 1962; B.D., Duke Divinity School, 1965; Ph.D., Duke Graduate School of Religion, 1967; Undertook further studies at the University of Edinburgh, 1968, and École

Biblique de Jerusalem, 1969. Career: Fulbright Fellow, University of Edinburgh; Thayer Fellow, American Schools of Oriental Research; Assistant Professor of Religion, Duke University, 1969-74; Associate Professor of Religion, Duke University, 1975 to present; Director, International Center on Christian Origins, Duke University. Organizational Memberships: New Testament Studies (editorial board); Society of Biblical Literature (pseudepigrapha project secretary); *Studiorum Novi Testamenti Societas* (chairman of the pseudepigrapha seminar); American Schools of Oriental Research (ancient manuscript committee); American Academy of Religion; Gazelam Foundation (incorporator, trustee); American Association of University Professors; Kappa Kappa Psi; Phi Beta Kappa; Elève Titulaire de l'École Biblique avec la mention "Tres Honorable". Community Activities: Welch Lectures, Brigham Young University; Staley Lectures, Pembroke State University, 1979, 1981; Distinguished Visiting Lecturer at seven universities in South Africa. Religion: Minister in Residence, Duke Memorial United Methodist Church; Member, Western North Carolina Conference; Ordained Methodist Minister. Published Works: Editor of *John and Qumran* and of books on the Dead Sea Scrolls and related subjects; Biblical Consultant for the major CBS movie "The Lives of Peter and Paul", 1981; Numerous articles, chapters or sections in professional works; Books include *The Odes of Solomon* and *The Pseudepigrapha and Modern Research.* Honors and Awards: Phi Beta Kappa; Fulbright Fellow; Thayer Fellow; Outstanding Educator of America, 1975; Inducted into Duke University's Old Trinity Club; Fellow, American Council of Learned Societies; Listed in *Who's Who in America, Who's Who in Religion, The British National Bibliography, Directory of American Scholars, Men of Achievement, International Who's Who in Education, The Book of Honor, Personalities of America, Community Leaders of America.* Address: 4022 West Cornwallis Road, Durham, North Carolina 27705.

Charner, Ivan

Director of Research, Educational Sociologist, Author. Personal: Born May 11, 1949, in New York City; Son of Hilliard Daniel and Geraldine Resnick Charner; Married Kathleen Hammond, May 7, 1971; Father of Megin Hammond. Education: B.A., Harpur College, 1970; M.A. (fellow), Ontario Institute for Studies in Education, 1972. Career: Research Assistant, Ontario Institute for Studies in Education, 1970-73; Research Associate, National Institute of Education, 1973-78; National Institute for Work and Learning, Senior Research Associate 1978-79, Director of Research 1979 to present; Consultant, Office of Education, Boystown Center for the Study of Youth Development, Appalachian Educational Laboratory, 1978 to present. Organizational Memberships: American Educational Research Association; American Sociological Association; American Society for Training and Development. Published Works: Author, *Greater Resources and Opportunities for Working Women, Union Subsidies to Workers for Higher Education, Patterns of Adult Participation in Learning Activities;* Editor, *Education and Work in Rural America: The Social Contest of Early Career Decisions and Achievement;* Research, Employment in Fast Food Industry, Worker Education and Training, Career Development. Honors and Awards: Grant, Department of Health, Education and Welfare, 1978-80; Grant, Department of Labor, 1979 to present; Grant, Women's Educational Equity Act, 1979 to present; Listed in *Personalities in America, Who's Who in the East.* Address: 8406 Cedar Street, Silver Spring, Maryland 20910.

Charry, Michael

Music Director and Conductor. Personal: Married Jane; Father of Stephen, Barbara. Education: Attended Oberlin Conservatory of Music, 1950-52; B.S., M.S., Orchestral Conducting, Juilliard School of Music, 1956; Studies at the Monteux School for Conductors, 1952-55; Hochschule fur Musik, Hamburg, Germany, 1956-57. Military: Served in the United States Army, 1958-60. Career: Apprentice and Assistant under Conductor George Szell, Cleveland Orchestra, 1962-72; Music Director, Canton Symphony, 1973-74; Principal Guest Conductor, Kansas City Philharmonic, 1972-74; Music Advisor, Savannah Symphony, 1973-74; Assistant Conductor, Rhode Island Philharmonic, 1960-61; Conductor and Pianist, Jose Limon Modern Dance Company, World Tours, 1957-63; Assistant Conductor, Sante Fe Opera, 1960; Music Director and Conductor, Nashville Symphony Orchestra; Music Director and Conductor, Peninsula Music Festival, Ephraim, Wisconsin; Music Advisor, San Antonio Chamber Players. Community Activities: Nashville Institute for the Arts (founding chairman); Nashville Music Consortium (founding chairman); John Work Foundation (board member). Honors and Awards: Kulas Foundation; Apprentice Conductor, Cleveland Orchestra under George Szell, 1961-72; Martha Baird Rockefeller Grant, 1973; Alice M. Ditson Award, Columbia University, 1981; Listed in *International Who's Who of Musicians, Who's Who in the South and Southwest, Who's Who in America.* Address: 2206 Chickering Lane, Nashville, Tennessee 37215.

Chartock, Hyman

Psychiatrist, Neurologist. Personal: Born August 26, 1912; Married Laurette Y.; Father of Robert Bruce, David Seth. Education: Graduate of Washington Square College, New York University, 1933; M.D., Royal College of Physicians and Surgeons, Edinburgh, Scotland, 1939; Triple Qualifications, Licentiate, Royal College of Physicians, Royal College of Surgeons, Edinburgh, Royal Faculty of Physicians and Surgeons, Glasgow, 1939; Licensed to Practice Medicine, State of New York, 1939; Internship, Israel Zion Hospital, 1939-40; Staff Member, Brooklyn State Hospital, 1940-41; Residency, Neurology, Psychiatry, Neurosurgery, City Hospital, Welfare Island, 1941; Postgraduate Work in Neurology and Psychiatry, Columbia University, 1946-48. Military: Served in the United States Army during World War II, attaining the rank of Major; Served as Chief Neurologist, Fort Monmouth, as Activating Regimental Surgeon, Engineers Amphibian Brigade; Medical Director, "This is the Army"; Chief Psychiatrist, Camp Ritchie, Maryland, Valley Forge General Hospital Psychiatric Service, Chief of Rehabilitation and Occupational and Recreational Therapy; Chief Psychiatrist, New Cumberland Disciplinary Barracks. Career: Assistant Chief, Neuropsychiatric Service, City Hospital, Welfare Island, 1946-57; Staff Neurologist, Psychiatrist, Presbyterian Medical Center, 1949-64; Neurologist, Long Island Jewish Hospital, 1954-55; Faculty, College of Physicians and Surgeons, Columbia University, 1949-64; Adjunct Professor, Union Graduate School, Yellow Springs, Ohio, 1972; Fellow, Academy of Orthomolecular Psychiatry; President, Bio-Phoresis Research Foundation, Inc., 1979-81; Consultant, B'nai B'rith Vocational Guidance Division, New York, 1961; Consultant, Psychiatrist, Neurologist, Commission of the Blind, New York State Department of Social Welfare, 1958; Vocational Rehabilitation Division, New York State Board of Education 1957, City of New York Compensation and Negligence 1958 to present; Author; Lecturer; Television and Radio Appearances; Specialist Rating, Workmen's Compensation Board (S.I.); Qualified Psychiatrist, Department of Mental Hygiene, State of New York, 1958. Published Works: Author *Road to Normalcy.* Honors and Awards: Listed in *American Men of Medicine, Who's Who in the East.* Address: 18-65 211th Street, Bayside, New York 11360.

Chase, Ramon LeRoy

Administrator. Personal: Born June 19, 1933; Son of Mr. and Mrs. Victor J. Chase; Married Arlene H.; Father of Kirt Allen, Diane Ranee, Rodney Ramon. Education: A.A., Graceland College, 1953; B.S.A.E., University of Michigan, 1956; M.B.A., University of California, 1975. Career: Director, Space Technology Division, Analytical Services, Inc.; Aeronautics and Astronautics Engineer; College Administrator, Riverside Community College; Consultant, Military Systems, Public Administration. Organizational

Memberships: American Institute of Aeronautics and Astronautics, 1957 to present; A.A.S., 1960 to present. Community Activities: Zionic Enterprises, Inc. (director, 1979 to present); Cub Scouts (cubmaster, 1968-70); Boy Scouts of America (assistant scoutmaster, 1970-72); Little League Baseball (assistant coach, 1970-80). Religion: Presiding Elder, 1967-71, 1976-77; Treasurer, 1971-75. Address: 2581 Huntington Drive, Herndon, Virginia 22071.

Chaudhuri, Tapan Kumar

Medical Researcher, Administrator, Teacher, Clinician. Personal: Born November 25, 1944; Son of Taposh K. and Bulu R. Chowdhury; Married Chhanda; Father of Lakshmi. Education: I.Sc., 1966; M.B.B.S., 1966; M.D.; F.A.C.P. and F.A.C.G., 1975; F.I.B.A. Career: Professor of Radiology, Nuclear Medicine, Eastern Virginia Medical Center, 1979 to present; Chief, Nuclear Medicine, Veterans Administration Medical Center, 1974 to present; Assistant Professor, Nuclear Medicine, University of Iowa, 1971-74. Organizational Memberships: Society of Nuclear Medicine; Biophysics Society; American Physiology Society; American Medical Association; American Federation of Clinical Research; American College of Physicians; American College of Nuclear Physics; American College of Gastroenterologists; Bengal and British Medical Councils; American Association for the Advancement of Science; American Heart Association; Former Member: Johnson County Medical Society; Iowa State Medical Society; Radiological Society of North America; American Geriatrics Society; American Society of Military Surgeons; American College Nuclear Physicians; Computerized Tomography Society. Community Activities: Chairman and Member of Various Committees. Religion: Hindu. Honors and Awards: Gold Medal; Silver Medal; Certificate of Honor; Honors in Internal Medicine, Obstetrics and Gynacology; Calcutta University Honors; Best Performance in Autopsy Prize; Fellow, American Biographical Association; Listed in *Notable Americans, International Who's Who in Community Service, Book of Honor.* Address: 304 Rudisill Road, Hampton, Virginia 23669.

Chen, Janey C

Director, Chinese Ministry and Language Classes. Personal: Born February 5, 1922; Daughter of Ching Choy Chou and Ski Yu Lee (both deceased); Married Jesse T. Chen; Mother of David, Julia Leong, Helen Law. Education: B.S., National Southwest Universities, 1944; M.R.E., Heavenly People Theological Seminary, 1968; M.R.E., Golden Gate Baptist Theological Smeinary, 1980. Career: Senior Instructor, Taipei Institute, Taiwan, 1957-64; Senior Instructor, Chinese University, Hong Kong, 1964-71; Founder and Principal, Hong Kong Language Institute, 1971-75; Teacher, German Swiss International School, 1975-78; Director, Hong Kong World Home Bible League, 1972-77; Owner, J. C. Publications, 1968-78; Director, Chinese Ministry, Language Classes, present. Organizational Memberships: Hong Kong Evangelical Fellowship, 1966-78; Hong Kong C. & M. A., 1964-78; World Home Bible League, 1972-77. Community Activities: Salvation Army Interpreter and Translator; Writer, Text Books for the Public Use; Any Volunteer Activities Relating to Chinese Language; Training, Teaching Missionaries to Work in Orphanages, Hospitals, Drug Addicts Hospitality House. Religion: Tiburen Baptist Church, 1978 to present; Principal, Sunday School, C. & M. A. Churches, Taiwan; Helping Missionaries to set up Churches and Train Local People to Work in Churches, 1953-78; Director of Chinese Ministry, 1978 to present. Honors and Awards: Contemporary Author, 1973-76l Listed in *Who's Who Among Students in American Universities and Colleges, Who's Who in American Women, Personalities of America, Personalities of the West and Midwest, Directory of Distinguished Americans, World's Who's Who of Women, Prominent Americans of the Eighties.* Address: 19 Miwok Way, Shelter Hill Apartments, Mill Valley, California 94941.

Chernoff, Robert

Rabbi. Personal: Born September 4, 1922, in New York City, New York; Son of Louis and Sarah Chernoff; Maried Lea Rosen; Father of Howard Chernoff, Shira Oler, Frances Kensky. Education: Studied at the University of Southern California, the Air Force Institute of Technology, and Ohio State University; B.A., Ph.D., Elysion College; Ordained Rabbi, Rabbinical Academy of America, 1972; Extraordinary Ordination as Rabbi, Philadelphia, Pennsylvania, 1979; Pre-Rabbinic Work, Yeshiva of Brooklyn, 1940. Career: Military-Civilian Career with United States Department of the Air Force, including the position of Chief, Maintenance Management Division, Directorate of Aerospace Maintenance, DCS/Logistics, Air Force Systems Command, Andrews Air Force Base, Maryland; Rabbi: Congregation Beth Knesset Bamidbar, Lancaster, California, 1950-56; Har Brook Hebrew Congregation, Baltimore, Maryland, 1956-68; Congregation Shaare Tikvah of Temple Hills, Maryland, 1968-69; Har Brook Hebrew Congregation, 1971-74; Congregation Sons of Israel, Chambersburg, Pennsylvania, 1974 to present. Organizational Memberships: Greater Carolinas Association of Rabbis; American Association of Rabbis (secretary 1979 to present); Chambersburg Area Ministerium (president 1978-79); Jewish Chaplains Organization of Pennsylvania; Association of Mental Health Clergy; South Mountain Restoration Center (Jewish chaplain). Community Activities: Kiwanis Club of Chambersburg-Downtown (president 1978-79); Cumberland Valley Torch Club; Children's Aid Society of Franklin County, Pennsylvania (board of directors); Mayor's Advisory Committee, Borough of Chambersburg, 1978-79; Lutheran Social Services (hospice committee); Coyle Free Library Committee; Occupational Services Inc. Religion: Jewish; Permanent Member, Holocaust Committee, Chambersburg Area Ministerium; Lecturer at Wilson College; Lecturer at various schools, churches, service clubs and professional clubs on various aspects of Judaism. Published Works: Author of *Schechitah; Aspects of Judaism; Biblically Inspired Dietary Laws: Recast in Contemporary Society;* Contributor to various journals. Honors and Awards: Meritorious Service Award, Department of the Air Force, 1954; Award of Merit, Department of Defense, 1973; Distinguished Presidential Award, Kiwanis International, 1979; Distinguished Service Award, American Association of Rabbis, 1981; Listed in *Who's Who in Religion, Men of Achievement, Who's Who in American Jewry, International Biographical Dictionary.* Address: 116 Grandview Avenue, Chambersburg, Pennsylvania 17201.

Childress, Charles C

Executive. Personal: Born November 10, 1939; Son of Kenneth A. and Waneta Childress; Married Marjorie Ann Brumfield; Father of Kenneth, Mark, Mary, Michael. Education: B.S., College of Great Falls, 1961; M.S., Kansas State College, 1964; Ph.D., Johns Hopkins University, 1968. Military: United States Air Force, 1958-61. Career: Director of Laboratories, Upsher, Kansas City, Missouri, 1968-71; President, Midwest Scientific Instruments, Inc. Organizational Memberships: Association of Clinical Chemists, 1968 to present. Religion: Methodist. Honors and Awards: Outstanding Educational Achievement Award, for completion of B.S. degree while on active duty, Strategic Air Command, United States Air Force, 1961; Outstanding Performance and Achievement Award, United States Army Chemical Research and Development Laboratories, Edgewood Arsenal, Maryland, 1965; Outstanding Young Alumni Award, Kansas State College, 1975. Address: 1203 Willow Drive, Olathe, Kansas 66061.

Chilton, Howard Goodner

Director, Advisor, Financial Corporation. Personal: Born November 3, 1910 in Dallas, Texas; Married Margaret H.; Father of Howard Goodner Jr., Margaret Anne Wynne Owen, Evalyne Wynne Baxter. Education: B.B.A., University of Texas, 1932. Military: Served in the United States Navy during World War II, attaining the rank of Lieutenant Junior Grade. Career: Instructor, Credit Management Institutes, Various Universities; Management Instructor, University of Kansas 1953-54, University of Illinois 1957; Instructor, Princeton University, University of North Carolina, University of Texas; Director, Associated Credit Bureaus; Chilton Corporation, President until 1947, Partner 1952 to present, Director and Advisor 1975 to present, Past Chairman of Executive Committee; Vice-President, Credit Bureau Management Company, 1964-68; Vice-President, Credit Bureau Services, 1968-69; Vice-President, Credit Bureau Management East Texas Inc., Central Texas Inc., South Texas Inc., South Arkansas Inc., Arizona Inc., Nevada Inc., Mesa Inc., Hawaii Inc., Pacific Ltd.; Vice-President, Merchant Retail Credit Association, 1928-64. Organizational Memberships: Retail Merchants Association of Texas (president, 1952); Associated Credit Bureaus of America (director, president, 1953-54; advisory board); Associated Credit Bureaus of Texas (director, president, 1950). Community Activities: Fort Worth Retail Credit Executives (secretary-treasurer, 23 years); Tarrant County Crime Committee, 1960; Chapter Plan United Fund (community vice-chairman); Dallas Junior Chamber of Commerce; Fort Worth Chamber of Commerce (life member); Phi Kappa Psi Fraternity; Rotary Club; Thalia Club; Dallas Sailing Club (past commodore). Religion: St. Michael's All Angels Episcopal Church; First Treasurer, Men's Bible Class; Money-Counting Team. Honors and Awards: Outstanding Credit Bureau Manager in Large Cities in the United States and Canada with his brother, J. E. R. Chilton, 1950; Dallas Junior Chamber of Commerce Diamond Award, 1942; International Service Awards, Credit Bureaus of America, 1955, 1956, 1957; Intermural Baseball Championship, University of Texas, 1931; Winner, Corpus Christi Bay Races, 1936; Gulf States Snipe Championship, Biloxi, Mississippi, 1936; Winner, Long Island Snipe Races, 1937; *Quest 80* Award, 1980; Member, American Biographical Institute Research Association; Commissioned Honoarary Admiral of the Texas Navy by Governor of Texas, Allan Shivers, 1956; Listed in *Who's Who in the World, Who's Who in America, Who's Who in Finance and Industry, Who's Who in the Southwest, Men of Achievement, Royal Blue Book, Who's Who in Commerce and Industry, Who Knows and What, Dictionary of International Biography, Who's Who in Texas, Notable Americans, Personalities of America, Community Leaders and Noteworthy Americans, Personalities of the South, Book of Honor.* Address: 4226 Arcady Avenue, Dallas, Texas 75205.

Howard G Chilton

Chin, Sue Suchin

International Conceptual Painter, Photographer, Occult Diviner, Palmist, Clairvoyant. Personal: Born in San Francisco, California; Daughter of William W. and Soo-Up Sweebe Chin. Education: Graduate, California College of the Arts, Los Angeles; Minneapolis Art Institute; Schaeffer Design Center; Student Yasuo Ku-niyo-shi, Rico LeBrun; Accadamia Italea; Studied directly with Cheiro. Career: Photojournalist, All Together Now Art Show, KPIX-TV, 1973; Channel 4, Live on 4, August 1981; Channel 7, September 1981; East West News, Third World Newscasting, 1975-81; KNBC Sunday Show, Los Angeles, 1975-76; Designer, Painter of Textiles, Wallcoverings, Hangings; International Photographer; Artist; Portrait Painter; Occult Diviner; Ordained Doctor of Divinity; One-Woman Show: Lucien Labaudt Gallery, San Francisco, 1975; Group Shows include: Los Angeles County Museum of Art (1975-77), California Museum of Science and Industry in Los Angeles (1975-78), Capricorn-Asunder in San Francisco (1972), Peace Plaza, Japan Center, Kaiser Center; Also Exhibited in Hong Kong and Australia; Represented in Permanent Collections: Los Angles County Federation of Labor, California Museum of Science and Industry and in Corporate and Private Collections. Organizational Memberships: Asian Women Artists (founding vice president, 1978-79); California Chinese Artists (secretary-treasurer, 1978-81); Japanese American Art Council (co-chairman, 1978-81; director); San Francisco Women Artists; Artists in Print; San Francisco Graphics Guild; Pacific Association American Women, Bay Area Coalition (psychic adviser); Chinatown Council of Performing and Visual Arts. Community Activities: National Women's Political Caucus (delegate to state convention, 1977-81; San Francisco affirmative action chairman, 1978-81). Honors and Awards: Life Fellow, American Biographical Institute; Honorarium, A.F.L.-C.I.O. Labor Studies Center, Washington, D.C., 1976; Bicentennial Award, Los Angeles County Museum of Art, 1975-76, 1977, 1979; First Award for Conceptual Painting and Photography of Far East, Asian Women Artists, 1978; Chinese Culture Centre Galleries Culture, 1979. Address: Fox Plaza, Ste. 903, San Francisco, California 94101.

Christensen, Larry Williams

Educator. Personal: Born April 9, 1945; Son of Ove L. Christensen; Father of Ronnie William, Matthew Larry, John Andrew. Education: Graduate of Cyprus High School, Magna, Utah, 1963; Language Training Mission, Provo, Utah, 1964; B.A., Brigham Young University, 1971. Career: Cotton Farmer, 1979-81; Patrolman, Utah Highway Patrol, 1970-79; Science Teacher, Ackerly High School, present. Organizational Memberships: Big Spring Art Association, 1981-82. Community Activities: Ogden, Utah Jaycees, 1975-76; Weber County Republican Committee (artist, illustrator of original filmstrips, 1975-76); Youth Conference Chairman (involved approximately 3000 youths, 1968); Church of Jesus Christ of the Latter Day Saints, (two year mission to Brazil, 1964-66). Religion: Church of Jesus Christ fo Latter Day Saints (seventy, 1972 to present; one of stake 7 presidents of seventy, two terms; ward mission leader, hometeacher, Sunday school teacher, present). Honors and Awards: Grand Champion Artist, Howard County, Texas, Art Show, 1980, 1981; "Sterling Scholar" in Art, High School; Scholarship, Leadership, Brigham Young University, 1966; Listed in *Personalities of the South.* Address: P.O. Box 171, Provo, Utah 84601.

Sae-il Chun

Chun, Sae-Il

Physician. Personal: Born September 25, 1936; Son of Jin-Kun and Yongwha Chun; Married Soon Ok; Father of Joseph H., Scott H., Sam H. Education: M.D., Yonsei University Medical College, Seoul, Korea, 1961; Resident in Physical Medicine, Hospital of University of Pennsylvania, 1972. Military: Served in the R.O.K., 1961-67, achieving the rank of Captain. Career: Physician; Director, Physical Medicine and Rehabilitation, St. Agnes Medical Center, 1979 to present; Editor in Chief, *International Journal of Acupuncture,* 1979 to present. Organizational Memberships: American Academy of Physical Medicine and Rehabilitation; American Congress of Rehabitative Medicine; International Rehabilitative Medicine Association; American College of International Physicians (board of trustees, 1978-79); American Academy of Acupuncture; International Acupuncture Association (president, 1980 to present). Community Activities: Deleware Curative Workshop (medical director, 1974-79; board of directors, 1974-79); Bureau of Vocational Rehabilitation (consultant, 1976-77); Acupuncture Advisory Board to State of New Jersey, 1977 to present; St. Agnes Medical Center (director, physical medicine and rehabilitation, 1979 to present). Religion: Christian Affairs Union (president, nonsan district, 1965-67). Published Works: Editor in Chief, *International Journal of Acupuncture,* 1978 to present. Honors and Awards: Recognition Award for Scientific Achievements in Acupuncture, Indonesian Acupuncture Association, 1977; Recognition Award for International Promotion of Art of Acupuncture, Philippine Acupuncture Association, 1977. Address: 516 Eaglebrook Drive, Moorestown, New Jersey 08057.

Chung, May E

Philanthropist, Health Care Worker, Investments Executive. Personal: Born February 15; Daughter of Ivah Kirkpatrick Parizo; Married Dr. Robert Chung; Mother of Keven, Cherie, Mark, Laurie, Leilani, Kirk. Education: Teaching Certificate, Pacific Union College; B.A., University of Oregon, 1969; Masters Degree in Public Health, University of Hawaii, 1970. Career: Philanthropist, Health Care Worker, Investment Executive. Organizational Memberships: Cosmopolitan Land Company (president, 1973-81); Windward Land Company (president, 1973 to present); Hawn Health Foundation (president). Community Activities: Castle Memorial Hospital (co-founder); Hawaiian Health Foundation (founder, director); World Wide Seventh Day Adventist Health Services (special assistant, 1974 to present); Junior Chamber of Commerce Auxiliary (president, 1953-54); Castle Hospital Auxiliary (president, 1980-82). Religion: Seventh Day Adventist Church, 1945 to present; Kailua Mission School Board; Hawn Mission Association of Seventh Day Adventists, 1981 to present. Honors and Awards: Presidential Award for Work Done for Civil Defense in Hawaii from President John F. Kennedy; Listed in *World Who's Who, Who's Who in Hawaii, Personalities of the West and Midwest.* Address: 625 Kaimalino Street, Kailua, Hawaii 96734.

Church, Avery Milton

Born January 9, 1909, Wilkesboro, North Carolina; Son of Noah Cleveland and Frances Caroline Yates Church (both deceased); Married Eulah May Lowe, daughter of the late Carl Arthur and Velona Stamey Lowe of Wilkesboro, North Carolina. Children: Milton Lowe, Dr. Avery Grenfell, John Whiteford, Martha Eulah. Education: B.A., Wake Forest University, 1930; Th. M., Southern Baptist Theoogical Seminary, 1939; Th.D., Southern Baptist Seminary, 1944; Fellowship, Hebrew University, Jerusalem, 1962; Ward Chairman, World War II, Served from 1942-43. Career: Pastor, Wilkesboro Baptist Church, 1931-37, New Hope and Beaver Creek Baptist Churches 1931-34, Oakwoods Baptist Church 1933-34, Jonesville Baptist Church 1934-37; Student Pastor, Bedford and Mount Zion Baptist Churches, Kentucky, 1938-40; Pastor, Waughtown Baptist Church, 1940-64, Parkway Baptist Church 1965-74, Winston-Salem North Carolina; Interim Pastor, First Baptist Church, Arlington, 1976-77; Pastor, Zion Hill Baptist Church 1978, Beaver Creek Baptist 1979, Little Rock Baptist Church 1980-81, Oakwoods Baptist Church 1981. Community Activities: Baptist State Convention (Member, General Board, 1946-50); Rural Church Committee, 1948-50; Program and Worship Committees, 1950; Pilot Mountain Executive Committee, 1941-74; Interracial Committee (President, 1973-74); Winston-Salem Baptist Ministers Conference (President, 1943); Pilot Mountain Association (Vice Moderator, 1945-46); Devotional Programs, WSJS, WAIR, WSJS Television; Old Hickery Council (Executive Committee 1953-55); Forsyth Allied Church League (Chairman, 1960). Southwest Community of Churches (Chairman, 1973-74). Honors and Awards: Varsity Letters, Wake Forest University, Track 1929-30, Debater 1929-30; Listed in *Who's Who in Religion, Community Leaders and Noteworthy Americans, Personalities of America.* Address: 656 Sunset Drive, Winston-Salem, North Carolina 27103.

Church, Irene Zaboly

Personnel Executive. Personal: Born February 18, 1947; Daughter of Bela and Irene Zaboly; Mother of Elizabeth Anne, Irene Elizabeth. Education: Graduate of Public Schools, 1965. Career: Chairman of the Board and President, Oxford Personnel, Euclid, Ohio; Chairman of the Board and Vice President, Oxford Temporaries, Inc., Euclid; Personnel Consultant, 1965; Secretary, 1966-68; Personnel Consultant, 1968-70. Organizational Memberships: The Greater Cleveland Association of Personnel Consultants, Inc. (member, 1973 to present, state trustee, 1975-80, 2nd vice president and chairperson of business practices and ethics, 1974-75, 1st vice president and chairperson of business practices and ethics, 1975-76, president, 1976-77, board advisor and chairperson of Vi Pender award, 1977-78, chairperson of Vi Pender award, 1980, chairperson of arbitration and fund raising, 1980 to present, committee member of Pi Vender award, 1981); The Ohio Association of Personnel Consultants, Inc. (member, 1973 to present, trustee and board member, 1975-80, secretary and chairperson of business practices and ethics, 1976-77, 1st vice president and chairperson of business practices and ethics, 1977-78, chairperson of resolutions committee, 1981 to present); The National Association of Personnel Consultants, Inc. (member, 1973 to present, ethics committee, 1976-77, co-chairperson of ethics, 1977-78, member of C.P.C. society and committee on business practices and ethics, 1980-82); National Association of Temporary Services, 1980-81; American Business Women's Association, 1980 to present. Community Activities: Guest lecturer and program guest for consumerism, market, ethics, government relations, business practices and work as it affects family life, 1975 to present; Generated and assisted in the implementation of a consumer/industry self-improvement ethics program for local, state and national use; Member of Better Business Bureau, 1973 to present; Member of Euclid Chamber of Commerce, 1973 to present; Girl Scout Leader, Lake Erie Girl Scout Council, 1980 to present; Small Business Committee, Euclid Chamber of Commerce, 1981 to present; Chaiperson on Task Force Committee on Federal Funds in Social Security and Veterans Benefits, Euclid Chamber of Commerce, 1981. Religion: Member of Federated Church (Christian action committee, 1981 to present, fund raiser for new iniatives in church development, 1981, Mary Martha Circle of Women's Fellowship, 1981 to present). Honors and Awards: Awarded designation of "Certified Personnel Consultant", 1975; Received Vi Pender Award for outstanding contributions to personnel industry. Address: 8 Ridgecrest Drive, Chagrin Falls, Ohio, 44022.

Church, James G

Insurance Agent. Personal: Born April 24, 1934; Son of Mrs. Carl Church; Married Nelda; Father of Gregory W., Laura G. Education: East Tennessee State University, Johnson City, Tennessee. Career: Factory Representative, Pillsbury Company; Advertising Executive, L. M. Barry Company; Dance Band Leader, Band Playing Local Country Clubs and Fraternal Organizations; Agent, State Farm Insurance Company, 20+ years. Organizational Memberships: American Federation of Musicians (past officer); National Association of Life Underwriters. Community Activities: Midfield Ruritan Club, Kingsport, Tennessee (past president); Kingsport Optimist Club (past president); Youth Committee; Businessman's Club of Kingsport (former member); Loyal Order of Moose, F.O.E; American Legion; Kingsport Chamber of Commerce. Honors and Awards: Optimist of the Year, 1978; Service Award, Salvation Army, 1977; Golden Circle Award, 1978-79; Health Insurance Quality Award, 1979; National Quality Award for Life Insurance, 1979-80; Top 1000 Agents in Automobile Insurance Production, 1980; Legion of Honor Award, Highest Honor Bestowed by State Farm Insurance, Twice. Address: 1213 Jerry Lane, Kingsport, Tennessee 37664.

Church, Lloyd E

Dentist, Oral Surgeon, Educator. Personal: Born September 25, 1919; Married Hildegard Cascia; Father of Pamela Gail. Education: A.B., West Virginia University, 1942; D.D.S., University of Maryland, 1944; M.S., George Washington University, 1953; Ph.D., George Washington Medical Center, 1959. Military: Served in Japan and China as Captain in the Dental Corps, 1946-48. Career: Researcher; Administrator; Dentist, Oral Surgeon, Teacher. Organizational Memberships: American Dental Association; American

Medical Association; American Association of Anatomy; American Association for the Advancement of Science (fellow); A.S.O.S.; American Society of Experimental Biology and Medicine; F.D.L.; New York Academy of Science; Royal Society of Health (fellow); Royal Medical Society (fellow); A.H.A.; F.A.C.D.; F.L.C.D.; Acr./Med. Washington Academy of Sciences. Community Activities: B-CC Chamber of Commerce; Montgomery County Chamber of Commerce; Washington Speech and Hearing Council (board of directors); Health and Welfare Council, National Capital Area; American Legion; A.C. Society (board of directors, Montgomery County division); Red Cross (cardio-pulmonary resuscitation instructor); American Heart Association (board of directors); Regional Law Enforcement and Planning Board (board of directors). Religion: Methodist Church; President, Men's Club; Official Board; Usher; Board of Stewards; Administrative Board. Honors and Awards: B'nai B'rith Awards for Community Achievement and Community Service; Presented Key to Miami Beach by Mayor, 1963; Potentate, Almas Shrine Temple, 1972; President, Washington Chapter #3, National Sojourners, 1961-62; Distinguished Citizen of Maryland, Presented by Governor Tawes, 1965; Sword of Hope, A.C.S., 1966; B'nai B'rith Award of Merit, 1969; Governor's Citation, 1952; Recognition, 25 Years on Faculty, George Washington Medical Center, 1975. Address: 7005 Glenbrook Road, Bethesda, Maryland, 20814.

Churchill, Arthur Chester

Book Collector, Reviewer. Personal: Born December 29, 1911; Son of Herman Churchill (deceased); Married Ruth Mae Hudson; Father of Kathryn, Marilyn, Jean, Alice. Education: B.S., University of Rhode Island, 1934; Attended Brown University 1934-35, Syracuse University 1935-37, Oberlin Graduate School of Theology 1943-45, Chicago Theological Seminary 1945-46; M.A., Political Science, American University, 1966. Military: Attended Reserve Officer Training School, 2 years. Career: High School Teacher; High School Principal; Government Researcher; College Lecturer; College Teacher; Educational Missionary; Labor Union Official; Private Organization Researcher; Museum Security Guard; Teacher of English to the Japanese, 1973-74; Death Records Clerk, City Hospital, 1959-60; Book Collector, Reviewer. Organizational Memberships: Sigma Alpha Epsilon; American Association of University Professors (president, Defiance College Chapter). Community Activities: Optimist Club (member, Williamsburg, Kentucky, Chapter; one of founders, Defiance Chapter); Community Industrial Development Committee (corresponding secretary, Williamsburg, Kentucky); Cumberland College, Williamsburg, Kentucky (adult education committee); Batzler for Congress Committee (chairman, 1968). Religion: Student Pastor, Kirtland Congregational Church, 1943-45; Minister to Farm Labor, Delmo Homes, Southeastern Missouri, 1946-48; Minister to Agricultural Workers, Mid-South Area, 1948-56; Religion Committee, Defiance College; Youth Education Committee, Adult Education Committee, First Congregational Church, Columbus, Ohio, 1978-80; Teacher, Adult Class, St. John United Church of Christ, Defiance, Ohio. Published Works: Co-Author, References on the Great Lakes-St. Lawrence Waterway, United States Department of Agriculture Publication; Writing on Waste in Federal Government Departments; Comparison Study of United States/Soviet Handling of Scientific Information. Honors and Awards: Kellogg-Briand Peace Prize, South Kingstown, Rhode Island, High School; Sachems, Honorary Student Government, University of Rhode Island; Phi Kappa Phi Scholastic Honorary Society; Tau Kappa Alpha Honorary Debating Society; Honorable Order of Kentucky Colonels; Professor Emeritus, The Defiance College, 1977 to present. Address: 203 East Sessions Avenue, Defiance, Ohio 43512.

Chyzowych, Eugene S

Educator, Coach. Personal: Born January 27, 1935; Son of Walter and Helen Chyzowych; Married Anna; Father of Eugene Jr., Michael. Education: B.S.Ed., Temple University; Graduate Work at New York University, Seton Hall, Montclair College. Military: Former Member of the United States Military Intelligence Detachment. Career: Coach, United States World Cup Team; Assistant Coach, United States Olympic Team; Instructor, Physical Education; Coach, Soccer, Volleyball; "A" License, Soccer Coach, U.S.S.F. Organizational Memberships: National Soccer Coaches Association of America; American Professional Soccer League (past president); U.S.S.F. Coaching Staff. Religion: Ukrainian Catholic Church. Honors and Awards: Coach of the Year, Both Soccer and Volleyball, Last Eight Years; Selected Coach, New Jersey All-Star Teams. Address: 61 Whiteoak Drive, South Orange, New Jersey 07079.

Emma V Cintron

Cintron, Emma V

Counselor and Educator. Personal: Born August 8, 1926; Daughter of Jose Vargas-Bocheciamppi and Maria Teresa Rivera (deceased); Married to Dr. Jorge C.; Mother of Dr. Lisi C, Dr. Leary C. Education: B.A., summa cum laude, M.A., Inter-American University; Candidate for Doctorate in Clinical Psychology, Caribbean Center for Graduate Studies. Career: Columnist for newspaper, *El Mundo;* Part-time Professor of Education, University Counselor, Inter-American University; Assistant to Dean of Admissions, Boston University; Advisor to Dormitories, and Manager of *Law Review*, University of Puerto Rico. Organizational Memberships: Phi Delta Kappa (newspaper editor); Puerto Rican Psychological Association; Puerto Rico Personnel and Guidance Association (president, committee on public relations); American Personnel and Guidance Association. Community Activities: Grandmothers Club of San German; Lions Wives Club; Hogar Del Nino, Cupey, Rio Piedras (board of directors). Religion: Member of United Methodist Church. Published Works: Currently working on book. Honors and Awards: Distinguished Kappan of the Year, Phi Delta Kappa, 1980; Award for her work with elderly people, signed by the Mayor of San Juan, Puerto Rico, 1981; Listed in *Who's Who in the South and Southwest, Personalities of the South, The Directory of Distinguished Americans, Book of Honor, Personalities of America, The World Who's Who of Women, International Who's Who of Intellectuals.* Address: Campus of Inter-American University, San German, Puerto Rico 00753.

Cissell, William Bernard

Educator. Personal: Born April 21, 1941; Son of James S. and Lucille Marie Cissell; Married Mary Ellen Siebe; Father of Lisa Kyung Mi. Education: B.S. 1967, Ph.D. 1977; Southern Illinois University, Carbondale; M.S.Ph., University of California at Los Angeles, 1970. Military: Served in the United States Marine Corps from 1961-64. Career: Principal, Byrd Elementary School; Assistant Principal, Taegu American School; Curriculum Supervisor, Department of Defense Overseas Dependents Schools, Pacific. Organizational Memberships: A.P.H.A. (section council, S.H.E.S. section, 1980-83); A.A.H.P.E.R. (editorial board for *Health Education*, 1979-82); S.O.P.H.E., Inc. (board of trustees, 1979; review panel for *Health Education Quarterly*, 1980 to present); T.P.H.A. (secretary-elect, 1979); T.S.O.P.H.E. (chairman, by-laws committee, 1980-81). Community Activities: Partners of the Americas (member, board of directors, 1980 to present); American Heart Association (Tennessee affiliate; chairman, committee to develop 5-year plan for heart health education, 1981); Tennessee Statewide Health Education Curriculum (writing team, 1980); Washington County International Year of the Child Health Committee, 1979-80; Task Force on Nutrition Education, 1979; American Cancer Society (public education committee, area II, 1979). Religion: Attended St. Henry's Seminary, 1955-56; Acolyte, 1952-59. Honors and Awards: Outstanding Health Educator Award, T.S.O.P.H.E., 1982; High Flyers Award, 1982; High Flyer Award, Tennessee Affiliate, American Heart Association, 1982; Numerous Other Certificates of Appreciation and Recognition for

Community Services; Guest Coach, University of Texas at Austin Football Team, 1979; Phi Kappa Phi, 1971 to present; Special Doctoral Fellowship, Southern Illinois University, 1969-71; United States Public Health Service Traineeship, 1967-69; Listed in *Dictionary of International Biography, Personalities of the South.* Address: 1418 Meadowbrook Drive, Johnson City, Tennessee 37601.

Cissik, John Henry

Aerospace Physiologist. Personal: Born August 18, 1943; Son of Mr. and Mrs. John P. Cissik; Married Dorothy Paulette Allen; Father of John Mark. Education: B.A., M.A., University of Texas-Austin, 1961-67; Ph.D., University of Illinois-Urbana, 1972; Studies in Management at the Industrial College of the Armed Forces. Military: Service in the United States Air Force, 1967 to present, with the current rank of Lieutenant Colonel. Career: Aerospace Physiologist, United States Air Force Medical Center, Wright-Patterson Air Force Base, Ohio, 1967-69; Aerospace Physiologist, United States Air Force Medical Center, Andrews Air Force Base, Maryland, 1969-70; Chief, Cardiopulmonary Laboratory, United States Air Force Medical Center, Scott Air Force Base, Illinois, 1972-80; Aerospace Physiologist/Chief, Cardiopulmonary Laboratory. Organizational Memberships: *Journal of Cardiovascular and Pulmonary Technology* (editorial committee, 1974 to present); *Journal of Allied Health* (editorial committee, 1978 to prsent); National Society of Cardiopulmonary Technology (chairman, editorial committee, 1976-78); American Association for Respiratory Therapy, 1974 to present; Air Force Association, 1967 to present. Community Activities: Evans Elementary School Parent-Teacher Association, 1976-79; Cardiopulmonary Instructor, Community and School Organizations, 1977 to present; Belleville Area College/St. Elizabeth Medical Center, Granite City Illinois (R.T. coordinating committee, Territory 14, 1979-80); Belleville's Belle Valley North Elementary School Parent-Teacher Association, 1979-80; St. Martin East Elementary School Parent-Teacher Association, 1980 to present. Honors and Awards: United States Air Force Chief Biomedical Scientist Rating, 1980; United States Air Force Meritorious Service Medal, 1980; Listed in *Who's Who in the Midwest, Dictionary of International Biography, American Registry Series, Book of Honor.* Address: 12316 Marlowe Place, Ocean Springs, Mississippi 39564.

Clague, Ann F

Health and Wellness Center Director. Personal: Born May 31, 1928; Daughter of Mr. and Mrs. Roscoe Eliason; Married Thomas E. Clague; Mother of Karen, Brian, Candace, Kevin. Education: B.S., Home Economics, Iowa State University, Ames, 1950; Ph.D., Nutrition, Donsbach University, Huntington Beach, California, 1979. Career: Supervisor, Managerial Level, Shaklee, Direct-Selling Organization, 1971-78; Commercial Artist, Jostens, Ring Manufacturers, 1974-76; Manager, Nutrition World, Health Food Store, Owatonna, Minnesota. Organizational Memberships: International Academy of Nutritional Consultants (charter member); American Academy of Medical Preventics. Community Activities: Parent-Teacher Association (active member, many and varied projects, 1958-77); Woman's Club of Owatonna, Minnesota (vice president, publicity; editor, newsletter, 1966-69). Religion: Faith Congregational Church, Glen Ellyn, Illinois, Choir Member, Founding Director, Organist; Founding President, Interdenominational Coffee House for High Schoolers, 1966-67; President, Women's Assembly, Associated Church, Federation of Presbyterian and United Churches of Christ Congregations, 1967-69; Founding Member, Charter Member, Owatonna Ecumenical Choir, 1968-78. Address: 7808 West 103rd Street, Bloomington, Minnesota 55438.

Fred Clark

Clark, Bill P

Senior Principal Engineer/Scientist. Personal: Born May 15, 1939; Son of Lloyd A and Ruby Laura Holcomb Clark. Education: B.S. 1961, M.S. 1964, Ph.D. 1968, Physics, Oklahoma State University; Postdoctoral Research Fellow, Theoretical Solid-State Physics, Department of Theoretical Physics, University of Warwick, Coventry, Warwickshire, England, 1968-69. Career: Senior Principle Engineer/Scientist, Systems Sciences Division, Computer Sciences Corporation, present; Senior Systems Scientist, Computer Sciences Technicolor Associates (Landsat Program), 1976-82; Senior Scientist, Computer Sciences Corporation, N.A.S.A. Langley Research Center Operation 1973-76, Computer Sciences Corporation Fort Leavenworth Operation 1970-73; Senior Analyst, Many Sites, Booz Allen Applied Research, Inc., 1969-70. Organizational Memberships: American Association for the Advancement of Science, 1970 to present; American Physical Society, 1968 to present; New York Academy of Science, 1968 to present. Community Activities: Oklahoma State University (life member, alumni association). Published Works: Co-Author, Over Fifteen Professional Papers, Two Monographs, Two Books; Areas covered in papers and monographs are physics, remote sensing, digital image processing, quality control, radar, elementary particles, quantum field theory, electro-optics and statistics. Honors and Awards: Postdoctoral Fellowship, 1968-69; Phillips Petroleum Company Scholarship, 1957-61; Oklahoma State Institutional Scholarship, 1957-58; Numerous Group and Individual Awards for Outstanding Achievement from N.A.S.A. Relative to the Landsat Program; Listed in *Community Leaders and Noteworthy Americans, Men of Achievement, Dictionary of International Biography, Notable Americans, American Men and Women of Science, International Who's Who of Intellectuals, National Social Directory, International Scholars Directory, Who's Who in the South and Southwest, Who's Who in the East, International Register of Profiles (North American Edition), International Register of Profiles (World Edition), Personalities of the South, Notable Americans of the Bicentennial Era, Book of Honor, Who's Who in Technology Today, Personalities of America.* Address: 5811 Barnwood Place, Columbia, Maryland 21044.

Clark, Fred

Senior Legal Editor. Personal: December 12, 1930; Son of Thomas and Irene Clark (both deceased); Father of Paul, Rodion. Education: Central American Academy, 1944-49; University of Costa Rica, 1950-51; Stafford College, 1956-57; Inner Temple, 1957-60; University of London, 1961; Litt. B., Barrister-at-Law. Military: Served in the Royal Air Force attaining the rank of Airman. Career; Consultant in Commonwealth Law and International Operations; Private Law Practice; Trust Officer; Master of Languages; Senior Legal Editor, present. Organizational Memberships: International Commission of Jursists (life member); American Management Association. Community Activities: Special Advisor, United States Congressional Advisory Board, 1982 to present; Inter-American Society, 1974 to present; American Museum of Natural History, 1971 to present; Smithsonian Associates, 1979 to present; National Geographic Society, 1979 to present; Amateur Astronomers Association, 1980 to present; International Platform Association; American Association for the Advancement of Science; United States Power Squadron (assistant secretary, 1981 to date); American Ballet Theatre, 1979; Metropolitan Opera Guild, 1979. Religion: United Church of Christ, Trustee, 1970-78. Address: 39 West Fourth Street, Freeport, New York 11520.

Clark, Steven

Student. Personal: Born August 22, 1946; Son of R. W. Clark; Married Sharon K. Clark; Father of Lori Jean, Jenny Ann. Education:

Graduate of United States Air Force Schools, 1966-69 (U.S.A.F. Technical School, Supply and Computer, 1966; Inventory Management Specialist Course, 1967; Functions of Inventory Management, 1967; Equipment Management, 1967; Standard Base Supply Proceduces, Part I and II, 1968); Attended General Electric Company Schools, 1970-71 (Volunteer Fireman School, Blue Print Reading I and II); B.S., Indiana University, 1978; A.A.S., Purdue University, 1980; Attending Saint Francis College, M.S. Candidate in Business Administration. Military: Served with the United States Air Force, achieving the rank of Staff Sergeant, 1966-69. Career: General Electric: 10 years in Distribution Area, 2 years Manufacturing, 1 year Quality Control; Inventory Manager, Supervisor of Warehouse, U.S.A.F. Equipment; Staff Sergeant in charge of Coordination and Training, Training Instructor, Research Section, U.S.A.F.; Teacher and Supervisor for 200 Seniors, Carrol High School, Fort Wayne, Indiana (Student Teacher). Organizational Memberships: Indiana University Alumni Association of Indiana; Indiana University Alumni Association of Allen County; Purdue University Alumni Association of Indiana; Purdue University Alumni Association of Allen County; Madison-Marion Consolidated Alumni Association of Allen County. Honors and Awards: Certificate of Award, Excellence in Student Leadership, Indiana-Purdue University, 1978; Listed in *Personalities of America, Book of Honor, The Directory of Distinguished Americans, Personalities of the West and Midwest, International Youth in Achievement, Who's Who Among Students in American Universities and Colleges.* Address: 425 Franklin Street, Convoy, Ohio 45832.

Clatanoff, Doris Ann

Educator. Personal: Born January 29, 1932; Daughter of Fred and Marie Goeller Risch; Married Duane B. Clatanoff; Mother of Dwight (deceased), Clark, Craig. Education: B.A. magna cum laude, Midland Lutheran College, Fremont, Nebraska, 1966; M.A., Education, Wayne State College, Nebraska, 1967; Ph.D., English, University of Nebraska-Lincoln, 1973. Career: Elementary and Secondary Teacher in Nebraska Schools (Wayne, Wisner, Norfolk, District 75, Cuming County); Associate Professor of English, Chairman of Humanities Division, Concordia College, Seward, Nebraska. Organizational Memberships: American Association of University Women (branch president; education representative, division level); Modern Language Association; National Council of Teachers of English; Sigma Tau Delta (faculty advisor, Concordia chapter). Community Activities: Nebraska Federation of Women's Clubs (president, District III, 1965-67); Midland Lutheran College (board of trustees, 1974-80; executive committee, alumni association, 1974-80); National Council of Teachers of English Writing Awards for High School Students (judge, 1975, 1976); Miss Nebraska National Teenager Pageant (state director, 1975-81). Religion: St. John Lutheran Church, Seward, Nebraska. Honors and Awards: Admiral in the Navy of the Great State of Nebraska, 1949; Cardinal Key National Honor Society, 1951; Magna Cum Laude Graduate, Midland Lutheran College, 1966; Graduate Assistantship, English, Wayne State College, Nebraska, 1966. Address: 1278 North 6 Street, Seward, Nebraska 68434.

Claudel, Alice Moser (deceased)

Poet, Editor. Personal: Died April 7, 1982; Daughter of Jeanette Moser; Married Calvin Claudel. Career: Poet, Editor, *New Laurel Review;* Former Teacher, Elementary to University Level. Published Works: *Three Lyric Poets, Southern Season.* Honors and Awards: Prizes for Poetry, including "Sestina for a Piano" (Helen Wood Rogers Prize for Traditional Verse). Address: c/o Calvin Claudel, New Laurel Review, P.O. Box 1083, Chalmette, Louisiana 70043.

Clayton, Robert L

College Administrator. Personal: Born February 25, 1934; Married Minnie H.; Father of Robert Joel, Myrna Audenise. Education: A.B., Talladega College, 1955; B.D., Hood Seminary, 1959; S.T.M., Interdenominational Theology Center, 1965; Further Study Undertaken at the University of Oregon, Rutgers, Michigan State University, Emory University. Career: Director of Marketing and Planning, Talladega College; National Director, Minority Programs, American College Testing Program; National Director, C.P.S. Consortium; College Minister; Special Assistant to President; Chairman of Sociology Department; Consultant to Department of Education. Organizational Memberships; A.C.P.A.; A.M.E.G.; A.N.W.C. (incorporator, president); N.V.G.A.; A.C.E.S.; A.S.C.A.; N.A.C.A.D.A.; N.A.C.D.R.A.O.; N.A.C.A.C.; N.A.C.U.C. Community Activities: Concerned Citizens of Southwest Atlanta (vice-president); Boy Scouts of America; Huntsville Recreational Commission (committee on testing legislation and minorities); Consultants in Evaluating and Surveying Higher Education Programs, Ltd. (president, senior evaluator); Lecturer on College Campuses in the United States, Canada, Virgin Islands. Religion: A.M.E. Zion Pastor; College Minister, Spelman College, Livingstone College, Dillard University. Honors and Awards: Danforth Seminary Intern; Danforth Campus Ministers Grant; Listed in *Who's Who in the South and Southwest, Two Thousand Men of Achievement, Who's Who in Black America.* Address: 668 Waterford Road N.W., Atlanta, Georgia 30318.

Emma Cleveland

Clemmons, Vincent Burton

Accountant, Writer. Personal: Born May 9, 1938; Son of Vincent S Clemmons; Married Christel Cross; Father of Brent Hayes. Education: Studied at De La Salle Institute, De Paul University. Military: College R.O.T.C., 1956-58. Career: Accountant; Writer; Former Positions: Library Page, Lab Assistant, Salesman, Clerical Worker, Day Camp Counsellor, Busboy. Organizational Memberships: International Academy of Poets (fellow); The Col, Poets and Writers Inc. Community Activities: Donated Sketches by Vince to Du Sable Museum, 1973; Projects to further recognition of endeavors in literature, art, music, poetry and other cultural programs. Religion: Catholic. Honors and Awards: Certificate of Merit, Poetry, Nashville Newsletter, 1979, 1980; Listed in *International Who's Who in Poetry Anthology.* Address: 9023 S Elizabeth, Chicago, Illinois 60620.

Cleveland, Emma Walker

Educator. Personal: Born July 24, 1931; Daughter of Mr. and Mrs. L. A. Walker; Married Earthy F. Cleveland; Mother of Constance Elaine. Education: A.B., Miles College, 1952; M.A., New York University, 1960; Postgraduate Study, University of Alabama. Career: Associate Professor of English and Speech; Former English and Speech Instructor, Lawson State Community College, Jefferson County Public Schools. Organizational Memberships: National Council of Teachers of English (essay award judge, 1976-81); American Association of University Professors; American Association of University Women; Association for Supervision and Curriculum Development; Institute for Services to Education (Miles College chairperson, Cooperative Academic Planning Curriculum Development Workshops, 1972-74); Spelman College (participant, consultant, Danforth Foundation teaching and learning workshops, 1975-77); Innovative and Non-Traditional Techniques for Teaching the Disadvantaged (conference consultant, 1978); Community Activities: Birmingham Human Relations Council (coordinator, Task Force, 1976-77); Titusville Civic League (secretary); League of Women Voters. Religion: Westminster Presbyterian Church, Elder; Birmingham Presbytery, Chairperson of Christian Community Action Committee 1978-79, Christian Education Committee 1981; Christian Education Shared Approaches

Planning Task Force, 1979-80. Honors and Awards: Listed in *World Who's Who of Women in Education, Dictionary of International Biography, Notable Americans of the Bicentennial Era, Book of Honor, Personalities of the South.* Address: 944 Center Place Southwest, Birmingham, Alabama 35211.

Cleveland, Lynda Gail

Director of Communications. Personal: Born October 26, 1946 in Austin, Texas; Daughter of Mr. and Mrs. Ray O. Cleveland. Education: Graduate of Lake Highlands High School, Dallas, Texas, 1964; B.A. Speech, Drama, English, Baylor University, 19678; M.S. Oral Interpretation, Rhetoric, Texas Tech University, 1973; Ph.D. Humanities and Business Management, A.B.D., University of Texas System, 1980; College Abroad, European Study Tour, 1971. Career: Teacher of Speech, Director of Forensics 1973-77, Teacher of Speech and English 1968-71, Head of English Department 1970-71; Assistant Professor of Speech & Communications, Texas Tech University, Lubbock, 1971-73; Student Teacher of Speech, Drama, English, University High School, Waco, Texas, 1968; Current Director of Communications, Faber Reed, Australia; President, Creative Visions Corporation, Dallas, Texas, 1977-80; Freelance Consultant, Multi-Media, Wynne Audio-Visual, 1973-78; Secretary of Division of Choirs, School of Music, Baylor University, 1966-68; Counselor, Various Camps, 1965-70; Secretary, New York Life Insurance, 1963-70; Creator, Director/Coordinator/Producer/Performer, "Sing Out America" Patriotic Variety Show 1975, Ann Criswell Jackson Concert Tour 1974-75, World Premiere, "I Love America", Alabama 1975, Media for "I Love America" National Road Company 1975, "I Am Old Glory" Cotton Bowl, Dallas 1975, Multi-Media Presentation for Home Interiors and Gifts, Dallas 1976, Old City Park Dedication 1976, Media 1776 at State Fair Bandshell 1976, Freedom Company Dallas-Based Performing Tour Group of Young People/Musical Revue 1977, Oratory on Positive Thinking Rallies 1978, Special Programming for Horatio Alger Awards, New York City 1978, Numerous Other Slide/Tape and Video Productions for Documentary, Commercial, and Training Purposes, 1978-80; Program Coordinator, Freedoms Foundation National Awards Program, City of Dallas, 1976-77; Public Speaker for Various Groups, 1980. Organizational Memberships: American Association of University Women, 1968; Texas Teachers Association, 1968; Speech Community Association, 1972; Texas Speech Association, 1972; American Association of University Professors, 1972; Texas Association of College Teachers, 1972; International Television Association, 1978; Direct Selling Association (chairman, associate advisory committee, 1979; audio-visual director, annual meeting, 1980; associate member representative, board of directors, 1980). Community Activities: National Forensic League, 1974; North Dallas Chamber of Commerce, 1978; Dallas Chamber of Commerce (membership committee); Texas Mid-Cities Clown Alley, 1980; Freedoms Foundation (program chairman, Dallas chapter); Dallas County Heritage Society (director, old city park); Director, Special Community Service Programs for 44 Convalescent Residences, Children's Hospitals and Homes Each Year, 1973-77. Religion: First Baptist Church, Sanctuary Choir 1968 to present, Chapel Choir 1962-68, Technical Director of Choir Program at State Fair Music Hall 1973-78, Assistant to Director of "Messiah" 1973, Live Telecast of Sunday Worship Services 1977; First Baptist Church, Lubbock, Texas, Choir, 1971-73; Director of "The Promise of America", First Baptist Church, Dallas, Texas, 1976; Media Presentation for Christian and Missionary Alliance, St. Louis, Missouri, 1976; Media Coordinator, Bill Glass Evangelistic Association Tour, 1977. Published Works: Novel in Progress, compiled from teaching experiences; Textbook, *How to Direct Readers Theatre;* Several Journal Articles. Honors and Awards: Pi Kappa Delta Communications Honorary Society, 1964; Sigma Tau Delta English Honorary Society, 1967; P. Merville Larson Debate and Interpretation Society, 1972; Phi Kappa Phi Scholastic Honorary Society, 1972; National Speakers Association, 1979; National Honors, Narration/Media Presentation, "Up with America" 1976, George Washington Medals of Honor for Media, Stage Production and Public Address, Freedoms Foundation, 1976; Outstanding Teacher, Northlane Exchange Club, 1970; Outstanding Teacher of the Year 1975, Certificate of Honor for Address 1976, Valley Forge; Sons of the American Revolution Outstanding Citizen, 1977; State Fair of Texas Outstanding Contribution, 1977; Martha Washington Award of Outstanding Service to Country, 1977; McCullough Junior High School Teacher of the Month, 1977; Spirit of '76, Outstanding Citizen, City of Dallas, 1976; Top 2%, Graduate School 1973, Selected by Speech Faculty for Faculty Membership in Speech Communication Association 1971, Teaching Assistant in Department of Speech and Theatre Arts 1971, Texas Tech University; Invited to Present Paper, Texas Speech Association Convention, 1972; Listed in *Who's Who Among Students in American Universities and Colleges, Outstanding Young Women of America, Personalities of America, Book of Honor, Community Leaders of America.* Address: 7006 Kingsbury Drive, Dallas, Texas 75231.

Clinton, John Hart

Lawyer, Publisher. Personal: Born April 3, 1905, in Quincy, Massachusetts; Son of John Francis and Catherine Veronica Hart Clinton (both deceased); Married First Wife Helen Alice Amphlett, February 18, 1933 (deceased), Second Wife Mathilda A. Schoorel van Dillen; Father of Mary Jane, Mary Ann, John Hart Jr. Educaton: A.B., Boston College, 1926; J.D., Harvard University, 1929. Career: California Bar, 1930; Massachusetts Bar, 1930; Law Practice, San Francisco; Associate, Morrison, Hohfield, Foerster, Shuman & Clark, 1929-41; Partner, Morrison, Foerster, Hollaway, Clinton & Clark, 1941-72; Of Counsel, Morrisson & Foerster, 1972 to present; Vice-President, General Counsel, Industrial Employers and Distributors Association, Emeryville, 1944-72; President, Leamington Hotel, Oakland, California 1933-37; President, Amphlett Printing Company, San Mateo, California, 1943 to present; *San Mateo Times,* Publisher 1943 to present, Editor 1960 to present. Organizational Memberships: Federal Communications Commission; American Bar Association; San Francisco Bar Association; San Mateo County Bar Association; State Bar California (chairman, state bar committee, fair trial/fair press; co-chairman, California bench/bar media committee); American Judicature Society; National Lawyers Club; American Law Institution; California Press Association; American Newspaper Publishers Association (government affairs committee; press/bar relations committee; American Bar Association-American Newspaper Publishers Association Task Force; California Newspaper Publishers Association (president, 1969); American Society of Newspaper Editors; Association of Catholic Newsmen; National Press Photographers Association. Community Activities: Boy Scouts of America (honorary member, executive committee, San Mateo council); California Jockey Club Foundation; Notre Dame College, Belmont, California (regent emeritus); Equestrian Order of Holy Sepulchre of Jerusalem (decorated knight); San Mateo County Development Association (president, 1963-65); San Mateo County Historical Association (president, 1960-64); International Platform Association; Newcomers Social Clubs, Commonwealth of California (past president), San Francisco Commonwealth, Bohemian; San Mateo Rotary Club (past president); Elks. Address: 131 Sycamore Avenue, San Mateo, California 94402.

Clogan, Paul Maurice

Educator. Personal: Born July 9, 1934; Father of Michael Rodger, Patrick Terence, Margaret Murphy. Education: B.A. 1956, M.A., 1957, Boston College; Ph.D., University of Illinois, 1961; F.A.A.R., American Academy in Rome, Italy, 1966. Career: Associate Professor of English, Duke University; Associate Professor of English, Case Western Reserve University; Professor of English, North Texas State University, present. Organizational Memberships: Modern Language Association (executive committee, 1980-84); Medieval Academy of America (nominating committee, 1974-75; John Nicholas Brown Prize committee, 1981-83); Linguistic Society of America. Community Activities: Delegate, People-to-People International to the People's Republic of China, 1982. Honors and Awards: Duke Endowment Grant, 1961-62; American Council of Learned Societies Fellowship, 1963-64; American Philosophical Society Grants, 1964-69; Senior Fulbright-Hays Postdoctoral Research Fellowship, Italy, 1965-66; *Prix de Rome* Fellowship, 1966-67; Bollingen Foundation Grant, 1966; National Endowment for the Humanities Fellowship, 1969-70; North Texas State University Faculty Research Grants, 1972-75, 1981-82; Senior Fulbright-Hays Research Grant, France, 1978. Address: P.O. Box 13348, North Texas Station, Denton, Texas 76203.

Cloke, Wilma Jean

Businesswoman, Educator. Personal: Born December 1, 1928; Daughter of Clarence William (deceased) and Mary Anita Taylor Newsom; Married Arthur L Cloke (deceased); Mother of Linda C Hettick, Victoria Lynn. Education: B.S., Texas Christian University, 1950; M.A., University of Redlands, 1964; Attended Claremont Graduate School; Honorary Ph.D., Colorado State Christian College, 1973. Career: Businesswoman; Educator. Organizational Memberships: Alpha Delta Kappa; San Bernadino, California, and National Education Associations; American Association of University Women; Norton Air Force Base Officers Wives Club. Community Activities: Chamber of Commerce; White House Conference on Education, 1960; Local & State Curriculum, Career Editor, Text Book Task Force; Rainbow Girls (past mother advisor); Furnished I.C.U.-C.C.V. Waiting Room, Saint Bernardine Hospital. Religion: First Christian Church. Honors and Awards: Distinguished Community Service Award, 1972; Order of Eastern Star; Numerous Biographical Listings. Address: 901 Frontier Ave, Redlands, California 92373.

Florence Cloudt

Closser, Patrick Denton

Radio Evangelist, Television/Radio Broadcaster, Filmmaker. Personal: Born April 27, 1945; Son of Mr. and Mrs. Edward B. Thompson. Education: Diploma, 16mm Filmmaking, American Schools of Cinema, 1970; First, Second, Third Class Radiotelephone License, Restricted. Career: Mission Field Work; Television/Radio Broadcasting; Religious Broadcasting; Radio Evangelist; Filmmaker; Sends Reception Reports to WINB, WYFR, HCJB. Organizational Memberships: Society of Motion Picture and Television Engineers; N.A.B.E.T. (member local #441); I.B.E.W. (member local #1257); International Christian Broadcasters. Community Activities: Ham Radio Operator (call letters KA5NKL); HCJB "Andex"; Civil Air Patrol, 1963; Dallas Jaycees, 1968; Money Raiser, KERA Channel 13, Dallas; Money Raiser for Religious Radio Stations, Pledge Drive Telethons, Easter Seals Telethon; Donated Equipment to Texas Broadcast Museum; North Texas Radio for the Blind; Two Half-Hour Specials over KXVI; 200-Page Autobiography, Life History Center, Houston/Conroe/Library of Congress. Religion: Radio Evangelist, KDTX-FM 1975-77, KBFI 1972, KVTT 1977-78, KXVI 1980-81, KTER 1981-82; Church Usher, Acolyte. Honors and Awards: Letter of Thanks, Texas Broadcast Museum; Award, Republican Party, 1962; Various Commemorative Awards, International Biographical Centre (Cambridge, England), American Biographical Institute; Life Fellow, International Biographical Association; Advisory Board, American Biographical Institute; Listed in *Who's Who of Intellectuals, Who's Who in the South and Southwest, International Who's Who in Community Service, Anglo-American Who's Who*. Address: 3514 Nogales Street, Dallas, Texas 75220.

Cloudt, Florence Ricker

Educator, Executive. Personal: Born July 12, 1925; Daughter of Norman Hurd Ricker (deceased); Married Frank Winfield Cloudt; Mother of Norman Sandford Pottinger, Margaret Halliday Pottinger. Education: B.F.A., Sophie Newcomb College, Tulane University, Louisiana, 1946; Post-graduate Courses in Childhood Education, University of Maryland, 1956-58. Career: Owner/Teacher, Nursery School, Atlanta; Kindergarten Teacher, Montgomery County School System, Maryland, 1956-60; Teacher, National Cathedral School, Washington, 1960-62; Founder 1963, Manager 1963-78, Florence Pottinger Interiors; Vice President 1970-78, President/General Manager 1978 to present, Focal Point Inc., Smyrna, Georgia; Writer, Producer, Award-Winning Monthly Television Program, Washington. Organizational Memberships: Institute of Business Designers; Association of Preservation Technology; Women Business Owners; Sophie Newcomb College (class officer, four years; vice president, art school; honor board). Community Activities: National Trust for Historic Preservation; Victorian Society in America; Historic House Association of America; Georgia Trust for Historic Preservation; Atlanta Historical Society; Atlanta Junior League; High Museum of Art (past vice chairman, women's committee; organizer, members guild); Atlanta Preservation Center (board of directors; ways and means committee); Atlanta Landmarks (trustee; writer, producer, 30-minute slide talk, facilities of Fox Theater, progress in saving movie palace; recruiter, volunteer and secretary trainer; narrator, "Tour of the Fabulous Fox", elementary and civic groups); Theater Atlanta (public relations); Young Matrons Circle, Tallulah Falls School (past president); Atlanta Woman of the Year (board member). Religion: Episcopalian. Honors and Awards: Selected One of 100 Contemporary Atlantans Whose Influence was Being Felt and of Whom More was Expected, 1977; Selected to Appear in Beauty Section of Georgia Tech Yearbook *Blueprint*; Listed in *Who's Who Among Students in American Universities and Colleges, Who's Who in the South and Southwest, Who's Who in the South, Personalities of the South.* Address: 137 Huntington Road, N.E., Atlanta, Georgia 30309.

Wesley S Coffman

Clunie, Robert

Painter. Personal: Born June 29, 1895; Married Myrtle Ireland (deceased); Father of Robert Kent. Military: Director of Camouflage for the United States Navy, 1942. Career: China Painting, New York, 1914; Painting and Varnishing, Ferrell County, Saginaw, Michigan; Head, Painting Department, World War I, 1918-19; Artist, Metro in Hollywood; Exhibits for Forest Service, Soil Conservation, County of Ventura Fair Exhibits and Sun Kist, as well as a number of others. Organizational Memberships: Painters & Sculptures; Los Angeles, California Art Club; Academy of Western Painters (governor of board); Sierra Club (honorary member); International Alpine Club (honorary member); Los Angeles County Museum (jury member); State Museum, Los Angeles (jury member). Community Activities: International Order of Odd Fellows. Honors and Awards: A-1 Man Show; Silver Cup, 1945; Marine Award, 1944; Winner over 30 Awards in Art. Address: 2399 N Sierra Hwy., Bishop, California 93514.

Coffman, Wesley Surber

Educational Administrator. Personal: Born June 17, 1927; Son of George Wesley and Mayme Rebecca Surber Coffman; Married Patricia Elaine Russell; Father of Russell Surber, Nancy Catherine, Rebecca Leone. Education: B.Mus. 1950, M.Mus. 1953, North Texas State University; Ph.D., Florida State University, 1968. Military: Served in the United States Navy, 1945-46. Career: Organist, Minister of Music, First Baptist Church, Sherman, Texas, 1949-58; Choral Director, Sherman High School, 1950-58; Minister of Music, Second Baptist Church, Houston, 1958-66; Choral Assistant, Florida State University, 1966-68; Professor of Music 1968-80, Chairman of Music Department 1968-74, Chairman of Arts Division 1974-80, Dallas Baptist College; Coordinator of Music, University of Texas-Arlington, 1980; Dean, School of Music, Hardin-Simmons University, Abilene, Texas, 1980 to present.

Organizational Memberships: Pi Kappa Lambda; Alpha Chi; Phi Mu Alpha; American Guild of Organists (executive committee, Dallas, 1970-73); Texas Choral Directors Association (director, 1954-56); Committee on Standards for Teacher Education in Texas, 1981; Texas Music Educators Conference (member-at-large, 1978-79); Texas Student Music Educators (state sponsor, national conference, 1979-81). Community Activities: Dallas Symphony (Oak Cliff board, 1976); Oak Cliff Fine Arts Festival (board member, 1975-76). Religion: Baptist, Deacon, Organist, Minister of Music, Choir Member. Address: 1281 Canterbury, Abilene, Texas 79602.

Cohan, George Sheldon

Advertising Executive. Personal: Born May 30, 1924; Son of Charles and Ann Cohan; Married Natalie Holmes; Father of Barry W., Gail J. Waferling, Charles F. M., Victoria. Education: B.S.M.E., University of Cincinnati, 1948; John Marshall Law School, 1954-56. Military: Served in the United States Army Corps of Engineers from 1943-46, attaining the rank of 1st Lieutenant. Career: Field Engineer, Industrial Erectors, Inc., Chicago; Sales Engineer, Fairbanks-Morse & Company, Chicago; Vice President, Accounts Supervisor, Hoffman-York Advertising Agency, Milwaukee; Tobias & Olendorf, Chicago; Senior Vice President, General Manager, Bozell & Jacobs, Inc., Chicago; Chairman of the Board, President, Cohan & Paul, Inc., Chicago; Director, Forest Labs, New York City; Director, C.I.M.; Director, Universal Gift Certificate, Inc.; Advertising Executive, present. Organizational Memberships: Business and Professional People in the Public Interest (board of directors, 1978 to present); International Presidents of Business/Professional Advertising Association, 1976-77; P.R.S.A., 1966 to present. Community Activities: Boy Scouts of America (board member, central Indiana council, 1965-69); March of Dimes (executive committee, 1965-69); Indiana Junior Achievement, 1965-69; A.N.T.A., 1948-51; B.G.A., 1969-71; Screen Actors Guild, 1962 to present; American Legion. Honors and Awards: 15th Annual G. D. Crain Award, 1981; Advertising Hall of Fame, 1981; Outstanding Merit, 8th Pan-American Railway Congress, 1954; 1st Place, National Lithographic Society, 1955; A.I.A. Best Seller Award, 1954; A.B.P. Award, 1971; A.I.A. Best of Show, 1962; B.P.A.A. Gold Award, 1979, 1980; C.A.D.M. Gold Award, 1980, 1981; Addy Gold Award, 190. Address: 3740 North Lake Shore Drive, Chicago, Illinois 60613.

Anita M Cohen

Cohen, Anita M

Attorney. Personal: Born December 4, 1945; Daughter of Dr. Rosalie A. Cohen. Education: B.A., University of Pittsburgh, 1967; J.D., Duquesne University, 1970. Career: Assistant District Attorney, All Trial Divisions, Philadelphia County, Pennsylvania; Assistant Public Defender, Allegheny County, Pennsylvania (Master in Divorce Matters); Chairperson, Panel Member, Small Claims Arbitration Cases, Dynamic Broadcastings Systems, Inc., Employee to Monitor for Federal Communications Commission Compliance; Attorney, Private General Practice, Divorce Master, Arbitration Hearing Examiner; Guest Lecturer, Seminar on Deviants and Society, Temple University College of Liberal Arts, Department of Sociology, 1979, 1982. Organizational Memberships: American Bar Association, 1970 to present; American Judicature Society, 1973 to present; National District Attorney's Association, 1971 to present; Fraternal Order of Police and Shomrim, 1975 to present; Pennsylvania Bar Association, 1970 to present; Allegheny Bar Association, 1970-80. Community Activities: Planned Parenthood of Southeastern Pennsylvania (board of directors, 1980 to present; public affairs committee, 1980 to present; finance committee, 1980-81); Girls Coalition of Southeastern Pennsylvania (board of directors, 1980 to present); Boosters Association of Philadelphia, 1980 to present; American Businesswomen's Association (speaker, 1973). Published Works: Author of Number of Papers with R. Cohen for Books, Professional Journals and Meetings, including "Compulsory Sterilization Statutes: Public Sentiment and Public Policy" in *Research in Community and Mental Health, Volume II;* Professional Paper Read at Meetings in Uppsula, Sweden, 9th World Congress of Sociology, 1978; "Resistance to Contemporary Mental Health Developments: Compulsory Sterilization Statutes as Indicators of Public Sentiment"; "Neglected Legal Dilemmas in Community Psychiatry" in *Sociological Perspectives on Community Mental Health.* Honors and Awards: Certificate of Achievement, 4th National Institution on Narcotics and Dangerous Drugs 1972, Delegate to National Convention 1973, National District Attorney's Association; Quarter Finalist, Appallate Moot Court, 1969; Semi-Finalist, Trial Moot Court, 1970; Participant, Bi-National Sociology Conference, 1980. Address: 4024 Woodruff Avenue, Lafayette Hill, Pennsylvania 19444.

Cohen, Gerson David

Chancellor, Professor. Personal: Born August 26, 1924; Son of Nehama G. Cohen; Married Naomi Wiener; Father of Jeremy, Judith. Education: B.A., City College of New York, 1944; B.H.L., 1943, and M.H.L., 1948, both from The Jewish Theological Seminary of America; Ph.D., Columbia University, 1958. Career: The Jewish Theological Seminary of America: Librarian (1950-57), Lecturer in Jewish Literature and Institutions (1957-60), Assistant Professor of Jewish Literature and Institutions (1960-64), Jacob H. Schiff Professor in Jewish History (1970 to present), Chancellor (1972 to present); Columbia University: Lecturer in Semitic Languages (1950-60), Assistant Professor of History (1960-63), Associate Professor of History (1963-67), Professor of Jewish History (1967-70), Director of the Center of Israel and Jewish Studies (1968-70), Adjunct Professor of History and Seminar Associate (1970 to present). Organizational Memberships: American Academy for Jewish Research (fellow, editor of proceedings 1969-72); Alliance Israelite Universelle (board of directors 1967 to present); Conference on Jewish Social Studies, 1967 to present; Jewish Publication Society, 1970 to present (chairman of publication committee 1970-72). Community Activities: Harvard Divinity School (board of visitors, 1976 to present); Legal Aid Society (board of sponsors 1978 to present). Honors and Awards: Townsend Harris Medal, City College of New York, 1975; Doctor of Divinity, *honoris causa,* Princeton, 1976; Doctor of Humane Letters, *honoris causa,* New York University, 1978; Doctor of Human Letters, *honoris causa,* City University of New York, 1979. Address: 416 West 255th Street, Riverdale, New York 10471.

Genson D Cohen

Cohen, Irving David

Environmental Consultant. Personal: Born May 12, 1945; Son of Harry and Fay Cohen; Married Dorothy; Father of Miriam Susan, Esther Heidi, Daniel Marc, Aaron Michael. Education: B.E., Chemical Engineering, City College of New York, 1967; M.E., Chemical Engineering, New York University, 1970. Career: Senior Process Engineer, Cardford and Russell, Inc.; Associate Chemical Engineer, Hoffman-LaRoche; Senior Project Manager, Woodward-Envicon Inc.; Environmental Consultant; Certified Environmental Professional. Organizational Memberships: American Institute for Chemical Engineers, New Jersey Section; International Association for Pollution Control; American Industrial Hygiene Association; National Association for Environmental Professionals; Air Pollution Control Association; New York Academy of Sciences. Honors and Awards: Listed in *Who's Who in Engineering, Who's Who in the East, Who's Who in Technology Today.* Address: 19 Copeland Road, Denville, New Jersey 07834.

Cohen, Rosalie Agger

Educator. Personal: Born February 2, 1923; Daughter of Benjamin and Pauline Agger (both deceased); Mother of David, Anita,

Michael, Joel, Brian. Education: B.A., Indiana Central College, 1951; M.Ed., Duquesne University, 1958; Ph.D., University of Pittsburgh, 1967. Career: Associate Professor of Sociology and Foundations of Education 1970 to present, Chairman of Foundations of Education Department, 1974-77, Temple University, Philadelphia, Pennsylvania; Guest Professor, Institute for Advanced Studies and Scientific Research, Vienna, Austria, Summer 1970; Assistant/Associate Research Professor G.S.S.W. 1967-69, Chairman of Ph.D. Program 1969, University of Pittsburgh; Research Assistant, Learning Research and Development Center, 1965-67. Organizational Memberships: American Sociological Association; Society for the Study of Social Problems (co-chairman, poverty and human relations section, 1968-71; session organizer, 1972; chairman, committee on standards and freedom of research, publication and teaching, 1973-76; organization of sessions, open sessions, plenary sessions, 1974-76); American Judicature Society; Society for Applied Anthropology (fellow); Eastern Sociological Society (committee on the professions, 1970); *Journal of Health and Social Behavior* (associate editor, 1969-72). Community Activities: N.I.E. Field Consultant, 1974; 3rd International Congress on Social Psychiatry (advisory council, 1970); Colleague Consultancies, 19687 to present; Mon-Valley Coordinated Health and Welfare Center, Monessen, Pennsylvania (research consultant, 1969-73); Organizer, Research Conference on Urban Sub-Cultural Differences with Interdisciplinary, University, Community, International Participation, Pittsburgh, Pennsylvania, 1969; Testified for School Governence and Management, Representative, College Task Force on Basic Education, Legislative Sub-Committee on Basic Education, Harrisburg, 1974. Published Works: Book Reviews for Publications and for Publishers of Research Centers; Writer, Working Papers, Position Papers for Presentation by University Deans and Committees. Honors and Awards: Outstanding Graduate Woman of the Year, Kappa Chapter, Phi Delta Gamma, 1967 Outstanding Faculty Woman of the Year, Temple University Women, 1978; International Dimensions Grants, Ford Foundation, 1968, 1970; Study Leave Award, Federal Impact on Education, Temple University, 1975; Listed in *American Men and Women of Science, Who's Who in the East, International Directory of Behavior and Design Research.* Address: 4024 Woodruff Avenue, Lafayette Hill, Pennsylvania 19444.

Cokinos, Geneos Pete

Oil Producer, Petroleum Engineering Consultant. Personal: January 7, 1916; Son of Panayotis and Elizabeth Cokinos (both deceased); Married Lula Pelias; Father of Peter, Elizabeth, Natalia, Nena, Katie. Education: B.S., Petroleum Engineering. Military: Served in the United States Air Force as Cadet. Career: District Petroleum Engineer, Texas Oil and Gas Commission, 1946-63; Oil Producer Petroleum Engineering Consultant, 1963 to present; Registered Professional Engineer, Texas, Louisiana. Organizational Memberships: Society of Petroleum Engineers; A.I.M.E. (president, Beaumont-Spindletop section, Society of Petroleum Engineers); Oil Information Committee (chairman, southeast Texas area). Community Activities: Downtown Young Men's Christian Association, Beaumont, Texas (president). Religion: President, Saint George's Greek Orthodox Church, Port Arthur. Honors and Awards: Tennis Championships, 55 Age Group, 60 Age Group. Address: 4675 Gladys Street, Beaumont, Texas 77706.

Col, Jeanne Marie

Educator. Personal: Born April 18, 1946; Daughter of Raymond T. and Elizabeth P. Col. Education: B.A. 1966, M.A. 1969, University of California-Davis; Ph.D., University of South Carolina, 1977. Career: Associate Professor of Public Administration, Sangamon State University, Springfield, Illinois; Former Positions include Assistant Professor of Public Administration State University of New York-Albany; Lecturer in Political Science and Public Administration, Makerere University, Kampala, Uganda. Organizational Memberships: American Political Science Association (women's caucus for political science, president, 1982-83; editor, *Quarterly*, 1980-81); American Society for Public Administration; African Studies Association; International Political Science Association (research committee, sex roles and political editor, *Newsletter*, 1979 to present); Coalition for Labor Union Women; American Federation of Teachers; National Organization for Women; National Committee for Women in Public Administration (coordinator, region II, 1980-81; workshop on affirmative action, 1982); Institute for Managerial and Professional Women; National Conference on Women's Networks (workshop leader, 1980); National Commission on Working Women (facilitator, regional dialogue, 1979). Community Activities: United Nations Industrial Development Organization (consultant, women in public administration, 1981); United States Military Academy (roundtable co-chairperson, conference on United States affairs, Africa, 1981); Association of Metis and Non-Status Indians of Saskatchewan (consultant, administrative reforms, 1981); New York State School of Industrial and Labor Relations, Cornell University (consultant, program for upwardly mobile clerical women, 1977-81); United States Agency for International Development (consultant on women's cooperatives); Center for Environmental Options, Inc. (board of directors, 1978-81); University Commission for Affirmative Action, State University of New York-Albany, 1979-81; Women in Public Administration Meetings (founder; member, Springfield, Illinois 1981 to present, Albany, New York 1978-81); New York State Civil Service Commission (lecturer; public administration trainee program, 1980-81); International Women's Year, United States Conference, Houston, Texas, Oral History Project, 1977; Various University and Public Lectures on Women's Issues and African Government and Public Policy, United States and Uganda; Radio Interviews, Legislative Politics, Administration Development, United States-Uganda. Honors and Awards: Listed in *Who's Who in the East, Community Leaders of America.* Address: 3217 Calredon Drive, Springfield, Illinois 62704.

Colanto, Emelda Trujillo

Microbiologist. Personal: Born September 12, 1935; Daughter of Josue and Laura Trujillo; Married Joseph D. Colanto; Mother of Daniel, Evelyn. Education: B.A., Adams State College, Alamosa, Colorado; M.A., New Mexico Highlands University, Las Vegas, New Mexico. Career: Microbiologist; Chemist; Hispanic Employment Program Manager. Organizational Memberships: National IMAGE (national women's action committee representative, 1979-81; southeastern Arizona Chapter president, 1976 to present; state vice president, 1980); Hispanic Employment Committee (chairperson for headquarters, Fort Huachuca, Arizona). Community Activities: Sierra Vista Human Relations Council, 1979 to present. Honors and Awards: Outstanding Performance Award 1977, 1978, 1979, 1980, for Work Performed for E.P.G. as Hispanic Program Manager; Sustained Superior Award, 1980, U.S.A.E.P.G.; Special Acts Award, 1974; Outstanding National IMAGE Award for Community Involvement, 1980; IMAGE Chapter Award for Community Involvement, 1979, 1980; National Women's Award, 1980. Address: Box 444, Huachuca, Arizona 85613.

Cole, Eddie-Lou

Poetry Editor. Personal: Daughter of Mr. and Mrs. J. R. Neill (both deceased); Married L. A. Cole (deceased), Second Husband Ray W. Howard; Mother of David L., Donna R. Stalling. Education: Attended Sacramento City College, University of California-Berkeley Extension. Career: Editor, State Employee's Magazine, *Fort Sutter Clutter;* Column Editor, Harlequin Press; Art Editor, Promethian Press; Poetry Editor, World of Poetry Press. Organizational Memberships: El Camino Poets Workshop; California Federation of Chaparral Poets (president); California State Poetry Club; National Federation of Poetry Clubs; Ina Collbrith Circle; New York Poetry Forum; Florida Poetry Society of Major Poets. Religion: St. Luke's American Lutheran Church. Published Works:

Poetry, *Of Winter, Shadows in Sundials, Pinions to the Sun, The Great Wall, Strange*; Textbook, *New Techniques for Today's Poets*; Co-Author, *Ballads and Story Poems*; Poems Published in *Yearbook of Modern Poets, Voices International*. Honors and Awards: 175+ Awards for Poems; Life Fellow, International Biographical Association, 1978; Life Patron, American Biographical Institute Research Association, 1981; Listed in *Contemporary Authors, Royal Blue Book, Who's Who, Notable Americans, International Who's Who, Personalities of the West and Midwest, Yearbook of Modern Poetry, Great American World Poets, Noteworthy Americans*. Address: 1841 Garden Highway, Sacramento, California 95833.

Cole, Lois Helen

Certified Public Accountant, Retired Educator. Personal: Born December 12, 1913; Daughter of Mr. and Mrs. Tom Durham (both deceased); Married Grady A. Cole (deceased). Education: B.A., North Texas State University, Denton, 1934; M.A., Southwest Texas State University, San Marcos, 1959; Ph.D., University of Texas-Austin, 1954. Career: Computer Programmer and Senior Analyst, Atomic Energy Commission, 1963-64; Dean of Women; Counselor; Office Manager, Government Office, Dallas; Chairman, Business Administration Department, Midwestern University; Principal, Blanco High School; University Professor until 1981; Certified Public Accountant, Certificate and License, Texas State Board of Accountancy, 1982. Organizational Memberships: American Association of University Women; American Association of University Professors; Delta Kappa Gamma International; American Institute of Certified Public Accountants; Texas Association of College Teachers; Texas Society of Certified Public Accountants. Community Activities: Alpine Women's Club Member, General Federation of Women's Clubs (secretary, two years); Sul Ross Women's Organization; Teacher for the United States Government, Rochefort, France, 1954-55. Religion: Methodist. Honors and Awards: Visiting Professor, Western New Mexico University, Silver City, 1976; Grants-in-Aid, Pioneer Title Insurance Company, for Study of Electronic Data Processing, 1965; Listed in *World Who's Who of Women, Who's Who of American Women, Dictionary of International Biography, World's Who's Who of Women in Education, Who's Who in American Law, American Men and Women of Science, Social and Behavioral Sciences, International Scholars Directory, Personalities of the South, Trustees, Presidents and Deans of American Colleges and Universities, Creative and Successful Personalities of the World, Who's Who in American Education, Who's Who in Texas Today, International Who's Who of Intellectuals, Personalities of America, Directory of Distinguished Americans, International Book of Honor*. Address: 411 June Street, Alpine, Texas 79830.

Lois H Cole

Colemon, Johnnie

Minister. Personal: Born February 18; Daughter of John (deceased) and Lula Parker Haley; Married Rev. Don Nedd. Education: Graduate of Rust College High School, Holly Springs, Mississippi; B.A. 1943, D.Div. 1977, Wiley College, Texas; Teaching Certificate, Ordained Minister, Unity School of Christianity, Lee's Summit, Missouri. Career: Teacher, Chicago Public School System; Price Analyst, Chicago Quartermasters, Chicago Market Center; Founder, Minister, Teacher, Christ Universal Temple for Better Living, Chicago; Speaker; Consultant; Television and Radio Appearances. Organizational Memberships: Universal Foundation for Better Living (composed of eighteen churches in Chicago, Detroit, Brooklyn, Benton Harbor, Michigan, Trinidad and Guyana, South America, Miami, Toronto, Las Vegas, Evanston and Hempstead; study groups in New Haven, Connecticut, Atlanta and Beverly Hills); International New Thought Alliance (district president; chairperson, 60th anniversary congress, Chicago). Community Activities: Community Speaker; Weekly Radio Broadcasts, "Tower of Power", WVON Radio Station, Chicago; Guest Speaker, Festival of Mind and Body, London, England; Chicago Port Authority (past director); Television Appearances, NBC-TV "Eyewitness News", "On Q" with Carol Cartwright, Channel 5, Chicago; Planning Christ Universal City, South Side, Chicago (complex to include 10,300 seat auditorium, residential housing units, The Johnnie Colemon Institute, a private school, retreat house, senior citizen housing, and a business section). Honors and Awards: Class Valedictorian, Rust College High School; Most Versatile Student on Campus, Wiley College; First Black Elected President, Association of Unity Churches, Unity School of Christianity. Address: 5008 South Greenwood Avenue, Chicago, Illinois 60615.

Coligado, Eduardo Ylanan

Physician. Personal: Born April 18, 1936; Son of Josie B. and Pacita Ylanan Coligado; Married Eladia Clemente; Father of Eric, Edwin, Edward-David, Emy-Lee. Education: M.D., University of Philippines, 1962; Internship, Philippine General Hospital; Resident in Internal Medicine, St. Vincent Charity Hospital, Cleveland, Ohio, 1963-64; Resident in Internal Medicine, Lutheran Hospital, Cleveland, Ohio, 1964-65; Fellow, Cleveland Metropolitan Hospital, 1965-67. Career: Demonstrator in Medicine, Highland View General Hospital, Cleveland, Ohio, 1967-70; Private Practice in Internal Medicine, Geneva, Ohio, 1970-76; Private Practice in Internal Medicine, Borger, Texas, 1976 to present. Organizational Memberships: Cuyahoga Medical Society, 1963-70; Ashtabula Medical Society, 1970-76; Top of Texas Medical Society, 1980-81. Community Activities: Geneva Kiwanis Club (member, 1970-76, board of directors, 1971-73). Religion: Roman Catholic. Published Works: "Reversible Vascular Occlusion of the Colon", *Radiology*, Volume 89 #3, page 432, September 1967; *Neutral Amino Acid Absorption in Humans: The Effect of Side Chain Length*. Honors and Awards: Listed in *Who's Who in the South and Southwest, Personalities of the South, The Book of Texas Pan-Handle*. Address: #7 Altamira, Borger, Texas 79007.

Johnnie Colemon

Collier, Gaylan Jane

Educator. Personal: Born July 23, 1924; Daughter of Mr. and Mrs. Ben Collier (both deceased). Education: B.A. Speech/Drama, Abilene Christian University, 1946; M.A. Drama, University of Iowa, 1949; Advanced Study, Cornell University, 1953; Ph.D. Theatre, University of Denver, 1957. Career: Instructor, Speech/Drama, University of North Carolina-Greensboro, 1947-48; Assistant Professor of Speech/Drama, Acting Chairperson, Greensboro College, 1949-50; Abilene Christian University, Assistant Professor and Director of Theatre 1950-57, Associate Professor 1957-60; Idaho State University, Associate Professor and Head of Acting Studies 1960-63; Sam Houston State University, Associate Professor of Drama, 1963-65, Professor of Drama 1965-67; Professor of Theatre and Coordinator of Acting/Directing Program, Texas Christian University, 1967 to present. Organizational Memberships: American Theatre Association (past secretary, committee on academic and production standards); Children's Theatre Association (governor, Region 4, 1962-63; administrative assistant to national director, 1965-67); Southwest Theatre Conference; Rocky Mountain Theatre Conference (vice president, 1962-63). Community Activities; Scott Actor's Repertory Company (director, summers 1968, 1969); Town and Gown (director, 1970); *The Imaginary Invalid* (director, chosen to represent the United States, American festival in Britain, summer 1970); Fort Worth Repertory Theatre (director, summer 1972); Fort Worth Community Theatre (guest director, summer 1976, judge, acting awards 1978-79); Frequent Speaker for Clubs, including Woman's Club of Fort Worth. Honors and Awards: Best Actress, Abilene Christian University, 1943-44, 1944-45, 1945-46; Director of Play Chosen to Represent the United States in American Festival in Britain, Summer 1970; Director, *You Can't Take it With You*, Chosen for Presentation, Regional Festival, American College Theatre Festival, 1979; Listed in *Who's Who in America, Who's Who in American Women,*

Directory of American Scholars, Notable Names in the American Theatre, Community Leaders of America, Who's Who in the Southwest. Address: 2616 South University Drive, Fort Worth, Texas 76109.

Collins, Marcus E Sr

State Representative; Farmer. Personal: Born January 25, 1927; Son of John Sr. and Emma Woodruff Collins; Married Elizabeth Griffin; Father of Elizabeth Ann, Marcus Eugene, James Edwin, David Almond, Jennifer, Rebecca. Education: High School Graduate, 1943. Military: Served in the United States Army, 1945-46. Career: Farmer. Organizational Memberships: Georgia Farm Bureau Federation (tobacco advisory board); Pesticide Advisory Board of the Department of Agriculture; Tobacco Advisory Board for Commissioner of Agriculture; Georgia Association of Retarded Citizens (advisory board); National Conference of State Legislatures (rural development committee). Community Activities: Representative, 144th District, Georgia House of Representatives, Elected 1961-62, 1964 to present; Chairman, House Ways and Means Committee; Ex-Officio Member, Appropriations Committee of the House; Agriculture and Consumer Affairs Committee; Highways Committee of the House; Joint House/Senate Legislative Services Committee; Special Rules Committee; Metropolitan Atlanta Rapid Transit Overview Committee; House Policy Committee; Vice-Chairman, Tax Reform Commission, 1978-80; State Board of Equalization, Department of Revenue; Tax Settlement Board, Department of Revenue; Joint House/Senate Overview Committee; Tobacco Advisory Board for the Commissioner of Agriculture; Chairman of the Resolutions Committee, Council of State Governments, Southern Legislative Conference, 32nd Annual Meeting. Religion: Board of Deacons, Lake Pleasant Baptist Church. Honors and Awards: Liberty Bell Award, Mitchell County Bar Association, 1978; Man of the Year, Friend of Vocational Education, 1978; Friend of County Agent's Award, University of Georgia Extension Service. Address: Route 12, Pelham, Georgia 31779.

Collins, Marva Deloise

Teacher. Personal: Born August 31, 1936; Daughter of Bessie Maye Johnson; Married Clarence Collins; Mother of Patrick, Eric, Cynthia Beth. Education: B.S., Clark College, 1957; Attended Northwestern University 1975, Chicago Teachers College. Career: Teacher, Westside Preparatory School; Teacher, 14 years, Chicago Board of Education. Organizational Memberships: Right to Read (director, 1975); White House Fellowships (president's commissioner), 1981-85. Religion: Baptist. Honors and Awards: Thomas Jefferson National Award, 1981; Movie of Her Life, starring Cicely Tyson, "The Marva Collins Story", 1981; Listed in *Who's Who in America, Who's Who in the Midwest.* Address: 3819 West Adams, Chicago, Illinois 60624.

Collins, Nancy Whisnant

Assistant to the President. Personal: Born December 20, 1933; Daughter of Mr. and Mrs. W.W. Whisnant; Married Richard F. Chapman M.D. on May 29, 1982; Mother of James Q., III, Charles L., and William R. Education: Attended Queens College, Charlotte, North Carolina; A.B. Journalism, University of North Carolina at Chapel Hill, 1955; M.S. Personnel Administration, Graduate School of Business, 1967, University of North Carolina; Graduate Fellowship, Cornell University, New York. Career: Personnel Assistant, Macy's, New York City; Junior Executive Placement Director, San Francisco; Free-Lance Journalist; Certified Military Correspondent, Europe; Program Director Girl Scouts of America, Virginia; Oriental Tour Director, Hong Kong, Bangkok, Singapore; Writer, Short Stories, Poems; Stanford University, Graduate School of Business, Corporate Development Officer, Assistant Director, Sloan Program, Hoover Institution, Assistant Director 1979-82, Assistant to the President, Palo Alto Medical Foundation 1982 to present. Organizational Memberships: Coro Foundation (board of directors, women's programs); Peninsula Professional Women's Network (founding board member; past membership director; conference manager, 1980 national network conference for professional women); Hoover Institution, Stanford University (manager, Mont Pelerin Conference, 1980). Community Activities: City of Menlo Park (personnel board); San Mateo County Charter Review Committee; Commonwealth Club; Menlo Park Women's Soccer League. Religion: Trinity Episcopal Church Council. Published Works: Book, *Professional Women and Their Mentors;* Numerous Articles, Other Publications; "The Collins Study of Creativity", "A Guide to San Francisco and the Bay Area". Address: 1850 Oak Avenue, Menlo Park, California 94025.

Gaylan Collier

Collins, William Edward

Laboratory Administrator. Personal: Born May 16, 1932, in Brooklyn, New York; Son of Mrs. L. Collins; Married Corliss Jean; Father of Corliss Adora. Education: B.A., St. Peter's College, 1954; M.A. Psychology 1956, Ph.D. Experimental Psychology 1959, Fordham University; Number of Post-graduate Courses, 1960-80. Career: Psychological Research Assistant 1954-56, Teaching Fellow 1958, Research Assistant 1958-59, Graduate Instructor in Experimental Psychology 1958-59, Fordham University; Research Psychology, United States Army Medical Research Laboratory, 1959-61; Research Psychologist 1961-63, Chief Sensory Integration Section 1963-65, Chief of Aviation Psychology Laboratory 1965 to present, Lecturer for Medical Examiners Seminars in Aeronautical Center 1969 to present, Aviation Psychology Laboratory, Federal Aviation Administration, Civil Aeromedical Institute; Adjunct Associate Professor 1963-70, Adjunct Professor 1970 to present, University of Oklahoma-Norman Department of Psychology; Adjunct Associate Professor 1965-70, Adjunct Professor 1970 to present, University of Oklahoma Health Sciences Center Department of Psychiatry and Behavioral Sciences; Licensed by Oklahoma State Board of Examiners of Psychologists, 1966 to present; Rating Panel Member, Interagency Board, United States Civil Service Examiners, State of Oklahoma, 1967 to present; Evaluator of Proposals, National Science Foundation 1968 to present, Department of Health, Education and Welfare 1971 to present; Lecturer, Railroad Accident Investigation Course, 1972 to present; Chairman, Discussant, Participant, Numerous Scientific Meetings, 1965 to present; Educational and Research Films, 1964, 1969. Organizational Memberships: American Psychological Association (fellow; division of experimental psychology; division of comparative and physiological psychology); American Association for the Advancement of Science (fellow); Sigma Xi; Psychonomic Society; Aerospace Medical Association (fellow); N.A.S.-N.R.C.; New York Academy of Sciences; Association of Aviation Psychologists (past president); Barany Society; International Research Group on Colour Vision Deficiencies; Associate Editor, *Aviation, Space and Environmental Medicine;* Oklahoma State Board of Examiners of Psychologists (1982-83 chairman). Community Activities: Oklahoma Science Fair (judge, 1964); Oklahoma Psychological Association (judge, graduate and undergraduate competitions, 1973, 1975, 1979); Oklahoma State Science and Engineering Fair (judge, 1980, 1981, 1982). Published Works: Numerous Articles, Professional Journals, Presentations, Professional Meetings (these include "Spatial Disorientation in General Aviation Accidents", "Performance Effects of Alcohol Intoxication and Hangover at Ground Level and at Simulated Altitude", "The Selection of Air Traffic Control Specialists: History and Review of Contributions by the Civil Aeromedical Institute"). Honors and Awards: Quality Performance Award 1964, 1969, 1970, 1974, Outstanding Performance Rating 1966, 1967, 1968, 1969, 1970, 1971, 1974, Sustained Superior Performance Award 1966, 1967, Expert Witness, Disorientation and Visual Illusions Public Civil Aeronautics Board Hearings 1966, Award for Employee Invention 1966, Special Achievement Award 1971, Federal Aviation Administration; Appointed Abstractor, *Psychological*

Abstracts, 1962 to present; Raymond F. Longacre Award, Aerospace Medical Association, 1971; Abstractor Citation, American Psychological Association, 1973; United States Patent for Caloric Irrigation Receptacle, 1968; Listed in *Who's Who in America, World Who's Who in Science, American Men of Science, Leaders in American Science, International Directory of Research and Development Scientists, Who's Who in the South and Southwest, Two Thousand Men of Achievement, Creative and Successful Personalities of the World, Dictionary of International Biography, United States Department of Health, Education and Welfare's Office of Education Final Report of Project #9-D-046, Community Leaders of America, Personalities of the South, American Men and Women of Science, International Who's Who in Community Service, Community Leaders and Noteworthy Americans, Notable Americans of the Bicentennial Era, Notable Americans of 1976-77.* Address: 8900 Sheringham Drive, Oklahoma City, Oklahoma 73132.

Comas, Joan Murphree

Educator. Personal: Born December 22, 1940; Daughter of Floyd and Lorena Murphree; Married Dr. Robert E. Comas; Mother of Michele Scott, Shannon Elizabeth. Education: B.A. English, Psychology, University of Montevallo, 1972; M.A. Counseling and Guidance 1974, Ph.D. Counselor Education 1981, University of Alabama. Career: English Teacher, Pensacola High School, Florida; University of Alabama, Counselor, New Student Orientation, Counselor, Freshman Outreach Program, Coordinator, Women Emerging Program, Director, Women's Career Service, Counselor, University Counseling Center, Assistant Professor of Behavioral Studies/Counselor. Organizational Memberships: Alabama Personnel and Guidance Association (editorial board member, *Journal*; member, district III); Alabama College Personnel Association; Capstone Women's Network; Alabama Association of Women Deans, Administrators and Counselors. Community Activities: Parent-Teacher Association, Alberta Elementary School (president, vice-president); University Newcomers Associatoin (president, secretary); Tuscaloosa Community Action Program (founding board member); Junior Great Books Program Leader; Tuscaloosa Women's Center; University Women's Club. Religion: Member, Church School Teacher, Covent Presbyterian Church; Leader, Youth Group's Career Exploration Activities; Tuscaloosa Community Ministries (executive board). Honors and Awards: Daughters of the American Revolution Citizenship Award; Honor Scholar; Miss Alabama College; Outstanding Psychology Student; Outstanding Student in Counselor Education Program; Birmingham's Citizen of the Month; Senior Elite Award; Alabama Congress of Parents and Teachers Scholarship; Listed in *Who's Who Among Students in American Universities and Colleges, Who's Who in the South and Southwest, Peronalities of the South, Men and Women of Distinction, Personalities of America, Dictionary of International Biography, Notable Americans, Who's Who of Intellectuals, International Book of Honor.* Address: 480 Woodland Hills, Tuscaloosa, Alabama 35405.

Combs, Douglas Lee

Division Manager. Personal: Born December 16, 1946, in Cincinnati, Ohio; Son of Francis G. and Nellie Marie Lauterwasser Combs. Education: B.S. with honors, Advertising, University of Florida, 1972; M.B.A., University of Alabama 1979. Military: Served in the United States Army, Intelligence Corps, from 1964-68, Vietnam. Career: Director, Combs and Associates, Gainesville, Florida, 1971; Communications Director, Gainesville Chamber of Commerce, 1972; Director of Public Relations, Blount Brothers Corporation, Montgomery, Alabama, 1973-77; Director of Promotions, *Southern Living, Progressive Farmer, Decorating and Craft Ideas* Magazines, Birmingham, 1977-Division Manager, Southern Progress Corporation, Birmingham, 1981-82; Circulation Director, Omega Group, Ltd., Boulder, Colorado (1982 to present). Organizational Memberships: Public Relations Society of America; Public Relations Council of Alabama; Society of Professional Journalists; American Society of Personnel Administrators; Alpha Delta Sigma; Association of M.B.A. Executives, Direct Mail Marketing Association. Community Activities: United Appeal (board of directors, 1975-76); Republican. Honors and Awards: Outstanding Industrial Photography Award, Montgomery Advertising Club, 1976; D.M.M.A. Echo Award, 1982. Address: P.O. Box 12154, Boulder, Colorado 80303.

Lewis H Conner

Combs, Janet Constance

Clinical Social Worker. Personal: Born November 25, 1949; Daughter of Eugene Columbus and Lillian Bunn Combs. Education: B.A., Morgan State College, 1971; M.S.W., University of Utah Graduate School of Social Work, 1973; Certificate, The John Marshall Law School, 1979. Career: Clinical Social Worker. Organizational Memberships: National Association of Social Workers, 1972 to present; State of Illinois Continuity of Care Organization, 1978 to present; National Association of Social Workers Liaison, Social Work Service, Veterans Administration West Side Medical Center, Chicago, Illinois. Community Activities: Girl Scouts, 1963-67; Blue Bird Organization (volunteer), Saint Vincent Hospital, Birmingham, Alabama, 1965-66; Junior Imperial Club, Birmingham, 1964-67; Reporter, *The Spokesman*, Morgan State College, Baltimore, 1970-71; Women's Auxiliary, University of Alabama Hospitals and Clinics (volunteer), Birmingham, Summers 1970-73; School and Concert Choirs, 1964-71; Morgan State College Alumni Association. Religion: Baptist. Honors and Awards: Miss Baptist, Morgan State College, 1968-69; Choir Plaque Award, Morgan State College, 1970-71; Social Rehabilitation Services Trainee Award, University of Utah, 1972-73; Volunteer Service Certificates, Newswriting Certificate, 1970-71; Honor Roll and Dean's List, 1963-71; Listed in *Who's Who of American Women, The World Who's Who of Women*; Other Service Certificates and Biographical Nominations. Address: 505 North Lake Shore Drive, #807, Chicago, Illinois 60611.

Combs, Willie Bernice

Information Clerk. Personal: Born May 7, 1949; Daughter of Louis and Peachella Bennett; Mother of Angela Michael and Kelly, Diann, Christina, Christopher. Education: Graduate of Eastern High School, 1967. Career: Procurement Clerk, United States Department of State; Information Clerk, United States Department of Commerce. Organizational Memberships: National Association of Female Executives; National Secretary Association. Community Activities: Toastmasters International. Religion: Secretary, Church of God, Washington, D.C., 1981 to present. Honors and Awards: Four Scholastic Awards, United States Department of Agriculture Graduate School; Listed in *Community Leaders of America, Personalities of America, Who's Who in the East*. Address: 4926 78th Avenue, Hyattsville, Maryland 20784.

Conner, Lewis H Jr

Judge. Personal: Born March 21, 1938; Son of Mr. and Mrs. Lewis H. Conner, Sr.; Married Ashley Whitsitt; Father of Holland Ashley, Lewis Forrest. Education: B.A., Vanderbilt University, 1960; J.D., Vanderbilt University School of Law, 1963. Military: Served in the Judge Advocate General's Corp, United States Army Reserve, 1963-66, achieving the rank of Captain. Career: Practicing Attorney, (Nashville, Tennessee) Partner, Bailey, Ewing, Dale & Conner, 1966-72; Founding Partner, Dearborn & Ewing,

1972-80; Appointed to the Court of Appeals by Governor Alexander, November 1980. Organizational Memberships: Tennessee Judicial Conference, 1980-81; American, Tennessee & Nashville Bar Associations, 1963-81; American College of Mortgage Attorneys (fellow); American, Tennessee & Nashville Trial Lawyers Associations, 1977-80 (treasurer, 1978-79); Lawyers Involved for Tennessee (trustee, 1979-80). Community Activities: Alexander for Governor campaign (state finance coordinator, 1974, 1978); Republican Party, State of Tennessee (finance committee, 1976); Nashville Quarterback Club (president, 1971; board of directors, 1966-81); Nashville Boy's Club (board of directors, 1981); Tennessee Golf Association (board of directors, 1968-80); Richland Chamber of Commerce, 1960-81 (board of directors, 1976-79; president, 1978-79); Nashville Exchange Club, 1975-81; Nashville Junior Chamber of Commerce, 1966-73. Religion: Presbyterian; Deacon, Elder, Sunday School Teacher. Honors and Awards: Alpha Tau Omega, President 1960; Raven Society; Order of the Coif, Vanderbilt Law School, 1963; *Vanderbilt Law Review*, Managing Editor, 1962-63; Phi Delta Phi; Outstanding New Member, Junior Chamber of Commerce, 1967; Honorary Member, Tennessee Section Professional Golfers Association, 1975; Tennessee Amateur Golfer of the Year, 1973; Winner of Over 20 State, Regional and Local Amateur Golf Championships; Special Chief Justice, Supreme Court of Tennessee, 1980-81; Honored by Joint Resolution of State of Tennessee Senate & House of Representatives, 1981. Address: 2005 Otter Valley Lane, Nashville, Tennessee 37215.

Connors, John Keith

Administrator, Professional Counselor. Personal: Born March 5, 1952; Son of William K. Connors. Education: B.S. Education, 1974; M.Ed. Human Services Counseling 1979, University of Virginia. Career: Substance Abuse Specialist, Valley Mental Health Services; Alcoholism Counselor, Alcoholism Treatment Center; Instructor, Alcohol Safety Action Project; Director, Charlottesville Honor Court; Director, Community Diversion Incentive Program, Licensed Professional Counselor, present. Organizational Memberships: Substance Abuse Program Directors Association (secretary, 1980-81); American Personnel and Guidance Association; Phi Delta Kappa; Virginia Association of Alcoholism Counselors, 1975-79. Community Activities: Albemarle County Democratic Committee, 1981 to present; Batesville Ruritans (board of directors, 1981 to present); Charlottesville Mental Health Association (president 1982); Planned Parenthood of Charlottesville (publicity chairman, 1975); Jefferson Literary and Debating Society, 1970 to present; *Declaration* Newmagazine (founding staff, 1974); Volunteers in Service to America (University Year for Action, 1973-74). Honors and Awards: DuPont Regional Scholar, University of Virginia, 1970-74; Listed in *Who's Who in the South and Southwest*. Address: P.O. Box 48, Batesville, Virginia 22924.

Conrad, Jerome Charles

Executive. Personal: Born March 20, 1947, in Chicago, Illinois; Son of William G. Conrad and Patricia T. Nicol; Married Judith Brudek; Father of Matthew Jerome, Daneen Judith. Education: A.A., Chicago City University, 1972; B.F.A., Northern Illinois University, DeKalb, 1976. Military: Served in the United States Navy Reserve, 1965-74, as an Air Crew Survival Instructor. Career: Various Positions in the Accounting Field with Libbey, McNeil and Libbey, a Major Food Processing Firm, and for United Airlines, One of Nations Largest Commercial Airline Corporations, Eight years; Principal Owner, Custom Furniture Manufacturing Firm, Sycamore, Illinois; Assistant to Chief Officer, EMCO, Restaurant Design and Manufacturing Firm, Chicago; Vice President, General Manager, Fulton & Partners, Inc., Toledo, Ohio; Purdue University Director of Research, Environmental Design Institute, Environmental Design Advisory Council, School of Consumer Sciences and Retailing; Environmental Design Advisory Council, Western Carolina University. Organizational Memberships: Office Landscape Users Group; Organization of Facility Managers and Planners Industrial Designers Society of America; Institute of Business Designers; Constructions Specifications Institute. Community Activities: Toledo Rotary Club; Toledo Museum of Art; Toledo Zoological Society; National Trust for Historic Preservation; Ohio Arts Council; Northern Illinois University (founding member, various executive offices, student art association, ARS NOVA; university council; college of visual and performing arts academic standards committee); Toledo Area Chamber of Commerce. Honors and Awards: Phi Theta Kappa; Listed in *Who's Who in the Midwest, Men of Achievement, Personalities of the West and Midwest, Personalities of America, International Who's Who of Intellectuals, Who's Who in Finance and Industry*. Address: 2055 South Avenue, Toledo, Ohio 43609.

David H Cook

Constans, H Philip Jr

Educator. Personal: Born February 6, 1928; Son of H. P. Constans; Married Evalyn Louise Simmons; Father of Cathy Cheak, Deborah Thompson, Leigh Pierce, Phyllis Evalyn. Education: B.S.P.H. 1950, M.A.E. 1953, Ed.D. 1962, University of Florida. Military: Served in the United States Army Corps of Engineers from 1946-47, attaining the rank of Corporal. Career: Teacher and Coach, Florida Public Schools; Supervising Pricipal, Live Oak Schools, Florida; Principal, Kirby-Smith Elementary Schools, Florida; Principal, Cocoa Beach High School, Florida; Executive Secretary, Florida Education Association; Professor of Educational Leaderships, Western Kentucky University, present; Visiting Fulbright Professor, University of Ilorin, Nigeria, 1981-82. Organizational Memberships: National Education Association (director, 1963-66); Florida Education Association (president, 1958-59; director, 1954-57); Florida Professional Practices Commission (chairman, 1964); Western Kentucky University Faculty Senate (chairman, 1976-78); Philosophy of Education Society (fellow); A.E.S.A. Community Activities: Bowling Green, Kentucky Kiwanis Club (director, 1975-78; president, 1980-81); American Cancer Society (president, Warren county unit, 1975-78); Kentucky Division (executive committee, 1978-81; chairman of the board); University of the South (trustee, 1979-81). Religion: Episcopal Church, Vestryman Christ Church 1972-75, Junior Warden 1976, Senior Warden 1977; Diocese of Kentucky Task Force on Christian Education, 1979-81. Honors and Awards: Phi Delta Kappa; Kappa Delta Pi; National Education Association PR & R Distinguished Service Award. Address: 642 Cottonwood, Bowling Green, Kentucky 42101.

Cook, David Hall

Training Manager. Personal: Born October 4, 1930; Son of Mrs. Jennie Hall Cook; Married Joyce Fralic; Father of David II, John. Education: B.B.A., 1974, and M.A. Ed., 1977, both from The George Washington University. Military: Served as an Airman, Mariner, United States Navy, 1947-67; Naval Science Instructor, High School R.O.T.C. Program, 1974-77; Computer Sciences Corporation: Engineer 1967-79, Senior Engineer 1971-74, Section Manager 1977-79, Training Manager of Control Systems Activity 1979 to present. Organizational Memberships: American Association for the Advancement of Science; Society for Interdisciplinary Studies (London); United States Naval Institute; American Society for Training and Development; Phi Delta Kappa (George Washington University chapter quarterly newsletter editor, 1977-81; editor of annual publication *Educational Perspectives*, 1977-81; George Washington University chapter president elect, 1981). Community Activities: Kiwanis Club (institutional representative to boy scout troop, 1970-73); Boy Scouts of America (troop committeeman, 1964-66; scoutmaster, 1966; neighborhood commissioner, 1966-73); Naval Sea Cadet Corps (training officer, 1976; administrative officer, 1977); Anchor Lodge #182, A.F. & A.M., 1952 to present; Key West Consistory, 1953 to pesent; Kena Temple Shrine, 1969 to present; The George Washington University Club, 1975 to present; Smithsonian Associates, 1972 to present; National Rifle Association, 1980 to present. Honors and Awards: Boy Scouts of America Wood Badge, 1967; American Defense, Commendation and Good Conduct Medals, 1947-67; Meritorious Service Award, Defense Communication Agency, 1967; Kiwanis Club Outstanding Service Award, 1973; U.S. Air Force Letter of Appreciation, 1981; American Biographical Institute Certificates, 1979-81; Letter of Appreciation, Harvard School of Dental Medicine, 1981. Address: 6217 Dana Avenue, Springfield, Virginia 22150.

Cooley, Carolyn A

Executive Secretary. Personal: Born June 28, 1956, in Farmerville, Louisiana; Daughter of Eddie and Ruby Butler; Married Dr. J. F. Cooley; Mother of Stephen Lamar. Education: Studied at Louisiana Technical University and Arkansas Baptist College. Career: Clerk-Typist, Louisiana Technical University, Ruston Louisiana, 1975-76; Typist, Arkansas Baptist College, 1976 to present; Currently, Executive Secretary, County Contact Committee, Inc.; Ex-Inmate Mission & Talent Center, Prison Rehabilitation Center, 1980 to present. Community Activities: Order of Eastern Star; Deputy Sheriff, Pulaski County; Deputy Constable, Pulaski County, District 3-A; National Sheriff's Association, 1978-79; Arkansas Constable's Association (associate member); Assistant Legislative Prison Aide to Chief Legislative Aide Dr. J. F. Cooley, 1980 to present; Secretary and Editor for Women, Children and Society Columns, *Arkansas Weekly Sentinel*, 1978 to present; Mothers' Prayers and Answers Auxiliary (secretary, 1980). Honors and Awards: Certificate of Merit, Governor Dale Bumpers, 1974; Certificate of Merit, Governor David Pryor, 1976; National Historical Society, 1975-76; Probation Officer, North Little Rock Municipal Court (honorary), 1973, 1979; Certificate of Merit, Cooley's Athletic and Teenage Club, Inc., 1973; Certificate of Honor, Cooley's Athletic and Teenage Club, Inc., 1973; Nominated for International Platform Association, 1974; Certificate of Participation, Literary High School Rally, Farmerville High Scool, 1974; I Dare You Award, Farmerville High School, 1974; Society of Outstanding American High School Students, 1974; Outstanding Teenager of America, 1974; Arkansas Travelers Certificate, 1977; Certificate of Recognition, Governor D. Pryor, 1977; Certificate of Membership, County Contact Committee; Certificate of Recognition, Constable's Office, District 3-A; Arkansas Volunteer Award, Governor's Office of Volunteer Services, 1980; Arkansas Certificate of Merit, Governor Frank White, 1981; Arkansas Certificate of Award for Outstanding Volunteer Services, Governor Frank White, 1981; Special Deputy Sheriff of Pulaski County, Sheriff Tommy Robinson, 1981; Listed in *Community Leaders and Noteworthy Americans, Dictionary of International Biography, Men and Women of Distinction, Personalities of America, Outstanding Young Women of America, Personalities of the South, International Youth in Achievement, Notable Americans of the Bicentennial Era, The World Who's Who of Women*. Address: P.O. Box 4520, Little Rock, Arkansas 72214.

Cooley, J F

J F Cooley

Minister, Educator, Civil Rights Activitist. Personal: Born January 11, 1926, Rowland, North Carolina; Son of James F. and Martha Buie Cooley (both deceased); Married Carolyn Ann Butler; Father of Virginia M., James Francis, Gladys M., Franklin Donell, Stephen Lamar. Education: Graduate of Southside High School; A.B. Social Sciences 1953, B.D. Theology 1956, M.Div. 1973, Johnson Smith University; M.A., Sociology, Eastern Nebraska Christian College; D.D., Life Science College, Rolling Meadows, Illinois; Cultural Doctorate in Social Science, Tuscon, Arizona. Military: Served as Chaplain in the United States Army, 1944-46, attaining the rank of Lieutenant. Career: Minister, Grant Chapel Presbyterian Church (Georgia) 1956-57, St. Andrews Presbyterian Church (Arkansas) 1957-69; Juvenile Probation Officer 1953-64, Associate Juvenile Judge 1963-64, St. Francis County; Political Science Director, Minister of Service, Dean of Men, Academic Dean, Shorter College, 1969-73; Press Agent; Private Investigator, North Little Rock; Public Relations Officer, Consumer Protection Division, State Attorney General's Office, Arkansas Baptist College, 1975-82. Organizational Memberships: Arkansas Teachers Association; International Platform Association; S.A.N.E.; American Security Council; National Committee of Black Churchmen; Omega Psi Phi; National Association for the Advancement of Colored People; Arkansas Council on Human Relations; Committee for Peaceful Co-Existence; Welfare Rights Organization; A.C.O.R.N.; National Sheriffs Association; Arkansas Law Enforcement Association; Ministerial Alliance of Greater Little Rock; Juvenile Correctional Association; National Conference of Christians and Jews. Community Activities: Established More Than Fifteen Community Organizations; Co-Sponsor, Community Reading and Development Center, 1976; Founder/Executive Director, County Contact Committee, Inc., 1977; Founder/Editor, *Arkansas Weekly Sentinel*, 1978; Founder/Executive Director, Ex-Inmate Mission Talent Center, 1980; Editor, *State Weekly News;* Bi-Monthly Column Writer, Associate Editor, *Baptist Vanguard Magazine and Newspaper;* Deputy Sheriff 1977-80, 1969-73, Special Deputy Sheriff 1981, Pulaski County; Justice of the Peace 1973-74, 1975-76, District #3 Constable 1978-80, Chaplain Corps and Instructor for Night Classes 1977, Pulaski County Correctional Facilities; St. Francis County Deputy Sheriff, 1961-62; Visiting Teacher and Juvenile Officer, Juvenile Court, St. Francis County, 1963-65; Chairman, Recruitment Committee on Minorities; A.F.&A.M. Masons; National Historical Society; State Democratic Party; Veterans Organization; Urban League; Early American Society; Inspirational Trio, Singing Group; Postal Commemorative Society; National Black Veterans Organization, Inc. Honors and Awards: First Black Lieutenant, North Little Rock Police Department, 1975; Honorary D.D., Shorter College 1971, Life Science College 1972; Honorary Doctor of Civil Law, Eastern Nebraska Christian College, 1971; Honorable Lieutenant Colonel, Retired Lieutenant Colonel, 1978; Two Certificates from the Federal Bureau of Prisons, Jail Operator and Jail Administrator, 1971, 1972; Five Certificates, Basic, General, Intermediate, Senior and Advanced, as Certified Law Enforcement Officer, 1980, Arkansas Commission on Law Enforcement Standards and Training; Course Certificate, National Rifle Association of America, 1971; Guest of President Lyndon B. Johnson, 1963; United Supreme Council's Thomas J. Stone Award, 1974; 33° Mason; Numerous Citations for Crime Prevention; Number of Honors, Recognitions, Certificates, Plaques from Federal, State, Local Government Officials, Private Individuals, Law Enforcement Agencies; Certificate of Membership, Prison Jaycees; January 11, 1977, Proclaimed as Dr. J. F. Cooley Day, in Arkansas; 60 Trophies and Plaques Given over 10-Year Period for Promoting Recreational Activities for Young People in Arkansas; Honorary Alumnus, Louisiana Tech University; Certificate of Eligibility, Veterans Administration; Certificate of Appreciation, Prison Inmates, 1970; Jury Commissioner, 1977; Community Service Award, Community Welfare Club of North Little Rock, 1978; Month of September 10 through October 10, 1978, Proclaimed Dr. J. F. Cooley Month, North Little Rock; Letter of Recognition, Prison Reform and Rehabilitation, 1978; March 28 through April 3, 1977, Proclaimed as Dr. J. F. Cooley Week; Honorary Citizen, Little Rock, 1977; Work Placed in Congressional Records, 1977; Arkansas Volunteer Award, 1980; "A Salute to a Champion", Cummins Prison Inmates, 1978; Arkansas Certificate of Merit for Outstanding Volunteer Services, 1981; Arkansas Certificate of Merit, 1981; Featured in Numerous National, State, Local Publications; First Black Certified Law Enforcement Instructor, State of Arkansas, 1981; Dr. J. F. Cooley Day, City of Little Rock, December 29, 1982. Address: P.O. Box 4520, Little Rock, Arkansas 72214.

Coolidge, Harold Jefferson

Administrator of International Conservation. Personal: Born January 15, 1904, in Boston, Massachusetts; Son of Harold J. and Edith Lawrence Coolidge (both deceased); Married Martha T. Henderson, in 1972. Education: Attended the University of Arizona, 1922-23; B.S., 19th Century History and Literature, Harvard University, 1927; Further Studies at Cambridge University, Corpus

Christi College, 1927-28. Military: Served in the United States Army, attaining the rank of Major; Served with O.S.S. in Washington, D.C., England, France, Italy; Organized and Headed Emergency Rescue Equipment Section of O.S.S.; Research on Chemical Shark Repellants, Signaling Mirror Credited with Saving 1000 Lives, Preparation of Survival Manuals and Other Rescue Equipment. Career: Harvard University, Assistant Mammalogist on Medical Expedition to Liberia and Belgian Congo 1926-27, Director of Harvard Film Service 1936, Leader of Asiatic Primate Expediation to Siam, Borneo and Sumatra 1937; Assistant Curator of Mammals 1929-46, Associate in Mammalogy 1946-70, Museum of Comparative Zoology; Executive Director, Pacific Science Board, National Academy of Sciences, National Research Council, 1946-70; International Union for Conservation of Nature and Natural Resources, Vice President 1948-54, Founding Chairman of Survival Service Commission of Commission of Natural Parks, Chairman of First World Conference on National Parks (Seattle) 1962, President 1966-72, Honorary President 1972 to present. Organizational Memberships: African Wildlife Leadership Foundation (founding director); American Committee for International Conservation (founder, secretary 1930-42, chairman 1951-71); American Society of Mammalogists (life member, past officer); Boston Museum of Science (life member of corporation); Charles Darwin Foundation for Galapagos Islands (founding trustee); Fauna Preservation Society, United Kingdom (vice president); Cultural Survival, Inc. (advisory board); Island Resources Foundation (vice chairman); Charles A. Linbergh Fund (wildlife preservation advisory committee); L.S.B. Leakey Foundation (director); National Parks and Conservation Association (secretary, 1946-59; director, 1959-74); United States National Park Service (collaborator, 1948 to present); New York Zoological Society (fellow); Pacific Science Association (United States Council member, 1961-72; secretary-general, 10th Pacific Science Congress, Honolulu, 1961); Pacific Tropical Botanic Garden Foundation (director emeritus); Research Ranch, Inc. (director); Threshold Inc. (founding director); Zoological Society of London (corresponding member, 1928 to present); William P. Wharton Conservation Trust (trustee); World Wildlife Fund (director, international fund, founding director, United States appeal). Community Activities: Boone and Crockett Club; Cosmos Club; Explorers Club (fellow chairman, education committee, 1976); Harvard Travellers Club (fellow, president, 1939-42); Tavern Club; Boston Society of Natural History (fund raiser, 1938-39); Originator of Ideas Leading to Endangered Species Act, World Heritage Trust of UNESCO; Worker, National Parks Development, Japan, Korea, Taiwan, Philippines, New Caledonia, Vietnam, Cambodia, Laos, Malaysia, Indonesia. Religion: Past President, Chocorua Island Chapel Association, Squam Lake, New Hampshire. Published Works: Co-Author, *Three Kingdoms of Indo-China;* Two Harvard Museum of Comparative Zoology Memoirs; Numerous Scientific Articles and Published Speeches. Honors and Awards: C. Phillips Medal 1978, Honorary President 1972 to present, Honorary Member, Survival Service Commission and Commission on National Parks and Reserved Areas 1976 to present, International Union for Conservation of Nature and Natural Resources; Edward W. Browning Conservation Award, Smithsonian Institute and New York Commission Trust, 1978; Honorary Director, Institute Nationale pour la Conservation de la Nature, Zaire, 1975 to present; Honorary Advisor on Pacific Studies, Peabody Museum of Salem, 1973 to present; Honorary Chairman, American Committee on International Conservation, 1971 to present; Silver Medal of International Achievement Award, United States National Park Service Centennial Committee, 1972; Commander Order of Golden Ark, the Netherlands, 1972; Honorary Member, National Resource Council of Philippines, 1970; Honorary Life Fellow, Pacific Science Association, 1969 to present; Gold Medal, New York Zoological Society, 1969; Albright Medal, Scenic and Historical Preservation Society, 1968; Hutchinson Medal, Garden Club of America, 1963; 75th Anniversary Medal, University of Arizona, 1960; Honorary Cons., Bishop Museum, Honolulu, 1953 to present; United States Legion of Merit, 1945; Decorations from Governors of Laos 1929, 1947, Annam 1929, Cambodia 1945, France 1954, Belgium 1958, Ecuador 1964; Honorary Life Member, Chicago Museum of Natural History, 1929 to present; Honorary Member, Cercle Zool. Congolaise, Belgium, 1928; Sigma Xi, 1929; Hon.D.Soc., George Washington University 1959, Seoul National University 1965, Brandeis University 1970; Listed in *Who's Who in America, Who's Who in the World, American Men of Science, Harvard Class 1927 Reunion Reports, Harvard Travellers Club Yearbooks.* Address: 38 Standley Street, Beverly, Massachusetts 01915.

Coombs, C'Ceal Phelps

C'Ceal P Coombs

Business Administrator, Educator. Personal: Mother of Two Children. Education: Attended Reed College; B.S., University of Idaho; Graduate Studies, Washington State University. Career: Business Administrator; Educator, City Councilwoman, Yakima, Washington, 1958-62. Organizational Memberships: National Society of Literature and the Arts; California Historical Society; Connecticut Historical Society; Dorchester (Massachusetts) Antiquarian and Historical Society; Elmore County (Idaho) Historical Society; Fort Somcoe at Mool-Mill Restoration Society (life member); Oregon Historical Society; Washington County (Oregon) Historical Society (life member); Windsor (Connecticut) Historical Society (life member); American Library Association (council member, 1968, 1970-72); American Library Trustee Association (board of directors, 1963-70; president, 1967-68; member, 1960 to present; vice-president for region, 1962-67); College and Research Libraries Association and Rare Books Section; International Federation of Library Associations, 1967 to present; Pacific Northwest Library Assocation, 1960 to present; Pacific Northwest Library Trustee Association (organizer, 1962 to present); Washington Library Trustee Association (past chairman); Washington Library Association (honorary life member); Yakima Valley Regional Library (honorary life member); New England Historic Genealogical Society; National Genealogical Society; Connecticut Society of Genealogists; International Council on Crime and Delinquency; International Biographical Association (life fellow); National Council on Crime and Delinquency (board member, 1956-76); National Book Committee (board member, 1969-74); Ford Foundation (western states regional scholarship committee, 1955-57); Yakima Valley Museum; Yakima Valley Museum Guild. Community Activities: Allied Arts Council (organizing committee); Community Concert Association; English-Speaking Union (San Francisco, Seattle, Commonwealth); Knife and Fork Club; Larson Gallery Guild; Patron of Music, Symphony; Town Hall; Capital Theatre (patron); Airline Passengers Association; Clipper Club; Red Carpet Club; Third House, Washington State Legislature, 1953 to present; Washington Council on Crime and Delinquency (founding and past chairman); Political Party and Club Activities; Washington State 4-H Foundation (founding and past chairman); Political Party and Club Activities; Washington State and International Flying Farmers; Yakima Chamber of Commerce; Yakima Country Club; Friends of Washington Libraries Foundation (life member; state board incorporator, president, 1976 to present); Friends of Whitman College Library; Colonial Dames of the XVII Century (state recording secretary, 1977 to present; president, local chapter); Daughters of the American Colonists; Daughters of Founders and Patriots; New England Women; Friends of Tewesbury Abbey, England; Washington Congress of Parents and Teachers (state board member, state vice-president, 1949-53; president, Franklin Junior High School, 1948-49; state conference chairman, 1949 to present) Allied School Council, 1949-55; Washington State Association of Cities (state legislature chairman, 1957-62); Federated Women's Clubs (member, 1949-70; Washington state, member, board member, legislative chairman, 1950-64); Advisor to Youth Legislatures, 1960-70; Yakima County Parents and Teachers Assocaition (president, 1949-50); Yakima County Health Board, 1959-60; Yakima County Law and Justice Committee, 1974-78; City Council, Parents and Teachers Association (president, 1949-50); Yakima Chamber of Commerce (member, several committees; past president, government affairs committee, 1950 to present); Yakima Education Committee for Four-Year College, 1954 to present; Committee for Yakima Public Schools (vice-chairman, 1954-55); League of Women Voters (among organizers, 1955; member, 1955 to present); Mayor's Surveys on Water Development and Urban Renewal, 1962-64; Washington State Allied School Council, 1951-53; Yakima County School Board, 1957-59; Notary Public, Washington State, Gubernatorial Appointment, 1960 to present; City of Yakima (acting mayor, 1960-61; assistant mayor, 1961-62); Washington State Library Commission, 1960-76. Religion: President, Church Guild, 1950-60. Honors and Awards: Citations, Washington State Council on Crime and Delinquency, 1971, 1978; Outstanding Citizen Award, Western Correctional Association, 1974; International Trustee Citation 1966, Citation of Merit 1967, Honorary Life Member 1975, Special Bicentennial Award 1976, Washington Library

Association; Yakima Valley Woman of Achievement, 1954; Honorary Life Member, Yakima Valley Regional Library, 1959; Citation, Yakima City Council, 1960; Zonta's State Woman of Achievement, 1964; Governor's State Recognition, 1976; Honorary Life Member, National Congress of Parents and Teachers; Citations, Washington Library Trustee Assocaiton; Yakima's First City Councilwoman, 1958-62; Listed in *Who's Who of American Women, Who's Who in the West, Who's Who in Washington, International Who's Who of Intellectuals, International Profiles, World Who's Who of Women, Two Thousand Women of Achievement.* Address: Route 1, Box 1055, Yakima, Washington 98901.

Cooper, Danielle Chavy

Educator. Personal: Born December 11, 1921; Daughter of Henri Paul (deceased) and Jeanne Chavy; Married Wilmer Albert Cooper (deceased); Mother of Laurel Martine. Education: Licence es Lettres, Diplôme d'Etudes Superieures de Lettres, with honors, Université de Paris, France, 1939-43; Teaching Fellow in French, Bryn Mawr College, Pennsylvania, 1946-47; Ph.D., University of Southern California, 1963. Military: Served in the French Air Force, 1944-46, attaining the rank of Second Lieutenant, with the position of Interpreter/Liaison Officer in the Mediterranean Air Transport Command. Career: Journalist/Editor, *The Topanga News,* California, 1951-55; Teaching Positions, Immaculate Heart College (Los Angeles) 1957-63, University of Colorado (Boulder) 1963-65, Keuka College (New York) 1964-70; Professor of French and Humanities, Monterey Institute of International Studies, 1970 to present. Organizational Memberships: Federation of French Alliances in the United States (national council, 1980 to present); Association of Independent Colleges and Universities (articulation council, foreign language liaison committee, 1980-83); American Association of Teachers of French (president, Southern California chapter, 1958-62). Community Activities: French Alliance of the Peninsula (president, 1971-76, 1978-81); Alpha Mu Gamma National Collegiate Foreign Language Honor Society (national president, 1973-75; regional vice president, Pacific states, 1975 to present; national scholarship chairman, 1975-77; faculty sponsor, Delta Epsilon Chapter, M.I.I.S., 1970 to present); The Modern Language Association of Southern California (member, 1957-63; chairman, French section; research council, 1958-60); Ballet Fantasque, Monterey, California (board of directors, 1982 to present); United States Consultant, *Le Français dans le Monde,* Pedagogical French Review, 1954 to present. Honors and Awards: Chevalier de l'Order des Palmes Académiques, French Government Cultural Award, 1972; Medaille de la Résistance, Medal of Liberated France, World War II; Marcelle Parde Fellowship, Bryn Mawr College, 1946-47. Address: 1146 Sea View Avenue, Pacific Grove, California 93950.

Herbert P Cooper

Cooper, Herbert Press

Dean Emeritus. Personal: Born February 18, 1887, near Ridgeway, South Carolina; Son of Mars Lafayette and Isabel Van Brackle Smith Cooper (both deceased); Married Sara Louise McCrary; Father of Sara Louise Cooper Shigley, Herbert Press Jr., Mary Elizabeth Cooper Acock, Thomas Reid. Education: Graduate, Clemson College, 1911; Master's Degree, University of Wisconsin, 1916; Ph.D., Cornell University, 1922. Career: Assistant Professor of Agronomy, Cornell University, 7 years; Head, Department of Agronomy, Clemson, 1930-36; Dean, School of Agriculture and Director of South Carolina Experiment Station, Clemson, 1936-54; Retired, 1957; Presently, Dean Emeritus, Clemson University College of Agriculture and Director of South Carolina Agricultural Experiment Station. Organizational Memberships: Association of Southern Agriculture Workers (president, 1939); American Society of Agronomy (president, 1950). Religion: United Methodist. Honors and Awards: South Carolina's Man of the Year, *Progressive Farmer* magazine, 1938; 1 of 10 Ablest Chemists or Chemical Engineers in U.S., American Chemical Society, 1947; First to Receive the Distinguished Agronomist Award, Agronomy Society of South Carolina, 1975; Distinguished Alumni for 1980, Clemson Alumni Association of Clemson University; Listed in *Two Thousand Men of Achievement, Men of Achievement, International Who's Who of Intellectuals.* Address: 114 Riggs Drive, Clemson, South Carolina 29631.

Cooper, Jimmy Lee

Registered Pharmacist, Store Manager. Personal: Born March 22, 1942; Son of Mitchell and Ocella Cooper; Married Diana Hightower; Father of James Sebestain Cabot Cooper. Education: B.S., Texas Southern University, 1965. Career: Pharmacist; Store Manager. Organizational Memberships: American Management Association. Texas Pharmaceutical Association. Community Activities: Rotary Club; Texas Southern School of Pharmacy Alumni Association (president); Southeast Rotary Club (director). Religion: Baptist. Honors and Awards: Chi Delta Mu; Manager of the Year, 1980; Listed in *Who's Who in the South and Southwest, Personalities of the South.* Address: 9413 Bentwood, Houston, Texas 77016.

Cooper, Luther Grady

Educator (retired). Personal: Born July 10, 1902; Son of John Francis and Martha Jane Page Cooper (both deceased); Married Miriam Greever; Father of Kathryn Link, John Walton, Roberta Schott. Education: A.B., Roanoke College, 1922; A.M., University of South Carolina, 1924; B.D./M.Div., Lutheran Theological Southern Seminary, 1925; Ph.D., Hartford Theological Seminary, 1927; S.T.M., Union Theological Seminary, 1936; Honorary D.D., Newberry College, 1977. Career: Ordained Lutheran Minister; President, American Lutheran Mission, Tsingtao, Shantung, China; Professor, Head of Philosophy and Religion Department, Professor Emeritus (retired), Newberry College. Organizational Memberships: American Academy of Religion, 1960-75; Council on Aging (board of directors, 1974-80). Community Activities: Committee on Retired Senior Citizens Program (advisory member); Newberry Civic League; Rotary Club (past member, Tsingtao, China); Lions Club, Elloree, South Carolina (past member); Volunteer Advisor, Newberry County Students Sent to Youth Centers; Volunteer Teacher, Greek, Students Entering Theological School; Volunteer Teacher, English, Vietnam Refugees, Newberry. Religion: Volunteer Chaplain, Newberry Memorial Hospital, 1975 to present; Supply Pastor, Newport-Pembroke Lutheran Parish, Virginia 1923-24, Timberville Lutheran Parish, Virginia 1924, Grace Lutheran Church, Prosperity, South Carolina 1925-26; Missionary in China, 1928-48; Pastor, Holy Trinity Lutheran Church, Little Mountain, South Carolina 1948-53, Trinity Lutheran Church, Elloree, South Carolina, 1953-57; Professor of Religion, Greek and Philosophy, 1957-72; Mission Study Classes, New York, Pennsylvania, New Jersey Lutheran Churches, 1942-45. Honors and Awards: Jacobus Fellowship, Hartford Theological Seminary, 1926-27; German Exchange Student Scholarship, Study in Marburg University, Gern any, 1927; Called to American Lutheran Mission, Tsingtao, China, 1928; Prisoner of the Japanese, China, 1941-42; Repatriated, Gripsholm, 1942; Honorary Doctor of Divinity, 1977; Made Professor Emeritus, Newberry College, 1972; Gift of Sister Mary Cooper Williams $10,000 Scholarship for Students, Newberry College, in Honor of Dr. L. Grady Cooper. Address: 1800 College Street, Newberry, South Carolina 29108.

Ray B Copple

Copple, Dr Ray B

Civil Engineering Consultant, Counselor, Public Speaker. Personal: Born October 3, 1919; Son of Floyd J. Copple; Married Jean J.

Raymond; Father of Kenneth R., Carol J., (Stepfather to) Debra, Kurt, Tod. Education: Teacher's Certificate, University of Southern Illinois, 1935; Civil Engineering Degree, Pennsylvania College, 1954; Real Estate Broker, 1964; Ministerial Degree, 1964; D.Div., 1980. Military: Served in the United States Army. Career: Department of Transportation, Resident Engineer 1964, District Safety Engineer 1974, District E.E.O. Officer 1974, District Training Officer 1974; Civil Engineering Consultant, Counselor, Public Speaker. Organizational Memberships: Arizona Society of Professional Engineers (president, 1973; state director, 1974; state board, 1974-75); National Society of Professional Engineers; American Society of Professional Engineers; Order of the Engineer. Community Activities: Arizona Public Employment Association (state board, 1972-80); Full Gospel Businessmen's Fellowship; Elks Club; American Legion; Varoius Public Relations Committees. Religion: Christian Crusade Evangelist Counselor. Published Works: Co-Author *My Heaven to Hell*, 1979; Articles in *Engineering Construction Magazine*. Honors and Awards: Extra Mile Awards, Department of Transportation, 1974; Outstanding Service Award, Arizona Society of Professional Engineers (Northern), 1975; Defensive Driving Instructor Award, 1978; Listed in *Who's Who, Who's Who in Technology, Men of Achievement, Who's Who of Intellectuals, Personalities of America*. Address: P.O. Box 271, Flagstaff, Arizona 86002.

Coran, Arnold Gerald

Arnold G Coran

Pediatric Surgeon. Personal: Born April 16, 1938; Son of Charles Coran; Married Susan W.; Father of Michael Kenneth, David Lawrence, Randi Beth. Education: A.B. 1959, M.D. 1963, Harvard University. Military: Served in the United States Navy from 1970-72, attaining the rank of Lieutenant Commander. Career: Instructor in Surgery, Harvard Medical School, 1967-69; Associate Professor of Surgery, University of South Carolina Medical School, 1972-74; University of Michigan Medical School, Professor of Surgery 1974 to present, Pediatric Surgeon, Chief of Pediatric Surgery, present. Organizational Memberships: American College of Surgeons; American Academy of Pediatrics; American Pediatric Surgical Association; Society of University Surgeons; American Surgical Association. Community Activities: Washtenaw County United Jewish Appeal (board of directors). Honors and Awards: Bronze Medal for Scientific Exhibit, American Medical Association, 1972; American Medical Writers Award, 1978. Address: 3450 Vintage Valley Road, Ann Arbor, Michigan 48105.

Cordaro, John Benedict

Executive Director. Personal: Born October 7, 1941; Son of Mrs. Joseph B. Cordaro; Married Elizabeth Ann Dewton; Father of Susan Marie, Gregory Edward, Michael Patrick. Education: B.S.S., Loyola of New Orleans, 1963; Undertook studies in International Economics, Georgetown School of Foreign Service, 1963-65; M.S., Cornell University, 1972. Career: Food-Nutrition Economist, U.S. Department of State; Food Program Manager, U.S. Congress/O.T.A.; Staff, Senator Hubert Humphrey; Executive Director of Food Safety Council. Organizational Memberships: American Association for Advancement of Science; Institute of Food Technology; Food Safety Council (trustee); National Meat and Poultry Advisory Board; Washington Nutrition Group. Honors and Awards: Louisiana Knights of Columbus Fellowship for Graduate Study at Georgetown University, 1963; A.I.D. Outstanding Performance Awards; Congressional Staff Observer, 1974 World Food Conference; Leader, U.S. Delegation Expert F.P.C. Conference, Morocco, 1969; Listed in *Men of Achievement, Personalities of the South, Community Leaders and Noteworthy Americans, Personalities of America, Notable Americans, Dictionary of International Biography, Community Leaders of America.* Address: 1336 Buttermilk Lane, Reston, Virginia 22090.

Corkery, Charles Thomas

Educator. Personal: Born October 26, 1922; Died March 23, 1982; Son of Mrs. Eve Corkery; Married Anne Marie Cox; Father of Kathleen, Thomas, James, Maribeth, Therese, Patricia. Education: B.A., St. Mary's College, Minnesota, 1949; M.B.A., DePaul University, 1954. Military: Served in the United States Army from 1944-46, attaining the rank of Staff Sergeant, and from 1950-52, attaining the rank of 1st Lieutenant. Career: Chairman, Department of Business, Chicago State University, 1957-67; Lecturer, De Paul University, 1960-67; Professor of Accounting/Business Administration, The Loop College, Chicago, Illinois, 1967-82. Organizational Memberships: American Association of University Professors; Chicago Business Teachers Association (vice-president, 1970); Illinois Business Education Association (president, 1963); American Vocational Association (membership chairman, 1964). Community Activities: Chicago Vocational Advisor, 1966-68; Director, Cook County Internship Program for Experienced Teachers, 1970-71; North Central Visitation Teams, 1969-70; Staff Member, Chicago Board of Education "General Business Curriculum Guide". Honors and Awards: Enos C. Perry Distinguished Service Award, Chicago Business Teachers Association, 1975; Citation, Outstanding Area President, American Vocational Association, 1964; Listed in *International Who's Who in Education, International Book of Honor, Outstanding Secondary Educators of America.*

John Cordaro

Cornelius, Ira E

Executive. Personal: Born February 29, 1916; Son of Jacob E. Cornelius; Married Lois Margaret. Education: B.A., Central University of Iowa, 1947; Graduation Certificate, Industrial College of the Armed Forces, 1963; Ph.D., St. Andrews Episcopal University, 1967; Special Certificate, University Extensions, Lasers, University of California-Los Angeles, 1971. Military: Served in the United States Signal Corps during World War II, attaining the rank of First Sergeant. Career: Various Positions with Montgomery Ward Company, 1947-53; Budget Group Supervisor, Indirect Methods Analysis, Northrop Aircraft Corporation, 1953-54; Engineering Specialist, Group Leader, North American Aviation Company, 1954-57; Various Management Positions, Hughes Aircraft Corporation, 1957-60; Senior Corporate Planner, Lockheed Corporation, 1960-61; Senior Corporate Planner, Rockwell International, Various Locations, 1961; Senior Executive, Resource Analyst, 1965-70; Senior Executive Advisor, Advanced Space Programs, 1970 to present; Instructor, West Coast University Graduate School, 1974-75; Registered Professional Engineer, State of California. Organizational Memberships: American Institute of Astronautics and Aeronautics; American Institute of Industrial Engineers (senior member). Community Activities: Republican Party; World Affairs Council. Religion: Episcopal Church. Honors and Awards: Doctoral Dissertation Citation, 1967; Tau Epsilon Pi; Sigma Tau Delta; Various N.A.S.A. Award Certificates, Medallions, N.A.S.A. Pin for Contribution to National Space Programs, *Apollo* Lunar Landings, Skylab Missions, *Apollo-Soyuz* Mission, Space Shuttle Launch and Landing Mission, Company Letters of Commendation, Other Special Commendations. Address: 1334 West Orangethrope Avenue, Fullerton, California 92633.

Cornell, David A

Consultant. Personal: Born May 17; Father of Sara Ann. Education: B.A., Alma College; Special Study, McCormick Theological Seminary; M.Div., Western Theological Seminary; Special Study, Hope College; M.A., Western Michigan University; Th.D.,

American University; Special Study, Grand Valley State College. Community Activities: Interseminary Delegate, 1956; Lions Club (education co-chairman, 1958); Rotary Club (president, 1963); College Students Characteristics (co-chairman, 1968); College Library Board of Trustees, 1969-72; College Student Speaker's Bureau (director, 1964-72); Civil Air Patrol (advisory board, 1974-81); Nursing Home Trustee. Religion: Inter-Church Committee; Boy Scout Chaplain, 1956; National General Council Delegate, 1960; Church Health and Welfare Accreditation, 1975. Honors and Awards: Herp Scholarship, 1949; Celtic Cross, 1948; Seminary Preaching Award; Church Fine Arts Awards, 1969-72; GRACE Award, 1980; GRACE Honorable Mention, 1979; American Cancer Award, 1978; Michigan Department of Social Services Merit Award, 1978; R.S.V.P. Award, 1976; Inter-Church Award, 1975; Red Cross Merit Award, 1974; Grand Valley State Colleges Mental Health Lecture Award, 1973; Pi Kappa Delta Chapter Award, 1972; Forensic Teaching Awards, 1971, 1972; Interseminary Award, 1956; Tau Kappa Alpha Achievement Awards, 1950-53. Address: 2231 Sylvan Southeast, Grand Rapids, Michigan 49506.

Cornelson, George Henry

George H Cornelson

President. Personal: Born July 12, 1931, in Spartanburg, South Carolina; Son of George Henry III and Elizabeth Miller Woodward Cornelson (both deceased); Education: Graduate of McCallie School, Chattanooga, Tennessee, 1949; Attended Davidson College, North Carolina, 1949-51; B.S. Textiles, North Carolina State University, 1953; Harvard Graduate School of Business Administration, 1953-54; Air Force Contracting Officers School, F. E. Warren Air Force Base, Cheyenne, Wyoming, 1955-56; A. M. A. Senior Management Program, 1979. Military: Served in the United States Air Force as Government Contracting Officer, Headquarters Air Material, Research and Development Command, Rotary Wing and Liaison Aircraft Section, Wright Patterson Air Force Base, Dayton, Ohio, 1955-57. Career: Position with Clinton Mills, Industrial Engineering Department, 1954; 1955-57, Vice President, Clinton Mills, Clinton Mills Sales Corporation, 1958, Executive Vice President, Clinton Mills, Inc., 1970, President, 1979; Director, M. S. Bailey and Son, Bankers, 1955; Director, Elastic Fabrics of America, Fort Washington, Pennsylvania, 1970; President, Director, Clinton Mills of Geneva, Alabama, 1979. Organizational Memberships: Presbyterian College, Clinton, South Carolina (trustee, 1959-68); South Carolina Foundation of Independent Colleges (trustee, 1971-82); American Textile Manufacturers Institute (research and technical service committee, 1964-71; vice chairman, education committee, 1975-76; South Carolina Textile Manufacturers Association (president, 1979-80; board of directors, 1973-82). Community Activities: Thornwell Home for Children, Clinton, South Carolina (trustee, 1968-76; executive committee, 1973-74; secretary, board of trustees, 1974); Carolinas Community Chest Fund (director, 1958-61, 1963); Clinton Lions Club (director, 1958-60; president, 1962-63; zone chairman, district 32A, 1963-64; deputy district governor, 1969-70); Greater Clinton Planning Commission (organizing chairman, 1967; Clinton Chamber of Commerce (director, 1959-61; 1966; vice president, 1968; president, 1969; South Carolina Chamber of Commerce, (director, executive commmittee, 1975-79); Clinton Community Chest and United Fund (president, 1963-64); Boy Scouts of America (chairman, Laurens County district, 1973; executive board, Blue Ridge council, 1974); Kappa Alpha Order Social Fraternity (president, alpha omega chapter, 1952-53); Bailey Foundation, Clinton, South Carolina (advisory committee). Religion: Deacon 1959-67, Elder 1967-73, 1976-81, First Presbyterian Church, Clinton, South Carolina. Honors and Awards: Phi Psi Textile Fraternity; Junior Chamber of Commerce Distinguished Service Award, 1962; Outstanding Young Alumnus Award, North Carolina State University, 1965. Address: Merrie Oaks, Clinton, South Carolina 29325.

Coronado, Rosa

Food Manufacturing Executive. Personal: Born July 27, 1938; Daughter of Arturo and Elvira Coronado. Education: Graduate of Humboldt Senior High School, 1956; Public Relations Studies at the University of Mexico, Mexico City, 1960. Career: Officer 1960-74, President 1975-79, La Cara Coronado Restaurant; Officer 1960-74, Executive Manager 1975 to present, Mama Coronado Food Products; Lecturer, Instructor, Ethnic Foods, Mexican. Organizational Memberships: Minneapolis Restaurant Association, 1965-78; National Restaurant Association, 1977-79; International Geneva Executive Chefs (Minnesota Chapter, member, 1975 to present; chairperson, membership committee, Geneva Executive, 1976-79); Midwest Chefs Association (member, 1975 to present; recording secretary, 1976-78); American Culinary Federation, New York chapter); Metropolitan Economic Development Association of Minneapolis (board of directors, 1975 to present). Community Activities: Democratic Party; Minneapol City Center (advisory board, redevelopment, 1973-78); Small Business Task Force, State of Minnesota; Minnesota Hispanic Chamber of Commerce; Volunteer Resources, Department of Education, Twin Cities; Geneva Ball (co-chairperson, 1977). Religion: Parish Church Council 1980-81; President of Ladies Society 1976-78, Our Lady of Guadalupe Catholic Church. Published Works: Author of Children's Cookbook; Board of Directors, West Side/West St. Paul *Voice* Newspaper, 1982 to present. Honors and Awards: First Woman to be Elected into International Geneva for State, First to be Elected into Geneva Executive Chefs; Certificate, Research and Seminar, Mexican Foods, General Mills; Culinary Awards for Exhibits, 1970-80; Special Recognition Plaque, Minnesota International Geneva, 1979; Certificate of Recognition, Amoco, Research, New Food Ingrediant, 1970; Subject of Special Feature on Women in Business, *Chamber of Commerce Magazine*, 1977; Listed in *Who's Who of American Women, Who's Who in the Midwest*. Address: 949 16th Avenue North, South St. Paul, Minnesota 55075.

Corsello, Lily Joann

Lily J Corsello

Guidance Counselor, Author, Lecturer. Personal: Born March 30, 1953; Daughter of Rev. and Mrs. J. Corsello. Education: B.A., Florida State University, 1974; M.Ed., Florida Atlantic University, 1977. Career: Educator of Language Arts, Journalism and Mass Media; Guidance Counselor; Author; Lecturer. Organizational Memberships: American Personnel and Guidance Association, 1978 to present; National Education Association, 1974 to present; National Educators Fellowship, 1974-77; National Council of Teachers of English, 1974-80; Florida Teaching Profession and Classroom Teachers Association, 1974-77; International Platform Association, 1981. Community Activities: Pilot International, 1978 to present; Republican Executive Committee (precinct chairman, 1980); Broward County Young Republicans, 1980. Religion: Lecturer, National Single Adult Conferences, The Southern Baptist Convention, Nashville, Tennessee, 1979 to present. Published Works: Author of articles in *Christian Single* magazine, 1979 to present. Honors and Awards: Lambda Iota Tau, Life Member; Citizenship/History Award, Daughters of the American Revolution, 1968; Listed in *Who's Who in the South and Southwest, Personalities of the South, Personalities of America, The World Who's Who of Women, The Directory of Distinguished Americans, The International Who's Who of Intellectuals, Book of Honor*. Address: 4521 N.E. 18 Avenue, Ft. Lauderdale, Florida 33334.

Costantino, Raymond Valentino

Insurance Company Executive. Personal: Born August 13, 1927; Son of Mr. and Mrs. Carmello Costantino; Married Betty Cook; Father of Sharon, Valerie, Raymond Scott. Education: Graduate of Johnstown High School, New York, 1943; C.L.U. Designation, American College of Certified Life Underwriters, 1970; Graduate, Dale Carnegie Course in Management; Life Underwriters

Certification, Parts I, II, III. Career: Agent 1945, Staff Manager 1948, District Manager 1964, Division Manager 1975, Assistant Vice President 1977, Vice President 1979 to present, Independent Life Insurance. Organizational Memberships: National Association of Life Underwriters (trustee, 1977; vice chairman, committee on field practice; public service committee); Albany Association of Life Underwriters, Georgia (past president); Georgia State Association of Life Underwriters (past president); L.I.M.R.A. Combinational Companies (vice chairman, development committee); Southeastern Training Directors Association (secretary); American Society of Certified Life Underwriters, Jacksonville Chapter; Jacksonville Life Underwriters Association; Jacksonville General Agency Managers Association. Community Activities: Jacksonville Chamber of Commerce, Florida; Doughtery Civitan Club (past president); Albany Toastmasters Club; Albany Masonic Lodge #24; Scottish Rite Lodge, Jacksonville Consistory Morocco Temple of Jacksonville, Florida. Religion: Deacon, First Baptist Church, Jacksonville, Florida. Honors and Awards: George Connor Award for Outstanding Service to Life Insurance Industry, Georgia Association of Life Underwriters, 1973. Address: 4204 San Servera Drive North, Jacksonville, Florida 32217.

Costin, Yvonne Marie Lipira

Account Executive. Personal: Born January 25, 1940, in Buffalo, New York; Daughter of Mary C. Lipira Guidice; Married Theron L. Costin; Mother of Andrea Marie Morsicato, Steven Nunzio Morsicato, Vincent Andrew Morsicato. Education: Studies Business Administration/Accounting, Bryant & Stratton Business Institute, 1959. Career: Worked for various corporations in Buffalo, New York, 1959-66; Manhardt Advertising, Inc., Buffalo, 1967-68; Account Executive/Copy Chief, Finley Greene Advertising Agency, Buffalo, 1969-70; James Curd Advertising, Denver, Colorado, 1972; Media Buyer, Tallent/Yates Advertising, Denver, 1973; Account Executive, "Adcon" Advertising, 1976 to present; Costin & Company, Inc., 1976 to present; Director, S.V.L. Concrete Construction, Inc., 1976-80; Director, Colorado Pain Rehabilitation, Inc., 1980 to present. Organizational Memberships: The Denver and American Advertising Federation, 1976 to present; The Rocky Mountain Motion Picture Association, 1971 to present; American Mensa Society, 1979 to present (Denver Mile High Mensa program chairman 1979-81); Intertel, The International Legion of Intelligence, 1980 to present (steering committee for the 1981 international annual general assembly). Community Activities: Comitis Crisis Center, Inc. (emeritus board); Ladies of Variety, Tent #37 (executive board); Foundation for the Advancement of Talent in Education, Inc., 1981 to present (vice president 1981-82); Delta Theta Tau, Beta Omega Chapter (chapter president 1980-81). Honors and Awards: Listed in *Foremost Women in Communications, Who's Who in the West, Personalities of the West and Midwest, The World Who's Who of Women, Dictionary of International Biography, International Who's Who of Intellectuals, Directory of Distinguished Americans, Book of Honor, Personalities of America.* Address: 3840 S. Helena St., Aurora, Colorado 80013.

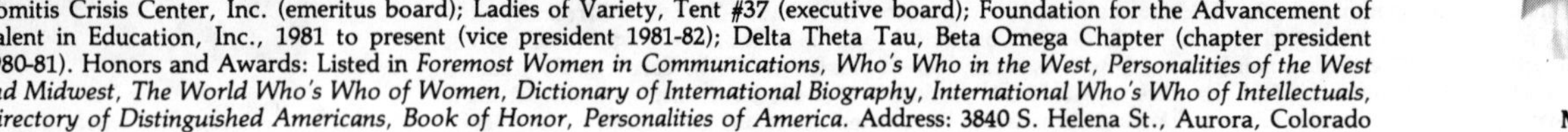

Magdalen Coughlin

Coughlin, Sister Magdalen

College President. Personal: Born April 15, 1930; Daughter of William J. and Cecilia Coughlin. Education: B.A., The College of St. Catherine, St. Paul, Minnesota, 1952; Postgraduate Fulbright Scholar, University of Nijmegen, The Netheralnds, 1952-53; M.A., Mount St. Mary's College, Los Angeles, California, 1962; Ph.D., University of Southern California, 1970. Career: Mount St. Mary's College, Los Angeles, President 1976 to present, Dean for Academic Development 1970-74, Assistant Professor of History 1963-70; Provincial Councilor/Regional Superior, Sisters of St. Joseph of Carondolet, Los Angeles Province, 1974-76; Teacher of History, St. Mary's Academy, San Fernando, 1960-61. Organizational Memberships: California Historical Society; American Historical Society; Fulbright Alumni Association: Community Activities: Council of Presidents of C.S.J. Colleges (chairman, 1980); *Educational Record* (advisory board); Association of Catholic Colleges and Universities (board of directors, 1979 to present; task force on minorities); Association of Independent California Colleges and Universities (executive board, 1979 to present); Carondolet High School (board of directors, 1976-78); Marianne Frostig Center for Educational Therapy (board of trustees, 1976 to present); Independent Colleges of Southern California (board of directors, 1976 to present). Honors and Awards: Haynes Dissertation Fellowship, 1969-70; Teaching Assistant, University of Minnesota, 1953-54; Fulbright Scholarship, University of Nijmegen, The Netherlands, 1952-53; Phi Alpha Theta; Delta Epsilon Sigma; Kappa Gamma Pi; Lambda Iota Tau. Address: 12001 Chalon Road, Los Angeles, California 90049.

Counter, Benjamin Frink

Executive Board. Personal: Born May 16, 1912; Son of B. T. and Marguerite F. Counter (both deceased); Married Marjorie L. Little; Father of Ann Tate, Benjamin T., James Dana, Karna Wells. Education: Attended the New Mexico Military Institute, 1931; B.S., Colorado State University, 1934. Military: Served with the United States Army, achieving the rank of Major, 1941-46. Career: Ft. Lupton Canning Company, Chairman of the Board (1956), President (1976). Organizational Memberships: National Food Processors Association (board of directors); Rocky Mountain Canners Association (past president); Old Guard Society (past president). Community Activities: Ft. Lupton School Board, 1940-41; Weld County (Colorado) Executive Committee, 1956 to present; Weld County Board of Health (president 1952-61); Platte Valley Soil Conservation District Board (secretary 1957-59); Colorado State University (advisory board 1970 to present); Rotary Club (past president); American Legion. Religion: Methodist. Honors and Awards: Ft. Lupton Outstanding Citizen Award, 1981; Bronze Star for Bravery. Address: P. O. Box 208, Ft. Lupton, Colorado 80621.

Naomi Miller Coval

Coval, Naomi Miller

Specialist in Orthodontics. Personal: Born Bayonne, New Jersey; Daughter of Dr. Jacob Paul and Bertha Blumstein Miller; Mother of Payson Rodney, Mark Lawrence, Ilya Sandra. Education: B.A., University of Chicago, 1939; D.D.S., Columbia University, 1943. Career: Lectured all over the World at Local, National and International Congresses, Conventions and Universities, 25 Years; Instructor, New York University Dental School; Editor, *International Journal of Orthodontics*, 1962-65, *Dentistae*, 1948. Organizational Memberships: International Academy of Orthodontics (vice president, secretary); New York Association of Women Dentists (vice president); American Association of Dental Editors, 1963-66; Society of Oral Physiology and Occlusion (fellow); Royal Society of Health (fellow); Long Island Committee for Flouridation of Water (chairperson); Federation Dentaire Internationale; Pan American Medical Association; American Dental Association; First District Dental Society, 1943-59; Tenth District Dental Society; Nassau-Suffolk Academy of Dentistry; American Academy of Oral Medicine; New York Association for the Professions (charter member); American Society for the Study of Orthodontics; Columbia University Dental Alumni Association; National Association of Women Dentists; Federation of American Orthodontists (charter member); Begg Society for Study of Orthodontics; British Society for Study of Orthodontics; New York Infirmary (attending dentist, 1946-51); Peninsula Hospital Center (attending dentist, 1967-); American Society of Preventive Dentistry; New York Academy of Sciences. Community Activities: Five Towns Auxiliary of Peninsula General Hospital (president, 1964); Five Towns American Jewish Congress (president, 1969-71); Lawrence High School Parent Teacher Association (president, 1966); B'nai B'rith Five Towns (vice president); Sisterhood Temple Israel Lawrence (vice president, 1973-75); National Women's Political Caucus (charter member, board member); Pulse of Women (vice president; charter member, 1970); International Platform Association (charter member); American Cancer Society (board member; chairman, art show); United Nations Association of U.S.A.; American Red Cross; American Field Service; Island Concert Hall (patron, sponsor); Wayfarer's Club; Rap Nui Society for Easter Islanders; American Red Mogen-David Society; Wildlife Society of Kenya; Lawrence Association; Union Temple Brooklyn, 1950-59; Temple Israel Lawrence, 1959-; Jane Addam's Hull House, Chicago (volunteer, 1931-34); Girl Scouts (leader, 1950-58); National Geographic Society; Natural History Society; National Council of Jewish Women, 1960-; Hadassah; National Social Directory; American Association for the Advancement of Science; Fellowship of Reconciliation; National Organization of Women; Metropolitan Opera Guild; American Association for the Study of Psychoanalysis (charter member); Jacques Cousteau Society; Intrepids Club; Atrium Club (charter member); Wilderness Society; Common Cause; National Association of Female Executives. Published Works: Articles: "Effect of Thyroid Ablatin on Dentin Apposition of Albino Rats", "Rapid Correction of Crowded Adult Malocclusion via Tooth Recarving", "Dental Report From Antarctica", Others. Honors and Awards: William Jarvie Society for Dental Research, 1942; First Woman Selected to Represent Official Dentistry on Television, 1964; Elected Delegate to Oral Hygiene Committee, 1948-51; First Woman Dentist Invited to Give University Seminars in Soviet Socialist Bloc; Listed in *Who's Who in America, Who's Who of American Women, Who's Who in the East, Who's Who in U.S.A.; Library of Human Resources, American Bicentennial Research Institute, International Who's Who of Community Service, Community Leaders of America, Community Leaders of the World, Two Thousand Women of Achievement, Dictionary of International Biography, National Register of Prominent Americans and International Notables, Directory of Public Affairs, The World Who's Who of Women, Community Leaders and Noteworthy Americans, International Biographical Yearbook, Intercontinental Biographical Association Directory, Notable Americans of the Bicentennial Era, Who's Who in World Jewry.* Address: 30 Westover Place, Lawrence, New York 11559.

CoVan, James Parker

Staff Industrial Hygienist. Personal: Born August 23, 1940; Son of Jack P. CoVan; Married Brenda Sample; Father of Cynthia Faith, Candace Hope, Heather Alisa. Education: Attended the United States Naval Academy, 1958-59; B.S. Chemistry 1962, M.E. Industrial Engineering (System-Safety Engineering, Industrial Hygiene) 1974, Texas A.&M. University. Military: Service in the United States Naval Reserve, 1958 to present, with the rank of Commander. Career: Industrial Hygiene Engineer; Project Engineer; Synthetic Detergent Manufacturing Shift Supervisor; United States Navy, Transport Pilot, Anti-Submarine Pilot; Staff Industrial Hygienist, Tenneco, Inc., Houston; Commanding Officer, Flag Operations, VR24 Component 182, Naval Air Station, New Orleans, Louisiana, 1983 to present. Organizational Memberships: System Safety Society (president, Houston Chapter, 1982 to present; editor, industrial hygiene, 1981 to present); American Industrial Hygiene Association (secretary, Gulf Coast Section, 1982 to present); American Society of Safety Engineers, 1976 to present; American Chemical Society (member, 1962 to present; chairman, safety and health committee, 1976-77). Community Activities: Safety and Health Seminars for High School Chemistry Teachers, Sponsored by the American Chemical Society, 1976; Volunteer Teacher, Review Course on Industrial Hygiene and Safety Engineering, American Society of Safety Engineers, 1979-81. Religion: Ordained Deacon, Southern Baptist Church, 1978 to present; Family Minister, 1979 to present. Honors and Awards: All-Ohio Boys Band, 1955; National Honorary Society, 1957; John Philip Sousa Award, 1958; Dean's List, 1962; Alpha Pi Mu Honorary Society, 1974; Comprehensive Certification, 1978; B.C.S.P. Comprehensive Certificate, 1979. Address: 15319 Torry Pines, Houston, Texas 77062.

Covin, Theron Michael

Psychologist. Personal: Born February 27, 1947; Son of Doris S. Knight; Married Charlotte. Career: University Professor; Social Worker; School Psychologist; Mental Health Counselor; Mental Health Project Director; Author; Editor; Researcher; Psychologist. Organizational Memberships: Kappa Delta Pi; American Association of University Professors; American Personnel and Guidance Association; N.A.S.P. Address: Route 3, Box 217, Abbeville, Alabama 36310.

Coward, Raymond

Attorney, Educator, Writer, Lecturer, Poet. Personal: Born February 10, 1909, in Searcy, Arkansas; Son of Emmett Timothy and Mary Alice Gentry Coward (both deceased); Father of Raymond Lynn, Janet Anne. Education: B.A., Coe College, Cedar Rapids, Iowa, 1933; J.D., University of Iowa, 1935; Postgraduate Study, International Law and Relations, University of Michigan, 1943, University of Vienna, Austria 1946; M.B.A., University of Alabama, 1966; Graduate, Federal Bureau of Investigation Academy, Quantico, Virginia, 1941; Graduate, Numerous Army Service Schools, including The Cavalry School, Fort Riley, Kansas, Command Management School, Command and General Staff College, Fort Leavenworth, Kansas, 1949. Military: Served in the United States Army Cavalry, 2nd Lieutenant to Colonel, Judge Advocate General's Corps, United States Army, Active Duty, 1943-63; World War II, Captain, Cavalry, Entered Normandy, France with General George S. Patton's Third United States Army, until End of War; Chief Legal Officer, American Sector, Vienna, Worked with British, French, Russians, Military Government of Austria, 1½ Years; Legal Advisor to Military Governor, Germany in Berlin, Worked with Three Powers; Four Years in Europe; Chief, Procurement Law Division, United States Army Forces, Far East, Two Years; Three Tours Duty, Pentagon, Washington, D.C., Counsel for Witnesses, Department of Defense, Appearances before Congressional Committees, General Counsel to the Surgeon General of the Army, Three Years, Member, Board of Review, Department of the Army, 1958-59; Voluntary Retirement as Colonel, JAG Corps, United States Army, 1963. Career: Admitted Iowa Bar, 1935, D.C. Bar 1956, Bar of United States Supreme Court, 1948; Law Practice, State, Federal Courts, Cedar Rapids, Iowa, 1935-41; Special Agent, Federal Bureau of Investigation, 1941-43; Teacher, Business Law, Louisiana State University, Baton Rouge 1963-65, University of Alabama, Tuscaloosa 1965-66, University of Texas, Arlington 1966-67; Teacher, Political Science, Economics, Texas Wesleyan College, Fort Worth, 1968-69; Weekly Columnist, National International Affairs, Editorial Page, Fort Worth *Star-Telegram*, Two Years; Teacher, International Law, University of Texas, Arlington, 1979 to present. Organizational Memberships: American Bar Association (section of international law; advisory committee to the standing committee on law and national security, formerly committee on education about communism). Honors and Awards: Combat Infantryman's Badge; Bronze Star; Purple Heart; Five Battle Stars; Various Other Military Medals and Awards; Freedoms Foundation at Valley Forge, Pennsylvania Award, 1973, 1974; American Bar Association Merit Award, 1974; Gold, Three-Gallon Donor's Pin, Blood Donations, American Red Cross; Listed in *Who's Who in the South and Southwest, Dictionary of International Biography, Men of Achievement, Who's Who in American Law.* Address: 1022 South Cooper, Suite 202, Arlington, Texas 76013.

Cowen, Donald Eugene

Physician, Allergist. Personal: Born October 8, 1918, in Fort Morgan, Colorado; Son of Frank and Edith Cowen; Married Hulda

Helling, December 24, 1942; Father of David L., Marilyn Marie, Theresa Kathleen, Margaret Ann. Education: Graduate of Senior High School, Fort Morgan, Colorado; B.A., University of Denver, 1940; M.D., University of Colorado School of Medicine, 1943; General Rotating Internship, United States Naval Hospital, Oakland, California, 1944; Residency, Internal Medicine, University of Colorado Medical Center, 1952-54. Military: Served in the United States Navy Medical Corps, 1944-47, attaining the rank of Lieutenant. Career: Family Practice, Fort Morgan, Colorado, 1947-52; Private Practice, Allergic Diseases, 1954 to present; Clinical Assistant Professor of Medicine, University of Colorado Medical Center, Denver; Faculty, Postgradaute Course, Fundamentals of Otolaryngologic Allergy, University of Tennessee College of Medicine, Department of Continuing Education, 1960 to present; Instructor, American Academy of Otolaryngologic Allergy Post-graduate Courses; Accredited Staff, Porter-Swedish Medical Center, Englewood, Colorado, Presbyterian Medical Center, Denver; Courtesy Staff, Children's Hospital and St. Joseph's Hospital, Denver. Organizational Memberships: American College of Physicians (fellow); American College of Chest Physicians (fellow; vice chairman, steering committee on allergy, 1968-72, 1976-77; member 1959 to present, secretary 1975-77, committee on allergy; secretary/treasurer 1971-77, president 1978-79, Colorado Chapter); American College of Allergists (fellow; committee on Ophtho-otolaryngology, 1964-74); American Association for Clinical Immunology and Allergy (fellow); Academy International of Medicine (fellow); West Coast Allergy Society (fellow); American Academy Otolaryngologic Allergy (fellow; council member, 1980-83; appointment, assistant to president, 1981-82); Rocky Mountain Allergy Society (past president); Denver Medical Society (chairman, library and building committee, 1963-73); American Society of Internal Medicine; Colorado Society of Internal Medicine; American Thoracic Society; Southwest Allergy Forum; Colorado Allergy Society; Illinois Society of Ophthalmology and Otolaryngology (honorary member). Community Activities: Community Arts Symphony Foundation (patron; honorary board member; president, 1980-82); Lions International (key member, past director, Denver Club; board of directors, Englewood Club); Community Classic Chorale of Denver (past director; patron). Religion: President, Board of Trustees, First Presbyterian Church, Fort Morgan, Colorado; Vice President of Board of Deacons, President of Chancel Choir, Chairman of Worship Service Committee, Central Presbyterian Church; Committee on Church Extension, Denver Presbytery. Published Works: Numerous Articles for Professional Journals, including "Serial Dilution Titration, Technique and Application", "Physiology and Symptomatology of Allergy", and "Clinical Symptomatology of the Allergic Response"; Two Chapters in *Otolaryngologic Allergy*. Honors and Awards: Consultant to Her Royal Majesty, The Queen of Thailand, 1973, 1975, 1979; Listed in *Who's Who in Colorado*, *Who's Who in the West*, *Who's Who in America*, *Dictionary of International Biography*, *Men of Achievement*, *Personalities of the West*. Address: 1501 East Quincy Avenue, Englewood, Colorado 80110.

Norman J Cowen

Cowen, Norman Jay

Physician, Hand Surgeon. Personal: Born June 7, 1934; Son of Everett and Rose Cowen; Married Sheila Israel; Father of Benjamin Ring, Rosemary. Education: A.B. summa cum laude, Brown University, 1956; M.D., University of Pennsylvania, 1960; Intern, Delaware Hospital, Wilmington 1960, Episcopal Hospital, Philadelphia 1961; Resident in Orthopaedics, Philadelphia Naval Hospital 1963-64, Philadelphia General Hospital 1965-68; Fellow in Hand Surgery, Thomas Jefferson Medical Center, 1967; Annie C. Kane Fellow in Hand Surgery, Columbia Presbyterian Hospital, New York City, 1968-69. Military: Served in the United States Navy, 1961-65, attaining the rank of Lieutenant. Career: Medical Practice, Specializing in Birth Defects, Washington, D.C. 1971 to present, McLean (Virginia) 1972-81, Fairfax (Virginia) 1981 to present, Bowie (Maryland) 1981 to present, Pawtucket (Rhode Island), Fall River and New Bedford (Massachusetts) 1969-71; Director, Hand Service, Georgetown University Hospital, 1972-78; Head, Hand Clinic, Arlington Hospital, Virginia, 1973-76; Lecturer in Hand Surgery, Massachusetts General Hospital, Chelsea Naval Hospital, 1969-71; Assistant Clinical Professor of Orthopaedics, George Washington University, 1972-73; Clinical Instructor in Orthopaedic Surgery, Georgetown University, 1972-78; Consultant, Hand Clinic, Truesdale Hospital, Fall River, Massachusetts 1971-77, National Upper Extremity Rehabilitation Clinic 1973 to present, Veterans Hospital, Providence, Rhode Island 1969-71; Guest Consultant, Hand Surgery, Tel Hashomer Medical Center, Tel Aviv, Israel, 1975 to present; Program Chairman, Annual Washington Hand Symposium, 1973 to present; Staff Member, Capitol Hill Hospital, Children's Hospital/National Medical Center, Commonwealth Doctor's Hospital, Alexandria Hospital, Prince George's Doctor's Hospital, Prince George's General Hospital, Many Others. Organizational Memberships: National Hand Research and Rehabilitation Fund, Inc., Washington, D.C. (president, chairman of the board, 1973 to present); American Board of Orthopaedic Surgery (diplomate, 1971); American College of Surgeons (fellow); American Association for Hand Surgery (chairman, ad hoc committee, resident training, 1979); Robert E. Carroll Hand Club; Jefferson Hand Club; Washington Medical Society; Virginia Medical Society; Arlington County Medical Society; Fairfax County Medical Society; Prince George's County Medical Society; Bowie Medical Society; Washington Orthopaedic Club; Virginia Orthopaedic Club. Community Activities: Brown University Club; Phi Beta Kappa Club of Washington, D.C.; Arlington Tennis and Squash Club. Published Works: Author/Contributor, Articles for Professional Periodicals; Editor, *Practical Hand Surgery*. Address: 704A Street, Southeast, Washington, D.C. 20003.

Eric Cox

Cox, Eric Frederick

National Field Director, Legislative Director. Personal: Born July 20, 1932, in Baltimore, Maryland; Son of C. R. and Elvira Cox. Education: Graduate of Eastern High School, 1950; B.A., Dickinson College, Carlisle, Pennsylvania, 1954; Graduate Work in Economics and Sociology. Military: Served in the United States Army, 1954-56. Career: Real Estate Salesman, Broker in Family Real Estate Business, Washington, D.C.; Community Organizer, Washington, D.C.; Radio Broadcaster for American Veterans Committee on District of Columbia Station WOOK and Weekly Radio Programs on Educational Radio WAMU-FM, Washington, D.C. ("Issues and Ideas" and "Eric Cox Interviews"); Free-lance Lecturer at Colleges; Teacher, Graduate School, United States Department of Agriculture, Free University of Georgetown University and the New School for Social Research in New York; College Administrator, Bronx Community College; Political Activist; Consultant in Politics and Community Development; Currently National Field Director for the World Federalists Association and Legislative Director for Campaign for United Nations Reform. Organizational Memberships: International Platform Association (publicity chairman, one year); Sierra Club; National Peace Academy (former national board member); Metropolitan Athletic Association (co-founder and past president); D.C. Citizens for Clear Air (co-founder). Community Activities: Founder of Local Committee for Self-Government for Washington, D.C.; D.C. Commissioners Crime Council; Washington, D.C. Jaycees (committee chairman); Dickinson College Alumni Club (past president); Organizer of Many Recreational, Athletic and Educational Programs for Inner-city Youth in Washington, D.C., made possible by Volunteers and Foundation Grants; Officer of D.C. Young Democrats, 3 years; International Affairs Committee of Young Democrats (national chairman); Democratic Precinct Chairman for Washington, D.C.; Atlantic Association of Young Political Leaders (advisory committee); Volunteer Worker in Five Presidential Campaigns; Occasional Speech Writer for Presidential Candidates; Presidential Inaugural Committees, 1961, 1965; New York City Voluntary Action Council under Mayor Lindsay, 1972; Testified Three Times before Committees of United States Senate on Poverty 1965, Foreign Relations 1965 and 1966; Speaker at State Caucuses at G.O.P. National Conventions in Kansas City and Detroit and before State Caucuses of Democractic Conventions in New York City. Religion: Unitarian; Past President, Young Adult Organization of All Souls Unitarian Church, Washington D.C.; Participant in National General Assemblies of Unitarian-Universalist Church. Published Works: Author, *5D.C. Jaycee Report on Juvenile Delinquency in the Nations Captial;* Over 30 Other Publications, including Op-Ed Pieces in Major Newspapers and Articles in *The*

Educational Record, The Colorado Quarterly, The Churchman, Journal of the American Red Cross, and Numerous Letters to the Editor in Major Papers and Magazines. Honors and Awards: National Honor Society; Five Hundred Dollar Award, National Jaycees, for Study on Delinquency which he Authored for D.C. Jaycees; Special Citation, D.C. Chapter, Recreation Society, 1964; Certificate of Achievement from Commanding General, Fort Jackson, South Carolina, 1954; Various Civic Awards in Washington, D.C.; Listings in Various Reference Directories, including the *Encyclopedia of Meeting and Convention Speakers*. Address: 3133 Connecticut Avenue, N.W., Washington, D.C. 20008.

Cox, Hollis Utah

Veterinarian, Educator. Personal: Born March 4, 1944; Son of Hollis and Molinda Cox; Married Debra Campbell; Father of Lindy Belle, Hollis Utah Jr., Matthew Christopher, Lauren Dawn. Education: B.S. 1965, D.V.M. 1967, Oklahoma State University; Ph.D., Louisiana State University, 1973. Military: Served in the United States Air Force from 1967-69 in Panama and Vietnam, attaining the rank of Captain. Career: Veterinarian, present; Professor of Bacteriology, present; Private Practice, Veterinary Medicine, Choctaw, Oklahoma, 1969-70; Educator, 1970 to present. Organizational Memberships: Baton Rouge Area Veterinary Medical Association (president, 1980; vice president, 1979; secretary-treasurer, 1977-78); American Association of Veterinary Medical Colleges (delegate, council of educators, 1976-82). Community Activities: Louisiana State University (chief, clinical diagnostic section, veterinary teaching hospital, 1980 to present; faculty senate committee on committees, 1980-83; faculty senator, 1978-80; curriculum committee, 1979 to present; admissions committee, 1975-79; chairman, faculty council, 1976-77); Louisiana State Science Fair (judge, 1980, 1981); United Way (section chairman, veterinarians, 1978 campaign). Religion: Trinity Episcopal Church, Baton Rouge, Louisiana. Honors and Awards: N.D.E.A. Postdoctorial Research Fellow, 1972-73; Phi Eta Sigma, 1962; Alpha Psi, 1964; Diplomate, American College of Veterinary Microbiologists, 1974; Sigma Xi (member, 1973; research award, 1974); Phi Zeta, 1979; Phi Kappa Phi, 1981; Pitman-Moore Research Award, 1966; Specialist in Microbiology, American Academy of Microbiology 1976, American Society of Clinical Pathology 1978. Address: 2925 Valcour Aime Avenue, Baton Rouge, Louisiana 70808.

Cox, Irene Dickson

Educator (retired). Personal: Born October 12, 1917; Daughter of John and Ruby Thompson Dickson; Married George Dewey Cox; Mother of Bill Dickey, Nathalia Sue Cox Strong. Education: Graduate of Virginia-Carolina High School, 1934; B.S., Appalachian State University, 1938; Certificate in Special Education, Radford Teachers College, Virginia, 1973. Career: Teacher, English and French, Lansing High School, North Carolina, 1938-39; Teacher, Mountain Park Elementary School, 1939-40; Virginia-Carolina High School, Grassy Creek, North Carolina, English Teacher 1940-60, Girls Varsity Basketball Coach 1940-57, Organizer, *Eagle-Lite* Annual 1950, Organizer, *Highlights* Newspaper 1950; Ashe Central High School, Jefferson, North Carolina, English Teacher 1961-67, Organizer, *Hilltopper* Newspaper 1961; Special Education Teacher, Mount Rogers High School, Whitetop, Virginia, 1971-76. Organizational Memberships: Retired School Teachers Association, Ashe County, 1980. Community Activities: Girl Scouts (sponsor, intermediate troop, 1945-50); Registrar, Grassy Creek Precinct, 1967-81; North Carolina Extension Homemakers Association (member, 1945-78; president, 1945-49, 1968-71; citizenship chairman, 1978; chairman, district program of work, 1978-79; publicity chairman, 1978-80); Grassy Creek Club (president, 1979-80); Virginia-Carolina Community, Inc. (one of ten initial directors, organizer, president, 1970-74); Daughters of the American Revolution (member, 1970 to present; national defense chairman, 1970-76); United Daughters of the Confederacy (charter member, 1974 to present; vice president, 1974-76; president, 1976-77; education committee, North Carolina division, 1977-80; 3 supplemental (collateral) lines, 1977; chairman, awards committee, Ashe County, 1978-81; director, North Carolina division, district III, 1980-82); Grassy Creek Community Watch (organizer; chairman, 1981-82); Ashe County Friends of Library, Jefferson, North Carolina (president, 1979-80). Religion: Grassy Creek Baptist Church (member, 1941-81; church clerk, 1943-50; former young people's teacher). Honors and Awards: Certificate of Appreciation for Sponsoring Local Chapter for Nineteen Years, National Beta Club, Spartanburg, South Carolina, 1966; Scholarship, Appalachian State University, Boone, North Carolina, 1972; Scholarship, Radford Teachers College, Virginia, 1973; Ashe County Homemaker of the Year, 1980; Listed in *Who's Who in Child Development Professionals, Personalities of the South, World Who's Who of Women, Who's Who in the South and Southwest, Dictionary of International Biography, Personalities of America, International Who's Who of Intellectuals*. Address: Route 1, Box 81, Grassy Creek, North Carolina, 28631.

Irene Cox

Cox, Joseph Mason Andrew

Poet, Writer, Lecturer, Television Producer. Personal: Son of Hiram and Edith Henderson Cox (both deceased); Father of Egypt Hosanna. Education: B.A. 1951, LL.B. Law School 1954, Columbia University; Ph.D. Art Psychology, China Art College, World University, Hong Kong, 1972. Career: Poet, Writer, Lecturer, present; Television Producer, *Focus on Thought Profound*, Sponsored by Community Crime Protection Agency, New York, 1979-81; Consultant on Security, International Bureau of Protection and Investigation, New York, 1977-79; Professor, Department of English, City University of New York, 1973-77; Consultant on Education, New York City Board of Education, 1971-73; Law Clerk, Pomerantz, Levy, Schreiber, Haubek, New York. Organizational Memberships: Columbia University (president, The Writers Guild, 1951); Poetry Society of America (executive board, 1974-76); Authors League of America, 1969 to present; Academy of American Poets; International Academy of Poets, England, 1978 to present; United Poet Laureate International, 1976 to present. Community Activities: Manhood Foundation, Inc. (executive board, 1977-78); Prince Hall Masonic Order (F.A.M.) (historian, 1980 to present). Religion: Unitarian, Universalist (chairman, speaker's bureau, 1974-76). Published Works: *Land Dimly Seen; Bouquet of Poems; Collected Poetry; Profound Fantasy and Reality Remembered; Ode to Dr. Martin Luther King*, Drama in Three Acts; *New and Selected Poems (1966-78); Great Black Men of Masonry*. Honors and Awards: Nominee, Pulitzer Prize in Letters for *Great Black Men of Masonry*, 1982; First Prize, Daniel S. Mead International Writers Contest, 1969; Fourth Prize, World Poetry Contest, Cambridge, England, 1970; United States Representative, World Poetry Conference, Expo 67, Montreal, Canada, 1967; Gold Medal, International Poets Shrine; Gold Medal, United Poet Laureate International, 1976. Address: Tilden Towers II, 801 Tilden Street, Bronx, New York 10467.

Cox, Mary E

Educator, Administrator. Personal: Born November 11, 1937; Married Kendall B. Cox; Mother of Kendall M. Education: A.B. Physics, Mathematics, Philosophy, Albion College, 1959; M.A. Physics, University of Michigan, 1961; National Science Foundation Summer Institutes, Apparatus in Physics Teaching, Lake Forest College 1966, Coherent Optics, Institute of Optics, University of Rochester 1971; P.S.I. Summer Workshop, McAlister College, 1975; Institute for Administrative Advancement, University of Wisconsin-Madison, 1980. Career: University of Michigan-Flint, College of Arts and Sciences, Acting Dean 1981 to present, Associate Dean 1980-81, Acting Associate Dean for Curriculum and Program Development 1980, College of Arts and Sciences; University of Michigan-Flint, Associate Professor of Physics 1976 to present, Chairman, Department of Physics and Astronomy

1976-77; University of Oxford, Tutor in Physics, Sommerville College 1977-78, Demonstrator, Clarendon Laboratory 1977-78; University of Michigan-Flint, Acting Director, Computing Center 1972-73, Assistant Professor of Physics 1971-76, Acting Director of Institutional Research, 1971-73, Instructor in Physics 1966-71; Lecturer, Instructor in Physics, University of North Dakota-Grand Forks, 1962-66; Tutor, Lab Instructor, University of Michigan-Ann Arbor, 1960-62. Organizational Memberships: American Association of Physics Teachers (referee, *American Journal of Physics*, Michigan section, executive council 1974-75, president 1973-74, program chairman 1972-73); Optical Society of America; Society of Photo-Optical Instrumentation Engineers. Community Activities: University of Michigan-Flint (C.A.S. executive committee, 1979-80; C.A.S. nominating committee, member 1979, chairman 1976-77; science building subcommittee, 1976-77; chancellor's advisory committee, 1974-76; computer study group, 1973-75; chairman, executive committee; chair, college of arts and sciences monthly faculty meetings). Published Works: Numerous Articles in Professional Journals, including "Holographic Study of Bubble Dissolution in Human Plasma" with R. G. Buckles, M. E. Cox and J. B. Eckenhoff, "The Lens-Pinhole Spatial Filter", "Image Plane Holograms for Introductory Physics Students"; Numerous Book Reviews; Numerous Papers Presented at Professional Meetings and Conferences. Honors and Awards: Presidor, Holography Session, Optical Society of America Spring Meeting, 1974; Presidor, Holographic Microscopy Session, Gordon Conference on Coherent Optics and Holography; University of Michigan Faculty Research Grants, 1979, 1978, 1976, 1974; National Institutes of Health Research Grants, 1977, 1976; National Institutes of Health Biomedical Research Support Grants Funded from N.I.H. Biomedical Parent Account to Vice President for Research, University of Michigan-Flint, 1978, 1977; Office of Naval Research Grants, 1970, 1969; National Science Foundation Science Faculty Professional Development Grant, 1977-78; Listed in *Who's Who of American Women, World Who's Who of Women, World Who's Who of Women in Education, Dictionary of International Biography, Personalities of America, International Who's Who in Community Service, Community Leaders and Noteworthy Americans.* Address: University of Michigan-Flint, Flint, Michigan 48503.

Crafton-Masterson, Adrienne Leona Ann

Executive, Real Estate Broker. Personal: Born March 6, 1926, in Providence, Rhode Island; Daughter of John Harold and Adrienne Fitzgerald Crafton; Mother of Mary Victoria, Kathleen Joan, John Andrew, Barbara Lynn. Education: Graduate of Saint Xavier's Academy; Courses Leading to Real Estate Licensing, 1962; College Courses, Philosophy, Anthropology, English, 1971 to present; Studies, Dramatic Soprano Singing. Career: Assistant Secretary, United States Senator Theodore Francis Green of Rhode Island, 1944; Staff Member, United States Senate Committee on Campaign Expenditures, 1944-45; Assistant Clerk, House Government Operations Committee, 1944-45; Clerk, House Campaign Expenditures Committee under Chairmanship of Congressman Mike Mansfield of Montana, 1950; Assistant Appointment Secretary under Harry S Truman and Dwight D. Eisenhower, 1951-53; Staff Member under Senator Theodore Francis Green of Rhode Island (then Chairman, Senate Foreign Relations Committee), 1954-60; Licensed Real Estate Broker, 1968; Establisher, Adrienne C. Masterson Real Estate, Alexandria, Virginia, 1968; Owner/Manager, Adrienne Investment Real Estate, Alexandria, Virginia, present. Organizational Memberships: International Investment & Business Exchange, London; National Association of Realtors; Virginia Association of Realtors; Northern Virginia Board of Realtors (chairman, commercial & industrial committee); National Association of Industrial & Office Parks; American Society of Professional & Executive Women; National Association of Female Executives; Alexandria Chamber of Commerce. Community Activities: Kennedy Center (founding member); National Historical Society; National Trust for Historic Preservation; Dramatic Soprano Singer. Address: P.O. Box 1271, Alexandria, Virginia 22313.

Craig, Robert John

Associate Professor. Personal: Born July 6, 1943; Son of Mr. and Mrs. Robert H. Craig. Education: Graduate, Noblesville High School, 1961; B.S.C.E. 1966, M.S.C.E. 1969, Ph.D. 1973, all from Purdue University. Career: Assistant Professor, Pennsylvania State Capitol Campus, Harrisburg, 1972-75; Associate Professor, Civil and Environmental Engineering Department, New Jersey Institute of Technology. Organizational Memberships: American Concrete Institute (committee E-801, chairman 1979 to present; committee 444, bibliography subcommittee, 1975 to present; committee 544, 1979 to present; New Jersey chapter, education committee, 1979 to present); American Society of Civil Engineers (North Jersey branch: history and heritage committee, chairman, 1977-80; student affairs committee, chairman, 1976-80; programs committee, chairman, 1979-80; vice president, 1979-80; president, 1980-81; New Jersey section: associate member, director, 1978-80; student committee, chairman, 1977 to present; board member, 1978 to present; secretary, 1981-83; national: student services committee, 1981-84); Sigma Xi (N.J.I.T. chapter, secretary, 1977-79; N.J.I.T. chapter president, 1979-83); Society for Experimental Stress Analysis (paper review committee, 1975 to present); American Society for Engineering Education (dow award committee, 1978-80); Omicron Delta Kappa (member, 1978 to present; faculty secretary, 1981-86); Tau Beta Pi (member, 1978 to present; faculty advisor, 1981 to present); New Jersey Society for Professional Engineers, 1981 to present; American Society for Testing Materials. Community Activities: Boy Scouts of America (cub, boy and explorer, 1951-61; assistant scoutmaster, 1961-72 & 1975-78; summer camp counselor, 1957-64; explorers advisor, 1967-69; merit badge counselor, 1978 to present). Religion: Catholic; Newman Center-Catholic Campus Ministry, 1978 to present. Honors and Awards: Boy Scout of America: Eagle Scout, Ad Altare Dei, St. George Award, Scouter's Key; Outstanding Young Faculty, Mid-Atlantic Region, Dow Award, A.S.E.E., 1978; James M. Robbins Award, Civil Engineering Department, New Jersey Institute of Technology, 1978; Listed in *Who's Who in the East.* Address: 128 Newark Avenue, Apt. 3, Belleville, New Jersey 07109.

Cralley, Elza M

Artist. Personal: Born November 20, 1905; Son of John W. and Martha Jones Cralley (both deceased); Married Cleda Ann Renner; Father of Barbara Ann Shaw, Patricia Sue Duncan. Education: B.S., McKendree College, Lebanon, Illinois, 1928; Ph.D., University of Wisconsin, 1931. Career: University of Arkansas, Instructor, Assistant Professor, Associate Professor, Professor, Department of Plant Pathology, 1931-46, 1948-52, 1953-72, Head of Department, 1953-59, Emeritus Professor 1973 to present; Director, Agricultural Experiment Station, 1959-72; Pathologist, United States Military Government, Korea, 1947; Point 4 Program, Panama, 1952; Consultant Pathologist, Cuba, 1955; Ford Foundation, India, 1959; Exhibited Landscapes in Local and Regional Shows, 1973 to present; Represented in Private and Government Collections. Community Activities: Arkansas State Plant Board, 1953-59; Rotary Club. Religion: Episcopalian. Published Works: Continuosly Contributed Articles to Scientific Journals. Honors and Awards: Arkansas Man of the Year, Progressive Farmer, 1970; Gamma Sigma Delta (Alpha Zeta); Distinguished Service Award, Rice Technical Working Group, 1972; Recognition for 42 Years of Service to Arkansas Agriculture, Arkansas Agricultural Pesticide Association, Arkansas Plant Food Education Society, 1973; Honorary Member, Arkansas Seed Dealers Association, 1973; Recognition for Distinguished Service to Arkansas Agriculture and the Food Industry, Ozark Canners and Freezers Association, 1973. Address: 1502 Cedar Street, Fayetteville, Arkansas 72701.

Crandall, Ira Carlton

Professional Engineer, Entrepreneur. Personal: Born October 30, 1931, in South Amboy, New Jersey; Son of Carlton Francis

Crandall and Claire Elizabeth Harned; Married Jane Leigh Ford, January 1, 1954; Father of Elizabeth Anne, Amy Leigh, Matthew Garrett. Education: Graduate of South River High School, New Jersey, 1949; B.S. Radio Engineering 1954, B.S. Electrical Engineering 1958, Indiana Institute of Technology; B.S. Engineering Electronics, United States Naval; Postgraduate School, 1962; Ph.D., University of Sussex, 1964; M.A., Piedmont University, 1967; Bachelor of Law, Blackstone School of Law, 1970; Associate of Business Administration, La Salle University, 1975. Military: Served in the United States Naval Reserve, 1949-53; Re-Enlisted, Commissioned Ensign 1955, Retiring in 1972 with the rank of Lieutenant Commander. Career: Elementary School Teacher, 1954-55; Naval Officer, Technical and Engineering Duties, 1955-72; President, 7C-s Enterprises, 1972 to present; Vice President, Dickinson Enterprises, 1973-76; Executive Vice President and Chief of Engineering, Williamson Engineering, Inc., 1972-82; Engineering Consultant, President and Board Chairman, I. C. Crandall and Associates, Inc.; Professional Engineer, N.C.E.E., North Carolina, Florida; Energy Manager, A.E.E., Professional Electrical Engineer, Professional Control Systems Engineer, Certified Energy Auditor, California; Professional Electrical Engineer, Oregon, Nevada. Organizational Memberships: American College of Engineers (fellow); American Institute of Technical Management (senior member); Association of Energy Engineers (charter member); Institute of Electrical and Electronics Engineers; Society of American Military Engineers; United States Naval Institute; Association of Naval Aviation; American Biographical Research Association. Community Activities: Optimist Club (past charter president); Century Club; Boy Scouts of America; Neptune Society; Concord Parade and Field Association; Concord Blue Devils (past vice president); Concord Chamber Singers; Young Men's Christian Association (youth group organizer); Parent-Teacher Association (past president); Diablo Valley Band Review Association; Mount Diablo Unified Schools Interested Citizens (past president); Concord Homeowners' Association; Clayton Valley Music Boosters (past president; board member); Pine Hollow Band Aides (board member); Optimist International; International Platform Association; Sons of the American Revolution; Reserve Officers' Association; Republican Party (member; business advisory council, national republican congressional committee). Religion: United Methodist Church (board member; past president, choir). Published Works: Articles on Engineering Management, *Journal of the American Institute of Technical Management*; Articles on Control Systems and Electronics, *Journal of the American College of Engineers*. Honors and Awards: Pioneered Use of Solid-State Electronics in Industrial Process Control Sysytems; Assisted in Development of Radar Systems for Ground Control of Aircraft Traffic; Responsible for Research, Development and Design of First Fully Engineered Two-Way Cable Television System in the United States; Military Decorations, Navy Unit Citation, Navy Expeditionary Medal, National Defense Service Medal, Armed Forces Expeditionary Medal, Vietnam Service Medal, Vietnam Campaign Medal, Vietnam Cross of Valor, Armed Forces Reserve Medal, Expert Rifle Shot Medal, Expert Pistol Shot Medal; Fellowships, International Biographical Association 1979; American Biographical Institute 1978; American College of Engineers 1975, University of Sussex 1964; Honorary Degrees, D.S.Sc. Piedmont University 1968, D.Litt. Saint Matthew University 1970, Ed.D. Mount Sinai University 1970; Pi Upsilon Eta, 1967 to present; Gamma Chi Epsilon, 1970 to present; Sons of the American Revolution, War Service Medal 1972, Silver Good Citizenship Medal 1975; Presidential Citation, Optimist International, 1976; Zero Defects Award, Navy Department, 1970; Listed in *Men of Achievement, International Who's Who of Intellectuals, Book of Honor, International Biographical Association Yearbook, Men and Women of Distinction, Dictionary of International Biography, Personalities of America, International Who's Who in Community Service, Community Leaders and Noteworthy Americans, Personalities of the West and Midwest, Notable Americans, Who's Who in the West, Who's Who in the United States, Who's Who in North America, Hereditary Register of the United States of America, National Social Directory, Who's Who in California, American Scientific Registry, Who's Who in California Business and Finance, American Patriots of the 1980's, Directory of Distinguished Americans, Who's Who in Technology Today, Industry's Directory of Technical Consultants, International Register of Profiles, People Who Matter, Ernest Kay's Personal Hall of Fame*. Address: 5754 Pepperridge Place, Concord, California 94521.

Crawford, James Franklin

Director, Industrial Relations Institute, Educator. Personal: Married Miriam Crawford. Education: A.B., Peru College, 1941; M.A. Economics, University of Colorado, 1952; Ph.D. Economics, University of Wisconsin, 1957. Military: Served in the United States Navy and Naval Reserve from 1942-46, attaining the ranks of Mus. 2/C and Lieutenant Junior Grade, Gunnery. Career: Director, Institute of Industrial Relations (present); Georgia State University, Chairman, Department of Economics 1962-80, Professor of Economics 1960 to present, Associate Professor of Economics 1958-60, Assistant Professor of Economics 1956-58; University of Wisconsin, Program Director, United States State Department Program for German Industrial Relations Trainees 1955-56, Instructor in Economics 1955-56; Dissertation Supervisor; Course Developer; Reviewer for Publishers and Journals. Organizational Memberships: American Arbitration Association (member, community disputes panel, 1970 to present); Office of Emergency Planning (member, region 3 economic stabilization committee, 1970 to present); Georgia Council on Economic Education (member, board of trustees, 1972 to present); Governor's Joint Full Employment in Georgia Study Committee (member, 1976-77; chairman, subcommittee on economic development for Georgia; 1976-77); Industrial Relations Research Association (president, Atlanta chapter, 1978 to present; member, nominations committee, 1980-81; local arrangements chairman for 1979 national meetings); National Association of Business Economists (Atlanta economics club, local affiliate, president 1976-77, panel moderator, financial problems of the cities 1975, nominations committee 1978-1979; vice president, program chairman, 1975-76; moderator, seminar, 1974; secretary, liaison with national organization, 1974-75; member, executive committee, present; general chairman, national seminar, 1977); Southern Economic Association (local arrangements chairman for 1970 annual meetings); Society of Federal Labor Relations Professionals; American Economic Association. Community Activities: Presentations at 40 Economic Education Workshops; Atlanta Chamber of Commerce (task force on unemployment, 1978); Administrative Management Society (presentation, Atlanta chapter, 1974); Organized Labor and Workmen's Circle (presentation, 1974); International Alliance of Postal and Federal Employees (presentation, training conference, 1974); National Alliance of Postal and Federal Employees (presentation, labor education conference, 1972); Equitable Life Assurance Society Economic Seminar (panel member, 1967); Atlanta Mailers Union Annual Seminar (presentation, 1967); Southern Bell Telephone and Telegraph Company (presentation, seminar, economics of public utilities, 1961; presentation, meeting of chief operators, 1957); Leadership Atlanta (panelist, seminar, urban employment, 1970); Georgia State University (moderator, quarterly forecasting conference, economic forecasting project 1974, seminar 1974, seminar 1975, conference on public sector labor relations 1978); Conference on Occupational Safety and Health (presentation, 1977); Life Insurers Conference Seminar (presentation, 1976); National Bank Examiner Trainees Seminar (presentation, 1966); Atlanta Society of Residential Appraisers (presentation, 1961); Georgia Executive Management Seminar (presentation, 1965); University of Georgia (committee on human research, 1974-78; interdepartmental committee on industrial and labor relations, 1974-78; faculty study coordinating committee, 1975-76; ad hoc dean's committee on revision of the business school statutes and bylaws, 1975; search committee for director of industrial relations center, 1976-78; university center in Georgia advisory council, 1976 to present; gerontology center faculty bylaws committee, 1978-79; search committee for director of labor education studies program, 1978; urban life faculty, 1970 to present; speaker's bureau; task force for industrial relations and labor studies cooperative endeavors, 1980 to present; curriculum committee 1970 to present, executive committee 1979 to present, academic procedures committee, 1979; search committee for dean, 1968). Religion: Central Congregational Church of Atlanta (presentation, 1974). Published Works: Interviews, *Newsweek* Magazine 1974, *The Oslo Aften Posten* 1975, *Atlanta Journal-Constitution* 1976, *Atlanta Journal* 1976; *Readings in Modern Economics; Principles of Economics;* Co-Author, *Automation and Technical Change;* Book Review; Numerous Articles Published in Professional and Other Journals including, "Productivity and Collective Bargaining", "Why So Much Unemployment?"; Numerous Research Papers Presented at Conferences. Honors and Awards: Pi Gamma Mu; Kappa Delta Pi; Alpha Kappa Psi;

Omicron Delta Epsilon; Listed in *Who's Who, American Men and Women of Science, Dictionary of International Biography, International Who's Who in Community Service, Men and Women of Distinction, Men of Achievement, Notable Americans, Outstanding Educators of America, Personalities of America.* Address: Institute of Industrial Relations, Georgia State University, Atlanta, Georgia 30303.

Crim, John Winthrop

Educator. Personal: Born November 9, 1924; Married Jean Beresford; Father of Lucinda Hill, Martha Winthrop Wilson. Education: B.M.E., Marquette University, 1946; M.B.A., University of Buffalo, 1955; Ph.D. Business Administration, Georgia State University, 1975. Military: Served in the United States Navy, 1943-46, attaining the rank of Lieutenant; Served in the United States Naval Reserve for Seventeen Years. Career: Professor of Business Management; Manufacturing Manager, Columbus Iron Works; Director of Engineering, True Temper Corporation; General Manager, Commercial Forging Corporation. Organizational Memberships: Academy of Management; Southern Management Association; American Society for Personnel Administrators; American Compensation Association; American Society of Mechanical Engineers. Community Activities: Kiwanis International (past club president; club secretary; member, board of directors); Springer Theatre Company, Columbus, Georgia, (state theatre of Georgia), (former secretary; member, board of directors); United Fund (campaign worker, annual fund drive). Religion: Episcopal Church (layreader; surrogate minister; usher; former vestryman; former senior warden). Honors and Awards: Certified Professional Manager, Institute of Certified Professional Managers, San Antonio, Texas; Sigma Iota Epsilon Honorary Management Fraternity. Address: 3421 Seminole Drive, Columbus, Georgia 31907.

Cromartie, Ernest William II

Attorney. Personal: Born June 6, 1945; Son of Ernest William Cromartie; Married Raynette White; Father of Antoinette Bouvier, Ernest William III. Education: Graduate of C. A. Johnson High School, 1963; B.A., Michigan State University, 1968; J.D., cum laude, George Washington National Law Center, 1968. Career: Practicing Attorney. Organizational Memberships: South Carolina Bar Association; American Bar Association; South Carolina Trial Lawyers Association; American Trial Lawyers Association; Richland County Bar Association. Community Activities: East Columbia Jaycees; Optimist Club; Kiwanis Club; City of Columbia Zoning Board of Adjustments and Appeals (appointed by Mayor of Columbia, 1976, first black chairman 1980, 1981); South Carolina Department of Youth Service Board for State of South Carolina (appointed by governor, July 1980, appointed to combined juvenile placement and aftercare, 1981); Inaugural Committee for Governor Dick Riley, 1978. Religion: African Methodist Episcopal Church; Chairman of the Junior Trustee Board, 1976-78; Senior Trustee Board, 1978 to present; Sunday School Teacher; Chairman, Usher Board; Youth Day Speaker, 1976; Chairman, Renovation and Building Fund, 1979 to present. Honors and Awards: Sigma Gamma Rho Outstanding Attorney Award, 1975; Outstanding Young Man of America, 1975; Listed in *Who's Who in the South and Southwest.* Address: 2213 Lorick Avenue, Columbia, South Carolina.

Cromer, Charles Marion

Poet. Personal: Born September 15, 1943; Son of Hiram (deceased) and Mary Cromer. Education: Graduate, Hallsville High School, 1962; Attended Letourneau College, 1963. Career: Poet; Musician. Organizational Memberships: International Platform Association, 1969-70; Poetry Society of Texas, 1966-73; Councillor in Poetry Society, 1967. Community Activities: Donations to Letourneau College, 1975 to present; Loaned Piano to Letourneau College, August 1974 to present. Religion: Assembly of God. Honors and Awards: Second Prize, District Spelling Contest, 1961, 1962; Scholarship, Letourneau College, 1962; Listed in *Royal Blue Book, Dictionary of International Biography, International Who's Who in Poetry, Personalities of the South.* Address: 117 Bostick Drive, Longview, Texas 75602.

Cronin, Donald Joseph

Law Partner. Personal: Born July 1, 1925. Education: B.S., University of Alabama School of Commerce; M.B.A., J.D., University of Alabama School of Law. Career: Assistant Professor (School of Commerce), Research Assistant (Bureau of Business Research), Scholastic Advisor to the Athletic Department, University of Alabama; Administrative Assistant to United States Senator Lister Hill of Alabama (Chairman, Senate Appropriations Committee on Health, Education and Welfare and Appropriations Committee for Atomic Energy Commission and Tennessee Valley Authority), 1953-69; Law Partner, Corcoran, Youngman and Rowe, Washington, D.C. Organizational Activities: University of Alabama (former member, board of publications; president's cabinet); University College, Buckingham, England (board of governors); Association of Administrative Assistants of the United States Senate (past president); Alabama Bar; District of Columbia Bar; Bar of the Supreme Court of the United States; Inter-American Bar; American Bar Association. Community Activities: University of Alabama Chapter, Alpha Sigma Phi Social Fraternity (past president); Editor, Campus Yearbook; University of Alabama Cotillion (president, elected by student body); University of Alabama Alumni Association (national president). Religion: St. David's Episcopal Church, Washington, D.C. (senior warden); National Cathedral School (past vice president; chairman, giving fund; chairman, continuing education). Honors and Awards: Omicron Delta Kappa, National Senior Leadership, Beta Gamma Sigma, National Senior Scholarship, Phi Delta Phi International Legal Fraternity, Phi Beta Kappa, Undergraduate and Law School, National Alumni Award 1977, University of Alabama; One of the Original Drafters of the National Defense Education Act (making it possible for thousands of deserving young men and women to attend college); Senate Distinguished Citizen Award; Senate Distinguished Service Award; Listed in *Who's Who in America, Dictionary of International Biography.* Address: 5406 Blackstone Road, Bethesda, Maryland 20016.

Crookshanks, Betty Dorsey

State Legislator, Educator. Personal: Born October 27, 1944; Daughter of Gilda S. Buckley; Married Donald E. Crookshanks. Education: B.A., West Virginia Tech, 1968, M.A., West Virginia University, 1973. Career: West Virginia House of Delegates, State Legislator 1976 to present; Educator (present); Life Insurance Underwriter (present); Secretary, National Institutes of Health; Girls' Coach. Organizational Activities: Delta Kappa Gamma (secretary 1980-81; first vice president, 1981-82); Greenbrier County Farm Bureau; West Virginia Education Association; Greenbrier Valley Life Underwriters; Business and Professional Women's Club; Greenbrier Valley Quota Club (board of directors, 1981); Fayette County Education Association (treasurer, 1973-74); Order of Women Legislators; Member, Standing Committees, Judiciary, Health and Welfare, Roads and Transportation; Co-Chairman, House Democratic Caucus; Member, Interim Committees, Health and Welfare Visitation, Coal Mining and Safety, Judiciary. Community Activities: Rupert Woman's Club (president, 1978-80); Cancer Society (Greenbrier president, 1981; board of directors,

West Virginia division, 1981 to present); Order of the Eastern Star (Electa, 1980-81); Rebekaks; West Virginia Health Systems Agency (board of directors, 1980 to present); Rupert Community Library (board of directors; treasurer, 1977 to present); Seneca Mental Health Council (treasurer, 1979; president, board of directors, 1980-81); West Virginia Women's Commission (advisory council, 1977 to present); Greenbrier County Committee on Aging (member, 1980 to present; transportation committee, 1980-81); Greenbrier Valley Domestic Violence Council, 1978-80; Governor's Golden Mountaineer Card Program, 1980 to present; Rainelle Medical Center Black Lung Clinic, 1980 to present; Delegate, State Democratic Convention, 1976, 1980; Delegate, Southern Legislators Convention, 1980, 1981, 1982; Delegate, National State Legislators Convention, 1981; West Virginia Tech Alumni Association; West Virginia University Alumni Association; Marshall University Alumni Association. Religion: Big Clear Creek Baptist Church,Treasurer, 1981-82; Bays Chapel Methodist Church, Sunday School Teacher. Honors and Awards: Outstanding Young Woman of the Year, West Virginia, 1980; Meritous Award for Conservation of Natural Resources, West Virginia Division, Issac Walton League of America, 1978; Outstanding Personality of Western Greenbrier, *Meadow River Post* Newspaper, 1977; Fayette County Young Teacher to Leadership Camp, 1969; Claude Bemedum Scholarship, 1963, 1964. Address: Box 370, Rupert, West Virginia 25984.

Cross, Rose Harris

School Social Worker. Personal: Born March 17, 1945; Daughter of Rev. Dr. and Mrs. R. B. Harris; Mother of Una-Kariim Alencia, Kha-Lihah DaVida. Education: B.A., Jackson State University, 1967; M.S.W., Michigan State University, 1973. Career: School Social Worker, Lansing, Michigan; Former Assistant Head Advisor of Student Housing, Michigan State University; Former Medical Social Worker, St. Lawrence Hospital, Lansing; Former Field Coordinator, Mississippi Action for Progess, Jackson, Mississippi. Organizational Memberships: National Association of Social Workers (social action chairperson, 1974-76, programs chairperson, 1976-78, president, 1978-79); National Association of Black Social Workers; Lansing School Education Association (representative assembly, 1974-75, negotiating committee, 1976-79); Minority Educators Association. Community Activities: Brownie Troop Leader, Girl Scouts of America, 1979-80; Delta Sigma Theta Sorority, Inc., Lansing Alumnae (past secretary, chaplain, 1981-82); Y.W.C.A. Committee to evaluate minority participants in the organization, 1981; Council for Stronger Government vs. Mayor Control, 1975-76; Public-Camp Scholarships, parenting classes, transportaion, 1975 to present. Religion: Summer Missionary, Southern Baptist Seminary, 1966 (vacation bible school, 1967, 1970, and 1981; woman day speaker, 1968; presenter, first national school social workers conference, 1978). Honors and Awards: Listed in *Who's Who of American Women, The World Who's Who of Women.* Address: 6435 Norburn Way, Lansing, Michigan 48910.

Crow, Lester Donald

Educator, Author. Personal: Born March 31, 1897, in Dundee, Ohio; Son of William and Mary Olmstead Caldwell; Married Alice von Bauer, June 11, 1927 (deceased); Second Wife, Rosamond M. Hardy, July 9, 1969. Education: A.B., Ohio University, 1923; M.A. 1924, Ph.D. 1927, New York University; LL.D., St. Lawrence University, 1975; Litt.D., Mount Union College, 1976. Career: Teacher, High Schools, Ohio 1919-22, New York 1924-26; Professor of Education, Mary Washington University, Fredericksburg, Virginia, 1926-27; Assistant Professor of Education, Leigh University, Bethlehem, Pennsylvania, 1927-28; Professor, New York University, 1929-30; Director of Education, Pelham Institute, New York City, 1930-32; Brooklyn College, Faculty Member 1932-67, Professor 1958-67, Emeritus Professor of Education 1967 to present. Organizational Memberships: Middle Atlantic States Colleges and Secondary Schools (member, committee to evaluate secondary schools, 1947-49); United States Commission for Teacher Education Program, Japan, 1950-51; American Personnel and Guidance Association (life member); New York Academy of Science (life member); New York Schoolmaster's Club (past president). Community Activities: Midwood Park Property Association, Brooklyn (president, 1955-65). Published Works: Author, Numerous Books, including *An Introduction to Education, Educational Psychology, Introductin to Guidance, Child Psychology, Readings in General Psychology, Sex Education in a Growing Family, How to Study, Psychology and Human Adjustment, General Psychology, Human Development and Adjustment, Development of Self-Discipline, Psychology of Childhood*; Author, Autobiography, *As the Crow Flies, Adjustment*; Contributor, Numerous Articles to Professional Journals. Honors and Awards: Certificate of Merit, Ohio University Alumni Association, 1970; Alumni Award, Mount Union College, 1974; Kappa Delta Pi (honorary life member); Phi Delta Kappa (life member); Honorary L.H.D., 1972. Address: 5300 Washington Street, Apartment 301D, Hollywood, Florida 33021.

Joe G Crowell

Crowell, Joe George

Dentist. Personal: Born April 9, 1919; Son of Mr. and Mrs. Ernest Benjamin Crowell; Married Buris Franks; Father of Dianne Buris House, Wanda Joelene White, Joe Robert. Education: Graduate of Hoquiam High School, 1937; Attended Brevard College 1939-40, Western Carolina University 1940-42; D.D.S., Emory University School of Dentistry, 1945. Military: Served in the United States Air Force from 1953-55, attaining the rank of Captain, and in the United States Army as Private First Class from 1942-45. Career: Dentist. Organizational Memberships: Henderson County Dental Society (president); American Dental Society; Academy of General Dentistry. Community Activities: Hendersonville Rotary Club (past president); Brevard College Alumni Association (past president); North Carolina Apple Society (past president); Henderson County Health Department (past director); Hendersonville Country Club (past director); Bald Head Island Property Owners Association (past president). Religion: Methodist Church. Honors and Awards: Recognition, Scientific Program, Ninety-Fourth Annual Session, American Dental Association, 1953; Alpha Psi Omega International Dramatics Fraternity; Listed in *Who's Who in the South and Southwest, Who's Who in America, Who's Who in North America, Men of Achievement, Dictionary of International Biography, Community Leaders and Noteworthy Americans, Book of Honor.* Address: 16 Lake Drive, Hendersonville, North Carolina 28739.

Crump, Mary Quinn

Businesswoman. Personal: Born July 31, 1939; Daughter of Mr. and Mrs. Hubert White; Mother of Carla Genetta. Education: Graduate, Patricia Stevens Finishing and Career College, Jacksonville, Florida, 1963; Graduate, Savannah School of Interior Decorating and Designing, Savannah, Georgia, 1976. Career: President, Mary Quinn's Interiors, Inc., Waycross, Georgia; President, Mary Quinn's Finishing and Modeling School, Waycross; Former Owner, Turnpike Mobile Homes, Inc.; Former Owner, Southern Sales and Service (retail carpet store); Former Secretary, General Motors Acceptance Corporation. Organizational Memberships: International Talent and Modeling School Association (member, board of directors, 1979-80); International Method Models Training School. Community Activities: Coordinator, Waycross-Ware County Clean Community Commission (keep America beautiful), 1980; Waycross-Ware County Chamber of Commerce (nominating committee, 1980, public relations committee, 1980); Advisory Panel, *Interior Design Magazine*, 1977. Religion: Member of Grace Episcopal Church, Waycross, Georgia. Honors and Awards:

Nominated for Mrs. Lyndon B. Johnson Outstanding Woman of the Year, 1980; Listed in *Personalities of the South*. Address: P.O. Box 944, Waycross, Georgia 31501.

Cruse, Irma Russell

Telephone Company Supervisor (retired), Free-lance Writer, Public Speaker. Personal: Married J. Clyde Cruse; Mother of Allan Baird, Howard Russell. Education: M.A., English, Samford University, 1981; Bell System Speaker's Training Class; Photography, Editing and Writing Workshops, University of Georgia; Famous Photographers Course; Writing Courses, Christian Writers School, Newspaper Institute of America, Famous Writers School, University of Chicago, University of Wisconsin, University of Minnesota, University of Alabama's New College. Career: Southern Bell and South Central Bell Telephone 36 years, Public Relations 4 years, Editor *Bell Tel News*, Advertising Editor *Bama Bulletin*, Alabama Area Rate and Tariff Organization, Coordinator, Share Owner-Management Visit Program 1 year, Traffic and Commercial Departments, Toll Operator, Toll Supervisor, Toll Training Supervisor, Sales Clerk, TWX Instructor, Service Representative, Training Coach 14 years, Rate Supervisor, Marketing Department until 1976; Stenographer for Director of Public Welfare, St. Clair County; Secretary to Public Works Officer; Naval Air Station, Birmingham; Chief of Planning, Anniston Ordnance Depot; Free-Lance Writer, Articles, Playettes, Skits, Public Relations, 1956 to present. Organizational Memberships: Alabama Writers Conclave (corresponding secretary, 1971-72; recording secretary, 1972-73, 1979-80; president, 1973-74); Alabama State Poetry Society (program chairman, 1972-73, 1973-74; Editor, *The Muse Messenger*, 1976-77, 1977-78); Women in Communications (corresponding secretary, 1968-70; president, 1970-71; first vice-president and program chairman, 1975-76; recording secretary, 1978-79; historian, 1979-80, 1981-81); Birmingham Business Communicators (now IABC/B'ham; corresponding secretary, 1967-68; president, 1968-69; national representative to ICIE, 2 years); American Association of University Women; International Platform Association, 1971-72, 1974-75; Telephone Pioneers of America (numerous positions). Community Activities: Public Speaker, Service and Civic Groups, School and Church Groups; Alabama Baptist Historical Commission; Alabama Baptist Historical Society (treasurer, 1980-81; assistant editor, *The Alabama Baptist Historian*, 1979, 1980, 1981 to present); Alabama Historical Society; Birmingham Historical Society; Birmingham-Jefferson Historical Society; St. Clair County Historical Society; Birmingham-Southern College Alumni Committee; Freedoms Foundation of Valley Forge, Birmingham Chapter; Women's Chamber of Commerce (second vice president, 1978-79; by-laws chairman, 1978-79, 1979-80, 1980-81); Birmingham Festival of Arts (board of directors, 1970-75); Birmingham Council of Clubs (formerly Inter-Club Council; first vice-president, 1971-72; board of directors, 1972-73, 1975-81; recording secretary, 1973-75); Metropolitan Business and Professional Women's Club of Birmingham (numerous positions); Quota Club of Birmingham (president, 1976-77); Jefferson County Radio and TV Council (president, 1971-72; corresponding secretary, 1975-76); Project Volunteer Power; United Way Speakers Bureau; Salvation Army Women's Auxiliary (chaplain, 1978-79); Alabama Women's Political Caucus; Birmingham-Jefferson Women's Center; Alabama Citizens for E.R.A.; Town and Gown Players. Published Works: Writer, Producer, Director, Plays, Playlets; Numerous Articles, including (most recently) "Proclaiming the Possibilities of Life" and "Don't Be Afraid". Honors and Awards: Phi Kappa Phi Scholastic Honor Society, 1982; Birmingham Branch, National League of American Pen Women, 1982; B.P.W. Member of the Week, Metro B.P.W. Club of Birmingham, 1965; Woman of Achievement, Twice; Liberty Bell Award, Birmingham Bar Association, 1973; David Daniel Eleemosynary Award for Community Service Activities, American Red Cross, 1973; One of "Beautiful Activists" for Alabama, 1972; Best All-Around Teletalker, Birmingham Teletalker Club; Annual Scholarship to be Named for Irma Cruse, Metropolitan Business and Professional Women's Club, 1982; Appointed by Governor Fob James to Governor's Commission on Employment of the Handicapped; Nine Awards, Birmingham Ad Club; Best Photograph, Award of Achievement for Writing, Southern Council of Industrial Edirotrs; Honorable Mention, International Association of Industrial Editors; First Place, Association of Writers for Technical Publications; First Place for Best Feature, Joint Commission Competition, Jefferson County United Appeal; Outstanding Chapter President, Birmingham Business Communicators, 1968; Simga Tau Delta; Listed in *Foremost Women in Communications, Who's Who of American Women, Who's Who in Alabama-Notable Women, Personalities of the South, Two Thousand Women of Achievement, World's Who's Who of Women, Dictionary of International Biography, Community Leaders and Noteworthy Americans, International Who's Who in Community Service, Alabama's Distinguished, Notable Americans of the Bicentennial Era, Who's Who in the South and Southwest, Contemporary Anericans*. Address: 136 Memory Court, Birmingham, Alabama 35213.

Cruthers, Larry Randall

Senior Research Parasitologist. Personal: Born March 15, 1945; Son of Harold and Irene Cruthers; Married Susan Margaret; Father of Carrie Lyn, Polly Jane. Education: B.S. Zoology, University of Wisconsin-Stevens Point, 1967; M.S. 1971, Ph.D. 1973, Parasitology, Kansas State University, Manhattan. Military: Served as Captain, Medical Services Corps, Honorable Discharge, 1978. Career: Senior Research Parasitologist, Diamond Shamrock Corporation, Painesville, Ohio (present); Senior Research Parasitologist, Squibb Institute for Medical Research, Princeton, New Jersey; Senior Research Parasitologist, Squibb Agricultural Research Center, Three Bridges, New Jersey; Instructor of Biology, Kansas State University, Manhattan, Kansas. Organizatonal Memberships: American Society of Parasitology; New Jersey Society for Parasitology (secretary/treasurer, 1976-79; president, 1979-80); Helmintholigical Society of Washington; American Association of Veterinary Parasitologists; American Heartworm Society; Conference of Research Workers in Animal Diseases; Sigma Xi. Community Activities: Kiwanis Club (president-elect, 1979-80); Society for the Prevention of Cruelty to Animals (member, board of directors, Hunterdon County, New Jersey); Church School Superintendent, 1977-80. Honors and Awards: Nominee, Outstanding Undergraduate Teacher Award in Biology, Kansas State University, 1969-70. Address: 10268 Cherry Hill Drive, Painesville, Ohio 44077.

Cucin, Robert Louis

Plastic Surgeon. Personal: Born April 17, 1946; Son of Julia Cucin. Education: B.A., Cornell University, 1967; M.D., Cornell University Medical College, 1971. Military: Served in the United States Air Force from 1976-77 as Berry Commitment-Major, Chief of Surgery, Misawa Air Force Base, Northern Japan. Career: Plastic Surgeon. Organizational Memberships: American Medical Association; American Association of Abdominal Surgeons (fellow); American Association of Tissue Banks; New York Academy of Science; Society of Cryobiology; Medical Society of County of New York (grievance subcommittee, peer review); International College of Surgeons (fellow); American College of Surgeons (candidate). Honors and Awards: Physicians Recognition Award, American Medical Association, 1978-83. Address: 425 East 58th Street, New York, New York 10022.

Culbertson, John Dennis

Counselor, Guidance Counselor. Personal: Born August 18, 1947; Son of John B. Culbertson and Ellie Barbare Culbertson (deceased); Married E. Virginia Watson; Father of John David, Ellen Barbare. Education: B.S., University of South Carolina, 1969;

M.S., North Dakota State University, 1978; Ph.D., Counseling & Guidance, University of North Dakota, 1982. Military: Served in the United States Air Force, Commissioned 2nd Lieutenant, United States Air Force Reserve, rose through ranks to Captain, served from 1969-77. Career: Counselor, Private Practice (present); Elementary School Guidance Counselor (present); Officer, United States Air Force. Organizational Memberships: American Personnel and Guidance Association; South Carolina Personnel and Guidance Association; A.M.E.G.; S.C.A.M.E.G.: A.S.C.A.; S.C.S.C.A.: A.S.G.W.; South Carolina Association for Humanistic Education & Development; S.C.A.N.W.C.; National Education Association; South Carolina Education Association; Florence Educational Association; American Biographical Institute (national board of advisors). Community Activities: Parents Anonymous (sponsor, Florence chapter, 1981 to present; member, state board of directors, 1981 to present); Boy Scouts of America (institutional representative, Minot, North Dakota, 1971-72, 1975-78). Religion: United Church of Christ (youth representative, national synod, 1977-78); Joint United Church of Christ-Presbyterian Educational Commission, North Dakota-Minnesota (member; 1977-78; member, executive committee, 1977-78); Highland Park United Methodist Church (member, administrative board, 1981 to present). Honors and Awards: Certificate of Appreciation: Dedicated Service to Florence, South Carolina, Public Schools District 1, 1981; Participant, South Carolina Department of Education-South Carolina ETV Production Depicting Guidance in Public Schools, 1981; Recipient, North Dakota Graduate Scholarship, 1978-79; Outstanding Contribution as Executive Spt. Officer, 91st OMMS, MAFB, North Dakota, 1975-77; Outstanding Performance as Executive Spt. Officer, 56th CAMS, PACAF, 1974-75; Executive Spt. Officer, 363 Supply Squadron, SAFB, South Carolina, 1973-74; Listed in *Personalities of America, Who's Who in the South and Southwest.* Address: 1886 Westmoreland Avenue, Florence, South Carolina 29501.

Culpepper, Charles L Sr

Emeritus Foreign Missionary. Personal: Born March 10, 1895; Son of John Thomason J. Culpepper (deceased); Married Ola Lane; Father of Charles Lee Jr., Mary Frances Culpepper Walker. Education: Graduate of Floresville High School, Texas; A.B., Baylor University, Waco, Texas; Th.M. 1922, Th.D. 1945, Southwestern Baptist Theological Seminary, Fort Worth, Texas. Military: Served in the United States Navy from 1918-19, attaining the rank of Quartermaster. Career: Emeritus Foreign Missionary (present); Foreign Missionary under the Foreign Mission Board of the S.B.C., Richmond, Virginia. Organizational Memberships: Foreign Mission Board (president of seminary, North China Mission, 1923-45; president of all-China seminary, Central China Mission, 1946-49); China Missions of Foreign Missions (treasurer, 1950-52); Taiwan Mission (treasurer, 1952-61; president of seminary, 1952-65). Community Activities: Liaison Officer, United States Armed Forces and China Armed Forces, 1945. Religion: Foreign Missionary; Theological Teacher, Mid-America Baptist Theological Seminary, 1975-80. Honors and Awards: Cloud and Banner Award, Chinese Army, 1945; Scroll of Honor, Foreign Mission Board, 1965; Distinguished Alumni Award, Southwestern Baptist Theological Seminary, 1966; Emeritus Distinguished Professor of Missions and Theology, Mid-America Baptist Theological Seminary, 1981 to present. Address: 609 Oblate Drive, San Antonio, Texas 78216.

Cummings, Conrad M

Executive. Personal: Born July 1, 1933; Married Beverly A. Arrant; Father of Constance Blain, Ross Martin, Leigh Cummings Ford. Education: Graduate, Byrd High School, Shreveport, Louisiana, 1951; B.S., Texas Agricultural and Mechanical University, 1955. Military: Served with the United States Army, achieving the rank of First Lieutenant, 1956-58. Career: Jr. Engineer, Lion Oil Company (now Monsanto), 1955-56; Monsanto: Staff Engineer (1958-60), District Engineer (1960-64), Regional Engineer (1964-68), Planning Coordinator (1968-70); President, McRae Oil Corporation, McRae Exploration Inc., and Petrofunds Inc.; Senior Vice President, McRae Consolidated Oil and Gas, Inc.; Director McRae Exploration Inc, Petrofunds Inc., Louisiana Gas Purchasing Corp., and Louisiana Gas Intrastate, Inc. Organizational Memberships: Society of Petroleum Engineers; Independent Petroleum Association of America; Louisiana Association of Producers & Royalty Owners; Texas Independent Producers & Royalty Owners; Mid-Continent Oil & Gas Association. Religion: Presbyterian; Deacon, 1966-69; Elder, 1969-71. Address: 10626 Glenway, Houston, Texas 77070.

Anne B S Cunningham

Cunningham, Anne Bernice Smith

Education Administrator. Personal: Born February 14; Daughter of Mr. Ernest Smith (deceased) and Mrs. Ernest Smith; Married James Clinton Cunningham; Mother of Dr. Evangeline Cheryl Cunningham, M.D. Education: B.S. with Honors, Alabama A. & M. University; M.A., Case-Western Reserve University; Ph.D., Walden University. Career: Elementary School Principal (present); Social Worker, Division of Aid for Aged; Teacher of English; Teacher of Home Economics; Elementary Teacher. Organizational Memberships: Cleveland Council of Administrators and Supervisors; Ohio Association of Elementary School Principals; Council on Human Relations; National Council of Women in Administrative Education. Community Activities: First Anti-Basilius, Alpha Kappa Alpha Sorority; Phi Delta Kappa Sorority; Tots and Teens, Inc. (past president; national chairman of publications); Alabama A. & M. Alumni Association (life member); Glenville Young Men's-Young Women's Christian Association (past member, board of management); Kathryn Tyler Community Center (member, board of directors); Women's City Club of Cleveland. Religion: Bethany Baptist Church (member, board of Christian Education; past secretary, women's council). Honors and Awards: Marth Holden Jennings Scholar; Listed in *Instructor* Magazine as Principal of a School Where Creativity Flourishes under an Atmosphere Which Encourages Students and Teachers to Think and to Experiment. Address: 21950 Shaker Boulevard, Shaker Heights, Ohio 44122.

Cunningham, David Surmier

Legislator. Personal: Born June 24, 1935; Son of Reverend and Mrs. David S. Cunningham, Sr.; Married Sylvia A. C. Kapel; Father of David S. III, Leslie J., Robyn. Education: B.A. Economics, Political Science, University of California-Riverside; M.A. Urban Studies, Occidental College. Military: Served in the United States Air Force from 1956-60, attaining the rank of Sergeant, and in the United States Navy from 1952-54. Career: Management Consultant, Founder, Cunningham, Short & Berryman, Management Consultant Firm; Legislator (present). Community Activities: California Minority Employment Council (past president); C.O.R.O. Alumni Association; Interracial Council for Business Opportunity (chairman, executive committee; board member); World Affairs Council; National Urban League; Los Angeles Brotherhood Crusade (chairman, 1976-77). Religion: Lewis Metropolitan Church. Honors and Awards: Honorary Chairman, Greater Pico Union Chamber of Commerce; 1981 Black Probation Officer; Outstanding Contribution to the Community; Honorary Member, Korean Military Corps Veteran's Association, 1981; Seventh Korean Festival of Los Angeles Award of Appreciation, 1980; Outstanding Community Service Award, Oscar Joel Bryant Association, 1976; Tree Planted in Honor of Dave Cunningham Trees for Israel, Jewish National Fund, 1981. Address: 2323 Buckingham Road, Los Angeles, California 90016.

Cunningham, Ernest Bernard

Pastor. Personal: Born October 31, 1927; Married to June D.; Father of five children. Education: Bachelor of Law, LaSalle University, 1971; Bachelor of Theology, 1947, Master of Theology, 1950, Northwestern University; Diploma in Music, Howard University, 1943. Military: Served with United States Army; National Chaplain, AMVETS, 1976-77. Career: Pastor, Unity Baptist Church, Washington, D.C., 1961 to present; Instructor, Washington Baptist Seminary, 1971 to present; Pastor, Mt. Zion Baptist Church, 1950-61; Former Equal Employment Opportunity Attorney for Naval District of Washington, D.C. Organizational Memberships: Mt. Bethel Baptist Association (executive board secretary, 1976); Ministers and Laymen's Educational Conference (president, 1972-74); Baptist Ministers' Conference, 1947 to present; Imperial Council A.E.O.N.M.S. (shriners - chaplain of 75,000 shriners, 1978 to present); Fraternal Order of Police (chaplain, 1977 to present). Community Activities: Police Chaplain of P.G. County, Maryland, 1973; Volunteer Protestant Chaplain at Greater S.E. Community Hospital, 1979 to present; Instructor for American Red Cross 30 years; Chaplain, District 22-C of Lions International, 1978 to present. Religion: Member Unity Baptist Church, Washington, D.C.; Honors and Awards: Received Medal for 2000 hours of volunteer service, Greater S.E. Community Hospital; E.B. Cunningham Annex in Unity Baptist Church named in his honor, 1981; Life time membership, American Legion, 1981; Awarded 100% President Award on club level from Lions International, 1977; Honorary D.Div., Rutgers University; 3rd degree Black Belt in Tae-kwon-do, 1978. Address: 1313 Centaur Drive, District Heights, Maryland 20028.

Cunningham, Irma Ewing

Irma E Cunningham

Associate Professor. Personal: Born September 19, 1940; Daughter of Linnie Thomas; Mother of Anthony Cunningham. Education: B.A., Le Moyne College, 1962; M.A., Indiana University, 1964; Ph.D., University of Michigan, 1970; Attended Unity School of Christianity, Detroit, Michigan, 1962-71. Career: Instructor of English and Linguistics, Southern University, Baton Rouge, Louisiana, 1963-64; Instructor of English and Linguistics, Macomb County College, Warren, Michigan, 1965-66; Assistant Professor of English (Sociolinguistics), State University of New York, Cortland, New York; Assistant Professor of Linguistics, Purdue University, West Lafayette, Indiana; Administrative Director of Curriculum and Associate Professor, Benedict College, 1975-77; Associate Professor of Linguistics, North Carolina Agricultural and Technical State University, 1978 to present. Organizational Memberships: Modern Language Association, 1970 to present; South Atlantic Modern Language Association, 1981 to present; President Carter's Commission on Foreign Language and International Project, 1979; North and South Carolina Association of Linguists (executive committee, 1976-77). Community Activities: Zeta Phi Beta; Attended Grantsmanship Workshop, National Endowment for the Humanities, 1981; Sea Island Language ("Gullah") Project, U.S. Department of Labor (consultant 1977-79); Resource person on linguistic matters for general public, public school systems and colleges and universities; Volunteer counselor in assertive training for battered wives, Frankfort, Indiana, 1978. Religion: Attends weekly Bible class. Published Works: Author of several articles including "What You Say Is More Than Just Words" and "Black English Reaches Dangerous Level"; *A Syntactic Analysis of Sea Island Creole ("Gullah")*, 1971. Honors and Awards: Le Moyne Honor Society; Florina Laska Fellowship; American Missionary Association Fellowship; Ford Foundation Grant; 3 University of Michigan Fellowships; Most Outstanding Member of Undergraduate Class, 1972; Nominated Most Outstanding Teacher by students in Humanities, Social Science and Education, Purdue University, 1975; Invited to attend conference, International Biographical Center, Holland, 1980; Certificate of Participation, "Tribute to Black Womanhood", *Ebony Magazine*, 1980; Listed in *Who's Who in American Colleges and Universities, Outstanding Young Women of America, Directory of American Scholars, Dictionary of International Biography, International Who's Who of Intellectuals, Personalities of the West and Midwest, American Registry Series, International Who's Who in Community Service, The International Register of Profiles, Directory of Distinguished Americans.* Address: 20123 Pinehurst Street, Detroit, Michigan 48221.

Curran, Louis Jerome Jr

Choral Master. Personal: Born June 13, 1934; Son of Louis Jerome and Gertrude Marie Frederick Curran, (both deceased). Education: B.Mus., Yale University, (H. B. Jepson Scholar), 1956; Undertrook graduate study, New England Conservatory of Music, 1956-57 and Yale University, 1959-62; M.Mus., summa cum laude, University of Tulsa, 1963; Fulbright Scholar, Linacre College, Oxford University, 1963-65. Military: Served with the United States Army, Military Intelligence, 1957-59. Career: Organist and Choirmaster, Emmanual Episcopal Church, Ansonia, Connecticut, 1954-56; Organist and Master of the Choristers, Cathedral Church of St. Mary, Fall River, Massachusetts 1956-57; Director of Music, First Congregational Church, Wallingford, Connecticut, 1960-62; Central Congregational Church, Worcester, Massachusetts, 1966-67; Organist, Grace Church, Amherst, Massachusetts, 1967-68; Director of Music and Master of the Choristers, Church of St. Peter, Worcester, Massachusetts, 1969 to present, Director of the Choir School, 1981 to present; Associate Professor Music, Northeast Missouri State College, Kirksville, Missouri, 1965-66; Assistant Professor of Music and Director of Music, Worcester Polytechnic Institute, 1966 to present; Director of Music and Master of the Choristers, Church of St. Peter, Worcester, Massachusetts, 1970 to present; Concert Tours with the Worcester Polytechnic Institute Glee Club and the Choir of Men and Boys of Church of St. Peter, Twice in California, throughout East-Coast USA and Canada, Twice throughout England; Worcester Polytechnic Institute and Regis College toured Germany and Austria; Organizational Memberships: Worcester Intercollegiate Chorale (founding member); Worcester Cultural Commission, 1978-80; American Boys Choir Federation; Organ Historical Society; Intercollegiate Musical Council (national board 1977-80); American Guild of Organists; American Musicological Society; Royal School of Church Music; American Choral Directors Association; Tau Kappa Epsilon. Honors and Awards: Fulbright Scholar, Musicology, Oxford University, 1963-65; Commendation, Ministry of Education, Tyrols, Austria. Address: 5 Einhorn Road, Worcester, Massachusetts 01609.

Louis J Curran Jr

Curran, Robert

Newspaper Columnist. Personal: Born October 4, 1923; Son of Sylvester and Ann Curran (both deceased); Married May Sullivan; Father of Robert Jr., Mark Sullivan, John Francis. Education: Graduate of Boston Latin School; B.A. English, Cornell University, 1949. Military: Served in the United States Army from 1943-45, attaining the rank of Staff Sergeant. Career: Newspaper Columnist (current); Magazine Editor; Director of Sports Publicity, NBC-TV; Syndicated Sports Columnist; Author. Organizational Memberships: Sigma Delta Chi; Overseas Press Club; American Society of Journalists and Authors. Published Works: Author, *$400,000 Quarterback or League That Came In From The Cold, The Violence Game, Pro Football in the Rag Days, The Kennedy Women.* Honors and Awards: Associated Press Award; Best Column, New York State, 1971; Freedom Foundation Best Column, United States, 1971; Most Outstanding Individual, Western New York, 1972; Silver Star; Bronze Stars; Two Purple Hearts; Combat Infantry Badge. Address: 261 Kings Highway, Snyder, New York 14226.

Currie, Charles Leonard

Educator. Personal: July 9, 1930; Son of Mrs. Charles L. Currie. Education: A.B. 1955, M.A. 1956, Boston College; Ph.L., Weston

College, 1956; Ph.D., Catholic University of America, 1961; S.T.B., Woodstock College, 1962, 1964. Career: President, Xavier University, Cincinnati; President, Wheeling College; Assistant Professor of Chemistry, Georgetown University; Postdoctoral Research, Cambridge University, England, 1972-82. Organizational Memberships: Xavier University (board of directors, 1978 to present); St. Joseph's University (board of directors, 1968-78); Council of Independent Colleges, 1981 to present; Association of Jesuit Colleges and Universities, 1972 to present; West Virginia Association of Private Colleges (member, 1972-82; chairman, 1975-82). Community Activities: West Virginia Board of Miner Training, Education and Certification (chairman, 1974-82); United Way of Upper Ohio Valley (board of directors); Olgebay Institute; West Virginia Chamber of Commerce, 1975-82; Wheeling Area Chamber of Commerce, 1973-82; West Virginia Humanities Foundation, 1978-81. Religion: Ordained Roman Catholic (Jesuit) Priest, 1963. Honors and Awards: Honorary Doctor of Science, Bethany College, 1975; Honorary Doctor of Laws, West Virginia Wesleyan College, 1982; Ignatian Award, St. Joseph's College High School, Philadelphia, Pennsylvania, 1975; Graduation Citation, St. Joseph's High School, Huntington, West Virginia, 1981; Citizen of the Month, Upper Ohio Valley, 1973. 1978. Address: 3800 Victory Parkway, Cincinnati, Ohio 45207

Cushing, Eva Ireta

Teacher, Workshop Clinician. Personal: Born July 12, 1920; Daughter of Arnold Vane Johnson; Mother of Reneta Arlene Peterson, Madaline Phyllis Given. Education: Attended University of Southern California, Los Angeles City College; B.A., 1953, and M.A., 1960, both from California State University; Undertook post-graduate work at Claremont, Idyllwild School of Music and Art, Brigham Young University, and California State University-Fullerton. Career: Music Consultant, Downey, La Hambra and Anaheim School District; Instructor, Pepperdine University; Clinician, Los Angeles and Orange Counties; State Music Conference Clinician; Private Music Teacher. Organizational Memberships: Music Education National Conference (workshop chairman, 1973; western division elementary chairman, 1979); California Music Education Association (southern section secretary, 1974-76); Orange County Music Education Association (consultant representative, 1974-76; advisor, 1977-78; treasurer, 1978-82); Orange County Music Administration (past president, past secretary, workshop chairman, 1973 & 1979); A.C.S.A.; Orange County Philharmonic Society; California Teachers Association; National Education Association; Sigma Alpha Iota; Beta Upsilon (charter member, secretary, 1953). Community Activities: Anaheim Carrousel of Music and Art (produced and directed annual Anaheim district patriotic program, 1967-77); Writer and Director Countless Programs and Choruses for Various Civic Clubs and Functions, including: Rotary, W.D.C.C., Parent Teacher Association Council, California Elementary Education Association, O.C.P.S., Hospitals, Senior Citizens, Churches, etc. Religion: Church of Jesus Christ of Latter Day Saints: Stake Board Jr. Sunday School Music and/or Coordinator, 26 Years; Director Youth Choruses; Teacher, children, youth, R. S. Spiritual Living; Ward Organist; Accompanist for Soloists; Clinician for Musical Seminars for Various Stakes and Regions in Southern California; Writer and Director "Christmas with the Apostles". Honors and Awards: Freedom Foundation Medal and Award, 1972; Orange County Outstanding Music Education Award, 1980; Orange County Philharmonic Society Honorary Member Award, 1975; Anaheim Carrousel Achievement Awards, 1966-77; Parent Teacher Association Council Life Member and Honorary Award; Listed in *World Who's Who of Women, Community Leaders and Noteworthy Americans, World Who's Who of Intellectuals, American Registry of Musicians and Educators, Dictionary of International Biography, The Directory of Distinguished Americans, Men and Women of Distinction, Book of Honor*. Address: 3994 San Bonito Avenue, Los Alamitos, California 90720.

Dailey, Mae Hileman

Social Worker (retired). Personal: Born October 19, 1907; Daughter of Richard Hileman (deceased); Married Earl Dailey; Raised Two Orphans, Sheila and Tom Trotter. Education: B.A., University of Oregon, 1929; Graduate Work, University of Chicago, Chicago Theological Seminary, Two Years. Career: Executive Director, Children's Home, Seventeen Years; Mothers' March Director, March of Dimes National Foundation, Ten Years. Organizational Memberships: Registered Social Worker; Regional Vice President, California Conference of Social Work, Two Years; President, Executives of Children's Homes of California and Nevada, Four Years; President, Community Social Workers, One Year. Community Activities: Board of Appeals for San Jose, Five Years; Young Women's Christian Association (board of directors, sixteen years; president, three years; member, national nominating committee, three years); Children's Home Board of Directors, Two Years; Quota International Board of Directors, Two Years; President, Willow Glen Business and Professional Women; President, American Business Women; President, Co-ordinating Council of Women's Clubs; Governor, Quota District Twelve. Religion: Teacher, Congregational Neighborhood House, 1934-36. Honors and Awards: Woman of the Year, 1970, Woman of Achievement, 1973, Willow Glen Business and Professional Women; Woman of the Year, American Business Women of San Jose; Honorary Life Member, Parent-Teacher Association; Woman of Achievement, Board of Supervisors, 1980; Included in *Women Of Our Valley*, by Bertha Rice. Address: 1127 Delynn Way, San Jose, California 95125.

Daly, Jane B

Executive. Personal: Born December 11, 1942; Married Patrick H. Daly; Mother of Anne, Suzie, Cindy, Tom. Education: B.A., University of Idaho, 1965; Business Management Study, Boise State University. Career: Young Women's Christian Organization, Executive Director 1979 to present, Program Director 1975-79, Volunteer Co-ordinator 1972-74; Teacher, Junior High Level, 1968-72; Paid Consultant in Communications for Federal Government, Corporations and Non-Profit Organizations, 1977 to present. Community Activities: Beaux Arts Board Member, 1972-77; Chairperson, Three of the Largest Fund Raisers for Art Gallery, 1976-78; Co-Chairperson, Task Force to Develop First Women's Center in Boise, 1974; Served on Committee that Testified and Co-ordinated Passage of the Equal Rights Amendment in Idaho, 1973; One of Thirty Idaho Women to Co-ordinate the Idaho Women's Conference, 1977; One of Fourteen Idaho Delegates to the National Women's Conference, Houston, Texas, 1977; Chairman, Affirmative Action Council, Boise City, 1976-78; Chairman, Ada County C.E.T.A. Board, 1978 to present; Co-Chairperson, Art for Downtown Committee, 1979; Organizer (with the Young Women's Christian Organization and the Labor Bureau), National Jobs Network for Women, 1979; Junior League (Boise board member, 1977 to present; national council, 1980-81); State Employment and Training Council (board member, 1980 to present); Office of Voluntary Citizen Participation (task force, 1980-81); Soccer Coach, Optimist Youth Soccer League, 1980. Honors and Awards: Awarded Only Lifetime Membership in Beaux Arts Society for Outstanding Volunteerism, 1977; Outstanding Young Woman of America, 1978; Boise Capital Jaycettes Dinstinguished Young Woman, 1980. Address: 1008 Johnson, Boise, Idaho 83705.

Maxima A Dandoy

Dandoy, Maxima Antonio

Educator. Personal: Born in the Philippines. Education: Attended Ilocos Sur Normal School; Elementary Teaching Certificate, Philippine Normal College, Manila, 1938; A.B., National Teachers College, Manila, 1947; M.A., Arellano University, Manila, 1949; Ph.D. Education, Stanford University, California, 1952. Career: Elementary School Teacher, Philippines, 1927-37; Laboratory School Teacher, Philippine Normal College, Manila, 1938-49; Part-Time Instructor, Arellano University, Manila, 1947-49; Curriculum Writer, General Office Supervisor, Entire Country, Department of Education, Manila, 1944-45; University of the East, Manila, Laboratory School Principal 1953-54, Associate Professor of Education 1952-55; Visiting Professor, University of California, Los Angeles, Summer 1956; Professor of Education, California State University, Fresno, 1956 to present. Organizational Memberships: California Federation of Business and Professional Women's Clubs (treasurer, international relations chairperson, Fresno Club; international relations chairperson, San Joquain Valley Central District; state chairperson, California state scholarships, California State Federation); American Association of University Women (liaison officer, California State University-Fresno); Section Chairperson, National Convention, National Council for the Social Studies, 1962; Pi Lambda Theta Honor Society in Education, Stanford University; Kappa Delta Pi, Gamma Psi Chapter of California State University-Fresno (counselor, 1972-77, 1978-79; co-counselor, 1977-78; national committee on attendance and credentials, 1975; national committee on regional conferences, 1976); One of First Women Members, Phi Delta Kappa Honor Society in Education; Organization of Filipino-American Educators of Fresno (vice president, 1975-76; president, 1977-82). Community Activities: California Governor's Committee on Juvenile Delinquency, 1958; California Governor's Committee on Traffic Safety, 1959; Counselor, Committee on Scholarships, Filipino-American Women's Club of Fresno; Resource Person, State Filipino-American Co-ordinating Council, 1968; Bank of America Scholarship Award Panel, 1968; Committee for the Selection of Social Studies Textbooks, State of California. Honors and Awards: John M. Switzer Scholarship, Stanford University, 1950; Newhouse Foundation Scholarship, Stanford University, 1951; Philippine Scholarship, California Federation of Business and Professional Women's Clubs, 1952; Distinguished Professional Woman of the Year 1957, Woman of Achievement 1973, Fresno Business and Professional Women's Club; Bicentennial Outstanding Service Award, "Compatriot in Education", Gamma Psi Chapter, Kappa Delta Pi Honor Society in Education, 1976; "Human Resource of America" Certificate, Library of Human Resources, American Bicentennial Research Institute, 1976; First Floro Crisologo Memorial Lecturer, University of Northern Philippines, Vigan, Ilocos Sur, Philippines, 1977; International Platform Association, 1979; Dr. Jose Rizal Outstanding Filipino Award, Filipino-American Association of Fresno, 1981; Listed in *Who's Who in the West, Leaders in Education, Dictionary of International Biography, Who's Who of American Women, The World Who's Who of Women, Notable Americans, The World Who's Who of Women in Education, Community Leaders and Noteworthy Americans, International Who's Who of Intellectuals, International Register of Profiles, Who's Who in California, Book of Honor, Who's Who in America*. Address: 1419 West Bullard Avenue, Fresno, California 93711.

Danesi, Barbara E

Financial Analyst. Personal: Born September 12, 1952; Daughter of Victor and Lydia A. Paglio; Married Paul C. Danesi. Education:

Attended St. Francis Xavier Academy, 1966-70; B.A., University of Rhode Island, 1974; M.B.A., Bryant College, 1978 to present. Career: Financial Anaylst, I.T.T. Grinnell-Pipe Hanger Division; Credit Analyst; Accounts Receivable Analyst. Organizational Memberships: Rhode Island Federation of Business and Professional Women; Young Career Women (chairman, Warwick club, 1981-82; finance committee). Honors and Awards: Rhode Island Honor Society, 1970; Dean's List, University of Rhode Island and Bryant College; Theatre Mask Award, St. Francis Xavier Academy, 1969. Address: 79 Ravenswood Avenue, Providence, Rhode Island 02908.

Danforth, Frances Mueller

Civic Worker. Personal: Born March 23, 1914; Daughter of Rudolph and Laura Mueller (both deceased); Married William P. Danforth; Mother of William Paul Jr., Douglas Mueller, Donald Lee. Education: Bachelor of Journalism Degree 1935, B.A. 1936, University of Texas-Austin; M.S. Journalism, Columbia University, New York City, 1938. Career: University of Texas-Austin, Grader in Journalism Department 1934, Assistant Director to Interscholastic League Press Bureau 1936-37, Assistant Editor, *Alcalde*, Monthly Alumni Magazine 1936-37, 1938-42; Editor, *Star Points*, National Paper, Delta Delta Delta, 1968-70; Reporter, *Austin American-Statesman;* Business Manager, Danforth's Antiques and Gifts, Austin. Organizational Memberships: Theta Sigma Phi Honorary Society (now Women in Communication; president); Austin Mortar Board Alums, Austin (president, 1978-82). Community Activities: Austin Symphony League (president, 1967-68); Texas Women's Association of Symphony Orchestras (state vice president, 1969-70); Austin Volunteer Bureau (president, 1966-68); Symphony Orchestra Society (board of Directors); American Red Cross, Central Texas Chapter (board of directors, secretary, 1970-72); Altenheim (president, 1961-62); Delta Delta Delta Austin Alums (president, 1968-69); Settlement Club; Lawyers' Wives (secretary, 1973-74); Women's Forum (secretary, 1972-74); Austin Woman's Club (vice president, 1977-79); Speaker, Chinese Cloisonne and Antiques, Numerous Art Groups and Clubs. Religion: St. Martin's Lutheran Church (member, 1914 to present; president 1972-74, secretary 1970-72, church women; publicity committee, 1978 to present). Honors and Awards: Honored as Fifty-Year Member, Delta Delta Delta, 1982. Address: 1400 West Avenue, Austin, Texas 78701.

Frances M Danforth

Daniel, Arthur III

Educator. Personal: Son of Willie Daniel; Married Denise Bembry; Father of Sterling, Jamie, Tracia. Education: Graduate of Polytechnic High School; Undergraduate Study in Business Administration, University of Iowa; B.S. Computer Systems Technology, Pacific Western University; Coast Guard Certification, Ordinary Seaman and Oiler; Certificate, Radar and Missile School, Fort Bliss, Texas; Certificates, Radio Repair School, Artillery Communication Supervisor School, Batallion Training Management System Trainers Workshop and Platoon Leaders Training, Advanced Non-Commissioned Officers Course, Fort Sill, Oklahoma; Certificate, U.H.F. and V.H.F. School, Fort Winfield, Scott, California; Certificate, Digital Computer Programming, I.B.M. Company; Certificate, School Community Worker Training, San Fernando State College; Certificate, Hybrid Computer Operation and Programming, United States Navy; Leadership Certificate, McGraw-Hill Continuing Education Center; Certificate, Computer Systems Technology, Electronics Engineering Technology, Nuclear Engineering Technology, McGraw-Hill, Washington, D.C.; Certificate, Technical Mathematics and Advanced Engineering Mathematics; Certificate, United States Army Recruiter School, Fort Benjamin Harrison, Indiana; Certificate, Career Insurance Agent Institute, Bankers Life and Casualty, Chicago, Illinois; Race Relations/E.E.O. Certificate, U.S.A. D.R.R.I.; Certificate U.S.A. Qm School, Petroleum Quality Assurance Representative Course; Advanced Electronic Cryptology Warfare Training, Fort Devens, Virginia; Stationary Engineering License Training, University of Toledo; Equal Opportunity Management Institute, United State Department of Defense; Methods of Learning Phases One and Two, United States Army Reserve Center, Inkster, Michigan. Military: Served in the United States Army Reserve for seventeen years, attaining the positions of Human Relations Staff Assistant, Computer Section Chief, Automatic Data Processing Section Chief, Radio Section Chief, Communication Chief, Radar Section Chief. Career: Hybrid Computer Systems Operator, United States Navy Laboratory, Pasadena, California; Operations Technician, Process Flow and Temperature Adjustment, Gulf Oil Refinery, Toledo, Ohio; Defense Technician, Calibrated Radar and Communication Equipment and Sections, State of California; Vocational Electronics Teacher, General Shop, Mathematics, Electronics, Blueprint Reading, A.C. Theory, Toledo Public Schools, Ohio; School Community Worker, Liaison between School and Community, Long Beach Public Schools, California; Salesman, Electronic Engineering Technology Employee-Training Programs, McGraw-Hill, Washington, D.C. and The Cleveland Institute of Electronics. Religion: Member of the Protestant faith. Honors and Awards: International Platform Association; Listed in *Community Leaders in America, The American Registry of Achievement, Men of Achievement.* Address: 3327 Collingwood, Toledo, Ohio 43620.

Dante, Sharon E

Founder, Director, Ballet Company. Personal: Born January 8, 1945; Daughter of Mr. and Mrs. James Dante. Education: Graduate of Torrington High School; A.S., Endicott Junior College, 1964; B.S., University of Hartford, 1966; Attended Connecticut College School of Dance, Summer 1965, 1967; Two Certificates, Connecticut College for Women's American Dance Festival; Dance Training with Yolan Szabo, Torrington and Joseph Albano, Hartford Ballet; Dance Study, Martha Graham School, New York; Leningrad Pedagogical Method of Dance Training. Career: Soloist, Charles Weidman Dance Company, Rudy Perez Dance Company, Jose Limon Dance Company; Dancer, Principle Roles, Larry Richardson Dance Company, Performances throughout the United States and Europe; Founder, Torrington School of Ballet, 1969; Performer, Faculty Member, Assistant to the Director, Hartford Ballet (joined 1969), Instrumental in the Development of Educational Programs in Hartford and Waterbury, Advisor and Teacher to Faculty, Principles of Leningrad Pedagogical Method of Dance Training, 1976-77; Instructor, Periodic Seminars, Principles of Leningrad Pedagogical Method of Dance Training; Participant, World Dance Competitions, Soviet Union (one of few Americans allowed to participate); Founder , Director, Nutmeg Ballet Company, Inc., 1971 to present. Organizational Memberships: National Association of Regional Ballet; National Association of Executive Females. Community Activities: Litchfield County Women's Network (founding board member); National Endowment for the Arts (Connecticut's dance co-ordinator, dance program, Litchfield school systems, 1974); Northwest Connecticut Arts Association (board member). Honors and Awards: De Rothchild Scholarship, Dance Study, Martha Graham School, New York; Received Outstanding Reviews for Performances with the Larry Richardson Dance Company; Listed in *Dance World* annually; biographed in *Who's Who of American Women, Who's Who in World Women, Outstanding Community Leaders.* Address: Clearview Avenue, Harwinton, Connecticut 06790.

Sharon E Dante

Darden, Edward LaFayette

Retired Architect and Educator. Personal: Born April 13, 1901; Son of Addison and Malissa Calaway Darden (both deceased); Widower; Father of Betty Darden Thompson, Paul Albert. Education: Graduate of Coast Artillery School, Fort Monroe, Virginia,

1918; Attended Alabama University and Auburn University, 1928-41; Special Course, University of Georgia, 1955. Military: Served in the United States Army, attaining the rank of Staff Sergeant. Career: Retired Architect and Educator; Former Positions include President, Alabama Vocational Association; President, Alabama Writers Conclave; Director, Alabama School of Trades, Gadsden, Alabama, 1951-70; Guest Feature Writer, *The Gadsden Times*. Organizational Memberships: United States Army Association. Community Activities: Gadsden Area Development Committee (president, 1951). Religion: Methodist. Honors and Awards: Gadsden State Technical School Man of the Year, Second Founders Day Award, 1967; Honorary Lieutenant Colonel, Alabama State Militia, 1962. Address: 527 Dumas Drive, Auburn, Alabama 36830.

Dasher, Charlotte Ann

Senior Vocational Rehabilitation Counselor. Personal: Born September 11, 1948; Daughter of Mr. and Mrs. Johnny V. Dasher. Education: A.A., DeKalb Junior College, 1972; B.S., Georgia State University, 1974; M.Ed., University of Georgia, 1977. Career: Encode Operator, 1966-67; Stenographer I, 1967-68; Typist I, 1968-69; Stenographer III, 1969-70; Stenographer III, 1970-71; Rehabilitation Intern, 1974-76; Counselor I, 1976-80. Organizational Memberships: Southwest Georgia Chapter, Georgia Rehabilitation Counseling Association (president elect, 1979; president, 1980). Community Activities: Georgia Association of Retarded Citizens (special education advisory committee, 1977 to present); Council of Exceptional Children; Ben Hill-Irwin Technical School (advisory committee for the handicapped); Tiftarea Civitan Club (project chairman, 1981 to present). Religion: Baptist. Honors and Awards: Nominated by Tifton Jaycettes to Pilot Club for Woman of the Year, 1981; Listed in *Community Leaders of America, Personalities of the South*. Address: 1478 Twila Drive, Tifton, Georgia 31794.

Charlotte Dasher

Dauber, Catherine Mary

Homemaker. Personal: Born January 30, 1908; Daughter of Mr. and Mrs. Michael C. Yeagle (now deceased); Married Clarence A. Dauber; Mother of Mrs. Grady Guye, Mrs. John Mosher, Dr. James Dauber. Education: R.N., B.S., Case Western Reserve University, 1930. Career: Head Nurse, Lakeside Hospital, Western Reserve University, Cleveland, Ohio, 1930-33. Community Activities: Parent Teacher Association (president in Oxford 1946-47, president in Monticello 1953-54); Cleveland Heights League of Women Voters (president, 1953-54); Volunteer at New England Medical Center, 1961-81; Member, Ladies Committee of New England Medical Center (chairman of hospitality, volunteer, member of numerous committees); Boston University Women's Council (vice president, 1980-82); College Club (vice president, 1981-82). Religion: Old South Church, Moderator 1973-76, Trustee 1978-83, Church Women United President in Cleveland 1960-61 & President in Massachusetts 1966-70, Vice President of Massachusetts Council of Churches 1968-70. Honors and Awards: Recipient, Brotherhood Award of the National Conference of Christians and Jews, 1977; Recipient, Churchman's Award, Churchman's League for Civic Welfare, 1970. Address: 780 Boylston Street 17B, Boston, Massachusetts 02199.

Daugherty, Frederick A

Judge. Personal: Born August 18, 1914, in Oklahoma City, Oklahoma; Married Marjorie E. Green, March 15, 1947 (deceased February 17, 1964); Married Betsy F. Amis, December 15, 1965. Education: Graduate of Central High School, Oklahoma City, Oklahoma, 1932; L.L.B., Cumberland University, 1934; Attended Oklahoma City University; Attended Oklahoma University. Military: Private Enlisted, Hq. Company, 1st Battalion, 179th Infantry, 45th Division, Oklahoma National Guard, 1934; Active Duty, 1st Lieutenant, 45th Infantry Division, 1940; Sixth United States Army, Asiatic-Pacific Theatre, World War II, 1943-45; Commanding Officer, 179th Infantry Regiment, 45th Infantry Division, 1946; Active Duty, Commanding Officer, 179th Infantry Regiment, 1950, Commanded Regiment at Camp Polk, Louisiana and Hokkaido, Japan and in Combat in Korea, 1951-52; Assistant Division Commander, 45th Infantry Division, 1952-60; General of Line, Brigadier General, 1952; Commanding General, 1960-64, Major General of Line, 1960, 45th Infantry Division; Campaigns, Bismarck Archipelago, New Guinea, South Philippines, Luzon, Leyte, Second Korean Winter, Korean Spring-Summer, 1952; Chairman, 45th Infantry Division Museum Board of Directors, 1974 to present. Career: Admitted Oklahoma State Bar, 1937; General Practice, Oklahoma City, 1937-40; Member, Firm of Ames, Ames & Daugherty, Oklahoma City, General Practice, 1946-50; Member, Firm of Ames, Daugherty, Bynum & Black, Oklahoma City, General Practice, 1952-55; Appointed Judge of District Court for Seventh Judicial District (Oklahoma and Canadian Counties), State of Oklahoma, 1955-61; Appointed United States District Judge for the Western, Eastern and Northern Districts of Oklahoma, 1961 to present; Chief Judge, Western District of Oklahoma, 1972 to present; Member, Judicial Conference of United States, 1973-76; Member, Advisory Committee of Judicial Conference on Judge Codes of Conduct, 1979 to present; Member, Judicial Panel on Multidistrict Litigation, 1980 to present; Member, Foreign Intelligence Surveillance Court, 1981 to present; Judge, Temporary Emergency Court of Appeals, 1982 to present. Organizational Memberships: Oklahoma Bar Association; American Bar Association; Federal Bar Association; Phi Delta Phi Legal Fraternity. Community Activities: Kiwanis Club of Oklahoma City (Downtown) (member, 1947 to present; president, 1957; lieutenant governor, division 19, Texas-Oklahoma district, 1959); American National Red Cross (national fund vice-chairman for Oklahoma, 1956-57, 1957-58; regional vice-chairman for Oklahoma, 1958-59, 1959-60; chairman, Oklahoma county chapter, 1958-60; member, midwestern area advisory council, 1959-62; chairman, resolutions committee, national convention, 1962; member, national board of governors, 1963-66, 1966-69; third vice-chairman, 1968-69); Oklahoma City Chamber of Commerce (vice-chairman, military affairs committee, 1958-60; member, board of directors, 1960-61, 1966-67, 1971-72, 1975-77, 1980 to present; member, corporate board of directors, 1969-70); United Fund of Greater Oklahoma City (chairman, public employees division, 1957, 1958 campaigns; member, board of directors, 1958-62; vice-chairman, 1959 campaign; vice president, 1960; member, executive committee, 1960-61; president, 1961; member, board of trustees, 1963 to present); Community Council of Oklahoma City and County (member, board of directors, 1962-66; vice president, 1965-66; president, 1967-69); Oklahoma City Council on Alcoholism (member, executive committee, 1964 to present); Oklahoma Medical Research Foundation (member, executive committee, 1966-69); Men's Dinner Club of Oklahoma City (member, executive committee, 1963-70; president, 1966-69); Oklahoma Heritage Association (member, board of directors, 1970-74); Guthrie Scottish Rite, A.A.S.R.F.M. (president, charitable and educational foundation, 1971-82; member, board of directors, building company, 1971-82; member, advisory conference, 1975-82; member, Oklahoma Scottish Rite Council, 1975-82; 33rd Degree Mason); Shriner, India Temple, Oklahoma City; Court 78, Oklahoma City (jester; director, 1967); Appointed Deputy, Supreme Council in Oklahoma, 1982 to present; Sigma Alpha Epsilon. Religion: All Souls Episcopal Church, Oklahoma City (member; senior churchwarden, 1957). Honors and Awards: Oklahoma City Sertoma Club Award to Mankind, 1962; Oklahoma City Junior Chamber of Commerce Outstanding Citizen Award, 1965; Big Brothers of Oklahoma County Citizenship Award, 1968; Oklahoma Hall of Fame, 1969; King of Beaux Arts Ball, 1972; University of Oklahoma Distinguished Service Citation, 1973; Oklahoma City University, Honorary L.L.B., 1974; Distinguished Alumni Citation, Cumberland School of Law, Samford University, 1974; Oklahoma Christian College Honorary Doctor of Humanities Degree, 1976. Address: 1800 Coventry Lane, Oklahoma City, Oklahoma 73120.

Catherine Dauber

D'Auria, Richard E

Educator. Personal: Born September 19, 1938, in Brooklyn, New York; Son of Josephine Arrigali; Married Maria Gavera Morciles; Father of Ricardo Enrico, Bianca Maria. Education: Graduate of Stuyvesant High School; B.S., New York University, 1962; M.A. 1968, Ph.D. 1974, University of Puerto Rico. Career: Associate Professor, University of Puerto Rico (present); Spanish Teacher, Junior and Senior High School. Organizational Memberships: American Association of Teachers of Spanish and Portugese; Modern Language Association; Latin American Association of Philology and Linguistics; International Platform Association; Puerto Rican Teachers Association; National Geographic Society. Community Activities: Alumni Association, Stuyvesant High School, 1978 to present; Spanish Heritage Society, 1975 to present; Sigma Delta Pi National Honor Society, 1960. Religion: Christian Family Movement, 1963-80; Cursillo Movement, 1966-75; Charismatic Renewal, 1979 to present. Honors and Awards: Founders Day Award, New York University, 1962; Huntington Foundation Grant, 1961; Certificate of Merit, Distinguished Service to the Community, Cambridge, England, 1976; Fellow, International Biographical Association, 1980-82; Listed in *Community Leaders and Noteworthy Americans, Notable Americans, Personalities of the South*. Address: Calle 24, Biq. 42-8, Sta. Rosa, Bayamon, Puerto Rico 00619.

Daut, Kenneth R

Industrial Engineer. Personal: Born August 3, 1952. Education: A.A., West Los Angeles Junior College, 1973; B.A., University of California-Los Angeles, 1975. Career: Northrop Corporation, Industrial Engineer, Budget Analyst 1978; Business Development Officer, Community Bank, 1977; Account Executive, Metropolitan Life Insurance Company, 1976. Organizational Memberships: American Institute of Industrial Engineers. Community Activities: Youth Motivation Task Force. Honors and Awards: Youth Motivation Task Force Award, Los Angeles County; Listed in *Who's Who in Finance and Industry, Who's Who in the West, American Personalities*. Address: 5816 Stratmore, Cypress, California 90630.

Davenport, Beatrice Josephine Hartman

Educator (retired). Personal: Born April 4, 1897, in Levy County, Florida; Daughter of Samuel and Nellie Hartman (deceased); Married John A. Davenport (deceased); Mother of Pauline, John Paul, Juanita, Ruth, Thomas. Education: Graduate of Morriston High School, Levy County Florida, 1914; Teacher's Institute, Cedar Keys, Florida, 1915; 2nd Grade Certificate, Cates Normal Institute, Madison, Florida. Career: Public School Teacher, Kindergarten (retired); Teacher, Five Mile Lake Butler, Bradford County, Two Years; Teacher, Guilford Bradford County, One Term; Assistant Teacher, Cherry Lake, Florida and Bell, Florida, 1916-17; Teacher, Little River Elementary School, Edison High School, 1931-70; Builder (homes, grocery store, nine furnished apartments); Opened Fire Hospital in Lake City, Florida with her husband, 1917-20; Deputy Clerk, Local Precinct; Sunday School Teacher; Maid Work, Sixteen Years; Private Helper, Aged Person, 1976-80. Organizational Activities: Parent-Teacher Association, Little River Elementary School. Community Activities: North Miami Beach Woman's Club (member, 1976-79; staff member); Lion's Club (worked with state nurse giving eye tests and glasses, five years). Religion: United Methodist Church (Sunday school teacher; United Methodist Women; all educational courses, 1930-80); Seller Methodist Church, Miami, Florida (United Woman's Society; kindergarten teacher, 1972-78). Address: 8028 Northwest 13 Court, Miami, Florida, 33147.

Mabel E Davidson

Davidson, Joeline Dillard

Laboratory Manager. Personal: Born October 4, 1942; Daughter of J. A. and Laura Christine Dillard; Married John Pratt Davidson. Education: B.S. Chemistry 1963, B.M. Voice 1967, University of Alabama; M.T., Birmingham Baptist School of Medical Technology, 1964; M.B.A. (Expected), Georgia State University. Career: Medical Technologist; Choir Director; Clinical Laboratory Manager. Organizational Memberships: Alabama State Association Blood Banks (board of directors, 1971-73); American Society of Medical Technology; Georgia Society of Medical Technology (chairman, administrative section, scientific assembly, 1978-80; program chairman, convention, 1981); Georgia Department of Human Resources (laboratory advisory council); West Central Georgia Society for Medical Technology (charter vice president, 1980); Chattahoochee Valley Clinical Laboratory Management Association (charter chairman, 1978). Community Activities: Bessemer Civic Chorale; Tuscaloosa Civic Chorale; University of Alabama Opera; Advisor to Medical Explorer Scout Troop, La Grange, Georgia; Festival of Fine Arts (board member, 1959-60); Bryce Hospital (volunteer teacher). Religion: First Methodist Church, Bessemer, Alabama (director, junior Methodist youth fellowship, 1959-60; accompanist, junior choir, 1958-60); Oak Grove Methodist Church, Mulga, Alabama (choir director, 1962); Martin Memorial Methodist Church, Birmingham, Alabama (choir director, 1964-68). Honors and Awards: Girl's State, 1959; Outstanding Student Award, Optimist International, 1960; Bessemer Music Club Scholarship, 1958; President's Honor Roll, American Society of Medical Technology, 1981; Listed in *Who's Who in the South and Southwest; International Who's Who of Intellectuals; The World's Who's Who of Women; The Book of Honor; The Directory of Distinguished Americans*. Address: P.O. Box 1786, La Grange, Georgia 30241.

Davidson, Mabel Elizabeth Farlow

Author, Lecturer, Researcher. Personal: Born May 20, 1901, in Rush County, Indiana; Married Dwight L. Davidson, 1920; Mother of Evelyn Mae Potvoricky. Education: Attended Milroy School, Indiana; Attended Purdue University and Indiana University; Graduate of The Famous Writers' School, Westport, Connecticut. Career: Free-lance Writer, Books and Articles; National Sales Manager, Clinton County Book Company; Lecturer; Researcher; Book Reviewer for Various Groups and Organizations. Organizational Memberships: Clinton County Historical Society; Indiana Historical Society; American Biographical Research Association (annual associate). Community Activities: International Platform Association; International Toastmistress Club; Quill and Gavel Toastmistress Club of Indianapolis; Indiana Roadside Council; Colfax Travel-Study Club; International Travel-Study Club; Daughters of the American Revolution (member, Captain Harmon Aughe chapter); Isaac Walton Auxiliary (chorister, thirteen years); Cancer Research, Handicapped Children Organizations (all of the profits from her books go to these causes); Clinton County Chorus; Home Demonstration Club. Religion: United Methodist Church (various offices; member, women's society; Sunday school teacher, 25 years). Published Works: Various Articles, *Indianapolis Sunday Star* Magazine, *The Indianapolis News*; Historical Articles, *The Franklin Times*, Other Publications; *Legend and Lore from America's Crossroads; Recollections of a Country Gal; Out of the Past and Into the Future*. Honors and Awards: Charter Member Certificate and Honorary Letter, Listed as One of All-Time Outstanding Graduates, Featured in Bicentennial Year Promotional Materials, The Famous Writers' School; *Legend and Lore from America's Crossroads* Selected One of the Most Distinguished Books of the Year, Author's Day, Indiana University; Listed in *The Directory of Notable Americans, The Book of Honor of Our Country's 200th Year, Community Leaders and Noteworthy Americans, Partiots of the 1980's, International Dictionary of Biographies, World's Who's Who of Women, World's Who's Who of*

Intellectuals. Address: Route 2, Colfax, Indiana 46035.

Davies, James Gerald

Director of Data Processing. Personal: Born October 18, 1947; Son of Glyndur J. and Maletha M. Davies. Education: B.S. Math, Evangel College, 1970. Military: United States Army Sergeant, 1971-73; United States Army Reserves, 1977 to present; Staff Sergeant, 1979 to present. Career: Evangel College, Director of Data Processing 1975 to present; Computer Programmer 1974-75; Computer Programmer, American Telephone & Telegraph, 1973-74; Computer Operator, Univac Division of Sperry Rand, 1970-71. Organizational Activities: N.C.R. Educational Users Group (president, 1979-80; vice president, 1978-79; director-at-large, 1977-78); Data Processing Management Association, Ozark Empire Chapter (international director, 1979-80; president, 1978-79; member of board of directors, 1977-78); Federation of N.C.R. Users (member, board of directors, 1980 to present). Honors and Awards: Outstanding Achievement Award, United States Army Reserve Duty, *St. Louis Globe-Democrat; Listed in Who's Who, Notable Americans, Community Leaders, Personalities of the West and Midwest; Men of Achievement.* Address: 1406 Blaine, Springfield, Missouri 65803.

Davis, C Neal

Administrator. Personal: Born November 3, 1936; Son of Mr. and Mrs. Claud Davis; Married Pat Duncan; Father of Cathy, Mike, Mark, Carol Kim, Connie Beth, Mitch. Education: A.B., William Jewell College, Liberty, Missouri, 1958; M.A., Northeast Missouri State University, Kirksville, 1963; Ph.D., University of Missouri-Kansas City, 1970; Certification, Institute for Educational Management, Harvard University, Cambridge, Massachusetts, 1975. Career: Vice President, Dean for Development and Public Relations, Hannibal-LaGrange College, Hannibal, Missouri, 1982 to present; President, Judson Baptist College, Portland, Oregon, 1973-80, The Dalles, Oregon, 1980-81; Dean of Students, Elmhurst College, Illinois, 1967-73; William Jewell College, Liberty, Missouri, Dean of Men 1963-67, Director of Yates College Union and Student Activities 1964-67. Organizational Memberships: American Association for Higher Education (lifetime member); American College Personnel Association (former officer); National Vocational Guidance Association; American Personnel and Guidance Association. Community Activities: Parent-Teacher Associations (president, 1969-70, 1972-73); Holt Adoption Program (board member); Holt International Children's Services, Eugene, Oregon (board member); Rotary Club (perfect attendance since 1964; member, Liberty, Missouri, 1964-67; member, Elmhurst, Illinois, 1967-73; member, Northeast Portland, Oregon, 1973-80; member, The Dalles, Oregon, 1980-82; past president; district governor, Oregon-Washington, 1981-82; member, Hannibal, Missouri, 1982 to present). Religion: Member, Ten Baptist Churches in Four States (active in all of them); Deacon; Sunday School Teacher; Lay Minister in Various Denominations. Honors and Awards: Western Auto Supply Company Career Scholarship; Phi Delta Kappa; Leader of Six International Study Tours; Paul Harris Fellow; Rotary Foundation Award, 1981; Listed in Various *Who's Who* Publications, 1958 to present. Address: Four Woodland Trail, Hannibal, Missouri 63401.

Evelyn M B Davis

Davis, Evelyn Marguerite Bailey

Musician and Artist. Personal: Born in Springfield, Missouri; Daughter of Philip Edward Bailey and Della Jane Morris Bailey Freeman (both deceased); Married James Harvey. Education: Secretarial Training; Private Student of Organ and Piano for Twelve Years, Webster Grove, Missouri; Special Classes at Drury College. Career: Secretary, Shea and Morris Monument Company; Soloist Mem, Sextet, Radio Station KGBX; Bible Teacher, Pianist, East Avenue Baptist Church; Teacher, Bible Class, Third Baptist Church, St Louis, Missouri; Engaged to Paint 12 by 6 Foot Mural of Jordan River, Bible Baptist Church, Maplewood, Missouri, 1954; Church Organist, Bible Teacher, Bible Baptist Church, 1956; Teacher of Organ and Piano, Voice and CromaHarp; Assistant Organist, Pianist and Soloist, Bible Church, Arnold, Missouri, 1969; Temple Baptist Church, Kirkwood, Missouri: Organist, Pianist, Soloist, Bible Teacher, Youth Orchestra Director, Music Arranger; Faculty Member, Bible Baptist Christian School, 1976-77; Organist, Vocal Soloist, Floral Arranger, Bible Teacher, Faith Missionary Baptist Church, St. Charles, Missouri, 1978 to present. Organizational Memberships: National Guild of Piano Teacher Auditions; St. Louis Chapter of National Guild of Organists. Compositions: "I Will Sing Hallelujah"; "I Am Alpha and Omega"; "Prelude to Prayer"; "My Shephard"; "O Sing Unto the Lord a New Song"; "O Come Let Us Sing Unto the Lord"; "The Lord is My Light and My Salvation"; Num Hymn Arrangements for Organ and Piano. Honors and Awards: Descendant of the Sixteenth Century Christian Leader John Knox and Dr. John Witherspoon (only minister to sign the Declaration of Independence); Life Fellow, International Biographical Association; International Platform Association; Life Fellow, American Biographical Institute; Listed in *International Who's Who in Music and Musicians Directory, International Register of Profiles, Dictionary of International Biography, Who's Who of American Women, Personalities of the West and Midwest, World Who's Who of Women, International Who's Who of Intellectuals, Community Leaders and Noteworthy Americans, Men and Women of Distinction, American Patriots of the 1980s, Personalities of America, Book of Honor, The Directory of Distinguished Americans, Who's Who in the Midwest, Notable Americans, Contemporary Americans, Contemporary Personalities.* Address: No. 4 Ranchero Drive, Edgewood Acres, St. Charles, Missouri 63301.

Davis, Gordon William

Educator. Personal: Born October 7, 1910, in Galva, Illinois; Son of William George and Beatrice Gordon Davis. Education: A.B., Knox College, 1934; M.S., Washington University, 1938. Military: Served in the United States Army Reserves from 1942-57, advancing from the rank of Commanding Captain in 1942 to Lieutenant Colonel in 1953, and holding such positions as Civil Affairs Officer 1944-45, Military Governor 1945-47, Branch Advisor of the Chemical Corps and Reserves for New York State 1951-53, Chemical Corps Branch Advisor for the South Carolina District and Chemical Reserve Units in Charleston 1953-57. Career: Associate Professor, Physical Science, Miami-Dade Junior College, 1963 to present; Assistant Professor, Chemistry and Math, Ferris State College, Big Rapids, Michigan, 1959-63; Professor of Biology and Chemistry, Chairman, Science Department, Frederick College, Portsmouth, Virginia, 1959; Assistant Professor, Scientific Supervisor, Winthrop College, Rock Hill, South Carolina, 1957-58; Head of Science Department, Elkader Junior College, Iowa, 1941-42. Organizational Memberships: American Association of University Professors (delegate, Florida Conference, 1966 to present; Miami-Dade Junior College chapter, founder, president, 1966 to present); Missouri Academy of Science; American Chemical Research Society; Dade County Classroom Teachers Association; American Association of Junior Colleges; Florida Education Association; Association for Higher Education; University Professors of Academic Order; Florida Academy of Science; Phi Sigma; National Science Teachers Association (lifetime member); American Ordnance Association (lifetime member); Sigma Xi (lifetime member); Reserve Officers Association; Armed Forces Chemistry Society; Chemist Club. Religion: Member of the Congregational Church. Honors and Awards: Intercontinental Biographical Association (life fellow); Presidential Citation, late President Harry F. Truman, 1948; National Honor Society; Listed in *Dictionary of International Biography, Royal Blue Book, National Social Directory, Who's Who in the East, Who's Who in the Midwest, Who's Who in*

America, Who's Who in the South and Southwest, International Who's Who in Community Service, Two Thousand Men of Achievement, U.N.A.-U.S.A., Greater Miami Area Social Register. Address: 1211-B Northwest 101st Street, Miami, Florida 33147.

Davis, Joy Lynn

Executive. Personal: Born February 4, 1945; Daughter of Irving and Irene Davis. Education: Graduated from Miami Norland Senior High School, 1962. Career: Vice President, Investments, Bache Halsey Stuart Shields Inc., Fort Lauderdale, Florida, 1980 to present; 2nd Vice President, Investments, Shearson Loeb Rhoades Inc., 1966-80. Organizational Memberships: Fort Lauderdale Bond Club (member, board of directors, 1980); Miami/Fort Lauderdale Stockbrokers Society (member, 1979). Address: 806 Northwest 79 Terrace, Plantation, Florida 33324.

Davis, Kenneth Penn

Management Analyst. Personal: Born August 5, 1942, in Charleston, South Carolina; Son of William Alexander and Alice Cummings Mears Davis; Married Diane Cecilia Leonard; Father of Carol Lee. Education: B.A., Oglethorpe University, 1964; M.A., Georgia State University, 1968; Ph.D., University of Virginia, 1975. Military: United States Army Officer Candidate School, Fort Benning, Commissioned 1969, Ranked 1st Lieutenant 1970; United States Army Southeastern Signal Corps School, Office of Commandant, 1969-70; 12th Signal Group, Asst. S-4 and H.Q. Detachment Commander, Danang, Vietnam; Signal Officer Basic Course, Signal Officer Advanced Course; Command and General Staff College; Ranked Captain, 1974; Ranked Major, 1981; Assigned to Alexandria, Virginia Office of Emergency Preparedness (present). Career: District Counselor, Circulation Department, *Atlanta Journal* Newspaper, 1964-65; Management Trainee, All-State Insurance Company, Atlanta, 1965-66; Program Analyst, National Archives, Washington, D.C., 1974-78; Part-Time Instructor, American History, Northern Virginia Community College, Alexandria, 1978; Management Analyst, General Services Administration, Washington, D.C., 1978 to present. Organizational Activities: G.S.A. Region Three Credit Union (board of directors, 1979 to present); American Humanics Foundation for Youth Leadership, Kansas City, Missouri; Combined Federal Campaign, National Archives (chairman, 1978); Boy Scouts of America (active member, 1955 to present; district commissioner, 1979-80; National Order of the Arrow committee, 1974-82; member-at-large, national council, 1974 to present; member, national events committee, 1974 to present; chairman, southeastern region Order of the Arrow committee, 1974 to present; National Camp School, director, 1974-78, director, wood badge leadership course, 1973 to present, camp inspector; associate advisor; assistant scoutmaster; training chairman; advisor for training, National Order of the Arrow conferences, 1975, 1977, 1979; staff member, Philmont scout ranch, six years; staff member, 1967 world jamboree, 1973 national jamboree); American Historical Association; Organization of American Historians; Society of Historians of American Foreign Relations; American Society of Public Administration; Phi Alpha Theta; Blue Key; Omicron Delta Kappa. Religion: Methodist. Published Works: Articles on the Cherokee Indians; Contributed Chapter to *The Cherokee Indian Nation.* Honors and Awards: National Defense Service Medal; Vietnam Service and Campaign Medals; Bronze Star with Oak Leaf Cluster; Army Reserve Components Achievement Medal; Presidential Sports Award for Jogging 200 Miles, 1981; Boy Scouts of America, Eagle Scout Award, God and Country Award, Silver Beaver, Silver Antelope, Order of the Arrow National Distinguished Service Award, Award of Merit, Vigil Honor of the Order of the Arrow; Lowry Scholar, 1960-64; Colonial Dames Georgia Graduate Scholar, 1967; Governor's Fellow, Virginia, 1973-74. Address: 6320 Phyllis Lane, Alexandria, Virginia 22312.

Kenneth P Davis

Davis, Lowell Livingston

Surgeon. Personal: Born December 14, 1922, in Urbanna, Virginia; Married Barbara Helen Allen. Education: Graduated from Montgomery Training School, Waugh, Alabama, 1940; B.S. Biology, Morehouse College, Atlanta, Georgia, 1949; M.S. Zoology, Atlanta University, Georgia, 1950; Attended University of Pennsylvania Graduate School of Medicine, Philadelphia; M.D., Howard University, Washington, D.C., 1955; Rotating Internship, Jersey Medical Center, New Jersey, 1955-56; Residencies 1956-69, Obstetrics, Margaret Hague Maternity Hospital, Jersey City 1956-57, Obstetrics and Gynecology, Elmhurst General Hospital, New York 1957-59, General Surgery, United States Veterans Administration Hospital, Tuskegee, Alabama 1960-61, General Surgery, Nassau County Medical Center, Meadowbrook General Hospital, Hemstead, New York 1961-64, Cardiothoracic Surgery, Cook County Hospital, Chicago, Illinois 1967-69. Military: United States Navy, 1943-46, Discharged as Pharmacist's Mate, Third Class; Active Duty, United States Naval Reserve Medical Corps, Commander, 1965-67 (served as general surgeon), 1969-71 (served as thoracic and cardiovascular surgeon), Discharged 1978 as Captain (M.C.). Career: Fellowships 1972-75, Cardiopulmonary Surgery, University of Oregon Medical School Hospitals and Clinics, Portland, Oregon 1972, Cardiovascular Surgery, St. Vincent Hospital, Portland, Oregon 1972, Coronary Revascularization Surgery, Medical College of Wisconsin, Milwaukee 1973, Cardiovascular Surgery, Pacific Medical Center, Institutes of Medical Sciences, Heart Research Institute, San Francisco, California 1974, Cardiac Surgery Research, Allen-Bradley Medical Science Research Laboratory, Medical College of Wisconsin 1975, Visiting Surgeon in Thoracic and Cardiac Surgery, Hospital for Sick Children, London, England 1977-78; Licensure, Maryland, New Jersey, Maine, New York, Pennsylvania, Illinois, Wisconsin, California, Georgia, Federal Narcotic, D.E.A.; Board Certifications, Diplomate, American Board of Surgery, American Board of Thoracic Surgery; Film Writer, with A. J. Tector, R. Flemma, D. Lepley et al, *Rapid Takedown of Internal Mammary Artery* 1974, with A. J. Tector et al, *Rapid Technique of Taking Down the Internal Mammary Artery;* Instructor, Embryology, Histology, Neuro-Anatomy, Gross Human Anatomy, Meharry Medical College, Nashville, Tennessee, 1950-51; Instructor, Surgery, College of Medicine, University of Illinois, 1969; Clinical Instructor, Thoracic Surgery, University of Southern California-Los Angeles, Los Angeles County General Hospital, 1981 to present; Private Practice, General Surgery, New York City, 1964-65; Military Practice, United States Naval Hospital, St. Albans, New York, Senior Surgeon 1965-67, Chief, Department of Thoracic asnd Cardiovascular Surgery 1970-71; Staff Thoracic Surgeon, 1969-70; Private Practice, Thoracic and Cardiovascular Surgery, 1975 to present; Staff Surgeon, Beth Israel Medical Center, Beth Israel Hospital, New York City, 1965-71; Staff Thoracic and Cardiovascular Surgeon, St. Luke's Hospital, Milwaukee, Wisconsin, 1976-78; Active Staff, Thoracic and Cardiovascular Surgeon, Hospital of the Good Samaritan, California Lutheran Hospital Medical Center, Los Angeles, California (present). Organizational Activities: Association of Military Surgeons f the United States, 1966; International College of Angiology, 1966; American College of Angiology, 1967; International College of Surgeons, 1967; New York Academy of Medicine, 1970; American College of Surgeons, 1971; American College of Cardiology, 1972; Society of Thoracic Surgeons, 1973; American Association of Thoracic Surgeons, 1973; The Albert Starr Cardiac Surgical Society (founding member, 1974); American College of Emergency Physicians, 1976; Cardiac Surgery Committee, Hollywood Presbyterian Hospital, Los Angeles, California (chairman, 1982); American Heart Association, 1981-82; Independent Medical Examiner (thoracic surgery), State of California, Department of Industrial Relations, Division of Industrial Accidents, 1981-83. Published Works: Contributor to *Obstetrics and Gynecology, New York State Journal of Medicine* (three articles), *Journal of the American Geriatrics Society, Surgery Digest, Chest, Annals of Thoracic Surgery.* Honors and Awards: American Campaign Medal, American Theater, Medal with One Gold Star, Asiatic-Pacific Theater, World War II Victory Medal, Presidential Unit Citation (Navy-Marine Corps), Okinawa, Presidential Letter of Thanks from Harry S. Truman, Personal Letter of Thanks from Secretary of the Navy James Forrestal, Certificate of Service with Task Force 31, World

War II; Occupational Medal, Asia, Post World War II; National Defense Medal; Certificate of Appreciation, signed by then-President Richard M. Nixon, 1971; Listed in *Who's Who in the West, Who's Who in California, Personalitiies of the West and Midwest, International Who's Who in Community Services, Community Leaders and Noteworthy Americans, Dictionary of International Biography, The International Who's Who of Intellectuals.* Address: 4267 Marina City Drive, WTS-310, Marina del Rey, California 90201.

Davis, Marjorie

Associate Professor. Personal: Born March 13, 1935; Daughter of Harry (deceased) and Lean Smith; Mother of Roger. Education: B.S., Panhandle State University, 1959; M.A., University of Kansas, 1962; Ph.D., Kansas State University, 1970. Career: Instructor in Biology, Mankato State University, Mankato, Minnesota; Instructor in Biology, Kansas State University, Manhattan; Assistant Professor in Biology, Missouri Western University, Joseph; Visiting Assistant Professor in Biology, Kansas State University, Manhattan; Associate Professor of Anatomy, Oklahoma Osteopathic College of Medicine and Surgery. Organizational Memberships: Sigma Xi; American Association of Zoologists; Society for the Study of Reproduction; New York Academy of Science; Oklahoma Academy of Science; Kansas Academy of Science; American Association of University Professors; American Association for the Advancement of Science. Community Activities: M.O.R.A.L. (president, 1980-81); Planned Parenthood (local educational committee; volunteer educator); "What's It All About" Program (curriculum committee); National Organization of Women; Parent Teachers Association (past president). Religion: United Methodist. Honors and Awards: Listed in *American Men and Women of Science; World Who's Who of Women in Education; World Who's Who of Women; Community Leaders and Noteworthy Americans, Who's Who in the South and Southwest.* Address: 3816 E 105th Street, Tulsa, Oklahoma 74136.

Davis, Marylee

Administrator, Educator. Personal: Born September 17; Daughter of Harold J. Davis (deceased) and Mrs. Harold J. Davis. Education: Attended Furman University, East Tennessee State University; B.S. Education 1965, M.S. College Student Personnel 1970, University of Tennessee-Knoxville; Ph.D. Administration and Higher Education, Michigan State University, 1974. Career: Michigan State University, Assistant Vice President, Associate Professor, Administration and Higher Education 1978 to present, Special Assistant to the Executive Vice President, Secretary to the Board of Trustees, Assistant Professor of Administration and Higher Education 1974-78, Division of Residence Hall Programs, Assistant Director, Owen Graduate Center 1972-74, Residence Hall Head Advisor (Rather Hall) 1971-72, Graduate Assistant, Research and Administration, Division of Judicial Programs, Dean of Students Office 1970-71; Congressional Staff Assistant, Office of the Honorable James H. Quillen, M.C., United States House of Representatives, Washington, D.C., Summer 1971; Carrick Hall South, Division of Residence Halls, University of Tennessee-Knoxville, Assistant Head Resident 1970, Resident Assistant 1969-70; Teacher, Madison School, Kingsport Public School System, Tennessee. Organizational Activities: Statewide Taskforce to Explore the Feasibility of an External Degree Program for the State of Michigan (chairperson, 1974-75); Non-Academic Women Employees (advisor, ad hoc member, advisory committee, 1975 to present); Council of Graduate Students (faculty advisor, 1979 to present); Mildred Erickson Scholarship Fund for Lifelong Education (board member, publicity committee chair, 1975-79; finance committee, 1979-80; chair of the board, 1980-81); Michigan State University (faculty council member, academic council, 1976-78, 1979-80; member, committee on academic governance, 1976-78; member, sub-committee on university by-law revision, 1976-78; member, faculty tenure committee, 1979-81; chair, career planning and placement council, 1978 to present; faculty women's association, treasurer 1975-76, vice president 1976-77, president 1977-78). Community Activities: United Way (chair, 1980 campaign, chair, campaign executive vice president's division 1974-79, Michigan State University; budget panel allocation committee 1977-80, budget steering committee, panel vice chair 1979-80, panel chair 1980-81, 1981-82, general vice chair 1982 campaign, capital area); Michigan's Statewide Extension Council for Family Living Education Program (charter member, 1977 to present); Michigan Capital Girl Scout Council (board member, 1977; first vice president, 1980-83); Zonta International, Zonta Club of East Lansing Area (charter member, 1975 to present; vice president, 1975-77; president, 1977-79; program chair, 1979-80, service committee co-chair, 1980-81; district XV public affairs chair, 1980-82; district XV nominating committee chair, 1980-82); Greater Lansing Chamber of Commerce, 1974 to present (East Lansing-Meridian Chamber of Commerce, university representative, legislative action committee, 1979-80; state taxation task force, 1980-81); M.S.U. Women's Sports Booster Club (board member, 1978-82; vice chairperson, 1979-80; president, 1980-81); Appalachian Girl Scout Council (advisor, Wing scout senior troop, 1966-70); Community Volunteers for International Programs, Lansing, Michigan (advisor, 1972-82); University of Tennessee, 1969-70 (chair, judicial board; student discipline specialist, first in the history of the institution). Honors and Awards: Dean's List, E.T.S.U. and University of Tennessee, 1962-65; Dean's Award for Outstanding Scholarship, E.T.S.U., 1964; Magna Cum Laude Graduate, University of Tennessee, 1965; Service Award, M.S.U. Co-operative Extension Service, 1977; Certificate of Merit, Y.W.C.A. Diana Dinner, Lansing, Michigan, 1977; Award for Excellence, Faculty Women's Association, M.S.U., 1980; Statewide Co-operative Extension Honorary Friend of Extension Award, M.S.U., 1980; Listed in *Outstanding Young Women of America, World's Who's Who of Women, Who's Who of American Women, Who's Who in the Midwest.* Address: 6223 Cobblers Drive, East Lansing, Michigan 48823.

Marylee Davis

Davis, Robert H

Secretary/Treasurer and Controller. Personal: Born March 26, 1943, in Philadelphia, Pennsylvania; Son of Dorothy P. Davis/Jenson; Father of Michelle R. Davis. Education: Attended Stanford University Graduate School of Business, 1978-80; Pepperdine University School of Law, 1981; University of San Francisco School of Law, 1982; Los Angeles Valley College, 1965-67; Alexander Hamilton Executive Training Program Institute; Dun and Bradstreet Basic Credit and Financial Analysis Course; Other Courses and Seminars. Military: Served with the United States Naval Reserve, 1961-66. Career: Financial Consultant: Western Energy Corporation, Trans-Equipment Company Inc., Huey's BBQ Inc., Three Percent Inc., Burn's Rathole Drilling Co., Inc., J & R Properties, Wyo Natrona Air; Controller, Secretary/Treasurer, John E. Burns Drilling Co., 1979-; Corporate Credit Manager, Caterpillar Heavy Machinery and Equipment, Wyoming Machinery Co., 1978-79; Great West Auto Dealers Service Inc., 1976-77; General Manager, L. P. Transport Inc., 1975-76; Corporate Credit Manager, Assistant Controller, Marfred Wholesale Paper Company Inc., 1974-76; Owner, Special Comodities, Explosives, R. H. Davis Trucking, 1970-74; Senior Analytical Analyst, Dun & Bradstreet Inc., 1965-70. Organizational Memberships: Casper Industrial Credit Group, National Association of Credit Management (founder, chairman); Alumni Association, Stanford University Graduate School of Credit and Financial Management; National Association of Credit Management (honorary member board of directors, state representative for Wyoming); Rocky Mountain Association of Credit Managers (conducted credit management seminars in Casper, Wyoming); Research Institute of America; American Management Association; National Association of Credit Management; U.S. Chamber of Commerce; International Platform Association; Alumni Association of Stanford University. Community Activities: United Fund Drive, Casper, Wyoming, 1980; Junior Achievement Program (counselor 1967); Citizenship Committee of Natrona County, 1980-81; Democratic Political Committee "Art Terry for Sheriff", 1982. Religion: Highland Park Community Church and Grace Lutheran Church: Finance and

Stewardship Committees; Active in World Vision Program and Jimmy Swaggart Ministries. Published Works: *Leasing As a Secondary Source of Financing In the Heavy Equipment Industry.* Honors and Awards: Senior DeMolay Award, 1963; National Association Award of Achievement, 1980; Runner-up, American Petroleum Award for Thesis, 1980; Listed in *Who's Who in Business and Finance, Who's Who in the West, International Platform Association,* American Biographical Institute Publications. Address: P.O. Box 1091, Mills, Wyoming 82644.

Davis, Samuel Adams

Retired. Personal: Born June 7, 1917; Son of Samuel P. and Eleanor Davis (both deceased); Married Mary Lona Forgy; Father of Lona Davis Spencer, Mary Dee Davis (deceased). Education: B.S., University of Florida, 1950. Military: Served with the United States Navy: Seaplane Pilot, 1942-47; Korean Conflict, 1952-55; Lieutenant Commander, Retired. Career: Hillsborough County Forester, Florida State Division of Forestry, Department of Agriculture, 1969-79; Area Forester, St. Regis Paper Company, 1955-58; Air Controller, Federal Aviation Agency, 1958-59; Pole Inspector, Koppers Company, 1950-52. Organizational Memberships: International Society of Argriculture (president, southern chapter, 1977); Flordia Section of Society of American Foresters (chairman, Caribbean chapter); Florida Farm Bureau; Florida Forestry Association; American Forestry Association; American Wildlife Federation; Audubon Society; State Cattlemen's Association. Community Activities: Rotary International; Tampa City Tree and Landscape Board, 1980-81; Florida Board of Registration for Foresters, 1978-79; Hillsborough County Children's Services Volunteer League (board of directors, 1981); Military Order of World Wars (staff of Florida department); Naval Reserve Association; Reserve Officers Association; National Geographic Society; U.S. Naval Institute; Smithsonian Institution; National Association of Retarded Citizens. Religion: Southern Baptists; Deacon, Sunday School Teacher. Honors and Awards: Navy Cross and Air Medal; Pacific Area with 2 Battle Stars, 1945; Special Commendation, Hillsborough County Commissioners. Address: 2138 W. Minnehaha Ave., Tampa, Florida 33604.

Dawson, Robert Edward

Robert E Dawson

Ophthalmologist, Assistant Clinical Professor. Personal: Born February 23, 1918, in Rocky Mount, North Carolina; Married Julia Davis; Father of Diane Elizabeth, Janice Elaine, Robert Edward, Melanie Lorraine. Military: Served in the United States Air Force, 1955-57, achieving the rank of Major. Career: Attending Staff, Ophthalmology, Durham County General Hospital, 1976 to present (Vice President of Staff; Vice President of Medical Council, 1976-78; Board of Trustees, 1978 to present); Assistant Clinical Professor of Ophthalmology, Duke University Medical Center, Durham, North Carolina, 1977 to present; Clinical Associate in Ophthalmology 1971-77, Duke University Hospital, Clinical Instructor in Ophthalmology 1968-70; Medical Director, Lincoln Hospital, Durham, North Carolina, 1968-70; Consultant, Division of Disability Determination, North Carolina Department of Human Resources, 1971 to present; Attending Staff, Ophthalmology, Watts Hospital, 1966-76; Chief, Ophthalmology and Otolaryngology, Lincoln Hospital, 1958-76; Post-Graduate Training, New York Eye and Ear Infirmary, 1963; New York University Institute of Ophthalmology, 1962; Chief, Ophthalmology and Otolaryngology, 3310th Hospital, Scott Air Force Base, Illinois, 1955-57; Pathology (Ophthalmic) Armed Forces Institute of Pathology, 1956; North Carolina Central University Health Service Consultant, Ophthalmology, 1950-64; Attending Staff, Ophthalmology, Lincoln Hospital, 1946-55. Organizational Memberships: American College of Surgeons (fellow); American Board of Ophthalmology (diplomate, 1963; examiner, 1979-82); Academy of Ophthalmology and Otolaryngology (fellow); American Association of Ophthalmology; Pan American Medical Association (diplomate); National Medical Association; Chi Delta Mu Scientific Fraternity; Society of Eye Surgeons; American Medical Association; Meharry Medical College (board of trustees 1971 to present; executive committee; chairman, hospital and health affairs committee; chairman, presidential search committee); National Medical Association (board of trustees, 1970 to present; chairman, constitution committee; chairman, council on financial aid to students; chairman, insurance committee; council on scientific assembly; budget committee; council on awards; publication committee; management committee; executive committee; chairman, student national medical association liaison committee; president, 1979-80); North Carolina Central University, Durham, North Carolina (board of trustees; executive committee; chairman, faculty-trustee relations committee; chairman, buildings and grounds committee; nominating committee); National Society to Prevent Blindness, North Carolina Chapter (board of directors, 1967 to present); Foundation for Better Health, Durham County General Hospital (board of directors, 1975-79); National Society to Prevent Blindness (board of directors, 1976 to present; vice president, 1981 to present); Clark College, Atlanta, Georgia (board of visitors, 1973 to present); Mutual Savings and Loan Association (board of trustees, 1975 to present); Durham United Fund (board of directors, 1975 to present). Community Activities: Lincoln Community Health Center (board of directors); Durham Academy (board of trustees, 1969-72); American Cancer Society (board of directors); North Carolina State Commission for the Blind (advisory board); Eye Bank Association of America, Inc. (regional surgical director); Governor's Advisory Committee on Medical Assistance, 1978 to present; Toastmasters International (past president, Durham chapter); Meharry National Alumni Association (president, 1968-69, 1969-70; board of management); Durham County Tuberculosis Association (board of directors, 1950-54); Chamber of Commerce (operation committee, 1975); Old North State Medical Society (past president); Alpha Phi Alpha (past president); Sigma Pi Phi (treasurer, past president); Democratic Party; 32° Mason and Shriner; Durham Community House (board of directors, 1966-68); Durham Council on Human Relations; National Association for the Advancement of Colored People (life member); Durham Business and Professional Chain; President's Committee on Employment of the Handicapped in America; Durham County Mental Health (board of directors, 1969-80); Association of Governing Boards Commission on Boards of Trustees of Single Campus State Supported Institutions, Their Scope and Future. Religion: St. Joseph's A.M.E. Church, Board of Stewards 1966 to present. Published Works: "Federal Impact on Medical Care" June 1980, "Bedside Manner of a Computer" March 1980, "Crisis in the Medical Arena: A Challenge for the Black Physician" December 1979, *Journal of the National Medical Association.* Honors and Awards: Distinguished Service Award, National Medical Association; Alpha Omega Alpha Honor Medical Society; Physician of the Year Award, Old North State Medical Society, 1969; Toastmaster of the Year, Durham-1206; Alpha Delta Alpha Honor Scientific Society; High School Valedictorian, Class of 1935; Listed in *Who's Who in Black America, Dictionary of Medical Specialists, International Who's Who in Community Service, International Who's Who of Intellectuals, Who's Who in the South and Southwest, Personalities of the South, North Carlina Lives.* Address: 817 Lawson Street, Durham, North Carolina 27701.

Day, Richard Robert

Director of Research and Training. Personal: Born January 2, 1944; Son of Robert W. Day; Married; Father of Lisa Denise, Leslie Diann, Lori Danielle. Education: B.S. Economics 1965, M.S. Psychology 1972, Auburn University; Ph.D. Counselor Education, University of Virginia, 1974. Military: Served in the United States Army Reserves from 1965-71, attaining the rating of E-5. Career: Director, Research and Staff Development, Arkansas Enterprises for the Blind, Little Rock, Arkansas; Assistant Professor of Human Development Counseling, George Peabody College; Assistant Professor, Counseling and Guidance, Troy State University. Organizational Memberships: American Psychological Association; American Personnel and Guidance Association, Phi Delta Kappa. Community Activities: Lions Club (member, 1978 to present); Georgia Task Force on Blindness (chairman). Religion:

Baptist. Honors and Awards: Licensed Psychologist, Arkansas, 1981; Licensed Professional Counselor, Arkansas, 1981; Listed in *Who's Who in the South and Southeast, Personalities of the South, The Directory of Distinguished Americans.* Address: 504 Oak Road, Warm Springs, Georgia 31830.

Day, Wallace Edwin

Plant Manager, Management and Systems Analyst. Personal: Born June 7, 1940; Son of Mrs. Les Stouffer; Married Sandra Lou McDonald; Father of Wallace Edwin Jr., Joseph Cristian. Education: Studies at the American Institute of Laundry; International Fabric Institute; United States Army Logistics Management Center. Military: Served in the United States Navy, 1959-63, and in the United States Navy Reserve, 1963-65; Commander, District 2, Maryland State Naval Militia, 1981 to present. Career: Laundry and Drycleaning Plant Manager, Staff Specialist and Management and Systems Analyst, Department of the Navy, United States Naval Academy, Annapolis, Maryland, 1976 to present; Laundry and Drycleaning Plant Manager, Staff Specialist, Supply Officer, Department of the Army, Nuernberg Military Community and VII Corps, Nuernberg, Germany, 1973-76; Laundry and Drycleaning Plant Manager, Linen Exchange Officer, Department of the Army, United States Army Training Center, Fort Jackson, Columbia, South Carolina, 1971-73; Laundry and Drycleaning Plant Manager, Staff Specialist, Member of Commander's Non-Appropriated Fund Audit and Advisory Board, Department of Army, Headquarters Rheinland-Pfalz Support District, Kaiserslautern, Germany, 1970-71; Laundry and Drycleaning Plant Manager, Transportation Officer, Accountable Property Book Officer, Theatre Officer, Property Disposal Officer and Member Commander's Non-Appropriated Fund Audit and Advisory Board, Department of Army, Headquarters Support Activity, Bad Kreuznoch, Germany, 1969-70; Laundry and Drycleaning Plant Manager, Mortuary Officer, Member Commander's Non-Appropriated Fund Audit and Advisory Board, Department of the Air Force, Headquarters Turkish-United States Logistics Group, Adana, Turkey, 1966-69; Laundry and Drycleaning Plant Superintendent, Department of the Army, Headquarters, United States Army Alaska, Fort Richardson, Anchorage, Alaska, 1965-66; Laundry and Drycleaning Plant General Foreman, Department of Army, Headquarters Yukon Command, Fort Greely, Alaska, 1963-65. Organizational Memberships: National Association of Institutional Laundry Managers; Tri-State Launders and Cleaners Association; Maryland Textile Maintenance Association; Alumni International Fabric Institute. Honors and Awards: Outstanding Performance Award, 1969, 1970, 1971, 1972, 1979, 1980; Certificate of Achievement, 1971; Outstanding Performance Award and Sustained Superior Performance Award, 1973, 1981; Certificate of Achievement Award, 1971-73; Outstanding Performance Award and Quality Step Increase, 1976, 1978; Quality Step Increase, 1977; Letter of Appreciation from Commandant of Midshipmen, United States Naval Academy, 1979; Baltimore Federal Executive Board Outstanding Professional Employee Award, Category Two, 1979; Letter of Commendation from Commander David W. Taylor Naval Ship Research and Development Center, 1979; Arthur S. Flemming Award, 1979; Listed in *Who's Who in the East, Personalities of America.* Address: 3009 Traymore Lane, Bowie, Maryland 20715.

Wallace E Day

Dean, Anne Frey

Registered Nurse, Administrator. Education: Graduate of Piketon-Scioto Rural High School, Piketon, Ohio, 1960; Attended Colorado College; Attended Ohio University; A.D.N. Nursing, San Antonio College, 1974; B.S. Nursing, University of Texas Health Science Center at San Antonio School of Nursing, 1979; Internship, Critical Care Nursing, Bexar County Hospital, 1974; Seminars, Texas Association Post-Anesthetic Nurses 1976, Florida Association Post-Anesthetic Nurses 1977, Association of Operating Room Nurses, Open Heart Surgical Patient, Corpus Christi, Texas 1979; A.O.R.N., Congresses 1978-81, Symposiums, San Antonio, Texas 1979, 1980. Career: Art Consultant, Division of Plastic and Reconstructive Surgery, U.T.H.S.C., 1977; Guest Lecturer, R.N., Neurosurgery, Anesthesia, Recovery Room Care, Critical Care Course, Bexar County Hospital 1974, U.T.H.S.C. Telecomference Network, Metropolitan General Hospital; Lecturer, Galveston Branch, U.T.H.S.C., Recovery Room Seminar, 1978; Panel Member, Operating Room Research Institute; Developer, Day Surgery Program, Autotransfusion Course with Anesthesiology; Orientation Program for Operating Room Personnel, E.M.T. Training Program in the Operating Room, Position of Inservice Instructor-Operating Room; Designer, Renovation of Endoscopy Suite; Relief Nursing Supervisor; Worked in P.R.N. Specialty Pool for E.R., M.I.C.U., S.I.C.U., R.R. and Gynecology; Bexar County Hospital, Staff Nurse, Surgical Intensive Care 1974-75, Charge Nurse, Assistant Supervisor, Post-Anesthetic Recovery Room 1975-78, Operating Room Supervisor 1978; Director, Outpatient Surgery Center, Southwest Texas Methodist Hospital, San Antonio, Texas, 1980. Organizational Activities: San Antonio College (vice president, Student Nurses' Association, 1973-74; state chairperson, Texas Student-Nurse Association convention, entertaining committee, 1974; member, dean's committee on admissions, 1973-74); Inservice Education Committee, Bexar County Hospital (chairperson, 1977); Texas Association Post-Anesthetic Nurses (member); National League of Nurses (member); Association of Operating Room Nurses (chairperson, publicity committee, symposium, Nurses' Day 1980; president, 1981); Sigma Theta Tau Professional Sorority (member). Religion: Methodist Church, Piketon, Ohio (president, women's society, 1969; lead soprano, choral assistant, mixed choir, 1969-72; assistant director, youth group, 1969-72; school instructor, 1969-72). Published Works: Co-Author, Bedside Flow Sheet-S.I.C.U., Operating Room Nursing Record, Operating Room Policy/Procedure Manual; Author, Recovery Room Nursing Record/Policy Manual; Honors and Awards: Listed in *Who's Who in American Women, Personalities of the South, The American Registry, Who's Who in the World of Women, Who's Who in the World of Intellects, Who's Who in the South and Southwest, Distinguished Americans.* Address: 2102 Orange Blossom, San Antonio, Texas 78247.

Bennett W Dean Sr

Dean, Bennett Wayne Sr

Community Relations Coordinator, Author. Personal: Born December 11, 1942; Son of Bennett and Dorothy Lucile Dean; Married Doris Jean Allinson; Father of Lillian Doris, Timpy Anna, Bennett Wayne Jr. Education: B.S. Biology 1965, B.S. Psychology 1966, University of Alabama-Tuscaloosa; Graduate Work: University of Arkansas, Mississippi State University. Military: Served with the United States Army as a Biologist Scientist Assistant at U.S. Army Natick Laboratories, Natick, Massachusetts, 1967-69. Career: Community Relations Coordinator; Former Employment Counselor; Author *A Mobile Mardi Gras Handbook* 1967, *Mardi Gras: Mobile's Illogical whoop-de-doo* 1971, *The Swarming Beehive* 1983, Others; Actor in "Close Encounters of the Third Kind", "Back Roads"; Director "Mardi Gras: Mobile's Big Blast!", United States Navy, 1981. Organizational Memberships: International Association of Personnel in Employment Security (president Alabama chapter 1974-75; district VIII representative 1978-79; past president's club, president 1981-82; associate editor *Guardian*, publication of the Alabama chapter, 1979-81; chairman, international public relations committee, 1982-83); Advertising Federation of Greater Mobile; Mobile Press Club (charter member). Community Activities: Gulf Coast Area Childbirth Education Association (president 1973-74); Mobile Area Community Action Committee (treasurer 1972--73); Mobile Public Relation Practioneers (president 1973-74); Mobile Jaycees (vice president, 1973-74; board of directors 1974-76); Alabama-Gulf Railroad Club (president 1975); Mobile Mardi Gras Doubloon Collector's Club Inc. (president 1977-78); City of Mobile's Mardi Gras Special Events Committee (vice chairman 1978 to May 1982); Society for the Restoration and Beautification of the Church Street Graveyard (The Joe Cain Society) (vice president 1977 to present); Abba Temple Shrine Bowl Football Classic (officer 1978-80); Toy Bowl Classic (board of directors 1976-78); Athelstan Lodge #369, F.&A.M.; Mobile Scottish Rite Bodies: Mobile Lodge of Perfection, Mobile Chapter of Rose Croix, Mobile Council of Kadosh, Mobile Consistory; Abba

Temple Shrine; Friendly Sons of St. Patrick; Oakleigh Garden Society; Mobile Sister Cities Federation (charter member); Historic Mobile Preservation Society; The National Trust for Historic Preservation; The Victorian Society in America; Live-in-a-Landmark Council, Alabama Historical Commission. Religion: Member of the Government Street United Methodist Church: Administrative Board 1982, Council on Ministries 1981-82, Chairman of the Ecumenical and Interreligious Concerns and Religion and Race Committee 1982, Co-Editor *Beehive* 1982, Parish Development Committee 1979; Former Member, Broad Streeet Methodist Church and Fulton Heights Methodist Church. Honors and Awards: City of Mobile and State of Alabama Senior Bowling Champion, 1961; Presented as One of the Honored Guests at "An Evening with Alabama Writers", State Librarians Convention, 1970; Certificate of Distinguished Service, Abba Temple, A.A.O.N.M.S., 1977; Award of Merit, International Association of Personnel in Employment Security, Portland, Oregon, 1973; Outstanding Jaycee Officer, Portland, Oregon, 1973-74; M. O. Beale Scroll of Merit, Mobile Press Register, 1975; Elected to Knight Commander Court of Honour, Supreme Council of the Scottish Rite, 1975; International Group Award of Merit, International Association of Personnel in Employment Security, "Greater Mobile ES/UC Disaster Operations", Wichita, Kansas, 1980 and "Cinema Talent Recruiting Service", Toronto, Canada, 1981; Patriot Award, City of Mobile, 1981; Listed in *Personalities of the South, International Book of Honor.* Address: 1064 Palmetto Street, Oakleigh Garden District, Mobile, Alabama 36604.

Deaver, Hazel V

Hazel V Deaver

Administrative Assistant. Personal: Born August 29, 1929; Daughter of Russell E. Deaver (deceased June 13, 1981) and Christine J. Reeder Deaver (deceased May 12, 1981). Education: Graduate of Lemasters High School, 1947; Chambersburg School of Business, 1949; Various Courses and Seminars. Career: Administrative Assistant in Charge of Finance, Board Secretary, Tuscarora School District, 1952 to present. Organizational Memberships: National Association of Educational Secretaries (life member; general chairman, national regional, 1976); Pennsylvania Association of Educational Secretaries (president, 1973-75); Tuscarora School District Secretarial Association; Pennsylvania Association School Boards Secretaries Association; National Association of Education Office Personnel; Child Accounting Professional Association; Pennyslvania School Business Officials; Franklin County School Managers Association. Community Activities: Franklin County Republican Women's Group (office holder). Religion: Lemaster's United Methodist Church (treasurer, 1950 to present; Sunday school teacher, 1952 to present; church pianist). Honors and Awards: Various Gregg Awards, Chambersburg School of Business; Outstanding Service in School Business Plaque, Pennsylvania Association of Educational Secretaries; Listed in *Who's Who in the East.* Address: 3753 Mercersburg Road, Mercersburg, Pennsylvania 17236.

DeBakey, Lois

Educator, Writer, Lecturer, Editor. Personal: Born in Louisiana. Education: B.A. Mathematics, Newcomb College, Tulane University, 1949; M.A. 1959, Ph.D., 1963, Literature and Linguistics, Tulane University. Career: Professor, Scientific Communication, Baylor College of Medicine (present); Tulane University School of Medicine, Scientific Communication, Assistant Professor 1963-65, Associate Professor 1965-66, Professor 1966-68, Adjunct Professor and Lecturer (present); Faculty, English Department, Tulane University; Director, Numerous Workshops and Courses. Organizational Memberships: Plain Talk, Inc. (director, 1979 to present); Council for Basic Education (member, special committee on writing); Council of Biology Editors (director, 1973-77; committee on graduate training in scientific writing; chairman, committee on editorial policy, 1971-75); National Council of Teachers of English (member, committee on technical and scientific writing; conference on college composition and communication); American Medical Writers Association (member, awards, publications, style and standards committees, chairman, education committee); National Association of Standard Medical Vocabulary (consultant); Association of Teachers of Technical Writing; Committee of a Thousand for Better Health Regulations; Institute of Society, Ethics, and Life Sciences; International Society for General Semantics; National Association of Science Writers; National Institutes of Health Alumni Association; Society for Health and Human Values; Society for Technical Communication (member, board of directors, Houston chapter); National Advisory Council of the University of Southern California Development and Demonstration Center in Continuing Education for Health Professionals (member). Community Activities: *The American Heritage Dictionary* (usage panel, 1980 to present); National Library of Medicine (member, biomedical library review committee, 1973-77; member, board of regents, 1982 to present); Southern Association of Colleges and Schools (member, 1975-80; executive council, commission on colleges, chairman, special committee to review accreditation of Ph.D. level nontraditional and extended educational programs); American Academy of Family Physicians (panel of judges, writing awards); Editorial Boards, *International Journal of Cardiology* 1981 to present, *Health Communications & Biopsychosocial Health* 1981 to present, *Grants Magazine* 1978-81, *Cardiovascular Research Center Bulletin* 1971 to present, *Forum on Medicine* 1977-80, *Health Communications and Informatics* 1976-80, *Tulane University Studies in English* 1966-68, Excerpta Medica's *Core Journals in Cardiology* 1981 to present. Published Works: Senior Author, *The Scientific Journal: Editorial Policies and Practices;* Editor (thousands of medical and scientific articles, chapters, books); Author (articles on biomedical communication, scientific writing, public speaking, audiovisual communication, editing, publishing, on ethical, philosophical, medico-political aspects of science, on journalism, on the fictional treatment of physicians and scientists, on literacy and its relation to the state of society). Honors and Awards: Distinguished Service Award, American Medical Writers Association, 1970; Bausch and Lomb Science Award for Outstanding Academic Performance; Phi Beta Kappa; Golden Key National Honor Society, 1982; Has been Subject of Articles in *Time, The Journal of the American Medical Association, Bulletin of the American College of Surgeons, Medical World News, Medical Tribune, Saturday Review, People, Los Angeles Times,* Publications of the United States Information Agency, and Numerous Other Lay and Medical Newspapers, Magazines and Periodicals; Listed in *Who's Who in America, Dictionary of International Biography, American Men and Women of Science, American Registry Series, Book of Honor, Creative and Successful Personalities of the World, International Who's Who in Community Service, International Who's Who in Education, Men and Women of Distinction, Men of Achievement, Notable Americans, Notable Americans of the Bicentennial Era, Personalities of America, Personalities of the South, Personalities of the West and Midwest, Who's Who in American Education, Who's Who in Health Care, Who's Who in Library and Information Service, Who's Who in the South and Southwest, Who's Who in the World, Who's Who of American Women, World Who's Who of Women, World's Who's Who of Women in Education, Community Leaders and Noteworthy Americans, International Book of Honor, Who's Who in Education.* Address: Baylor College of Medicine, 1200 Moursund Avenue, Houston, Texas 77030.

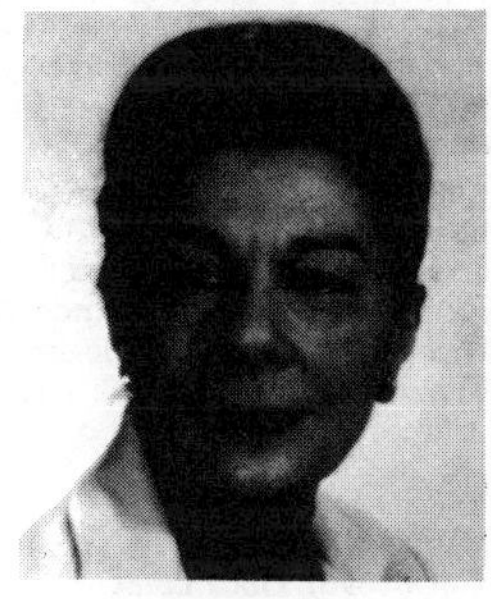
Lois DeBakey

DeBakey, Michael E

Surgeon, Educator. Personal: Born September 7, 1908; Married Katrin Fehlhaber; Father of Four Sons, One Daughter. Education: B.S. 1930, M.D. 1932, M.S. 1935, Tulane University, New Orleans, Louisiana. Military: Colonel, U.S. Army Reserve; Chief of General Surgery, Branch of Surgical Consultants Division; Office of Surgeon General. Career: Surgeon; Chancellor, Professor, Baylor College of Medicine. Organizational Memberships: (advisory appointments) American College of Surgeons, National Institutes of Health, American Institute of Stress, China-American Relations Society, Committee of A Thousand for Better Health

Regulations, The Draper World Population Fund, Thomas Alva Edison Foundation, Father of the Year, Foundation for Biomedical Research, The Hospital for Sick Children, Institute for Advanced Research in Asian Science and Medicine, International Medical Complex of Iran, The Living Bank International, Muscular Dystrophy Association of America, Inc., National Council of Drug Abuse, National Academy of Sciences, Office of Technology Assessment, Pennsylvania Regional Tissue and Transplant Bank, Inc., Recontres Culturelles Internationales, Religious Heritage of America, Inc., St. Jude Children's Research Hospital, Task for Mechanical Circulatory Assistance, Texas Education Agency, Transylvania University, Tulane University Delta Regional Primate Research Center, United States Government Promotion of Conquest of Cancer, Stroke, and Heart Disease, University of Aviation Foundation, Inc., White House Conference on Aging, Academy of Medical Sciences, U.S.S.R., Academy of Medicine of Sao Paulo, Brazil, American Association for the Advancement of Science, American Association for Thoracic Surgery, American Heart Association, American Medical Association, American Trauma Society, Asociacion Mexicana de Cirugia Cardiovascular A.C., Association for the Advancment of Medical Instrumentation, Bio-Medical Engineering Society, British Medical Association, Cuban Medical Association in Exile, Michael E. DeBakey International Cardiovascular Society, International Cardio-Pulmonary Academy, International Committee Against Mental Illness, International Platform Association, Israel Surgical Society, Peripheral Vascular Society of Great Britain and Ireland, Phliosophical Society of Texas, Royal Society of Medicine, Sociedad Cirujana de Chile, Society for Biomaterials, Society for Cryobiology, Society for Experimental Biology and Medicine, Society of Medical Consultants to the Armed Forces, Southern Association for Vasacular Surgery, Southern Society for Clinical Investigation, Surgical Society of Langobard, Milan, Italy, Udruzenje Kirurga Jugoslavije, Western Surgical Association, World Medical Association, Inc. Honors and Awards: (honorary degrees) Doctor of Science, Albany Medical College, Florida State University, Fort Lauderdale University, Hahnemann Medical College & Hospital of Philadelphia, MacMurray College, Medical College of Ohio at Toledo, Roger Williams College, St. John's University, University of Michigan; Doctor of Science, Honoris Causa, Assumption College, D'Youville College, Long Island University, Loyola University of the South; Doctor of Medicine, Aristotelian University of Thessaloniki; Doctor of Medicine, Honoris Causa, University of Ottawa; Faculty of Medicine, University of Chile; Doctor of Humanities, Centenary College; Doctor of Laws, LaFayette College, McNeese State University, Southwestern University, Tulane University, University of Belgrade Medal, University of Cincinnati; Doctor Honoris Causa, Ljubljana University, Yugoslavia, Universite Catholique de Louvain, University of Athens, University of Brussels, University of Ghent, University of Lyon, University of Turin; Fellowship, Institute of Medicine of Chicago; Numerous Awards, including Marian Health Care Award, St. Mary's University 1981, Gran Collare d'Oro, Accademia Internazionale di Pontzen di Lettere, Scienze ed Arti 1969, First Annual American Bicentennial Awrd in Medicine 1972, Certificate of Appreciation for Scientific Exhibit, American College of Surgeons 1970, Hektoen Gold Medal Award, American Medical Association 1954, 1970, Distinguished Service Award, American Surgical Association 1981, Baylor College of Medicine, Alumni Distinguished Faculty Award 1973, Faculty/Staff Recognition Award 1977, Olga Keith Wiess Chair of Surgery 1981, Michael E. DeBakey Day 1976, Michael E. DeBakey Professorship in Pharmocology 1977, DeBakey Scholar Program 1972, Britannica Achievement in Life Award for 1980, "Al Merito della Repubblica Italiana", Commendatore nell 'Ordene 1972, Presidential Citation for Humanitarian Services, Government of Ecuador 1970, Harris County Hospital District 30-Year Service Award 1978, Hellenic Red Cross, Gold Cross with Laurel 1972, Supreme Red Cross 1977, Independence of Jordan Medal, First Class 1980, International Prize "LaMadonnina" 1974, Lions International Special Award 1973, Merit Order of the Republic, Egypt 1980, Panhellenic Medical Association Gold Cross Award 1972, Rotary Club Distinguished Citizens Award 1972, Secretary of Defense Meritorious Civilian Service Medal 1970, Texas Scientist of the Year, Texas Academy of Science 1979, Tulane Distinguished Alumnus of the Year 1974, U.S.S.R. Academy of Science 50th Anniversary Jubilee Medal 1973, Veterans of Foreign Wars Commander-in-Chief's Medal and Citation 1980. Address: 5323 Cherokee, Houston, Texas 77005.

Michael E DeBakey

DeCelles, Charles Edouard

Educator. Personal: Born May 17, 1942, in Holyoke, Massachusetts; Son of Fernand and Stella DeCelles; Married Mildred Manzano Valdez; Father of Christopher Emanuel, Mark Joshua. Education: B.A. Philosophy, University of Windsor, Ontario, 1964; M.A. Theology, Marquette University, Milwaukee, 1966; Ph.D. Theology, Fordham University, New York, 1970; M.A. Religion (Non-Christian World Religions), Temple University, Philadelphia, 1979. Career: Instructor, Department of Theology, Dunbarton College of the Holy Cross, 1969-70; Marywood College, Department of Theology, Instructor 1970-72, Department of Religious Studies, Assistant Professor 1972-75, Associate Professor 1975-80, Professor 1980 to present. Organizational Activities: College Theology Society of America. Community Activities: United Nations Day, Scranton, Pennsylvania (chairman, 1974); United Nations Association of Scranton (member, board of directors, 1974-75); Sponsor, Vietnamese Refugee Family, 1975-76. Religion: Charismatic Prayer Group, Marywood College (leader). Published Works: Books, *Psyche and Spirit* (one of numerous contributing authors), *Paths of Belief, Volume 2;* Numerous Journal and Professional Articles, including "Reincarnation: A Maturation Process Like Purgatory?", "The Importance of Dialoguing on the Holocaust", "A Neglected Apostolate: Writing for the Secular Newspaper"; Opinion Magazine Article, "Conservatives and Liberals on Prolife Issues"; Numerous Popular Magazine Articles, including "The Intelligence Beyond", "Africa: A Land of Suffering", "Church of Brambles, Church of Fire"; Several Newspaper and Series Articles, including "Dorothy Day: A Contemporary Saint?", "Divorce and Remarriage in the Catholic Church", "Global Starvation". Honors and Awards: Distinguished Service Award, United Nations Association of the United States of America; Certificate of Appreciation for the Sponsorship of Indo-Chinese Refugees, United States Catholic Conference; Honorable Mention, Best Magazine Article Originating with the Magazine, Catholic Press Association of America Essay Competition, 1975, for his essay "Ecology: A Theological Perspective"; Listed in *Dictionary of International Biography, Directory of American Scholars, International Who's Who in Education, Men of Achievement, Who's Who in the East.* Address: 923 E. Drinker Street, Dunmore, Pennsylvania 18512.

DeDobeau, Tibor Louis

Executive. Personal: Born December 15, 1934; Son of Louis Michael (deceased) and Elisabeth DeDobeau. Education: A.S., Hamburger Fern-Lehrinstitut, Hamburg, West Germany, 1964; B.S., Institut-Berufsbildung Zurich, Zurich, Switzerland, 1968; M.E., Studien-Gemeinschaft Darmstadt, Darmstadt, West Germany, 1970. Career: Machine Designer and Design Engineer, Switzerland and Lebanon, 1957-67; Design Engineer, Rotodyne Manufacturing Corporation, Brooklyn, New York, 1968-69; Design Engineer, Midland Ross Corporation, New Brunswick, New Jersey, 1969-74; Structural Engineer, Research Cottrell Inc., Bound Brook, New Jersey, 1974-75; President, Deltanova Corporation, 1975 to present. Organizational Memberships: A.S.M.E.; A.M.A.; American Association for the Advancement of Science; A.S.I.; New York Academy of Science; N.S.P.E. Community Activities: Personal Adviser to Harry Dreier (assemblyman aspirant for democratic election campaign, 1979). Religion: Roman Catholic. Honors and Awards: Listed in *Roster of the Board of Advisors* (American Biographical Institute), *Biographical Roll of Honor, A.B.I.R.A. Membership Roster, Who's Who in the East, Personalities of America, Community Leaders of America, International Who's Who of Intellectuals, Directory of Distinguished Americans, Registry of American Achievement, International Register of Profiles, International Book of Honor, Personalities of the East, Personalities of America, Men of Achievement, Book of Honor.* Address: P.O. Box 762, Somerville, New Jersey 08876.

Degerstrom, Ann Blandford

Educator. Personal: Born June 6, 1929, in Kentucky; Daughter of James D. Blandford (deceased) and Nell Blandford; Married James M. Degerstrom. Education: A.B., Webster College, 1952; Professional Dietetic Internship, Cook County Hospital, 1955; M.B.A., University of Chicago, 1962; Ed.D., Nova University, 1979. Career: Instructor of Clinical Dietetics to Interns and Nurses, Presbyterian, Cook County Hospitals; Associate Director, Department of Dietetics, Cook County Hospital; Director of Dietetics, Belmont, Edgewater Hospitals; City Colleges of Chicago, Professor, Food Systems Management and Clinical Nutrition, Loop Campus 1966-79, Malcolm X Campus 1979 to present, Chairperson, Allied Health Department, Malcolm X Campus 1980-82; Chairperson, Institute of Health Sciences, Fall 1981. Organizational Memberships: American Dietetic Association (member, 1955 to present; registered dietitian, 1969-84), Illinois Dietetic Association, 1955 to present; Chicago Dietetic Association (member, 1959 to present; professional education committee, 1980-81); Society for Nutrition Education, 1973 to present; Chicago Nutrition Association (member, 1973 to present; education committee, 1978-80; speakers bureau); American Home Economics Association, 1974-80; Chicago Restaurant Women's Club (member, 1970 to present; scholarship committee, 1978-79); Chicago-Illinois Restaurant Association, 1971-74; American School Food Service Association (member, 1976 to present; certified specialist II); State of Illinois School Food Service Association (member, 1976 to present; certification committee, 1976-80); Malcolm X Campus, City College of Chicago, Student Achievement Recognition Co-ordinating Committee, Faculty Advisor, Dietetic Technology Club, Faculty Council Committee M Chairperson, Educational Excellence Competitions Awards Committee, Student Recruitment and Retention Committee, Cook County College Teachers Union (chairperson, educational policies committee; executive board; house of representatives; chairperson, working conditions committee 1981-82, chairperson, social committee 1982-83, Malcolm X chapter). Community Activities: Examination Proctor, University of California-Berkeley, Nutrition and Food Service Management Courses, 1979-81; Educator, Respiratory Therapy Program Community Advisory Board (present). Religion: Has Studied Six Religions (the effects of cultural beliefs and religious habits on nutritional status). Published Works: "Student Self-Instructional Guide in Basic Nutrition", "Development of Comprehensive Food and Nutrition Management Examination for Assessment of Experiential Learning", "Synthesis of Health Learning Theories". Honors and Awards: Award for Distinguished Service, National Institute for the Food Service Industry, 1977; "Outstanding Service" Chairperson Allied Health Plaque 1980-81, Versatility of Services Plaque 1982, Malcolm X Chapter, Certificate of Service Recognition 1981, Cook County College Teachers Union; Certificate of Merit, Faculty Advisor, Dietetic Technology Club, 1980; Listed in *Personalities of the West and Midwest, International Who's Who of Intellectuals, World Who's Who of Women, Personalities of America, Book of Honor, Community Leaders of America.* Address: 8650 North Elmore Street, Niles, Illinois 60648.

de la Sierra, Angell

Biophysicist, Educator, Writer. Personal: Born February 28, 1932, in Santruce, Puerto Rico; Married Judith Ann Sheffer-La Valle; Father of Angell II, John Arthur, Daniel Gerard, Barbara Grace, Dennise Roxanne. Education: B.S. Chemistry, University of Puerto Rico, 1954; M.S. Chemistry-Physiology, City University of New York, 1958; Ph.D. Biophysics, St. John's University, 1963; Various Post-Graduate Courses, Workshops. Career: Cornell University, New York, Research Associate, Experimental Surgery, Biophysicist, Sloan-Kettering Institute; Research Analyst, Smithsonian Institution, Washington, D.C.; Research Chemist, Molecular Biology Studies, Department of Defense of the Armed Forces' Radiobiology Research Institute; Professor of Biophysics, Georgetown University Medical School, Washington, D.C.; Visiting Professor, Faculty of Medicine, University of Puerto Rico; Chairman, Faculty of the Natural Sciences, University of Puerto Rico-Cayey. Organizational Memberships: Sigma Xi Honor Society; New York Academy of Sciences; Biophysical Society; Radiation Research Society; Consulting Board on Technology and Vocational Training, Cayey (president). Community Activities: Founder, Organization to Promote the Performing Arts. Religion: Roman Catholic. Published Works: Many Publications and Papers. Honors and Awards: Jules Ochs Adler Scholarship, Sloan-Kettering Institution, 1960-63; First Puerto Rican Scientist to Visit Akadem Gorod (Academic City) in Siberia; Listed in *Who's Who in America, Personalities of the South, International Who's Who in Community Service.* Address: University of Puerto Rico, Box 5051, Cayey, Puerto Rico 00633.

Ann B Degerstrom

Demchevsky, Margaret Spaska

Library Specialist, Author, Translator (retired). Personal: Born November 30, 1892, in Samokov, Bulgaria; Daughter of Manol and Spaska Demchevsky (deceased). Education: B.A., American College for Girls, Constantinople, Istanbul, 1914; Librarianship Diploma, University College, School of Librarianship, University of London, 1925. Career: Librarian, American College for Girls, 1914-21; Head of Foreign Division, National Library of Bulgaria, Sofia, 1925-26; Librarian, School of Co-operative Studies, Sofia, 1926-34; Library Specialist, Ministry of Public Education, Sofia, 1926-34; Organizer, Conductor and Single-Handed Lecturer of First (and Second) Library Course in Bulgaria for Librarians of Gymnasiums in Sofia, 1928, and 1931; Lecturer, Library Economy, Sixth Library Course, Popular Libraries Union, 1928; Introduced Annual National Holiday, "Good Book Day" 1929, Organizer for Entire Country, Four Successive Years; Official Delegate, Ministry of Education, First International Library Conference, Rome-Venice, 1929; Member, Supreme Public Library Council, 1929; Organizer, First Bulgarian International Library Exhibit, 1930; Single-Handed Lecturer, Library Course for Librarians, Popular Libraries, County of Lovetch Union, 1932; National Library of Bulgaria, Acting Director 1934-35, Chief Librarian 1934 (dismissal 1943 as non-Nazi); Preparer, Library Project for Entire Country, Requested by Government, 1934; Organizer, Fra Paisi Exhibit, National Library, Shown to the General Public for the First Time, 1935; Obtained Grant from Rockefeller Foundation for Three Bulgarian Architects and One Librarian to Visit and Study American and European Library Architecture (cancelled because of commencement of World War II); Introduced Bookbinding Department, National Library, 1934-35; Head, Division for Administrative Efficiency, 1943-50; Founder, Organizer and Head of the Administrative Efficiency Division, Private Institute for Business Efficiency, 1943-50; Author, Various Reports to the Bulgarian Government, 1943-50; Teacher, Office Efficiency Course, Labor Regiments, 1947-48. Published Works: Annotated Bibliography, Bulgarian Book on Co-operation, Acclaimed as Only National Bibliography on Co-operation in Existence, 1931; Chapters on Bulgaria in Various Compilations and Anthologies; Report, Rationalization of Typewriting Services of the State Departments in Sofia; Alphabetical Card Index Cataloguing Rules in Print, Presented to the American Library Association, Transferred to Library of Congress, Washington, D.C.; List of Bulgarian Pseudonyms to 1942; "Building Principles in American and English Library Buildings", Numerous Articles Published in Library Magazines and Newspapers; Translations, Bulgarian Proverbs, Gurney Champion's Book on Proverbs, E. Marshall's Novel *The Girl from India;* Concise Dewey Decimal Classification, Adapting Special Number for Bulgaria, (by permission of Melvil Dewey; not published), Edited the English Translations of Several Books, Fourteen Film Scripts, Kahlil Gibran's *The Prophet.* Honors and Awards: Director's Annual Prize for Best Work in Book Selection, 1924; Sir John Mac Alister's Annual Prize, Best Results, Diploma Examination, 1925; Carnegie Endowment for International Peace Grant, Study of 243 Libraries in the U.S.A. and Canada, with American Library Association, 1930. Address: 301 Garfield Street, Denver, Colorado 80206.

DeMichele, Margaret Mary

Administrative Assistant (retired). Personal: Born March 3, 1921; Daughter of Lawrence and Elizabeth Connelly (deceased); Married

Joseph A. DeMichele. Education: Graduate of St. Patricks Academy, Washington, D.C., 1939. Career: Administrative Assistant to Senator Mike Mansfield (D-Montana), 1955-76; Secretary to Senator and Congressman Mansfield, 1945-55; Secretary to Congressman James F. O'Connor (D-Montana), 1940-45. Organizational Memberships: Administrative Assistants and Secretaries Associations (member; secretary, 1962); Democratic Women of Montana; State Democratic Central Committee of Montana. Community Activities: Benevolent Patriotic Order of Does of the United States of America (secretary, 1979 to present, Forestville Drove 235). Religion: Catholic Church; Catholic Student Mission; Crusde Veteran Unit (member, 1939-42; secretary and delegate). Address: 9409 Old Marlboro Pike, Upper Marlboro, Maryland 20772.

Demos, Aryola Marieanne

School Psychologist and Family Therapist. Personal: Born February 26, 1924; Daughter of William and Molly Passodelis (both deceased); Married Andrew Peter Demos. Mother of Terria Ann, Norman William. Education: Ph.D. Cand., University of Pittsburgh; D.Div., Lagos, Nigeria; Master's Equivalence, Medical Social Work, School Psychology. Career: School Psychologist and Family Therapist; Coordinator of Special Education and Rehabilitation; Lecturer of Continuing Education Courses: Pennsylvania State University; University of Pittsburgh, Carlow College, La Roche College, Duquesne University, Cornell Schools, Upper St. Clair Schools, Pittsburgh Board of Education. Organizational Memberships: National Education (membership chairwoman of Upper St. Clair school district); American Personnel and Guidance Association (steering committee to plan convention programs for the gifted student); Adult Basic Education Commission (speaker for program advocacy); International Platform Association (membership and social committee); Phi Delta Gamma. Community Activities: Lions Club (speaker on education issues); Kiwanis; Disabled American Veterans Auxiliary (president and organizer); Greek Orthodox Church (organized English classes for presentation to American/Greek students); Helped to inaugurate hospital in Lagos, Nigeria and organized Health Care Units for Mothers of Children. Religion: St Nicholas Greek Orthodox Church. Honors and Awards: Notary Public, Commonwealth of Pennsylvania; D.Div., Conferred by His Emminence, Archbishop Solomon Ola Gbodabo, Nigeria; Listed in *World Who's Who of Women, International Biographical Register, American Biographies and Notables in Community Services, World's Who's Who in Community Service.* Address: 1006 Bramble Bush Dr, Hutchinson, Kansas 67501.

Aryola M Demos

Denise, Margaret Ethel

Musician, Civic Worker. Personal: Born September 30, 1887, in Arlington Township, Michigan; Daughter of Franklin and Sidney Ann Pierson Lawrence; Married Malcolm F. Denise, October 4, 1912; Mother of Malcolm Lawrence, Theodore Cullom, Warren Pritchard (deceased). Education: Attended Ferris State College, Detroit Conservatory, Cincinnati Conservatory; Private Music Studies in Milwaukee and Philadelphia. Career: Contralto Soloist, Recitalist, Churches and Synagogues; Active in Music as a Therapy, 1947 to present. Organizational Memberships: Michigan Federation of Music Clubs (president, southeast Michigan district, 1944-45; honorary life member, advisory council); National Federation of Music Clubs (life member; president, past president's assembly, chapter #34, 1948-49); Sigma Alpha Iota National Music Sorority (patroness, over 25 years). Community Activities: Lansing, Michigan Symphony Orchestra (president, 1934-36); Greater Lansing Community Concerts Association (president, 1945-57); Grinnell Foundation Piano Scholarship, (co-founder, chairman, 1955-76); Lansing Matinee Musicale (president, 1945-47); Edward W. Sparrow Hospital Women's Association (life member); Kresge Art Gallery, Michigan State University; Metropolitan Opera Guild; Denise Alumni Business and Professional Women (sponsor); Golden Eagle Alumni Society of Ferris State College (honorary life member); Lansing Town Hall Association (honorary life member). Religion: Presbyterian Church; Contralto Soloist, Recitalist, Various Churches and Synagogue. Honors and Awards: Affiliated as Friend of the Arts, Lansing-East Lansing, Michigan Alumnae Chapter, Sigma Alpha Iota, Founders Day Celebration, 1981; Awards Annual Piano Scholarship, Greater Lansing Area, Funded by Anonymous Donor in her name by Irrevocable Trust, 1976. Address: 1229 Chester Road, Lansing, Michigan 48912.

Denson, Gail

Certified Public Accountant. Personal: Born March 26, 1939; Son of John M. Denson; Married Onie Lee; Father of Christiana Y., William S., Monte W. Miller, Michael D. Miller, Martin E. Miller. Education: A.A., Los Angeles City College, 1961; B.A., University of Redlands, 1963. Career: Nursing Home Administrator; Certified Public Accountant (present). Organizational Memberships: American Institute of Certified Public Accountants; California Society of Certified Public Accountants; Home Administrators; California Associates of Health Facilities. Religion: Church of the Latter Day Saints (Sunday school president, 1973; ward executive secretary, 1973-76; ward clerk, 1976-81; assistant stake clerk, 1981 to present). Address: 165 West Arthur, Arcadia, California 91006.

Margaret E Denise

Densen-Gerber, Judianne

Psychiatrist, Lawyer. Personal: Born November 13, 1934; Married Michael B. Baden; Mother of Judson Michael, Lindsay Robert, Trissa Austin, Sarah Densen. Education: B.A., cum laude, Bryn Mawr College, 1956; LL.B., Columbia University Law School, 1959; M.D., New York University Medical School, 1963; J.D, Columbia University Law School, 1969; Rotating Internship, French Hospital, 1963-64; Psychiatric Residency, Bellevue and Metropolitan Hospitals, 1964-67. Career: Admitted to New York State Bar, 1961 to present; Admitted to practice Medicine and Surgery: New York, 1967 to present; New Jersey, 1971 to present; Utah, 1971 to present; Michigan, 1973 to present; Connecticut, 1973 to present; Louisiana, 1974 to present; New Mexico, 1975 to present; New South Wales, Australia, 1977 to present; Texas, 1978 to present; Pennsylvania, 1978 to present; Founder and Executive Director, Odyssey House, Inc., 1967-74; Founder, President, Chief Executive Officer, Chief of Psychiatry, Odyssey Institute of America, Inc., 1974 to present; Founder, President, Chief Executive Officer, Chief of Psychiatry, Odyssey Institute International, 1978 to present; Visiting Associate Professor of Law, University of Utah Law School, 1974-75; Adjunct Associate Professor of Law, New York Law School, 1973 to present; Founder and President, Institute of Women's Wrongs, 1973 to present. Organizational Memberships: White House Conference on Youth (delegate 1971); Law Enforcement Assistance Administration (national advisory commission on criminal justice standards and goals, 1971-74); National Center for Health Research and Development, Department of Health, Education and Welfare, Public Health Services (consultant, 1972 to present); United States Army, Fort Meade (consultant, 1972-73); Department of Health, Education, and Welfare (drug experience advisory committee, 1973-76); New York State Crime Control Planning Board, 1975-79; Governor's Task Force on Crime Control, 1977-79; Society of Medical Jurisprudence, 1967 to present; American Medical Association, 1968 to present; New York State Medical Society, 1968 to present (sub-committee on drug abuse, sub-committee on delivery of health care, sub-committee on prescription practices, sub-committee on child welfare); New York Women's Bar Association, 1969 to present; American Academy of Forensic Sciences (member 1969-72, fellow 1972 to present); American Psychiatric Association, 1970 to present; American Academy of Psychiatry and the Law, 1970 to present; American College of Legal Medicine (fellow 1971 to present, annual convocation committee 1973-74); American Bar Association, 1972 to present; The National

Coalition for Children's Justice (board of directors 1975 to present); Daitch Shopwell, Inc. (board of directors 1976 to present); American Society for the Prevention of Cruelty to Children (board of directors 1979 to present); Mary E. Walker Foundation (board of directors 1978 to present); New York Council on Alcoholism (president, A.C.C.E.P.T. board of directors 1978 to present); Paga House (president, board of directors 1978 to present); Harmony School (president, board of directors 1979 to present); *Contemporary Drug Problems* (board of advisors 1971 to present); Hospital Audiences Inc. (board of advisors 1971 to present); Institute for Child Mental Health (board of advisors, professional advisory committee for the study of drug use among children and adolescents, 1972 to present); First Women's Bank of New York (board of Advisors 1974 to present); President's Council of the School of Social Work of New York University (board of advisors 1977 to present); Beard's Fund for the Arts (board of advisors 1978 to present); National Forensic Center (advisor for law and medicine 1980 to present); *Focus on Women* (editor, board of advisors, 1980 to present). Community Activities: Women's City Club of New York, 1956 to present; Women's Forum, 1976 to present. Religion: All Souls Unitarian Church, 1958 to present. Published Works: *Drugs, Sex, Parents and You; We Mainline Dreams: The Odyssey House Story; Walk in My Shoes: An Odyssey into Womanlife; Child Abuse and Neglect as Related to Parental Drug Abuse and Other Anti-Social Behavior.* Honors and Awards: American Association of University Women, 1970; Myrtle Wreath Award, Hadassah, 1970; Women of Achievement Award, B'nai B'rith Women, 1971; B'nai B'rith Women of Greatness Award, 1971; Honorable Order of Kentucky Colonels, 1973; Honorary New York State Fire Chief Award, 1974; Dame of Malta, Knights of Malta, America, 1974; Outstanding Teacher of the Year, Service to New York City, Our Town Newspaper, 1977; Nobless, Order of the White Cross, Australia, 1977; Dame Commander, Knights of Malta, America, 1980; Listed in *National Social Directory, Outstanding Young Women in America, Who's Who of American Women, Dictionary of International Biography, Community Leaders of America, Who's Who in the East, Who's Who in America.* Address: 656 Avenue of the Americas, New York, New York 10010.

Denton, Thomas S

Petroleum Producer. Personal: Born October 12, 1945; Son of Stewart B. Denton; Jane Alma Denton. Education: Attended the University of Mississippi, 1964-68; B.S., Murray State University, 1969; Pre-Veterinary and Post Graduate Studies, Murray State University, 1974-77. Military: Served with the United States Air Force, 1969-73, achieving the rank of Staff Sergeant; Served with the United States Air Force Reserves, 1973-74, also achieving the rank of Staff Sergeant. Career: Numismatist; Petroleum Producer; Investment in Council of Agricuture. Organizational Memberships: American Numismatic Association (life member). Community Activities: Murray State Alumni Association, Century Club, 1980; Murray State Super Racer Club, 1978; Big M Club, 1979-80; Washington Legal Foundation; Masons; Public Service Research Council; Americans Against the Union Control of Government; American Security Council (national advisory board); Liberty Lobby (board of policy); National Conservation Political Action Committee; Biblical Archaeological Society; Citizens Committee for the Right to Keep and Bear Arms; Conservation Caucus; Congressional Club. Religion: Presbyterian. Honors and Awards: Life Patron, American Biographical Institute Research Association; International Platform Association; Listed in *Men of Achievement, Who's Who in the South and Southwest, Personalities of the South, The Book of Honor, Who's Who in Finance and Industry, International Who's Who of Intellectuals, The Directory of Distinguished Americans, Personalities of America, International Register of Profiles, Community Leaders and Noteworthy Americans.* Address: 812 N 20th Street, Murray, Kansas 42071.

dePaolis, Potito Umberto

Food Company Executive. Personal: Born August 28, 1925, in Mignano, Italy; Son of Giuseppe A. and Filomena Macchiaverna dePaolis; Married Marie A. Caronna, April 10, 1965; Naturalized U.S. Citizen, 1970. Education: D.V.M., University Naples, 1948; Libera Docenza. Minister Pubblica Istruzione, Rome, Italy, 1955. Career: Professor, Food Service, Veterinarian School, University Naples, Italy, 1948-66; Retired 1966; Assistant Professor, A titre Benevole Ecole Veterinaire Alfort, Paris, France, 1956; Veterinary Inspector, U.S. Department of Agriculture, Omaha, Nebraska, 1966-67; Senior Research Chemist, Grain Processing Corporation, Muscatine, Iowa, 1967-68; Vice President, Director, Product Development, Reddi Wip Inc., Los Angeles, 1968-72; President, Vegetable Protein Co., Riverside, California, 1973-75; Vice President, Shade Foods-Chocolate International, Belmont, California, 1975-77; President, Tima Brand Co., Los Angeles, 1977 to present. Organizational Memberships: Institute of Food Technologists; Italian Association for the Advancement of Science; American Association for the Advancement of Science; Veterinary Medical Association; Biological Science Association, Italy; Italian Press Association; Greater Los Angelels Press Club; Published Works: Patentee in Field; Contributor of Articles in Field to Professional Journals. Honors and Awards: Fulbright Scholar, Cornell University, Ithaca, New York, 1954; British Council Scholar, University of Reading, England, 1959-60; Postdoctoral Research Fellow, N.I.H., Cornell University, 1963-64. Address: 131 Groverton Place, Bel Air, California 90024.

Desai, Veena Balvantrai

Obstetrician, Gynecologist. Personal: Born October 5, 1931; Daughter of Dr. Balvantrai P. Desai (deceased) and Maniben Ond Gujarat; Married Vinay D. Gandevia; Mother of Vijay Gandevia. Education: M.B.B.S., 1957; M.D. Obstetrics/Gynecology, 1961; M.R.C.O.G., London, 1966; F.A.C.O.G., U.S.A., 1974; D.A.B.O.G., U.S.A., 1976; F.A.C.S. , 1979; F.I.C.S., 1980; Honorary Ph.D., World University, 1981. Career: Obstetrician and Gynecologist; Delegate, American Medical Delegation to China, 1981; Reporter, *Journal of the American Medical Delegation to China*, 1981-82. Organizational Memberships: American Society of Colcoscopy and Cervical Pathology (fellow); New Hampshire Medical Society; American Medical Women's Association. Portsmouth Hospital (cancer care committee, 1978 to present; quality assurance committee, 1981 to present; chairperson, dietary committee, 1978-81); American Biographical Institute (editorial advisory board). Community Activities: Portsmouth Hospital Guild (patron, 1981); Portsmouth Community Health Services (patron, 1981); Greater Chamber of Commerce, 1982; Free Health Fairs for Senior Citizens (volunteer); Prepared Childbirth Classes (volunteer lecturer, 1975-79); International Platform Association, 1979-82; World University (member, round table); Donations, Portsmouth Hospital Development Fund, Portsmouth Community Services, Young Women's Christian Organization, Portsmouth Junior High School, Disabled Veterans, Various Police Organizations, Phillips-Exeter Academy, National Republican Committee. Honors and Awards: Honorary Ph.D., World University, 1981; Listed in *Who's Who of American Women, World's Who's Who of Women, Directory of Distinguished Americans, International Book of Honors, Personalities of America, International Register of Profiles, International Who's Who of Intellectuals.* Address: 12 Harborview Drive, Rye, New Hampshire 03870.

DeSomogyi, Aileen Ada

Librarian (retired). Personal: Born November 26, 1911; Daughter of Harry Alfred and Ada Amelia Taylor (both deceased); Widow. Education: B.A., London, 1936; M.A., London, 1938; A.L.A., British Library Association, 1946; M.L.S., U.W.O., 1971; Certificate of Proficiency in Archive Management, 1969; Diploma in Computer Programming, Career Learning Centre, Toronto, 1980. Military:

Served with the W.R.A.C., 1955-56, achieving the rank of Corporal. Career: Librarian. Organizational Memberships: American Library Association, 1967 to present; Ontario Genealogical Society (secretary, London branch, 1967-71); East York Historical Society, 1975 to present. Community Activities: N.A.L.G.O. (committee, Enfield branch, 1949-52); C.U.P.E. (committee, East York branch, 1971-74). Address: 9 Bonnie Brae Boulevard, Toronto, Ontario, Canada M4J 4N3.

De Veau, Violet D Young

Personal: Daughter of Samuel A. Young and Lillian Baker (both deceased); Married; Mother of Courtenay Gentry McWhinney. Education: Transylvania College, Lexington, Kentucky; Post Graduate University of Kentucky; Alliance Francais, New York; School of Interior Design, New York. Community Activities: National Panhellenic Conference (president, 1936-38); Spence Chapin Adoption Service (board member, 1939-42); Blue Ridge Auxilliary, St. James Diocese, New York (board member); Panhellenic House, Beekman Place, New York (member, board of directors); Kentucky Women's Foundation (board member); Society of Mayflower Descendants (secretary, state of New York); Bath and Tennis Club; Everglades Club; Beach Club; Sail Fish Club; Society of Four Arts; Flagler Museum. Honors and Awards: National Society of Colonial Dames of America; Society of Mayflower Descendants; Daughters of the American Revolution. Address: 198 Via Linda, Palm Beach, Florida 33480.

DeVere, Julia Anne

Teacher. Personal: Born November 2, 1925; Daughter of Goodlet C. (deceased) and Anna R. Bonjour; Married Robert E. DeVere; Mother of David E. Education: Attended: Emporia State Teachers College, University of Kansas-Lawrence, Kansas State University-Manhattan; B.A., University of Denver, 1957; M.A., University of Denver, 1961; Undertook Postgraduate Studies at University of Maryland, University of the Pacific, San Jose University, University of San Cruz, Sacramento State University, Others. Career: Teacher, One Room School, Jackson County, Kansas, 1943-45; Teacher, Upper Elementary, Bancroft, Kansas, 1946-47; Teacher, Primary Grades, 1947-52; Teacher, Second Grade, Westmoreland, Kansas, 1953-55; Teacher, Elementary Class of Mentally Retarded Students, Stockton, California, 1957-64, Teacher, Handicapped Children, Cupertino School District, 1964 to present. Organizational Memberships: National Education Association; California Teachers Association; Cupertino Education Association; Council for Exceptional Children; Foundation for Exceptional Children, Behavioral Disorders, Mentally Retarded, Visually Handicapped and Learning Disabilities; Educational Diagnostic Service. Community Activities: Walked Block for Cancer, Leukemia, Muscular Dystrophy, Heart Fund. Religion: United Brethern Church. Honors and Awards: Delta Kappa Gamma Scholarship, 1955; International Biographical Center and American Biographical Institute Awards and Honors; Listed in *Who's Who of Women, Who's Who in the West and Midwest, Who's Who of Community Service, Notable Americans*, Others. Address: 950 Chehalis Dr., Sunnyvale, California 94087.

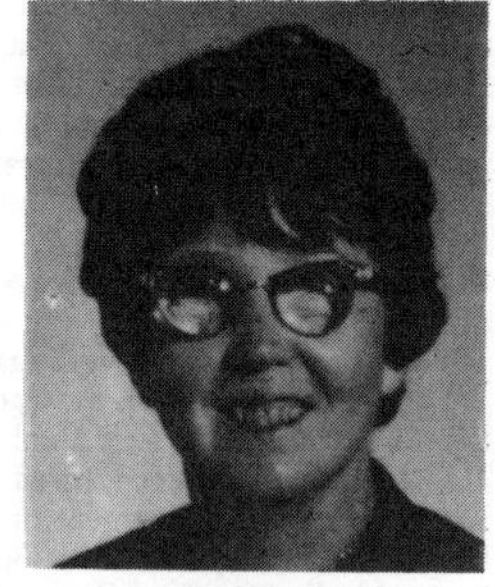

Julia DeVere

De Vito, Albert Kenneth

Musician, Composer, Editor, Publisher. Personal: Born January 17, 1919, in Hartford, Connecticut; Son of Ralph and Rose Abronze De Vito. Education: Attended Hartford Federation College, Columbia University; B.S. 1948, M.A. 1950, New York University; Ph.D., Midwestern University, 1975; Mus.D. (honorary), East Nebraska Christian College, 1974. Military: Served in the Infantry, Special Services, United States Army, 1942-46. Career: Manager, G. Schirmer, Inc., New York City, 1948-52; Instructor, Westbury Public Schools, New York, 1952-55; Author; Composer; Compiler; Member, Board of Directors, Long Island Chapter, Spiritual Frontier Fellowship. Organizational Memberships: Intercontinental Biographical Association (life fellow); American Choral Directors Association; International Platform Association; American Music Center, Inc.; New York State Music Teachers Association; American Society of Composers, Authors and Publishers; New York State School Music Teachers Association; Music Teachers National Association, Inc.; Associated Musicians of Greater New York; Associated Music Teachers League; Music Educators National Conference; International Association of Organ Teachers; Piano Teachers Congress (president); Phi Mu Alpha Sinfonic; Piano Teachers of New York, Inc. (president, honorary member); National Geographical Society; Screen Actors Guild; American Federation of Television and Radio Artists; Dramatic Artists Guild; National Academy of Television Arts and Sciences (New York chapter). Published Works: Eleven Chord Books; Fourteen Chorals (original and arrangements); Twelve Chord Organ Books; *Pocket Dictionary of Music Terms;* Two Organ Methods; Thirteen Organ Collections; Twelve Piano Collections; Three Piano Methods; Thirty-two Piano Solos; Piano Solo (for two pianos); School Series; Two Technical Books; Two Vocal Solos; Numerous Articles on Music and Teaching, appearing in *Choral Journal, Clavier, Modern Keyboard, Music Educators Journal, Piano Guild Notes, Songwriters Review.* Honors and Awards: A.S.C.A.P. Panel Awards; Certificate of Merit Proclaimed Throughout the World for Distinguished Service to Community, 1975; Merit Award, National Federation of Music Clubs, 1974; Parade of American Music Award of Merit; Victory Medal; American, European, African, Middle East Theatre Campaign Ribbons; Listed in *A.S.C.A.P. Biographical Dictionary, Book of Honor, Community Leaders and Noteworthy Americans, Contemporary American Composers; Dictionary of International Biography, International Who's Who of Intellectuals, International Who's Who in Community Service, International Who's Who in Music and Musician's Directory, Men and Women of Distinction, Men of Achievement, Notable Americans, Personalities of America, Who's Who in the East.* Address: 361 Pin Oak Lane, Westbury, New York 11590.

De Witt, Susan Pierson

Attorney. Personal: Born May 15, 1947; Daughter of Mr. and Mrs. George W. Pierson; Married James A. De Witt (deceased). Education: A.A., Joliet Junior College, 1967; B.S., University of Illinois, 1969; J.D., John Marshall Law School, 1973. Career: Partner in Law Firm of O'Brien, Garrison, Berard, Kusta, & De Witt, Joliet, Illinois, 1973-77; Assistant Attorney General, Litigation Section, Chicago Office of the Attorney General, 1977-78; Assistant Attorney General and Chief, Consumer Protection Division, Springfield Office of the Illinois Attorney General, 1977 to present. Organizational Memberships: Consumer Advisory Council to the Federal Reserve Board (chairman); National Association of Attorneys General Consumer Protection Committee (secret warranties subcommittee); American, Illinois, Sangamon County Bar Associations; American Association of University Women. Community Activities: Zonta Club of Springfield (president); Land of Lincoln Girl Scout Council (board of directors); International Organization of Women Executives (board of advisors; executive committee); Family Service Center; Aid to Retarded Citizens; Capital Campaign. Religion: Protestant. Honors and Awards: Leadership Award, International Organization of Women Executives, 1980; Young Career Woman, Business and Professional Women's Organization, 1974; Featured in *Illinois Issues*, January 1981; Young Republican of the Year, 1973. Address: 849 Roanoke Drive, Springfield, Illinois 62702.

DiAiso, Robert J

Civil Engineer and Professional Planner. Personal: Born January 3, 1940; Son of Dominick and Marie DiAiso; Father of Michael. Education: B.S., United States Naval Academy, 1962; M.C.E., New York University, 1964; M.U.R.P., University of Pittsburgh, 1970; Ph.D., University of Pittsburgh, 1971. Career: Civil Engineer; Professional Planner. Organizational Memberships: American Society of Civil Engineers; National Society Professional Engineers; American Institute Civil Planners; American Planners Association; National Association of Home Builders; Home Builders of Anne Arundel County (director, 1978-81). Community Activities: Anne Arundel Community College (trustee, 1974-80, 1980-86; chairman, 1976-78); Crofton Civic Association (president, 1973; director, 1974); Public Works Review Board of Anne Arundel County (chairman, 1980-82); Anne Arundel County Council on Adequate Facilities Board, 1976; Anne Arundel County Bicentennial Committee, 1974-75. Religion: Vice Chairman, St. Elizabeth Ann Seton Building Committee, 1976-80; Advisor, Archdiocese of Baltimore Building Committee. Honors and Awards: U.S. Air Force Commendation Medal, 1969; Honor Award, Maryland Homebulders Association, 1980; Academic Fellowship, 1969-70; Distinguished Service Award, Anne Arundel Community College, 1979; Outstanding Service Award, Crofton Civic Association, 1974. Address: 1544 Farlow Avenue, Crofton, Maryland 21114.

DiCasimirro, Donna Marie

Unit Manager. Personal: Born December 24, 1954; Daughter of Wassil F. and Geraldine A. DiCasimirro. Education: Graduate of Marian High School, Tamaqua, Pennsylvania, 1972; B.S. magna cum laude, Communication Disorders, Marywood College, Scranton, Pennsylvania, 1976; M.A., Audiology, University of Florida-Gainesville, 1977. Career: Mental Retardation Unit Manager, 1981 to present; Clinical/Rehabilitative Audiologist, Hamburg Center, 1978-81; Clinical Audiologist, ENT Surgical Group, Kingston, Pennsylvania, 1978; Hearing Consultant, Wyoming Valley Crippled Children's Center, Wilkes-Barre, Pennsylvania, 1978. Organizational Memberships: American Speech-Language-Hearing Association; Pennsylvania Speech & Hearing Association; Northeastern Speech & Hearing Association of Pennsylvania; Centurions of Deafness Research Foundation; Alexander Graham Bell Association for the Deaf; *Amer-Ind Code* International League. Community Activities: National Federation of Business and Professional Women's Clubs (member, 1979 to present; chairperson, young careerist, Schuylkill Haven chapter, 1980-81; chairperson, ways/means 1981-82, first vice president 1982-83, Hamburg chapter). Religion: Sacred Heart Church, Mahanoy City, Pennsylvania (Sacred Heart society; parish charity solicitation). Honors and Awards: Delta Epsilon Sigma, 1976 to present; Kappa Gamma Pi, 1976 to present; Young Careerist, Schuylkill Haven Business and Professional Women's Club, 1980; Listed in *Who's Who of American Women, Personalities of America.* Address: 508 New Boston, Mahanoy City, Pennsylvania 17948.

Dickinson, Charles Cameron III

Charles C Dickinson III

Curatorial Associate. Personal: Born May 13, 1936; Son of Mr. and Mrs. Charles C. Dickinson, Jr., (both deceased); Married Janell Truly; Father of Tena Truly, Michael Truly. Education: Attended Phillips Academy, 1950-54; B.A., cum laude, Dartmouth College, 1958; Undertook futher studies, Chicago Theological Seminary, 1962, and University of Chicago Divinity School, 1962-63; B.D., Pittsburgh Theological Seminary, 1965; Attended Kirchliche Hockschule (West Berlin), 1965-66, Ernst Mortiz Arndt-Universitat (Greifswald, German Democratic Republic), 1966, University of Pittsburgh, 1966-68, Yale University and Divinity School, 1968-69, Union Theological Seminary, 1969-72; Ph.D., University of Pittsburgh, December 1973. Military: Served with the United States Marine Corps, Private and Private First Class, Communicator, 1958-59, 2nd and 1st Lieutenant, Communications Officer, 1959-61. Career: Visiting Professor of Theology and Philosophy, Union Theological Seminary in Virginia, 1974-75; Assistant Professor of Religion and Philosophy, Morris Harvey College, 1975-79; Professor of Religion and Philosophy, American College of Rome, 1979; Research Professor of Theology and Philosophy, The University of Charleston, 1980-81; Lecturer in Medical Ethics, West Virginia University Medical Center at Charleston, Fall 1978; Curatorial Associate for Manuscript Collections, Andover-Harvard Theological Library, Harvard University. Organizational Memberships: American Academy of Religion; Society of Biblical Literature; American Theological Society (Midwest); American Philosophical Association; American Association for the Advancement of Humanities; American Association for the Advancement of Science; International Platform Association; West Virginia Philosophical Society; West Virginia Association for the Humanities; University Press Edition, Mountain State Press (general editor); Karl Barth Society of North America (executive board); International Bonhoeffer Society; Royal Society of Arts (fellow). Community Activities: Charleston Rotary Club (past chairman of student exchange committee, member of program committee); The River School (past member board of directors, member of educational council); University of Charleston (advisory council); Union Theological Seminary (trustees' council). Religion: Occasional Preaching. Honors and Awards: B.A., cum laude, Dartmouth College, 1958; Entrance Fellowship, Chicago Theological Seminary, 1962; First Semester Scholarship, University of Chicago Divinity School, 1962. Address: 1200 Johnson Rd., Charleston, West Virginia 25314.

Dickinson, Kandice Ruth

Educator. Personal: Born June 22, 1939; Mother of Jerard, Charles, Nona. Education: A.S. Spanish, Essex County College, Newark, New Jersey, 1972; B.A. English, Spanish, Bloomfield College, New Jersey, 1975; M.A. Reading, Montclair State College, 1979; Attended New York University; Certificate, Intensive Foreign Language Workshop; Certificate, Leadership Development Group, National and International Affairs, Essex County College, 1981; Enrichment Courses, Bilingual, Holistic Testing, Reading Workshops, Educational Improvement Center. Career: American Red Cross Licensed Practical Nurse, Bitburg, Germany, 1959-61; Operator, Service Assistant (bilingual), New York, New Jersey Telephone Companies, 1961-70; Essex County College, Adult Basic Education Specialist, College Work-Study Supervisor 1970-1975, Adjunct Faculty Member, Instructional Intern, Tutorial Faculty, Tutor 1976-78; Instructor/Consultant, Department of Civil Service, Northern New Jersey Civil Service Training Center, 1976-78; Essex County College, Language Laboratory Supervisor/Instructor 1978 to present, Coordinator/Counselor, Project WHY-Leaguers Center 1978-79, English as Second Language Course Coordinator/Language Lab Supervisor 1979-80, Coordinator of English as a Second Language and Foreign Languages, Administratvie Supervisor, C.E.T.A. Basic Skills 1980-81; Supervisor, Prudential Life Insurance Company, Newark, Summer 1980. Organizational Memberships: New Jersey Congress of Parent-Teacher Associations (life member, Abington Avenue School executive committees); Science and Arts Highs Parent-Teacher Associations; Essex County Advisory Board, 1981; N.J.E.A. (former senator); Essex County College (evening students advisor; commencement chairperson, 1980, 1981; bilingual research committee; senator, faculty association, 1979); New Jersey Foreign Language Teachers Association; New Jersey T.E.S.O.L.; Parent-Teacher Association (executive committees); Bilingual and English as a Second Language Coordinator (state committee); Essex County Women's Advisory Board (secretary, 1980). Community Activities: National Urban League; National Association for the Advancement of Colored People; League of Women Voters (by-laws chairperson); Women's Political Caucus (educational chair); National Association of Negro Business and Professional Women's Clubs, Inc. (life member, co-chair, education committees; secretary, international committee); Daycare Coordinating Council of Essex County (chairperson, board of trustees, 1979-81); Montclair State College (advisory board, 1980 to present); American Red Cross Volunteer, 1959-65;

Newark Board of Education (parent volunteer, 1965-75); Boy Scouts of America (den mother chief, 1970-72). Religion: St. James A.M.E. Church (Sunday school teacher, member, Sunday school board, speaker, parent-teacher dinner); U.N.I.C.E.F. Volunteer, N.J.E.A. Convention, Atlantic City, New Jersey, 1981. Published Works: Contributing Writer, Communications Skills Lab; Abstracts, "Accurate Placement of L.E.P. Students", "Linguistically Different Students"; Paper, "Factors Relating to the Incorrect Analyses of Miscues Relate to Dialect Errors". Honors and Awards: Essex County College, Dr. Martin Luther King Scholarship 1972, Ford Foundation Scholarship 1972, Student of the Month 1971; Volunteer of the Quarter, United States Air Force, Bitburg, Germany; 500 Hour Volunteer Certificate, American Red Cross, Germany; Seven Volunteer Certificates, Newark Board of Education, 1970-77; Community Service Award, North Jersey Unit, National Association of Negro Business and Professional Women's Clubs, Inc., 1981; Certificate of Appreciation, New March of Dimes, 1970; Listed in *Outstanding Young Women of America, Community Leaders and Noteworthy Americans, Who's Who Among Students, Personalities of America.* Address: 215-2B West Market Street, Newark, New Jersey 07103.

Diggs, Steven Franklin

Executive, Composer, Recording Artist, Radio Personality. Personal: Born July 3, 1952, Oak Ridge, Tennessee; Married Bonita Louise, August 8, 1976; Father of Megan Ruth, Joshua Franklin. Education: Graduate of Oak Ridge High School, Oak Ridge, Tennessee, 1970; B.A., David Lipscomb College, Nashville, Tennessee, 1974. Career: Radio Personality, Three Radio Stations, 1970-74; Radio Personality and Announcer, 1971-73; Recording Artist, Dot Records, 1973; Sales Manager/Salesman, Dave Floyd and Associates, Realtors, 1974-76; Public Relations Director, Lloyd White Company, 1976; President/C.E.O., The Franklin Group, Inc. (owner of Steve Diggs & Friends Advertising, Bonner Jingles Radio and Television Commercial Production Firm, Bonnie-Lou Music Publishing Company, Kyte Record Label), 1977 to present. Organizational Memberships: Business Advisory Board, David Lipscomb College; American Society of Composers, Authors and Publishers; National Academy of Recording Arts and Sciences. Community Activities: Tennessee Volunteers for Life; Republican Party; Omega Chi Social Club. Religion: Church of Christ. Published Works: Musical Compositions, "Flight 408", "Raggedy Ann". Honors and Awards: Honorary Tennessee Colonel, Awarded by Governor Winfield Dunn, 1975; Club 100 Award 1970, Top 30 Crew Award 1970, Southwestern Company; Salesmanship Award, Dave Floyd Realtors, 1976; Forensic Award, David Lipscomb College, 1973; Listed in *Who's Who in the South and Southwest, Personalities of the South, Men of Achievement.* Address: The Franklin Group, Inc., 1110 Music Square East, Nashville, Tennessee 37212.

Dilley, William G

Manufacturer. Personal: Born June 6, 1922; Son of Ethel M. Dilley; Married M. Jean Dilley; Father of Gregory D., Karen K. Education: B.S., University of Colorado, 1951; Undertook Post Graduate Studies, University of Southern California, 1957. Military: Served in the United States Air Force and the United States Air Force Reserve. Career: Founder, Principal, Spectra Sonics; Previously Chief of Electronics Engineering, Thor, Atlas D, Atlas E, Atlas F, Titan I, Titan II, Intercontinental Ballistic Missile Systems; Chief of Engineering, Minuteman Engineering Test Facilities. Organizational Memberships: Audio Engineering Society Inc. (fellow); National Association of Broadcasters (designated senior broadcast engineer); Society of Motion Picture and Television Engineers; Society of Registered Inventors; Aircraft Owners and Pilots Association; National Aeronautic Association; Caterpillar Club; International Platform Association. Honors and Awards: Distinguished Flying Cross; Air Medal with 9 Oak Leaf Clusters; Army Commendation Medal; Belgian Fourraguerre; Holder of the United States and World Aircraft Speed Records; University of Colorado Distinguished Engineering Alumnus Award; Holder of 14 U.S. and Foreign Patents; Listed in *Who's Who in the World, Who's Who in Technology Today, Who's Who in Finance and Industry, Who's Who in the West, International Who's Who of Intellectuals, International Who's Who in Community Service, The International Register of Profiles, Dictionary of International Biography, International Gold Award Book, Men of Achievement, Men and Women of Distinction, Engineers of Distinction, Book of Honor, Notable Americans, Notable Americans of the Bicentennial Era, Community Leaders and Noteworthy Americans, The American Registry, Directory of Distinguished Americans, Personalities of America, Personalities of the West and Midwest, National Social Directory.* Address: 3750 Airport Road, Ogden, Utah 84403.

G Benjamin Dillow

Dillow, G Benjamin

Director of Human Resources. Personal: Born February 26, 1940; Son of Mr. and Mrs. B. L. Dillow; Married Cherie A. Fitting; Father of Scott B., Steven K., Shane M. Education: A.B. Education, Sheperd College, Sheperdstown, West Virginia, 1962; M.S. Counseling, Virginia Commonwealth University, Richmond, Virginia, 1969. Career: Howmet Corporation, Director, Human Resources 1979 to present, Manager, Employee Relations 1977-79, Personnel Manager 1973-77; Counselor, District of Columbia Government, Washington, D.C., 1969; High School Instructor, Washington County, Maryland, 1962-66. Organizational Memberships: American Society of Personnel Administrators (member, 1975 to present); Lancaster County Personnel Association (member, 1973 to present; vice president, 1977-78; president, 1978-79; board of directors, 1979-80); Lancaster Association of Commerce and Industry (member, 1978 to present). Community Activities: United States Jaycees, 1970-73; Lancaster County Community Employment of the Handicapped (member, 1974-80; chairperson, executive committee, membership). Honors and Awards: Outstanding Freshman Student, 1958; Outstanding Senior in Art Department, 1962; Woodrow Wilson Fellowship Nominee, 1962; Listed in *Who's Who Among Students in American Universities and Colleges, Who's Who in the East, Community Leaders of America, Men of Achievement, Dictionary of International Biography, Directory of Distinguished Americans, Registry of American Achievememt.* Address: Route 1, Box 413, Mount Joy, Pennsylvania 17552.

Dimitry, John Randolph

Executive, Educator. Personal: Born February 15, 1929; Married Audrey Oktavec; Father of Mark, Jane, Kate. Education: Attended Spring Hill College, 1948-49; B.A. 1952, M.S. 1954, Ed. D. 1966, Wayne State University. Military: Served in the United States Army, 1947-48 and 1952-53. Career: Teacher, Highland Park Junior College, Michigan, 1954-61; Instructor, Wayne State University, Part-Tine, 1957-61; Macomb County Community College, Research Associate 1962-63, Administrative Assistant 1963, Assistant to the President 1963-65, Director of Division of Research and Development 1965-66, Dean of Center Campus 1966-67, President 1967-75; President, Northern Essex Community College, Haverhill, Massachusetts, 1975 to present. Organizational Memberships: Governor's Committee on Higher Education, 1973; Michigan Community College Association (president, 1972-73); State Advisory Council on Higher Education, 1972; Massachusetts Commission for Occupational Education, 1981 to present; New England Board of Education Student Exchange Commission, 1981 to present. Honors and Awards: Kellog Foundation; Fellow, Community College Administration, 1961-63. Address: Old Wharf Road, West Newbury, Massachusetts 01985.

Di Ponio, Concetta Celia

Systems Security Coordinator. Personal: Daughter of Antonio and Mary Franciosi Di Ponio. Education: A.C., magna cum laude, Henry Ford Community College, 1969; B.B.A., magna cum laude, 1973, M.A., 1974, and M.B.A., 1975, all from the University of Detroit; Expertise Certificates in Electronic Computer Language, 1974-80. Career: Italian Translator, Ford Motor Company, 1960; Elected at Large Member to the Board of Directors, University of Detroit Alumni, 1974 to present; Teacher of Business-Data Processing, Detroit College of Business, 1974 to present; Founder/Advisor, University of Detroit National Evening B&A Alumni Council, 1975 to present; Instructor/Teacher of Management Subjects, Henry Ford Community College, 1978 to present; President, University of Detroit National Alumni Association, 1978 to present; President, University of Detroit Board of Directors, 1978 to present; Systems Security Coordinator, Ford Parts and Service Division, Ford Motor Company, 1981 to present; Ford Motor Company: Electronic Computer Programmer-Analyst 1974-81, Parts Program Coordinator 1966-74, Divisional Production Surplus Liaison 1955-66, Statistical Analytical Coordinator 1952-55, Service Parts Stock Distributor 1949-52, Confidential Superintendent Assistant of the Tank/Bomber Division 1942-52; Owner, Manager, Civil Engineer, Tri-D Construction Company, 1955-69; Office Manager, Instructor, Design and Engineering Institute, 1940-41. Organizational Memberships: American Management Association (national management association for training professionals); Phi Gamma Mu (has held all offices); Alpha Kappa Psi (first woman honorary member); Beta Gamma Sigma (induction officer); Metropolitan Detroit Alumnae; National Association of Female Executives; National Business Education Association; American Society of Professional and Executive Women; American Association of University Women. Community Activities: Alpha Sigma Nu (president, 9 terms; first female inducted); Metropolitan Detroit Girl Scouts (scout leader, junior troop #1222, 9 years); Alpha Sigma Lambda; Ford Motor Girls Club (president, 2 terms; all other offices); Ford Employee Recreation Association (board member, 10 years); University of Detroit B&A National Alumni Council (founder, advisor). Honors and Awards: Greater Metropolitan Detroit Chamber of Commerce Top Ten Working Woman Award, 1969; Alpha Kappa Psi Service Award (first woman to receive this award), 1972; Phi Gamma Nu Scholastic Key, 1973; Ford Motor Company: Divisional Community Service Award 1973, National Citizen of the Year Award 1973, National Town Crier Bell for Community Services 1973; The Dow Jones *Wall Street Journal* Student Achievement Award, 1973; The Lawrence Canjar Woman of the Year Award (first graduate student to receive this award), 1974; National Centennial Award, University of Detroit National Alumni Association, 1976; M.B.A. Award, Masters of Business Administration Society, 1976; Board of Directors Award for Services, University of Detroit, 1977; Presidential Award, University of Detroit, 1980; Listed in *Who's Who Among Students in American Colleges and Universities, Who's Who in America, Who's Who of American Women, The World Who's Who of Women, Dictionary of International Biography, International Who's Who of Intellectuals.* Address: 22204 West Seven Mile Road, Detroit, Michigan 48219.

Dolciamore, John V

Priest, Officialis. Personal: Born April 26, 1926; Son of Luigi and Cecilia DePalo Dolciamore (both deceased). Education: B.A., St. Mary of the Lake Seminary, 1948; M.A., S.T.L., St. Mary of the Lake Seminary, 1952; J.C.L., Pontifical Gregorian University, Rome, Italy, 1956. Career: Officialis (Chief Judge), Metropolitan Tribunal of the Archdiocese of Chicago; Pastor, Divine Providence Parish, Westchester, Illinois. Organizational Memberships: Canon Law Society of America (consultor to board of governors, 1975-78); Midwest Canon Law Society (president, 1975 to present); Archdiocese of Chicago (consultor, 1978 to present); National Conference of Catholic Bishops (consultant, canonical affairs committee, 1978-81); Proviso Township Clergy Group. Community Activities: Committee for Tribunal Assistance, 1973-76; Cursillo Movement (spiritual director, 1963 to present); Committee for Revision of American Procedural Norms for Processing of Marriage Cases, 1977; International Graphoanalysis Society, 1974-81; Illinois Div, International Graphoanalysis Society, 1974-81; Matrimonial Jurisprudence (editor, 1968-72). Religion: Ordained to Priesthood of Roman Catholic Church, May 1, 1952. Honors and Awards: Role of Law Award, Canon Law Society of America, 1981. Address: 2550 Mayfair Avenue, Westchester, Illinois 60153.

Dennis E Dollar

Dollar, Dennis Earl

State Legislator, Real Estate Broker, College Instructor. Personal: Born August 22, 1953; Son of Mr. and Mrs. Bennie Dollar; Married Janie Sullivan; Father of Christopher Ryan. Education: A.A., Mississippi Gulf Coast Jr. College, 1973; B.A., University of Mississippi, 1975; Undertook further studies at the University of Southern Mississippi. Career: State Legislator; Real Estate Broker; College Instructor; Public Relations Manager; Sales Representative. Organizational Memberships: Council of State Governments; National Council of State Legislators; Board of Realtors; Homebuilders Association. Community Activities: Lions Club, 1975 to present; Jaycess, 1973 to present; Goodwill Industries (board of directors 1981); Gulf Coast Employment and Training Council, 1976 to present; United Way, 1977-79; Heart Fund (chairman 1978); Chamber of Commerce, 1976-79; Boys Club (board of directors 1977-77); Mississippi Arts Fair for the Handicapped (board of directors 1977 to present); Gulf Coast Mental Health Center (advisory board 1977-80). Religion: Baptist; Deacon, 1975 to present; Sunday School Teacher; Lay Music and Youth Director. Honors and Awards: Margaret Dixon Freedom of Information Award, 1981; Distinguished Service Award, 1976; Listed in *Notable Americans, Personalities of the South, Who's Who in American Politics, Outstanding Young Men of America.* Address: 4925 Courthouse Road, Gulfport, Mississippi 39501.

Donaldson, Marceline M

Aspirant, Holy Orders, Episcopal Church. Personal: Mother of Elise, Karen, Malica, Michelle, Jacqueline. Education: Bachelor's Degree, Mathematics, Physics, New York University, New York, New York; Program for Management Development, Harvard Graduate School of Business, Boston, Massachusetts; Stock Brokerage Training Program, Dain, Kalman & Quail, Inc.; Training Program, International Business Machines. Career: International Business Machines, General Systems Division, Cincinnati, Ohio, Marketing, General Systems Division, Madison, Wisconsin, Marketing; Owner-Manager, Donaldson & Associates, Consulting Firm Specializing in Marketing and Affirmative Action Accounts, Minneapolis, Minnesota; Assistant Manager Manpower Planning, Marketing, Consumer Export Division, Cooperative Marketing Program, The Pillsbury Company, Minneapolis, Minnesota; Stockbroker, Dain, Kalman & Quail, Inc., Minneapolis, Minnesota; Owner, Manager, Ma-Li-Kai, Inc., Antiques, Auction Gallery, Interior Design Studio, Minneapolis, Minnesota; Junior Engineer, Programmer, Western Union Telegraph Company, New York, New York; Research Assistant to Dr. Bazer (pioneer in the field of magneto-hydrodynamics), New York University, New York, New York. Community Activities: Harvard Business School Club (Minnesota club, board member, vice president, chair, international seminar, 1975; present member, Cincinnati club); "Annual Honored Company Night" Awards Dinner (chair, 1975); Minneapolis Urban Coalition (board member, three years); National Organization for Women (board member, two years); National Association for the Advancement of Colored People (establisher, coordinator, fund raising activities, legal defense fund in Minnesota); Republican Party (precinct chair, Minnesota and Wisconsin); Ripon Society (board member); Academy of Management; Friends of Amistad (supporters of the Roy Wilkins Research Library, New Orleans, Louisiana). Honors and Awards: Finished Year with 140%

of Assigned Quota with All Customer Problems Solved, International Business Machines; First Person in Training Class of Twenty-One to Go off Draw onto Straight Commission because of High Level of Sales Attained Very Quickly; First Person to Sell Several Hundred Thousand Dollars of Bonds within Two Months of Being Registered; First Minority Female Elected to Membership, Academy of Management; Dean's List, New York University; Listed in *World's Who's Who of Women, Who's Who of American Women, Notable Americans, Women in Business, Women Organizations and Leaders*. Address: 37 Kirkland Street, Apartment 302, Cambridge, Massachusetts 02138.

Donnelly, Anne Marie

Catering Consultant. Personal: Born November 28, 1938; Daughter of William L. and Anne E. Earth, (both deceased); Married Maurice Lee Donnelly (deceased); Mother of Patricia Anne, Michael Jude. Education: Graduate of St. Brides, 1952, and Loretto Academy, 1956; Attended De Paul University, 1956-59. Career: Catering Consultant, D'Masti Custom Catering, 1977 to present; Owner, Annette's Catering, 1966-73; Assistant Catering Manager, South Shore View, 1960-66; Employee, South Shore View, 1953-66. Organizational Memberships: National Business and Professional Women; National Female Executives; North Illinois Food Executives; National Restaurant Association; Smithsonian Institution; National Historical Society; Policemen's Annuity; Retired Police Association. Community Activities: Chicago Council Cub Scouts (den mother, 1975-78); Mount Greenwood Youth Baseball (manager, Kitty Kats, 1976-78, coach, Mohawks, 1979-81); St. Christina Band Boosters, 1975-80 (officer, 1976-79); Chicago Council Girl Scouts (cookie chairman, 1973-75). Religion: Catholic; St. Christina's Altar & Rosary, 1974-81; Executive Board; Choir Member, 1980 to present; Mt. Carmel's Mother's Club; Mt. Assisi Parent's Association, Raffle Chairman. Honors and Awards: Honorary Appointment, National Board of Advisors, American Biographical Institute; Listed in *Who's Who of American Women, Personalities of America, World Who's Who of Women, International Register of Profiles*. Address: 3450 W. 115th Place, Chicago, Illinois 60655.

Sharon Dorner

Dooley, Mary Agnes S S J

Executive, Educator. Personal: Born March 5, 1923; Daughter of Mr. Dooley (deceased) and Mary A. O'Neill Dooley. Education: B.A., Our Lady of the Elms College, Chicopee, Massachusetts, 1944; M.A., Assumption College, Worcester, Massachusetts, 1960; Doctorat d'Universite, University of Paris (Sorbonne), 1968. Career: Teacher, St. Joseph High School, North Adams, Massachusetts, 1946-65; Chairperson, Language Department, Elms College, 1968-70; President, Congregation of the Sisters of St. Joseph of Springfield, 1971-79; President, Elms College, present. Organizational Memberships: Leadership Conference of Women Religious of the United States (member, 1978-80; president; vice president; past president); Association of Catholic Colleges and Universities (board member, 1980 to present); Delegate, Second, Third, Fourth Inter-American Conference, 1974, 1977, 1980. Community Activities: Official Delegate, Installation of Popes John Paul I and II, 1978; Delegate, White House Reception for Pope John Paul II, 1979; Delegate, U.J.A. Ecumenical Leadership Mission to Israel, 1975; Interfaith Council of Springfield, Massachusetts (chairperson, 1975-77); Frequent Speaker to Religious and Educational Organizations. Religion: Delegate, International Union of Superiors General, Rome 1975, 1977, 1979, Montreal 1977, 1978, Rio De Janeiro 1980. Honors and Awards: Chevalier dans l'Ordre des Palmes, French Government, 1981; Honorary Degree, Doctor of Letters, American International College, Springfield, Massachusetts, 1981; Distinguished Alumna Award, Elms College, 1979. Address: 291 Springfield Street, Chicopee, Massachusetts 01013.

Dorner, Sharon A

Educator. Personal: Born November 3, 1943; Daughter of William and Eleanor Haddon; Mother of Wendy Ann, Meredith Lynn. Education: Graduate of Parsippany High School, 1961; B.A. 1965, M.A. Business Education 1970, M.A. Guidance 1978, Montclair State College; Ed.D. Vocational Education and Administration, Rutgers University, 1982. Career: Business Teacher, Morris Knolls High School, Denville, New Jersey, 1965-70; Adult Education Teacher, Sussex Vocational School, Sparta, New Jersey, 1969-70; Business Teacher, Katherine Gibbs Secretarial School, Montclair, New Jersey, 1972-73; Business Teacher, Kimberely Academy, Montclair, New Jersey, 1972-73; Business Teacher, County College of Morris, Randolph, New Jersey, 1973; Business Teacher, Leonia High School, New Jersey, 1974-75; Business Teacher, Montville High School, New Jersey, 1976; Woodcliff School, Woodcliff Lake, New Jersey, Administrative Intern to Superintendent 1980, Business Teacher, 1976 to present. Organizational Memberships: National Education Association; New Jersey Education Association; Bergen County Education Association; Woodcliff Lake Education Association (secretary, 1976 to present); National Business Education Association; New Jersey Business Education Association; Eastern Education Teachers Association; American Vocational Association; New Jersey Vocational Association; American Research Association; American Vocational Research Association; Delta Pi Epsilon National Business Education Graduate Honorary Society (national inter-chapter activities standing committee, 1980-83; national committee member, 1980-84; chairperson, 1982-84; national council representative, 1981-85; Beta Phi chapter, president 1979-80, vice president 1978-79, corresponding secretary 1976-78, newsletter editor, 1974-76); Phi Delta Kappa National Graduate Honorary Society for Educational Leadership (president, Montclair state chapter, 1980-82; vice president of program, 1979-80; treasurer, 1975-79, 1982 to present; national council delegate, 1977-80; national council alternate, 1980-82; national district VI newsletter editor, 1977-79); Omicron Tau Theta National Graduate Honorary Society for Vocational Education; Association for Supervision and Curriculum Development; Kappa Delta Pi Educational Honorary Society; Pi Omega Pi Business Education Honorary Society. Community Activities: Sigma Kappa Sorority (alumnae province officer for New Jersey and New England, 1977-81; alumnae district director, northern United States, 1981 to present); Byram Board of Education, 1968-70; Lenape Valley Board of Education, 1969-72; Consumer's League of New Jersey (board of directors, 1974 to present); National Advisory Board for *Today's Secretary* Magazine, 1981-82; Order of the Eastern Star, 1963 to present; Daughters of the Nile, 1976 to present. Religion: First Presbyterian Church of Upper Montclair, 1972 to present. Honors and Awards: Magna Cum Laude Graduate, Montclair State College, 1965; Listed in *Who's Who of American Women, World's Who's Who of Women, Who's Who in the East, Personalities of America, Directory of Distinguished Americans*. Address: 28 College Avenue, Upper Montclair, New Jersey 07043.

Virginia A Dorough

Dorough, Virginia Ann

Systems Programmer. Personal: Born December 26, 1930; Daughter of Joe S. and Gladyce W. Dorough. Education: B.S., University of Alabama, 1952; Graduate Certificate, School of Banking of the South, Louisiana State University, 1973; Certificates from the American Institute of Banking: Basic 1967, Standard 1969, General 1971, Advanced 1975; Undertook Post-graduate Studies at Georgia State University 1964, University of Alabama at Birmingham 1964-65. Career: Systems Programmer, Akra Data Inc., 1980 to present; Programmer/Analyst, Central Computer Services Inc., 1978-79; Manager of Systems, First Alabama Bancshares, 1977-78; First Alabama Bank of Birmingham: Programmer 1965-67, Systems Analyst 1967-75, Assistant Cashier 1969-76, Manager of Systems 1975-76; Reservations Agent, Eastern Air Lines, 1955-64; Loan Clerk, First National Bank of Birmingham, 1952-53; Science

Teacher, Cahaba Heights Junior High School, 1952-53; Science Teacher, Munford High School, 1952. Organizational Memberships: Association for Computing Machinery (treasurer of southern region conference, 1976); Data Processing Management Association; American Society of Women Accountants (president, 1972-73); Business and Professional Women's Club (president, Mountain Brook club, 1973-74; co-director, district V, 1981-82). Community Activities: Soroptomist International of Birmingham (president, 1975-76); Bluff Park Order of the Eastern Star (worthy matron, 1957-58); Xi Upsilon Chapter, Beta Sigma Phi (president, 1976-77); American Association of University Women; Birmingham Museum of Art; Freedoms Foundation at Valley Forge; Arlington Historical Association; Smithsonian Associates; International Biographical Association, 1975-77; Birmingham Historical Association; Red Mountain Museum. Religion: United Methodist. Honors and Awards: Bausch & Lomb Science Award, 1948; American Institute of Banking, District V, Official Family Award, 1967; National Association of Bank Women Inc., Southern Region Scholarship, 1970. Address: 2140 Shadybrook Lane, Birmingham, Alabama 35226.

Dorta-Duque, Jorge E

Architect, General Contractor, Developer, Executive. Personal: Born June 4, 1932, in Havana, Cuba; Married Maria L., 1958; Father of Maria L., Carmen, Jorge J. Education: Graduate of Belen Catholic School, 1946; B.S., Marianao Institute, 1951; Bachelor in Sciences and Letters, Belen Catholic College, Havana, Cuba, 1951; Architect, School of Architecture and Planning 1960, Doctorate in Sciences, Physics-Mathematics, School of Sciences 1961, University of Havana, Cuba; Continuing Education Courses in Business, Business Administration, Tax Procedures, Real Estate and Mortgages, Environmental Impact, Engineering, Structural Design, Planning and Zoning. Career: President, Chief Operating Officer, Southeast Enterprises, Inc., 1977 to present; General Contractor, Architect/Planner, Jorge Dorta-Duque, A.I.A., Miami, Florida, 1970-77; Architect/Office Manager, Associate, C. M. Fein & Associates, Miami, Florida, 1964-70; Chief Designer, Planner, Associate, E. Abraben Associates, Miami, Florida, 1961-64; National Director of School Construction, Ministry of Public Works, Havana, Cuba, 1959-61; Member, Architect/Owner, J. Dorta-Duque, Arquitecto, Havana, Cuba, 1959-61; Chief Designer, A. Fojo, Arquitecto, Havana, Cuba, 1954-58; Draftsman/Designer, J. Vila & Associates, Havana, Cuba, 1952-54; Associate Professor of Design, University of Havana School of Architecture, 1959-61; Professor of Drafting, Belen Electromechanic University, Marianao, Cuba, 1955-59; Professor of Mathematics, Physics and Drafting, Saint George's College, Havana, Cuba, 1953-59; Registered Architect, Havana Provincial Board 1959, Cuba National Board 1959, Florida State Board 1965; Registered Civil Engineer, Florida State Board (E.I.T.) 1976; Registered General Contractor, Havana, Cuba 1956, Dade County 1968, State of Florida 1974. Organizational Memberships: American Institute of Architects; American Association of Registered Architects; Society of American Reistered Architects (fellow); Sociedad Colegio de Arquitectos de Cuba (Miami); Florida Planning and Zoning Association; International Association for Housing Science; Society of Cuban Engineers; National Planning Board, Havana, Cuba, 1960-61. Community Activities: Technical Committee on South Shore Development Plan, Miami Beach; A.I.A. Legislative Minutemen; Land and Water Conservation Act (golden eagle operation); Florida Democratic Party (state delegate); Architectural Delegation to the People's Republic of China (delegate); People to People International Citizen Ambassador Programs; Big Five Club; Home and School Association (vice president); International Platform Association. Religion: Holy Rosary Parish (chairman, building committee); Catholic Mission (consultant to South Florida migrant workers); Epiphany Church (president, liturgy committee). Published Works: Collaborator, "The Resort World"; Author, "The Planning World"; Editor, Architectural Review, "Espacio", School of Architecture, University of Havana, Cuba. Address: 5645 Southwest 87th Street, Miami, Florida 33143.

Marguerite R Dow

Dow, Marguerite Ruth

Educator. Personal: Born June 13, 1926; Daughter of Gordon Russell and Beatrice Bott Dow (both deceased). Education: B.A. 1949, B.Ed. 1971, M.A. English 1970, University of Toronto; Senior Certificate in Drama, Banff School of Fine Arts, University of Alberta, 1956; Ontario High School Specialist's Certificate in English, 1952. Military: Served as Cadet, Governor General's Foot Guards, Ottawa, 1943-44. Career: Professor, English and Drama in Education; Teacher, English and Drama, Librarian, Ontario High Schools, 1950-65; Head of English Department, Laurentian High School, Ottawa, 1959-65; Librarian, Government of Canada, 1947-50; Laboratory Assistant, National Research Council of Canada, 1944-46. Organizational Memberships: Canadian Heritage Writing Competition Committee (founder; chairman, 1974-81); Canadian College of Teachers (elected member, 1972); Canadian Council of Teachers of English; National Council of Teachers of English. Community Activities: Ontario Secondary School Teachers' Federation (vice president, Brockville local 1953-55, Ottawa district 1960-62); Theatre Foundation of Ottawa (board of directors, 1961); University Women's Club, Ottawa (chairman, scholarship committee, 1961-62); Ontario Ministry of Education (seven consultative and research committees, 1959-64); Ontario Institute for Studies in Education (creative arts committee, theatre arts committee, 1966-69); United Empire Loyalists' Association of Canada (president, London & western Ontario branch, 1977-79; dominion councillor, 1976-82; dominion chairman, membership committee, 1981-82); Monarchist League of Canada (chairman, London branch, 1979-81; secretary-treasurer, 1977-79). Religion: Baptist. Honors and Awards: Intercontinental Biographical Association (life fellow, 1974; life patron, 1976); International Institute of Community Service (life fellow, 1975); World Academy (fellow, 1976); American Biographical Institute (life fellow, 1979); Biographical Academy of the Commonwealth (honorary fellow, 1981); Founder-Fellow Silver Medal 1975, Silver Medal 1976, International Institute of Community Service; Granted Armorial Bearings, Kings of Arms, England, 1974. Address: 1231 Richmond Street, Apartment 909, London, Ontario N6A 3L9 Canada.

Line B Draper

Draper, Line Bloom

Painter, Educator, Enamelist. Personal: Daughter of Leopold and Mathilde Voisin, (both deceased); Married Glen C. Draper; Mother of Andre L. Education: Ecole des Arts Decoratifs, Verviers, Belgium; Academie Royale des Beaux Arts, Tournai, Belgium; Bowling Green State University, Ohio. Career: Has appeared on Television and Radio Programs; Member Panel Discussion Groups; Lecturer; Judge for Professional and Amateur Art Exhibitions; Conductor of Classes, Defiance College, Adult Board of Education at Monroe, Michigan, and Sylvania, Ohio, Findlay, Bowling Green, Fremont, Napoleon, Tiffin, Waterville, Fostoria, Fayette, Montpelier, Others; Number of One-Man Shows including Elliott Museum, Stuart, Florida, 1977 and McInnis Galleries, 1970; Work in Private Collections including Stuart Historical Museum and Miami Childrens Center. Organizational Memberships: Toledo Artists' Club (life member, president 1963-66); Founder: Ohio Gold Medal Exhibition, Port of Toledo Art Exhibition, TAC Westgate Annual Inviational Art Exhibition; American Watercolor Society; Athena Art Society (life member, president, 1967-69 and 1973-74, vice president, 1972-73); Toledo Women's Art League; Zonta of Toledo, 1974-77; Zonta of Delray Beach Area, 1977 to present; Toledo Federation of Art Societies (past vice president, recording secretary); National League of American Pen Women, 1979; International Society of Artists (charter member); Centro Studi E Scambi Internazionaldi. Community Activities: Boca Raton Music Study Club, 1977 to present; Boca Raton Center for the Arts, 1977 to present; Boca Raton Exhibiting Artists Guild, 1977 to present; Soroptiminst International of Toledo (charter member, past president, 1957-67); Spectrum, Friends of Fine Art Inc (charter president, 1975, 1976, life member). Honors and Awards: Numerous Best of Show, 1st Prize and Other Awards in Regional, State and National Exhibitions; Spectrum, Friends of Fine Arts Honor Award for founding & fostering the growth of the organization, 1978; Special Honor Award for Art Achievement and Leadership, Athena Art Society 1969; Honor Award for excellence and achievement in the field of art, Athena Art Society, 1975; Gold Medal and Special Award for Outstanding Achievement in raising standards of Artistic Endeavor, Toledo Artists Club, 1965; Honor Award for Outstanding Contribution to Art and Service in fostering Art Activities in the Community, Toledo Federation of Art Societies, 1964, 1966; Listed in *Who's Who in American Art, Who's Who of American Women, Who's Who in the Midwest, National Register of Prominent Americans & International Notables, Community Leaders of America, The World Who's Who of Women, Two Thousand Women of Achievement, International Who's Who in Community Service, International Men & Women of Distinction, Personalities of the South, Dictionary of International Biography*. Address: 3134 Lakeview Drive, Delray Beach, Florida 33445.

Drewry, John Eldridge

Educator, Author, Columnist. Personal: Born June 4, 1902, Griffin, Georgia. Education: Graduate of Griffin Grammar and High School, 1918; A.B. 1921, B.J. 1922, A.M. 1925, University of Georgia. Career: Reporter, News Editor, *Athens Banner-Herald;* Capitol Reporter, State Editor, Associated Press, Atlanta; Correspondent, *Atlanta Constitution, Atlanta Journal, Christian Science Monitor;* Lecturer, Journalism, Lucy Cobb Institute; University of Georgia, Instructor, Journalism 1922-24, Adjunct Professor 1924-26, Associate Professor 1926-30, Professor 1930 to present, Director, School of Journalism 1932-40, Organizer, University Press Bureau 1921, University Publicity Director 1921-28, 1930-32, Supervisor, *University Items*, Weekly Campus Newspaper Summers 1927-32, Associate Editor, Georgia Alumni Record 1925-39, Henry Grady School of Journalism, Dean 1940-69 (duties included Director, Georgia Press Institute, Southern Industrial Editors Institute, Georgia Radio and Television Institute, Georgia Scholastic Press Association, Georgia Collegiate Press Association, Education-Industry Conference on Public Relations, Education-Industry Conference on Advertising, George Foster Peabody Radio and Television Awards; Chairman, Red and Black Board of Control; Administrative Council; Chairman, Faculty Committee on Special Lectures and Convocations), Dean Emeritus 1969 to present. Organizational Memberships: Phi Beta Kappa (president, Georgia Alpha chapter, two terms); Kappa Tau Alpha Scholastic Honor Society for Communications Majors (president); American Association of Teachers of Journalism (secretary; vice president; president; chairman, secretary, joint committee with American Society of Newspaper Editors and National Editorial Association on education for journalism); American Association of Schools and Departments of Journalism (vice president); National Editorial Association (journalism committee); Georgia Bicentennial Commmission; Chairman, Member, Contest Judging Committees, Associated Press, National Editorial Association, International Council of Industrial Editors; Columbia University (president, Georgia Club); Newcomen Society. Community Activities: Rotary Club (president; program chairman; board member; governor's council); Clarke County Welfare Board; American Cancer Society (publicity chairman, Athens chapter). Religion: First Baptist Church, Griffin (member until 1921; president, junior B.Y.P.U.; president, senior B.Y.P.U.; treasurer; usher; Sunday school); First Baptist Church, Athens (member since 1921; usher; associate deacon; deacon; chairman, board of deacons; member, finance committee; chairman, committee on selection of pastor; consultant on design of church calendar); Visiting Lecturer, Annual Covention , Southern Baptist Press Association, Tampa, Florida, 1951. Published Works: Author, Numerous Books and Brochures, including *A Forward Look for Communications, Journalistic Escalation, New Heights for Journalism;* Weekly Column, "New Book News", *Athens Banner-Herald, Atlanta Constitution, Publishers' Auxiliary;* Numerous Articles in General and Professional Magazines. Honors and Awards: Phi Kappa Phi; Sigma Delta Chi; Omicron Delta Kappa; Gridiron; Blue Key; Phi Eta Sigma; Gold Key Award; Columbia Scholastic Press Association; Distinguished Service Awards, University of Georgia Alumni Society, Georgia Press Association, Georgia Association; South's Hall of Fame for the Living; Georgia Press Association President's Award; Brenda Award, Atlanta Professional Chapter, Theta Sigma Phi; Resolution of the Georgia State Legislature in Appreciation of "Outstanding Work to the School of Journalism, University of Georgia, and State of Georgia"; Creation of Bench Honoring John E. Drewry in Front of Old Journalism Building, Sigma Delta Chi; Creation of John E. Drewry Scholarship by Gamma Alpha Chi; *Anderson Daily Mail* (South Carolina) Distinguished Citizen Public Service Award; Proclamation by Mayor of Athens and President of University of Georgia Creating John E. Drewry Day "In Recognition of His Outstanding Service to Both"; Wisdom Hall of Fame, Wisdom Award of Honor; Honorary Life Membership, International Council of Industrial Editors (honorary life membership); Listed in *Who's Who in America, Leaders in Education, Directory of American Scholars, Dictionary of International Biography*. Address: 447 Highland Avenue, Athens, Georgia.

Drisko, Barbara Lucille

Realtor. Personal: Born October 16, 1932; Daughter of Rev. Dr. Ralph J. Barron; Married to Shapleigh M.; Mother of Shapleigh M., Jennifer Elizabeth, James Coburn, Jonathan Tabbutt. Education: Graduate, Bangor (Maine) High School; B.A., West Virginia Wesleyan College; M.A., M.Mus.Ed., Peabody (Vanderbilt) University. Career: Broker of Real Estate Agency, Bridgeport, Connecticut; Former Director of Music and instructor. Organizational Memberships: Greater Bridgeport Board of Realtors (board of directors, 1975 to present, vice president, 1979-81); Eastern Fairfield County Commercial Investment Division of Connecticut Association of Realtors (president, 1980); Connecticut C.I.D. of Connecticut Association of Realtors (secretary, 1981); Women's Council of Realtors of Eastern Fairfield County (president, 1975); Connecticut Women's Council of Realtors (governor, 1975 to present, chairman of committees on legislation, education, program and membership, 1975 to present). Community Activities: Connecticut Republican State Central Committee, 1977-81; Board of Education, City of Shelton, Connecticut, 1978 to present; Shelton Republican Town Committee, 1976 to present; President, Officers Wives Clubs in Schwebach, Germany, 1957; Chairman of Army Community Service, Fort Bliss, Texas, 1969; Advisory Committee of State of Connecticut (treasurer, 1981). Religion: Member of United Methodist Church (delegate to New York annual conference, 1978-81, member of board of trustees, 1979-81, commissioner of education, 1973-76). Honors and Awards: Graduate of Realtor Institute, 1976; Realtor Associate of the Year, 1976; Realtor of the Year Candidate, 1978-80; Certified Residential Broker Candidate, 1980; Carnegie Foundation Fellow, 1955. Address: 28 Sorghum Road, Huntington, Connecticut 06484.

Drown, Eugene Ardent

Forest Management Specialist. Personal: Born April 25, 1915, Ellenburg, New York; Married Florence Marian Munroe, 1938; Father of Two Daughters. Education: B.S., Utah State University, 1938; M.S., Command & General Staff College, 1961; Postgraduate Work, Industrial College of Armed Forces, 1956-58; Ph.D. Public Administration, University of Beverly Hills, 1979. Career: Park Ranger, Yosemite National Park, 1940-47; Forest Ranger, United States Forest Service, 1948-56; Forest Management and Development Specialist, United States Bureau of Land Management, 1956 to present. Organizational Memberships: American Institute of Biological Scientists; American Forestry Association; National Society of Professional Engineers; Reserve Officers Association of the United States of America; Society of American Foresters. Community Activities: Ecological Society of America; International Rescue and First Aid Association; International Platform Association; Masonic Orders, Idaho and California. Published Works: Contributor to *Journal of Forestry, Manual of the Bureau of Land Management*. Honors and Awards: Numerous Military Awards; National Service Medal, American Red Cross, 1964; Superior Performance Award, 1970; Phi Kappa Phi; Xi Sigma

Xi; Listed in *Community Leaders of America, Personalities of the West and Midwest, Who's Who in America, Men of Achievement.* Address: 524 Bonniemae Way, Sacramento, California 95824.

DuBroff, Diana D

Attorney, Television Show Producer. Personal: Born March 4, 1919 in New York City, New York; Daughter of Meyer and Gussie Ginsburg Leibow (both deceased); Married Alexander DuBroff (deceased); Mother of Elinor, Dean, William. Education: B.S., Hunter College, 1928; LL.B., Brooklyn Law School, 1931. Career: Educator, 1928-61; Practicing Attorney, Specializing in Family Law and Equal Employment Claims and Litigation, Designed Concept of Divorce Insurance and Homemaker's Insurance; Founded Institute for Practical Justice; Producer, Cable Television Series "Practical Justice by a Creative Lawyer"; Writes Column, "Let's Look at the Law". Organizational Memberships: National Organization to Insure Survival Economics (president); Institute of Practical Justice. Community Activities: Organized Forest Hills Nursery School, 1941-42; Star Civic League, 1932; Bar Association Committees. Honors and Awards: Described as "The Holistic Lawyer" and "The Renaissance Lawyer". Address: 12 West 72 Street, New York City, New York 10023.

Duerksen, Mable

News Reporter, Teacher, Diamond Wholesaler. Personal: Born January 4, 1928; Daughter of J. C. and Lena Vogt; Mother of Sharon Flaming, Tim, John, Deb. Education: A.A., Freeman Junior College, Freeman, South Dakota, 1970; B.A. English 1972, Teacher Education 1973, Southwestern Oklahoma State University. Career: News Reporter, Teacher, Diamond Wholesaler; Writer, Reporter, Sunday School Teacher, Thirty Years. Community Activities: Oklahoma Extension Homemakers (safety chairman, 1978-80; handbook author, 1981-82; southwest district representative, 1983-84); Oklahoma Safety Board, 1980; Washita County Historical Society (president, 1980 to present); Alternatives Club for Singles (president, 1981-82); Washita County Extension Homemakers Council (president, 1982-83); Community Red Cross (chairman, 1976 to present); Oklahoma Delegate to A.C.W.W., Hamburg, Germany, 1980; Town Board, 75th Anniversary of Corn. Religion: W.M.S.-Mennonite Brethren Conference (program chairman, 1969-70). Honors and Awards: National E.H. Council, First Place, Safety Awards 1977, Home, Farm and Traffic Safety 1979, Farm, Recreational, Traffic, Emergency Preparedness and Home 1980; National Safety Council, Home Safety, Citation of Meritorious Service 1977, Farm Safety 1979, Award of Honor 1979. Address: Box 147, Corn, Oklahoma 73024.

June L Duke

Duke, June L Conway

Director of College Events. Personal: Born June 4, 1936; Daughter of Mr. and Mrs. George L. Laber; Married Robert G. Duke; Mother of Deborah Lynn Conway, Stephen J. Conway, Diane R. Conway, Kathleen H. Conway, J. David Conway; (Stepchildren:) Lawrence G., Stacey M., Randall C. Education: R.N., University of Maryland, 1956; Undertook post-graduate studies, Johns Hopkins University, 1975-78; Attending Notre Dame College. Career: Director of College Events; Director of Public Relations; Entrepreneur-Owner of Various Businesses and Real Estate Firms; Fashion Model since the age of 15; Hospital Co-Ordinator, University of Maryland Hospital, 1956-58; Community Activities: Maryland General Hospital (executive committee, board of trustees); Maryland General Hospital Auxiliary Inc (president, 1972-74, 1976-79); Long Quarter Association (president, 1976-79); Maryland Health Care System (board member, 1978-79); American Field Service (public relations chairman, 1977); Baltimore Opera Guild (ball chairman, 1978); American Cancer Society (vice president, metro-centre unit, 1977); Organized Republican Campaigns on County, State and National Levels; Chaired Many Fund Raisers for Private and Public Schools and Organizations; Opened Home for Charity; House and Garden Tour, 3 Years.

Dula, Joanne Christine

Management Analyst. Personal: Born August 10, 1944; Daughter of Daniel F. and Florence C. Dula. Education: B.A. magna cum laude, Notre Dame College, Ohio, 1967; M.A., University of Cincinnati, 1971; M.P.F.M., The American University, Washington, D.C., 1979. Career: Management Analyst, Navy Accounting and Finance Center, Washington, D.C., 1976 to present; Program Analyst, Navy Finance Center, Cleveland, Ohio, 1972-76; Mathematics Instructor, Cuyahoga Community College, Cleveland, Ohio, 1974-76; Mathematics Teacher, Central Catholic High School, Canton, Ohio 1971-72, Lourdes Academy, Cleveland, Ohio 1967-69; Graduate Teaching Assistant, University of Cincinnati, 1969-71. Organizational Memberships: American Society of Military Comptrollers, 1978 to present; Federally Employed Women, 1977 to present; Various National, State and Local Mathematics Teachers Associations, 1967-72; Phi Delta Gamma (member, alpha chapter, 1978 to present; chairman, educational services, 1979-80; first vice president, programs, 1980-81; president, 1981-82). Community Activities: Pinewood Lawns Council of Co-Owners (communications committee, 1979-80; board of directors, 1979-80). Religion: St. Jerome Church, Cleveland (liturgy committee, musician, 1975-76); Blessed Sacrament Catholic Community (lay reader, 1978); Good Sheperd Catholic Church (lay reader, 1978-81; adult education committee, 1979-80); Prime Time Single Catholics Parish Representative, 1978-80. Honors and Awards: Commendation for Service as E.E.O. Committee Chairperson, Navy Accounting & Finance Center, 1978; Department of Defense Graduate Financial Management Program Selectee, 1977-79; Graduate Teaching Assistantship, Scholarship, University of Cincinnati, 1969-71; National Science Foundation Summer Study Grant, 1968. Address: 2726 Hickory Street, Alexandria, Virginia 22305.

Gertrude B Dunbar

Dunbar, Gertrude Ballou

Writer. Personal: Born April 27, 1908; Daughter of James Wesley and Anna Elizabeth Stoner Ballou (both deceased); Married William Lewis Dunbar (deceased). Education: Attended Maryland Institute of Art, Johns Hopkins University 1931-33, St. Gall (Switzerland) 1935-36, Columbia University 1935-36; Private Tutoring in Languages, Interior Decorating. Military: American Red Cross, European Theater of Operations, Served on War Bride Ships, 1943-46. Career: Secretary and Assistnt to Librarian, Welch Medical Library, Johns Hopkins University, Baltimore, Maryland, 1929-35; Library of Congress; Army Medical Library; Army Specialist Corps, The Pentagon; American Red Cross, Librarian; Medical Library Consultant, Office of the Surgeon General, United States Air Force, Far East Command. Community Activities: Assistant to the Chief Air Raid Warden, Washington DC, 1941-43. Religion: Episcopalian. Honors and Awards: Presidential Citation (President Harry S. Truman), Far East Command; Certificate of Achievement, General Headquarters, Far East Command. Address: 2413 Brook Road, Charlottesville, Virginia 22901.

Duncan, Bert Logan

Retired Parish Minister. Personal: Born September 12, 1913; Son of Johnathan Marshall and Mary Elizabeth Logan Duncan (both deceased); Married Edith Halsey; Father of Beverly Duncan Johnson (Mrs. Dennis Johnson). Education: A.B., William Jewell College, 1936; Th.M., Southern Baptist Theological Seminary, 1939; Undertook postgraduate work: Divinity School of the University of Chicago, 1946-47; University of Virginia, summer of 1949; Indiana University Department of Sociology, 1950-53; Attended Select Conferences. Military: Served in the rank of Lieutenant, Chaplain Corps, with the United States Naval Reserve, 1943-46. Career: Instructor in Bible, Oak Hill Academy, Mouth of Wilson, Virginia, 1939-40; Pastor, Rural Baptist Churches in Eastern Virginia, 1941-43; Chaplain, United States Naval Reserve, 1943-46; Instructor in English, Fork Union Military Academy, Virginia, 1948-50; Parish Minister, Congregational Churches: Michigan (1958-67), Ohio (1967-70), New York (1970-71); Work with Clark County Council for Retarded (Indiana), 1972-76. Organizational Memberships: Active in Ministerial Associations in Constantine, Michigan, Traverse City, Michigan, and Amherst, Ohio, 1958-70; Counselor for summer youth church camps in Michigan, 1958-65; Michigan United Church of Christ Churchmen's Fellowship (pastoral advisor, 1965-67); Lorain County Ohio Conference of Religion and Society, 1967-70; Cleveland Area Peace Action Council, 1967-70. Community Activities: Older Americans Center (advisory council); Area 10 Agency on Aging (advisory council); Bloomington Track Club; Supporting Member: American Humanist Association, World Future Society, International Platform Association, American Civil Liberties Union, S.A.N.E. (a citizen's committee for a sane nuclear policy); Others. Religion: Unitarian-Universalist Church. Honors and Awards: Winner of 1st and 2nd places in road races in Indiana in his age division (over 60); Listed in *Who's Who in the Midwest, Dictionary of International Biography, Men of Achievement, International Who's Who of Intellectuals, Personalities of America, Personalities of the West and Midwest, Community Leaders of America, International Who's Who in Community Service,* Others. Address: 2531 E. 7th Street, Bloomington, Indiana 47401.

Bert L Duncan

Duncan, Dyna

United States Army Captain. Personal: Born March 27, 1952; Daughter of Mr. and Mrs. Dwyer Duncan. Education: B.S. Wildlife Ecology, Oklahoma State University, 1974; Signal Officer Basic Course, 1976; Signal Officer Advanced Course, 1980; Field Artillery Officer Basic Course, 1982. Military: Captain, United States Army, 1975 to present. Career: Captain, 3D Support Command, APO New York. Organizational Memberships: Association of the United States Army; Reserve Officer Association; National Association of Uniformed Services; Signal Corps Association; Armed Forces Communication & Electronics Association; Oklahoma State University Bar Association; American Biographical Institute Research Association; International Biographical Association. Community Activities: National Wildlife Association; American Association of University Women; Oklahoma State Alumni Association; National Rifle Association. Honors and Awards: 1979 Army Commendation Medal; Listed in *Who's Who of American Women, World's Who's Who of Women, Dictionary of International Biography.* Address: 10724 North Kelley, Oklahoma City, Oklahoma 73114.

Duncan, William Adam Jr

Consulting Specialist. Personal: Born April 27, 1918; Son of William A. and Milner Sammone Duncan; Married Edna Shaw. Education: B.A.; M.Div.; D.Div. Military: Served as a Chaplain in the United States Army and the United States Air Force Reserves-Civil Air Patrol. Career: Pastor; Director of Missions and Church Development, 24 Years; Consulting Southern Baptist Church Planning and Development Specialist. Community Activities: Greensboro Community Council; Co-Founder, Second Amendment Foundation; Civil Air Patrol. Religion: Southern Baptist. Honors and Awards: Life Membership, American Radio Relay League; Endowment Member, National Rifle Association; Conservation Caucus. Address: 2239 Headland Drive, East Point, Georgia 30344.

Dunlap, Estelle Cecilia Diggs

Retired Educator, Civic Leader. Personal: Born September 26, 1912; Daughter of John F. and Mary F. Diggs (both deceased); Married Lee A. Dunlap; Mother of Gladys Cecilia D. Kimbrough, Dolly Ann D. Sparkman. Education: Graduate, Dunbar High School, 1932; B.S., District of Columbia Teachers College, 1937; M.S., Howard University, 1940; Undertook further studies, Catholic University, 1941. Career: Garnet Patterson Jr. High School: Instructor, Head of Math Department 1941-56; Math-Science Instructor, MacFarland Jr. High School, 1956-72; Visiting Lecturer of Mathematics, District of Columbia Teachers College, 1963. Organizational Memberships: American Mathematical Society; National Council of Teachers of Mathematics; American Association for the Advancement of Science; Benjamin Banneker Mathematics Club (vice president); National Education Association; National Defense and Preparedness Association; American Association of University Women; Howard University Alumni Association; National and District of Columbia Retired Teachers Associations; American Association of Retired Professors. Community Activities: Northwest Boundary Civic Association (recording secretary, 1964-69); Smithsonian Resident Association; International Platform Association; American Museum of Natural History; The National Historical Society (founding member); Washington Educational Television Association; Petworth Block Club (treasurer, 1965-70); National Urban League; The Marquis Biographical Library Inc.; American Security Council (advisory board); National Parks and Conservation Association; Republican Congressional Club (charter member); United Nations Association of the United States; American Biographical Research Institute (life member); International Biographical Association (fellow); Academy of Political Science; National Audubon Society; International Institute of Community Service; U.S. Senatorial Club (founding member); National Police and Firefighters Association; Boys' and Girls' Clubs of Metropolitan Police; The Salvation Army Association; American Film Institute; Washington Performing Arts Society (charter member); Arena Stage Association; National Symphony Orchestra Association; Metropolitan Opera Guild; Washington Opera Society; United States Olympic Society; National Association of Negro Musicians; Brunswick Bowling Clubhouse; National Council of Senior Citizens; 1980 Campaigner Member, Republican National Committee; American Council for the Arts; New York City Opera Guild; Friends of the Kennedy Center; Johns Hopkins Hospital Committee of Friends; National Travel Club; Corcoran Gallery of Art; The Jacques Cousteau Society; Donations to: Help Hospitalized Veterans, Red Cross, Young Women's Christian Association, Howard University Development Fund, Goddwill Industries, The Schomburg Center in New York, The New York City Library, National Conservative Political Action Commission, The Sloan-Kettering Cancer Center, The Vietnam Veterans Memorial Fund, Young American's Federation, National Shrine of the Immaculate Conception. Religion: Member St. Gabriel's Church, Church Women United. Honors and Awards: National Science Foundation Fellowships, 1959-62; Diploma of Honor, Advisory Board of Who's Who in Community Service, 1973; Certificate of Appreciation: U.S. District Court 1975, Superior Court of the District of Columbia 1971, Institute for American Strategy; Honorary Fellow, Anglo-American Academy; Honorary Member, 1980 Inaugural Committee, 1980; Certificate of Award: U.S. School of Music, Library of Human Resources of the American Bicentennial Research Institute, Junior Citizens Corps Inc.; Certificate of Merit, Editorial and Advisory Board of the Dictionary of International Biography. Address: 719 Shepherd Street, N.W., Washington D.C. 20011.

Estelle C Dunlap

Dunlap, E T

Chancellor. Personal: Born December 19, 1914, in Cravens, Oklahoma; Son of C. C. and Ida McWhirter Dunlap (both deceased);

Married Opal Jones, 1934; Father of Tom. Education: Attended Eastern Oklahoma State College; B.S., Southeastern Oklahoma State University, 1940; M.S. 1942, Ed.D. 1956, Oklahoma State University. Career; Chancellor, Oklahoma State System of Higher Education, 1961 to present; President, Eastern Oklahoma State College, 1952-61; Superintendent of Schools, Red Oak, Oklahoma, 1945-52; High School Inspector, Oklahoma State Department of Education, 1942-45; County Superintendent, Latimer County, 1938-42; Teacher, Latimer County Public Schools, 1936-38. Organizational Memberships: Education Commission of the States (steering committee; executive committee; treasurer; James B. Conant selection committee); Federal Student Loan Marketing Association (chairman, board of directors); Oklahoma Educational Television Authority; Oklahoma State Accrediting Agency (chairman); Oklahoma Professional Standards Board; Oklahoma Education Council; Oklahoma Board of Private Schools; Oklahoma Health Planning Council; Oklahoma Prime Sponsor Planning Council on Manpower; Oklahoma Emergency Medical Services Advisory Council; Oklahoma University Hospital Advisory Council; Governor's Committee on Employment of the Handicapped; Oklahoma Frontiers of Science Foundation (executive comittee); Oklahoma Health Sciences Foundation (executive committee); Oklahoma Energy Extension Service Advisory Council; Oklahoma Industrial Recreation and Fitness Council; Oklahoma Council on Economic Education; Oklahoma Manpower Services Council; American Council on Education (commission on women in higher education); Governor's Cabinet (education member); State Higher Education Officers Association (past president; chairman, budget and finance committee; chairman, planning board of inservice education project; federal regulations committee); Commission on Colleges and Universities of the North Central Association of Colleges and Schools (past member; consultant; examiner); United States Office of Education (past member, advisory committee on graduate education); Oklahoma Junior College Association (past president); Oklahoma Education Association (past member, board of directors; present member); National Education Association; American Association of School Administrators; Oklahoma Association of School Administrators; American Association for Higher Education; National Society for the Study of Education; Oklahoma Political Science Association; Oklahoma Historical Society; Red Red Rose; Phi Delta Kappa; Pi Kappa Alpha; Masonic Lodge (master mason, consistory 33°, shrine, jester, grotto); Men's Dinner Club of Oklahoma City. Community Activities: Lions Club (past president, North Lincoln club, Oklahoma City); Boy Scouts (executive committee; Last Frontier council); Oklahoma City Chamber of Commerce. Religion: Protestant; Wesley Methodist Church, Oklahoma City (member, official board). Published Works: Author, Ten Books and Monographs, including *State Level Perspectives on Student Financial Aid, Chancellor's Report of Progress: The University of Oklahoma Sciences Center, Educational Program Budgeting: Key to Accountability in Oklahoma Higher Education;* Author, Over 600 Articles, Formal Papers, and Addresses Presented during the Past Decade, including "Education: Prerequisite to Freedom", "The Politics of Board, Staff, and Public Relations", "Talkback Television: Oklahoma State Regents for Higher Education". Honors and Awards: Honorary Degrees, Doctor Humane Letters, Oklahoma City University 1962, Doctor of Laws, John Brown University 1968, Oral Roberts University 1979, Pepperdine University 1979; Henry G. Bennett Distinguished Service Award 1980, Alumni Hall of Fame 1977, Oklahoma State University; Senate Concurrent Resolution No. 89 Commending Contribution to Oklahoma Education, 1976; Oklahoma State Dental Association (honorary member); Medical Ambassador Award, University of Oklahoma, Health Sciences Center, Oklahoma Medical Association; Distinguished Public Service Award, The Oklahoma College of Osteopathic Medicine and Surgery, 1974; Certificate of Achievement, United States Army, Europe and Seventh Army, 1972; Distinguished Service Award, Education Commission of the States 1980, State Higher Education Executive Officers Association 1980; Oklahoma Hall of Fame, 1981; Silver Beaver Award, Boy Scouts of America; Listed in *Who's Who in America, Who's Who in American Education, Who's Who in Education in the Southwest, Who's Who in American Political Science.* Address: 5304 Stonewall Drive, Oklahoma City, Oklahoma 73111.

Helen E Dunn

Dunn, Helen Elizabeth Joos

Educator. Personal: Born July 14, 1930; Daughter of Mrs. Albert E. Joos; Married to Dr. Harry Christie; Mother of Pamela Elizabeth Baumann, Patricia Louise. Education: Attended Peoria Public Schools, 1935-48; B.S., 1951, M.A., 1970, Bradley University. Career: Teacher in elementary schools of Peru, Illinois; Former high school and grade school teacher in Hawaii; Former elementary school teacher in Peoria; Former teacher and counselor in high schools and grade schools in Peru. Organizational Memberships: National Education Association (life member, delegate to national convention, 1955); Peoria Education Association (secretary, 1957-58); Delta Kappa Gamma (member, 1957-81, president of Nu chapter, 1968-69, president of Gamma Delta chapter, 1978-79, state nominating committee, 1979-81, state expansion committee, 1981 to present). Community Activities: Newcomers Club (president of Illinois Valley, 1970); Epsilon Sigma Alpha (president, 1971-72); League of Women Voters (board of directors, 1974-79); United Way of Illinois Valley, Inc. (board of directors, 1975-79); Host Family for Costa Rican student, 1975-76; American Field Service (secretary, 1976, president, 1977); Sweet Adelines, Inc. Religion: Member of First Congregational United Church of Christ (board of Christian education, 1975-78, chairperson, 1978). Honors and Awards: Member of Federation of Scholars, 1949-51; Delta Kappa Gamma, 1957-82; Pi Lambda Theta, 1969-82; National Epsilon Sigma Alpha pledge of the year, 1970. Address: 2604 Rock Street, Peru, Illinois 61354.

Ross Dunn

Dunn, Ross

Educator, Administrator. Personal: Born September 19, 1931; Son of Petronia Dunn; Married Rosa; Father of Martin DeRosseau, Rosephanye Tolandra, Kennedy Fitzgerald, Wilfred Julian. Education: Graduate of Lanier High School; B.S., Master's Degree in Administration Supervision, Alabama State University, Montgomery, Alabama; Postgraduate Study; Attended University of Georgia, Tuskegee Institute, Troup Vocational School; Certificate, Management, Patrick Comer School, Greensboro, North Carolina; Camping Certificate, Boy Scouts of America, National Camping School, New Jersey; Philmont Boy Scouts Training Center Certificate, Cimarron, New Mexico; Certificate, Management Update; Certificate, Personnel Seminar; Certificate, Executive Conference on Personnel Relations, 1980; Certificate, Managing with Interference, West Point Pepperell, 1980; Certificates, Class A-GL Superintendent-Principal, DA-5 Administration-Professional, CS-1 Custodial Services, SL-1 Foundation in School Lunch, SL-2 Menu Planning, SL-3 Nutrition. Career: Teacher, Laney Elementary School, Waverly Hall, Georgia One Year; Johnson Elementary School, Whitesville, Georgia, Teacher Nine Years, Principal Three Years; Teacher, Dunbar Elementary School, Tuskegee, Alabama, One Year; Principal, Dunbar Elementary School, Pine Mountain, Georgia, One Year; Assistant Superintendent, Macon County School System, Tuskegee, Alabama, One Year; Administrator Assistant, Muscogee County School District, Columbus, Georgia, Two Years; West Point Pepperell, Personnel Assistant-Personnel Relations Four Years, Employee Relations Specialist, Personnel Relations Department Three Years (current). Organizational Memberships: Alabama Education Association (member, Montgomery chapter); National Education Association (member, Montgomery chapter). Community Activities: West Point Parent-Teacher Association; West Point Quarterback Club; West Point Band Booster Club; Huguley Water System, Huguley (president); Drew Recreation Center, Shawmut (advisor); Goodwill Industries, Columbus, Georgia (former board member); Health Systems Agency, Gadsden (board member); Chattahoochee Valley Area Association for Retarded Children, Fairfax, Alabama; Magnolia Civic Club, Shawmut (president); National Association for the Advancement of Colored People (former president, Chamber County Valley branch, Lanett; lifetime member, New York); Chambers County Pensions and Security, LaFayette; Chambers County Child Abuse, LaFayette (co-chairman); Notary Public, State of Alabama, State of Georgia; Boy Scouts of America (assistant scout master, troop #15, West Point; former chairman, Valley district, West Point; member, executive board, George H. Lanier council, West Point);

Master Mason F. & A.M., Alabama; Valley Chamber of Commerce, Lanett; Junior Achievement, Lanett; American Red Cross (member, West Point); Lurleen Allace Courage Crusade, Birmingham (collected $19,000 in pledges); Valley Human Relations Forum, Lanett (former member); Alabama Democratic Conference, Montgomery; Chambers County Democratic Executive Committee, LaFayette; Alabama Democratic Club (member, Birmingham); Governor Staff, (honorary member, Montgomery, Atlanta); Alabama State University (member, Valley chapter, alumni association; member, board of trustees, Montgomery); East Alabama Sickle Cell Association, Inc., Opelika (former board member); Chambers County Industrial Development Board, LaFayette; Secretary of the State of Alabama Election Law Commission; Pine Valley Girl Scout Council, Griffin, Georgia; Chambers County Education Advisory Council, LaFayette. Lanett). Religion: Methodist; Hall Memorial C.M.E. Church, Fairfax, Alabama (member; steward; Sunday school advisor; chairman, trustee board). Honors and Awards: Outstanding Service 1968, District Award of Merit 1977, Silver Beaver Award 1978, Boy Scouts of America; Outstanding X-H Leader, 1969; Man of the Year, 1970, 1971; Essie Handy Award, 1971; Administrator Spirit Award, 1972; Citizen Award 1973, President's Award 1975, 100 Membership Award 1976, 1977, 1978, 1980, National Association for the Advancement of Colored People; Democratic Club of Alabama Award, 1974; Huguley Water Systems Award, 1979; Listed in *Who's Who Among Black Americans, Men of Achievement, Personalities of the South*, Publications of the American Biographical Institute. Address: Route 2, Box 923, Drew Lane, Lanett, Alabama 36863.

Dupin, Clyde

Clyde Dupin

Preacher, Crusade Evangelist, Columnist. Personal: Born February 22, 1933, in Elizabethtown, Kentucky; Married Grace Spencer; Father of Ken, Wes, One Daughter. Education: Theological Training, United Wesleyan College; Attended University of Evansville, Evansville, Indiana. Career: City-Wide Crusader, Age Nineteen; Pastor, Ten Years; Evangelist, Eighteen Years (has traveled more than one million miles and conducted more than two hundred interdenominational crusades, church revivals, camps and Bible conferences). Published Works: Author, Weekly Newspaper Column, "Religious Viewpoint". Honors and Awards: Biographed in *The Evangelist*, by Bob Hill, Cross Roads Books, 1980. Address: Kernersville, North Carolina.

Dupree, Kathryn Joyce

Captain, United States Army. Personal: Born April 22, 1940; Daughter of Gordon P. Dupree Sr.; Sara W. Booth. Education: Graduate, with honors, Alameda High School 1958; A.A. Merritt College 1967; Certificate, American Institute of Banking 1962; B.A. University of California, Berkeley 1969; Diploma, Women's Army Corps Basic Officer Course, Ft. McClellan, Alabama 1969; Diploma, with honors, Chemical, Biological, Radiological Instructor Course, Ft. Gordon, Georgia 1970; Diploma-Honor Graduate: Military Police Officer Advanced Course, Correctional Administration Course, Civil Disturbance Orientations Course, Security Management Course, all from the U.S. Army Military Police School; Certificate, Safe and Burglary Investigator's Seminar 1977; Certificate/Diploma, St. Louis University School of Medicine; Further Courses, University Colorado and Denver University. Military: Served with the U.S. Army, achieving the rank of Captain in the Military Police Corps; Retired 1978. Career: Newspaper Route Captain 1955-58; Cashier, Clerk, American Embassy Commissary, Tehran, Iran 1958-59; Accounting Clerk, Navy Exchange Accounting Office, Alameda, California 1959-60; Laboratory Assistant, Borden Laboratories 1961; Head Resident, Westminster House, Presbyterian Student Center, University of California, Summer 1961; Loan Clerk, Computer Reconcilor, Bank of America 1962-66; Intensive Care Unit Technician, Kaiser Foundation Hospital, Oakland 1966-69; Corporal Cadet, W.A.C. College Junior Program, U.S. Army, Summer 1968; Student Officer, First Lieutenant, Officer Training Detachment, U.S. Women's Army Corps School and Center, Ft. McClellan 1969; Executive Officer, Headquarters Company, W.A.C., U.S. Army School Training Center, Ft. Gordon 1969-71; Battery Commander, W.A.C. Battery, Ft. Sill, Oklahoma 1971-73; Recruiting and Induction Officer/Coordinator of Project A.H.E.A.D., U.S. Army District Recruiting Command, Minneapolis 1973-76; Student, Military Police Officer Advanced Course, U.S. Army Military Police School, Ft. McClellan 1976; Provost Marshal/Chief, Security Office, Tripler Army Medical Center, Health Services Command, Hawaii 1976-77; Patient-Fitzsimons Army Medical Center, Denver 1977-78; Temporary Disability Retired List, U.S. Army 1978 to present; Retired Captain, U.S. Army; Retired Provost Marshal, U.S. Army. Organizational Memberships: International Association of Chiefs of Police; Hawaiian Joint Police Officer's Association; International Academy of Criminology; American Law Enforcement Officer's Association; National Council on Crime and Delinquency; Child Protection and Case Management Team (law enforcement representative); Association of the U.S. Army; American Institute of Banking; Retired Officer's Association; American Association for the Advancement of Science. Community Activities: American Association of University Women; California Alumni Association, University of California-Berkeley; Veterans of Foreign Wars Auxiliary #939; Tower and Flame Honor Society, University California-Berkeley; Alpha Gamma Sigma; Merritt College Judicial Council (judge 1966-67); Premedical Society, University of California-Berkeley (editor, treasurer, 1960-63, 1967-69); Acorn Yearbook (administrative editor 1957-58); Big Sister Program, Lawton, Ohio (co-founder and council member 1971-73); Lawton Tutorial Program (co-founder and council member 1971-73); Fitzsimons Army Medical Center Chapel (choir director 1977-78); Bay Farm Island Baptist Mission (Sunday school teacher 1960-68; superintendent, choir director); Chemistry Club (president, editor, treasurer); California Scholarship Federation (life member); Star and Key Honor Society (life member); Volunteer Reader for the Blind, University of California-Berkeley, 1960-62, 1967-69; California State Junior College, Area 7 (representative for Merritt College 1965-67); Merritt College Bond Raising Committee; Merritt College Glee Club; Merritt College Marching Band; Merritt College Orchestra; California School for the Deaf; Kaiser Hospital (volunteer worker); Armed Forces Day Parade Committee, Lawton, Oklahoma; Human Relations Council, Ft. Sill, Oklahoma; Girls Association, Alameda, California; Girls Athletic Association, Alameda; National Education Association; American Association for the Advancement of Science. Honors and Awards: Gold Pin 1954; First Chair Viola, California State Competition 1955; Life Member, California Scholarship Federation and Star and Key Honor Society 1958; Certificate of Excellence, Navy Exchange Accounting Office 1960; Delta Zeta Award 1961; Award for Efficiency Study, Bank of America 1965; Faculty Scholarship Award, Merritt College 1966; Irene Purington Scholarship Award, University of California-Berkeley 1967; Distinguished Grad of the Women Officer's Basic Course and Letter of Commendation 1969; Graduation Parade Commander 1969; National Service Defense Medal, U.S. Army 1969; Army Commendation Medal, U.S. Army 1971; Army Commendation Medal w First Oak Leaf Cluster 1973; Army Commendation Medal with Second Oak Leaf Cluster 1976; Marksman Badge, Military Police School 1976; Listed in *World Who's Who of Women, Who's Who in American Law Enforcement, Book of Honor, Community Leaders and Noteworthy Americans, Personalities of America, International Register of Profiles*. Address: 6192 Pitkin Way, Denver, Colorado 80239.

Kathryn J Dupree

Durham, Peggy J

Journalist, Executive. Personal: Born August 19, 1941, in Boise City, Oklahoma; Daughter of John and Mildred Durham; Mother of Erin Christine Phillips. Education: Attended Southwestern State College, Weatherford, Oklahoma; B.A. Journalism, News Advertising, University of Oklahoma-Norman, 1963. Career: President, Board Chair, The WORD Place Company, 1978 to present; Board Chair/Half Owner, Metro Media, Ltd., 1977-78; Director of Public Information, Oklahoma Bar Association, 1975-77; Manager, Communications and Community Relations 1974-75, Communications Specialist 1970-74, Honeywell Information

Systems; Director of Public Information, St. Gregory's College, 1969-70; Director of Public Information, University of Tulsa, 1968-69; Reporter, Editor, *The Oklahoma Journal* Daily Newspaper, 1966-68; Editor, *Briston News and Record Citizen*, 1966; Assistant Director of Public Relations, World Neighbors, 1965-66; Special Publicist for Mexican National Fair, Juarez, Mexico, 1964; Associate Editor, Oklahoma Gas and Electric Company, 1963-64. Organizational Memberships: Business Professional Advertising Association, 1981; Oklahoma Press Club, 1970-81. Community Activities: Paseo Drug Information Center (member, board of directors, 1970-73; editor, volunteer newsletter, 1971-73; volunteer drug counselor, 1970-73); Tutor to Child with Dyslexia, 1971-73; National Organization for Women; Oklahoma Women's Political Caucus; Democratic Ward 8, Precinct 16 (chair, 1976-77); Oklahoma Halfway House (editor, *Alternatives*, 1974); Oklahoma Women's Center (board member, public information officer, 1973-74); The Oklahoma *New Woman* (editor, publisher, 1975-77); *Sister Advocate*, Oklahoma's Only Feminist Newspaper (editor, 1977-80); Democratic House District #87 (chair, 1976-77); Planned Parenthood Association (member, public information committee, 1980 to present); The Production Company, Women's Music (board member, promotion chair); *The Oklahoma Observer* (columnist, political commentary); Oklahoma County Democratic Party. Honor and Awards: First Bar Association Public Relations Official Ever Invited to Address the National Association of Bar Presidents; One of Ten "Movers & Shakers" in the Oklahoma Women's Movement, Oklahoma *Monthly* Magazine; One of "80 Women to Watch in the 80's", Oklahoma Women's Political Caucus; Developed an Award-Winning $100,000 Public Information Program for the Oklahoma Legal Profession Involving Radio and Television Spots and News Releases (while director of public information, Oklahoma Bar Association); Delta Zeta; Listed in *Foremost Women in Communication, Who's Who in American Women, Who's Who in the Southwest, Directory of International Biography, Personalities of the South, World Who's Who of Women, Community Leaders and Noteworthy Americans, Personalities of America*. Address: 1308 Northwest 10th Street, Oklahoma City, Oklahoma 73106.

Dworski, Sylvia

Educator. Personal: Born April 10, 1915; Daughter of Louis and Ida Dworski (both deceased). Education: B.A. with Highest Honors, Connecticut College, 1935; M.A. with Distinction 1937, Ph.D. 1941, Yale University; Certificat d'études pratiques de prononciation française, Institut de Phonétique de l'Université de Paris, 1939; Spanish Language Institute for Teachers of Spanish, University of Mexico, Summer 1944. Career: Professor Emeritus of Modern Languages (current); Saint Mary's College, Notre Dame, Indiana, Associate Professor 1963-64, Professor 1964-80, Co-Chairperson, Department of Modern Languages 1963-65, Chairperson, Department of French 1965-67; Visiting Faculty Member, University of Notre Dame Graduate School, Summers of 1967 and 1968; Wilkes College, Associate Professor 1954-63, Assistant Professor 1948-54; Instructor in Romance Languages, Saint Helena Extension, College of William and Mary, 1946-48; Instructor in Romance Languages, Sweet Briar College, 1944-46; Teacher of French, Spanish and English, East Haven High School, 1942-44; Instructor in Spanish, New Haven State Teachers Evening College, 1941-44. Organizational Memberships: American Association of Teachers of French (1940's to present); American Council of Learned Societies; American Association of University Professors (member, 1940's to present; Saint Mary's College chapter, founding member, first secretary/treasurer 1965-66, 1978-79, executive board member 1979-80). Community Activities: Alliance Francaise; Connecticut College Library (friend); Common Cause; Public Citizen; Donations to The Carol Satosky Druckman Memorial Scholarship Fund, The Rabbi Maurice Parzen and Sheldon Parzen Memorial Fund. Religion: Jewish; Donations to Synagogues in Moodus and New Haven, Connecticut, South Bend, Indiana, Hadassah. Honors and Awards: Sabbatical Study of Modern French Theater, France, 1969-70; United States Grant to Attend Spanish Language Institute, Mexico City, Summer 1944; Visiting Fellow in Romance Languages, Yale University, 1941-42; Yale University French Traveling Fellow, 1938-39; Phi Beta Kappa (charter member, Connecticut College chapter, 1935); Connecticut College Winthrop Scholar, 1934; Honor Graduate, Connecticut College, Yale University; Listed in *Who's Who of American Women, Men and Women of Distinction, World's Who's Who of Women, Personalities of America, Community Leaders of America*. Address: 70 Byron Place, New Haven, Connecticut 06515.

Marie R Dwyer

Dwyer, Marie Rita Rozelle

Director of Community Relations, Educator. Personal: Born September 4, 1915, in New York City; Daughter of Charles W. and Agnes Coyle Rozelle (both deceased); Married Dr. John D. Dwyer, September 8, 1942; Mother of John Duncan, Joseph Charles, James Gerard, Jerome Valentine. Education: Attended Notre Dame Academy of Staten Island, New York City, Convent de L'Assomption, Paris, France; B.A., Notre Dame College of Staten Island, New York City, 1936; M.A. 1938, Ph.D. Candidate 1942, Fordham University, New York City; Postgraduate Study, St. Louis University; Attending Student, Summers 1933-37, 1952, Diplômes d'Études Françaises, Certificat de la Sorbonne 1952, Sorbonne, Paris; Certificat, Institut de Phonetique, Paris, 1952; Teaching Certificates, New York, Missouri. Career: Teacher of French, School of Education, Fordham University, New York City College, 1938-42, Notre Dame College, New York City 1939-40, College of St. Rose, Albany, New York 1949-53, Washington University, St. Louis 1959-60; Faculty Member, French Department, Webster College, 1966-74; Professor of Biology, 1953 to present, Director of Community Services, International Office, Educational, Cultural, Social, 1974-82, Assistant to Dean of Student Affairs, 1982 to present, St. Louis University; Faculty Member, Meramac Community College, St. Louis, 1968-70; Extensive Travel for Educational and Linguistic Research. Organizational Memberships: American Association of Teachers of French (member; president, St. Louis chapter, 1954-55); Association of Foreign Language Teachers of Greater St. Louis (records secretary, 1970); Teachers of French Association (president, St. Louis chapter, 1955); National French Contest (president, St. Louis area, one year); Missouri Academy of Sciences (life member; editorial staff transactions, 1969-72; chairman, linguistics section, 1970-76; past member, executive board; representative, American Academy for the Advancement of Science convention, Mexico City, 1973); American Academy for the Advancement of Science; American Association of University Professors; Modern Language Association; Missouri Modern Language Association (president, 1961-63); Central States Conference on Teaching Foreign Languages; Societe International de la Linguistique; Linguistic Society of America; Foreign Language Association of Missouri (vice president, 1973; secretary, 1970; 4-college consortium, including Webster, Fontbonne, Maryville, Lindenwood, 1972-73); Centro Studie Scambi Internazionali (member, international committee); National Association of Foreign Student Affairs (member, 1974 to present; registration committee, national convention, St. Louis, 1980); COMSEC, Community Section (chairman, region 4, five states, 1978-79). Community Activities: Community Fund Drives, including Greater St. Louis Fund for Arts and Education (board of directors, 1962-64), Christmas Carols Association 1962-64; Alliance Francaise (past secretary, St. Louis chapter); La Société Francaise (secretary, 1955); Knights of Columbus (president, Women's Auxiliary, 2119 Webster Groves, 1956-57); Notre Dame College Alumni Association (president 1942-43); Smithsonian Institution National Associations; International Platform Association (member, 1968); St. Louis University Faculty Women's Club (president, 1956-58; director, 1959 to present); International Federation of Catholic Alumnae (president, Albany Circle, New York, 1945-49). Religion: Catholic; Parish Council, 1966-67; Archdiocean Council-Catholic Youth (adult advisor, cultural program for young adults, 1961-67); Archdiocean Council of Laity (member, committees, family life, teenage code, corresponding secretary 1963-64, president 1964-66, south central district, Catholic women; advisory council, member 1968, nominated vice president 1969, president 1969); Jesuit Mothers' Guild (president, Missouri province, 1963-65); Catholic Women's League (president, Holy Redeemer parish, St. Louis, 1964-66). Published Works: Master's Thesis on the 17th Century; Three Papers Presented at Missouri Academy of Science. Honors and Awards: Pi Delta Phi National French Honor Society (member, Beta Kappa chapter, 1966 to present); Alpha Sigma Nu Jesuit Honor Society (member, 1981 to present); Listed in *National Social*

Directory, Who's Who of American Women, Who's Who in the Midwest, Who's Who of the West and Midwest, Dictionary of International Biography, 2000 Women of Achievement, American Catholic Who's Who, World Who's Who of Women. **Address: 525 Oakwood Avenue, St. Louis, Missouri 63119.**

Eads, Sherry Lynn

Medical Administrator. Personal: Born July 3, 1946; Daughter of Mrs. Erlene Pope Smith; Married Major James Robert Eads; Mother of Judi L. Wood, Dawn Michelle Eads. Career: Medical Administrator. Religion: First United Methodist Church, Temple, Texas. Honors and Awards: Listed in *Personalities of the South, Personalities of America.* Address: 4117 Antelope Trail, Temple, Texas 76501.

Eakin, Thomas Capper

Thomas C Eakin

Sports Promotion Executive. Personal: Born December 16, 1933, in New Castle, Pennsylvania; Son of Frederick William and Beatrice Capper Eakin (both deceased); Married Brenda Lee Andrews, October 21, 1961; Father of Thomas Andrews, Scott Frederick. Education: B.A., History, Denison University, 1956. Military: Served in the United States Army, 1956-58, attaining the rank of Specialist 4th Class. Career: Life Insurance Consultant, Northwestern Mutual Life Insurance Company, Cleveland, Ohio, 1959-67; Regional Director of Sales, Empire Life Insurance Company of Ohio, 1967-68; District Manager, Putman Publishing Company, Cleveland, Ohio, 1968-69; Regional Business Manager, Chilton Publishing Company, 1969-70; District Manager, Hitchcock Publishing Company, Cleveland, 1970-72; President, TCE Enterprises, Shaker Heights, Ohio, 1973 to present; Founder, President, Golf International 100 Club, 1970 to present; Founder, Director, Cy Young Museum, 1970 to present; Founder, Director, "TRY", Target/Reach Youth, 1971 to present; Founder, Director, Interact Club of Shaker Heights, Ohio, 1971 to present; Founder, President, Ohio Baseball Hall of Fame, 1976 to present; Founder, President, Ohio Baseball Hall of Fame "Celebration", 1977 to present. Community Activities: Shaker Heights Rotary, International Student Exchange Program, United States and Canada (founder and chairman, 1965-70); Shaker Heights Rotary Club (president, 1970-71; vice-president, 1969-70; secretary, 1964-65; board of directors, 1963, 1965, 1968, 1972); Phi Delta Theta Alumni Club of Cleveland, Ohio (president, 1970; vice-president, 1969; board of directors, 1971-75); Phi Delta Theta National Fraternity; Cleveland Council on Corrections, 1971 to present; Cuyahoga Hills Boys School (advisory board, 1971 to present); Camp Hope (advisory board, 1973 to present); Cleveland Indians Old Timers Committee, 1966-67; Cy Young Centennial (organizer and national chairman, 1967); Cy Young Golf Invitational (founder, national chairman, 1967 to present); Tuscarawas County American Revolution Bicentennial Commission (executive committee, 1974 to present); Intercontinental Biographical Association (fellow, 1973); Tuscarawas County Old Timers Baseball Association (honorary director, 1972 to present); National Lou Gehrig Award Committee, Phi Delta Theta (executive committee, 1975 to present); Newcomerstown Sports Corporation (trustee, 1975-80); Wahoo Club (board of directors, 1975); Tuscarawas County Historical Society (trustee, 1978-81); Shaker Heights Youth Center Inc. (board member, 1975); Fitness Evaluation Services Inc. (advisory board, 1977-79); International Platform Association (member, 1978 to present); World Golf Hall of Fame, Pinehurst, North Carolina (Ohio executive sponsor chairman, 1979 to present); Tuscarawas Valley Tourist Association (director, 1979-81); Ohio Iota, Phi Delta Theta, Denison University Chapter (trustee, 1979-81); Buckeye Tourist Association (director, 1979-80); The Shaker Historical Society (trustee, 1980-82). Religion: First Baptist Church of Greater Cleveland (board member, 1966-69). Honors and Awards: Presidential Commendation, President, Richard M. Nixon, 1973; State of Ohio Commendation, Governor James A. Rhodes 1968 and 1975, Governor John J. Gilligan 1972; Baseball Commissioner Commendation, William D. Eckert, 1967; Baseball Commendation, The Sporting News, 1968; Citation of Merit, Louisiana Stadium and Exposition District, Louisiana Superdome, 1972; Civic Service Award, Cuyahoga Hills Boys School, 1970; Commendation Award, Cy Young Centennial Committee, 1967; Tuscarawas County, Ohio, Chamber of Commerce Commendation, 1967; Newcomerstown, Ohio, Chamber of Commerce Commendation, 1967; Sport Service Award, *Sport Magazine*, 1969; Outstanding Young Rotarian Award, Shaker Heights Rotary Club, 1962; Appreciation Award, Phi Delta Theta Alumni Club of Cleveland, Ohio, 1971; Distinguished Service Award, Camp Hope, 1974; Founder's Award, Interact Club of Shaker Heights, Ohio, 1974; Proclamation Award, "Thomas C. Eakin Day", City of Cleveland, 1974; Governor's Award for Community Action, Ohio Governor John J. Gilligan, 1974; Award of Achievement, Ohio Association of Historical Societies, 1975; Chief Newawatowes Award, Newcomerstown, Ohio Chamber of Commerce, 1975; Outstanding Alumnus Award, Phi Delta Theta Alumni Club of Cleveland, 1975; Ohio Senate Commendation Award, Ohio Senate, 1976, 1979; Ohio American Revolution Bicentennial Advisory Commission Commendation, 1976; Tuscarawas County American Revolution Bicentennial Commission, Certificate of Merit, 1976; American Revolution Bicentennial Administration, Appreciation Award, 1977; State of Louisiana, Certificate of Merit, 1978; Honorary Citizen of New Orleans, 1978; Ohio House of Representatives Commendation, 1978; Governor's Award, State of Ohio, 1978; Founder's Award, "TRY", 1979; Listed in *Who's Who in America, Men of Achievement, Dictionary of International Biography, Community Leaders of America, International Who's Who in Community Service, Who's Who in Ohio, Two Thousand Men of Achievement, Outstanding Young Men of America, Who's Who in the United States, Who's Who in the Midwest, Who's Who in the World, Personalities of America.* Address: 2729 Shelly Road, Shaker Heights, Ohio 44122.

Eakins, Rosemary Louise

Executive and Research Manager. Personal: Born March 22, 1931; Daughter of Princess Lona-Marie di Gravina; Mother of Nancy Louise Eakins Hope. Education: B.Sc. Honors Geological Sciences 1956, M.A. English Literature 1960, McGill University, Montreal; D.Phil. English Literature, St. Anne's College, Oxford University, England, 1972. Career: Vice President, Research Manager, Research Reports, New York City; Tutor, St. Anne's, St. Hilda's and Somerville Colleges, Oxford, 1967-70; Lecturer in English, McGill University, 1959-64; Geologist, Mineral Management Ltd., Montreal, 1956-59; Geologist and Geochemist, Cerro de Pasvo Corporation, Arequipa, Peru, 1952-55. Organizational Memberships: American Society of Picture Professionals. Community Activities: Friends of Alice Austen House, Inc. (executive committee, 1976 to present). Address: Box 80, New Lebanon Center, New York 12126.

William E East

East, William Eugene

Director of Missions. Personal: Born May 25, 1929; Son of Henry Melton East and Jackie V. White; Married to Shirley Jean Eddy;

Father of Carol Maxine, David Eugene, Virginia Inez, Donna Sue, Melton Earl; Foster father of Robert Wagoner, Ginger Oliver, Brad Oliver. Education: A.B., Oklahoma Baptist University, 1951; B.D., 1957, Th.M., 1960, Doctor of Ministry, 1973, Golden Gate Baptist Theological Seminary, Mill Valley, California. Career: Director of Missions, Kern County Southern Baptist Association of Churches, Bakersfield, California; Pastor at First Baptist Church (Newark, California), 1951-54, Calvary Baptist Church (Auburn, California), 1954-55, First Baptist Church (El Sobrante, California), 1956-58, First Baptist Church (Folsom, California), 1958-62. Organizational Memberships: Ministers Association at El Sobrante (president, 1957), and at Folsom (president, 1960); Greater Bakersfield Ministers Association (president, 1972, vice president, 1970). Community Activities: Suicide Prevention Center Board of Bakersfield (president, 1974); Baptist Association for Sacramento, California (moderator, 1961); Volunteer Chaplain, Kern Medical Center, 1978; Bakersfield Rescue Mission Board Member, 1970-72; Church of Sequoia Board Member (a ministry to national parks), 1968-79. Honors and Awards: Listed in *Personalities of the West and Midwest, Who's Who in Religion.* Address: 3500 Akers Road, Unit #52, Bakersfield, California 93309.

Ebersole, J Glenn Jr

Engineering and Marketing Executive. Personal: Born February 8, 1947; Son of J. Glenn Ebersole, Sr. Education: B.S.C.E., Pennsylvania State University, 1970; M.Eng., 1973. Career: Engineering and Marketing Executive, Self-Employed Consultant; Executive Engineer, Account Executive, Gilboy, Stouffer, Giombetti, Skibinski and Bellante; Chief Transportation Engineer, Huth Engineers, Inc.; Assistant Chief Engineer, Traffic, Pennsylvania Turnpike Commission; Head of Research and Special Studies, Pennsylvania Department of Transportation Bureau of Traffic Engineering. Organizational Memberships: American Society of Civil Engineers; National Society of Professional Engineers; Pennsylvania Society of Professional Engineers; International Platform Association; American Marketing Association (president, Central Pennsylvania Section); T.R.B.; I.T.E. (national technical program, 50th annual meeting, 1980). Community Activities: Lancaster Chamber of Commerce; Harrisburg Chamber of Commerce; Rapho Township Planning Commission (chairman, 1973-79); Advisory Committee of Local Governments to Lancaster County Planning Commission; Casiphia Lodge #551 (worshipful master, 1983); Lancaster Lodge of Perfection; Harrisburg, Consistry, Zembo Temple Shrine; United Way Campaigns (account executive). Religion: Zion Lutheran Church, Vice President of Church Council, Lay Preacher, Chairman of Stewardship Committee, Adult Sunday School Teacher, Parish Life Development Committee. Honors and Awards: Gil Shirk Trophy as Outstanding Senior Athlete, E-town Area High School, 1965; Varsity Club Trophy, Best All Around Athlete, E-town High School, 1965; Chosen as Speaker, I.T.E. National Meetings, 1976, 1978, 1981. Address: R.D. 2, Box 305, Manheim, Pennsylvania 17545.

Ebersole, Priscilla Pierre

Field Director. Personal: Born August 17, 1928; Daughter of Joseph and Miriam Pierre; Married Raymond V. Ebersole; Mother of Lorraine Kester, Raymond Jr., Randolph, Elizabeth Tanti. Education: Attended Cascade College, 1947-48; A.A., College of San Mateo, 1971; B.S. magna cum laude, San Francisco State University, 1971; M.S. 1972, Post Graduate Study 1972-73, University of California-San Francisco; Certificate of Gerontological Nursing Summer Institutes, University of Southern California, 1973-78. Career: Field Director, Geriatric Nurse Practitioner Project, Mountain States Health Corporation, Boise, Idaho, 1981 to present; Faculty, Department of Nursing, San Francisco State University, 1973-81 (granted doctoral equivalency and promoted to associate professor, 1978); Faculty, Summer Institute, Andrus Gerontology Center, University of Southern California, 1977-81; Intermittent Consultation, Palo Alto Veterans Hospital (California), Peninsula Hospital and Mental Health Center (Burlingame, California), County of Santa Clara Public Health Department (San Jose, California), 1973-81; Affiliated with Geriatric Screening Unit, City and County of San Francisco, 1973; Conducted Workshops, Seminars and Lectures in Nation-wide Locations on Various Psychosocial Aspects of Aging, 1973-81; Thesis Advisor, University of Southern California, 1978; Curriculum Project Director, San Francisco State University, 1978; Survey of Board and Care Operators in San Francisco Bayview District, 1973; Developed Video Teaching Aides, 1975-81; Professional Presentations at Regional, National and International Gerontology Meetings, 1975-81. Organizational Memberships: American Nurses Association; Gerontological Society of America; Western Gerontology Society. Community Activities: American Association of University Women; California Commission on Aging, San Mateo County. Published Works: Author of Numerous Professional Articles including "Mental Health and Illness in Old Age", "Middle Age Family", "A Theoretical Approach to the Use of Reminiscence"; Contibuting Author to Several Texts of Gerontological Nursing; Author of Nursing Text *Toward Healthy Aging: Human Needs and Nursing Response.* Honors and Awards: Book of the Year Awards, *American Journal of Nursing,* 1979, 1982. Address: 1112 Abbey Circle, Boise, Idaho 83705.

Trudy Ebert

Ebert, Kathryn

Interior Architect. Personal: Born September 22, 1949; Daughter of Robert A. and Trudy M. Ebert; Married Timothy J. Hilger; Mother of Caroline Ebert Hilger. Education: Graduate of Derham Hall High School, St. Paul, Minnesota, 1967; B.A., Interior Architecture and Design, Northwestern University, Evanston, Illinois, 1971; Summer Studies at University of Montreal 1967, Macalester College 1968, Chicago Lighting Institute 1970, University of Oslo (Norway) 1970. Career: Minnesota State Bar Association, 1967; Ellerbe Architects, 1969; Northwestern University Art Department, 1969-71; Commercial Interior Architect, Daytons Contract Division, 1971 to present. Community Activities: Northwestern University (director of alumni admission, 1975 to present; vice-president of alumni club, 1976 to present); Minneapolis Jaycess (vice-president, 1976 to present); Pi Beta Phi (vice-president, 1970-71); Word Processing Association; Camp Fire Girls Inc.; Derham Hall Alumni; Walker Art Institute; Minneapolis Institute for Art; Hennepin Center for the Arts (board of directors, 1978 to present); Institute of Business Designers, 1979 to present. Religion: Catholic. Honors and Awards: Honours Class, Derham Hall, cum laude; National Honour Society; Northwestern University Dean's List; Minnesota Society of Architects Recipient of Special Honor Award for Rockford Road Library, 1973; Minnesota and Minneapolis Jaycee Build a Better You Award, 1976; Minnesota Jaycee Internal Vice-President Award, 1976; Minnesota Jaycee Division of the Quarter Award, 1978. Address: 2054 Louisiana Avenue South, St. Louis Park, Minnesota 55426.

Ebert, Trudy Mary

Civic Worker. Personal: Born February 15, 1925, St. Paul, Minnesota; Daughter of Edward M. and Gertrude C. O'Leary; Married Robert A. Ebert, February 8, 1947; Mother of Kathryn Ebert-Hilger, Richard Friess. Education: Attended the University of Minnesota 1948-49, St. Catherine's College 1967-68. Community Activities: Disaster Driver Unit, Ramsey County Chapter, American Red Cross, 1947-58; Parent-Teacher Association, Derham Hall, St. Thomas Military Academy, 1957-71; St. Croix Valley Council of Camp Fire Girls of America (national board of directors, president, 1956-82); Community Chest, St. Paul (chairperson, 1958); Ramsey County Bar Association Auxiliary (president, board of directors, 1961-82); Inter Club Council, St. Paul (board of directors, president, 1966-81); Lawyers Wives of Minnesota, St. Paul (treasurer, 1968-70); Women's Organization of Decathalon Athletic Club, Bloomington, Minnesota (president, 1969); National Lawyers Wives Auxiliary, American Bar Association (president, 1974); Minnesota Governor's Volunteer Task Force, 1975-79; Minnesota Historical Society Women's Organization (president, 1977-80; Children and Law (Minnesota organizer, 1968; national organizer, 1970); Republican Precinct, St. Paul (chairperson); Minnesota Historical Society; Ramsey County Historical Society; Good Old Girls of Minnesota; St. Paul Athletic Club (auxiliary president, 1970); St. Paul's Women's Club; St. Paul Pool and Yacht Club. Religion: Roman Catholic. Honors and Awards: Outstanding Community Service Award, National Camp Fire Girls, 1966; Volunteer Service Award, Minnesota Governor, 1979; Other Service Awards; Listed in *Who's Who of American Women*. Address: 1163 Edgcumbe Road, Saint Paul, Minnesota 55105.

Edelen, Mary Beaty

State Representative. Personal: Born December 9, 1944; Daughter of Mr. and Mrs. D. W. Beaty; Married Joseph R. Edelen, Jr.; Mother of Audra Angelica, Anthony Callghan, Jerrod Arthur. Education: Attended Cohey College, 1963-64; B.A., University of South Dakota, 1967; Attended Trinity University, 1967-68; M.A. 1971. Career: South Dakota House of Representatives, 1972-81, 1983-85; Lecturer, Department of History, University of South Dakota; Lecturer, Department of Social Sciences, Yankton College. Organizational Memberships: Organization of Women Legislators (legislative chairperson); South Dakota/National Women's Political Caucus (state chairperson). Community Activities: Southeastern Council of Governments (executive board, 1976 to present); Foster Care Task Force, Department of Social Services for the State of South Dakota; Clay County Republican Party (vice chairman, 1981-82); South Dakotans for Modern Courts (secretary, 1973 to present); University of South Dakota Medical Advisory Committee, 1973-80; American Association of University Women (past president); University of South Dakota Alumni Association (recorder). Religion: United Church of Christ. Honors and Awards; Grace Burgess Book Award, 1965. Address: 311 Canby Street, Vermillion, South Dakota 57069.

Edwards, Ray Conway

Executive. Personal: Born September 1, 1913; Son of Ernest Alfred and Augusta Edwards (both deceased); Married Marjorie Baisch; Father of David, Douglas, Ruth, Helen, Diane, Robert (deceased). Education: B.A., University of California-Los Angeles, 1935; Licensed Professional Engineer, New York, New Jersey, Virginia, Pennsylvania. Career: Engineer, Carrier Corp., Syracuse, New York, 1935-42; Physicist, General Laboratories, U.S. Rubber Company, Passaic, New Jersey, 1942-46; Accoustical Consultant, Founder, Chairman of the Board, Spi-Rol-Fin Corp., 1954-58; President, Edwards Engineering Corporation, Manufacturer of Air Conditioning and Refrigeration Equipment and Gas Treatment and Pollution Control Equipment for the Petroleum Industry. Organizational Memberships: American Society of Heating, Refrigeration and Air Conditioning Engineers; Theta Delta Chi. Community Activities: Smoke Rise Club, Kinnelon, New Jersey. Honors and Awards: Patentee in Field; Member of United States Masters Track and Field Club, Holds Track Meet Record for Age Group. Address: 396 Ski Trail, Smoke Rise, Kinnelon, New Jersey 07405.

Edwards, Robert A

Robert A Edwards

Landscape Designer. Personal: Born January 28, 1906, Beverly, Massachusetts. Education: Attended the Boston Museum of Fine Arts School, Child-Walker Art School, New England Conservatory of Music, Faelton Pianoforte School; Studied Architecture under Howard Walker and John P. Brown. Career: Director, Anna Coleman Ladd Sculpture Collection, 1941 to present; Executive Director, Wenham Museum, Massachusetts, 1952-61; Designer Arboretum of the John T. Berry Rehabilitation Center, North Reading, Massachusetts, 1970 to present. Organizational Memberships: Guild of Beverly Artists (founder, honorary life president); Salon of Allied Arts, Boston (past president, only living honorary member); Wenham Historical Association and Museum (life benefactor); Beverly Historical Society (life member); Essex Agricultural Society (life member); Peabody Museum, Salem (fellow). Published Works: *History of International Contemporary Personalities;* Currently Writing his Autobiography and Family History. Honors and Awards: Honorary Degree in Art, International Institute of Arts and Letters, Switzerland; Silver Medal Award, Massachusetts Horticultural Society, 1976; Maharishi Mahesh Yogi Award for Most Qualified Artist of the Area, 1978; Honorary Fellow, Anglo-American Academy, Cambridge, England, 1980; Honorary Nomination with Gold Medal, Accademia Italia delle Arti, Parma, Italy, 1981; Diploma of Merit, University of Arts, Parma, Italy, 1981; Listed in *Who's Who in the East, International Directory of Arts, Dictionary of International Biography, Who's Who in Art, International Who's Who of Intellectuals.* Address: "Paradise", 13 Foster Street, Beverly, Massachusetts 01915.

Edwards, Ward Dennis

Institute Director, Professor, Researcher. Personal: Born April 5, 1927; Son of Corwin D. Edwards (deceased); Mrs. Francis Edwards Ferriss; Married Silvia Edwards; Father of Page, Tara. Education: B.A., Swarthmore College, 1947; M.A. 1950, Ph.D. 1952, Harvard University. Military: Served in the United States Navy as Seaman First Class and Yeoman Third Class. Career: Director of Social Science Research Institute, Professor of Psychology and Industrial & Systems Engineering, University of Southern California; Research in Field of Behavioral Decision Theory and Analysis. Organizational Memberships: W.P.A.; A.P.A.; Psychonomic Society; O.R.S.A./S.I.G. Council. Honors and Awards: Franklin V. Taylor Award, American Psychological Association, 1978. Address: 11466 Laurelcrest Drive, Studio City, California 91604.

Egan, Eileen M

College President. Personal: Born January 11, 1925, Boston, Massachusetts; Daughter of Eugene O. and Mary B. Condon Egan (both deceased). Education: B.A., Spalding College, 1956; M.A., The Catholic University of America, 1963; Institute of International Education Fellow, Oxford University, England, 1963; Ph.D., The Catholic University of America, 1966; Academic Administration Internship Program, Smith College, 1967-68; J.D., University of Louisville School of Law, 1981. Career: Secondary School Teacher and Administrator, 1956-63; Teacher, English Department, The Catholic University of America, 1963-66; Chairman, English Department, Spalding College, 1966-67; Administrative Intern, Smith College, 1967-68; Vice President 1968-69, President 1969 to present, Spalding College. Organizational Memberships: American Council on Education; Association of American Colleges; Council for the Advancement of Small Colleges; Council of Independent Kentucky Colleges and Universities; Kentuckiana Metroversity; Kentucky Independent College Fund; Kentucky State Commission on Higher Education; National Catholic Education Association; Southern Association of Colleges and Schools; National Association of Independent Colleges and Universities; American Association for Higher Education; American Association of University Women; The English-Speaking Union, Kentucky

Branch. Community Activities: Archdiocese of Louisville; Better Business Bureau of Greater Louisville; Federal Reserve Bank of St. Louis, Louisville Branch; Louisville Area Chamber of Commerce; Louisville Center City Commission; Louisville Central Area, Inc.; Louisville Committee on Foreign Relations; Louisville and Jefferson County Human Relations Commission; Louisville and Southern Indiana Chapter, National Conference of Christians and Jews; Louisville Unit of the Recording for the Blind; Louisville's Open Spaces and Advisory Committee; Metro United Way; Old Kentucky Home Council of the Boy Scouts of America; International Center, University of Louisville; St. Joseph Infirmary; Cultural Action Plan for Louisville and Jefferson County; Jefferson County Board of Education. Religion: Member of the Sisters of Charity of Nazareth. Honors and Awards: Board of Trustees Scholar, The Catholic University of America, 1963-66; Equality Award, Louisville Urban League, 1978; Blanche B. Ottenheimer Award, Louisville Jewish Community Center, 1978; Brotherhood Award, National Conference of Christians and Jews, 1979: Phi Delta Kappa Award, 1979; Listed in *Biographical Directory of American Education, Personalities of America, Pesonalities of the South, The American Catholic Who's Who, The World Who's Who of Women, Who's Who in America, Who's Who in the U.S.A.* Address: 2511 River Bend Drive #15, Louisville, Kentucky 40206.

Egan, Lorraine AnnaMarie

Office Manager. Personal: Born June 20, 1938; Daughter of Anna Hummel; Married Richard T. Egan; Mother of Randolph E. Education: Graduate of Albany High School; B.A., History-Social Studies & German, New York State University-Albany, 1960. Career: Office Manager, Periodontal Office; Teacher, High School History and German; Teacher, Foreign Language in Elementary School Program; Substitute Teacher, Montgomery County Field Supervisor for Media Trends. Community Activities: Montgomery County Democratic Central Committee; District 14-A Democratic Club; Campaign Chairman, Joel Chasnoff 1978 Campaign for Maryland House of Delegates; District 14-A Coordinator, Lanny Davis 1976 Campaign for Congress; Communications Coordinator, Joel Chasnoff 1974 Campaign for Maryland House of Delegates; Chairperson, Precinct 5-8, Democratic Party, Montgomery County; Co-Founder, First President, District 14-A Democratic Club, Montgomery County; Springbrook Senior High Parent-Teacher Association; Albany Chapter #12 Order of the Eastern Star; Tamarack Triangle Civic Association. Religion: Methodist Women's Circle. Honors and Awards: Listed in *Who's Who Among American Women, Who's Who Among World's Women, Who's Who Southern Biographies.* Address: 17537 Roseland Boulevard, Lathrup Village, Michigan 48076.

Eggert, Robert John

Robert J Eggert

Economist. Personal: Born December 11, 1913, in Little Rock, Arkansas; Son of John and Eleanora Fritz Lapp; Married Elizabeth Bauer, November 28, 1935; Father of Robert John, Richard F., James E. Education: B.S., University of Illinois, 1935; M.S. 1936, Candidate in Philosophy 1938, University of Minnesota. Career: Research Analyst, Bureau of Agricultural Economics, United States Department of Agriculture, Urbana, Illinois, 1935; Principal Marketing Specialist, War Meat Board, U.S. Department of Agriculture, Chicago, Illinois, 1943; Research Analyst, University of Illinois 1935-36, University of Minnesota 1936-38; Assistant Professor of Economics, Kansas State College, 1938-41; Assistant Director of Marketing, American Meat Institute, Chicago, 1941-43; Economist, Association Director, American Meat Institute, 1943-50; Ford Division, Ford Motor Company, Dearborn, Michigan - Manager Department of Marketing Research 1951-53, Manager Program Planning 1953-54, Manager Business Research 1954-57, Manager Marketing Research Marketing Staff 1957-61, Manager Marketing Research Ford Division 1961-64, Manager International Marketing Research Marketing Staff 1964-65, Manager Overseas Marketing Research Planning 1965-66, Manager Marketing Research Lincoln-Mercury Division 1966-67; Director, Agri-business Programs, Michigan State University, 1967-68; Staff Vice-President of Economics and Marketing Research 1968-73, Staff Vice-President and Chief Economist 1974-76, R.C.A. Corp., New York City; President, Chief Economist, Eggert Economics Enterprises, Inc., Sedona, Arizona, 1976 to present; Lecturer, Marketing, University of Chicago, 1947-49; Adjunct Professor, Business Forecasting, Northern Arizona University, 1976 to present; Economic Advisory Board, United States Department of Commerce, 1969-71; Census Advisory Committee, United States Department of Commerce, 1975-78; Panel Economic Advisors, Congressional Budget Office, 1975-76; Arizona Economic Estimates Commission, 1978 to present. Organizational Memberships: Council of International Marketing Research and Planning Directors (chairman, 1965-66); American Marketing Association (director, vice-president, 1949-50; president, Chicago chapter, 1947-48; vice-president, marketing mangement division, 1972-73; national president, 1974-75); American Statistical Association (chairman, business and economic statistics section, 1957 to present; president, Chicago chapter, 1948-49); Federal Statistics Users Conference (chairman, trustees, 1960-61); Conference Business Economists (chairman, 1973-74); National Association of Business Economists (council member, 1969-72); Arizona Economic Roundtable; American Farm Economics Association; American Economics Association; American Quarter Horse Association (director, 1966-73); Alpha Zeta. Community Activities: Republican; Poco Diablo Country Club. Religion: Congregationalist. Published Works: Contributor of Articles to Professional Publications; Editor of Monthly *Blue Chip Economic Indicators* and *Blue Chip Financial Forecasts.* Honors and Awards: Economic Forecast Award, Chicago Chapter, American Statistical Association, 1950, 1960, 1968; Seer of the Year Award, Harvard Business School of Industrial Economics, 1973; Listed in *Who's Who in the World.* Address: Schnebly Hill Road, P.O. Box 1569, Sedona, Arizona 86336.

Eidson, John Olin

Retired. Personal: Born December 10, 1908; Son of Olin Marvin and Margaret Rushton Eidson (both deceased); Married Perrin Cudd. Education: A.B., Wofford College, 1929; M.A., Vanderbilt University, 1930; Ph.D., Duke University, 1941. Military: Served in the United States Army Infantry, 1942-46, attaining the rank of Major; Serving as Lieutenant Colonel in the United States Army Reserves, 1973 to present. Career: Retired Professor and College Administrator; Fulbright Professor, University of Freiburg, Germany, 1945; Visiting Professor, University of Bonn, Germany, 1977-78; Vice Chancellor, University System of Georgia, 1971-76; President, Georgia Southern College, 1968-71; Dean's College of Arts and Sciences, University of Georgia, 1957-68; Editor, *Georgia Review*, 1950-57. Organizational Memberships: Southeastern American Studies Association (president, 1966-68); Conference of Academic Deans of Southern States (secretary-treasurer, 1965-66; vice-president, 1966-67; president, 1967-68); National Association of State Universities and Land Grant Colleges (senate, 1963-66); South Atlantic District Phi Beta Kappa (chairman, 1958-61); National Council of Colleges of Arts and Sciences (board of directors); Delta Phi Alpha Honorary German Fraternity (national secretary); Coastal Georgia-Carolina Association of Phi Beta Kappa (president, 1970-71); English Association of London; The Tennyson Society; S.A.M.L.A. (chairman, American literature section); Modern Language Association (chairman, southern literature section, 1964-65). Community Activities: Boy Scouts of America (vice-president, coastal empire council, 1970-71; executive board, Atlantic area council, 1971 to present); Institute of International Education (southeastern regional advisory board, 1976 to present); Friends of the University of Georgia Botanical Garden (president, 1981 to present); Rotary Club, 1968 to present. Religion: Methodist. Honors and Awards: M. G. Michael Award for Research, 1950; Honorary Degree, Litt.D., Wofford College, 1954; WSB Radio Award for Outstanding Name in News, 1968; W. S. Beaver Award for Outstanding Achievement, 1968; John Olin Eidson Day, Athens, Georiga, April 19, 1968; Honorary Citizen, Statesboro, Georgia, Presented Key to the City, 1971; Award of

Appreciation, Georgia Southern College and Georgia College Foundation, 1979. Address: 362 Valley Green Drive, N.E., Atlanta, Georgia 30342.

Eie, Leif D

Area Manager. Personal: Born July 12, 1929; Son of Lars (deceased) and Aagot Eie; Married Patricia Eie; Father of Lisa Britt, Christian. Education: Diploma, Ringards College, 1947; Diploma, Flekkefjord Business and Trade School, 1949. Military: Served in the Norwegian Air Force, 1949; Served with the United States Army, 1953-55. Career: Actor/Singer, Jens Book-Jenssen Revy, Oslo, Norway, 1950-52; Area Manager, North American Division, Scandinavian Airlines, 1952-; Recorded 2 LP's on Standard and Colonial Records. Organizational Memberships: The Travel Committee (founder, 1960); Norwegian Chamber of Commerce (founder, 1968; vice president); Washington State Trade Fair (director, 1977-79; trustee, world affairs council, 1973-76); Seattle Visitor Bureau (director, 1970-81). Community Activities: Nordic Festival (chairman, 1965); Seattle Begen, Norway Sister City (founder and chairman, 1976); Seattle Tashkent Sister City (founder, 1974); Ski for Light, Cross County Skiing for Blind Persons (founder and director, 1975); Nordic Council, Seattle (founder and director, 1975); Nordic Heritage Museum, Seattle (founder and trustee, 1979); Pacific Lutheran University (board of regents, 1980-83). Religion: Lutheran. Honors and Awards: American Spirit Honor Medal, Presented Jointly by the Army, Navy and Air Force, 1953; International Readers Digest Award for Best Sister City Program, 1969; Man of the Year, Norwegian Chamber of Commerce, 1969; Washington State Senate Resolution "contributed greatly to the cultural and economic growth of the state", 1972; St. Olav Medal, Norway, 1973; Order of the Northern Star, Sweden, 1977. Address: 17428 - 93rd Ave. N.E., Bothell, Washington 98011.

Leif D Eie

Eigel, Thomas John

Manager. Personal: Born August 30, 1934; Married to Gail Keenan; Father of Thomas J. Jr., Kathleen R., Victoria A., Andrea S., Christina M. Education: B.S., St. Louis University, 1956; M.S., San Diego State University, 1972. Military: Served with United States Air Force with rank of 2nd Lieutenant to Lieutenant Colonel, 1956-79; Command Pilot. Career: Manager of Program Services, Rolling Meadows, Illinois; Former Manager of Configuration and Data Management, Northrop Defense Systems Division; Former Deputy Director, Directorate of Configuration Management A-10 System Program Office, U.S.A.F. Organizational Memberships: A.D.P.A.; A.F.A.; Association of Old Crows; S.O.L.E. Community Activities: Republican Senatorial Club, 1979-81; Republican National Committee sustaining member, 1980; Illinois Republicans, 1981; Chuck Percy Senate Club, 1981. Religion: Member of Roman Catholic Church (Knights of Colombus). Honors and Awards: Beta Gamma Sigma, 1971; Sigma Iota Epsilon, 1971; Meritorius Service Medal, U.S.A.F., 1979; Distinguished Flying Cross, U.S.A.F., 1968; Air Medal (21 awards), U.S.A.F., 1968. Address: 772 Harvard Court, Palatine, Illinois, 60067.

Eisenhart, Charles Robert

Town Councilman. Personal: Born March 12, 1919; Son of Mr. and Mrs. John A. Eisenhart (both deceased); Married Judith A. Russell; Father of Charles R. Jr., Judith A. Smullen, John B. Education: Ph.B., Muhlenberg College, 1933; M.A., State University of New York at Albany, 1940; Ed.D., Columbia University, 1954. Military: Served in the United States Air Force, retiring with the rank of Colonel. Career: Former Teacher, Administrator, College President; Founding President, Adirondack Community College, 1961 (now President Emeritus); Dean of Men, Hartwick College; Dean, Jacksonville (Florida) University; Dean, Defiance College. Organizational Memberships: Phi Sigma Iota; Kappa Phi Kappa; Phi Delta Kappa; R.O.A.; T.R.O.A.; American Meteorological Society; American Legion. Community Activities: Oneonta (New York) Commission on Public Schools (chairman); Boy Scouts of America (district commissioner); Tri-County United Way (president, 1981); Mohican Council, Boy Scouts of America (executive board); Adirondack Chapter, R.O.A. (past president); Americans Concerned with Peace and Stablility in Asia-Pacific (national chairman ad hoc committee); White House Conference on Aging (Ohio delegate, 1961); Hyde Collection (board member); New York State Balance of State Advisory Council (chairman, program committee). Religion: Ordained Elder, Presbyterian Church. Honors and Awards: Doctor of Humanities, Defiance College, 1961; Special Citation, United States Air Force Reserve, 1961; "Dr. Charles R. Eisenhart Day", Warren County, Washington County, 1978. Address: 238 Bay Street, Glens Falls, New York 12801.

Eisenstein, Alfred

Composer. Personal: Born November 14, 1899; Son of Marcus and Louise Eisenstein (both deceased); Married Mercedes Malespin Felix. Education: Attended the Technical University, Vienna, Austria, and Berlin, Germany; Civil Engineering Degree, Technical University, Vienna; Diploma in Civil Engineering, Berlin; Private Piano Studies, Vienna. Career: Composing Classical and Semi-Classical Music and Producing Benefit Concerts of His Music; Former Engineer, Building Construction and General Contracting, President, Alfred Eisenstein, Inc., Consulting Engineers and Builders; Manager, Music Publishing Company. Organizational Memberships: American Society Composers, Authors and Publishers; Professional Engineers, Civil Engineers and Military Engineers (past member). Community Activities: All-Eisenstein Symphonic Concerts with Ballet for the Benefit of Variety Children's Hospital, 1974; Benefit for Archbishop Curley High School, 1980; Public Service Contributions through Appearances on Radio and Television with Pesonal Performances in Piano Recitals and Interviews on Most of Local Television Stations. Honors and Awards: Special Standard Award, American Society of Composers, Authors and Publishers; Special Plaque, New York Audio Society, 1967; Bronze Plaque, Chamber of Commerce, Queens, New York, 1968; Listed in *Who's Who in the South and Southwest, Men of Achievement, Dictionary of International Biography, Personalities of the South, Book of Honor.* Address: 18900 N.E. 14th Avenue, North Miami Beach, Florida 33179.

Alfred Eisenstein

Elian, Arthur Joseph

Associate Professor. Personal: Born March 21, 1924; Married Katherine Mary Rogers; Father of Elizabeth Ann, Mary, Diane, John, Nancy. Education: Attended University of Maine, Orono, 1950; B.S.F., Ohio State University, 1953-54; Further study at the Institute of Geodesy, Photogrammetry and Cartography; Military Studies, Engineers Officers Advanced Course, Ft. Belvoir, Virginia, 1957; M.A., 1961, Ph.D. Candidate, 1967-68, Rutgers. Military: Served in the Infantry, 1943-46; Advanced from rank of 2nd Lieutenant to Lieutenant Colonel, 1950-67. Career: Forest Service, United States Department of Agriculture, 1949; Officer, Corps of Engineers, United States Army, 1950-67; Associate Professor of Modern Languages. Organizational Memberships: Retired Officers Association (founding member, Chapala, Mexico chapter); Society of Photogrammetry; Society of American Foresters; American Translators Association; National Education Association; New Jersey Educators Association; Interamerican Geodetic Survey, La Paz, Bolivia (officer-in-charge, 1963-65); U.S. Embassy, U.S. Aid Program, La Paz (mapping advisor, 1963-65); American Cooperative School,

La Paz (chairperson, board of education, 1964-65); Study Group for Future Mapping Systems, Office of the Chief of Engineers, U.S. Army, Washington D.C. (committee chairperson, 1966-67); Montclair State College (educational planning committee, 1968); County College of Morris, New Jersey (committee chairperson on bilingual education). Religion: Catholic. Honors and Awards: Combat Infantry Badge, 1943; Bronze Star Medal, 1953; Unit Citation, Tokyo, Japan, 1957; Army Commendation Medal, 1965; Condor de Los Andes Medal, Bolivian Government, 1965; Army Commendation Ribbon with Oak Leaf Cluster, Office Chief of Engineers, U.S. Army, 1967; Listed in *Who's Who in the East, Who's Who in International Education*. Address: P.O. Box 452, Canadensis, Pennsylvania 18325.

Eliot, Alexander

Author. Personal: Born April 28, 1919; Married Jane Winslow; Father of May Rose, Jefferson, Winslow. Education: Attended Loomis Institute, Black Mountain College, Boston Museum School. Career: Author; Art Editor, *Time* Magazine, 1945-60. Organizational Memberships: Century Association; Dutch Treat Club; Society of American Travel Writers; Authors Guild; P.E.N.; Bay State Circle; Northampton Historical Commission; Northampton Arts Council. Published Works: Author of *Proud Youth; 300 Years of American Painting; Sight and Insight; Greece; Concise History of Greece; Socrates, the Person and the Portent; Love Play; Creatures of Arcadia; Myths; Zen Edge*. Honors and Awards: Guggenheim Fellow, 1960; Japan Foundation Senior Fellow, 1974. Address: 12 Hampton Terrace, Northampton, Massachusetts 01060.

Alexander Eliot

Ellerbee, Estelle

Evangelist, Healer, Psychic. Personal: Born September 16, 1924; Married Ellis Ellerbee; Mother of Clarence, Cathy, Ellis Jr., Carol, Annie (adopted). Education: Graduate of Bennetsville High School, 1939; Completed Standard Red Cross Course and Nursing Course, 1961-62. Career: Practical Nurse; Gospel Singer; Evangelist and Healer, conducts world-wide services; Pastor, Miracle Chapel Deliverance Church, Inc.; Psychic. Community Activities: Volunteer Nurse, once a week, 1962. Religion: Founder, President, Pastor, Miracle Chapel Deliverance Church, New York City, 1964 to present. Honors and Awards: In her words, her Greatest Honor is that "God has anointed [her] from [her] mothers womb with a Holy Gift of Laying Hands on the sick. Foretelling the future and preaching the Gospel. [Her] spirit can move out of [her] body. [She has] been told that [she has] appeared in many homes through the Spirit. Many people have been Healed and set free, as God has led [her] to stretch forth [her] hands, also through [her] eyes many have been Saved and Baptized with the Holy Spirit. God has also anointed [her] son to preach the Gospel, and with the Laying on of hands, through [her] prayers."; Citation of Outstanding Achievement in Fields of Endeavor; Listed in *Who's Who in the East*; Nominated for *Personalities of America*. Address: 147-11 Sutter Ave., Queens, New York, 11436.

Ellis, Susan Gottenberg

Psychologist. Personal: Born January 24, 1949; Daughter of Sam and Sally Gottenberg; Married David Roy Ellis; Mother of Sharon Rachel, Dana Michelle. Education: B.S., Cornell University, 1970; M.A., Columbia University, 1971; M.A. 1975, Ph.D. 1976, Hofstra University. Career: Psychologist in Private Practice; Former School Psychologist, Clinical Psychologist, Health Education Instructor. Organizational Memberships: American Psychological Association; Florida Psychological Association; Pinellas Psychological Association (treasurer, 1978; political action chairman, 1979); Mental Health Association of Pinellas County. Community Activities: Cornell Suncoast Club (vice president, 1979-80); Hadassah; B'nai B'rith; O.R.T. Honors and Awards: Teachers College Tuition Scholarship, Columbia University, 1970-71; Kappa Delta Pi, Columbia University, Spring 1971; New York State Regents Scholarship; Home Economics Alumnae Martha Van Rensselaer Scholarship, 1968-69; Nassa County Homemakers Council Scholarship, 1969-70; Dean's List, Four Semesters. Address: 1904 Oakdale Lane North, Clearwater, Florida 33516.

Elmaghraby, Salah E

Professor, Program Director. Personal: Born October 21, 1927; Son of Leila O. Elmaghraby; Married Amina Ishac; Father of Leila, Wedad, Karima. Education: B.S.M.E., Cairo University, 1948; M.Sc., Industrial Engineering, Ohio State University, 1955; Ph.D., Industrial Engineering, Cornell University, 1958. Career: Professor and Director of Operations Research Program, North Carolina State University; Associate Professor, Yale University, New Haven, Connecticut, 1962-67; Visiting Associate Professor, Industrial Engineering, Cornell University, Spring 1967; Research Leader, Western Electric Company, Princeton, New Jersey, 1958-62; Engineer, Foreign Inspection Office of the Egyptian State Railways in London, Brussels and Budapest, 1948-54. Organizational Memberships: American Institute of Industrial Engineers; American Association of University Professors; Operations Research Society of America; The Institute of Management Science. Honors and Awards: Distinguished Research Award, American Institute of Industrial Engineers, 1970; Operations Research Division of A.I.I.E. Award, 1980. Address: 124 Perquimans Drive, Raleigh, North Carolina 27603.

Estelle Ellerbee

Emmons, Tetta Wanda

Retired Laboratory Technician. Personal: Born August 11, 1914; Daughter of William and Sarah Ada West (both deceased); Widow of Leroy G. Education: Attended University of Texas, 1934-35. Career: Laboratory Technician for Neches Butane Products Company 19 years; Freelance Photographer; International Salon Exhibitor with 3 stars in pictorial color slides and 3 in nature; Has prepared and presented slide programs for local camera club and for schools and various civic groups; Has given instructional programs on photography to local camera club and civic clubs; Judge for P.S.A. international photographic exhibitions in pictorial color slides and nature slides. Organizational Memberships: National Association of Retired Federal Employees (secretary for chapter 864, 1981-82); Photographic Society of America (various positions including area representative, 1975 to present, central zone distributor of instructional slide sets for individuals, 1976); Port Arthur Camera Club (member 1956 to present, color slide division chairman 2 years, president, 1961 and 1973); CavOILcade International Photographic Salon (chairman of color slide division, 1960, 1965 and 1981, director, 1970, co-director, 1972); Gulf Coast Camera Club Council (financial chairman, 1965, color slide consulting serice, 1965, director, 1966, secretary-treasurer, 1971-72, 1st vice president, 1973-74, president 1974-75). Community Activities: Has presented numerous slide shows to civic groups; Former member of Parent-Teacher Association; Past member of Garden Club; Charter member of Sabine's Explorers Club; Charter member of First Ladies of Port Arthur; Charter member of Women's Club of Allied Merchants Bank; National Trust for Historic Preservation, 1980. Religion: Member of Church of Christ. Honors and Awards: Won photography contest sponsored by Port Arthur Chamber of Commerce; Received several honorable mentions in International exhibitions; Received a Silver Medal, New York Salon and CavOILcade Gold Medal; Chicago Nature Photograhic Salon requested permission to use one of her slides for its Nature Travel Slide Set, 1972; Has 2 slides in Sierra Club's 1981 Golden Triangle Nature Calendar; Wilmington International Exhibition of Photography requested permission to use one of her H.M. slides in an instructional slide set for camera clubs and P.S.A., 1981; Associate of the Photographic Society of America, 1981; Listed in *World Who's Who of Women, Community Leaders and Noteworthy Americans, Personalities of the South.* Address: 3629 Drexel Avenue, Port Arthur, Texas 77640.

Engelhardt, Sister M Veronice

Reading Clinic Director. Personal: Born March 29, 1912; Daughter of Herman and Ella Engelhardt (both deceased). Education: B.S.Ed. 1937, M.A. 1938, Ph.D. 1962, The Catholic University of America; Post-Doctoral Studies at Temple University, University of Pittsburgh, Notre Dame University. Career: Director, Reading Clinic, Franciscan Academy, Syracuse, New York; Formerly, Elementary and Secondary Teacher, Diocesan and Community School Supervisor; Instructor in Education and Psychology, St. Francis Normal School, Syracuse; Dean of Women and Head, Department of Education and Psychology, Chaminade College, Honolulu; Clinical Instructor, Child Center; Catholic University; Supervisor of Student Teaching, Catholic University; Head, Department of Education and Psychology, Maria Regina College, Syracuse; Founder and Director, Reading and Speech Clinics, Maria Regina. Organizational Memberships: American Psychological Association; American Educational Research Association; International Reading Association; International Platform Association; International Biographical Association (fellow); National League of American Pen Women (recording secretary, 1980-81; first vice-president, 1981-83); Consultant-Evaluator for Catholic University for Affiliations of Catholic Colleges in the United States; Educational Developmental Laboratories of Huntington, New York (reading consultant). Community Activities: Lecturer at Many Teacher's Institutes in Eleven States; Religious Community (assistant Mother General, 1965-71; chairman of personnel board, 1972-75; chairman of communications board, 1971 to present; editor of community newsletter, 1972 to present). Religion: Catholic Nun. Honors and Awards: Listed in *Dictionary of International Biography, Community Leaders of America, Notable Americans.* Address: 1024 Court Street, Syracuse, New York 13208.

Wanda Emmons

Elrod, Linda Diane Henry

Law Professor. Personal: Born March 6, 1947; Daughter of Lyndas and Jane Allen Henry; Married Mark Douglas Elrod; Mother of Carson Douglas, Bree Elizabeth. Education: B.A., Departmental Honors English, Washburn University, 1969; J.D. cum laude, Washburn University of Topeka School of Law. Career: Professor of Law, Washburn University School of Law; Research Assistant, Kansas Judicial Council; Secondary School Teacher. Organizational Memberships: American Bar Association (member, 1972 to present); Kansas Bar Association (coordinator of several continuing legal education programs); Topeka Bar Association (chairman, title standards committee, 1977-78; chairman, program committee, 1978-79; secretary, 1979 to present). Community Activities: Kansas Public Disclosure Commission (elected vice-chairman, 1981); Kansas Governmental Ethics Commission, 1978-81; Young Women's Christian Association (board of directors, 1978 to present; president, 1982-83; chairman, adult committee, 1978-79; chairman, health, physical education, recreation, 1979-81; executive board, 1981 to present); Kappa Alpha Theta (advisory board, 1981-82); University Child Development (board of directors, 1976-78); Colonial Park Townhouse (board of directors, 1972-74); Topeka Friends of the Zoo, 1974 to present; Shawnee County Historical Society, 1974 to present. Religion: Westminster Presbyterian Church; Speaker on "Law and the Family", April 1981. Honors and Awards: William O. Douglas Outstanding Professor Award, 1978-79. Address: 231 Edgewood, Topeka, Kansas 66606.

Englert, Robert Dixon

Vice President and General Manager. Personal: Born February 11, 1920; Son of Robert Lincoln (deceased) and Blanche Englert; Married Patricia Duff; Father of Janice, Jolene, Nancy. Education: B.S. Chemistry, University of Portland, 1942; B.S. Chemical Engineering, Oregon State University, 1944; M.S. Chemistry, Oregon State University, 1944; Ph.D. Chemistry, University of Colorado, 1949. Military: Served in the United States Naval Reserve, 1944-46. Career: Vice President and General Manager, Advanced Technology Center, Dresser Industries, Inc.; Vice President and General Manager, Environmental Technology Division, Dresser Industries, 1970-76; Executive Director, Southern California Laboratories, 1968-70; Director of Sciences, Southern California Laboratories, 1955-68; Organic Chemist to Senior Organic Chemist, Stanford Research Institute, 1949-55. Organizational Memberships: American Chemical Society; American Association for the Advancement of Science; Sigma Xi; Research Society of America; American Oil Chemists Society; California Academy of Sciences; Phi Lambda Upsilon; Los Angeles County Air Pollution; American Institute of Chemists; Balboa Bay Club; New York Academy of Sciences; Air Pollution Control Association. Religion: Protestant. Honors and Awards: Fellowship, Chemical Foundation, University of Colorado and United States Public Health Service; University of Colorado Graduate Scholarship, Graduate Assistantship, Oregon State College. Address: 1312 Sandcastle Drive, Corona del Mar, California 92625.

Jean H Erwin

Erskine, Kathryn A

Public Accountant. Personal: Born September 19, 1934; Daughter of Griff and Oneita Adkins; Married William Jack Erskine; Mother of Michael. Education: Graduate of Hamlin High School, Hamlin, West Virginia, 1951; Studies in Secretarial Science, Marshall University, 1953-54; A.A. 1977, B.A. 1979, West Virginia State College; C.P.A. Review Course, Parkersburg Community College; Graduate of Dale Carnegie Associates, 1980. Career: Deputy Clerk, Lincoln County Court House, Hamlin, West Virginia, 1953; Vacation-Relief Clerk, Main Distribution Department, Columbia Gas, Charleston, West Virginia, 1954; Bookkeeper, United Insurance Company of America, Scottsman of West Virginia, West Virginia Department of Welfare, 1956-58; Receptionist, Secretary Service and Parts Department, Ray C. Call Inc., South Charleston, West Virginia, 1958; Ogden Insurance and Realty Company, 1959-60; Secretary, Bookkeeper, Office Manager, Davis Agency, Hurricane, West Virginia, 1961-71; President, Owner, Public Accountant, Davis-Erskine, Inc., 1973 to present. Organizational Memberships: National Association of Tax Consultors; National Association of Accountants; National Federation of Independent Businesses; National Female Executives; West Virginia Association of Executives; Entrepreneurs Association. Community Activities: West Virginia Coalition for Small Businesses; Hurricane Business Women (network director); Putnam County Chamber of Commerce; Y.M.C.A.-St. Albans; West Virginia State College Alumni; Commodore Ship of State; West Virginia All-Stars; Community Education Teacher. Religion: Pine Grove Church of Christ. Honors and Awards: Listed in *Who's Who of American Women.* Address: 1072 Springdale Road, Hurricane, West Virginia 25526.

Erwin, Jean Hocking

Professor. Personal: Born December 15, 1920; Daughter of William Jo and Margaret Pearl Hocking (deceased); Widow. Education:

B.A., University of Toronto, 1942; Specialist Teaching Certificate, Ontario College of Education, 1943; M.S., Iowa State University, 1960; Ph.D., Iowa State University, 1969. Career: Professor, Child Development Family Relations, University of Tennessee-Martin; Associate Professor, Washington State University, 1969-71; Instructor, Iowa State University, Summer 1959; Instructor, College of Education, Toronto, Summer 1948; Head, Home Economics Department, Winston Churchill Collegiate, Scarborough, Ontario, 1954-66; Head, Home Economics Department, London South Collegiate, Ontario, 1952-54; Glebe Collegiate, Ottawa, 1943-52. Organizational Memberships: American Association of University Professors (executive member, University of Tennessee-Martin branch); Canadian Home Economics Association (life member); Century Club, University of Tennessee-Martin; Consumers Association of Canada; Iowa State Alumni Association (life member); International Federation for Home Economics; National Association for Education of Young Children; National Council on Family Relations; Society for Research in Child Development; Southern Association on Children Under Six; Southeastern Council on Family Relations; Tennessee Association for Education of Young Children; Tennessee Home Economics Association (life member); West Tennessee Education Association; University of Tennessee-Martin: Academic Senate, Agenda Committee, Nominating Committee (chairman), Financial Aids Policy Committee, Graduate Council, Graduate Affairs Committee, Promotion and Tenure Committee, Scholarship Awards Committee (chairman), Protection Form Human Rights Committee (chairman for home economics). Community Activities: Northwest Association for Young Children (secretary, steering committee); Easter Seal Society for Northwest Tennessee (advisory committee, secretary and past president); Easter Seal Center, Martin, Tennessee (human rights committee). Religion: First United Methodist Church: Board of Trustees, United Methodist Women (past president). Honors and Awards: Life Fellow, International Biographical Association; Life Fellow, American Biographical Institute; Omicron Nu, Life Fellow; Phi Kappa Phi; General Foods Awards; Iowa State University Grant, 1968-69; Faculty Research Grant, University of Tennessee at Martin, 1980; Listed in *Who's Who Biographical Record - Child Development Professionals, Who's Who in the South and Southwest; International Who's Who in Community Service, World Who's Who of Women in Education, Personalities of America, Notable Americans, Dictionary of International Biography, Men and Women of Distinction, Book of Honor, International Who's Who in Education, Ernest Kay's Personal Hall of Fame, The American Registry Series, Who's Who in America, Directory of Distinguished Americans, Personalities of the South, World Who's Who of Women, International Register of Profiles.* Address: 162 Glenwood Drive, Glenwood Estates, Martin, Tennessee 38237.

Espinoza-Gala, Lillian R

Technical Writer. Personal: Born December 5, 1948; Daughter of Charles and Marjorie Miller; Married Carlos Espinoza-Gala. Education: Associate Degree in Petroleum Technology, Nichols State University, 1977. Career: Self-Employed Technical Writer; Former Positions include Gauger, Offshore Production Supervisor, Ocean Drilling and Exploration Company; Project Coordinator, Spyder Sales and Service, Buyer, Alboa Company. Organizational Memberships: Leader of Offshore Training Committee, OPCO, 1980; Terrebonne Writers Guild. Community Activities: Friends of the Library, Lafourche Parish (publicity committee); Society of Mayflower Descendants, State of Iowa; Daughters of the American Revolution, Lafourche Chapter; Prison Fellowship (inmate counsellor and work-release counsellor); United Way Campaign; SPEC International, Inc. (director); Americans Against Unions (charter member); National Anti-Drug Coalition; Captain Daniel Little Fly Inc. Religion: First Baptist Church, Houma; Outreach Leader for Sunday School Class; Chairman of Publicity Committee, Together We Build Program. Honors and Awards: Went Offshore with One of First Groups of Women to be Employed in Galley Offshore, 1973; First Female Roustabout to Work in that Capacity Offshore for Any Company in the World. Address: P.O. Box 956, Gray, Louisiana 70359.

Mary E Ester

Esquivel, Clara Beth

Executive. Personal: Daughter of James C. Lay, Stella Ihle. Career: President/Owner, Galen College of Medical/Dental Assistants. Community Activities: Chamber of Commerce. Address: 13591 East Shaw, Sanger, California 93657.

Essenwanger, Oskar M

Supervisory Research Physicist and Adjunct Professor. Personal: Born August 25, 1920; Married Katharina D. Essenwanger. Education: Dr.rer.nat. (Ph.D. equivalency), University of Wuerzburg, West Germany, 1950. Military: Served in the German Air Force, 1939-45. Career: Supervisory Research Physicist and Adjunct Professor of Environmental Science; Research Meteorologist, 1945-57; Principal Investigator, 1957-60. Organizational Memberships: Sigma Xi (president, University of Alabama-Huntsville Club, 1977 to present); American Institute of Aeronautics and Astronautics (associate fellow); American Society of Quality Control (senior member); International Biographical Association (fellow). Community Activities: German Weather Service, 1946-57; United States Government, 1957 to present; University of Alabama-Huntsville, 1961 to present. Religion: Roman Catholic. Honors and Awards: Missile Command Scientific Achievement Award, 1965; Certified Quality Engineer, 1966; Certified Consulting Meteorologist, 1967; Fellow, Intercontinental Biographical Association, 1970; Outstanding Research, Sigma Xi-University of Alabama, Huntsville Club, 1977; Herman Oberth Award, Alabama Section, A.I.A.A., 1981; Life Fellow, American Biographical Association, 1979. Address: 610 Mountain Gap Drive, Huntsville, Alabama 35803.

Ester, Mary Ellen

Cosmetologist, Esthetician, Writer. Personal: Born April 26, 1926; Daughter of John Cleveland and Flora Effie Ellen Snider Leasure, (both deceased); Married Henry Ester on August 25, 1946; Mother of Barbara Rosanne Ester Christensen. Education: Licensed, Cleveland Academy of Cosmetology, 1945; Graduate of the Realtor's Institute, University of Michigan, 1975; Certificate, Newspaper Institute of America, 1980. Career: Owner-Manager, Fair Lady Beauty Salon, Fairview Park, Ohio, 1960-70; Teacher of Cosmetology, American Beauty School, 1969-70; Real Estate Salesperson, Martin-Ketchem & Martin Inc., Realtors, Livonia, Michigan, 1972-76; Esthetician, Adrien Arpel Skin Care and Cosmetics, Halles-Westgate Beauty Salon, Fairview Park, Ohio, 1977 to present; Teacher, Adult Education, Lakewood High School, Lakewood, Ohio, 1979 to present, and Rocky River High School, Rocky River, Ohio, 1980 to present; Skin Care Consultant, Halles and *Seventeen* magazine, 1981 to present. Organizational Memberships: National Hairdressers and Cosmetologists Association; Business and Professional Women's Club; Women's Council of Realtors (secretary). Honors and Awards: Listed in *Who's Who of American Women, The World Who's Who of Women, Personalities of America, Personalities of the West and Midwest, Distinguished Americans.* Address: 18849 Timber Lane, Fairview Park, Ohio 44126.

Eu, March K Fong

Secretary of State of California. Personal: Born March 29; Daughter of Yuen and Shiu Kong; Married Henry Eu; Mother of Matthew Kipling Fong, Marchesa Suyin You. Education: B.S., University of California-Berkeley; M.Ed., Mills College, 1951; Ed.D., Stanford

University, 1956; Post-Graduate Study, Columbia University, California State University-Hayward. Military: Served during World War II as a Dental Hygienist, Presidio, San Francisco. Career: Secretary of State of California; Former Dental Hygienist; Chairman of Dental Hygiene Division, University of California Medical Center; Dental Hygienist, Oakland Public Schools; Supervisor of Dental Health Education, Alameda County Schools; Lecturer in Health Education, Mills College; Member of California Assembly, 1966-74. Organizational Memberships: American Dental Hygienist Association (life member); Business and Professional Women's Club; American Association of University Women; California Teacher's Association; Delta Kappa Gamma; Northern California Dental Hygienist Association (life member). Community Activities: Parent-Teachers Association (life member); Oakland League of Women Voters; Alameda County School Board Association; Alameda County Board of Education (member, 1956-66; president, 1961-62; legislative advocate, 1963); Assembly Committees (chairman, committee on employment and public employees, 1973-74; chairman, select committee on agriculture, foods and nutrition, 1973-74); Chinese Young Ladies Society; National Commission on Observance of International Women's Year, 1977; University of Southern California School of Dentistry (board of councillors, 1976); Number of Positions in Democratic State and County Central Committees. Religion: Unitarian. Honors and Awards: Outstanding Woman Award, Number of Awards for Public Service and Professional Achievement, National Women's Political Caucus, 1980. Address: 1230 J Street, Sacramento, California 95814.

Euler, Arthur Ray

Research Physician, Administrator. Personal: Born October 20, 1942; Son of Mr. and Mrs. John S. Biestek; Married Dana Mary; Father of Elizabeth Suzanne, Katherine Anne. Education: B.S., Microbiology, Purdue University, 1965; Attended Indiana University School of Medicine, 1965-69; Intern in Pediatrics, Riley Hospital, Indiana University Medical Center, 1969-70; Resident in Pediatrics, Riley Hospital, Indiana University Medical Center, 1970; Resident in Pediatrics, Harbor General Hospital, Torrance, California, 1973-74; Cystic Fibrosis Foundation Fellow in Pediatric Gastroenterology, University of California at Los Angeles Center for Health Sciences, 1974-76. Military: Served in the United States Navy, 1970-73; attaining the rank of Lieutenant Commander. Career: Research Physician, Head of Gastrointestinal Sub-program, Medical Development, The Upjohn Company; Assistant Professor of Pediatrics, University of Arkansas for Medical Sciences, 1977-81; Acting Assistant Professor of Pediatrics, University of California-Los Angeles Center for the Health Sciences, 1976-77. Organizational Memberships: North American Society of Pediatric Gastroenterology; Southern California Society of Gastrointestinal Endoscopy; Western Gastroenterological Association; Southern California Society of Gastroenterology; American Society for Parenteral and Enteral Nutrition; Central Arkansas Pediatric Society; Midest G.U.T. Club; Southern Society for Pediatric Research; American Academy of Pediatrics; American Federation for Clinical Research; American Gastroenterological Association; American Association for the Advancement of Science; New York Academy of Sciences; American College of Gastroenterology; Society for Pediatric Research; American Motility Society. Honors and Awards: Citation of Meritorious Service from Commanding General, United States Marine Corps, El Toro Marine Corps Station, Santa Ana, California, 1973; Southern California Society for Gastrointestinal Endoscopy Olympus Prize Essay, 1978; Listed in *Outstanding Young Men of America, Who's Who in the South and Southwest, Personalities of the South, Personalities of America, Book of Honor, Men of Achievement.* Address: 2101 Bronson, Kalamazoo, Michigan 49001.

Alta M Evans

Evans, Alta Marie

Freelance Writer, Artist, Homemaker. Personal: Born April 22, 1930; Daughter of Virgil Alva and Ines Roe Davis Smith (both deceased); Married Lynn E. Evans (deceased); Mother of Charles Lynn, Vernard Dale, Mark Duane, Lynn Everett Jr., Johnny Rufe, Brent Lee, Lynnetta Marie. Education: Attended Draughon's Business College, 1948-49; Art Lessons in Oil from Richard Goetz, Oklahoma City, Oklahoma, 1966, 1967, 1968; Undertook an Oklahoma University Off-Campus Journalism Class, 1938-39. Career: Freelance Writer; Songwriter; Artist; Formerly a Farmer. Organizational Memberships: Kingfisher Brush and Palette Club, Kingfisher, Oklahoma (charter member; president, 1968-69; exhibiting committee chairman, 1966-67); National Writers Club, 1980-82; Writers of the Purple Sage (historian, 1980-81); Oklahoma Writers Federation (reporter, 1981-82). Community Activities: Vici Art Guild (president, 1976; charter member; vice president, 1977); Oklahoma Rural Letter Carrier Auxiliary (member 1960-; northwest district president, 1977-); International Society of Artists (charter member); Helped with Story Time, Vici Youth Center, 1981. Religion: Member, General Assembly, Church of the First Born, Vici, Oklahoma. Honors and Awards: Invited to Oklahoma Statewide Art Guild to Hang "Sketching at Schafenberg Lake" and "Coffee and the Birds", November 1968; "Coffee and the Birds" Accepted at Seventh Annual Artist Salon, Oklahoma Museum of Art at Red Ridge, June 1968; Honorable Mention Ribbon, "Pine Trees", Spring Art Festival, Tulsa, Oklahoma, 1968; "Lonesome Pine Lake" Accepted by Juror for the Oklahoma Museum of Art, 1969; 1 of 200 Oklahoma Artists invited to Mayo Hotel, Tulsa, Oklahoma, June 7 & 8, 1978, to Humanities Convention Invitational Conference; Invited by Oklahoma Governor, David Boren and his Wife to Attend Women's Day at State Capitol Building, October 14, 1978; Nominated for Italy's Gold Medal Award; Diploma of Distinction, International Biographical Centre, Cambridge, England; Honorary Member 250 Port Company, 497th Port Batallion A Company of World War II; Listed in *Who's Who in American Politics, Personalities of America, Directory of Distinguished Americans, Personalities of the South, Anglo-American Who's Who, International Directory of the Arts, American Registry, American Artists of Renown, Book of Honor, Dictionary of International Biography, Men and Women of Distinction;* Nominated for *International Who's Who of Intellectuals.* Address Paradise Acres, Rt. 2 Box 169, Vici, Oklahoma 73859.

Jo B Evans

Evans, Jane

Executive Vice President. Personal: Born July 26, 1944; Daughter of Mrs. C. M. Pierce; Mother of One Son. Education: B.A., Vanderbilt University, 1965; Attended L'Universite d'Aix-Marseille, Aix-en-France, 1962; Post-Graduate Courses in Fashion Merchandising, Fashion Institute of Technology, New York City, 1965, 1966. Career: Executive Vice President, General Mills; Group Vice President, Apparel, General Mills, 1980-81; Vice President, Administration and Corporation Development, Fingerhut Corporation, Minnesota, 1977-79; President, Butterick Fashion Marketing Co., New York City, 1974-77; President, I. Miller, New York City, 1970-73. Organizational Memberships: Young President's Organization (executive committee, New York chapter); The Fashion Group of New York. Community Activities: Vanderbilt University (alumni board of directors, visiting committee); Laboratory Institute of Merchandising (advisory board); National Association of Women Business Owners (advisory board); Guthrie Theatre, Minneapolis (board of directors). Address: 507 Trinity Pass Road, New Canaan, Connecticut 06840.

Evans, Jo Fred Burt

Business Manager. Personal: Born December 18, 1928; Daughter of John Fred and Sadie Oliver Burt; Mother of Charles Wayne III, John Burt, Elizabeth Wishart Burt. Education: B.A. Mary Hardin-Baylor College, 1948; Attended University of Houston School of Law; M.A., Trinity University, 1967. Career: Owner, Manager, Radio Station KMBL, Junction, Texas, 1957-59; Real Estate Broker,

1966-74. Organizational Memberships: National Translater Association; Business and Professional Women (secretary, 1979-81; president, 1981). Community Activities: Daughters of the Republic of Texas, Alamo Mission Branch, 1967-; Sheriff's Association of Texas; Troup 410, Boy Scouts of America (cub scout den mother, 1958-60; publicity chairman 1959-62); American Association of University Women (book fair chairman of San Antonio Branch, 1968-70; We the People study group chairman, 1971-72; your money's worth chairman, 1972-73; volunteer for citizens, 1973-74; speakers committee); Citizens for Texas (treasurer and co-coordinator); Nelson Wolff Congressional Campaign (volunteer, 1973; advisor of West Texas water problems); Committee for a New Constitution (treasurer and co-coordinator, 1974); Brighton School Council (president, 1972-75); Committee to Save the Edwards Aquifer (finance chairman, 1973); Kimble County Historical Survey Commission (historian, 1979-81; preservation committe, 1981-82); Junction High School Ex-Students Association (chairman). Religion: St. Marks Episcopal Church: Sunday School Teacher, 1954; Altar Guild, 1954; Junior Altar Guild, 1955-56. Honors and Awards: American Association of University Women Fellowship Named in Her Honor, 1972; Senate Resolution Designating Outstanding Service to the State of Texas, 1973; Listed in *Who's Who of Women in America, World Who's Who of Women*. Address: P.O. Box 283, Junction, Texas 76848.

Evensen, Barbara Ann

Computer Educator. Personal: Born July 12, 1942; Daughter of Albert and Hazel Evensen. Education: B.B.A, Pace University, 1974. Career: Professional Theatre, 7 years; Film Researcher, United Artists, New York City, 1965-66; Teacher/Lecturer, Italo-American Association, Genoa, Italy, 1966-67; Chemical Bank, New York City - Computer Programmer 1967-70, Coordinator Technical Training 1971-75, Assistant Manager of Long Range Automation Planning 1976-78, Assistant Treasurer for Mini-Computer Services 1978-79, Director of Academic Computing on Special Assignment to Pace University 1979-80, M.I.S. Consultant-International Division 1980-82; Graduate of Credit Training Program, 1982; Training Director of Information Center, 1982 to present. Organizational Memberships: New York Chapter, Data Processing Management Association, 1972-73; Greater New York Chapter, Association for Women in Computing (founding member; secretary and board of directors, 1979-80); GUIDE International, Inc. (world's largest computer users group; corporate secretary, 1975-77, 1977-79; director, board of directors, 1973-75; manager of computer operations training project, 1970-73; divisional educational coordinator, 1972, 1973; representative at 19th European GUIDE conference, Bologna, Italy, June 1978; speaker/representative, 13th European GUIDE conference, Madrid, Spain, June 1972); VUE Group (president, New York, 1972, 1973; executive vice-president, New York, 1971; national secretary in United States and Canada, 1972, 1973; columnist for quarterly *Advanced Systems Incorporated Newsletter*; speaker, third national VAI users conference, Chicago, 1971; workshop coordinator); Pace University (board of trustees; alumni association, president 1981-83, vice-president 1979-81, secretary 1978-79, director, board of directors 1975-81, led guidelines for EDP college courses project 1971); Chaired and Organized Educational Advisory Board Determining Needs of the EDP Industry, Underwritten by a Grant from Edutronics Systems International, Inc., and Control Data Corporation, 1973. Community Activities: Teacher of Arts and Crafts, Dramatics, Nature Study, Specializing in Occupational Therapy, Pediatrics, Child Care; Over 1000 Hours Community Service, 1957-60, as Instructor, Discussion Leader, Guest Speaker for Girl Scouts, Long Island Jewish Hospital, Various Community Organizations. Honors and Awards: Listed in *Who's Who of American Women, Who's Who in Finance and Industry, Who's Who in the East, World Who's Who of Women*. Address: 70 Sherman Street, Brooklyn, New York 11215.

Faatz, Jeanne Ryan

State Legislator. Personal: Born July 30, 1941; Daughter of Charles Keith and Elizabeth M. Ryan, Evansville, Indiana; Mother of Kristin B., Susan E. Education: Graduate of Evansville Bosse High School, 1958; Bachelor's Degree, Indiana University, 1962; Graduate Credit, University of Northern Colorado, 1975. Career: State Legislative Representative, Two Terms; Teacher of English and Speech. Organizational Memberships: Council of State Governments (transportation committee, western conference); Colorado House Transportation and Energy Committee (chairman); Regional Transportation District Legislative Oversight Committee (chairman). Community Activities: Harvey Park Improvement Association (past president); Southwest Y.W.C.A. Adult Education Club (past president); United Nation's Children's Fund (past southwest metro area coordinator); Ft. Logan Mental Health Center Citizen's Advisory Board (board member); Southwest Y.M.C.A. (board of managers). Honors and Awards: Women's Scholastic Award, Indiana University; Magna Cum Laude, Graduate with College Honors, Top 3% of Class, University of Illinois; Gallery of Fame for Community Work, *Denver Post*, 1978. Address: 2903 South Quitman Street, Denver, Colorado 80236.

Fabrizio, Tuula Irja Jokinen

Physician and Medical Writer. Personal: Born May 13, 1931; Daughter of Arne Valfrid and Jenny Lydia Jokinen (both deceased); Married John Arthur Fabrizio; Mother of John Arne, Robert Arthur. Education: M.D. 1957, Sc.D. 1958, University of Helsinki Medical School, Finland. Career: Physician, Medical Writer, Editor of *Medical News, The Finnish Medical Journal*, 1971 to present; Emergency Room Physician, St. Vincent's Medical Center, Bridgeport 1977-79, Milford Hospital 1973-77, Norwalk Hospital 1966-69; School and Well Baby Clinic Physician, City of Norwalk, 1969-73. Organizational Memberships: Connecticut Academy of Family Physicians (education committee 1979 to present); American Medical Association; Fairfield County Medical Association; Connecticut State Medical Society; American Board of Family Practice (diplomate); American Academy of Family Physicians (fellow); American College of Preventive Medicine (fellow); American Public Health Association; American Medical Writers Association; American Association for Automotive Medicine; New York Academy of Sciences; American Association for the Advancement of Science; Finnish Medical Association. Religion: St. Peter's Lutheran Church, Norwalk (member 1963 to present). Honors and Awards: Bronze Plaque, Finnish Medical Association, 1980; Elected to World Academy of New Zealand, 1976; Medal Award, Listed in *International Who's Who in Community Service*, 1971. Address: 42 Stevens Street, Norwalk, Connecticut 06850.

Harold V Fairbanks

Fairbanks, Harold Vincent

Professor of Metallurgical Engineering, Research Fellow, Associate Chairman. Personal: Born December 7, 1915, in Des Plaines, Illinois; Son of Oscar William and Muriel Hullet Fairbanks; Married Marilyn Elizabeth Markussen; Father of Elizabeth Muriel, William Martin. Education: B.S.Ch.E 1937, M.S. 1939, Michigan State University; Undertook Studies in Metallurgy, Massachusetts Institute of Technology, 1939-40. Career: Teaching Graduate Assistant, Chemistry Department, Michigan State University, 1937-39; Instructor, Chemical Engineering Department, University of Louisville, 1940-42; Assistant Professor, Chemical Engineering Department, Rose Polytechnic Institute, 1942-47; West Virginia State University - Associate Professor of Metallurgical Engineering, Chemical Engineering Department and Associate Metallurgical Engineer 1949-55, Professor of Metallurgical Engineering and Metallurgical Engineer 1955-78, Research Fellow in the Coal Research Bureau 1970 to present, Professor Emeritus and Research Fellow in the Department of Chemical Engineering, Coal Research Bureau 1978 to present; Advisor for Mining and Metallurgical Engineering Department, Taiwan Provincial Cheng University, Tainan, Taiwan, Free China, Purdue-Taiwan Engineering Education Project, 1957-59; Consultant to State Geology Department of Michigan 1938, Reclaiming of Oil (Lansing, Michigan) 1939, Columbian Enameling and Stamping 1946, Bus Company (Charleston, West Virginia) 1948, West Virginia State Road Commission 1949, Brown and Neil Corporation 1952 and 1955, United States Bureau of Mines 1964-67, Morgantown Machine and Hydraulic Inc. 1965 to present, Continental Can Corporation 1972, Preiser and Wilson 1974, Others. Organizational Memberships: Acoustical Society; American Chemical Society (member, 1941-61; chairman, Wabash Valley section, 1945-46; chairman, West Virginia section, 1954-55; national committee member, 1955-57); American Association for the Advancement of Science (fellow); American Institute of Chemical Engineers; American Institute of Metallurgical Engineers; American Ordinance Association, 1961-78; American Powder Metallurgy Institute (charter member); American Society for Engineering Education, 1941-77; American Society for Metals; American Society for Testing and Materials; Chinese Institute for Engineers (honorary member); International Association for Hydrogen Energy; International Metallorgraphic Society (charter member); International Solar Energy Society, American Section; Institute of Electrical and Electronic Engineers (sonic and ultrasound group); Instrument Society of America, 1973-76; National Association of Corrosion Engineers; National Society for Professional Engineering; West Virginia Academy of Science (chairman, engineering science section, 1969); West Virginia Society for Professional Engineering, 1948-75; Morgantown Chapter of Professional Engineers (president, 1962-64); Professional Engineers in Education (state chairman, 1966-69). Religion: Elder, First Presbyterian Church, Morgantown, West Virginia, 1960 to present. Published Works: Author/Co-Author Numerous Professional Publications including (most recently) "Selective Fracturing: A Method of Dry Separation of Unwanted Material from Coal", "Ultrasonic Assist in Rotary Kiln Drying of Temperature Sensitive Powders", "Melting of Heterogeneous Mixture with the Aid of Ultrasound", Others. Honors and Awards: Research Grants and Contracts from Armstrong-Cork 1947-52, National Science Foundation 1955-58, National Steel Corporation 1960-62, N.A.S.A. Space Oriented Research 1964-66, Senate Research Grants 1960 & 1964, National Steel Fellowship 1951-66, National Science Foundation 1975 to present; Sigma Xi, President of West Virginia Chapter 1965-66; Tau Beta Pi; Phi Kappa Phi; Phi Mu Alpha; Tau Beta Pi Scholarship, Michigan State University; Graduated with High Honors, Michigan State University; Cheng Kung University Laboratories Named in Honor for Advisory Service Given to University, 1957-59; Fairbanks Applied Metallurgical Enginering Laboratory; Fairbanks Quality Control Laboratory; Listed in *American Men of Science, Dictionary of International Biography, International Register of Profiles, Leaders in American Science, Men of Achievement, Notable Americans, Outstanding West Virginians, Personalities of the South, People Who Matter, Who's Who in America, Who's Who in American Education, Who's Who in the East, Who's Who in the South and Southwest, Who's Who in Technology*. Address: 989 Riverview Drive, Morgantown, West Virginia 26505.

Fales, DeCoursey Jr

Professor of History. Personal: Born March 9, 1918; Son of Mr. and Mrs. DeCoursey Fales (both deceased); Married Iten N. Fales. Education: Graduate of St. Paul's School, Concord, New Hampshire, 1937; A.B., Harvard University, 1941; M.A. 1947, Ph.D. 1957, Classical Archaelogy, Harvard Graduate School; United States Army Command and General Staff College, 1959. Military: Served in the Panama Coast Artillery Command from October 5, 1942, until November 7, 1945, attaining the rank of T/Sgt.; Served in the United States Army Reserve, 1946-71, attaining the rank of Lieutenant Colonel. Career: Professor of History; Field Archaeologist, Circum Excavations, University Museum, University of Pennsylvania, 1948-51; Junior Fellow, Dumbarton Oans Research Center, Washington, D.C., 1951-53. Organizational Memberships: American Institute of Archaeology; American Philological Association; Association of United States Army. Community Activities: Greek, Roman and Byzantine Studies (business manager, treasurer); Boston Museum of Fine Arts, Department of Greek and Roman Art (overseer). Honors and Awards: George Emerson Lowell Prize Scholarship, 1973; Distinguished Educator, 1971; United States Army Commendation Medal. Address: 11 Hilliard Street, Cambridge, Massachusetts 02138.

Famarin, Sally Basiga

Real Estate and Insurance Executive. Personal: Born, November 11, 1923, Mandaue City, Philippines; Daughter of Severo and Serapia Basiga (deceased); Married Carsiolo Tagle Famarin; Mother of Sally Anne, Catherine, Rodolfo Carlite, Rose Marie. Education: Graduate of University of Visayas, Cebu, Philippines, 1941; Post-Graduate Study, Chamberlain Real Estate School 1961, Harlowe Real Estate School 1962, Income Tax Service 1975, San Francisco, California. Career: Director-Owner, Famarin Realty, United Homes Realty, United Homes Insurance Service, Far East America Travel, Income Tax Service; Business Opportunity, Mortgage, and Real Properties Securities Dealer; Owner-Operator, Sally's Sunset Villa Ambulatory Home for the Aged, 1972-74; Real Estate Saleswoman, 1962 to present; Accountant, Bookkeeper, and Manager of Ladies Home, Philippines. Organizational Memberships: National Real Estate Association; National Association of Real Estate Board; The National Salesman's Association; The California Real Estate Association; The San Francisco Board of Realtors; The Multiple Listing Service of San Francisco; The American Society of Notaries; National Historic Preservations of America. Community Activities: City and County of San Francisco (advisory board, child health and disability prevention program, Mayor George Moscone's screening committee on boards and commissions, commissioner on landmarks preservation advisory board); Philippine Gardens, Golden Gate Park, San Francisco (initiator, 1976); International Hotel Landmark, 1st Filipino Landmark in United States National Register of Cultural and Historical Places (author, endorser, 1977); Regular Veterans Association Auxiliary (president, 1953-60); Cebu Association of California, Inc. (founder, president emeritus, world emissary); Mandaue Association de Santo Nino, Philippines (founder); American Legion Bataan Post 600; Filipino-American Senior Citizens of San Francisco and Bay Area of St. Joseph's (advisor); National Housing Conference Committee, Washington, D.C., 1981. Religion: St. Joseph's Church (member, parish council president). Honors and Awards: Robert C. Howe Memorial Plate Award for Patriot of the United States of America, 1977; Famarin Bicentennial Commemorative Flag, American Biographical Institute; Most Successful Woman Award; Mandaue's Pride Abroad; Resolution from Mandaue City Council; Certificate of Honor, San Francisco Board of Supervisors for Exemplary Leadership in the Community, Three Times; California State Senate and State Assembly for Exemplary Leadership in the Philippine-American Community of San Francisco and Distinguished Professional Achievements, Twice; Only United States Awardee, Fourth Centenary Celebration of Cebu's Republic of the Philippines, 1975; Gold Pin Award, Cebu Association, 1971; Gold Medal Award, 1980; Best of the Best and Honoring the Honored, Cambridge, England; City Planning Resolution 8621 of San Francisco for Dedication in Preserving San Francisco's Architectural and Historical Heritage, 1980. Address: 2207 - 28th Avenue, San Francisco, California 94116.

Sally B Famarin

Farha, William Farah

Food Company Executive. Personal: Born November 27, 1908, in Lebanon; Son of Farah Farris and Nahima (Salamy) Farha; Married Victoria Barkett, April 15, 1934; Father of William George. Education: Graduate of United States Industrial College, 1948; Brooking Institute, 1968. Career: President, River Bend Shopping Center, Wichita; William F. Farha and Son Enterprises. Organizational Memberships: Rotary Club; Wichita Chamber of Commerce (board of directors); National Board of Institute of Logopedics. Community Activities: National Conference of Christian and Jews (board of directors); Kansas Foundation for the Blind (board of directors); Salvation Army (board of advisors); Young Men's Christian Association World Service (international board); Wichita Leadership Prayer Breakfast (chairman); Wichita Police and Fireman Pension Plan (chairman); Wichita Symphony Society (board of trustees); American Security Council (national advisory board); United States Congressional Advisory Board; President Reagan's Republican Presidential Task Force (charter member); Republican National Committee. Religion: Saint George Church (board of trustees president). Honors and Awards: Wisdom Hall of Fame, Beverly Hills, California, 1970; Doctors Degree Conferred by Hamilton State University of Tuscon, Arizona, Business Administration, 1973; Honorary Colonel on Governor's Staff of the State of Oklahoma, 1956; Gold Medallion for Outstanding Service to Orthodoxy, Antiochian Patriarch Alexander of Damascus, Syria; Antonian Gold Medal of Merit, The Antiochian Orthodox Christian Archdiocese of New York and All North America; Invited by Presidents Eisenhower, Kennedy, Johnson, Nixon and Ford to Washington, D.C., to Attend Presidential Prayer Breakfast; Brotherhood Award of National Conference of Christians and Jews; Listed in *International Who's Who of Intellectuals.* Address: 8630 Shanon Way, Wichita, Kansas 67206.

Farmer, Barbara May

Social Worker. Personal: Born May 18, 1931. Education: Graduate of Rahway High School, Rahway, New Jersey 1949; B.S., Certified for Teaching of Handicapped, New Jersey State Teacher's College, Newark, New Jersey, 1953; M.S.S.W., Columbia University School of Social Work, New York, New York, 1957; Certified in Practice of Social Work, New York State, 1968. Career: Albert Einstein College of Medicine, Assistant Professor of Community Health 1979 to present, Associate Director of Evaluation Unit in Department of Community Health 1974 to present, Principal Associate of Department of Community Health 1974-79, Instructor of Medicine 1974-76, Assistant Director/Director of Family Therapy of Van Etten Home Care 1967-70, Department of Medicine Instructor 1967-70; Consultant, Amron Management Consultants, Inc., 1977 to present; Bronx Professional Standards Review Organization, Organizational Reviewer of Services for Shared Health Facilities 1978 to present, Social Services Consultant 1977 to present, Assistant Project Director for Technical Assistance in Development and Testing of Project Assessment Methodology of Bureau of Quality Assurance 1976-79; Assistant Project Director, Study of Impacts of N.I.M.H./R.O. Management and Quality Control Activities on Changes in Community Mental Health Centers, 1977-79; Study of Psychosocial Services of Prepaid Health Plan in Los Angeles for California Department of Health, 1976; Team Coordinator/Psychosocial Review for Evaluations of 314(e) Community Health Centers and Family Planning Programs, 1973-77; Reviewer of Psychosocial Service for Health and Hospitals Corporation of New York in Conjunction with Quality of Care Students, 1972-75; Team Coordinator of Site Evaluations of O.E.O. Neighborhood Health Centers/Evaluator of Psychosocial Service, Quality of Care, 1971-73; City of New York Department of

Hospitals, Director of Social Service for Van Etten Hospital 1957-67, Clinical Instructor in Department of Medicine 1964-67; Consultant, Berkshire County Rehabilitation Center, 1965-67; Private Practice, 1964-65; Caseworker, Therapeutic Community Research Program in Rehabilitation Medicine at Bronx Municipal Hospital Center 1961-64, Bird S. Coler Hospital Rehabilitation Service 1957-61; Part-Time Group Work, Association for Help for Retarded Children, 1957-61; Special Education/Remedial Education, St. Christophers School for Disturbed Children, 1954-55; Third, Fourth, and Retarded Grades Teacher, Rahway (New Jersey) Public Schools, 1953-54; Presentation of Paper with Grace G. Eddison, M.D., "A Control Study of Home Versus Hospital Treatment of Tuberculosis" Preliminary Results, 20th International Union Against Tuberculosis Conference 1969, Three Year Study Results, American Thoracic Society Annual Meeting, 1971, and 21st International Union Against Tuberculosis Conference, Moscow, 1971. Organizational Memberships: National Association of Social Workers (northeastern regional representative 1969-70); Academy of Certified Social Workers; American Group of Psychotherapy Association (eastern division); American Public Health Association; Community Council of Greater New York Services to Family, 1968; American Association of University Professors; Physicians Forum. Published Works: Co-Author with G. G. Eddison, "The Development of a Comprehensive Health Care Program for Patients with Active Tuberculosis," *M.C.V. Quarterly*, "A Control Study of Home Versus Hospital Treatment of Tuberculosis: 3 Year Study Results," submitted to *American Review of Respiratory Disease; Contributor to Ambulatory Health Care Services Review Manual* and *Manual for Assessment of Functions of Ambulatory Care Facilities.* Address: 48 Woodlake Drive, Charlottesville, Virginia 22901.

Farr, Charles Lester Jr

Plant Manager. Personal: Born September 21, 1926; Son of Mr. and Mrs. Charles L. Farr, Sr.; Married to Helen E. Airy; Father of Thomas B., Candace E., Charles L. III. Education: A.B., Colgate University, 1948. Military: Served with United States Naval Corps and R.O.T.C. (cadet), 1944-46. Career: Plant Manager of Fiber Glass Manufacturing (Berlin, New Jersey), 1974 to present, Plant Manager (Parkersburg, West Virginia), 1972-74, Plant Manager (Defiance, Ohio), 1967-72, Product Superintendent (Waterville, Ohio), 1963-67, Division Staff Industrial Engineer (Toledo, Ohio), 1962-63, Corporate Supervisory Industrial Engineer (Toledo), 1956-62, and Industrial Engineer, 1947-56, Johns-Mansville Sales Corporation. Organizatonal Memberships: American Management Association. Community Activities: Mason Lodge, Cranford, New Jersey, 1950 to present; South Jersey Chamber of Commerce (member and director, 1975 to present, chairman labor relations committee, 1977 to present); Camden County, New Jersey Heart Association (trustee, 1977 to present); Member, PENJERDEL Council, Philadelphia, Pennsylvania; Member, Southern New Jersey Development Council; Bernards Township, New Jersey Recreation Committee, 1958-61; Bernards Township Board of Education, 1958-62; Bernards Township Police Reserve, 1958-61; Bernards Township Kiwanis Club (chairman, youth committee, 1958-61). Religion: Vestryman and Warden, St. Marks Episcopal Church (Basking Ridge, New Jersey), 1960-62; Vestryman, St. Paul's Episcopal Church (Maumee, Ohio), 1965-68; Vestryman and Warden, Grace Episcopal Church (Defiance, Ohio), 1969-74; Vestryman and Warden, St. Peters Church (Medford, New Jersey), 1977-80. Honors and Awards: Received Commendation from Camden County Board of Freeholders, 1979; Listed in *Who's Who in the East, Personalities of America.* Address: 102 Ramblewood Lane, Medford, New Jersey 08055.

Fatiadi, Alexander Johann

Research Chemist. Personal: Born October 22, 1923, in Merefa, Ukraine, U.S.S.R.; Emigrated to the Unites States, 1952; Son of Johann and Maria Goncharehko Fatiadi; Married Irina Matussevich; Father of Elena, Irina, Tamara, Julia. Education: Graduate with Distinction from High School; Attended the Kharkov State Univeristy; Ph.D., Johannes Guttenberg University, Mainz, 1950; B.S., 1957, and M.S, 1959, both from George Washington University. Career: Locomotive Engineer, 3 years; Research Associate in Chemistry, George Washington University; Research Chemist in Organic Chemistry, National Bureau of Standards, Washington, D.C., 1959 to present. Organizational Memberships: The American Chemical Society, The Chemical Society (London); The New York Academy of Science; The German Chemical Society. Published Works: "The Reaction Between Molten Potassium and Carbon Monoxide", 1959; "Electron Spin Resonance Studies of Chemical Changes of Phenylhydrazones and Osazones in Alkaline Solution", 1973; "Active Manganese Oxidation in Organic Chemistry", 1982, and "Permanganate Oxidation in Organic Chemistry", 1982, among others. Honors and Awards: Certificates of Recommendation, 1965, 1966, 1968, 1970, and a Special Achievement Award, 1973, all from the National Bureau of Standards; International Scholars Award, 1973; Listed in *Community Leaders of America.* Address: 7516 Carroll Avenue, Takoma Park, Maryland 20912.

Fawcett, James Davidson

Educator, Herpetologist. Personal: Born January 10, 1933; Son of James (dec) and Edna Catterick Fawcett; Married Georgene Ellen Tyler. Education: B.S., University of New Zealand, 1960; M.S., University of Auckland, 1964; Ph.D., University of Colorado-Boulder, 1975. Career: High School Teacher, Auckland, New Zealand, 1953-59; Head, Department of Biology, King's College, Auckland, 1960; Senior Demonstrator, Department of Zoology, University of Auckland, 1963-64; Graduate Teaching Assistant, University of Illinois, 1965-67; Graduate Teaching Assistant, Department of Biology, University of Colorado, 1969-72; Department of Biology, University of Nebraska at Omaha: Instructor 1972-75, Assistant Professor 1975-81, Associate Professor 1981 to present. Organizational Memberships: American Association for the Advancement of Science; American Society of Zoologists; Royal Society of New Zealand; Herpetologists League; New Zealand Association of Scientists; Society of Systematic Zoology; Omaha Sigma Xi Club (president, 1980-81). Community Activities: Nebraska Herpetological Society (president, 1979-80); Lecturer at Regional Herpetological Societies. Honors and Awards: Outstanding Graduate Student, Alpha Pi Chapter, Phi Sigma, 1972; Great Teacher Award, University of Nebraska at Omaha, 1981.

Fawcett, Marie Ann Formanek

Volunteer Civic Leader. Personal: Born March 6, 1914, Minneapolis, Minnesota; Daughter of Peter Paul and Mary Ann Formanek; Married Roscoe Kent Fawcett, March, 1934; Mother of Roscoe Kent Jr., Peter Formanek, Roger Knowlton II, Stephen Hart. Education: Graduate, Washburn High School; Attended Harvard University; Certificates from Harvard Alumni College, 1976-77, 1978-79, 1980-81. Community Activities: Weekend Volunteer Chairman, Greenwich Hospital; Board of Directors: Merry Go Round for the Aged, Merry Go Round Mews for the Elderly, Multiple Sclerosis Society, Nathaniel Witherell Auxiliary, Greenwich Philharmonia; Fund Raising: Red Cross, Leukemia, Community Chest, Muscular Dystrophy, Mental Health, Mentally Retarded Children at Milbank School; Women's Club of Greenwich; 24 Weeks Superiour Court Jury Duty; Marquis Biographical Library Society (advisory member); Huxley Institute for Biosocial Research; York Club of New York. Religion: Roman Catholic. Honors and Awards: Citation for Outstanding Service to Greenwich Hospital; Citation from Connecticut State Department of Health for Volunteer Services in Recreational Service Program at Nathaniel Witherell Hospital, 1974; Certificate of Achievement, Connecticut

State Department of Health, 1977; Woman of the Year, Soroptimist Club, 1967; Award, United Cerebral Palsy Association of Fairfield County Incorporated; Selected by the American Bicentennial Research Institute to Appear As a Reference Source in its Library of Human Resources; Listed in *Contemporary Personalities, World Who's Who of Women, International Platform Association Directory, Community Leaders and Noteworthy Americans, Book of Honor,* Others. Address: North Street and Hawkwood Lane, Greenwich, Connecticut 06830.

Fedelle, Estelle

Artist, Author, Educator, Lecturer. Personal: Born July 21. Education: Attended the Art Institute of Chicago, Northwestern University, Institute of Design, American Academy of Fine Arts; Studied Under 8 Private Teachers. Career: Art Instructor, Fedelle Art Studio, Chicago and Park Ridge, Illinois; Lecturer and Demonstrator of Painting Techniques, Eastern and Midwestern United States; Regent Art League (honorary director); Laurel Art League (honorary director); Municipal Art League; National League of American Penwomen; International Platform Association; Group Shows: Visual Arts Center (Chicago), Illinois State Fair, Chicago Public Library, Kenosha Public Museum, Barron Galleries (Chicago and Las Vegas); Grand Central Galleries (New York), American Artists Professional League. Published Works: *How to Begin Painting for Fun;* Weekly Column, *The Leader Newspaper,* Chicago, Illinois, "Art and You", 1974 to present. Honors and Awards: Winner 66 Awards for Painting; 50 One Man Shows; Certificate of Merit for Distinguished Service in Art, 1967; Certificate of Registry of Prominent Americans; Honorary Doctor of Philosophy, Colorado State Christian College, 1973; Listed in *Who's Who in the Arts, Who's Who of American Women, Who's Who in the Midwest, Creative and Successful Personalities, Royal Blue Book, National Social Registry, Personalities of the West and Midwest, 2000 Women of Achievement, Permanent Record-Illinois Lives, Writers Directory, National Register of Prominent Americans and International Notables, Register of United States Living Artists.* Address: 1500 S. Cumberland, Park Ridge, Illinois 60068.

Fehr, Lola M.

Nursing Administrator. Personal: Born September 29, 1936; Married to Harry E. Fehr; Mother of Dawn M. Murphy, Cheryl L. Murphy, Michael P. Murphy. Education: Diploma, St. Luke's Hospital, Denver, 1958; B.S.N., University of Denver, 1959; M.S., University of Colorado, 1975. Career: Executive Director, Colorado Nurses Association; Director of Nursing Service 1976-80, Director of Staff Development 1972-76, Medical Unit Staff Nurse 1970-72, Weld County General Hospital, Greeley, Colorado; Director of Christian Education, First United Methodist Church, Greeley, Colorado, 1967-71; Volunteer, Teaching and Leadership Activities, Local and Regional Churches, 1960-67; Staff Nurse and Head Nurse, St. Luke's Hospital, Denver, Colorado, 1959-60; Professional Presentations, Colorado Chatauqua Continuing Education Symposium for Nurses 1976-78; Conference Speaker on "The Effects of Primary Care Preparation in Baccalaureate Education and Its Utilization in Job Performance," Sponsored by H.E.W., Denver, 1978; Teacher of Six-Hour Session, Nursing Management Class, University of Northern Colorado, 1978; Interviewing Workshop for Head Nurses, St. Luke's Hospital, Denver, 1979; Annual Radio Interview Programs, 1976-80; Affiliate Professor, University of Northern Colorado; Preceptor for Students in Summer Field Study, University of Colorado Nursing Administrative Program, 1977-79. Organizational Memberships: American Society for Nursing Service Administrators; Colorado Society for Healthcare Nursing Service Administrators (president, 1977-78); Western Council for Higher Education in Nursing; American Nurses Association; Colorado Nurses Association (member and chairperson of commission on nursing service and education 1976-79; member 1979, chairperson 1980, Chautauqua planning committee; delegate to A.N.A. convention 1980; district president 1978-79). Community Activities: Welco Credit Union (board of directors, secretary 1977-78; president 1979-80); Greeley Chorale, 1970 to present; American Association of University Women; League of Women Voters, Campfire Girls Leader. Religion: First Congregational Church, Greeley (member, 1970 to present; chancel choir). Honors and Awards: Phi Beta Kappa, 1956; Sigma Theta Tau, 1979; Colorado Nurses Association Professional Nurse of the Year, 1979; Certified by American Nurses Association in Nursing Administration Advanced, 1980; Nominee, Recognition Program for Excellence, American Society of Nursing Service Administrators, 1980. Address: 1321 15th Street, Greeley, Colorado 80631.

Feindt, Mary Clarissa

Executive. Personal: Born March 9, 1916; Daughter of Ernest H. and Lila M. Bastian (both deceased); Married John L. Feindt; Mother of Lawrence R. Education: A.B., Albion College, 1937; B.S. Geodesy and Surveying 1938, M.S. Civil Engineering 1944, University of Michigan. Career: President, Charlevoix Abstract and Engineering Company. Organizational Memberships: Michigan Land Title Association (past president); American Land Title Association (governor; past secretary of asbtractor's section); American Congress on Surveying and Mapping (life member); Michigan Engineering Society (life member); Michigan Society of Registered Land Surveyors (past director); Society of Women Engineers; American Society of Civil Engineers; Michigan Association of the Professions; National Engineering Council; National Council of Architectural Registration Board. Community Activities: Michigan State Board of Land Surveyors (past chairperson); Michigan State Board of Architects; Charlevoix County Surveyors, 1944 to present. Religion: Congregational Church, Charlevoix. Address: 413 Prospect Street, Charlevoix, Michigan 49720.

Feist, Marian Jean

Director of Nutrition. Personal: Born March 23, 1921; Daughter of Harlan Oscar and Bridget Matilda Hagan Mock (both deceased); Married Arthur W. Feist. Education: Graduate of Ferndale High School, Johnstown, Pennsylvania, 1938; B.S. Foods and Nutrition, Seton Hill College, Greensburgh, Pennsylvania, 1942; Dietetic Internship, Good Samaritan Hospital, Cincinnati, Ohio, 1942-43; Post-Graduate Courses, University of Cincinnati School of Education, Foods and Nutrition; Registered, A.D.A., 1969 and Current. Career: Director of Nutrition 1969 to present, Acting Director, Assistant Director, Purchasing Dietitian 1948 to 1969, Good Samaritan Hospital, Cincinnati, Ohio; Assistant Administrative Dietitian, Conemaugh Valley Memorial Hospital, Johnstown, Pennsylvania, 1948; Dietitian in Administration, Therapeutics and Teaching, Allegheny General Hospital, Pittsburgh, Pennsylvania, 1943-48; Presided Over Session at Ohio Hospital Association-Hospital Institutional and Education Food Service Society, Cincinnati, Ohio, 1971; Teacher for Daycare Cooks, Foods and Nutrition Purchasing and Menu Planning, Cincinnati, Ohio, 3 Years; Presentation of Paper, "Purveyors - How They Can Help," Development of a Computerized Food Service System and the Dietitian Seminar, Cincinnati Dietetic Association, Good Samaritan Hospital, 1967; Lecturer, "Menu Planning and Purchasing," Xavier University, Cincinnati, Ohio 1963, University of Cincinnati Evening College 1967. Organizational Memberships: Greater Cincinnati Dietetic Association (president, 1971-72; president's advisory committee, 3 terms; treasurer, administrative section chairman, legislation and consultation, recruitment and career guidance, representative for the Sisters of Charity, chairman of computer action committee, 2 terms; food parade, president-elect, co-chairman of national nutrition week, 1 term; participating member in speakers bureau and consultant service); Pittsburgh Dietetic Association (recording secretary, chairman of therapeutic section, 1 term); Ohio Dietetic Association (administrative section committee, co-chairman of exhibits annual convention, 1976; "food purchasing" panel participant at Ohio Dietetic Workshop, 1951; lecturer on "Two Plus Three and Convenience Food," for Institute for Dietitians in Nursing Homes, University of Dayton, 1967); American Dietetic Association (life member); American Diabetic Association; Cincinnati Restaurant Association; Ohio Restaurant Association; National Restaurant Association; Nutrition Today Society; American Society for Food Service Administration; Society for Advancement of Management. Religion: Roman Catholic. Published Works: Co-Author, "Food Freezers," *Hospital Progress*, 1956. Honors and Awards: Daughters of the American Revolution, 1938; Sigma Kappa Pi, 1942; G.S.H. Employee Awards, 1953, 1958, 1963, 1968, 1973, 1978; International Platform Association, 1980-82; Listed in *Who's Who Among Students in American Universities and Colleges; Who's Who in the Midwest; World's Who's Who of Women; International Who's Who of Intellectuals, Personalities of the West and Midwest.* Address: 231 Deblin Drive, Cincinnati, Ohio 34239.

Felton, Gary Spencer

Clinical Psychologist/Author. Personal: Born March 8, 1940, San Francisco, California; Son of Dr. J. S. Felton, Pacific Palisades, California; Married Lynn Sandell; Father of Colin Spencer, Megan Ariana. Education: B.A. General Science, Grinnell College, 1961; M.S. Clinical Psychology, California State University-San Francisco, 1966; Ph.D. Clinical Psychology, University of Southern California, 1970; Internship, Los Angeles County-University of Southern California Medical Center, 1968-69. Career: Director of Special Education Programs and Associate Professor of Psychology, Los Angeles City College; Director/Licensed Clinical Psychologist in Private Practice, Center for Interpersonal Studies, Los Angeles, California; Consultant to Several Mental Health and Human Services Community Advisory Committees, Greater Los Angeles Area; Director of Allied Health/Coordinator of the Child Health Care Worker Training Program, University-Affiliated Program of Childrens Hospital, Los Angeles, 1972-75; Coordinator of Human Services Worker Training Program, Brentwood Veterans Administration Hospital, Los Angeles, 1971-72; Coordinator of Counseling Services/Co-Director of Research Programs, Mount St. Mary's College Student Development Center, 1969-71; Part-Time Consulting Psychologist, Adult Back Clinic of Orthopaedic Hospital, Los Angeles, 1967-69; Research Psychologist/Project Writer, American Heart Association Program, California State University, San Francisco, 1965-66; Psychiatric Fellowship Recipient, University of California-Los Angeles School of Medicine and Neuropsychiatric Institute, 1963; Academic Appointments, Los Angeles City College, 1971 to present, Mount St. Mary's College 1969-71; Instructor in Psychology, California State University-San Francisco, 1965-66; Editor, Three Academic Journals and Publications. Organizational Memberships: *College Student Journal* (editorial board member); *Journal of Educational Psychology* (ad hoc consultant to editorial review board); Public Advertising Council, Los Angeles (board of directors); American Psychological Association; Western Psychological Association; California State Psychological Association; Los Angeles County Psychological Association; Los Angeles Society of Clinical Psychologists; Association for Humanistic Psychology; American Name Society; American Humanist Association; American Federation of Teachers. Published Works: *The Record Collector's International Directory*, 1980; *Up from Underachievement*, 1977; One Monograph, More than 75 Professional Articles and Book Chapters in Various Areas of Psychology, Education, Language, and Names. Honors and Awards: Listed in *International Register of Profiles, People Who Matter, International Who's Who of Intellectuals, International Who's Who in Community Service, Who's Who in the United States, Dictionary of International Biography, Men of Achievement, Personalities of the West and Midwest, Who's Who in the West, Community Leaders and Noteworthy Americans, Notable Americans of the Bicentennial Era, The Compendium-International Directory of Eminent Persons in the Field of Exceptional Children, International Directory of Outstanding Teachers in Exceptional Education, Men and Women of Distinction, Personalities of America, Who's Who in California, The Book of Honor, The Anglo-American Who's Who, The Directory of Distinguished Americans, Community Leaders of America, Who's Who in Community Service, International Book of Honor.* Address: 2739 Forrester Drive, Los Angeles, California 90064.

I L Ferguson

Ferguson, Ira Lunan

Clinical Psychologist. Personal: Born January 27, 1904; Son of Rev. Edwin and Clarice Ferguson, (both deceased); Married Sarah Elizabeth; Father of David Ferguson, Clarice Ferguson Sebastian. Education: B.A., 1937, M.S., 1941, both from the University of Minnesota; M.A., 1949, Ph.D., 1950, both from Columbia University; LL.B., LaSalle Extension University, Chicago, Illinois, 1970. Carrer: Associate Professor of Health Education, Education, Psychology, Southern University, Baton Rouge, Louisiana, 1944-48; Professor of Bacteriology, Education, Hygiene, Psychology, Tuskegee Institute, Alabama, 1950-57; President, Lunan-Ferguson Library, Publishers of Lunan-Ferguson Books; Licensed Clinical Psychologist; Licensed Marriage & Family Counselor. Organizational Memberships: American Association of University Professors; New York Academy of Sciences; The Royal Society of Health (England); California State Psychological Association; American Publfc Health Association; The Gerontological Society; International Academy of Law & Science. Community Activities: California Republican Equal Opportunity Council (president, 1957-60); California Republican State Central Committee, 1958-62; San Francisco County Republican Central Committee, 1958-62; San Francisco Citizens Political Advisory Board, 1957-65; World Affairs Council, 1957-66; Graduate Interfraternal Council, Tuskegee Institute (president, 1954-57). Published Works: *The Interfraternal Review* (founder & editor, 1953-57); Author of 16 books, including social psychology/social philosophy textbooks, romantic novel with happy ending, travelogue, autobiography, satirical novel, marriage book for men, marriage book for women and others. Honors and Awards: Beta Kappa Chi, 1945; Phi Delta Kappa, 1944; President's Scholar, Columbia University, 1949; Award Letter of Commendation, signed by President and Chairman of the Board of Regents, University of Minnesota, 1979; Publications and Memorabilia requested by University of Wyoming for Archive of Contemporary History, now exhibited as "Dr. Ira Lunan Ferguson Collection". Address: 2219 Clement Street, San Francisco, California 94121-2096.

Ferguson, Robert William

Business Executive. Personal: Born February 1, 1923, Newark, New Jersey; Son of Elbert W. and Henrieete F. Ferguson (both deceased); Married Jeanne Kathleen Ferguson; Father of Robert William, John William, Thomas William, Bruce William, Jeanne Marie, Elizabeth Marie, Emily Marie, Kathleen Marie, Frank William, Christine Marie. Education: B.S., Rutgers University, 1947; Post-Graduate Studies in Industrial Relations, Princeton University Graduate School, 1952; Postgraduate Studies, University of Pennsylvania Institute on Humanistic Studies for Executives, 1956-57. Military: Served in the United States Army during World War II. Career: Business Executive in Organizational Development, American Telephone and Telegraph Company, Basking Ridge, New Jersey; Director, Mercantile Trust Company, St. Louis, Missouri; Director, Mercantile Bancorporation, Inc., St. Louis, Missouri; Director, Marine Bank Corporation, Milwaukee, Wisconsin; Executive Committee, Southwestern Bell Telephone Company. Community Activities: Pennsylvania Council on Crime and Delinquency (director); Pittsburgh Chamber of Commerce (director); Allegheny Roundtable (director); Family and Children's Service of the United Fund (director); Americans for the Competitive Enterprise System (director); Delaware Valley Council (director); Pittsburgh Rotary Club (vice president); Boy Scouts of America (organizational and extension chairman, General Wayne district, Valley Forge Council); Philadelphia Suburban Counties United Fund (vice chairman, 1969); Vocational Education Survey of Public Schools, Pittsburgh (executive committee); Civic Club; Delta Phi (board of governors); College of St. Elizabeth, New Jersey (board of trustees, development committee); Epsilon Chapter of Delta Phi, Rutgers University, New Jersey (board of governors); Greater Philadelphia Chamber of Commerce; Canoe Brook Country Club, Summit, New Jersey; Seaview Country Club, Absecon, New Jersey; Delray Beach Country Club, Florida; Citrus Club, Orlando, Florida. Religion: Catholic. Honors and Awards: Meritorious Service Award, Bell System; Businessman of the Day. Address: Green Hills Road, Mendham, New Jersey 07945.

Ferraro, Geraldine Anne

Member of Congress. Personal: Born August 26, 1935; Daughter of Antonetta Ferarro, Forest Hills, New York; Married John Zaccaro; Mother of Donna Zaccaro, John Zaccaro, Jr., Laura Zaccaro. Education: B.A., Marymount College; J.D., Fordham Law School. Career: Member of United States House of Representatives; Attorney in Private Practice; Assistant District Attorney, Queen County District Attorney's Office; Teacher, New York City Public School System, 1956-60. Organizational Memberships: Queens County Bar Association; Queens County Women's Bar Association (past president). Community Activities: Advisory Council for the Housing Part of the Civil Court of the City of New York (appointee). Address: 22 Deepdene Road, Forest Hills, New York 11375.

Ferrer, Deborah Ann Boone

Recording Artist. Personal: Born September 22, 1956; Daughter of Mr. and Mrs. Charles Eugene (Pat) Boone; Married Gabriel Vicente Ferrer; Mother of Jordan Alexander. Education: Graduate, Marymount High School, 1974; Attended the Vineyard School for Discipleship, 1975-76. Career: Recording Artist. Organizational Memberships: A.F.T.R.A.; S.A.G.; Academy of Country Music; NARAS. Community Activities: Volunteer, Hathaway House School for Autistic Children, 1974-76; Youth With a Mission, Summer Missionary Training School, 1976. Religion: Church on the Way, First Foursquare Church of Van Nuys, 1970-81. Honors and Awards: Grammy Award as Best New Artist, 1977; Gold and Platinum Single and Album, "You Light Up My Life", 1977; American Music Award, Song of the Year, 1977; National Theatre Owners Award, Best New Personality, 1977; Grammy Award, Best Inspirational Performance, "With My Song. . . ", 1980; Country Music Association Award, Best New Country Artist, 1977; A.G.V.A., Singing Star of the Year, 1978; Dove Award, "With My Song. . . " Album, 1980. Address: 9255 Sunset Blvd., Suite 519, Los Angeles, California 90069.

Ferrier, Dale O

Executive. Personal: Born October 14, 1936; Married Patty Jane Ferrier; Father of Jeffrey Eugene, Edward Dale, Ruth Elaine. Education: B.S., Fort Wayne Bible College, 1969; M.S.B.A., Indiana University, 1973; Ph.D., Walden University, 1982. Career: Supervisor of Northern Indiana Instructors 1979 to present, Management Seminar Leader 1971 to present, Instructor 1966 to present, Dale Carnegie Courses; Indiana Wire Die Company, Inc., President 1965 to present, General Manager 1960-65, Supervisor 1958-60. Organizational Memberships: A.M.A., 1959 to present; American Diamond Die Manufacturers Association (secretary/treasurer, 1966 to present); National Speakers Association, 1979 to present; International Platform Association, 1981 to present. Community Activities: Fort Wayne Bible College (chairman, governing board, 1969-81); Youth for Christ International Board (secretary, 1969-77); Y.M.C.A. (board member, 1979 to present); Fort Wayne Rotary Club (board member, 1981 to present). Religion: Missionary Church (general board, 1981 to present); Harvester Missionary Church Council (chairman, 1971 to present); F.W.B.C. Governing Board, 1969 to present; Y.F.C.I. Board, 1969-77; M.C. General Board, 1981 to present; Church Council, 1965 to present; Lifeline Homes Board, 1971 to present; Student Minister, 1956-63. Honors and Awards: Youth for Christ International "Distinguished Trustee" Award, 1978; Third Place, Toastmaster International World Championship of Public Speaking, 1981. Address: P.O. Box 10539, Fort Wayne, Indiana 46852.

David M Fetterman

Fetterman, David Mark

Anthropologist/Educational Evaluator. Personal: Born January 24, 1954; Son of Irving and Dr. Elsie Fetterman, Willimantic, Connecticut. Education: B.A. Anthropology/B.S. History, University of Connecticut, 1976; A.M. Anthropology 1977, A.M. Education 1979, Ph.D. Medical and Educational Anthropology 1981, Stanford University. Career: Anthropologist, Educational Evaluator and Project Director; Lecturer, Stanford University; Assistant Director, Palo Alto Senior Citizen Day Care Center; Director of Office of Economic Opportunity Anti-Poverty Program; High School Teacher. Organizational Memberships: American Anthropological Association (chairman of committee on ethnographic approaches to evaluation); Council on Anthropology and Education (liason to American Educational Research Association); American Educational Research Association; Society for Applied Anthropology. Community Activities: California Arts Council Evaluation Study (director, 1982); Stanford Geneological Society (president); Contemporary Chinese Studies Association (chairman); Charitable Organizations (coordinator of fund-raising activities). Religion: Religious Educator, Ethics and Judeo-Christian Historical and Cultural History. Honors and Awards: Praxis Publication Award, American Anthropological Association; Evaluation Research Society, 1981; Distinguished Scholarship Service to the Nation Award, 1981; Richard M. Weaver Fellow, 1980; Josephine de Kamin Fellow, 1979; Irish Institute of Studies Award, 1975; International Studies Award, 1973; University Scholar, 1976; Phi Beta Kappa, 1976; Phi Kappa Phi, 1976; Phi Alpha Theta International Honor Society in History, 1976. Address: 3208 Alameda de las Pulgas, Menlo Park, California 94025.

Fields, Clyde Douglas

Hospital Adminsitrator. Personal: Born June 6, 1932, Owen County, Indiana; Son of Rev. Arthur LaVerne and Mary Elizabeth Fields, Connersville, Indiana; Married Barbara Marie Ott, August 25, 1956; Father of Gayla Jean (deceased), Douglas Jay, Angela Kay. Education: B.S.B.A., Indiana Central University, 1963; M.B.A., Butler University, 1968. Military: Served in the United States Navy, 1952-56. Career: Senior Vice-President and Treasurer 1981 to present, Vice-President of Administration and Assistant Treasurer 1978-81, Vice-President of Finance and Assistant Treasurer 1973-77, Methodist Hospital of Indiana, Inc.; Assistant Executive Director 1972, Director of Financial Affairs 1969-71, Bartholomew County (Indiana) Hospital; Linde and Materials Systems Divisions, Union Carbide Corporation, 1964-69; Allison Division, General Motors Corporation, 1951-64; Crosley Division, Avco Manufacturing Company, 1950-51; Faculty Member, American Medical Association Medical Staff Leadership Conferences, 1979; Adjunct Faculty, Master of Health Care Administration Program, Indiana University School of Medicine, 1980 to present. Organizational Memberships: Association for Systems Management (member, 1965-77; president of South Central Indianapolis chapter, 1971-72); South Central Indiana Chapter of National Association of Accountants, 1970-72; Indiana (Pressler Memorial) Chapter of Hospital Financial Management Association (member, 1969 to present; board of directors, 1973-74; advanced member status, 1974; eligible for fellowship examination); Indiana Hospital Association (council on finance, 1973-79; public relations advisory committee, 1977 to present; council on government relations, 1980 to present); Spectrum Research, Inc., Denver, Colorado (advisory group member, 1974-78); Indiana State Board of Health Section 1122 (financial feasibility committee, chairman of hospital subcommittee, 1977); American Hospital Association Task Force to Develop Interpreting Language Regarding Operating Margin Requirements, "Statement of Financial Requirements of Health Care Institutions and Services," 1978; Indiana Chapter of Midwest Pension Conference, 1979-81; Nominee, American College of Hospital Administrators, 1980. Community Activities: Community Action Program of Bartholomew, Brown and Jackson Counties, Indiana (board of directors, chairman of economic development committee, 1972); Bartholomew County (Indiana) Chapter of Indianan Association for Retarded Children (board of directors, treasurer, 1971-72); South Indianapolis Kiwanis Club (member, 1973 to present; secretary, 1973-74; vice-president, 1974-75; president-elect, 1975-76; president, 1976-77); Methodist Hospital Foundation (board of directors, assistant treasurer, 1973-83); Indiana Central University Business Association, 1973 to present; Indiana Central University Alumni Association (board of directors, 1975 to present; president-elect, 1978-79; president, 1979-80); Perry Senior Citizens' Services (board of directors, 1977-80); Wesley Manor, Inc. (board of directors, 1980 to present); Indiana Central University (board of trustees, 1981 to present). Religion: United Methodist Church Member, 1945 to present; Center United Methodist Church, Administrative Board, Council on Ministries and Finance Committee; Chairman of Staff-Parish Relations Committee; Lay Delegate to Annual Conference; Certified Lay Speaker; Ecumenical Assembly of Bartholomew County (Indiana) Churches, Board of Directors 1970-72, Treasurer 1971; Church Federation of Greater Indianapolis, Member 1974-80, Chairman of Finance Committee 1978-79, Board of Directors, 1978-80; South Indiana Conference, Indiana Area, United Methodist Church, Member 1976 to present, Planning and Research Committee 1980 to present, Chairman of Committee on Clergy Support 1980-83; Indiana Council of Churches, Board of Directors, 1980 to present. Honors and Awards: Gold Achievement Award, Indianapolis Chapter 1969, Merit Award 1975, Association for Systems Management; William G. Follmer Merit Award for Outstanding Service in Chapter Activities, Indiana (Pressler Memorial) Chapter of Hospital Financial Management Association, 1974; Indiana District's Distinguished Club President Award, South Indianapolis Kiwanis Club, 1976-77; Listed in *Who's Who in Finance and Industry, Who's Who in the Midwest, Who's Who in the World, Personalities of the West and Midwest, Community Leaders of America, Book of Honor, The American Registry, The Directory of Distinguished Americans, Personalities of America, Men of Achievement, International Who's Who of Intellectuals, Dictionary of International Biography.* Address: 540 Ho Hum Court, Greenwood, Indiana 46142.

Filar, Donald A

Accountant. Personal: March 29, 1947; Son of Adam and Wands Filar, Baltimore, Maryland; Married Karen Robiñette. Education: Diploma in Accounting and Computer Programming, Baltimore Institute, 1967; B.S. Accounting, Baltimore College of Commerce, 1969. Career: Accountant, D. A. Filar and Company Bookkeeping and Tax Service; also, Accountant, Western Electric Company. Organizational Memberships: Essex Businessman Association, 1978; Point Breeze Club (treasurer, 1975-76). Community Activities: Junior Achievement (advisor, 1975, 1976, 1977, 1979); Joseph Lee Recreation Center (advisor, 1976-77); Notary Public (1978-82); Infant Hearing Assessment Program (volunteer, 1981); International Platform Association, 1981, 1982; Planetary Society. Honors and Awards: Listed in *Who's Who in the East; Directory of Distinguished Americans; Community Leaders of America.* Address: 309 Tartan Green Court, Joppa, Maryland 21085.

Finch, Thomas Wesley

Area Manager, Cathodic Protection Engineer. Personal: Born December 17, 1946; Son of Mr. and Mrs. Charles P. Finch; Married Jinx Lynn Heath; Father of Wesley Phillip and Dennis Lee. Education: Graduate, West Covina High School, 1964; Attended Colorado School of Mines, Golden, Colorado, 1964-68. Military: Served with the United States Army Corps of Engineers, 1968-72, achieving the rank of Captain. Career: Officer in the United States Army Corps of Engineers; Area Manger, Cathodic Protection Services Inc. Organizational Memberships: National Association of Corrosion Engineers, 1973 to present; Reserve Officers Association, 1972 to present; Society of American Military Engineers. Religion: Lutheran. Honors and Awards: American Biographical Institute, 1980 to present; International Biographical Association, 1980 to present; Listed in *Who's Who in the West, Who's Who in Technology Today, Who's Who in the Southeast.* Address: 2629 Cliffside Drive, Farmington, New Mexico 87401.

Finkelstein, Ruth Margaret

Senior Administrator. Personal: Born March 26, 1930; Daughter of Mr. and Mrs. John Knarr, Tavistock, Ontario, Canada; Married Bernard Finkelstein; Mother of Craig Edward Uhrich. Education: B.A., Valparaiso University, 1951; M.S.W., Syracuse University, 1964; Licensed Clinical Social Worker, State of California. Career: Senior Program Administrator, San Francisco Housing Authority; Assistant Executive Director, Lutheran Care for the Aging; Senior Supervisor of Adoption, Santa Clara County, San Diego County; Social Service Specialist, Social Caseworker, State of Nevada Welfare Division; Consultant, Long-Term Care Facilities for the Aged. Organizational Memberships: Academy of Certified Social Workers, 1969 to present; National Association of Social Workers, 1964 to present; National Council on the Aging, 1971 to present; Western Gerontological Association, 1974 to present. Community Activities: Good Shepherd Lutheran Home (chairperson, Christian habilitation committee, 1956 to present; board of directors, 1956 to present); Good Shepherd Residence Inc. (incorporator, secretary, 1979 to present); Federation of North California Aid Association for Lutherans (fraternal life insurance company, 1977-82); Creative Ministries Committee, 1973-79; Lutheran Church, Missouri Synod, North California District (salary review committee, 1979 to present). Religion: Lutheran Church, Life Member, Sunday School teacher 1966-72, Parent-Teacher League 1968-72; Cub Scout Den Mother, 1966; Deaconess in Youth and Visitation to the Elderly, 1951-56. Honors and Awards: Honored for Ten Years' Service to Lutheran Care for the Aging, 1980; Recognition of Five Years' Service as Leader of Pre-Retirement Training Workshops for Aid Association for Lutherans, 1981; Listed in *Who's Who of American Women.* Address: 4283 George Avenue #2, San Mateo, California 94403.

Finley, Joanne Elizabeth

State Commissioner of Health. Personal: December 28, 1922; Daughter of Frank Robert and Margaret Matthews Otte; Married Joseph Finley; Mother of Scott, Ethan, Lucinda, William. Education: B.A. Public Administration/Economics, Antioch College, Yellow Springs, Ohio, 1944; M.S. Public Health, Yale University School of Medicine, 1951; M.D., Case-Western Reserve University School of Medicine, 1962. Career: New Jersey State Commissioner of Health, 1974 to present; Administrative Assistant to Congressman George Outland of California; Research Director, Cleveland, Ohio, Health Goals Project; Acting Commissioner of Health, Cleveland, Ohio; Director of Health Planning, Philadelphia Department of Public Health; Vice-President of Medical Affairs, Blue Cross of Greater Philadelphia; Director of Public Health, New Haven, Connecticut. Organizational Memberships: Association of State and Territorial Health Officers; American Public Health Association; American Society for Public Administration; Kellogg Commission on Education for Health Administration. Community Activities: University of Medicine and Dentistry of New Jersey (board of trustees); New Jersey Health Care Facilities Financing Authority; New Jersey Health Care Administrators Board; New Jersey State Health Coordinating Council; New Jersey Board of Institutional Trustees; New Jersey Council on Post-Graduate Medical Education; The Medical College of Pennsylvania (assistant clinical professor); Philadelphia Mayor's Committee on Hospital Services (staff director, 1972-73); Philadelphia Experimental Health Services Delivery System Project (director, 1972); Parent and Child Inc., Washington, D.C. (executive director, 1957); Yale University School of Medicine (department of epidemioloy and public health, lecturer, 1974). Honors and Awards: Diplomate, American Board of Preventive Medicine, 1972. Address: 57 Brookstone Drive, Princeton, New Jersey 08540.

Finn, William F

William F Finn

Obstetrician/Gynecologist. Personal: Born July 23, 1915, in Union City, New Jersey; Son of Neil and Catherine Hearn Finn; Married Doris Ida Henderson; Father of Neil Charles, Sharon Ruth, David Stephen. Education: Graduate of St. Peter's Preparatory School, 1932; B.A., Holy Cross College, 1936; M.D., Cornell University Medical College, 1940; Internship, Albany Hospital, 1940-41; Internship, Obstetrics and Gynecology, New York Hospital, 1941-42; Residencies, New York Hospital, 1942-44. Military: Commissioned First Lieutenant 1943, Captain 1945-46; Active Duty from October 7, 1944 to October 24, 1946; Awarded Okinawa Battle Star in Pacific Theater, World War II Victory Medal, Occupation Medal. Career: Assistant/Associate Attending Obstetrician/Gynecologist, New York Hospital, 1948-1966; Director of Obstetrics/Gynecology, North Shore University Hospital, 1952-59; Courtesy Staff, Manhasset Medical Center, 1959-70; Associate Attending Obstetrician/Gynecologist, 1973-78; Attending Obstetrician/Gynecologist, North Shore University Hospital, 1959 to present; Consultant in Obstetrics/Gynecology, Mercy Hospital, 1959 to present; Attending Obstetrician/Gynecologist, St. Francis Hospital, 1979 to present; Cornell University Medical College, Assistant Instructor Obstetrics/Gynecology of 1942-43, Instructor of Obstetrics/Gynecology 1944, Assistant Professor of Obstetrics/Gynecology 1948-50, Associate Professor of Clinical Obstetrics and Gynecology 1950-66, 1971 to present; J. Whitridge Williams Fellowship in Obstetrics and Gynecology, New York Hospital, 1946-47; American Cancer Society Fellowship in Gynecology, New York Hospital, 1950-51. Organizational Memberships: Diplomate, American Board of Obstretrics/Gynecology 1949, Recertified 1979; American College of Surgeons, 1950; American College of Obstetricians/Gynecologists, 1951; American Board of Quality Assurance and Utilization Review, 1980; Lying-In Alumni Association, 1943; New York Hospital Alumni, 1944; A.M.A., 1949; New York State Medical Society, 1947; New York County Medical Societies, 1949; Queens Gynecology Society (past president, 1951); New York Obstetrical Society, 1952; Nassau County Medical Society, 1953; Nassau Obstetrical and Gynecological Society (past president, 1953); New York Academy of Science, 1956; American Fertility Society, 1960; New York Gynecological Society, 1960; American Association of Gynecological Laparoscopists, 1972; American Association of Colposcopists, 1973; American Geriatrics Society, 1974; Nassau Academy of Medicine, 1980; Foundation of Thanatology, 1966; Institute for Society, Ethics and Life Sciences, 1968; Society for Life and Human Values, 1973; American Philosophical Association, 1973. Community Activities: Boy Scouts of America (district committee); North Shore University Hospital (medical board president, 1958-59); New York State Medical Society (obstetrics/gynecology section chairman, 1971); Manhasset Interfaith Council; Maternal Welfare Committee (chairman); New York State Maternal and Child Welfare Committee; Nassau County Medical Society; Abortion Review Committee (chairman); Nassau Obstetrical and Gynecological Society; Commissions on Ministry, Human Life and Health; National, Interntaional And Social Relations; Episcopal Diocese of Long Island; Church Charity Foundation (board manager); Village of Plandome Manor (trustee); Foundation of Thanatology (executive committee). Religion: Zion Episcopal Church, Douglaston, New York, Christ Episcopal Church, Manhasset, New York (church warden). Published Works: Contributor of Numerous Articles to *American Journal of Obstetrics and Gynecology, American Journal of Surgery, Cancer, Texas State Journal of Medicine, New York State Journal of Obstetrics and Gynecology, Archives of the Foundation of Thanatology, North Shore University Hospital Clinical Journal*, and Others. Honors and Awards: Awards for 25 Years of Service, North Shore University Hospital, New York Hospital, Department of Obstretrics and Gynecology of North Shore University Hospital; Physician Recognition Award, American Medical Association; Medical Education Award, American College of Obstetricians and Gynecologists. Address: 3 Aspen Gate, Manhasset, New York 11030.

Fiorentino, Carmine

Carmine Fiorentino

Private Practice Lawyer. Personal: Born September 11, 1932, in Brooklyn, New York; Son of Pasquale and Lucy Coppola Fiorentino. Education: Graduate of Franklin K. Lane High School, 1950; Studied Court Reporting, Hunter College, 1951; Studied Radio Announcing, Columbia Broadcasting School, 1952; LL.B., Blackstone School of Law, Chicago, 1954; LL.B., John Marshall Law School, Atlanta, 1957; Studied Fiction and Non-Fiction Writing, Famous Writers School, Connecticut, 1962. Career: Private Law Practice; Acting Director, Elmira New York Disaster Field Office, United States Department of Housing and Urban Development, 1973; Attorney-Advisor, Trial Attorney, United States Department of Housing and Urban Development, Atlanta, Georgia and Office of HUD General Counsel, Washington, D.C., and Legal Counsel, The Peachtree Federal Credit Union, 1963-74; Private Law Practice, Atlanta, 1959-63; Secretary, Import-Export Firm, Atlanta, 1956; Legal Stenographer, Researcher, Law Clerk for Various Law Firms, Atlanta, 1955, 1957-59; Public Relations Secretary, The Industrial Home for the Blind, Brooklyn, 1953-55; Court Reporter-Hearing Stenographer, Governor Thomas E. Dewey's Committee of State Counsel and Attorneys, 1953; New York State Department of Labor, 1950-53; New York State Workmen's Compensation Board. Organizational Memberships: Licensed to Practice Before State of Georgia Bar, District of Columbia Bar, United States Supreme Court, United States District Court in the District of Columbia, United States Second Circuit Court of Appeals, United States District Court (Northern District of Georgia), United States Fifth Circuit Court of Appeals, Georgia Supreme Court, Georgia Court of Appeals; Practiced Before United States Court of Claims; American Bar Association; Federal Bar Association; Atlanta Bar Association; Decatur-DeKalb Bar Association; American Judicature Society; Old War Horse Lawyers Club; Association of Trial Lawyers. Community Activities: Junior Chamber of Commerce; Toastmasters International; International Platform Association; The Smithsonian Institute; Century Club of the Republican National Committee (founding member); Brooklyn Republican Assembly District Political Organization; Columbian Republican League; The National Historical Society; Atlanta Historical Society; Atlanta Botanical Gardens; American Museum of Natural History; Gaslight Club; National Audubon Society; Assistant, Banquet and Meetings Preparation for President Dwight D. Eisenhower, President Richard M. Nixon, Senator Irving Ives of New York, Senator Jacob Javits of New York, Governor Thomas E. Dewey, and Governor Nelson A. Rockefeller, New York; Served as Tutor and Monitor for Georgia State Bar Examinations, 1959-61; Appeared on Network Television, Local Television, and Radio Broadcasts; Appeared in Motion Pictures Narrated by Eva Le Gallienne and John C. Daly, Aired Nationally and Produced for the Blind and the Deaf-Blind; Acted as Public Relations Director for Robert J. Smithdas, First Deaf-Blind Person in the World to Earn a Master's Degree; Served on Atlanta Lawyer Reference Panel, 1959-63; Instructed Students in District of Columbia Public School System on United States Constitution (Bill of Rights) in Conjunction with Annual Program Sponsored by Federal Bar Association and Assisted by United States Supreme Court Justice Tom Clark; Served on Committee Honoring Special Assistant to the Secretary of State of the United States. Religion: Presbyterian. Published Works: Non-Fiction Works; Words and Music, Popular Songs and Hymns; Published in *The National Observer* and *The Evening Star*, Washington, D.C. Honors and Awards: Most Progressive Commercial Student Award, New York City Public School System, 1950; Pitman Shorthand Achievement Awards, 1948-50; Commendation, United States Crusade for Freedom, 1951; Commendation, United States House Un-

American Activities Committee, 1951; Recommendation for Policy-Making Position, Administration of President Dwight D. Eisenhower, 1953; Recommendation for White House Position in Administration of President Richard M. Nixon, 1971; Commendation for Excellence in Disaster Relief Work during 1972 Tropical Storm Agnes Flood Disaster, Director of United States Department of Housing and Urban Development, Elmira (New York) Disaster Field Office; Listed in *History of the Atlanta Bar Association 1888-1962, Georgia Legal Directory, Martindale Hubbell Law Directory, Outstanding Atlantans, Personalities of the South, Community Leaders and Noteworthy Americans, Notable Americans of 1978-79, Who's Who in American Law, Dictionary of International Biography, Men and Women of Distinction, Men of Achievement, Book of Honor, The International Who's Who of Intellectuals, International Register of Profiles, International Platform Association Directory, International Who's Who in Community Service, The American Cultural Arts Registry, The American Business Registry, The Anglo-American Who's Who, The Directory of Distinguished Americans, Personalities of America, Community Leaders of America, Contemporary Personalities, Personnaes Contemporains, Zeitgenossische Personlichkeiten.* Address: 2164 Medfield Trail Northeast, Atlanta, Georgia 30345.

Fischer, Roger Raymond

State Representative. Personal: Born June 1, 1941, in Washington, Pennsylvania; Son of Raymond and Louise Fischer; Married Catherine Louise Trettel on August 13, 1972; Father of Roger Raymond II, Steven Gregory. Education: Graduate, Washington High School, 1959; B.A., Washington and Jefferson College, 1963; Undertook graduate work, Carnegie Institute of Technology. Military: Served with the United States Air Force Reserve, achieving the rank of Major; presently serving with the United States Air Force Reserve 911th U.S. Air Tactical Airlift Group, Greater Pittsburgh International Airport; Former U.S. Air Force Academy Liaison Officer. Career: Research Engineer, Jones and Laughlin Steel Research; Legislator, Pennsylvania House of Representatives, Elected 1966, 1968, 1970, 1972, 1974, 1976, 1978, 1980. Organizational Memberships: Education Committee (chairman); Veterans Affairs Committee (former minority chairman, former vice chairman); Basic Education Sub-committee (former chairman); House Committees on Appropriations, Military, and Veterans Affairs, Industrial Development, Professional Licensure Public Utilities, Law and Order and Conservation (former member); Joint State Government Commissions Task Forces on Veterans Benefits to Investigate Prisons, Aid Black Lung Victims and Study Cost of Education (former member); Police Sub-Committee on the Pennsylvania Crime Commission's Regional Planning Council (former chairman). Community Activities: Washington School Board (advisory member 1965-71); City Mission (board of directors); Boy Scout Merit Badge Counselor; Washington, Canonsburg, and Planka Sportmen's Clubs; Local 1141 U.S. Steel Workers; American Legion Post #175; Department of Pennsylvania American Legion 40 et 8, Voiture #676 (vice chairman for legislation); Reserve Officers Association (vice president chapter #27, 1970-71; life member); Washington Lodge #164 F&AM; Washington Royal Arch Chapter #150; Jacques Demolay Commander #3; Washington Council #1; Washington-Greene Shrine Caravan; Syria Temple A.A.O.N.M.S.; Appalachian Trail Conference (life member); Potomac Appalachian Trail Club; Keystones Trails Association; Warriors Trails Association (life member); Pennsylvania Appalachian Trail Committee. Religion: Lay Assistant, Lutheran Church in America. Honors and Awards: Delta Epsilon; Physics Achievement Award, Chemical Rubber Company, 1961-62. Address: Overlook Drive, Washington, Pennsylvania 15301.

Robert T Fish

Fish, Robert Jay

Doctor of Dental Surgery. Personal: Born June 4, 1947; Son of Sidney, and Sara Fish; Married Lana Joy Halperin on May 24, 1981. Education: B.S., The Ohio State University, 1969; D.D.S., The Ohio State University College of Dentistry, 1973. Career: Externship, Department of Oral Surgery, Jackson Memorial Hospital; Licensed to Practice Dentistry in Florida, Ohio, Massachusetts, Washington D.C., New York, Michigan; Former Owner Innerspace Concepts, Inc.; Staff Member, Broward Community College of Allied Medicine, 1974; Lecturer, Dental Practice Management and Administration, Dental Health Services of Florida, 1975; Began a Charter and Air Taxi Service, Flying Fish, 1976; RJF Enterprises, 1978; Owner Fish Realty; U.S. Representative to Paletta Cosmetics, Paris; Member of Staff of Pennsylvania Hospital Institute and Florida Medical Center Hospital; Guest Speaker and Radio Guest Apppearances on Topics of his Special Interests; Weekly Program, "Ask the Dentist"; Sole Importer for U.S. and Canada of fine French wine from Domaine de Saint Jean; Owner, Robert Jay Fish & Company, U.S. Representative for Sandri, S.R.L. of Genoa, Italy, manufacturers of sophisticated dental equipment. Organizational Memberships: Alpha Omega Dental Fraternity; American Analgesia Society; Board of Certified Hypnotists; Dental Health Services of Florida (board of directors). Published Works: *Cosmetic and Reconstructive Dentistry.* Honors and Awards: Listed in *Who's Who in the South and Southwest, Men of Achievement; Personalities of America.* Address: 10237 N.W. 2nd Street, Coral Springs, Florida 33065.

Fisher, Charles Frederick

Education Administrator. Personal: Born March 20, 1936; Son of Helen D. Fisher. Education: B.A., Lawrence College, 1958; M.A. 1966, Ed.D. 1973, Columbia University. Military: Served as Lieutenant and United States Navy Mine Countermeasures Officer, Seventh Fleet, Western Pacific, 1958-62; Served as Naval Reserve Officer Recruiting Officer. Career: Currently Director of Council Affairs, American Council on Education, Washington, D.C.; Assistant to President, Lawrence University, Wisconsin; American Council on Education, Assistant Director of Academic Administration Fellows Program, American Council on Education, Director of Institute for College and University Administrators, Director of Higher Education Management Improvement Program, Director of Higher Education Leadership Development Programs. Organizational Memberships: Phi Delta Kappa; American Association for Higher Education; Association for the Study of Higher Education; American Society for Training and Development; American Association of University Administrators (board of directors, 1981-84); Commission on Leadership Development in Higher Education; National Center for College and University Planning (board of directors, 1979-81). Community Activities: Beta Theta Pi (chapter and alumni president); Reserve Officers Association of the United States; Lawrence University Alumni Association (Vice-President, 1971-73); National Executive Service Corps; Washington International Visitors' Center (lecturer); United States-Japan Culture Center (board of directors, 1980-); Episcopal Church Vestry; Palladium Association, 1976-); Adjunct Professor, University of Pennsylvania and Union of Experimenting Colleges and Universities; Lawrence University Board of Trustees (1982-86); United Charities (chairman); Council on Religion and International Affairs (chairman); White House Conference on Youth (delegate); National Academy for Human Resource Development; National Identification Program for Women in Higher Education; World Affairs Council. Religion: Episcopal Church, Acolyte, Lay Reader, Committee Member, Vestryman. Published Works: "Behind the Iron Curtain," 1963; *The Remaining Steps,* 1964; *Mini Cases in College and University Administration,* 1975; *The Evaluation and Development of College and University Administrators,* 1977; "Being There Vicariously by the Case Study Method, " *On College Teaching,* 1978; *A Guide to Leadership Development Opportunities for College and University Administrators,* 1976-80. Honors and Awards: Bausch and Lomb Science Award, 1952; Phi Beta Kappa Award, 1954; Pullman Foundation Award, 1954-58; Mace Honorary Society, 1957; Senior Class President, 1958; Outstanding Graduate Award, 1958; Navy People-to-People Award, 1961; New York Regents Fellowship, 1966; Heft and Delta Alpha Pi Scholarships, 1966-67; Alumni Fellowship, 1967; American Council on Education Institute Faculty Appreciation Award, 1979; Listed in *Outstanding Young Men of America, Leaders in Education, Who's Who in America, Notable Americans of the Bicentennial Era; International Men of Achievement, International Who's Who of*

Intellectuals, Who's Who in the World. Address: 1325 - 18th Street Northwest, Suite 906, Washington, D.C. 20036.

Fisher, Charles Harold

Research Professor and Technical Consultant. Personal: Born November 20, 1906 in Hiawatha, West Virginia; Married Lois C. Fisher, 1968. Education: B.S., Roanoke College, Salem, Virginia, 1928; M.S. 1929, Ph.D. 1932, University of Illinois-Urbana; Certificate, American Management Association, 1961. Career: Adjunct Research Professor, Roanoke College, Salem, Virginia, 1972 to present; Consultant, Paper Technology for the Library of Congress 1973-76, Food Technology for Pan-American Union 1968, Textile Research to the Republic of South Africa 1967; Director, United States Department of Agriculture Southern Utilization Research Division, New Orleans, Louisiana, 1950-72; Research Group Leader, United States Department of Agriculture Eastern Regional Laboratory, Philadelphia, Pennsylvania, 1940-50; Research Group Leader, United States Bureau of Mines, Pittsburgh, Pennsylvania, 1935-40; Instructor, Chemistry, Harvard University, 1932-35. Organizational Memberships: American Chemical Society (board member, 1969-71); American Institute of Chemists (president, 1962-63; chairman of the board, 1963, 1973-75); American Institute of Chemical Engineers; The Chemical Society, London; American Association for the Advancement of Science; Chemists Club, New York. Community Activities: Established Lawrence D. and Mary A. Fisher Scholarship Fund, Roanoke College, Salem, Virginia; Cosmos Club, Washington, D.C.; Chamber of Commerce, New Orleans; International House, New Orleans; Round Table Club, New Orleans; Roanoke College Alumni Association (president, 1978-79). Published Works: Author or Co-Author of More than 150 Publications; Inventor or Co-Inventor with 72 Patents. Honors and Awards: Honorary D.Sc. Degrees, Tulane University 1953, Roanoke College 1963; Southern Chemists Award, 1956; Herty Medal, 1959; Chemical Pioneer Award, 1966; Honorary Member, American Institute of Chemists, 1973; Named Polymer Science Pioneer by *Polymer News* Periodical, 1981; Listed in *Who's Who in the World, Who's Who in America, Who's Who in the South and Southwest, Who's Who in Government, Dictionary of International Biography, Two Thousand Men of Achievement, American Men and Women of Science, The Blue Book of Leaders of the English-Speaking World, Engineers of Distinction Including Scientists in Related Fields, Leaders in American Science, Personalities of the South.* Address: Chemistry Department, Roanoke College, Salem, Virginia 24153.

Fisher, Francenia Eleanore

Plant Pathologist. Personal: Born September 23, 1924; Daughter of Roy Dexter and Daisy Sparkman Fisher. Education: B.S., Florida State College for Women, 1945; M.S., Michigan State University, 1946; Post-Graduate Studies, University of Chicago. Career: Plant Pathologist, Private Practice and Consultant; Plant Pathologist, University of Florida, Citrus Experiment Station, Lake Alfred, Florida, 1946-79. Organizational Memberships: American Phytopathological Society; International Organization of Citrus Virologists; International Society for Plant Pathology; International Congress of Plant Protection; Mycological Society of America. Community Activities: Red Cross Water Safety Instructor, 1944-1958; World Directory of Plant Pathologists, 1973 to present. Religion: Episcopalian. Honors and Awards: Ancient Order of Ranales, 1944; Sigma Xi, 1948; Listed in *Who Knows and What, American Men of Science, Who's Who of American Women, Who's Who in the South and Southwest.* Address: 1507 West Lake Cannon Drive, Winter Haven, Florida 33880.

Fishman, Charles M

Educator. Personal: Born July 10, 1942; Son of Murray and Toby Fishman; Married Ellen Fishman; Father of Jillana, Tamara. Education: B.A. English 1964, M.A. English 1965, Hofstra University; D.A. English, State University of New York-Albany, 1982. Career: Associate Professor of English, State University of New York-Farmingdale. Organizational Memberships: Poetry Society of America; Modern Language Association; United University Professionals; Poets and Writers. Community Activities: Wantagh Chess Club (founder and first president, 1972); The Long Island Poetry Collective (co-founder, 1973); Blood Program Drive, Suburban Temple (volunteer, 1979 to present); Big Brother Program, 1979 to present; Campaigner for McGovern; Anti-War Activist in Vietnam Era; Pro-Conservation Movement/Anti-Nuclear Power Activist. Religion: Suburban Temple; Religious Services Committee, 1981 to present; Brotherhood, 1979 to present. Honors and Awards: Poet in the Community Award, C. W. Post College, 1979, 1982; National Endowment for the Humanities Fellowships, 1974, 1978, Yale University 1982; America the Beautiful Fund Grant, 1973; Doctoral Fellowship, State University of New York-Albany, 1980; First Prize, *Writer's Digest* Creative Writing Competition, 1972. Address: 2956 Kent Road, Wantagh, New York 11793.

Fite, James Bateman III

Management Consultant. Personal: Born June 16, 1945, in Roosevelt, Utah; Son of James Bateman II and Boneta (LeBeau) Fite; Married Carolyn Louise Barton, August 25, 1973. Education: B.A. 1974, M.B.A. 1975, Central State University. Career: Sales Representative, South Coast Life Insurance Company, Oklahoma City, 1967-68; State Sales Manager, Horace Mann Insurance Company, Oklahoma City, 1968-71; President, J. B. Fite, Inc. and J. Bateman Fite Agency, Oklahoma City, 1971-72; Management Consultant, Fite-Davis Consulting Firm, Oklahoma City, 1971 to present; Marketing and Management Faculty, Oklahoma State University, 1976; Business Faculty, Central State University, 1978 to present; Coordinator of Management Assistance Program S.B.A., 1975 to present; Oklahoma City Metropolitan Area Trainer, National Alliance of Businessmen, 1976 to present. Organizational Memberships: American Marketing Association; American Management Association; Oklahoma Lumbermans Association; Association of M.B.A. Executives; International Platform Association. Religion: Church of Christ. Address: 2701 Drakestone Avenue, Oklahoma City, Oklahoma 73120.

Fitts, Leonard Donald

Education Administrator. Personal: Born August 19, 1940 in Montgomery, Alabama; Son of William Leonard Fitts and Mary Alice Brown; Married Sherrell Adrienne Thomas, June 4, 1966. Education: B.S. 1961, M.Ed. 1964, Tuskegee Institute; N.D.E.A. Fellow, Boston University, 1965-66; Postgraduate Study, University of Wisconsin, 1966-67; Ed.D., University of Pennsylvania, 1972; H.B.A., Drexel University, 1981. Military: Served in the United States Air Force as Communications Officer, 1961-63. Career: Assistant Superintendent of Education, Lower Camden County Regional School District Number One, Atco, New Jersey, 1981 to present; Director of Special Services, Camden City Board of Education, Camden, New Jersey, 1975-81; Psychologist of the Florida Parent Education Follow Through, Philadelphia Board of Education, 1971-75; Teaching Fellow and School Psychologist, University of Pennsylvania-Philadelphia, 1969-71; Chief of Guidance Counselors and Administrator-Staff-Equal Employment Opportunity Programs, Radio Corporation of America, 1968-69; Guidance Counselor, University of Wisconsin, 1967; School Psychometrist, Boston University, 1965-66; Graduate Assistant, Mathematics Coordination and Associate Education Director, Tuskegee Institute,

1963-5. Organizational Memberships: National Association of School Psychologists; American Psychological Association; American Personnel and Guidance Association; Association of Special Education Administrators; Camden County Guidance and Personnel Association; Council of Exceptional Children; New Jersey Association of Pupil Personnel Administrators. Community Activities: Phi Delta Kappa; Lions Club; Advisory Council of Learning Resources Center; Al-Assist Recovery and Counseling Program, Southeast Neighborhood Health Center (advisory chairman); Lincoln Day Nursery (board member); The National Foundation March of Dimes, Southwest New Jersey Chapter (board of directors). Published Works: Author of Papers including "The School Psychologist and Drug Problems in the Schools," Published in *International Encyclopedia of Neurology, Psychiatry, Psychoanalysis, and Psychology*, 1977. Honors and Awards: Appreciation Award, The White House Conference on Handicapped Individuals, 1977; Region III Outstanding Citizens Award, United States Department of Health, Education and Welfare; The Chapel of Four Chaplains Legion of Honor Certificate Citation, 1977; Project Follow Through Certificate of Appreciation, 1975; National Association of School Psychologists Certificate of Recognition, 1973; Delta Airline Service Award, 1970; Vice-President's (Hubert Humphrey) Task Force on Youth Motivation Certificate of Appreciation, 1969; Watson Kinter Scholarship, Psychological Services Assistantship, University of Pennsylvania, 1969-72; Various Scholarships; Listed in *Who's Who in the East, Men and Women of Distinction.* Address: 1105 Hudson Avenue, Voorhees, New Jersey 08043.

Henry J Flanders Jr

Fitzgerald, Janet Anne

Professor, Administrator. Personal: Born September 4, 1935. Education: B.A. Mathematics magna cum laude 1965, M.A. Philosophy of Science 1967, Ph.D. 1971, St. John's University, Jamaica, New York; New York State Permanent Certification. Career: President and Philosophy Professor, Molloy College, 1969 to present; Regional Director and Member of Executive Board of Dominican Community, 1971-72; Math Teacher, Bishop McDonnell Memorial High School, 1965-69; Teacher of Grades 5-8, St. Thomas Apostle School, 1956-65; Teacher of Primary Grades, St. Ignatius School, 1955-56. Organizational Memberships: Long Island Regional Advisory Council on Higher Education (chairman); Commission on Independent Colleges and Universities (board of trustees); American Catholic Philosophic Association; Philosophy of Science Association; American Association of University Administrators; American Philosophical Association; American Association of Presidents of Independent Colleges and Universities; American Council of Education; American Association of Higher Education. Community Activities: St. John's University, Jamaica, New York (board of advisors); Management Institute for Religious Organizations (board of advisors); Fellowship of Catholic Scholars; St. Francis Hospital, Roslyn, New York (member of education committee, advisory committee, board of directors); St. John's University, Jamaica, New York (institutional review board); National Congress of Church-Related Colleges and Universities (Catholic delegate). Religion: Roman Catholic; Dominican Nun. Honors and Awards: Post-Doctoral Fellowship from National Science Foundation to Institute on History, Sociology, Philosophy of Science, Catholic University of America, Washington, D.C., 1971; Honorary Doctor of Laws Deree, St. John's University, 1982; Award for Post-Doctoral Work, Carnegie Institute of Philosophy, Notre Dame University, Indiana, 1971; National Science Foundation Teaching Fellowship, 1965-67; Manhattan College Graduate Scholarship in Math 1965, M.A. and Ph.D. 1965-71, St. John's University School. Address: 1000 Hempstead Avenue, Rockville Centre, New York 11570.

Flanders, Henry Jackson Jr

University Department Chairman. Personal: Born October 2, 1921; Son of Mr. and Mrs. H. J. Flanders Sr.; Married Tommie Lou Pardew; Father of Janet Mitchell, Jack. Education: B.A., Baylor University, 1943; B.D. 1948, Ph.D. 1950, Southern Baptist Theological Seminary. Military: Served in the United States Army Air Corps, 1942-45, as First Lieutenant with 50 Combat Missions in Europe. Career: Baylor University Department of Religion, Chairman, Professor of Religion, Baylor University, 1969 to present; Pastor, First Baptist Church, Waco, Texas, 1962-69; Furman University, Greenville, South Carolina, Department Chairman and Chaplain 1955-62, Professor, 1950-55. Organizational Memberships: Society of Biblical Literature; American Academy of Religion; Society for Religion and Ethics; Association of Baptist Professors of Religion (past president); Council on Religion and Law; American Association of University Professors (Baylor University chapter president). Community Activities: Hillcrest Hospital (trustee); Baylor University (trustee); Weekly Television Program, "Lessons for Living," WFBC-TV; South Carolina Board of Mental Health; South Carolina Christian Action Council; Heart of Texas Red Cross (chairman of the board); Texas Ranger Commission (chaplain); Executive Board BGCT; Texas Supreme Court Grievance Oversight Committee; Waco Rotary Club (director); Opportunities Advancement Corporation (president). Religion: Pastor, First Baptist Church, Waco, Texas, 1962-69; Chairman, Trustees, Golden Gate Baptist Seminary, 1971-76; Waco Ministerial Alliance. Published Works: *People of the Covenant; Introduction to the Bible* Numerous Articles. Honors and Awards: International Platform Association; Top Professor, Baylor University, Several Years; Favorite Professor, Furman University, Several Years; Listed in *Directory of American Scholars, Notable Americans of the Bicentennial Era, International Who's Who of Intellectuals, International Scholar Directory, Contemporary Authors, Dictionary of International Biography; Who's Who in American Education; Personalities of the South.* Address: 3820 Chateau, Waco, Texas 76710.

Milo J Fleming

Flaster, Donald J

Medicolegal Consultant. Personal: Born August 29, 1932; Son of Murray and Theresa Flaster (both deceased); Father of Elisabeth Ann, Andrew Paul. Education: A.B., The Johns Hopkins University, 1953; M.D., University of Naples, 1959; LL.B., Blackstone School of Law, 1970. Career: President, Scientific and Regulatory Services Consulting, Inc.; Medicolegal Consultant; Family Physician. Organizational Memberships: New York Academy of Family Physicians; American Academy of Family Physicians (fellow); Medical Society of New Jersey. Community Activities: Valley Cottage, New York Fire Department (assistant chief and fire surgeon, 1961-66); Nyack Community Ambulance Corps (medical advisory); "Y" Indian Guides; Morris School District Boy Scouts/Cub Scouts (pack committee, instructor of health-related courses). Honors and Awards: New York State Regents Scholarship, 1949; Mead Johnson Fellowship for General Practice Residency Training, 1960; Featured as "Businessman of the Week", *Morristown Daily Record*, January, 1981; Listed in *Who's Who in the East.* Address: 22B Foxwood Drive, Morris Plains, New Jersey 07950.

Fleming, Milo Joseph

Attorney at Law, Municipal Attorney. Personal: Born January 4, 1911; Son of Mr. and Mrs. John E. Fleming (both deceased); Married Lucy Anna Pallissard; Father of Michael Bartlett Russell (Stepson), JoAnn Clemens (Stepdaughter), Elizabeth Charlene Fleming. Education: A.B. 1933, L.L.B. 1936, both from University of Illinois-Urbana; Undertook Post-graduate courses at John Marshall Law School. Military: Participated in the Reserve Officers Training Corp, University of Illinois, 1929-31, Graduating with the Rank of Sergeant. Career: Clerical, Universitv of Illinois Health Service, 1930-36; Attorney at Law and Municipal Attorney.

Organizational Memberships: American Bar Association (chairman, committee on ordinances and administrative regulations, local government section, 1969-72 and 1975-78; member of the council of local government section, 1976-80); Iroquois County Bar Association, State of Illinois (president, 1966-67); University of Illinois Health Service (chief clerk, 1934-36). Community Activities: Iroquios County Universities Bond Issues Campaign (chairman, 1960); Assistant Attorney General of Iraquois County, 1964-69; State of Illinois Employees Group Insurance Advisory Commission, 1975-78; Independent Order of Odd Fellows, State of Illinois (grand master, 1964-65); Odd Fellows Old Folks Home, Mattoon, Illinois (board of trustees, 1966-71); Mason (Shriner); Prepared Eight Municipal Code Books for the following Illinois Municipalities: Watseka, Milford, Martinton, Crescent City, Woodland, Cissna Park, Papineau; New Sewage Disposal Plant, New Industrial Plant of Life Time Doors, New Water Tower for Watseka; New Municipal Gas Plant for Milford; New Water Systems for Martinton and Willington; Assisted in Rebuilding Business Area of Crescent City; New Sewage Disposal Plant at Cissna Park; Developer of Belmont Acres; Belmont Water Company (president, 1976-81); Iroquois County Development Corporation (president, 1961-68). Religion: Methodist. Honors and Awards: First Place in State of Illinois, Examination of League of Nations, 1928; Third Place, United States in Competiton for the Baldwin Prize in the Field of Municipal Government, 1932, 1933; Phi Eta Sigma, 1930; Gregory Scholarship Award, 1932; Meritorious Service Jewel, Grand Encampment of the Independent Order of Odd Fellows, 1980; 1 of 10 Finalists for Dad of the Year, University of Illinios, 1970; International Platform Association, 1980; Life Member, University of Illinios President's Council, University of Illinios Alumni Assciation, International Biographical Association, Iroquois County Historical Association, Danville Consistory; Listed in *Personalities of America, Personalities of the West and Midwest, Dictionary of International Biography, Who's Who in the World, Who's Who in American Law, Who's Who in Finance and Industry, Who's Who in the Midwest.* Address: 120 West Jefferson Avenue, Watseka, Illinois 60970.

Fletcher, Louise Mary

Executive Vice President. Personal: Born May 3, 1926; Daughter of Jakov and Vica; Mother of Jack B. and William J. Education: Attended University of Southern California. Career: Owner, Trojan Shop; Airline Hostess; Buyer, Jeanine's Boutique; Vice President, Fletcher Engineering; Executive Vice President, Eze-Lap Diamond Company. Community Activities: Parent Teacher Association (honorary member); H.V. Juniors; Charity League; Assistance League (board of directors); Los Cabelleros Country Club. Honors and Awards: Woman of the Year, Parent Teacher Association; Listed in *Who's Who in Finance and Industry, Who's Who in the West, Who's Who in Orange County, Who's Who of Women of the World, Who's Who in California.* Address: 15164 Weststate Street, Westminster, California 92683.

Louise M Fletcher

Fletcher, Paul Louie

Executive. Personal: Born April 18, 1930; Son of Mrs. Pearl Fletcher; Married Ying-Lun; Father of James, Raymond, Pearl, Dana, Paul II, England. Education: Degree in Mechanical and Architectural Drawing, McKee Vocational Trade School, 1958. Military: Served in the United States Air Force from 1947-50. Career: Executive Vice-President and Secretary, United Trading and Fletcher Incorporated. Community Activities: Boy Scouts of America (scoutmaster of troop 150, 1950-52); Independence Battalion of Island Cadet Corps (commander, 1955-63); Lions International (district 20-R2 zone 9, blood bank chairman 1973-74, chairman, 1976-77, CARE chairman, 1977-78, cabinet secretary-treasurer 1980-81, extension chairman and deputy district governor 1981-82, district governor 1982-83; New York Chinatown Lions Club president, 1975-76; charter president of New York Chinese-American Lions Club, 1978-80); Soo Yuen Benevolent Association (president, 1977; re-elected president, 1978, 1984); Mei Wah Chinese School (chairman, 1977-78); Mei Wah Day Care Center (chairman, 1977-78). Religion: Chinese Methodist Community Center, Day Care Center and Chinese School, President and Chairman of the Board 1977-78, 1979-80; Chinese United Methodist Church Board of Indigenous Community Developer, President and Chairman 1979 to present; United Methodist Churches National Division of the Board of Global Ministries, National Indigenous Community Developer Policy Committee, 1980-84. Honors and Awards: Lions International, Key Award 1972, Membership Development Award 1973, 1974, 1976-78, 1980, Advancement Key Award 1973, Master Key Award 1974, Presidents Award 1976, 1977, 1980, Melvin Jones Award 1976, Sight Conservation and Work for the Blind 1976, Lions Presentation to Manilla Chinatown Lions 1977, Senior Master Key 1977, Honorary Member Service Award from the Manhattan South Lions Club 1979, Hearing and Speech Medal Award 1980, Extension Awards #1-4 1980-82; March of Dimes, 1960-64; Chinese Methodist Community Center, Presidents Award 1977; Soo Yuen Benevolent Association, Presidents Award 1978; The Manhattan Division of the Council of Churches, New York City, New York, Distinguished Service Award in Community Service 1978; Listed in *Who's Who in Finance and Industry, Personalities of America, Personalities of the East.* Address: 77 Lynhurst Avenue, Staten Island, New York 10305.

Paul L Fletcher

Floyd, John Alex Jr

Horticulturalist and Journalist. Personal: Born February 21, 1948; Son of John A. Floyd, Selma, Alabama. Education: B.S. Ornamental Horticulture, Auburn University, Alabama, 1970; M.S. Horticulture 1972, Ph.D. Plant Physiology/Horticulture 1975, Clemson University, South Carolina. Career: Senior Horticulturist, *Southern Living* Magazine; Horticulturist, Jefferson State Junior College, Birmingham, Alabama, 1975-77; Clemson University, Agricultural Science Assistant 1972-75, Landscape Designer 1970-75. Organizational Memberships: G.W.A.A.; Alabama Nurserymen Association; American Society of Horticultural Science; American Horticultural Society. Community Activities: Birmingham Botanical Gardens (board member). Honors and Awards: Sigma Xi, 1981; Project Director of C.A.U.S.E.; National Science Foundation, 1977; Personality in America Award, 1978; Outstanding Civic and Community Leader in South, 1978; Pi Alpha Xi; Gamma Sigma Delta; Listed in *Outstanding Young Men in America.* Address: 8604 Fourth Avenue South, Birmingham, Alabama 35206.

Flume, Violet Bruce Sigoloff

Gallery Owner. Personal: Daughter of Rufus Otho, (deceased), and Rachel Witt Bruce; Married Samuel Sigoloff, (deceased); 2nd marriage to Lawrence Flume; Mother of Bruce Myron Sigoloff, Nelson Witt Sigoloff. Education: Studied at Huntington University, 1964-65, and Trinity University, 1964-65; Studied with Portrait Artist, David Wilson, 1963-64. Career: Owner, Wonderland Gallery; Owner Sigoloff Gallery. Organizational Memberships: Texas Fine Arts Association; San Antonio Art League; San Antonio River Art Group. Community Acitivities: Parent Teacher Association (vice president, 1965-65, chairman of education for family living, 1964-65). Honors and Awards: Art Judge, Hallmark Contest, 1969; 1st Prize Award in Miniatures, Composers, Authors and Artists of American National Exhibit, New York City, 1965; San Antonio Outstanding Women in Art, *San Antonio Express* and San Antonio Evening News, 1967; Named Today's Women, *San Antonio Light*, 1980. Address: 8410 Tiffany Dr., San Antonio, Texas 78230.

Fly, Anderson B

Executive. Personal: Born November 27, 1923, in Caddo, Oklahoma; Married Celia Patterson, 1947; Father of Two Sons. Education: Graduate of Cotton Center High School, Cotton Center, Texas, 1940; United States Navy Aviation Radio School, Aviation Radar School, Aerial Gunnery School, and Operational Training in Dive Bombers, 1943; B.S. Agriculture with major in Animal Husbandry and minor in Organic Chemistry, Texas Technological College, Lubbock, Texas, 1951; United States Air Force, Technical Instructor Course Number IT57100 completed 1955, Guidance Missile Familiarization Course completed 1956, Curricula Course in Technical Writing completed 1957; Northrop Aircraft, Inc., SM-62 Snark Guided Missile Weapons System, Guidance System Repair Technician, Electronic 31170B completed December 1957. Military: Served in the United States Navy from 1943 to 1945 as a Combat Aircrewman in Dive Bombers and Patrol Bombers; Awarded Two Distinguished Flying Crosses and Two Air Medals as Aviation Radioman 1/c While Serving in the South Pacific. Career: President and General Manager, Hydro-Jet Services Incorporated, Amarillo, Texas 1959 to present, Tuff-N-Lite Incorporated, Amarillo, Texas 1981 to present, Marine Metals Incorporated, Amarillo, Texas 1977 to present; Vice-President, Tuff-N-Lite Incorporated, Amarillo, Texas 1981 to present; Chief Civilian Instructor of Guidance System Electronics Repairman Course on the SM-62 Snark Guided Missile, United States Air Force, 1955-59; Automotive Mechanics Instructor in the Night School Adult Vocational Program, Amarillo Junior College, Amarillo, Texas, 1956-57; Instructor in the Veterans On-Farm Training Program, Dora, New Mexico, State Department of Vocational Education, Las Cruces, New Mexico, 1951-55; Heavy Equipment Operator, Sanders Construction Company, Portales, New Mexico, 1954-55; Derrickman, Motorman, and Roughneck on Deep Oilwell Drilling Rigs, Makin Drilling Company, Hobbs, New Mexico, 1952-54; Instructor in Veterans On-Farm Training Program, Encino, New Mexico, State Department of Vocational Education, State College, New Mexico, 1948-50; Instructor of Farm Mechanics and Welding, Hale County Vocational School, Plainview, Texas, 1948. Organizational Memberships: Society of Mining Engineers of A.I.M.E. (presented paper, "Subsurface Hydraulic Mining though Small Diameter Boreholes", 98th annual meeting, Washington, D.C., February 1969); . Published Works: "Subsurface Hydraulic Mining through Small Diameter Boreholes", Published in *British Hydromechanics Research Association* 1970, *Mining and Minerals Engineering* 1969, *Mining Journal* 1970, Presented at First Conference on the Hydraulic Transport of Solids in Pipes, University of Warwick, Cranfield, Bedford, England, September 1970; Presented Paper, "The Hydro-Jet Mining System", Idea Conference of the 1970 Uranium Symposium sponsored by the New Mexico Institute of Mining and Technology, Socorro, New Mexico, May 1970; "Mining by Water Jet", *The Australian Miner*, 1969; "Hydro-Blast Mining Shoots Ahead", *Mining Engineering*, 1969; *Solids Pipelining Seen Around Corner", Mid-America Oil and Gas Reporter*, 1966; Two United States Patents and One Canadian Patent on Hydro-Jet Bore Hole Mining System; Three United States Patents and One Canadian Patent on Hydro-Torq Pumping Systems; One United States Patent on Subsurface Fluid Control Systems; Other Patents Pending. Honors and Awards: Listed in *Who's Who in the South and Southwest, Personalities of the South; Dictionary of International Biography, Who's Who in Finance and Industry, Notable American of 1978-79, Men of Achievement, International Who's Who of Intellectuals.* Address: Post Office Box 30400, Amarillo, Texas 79120.

Fly, Claude L

Executive. Personal: Born June 23, 1905; Son of A. B. and Josephine Lowery Fly (both deceased); Married Miriam R. Fly; Father of Maurita Ellen Kane, John M. Education: B.S. Agronomy/Soils/Chemistry 1927, M.S. Chemistry and Soils 1928, Oklahoma State University; Ph.D. Chemistry and Soils, Iowa State University, 1931; Postgraduate Studies in Personnel Management and Communications. Military: Served in the Oklahoma National Guard, 1923-25. Career: President, Claude L. Fly and Associates Consultants in Soil and Water Resource Development, 1963 to present; Assistant Administrator and Research Leader, U.S.D.A.-A.R.S.-S.W.C., 1958-63; Chief Agronomist and Head of Land Development, Morrison-Knudsen Company, 1953-58; Soil Scientist, U.S.D.A. Soil Conservation Service, 1935-53; Head of Chemistry and Sciences Department, Panhandle A. & M. College, 1931-35. Organizational Memberships: American Chemical Society (chapter chairman); Soil Conservation Society (chapter president); American Society of Agricultural Consultants (president); American Society of Agricultural Engineers; American Society of Agronomy and Soil Sciences; American Institute of Chemists. Community Activities: Ft. Collins Lions Club (active member; drives for the blind); Republican Party (precinct chairman, 1979; state caucus representative); Salvation Army (donations and Christmas bells ringer); Condominium Association (executive board; rules committee chairman). Religion: Methodist Church, Member and Supporter. Honors and Awards: Honorary Life Member, American Society of Agronomy; Fellow of the Soil Conservation Society; Fellow of the American Institute of Chemists; Distinguished Service Award, Gamma Sigma Delta; Golden Medal of Honor, Sons of the American Revolution; National 4-H Alumni Award; Listed in *Who's Who in the West, World's Who's Who in Business and Commerce, Dictionary of International Biography, Men of Science, Community Leaders and Noteworthy Americans, Book of Honor.* Address: 415 South Howes Street, Fort Collins, Colorado 80521.

Nina Foch

Foch, Nina

Actress, Director, and Educator. Personal: Born in The Netherlands; Daughter of Dirk Fock the younger and Consuelo Flowerton; Married Michael Dewell; Mother of Schuyler Dirk Dewell. Education: Miss Hewitt's Classes; The Lincoln School of Columbia University; Studied Painting at the Arts Students League and the Parsons School of Design; Studied Extensively with Stella Adler. Career: Columbia Pictures, Film Actress in Eighteen Features including *A Song to Remember, I Love a Mystery, My Name is Julia Ross, Escape in the Fog, Johnny O'Clock, The Dark Past, Johnny Allegro,* and *Undercover Man,* Playing Opposite Such Leading Men as William Holden, Glenn Ford, Dick Powell, Lee J. Cobb, and George Raft until 1948; Starred in More than Twenty Features for M.G.M., Paramount, Universal, 20th Century Fox, United Artists and Warner Brothers, Under Directors such as Vincente Minnelli (*An American in Paris),* Cecil B. De Mille (*The Ten Commandments),* Charles Vidor (*A Song to Remember),* Norman Taurog, (*You're Never Too Young),* Phillip Dunn, (*Three Brave Men),* Stanley Kubrick (*Spartacus),* Otto Preminger (*Such Good Friends),* Robert Wise (*Executive Suite),* and Tony Richardson (*Mahogany);* Associate Director, 20th Century Fox's *The Diary of Anne Frank;* Stage Actress, Broadway Productions such as *John Loves Mary, Twelth Night, King Lear;* Stage Actress, American Shakespeare Festival with Eva LeGallienne and Margaret Webster in *An Evening With Will Shakespeare* Fundraiser for Stratford (Connecticut) Theatre; Stage Actress, Stratford (Connecticut) Theatre, with John Houseman, *The Taming of the Shrew, Measure for Measure;* Stage Actress, The Los Angeles Theatre Group at U.C.L.A., Chekhov's *Three Sisters,* Dos Passos' *U.S.A., Brecht on Brecht* and Works by Tennessee Williams, Murray Shisgal and Others; Stage Appearances, Los Angeles, *Shakespeare's Women,* Becket's *Happy Days;* Special Guest of the Company, Seattle Repertory Theatre, Albee's *All Over,* Chekhov's *Seagull;* Television Actress, Several Hundred Plays for All Major Networks; Co-Hostess with Walter Cronkite, C.B.S. News Series, Three Consecutive Seasons; Lecturer at Many Universities; Artist-in-Residence, University of Ohio-Columbus, University of North Carolina-Greensboro, California Institute of Technology-Pasadena; Adjunct Professor, University of Southern California, 1966-68; Senior Faculty, American Film Institute's Center for Advanced Film Studies, 1974-77; Adjunct Professor of Drama, School of Performing Arts of the University of Southern California, 1979-81; Acting Teacher, The Nina Foch Studio. Organizational Memberships: Academy of Motion Picture Arts and Sciences (executive committees for foreign film award and for student film awards; special projects committee); Hollywood Academy of Television Arts and Sciences (former governor). Community Activities: American Cancer

Society (Honorary Crusade Chairman for Los Angeles chapter); The Los Angeles Theatre Group (fund raiser). Honors and Awards: Listed in *Who's Who in America, Who's Who in the World, Who's Who of America Women, Who's Who in the Theatre, Notable Names in The American Theatre, Who's Who in California.* Address: Post Office Box 1884, Beverly Hills, California 90213.

Ford, Lee Ellen

Attorney-at-Law. Personal: Born June 16, 1917; Daughter of Arthur and Geneva Ford. Education: Ph.D., Iowa State College, 1952; J.D., University of Notre Dame Law School, 1972. Career: Attorney in individual practice, Auburn, Indiana; Former Writer, Professor, Auditor, Manpower Economist, Researcher and Editor. Organizational Memberships: American Bar Association; National Association of Women Lawyers; Indiana Bar Association; DeKalb County Bar Association; Association of Trial Lawyers of America, 1972-75. Community Activities: Aide to Governor of Indiana, 1973-75; Member, Board Association of Migrant Opportunity Services, 1975-80; Board Member of Indiana Federal Humane Societies, 1975 to present; Board member of DeKalb County Humane Society, 1974-80; Butler City Planning Commission (board member, 1973-75); Butler City Park Board, 1973-75; C.O.V.O.H., handicapped Indiana, 1975 to present. Religion: Member of Lutheran Church of America (board of Indiana-Kentucky synod, 1976 to present, Indiana council of churches, 1975-80, Indiana inter-religious council on human equality, 1975-80). Published Works: Has published over 1000 volumes of research papers, articles, etc., in the fields of cytogenetics research, dog genetics and breeding, guide dogs for the blind, women's legal rights, animal legal rights, family law, etc. Address: 824 East Seventh Street, Auburn, Indiana 46706.

Lee E Ford

Ford, Ruth VanSickle

Painter and Teacher. Personal: Born August 8, 1897 in Aurora, Illinois; Daughter of Charles and Anna VanSickle (both deceased); Married Albert G. Ford; Mother of Barbara Jane Turner. Education: Graduate of Chicago Academy of Fine Arts; Studied at Art Students League and Privately, with George Bellows, Guy Wiggins, Jonas Lie, and Bruce Crane. Career: President-Director, Chicago Academy of Fine Arts, 1937-60; One-Man Shows, Art Institute of Chicago, Grand Central Galleries of New York City, Mexico City Country Club, Centre d'Art of Port-au-Prince, Haiti. Organizational Memberships: American Watercolour Society, 1954 to present; American Artists Professional League, 1964 to present; Connecticut Academy; Grand Central Galleries; Chicago Painters and Sculptors; Salon of Women Painters; National Association of Women Artists of New York; Philadelphia Water Colour Club; Chicago Society of Artists; Artists Guild of Chicago (honorary member); Palette and Chisel Academy (first woman member). Honors and Awards: Fine Arts Building Prize; Awards, Art Institute of Chicago and Shows in the Vicinity; Connecticut Academy Show; National Association of Women Artists; Bellas Artes Show, Havana, Cuba; Palette and Chisel Academy and Springfield Professional Show; Works Features in Collections of Aurora College, Illinois and Other Civic and Charitable Institutions in Aurora, and in Various Private Collections including that of Henry Fonda; Listed in *Who's Who in American Art, Who's Who of American Women, 2000 Eminent Women, Who's Who in the Midwest, Community Leaders and Noteworthy Americans, Artists U.S.A., World's Who's Who of Women, International Who's Who in Community Service, Dictionary of International Biography.* Address: 69 Central Avenue, Aurora, Illinois 60506.

Ford, William B

Surgeon. Personal: Born May 31, 1917; Son of Mr. and Mrs. N. B. Ford; Married; Father of Three Children. Education: B.S., Purdue University, 1939; M.D., Indiana University, 1943. Military: Served in the United States Navy as Lieutenant J.G., 1943-46, and as Lieutenant S.G., 1946-48. Career: Thoracic and Cardiovascular Surgeon, Director of Thoracic Surgical Division, Shady Side Hospital of Pennsylvania, 1965 to present; Engineer. Community Activities: Pittsburgh Athletic Association (director); Board of Industrial Maintenance Systems of Pittsburgh (director). Honors and Awards: Election to Association of Thoracic Surgeons, 1957; Election to Order of Ahepa, Aristotle Chapter, 1977; Listed in *Who's Who in Pittsburgh, Book of Honor, Who's Who in the East.* Address: 1700 Grandview Avenue, Pittsburgh, Pennsylvania 15211.

Forest, Joseph Gerard

Food Company Executive. Personal: Born October 3, 1914 in Joliette, Quebec, Canada; Son of Joseph Edward and Marie Diana (Croteau) Forest; Married Marie Anita Babin, September 5, 1938; Father of Jacques, Andre, Monique, Robert, Charles. Education: Attended Dale Carnegie School, 1946; Attended Laval University, 1947-48. Career: International Stock Food Corporation, Waverly, New York, Founder, President 1949 to present, Chairman of the Board 1960 to present, Treasurer 1970 to present; Salesman and Assistant Sales Manager, International Stock Food Company Limited, Toronto, 1944-49; Machinist, War Plant, Montreal, Quebec, 1940-44; Owner, Forest and Feeres Electrical Appliances, Joliette, 1935-40. Organizational Memberships: International Stock Food Company, Limited (director); Valley Economic Development Association; American Institute of Management; American Management Association. Community Activities: Knights of Columbus; Elks; Inventor in Field. Religion: Roman Catholic. Address: 303 Chemung Street, Waverly, New York 14892.

Ruth L Forman

Forester, J Darlene

Food and Nutrition Specialist. Personal: Born June 9, 1946; Daughter of D. R. and Geneva Riggs. Education: B.S. with distinction Home Economics (Nutrition), Wayne State University, 1968; M.S. Home Economics (Nutrition) 1971, Ph.D. Animal Science (Nutrition) 1977, University of Kentucky. Career: Assistant Extension Professor and State Extension Specialist in Food and Nutrition, University of Kentucky College of Agriculture; Assistant Professor of Home Economics, Berea College. Organizational Memberships: Kentucky Dietetic Association (president, 1977-78; delegate to A.D.A., 1981-84; registered dietitian). Community Activities: Mt. Maternal Health League Board, 1974-79; Council on Higher Education in Kentucky (disciplinary advisory group, 1979 to present); Phi Upsilon Omicron of the University of Kentucky (advisor for undergraduates, 1981). Honors and Awards: Outstanding Dietitian of the Year for Kentucky, 1981; Borden Undergraduate Nutrition Award, 1968; Phi Upsilon Omicron Home Economics Honor Society, 1970; Phi Kappa Phi, 1977; Fellowship, University of Kentucky, 1978. Address: 3100A High Ridge Drive, Lexington, Kentucky 40502.

Forman, Ruth Love

Elementary School Teacher. Personal: Born August 20, 1938; Daughter of Willie James, and Gertie Lou Pippen; Married Wilbert

James Forman. Education: Graduate of Dunbar High School; B.S., Alabama A. & M. University. Career: Elementary School Teacher. Organizational Memberships: Alabama Education Association; National Education Association; Parent Teacher Association; A.F.T.; J.C.E.A.; National Dunbar Alumni Association. Religion: Member Ebenezer Baptist Church; Narrator, Rev. T. Thornes Ministry, WSMQ Radio. Honors and Awards: 4-H Female Award, 1972; Miss Washington, 1975; Plaque for Outstanding and Dedicated Service, Ebenezer Baptist Church, 1981; Certificate of Membership, American Biographical Institute Research Association; Listed in *Two Thousand Notable Americans, Personalities of the South, Book of Honor.* Address: 3012 Wenonah Circle, Birmingham, Alabama 35211.

Formanek, Luella Helen

Federal Government Employee. Personal: August 11, 1924 in Minneapolis, Minnesota; Daughter of Peter Paul and Mary Ann Stepanek Formanek (deceased). Education: Graduate of Washburn High School; University of Minnesota. Career: Federal Government Employee, Minneapolis, Minnesota, 1967; Traffic Expert, Illinois Central Railroad, Minneapolis, Minnesota, 1957-64; Model, New York, New York, 1946-55. Community Activities: U.S.O. and Semper Fidelis (volunteer, 1943-45); Community Chest, 1945-46; Merry Go Round Gold Ring Club, Greenwich, Connecticut (chairman, 1950-53); Greenwich Hospital (volunteer 1952-54); American Red Cross (volunteer); Multiple Sclerosis (volunteer); Cerebral Palsy (volunteer); Leukemia (volunteer); Muscular Dystrophy (volunteer); Mental Health (volunteer); Junior Woman's Club; Jury Duty; St. Mary Hospital, Minneapolis (auxiliary member, 1963 to present); Organization of Women in Service to Education (volunteer tutor, 1974 to present); National Council of Catholic Women (volunteer tutor, 1974 to present); March of Dimes, 1974 to present; The Catholic Junior League, 1964 to present; Trust Program for the Aged, 1975 to present; American Heart Association, 1974 to present; Kidney Foundation of Upper Midwest, 1978 to present; Epilepsy Foundation; Leukemia, The City of Hope, 1978 to present; Lioness Club. Honors and Awards: Listed in *National Social Directory, Notable Americans of the Bicentennial Era, Community Leaders and Noteworthy Americans, Dictionary of International Biography, World Who's Who of Women, Who's Who of American Women, International Who's Who of Intellectuals, International Register of Profiles, Who's Who in the Midwest, National Register of Prominent Americans and International Notables, Notable Americans, Who's Who in Community Service, Personalities of America, Men and Women of Distinction, Book of Honor, Personalities of America, Personalities of the West and Midwest, Community Leaders of America, Two Thousand Notable Americans, Contemporary Personalities.* Address: 4452 Portland Avenue, Minneapolis, Minnesota 55407.

Luella H Formanek

Forward, Dorothy Elizabeth

Legal Assistant. Personal: Born October 12, 1919; Married Winston W. Forward. Education: Graduate of Medford High School, Medford, Massachusetts, 1937; Attended Los Angeles City College, Pasadena City College, University of California-Los Angeles. Career: Director, California Probate Institutes, 1969 to present; Legal Secretary and Legal Assistant, John M. Podlech, Esq., 1964-79; Office Manager, Winston W. Forward, Insurance Adjusters, 1956-64; Legal Secretary, William W. Waters, Esq., 1953-56; Adv. Office Manager, *American Home* Magazine, New York; Secretary, National Director of Fund Raising, American Red Cross, Washington, D.C. Organizational Memberships: California Association of Legal Secretaries, Inc. (charter parliamentarian, 1982-83); Pasadena Legal Secretaries Association (president, 1976-78); Legal Secretaries Incorporated of California; National Association of Legal Secretaries; Los Angeles County Forum of Legal Secretaries (chairman, 1978-80); National Association of Legal Assistants (charter member). Community Activities: Los Angeles County Forum of Legal Secretaries (education committee in cooperation with the University of California-Los Angeles, basic probate class teacher, 1977-80). Honors: Legal Secretary of the Year Award, 1974, 1975, 1977; Freedom through Education Award, Pasadena Legal Secretaries Association, 1975; Meritorious Personal Service Award, American National Red Cross, World War II; Listed in *Who's Who of American Women.* Address: 903 Alta Vista Avenue, Arcadia, California 91006.

Fowler, Leon Jr

Dentist. Personal: Born April 28, 1943; Son of Leon Fowler Sr. (deceased) and Belle Dunn; Married Kay O.; Father of Roderic Lloyd, Lauren Onell. Education: B.A. Chemistry, Hampton Institute, 1965; D.D.S., Howard University College of Dentistry, 1969. Career: Dentist; Private Practice, General Dentistry, Winston-Salem, North Carolina, 1970-80; Clinical Instructor, Howard University College of Dentistry. Organizational Memberships: National Dental Association, 1974 to present; International Analgesia Society, 1979 to present; North Carolina Dental Society, 1970-76; Academy of General Dentistry, 1973 to present; American Dental Association, 1965 to 1976; Old North State Dental Society, 1970 to present; American Federation of Physicians and Dentists, 1975 to present; American Professional Practice Association, 1969 to present; Forsyth County Dental Society, 1970 to present; Twin City Dental Society, 1970 to present. Community Activities: Sickle Cell Anemia Foundation of Forsyth County (chairman of the board, 1972-80); Salvation Army Boy's Club, Winston-Salem, North Carolina (board of directors, 1974-77); Y.M.C.A., Patterson Avenue, Winston-Salem, North Carolina (century club), 1970-72; Forsyth County Economic Development Corporation (board of directors, 1974-75). Religion: Kyles Temple A.M.E. Church, Durham, North Carolina, Member 1956-65. Honors and Awards: Listed in *Who's Who Among Black Americans, International Who's Who of Intellectuals, Directory of Distinguished Americans, Personalities of America, Community Leaders of America, Book of Honor, International Register of Profiles.* Address: 3101 Poole Road, Raleigh, North Carolina 27610.

Sandra Fowler

Fowler, Sandra Lynn

Poet and Writer. Personal: Born February 4, 1937; Daughter of Mr. and Mrs. Okey O. Fowler. Education: Graduate, Wahama High School, Mason, West Virginia, 1954; Studied poetry with Lilith Lorraine in the early 1960's; Diploma, Palmer Institute of Authorship, 1966. Career: Associate Editor, *Ocarina,* 1978 to present; Contributing Editor, *Ocarina,* 1972-78. Organizational Memberships: Avalon (life member); World Poetry Society (representative-at-large); American Biographical Institute Research Association; Anglo-American Academy (honorary fellow); C.S.S.I. (honorary representative); Leonardo Da Vinci Academy (honorary representative, editorial advisory board); American Biographical Institute (honorary member editorial advisory board). Religion: Protestant Fundamentalist. Honors and Awards: Medal of Honor, C.S.S.I., 1967; Certificate of Merit, Personal Poetry Radio Program, 1967; Certificate of Merit, Leonardo Da Vinci Academy, 1968 and 1971; Represented West Virginia in Poet Laureates Edition of *World Poet,* Madras, 1981; Poet Laureate for the month of May, 1981, C.S.S.I.; Distinguished Service Citation, World Poetry Society, 1981; Awarded a Cultural Doctorate in Literature, World University Roundtable in Corporate Affiliation with World University, 1981; Listed in *The Directory of Distinguished Americans.* Address: West Columbia, West Virginia 25287.

Fox, Judith Ellen

Company Executive. Personal: Born August 2, 1941; Daughter of Murray and Harriette Schneider; Married Jerome Fox; Mother of

Brian Spencer, Jennifer Leslie. Education: Attended Pennsylvania State University, Dean's List, 1959-60. Career: President and Co-Owner, Fox-Huber Temporaries; Manager, Forbes Temporaries; Free-Lance Writer, National Magazines; Co-Owner, J. Fox Photographers; Assistant Personnel Director, Wallachs, Inc.; Assistant Personnel Director, Miles Shoe Company. Organizational Memberships: Virginia Association of Temporary Services (vice-president, 1981 to present); National Association of Temporary Services; Professional Association of Temporary Services; International Platform Association; National Association of Female Executives. Community Activities: Virginia Electric Power Company Customer Advisory Board (chairman); Metro Richmond Chamber of Commerce (chairman, small business council; ex-officio member, board of directors); Governor's Advisory Committee on Small Business, 1982; Metro Young Men's Christian Association (board of directors); Women's Bank (advisory board; women in business committee chairman); Richmond Women's Network (co-founder, 1978); Multiple Sclerosis Society, Central Virginia Chapter (board of directors, 1979); Virginia Gubernatorial Campaign (district chairman, 1977). Honors and Awards: Listed in *Who's Who of American Women, The World's Who's Who of Women.* Address: 5006 Monument Avenue, Richmond, Virginia 23230.

Fox, Lauretta Ewing

Pharmacology Professor (retired). Personal: April 25, 1910; Daughter of Leslie Evans and Mary Ellen McMaster Fox (deceased). Education: B.S magna cum laude, salutatorian, Westminster College, 1931; M.S. 1932, Ph.D. 1934, University of Illinois; Postdoctoral Study, Vanderbilt University School of Medicine, 1945-46. Military: Civilian Teacher, Preparation School for United States Naval Cadets, Northwestern State College. Career: Associate Professor of Pharmacology, College of Medicine, University of Florida, 1966-76; Assistant Associate Professor of Pharmacology, University of Florida College of Pharmacy, 1949-66; Associate Professor and Head of Biological Sciences, University of Cincinnati College of Pharmacy, 1947-49; Associate Professor of Chemistry, Mississippi State College for Women, 1946-47; Assistant Professor of Biological Chemistry, Vanderbilt University School of Medicine, 1945-46; Assistant Associate Professor of Biology, Northwestern State College, Louisiana, 1936-49; Head of Science Department, Dodd College, 1935-36; Professor and Head of Biology Department, Aldercon-Broaddies College, 1934-35. Organizational Memberships: American Association for the Advancement of Science (fellow); American Institute of Chemists; American Nuclear Society; American Pharmacy Association; Phi Sigma; Sigma Xi; Sigma Delta Epsilon; Delta Kappa Gamma; Iota Sigma Pi; Delta Sigma Epsilon; Kappa Epsilon (chapter advisor, 1952-69; grand council, 1958-59); Rho Chi; Retired Faculty of the University of Florida, 1976 to present. Community Activities: American Rose Society. Religion: Elementary Diploma, Pennsylvania State Sabbath School Association, 1926. Publications: More Than 100 Articles in Scientific Journals; Research on Toxicities of Estrogens and Related Anticholesterol Drugs and Toxic Constituents of Plants. Honors and Awards: Pennsylvania State Scholarship, 1927-31; Scholar, University of Illinois, 1931-32; Arthur D. Little Fellow, Vanderbilt University School of Medicine, 1945-46; Rose Test Panel. Address: 1410 Southwest 35 Place, Gainesville, Florida 32608.

Fox, Mary Elizabeth

Mary E Fox

Journalist and Retired Professor. Personal: Born in Williamson County, Texas; Daughter of Mr. and Mrs. J. S. Fox (both deceased). Education: Attended Southwestern University and University of Texas at Austin. Career: Journalist and lecturer; Associate Professor of government, history, English, drama, speech and journalism (served as head of journalism department) and served as Director of Publicity, Southwestern University, 1944-77; Head of Public Relations Bureau in Washington, D.C., 1952-54; During the summer of 1968, assumed position of Dean's Assistant, School of Fine Arts, Southwestern University (retired from education in 1977); Served as Accredited Correspondent to the United Nations since its founding in 1945, and attended numerous sessions of the organization; Frequent speaker on international affairs; Popular book reviewer. Organizational Memberships: Women in Communications, Inc.; Writers and Press Club of England; American Judicature Society; American Association of University Women; American Newspaper Women's Club; Pi Delta Epsilon; Sigma Tau Delta; Sigma Phi Alpha; Delta Omicron; Pi Epsilon Delta; National Collegiate Players; Delta Delta Delta; Mask and Wig Players; Bell County New Media Club; P.E.O. Community Activities: British Horse Society; Texas Historical Society; Stagecoach Country Club; Democratic delegate to county, state and national conventions. Published Works: Working on several projects to be published. Honors and Awards: Listed in *International Who's Who in Public Relations, Who's Who in the United States, National Register of Prominent Americans and International Notables, Dictionary of International Biography, World Who's Who of Women, Who's Who in Texas, Who's Who in Politics,* and others; Member of International Platform Association; Named to the Advisory Board of Marquis Biographical Library Society. Address: Plantation Square #C-3, 2411 South 61st Street, Temple, Texas 76502.

Fox, Paul John

Chiropractic Physician and Dairy Farmer. Personal: August 22, 1945; Son of Dan and Bertie Cheshire; Married Patricia Ann; Father of Paul Jason, Debra Ann, John Matthew, Trisha Ann, Jared Keith. Education: Pre-Medicine, University of Tampa, Florida, 1963-64; Doctorate Degree of Chiropractic, Palmer College of Chiropractic, Davenport, Iowa, 1969; Florida Basic Science Certificate, 1968; License to Practice Chiropractic, Florida State Board of Chiropractic Examiners, 1969. Career: Chiropractic Physician and Dairy Farmer; Owner-Operater, Creamy and Jersey Farms, Gainesville and Grandin, Florida. Organizational Memberships: Dade County Chiropractic Society (director, 1972); Dade County Chiropractic Childrens Clinic (vice-president, 1973); Chiropractic Intensive Day Care Centers (director, 1972-75); Paul J. Fox Day Care, P.A., 1970; Chiropractic Associates, P.A. (president, 1972-73); Pain Correction Clinic, Inc. (president, 1974 to present); Florida Jersey Cattle Club (board director). Community Activities: Kiwanis Club of Kendall, Florida (charter member, 1970; board director, 1971); Florida Chiropractic Association; American Chiropractic Association; Palmer College of Chiropractic Alumni Association; The Florida Club, 1965-69; Parker Chiropractic Research Foundation; American Jersey Cattle Club; Florida Jersey Cattle Club; County 4-H Club (leader). Religion: Southside Baptist Church, Sunday School Teacher Junior-Senior High School Class 1979-80, Church Council 1980. Honors and Awards: District Co-Op Award, Perrine Boys 4-H Club, 1960; Ambassador Award, Palmer College of Chiropractic, Davenport, Iowa, 1977; Award of Dedicated Service, Southside Christian School, Gainesville, Florida, 1978-79; Notable American Award, 1978-79; Personalities of the South Award, 1976-77, 1978-79; Outstanding Jersey Dairy Herd, Florida, 1981; Listed in *Who's Who in the South and Southwest.* Address: State Road 241 North, Gainesville, Florida 32601.

Fox, Pauline

Private Music Teacher. Personal: Born April 8, 1914; Daughter of Frank Adelbert and Della Alexander Butler (both deceased); Married Ray W. Fox. Education: Studied Piano with Mrs. H. O. Pope, 1950-54; Organ Lessons, Mrs. Lularose Wilson; Studied Piano and Accordion Classic Music, Marquette Music Conservatory, 1954-56; Diploma in Violin Studies 1959, Diploma in Choral Conducting 1958, University Exten. Conservatory; Dale Carnegie Course in Public Speaking and Public Relations, 1974; Voice Studies with Norma Steinheimer, West Frankfort, Illinois, 1972-74, Italian Art Songs and German Leider 1974-77; Piano Classic

Repertoire, 1973-75; Art Major, Southern Illinois University, Carbondale, Illinois, 1981; Kachina School of Art, 1981 to present; New York Institute of Photography, New York, 1982 to present. Career: Affiliated Teacher, Sherwood Music School, 1973 to present; Owner-Teacher, Fox Music Studio, 1961. Organizational Memberships: Illinois Associated Band Activities, 1970 to present; Music Teachers National Association, 1969 to present; Illinois State Music Teachers Association, 1966 to present; American College Musicians National Guild of Piano Teachers, 1976 to present; Egyptian Area Group of Piano Teachers (membership chairman, 1968). Community Activities: Business and Professional Women's Club, 1969 to present. Religion: Protestant. Honors and Awards: Albert Malsin Scholarship Award, 1949-50. Address: 323 Smith Avenue, DuQuoin, Illinois 62832.

Fox, Stephen Cary

Medical Researcher. Personal: Born June 3, 1951; Son of Harold and Betty Fox. Education: B.A. 1970, M.D. 1974, Boston University; Residency, Metropolitan Hospital Center, 1974-77. Career: Medical Oncology Research, Working on Targeting Anticancer Agents to the Sites of Cancer Using Carrier Molecules, Increasing the Efficiency of Known Anticancer Drugs. Honors and Awards: Listed in *Who's Who in the East, The International Who's Who of Intellectuals, International Book of Honor.* Address: Charleston Greene House #915, King and Sugartown Road, Malvern, Pennsylvania 19301.

Fox, Vivian Estelle

Education Administrator (retired). Personal: Born January 3, 1914; Daughter of William Augustus Scrutchin (deceased) and Attala Winn Fleming Scrutchin; Married Vilous Bertis Fox. Education: B.A., University of Corpus Christi, 1963; M.A., Texas A. & I. University, 1965; Professional Supervision Certificate, 1965; Professional Elementary Certificate, Southwest Texas State Teachers College, 1934; Professional High School, 1965; Language Learning Disabilities, 1975. Career: Director of Special Education, 7 Years; Public School Teacher, 18 Years; Secretary, Department of Public Safety, 3 Years; Secretary, Corpus Christi Police Department, 3 Years; Office/Credit Manager, Automobile Finance Company, 3 Years; Real Estate Broker, 10 Years. Organizational Memberships: Council for Exceptional Children; Association for Supervision and Curriculum Development; Council of Administrators of Special Education; Association for Children with Learning Disabilities; Texas State Teachers Association; National Education Association; Calallen Chapter of Texas State Teachers Association (vice-president, 1980-81); American Association of University Women; American Association of Retired Persons; Corpus Christi Retired Teachers Association. Community Activities: Order of Eastern Star; Worthy Matron Chapter 354, 1957-58; Past Matron Club. Religion: United Methodist Church; Pianist, Businessmen's Bible Class. Honors and Awards: Retirement Plaque in Appreciation of 25 Years Outstanding Service to the Youth of Texas as a Teacher and Director of Special Education, Calallen Independent Schools District, 1981. Address: Route 3 Box 472, Corpus Christi, Texas 78415.

Pauline Fox

Foxe, Arthur Norman

Doctor of Medicine. Personal: Born June 28, 1902, in New York City, New York; Son of David and Jennie Nash Foxe (both deceased); Married Jane Millicent; Father of Jon. Education: B.S., Townsend Harris Hall, New York City College, 1923; M.D., Jefferson Medical College of the University of Philadelphia, 1927; Expert Figure Skating; Wild Flower Photography of 400 Species. Military: S.X.T.C. at Age 14; R.O.T.C. in College; Served as 1st Lieutenant in the United States Army; University of Ohio Medical Reserve. Career: Attending Psychiatrist, Gracie Square Hospital, 1961 to present; Consultant Psychiatrist, Mary Manning Walsh Home 1956-62, Trinity Chapel Home 1957-62, Mt. Carmel Home 1947-57; Physician, St. Lawrence State Hospital; Psychiatrist and Director of Classification, Great Meadow Prison; Assistant Visiting Physician, Instructor in Neurology, Bellevue Medical College; Intern, Bellevue Hospital; Private Practice, New York City and Glen Falls, New York, 1933 to present. Organizational Memberships: Many Medical Associations and Societies. Community Activities: Florida State Poetry Society. Religion: Episcopal Church, Baptized at Birth. Published Works: Editor of Several Journals in Field of Psychiatry; Published over 325 Articles, Editorials, Book Reviews and Encyclopaedia Chapters in Various Scientific Journals and Other Publications; Three Volumes of Poetry; Book About a Portrait by Gainsborough; *Skating for Everyone*; Psychiatry Books. Honors and Awards: International Poetry Society Fellow; World-Wide Academy of Scholars Fellow; Founder Fellow Medal, International Institute of Community Service, 1976; Medal, National Poetry Day Committee; Medal, American Security Council; Listed in Nearly Thirty Biographical Directories and Encyclopedias, Including *National Cyclopedia of American Biography, Who's Who in New York, American Men of Medicine, Contemporary Authors, Two Thousand Men of Achievement, International Who's Who in Community Service, International Authors and Writers Who's Who.* Address: 9 East 67th Street, New York, New York 10021.

Foxman, Paul

Mental Health Program Director. Personal: Born August 7, 1946; Son of Arun Foxman and Doris Greene; Married Sheryl Anne Melcer. Education: B.A. Psychology, Yale University, 1968; Ph.D. Clinical Psychology, Vanderbilt University, 1974. Military: Conscientious Objector Service in Clinical Psychology, Miami, Florida, 1968-69. Career: Mental Health Program Director, United Counselling Service, Bennington, Vermont; Private Practice in Clinical Psychology, Beverly Hills, California, 1979-80; Clinical Psychologist, St. John's Community Mental Health Center, Santa Monica, California 1974-80, Dade Wallace Community Mental Health Center, Nashville, Tennessee 1972-74, Mt. Zion Hospital Department of Psychiatry, San Francisco, California 1970-71. Organizational Memberships: American Psychological Association; National Register of Health Service Providers in Psychology. Community Activities: Yale University Community Council, 1966-67; Staff Psychologist, St. John's Community Mental Health Center, Santa Monica, California, 1974-80; Staff Psychologist, Dede Wallace Community Mental Health Center, Nashville, Tennessee, 1972-74; Adult and Emergency Service Director, United Counselling Service, Bennington, Vermont, 1980 to present. Honors and Awards: Ranking Scholar 1966, Dean's List 1965, 1966, Cum Laude Honors in Psychology 1968, Yale University; National Institute of Mental Health Fellow, 1970-71; Listed in *Who's Who in the East.* Address: 132 Monument Avenue, Bennington, Vermont 05201.

Franchino, Dorothy Killian

Consultant and Lecturer. Personal: Born August 12, 1921, in Lancaster, Pennsylvania, U.S.A.; Daughter of Howard Garfield Killian and Margaret Williams; Married to Domenic Franchino in 1935; Mother of Dorothy F. Watkins, Anthony Dale, Maryann E. Van Dorn. Education: Attended William Paterson College, Rutgers University, Temple University, University of Miami and Scarborough College in England; Holds M.S., 1960, M.A., 1965, Ed.S., 1970, Eg.A. and Mg.A., 1975. Career: Teacher, 1945-60, Regional Coordinator, 1960-65 and 1965-80, Assistant Professor at William Paterson College (retired in 1980); Teacher for New Jersey

Paterson School System, 1945-60; Teacher, Reading Consultant and Director of Summer Schools, 1960-66; Consultant to day-care and nursery schools; Counseling Psychologist; Learning Disabilities Specialist. Organizational Memberships: New Jersey Reading Association (past president); Psychology, Administration and Supervision Associations; Pi Lambda Theta; International Reading Association. Community Activities: Board of Directors, Wildwood Shores, Hopatcong Board of Education. Published Works: *Using Charts with Language Arts, Welcome Dori, The Development of a Child, Handwriting and You*, plus other books and textbooks; Has published poetry, short stories and professional articles; Authored a documentary on creative writing in Washington, D.C. Honors and Awards: First Woman President of Hopatcong Board of Education; Received yearly awards from the Mayor of Paterson, New Jersey for her work with senior citizens, as a William Paterson College volunteer, and for creative writing on aging; Listed in *Who's Who, International Who's Who of Community Leaders, Men and Women of Distinction, International Who's Who of Intellectuals*. Address: Box 604, Hopatcong, New Jersey, 07843.

Frank, Patricia Anne Collier (Pat)

Legislator. Personal: Born November 12, 1929, Cleveland, Ohio; Daughter of Paul Conrad and Mildred Patricia Roane Collier; Married Richard H. Frank; Mother of Stacy, Hillary, Courtney. Education: Graduate of Rosarian Academy, West Palm Beach, Florida, 1947; B.S.B.A. Finance and Taxation, University of Florida-Gainesville, 1951; Attended Georgetown University School of Law, Washington, D.C., 1951-52. Career: Member of Florida Senate, Two Terms, 1978 to present; Member of Florida House of Representatives, 1976-78; Member, Staff of Congressman John R. Foley, U.S. Capitol, 1959-60; Business Economist, Department of Justice, Anti-Trust Division, Washington, D.C., 1951-53. Organizational Memberships: Florida Senate (education committee chairman; agriculture committee, judiciary-criminal committee, subcommittee B of the appropriations committee, rules committee). Community Activities: Appointee, Office of Member of the Governor's Commission on Secondary Schools, 1981; School Board of Hillsborough County (member, 1972-76; chairman, 1975-76); Florida Phosphate Land Reclamation Study Commission, Appointed by Governor Askew; Southern Regional Education Board; Special Ambassador for the United States to the Independence of St. Vincent's Island, 1979; City of Tampa Election Board; Health and Rehabilitative Services, District VI, Appointed by Governor Askew (advisory council); Tampa Y.M.C.A. (board of directors); Federal Relations Network of National School Board Association, Congressional District #7 (representative); Region VIII Drug Advisory Council; Florida School Boards Association (legislative committee); Georgetown University Alumni Association for Central Florida (secretary-treasurer); Hillsborough County Advisory Council on Aging; Florida Association for Gifted Education (board of directors; state legislative chairman); League of Women Voters (board member); Hillsborough County Council of P.T.A.'s (first vice-president); Hillsborough County Bar Auxiliary (director); St. Andrew's Episcopal Churchwomen (vice-president); Gorrie Elementary P.T.A. (president). Honors and Awards: First Woman Admitted to Georgetown University School of Law, 1951; Hall of Fame, Mortar Board, University of Florida-Gainesville; Valedictorian 1947, Student Body President 1945, Rosarian Academy; Appointment to National Conference of State Legislatures Committee on Education, 1981; Membership in National Advisory Panel for the Advanced Leadership Program Services of the National Conference of State Legislatures, 1981; Participation in United States-Caribbean Legislative Symposium of National Conference of State Legislatures, St. Lucia, 1981; Selection as Member of Advanced Leadership Program Services National Planning Committee, 1981; Selection as Speaker at Joint Meeting of State Higher Education Executive Officers and Council of Chief State School Officers, Colorado Springs, Colorado, 1981; Selection to Participate in First National Invitational Advanced Leadership Program Services Seminar, Co-Sponsored by the Education Commission of the States and the National Conference of State Legislatures, Houston, Texas, 1980; Tiger Award, F.E.A./United-A.F.T., 1977, 1978, 1979, 1981; Athena Award, Women in Communication, 1980; Outstanding Service Award, Florida Council of Handicapped Organizations, 1980; Educator of the Year Award, Kappa Delta Pi, Tampa Chapter, 1979; Florida N.O.W. Award, 1979; Award from Board of County Commissioners of Pasco County for Outstanding Service during 1979 Session of the Florida Legislature; Award from the School Board of Pinellas County for Contributing to Public Education during the 1979 Legislative Session; Community Leadership Award, Mental Health Association of Hillsborough County, 1979; Tampa Jaycee's Good Government Award, 1979; Allen Morris Award, Most Effective First Term Member of the House, 1978; Selection by Colleagues as Most Promising Freshman Legislator of the 1977 Legislative Session; Friends of Education Award, N.E.A.-F.T.P., 1977; Honorary Life Membership in Florida Congress of Parents and Teachers, Awarded by Hillsborough County Council of P.T.A.'s, 1976; Outstanding Service Award, Adult Education, Hillsborough County, 1974; Educational Leadership Award, Hillsborough County C.T.A., 1973; Gorrie School Bell Award; Honorary Member, Delta Kappa Gamma Women Educator's Honor Society. Address: 4141 Bayshore Boulevard, Tampa, Florida 33611.

Loyd D Frazier

Frazier, Loyd Derwood

Administrator. Personal: Born August 12, 1912; Married Marjorie L.; Father of Larry, Robert L., Carla Stewart, Melinda Smith, Connie Doss. Education: Graduate of Corsicana High School, 1930; Fingerprint Identification, American Institute of Applied Science, Chicago, Illinois, 1930; B.S., Oklahoma University, 1934. Career: Administrative Director, Harris County District Attorney's Office, 1972 to present; Chief Deputy, Harris County Sheriff's Office, 1949-72; Instructor of Criminology, University of Houston, 1947; Assistant Superintendent, Bureau of Identification, Houston Police Department, 1940; Druggist, Memorial Hospital, 1936, P.R.B. Drug Company 1935. Organizational Memberships: National District Attorneys Association; Texas District and County Attorneys Association; Texas Police Association International Association for Identification; Texas Division for Association of Identification; Texas Crime Prevention Association; Texas Police Association; Texas State Bar (committee on revision of the penal code); Harris County Mental (board of directors); Houston-Galveston Area Criminal Justice Advisory Committee; Texas Narcotic Association; Pharmaceutical Society. Community Activities: Masonic Lodge; Scottish Rite; York Rite; Order of Demolay; The Royal Order of Scotland; China Grotto; Arabia Temple Shrine (assistant marshal); Houston P.T.A.; Harris County Federal Credit Union (board of directors); Houston Livestock Association (life member); Houston Farm and Ranch Club; Law Enforcement Advisory Committee, College of the Mainland, Texas City, Texas, 1974-76; National Republican Congressional Committee; President Ronald Reagan's Talk Force; Governor Clements of Texas Committee; Harris County Traffic Safety Advisory Committee. Address: 24600 Clay Road, Katy, Texas 77449.

Freeman, Ernest E

Tanner. Personal: Born April 13, 1935; Son of Harvey C. and Cora S. Bressler Freeman; Married Shirley A. Brown; Father of Scott Alan, David Alan. Education: Graduate of Cressona High School, 1952; Continuing Education in Commonwealth of Pennsylvania in Fire-Fighting; Continuing Education in Religious Activities. Military: Served in Company B of the 38th Infantry, 3rd Infantry, Division E-4, of the United States Army, Honorably Discharged; Served in the Army National Guard, 1959-62, Honorably Discharged. Career: Tanner, Garden State Tanning, Inc., and Subsidiaries, 30 Years to Date; Past President and Fire Chief, Assistant Fire Chief, Past Financial Secretary, Summit Station Fire Company #1, Summit Station, Pennsylvania. Community Activities: AGWAY, Inc. (stockholder); Wayne Township Lions Club (charter member with 10 years perfect attendance; past president;

delegate, 2 state conventions). Religion: St. Mark's United Church of Christ; Council, 16 Years; President, 10 Years. Address: Rural Delivery #2 Box 1052, Schuylkill Haven, Pennsylvania 17972.

Freund, E(mma) Frances

Medical Laboratory Supervisor. Personal: Born October 8, 1922; Daughter of Walter Russell and Mabel Loveland Ervin (both deceased); Married Frederic Reinert Freund; Mother of Frances R. F. Taylor, Daphne R. F. Robertson, Fern R. F. Matheny, Frederic R. Education: B.S., Wilson Teachers College, Washington, D.C., 1944; M.S. Biology, Catholic University, Washington, D.C., 1953; Certificate in Management Development, Virginia Commonwealth University, Richmond, Virginia, 1975; Certificate in Electron Microscopy, State University of New York-Paltz, 1977. Career: Supervisor of Histology Laboratory of Surgical Pathology Department, Medical College of Virginia; Clinical Laboratory Technician, Kent and Queen Anne's County Hospital, Chestertown, Maryland, 1949-51; Histologic Technician, Pathology Department, Georgetown University Medical School, Washington, D.C., 1948-49; Technician, Parasitology Laboratory, Zoology Division, United States Department of Agriculture, Beltsville, Maryland, 1945-48. Organizational Memberships: American Society for Medical Technology (representative to scientific assembly, histology section 1977-78, histology and cytology section 1980-82; vice-chairman of histology section, 1981-83); Virginia Society for Medical Technology; Richmond Society of Medical Technologists (corresponding secretary, 1977; chairman of publicity, 1981-82); National Society for Histotechnology (charter member; house of delegates, 1979-82; by-laws committee, 1981-82); Virginia Society of Histology Technicians (charter member; board of directors, 1979-81, 1981-83; by-laws committee, 1975, 1979-81); American Society of Clinical Pathologists (affiliate); American Association for the Advancement of Science; Association for Women in Science. Community Activities: Robert E. Lee Council of Boy Scouts of America (assistant cub scout den leader, 1967-68; den leader, 1968-70). Honors and Awards: Phi Beta Rho, 1940; Kappa Delta Pi, 1944; Phi Lambda Theta, 1946; Helminthological Society of Washington, D.C., 1948; Sigma Xi, 1953; New York Academy of Sciences, 1979; American Biographical Institute Research Association, Life Member Since 1981; Listed in *Who's Who in the South and Southwest, Personalities of the South, The World Who's Who of Women, International Who's Who of Intellectuals.* Address: 1315 Asbury Road, Richmond, Virginia 23229.

Friedman, Alan Warren

Professor of English. Personal: Born June 8, 1939; Son of Mr. and Mrs. Leon Friedman; Father of Eric Lawrence, Scot Bradley, Lorraine Eve. Education: B.A., Queens College, New York, 1961; A.M., New York University, New York City, 1962; Ph.D., University of Rochester, New York, 1966. Career: Professor of English, University of Texas-Austin. Organizational Memberships: American Association of University Professors (University of Texas chapter president, 1980-82); Modern Language Association (member of delegate assembly, 1977-79, 1982-84); Texas Association of College Teachers. Community Activities: Neighborhood Association (founder, first president); Hillel Foundation (board member); Democratic Precinct Convention (chairman; delegate to county and state conventions). Honors and Awards: Senior Fulbright Professor, University of Lancaster, England, 1977-78; National Endowment for the Humanities Fellowship, 1970-71; Elected to Omicron Delta Kappa National Leadership Society; Grants from University of Texas Research Institute. Address: 1908 Stamford Lane, Austin, Texas 78703.

Friedman, Richard N

Lawyer. Personal: Born June 13, 1941; Son of Caroline Shaines (father deceased); Married Catherine H. Friedman; Father of Melissa Danielle. Education: B.A. 1962, J.D. School of Law 1965, University of Miami, Coral Gables, Florida; LL.M. Taxation, Georgetown Law Center, Washington, D.C., 1967. Career: Private Practice Lawyer; Arbitrator, New York Stock Exchange, Inc., 1973 to present; Adjunct Professor of Law, University of Miami School of Law, 1972-76; Feldman and Warner, Attorneys at Law, Washington, D.C., 1966-67; Staff Attorney, S.E.C., Washington, D.C., 1965-66. Organizational Memberships: The Florida Bar, 1965 to present; Unified Bar of District of Columbia, 1966 to present. Community Activities: American Stockholders Association, Inc. (founder-president, 1971-74); Stop Transit Over People, Inc. (founder-president, 1975 to present); Society of University Founders, University of Miami, 1980 to present; President's Club, University of Miami (charter member, 1976 to present); Endowment Committee, University of Miami, 1970 to present. Honors and Awards: Certificates of Merit, Dade County Bar Association, 1972, 1973; Certificates of Appreciation, Opa Locka-Carol City Jaycees 1977, Ponce de Leon Development Association 1976, Kiwanis Breakfast Club of Miami 1977, Kiwanis Club of South Miami 1977, Kiwanis Club of North Miami 1977, Kiwanis Club of Miami-Midtown 1977, The Allapattah Lions Club of Miami 1977, The Bayshore Service Club of Miami Beach 1970, The 100 Club of Dade County 1978, Optimist Club of North Shore 1977, North Dade Chamber of Commerce 1977, The Exchange Club of Miami 1978, The Exchange Club of Miami Lakes 1978, Southwest Miami Jaycees 1978; Honorary Citizen, State of Tennessee, 1970; Richard N. Friedman Week, City of Homestead, Florida, April 1978; Citizen of the Day for South Florida, Citizens Federal Saving and Loan Association and WINZ Radio, 1980; Performance as San Francisco Prosecutor in Film, *Lenny*, 1974 and Featured in Other Television and Theatrical Films; Listed in *Who's Who in the South and Southwest, Who's Who in American Law, Dictionary of International Biography.* Address: 100 North Biscayne Boulevard, Suite 616, Miami, Florida 33132.

Friedman, Ronald Marvin

Research Scientist. Personal: Born April 26, 1930; Son of Joseph and Helen Plotkin Friedman, Brooklyn, New York; Father of Philip Max, Joelle Norma. Education: B.S. Zoology, Columbia University, 1960; M.S. Physiology 1967, Ph.D. Cell Biology 1976, New York University. Career: Scientific Advisor to Royal Area Medical Research Foundation, Inc., 1982 to present; Research Scientist; Coordinator, Medicade Centers, South Bronx, New York. Organizational Memberships: Sigma Xi; American Society of Cell Biologists; Harvey Society; New York Academy of Sciences. Community Activities: Emergency Home Medical Call Survey, Bronx County, New York, 1971-72; Volunteer on Human Nutrition and its Relation to Pathology, Secretary of Agriculture's Office, Washington, D.C., 1970-71. Published Works: "Life Objectives of Dr. Ronald Friedman," a Thesis on the Global Implications of Raising Human Dignity, Submitted to and Accepted by United Nations, Translated and Sent Around the World 1981, Submitted to United States Senate 1981; Encouraged and Publicized Nationally the Fact that the Human Pediatric Neoplasm Neuroblastoma sometimes matures to a Benign State called Ganglioneuroma before the Age of Four, 1973-80; Pioneering Experiments Showing that Neoplastic Disease under Certain Conditions may exist or be induced in all Cellular Forms of Life, 1973-75; Pioneering Efforts Showing that Human Nutrition may have an Important Effect in the Induction of Pathology, 1970-71; Pioneering Efforts Showing the Effect of Internal Trauma to Elastic Arteries with Respect to the Induction of Cerebral Vascular Accidents and Coronary Heart Disease, 1963-66. Honors and Awards: Knights Templar Fellow, 1973-81; National Institute of Health Fellow, 1981; Listed in *Who's Who in the East.* Address: 3210 Arlington Avenue, Riverdale, New York 10463.

Fromme, Arnold

Professor of Music. Personal: Born December 2, 1925; Son of Samuel and Jeanette Fromme (both deceased); Married Catherine M. Thomasian; Father of Gregory A., Vanessa C. Education: Juilliard School of Music, 1942-48; American School of Fontainebleu, 1949; Accecit, Paris Conservatory, 1949-50; B.M., M.M., Manhattan School of Music, 1966-69; Ph.D., New York University, 1980. Military: Served in the United States Army as a Private, 1943-45. Career: Assistant Professor of Music, Jersey City State College; Trombonist and Founder, American Brass Quintet; New York Pro Musica-Sackbut; Principal Trombone, R.C.A. Victor Symphony, Columbia Records Symphony, New York City Ballet Orchestra, Little Orchestra, Esterhazt Orchestra; Trombone Extra, New York Philharmonic. Organizational Memberships: American Musical Institute Society (founder; vice-president, 1971-74); International Trombone Association Research Committee; American Musicological Society; Galoin Society A.F. of M.; American Association of University Professors; M.E.N.C.; College Music Society; National Association of College Wind and Percussion Instructors. Religion: The Unitarian Church in Summit, Music Director, 1979-81. Published Works: Original Musical Work, "3 Studies for Brass Quintet"; Editings of Renaissance Music by Gabrieli, Scheidt, Reiche, East and Others; Articles for Scholarly Journals, Music Education Journals and Popular Music Magazines, such as *M.E.N.C. Research Journal, I.T.A. Journal, Music Journal Magazine, Conn Chord Magazine;* Recor Album Program Notes, Desto Records; Performance on Numerous Record Albums with New York Pro Musica, American Brass Quintet, Igor Stravinsky and Others. Honors and Awards: Diploma, *International Who's Who in Music,* 1976; Martha Baird-Rockefeller Foundation Award as Member of the American Brass Quintet, 1968. Address: 4 Janet Lane, Berkeley Heights, New Jersey 07922.

Frost, Bruce W

Superintendent of Schools. Personal: Born December 4, 1941; Son of Pat and Louveda Frost; Married Nell Frost; Father of Bruce Jr., Kim, Kandi, Kevin. Education: B.S., Arkansas Tech University; M.S., Additional Graduate Work, East Texas State University. Career: Superintendent of Schools, Fourche Valley, Arkansas, Miller Grove High School; Principal, Yantis High School; Coach, Como-Pickton High School. Organizational Memberships: Texas Association of School Administrators; Association of Texas Professional Educators. Community Activities: Parent-Teacher Association (officer); 4-H Leader; Elementary Education Council; Cub Scouts (head). Honors and Awards: Plaque for Work with Cub Scouts, Cub Scout Organization, 1981-82; Listed in *Who's Who Biographical Record of School District Officials, Who's Who in Community Service.* Address: Box 1093, Waxahachie, Texas 75165.

Fuentes, Martha Ayers

Writer. Personal: Born December 21, 1923; Daughter of William Henry and Elizabeth Pearl Dye Ayers (both deceased); Married Manuel Solomon Fuentes. Education: B.A. English, University of South Florida, Tampa, 1969. Career: Writer, 1953 to present; Teacher at Writer's Workshops; Clerk Typist, Bookkeeper, Western Union, Tampa, Florida, 1943-48; Jewelry Sales Clerk, Department Store, Tampa, Florida, 1940-43. Organizational Memberships: Authors Guild; Authors League of America; Dramatists Guild; Society of Children's Book Writers; Southeastern Writers Association (teacher); Florida Library Association; International Women's Writing Guild. Community Activities: All Phases of Theatre Work from Backstage to Acting, Tampa Community Theatre, 1950-60. Religion: Blue Army; Association of the Miraculous Medal; Missionhurst; League of the Miraculous Infant Jesus of Prague; Prayer Affiliation of the Sisters of St. Francis; Shrine of St. Jude Thaddeus. Honors and Awards: George Sergel Drama Award for *Go Stare at the Moon* Full-Length Play, University of Chicago, Illinois, 1969; Scholarship Award, Fiction, University of South Florida, 1966. Address: 102 3rd Street, Belleair Beach, Florida 33535.

Quint E Furr

Fukushima, Barbara Naomi

Certified Public Accountant and Entrepreneur. Personal: Born April 5, 1948 in Honolulu, Hawaii; Daughter of Harry Kazuo and Misayo (Kawasaki) Murakoshi; Married Dennis Hiroshi Fukushima, March 23, 1974; Mother of Dennis Hiroshi. Career: Realtor-Associate, Carol Ball and Associates, Kahului, 1981 to present; Hotel Auditor, Hyatt Regency Maui, Kaanapali, 1980-81; Representative, Equitable Life Assurance Society of the United States, Wailuku, 1980; Realtor-Associate, Stapleton Associates, Kahului, 1980; Franchisee, Audit-Guard (Maui), Wailuku, 1980-81; President, Barbara N. Fukushima C.P.A., Inc., Wailuku, 1979 to present; Secretary/Treasurer, Target Pest Control, Inc., Wailuku, 1979 to present; President, Book Doors, Incorporated, Pukalani, 1977 to present; Partner, D & B International, Pukalani and Wailuku, 1976 to present; Internal Auditor, Accountant, Maui Land and Pineapple Company, Inc., Kahului, 1977-80; Auditor, Haskins and Sells, Kahului, Hawaii, 1974-77; Intern, Coopers and Lybrand, Honolulu, 1974. Organizational Memberships: American Institute of C.P.A.'s; Hawaii Society of C.P.A.'s; National Association of Accountants; American Womens Society of C.P.A.'s; Hawaii Association of Public Accountants; Business and Professional Women's Club. Community Activities: Donation to University of Hawaii Foundation, Harry K. Murakoshi Memorial Scholarship for Cardiology Student of the John A. Burns School of Medicine, 1980. Religion: Aloha Church (Tenrikyo), Waipahu, Hawaii. Honors and Awards: Phi Beta Kappa Book Award, 1969; Phi Kappa Phi Prize, 1970. Address: 200 Aliiolani Street, Pukalani, Hawaii 96788.

Furr, Quint Eugene

Textile Leasing Company Executive. Personal: Born September 21, 1921 in Concord, North Carolina; Son of Walter Luther and Mary Barnhardt Furr; Married Helen Wilson, December 30, 1961; Father of Tiffany Grantham, Quentin, Robert, (Stepfather of:) Pamela Shotwell, Erik Erickson. Education: Belmont Abbey College; B.A. Political Science 1943, Postgraduate Law School 1946-47, University of North Carolina-Chapel Hill. Military: Served in the United States Naval Reserve, World War II and Korean Conflict, attaining the rank of Lieutenant. Career: Vice-President of Corporate Marketing, Textilease Corporation, Beltsville, Maryland, 1967 to present; Regional Manager, Top Value Enterprises, Washington, 1965-67; General Manager, Hogan Rose Advertising, High Point, North Carolina, 1963-65; Regional Manager, J. F. Pritchard Company, Charlotte, North Carolina, 1961-63; National Advertising and Sales Promotion Manager, Western Auto Supply Company, Kansas City, Missouri, 1949-61; Promotion Representative, Sears, Roebuck & Co., Atlanta, Georgia and Greensboro, North Carolina, 1947-49. Organizational Memberships: Sales and Marketing Executives International; Institute of Industrial Laundries (past chairman of marketing committee). Community Activities: American Legion; Veterans of Foreign Wars; Pi Kappa Alpha; Moose Club; Elks. Religion: Roman Catholic. Honors and Awards: Marketing Award, Textile Leasing Industry, 1970-74; Listed in *Who's Who in Advertising, Community Leaders and Noteworthy Americans, Dictionary of International Biography, Notable Americans, Men of Achievement, People Who Matter, International Register of Profiles, Personalities of the South, Who's Who of Intellectuals, Personalities of America, Who's Who in Community Service, Who's Who in the East.* Address: 9232 Three Oaks Drive, Silver Spring, Maryland 20901.

Fye, Rodney Wayne

Property Investor, Redeveloper, and Manager. Personal: Born August 3, 1928; Son of E. T. (Ben) and Pearl Combs Fye. Education: Graduate of Sutherland (Nebraska) High School, 1946; Diploma, Chillicothe (Missouri) Business College, 1948; B.S., Brigham Young University, Utah, 1959; M.A., San Francisco (California) State University, 1964; Secondary Teaching Certificate, University of Utah, 1962. Military: Served as Special Investigator for the United States Army and United State Marine Corps, 1953-56. Career: Vice-President, Pan-American Investments, Inc., United States Virgin Islands, 1980 to present; Vice-President, Casa Loma Properties, Inc., 1979 to present; Owner, Manager, Keycount Properties, San Francisco, 1975-79; Instructor, Reading Dynamics, Northern California, 1967-75; Executive Vice-President, Nu Face of America, Los Angeles, 1970-73; Administrator, Millcreek Terrace Nursing Home, Salt Lake City, 1962-63; Teacher, Granite District High Schools, Salt Lake City, 1960-63; Secretary to President, Hughes Tool Company, Los Angeles, 1958-59; Clerk, Union Pacific Railroad, Company, Utah, 1948-57. Community Activities: Commencement Speaker, San Francisco State University, 1964; Brigham Young University Inter-Organizational Council (president, 1958); San Francisco Safety Council, 1980 to present; Various Academic Review Committees, Cogswell College, San Francisco, 1981-82. Religion: Latter-Day Saints Church, Mission 1949-51, Servicemen's and Korean Branch Coordinator 1954-55, Editor of *Outreach* Publication 1973; State or Regional Officer, San Francisco Special Interest (Adult Singles) Groups, 1972-76; Adult Sunday School Teacher, 1973 to present. Published Works: *Gandy*, Musical Comedy, 1959; *Absinthe and Wormwood*, Dramatization, 1964; Contributor of Articles to Magazines. Honors and Awards: Heber J. Grant Oratorical Award, 1958. Address: Post Office Box 15283, San Francisco, California 94115.

Gabbard, Bessie Flannery

Educator (retired). Personal: Born May 26, 1905; Daughter of Meredith F. and Loucinda F. Gabbard (both deceased). Education: B.S. 1927, B.Ed. 1928, M.Ed. 1945, University of Cincinnati; Graduate Work, University of Chicago. Career: Retired Educator; Lecturer, Board of Governors, Phi Delta Kappa; Faculty Member, University of Cincinnati 1952-65, Ohio State University 1961; Cincinnati Public Schools, Supervisor 1952-65, Principal 1942-52, Teacher 1928-42. Organizational Memberships: National Education Association (life member); National Retired Teachers Association; Ohio Association for Childhood Education (president); Ohio Council for Social Studies (treasurer); Xi Chapter of Delta Kappa Gamma (charter member); Pi Theta (president); Ft. Lauderdale Branch of National League of American Pen Women (president; former vice-president). Community Activities: Story Lady, W.L.W., Cincinnati, Sponsored by Ohio Department of Education, 1929-42; Cincinnati Branch of Y.M.C.A. (secretary); President's Club, Berea College, Kentucky; Mellow-Dears Musical Group (volunteer playing in hospitals in nursing homes). Religion: Coral Ridge Presbyterian Church, Ft. Lauderdale, Florida (Bible Study Teacher, 3 Years). Honors and Awards: First Woman Elected to Phi Delta Kappa with Membership of 90,000 Men at That Time, 1973; Distinguished Service Award for Service to Phi Delta Kappa, Ohio State University, 1975. Address: 26952 North Lewisburg Road, North Lewisburg, Ohio 43060.

Gainer, Ruby Jackson

English and Reading Teacher. Personal: Born March 9, 1915; Daughter of William B. and Lovie Jones Jackson (both deceased); Married to Herbert P.; Mother of James Herbert, Ruby Paulette, Cecil P. Education: Graduate, Parker High School, Birmingham, Alabama; Attended Miles College, Vinesville; B.S., Alabama State University; M.A., Atlanta University; Holds 6 honorary degrees, including a Ph.D. Career: Instructor of English and Reading, Woodham High School, Pensacola, Florida; Former Guidance Counselor, Administrative Dean and Teacher, Jefferson County (Alabama), Santa Rosa, Milton (Florida), Escambia County (Florida), Pensacola, Washington Senior High School, Wedgewood Junior-Senior High School and W.J. Woodham High School. Organizational Memberships: National Education Association; Association of Classroom Teachers (vice president, 1972); Florida Teaching Profession; Escambia Education Association (minority affairs, 1981). Community Activities: Delta Iota Omega chapter of Alpha Kappa Alpha; Basileus, organizer and first president of Pensacola chapter of Top Ladies of Distinction; Appointed to National Parlia-Men Top of T.L.O.D.; Democratic Executive Committee; Alabama State University Alumni Executive Committee; American Association of University Women; Phi Delta Kappa; United Negro College Fund; League of Women Voters; N.A.A.C.P.; S.C.L.C.; Cancer Fund; Heart Fund; Woodham Parent Group; Minority Affairs; Toastmasters International. Religion: Member of Sardis Baptist Church, Birmingham, Alabama; Mt. Zion Baptist Church, Pensacola ("Mrs. Mt. Zion of the Year" 3 times, Soveriety of the Year, 1979). Honors and Awards: Woman of the Year; Pensacola's Top Lady of the Year; Teacher of the Year 3 times; Educator of the Year; Top Teacher-Leader of the Year; Mother of the Year; Distinguished Mother of the Year; Soror of the Year; American Women's Service Awards, A.K.A. Boule, 1976; Honorary Citizen's Award, Dallas, Texas, 1976; Most Progressive Black Woman; Distinguished Service Award, Florida Human Relations Award in Education, Southeast Human Relations Award, Parent Leadership Award, Alpha Kappa Alpha; Received over 469 awards, 1971-81. Address: 1516 West Gadsden Street, Pensacola, Florida 32501.

Ruby J Gainer

Gallagher, Anna Helen

Nursing Consultant. Personal: Born July 6, 1913; Daughter of Filippo and Maria Antonia Giordano (both deceased); Married John Joseph Gallagher. Education: Nursing Diploma, Philadelphia General Hospital, 1939; B.S. 1950, M.S. 1951, Ed.D. 1956, University of Pennsylvania; Visiting Scholar, Columbia University, Summer 1963. Military: Served as Nurse Faculty Member Training Nurses for United States Nurse Cadet Corps, 1942-45. Career: Consultant in Nursing Education/Administration; University of Massachusetts-Amherst, Founder and First Chairman of Continuing Education in Nursing 1975-76, Chairman of Undergraduate Nursing 1974-75; First Dean/Director and Founder of School of Nursing, Lewis University of Lockport, Illinois 1971-74, State University of New York College at Brockport 1967-71, Northeast Louisiana State University at Monroe 1960-67. Organizational Memberships: American Nurses Association; National League for Nursing; Western Regional Council of the State Leagues for Nursing (board of directors, 1958-60); Genesee Valley Regional Planning for Nursing (steering committee, 1968-71). Community Activities: Woman Power Conference (nurse participant, 1957); Will-Grundy-Kankakee County (Illinois) Comprehensive Health Planning Council and Health Services Manpower Committee, 1971-74; Central Shenandoah Health Advisory Council (board of directors, 1977-78); Ivy Twig Branch of Twigs Organization, 1967-71; Altrusa, 1957-60; Pi Lambda Theta; American Association of University Women. Published Works: Author, *Educational Administration in Nursing*, 1965; Co-Author with Dr. John J. Gallagher, "A Phantasy - With References", *American Journal of Nursing*, 1970. Honors and Awards: Listed in *World Who's Who of Women, Who's Who of American Women, Leaders in American Science, Outstanding Educators of America.* Address: 952 Agate Street, San Diego, California 92109.

Galluzzo, Domenick K

Health Administrator and Pediatrician. Personal: Born April 22, 1923 in Italy; Son of Vincent and Maria Teresa Nigro (both deceased); Married Ingrid Maria Karaus. Education: M.D. 1951, Pediatric Residency 1951-53, Specialist in Pediatrics 1953, University of Turin, Italy; Rotating Internship 1953-54, Residency in Medicine 1955, Fordham Hospital, New York, New York; Resident in Child Psychiatry, Willowbrook State School, Staten Island, New York, 1955-56; Intern in Pediatrics 1957, Assistant Resident and Resident in Pediatrics 1959-60, St. Luke's Hospital, New York City, 1957; Postgraduate Course in Comprehensive Medicine, New York University, 1957-58; New York State License to Practice Medicine, 1959; Ohio State License to Practice Medicine, 1960; New Jersey State License to Practice Medicine, 1970; Passed Second Part of National Board Examination as Pre-Requisite for Eligibility to Pediatric Board, 1959; Diploma, American Board of Pediatrics, 1961. Career: Assistant Clinical Professor, Mental Retardation Institute, New York Medical College; Deputy Commissioner of Health and Director of the Office of Quality Assurance, 1979 to present; Deputy Commissioner for Professional Services, 1978; Deputy Commissioner for District Services and Liaison Public Health

Officer for Commissioner's Office with Local Governments, 1976-77; Deputy Commissioner of Health, Westchester County Health Department, White Plains, New York, in charge of Mount Vernon Health District Office and Director of Maternal and Child Health and Family Planning, 1970-75; District Health Director, Westchester County Health Department, White Plains, New York, 1967; Assistant Attending Pediatrician, St. Luke's Hospital, New York City, 1964-67; Private Practice Pediatrician. Organizational Memberships: New York State Medical Association; Westchester County Medical Association; New York State Public Health Association; American Public Health Association; Pan-American Medical Association (diplomate member section of pediatrics); American Academy of Political and Social Science. Community Activities: New York Chapter 3 of District II of American Academy of Pediatrics (committee on children with handicaps); Westchester County Health Department (former chairman of maternal and child health committee); Developmental Service Coordinating Council of Community Mental Health Board (former chairman of health committee); Community Advisory Council of New York City Information and Counselling Program for Sudden Infant Death; Child Health Assurance Program, New York Chapter 3 of American Academy of Pediatrics; American Academy of Political Science (former member); Capitol Hill Club, Washington, D.C. Honors and Awards: Fellow, American Academy of Pediatrics, American College of Preventive Medicine, Royal Society for the Promotion of Health, London, England, International Biographical Centre, Cambridge, England; Listed in *Men of Achievement, Community Leaders of America, Book of Honor, Who's Who in Health Care.* Address: 25 Parkway East, Yonkers, New York 10701.

Ganas, Perry Spiros

Professor of Physics. Personal: Born June 20, 1937 in Australia; Son of Lula Ganas. Education: B.Sc., University of Queensland, Australia, 1961; Ph.D., University of Sydney, Australia, 1968. Career: University of Florida, Visiting Research Professor 1979-80, Summer 1978, Postdoctoral Research Associate Instructor 1968-70; California State University-Los Angeles, Professor of Physics 1982 to present, Associate Professor of Physics 1974-82, Assistant Professor of Physics 1970-74. Organizational Memberships: American Physical Society; American Association of University Professors; Congress of Faculty Associations; Sigma Xi Scientific Research Society. Honors and Awards: Referee, *The Physical Review* and *Physical Review Letters;* Listed in *Who's Who in the West, Personalities of the West and Midwest, Who's Who in Technology Today, International Who's Who of Intellectuals, Men of Achievement, Dictionary of International Biography.* Address: 11790 Radio Drive, Los Angeles, California 90064.

Gannon, Robert

Professor of English. Personal: Born March 5, 1931; Son of John and Dorothy Gannon, Plainfield, New Jersey. Education: Attended Miami University, 4 Years. Military: Served in the United States Army, 1953-55, attaining the rank of Corporal. Career: Associate Professor, Pennsylvania State University Department of English; Contributing Editor, *Popular Science* Magazine; Free-Lance Writer of 8 Books, Hundreds of Articles, 15 Years. Organizational Memberships: Member of Various Career-Related Organizations. Community Activities: High Falls (New York) Civic Association (former president); Sigma Tau Alpha of Miami University (former president); D. & H. Canal Society, Inc., High Falls, New York (co-founder); Hudson River Sloop Association, Clearwater (former member, board of directors). Address: 127 East Curtin Street, Bellefonte, Pennsylvania 16823.

Gantman, Carol A

Clinical Psychologist. Personal: Born April 3, 1949; Daughter of Jack and Sylvia Gantman. Education: B.A. Psychology, B.S. Education, University of Pennsylvania, 1970; M.A. 1972, Ph.D. 1976, Bryn Mawr College. Career: Clinical Psychologist in Private Practice; Consultant, Friends Hospital and ACORN, Philadelphia, Pennsylvania; Director of Internship 1981, Senior Staff Psychologist 1976-80, Friends Hospital, Philadelphia, Pennsylvania; Clinical Assistant Professor, Nahnemann Medical College, Philadelphia, Pennsylvania; Psychological Assistant, Life Guidance Services, Broomall, Pennsylvania. Organizational Memberships: American Psychological Association; American Group Psychotherapy Association; Philadelphia Society of Clinical Psychologists; Human Services Center (board member, 1980-81). Community Activities: Federation of Jewish Agencies (board of trustees, 1980 to present; executive committee of leadership development committee, 1977 to present; vice-chairperson of leadership development committee, 1981-82; chairperson of leadership training program). Honors and Awards: Bryn Mawr College Fellowship, 1972-73; Myer and Rosalie Feinstein Award, Outstanding Young Leader, 1979; Outstanding Person to Watch, *Philadelphia* Magazine, 1981; Listed in *Who's Who of American Women.* Address: 612 Carpenter Lane, Philadelphia, Pennsylvania 19119.

Garcia-Palmieri, Mario R

Physician. Personal: Born August 2, 1927; Son of Rafael Garcia and Mercedes Palmieri (deceased); Father of Maria Mercedes. Education: B.S. magna cum laude, University of Puerto Rico, 1947; M.D., University of Maryland, 1951; Internship, Fajardo District Hospital, 1951-52; Residency in Medicine, Bayamon District Hospital 1952-53, San Patricio V.A. Hospital, 1953-54; Fellowship in Cardiology, National Heart Institute, School of Medicine, University of Puerto Rico, 1954-55; License to Practice Medicine, State of Maryland 1951, Puerto Rico 1953, State of Alabama 1981; Certified as Diplomate in Medical Specialty, American Board of Internal Medicine 1958, American Board of Cardiovascular Disorders 1962. Career: Head of Department of Medicine and Section of Cardiology, University Hospital, 1961 to present; Head of Department of Medicine, Fajardo District Hospital, 1955-56; Visiting Professor in Medicine and Cardiology, University of Alabama-Birmingham School of Medicine, 1981; Professor Ad-Honorem, University of Puerto Rico School of Dentistry, 1975; Department of Medicine of University of Puerto Rico School of Medicine, Lecturer in Cardiovascular Epidemiology for Department of Preventive Medicine and Public Health, Department Head 1968 to present, 1961 to 1966, Chief Section of Cardiology 1961 to present, Professor of Medicine 1961 to present, Associate Professor of Medicine 1958-60, Associate in Medicine 1956-58, Instructor in Medicine Ad-Honorem 1955-56, Assistant in Medicine 1953-54; Consultant to Presbyterian, San Jorge, San Juan City, Auxilio Mutuo, Doctors, Teachers, and San Patricio V.A. Hospitals, San Juan, Puerto Rico; Secretary of Health, Commonwealth of Puerto Rico, 1966-67; President of Board of Directors, Puerto Rico Medical Center, 1976-77. Organizational Memberships: Association of University Cardiologists, 1971 to present; Association of American Physicians, 1971 to present; American Association for the Advancement of Science; Southern Society for Clinical Investigation; Association of Professors of Medicine; American Federation of Tropical Medicine and Hygiene; Association of American Medical Colleges; Puerto Rico Chapter of American Society of Internal Medicine; Section of Internal Medicine of the Puerto Rico Medical Association; Puerto Rico Medical Association; Puerto Rico Society of Cardiology; Puerto Rico Society of Gastroenterology; Section of Cardiology of the Puerto Rico Medical Association; American Public Health Association; Puerto Rico Public Health Association; Society for Epidemiologic Research; Royal Society of Health, 1972 to present; International Epidemiological Association, 1976 to present; Sociedad Mexicana de Cardiologia; Puerto Rico Academy of Arts and Sciences. Published Works: Numerous Articles; Co-author with R. C. Rodriguez, and C. Girod, *The Electrocardiogram and Vectorcardiogram in Congenital Heart Disease*, 1965. Honors and Awards: Fellow, American College of Physicians 1961, American College of Cardiology 1962, Council of Clinical

Cardiology of American Heart Association 1963, Council on Epidemiology of American Heart Association, Royal Society of Health 1972; Alpha Omega Alpha Honorary Medical Fraternity; Governor for 38th Anniversary Congress of Pan-American Medical Association, 1963; Certificate of Merit, Fajardo District Hospital 1965, Puerto Rico Medical Association 1965; Governor of Puerto Rico Chapter of American College of Cardiology, 1966-69; Honorary Citizen, Aguadilla, Puerto Rico, 1967; Latin American Vice-President, Section of Cardiovascular Diseases, P.A.M.A., 1967-70; Certificate of Merit, Puerto Rico Society of Sanitary Engineers, 1968; Recognition Award, Puerto Rico Instutite of the Blind, 1967; Honorary Member, Dominican Society of Cardiology, Dominican Republic, 1969; Distinguished Citizen Award, Adjuntas, Puerto Rico, 1970; Certificate of Distinction, Puerto Rico Hospital Association, 1970; Honorary Member, Alumni Association, University of Puerto Rico School of Medicine, 1973; Recognition Award, Puerto Rico Medical Association, 1972; Associate Member by Invitation, Mexican Society of Cardiology, Mexico, 1977; Gran Premio de Ciencias, Puerto Rico Academy of Arts and Sciences, 1978; Plaque of Recognition, Puerto Rico Medical Association 1978, Puerto Rico Chapter of Cuban Society of Surgery 1979; Distinguished Scholar of School of Medicine, University of Puerto Rico, 1979; Honorary Member, Dominican Medical Society, Dominican Republic, 1980; International Achievement Award, American Heart Association, 1980; President, Inter-American Society of Cardiology, 1980-85; Miembro Correspondiente Extranjero, Argentinian Medical Society, 1980. Address: Box DG, Caparra Heights Station, San Juan, Puerto Rico 00922.

Gardner, Virginia Dickens

Extension Agent. Personal: Born in Marianna, Florida. Education: B.S. Home Economics, Florida Agricultural and Mechanical University, Tallahassee, Florida; Graduate Study at Howard University, Prairie View Agricultural Mechanical College, Tuskegee Institute, Cornell University, University of Florida-Gainesville, University of North Carolina-Greensboro; M.Ed., North Carolina State University, Raleigh; Certificate, Psychology and the Management of Human Resources Course, The Atlanta Region, United States Civil Service Commission; Participation in More Than 450 In-Service Training Programs. Career: Treasurer, The Florida Parent-Child Center, Incorporated; United States Department of Agriculture Federal Extension Service, Science and Education Administration-Extension Agent, Extension Service Agent III in Home Economics, Supervising Agent for Expanded Nutrition Program, Home Economics Extension Agent II, Home Economics Extension Agent I, Assistant County Extension Home Economics Agent, 4-H Club Agent, Assistant Home Demonstration Agent, Negro Home Demonstration Agent, Pinellas, Columbia and Jackson Counties, Largo, Clearwater, Lake City and Marianna, Florida; United States Department of Agriculture Extension Service, Associate Professor of Home Economics, University of Florida-Gainesville. Organizational Memberships: National Negro Home Demonstration Agents Association; Florida State Association of Negro County and Negro Home Demonstration Agents; Florida State Association of Negro Home Demonstration Agents; Florida Home Economics Agents Association; Social, Educational and Recreational Club; The Black Caucus of Univerity Professors; National Association of Extension Home Economists; Florida Home Economics Association; West Coast Home Economics Association; Florida Association of Extension Home Economics Agents; Alpha Delta Chapter of Epsilon Sigma Phi National Honorary Extension Fraternity, Inc.; American Home Economics Association. Community Activities: Beta Sigma Zeta Chapter of Zeta Phi Beta Sorority, Inc. (committee member); Pinellas County Adult Vocational Home Economics (advisory committee); Home Economics Consumer Education Advisory Committee of Pinellas County Public Schools, Clearwater, Florida; Health Committee of Jackson County, Marianna, Florida (chairman); Jackson County Training School Parent-Teachers Association (former secretary); Educational Exhibit Division for Individual, Club and Community Exhibits for Negro Girls, Women, and Community Groups, The Jackson County Fair, Jackson County, Marianna, Florida (former chairman, 7 years); March of Dimes Drive, Pinellas County, Clearwater, Florida (former chairman, 1 year); Neighborhood Organization, Pinellas County (former president, 3 years); County Health Education Council; South Clearwater Organization (guest speaker, citizenship address); Summer Project Program Sponsored by Upper Pinellas Churches and Florida Council on Human Relations (elected representative); American Education Week, Pinellas County, Clearwater, Florida (guest speaker at Williams Elementary School); Upper Pinellas County Council on Human Relations (board of directors, 4 years; advisory committee, 4 years; nominating committee, 1 year); The Leadership Institute (former discussion leader); Conducted Home Improvement Workshop; Dairy Days Contest, Alachua County, Gainesville, Florida (judge, 1 year); State of Florida 4-H Record Review Team (judge, 1 year); Mobile Home All-Electrical Home Award, Tampa, Florida (judge, 1 year); Stress and Time Management in the Home for Health Care Professionals, St. Petersburg Junior College Program (guest instructor); Recreational Project for Youth, Dunedin, Florida (organizer, director). Religion: Mt. Carmel Progressive Missionary Baptist Church, Clearwater, Florida; Women's Day (co-chairman, 2 years; guest speaker, 6 years; chairman, 3 years); Young People's Religious Emphasis Week (co-sponsor, 2 years); Girls' Acteens Group (former advisor, 4 years); Junior Women (former treasurer, 3 years); Committee of Trustees, 3 Years; Class of Median Adults, Sunday School (former teacher, 1 year); Former Church Clerk, 1 Year; Vacation Bible School (instructor, 2 years). Honors and Awards: Letters of Congratulations from Numerous Extension Service Administrators; Distinguished Service Award Plaque for Distinguished Service State and National, Agent of the Year Certificate; Citation for Distinguished Service and Leadership to Florida Agricultural Extension Service, National Negro Home Demonstration Agents Association; Agent of the Year, Citation for Distinguished Service in the Community as Home Demonstration Agent and Leadership in the Flrida Cooperative Extension Service, Florida State Association of Negro Home Demonstration Agents; Plaque and Gift for Dedicated Service as President, National Negro Home Demonstration Agents Association; Listed in *Who's Who of American Women, Dictionary of International Biography*. Address: Post Office Box 15353, St. Petersburg, Florida 22733.

Virginia D Gardner

Garmo, John Charles

Minister, Educator and Musician. Personal: Born June 9, 1947; Son of Mr. and Mrs. Bud Garmo; Married Janice; Father of Byron, Krista, Kara. Education: Diploma, Moody Bible Institute, 1965-68; B.Mus., Biola College, La Mirada, California, 1971; M.A., California State University-Los Angeles, 1974; Ph.D. Candidate, Psychomusicology, University of Washington-Seattle, 1978 to present. Career: Minister, Educator and Musician. Organizational Memberships: American Society of Composers, Authors and Publishers; Lifetime Standard Teaching Credential, California; Ordained Minister of the Baptist General Conference. Community Activities: Contributions to the Public Through Work as Minister, Public School and College Educator, and Touring Music Conductor. Religion: Ordained Minister of the Baptist General Conference. Honors and Awards: California Scholarship Federation (life member; sealbearer); Ephebian Society (life member); National Church Music Fellowship Anthen Contest (winner, 1975); Listed in *The Book of Honor, Dictionary of International Biography, International Who's Who of Intellectuals, Who's Who in the West, Directory of Distinguished Americans, Men of Achievement*. Address: 4047 Soundview Drive, Tacoma, Washington 98466.

Garrett, Carol Ann

Speech/Language Pathologist. Personal: Born June 24, 1940; Daughter of James C. Garrett (deceased) and Hilma H. Garrett. Education: A.A. third honor graduate, Averett College, 1960; B.S. Speech Therapy magna cum laude, Mississippi University for Women, 1962; M.Ed. Speech Pathology, University of Virginia, 1966. Career: Speech/Language Pathologist, Lynchburg Public

Schools 1962 to present, Private Practice 1963 to present; Consultant in Speech and Hearing, Rockbridge County Schools, 1972. Organizational Memberships: American Speech-Language-Hearing Association, 1962 to present; Speech and Hearing Association of Virginia, 1962 to present; American Association of University Women, 1963 to present; Central Virginia Speech-Language-Hearing Association, 1979 to present; Eastern Communication Association, 1963-75; Virginia Education Association, 1962-70; Lynchburg Education Association (member, 1962-70; handbook committee chairman, 1967-68); International Council for Exceptional Children, 1963-68; Lynchburg Chapter of Council for Exceptional Children (member, 1963-68; secretary, 1966-67; publicity chairman, 1967-68); Board of Central Virginia Speech and Hearing Center, Inc. (advisory committee, 1970-74); Lynchburg Public Schools Special Education Advisory Committee, 1975-79. Community Activities: Beta Sigma Phi International Sorority, 1959 to present; Xi Alpha Kappa Chapter of Beta Sigma Phi (member, 1963-77; president, 1965-66, 1968-71; vice-president, 1971-72, 1976-77; recording secretary, 1973-74; treasurer, 1975-76; extension officer, 1967-68; social committee chairman, 1971-72; publicity chairman, 1965-77; service committee chairman, 1972-73; yearbook committee chairman, 1965-66, 1968-71, 1973-75); Lynchburg Beta Sigma Phi City Council (president, 1964-65; vice-president, 1974-75; Founder's Day committee chairman, 1971-72, 1974-75; Mother's Day tea committee chairman, 1970-71; service committee chairman, 1965-66); Welfare Staff Agencies Club (member, 1963-67; treasurer, social committee chairman, 1965-66); Reorganized Speech Therapy Program for Lynchburg Public Schools, 1968; Participated in A.S.H.A. Speech Survey, 1968, 1981. Religion: Court Street United Methodist Church, 1963 to present. Honors and Awards: Lynchburg Beta Sigma Phi Valentine Queen, 1965; Girl of the Year Award, Xi Alpha Kappa, 1969-71, 1973-75; Order of the Rose Degree, Beta Sigma Phi, 1975; Listed in *Outstanding Young Women of America, Community Leaders of America, Personalities of the South, Dictionary of International Biography, Who's Who in Virginia, Community Leaders of Virginia, The World Who's Who of Women, Anglo-American Who's Who, The International Who's Who of Intellectuals, The Directory of Distinguished Americans, Personalities of America.* Address: 723 Custer Drive, Lynchburg, Virginia 24502.

Garrett, James Herschel

Hospital Administrator. Personal: Born November 26, 1943; Son of Helen Garrett; Married Wilda Lee Reeves; Father of Kyle Connell, Kristin Brooke. Education: B.A., Texas Christian University, 1966; M.A., Texas Christian University, Ft. Worth, 1969; M.H.A., Washington University School of Medicine, 1971. Military: Served in the United States Army Medical Service Corps to the rank of Captain, 1966-71. Career: Hospital Administrator; Medical Education Faculty, Washington University; Development Director. Organizational Memberships: American Society for Health Education (training board member); American Hospital Association; American Public Health Association; American Management Association; Texas Hospital Association; Texas Society for Hospital Education (president). Community Activities: Optimist; Rotary; Kiwanis; Lions; Masons (2nd degree); National Exchange. Religion: Presidential Overseas Award, United States Army; Teacher of the Year; Man of the Year, Fort Smith, Arkansas; 10 Outstanding Young Men of Arkansas. Address: 2550 Shirley Avenue, Ft. Worth, Texas 76109.

Carol A Garrett

Garrison, George Carter

Assistant Staff Manager. Personal: Born January 25, 1945; Son of George and Gladys Garrison, Montclair (both deceased); Married Patricia Medley; Father of Renett, George III, D'Vell. Education: B.S. Electrical Engineering, Howard University, 1967; Graduate Study in Computer Science, Moore School of Engineering, University of Pennsylvania, 1969-71; M.A. Education, Seton Hall University, 1974; Postgraduate Courses in Education Administration, Seton Hall University, 1977-79. Career: Assistant Staff Manager, New Jersey Bell Telephone Company; Assistant Professor, Mathematics Department, Seton Hall University; Acting Director and Director of Summer Program, Educational Opportunity Program; Product Engineer, Philco-Ford; Design Engineer, R.C.A.; Systems Equipment Engineer, Western Electric Company. Organizational Memberships: Institute of Electrical and Electronics Engineers, 1964-67. Community Activities: Omicron Chi Chapter of Omega Psi Phi Fraternity, Inc. (vice-basileus, 1978 to present); Committee for Minorities in Engineering of New Jersey Bell (speaker, 1980 to present); Adult Education Advisory Committee of Plainfield, New Jersey, 1975-78; Undergraduate Chapter of Omega Psi Phi Fraternity, Inc., Seton Hall University (advisor, 1974-79); Garrison Memorial Scholarship (administrator, 1978 to present); George Garrison Singers (director, 1975 to present); Garrison Music, Inc. (president, 1981 to present). Religion: Calvary Baptist Church, Plainfield, New Jersey, Board of Trustees Secretary 1976 to present, Organist and Director of Young Adult Choir 1977 to present, Organist and Director of Gospel Choir 1980 to present; Fountain Baptist Church, Summit, New Jersey, Organist and Director of Young Adult Choir 1973 to present; Mount Hermon Baptist Church, Philadelphia, Pennsylvania, Pianist and Director of Voices of Mount Hermon, 1968-72. Published Works: Article Contributor, *Journal of Business*, Seton Hall University, 1975. Honors and Awards: Captain, Howard University Varsity Track Team, 1966; Father of the Year, Calvary Baptist Church Sunday School, 1978; Gurry Huggins Award, 1962; Listed in *Personalities of America, Book of Honor.* Address; 920 Carnegie Avenue, Plainfield, New Jersey 07060.

Garrison, Patricia Medley

Speech Pathologist. Personal: Born October 5, 1944; Daughter of Rev. Thomas S. Medley (deceased) and Cassie R. Medley; Married George C. Garrison; Mother of Renette, George III, D'Vell. Education: Graduate of John Bartram High School, 1962; B.A., Howard University, 1966; Reading Instruction, Temple University, 1967; M.S., Rutgers University, 1978. Career: Speech Pathologist, Co-Adjunct Instructor, Lecturer; Comprehensive English Teacher, 1966-67; Counselor, Y.W.C.A., Washington, D.C., 1966; Counselor, Family and Child Services, Washington, D.E., 1964. Organizational Memberships: Alexander Graham Bell Association for the Deaf Inc., 1981 to present; Orton Society, 1981 to present; National Black Association for Speech, Language and Hearing, 1981 to present. Community Activities: Central Jersey Network of Black Women, 1981 to present; Black Women's Agenda, 1981 to present. Religion: Essential Christianity for Women, 1981 to present; Christian Workshops, Inc., 1979 to present; George Garrison Singers (performer and soloist, Madison Square Garden, television, radio, universities, churches, 1974 to present); Calvary Baptist Church, Member 1973 to present, Woman's Day Captain 1979, Young Adult Choir 1977-79, Junior Church Advisor and Speaker 1980 to present, Gospel Choir 1980. Honors and Awards: Certificate of Clinical Competence in Speech-Language Pathology, 1980 to present; New Jersey Department of Human Services, 1979 to present; Speech Correctionist Consultant for Educational Specialists, Inc., 1979 to present; Evergreen School Parent-Teacher Association Service Awards, 1974-77; Listed in *Book of Honor, Community Leaders of America, Personalities of America, The World Who's Who of Women, Distinguished Americans, Who's Who of American Women, Outstanding Young Women of America.* Address: 920 Carnegie Avenue, Plainfield, New Jersey 07060.

Gary, Gayle Harriet Margaret

Communication Executive. Personal: Born December 23, 1920 in New York, New York; Daughter of Michael H. and Lilian E. Robbins Summers; Married Arthur John Gary, October 28, 1943; Mother of Sandra G. M. Education: Attended University of Miami, 1939; New York University, 1940-43. Career: President, Owner, Gayle Gary Associates Radio and Television Consultants,

1954 to present; Interviewer, Producer of Syndicated Radio Program, *Views and People in the News.* Organizational Memberships: Public Relations Society of America; International Radio and Television Executives Society; National Institute of Social Sciences; Religious Public Relations Society of America; American Women in Radio and Television. Community Activities: New York Infirmary Debutante Cotillion and Christmas Ball (prize committee, patron, activities committee, 1945 to present); Friends of Philharmonic Committee, 1950 to present; United Hospital Fund (fund raising committee for women, 1950 to present); Medico (national advisory committee, 1958 to present); Thrift Shop (board, 1958-84); Parents League (special events member, 1958-64); New York University-Bellevue Medical Center (board member, special social service); Horticultural Society of New York; Churchwomen's League for Patriotic Service (board member, 1970 to present); Navy League; Hubbard Association; Scientologists International; English-Speaking Union; Women's National Republican Club. Religion: St. Bartholomew P. E. Church, Guild President 1954-56, Convocation and Diocesan Officer 1954 to present. Address: 1212 Fifth Avenue, New York City, New York 10029.

Gaudieri, Alexander V J

Director. Personal: Born May 23, 1940; Son of Mr., (deceased), and Mrs. Alexander V. Gaudieri; Married Millicent Hall; Father of Alexandre Barclay Everson. Education: B.A., Ohio State University, 1962; Diplôme, University of Paris, 1962; Undertook further studies at Colgate University; M.B.A., American Graduate School of International Management, 1965; M.A., Institute of Fine Arts, New York University, 1976. Career: International Banking Officer, Marine Midland Bank, New York; Director, Telfair Academy of Arts and Sciences, Inc. Organizational Memberships: Association of Art Museum Directors; American Associations of Museums; British National Trust. Community Activities: Young Concert Artists (vice chairman and board of directors); Harlem School of the Arts (chairman, junior council). Address: 311 West York Street, Savannah, Georgia 31401.

Gavey, James Edward

Real Estate Executive. Personal: Born June 6, 1942; Son of George W. and Clara E. Hanley Gavey; Married Joan E. Moran; Father of Philip W., Peter J., John P. Education: B.A., LeMoyne College, 1964; M.B.A., Columbia University, 1965. Career: Real Estate Executive, 1973 to present; Business Consultant, 1965-73; Certified Public Accountant, 1960-65. Organizational Memberships: American Institute of Certified Public Accountants; International Institute of Valuers; New York State Society of Certified Public Accountants; National Association of Review Appraisers; National Apartment Association; National Association of Home Builders. Community Activities: Community United Fund, Bronxville, New York (chairman, 1970); Tuckahoe Housing Authority, Tuckahoe, New York (commissioner, 1974-76; chairman, 1976-81); Fordham Prep, New York Annual Fund (captain, 1980-81); New York Diocesan Cardinal's Appeal, 1981. Religion: Roman Catholic; St. Joseph's Church, Bronxville, New York; Blessed Sacrament Church, Springfield, New York. Honors and Awards: Outstanding Accounting Achievement, Carrier Corporation, 1964; Community Achievement Proclamation, Tuckahoe, New York, 1981. Address: 98 Park Avenue, Bronxville, New York 10708.

James E Gavey

Gayles, Joseph N Jr

Education Administrator. Personal: Born August 7, 1937; Father of Johnathan Ifeanyi-Chukw, Monica Saliyeka. Education: Graduate of Ullman High School, 1954; A.B. Mathematics and Chemistry summa cum laude, Dillard University, New Orleans, Louisiana, 1958; Ph.D. Chemistry, Brown University, 1963; Career: President, Talladega College, 1977 to present; Morehouse College, Associate Program Director of School of Medicine 1975-77, Program Director of Medical Education Program 1972-75, Health Professions Advisor 1971-77, Tenured Professor of Chemistry 1971-77, Associate Professor of Chemistry 1969-71, Woodrow Wilson Teaching Associate 1963-66; Staff Scientist and Project Director, I.B.M. Research Laboratory, 1966-69; Research Assistant, Brown University, 1961-62; Demographic Statistician, Bureau of the Census, 1957-58. Organizational Memberships: Alpha Phi Alpha, 1956; American Physical Society, 1960 to present; American Chemical Society, 1965 to present; Beta Kappa Chi Scientific Honor Society; The Georgia Conservancy, 1970-75; American Association of Political and Social Scientists, 1970 to present; Society of the Sigma Xi, 1969 to present; Sigma Pi Phi; American Association of University Professors. Community Activities: Project Discovery (volunteer math teacher using "discovery method", 2nd-4th grades of Palo Alto school district, 1965-66); Metropolitan Atlanta Counsel on Alcohol and Drug Abuse (board of directors, 1972-74); Georgia Mental Health Association, 1974-76; Ole Fairburn Village Community Club (president, 1973-77); Talledega County Red Cross (board of directors); Kiwanis International, Talledega, Alabama, 1978 to present. Published Works: Contributor to *Journal of Chemical Physics, Spectrochimica Acta, Applied Physics Letters, I.B.M. Journal of Research and Development, The Sphinx Magazine.* Honors and Awards: Summer European Travel Fellowship, 1965; American Men of Science Award, 1967; Camille and Henry Dreyfus Teacher-Scholar Award, 1970-77; Powers European Travel Fellowship, 1975; Teacher of the Year Award, Morehouse College 1976, Dillard University 1977; Educator of the Year Award, Omega Psi Phi, Birmingham, 1978; Educational Achievement Award, Emancipation Day Committee, Birmingham, 1980; Summer Scholarship, Phillips Acadmey, Andover, 1953; Class Valedictorian, Exchange Club Cup Scholar, Samuel Ullman High School; Full 4-Year Tuition Scholarship, Benjamin Brawley Literature Award, Davage Award for Ranking Male Student 4 Years, Dillard University; Listed in *Who's Who in America.* Address: 702 West Battle Street, Talladega, Alabama 35160.

Gebo, Robert Duane

Numbered Air Force Disaster Preparedness Officer. Personal: Born June 10, 1938; Son of Melvin S. and Iris C. Gebo; Father of David G., Duane M., Kevin L. Education: B.S. Social Science, Portland State College, Oregon, 1963; M.S. Industrial Management, University of North Dakota, Grand Forks, 1972. Career: Numbered Air Force Disaster Preparedness Officer, March Air Force Base, California, 1981 to present; Chief, Disaster Preparedness Division, Whiteman Air Force Base, Missouri, 1979-81; Minot Air Force Base, North Dakota, Chief of Missile Procedures Trainer Branch 1972-79, Wing Standardization Missile Combat Crew Commander 1971-72, Wing Instructor Missile Combat Crew Commander 1967-71; Personnel Officer, Japan 1963-64, Okinawa 1964-66, Roanoke Rapids Air Force Station, North Carolina 1966-67; Plywood Worker, Dwyer Lumber and Plywood Company, Portland, Oregon, 1959-63; Logger, Clackamas Logging Company, Portland, Oregon, 1958-59. Organizational Memberships: Air Force Association, 1967 to present; Sedalia-Pettis County Civil Defense Agency, 1979-81; Air Command and Staff Program (seminar leader, 1978). Community Activities: Boy Scouts of America (Order of the Arrow, 1955 to present; Portland Area Council, assistant scoutmaster of troop 30, 1956-57; Northern Lights Council, pack 435 cubmaster 1974-78, pack 435 WEBELOS den leader 1973-75 and cubmaster 1974-78, cub scout POW WOW chairman of WEBELOS section 1974-75 and of pack administration section 1976-78, advancement chairman and committee member of troops 436 and 431 1974-79, unit commissioner and merit badge counselor 1973-79, Tomahawk District scout roundtable staff 1975-79, assistant scoutmaster of troop leadership development program 1976, board of directors 1976-79, silver beaver selection committee 1977, scout woodbadge staff for north central region 1977-79; Heart of America Council, unit commissioner and merit badge counselor 1979-81, advancement chairman and committee member of troop 401 1979-81, guest

:hairman of eagle scout board of reviews 1979-81, Lone Bear District leadership training chairman 1979-81, training committee 1979-81, assistant scoutmaster of Brownsea II program 1980, chairman of skits and costumes section of cub scout POW WOW staff 1980, Order of the Arrow chapter advisor 1980-81; Far East Council, Japan, scoutmaster of troop 78 1964-65; California Inland Empire Council, advancement chairman and committee member of troop 100 1981 to present, assistant cubmaster of pack 700 1981 to present; National Eagle Scout Association, 1974 to present); Volunteer High School Varsity Football Coach, Okinawa, 1966; Minot Fin and Gill Society, 1970-74; American Red Cross (first aid instructor, 1971-81); Parents without Partners (family activities committee 1976-79); Minot Air Force Base Youth Advisory Council, 1977-79. Religion: Assembly of God Church. Honors and Awards: United States Treasury Department Award, 1965; Tomahawk District Award of Merit Northern Lights Council, Boy Scouts of America, 1975; Silver Beaver Award, Boy Scouts of America, 1976; Air Force Commendation Medal, 1974; Meritorious Service Medal, 1979. Address: 14569 Perham Drive, Sunnymead, California 92388.

Geck, Francis Joseph

Francis J Geck

Interior Designer (retired). Personal: Born December 20, 1900 in Detroit, Michigan; Married Evelyn Marie Sturdyvin. Education: Studied Painting with John P. Wicker, Detroit, Michigan; Diploma, Interior Design, Paris Atelier, France, New York School of Fine and Applied Art (now Parson's School of Design), 1924; M.F.A. Interior Design, Syracuse University, 1946. Career: University of Colorado-Boulder, Professor Emeritus 1969, Visiting Lecturer 1969, Professor, 1930-69; Director of Exhibits, Pioneer Museum, Boulder Colorado, 1958-79; Interiors and Furniture for Fred Fisher's Yacht "Nakhada" and Furniture for Walter O. Brigg's Yacht "Cambriona"; Interior Architect and Designer of 360 Pieces of Furniture for Distinguished Detroiters and 17 Private and Related Offices for the Fisher Brothers in their Fisher Building in Detroit, William Wright Company, Detroit, Michigan, 1927-30; New York School of Fine and Applied Art (Paris Atelier), Director of Research Classes in England During Summers 1926-27, Director of Research Classes in Italy During Winters 1925-26, Instructor of Interior Architecture and Decoration 1925-27, Teaching Fellow in Interior Architecture and Decoration 1924-25; Romantic Architectural Settings as Background for Gloria Swanson, Neada Nauldi, Theda Bara, and Pola Negri, Long Isle Student of Famous Players; Internship, Stage Settings for Jessie Bonstelle's Summer Stock, Detroit, Michigan, 1922. Community Activities: Art Association of Boulder (president 1935-42); Delta Phi Delta National Honorary Art Fraternity (first vice-president, 1948-54; national president, 1954-58); Boulder Historical Society (president, 1948-50, 1952-53, 1970; first vice-president, 1944-46, 1956, 1969-71; trustee, 1944-79; chairman, 1937-44); American Institute of Interior Designers (education associate, 1954-72); Interior Design Educators Council (member, 1963-69; executive committee, 1963-66; emeritus, 1969). Published Works: *Bibliographies of Italian Art* (6 Volumes), 1932-41; *Interior Design and Decoration*, 1967; Honors and Awards: Florida International Art Exhibition Honorable Mention Award, 1952; Invited to Exhibit, Pavilion of American Interiors, New York World's Fair, 1965; Participant in Washington Watercolor Club's 54th Annual Juried Exhibit, Smithsonian Institution, Washington, D.C., 1950; Benedictine Art Award and Certificate of Merit, 1971; Honorary Fellow, American Society of Interior Designers, 1974; Listed in *Who's Who in American Art, America's Young Men, American Catholic Who's Who, American Art Annual, International Blue Book, Directory of American Scholars, An Index of Artists, Who's Who in the Western Hemisphere, Who's Who in the Northwest, Who's Who on the Pacific Coast, Who Knows--and What, Who's Who in the West, Who's Who in American Education, The Blue Book, Who's Who in Colorado, International Directory of Arts, Contemporary Authors, International Who's Who in Art and Antiques, International Scholars Directory, Personalities of the West and Midwest, Dictionary of International Biography, Men of Achievement, International Register of Profiles, Community Leaders of America, International Who's Who in Community Service*. Address: 407 - 16th Street, Boulder, Colorado 80302.

Geise, Harry Fremont

World Traveller and Investor. Personal: Born January 8, 1920; Married Juanita; Father of Gloria, Marian, and Gary, Barry and Harry. Education: Attended University of Chicago, 1938-39; Navy Meteorological Service School, Lakehurst, New Jersey, 1943-44. Military: Served as Staff Sergeant in United States Marine Corps, 1943-45. Career: Meteorologist, 45 Years; Private Consultant, Pioneer in Weather Services, 1937 to present; Television and Radio Meteorologist, Coast to Coast, 1941 to present; Short-and Long-Range Forecasts to Business, Industry, Agriculture and State and Federal Agencies; Numerous Discoveries, Such as Use of Sferics in Severe Storm Forecasting for Ordnance Plants, 1943, and 72-Day Weather Cycle Revealing Major Weather Pattern Chances; Recognized Solar-Earth Weather Relationship, Including Periodic Plains States Drought, 1936, and Specific Earth Pattern Resulting from Solar Activity, 1955. Honors and Awards: California's First Teaching Credential for Eminence in Meteorology, 1964; Discovered Weather Pattern Responsible for Rash-Type Tornado Outbreaks in Nation's Midsection, 1965; Established C.B.S. Weather Center in New York. Address: 566 Rainbow Drive, Napa, California 94558.

Geizer, Robert Charles

Robert C Geizer

Psychotherapist. Personal: Born August 6, 1949; Son of G. J. Geizer. Education: B.A. Psychology/Psychophysiology Research, California State University-Long Beach, 1973; M.A. Clinical-Community Psychology, Chapman College, Orange, California, 1979; J.D. Candidate, Western State University School of Law, Fullerton, California; Ph.D. Coursework, Clinical Psychology, United States International University-San Diego, California. Career: Psychotherapist in Child Abuse and Criminal Behavior, Robert C. Geizer, M.A., M.F.C.C. & Associates, Inc., 1980 to present; Consultant, Hillside Strangler Case-Bianchi Murder Trial, Forensic Evaluation, 1980; Registered Psychological Assistant, Everett S. Jacobson, Ph.D. and Associates 1978 to present, M. David Riggs, Ph.D. 1978-79, William Hartman, Ph.D. 1978; Medical Sales and Hospital Contract Negotiation, Cutter Laboratories, 1978-79; Hospital Medical Sales, Abbott Laboratories, 1974-78; Emergency Paradémic Cardiovascular Technician, Long Beach Community Hospital, 1970-74; Emergency Ambulance Assistant, Goodhew Ambulance Company, 1968-69; Technical Advisor Concurrent with Sales for Motion Picture Property Design. Organizational Memberships: California State Psychology Association, 1979 to present; American Psychology Association, 1979 to present; Public Offender Counselors Association 1979 to present; California State Student Bar Association, 1979 to present; California Association of Marriage Counselors, 1979 to present; American Association of Marriage Counselors. Community Activities: Department of Social Services Child Abuse Treatment Team, 1978-81; Human Services of Orange County Mental Health, 1978; American Personnel Guidance Association, 1979; Public Offender Counselors Association, 1979; Psychiatry and Law Interest Group, University of Southern California School of Medicine; Orange County Supreme Court (domestic law, evaluation referral list, child custody). Religion: Catholic; Speaker on Topics in Parent-Child Relations to Different Men's and Women's Church Organizations. Published Works: Contributor of Articles on Psychopathology of Criminal Behavior, America Personnel Guidance Association, 1979. Honors and Awards: Human Services Award, Orange County Mental Health Services, 1978; Awards for Therapy in Child Abuse, Department of Social Service Child Protection Service; Listed in *Who's Who in the West, Distinguished Americans, Forensic Psychology*. Address: 710 Park Center Drive #43, Santa Ana, California 92705.

Geltz, Charles Gottlieb

Distinguished Professor of Silviculture Emeritus. Personal: Born February 21, 1896; Son of William and Mary D. Geltz (deceased);

Married Mildred Hardy; Father of Jane Keenan, Helen Reiley, Charles G. Jr., Betty Anne Swanson. Education: B.S.F., Pennsylvania State Forest School, 1924; M.S.F., University of California-Berkeley, 1927; Silvicultural Specialist, Duke University, 1940-41. Military: Served with the United States Army, 13th Cavalry, during World War I (1919-20); Served with the Army Cavalry Reserves, 1922-41; Duty during World War II, 1942-46; Served with the Adjutant General's Cavalry Reserve, 1946-56; Retired Major (Life). Career: Assistant-Associate Professor, Director Forestry Summer Camp, Purdue University, 1930-41; Pennsylvania State College, 1929-30; Visiting Professor, Consultant, University of Kentucky, 1967-68; Professor of Silviculture, University of Florida, 1946-66; Retired Emeritus Professor. Organizational Memberships: Society of American Foresters; American Forestry Association; Florida Forest Association (secretary, 1949-63); Florida Forest Council (secretary-treasurer, 1949-66); Audubon Society; Wilderness Society; National Park and Recreation Association; Association of Emeriti. Community Activities: Pennsylvania Department of Forests and Waters (assistant district forester); Alabama Commission of Forestry, 1924-25; New York Forest Ranger School, 1925-26; University of California (graduate research assistant, 1926-27); U.S. Forest Service (junior assistant for silvicultural management, 1927-29); Boy Scouts of America (commissioner for soul and tan center); American Security Council (advisor to the president); U.S. Congressional Advisory Board; Military Order of World War Veterans. Religion: Episcopalian. Honors and Awards: Phi Sigma; Xi Sigma Pi; Phi Kappa Delta; Kappa Delta Pi; Wisdom Award of Honor, Wisdom Society, 1970; Silver Beaver Award, Boy Scouts of America, 1954; Distinguished Professor Silviculture Emeritus, American Association of Emeriti; Commendation Ribbon; Distinguished Service Plaque; 32° Mason and Shriner; Life Member, Retired Officers Association; Awarded the Silver Beaver, Boy Scouts of America; Listed in *International Book of Honor, Directory of Distinguished Americans*. Address: 1521 Northwest 7th Avenue, Gainesville, Florida 32603.

Gerjouich, Michael William

Artist, Painter, Photographer. Personal: Born December 15, 1944; Son of Henry J. Gerjouich (deceased). Education: A.A., York Academy of Art, 1968; Cleveland Institute of Art, 1969-72; Cleveland State University, 1969-72; B.S., University of Delaware, 1973. Military: Served in the United States Coast Guard Reserve as CS/3, 1965-71. Career: Artist, Painter, Photographer; Art Teacher; Commercial Artist Affiliated with Numerous Prestigious Galleries, Museums, Art Centers; Numerous Public and Private Collections. Organizational Memberships: Philadelphia Sketch Club (board of directors, 1981); Council of Delaware Artists (vice-president, 1980). Community Activities: Les Surindependents, Luxembourg Musee; Philadelphia Watercolor Club; International Committee of Raymond Duncan Gallery, Paris; Philadelphia Art Alliance; Society of Marine Painters; Rehoboth Art League; Society of North American Artists; Chester County Art Association; American Society of Artists; Brandywine River Museum; Society of New Jersey Artists. Religion: Catholic. Honors and Awards: Bronze Medal of Honor, Republic of France; Rubens Medal of Honor, Holland; Philadelphia Sketch Club Awards; Numerous Honorable Mentions; Listed in 15 International and National Biographical References. Address: 1420 North Clayton Street #1A, Wilmington, Delaware 19806.

German, Finley LaFayette

Retail Sales. Personal: Born May 30, 1910; Son of John Finley and Malona Eller German; Married Gladys Bell German; Father of John Walker, Anita G. Denius. Education: Graduate of Wilkesboro High School, 1931; Special Courses, University of North Carolina-Chapel Hill; Attended Chrysler Sales Institute. Career: Manufactured Housing; Farm Machinery Retail; North Carolina Deputy Commissioner of Revenue Attached to Field Forces; President, F. L. German Motor Company Inc., Granite Falls, North Carolina, 1946 to present; Owner, Operator, Caldwell Insurance Agency, Granite Falls, North Carolina. Organizational Memberships: Carolina Mobile Home Association (North and South Carolina two-state association president); North Carolina Manufactured Housing Institute (president). Community Activities: Upper Yadkin Valley Citizens Association of North Carolina (former president); Dr. Robert L. Isbell Memorial Foundation, Lenoir, North Carolina (president); Lenoir Kiwanis Club (member, 42 years); Kiwanis International (life member). Religion: Tabernacle Advent Christian Church, Lenoir, North Carolina; Bible Class Teacher, 30 Years; Chairman of Board of Trustees. Address: 104 Auld Farm, Lenoir, North Carolina 28645.

Gershowitz, Sonya Ziporkin

Administrator. Personal: Born July 30, 1940; Daughter of David and Rose Ziporkin (deceased); Mother of Benjamin, Sharon. Education: Graduate of Monticello High School, New York, 1957; R.N. Maryland, Sinai School of Nursing, 1960; A.A. Education, Catonsville Community College, 1972; B.S.N. 1973, Master's in Nursing Administration 1978, University of Maryland. Career: Federal Hill Nursing Center, Owner 1978 to present, Acting Administrator 1980 to present, Administrative Director of Chai Management, 1978 to present; Owner, Lafayette Square Nursing Center, 1976 to present; Greater Pennsylvania Avenue Nursing Home, Owner 1975 to present, Administrator, 1975-76; D.N., Multi-Medical Convalescent and Nursing Center, 1974-75; Consultant to Harper View Nursing Home upon Salmonella Outbreak, 1973; D.N., Mt. Sinai Nursing Home 1968-71, 1973-74, Ashberton Home 1963-64; Evening Supervisor, Happy Hills Convalescent Home, 1963-64; Staff Nurse, Sinai Hospital, 1960-63. Organizational Memberships: President's White House Conference on Aging, 1971; American Nurses Association; Sinai Hospital Nurses Alumni; State Task Force on Nosocomial Infections, 1974 to present; American College of Nursing Home Administrators (member, 1977 to present; education comittee, chairman, president-elect 1978); Labor Market Advisory Committee; The Mayor's Office of Manpower Resourses (advisory committee on nursing home aide/orderly training 1978); Senator Humphrey's Washington Legal Foundatioin, 1980-81; Governor's Conference on Aging, 1980. Community Activities: Appointed by State of Maryland to Department of Health and Mental Hygiene (chairperson of subcommittee on innovation survey procedures dealing with compliance with federal, state and local laws, 1977); South Baltimore Businessmen's Associatoin; Mt. Royal Improvement Association; The League of Maryland Horsemen (board member 1973-75). Honors and Awards: Fellow, American College of Nursing Home Administrators; Honoree, The American Heart Association, 1980; Honor Roll Certificate, National Foundation for Cancer Research, 1980. Address: 2307 Hidden Glen Drive, Owings Mills, Maryland 21117.

Gewirtz, Gerry

Editor and Associate Publisher. Personal: Born December 22, 1920; Daughter of Dr. and Mrs. Max Gewirtz; Married Eugene W. Friedman; Mother of John Henry Friedman, Robert James Friedman. Education: B.A., Vassar, 1941; Graduate Courses, New York University School of Merchandising. Career: *Executive Jeweler* Magazine, Editor-in-Chief and Associate Publisher, Editor and Associate Publisher; Editor, *Jeweler's Forecast;* Fashion Editor, *National Jeweler;* Editor *National Jeweler* "Annual Fashion Guide"; Contributing Editor, *Club Living;* Editor, *Package Store Management* Magazine, *Jewelry* Magazine; Free-Lance Fashion and Gift Editor, *Jeweler's Circular Keystone;* Free-Lance Editor in Promotion Departments of *McCall's* and *Esquire* Magazines; Editor and Publisher, *The Fashionables;* Free-Lance Public Relations and Marketing. Organizational Memberships: The Fashion Group; National Home Fashions League; National Association of Television Arts and Sciences; Overseas Press Club. Community Activities:

Cardinal Cooke's Inner City Scholarship Fund (executive committee); Central Synagogue (board of trustees); Israel Cancer Research Fund (secretary; board of trustees); Women's Auxiliary of Phi Delta Epsilon Medical Fraternity (former president); American Jewish Committee (chairman of jewelry division); Israel Bonds (co-chairman of jewelry division); Women's Task Force (chairperson); U.J.A.-Federation (diamond, jewelry and watch division); Brandeis University (executive committee); Ort (executive committee of jewelry division); Marymount College, Tarrytown, New York (board of directors). Religion: Central Synagogue. Honors and Awards: Graphic Excellence Award for *The Fashionable*, 1971; Human Relations Award, American Jewish Committee, 1976; Woman of the Year, Israel Cancer Research, 1981. Address: 55 East 86th Street, New York, New York 10028.

Geyer, Georgie Anne

Syndicated Columnist, Author, Speaker, Teacher. Personal: Born April 2, 1935; Daughter of Robert and Georgie Hazel Geyer (both deceased). Education: B.S. Journalism/History, Northwestern University, 1956; Fulbright Scholarship, University of Vienna, Austria, 1956-57. Career: Syndicated Columnist, Universal Press Syndicate and *The Washington Star;* Author, Speaker, Teacher; Television Appearances, Semi-Regular on P.B.S. *Washington Week in Review*, B.B.C. Overseas Broadcasts, *Meet the Press, Kup's Show, Panorama* Television Show in Washington, D.C., Regular on Voice of America Press Review, Many Appearances on *William Buckley's Firing Line;* Syndicated Columnist, *Los Angeles Times* Syndicate, 1975-80; *Chicago Daily News*, Foreign Correspondent 1964-75, General Assignment Reporter, 1960-64. Organizational Memberships: International Institute for Strategic Studies, London; Women in Communications; Sigma Delta Chi; The Women's Institute for Freedom of the Press. Community Activities: Lyle Spencer Professor of Journalism, Newhouse School of Communications, Syracuse University, 1977; Courses by Newspaper Project, University of California, Sponsored by National Endowment for the Humanities (national board member); John J. Fitzpatrick Lecturer, University of Utah, 1977; Chicago Council on Foreign Relations (board member, 1972-75); Conferences at Army, Navy and Air War Colleges; American Enterprise Institute Latin America Group; Aspen Institute's Latin American Governance Project (steering committee); Lecturer on Press Ethics, Foreign Service Institute Executive Seminar; International Communications Agency Speaking Tour of Africa on Press Problems and Ethics, 1979; Commencement Speaker at Rosary College, River Forest, Illinois, 1978; Speaker to Groups such as Chicago Committee of Chicago Council on Foreign Relations, Finnish-American Chamber of Commerce in Helsinki, Finland, National Journalism Education Association, American Supply Corporation, Bank Administrators Convention, International Seminar at Lewis and Clark College, Institute for International Education in Denver, Colorado. Published Works: *The New Latins*, 1970; *The New 100 Years' War*, 1972; *The Young Russians*, 1976; *Buying the Night Flight* (Autobiography), 1983; Contributor to *The Saturday Review, The Atlantic, The New Republic, The Progressive, Look, The Nation, Playgirl, Ladies Home Hournal, Encyclopedia Britannica, People, Signature.* Honors and Awards: Chicago Newspaper Guild Prize for Best Human Interest Story for Masquerading as a Waitress at a Mafia Wedding, 1962; Overseas Press Club Latin America Award for Series on Living in the Mountain in Guatemala with Guerrillas and for Exclusive Interviews with Fidel Castro, 1967; National Council of Jewish Women's Hannah Solomon Award for Public Service, 1971; Maria Moors Cabot Award for Improving Relations Within the Hemisphere, 1971; *Who's Who of American Women* Award for Outstanding Woman Journalist in the Country, 1971; One of Four Outstanding Women Journalists in the Country, *Newsweek Magazine*, 1967; Illinois State Merit Award, 1975; Northwestern University Merit Award, 1968; Honorary Degree of Doctor of Letters, Lake Forest College, Illinois, 1980; Mortar Board. Address: 800 - 25th Street Northwest, Washington, D.C. 20037.

Gibson, Curtis A

Curtis A Gibson

Aircraft Systems Engineer. Personal: Born November 5, 1929 in Springfield, Ohio. Education: C.H.E., University of Cincinnati, 1952; Ph.D. Religion, Universal Life Church, Modesto, California, 1979. Career: United States Air Force, Wright-Patterson Air Force Base, Ohio, Aircraft Systems Engineer 1979 to present, Life Support Systems Engineer 1970 to 1979, Mechanical Engineer 1959-70, Chemical Engineer 1956-59; Chemical Engineer, Sylvania Electric Products, Emporium, Pennsylvania, 1952-54. Organizational Memberships: American Defense Preparedness Association; International Academy of Professional Business Executives; Air Force Association. Community Activities: Boy Scouts of America (scout leader). Honors and Awards: Silver Beaver Award, Boy Scouts of America, 1973; Honorary D.D. Degree for Religious Studies, Universal Life Church, Modesto, California, 1979. Address: 2806 Oxford Drive, Springfield, Ohio 45506.

Gibson, Weldon Bailey

Executive. Personal: Born April 23, 1917 in Eldorado, Texas; Married Helen Mears; Father of David Mears. Education: A.B., Washington State University, 1938; M.B.A. 1940, Ph.D. 1950, Stanford University. Military: Served in the United States Air Force as Director of Materiel Requirements During World War II, Discharged with Rank of Colonel. Career: S.R.I. International, Senior Director 1982 to present, Executive Vice-President 1960-82, Member of Board of Directors, Vice-President 1959-60, Associate Director 1955-59, Director of Economics Research 1947-55; Assistant Director, United States Air Force Institute of Technology, Dayton, Ohio, 1946-47; Employee, Burroughs Corporation, San Francisco, California, 1940-41. Organizational Memberships: American Economic Association; Society for International Development. Community Activities: Plantronics Inc. (director); The Valley National Bank, Arizona (director); The Vendo Company (director); Technical Equities Corporation, Inc. (director); Acmil Limited, Australia (director); Group 800 N.V., The Netherlands (director); Callog Limited, England (director). Published Works: Author and Co-Author of Several Books and Other Publications in Fields of Economic Geography and International Economic Affairs; *S.R.I. - The Founding Years*, 1980. Honors and Awards: International Associate of the Hoover Institution, Stanford University; Medal of the Legion of Merit, 1946; Order of Commander of the British Empire, 1947. Address: 593 Gerona Road, Stanford, California 94305.

Gieck, Joe Howard

Physical Therapist. Personal: Born December 15, 1938 in Hollis, Oklahoma; Married Sally; Father of Betsy, Katherine. Education: Graduate of Altus High School, Oklahoma, 1957; B.S. Physical Therapy, University of Oklahoma, 1961; M.Ed. Physical Education 1965, Ed.D. Counselor Education 1975, University of Virginia; Registered Physical Therapist; Certified Athletic Trainer D3-12. Career: Trainer, Virginia All-Star Baseball Team 1976, United States Olympic Basketball Development Camp 1971, United States Pan-American Games 1971; N.C.A.A., All-Star Lacrosse Trainer 1976, 1963, Host Trainer 1977 Finals; Physical Therapist, University of Virginia Student Health 1962 to present, Private Practice 1961 to present; Physical Fitness Consultant, Federal Executive Institute; University of Virginia, Head Trainer 1962 to present, Assistant Professor in School of Education, Director of Athletic Training Master's Program, Director of Adapted Service Education Program, Service in Physical Education; Assistant Trainer, United States Military Academy-West Point, New York, 1961-62; University of Oklahoma, Clinical Instructor in Physical Therapy Department, Student Trainer 1957-61. Organizational Memberships: National Athletic Trainers Association (district secretary-treasurer, 1966-68; board of directors, 1968-73; chairman, 1969-70; 25-year awards committee, 1968-70; certification committee, 1974 to present; editorial board of *N.A.T.A. Journal* 1976 to present; liaison to American Orthopaedic Society of Sports Medicine, 1979 to present); American College of Sports Medicine; American Physical Therapy Association; Virginia and Oklahoma Physical Therapy Associations; Phi Delta Kappa Honorary Education Society; American Association of University Professors; American Orthopaedic Society for Sports Medicine; American Personnel and Guidance Association; Virginia Athletic Trainers Association (president, 1981-83). Community Activities: Virginia Athletic Training and Licensing Bill (coordinator). Published Works: Contributor to *Scholastic Coach, Coach and Athlete, Athletic Journal, National Athletic Trainers Journal, Encyclopedia of Sports Sciences and Medicine, Journal of American Physical Therapy Association, Journal of Bone and Joint Surgery, International Surgery, Medical Tribune and Medical News, Athletic Training, American Physical Therapy Association Sportsmedicine Newsletter, Track and Field News, American Journal of Sports Medicine*; Contributing Editor, *Modern Athletic Training.* Honors and Awards: Distinguished Service Award, Virginia High School Coaches Association, 1976; Personalities of the South Award, 1978-79; College Athletic Trainer of 1979, National Athletic Trainers Association; National Distinguished Service Award, National High School Athletic Coaches Association, 1980; Certificate of Appreciation in Sports Medicine, Medical Society of Virginia, 1979; Listed in *Who's Who in the South and Southwest.* Address: Wentworth Farm, Route 9 Box 238, Charlottesville, Virginia 22901.

Gilbert, Robert Frank

United States Army Surgeon. Personal: Born July 19, 1935; Son of Frank and Eleanor H. Marshall Gilbert; Married Ihn Jae Byun; Father of Evelyn, Aimee, Andrew, Terence, Diane, Catherine, Elizabeth. Education: B.A., Miami University, 1957; M.D., Ohio State University of Medicine, 1962. Military: Served in United States Army Medical Corps, 1969 to present, with rank of Colonel; Served as Army Surgeon in Korea, 1969-71 and 1972-74; Served as Surgical Advisor, A.R.V.N. Airborne Division in Viet Nam 1971-72 and Senior Medical Advisor, M.R. IV Republic of Viet Nam 1972. Career: Medical Doctor, General Surgeon, United States Army. Professional Memberships: American Board of Surgery (diplomate); American College of Surgeons (fellow). Community Activities: Volunteer Physicians for Viet Nam, 1967. Honors and Awards: Military Decorations including Legion of Merit, Bronze Star. Address: 982 Sycamore Avenue, Tinton Falls, New Jersey 07724.

Gilde, Louis Charles Jr

Executive. Personal: Born March 23, 1924; Son of Louis Charles and Therese May Gilde, (both deceased); Married Patricia Ann Gilde; Father of Lisa, Mark, Patty, Susan, Troy, Sam. Education: B.S., Rutgers University, 1950. Military: Served with the United States Army, 1943-45. Career: Director of Environmental Programs, Campbell Soup Company, 1970 to present; Vice President and Member of the Board of Directors, Technological Resources Inc., subsidiary of Campbell Soup Company, 1978 to present. Organizational Memberships: National Environmental Development Association (director 1974 to present); National Food Processors Association (chairman environmental research committee 1968-74); American Frozen Food Institute; N.A.M. (chairman water task committee 1975-79); Water Pollution Control Federation; American Water Works Association; Academy of Natural Sciences, Philadelphia. Community Activities: National Technical Task Committee on Industrial Waste, 1960-64; National Industrial Pollution Control Council, U.S. Department of Commerce, 1970-72; Camden City Environmental Commission (commissioner and vice chairman 1977 to present). Religion: Lutheran; Past Vice President Martin Luther Chapel, Pennsauken, New Jersey. Published Works: Author of chapters in four environmental engineering handbooks and over 35 publications. Honors and Awards: Designer, Waste Treatment System that received National Gold Medal Award of Sports Foundation, 1970; Industrial Development Research Council Award for Distinguished Service in Environmental Planning, 1979; E.P.A. Certificate of Appreciation for Efforts to Improve the Environment, 1979. Address: P.O. Box 436, Haddonfield, New Jersey 08033.

Robert F Gilbert

Gilman, Benjamin A

United States Congressman. Personal: Born December 6, 1922; Father of Jonathan, Harison, David, Susan. Education: Graduate of Middletown High School, 1941; B.S., Wharton School of Business and Finance, University of Pennsylvania, 1946; LL.B., New York Law School, 1950. Military: Served in the United States Air Force during World War II as a Staff Sergeant in the 19th Bomb Group of the 20th Air Force; Flew 35 Missions over Japan, Earning the Distingiushed Flying Cross and the Air Medal. Career: Congressman, United States House of Representatives, Five Terms, 1973 to present; Assemblyman, New York State Assembly, 1967-72; Advisory Committee of the New York State Youth Division's Start Center in Middletown, 1962-67; Counsel to Assemblyman Wilson VanDuzer's Committee on Local Finance, New York State Legislature, 1956-67; Attorney, New York State Temporary Commission on the Courts, 1955-57; New York State Department of Law, 1953-55. Professional Memberships: United States House of Representatives (house foreign affairs committee; post office and civil service committee; select committee on missing in action; select committee on narcotics and drug abuse; congressional representative, United Nations law of the sea conference; delegate, United States Mexican Inter-Parliamentary Conference; congressional energy task force; presidential commission on world hunger; ad-hoc committee on Irish affairs; Republican task force on the handicapped; United States Mexico consultative mechanism sub-committee on narcotics trafficking; board of visitors of United States Military Academy); United Nations General Assembly 36th Session (member, United States delegation); International Narcotic Enforcement Officers Association; Middletown, Orange County, New York State and American Bar Associations; Association of the Bar of the City of New York; Washington D.C. Bar; American Trial Lawyers Association. Community Activities: Columbia University's Advisory Council of the Lamont-Doherty Geological Observatory, 1979-82; 11th Special Session of the United Nations (congressional delegate); Federal Correctional Institute (Otisville board of visitors); Middletown Little League (former board chairman); Orange County Mental Health Association (past vice-president); Goldenarea Hospital Funds (former member of the board of directors); Orange County Heart Association (former member of the board of directors); Temple Sinai; Veterans of Foreign Wars Post #692 (County and Post Commander); Masonic War Veterans Beth El Post #29 (Lieutenant Commander); American Legion Post #151; Jewish War Veterans of Monroe, B.P.O.E. #1097; Orange County Republican Committee; Hoffman Lodge #523; F. & A.M.; A.A.O.N.M.S. of Cyprus Temple; Capitol Hill Shrine Club (president); Zeta Beta Tau Fraternity; Otisvile Grange; Hudson-Delaware Boy Scout Council (honorary vice-president); New York Society in Washington (president); Air Force Association; Civil Air Patrol (lieutenant colonel, congressional branch); La Societe des 40 Hommes et 8 Chevaux. Honors and Awards: Medal of Merit for Administering to the Needs of Veterans, United States Veterans of Foreign Wars, 1972; Man of the Year Award, Citizens for Clean Government, 1976; Award for Outstanding Loyalty and Contribution to the Field, International Narcotic Enforcement Officers Association, 1976; Leadership Award, American Security Council, 1977; Honorary Degree of Doctor of Laws, St. Thomas Aquinas College, 1977; Distinguished Service Award, Marine Corps League, 1977; Certificate of Appreciation, President's Committee on Mental Retardation, 1977; King of Hearts Award for Service, Orange and Rockland Division of the American Heart Association, 1978; Dean's Medal for Contributions to the Profession and the Nation, New York Law School Alumni Association, 1979; Humanitarian Award, Lt. Walter Lipman Post #756, Jewish War Veterans and Ladies Auxiliary, 1979; Certificate of Honorary Apprenticeship in Appreciation and Recognition of Services Unselfishly Rendered, Carpenters Joint Apprentice Ship Committee of Rockland and Orange Counties, Local 964; Admission to Washington

D.C. Bar, 1979; Award of Appreciation for Service to the Families of Americans Missing in Action, National League of Families of American Prisoners and Missing in Southeast Asia, 1979; The Cardinal Aloysius Stepinac Justice Award, American Friends of Croatia, 1979; Anatoly Scharansky Humanitarian Award, Rockland County Committee for Soviet Jewry, 1979; Man of the Year, Builders Association of the Hudson Valley, Inc., 1979; Distinguished Service Award, Administrative Law Judges of the Department of Health and Human Services, 1980; Honorary Warden, Noraman A. Carlson, Director of Federal Prison System, 1980; Patriot of the Year, Department of New York Reserve Officers Association of the United States; Distinguished Service Award, Yeshiva University, 1981; Humanitarian Award, RAV TOV International Jewish Rescue Organization, 1981. Address: 16 Orchard Street, Middletown, New York 10940.

Girard, Charles Martin

Federal Administrator. Personal: Born February 3, 1943; Son of Charles and Meta Girard; Married Roberta Carole Jeorse; Father of Charles John. Education: B.A. Political Science, Economics and Business, Park College, Parkville, Missouri, 1965; Master of Governmental Administration, University of Pennsylvania Wharton School, Fels Institute of Local and State Government, Philadelphia, Pennsylvania, 1967; Ph.D. Management, Administration, Organizational Theory and Resource Methodology, Wayne State University, Detroit, Michigan, 1971. Career: Associate Director, Federal Emergency Management Agency, Washington, D.C., 1981 to present; Director of Human Resources, Public Technology, Inc., Washington, D.C., 1980-81; President, International Training, Research and Evaluation Council, Fairfax, Virginia, 1971-80; Assistant to the Director, Southeast Michigan Council of Governments, Detroit, Michigan, 1969-71; Instructor/Training Coordinator, Wayne State University, Detroit, Michigan, 1967-69; Assistant to the City Manager, City of Port Huron, Michigan, 1966-67; Part-Time Hourly Employee, Management Trainee, Ford Motor Company, Dearborn, Michigan, 1961-65. Organizational Memberships: American Society of Public Administration; International City Management Association; International Society of Law Enforcement and Criminal Justice; Technology Transfer Society. Community Activities: National Association of Clock and Watch Collectors; National Crime Prevention Institute of the University of Louisville, Louisville, Kentucky (first national advisory board); Motorola Teleprograms, Inc., Schiller Park, Illinois (security management training board); American University, Washington, D.C. (adjunct professor); Law Enforcement Assistance Administration, United States Department of Justice, Washington, D.C. (reviewer, national criminal justice reference service); Villa Lee Community Association, Fairfax, Virginia (chairman, architectural review and audit committees); Federal Emergency Management Agency, Washington, D.C. (director, nominee's reorganization task force). Published Works: Author of Over 200 Published Professional Reports; "The Principles of Contemporary Crime Prevention Techniques", *Security Techniques for Complexes Accessible to the Public and Special Use Facilities*, Edited by L. Fennelly, 1982; "Planning, Management and Evaluation: Important Tools to the Crime Prevention and Security Officer", *Handbook of Loss Prevention and Crime Prevention*, Edited by L. Fennelly, 1982; "Community-Based Child Care Programs: An Evaluation System", *Criminal Justice Research: New Models and Findings*, with K. Johnson and W. Rusinko, 1980; "Job Satisfaction and Burn-Out: A Double-Edged Threat to Human Services Workers", *Theory and Research in Criminal Justice: Current Perspectives*, with K. Johnson, W. Rusinko, et al., 1979; *Small Police Agency Consolidation: Suggested Approaches*, with T. W. Koepsell, 1979; "Single Family Homes", with R. Bray in *Handbook of Building Security, Planning and Design*, 1979; *Pro-Cop: Professional Growth Exercises*, 1978; *Crime Prevention Security Surveys: Phase I Report*, 1977; "A Survey of the Utilization of Civilians by Maryland Law Enforcement Agencies, *Maryland Municipal Review*, 1977; "Crime Prevention, the Citizen and the Security Survey", with T. Koepsell, *California Crime Prevention Review*, 1977; *Instructor's Guide for Two Cops* Training Manual Accompanying Film on Job Street; *A Short Course in Crime Prevention*, 1975; "The Automatic Digital Computer and Binary Notation: The Sophisticated and the Simple", *Research News Notes*, 1969; "The Defunct Service Bureau", *Midwest Review of Public Administration*, 1969. Honors and Awards: Fels Scholarships and Fellowship, University of Pennsylvania, 1965-67; Spark Plug Award, United States Junior Chamber of Commerce, 1967; Phi Sigma Alpha National Honor Society for Political Science, 1968; Honorary Texas Citizen, Governor Dolph Briscoe, 1974; Certificate of Appreciation, El Paso Police Department, 1976; Honorary Colonel, Salt Lake City Police Department, 1978; Listed in *Who's Who in the South and Southwest*, *Men of Achievement*, *International Who's Who of Intellectuals*, *Personalities of the South*, *Two Thousand Distinguished Southerners*, *Federal Staff Directory*. Address: 2928 Espana Court, Fairfax, Virginia 22031.

Giraudier, Antonio

Poet, Writer, Artist, Musician. Personal: Born September 28, 1926; Son of Antonio and Dulce M. de Giraudier. Education: Graduate of Deutsche Schule, Havana, Cuba; B.L., Institute 2, Vedado, Havana, Cuba, 1944; B.L., Belen Jesuits, Havana, 1944; LL.B., Havana University Law School, 1949; Culver S. Naval School, Indiana; Admiral Bellard Academy, New London, Connecticut; Private Art Studies. Career: *Modern Images* Publication of the American Poets Fellowship Society, Editor 1978-81, Poetry Critic 1978-80; Poetry Critic of *Arbol de Fuego*, Caracas, Venezuela, 1971-76; Around 900 Poetry Readings and Musical Recitals, including Readings at the New York Poetry Forum; Over 700 Performances in the United States and Europe, Piano Solo, Piano Accompaniment for Singing, and Singing and Accompanying Himself on Guitar; Has had 167 Exhibits; One-Man Exhibitions, Smolin Gallery New York 1965, New Masters Gallery, New York 1967, Avanti Galleries, New York 1968, 1969, 1971, 1973, 1975, Palm Beach Towers, Florida 1969, University of Palm Beach 1970, Eastern Illinois University 1975, Senior Advisory Exhibition, Charleston, Illinois 1977; Two-Man Exhibitions, Welfleet Gallery, Cape Cod, Massachusetts 1967, Avanti Galleries 1972; Group Exhibitions in the United States and Europe Since 1964; Creator of Around 7000 Art Works, Owner of Over 5000 of Own Works and Some of Other Artists; Over 1700 Art Works Among Private and Public Collections Throughout the United States and Europe, Fordham University, Lincoln Center in New York City and the Bronx, University of Palm Peach, Greenville Museum of Art, South Carolina, Maryhill Museum of Fine Arts in Washington State, Marshall Public Library, Illinois, Eastern Illinois University, Museum of Literature and the Royal Library, Brussels, Belgium, and Others; Author of 55 Published and 65 Unpublished Titles. Organizational Memberships: American Poets Fellowship Society (life member); International Biographical Association (life patron); Amsterdam International Congress (Eastern United States representative, 1980); New York Poetry Forum (Big Apple festival, 1982). Published Works: Art Work Reproduced in Over 50 Publications in the United States, Switzerland, Spain, Germany, Italy, and France; Author of Numerous Books of Poetry Published in the United States, Venezuela, Cuba, France, and Spain since 1957, including 41 Definitive Works in English, 12 Definitive Works in Spanish, and 2 Definitive Works in French; Published in 6 Languages; Author of Over 6,000 Poems and Prose Works; Contributor to Over 100 Books including Over 80 Anthologies; Publications Appear in More than 60 Libraries; Completed Over 30 Musical Compositions and Arrangement Entitled "Musical Salutes and Remembrances to Composers". Honors and Awards: Over 800 Reviews on Works, Many Positive Reviews Internationally for Poetry and Art Works; Premier Prix de Printemps, Paris, 1959; Laureat Margerite d'Or, Paris, 1960; Honorary Member, L'Orientation Litteraire, Paris; Danae Literary Designate, 1973; Golden Laurel Cup, American Poets Fellowship Society; Golden Laurel Crown for Arts and Letters, United Poets International; Academician of Italy with Gold Medal, 1980; American Biographical Institute Research Association, Gold Plaque of Outstanding Membership 1981, Gold Plaque of Distinction for Multiple Accomplishments 1982; International Biographical Centre, Certificates and Dictionaries, England; Master of Painting Honoris Causa, Italy, 1982; Listed in *Book of Honor*, *Dictionary of International Biography*, *International Who's Who of Intellectuals*, *People*

Who Matter, Who's Who in American Art, International Who's Who in Poetry, Personalities of America. Address: 215 East 68th Street, New York City, New York 10021.

Gissberg, John Gustav

Assistant Attorney General. Personal: Born May 6, 1943; Son of G. H. and Claudia Gissberg; Married Choko Y. Gissberg, December 23, 1967; Father of Eron Thomas, Christena. Education: Graduate of Juneau-Douglas High School, 1961; B.Sc., University of Washington College of Fisheries, Seattle, Washington, 1965; Stanford Interuniversity Center for Foreign Studies/University of Tokyo School of Fisheries, Tokyo, Japan, 1966-67; J.D., University of Michigan Law School, Ann Arbor, Michigan, 1970; Ph.D. Fisheries, University of Michigan School of Natural Resources, Ann Arbor, Michigan, 1971. Military: R.O.T.C., University of Washington, 1961-63. Career: Assistant Attorney General, Fisheries and International Affairs, Anchorage and Juneau, Alaska, 1976 to present; Legal Consultant, The Conservation Foundation, International Land Use Planning Program, Tokyo, Japan, 1974-76; Associate, Cole, Hartig, Nunley, Rhodes and Norman, Attorneys at Law, Anchorage, Alaska, 1972-73; Postdoctoral Associate and Lecturer, University of Singapore, Faculty of Law, 1972; Guest Investigator, Marine Policy Affairs and Ocean Management Program, Woods Hole Oceanographic Institution, Woods Hole, Massachusetts, 1971. Organizational Memberships: American Fisheries Society (member, 1963 to present; international fisheries committee, 1969; chairman, student foreign study committee, 1970; internationalism committee, 1977, 1980-82); American Bar Association (member, 1968 to present; natural resources law section, 1968 to present; international law section, 1973 to present, young lawyers section, 1972-74; chairman, environmental quality committee, Alaska section, 1973-74); Alaska Bar Association (member, 1971 to present; co-chairman, environmental law committee, 1973-74); Anchorage Bar Association (1972 to present, chairman, lawyers referral service committee, 1973-74); Michigan Bar Association, 1971 to present; *Marine Fisheries Management Reporter* (advisory board, 1981); International Academy of Fisheries Law/Academia Internacional de Derecho Pesquero, Mexico City (charter invitee, 1981); National Academy of Sciences, Washington, D.C. (ocean policy committee, 1979-82); International North Pacific Fisheries Commission (United States advisory committee, Tokyo 1979, 1982, Anchorage 1980); Governor's Commission on the Conference of the Law of the Sea, Juneau, Alaska (commissioner, 1973-74). Honors and Awards: Territorial Sportsmen's Scholar, 1961; University of Washington, Phi Eta Sigma Honorary Society 1962, William F. Thompson Award of the College of Fisheries 1964, N.D.E.A. Fellow 1967-71; Ministry of Foreign Affairs Award, All-Japan Japanese Speech Contest for Foreign Residents, 1966; Certified Fisheries Scientist, American Fisheries Society, 1973. Address: Box 1225, Juneau, Alaska 99801.

Giuliani, Emilio Romolo

Professor of Medicine. Personal: Born January 26, 1927 in Williamsport, Pennsylvania; Married Georgene; Father of Four Daughters and Two Sons. Education: B.S. cum laude, Notre Dame University, Indiana, 1949; M.D., Georgetown University, Washington, D.C., 1953; M.S. Medicine, University of Minnesota-Minneapolis, 1962; Internship, Geisiner Memorial Hospital, Danville, Pennsylvania, 1953; Residencies in Internal Medicine, Geisiner Memorial Hospital, Danville, Pennsylvania, 1954; Fellowship in Internal Medicine, Mayo Graduate School, Rochester, Minnesota, 1957; Certification, National Boards, 1954, Internal Medicine 1962, Cardiovascular 1967; Recertification, Internal Medicine, 1974. Military: Served in the United States Army at the Manhattan Atomic Project, Los Alomos, 1945. Career: Private Practice, Williamsport, Pennsylvania, 1955; Assistant to the Staff, Mayo Graduate School, Rochester, Minnesota, 1960; Mayo Clinic, Rochester, Minnesota, Consultant in Cardiology 1961, Instructor in Internal Medicine 1964, Vice-Chairman of Division of Cardiovascular Diseases 1972, Associate Director of Cardiovascular Training Program 1972, Associate Professor of Medicine of Mayo Medical School 1973, Co-Director of Congenital Heart Clinics 1973, Representative to American Group Practice Association 1975, Director of Echocardiographic Laboratory 1977, Professor of Medicine of Mayo Medical School 1979; Co-Director of Intensive Care Unit, St. Mary's Hospital, Rochester, Minnesota, 1964; Director of Cardiac Intensive Care Unit, Methodist Hospital, Rochester, Minnesota, 1968; Assistant Professor of Medicine, Mayo Graduate School, University of Minnesota-Minneapolis, 1968; Northlands Regional Medical Program, Director of Professional Education of Minnesota Heart Association 1969, Board of Trustees 1972; American Heart Association, Board of Directors 1972, North Dakota and Minnesota Representative 1976; American Medical Association, Residency Review Committee and Specialist Site Visitor, 1973; Professional Standard Quality Control Minnesota, Board of Directors 1976, Secretary 1979. Organizational Memberships: Professional Services Quality Council of Minnesota (president, 1981-83); Mayo Clinic Cardiovascular Society (president, 1981-83); Minnesota Heart Association (chairman of summer scholarship award, 1963; chairman of community service committee, 1964; board of governors, 1964; executive committee, 1965; chairman, long range planning committee, 1969; secretary, 1969; president-elect, first vice-president, 1970; president, 1971; immediate past president, chairman of membership and nominating committees, 1972); Sigma Xi (member, 1964 to present; executive committee, 1970, vice-president, 1973; president, 1974); American Heart Association (fellow, council clinical cardiology, 1964; fellow, council thrombosis, 1970; board of directors, 1972; council representative for Minnesota and North Dakota, 1975); Lambda Phi Mu Medical Fraternity, 1960; Society of Nuclear Medicine, 1962; Minnesota Society of Internal Medicine, 1963; American Federation for Clinical Research, 1963; American College of Physicians (fellow, 1963); American College of Angiology (fellow, 1964); American College of Cardiology (fellow, 1967); American College of Chest Physicians (fellow, 1969); Royal Society of Medicine (fellow, 1973); American Institute of Ultrasound, 1974; Society of Pediatric Echocardiography, 1975; Society of Clinical Ultrasound, 1976; Mayo Clinic (chairman, medical care evaluation and medical audit; chairman, coordinating committee; chairman, clinical society; chairman, advisory committee on epidemiology and statistics; chairman, review committee on epidemiology and statistics; department of international medicine, chairman of evaluation of medical residents, chairman of cardiovascular practices committee, chairman of ad hoc committee on ultrasound). Honors and Awards: A. Ashley Rousuck Award for Outstanding Achievement, Fellow in Internal Medicine, Mayo Foundation, 1962; Outstanding Leadership Awards, Director of Continuing Education for Northlands Regional Medical Program 1969, N.R.M.P. Minnesota Heart I.C.C.U. Project 1969; Outstanding Teacher Award, Mayo Clinic, 1970; Honorary Membership, Milwaukee Dental Forum, 1971; Distinguished Service Award, Minnesota Heart Association, 1972; Certificate of Appreciation for Dedicated Leadership and Voluntary Services, Northlands Regional Medical Program, 1973; International Registry of Who's Who, 1975; Award for Excellence, American Medical Association Advanced Seminar on Negotiations, 1977. Address: 330 - 16th Avenue Southwest, Rochester, Minnesota 55901.

John G Gissberg

Given, Barbara Knight

Associate Professor. Personal: Born July 17, 1935; Daughter of Henry and Lucile Knight; Married Bruce W. Given; Mother of Bryce W., Bethany K. Education: A.A., Colorado Women's College, 1955; B.S., Kansas State University, 1958; M.Ed., University of Oregon, 1967; Ph.D., Catholic University of America, 1974. Career: George Mason University, Fairfax, Virginia, Associate Professor, Coordinator of Learning Disabilities Teacher Preparation Program, Coordinator of Special Education Program; Teacher of Learning Disabled Children and Adults, Mentally Retarded and Second Grade; Principal and Director, Johns Hopkins University Affiliated Center School of Baltimore. Organizational Memberships: The Council for Exceptional Children, Division for Children with Learning Disabilities and Council for Educational Diagnostic Services; Phi Delta Kappa; Association for Children and Adults with Learning Disabilities; Association for Learning Disabled Adults. Community Activities: Association for Learning Disabled Adults (executive committee, 1980 to present); Northern Virinia Literacy Council (advisory board, 1981 to present); Alexandria City Public Schools (special education committee advisory board); Fairfax County Schools (past special education advisory board alternate); Central Fairfax Services for Adult Retardates (advisory board, 1975-79); Public School Systems (consultant to Stafford, Arlington, Loundoun, Prince William and Faquair Counties, Manassas Park, and Alexandria); Testing Program for Adults with Learning Problems. Religion: Presbyterian Church. Honors and Awards: Certificate of Award in Recognition of Meritorious Service to the Mentally Retarded Children of Lane County, Eugene, Oregon, 1962; Listed in *Who's Who of American Women, Who's Who Women of the World, Community Leaders and Noteworthy Americans, Directory of Women for Corporate Boards and Appointive Offices.* Address: 3113 Shadeland Drive, Falls Church, Virginia 22044.

Glass, Wendy D

Art Dealer. Personal: Born August 28, 1925; Daughter of A. W. Davis and Mrs. Joseph Obstler; Mother of Roberta Chess, Timothy. Education: Graduate of Scarborough Boarding School, 1944; B.A., Bard College, 1948. Career: Art Dealer; Group Worker with Children, Settlement Houses; Art Coordinator of Charity Shows or Exhibits in Schools. Organizational Memberships: Professional Women's Organization of New York City. Community Activities: Franklin Delano Roosevelt-Woodrow Wilson Democrats (volunteer worker, early 1960's); Hadassah Board of Kadimah Chapter; Art Shows, Walden School; Parent-Teacher Association Meetings, Walden School, New York City, New York. Religion: Temple Shearay Tefila Synaogue, New York City, New York. Address: 315 Central Park West, New York City, New York 10825.

Glenn, Helen Irene

Assistant Director. Personal: Born August 17; Daughter of Harry James and Edna Montanye Glenn. Education: B.A., Mercer University, 1938; M.A., Indiana University, 1942; Graduate Work, Auburn University, Michigan State University, Middle Tennessee State University, Wheeling College. Military: Served in United States Women's Army Corps, 1942-46, from Officer Candidate to Major, with Principle Assignment Overseas. Career: Jacksonville University, Assistant Director of Development 1977 to present, Director of Student Financial Aids 1971-77; Advisor to Married Students, Auburn University, 1970-71; Dean of Women and Assistant Professor of Journalism, Mercer University, 1961-70; Director of Public Relations and Associate Professor of Journalism, Wesleyan College, Macon, Georgia, 1957-61; International Secretary-Treasurer and Director of Executive Office, Alpha Delta Pi Sorority, 1948-57; Director of Public Relations and Associate Professor of Journalism, Brenau College, 1946-48. Organizational Memberships: Southern College Personnel Association (former president); Florida Association of Student Financial Aid Administrators (former president); Delta Kappa Gamma Professional Society (chapter president, 1980-82; district director, 1981-82); American Association of University Women (former chapter president). Community Activities: Y.W.C.A. (personnel committee, 1976 to present); Quota International Service Club (former president of 2 chapters; former district governor); Jacksonville Alumnae Panhellenic Association (former chairman, scholarships committee; former secretary; N.P.C. and J.U. liaison officer); Girl Scouts of America (sustaining member). Religion: Southside United Methodist Church, Education Commission Member 1978 to present. Honors and Awards: Algernon Sydney Sullivan Award, 1938; Among First Financial Aid Administrators to be Certified in State of Florida, 1976; Listed in *Who's Who of American Women, World Who's Who of Women, Who's Who in the South and Southeast, Who's Who in Education, Personalities of the South, Dictionary of International Biography, National Registry of Prominent Americans.* Address: 3830 University Boulevard South, Apartment 49, Jacksonville, Florida 32216.

Perry A Glick

Glenn, William Allen

Teacher, School Administrator, Research Historian (retired). Personal: Born March 28, 1925; Son of Mrs. C. G. Glenn; Married Ruth McClendon; Father of Bryan C., Phyllis G. Kelly. Education: A.B. Sociology 1951, M.A. Counseling and Guidance 1965, University of Alabama; Postgraduate Work in International Relations, American University, Washington, D.C., 1967; Postgraduate Work in Aerospace Education, Samford University, Alabama, 1976. Military: Served in the United States Navy as Radioman 3rd Class, 1943-46. Career: Writer of Weekly History Article, *North Jefferson News*, Gardendale, Alabama, 1981; Consultant, Cullman Museum, Alabama, 1978-79; Research Project on Abraham Lincoln Family Bible, United States National Park Service, 1976-77; Editor of Filmstrip Script, *History of South Carolina*, 1968-69; Author of Biographies of Famous Americans Freedoms Foundation Radio Narration, 1967-69; Teacher, Counselor, Principal and Supervisor, Jefferson County Schools, Birmingham, Alabama, 1965-77; Principal, Plainview Junior High School, Hartselle, Alabama, 1962-64; History and Government Teacher, Priceville High School, Decatur, Alabama, 1959-62; Research Analyst, United States Air Force and United States Army, 1952-58. Organizational Memberships: Alabama Education Association; Alabama Retired Teachers Association; Alabama Historical Association; National Historical Society; North Jefferson Historical Society (vice-president, 1979-81); Gardendale Band Boosters Club (secretary, 1981-82); Alpha Kappa Delta; Phi Delta Kappa; Kappa Phi Kappa; International Platform Association. Community Activities: Alabama Committee on Intergovernmental Cooperation (subcommittee on air and water pollution, 1972-76); Alabama Nixon Inaugural Committee (chaplain, 1969); Alabama Reagan-Bush Campaign Committee (advisor, 1980). Religion: Licensed Baptist Minister; Ordained Deacon; Sunday School Teacher; Contributor of Articles to *The Alabama Baptist.* Honors and Awards: Freedoms Foundation, Schoolmen's Medal 1966, Honor Certificate for Sermon 1967, Honor Certificate for Newspaper Editorial 1968; Governor's Citation for Work with Freedoms Foundation at Valley Forge, 1967. Address: 1319 Columbia Avenue, Gardendale, Alabama 35071.

Glick, Perry A(aron)

Entomologist (retired). Personal: Born December 21, 1895; Son of M. M. and Eva Alice Moran Glick (both deceased); Married Jessie Odum Kayser (deceased); Stepfather of Dorothy Provine. Education: Attended Park College and the University of Kansas; A.B. 1921, M.S. 1922, University of Illinois. Military: Served in the Texas State Guard, 1941-44. Career: Entomologist-Ecologist, United States Department of Agriculture, A.R.S., Cotton Insects Branch, and Others. Organizational Memberships: Royal Entomological Society of London (fellow); The Explorers Club of New York (fellow, 1979); Texas Chapter of the Explorers Club, 1981. Community Activities: Lions Club International, Waco Texas; National Association of Retired Federal Employees, American Advisory Council, International Good Neighbor Council; K.L.M. Royal Dutch Airlines and Allyn Museum of Entomology's "Adventure in Butterflies" Safari, South Africa (special invitee, 1978); Worldwide Travels. Published Works: 31 Publications, including "Cultural Practices and Their Influence on the Arthropod Populations in Cotton", 1981. Religion: Presbyterian Church, Ruling Elder. Honors and Awards: United States Department of Agriculture, Nominee for Superior Service Award 1963, 42 Years of Service Award 1964, Certificate of Appreciation 1965; Distinguished Alumnus Award, Park College Alumni Association, Kansas City, Missouri; Anglo-American

Academy, Cambridge, England, 1980; Photographer of Merit in Pictorial Composition; Fellow, American Association for the Advancement of Science. Address: Los Cedros Apartments #901A, 1025 Wildrose Lane, Brownsville, Texas 78520.

Glines, Don Eugene

Futurist. Personal: Born November 25, 1930; Son of Charles and Helen Porter; Married Ruth; Father of Laurie, Harlan. Education: B.A., Springfield College, Massachusetts, 1952; M.S. 1956, Ph.D. 1960, University of Oregon-Eugene. Military: Served as 1st Lieutenant in the Medical Service Corps of the United States Army, 1952-54; Served in the United States Army Reserves, 1956-68. Career: Futurist, California State Department of Education; Professor of Education, Mankato State University, Minnesota; Director, Wilson Campus School, Mankato, Minnesota; Principal, Tucson, Arizona; Superintendent, Port-au-Prince, Haiti; Assistant Superintendent, Taipei, Taiwan; Consultant, State of South Dakota; Teacher, Seville, Spain. Organizational Memberships: National Council on Year-Round Education (president, 1975-76); American Association of Social Psychiatry (fellow); Association for Curriculum Development; World Future Society. Community Activities: Cousteau Society; Phi Delta Kappa; Given Over 700 Major Addresses in 42 States and Several Foreign Countries; Consulted with Over 400 School Districts; Served as Advisor to Several Major Projects, such as California 2000; Volunteer Work in Field of Clinical Ecology. Published Works: Published 7 Books; Published 72 Articles. Honors and Awards: Service Awards, Several Local Phi Delta Kappa Chapters; Listed in *Who's Who in American Education* and 9 similar publications. Address: 1501 - 3rd Street, Sacramento, California 95814.

Gloe, Donna Sue

Family Counselor. Personal: Born April 24, 1951; Daughter of James Osborn; Married Lloyd R. Gloe; Mother of Darin Robert, Leslie Renee. Education: B.A. Psychology, University of Missouri; M.Ed. Counseling, Lincoln University. Career: Family Counselor; Histologic Technologist, A.S.C.P.-Registered. Community Activities: Women Helping Women (steering committee, 1979); Webster County Family Services Advisory Board, 1978 to present. Religion: Elkland Christian Church; Worship Committee Chairman; Program Chairman of Christian Women's Fellowship. Honors and Awards: National Merit Certificate of Scholastic Recognition, University of Missouri, 1969; Regents Scholar, Central Missouri State University, 1969; Listed in *Who's Who in the Midwest*. Address: Route 2 Box 171, Marshfield, Missouri 65706.

Gneuhs, Charles Oscar

Credit Union Executive. Personal: Born February 16, 1949; Son of Dr. and Mrs. Robert E. Gneuhs; Married Pamella K. Gneuhs; Father of Faith Ann. Education: B.A., Cleveland State University, 1973; Institute for Credit Union Personnel, Ohio University, 1976; Financial Counselling Seminar, Bowling Green University, 1976. Career: President and Chief Operating Officer, Sears Employees Credit Union; President, Northwest Parishes Credit Union; Manager, Norwalk Area Federal Credit Union; Loan Service Manager, American Savings and Loan; Loan Manager, G. E. Evendale Federal Credit Union. Organizational Memberships: Credit Union Executives Society; International Platform Association; Foundation of Economic Education. Community Activities: Foundation for Economic Education; Cleveland Jaycees (board member, 1974-78); Cincinnati Jaycees (board member, 1977-79); Elderlot Inc. (board member, 1974-79); Lake Erie Chapter of the Ohio Credit Union League (board member, 1980); Norwalk Chamber of Commerce, 1980; Norwalk Board of Education (advisory board). Honors and Awards: Cleveland Jaycees Keyman; Listed in *National Student Register, Who's Who in American Colleges and Universities, Outstanding Young Men of America, Who's Who in the Midwest, Men of Achievement, International Who's Who of Intellectuals, Book of Honor, Personalities of the West and Midwest, The American Registry*. Address: Olde Ways, Post Office Box 587, Middletown, Ohio 45042.

Godbold, Jake M

Mayor. Personal: Born March 14, 1934; Son of Irene Whitfield; Married Jean J. Godbold; Father of Ben. Education: Graduate Andrew Jackson High School, 1953. Military: Served with the United States Army during the Korean Conflict, 1953-55. Career: Mayor, City of Jacksonville, Florida; Owner, Gateway Chemical Company. Community Activities: Jacksonville Jaycees (past president); Big Brothers (past president); Boy's Clubs of Jacksonville (past president); Muscular Dystrophy Association (board member); Rotary Club; Northside Businessmen's Club; Springfield Businessmen. Religion: Member of St. Marks Methodist Church. Honors and Awards: National Defense Service Medal; United Nations Service Medal; Good Conduct Medal; Distinguished Service Award, Jacksonville Area Chamber of Commerce, 1968. Address: 14667 Capstan Drive, Jacksonville, Florida 32226.

Goff, Doyle Roger

Marriage and Family Therapist. Personal: Born June 19, 1950; Son of Mr. and Mrs. Vernon H. Goff, Sr.; Married to Terrie Lane Roberts; Father of David Roger, Duane Richard. Education: Attended Lee College, 1968-71; B.A., 1974, M.S., 1979, Florida International University; Ph.D. Candidate, Florida State University. Career: Minister, Licensed with Church of God, 1975; Ordained in 1980; Pastor at Carrabelle, Florida, 1974-76; Pastor at Chokoloskee, Florida, 1977-80; Director, District Youth and Christian Education, 1977-79. Organizational Memberships: American Personnel and Guidance Association; American School Counselor Association; American Mental Health Counselor Association; American Association of Marriage and Family Therapy. Community Activities: Cystic Fibrosis Foundation (campaign chairman, 1978 and 1980); Florida Chapter, Lee College Alumni Association (secretary-treasurer, 1976-80, vice president, 1980 to present). Honors and Awards: Listed in *Who's Who in the South and Southwest, Personalities of the South, Directory of Distinguished Americans, International Who's Who of Intellectuals*. Address: 2428 Ramblewood Court, Tallahassee, Florida 32303.

Gogick, Kathleen Christin

Editorial Director. Personal: Born August 3, 1945; Daughter of Emeline Wadowski; Married Robert Joseph Gogick; Mother of Jonathan Robert. Education: Attended Emmanuel College, Boston, Massachusetts; B.S., Fairleigh Dickinson University, Rutherford, New Jersey, 1967. Career: Editorial Director, Scholastic Inc.; Beauty Editor, *Town and Country*; Creative Manager, Estee Lauder Inc.; Assistant Editor, *Cosmopolitan*. Organizational Memberships: American Society of Magazine Editors; Women in Communications; Fashion Group. Community Activities: Fairleigh Dickinson University (board of directors). Honors: Numerous Editorial Awards, 1977-81. Address: 2 Pierrepont Place, Brooklyn, New York 11201.

Goktepe, Janet Yeager

Financial Analyst. Personal: Born November 27, 1950; Daughter of Clifton F. Yeager (deceased) and Bertha Yates Yeager; Married Omer F. Goktepe; Mother of Katherine Emel Goktepe. Education: B.S. Business/Management magna cum laude 1976, M.B.A. summa cum laude 1979, Doctoral Candidate in Business/Management 1979 to present, University of Maryland. Career: United States Government, Financial Analyst 1979 to present, Financial Research Analyst 1975-79, Secretary 1969-75; Part-Time Faculty Member, Montgomery College, Rockville, Maryland 1979 to present, University of Maryland 1979 to present; Financial Analyst, I.C.C., 1978 to present; United States Treasury Department, Financial Analyst 1977, Research Analyst 1974-77, Secretary 1972-74; Secretary, United States Justice Department, 1969-72. Organizational Memberships: Toastmasters International (member 1979 to present; president I.C.C. Toastmasters, 1980; education vice-president, 1980; administrative vice-president, 1979); Washington Society of Investment Analysts; Financial Analysts Federation. Community Activities: Federal Women's Program (volunteer, 1980 to present). Religion: Church of Jesus Christ of Latter-Day Saints (Mormon), 1964 to present. Honors and Awards: Beta Gamma Sigma National Honor Society, 1979 to present; Phi Kappa Phi National Honorary Society, 1977 to present; Listed in *Who's Who of American Women*. Address: 7604 Bells Mill Road, Bethesda, Maryland 20817.

Golany, Gideon S

Urban and Regional Planner. Personal: Born January 23, 1928; Married; Father of Ofer, Amir. Education: B.A. Geography/Middle-Eastern Studies 1956, M.A. 1962, Ph.D. 1966, Hebrew University, Jerusalem, Israel; Diploma in Comprehensive Planning, The Institute of Social Studies, The Hague, The Netherlands, 1965; M.Sc., Faculty of Architecture and Town Planning, Technion-Israel Institute of Technology, Haifa, Israel, 1966; New Communities Masters Program, University of Northern Colorado, Center for Special and Advanced Programs, 1971-73; Summer Seismic Institute for Architectural Faculty, A.I.A., 1978. Military: Served in Hagana, and Israeli Underground Movement, 1946-48; Served in the Israeli Army, 1948-50, during the War of Independence 1948, Sinai War 1956, and Six Day War 1967. Career: Pennsylvania State University Division of Environmental Design and Planning, Professor of Urban and Regional Planning 1970 to present, Chairman of the Graduate Program 1970-76; Associate Professor of Urban and Regional Planning, Graduate Division of Environmental and Urban Systems, College of Architecture, Virginia Polytechnic Institute and State University, 1968-70; Cornell University, Research Planner in Office of Regional Resources and Development 1968, Lecturer in Department of City and Regional Planning 1967-68; Technion-Israel Institute of Technology, Haifa, Israel, Faculty of Architecture and Town Planning, Visiting Professor 1979-80, Lecturer 1963-67; Visiting Professor, College of Architecture, University of Western Australia, Perth, 1980; Visiting Professor, Environmental Quality Program, The Hebrew University of Jerusalem, 1980; Visiting Professor of Urban and Regional Planning, Institute for Desert Research, Ben-Gurion University of the Negev, Beer Sheva, Israel, 1975-76; New Town Planner, Natural Resources Economics Specialist, Urban and Regional Planner, Golany Associates, 1970 to present; Consultant to Numerous Cities and Governmental Offices, Urban and Regional Planning, 1964-80; Partner, Planning Team Office, Haifa, Israel, 1964-69; Ministry of Interior, Main Office, Jerusalem, Israel, Senior Planner for Department of Regional and National Planning 1962-63, Principal Assistant of Village Planning 1960-62, Principal Assistant of the General Director 1958-60; General Secretary, Scout Union Organization, Youth Department, Ministry of Education and Culture, Jerusalem, Israel, 1956-58; Member and Founder, Building Firm, Kibbutz Bea'ri, Negev, Israel, 1946-52. Organizational Memberships: American Planning Association; American Society of Planning Officials; Canadian Institute of Planners; Association of Engineers and Architects in Israel (overseas member); American Underground Space Association; International New Towns Association; International Center for Arid and Semi-Arid Land Studies; Association for Arid Lands Studies. Community Activities: Pennsylvania State University (steering committee of the interdisciplinary graduate program in the humanities; departmental curriculum committee; college sabbatical committee; departmental tenure and promotion committee; chairman, committee on urban and regional planning program; advisory committee on the department of architecture; chairman, departmental committee on the M.Sc. graduate program; departmental independent project and thesis committee); Attended and presented papers at many international conferences. Published Works: *Design for Arid Regions*, 1983; *Earth-Sheltered Habitat: History, Architecture and Urban Design*, 1982; *Desert Planning*, 1982; *Housing in Arid Lands: Design and Planning*, 1980; *Arid Zone Settlement Planning: The Israeli Experience*, 1979; *Urban Planning for Arid Zones: American Experiences and Directions*, 1978; *International Urban Growth Policies: New-Town Contributions*, 1978; *New-Town Planning: Principles and Practice*, 1976; Author of Numerous Other Published Books, Monographs, Papers, and Other Works; Contributor to Books and Journals. Honors and Awards: Grant to Travel and Study Comprehensive Planning in The Netherlands, Government of The Netherlands, 1965; Prize of the Committee for Encouragement Towards Research and Higher Studies, Executive Committee of the Histadrut, Tel-Aviv, 1963; National Science Foundation Grant for Development of Method of New Town Site Selection, 1972-74; Listed in *Dictionary of International Biography, Men of Achievement, International Who's Who in Community Service, Who's Who in America; International Who's Who of Intellectuals, Who's Who in the East, Community Leaders and Noteworthy Americans, Personalities of America, Notable Americans, Dictionary of Distinguished Americans, Who's Who in American Jewry, Who's Who in the World, Who's Who in Israel, Who's Who in the World Jewry*. Address: 292 Douglas Drive, State College, Pennsylvania 16802.

Leo M Goldberg

Goldberg, Leo Monroe

Attorney-at-Law. Personal: Born February 28, 1907; Son of Harris and Sarah Gere Goldberg (both deceased); Married Ruth S. Shartenberg. Education: A.B. magna cum laude, Brown University, 1928; LL.B., Yale University, 1931. Military: Served in the United States Air Force, 1941-45, as a member of the Headquarters Company, Eastern Base Section, Division of A.F.H.Q. APO763 Engineering Section and Office of Town Majors. Career: Public Defender, Rhode Island Superior Court, 1936-37; Attorney-at-Law, Goldberg & Goldberg, Providence, 1935 to present; Associate, Voigt, O'Neil & Monroe and their Predecessor Firm, Providence, 1931-34. Organizational Memberships: American, Rhode Island, Massachusetts Bar Associations; American Judicature Society; Association of Trial Lawyers of America. Community Activities: Admitted to Rhode Island Bar 1931, Massachusetts Bar, 1936, United States District Court of Rhode Island 1932, United States District Court of Massachusetts 1949, United States 1st Circuit Court of Appeals 1952; F. Ronci Company Inc. (general counsel); Turks Head Club; University Club. Religion: Sons of Jacob Synagogue, Providence, Rhode Island, Chairman of the Board, 1935-40; Temple Beth El. Honors and Awards: American Economic History; Phi Beta Kappa; Francis Wyland Scholar; James Manning Scholar; Listed in *Who's Who in American Law, Men of Achievement, Dictionary of International Biography, International Who's Who of Intellectuals*. Address: 52 Lorraine Avenue, Providence, Rhode Island 02906.

Golden, Constance J

Manager of Aerospace Mission Operations. Personal: Born June 8, 1939; Daughter of Herman and Chrystle Leuer; Married Charles J. Golden; Mother of Kerri Lynn. Education: B.S. Mathematics/Physics, Beloit College, 1961; A.M. Mathematics, Harvard University,

1962; Stanford University, Ph.D. Course Work in Mathematics and Aerospace Engineering 1966, M.S. Operations Research 1970. Career: Manager, Aerospace Mission Operations; Manager, Corporate Strategic Planning; Program Manager, Various Aerospace Projects; Engineer, Development of Computer Models of Aerospace Projects. Organizational Memberships: Society of Women Engineers (San Francisco Bay Area section president, 1974-75; national scholarship chairman, 1976); A.F.C.E.A. (Santa Clara Valley chapter board of directors, 1979-80). Community Activities: A.I.A.A. (public policy committee); O.R.S.A.; Mills College (science advisory council); Toastmasters International (past president of local club and A.T.M.). Honors and Awards: Phi Beta Kappa Award, 1960-61; N.S.F. Fellowship, 1961-62; Lockheed's Most Distinguished Woman, 1976; Featured in *Business Week* Article on Corporate Women, 1981; Featured on *60 Minutes* Television Program, 1981; Listed in *World Who's Who of Women, Who's Who in the West.* Address: 1260 Crossman Road, Sunnyvale, California 94086.

Golden, Martha (Marti) A

Telecommunications Analyst. Personal: Born November 27, 1945 in Laurel, Mississippi; Daughter of Mr. and Mrs. Cleveland Golden. Education: B.S. Administrative Management, 1976; M.B.A. Marketing Management, 1979. Career: Telecommunications Specialist, Port Authority, 1981 to present; Account Executive, New York Telephone, 1980-81; Director of Conference Planning and Management, Kaaren Johnson and Associates, 1978-80; Vice-President, Borcar Enterprises Inc., 1977-80; Systems Analyst, COBOL Programmer, Computing and Software Company, Los Angeles, 1972-74; Assistant Personnel Manager, Aetna Maintenance Company, Los Angeles, 1964-67. Organizational Memberships: International Platform Association; Meeting Planners International; Thousand Oaks Investment Club (vice-president); National Organization of Women (board of directors); League of Women Voters; National Association of Female Executives; Coalition of 100 Black Women; A.M.A.; National Association of M.B.A.'s; Public Education Association. Community Activities: United Fund (donor); Easter Seals (donor); American Cancer Society (donor); U.N.I.C.E.F. (donor); American Folk Theatre (director of audience development); Toastmasters International. Religion: Protestant; Sunday School Teacher, Usher. Honors and Awards: Gold Dictionary in Spelling Match; Winner, C.P.A. Toastmaster; Shorthand Awards. Address: 41 West 86th Street, 14F, New York City, New York 10024.

Goldkorn, Isaac

Writer. Personal: Born October 1, 1911; Son of David and Chaya Goldkorn (both deceased); Married Irene; Father of David. Education: Attended Hebrew Religious School (mainly self-educated). Career: Editor, *Unzer Haint*, Munich, Germany, 1951; Editor, *Widerstand*, Montreal, Quebec, Canada, 1957-59; Editor, Israelite Press, Winnipeg, Canada, 1960-64; News Editor, *Canadian Jewish Eagle*, Montreal, 1965; Staff Writer, *Unzer Express*, Warsaw, Poland, 1939; Staff Writer, *Jewish Daily Forward*, New York, New York, 1967-77. Organizational Memberships: Yiddish P.E.N. (affiliated with International P.E.N. Clubs); World Union of Jewish Journalists. Religion: Jewish. Published Works: Contributor of Articles, Essays, Book Reviews and Poems to Yiddish Newspapers and Magazines in Poland (1930-39) and in Western Europe, Canada, United States and Other Countries; Author, *Nocturns* (Lodz, 1938), *Lit. Silhouetten* (Munich, 1949), *Lieder* (1950), *Epigramatish* (Montreal, 1954), *Fun Welt-Kval* (Tel Aviv, 1963), *Lodzher Portreten* (Tel Aviv, 1963), *Zingers un Zogers* (Tel Aviv, 1971), *Heimishe un Fremde* (Buenos Aires, 1973), *Yellow Letters, Green Memories* (Cornwall, 1979), *Kurts un Sharf* (Toronto, 1981). Honors and Awards: Received Jacob Gladstone Prize, World Congress for Jewish Culture in New York, 1976; Listed in *Encyclopedia Britannica Year Book*, 1971 and 1973. Address: 122 Clanton Park Road, Downsview, Ontaria M3H 2E5, Canada.

Issac Goldkorn

Goldstein, Jack C

Attorney. Personal: Born May 11, 1942; Married Leslie Silber; Father of Jason Brent, Jill Paige. Education: B.S.M.E., Purdue University, 1964; J.D. with honors, George Washington University, 1968. Career: Attorney, Arnold, White and Durkee, Houston, Texas, 1969 to present; Law Clerk, Judge Phillip B. Baldwin, United States Court of Customs and Patent Appeals, Washington, D.C., 1968-69; Patent Advisor, Office of Naval Research, Washington, D.C., 1967-68; Patent Examiner, United States Patent and Trademark Office, 1964-67. Organizational Memberships: American Patent Law Association (board of directors, 1980-82); Houston Patent Law Association (president, 1979-80); Copyright Society of the United States of America (trustee, 1978-82); American Bar Association (member of council, section of patent, trademark and copyright law, 1982 to present); Houston Bar Association; Federal Bar Association; Texas Bar Association; Texas Bar Foundation. Address: 6231 South Braeswood Boulevard, Houston, Texas 77096.

Goldstein, Jeffrey Marc

Psychopharmacoloist. Personal: Born May 9, 1947; Son of Joseph and Shirley Goldstein; Married Robin Goldstein; Father of Kevin Alan, Neal David. Education: Graduate of Martin Van Buren High School, Queens, New York, 1965; B.S. Biology, Colorado State University, Fort Collins, Colorado, 1970; M.S. Biology, Seton Hall University, South Orange, New Jersey, 1973; Ph.D. Neuroscience, University of Delaware, Newark, Delaware, 1980. Career: Research Pharmacologist, Biomedical Research Department, I.C.I. Americas Inc., Wilmington, Delaware, 1976 to present; Associate Scientist, Pharmacology Department, Shering Corporation, 1970-76. Organizational Memberships: American Association for the Advancement of Science; New York Academy of Sciences; American Society for Pharmacology and Experimental Therapeutics; Society for Neuroscience; Sigma Xi. Published Works: Reviewer for Science Books and Films; Reviewer for National Science Foundation Grants; "Electrophysiological Demonstration of Both Alpha-2 Agonist and Antagonist Properties of RX781094", with L. C. Knobloch and J. B. Malick, *Neuroscience Abstracts*, 1982; "Animal Pharmacology of Endorphins", with J. B. Malick, *Endorphins: Chemistry, Physiology, Pharmacology and Clinical Relevance*, 1982; "An Automated Descending Rate-Intensity Self-Stimulation Paradigm: Usefulness for Distinguishing Antidepressants from Neuroleptics", with J. B. Malick, *Drug Development Research*, In Press; "Stimulation of Ventral Tegmental Area and Nucleus Accumbens Reduces Receptive Fields for Hypothalamic Biting Reflex in Cats", with J. Siegel, *Experimental Neurology*, 1981; "Stimulation of Mesolimbic Dopamine System Reduces Receptive Fields for Hypothalamic Biting Reflex in Cats", with J. Siegel, *International Congress of Physiological Science*, 1980; "The Role of Gabaergic Systems in the Modulation of Intracranial Self-Stimulation in the Rat", with K. Leszczynska and J. B. Malick, *Brain Research*, 1980; "Suppression of Attack Behavior in Cats by Stimulation of the Ventral Tegmental Area and Nucleus Accumbens", with J. Siegel, *Brain Research*, 1980; "Suppression of Medial Forebrain Bundle Self-Stimulation Following Intrecerebral Administration of Muscimol in Rats", with K. Leszczynska and J. B. Malick, *Brain Research Bulletin*, 1979; "Lack of Analgesic Activity of Substance P Following Intraperitoneal Administration", with J. B. Malick, *Life Sciences*, 1979; "Suppression of Emotional Behavior in Cats by Stimulation of Ventral Tegmental Area and Nucleus Accumbens", with J. Siegel, *Neuroscience Abstracts*, 1978; "Effects of Psychoactive Drugs on a Descending Rate-Intensity Model of Self-Stimulation in Rats", with J. K. Karpowicz and J. B. Malick, *Pharmacologist*, 1978; "Analgesic Activity of Substance P Following Intracerebral Administration in Rats", with J. B. Malick, *Life Science*, 1978; "Evaluation of Naloxone in Laboratory Tests Predictive of Clinical Antipsychotic Activity", with J. B. Malick, M. L. Billingsley and

R. K. Kubena, *Communications Psychopharmacology*, 1977; "Effects of Substance P on Medial Forebrain Bundle Self-Stimulation in Rats Following Intracerebral Administration", with J. B. Malick, *Pharmacology Biochemistry and Behavior*, 1977; "The Effects of Substance P on Self-Stimulation Behavior in Rats Following Intracerebral Administration", with J. B. Malick, *Pharmacologist*, 1977; "Substance P: Analgesia Following Intracerebral Administration in Rats", with J. B. Malick, *Federation Procedures*, 1977; "Analgesic Activity of Enkephalins Following Intracerebral Administration in the Rat", with J. B. Malick, *Life Science*, 1977; "Intravenous Infusion System for Chronic Drug Administration in Unrestrained Rats", with J. B. Malick, *Pharmacologist*, 1976; "Gamma-Aminobutyric Acid: Selective Inhibition of Electrically-Induced Head-Turning Following Intracaudate Administration", *Pharmacology Biochemistry and Behavior*, 1976; "Head-Turning Induced by Electrical Stimulation of the Candate Nucleus and Its Antagonism by Anti-Parkinson Drugs", with A. Barnett, *Journal of Pharmacology and Experimental Therapeutics*, 1975. Honors and Awards: Listed in *Who's Who in the East*. Address: 4 Curry Court, Wilmington, Delaware 19810.

Goldstein, Maxine Shapiro

Civic Worker. Personal: Born August 25, 1926 in Augusta, Georgia; Daughter of Harry and Sadie Rabinowitz Shapiro; Married Jacob Louis Goldstein, September 1, 1947; Mother of Marcia G. Stein, Harriet G. Greenhut. Education: Junior College of Augusta, 1945; Radio, University of Georgia, 1946; Hedgerow Theatre School of Dramatic Art. Community Activities: Georgia Status of Women Commission, 1962-70; Democratic Party, 1974 to present; Affirmative Action Committee (charter commission, executive committee, 1974 to present); Women for President Carter (state campaign coordinator, 1976); National Credentials Committee, 1976; Georgia Federation of Democrat Women (8th district director, 1976-78); Georgia Commission on Indian Affairs, 1978-80; Georgia Judicial Selection Committee, 1978; Georgia Federation of Democratic Women (president, 1980 to present); Democratic Party of Georgia (vice-chair, 1982 to present; 8th Congressional district chairman, 1978 to present); Fair Employment Practices Commission, 1980 to present; Georgia Cooperative Services for the Disabled, 1980 to present; National Platform Committee of Democratic Party, 1980; National Democratic Convention (delegate at large, 1980); Georgia Presidential Elector, 1981; Georgia Federation of Democratic Women (state president, 1980-82); Georgia Federation of Women's Clubs (district director; mental health chairman; awards chairman; international affairs chairman); Jewish Patients Benefit Fund of Central State Hospital (treasurer); Garden Club of Georgia (garden therapy chairman; scrapbook chairman; reclamation and recyling chairman, 1981-83); Milledgeville Junior Women's Club (co-founder; president); Milledgeville Civic Women's Club (co-founder; president); Milledgeville Little Theatre (co-founder; president); Milledgeville Hadassah (co-founder; president); Designers Critique, Macon (co-founder; president); Mayor's Commission on Downtown Revitalization; Recreation Department Allied Arts Council; American Red Cross (past board member); American Cancer Society (past board member); Mental Health Association (past board member); Heart Fund (past board member); Eastern Star; Temple Beth Israel Sisterhood; Town and Country Garden Club; B'nai B'rith; Old Capitol Historical Society; American Guild of Flower Arrangers; American Land Trust; Nature Conservancy; Middle Georgia Flower Show Judges (president, 1979-81); Baldwin County Democratic Women (founder); Delta Phi Epsilon Sorority; Pi Gamma Kappa National Radio Fraternity; Zeta Phi Eta National Speech Fraternity. Religion: Jewish. Honors and Awards: Master Judge, Amateur Flower Show; Family of the Year, Baldwin County, 1979; Listed in *Notable Americans, International Who's Who in Community Service, Personalities of America, Personalities of the South, Who's Who in American Politics, International Biography, World Who's Who of Women, Book of Honor*. Address: Post Office Box G, Milledgeville, Georgia 31061.

Norman Goldstein

Goldstein, Norman

Dermatologist. Personal: Born July 14, 1934; Son of Mr. and Mrs. Joseph H. Goldstein; Married Ramsay; Father of Richard David, Heidi Lee. Education: B.A., Columbia College, 1955; M.D., State University of New York Downstate Medical Center, 1959; Internship, Maimonides Hospital, 1960; Dermatology Residency, New York University Skin and Cancer Unit 1961, Bellevue Hospital 1962, New York University Postgraduate Medical Center 1963; Preceptorship, New York, 1963. Military: Served in the United States Army Reserve, New York City 1960-61; Chief of Dermatology Services, United States Army Hospital, Ft. Gordon, Georgia, 1963-64; United States Army Tripler General Hospital, Honolulu, Hawaii, Dermatology Service, Assistant Chief 1964-66, Chief 1966-67, Dermatology Consultant, 1967 to present; Career: Private Practice Dermatologist, 1972 to present; Partner, The Honolulu Medical Group, Honolulu, Hawaii, 1967-72. Organizational Memberships: American Medical Association; Society for Investigative Dermatology; International Society for Tropical Dermatology; Association of Military Dermatologists; Hawaii Dermatological Society Honolulu County Medical Society; Hawaii Medical Association; Micronesian Medical Association (honorary member); Hawaii Public Health Association; American Association for the Advancement of Science; American Society for Photobiology (charter member); Environmental Health and Light Research Institute; American Association of Clinical Oncology; Pacific Dermatological Association; Hawaii Association for Physicians for Indemnification; Pacific Health Research Institute; Biologic Photographic Association; Health Sciences Communications Association; Hawaii Association for Protective Indemnities; International Pigment Cell Society; American Society of Preventive Oncology; American Medical Writers Association, 1979 to present; Pan-Pacific Surgical Association, 1979 to present; American College of Cryosurgery, 1979 to present; International Society for Dermatologic Surgery, 1979 to present; American College of Physicians; International Society of Cryosurgery, 1980; Society for Computer Medicine, 1981 to present; American Association for Medical Assistants and Informatics, 1982; American College of Sports Medicine, 1982. Community Activities: Hawaii Planned Parenthood; International Solar Energy Society; Photographic Society of America; Tokai Tattoo Club of Japan (honorary member, 1979); North American Tattoo Club, 1980; Tattoo Club of Japan (life member, 1980); Tattoo Club of Deutschland, 1981 to present; New York Academy of Science, 1980; National Space Institute, 1980; The Friends of Photography, 1981; La Societe Internationale de la Photographie, 1981; International Platform Association, 1981 to present; Outrigger Canoe Club; Honolulu Rotary Club; Honolulu Symphony Society; Metro Opera Guild; Smithsonian Institution; Honolulu Art Academy; Hawaii Council for Culture and Arts; Hawaii Jewish Welfare Board (trustee, 1976-79); Historic Hawaii Foundation; American Institute of Architects (liaison to national meeting, 1982); National Trust for Historic Preservation; Hawaii Visitors Bureau; Chamber of Commerce, 1979 to present; Hawaii Historical Society; University of Hawaii Art Department (partner); Plaza Club of Honolulu; The Honolulu Club; Chancellor's Club of the University of Hawaii, 1980 to present; Downtown Improvement Association; Friends of Alexander Young Building. Religion: Jewish; Jewish Welfare Board of Trustees, 1976-79. Published Works: Contributor to *Cosmopolitan, Glamour, Mademoiselle, Self*. Honors and Awards: Illuminating Engineer Society of North American Office Lighting Design Award, Hawaii, 1982; Special Award, World of Tattoos Exhibit, Western Section of American Urologic Association, 1980; Historical and Cultural Award, World of Tattoos Exhibit, International Society of Tropical Dermatology 4th Congress, New Orleans, 1979; 3rd Place Photography Award, Art in Dermatology, American Academy of Dermatology, 1979; Leadership Award, Outstanding Service, United Jewish Appeal, 1976; Silver Award, Original Research in Prevention of Skin Cancers Exhibit, American Academy of Dermatology, 1972; CUTIS Manuscript Contest, 3rd Prize 1971, 1st Prize 1968; Special Award, *Dermatologia Hawaiiana*, Academy of Dermatology, 1971; Department of Army Commendation Medal, 1967; The Husik Award, Dermatology Research, 1963; Henry Silver Award, Research, The Dermatologic Society of Greater New York, 1963; Listed in *Who's Who in Frontier Science and Technology, Directory of Distinguished Americans, Personalities of America, Leaders of Hawaii, International Authors and Writers Who's Who, International Who's Who of Intellectuals, The Best Doctors in America, International Men of Achievement, Dictionary of International Biography, Community*

Leaders of America, Who's Who in the West, Directory of Medical Specialists. Address: 119 Merchant Street, Suite 504, Honolulu, Hawaii 96813.

Gollub, Monica

Monica Gollub

Commissioner. Personal: Born July 5, 1943; Daughter of Dr. Gerda Schulman; Married Gerald Gollub; Mother of Michael Scott. Education: Attended the University of Wisconsin, 1961-63; B.A. cum laude, City University of New York, 1965. Career: Commissioner, Workers Compensation Board, New York State; Former Director of Operations, New York State Workers Compensation Board. Community Activities: Metropolitan Council American Jewish Congress (former member-at-large; past chairperson, women's committee; governing council); Fund Raising Activities for Numerous Causes and Political Candidates. Honors and Awards: Phi Beta Kappa; Pi Delta Phi; Société d'Honneur Francaise; Cum Laude Graduate; Listed in *World Who's Who of Women, Personalities of America, Who's Who in World Jewry.* Address: 125 East 72 Street, New York, New York 10021.

Gonas, John S

John S Gonas

Judge (retired). Personal: Born May 14, 1907; Son of Samuel and Hazel Gonas (both deceased); Married Theodosia B. Gonas; Father of John S. Jr., Roy B. Education: B.S.C.E., Tri-State University, 1930; LL.B., Blackstone College of Law, 1930; Master of Law, Chicago Law School, 1933; Graduate Work in Social Psychiatry, Patent Law and Foreign Languages. Career: Presiding Judge and Chief Justice, Indiana Appellate Court (retired); Judge of County Probate-Juvenile Court; Public Defender; State Senator; State Representative; Justice of the Peace; Assistant Prosecuting Attorney; Assessor of Voters. Organizational Memberships: American and Indiana Bar Associations; Appellate Judges Conference; Juvenile Court Foundation. Community Activities: State Budget Committee, 1940; Senate Leader, 1943; Democratic Conventions (delegate); International Congress of Juvenile Court Judges, Brussels, Belgium (delegate, 1954); First United Nations Conference on Crime and Delinquency, Geneva, Switzerland (delegate upon invitation of Dag Hammarskjold, secretary general of United Nations). Religion: Catholic Church. Honors and Awards: Kentucky Colonel, 1955; Oklahoma Colonel, 1962; Alabama Colonel, 1964; Chieftain on the Staff of Sagamores of the Wabash, Governor of Indiana, 1961; Admiral of Great Navy of Nebraska, Governor of Nebraska, 1959; Certificate of Award, Juvenile Court Institute; Man of the Year, South Bend Optimist Club; Alumni Distinguished Award, Tri-State University; Certificate of Appreciation, United States Navy; Certificate of Appreciation, Lions Club of South Bend; Certificate of Achievement for Demonstrating Vision, Resourcefulness, Hard Work, Integrity, Patience, Understanding, and Common Sense as Hallmarks of American Way of Life, American University of Experience; Listed in *International Who's Who of Intellectuals, Men of Achievement.* Address: 1512 East Wayne, South Bend, Indiana 46615.

Gonzales, Lucille Contreras

Lucille C Gonzales

Administrator of Special Projects. Personal: Born November 30, 1937; Married to Enrique; Mother of Leticia Maria, Cecilia Maria. Education: A.A., San Bernardino Valley College, 1958; B.A., University of California at Santa Barbara, 1960; M.A., Claremont Graduate School, 1969; Administrative Credential, California State University at Fullerton, 1977. Career: Supervisor of Special Projects, 1978; Coordinator of Consolidated Application and Intergroup Relations, 1976-78; Bilingual Coordinator, 1974-76; Bilingual Classroom Teacher, 1970-74; Classroom Teacher, 1960-70. Organizational Memberships: Association of Chino, California Teachers, 1960-74; Employees Council (certified representative, 1972); National Education Association, 1960-74; Chino Association of Management Personnel, 1974-81; Association of California School Administrators, 1974-81; Pi Lambda Theta, 1966-81; Delta Kappa Gamma, 1972-81; Association of San Bernardino County Administrators of Consolidated Programs (vice president, president, 1981-82); National Association of Female Executives, 1979-81; Migrant Executive Board, 1978-81; San Bernardino County Bilingual Task Force, 1974-81; State of California Department of Education Representative in Program Reviews and School Plan Reivews, 1980-81; Association of Secondary Special Projects, 1980-81. Community Activities: Educational and Cultural Organization (treasurer, 1970); P.E.O. Chapter, C.S. (chaplain, 1969); Community Organization of Social Service (board member, 1977). Religion: Member of St. Margaret Mary Catholic Church (annual festival fund raising volunteer). Honors and Awards: Outstanding Elementary Teacher, 1972; Friend of Magnolia Junior High School for contributions to students, 1980; Listed in *Who's Who of American Women, The Directory of Distinguished Americans, Who's Who in the West, Personalities of America, The World Who's Who of Women, Book of Honor.* Address: 4955 Tyler Street, Chino, California 91710.

Gonzalez, Rafael A

Rafael A Gonzalez

College Professor and Author. Personal: Born December 17, 1922; Son of Enrique Gonzalez and Emilia Torres (both deceased); Married to Josefina Hermandez; Father of Marta Josefina, Milagros Maria (twins). Education: Graduate, Utuado High School; B.A., 1953, M.A., 1956, Ph.D., 1970, University of Puerto Rico; Graduate work at University of Munich, 1957-58, Madrid University, 1958-59, and in Arizona, summer of 1965. Career: Professor of Spanish and Humanities, University of Puerto Rico, 1955 to present; Founder and Chairman of Spanish Department, Cayey College, 1967-72; Editor, *Revista Cayey*, 1969-72. Organizational Memberships: Modern Language Association; Sociedad de Autores Puertorriquenos (secretario, 1977-79); Ateneo de Puerto Rico; Asociacion Europea de Profesores de Espanol; Asociacion de Maestros de Puerto Rico. Published works: *Un hombre se ha puesto de pie*, novel, 1967, 3rd edition, 1973, *El retrato del otro*, novel, 1976, "Los cuentos de Emilia Pardo Bazan", essay, 1977, "La busqueda de lo absoluto o La poesia de F. Matos Paoli", essay, 1978, "La obra poetica de Felix Franco Oppenheimer", essay, 1981. Honors and Awards: Received Premio Bolivar Pagan Awards for *El Retrato del Otro* and "Los cuentos de Emilia Pardo Bazan"; Received the Premio Mobil Oil Award for "La Busqueda de lo absoluto", 1978. Address: Josefa Mendia 500, Urb. Los Maestros, Rio Piedras, Puerto Rico 00923.

Good, Mary Lowe

Research Chemist. Personal: Born June 20, 1931; Daughter of Mr. and Mrs. John W. Lowe; Married Bill J. Good; Mother of Billy John, James Patrick. Education: Ph.D. Inorganic Chemistry, University of Arkansas-Fayetteville. Career: Vice-President and Director of Research, U.O.P. Inc., Des Plaines, Illinois, 1981 to present; Boyd Professor of Materials Science, Louisiana State University, 1979-81; Associate Professor, Professor and Boyd Professor of Chemistry, University of New Orleans, 1958-78; Instructor and Assistant Professor of Chemistry, Louisiana State University, 1954-58. Organizational Memberships: Oak Ridge National Laboratory (chemistry division review committee); Harvard Board of Overseers (committee for chemistry department review); National Resource for Computation in Chemistry of Lawrence Berkeley Laboratory (policy board); International Union of Pure and Applied Chemistry (chairman of inorganic section); President's Committee on National Medal of Science (chairman);

A.C.S. (chemical abstracts committee); *Inorganic Chemistry* (editorial board); National Research Council (advisory committee for office of chemistry and chemical technology); National Science Board. Community Activities: Zonta International (chairman, Amelia Earhart fellowship committee); Oak Ridge Associated Universities (past member, board of directors, 1976-76); American Chemical Society (past chairman, board of directors, 1978, 1980); National Advisory Panels (past member, chemistry section N.S.F., 1972-76); N.I.H. Committee on Medicinal Chemistry, 1972-76; Office of Air Force Research, 1974-78; Brookhaven National Laboratory (chemistry committee, 1973-77); Science Information Task Force N.S.F., 1977. Published Works: Approximately 100 Articles in Referred Technical Journals; One Book. Honors and Awards: Agnes Faye Morgan Research Award, Iota Sigma Pi, 1969; Distinguished Alumni Member, Phi Beta Kappa, 1972; Garvan Medal of the American Chemical Society, 1973; Distinguished Alumni Citation, University of Arkansas, 1973; A.I.C. Honor Scroll, Louisiana Chapter, 1974; Teacher of the Year Award, Delta Kappa Gamma, 1974; Herty Medal, Georgia Section of the American Chemical Society, 1975; Florida Section Award for Outstanding Research, Teaching and Public Service, A.C.S., 1979; Honorary Doctor of Laws Degree, University of Arkansas, 1979; Listed in *Outstanding Educators*. Address: 295 Park Drive, Palatine, Illinois 60067.

Goode, Wade Calvin

Wade Goode

Teacher. Personal: Born November 30, 1925; Son of Calvin and Lela Goode; Married Bettie Christina Goode; Father of Vicki Sharon Floyd. Education: Graduate of Bradley High School; Florida State University; University of California; University of Maryland; East Carolina College; B.S. History/Religion 1970. M.S. Elementary Education 1973, M.S. 1975, University of Tennessee. Military: Served in the United States Marine Corps, 1942-45; Served in the United States Army, 1946-48; Served in the United States Air Force, 1948-64, Retiring with the Rank of Technical Sergeant; Served in the Armed Forces 21 Years, Mostly in Electronics and Security. Career: 5th Grade Teacher, E. L. Ross School 1977 to present, Blythe Avenue School 1969-76; First Aid and Swimming Teacher, American Red Cross, 1950-52; Marine Aircraft Mechanic, 1942-45. Organizational Memberships: National Education Association; Tennessee Education Association (representative, 1972, 1973, 1980); Cleveland Education Association (president, 1974; faculty representative, 1970, 1971, 1973, 1976, 1980); Eastern Tennessee Education Association; Parent-Teacher Association. Community Activities: Air Force Sergeants Association (chaplain, historian, 1979-81); Disabled American Veterans (life member; Tennessee department, Chaplain 1974, 1975, 1981, commander 1978; East Tennessee division commander, 1976; senior vice-commander, 1977); Commanders and Adjutants Association; United Tennessee Veterans Association (charter member); Veterans of Foreign Wars; American Legion; International Platform Association; Smithsonian Institution; Toastmasters International. Religion: Church of Christ; Adult Bible Teacher, Many Years; Part-Time Songleader and Speaker. Honors and Awards: National Republican Victory Certificate Signed by President Reagan, Mr. Brock, and Mr. Richards, 1979; Presidential Unit Citation, Bronze Star for Service in Okinawa, Military Ribbons including Good Conduct Medal with 4 Loops, Several Military Education Certificates and Awards; Bradley County Bicentennial Certificate; Service Certificate, Disabled American Veterans; Certificate for Service, E. L. Ross School; Dinner Bell Award, Parent-Teacher Association, 1977; United Veteran Citation, 1978; Colonel Aide de Camp, Governor's Staff, 1979. Address: Post Office Box 3322, Cleveland, Tennessee 37311.

Goodman, Jess Thompson

Quality Assurance Manager. Personal: Born January 18, 1936, in Joplin, Missouri; Son of Walter Raymond and Opal Mae Goodman (both deceased); Married Yvonne Vasquez; Father of Walter Raymond II. Education: Graduate of Joplin High School, 1954; Attended Joplin Jr. College, 1955; A.B., Political Science, University of Missouri, 1959; Studies in Personnel Management undertaken at George Washington University, 1968; M.A., National Security Affairs, Naval Postgraduate School, 1975; Naval War College, 1977; Ph.D. Candidate, International Relations, University of Hawaii, 1978; Studies in Manufacturing Engineering, Missouri Southern College, 1981. Military: Served in the United States Navy, 1959-79, achieving the rank of Lieutenant Commander. Career: Quality Assurance Manager, Eagle-Picher Industries Inc., Electronics Division, Precision Products Department, 1980 to present; Naval Science Instructor, Carl Junction School District, Missouri, 1979-80. Organizational Memberships: World Affairs Forum of Hawaii, 1975-79; World Affairs Council of Pittsburgh, 1978-79; Mensa Special Interest Group in International Affairs (national coordinator, founder, 1978-79); Air Force Association; Academy of Political Science; American Society for Quality Control; Society of Manufacturing Engineers; American Association for the Advancement of Science; American Academy of Political and Social Science; American Defense Preparedness Association; American Film Institute; American Legion; American Management Association; American Mensa Ltd.; American Military Institute; American Museum of Natural History; American Political Science Association; American Security Council Education Foundation; American Society of International Law; American Universities Field Staff. Community Activities: National Archives (associate); Arms Control Association; Centre for Study of Presidency; Common Cause; Federation of American Scientists; Foreign Policy Association; Humanist Association; International Institute for Strategic Studies; International Platform Association; Foreign Policy Research Institute; International Studies Association; National Geographic Society; National Military Intelligence Association; National Rifle Association; Overseas Development Council; Retired Officers Association; Security and Intelligence Fund; Smithsonian Institute; University of Missouri Alumni Association; United States Naval Institute; United States Strategic Institute; Veterans of Foreign Wars; Military Order of the World Wars; World Future Society; Pi Kappa Alpha; Planetary Citizens; Kiwanis International; Mason; Democrat. Religion: Methodist. Published Works: Editor *The Mintas' Hoot*, 1970; Author, *The Chinese Perception of the Spectrum of the Sino-Soviet Territorial Conflict*, 1975. Honors and Awards: Navy Commendation Medal; Navy Achievement Medal with One Gold Star; Navy Meritorious Unit Commendation Medal with Two Bronze Stars; Navy Expert Rifleman Medal; Navy Expert Pistol Shot Medal; Vietnam Service Medal; One Silver Star; Vietnam Campaign Medal; Armed Forces Expeditionary Medal; Vietnam Cross of Gallantry. Address: 2725 Schifferdecker, Joplin, Missouri 64801.

Goodrich, James Tait

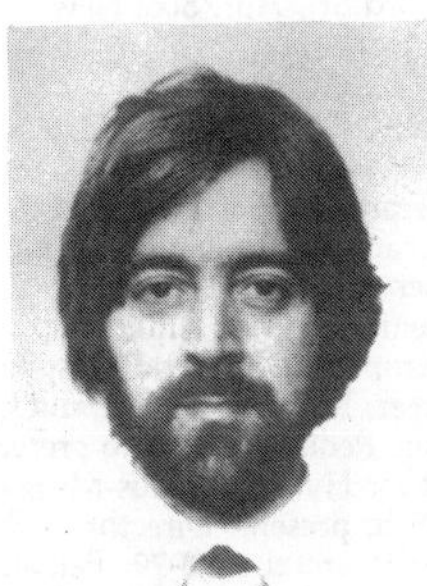
James T Goodrich

Neuroscientist and Physician. Personal: Born April 16, 1946, in Portland, Oregon, U.S.A.; Son of Gail J. Goodrich; Married to Judy Loudin. Education: Attended Fort Buckner Army Language Center (Japan), 1968; A.A., Orange Coast College, 1972; Attended Golden West College, Huntington Beach, California, 1971-72; B.S., cum laude, University of California at Irvine, 1974; M.Phil., 1979, Ph.D., 1980, Columbia University Gradaute School of Arts and Sciences; M.D., Columbia University College of Physicians and Surgeons, 1980. Military: Served with United States Marine Corps Reserve, 1964; Served with U.S.M.C., active duty in Vietnam, 1967-68. Career: Researcher and Physician, New York Neurological Institute (neurosurgery), 1981 to present; Associate Research Consultant, University of California at Irvine Education Plan, 1974; S.C.U.B.A. salvage diver, 1969; Computer Operator, I.B.M. 360 systems, 1966; Store Detective, 1965-66; Participant in numerous professional conferences. Organizational Memberships: American Association for the History of Medicine; American Medical Association; British Brain Research Association; European Brain and Behavior Society; New York Academy of Medicine; New Jersey Medical History Society; Columbia Presbyterian Medical Society; Society for Ancient Medicine. Community Activities: Friends of the Columbia University Libraries; Friends of the Osler Library, McGill University; Society for Bibliography of Natural History; University of California Alumni Association; Les Amis du

Vin; South Coast Wine Explorers Club (past chairman); Friends of Bacchus Wine Club (past chairman); Dionysius Council of Presbyterian Hospital in the City of New York. Published Works: Contributor of articles to numerous professional journals, including *Connecticut Medicine, Gastroenterology, Anatomical Record, Journal of Pediatric Surgery, Journal of Comparative Neurology, Bulletin of New York Academy of Medicine, American Journal of Pathology.* Honors and Awards: Kiwanis Club Scholarship; Willamette Industries Scholarship; University of California President's Undergraduate Research Fellow, 1973-74; National Institute of Health Medical Scientist Trainee; Orange Coast College Class Valedictorian, 1972; Sir William Osler Medal, American Association for History of Medicine, 1977-78; Participated in National Student Research Forum, Roche Laboratories; Mead-Johnson Award for overall excellence of research, National Student Research Forum, 1978; Sandoz Award for outstanding research, 1980; Melicow Award, New York Academy of Medicine; Listed in *Who's Who in the East, Who's Who Among Students in American Universities and Colleges,* and others. Address: 214 Everett Place, Englewood, New Jersey 07631.

Gordon, Donnie E

Marketing Coordinator. Personal: Born March 9, 1947; Married; Mother of Two Children. Education: English Major/Art Minor, University of Alabama, 1965-67; Courses in Business Administration, Management, Creative Writing and Business Law 1978-80, Women in Management and Personal Development Seminars 1980, University of Nevada-Las Vegas. Career: American International Vacations, Inc. Resort Timesharing, Las Vegas, Nevada, Marketing Coordinator to Vice President of Marketing 1981, Executive Assistant 1979-81, Manager of the Administration Department and Creator/Manager of In-House Publications Department 1978-79; Lead Technical Documentation Typist, Northrop Services, Inc., Huntsville, Alabama, 1974-77; Free Lance Publications and Parachuting, 1972-74; Administrative Manager, XI World Parachuting Championships, Tahlequah, Oklahoma, 1972; Special Projects Secretary, United States Parachute Association, Monterey, California, 1969-72; Manager, Instant Type Services, Monterey, California, 1969-72; Senior Secretary, Northrop Space Labs, Huntsville, Alabama; Part-Time Secretary, Alabama State Highway Department, Tuscaloosa, 1965. Address: Route 2 Box 23X, State Road 3028, Apex, North Carolina 27502.

Gorman, Timothy John

Public Relations Executive. Personal: Born January 19, 1939; Son of Mary W. Gorman; Married Mary Daly; Father of Timothy John Jr., Tara Kathleen, Maureen Daly. Education: B.S. Public Relations, University of Maryland, 1961; Master of Communications Studies, The American University, 1968-70. Military: Serves in the United States Naval Reserve with Rank of Commander and Saw Active Duty, 1961-64. Career: Senior Vice-President and Public Relations Counselor, The Adams Group, Inc.; Vice-President of Client Services; Advertising and Public Relations Account Executive; Copywriter. Organizational Memberships: National Press Club; American Society of Association Executives (associate member, advisory committee); Public Relations Society of America; National Public Relations Network. Community Activities: Montgomery County, Maryland, Chamber of Commerce (public relations chairman, economic development committee, 1979-82); Chevy Chase Section 3 (board member, 1975-77). Honors and Awards: Listed in *Who's Who in the East.* Address: 7000 Georgia Street, Chevy Chase, Maryland 20815.

Gary A Gosky

Gorup, Gregory James

Executive. Personal: Born March 27, 1948; Son of Mr. and Mrs. Mike Gorup. Education: B.A., St. Benedict College, 1970; M.B.A., University of Pennsylvania, 1972. Career: Citibank, New York City, 1972-75: Market Planning and Development (1972-73), Product Planning and Development (1973), Marketing Officer (1973); Division Staff Corporate Product Management Division (1973-74), Product Manager for Dividend Reinvestment and Corporate Stock Transfer Services (1974-75); Irving Trust Company, New York City, 1976 to present: Assistant Vice President, Director New Product Development (1975), Vice President (1977 to present), Manager, Product Management Department (1980 to present). Organizational Memberships: American Management Association; Bank Administration Institute; Marshall D. Sokol & Associates (Adjunct Facility). Community Activities: Knights of Columbus, Council #4708 (grand knight, 1968-70); New York East Side Lions Club (treasurer, 1975-76, president, 1977-80); Big Brothers of New York (fund raising committee, 1974-76). Religion: Archdiocese of New York; Adult Education Program, Volunteer Teacher, 1972-75. Honors and Awards: Listed in *Who's Who in Industry and Finance, Who's Who in the World, Who's Who in the East.* Address: 245 E. 63rd St., Apt. 806, New York, New York 10021.

Gosky, Garry Alan

Doctor for the Underprivileged. Personal: Born July 13, 1946 in Cleveland, Ohio; Married Patricia; Father of Ross, Brad, Jill, Paul. Education: Graduate with multiple honors of St. Ignatius High School, 1964; B.A. Religion with multiple honors, Case Western Reserve University, 1968; M.D., Ohio State University School of Medicine, 1972; Licensed in Ohio, 1972; Licensed in New York (inactive), 1974; Internship, Residency, Chief Residency, Rainbow Babies' and Children's Hospital; Residency, Cleveland Metropolitan General Hospital; Board Certification, American Board of Pediatrics; Certification, Crippled Children's Services. Career: Rainbow Babies' and Children's Hospital Department of Pediatrics, Case Western Reserve University, Assistant Professor of Clinic Pediatrics 1977 to present, Assistant Professor 1976-77, Senior Instructor of Pediatrics 1975-76; Pediatrician, Private Practice and for Hydrocephalus-Myelodysplasia Clinic, 1974-77; Pediatrician, Case Western University Department of Community Health, 1975 to present; Director of Pediatrics, St. Vincent Charity Hospital 1977-81, Cleveland Metropolitan General Hospital, Massilon City Hospital 1978-79; Pediatric Director of Child Development Units, Valley Springs 1976-81, Roseland Extended Care Facility 1977-80, Charlotte Village Extended Care Facility 1977-80; Pediatric Medical Director, Aristocrat South Extended Care Facility 1976 to present, Aristocrat West Skilled Nursing Facility 1978 to present, Children's Aid Society 1975 to present, Cleveland Developmental Center 1980-81, Ohio Residential Services, 1980 to present, P.V.A. Group Home 1977 to present. Community Activities: Federation for Community Planning (consultant); P.S.R.O. of Cleveland; Marcare Corporation of Health Delivery Systems (national pediatric advisor, 1976-81); Birthright of Cleveland (advisory board); Health Education Learning Progams, Inc. (medical consultant); Marriage Encounter (west side coordinator); Eucharistic Minister to Patients, 1981; Our Lady of Angel's Parish (parish renewal program; football and basketball coach; consultant, parents support league; annual festival worker); St. Ignatius President's Club. Religion: Our Lady of Angel's Parish. Honors and Awards: Buckeye Award for the Care of the Mentally Retarded, Team Award, Won Twice; First Alumneye Spotlight, St. Ignatius High School, 1979; Roche Award for Student Who Best Exemplifies the Ideals of the Modern American Physician on the Basis of Scholarship, Character, Personality, and Seriousness of Purpose; Alpha Omega Alpha Honor Society; Landacre Research Honor Society; Guest Speaker, Association for Practitioners in Infection Control; Case Western Reserve University Honoree, Alumni Directory; Listed in *Who's Who in the Midwest, Community Leaders of America, Directory of American Medical Specialists, International Who's Who of Intellectuals, Directory of Distinguished Americans, International Register of Profiles, Dictionary of International Biography, Book of Honor, Men of Achievement, Personalities of the West and Midwest.* Address: 17301 Fernshaw Avenue, Cleveland, Ohio 44111.

Gosselin, Raymond A

Pharmacy College President. Personal: Born July 28, 1922 in Manchester, New Hampshire; Married Christine; Father of John, Christine, Paul. Education: B.S. 1943, M.S. Pharmacy Administration 1948, Sc.D. (honorary) 1970, Massachusetts College of Pharmacy; M.B.A. Statistics, Boston University College of Business Administration Graduate School, 1951; Registered Pharmacist, Massachusetts and New Hampshire. Military: Served in the United States Navy as an Officer in the Amphibious Forces during World War II; Awarded Silver Star Medal and Purple Heart. Career: President, Massachusetts College of Pharmacy and Allied Health Sciences, 1972 to present; R. A. Gosselin and Company, Inc., Founder and President as Research Society, Inc. 1952, President 1956-72; Faculty Member, Business Administration, Massachusetts College of Pharmacy, 1946-56. Organizational Memberships: American Association of Colleges of Pharmacy (chairman, finance committee, 1973-75); American College of Apothecaries; American Pharmaceutical Associaiton (policy committee on professional affairs, 1974); Academy of Pharmaceutical Sciences (public policy committee, 1975-79); American Society of Hospital Pharmacists (commission on goals, 1976-79); American Statistical Association; Massachusetts State Pharmaceutical Association; Massachusetts Society of Hospital Pharmacists; Maine Pharmaceutical Association; Market Research Managers Association (life member); New Hampshire Pharmaceutical Association. Community Activities: Massachusetts College of Pharmacy (secretary, vice-president of board of trustees, 1967-72); Pharmaceutical Reimbursement Advisory Committee Dealing with the M.A.C./E.A.C. Implementation (appointed by secretary of H.E.W. to 2-year term, 1976); Institute of Medicine, Washington, D.C. (member of study committee on pharmaceutical innovation and the need of developing countries, 1978-79); Astra Pharmaceutical Company (director); Retired Officers Association; Kappa Psi Pharmaceutical Fraternity; Phi Delta Chi Fraternity; Rho Chi and Beta Gamma Sigma Honor Societies. Published Works: Author of Numerous Published Articles and Textbook Chapters Dealing with Pharmaceutical Marketing, Marketing Research, Statistics and the Health Care System; Lecturer in Industry and Academic Programs. Address: Masschusetts College of Pharmacy and Allied Health Sciences, 179 Longwood Avenue, Boston, Massachusetts 02115.

Gowens, Verneeta Viola

Freelance Writer. Personal: Born March 19, 1913; Daughter of Mr. and Mrs. William Gibson (both deceased); Married; Mother of Victoria Ann Utke, Mary Ann Weiss. Education: Graduate of Thornton Township High School; Bryant and Stratton Business College; Journalism Workshops and Courses at Various Universities. Career: Freelance Writer; Women's Editor, *Star-Tribune* Publications. Oranizational Memberships: Illinois Women's Press Association; National Federation of Press Women (corresponding secretary). Community Activities: Parent-Teacher Association (district 150 president, 1965-66); Thornton High School (advisory council for program in limited occupational training, 1963-69); South Holland Industrial Commissioner, 1965-68; Family Services and Mental Health Center of South Cook County (board of directors, 1974-77); South Holland Salvation Army Unit, 1958 to present; South Holland Community Chest, 1978 to present; Thornton Community College Nursing Program (advisory board, 1976 to present); South Holland Diamond Jubilee Committee, 1969. Religion: Sunday School Teacher, 1955-70; Youth Leader, 1966-72; Editorial Council, *Church Herald* National Magazine of Reformed Church in America, 1976 to present; Editor, Church Newsletter, 1981 to present. Honors and Awards: South Holland Chamber of Commerce Award, 1970; Woman of the Year, Illinois Women's Press Association, 1974; General Council Award, 1974; South Holland Village Award, 1969; Top Awards in Journalism, National Federation of Press Women, 1976; 50 Other Journalistic Awards, National Federation of Press Women, Northern Illinois University, Illinois Press Association, Sub. Press Foundation. Address: 16830 South Park Avenue, South Holland, Illinois 60473.

John W Grace

Grace, John William

Engineering Manager. Personal: Born May 29, 1921; Married Ruth Delores Schroeder; Father of Martha Ann G. Winters, Joan Ruth G. Chatfield, Nancy E., John W. Jr. Education: American Television Institute of Technology, 1950; B.S.E.E., Drexel University, 1960. Military: Served in the United States Navy as Fire Controlman, 1941-45. Career: E.G. & G. Inc., Engineering Manager in Idaho Falls, Idaho 1977 to present, Manager of Business Development Operational Test and Evaluation in Albuquerque, New Mexico 1973-77, Scientific Executive and Manager of Engineering at Special Projects Division in Las Vegas, Nevada 1966-73; Instrumentation Programs, R.C.A. Missile and Surface Radar Division, Moorsetown, New Jersey, Project Engineer 1960-66, Design Engineer 1956-60, Technician 1950-56. Organizational Memberships: Institute of Electrical and Electronics Engineers (member, 1950-73; professional groups including microwave technology, antennas and propagation); Association of Old Crows, 1969-77; Instrument Society of America (senior member, 1980 to present; director of scientific and instrumentation research division). Community Activities: American Legion (member, 1945 to present; adjutant and vice-commander, 1950); Boy Scouts of America, 1969-71; Episcopal Couples Retreat (president couple, 1969-70); Little League Baseball, 1968-73; Young American Football Association, 1973-75; New Mexico Energy Research Resource Registry, 1974-77. Religion: Episcopal. Honors and Awards: Patentee, Contradirectional Wave Guide Coupler; Listed in *Who's Who in the West, Who's Who Honorary Society of America, Men of Achievement, Who's Who in Finance and Industry*. Address: 1270 Riviera Drive, Idaho Falls, Idaho 83401.

Graham, Amanda Lola

Poet, Photographer, Writer. Personal: Born November 12, 1896; Daughter of John Gainer and Della Beall; Widow; Mother of Billy Duane, John Thomas, Helen Marie G. Hall, Donald Jackson, Beverly Ann G. Forson. Education: Teacher's Certificate, Florence Normal, Florence, Alabama, 1914. Career: Poet, Photographer, Writer; Teacher, Primary Grade School. Organizational Memberships: Ina Coolbrith Poetry Circle; Chaparral Poets (local chapter; state chapter); State Poetry Society; National Writers Club. Community Activities: Active in Schools, Parks, Church and Other Organizations; Donor to Current Needs. Religion: Covenant Church. Published Works: Nature and Wildlife Pictures Published in Many Magazines and Books. Honors and Awards: Winner, Local, State and National Awards in Poetry, 30 Years; National Grand Prize, Crossroads 5th National Contest, 1980; Many Prizes in Photography. Address: 225-93 Mt. Hermon Road, Scotts Valley, California 95066.

Graham, Daniel Robert

Governor of the State of Florida. Personal: Born November 9, 1936; Son of Ernest and Hilda Graham; Married Adele Khoury; Father of Gwen, Cissy, Suzanne, Kendall. Education: B.A., University of Florida, 1959; Law Degree, Harvard Law School, 1962. Career: Governor of the State of Florida, 1978 to present; Florida Senator, 1970-78; State Representative, 1966-70; Vice-Chairman of the Board, The Sengra Corporation; Vice-President, The Graham Company; Attorney. Organizational Memberships: Education Commission of the States (chairman, 1980-81); Southern Regional Education Board (chairman, 1980-81); Intergovernmental Advisory Council to the Department of Education (chairman). Community Activities: United States Intergovernmental Advisory Council on Education; 4-H Youth Foundation; National Commission on Reform of Secondary Education; National Foundation for

Improvement of Education; Southern Regional Education Board (chairman); National Committee for Citizens in Education; Senior Centers of Dade County, Florida. Religion: United Church of Christ. Honors and Awards: One of Five Most Outstanding Young Men in Florida, Florida Jaycees, 1971; Allen Morris Award for Outstanding First Term Member of the Senate, 1972; Allen Morris Award for Most Valuable Member of the Senate, 1973; Allen Morris Award for Second Most Effective Senator, 1976; Named by Jimmy Carter to Head the Carribean Central American Action Group; Conservation '70's Florida Wildlife Federation and Sierra Club Legislative Awards. Address: 700 North Adams, Tallahassee, Florida 32302.

Graham, Francis G

Astronomer. Personal: Born June 1, 1951. Son of Francis E. Graham (deceased) and Marlene Miller; Married Charmaine Graham; Father of Kathryn K. Education: B.A. 1975, M.S. 1981, University of Pittsburgh; Honorary D.D., 1981. Career: Astronomer, Halo Star Research 1980, Sounding Rocket Testing 1968-71, Lunar Mapping Program; Solar Energy Consultant; Science and Mathematics Instructor; Hydrologist; Physics Instructor. Community Activities: Tripoli Science Association (secretary, 1964 to present); A.I.A.A. Publications Committee, 1979-81; *Tripolitan Journal* (editor, 1978-80). Religion: Committee on Science and Religion. Honors and Awards: Bausch and Lomb Science Award, 1969; Young Men's Christian Association Service Award, 1975. Address: 417 Franklin Street, East Pittsburgh, Pennsylvania 15112.

Gratton, Marilyn

Documentation Services Manager. Personal: Born January 26, 1948; Daughter of Robert and Celia Gratton. Education: B.A. English/History, University of California-Los Angeles, 1969; Standard Secondary Education Teaching Credential, Life Issue, State of California, 1970; Miscellaneous Courses, Various Colleges. Career: Manager of Documentation Services; Owner and Operator, Gradan Consulting Company; Owner/Operator, Professional Resume Preparation Service, 1977 to present; Technical Writer/Editor, Including Experience in United States Navy Technical Manuals, Aerospace, Integrated Logistic Support and Computer Software. Organizational Memberships: Society of Logistic Engineers; Society for Technical Communication; National Writers Club; American Mensa Society; University of California-Los Angeles Alumni Association. Published Works: "The Leopard and His Brother", *Lighted Pathway*, 1982; *It's a Good Thing I'm Not Married*, 1975; "I'd Do It Again", *Slimmer*, 1981; "Write Your Own Resume", *Modern Secretary*, 1980; 7-Month Column, American Mensa Society; Numerous Articles, *Update* Journal of Society for Technical Communication; "From Creative Script Writing to Finished Tape Production", *California English*, 1975; "I.A. and English Team Up for Television", *School Shop*, 1974; "I.Q. Testing", *Classroom Practices in Teaching English-MEASURE FOR MEASURE*, 1972-73; "Harry", *Classroom Practices in Teaching English-THROUGH A GLASS DARKLY*, 1971-72; "The Monroes" Television Review, *Independent Star-News*, 1966. Honors and Awards: 3rd Place, Articles Contest, National Writers Club, 1976; Honorable Mention Poetry Contest, National Writers Club, 1976; 2nd Place, Port Hueneme Harbor Days Photography Contest, 1976; Young Careerist, Hueneme Business and Professional Women, 1975; Listed in *Who's Who in the West, Who's Who of American Women, Personalities of the West, World Who's Who of Women*. Address: Gradan Consulting Company, Post Office Box 3594, Thousand Oaks, California 91359.

Gravina, Robert Michael

Robert Gravina

Central Quality Control Staff Member. Personal: Born March 16, 1943; Son of Florence L. Gravina; Father of Michele Suzanne. Education: Graduate with honors of Somerville High School, Somerville, Massachusetts, 1961; A.B. Mathematics 1966, M.S. Mathematics 1968, Ph.D. Candidate, Northeastern University, Boston, Massachusetts. Military: Served in the United States Army Ordnance Branch, Attaining the Rank of Captain and Honorably Discharged, 1966-80. Career: Quality Control Engineer, Wang Laboratories, Tewksbury, Massachusetts, 1982 to present; Staff Member, Sensor Processing Technology, M.I.T. Lincoln Laboratory, 1981-82; University of Lowell Mathematics Department, Massachusetts, Associate Professor 1969-81, Full Member of Graduate Faculty 1980-81; Teaching Assistant, Northeastern University Department of Mathematics, 1967-69; Senior Programmer/Reliability Engineer, Project Apollo, M.I.T. Instrumentation Laboratory, Cambridge Massachusetts, 1964-68; Mathematician for Graphic Analysis of Heat Shield, Avco Corporation, Lowell, Massachusetts, 1963-64; Chemist, Dennison Manufacturing Company, Framingham, Massachusetts, 1962-63. Organizational Memberships: Armed Forces Communications and Electronics Association (member, 1962-66; president, 1964-65); Mathematical Association of America, 1965 to present; National Council of Teachers of Mathematics (member, 1969 to present; conference delegate, 1971-78); Computers and Education, 1978 to present. Community Activities: Lowell Mathematics Fair (judge, 1972, 1973); Tewksbury Junior High School Mathematics Fair (judge, 1975-79); Wadsworth Publishing Comany (text reviewer); Presentation of Mary Academy, Hudson, New Hampshire (advisor and consultant, mathematics department); Upward Bound Program, Northeastern University, 1967-69; Lowell State College and University of Lowell Mathematics Department (chairperson, departmental affairs committee, 1973-74; departmental personnel committee, 1973-74, 1976-79; co-acting department chairperson, 1973; curricula committee, 1973-75; coordinator of south campus courses offered by department, 1970 to present; course assignment and scheduling assistant, 1971-79; department chairperson, 1974-75; coordinator, south campus mathematics department, 1975 to present; executive officer, mathematics department, south campus, 1975-79; department work load committee, 1976-78; department promotion and tenure committee, 1976-78; department evaluation committee, 1979). Religion: Roman Catholic. Published Works: *The Articulate Computer*, In Progress; "How Computers Have Developed and Changed", *Computer Education*, 1979; "Computer Program Analysis", *Computers and Education International Journal*, 1979; "The Modern Computer and Microelectronics", *Association of Field Service Managers*, 1979; "Computer Simulations", *International Journal of Mathematical Education in Science and Technology*, 1979; "Thinking, Learning, and Intelligence", *International Journal of Mathematical Education in Science and Technology*, 1980; "How Computers Have Developed and Changed" (reprint), Aberdeen College of Educaiton, Scotland, 1979; "Learning, Teaching and Mathematics", *Computer Education*, 1979. Honors and Awards: Sigma Xi Scientific Research Society of North America (full member, 1979 to present); Pi Mu Epsilon National Honorary Mathematics Fraternity (full member, 1979 to present); Sabbatical Leave, University of London, Institute of Education, England, 1978; Dean's List, Top Tenth of Liberal Arts Science Majors, Northeastern University; Academy Honor Society, 1965; Distinguished Military Student Award, 1965; Professor of Military Science Award, 1964; Distinguished Military Graduate Award, 1966; Listed in *Who's Who in the East, Personalities of America*. Address: 156 Westwood Drive, Hashua, New Hampshire 03062.

Gray, Dora E Clyburn

Warehouse Accountant. Personal: Born March 26, 1924; Daughter of Mr. and Mrs. H. E. Clyburn (both deceased); Married Harvie A. Gray (deceased); Mother of Dennis H., Ladell L. Green. Education: Graduate of Federal Institute, Tyler, Texas, 1944; Courses, University of Texas-Austin, 1953-54; Courses, Texas Christian University, Ft. Worth, 1963. Career: Warehouse Accountant, 1975 to present; Loan Officer, Concho Educators Federal Credit Union, 1972-75; Assistant Treasurer, Pool Company, Inc., 1962-72; Assistant Manager and Treasurer, Wagner Office Equipment, 1948-61. Organizational Memberships: Business and Professional Women's Club (member, 1955 to present; state board, 5 years; all district and local offices); Desk and Derrick Club, 1963-72; International Platform Association, 1979 to present. Community Activities: Salvation Army (Christmas Bell Ringer, 1955 to present); United Way (metro committee, 1972-76); Fort Concho Museum, 1978 to present; West Texas Boys Ranch, 1964-68; E.R.A., 1955 to present; Girl Scouts of America, 1978 to present; Jerry Lewis Telethon, 1980; Marguire Rawalt National Foundation (state chairman, 1974; committee member, 1981-82); Democratic Party (precinct delegate to county, 1978, 1980; alternate, state convention, 1978). Religion: Johnson Street Church of Christ. Honors and Awards: Texas Committee for E.R.A. Award, 1972; Legislation Certificate, 1963; National Foundation Award, 1972; United Way Award, 1972; Woman of the Year, San Angelo Business and Professional Women's Club, 1979; Listed in *Who's Who in the South and Southwest, Who's Who in Finance and Industry, Community Leaders of America, Directory of Distinguished Americans, Notable Americans, Personalities of the South, Personalities of America, Who's Who of American Women, International Who's Who in Community Service, Dictionary of International Biography, World's Who's Who of Women.* Address: 915 North Adams, San Angelo, Texas 76901.

Green, Albert W

Pastor and Educator. Personal: Born August 12, 1929; Son of Levallia C. Green; Married; Father of Vicki, James, Lisa. Education: A.B. Sociology, Virginia Union University, Richmond, Virginia. Military: Served in the United States Armed Forces, 1951-53. Career: Pastor, Second Baptist Church of Danville, 5 Years; Educator, Danville, Illinois, School District 118, 13 Years. Community Activities: O.I.C. (board of directors); Vermillion County Emergency Service; Vermillion County Region Diabetic Association (board member); Danville Senior High School Human Relations Club (sponsor). Religion: Woodriver Baptist District Association (secretary); Congress of Christian Education (founder; assistant dean); Committee on Church Extension of General Baptist State Convention. Honors and Awards: Saudsow Staff Teacher of the Year Award, 1978; Danville Black Ministerial Alliance Certificate, 1978; Listed in *Personalities of the West and Midwest, Who's Who Among Black Baptist Ministers in America.* Address: 1001 North Grant Street, Danville, Illinois 61832.

Green, Alma J

Housing Coordinator. Personal: Born April 19, 1932; Daughter of Will and Ophelia James (both deceased); Married Ben Green; Mother of Tommy E., Lois G. McCray, A. Elaine, Bennie G. Robinson, Chandra R., Benja E. Education: A.A., Lawson State Junior College. Career: J.C.C.E.O., Job Developer 1982 to present, Family Worker; Notary Public State-at-Large, 1982-86; Housing Coordinator, Social Services; Family Counselor. Organizational Memberships: Social Workers Club of Jefferson County, 1970-78; Family Workers Club, 1967-70. Community Activities: Order of Eastern Star, 1957 to present; Town of Mulga (member and secretary, water and gas board, 1982-86; councilwoman, 1976 to present); Parent-Teacher Associatoin (Minor High School 2nd vice-president, 1976-77; Mulga Junior High School president, 1960-65); Ensley Federal Credit Union (chairperson of credit committee, 1969 to present); Westfield Alumni Association, 1974 to present; Alabama League of Municipalities, 1976 to present; *Birmingham Times Newspaper* (reporter, weekly column, 1966 to present). Religion: Peace Baptist Church; Church Clerk, 1976 to present, Sunday School Teacher, 1965 to present; Board of Ushers Secretary; Deaconess Board Secretary; District 5 Sunday School Secretary. Honors and Awards: Mother of the Year, 1967; Recognition Awards, Alabama Federation of Women's Clubs; Outstanding Service Award, Zeta Phi Lambda Sorority, 1973. Address: 219 First Street, Mulga, Alabama 35118.

Alma J Green

Green, Edith

United States Congresswoman (retired). Personal: Mother of James S., Richard A. Education: Graduate of Salem, Oregon, Public Schools; Attended Willamette University, 1927-29; B.S., University of Oregon, 1939. Career: United States Congresswoman, 1955-75; Educator. Organizational Memberships: United States Congress (appropriations committee; subcommittee on labor, health, education and welfare; legislative subcommittee; education and labor committee; chairman, subcommittee on secondary education); Legislation Authored in Congress (higher education acts, 1965, 1967; higher education facilities act; higher education act, 1972; amendments to end sex discrimination in education and health manpower training; social security improvements; equal pay for equal work; vocational rehabilitation; national quality education act, 1972; juvenile delinquency prevention and control act; bill to compensate victims of crime; library service act; bill requiring improved financial management of federal programs; war powers act, limiting powers of a President; narcotic addict rehabilitation act; hospital and nursing home care for the aged; Constitutional amendment to provide for special presidential election in case of "no confidence" vote); Henry M. Jackson Oregon Presidential Primary Campaign (chairman, 1972); Robert F. Kennedy Oregon Presidential Primary Campaign (chairman, 1968); John F. Kennedy Oregon Presidential Campaign (chairman, 1960); Democratic National Convention (asked by John F. Kennedy to second his nomination, first woman chairman of a state delegation, 1960; asked by Adlai E. Stevenson to second his nomination, 1956; delegate, 1956, 1960, 1964, 1968, 1972); World Population Conference, Bucharest (congressional delegate, 1974); World Health Organization, Switzerland (congressional delegate, 1973); U.N.E.S.C.O. General Conference, Paris (congressional delegate, 1964, 1966); N.A.T.O. Conference, London (congressional delegate, 1958); Parliamentary Conference, Switzerland (congressional delegate, 1958); Non-Government Sponsored International Conference on Higher Education, Japan (one of two delegates invited, 1974). Community Activities: Benjamin Franklin Savings and Loan, Portland, Oregon (board of directors); Linfield College, Oregon (board of trustees); University of Oregon Health Sciences Center, Portland (advisory board); Oregon Community Foundation (board member). Honors and Awards: Honorary Doctor of Laws Degrees, Beloit College, Wisconsin 1971, Oberlin College, Ohio 1966, Reed College, Oregon 1966, Georgetown University, Washington, D.C. 1966, Yale University, Connecticut 1965, Gonzaga University, Washington 1964, Linfield College, Oregon 1964; Honorary Doctor of Public Administration Degree, Willamette University, Oregon, 1970; First Citizen Award, Portland, 1978; Annual Achievement Award, American Association of University Women, 1974; Simon LeMoyne Medal, LeMoyne College, Syracuse, New York, 1973; Annual Award, Oregon Public Health Association, 1973; Abram L. Sachar Award, National Women's Committee, Brandeis University, 1972; Distinguished Service Award, Oregon State University, 1972; Outstanding Service Award, National Association of Student Personel Administrators, 1972; Portland Women of Accomplishment, One of Ten Named by *Oregon Journal*, 1972; Citation of Appreciation, American Legion, 1972; Award of Distinction, National Council of Administrative Women in Education, 1971; Distinguished Service Award, National Association of Trade and Technical Schools, 1971; Citation, World Convention of Churches of Christ, Sydney, Australia, 1970; Conde Nast Award, Georgetown University Student Body, 1969; Distinguished Service Award, National Education Association, 1967; Distinguished Service Award, Council of Chief State School Officers, 1967; Outstanding Woman in the Field of Government, *Who's Who of American Women*, 1967; President's Award, National Rehabilitation Association, 1967; Award for Distinguished Services, University of Oregon, 1967; E. B. McNaughton Award, Oregon Chapter of American Civil Liberties Union, 1966; Top Hat Award, Business and Professional Women's Clubs of America, 1965; Distinguished Achievement Award, The American College Public Relations Association, 1964;

Eleanor Roosevelt - Mary McLeod-Bethune World Citizenship Award, National Council of Negro Women, 1964. Address: 8031 Sacajawea Way, Wilsonville, Oregon 97070.

Green, Lori Beth

Senior Budget Analyst. Personal: Born March 27, 1944; Daughter of Emanuel and Selma Green. Education: B.A. French and Psychology, Western Reserve University, 1964; M.A. International Relations, Syracuse University, 1967. Career: Senior Budget Analyst, Office of Management and Budget, Mayor's Office, New York City, 1981 to present; Associate Planning and Operations Officer, United Nations Fund for Population Activities, 1978-80; Coordinator of Medical Affairs, Ayerst International, 1972-78; Assistant to Chairman, Microbiology Department, Cornell University Medical College, 1971-72; Personnel Officer, World Health Organization, Geneva, Switzerland, 1968-71. Organizational Memberships: World Federation of Public Health Associations; American Society of Public Administration; American Public Health Association; Pi Sigma Alpha. Address: 315 East 65th Street, New York City, New York 10021.

Green, Virginia Mae Hicks

Virginia G Green

Retired Educator. Personal: Born March 24, 1912; Daughter of Nelson H. and Carrie Wyche Hicks; Married to Rhodes Green; Mother of Carrie Rowena Waiter, Rhodes Nelson Green (deceased). Education: Graduate, Henderson Institute, Henderson, North Carolina, 1929; Attended Knoxville College, Knoxville, Tennessee; B.S., Virginia State College, 1939; M.A., North Carolina Central University, 1953; Undertook further graduate study at Atlanta University, Columbia University, East Carolina University and University of North Carolina at Chapel Hill. Career: Teacher and elementary school Principal, Vance County Schools, 1931-34 and 1941-53; Junior high school Teacher, Creedmore High School, Creedmore, North Carolina, 1936-39; Supervisor of elementary schools, Anson County, North Carolina, 1954-57; Supervisor of Wayne County Schools and Supervisor of Compensatory Education Program, Goldsboro, North Carolina, 1957-77. Organizational Memberships: Vance County Schoolmasters Club (secretary, 1948-50); Vance County Home Extension Council (president, 1947-50); Headstart Advisory Council of Wayne County (president, 1960-62); Interagency Council of Goldsboro (president); N.R.T.C. of Goldsboro and Wayne County (vice president, 1980). Community Activities: Epsilon Phi Omega chapter of Alpha Kappa Alpha Sorority (epistoleus, 1962-63); Former Girl Scout Leader. Religion: Member of Nun Bush Baptist Church, Henderson, North Carolina (Sunday school teacher, chairman of founder's day activities, 1977-81). Honors and Awards: Received Scholarship to Knoxville College, 1929-30; Received numerous local community awards through the years; Listed in *Personalities of the South, Community Leaders and Noteworthy Americans*. Address: 119 Neuse Circle, Goldsboro, North Carolina 27530.

Greenberg, Lewis Mitchell

Educator. Personal: Born February 4, 1938; Son of A. Byron and Pearl S. Greenberg. Education: B.A., Rutgers University, 1961; M.A., 1965, A.B.D., 1968, University of Pennsylvania. Career: Professor of Art History, Moore College of Art; Editor-in-Chief, *Kronos;* Associate Editor, *Pensee*, 1972-75; Editorial Advisor, Greystone Press, 1968. Organizational Memberships: College Art Association, 1963-70; Innovative Concepts Associates, 1972-79; Society for Interdisciplinary Studies, 1975 to present; Cosmos and Chronos (vice president, 1975 to president); Center for Velikovskian and Interdisciplinary Studies, Glassboro State College (chairman, 1975 to present); Institute for Collective Behavior and Memory (advisory board, 1980 to present); Editorial Advisory Board Member, *Frontiers of Science*, 1980 to present. Honors and Awards: Dean's List, 1959-61; Henry Rutgers Scholar in Art History, 1960-61; Classics Prize, 1961; Member of Pi Mu Epsilon; Teaching Fellow, University of Pennsylvania, 1961-63; Head Teaching Fellow, 1963-64; Kress Fellow, 1964-65; Nominated for Lindbach Award, Villanova University, 1967; Nominated for Honorary Doctor of Humanities, Glassboro State College, 1976; Listed in *Who's Who in the East, Personalities of America.* Address: 300 East Lancaster Avenue, Wynnewood, Pennsylvania 19096.

Greenberger, Ellen

Professor of Social Ecology. Personal: Born November 19, 1935; Daughter of Dr. and Mrs. Edward M. Silver; Married Michael Burton; Mother of Kari, David. Education: A.B., Vassar College, 1956; M.A. 1959, Ph.D., 1961, Harvard University. Career: Professor of Social Ecology, Interdisciplinary Psychologist, University of California-Irvine; Assistant Professor of Psychology, Wellesley College, Massachusetts; Principal Research Scientist, The Johns Hopkins University, Baltimore, Maryland. Honors and Awards: Phi Beta Kappa; Margaret Floy Washburn Fellowship, 1956-58; United States Public Health Service, Pre-Doctoral Fellowship 1956-58, Post-Doctoral Fellowship 1961-62. Address: Program in Social Ecology, University of California, Irvine, California 92717.

Lewis M Greenberg

Greenburg, Stan

Cardiovascular Pharmacologist. Personal: Born September 14, 1945; Son of Louis and Anna Greenberg; Married Patricia Ann; Father of Jonathan Michael and Kristen Ann. Education: B.S. magna cum laude, Brooklyn College of Pharmacy, 1968; M.S. 1970, Ph.D. 1972, Clinical Fellowship, 1972-73, Department of Pharmacology, College of Medicine, University of Iowa. Military: Served in the United States Armed Forces. Career: Cardiovascular Pharmacologist. Organizational Memberships: American Society of Pharmacological Experimental Therapy, 1974 to present; American Heart Association; American Physioloical Society, 1978 to present; Microcirculatory Society, 1979 to present; Shock Society, 1978 to present; American Association for the Advancement of Science, 1974 to present. Community Activities: Mobile Area High Blood Pressure Council (vice-president, 1977-80). Religion: Mobile Jewish Community Center and Congregation, 1977 to present. Honors and Awards: Past Doctoral Fellow, N.I.H., 1973-74; Career Development Award, N.I.H.-N.H.L.B.I., 1976-77, 1978-82; Research Citation, Central Ohio Heart Association, 1972; Fellow, Medical Advisory Board, American Heart Association Council on High Blood Pressure Research, 1981. Address: 3651 Sprucewood Lane, Mobile, Alabama 36608.

Greene, John Thomas

Marital and Family Therapist. Personal: Born August 31, 1911; Married Nellie Lillie Pell; Father of John Elbert, Harold Pell. Education: A.B. 1936, B.D. 1938, M.A. 1940, Duke University; Ph.D., University of North Carolina, 1955. Career: Private Clinical and Supervisory Practice Marital and Family Therapist; Florida State University, Emeritus Professor 1976 to present, Professor, 1958-76; Professor, Boston University, 1953-59; Director, Family Life Education Department, The North Carolina Methodist

Conference, 1949-53; Methodist Minister, 1936-49. Organizational Memberships: Southeastern Council on Family Relations (president, 1975-77; newsletter editor, 1970-76; annotated and classified bibliography editor, 1971-80); National Council on Family Relations (chairman, counseling section, 1972); American Association of Marriage and Family Therapy; Florida Association of Marriage and Family Therapy. Community Activities: Family Life Institute (summer church-sponsored courses and workshops for various age groups); Youth Camps (counselor); Boy Scouts of America (North Carolina and Massachusetts scoutmaster and scouter); Mental Health Groups and Various Other Community Organizations (lecturer); Robert Butler Lodge #305; Eastern Star, Tallahassee, Florida; Sons of Confederate Veterans. Religion: Methodist; Pastor, Columnist, and Writer for Various Church Publications, Both Denominational and Inter-Denominational. Published Works: Author of Books, Chapters of Books, and Articles in Professional Journals. Honors and Awards: Award for Service to Families, Southeastern Council for Family Relations, 1980; Award for Dedicated Service in Achieving the First Florida Licensing of Marriage and Family Therapists, Florida Association for Marital and Family Therapy, 1982. Address: Post Office Box 43, Pomona Park, Florida 32081.

Greene, Sharon Elizabeth

Secretary. Education: Liberal Arts Major, Stevens Junior College of Business, 1967-68; Executive Secretarial Diploma, Berkeley Secretarial School, White Plains, New York, 1970; Associate of Applied Secretarial Sciences 1975, Diploma in Word Processing 1982, Berkeley-Claremont School, New York, New York; B.B.A., Pace University, 1975-80; A.A.S. Marketing, Berkeley Secretarial School, New York, New York, expected 1983. Career: Secretary, Chemical Coatings Division, Central Distribution Department, Mobil Oil Corporation, New York, New York, 1971 to present; Secretary, Financial Department, Mutual of New York, 1970-71. Organizational Memberships: Professional Secretaries International, New York Chapter (co-chairman, membership committee, 1977-78; arrangements committee, member 1977-78, chairman 1978-79; hostess committee, 1977-78; delegate, northeast district conference, Hershey, Pennsylvania, 1977; delegate, New York State Division Meeting, Syracuse, 1978; New York State division outstanding member of the year committee, 1978-79; recruiting sub-committee, 1978-80; executives night committee, 1978-80; secretaries week committee, 1979-80; corresponding secretary, 1980-81; international convention delegate, New York 1980, New Orleans 1981; vice-president, 1981-82); The National Association of Negro Business and Professional Women's Clubs, Inc. (assistant recording secretary, 1976-77; recording secretary, 1977-78; chairperson, hostess committee Sojourner Truth awards luncheon, 1977; co-chairperson, sub-debs, floral cotillion, 1977; safari weekend, Summit Hotel, 1977; delegate, northeast district conference, New York, 1978; co-chairperson, journal committee, poinsettia debutante's dinner-dance cotillion, 1981). Community Activities: The National Council of Negro Women, Bronx, New York (recording secretary, 1977-79; international chairperson, 1977-80; theatre party committee, 1978; membership committee, 1978; awards luncheon committee, 1978; invitations coordinator, Mary LcLeod Bethune recognition luncheon, 1979; second vice-president, 1979-81; delegate, national convention, Washington, D.C., 1979, 1981; awards chairperson, past presidents' luncheon, 1981; first vice-president, 1981-82; New York State recording secretary, Bethune recognition program, 1981-82); New York City Junior Chamber of Commerce (Macy's Jaycees Christmas shopping tour for underpriviledged children, 1977-81; Leukemia Society phonothon committee, 1978-81; Leukemia Society WOR radiothon committee, 1981; Pace University alumni phonothon, 1981); International Toastmistress Clubs, Innovators Club (ways and means committee, 1980-81; membership committee, 1980-81; sick committee, 1980-81; secretary, 1981-82; representative, area speech contest, Woodbridge, New Jersey; council #2 nominating committee, 1981); New York Toastmistress Club, September 1982 to present; New York League of Business and Professional Women, Inc.; International Platform Association; American Biographical Institute Research Association (associate member); American Biographical Institute National Board of Advisors. Published Works: "What's on Your Mind?" Monthly Column March 1981, " 9 to 5 Lifestyle" Monthly Column February 1981, *Today's Secretary Magazine.* Honors and Awards: Mary McLeod Bethune Achievement Award, National Council of Negro Women, Bronx, New York, 1977; Winner, Speech Contest, Local Chapter, International Toastmistress Club; Listed in *Who's Who of American Women, World Who's Who of Women, Community Leaders of America, Book of Honor, International Who's Who of Intellectuals, Register of Distinguished Americans, Personalities of America, Two Thousand Notable Americans.* Address: 54 Lytton Avenue, Hartsdale, New York 10530.

John Greene

Greenlee, M(ary) Elysia

Conservation Corporal. Personal: Born January 1, 1950; Daughter of Paul C. Greenlee Sr. (deceased) and Mrs. Jackie Stapp Raven. Education: B.A. English, Presbyterian College, Clinton, South Carolina, 1971; M.Ed. Student Personnel, University of Georgia, 1976; 600 Hours of Law Enforcement Training, Operation Catchup, 1975-76, University of Georgia. Career: Conservation Corporal; Teacher of English and Reading, 1971-74. Organizational Memberships: Peace Officers Association of Georgia; Southeastern Association of Fish and Wildlife Agencies, Law Enforcement Section. Religion: Presbyterian. Honors and Awards: 1st Woman Conservation Ranger in Georgia, 1976; Award for Best Paper Presented at Southeastern Association of Fish and Wildlife Agencies, 1979; Ranger of the Year, 1st in Calhoun District, 3rd in State, 1979; Academic and Physical Fitness Awards, Operation Catchup Program, 1976; Listed in *Personalities of the South, Who's Who in the South and Southwest, Who's Who Among American High School Students, Who's Who Among Students in American Colleges and Universities.* Address: 9106 Woodgreen Way, Jonesboro, Georgia 30236.

Griffin, Joseph Wayne

Investment Counseling Executive. Personal: Born December 10, 1937; Son of Joseph Hassell Griffin (deceased) and Ila Mae Nelson; Married Betty Fuller; Father of Michael J. Education: B.A., Greensboro College, 1963; University of North Carolina Law School, 1964; Law, LaSalle Extension University, 1967; Executive M.B.A. Program, Pace University, 1969. Military: Served in the United States Army as a Specialist, 1956-59; Awarded United States Army Good Conduct Medal and Outstanding Performance Commendation. Career: General Partner, Investment Counsel, Century Capital Associates, 1975 to present; Wall, Patterson, McGrew & Richards, 1974; Paine, Webber, Jackson & Curtis, 1971-74; Hayden, Stone, Inc., 1968-70. Organizational Memberships: Association of Investment Management Sales Executives. Community Activities: Walden School (board of trustees, vice-president of fund raising, 1980 to present); Saint Mary's Hospital for Children (fund raising committee, 1982 to present); Toastmaster's International, 1967-69; Greensboro United Fund Pace Setter Group, 1963-64. Religion: Saint Mark's Episcopal Church; Vestry, 1978-81. Honors and Awards: Listed in *Outstanding Young Men of America, Who's Who in Finance and Industry, Personalities of America, Personalities of the East.* Address: 245 East 87th Street, New York, New York 10028.

Grigory, Mildred A

Business Executive. Education: B.A. magna cum laude Business Management, College of William and Mary; Doctorate in Humanities and Sciences, Harvard University; Certificate in Data Processing, 1977. Career: President, Certified Resources Corporation, 1979 to present; Principal and Director of Data Processing, Judd, Thomas Beasley & Smith, C.P.A.'s; Director of Data Processing, Parish Murrel and Company; Corporate Director of Data Processing, Best Products Company. Organizational Memberships: Association for Systems Management; Data Processing Management Association; International Entrepreneurs Association; Business and Professional Women; Electronic Data Processing Auditors Association. Community Activities: National Historical Society; National Trust for Historic Preservation; The Smithsonian Associates; Fellowship of Christian Athletes (national lecturer). Honors and Awards: Professional Public Speaker, International Platform Association; Chamber of Commerce of the United States of America; Outstanding Woman of the Year in America, *Who's Who of American Women*, 1980; President's Advisory Council for Small Business Reform, 1978, 1979, 1981; Woman of the Year, Data Processing Management Association, 1973, 1976, 1978; American Film Institute; Distinguished American, American Biographical Institute, 1981; Listed in *Directory of Distinguished Americans, Who's Who in the World, Personalities of the South, Community Leaders of America, Book of Honor*. Address: 8730 King George Drive, Suite 115, Dallas, Texas 75235.

Grigsby, Robert L "Buck" Jr

College President. Personal: Born January 25, 1924 in Saluda, South Carolina; Son of Mr. and Mrs. Robert L. Grigsby; Married Martha L. Grigsby; Father of Robert L. III. Education: Manufacturing Training Program, General Electric Company, 1957-59; Methods Analysis Improvement Program, Union College, 1956; M.S. Vocational Education with honors, North Caroina State College, 1952; Studies 1941-43, B.S. 1947, Vocational Agriculture Education, Clemson College; United States Army Specialized Training Program in Industrial Engineering, Purdue University, 1944. Military: Served in the United States Army during World War II. Career: President, Midlands Technical College, 1974 to present; Executive Director, Midlands Technical Education Center, 1969-74; Director, Richland Technical Education Center, 1962-69; Manufacturing Supervisor, General Electric Company, Irmo, South Carolina, 1962-56; Assistant Principal, Irmo High School, South Carolina, 1952-56; Assistant Principal, Gilbert High School, South Carolina, 1947-51. Organizational Memberships: American Council on Education; American Society of Engineering Education (national vice-president, technical institute division, 1964-69); American Vocational Association; Lexington, South Carolina, Board of Education (member, 1961-76; secretary, 1965-76); South Carolina State Employees Association; South Caroina Technical College Presidents Association (secretary-treasurer, 1980-81); South Carolina Technical Education Association; Southern Association of Colleges and Schools (trustee, 1968-74; chairman of visiting committees for Commission on Colleges to recommend initial membership or reaffirmation of membership); Wardlaw Club. Community Activities: American Legon Post 142, South Carolina (organizer; commander); Ruritan Club (Gilbert, South Carolina, organizer and member of board of directors; Irmo, South Carolina, past president); Rotary International (past district governor and secretary; Columbia, South Carolina, Five Points club past president); South Carolina Crippled Children's Association (past state director; past Lexington County director); United Methodist Church Conference (all committees; past conference director; past member, board of laity; past chairman, pastor-parish relations committee; past chairman, building committee). Religion: United Methodist Church; Past Chairman, Officer Board; Past Chairman, Administrative Board; Past Chairman, Pastor-Parish Relations Committee; Past Chairman, Building Committee. Published Works: *Beef Cattle in South Carolina*, 1952; Contributor to *The Young Farmer, The Progressive Farmer, South Carolina Vocational Agriculture Newsletter*, 1946-56; Editor, American Technical Association Newsletter 1969-71, Technical Institute Division of American Society for Engineering Education Newsletter 1963-65. Honors and Awards: "40 & 8" Award, American Legion; Phi Kappa Phi, 1952 to present; Listed in *Who's Who in the Methodist Church, Who's Who in the South and Southwest, Who's Who in American Colleges and University Administration, International Notables, Personalities of the South, Community Leaders of the South, Distinguished Educators of America*. Address: Route 2 Box 344, Leesville, South Carolina 29070.

Grimmer, Margot

Dancer, Choreographer, Director, Teacher. Personal: Daughter of Vernon and Ann Grimmer. Education: Attended Lake Forest College and Northwestern University, 1964-68. Career: Dancer, Choreographer, Director, Teacher, The American Dance Company and School; Dancer, New York City Ballet's *Nutcracker*; Dancer, Kansas City Starlight and St. Louis Municipal Theatres; Dancer, Chicago Tenthouse and Music Theatres; Dancer, Chicago Lyric Opera Ballet; Dancer, Ballet Russe de Monte Carlo, New York City; Dancer/Choreographer, Ravinia Festival, Ruth Page International Ballet; Dancer, Chicago Symphony Orchestra Ballet; Dancer, Bob Hope Show, Milwaukee; Dancer, Washington, D.C., Bicentennial Celebration at the Kennedy Center; Dancer, Assyrian Cultural Foundation-and Iranian Consulate-Sponsored Performances, Chicago. Honors and Awards: Grantee, Illinois Arts Council, 1972-75, 1978; Grantee, National Endowment for the Arts, 1973-74. Address: 970 Vernon, Glencoe, Illinois 60022.

Grimstad, Kirsten Julia

Editor. Personal: Born November 17, 1944; Daughter of Mr. and Mrs. James Grimstad. Education: B.A., Barnard College, 1968; Postgraduate President's Fellowship 1969-73, M.A. 1969, Columbia University. Career: Editor, J. P. Tarcher Publishing Company, Los Angeles, California; Founder, Publisher, Executive Editor, *Chrysalis Magazine*, Los Angeles; Instructor of Germanic Languages and Literature, Columbia University, New York, New York, 1969-73. Organizational Memberships: Feminist Writers Guild; Western Magazine Publishers Association; Women's Institute for Freedom of the Press. Published Works: *Women's Work and Women's Studies*, 1971, 1972; *The New Woman's Survival Sourcebook*, 1975; *The New Woman's Survival Catalog*, 1973. Honors and Awards: Excellence Award, American Institute of Graphic Arts, 1974; President's Fellow, Columbia University, 1969-73. Address: 267 Mabery Road, Santa Monica, California 90402.

Grosvenor, Geraldine R

Personal: Born August 21, 1918 in Oakland, California; Daughter of William Bennett and Ruth Lay Grosvenor; Mother of Larry Dennis, Richard Lynn. Education: Graduate and Honor Scholar of High School; Studies in Languages, Creative Writing and Psychology. Career: Clerk Typist, Federal Government Disaster Loans; Researcher, Ancient History and Languages, Early American History, Physics, Astronomy, and Science; American Foreign Service, 1967-76; Former Part-Owner, Hunn Engineering and Manufacturing. Organizational Memberships: American Academy of Political and Social Service; American Public Health Association; American Scholars; Atlantic Council of the United States, Inc.; N.A.T.O.; American Society of International Law; Institute of World Affairs, University of Southern California and March Air Force Base; Los Angeles World Affairs Council; United Nations Organization; Daedalus; Ensalen Institute; Carnegie Endowment for International Conciliatory Peace; California Pan-American Association; Pan-American Union; Los Angeles Area A.B.M.A.C.; International Society for General Semantics (D.A.T.A.); University of Denver Graduate School of International Studies, Africa; American College of Arms; American Judicature Society; Columbia University Academy of Political Science; Hollywood Pen Women; Santa Monica Writers Club;

California Federation of Chaparral Poets; Poets Haven; University of California-Los Angeles Extension of Painters, Poets and Authors. Community Activities: American Academy of Arts and Sciences; Town and Gown of University of Southern California; American Forestry Association; Propylean Society; Royal Society of St. George, England; *Psychedelic Review*; Variety Club; W.A.I.F.; Augustan Society; United Inventors and Scientists; National Travel Club; Genealogical Societies of New England, Texas, Southern California, and Long Beach; San Souci Celebrity Club; Celebrity and Culture Clubs of California; Music Center Founders Circle; Save the Redwoods League; Mayor's Council for International Visitors and Sister Cities; International Society of Toastmistresses; Huntington Library Rare Books Readers Club; Franklin Mint and Archives Associations; Hollywood Wilshire Symphony (supporter); Children's Baptist Home of Southern California (supporter); American Museum of Natural History (supporter); Union Rescue Mission (supporter); Evangelism Crusades, Inc. (supporter). Published Works: *The Etude of Agamemnon-Zeus - A Saga; The Song of Elatra; Tales from King Arthur's Court;* Poems in Ten Different Anthologies and Currently Writing Sonnets and Lyrics for Several Books including *Songs to the Immortals* and *The Mountain Song (The Afternoon La Faun).* Honors and Awards: Bronze Presidential Medal and Honorary Fellowship, Truman Library; I.P.A. Fellow; Numerous Merit and Service Citations; Award, California Historical Society; Honorary Appointment, American Biographical Institute Advisory Board; Fellow, American Biographical Institute Research Association; Member, Academia Italia delle Arti & del Lavoro; Member and Diploma of Honor, International Order of Volunteers for Peace, 1981-82; Listed in *Comtemporary Personalities, Dictionary of International Biography, The International Register of Profiles, International Who's Who in Community Service, Men and Women of Distinction, Personalities of the West and Midwest, Who's Who of American Women, Who's Who in Technology Today, Who's Who in the West, The Worlds Who's Who of Women, International Register of Distinguished Men and Women, International Who's Who of Intellectuals, Encyclopedia of Contemporary Personalitites, Who's Who in California, Who's Who in Historical Societies.* Address: 10799 Sherman Grove Avenue #39, Sunland, California 91040.

Gruver, William Rand II

Journalist. Personal: Born June 18, 1936; Son of Henry and Anne Gruver (both deceased). Education: Alexander Hamilton School; Professional Children's School, Rhodes Preparatory School; B.S., M.A. Journalism, Columbia University. Military: Served in the United States Navy, 4 Years, as an Ensign, Newspaper Editor, and Foreign Language Interpreter. Career: Journalist; Radio and Television Commentator; Public Affairs Advisor to Industry, Foreign Governments, and United States Cities and States; Press Secretary to 2 United States Senators and 2 Presidential Candidates. Organizational Memberships: Beta Sigma Tau; National Writers Union; International Platform Association; P.R.S.A.; Navy League of the United States. Community Activities: California-Nevada Parks Commission, 1964-65; California Trade Council; Press Secretary to United States Senators Vance Hartle and Robert F. Kennedy and to Presidential Candidates Hubert Humphrey, Lyndon Johnson and Robert F. Kennedy; Advisor to Mayors of Los Angeles and Detroit. Religion: Marble Collegiate Methodist Church. Honors and Awards: Presidential Unit Citation, United States Navy; Bishop Buckley Scholarship; Community Service Award, Veterans Organization. Address: Post Office Box 3276, Paterson, New Jersey 07509.

Harold J Gryting

Gryting, Harold Julian

Consultant. Personal: Born December 31, 1919; Son of Reier and Julia Gryting (both deceased); Married Barbara Jean Ruggles; Father of Corri, Paul. Education: B.A. cum laude, St. Olaf College, 1941; Attended North Dakota State University, 1941-42; Ph.D., Purdue University, 1947. Career: Consultant, Department of Ballistics and Explosives Research, Southwest Research Institute, 1980 to present; Naval Weapons Center, Research Chemist 1976-80, Safety Advisor and Technical Coordinator 1975-76, Associate Head of Applied Research and Processing Division 1972-75, Technical Assistant for Explosives 1965-72. Organizational Memberships: Sigma Xi; R.E.S.A.; A.I.A.A.; American Association for the Advancement of Science (fellow); Phi Lambda Upsilon; New York Academy of Science; American Chemical Society (chairman, Mohave Desert section, 1959-60, 1970); American Institute of Chemistry (fellow); Certified Professional Chemist. Community Activities: Boy Scouts of America (scoutmaster, 1975-80). Religion: Grace Lutheran Church, Ridgecrest, California, 1955-81; Hope Lutheran Church, San Antonio, Texas, 1981 to present. Honors and Awards: Alrose Research Fellow, Purdue University, 1943-46; Westinghouse, Air Force and Mallinckrodt Fellow, 1946-47. Address: 1324 Klondike Drive, San Antonio, Texas 78245.

Gubanc, David Michael

Personal: Born October 31, 1949; Son of Robert and Louise Gubanc; Married Phyllis Hammer. Education: B.S. Chemical Engineering, Northwestern University, 1971; M.B.A., Cleveland State University, 1979. Military: Served in the United States Navy to the Rank of Lieutenant, 1971-75. Career: Senior Solid Waste Management Engineer; Naval Officer; Combustion Technologist, Staff Environmental Engineer. Organizational Memberships: American Institute of Chemical Engineers, 1973 to present; Water Management Association of Ohio (trustee, 1978 to present); Republic Steel Environmental Speakers Bureau, 1979 to present; Association of Iron and Steel Engineers, 1977 to present. Community Activities: Parma Heights (Ohio) Planning Commission (member, 1979-81; vice-chairman, 1980-81); Garden Valley Neighborhood House (trustee, 1977-80); Northwestern University Alumni Club of Cleveland (trustee, 1977-80); State Senate Campaign Committee for Senator Gary Suhadolnile, R-Parma Heights (treasurer, 1979 to present); Fresh Start Incorporated Halfway House (trustee, 1981 to present). Religion: Calvary Presbyterian Church, 1975-80. Honors and Awards: Meritorious Unit Commendation Ribbon, United States Navy, 1973; Outstanding Young Man of America, United States Jaycees, 1981; Listed in *Who's Who in Finance and Industry, Personalities of America.* Address: 1533 Waterbury Road, Lakewood, Ohio 44107.

Dave Gubanc

Gunnarshaug, Dagfinn

Business Executive. Personal: Born February 21, 1933; Married; Father of Oistein Lande, Aagot Elisabeth, Tore Kristian, Inger-Elin. Education: Graduate of Haugesund Gymnas College, Norway, 1951; Haugesund Handels Gymnas Business College, 1952; Industrikonsulent A/S, Oslo Ocean Shipping Course. Military: Served in the Norwegian Army to the Rank of Second Lieutenant, 1953-54. Career: Director and Vice-President, Merzario Maritime Agency, Inc.; Vice-President, Viking Steamship Corporation, Inc.; Vice-President, Ugland Management Company, Inc.; Chairman of the Board and President, Boise-Griffin Agencies, Inc., New York; Chairman of the Board and Chief Executive Officer, Boise-Griffin Steamship Company, Inc., New York; Director and Managing Director, Saudi Concordia Shipping Company, Limited, Jeddah, Saudi Arabia, 1969 to present; United States Director, Concordia Line and Saudi Concordia Line, New York, 1969 to present; Christian Haaland, Haugesund, Norway, 1956-68; Northern State Power Company, Minneapolis, Minnesota, 1955; Haugesund Sjo Insurance Company, Haugesund and Oslo, Norway, 1952-53. Organizational Memberships: New York Shipping Association (director); Job Security Program (director); American-Norwegian Chamber of Commerce (director); Security Bureau (director); Board of Shipping Industry Mutual Assurance Association Limited of

Bermuda (director); Breakbulk Committee, New York (chairman); I.L.A.-N.Y.S.A. Contract Board, New York. Community Activities: Negotiating Team on Behalf of All Ocean Shipping Lines Serving the East Coast of the United States and the United States Gulf; Norwegian Student Association, New York (president, 1977-78; secretary, 1981); Board of Galleria Condominium, New York (member, 1977-81; president, 1981). Address: 117 E. 57th Street Apt. 27-H, New York, New York 10022.

Gupta, Venu G

Venu G Gupta

College Professor. Personal: Born April 3, 1934 in Hoshiarpur, Punjab, India; Married Sunita Gupta; Father of Sunil, Sanjiv. Education: B.A. with honors, first class 1953, M.A. first class first 1955, M.Ed. first class first with highest academic distinction, 1959, Punjab University; B.Ed., Central Institute of Education, Delhi University, 1958; Ph.D. with 4.0 grade point average, Georgia State University, 1974. Career: Kutztown State College, Pennsylvania, Professor of Counseling and Psychology 1977 to present, Associate Professor, 1974-77; Teaching and Research Fellow, Georgia State University, 1972-74; Assistant Professor of Psychology and Counseling, Eastern Kentucky University, 1968-72; Assistant Professor of Psychology, University of Wisconsin-Stevens Point, 1966-68; Teaching and Research Fellow, University of Alberta, Canada, 1964-66; Lecturer, Colleges of Punjab and Kurukshetra Universities, India, 1955-63. Organizational Memberships: American Psychological Association; American Educational Research Association; American Personnel and Guidance Association; Association for Counselor Education and Supervision; American Mental Health Counselors Association; American Association for the Advancement of Science; American Association of University Professors; Phi Delta Kappa; International Council of Psychologists; International Association of Applied Psychology; International Association for Cross-Cultural Psychology; International Council on Education for Teaching. Community Activities: Radio and Television Appearances for Interviews; Lecturer on Hinduism, Various Interested Groups; World Travel; Languages and Literature. Religion: Hindu. Published Works: "Intercorrelations of W.I.S.C. Subtest-Scores of Seventy Children, Tested Two Years Apart"; "Self-Actualization--East and West: A Counselor's Viewpoint"; Students' Perception of College Instructors Based on Faculty-Evaluation Ratings"; "Piaget: A Human Learning Theory"; " Effects of Varied Instruction on Student Ratings of University Faculty"; Research Studies Published and Presented at National and International Professional Conventions. Honors and Awards: Commendation Award, American Society of Distinguished Citizens, Beverly Hills, California, 1976; Diploma of Honor for Community Service, *International Who's Who in Community Service*, 1973; Creativity Recognition Award, International Personnel Research, Los Angeles, 1972; Outstanding Educator of America Award, Chicago, 1971; Award for Distinguished Service to the Teaching Profession, *Dictionary of International Biography*, 1970; Distinguished Achievement Award, London, 1970; Dean's Special Graduate Studies Scholarship, University of Alberta, Canada, 1963; Gold Medalist, Punjab University, India, 1959; Winner, Several Academic Prizes and Certificates of Merits; Listed in *Outstanding Educators of America, Dictionary of International Biography, Creative and Successful Personalities, Community Leaders of America, International Directory of Scholars Interested in Human Development in Cross-Cultural Perspective, Distinguished Citizens of America Directory, American Men and Women of Science: Social and Behavioral Sciences, Who's Who in the East, Who's Who in America, Who's Who in Education: The Seventies, International Who's Who of Intellectuals.* Address: 744 Highland Avenue, Kutztown, Pennsylvania 19530.

Guzman, Lorenzo G

L G Guzman

Physician. Personal: Born September 18, 1919; Son of Philip and Maria T. Guzman (both deceased); Married to Lucrecia; Father of Philip A., Theresa A. Education: A.B., B.S., Long Island University, 1950; M.A., New York University Graduate School of Arts and Sciences, 1951; Attended Webb Institute of Engineering, 1952-53; M.D., University of Puerto Rico School of Medicine, 1957. Military: Served with United States Army as a technician, 1942-46; Active in U.S. Army Reserve, 1946-48; U.S.P.H.S. Colonel, 1959 to present. Career: Medical Officer in charge, Chamberlain, South Dakota; Medical Officer in charge, Rosebud, South Dakota; Chief of Surgery, Talihena, Okaah; Deputy Chief of Surgery, Galveston, Texas; Deputy Chief of Surgery, Staten Island, New York; Chief of Surgery, Staten Island, New York; Director of San Juan O.P.D Clinic. Organizational Memberships: American Medical Association; Royal Society of Health; Royal College of Surgeons; New York State Cancer Programs Association; Association of Military Surgeons; American Association for the Advancement of Science; American Academy of Family Physicians; American Society of A.B.D. Surgeons; Veterans of Foreign Wars (commissioned officer); Association of A.P.H.S.; Staten Island P.S.R.O. committee, 1977-79; Southwestern Council of Biological Sciences, 1965; Triboro Association of Directors of Surgery, 1975-79; National Medical Historical Society, 1970-79; Cancer Treatment subcommittee, Washington, D.C., 1978-79; Cancer and Leukemia Treatment Group, 1977-79. Religion: Member of Roman Catholic Church (member of catholic brothers, 1970-79). Honors and Awards: Elected to Society of Optimates, L.I.U., 1949; Received Physicians' Recognition Award, American Medical Association, 1973, 1976, 1979 and 1982; Received U.S.P.H.S. Plaque, 1979, and Commendation, 1966; President of U.S.P.H.S. Commissioned Corps Association Chapter, 1980-81; Listed in *Who's Who in the East*. Address: P.O. Box 3788, Old San Juan, Puerto Rico 00904.

Haas, Charles David

Dentist. Personal: Born January 3, 1941; Son of Mr. and Mrs. Milton Haas; Married Sheila Carole Greenberg; Father of Andrew Scott, Gary Adam. Education: A.B., Biology, Boston University; D.M.D., Tufts University School of Dental Medicine. Military: Served as a Forensic Dental Officer in the United States Army Dental Corps, 1967-69, attaining the rank of Captain. Career: Dentist. Organizational Memberships: American Dental Association; Royal Society of Health; Academy of General Dentistry; Academy of Forensic Odontology; Alpha Omega Fraternity; Alpha Epsilon Pi Fraternity. Community Activities: Migrant Education Project, State of Massachusetts (dental consultant, 1961-67); Consultant to Numerous Nursing Homes and Hospitals, 1978 to present. Religion: Temple Sinai, North Dade, 1976 to present. Honors and Awards: Elected Fellow, Royal Society of Health, London, England, 1975; Listed in *Who's Who in the Southeast, Who's Who in America, Best Dentists in America, Personalities of the South.* Address: 2220 N.E. 201 Street, North Miami Beach, Florida 33180.

Charles D Haas

Haas, Merrill Wilber

Petroleum Consultant. Personal: Born July 9, 1910; Married Maria Haas; Father of Mariella Allard, Merrill Jr., Maria Cecilia, Frederick. Education: Attended the University of Kansas, 1928-31; B.A., University of Michigan, 1932; Undertook Post-Graduate Studies, Harvard University, 1932-33. Career: Paleontologist, Humble Oil and Refining Company; District Geologist and Director of Paleontological Laboratory, Lago Petroleum Corporation, Venezuela; Division Geologist, Creole Petroleum Corporation, Venezuela; Area Geologist, Standard Oil Company, New Jersey, New York; Chief Geologist, Exploration Manager, Vice President, Director, The Carter Oil Company, Tulsa; Vice President for Exploration, Exxon, U.S.A. Organizational Memberships: Geological Society of America (fellow); Houston Geological Society; Tulsa Geological Society; American Association of Petroleum Geologists (president, 1974-75); Paleontological Research Institute (trustee, president, 1970-75); American Association of Petroleum Geologists Foundation (trustee). Community Activities: American Geological Institute (chairman, manpower committee, 1967-69); American Petroleum Institute (chairman, reserves and productive capacity committee, 1971-73); University of Kansas Geology Associates (advisory board chairman, 1971 to present). Religion: Methodist. Honors and Awards: Erasmus Haworth Distinguished Alumni Award, University of Kansas, 1961; University of Kansas Distinguished Service Citation, 1966; The Merrill W. Haas Distinguished Visiting Professorship in Geology, University of Kansas, 1973; Honorary Member, American Association of Petroleum Geologists, 1979; Honorary Member, Houston Geological Society, 1980; Outstanding Achievement Award, University of Michigan, 1981. Address: 10910 Wickwild, Houston, Texas 77024.

Hackerman, Norman

College President, Professor. Personal: Born March 2, 1912, in Baltimore, Maryland; Son of Jacob and Anna Raffel Hackerman (both deceased); Married Gene Allison Coulbourn, August 25, 1940, Baltimore, Maryland; Father of Patricia Gale, Stephen Miles, Sally Griffith, Katherine Elizabeth. Education: A.B. 1932, Ph.D. 1935, Johns Hopkins University; LL.D. (honorary), Abilene Christian University, 1978; D.Sc. (honorary), Texas Christian University, 1978; D.Sc. (honorary), Austin College, 1975; LL.D. (honorary), St. Edward's University, 1972. Career: Rice University, President 1970 to present, Professor of Chemistry 1970 to present; The University of Texas at Austin - President 1967-70, Vice Chancellor for Academic Affairs 1963-67, Vice President and Provost 1961-63, Dean of Research and Sponsored Programs 1960-61, Director of the Corrosion Research Laboratory 1948-61, Chairman of Chemistry Department 1952-61, Professor of Chemistry 1950-70, Associate Professor Chemistry 1946-50, Assistant Professor of Chemistry 1945-46; Research Chemist, Kellex Corp., 1944-45; Assistant Professor of Chemistry, Virginia Polytechnic Institute, 1941-43; Assistant Chemist, United States Coast Guard, 1939-41; Research Chemist, Colloid Corp., 1936-40; Assistant Professor of Chemistry, Loyola College, 1935-39. Organizational Memberships: American Academy of Arts and Sciences (fellow, 1978); American Philosophical Society, 1972; National Academy of Sciences, 1971; American Chemical Society (executive committee, colloid division, 1955-58; board of editors, *American Chemical Society Monograph Series*, 1956-62; honorary member, 1975); National Association of Corrosion Engineers (board of directors, 1952-55; chairman, A. B. Campbell young authors award committee, 1960 to present); Electrochemical Society (chairman, corrosion division, 1951; vice-president, 1954-57; president, 1957-58; interim editor, *Electrochemical Technology*, 1965-68; technical editor, *Journal of the Electrochemical Society*, 1950-68; editor, 1969 to present; honorary member, 1973); American Association for the Advancement of Science (fellow); New York Academy of Sciences (fellow); International Society of Electrochemistry. Community Activities: Solar Advisory Committee, State of Texas, 1980 to present; American Chemical Society Joint Board (council committee on chemistry and public affairs, 1980 to present); Energy Research Advisory Board, Department of Energy, 1980 to present; Defense Science Board, Department of Defense, 1978 to present; CO_2 Study Group, Department of Energy, 1977-80; University of California-Berkeley, Lawrence Berkeley Laboratory (scientific and educational advisory committee, 1977-81; MITRE Corporation (board of trustees, 1980 to present); American Council on Education (board of directors, 1980 to present); Oak Ridge Associated Universities (board of directors, 1975-81); Independent Colleges and Universities of Texas (president, 1974 to present); National Board of Graduate Education, 1971-75; Board on Energy Studies, National Academy of Sciences/National Research Council (chairman, 1974-77); National Science Board (member, 1968-80; chairman, 1974-80); Environmental Pollution Panel (president's science advisory committee, 1965-66); Association of Universities for Research in Astronomy (consultant, 1964-78); Argonne National Laboratory (chemical engineering division review committee, 1963-69; chairman, board of trustees, 1969-73); Intersociety Corrosion Committee (chairman, 1956-58). Published Works: Author/Co-Author 190 Publications. Honors and Awards: American Institute of Chemists Gold Medal, 1978; Honor Scroll, Texas Institute of Chemists, 1975; Palladium Medalist of the Electrochemical Society, 1965; Southwest Regional Award, American Chemical Society, 1965; Joseph L. Mattiello Award, 1964; Whitney Award of National Association of Corrosion Engineers, 1956; Mirabeau B. Lamar Award, Association of Texas Colleges and Universities, 1981; Alpha Chi Sigma; Phi Kappa Phi; Phi Lambda Upsilon; Sigma Xi. Address: President's House, Rice University, Houston, Texas 77001.

Merrill W Haas

Hacklander, Effie Hewitt

Assistant Professor, Assistant Dean. Personal: Born October 10, 1940; Daughter of Kenneth Hewitt; Married Duane Hacklander;

Mother of Jeffrey, Alan, Craig. Education: B.S., University of Minnesota, 1962; M.A. 1968, Ph.D. 1973, Michigan State University. Career: Assistant Professor, Assistant Dean, College of Human Ecology, University of Maryland; Acting Assistant Provost, Division of Human and Community Resources, University of Maryland, College Park; Lecturer, Wayne State University, 1969; Secretary/Special Assistant, Marriott Corporation. Organizational Memberships: American Home Economics Association (technical consultant, 1977-82); American Marketing Association; Association for Consumer Research; Eastern Economics Association; World Future Society. Community Activities: Maryland Home Economics Association Research Committee, 1979-82. Religion: Music Committee Chairperson, Congregational Christian Church, Fairfax, Virginia, 1975-80. Honors and Awards: Augusta L. Searles Academic Scholarship, University of Minnesota, 1958; General Research Board Proposal Writing Grant, 1981. Address: 4211 Ann Fitz Hugh Drive, Annandale, Virginia 22003.

Hackney, Howard Smith

County Executive Director, Farmer. Personal: Born May 20, 1910, Clinton County, Ohio; Married Lucille Morrow; Father of Albert M., Roderick Allen, Katherine Ann Hackney Becker. Education: Graduate of Chester Township High School, 1928; B.S. cum laude, Wilmington College, 1932. Career: County Executive Director, A.S.C.S.; Farmer, Breeding of Duroc Swine and Southdown Sheep (Bred Premier Sire for Ohio in Doroc Swine, 1962); Positions with United States Department of Agriculture Farm Programs, (reporter, community committeeman, county committeeman, county chairman, office manager, county executive director), 1934 to present. Organizational Memberships: Ohio State Duroc Breeders Association (president, director); United Duroc Swine Registry; Ohio State Southdown Breeders Association; American Southdown Breeders Association; American Association for the Advancement of Science; Ohio Academy of Science; Ohio Academy of History; Clinton County Lamb and Fleece Improvement Association (director). Community Activities: Farmers Union, Grange and Farm Bureau; Clinton County Farm Bureau (secretary/treasurer); Clinton County Community Action Council (treasurer, director); Clinton County Agricultural Society (treasurer, director); Clinton County Council of Churches (treasurer); Wilmington College Agricultural Advisory Committee; Ohio Historical Society; Clinton County Historical Society (board of trustees); Soil Conservation Society of America; N.A.S.C.O.E.; Mason; Wilmington College (board of trustees). Religion: Quaker, Presiding Clerk, Chester Monthly Meeting; Executive Committee, Miami-Center Quarterly Meeting; Permanent Board, Wilmington Yearly Meeting; Chairman, American Young Friends Fellowship; Board Member, American Friends Service Committee; Board Member, Friends National Committee on Legislation. Honors and Awards: Ohio State and Midwest Area N.A.S.C.O.E. Awards for Service to Agriculture; Clinton County Agricultural Society Award for Service to Agriculture; International Platform Association; Listed in *Who's Who in Religion, Personalities of America, Personalities of the South, Personalities of the West and Midwest, Community Leaders and Noteworthy Americans, Book of Honor, Notable Americans of 1976-77; International Who's Who in Community Service, Dictionary of International Biography, International Who's Who of Intellectuals, International Register of Profiles, Men of Achievement, Men and Women of Distinction, The Directory of Distinguished Americans, Who's Who in the Midwest*. Address: 2003 Inwood Road, Wilmington, Ohio 45177.

Effie H Hacklander

Hafer, William Keith

Marriage and Family Counselor. Personal: Born January 16; Son of Warren Lavere Hafer and Helena Himes Keith; Married Joyce Pennington; Father of Lindsay Burgoyne Hafer Carpenter, Alexander Keith. Education: J.D., George Washington University, 1941; Graduate Work in Psychology, Harvard University, University of Virginia; M.A., Counseling Psychology, New York University, 1974; Undertook Doctoral Work in Counseling Psychology, University of Georgia, University of Texas; Ph.D., Counseling Psychology, Walden University, 1977. Military: Served in the United States Army General Staff Corps, 1942-55, rising through the ranks from Lieutenant of Infantry to Lieutenant Colonel; Retired from the United States Air Force with the rank of Lieutenant Colonel. Career: Marriage and Family Counselor; Personnel Director, International Cellu-cotton Production Company; Superintendent of Industrial and Public Relations, International Minerals and Chemical Corporation; Managing Partner, Sadler, Hafer and Associates (personnel management and vocational guidance); Vice President, Director of Human Relations and Communications, Board Member, Fischer and Porter Company; President, Chalfont Crafts, Inc.; Business Development Manager, Account Group Supervisor, N. W. Ayer and Son, Inc.; Faculty Member, Universities of Virginia, Texas, Georgia. Community Activities: Family Service Association of Bucks County, Pennsylvania (co-founder, president); Tri-Counties Mental Health Clinics, Norristown State Hospital, Pennsylvania (director); Family Service of Santa Monica, California (director); Family Service of Greater Boston, Massachusetts (board of trustees); Family Service of Norfolk, Virginia (marriage and family counselor); United States Foreign Service Officer, American Embassay, Paris, France, 1945-46. Published Works: *Psalm of Life*, 1962; *History of Our Presidents*, 1963; *Things I Love*, 1968; *Advertising Writing*, 1977; *Understanding Texas Politics*, 1974; *Coping with Bereavement from Death or Divorce*, 1981. Address: 762 Poinsettia Street, Columbia, South Carolina 29205.

Hagan, Paul Wandel

Professor, Concert Artist, Composer. Personal: Born November 18, 1930. Education: B.Mus.Ed., University of Evansville, Indiana; M.Sc., Indiana State University; Postgraduate Studies undertaken at Indiana and Purdue Universities. Career: Organist, Cathedral of Immaculate Conception, Fort Wayne, Indiana; Professor, St. Francis College, Purdue Extension, Fort Wayne; Professor, St. Joseph College, Rensselaer, Inc.; Music Teacher, Brunnerdale Seminary, Canton, Ohio; Organ Recitals, United Kingdom, Scandinavia, Germany, France, the Netherlands, Greece, India, Others. Organizational Memberships: Phi Delta Kappa; Sinfonia Phi Beta. Published Works: Compositions include "Five Wounds of Christ"; "Life of Christ in Sound"; "Psalm Chorale Preludes"; "Sketches of Paris Churches"; "Petit Elegies"; "Swedish Suite for Organ"; "All American Suite for Cello-Flute". Honors and Awards: Commendations for Organ Works from Scotland, Sweden; Government Grants for Music Study in Paris, Vienna, Salzburg; Listed in *Dictionary of International Biography*. Address: Sacred Heart Seminary, 7335 South Lovers Lane, Hales Corners, Wisconsin 53130.

Howard S Hackney

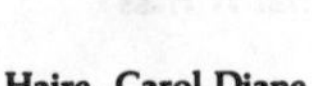

Haire, Carol Diane

Associate Professor, Director of Speech-Language Pathology and Audiology, Consultant. Personal: Born June 24, 1949; Daughter of Lloyd F. and M. Vera Smith Haire. Education: B.A., Speech Pathology, Texas Tech University, 1970; M.A., Speech Pathology, North Texas State University, 1971; Ed.D., Texas Tech University, 1976. Career: Associate Professor of Speech-Language Pathology and Special Education, Director of Speech-Language Pathology and Audiology, Hardin-Simmons University, Abilene, Texas, 1977 to present; Speech-Language Pathology Consultant, West Central Texas Home Health Agency, Abilene, 1980 to present; Consultant in Speech-Language Pathology, Learning Disabilities, and Special Education, Educational Diagnostician, West Texas Rehabilitation Center, Abilene, 1977 to present; Assistant Professor, Clinical Supervisor, Communicative Disorders Center, Howard Payne University, Brownwood, Texas, 1976-77; Part-Time Instructor, College of Education, Texas Tech University, 1974-76; Speech Pathologist, Muleshoe, Texas, Independent School District, Private Practice, Muleshoe, 1973-74; Speech Pathologist, Cooke County

Public Schools, Private Practice, Gainesville, Texas, 1972; Headstart Teacher, Cooke County Junior College, Gainesville, Summer 1972; Graduate Assistant, Speech and Hearing Clinic, North Texas State University, 1971; Language Development Aide, Migrant Summer Program, Muleshoe, Texas, Independent School District, Summer 1970. Organizational Memberships: International Platform Association; American Society of Allied Health Professions; American Speech-Language-Hearing Association; Texas Speech-Language-Hearing Association; Big Country Speech and Hearing Association (president, 1979-80); Phi Delta Kappa; Council for Exceptional Children; Division for Children with Communication Disorders, Council of Exceptional Children; National Student Speech-Language-Hearing Association (honorary member, sponsor of Hardin-Simmons University Chapter); Hardin-Simmons University General Faculty and Faculty Assembly Officer (secretary, 1980-81). Community Activities: American Heart Association, Taylor County Division (board of directors, youth education task force chairperson, 1981 to present). Religion: Work with American Children in Guadalajara, Jalisco, Mexico, Sponsored by the Texas Tech University Baptist Student Union and First Baptist Church of Lubbock, Texas, Summer 1968. Honors and Awards: Phi Kappa Phi; Certificate of Clinical Competence in Speech Pathology, American Speech-Language-Hearing Association; Texas Education Agency Certification in Speech and Hearing Therapy, Language and/or Learning Disabilities, Generic Special Education, Professional Educational Diagnostician, Professional Supervisor, Professional Special Education Supervisor, High School Speech, High School Psychology; Listed in *Who's Who in the South and Southwest, Personalities of the South, World Who's Who of Women, Directory of Distinguished Americans, International Who's Who of Intellectuals, Book of Honor, Personalities of America, Community Leaders of America.* Address: 4810 Stonehedge Road, Abilene, Texas 79606.

Hake, Don F

Professor of Psychology. Personal: Born June 28, 1936; Son of Mr. and Mrs. W. F. Hake; Married Elaine Bicknell; Father of Lisa, Holly. Education: B.A., DePauw University, 1958; M.A. 1962, Ph.D. 1963, Southern Illinois University. Career: Professor of Psychology, West Virginia University; Research Scientist, State of Maryland, State of Illinois; Professor, Southern Illinois University. Organizational Memberships: American Psychological Association (executive committee, division 25, 1978-81); Association of Behavior Analysis (executive committee, 1978-81). Published Works: Associate Editor, *Journal of Experimental Analysis of Behavior* (1973-77) and *Behavior Analyst* (1981-82); Board of Editors, *Behavior Modification* (1981-83) and *Journal Applied Behavior Analysis* (1972-77). Honors and Awards: Fellow, American Psychological Association, 1971; Listed in *Who's Who in America.* Address: 140 Poplar, Morgantown, West Virginia 26505.

Hakim-Elahi, Enayat

Physician. Personal: Born November 23, 1934; Son of M. Ali and Masoomeh (both deceased); Married to Renate; Father of Cristina. Education: B.A., Tehran, 1952; M.D., Tehran Medical School, 1959; Post-graduate training, Queens Hospital Center, New York City, 1960-65; Board Certified in Obstetrics and Gynecology, 1970, recertified, 1978. Career: Physician and Medical Director, Planned Parenthood of New York City, 1975 to present; Clinical Assistant Professor of Obstretrics and Gynecology, Cornell University Medical College, 1973 to present; Consultant in Obstetrics and Gynecology, Hillcrest General Hospital, Flushing, New York, 1968 to present; Attending Physician, The Jamaica Hospital, Jamaica, New York, 1969 to present; Assistant Attending Physician, New York Hospital, 1973 to present; Attending Physician, Booth Memorial Medical Center, Flushing, 1970 to present; Medical Director, Margaret Sanger Center, New York City, 1973-80; Formerly associated with French and Polyclinic Medical School and Health Center (New York City), Mary Immaculate Hospital (Jamaica, New York), and Parkway Hospital (Forest Hills, New York); Participant in numerous professional conferences. Organizational Memberships: American College of Surgeons (fellow, 1972); American College of Obstetricians and Gynecologists (fellow, 1971); International College of Surgeons (fellow, 1971); American Fertility Society (fellow, 1976); Royal Society of Medicine; American Society of Gynecological Laparoscopists; American Society for Colposcopy and Cervical Pathology; American Association of Planned Parenthood Physicians; American Medical Society; New York State Medical Society; Medical Society of County of Queens; Queens Gynecological Society; The World Medical Association; The Society of New York Hospital; American Public Health Association. Published Works: Contributor of numerous articles to professional journals, including *Obstetrics and Gynecology, American Journal of Obstetrics and Gynecology, Obstetrics and Gynecology Collected Letters, New York State Journal of Medicine, Advances in Planned Parenthood.* Honors and Awards: Named Best Intern, Queens Hospital Center, 1960; Listed in *Who's Who in the East, Directory of Medical Specialists, Directory of Distinguished Americans.* Address: 43-70 Kissena Blvd., Flushing, New York 11355.

Hall, Andrew Clifford

Lawyer. Personal: Born September 16, 1944, in Warsaw, Poland; Naturalized U.S. Citizen, 1954; Son of Edmund and Maria Hall; Married Suzanne; Father of Michael Ian, Adam Stuart. Education: B.A., 1965, J.D. with high honors, 1968, both from the University of Florida. Career: Admitted to Florida Bar, 1968, Georgia Bar, 1971, U.S. Supreme Court, 1973; Law Clerk, U.S. District Court, Southern Florida District, 1968-70; Associate, Firm of Haas, Holland, Levison & Gilbert, Atlanta, Georgia, 1970-72, and Frates, Floyd, Pearson & Stewart, Miami, Florida, 1972-75; Partner, Firm of Storace, Hail and Hauser, Miami, 1975-79, and Hall & Hauser, Miami, 1979 to present. Organizational Memberships: American Bar Association; American Judicature Society; Academy of Florida Trial Lawyers; American Trial Lawyers Association. Community Activities: Democratic Party; Order of Coif. Religion: Jewish. Honors and Awards: Phi Kappa Phi; Phi Alpha Delta. Address: 10951 S.W. 60th Avenue, Miami, Florida 33157.

Hall, David McKenzie

Officer, United States Air Force. Personal: Born June 21, 1928; Son of Mrs. Grace E. Hall; Married Jacqueline V. Branch; Father of Glen David, Gary Duane. Education: B.A., Howard University, 1951; M.S., The Agricultural and Technical State University of North Carolina, 1966. Military: United States Air Force, 1951 to present. Career: Brigadier General, United States Air Force. Organizational Memberships: Air Force Association, 1967 to present; American Society of Military Comptrollers, 1979 to present; Association for Systems Managers, 1978 to present; Data Processing Management Association (member, 1970-76, 1978-80; chapter president, 1972-73); Association for Computing Machinery, 1978-80. Community Activities: Tecumseh Council Boy Scouts of America, Springfield, Ohio (vice president, executive board, 1981 to present); Okaw Valley Council, Boy Scouts of America, Belleville, Illinois (executive board, 1974-76); Tecumseh Council (advancement chairman, 1980-81); Wright-Patterson Trail Fund, Wright-Patterson Air Force Base, Ohio (treasurer, 1976-81). Religion: Chapel 1, Wright-Patterson Air Force Base, Usher, 1976 to present; Chairman, Parish Council, 1979-80. Honors and Awards: Honorary Citizen, City of East St. Louis, 1976; Boy Scouts of America, Award of Merit 1976, Silver Beaver 1981. Address: 513 Johnson Drive, Wright-Patterson Air Force Base, Ohio 45433.

Hall, E Eugene

University President. Personal: Born June 19, 1932; Son of Mr. and Mrs. Alvin Hall Sr.; Married Reba; Father of David, Laurie, Steven. Education: B.A., Louisiana College, 1953; B.Div., Southern Baptist Theological Seminary, 1956; M.A. 1959, Ph.D. 1963, Louisiana State University; Undertook Post-Doctoral Studies, University of Kentucky, 1970. Military: Served in the United States Navy Chaplain Corps, 1956-58, attaining the rank of Lieutenant. Career: President, Oklahoma Baptist University; Louisiana College, Vice President for Academic Affairs 1976-77, Dean of the College 1973-76, Interim Administrator 1974-75, Associate Professor and Chairman, Department of Speech 1965-68; Western Kentucky University, Staff Assistant to the Dean of the College of Arts and Humanities, Associate Professor of Speech, 1971-73; Georgetown College, Associate Professor and Chairman, Department of Speech 1968-71, Assistant Professor, Department of Speech 1962-65. Organizational Memberships: Association of Southern Baptist College and University President; American Association of University Administators; American Association of Presidents of Independent Colleges and Universities; National Institute of Campus Ministries. Community Activities: Rotary; Shawnee Chamber of Commerce. Religion: Ordained Southern Baptist Minister; Member First Baptist Church, Shawnee, Oklahoma, Teacher of Single Adults Sunday School Class 1978 to present. Honors and Awards: Phi Kappa Phi National Honor Society, 1959; Distinguished Alumnus, Louisiana College, 1978; Listed in *Who's Who in America*, *Who's Who in the South and Southwest*. Address: 616 University Parkway, Shawnee, Oklahoma 74801.

George Hall

Hall, George Emerson

Manager, Semi-Retired. Personal: Born December 30, 1910; Son of Edwin Albert and Carrie Pearl Hall (both deceased); Married Hazel Marie Sampson; Father of Edwin Edsel, Madeline Ann, Melva Marie, Beverly Kay, Sherry Lee, Barbara Jean. Education: Studies in Engineering, Flint Junior College, 1931-33; Studies in Product Engineering, General Motors Technical Institute, 1934. Military: Served in the Michigan National Guard, Intelligence Section, Headquarters Division, Flint, Michigan, 1935-39. Career: Buick Motor Division, Tool and Die 1935-41, Tool and Fixture Engineer 1941-45, Tool and Die 1945-70; Hall Engineering and Manufacturing Company, 1945-80; Patented, Designed, Developed, Manufactured and Promoted Marketing of Several Inventions. Organizational Memberships: American Society of Tool and Manufacturing Engineers, 1943-60. Community Activities: Genesee Township Board of Review (chairman, vice-chairman, 1963-81); Genesee Township Democratic Club (treasurer, 1972-76); American Security Council (national advisory board member, 1978-81); Michigan Sheriff Association (associate member, 1978-81); Free & Accepted Masons Lodge #236, Davison, Michigan; Order of Eastern Star, #299, Davison, Michigan; Order of W.S.J., #56, Flint, Michigan; Amaranth Court, #2, Flint, Michigan; Lodge Council Chapter Consistory, Valley of Bay City, Michigan; Elf-Khurafoh, Saginaw, Michigan Shrine Temple. Religion: St. Mark's Lutheran Church, Men's Club and Board of Trustees, 1968-81. Honors and Awards: Listed in *Who's Who in the Midwest*. Address: 3039 Alcott Avenue, Flint, Michigan 48506.

Hall, Patricia DeLay

Accountant. Personal: Born December 24, 1930; Daughter of Byron N. (deceased) and Esther J. DeLay; Married Miles A. Hall, Jr.; Mother of Kathryn B. Finch, Andrew C. Barber III. Education: Graduate of Lutcher Stark High School, Orange, Texas, 1948; Attended Private Business School, 1948; La Salle Correspondence Course in Accounting, 1956; B.B.A, Lamar University, 1982. Career: Worked in Father's Accounting Firm, DeLay and Correa, Accountants, 1948-49; Accounting Clerk, American Bridge Division, U.S.S., 1949-59; E. I. duPont de Nemours, Stenographer 1959-65, Accounting Clerk 1965-76, Accountant 1976-79, Accounting Specialist 1979 to present. Organizational Memberships: Lamar University Accounting Society, 1980; Beta Gamma Sigma; University Honor Society of People in Business; American Society of Professional and Executive Women. Religion: St. Paul's Episcopal Church, Treasurer 1978, 1980; Diocese of Texas, Council Representative, 1979, 1980. Honors and Awards: Beta Gamma Sigma Membership Invitation, 1981. Address: 309 Sandy Drive, Bridge City, Texas 77611.

Hall, Sarah

Homemaker, Church Worker, Staff Writer. Personal: Born September 30, 1928; Daughter of A. B. Menton; Foster Mother of Franklin Alonzo. Education: Graduate of West Charlotte High School, 1946. Career: Certified (1982) Staff Writer, Creative Music Productions, Houston, Texas, present. Community Activities: Visits Rest Homes, Hospitals, Shut-Ins in the Community; Donations to P.T.L., Oral Roberts, Billy Graham, Foreign Mission Children's Home. Religion: Sunday School Superintendent, 25 years; Church Secretary, 15 years; Missionary Worker, 1949-81; 12 O'Clock Prayer, 9 years; Church School Teacher, 25 years. Honors and Awards: Woman of the Year, 1978; 25-Year Service, 1949-74, St. James United Church of God; Christian Women's Retreat, Pawling Island, New York; Gold Bond, Book Member Award, Dallas, Texas; Certificate of Appreciation, for Service Rendered in the Community as a Humanitarian, Noah's Ark Out Reach Ministries, 1982; Plaque, Bethlee Baptist Church, 1982; Cross, Presented by Young People Easter 1982, Appreciation Day Service Given Her 1982, St. James Church. Address; 937 Justice Avenue, Charlotte, North Carolina 28206.

Patricia A Halpern

Halleck, Constance Joyce

Executive. Personal: Born May 23, 1944; Daughter of Ruth Adams; Married Thomas M. Halleck; Mother of John R. Harvey. Education: A.S., St. Petersburg Junior College, 1964; B.S., University of Florida, 1965. Career: President, Sales Promotion Agency; Sales Representative, RAN Specialties; Sales Manager, NFC Marketing Association; Secretary/Treasurer, Trans-Global Corporation. Organizational Memberships: Specialty Advertising Association of Atlanta (treasurer, 1980-81; president, 1982-83); Specialty Advertising Association International (speakers bureau, 1981-82, 1982-83); National Association of Female Executives; American Business Women's Association (chapter vice-president, 1979); Women Business Owners (board of directors, 1979-80; vice-president, 1980-81; president, 1982-83); Atlanta Network; Georgia Small Business Council (board of directors, 1980-81); National Association for Professional Saleswomen (board of directors, 1980-81); Sales and Marketing Executives; Women's Forum; Women's Commerce Club (founding director, 1981-82; secretary, 1981-82; board of directors, 1982-83). Honors and Awards: Graduate Distributor Management Institute 1979, Graduate Management Development Seminar 1980, S.A.A.I.; Designated Certified Advertising Specialist, C.A.S., 1980. Address: 4741 Pine Acres Court, Atlanta, Georgia 30338.

Halpern, Patricia Ann

Account Executive. Personal: Born January 13, 1934; Daughter of William O'Shaughnessy and Alice Dewey (both deceased); Mother of Rebecca Lynn, Jay Alan. Education: Graduate of Park Ridge School for Girls, Park Ridge, Illinois; Attended the University of

Illinois and the New School, New York City. Career: Account Executive, Advertising Specialties and Promotions, ReAct Enterprises Inc.; Former Position with Advertising Agency, Commercials for Television, Fur Buying Office. Organizational Memberships: Advertising Specialty Association. Community Activities: NOW; Copa Girls of New York. Honors and Awards: Listed in *Who's Who of American Women, Personalities of America, World Who's Who of Women*. Address: 132 East 35 Street, New York, New York 10016.

Halverstadt, Robert D

Senior Staff Vice President. Personal: Born January 25, 1920; Son of Roscoe B. and Dorothy Grubbs Halverstadt (both deceased); Father of Marta J. Carmen, Linda A. Orelup, Sally J. Education: Marine Officer Training, United States Coast Guard Academy, 1943; B.S.M.E., Case Institute of Technology, 1951; Apprentice Course Graduate, Republic Steel Corporation, 1945. Military: Served in the United States Coast Guard, 1942-45, attaining the rank of Lieutenant (jg). Career: Allegheny International, Senior Staff Vice President, President of Materials Technology Group, President and Board Member Special Metals Corporation; Co-Chairman, Board Member, Titanium Metals Corporation of America; Vice President of Technology, Singer Company, 1973-74; Booz. Allen and Hamilton Inc., Group Vice President of Product and Process Design Group, Chief Executive Officer of Foster D. Snell Inc., President of Design and Development Inc., 1964-73; General Manager, Operations Engineering, Continental Can Company, 1963-64; General Electric Company, Manager of Thomson Engineering Laboratory, Supervisor of Metal Working Research Laboratory, Engineer in Turbojet Engine Development, 1951-63; Republic Steel Corporation, Journeyman Machinist, Apprentice Machinist, 1940-51. Organizational Memberships: American Society of Mechanical Engineers; American Society for Metals (fellow; board of trustees); American Institute for Chemical Engineers; Toastmasters International; Water Resources Association; Regional Plan Association; Chemists Club of New York; Oneida National Bank (board member); Centrex Laboratories (board member); Editorial Board *International Journal of Turbo and Jet Engine Technology*. Community Activities: Utica Chamber of Commerce; Utica Industrial Development Council (director); Industry Labor Education Council (director, president); National Alliance of Business (chairman); University Club of New York; Yahnandasis Golf Club; Fort Schuyler Club; New York Academy of Science. Religion: United Church of Christ, Church School Teacher, Church School Superintendent. Honors and Awards: Commendation, President, of the United States, 1976; Registered Professional Engineer, Ohio 1953, New York 1963; Three Patent Awards, General Electric Company, 1958; Fellow, A.S.M., 1977; Silver Anniversary Award, A.S.M., 1981; Tau Beta Pi; Sigma Xi; Listed in *Who's Who in Finance and Industry, Who's Who in the East, Who's Who in Technology Today, Who's Who in the World, Who's Who in Engineering*. Address: 7 Old Willow Road, New Hartford, New York 13413.

Hamill, Patrick James

Professor of Physics. Personal: Born April 29, 1939; Son of Mrs. Frank Hamill; Married Elsa Li; Father of Carla Alexandra, Candace Joy. Education: B.S., Physics, St. Edward's University, Austin, Texas, 1961; M.S. Physics 1968, Ph.D. Physics 1971, University of Arizona, Tucson; Undertook Post-Doctoral Studies, University of Chicago, 1972. Career: Professor of Physics, San Jose State University; Physicist, N.A.S.A. Ames Research Center, Mountain View, California; Physicist, N.A.S.A. Langley Research Center, Hampton, Virginia; Physics Professor, Universidad Nacional de Trujillo, Trujillo, Peru; Research Professor, Universidad Catolica Andres Bello, Caracas, Venezuela. Organizational Memberships: American Physical Society; American Meteorological Society; American Association of Physics Teachers; Sigma Xi. Community Activities: United States Peace Corps Volunteer in Peru, 1962-65. Honors and Awards: Outstanding Educator of America, 1973-74; Latin American Teaching Fellowship, 1973; N.C.A.R. Post-Doctoral Fellowship, University of Chicago, 1972; N.A.S.A.-A.S.E.E. Faculty Fellowship, 1974-76. Address: 580 Vista Avenue, Palo Alto, California 94306.

James G Hamilton

Hamilton, James G

Executive Director. Personal: Born June 22, 1939; Son of John Henry Hamilton, Ruth Hamilton Proctor. Education: A.A.S. 1970, B.S. magna cum laude 1972, Rochester Institute of Technology, New York; M.A., American History, University of Rochester, 1974. Military: Served in the United States Army as Public Information Supervisor, attaining the rank of Staff Sergeant. Career: Founder, Executive Director, Ankh-Mobile Project, Inc.; Senior Graphic Communications Consultant, Corporate Communications, Aetna Life and Casualty; Technical Sales Representative in Graphic Arts, Eastman Kodak Company; Veterans Representative on Campus, Rochester Institute of Technology; Employment Interviewer, Youth Opportunity Center, New York State Department of Labor; Community Consultant and Director of Urban Education, Rochester Museum and Science Center; Photographic Laboratory Technician, Eastman Kodak Company; Junior Federal Assistant, Drug Enforcement Administration; Reporter-Editor, Manager of Ayer Branch Office, Lowell Sun Publishing Company. Organizational Memberships: American Film Institute; Association for the Study of Afro-American Life and History, Inc. (founder; first president of Rochester, New York, branch; life member, 1976); Connecticut Historical Society; Connecticut Public Television; Disabled American Veterans (life member); International Platform Association; National Archives Trust Fund Association; National Association for the Advancement of Colored People (life member); National Geographic Society; National Historical Society; National Trust for Historic Preservation; Smithsonian Institution; Photographic Society of America. Religion: African Methodist Episcopal Zion. Honors and Awards: Doctor of African History, Universal Orthodox College, Nigeria, 1981; Listed in *Who's Who Among Students in American Universities and Colleges, Men of Achievement, Pesonalities of America, Directory of Distinguished Americans, Who's Who Among Black Americans, Directory of Speakers*. Address: P.O. Box 344, Ayer, Massachusetts 01432.

Hamilton, Madrid Turner

Executive. Personal: Married Norman Woodrow Hamilton (deceased); Mother of Alexander. Education: B.A., Spelman College; M.S.W., Atlanta University; Ph.D., Union for Experimental College and Universities, Cincinnati, Ohio. Career: President, Hamilton Enterprises, Inc.; Counties Coordinator, West Bay Health Systems Agency, San Francisco; Licensed Realtor; Associate Professor, Sociology and Ethics Studies, University of Redlands, San Francisco State University; Western Region Representative, Family Services Association of America; W. R. Director, Planned Parenthood; Consultant, Public Health Social Work, New York City Department of Public Health; Assistant Professor, Sociology, Morehouse College, Atlanta, Georgia. Organizational Memberships: National Association of Social Work; Academy of Certified Social Workers; American Academy of Political and Social Sciences; A.P.H.A. Community Activities: Y.W.C.A. of San Francisco (board of directors, vice-president, treasurer); Y.W.C.A. of the U.S.A., Western States Region (vice president, national board); Zeta Phi Beta Sorority; Northern California Coalition of 100 Black Women (founding coordinator); Community Chest of White Plains, New York (board of directors); United Way of Redlands (board of directors); Governor E. Brown's Population Study Commission; Urban League of Greater New York (chairman, community service committee; Manhattan and Bronx advisory committees); Spelman College Alumnae (regional coordinator); Altrusa Club of

San Francisco; Y.W.C.A. (national board member); Zeta Phi Beta (vice president, western states region). Published Works: Author of 3 Books; Newspaper Columnist. Honors and Awards: Human Resources Award, American Heritage Foundation; Listed in *Who's Who in the West, Who's Who Among Women of the World, Who's Who in California, Who's Who of American Women, Book of Honor, Dictionary of International Biography*. Address: 136 Geneva Avenue, San Francisco, California 94112.

Hammer, Lillian

Poet. Personal: Mother of Ruth, Helen. Education: University Courses in History, Far Eastern Arts, Humanities, Philosophy, Psychology, Science, Language, Others. Career: Writer and Poet, Published in Two Languages in the United States and Abroad. Organizational Memberships: C.S.E.S.I. (honorary representative, 1975; honorary vice-president, 1974); United Poet International, Philippines; I.A.O.P. U.K.; Academy Institute Leonardo da Vinci, Italy; Italy Poetry Society Hall of Fame; International Academy of Poets (founder, fellow). Community Activities: The Whale Protection Fund; Amvets; National Service Foundation; A.M.C. (contributing member, 1981); National Trust for Historic Preservation; Friends of Animals, Inc.; National Foundation for Cancer Research; Korean Relief, Inc. Published Works: Published in *Ideas of the Master Poets*, 1976. Honors and Awards: Honorary Cultural Doctorate in Literature in Recognition of Distinguished Achievement, World University; Belletrist Award, Life Membership, for Outstanding Contribution to the State of Poetic Arts; Diploma for Poetic Achievement, Leonardo da Vinci, 1980; Poet Laureate Award; Certificate of Appreciation; Poet Laureate of the Month; Award for Outstanding Work in the Field of Poetry, 1981; Listed in *Abbo D'Ore-Gold List*. Address: 15 Elmwood Street, Albany, New York 12203.

Hammett, Eugene Kirby

Ballet Master. Personal: Born April 24, 1932; Son of Irene Beatrice Norman, Sea Island, Georgia. Education: Studies at Black Mountain College, New York University, University of Santiago. Career: Ballet Master, Winston-Salem Civic Ballet, Chamber Opera Ballet, Norfolk Civic Ballet, Tidewater Ballet Association, Virginia Dance Company; Master Professor of Dance, Paul D. Camp College 1971, Chowan College 1972, Virginia State College 1981, Richmond Ballet 1975, Charlotte Ballet 1978, Richmond Dance Center 1979. Organizational Memberships: Winston-Salem Dance Forum (president); Norfolk Ballet (founder, 1961); Tidewater Ballet Association (founder, 1976). Religion: Moravian, 1952; Christian Science, 1980. Honors and Awards: White House Citation for International Azalea Festival, President Johnson 1965, President Nixon 1969, President Gerald Ford 1976. Address: 3216 Tidewater Drive, Norfolk, Virginia 23509.

Hammond, Ruth Kartchner

Ruth K Hammond

Educational Diagnostician and Therapist. Personal: Born February 24, 1911; Daughter of Asael Wain and Rosenea Heath Kartchner; Married Marion E. Hammond; Mother of Carl Wain, Bert Kartchner, Kendall Ray. Education: B.S. 1950, M.S. 1958, University of Utah; Ph.D., Purdue University, 1971; Special Training with Emmett A. Betts, Newell K. Kephart, Marianne Frostig, Elizabeth Freidus, Samuel Kirk and Ray Barsch. Career: Self-Employed Educational Diagnostician and Therapist; Brigham Young University, Appointed to Faculty 1964-76, to Faculty of Graduate School 1971-76, Associate Professor 1971-76, Director, Diagnostic Special Education Team for Service to Exceptional Children and Teachers in Rural Areas of Utah 1974-76; Consultant to Teachers in School Districts in Utah, Nevada, Idaho, 1964-76; Demonstration Teacher and Supervisor of Elementary Education, University of Utah, 1950-58; Public School Teacher, Davis County School District, Farmington, Utah 1943-44, Salt Lake City School District 1943-50, 1958-64. Organizational Memberships: National Education Association (life member); Utah Education Association, 1958-76; A.C.E., 1950-58; C.E.C. (member, 1958-76; board of trustees, Utah council); U.A.R.T., 1958-67; Utah Remedial Reading Teachers (board of trustees); A.C.L.D., 1967-76; International Learning Disabilities Association (board of trustees, 1974-76); International Reading Association, 1958-76; Business and Professional Women, 1963-66; Delta Kappa Gamma, 1954 to present; Alpha Theta State (vice president, 1961-63; president, Zeta chapter, 1964-66; state research chairman, 1980-83). Community Activities: White Community Memorial Chapel Foundation (board of trustees, 1977 to present); Director of 8 Workshops Conducted throughout Utah entitled "Oral and Family History - The Professionalization of Utah's Hobby", Sponsored by Community Memorial Chapel Foundation and Funded by Utah Endowments for the Humanities in Public Policy, 1978-79; Fiscal Officer for a Grant Awarded by U.E.H. to W.C.M.C. Foundation for Series of Lectures "The Religious Communities of Utah: An Historical Perspective", 1981-82; North County Company, Daughters of the Utah Pioneers (membership chairman); 33rd Ward Camp (historian, 1980 to present); John and Barbara Hulme Heath Family Organization (secretary, 1976 to present); Sweetwater Condominiums Development, Phase III (board member, 1982 to present). Religion: Church of Jesus Christ of Latter Day Saints, Teacher in Every Auxiliary Organization, Primary, Sunday School, Mutual and Relief Society. Published Works: Co-Author *Handbook for Remedial Reading in Utah Public Schools*; Co-Editor, U.A.R.T.'s Quarterly Publication; In Progress, Autobiography and Biographies of Parents and Grandparents. Honors and Awards: Woman of the Year, Business and Professional Women's Club, Ensign Chapter, 1965; Listed in *International Who's Who of Intellectuals* and 2 Biographical Dictionaries. Address: 429 South 13th East, Salt Lake City, Utah 84102.

Hampton-Kauffman, Margaret Frances

Senior Vice President. Personal: Born May 12, 1947; Daughter of William Hampton III and Dorothy Maples Hampton; Married Kenneth L. Kauffman. Education: B.A. summa cum laude with Honors, French, Florida State University, 1969; Study at L'école de l'été pour les étrangers dépendent de l'université de Nice, Nice, France, Summer 1969; M.B.A., Finance, Columbia University Graduate School of Business, 1974. Career: Senior Vice President, Corporate Planning, Bank South Corporation, Atlanta, Georgia; Vice President of Corporate Finance and Planning, Secretary for Asset/Liability Management Committee, National Bank of Georgia, 1976-81; A.V.P., Corporate Finance and Banking Industry Specialist, Manufacturers Hanover Trust Company, New York, 1975-76; Financial Analyst and Economist, Federal Reserve Bank, Washington, D.C., 1974-75. Organizational Memberships: Planning Executive Institute; Institute for Management Science; American Institute of Banking; Institute for Financial Education; American Finance Association; Phi Beta Kappa; Beta Gamma Sigma; Phi Kappa Phi. Community Activities: Georgia Chapter, Leukemia Society (trustee, 1980 to present; treasurer, 1981-82; vice president, 1982-83); Government Relations Subcommittee, Downtown Atlanta Chamber of Commerce, 1977; Angel Flight (Air Force R.O.T.C. Auxiliary Drill Team and Service Organization), 1966-68; Atlanta Women's Forum, 1981 to present; Women's Commerce Club, Atlanta (charter member, 1981); Georgia Executive Women's Network (member, 1981 to present; secretary, board of directors, 1982-83); Accent Enterprises, Inc. (director, 1979 to present); Atlanta Professional Women's Directory (director, 1981-82). Religion: Episcopalian. Honors and Awards: Alcoa Foundation Fellow, 1973; Florida State University Hall of Fame, 1969; National Alpha Delta Pi Scholarship Award of Excellence, 1969; Finalist, Dorothy Shaw Leadership Award, 1969; Mortar Board, 1968-69; Garnet Key, 1968-69; Listed in *Who's Who in Finance and Industry, Who's Who of American Women, Who's Who in the South and Southwest, Outstanding Young Women of America, Who's Who Among Students in American Colleges and Universities*. Address: 1065 West Paces Ferry Road, N.W., Atlanta, Georgia 30327.

Hance, Kent R

Congressman. Personal: Born November 14, 1942; Married Carol Hays; Father of Ron, Susan. Education: B.B.A., Texas Tech University, 1965; LL.B., University of Texas, 1968. Career: Member, United States House of Representatives, 1979 to present; Member, Texas Senate, 1974-78; Faculty, Texas Tech University, 1968-73; Law Practice in Lubbock, Texas, 1968-78. Organizational Memberships: 96th New Members Caucus (chairman, 1979); House Committee on Agriculture, Subcommittees on Cotton, Livestock & Grains, Conservation & Credit, 1979-80; Science and Technology Committee, 1979-80; Consent Calendar Committee, 1979 to present; Committee on Ways and Means, Subcommittees on Trade and Public Assistance & Unemployment Compensation, 1981 to present; Texas Bar Association; American Bar Association. Community Activities: West Texas State University (board of regents, 1972-74); Texas Boys' Ranch, Lubbock, Texas (original incorporator); Texas Tech Century Club; March of Dimes (Texas chairman, 1972-73); Water, Inc.; Southwest Lubbock Rotary Club; Lions Club; Chamber of Commerce. Religion: First Baptist Church. Honors and Awards: Best Freshman Congressman, *Texas Business Magazine*, 1980; Coalition for Peace through Strength Leadership Award; Outstanding Professor, Texas Tech University. Address: P.O. Box 1, Lubbock, Texas 79401.

Hancock, Joyce Ann

Consultant, Writer. Personal: Born January 30, 1945; Daughter of Mrs. F. D. Hancock. Education: B.A., Honors, University of Kentucky, 1967; M.A., High Distinction, University of Florida, 1968; Ph.D., University of Kentucky, 1978. Career: Associate Professor, Department of Literature, Kentucky State University, present; Director, Connections Unlimited, 1981 to present; Writer; Literary Consultant for the Mountain Association for Community and Economic Development in Berea, Kentucky, 1980-81; Research Consultant for Ohio Telecommunications Department, University of Ohio; Executive Secretary, Settlement Institutions of Appalachia, 1980-81; Research Director, Appalachian Folklife Project, Berea College, 1979-80; Photographer; Instructor of Literature; Editor, University Press of Kentucky; Faculty Aide, University of Kentucky; Oral Historian. Organizational Memberships: Modern Language Association; University Photographers Association; Folk School Society of Ameria; International Mediation Society. Community Activities: Henry County Historical Society (board of directors, 1977 to present); Governor's Task Force on Education, Kentucky, 1977-79; Regional Coordinator for Oral History Commission, Kentucky, 1977. Religion: Sulphur Baptist Church, 1955 to present. Published Works: "Appalachian Welcome: A Photographic Essay", "On the Rebuilding of Wheelwright", "the switch" (a poem), "Catching Magic", "Going Home to Sally", "Creative Energy in James Still's 'Mrs. Razor'", "A System of Conflicts in Tom Berger's *Little Big Man*", Others. Honors and Awards: Little Kentucky Derby Award, 1964; Phi Beta Kappa; N.D.E.A. Title IV Fellowship, 1971-74; Woodrow Wilson Fellowship, 1967; Delta Epsilon Upsilon; Oswald Award Winner, 1966. Address: Box 111, Sulphur, Kentucky 40070.

Kent R Hance

Hanf, James Alphonso

Naval Architect Technician, Poet. Personal: Born February 3, 1923; Married Ruth G.; Father of Maureen R. Career: Naval Architect Technician, Puget Sound Naval Shipyard, Bremerton; Lecturer on Writing Poetry for Clubs and Organizations. Organizational Memberships: New York Poetry Forum, Inc.; Stella Woodall Poetry Society; Literarische Union (Germany); California Federation of Chaparral Poets; Ina Coolbrith Circle; International Academy of Poets; National Poetry Day Committee, Inc.; World Poetry Society; Kitsap County Writers Club (president); Illinois State Poetry Society; Western World Haiku Society; International Biographical Association; International Platform Association. Religion: Baptist. Published Works: Poet, Specializing in Haiku (pseudonyms: James Alfred Wildwood, James Allen Wordsmith); Former Poetry Editor, *Coffee Break*; Author of Over 500 Poems Published in Books, Magazines and Anthologies, including *Washington Verse, Quickenings, Inky Trails, A.B.I.R.A. Digest, Poem, Adventures in Poetry*, and Others Published in Japan, Brazil, Argentina, Italy, India; Author of Journal Articles on Writing Poetry. Honors and Awards: Honorary Doctor of Literature, 1980; Poet Laureate, *Idaho* Magazine, 1978; Various Commendations, Awards and Prizes for Poetry; Diploma di Merito, Universita Delle Arti, Italy, 1982; Award of Recognition, *Inky Trails*, Magazine, 1982; Special Honorary Membership, Stella Woodall Poetry Society, 1982-83; Doctor of Literature, World University (expected 1983); Nominated Poet Laureate of Washington by International Poetry Society, 1981; Special Poetry Books given to Him by Government of Sweden, 1982; Recipient of 1981 Testimonial of Outstanding Memberships in Annual Associate Category from A.B.I.R.A.; Listed in *Community Leaders of America, Community Leaders and Noteworthy Americans, International Who's Who of Intellectuals, Personalities of the West and Midwest, Who's Who in the West, Men of Achievement, International Who's Who in Poetry*. Address: P.O. Box 374, Bremerton, Washington 98310.

Hanford, William Edward

Consultant. Personal: Born December 9, 1908; Son of Thomas Cook Hanford (deceased); Father of William E. Jr., Ruth Harwood (deceased). Education: B.Sc., Philadelphia College of Pharmacy and Science, 1930; M.S. 1932, Ph.D. 1935, University of Illinois; D.Sc. (honorary), Philadelphia College of Pharmacy and Science, 1956; D.Sc. (honorary), Alfred University, 1959. Career: Consultant to the Chemical Industry; Former Chemist, Rohm and Haas; Research Chemist, Group Leader, duPont; Research Director, General Anilive and Film Corporation; Vice President, Research and Development, M. W. Kellogg Company; Vice President, Research and Development, Olin Corporation; Consultant to World Water Resources. Organizational Memberships: American Chemical Society (North Jersey section, treasurer 1956-58, councilor 1956-58, 1960-61; chairman, division of polymer chemistry, 1952; chairman, sub-division of fluorine chemistry, division of industrial and engineering chemistry; executive committee, division of industrial and engineering chemistry; chairman, speakers bureau, 1952; special board committee on chemistry and public affairs, 1967-69; council committee on professional relations, 1961; canvassing committee for the E. V. Murphree award in industrial and engineering chemistry, 1957-59; advisory boards, *Industrial and Engineering Chemistry* 1954-55, *chemical reviews* 1951-53; finance committee, *Journal of Organic Chemistry*; regional director, second district, 1968-70; executive committee, A.C.S. board, 1969; chairman, A.C.S. board committee on public, professional, and member relations, 1968-69; A.C.S. board committee on chemical abstracts service, 1968; member, chairman, A.C.S. board committee on finance, 1968-70; committee on chemistry and public affairs, 1967-69; committee on investments, 1969-70); Society of Chemical Industry, American Section (member, 1957 to present; past honorary chairman, 1958-59); Board of Scientific Research Society of America (national chairman, 1964-65); Directors of Industrial Research (president, 1966-67); Industrial Research Institute (president, 1968-69); American Institute of Chemists (president, 1964-65; chairman of the board, 1965-66; board member); American Association for the Advancement of Science; Society for the History of Technology (director); American Management Association; New York Academy of Sciences; National Research Council; American Institute of Chemical Engineers; Philadelphia College of Pharmacy and Science (board of trustees, 1960); The Chemists Club (board of trustees); Alfred University (board of trustees, 1960). Community Activities: Advisor to United States Office of Naval Research, United States Air Force Research, United States Department of Defense C.B.W.; Team Member for United States Government to Taiwan and Russia to Advise on Management of Industrial Research and Development. Published Works: Granted Over 100 Patents, Mostly in Polymer Chemistry. Honors and Awards: Chemical Industry Medal, Society of Chemical

Industry, American Section, 1961; Ambassador's Award, State of Pennsylvania, 1955; Annual Alumni Award, Philadelphia College of Pharmacy and Science, 1963; Honor Scroll, American Institute of Chemists, New York Chapter, 1957; Chemical Pioneer Award, American Institute of Chemists, 1967; Gold Medal, American Institute of Chemists, 1974; Phi Beta Kappa; Sigma Xi, Membership-at-Large Committee; Phi Kappa Phi; Phi Lambda Upsilon; William Albert Noyes Lecturer, University of Illinois, 1965; Honorary Member, American Institute of Chemists. Address: 4956 Sentinel Drive, Bethesda, Maryland 20816.

Hanks, Jesse Mack

Superintendent Emeritus. Personal: Born October 8, 1901; Son of Jesse Palmer and Maggie Ruth Hanks (both deceased); Married Robbie Holloway. Education: B.S., Southwest State University, San Marcos, Texas; M.A., Sul Ross State University, Alpine, Texas; Ph.D. (honorary), New Mexico State University, Las Cruces; LL.D. (honorary). Military: Served in the United States Air Force as Liaison Officer (Major). Career: Principal, Teacher, Coach, Anderson County, Texas, Schools, 1920-26; Teacher/Coach, Ysleta High School, El Paso, Texas, 1926; Principal/Coach, Ysleta High School, 1927-29; Superintendent, Ysleta Common School District, 1929-37; Superintendent, Ysleta Independent School District, 1937-80; Superintendent Emeritus, 1980 to present. Organizational Memberships: East El Paso Educators Association; Trans-Pecos Teachers Association (past president, District XIX); Texas State Teachers Association; National Education Association (life member); State and National Congress of Parents and Teachers (life member); Texas Association of School Administrators; American Association of School Administrators; Southwestern Cooperative Educational Laboratory (original member of council and executive committees). Community Activities: Ysleta Lions Club (charter member, past president); Knife and Fork Club of El Paso (past president); Yucca Council of Boy Scouts of America; East El Paso Y.M.C.A.; National Conference of Christians and Jews; El Paso Museum of Art (past board member); El Paso Family Welfare Service (past board member); El Paso Safety Council (past board member); Masonic Lodge; El Paso Chamber of Commerce. Religion: Ysleta United Methodist Church (member, past president, administrative board; past president, board of trustees). Honors and Awards: Conquistador Award for Outstanding Service, City of El Paso; Outstanding Administrator Awards from Future Farmers of America, Future Homemakers of America, Distributive Education Clubs of Texas, Vocational Agriculture Teachers Association of Texas; Nominated for Educational Administrator of the Year, National Association of Educational Secretaries; Nominated for James Bryant Conant Award (one of most prestigious honors in education), East El Paso City Council of Parents and Teachers Association; Human Relations Award, Trans-Pecos Teachers Association, 1978-79; Honored Ex of Ysleta High School, 1978; Board of Trustees Named New High School "J. M. Hanks High School"; Inducted into Hall of Honor, El Paso Historical Society; Inducted into Hall of Fame, Ysleta Retired Teachers Association, 1980; Listed in *Personalities of the South*. Address: 9824 Eastridge, El Paso, Texas 79925.

Jesse M Hanks

Hannahs, James R

Executive. Personal: Born December 23, 1942; Son of James H. Hannahs; Married Mary E. Hemmert; Father of Tricia, Michael. Education: B.S., Welding Engineering, The Ohio State University, 1967. Career: President, Midwest Testing Laboratories; Formerly, Manager, Welding and Metallurgical Laboratory, Bowser-Morner Testing Laboratories; Development Engineer, Hobart Brothers Company. Organizational Memberships: Ohio State University Welding Engineering Alumni Club (director); Central Ohio Metallographic Society; Theta Tau Fraternity; National Society of Professional Engineers; Ohio Society of Professional Engineers; American Society for Testing and Materials; American Society of Mechanical Engineers; American Society for Metals; American Welding Society (director). Community Activities: Garfield Skill Center Machine Trades and Welding Advisory Committee, Dayton, Ohio; Western Ohio Youth Center (advisory committee); Edison State College Welding Technology Advisory Committee (chairman); Upper Valley Joint Vocational School District High School and Adult Education Welding Advisory Committee. Honors and Awards: Dayton Chapter, American Society for Metals Young Member of the Year, 1979; American Welding Society District Meritorious Award, 1979; Registered Professional Engineer; Certified A.W.S. Welding Inspector. Address: 8598 Industry Park Drive, Piqua, Ohio 45356.

Hanns, Christian Alexander

Vocational/Educational Consultant. Personal: Born September 12, 1948; Son of Christian J. Hanns. Education: Diploma, Career Academy of Broadcasting, 1966; B.A., M.A., Kean College of New Jersey, 1969-72; Diploma, Glassboro State College, 1979; A.B.D., Doctoral Candidate, Rutgers University. Military: Served in the United States Army, 1966-69, in the capacity of Specialist Fifth Class. Career: Vocational/Educational Consultant, Essex Clinic; Former Director, Counselling, Testing and Curriculum; Director, Career, Vocational, Counselling and Placement; Coordinator, C.L.E.P. Preparation Programs. Organizational Memberships: Association of Community Education; National Psychiatric Association; American Vocational Association; American Personnel and Guidance Association; American Council of Counselors, Therapists and Educators; Substance Abuse Counselors Association (state representative, 1976-77); Association of Adult Education of New Jersey (chairman, counselling adults, 1979-81); Association for Families in Crisis (representative, statewide protection service coalition); Cooperative Work Association. Community Activities: American Red Cross (board of directors, 1976 to present); Clara Barton Auxiliary (president, 1980 to present); Union County Psychiatric Clinic (secretary, board of directors, 1980 to present); International Platform Association; United Way of Union County (allocations committee, research chairman, 1980 to present); March of Dimes (board of directors, 1976-77); Veterans Administration, Newark, New Jersey (advisory council, joint planning committee on Vietnam era veterans); Union County Coalition for Human Services (coordinator, human delivery system assessment, 1975-77); Metropolitan Ecumenical Ministry (co-chairman, ways and means committee); Association for Community Education-New Jersey (secretary, board of directors; chairman, legislative caucus). Religion: Co-Chairman, Community/Pastoral Relations 1980 to present, Chairman, Special Projects, Fund-Raising, Linden United Methodist Church. Honors and Awards: Red Cross Volunteer of the Year, 1980; Special Achievement Award, State Department of Education, New Jersey, Pioneering G.E.D. Flexible Testing Concept; Fellow, International Biographical Association; Life Membership, American Biographical Institute Research Association; Listed in *Who's Who in the East*, *Who's Who in American Vocational Education*, *International Who's Who in Community Service*, *Community Leaders and Noteworthy Americans*. Address: 312 Jefferson Avenue, Linden, New Jersey 07036.

Hanser, Julie

Member of Daughters of Charity; Hospital Administrator. Personal: Born July 5, 1941; Daughter of Mr. and Mrs. Forrest Hanser. Education: B.S., Marillac College, St. Louis, Missouri, 1965; Studies in Accounting, University of Evansville, Indiana, 1974; Master's in Health Administration, Indiana University, 1976. Career: Chief Executive Officer, St. Mary's Hospital, Milwaukee, Wisconsin, 1981 to present; Chief Executive Officer, Providence Hospital, Mobile, Alabama, 1978-81; Assistant Administrator, Providence Hospital, 1976-78; Nursing Service Administrator, St. Mary's Hospital, 1970-74; Various Nursing Positions, New Orleans, Louisiana,

1965-70. Organizational Memberships: American College Hospital Administrators; Hospital Financial Management Association (advanced member); American Society of Law and Medicine; Providence Hospital, Southfield, Michigan (president of board); Providence Hospital, Mobile, Alabama (vice president of board). Community Activities: Health Systems Agency (board of directors; chairperson, by-laws committee; chairperson, appropriations review); Chamber of Commerce, Mobile, Alabama; United Fund (chairperson, health division); Mobile United (civic improvement organization). Religion: Daughters of Charity of St. Vincent Depaul, 1960 to present. Honors and Awards: Outstanding Leadership, Hurricane Fredric, Mobile, Alabama, 1979; Outstanding Career Woman, Mobile, 1980; Administrator of the Year, Alabama Society of Hospital Social Workers, 1981; Certificate of Merit, Health Systems Agency, 1981; Certificate of Merit, Alabama Kidney Foundation, 1981. Address: 2430 N. Lake, Milwaukee, Wisconsin 53211.

Bernold M Hanson

Hanson, Bernold M (Bruno)

Consulting Geologist, Executive. Personal: Born May 7, 1928, Mayville, North Dakota; Married Marilyn Miller, October 1951; Father of Karen, Gretchen, Eric. Education: B.S., Engineering Geology, University of North Dakota, 1951; M.A., Geology, University of Wyoming, 1954. Career: United States Geological Survey Fuels Branch, Grand Forks, North Dakota, 1948-49; Geologist, Magnolia Petroleum Company, Midland, Texas, 1951-52; First Lieutenant, United States Corps of Engineers, Topographic Branch, Alaska and Southern California, 1952-53; Graduate School and Petrology Laboratory Instructor, University of Wyoming, 1953-54; Humble Oil and Refining Company, New Orleans (District Geologist), Alaska (In Charge of Project), Texas (District Geologist), 1955-60; Consulting Geologist and Independent Oil Operator, 1960 to present; President, Hanson and Allen, Inc., 1966-74; President, Hanson Exploration Company, Inc., 1971-75; President, Hanson Corporation, 1974 to present. Organizational Memberships: American Association of Petroleum Geologists (chairman, professional standards committee; chairman, continuing education committee; secretary, professional section; environmental committee, industrial advisory committee; chairman, public relations committee; secretary, 1973, 1974); American Institute of Mining Engineers, Petroleum Section; American Institute of Professional Geologists (advisor of finance); Society of Economic Paleontologists and Mineralogists (Permian Basin Section, vice-president, 1961; president, 1962-63); Sigma Xi; Sigma Gamma Epsilon; West Texas Geological Society (secretary, 1961; president, 1965-66; honorary life member); Southwest Federation of Geological Societies; Society of Independent Professional Earth Scientists; Rocky Mountain Section, American Association of Petroleum Geologists; All-American Wildcatters (charter member). Community Activities: University of Wyoming Alumni Association (life member); Wyoming Science Camp Alumni Association (life member); Lectured at University of Wyoming 1972, University of North Dakota 1970; Midland Chamber of Commerce; Lions Club; National Rifle Association (life member); United Fund (captain, 1960-62); Y.M.C.A. (football and basketball coach, 1965-66); Boy Scouts of America (joined in 1940; P.L.; A.S.P.L.; S.P.L.; J.A.S.M.; originated canoe trails in Red River Valley, Council Wilderness Camp, 1946; assistant scoutmaster, Elks Troop, Laramie, Wyoming, 1953; assistant scoutmaster, Troop 51, 1967-69; institutional representative, Troop 51, 1966; scoutmaster, Troop 51, 1969-70; board member, Buffalo Trail Council, camping and activities chairman, 1970; Philmont leader, 1970; scoutmaster, World Jamboree, Japan, 1971; canoe trail leader, 1972, O-A Indian dance team assistant; council president, 1972, 1973; attended University of Scouting, Bemidji, Minnesota, 1974; Wood Badge training, 1970; chairman, South Central Region World Jamboree committee, World Jamboree, Norway, 1975; participation chairman, Boy Scout World Jamboree, Sweden, 1979; national camping chairman, 1981); President's Council, University of Wyoming, 1979 to present; University of North Dakota (trustee); Petroleum Club, Midland and Houston, Texas. Religion: Holy Trinity Episcopal Church, Midland, Texas, Member of Vestry, 1968-71. Published Works: *Permian Limestone on Pacific Side of Alaska Peninsula; Geology of Elkhorn Ranch Area, North Dakota; West Texas Oil and Gas Fields; Oil and Gas Development Paper, West Texas and Southeastern New Mexico; Geology of the Bar-Mar Devonian Field, West Texas.* Honors and Awards: Boy Scouts of America, Eagle Rank with 3 Palms, Order of the Arrow, Vigil Honor, Silver Beaver Award, Distinguished Eagle Scout, Silver Antelope Award; Sioux Award, University of North Dakota, 1978 (highest alumni award); Boss of the Year, 1981, Permian Basin, Professional Secretaries International; Life Patron, Department of Geology, University of North Dakota; Distinguished Service Award, American Association of Petroleum Geologists, 1981; Listed in *Who's Who in the Southwest, Personalities of the South, Who's Who 1979, Who's Who in Finance.* Address: P.O. Box 1212, Midland, Texas 79702.

Mable K Haralson

Haralson, Mable Kathleen

State Employee. Personal: Born May 8, 1935; Daughter of Ralph Q. (deceased) and Minnie Murphy Haralson. Education: B.S., University of South Carolina, 1974; M.P.H., University of Tennessee, 1976. Career: Administrative Assistant, Department of Health and Environmental Control Community Health Service, 1968-74; Health Educator, South Carolina Department of Health and Environmental Control 1974-75; District Director of Health Education (Appalachia I), 1976-79; State Director, Public Information and Education, South Carolina Water Resources Commission, 1979 to present. Organizational Memberships: Southern Branch, American Public Health Association (chairman, health education section, 1980); American Public Health Association; South Carolina Public Health Association (secretary); American Association of Sex Educators and Therapists (certified). Community Activities: State Employees Association (board of directors, 1980-81); South Carolina Governor's Beautification and Community Improvement Board, 1979-81; State Natural Resources Education Council, 1980-81; South Carolina State Environmental Association, 1980-81. Religion: Baptist. Published Works: "Health Education Delivererd the Goods", *American School Health Association Journal*, February 1980. Honors and Awards: Distinguished Service Award, Southern Branch Health Education Section, 1980. Address: P.O. Box 515, Abbeville, South Carolina 29620.

Joyce P Hardy

Hardy, Joyce Pounds

Poet and Writer. Personal: Born November 23, 1925; Daughter of Horace and Chris Pounds (both deceased); Married to Tom Charles Hardy, M.D.; Mother of Tom Hardy Jr., Lynn Hardy Brotherton, H.P. Buck, Mike, Larry. Education: B.A., Rice University, 1967. Career: Published Author; Teacher of English, Spring Branch Senior High School, 1967-68. Organizational Memberships: Texas State Teachers Association, 1967-70; Authors Unlimited of Houston, Inc., 1979 to present; Romance Writers of America, 1981. Community Activities: Society of Rice University Women (president, 1972-73); Association of Rice Alumni (executive board, 1973-76, elected first woman president, 1977); Alumni Division Chairman, Rice Fund Council, 1976; Associate of Jones College, 1977-82; First woman member of Board of Directors, Owl Club; Board of Directors, Rice Sports Foundation, 1977; Community Advisor to N.C.A.A. Volunteers for Youth, 1977-81; University Standing Committee on Athletics, 1979-81; Legislative Committeewoman for Harris County Medical Auxiliary, 1978-81; Active Scout Leader, Sam Houston Area Council, 1955-65. Religion: Member of St. Andrews Presbyterian Church (ruling elder, 1974 to present, chairman of elementary division of church school, 1980-82, president of school board, 1973-74, director of mother's day out program, 1967-71, circle chairman, 1960-62, chairman of session commitment committee, 1976 and 1979). Published Works: Co-author *Three Ingredient Cookbook*; Poetry published in *Touchstone, Adventures in Poetry, Dragonfly.* Honors and Awards: Member of Pi Delta Phi; Honorary Member of "R" Association, 1980; Winner of Hugh Scott Cameron Award for distinguished service to Rice University, 1978; 10-year Den Mother

Award, Boy Scouts of America, 1966; Winner of John and Elsa Holland Prize for best sports story, 1981; Winner Writers Recognition Award for Poetry, Texas Commission on Arts, 1981. Address: 4067 Merrick, Houston, Texas 77025.

Hardy, Mary Priscilla

Retired Air Force Nurse. Personal: Born June 2, 1937; Daughter of Cecil and Elsie Hardy (both deceased). Education: Attended Inter-American University, 1965-67; Philips University, 1965; R.N., Central Maine General Hospital School of Nursing, 1959-63; B.S.N., University of Massachusetts, 1973; Master's Candidate, Golden Gate University, California. Military: Served in the United States Army, 1956-59; Served in the United States Air Force, 1964-82, retiring with the rank of Lieutenant Colonel. Career: Retired Air Force Nurse. Organizational Memberships: National League of Nurses; Aeromedical Association, Nurse Division; American Business Women's Association; A.F.I.T.-A.O.G.; Emergency Room Nurses Association (secretary-treasurer, Las Vegas section, 1978); Clark County Health Educators, 1978. Community Activities: Grange, 1954 to present; American Legion, 1970 to present; Alumni Association, University of Massachusetts; Red Cross Nurse; Director of Nurses Council, Lubbock, Texas; Volunteer assisting with Blood Pressure Screening, Vandenberg Air Force Base, California, 1976; Provided Continuing Education Hours for Nurses in Local Communities of Lompoc (California) and Lubbock (Texas); Served on Air Force Promotion Boards, Randolph Air Force Base, Texas, 1981; Organized Women's Health Week for Retired and Active Dependents of Combined Services, 1978, 1979. Religion: Deer Isle Congregational Church, Choir Member, 1949-56; Thule Green Air Force Base, Choir Director, 1974. Honors and Awards: William H. Walter III Award for Excellence, 1978; Chief of Staff Award, Squadron Officers School, 1968; Air Force Commendation Medal; Meritorious Service Medal with 2 Oak Leaf Clusters; Listed in *World's Who's Who of Women, Dictionary of International Biography, Who's Who of American Women, Who's Who, American Academy of Human Services*. Address: General Delivery, Deer Isle, Maine 04627.

Hare, Robert Lee Jr

Evangelist. Personal: Born January 12, 1920; Married Ruth Bradley; Father of Reggy Lynn Hiller, Mary Lee, Linda Jean Glenn. Education: B.A., Harding University, 1950; M.A., Language Study, University of Munich, 1956; Studies at the University of Vienna, 1957-58. Military: Served in the United States Navy, 1944-46, as Radioman 3/C. Career: Evangelist, Church of Christ; Committee Member, Futherance and Preservation of Religious Freedom in Austria, 1973-81; Assistant to President, European Christian College, Vienna, Austria, 1979-81; Missionary, Munich, Germany 1950-55, Salzburg, Austria 1952-55, Vienna, Austria 1956-73, 1981, Yugoslavia 1958-79, Czechoslovakia 1960-81, Hungary 1960-81, East Germany 1961-62, Poland 1962-78, Russia 1965-79, Bulgaria 1964-79, Romania 1964-79, Wiener Neustadt, Austria 1974-80; Served Churches of Christ in Arkansas, 1946-50; Inspector, North American Aviation Company, Grand Prairie, Texas, 1941-44; Order Clerk, Haggar Pants Co., Dallas, Texas, 1938-41. Honors and Awards: Given Farewell Party by President of Austria for Service Rendered to Their Government in Working with Committee which Drew Up Laws and Regulations Governing Young Men Who Wanted to Serve Their Country in Civil Service Jobs Rather than in the Armed Forces, 1981; Outstanding Alumnus Award, Harding University's Bible Department, Searcy, Arkansas, 1981. Address: 307 South Harding, Breckenridge, Texas 76024.

Haren, James H

Executive. Personal: Born March 25, 1935; Son of Mrs. W. H. Haren; Married Kathryn Amy Marshall; Father of James H. Jr., D. Michael, Susan J., Jeffrey W., Gregory P., Jamie L. Education: B.S. , Virginia Tech, 1955; M.S., New Mexico State Universiy, 1958. Military: Served in the United States Army, 1946-58. Career: President, Safe Baby Products, 1960-70; President, International Inventors, Inc., 1971 to present; Chairman of the Board, International Bartending Institute, 1977 to present. Organizational Memberships: Virginia Private Trade Schools Association. Religion: Protestant. Published Works: *Blocking, The First Fundamental of Football* and *Who Motivates the Motivator*. Honors and Awards: Who's Who in Adult Continuing Education, Who's Who in the South and Southwest. Address: 208 Churchill Drive, Longwood, Florida 32750.

Jakob Harich

Harich, Jakob

Doctor. Personal: Born September 1, 1920; Son of Jakob and Eva Harich (both deceased); Married Elisabetha Kautt; Father of Franz P. Hermine Allen, Wilhelmina Weinstein. Education: B.S., M.A., Ph.D., University Liubliana, Yugoslavia, 1939-44; M.D., University Sorajevo, 1950; Undertook Post-Graduate Studies at the University of Heidelberg and Tubingen, Germany, Pharmacology LI University, 1968. Military: Served in the Germany Military during World War II. Career: Doctor in Science Research and Development; President, Chemic Research and Manufacturing Company, Inc. (development of organic products and research in South American jungle, new organic chemicals and cholesterol study on the natives of the jungle). Community Activities: Central Florida Research and Education Foundation; National Foundation of Independent Business; Orlando Chamber of Commerce; Contributions to Various Local Charities; Police Activities; Boys Ranch. Religion: Lutheran. Honors and Awards: Listed in *Who's Who in America, Who's Who in the World, Personalities of the South, International Register of Profiles, Book of Honor*. Address: 31 South Cortez Avenue, Winter Springs, Florida 32707.

Harrington, Michael Ballou

Senior Health Economist, Systems Engineer. Personal: Born September 26, 1940; Son of Theodore C. Ballou; Married Mary Lynn Kijanka. Education: B.A., Political Science, California State University, Fullerton, 1965; M.S. (Health Economics) 1969, Ph.D. (Public Administration) 1973, University of California-Irvine. Military: Served in the United States Marine Corps, 1958-61. Career: Senior Health Economist/Systems Analyst, The MITRE Corporation; Adjunct Professor of Health Administration, Southeastern University; Former Senior Health Scientist, GEOMET Technologies, Inc.; Senior Health Associate, Arthur Young and Company, Accountants; Foreign Service Officer, United States Department of State. Organizational Memberships: National Platform Association; Operations Research Society of America; United States Foreign Service Association, 1972-73; National Rural Primary Health Care Association, 1981-82. Community Activities: Graduate School of Management Alumni Association (charter member); Potomac Valley Seniors Track Club (proctor). Religion: First Unitarian Church, McLean, Virginia. Honors and Awards: National Defense Graduate Fellow, University of California-Irvine, 1969-72; Scholastic Athlete of the Year, Santa Ana College, 1963; Rhodes Scholarship Nominee, California State University, 1965; Man of the Year, Santa Ana College, 1963; Scholastic Athlete of the Year, Santa Ana College, 1963; Listed in *Who's Who in the East, Directory of Distinguished Americans, Men of Achievement*. Address: 8380 Greensboro Drive, McLean, Virginia 22102.

Harris, Bettye J

Administrator. Personal: Born February 24, 1934; Married Ernest J. Harris; Mother of Mark Anthony, Tanya Denise, Gregory Scott. Education: B.S. 1975, M.P.H. 1977, University of Hawaii. Career: Director, Kalihi Palama Immigrant Service Center; Former Positions include Health Educator, School of Public Health, University of Hawaii; Health Educator, Arthritis Foundation; Executive Director, National Association of Social Workers, Hawaii. Organizational Memberships: American Public Health Association; Hawaii Public Health Association. Community Activities: League of Women Voters (board member, 1962-69); Y.W.C.A. (board member, 1972-75); Board of Review, Appointed by Mayor, City and County of Honolulu; Wai Wai Nui Women's Club (president); Senior Warden, St. Christopher's Church. Religion: Episcopal Diocesan, Standing Committee, Urban Ministry and Social Concerns Committee. Address: 45-170 Ohaha Place, Kaneohe, Hawaii 96744.

Harris, Charles Edgar

Chairman of the Board and Chief Executive Officer. Personal: Born November 6, 1915, in Englewood, Tennessee; Son of Charles Leonard and Minnie Borin Harris; Married Dorothy Wilson, August 20, 1938; Father of Charles Edgar Jr., William John. Career: The H. T. Hackney Company, Knoxville, Tennessee, Treasurer 1958-72, Vice President 1964-71, Director 1962 to present, President 1971-81, Chairman of the Board and Chief Executive Officer 1972 to present; Chairman of the Board and Director, Hackney Caroline Company (Murphy, North Carolina), Hackney Jellico Company (Harlan, Kentucky), Haywood Wholesale Grocery Company (Waynesville, North Carolina), Dale Sanitary Supply Company (Knoxville, Tennessee), Jellico Wholesale Grocery Company (Oneida, Tennessee; Elizabethton, Tennessee; Corbin, Kentucky; Somerset, Kentucky), Tri-State Wholesale Company (Middlesboro, Tennessee), Brink's Inc. (Knoxville, Tennessee), Park Oil Company (Alcoa, Tennessee), Testoil Company (Harlan, Kentucky), Carolina Oil and Gas Company (Bryson City, North Carolina), Pride Markets Inc. (Knoxville, Tennessee), Foodservice Distributors Inc. (Knoxville, Tennessee), Central Oil Company (McMinnville, Tennessee), Mid-State Investment Corp. (McMinnville, Tennessee), Appalachian Realty Corp. (Knoxville, Tennessee); Park National Bank, Knoxville, Tennessee, Director 1976 to present, Trust Board 1980 to present. Organizational Memberships: United States Industrial Council (director, 1975-81; executive committee member, 1977-81); Knoxville Wholesale Credit Association (president, 1956-57); National Association of Wholesalers-Distributors (board of trustees, 1977 to present). Community Activities: Tennessee Taxpayers Association (director, 1976 to present); Tennessee Baptist Convention (executive board member, 1976 to present; administrative committee, 1980 to present; state missions committee, 1976 to present); Greater Knoxville Chamber of Commerce (director, 1973-76; vice-president, 1975-76); Metropolitan Y.M.C.A. of Knoxville (director, 1971-77; executive committee, 1971-76; treasurer, 1975); Knox County Baptist Association (treasurer, 1964-67; chairman of finance committee and executive board, 1973-77); Rotary Club of Knoxville (member, 1966 to present; director, 1973-76; vice-president, 1975-77); Great Smoky Mountain Council Boy Scouts of America (executive board director, 1956-67, 1981 to present); Downtown Knoxville Association (director, 1977 to present; vice president, 1979 to present; executive committee, 1979 to present); Laymen's National Bible Committee Inc. (associate chairman, 1977); Volunteers of America (director, 1981); United Way of Greater Knoxville (budget committee, 1974-79; chairman, finance committee, director, 1979); 1982 World's Fair (budget review committee, 1980 to present). Religion: Central Baptist Church, Deacon, Trustee. Honors and Awards: Outstanding Community Leadership Award, Religious Heritage of America, 1978; Y.M.C.A. Silver Triangle and Red Triangle Awards, 1979; Listed in *Who's Who in the South and Southwest, Who's Who in Finance and Industry, Who's Who in the World, International Who's Who in Community Service*. Address: 7914 Gleason Road, Unit 1071, Knoxville, Tennessee 37919.

Virgil W Harris III

Harris, George Carleton

Personnel Specialist, Consultant. Personal: Born October 14, 1941; Son of Eloise C. Harris; Married Doris Jean McCormick; Father of Raymond Carleton. Education: B.A. 1961, M.A. 1966, Post-Graduate Studies 1967-69, University of Georgia. Military: Served in the United States Naval Reserve in the capacity of Chief Warrant Officer, 1961 to present, Active Duty 1961-63. Career: Personnel Specialist; Consultant; Former Counselor, Professor, Social Insurance Representative. Organizational Memberships: American Society of Public Administration (professional development committee, 1978-79); United States Naval Institute; American Management Association; International Personnel Management Association. Community Activities: Northern Maine Vocational-Technical Institute, Presque Isle (board of advisors, 1975-77); Assistant to Governor's Efficiency Commission, Atlanta, 1965-66; Advisor to State and Local Law Enforcement Agencies, 1965 to present. Religion: Episcopal. Honors and Awards: Scholarships, 1959, 1960, 1961, 1965, 1967; Listed in *Who's Who in Finance and Industry, Personalities of the South, Distinguished Americans, Community Leaders of America, Who's Who in the World, Men of Achievement, Personalities of America*. Address: P.O. Box 42, Cheltenham, Maryland 20623.

Harris, Louise

Researcher, Writer. Personal: Son of Samuel P. and Faustine M. Borden Harris (both deceased). Education: A.B., Economics, Brown University, 1926; Private Study in Organ with T. Tertius Noble, New York, 1938-42. Career: Researcher and Writer; Former Teacher and Recitalist of Piano and Organ. Organizational Memberships: American Guild of Organists (life member); American Historical Association; American Heritage Association; National Historical Society; National Archives; American Historical Association. Community Activities: Rhode Island Hospital, Children's Department; Brown University Medical School. Religion: Church Organist, 1929-50. Honors and Awards: Library of Human Resources in American Research Institute and American Heritage Association; Fellow, American Biographical Institute; Life Patron, A.B.I. Research Association; Life Fellow, Intercontinental Biographical Association; Life Fellow, Life Patron, International Institute of Community Service (now International Biographical Association); Honorary Fellow, Anglo-American Academy, England; Numerous Diplomas, Certificates, Desk and Wall Plaques; 3 Medals Minted in Royal Mint, London; Two Articles on the Pledge of Allegiance Published in Congressional Record. Address: 15 Jay Street, Rumford, Rhode Island 02916.

Harris, Virgil William III

Private Practice in Behavioral Psychology. Personal: Born June 4, 1946; Son of Virgil William (deceased) and Mary Jeanne Millard Harris. Education: B.S. with distinction, 1968; M.A. with honors, Development and Child Psychology, 1970; Ph.D., Development and Child Psychology, 1972; Undergraduate Research Assistant, Psychology Department, 1966-67; Student Associate, Project Follow-Through, 1967-68; Graduate with honors, Teaching Assistant, 1968-71; Research Assistant, Project Follow-Through, 1969-70 (all of the above at University of Kansas-Lawrence). Career: Research Director, Midwest Training Center, Project Follow-Through, University of Kansas, 1970-71; Research Director, Southwest Indian Youth Center, Tucson, Arizona, 1971-74; Director of Program and Research, Southwest Indian Youth Center, 1973-74; Associate in Developmental Training, Department of Psychology,

University of Arizona, Tucson, 1973-74; Associate in Clinical Training, University of Arizona, Tucson, 1975-80; Director, Centers for Youth Development and Achievement, Tucson, 1974-80; Principal Investigator, N.I.M.H. Crime Delinquency Division, Grant Award, 1972-75; Associate in Psychology and Adjunct Assistant Professor, Educational Psychology, University of Arizona, Tucson, 1977-78; Associate in Salute America, Tucson, 1980 to present. Organizational Memberships: National Council of Crime Delinquency; American Society of Criminology; Western Psychological Association; National Teaching Family Association; Arizona Council Child Care Agencies, 1975-80. Community Activities: Pimo County, Arizona, Juvenile Justice Collaborator, 1976-80; Bureau of Indian Affairs, Department of the Interior, Arizona Area Office (consultant, 1973-80), San Carlos Apache Tribe 1975-80, Blackfeet Tribe 1976-80. Published Works: Guest Reviewer, *Journal of Applied Psychology*, 1972 to present; Board of Editors, *Journal Scholastic Applications Learning Theory*, 1976-80; Author of Articles in Professional Journals. Honors and Awards: Indian Health Service Award for Valued Guidance and Assistance, 1975; Kiwanis Club of Sunshine Award in Recognition of Valued Service, 1976; Field Instructor, University of Tennessee, 1977; Listed in *Community Leaders and Noteworthy Americans, Who's Who in the West, International Who's Who of Intellectuals, Book of Honor, International Who's Who*. Address: P.O. Box 42971, Tucson, Arizona 85773.

Harris, Wayne M

Attorney. Personal: Born December 28, 1925; Son of George H. and Constance M. Harris (both deceased); Married Diane C. Harris; Father of Wayne J., Constance M., Karen L. Clark, Duncan G., Claire M. Sunberg. Education: Graduate of East Rochester High School; Studies at the University of Rochester; Graduate of Albany Law School. Military: Served in the United States Army, Combat Infantry, 1944-46. Career: Attorney; Admitted to Practice before the United States Supreme Court, 1958; Conducts Extensive Practice in Corporate, Trial, Estate, Real Estate and Environmental Law. Community Activities: Author of New York State Law which Prohibits the Filling of Land Under the Waters of New York State Streams, Rivers and Lakes, and a New York State Law to Protect Nesting Blue Herons on Iron Island; Non-Paid President, Delta Laboratories, Inc., 1971 to present; Monroe County Conservation Council, Inc. (president, 1954-59); Genesee Conservation League (president, 1967). Honors and Awards: Bronze Star, United States Army; Sportsman of the Year, Genesee Conservation League, 1960; Conservationist of the Year, Monroe County Conservation Council, 1961; Kiwanian of the Year, Kiwanis Club, 1965; Lester P. Slade Award, Real Estate Board of Rochester, 1965; Livingston County Federation of Sportsmen Award, 1966; New York State Conservation Council National Wildlife Federation Water Conservation Award, 1967; Rochester Academy of Science Award, 1970; American Motors Corporation Conservation Award, 1971; Rochester Chamber of Commerce Award, 1972; Association of Trial Lawyers of America, 1978; Listed in *Who's Who in American Law*. Address: 60 Mendon Center Road, Honeoye, New York 14472.

John R Harvey

Harshbarger, Boyd

Retired Professor, Department Head. Personal: Born February 15, 1906, in Weyers Cave, Virginia; Son of John A. Harshbarger (deceased); Married Isabelle Hoge; Father of John Hoge, Barbara H. Church. Education: B.A. honors, Engineering, Bridgewater College, 1928; M.S. honors, Engineering, Virginia Polytechnic Institute, 1931; M.A., Mathematics, University of Illinois, 1935; Ph.D., Mathematical Statistics, George Washington University, 1941; D.Sc., Bridgewater College, 1955. Career: Consultant to Army Ordnance, 1952 to present; Head of Department of Statistics, Director of Statistical Laboratory, Professor of Statistics, Virginia Polytechnic Institute, 1949-76; Retired, 1976; Consultant to Various Industrial Organizations (Hercules Inc., Westinghouse Electrical Co., Various Army Installations); Chairman of Committee on Statistics, Southern Regional Education Board, 1954-59; Collaborator with the Eastern Regional Laboratory, 1953-55; Consultant to the Navy Electronic Laboratory, San Diego, California, 1950; Professor of Statistics, Virginia Polytechnic Institute, Statistician, Virginia Agricultural Experiment Station, 1941-49; Rockefeller Fellowship, 1939-41; Instructor, Assistant Professor of Mathematics, Virginia Polytechnic Institute, 1931-39; Taught Quality Control Courses, Princeton University, University of North Carolina, Virginia Polytechnic University during World War II. Organizational Memberships: Virginia Academy of Science (president, 1949; council member, chairman of finance committee, 1958 to present; organized statistical section, secretary 1945-46, vice chairman 1947, chairman, 1948); Virginia Polytechnic Institute Science Club (president, 1945); Local Chapter, American Association of University Professors (president, 1947-48); Virginia Polytechnic Institute Chapter, Sigma Xi (president, 1950); Academy Conference, American Association for the Advancement of Science (president, 1950); Institute of Mathematical Statistics (national committee); Biometrics Society (national committee); American Statistical Association (fellow; national committee); Eastern North American Region of the Biometric Society (president, 1957-59); Phi Kappa Phi; Sigma Xi; Virginia Educational Association. Community Activities: Denny Commission on Education in Virginia (statistician, 1944). Published Works: Founder, Editor-in-Chief, *Virginia Journal of Science*, 1950-55; Associate Editor, *American Institute of Biological Sciences Bulletin*, 1954-58; Collaborating Editor, *Journal of the American Statistical Association;* Number of Professional Articles. Honors and Awards: Organized Department of Statistics and the Statistical Laboratory, Virginia Polytechnic Institute (now one of the largest in the nation); Organized and Supervised First Regional Statistical Summer Session, Virginia Polytechnic Institute, 1957; Initiated Modern Statistical Designs in Engineering and Agriculture Research, Virginia Polytechnic Institute; Developed Efficient Sampling Method Utilizing Land Classes in Virginia, 1945-48; J. Shelton Horsley Awards, Virginia Academy of Science, 1946; Alumnus Award of Bridgewater College, 1950; Distinguished Service Award, Virginia Academy of Science, 1966. Address: 213 Country Club Drive, S.E., Blacksburg, Virginia 24060.

Harutunian, John Martin

Musician. Personal: Born August 29, 1948; Son of John and Karmille Harutunian. Education: B.Mus., Wheaton College, Illinois, 1969; Attended Harvard University, 1969-70; M.A., University of Pennsylvania, 1975; Ph.D., University of California-Los Angeles, 1981. Military: Served in the United States Army, 1970-73, attaining the rank of Specialist, 5th Class. Career: Former Teaching Associate, University of California-Los Angeles. Organizational Memberships: Arturo Toscanini Society, 1969-76; American Musicological Society, 1975 to present. Religion: Park Street Church, Boston, Massachusetts, 1970 to present. Honors and Awards: Piano Soloist, Boston Pops Orchestra, June 1965; Piano Soloist, Boston Symphony Orchestra, in Own Composition, *Fantasy-Gavotte*, Youth Concerts in Symphony Hall, Boston, March and April 1966; Paderewski Medal, 1966. Address: 355 Newtonville Avenue, Newtonville, Massachusetts 20160.

Harvey, John R

Associate Professor. Personal: Born May 23, 1930; Son of Edna Harvey; Married Delores Deane Hill; Father of James, Jay, Jeffrey, Jennifer. Education: B.S., Purdue University, 1952; Graduate Studies, Massachusetts State College-Bridgewater, 1964-66; M.P.H., University of Michigan, 1968; Ph.D., The Ohio State University, 1978. Career: Associate Professor, Department of Health Education, East Tennessee State University, 1980 to present; Director, Health Related and Helping Service Programs, Division of

Continuing Education, The University of Kansas, Lawrence, 1978-80; Health Commissioner, Butler County Health Department, Hamilton, Ohio, 1974-77; Director of School and Community Health Education, Washtenaw County Health Department, Ann Arbor, Michigan, 1967-74. Organizational Memberships: American Public Health Association; American School Health Association; International Union for Health Education; Association for the Advancement of Health Education; Tennessee Society for Public Health Education; American Association for Health, Physical Education and Recreation. Community Activities: American Lung Association of Upper East Tennessee (board member; chairman, regional smoking education program, 1981); Lawrence-Douglas County Emergency Preparedness Board (board member, 1978-79); 4th Annual Governor's Conference on Aging (program developer, "Older-Bolder", 1979); Operation "Drug Alert", Kiwanis Program (director, Ann Arbor 1964-67, Hamilton 1974-77); Swine Influenza Immunization Program, Bulter County, Ohio (chairman, 1976); Mental Hygiene Association, Ann Arbor (Michigan), Hamilton (Ohio), 1966-76; Special Committee of Disaster Services, Following Major Tornado; Michigan Public Health Association (professional development committee); Ohio Health Commissioner's Association (legislative committee, 1975-76). Honors and Awards: Kiwanian of the Year, Hamilton, Ohio, 1977; Leadership Award, Ohio Department of Health, 1975; Eta Sigma Gamma, East Tennessee State University, 1980. Address: 1504 Woodridge Drive, Johnson City, Tennessee 37601.

Harvey, Maria Luisa Alvarez

Professor and Program Director. Personal: Born January 20, 1938; Mother of Rogelio Vicente Solis. Education: B.A., Texas Western College, 1965; M.A., University of Texas at El Paso, 1966; Ph.D., University of Arizona, 1969; M.Sc.Ed., Jackson State University, 1972; Undertook postdoctoral studies, Harvard University, Summers 1972, 1973. Career: Professor of Modern Foreign Languages, Director Honors Program, Jackson State University. Organizational Memberships: Modern Language Association; A.A.T.S.P. (president of state chapter, 1974-79); National Collegiate Honors Council; Southern Regional Honors Council (faculty executive committee, 1980-83). Community Activities: American Association of University Women; Young Women's Christian Association; League of Women Voters; Council ón Human Relations; Mississippi Arts Association; Friends of the Arts in Mississippi; Mississippians for Educational Television; Jackson Committee for the Bicentennial Celebration of the American Revolution, 1974-77; Mississippi Authority for Educational Television (advisory council on minorities, 1974-80). Honors and Awards: Phi Beta Kappa; Danforth Associate, 1977-83; Teacher of the Year Award, 1978; Listed in *Directory of Women Scholars in the Modern Languages, Directory of American Scholars, Dictionary of International Biography, Contemporary Authors*, Others. Address: 1062 Robinson St., Jackson, Mississippi 30203.

Harvey, William Robert

Administrator. Personal: Born January 29, 1941; Son of W. D. C. and Mamie C. Harvey; Married Norma Baker; Father of Kelly Renee, William Christopher, Leslie Denise. Education: B.A., Talladega College, 1961; Ed.D., Harvard University, 1971. Military: Served in the United States Army, 1962-65. Career: President, Hampton Institute; Tuskegee Institute, Vice President for Administrative Services 1976-78, Vice President for Student Affairs/Director of Planning 1972-75; Administrative Assistant to the President, Fisk University, 1970-72; Assistant to the Dean, Harvard Graduate School of Education, 1969-70. Organizational Memberships: American Council of Education; American Association of Higher Education; Virginia Association of Higher Education; National Association for Equal Opportunity in Higher Education. Community Activities: United Virginia Bank (director); Newport News Savings and Loan (director); United Way (director); Peninsula Economic Development Council (director; executive committee); Peninsula Chamber of Commerce (director); President's National Advisory Council, E.S.EA. (member, vice chairman); Harvard Alumni Council; National Merit Scholarship Corp. (director). Honors and Awards: Woodrow Wilson "Martin Luther King" Fellowship; Woodrow Wilson Foundation Intern Fellowship; Harvard University Higher Education Administrative Fellowship. Address: 612 Shore Road, Hampton, Virginia 23669.

Harwell, Kenneth Edwin

Dean and Professor. Personal: Born November 22, 1936; Son of Kelly Edwin (deceased) and Etta Sasser Harwell; Married Sharon Elizabeth Hilton; Father of Kathryn Ruth, Karen Elizabeth, Kenneth Hilton. Education: B.S., Aeronautical Engineering, University of Alabama, 1959; M.S. 1960, Ph.D. 1963, California Institute of Technology. Military: Served in the United States Army Reserve, 1953-61, becoming Sergeant First Class in 1958. Career: Dean, Professor, present, Research Division Director, University of Tennessee Space Institute, 1976 to present; Professor, Aerospace Engineer, Auburn University, 1963-76; Assistant to the Director, United States Army Missile R.D.&E. Laboratory, 1973-74; Engineering Consultant to United States Air Force Armament Laboratory, 1972-73; Graduate Teaching Research Assistant, California Institute of Technology, 1960-63; Associate Engineer, Jet Propulsion Laboratory, 1960; Associate Engineer, CONVAIR (General Dynamics), 1959. Organizational Memberships: American Institute of Aeronautics and Astronautics; A.S.E.E. (graduate studies division, chairman 1980-81, director 1981-82, vice-chairman 1979-80, secretary-treasurer 1978-79, program chairman 1977-78); A.P.S.; N.S.P.E.; T.S.P.E. Community Activities: Auburn Community Transportation Service (director, 2 years); Rotary Club, 1978 to present; University of Tennessee Century Club, 1977 to present; University of Tennessee 10x10 Volunteer Club, 1976 to present; Lakeview Country Club, 1976 to present. Religion: First Baptist Church, Tullahoma, Tennessee, Director of Adult Sunday Evening Program 1980 to present, Teacher of Singles Sunday School Class 1979-80, Deacon 1976 to present; Auburn First Baptist Church, Deacon 1970-76, Teacher of College Student Sunday School Class 1964-76. Honors and Awards: Anchor Rome Mills Fellow, 1955-59; Theta Tau, Most Outstanding Engineering Graduate, University of Alabama, 1959; A.I.A.A. Scholastic Award, 1959; A.I.A.A. Lecture Award, 1959; Tau Beta Pi Fellow, 1959-60; Associate Fellow, A.I.A.A., 1976; United States Army Missile Scientific Advisory Group, 1974-78; General H. H. Arnold Research Award, A.I.A.A., 1981; Alumni Professor, Auburn University, 1968-71; Most Outstanding Research Paper, 1971-72; Most Outstanding Engineering Professor, Pi Tau Syna, 1964. Address: 1916 Country Club Drive, Tullahoma, Tennessee 37388.

Hassouna, Fred

Professor of Architecture. Personal: Married Verna Arlene Dotter. Education: Diploma in Architecture with First Class Honors, Higher School of Fine Arts, Cairo, Egypt, 1940; Diploma in Egyptology with First Class Honors, University of Cairo, Egypt, 1944; Diploma in Civic Design, University of Liverpool, England, 1946; M.Arch., University of Southern California, 1950; M.S., Public Administration, University of Southern California, 1950; Licensed Architect, Texas 1955, California 1956. Career: Architect, Curator, Director of Excavations, Cairo Museum, Egypt, 1940-44; Lecturer in Egyptology and Architecture, University of Alexandria, Egypt, 1944-45, 1947-48; Director of Planning, Huyton-with-Roby Urban District Council, Huyton, England, 1946-47; Lecturer in City and Regional Planning, University of Southern California, 1950-55; Architect with Kistner, Wright and Wright, Architects and Engineers, Los Angeles, 1952-53; Architect with Welton Becket and Associates, Architects and Engineers, Los Angeles, 1954-56; Project Architect with Albert C. Martin and Associates, Architects and Engineers, Los Angeles, 1956-58; Professor and Head, Department of Architecture, East Los Angeles College, 1958-75; Professor and Head, Department of Architecture, Saddleback College, Mission Viejo, California, 1975 to present. Organizational Memberships: California Council of Architectural Education (president, 1977; vice president, 1976; director, 1973-76); American Institute of Architects (held offices of chairman of education committee and students affairs committee, Pasadena, Foothills chapters); American Institute of Certified Planners. Community Activities: Industrial Technology Advisory Board, California State University-Long Beach, 1963 to present; Architectural Advisory Committee, Rio Hondo College, 1967-76; Advisory Committee on Environmental and Interior Design, University of California-Irvine, 1976 to present; Liaison Committee on Architecture, Landscape Architecture and Urban and Regional Planning in Higher Education in California; Advisory Board on Architecture, University of California-Irvine, 1981 to present. Honors and Awards: Fellow, International Institute of Arts and Letters, 1961; Listed in *Who's Who in the West, Who's Who in American Education, Dictionary of International Biography, National Register of Prominent Americans, American Architects Directory, Men of Achievement, Who's Who in the United States, International Registry of Who's Who, Notable Americans of the Bicentennial Era, International Who's Who in Community Service, Two Thousand Men of Achievement, Personalities of America, Personalities of the West and Midwest, Community Leaders and Noteworthy Americans, Men and Women of Distinction, Who's Who in California, Directory of Distinguished Americans, Who's Who in Orange County*. Address: 31242 Flying Cloud Drive, Laguna Niguel, California 92677.

Hastings, Robert Clyde

Research Physician. Personal: Born April 23, 1938; Son of Robert S. Hastings, Jr.; Married Virginia Ruth Thomas; Father of Cynthia Margaret, Robert Clyde Jr., Jeffrey Scott. Education: Attended Vanderbilt University, 1956-59; M.D., University of Tennessee College of Medicine, 1962; Ph.D., Pharmacology, Tulane University, 1971. Military: Medical Director (06) of the United States Public Health Service, 1964 to present. Career: Intern, City of Memphis Hospitals, Memphis, Tennessee, 1963-64; Staff Physician, United States Public Health Service, Carville, Louisiana, 1964-68; Adjunct Associate Professor of Pharmacology, Tulane University, Tulane Medical Center, New Orleans, 1974 to present; Clinical Associate Professor of Medicine, Tulane Medical Center, 1976 to present; Associate Staff, Tulane Medical Center Hospital, New Orleans, 1977 to present; Research Physician, Chief of Pharmacology Research Department, National Hansens Disease Center. Organizational Memberships: Central Clinical Investigations Committee, Division of Hospitals and Clinics, United States Public Health Service, 1976-81; Central Committee on Human Research, Division of Hospitals and Clinics, United States Public Health Service, 1980-81; United States Leprosy Panel, United States-Japan Cooperative Medical Science Program (member, 1977 to present; chairman, 1980 to present); International Leprosy Association; American Society of Tropical Medicine and Hygiene; American Association for the Advancement of Science; Reticuloendothelial Society; American College of Clinical Pharmacology (fellow); American Chemical Society; New York Academy of Sciences; American Society of Microbiology. Community Activities: Tulane University School of Medicine (human use committee, 1972 to present); Council of Biology Editors. Religion: First United Methodist Church, Covington, Tennessee, 1951-80; St. John's United Methodist Church, Baton Rouge, Louisiana, Member 1980 to present, Pastor-Parish Relations Committee 1980 to present. Published Works: Editor, *International Journal of Leprosy*, 1979 to present. Honors and Awards: Alpha Omega Alpha; Sigma Xi; Honorary Member, Mexican Society of Dermatology; Corresponding Member, Argentine Society of Leprosy; Vice President, Congress of Hansenology of the Endemic Countries; Physician's Recognition Award, American Medical Association, 1972, 1976, 1980; Foreign Duty Service Ribbon 1977, Special Assignment Service Ribbon 1977, Isolated Hardship Service Ribbon 1981, Meritorious Service Medal 1980, Public Health Service. Address: 9373 Fox Fun Avenue, Baton Rouge, Louisiana 70808.

Haulsee, Anne Louise

Career Effectiveness Consultant. Personal: Born December 21, 1946; Daughter of Russell and Louise Haulsee; Married Russell T. Boyle, Jr. Education: B.A., Sociology, Roanoke College, 1968; M.A., Sociology, West Virginia University, 1971. Career: Career Effectiveness Consultant, Self-Employed; Fairfax County Young Women's Christian Association Women's Network; Staff, Special Programs Division, United States Department of Agriculture Graduate School; Co-Founder, Administrative Director, Corporate Secretary, Martha Movement (national association devoted to recognition of homemakers); Consultant, Women's Program Division, TransCentury Corporation; Manager, Washington Office, Western Temporary Services; Program Assistant, National School Public Relations Association. Organizational Memberships: National Association of Women Business Owners, Capital Area Chapter (membership officer, 1978-79; president, 1979-80); National Council of Career Women; Washington Women's Network; Federally Employed Women; National Association for Female Executives; American Society of Professional and Executive Women. Community Activities: The Executive Club (founding member); Georgetown University Speaker's Bureau, 1977 to present; Johnson-Butler Agency Speaker's Bureau, 1980 to present; Northern Virginia Alumnae Panhellenic Association (vice president, 1981-82; president, 1982-83); Northern Virginia Alumnae Chapter, Delta Gamma (treasurer, 1971-73; president, 1973-75); Roanoke College Annual Fund Drive, 1971-74; New Priorities Campaign, 1974-75; National Organization for Women (coordinator, employment task force, Northern Virginia Chapter, 1974-75); Dolly Madison Towers Social Club (president, 1972-73). Religion: Little Falls Presbyterian Church, 1961 to present). Honors and Awards: Listed in *Who's Who of American Women, Personalities of America, World Who's Who of Women, The Directory of Distinguished Americans, Community Leaders of America*. Address: 205 Yoakum Parkway #1511, Alexandria, Virginia 22304.

Havilland, Ben

Policy and Procedure Specialist. Personal: Born March 11, 1924; Married Michele Drapeau; Father of Stephen, Lance. Education: A.B., W. Henberg University, 1948; J.D., University of Washington, 1953. Military: Served in the United States Navy, 1942-45; Served in the United States Marine Corps, 1945-59, attaining the rank of Major (disability retirement). Career: Policy and Procedure Specialist, Security Assistance; Attorney; Procurement and Contracts Administration; Business Law Professor; Contract Law Professor. Organizational Memberships: Pi Sigma Alpha. Community Activities: Boy Scouts of America (volunteer leader, 1942 to present); William T. Hornaday Conservation Trust (trustee, 1979 to present; secretary, 1981-83). Honors and Awards: Silver Beaver Distinguished Service to Youth; Outstanding Contribution to Conservation, Hartford Insurance Company; Honorary Pilot, Guatemalan Air Force; Peruvian Cross of Aeronautical Merit; United States Air Force Letter of Commendation. Address: 4214 River Road, N.W., Washington, D.C. 20016.

Hawes, Grace M

Assistant Director. Personal: Born February 4, 1926; Daughter of Clarence and Mabel Maxcy; Married John G. Hawes (deceased); Mother of Elizabeth H. Crane, John D., Mark W., Amy C. Education: B.A. (Library Science) 1963, M.A. (History) 1971, San Jose State University. Career: Assistant Director, Communications/Events, Stanford University; Former Archival Specialist, Hoover

Institution Archives. Organizational Memberships: Institute for Historical Study; Society for Scholarly Publishing; Society of American Archivists; Society of California Archivists. Community Activities: Montalvo Art Association, Saratoga, California (volunteer, gallery committee, 1975-77). Published Works: *The Marshall Plan for China: Economic Cooperation Administration, 1948-49;* Engaged in Research on Book of Sino-American Relations. Address: 410 Sheridan #220, Palo Alto, California 94306.

Hawkins, Dorothy Lee

Associate Professor. Personal: Daughter of Dave Hawkins (deceased) and Mrs. Lucille H. Hall. Education: B.A. cum laude 1944, M.A. 1950, Xavier University, New Orleans, Louisiana; Ed.D., Indiana University, Bloomington, 1968. Career: Associate Professor, Adult Continuing and Elementary Education, Jackson State University, Jackson, Mississippi; Former Elementary School Teacher, New Orleans Public Schools; Elementary School Principal, New Orleans Public Schools; Visiting Professor, College of Education, Southern University, Baton Rouge, Louisiana; Associate Professor of Education, Southern University, New Orleans. Organizational Memberships: Mississippi Higher Education Association (secretary-treasurer, 1978-80; vice-president, 1980-81; president-elect); Jackson State Higher Education Association (president, 1979-80); Phi Delta Kappa (corresponding secretary, Utica Chapter, 1976-78). Community Activities: Jackson Y.W.C.A. (board of directors, 1973-79); Cade Chapel Baptist Church's Sunday School Council (consultant, 1980-81); Jackson O.I.C. (advisory committee, 1977-79); Greater Mt. Calvary Adult Development Center (consultant, 1978-80); Adult Education Workshops, Utica Junior College (consultant, 1979-80); Presenter, 5th Annual Southern Regional Conference, National Association for Public Continuing and Adult Education, May 1981; Workshops of Governor's Office of Voluntary Citizen Participation (group leader and recorder, 1980-81). Religion: St. John Institutional Missionary Baptist Church, New Orleans, Member 1934 to present, Chairperson of Council of Christian Education 1970-73; Women's Day Speaker, New Hope Baptist Church, 1980; Women's Day Speaker, Farish Street Baptist Church, 1981. Honors and Awards: Scholastic Achievement Award, Indiana University, 1956; Ford Foundation Fellowship in Adult Education Indiana University, 1957-58; Neophyte of the Year, Southeastern Region, Alpha Kappa Alpha, 1978; Mayoralty Certificates of Merit, City of New Orleans, 1979, 1981. Address: P.O. Box 17087, Jackson State University, Jackson, Mississippi 39217.

Austin Hay

Hay, G Austin

Motion Picture Producer/Director. Personal: Born December 25; Son of Dr. George and Mary Austin Hay. Education: Attended the University of Rochester, 1939-41; B.S. 1938, M.Litt. 1948, University of Pittsburgh; M.A., Columbia University, 1948. Military: Served as Newscaster, Information and Education Director, Headquarters, 31st Division, United States Army, South Pacific, 1942-46. Career: Motion Picture Producer/Director, United States Department of Transportation; Formerly Casting Director, United States Army Films; Public Relations Coordinator, Metropolitan Group, New York; Producer/Director, Off-Broadway Productions; Actor in Feature Films ("Being There", "Child's Play"), on Broadway ("Inherit the Wind", "What Every Woman Knows") and for Network Television ("Adam's Chronicles", "As the World Turns"). Organizational Memberships: Screen Actors Guild; Actors' Equity Association; American Federation of Television and Radio Artists; Washington Film Council; National Academy of Television Arts and Sciences; The Players; Federal Design Council; National Press Club. Community Activities: Red Cross Fund Raising Programs, 1936; Hospital Volunteer Work, 1950; Veteran's Hospital Radio Guild, 1952; Donations of Original Paintings to Exhibitions, 1954; Benefit Piano Concerts, 1937; Christmas Benefit Presentations, 1963; Lectures as President James Monroe, 1981; Donor to Museum, Turn-of-the-Century Period Room, 1976; National Trust for Historic Preservation; Arts Club of Washington (board of governors, trustee); American Artists Professional League; Allied Artists; Shakespeare-Oxford Society; Music Library Association; Institute for Bach Studies; Cambria County Historical Society; Sons of the American Revolution; Sigma Chi; American Philatelic Society; St. Andrew's Society. Religion: Writer of Television Program for National Council of Churches, 1965. Honors and Awards: Junior League Loyal Service Award, 1953; St. Bartholomew's Silver Leadership Award, 1966; Noteworthy Americans Award, 1976; (Academia Italia) Academy Gold Medal, 1980; Smithsonian Institution Associates Award, 1982; Biographical Memorabilia Book, *The Career of Austin Hay*, in the New York Public Library. Address: 2202 Columbia Road, N.W., Washington, D.C., or Hay Avenue, Johnstown, Pennsylvania 15902.

Hay, Jess Thomas

Executive. Personal: Born January 22, 1931; Son of Mrs. Myrtle Hay; Married Betty Jo Peacock; Father of Deborah H. Werner, Patricia Hay Mauro. Education: B.B.A., Southern Methodist University, 1953; J.D. magna cum laude, Southern Methodist University School of Law, 1955. Career: Chairman and Chief Executive Officer 1969 to present, President and Chief Executive Officer 1965-69, Lomas and Nettleton Financial Corporation; Associate 1955-61, Partner 1961-65, Law Firm of Locke, Purnell, Boren, Laney and Neely. Organizational Memberships: American Bar Association; Texas Bar Association; Dallas Bar Association; American Judicature Society; Newcomen Society of North America (vice chairman, Dallas committee). Community Activities: Southern Methodist University (board of trustees; board of governors); University of Texas System (board of regents); Texas Arts Alliance (governing board); Dallas Citizens Council; Dallas Council on World Affairs; Texas Research League (board of directors); Greater Dallas Planning Council (treasurer); Dallas Community Chest Trust Fund (advisory council); March of Dimes (board of directors, 1981; women's auxiliary, metropolitan Dallas chapter); Exxon Corporation (board of directors); Greyhound Corporation (board of directors); Mercantile Texas Corporation (board of directors); Trinity Industries, Inc. (board of directors); Republic Financial Services, Inc. (board of directors); Lomas & Nettleton Mortgage Investors (board of directors). Religion: Ridgewood Park United Methodist Church. Address: 7236 Lupton Circle, Dallas, Texas 75225.

Marcie L Hayes

Hayes, Marcie L

Student and Private Music Instructor. Personal: Born May 6, 1951; Daughter of Leo G. May; Married to L. Dayne Jr. Education: Currently attending Illinois State University for B.Mus.; Pedagogy training at American Suzuki Institute, 1980. Career: Manager of Private Music Studio; Former Manager, Lewiston Plumbing and Heating. Organizational Memberships: Local I.S.M.T.A. Group (secretary-treasurer); S.A.A.; M.T.N.A. Honors and Awards: Attending Illinois State University on scholarship; Honors Student, Illinois State University; Member of Mensa; Listed in *Who's Who in the Midwest*. Address: 122 Exchange Street, Danvers, Illinois 61732.

Hayes, Martha Bell

Owner of Beauty Salon, Modeling School and Beauty School. Personal: Born October 20, 1943; Daughter of Otha James and Earlane Williams Bell; Married Dirk Lambert; Mother of 3 Daughters and 4 Sons. Education: C.C.D. High School Diploma; Graduate of

Forsyth Technical Institute, Wake Forest University, Winston-Salem, North Carolina, 1964; Graduate of Metropolitan Beauty School, Washington, D.C., 1966; Graduate of Harris Barber College, Raleigh, North Carolina, 1977; Attended Several Professional Courses. Career: President, Wildreds Inc., Fayetteville, North Carolina; Owner, Shades of Beauty Modeling School; Owner, Cape Fear Beauty Institute and Hairweaving College; Owner, Martha's Beauty Salon, North Carolina #2 and #3 1976 to present, North Carolina 1975 to present, Arizona #1 and #2 1974-75; Owner, Martha's Discount Beauty Salon, Fayetteville, North Carolina, 1970-74; Manager, Martha's Beauty Salon, Fayetteville, North Carolina, 1968-74; Night Manager, Continental Trailways, to 1968. Organizational Memberships: National Association of Cosmetology Schools, 1978 to present; First International Independent Hair Weavers Association, Inc., 1977; North Carolina Beauticians Annual Trade Show, Inc., 1969; Certified Hair Weaving Specialist, 1976; North Carolina State Board of Cosmetic Arts, Raleigh, North Carolina, 1968; Martha Hayes Fayetteville Cosmetologist Association, 1979. Honors and Awards: Highly Qualified Associated Technician and Master Hair Dresser, Alberto-Culver RCB Division, 1977; Certificate of Award, First International Independent Hair Weavers 2nd Annual Convention, 1975; Diploma of Trichology, Plus Fair Centers International Inc., 1976; Medallion Styling Guild, Bronner Brothers International Beauty Show, Atlanta, Georgia, 1976; Job Well Done as Vice-President, Martha Hayes Fayetteville Cosmetologist Association, 1979; Certificate in Recognition of Promotion in the Field of Cosmetology, 1979. Address: 315 Hay Street, P. O. Box 1811, Fayetteville, North Carolina 28301.

Martha B Hayes

Hayes, Teddie Narver

Technical Instructor. Personal: Born January 24, 1942; Son of Jake Hayes; Married Addie Adams; Father of Teddie Narver II. Education: Graudate of Carver High School, 1961; Attended North Carolina College, 1961-64; Diploma, United States Army Signal School, 1965; Associate's Degree in Aviation Instrument/Electronics 1979, Airframe and Powerplant 1981, Spartan School of Aeronautics. Military: Served in the United States Army, 1964-78, attaining the rank of SSG; Served in the United States Army National Guard and Army Reserve. Career: Technical Instructor of International Students; Avionics Instructor, Pilot and A&P Mechanic. Organizational Memberships: Civil Air Patrol (2nd lieutenant; command pilot and training officer); Negro Airmen International; Aircraft Owners and Pilots Association. Community Activities: U.S.O. Service (volunteer, 1968); Church Brotherhood (president). Religion: Asbury Mt. Olive United Methodist Church. Honors and Awards: U.S.O. Serviceman of the Year, 1972; Commander's Award, Civil Air Patrol, 1975; Honor Graduate, Spartan School of Aeronautics, 1979. Address: 7221 S.W. Greenview Terrace, Topeka, Kansas 66619.

Hazlehurst, Franklin Hamilton

Educator. Personal: Born November 6, 1925; Married Carol Foord; Father of Franklin Hamilton Jr., Robert Purviance, Mary Hadley, Abigail Norris. Education: B.A. 1949, M.F.A. 1952, Ph.D. 1956, Princeton University. Military: Served in the United States Army Combat Engineers, 1944-46, attaining the rank of Staff Sergeant. Career: Professor, Chairman, Department of Fine Arts, Vanderbilt University, 1963 to present; Associate Professor, Art History, Department of Art, University of Georgia, 1957-63; Lecturer, Princeton Theological Seminary, 1956-57; Lecturer and Research Assistant, The Frick Collection, New York City, 1956-57; Assistant Instructor, Instructor, Princeton University Department of Art and Archaeology, 1951-56. Organizational Memberships: American Archaeological Society; College Art Association of America; Southeastern College Arts Conference (past president); Societé de l'histoire de l'art français; Society of Architectural Historians. Religion: Episcopalian; Member of Christ Church, Nashville, Tennessee. Published Works: *Jacques Boyceau and the French Formal Garden*, 1966; *The French Formal Garden*, Editor with Elizabeth MacDougall of the Papers of the Third Colloquium on Landscape Architecture, Dumbarton Oaks, Washington, 1974; *Gardens of Illusion: The Genius of Andre Le Nostre*, 1980; Numerous Articles in Scholarly Journals. Honors and Awards: Fulbright Fellowship, Paris, 1953-54; Charlotte Elizabeth Proctor Fellowship, Princeton University Graduate School, 1954-55; Sarah H. Moss Fellowship, Paris, 1961-62; A.C.L.S. Grant-in-Aid, 1967; American Philosophical Society Grant, 1967, 1982; Millard Meiss Publication Grant of College Art Association of America, 1979; Madison Sarratt Prize for Excellence in Undergraduate Teaching, Vanderbilt University, 1970; Alice Davis Hitchcock Award for *Gardens of Illusion*, Society of Architectural Historians, 1982. Address: 4430 Shepard Place, Nashville, Tennessee 37205.

Head, William Iverson

Manufacturing Company Executive. Personal: Born April 4, 1925; Son of Mrs. D. R. Howard; Married to Mary Helen Ware; Father of William I. Jr., Connie Suzanne, Alan David. Education: B.S., Georgia Tech, 1950. Military: Enlisted as Air Crewman, Navy Dive Bombers in the Pacific Theatre 3 years during World War II; Member of Naval Reserve 38 years, with present rank of Captain; Reserve Liaison with Selective Service System, 1969-80. Career: Superintendent, Acetate Yarn, Tennessee Eastman Company, Chemicals Division, Eastman Kodak Company, Kingsport, Tennessee, 1976 to present; Textile Engineer (r&d and quality control), Tennessee Eastman Company, 1949-57; Senior Textile Engineer in charge of quality inspection and packing, Tennessee Eastman Company, 1957-66; Department Superintendent (various departments), Acetate Yarn, 1966-76. Organizational Memberships: American Association for Textile Technology; American Society for Quality Control; International Platform Association; Naval Reserve Association; Reserve Officers Association (past chapter president, past state vice president, state president, 1981-82). Community Activities: Consulting member, Radiological Unit, Civil Defense, 1962 to present; Kiwanis, 1968-77; Elks, 1957 to present; Veterans of Foreign Wars; Military Order of World Wars. Religion: Member of Unitarian Church. Honors and Awards: Honor Graduate, Georgia Tech; Charter member, Delta Kappa Phi; Navy Commendation Medal and Meritorious Service Award; Has been issued 5 U.S. patents of significant commercial impact; Holds 3 British patents, 3 French patents and 1 or more German and Japanese patents; Member of Mensa and Intertel; Member of International Society for Philosophical Enquiry (international personnel consultant, 1978-79, international vice president, 1979-80, elected senior fellow and international president, 1980). Address: 2026 Bruce Street, Kingsport, Tennessee, 37664.

Charles V Hearn

Hearn, Charles Virgil

Clergyman, Behavioral Scientist. Personal: Born September 4, 1930, in Westport, Indiana; Son of Forrest V. and Emma F. Hearn; Father of Debra Lynn, Charles Gregory, Martin Curtis. Education: Ph.D., Thomas A. Edison University, 1972; D.D., Trinity Hall College and Seminary, 1977; Diploma, Palm Beach Psychotherapy Training Center, 1976. Military: Served in the United States Army, 1951-53, attaining the rank of S.F.C. Career: Ordained to Ministry, Methodist Church, 1958; Pastor, Various Methodist Churches, Indiana, Texas, Wyoming, California, 1958-70; Interpersonal Minister, St. Albans Church of the Way, San Francisco, 1974 to present; Clergyman and Counselor, Green Oak Ranch Boys Camp, California, 1969-70; Director of Rehabilitation, Mary-Lind Foundation, Los Angeles, 1970-71; Medical Assistant, Fireside Hospital, Santa Monica, California, 1971-72; Director, Alcoholism Program, Patrician Hospital, Santa Monica, 1972-74; Proprietor, Executive Director, Consultation, Mediation, Referral,

Santa Monica, 1974 to present; Vice Chairman, Western Los Angeles Alcoholism Coalition, 1974-78. Organizational Memberships: American Ministerial Association (president); American Board of Examiners in Psychotherapy (diplomate); American Academy of Behavioral Science (fellow); Association for Social Psychology; Western Association of Christians for Psychological Studies; National Council on Family Relations; American College of Clinic Administrators; Association of Labor-Management Administrators. Community Activities: Western Los Angeles Alcoholism Coalition (vice chairman); Coastal Region Alcoholism Consortium (past chairman); Los Angeles County Alcoholism Alliance (various offices); Coastal Region Health Services (proposal review committee); Special Advisor to Various Private/Non-Profit Programs; Democrat. Published Works: Contributor of Numerous Articles on Psychotherapy to Professional Publications. Honors and Awards: Bronze Star, United States Army; Listed in *Who's Who in the West*. Address: 1248 11th Street, Suite B, Santa Monica, California 90401.

Hefflefinger, Clarice Mae

Realtor. Personal: Born October 5, 1937; Daughter of Ralph Wayne (deceased) and Wyota Anita Nashold Thorpe; Married Jack Kenneth Hefflefinger; Mother of Kevin, Deborah, Jack, Kenneth. Education: A.A., College of Sequoias, Visalia, California, 1967. Career: Real Estate Broker/Realtor, 1977 to present; Substitute Teacher, Tulare City Schools, 1979; Various Positions in Banking and Insurance, 1956-76. Organizational Memberships: National Association of Realtors; California Association of Realtors (director); Tulare Board of Realtors (director; vice president, 1981; president, 1982). Community Activities: Tulare Chamber of Commerce; Tulare Draft Board (chairman); Secretary to Don Rogers, State Assemblyman, 33rd District; Republican Club; Quota Club; AMVETS Auxiliary (president, 1981). Religion: Protestant. Honors and Awards: Listed in *Who's Who of American Women*. Address: P.O. Box 1213, Tulare, California 93275.

Heggers, John Paul

Professor of Surgery, Director of Research and Laboratories. Personal: Born February 8, 1933, in Brooklyn, New York; Son of Mr. and Mrs. J. Heggers; Married Rosemarie Niklas; Father of Arn, Ronald, Laurel, Gary, Renee, Annette. Education: B.A., Montana State University, 1958; M.S., University of Maryland, 1965; Ph.D., Washington State University, Pullman, 1972. Military: Served in the United States Army, 26 years, retiring with the rank of Lieutenant Colonel. Career: Director, Burn Center Laboratory, University of Chicago Burn Center, 1977 to present; Research Associate, Professor of Surgery, Department of Surgery, Section of Plastic and Reconstructive Surgery, The University of Chicago, 1980 to present; Instructor, Clover Park Vocational Technical Institute, Tacoma, Washington, 1977; Assistant Chief, Clinical Investigation Servics, Madigan Army Medical Center, April-October 1977; Chief Clinical Research Laboratory, Clinical Investigation Service, Madigan Army Medical Center, 1974-77; Special Assistant to the Director, Armed Forces Institute of Pathology, Washington, D.C., 1973-74; Microbiologist, Special Mycobacterial Disease Branch, Geographic Pathology Division, Armed Forces Institute of Pathology, April-October 1973; Laboratory Sciences Officer, Office of the Surgeon General, Pathology and Laboratory Sciences Consultant, 1972-73; Chief, Microbiology Division, Pathology Department, Brooke General Hospital, Fort Sam Houston, Texas, 1967-69; Chief, Diagnostic Bacteriology, 9th Medical Laboratory, Saigon, Vietnam, 1966-67; Chief, Virology and Rickettsiology Division, Department of Microbiology, Third U.S. Army Medical Laboratory, Fort McPherson, 1965-66; Chief, Clinical Laboratory, United States Army Hospital, Verdun, France, 1960-63. Organizational Memberships: American Medical Technologists (national secretary,1980-82; national vice president, 1982; national board of directors, 1979-80; chairman, nominations committee, I.S.S.A.M.T., 1978 to present; board member, I.S.S.A.M.T., 1979 to present; chairman, legislative committee); American Academy of Microbiology (fellow); American Society for Microbiology; American Society for Medical Technology; Chicago Society for Medical Technology; American Burn Association; American Society of Tropical Medicine and Hygiene; The American Geriatrics Society (fellow); The American Society of Clinical Pathologists (associate); American Veterinary Medical Association; Association of Military Surgeons of the United States; The Institute of Medicine in Chicago (fellow); New York Academy of Science (active member, fellow); Plastic Surgery Research Council; Royal Society of Tropical Medicine and Hygiene; Sigma Xi; Surgical Infection Society (charter member, 1980; local arrangement committee, 1981); Society of Armed Forces Clinical Laboratory Scientists (emeritus); American Public Health Association; American Society of Plastic and Reconstructive Surgeons (associate); International Society for Burn Injuries. Community Activities: Certified Y.M.C.A. Scuba Diver; United States Coast Guard Auxiliary (member of flotilla, 1974-77); Eagle Scout, Scout Masters Key; Explorer Post 405, Boy Scouts of America (committee chairperson, 1974-77); Health Systems Agency, DuPage County, 1978 to present; Our Lady, Mt. Carmel (finance, administration, maintenance committee, 1980 to present). Published Works: Author/Co-Author Numerous Professional Publications including (most recently) "Analysis of the Surface Morphology of Recovered Silicone Mammary Prostheses" and "Myth, Magic, Witchcraft or Fact *Aloe Vera* Revisited". Honors and Awards: Army Commendation Medal, Meritorious Service, 1963; Armed Forces Research Medal, 1963; Certificate of Achievement, Third U.S. Army, 1963; Suggestion Award Certificate, Third United States Army, Fort McPherson, 1966; Vietnamese Cross of Gallantry with Bronze Palm, 1967; Vietnam Conflict Medals, 1966-67; Bronze Star Medal, 1967; Fisher Award in Medical Technology, American Medical Technologists, 1968, 1982; Raymond Franklin Metcalfe Award for Surgical Research, 1968; Certificate of Appreciation, American College of Surgeons, 1969; Gerard B. Lambett Award, 1973; Freedoms Foundation Valley Forge Honor Certificate, 1974; Good Conduct Medal, United States Army, 1974; Letter of Commendation, Armed Forces Institute of Pathology, 1974; Joint Services Commendation Medal, 1974; Certificate of Appreciation, Armed Forces Institute of Pathology, 1974; Distinguished Achievement Award, American Medical Technologists, 1976; Exceptional Merit Award, American Medical Technologists, 1977; Letter of Commendation, Madigan Army Medical Center, 1977; Legion of Merit, 1977; American Medical Technologists Writing Award, 1980; Lancer Authors Award, 3rd Place, Sponsored by Lancer, Division of Sherwood Medical, 1981; Certificate of Recognition, I.S.S.A.M.T., 1981; Nominated to *Who's Who in Maryland, Who's Who in America, Who's Who in the World, Who's Who in Health Care, Who's Who in Technology Today;* Listed in *Directory of Medical Specialities, American Men and Women of Science, Directory of Distinguished Americans, Men of Achievement.* Address: 10S082 Lakewood Drive, Hinsdale, Illinois 60521.

Clarice M Hefflefinger

Heilman, Marilyn Patton Mangum

Retired. Personal: Born August 31, 1925; Daughter of Frank Mangum; Married Walter Ritter Heilman, Jr. (deceased); Mother of Walter Ritter III. Education: B.A., Lindenwood College, 1947; M.A., East Tennessee State University, 1970. Career: Special Instructor in Modern Dance, Wake Forest College, 1957; Visiting Instructor in Art Education, East Tennessee State University, Summer 1971; Teacher, Art, History and Humanities, Bearden High School, Knoxville, Tennessee, 1958-81; Art Work Exhibited at E. G. Fisher Library, Lindenwood College, Hyatt Regency Hotel, Slocumb Gallery of East Tennessee State University, Offices of Volunteer Knoxville, West Town Mall (Knoxville). Organizational Memberships: National Art Education Association (life member; vice president, 1982-84; director of secondary division, 1977-79); National Art Honor Society for High School Students (national director); Tennessee Art Education Association (president, 1971-73); East Tennessee Art Education Association (chairman, 1964-67); American Crafts Council, 1961-81; International Society for Education through Art, 1965-84; United States Society for Education through Art, 1974-84; National Education Association, 1958-81; Tennessee Education Association, 1958-81; East Tennessee

Education Association, 1958-81; American Association of University Women, 1948-81; Tennessee Arts Alliance, 1980-82; International Biographies Association. Published Works: "Report of the Secondary Division Sessions" *Carer Education and the Art Teaching Profession*. Honors and Awards: Award for Outstanding Contributions to the Profession of Art Education, Western Regional N.A.E.A.; Significant Contribution to American Education Award, National Study of School Evaluations; Outstanding Contributins to the Profession of Art Education Award, Southeastern Regional N.A.E.A.; Award in Appreciation for Dedicated Service as a Member of the Board of Directors of the National Art Education Association, 1979; Listed in *Outstanding Secondary Educators, International Who's Who of Intellectuals, World Who's Who of Women, Dictionary of International Biography, International Register of Profiles, Men and Women of Distinction, Notable Americans*. Address: Apt. 13, Ambassador Arms, Route 13, Crestview Drive, Greeneville, Tennessee 37743.

Heisler, Elwood Douglas

Hotel Executive. Personal: Born June 29, 1935; Son of Elwood D. and Laura H. Heisler. Education: Graduate of Pierre S. DuPont High School, 1953; B.A., Michigan State University, 1957; M.A.S. Candidate, Johns Hopkins University. Military: Served in the United States Army, 1957-60, attaining the rank of 1st Lieutenant. Career: General Manager, Quality Inn. Organizational Memberships: American Hotel and Motel Association; Baltimore Economics Society; Hotel Sales Management Association; Travel and Tourism Research Association; Maryland Hotel and Motor Inn Association; Michigan State University Hotel Association; Advertising Club of Baltimore (board of directors); Future Business Leaders of America (Northern High School advisory council); Maryland State Advisory Council, Phi Beta Lambda. Community Activities: Baltimore County Chamber of Commerce (vice president, small business council); Towson Rotary Club (board of directors); Maryland Press Club (board of directors); Maryland Travel Council; Greater Baltimore Committee; Baltimore Council on Foreign Affairs; Towson Business Association; Maryland Historical Society; Towson State University Tiger Club; Gunpowder Youth Camps (board of directors); Historical Society of Delaware; Association for the Preservation of Virginia Antiquities; National Trust for Historical Preservation; Flag House Association; Detroit Institute of Arts Founders Society; Supreme Court Historical Society; Capital Historical Society; Society for the Preservation of Maryland Antiquities; Nantucket Historical Association; Republican National Committee; Lockwood-Mathews Mansion of Norwalk, Inc.; Baltimore Museum of Art; Theta Chi Fraternity Alumni Association; Michigan State Business Alumni Association. Religion: Member, First Congregational Church, Nantucket, Massachusetts; National Cathedral Association, Washington, D.C.; St. Andrews Music Society, Madison Avenue Presbyterian Church, New York City; Friends of Kirk-in-the-Hills Presbyterian Church, Bloomfield Hills, Michigan, 1981; Membership and Outreach Committee, Baltimore Episcopal Cathedral of the Incarnation. Honors and Awards: Maryland Business Person of the Year, Maryland Chapter, Future Business Leaders of America, 1981; Business Person of the Year, National Future Business Leaders of America, 1981; Top Ten Percent Innkeeper, Holiday Inn System, 1975; Fifty-Seven Club, Michigan State University Service Honorary, 1957; Certificate of Recognition, Troy, Michigan, Chamber of Commerce, 1975; Award of Appreciation, Troy, Michigan, Optimist Club, 1972; Award of Merit, Baltimore County Chamber of Commerce, 1982; Listed in *Who's Who in the East, Who's Who in Finance and Industry*. Address: 620 Bridgeman Terrace, Towson, Maryland 21204.

Elwood D Heisler

Helinka, Ellen Marie (Bissert)

Editor. Personal: Born August 28, 1947. Education: B.A. cum laude, City College, 1970; M.A., City University of New York, 1973. Career: Editor, Feminist Literary Magazine, *13th Moon*. Honors and Awards: Phi Beta Kappa; Recipient of a Youthgrant, Naitonal Endowment for the Arts, 1974; Doctoral Scholarship to New York University, 1974; Fels Award for Editing, 1976; Editors Grant from the Coordinating Council of Literary Magazines, 1980. Address: 30 Seaman Avenue, New York, New York 10034.

Heller, Steven Ashley

Associate Professor. Personal: Born June 10, 1944; Son of Mr. and Mrs. J. Heller; Married Madolyn Carol Moutardier. Education: B.S., Business Administration, Florida State University, 1966; M.S., Management, University of Arizona, 1968; Ed.D., Administration, University of Tennessee, 1971. Career: Associate Professor of Management, Mississippi State University; Formerly, President, Management and Educational Consulting Associates, Inc.; Management Analyst, State of Florida, Department of H.R.S.; Project Director, Psychotherapy Project, Department of Psychiatry, University of Kentucky Medical Center; Program Evaluator, Innovative Education Project, Oglala Sioux Indian Reservation. Organizational Memberships: Academy of Management; Association for Business Simulation and Experiential Learning; International Registry of Organization Development Professionals; Organizational Development Network; Association for Specialists on Group Work; American Personnel and Guidance Association; American Society of Training and Development. Community Activities: Alternative Schools, Inc., Lexington, Kentucky (chairman, board of directors, 1973-74); Leon County Schools, Tallahassee, Florida (technical assistance advisor, 1977-78); Waukesha Day Care Center, Waukesha, Wisconsin (management advisory board, 1980-81). Honors and Awards: National H.E.W. Recognition and Commendation for Authoring Florida State Plan, 1976-77; President, Florida State University Chapter, Phi Delta Kappa, 1976-77. Address: 2301 Bittersweet Drive, Columbus, Mississippi 39701.

Hemleben, Sylvester John

Retired. Personal: Born February 25, 1902; Son of Albert Lawrence and Jeanette Elligen Hemleben (both deceased); Father of Sylvester John Jr., Scott Parker. Education: B.A. 1927, M.A. 1928, University of Iowa; Ph.D., Fordham University, 1931; LL.B. with distinction 1963, J.D. 1968, University of Mississippi; Post-Doctoral Studies at Columbia University, Harvard University, Cambridge University (England), Munich University (Germany). Career: Head, Department of Social Studies, School of Education, Fordham University, New York, 1931-45; Historical Branch, Chemical Corps, War Department, 1945-47; Professor of History, University of Southwestern Louisiana, Lafayette, 1947-61; Associate Professor of Law, University of Mississippi, 1963-65; Practice of Law, 1965-66; Professor of Political Science 1966-72, Professor Emeritus 1972 to present, Brevard Community College, Cocoa, Florida. Organizational Memberships: Mississippi State Bar; Phi Delta Phi; Pi Gamma Mu; Phi Alpha Theta; Phi Delta Kappa. Published Works: Author, *Plans for World Peace through Six Centuries; Mississippi Workmen's Compensation; The Voice of the People; Grass Roots Government*; Three Volume *History of the Hemleben Family;* Numerous Research Articles and Reviews in Learned Journals; Works of Poetry, Reflecting His Philosophy of Life. Honors and Awards: Dean Robert J. Tarley Award for Highest Scholastic Record in Law School Graduating Class; Articles Editor, *Mississippi Law Journal;* Award for Best Comment Published in the Year 1913, *Mississippi Law Journal;* Fellow, Royal Historical Society. Address: 201 St. Lucie Lane, Apt. 105, Cocoa Beach, Florida 32931.

Henderson, Douglas James

Theoretical Physicist. Personal: Born July 28, 1934, Calgary, Alberta, Canada; Son of Evelyn L. Henderson; Married Rose-Marie Steen-Nielssen; Father of Barbara, Dianne, Sharon. Education: B.A., 1st Class Honors, University of British Columbia, 1956; Ph.D., University of Utah, 1961. Career: Teaching Assistant, Department of Physics, University of Utah, 1956-57; Instructor, Department of Mathematics, University of Utah, 1960-61; Assistant Professor of Physics, University of Idaho, 1961-62; Assistant Professor of Physics, Arizona State University, 1962-64; Associate Professor of Physics, University of Waterloo, Canada, 1964-67; Professor of Applied Mathematics and Physics, University of Waterloo, 1967-69; Research Scientist, I.B.M. Research Laboratory, San Jose, California, 1969 to present. Organizational Memberships: American Chemical Society; American Institute of Chemists (fellow); American Physical Society (fellow); Institute of Physics (fellow); Canadian Association of Physicists; New York Academy of Science; Mathematical Association of America; Sigma Xi; Phi Kappa Phi; Sigma Pi Sigma. Religion: Missionary to South Africa, Church of Jesus Christ of Latter Day Saints, 1957-59. Published Works: Author of More Than 150 Research Papers in Physics, Chemistry and Mathematics; Co-Author, *Statistical Mechanics and Dynamics*; Co-Editor of 15 Volume *Advanced Treatise on Physical Chemistry* and *Theoretical Chemistry: Advances and Perspectives*; Board of Editors, *Utilitas Mathematica*; Reviewer, *Mathematical Reviews*; Associate Editor, *Journal of Chemical Physics*. Honors and Awards: University Great War Scholarship, 1953; Johnathan Rodgers Award, 1954; Province of British Columbia Bursary, 1954; Daniel Buchanan Scholarship for Highest Standing in Mathematics, 1955; Burbridge Scholarship for Highest Standing in Physics, 1955; National Research Council of Canada Bursary, 1956; Corning Glass Foundation Fellowship, 1959; Arizona State University Faculty Award, 1963; Alfred P. Sloan Foundation Fellowship, 1964, 1966; Ian Potter Foundation Fellowship, 1966; C.S.I.R.O. Research Fellowship, 1966; Visiting Scientist, C.S.I.R.O. Chemical Research Laboratories, Melbourne, Australia, 1966-67; Visiting Professor of Physics, National University of La Plata, Argentina, 1973; I.B.M. Outstanding Research Contribution Award, 1973; Visiting Scientist, Institute of Physical Chemistry, Polish Academy of Sciences, 1973; Sabbatical Visitor, I.B.M. Thomas J. Watson Research Center, Yorktown Heights, New York, 1973-74; Visiting Scientist, Korea Advanced Institute of Science, Seoul, Korea, 1974. Address: 23454 Skyview Terrace, Los Gatos, California 95030.

Hendricks, Robert Michael

Executive. Personal: Born August 23, 1943; Son of Chester Eugene and Reba Eileen Leake Hendricks; Married Yvonne Sharon McAnally; Father of Robert Christian. Education: B.A., University of California-Berkeley. Career: President, Chief Executive Officer, ADCO Re Life Assurance Company; Board of Directors, Assurance Distributors Company, Inc.; Former Director of Agencies, Bankers United Life Assurance Company, Los Angeles. Organizational Memberships: Chartered Life Underwriters; National Association of Life Underwriters; Orange County Association of Life Underwriters; Life Underwriters Training Council. Community Activities: Rotary Club International; 32° Mason; Scottish Rite, Al Malaikah Shrine; Chamber of Commerce; California Young Republicans; Orange County Council, Boy Scouts of America; United States Senatorial Business Advisory Board. Honors and Awards: Recipient of Numerous Company and Civic Awards, including Company Leader/Man of the Year; Speaking Engagements Nation-wide, Certified Life Underwriters, Life Underwriters Training Council I & II; Distinguished Service Award, Republican Party; Presidents Club; Century Club, Boy Scouts of America. Address: 1611 LaLoma Drive, Santa Ana, California 92705.

Hendrickson, Benjamin S

Marriage, Family and Child Therapist. Personal: Born January 23, 1931; Father of Steven D., Sharon J. Welch, Wendy C. Curtier. Education: A.A., Antelope Valley College, 1963; S.T.D. 1969, Th.B. 1970, Life Bible College; B.A. 1971, M.A. 1972, Azusa Pacific College; Th.D., Florida State Theological Seminary, 1972; Ph.D., American International University, 1979. Military: Served in the New Jersey National Guard, 1947-50, attaining the rank of Sergeant; in the United States Air Force, 1951-68, attaining the rank of Lieutenant Colonel; and in the United States Air Force Civil Air Patrol, 1971 to present. Career: Marriage, Family and Child Therapist; Staff Member, Antelope Valley Hospital Medical Center, Palmdale General Hospital Mental Health Unit, 1973 to present; Teacher, All Local High Schools, Sex and Marriage Classes, 1973 to present; Former Director, Liquid Missile Propulsion Systems Inspection. Organizational Memberships: American Association of Psychotherapy (diplomate); American Board of Examiners in Pastoral Counseling (diplomate); American College of Clinic Administrators (fellow); American University (fellow) Sex Counseling and Therapy; American Association of Sex Educators and Therapists; California Association of Marriage Therapists; American Association of Marriage Therapists. Community Activities: Substance Abuse Coalition, North Los Angeles County, 1975-76; Teacher, Court Diversionary Program, Los Angeles County Substance Abuse, 1975; Hypnotist, Los Angeles County Sheriff, Suspect Identification, 1980 to present; President Reagan's Task Force; American Security Council; United States Congressional Advisory Board. Religion: Chaplain, United States Air Force Civil Air Patrol, 1971 to present. Honors and Awards: Th.D. magna cum laude, 1972; Alpha Psi Omega, 1972; Listed in *Who's Who in California, International Directory of Distinguished Psychotherapists, Community Leaders and Noteworthy Americans, Outstanding Community Leaders*. Address: 45800 N. 10th Street East #158, Lancaster, California 93535.

Hendrix, Ruth Ellen

Retired. Personal: Born December 21, 1894; Daughter of William and Mary Ellen Oelke (both deceased); Widow. Education: B.S., Home Economics, North Central College, Naperville, Illinois, 1919; Studies at Columbia University, New York City, Summer 1927; M.S., Home Economics Education, Iowa State University, 1933. Career: Teacher of Home Economics, Iowa 1919-24, Minnesota 1924-28; Teacher, Summer Session, Arizona University, Flagstaff, 1936; State Supervisor, Home Economics, Arizona, 1934-40; Teacher of Home Economics, Mesa High School, Mesa, Arizona, 1929-31. Community Activities: Soroptimist Club of Mesa (charter member; past president); American Business Women's Association (charter member, Mesa charter chapter; president, 1962); Donated Proceeds of Country Home to Sunshine Acres Children's Home, 1958; Donations Annually, Arizona Boys Ranch, Salvation Army. Religion: Presbyterian; President, United Presbyterian Church Women, 2 years; State President, Church Women United, 1957. Honors and Awards: Woman of the Year, American Business Women's Association, 1962; Honorary Woman, 1 year, First Presbyterian Church, Mesa; Delegate to A.B.W.A., Texas, 1962. Address: Mesa Christian Home, 255 West Brown Road, Mesa, Arizona 85201.

Henley, Melvin Brent

Mayor. Personal: Born August 25, 1935; Son of Jesse and Effie Henley (both deceased); Father of Sonny, Stanley, Stuart, Steven, Shane. Education: Attended the University of Nevada, 1955-56, and Valley College, 1957-58; B.S., Murray State University, 1961; Ph.D., University of Mississippi, 1964. Military: Served with the United States Air Force, achieving the rank of Sergeant, 1954-58. Career: Associate Professor, Murray State University; Mayor, City of Murray. Organizational Memberships: Kentucky Lake

Section, American Chemical Society (past chairman); Murray Civitan Club (past president); Purchase Area Development District (board of directors); Murray Airport (board of directors); Murray-Calloway County Hospital (board of directors); Kentucky Municipal League; Murray Headstart; Murray State University (faculty senate); Murray Headstart (board member). Community Activities: Kentucky Local Government Statutes Revision Commission (member by appointment of governor); National League of Cities (economic issues committee, human development committee, municipal development committee); Kentucky Historical Society. Address: Fox Meadows, Murray, Kentucky 42071.

Henn, Shirley Emily

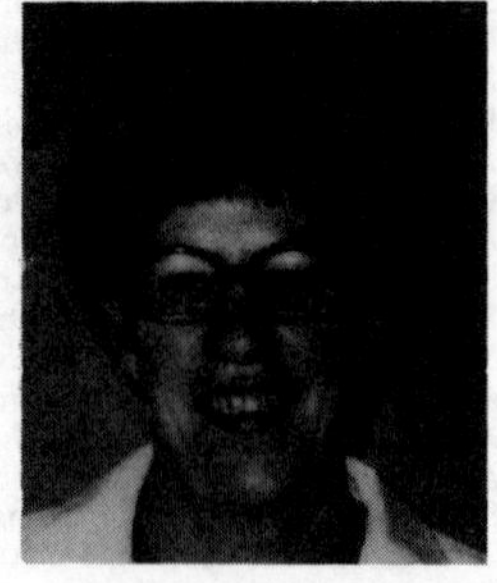

Shirley E Henn

Reference Librarian. Personal: Born May 26, 1919; Daughter of Albert R. and Florence M. Henn (deceased); Mother of Peter Albert (deceased). Education: A.B., Hollins College, 1941; M.S., Library Science, University of North Carolina, 1966. Career: Reference and Government Documents Librarian, Fishburn Library, Hollins College, 1965 to present; Library Assistant, Hollins College 1961-1964, 1943-44; Library Assistant, Collinwood High School, Cleveland, Ohio, 1941-43; Advertising Manager, R. M. Kellogg Company, Three Rivers, Michigan, 1946-47; Executive Secretary, Hollins College Alumnae Association, 1947-55; Real Estate Salesman, Roanoke, Virginia, 1955-61. Organizational Memberships: American Alumni Council (board of directors, 1952-54); American Library Association, 1965-78; Virginia Library Association, 1961 to present; Public Documents Forum, Virginia, 1977 to present; Roanoke Valley Library Association, 1970 to present; Alumnae Association, Hollins College, 1941 to present; Alumni Association, Library School, University of North Carolina, 1966 to present. Community Activities: Roanoke Valley Society for the Prevention of Cruelty to Animals (president, 1959-61, 1969-72; board of directors, 1972-81); National Daughters of the American Revolution, 1977 to present; Nancy Christian Fleming Chapter, Daughters of the American Revolution, Roanoke, Virginia, 1977 to present; Collie Club of America; Roanoke Valley Bird Club; Roanoke Kennel Club; Quota Club (chapter president, 1958-60); Early American Society; Association for the Preservation of Virginia Antiquities; Roanoke Valley Historical Society; National Wildlife Federation; Science Museum Association of Roanoke Valley; National Trust for Historic Preservation; Donor, Mary Williamson Award in the Humanities, Hollins College, 1947 to present. Published Works: Author and Illustrator, *Adventures of Hooty Owl and His Friends*, 1953. Honors and Awards: Editor, Hollins Alumnae Bulletin, 1947-56; Winner, 2 National Awards for Editorial Achievement, 1948; Citation from Library of Human Resources of American Bicentennial Research Institute as an "Important and Valuable Human Resource", 1974; Listed in *Who's Who of American Women, Who's Who in the South and Southwest, World Who's Who of Women*. Address: 6915 Tinkerdale Road, Hollins, Virginia 24019.

Herman, Charles Robert

Charles R Herman

Executive Director, General Manager. Personal: Born February 24, 1925; Son of Floyd Caves and Anna Merriken Herman. Education: A.B. summa cum laude, German, University of Southern California, 1949. Military: Served in the United States Army, 1944-46, attaining the rank of Lieutenant Colonel. Career: Executive Director, New World Festival, Inc.; General Manager, Greater Miami Opera Association; Assistant Manager, Artistic Administrator, Metropolitan Opera, New York City, 1953-72; Assistant to the Head of Opera Department, University of Southern California, 1949-53. Organizational Memberships: Dade County Cultural Executives Council (president, 1978-80; secretary, 1980); Opera America (treasurer, 1979 to present). Community Activities: National Endowment for the Arts (chairman, opera/musical theater policy and grants panels, 1981 to present); Florida Arts Council, 1977-81; Greater Miami Chamber of Commerce (chamber of the arts committee, 1978-80). Honors and Awards: Army Commendation Ribbon; Cavaliere, Order of Merit, Republic of Italy, 1969; Officers Cross, Order of Merit, Federal Republic of Germany, 1979; Austrian Honor Cross for Science and Art, First Class, 1981. Address: 3441 Poinciana Avenue, Coconut Grove, Florida 33133.

Herring, Michael Morris

Michael M Herring

Mineral Development. Personal: Born October 15, 1922; Son of Mike and Flossie Herring, (both deceased); Married Dorothy Eleene. Education: B.S., Oklahoma City University, 1948. Military: Served with the United States Air Force, World War II. Career: Lumberman; Property and Mining Development, Oklahoma City, Oklahoma; Originator and Designer of Businesses. Organizational Memberships: National Society of Literature and the Arts; Associate of MENSA; Smithsonian Associate. Community Activities: DeMolay (master councilor); Blue Lodge Mason 276; 32° Mason; Shriner; Beta Beta Beta; Kappa Alpha; Delta Psi Omega. Honors and Awards: U.S. Naval Award, Outstanding Businessman in 8th Naval District; North Atlantic Command Award; Cited by President and Congress; Citation from General Harmon; National Amateur and Professional Champion Athlete; Armed Forces Combat Commando Champion; National Write-Ups in Commerce and Industry; Safety Award in Manufacturing and Transportation; Honorary Admiral of the Fleet, State of Oklahoma; Honorary Commodore of the Navy, State of Oklahoma; Honorary Colonel of the Army, State of Oklahoma; Honorary Deputy Sheriff; Infantile Paralysis and Crippled Children Awards; Subject (with family) of: *Patriots of 1976, The Iron Men, Seven Volumes of Abraham Lincoln*; Listed in *Who's Who in the World, Who's Who in Finance, Who's Who in Commerce and Industry, Who's Who in Public Interest, Who's Who in the South and Southwest, Who's Who in Arkansas, Royal Blue Book, Two Thousand Men of Achievement, Men of Achievement, Dictionary of International Biography, National Social Directory, Community Leaders of America, Notable Americans of 1976-1977, Encyclopedia of Proud Bicentennial Americans, Personalities of America, Personalities of the South, International Who's Who of Intellectuals, International Who's Who in Community Service, International Register of Profiles, International Register of Business*. Address: 4309 N.W. 61st Terrace, Oklahoma City, Oklahoma 73112.

Hershey, Robert Lewis

Executive. Personal: Born December 18, 1941; Son of Maurice and Rose (deceased) Hershey. Education: B.S.M.E., Tufts University, 1963; M.S.M.E., Massachusetts Institute of Technology, 1964; Ph.D., Engineering, Catholic University of America, 1973. Career: Vice President, Science Management Corporation, Washington, D.C., 1979 to present; Manager of Acoustics Programs, Booz, Allen & Hamilton, Bethesda, Maryland, 1971-79; Senior Scientist, Bolt, Beranek & Newman, Arlington, Virginia, 1968-71; Manager of Acoustics, Weston Instruments, Poughkeepsie, New York, 1967-68; Member of the Technical Staff, Bell Telephone Laboratories, Whippany, New Jersey, 1963-67. Organizational Memberships: D.C. Council of Engineering and Architectural Societies (president, 1978-79); American Society of Mechanical Engineers (chairman, Washington section, 1978-79); D.C. Professional Council (secretary, 1975); D.C. Society of Professional Engineers (president, 1975-76; national director, 1980 to present); Acoustical Society of America (chairman, Washington chapter, 1982 to present); Professional Engineers in Industry Division, National Society of Professional Engineers (national secretary, 1972-74). Community Activities: Massachusetts Institute of Technology Club of Washington (president, 1979-80); Joint Board on Science and Engineering Education of Metropolitan Washington. Honors and Awards: National Capital Award for Professional Achievement in Engineering, 1974; Young Engineer of the Year Award, D.C. Society of Professional

Engineers, 1974; *Machinery Magazine's* Design Award, 1963; Tau Beta Pi, 1961; Sigma Xi, 1963. Address: 1255 New Hampshire Avenue, N.W., Apt. 433, Washington, D.C. 20036.

Herth, Kaye Ann

Assistant Professor of Nursing. Personal: Born September 9, 1945; Married Leonard Alvin Herth; Mother of Wendy Joye, Randy Scott. Education: Diploma, St. Luke's Hospital School of Nursing, 1966; B.S., Northern Illinois University, 1968; M.S., University of Minnesota, 1973. Career: Team Leader, Medical-Surgical, Trinity Memorial Hospital, Cudahy, Wisconsin, 1966-67; Staff Nurse, Pediatrics, Geneva Community Hospital, Geneva, Illinois, 1967-68; Fundamental's Instructor, Milwaukee County Hospital, Wisconsin, 1968-69; Nursing Coordinator Medical-Surgical, United Hospital-Miller Division, St. Paul, Minnesota, 1969-71; Medical-Surgical Instructor, Lutheran Deaconess Hospital School of Nursing, Minneapolis, Minnesota, 1971-73; Assistant Professor of Nursing, East Tennessee State University, 1973-77; Assistant Professor of Nursing, University of Tennessee, Memphis, 1977-78; Assistant Professor of Nursing, University of Texas-Houston, 1978 to present. Organizational Memberships: Texas Nurses Association; American Nurses Association; Tennessee Nurses Association (past member, executive board, district 5); American Association for the Advancement of Science (resource group); Nurses Christian Fellowship. Community Activities: Group Facilitator for Support Group of Cancer Patients and Their Families, American Cancer Society; Memphis Chapter, Make Today Count (advisor, member, 1977-78); Advisor to Senior Citizens Group Dealing with Problems Relating to Aging, Memphis, 1977-78; Counselor, Prospective Parents of Adopted Children, Memphis, 1978; Alexander Graham Bell Association (O.D.A.S. executive board); Red Cross (coordinator and teacher, "Preparation for Parenthood", 1974-76); Consultant to the Department of Special Education, East Tennessee State University, Working with Parents and Deaf Children, 1973-77; Women's Division of Johnson City Chamber of Commerce, 1974-77. Published Works: "Beyond the Curtain of Silence", "Please Reach Out to Me Your Elderly Patient", "Early Recovery", "The Therapeutic Use of Music"; Manuscript, "Dealing with Loneliness"; Chapter in Nursing Text *Introduction to Nursing Practice.* Honors and Awards: Sigma Theta Tau; Nominated for Tennessee Nurse in Action, 1975; Outstanding Graduate Nurse for the State of Wisconsin, 1969; Outstanding Graduating Senior, Northern Illinois University, 1968; Listed in *Distinguished Americans, Who's Who in the South and Southwest, International Who's Who in Education, World's Who's Who of Women in Education.* Address: 12806 Westmere, Houston, Texas 77077.

Hew, Ah Kewn

Anton Heyn

Consultant. Personal: Born November 5, 1912; Daughter of Sing Cha (deceased) and Ngun Moi Shinn Hew. Education: Graduate of Maui High School, Hawaii, 1930; B.A., University of Hawaii, 1934; Further Studies at the New York School of Social Work, Columbia University. Career: Consultant; Former Planner, Community Improvement and Development Director, Planning Coordinator, Coordinator for Manpower, Child Care, Home Management and Transportation Programs, Supervising Social Worker, Branch Administrator, Assistant Administrator, Child Welfare Worker, Caseworker, Housing Investigator, Stenographer, Medical Agent. Organizational Memberships: American Public Welfare Association. Community Activities: Alumni Association New York School of Social Work, Columbia University; Alumni Association New York International House; American Association of Retired Persons; Cameron Center Community Council; Friends of Maui County Library (president, 1964-65); Hawaii Chinese Historical Center; Hawaiian Government Employees Association (Retirees Chapter, secretary 1973-75, board of directors 1975-83); Lahaina Restoration Society; Maui Association, Girl Scouts of the Pacific (nominating committee); Maui Big Brothers/Big Sisters (secretary, 1973-74; chairman, service policy committee, 1972-75; evaluation committee); Maui Chinese Club (vice president, 1951; president, 1951-52; board of directors, 1952-54); Maui Community Human Services Coordinating Council (steering committee); Maui Community Mental Health Center (advisory board); Maui Historical Society; Maui Kokua Services Inc. (board of directors, vice president, 1981-82); Maui Mental Health Association (steering and planning committee); Maui Mental Health Coalition; Maui United Way (president, 1966; committee chairman, agency liaison, budget and allocation, long rang planning, agency admission committees; board of directors); Zonta Club of Maui (charter president, 1979-80; board of directors); Lioness Club of Kahului (president, 1981-82; 2nd vice president, 1980-81; 3rd vice president, 1979-80); Volunteer Leadership Development Project (statewide steering committee); State Health Planning and Development Agency, Tri-Isle Planning Council (review committee); American Cancer Committee (service committee). Honors and Awards: Outstanding Business Woman of the Year, National Business Women's Week, Board of Directors of Maui Business and Professional Women, 1956; 25 of Distinguished Service to State Department of Social Services and Housing, 1963; Participant by Invitation of the Secretary of State, United States State Regions Policy Conference, Los Angeles, California, 1963; Thanks Badge (highest award for adult volunteer for services above and beyond the call of duty), Girl Scout Council of the Pacific, 1966; One of Maui's Most Active Civic Workers, National Business Week, 1966; "Milady of the Week", *Maui News,* 1967; Certificate of Award in "Official Recognition and Appreciation for Exceptional Services to the Department of Social Services and Housing and to the Public of the State of Hawaii", D.S.S.H. and the State of Hawaii, 1970; Award for "Outstanding Service in the Fight Against TB, Asthma, Emphysema", American Lung Association, 1974; Special Commendation in "Recognition of Unselfish and Dedicated Services Rendered...for Meritorious Services and Valuable Contributions Made Toward the Betterment of Our Community", County of Maui, 1974; Nominated First Lady's Volunteer Award, 1980; I.B.A. Life Fellow, 1977; Listed in *Men and Women of Hawaii, Dictionary of International Biography, World Who's Who of Women, International Who's Who in Community Service, Notable Americans, Community Leaders and Notable Americans, Notable Americans of the Bicentennial Era, International Register of Profiles, Book of Honor.* Address: P.O. Box 895, Wailuku, Hawaii 96793.

Hewitt, Marvin Harold

Consultant. Personal: Born March 24, 1922; Son of Samuel Harrison and Anna Hewitt (both deceased); Father of Daniel, David, Richard Barry, Deborah Lynn, Kenneth. Education: Special Student, University of Pennsylvania, Temple University, during World War II; Graduate School, University of Colorado, 1958, 1959. Career: Consultant, 1968 to present; Technical Consultant, Radiation Systems Inc., 1966-68; Technical Staff, Mitre, 1963-66; Principal Engineer, Raytheon Company, 1961-63; Design Engineer, Martin Marietta Company, 1954-61. Organizational Memberships: British Interplanetary Society (fellow); American Astronautical Society (chairman, 1961); American Rocket Society (technical referee, 1961-62). Community Activities: American Security Council (national advisory board, 1978 to present). Honors and Awards: Special Recognition Award, American Security Council, 1972; Certificate of Merit, *Dictionary of International Biography,* 1975; Listed in *Men of Achievement, Who's Who in Technology Today.* Address: 5449 North Marvine, Philadelphia, Pennsylvania 19141.

Heyn, Anton Nicolaas Johannes

Professor Emeritus, Research Scientist. Personal: Born January 25, 1906; Son of A. Ch. Heyn (deceased); Married Frances Forbes. Education: B.Sc. 1927, M.Sc. 1929, Ph.D. 1931, (all degrees cum laude), University of Utrecht, Netherlands; Post-Doctoral Studies,

University of Paris 1931-32, University of Leeds 1932-33, NATO Advanced Studies Institute. Career: Professor Emeritus, Louisiana State University; Research Scientist, Touro Research Institute, New Orleans, Louisiana; Professor of Biology, Louisiana State University, New Orleans, 1963-76; Professor, Physics, Auburn University, Alabama, 1959-63; Professor, Clemson University, South Carolina, 1948-58; Scientific Advisor, Netherlands Governmnet, Netherlands East Indies, 1933. Organizational Memberships: American Chemical Society; Biophysics Society of America; American Physics Society; American Institute of Biological Science; American Crystllgr. Association; American Society of Cellular Biology; Electron Microscopy Society; American Society of Plant Physics; New York Academy of Sciences; Sigma Chi; American Institute of Chemists (fellow); American Association for the Advancement of Science (fellow); Royal Microscopy Society (fellow). Community Activities: United States Congressional Advisory Board. Honors and Awards: Rockefeller Fellowship, 1932-33; Teub Fellowship, Netherlands Indies, Netherlands Ministry Education, 1937; Several Research Grants, National Science Foundation, United States, 1963-76. Address: 2363 Killdeer Street, New Orleans, Louisiana 70122.

Heyward, Joseph Edward

Assistant Superintendent for Instruction. Personal: Born November 17, 1941; Married Evelyn Sargent; Father of Joseph E. II, Ryan C. Education: B.A., Hampton Institute; M.A., Morgan State University; Further Studies at Wake Forest University, South Carolina State University; Ed.D. Candidate, University of South Carolina. Military: Served in the United States Army as Tactical Control Director, 1964-66, attaining the rank of Lieutenant. Career: Assistant Superintendent for Instruction; Teacher, Assistant Principal and Principal, Florence School District One; Director of Smith College Center, Assistant Dean of Students and Professor of Mathematics, Francis Marion College; Area Representative for United States Senator Ernest Hollings, 1979-80. Organizational Memberships: Association of Supervision and Curriculum Development; Florence County Education Association; National Education Association; South Carolina Association of School Administration; American Association of School Administration; South Carolina College Personnel Association. Community Activities: South Carolina Board of Accountancy, 1981; Florence Boys Clubs of America (board of directors, 1972-79); "Fun for Funds, Fun with a Purpose" (chairman, annual meeting committee; chairman, basketball committee; stage director); Pee Dee Big Brother Association (board of directors, 1974); Pee Dee Area Council, Boy Scouts of America (vice president for relationships, 1977-80; vice chairman, Atakwa District, 1974-77; treasurer, 1980-81); Executive Committeeman, Florence Precinct #3, 1971-80. Religion: Cumberland United Methodist Church, Organist for Choir; Vice Chairman, Work Area on Worship, South Carolina Conference of United Methodist Churches, 1977. Honors and Awards: South Carolina Alpha Man of the Year, 1975; United Methodist Men Dedicated Service Award, 1978; President's Award, Southern Region of Alpha Phi Alpha, 1980; Listed in *Outstanding Young Men of America, Personalities of the South, Personalities of America, Dictionary of International Biography*. Address: P.O. Box 384, Florence, South Carolina 29503.

Hickrod, George Alan

Professor, Administrator. Personal: Born May 16, 1930; Son of Hershell Roy and Bernice Karnes Hickrod (both deceased); Married Lucy Jen Huang. Education: A.B., Wabash College, 1954; M.A.T. 1955, Ed.D. 1966, Harvard University. Military: Served in the United States Marine Corps during the Korean War. Career: Professor, Director of Center for Study of Education Finance, Illinois State University; Assistant Professor, Lake Erie College; Instructor, Muskingum College, Boston University. Career: American Education Finance Association; Phi Beta Kappa; American Education Research Association; American Economic Association. Community Activities: Member of Two Advisory Councils to the Governor of Illinois; Member, Two Advisory Councils to State Superintendent of Education of Illinois (on public education finance); Illinois School Problems Commission on School Finance (consultant); United States Office of Education on School Finance (consultant); Expert Witness on Constitutional Cases Regarding School Finance. Religion: Unitarian. Honors and Awards: Phi Beta Kappa; National Award for School Finance Research; Listed in *Outstanding Educators of America, International Who's Who of Intellectuals.* Address: #2 Turner Rod, Normal, Illinois 61761.

Hicks, Darrell Lee

Professor of Mathematics. Personal: Born July 3, 1937; Son of Jason and Winona Hicks; Married Kathryn Jean Chaney; Father of April Lee, Rachel Elizabeth, Jason Chaney. Education: B.S. 1961, Ph.D. 1969, University of New Mexico. Career: Professor of Mathematics, University of Colorado; Technical Staff, Sandia National Labs, 1969-81; Research Mathematician, Air Force Weapons Labs, 1963-69; Graduate Assistant, Mathematics Department, University of New Mexico, 1961-63. Organizational Memberships: American Mathematical Society; Mathematical Society of America; Society of Industrial and Applied Mathematics; Association of Computing Machinery; A.C.M./S.I.G.N.U.M.; American Physical Society; American Academy of Mechanics; Others. Community Activities: New Mexico Science Fair (judge in mathematics and computing, 1974-81). Honors and Awards: Certificate of Proficiency in Mathematics, National Council of Teachers of Mathematics, 1954; New Mexico Legislative Scholarship, 1955-56; Outstanding Performance Award, Air Force Weapons Laboratories, Albuquerque, New Mexico, 1967. Address 33190 Janelle Circle, Golden, Colorado 80403.

Hicks, Maryellen Whitlock

Chief Municipal Judge. Personal: Born March 10, 1949; Daughter of Mrs. Kathleen Butler; Married Arvid Hicks (deceased); Mother of Kathleen. Education: B.A., Texas Women's University, 1970; Law Degree, Texas Tech University, 1974. Career: Chief Municipal Judge; Attorney-at-Law. Organizational Memberships: State Bar of Texas; National Bar Association; Judicial Council; Tarrant County Young Lawyers; Tarrant County Women Lawyers; Tarrant County Black Lawyers. Community Activities: Delta Sigma Theta; U.N.C.F. (co-chairperson, 1981); Task Force 100 (co-chairperson, 1980); National Council of Negro Women (vice president, 1979); Forum Fort Worth. Religion: Board of Directors, Our Mother of Mercy, School Board 1981. Honors and Awards: Quad V Award, 1979; Human Relations Commission Award, 1979; Chairman's Award, Judicial Council, 1980. Address: 2318 5th Avenue, Fort Worth, Texas 76110.

Hill, George Blood

Consulting Professional Mechanical Engineer. Personal: Born February 1, 1914, in Riverdale, Idaho; Son of John E. (deceased) and Ivy Blood Hill; Married Thelma Orman, September 28, 1935; Father of Ruth Jane Hill Soper, Charles Philip. Education: B.S.M.E., Montana State University, Bozeman, 1935. Career: Registered Professional Engineer, Pennsylvania, Ohio, Utah; John Deere Works, Ottumwa, Iowa, Draftsman 1935-37, Junior Engineer in Design 1937-39, Senior Engineer in Design 1939-42, In Charge of Aircraft Production 1942-44, Design Engineer in Charge of New Design 1944-47, Chief Engineer in Charge of All Design and Experimental

Work 1947-48; Chief Engineer, Member Management Committee, New Holland Machine Division, Sperry, Pennsylvania, 1948-51; Director of Engineering, Chairman of New Products Committee, New Idea Division, Avco Corporation, Coldwater, Ohio, 1951-54; President, Owner, Hills Engineering Company, Celina (Ohio) 1954-56, Mansfield (Ohio) 1951-54, Salt Lake City (Utah) 1963 to present; President, Ute Manufacturing Company, Salt Lake City, 1966; President, General Manager, Brimco Manufacturing Company 1966-68, Western Research and Manufacturing Company 1968-70; Consultant, Perfection Steel Bocy Company, Galion, Ohio, 1955-60; Teacher, Management Classes, Utah Technical College, 1963-66; Coordinator of Engineering, in Charge of Manufacturing, Engineer, Eimco Corporation, Salt Lake City, 1964-65; General Manager, Eaton Metal Products Company, Salt Lake City, 1969-70; President, General Manager, McGee & Hogan Machine Works, Salt Lake City, 1970-72; Newspaper Equipment Company, Inc., Salt Lake City, Vice President 1973-74, President 1974 to present; Director, Numerous Companies. Organizational Memberships: American Society of Automotive Engineers; American Society of Mechanical Engineers; American Society of Agricultural Engineers (past chairman, power machinery division); Tau Beta Pi; Lambda Chi Alpha. Community Activities: Lions Club (president, Celina Club, 1955-56); Boy Scouts of America, 1935-48. Religion: Church of Jesus Christ of Latter-Day Saints; Ordinance Worker, Salt Lake Temple, 1976 to present; Guide on Temple Square, Salt Lake City, 1976-80; President, Eastern Atlantic States Mission, 1960-63; First Counselor, Great Lakes Mission Presidency, 1951-60; First Counselor, Mission Presidency, Eastern States Mission, 1948-51. Honors and Awards: 62 Issued American Patents and Several Canadian Patents, Developed First Automatic Wire Tie and Twine Field Operated Pickup Hay Baler that Operated without Stopping the Feeding Mech, Developed the Field Forage Harvester that would Harvest Both Hay and Corn by simply Changing the Gathering Attachment; Listed in *Who's Who in America, Leaders in American Science, Who's Who in Engineering*. Address: 4610 Locust Lane, Salt Lake City, Utah 84117.

Hill, Mary Alice

Associate Athletic Director. Personal: Born May 6, 1940; Daughter of Mrs. Laurina Hill. Education: Graduate of Missouri State Teachers College, 1967; M.A., Texas Women's University, 1972; 42 Hours toward a Ph.D. Career: Associate Athletic Director, San Diego State University, 1979 to present; Associate Director of Women's Athletics, San Diego State University, 1976-79; Director of Women's Athletics, Colorado State University, 1972-75; Assistant Professor, Colorado State University, 1972-75; Graduate Teaching Assistant, Texas Women's University, 1969-72; Instructor, Fort Zumwalt High School, O'Fallon, Missouri, 1967-69. Organizational Memberships: Western Collegiate Athletic Association (vice president; chairperson); Western Association for Intercollegiate Athletics for Women (chairperson, television committee); N.C.A.A. (subcommittee on eligibility appeals; Division I steering committee; chairman, cross country/track & field committee for women's championships). Religion: Catholic. Honors and Awards: Outstanding Professor, Colorado State University, 1974; Top Fund-Raiser Award, San Diego State University Aztec Athletic Foundation, 1979, 1980; Listed in *Who's Who in the West, Personalities of the West and Midwest, World Who's Who of Women, International Who's Who of Intellectuals, Directory of Distinguished Americans, Personalities of America, Who's Who in California, Dictionary of International Biography*. Address: 10150 Campo Road, Spring Valley, California 92177.

Hill, Ruth Beebe

Ruth B Hill

Writer, Lecturer. Personal: Born April 26, 1913; Daughter of Hermann and Flora Beebe (both deceased); Married; Mother of Reid. Education: Attended Oberlin College, 1931-32; B.S., Western Reserve University, 1935; Further Study at the University of Colorado, 1939-40. Career: Bridal Consultant, Denver, Colorado, and Boston, Massachusetts, 1941-43; Assistant, Department of Geology, Western Reserve University, 1935-37; Book Dramatist, 1947-52; Founder, Gull Hill (Private) Children's School, New Orleans, 1947; Assistant, Books and Authors, Los Angeles, 1950-54; Writer, Lecturer. Organizational Memberships: National League of American Pen Women, 1979 to present; National Writers, 1979 to present; American Academy Achievement Council, 1980 to present; Ohioana Library Association, 1980 to present. Community Service: California Institute of Cancer Research, Los Angeles (ways and means chairman, 1951-55); American Association of University Women, 1945-49; San Juan Island Historical Society, Friday Harbor, Washington, 1970 to present; Daughters of the American Revolution, San Juan Island Chapter (member, 1979 to present; American Indians chairman, 1979 to present). Published Works: Author *Hanta Yo*, Documentary Novel, 1979. Honors and Awards: Pulitzer Nomination, Books Across the Sea Award 1979, Cowboy Hall of Fame and Western Heritage Award 1980, American Academy of Achievement Honoree 1979, Northwest Booksellers Association Excellence in Writing Award 1980, Ohioana Book Award 1980, all for *Hanta Yo*. Address: Watershed Acres, Friday Harbor, Washington 98250.

Hilton, Bonnie A

Regional Marketing Director. Personal: Born December 18, 1945; Daughter of Mr. and Mrs. Allen Auerr. Education: B.A. magna cum laude, History, State College, Framingham, Massachusetts, 1967; M.S. (Home Economics) 1976, Ph.D. (Family Management) 1977, Ohio State University. Career: Social Science Teacher, Fremont, California, 1967-70; Ohio State University, Graduate Research Associate 1972-74, Graduate Teaching Associate 1974-75, Graduate Research 1975-76; United Van Lines, Manager of Consumer Services 1977-80, Director of Consumer Affairs 1980-81, Regional Marketing Director 1982 to present. Organizational Memberships: Society of Consumer Affairs Professionals (national board of directors, 1982 to present); Central Midwest Chapter, Society of Consumer Affairs Professionals (vice president, 1981; president, 1982); Home Economists in Business (St. Louis executive board, 1978-79, 1980-81); American Council on Consumer Interests (career competencies committee, 1981 to present); American Society for Training and Development; American Home Economics Association; American Women in Radio and TV; Phi Kappa Phi; Kappa Delta Pi; Omicron Nu; Phi Upsilon Omicron; National Association for Female Executives; Society of Consumer Affairs Professionals (president, Central Midwest chapter, 1982, 1983). Community Activities: National Council on Family Relations; Missouri Coalition for the Equal Rights Amendment (past project and district coordinator). Religion: Ministry to the Sick; Liturgical Council (coordinator); Eucharistic Minister; Lector; Liturgical Dancer. Honors and Awards: Young Professional Award, Ohio State University, 1980; Listed in *Who's Who in American Women*. Address: 418 E. Madison Avenue, Kirkwood, Missouri 63122.

Himelick, Eugene Bryson

Plant Pathologist, Professor. Personal: Born February 11, 1926; Son of Virgil B. Himelick; Married; Father of David E., Kirk J., Douglas N. Education: B.S., Ball State University, 1949; M.S., Purdue University, 1952; Ph.D., University of Illinois, 1959. Military: Served in the United States Navy as an Electronics Technician, 1945-50. Career: Plant Pathologist, Professor of Plant Pathology, Illinois National History Survey and University of Illinois. Organizational Memberships: International Society of Arboriculture (executive director, 1969-79); Midwestern Chapter, International Society of Arboriculture (president, 1969). Community Activities: Scoutmaster, Troop 10, 1961-75; Urbana Tree Commission (chairman, 1976 to present); Champaign County Development Council, 1973-77. Religion: First United Methodist Church, Urbana, Illinois; Board of Trustees, 1976; Administrative Board, 1980 to present; Chairman, Parsonage Committee, 1980 to present. Honors and Awards: Scouters Key, Ken Fredricks Award, Vigil Honor, Silver

Beaver, Boy Scouts of America; Authors Citation, Honorary Life Award, Past Presidents Award, International Society of Arboriculture. Address: 601 Burkwood Court East, Urbana, Illinois 61801.

Hipscher, Jerome Jay

Political Scientist. Personal: Born May 9, 1932; Son of Charles and Helen Hipscher; Married Joan Miller; Father of Phillip, Hara, Marla and Joseph Wolfe. Education: Business School Degree, 1956; A.A., Queensborough Community College, 1976; B.A., Political Science, Florida International University, 1981. Military: Served in the United States Army, 1950-52, attaining the rank of Private First Class. Career: Political Scientist, Florida International University; Former Community Leader/Government Clerk; Executive Director, Jamaica Bay Council; Senate Legislative Assistant to John Santucci; Administrative Officer, A.P.W.U. Organizational Memberships: Advisor to N.Y.S. D.E.C., 1974-76; Community Planning Board Member, Queens, New York City, 1974-76; Intern for Dade County Court, 1981; Intern, United States Senator Richard Stone; Intern, Dade County Commission, 1981. Community Activities: New York City Mayor's Subway Watchdog Commission, 1970; Rockaway Health Council (transportation chairman, 1971-73); Muscular Dystrophy (Rockaway district chairman, 1972); American Cancer Society (vice president, Rockaway chapter, 1972); Rockaway Mental Health Association (advisor, 1972-73); District I Health Council; New York City 208 Environmental Council (advisor); Rockaway Arts Council (president); Queens Council on the Arts (board member); Rockaway Music and Arts Council (board member); Other Community and Civic Memberships. Religion: Board Member, Arverne-Edgemere Jewish Center; President, D.O.A.R. A.V.I.R., 1970-72; Vice President, D.O.A.R. A.V.I.R., 1973-75. Honors and Awards: Presidents Youth Award, 1978; United States Environmental Commendation Award, 1975; United States Post Office Bicentennial Award, 1976; Mayors Citation, 1970; Borough President of Queens Citation Awards, 1972, 1978; Jamaica Bay Council Certificate, 1976; Florida International University Plaque for Outstanding Student Service, 1981; Florida International University Certificates for Political Science, Budget Committee, Senate, Social and Cultural, 1981. Address: 1990 N.E. 181 Street, North Miami Beach, Florida 33162.

Hirsch, Maurice

Lawyer. Personal: Born January 13, 1890, in Houston, Texas; Son of Jules and Theresa Meyer Hirsch; Married Winifred Busby, January 25, 1947. Education: B.A., M.A., University of Virginia, 1910; J.D., Harvard University, 1913; LL.M., University of Texas, 1914; LL.D. (honorary), Northwood Institute, 1971. Military: Served in the United States Army, 1944-47, rising through the ranks to Brigadier General. Career: Practiced Law in Houston, Texas, 1914-17, 1918-42, 1947 to present, Counsel Firm of Hirsch and Westheimer; Chairman of the Board, Wald Transfer and Storage Company; Chairman Emeritus, Republic Bank, Houston; Chairman, City of Houston Civil Service Commission, 1915-17; Secretary, Priorities Committee, War Industries Board, 1917-18; Expert Consultant, War Department Price Adjustment Board, 1942; Chief of Settlements Division, War Department Price Adjustment Board, 1942; Vice Chairman, Price Adjustment Board, Deputy Director of Renegotiation Division, Headquarters A.S.F., 1943; Director, Renegotiation Division, and Chairman, War Department Price Adjustment Board, 1944-47; Chairman, Joint Price Adjustment Board (War, Navy, Treasury Departments, R.F.C., Maritime Commission and War Shipping Administration), 1944-47; War Contracts Price Adjustment Board, 1945-47. Organizational Memberships: American Bar Association; Texas Bar Association; Harris County Bar Association. Community Activities: Sam Houston Area Council, Boy Scouts of America (honorary life member, executive board; honorary Eagle Scout); Salesmanship Club Camp for Children (life trustee); International Council Museum of Modern Art, New York City; U.S.O. Council of Houston and Harris County (past chairman; honorary life member); Shrine Hospitals for Crippled Children (member emeritus, board of governors); Metropolitan Opera National Council; Museum of Fine Arts, Houston (honorary life trustee); Houston Society for the Performing Arts (board of directors); Shepherd School of Music (governing council); Houston Grand Opera (governing board; vice chairman); Orpheus Society, University of Houston School of Music (honorary member, directors committee); Junior Chamber of Commerce (honorary life member); Houston Symphony Society (president, 1956-70; president emeritus, 1971 to present); Confrerie des Chevaliers du Tastevin; Committee on Foreign Relations; Confrerie de la Chaine des Rotisseurs; Rice University Associates (life member); Japan-American Society of Houston (past president; president emeritus); American Legion; Houston Chamber of Commerce (military affairs committee; cultural commttee); Retired Officers Association; Raven Society, University of Virginia; Phi Beta Kappa; Delta Sigma Rho; Mason (32°, Shriner); Kiwanis (life member); Rotarian (honorary member; distinguished citizen award, 1978); Elk (honorary life member); B'nai B'rith (past district president); Houston Press Club (honorary life member); Petroleum Club; Coronado Club; Allegro Club; Army and Navy Club, Washington, D.C.; National Aviation Club, Washington, D.C. Honors and Awards: Silver Beaver, Boy Scouts of America; Decorated Distinguished Service Medal, United States; Stella Della Solidariata Italiana; Distinguished Service Medal, Texas Heritage Foundation; Brotherhood Award, N.C.C.J.; Distinguished Citizen Award, Goodwill Industries; Cultural Leader Award, Houston Youth Symphony and Ballet; Medal of Grand Order, Dr. Mazzei of Unico National Honor Society. Address: Suite 2020, Niels Esperson Building, Houston, Texas 77002.

Hislop, Anne H

Counselor and Administrator. Personal: Born November 13, 1918; Married Gordon D. Hislop; Mother of Anne H. Gove, Allan D., Sally H. Comegys, Albert S., Gordon D. Jr. Education: A.B., Sociology, Radcliffe College, 1939; M.Ed., Education Psychology, University of New Hampshire, 1961; N.D.E.A., Advanced Counseling, University of Maine, 1967; C.A.G.S., Advanced Counseling, University of New Hampshire, 1968. Career: Director of Counseling Center, University of Bridgeport, Connecticut, 1971 to present; Dean of Women and Director of Women's Housing, Mauno Olu College, 1970-71; Director of Guidance and Counseling, Exeter School District, Exeter, New Hampshire, 1961-70; Guidance Counselor, Portsmouth Junior & Senior High School, Portsmouth, New Hampshire, 1958-61; Instructor, University of New Hampshire Graduate College of Education, 1964-66. Organizational Memberships: American Personnel and Guidance Association (panelist and recorder); Connecticut Personnel and Guidance Association (governing board); N.A.C.A.C. (national committee on research, 1969-70); N.E.P.G.C. (co-chairman, annual conference; executive council; panel chairman); New Hampshire Guidance Council (president, 1957-62); New Hampshire Personnel and Guidance Association (executive committee; chairman, school and college relations). Community Activities: Exeter Area Youth Resource Council (co-chairman, 1968-70); Maui Mayor's Youth Council, 1970-71; New Hampshire State Department of Education (chairman, committee to establish guidelines for elementary education); University of New Hampshire Department of Education (steering committee to plan graduate programs in counselor education); New Hamphire Education Association (division chairman, T.E.P.S. commission representative for N.H.P.G.A.); Women and the World of Work (charter board member, seminar leader, annual conference). Published Works: Assistant Editor, *The School Counselor*, The A.S.C.A. Journal, 1973-77. Honors and Awards: Outstanding Educator of America, 1972; New Hampshire Personnel and Guidance Award, Outstanding Woman Counselor in New Hampshire, 1967; Listed in Who's Who of American Women, 5000 Women of the World, Dictionary of International Biography. Address: 595 Atlantic Street, Bridgeport, Connecticut 06604.

Hoffberg, Alan Marshall

Executive. Personal: Born April 15, 1940; Son of Nathan Hoffberg (deceased), Gerald and Evelyn Hoffberg Gottlieb; Married Janet Glunts; Father of Amy, Donna, Wendy. Education: Attended DePaul University Law School, 1961-63; B.S., Commerce/Accounting, DePaul University, 1962; M.B.A. with honors, Roosevelt University Graduate School of Business, 1966. Career: Certified Public Accountant, Illinois 1961, New York 1969; Auditor, Certified Public Accountant, David Himmelblau and Company, C.P.A.s, Chicago, 1963; Director of Management Services, Schultz & Chez, C.P.A.s, Chicago, 1964-66; Auditor 1966, Management Consultant 1967-69, S. D. Leidesdorf & Company, C.P.A.s, New York; Administrative Vice President, Director of Management Information Systems, Williams Real Estate Company, Inc., New York, 1969-80; Administrative Vice President, Williams & Company, Inc., New York, 1969-79; Executive Vice President, Realty Programs Sales Corporation, New York, 1978-80; Executive Vice President, Realty Programs Corporation, New York, 1976-80; President, Chief Executive Officer, Information Resource Management, Inc., New York, 1980 to present. Organizational Memberships: Association for Systems Management (past president, treasurer, vice president; board of directors, 1974 to present). Community Activities: The Suburban Temple, Wantagh, New York (board of directors, 1981 to present); Boy Scouts of America (advisory committee on management systems, 1980 to present); Broadview Police Pension Fund, Broadview, Illinois (board of directors, treasurer, 1964-66). Published Works: *FORTRAN IV; Apple Computer Supplement to FORTRAN IV; Contributing Editor, Administrative Management Magazine*, 1978 to present; Various Articles Published in *The CPA Journal*. Honors and Awards: Distinguished Service Award, Association for Systems Management, 1979; M.B.A. with Honors, Roosevelt University, 1966; Listed in *Who's Who in the East*. Address: 1644 Jane Street, Wantagh, New York 11793.

Hoffman, Howard Torrens

Multi-Industry Executive. Personal: Born December 30, 1923, East St. Louis, Illinois; Son of Mrs. B. E. Hoffman; Married Ruth Ann Gisela Koch; Father of Howard T., Jean Gisele, Glenn Kevin. Education: B.S.E.E., Iowa State University, 1950; M.S.E.E. 1972, Ph.D. 1977, Thomas University; Registered Professional Engineer. Military: Served in the Office of Military Government, United States Zone, Berlin, Germany, 1943-46. Career: President, Chief Executive Officer, Hoffman Associates; Executive Director, H&R Associates; Division Manager, Teledyne-Ryan, San Diego, California, 1960-66; Manager, Missile Systems, Litton Industries, College Park, Maryland, 1959-60; Executive Engineer, I.T.T. Labs, Fort Wayne, Indiana, 1957-59; Missile Systems Engineer, McDonnell Aircraft Corporation, St. Louis, Missouri, 1955-57; Engineering Section Head, Joy Manufacturing Company, St. Louis, Missouri, 1950-55. Organizational Memberships: Institute of Electrical and Electronic Engineers; American Institute of Aeronautics and Astronautics; National Society of Professional Engineers; American Management Association; National Management Association; Armed Forces Communications and Electronic Association; International Platform Association. Community Activities: Association of the United States Army; D.A.V.; University City Civic Association; Boy Scouts of America; United Crusade. Published Works: Articles on DC Amplifiers, Intrinsic Safety, Lunar Landing Radars, Space Radars and Program Control. Honors and Awards: Bronze Star Medal, 1945; Combat (Medical) Badge, 1945; United Crusade Community Service Award, 1972; Community Leaders Award, 1975; Listed in *Who's Who in America, Who's Who in the West, Who's Who in Finance and Industry, Who's Who in Aviation, Dictionary of International Biography, Pesonalities of America, Notable Americans, Personalities of the West and Midwest, Community Leaders and Noteworthy Americans, International Who's Who in Community Service, Men of Achievement*. Address: 5545 Stresemann Street, San Diego, California 92122.

George H Holdaway

Hoffman, Julius Jennings

Senior United States District Judge. Personal: Born July 7, 1895; Son of Aaron and Bertha Hoffman (both deceased); Married Eleanor H. Greenebaum (deceased), September 20, 1928; Stepfather of William E. Gardner. Education: Attended Lewis Institute, Chicago, Illinois; Ph.B. 1912, LL.B. 1915, LL.D. (honorary) 1955, Northwestern University. Career: Admitted to Illinois Bar, 1915; Practiced in Chicago, 1915-47; Past Vice President, General Council, Brunswick-Balke-Collender Company; Faculty Member, Northwestern University Law School; Associate Editor, *American Journal of Criminal Law and Police Science*; Judge, Superior Court of Illinois, Cook County, 1947-53; Judge, United States District Court for Northern District Illinois, 1953-72; Senior Judge, 1972 to present; Designated Judge, United States Court of Appeals; Presided Over Numerous Civil and Criminal Cases including Krebiozen Case and Chicago 7 Case. Organizational Memberships: American Bar Foundation (fellow); American Law Institute; Federal Bar Association; American Bar Association; Illinois Bar Association; Chicago Bar Association; Bar Association 7th Judicial Circuit; Patent Law Association of Northern District Illinois; Decalogue Society of Lawyers; American Judicature Society. Community Activities: Northern Illinois University Alumni Association (president); Illinois State Housing Board; Wigmore Club of Northwestern University; Northwestern University Associates; Republican; Standard Club; Tavern Club; Union League; Mid-Day Law Club, Chicago; Lake Shore Country Club; Post and Paddock. Published Works: Past Editor, *American Journal of Criminology and Criminal Law*; Contributor of Articles to Professional Publications. Honors and Awards: Gold Good Citizenship Medal, Sons of the American Revolution; Gold Medal of Merit, Veterans of Foreign Wars; Award of Merit 1954, Service Award 1962, Northwestern University Alumni Association; Man of the Year, Patent Law Association of Northern District Illinois; Certificate of Honor, Decalogue Society of Lawyers; Listed in *Who's Who in the World*. Address: 179 East Lake Shore Drive, Chicago, Illinois 60611.

Hoffnung, Audrey Sonia

Associate Professor. Personal: Born March 15, 1928; Daughter of Nathan and Gussie Karp Smith (both deceased); Married Joseph Hoffnung; Mother of Bonnie Fern Hoffnung Loewenstein, Tami Lynn Hoffnung Schwartzman. Education: B.A., Brooklyn College, 1949; M.A., Teachers College, Columbia University, 1950; Ph.D., City University of New York, 1974. Career: Associate Professor of Speech-Language Pathology, St. John's University; Adjunct Lecturer, Brooklyn College, 1973-77; Lecturer, Queens College, 1970-72; Consultant and Therapist, South Nassau Communities Hospital, 1964-65; Diagnostician and Therapist, Brooklyn College, 1958-62, 1963-64; Diagnostician, Consultant, Therapist, Morris J. Colomon Clinic for Mentally Retarded and Emotionally Disturbed, Brooklyn Jewish Hospital; Director of Speech-Language Therapy, Kingsbrook Medical Center, 1950-55; Speech Therapist, Ridgewood Cerebral Palsy Center, 1949-50. Organizational Memberships: Aphasia Study Group; American Speech-Language-Hearing Association; Long Island Speech-Language-Hearing Association; New York State Speech-Language-Hearing Association; New York City Speech-Language Hearing Associaton; New York State English as a Second Language-Bilingual Education Association. Honors and Awards: Vocational Rehabilitation Administration Traineeship, 1971; Listed in *Who's Who of American Women*. Address: 3282 Woodward Street, Oceanside, New York 11572.

Holdaway, George Harmer

Aerospace Engineer/Planning Consultant. Personal: Born October 10, 1921; Son of Hugh Holdaway (deceased); Married Lorna Lee;

Father of Larry Lee, Sheryl Lee, Steven Lee, George Lee. Education: B.S., Engineering, University of Utah, 1944; Master of Engineering Science, Stanford University, 1956. Military: Served in the United States Naval Reserve, 1944-46, attaining the rank of Lieutenant (j.g.). Career: Aero Research Project Engineer, N.A.S.A. and N.A.C.A., 1944-63; N.A.S.A., A.R.C., Chief of Development Projects Office 1963-66, Staff Assistant on Director's Staff 1966-71, Chief of Facilities Planning Office 1971-80, Retired August 1980, Re-employed Annuitant 1980, Assistant to Director of Research Support; Technical Management, N.A.S.-Ames Research Center, 1980-81; Aerospace Engineer/Planning Consultant. Organizational Memberships: American Institute of Aeronautics and Astronautics (associate fellow, 1964); International Right of Way Association (chairman of property management, 1977, 1978); American Association for the Advancement of Science; The Planetary Society. Community Activities: Scouting Leadership Positions (Cub, Boy, Explorer), 1948 to present; Stanford Area Council (executive board, 1969 to present); Committee for Handicapped (chairman); Regular Contributor to Boy Scouts of America, Latter Day Saint Church, Handicapped Groups; Leadership Positions in Local Organizations of the Latter Day Saint Church (including first counselor in Bishopric, high priest group leader, elders quorum president, 70's group leader, ward mission leader, stake missionary, ward clerk). Religion: Church of Jesus Christ of Latter Day Saints. Honors and Awards: N.A.S.A. Group Achievement Award, Lifting Body Research Team, 1970; N.A.S.A. Special Achievement Award, 1973; Boy Scouts of America Silver Beaver Award, 1976. Address: 3861 Grove Court, Palo Alto, California 94303.

Ray G L Holland

Holland, Ray G L

Psychiatrist, Assistant Clinical Professor. Personal: Born October 30, 1931, in Belfast, Northern Ireland; Son of John (deceased) and Mary Holland; Married Mary Kennedy; Father of Sean. Education: Matriculated, London University, England, 1949; Interscience Degree, London University, 1952; Attended Lectures at London School of Economics, 1953; B.A. 1959, Bachelor of Medicine and Surgery 1963, M.A. 1964, Oxford University; Licentiate of the Medical Council of Canada; Diplomate, American Board of Psychiatry and Neurology, 1980; Fellow, Royal College of Physicians and Surgeons of Canada in Specialty of Psychiatry, 1978. Military: Served in the Royal Canadian Navy as Senior Medical Officer and Flight Surgeon, 1964-69, with the rank of Lieutenant Commander. Career: Assistant Clinical Professor, Department of Psychiatry, State University of New York at Buffalo; Private Practice in Psychiatry, New York; Fellowship in Child Psychiatry, State University of New York at Buffalo, 1977-78; Senior Medical Officer and Flight Surgeon, Royal Canadian Army, 1964-69. Organizational Memberships: American Psychiatric Association; Canadian Psychiatric Association. Community Activities: Canadian Civil Liberties Association; Voluntary Teaching, State University of New York at Buffalo. Published Works: Preparing *The Psychotherapies - An Integrative Approach; Psychiatry - From Basic Facts to the Growing Edge; Child Development, Psychiatric Diagnosis and Treatment in Relation to Home, School and Community*. Honors and Awards: Fellow, International Biographical Association, 1979; Listed in *Who's Who of Intellectuals, Community Leader of America*. Address: 57 Elgin Street, Port Colborne, Ontario L3K 3J9 Canada.

Sandra G Holland

Holland, Sandra Gunter

Journalist, Free-lance Writer. Personal: Born January 12, 1952; Daughter of J. B. and Rondalene S. Gunter; Married Gasper O. Holland. Education: B.S., Journalism, Virginia Commonwealth University, 1973; Undertook Graduate Studies at North Texas State University, University of Texas-Austin. Military: Service in the United States Army Reserve, 1977 to present. Career: Journalist, Free-Lance Writer. Organizational Memberships: Women in Communications, Inc.; Society of Professional Journalists/Sigma Delta Chi; Business and Professional Women's Club. Community Activities: Civil Air Patrol (public information officer); Media Representative for United States Congressional Candidate, 1979; Various Committee Chairmanships for Professional and Civic Clubs. Religion: Southern Baptist. Honors and Awards: Danforth Award, 1970, for Scholarship, Citizenship and Leadership; Freedoms Foundation at Valley Forge George Washington Honor Medal, 1980, for Patriotic Essay in Military Competition Category; United States Fifth Army Minaret Award for Public Service, 1982, for Newspaper Article; Honorable Mention in Short Story Writing Contest, 1973; Certificate of Appreciation, National Committee for Employer Support of the Guard and Reserve, 1982; Senior Member of the Month Award, Civil Air Patrol, 1978. Address: 529 Oakhaven, Pleasanton, Texas 78064.

Hollingsworth, Wyla Jean

Private Piano Teacher, Artist, Secretary. Personal: Born December 8, 1929; Daughter of Charles Norman and Clara Henderson Nelson; Married Howard Earl Hollingsworth; Mother of Rebecca (deceased), Norman Earl, Daniel Dee, David, Cynthia, Theresa H. Hafen, Richard. Education: B.A., Secondary Music Education, Idaho State University; Studies in Oil Painting, 1979-80, 1980-81. Career: Private Piano Teacher, Artist, Secretary; Formerly an Elementary Music Teacher, Public Schools in Idaho; Accompanist for Dance Studio; Doctor's Receptionist; Assistant Office Manager, Swift and Company Wholesale House. Organizational Memberships: Phi Beta Sigma, 1949-50; Music Teachers National Association (monitoring committee, national convention, 1981); Sigma Beta Mu, 1949-51; Nevada Music Teachers Association (vice president, 1980-82; treasurer, 1971); Allied Arts Council (representative, 1965); Las Vegas Music Teachers Association (first vice president 1979-80); Community Concert Association (board of directors, 1973-81; north Las Vegas chairman, 1976-81); Sigma Beta Mu (historian, 1949-50). Community Activities: Allied Arts Council (representative, 1964-65); Political Campaign Volunteer Worker, 1970 to present; Bicentennial Committee representing Church, 1976; Community Concert Association (volunteer worker, 1960 to present). Religion: Church of Jesus Christ of Latter Day Saints; Pianist for Primary and Mia. Young Women's Mutual Improvement Association; Mia. Maid Teacher, Laurel Teacher, Ward and Stake; Stake Y.W. President; Age Group Counselor; Activity Counselor; Pianist, Music Director, 1961-79; Councilor in Relief Society; Cultural Refinement Leader; Spiritual Living Leader; Ward Choir Director; Stake Music Chairman, 1979 to present. Honors and Awards: Lambda Delta Sigma, Omega Chapter President 1949-50, Inter-Chapter Officer 1950-51; Piano Soloist, Idaho State University Choir Tour, 1950; School Merit Award for Outstanding Activitiy Participation, 1943; Golden Gleaner Award, 1959; Young Woman's Award, 1979; Queen Gold and Green Ball, 1947; Listed in *Directory of Distinguished Americans*. Address: 1700 Arrowhead Street, North Las Vegas, Nevada 89030.

Wyla J Hollingsworth

Hollis, Sheila S

Attorney. Personal: Born July 15, 1948; Married John Hollis; Mother of Windsong. Education: B.S., University of Colorado; J.D., University of Denver College of Law. Career: Attorney, Office of Butler, Binion, Rice, Cook and Knapp; Professorial Lecturer in the Law, George Washington University National Law Center; First Director, Office of Enforcement, Federal Energy Regulatory Commission, 1977-78; With Firm of Wilner and Scheiner, 1975-77; Trial Attorney, Federal Power Commission. Organizational Memberships: Federal Energy Bar Association (executive committee, 1981-82); American Bar Association (vice-chairman, natural gas committee, natural resources section, 1979-82; administrative law judge's committee, administrative law section, 1981-82); Colorado Bar Association; District of Columbia Bar Association; Bar Association of the District of Columbia. Published Works: Numerous

Articles on Energy Policy, the Federal Power Commission, the Federal Energy Regulatory Commission, the Enforcement Program, the Natural Gas Act and the Natural Gas Policy Act; Co-Author Book *Energy-Decisionmaking*. Honors and Awards: B.S cum laude and with honors, University of Colorado, 1971; Listed in *Who's Who in American Women, Who's Who in the East*. Address: 2415 Sandburg Street, Dunn Loring, Virginia 22027.

Holloway, Ernest Leon

University President. Personal: Born September 12, 1930; Widower; Father of Ernest Jr., Reginald, Norman. Education: B.S., Langston University, 1952; M.S., Oklahoma State University, 1955; Ed.D., University of Oklahoma, 1970. Career: Langston University, President, 1979 to present, Assistant Registrar, Dean of Student Affairs, Professor, Vice President for Administration, Acting President, 1963 to present; Science Teacher, Principal, Boley High School, 1952-62. Organizational Memberships: Oklahoma Higher Education Alumni Council; National Association of State Universities and Land-Grant Colleges; National Association for Equal Opportunities in Higher Education. Community Activities: Logan County Health Center (authority and board); Committee on Veteran Affairs; Research Achievement Committee; Langston University Alumni Association; Lions Club International; Imperial Council; Shriners; Northwest Consistory, 32° Mason; Alpha Phi Alpha (life member); Phi Delta Kappa; Consultant for Many Educational and Civic Groups. Religion: Young Men's Christian Association. Honors and Awards: Listed in *Who's Who in American College and University Administration, Personalities of the South, Leaders in Education*. Address: P.O. Box 666, Langston, Oklahoma 73050.

Lawrence M Holloway

Holloway, Lawrence Milton Jr

Executive. Personal: Born January 14, 1946; Son of Dr. and Mrs. L. M. Holloway; Married Charlotte Jane; Father of Tiffany Jane, Marque Spiter. Education: B.S., Michigan State University, 1968; M.A., Drake University, 1977; D.D., Church of Gospel Ministry, 1981. Career: President, Holloway House; Collection Supervisor, Owosso Finance Company; Supervisor, Medical Laboratory; Teacher; Financial Consultant; Vice President, National Potential Development Company. Organizational Memberships: National Association of Federal Licensed Firearms Dealers; American Chemical Society; American Institute of Hypnotists; Iowa Academy of Science; The Cranial Academy. Community Activities: Masonic Lodge; Shriners; Boy Scouts of America (scoutmaster, 1971); Iowans for L.I.F.E., Inc. (board of directors, 1979 to present; executive committee, 1980 to present; central regional coordinator, 1981 to present); Pro Life Action Council (board of directors, 1980 to present); Variety Club, 1980 to present. Religion: Sunday School Director, 1964-67; Stage Crew Director, 1979-80; Social Action Committee, 1980 to present. Honors and Awards: National Honor Society, 1962; Eagle Scout, 1961; Notable Americans Award, 1976. Address: 818 15th, Des Moines, Iowa 50314.

Holman, B Leonard

Physician and Educator. Personal: Born June 26, 1941; Son of Max and Sophie Holman; Married to Dale Elyse Barkin; Father of Amy Lynn, Allison Stacy. Education: B.S., University of Wisconsin, 1963; M.D., Washington University School of Medicine, 1966; Intern, Mt. Zion Hospital Medical Center, San Francisco, California, 1966-67; Resident, Edward Mallinckrodt Institute of Radiology, St. Louis, Missouri, 1967-70. Career: Professor of Radiology, Harvard Medical School, 1982 to present; Director of Clinical Nuclear Medicine Services, Brigham and Women's Hospital, Boston, Massachusetts, 1980 to present; Radiologist, Children's Hospital Medical Center, Boston, 1970 to present; Attending Physician, West Roxbury V.A. Hospital, Boston, 1974 to present; Radiologist, Sidney Farber Cancer Institute, Boston, 1976 to present; Chief of Clinical and Nuclear Medicine, Peter Bent Brigham Hospital, Boston, 1970-80; Instructor 1970-73, Assistant Professor of Radiology 1973-76, Associate Professor of Radiology 1976-81, Harvard Medical School; Associate Editor, *Cardiovascular and Intervention Radiology*, 1977 to present; Editorial Board, *American Journal of Cardiology*, 1978 to present; Editorial Board, *Journal of Cardiovascular Medicine*, 1979 to present; Editor, Diagnostic Imaging Section, *Medical Instrumentation*, 1980 to present; Editorial Board, *Post-graduate Radiology*, 1981 to present; Consulting member of Editorial Board, *Journal of Nuclear Medicine*, 1973-81. Organizational Memberships: Society of Nuclear Medicine (trustee, 1976-77 and 1980 to present, president of New England chapter, 1978-79); American Heart Association Council on Cardiovascular Radiology (executive committee); American College of Cardiology (trustee, 1981 to present); American College of Chest Physicians; American College of Radiology; American College of Nuclear Physicians; Massachusetts Radiological Society; American Federation for Clinical Research; Association of University Radiologists; Panel on Radiopharmaceuticals for the committee on Scope, U.S. Pharmacopeia, 1970 to present; Nuclear Cardiology Review Panel (intersociety commission on heart disease resources); United States Nuclear Regulatory Commission (advisory committee on medical uses of isotopes, 1979 to present); American Board of Nuclear Medicine (representative to the American Board of Radiology, 1980); Residency Review Committee for Nuclear Medicine, Liaison Committee for Graduate Medical Education, 1980; Consultant to Boards of Nuclear Medicine, Israel Medical Association, 1981. Published Works: *Regional Pulmonary Function in Health*, 1973, *Principles of Cardiovascular Nuclear Medicine*, 1974, *Cardiac Nuclear Medicine*, 1979, *Computer-assisted Cardiac Nuclear Medicine*, 1981, *Computed Emission Tomography*, in press. Honors and Awards: N.I.G.M.S. Fellow in Radiology; Elected to Phi Beta Sigma, Sigma Xi and Phi Kappa Phi; Fellow, International Bibliographic Association, 1980; Fellow, American College of Cardiology, 1976; Fellow, Council on Cardiovascular Radiology, 1977; Fellow, Council on Circulation, American Heart Association, 1981; Established Investigator, American Heart Association, 1977; Diplomate, American Board of Radiology, 1972; Diplomate, American Board of Nuclear Medicine, 1972; Fellow, American College of Chest Physicians; Listed in *Men and Women of Science, Best Doctors in the U.S.* Address: 25 Nancy Road, Chestnut Hill, Massachusetts 02167.

B Leonard Holman

Hoof, David Lorne

Physical Scientist. Personal: Born December 2, 1945; Son of Wayne and Mary Hoof; Married Bethea L. Giedhill; Father of Laura Louise, Emily Joy. Education: A.B., Chemistry, Cornell University, 1969; M.S. (Chemistry) 1971, Ph.D. (Inorganic Chemistry) 1974, Purdue University. Career: Physical Scientist, Office of Nuclear Fuel Cycle, United States Department of Energy; Previous Positions include Chemist, Chemical Engineer, Lecturer in Chemistry, N.S.F. Post-doctoral Fellow in Research Chemistry. Organizational Memberships: American Chemical Society, 1972-76; American Nuclear Society, 1978-80; Sigma Xi; American Association for the Advancement of Science, 1978-80; New York Academy of Sciences, 1978-80; Planetary Society, 1981-82. Community Activities: Episcopal Youth Fellowship Program (leader, 1975-76); District Architectural Control Committee, 1979-80. Religion: Saint Mary Magdalene Episcopal Church, 1974-82; Christ Church Episcopal, 1982 to present. Honors and Awards: All-American Interscholastic Swimming Team, 1962-64; N.S.F. Post-doctoral Fellowship, 1974-75; Sigma Xi, Research Society of North America, 1974; Listed in *Who's Who in the East, Community Leaders of America, Dictionary of International Biography*. Address: 11604 Silent Valley Lane, Gaithersburg, Maryland 20878.

Hoover, Theressa

Associate General Secretary. Personal: Born September 7, 1925; Daughter of James Cortez and Rissie Vaughn (both deceased). Education: B.A., Philander Smith College, 1946; M.A., New York University, 1962. Career: Associate Director, Little Rock Methodist Council, 1946-48; Field Worker, Women's Division, Methodist, 1948-58; Christian Social Relations Worker, 1958-65; Head of Section of Program and Education, 1965-68; Associate General Secretary, The Women's Division, General Board of Global Ministries, The United Methodist Church. Organizational Memberships: Y.W.C.A. (board of directors, 1964-76); Church Women United (board of managers, 1968 to present); The World Council of Churches Commission on Churches Participation in Development (officer); National Council of Churches (general board); Association of National Executives of Denominational Women's Organizations. Community Activities: National Board, Y.W.C.A. Task Force on Racial Justice (chairperson); National Council of Negro Women (executive board; personnel committee, chairperson; commission on N.C.N.W.'s future, chairperson); Delta Sigma Theta; Society for International Development Roundtable; Board of Trustees of Paine College; Board of Associates of Adrian College. Religion: Salem United Methodist Church; Joint Commission of Church Union; Chairperson, Council of Secretaries of United Methodist Church; Delegate to 1968, 1975, 1983 Assemblies of the World Council of Churches. Honors and Awards: Quality of Life Award, National Welfare Rights Organization; Distinguished Alumni Achievement Award, Philander Smith College; Citation in Recognition of Service to Religious Community, The Women's Missionary Council of the Christian Methodist Episcopal Church; Mary McCloud Bethune Award, National Council of Negro Women; Listed in *Who's Who of American Women, World's Who's Who of Women, Who's Who Among Black Women, Directory of Distinguished Americans.* Address: 90 La Salle Street, New York, New York 10027.

Hopson, William Briggs Jr

General and Peripheral Vascular Surgeon. Personal: Born September 20, 1937, Delhi, Louisiana; Son of William Briggs Hopson Sr.; Married Patricia Spearman; Father of Karen Renee, Mary Kathryn, William Briggs III, James Walter. Education: Graduate, Delhi High School, 1955; B.S., University of Mississippi, 1958; M.D., University of Tennessee, 1961; Internship, City of Memphis Hospitals, 1961-62; Residency, University of Tennessee, 1962-66; Teaching Appointment, Instructor in Surgery and Chief Resident, 1966-67. Career: General and Peripheral Vascular Surgeon, The Street Clinic and Mercy Regional Medical Center, Vicksburg, Mississippi; President, The Street Clinic; Chief of Surgery, Mercy Regional Medical Center. Organizational Memberships: American Board of Surgery (diplomate); American College of Surgery (fellow); Southeastern Surgical Congress (fellow); American Medical Association; West Mississippi Medical Association; American Trauma Society; Mississippi State Medical Association (past president, surgical section; vice president); Society of Clinical Vascular Surgeons; American College of Sports Medicine; American College of Surgeons (secretary-treasurer, president, Mississippi Chapter). Community Activities: Delta Kappa Epsilon; Phi Chi; Warren County Ole Miss Alumni Association (past president); American Cancer Society, Warren County Section (board of directors); State Trauma Committee; Governor's Highway Safety Program; Vicksburg Chamber of Commerce; Y.M.C.A.; Vicksburg Country Club; Rivertown Club; Catholic Home School Association (past president); Catholic School Board; Merchants National Bank (advisory board); American Trauma Society (Mississippi Chapter, president, founder); Warren County Campaign Manager for Thad Cochran, 1974; Warren County Campaign Manager for Brad Dye, 1975, 1979; Red Carpet Bowl (president); Mercy Regional Medical Center (president of staff); Vicksburg Hospital (courtesy staff); Ad Hoc Committee for Categorization of Emergency Rooms (chairman); State Peer Review Committee; Central Mississippi Health Planning Council (E.M.S. task force); Warren County Ambulance Service (co-director, medical consultant); Merchants National Bank (board of directors); E.M.S., State of Mississippi (medical control director); Miss Mississippi Pageant Board (board of trustees). Religion: Crawford Street United Methodist Church, Administrative Board, Sunday School Teacher. Published Works: Articles in *Southern Medical Journal, Annals of Surgery, The American Surgeon, Archives of Surgery, Journal of Surgical Research, Journal of the Mississippi State Medical Association, Emergency Medical Service Informer.* Honors and Awards: Gamma Sigma Epsilon; Alpha Epsilon Delta; Listed in *Who's Who in the South.* Address: 3320 Indiana Avenue, Vicksburg, Mississippi 39180.

Horan, Linda McDonald

Army Officer, Helicopter Pilot. Personal: Born April 14, 1944; Daughter of Mr. and Mrs. C. Bruce McDonald. Education: A.A., Sierra Junior College, 1964; B.A., Art/Design, San Jose State University, 1966; Teaching Degree, Chico State University Graduate School, 1967; M.F.A., Ceramics/Design, University of Montana, 1969. Military: Captain, Transportation Corps, United States Army, 1972 to present. Career: Commander, Helicopter Pilot, United States Army; Art Specialist, United States Army Asia Project Analyst, Human Factor Department. Organizational Memberships: Korean American Asiatic Society, 1969-71; Delta Phi Delta Honorary Art Fraternity (life member); Delta Phi Epsilon Honorary Education Fraternity (historian, 1966-69); Business and Professional Women, 1975-78; Army Aviation Association of America (vice president publicity, 1978-80; vice president membership, 1981); National Helicopter Association; United States Army Association; Whirlygirls, International Association of Women Helicopter Pilots. Community Activities: Daughters of the American Revolution; University of Montana Alumni Association; San Jose State University Alumni Association; Schwaebisch Hall Women's Advisory Council (president, 1980 to present). Honors and Awards: Young Craftsman of America National Tour, 1968; Given Key to the City of Dothan, Alabama, on "Linda Horan Day" for Fostering Relations between Military and Civilian Communities, 1978; Army's Woman of the Year, Southeastern Region, 1978; Only Female Military Member, United States International Competition Helicopter Team competing in Vitesk, Russia, 1978; Nominated as Distinguished Graduate, University of Montana, 1978; Member, United States Army Battalion selected as Outstanding Aviation Support Unit of the Year, Army Aviation Association, 1979; Outstanding Young Woman of America, 1980; Member, Battalion selected as Outstanding Aviation Unit of the Year, Army Aviation Association, 1981; United States Army's First Aviation Maintenance Test Pilot Graduate, 1975; Listed in *World's Who's Who of Women.* Address: 15038 Colfax Highway, Grass Valley, California 95945.

Hornbaker, Alice

Writer, Editor. Personal: Mother of Three. Education: B.A. cum laude with honors, Journalism, San Jose State University. Career: Columnist, Copy Editor, Reporter, Feature Writer, Free-lance Author, Magazine Writer. Organizational Memberships: Blue Pencil of Ohio State University (president, 1981-81); Ohio Newspaper Women's Association (vice president, 1981-83); Sigma Delta Chi, Society of Professional Journalists, Queen City Chapter (treasurer, 1980-82); Women in Communications, Inc. Community Activities: Teacher of Creative Writing, Thomas More College, Forest Hills Adult Education Center. Published Works: Book *Preventive Care: Easy Exercise Against Aging,* 1974; Author of Numerous Magazine Articles in *Modern Maturity, New York Times Sunday Magazine, N.A.T.R. Journal, Cincinnati Magazine,* and other nationally published magazines. Honors and Awards: Two Time Holder, Bronze Award, American Chiropractic Association 1976, 1977; First Place, Second Place, Honorable Mentions, Ohio

Newspaper Women's Association for Feature Stories to Columns, 1977-82; First Place, Feature Writers, Cincinnati Editors Association, 1973; "Aging", Best Column in Ohio, Ohio Newspaper Women's Association, 1982. Address: 485 McIntosh Drive, Cincinnati, Ohio 45230.

Horvath, Dorothy M

Banking Executive. Personal: Born November 24, 1946; Married Joseph Dean Horvath; Mother of Joseph Dean II. Education: Bachelor's Degree in Finance. Career: BancOhio National Bank, Vice President and Corporate Banking Team Manager, Columbus present, formerly Vice President, Senior Lending Officer, Dayton Area. Organizational Memberships: Robert Morris Associates (chairperson, Miami Valley Group, 1981-81; national committee on cooperation with N.A.C.M. and other credit associations, 1980-82; director, Ohio Valley chapter, 1980-82); Dayton Association of Credit Management (president, 1980-81; director, 1976-82). Community Activities: Miami Valley Regional Transit Authority (trustee, 1981 to present; chairperson, finance committee, 1981 to present); Dayton Women's Network (treasurer, 1980-82); Altrusa Club of Dayton (treasurer, 1979-80); United States Representative Hall's Advisory Board of Business, 1980-82; National Association of Bank Women, Greater Cincinnati Chapter (vice chairperson, 1980; director, 1977-80). Honors and Awards: Robert Morris Associates Loan Management Seminar, 1978; Golden Coin Award, Bank Marketing Association for Outstanding Marketing Program in the United States, 1976; BancSystems Award for Outstanding MasterCharge Marketing Program for State of Ohio, 1975; Member, American Banker's Association Advisory Board on Instalment Credit, 1974. Address: 115 Lyndale Drive, Westerville, Ohio 43081.

Hillaine A Hoste

Horwitz, Louis Aaron

Chairman of the Board/Chief Executive Officer. Personal: Born April 29, 1899, in Newark, New Jersey; Son of Samuel H. and Sara Glass Horwitz (both deceased); Married Rose Estelle; Father of Barbara Syma Goldfarb. Education: B.S., M.Ed., Doctorate Credits, Rutgers University; Studies in Education and Coaching, Tufts College, Bucknell University; Graduate of Panzer College of Physical Education and Health. Military: Served in the United States Navy during World War I. Career: Mayflower Savings and Loan, Director 1939-49, President 1949-71, Chairman of the Board/Chief Officer 1971 to present; Director, Justice Building and Loan Association (now Mayflower Savings and Loan), 1923-39; Teacher, Secondary Education, Football, Basketball, Track Coach, Newark (New Jersey) School System. Organizational Memberships: American Football Coaches Association; New Jersey Teachers Association; New Jersey Savings and Loan League (economic and budget committees); American Platform Association. Community Activities: Masonic Order; Tall Cedars; St. Barnabas Hospital (chairman of cryosurgery and hyperbaric chambers); Elks; Rotary Club (past president); Chamber of Commerce; Zionist Organization of America (past president; New Jersey state vice president). Honors and Awards: Kappa Delta Phi; Listed in *Dictionary of International Biography, Who's Who in the East, Notable Americans of the Bicentennial Era, Who's Who in Finance and Industry, World Who's Who in Commerce and Industry, Who's Who in American Jewry, Men of Achievement, Book of Honor, Community Leaders of America, Notable Americans, Who's Who in America, Who's Who in World Jewry.* Address: 320 South Harrison Street, East Orange, New Jersey 07018.

Hoskins, Robert Lee

College Dean. Personal: Born September 24, 1941; Son of Ralph H. (deceased) and Annamae Hoskins; Married Andrea Wallace; Father of Leslie Ann, Charlotte Leigh, Zachary Wallace. Education: B.J. 1962, M.A. 1963, University of Missouri-Columbia; Ph.D., North Texas State University, 1972. Career: Reporter/Editorial Writer, *Daily Enterprise*, Beaumont, Texas, 1963-65; Director of Public/Community Relations, Alice Lloyd College, Pippa Passes, Kentucky, 1965-68; Registrar/Director of Admissions, Texas Southmost College, Brownsville, Texas, 1968-70; Director, Continuing Education, Navarro Junior College, Corsicana, Texas, 1972; Director, Community Medical Manpower Research Project, Arkansas State University, 1972-73; Dean of College of Communications, Arkansas State University, 1973 to present. Organizational Memberships: Arkansas Chapter, S.P.J.-S.D.X.; American Association of University Administrators (chairman, nominations committee, 1980-81); American Society of Journalism School Administrators (resolutions committee, 1977-78; chairman, awards committee, 1979-80, 1980-81); Association for Education in Journalism and Mass Communications; Phi Delta Kappa; International Newspaper Advertising Executives. Address: P.O. Box 24, State University, Arkansas 72467.

Hoste, Hillaine Adeline

Medical Record Technician. Personal: Born March 20, 1930; Married Raymond A. Hoste; Mother of Mark Alan Becker. Education: Attended Clery College, Ypsilanti, Michigan, 1965-68; Monroe County (Michigan) Community College, 1968-72; B.A., Allied Health Science, Stephens College, Columbia, Missouri, 1980. Career: Medical Record Technician; Former Traffic Analyst. Organizational Memberships: American Medical Record Association; Michigan Medical Record Association (member consultant group); Faculty Joint Commission Accreditation Hospitals; Southeastern Michigan Medical Record Association. Community Activities: Michigan Association of Quality Assurance Professionals (board of directors, 1982-84); National Organization of Women; Federally Employed Women (secretary, 1982); Dundee Community Council (secretary, 1954); Dundee Business and Professional Women (past president). Religion: Presbyterian Church, Dundee, Michigan, Session, Property and Stewardship Committee, Personnel Committee. Honors and Awards: Superior Performance Award, Veterans Administration, 1974; Certificate of Appreciation for Service on E.E.O. Committee, 1981. Address: 366 Main Street, Dundee, Michigan 48131.

Lewis D Houck

Houck, Lewis Daniel Jr

Executive. Personal: Born July 9, 1932; Son of Mr. and Mrs. Lewis D. Houck; Father of Marianne Jennifer, Leland Daniel. Education: A.B., Princeton University, 1955; M.B.A., with distinction, 1964, Ph.D., 1971, New York University Graduate School of Business Administration. Military: Served with United States Army Reserve to rank of 1st Lieutenant, 1955-57. Career: President, Houck Marketing and Management Consultants, Inc., Kensington, Maryland, 1979 to present; Project Leader, Economic Research Service, U.S. Department of Agriculture, 1973-78; Special Consultant, U.S. Department of Agriculture, Washington, D.C., 1971-73; Educational Projects Manager, National Assciation of Accountants, New York City, 1969-71; Instructor, New York University Graduate School of Business, New York City, 1966-69; Management Consultant to private industry, New York City, 1962-64; Marketing Manager, Selling Research, Inc., New York City, 1959-62; Manager of Special Research, Young and Rubicam, Inc., New York City, 1957-59. Organizational Memberships: Academy of Political Science; International Platform Association; American Institute of Management; American Accounting Association; American Economic Association; American Academy of Political and Social Science; American Marketing Association. Community Activities: District Chairman of Committee to Re-elect John Lindsay (mayor of New York City), 1969. Published Works: *A Practical Guide to Budgetary and Management Control Systems*, 1979. Honors and Awards: Fellow, Ford Foundation, 1964-66; Founders Day Award, New York University, 1971; Fellow, American Biographical Institute, 1977 to present (honorary member of editorial advisory board, 1980 to present); Life Fellow, International Biographical Association, 1980 to present (chairman of marketing and communications discussion seminars, 4th I.B.C. Congress, London, England, 1977); Honorary Fellow, The Anglo-American Academy, 1980 to present. Address: 11111 Woodson Avenue, Kensington, Maryland 20895.

Houck, W Margaret (Midge)

Administrator. Personal: Born August 20, 1938; Daughter of Mr. and Mrs. James R. Harrison; Mother of Stan, Jim, Lisa. Education: B.A., M.A., Work toward Ed.D., University of Oregon. Career: President/Broker, Real Estate 100, 1982 to present; Hostess, "Conversations with Midge Houck" on Radio Station KSLM/KSKD, 1982 to present; Chemeketa Community College, Director of Work Related Experience 1971-82, Executive Director 1976-77; Assistant Dean of Women, University of Oregon, 1958-60. Organizational Memberships: Salem Board of Realtors; Oregon Association of Realtors Board, 1982 to present; National Association of Realtors, 1982 to present; National Cooperative Education Board (region 7 representative, 1982 to present); Adventures in Living Corporation (board of directors, 1981 to present); Western Regional Training Center; Rocky Mountain States Training Center (advisory committee, 1977 to present); Northwest Cooperative Education Center; Pacific Northwest Training Center (advisory committee, 1978 to present); Special Task Force To Advise United States Office of Education and National Commission for Cooperative Education, 1977 to present; Northeastern Training Center (consultant, 1977 to present); Work Experiences Congresses of Oregon (master planning committee, 1973 to present); Reader of Federal Cooperative Education Grants, Washington, D.C., 1977-78; Chemeketa Community College (chairman, college affairs committee, 1977-78; chairman, ad hoc committee to rewrite Code of Conduct, board of directors, 1977); Advisory Committee for Career Education, 24-J School District, 1975 to present; Work Related Experience Coordinators of Oregon (charter president, 1973); Northwest Placement Association Conference (chairman, 1975); Oregon Community College Administrators (delegate for Chemeketa, 1973-75); Oregon Vocational Association (board member, 1973-75); Ad Hoc Committee for Development of Oregon State Plan for Vocational Education, 1974-76; Eleven Western States Regional Work Experience Seminar (chairman, 1975). Community Activities: Young Men's Christian Association (chair, fund drive, 1982 to present); "Save Our Symphony" Drive (chair, 1981-82); Mid Valley Arts Council (chair, 1982-83); Friends of Chemeketa (originator, chairman, 1972-76); Salem Area Chamber of Commerce, 1971 to present; Women's Auxiliary to Oregon Symphony Society (chairman, 1972); American Association of University Women, 1963-72; Alpha Delta Pi Sorority Alumni (president, 1966-68); Terrace Dance Club (board of directors, 1965-66); Salem Area Panhellenic (treasurer, 1968-89); Boys and Girls Aid Society (president, 1969-70); Salem Area Hi-Y Mother's Club (president, 1971-72); Salem Art Association, 1968-74; Western Oregon Open Tennis Tournament. Religion: Episcopalian, Junior High Sunday School Teacher, Community Action Committee. Honors and Awards: Kwama, University of Oregon Activities and Scholarship Honorary; Phi Theta Upsilon, University of Oregon Activities and Scholarship Honorary; Mortar Board; Secretary, University of Oregon Student Body; University of Oregon Rally Squad. Address: 3595 Cherokee Drive, South, Salem, Oregon 97302.

Houseal, Reuben A

Pastor, Educator, Writer. Personal: Born January 6, 1910, in York, Pennsylvania; Son of John Franklin and Beatrice Vervean Dellinger Houseal; Married First Wife, Jennie Belle Kinkle, June 1, 1929; Married Second Wife, Marguerite Edna Ruth Arnold, on November 26, 1964; Father of Reuben John, Elisabeth H. Honecker, Lawrence Garrison, (Stepfather of) John A. Johnson, Marguerite Johnson Redmond. Education: Graduate of Philadelphia College of Bible, 1932; B.A., M.A., University of Pennsylvania; Undertook Post-graduate Studies, Reformed Episcopal Theological Seminary, 1934-37; Th.D. 1973, Ph.D. 1977, LL.D. (honorary), Clarksville School of Theology, Clarksville, Tennessee. Career: Pastor, Several Churches, including Bethany Community Church (Dayton, Ohio), Olive Branch Congregational Church (St. Louis, Missouri), Central Baptist Church (Erie, Pennsylvania), 1937-57; Founder, Director, Gospel Lite House of the Air (a broadcast ministry in Pennsylvania, Ohio, Illinois, Missouri and Michigan), 1942; Executive Board, Faculty, Greenburg Bible Institute, Pennsylvania, 1960-71; Institutional Chaplain, Mercer County, Pennsylvania, 1967 to present; Bible Conference/Evangelist Ministry, Mercer County, Pennsylvania, 1967 to present. Organizational Memberships: Independent Fundamental Churches of America (member, 1938 to present; chairman, national commission on institutional chaplains, 1972 to present); Calvary School of Theology, Mercer, Pennsylvania (co-founder, vice president, academic dean); York Gospel Center, York, Pennsylvania (constituent member). Honors and Awards: Life Member, Mercer County Historical Society; Life Fellow, International Biographical Association; Life Patron, A.B.I.R.A.; Outstanding Alumnus Award, Philadelphia College of Bible; Honorary M.S., Conferred by the *Encyclopaedia Britannica;* Commissioned a Kentucky Colonel by that State's Governor, October 1977; Listed in *Who's Who in Religion, International Register of Profiles, International Men of Achievement, International Who's Who of Intellectuals, International Who's Who in Community Service, International Men and Women of Distinction, Dictionary of International Biography, Book of Honor, Notable Americans, Personalities of America, Community Leaders and Noteworthy Americans, American Registry Series, Community Leaders of America, Directory of Distinguished Americans, Personalities of the East, Biographical Roll of Honor, Who's Who in the East, Encyclopaedia of Contemporary Personalities, Who Is Who*. Address: 132 South Erie Street, P.O. Box 132, Mercer, Pennsylvania 16137.

Reuben & Ruth Houseal

Houseal, Ruth Arnold

Retired Teacher. Personal: Born November 23, 1904, in Mercer, Pennsylvania; Daughter of Samuel B. McAle and Mary Edna Williams Arnold; Married First Husband, 1932; Married Second Husband, Reuben Arthur Houseal, November 26, 1964; Mother of John A. Johnson, Marguerite Johnson Redmond. Education: B.S., Slippery Rock State College, Pennsylvania, 1958; M.S.Ed., Westminster College, New Wilmington, Pennsylvania, 1963; Diploma for completing the Schofield Bible Course, Moody Bible Institute, 1966; D.R.E. 1973, L.H.D. (honorary) 1974, Clarksville School of Theology, Clarksville, Tennessee. Career: Teacher, Building Principal, Art Supervisor on Elementary Level, 27 years; Worked with and Successfully Educated Exceptional Children, 15 years. Organizational Memberships: National Education Association (life member); Pennsylvania State Education Association (life member); Mercer County Historical Society (life member); International Biographical Association (life fellow). Published Works: Textbook *A Survey of Christian Education*. Honors and Awards: Certificate of Merit and Distinguished Achievement for Meritorious Work and Citizenship, International Biographical Association; Life Patron, A.B.I.R.A.; Listed in *Who's Who in Religion, Dictionary of International Biography, International Register of Profiles, International Who's Who in Community Service, Book of Honor, Notable Americans, American Registry Series, Personalities of America, Community Leaders and Noteworthy Americans, Notable Personalities of America, International Men and Women of Achievement, World's Who's Who of Women, Community Leaders of America, Directory of Distinguished Americans, Personalities of the East, Biographical Roll of Honor, World Who's Who of Women, Who's Who in Community Service, Who's Who of American Women, International Men and Women of Distinction, International Who's Who of Intellectuals, Who's Who in the East, Encyclopaedia of Contemporary Personalities, Who Is*

Who. Address: 132 South Erie Street, Mercer, Pennsylvania 16137.

Houser, Ronald Edward

Veterinarian. Personal: Born August 11, 1949; Son of E. Erle and Lois Houser; Married Linda Marie Webber; Father of Angela Marie, Brian Edward. Education: D.V.M., University of Missouri, 1974; M.S., The Ohio State University, 1979. Military: Served in the United States Air Force, 1974-76, attaining the rank of Captain. Career: Veterinarian. Organizational Memberships: American Veterinary Medicine Association; Nebraska Veterinary Medicine Association (district president); Christian Veterinary Mission; American College of Veterinary Preventive Medicine. Community Activities: National Agricultural Youth Institute (counselor, 1968-70); Northern Virginia Youth Science Fairs (United States Air Force judge, 1975-76); Advisory Committee on Health Education Services, The Ohio State University, 1978-79; Graduate Professional Commission, Ohio State University, 1978-79; Nebraska State Board of Health, 1981-83. Religion: Rockbrook United Methodist Church, Omaha, Nebraska, Administrative Board, 1979-82. Honors and Awards: Gamma Sigma Delta Agricultural Honorary; Phi Zeta Veterinary Medicine Honorary; Sigma Xi Scientific Honorary; Listed in *Community Leaders and Noteworthy Americans, Personalities of the West and Midwest*. Address: 3218 Cornhusker Drive, Omaha, Nebraska 68124.

Colleen J Howe

Houston, Vivian McCoy

Administrator. Personal: Born January 30, 1943; Daughter of Charles L. McCoy; Married Mark T. Houston; Mother of Jennifer M. Education: Studies at Park College, Temple University, Creighton University; Dale Carnegie Courses; Marriott Management Courses. Career: General Manager, Marriott Worldwide Reservations System; Assistant Manager-Manager, Marriott Communications Center, Omaha, Nebraska, 1974; Reservation Manager, Marriott, New Orleans, Louisiana, 1972-74; Reservation Manager, Marriott, Washington, D.C., 1971-172; Reservation Manager, Marriott, Arlington, Virginia, 1969-71; Desk Clerk, Marriott, Philadelphia, Pennsylvania, 1967-69; Teller, Fidelity Bank, Philadelphia, Pennsylvania, 1964-67; Proof Reader, Pennland Printing, Yeadon, Pennsylvania, 1964; Waitress, Howard Johnson, 1964; Counselor, Girl Scout Camp, Pocono Mountains, Pennsylvania, 1961-62. Organizational Memberships: American Business Women (treasurer, 1978-79); Society for the Advancement of Management, Division of American Management Association. Community Activities: Omaha Chamber of Commerce. Religion: Hancock Methodist Church, 1964-67; Unity Church. Honors and Awards: Dale Carnegie Awards; Listed in *Who's Who of American Women*. Address: 9904 Pasadena Avenue, Omaha, Nebraska 68124.

Howard, Gene C

Attorney, State Senator. Personal: Born September 26, 1926, Son of Joe W. and Nell Howard; Married Belva J. Prestidge; Father of Joe Ted, Jean Ann Peterson. Education: LL.B., University of Oklahoma, 1951. Military: Served in the United States Air Force, 1944-46, 1961-62, attaining the rank of Lieutenant Colonel. Career: Attorney; Senator, State of Oklahoma, 1964 to present; Representative, State of Oklahoma, 1958-62. Organizational Memberships: Tulsa Bar Association; Oklahoma Bar Association; Phi Delta Phi. Community Activities: Oklahoma Senate (president, pro tem, 1975-81). Religion: Disciples of Christ. Honors and Awards: Outstanding Young Attorney for 1953, Tulsa County Bar Association; Honorary Member, O.C.U. Law School Alumni Association, 1977. Address: 1742 South Erie, Tulsa, Oklahoma 74112.

Howe, Colleen Janet

Executive. Personal: Born February 17, 1933, in Detroit, Michigan; Married Gordon Howe; Mother of Marty Gordon, Mark Steven, Cathleen Jill, Murray Albert. Education: Graduate, Mackenzie High School, Detroit, Michigan, 1950. Career: President, Howe Enterprises, 1954 to present; Consultant, Hartford Whalers Hockey Club, Hartford, Connecticut, 1977 to present; President, Howe International Marketing; Investor/Manager; Licensed Life Insurance Agent, Connecticut; Consultant, Houston Aeros Hockey Club, Inc., Houston, Texas, 1973-77; Director, Howe Travel, Inc., Southfield, Michigan, 1975-79; Receptionist, Secretary, Ferd Prucher Art Studios, Detroit, Michigan, 1952-53; File Clerk, Receptionist, Recorder, Bethlehem Steel Company, Detroit, Michigan, 1950-52. Organizational Memberships: Hartford Life Underwriters Association; A.D.A.U.S.; Advertising Club of Greater Hartford; Convention and Visitors Bureau. Community Activities: Republican Candidate for First District Nomination for Congress; March of Dimes, Northern Connecticut Chapter (executive committee); Newington Children's Hospital (director); Sports Medicine Council, University of Connecticut; Colonial Bank Advisory Board; Michigan 4-H Foundation (board member); Detroit Jr. Wings, Michigan Amateur Hockey Program (board member; spearheaded the formulation of and managed this first successful Jr. A hockey club in the United States). Published Works: Book *My Three Hockey Players;* Articles in Face-Off Hockey Publication and the *New York Times*. Religion: First Church of Christ Congregational. Honors and Awards: Honored for Outstanding Achievements in Insurance Field, Aetna Life Insurance Company; Voted Sportswoman of the Year, Sportcasters/Sportwriters of Detroit, 1972; Charter Oak Medal for Outstanding Community Achievement, Hartford Chamber of Commerce, 1979; Executive of the Year, *Connecticut Journal;* Listed in *Who's Who of American Women*. Address: 32 Plank Lane, Glastonbury, Connecticut 06033.

Henry Howell

Howell, Henry G

Retired Auto Electro-Plating Line Operator, Evagelical Vocalist. Personal: Born August 31, 1920; Son of Henry and Ottie Bowling Howell (both deceased); Married Audrey Louise Lemaster (deceased); Father of Carlin Sue Howell Wright, Gereda Myra Howell West. Education: High School in Louisa, Kentucky, and Webbville, Kentucky, 1939-40; Further Studies at the Louise E. Chandler Studio of Music and Voice. Military: Served in the United States Army, 1941-43, attaining the rank of Private First Class; Survived the Pearl Harbor Attack. Career: Retired 1978; Automotive Electro-plating Line Operator, Houdaille Industries, Inc., Huntington, West Virginia; Professional Evangel Vocalist, Church and Radio; Featured in Religious Program "Forward in Faith, Meditations and Songs of Higher Ground"; Nursery and Orchard Salesman, assisting with Landscaping, 1940-41. Organizational Memberships: Pearl Harbor Survivors Association, Inc. Community Activities: Masonic Lodge 626, F.&.A.M., Willard, Kentucky; Kentucky State Bluegrass Chapter #1. Religion: Catlettsburg (Kentucky) United Methodist Church. Published Works: Written Recollections of the Pearl Harbor Bombing in Several Publications. Honors and Awards: Kentucky Colonel, Commissioned Admiral, Commonwealth of Kentucky, Department of Natural Resources, 1969; Featured in *Mass Media*. Address: 3430 Floyd Street, Ashland, Kentucky 41101.

Hoye, Robert Earl

Director of Instructional Technology, Professor. Personal: Born January 12, 1931; Son of Alice M. Hoye; Married Patricia B.; Father of Robert E. Jr., Joanne D., Peter M., Kathleen B. Education: A.B., Providence College, 1953; M.S., St. John's University, 1955; Ph.D., University of Wisconsin, 1973. Career: Director of Instructional Technology, Professor, University of Louisville, Kentucky; Director, Instructional Media Laboratory, University of Wisconsin-Milwaukee; Director, Learning Systems Division, Xerox Corporation; New England Director, Science Research Associates, I.B.M.; Superintendent of Schools, Deerfield, Massachusetts; Dean, Champlain College, Vermont. Organizational Memberships: American Psychological Association; Association for Educational Communication and Technology; American Association of Clinical Counselors. Community Activities: Office of Technology Assesment of the United States Congress (panel member); Consultant to Numerous Public Service Organizations. Published Works: Former Editor of Educational Journal; Author of 29 Articles in Professional Journals and of 1 Book. Religion: St. Lou's Bertrand Church (Catholic), Third Order of St. Dominic. Honors and Awards: Commission on Academic Excellence, University of Louisville; Honorary Citizen, City of Louisville; Honorary Kentucky Colonel; Outstanding Educator Award, Freedom Foundation; I.B.M./S.R.A. Man of the Year, 1964. Address: 2238 Wynnewood Circle, Louisville, Kentucky 40222.

Hsu, Shao Ti

Educator. Personal: Born May 28, 1916; Son of Mr. and Mrs. T. S. Hsu; Married to Charlotte Chien; Father of William, Vincent, Lillian. Education: B.S., Chiao Tung University, 1937; M.S., Massachusetts Institute of Technology, 1943; D.Sc., Swiss Federal Institute of Technology, 1954. Military: Served in Mechanical Division as Air Force Captain, 1939-44. Career: Professor of Mechanical Engineering, University of Maryland (student affairs committee, 1969-71, executive committee of mechanical engineering department, 1970-72); Professor of Mechanical Engineering, Virginia Polytechnic Institute, 1961-67; Associate Professor of Mechanical Engineering, University of Wisconsin, 1954-61; Production Engineer, Central Aircraft Factory, 1940-44; Production Engineer, China Motor Corporation, Hong Kong, 1939-40; Operating Engineer, Hankow Water Works, 1937-39. Organizational Memberships: American Society of Mechanical Engineers; Solar Energy Society; American Society of Heating, Refrigeration and Air Conditioning Engineers (research committee, 1967-69); American Society of Engineering Educators. Community Activities: Chairman, Anacostia Housing Corporation, 1978 to present. Religion: Member of Methodist Church. Honors and Awards: Registered Engineer, State of Ohio, 1956 to present; Honorary member, Tau Beta Pi and Pi Tau Sigma; Elected to Sigma Xi; Listed in *Community Leaders and Noteworthy Americans.* Address: 11 Tanager Court, Potomac, Maryland 20854.

Hubbard, Harvey Hart

Consultant. Personal: Born June 17, 1921; Son of H. W. Hubbard; Married Sadie Miller; Father of Thomas Waite, Susan Hart, Pamela Lynn, Walter Raleigh. Education: B.S.E.E., University of Vermont, 1942; Graduate Work at the University of Virginia, Massachusetts Institute of Technology, University of Alabama, 1946-67. Military: Served in the United States Air Force, 1942-45, attaining the rank of Lieutenant Colonel. Career: Consultant in Noise Control Engineering; Assistant Chief, Acoustics and Noise Reduction Division, National Aeronautics and Space Administration. Organizational Memberships: Acoustical Society of America (member, 1963 to present; executive council, 1975-78; chairman for May 1984 national meeting); Institute of Noise Control Engineering (member, 1972 to present; president, 1979; executive vice president, 1978; board of directors, 1972-81); American Institute of Aeronautics and Astronautics, 1973 to present. Community Activities: United States Department of Transportation (noise research panel, 1971); Institute of Sound and Vibration Research, England (science advisory committee, 1968-70); I.C.A.O. Sonic Boom Panel, 1970; American Health Society (committee on rotor aeroacoustics, 1969-70); S.A.E., A-21 (committee on aircraft noise measurement, 1962-79); National Academy of Science Committee on Hearing and Acoustics, 1970-72. Published Works: Editorial Board *Noise Control Engineering*, 1973-81; Editorial Board, *Journal of Sound and Vibration*, 1970-73. Religion: Presbyterian Church, Elder, 1960 to present. Honors and Awards: University of Vermont Honor Graduate in Military Science and Tactics, 1942; Aeroacoustics Medal, A.I.A.A., 1979; Silver Medal, Acoustical Society of America, 1978; Gold Medal for Exceptional Science Achievement, N.A.S.A., 1969; Group Achievement Award, N.A.S.A., 1968; N.A.S.A.-Langley Special Service Award, 1967, 1968; Apollo Achievement Award, N.A.S.A., 1969; Certificate of Recognition, George Washington University, 1980. Address: 23 Elm Avenue, Newport News, Virginia 23601.

Hubbard, Kristin Kuhns

Public Relations Executive. Personal: Born July 15, 1950; Daughter of James and Faith Kuhns. Education: B.A., Sweetbriar College. Career: President, Kristin Hubbard Public Relations; Writer, Press Officer, The Government of Puerto Rico; Writer, *House Beautiful* Magazine; Pubic Relations Department, Champion International; Newscaster, Channel 13, New York City; Reporter, Channel 5, New York City; Public Relations Department, C.I.T. Financial Corporation. Organizational Memberships: Women in Communications; New York Junior League (public relations committee); City Club of New York. Community Activities: Established Video Class in East Harlem, New York Junior League; One of Founders of Earth Day 1970 and the Environmental Action Coalition; Daycare Worker, East Harlem. Religion: Episcopal. Published Works: Features for *House Beautiful, The Christian Science Monitor, Daily News, Town and Country, Ingenue, Dayton Journal Herald.* Honors and Awards: Listed in *Who's Who of American Women, Who's Who in the East, The World's Who's Who of Women.* Address: 517 East 82nd Street, New York City, New York 10028.

Hubbard, L(afayette) Ron(ald)

Writer/Author. Personal: Born March 13, 1911; Son of Harry Ross and Dora May Hubbard (both deceased): Married Mary Sue Whipp; Father of Diana Meredith de Wolfe (Mrs. Jonathan Horwich), Mary Suzette Rochelle (Mrs. Michael Titmus), Arthur Ronald Conway. Education: Graduate of Swavely Prep School 1928, Woodward Prep School 1930; Attended George Washington University, 1930-32; Princeton School of Government, 1945. Military: Served in the United States Naval Reserve, 1941-46, attaining the rank of Lieutenant. Career: Writer/Author, 1932 to present; Screenwriter, Hollywood, 1937-38; Explorer, Leader, Caribbean Motion Picture Expedition, 1932; Leader, West Indies Mineralogical Expedition, 1933; Leader, Alaskan Radio-Experimental Expedition, 1940. Organizational Memberships: Authors Guild of America; Writers Guild of Great Britain; International Oceanographic Foundation; Explorers Club; Cruising Association; Capital Yacht Club. Community Activities: Research and Technology for Improved Education, 1964-71; Research and International Programs to Resolve Drug Abuse, 1966 to present. Published Works: Research and Development of Technology for Increase in Human Ability including *Dianetics: The Modern Science of Mental Health*, 1950; *Science of Survival*, 1951; *Fundamentals of Thought*, 1956; *Scientology: A New Slant on Life*, 1966; *Self Analysis*, 1968; *Dianetics Today*, 1975; *Volunteer Ministers Handbook*, 1976. Religion: Director, Church of Scientology, 1952-66. Honors and Awards: 17 Awards and Recognitions, 1923-77, including Explorers Club Flag 3 Times, 1940-66; Eight Proclamations from Various United States Cities, 1974-76; 25 Keys to United States Cities, 1970-76; San Antonio Alcalde Award, 1975; California Assembly Award, 1975: International Social Reform Award, 1976. Address: c/o Explorers Club, 46 East 70th Street, New York, New York 10021.

Hubbard, Margaret Eleanor

News/Public Affairs Director. Personal: Born November 8, 1931; Daughter of Percil Cameron and Harriet Ellen Wilson Muncie (both deceased); Married; Mother of Cameron Munsie, Harriet Katherine. Education: High School Graduate, Trenton, Nova Scotia; Johnson & Wales Business School, 1953; Studies in Public Speaking 1976, Journalism 1978, Providence College; Barbara's Modeling and Finishing School, 1976-77; Rhode Island School of Broadcasting, 1978. Career: News/Public Affairs Director, WARV; Edgewood Electronics Company, Warwick, 1960-76; Automobile Mutual Insurance Company, Providence, 1955-60; Brown and Sharp Company, Providence, 1951-55. Organizational Memberships: Rhode Island Press Club; Rhode Island Advertising Club. Community Activities: Harmony, Inc. (publicity chairman, Providence Chapter, 1968-70); Communications Department, Rhode Island State Council of Churches, 1973 to present; Ruth Rebekah Lodge #8 (past noble grand); Rhode Island Association of Evangelical Churches (media committee). Religion: First Presbyterian Church, Providence, Deaconess. Honors and Awards: Listed in *Who's Who of American Women, Personalities of America.* Address: 52 Park View Avenue, Warwick, Rhode Island 02888.

Huber, Joan Marie

Military Nurse. Personal: Born September 15, 1951; Daughter of Mr. and Mrs. Fred Huber. Education: B.S.N., Villanova University, 1973; M.S., University of California at San Francisco, 1982; C.C.R.N., certified by American Association of Critical Care Nurses. Military: Serving with United States Navy as Lieutenant Commander, 1971 to present. Career: Nurse Corps Officer, N.R.O.T.C. Unit, University of California at Berkeley. Organizational Memberships: American Association of Critical Care Nurses; American Association of Nephrology Nurses and Technicians; American Nurses Association; Association of Military Surgeons of U.S.; National League for Nursing; Sigma Theta Tau. Honors and Awards: National Defense Service Medal, 1971; Young Career Woman of the Year, Groton, Connecticut, 1978; Navy Commendation Medal, 1979. Address: 428 Sherwood Drive, Apartment 201, Sausalito, California 94965.

Hudgins, Dudley R

Administrator. Personal: Born November 4, 1937; Son of Helen Hudgins; Married; Father of Brian W. Randall W., (Stepfather of) Mianne Woods, Todd Woods. Education: B.A, Psychology, Kansas University, 1959. Military: Served in the United States Army, 1960. Career: Director of Sales and Training Development, Marion Laboratories; Sales Representative, San Antonio, Texas, Marion Labs. Organizational Memberships: National Society Pharmaceutical Sales Trainers (midwest treasurer, 4 years; chapter president, 1978-79; national president, 1979-80). Community Activities: Consultant to Field; Speaker/Consultant, School, Civic Organizations; Honorary Director, Rockhurst College, Kansas City, Missouri. Religion: Zion Lutheran Church, Sunday School Teacher, Congregational President 1980. Honors and Awards: Salesman of the Year (National), 1964, 1968; Salesman of the Year, Southwestern Region, 1966; Marion Builder's Award, Developing Managers, 1979; Listed in *Who's Who in the World, Who's Who in Finance and Industry*. Address: 12817 Sagamore, Leawood, Kansas 66209.

Margaret E Hubbard

Hudgins, William Robert

Neurosurgeon. Personal: Born March 10, 1939; Son of Rev. and Mrs. W. Douglas Hudgins; Married Cynthia Kite; Father of Catherine, David, Anne, Lauren. Education: Studies in Pre-Med, University of Oklahoma, 1957-60; M.D., University of Mississippi School of Medicine, 1964; Surgery Internship, Duke University Hospital, 1964-65; Neurosurgery, University of Tennessee, 1964-68. Military: Served in the United States Navy as a Neurosurgeon for Hospital Ship *U.S.S. Sanctuary* in Vietnam, 1969-71, attaining the rank of Lieutenant Commander, M.C. Career: Neurosurgeon in Private Practice; Former Staff Neurosurgeon, Scott and White Clinic, Temple, Texas; Assistant Professor of Neurosurgery, University of Texas Southwestern Medical School, Dallas. Organizational Memberships: Congress of Neurological Surgeons; American Association of Neurosurgeons; Society of Military Surgeons; American College of Angiology; American Geriatrics Society. Community Activities: Chairman of Neuroscience Section, St. Paul Hospital, 1980-81; American Heart Association Stroke Council, 1978 to present; Dallas Neuroscience Foundation (board member, 1980 to present); Dallas Epilepsy Association, 1977 to present; Dallas Symphony Orchestra Guild, 1979-80; Course Director of Laser Neurosurgery Workshops in Dallas, Quarterly, 1980 to present; Developed Computer Program for Diagnosis of Back Pain, Appeared on Panel to Discuss "Artificial Intelligence", National Computer Conference, 1981. Religion: Ordained Deacon, Baptist Church, 1973. Published Works: Editor, *Clinical Neurosurgery*, 1973; Author of 27 Articles in Medical Journals. Honors and Awards: Dean's Scholarship, University of Mississippi School of Medicine, 1960; Alpha Omega Alpha Medical Scholarship Society, 1964; Vietnamese Cross of Gallantry with Bronze Star, 1970; Diplomate, American Board of Neurological Surgery, 1972. Address: 5111 Park Lane, Dallas, Texas 75220.

Hudson, Edward V

Businessman. Personal: Born April 3, 1915, Seymour, Missouri; Son of Marion and Alma Hudson (both deceased); Married Margaret Greely, December 24, 1939; Father of Carolyn K., Edward G. Education: Graduate of Harmony High School, Salutatorian, 1932; Attended Bellingham Normal College, 1933-36; Studies in Electrical Engineering, University of Washington, 1934-38. Career: Owner and Operator of Milk Route, 1933-36; Meter Tester, Puget Sound Power and Light Company, 1937; Assistant to the Manager, Natural Hard Metal Company, Bellingham, 1935-37; Partner, Metropolitan Laundry, Tacoma, 1938-39; Owner, Manager, Peerless Laundry and Linen Supply, 1939 to present; Partner, Tacoma Electric Company, 1942-44; Owner, Independent Laundry and Everett Linen Supply, 1946-74; Owner, 99 Cleaners and Launderers since 1957. Organizational Memberships: Tacoma Sales and Marketing Executives (president, 1957-58); Pacific Northwest Laundry, Dry Cleaning and Linen Supply Association (president, 1959; treasurer); International Fabricare Institute (director, district #7; treasurer, 1979; president, 1981); Northwest Laundry and Dry Cleaning Health and Welfare Trust (trustee). Community Activities: Tacoma Public Utilities, 1959-60; Small Business Administration (advisory board, 1960); Tacoma-Pierce County U.G.N. (president, 1962; campaign manager, 1965); Tacoma Knife and Fork Club (president, 1964); Tacoma Chamber of Commerce (president, 1965); Rotary Club of Tacoma (president, 1967-68); Puget Sound Industrial Development Council (chairman, 1967); Tacoma Boy's Club (president, 1970); Tacoma-Pierce County U.S.O. (president, 1970); Tacoma-Fort Lewis-Olympia Chapter, A.U.S.A. (president, 1970-71); Active Club of Tacoma (secretary, 1939); Washington Conference on Unemployment Compensation (president, 1975-76); Tacoma Chapter, Air Force Association (president, 1976-77);

Puget Sound Area U.S.O. (vice president); United Mutual Savings Bank (trustee); Tacoma Better Business Bureau (board member); Afifi Shrine Temple (Divan member); Masonic Lodge; Scottish Rite; York Rite; Afifi Shrine (potentate); Elks; Navy League, Air Force Association; A.U.S.A.; Tacoma Club; Tacoma Country and Golf Club; Tacoma Chamber of Commerce; American Security Council (board member); Republican. Religion: Emmanuel Presbyterian Church, 1974 to present. Honors and Awards: Distinguished Citizens Certificate, United States Air Force Military Airlift Command, 1977; United States Department of Defense Medal for Outstanding Public Service, 1978. Address: 3901 North 37th Street, Tacoma, Washington 98407.

Hudson, Grace Powers

Free-lance Writer, Editor. Personal: Born July 9; Daughter of Mr. and Mrs. James E. Powers (both deceased); Married Print Hudson. Education: A.B., Union University, Jackson, Tennessee, 1923; M.S., Iowa State University, Ames, 1928; Diploma in Violin, Union University, 1924; Advanced Studies in Violin, Athens, Greece; Graduate Studies, University of Tennessee-Knoxville, Iowa State University; Art Courses, Corcoran Art School. Career: Free-lance Writer; Editor, Goodwill Guild Newsletter; Currently Exhibiting Paintings in Washington, D.C., Jackson, Tennessee, Nutley, New Jersey; Dean, Home Economics, Union University; Teacher Trainer, Iowa State University; Ball State Teachers College; Lecturer, George Washington University; Specialist in Plant and Equipment for Home Economics, United States Department of Interior; Assistant in Home Economics and Family Relations, American Home Economics Association; Head, Department of Art, Union University. Organizational Memberships: American Home Economics Association (past president; state chairman, Tennessee, Iowa); American Newspaper Women's Club (board of governors, 1978-79, 1980-82); American Opera Scholarship Society (president, 1973-79); National Press Club, Washington, D.C.; National League of American Pen Women (vice president, D.C. branch; national corresponding secretary, 1976-78; national 3rd vice president, 1978-80; national 2nd vice president, 1980-82). Community Activities: National Symphony Orchestra Women's Committee; Wolftrap Farm Association Women's Committee; Association of American Foreign Service Women (chairman of various committees); Goodwill Guild (board member, editor of newsletter); American Cancer Society; Hellenic-American Club (one of three American women chosen by Greek women's committee to be founding member, 1953-57); Foreign Friends of the Creche, Athens, Greece (founder; life president, 1954 to present); Y.W.C.A., Washington, D.C. (governing board; membership chairman, 1958-62); Washington Club (governing board; chairman, international, membership, Tuesday educational lecture programs, 1972-75); Capital Speakers Club (president, chapter I, 1972-73; governing board; club president, 1978); Upsilon Chapter, Chi Omega (president, charter member); Honorary Member of Several Welfare Boards in Athens, Greece, 1953-55; Tennessee State Society in Washington; Iowa State Society in Washington, Iowa State University Society in Washington; Wesley Heights-Spring Valley Garden Club; Wesley Heights-Spring Valley Art Club; Wesley Heights-Spring Valley Book Club; First Families of Virginia; National Society of Colonial Dames in America, Commonwealth of Virginia; Jamestown Society; National Society of Daughters of the American Revolution; United Daughters of the Confederacy. Religion: Metropolitan Memorial Methodist Church, 1977-81. Published Works: Revised Textbook for High School Teachers on Family Relations; Originated and Edited Quarterly Prospectus on Research in Home Economics and Related Fields; Editor/Writer, *Leaves* Magazine, 1972-77. Honors and Awards: Emily Gates National Award for Outstanding Leadership (first winner), Tri-Sigma Sorority, 1938; Award for Unselfish Service in the United States and Abroad, Union University, 1957; Citation for Services to the Y, Y.W.C.A., Washington, D.C.; Citation from National Board of Children's Shelters, Athens, Greece, 1957; Distinguished Achievement Citation as Educator, Humanitarian, Artist, Iowa State University, 1978; Building at Union University Named after Her, 1976; National League of American Pen Women, First Prize Non-Fiction 1975, First Prize Water Colors 1977, Branch Award of Merit in Watercolors (state competition) 1979, National Award in Public Relations/Publicity, "Goodwill Guild Embassy Tour Book" 1978; Listed in *Who's Who of American Women, World Who's Who of Women, Community Leaders and Noteworthy Americans, Hereditary Register of the United States, Who's Who in the East, International Men and Women of Distinction, Southern Artists Directory* (unpublished), *National Society Directory of New York, The Green Book* (Social Listing of Washington, D.C.), *The Blue Book* (Social Listing of Washington, D.C., and Maryland). Address: 5165 Rockwood Parkway, N.W., Washington, D.C. 20016.

Grace P Hudson

Huebschman, Eugene Carl

College President. Personal: Born October 31, 1919, in Evanston, Indiana; Married Edna Arldt; Father of Donald, Mike, Ruth, Jo Anna. Education: B.S, Philosophy, Concordia Teachers College, Illinois, 1941; M.S., Physical Chemistry, Purdue University, 1946; Ph.D., Theoretical Physics, University of Texas, 1957. Career: President, Nathaniel Hawthorne College, Antrim, New Hampshire; Professor of Electrical Engineering, University of Tennessee; Previous Positions include Coach, Football, River Forest College; Science Professor 10 years, Head of Science Department and Athletic Director, Concordia College, Austin, Texas; Air Force Missile Development Center, Holloman Air Force Base, New Mexico; Technical Advisor to the Guidance Division, Wright Field, Dayton, Ohio; Has Made 20+ Patent Proposals in Inertial Guidance; Teacher, Purdue University 1942-44, University of Texas 1946-54, University of New Mexico 1956-58, Sinclair College 1958-59, San Diego State University 1960, University of California 1961, University of Tennessee 1965-71; Chairman, Brevard Engineering College's Graduate Physics Department. Organizational Memberships: American Physical Society; Institute of Electrical and Electronic Engineers; American Institute of Aeronautics and Astronautics; Sigma Pi Sigma; Gamma Delta; Beta Sigma Psi; Southwest Basketball Officials Association; Southwest Football Officials Association. Community Activities: American Cancer Society (educational committee); Boy Scouts of America (board member); University of Tennessee Senate; Southwest Academic League (president); Oceanography and Pollution Corporation (board member, founder); Comtel, Advanced Research, Computer Science and Mineiva Electronics (board member); International Platform Association. Religion: Christ Lutheran Church. Honors and Awards: Certificate of Accomplishment, Air Research and Development Command, Conferring upon him the Honorary Title of Outstanding Inventor; Solicited by Library of Congress to serve as Physical Science Advisor to Congress; Fellow, Explorer's Club, 1979; Listed in *International Scholars Directory, Silver Wings Fraternity, Creative and Successful Personalities, Dictionary of International Biography, International Register of Profiles.* Address: Nathaniel Hawthorne College, Antrim, New Hampshire 03440.

Cherry I Huff

Huff, Cherry Irby

Retired. Personal: Born March 23, 1924; Daughter of Raymond Guerry and Lila Sue Godwin Irby (both deceased); Married William Beausegneiur Huff; Mother of William Godwin. Education: Graduate of Eufaula High School, 1944; Studies in Journalism, Columbia University, 1947-48; Studies in Spanish, City College of New York, 1950; Medical Technology Course, 1971; Medical Assistants Course, 1972. Career: Advertising, New York City; Medical Secretary and Assistant, 18 years; Now Retired. Organizational Memberships: American Business Women's Association (vice president, 1966); Bethania Hospital Auxiliary (volunteer coordinator, 2½ years; 1st vice president, 2 years). Community Activities: American Cancer Society (lay director, 1979-80; lay director-at-large, 1980-82; vice president; secretary; local and district public education chairman; state board of directors); Helping Smokers Quit State Committee, 1977-82; Employee Education Chairman, 1981-82; Special Olympics Executive Committee, 1974-78; Teens Aid the Retarded (advisor, 1975-78); Wichita County Association of Retarded Citizens (secretary, 1975-76); Denton State School Parents

Group (executive committee, 1981-82); Parents of Retarded in State Schools. Religion: Baptist. Honors and Awards: Woman of the Year, American Business Women's Association, 1968-69; Volunteer of the Year, American Cancer Society, 1976; Outstanding Member of the Year, Wichita County Association of Retarded Citizens, 1976. Address: Route 1 Box 100, Eufaula, Alabama 36027.

Huff, Norman Nelson

Computer Consultant, Educator. Personal: Born April 22, 1933; Son of George Peabody Huff and Norma Rose Demetz; Married to Sharon Kay Lockwood. Education: B.S., San Diego State University, 1957; A.A., Victor Valley College, 1971; Attended University of California at Los Angeles; M.B.A., Golden Gate University, 1972. Career: Professor and Chairman of Computer Science and Information Science. Religion: Attends Catholic Church. Honors and Awards: Listed in *Notable Americans*. Address: 16746 Sunset Drive, Victorville, California 92392.

Norman N Huff

Hug, Richard Ernest

Executive. Personal: Born January 11, 1935; Son of Gustave T Hug; Married Lois-Ann Schack; Father of Donald R., Cynthia A. Education: B.S., 1956, and M.F., 1957, both from Duke University. Career: Manager, Product Development, Koppers Company, Inc., 1970-72; General Manager, Laminated Products, Koppers Company, Inc., 1972-73; President, Environmental Elements Corporation, 1973 to present; Vice President, Koppers Company, Inc., 1973 to present. Organizational Memberships: Forest Products Research Society, 1955 to present; American Wood Preservers Association, 1957 to present; Industrial Gas Cleaning Institute, 1973 to present (board of directors 1980 to present). Community Activities: Greater Baltimore Committee (board of directors 1978); Economic Development Council, 1978 to present; Blue Cross of Maryland (secretary 1981, board of directors 1973 to present); Boy Scouts of America (Baltimore council executive board 1976 to present); United Way of Central Maryland (board of directors and executive committee 1978 to present, general campaign chairman 1979); Loyola College (board of trustees and executive committee 1979 to present); Independent College Fund of Maryland (board of trustees 1979 to present); National Aquarium of Baltimore (board of directors 1976 to present); John F. Kennedy Institute (board of directors and first vice president 1979 to present); Religion: Presbyterian. Honors and Awards: Chairman, Young Presidents Organization, 1980; Man of the Year, Laminated Structures Department, 1970; Chairman, Baltimore Colt Touchdowners, 1980 to present. Address: 247 Oak Court, Severna Park, Maryland 21146.

Richard E Hug

Huggins, Cannie Mae

Corporation Executive. Personal: Born July 16, 1916; Daughter of Jesse D. and Mary Alice Cox; Married Bertrand E. Huggins; Mother of Darline Hunter Gamble, Bob Roy Hunter. Education: B.S., Mary Hardin Baylor University, 1940; M.A., San Marcos State University, 1942; Graduate Studies at the University of Texas, Baylor University, University of Arizona, University of San Diego, St. Mary's University of San Antonio, Texas Tech University, Stephen F. Austin University. Career: Bilingual First Grade Education Classroom Teacher, 1935-41; Staff Testing Department, University of Arizona, 1941-43; Reading Consultant, Phoenix, Arizona, 1943-45; Junior High School Science Department, Killeen, Texas, 1946-54; Counselor, Westernlife Girls Camp, New Mexico, Summers 1956-60; Assistant Tour Director of Europe and the Greek Islands, 1964-65; Vice President, Killeen Housing Corps, 1954-74; President, C.M.C. Corporation, Killeen, Texas, 1974 to present. Organizational Memberships: Texas State Teachers Association; National Association for Supervision and Curriculum Development; International Platform Association; Association for Child Education International; National Association for Bilingual Education; American Association of University Women. Community Activities: Lubbock County American Red Cross (first aid chairman, 1964-65); Life Line International; American Business Women's Association; March of Dimes (group chairman); Contact Teleministries International. Religion: First Baptist Church, Youth Division 1960 to present, Co-Director of 12th Grade Department, Outreach Leader, Youth Council, Teacher. Honors and Awards: Texas Certified Public Educator Award, 1972; Life Line International Certificate of Award, 1973; American Red Cross Outstanding Service Award, 1966; Contact Teleministry International Bronze Honor Roll, 1976; Listed in *Who's Who of American Women, Personalities of the South, World Who's Who of Women, Community Leaders of America, Directory of Distinguished Americans*. Address: 4626 30th Street, Lubbock, Texas 79410.

Hughes, Inez Hatley

Teacher. Personal: Born January 29, 1903; Daughter of Tapley Bynum and Daisy McPherson Hatley (both deceased); Married Solon Greene Hughes (deceased), in 1939. Education: A.A., College of Marshall, 1921; B.A., Baylor University, 1924; M.A., University of Texas-Austin, 1936; Summer Sessions at Oxford University, Cambridge University, Harvard University, Columbia University, University of Madrid, Spain; Attended the Greek Heritage Symposium, Athens, Greece, 1964. Career: Teacher, Grades 1-8, Terlingua, Texas, 1921-23; Teacher of English, Karnes City (Texas) High School 1924-27, Marshall (Texas) High School 1927-64, College of Marshall (Summer) 1933, Sul Ross State College (Summer) 1938. Community Activities: Harrison County Historical Society (first vice president, 1964-66; 2nd vice president, 1967 to present); Harrison County Historical Commission; Texas State Historical Association; Society of Southwest Archivists; Texas Association of Museums; Texas State Genealogical Society; National Genealogical Society; Museum Volunteer, 1965 to present; Alpha Zeta Chapter, Delta Kappa Gamma (charter member, first president) Marshall Cultural Affairs Council (board member; charter member, 1981); Marshall American Association of University Women (secretary); Marshall Teacher's Club (secretary). Honors and Awards: Business and Professional Women "Woman of Achievement", 1974; One of 25 Senior Citizens Chosen for *The Texas Sampler* 224 Page Book, Bicentennial Project, Governor's Committee on Aging, 1976; One of 20 Chosen for Winedale Fun Seminar for Museum Personnel; Inez Hatley Hughes Scholarship Established 1977; Inez Hatley Hughes Research Center in Harrison County Historical Museum, 1981. Address: P.O. Box 23, Marshall, Texas, 75670.

Inez Hughes

Hunt, Edward Hatcher

County Extension Director. Personal: Born March 5, 1923; Son of Mr. and Mrs. James Daniel Hunt; Married Daisy Adele Broadhurst; Father of Susan Elizabeth, Jane Marie, John Edward. Education: Graduate of Harlem High School, Harlem, Georgia, 1941; B.S.A. 1949, M.S.A. 1950, University of Georgia; Summer Study, University of Arkansas, 1956. Military: Served in the United States Army, 1943-45, as a Corporal Technician 5th Grade. Career: Newton County Extension Director; Teaching Assistantship, University of Georgia, 1949-50; Staff Member, Berry College, Mt. Berry, Georgia; Assistant County Agent, Polk County, Cedartown, Georgia; Assistant County Agent, Meriwether County, Greenville, Georgia. Organizational Memberships: Georgia Master 4-H Club (director, 1972-78); ETERNA Club, University of Georgia (charter member); Piedmont Cattlemen's Association;

Georgia Cattlemen's Association; Georgia Association of County Agricultural Agents (director, 1961-63); National Association of County Agricultural Agents; Epsilon Sigma Phi, Alpha Beta Chapter (president, 1980-81); Georgia Association of Extension 4-H Agents; National Association of Extension 4-H Agents; Atlanta Farmers Club; Atlanta Metro Agribusiness Council; Newton County, Georgia, Farm Bureau; National Farm Bureau; Georgia Agribusiness Council; Georgia Agricultural Alumni Association; University of Georgia Alumni Association; Newton County Dairy Association. Community Activities: Kiwanis Club of Covington, Georgia (board of directors, 9 terms; distinguished president, 1974-75; 12th division lieutenant governor, 1976-77; district chairman of administration, 1977-78; district chairman of youth services, 1978-79; district chairman inter-club, 1979-80; district chairman of public relations, 1980-81; district chairman of finance and fund raising, 1981-82; district chairman of public relations, 1982-83; life membership, Kiwanis International; 24 years perfect attendance; trustee, Georgia Kiwanis Foundation, 1976-79); American Legion Post 32, Covington; Harlem American Legion Post (charter member, 1946); Veterans of Foreign Wars Post #2933; Cousins School Band Parents (president, 1978-79): National Association of Retired Federal Employees Chapter 1829. Religion: First Baptist Church, Athens, Georgia, 1948-50; First Baptist Church, Rome, Georgia; Mt. Lavender Baptist Church, Mt. Berry, Georgia, 1951-53; West Rome Baptist Church, 1953-55; First Baptist Church, Cedartown, Georgia, 1955-56; First Baptist Church, Warm Springs, 1956-58; First Baptist Church, Covington, Georgia, Member 1958 to present, Deacon, Training Union Director 1964-66, Sunday School Teacher 16 years. Honors and Awards: Named a Master 4-H'er, 1971; Distinguished Service Award, Georgia Association and National Association of County Agricultural Agents, 1961; Farmers Club Atlanta Metro Agribusiness Council Outstanding Government Employee Award, 1976; Distinguished Service to National 4-H Agents Association, 1981; State Distinguished Service Award, Epsilon Sigma Phi, 1980; Distinguished Service Award, Newton County Agriculture, 1981; District Award in Leadership, Georgia Agribusiness Development, 1981; 25 Year Service Award to 4-H, 1978; County Agent of the Year, Commercial Cattleman in County, 1980; Joint Man of the Year Award, Georgia Association of County Commissioners, 1970; Life Member, Kiwanis International, 1977; U.S.D.A. Service Award, 5, 10, 15, 20, 25 Years; District Award for Outstanding Leadership in Agribusiness Development 1982, Georgia Agribusiness Council, Georgia Power Company, and Georgia Cooperative Extension Service; 25 Years Professional Assistance Award, Upper Ocmulgee River Soil and Water Conservation District, 1982. Address: P.O. Box 68, Covington, Georgia 30209.

Edward H Hunt

Hunt, Gordon

Attorney. Personal: Born October 26, 1934, in Los Angeles, California; Son of Howard Wilson and Esther Nita Dempsey Hunt; Married Marie Ann Agosta, June 21, 1958; Father of Marianne, Stephanie. Education: B.A., University of California-Los Angeles, 1956; J.D., University of Southern California, 1959. Career: Admitted to California Bar, 1960; Law Clerk, Appellate Department, Superior Court of Los Angeles County, 1959-60; Member, Firm of Behymer and Hoffman, Los Angeles, 1960-65; Partner, Firm of Behymer, Hoffman and Hunt, Los Angeles, 1965-68; Partner, Munns, Kofford, Hoffman, Hunt and Throckmorton, Pasadena, 1969 to present; Lecturer, Author, University of California, Los Angeles, 1971, 1977, 1980, 1981; Consultant to Real Property Subcommittee of Joint Advisory Committee for Continuing Education of the Bar, 1977 to present; Arbitrator for Los Angeles Superior Court, American Arbitration Association, California State Construction Arbitration Panel. Organizational Memberships: American Bar Association; California Bar Association (convention delegate, 1964-69; executive committee, real property section, 1979-80); Los Angeles County Bar Association (executive committee, real property section, 1970-72; secretary, 1972-73; vice chairman, 1973-76; chairman, 1976-77); American Arbitration Association. Community Activities: Republican. Religion: Methodist. Published Works: *California Construction Law Handbook*, 1981-82; Contributor of Articles to Legal Journals. Honors and Awards: Listed in *Who's Who in America, Who's Who in American Law, Who's Who in the World, Who's Who in the West, Who's Who in California*. Address: 199 North Lake Avenue, Suite 300, Pasadena, California 91101.

Huraj, Helen I

Social Worker. Personal: Born July 13, 1926. Education: B.A., Concordia University, Montreal, Canada, 1956; M.S.W., Smith College, Northampton, Massachusetts, 1966. Career: Social Worker; Lecturer. Organizational Memberships: Academy of Certified Social Workers; National Association of Social Workers; Ontario Association of Social Workers; La Corp. Professionnelle des Travailleurs Sociaux du Quebec (editorial board of intervention, 1968; board of examiners, 1968-75; admissions committee, 1967-70); American Association for Marriage and Family Therapy; New York State Chapter, National Association of Social Workers; Dawson College Advisory Board, 1967; Family Foster Home Association, 1967-69. Community Activities: Montreal Boys Club (charter and life member); Buena Vista on the Rideau (life member; past president); United Way (representative); Ministerial Association of the Province of Quebec (provincial representative); Park Extension Recreation Association (president); Mental Health Association of Brockville (president); Mental Health/Ontario (vice president); Mental Health/Canada (provincial representative); Mental Health/Elgin (president); Jaycees (outstanding citizen award chairman). Honors and Awards: Venerable Order of the Hos of St. John of Jerusalem, The Priory in Canada; Order of Canada Medal, 1974; Queens Silver Jubilee Medal, 1978; Mental Health/Elgin Plaque for Outstanding and Selfless Service, 1977; Certificates of Appreciation, St. Thomas Jaycees, 1976; Special Award, City of St. Thomas, 1979; Lifestyle Award, 1982 (a most distinguished award). Address: 55 Bailey Avenue, St. Thomas, Ontario, Canada N5R 4Z8.

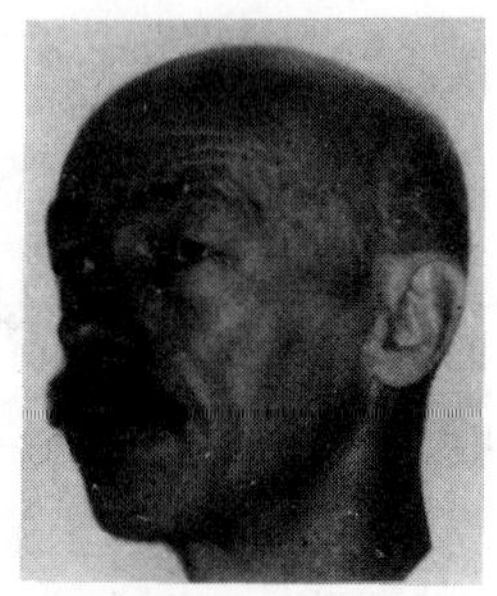

Harvey D Hurtt

Hurt, Allie Teague

Real Estate Executive. Personal: Daughter of Lucious and Mary L. Teague (both deceased); Married Charles E. Hurt (deceased); Mother of Eric Charles, Gregory Bernard, James E. Taylor, Daniel McLane Jr., Gwendolyn McLane, Winfred R. McLane. Education: B.S., Bishop College, 1973; Completed the Requirements in the Real Estate Program, El Centro Community College, 1969; Post Graduate Studies, North Texas State University, 1973-74, and at Cedar Valley College, 1979. Career: Secretary, Excelsior Life Insurance Company, 1957-59; Manager, Pruitt Insurance Agency, 1959-62; Society Editor at Dallas, Home Office in Houston, Texas, 1962-66; Sales Associate, H. J. Watts and John W. Giddings Real Estate Company, 1967-77; Teaching, Dallas Independent School District, 1973-74; Real Estate Executive. Organizational Memberships: Real Estate Realtist Association, 1980-82. Community Activities: American Cancer Society; Texas March of Dimes; American Lung Association. Religion: Good Street Baptist Church, Usher 1945-52. Honors and Awards: Certificates of Recognition, Iota Phi Lambda, Eta Phi Beta (Epsilon Chapter); Listed in *Who's Who in the South and Southwest, Who's Who in Finance and Industry, Golden Profiles of the Dallas/Fort Worth Area*. Address: 5324 Mystic Trail, Dallas, Texas 75241.

Hurtt, Harvey Duane

Educator. Personal: Born January 5, 1928; Son of Robert Filewood Hurtt and Mamie Alfield Huset (deceased); Married Beverly Hurtt (deceased); Father of John Henry, Conrad Marlow. Education: B.A., The New School for Social Research; Undertook graduate studies: University of Washington, University of California, Columbia University Teachers College, Walden University (doctoral fellow); M.A., San Francisco State University. Career: Publisher, Century 21 Publications; Editor, *Firland Magazine*; Publisher, *Ancient Coins*; Editor, *Civil Liberties in Washington State*; Publisher, Society of Spanish Studies; Photographer, *America's Many Faces*; Editor, *University of Washington Magazine*. Organizational Memberships: Montana Association for Community Education (founding member, board of directors and chairman, membership committee); Montana School Administrators Association; Montana Association for Environmental Education.

Husting, Edward Lee

Professor, Epidemiologist. Personal: Born February 25, 1939, in Madison, Wisconsin; Son of Frank and Margaret Husting (both deceased); Father of Sheila Renee, Ian Aims, Mark Andrew. Education: B.S., Zoology, University of Michigan, 1963; Ph.D., The Epidemiology of Bilharziasis (Schistosomiasis), University of London, England, 1968; M.P.H., University of Pittsburgh, 1970. Career: Research Assistant, Department of Zoology, University of Michigan, 1960-63; Fishery Aide, United States Bureau of Commercial Fisheries, Ann Arbor, Michigan, 1963-64; Research Fellow, University College of Rhodesia, Salisburg, Rhodesia, Africa, 1964-66; Consultant, Cornell Medical School, New York Hospital, New York City, 1967; Research Fellow, Bureau of Biological Research, Rutgers - The State University of New Jersey, 1967-68; Professional Officer, Mininstry of Health, Rhodesia, 1968-69; Senior Science Instructor, Chisipite School, Rhodesia, 1969; Postdoctoral Trainee, Department of Epidemiology, Graduate School of Public Health, University of Pittsburgh, 1969-70; Professional Fellowship in Tropical Medicine, Louisiana State University Medical Center, 1970; Postdoctoral Trainee, Department of Public Health Practice, Graduate School of Public Health, University of Pittsburgh, 1970; Visiting Lecturer, Department of Social and Preventive Medicine, University of West Indies, and Consultant to Jamaica National Family Planning Board, Kingston, Jamaica, 1970-72; Assistant Research Professor, Maternal and Child Health 1972-73, Epidemiology/Population 1970-72, Graduate School of Public Health, The University of Pittsburgh; Director, Health and Environmental Studies, Associate Director, Occupational Health Research, Equitable Environmental Health, Inc., Berkeley, California, 1973-75; Professor and Director, Health Science Program, California State University, Hayward, California, 1975-76; Manager, Health and Safety Programs, Flow Resources Corporation, San Rafael, California, 1976-78; Consultant and Associate on Occupational and Environmental Health Projects, 1975-81; Lecturer, Adjunct Professor, Health Sciences Program, California State University-Hayward, 1973-81; Professor and Epidemiologist, Department of Comprehensive Medicine, University of South Florida, 1981 to present. Organizational Memberships: Royal Society of Tropical Medicine and Hygiene (fellow); American Industrial Hygiene Association (full, national); American Public Health Association; Association of Teachers of Preventive Medicine; International Epidemiological Association; Pan American Medical Association; Society of Epidemiological Research; World Safety Organization. Published Works: Number of Professional Articles including "Macdonald's model for Transmission of schistosomiasis - availability of data", "Human water contact activities related to the transmission of bilharziasis", and "University of Pittsburgh -Studies in Adolescent Pregnancy"; Author/Co-Author Several Chapters in Books, Technical Reports, Other Publications. Honors and Awards: United States Public Health Service Traineeship, 1970; Professional Fellowship in Tropical Medicine, Louisiana State University International Center for Medical Research and Training, 1970; Rockefeller Foundation Fellowships, 1964-68; Listed in *Who's Who in Health Care, Who's Who in the West, Personalities of the West and Midwest, Book of Honor, International Who's Who in Community Service, Dictionary of International Biography, Men of Achievement*. Address: P.O. Box 290002, Temple Terrace, Florida 33687.

Ira K Hutchinson

Hutchinson, Ira Kamahalo

Certified Review Appraiser. Personal: Born September 7, 1911; Son of Edson L. and Lani Wong Kong Hutchinson (deceased); Married Gwendolyn L.; Father of Edson B., Darlene L., Lisa L. Education: Graduate of the Military School for Boys (Kamehameha School), 1932. Military: Served in the Armed Forces during World War II. Career: Certified Review Appraiser; Appointed Land Consultant to the Office of Hawaiian Affairs; Elected Sub-District #4 Representative, Neighborhood Zone; Land Consultant to Hawaiian Homes Commission and B.P. Bishop Trust Estate; Registered Land and Land Court Surveyor; Professional Property Appraiser. Organizational Memberships: American Congress on Surveying and Mapping (fellow; first president, Honolulu chapter, 1940); American R/W Association (established Honolulu chapter in 1943); American Society of Appraisers (fellow; charter member, Honolulu chapter; regional governor for area #14, Pacific Basin area); National Society of Review Appraisers; American Institute of Real Estate Appraisers; Society of Real Estate Appraisers. Community Activities: National Security Council; International Platform Association (panel member); Smithsonian Institution (panel member); President and Governor's Land Use Committee; Civil Defense Agency; Kapalama Industrial Development Company (manager, 1960); Department of Land and National Resources (chief appraiser, 1968-76); Land Surveys for Territorial Transportation Department, 1947-53, 1963-68; Research for Hawaii Irrigation Authority, Hawaii Water Authority and Hawaii Water and Land Development, Divison of Department of Land and Natural Resources. Religion: Protestant, Member of St. Andrews Church. Honors and Awards: Senior Designations and Certificates of Achievement; Listed in *Who's Who in the West and Midwest, Men of Achievement, Notable Americans*. Address: 993 Waiholo Street, Honolulu, Hawaii 96821.

Hutto, Earl

Congressman. Personal: Born May 12, 1926, in Midland City, Alabama; Married Nancy Myers; Father of Lori Keeffe, Amelia Ann. Education: Graduate of Dale County High School, Ozark, Alabama; B.S., Troy State University; Graduate Studies in Broadcasting, Northwestern University. Military: Served in the United States Navy. Career: Former Owner and President, Earl Hutto Advertising Agency; Founder and Former President, WPEX-FM, Pensacola, Florida; Former Sports Director, WEAR-TV, Pensacola (Florida), WSFA-TV, Montgomery (Alabama), WJHG-TV, Panama City (Florida); Elected to Florida House of Representatives, 1972, Reelected 1974, 1976, Served on Governmental Operations Committee, Education Committee (Chairman, Post-Secondary Education Subcommittee), Select Committee on Paperwork Reduction; Elected to 96th Congress, November 7, 1978, Reelected to 97th Congress, November 4, 1980, Serves on Armed Services Committee, Merchant Marine and Fisheries Committee. Community Activities: Panama City Civitan Club (past deputy governor); Alabama-West Florida Distrist, Civitan International; Mary Mackin School for Retarded Children (advisory council); Girl Scout Council of Apalachee Bend (board of directors); Florida Easter Seal Society; United Way Campaign (chairman, state government division, 1976, 1977); Troy State Alumni Association; Gulf Coast Council, Boy Scouts of America (executive board); Haney Vocational-Technical Center (advisory committee); Christian Business Men's Committee of the United States. Honors and Awards: State Leadership Award, Sunshine State Association for the Blind, 1973; Legislator of the Year, Florida Association for Retarded Children, 1974; Woodmen of the World Conservation Award, 1974; Conservationist of the Year, Bay County Audubon Society, 1975; Legislative Award, Florida Association of Community Colleges, 1978; National Associated Businessmen's Watchdog of the Treasury Award, 1979-80; Alumnus of the Year Award, Business and Government, Troy State University, 1980. Address: Panama City, Florida 32401.

Ibranyi, Francis Joseph

Professor and Chaplain. Personal: Born April 30, 1901; Son of Francis Ibranyi and Emilia Pacsesz (both deceased). Education: B.A., Piarists' College, Budapest, Hungary, 1919; S.T.D., University of Pazmany Peter, Budapest, Hungary, 1925; Ph.D., University of Angelicum, Department of Philosophy, Rome, Italy, 1929; Summer Course in Modern French Literature, University of Lausanne, Switzerland. Career: Professor and Chaplain to the Convent and Conference, Guidance Counselor; Professor of Philosophy and Comparative Religion, Mount St. Joseph College, Wakefield, Rhode Island, 1970-76; Visiting Professor, School of Theology, Pontifical College "Josephinum", Columbus, Ohio, 1967-70; Professor of Metaphysics and History of Philosophy, Ursulines' College, Quebec, 1956-67; Full Professor of Ethic, Laval University, Quebec, 1950-70; University of Pazmany Peter, Budapest, Full Professor 1939-49, Dean of the Department 1946-48, Member of University Senate 1946-48. Organizational Memberships: Thomas Aquinas Society, Budapest (secretary); St. Stephen Academy of Sciences, Budapest; Hungarian Academy "Scientiis et Artibus", Rome, Italy; Ohio Theological Colloquium; Central Ohio Academy of Theology. Community Activities: Sessions of the Catholic Council of International Relations (Hungarian delegate, Dublin 1937, the Hague 1938); Sheltered Around 150 People during Siege of Budapest (shelter commandant, 1945); Council of Christians and Jews (Hungarian Catholic Ep-iscopacy representative); Goethe Club, Quebec, Canada; International Institute of Rhode Island, Providence. Religion: Ecclesiastical Tribunal, Esztergom Hungary, Judge, 1930-39; Conducts Ecuminical Meetings and Religious Celebrations in Hungary, Austria, Quebec, Columbus (Ohio). Honors and Awards: Doctor Collegiatus, University of Budapest, 1933; Papal Chamberlain (Holy See), 1945; Papal Domestic Prelate, 1970; Fellow, American Biographical Institute, 1977. Address: Mount St. Joseph Convent, Box 32, Wakefield, Rhode Island 02880.

Ilvento, Barbara Kautz

Company Executive. Personal: Born September 6, 1941; Daughter of Palmy Kautz; Mother of Lauren, Charles II. Education: B.A., Florida International University, Miami, Florida; M.Ed., University of Miami. Career: Vice-President of Sales, Bengis Associates, Inc.; Vice-President, International Research Institute of America; Owner/Operator, Appleby's Eatery; Office Manager, Penta and Ilvento, C.P.A.'s; Executive Secretary, Beech-Nut Life Savers Inc.; Medical Assistant, L. Melvin Elting Diagnostic Center, Allen B. Kendall M.D. F.A.C.S. Organizational Memberships: Monmouth County Medical Assistants Association (founder; charter member, 1962-68; president); New Jersey Medical Assistants Association (chairperson, state convention, 1964); Mental Health Task Force on Child Abuse (assistant to chairman, 1975). Community Activities: Progress Club of Miami, Florida (member, 1978-81; first woman board member, 1979); South Dade Chamber of Commerce (board of directors; chairperson, membership committee). Honors and Awards: Psi Chi Psychology National Honor Society; Charter Member, Certificate of Distinction, Psychology Department, Florida International University. Address: 16923 Southwest 87th Avenue, Miami, Florida 33157.

June K Inglima

Ingels, Marty

Celebrity Broker. Personal: Born March 9, 1936; Son of Jack and Minnie Ingerman; Married Shirley Jones; Stepfather of David Cassidy, Shaun Cassidy, Patrick Cassidy, Ryan Cassidy. Education: P.S. 167, Brooklyn, New York; Graduate of Erasmus Hall High School, Brooklyn, New York; Forest Hills High School, Forest Hills, New York. Military: Served in the United States Army as a member of the Infantry Division of Special Services to the Rank of Sergeant. Career: World's Largest Celebrity Broker, Packaging Celebrity Events Internationally; Motion Picture and Television Producer; Comedian. Community Activities: Youth Drug Abuse Campaign (national chairman); Leukemia Foundation (national chairman); Association for National Sanity Again (national chairman). Honors and Awards: Meritorious Community Service Citations, United States Congress, Los Angeles City Council, American Jewish Congress, Muscular Dystrophy Association, Boy Scouts of America, United States Anti-Defamation League. Address: 8322 Beverly Boulevard, Hollywood, California 90048.

Inglima, June King

Regional Training Director. Personal: Born November 27, 1925; Daughter of Gladys P. Ayers; Married John N. Inglima (deceased); Mother of Michael. Education: Received a Degree in Voice, Juilliard School of Music, 1948; B.M.E., Mt. Union College, 1958; M.A., Kent State University, 1962; Certificate in Business. Career: Singer on Broadway and Model in New York City, 1948 53; English Teacher, Lakewood High School, Lakewood, Ohio, 1962-65; Consultant and Program Director in U.S. Government, 1965-68; Director of Sales Training and Communication, Society for Savings, Hartford, Connecticut, 1968-69; Senior Training Specialist, Citibank, New York City, 1969-71; Senior Training Specialist, Royal-Globe Insurance Co., New York City, 1971-74; Regional Training Director, U.S. Customs Service, Los Angeles, California, 1974 to present; Visiting Professor, University of Southern California. Organizational Memberships: National Society of Arts and Letters (corresponding secretary, music chairperson); Ebell of Los Angeles; Adrians of Ebell (newsletter writer, 1978-81); A.S.T.D.; A.M.A.; Wilshire Business and Professional Women's League; National Association for Female Executives; Phi Beta Kappa; National Organization of Women; American Society of Professional and Executive Women; International Platform Association. Religion: Crystal Cathedral, Garden Grove, California; Sang in the Televised "Hour of Power" Choir for 5 Years. Honors and Awards: U.S. Customs Service Award for Superior Job Performance, 1977; A.S.T.D. Award, 1977; Featured in National Publication *Customs Today* for Outstanding Training Program; Certificate of Recognition, Los Angeles Chamber of Commerce and the Los Angeles Unified School District for Outstanding Support of the Youth and Industry in the Business-Education Exchange Program, 1977; 2 Commendations and a U.S. Customs Service Award for Outstanding Service in Special Assignments at Customs Headquarters in Washington, D.C., 1981. Address: 1708 Aspen Village Way, West Covina, California 91791.

Ingram, Arbutus Boyd

Executive Assistant. Personal: Born March 29, 1930; Daughter of Ted L. Boyd and Gladys Spencer Boyd (deceased); Married.

Education: Attended Ferrum College 1947, Cornett Business School 1947-48. Career: Double Envelope Corporation, Assistant to Chairman of the Board 1978 to present, Vice-President and Assistant to the President 1975-78, Secretary to the President 1950-75; Secretary to Vice-President, Clover Creamery Company, 1948-50. Organizational Memberships: Professional Secretaries International (local board; chairman, several committees); Business and Professional Women's Club (past member). Community Activities: North Roanoke Civic League (secretary). Religion: St. James Episcopal Church; Vestry, 3-Year Term, 1981 to present; Flower Chairman, 3 Years; Assistant Chairman, Altar Guild, 3 Years; Budget and Finance Committee. Honors and Awards: Listed in *Who's Who in Virginia Communities, Who's Who in the South and Southwest.* Address: 7823 Alpine Road, Roanoke, Virginia 24019.

Inman, Franklin Pope Jr

Professor and Department Chairman. Personal: Born August 2, 1937 in Hamlet, North Carolina; Son of Mrs. Aieleen Inman; Married Barbara Jean Bullock; Father of Jody Lin, James Walter. Education: A.B. Chemistry 1959, Ph.D. Biochemistry, University of North Carolina-Chapel Hill; Postdoctoral Fellow, Department of Microbiology, University of Illinois-Urbana, Research in Immunochemistry with Dr. Alfred Nisonoff, 1964-66; American Cancer Society Scholar, Department of Medicine, R. B. Brigham Hospital, Harvard Medical School, Boston, Massachusetts, Research in Cellular Immunology with Drs. John David and Heinz Remold, 1975-76. Career: Professor and Chairman, Department of Biochemistry, Quillen-Dishner College of Medicine, East Tennessee State University, Johnson City, Tennessee, 1977 to present; Visiting Lecturer in Immunology, Harvard Medical School, 1975-76; University of Georgia, Professor of Biochemistry 1975-77, Professor of Microbiology 1975-77, Associate Professor of Biochemistry 1970-75, Associate Professor of Microbiology 1970-75, Assistant Professor of Biochemistry, 1966-70, Assistant Professor of Microbiology 1966-70. Organizational Memberships: American Association of Immunologists; American Society of Biological Chemists; American Society of Microbiology; American Chemical Society; Association of Medical School Departments of Biochemistry; New York Academy of Sciences. Community Activities: Jaycees, 1970-74; Forest Heights Pool, Inc. (board of directors, 1968-72). Published Works: Personal Research on "Structure of IgG" 1964-66, "Structure of IgM" 1965-75, "Purification and Characterization of Lymphokines" 1976 to present. Honors and Awards: American Cancer Society Scholar, 1976; A.A.I. Travel Award for Second International Congress in Immunology, Brighton, England, 1974; M. G. Michael Award for Research, University of Georgia, 1969; John Motley Morehead Scholarship, University of North Carolina-Chapel Hill, 1955-59; Listed in *Who's Who in America, Dictionary of International Biography, Men of Achievement, American Men and Women of Science, Personalities of America, American Men of Science.* Address: 707 Wilmar Street, Johnson City, Tennessee 37601.

Irons, William Lee

Lawyer. Personal: Born June 9, 1941 in Birmingham, Alabama; Son of Dr. George V. Irons Sr. and Velma Wright Irons (deceased); Married Karen Phillips. Education: Graduate of Woodlands High School, 1959; B.A., University of Virginia, 1963; J.D., Samford University School of Law, 1966; Graduate, Staff Officer Course, Lackland Air Force Base, Texas, 1966. Military: Appointed to United States Military Academy, West Point, Declined, 1959; Served in the United States Air Force 1966-67, with Commission as First Lieutenant 1966; Commissioned from Private Law Practice to Judge Advocate General's Staff, 1966-70; Promoted to grade of Captain. Career: Partner, Law Firm of William L. Irons, 1972 to present; Partner, Law Firm of Speir and Irons, 1971-72; Partner, Law Firm of Speir, Robertson, Jackson & Irons, 1970-71; Law Clerk to Presiding Judge, Alabama Court of Appeals; Trustee in Bankruptcy, United States District Court, Northern District of Alabama; Law Clerk, 1964-65. Organizational Memberships: Birmingham Bar Association; Alabama Bar Association; American Trial Lawyers Association; Sigma Delta Kappa Legal Fraternity; American Bar Association; National Association of Certified Judge Advocates; Governor's Staff of the State of Alabama; Federal Bar Association; Bar of Court of Military Appeals, Washington, D.C.; National Association of Judge Advocates; American Judicature Society; National Feserve Officers Association; National Lawyers Club, Washington, D.C.; American Law School Association. Religion: Baptist. Honors and Awards: DuPont Regional Scholar, University of Virginia, 1959-63; National Officer, Sigma Delta Kappa Legal Fraternity, 1965; Air Force Commendation Medal and Citation, 1968; Scholarship to Work on Congressional Medal of Honor Project for the United States Air Force, Medal of Honor Grove, Freedoms Foundation, Valley Forge, Pennsylvania; Outstanding Junior Officer of Command, Air University, Maxwell Air Force Base, Alabama, 1969; *Who's Who* Honorary Society; Listed in *National Social Directory, Martindale-Hubbell Law Directory; Who's Who in Alabama, Distinguished Personalities of the South, Who's Who in the South and Southwest.* Address: 3855 Cove Drive, Birmingham, Alabama 35213.

M Ali Issari

Irvine, Reed

Chairman of the Board. Personal: Born September 29, 1922; Son of William J. and Edna May Irvine (both deceased); Married Kay Araki; Father of Donald Irvine. Education: B.A., University of Utah, 1942; B.Litt., St. Catherine's, Oxford University, 1951. Military: Served in th United States Navy and United States Marine Corps, 1942-46. Career: Chairman, Board of Accuracy in Media; Advisor to Division of International Finance, Board of Governors, Federal Reserve System, Washington, D.C., 1951-77. Organizational Memberships: National Press Club, Washington, D.C. Honors and Awards: Phi Beta Kappa, Phi Kappa Phi, 1942; George Washington Honor Medal, Freedoms Foundation, Valley Forge, 1981; Annual Americanism Award, American Legion, Westchester, New York, 1981. Address: 11120 Nicholas Drive, Silver Spring, Maryland 20902.

Issari, M Ali

Educator, Filmmaker and Administrator. Personal: Born August 13, 1924, in Esfahan, Iran; Son of Mrs. Qamar Issari; Married to Joan A.; Father of Scheherezade, Katayoun, Roxana. Education: B.A., University of Tehran, 1963; M.A., 1968, Ph.D., 1979, University of Southern California. Career: Professor of Cinema, Department of Telecommunication, College of Communication Arts and Sciences, Michigan State University, 1978-81; Director of Instructional Film and Multimedia Production Service and Professor, 1975-78; Co-director, N.I.R.T. (national Iranian radio television) Staff Training Project, Michigan State University, 1975-78; Project Director and Executive Producer, Iran Film Series Project, 1975-78; Director, M.S.U.-N.I.R.T. Program Coordinating Office, 1975-78; Head of Film Production Division and Associate Professor, Michigan State University, 1969-75; Presented special film production workshops in Cranbrook Institutions, Detroit, 1973-74; Helped organize and present various local and international film festivals at M.S.U., 1970-73; Served as Judge for Midwest Film Festival (1st international film festival organized and run by students, 1972-73); Served as Special Consultant on educational television with the Saudi Arabian Ministry of Information, 1972; Assistant Motion Picture Officer (production), United States Information Service, Tehran, Iran, 1955-65 (distribution, 1950-55); Acted as Liaison Officer and Interpreter between American and Iranian government officials, 1950-65; Motion pictures and public relations advisor to Iranian oil operating companies, 1963-65; Freelance cinematographer and reporter in Iran for Telenews and Visnews (B.C.I.N.A.) and United Press International, 1959-63; Initiated and presented the first American Film Festival in Iran under the auspices of U.S.I.S.-Tehran, 1951; Films Officer, British Council in Tehran, 1945-50; Produced a number of stage plays in English and Persian (performed in some of these), Tehran; Translator and Interpreter, British Embassy in Tehran, 1943-45. Organizational Memberships: Michigan Film Association (co-founder and member of first board of directors, 1974-75); Iran-America Society (served on various cultural and entertainment committees, 1950-64); Audio-Visual Society of Iran (founder and member of board of directors, 1953); Anglo-Iranian Dramatic Society (board of directors, 1945-49); Association for Educational Communication and Technology, 1966 to present; Society of Motion Picture and Television Engineers (member of progress committee, 1960-65), 1959 to present; Middle East Studies Association of North America, 1976 to present; Society for Cinema Study, 1977 to present; The American Academy of Political and Social Sciences, 1976 to present; Delta Kappa Alpha (vice president, 1967), 1966-69; University Film Association, 1959 to present. Community Activities: Youth Organization of Iran (founder, 1951); Introduced rugby football to Iran and organized Rugby Football Federation, 1949 (secretary, vice president and president, 1949-52). Published Works: *What is Cinema Verite?*, with Doris A. Paul, 1979, *A Picture of Persia*, with Doria A. Paul, 1977; Contributor to professional journals, including *Audio Visual Instruction, Journal of the University Film Association;* Has designed, written, produced, directed, photographed and edited over 1000 documentaries, slide tapes and multi-image presentations. Honors and Awards: Received the Cine Eagle Award, 1976; University Film Association/McGraw-Hill Scholarship Award, 1968; Meritorious Honor Award, U.S. Information Agency, 1965; Order of Mahnum Cap. ; Order of Esteghlal, Hashemite, Jordan, 1959; Order of Oranje Nassau, Holland, 1959; Order of Ordinis Sancti Silvestri Papae, Pope John 23rd, Vatican, 1959; Order of Cavalieres, Italy, 1958; Orders of Pas and Kooshesh, Iran, 1957 and 1951; Listed in *Who's Who in America, Who's Who in the Midwest, Notable Americans, Men of Achievement, Dictionary of International Biography, Leaders in Education.* Address: 4454 Seneca Drive, Okemos, Michigan 48864.

Ituen, Edet Bassey

Edet B Ituen

Professor of Political Science. Personal: Born October 11, 1939; Son of Chief and Mrs. Bassey Ituen; Married to Lucy; Father of Ubong, Emem, Ifiok, Eno. Education: B.A., University of Portland, 1963; M.A., 1965, M.Sc., 1966, University of Oregon; Diploma in Economics and Social Development, Claremont Graduate School, 1966; Ph.D., St. Louis University, 1970. Career: Professor of Political Science, Florissant Valley College, University of Missouri at St. Louis; Former School Administrator, Lutheran School in Nigeria; Former Assistant Personnel Officer, First National Bank of Oregon. Organizational Memberships: American Political Science Association; International Studies Association; African Studies Association; United Nations Association. Community Activities: Board member of St. Louis Nursery Foundation, 1967-70; Director of Model United Nations Program at Florissant Valley College; World Affairs Council of Greater St. Louis, 1978 to present; Member and supporter of St. Louis International Institute, 1973 to present; Member and supporter of St. Louis Committee on Africa, 1968 to present; Active participant in Foreign Policy Association, 1970 to present; Member and supporter of American Academy of Political and Social Science, 1967 to present; Appointed to curriculum committee, St. Louis Board of Education, 1973; Member and supporter of Royal Geographical Society of London, 1962-70. Religion: Life member of Lutheran Church, Missouri Synod. Honors and Awards: Cited for 10 years outstanding teaching, 1978; Received award for outstanding fund drive, United Way, 1978; Listed in *Personalities of the West and Midwest, International Who's Who of Intellectuals, International Register of Profiles.* Address: 210 Cardinal Place, St. Louis, Missouri 63103.

J

Jack, Elizabeth Stephens

Elizabeth Jack

Administrator. Personal: Born June 10, 1927; Daughter of Alfred E. (deceased) and Minnie Hammett Stephens; Married James Ward Jack. Education: Diploma in Nursing, Spartanburg, South Carolina, General Hospital, 1947; B.A., Furman University, 1961; M.P.H., University of North Carolina-Chapel Hill, 1966. Military: Served in the Cadet Nurse Corp, 1944-47. Career: District Director of Public Health Nursing, Appalachian III Public Health District; Former Positions include Director of Nursing Services, Spartanburg County Health Department; Coordinator, Maternal and Infant Project, Greenville County Health Department; Staff Nurse, Coordinator, Stroke Rehabilitation Project, Spartanburg County Health Department; Staff Nurse, Shriners Hospital, Greenville, South Carolina. Organizational Memberships: American Nurses Association; South Carolina Nurses Association (council on practice, 1968-76; served on various district boards and committees); National Leauge of Nursing (chairperson, C.H.H.A./C.H.S. accreditation standards committee, 1975-81); American Public Health Association; South Carolina Public Health Association. Community Activities: National Multiple Sclerosis Foundation (board member, Piedmont Chapter, 1974-80); Heart Services of Spartanburg County (board member, 1973-81); Spartanburg County Hospice Association (steering committee, 1979-81); South Carolina Long Term Care Project, 1978-80; Spartanburg County Health Planning Committee (board member, 1976-81); United Services Council of Spartanburg County (board member, 1979-81); Mary Black School of Nursing, University of South Carolina-Spartanburg (advisory committee, 1978-81). Religion: Oak Grove Baptist Church, Sunday School Teacher 1967-81. Honors and Awards: Fellow, American Public Health Association, 1969; Graduated magna cum laude, Furman University, 1961; Sigma Theta Tau; Delta Omega; Marion Sims Award, South Carolina Public Health Association, for Meritorious Achievement in Public Health, 1981. Address: 120 Longwood Drive, Spartanburg, South Carolina 29301.

Jackson, Anna M

Associate Professor. Personal: Born April 10, 1934; Mother of Sean William, Stevan Mitchell. Education: B.A., Bowling Green State University, 1959; M.A., University of Denver, 1960; Ph.D., Colorado State University, Fort Collins, 1967. Career: University of Colorado School of Medicine, Director of Student Advisory Office 1979-81, Associate Professor of Psychiatry 1976 to present, Acting Director of the Clinical Child Psychology Section 1978, Director of Children's Diagnostic Center 1973-79, Assistant Professor of Psychiatry 1970-76, Instructor in Psychiatry 1968-70, Graduate Faculty Member 1978 to present; Interim Director, Minority Student Affairs Office, University of Colorado Health Sciences Center, 1979-80; Adjunct Professor, School of Professional Psychology, University of Denver, 1976; Visiting Lectureer, Afro-American Studies Department, Metropolitan State College, Denver, Colorado, 1971-72; Lecturer, University of Colorado-Boulder Campus, Northeast Denver Higher Education Program, 1970; Chief Psychologist, State Home and Training School, Wheatridge, Colorado, 1962-68; Consultation Experience with Pike's Peak Mental Health Center, Veteran's Administration Hospital, Medical Student Advisory Office, Colorado Department of Social Services, Colorado Vocational Rehabilitation Department, Denver U.S. Homes Inc., Park East Mental Health Center. Organizational Memberships: Association of Black Psychologists (associate editor, *Journal of Black Psychology*); American Psychological Association; Rocky Mountain Psychological Association; Society for Psychotherapy Research. Community Activities: College of Natural Sciences, Colorado State University (alumni advisory board); Colorado Christian Home (board of directors); East Motivation Cooperative Action Program (board of directors); School of Professional Psychology, University of Denver (advisory board). Honors and Awards: Outstanding Service Award, Denver-Rocky Mountain Chapter, Association of Black Psychologists, 1981; Distinguished Service Award, Intermountain Regional Board of the American Board of Professional Psychology, 1980; Minority Affairs Committee Award, University of Colorado School of Medicine, 1980; Honorary Member, Editorial Advising Board, American Biographical Institute, 1980; Woman of the Year, Regina Social and Civic Club, 1977. Address: 6950 West Bear Creek Drive, Lakewood, Colorado 80227.

Jackson, Graham Washington Sr

Graham Jackson

Personal: Born February 22, 1908, in Portsmouth, Virginia; Son of Graham Wilson and Pauline Jackson (both deceased); Married Helen Balton; Father of Graham Washington Jr., Gerald Wayne. Education: Graduate of Norcom High School, Portsmouth, Virginia, 1923; Attended Morehouse College, Atlanta, Georgia, 1923-24; Chicago Musical College, 1927-29, Summer 1931; Hampton Institute, Summers 1930-32; Loyola University, Chicago, Summers 1927-29; Atlanta University, Atlanta, Georgia. Military: Served in the United States Navy, 1942-45, attaining the rank of Chief Petty Officer. Career: Taught Piano, Voice, Instrumental and Organ, 1923-27; Orchestra Leader, 81 Theatre, Atlanta, Georgia, 1923-27; Teacher, Booker T. Washington High School, Atlanta, Georgia, 1928-40; Classical Concerts, Personal Appearances, Recorded for OK Record Company, 1940; Organist, Radio Station WERD, Atlanta, 1948; Official Entertainer for President Franklin D. Roosevelt, 1933-45 (24 Command Performances in White House and at Litle White House in Warm Springs, Georgia); Entertained for President Harry S. Truman; Command Performances for President Dwight D. Eisenhower in Washington, D.C., November 7, 1953, and at Augusta National Golf Club and Mamie's Cabin, November 27, 1953; Command Performance for Chief Justice Earl Warren, for Adlai Stevenson and Other High-Ranking Diplomatic Officials, for Secretary of the Treasury, George M. Humphrey, for Former Secretary of the Navy John L. Sullivan; Served as Official Entertainer for Five Consecutive Governors of the State of Georgia; Played for Lord and Lady Halifax, the Biffles, Rockefellers, Firestones, Callaways, Robert Woodruffs, Clays and Others; Played for Opening of World Monetary Conference; Has Appeared in All Leading Cities of America; Has Appeared at the Waldorf Astoria in New York with Madame Jarmila Novotna, Vladimir Horowitz, Joseph Szigeti, Deems Taylor, Frederic March, Mack Harell, John Finley Williamson; Appeared on Ed Sullivan's "Toast of the Town", June 1951; Has Entertained for Seven Consecutive Presidents of the United States; Appearance for National Bankers Association Convention, Los Angeles, 1956; Official Entertainer for National Bar Association, 1956; Advertising Staff, Coca-Cola Company; Taught Vocal and Instrumental Music in Atlanta Public Schools for 12 Years; Radio and Television Artist; Entertains Nightly at Pittypat's Porch, Atlanta; Known as "The Ambassador of Good Will". Organizational Memberships: Georgia Board of Corrections (first Black ever to be appointed to major state post); American Guild of Organists. Community Activities: 33° Mason; Kappa Alpha Psi; Gate City #54, Elks. Religion: Saint Paul of the Cross Catholic Church, Organist. Honors and Awards: Name of Street on Which he Resides Changed to White House Drive in Recognition of His Home (which is a replica of the Little White House in Warm Springs, Georgia); Made Official Entertainer for the State of Georgia by Appointment of Former Governor Herman Taldmadge; 7 Citations for Outstanding Service while in the Navy; Featured in *Life* Magazine Nine Times; Received Several Awards in the Field of Music; 2 Cups of Achievement in the field of Music, Citizenry of Portsmouth, Virginia and Surrounding County, 1928; Cup for Piano Playing, Southern Piano Championship, 1927; Kappa Alpha Psi Award for Achievement, 1952; Urban League Award for Public Relations. Address: 60 White House Drive, S.W., Atlanta, Georgia 30314.

Jackson, Rodney Newland

Chief Cytotechnologist, Histotechnologist, Medical Photographer, Section Head. Personal: Born October 30, 1936; Son of Virginia Huisinga; Married Charlotte Elaine Kochendorfer; Father of Carol Ellen, Beth Ann. Education: Attended Lincoln College, Lincoln, Illinois, 1955-56; Illinois Wesleyan University, Bloomington, Illinois, 1956-57; Illinois State University, Normal, 1957-58; Millikin University, Decatur, Illinois, 1959; Histology/Cytology Training, Memorial Hospital, Springfield, Illinois, 1959-63. Career: Chief Cytotechnologist, Histotechnologist, Medical Photographer, Technical Section Head, Anatomic Pathology, Passavant Memorial Hospital, Jacksonville, Illinois; Staff Histotechnologist 1959-65, Chief Cytotechnologist 1963-65, Memorial Hospital, Springfield, Illinois. Organizational Memberships: American Society of Clinical Pathologists (associate member); American Society of Cytology (associate member); American Society for Cytotechnology; Illinois Society of Cytology; St. Louis Society of Cytology (parliamentarian, corresponding secretary, vice president, president). Community Activities: Jacksonville Amateur Radio Club (member, 1965 to present; secretary; treasurer; vice president; president; board of directors); Passavent Memorial Hospital (board of governors, 1968, 1970); Pavilion Players of Jacksonville (board of directors, 1978); American Cancer Society, Local Chapter, 1980-81; Morgan, Scott, Cass Counties Emergency Weather Network (net manager, 1966-70); Council of Local Advisors, Explorer Scouts, 1970-71; Illinois Junior Academy of Science Regional Science Fairs (judge, 1967-82). Religion: First Presbyterian Church of Jacksonville, Illinois, Member 1965 to present, Board of Deacons 1969-70. Honors and Awards: Public Service Award, American Radio Relay League, 1969, 1973; Public Service Award, United States Corps of Engineers, 1969; Listed in *Outstanding Young Men of America, Personalities of the West and Midwest, Who's Who in the Midwest, Notable Americans, Men of Achievement*. Address: 429 Pendik Road, Jacksonville, Illinois 62650.

Rodney Jackson

Jackson, Rosalee

Homemaker, Writer. Personal: Born April 12, 1926; Daughter of Floyd and Eunice Kepford (both deceased); Married Charles William Jackson; Father of William Charles, Dana Andrew, Kevin Lee. Education: Graduate of the American School, Chicago, Illinois, 1965; Famous Writers School, 1967; Oklahoma University Short Course on Professional Writing, 1980. Community Activities: Hospital Volunteer, 1950's; Women's Political Caucus, 1970's; Oklahoma E.R.A., 1981. Religion: Disciples of Christ; Various Offices 1962 to present, Church Women United. Honors and Awards: Certificates from Famous Writers School 1967, Studio of Rhetorical Arts 1980; Attestation of Pilgrimage, Jerusalem, 1973, 1980. Address: 2542 N.W. 44th Street, Oklahoma City, Oklahoma 73112.

Jackson, Wilma (Darcy DeMille)

Writer, Columnist. Education: Baccalaureate Degree, University of Michigan, 1977; Certificate, Urban Studies-Substance Abuse, Michigan State University, 1976; Advanced Study, Creative Writing, Oakland University, 1974-75, 1976-77. Career: Feature Writer and Columnist, *Sepia* Magazine, 1961 to present; Columnist, *Hip* Magazine, 1963 to present; Columnist, *Soul-Teen Magazine*, 1973 to present; Feature Writer, Columnist, *Bronze Thrills Magazine*, 1957 to present; News Reporter, *Chicago Daily Defender*, 1956-59; Columnist, National Editions and Chicago Edition, *Daily Defender*, 1956-59; Women's Editor, Associated Negro Press, 1959-61; Syndicated Columnist, 173 Newspapers, United States, Virgin Islands, Ghana, Kenya, Jamaica, Bahamas, 1959-64; Reporter, Feature Writer, Negro Press International, 1964-65; Executive Editor, *The Circle*, Urban League Newspaper, 1960-61; Market Research Interviewer, Barlow Survey Service, Chicago, 1958-59; Promotions/Publicity, Holiday Inn, Flint, Michigan, 1976; Guest Lecturer, Creative Writing, University of Michigan, Flint Campus, 1977-78; Coordinated Writers and Composers Day at the Artrain, Flint, Michigan, 1978; Moderator/Writing Seminar, Howard University, Communications Conference, 1979; Working Press, President Carter's Inauguration; Working Press, International Women's Year Confab, Houston, Texas, 1977; Counselor, State of Michigan, Case Aide, 1976-78; Advisor, Black Fashion Museum, New York City, 1979 to present; Recruiter, Manufacturers Life Insurance Company, 1979 to present; Evaluation Specialist, Instructor, The Kennedy Center, 1979 to present; Instructor, Creative Writing, Mass Communications, Job Seeking Skills, MOIS Computer, The Kennedy Center, Flint, Michigan; Entertainment Writer, *The Flint Journal*, 1981 to present; Consultant, TimeShares, Inc.; Instructor, Psychology, Counseling, Jordan College, 1982-83; Columnist, "Dear Wilma", *The Flint Journal*, 1982-83. Organizational Memberships: National Association of Media Women (founder, past president; public relations, 1981-82); The Links, Inc. (memberships chairman, 1981-82). Published Works: Column "Confidentially Speaking" *Hep* Magazine, 1957-60; Article "Ten Things I'll Always Remember" (series), *Ebony* Magazine, 1958; Column "Just Ask Me", "Darcy DeMille's Data 'N Chatter", "Dear Soul Sister", "Star-O-Scope"; Article "New Champion of Black Brainpower/M.S.U.'s President Wharton", *Sepia* Magazine, 1976. Honors and Awards: Listed in *Contemporary Authors, Who's Who Among Black Americans, Who's Who of Intellectuals, Index to Periodical Articles, International Who's Who in Community Service, Who's Who of American Women, Who's Who in the Midwest*. Address: 2018 Whittlesey Street, Flint, Michigan 48503.

Wilma Jackson

Jacobs, Gordon Waldemar

General Surgeon. Personal: Born May 30, 1933; Son of Rev. and Mrs. Elmer Jacobs; Married Lorraine Maria; Father of Mary Lou, Melanie Ann (deceased), Kristen Clara, Damien. Education: B.S. 1955, M.D. 1958, University of Iowa; Rotating Intern, Sacramento County Hospital, Sacramento, California, 1958-59; Resident, General Surgery, Veterans Administration Hospital, Oakland-Martinez, California, 1962-66; Fellow in Surgery, Lahey Clinic, Boston, Massachusetts, 1969-70. Military: Served in the United States Army Medical Corps, 1960-62, attaining the rank of Captain. Career: Staff Surgeon and Medical Missionary, Lutheran Mission Hospital, Madang, New Guinea, 1966-68; Staff Surgeon, Somerville Surgical Associates, Central and Somerville Hospitals, Somerville, Massachusetts, 1970-75; Acting Chief of Surgery, Instructor in Surgery, Haile Selassie Medical School, Addis Abba, Ethiopia, 1973-74; Staff Surgeon, Alta Bates, Herrick, Children's Hospital, Merritt, Providence and Peralta Hospitals, Berkeley-Oakland; General Surgeon in Private Practice, Berkeley-Oakland. Organizational Memberships: California Medical Association (chairman, committee on medicine/religion, 1980 to present; program planner and moderator, Healing the Whole Person, 1981; program planner and moderator, How to Apply Spiritual Care in Modern Society, 1982); Christian Medical Society; East Bay Surgical Society; International College of Surgeons (fellow); American College of Emergency Physicians (fellow); Herrick Hospital (credentials, tissue, cancer, continuing education committees); Alta Bates Hospital (tissue and disaster committees). Community Activities: Oakland Uptown International, Toastmasters International (past president, 1980); Big Brother, Boston, 1969-73; Hospital

Chaplains Ministry of America (guest speaker, annual seminar, Pasadena, California, January 1981). Religion: Trinity Lutheran Church, Oakland, California, President 1979-81. Honors and Awards: Listed in *Who's Who in the West, Community Leaders and Noteworthy Americans, Book of Honor, Men of Achievement, Personalities of America, Personalities of the West and Midwest, Notable Americans, International Reigster of Profiles, International Who's Who in Community Service, Dictionary of International Biography*. Address: 1130 Harvard Road, Piedmont, California 94610.

Jacobs, Patricia Dianne

Executive. Personal: Born January 27, 1950; Daughter of Felix and Helen Jacobs. Education: B.A. magna cum laude, Lincoln University, Pennsylvania, 1970; J.D., Harvard Law School, 1973. Career: President and Chief Executive Officer, The American Association of Minority Enterprise Small Business Investment Companies, Washington, D.C.; Congressional Liaison Officer, Secretary of the United States Commerce Department, 1977; Assistant Minority Counsel, Small Business Committee, United States Senate, 1975-77; Instructor, Federal City College, Institute of Gerontology, 1976; Assistant Professor and Director of Legal Services Counseling, John Jay College of Criminal Justice, New York, 1974-75; Associate Professor (adjunct), Borough of Manhattan Community College, Center for African and African-American Affairs, New York, 1973-75; Lecturer in Administrative and Legislative Law, Seton Hall Law School, 1974-75; Associate (Partner/Co-Founder), Pickett and Jennings, P.C., Newark, New Jersey, 1974-75; Associate, Tax Department, Exxon Corporation, New York, 1973-75: Legal Clerk, General Motors Corporation, New York, 1972; Legal Intern, Walker, Kaplan and Mays, P.A., Little Rock, Arkansas, 1971-72; Assistant Director of Financial Aid, Lincoln University, Pennsylvania, 1970. Organizational Memberships: American Bar Association; National Bar Association; N.C.B.L.; Association of University and College Professors; Council of New York Law Associates; Potomac Fiscal Society; Lawyer's Study Group; Federal Bar Association; Harlem Lawyer's Association. Community Activities: Women's League of Voters; N.W.B.D.C.; Lincoln Alumni Club; Coalition of 100 Black Women of D.C.; Alpha Kappa Alpha. Honors and Awards: National Finalist, White House Fellows Program, 1975; Business Award, National Association of Black Manufacturers, 1976; Board of Directors of Winthrop Rockefeller Foundation, 1976; Cooperative Assistant Fund, 1976; Center for Youth Services, 1976; Southwest Day Care Center, 1976; Caribbean Capital Corporation, 1976; Phoenix Services Corporation, 1976; Council on Foundations, 1976. Address: 5016 3rd Street, Northwest, Washington, D.C. 20011.

Jaeger, Sharon Ann

Poet, Editor, Translator, Administrator. Personal: Born January 15, 1945; Daughter of Paul Jaeger, Catherine S. Jaeger. Education: B.A. summa cum laude, University of Dayton, 1966; M.A., English, Boston College, 1971; D.A., English, State University of New York-Albany, 1982. Career: Co-Editor, Sanchem Press; Director, Intertext; Translator; Poet; Instructor, Writing Workshop, State University of New York, Albany; Instructor, Writing Center, Rensselaer Polytechnic Institute; Assistant to Editor-in-Chief, *Foundation* Magazine; Faculty Secretary and Records Specialist, School of Nursing, University of Alaska-Anchorage; Graduate Assistant, Department of English, Boston College; Graduate Assistant, Department of English, University of Dayton. Organizational Memberships: Academy of American Poets; American Literary Translators Association; American Comparative Literature Association; Modern Language Association; New England Modern Language Association; National Council of Teachers of English; C.C.C.C.; Society for Textual Scholarship; Society for Critical Exchange; Mensa, 1969-70; International Society for the History of Rhetoric; International Association of Philosophy and Literature; Rhetoric Society of America; American Studies Association; American Association of University Women; Philological Association of the Pacific Coast; Semiotic Society of America; Appalachian Writers Association; Cambridge Footnote Society (co-founder, 1969-71). Community Activities: Community Volunteer, 1970-77; Volunteer Work with the Elderly, 1973-75; Save the Children (sponsor, 1980 to present); Sigma Tau Sigma, 1966. Religion: Full-Time Minister, 1970-77. Honors and Awards: Presidential Fellowship, 1979-82; First Place Award in Poetry, Graduate Division, McKinney Literary Competition, 1979; Austrian Government Scholarship for German Study, University of Salzburg, Summer 1966; Alpha Sigma Tau Honor Key, 1966; Chaminade Award for Excellence, 1966; Boston College Graduate Assistantship, 1969-70; University of Dayton Graduate Assistantship, 1966-67; Listed in *Outstanding Young Women of America, World Who's Who of Women, International Who's Who of Poetry*. Address: P.O. Box 14, Anchorage, Alaska 99510.

Sharon A Jaeger

Jafri, Alhaj Saiyed Qamar

Senior Associate Head Engineer. Personal: Born July 16, 1940; Son of Syed Alay Hasan (deceased), Safdari B. Jafri, Streamwood, Illinois; Married Najma Qamar Jafri; Father of Zaineb Saiyeda, Alay Safdar (Hur), Alay Haani. Education: B.S., Physics, Statistics, Mathematics, Lucknow University, 1957; M.S., Mathematics, Aligarh Muslim University, 1961; B.S.M.E. (honors), Amu-India, 1963; M.S.M.E., Tuskegee Institute, Alabama, 1968; M.B.A., Management, Northern Illinois University, DeKalb, 1978. Military: Served in the Indian Military Engineering Service as Assistant Executive Engineer. Career: Product Engineering, I.B.M.; Product Evaluation Engineer, Memorex Corporation, Cupertino, California, 1981; Product Evaluation Engineer, N.C.R. Corporation, Sunnyvale, California, 1979-81; Manager, Research and Development, F.M.C. Corporation, San Jose, California, 1979; Supervisor, Marketing, International Harvester Company, Schaumburg, Illinois, 1968-78. Organizational Memberships: American Society of Quality Control (senior member; secretary, San Francisco section, 1980-81; treasurer, San Francisco section, 1981-82); American Society of Mechanical Engineers (member, 1968 to present; publicity chairman, assistant editor of newsletter, operating board, 1973-74; chairman of biomechanical and human factors professional division, operating board, 1972-73; chairman of associate committee, operating board, 1971-72; vice chairman, associate committee, operating board, 1970-71; associate committee, 1968-70); Society of Automotive Engineers (member, 1974 to present; member "Belleville Spring" subcommittee, 1974-75; arrangement chairman, Mid-California section, 1979-80); American Management Association, 1976 to present; Association of M.B.A. Executives (member, 1974 to present); Sigma Iota Epsilon (secretary, Rho chapter, Northern Illinois University, 1976-77); Illinios Society of Professional Engineers (member, 1973-76; chairman, Illinois state chapter activities committee, 1975-76; editor *Brine*, membership communicator of Salt Creek chapter, 1975-77; vice president, Salt Creek chapter, 1974-75; chairman, education and scholarship committee, Salt Creek chapter, 1973-74); National Society of Professional Engineers (member, 1973-76; professional engineers in industry committee, 1975-76; Young Engineers list, 1975-76). Community Activities: Foster Parent, State of California; Volunteer, Dupage County, 1978; Two-Way Communicator, College of Dupage, Glen Ellyn, Illinois; Republican. Religion: Shia-Ithna-Ashri; Secretary, Husaini Association of Greater Chicago, 1977-78; Trustee, Shia Association of Bay Area, San Jose, California. Honors and Awards: Outstanding Service Certificate, Illinois Society of Professional Engineers; Certified Reliability Engineer 1981, Certified Quality Engineer 1980, American Society of Quality Control; Outstanding New Citizen of the Year, 1975-76; Illinois Young Engineer of the Year, Illinois Society of Professional Engineers, 1974; Professional Engineer, State of Illinois, 1973; Professional Engineer (M.E.), State of California, 1979; Professional Engineer (W.E.), State of California, 1980; Ziauddin Gold Medal for Obtaining First Position in Master in Maths, 1961; Listed in *Who's Who in the Midwest, Who's Who Among Indian Immigrants, Who's Who in California*. Address: 114 Mayland Court, San Jose, California 95138.

James, Jeannie Henrietta

Lecturer, Consultant, Writer. Personal: Born December 5, 1921; Daughter of Portice J. (deceased) and Essie Ross James. Education: Graduate, Valedictorian, Ashwood High School, 1938; B.S., Berea College, 1945; M.S., Home Economics Education, University of North Carolina-Greensboro, 1949; Graduate Assistant, Iowa State College, 1947; Ed.D., Penn State University, 1965. Career: Nutrition and Education Consultant, Lecturer and Writer on Child Development and Home Economics; Associate Professor, Spartanburg Methodist College, 1979; Associate Professor, Early Childhood Education, University of South Carolina, 1975-79; Assistant/Associate Professor, Home Economics, Illinois State University, 1959-75; Assistant Professor, Home Economics, Lincoln Memorial University, 1949-59; High School Home Economics Teacher, Stowe High School, Stowe, Vermont, 1945-48. Organizational Memberships: American Home Economics Association (sectional program chairman, 1977-79); N.A.E.Y.C.; S.C.A.E.Y.C.; American Association of University Women (local president); American Association of University Professors (local president, secretary); Society for Research in Child Development; Illinois Association for the Education of Young Children (state co-chairman of Week of the Young Child). Community Activities: Women's Club (president, local group); Free Consultant for Child Care Centers for Department of Social Services, Illinois, South Carolina; Lecturer in Vocational Home Economics, Kindergarten and Other Group Workshops. Religion: Sunday School Teacher; Membership Committee Drive of Church; Church Pre-School Programs Committee. Pubilshed Works: Articles in *Journal of Home Economics; Reading; What's New in Home Economics;* Booklets Based on Research. Honors and Awards: Honorary Member, Society for Research in Child Development, 1965; Elected to Graduate Council, Curriculum Committee, Illinois State University; Masters Craftsman, Southern Highland Handicraft Guild, 1941-81; Phi Kappa Delta; Zeta Tau Alpha; Listed in *Who's Who in American Education, Who's Who of Women Who's Who in the South and Southwest.* Address: Belmont Estates, Belmont Drive, Route 2, Box 538, Fountain Inn, South Carolina 29644.

Jary, Roland Saunders

Civil Engineer. Personal: Born January 26, 1936; Son of Mrs. Jane S. Jary; Married to Linda Ann Gordanier; Father of Janiece Lorraine, Matthew Saunders. Education: B.A., Texas Christian University, 1959; B.S., Texas A & M University, 1965; Army Command and General Staff College, 1974; M.S., Texas Christian University, 1977. Military: Served as Major with Corps of Engineers, 1959-74. Career: Registered Professional Engineer; Former Army Engineer in construction; Former college faculty member in the Canal Zone. Organizational Memberships: American Society of Military Engineers (vice president, Fort Worth Post, 1976); Texas Society of Professional Engineers (secretary, treasurer, vice president, president-elect, Fort Worth chapter, 1976-81); American Society of Civil Engineers (chairman of publications committee, Fort Worth chapter, 1981); Texas Council of Engineering Laboratories (director, 1981); American Water Works Association. Community Activities: Appointed by mayor as City Councilman, Town of Pantego, Texas, 1979-80; Advisor to Tarrant County Junior College in civil/construction courses; MayFest volunteer, 1976; Ambassador's "Country Team" to Chile and Ecuador, 1971-73. Religion: Member of Calvary Presbyterian Church (deacon, 1975 to present, director of English Fellowship Church in Quito, Ecuador, 1972-73). Honors and Awards: Bronze Star; Meritorious Service Award; Army Commendation; National Defense Award; Vietnamese Campaign Award; Vietnamese Defense Award; Vietnamese Cross of Gallantry. Address: 1600 Trail Glen Court, Arlington, Texas 76013.

Jeannie H James

Jascourt, Hugh Donald

Labor Law Counsel. Personal: Born March 25, 1935; Son of Jack and Gladys Jascourt (both deceased); Married Resa Zall; Father of Stephen D., Leigh R. Education: A.B. honors, University of Pennsylvania, 1956; J.D., Wayne State University Law School, 1960. Military: Served in the United States Army, 1956-57, with the rank of Lieutenant. Career: Labor Law Counsel, United States Department of Commerce; Assistant Solicitor, Labor Law, United States Department of the Interior; Director, Public Employment Relations Research Institute; Professor, George Washington University Law School; House Counsel, American Federation of State, County and Municipal Employees; Labor Relations Counsel, Federal Reserve Board; Executive Director, Federal Bar Association; Attorney-Advisor, National Labor Relations Board; Assistant Director, Employee Management Relations, American Federation of Government Employees. Organizational Memberships: Industrial Relations Research Association, D.C. Chapter (board of governors, 1979 to present); American Bar Association (chairman, various subcommittees); Society of Professionals in Dispute Resolutions; Society of Federal Labor Relations Professionals; American Society for Public Administration; International Personnel Management Association. Community Activities: Unfair Labor Practice Panel, Prince George's County P.E.R.B., 1973-81; Greenbelt Employee Relations Board, 1977 to present; National Jogging Association (vice president, 1980 to present; board of directors, 1969 to present); Road Runners Club of America (president, 1961-65); Maryland Public Sector Conference Board, 1973 to present; Prince George County Federation of Park and Recreation Councils (president, 1969-71); Prince George County P.T.A.s (regional vice president, 1981); Maryland Congress of Parents and Teachers (chairman, curriculum committee). Published Works: Labor Relations Editor, *Journal of Law and Education,* 1973 to present; Author of Collective Bargaining Chapter, *Yearbook of School Law,* 1978 to present; *Government Labor Relations,* 1979; *Trends in Public Sector Labor Relations,* 1974; *Public Sector Labor Relations,* 1974. Religion: Religious School Committee of Congregation, 1974 to present. Honors and Awards: Coach/Manager, United States Team, International Cross Country Championship 1966, Southern Games (Trinidad) 1964; Maryland's Outstanding Volunteer Recreation Leader, 1968; Maryland's Outstanding Physical Fitness Leader, 1967; 1 of 5 Maryland Outstanding Young Men of the Year, 1969; Editor-in-Chief, *Wayne Law Journal,* 1959-60; Robbins Award for Best Brief in Moot Court, 1960; Listed in *Who's Who in American Law, Who's Who in the East.* Address: 7 Maplewood Court, Greenbelt, Maryland 20770.

Jasek, Diane Martha

Administrator. Personal: Born June 24, 1955; Daughter of Martha Rychlik and Edward Thomas Jasek. Education: Graduate of Taylor High School, Taylor, Texas, 1972: Attended Temple Junior College, Temple, Texas, 1972-74; B.S., American Studies-Government, University of Texas-Austin, 1978. Career: Director of Educational Institutes; Legal Secretary/Assistant, Attorney General's Office, Prosecutor's Assistance Section, 1980-81; Staff Assistant, State Pension Review Board, Representative Bill Blythe, August 1890; Meetings and Exhibits Coordinator/Convention Planner, State Bar of Texas, Special Events Section, 1979-80; Administrative Assistant to Representative Paul Ragsdale; Personal Staff, Senate Independent Research Group, Texas Senate, Senator Chet Brooks, 1979; Senate Committee Coordinator, Texas Senate, 1977-78; Counselor, International Children's Camp, San Martino, Switzerland, Summer 1974-75. Community Activities: Williamson County Democrats; Youth Advisory Committee, District 18, 1974. Religion: Roman Catholic. Honors and Awards: Delegate, Democratic State Convention, 1974, 1976, 1978, 1980; Delegate, Democratic National Convention, 1976: Goodwill Ambassador for the State of Texas, Appointed by Governor Briscoe; Listed in *Book of Honor, Personalities of America, Outstanding Young Women of America, Notable Americans, World's Who's Who of Women, International Youth in Achievement, Who's Who in American Politics, Personalities of the South.* Address: 915 Vance Street, Taylor, Texas 76574.

Jasper, Martin Theophilus

Professor of Mechanical Engineering. Personal: Born March 19, 1934; Son of Thomas Theophilus and Alice Maie Jasper (both deceased); Married Mary Altha Ledbetter; Father of Nellie Rebecca, Alice Hesta, Martin Theophilus Jr., Mary Margaret, William Richard. Education: B.S.Ch.E. 1955, M.S.M.E. 1962, Mississippi State University; Graduate Studies at Stevens Institute of Technology, 1963: Ph.D., Mechanical Engineering, University of Alabama, 1967. Military: Served in the United States Army Medical Service Corps, 1956-57, attaining the rank of 2nd Lieutenant. Career: Professor of Mechanical Engineering, Mississippi State University; Design Engineer, Chrysler Corporation Missile Division; Plant Metallurgist, Vickers Inc.; Engineer, American Cast Iron Pipe Company. Organizational Memberships: American Society for Engineering Education; American Society of Mechanical Engineers (secretary-treasurer 1968-69, 1969-70, chairman 1971-72, director 1972-75, Mississippi Section; region XI committee on relations with colleges and universities 1970-72, committee on membership development 1972-74); Society of Manufacturing Engineers (Tombigbee Warrior Chapter, organizational chairman, 1969-70; 1st vice chairman 1967-70, chairman 1970-71, Mississippi Chapter; chairman, Region V education committee, 1971-72; member 1971-75, chairman 1974-75, national committee for research and educational grants; charter member, president's club, 1974 to present); New York Academy of Sciences; Registered Professional Engineer, Mississippi, 1962 to present. Community Activities: Starkville Kiwanis Club (director, 1972-74; chairman, major emphasis committee, 1974-75); Advisory Council to Webster County Superintendent of Education, 1980. Religion: First Baptist Church of Mathiston, Mississippi; Sunday School Teacher; Deacon, Vice Chairman of the Board of Deacons, 1980-81. Honors and Awards: Sigma Xi; Tau Beta Pi; Pi Tau Sigma; Pi Mu Epsilon. Address: P.O. Box 77, Mathiston, Mississippi 39752.

Hilda L Jay

Jay, Hilda Lease

Library Media Specialist, Teacher. Personal: Born December 29, 1921; Daughter of Frank and Hilda Whitton Lease; Married John Jay; Mother of Sarah Louise, Margaret Ellen. Education: B.S.Ed., Indiana University, 1945; M.S.Ed., Danbury State College, 1960; Sixth Year Studies, University of Bridgeport, 1964; Ed.D., New York University, 1970. Career: Library Media Specialist, Teacher; Former Public Librarian. Organizational Memberships: Connecticut School Library Association (executive board, 1963-66, 1970-76; secretary, 1974-75; chairman, library skills committee, 1964-66); State Department of Education Study Group for Accreditation of Public Schools, 1963-64; Connecticut Educational Media Association (president, 1975-77; secretary, 1978); Association for Educational Communications Technology (certification committee, 1979-81; board of directors, school media specialists, 1981 to present); American Association of School Librarians; Association of Supervision and Curriculum Development. Community Activities: Governor's Task Force Advisory Committee for Equity of Educational Opportunity, 1978-80; Bridgeport Area Girl Scout Council (president, 1955-58); Norwalk Symphony, 1960-65; Norwalk Youth Symphony (secretary, advisory board, 1959-65). Religion: Episcopalian. Published Works: Author of United Fund Teen Column, *Bridgeport Post*, 1951-56. Honors and Awards: Girl Scout Thanks Badge, 1956; Connecticut Representative, Okoboji Leadership Conference, 1977; New Spirit Conference, Okoboji, 1980; Rheta A. Clark Award, 1981; Kappa Delta Pi; Phi Delta Kappa; Pi Lambda Theta. Address: P.O. Box F, Sandy Hook, Connecticut 06482.

Jenks-Jordal, Mary Ellen

Executive. Personal: Born October 4, 1933; Daughter of Mrs. Emma Jenks; Married Douglas R. Jordal; Mother of Joyellyn Jenks, Jared Brent, Juliette Leslie. Education: B.S.Ed. 1956, M.S. 1957, University of Wisconsin-Madison. Career: Vice President, Consumer Affairs, The Pillsbury Company; Director, Consumer Services and Affairs, Green Giant Company, 1976-79; Director, Consumer Services, Green Giant Company, 1962-76; Editorial Writer, American Dairy Association, 1961; Director, Consumer Services, Salada Foods, 1957-61; Director, Speech Department, Monona Grove High School, 1956-57. Organizational Memberships: American Women in Radio and Television; Society for Nutrition Education; Society of Consumer Affairs Professionals in Business; Grocery Manufacturers of America; American Frozen Foods Institute (chairperson, program planning committee); Home Economists in Business. Community Activities: Better Business Bureau of Minnesota (board of directors). Honors and Awards: Publicity Chairperson, American Women in Radio and Television National Convention, 1977; Publicity Chairperson, American Home Economics Association National Convention, 1968; Publicity Chairperson, Home Economists in Business Microwave Seminar, 1975; Chairperson, Professional Women's Seminar, 1974. Address: 6624 Dovre Drive, Edina, Minnesota 55436.

Dolores V Jimenez

Jimenez, Dolores Vasquez

Retired Businesswoman. Personal: Born March 27, 1916; Daughter of Gregorio and Lucia Vasquez (deceased); Married to Louie; Mother of Eleanor Vetter, Dolores Thompson, Beatrice Jimenez, Robert Jimenez, Lucille Olivas, Michael Jimenez. Education: Attended Liberty Union High School, 1930-32; Graduate, Adrian's Beauty College, 1957. Career: Beautician, 1958-68, and Owner/Operator, 1968-78, Hartley's Beauty Salon. Community Activities: Soroptimist International of Stockton, California, 1969 to present; Girl Scout Leader, 1953-56; Cub Scout Den Mother, 1956-59; Lincoln City Elementary School Parent-Teacher Association (president, 1954-56); Edison Senior High School P.T.A. (president, 1956-58); Hamilton Junior High School P.T.A. (president, 1963-65); Stockton Grange (master, 1973); Rainbow Rebekah Drill Team (president, 1977); El Circulo Espanol De Stockton (founder and president, 1978 to present); Toasmasters International (charter member "Bohemio", 1980 to present); Stockton Council P.T.A. (financial secretary, 1981). Religion: Attends Catholic Church. Honors and Awards: Honorary Life Member, California Congress of Parents and Teachers Inc., 1967. Address: 618 South Eugenia Street, Stockton, California 95205.

Jobst, Caroline Briggs

Manufacturing Executive. Personal: Born May 7, 1919, in Asheville, North Carolina; Daughter of Horace Gladstone and Erma Parham Briggs; Married Conrad Jobst, (deceased), on June 16, 1941. Education: Attended Cecil College, 1937-38. Career: President, Chief Executive Officer, Jobst Institute, Inc., Toledo, Ohio, 1957 to present; Director, Toledo Trust Company. Organizational Memberships: American Management Association; Aerospace Medicine Association; National Management Association (advisory board); National Association of Hosiery Manufacturers; Employers Association of Toledo; Toledo Area Chamber of Commerce (board of directors). Community Activities: Community Chest (board of directors); Toledo Museum of Art (president's council); Golden Baton Association; Toledo Symphony Orchestra. Religion: Episcopal. Honors and Awards: Silver Knight Award, National Management Association, 1980. Address: 418 Riverside Drive, Rossford, Ohio 43460.

Johnson, Arlene Lytle

Administrative Assistant. Personal: Born January 20, 1937; Daughter of Minnie L. Blackman; Married William Dalois; Mother of

Robin G. Lytle, Cheryl R. Campbell. Education: Graduate of Mapletown High School, Mapletown, Pennsylvania. Career: Administrative Assistant to Deputy Assistant Secretary for Human Development Services, D.H.H.S., Washington, D.C.; Secretary to the Chief, Health Economics Branch, Secretary to Director, Deputy Director, Assistant Director, Division of Medical Care Administration; Secretary to Deputy Director and Director, Bureau of Community Health Services, Department of Health and Human Services, 1961-81; Clerk Stenographer, Pennsylvania State Employment Service, 1960-61. Community Activities: Bible Education Work, 1971 to present. Religion: Jehovah's Witness, 1971. Honors and Awards: Public Health Service Special Recognition Award, 1976; H.S.M.H.A. Superior Service Award, Department of Health, Education and Welfare, 1973; Numerous Cash Awards and Quality Increases, 1954 to present; Listed in *Who's Who of American Women*. Address: 5945 Addison Road, Capitol Heights, Maryland 20743.

Johnson, Arthur M

Consultant to President. Personal: Born February 22, 1923; Married Nell Johnson; Father of Nedra Sue Cook. Education: Graduate of Redwater High School, 1940; A.S., Texarkana College, 1946; B.S. 1948, M.S. 1949, East Texas State University. Military: Served in the United States Army and the United States Air Force, 1943-46. Career: Panola Junior College, Consultant to the President, President 1974-81, Dean 1966-74, Registrar 1964-66, Coach and Instructor 1950-64; Instructor, Talco High School, 1949-50. Organizational Memberships: Texas State Teachers Association (life member); Panola County Texas State Teachers Association (president, 1965); East Texas Council of Higher Education (chairman, 1977-79); Texas Public Community/Junior College Association (legislative committee, 1978). Community Activities: Carthage Lions Club (president, 1970; deputy district governor, 1972-74); Panola County Chamber of Commerce (president, 1978); Panola County Industrial Foundation (secretary-treasurer, 1972-73); Panola County United Fund (drive chairman, 1968; president, 1969). Religion: First United Methodist Church, Administrative Board, Trustee. Honors and Awards: Panola County Citizen of the Year, 1974; Arthur M. Johnson Gymnasium Dedicated February 1982 on the Campus of Panola Junior College; Listed in *Who's Who in Texas*. Address: 836 Crawford, Carthage, Texas 75633.

Johnson, Beverly Kim

Teacher, Coach. Personal: Born November 12, 1955; Daughter of Beverly and Nelle Johnson. Education: B.S.Ed., Southern Arkansas University, 1978. Career: Teacher of Physical Education and Science, Coach of Girls Volleyball and Basketball Teams, North Heights Junior High School. Organizational Memberships: American Alliance of Health, Physical Education and Recreation; Physical Education Majors and Minors Club (president). Religion: Baptist. Honors and Awards: Youth in Achievement, 1979; National Honor Society, Alpha Chi, 1978; Listed in *Who's Who in American Colleges and Universities, Outstanding Young Women of America*. Address: Magnolia, Arkansas.

Johnson, Elsa L

Adjunct Professor, Psychiatrist. Personal: Born June 13, 1921; Daughter of Karl Axel and Anna Ahlberg Johnson (both deceased). Education: Attended Eveleth Junior College, Eveleth, Minnesota, June 1940; D.O., Chicago College of Osteopathic Medicine. Career: Private Practice in Psychiatry; Adjunct Professor of Psychiatry, Chicago College of Osteopathic Medicine; Full Professor of Psychiatry, Chicago College of Osteopathic Medicine, 1957-80. Organizational Memberships: American Osteopathic Association; American College of Neuropsychiatry; Illinois Association of Osteopathic Physicians and Surgeons; Delta Omega Sorority (treasurer). Community Activities: Participated in Scholarships for Young Women Sponsored by American Daughters of Sweden, Delta Omega, Zonta Club of Chicago South Side; Former Member, Hyde Park Council of Seniors; Volunteer Physician, Clinic of the Pacific Garden Mission, 1968 to present. Religion: Trinity Evangelical Covenant Church, Oak Lawn, Illinois, Sunday School Teacher, Board of Christian Education 1960-64. Honors and Awards: Fellow, American College of Neuro-Psychiatry, 1970; N.I.H. Senior Stipend in Psychiatry, University of Chicago, 1967-68; High School Valedictorian; Scholarship Honors in Pre-Medicines and at the Chicago College of Osteopathic Medicine. Address: 5435 South Woodlawn Avenue, Chicago, Illinois 60615.

Lonnie L Johnson

Johnson, June Linnea

Independent Fee Appraiser. Personal: Born June 29, 1931; Daughter of Bertha L. Pearson; Married Norman Frank Johnson; Mother of Nona Linnea Bender (Mrs. Robert S.). Education: B.S., University of Illinois, 1952. Career: Antiques Dealer and Shop Owner, 1954 to present; Partner in Show Promotion, 1965-73. Organizational Memberships: National Associaton of Dealers in Antiques, 1975 to present; American Society of Appraisers (associate, 1976; senior member and second designation, October 1979; only 59 so tested A.S.A. appraisers in the United States as of 1981). Religion: St. Paul Lutheran Church, Mt. Prospect. Illinois (Missouri Synod). Honors and Awards: Listed in *Who's Who of American Women*. Address: 1003 East Camp McDonald Road, Prospect Heights, Illinois 60070.

Johnson, Kenneth Leroy Sr

E.R.A. Realtor, Program Manager Executive. Personal: Born January 24, 1922, in Chicago, Illinois; Son of Stanley C. and Nell L. Lundberg Johnson; Married Tran Thi Phuong, July 3, 1949; Father of Jeffrey John, Candy Ann, James John, (by previous marriage) Kenneth LeRoy Jr., Terri Ann, Jeff J. Education: Attended Kansas State College, 1940-42, University of Southern California, 1956-57; B.S., University of Omaha, 1959. Military: Served in the United States Air Force, 1942-69, advancing though the grades to Colonel, Retired 1969. Career: Contract Manager and Manager, Air Department, Pacific Architects and Engineers Co., Vietnam, 1970-75; Program Manager, Bell Helicopter International, Tehran, Iran, 1977-79; E.R.A. Realtor Associate, 1980 to present. Organizational Memberships: National Association of Security Dealers; National Association of Realtors. Community Activities: Republican; Mason. Honors and Awards: Distinguished Flying Cross with One Oak Leaf Cluster; Bronze Star; Purple Heart; Air Medal with Seven Oak Leaf Clusters; 24 Other Campaign Medals. Address: 3020 South Sheridan, Wichita, Kansas 67217.

Johnson, Lonnie L

Union Executive. Personal: Born December 23, 1932, in Hickory, Mississippi; Married to Gwendolyn, in 1967; Father of Derian, Jocelyn, Andrea, Lonnie II. Education: Attended 2 years of college, Chicago, Illinois; Earned 22 credits in labor relations, Roosevelt University, 1957. Military: Served with United States Army 2 years; Discharged with rank of Corporal, 1954. Career: E.K.G. Technician, Chicago Veterans Administration, 1954-62; Began working in a Chicago Post Office in 1962. Organizational

Memberships: National Post Office Mail Handlers Union which merged with the Laborers' International Union of North America in 1970 (national director, 1970 to present, president, 1969-70, elected central regional representative in 1967, national education director for mail handlers union, 1965-69, local president for 1 year, local vice president for 1 year, shop steward for 6 months); American Civil Liberties Union. Community Activities: National Association for the Advancement of Colored People; Urgan League; Leadership on Civil Rights; Congressional Black Caucus; Operation P.U.S.H. Honors and Awards: Became the first Black National President of an A.F.L.-C.I.O. affiliated Postal Union, 1969; Became the first National Director of the National Post Office Mail Handlers Union, 1970; Successfully negotiated the first contract for the National Post Office Professional Nurses affiliation with the Mail Handlers Union, 1980; Received a Special Key to the City of New Orleans, 1970, and Kansas City, 1975; Received numerous honors and recognitions from affiliated labor locals; Listed in *Who's Who Among Black Americans, Who's Who in Labor, International Who's Who of Intellectuals, Community Leaders and Noteworthy Americans.* Address: 14115 Flint Rock Road, Rockville, Maryland, 20853.

Marilyn Johnson

Johnson, Marilyn

Obstetrician/Gynecologist, Semi-Retired. Personal: Born May 7, 1925; Daughter of William Walton and Marilyn Henderson Johnson (both deceased). Education: B.A., The Rice Institute, 1945; M.D., Baylor University College of Medicine, 1950; Intern, New England Hospital, Boston, Massachusetts, 1951-52; Fellow in Gynecological Pathology, Harvard Medical School, 1952-53; Fellow, M. D. Anderson Cancer Institute, 1954; Resident Physician, Methodist Hospital, Houston, Texas, 1951. Career: Obstetrician/Gynecologist, Semi-Retired for One Year to Write Medical Book; Federal Drug Research, Sandoz, Schering, Delbay Pharmaceuticals; Bentex Clinical Instructor, Obstetrics and Gynecology, Baylor University. Organizational Memberships: American College of Obstetrics and Gynecology (fellow); American Medical Women's Association; American Medical Association (membership chairman, 1950 to present); Texas Medical Association; Harris County Medical Association; Houston Obstetrical and Gynecological Society; International Infertility Association. Community Activities: Gynecologist for DePelchin Faith Home, Houston, Texas, 1954-80; Gynecologist for Rice University, 1957-80; Birthright, Houston, Texas (medical director, 1976-81); Houston Right to Life (board of directors); Life Advocates (board of directors); Expert Witness for Committee on Human Resources, Texas State Legislature, 1973-79; Public Speaker, Television, Radio, College Campuses; Foundation for Life (board of directors). Religion: Baptist; Social Vice President, Baptist Student Union, Rice Institute and Baylor University College of Medicine, 1943-50; Sunday School Teacher; Choir. Honors and Awards: George Washington University Medal for Excellence, 1942; Listed in *Who's Who in American Women, Who's Who in Houston.* Address: 205 South Orange Street, Fredericksburg, Texas 78624.

Mary R Johnson

Johnson, Mary Rose

Retired Educator. Personal: Born May 31, 1916, in Evansville, Indiana, U.S.A.; Daughter of Charles Frederick Heilman and granddaughter of U.S. Congressman William Heilman; Married to Fred Lambert Johnson. Education: B.Ed., National College of Education; Graduate studies at Florida State and Florida Atlantic Universities. Career: Kindergarten Director, Evansville Public Schools, prior to 1955; Principal, private nursery-kindergarten, Fort Lauderdale, Florida, 1955-57; Teacher, Broward County Schools, 1958-72. Organizational Memberships: Fort Lauderdale Branch of American Association of University Women (president, 1959-63); Broward County, Florida Association for Childhood Education (president, 1969-71); National College of Education Alumni Association (president Florida East Coast Chapter, 1969 to present); Broward County Classroom Teachers Association (parliamentarian, 1968-71); National Professional Honorary Teachers Sorority, Fort Lauderdale (conclave president, 1963-65, Florida state president, 1965-67). Community Activities: Royal Dames of Cancer Research, Inc. (1st vice president and parliamentarian, 1979 to present); Fort Lauderdale Symphony Society; Fort Lauderdale Oral School Auxiliary; Coral Ridge Yacht Club (parliamentarian); Landings Boat Club. Honors and Awards: Nominated Broward County Woman of the Year, 1961, 1962, 1965; Named to American Association of University Women Florida Honor Roll Register, 1963; Teacher of the Year Award, Pompano Beach Junior Women's Club, 1969; Teacher of the Year Award, District 13 Florida Federation of Women's Clubs, 1969; $500 Grant named for Mary Rose Heilman by Fort Lauderdale Branch of A.A.U.W., 1964; Distinguished Service Award, Norcrest School Parent-Teacher Association, Pompano Beach, 1967; Certificate of Life Membership, Florida Congress of Parents and Teachers, 1971; Outstanding Alumni Achievement Award, National College of Education Board of Trustees, 1969. Address: 3900 Galt Ocean Drive, Apartment 1017, Playa del Mar, Fort Lauderdale, Florida 33308.

Johnson, Mohamed Ismail

Investigative Research Consultant. Personal: Born January 20, 1947; Son of Mrs. Charles C. Johnson; Father of Sadiga Bahiya. Education: M.P.H., Yale University School of Medicine, 1971. Military: Served in the United States Naval Reserve, 1973-75, attaining the rank of Lieutenant (j.g.). Career: Investigative Research Consultant; Former Health Education Consultant. Organizational Memberships: American Public Health Association; Islamic Medical Association of North America. Community Activities: Citizens Crime Commission of Philadelphia, 1980-81; Donations to Islamic Community Center School of Philadelphia; Share Holder, Islamic Banking System, 1980 to present. Religion: Certificate of Shahada, Al Azhar University, 1973; Umra Pilgrimage, Mecca, Saudi Arabia, 1974. Honors and Awards: Inter-Faith Studies Award, 1969; Listed in *Biographical Directory of the American Public Health Association, Dictionary of International Biography.* Address: 6219 North 16th Street, Philadelphia, Pennsylvania 19141.

Mohamed I Johnson

Johnson, Norma Jeanette

Producer of Specialty Wools, Angus. Personal: Born August 30, 1925; Daughter of Jasper Crile and Mildred Catherine Russell Johnson (both deceased); Mother of Susan Kay Covey. Education: Attended Heidelberg College, 1943; Certificate, Drafting Techniques, Case School of Applied Science, 1944; Attended Western Reserve University 1945-47, Ohio State University 1951, Muskingun College 1965; A.A., Kent State University, 1979; Adult Education, Buckeye Joint Vocational School. Career: Owner, Operator, Sunny Slopes Farm; Instructor, Arts and Crafts, University Settlement House, Cleveland, Ohio, 1944; Mechanical Draftswoman, National Association Aeronautics, Cleveland, 1944-46; Manufacturer's Representative, National Spice House, 1947-49; Teacher, Economics, English, Mathematics, Home Economics, History, Tuscarawas County School System, New Philadelphia, Ohio, 1962-69. Organizational Memberships: Mid-States Wool Growers; Select-Sires, Inc.; American Angus Association; National Grange; International Platform Association. Community Activities: Winfield Parent-Teacher Association (chaplain 1960); Brandywine Grange (program director 1960-62); Girl Scouts (leader 1961-70); Jail Committee of Tuscarawas County, 1981. Religion: Teacher, Methodist Sunday School, 1956-61. Honors and Awards: Scholastic Honorable Mention, State of Ohio, 1939; Herbster Oration Award, 1943; Certificate, Voluntary Trainer, Girl Scouts, 1967; Certificate of Merit, Tuscarawas County Schools, 1965; Ohio Wildlife Conservation Award for Tuscarawas County, 1972; Listed in *Who's Who of American*

Women. Address: Route 1, Box 398, Dover, Ohio 44622.

Johnson, Paul Robert

Lawyer. Personal: Born June 16, 1941; Son of George W. Johnson, Mary Bess Osteen. Education: Attended Florida Southern College 1960-62, Jacksonville University 1963; B.A., Florida State University, 1964; J.D., North Carolina Central University School of Law, 1971. Military: Served in the United States Army, 1964-66, attaining the rank of 1st Lieutenant. Career: School Teacher, 8th Grade English, Jacksonville Beach, Florida; Lawyer. Organizational Memberships: Florida Bar Association; American Bar Association; Florida Trial Lawyers Association; Phi Alpha Delta Law Fraternity; United States Supreme Court Historical Society; Duval County Teachers Association. Community Activities: Trenton Rotary, 1973-74; Capitol City Kiwanis, 1975-76; International Christian Leadership Conference, 1975-77; Dialogue of the Arts, 1975-77; Girl Scouts of America, 1975-76; Democratic Party; Patron of the Theatre, Florida State University, 1975-77; Tennessee Performing Arts; Sons of Confederate Veterans, 1973-77. Religion: Episcopal Church. Honors and Awards: J.D. Degree magna cum laude; Army Certificate of Achievement; Honorary Army Recruiter; Listed in *Who's Who in the South and Southwest, International Men of Achievement, International Who's Who of Intellectuals, One Thousand International Profiles.* Address: 5539 Stanford Road #B, Jacksonville, Florida 32207.

Norma J Johnson

Johnson, Richard Alvin

Oil Company Superintendent. Personal: Born July 8, 1934; Son of Elma B. Ryan; Married Linda Covington; Father of Richard, William, Terry. Education: B.S., Michigan State University, 1963. Military: Served in the United States Army Signal Corps as Chief Enlisted Instructor, Radar School, 1955-58. Career: Superintendent, Program Control Division, Arabian American Oil Company, Dhahran, Saudi Arabia, 1977 to present; Senior Partner, Johnson and Associates, Gulfport, Mississippi, 1976-77; Vice President and Principal, Amco Construction Company Inc., 1974-76; Director, M.S.U.-M.T.F. Research Center, Mississippi State University, 1971-74; Research Coordinator, Program Analysis Engineer, General Electric Company, 1966-71; Manager, Engineering Systems Test, I.T.T. Federal Laboratories, Nutley, New Jersey, 1965-66; Senior Field Engineer, A.N./G.L.R-1 Maintenance Training Installation, General Dynamics/Electronics, Rochester, New York, 1959-65; Field Engineer, A.N./G.L.R.-1 Overseas Installation; Engineering Aide, Antenna Laboratory, MELPAR Inc., 1958-59. Published Works: Author "Visual Display of Transistor Characteristic Curves", "Proposal, Contract, and Program Management", "Data Acquisition System for Marine and Ecological Research", Others; Co-Author "Application of Aerospace Data Acquisition Technology to Atmospheric and Meteorological Investigations", "Airborne Data Acquisition System for Atomospheric and Meteorological Research", "A Tidal Simulation System for Marine Ecosystems Research in Salt Water Impoundments", Others. Honors and Awards: Has Appeared Before National and International Conferences to Deliver Presentations on Instrumentation Engineering and Technology Utilization, including the American Astronautical Society Award Conference, Little Rock, Arkansas, November 1970; International Aerospace Instrumentation Conference, Las Vegas, Nevada, May 1971; N.A.S.A. Space Benefits Conference, Huntsville, Alabama, November 1971; Mississippi Engineering Society, Jackson, Mississippi, July 1973. Address: 17 Poplar Circle, Gulfport, Mississippi 39501; Aramco Box 5734, Dhahran, Saudi Arabia.

Johnson, Robert Leland

Lawyer. Personal: Born May 1, 1933, in Denver, Colorado; Married Pamela Gay Stearns, June 6, 1964; Father of Mary Morris (deceased), Anthony Morris. Education: Graduate of East High School, 1951; Class of 1955, Yale University; J.D., University of Denver College of Law, 1958; B.A., English, University of Denver, 1962; Human Development Certificate, The Institute for the Achievement of Human Potential, Philadelphia, Pennsylvania, 1978. Career: Admitted to the Bar of the State of Colorado, Federal District Court for the District of Colorado, Tenth Circuit Court of Appeals, Inter-state Commerce Commission, Supreme Court of the United States; Admitted to United States Tax Court; Former Law Clerk to Justice O. Otto Moore, Colorado Supreme Court; Former Assistant Regional Counsel, United States General Services Administration, Region 8; One of Three Commissioners in Urban Renewal Condemnation; One of Three Deliberative Panel Members for Denver Bar Association Legal Fee Arbitration Committee; Sole Practitioner in Private Law Practice, Denver, Colorado. Organizational Memberships: American Bar Association; American Judicature Society; Colorado Trial Lawyers Association; Denver Bar Association (legal aid and public defender committee; family law committee; interprofessional committee; economics of law practice committee; lawyer referral committee; law day, U.S.A. committee); Adams County Bar Association; Colorado Bar Association (medical-legal liaison committee; defense of indigents committee; legal services for the poor committee; public relations committee; lay assistants to lawyers committee; mental health committee; grievance policy committee). Community Activities: Chi Phi Fraternity; Colorado Council for the Experiment in International Living; Colorado Press Association; Colorado Society of the Sons of the American Revolution (state secretary, 1971-72; state president, 1972-74); Colorado Yale Association; Elks; International Platform Association; Louisa County, Iowa, Historical Society; Military Order of the Loyal Legion of the United States; Moose; National Genealogical Society; National Historical Society; National Society of the Sons of the American Colonists (national chancellor, 1974; acting Colorado state regent, 1974 to present); National Society of the Sons of the American Revolution (vice president general, 1975; national trustee, 1977); Smithsonian Institution Associates; Sons of Union Veterans of the Civil War (junior vice-commander, Colorado-Wyoming department, 1971-72); The Historical Society of Pennsylvania; Yale Alumni Representative to Northglenn High, 1967-68. Religion: Society of Friends (Quaker). Published Works: Author, *The Newspaper Accounts of B. F. Wright, Esq., and Others of Louisa County, Iowa,* 1967; *Trial Handbook for Colorado Torts Lawyers,* 1967; *Matrimonial Practice in Colorado Courts,* 1969; *The American Heritage of James Norman Hall,* 1970; *Colorado Mechanic's Liens,* 1971; *Statute Annotations,* 1969-78; *A Genealogical Excursion through Historic Philadelphia,* 1976; Co-Author, *A Mother's Love,* 1977; Author, *Letters to Glenn Doman: A Story of Enriched and Accelerated Childhood Development,* 1980; *Super Babies: A Handbook of Enriched and Accelerated Childhood Development,* 1982. Honors and Awards: High School Valedictorian; Certificate of Merit, University of Denver College of Law, 1958; Denver Opportunity Certificate of Merit, 1967; Patriot Medal, Colorado Society of the Sons of the American Revolution, 1976; Listed in *Who's Who in American Law, Who's Who in the West, Who's Who in Finance and Industry, Who's Who in Colorado, Who's Who in the World, Community Leaders of America, Dictionary of International Biography, Two Thousand Men of Achievement, Personalities of the West and Midwest, National Register of Prominent Americans, National Social Directory, Royal Blue Book, Hereditary Register of the United States, International Who's Who in Community Service, Contemporary Authors, Social Directory of Colorado, Library of Human Resources, Community Leaders and Noteworthy Americans, International Who's Who of Intellectuals, People Who Matter, Personalities of America, Men and Women of Distinction, The Best Lawyers of America, Community Leaders of America, Anglo-American Who's Who, Honor Book, Directory of Distinguished Americans.* Address: 705 West Eighth Avenue, Denver, Colorado 80204.

Richard A Johnson

Johnson, Rufus Winfield

Attorney-at-Law (semi-retired); Creative Writer. Personal: Born May 1, 1911; Son of Charles L. Sr. and Margaret Smith Johnson (both deceased); Married Vaunda Louise Griffith. Education: A.B. 1934, Graduate School 1934-36, School of Law 1936-39, LL.B. 1939, Howard University, Washington, D.C. Military: Graduated from the Reserve Officers Training Corps with Commission as Second Lieutenant, 1934; Served in the United States Army with the 92nd Infantry Division in Action in Italy as a Combat Infantry Company Commander during World War II; Served during the Korean Crisis, 3 Years; Served as Staff Judge Advocate of Fort McArthur, San Pedro, California upon return from overseas; Retired from United States Armed Forces Reserve Program with the rank of Lieutenant Colonel. Career: Private Practice of Law, Branch Office in San Bernardino, Santa Barbara 1956-58, San Bernardino 1954-78, Los Angeles 1952-54, Washington, D.C. 1945-48; Represented Navajo Indians in the Case of People vs. Woody in which California Supreme Court ruled use of peyote as a religious sacrament by American Indians protected by First Amendment of United States Constitution. Organizational Memberships: California State Bar Association; San Bernardino County Bar Association; American Judicature Society; Judge Advocates Association; Admitted to Practice before United States Supreme Court Bar, Bar of the Supreme Court of South Korea, Washington, D.C. District Court of Appeals Bar, Bar of the Supreme Court of California, Bar of the United States District Court for the Southern District of California, Bar of the Supreme Court of Arkansas. Community Activities: American Academy of Political and Social Science; National Association for the Advancement of Colored People; American Civil Liberties Union; Masonic Lodge; Consistory; Shriners; 32nd Degree Mason; 4th Degree Black Belt, Shorin-Ryu Karate. Religion: Baptist Church. Published Works: Transcription of the Memoirs of his Military Experiences and of Cases involving his Private Practice (in progress). Honors and Awards: CIB, Bronze Star, Purple Heart and Special Regimental Citation for Bravery, United States Army; First Black Officer to Serve as Staff Judge Advocate of any Military Base in the United States; First Civilian Employee from the White House Staff to enter the United States Armed Forces during World War II. Address: Route 2 Box 220A, Hogeye, Prairie Grove, Arizona 72753.

Johnson, Scott Edwin

Retired School Principal. Personal: Born October 14, 1894; Son of Scott and Caroline Johnson (both deceased); Married Ethel Mae Downs; Father of Ethel Ruth Daniels. Education: Trade Certificate, B.S., M.A., Hampton Institute, Virginia; Advanced Studies undertaken at the University of Colorado, Columbia University. Military: Served in the United States Army, 1917-18, with the rank of Private First Class. Career: Retired High School Prinicipal; Supervision Teacher. Organizational Memberships: Teachers Association, 1941-55. Community Activities: Chamber of Commerce, 1939-42; Day Care Center; Cancer Drive (chairman); U.S.O. (chairman, 1943-44); Walker County Resource Commission (board member); Walker County Council of Organizations (board member); Bi-Racial Organization (chairman). Religion: Baptist, Deacon. Honors and Awards: City Councilman, 1966-74; Mayor for a Day, 1968; Awards from City, Fire Department, Alumni Association, Chamber of Commerce, Church, Texas Teachers Association, National Education Association, Teachers Credit Union, School Board, Texas Principal's Association, Texas Schoolman's Organization. Address: 716 10th Street, P.O. Box 1400, Huntsville, Texas 77340.

Johnson-Masters, Virginia

Institute Director. Personal: Born February 11, 1925, in Springfield, Missouri; Married William H. Masters; Mother of Scott F. Johnson, Lisa E. Johnson. Education: Attended Missouri University (Columbia) 1944-46, Washington University (St. Louis) 1964; D.Sc. (honorary), University of Louisville, 1978. Career: Missouri State Insurance Department, Missouri State Legislature, 63rd General Assembly, 1942-44; Editorial Writer and Administrative Secretary, *St. Louis Daily Record*, 1947-50; Advertising Department, Columbia Broadcasting System, KMOX, St. Louis, 1950-51; Washington University School of Medicine, Division of Reproductive Biology, Department of Obstetrics and Gynecology, St. Louis, Missouri, Research Staff 1957-64, Research Assistant 1960-62, Research Instructor 1962-64; Reproductive Biology Research Foundation, St. Louis, Missouri, Research Associate 1964-69, Assistant Director 1969-73; Co-Director (with William H. Masters), Masters & Johnson Institute (formerly Reproductive Biology Research Foundation), St. Louis, 1973-80; Director, Masters & Johnson Institute, 1981 to present; Certified Sex Therapist, American Association of Sex Educators, Counselors, and Therapists, 1975. Organizational Memberships: American Association for the Advancement of Science; American Association of Sex Educators, Counselors and Therapists; Author's Guild, Inc.; Colombian Sexological Society (honorary); Eastern Association for Sex Therapy (life member); Eastern Missouri Psychiatric Society (honorary); Homosexual Community Counseling Center (advisory board); International Academy of Sex Research (member; treasurer, 1975-76); International Platform Association; Pastoral Psychology Advisory Committee; Sex Information and Education Council of the United States; Society for the Scientific Study of Sex (fellow). Community Activities: Friends of the City Art Museum; Jewish Hospital Auxiliary; Missouri Botanical Garden; The Women's Association of the St. Louis Symphony Society; Bridlespur Hunt Club; The Saint Louis Club. Published Works: Co-Author *Ethical Issues in Sex Therapy and Research, Textbook of Sexual Medicine, Homosexuality in Perspective*, Many Other Books and Articles. Honors and Awards: Alpha Sigma Lambda; Paul H. Hoch Award, American Psychopathological Association, 1971; Citation Award, Sex Information and Education Council of the United States, 1971; World Almanac 25 Most Influential Women in America, 1975, 1978, 1979, 1980; Rotary International Paul Harris Fellow, 1976; Distinguished Service Award, American Association of Marriage and Family Counselors, 1976; Modern Medicine Award for Distinguished Achievement, 1977; American Association of Sex Educators, Counselors and Therapists Award, 197; World Association for Sexology Biomedical Research Award, 1979; Edward Henderson Lecture Award, American Geriatrics Society, 1981. Address: 4529 Pershing Place, St. Louis, Missouri 63108.

Ruth L Johnston

Johnston, Ruth Le Roy

Retired Nosologist, Medical Record Administrator. Personal: Born June 19, 1915, in Elizabeth, New Jersey; Daughter of James Archibald and Frances Ione Davis Austin Le Roy; Married Earl B. Johnston (deceased), in 1944; Mother of Jonathan Bruce Johnston (deceased). Education: Graduate of Battin High School, Elizabeth, New Jersey, 1934; B.A., Bob Jones University, 1945; R.R.A., Emory University, 1953; I.B.M. Computer Systems and FORTRAN, 1962-65; D.H.E.W., S.S.A., and Various I.D.C. Disease Nomenclature Workshops through 1979. Career: Assistant to Chief Medical Record Librarian, Grady Memorial Hospital, Atlanta, Georgia, 1948-53; Chief Medical Record Librarian, Georgia Baptist Hospital 1953-54, Memorial Mission Hospital (Asheville, North Carolina) 1954-55, Veterans Administration Hospital (Richmond, Virginia) 1955-60, Veterans Administration Center (Wood, Wisconsin) 1960, Veterans Administration Hospital (Hines, Illinois) 1960-62; Supervisory Medical Classification Specialist, Nosologist, Research and Statistics, Social Security Administration, Department of Health, Education and Welfare, Baltimore, Maryand, 1962-68; Consultant, Medical Records, Prince George's Hospital, Cheverly, Maryland, 1965-67; Medical Record Consultant, Health Data Service, Maryland Blue Cross-Blue Shield, Baltimore, Maryland, 1969-71; Chief Medical Record Administrator, Good Samaritan Hospital, West Palm Beach, Florida, 1971-74; Chief Medical Record Administrator, Gorgas Hospital, United States Canal Zone, Panama, 1974-77; Consultant to Coco Solo Hospital, 1974-77; Retired, Working Part-Time in Office of Arthur W. Yount, M.D., P.A., North Palm Beach, Florida. Organizational Memberships: American Medical Record Association; Maryland Medical Record Association (chairman, education committee; past vice president); Virginia Medical Record Association (president, treasurer); Veterans Administration (area medical record consultant; speaker at national conference);

Member Various Other State Medical Record Associations. Community Activities: International Platform Association; National Audubon Society; National Republican Congressional Committee; Congressional V.I.P. Memberships; Republican National Committee; Republican Presidential Task Force (charter member); United States Senatorial Club; Panama Canal Club; National Association of Federal Retired Employees; A.A.R.P. Religion: First Baptist Church, West Palm Beach, Florida, Adult Jubilee Choir. Published Works: Contributor to Professional Journals. Honors and Awards: Various Veterans Administration and Civil Service Awards, 1960-68; Listed in *Notable Americans, Who's Who, American Registry Series, World's Who's Who of Women, Marquis Who's Who, Dictionary of International Biography, International Who's Who of Intellectuals.* Address: 100 Paradise Harbour Blvd., North Palm Beach, Florida 33408.

Jones, Ed

Farmer. Personal: Born April 20, 1912; Married Llewellyn Wyatt; Father of Mary Lew Jones McGuire (deceased), Jennifer Jones Kinnard. Education: Attended the University of Tennessee; D.Lit. (honorary), Bethel College. Career: Farmer; Former Dairy Inspector, Railroad Agriculture Representative; Tennessee Commissioner of Agriculture, 1949-53. Organizational Memberships: Tennessee A.S.C.S. Committee (chairman, 1962-69); House Administration Subcommittee on Services (chairman); House Committee on Agriculture; Subcommittee on Conservation Credit and Rural Development (chairman). Community Activities: Gibson County Board of Education, 1948-69; Mid-South Fair (board of directors); Bethel College (board of trustees, 1952-69). Honors and Awards: Award for Distinguished Service to Southern Agriculture of the *Progressive Farmer Magazine*, 1980; Award for Distinguished Service to Agriculture of Gamma Sigma Delta, 1980; Distinguished Alumnus Award of the University of Tennessee at Martin, 1980; Distinguished Service Award of the National Limestone Institute, 1979; Leadership Service Award of the National Telephone Cooperative Association, 1978; Man of the Year Award of the Memphis Agriculture Club, 1957; Man of the Year Award of the *Progressive Farmer Magazine*, 1951; Number of Other Awards and Honors. Address: Post Office Box 128, Yorkville, Tennessee 38389.

Jones, James Robert

Barber. Personal: Born June 28, 1937; Son of Sallie Jones; Married Mamie Johnson; Father of Crystal, Patricia. Education: Attended Durham Business College (Durham, North Carolina), Kittrell College (Kittrell, North Carolina), Louisburg College (Louisburg, North Carolina), Harris Barber College (Raleigh, North Carolina). Military: Served in the United States Air Force, 1957-65. Career: Barber. Community Activities: Franklinton Elementary School Parent-Teacher Association (president, 1970-72); Franklin County Branch, National Association for the Advancement of Colored People (treasurer, 1976-80); Thrifty Sons Lodge #284 (worshipful master, 1977-79); Thrifty Daughters, Order of the Eastern Star (patron, 1975-81). Religion: Ordained Deacon, 1966; Treasurer, Sunday School, 1975-81; Senior Choir; Assistant Adult Teacher. Honors and Awards; Plaque from Franklinton Elementary School P.T.A., 1972; Listed in *Personalities of the South.* Address: Route 2 Box 164A, Franklinton, North Carolina 27529.

Jones, Leander Corbin

Associate Professor. Personal: Born July 16, 1934; Son of L. C. and Una Bell Jones; Married Lethonee Angela Hendricks; Father of Angela Lynne, Leander Corbin Jr. Education: A.B., Speech and Drama, University of Arkansas-Pine Bluff, 1956; M.S., Radio/TV, University of Illinois, 1968; Ph.D., Mass Communications, Union Graduate School, 1973. Military: Served in the United States Army, 1956-58, with the rank of Private First Class. Career: Associate Professor of Black Studies, Western Michigan University; Previous Positions include Communications Media Specialist, Television Producer and Director, Teacher of English as a Foreign Language, Teacher of English, Writer of Telescript. Organizational Memberships: Theatre Arts and Broadcasting Skills Center (president); Popular Culture Association; Black Theatre Group, Kalamazoo (chairman); Du Sable Museum of African-American History; National Association for the Advancement of Colored People. Community Activities: African Studies Program (chairman); Parent-Teacher Association (chairman); P.T.S.A. (vice chairman); Theatre Director/Actor; Council on Black Studies; Michigan Council on Black Studies; Michigan Commission on Crime and Delinquency; American Youth Soccer Organization (coach, referee). Religion: Unitarian. Honors and Awards: Dramatic Merit 1954, Highest Drama Award 1955, A.B. cum laude 1956, University of Arkansas-Pine Bluff; Listed in *Dictionary of International Biography, Personalities of the West and Midwest, Who's Who in the Midwest, Notable Americans.* Address: 2226 S. Westnedge, Kalamazoo, Michigan 49008.

Mallory M Jones

Jones, Mallory Millett

Actress. Personal: Born in St. Paul, Minnesota; Daughter of James and Helen Millett; Mother of Kristen Vigard. Education: B.A., University of Minnesota; Specialized Language Studies at the University of Mexico, Mexico City; Studied with Charles Conrad in Los Angeles, Frank Corsaro and Lee Strasberg in New York City. Career: Active in New York Theatre for 10 Years, Working in Plays at LaMama, Theatre for the New City, W.P.A., Theatre Genesis; Appeared on Television in the United States and Europe; Appeared with the Living Theatre in America; Toured Europe with John Vaccaro's Playhouse of the Ridiculous; Member of Original Companies of "Annie" and "The Best Little Whorehouse in Texas"; Portrayed Roles of Hedda Gabler, Carla, "Kennedy's Children", Daughter of Jan Sterling and John McMartin in Berkshire Theatre Festival's "Dodsworth", Corinna Stroller in "The House of Blue Leaves"; Played Role of Kathy Smith on C.B.S. Daytime Drama "Love of Life" and Gena Venucci on N.B.C.'s "Another World"; Role of Louise Sniffin in Movie of the Week "Eischeid"; Five One-Woman Photography Shows, New York City; With Lisa Shreve, Has Written and Photographed Four Film Strips on Infant Care and Development and Co-Author Screenplay "Canberra". Published Works: Currently Writing Novel *A Leap of Faith.* Address: 484 West 43rd Street, New York City, New York 10036.

Jones, Mildred Lucille Singleton

Administrator. Personal: Born January 8, 1927; Daughter of Arthur F. and Media Jordan Singleton (both deceased); Married Bobby H. Jones; Mother of Randall H., Gerald W. Education: Attended Southern Methodist University, 1971, 1973; Studies at the University of Texas-Dallas, 1978, 1979. Career: Dallas Child Guidance Clinic, Administrative Director 1980 to present, Acting Executive Director 1980-81, Administrative Assistant 1957-80, Office Manager 1951-56, Secretary 1949-51. Organizational Memberships: American Association of Psychiatric Services for Children; American Management Association; Business and Professional Women; Mental Health Association (committee on adolescent foster care, 1979; planning committee for parenting conferences, 1978, 1979, 1980); Association for Volunteer Directors. Community Activities: P.T.A. (officer, 1975-77); Cub Scout (leader, 1968-70; den mother's trainer, 1970); United Way (campaign worker, member of speaker's bureau, 1970 to present). Religion: Park Cities Baptist Church, Sunday School Teacher 1965-77. Honors and Awards: Listed in *Who's Who of American Women,*

Personalities of the South, Who's Who in the South and Southwest, World Who's Who of Women. Address: 9909 Elmada Lane, Dallas, Texas 75220.

Jones, Myrtis Idelle

Retired. Personal: Born May 16, 1908; Daughter of A. B. and Ethel Hardwick Barham (both deceased); Married B. H. Harrison, J. W. E. Moore, C. W. Jones (all deceased); Mother of Jack Barham Harrison, Charles Ray Harrison, Mary Anna Harrison Scheie, William Robert Moore, Jonathan Edward Moore, Ethel Rachel Moore Hubka, Paul David Moore. Education: A.A., Little Rock Junior College, 1952; B.S.Ed., Arkansas State Teachers College, 1958; M.L.S., George Peabody College for Teachers, 1965. Career: Library Assistant, Little Rock Junior College, 1950-53; Librarian, Holly Grove High School (Arkansas) 1955, Vanndale High School (Arkansas) 1955-56, Stuttgart Senior High School (Arkansas) 1956-59; Supervisor, Libraries, Stuttgart Public Schools, 1956-59; Librarian, Arkansas School for the Blind, 1959-74; Member, Retired Senior Volunteer Program. Organizational Memberships: Arkansas Student Librarians Association (sponsor, executive council, 1957-74); American Library Association; Arkansas Education Association; National Education Association; Southwest Library Association; Council on Exceptional Children; Educators of Visually Handicapped (chairman, library workshop, 1964-68); Arkansas Association of Classroom Teachers; Arkansas Library Association (vice president, 1966-67; chairman, special library section, 1963-64); A.L.A. Roundtable for the Blind (secretary, 1973-74); Alpha Beta Alpha. Community Activities: Commission on Standards and Accreditation of Services for the Blind, 1963-66; Pulaski County Council on Aging (coordinator of activities, 1977-80). Religion: Soloist, Pianist, Organist, Choir Director, 1920 to present; Sunday School Teacher, 1925 to present; Pastor, Children's Church, 1939-42; Director, Intermediate Youth Program, 1943-46; Vacation Bible School Director, 1940-50; Senior Adult Ministries Director, 1981 to present. Honors and Awards: John Cotton Dana Library Publicity Award, 2nd Place in High School Division, 1957; Citation for Contribution to American Association of Educators of the Blind, 1962; Outstanding Achievement Award, C.O.M.S.T.A.C., 1966; Honorary Life Member, Arkansas Gerontological Society, 1979; Outstanding Service Award, Pulaski County Council on Aging, 1981. Address: 5608 Geyer Springs Road, Little Rock, Arkansas 72209.

Jones, Ruthanne Marr

Physical Therapist, Civic Worker. Personal: Born October 9, 1935, in Warrensburg, Missouri; Daughter of J. Kenneth and Ruth A. Noble Marr; Married Keith D. Jones, January 31, 1964; Mother of Brian Kent, Stephen Dennis. Education: Attended the University of Missouri 1953-54, University of Colorado 1954; B.A. Psychology, B.S. Physical Therapy, University of Southern California, 1958; Graduate Studies at London School of Economics, 1956-57; M.A. English, Central Missouri State University, 1962. Career: Physical Therapist, Cerebral Palsy Nursery School, University of California-Los Angeles, 1958-59; Chief Physical Therapist, Warrensburg Nursing and Medical Center, 1966-76; President, Jones and Associates, Rehabilitation Specialists, 1970 to present; President, Ruthanne Jones and Associates, Rehabilitation, Inc., 1977 to present; Former Vice President, Holiday Inn, Warrensburg; Assistant Secretary, Volunteer Therapist, Johnson County Memorial Hospital, Warrensburg, 1964-66; Volunteer Instructor, Physical Therapy, Jordan for Medico, 1962-63; Organizational Memberships: Johnson County Medical Auxiliary (president, 1965-66; 6th district director, 1968-70); Missouri State Medical Auxiliary (3rd vice president, 1970-71; president, 1972-73); Missouri State Medical Association (Missouri councilor, 1967-69; historian, 1973-74; treasurer, 2nd vice president, 1976); Johnson County Memorial Hospital Guild (founder, 1967); American Association of Physical Therapy; National Association of Parliamentarians; Women's Auxiliary to Missouri State Medical Association (president, 1972-73); Missouri State Physical Therapy Association (legislative chairman, 1976 to present); American Contract Bridge League; Chi Omega. Community Activities: Order of the Eastern Star; Socunda Study Club (president, 1966-68); Johnson County Parliamentarian Club (secretary, 1969; historian, 1979-71; president, 1971-72); Arts Book and Craft Club. Religion: Presbyterian. Address: 711 South Holden Street, Warrensburg, Missouri 64093.

Myrtis B Jones

Jones, Virgil Carrington

Writer. Personal: Born June 7, 1906; Son of Alonzo Lewis Jones (deceased); Married Geneva Peyton; Father of Virgil Carrington Jr., Judith Watkins. Education: Attended Virginia Polytechnic Institute, 1924-26; B.A. magna cum laude, Journalism, Washington and Lee University, 1927-30. Career: Newspaper Reporter; Public Relations Director, The Curtis Publishing Company; Administrative Assistant to Congressman William M. Tuck of Virginia; Professional Writer for the National Aeronautics and Space Administration. Published Works: Author of *Ranger Mosby; The Hatfields and the McCoys; Gray Ghosts and Rebel Raiders; Eight Hours Before Richmond; The Civil War at Sea* (3 volumes); *Birth of Liberty; Roosevelt's Rough Riders; Log of Apollo 11* (first official government account of the moon landing). Honors and Awards: Sigma Delta Chi Scholarship Award; District of Columbia Civil War Round Table's Gold Medal Award for Meritorious Writing. Address: 15000 Lee Highway, Centreville, Virginia 22020.

Jones-Flake, Judy Carol

Administrative Assistant. Personal: Born November 27, 1946; Daughter of Roy M. and Viola Mae Jones. Education: Attended Universal Business College, 1965; American Institute of Banking, 1967-69; A.A., Austin Community College, 1977; B.A., 1979, and M.A., 1980, University of Texas at Austin. Career: Clerk-Secretary, Texas Southern University; Senior Bookkeeper, Texas Commerce Bank; Administrative Technician I, State Senator Chet Brooks; Administrative Assistant, State Representative Ron Wilson. Community Activities: Ms. Black Austin Community Project (chairman of the board 1978-79); Guest Lecturer; Consultant, Management and Governmental Affairs, Human Resources Management and Employment Practices. Honors and Awards: The Organizational Management Special Project, University of Texas, 1979; Community Outreach Award, The Austin Women's Center, 1979; Listed in *Who's Who of America, Who's Who of American Women.* Address: 9401 Hunters Trace, Austin, Texas 78758.

Jordan, Gary Blake

Administrator. Personal: Born February 3, 1939; Son of Lt. Col. Robert Leslie and Lois Evelyn Jordan; Married Gloria Jean Heppler; Father of Gareth Kylae, Glynis Jerelle. Education: B.S.E.E., College of Applied Science, Ohio University, 1961; Ph.D. (H.C.), Electrical Engineering, Sussex College of Technology, England, 1977; Doctor of Electrical Enigneering, Pacific Southern University, 1977. Career: Director, National Intelligence Agency; Former Executive Vice-President, The Electronic Warfare Organization. Organizational Memberships: Institute of Electrical and Electronic Engineers; American Defense Preparedness Association; Armed Forces Communications and Electronics Association; United States Naval Institute. Community Activities: Society for Technical Communication (senior member); Society for Scholarly Publishing (charter member); Radio Society of Great Britain (corporate member); American Radio Relay League (full member); Washington Academy of Science (member-at-large); Northern California DX

Foundation; International Amateur Radio Club, Geneva, Switzerland; Association of Old Crows (life member); American Association for the Advancement of Science; Professional Association of Diving Instructors. Honors and Awards: Life Fellow, Lambda Xi Pi, 1961; Fellow, American Biographical Institute, 1980. Address: 1012 Olmo Court, San Jose, California 95129.

Jordan, Lucille Galloway

Associate State Superintendent. Personal: Daughter of Mr. and Mrs. T. P. Galloway; Married F. L. S. Jordan; Mother of Noelle Jordan. Education: Undergraduate Studies at Asheville College, University of Tennessee; Master's Degree, University of Georgia; Ed.D., University of Georgia. Career: Associate State Superintendent of Schools, Office of Instructional Services, Georgia Department of Education; Directed following programs in Atlanta Public Schools--Title III, Teacher Corps Consortium of Eight Colleges and Universities, Elementary Curriculum and Program Development, (1966-78); Classroom Teacher for 15 years, North Carolina, Tennessee, Georgia. Organizational Memberships: National Association for Supervision and Curriculum Development (president); Phi Kappa Phi Honorary Scholastic Society; Pi Kappa Delta Honorary (president); Georgia Association of Educational Leaders; American Association of University Women. Community Activities: Advisory Board to C. B. S. Television Specials; Teacher's Guide to Television (advisory board); Atlanta Teacher Educational Teacher's Guides to Television (advisory board); Atlanta Teacher Educational Services (advisory board); Atlanta Journal and Constitution (educational advisory board). Religion: Sandy Springs First Baptist Church. Honors and Awards: National Science Foundation Fellow, 1973; Listed in *Who's Who of American Educators, Who's Who of American Women, World Who's Who of Women, International Biographies of Two Thousand Women of Achievement*. Address: 2310 North Peachtree Way, Dunwoody, Georgia 30338.

Lucille G Jordan

Jorgensen, Kay S

Museum Administrator. State Representative. Personal: Born March 25, 1951; Daughter of Arnold and Twyla Jorgensen; Married Michael R. Pangburn. Education: B.S.Ed., Black Hills State College, 1974; One Semester of Study, World Campus Afloat, Chapmon College; Auctioneer, Fort Smith Auction School. Career: Executive Director of Museum; South Dakota Legislator, House of Representatives; Former Positions include Auctioneer, Educator. Organizational Memberships: State History Association; Local History Association; Le Case Library Association; American Legislative Exchange Council; National Council of State Legislators. Community Activities: Select Committee on Mining, 1981-82; Governors Ad Hoc Water Committee, 1981; High-Plains Heritage Society, 1976 to present; Business and Professional Women; American Association of University Women; National Federation of Independent Businesses. Honors and Awards: Outstanding Alumnus, 1981. Address: 840 West Jackson, Spearfish, South Dakota 57783.

Sylvia Joure

Joure, Sylvia Ann

Executive. Personal: Born October 15, 1945; Daughter of Patrick and Martha Joure. Education: B.S. 1966, M.S. 1969, Ph.D. 1970, Memphis State University. Career: President, Senior Partner, Frye/Joure and Associates, Memphis, 1973 to present; Operating Vice President, Frye/Timmons and Associates, Memphis, 1973 to present; Assistant Professor of Psychology, University of Arkansas-Little Rock, 1970-71; Industrial/Organizational Psychologist, Frye/Timmons and Associates, 1968 to present; Teaching and Research Assistant, Memphis State University, 1967-70. Organizational Memberships: American Psychological Association; Southeastern Psychological Association; Southwestern Psychological Association; Tennessee Psychological Association; International Association of Applied Psychology; A.S.T.D. Community Activities: National Organization of Women (board of directors, task force); Sexual Harrasment Project (chairperson); Memphis Girls Club (board of directors; vice president); League of Women Voters. Honors and Awards: Diplomate, Highest Distinction Awarded Practitioners by the American Board of Professional Psychology; University of Arkansas-Little Rock "Biographical Study of Achieving and Non-achieving Females" Grant: Psi Chi Honor Society; Regional Finalist, White House Fellowship, 1981, 1982; Listed in *Young Women of America, Who's Who in American Women, Who's Who in the South and Southwest*. Address: 367 Caraway Cove, Memphis, Tennessee 38117.

Joyce, Edwin Anthony Jr

Edwin A Joyce Jr

Administrator. Personal: Born February 23, 1937, in Hampton, Virginia; Son of Edwin Anthony (deceased) and Leah Bell Gates Joyce; Married Mary Dale Smith; Father of Edwin Anthony, William Christopher, Kathy Smith, Kim Smith, Beth Smith, Kelly Smith, Carson Smith. Education: Graduate of Broadripple High School, Indianapolis, Indiana; B.A. Botany, Butler University, 1959; Graduate Level Course in Marine Invertebrate Zoology, Duke University, Summer 1958; M.S. Marine Biology, University of Florida, 1961; Graduate Level Course in Marine Algology, University of South Florida, 1966. Career: Director, Division of Marine Resources, Florida Department of Natural Resources, 1975 to present; Chief, Bureau of Marine Science and Technology, 1972-75; Supervisor, Marine Research Laboratory, 1968-72; Senior Fisheries Biologist, 1967-68; Other Former Positions. Organizational Memberships: National Shellfisheries Association; Gulf and Caribbean Fisheries Institute (board of directors); South Atlantic State-Federal Fisheries Management Board; Governor's Appointee to Coastal Plains Regonal Commission; Coastal Plains Center for Marine Development Services (board of directors); Atlantic States Marine Fisheries Commission (scientific advisory committee); Gulf States Marine Fisheries Commission (technical coordinating committee); Capital City Kiwanis Club of Tallahassee; Gulf of Mexico and South Atlantic Fishery Management Councils (designee for executive director); American Institute of Fishery Research Biologists; Sigma Xi; American Fisheries Society; Certified Fishery Scientist. Honors and Awards: Listed in *American Men of Science, Who's Who, Who's Who in the South and Southwest, Dictionary of International Biography, American Malacologists*. Address: Route 1 Box 180-H, Tallahassee, Florida 32312.

Kael, Pauline

Movie Critic. Personal: Born June 19, 1919; Daughter of Issac Paul and Judith Friedman Kael (both deceased); Mother of Gina James. Education: Attended University of California-Berkeley, 1936-40. Career: Movie Critic, *The New Yorker*; Freelance Writer; Author, Numerous Books. Published Works: Contributor to *Partisan Review, Vogue, The New Republic, McCall's, The Atlantic, Harpers,* and Many Other Magazines; *I Lost it at the Movies*, 1965; *Kiss Kiss Bang Bang*, 1968; *Going Steady*, 1970; "Raising Kane", *The Citizen Kane Book*, 1971; *Deeper into Movies*, 1973; *Reeling*, 1976; *When the Lights Go Down*, 1980; *5001 Nights at the Movies*, 1982. Honors and Awards: Guggenheim Fellow, 1964; George Polk Memorial Award for Criticism, 1970; The National Book Award (Arts and Letters) for *Deeper into Movies*, 1974; Front Page Award for Best Magazine Column, Newswomen's Club of New York, 1974; Honorary Doctor of Laws Degree, Georgetown University, 1972; Honorary Doctor of Arts and Letters Degree, Columbia College, Chicago, Illinois, 1972; Honorary Doctor of Letters Degree, Smith College 1973, Allegheny College 1979; Honorary Doctor of Humane Letters Degree, Kalamazoo College, 1973, Reed College 1975, Haverford College 1975; Honorary Doctor of Fine Arts Degree, School of Visual Arts, New York 1980. Address: The New Yorker, 25 West 43rd Street, New York, New York 10036.

Kahn, Edward

Gynecologist, Obstetrician, Researcher, Inventor. Personal: Born September 16, 1913; Son of Emile Kahn and Pauline Andorn (both deceased); Married Faith-Hope Green; Father of Ellen Leora, Faith Hope II, Paula Amy. Education: B.S., University College of Arts and Pure Science, New York University, 1934; M.D., Long Island College of Medicine, 1939; Assistant, Pathology, Long Island College of Medicine, Kings County Hospital Division, Brooklyn, New York, 1939-40; Internship and Residency, Knickerbocker Hospital, New York, New York, 1940-42. Military: Served in the United States Army to the Rank of First Lieutenant, 1942-44. Career: Sydenham Hospital, New York, Consultant in Obstetrics and Gynecology 1974 to present, Coordinator of Hysterography for Hysterosalpingography Clinics 1950 to present, Culdoscopist for Gynecological Services 1954 to present, Associate Visiting Obstetrician and Gynecologist 1955, Assistant Adjunct in Obstetrics and Gynecology 1944-47; Chief Female Gynecologist, Specialty Clinics, 1950 to present; Assistant Visiting Obstetrician and Gynecologist, Department of Hospitals, Sydenham, New York, 1949-55. Organizational Memberships: American College of Obstetricians and Gynecologists (founding fellow); International College of Surgeons (fellow; examiner, obstetrics and gynecology, 1964; North American Federation, lecturer, instructional courses on female sterility, 1962; New York State surgical section, lecturer, 1957); Medical Jurisprudence Society, 1963, 1965; International Fertility Association (teaching clinics, 1953); New York State Medical Society; Queens County Medical Society. Community Activities: Kings County Hospital, New York (volunteer assistant, Long Island College of Medicine division of pathology, 1939-40); American National Red Cross (instructor of junior, standard and advanced courses, emergency medical service, 1942); Knickerbocker Hospital Disaster Casualty Station (originator, designer, chief, mobile emergency units, 1942); Sydenham Hospital Hysterography and Hysterosalpingography Services (director of teaching program for residents and interns, 1950 to present); C.B.S. *Coast-to-Coast Calendar Show* (panelist on female infertility and sterility, 1963). Religion: Lecturer, Invitational, All Denominations, Professional and Lay Groups. Honors and Awards: Special Recognition for Knickerbocker Disaster Mobile Units, 1942; Inventor and Patent Holder, Kahn Self-Retaining Uterine Trigger Cannula 1949, Kahn-Graves Open Side Vaginal Speculums 1957; Inventor, Traction Tenaculum with Offset Teeth and Curved Shaft 1949, Cannula Stand 1946, Kahn Giant Rubber Cervical Acorn and Kahn Surgical Dissecting Scissors, Curved and Straight 1952, Kahn One-Piece Office Model Cannula 1954; Listed in *Leaders in American Science, Two Thousand Men of Achievement, Dictionary of International Biography, Community Leaders and Noteworthy Americans, Who's Who in the East, Wisdom Hall of Fame.* Address: 213-16-85th Avenue, Queens Village, New York 11427.

Faith H Kahn

Kahn, Faith-Hope

Registered Nurse, Educator, Lecturer, Author, Inventor, Researcher, Administrator. Personal: Born April 25, 1921; Married Edward Kahn; Mother of Ellen-Leora, Faith-Hope II, Paula Amy. Education: Graduate of Beth Israel School of Nursing, 1942; Attended New York University, I.T.T. Educational Services; Special Courses and Continued Education, 1943 to present. Military: Served in the Civil Defense Emergency Medical Service since 1942; Served in the American Red Cross Disaster Service in the Field as a Supervisor of Nurses and Set-Ups and as Operating Room Supervisor, Phoenixville General Hospital, Pennsylvania, 1942-43. Career: Manager, Team Coordinator and Registered Nurse, Dr. Edward Kahn, 1945 to present; Researcher, Obstetric and Gynecological Reconstruction Procedures, 1945 to present; American Red Cross, Visiting Instructor for Upjohn and Rehab. 1977-78, Disaster Field Hospital Supervisor 1950; Executive Director of Publicity and Applied Arts, St. John's Hospital, Smithtown, New York, 1942; Operating Room First Scrub Nurse, Beth Israel Hospital, 1942. Organizational Memberships: National Association of Physician Nurses Association; American Society of Abdominal Surgeons; National Critical Care Institute of Education; National League of Nurses; American League of Nurses; American Academy of Ambulatory Nursing Administration; *American Journal of Nursing* (advisory panel); New York Academy of Sciences; National Medical Society; American Law Enforcement Association; American Police Academy; National Association of Female Executives; International Platform Association; Nurses Association American College of Obstetrics and Gynecology; American Organization of Registered Nurses (lecturer and scientific exhibitor, 1953; women's convention committee; first world congress on fertility and sterility, 1953). Community Activities: Woodhull Schools (past president, Parent-Teacher Association; director and coordinator of advisory education, 1950-64; past executive director, publicity); American Security Council (educator and founder, Center for International Studies; national advisory board member); Smithtown Historical Society; American Red Cross (disaster service); Civil Defense, Queens, New York (chairman and lecturer, health education classes, 1951; director and coordinator, Sterlingshire sector, 1951); Paul Revere Club, Washington, D.C., 1980; The American Shooter (international development fund gold club, 1979); American Law Enforcement Officers Association; American Police Academy, 1970 to present. Religion: St. Gabriels Episcopal Church of Hollis, Building Fund Committee, 1959; Contributor of Religious Crossword Puzzles, Lutheran School Chapel of the Redeemer, St. Gabriels Episcopal Church of Hollis. Honors and Awards: Patent Holder, Kahn Surgicap for Operating Room and Applied Fields; Poet Laureate, Sterlingshire Women's Club, 1951; Honored Operating Room Supervisor, Sydenham Hospital, 1942; Memorial Place, 1976; American Security Council Education Foundation and the Pentagon Education Center, 1979; Special Recognition Award, Center for International Studies, Washington, D.C., 1979. Address:

213-16-85th Avenue, Hollis Hills, New York 11427.

Kailian, Aram H

Architect, Builder, Developer. Personal; Born October 23, 1949; Son of Harry G. Kailian (deceased) and Louise Caily Kailian; Married Kathryn Zakian; Father of Arsine K., Aram E. Education: Attended 1967-69, B.S. Architecture, College of Engineering 1973, Temple University; Drexel University, 1969-70. Career: Architect, Builder, Developer; Draftsman; Designer; Planner. Organizational Memberships: American Institute of Architects; Pennsylvania Society of Architects; International Solar Energy Society (American section); Construction Specifications Institute; American Arbitration Association; National Academy of Conciliators; National Trust for Historic Preservation; Urban Planning Institute; Solar Lobby; Grass Roots Alliance for Solar Power; Temple University Alumni; Registered Architect, Pennsylvania, New Jersey, New York; N.C.A.R.B. (certification). Community Activities: Armenian National Committee, Boston, Massachusetts (national steering committee, 1978 to present); Armenian National Committee (chairman, 1982 to present); Armenian Assembly, Washington, D.C. (executive member, 1979-81); A.R.F. (central committee member, 1982 to present); Democratic Nationlities Council, 1976 to present; Armenian Sisters Academy, Radnor, Pennsylvania (board member, 1981 to present; service volunteer, 1974); National Republican Heritage Groups Council, 1976 to present; St. Gregory's Armenian Apostolic Church, Philadelphia, Pennsylvania (donation of master plan and community center, 1979-81); Senior Citizens Housing, Watertown, Massachusetts (service volunteer, 1981); Armenian Community Center, Toms River, New Jersey (donation of master plan and community center, 1981). Honors and Awards: Listed in *Who's Who in the East, Who's Who in Real Estate, Personalities of America, Personalities of the East, World Leaders*. Address: 2249 Menlo Avenue, Glenside, Pennsylvania 19038.

Kalb, Roland J

Management Consultant. Personal: Born June 16, 1916; Married Lore; Father of Linda Susan, Richard Oskar. Education: Degree in Electrical Engineering, Tech. Lehranstalt, Vienna, 1938; Postgraduate Studies undertaken at the Ecole Radio Technique, Paris, France, 1938-39. Career: Manager, Quality Control, Minerva Radio, Vienna, 1937-38; Chief Engineer, Minerva Radio, Paris, 1938-39; Plant Manager, Air King Products, New York City, 1941-47; General Manager, Teletone Radio, New York City, 1947-50; Chairman of the Board, Herold Radio and Electronics, Yonkers, New York, 1950-61; President, Roland Radio Corporation, 1950-61; Group Vice President, Fairbanks Morse and Company, Yonkers, 1961-63; Chief Executive, Pilot Radio Corporation, 1963-64; Group Vice President, Harmon Kardon and Jerrold Corporation, 1963-65; President, Roland Electronics Corporation, New York City, 1965 to present; Management Consultant, Roland J. Kalb Associates, Inc., 1965 to present; Vice Chairman, Board of Trustees, Center for Preventive Psychiatry, 1968-72, Chairman, 1972-79, Honorary Chairman, 1979 to present; President, Oskar Kalb Memorial Foundation, 1964 to present. Organizational Memberships: International Consulting Association; American Management Association; American Hospital Association; American Public Health Association; Weitzman Institute of Science. Honors and Awards: Numerous Leadership and Appreciation Awards; Congressional Record, 1964, Pilot Record Corporation, Pioneering Free Enterprise. Address: 2 Eaton Lane, Scarsdale, New York 10583.

Kalins, Dorothy G

Magazine Editor-in-Chief. Personal: Born November 9, 1942; Daughter of Mrs. Gil Kalins. Education: Attended Skidmore College, 1960-62; Sorbonne University, Paris, 1962-63; Columbia University, 1965. Career: Editor-in-Chief, *Metropolitan Home* Magazine, 1974 to present; Freelance Writer, 1969-76; Design Writer, *Home Furnishings Daily*, 1965-68. Organizational Memberships: American Society of Magazine Editors. Published Works: *The New American Cuisine*, 1981; *The Apartment Book*, 1979; *Cutting Loose*, 1972; *Researching Design in New York*, 1968; Contributor to *Cosmopolitan* Magazine. Address: 136 East 56th Street, New York, New York 10022.

Kalsem, Millie E

Retired Dietician. Personal: Born December 12, 1896; Mr. and Mrs. O. J. Kalsem (both deceased). Education: Attended Iowa State University, 1921; University of Illinois Medical School Dietetic Internship, Chicago, Illinois. Career: Hospital Dietetic Administrator, Head of Dietetics Department, Cook County Hospital, Chicago, Illinois; Executive, All American Manufacturing Company, Des Plaines, Iowa, 1923-29. Organizational Memberships: American Dieticians Association, 1923 to present; Chicago Dieticians Association, 1927 to present; Illinois Dieticians Association (member, 1931 to present; organizer; first president). Community Activities: Altrusa Club (member, Des Moines chapter, Iowa; Chicago, Illinois chapter, member 1927 to present, former president). Religion: American Lutheran Church. Honors and Awards: Senior Jack O'Lantern, Omicron Nu Junior Home Economics Honorary; Phi Kappa Phi; One of 100 Women in United States Development, Selected by Carrie Chapman Catt, Ahenie Merit Award, 1956; Order of the Knoll (member; board member); Chi Omega Social Sorority; Dean's Home Economics Development Fund, 1980. Address: 111 Lynn Avenue, Ames, Iowa 50010.

Kane, Flora

Real Estate Agent, Investor, Entrepreneur. Personal: Born April 2, 1948; Daughter of Henry and Rochelle Greenbaum; Mother of Dawn Elizabeth. Education: Paralegal Degree, 1980; Real Estate License, 1981; Notary Public License, 1981. Career: Real Estate Agent, Investor, Entrepreneur; Owner, Office Manager, Ditto of California, Inc. Organizational Memberships: San Fernando Valley Board of Realtors; National Notary Association. Community Activities: American Society of Professional and Executive Women, 1981; National Republican Congressional Committee; The Academy of Magical Arts (member). Honors and Awards: National Republican Victory Certificate, 1980; Listed in *Who's Who of American Women, Directory of Distinguished Americans-Services to the Community*. Address: 3410 San Martin Circle; Palm Springs, California 92262.

Kane, Katharine Daniels

Deputy Mayor. Personal: Born April 12, 1935; Daughter of Joseph J. and Katharine H. Daniels; Married Louis Isaac Kane; Mother of Elizabeth Holliday, Jennifer Johnson, Joseph Daniels. Education: B.A. summa cum laude American Government and Constitutional Law, Smith College, 1956. Career: Deputy Mayor, City of Boston, Massachusetts, 1975 to present; Chairman, Jubilee 350 Commission, 1979-80; Director, Office of the Boston Bicentennial, 1972-75; Director, Mayor's Office of Cultural

Affairs/Summerthing; State Representative, Massachusetts House of Representatives, 1964-68; President, League of Women Voters of Boston, 1961-64. Organizational Memberships: Greater Boston Convention and Tourist Bureau (director); United States Trust Company (director, 1974-76). Community Activities: Tufts-New England Medical Center (board of governors); Massachusetts Committee on Children and Youth (vice-president); United Way of Massachusetts Bay (director); Boston Natural Areas Fund (director); Boston Ballet Company (trustee); Boston Center for the Arts (director); Boston Symphony Orchestra (overseer); Arts Boston, Inc. (director); Boston Repertory Company (advisory board); Institute of Contemporary Art (council member); Boston University Department of Art History (visiting committee); Citizens Housing and Planning Association (charter director); Ellis Memorial Settlement House (director); Governor's Committee on Accessibility of the Arts (chairman, 1972); Young Audiences of Boston (charter director); Metropolitan Cultural Alliance (executive committee); Massachusettts Association on Mental Health (director); United Community Services (director; public policy committee); Democratic National Convention (delegate, 1972); Boston Ward 5 Democratic Committee; Smith College Alumnae Association (director, 1971-74); Miss Porter's School, Farmington, Connecticut (trustee, 1969-74); Commonwealth School, Boston, Massachusetts (trustee, 1973-76); The Winsor School, Boston, Massachusetts (corporation member, 1971-74). Honors and Awards: Outstanding Contributions Award, Bicentennial Council of the 13 Original States Great American Achievement Program, 1977; Special Citation, Simmons College, 1976; Myron Glazer Award/Woman of the Year in Travel-Discover America Travel Organization and *Southern Living Magazine*, 1976; Presidential Bicentennial Award, Boston College, 1976; Honorary Doctor of Humane Letters Degree, Franklin Pierce College, 1976; Woman '76 Award, Boston Young Women's Christian Association, 1976; Phi Beta Kappa. Address: Ten Chestnut Street, Boston, Massachsetts 02108.

J Kapacinskas

Kapacinskas, Joseph

Engineer, Author. Personal: Born October 20, 1907 in Mazuciai, Kybartai, Lithuania; Son of George and Teofile Baskeviciute Kapacinskas; Married Marie Kulikauskas, December 27, 1952; Father of Joseph-Vytautas. Education: Graduate of Technical College, Augsburg, Germany, 1948; Bachelor's Degree, Allied Institute of Technology, Chicago, Illinois, 1960. Career: Engineer, Author; Editor, *Sandara* Weekly Lithuanian Newspaper, Chicago, Illinois, 1973-76; Electrician, Burlington Northern Railroad, Inc., 1951-72; Instructor and Chief Electrician, U.N.R.R.A., Weissenburg, Germany, 1946-47; Employee, National Railroad, Treuchtlingen, Germany 1944-45, National Railroad Lithuania 1940-44, City of Kaunas Municipal Administration in Lithuania 1929-39. Organizational Memberships: Lithuanian Engineers and Architects Association; Lithuanian Journalists Association (Chicago chapter secretary); American Society of Tool and Manufacturing Engineers. Community Activities: Lithuanian-American Council of Chicago; Lithuanian Alliance of America; American Association for the Advancement of Science; International Platform Association. Published Works: *Siaubingos Dienos--Horrifying Days*, 1965; *Iseivio Dalia--Emigrant's Fate*, 1974; *Spaudos Baruose--Within the Press*, 1979. Listed in *Dictionary of International Biography, International Register of Profiles, Community Leaders and Noteworthy Americans, Notable Americans of the Bicentennial Era, Leaders in American Science, Lithuanian Encyclopedia, History of Chicago Lithuanians, Men of Achievement.* Address: 6811 South Maplewood Avenue, Chicago, Illinois 60629.

Ken Kaplowitz

Kaplowitz, Ken

Department Chairman. Personal: Born June 29, 1941; Son of Rose Kaplowitz. Education: B.A., Montclair State College, 1963; M.A., New York University, 1969; M.F.A., Rutgers University, 1970. Career: Special Education Art Teacher, Newark School System, 1964-68; Instructor, William Paterson College, 1968-70; Trenton State College: Television Coordinator 1970-72, Assistant Professor of Media Communications Science 1972-70, Media Communications Science Department Chairman 1979 to present. Organizational Memberships: Friends of Photography; Society for Photographic Education; Kappa Delta Pi; Association for Humanistic Psychology; International Center for Photography. Community Activities: Five Community Photographic Exhibitions, 1975-79; Volunteer Work for State Museum, 1977 to present; Princeton Art Association (volunteer film making instructor, 1978-79); Community Multi Media Performances, 1975-79; Hopewell Fire & Rescue Squad, 1980; Photo Judge for Community Photographic Exhibitions, 1978-80. Religion: Member & Soloist in Professional Religious Choir, 1954-55; Exhibition of Religious Photographs, 1977-79. Honors and Awards: Painting Scholarship, New York University, 1959; Purchase Award, New Jersey State Museum, 1977; Purchase Award, Mercer County Photo Show, 1981; Listed in *Who's Who in the East, Personalities of America.* Address: 27 Hart Ave., Hopewell, New Jersey 08525.

Karampelas, Napoleon Demetrius

Arch Priest. Personal: Born December 31, 1904; Son of Mr. and Mrs. Demetrius Karampelas; Married to Panagoula; Father of Angelos, Panagiotes. Education: Diploma, Theological Eclesiastic School of Corinth, Greece, 1932. Military: Soldier with the Greek Army, 1924-26. Career: Arch Priest, Marquette, Michigan. Organizational Memberships: Clergy Association of Marquette; Professional Association of America. Religion: Arch Priest, Greek Orthodox Church. Published Works: Published over 300 Articles in Greek and American Newspapers. Honors and Awards: Listed in *Personalities of the West and Midwest, Men of Achievement, International Who's Who in Community Service, Dictionary of International Biography, Who's Who in Religion.* Address: 237 West Ridge, Marquette, Michigan 49855.

Napoleon D Karampelas

Kaslow, Florence W

Family Therapist and Psychologist. Personal: Born January 6; Daughter of Mr. and Mrs. Irving Whiteman; Married Solis Kaslow; Mother of Nadine Joy, Howard Ian. Education: A.B., Temple University, 1952; M.A., Ohio State University, 1954; Bryn Mawr College, Ph.D., 1969; Licensed Psychologist, Pennsylvania, 1973 to present; Registered, National Registry of Health Service Providers in Psychology 1975 to present, National Register of Providers in Marital and Family Therapy 1978 to present; Diplomate, Forensic Psychology and Family Psychology, American Board of Forensic Psychology and American Board of Family Psychology; Diplomate, Clinical Psychology, American Board of Professional Psychology. Career: Consultant, Forensic Psychology Associates, Inc., Tampa, Florida, 1981 to present; Family Therapy Principal Workshop Leader, Psychological Seminars, Inc., 1980 to present; Consultant in Family Therapy, Center Psychiatrists, Portsmouth, Virginia, 1980-81; Consultant in Marital and Family Therapy, Naval Regional Medical Center Departments of Psychiatry, Philadelphia, Pennsylvania, Portsmouth, Virginia and San Diego, California, 1976 to present; Visiting Professor and Board Member, Wisconsin Family Studies Institute, Madison, Wisconsin, 1980 to present; Visiting Professor, Southwest Family Institute of Dallas, Texas 1979 to present, Galveston Family Institute, Texas 1979 to present; Editor, *Journal of Marital and Family Therapy*, 1976-81; Private Practice Individual, Marital, Family and Sex Therapist, 1964 to present. Organizational Memberships: American Board of Forensic Psychology, Inc. (president, 1978-80; board member, 1978-81; Mid-Atlantic regional examination chair, 1979-80; Florida regional examination chair, 1981 to present); American Psychological Association (member, 1974 to present; fellow, 1981; division of teaching of psychology, division of industrial and organizational psychology; division of psychotherapy; division of psychoanalysis; division of psychology and law; division of independent practice); American Association for Marital and Family Therapy (clinical member, 1971 to present; approved training supervisor, 1973 to present; national legislation and licensing committee, 1976-79; editor, *Journal of Marital and Family Therapy*, 1976-81; fellow, 1976 to present); American Family Therapy Association (charter member, 1978); Pennsylvania Association of Marriage and Family Therapists (member 1973-80; chair, licensing committee, 1974-76; treasurer, 1974-75; vice-president, 1976-77); Pennsylvania Psychological Association (member, 1974 to present; fellow, chair, program committee, fall conference, 1975; chair, awards committee, 1976; chair, academic division program, spring conference, 1978; president, academic division, 1978-79); Philadelphia Society of Clinical Psychologists (member, 1974 to present; fellow, program chair, 1975-78; executive board, 1975-78; member at large, board, 1976-78); Family Institute of Philadelphia (member, 1971 to present; faculty of training program; annual conference committee, 1972-75); Eastern Psychological Association, 1973-80; American Psychology-Law Society (member, 1975 to present; chair, certification committee, 1977-78); International Transactional Analysis Association, 1972-75; Philadelphia Community Service Institute, 1976-80; American Association of Sex Educators, Counselors and Therapists, 1977 to present; Florida Association of Marital and Family Therapists, 1981 to present; Southeastern Psychological Association, 1981 to present; Florida Psycholgical Association, 1981 to present. Community Activities: Business and Professional Women's Group of Federation of Jewish Agencies, Philadelphia, Pennsylvania (steering committee, 1979-80). Religion: Keneseth Israel Synagogue, Elkins Park, Pennsylvania, Teacher of Confirmation and Post-Confirmation Classes, 1972-76. Honors and Awards: Order of the Owl Award, Temple University Montgomery County Club, 1979; Outstanding Liberal Arts Alumnus of Temple University, 1966; Pi Gamma Mu National Social Science Honorary Society; Phi Alpha Theta National History Honorary Society; Temple University English Honorary Society; Traineeship, National Institute of Mental Health, Bryn Mawr; Fellowship, Ohio State Graduate School; Women's Club Scholarship, Alumni Prize for Outstanding Senior, Graduation with Distinction in Sociology, Temple University; Listed in *Men and Women of American Science, Compendium, Community Leaders and Noteworthy Americans, Outstanding Professionals in Human Services, Contemporary Authors, International Who's Who in Community Service, World Who's Who of Authors, World Who's Who of Women, Notable Americans of the Bicentennial Era, Who's Who of American Women, Dictionary of International Biography, International Register of Profiles, International Who's Who of Intellectuals, Who's Who in the East, Personalities of America, Men and Women of Distinction, Contemporary Personalities.* Address: 1900 Consulate Place, Apartment 1903, West Palm Beach, Florida 33401.

Katz, Menke

Poet, Editor, Publisher. Personal: Born April 12, 1906; Son of Badana and Heershe-Dovid Katz; Married Ruth Rivke Feldman; Father of Heershe-Dovid, Troim Handler. Education: Columbia University; Brooklyn College; University of Southern California. Career: Poet; Editor and Publisher, *Bitterroot* Poetry Magazine, 1962 to present; Lecturer; Teacher. Organizational Memberships: P.E.N.; Poetry Society of America; World Poetry Society; United Poets Laureate International. Community Activities: Conducted Poetry Workshops in Prisons in New York State, Eastern Correctional Facility at Napanoch and Green Havan. Published Works: 9 Books of Poetry in Yiddish, including *Three Sisters* 1932, *Dawning Man* 1935, *Burning Village* Volumes 1 and 2 1938, *My Grandma Myrna* 1939, *To Happier Days* 1941, *The Simple Dream* 1947, *Midday* 1954, *Safad* 1979; 4 Books of Poetry in English, *Land of Manna* 1965, *Rockrose* 1969, *Burning Village* 1972, *Two Friends* 1981; One Book of Prose, *Forever and Ever and a Wednesday* 1981. Honors and Awards: Stephen Vincent Benet Award, 1st Prize, 1969, 1973; Poet Lore Narrative Award, 1st Prize, 1967; Poet Lore, Descriptive Poem, 1st Prize, 1972; Nominee, Pulitzer Prize, 1965, 1969, 1972. Address: Post Office Box 453, Spring Glen, New York 12483.

Kaufer, Gerald Ira

General and Vascular Surgeon. Personal: Born October 16, 1937; Son of Esther Kaufer; Married Virginia Gross Kaufer; Father of Michael David, Jill Frances, Jonathan Bradley, Wendy Rachel, Elizabeth Rebecca, Abigail Debra, Amy Heather. Education: B.S. Chemistry 1959, M.D. School of Medicine 1963, University of Pittsburgh. Military: Served in the United States Navy on Active Duty, 1968-70; Recipient of Navy Achievement Medal; Served Aboard U.S.S. Ticonderoga as Ship Surgeon. Career: Chief, General and Vascular Surgery, Central Medical Center; Clinical Instructor in Surgery, University of Pittsburgh School of Medicine. Organizational Memberships: American Medical Association; Pennsylvania Medical Association; Allegheny County Medical Society; Pittsburgh Surgical Society; Phi Delta Epsilon Fraternity; American College of Surgeons (fellow); American College of Angiology (fellow); American College of Surgeons (southwest chapter). Community Activities: B'nai B'rith. Religion: Beth El Synagogue; School Board Chairman, Executive Committee. Address: 1574 Tiffany Drive, Pittsburgh, Pennsylvania 15241.

Kawahata, Henry Hajime

Personal: Born August 11, 1919; Son of Minofu and Toku Kawahata, Hidalgo, Texas; Married Elsie S. Sueyasu; Father of David, Joyce E., Gaily, Ann S. Education: B.S. Agriculture Administration, Texas A.&M. University. Organizational Memberships: Valco Oil Mill, Harlingen, Texas (director, 1950-57); 281 Cotton Gin, Pharr, Texas (director, 1950-57); McAllen Farm Bureau (president, 1951-52). Community Activities: City of Hidalgo (alderman, 1960-64, 1968-70, 1972-73); McAllen International Museum (board of directors, 1969-73); McAllen Botanical Gardens (board of directors, 1970-72); Region One Education Service Center (board of directors, 1979-82); Texas A.&M. Research Foundation Center (counselor, 1976-82); McAllen Cemetery Association (board of directors, 1978-80, 1980-83). Address: P.O. Box 206, Hidalgo, Texas 78557.

Kawecki, Leon Stanley

Art Director. Personal: Born in Chojnice, Poland; Son of Adam and Elisabeth Link Kawecki; Married First Wife Jacqueline Salamey on April 25, 1953, Second Wife Inge Moeller on December 29, 1975; Father of Raymond Mark, Steven James, Daniel Noel, Barbara Rachelle. Education: Graduate of State College of Fine Arts, Poznan, Poland, 1939; Studied at Pittsburgh Art Institute 1952-54, Otis Art Institute, Los Angeles, California 1964, California Art Institute 1966-67, Art Center College of Design, Los Angeles, California 1968, University of California-Irvine 1968-71. Military: Served in the Polish Armed Forces, 1939-47. Career: Art Director, Mead Packaging, Buena Park, California, 1960 to present; Packaging Designer, Standard Packaging Corporation, Pittsburgh, Pennsylvania, 1957-60; Commercial Artist, Fuller Label & Box Company, Pittsburgh, Pennsylvania, 1952-57; Exhibited in Shows in Warsaw, Poland, Dusseldorf, Germany, Pasadena, California, Los Angeles, California, Brno, Czechoslovakia, Mexico City, Mexico; Designer of United States Bicentennial Commemorative Medal "Freedom Founders"; Designer, Polonus Commemorative Medal, International Philatelic Exhibition, 1979; Designer, Commemorative Medal "John Paul II - A Son of Poland"; Designer, Commemorative Medal "300th Anniversary Relief of Vienna - King John III" for Polish American Numismatic Association. Organizational Memberships: Pasadena Arts League; Fountain Valley Arts Association (founding member); American Philatelic Society; National Society of Art Directors; Art Directors Club of Los Angeles; Polonus Philatelic Society; Town Hall of California.

Community Activities: Pittsburgh Symphony Orchestra (supporting member, 1957-58); Arizona-California National Copernicus Committee (executive officer, 1971-73); Polish American Historical Association, California Chapter (vice-president, 1980-81). Honors and Awards: Silver Medal, All Polish Scholastic Art Exhibition, 1936; Grand Award, University of Pittsburgh, Pennsylvania, 1960; Gold Medal, International Folding Box Competition, 1963; Silver Medal, National Folding Box Competition, 1966; Gold Medal, 500th Anniversary Copernicus Celebration U.S.A., Adler Planetarium, Chicago, Illinois, 1973; Silver Medal, 500th Anniversary Copernicus Celebration, Warsaw, Poland, 1973; Commendation from President Gerald Ford, American Bicentennial, 1976; Grand Prix, International Folklore Exhibition, Chicago, Illinois, 1978; State Order "Merite Culturel", Ministry of Culture and the Arts, Warsaw, Poland, 1979; Award of Excellence, Graphic Arts, Orange County Chapter of American Advertising Federation, 1978. Address: 6400 Valley View Street, Buena Park, California 90620.

Kay, Stanley Robert

Stanley R Kay

Clinical Psychologist and Research Scientist. Personal: Born June 7, 1946; Son of Leslie L. and Anne Kay; Married Theresa Maria De Monte Kay; Father of Lisa Paula, Stacy Lynn. Education: B.A., Psychology, New York University, 1968; M.A. cum laude, Psychology, Fairleigh Dickinson University, 1970; Ph.D. Studies, Psychology, New School for Social Research, 1971-73; Ph.D., Psychology, State University of New York-Stony Brook, 1980. Career: Department of Psychiatry, Albert Einstein College of Medicine, 1980 to present; Bronx Psychiatric Center, Clinical Psychologist 1976 to present, Clinical Research Psychologist in Clinical Psychopharmacology Unit 1970-76; Psychotherapist in Private Practice, 1975 to present; Consulting Psychologist, Green Chimneys Children's Services, 1980-81; Psychometrist, The Klein Institute for Aptitude Testing, 1970. Organizational Memberships: Eastern Psychological Association, 1973 to present; New York Psychologists in Public Service, 1975 to present; American Psychological Association (member, 1972 to present; member, Task Force on Health Behavior Research, 1974); Bronx Psychiatric Center (Research Committee, 1973). Published Works: Author of Over 40 Articles in Scientific Journals and 20 Professional Conference Papers since 1973; *The Cognitive Diagnostic Battery: Evaluation of Intellectual Disorders*, 1982; *Conceptual Disorder in Schizophrenia as a Function of Coding Processes*, 1980; Author of 5 Psychological Tests: Color-Form Preference Test 1975, Color Form Representation Test 1975, Egocentricity of Thought Test 1975, Span of Attention Test 1974, Progressive Figure Drawing Test 1980; Editorial Consultant *The Behavioral and Brain Sciences, The Journal of Nervous and Mental Disease, Psychiatry Research, Child Development, Perceptual and Motor Skills, Psychological Reports.* Honors and Awards: Certificate for Outstanding Scientific Achievement, American Biographical Institute, 1981; Certificate for Distinguished Contribution to Psychology, American Biographical Institute, 1981; Certificate for Outstanding Employee of the Year, Bronx Psychiatric Center, 1978; Honorary Member, American Society of Distinguished Citizens, 1977; Awarded Master of Arts Degree in Psychology with Honors, 1970; New York University Coat of Arms Society, 1968; Listed in *Who is Publishing in Science.* Address: Kirkwood Road, R.F.D. 2, Mahopac, New York 10541.

Kazmerski, Lawrence L

Principal Scientist and Branch Chief. Personal: Born June 9, 1945; Son of Natalia Kazmerski; Married Kathleen E. Scanlan; Father of Keira Elisabeth, Timothy Lawrence. Education: B.S.E.E. 1967, M.S.E.E. 1968, Ph.D. 1970, University of Notre Dame. Career: Solar Energy Research Institute, Principal Scientist and Branch Chief 1979 to present, Senior Scientist 1977-79; University of Maine, Associate Professor of Electrical Engineering 1974-77, Assistant Professor of Electrical Engineering 1971-74; Thin Film Specialist, University of Notre Dame Radiation Research Laboratory, A.E.C., 1970-71. Organizational Memberships: Institute of Electrical and Electronic Engineers; A.P.S.; Electrochemistry Society; I.S.E.S.; Eta Kappa Nu; Sigma Xi; Phi Kappa Phi; A.V.S. (chairman of thin films division, 1980-81; chairman of national symposium, 1982). Community Activities: Young Men's Christian Association Youth Basketball Program; Green Mountain Little League Baseball. Honors and Awards: Peter Mark Memorial Research Award for Demonstrating the Correlation Between the Electrical and Chemical Properties of Interfaces in Poly-Crystalline Photovoltaic Devices, American Vacuum Society, 1981; Outstanding Performance Award for Outstanding Research Leadership and Sustained Personal Contributions to the Characterization of Photovoltaic Materials and Devices, Solar Energy Research Institute, 1982. Address: 12799 West Atlantic Avenue, Lakewood, Colorado 80228.

Kedia, Prahlad Ray

Evelyn M D Keefer

Professor and Department Chairman. Personal: Born July 4, 1937; Son of Kaluram Shrinarayan and Kanchandevi Kedia (both deceased); Married Sushila Podar; Father of Kavita, Sarita, Anita. Education: International Science, University of Rajasthan, 1957; LL.B. 1961, LL.M. 1965, University of Bombay, India; Postgraduate Institute for the Humanities and Criminal Justice, Boston University, Summer 1981; Ph.D. Candidate, University of Southern Mississippi, 1982-83. Career: Grambling State University, Associate Professor and Chairman of Department of Criminal Justice 1979 to present, Director of Criminal Justice and Law Administration Center 1978 to present, Director of Criminal Justice Center 1975-78, Associate Professor of Law 1971-79; Practicing Attorney, High Court of Bombay, 1965-71; Indore Malwa United Mills, Limited, Bombay, Assistant Accountant and then Accountant, 1958-65. Organizational Memberships: Bombay Bar Association, 1965 to present; Academy of Criminal Justice Sciences, 1976 to present; American Criminal Justice Association, 1978 to present; Louisiana Criminal Justice Educators Association, 1980 to present. Community Activities: Pilot Projects for Off-Campus Courses and Seminars for Local In-Service Criminal Justice Officers (director, 1976 to present); Fifth through Ninth National Conferences on Juvenile Justice (president, 1978-82; presented seminars as a conference faculty, 1978-82); Louisiana Governors Conference on Juvenile Justice (presented seminar on transcendental meditation as behavior modality for juveniles, 1982); Conferences and Seminars in Criminal Justice (organizer and presenter, community, student and criminal justice officer programs 1976-81, Ruston Peach Festivals, Louisiana 1972-77). Honors and Awards: First Prize, Bicycle Race, Law College Annual Sports, 1959; First Prize, Article in *The Young Lawyer* Law College Journal, 1960; Listed in *Who's Who in the South and Southwest, Men of Achievement, Personalities of the South, International Who's Who of Intellectuals.* Address: Route 2 Box 507, Choudrant, Louisiana 71227.

Keefer, Evelyn M Denney

Company Executive. Personal: Born March 24, 1925 in Greenway, Arkansas; Daughter of Louis Delbert and Lucy Jane Milde Denney (both deceased); Married Howard Eugene Keefer; Mother of Janice Kay K. Diamond, Paul Eugene. Education: Graduate of Garland High School, Arkansas, 1942; Four State Business College, Texarkana, Texas. Career: Co-Owner, Secretary and Treasurer, Keefer Supply Company and Keefer Oil, Ada, Oklahoma, 1951 to present; Secretary, Jarecki Oilfield Supply Company, Seminole, Oklahoma, 1944-45; Inventory Clerk, Larkin Packer Company, St. Louis, Missouri, 1943-44; Receptionist, Brown Root Construction Company, Texarkana, Texas and McAlester, Oklahoma, 1942-43. Community Activities: Fine Arts Department of Tanti Study Club (chairman, 1971-72; parliamentarian, 1972-73; civic and social chairman, 1970-71, 1963-64; secretary and treasurer,

1969-70; nominating committee chairman, 1965-66); Tanti Study Club (president, 1976-77; parliamentarian, 1977-78); Garden Club (Ada Council, president 1973-74, parliamentarian 1975-79, reporter 1980-84; chairman, Hays Indian Cemetery Committee, 1973-80; chairman, yearbook committee, 1973-75; historian, gladiolus unit, 8 years; south central district, garden pilgrimage chairman 1973-75, nominating committee 1975-77, national council books and national gardener promotion 1977-79, historian 1981-83); Sigma Tau Mothers Club (treasurer, 1969-72); Ada Parent-Teacher Association (Ada council president, 1960-61; junior high president, 1962-63; home room mother, many years); Camp Fire Girls (leader, many years); Heart Fund (fund raiser); Cancer Society (fund raiser); March of Dimes (fund raiser); Red Cross (fund raiser); Community Chest (fund raiser); Order of Eastern Star; American Numismatic Association; Oklahoma Heritage Association; Pontotoc County Historical and Geneaological Society. Religion: First Baptist Church; Women's Missionary Union, Director 1969-70, Treasurer 1968-71; Baptist Women, Chairman of Current Mission Group, 1972-73, 1973-74, 1978-80; Berean Class, Assistant Outreach Leader, 4 Years; Five-Year-Olds Sunday School Class Teacher, 6 Years. Honors and Awards: Nominee, Woman of the Year for Ada, Oklahoma, 1975; Listed in *Who's Who in the South and Southwest, Personalities of the South, Dictionary of International Biography, Who's Who in America, Community Leaders and Noteworthy Americans, Notable Americans of the Bicentennial Era, Personalities of America, Who's Who in Finance and Industry, National Social Directory, The Blue Book, International Register of Profiles, Men and Women of Distinction, Who's Who in the World, International Who's Who in Community Service, Anglo-American Who's Who.* Address: 2420 Timber Terrace, Ada, Oklahoma 74820.

Keene, Ruth Frances

Supply Systems Analyst. Personal: Born October 7, 1948; Daughter of Sally and Seymour Keene. Education: B.S., Arizona State University, 1970; M.S., Fairleigh Dickinson University, 1978. Career: Supply Systems Analyst, Headquarters, 60th Ordnance Group, Zweibrucken, West Germany, 1980 to present; Chief, Inventory Management Division, Crane Army Ammunition Activity, Crane, Indiana, 1979-80; Inventory Management Specialist, United States Army Communications-Electronics Materiel Readiness Command, Fort Monmouth, New Jersey, 1974-79; Inventory Management Specialist, United States Army Electronics Command, Philadelphia, Pennsylvania, 1970-74. Organizational Memberships: Federally-Employed Women (member, 1971 to present; chapter president, 1977-78, 1979-80; chapter vice-president, 1976-77; chapter program chair, 1976-77; chapter newsletter editor, 1974-77); Society of Logistics Engineers (member, 1976 to present; bylaws chairman, 1978; program chair, 1976-77); American Association for the Advancement of Science, 1979 to present; National Association for Female Executives, 1979 to present; American Society for Public Administration, 1981 to present; Society of Professional and Executive Women, 1980 to present; Association for Computing Machinery, 1966 to present; International Information/Word Processing Association, 1981 to present. Community Activities: Fort Monmouth Commanding General's Equal Employment Opportunity Advisory Committee, 1978. Honors and Awards: Outstanding Performance Award, United States Army Electronics Command, 1973; Letter of Commendation, Crane Army Ammunition Activity, 1980; Listed in *Who's Who of American Women, Who's Who in the West, Directory of Distinguished Americans.* Address: 4916 West Pinchot Avenue, Phoenix, Arizona 85031.

Ruth F Keene

Kefauver, Elizabeth McGee

Supervisor of Art. Personal: Born August 11, 1923; Daughter of Mr. and Mrs. Morris George McGee; Married John Moody Kefauver; Mother of Alexander Tedford Barclay III, Christopher Morris Barclay, Benner McKee Barclay. Education: B.F.A., University of Oklahoma, 1945; M.Ed., Trinity University, 1965. Career: Supervisor of Art, San Antonio Independent School District, 11 Years; Art Teacher, Fox Technical High School, 8 Years; Head of Photography Department, University of Oklahoma Extension Division, 1947-48. Organizational Memberships: National Art Education Association (life member); University of Oklahoma Alumni Association (life member); National Education Association; Texas State Teachers Association; Administrators and Superintendents Association; Texas Art Education Association (local chairman, state convention in San Antonio, 1978). Community Activities: Southwest Craft Center (board of trustees, 1970 to present); Ruth Taylor Fine Arts Center, Trinity University (vice-president); Dance Art of San Antonio Interpretive Dance Group (founder; executive board member); San Antonio Symphony (opera board; women's board; Joeffry Workshop advisory board). Religion: St. Luke's Episcopal Church; President, St. Francis Guild; Chairman, Decorating Committee. Honors and Awards: Listed in *Who's Who of School District Officials, Who's Who in the Southwest, International Who's Who of Women.* Address: 216 Lilac Lane, San Antonio, Texas 78209.

Keith, David Box

Corporate Vice-President. Personal: Born May 26, 1934 in Brownwood, Texas; Son of G. E. Keith; Married Susan Prim; Father of Lynda, Laurabeth. Education: B.B.A. Advertising, University of Houston, 1957. Military: Served in the Army Reserve 24 Years, Retiring as Major in 1975. Career: Houston Natural Gas Corporation, Employee 1960 to 1975, Vice-President of Corporate Communications 1975 to present. Organizational Memberships: Public Relations Society of America; Texas Public Relations Association; National Investor Relations Institute; Association of Petroleum Writers, National Press Club, Washington, D.C.; Houston Press Club; Sigma Alpha Epsilon Alumni (past president). Community Activities: Houston Club; American Advertising Federation (president of Houston Advertising federation, 1968; governor, 10th district, 1977; chairman 1982); American Red Cross (volunteer, past chairman, national public affairs advisory committee; director and member, executive committee of Greuler Gulf Coast chapter); Girl Scouts of America (volunteer, 1969 to present; executive committee, San Jacinto Council); National Coal Association (public relations committee); Harris County Heritage Society (executive committee); University of Houston Alumni Organization (chairman, University of Houston Annual Fund; director). Religion: Park Place United Methodist Church. Honors and Awards: American Advertising Federation, Silver Medal 1980, 10th District Sterling Service Award 1981; Friends Badge, San Jacinto Girl Scouts, 1980. Address: 11011 Sagemeadow Lane, Houston, Texas 77089.

Kellar, Elizabeth Kaenzig

Communications Director. Personal: Born November 9, 1948; Daughter of Joseph and Mary Kaenzig; Married Kenneth Jon Kellar; Mother of Joshua Aaron, Amanda Marin. Education: B.A., Muskingum College; M.A., Ohio State University. Career: Communications Director, International City Management Association; Public Relations Director, Central Ohio Heart Association; Community Relations Officer, Sunnyvale, California. Organizational Memberships: Public Relations Society of America (executive committee, government section, 1980-83); Women in Communications. Community Activities: Presidential Management Intern Program (resource leader, 1980-82). Honors and Awards: Fellowship, National Music Critics Institute, 1972; Public Relations Awards, Ohio Heart Association, 1974; Listed in *Who's Who of American Women.* Address: 7109 Braeburn Place, Bethesda, Maryland 20817.

Kelley, Vincent Charles

Professor and Division Head. Personal: Born January 23, 1916; Son of Charles Enoch and Stella May Ross Kelley (both deceased); Married Dorothy Jean MacArthur; Father of Nancy Jean, Thomas Vincent, Richard Charles, William MacArthur, Robert Kenneth, Jean Elizabeth, James Joseph. Education: B.A. Chemistry 1934, M.S. Physical Chemistry 1935, University of South Dakota; B.S. Education 1936, Ph.D. Biochemistry 1942, B.S. Medicine 1944, M.B. Medicine 1945, M.D. 1946, University of Minnesota. Military: Served in the United States Army as Pfc A.S.T.P., 1943-45, and from 1st Lieutenant to Captain, 1946-48, at A.A.F. School of Aviation Medicine, Research Division, Randolph Field, Texas; Served Successfully as Chief of Department of Biophysics, Assistant Chief of Department of Biochemistry, and Chief of Research Medicine. Career: University of Washington-Seattle, Head of Division of Endocrinology, Metabolism and Renal Disease 1958 to present, Professor of Pediatrics 1958 to present; Children's Orthopedic Hospital and Medical Center, Seattle, Washington, Director of Research 1959-65, Associate Director of Medical Education 1958-63; Consultant in Pediatrics, Madigan Army Hospital, Tacoma, Washington, 1958-69; Visiting Professor in Pediatrics, Kauikeolani Children's Hospital, Honolulu, Hawaii, 1958; Director, Utah State Department of Health, 1953-58; University of Utah, Associate Professor of Pediatrics 1952-58, Assistant Professor of Pediatrics 1950-52; University of Minnesota, Instructor in Pediatrics 1949-50, Swift Fellow in Pediatrics 1948-50, Rockefeller Research Fellow in Physiological Chemistry 1941-42, Teaching Assistant in Biochemistry 1940-41; A.A.F. School of Aviation Medicine, Randolph Field, Texas, Chief of Department of Biophysics, Assistant Chief of Department of Biochemistry, and Chief of Research Medicine Successively, 1946-48; University of Minnesota Hospitals, Assistant Resident in Pediatrics 1946, Intern in Pediatrics 1945-46; Assistant Professor of Organic Chemistry, College of St. Thomas, St. Paul, Minnesota; Professor of Chemistry, Emory and Henry College, Emory, Virginia, 1941; University of North Dakota, Graduate Assistant in Chemistry 1934-35, Undergraduate Assistant in Chemistry 1933-34. Organizational Memberships: American Academy of Pediatrics; American Association for the Advancement of Science; American Association of University Professors; American Chemical Society; American College of Clinical Pharmacology and Chemotherapy; American Heart Association; American Institute of Biological Sciences; American Medical Association; American Pediatric Society: American Rheumatism Association; American Society of Nephrology; American Therapeutic Society; King County Medical Society; Lawson Wilkins Pediatric Endocrine Society; New York Academy of Sciences; North Pacific Pediatric Society; Pan-American Medical Association; Puget Sound Endocrine Society; Seattle Pediatric Society; Society for Experimental Biology and Medicine; The Endocrine Society; The Society for Pediatric Research; Washington Heart Association; Washington State Medical Association; Washington State Pediatric Society; Western Society for Clinical Research; Western Society for Pediatric Research (past president). Published Works: Editor-in-Chief, *Practice of Pediatrics*, 10 Volumes with Annual Revisions, 1960 to present; Editor, *Metabolic, Endocrine and Genetic Disorders of Children*, 3 Volumes, 1974; Chief Editor, *Pediatrics: International Medical Digest*, 1960-71; Editor, *American Journal of Diseases of Children*, 1958-68; Consultant Editor, *Pediatrics* Medical Digest, 1956-75; Editor and Advisory Board Member, *Audio-Digest*, 1956-72; Author and Contributor of Over 200 Articles and Book Chapters. Honors and Awards: Phi Beta Kappa; Sigma Xi; Phi Lambda Upsilon; Phi Eta Sigma; Kappa Kappa Psi; L. Mead Johnson Award for Pediatric Research, 1954; Ross Pediatric Education Award of the Western Society for Pediatric Research, 1971; Listed in *Who's Who in America, Who's Who in the West, Who's Who in the World; American Men and Women of Science*. Address: 8611-45th Avenue Northeast, Seattle, Washington 98115.

Kelly, Margaret Ricaud

Teacher (Retired). Personal: Daughter of Robert Barry Ricard (deceased) and Leslie Mowry Crosland; Married Thomas W. Kelly, 1950. Education: B.A., Winthrop College, Rock Hill, South Carolina; Part-Time Graduate Work, Duke University, Durham, North Carolina, University of North Carolina-Chapel Hill, Coker College, Hartsville, South Carolina, University of South Carolina-Columbia, University of Florida-Gainesville, University of Miami, Coral Gables, Florida. Career: School Teacher in North Carolina, South Carolina, and Florida, 39 Years. Community Activities: Magna Charta Dames; Colonial Order of the Crown; Descendant of Knights of the Most Noble Order of the Garter; French Huguenot Society; Colonial Dames of the XVII Century (registrar, 1979 to present; charter member); Daughters of the American Revolution; United Daughters of the Confederacy; National Geneological Society, Washington, D.C.; Registered Geneologist; South Carolina Historical Society; Marlboro County Historical Society; Oak Ridge Cemetery, Bennettville, South Carolina; McCall Cemetery Association; Crosland Family Association (secretary, 23 years). Religion: Methodist. Address: 402 Fayetteville Avenue, Bennettville, South Carolina 29512.

Eugene E Kenega

Kenaga, Eugene E

Chemical Ecologist. Personal: Born July 15, 1917; Son of Mr. and Mrs. Ivan Kenaga (both deceased); Married First Wife Joan Elizabeth Bailey, Second Wife Kathleen Virginia Walker; Father of Dennis Kipton, Marcia Bailey, David Ellis. Education: B.S., Zoology, University of Michigan, 1939; M.A., Entomology, University of Kansas, 1940; Ph.D., Agricultural Chemistry, Tokyo University of Agriculture, 1977. Military: Served in the United States Navy, 1944-46, attaining the rank of Lieutenant (j.g.). Career: Chemical Ecologist, The Dow Chemical Company; Former Jobs include Taxonomist (Entomology), Insecticidal Researcher, Pesticide-Wildlife Toxicologist, Ecotoxicologist, Inventor (30 patents), Author (over 100 publications). Organizational Memberships: Society of Environmental Toxicology and Chemistry (founding president, 1979-81); Entomological Society of America; Ecological Society of America; American Chemical Society; American Ornithologist Union; National Agricultural Chemical Association; American Society for Testing and Materials; American Institute of Biological Science (board of directors, 1980-82). Community Activities: Michigan Audubon Society (president, 1962-64); Michigan Natural Resources Council (president, 1972-73); Midland Nature Club (founding president, 1953-55); Chippewa Nature Center, Midland, Michigan (founding president, 1966-70); Blue Ribbon Pesticide Advisory Committee, Michigan Department of Natural Resources, 1966-70; Michigan Department of Agriculture, 1965-68; Agriculture and/or Wildlife Consultant, N.A.T.O. 1974, W.H.O. 1971, I.U.P.A.C. 1967-71, N.R.C. 1964, 1971, 1976; Natural Resources Council, Canada, 1973-78; United States-Japan Science Seminar, 1971; U.S.-U.S.S.R. Joint Symposium, 1977. Religion: Life Member, Methodist Church. Honors and Awards: Emeritus Life Member 1981, Service Award 1982, Society of Environmental Toxicology and Chemistry; Honorary Board Member, Chippewa Nature Center, 1981; Research Scientist, Dow Chemical, 1978; Photographic Society of American International Ern. Exhibit Award Medals, Best of Show, 1961-67; University of Michigan Alumni Award, Midland High School, for Leadership, Scholarship, Athletics, 1934. Address: 1281 N. Wagner Road, Essexville, Michigan 48732.

Kennedy, William Thomas

Psychotherapist and Consultant. Personal: Born May 21, 1932; Married Brenda Kennedy; Father of Todd, Jennifer, Shawn, Lisa, Christina. Education: B.A. Chemistry, Adelphi University, 1955; M.A. Education, Columbia University, 1959; M.A. Psychology, New School for Social Research, 1972; Ph.D. Psychology, Humanistic Psychology Institute, 1979. Career: Psychotherapist and Consultant; Chemist; Teacher of Elementary and Secondary School and College; Educational Sales Consultant. Organizational Memberships: American Psychological Association; American Association of Marriage and Family Therapists; New York State

Association of Practicing Psychotherapists; New York Society of Clinical Psychologists; American Orthopsychiatric Association; Canadian Psychological Association; Federation of American Scientists; National Council on Family Relations; Association of Labor-Management Administrators and Consultants on Alcoholism. Address: 341 Latham Road, Mineola, New York 11501.

Kenny, Bettie Ilene Cruts (Bik)

Author, Artist, Diamond-Point Engraver. Personal: Born June 5, 1931; Daughter of Lester Arthur and Ruby Doris Harmon Cruts; Married Donald Keith Kenny. Education: Attended Pacific Lutheran University, Seattle Community College, Edison Technical and C.R.E.I. School; B.A. with honors, English Writing and Composition, University of Washington. Career: Partner, Bettie Kenny Diamond-point Engraving Company; Former Positions include Talcott's Jewelers, Olympia, Washington; Data Transcriber, Administrative Assistant, Boeing; Wrote Her First Poem at Age Eight; Sold Her First Painting at Age Sixteen; Submitted Her First Short Story to *Collier's Magazine* at Age Seventeen; Works in Numerous Private and Public Collections including Lawrence Welk, Janie Blalok, Governor and Mrs. Evans, Mayor and Mrs. Wes Uhlman, Mrs. Sydney Gerber, Mr. and Mrs. Ivor Crips of Friedlander's Fifth Avenue Jewelers in Seattle, Pioneer Museum (Longmont, Colorado), Seattle Museum of History and Industry, Washington State Historical Museum (Joshua Green Collection), President Nixon Commemorative at the White House, President John F. Kennedy (Smithsonian Institute), President Abraham Lincoln Memorial (Corning Museum of Glass); Drawings, Paintings, Crystal Drawings and Sculpture Exhibited in Numerous Shows including Washington State Museum, Rhodes International Gallery, Seattle Art Museum and 11th Annual Exhibit at the Frye Art Museum; Resident Artist, Seattle Museum of History and Industry (first artist-in-residence on record in any museum); Writing Assignments with Boening Aircraft. Community Activities: Senior Visions Council of Good Shepherd (cultural arts center); Helped Obtain One Percent Funding for Artists in City of Seattle; Rainier Chapter, N.S.D.A.R. Religion: Pianist for Various Presbyterian Churches; United Church of Christ, Choir Member, Deaconness, Youth Fellowship Director, Bible Camp Counsellor, President of Women's Missionary Fellowship, Committee to Select Pastors at Turnwater G.A.R.B.C. Baptist Church. Published Works: Numerous Articles to Various Professional Journals and Magazines, including *Keyboard, Jr.; Young Keyboard, Jr., Organic Gardening and Farming, Birches to Brag About, Apricots by the Bushful.* Honors and Awards: Numerous Letters of Commendation; Four Merit Awards from Boeing Engineering Departments; Gold Medal and Pro Mundi Benefeci Award from Brazil; Several Gold Medals, Special Awards and Prizes in Painting; Listed in Many Biographical Reference Publications. Address: 5610 44th Avenue S.W., Seattle, Washington 98136.

Kenny, Donald Keith

Businessman and Mathematician. Personal: Born November 20, 1928, in Cannon City, Colorado; Son of Carl Marshall and Grace Tuller Kenny (both deceased); Married Bettie Ilene Cruts. Education: B.A., Pacific Lutheran University; M.A., Reed College; Attended the University of California-Berkeley, University of Washington-Seattle. Career: Partner, Bettie Kenny Diamond Point Engraving Company; Mathematician; Teacher and Lay Minister, Grace Baptist Church. Organizational Memberships: S.C.E.A. (president; vice-president; treasurer); Fellow, Washington Heart Association. Community Activities: Chess Club (advisor); Youth for Christ Club; Honor Society. Religion: Deacon, Tumwater Baptist Church, Bible Youth Leader, Teacher, Pastor Selection Committee, Choir; Highline Baptist Church, Pastor Selection Committee, Youth Leader; Alki Church of Christ, Treasurer of Men's Fellowship, Choir. Honors and Awards: Listed in *Community Leaders and Noteworthy Americans, Personalities of America, Dictionary of International Biography, International Who's Who in Community Service, Who's Who in International Arts and Antiques, Who's Who in American Arts, World Who's Who of Women, Men and Women of Distinction, Men of Achievement.* Address: 5610 - 44th Avenue S.W., Seattle, Washington 98136.

Odis W Kenton

Kenton, Odis Wilson

Logistics Engineer. Personal: Born May 1, 1943, in Camden, New Jersey; Son of Edgar J. and Jessie E. Smith (both deceased); Father of Odis Wilson, Darnela Renee, Celeste Sheree. Education: A.B.B.A. Management and Accounting/Economics, Rutgers University, 1978; Attended United States Air Force Training Centers. Military: Served in the United States Air Force to the rank of Staff Sergeant (E5), 1961-69; Served in the United States Army National Guard to rank of Staff Sergeant (E6), 1976-78. Career: Logistics Specialist and Assistant Office Manager, Lockheed Electronics Company, Inc., Product Support Division, Arlington, Virginia, 1980 to present; Senior I.L.S. Engineer, Taurio Corporation, Alexandria, Virginia, 1979-80; Lead Systems Engineer, American Communications Corporation, 1974-78; Applied Metro Technology Inc., Senior R&D Lab Technician, Chief Technician, Field Service Representative, Manager of Field Service and Customer Relations Departments, 1970-74; Owner/Consultant, ODO Enterprises, Camden, New Jersey, 1970; Radio Communications Systems Field Installation Engineer, Melpar Inc., Falls Church, Virginia, 1970; Engineering Associate, Westinghouse DECO, McLean, Virginia, 1969-70. Organizational Memberships: American Society of Certified Engineering Technicians; Society of Logistics Engineers. Community Activities: Howard W. Brown Y's Men's Club, 1970-78; Greater Camden Jaycees, 1970-78; Vietnam Veterans Association, Washington, D.C., 1979-80; Rutgers University Alumni Association, 1978 to present; Special Services to Camden County O.I.C., 1977. Honors and Awards: Dean's List, Rutgers University; Honor Student, United States Air Force Technical Schools; Honor Graduate, 210th F.T.D. (KC-135); Airman-of-the-Month, 380th F.M.S., 380th Bomb Wing, 820th Air Division; Achievement Award, S.A.C. (educational); Certificate of Achievement, K.T.T.C.-United States Air Force (shift leader); Cost Reduction Award, Headquarters United States Air Force, A.F.S.C.-United States Air Force; Department of the Air Force, Air Force Commendation Medal, Good Conduct Medals, Air Force Longevity Ribbon for Eight Years of Service; Expert Marksman Ribbon; Department of Defense, Presidential Unit Citations, National Defense Medal, Vietnam Campaign Medal w/3CC; Department of the Army, Expert Marksman Medal, Marksman Medal; Vietnam Service Medal, Republic of Vietnam; 25 Memberships Award, South Camden Branch Young Men's Christian Association; Merit Award, Howard W. Brown Y's Men's Club G.C., Young Men's Christian Association. Address: 4508 Commons Drive 201, Annandale, Virginia 22003.

Keogh, Frances Troxler

Supervisor of Corporate Benefits Administration. Personal: Born January 28, 1926; Daughter of Pearl S. Troxler; Married John Milton Keogh; Mother of James Robert. Education: Business Certificate of Achievement 1945, Business Administration 1958, Elon College; Western Electric Company Training in Psychology and Computer Concepts, Princeton University, 1975-80. Career: Western Electric Company, Supervisor of Corporate Benefits Administration 1980 to present, Corporate Benefit Specialist in Policy Interpretation 1977-80, Methods Specialist in Government Systems Division 1972-76, Industrial Relations Associate for Benefit Service 1967-77, Supervisor of Technical Services at Kwajalein, Marshall Islands and White Sands Missile Range 1962-66, Executive Secretary 1951-62. Organizational Memberships: Telephone Pioneers of America (director of women's activities, 1975); Wenoca Club (vice-president, 1975); Nat Greene Secretarial Explorer Post (advisor, 1976). Community Activities: International Platform Association (red carpet committee, 1979-82); American Business Women's Association (chapter president, 1959, 1974, 1975); Inter-

Club Council, City of Greensboro (secretary, 1975); Beta Sigma Phi Sorority (treasurer, 1975); Small Business Administration Score Chapter, Greensboro (chairman, 1980-81). Religion: Maple Springs Methodist Church, Winston-Salem, North Carolina, Member, 1968-81; Faith Methodist Church, Burlington, North Carolina, Member 1951-68; Youth Sunday School Teacher and Counselor, Kwajalein, Marshall Islands, 1962-64; Young Adult Sunday School Teacher, Secretary of North Carolina Conference on Student Work, Secretary of North Carolina Methodist Conferency Young Adult Council, President of Local Women's Society of Christian Service 1951-58. Honors and Awards: Woman of the Year, American Business Women's Association; Candidate, Greensboro Citizen of the Year, 1975; Top Ten Best Dressed Women, 1962. Address: 1 Hastings Circle, Greensboro, North Carolina 27406.

Ethel M Kerchner

Kerchner, Ethel Marie

Homemaker, Farmer, Township Supervisor, Substitute Rural Letter Carrier. Personal: Born October 27, 1927; Daughter of Earl W. and Marie C. Jeanblanc Mellott (both deceased); Married Oscar A. Kerchner; Mother of Betty J. K. Higby, Bonnie J. K. Hancock Kersten, Joy A. K. Doyle Meyer, Joan L. K. Jacobs. Education: Graduate of Lee Center High School, 1945. Career: Homemaker, Farmer, Township Supervisor, Substitute Rural Letter Carrier; Cashier, Grocery Chain. Organizational Memberships: Township Officials of Lee County (president, 1978-80); Township Officials of Illinois, 1974 to present; Lee County Health Improvement Association (vice-president, 1976-80; president, 1980 to present); National Rural Letter Carriers Association, 1981-82; Lee County Rural Letter Carriers Association, 1981-82. Community Activities: Diabetic Clinic, Lee County, Illinois (chairman of first clinic); Lee County Health Department (past school volunteer); Lee County Health Improvement Association (past vice-president; president); Juror; Election Judge; Notary Public; Family Genealogist; Numerous School Activities (chairman); University of Illinois College of Agriculture (community resource council for Lee County, member 2 years, chairman 1 year); Northern Illinois University Alumni Association. Religion: Immanuel Lutheran Church of Amboy; Secretary, 110th Anniversary Church Committee and 35th Anniversary Ordination Committee, 1980; Archivist and Historian, Several Years; Sunday School Teacher; Organist; Secretary-Treasurer, Sunday School; President and Secretary, Ladies Aid of Immanuel. Published Works: Contributor of Articles to Lee County Historical Society Historical Yearbook, 1976. Honors and Awards: Listed in *Women in Public Service, Community Leaders and Noteworthy Americans, Book of Honor, Notable Americans*. Quiet Acres, Route 2 Box 253, Amboy, Illinois 61310.

Kernaleguen, Anne Paule

Professor. Personal: Born February 15, 1926; Daughter of Mr. and Mrs. Pierre Kernaleguen (deceased). Education: B.H.Sc., University of Saskatchewan, 1948; B.Ed., University of Alberta, 1957; M.A., Michigan State University, 1963; Ph.D., Utah State University, 1968. Career: Professor, University of Alberta; Academic Appointment, Michigan State University and University of Saskatchowan; High School Teacher, Red Deer Composite High School, Alberta; Canadian Bilingual Educational Representative, McCall's Corporation, New York; Extension Work, Ontario and Alberta Agriculture. Organizational Memberships: Home Economics Organizations (local, provincial, and national); Provincial, National and American Gerontological Associations; National and American Clothing Organizations; Canadian and American Psychological Associations. Community Activities: A.C.P.T.C. American Clothing Association (president, 1982; western president, 1978); A.S.A.C. (past president); American Home Economics (textiles and clothing chairman, 1971-73); C.H.E.A. (research editor, 1973-81; chairman of 50th anniversary publication); Alberta and Edmonton Home Economics Association (various offices); Westcliffe and Claridge House Condominium Association (secretary); Handicapped Housing and Communications Society (board of directors). Religion: Roman Catholic. Honors and Awards: Omicron Nu; Phi Upsilon Omicron; Phi Kappa Phi; Listed in Several British and American Biographical References. Address: 605 Claridge House, 11027-87 Avenue, Edmonton, Alberta, Canada T6G 2P9.

Latif S Khayyat

Kessler, Minuetta

Pianist, Composer, Teacher. Personal: Married Myer M. Kessler; Mother of Ronald, Jean K. Brenner. Education: Licentiate, Associate Board of the Royal College and Royal Academy of Music, London, England; Diploma in Piano, Postgraduate Diploma in Piano as Teacher and Artist, Juilliard School of Music, New York City, New York. Career: Pianist; Composer; Teacher. Organizational Memberships: Massachusetts Music Teachers Association (Boston chapter president, 1982; state president, 1979-81); New England Pianoforte Teachers Association (president, 1965-67). Community Activities: Friends of Young Musicians, Inc. (founder and artistic director, 1968); Concerts in the Home (founder and director, 1964); Boston Juilliard Alumni Association (founder and president, 1958); New England Jewish Music Forum (founder and vice-president, 1958). Honors and Awards: Two Canadian A.S.C.A.P. Awards for Serious Composition, 1945, 1946; Brookline Library Music Association Prize for Composition, 1957-58; Golden Key to the City of Calgary, Alberta, Canada, 1951. Address: 30 Hurley Street, Belmont, Massachusetts 02178.

Khayyat, Latif Shimon

Associate Professor. Personal: Born December 13, 1938; Son of Georgiyya Shabat Khayyat; Married Vita Glassman; Father of Haskel, Devorah. Education: B.A., 1966, and M.A., 1971, both from Hebrew University; Ph.D., Dropsie University, 1975. Career: Translator, Ministry of Justice, Israel, 1964; Teacher of Arabic, Israel, 1967-70; Research Assistant, Department of Geography, Hebrew University, 1969-70; Research Assistant, Department of Arabic, Hebrew University, 1970; Deparment of Music, Hebrew University, 1972; Associate Professor of Arabic, Dropsie University. Organizational Memberships: Research Fellow, Truman Institute, 1971-72; Professors for Peace in the Middle East, 1976. Community Activities: Council of the Sephardic Community, Jerusalem (translator of Arabic documents from Ottoman period 1969-71). Published Works: Contributor to various journals in Israel, United States and Europe, 1968 to present; Correspondent for Israeli weekly *al-Musawwar*, 1961-64; Prepared Bibliography of published Genizah fragments (Judeo-Arabic), Jewish Theological Seminary, 1976-79. Religion: Work with Jewish Theological Seminary, 1973, 1974. Honors and Awards: Scholarship for achievement in the study of Arabic folk songs of Iraqi Jews, Ben Zvi Institute, 1966 to present; Scholarship for achievement in study of Judeo-Iraqi literature, Memorial Foundation of Jewish Culture, 1974-76. Address: 504 Grand Street, Apt. H32, New York, New York 10002.

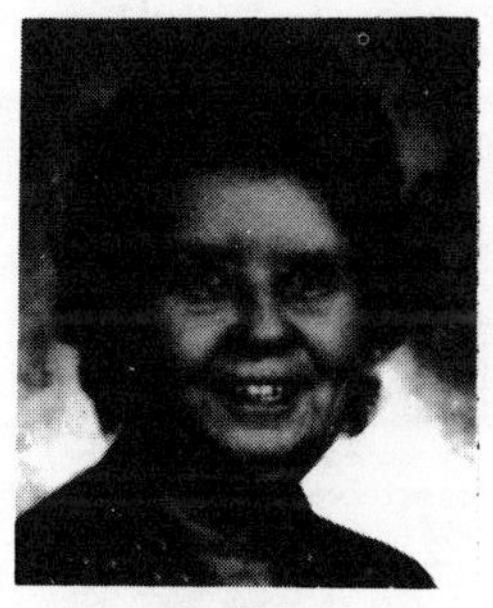

Alice Kimber

Kimber, Alice Mae

Retired Teacher and Social Worker. Personal: Born March 24, 1921; Daughter of James Dee and Buena New Perkins; Married Victor Daniel Kimber; Mother of Betty Simpson. Education: B.A., Southern Missionary College, 1947; Also attended LSU and Tulane in Louisiana for Social Work Courses. Career: Former Social Worker and Missionary Teacher, Social Worker in Mississippi and Florida for 15 Years; Home Economics Teacher in Rhodesia 1951-55; Volunteer Bible Missionary Teacher at Bethel College of S.D.A., 1979-80 in the Transkei in Africa; Dietician, Florida Hospital, S.D.A., 4 Years; Taught Home Economics to Indians at Holbrook,

Arizona S.D.A. Mission. Organizational Memberships: Home Economics Club President 1946; Social Workers Organization 1947-51; Head Start Committee 1970.Religion: Seventh-Day Adventist; Sabbath School Secretary for S.D.A. Church; Young People's Leader 1938; Health and Welfare Leader for S.D.A. Church in Florida 1971; Church Treasurer 1978. Honors and Awards: Listed in *Personalities of the South*. Address: 1421 Valencia Street, Sanford, Florida 32771.

Kimmel, Ellen Bishop

Ellen B Kimmel

Professor of Psychology and Educational Psychology. Personal: Born September 16, 1939; Daughter of Archer and Mary Ellen Bishop; Mother of Elinor, Ann, Jean, Tracy. Education: Graduate of National Cathedral School, 1957; B.A., University of Tennessee, 1961; M.A. 1962, Ph.D. 1965, University of Florida. Career: University of South Florida, Full Professor of Psychology and Educational Psychology 1966 to present, Director of Universities Studies College 1972-73, Current Director of Women and Administrator of Summer Institute; Freelance Consultant and Trainer; Distinguished Visiting Professor, Simon Fraser University, Vancouver, British Columbia, Canada, 1980-81. Organizational Memberships: Southeastern Psychological Association (president, 1977-80); American Psychological Association (fellow; council member); Eleven Other Professional Organizations. Community Activities: Democratic Executive Committee (precinct 52, elected member, 1973-76); Hillsborough County Status of Women Commission (vice-chair, 1977-79); Governor's Commission on the Status of Women, 1979-83; Blue Ribbon Committee on Juvenile Delinquency, Hillsborough; Stop Rape, Tampa (board member); Hillsborough County Kindergarten Committee; American Council on Education (national identification committee). Honors and Awards: Scholarship Awards for Highest Academic Achievement, University of Tennessee, 1958-60; Outstanding Senior Award, University of Tennessee, 1961; Phi Kappa Phi and Phi Beta Kappa Recognition, 1961; Florida Governor's Award for Outstanding Service to State, 1975; Faculty Honor Guard, University of South Florida, 1975, 1976; Special Contribution Award, American Personnel and Guidance Association, 1975; Dianna Award, Tampa Chapter of National Organization of Women, 1975; Women Helping Women Award, Soroptimist Clubs of America, 1977; Omega Delta Kappa Leadership Fraternity, 1977; Outstanding Professor Award, University of South Florida, 1978; Equal Opportunity Award, University of South Florida, 1979; Listed in 12 Biographical Reference Publications. Address: 8643 Lake Isle Drive, Tampa, Florida 33617.

King, Joseph Jerone

Joseph J King

Executive, Consultant. Personal: Born September 27, 1910, in Spokane, Washington; Son of Joseph J. Sr. and Alice E. Halferty King (both deceased); Married Irma Kathleen Martin, in 1937; Father of Sally Jo Thompson, Nikki Sue Ring, Cindy Lou Mullen. Education: Graduate of Salem High School, Oregon; A.B. Economics-Sociology (with great distinction), Stanford University, 1935; M.A. Economics-Sociology, Duke University, 1937; Research Fellowship on Doctoral Thesis, Brookings Institution, 1938-39. Career: Instructor in Economics, Black Mountain College, North Carolina, 1937-38; United States Department of Agriculture, Portland, Oregon, Headquarters (1939-51), Chief of Regional Migratory Farm Labor Program, Chief of Regional Community Services and Co-operative Program, Regional Personnel Officer, Regional Administrative Management Officer, National Administrator's Representative on the U.S.D.A. Field Committee of the Columbia River Basin; Oregon State Director, Christian Rural Overseas Program, sponsored jointly by Catholic Relief Life, Church World Service, Lutheran World Relief, late 1940's; Senior Civilian in charge of Industrial Relations, Puget Sound Naval Shipyard, Bremerton, Washington, 1951; Public Affairs Director, Executive Vice President, Association of Washington Industries, Olympia, Washington, 1958; Association of Washington Business, Olympia, 1966; President, King's Public Affairs, Ltd., Silverdale, Washington, 1978. Organizational Memberships: Governor's Committee for State Government Organization, 1950's; American Society for Public Administration (past president, Oregon state chapter; president, two terms, Washington state chapter); Chairman of Panels on Personnel Administration Leadership and Labor Relations for the Public Service; Society for Personnel Administration (past president, Puget Sound chapter); Governor's Council for Reorganization of Washington State Government, 1960's; State-wide Public Education Management Survey (director of manpower, 1970's); Tuition in Higher Education (select legislative committee); National Association of Secondary School Principals (Century III leaders scholarship program selection committee); State Department of Public Instruction (served on several advisory committees, including professional education, Title IV, urban, rural, racial and disadvantaged); Washington State Council on Economic Education (board of directors). Community Activities: Governor's Committee on Employing the Physically Handicapped; Founder with President of Central Washington University Project for High School Youth Business Week; The American Red Cross (chairman, Kitsap County chapter); Visiting Nurse Association (chairman, citizen county advisory committee); Bremerton Aquatics Show, Inc. (president); American Legion (honorary "forty and eight"; post mortem club); Elks Lodge; Masons; Scottish Rite; Shrine; Rotary; Kitsap Golf and Country Club; Washington Athletic Club; Washington Generals; Washington Admirals. Religion: Protestant; Served on Oregon Council of Churches to Several Annual National Rural Life Conferences. Published Works: Number of Articles including "F.S.A. Group Services in the Pacific Northwest", *Harvard Business Review*, 1944; "Cooperatives and Cutover Lands", *Sociology and Social Research*, 1944; "Rural Co-operative Self-Help Activites in the Pacific Northwest", *American Sociological Review*, 1943; "Back to the Land Movements", *Rural Sociology*, 1945; Guest Editorial Writer on Various Subjects including "Share the Tools", "Employees Plans Boost Efficiency", "Telling a Clerk about his Agency", *Portland Oregon Journal*; Book *Winning* reprinted 7 times, Association of Washington Industries. Honors and Awards: Phi Beta Kappa; A.B. with Great Distinction, Stanford University, 1935; *The Bremerton Sun* (daily), Featured an Editorial "Well Said" which Commended Development of a Code of Ethics for Public Servants; Award for Services Rendered in Promoting (and prompting of) Public Administration in State, American Society for Public Administration; Honorary Chief Journalist, 13th United States Naval District. Address: Ioka Beach, Hood Canal, 11655 Ioka Way N.W., Silverdale, Washington 98383.

King, Robert Daniel

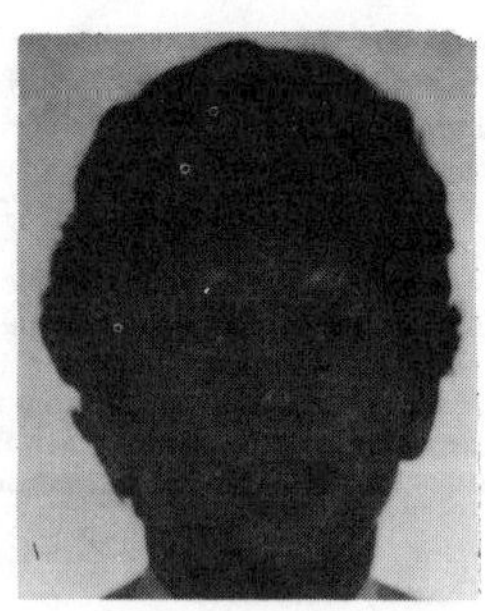

Robert D King

Executive and Microbiologist. Personal: Born February 5, 1944; Son of Katherine H. King; Married to Mary Josephine Daniel. Education: B.S., 1967, Ph.D., 1971, Oklahoma State University at Stillwater. Military: Served with United States Army in the Medical Service Corps, advanced through grades to Captain, 1967-76. Career: Chief Executive Officer, Director and President, Diversified Technology, Inc., San Antonio, Texas, 1978 to present; Assistant Professor of Microbiology, University of Texas Health Science Center, San Antonio, 1976 to present; Consultant to Department of the Army, Brooke Army Medical Center, San Antonio, 1976 to present; Research Microbiologist in Dermatology Division, Letterman Army Institute of Research, San Francisco, California, 1973-76; Chief of Microbiology Section, Pathology Department, Letterman Army Medical Center, San Francisco, 1971-73. Organizational Memberships: New York Academy of Sciences; Sigma Xi; American Society for Microbiology; American Association for the Advancement of Science; American Federation of Clinical Research; American Society of Lubrication Engineers (executive director, 1981). Community Activities: President's Club, Oklahoma State University Foundation, 1981. Published Works: Contributor of numerous articles to professional journals. Honors and Awards: Army Commendation Medal, 1973; Army Commendation Medal with Oak Leaf Cluster, 1976; Graduate Excellence Award, Oklahoma State University, 1969-70; Received National Institute of Health research grants, 1976-80; Patentee in field-related inventions, 1973; Guest Lecturer and Speaker, including International Conference in Germany, 1982; Listed in *Who's Who in the South and Southwest*. Address: 12710 Kings Forest, San Antonio, Texas 78229.

Kinney, Arthur F

University Professor, Author, Editor. Personal: Born September 5, 1933; Son of A. F. Kinney, Sr. Military: Served in the United States Army, 1956-58. Career: Professor, University of Massachusetts-Amherst. Published Works: *Faulkner's Narrative Poetics; Dorothy Parker; Elizabethan Backgrounds; Titled Elizabethans; William Faulkner; The Compson Family; Resources of Being: The Library of Flannery O'Connor (In Progress); Nicholas Hilliard's Treatise on Limning;* Essays on the American South and on Jazz Music; Editor, *English Literary Renaissance* Journal. Honors and Awards: National Endowment for the Humanities Senior Fellow, Senior Fellow, Huntington Library, California; Folger Fulbright-Hays Fellow, Oxford University, England; Folger Sheakespeare Library Fellow, Washington, D. C.; American Philosophical Society Fellowship; Morse Fellow, Yale University, 3 Years; Bread Loaf Scholar in Fiction and Criticism, Middlebury College; Avery and Jules Hopwood Award in Criticism, University of Michigan; Distinguished Lecturer, Nearly 50 Public and Private American Universities and 14 European Universities in England, Holland, and Belgium. Address: 25 Hunter Hill Drive, Amherst, Massachusetts 01002.

Nancy J Kinsler

Kinney, Rayner Haliimaile

Executive. Personal: Born April 26, 1929; Son of Ray and Hanakaulani Holt Kinney; Married to R. J. Leinani Kamai; Father of Leimana, Rayner, Melvin, Rhana-Mae. Education: Graduate of the Kamehameha Schools, Hawaii. Career: President of Resort Consultants, Inc., San Francisco, California; Vice President, Continental Hotels, Inc., Continental Airlines, Los Angeles, California, 1974-81; Vice President, C. Brewer Hotels, Hawaii, 1971-74; Project Manager and General Manager, A.I.T.S. Hotels, Hawaii, 1970-71; Resident Manager, Maui Hilton, 1968-70; Held all food and beverage positions with Hilton Hotels, 1961-68; Held various positions with Western International Hotels, 1957-61. Organizational Memberships: American Hotel and Motel Association; American Restaurant Association; California Restaurant Association. Community Activities: Lake County Chamber of Commerce. Honors and Awards: Listed in *Who's Who in the West, Pesonalities of the West and Midwest, International Who's Who of Intellectuals, Businessmen of California.* Address: 1355 Lombard Street, San Francisco, California 94109.

Kinsler, Nancy J

Corporate Controller and Treasurer, Certified Public Accountant. Personal: Born June 19, 1950; Daughter of William J. and Erna J. Kosek Kinsler. Education: B.S. Candidate, Villanova University, Villanova, Pennsylvania, 1968-70; B.S. summa cum laude Accounting, Pennsylvania State University, State College, Pennsylvania, 1971; Certified Public Accountant, Commonwealth of Pennsylvania, 1975. Corporate Controller/Treasurer, National Interior Contracting Organization, Inc., New York, New York, 1980 to present; IU Conversion Systems, Inc., Horsham, Pennsylvania, Controller 1979-80, Assistant Controller 1977-78, Manager of Planning and Analysis 1976-77, Manager of Accounting Services 1974-76; Auditor, Arthur Andersen & Co., Philadelphia, Pennsylvania, 1971-74. Organizational Memberships: Pennsylvania Institute of Certified Public Accountants, 1975 to present; Beta Gamma Sigma, 1970-71; Beta Alpha Psi, 1970-71. Religion: Roman Catholic. Honors and Awards: Summa Cum Laude Graduate, Pennsylvania State University, 1971. Address: 27 Log Pond Drive, Horsham, Pennsylvania 19044.

Gelsey Kirkland

Kirkland, Gelsey

Principal Ballerina. Personal: Born in Bethlehem, Pennsylvania. Education: Graduate of The School of American Ballet. Career: Principal Ballerina, American Ballet Theatre, 1974 to present; New York City Ballet, Principal Dancer 1972-74, Soloist 1970-72, Member of Corps de Ballet 1968-70; Ballet Choreographed for her by George Balanchine, *Firebird;* Created Roles in Jerome Robbins' *Goldberg Variations, An Evening's Waltzes, Four Bagatelles* and *Scherzo Fantastique,* John Clifford's *Stravinsky Symphony in C* and *Tchaikovsky Suite #1,* and John Taras' *Song of the Nightingale;* Repertoire includes Title Roles in *Giselle* and *La Sylphide,* Kitri in *Don Quixote, or Kitri's Wedding,* Princess Aurora in *The Sleeping Beauty,* Clara in *The Nutcracker,* and Odette-Odile in *Swan Lake,* and Leading Roles in *La Bayadere, Coppelia, La Fille Mal Gardee, Les Sylphides,* Balanchine's *Theme and Variations* and *Tarantella, Ben Stevenson's Three Preludes,* Glen Tetley's *Voluntaries,* and Antony Tudor's *Jardin Aux Lilas, The Leaves are Fading,* and *The Tiller in the Fields;* Starring Role, Television Production, *The Nutcracker,* Opposite Mikhail Baryshnikov; Starring Role, *Live from Lincoln Center* Public Broadcasting Service Broadcast, *Theme and Variations,* Opposite Mikhail Baryshnikov; Appearance with Stuttgart Ballet as Juliet, John Crank's Production of *Romeo and Juliet,* 1980; Appearance with The Royal Ballet, Covent Garden, London, as Juliet, Kenneth MacMillan's Production of *Romeo and Juliet,* 1980; Guest Artist with Ballet Companies and Orchestras Internationally. Address: New York, New York.

Kissane, Sharon Florence

Communications Consultant and Writer. Personal: Born July 2, 1940; Daughter of William and Agnes Mrotek; Married James Q. Kissane; Mother of Laura Janine, Elaine Marie. Education: B.A., De Paul University, 1962; M.A., Northwestern University, 1962; Ph.D., Loyola University, 1970. Career: Communications Consultant and Writer; Teacher; Editor. Organizational Memberships: National Association of Women Business Owners (board member, public relations officer, 1980-81); League of Women Voters; Barrington Area Arts Council (founder of writers' group). Community Activities: District 220 Gifted Program Task Force, 1979 to present; Barrington High School Curriculum Committee (parents' representative, 1981 to present); Crusade of Mercy (block chairman, 1966); South Barrington Annual Art Fair (founder, 1979); Northwestern University Alumni Association Telethon, 1979-80; League of Women Voters Fund Drive, 1980-81. Honors and Awards: Honorary Citizen of Korea, 1965; Prix de Paris Art Award, 1974; Chicago Sketch Club Honorary Award, 1973; Northwestern University Alumni Achievement Award, 1979; Illinois Arts Council Artist-in-Residence Grant, 1978; Listed in *Who's Who Among American Women, International Who's Who of Women, National Social Register, Who's Who in Education, Who's Who in Community Service, Who's Who in Education.* Address: 15 Turning Shore Drive, Barrington, Illinois 60010.

Sandra C Kittner

Kittner, Sabra Corbin

Media Specialist. Personal: Born November 1, 1922 in Federalsburg, Maryland; Daughter of George Edwin and Hilda Villars Corbin MacDorman; Mother of Sabra Corbin, Jo Corbin. Education: A.B. 1944, M.Ed. 1966, Western Maryland College; Postgraduate

Studies, Catholic University, Johns Hopkins University. Career: Associate Professor, Western Maryland College, 1968 to present; Supervisor of Media Services, Carroll County, Maryland, 1966 to present; Librarian, North Carroll High School, 1949-50, 1957-66; Teacher, Franklin High School 1950-51, Stemmers Run Junior High School 1949-50, Kenwood High School 1944-49. Organizational Memberships: Association of Education Communication and Technology; Maryland Educational Media Organization; National Association of Supervisors and Principals. Religion: Methodist. Address: 94 Willis Street, Westminster, Maryland 21157.

Kizer, Bernice Lichty

Chancery and Probate Judge. Personal: Born August 14, 1915 in Fort Smith, Arkansas; Daughter of Ernest and Opal C. Lichty; Married Harlan D. Kizer; Mother of J. Mayne Parker, Shirley Parker Wilhite, Karolyn Parker Sparkman, Mary K. Holt. Education: Graduate of Fort Smith High School; Attended Fort Smith Junior College (now Westark Community College) and Stephens College; LL.B. 1947, J.D. 1969, University of Arkansas. Career: Judge, Twelfth Judicial District Chancery and Probate Courts, 1975 to present; State Representative, House of Representatives, Arkansas State Legislature, 1961-74. Organizational Memberships: Sebastian County Bar Association; Crawford County Bar Association; Arkansas State Bar Association; Licensed to Practice before all Arkansas Courts, the United States Eighth Circuit Court of Appeals, United States Supreme Court. Community Activities: United Fund (women's division chairman); Governor's Commission for the Aging; Library Week (state chairman); Christmas Seals for Tuberculosis (state chairman); Mental Health Association (state chairman); Western Arkansas Counseling and Guildance Center (board of directors); City National Bank of Fort Smith (board of directors); Cottey College, Nevada, Missouri (board of directors); Western Arkansas Planning and Development District, Inc. (board of directors); Young Women's Christian Association; League of Women Voters; American Association of University Women; P.E.O.; Soroptimists; Business and Professional Women's Club. Honors and Awards: First Recipient, *Southwest Times Record* Woman Achiever Award; 1980 Horizons 100 Arkansas Women of Achievement, Arkansas Press Women; Listed in *Who's Who in America*, *Who's Who of American Women*, *Who's Who in Government*, *Who's Who in the South and Southwest*, *Personalities of the South*, *Who's Who in American Law*. Address: 1235 58 Terrace, Fort Smith, Arkansas 72904.

Klein, Barry Todd

Publisher and Author. Personal: Born December 7, 1949; Son of Bernard and Betty Klein; Married Laurie Kay. Education: B.S., New York University, 1971. Career: President, Todd Publications, Rye, New York; Author; Editor of Numerous Professional Reference Books; General Manager, Irvington Publishers, Inc., New York, New York. Community Activities: Organization for the Betterment of Mankind (president, 1975 to present); Association for the Development of Thought (chairperson, 1979 to present); Committee to Eliminate Criminal Minds in Politics (secretary); Council of Economic Futurism (honorary member). Published Works: *Reference Encyclopedia of the American Indian*, 1973-81 Editions; *Reference Encyclopedia of American Psychology and Psychiatry*, 1975; *Bibliography of American Ethnology*, 1976. Address: 400 East 77th Street Apt. 11A, New York, New York 10021.

Kleinrock, Susan Naomi

Psychologist. Personal: Born March 30, 1955; Daughter of Martin and Ruth Blum Kleinrock. Education: B.A., New York University, 1975; M.S., Syracuse University, 1976; Ph.D., Syracuse University, 1982. Career: Research Associate, Syracuse University, 1976-78; Regional Assessor, New York State Division for Youth, 1977-78; Industrial Consultant, 1978 to present. Organizational Memberships: American Psychological Association, 1973 to present; New York Academy of Science, 1973 to present; American Association of Psychiatric Services for Children, 1978 to present; Eastern Psychological Association, 1976 to present; National Rehabilitation Association, 1978 to present; Council for Exceptional Children, 1980 to present. Community Services: Girl Scout Leader, 1978-80; League of Women Voters; Zoological Society (supporting member); Medex-Coney Island Hospital (volunteer 1969-73); ASPCA; National Organization for Women; Women's Civic Club of New York; Advocate for Children's Rights in the New York and the United States; Supporting member and Patron of the Arts (Ballet) in New York. Honors and Awards: Outstanding Citizen 1972; Outstanding Community Service (volunteer for 1981-82); Outstanding Scholarship in Spanish and English 1972; Listed in *Who's Who of American Women*. Address: 958 Brady Avenue, Apt. 2, Bronx, New York 10462.

Klisch, Karen

Associate Professor and Director of Aquatic Center. Personal: Born June 12, 1941; Daughter of Roland and Marion Klisch. Education: B.S., Florida State University, 1962; M.A. 1968, Ph.D. 1980, Postdoctoral Work in Stress Management 1982, University of Maryland. Career: Associate Professor, Hood College, Frederick, Maryland; Director, Huntsinger Aquatic Center. Organizational Memberships: American Association of University Professors; A.A.H.P.E.R.; M.I.S.A.W. (president, 1975-76); American College of Sports Medicine. Community Activities: American Red Cross (volunteer instructor trainer, water safety instruction; aquatics committee, 1974-76); American Heart Association (volunteer); Equal Rights Amendment (fund raiser); National Organization of Women; U.S.S. Master's Swimmer. Honors and Awards: Phi Delta Pi, Florida State University; Phi Alpha Epsilon, University of Maryland. Address: 1704 Dahlgren Road, Middletown, Maryland 21769.

Kluckhohn, Florence Rockwood

Educator (retired). Personal: Born January 14, 1905. Daughter of Homer G. Rockwood and Florence McLaughlin Rockwood (both deceased). Married Clyde K. M. Kluckhohn, 1932 (deceased 1960); Married George Edward Taylor, 1968. Mother of Richard Paul Rockwood Kluckhohn (deceased). Education: B.A. University of Wisconsin, 1927; Ph.D. Radcliffe College-Harvard University, 1941. Career: Instructor, Wellesley College, 1942-48. Leave of absence for service in Office of War Information, 1944-46. Instructor and later Lecturer (Professional status), Harvard University, 1948-68. Organizational Memberships: American Anthropology Association; American Sociological Association; American Academy of Political and Social Science; Society for Applied Anthropology; Phi Beta Kappa. Community Activities: Highlands Guild of Orthopedic Hospital, Seattle, Washington, 1971-81; The Age Center of New England, Inc. (trustee); Office of War Information (analyst, 1944-45). Honors and Awards: Phi Beta Kappa, 1939; Honorary Position, Auxiliary Professor of Anthropology, University of Washington, 1974-81. Address: The Highlands, Seattle, Washington 98177.

Knepper, Eugene Arthur

Real Estate Executive, Investor, and Financial Counselor. Personal: Born October 8, 1926; Son of May C. Knepper; Married LaNel

Knepper; Father of Kenton Todd, Kristin Rene. Education: Bachelor of Commercial Science, Accounting, Drake University, Des Moines, Iowa, 1951. Military: Served in the United States Navy to Rank of Seaman First Class, 1945-46. Career: Owner, Real Estate Planning Associates; Investment Real Estate Syndicator, Investor and Financial Counselor; Controlling Partner, Various Limited Partnerships; Corporate and Public Accountant; Assistant Controller, United Fire and Casualty Insurance Company; Auditor, Certified Public Accounting Firm; Government Renegotiation Department, Collins Radio Company; Licensed in Life Insurance, 25 Years; Licensed in Real Estate Brokerage, Over 20 Years; Owner, Commercial Laundry; Small Business Management Consultant. Organizational Memberships: Eastern Iowa Executive Club (president, 1981-82); Iowa Real Estate Commission (accredited continuing education instructor, 1981); Iowa Association of Realtors (president, commerical investment division, 1973, 1980); Realtor's Political Action Committee (life member); National Association of Accountants; Real Estate Securities Syndication Institute; Iowa Association of Realtors and National Association of Realtors (various legislative committees, state and national levels). Community Activities: Cedar Rapids Symphony (patron, 1977-82); Oakhill-Jackson Outreach Fund Inc. (board of directors, 1970 to 1981; president, 1970-80); Consumer Credit Counseling Service of Cedar Rapids-Marion Area (president, 1974-81); International Platform Association, 1977 to present; Cedar Rapids Optimist Club (former board member and chairman of boy's work committee); Young Men's Christian Association, 1961 to present; Cedar Rapids Chamber of Commerce (housing committee); Various High Schools and Colleges (guest lecturer on personal money management and investments); Republican Party (life member). Religion: United Methodist Church; Sunday School Instructor, 10 Years; Various Committees; Finance Committee; Wills and Legacies Committee; Social Concerns Committee; Education Committee; Administrative Board. Published Works: "One Person's Financial Future--Yours!" Manuscript; "Real Estate vs. Wall Street", *Real Estate Today* 1973, *Selling Commercial Real Estate* (Republication). Honors and Awards: S. J. Storm Trophy for Best Accounting Manuscript of the Year, 1975-76; Cedar Rapids Chapter of National Association of Accountants Manuscript of the Year Award, 1975-76; Fellow, International Biographical Association; Listed in *Who's Who in Finance and Industry*, *Who's Who in Real Estate*, and Other Biographical References. Address: 283 Tomahawk Trail Southeast, Cedar Rapids, Iowa 52403.

Knoerle, Jeanne

College President. Personal: Born February 24, 1928. Education: B.A., Drama-Journalism, Saint Mary-of-the-Woods College, 1949; M.A. Journalism 1961, Ph.D., Comparative Literature/Asian 1966, Indiana University; Additional Work, Catholic University of America, Georgetown University. Career: Saint Mary-of-the-Woods College, President 1968 to present, Assistant to President and Associate Professor of Asian Studies 1967-68, Chairman of Department of Journalism 1954-63; Visiting Professor, Providence College, Taichung, Taiwan, 1966-67; Summer Seminar in Art, Culture and Society, Taiwan, Summer 1966; Teacher, Immaculata High School, Washington, D.C., 1953-54; Teacher, Central Catholic High School, Fort Wayne, Indiana, 1952-53; Teacher, Providence High School, Chicago, Illinois, 1952; St. Columbkille High School, Chicago, Illinois, 1952. Organizational Memberships: Association of Catholic Colleges and Universities (chairwoman, 1978-80; board member, 1976-82); Association of American Colleges (board member, 1976-80); American Council on Education (board member, 1978-82; Commission on Women in Higher Education, 1976-79); Council of Independent Colleges (board member, 1980-83); International Association of University Presidents (advisory council, North American council, 1977-79); National Catholic Educational Association (executive committee, 1978-80); Indiana Conference of Higher Education (president, executive committee, 1973-74); Associated Colleges of Indiana (president, 1982-84; vice president, executive board, 1980-82); Independent Colleges and Universities of Indiana (secretary/treasurer, 1979-80; executive board, 1976-82). Community Activities: Fund for the Improvement of Postsecondary Education, 1982 to present; Federal Home Loan Bank of Indianapolis (board member, 1975 to present); Grow Terre Haute (executive committee, 1981 to present); Aquinas College (board member, 1978-80); Union Hospital of Terre Haute (board member, 1973 to present); Wabash Valley Goodwill Industries (board member, 1971-78); Terre Haute Medical Education Foundation (board member, 1974-79); United Way of the Wabash Valley (board member, 1971-75); Mental Health Association of Vigo County (board member, 1971-78); Indiana Academy in the Public Service (board member, 1980-82); Center for Constitutional Studies of Notre Dame University Law School (board member, 1980-82); International Women's Year (Indiana coordinating commission, 1970); National Institutes of Health (Division of Research Resources advisory council, 1975-79); Women's College Calition (executive committee, 1973-77); Lilly-Poynter Project on "American Institutions and the Crisis of Confidence", Indiana University (regional chairperson, 1974-77); Series of Seminars on "The President as Creative Leader", Association of American Colleges (speaker, 1974-75); N.B.C. *Today Show* (participant, 1971; segment, 1980); *Phil Donahue Show* (segment); *Good Housekeeping* Women in Passage Program (participant, 1976-77); Symposium on "Evangelization in the American Context: The Pastoral Presence in an Open Society", Center for Continuing Education, University of Notre Dame (participant, 1976). Religion: Roman Catholic; Member, Congregation of Sisters of Providence, July 22, 1949 to present. Published Works: *The Dream of the Red Chamber, a Critical Study*, 1972; "The Poetic Theories of Lu-Chi - With a Brief Comparison with Horace's Ars Poetica", *Journal of Aesthetics and Art Criticism*, 1966; "Ezra Pound and the Literature of China", *Tamkang Review*, Tamkung College of Arts and Sciences, Taipei, 1973; "The Chinese College Woman", *Indiana University Alumni* Magazine, 1967; *Pius XII and Modern Communications Theory*, M.A. Thesis; Frequent Speaker, Service Clubs, Professional Organizations, Church and Educational Groups. Honors and Awards: Honorary Doctor of Letters Degree, Rose-Hulman Institute of Technology, 1971; Honorary Doctor of Laws Degree, Indiana State University 1972, Indiana University 1975, Saint Mary's College, Notre Dame, Indiana 1981; Honorary Doctor of Divinity Degree, Indiana Central University, 1978; Summer Seminar in Art, Culture and Society, Taipei, Taiwan, Fulbright Award, 1966; Educational Counselor, Purdue University's Old Masters Program, 1970; Advisor of the Year Award, Catholic School Press Association, 1960; Mother Theodore Guerin Medallions for Outstanding Alumna, Saint Mary-of-the-Woods College, 1975; Listed in *Who's Who of American Women*, *Who's Who Among Authors and Journalists*, *Who's Who in Religion*, *Who's Who of Women*, *Who's Who in the Midwest*, *Who's Who of Women in Education*, *American Catholic Who's Who*, *Dictionary of International Biography*, *Leaders in Education*, *Directory of American Scholars*, *Terre Haute's People of Progress*. Address: Saint Mary-of-the-Woods College, Saint Mary-of-the-Woods, Indiana 47876.

Ko, Yih-Song

Family Physician. Personal: Born March 31, 1941; Son of Lien-Chih and Shuang-Mei Ko; Married Hwan Chang; Father of Tina, Judy, David. Education: M.D., Kaoshiung Medical College, Taiwan, Republic of China, 1968. Military: Served as Medical Officer in the Chinese Air Force, 1968-69. Career: Active Staff Physician, United Community Hospital, Grove City, Pennsylvania, 1975 to present; Family Physician, Grove City, Pennsylvania, 1974 to present; Residency in General Practice, Good Samaritan Hospital, Pottsville, Pennsylvania, 1972-74; Internship, Catholic Medical Center of Brooklyn and Queens, New York, 1971-72; Internal Medicine Residency, Veteran General Hospital, Taipei, Taiwan, Republic of China, 1969-70; Medical Officer, Tai-Chung Air Force Hospital, Taiwan, Republic of China, 1968-69. Organizational Memberships: American Academy of Family Physicians, 1976 to present; American Medical Association, 1975 to present; Pennsylvania Medical Society. Community Activities: Child Health Clinic, Grove City, Pennsylvania (clinician, 1975-76); Allegheny General Hospital, Pittsburgh, Pennsylvania (preceptor, nurse practitioner program, 1979); Gannon University, Erie, Pennsylvania (preceptor, physician assistant program, 1979-80); Flo-Con System Inc. Grove City Plant (company physician, 1976-80); Equitable Insurance Company (appointed physician, 1978 to present). Honors and Awards: Diplomate, American Board of Family Practice, 1977; Fellow, American Academy of Family Physicians, 1978. Address: 421

Shady Drive, Grove City, Pennsylvania 16127.

Koehler, Wanda Mae

Social Worker. Personal: Born July 9, 1933 in Hennepin, Oklahoma; Daughter of James Clifford and Ila Mae McGaw (both deceased); Mother of Wesley Cannon, Valorie DeAnn C. Nordbye, Sandra Gail C. Westling. Education: Graduate of Pauls Valley High School, 1950; B.A. Education, East Central University, Ada, Oklahoma, 1956; M.A. Elementary Education, 1974, M.A. Community College Teaching 1975, M.A. Social Science 1976, Northern Arizona University, M.S.W. 1980, Masters of Human Relations Studies 1980 to present, Oklahoma University. Career: Social Worker III, Qualified Mental Retardation Professional Department of Human Services, Pauls Valley State School for the Mentally Retarded, 1976 to present; Part-Time Instructor, Central Arizona Community College, Coolidge, Arizona, 1973-76; Independently Contracted Consultant Work, Hopi, Walapai, Apache, and Navajo Reservations, Arizona and New Mexico, 1972-76; I.P.D.A. Project Instructor, 5-Week Summer Workshop, Northern Arizona University, 1972; Durfee School, El Rancho District, Pico Rivera, California, Kindergarten Teacher 1968-71, Summer Adult Education Teacher of Pre-School Education 1970, Summer School Teacher 1969; Summer Adult Education Teacher of Pre-School Education, Obregon School, Pico Rivera, California, 1971; Assistant Program Director, Summer Parks and Recreation Program, La Habra, California 1961, La Puente, California 1960-61; Substitute Teacher, Elementary, Junior High and High School, Hudson District, La Puente, California, 1960; High School and Junior High English Teacher, Jenks Public Schools, Janks, Oklahoma, 1956-57; Telephone Operator, Bell Telephone Company, Pauls Valley, Oklahoma City and Seminole, Oklahoma, 1951-53. Organizational Memberships: National Association of Social Workers (Oklahoma chapter, social policy committee, school social work task force); Oklahoma Health and Welfare Association; Oklahoma Public Employees Association (president, Garvin County chapter, 1980-81; vice-president, district council, 1981-82); American Association on Mental Deficiency. Community Activities: Court-Related and Community Services (district V practicum placement participant, 1980); Oklahoma Electric Co-Op, Norman, Oklahoma (summer practicum participant, 1979); Oklahoma Reading Council (state conference workshop leader, 1978); Arizona Bilingual Council (state conference workshop leader and member, 1976); El Rancho School District Curriculum Council, Pico Rivera, California (Durfee School representative, 1970-71); Santiago Council of Girl Scouts, California (volunteer consultant, 1968); Girl Scouts of America (Brea, California, assistant troop leader 1967, Brownie troop leader 1966; assistant Brownie troop leader, La Puente, California, 1960); Rainbow for Girls, 1946-50; Common Cause; American Civil Liberties Union; Garvin County Community Living Center Inc. (secretary and board member of group home); National and Oklahoma Women's Political Caucus; Environmental Action; League of Women Voters; Oklahoma Political Action for Candidate Election; National Organization for Women; Oklahoma N.O.W.; Sierra Club; Union of Concerned Scientists; Cousteau Society; The Nature Conservancy; Southern Poverty Law Center, Klanwatch; Oklahoma Alliance Against Racist and Political Repression; Environmental Policy Center; Coalition for Fair Utility Rates; Environmental Policy Center; People for the American Way; Council for a Livable World; Friends of the Earth; Planned Parenthood Association; World Federalist Association; Amnesty International U.S.A.; United Nations International Children's Emergency Fund (United States committee); National Peace Academy (charter member); Ada Citizens Concerned to End the Nuclear Threat; Oklahoma Peace Strategies; Tulsa Peace Fellowship; Clergy and Laity Concerned; Mobilization for Survival; Fellowship of Reconciliation; The Albert Einstein Fund. Honors and Awards: Certificate of Achievement, Oklahoma Public Employees Association, 1982; Certificate of Achievement, Democratic National Committee, 1982; Listed in *Who's Who in the South and Southwest, Personalities of America, International Who's Who of Intellectuals.* Address: 405 South Cherry, Pauls Valley, Oklahoma 73075.

Wanda M Koehler

Kogelschatz, Joan Lee

Psychotherapist. Personal: Born November 26, 1940, in Detroit, Michigan. Education: B.A., University of Florida, 1963; Undertook graduate studies, Wayne State University, 1964-65; M.S.W., Florida State University, 1967; Ph.D., Psychology-Marital and Family Therapy, Department of Psychology, Florida State University, 1975; Internship, Veteran's Administration Hospital, Bay Pines, Florida and Division of Child and Adolescent Psychiatry, University of Florida Medical Center, Shands Teaching Hospital and Clinics, 1966; Internships for Ph.D., Florida State University, Marital and Family Therapy Clinics, Apalachee Mental Health Center, and Leon County Health Department, 1972-75. Career: Instructor in Psychiatry, Department of Psychiatry, Division of Child & Adolescent Psychiatry, University of Florida Medical Center, Shands Teaching Hospital and Clinics, 1967-72; Field Supervisor/Instructor for Graduate and Undergraduate Students specializing in Individual & Group Psychotherapy with Children, Florida State University School of Psychiatric Social Work, 1973-74; Conducted Workshops, Florida State University, 1973-74; Private Practice Psychiatrist with E. P. Pruitt, Dothan, Alabama, 1975; Private Practice, Dothan, Alabama, 1975 to present. Organizational Memberships: Stop Child Abuse Today, 1978 to present; Law Enforcement Planning Agency (appointed to advisory board by Governor Fob James, 1980 to present); Alabama Society for Crippled Children & Adults (board member, 1981 to present); American Psychological Association; The Academy of Psychosomatic Medicine; American Orthopsychiatric Association; American Association of Psychiatric Services for Children; American Society of Clinical Hypnosis; American Association of Marriage and Family Therapists (clinical member); National Association of Social Workers; Academy of Certified Social Workers; National Council on Family Relations; Southeastern Council on Family Relations; American Association of Sex Educators, Counselors & Therapists; Gulf Coast Association for Marriage & Family Therapy. Religion: Episcopal Church of the Nativity. Published Works: "Family Styles of Fatherless Households", *The Journal of the American Academy of Child Psychiatry*, April 1972; "Teacher to Parent", *Early Childhood Education -An Interdisciplinary Approach*; Co-Author *Fatherlessness in Perspective*, with Paul L. Adams. Honors and Awards: Alpha Kappa Delta; Listed in *Who's Who of American Women, Distinguished Leaders in Health Care, Personalities of the South, Personalities of America, Community Leaders in America.* Address: 1514 Fern Drive, Dothan, Alabama 36301.

Kolbe, Stanley E Jr

Director of Government Affairs. Personal: Born February 1, 1953; Son of Mr. and Mrs. Stanley E. Kolbe Sr. Education: B.S. Management and Labor Relations/Government Policy, Cornell University, 1976; M.A. with honors Government Policy/Legislative and Public Policy Analysis, George Washington University Graduate School, 1978; M.B.A. Business Financial Management/Government Relations, George Washington University School of Business, 1982. Career: Director of A.I.A./P.A.C. and Government Affairs, The American Institute of Architects, 1979 to present; Research Analyst in Federal Relations, United States Conference of Mayors, 1978-79; Analyst and Writer on Federal Affairs, National League of Cities/United States Conference of Mayors, 1977-78; United States Senate Legislative Aide, Office of Senator John C. Culver (D-IA), 1976; New York State Senate Legislative Assistant, Office of Senator Linda Winikow (D-38th District), 1976; Cornell University Teaching Assistant, Business and Occupational Sociology, 1975. Organizational Memberships: American Political Science Association. Community Activities: Campaign Manager, Iowa 3rd Congressional Race, 1978; Iowa Newspapers (political writer); Phi Delta Theta National Fraternity (chairman, fund raising); Kennedy Presidential Campaign, 1980; Culver for Senate Campaign, Iowa, 1980. Honors and Awards:

National Honor Society of Academics; Cornell University Academic Award; Judge M. D. Tolles Academic Scholarship; Cornell University Academic Integrity Board, Listed in *Who's Who in America.* Address: 402 Constitution Avenue Northeast, Washington, D.C. 20002.

Kolman, Laurence Steven

Chief Exeutive Officer. Personal: Born November 24, 1940; Son of Mr. and Mrs. Sol Kolman; Married Elaine Susan Kolman (deceased); Father of Michele Blaine, Geoffrey Scott. Education: Polytechnic Institute of Brooklyn, 1957-58; B.A., Hofstra College, 1962; M.A./L.S., University of New York-Stony Brook, 1976. Military: Served in the United States Air Force to the rank of Captain, 1962-67; Received Air Force Commendation Medal, Armed Forces Expeditionary Medal, Vietnam Service Medal with 2 Bronze Service Stars, National Defense Service Medal, Republic of Vietnam Campaign Medal, Air Force Outstanding Unit Award with 1 Oakleaf Cluster. Career: Chief Executive Officer, Industrial Filtration; Chief Executive Officer, Home Food Industry; Sales Manager, Computer Industry; Registered Representative, Stock Brokerage; Officer, United States Air Force. Organizational Memberships: American Association for the Advancement of Science, 1981 to present; American Institute of Chemical Engineers (associate member, 1982 to present); American Association of Meat Processors, 1975-78; New York State Council of Retail Merchants, 1975-78; Society for Private and Commercial Earth Stations (S.P.A.C.E.), 1982 to present. Community Activities: Harborfields-Elwood Youth Development Association (president, 1970-74); Kiwanis Club of Elwood (president, 1970-73); Kiwanis International (chairman, Suffolk West division youth services, 1972-73); Elwood Friends of the Library Committee, 1972-74; Robertson Center for the Arts and Sciences, 1976-78; Planetary Society, 1980 to present; Sierra Club, 1982 to present; Gamma Rho Epsilon (president, 1959-62); Broome County Chamber of Commerce; Better Business Bureau of Westchester, Putnam and Dutchess Counties; Consumer Relations Bureau of the Capitol Area; Chemung Chamber of Commerce; Hornell Area Chamber of Commerce; Albany Area Chamber of Commerce; Poughkeepsie Area Chamber of Commerce, 1976-78. Honors and Awards: Horstra Alumni Association's George M. Estabrook Distinguished Service Award, 1966; Outstanding Achievement, Freedoms Foundation at Valley Forge, 1965; New York State Regents War Service Scholarship for Veterans, 1972; Pi Delta Epsilon National Honorary Journalism Fraternity, 1961; Life Fellow, American Biographical Institute; Listed in *Who's Who in Finance and Industry, Who's Who in the World, Personalities of America, Directory of Distinguished Americans.* Address: 3 Lodi Lane, Monsey, New York 10952.

A L Korenyi-Both

Konopka, Mary-Ann S

Project Control Supervisor. Personal: Born January 30, 1933; Daughter of Thomas S. and Mary I. Poltorak; Married Louis S. Konopka (deceased); Stepmother of Linda M. Orseno, Lorraine L. Capra. Education: Graduate of Parochial Grammar School 1946, Parochial Business School 1948 and Public High School 1952. Career: Inventory Control Supervisor; Project Control Supervisor. Organizational Memberships: National Association of Female Executives, 1979; American Society of Professional and Executive Women, 1980; Northwest International Trade, 1979; United States Citizens Band Radio Association, 1980. Honors and Awards: Listed in *Who's Who of American Women, Who's Who in the Midwest, The World Who's Who of Women.* Address: 526 E. Pomeroy, West Chicago, Illinois 60185.

Korenyi-Both, Andras Levente

Physician. Personal: Born March 30, 1937; Son of Ernone Korenyi-Both; Married Ildiko Korenyi-Both; Father of Andras, Gyorgy, Adam. Education: M.D., Szeged Medical University, Hungary, 1962; C.Sc. (Med.), Hungarian Academy of Science, 1972. Career: Associate Professor of Pathology, Thomas Jefferson University; Adjunct Professor of Microbiology and Cell Biology, State University of Pennsylvania; Former Senior Lecturer in Pathology, Semmelweis Medical University, Hungary. Organizational Memberships: International Academy of Pathology; Hungarian Medical Association of America; College of American Pathologists; American Association of Neuropathologists; American Association of Pathologists; European Society of Pathologists; New York Academy of Science; Federation of State Medical Boards; Pathology Society of Philadelphia; American Association for the Advancement of Science; International Platform Association. Published Works: Author and Co-Author of 75 Publications in the Field of Muscle Pathology in Neuromuscular Disease. Address: 202 Wickford Road, Havertown, Pennsylvania 19083.

Kosovich, Dushan Radovan

Director of Psychiatry. Personal: Born December 23, 1926 in Trepca, Niksic, Yugoslavia; Son of Radovan Dj and Djurdja Bacovic Kosovich; Father of Jasmina, Nicholas. Education: B.A. Equivalent, Higher Gymnasium, Yugoslavia, 1947; M.D., Belgrade University, 1954; Postgraduate Study in Psychology, 6 semesters, 1957. Military: Served in the Yugoslavian Army, 1944-46. Career: The Methodist Hospital, Director of the Department of Psychiatry 1978 to present, Acting Director of Psychiatry 1976-78, Chief of Psychiatric Inpatient Unit 1975-76, Teacher of Medical Residents and Paraprofessionals 1975 to present; Adjunct Professor, Long Island University, 1978 to present; Clinical Associate Professor, Downstate Medical Center, State University of New York, Brooklyn, 1976 to present; Teacher of Psychoanalytic View of Shifting Patterns in Love, Sex and Marriage, New School for Social Research, 1976; Albert Einstein College, Lincoln Hospital, Director of Inpatient Services for Department of Psychiatry 1973-75, Teacher of Psychiatric Residents and Paraprofessionals 1973-75; Assistant Professor of Psychiatry, Albert Einstein College of Medicine, 1973-75; Attending Psychoanalyst, Karen Horney Psychoanalytic Institute, 1975 to present; Bellevue Medical Center, New York University, Staff Psychiatrist 1967-73, Teacher of 3rd-Year Medical Students, Psychiatric Residents and Psychology Interns 1967-73, Resident in Psychiatry 1957-59; Resident in Psychiatry, McGill University, 1965-67; General Hospital of Titograd, Montenegro, Yugoslavia, Chief and Founder of Neuropsychiatric Services of Inpatient and Outpatient 1960-65, Teacher of Residents and Interns 1960-65; Resident in Psychiatry and Neurology, Neuropsychiatric University Clinic, Belgrade, Yugoslavia, 1954-57. Organizational Memberships: Certified Psychoanalyst, American Institute for Psychoanalysis, 1972; Association for the Advancement of Psychoanalysis, Karen Horney Psychoanalytic Institute (fellow); American Academy of Psychoanalysis (fellow); New York State Medical Society; American Medical Association; American Psychiatric Association; Psychiatric Outpatient Centers of America (board of directors); American Association for Social Psychiatry; World Association for Social Psychiatry; German Academy for Auricular Medicine; North American Academy for Auricular Medicine; *Engrams* Psychiatric Journal (editorial board); American Association for Sex Educators, Counselors and Therapists; American-Yugoslav Medical Society; International Platform Association; New York Academy of Science; American Academy of Clinical Psychiatrists; American College of Forensic Psychiatry; American Academy of Psychiatry and the Law. Community Activities: The American Academy of Psychoanalysis (committee for recognition of foreign medical graduates, 1975 to present); Republic of Montenegro, Yugoslavia Medical Association (general secretary), 1960-65; Federal Commission for Mental Health of Yugoslavia, 1960-65. Published Works: Contributor to *World Journal of Psychosynthesis, Psychiatric Opinion, Journal for Social, Cultural and Scientific Problems, Medicinski Zapisi;* Presenter of many professional papers. Honors and Awards: Award of City of Titograd for Best Scientific Achievement, 1964; Physician's Recognition

Dushan R Kosovich

Award for Continuing Medical Education, American Medical Association, 1978; Recognition Award for Continuing Medical Education, American Psychiatric Association, 1980; Listed in *Who's Who in America, Who's Who in the World, Men of Achievement, Book of Honor, International Directory of Distinguished Psychotherapists.* Address: 300 Mercer Street, New York, New York 10003.

Kourouma, Nichelle Doswell

Executive Director. Personal: Born March 15, 1943; Mother of Kesso. Education: B.S., State University of New York, Oswego, New York, 1964; M.P.A., Central Michigan University, Mt. Pleasant, New York, 1980 to present. Career: Executive Director, National Conference of Black Mayors, Inc.; Instructor, Fairleigh Dickinson University, Hofstra University, State University of New York-New Paltz; Community Development Specialist; Teacher, New York Public School System. Organizational Memberships: National Education Association, 1964-67. Community Activities: American Cancer Society (mid-Atlantic unit, board of directors, 1980 to present); National Association for the Advancement of Colored People, 1960 to present; Cowart Estates Civic Association (president, 1971-76); New York City Mission Society (Camp Minisink, 1950 to present); Tapawingo Honor Society, 1958. Religion: Saint Phillips Episcopal Church, 1950-60; National Conference of Christians and Jews, 1954-60; Hillside Truth Center, 1980 to present. Honors and Awards: Encampment for Citizenship Fellow, 1961; Operation Crossroads Africa Fellow, 1962; Kizzy Award, 1979; Alberta T. Kline Service Award, 1981; Listed in *Who's Who Among Black Women, Who's Who in America.* Address: P.O. Box 42578, Atlanta, Georgia 30311.

Koveleski, Kathryn Delane

Teacher. Personal: Born August 12, 1925; Daughter of Edward Albert and Delane Bender Vogt (both deceased); Married Casper Koveleski; Mother of Martha, Ann. Education: B.A., Olivet College, Michigan, 1955. Career: Teacher of the Learning Disabled; Classroom Teacher; Orthopedic Teacher; Emotionally and Mentally Handicapped Teacher. Organizational Memberships: Parent-Teacher Association; Council for Exceptional Children; National Education Association; Michigan Education Association; Garden City Education Association. Community Activities: Business and Professional Women's Club (president 1980-82, 1982-83); Wayne Literary Club (past president); Couples Bowling League (president 1982-83). Religion: Congregational Church; Former Sunday School Teacher. Address: 33411 Marquette, Garden City, Missouri 48135.

Krascheninnikow, Serhij

Protozoologist. Personal: Born October 25, 1895 in Sluzk, Byelorussia; Son of Mychailo and Lysaveta Krascheninnikow; Father of Alex. Education: Graduate in Natural Science, Kiev University, Ukraine, U.S.S.R., 1924; M.A., Board of Higher Education, Moscow, 1937; Ph.D. Zoology/Protozoology, Ukrainian Free University, Munich, Germany, 1949. Career: Principal Investigator, Sytochemical Study of Balantidium Coli, The Ukrainian Academy of Arts and Sciences, New York, 1964-67; University of Pennsylvania, Parasitology Professor in Division of Medical Technology 1964, Investigator of Morphology and Taxonomy of the Species of the Ciliate Genus Balantidium 1955-62; Research Assistant in Cytochemistry of Balantidium Coli, University of Miami, 1962-63; Scientific Assistant, Academy of Natural Sciences, Philadelphia, Pennsylvania, 1953-55; Professor of Zoology and Parasitology, Ukrainian Technical-Husbandry Institute, Veterinary Medical School, Munich, Germany, 1945-49; Professor, Veterinary Medical School of the Husbandry Institute, Bila-Tserkva, Ukraine, 1934-41; Assistant Professor, University of Kiev, 1936-37; Head of Protozoological Section, The Ukrainian Academy of Sciences, 1930-35; Instructor of Zoology and Parasitology, Veterinary Medical Institute, Kiev, 1930-34; Employee, Protozoological Laboratory Headed by Professor V. Dogiel, Leningrad University, 1927, 1929. Organizational Memberships: The Ukrainian Academy of Arts and Sciences; The Society of Protozoologists; Academy International Libre des Sciences et des Arts, Paris; The New York Academy of Sciences; The Ukrainian Scientific Shevchenko Society, New York; Societe Zoologique de France, Paris; The Ukrainian Veterinary Medical Association, Chicago. Published Works: Contributor of Over 43 Papers dealing mostly with Parasitic Ciliata (Protozoa) to Scientific Journals. Honors and Awards: Ciliatologist of the Year Award for Outstanding Achievement in the Field of Ciliatology, The Society of Protozoologists, 1969; Membership, The New York Academy of Sciences, 1976; Listed in *Notable Americans of 1976-77.* Address: P.O. Box 29561 Germantown Station, Philadelphia, Pennsylvania 19144.

Kraus, Anna Josephine

Administrator and Registered Nurse. Personal: Born April 11, 1927; Daughter of Alexander (deceased) and Bernadine L. Kraus. Education: B.S., Avila College, Kansas City, Missouri, 1959; A.A. Nursing, Pasadena City College, 1969; M.P.H. Medical Record Administration, University of California-Los Angeles, 1972; M.S. Teacher Preparation in Allied Health Professions, University of New York, Buffalo, New York. Career: Medical Record Administrator and Registered Nurse; Consultant in Medical Records for Hospitals and Long-Term Care Facilities; General Staff Nurse; Director, Assistant Director, Medical Records, Various Hospitals in California and Pennsylvania. Organizational Memberships: American Nurses Association; District 4 Nurses Association, West Virginia (2nd vice-president; planning and legislative council); American Medical Record Association (West Virginia delegate, 1981); West Virginia Medical Record Association (president; past treasurer and chairman, various committees); Southeastern Medical Record Association of Pennsylvania (president-elect); Southern California Medical Record Association (past president); American Association of University Women; American Association of University Professors; American Public Health Association; American Hospital Association. Community Activities: Nursing Homes (volunteer visitor); Various Interested Groups (guest lecturer); Church Donations; United Nations International Children's Education Fund; C.A.R.E.; Kidney Foundation; Cancer Foundation; Heart Foundation. Religion: Catholic Community Services Board of Directors, Wheeling, West Virginia, 1978-81; Sunday School Teacher, 1976-80; Organist, 1976-81; Altar and Rosary Society, 1976-81; Past Secretary. Honors and Awards: Leadership and Service Award, Student Nurses Association of Pasadena, 1969; Listed in *Who's Who in Allied Health Professions, Who's Who Among American Women.* Address: Route 1 Box 305, Bunker Hill, West Virginia 25413.

Krauth, Dorothy Colette

Real Estate Broker. Personal: Born October 26, 1938; Daughter of Edward V. and Ethel M. Sanford Walsh; Married Carl H. Krauth Jr.; Mother of Gerald C. McDonald Jr., Deborah L. McDonald, Gregory C. McDonald, (Stepmother of) Carl H. Krauth III. Education: Regis College, 1958; Associate of Secretarial Science, Chandler School for Women, 1958; B.S., Harvard University, 1960. Career: Real Estate Broker; Model; Artist; Fashion Coordinator; Guidance Counselor; Television Commercial Actress; Secretary. Community Activities: Montessori Club (vice-president, 1963); Mt. Alvernia M. Club (board of directors, 1970); Appointed

Television Facts Girl, 1974; Girls' Clubs of America (volunteer, 1965-67); Newton Schools (volunteer, 1969-72). Religion: Boston Catholic Charities (board of directors, 1966-73). Honors and Awards: Realtor of the Year, Wellesley Council, 1979; Designer of Winning Red Sox Program Covers, 1974-76; Personal Shopper, Filenes, Chestnut Hill, Massachusetts, 1974-78; Listed in *Who's Who of American Women*. Address: 151 Hampshire Road, Wellesley, Massachusetts 02181.

Krengel, Floyd

Osteopathic Physician. Personal: Born August 15, 1931; Son of Samuel and Frieda Krengel; Married Joan M. Krengel; Father of Sharon Jill, Maxine Hope. Education: A.B., Lehigh University, Bethlehem, Pennsylvania, 1953; D.O., Philadelphia College of Osteopathic Medicine, 1960. Military: Served in the United States Army Medical Service, 1953-55. Career: Osteopathic Physician. Organizational Memberships: American Osteopathic Association (president, 1980-81). Community Activities: Jersey Shore Medical Center, Neptune, New Jersey (director, department of ambulatory care). Address: 305 Lincoln Drive, Ocean, New Jersey 07712.

Kruger, Jeffrey Sonny

Entertainment Entrepreneur. Personal: Born April 19, 1931 in London, England; Son of Samuel Kruger (deceased) and Thela Shafran Kruger; Married Rene Fifer, October 12, 1958; Father of Howard and Loraine. Education: Graduate of Acton County School, London; Inter B.Sc., London University. Military: Served in the Royal Ordinance Corps of the British Army, 1948. Career: Promoter of Concerts and International Entertainers, such as Jack Benny, George Burns, Glen Campbell, Andy Williams, Gladys Knight and the Pips, Anne Murray, Wayne Newton, Charley Pride, Tony Bennett, Lena Horne, Billie Holiday, Sarah Vaughan, Billie Eckstine, Stan Kenton Orchestra, Illinois Jacques Band, Woody Herman Orchestra, Chet Baker, Gerry Mulligan, the Best Known of British Jazz Stars and Others; Music Publisher, Songs for Today Limited; Film and Video Producer and Distributer, Kruger Leisure Enterprises Limited; Record Distributor, Bulldog and Ember Records; Owner and Chief Executive Officer, The Temple Rock Venue, 1973; Owner and Chief Executive Officer, Flamingo Jazz Club, London, 1953-73; Pianist, Studied with Maestro Jules Ruben and Formed Own Band; Employee, Eros Films Limited 1952-53, Columbia Pictures Corporation 1949-52. Organizational Memberships: Country Music Association (director); Association of Motion Pictures Arts and Sciences (associate member). Honors and Awards: Honored in 25th Year of Business by the City of Beverly Hills, the City of Los Angeles, 1977; Commendation, President, Jimmy Carter, 1977; Special Award Winner, Country Music Association (Great Britain) Limited, 1978; Citation of Achievement, Broadcast Music Inc., 1973; Membership, Variety Club of Great Britain; Certificate of Merit for Distinguished Service, 1979; Listed in *Who's Who in the East, International Who's Who in Community Service, The International Who's Who of Intellectuals, Country Music Who's Who, Who's Who in Music, Who's Who in the World, Who's Who in World Jewry, Men of Achievement, Dictionary of International Biography*. Address: Post Office Box 130, Hove, East Sussex BN3 6QU England.

Krysiak, Joseph Edward

Mechanical Engineer. Personal: Born January 13, 1937; Son of Edward Aloysious (deceased) and Anna Margaret Molinski Krysiak. Education: B.M.E. 1964, M.M.E. 1973, University of Dayton. Military: Served in the United States Naval Reserve as Radioman 3, 1955-63. Career: Mechanical Engineer, Lewis Research Center of the National Aeronautical and Space Administration 1979 to present, Industrial Application International 1976-79, Specialist with Reliance Electric Company 1973-75, Air Force Flight Dynamics Laboratory of Wright-Patterson Air Force Base 1965-73. Organizational Memberships: American Society for Metals; Mathematical Association of America. Religion: Knights of Columbus, 1956 to present. Honors and Awards: Holder of Six United States Patents; Thirteen United States Air Force Invention Awards, 1967-73; United States Air Force Outstanding Laboratory Award, 1966-68. Address: 8990 Billings Road, P.O. Box 676, Willoughby, Ohio 44094.

Kubiak, Daniel James

State Representative. Personal: Born March 19, 1938 in Reagan, Texas; Son of Mr. and Mrs. John T. Kubiak; Married Zona Bassler; Father of Kelly Dan, Alyssa Lea, Kody Earl. Education: Graduate of Marlin, Texas, High School, 1957; A.A., Blinn College, 1959; B.B.A. 1962, Ph.D. Education, University of Texas-Austin; M.Ed., Midwestern University, 1968; Graduate Work, Georgetown University, Washington, D.C. Career: Texas State Representative, 27th District 1968-72, 36th District, 1972 to present; Teacher of Government, Economics and Mathematics Coach, Cypress-Fairbanks High School, Houston, Texas and Vernon High School, Texas; Semi-Professional Football Player, Vernon Vikings, Texas; Operator, Construction Business, Rockdale, Texas. Organizational Memberships: Texas State House of Representatives (legislature committees on education, agriculture, parks and wildlife, penitentiaries, special committee on 4-quarter school plan, 1970-72; legislature committee on energy, chairman of agriculture committee, 1976-78; chairman, joint interim committee to study ad valorem tax and effect on agricultural land, 1977; vice chairman for appropriations committee, 1978-80; agriculture and rural development committee of southern legislative conference, appointed by Speaker of the House, 1979; chairman for budget and oversight, legislature committees on agriculture and livestock, appropriations, and rules, 1980 to present. Published Works: *Ten Tall Texans*, 1967; *Monument to a Black Man*, 1972; "Youth and Their Vote: A New Day is Coming", *Theory into Practice* Magazine, National Education Association, 1970. Honors and Awards: Man of the Year, Agriculture, Texas County Agricultural Agents Association, 1981; Honorary Member, Limestone Company Union, 1980; Appointed Department Member of the Southwest Regional Energy Council by Speaker of the House Bill Clayton, 1980; Acknowlegement of Energy, Time and Interest as Member of Board of Directors, The University Cooperative Society, Inc.; Award of Appreciation, Central Texas Sports Center, Temple, Texas and Westphalia Public Schools; Certificate of Appreciation for Participation in Gasohol Know-How Conference 11; Special Award, Texas Chiropractic Association; Certificate of Recognition for Support During 66th Legislative Session, Good Neighbor Commission of Texas, 1979; Award of Appreciation for Outstanding Contribution to Compensatory Education in Texas, 1979; Special Award for Outstanding Service and Support, Texans for Equitable Taxation, 1978-79; Speical Award, Texas Industrial Vocational Association, 1976; T.I.V.A. Legislative Award, 1976; Award of Appreciation, Citizens of Buckholts, Texas, 1976; Spcial Award, Round Rock Lions Club, 1976; Certificate of Appreciation, Modernistic Social Club, 1976; Certificate of Appreciation, Dioceses of Austin Catholic Youth Organization, 1975; Certificate for Outstanding Service, 1975; Certiciate of Appreciation, Lee County T.S.T.A. Local Association; South Central Texas District Outstanding Service Award, Optimist Club of Rockdale, 1974; Citation for Contributions in Communications in Texas, Texas Council of Teachers of English, 1974; One of the Best Legislators and Best-Educated Education Chairman in Modern Times, *Texas Monthly* Magazine, 1973; Special Award, Texas Personnel and Guidance Association, 1973; Certificate of Commendation for Outstanding Achievement and Interest in Coastal and Marine Resources, 1973; Certificate of Appreciation, Calvert, Texas Chamber of Commerce, 1971; Honorary Appointment as Lifetime Member, 147th Fighter Group, Texas Air National Guard, 1970; Distinugished Service Award, 1970; Award for Excellence for Portraying Texas and its Past, Texas State Teachers Association, 1967;

John T. Burton Scholarship Award for Young Educators, 1963; Numerous Collegiate Elected Offices and Honors. Address: 135 Champions Drive, Rockdale, Texas 76567.

Kubose, Gyomay Masao

Senior Buddhist Minister. Personal: Born July 7, 1905; Son of Toiichi Kubose (deceased); Married to Minnie; Father of Don A., Sunnan K., Joyce T. Evans. Education: B.A., University of California at Berkeley; M.A., University of Otani, Kyoto, Japan. Career: Senior Minister of Buddhist Temple of Chicago, Illinois (founder of the temple and resident minister for over 37 years). Community Activities: Chicago Japanese American Resettlers Committee; Chicago Japanese American Citizens League; Chicago Japanese American Mutual Aid Society; Chicago Uptown Commission; Chicago Uptown Lions Club; Chicago Mayor's Committee for Senior Citizens; Member of numerous other community and civic organizations; Active in many community projects. Religion: Member and Founder of the Buddhist Temple of Chicago. Honors and Awards: Brotherhood Award, J.A.C.L.; Received award for outstanding service to the community; Received Buddhist Missionary Award from Japan; Honorary Life Member of Lions International. Address: 4641 North Raine Avenue, Chicago, Illinoos 60640.

Judith B Kuriansky

Kucharski, Jerry Stanley

Educator. Personal: Born November 16, 1940; Son of Stanley J. Kucharski (deceased) and Irene Borzyczkowski Kucharski. Education: B.S. Education, University of Wisconsin-Milwaukee, 1965; Graduate Studies, Jagiellonian University, Krakow, Poland. Career: Upper Elementary Educator; President, Marian Accessories Corporation. Organizational Memberships: American Council for Geographic Education, 1965-73; Wisconsin Council for Geographic Education, 1970 to present; Polish-American Historical Association, 1961 to present. Community Activities: Polish National Alliance (officer; co-chairman, youth committee, national convention, 1975); Pulaski Council of Milwaukee (director, 1976 to present); Polish American Congress (Wisconsin division, delegate 1974, treasurer 1981); Milwaukee Folk Council, 1959-69; Holiday Folk Fair General Committee (representative, 1958 to present); Polish Genealogical Society (charter member); Mazur Polish Dancers of Milwaukee, Inc. (member, 1957-59; dance director, 1959-69; member, board of directors, 1959 to present; executive director, 1978 to present); Polish Folk Dance Classes and Seminars (conductor, Polish National Alliance council 8, Federation Life Insurance of America, Polish Roman Catholic Union of America circuit 6, Polish Women's Alliance of America council 1, University of Wisconsin extension, University of Wisconsin-Stevens Point); General Casimir Pulaski High School Award Committee (chairman). Published Works: *A Polish Christiman Pageant--Polskie Jaselka*, 1962; *Our Polish Heritage*, 1964; Contributor to *Kuryer Polski, Polish American Journal, Historical Messenger, Polish American Studies*. Address: 2321 South 15th Street, Milwaukee, Wisconsin 53215.

Kuriansky, Judith B

Psychologist, Feature Reporter, Talk Show Host, Writer. Personal: Born January 31, 1947; Daughter of Sylvia Sporn; Married Edward J. Kuriansky. Education: University of Geneva, Switzerland, 1966; A.B., Smith College, 1968; Ed.M., Boston University, 1970; Ph.D., New York University, 1980. Career: Psychologist; Television and Radio Feature Reporter; Talk Show Host; Writer; Musician. Organizational Memberships: American Psychological Association, 1976 to present; Society of Sex Therapists and Researchers, 1975 to present; Association of Women in Radio and Television; Academy of Television Arts and Sciences. Community Activities: Benefits Committee for the Deaf, 1980 to present; American Psychiatric Association (nomenclature committee, 1976-79); Masters and Johnson Ethics Congress, 1979; Scientists Committee for Public Information (member, 1976-79; board of directors, 1977-78); Federal Trade Commission (testimony). Religion: Lecturer for Religious Groups. Honors and Awards: Sloan Foundation Science Research Grant, 1968; Listed in *Outstanding Young Women of America, Who's Who of American Women*. Address: 8 Thomas Street, New York, New York 10007.

Kuttner, Bernard A

Attorney. Personal: Born January 13, 1934; Son of Vera Kuttner; Father of Karen, Robert, Stacey. Education: A.B., cum laude, Dartmouth College, 1955; Attended University of Virginia Law School, 1956; J.D., Seton Hall University Law School, 1959. Military: Served with United States Naval Reserve, L.CDR., 1964-74. Career: Practicing Attorney in Livingston, New Jersey; Former Judge, State Court of Tax Appeals; Adjunct Professor of Civil Trial Litigation, Montclair State College. Organizational Memberships: Essex County (New Jersey) Bar Association (president, 1980-81, president-elect, 1979-80, treasurer, 1975-79); New Jersey State Bar Association; American Bar Association Community Activities: Lions Club of Irvington (president); Irvington Jaycees (president); Anti-Defamation League of New Jersey (president); Essex County Parks Commission (president). Religion: Member of Temple Abraham. Honors and Awards: Outstanding Young Man of New Jersey; Outstanding Civic Leader Awards; Listed in *Who's Who in the East, Who's Who in American Law*. Address: 321 Wyoming Avenue, Maplewood, New Jersey 07040 and Gregory Town, Eleuthera, Bahamas.

Lubomyr I Kuzmak

Kuzmak, Lubomyr Ihor

General and Vascular Surgeon. Personal: Born August 2, 1931; Son of Wolodymyr and Lidia Litynsky Kuzmak (both deceased); Married Roxana A. Smishkewych. Father of Roxolana M. Education: M.D., Medical Academy, Lodz, Poland, 1953; Sc.D., Silesian Academy of Medicine, Katowice, Poland, 1965; Diplomate, Polish Board of General Surgery, 1961. Career: St. Barnabas Medical Center, Livingston, New Jersey, Practicing General and Vascular Surgeon 1971 to present, Teaching Staff Member in Surgical Residency Program, Resident and Chief Resident in General Surgery 1966-71; Practicing General and Vascular Surgeon, Irvington General Hospital, New Jersey, 1971 to present; Silesian Academy of Medicine, III Surgical Clinic, Bytom, Poland, General Surgeon, Division Head and Associate Professor 1961-65, Resident and Chief Resident in General Surgery 1954-61. American Medical Association; New Jersey Medical Society; Essex County Medical Society; Ukrainian Medical Association (president-elect); Ukrainian Institute of America, American Society of Contemporary Medicine and Surgery; The Royal Society of Medicine, American Society of Abdominal Surgeons, The International Platform Association. Community Activities: Irvington General Hospital (member and chairman, various committees); New Jersey Gastroplasty Club for the Treatment of Morbid Obesity (founder and surgeon advisor); Various Charity and Church Organizations (contributor). Religion: Ukrainian Catholic Church. Honors and Awards: Physicians Recognition Award, American Medical Association, 1970-73, 1976-79; Listed in *Community Leaders and Noteworthy Americans*. Address: 657 Irvington Avenue, Newark, New Jersey 07106.

Kwik-Kostek, Christine

Medical Doctor. Personal: Born September 12, 1939; Daughter of Karl and Leonarda Kostek; Widow; Mother of Christine, Catherine. Education: Graduate with honors Liberal Arts, Junior College, Cracow, Poland, 1956; M.D. with distinction, Medical Academy, Cracow, Poland, 1962. Military: Serves in the United States Air Force as a Major on Active Duty, 1978 to present. Career: Medical Doctor. Organizational Memberships: American Medical Association; N.A.R.I.; A.C.E.P. Address: 4436 East San Muguel, Colorado Springs, Colorado 80915.

Kwon, Joon Taek

Principal Research Chemist. Personal: Born March 10, 1935; Son of Mr. and Mrs. Young Tae Kwon; Married Moon Ja Kwon; Father of Howard Albert, Daphne Elsa. Education: B.S. Chemistry Curriculum, University of Illinois, 1957; M.S. 1959, Ph.D. 1962, Inorganic Chemistry, Cornell University. Career: Principal Research Chemist, C-E Luminius, 1970 to present; Senior Research Chemist, Celanese Research Company, 1967-70; Research Chemist, Chemcell Limited, Edmonton, Alberta, Canada, 1965-67; Instructor II, Department of Chemistry, University of British Columbia, Vancouver, Canada, 1964-65; Postdoctoral Research and Teaching Fellow, Department of Chemistry, University of British Columbia, Vancouver, Canada, 1962-64. Organizational Memberships: American Chemical Society; Catalysis Society of New York; North American Thermal Analysis Society; The Royal Chemical Society, London; The Society of Chemical Industry, London; The Korean Chemical Society; Korean Scientists and Engineers in North America. Community Activities: Boy Scouts of America (scoutmaster; Order of the Arrow). Honors and Awards: Research Grants, National Council of Canada, 1964-67; Industrial Grants in Aid, National Research Council of Canada, 1965-67. Address: 142 Derby Drive, Freehold Township, New Jersey 07728.

La Cava, Carl

Professor. Personal: Born March 20, 1932; Son of Albert La Cava (deceased); Married Dorothy L. Graziano (deceased); Father of Sandra, Jude. Education: B.B.A., Dyke College, 1950; Two M.B.A. Programs, Temple University, of Philadelphia; Two Certification Courses at Penn State University; M.B.A. Degree, Baldwin-Wallace College, 1978. Military: Served in the United States Army, 1950, Field Promotion to Lieutenant, Army, Corps of Engineers; United States Army Reserve. Career: Professor of Marketing, Dyke College, Cleveland, Ohio; Loaned Executive, City of Cleveland; Growth Association, Jobs Council, National Alliance of Business; President, Custom Leasing Corporation. Organizational Memberships: Society of Automotive Engineers; American Management Association; Sales and Marketing Executives; Delta Mu Delta for Academic Achievement. Community Activities: Headed a Task Force Group to Aid Blacks, Hispanics, Ex-Offenders, Vietnam Veterans. Over 40 Unemployed, Handicapped, Youth Jobs Program and All Other Less Fortunate of the Community. Religion: Roman Catholic. Address: P.O. Box 741, Edgewater, Cleveland, Ohio 44107.

V Duane Lacey

Lacayo, Carmela G

Executive. Personal: Born June 28, 1943; Daughter of Enrique Luis Lacayo, Mary Louise Velasquez. Education: B.A., Immaculate Heart College; B.A., Regina Mundi International University; Graduate Work in Public Administration, University of California-Los Angeles. Career: President/Executive Director, A.N.P.P.M./N.A.H.E.-N.H.I.P.P.; Professor of Urban Development and Sociology, University of San Buenaventura, Colombia, 1973-74; Administrative Coordinator, Office of Mayor, Los Angeles, 1974-75. Organizational Memberships: National Council on Aging (board of directors); Gerontological Society of America W.G.S.; Continental Baking Company, I.T.T. (advisory panel for nutrition education for older Americans); European Values Systems Study, Center for Applied Research in the Apostolate (international advisory board for the Americas); National Policy Center on Housing and Living Arrangement for Older Americans, University of Michigan (advisory board); U.S.C. National Policy Center on Employment and Retirement; University of California-San Francisco Aging Health Policy Study Center (advisory board); Catholic Coordinating Committee for the White House Conference on Aging, United States Catholic Conference. Honors and Awards: Latina Woman of the Year, Los Angeles, 1976; National Woman of the Year, Latin American Professional Women's Association, 1977. Address: 1730 West Olympic Blvd., Los Angeles, California 90015-1964.

Lacey, V Duane

Health Care Executive. Personal: Born November 11, 1932; Son of John Lacey (deceased) and Leah Lacey; Married to Joan Marotta; Father of Lauren Joan, Duane Jr. Education: B.A., University of Washington at Seattle, 1960; M.A., State University of Iowa, 1962; Ph.D. Candidate, California Western University, 1982. Military: Served with United States Army as P.F.C., Medical Service Corps, 1952-53. Career: President, Health Development Corporation of America, Washington, D.C.; Health Care consultant, developer, investor; Former Vice President, American Health Services, Inc.; Former President, L.I.C.O., Health Care Consultants; Former Director, Medical Services Administration, International Nickel Company in Indonesia; Former Vice President, Chi Systems, Inc., (hospital planners and consultants); Former Administrator, Christ Hospital, Jersey City, New Jersey. Organizational Memberships: Commission for Responsible Health Policy, Washington, D.C. (member and treasurer, co-founder, 1980 to present); Health Services Committee of A.N.S.I., 1976-79; American College of Hospital Administrators, 1962 to present; Technical Advisor, World Health Organization, 1975 to present; National Geriatrics Society (trustee, 1971); M.A.C. Health (nursing homes services committee, chairman of subcommittee on standards, Atlanta, Georgia, 1971); New Jersey-Hudson County Heart Association (trustee, executive committee, finance committee, 1968-71); Hudson County Regional Health Facilities Planning Commission (trustee and secretary, 1968-71). Honors and Awards: Outstanding Citizen's Award, South Vietnam, 1968; Rotarian Membership Award, Bangkok, Thailand, 1966; Listed in *Who's Who in the East, International Who's Who of Intellectuals, Dictionary of International Biography, Men of Achievement, Book of Honor.* Address: 8626 Georgetown Pike, McLean, Virginia 22102.

Selma Lamkin

Lafferre, Bruce Allen

Market Planner. Personal: Born December 17, 1949; Son of Mr. and Mrs. J. A. Lafferre; Brother of Denise Kaye Lafferre; Married to Nancy Jean. Education: B.A., University of Louisville, 1971; M.B.A. candidate, University of Detroit, 1976-79; M.B.A., Michigan State University, 1981. Career: Market Planner for Detroit Edison Company, Detroit, Michigan; Insurance Agent, New York Life, 1972; Engineering Product Representative, Bruning Division of AMCORP, 1973-76; Microsystems Product Representative, Xerox Corporation, 1976-78; Microfilm Systems Analyst, Detroit Edison Company, 1978-79. Organizational Memberships: American Marketing Association; National Microfilm Association; Engineering Society of Detroit (hosted several conferences and shows). Community Activities: Detroit Athletic Club; Host to Georgia State Delegation for 1980 G.O.P. Convention, Detroit; Appointed to Advisory Committee for Economic Club of Detroit (past presiding officer); President's Club (which solicits memberships for the Detroit Chamber of Commerce); Served as host for Kentucky Delegation for the 1981 International S.P.E.B.Q.S.A. convention in Detroit. Religion: Member of St. Thomas More Catholic Church (served on several parish committees and fund drives). Honors and Awards: Olsten Award for Excellence in Records Management Programs, National Microfilm Association, 1979; Graduated with Honors from Michigan State University, 1981; International Champion Chorus member, S.P.E.B.Q.S.A., 1969; Listed in *Who's Who in Midwest, Who's Who in Finance and Industry.* Address: 1867 Derby, Birmingham, Michigan 48008.

Lamkin, Selma H

Accountant, Educator, Author. Personal: Born March 29, 1925; Daughter of Julia Hoffman; Widow; Mother of Barry D., Deborah L., Leonard. Education: Graduate of Bently College of Accounting and Finance, 1958; Attended Hebrew Teachers College, 1940.

Career: Public Accountant; Instructor in Accounting, Taxes and Money Management, Graham Junior College, Northeastern University, Roxbury Community College, Cambridge Y.W.C.A. Organizational Memberships: Federal Women in Government Contrast (steering committee); Northeast Women in Business (founder); Women's Athletic Club. Community Activities: Massachusetts Women's Political Caucus (treasurer, 1980 to present); Fanuiel Hall Business and Professional Women (legislative chairperson, 1981 to present). Religion: Vice President of Temple Sisterhood, 1965-77. Published Works: Author of *Money Management and Investment; Accounting; Self-Instruction Manual; Small Business Success Manual; Shoebox Syndrome; How to Start Your Business and Succeed.* Honors and Awards: Listed in *Who's Who in American Women, Personalities of America, Who's Who in the East.* Address: 698 River Street, Boston, Massachusetts 02126.

Landers, Newlin Jewel

Contractor. Personal: Born July 10, 1906; Son of DeLoy Landers (deceased); Married Vernette Trosper Landers; Father of Larry, Marlin. Education: Attended Contractors School. Career: Positions with Howard Hughes Multi-Color Laboratory, Hughes Development Company, Paramount Motion Picture Studios: Owner, Landers Machine Shop; Co-Owner, Selwyn-Landers Valve Company in Los Angeles; Invented, Developed, Tested, Patented and Manufactured High Pressure Valve; Bought and Improved Havasu Landing, Navajo Needles, California; Owner, Navajo Tract, Apple Valley 1950, Founded Community of Landers and Landers Air Strip; Donated Land and Building to Landers Volunteer Fire Department; Donated Land to Homestead Valley Women's Club; Owned, Operated Landers Gas Station and Water Delivery. Organizational Memberships: American Biographical Institute (life fellow); International Biographical Association (life member). Community Activities: Landers Volunteer Fire Department (honorary member); Landers Garden Club; Moose Lodge. Honors and Awards: Businessman of the Week, KSST Radio Station, 1969; Plaque and Badge for 13 Years of Search and Rescue Work with Yucca Valley Sheriff Rangers; International Diploma of Honor for Community Service; 1981 Landers Community Dinner honoring Newlin as its founding father on his 75th birthday; 1981 Plaque from Board of Directors of Landers Volunteer Fire Department in appreciation of his contributions. Address: 905 Landers Lane, Landers, California 92284.

Newlin Landers

Landers, Vernette Trosper

Author, Retired School Counselor, Volunteer Clerk-in-Charge. Personal: Born May 3, 1912; Daughter of LaVerne Trosper; Married Newlin J. Landers; Mother of Larry, Marlin. Education: A.B. with honors; M.A. 1935; Ed.D. 1953; Educational Credentials from the State of California (two of which are life diplomas). Career: Author, Nine Books of Poetry; Volunteer 22 years, Clerk-in-Charge, Landers Community Post Office; Guidance Project Director, 1967; Coordinator, Adult Education, 1965-67; District Counselor, Morongo Unified School District (California), 1965-72; Dean of Girls, 29 Palm High School, 1960-65; Assistant Professor, Los Angeles State College, 1950; Professor, Long Beach City College, 1946-47; Teacher, Secondary Schools, Montebello, California, 1935-45, 1948-50, 1951-59. Organizational Memberships: International Studies and Exchanges, Leonardo Da Vinci International Academy, Rome (titular member, 1981); International Academy of Poets, London (life fellow, 1981); International Biographical Association (life member); National League of American Pen Women; International Platform Association; N.R.T.A.; C.T.A.; American and California Personnel and Guidance Association; Phi Beta Kappa; Pi Lambda Theta; Sigma Delta Pi; Mortar Board; Prytanean Spurs. Community Activities: Montebello Business and Professional Women's Club (president, 1940); Soroptimist Club, 29 Palms, California (secretary, 1962); Landers Association, Inc. (vice president, secretary, 1965 to 1977); Landers Volunteer Fire Department (secretary, 1972 to 1975); Desert Emergency Radio Service (secretary); Hi Desert Playhouse Guild (life member); Hi Desert Memorial Hospital Guild (life member); Hi Desert Nature Museum (life member); Homestead Galley Women's Club (life member); Landers Area Chamber of Commerce; Landers Garden Club. Religion: Landers Community Church, Bible School Lecturer 4 Years. Honors and Awards: C.S.S.I. Poet Laureate, February 1981, Rome, Italy; International Diploma of Honor for Community Service, 1973; 1973 Certificate of Merit for Distinguished Service to Education; Creativity Award, International Personnel Research Association, 1972; Soroptimist of the Year, 29 Palms Soroptimist Club, 1969; 1982 International Winged Glory Diploma of Honor in Letters, Leonardo Da Vinci International Academy, Rome, Italy; 1982 Diploma of Merit in Letters, University of Arts, Parma, Italy. Address: 905 Landers Lane, Landers, California 92284.

Landgarten, Helen Barbara

Associate Professor and Director. Personal: Born March 4, 1921; Married Nathan Landgarten; Mother of Aleda Siccardi, Marc. Education: B.F.A., University of California-Los Angeles, 1963; M.A., Goddard College, Los Angeles, 1973. Career: Associate Professor and Director, Graduate Department, Clinical Art Therapy, Loyola Marymount, Los Angeles; Coordinator, Art Psychotherapy, Thalians Community Mental Health Center, Family and Child Department of Psychiatry; Author, *Clinical Art Therapy;* Film Producer, "Lori: Art Therapy and Self Discovery"; Artist; Former Positions include Radio Interviewer, Art Instructor, Director of Clinical Art Therapy Graduate Department at Immaculate Heart College. Organizational Memberships: American Art Therapy Association (public information, 1969-71; finance chairperson, 1971-75); Southern California Art Therapy Association (president, 1973-74). Community Activities: Council for Accreditation of Psychiatric Hospitals; Consultation and Education to Mental Health Centers in Western Region and Numerous Universities, Hospitals, Professional Organizations, Mental Health Facilities and to the Public through Television, Radio and the News Media; Public Service Extended to the United States, Europe, South America, South Africa, Canada. Honors and Awards: Honorary Life Member, American Art Therapy Association, 1975; Honorary Life Member, Southern California Art Therapy Association, 1974. Address: 2427 Arbutus Drive, Los Angeles, California 90049.

Vernette Landers

Lang, Gloria Helen

Tooling Engineer, Tool and Die Maker, Lecturer. Personal: Born March 15, 1932; Daughter of Mr. and Mrs. Michael Lang (both deceased). Education; Attended Kent State University 1961, Youngstown State University 1971; A.A., New York State University, 1982. Military: Served in the United States Army, 1951-54, attaining the rank of Sergeant First Class. Career: Tool and Die Maker, Tooling Engineer; President and Chief Executive Officer, Lang Industries, Inc. Organizational Memberships: National Association of Female Executives; National Association of Small Businesses; National Organization of Women; American Society of Professional and Executive Women. Community Activities: American Legion (past commander). Religion: Unitarian, Sunday School Teacher 1959-62. Honors and Awards: Listed in *Who's Who of American Women, Who's Who in the West and Midwest, Notable Americans, Community Leaders of America, Directory of Distinguished Americans, World Who's Who of Women, Book of Honor.* Address: 4793 Ardmore Avenue, Youngstown, Ohio 44505.

Langsam, Walter Consuelo

University President Emeritus. Personal: Born January 2, 1906; Married Julia Elizabeth Stubblefield; Father of Walter Eaton, Geoffrey Hardinge. Education: B.S., City College of New York, 1925; M.A. 1926, Ph.D. 1930, Columbia University. Military: Office Strategic Services 1944-45; Civilian Aide to Secretary of the Army, 1962-66; Chairman, Department of Army Historical Advisory Committee, 1968-72; Board of Consultants, National War College, 1972-76. Career: Columbia University, Instructor in History 1927-35, Assistant Professor of History 1935-38; Professor of History, Union College, 1938-45; President, Wagner College, 1945-52; President, Gettysburg College, 1952-55; President, University of Cincinnati, 1955-71; President Emeritus and Distinguished Service Professor, University of Cincinnati, 1971 to present. Organizational Memberships: North Central Association of Colleges and Secondary Schools Commission on Colleges and Universities (member, 1957-70; executive committee, 1963-70; vice chairman, 1966-68; chairman, 1968-70); Ohio College Association (president, 1965-66). Community Activities: Endicott College, Beverly, Massachusetts (trustee, 1949 to present); Hamma School of Theology, Springfield, Ohio (trustee, 1967-70); University of Cincinnati Foundation (trustee, 1978 to present); Cincinnati Institute of Fine Arts (trustee, 1955 to present); Cincinnati Historical Society (trustee, 1972 to present); Cincinnati Ballet Company (trustee, 1971-78; chairman of the board, 1975-77; honorary trustee, 1978 to 1982); Honorary Consul of Finland to Cincinnati, 1967-76; Cincinnati Branch, Federal Reserve Bank of Cleveland (director, 1961-66; chairman of the board, 1964-66); Greater Cincinnati Chamber of Commerce (board member, 1965-70; senior council member, 1972-76); Boy Scouts of America (region four executive committee, 1965-70; east central region advisory council, 1970 to present; national council, 1967-75). Religion: Lutheran Church of America, Vice President of the Board of Theological Education, 1962-72. Honors and Awards: Townsend Harris Medal as Outstanding Alumnus, City College of New York, 1952; George Washington Honor Medal, Freedoms Foundation, 1956, 1958, 1973; Governor's Award for Outstanding Service to the State of Ohio, 1968; Silver Antelope Award, Boy Scouts of America, 1970; Outstanding Civilian Service Medal, Department of the Army, 1968, with Laurel Leaf Cluster 1971, with second Laurel Leaf Cluster, 1972; Commander's Cross, Order of Merit, West Germany, 1970; First Appreciation Medal, Wagner College, 1971; City College of New York's 125th Anniversary Medal, 1972; "Great Living Cincinnatian" Award, Greater Cincinnati Chamber of Commerce, 1972; Good Neighbor Award, Issac M. Wise Temple, 1972; Silver Beaver, Boy Scouts of America, 1973; D.A.R. Americanism Medal; Author of 12 Volumes of History; 12 Honorary Doctorate Degrees. Address: 1071 Celestial Street, Cincinnati, Ohio 45202.

Langston, Dewey Francis

Professor, Graduate Coordinator. Personal: Born July 17, 1920; Married Dessie D. Rierson; Father of Jackie Frances, Judy Kaye. Education: Graduate of Wink High School, Wink, Texas, 1939; B.A., Eastern New Mexico University, 1943; M.Ed., Springfield College, Massachusetts, 1948; Director of Physical Education Degree, Indiana University, 1950; Doctor of Physical Education, Indiana University, 1950; Post-doctoral Studies, Stanford University, 1956. Military: Served in the New Mexico State Guard, 1942; Served in the United States Marine Corps Reserve, retiring as Captain in 1962; United States Army Reserve, retiring as Lieutenant Colonel in 1971; (wounded in Okinawa, 1945). Career: Graduate Assistant in History, Springfield College, 1946-47; Graduate Fellow, Physical Education, Indiana University, 1949-50; Assistant Professor of Physical Education, Eastern New Mexico University, 1951-53; Associate Professor of Physical Education, Eastern New Mexico University, 1953-57; Professor of Health and Physical Education, Eastern New Mexico University, 1957 to present; Other Positions at Eastern New Mexico University include Head of Professional Education Program 1967-71, Varsity Track Coach 1951-56, Assistant Football Coach 1952-56, Chairman of the Division of Health, Physical Education and Recreation 1970-75; Director of Intercollegiate Athletics 1970-75, Assistant to the Dean of Admissions 1977-79, Affirmative Action Officer 1977-79, Professor and Graduate Coordinator, School of Health, Physical Education and Recreation, 1979 to present; Instructor, Albuquerque United States Army Reserve and Other Military Schools, 1962-71. Organizational Memberships: New Mexico American Association of Health, Physical Education and Recreation (chairman, student section, 2 years; chairman, honor award, 1961, 1964; representative to southwest district representative assembly; constitutional revision committee, 1966-67; chairman, college section, 1962-63; vice president, 1965-67; president, 1967-68; past chairman, research section; president, N.M.C.Y.F., two terms); Southwest District American Alliance of Health, Physical Education and Recreation (chairman, honors awards, 1958; executive committee; honor awards committee, 1959-71; chairman, professional education section, 1961; chairman, boys and mens athletic section, 1957; chairman safety section, 1983); American Alliance of Health, Physical Education and Recreation (representative assembly; chairman, safety section, 1963; college physical education position paper, 1968-69; safety education council, 1969-70, 1977-78; graduate/professional preparation committee, 1966; vice president, A.S.C.S.A., 1977-78, president, A.S.C.S.A., 1978-79; board of governors, 1978-79; chairman, committee to study national convention, 1978-79; board of directors, A.S.C.S.A., 1968-74, 1977-80). Community Activities: Chamber of Commerce of Roosevelt County; Portales Rotary Club (president, 1958-59); Rotary International (district governor, 1963-64); Roosevelt County Oral Vaccine Drive (chairman, 1957); Portales Armory Board (chairman, 1965-83); Roosevelt County United Fund (board member and general fund chairman, 1968-74); Chairman of the Military Academy Review Board, Senator Schmidt, 1978-82. Religion: First Baptist Church, Portales, New Mexico, Member 1939 to present; Deacon 1976; Sunday School Teacher, 1953-81. Published Works: Number of Professional Articles including "Sports on Stamps", "Do You Gamble in Physical Education?", "Postage Stamps That Save Lives" and "History of New Mexico on Postage Stamps"; *Articles of Administraton; District Policies and Procedures* (Rotary International); *Brief History of the Portales Rotary Club.* Honors and Awards: Military Decorations include Asiatic-Pacific Theatre, American Theatre, American Defense, WWII Victory, Occupation of Japan, China Defense, Purple Heart, Recommended for Silver Star; Phi Delta Kappa Service Key, 1964; Alpha Phi Omega Service Key, 1958; Paul Harris Award, Portales Rotary Club, 1976; Phi Delta Kapa Distinguished Service Award, 1974, 1978; Distinguished Service Award, Eastern New Mexico University, 1973; Phi Epsilon Kappa Honor Key, 1958; Sigma Delta Psi; Honor Award, Southwest District, American Alliance of Health, Physical Education, and Recreation, 1968; Colonel Aide-de-Camp, Three Governors of New Mexico; Phi Kappa Phi; Professional Sevice Award, American School and Community Safety Association, 1980; Listed in *International Who's Who in Education, Personalities of America, International Who's Who of Intellectuals, Who's Who in the West, Who's Who in American Education, Who's Who in American Higher Education, Notable Americans, Dictionary of International Biography, National Social Directory, Book of Honor, Outstanding Educators of America, Personalities of the West and Midwest, Community Leaders of America, Men of Achievement, International Platform Association, Community Leaders and Noteworthy Americans, Notable Americans of the Bicentennial Era, American Society of Distinguished Citizens, Who's Who in Community Service.* Address: 1500 West 17th Lane, Portales, New Mexico 88130.

Gene D Lanier

Lanier, Gene Daniel

Professor of Library Science. Personal: Born March 13, 1934, in Conway, North Carolina; Son of Mrs. J. D. Lanier; Married Susan Roberts; Father of Leigh Katherine, Nicole McLean. Education: B.S., East Carolina University, 1955; M.S.L.S. 1957, Ph.D. 1968, University of North Carolina at Chapel Hill. Career: Teacher, Hillsborough (North Carolina) High School, 1956-57; Counterintelligence Specialist, Western Europe, 1957-59; Assistant Librarian, East Carolina University, 1959-60; East Carolina University, Head of the Acquisitions Department (Library) 1960-63, Associate Professor in the Department of Library Science

1963-64, Chairman and Professor of the Department of Library Science 1966-81; Professor, 1981 to present; Visiting Professor, School of Library Science, University of North Carolina-Chapel Hill, Summer, 1982; Part-time Instructor, School of Education, University of North Carolina-Chapel Hill, 1964-66. Organizational Memberships: American Library Association (White House conference state contract, 1974-77); Southeastern Library Association (committee on librarianship as a career, 1969-71; implementation committee, southeastern states cooperative library survey, 1974-76); North Carolina Library Association (education for librarianship committee, 1965-66; chairman, education for librarianship committee, 1967-68; first vice president, 1971-73; president, 1973-75; chairman, grievance committee, 1973-75; executive board, 1975-77; chairman, nominating committee, 1978-79; parliamentarian 1979, 1981; chairman, intellectual freedom committee, 1980-84; governmental relations committee, 1980-82); North Carolina Association of School Librarians (director, 1968-71; standards committee, 1979-81); North Carolina Learning Resources Association (program committee, 1979-80; district II director, 1980-81); *North Carolina Libraries* (director, southeastern student manuscript project; editorial board, 1975-79); Association of American Library Schools; Alpha Beta Alpha; Phi Sigma Pi; Phi Delta Kappa; Beta Phi Mu; Greenville/Pitt County Media Society. Community Activities: Benevolent and Protective Order of the Elks (lecturing knight, 1973-74); South Greenville Elementary School Parent Teacher Association (nominating committee, 1978-79). Religion: St. Paul's Episcopal Church; First Christian Church-Pastoral Oversight Committee, 1971-73; Pulpit Committee, 1974; Deacon, 1976-79; Executive Board, 1976-79; Music Committee, 1978-79. Published Works: *The Library and Television: A Study of the Role of Television in Modern Library Service; The Transformation of School Libraries Into Instructional Materials Centers;* Articles "Curricular Aids and the Materials Center"; "The Textbook-Major Curriculum Problem"; "Library Technical Assistants Bibliography"; "A Bibliographical Primer to Intellectual Freedom". Honors and Awards: Recipient of the 1982 Hugh M. Hefner First Amendment Award in Education, Chicago, The Playboy Foundation; Recipient of the 1982 Mary Peacock Douglas Award, Winston-Salem, North Carolina, Association of School Librarians; Listed in *Who's Who in Library Service, Who's Who in the South and Southwwest, Biographical Directory of Librarians in the United States and Canada; Personalities of the South, International Scholars Directory, Men of Achievement, Adult and Community Education Directory, Notable Americans of 1976-77, Who's Who in Library and Information Services, Directory of Distinguished Americans.* Address: 526 Westchester Drive, Greenville, North Carolina 27834.

Lanier, Ray Berry

Critical Care Instructor. Personal: Born 16 March 1952; Son of Mr. and Mrs. R. J. Lanier, Albany, Georgia. Education: A.D., General Education, Columbus College, 1975; B.S.N., Nursing, Medical College of Georgia, 1977; M.S. and Ph.D., Nursing Administration and Education, Columbia Pacific University, 1980; Additional studies at Hunter College (New York), Navajo Community College (Tsaili, Arizona), Veterans Administration Hospital (Albuquerque, New Mexico), St. Vincent Medical Center (Jacksonville, Florida), Medical College of Georgia, University of Georgia and training programs of the American Heart Association. Military: Served as certified senior operating room specialist with 2nd Combat Support Hospital, United States Army. Career: Critical Care Instructor, Veterans Administration Medical Center, New Orleans, Louisiana, 1981 to present; Nurse Educator, Gallup Indian Medical Center, Gallup, New Mexico, 1980-81; Emergency Medicine Instructor and National Faculty Member, U.S. Public Health Service, Indian Health Service, 1980-81; Clinical and Guest Faculty member, University of New Mexico, Gallup, 1980-81; Educational Coordinator, U.S. Naval Regional Medical Center, Jacksonville, Florida, 1977-80; Multiple Trauma Specialist, St. Vincent Medical Center, Jacksonville, 1978-80. Organizational Memberships: American Heart Association (chairman, McKinley County); American Nurses Association; National League for Nursing; Emergency Department Nurses Association; McKinley County Vocational Advisory Board; University of New Mexico Nursing Advisory Board; Western Interstate Council of Higher Education; Georgia Federation of Nursing Organizations (former executive member); Georgia Coordinating Council of Nursing (former executive member). Public Service: Former Chairman, Big Brother Program. Religion: Byne Memorial Baptist Church, Albany, Georgia. Honors and Awards: Named "Most Outstanding Teenager of the United States," 1968; Recipient, First Place in State Elk's Leadership Award, American Legion Oratorical Contest; Valedictorian, U.S. Army Surgical Specialist School; Recipient, "We Care Award," American Heart Association; Letter of Commendation, U.S. Public Health Service; Listed: *Personalities of America, Book of Honor.* Address: Veterans Administration Medical Center, 1601 Perdido Street, New Orleans, Louisiana 70140.

Leon Larimore

Lant, Jeffrey Ladd

Consultant, Educator. Personal: Born February 16, 1947; Son of Mrs. S. Lant. Education: B.A. summa cum laude, University of California-Santa Barbara, 1959; M.A., Harvard, 1975; Certificate of Advanced Graduate Studies in Higher Education Administration, Northeastern University, 1976. Career: Consultant, Educator. Published Works: Insubstantial Pageant: Ceremony and Confusion at Queen Victoria's Court, 1979; Development Today: A Guide for Nonprofit Organizations, 1980; The Consultant's Kit; Establishing and Operating Your Successful Consulting Business, 1982; Our Harvard: Reflections on College Life by Twenty-Two Distinguished Graduates (Editor); General Editor, J.L.A. Publications Nonprofit Technical Assistance Series and J.L.A. Publications "Get Ahead" Series. Honors and Awards: Sir Henry Jones Prize, Moral Philosophy, University of St. Andrews, Scotland, 1968; Woodrow Wilson's Fellow, 1969-75; Harvard Prize Fellow 1969-75; Harvard Travelling Fellow, 1972-73; Harvard College Master's Award, 1975; Official Citation, Boston City Council, 1978; Official Citation, Massachusetts House of Representatives, 1977; Official Citation, Governor of Massachusetts, 1978. Address: 50 Follen Street, Suite 507, Cambride, Massachusetts 02138.

Larimore, Leon

Pastor. Personal: Born July 22, 1911, in Hart County, Kentucky; Son of William C. and Myrtie D. Isenberg Larimore; Married Blanche Lile, July 13, 1929; Father of Marjorie Bell (Mrs. Levy Broady). Education: Graduate of Campbellsville College, 1946; Attended Georgetown College, 1946; A.B., Western Kentucky University, 1949; M.D., Southern Baptist Theological Seminary, 1952; D.D., Campbellsville College, 1962. Career: Ordained Baptist Minister, 1937; Pastored Churches in Hart, Edmonson, Metcalfe, Green and Monroe Counties, Kentucky, 1937-57; Moderator, Liberty Association of Baptists, 1942-49, 1952-57; State Mission Board, Kentucky Baptists, 1952-55; Trustee, Campbellsville College, 1953-70; Chairman of the Board, Campbellsville College, 1967-68; Recording Secretary, Kentucky Baptist Executive Board, 1960; Trustee, Carver School of Missions and Social Work, Southern Baptist Theological Seminary, 1961-63; Vice President, Kentucky Baptist Pastors Conference, 1961-63; Director, Baptist Homes for the Elderly, 1962-77; Vice President, Kentucky Baptist Convention, 1965; Trustee, Wigginton Home for Men, Louisville, Kentucky, 1967-77; Moderator, Long Run Baptist Association, 1971-72; President of the Executive Board, Long Run Baptist Association, 1971-72; Member of State Board, Kentucky Baptist Convention, 1972-73; Administrative Committee, Kentucky Baptist Convention, 1972-73; Vice-Chairman, Administrative Committee, Kentucky Baptist Convention, 1972-73; Chairman of the Board, Baptist Homes for the Elderly, 1976-77; Field Supervisor, Boyce Bible School, Southern Baptist Theological Seminary, 1976 to present; Pastor, Third Avenue Baptist Church, Louisville, Kentucky, 1957 to present. Community Activities: South Central Rural Telephone Cooperative (director, 1951-57); Economic Security Welfare Committee, 1951-57; American Cancer Society (chairman,

Hart County unit, 1952-56); Kentucky Colonel, 1955; Horse Cave Rotary Club (president, 1956); Mason, Bear Wallow Lodge #3231 Free and Accepted Masons; Glasgow Chapter #45 Royal Arch, York Rite; Grand Lodge, Kentucky Masons (grand chaplain, 1960); 32° Degree Scottish Rite, Valley of Louisville; Kentucky Admiral, 1972; Shriner. Homnors and Awards: Distinguished Service Award, American Cancer Society, 1954, 1956; Doctor of Divinity, Campbellsville College, 1962; Listed in *Who's Who of the South and Southwest, Dictionary of International Biography, Community Leaders and Noteworthy Americans, Who's Who in Kentucky, Library of Human Resourcers American Bicentennial, International Who's Who in Community Service, Men of Achievement, Notable Americans of the Bicentennial Era, Personalities of the South, Personalities of America, Men and Women of Distinction, Book of Honor, Directory of Distinguished Americans.* Address: 1041 Eastern Parkway, Louisville, Kentucky 40217.

Larkin, Gertie Mae

Registered Nurse. Personal: Born October 1, 1930; Daughter of Urbane Aaron Sr. (deceased) and Willie Mae Linkous; Married William Clayton Larkin Jr. (deceased) on August 14, 1949; Mother of Sue Ann. Education: Graduate of Temple High School, 1947; Graduate of Temple Junior College, 1949; B.S.N., University of Mary Hardin-Baylor, 1975; Undertook Post-Graduate Studies at Texas Women's University, Temple Campus, 1975-78. Career: EKG Technician, Scott and White Memorial Hospital, 1951-52; First Grade Teacher, Sinclair Elementary School, Hampton, Virginia, 1954-55; Private Secretary, First National Bank, Temple, Texas, 1956-58; Staff Nurse, Santa Fe Memorial Hospital, Temple, 1976-80; Charge Nurse, 3-11 Shift, Cameron Community Hospital, Cameron, Texas, 1980 to present. Organizational Memberships: American Nursing Association; Texas Nursing Association; District 7 Nursing Association; Scott and White Memorial Hospital School of Nursing Alumnae Association; American Biographical Institute (annual associate member, 1982 to present; contributing member of national board of advisors, 1982 to present). Community Activities: Volunteer for Harvest House, Center for Senior Citizens. Religion: Baptist. Honors and Awards: Listed in *Who's Who of American Women, World Who's Who of Women, Who's Who in the South and Southwest, Personalities of America, Directory of Distinguished Americans, Personalities of the South, Book of Honor, International Book of Honor, International Who's Who of Intellectuals, International Register of Profiles, Community Leaders of America.* Address: 3716 Robinhood Drive, Temple, Texas 17502.

Gertie M Larkin

Larsen, Gail

Executive. Personal: Born December 30, 1944; Daughter of Thomas S. and Gertrude Becker. Education: A.S., Palm Beach Junior College, 1965. Career: 2/8E Executive Vice President, National Speakers Association, Phoenix; President, Career Conventions, Inc., 1979-82; President, Gail Larsen and Associates, Inc., 1976-80; Employment Manager, Vanderbilt University Medical Center, 1973-76; Employment Manager, Werthan Industries, 1970-71; Former Executive Secretary. Organizational Memberships: National Speakers Association; Meeting Planners International; American Society of Personnel Administration; CABLE (vice president, 1980). Community Activities: Tennessee Commission on the Status of Women, 1980-81; Metropolitan Nashville Private Industry Council, 1980-81; Governor's Conference on Small Business (planning committee, 1981); Nashville State Technical Institute (advisory board, 1980 to present); United American Bank of Nashville (advisory director, 1980 to present); River Conservancy of Tennessee (board of directors, 1980 to present); Nashville Urban League (board of directors, 1981 to present); Tennessee Scenic Rivers Association (women's political caucus member). Religion: Christ Presbyterian Church, Nashville. Honors and Awards: Tennessee Small Business Person of the Year, 1981; Tennessee Woman on the Move, Women's Political Caucus, 1980. Address: 8045 Via de Los Libros, Scottsdale, Arizona 85258.

Marjorie S Larsen

Larsen, Marjorie Susan

Businesswoman. Personal: Born July 12, 1916; Daughter of William and Elizabeth Larsen (both deceased). Education: A.B., University of California-Berkeley, 1938; M.A., College of the Pacific, 1947. Career: Owner, Bee Beauty Salon and Gift Shop; Real Estate Associate; Teacher and Administrator, Stockton Unified School District, 1946-72; Teacher, Orestimba Union High School, 1940-46. Organizational Memberships: California Association of Health, Physical Education and Recreation; National Education Association; California Teachers Association; Stockton Retired Teachers Association; Stockton Board of Realtors; Delta Kappa Gamma. Community Activities: Stockton Women's Track Club (president 1967-68); Pacific Women's Club (president 1978-80); Stockton Recreation Department (volunteer services 1946-69); A.F.S., 1961-69; Donations for Scholarships, Edison Senior High School, 1975-80; Donations to Athletic Program for Women, University of the Pacific, University of California, San Jose State University, 1975-81. Honors and Awards: Others Award, Salvation Army, 1971; Distinguished Service Award, California Association of Health, Physical Education and Recreation, 1973; Susan B. Anthony Award, Women's Community Council, 1978; Certificate of Appreciation, Metropolitan Recreation Department, 1967; Life Member, Edison High School Parent Teacher Association, 1968; Originator of the Game "Speed-a-way"; Listed in *Who's Who of American Women, Who's Who in California, The World Who's Who of Women, Community Leaders of America.* Address: 1754 Middlefield, Stockton, California 95204.

LaRue, DeRette Sartain

Retired. Personal: Born December 20, 1917; Daughter of Robert C. and Birthday Thompson Sartain (both deceased); Married Eldon J. LaRue. Education: Graduate of Okmulgee High School, Oklahoma; Attended Okmulgee Junior College, 1935, 1936. Career: Mountain Bell Telephone Operator, 1937-40; Supervisor, 1940-43; Checker and Spotter, Color Classics Film Processing Laboratory, 1974; Counselor, Diet Center, 1978. Community Activities: Young Women's Christian Association (craft instructor, 1970; acting secretary, 1935-36); Camp Fire Girls, 1930's; Rainbow Girls, 1930's; Reserve Officers Ladies (state president, 1974; president, local chapter, 1973, 1976); Beta Sigma Phi Xi Eta Chapter (president); Xi Alpha Phi (founder, president); Xi Delta (president); Preceptor Alpha Lambda (president); Tucson City Council (president, vice president, corresponding secretary); Advisor to Gamma Pi, Beta Iota, Epsilon Epsilon Chapters. Religion: Methodist. Honors and Awards: Beta Sigma Phi State Convention Chairman, 1973; Valentine Princess, International Royal Court, Beta Sigma Phi, 1977; Xi Delta Girl of the Year, 7 times; 16 Years Perfect Attendance, Recipient of Order of the Rose; Princess, Xi Eta Chapter, 1971; Xi Delta, 1977. Address: 3319 East Waverly, Tucson, Arizona 85716.

Derette S Larue

Laska, Vera Oravec

Author, Lecturer, Professor, Columnist. Personal: Born in 1928; Married Andrew J. Laska; Mother of Thomas Vaclav, Paul Andrew. Education: Ph.D., American History, University of Chicago, 1959. Career: Foreign Student Counselor, University of Chicago; Consultant, Institute of International Education; Instructor, University of Illinois, Roosevelt University. Organizational Memberships: American Historical Association: New England Historical Association; New England History Teachers Association;

Pan American Society; National Association of Foreign Student Affairs; Czechoslovak Society of Arts and Sciences in America. Community Activities: Massachusetts Bicentennial Commission, 1971-76; Weston Historical Commission, 1968-75; Weston Public Library Trustee, 1979-80; Weston Measurer of Lumber, 1981 to present. Published Works: Author of 5 Books, Over 100 Articles. Honors and Awards: Masaryk Scholar, Prague, 1948; International Gouse Fellow, 1949; University of Chicago Fellow, 1949-50; Outstanding Teacher of America, 1972; National Endowment for the Humanities Grantee, 1974. Address: 50 Woodchester Drive, Weston, Massachusetts 02193.

Latimer, James H

Timpanist, Associate Professor. Personal: Born June 27, 1934; Son of Major (deceased) and Maria Latimer; Father of M. Clark, Catherine, Danielsen, Treater, Amani. Education: B.Mus., Indiana University-Bloomington, 1956; M.Mus., Boston University, 1964; Post Master's Study, Harvard University, 1968. Career: Timpanist, Madison Symphony Orchestra; Associate Professor, Music/Percussion, University of Wisconsin-Madison; Former Freelance Percussionist; Instructor of Percussion, Florida A&M University. Organizational Memberships: American Society of Composers, Authors and Publishers (contributing composer); Madison Symphony Orchestra (past president); Wisconsin Federation of Music Clubs (honorary life member); College Music Society; Percussive Arts Society (past president, vice-president, secretary/treasurer); National Black Music Colloquium, Kennedy Center, Washington, D.C. (state chairman). Community Activities: Wisconsin Youth Symphony Orchestras (music director and conductor, 1972-78); Duke Ellington Festival, University of Wisconsin-Madison (coordinator, 1972); Amateur Radio Relay League (life member); Citizens for a Civic Center Committee, 1973-75; Guest Conductor and Percussion Consultant/Clinician throughout the United States; Madison Symphony Pops Concerts (guest conductor, 1977, 1978); Madison Capitol City Band and V.F.W. Band (director, 1980, 1981, 1982). Honors and Awards: Florida A&M University Citation for Outstanding Service in Percussion, 1958; Florida A&M University Citation for Sustained Excellence as Director of Percussion, 1959; Wisconsin State Journal "Know Your Madisonian" Citation for Community Service, 1972; Certificate of Merit for Outstanding Performance at the Kennedy Center, Washington, D.C., Wisconsin Federated Music Clubs, 1977; Wisconsin Governors Proclamation "Wisconsin Artist of Distinction", 1978. Address: 3922 Hillcrest Drive, Madison, Wisconsin 53705.

Lattimer, Agnes Delores

Pediatrician. Personal: Born May 13, 1928; Daughter of Hortense Lattimer; Married Frank Daniel Bethel; Mother of Bernard Cassell Goss. Education: Graduate of Booker T. Washington High School, Memphis, Tennessee, 1945; A.B., Fish University, Nashville, 1949; M.D., The Chicago Medical School, Chicago, 1954; Intern, Cook County Hospital, Chicago, 1954-56; Resident, Pediatrics, Michael Reese Hospital, Chicago, 1956-58. Career: Pediatrician. Organizational Memberships: National Board of Medical Examiners (diplomate); Ambulatory Pediatric Association; American Association for the Advancement of Science; American Institute of Hypnosis; Chicago Pediatric Society; American Academy of Pediatrics (fellow; secretary/treasurer, president-elect 1980-81); International College of Applied Nutrition (fellow). Community Activities: Chicago Committee Against Lead Poisoning; Medical Consultant, Region V, Job Corps. Honors and Awards: Professor of the Year, The Chicago Medical School, 1968; Distinguished Alumnus Award, Chicago Medical School Alumni Association, 1971; Elected Memberships to Alpha Gamma Pi Honorary Sorority for Excellence in Community Service, 1969; Image Award, League of Black Women, 1974; Listed in *Men and Women of Distinction*. Address: 2138 East 75th Street, Chicago, Illinois 60649.

Lattimore, Caroline Louise

University Dean. Personal: Born May 12, 1945; Daughter of Earl R. Sr. and Mary Lattimore. Education: B.S. 1967, M.A. 1973, Hampton Institute; Ph.D., Duke University, 1978. Career: Dean of Minority Affairs, Duke University; Former Positions include Educational Consultant, Graduate Assistant, Psychological Testing Intern, Coordinator of the Senior Citizens Program, Secondary English Teacher, Counseling Intern. Organizational Memberships: Black Women in Higher Education; American Educational Research Association; Kappa Delta Pi Honor Society. Community Activities: North Carolina Black Educators Group (steering committee, 1981); North Carolina Black Legislative Caucus (secretary, 1982); WTVD-TV 11, Durham, North Carolina (advisory board, 1982); National Council on Negro Women (2nd vice-president, local chapter, 1981); Hampton Alumni, Durham-Chapel Hill Chapter (president, 1981); Alpha Kappa Alpha (national chairman, AKA Connection, 1982-84). Religion: Holy Week Speaker, Duke Chapel, 1979; Lector for Duke University Chapel, 1981-82. Honors and Awards: Award of Merit for Outstanding Achievement, Winston-Salem Junior Chamber of Commerce, 1963; National Fellowship Fund Recipient, Ford Foundation, 1976-78; Outstanding Young Woman of America, North Carolina State Winner, with Letters of Commendation from Governor James B. Hunt and Congressman Ike Andrews, 1979; Listed in *Who's Who Among Students in American Colleges and Universities, Who's Who Among Black Americans*. Address: 234 Overlook Avenue, Durham, North Carolina 27712.

Laudenslager, Wanda Lee

District Coordinator of Speech, Language and Hearing Department, General Building Contractor and Real Estate Broker. Personal: Born July 22, 1929; Daughter of Victor Vierra (deceased) and Florence Lorene Houck Silveira; Married Leonard E. Laudenslager; Mother of Leonard E. II, Dawn Marie. Education: A.A., College of San Mateo, 1960; B.A., San Jose State University, 1962; M.A. 1965; Certified in Standard Supervision, 1971; Certified in Teaching, 1962; Certified in Speech, Language and Hearing Pathology, 1962; California Licensed Audiometrist, 1966; Real Estate Broker, 1978; Certified General Building Contractor, 1979; National Certification of Clinical Competence in Speech Pathology, American Speech, Language and Hearing Association, 1963; Licensed by California State Board of Medical Examiners as Speech Pathologist, 1974. Career: Speech Pathologist, Newark (California) Unified School District, 1962-65; District Coordinator, Speech, Language and Hearing Department, 1965 to present; Self-Employed Real Estate Broker and General Building Contractor. Organizational Memberships: American Speech-Language-Hearing Association; Association of California School Administrators; Newark School Administrators Association; School Administrators Special Services; National Association of Realtors; California Association of Realtors; Southern Alameda County Board of Realtors. Honors and Awards: Phi Kappa Phi; Alpha Gamma Sigma; Pi Lambda Theta; Kappa Delta Pi; Congress of Parents and Teachers, Life Membership; Crown Zellerback Foundation, 1961; Honors, Department of Education, San Jose State University; International Biographical Association, Life Fellowship, 1981; Listed in *Who's Who in the West, World Who's Who of Women, International Who's Who of Intellectuals, Book of Honor, Directory of Distinguished Americans, International Register of Profiles, Dictionary of International Biography, Personalities of America, Who's Who in California*. Address: 37733 Logan Drive, Fremont, California 94536.

Lauer, Frances Louise Peacock

Consultant. Personal: Born February 20, 1942; Daughter of Eldred Giles Peacock, Roberta Shanks; Married Ralph E. Lauer J.D.; Mother of AnnaLisa, Ralph Edward III. Education: B.A. with honors, University of Washington, 1964; M.A., Pennsylvania State University, 1970. Career: Consultant, Ice Arena West Inc.; Guest Counselor, Eastern Washington State College of Education, 1967; Dean of Women's Staff, Pennsylvania State University, 1964-66; Research in Medieval Literature, Comparative Literature, German, Spanish Literature. Organizational Memberships: International Platform Association; American Personnel and Guidance Association; American College Personnel Association; Association for Humanistic Education and Development. Community Activities: Volunteer and Room Mother, Longfellow and Anderson's Schools' Parent Teacher Association; Early Childhood Education Association; Red Cross Backyard Swim Program (volunteer); Mid-City Senior Day Care Center (advisory board); Camp Fire Girls (leader); Society of Mayflower Descendants; Experiment in International Living; United States Figure Skating Association; San Diego Figure Skating Club; San Diego Civic Light Opera; Founder, Highline College Child Care Center, 1967; Soloist, Pennsylvania State Ice Show, 1966. Honors and Awards: Listed in *World Who's Who of Women, Personalities of America, Book of Honor, International Who's Who of Intellectuals*. Address: 4263 Mt. Castle, San Diego, California 92117.

Laughter, Mabel Young

Professor, Program Director. Personal: Born January 22, 1941; Daughter of Mr. and Mrs. Herman Young; Married Joseph A. Laughter; Mother of Tara Charleen, Alexander Joseph. Education: B.S.Ed. 1963, M.A. Education 1970, Western Carolina University; Ed.D., University of Mississippi, 1972. Career: Director, Developmental Reading Program, Professor, East Carolina University; Former Classroom Teacher, Raleigh, North Carolina City Schools, Winston-Salem/Forsyth County Schools, Henderson County Schools; Social Worker, Forsyth County Department of Social Services; Teaching Assistant, Supervisor of Student Teachers, University of Mississippi; Professor, University of Southwestern Louisiana. Organizational Memberships: International Reading Association; Association of Teacher Educators; Phi Kappa Phi; Alpha Delta Kappa. Community Activities: Governor's Task Force on Reading (Pitt County), 1976-78; Co-Author of Film Strip Showing Parents How to Help Their Children Read Better, 1977; Curriculum and Instruction Team for Development of the Middle Schools of Pitt County, North Carolina (member and chairman, 1978); Moore County Schools Experimental Middle School Program (consultant, 1977-80). Religion: President, Young Women's Bible Class, Presbyterian Church. Honors and Awards: Certificate of Commendation, National Right to Read Program and Moore County Schools; One of Fifteen Professors Chosen from Across the United States to Design Model Program for Training Teachers of Reading; Listed in *Who's Who in American Women, Dictionary of International Biography, Leader's in Education, Personalities of the South, Contemporary Personalities, World Who's Who of Women in Education*. Address: 3202 Ellsworth Drive, Greenville, North Carolina 27934.

Eula M T Lavender

Lavender, Eula Mae Taylor

Artist, Hand-crafter. Personal: Born April 4, 1923; Daughter of John Randolph and Ida Oma Marlowe Taylor; Married H. W. Morris, Second Marriage to Howard Lavender; Mother of William Randolph Morris, Gerald Lee Morris, Herman Taylor Morris (deceased), David Andrew Morris. Career: Paintings in Oil, Rock Crafts, Blue Prints; Formerly a Seamstress and Tailor, Electronic Worker, Farmer, Tile Setter, House Painter, Furniture Designer, Others. Community Activities: Numerous Public Donations. Religion: Clear Branch Pentecostal Holiness Church, Primary Sunday School Teacher and Youth Leader, 1940-55; West Palm Beach Pentecostal Holiness Church, Primary Sunday School Teacher and Youth Leader, 1956-58. Honors and Awards: Featured on "Carolina Camera", human interest program, WBTV Channel 3, Charlotte, North Carolina; Listed in *Personalities of the South, International Book of Honor, Community Leaders of America, The Directory of Distinguished Americans, Two Thousand Distinguished Southerners, The World Who's Who of Women*. Address: Star Route, Box 47, Black Mountain, North Carolina 28711.

Law, Beulah (Boo) Enfield

Geriatric Nurse. Personal: Born September 15, 1922; Daughter of John Henry and Minnie Jorgensen Enfield (both deceased); Married Melvin J. Law; Mother of Mona L. Pedersen, Jeanne L. Hale, John Albert. Education: Studies in Education, University of Nebraska-Curtis, 1941; Studies in Nursing, Glendale College and Los Angeles County General Hospital, 1949; Studies in Public Health Nursing, University of Maryland, 1963. Military: Built B17 Bombers for Lockeed Aircraft, Burbank, California, World War II. Career: Elementary School Teacher, Arthur County, Nebraska; Obstetric, Gynecology Nursing, Los Angeles County General Hospital; Industrial Nursing, Prudential Life Insurance Co., Los Angeles, and Department of Labor, Washington, D.C.; School Nurse, Holton-Arms School, Bethesda, Maryland; Research Nursing, National Institutes of Health, Bethesda, Maryland; Obstetrics-Gynecology, Johns Hopkins Hospital, Baltimore, Maryland; Geriatric Nursing, Army Distaff Hall, Washington, D.C. Organizational Memberships: Los Angeles County General Hospital Nurses Alumni Association; American Nurses Association; Professional Nurses Club of Suburban Maryland. Community Activities: Church School Teacher, 1960-68; Girl Scout Leader of Brownies, Juniors and Cadets, 1959-65; Girl Scout Advisor of Senior Troop #1978, 1965-75; Outdoor Consultant and Director for Girl Scouts of America, 1960-70; Petticoats, Pot and Politics (chairman, 1972); National Explorer President's Congress (special events chairman, 1971-75); Cohasset Garden Club (charter member; president, 1966; all other offices); Washington Hospice Society (volunteer). Religion: Reorganized Church of Jesus Christ of Latter Day Saints, Taught Church School Kindergarten Class, 1960-68. Honors and Awards: Certificate for Outstanding Service, Girl Scouts of America, 1969; Certificate of Recognition, Girl Scout Council of the Nation's Capital, 1971; Thanks Badge, Girl Scouts of America, 1972; Service Award Plaque, Boy Scouts of America, 1972; Queen of the May, Los Angeles County General Hospital Student Nurses, 1949. Address: "Ogallala", 7603 Winterberry Place, Bethesda, Maryland 20817.

Beulah E Law

Lawson, Archie David

Physician's Assistant. Personal: Born August 29, 1947; Son of A. D. and Helen Lawson (deceased); Married Judith Ann Reynolds; Father of Melissa Ann, Christopher David. Education: Attended Florence State University, 1965-67; Physician's Assistant Program, Bowman Gray School of Medicine, Wake Forest University, 1970-72; Board Certified Physician's Assistant, National Commission on Certification of Physician's Assistants, 1972. Military: Served in the United States Army Medical Services, 1967-70, attaining the rank of E-5; 311th and 17th Field Hospitals, Republic of South Vietnam, 1969. Career: Physician's Assistant. Organizational Memberships: Alabama Society of Physician's Assistants (vice president, 1976-77); American Academy of Physician's Assistants. Religion: Church of Christ, Former Sunday School Teacher. Honors and Awards: Candidate for Regent's External Bachelor of Science Degree, Spring, 1983, The University of the State of New York; Awarded Green Belt Tae Kwan do Karate, December 1982; Listed in *Personalities of the South, Directory of Distinguished Americans, Two Thousand Notable Americans, International Men of Achievement,*

Dictionary of International Biography, Personalities of America. Address: 206 Harding Street, Florence, Alabama 35630.

Lazerowitz, Morris

Author, Lecturer. Personal: Born October 22, 1907; Son of Max and Etta Lazerowitz (both deceased); Married Alice Ambrose. Education: A.B. 1933, Ph.D. 1936, University of Michigan. Career: Professor of Philosophy, Smith College 1938-73, Bedford College (University of London) 1951-52, University of Delaware 1975, Hampshire College 1977, 1979, 1981, Carleton College 1979. Organizational Memberships: Royal Institute of Philosophy; Aristotelian Society; American Philosophical Association; American Association of University Professors. Published Works: Author of *The Structure of Metaphysics*, 1955; *Studies in Metaphilosophy*, 1964; *The Language of Philosophy*, 1977; Co-Author *Fundamentals of Symbolic Logic; Logic: The Theory of Formal Inference; Philosophical Theories; Necesidad y Filosofia* (in progress); Co-Editor and Contributor to *Metaphysics; Readings and Reappraisals; Essays in Retrospect; Philosophy and Language; Psychoanalysis and Philosophy.* Honors and Awards: Rackham Postdoctoral Fellowship, University of Michigan, 1937-38; Fulbright Professorship, University of London, 1951-52; Sophia and Austin Smith Chair, Smith College, 1964-73; Distinguished Visiting Professor, University of Delaware, Hampshire College, Carleton College. Address: 126 Vernon Street, Northampton, Massachusetts 01060.

Leacock, Ingrid C

Communications Consultant, Journalist, Research Writer. Personal: Born April 23, 1947; Daughter of Mr. and Mrs. James Razack; Mother of Stephen Anthony. Education: Teachers Certificate, Secondary Education, Teachers College, Guyana, 1967; Certificate, School of Broadcasting and Announcing, New York, 1967; A.A., Borough Manhattan College, 1975; B.A., History and Communication, City College of New York, 1977; M.A., New School of Social Research, 1979; Candidate for Ph.D., Communications in Education, New York University. Career: Researching and Compiling Material on the Refugee and Migrant Problems in New York City; Tapings for Compilation of Materials on Terminal Cancer Patients, Their Families, Doctors and Nurses; Communicator, Campaign Communications Institute; Assistant Editor, Newsletter, International Center of New York; Reporter, *New York Graphic* (now known as *Downtown News*); Overseas Editor, Woman's Page Editor, *Pace Magazine;* Produced Information Tapes for Guyana Broadcasting Service. Organizational Memberships: International Institute of Communications (London); A.C.E.T.; International Platform Association; F.L.C.P.; United Nations Association; National Council of Women. Community Activities: Volunteer Projects, Channel 13's Telethons, Recording for the Blind, International Center; Blessed Sacrament English Conversation Program (organizer, administrator); Lincoln Square Community Council (director, board member). Religion: Catholic; Parish Council, Blessed Sacrament Church. Honors and Awards: Listed in *International Biographical Center Directory, Personalities of America, World Who's Who of Women.* Address: Beacon Hotel, 2130 Broadway, New York, New York 10023.

Lease, Sharon Albert

Assistant Coordinator. Personal: Born September 1, 1943; Daughter of Anita Albert; Married Kenneth T. Lease; Mother of Stephanie Renee, Elizabeth Gail. Education: B.A., Elementary Education, Oklahoma City University, 1965; M.Ed., Guidance and Counseling, Millersville State College, Pennsylvania, 1970; M.Ed., Administration/Supervision, University of Guam, 1975; Doctoral Program in Progress, University of Oklahoma. Career: Assistant Coordinator, Youth Re-Entry Program, Oklahoma City Public Schools; Reading Director, American School, Rio de Janeiro, Brazil; Assistant Principal/Principal, Passargad International School, Iran, and Department of Education, Government of Guam; School Counselor; Teacher/Elementary and Secondary Levels; Former Peace Corps Volunteer; Assistant Administrator, Curriculum Section, Oklahoma, State Department of Education. Organizational Memberships: American Personnel and Guidance Association; Phi Delta Kappa (treasurer, 1970); Pi Lambda Theta; International Reading Association; United States Professional Tennis Association (certified member). Community Activities: Served on Governor's Committee for the Exceptional Child, 1970-71; Served on Title III-A Projects Evaluation Committee, Government of Guam, 1970. Religion: International Church, Rio de Janeiro, Brazil, 1979; Metropolitan Baptist, Oklahoma City. Published Works: "School Drop-Outs Given an Alternative", *Oklahoma Educator*, 1981; "Dropouts-Alternative", *Manpower*, 1981. Honors and Awards: Varsity Cheerleader, Varsity Tennis Team, Oklahoma City University, 1961-65; Miss Oklahoma City University, 1963; Dean's Honor Roll, 1964-65; Miss Sarawak State Customs, Malaysia, 1968; Certificate of Appreciation, Governor of Guam, 1970; Certificate of Appreciation, State of Malaysia, 1965; Listed in *Outstanding Young Women of America.* Address: 6002 Northwest Expressway, Oklahoma City, Oklahoma 73132.

Leavitt, Jerome E

Executive. Personal: Born August 1, 1916; Married Florence E. Leavitt. Education: B.S., Newark State College, Union, New Jersey, 1938; Attended Teachers College, Columbia University, New York City, 1938-39; M.A., School of Education, New York University, 1942; University of Colorado, Boulder, 1949-50; Ed.D., Northwestern University, Evanston, Illinois, 1952; Visiting Scholar, Anthropology, University of Arizona, Tucson, 1958-59. Career: Elementary Teacher, Rosyln Heights, New York, 1938-42; Instructor, Sperry Gyroscope Co., Inc., Brooklyn, 1942-45; Elementary Principal and Supervisor, Los Alamos, New Mexico, 1945-49; Instructor in Education and Supervisor of Student Teaching, Northwestern University, Evanston, Illinois, 1952; Assistant Professor of Education and Director of Student Teaching, Oregon State System of Higher Education, Portland, 1952-55; Associate Professor of Education 1955-58, Professor of Education and Executive Assistant to the Dean, School of Education 1958-66, Portland State University, Oregon; Professor of Education, College of Education, University of Arizona, Tucson, 1966-69; Professor of Education and Chairman, Department of Elementary Education, School of Education, Fresno State College, 1969-71; Professor of Education, Department of Elementary Education, School of Education, California State University-Fresno, 1971-75; Professor of Education, Coordinator of Child Abuse Program, California State University-Fresno, 1975-81; President, Jerome Leavitt Publishing and Educational Services, 1981 to present. Organizational Memberships: Association Childhood Education International (life member); National Education Association (life member); Association for Supervision and Curriculum Development; National Society for the Study of Education; Society of Professors of Education; California Teachers Association; Professors of Curriculum; American Humane Association; Phi Delta Kappa, National Honorary Professional Fraternity in Education; Kappa Delta Pi, National Honor Society in Education; Epsilon Pi Tau, National Honorary Professional Fraternity in Arts. Community Activities: Oregon State Department of Education (research consultant, 1963-66); President Johnson's Advisory Council on the Education of the Disadvantaged Child (consultant, 1966-68); American Specialist in Education for the United States State Department in Cyprus, 1961; Portland, Oregon, United Fund Central Committee (executive board, 1957-59); Outdoor Education Workshop, HooDoo Ski Bowl, Oregon (director, 1955); Camp Columbus, New Jersey (camp counselor, arts and crafts, 1937-38); State of Oregon Science Fairs (judge, 1955-65); Video-Taped Public Service Announcements "You and Your Child" for Broadcast on KJEO-TV; Conducted Conservation Education Workshop for Elementary Teachers for the National Wildlife Federation, 1975; Directed NATO Advanced

Study Institute on "Research in Child Abuse", Les Ares, France 1982. Published Works: Number of Educational Books including *Readings in Elementary Education*, 1961; *Terrariums and Aquariums*, 1961; *By Land, By Sea, By Air*, 1969; *The Battered Child*, 1974; Articles include "Each One-Teach One Program Adapted to Head Start Training", 1977; "My Mother Writes Terrible", 1969; "Democratic Leadership of the School Principal", 1974; (over 100 articles published in all); Editorial and Publishing Consultant to Numerous Educational Periodicals. Honors and Awards: Listed in *Contemporary Authors, Dictionary of International Biography, International Authors and Writers Who's Who, Leaders in Education, Men of Achievement, Who's Who in America, Who's Who in the West*. Address: 39736 Pine Ridge Way, Oakhurst, California 93644.

Leba, Samuel

Samuel Leba

Social Work Supervisor. Personal: Born January 11, 1932; Son of Theodore Sr. and Sarafina Leba (both deceased). Education: B.A. Psychology, Washington Square College, New York University, 1953; Attended Hahnemann Medical College, Philadelphia, Pennsylvania, 1953-54. Career: Social Case Worker, City of Newark, Division of Public Welfare; Social Case Work Supervisor, City of Newark, Division of Public Welfare, 1972 to present. Organizational Memberships: Essex Council #1, New Jersey Civil Service Association; National Association of Social Workers (associate member); American Public Welfare Association (contributing member); Council for Human Services of New Jersey (supporting member); New York University Club. Community Activities: Urban League of Essex County (leadership training program, 1965); City of Newark Management Development (Rutgers program, 1973); Rutgers-New Brunswick Basic Management Techniques for the Public Supervisor, 1977; New York University Alumni Fund Worker, 1973 to present; National Geographic Society; Young Men's and Young Women's Christian Association of Newark and Vicinity. Honors and Awards: Certificates of Appreciation, New York University Alumni Fund Campaigns, 1977-82; Life Member, Psi Chi National Honorary Society of Psychology; Dean's List, New York University, Washington Square College of Arts and Science; Charles Hayden Memorial Scholar, New York University, 1949; National Honor Society, East Side High School, Newark, New Jersey, 1949; Bausch and Lomb Award, 1949; Listed in *Community Leaders of America, Directory of Distinguished Americans, Who's Who in the East*. Address: 57 Houston Street, Newark, New Jersey 07105.

LeCocq, Rhoda P

Rhoda P LeCocq

Author. Personal: Born January 31, 1926; Daughter of R. B. LeCocq. Education: M.A., English-Creative Writing; M.A., Philosophy; Ph.D., Comparative East/West Philosophy. Military: Served as a Lieutenant in the United States Naval Reserve, 1942-70. Career: Associate Professor; Information Officer/Legislative Liaison Officer; United States Naval Officer; Continuity/Production, Radio and Television; Columnist, Newspaper; Free-Lance Magazine Writer; Author; Associate Professor, California Institute of Asian Studies, San Francisco, 1972 to present. Organizational Memberships: Sacramento Chapter, Public Relations Society of America and Press Club (board of directors, 1975-78). Community Activities: Retired Officers Association, 1970 to present; International Platform Association; Smithsonian Associates; United States Naval Reserve Association; Armed Forces Writers League; Mensa; San Francisco Press Club; Marines Memorial (San Francisco); Kappa Alpha Theta; Theta Sigma Phi; Sponsor Tibetan Professor/Lecturers from India & Nepal, 1980; Lecturer on Comparative Religions, 1970 to present. Published Works: Author of *The Radical Thinkers*, 1972; Honors and Awards: Contributor to *East/West Understanding*, London, and Cultural Integration Center, San Francisco, 1973; Excellence Award, Cultural Integration Center, 1974; Two Awards of Excellence, National Association of Counties, 1974; Listed in *Who's Who of World's Women, Who's Who of American Women*. Address: P.O. Box 5025, Bellevue, Washington 98009-5025.

Lee, Gerald Francisco

Administrator, Cultural Activist. Personal: Born March 14, 1951; Son of Kyong Ho and Sunny Lee; Married Jung Soon; Father of Edward Y., Nancy M. Education: B.B.A. 1973, M.B.A. 1975, Ph.D. 1978, University of California-Berkeley; D.B.A. (honorary), Far Eastern Study Institute, Seoul, Korea, 1978; Honorary Doctor of Management Engineering, Far East Management Society, Tokyo, Japan. Military: Served in the United States Army, attaining the rank of First Lieutenant. Career: Established Conglomerate of Sic Manufacturing and Distributor Companies in South Korea, 1978-80; Established Subsidiary Land Transportation, Sea Transportation and Heavy Equipment Transportation Companies and Import/Export Trading Company in South Korea, 1978-80; Executive Director and Advisor to All Enterprises in Korea; Director, Far Eastern Studies Institute, Seoul, 1978-81; President, International Business Research and Management Consultants Institution Seoul/San Francisco. Organizational Memberships: East-West Studies and Cultural Exchange Association; Korean-American Friendship Association; American Institute of Industrial Engineers; Association of the United States Army; Veterans of Foreign Wars Pacific Area. Community Activities: National Orators Association (vice president/president); East-West Studies and Cultural Exchange Association (president); Korean-American Friendship Association (director); Far Eastern Study Institute (director, 1978 to present); Academy of Korean Studies (director). Religion: Buddhist. Published Works: *Korea 2000; Economic and Cultural Ties with Mainland China.* Honors and Awards: Good Conduct Medal; Korean Service Medal; United Nations Medal; Honor Graduate Certificate upon Graduation from Adjutant General School, Fort Benjamin Harrison, Indiana, with 99.48 Average (highest ever attained), 1974; 1975 Korea 8th United States Army Logistics Procurement Performance Award for Outstanding Operation and Control of Logistics Computer Program; Top Management Executive Awards, 1979, 1980. Address: U.S.A.C.C.J., Box 1061, A.P.O. San Francisco, California 96343.

Lee, Maria Berl

Maria B Lee

Free-Lance Writer. Personal: Born July 30, 1924; Daughter of Arthur and Gunda Berl; Married Ray E. Lee, Jr. Education: Early Education in Austria, Switzerland, France and the United States; B.A. magna cum laude, Nazareth College, Rochester, New York, 1946; M.A., Literature, Fordham University, New York, 1949. Career: Free-Lance Writer in English, German and French; Writes and Edits Books for International Institute of Rural Reconstruction, 1968 to present; Rare Books, John F. Fleming (Rosenbach), 1953-59; Interpreter and Translator, United States Embassy, Vienna, 1949-51. Organizational Memberships: PEN Club; Kappa Gamma Pi (writer); Austrian Forum (board member); National Writers Club; Society for German-American Studies; Society for German-American Authors; Nazareth College Alumni Association. Community Activities: Immigrants on Tape Program of United States Department of Interior, 1973-74; Poetry in Readings for the Blind and 9th Grade Literature Texts, 1979 to present; Invited to Read Works before American Association of Teachers of German, Atlanta, 1979; Invited as Observer/Delegate from United States to First Austrian Writers Congress, March 1981. Published Works: Writings for Kappa Gamma Pi, 1975 to present; Two German Books, *North American Mentor* (1973 to present), *Modus Operandi* (1974-80); Poetry in *Our Family* (1974), *Bitterroot* (1974 to present), *Poet Lore* (1977), *Reflect* (1981-82), *Echos* (1981), Others. Honors and Awards: Outstanding Alumni Award of Nazareth College, Rochester, New York, 1979; Novella Prize, Society of German-American Authors, 1976; Short Story Prizes, *Writers Digest* 1970 and *In a Nutshell* 1978; Citations of Merit, *North American Mentor* 1974, Society for German-American Studies 1974; National Writers

Club, 4 Poetry and Short Story Prizes, 1967-74; Second Prize, National Catholic Short Story Contest, 1945. Address: 69-46 Ingram Street, Forest Hills, New York 11375.

Lee, William J

Attorney, Administrator. Personal: Born January 13, 1924; Son of William J. Sr. and Arah A. Lee; Married Marjorie Y. Lee; Father of David W., James A. Education: Attended the University of Akron 1941-43, Denison University 1943-44, Harvard University Graduate School 1944-45; J.D., Ohio State University Law School, 1948. Military: Served in the Army Air Force 28th Combat Weather Squadron during World War II. Career: Research Assistant, The Ohio State University Law School, 1948-49; Attorney Examiner, Assistant Permit Chief, State Permit Chief and Ohio's Assistant State Liquor Control Director and Chief of Liquor Purchases, 1951-57; Assistant Counsel on Staff of Multi-Plant Manufacturing Corporation, Hupp Corporation, 1957-58; Part-time Instructor, College of Business Administration, Kent State University, Fall 1961, Winter 1961-62; Lawyer, General Practice, 1959-62; Admitted to Bar, State of Florida, 1962; Employed by Law Firm of Papy and Carruthers, 1962-63; Special Counsel, City of Ft. Lauderdale, 1963-65; Private Practice of Law, Fort Lauderdale, Florida, 1965-66; Assistant Attorney General, State of Ohio, 1966-70; Administrator, State Medical Board of Ohio, 1970 to present. Organizational Memberships: Broward County Bar Association; Akron Bar Association; Columbus Bar Association; Delta Theta Phi Legal Fraternity; Phi Kappa Tau; Ohio Association of Attorneys General. Community Activities: American Legion; Church Board, Melrose Park Methodist Church, Florida 1964-66; Pastoral Relations Committee, Epworth Methodist Church, Columbus, Ohio, 1977-78; Kiwanis International, Ravenna, Ohio (chairman, boys and girls committee, 1961-62); James D. Watson Chair, Ohio University College of Osteopathic Medicine (founder); Boy Scouts of America, Melrose Park Troop (awards chairman, 1965-66). Religion: Church of the Messiah United Methodist Church, Westerville, Ohio. Published Works: Served on the Editorial Board, *Ohio State Law Journal;* Author of Several Articles. Honors and Awards: American Legion School Award, 1937; American Legion Citation for Meritorious Service, 1966; Pi Kappa Delta; World War II Victory Medal, 1946; Jaguar Club of Central Ohio, Driving and Car Awards, 1979, 1980, 1981; Listed in *Who's Who in Ohio, Who's Who in Health Care, Who's Who in the Midwest, Who's Who in American Law, Personalities of the West and Midwest,* Publications of the International Biographical Institute, Cambridge, England. Address: 4893 Brittany Court West, Columbus, Ohio 43229.

Leedy, Emily L

State Government Official. Personal: Born September 24, 1921; Daughter of Raymond S. Foster; Married William N. Leedy; Mother of Dwight A. Education: B.S., Rio Grande College, 1949; M.Ed., Ohio University, 1957; Postgraduate Studies, Ohio State University, 1956; Michigan State University, 1958-59; Case Western Reserve University, 1963-65. Career: Teacher, Frankfort, Ohio, Public Schools, 1941-46; Teacher, Ross County Schools, Chillicothe, Ohio, 1948-53; Elementary and Supervising Teacher, Chillicothe City Schools, 1953-56; Dean of Girls, Secondary Teacher, Berea City Schools, Ohio, 1956-57; Visiting Teacher, Parma City Schools, Ohio, 1957-59; Teaching Fellow, Ohio University, 1960-62; Counselor, Homewood-Flossmoor High School, Flossmoor, Illinois, 1959-60; Associate Professor, Education, Ohio University; Counselor, Associate Professor, Cuyahoga Community College, Cleveland, 1964-66; Dean of Women, Cleveland State University, 1966-69; Director of Guidance, Cathedral Latin School, Cleveland, 1969-71; Director, Women's Services Division, Ohio Bureau of Employment Services, 1971 to present. Organizational Memberships: National Association of Women Deans, Administrators and Counselors (publications committee, 1967-69; continuing education committee, 1971-72; membership committee, 1971-72; professional employment practices committee, 1980 to present); Ohio Association of Women Deans, Administrators and Counselors (nominating committee, 1965-66; state program chairman, 1967; newsletter editor, 1976-81; status of women committee, 1969-71); American Personnel and Guidance Association (program national convention, 1962; delegate national assembly, 1959, 1962); National Vocational Guidance Association; Central Ohio Adult Education Association (board of directors, 1980 to 1982); Ohio School Counselors Association; Northeastern Ohio Personnel and Guidance Association (secretary, 1958-59; executive committee, 1963-64; public relations chairman, 1962-64); National Rehabilitation Counseling Association; Cleveland Counselors Association (secretary, 1964; vice president, 1965; president, 1964; secretary-treasurer, 1969). Community Activities: Council on Appalachian Women (vice president, board of directors, 1980 to 1981); League of Women Voters; American Association of University Women (Berea vice president, 1970-72); Cleveland Welfare Federation (group services council, 1964-76); Governor's Committee on the Status of Women (education subcommittees on counseling, continuing education); Southwest Cleveland Y.W.C.A. (board of management, 1964-70; youth committee chairman, 1964-70); Cleveland Metropolitan Y.W.C.A. (board of directors, 1966-72; chairman, youth committee, 1966; young adult study committee, 1967; program committee, 1966-70; public affairs committee, 1967-72; vice president, 1967; national convention delegate, 1967); Cleveland Council on the Status of Women (vice president, 1968-70; president, 1970-72); Ohio Commission on the Status of Women (board of trustees, 1970-72; vice president, 1970-71; president, 1971-72); Women's Equity Action League; Women's City Club of Cleveland; Zonta International (Berea Club: executive board, 1968-72; status of women chairman, 1967-72; alternate delegate, regional conference, 1968; treasurer, 1970-72; District V, Ohio, Kentucky and West Virginia: status of women chairman, 1971-73; international committee on the status of women, 1974-76; status of women chairman, 1980-82); Columbus Business and Professional Women's Club (finance chairman, 1976-77; legislative chairman, 1980 to 1982); Columbus Metropolitan Club; International Platform Association. Honors and Awards: Cleveland Area "Women of Achievement", 1969; International Certificate of Merit for Distinguished Service in Professional and Community Affairs, 1970; Ohio Business and Professional Women Nike Award, 1973; Atwood Achievement Award, Rio Grande College Alumni Association, 1975; Inducted into Ohio Women's Hall of Fame, 1979; Certificate of Merit from Agriculture, Home Economics and Natural Resources College Council, The Ohio State University, 1981; Alpha Kappa Delta; Phi Delta Gamma, Theta Chapter; Delta Kappa Gamma, Alpha Delta State Scholarship, 1971-73. Address: 580 Lindberg Blvd., Berea, Ohio 44017.

Leers, Wolf-Dietrich

Administrator. Personal: Born August 9, 1927; Son of Dr. W. R. Leers; Father of Ulrika, Dirk, Karen, Heiko. Education: Attended Medical School, University of Goettingen, Freiburg, Wuerzburg, Germany, 1949-55; M.D., University of Wuerzburg, West Germany, 1955; Diploma in Bacteriology, University of Toronto, 1967; Fellow, Royal College of Physicians and Surgeons, Canada. Military: Served in the German Navy, 1943-45, with the rank of Cadet. Career: Chief, Department of Microbiology, Wellesley Hospital, Toronto; Civil Aviation Medical Examiner for the Department of Transportation, Canada; Consultant for Microbiology, Extenicare Laboratories, Toronto. Organizational Memberships: Canada Society of Aviation Medicine; Canada Society of Microbiologists; Canada Society of Medical Microbiologists; Canada Public Health Association; American Society of Microbiologists; Canada Medical Association; Ontario Society of Medical Microbiologists (secretary/treasurer); Canada Society for Clinical Investigation; Canada Association of Infectious Disease and Medical Microbiology; Canada College of Microbiology. Community Activities: Counsellor for the Canadian Association of Clinical Microbiologists and Infectious Diseases. Honors and Awards: Fitzgerald Memorial Fellow, School of Hygiene, Faculty of Arts and Sciences, University of Toronto, 1963, 1964. Address: 1200 Royal York Road, Islington, Ontario, Canada.

Leeson, Janet Caroline

Company Executive, Artist. Personal: Born May 23, 1933; Daughter of Harold Arnold Tollefson (deceased); Sylvia Aino Makikangas (deceased); Married Raymond Harry Leeson; Mother of Warren Scott, Debra Dolores, Barry Raymond. Education: Attended Prairie State College and Cosmopolitan School of Business, 1973; Wilton Master School of Cake Decorating; Degree in Leadership Training. Career: President, Leesons Party Cakes, Inc., 1975 to present; Office Manager, Pat Carpenter Associates, 1975; Head of Foreign Trade Department, Wilton Enterprises, Inc., 1970-75; Co-Owner, Ra-Ja-Lee Television, 1962-68; Manager, Peak Service Cleaners, 1959-60; Teacher of Cake Decorating, J. C. Penney's, 1974-76. Organizational Memberships: Brementown Republican Organization; American Business Women's Association, Genesis Charter Chapter (public relations chairperson). Community Activities: Whittier Parent-Teacher Association, 1963-68; Cub Scouts (leader 1957-59); Girl Scouts and Brownies, 1962-66; Ingall Hospital Auxilliary, 1969 to present; Boy Scout Art Councellor, 1976 to present; C.A.R.B.A. Religion: Life Member, Lutheran Church Women, 1954 to present. Published Works: *Our Specialty Cakes*. Honors and Awards: Yearly Top Honors in Art, School Achievement Events; First Place in Portraits, Charcoal and Pencil, 1959-60; First Place, Sewing Adult, Third Place in Child Outfit, 1959-63; First Place, C.A.R.B.A. Convention, 1978; First Place, Wedding Cake Division, 1980; Listed in *Who's Who of American Women*. Address: 6713 W. 163rd Place, Tinley Park, Illinois 66477.

Janet C Leeson

LeGrand, Alberta Alane

Sales Associate. Personal: Born March 29, 1952; Daughter of Dr. and Mrs. F. E. LeGrand. Education: B.S., Oklahoma State University, 1974; M.A. 1975, Ph.D. 1982, University of Southern California. Career: Graduate Assistant and Assistant Basketball and Assistant Track Coach, University of Southern California, 1974-75; Instructor and Volleyball Coach, Biola University, 1975-76; Women's Athletic Director, Associate Professor, Women's Head Volleyball Coach, Azusa Pacific University, 1976-81; Head Counselor, Kanakuk Kamps, Branson, Missouri, Summers, 1970 to present; Century 21 Sales Associate, present. Organizational Memberships: National Association of Intercollegiate Athletics (vice president, women's national volleyball committee, 1980-81); Association for Intercollegiate Athletics for Women, Division III (chairman, women's All-American volleyball committee, 1980-81); California Collegiate Athletic Conference (president, 1979-81; Secretary, 1978-79); Azusa Pacific University (faculty athletic council, 1979-81; rank and salary committee, 1978-79). Community Activities: Youth Enterprises, Inc. (head volleyball coach for three week outreach tours to Mexico); La Mirada Volleyball Club (president and head volleyball coach, 1975-77); Kappa Delta Alumni Club (co-director, pledge class); Payne County 4-H Clubs (sponsor, bi-annual LeGrand Trophy at state livestock judging contests); California Interscholastic Federation (clinician director of volleyball and softball officials in West Covina area of Southern California); Easter Seals Campaign (garage sale and auction committee, 1982). Religion: Stillwater Christian Women's Club, 1981 to present; Athletes in Action, Women's Head Volleyball Coach, 1978-79; Evangelical Free Church, Fullerton, California, 1979; "I Found It" Campaign, Campus Crusade for Christ, Action Leaders Training, 1972-74, 1978; Sponsor Leaders on Campus. Honors and Awards: National N.A.I.A. Women's Volleyball Coach of the Year, 1980; N.A.I.A. National Championship Volleyball Team, Head Coach, 1980; A.I.A.W. Division III National Championship Volleyball Team, Head Coach, 1980; Top Six Outstanding Professors of Azusa Pacific University, 1981; Sigma Sigma Psi; Kappa Delta Pi; Oklahoma State University Alumni Association Award (top three graduating senior women), 1974; Mattie Ruth Gallagher Award, Outstanding Member of Kappa Delta Sorority, 1974; Gamma Gamma; Mary Ann Stewart Award, for Outstanding Leadership and Service to Oklahoma State University, 1973; Listed in *World's Who's Who of Women, Personalities of America, International Youth in Achievement, Directory of Distinguished Americans, Who's Who in California, Book of Honor, Outstanding Young Women in America, Personalities of the West and Midwest, Dictionary of International Biography*. Address: Route 3 Box 223, Stillwater, Oklahoma 74074.

Alberta A LeGrand

Lehrhoff, Irwin

Psychologist, Speech Pathologist. Personal: Born June 4, 1929; Married Barbara Lehrhoff; Father of Debra, Terri, Howard, Steven. Education: M.A. 1949, Ph.D. 1954, University of Southern California; Post-doctoral Training, Columbia University, New York; Studies at Rutgers and Princeton; Nine Years Training in Psychology and Communicative Disorders. Career: Certification from the State of California Board of Medical Examiniers and Board of Quality Assurance as Marriage, Family and Child Counselor (1964), Psychologist (1967), Speech Pathologist (1974); Certificate of Clinical Competence, American Speech and Hearing Association; Certified and Licensed in Speech Pathology, Psychology, and Marriage and Family Counseling; Director, Department of Communicative Disorders, Harbor General Hospital, Torrance, California, 1955-58; Private Practice, President of Irwin Lehrhoff and Associates, Practice Accredited by Board of Examiners of Speech, Pathology and Audiology, 1954 to present. Organizational Memberships: American Academy of Private Practice in Speech Pathology and Audiology (director and national president, 1974-78); American Association of Marriage and Family Counselors; American Orthophychiatric Association (fellow); Association for the Advancement of Science; American Psychological Association (member of four divisions); American Speech and Hearing Association; California Psychological Association; California Speech and Hearing Association; California Speech Patholigists and Audiologists in Private Practice (director and president, 1973-77); International Society of Mental Health; Los Angeles County Psychological Association; New York Academy of Science. Community Activities: American Academy of Child Psychiatry (advisory board); Reiss-Davis Child Study Center (board of trustees, 12 years; former chairman, Reiss-Davis budget, personnel and development committees; founder, women's division; former chairman, Reiss-Davis president's committee); Thalians Community Mental Health Center, Cedar-Sinai Medical Center (board of directors, first vice president, executive committee, executive vice chairman, chairman of nominating committee, chairman of hospital liaison committee); Thalians Presidents Club (founder, chairman); District Attorneys Advisory Council; Presidents Circle and Cardinal and Gold, University of Southern California. Published Works: "Speech Problems in Children" 1958, "An Experimental Study of Auditory Threshold Acuity in Children with Cerebral Palsy by PGSR and Other Techniques" 1958, "A Study of PGSR Testing of RH Athetoids" 1961, "Pathogenesis and Treatment of Vocal Nodules" 1962, "Speech Problems in Children", Numerous Other Articles Published in Speech, Psychology and Medical Journals. Honors and Awards: Listed in *American Men of Science, Who's Who in American Education, Who's Who in the West, Leaders in American Science, National Register of Prominent Americans and International Notables, Personalities of the West and Midwest*. Address: One Roxbury Plaza, Suite 1200, 9701 Wilshire Blvd., Beverly Hills, California 90212.

Leiferman, Irwin Hamilton

Consultant, Foundation Executive. Personal: Born January 8, 1907, in Chicago, Illinois; Son of Beril and Ida Rosenbaum Leiferman; Married Silvia Weiner. Education: Attended Crane Junior College 1923, Northwestern University 1924-29. Career: Consultant, Leiferman Investment Company; Co-Founder, President, Silvia and Irwin H. Leiferman Foundation; Founder, Greater Technion Israel Institute of Technology 1972, and Mt. Sinai Hospital 1969; Chairman of the Board, Hamilton Industries, 1964; Vice President, Comet Productions 1964, Bet-R-Lite Company 1940-46; President, Beaumont Electric Supply Company 1940-46, Leiferman Investment Company, Winston Lamp and Shade 1948-55, Illinois Wire Goods Company, Hamilton Industries 1931-64; Purchasing

Agent and Executive, Hamilton-Ross Coporations, 1924-30. Organizational Memberships: Brandeis University (executive advisory committee 1961-62); Bonds for Israel (national board of governors); B'nai B'rith, Temple Sholom, Brandeis University (life member); Lowe's Gala (honorary committee 1972); Art Institute of Chicago (life member); Miami Museum of Modern Art (life member); Nathan Goldblatt Society for Cancer Research (life member); United States Department of Labor (industry committee, 1940); Chicago Association of Commerce and Industry; Illinois Manufacturer's Association; B'nai B'rith; International Platform Association, 1968. Community Activities: Illinois Chamber of Commerce; Friends of Lowe's Museum; American Contract Bridge Association; Jewish Home for the Aged Men's Club; Bayshore Service Club; Executive Club, Chicago; Runaway Bay Club, Miami Beach; Jockey Club and Brickell Bay, Miami, 1974; Royal Ballet Society of Miami (patron); Lowe's Museum of Miami; Philharmonic Society of Miami; Greater Miami Cultural Art Center; Donations to Gift Shop and Seventh Floor Reception Room of Edgewater Hospital, Conference Room of Mary Lawrence Jewish Children's Bureau, Leiferman Award, City of Hope, Yeshiva University, University of Southern California, Waiting Room of the Radiology Building at Mt. Sinai Hospital. Honors and Awards: Army and Navy "E" Award 1945; Special Awards, Mt. Sinai Hospital (for patriotic cooperation with the nation's War Bond Program); Mighty Seventh War Loan; Recognition of Leadership and Achievement, Secretary Treasury, State of Israel; Award, United States Department of Labor; Listed in *Who's Who in Commerce and Industry, Who's Who in the Midwest, Who's Who in the South and Southwest, Who's Who in America, Who's Who in World Jewry, Who's Who in Finance and Industry, Dictionary of International Biography, Royal Blue Book, Community Leaders of America, Board of Governors of the Library of Who's Who, Personalities of the South, Book of Honor.* Address: 5445 Collins Avenue, Apt. 14B-C, Miami Beach, Florida 33140; La Costa Hotel and Spa, Carlsbad, California 92008; Standard Club, 320 South Plymouth Court, Chicago, Illinois.

Leiferman, Silvia Weiner

Artist, Foundation Executive. Personal: Born in Chicago, Illinois; Daughter of Annah Caplan Weiner; Married Irwin Hamilton Leiferman in 1947. Education: Studies at the University of Chicago, 1960-61; Studies in Design and Painting, Chicago, Rome, Mexico, Madrid, Massachusetts. Career: Chairman of the Board, Former Vice President and Secretary, Leiferman Investment Company; Co-Founder, Vice President, Silvia Leiferman Foundation; President, Active Accesories by Silvia, 1964 to present; One-Woman Shows, including the Miami Museum of Art, Schram Galleries of Fort Lauderdale, Contemporary Gallery of Palm Beach, D'Arcy Galleries of New York City; Group Shows, including Lowe Art Museum, Artist's Equity at Crystal House Gallery, Barry College, Gallery 99 of Miami, Hollywood Museum of Art. Organizational Memberships: Art Institute of Chicago (life member); International Platform Association, American Federation of Arts, Royal Society of Arts and Sciences, Artist Equity Association, International Council of Museums. Community Activities: Miami Ballet Society-Bal Masque (international chairman); Nathan Goldblatt Hospital (trustee, life member); Mount Sinai Hospital of Miami Beach (founder); Brandeis University (life board member); Lowe Art Museum, University of Miami (board member); Nathan Goldblatt Society for Cancer Research (former member, board of directors); Hebrew University (charter member, board for the women's division); State of Israel (former chairwoman for the special sales and special events Greater Chicago committee, originator of the Ambassador's Ball 1956, former chairwomen Dior-Israel fashion preview, originator and chairwoman of the Presentation Ball 1963-64, 1965); Bonds for Israel (national board of governors, Greater Chicago board of governors). Honors and Awards: Distinguished Service Award, Queen Elizabeth II, 1975; Woman of Valor, State of Israel, 1963; United States Government Citations for Defense Bond Sales; Donor Awards, Miami Heart Institute and Michael Reese Hospital of Chicago; 1969 Edition of *Two Thousand Women of Achievement* Dedicated in Her Honor; Listed in *Community Leaders and Noteworthy Americans, Notable Americans of 1976-77, Who's Who in Finance and Industry, Who's Who of American Women, Who's Who in America, Who's Who in American Art, Who's Who in International Art and Antiques, Book of Honor,* Others. Address: 5445 Collins Avenue, Miami Beach, Florida 33140; La Costa Hotel and Spa, Carlsbad, California 92008; Standard Club, 320 South Plymouth Court, Chicago, Illinois.

Silvia Leiferman

Leininger, Madeleine M

Professor, Administrator. Personal: Born November 13, 1925, in Sutton, Nebraska. Education: Diploma in Nursing, St. Anthony's School of Nursing, Denver, Colorado, 1948; B.S. 1950, Lh.D. (honorary) 1975, Benedictine College (formerly Mount St. Scholastica College), Atchison, Kansas; Graduate Studies in Nursing Administration, Creighton University, 1950-52; Graduate Studies in Curriculum and Social Sciences, University of Cincinnati, 1955-58; M.S.N., Psychiatric Nursing, Catholic University of America, Washington, D.C., 1954; Ph.D., Anthropology, University of Washington, Seattle, 1965; Post-Doctoral Workshops, Conferences and Studies in the United States and Abroad, 1965 to present. Career: Professor of Nursing and Anthropology, Wayne State University, Director of Center for Health Research, Detroit, Michigan, 1981 to present; Distinguished visiting Professor of Nursing, Anise J. Sorrell chairholder, Troy State University System, Troy, Alabama, 1981; Professor of Nursing, College of Nursing, Adjunct Professor of Anthropology, University of Utah, Salt Lake City, 1974 to 1981; Dean and Professor of Nursing, College of Nursing, University of Utah, Salt Lake City, 1974-81; Dean and Professor of Nursing, School of Nursing, Lecturer in Anthropology, University of Washington, Seattle, 1969-74; Professor of Nursing and Anthropology, University of Colorado, Boulder and Denver Campuses, and Director of Pscyhiatric Nursing Program, Nurse-Scientist Ph.D. Program, 1966-69; Research Associate, Department of Anthropology, University of Washington, Seattle, 1964-65; Research Fellow, Eastern Highlands of New Guinea, 1960-62; Associate Professor of Nursing and Director of the Graduate Program in Psychiatric Nursing, College of Nursing, University of Cincinnati, 1954-60; Instructor, Staff and Head Nurse of Medical-Surgical Unit, Supervisor of Psychiatric Unit, St. Joseph's Hospital, Omaha, Nebraska, 1950-54; Primary Care College Health Nurse, Mount St. Scholastica College, Atchison, Kansas, 1948-50; Staff Nurse in Medical-Surgical Nursing and Operating Room, St. Anthony's Hospital, Denver, Colorado, 1948. Organizational Memberships: Sigma Theta Tau, National Honor Society of Nursing. Published Works: Author of 14 books, the most recent being *Care: An Essential Human Need,* 1981; *Transcultural Nursing Theory, Research and Practice;* Author of 150 published articles and 15 video films in social sciences, nursing and health care. Honors and Awards: Given more than 330 public addresses; Field Visits since 1975 in Ten Countries including The People's Republic of China in 1982; First Distinguished Guest Speaker, Lucy Harris Linn Institute, 1976; Pi Gamma Mu; Fellowship, National League of Nursing, for Graduate Study at the University of Washington, 1960-63; Delta Kappa Gamma, National Honorary Society of Education; Outstanding Alumni Award, Catholic University of America, 1969; Alpha Tau Delta, Honorary Member, 1974; Honorary Doctorate of Humane Letters, Benedictine College, 1975; Nurse of the Year, District I, Utah Nurses Association, 1976; Utah Nurses Association Literary Award for Outstanding Achievement in the Area of Nursing Literature, 1978; Award of Recognition for Unique and Significant Contributions to the American Association of Colleges of Nursing, 1976; 1976 Books of the Year Award for *Transcultural Health Care Issues and Conditions,* American Journal of Nursing; First American Nurse to Give Keynote Address for the Annual Scholarly Nursing and the Victorian Order of Nurses, Winnipeg, Canada, 1978; Society for Sigma Xi, University of Utah, 1978; Keynote Presentation at the Second Annual Nurse Educator Conference, New York City, 1978; Fellow, American Anthropolgical Society; Fellow, American Academy of Nursing, American Nurses Association; Chosen as First American Nurse to give Annual Scholarly Nursing Lecture for the Victoria Order of Nurses, Manitoba, Canada, 1978; Listed in *American Men and Women of Science, Dictionary of International Biography, Leaders in Anthropology, A.A.A. Encyclopedia of Who's Who of Leaders and Their Contributions to the Discipline, Leaders in Education, Outstanding Educators of America, National Register of Prominent Americans and International Notables, National Register of*

Prominent Community Leaders, Who's Who in the West, Who's Who of American Women, Women Leaders in Higher Education, Who's Who in Health Care, World Who's Who of Women, Inernational Who's Who in Community Service, Who's Who of Community Leaders. Address: 333 Covington Drive 3-B, Detroit, Michigan 48203.

Leitner, Stanley Allen

Chairman of the Board. Personal: Born September 11, 1938; Son of Perry O. (deceased) and Ruth A. Leitner; Married Janet Sherman; Father of Stacy. Education: B.A., University of Bordeaux. Military: Served in the United States Army, 1955-58. Career: Chairman of the Board, Weapons Corporation of America. Religion: Protestant. Published Works: Author of Book *Last Chance to Live.* Honors and Awards: Most Humerous Businessman of the Year, Humor Society of America, 1977. Address: 1593 Foxham, Chesterfield, Missouri 63017.

LeMaster, David Ray

Petroleum Landman. Personal: Born December 4, 1935; Son of A. B. (deceased) and Ruth LeMaster; Married J. Mosolete (Mossie) Fowlkes; Father of Davey J., Marvin A. B. II, Chyree Mosolete. Education: A.A. Odessa College, 1956; B.Ş., West Texas State University, 1957; M.Ed., Sul Ross State University; Ed.D., Texas Tech University, 1982. Military: Served in the United States Air Force, 1961-70, and United States Air Force Reserve, 1970 to present, to Lieutenant Colonel. Career: Petroleum Landman, Gulf Oil Corporation; Former Educator, United States Air Force Officer. Organizational Memberships: American Association of Petroleum Landmen; Permian Basin Landman's Association; Reserve Officers Association; Air Force Association; National Education Association; Texas State Teachers Association; Classroom Teachers Association. Community Activities: Appointed by Governor to Texas Professional Practices Commission, 1980-81; President, John the Apostle Sunday School Class, 1980; Robert E. Lee (Frosh) High School Parent-Teacher Association (president, 1982; presented life membership, 1980); Circle K (vice president); International Club (president); Phi Theta Kappa (vice president). Religion: Midland (Texas) First Baptist Church, Deacon, Sunday School Teacher; Former Education Director, Calvary Baptist Church, Midland. Honors and Awards: Commendation by Korean Air Force Chief of Staff, 1968; Commendation by Korean Air Force Academy Superintendent, 1968; United States Air Force Commendation Medal, 1969 (presented at Georgia Tech). Address: 3312 West Michigan, Midland, Texas 79703.

Lemke, Arthur Athniel

Retired Engineer. Personal: Born February 26, 1913; Son of Frederick William and Ruth Hauser Lemke (both deceased); Married Rosalie Lyga. Education: B.S.C.E. 1934, M.S.C.E. 1935, C.E. 1946, University of Wisconsin. Career: Retired Hydraulic and Environmental Engineer, Consultations since 1978; Supervisor, Process Engineering and Senior Project Engineer, Patent Liaison and Consultant, Environmental Equipment Division, FMC Corporation, Chicago and Itasca, Illinois; also the following positions in the same company in chronological order: Sanitary Engineer, Senior Sanitary Engineer, Assistant Manager and Manager of Application Engineering; Manager of Hydraulic and Equipment Engineering 1942-78; Instrumentman, Chief of Party, Chicago Park District, 1940-42; Instructor of Civil Engineering, Lewis Institute, Chicago (later Illinois Institute of Technology), 1936-40; Junior Chemist, Engineering Aide, Wisconsin Highway Commission, 1935. Organizational Memberships: American Society of Civil Engineers (fellow, life member); American Academy of Environmental Engineers (life member); Water Pollution Control Federation (life member); International Association of Hydraulic Research. Religion: Protestant, Member of Church Choir Many Years. Honors and Awards: Phi Eta Sigma; Chi Epsilon; Patentee of Various Patents Relating to Waste Treatment, 1946-78; Professional Engineering Registration in States of Wisconsin and Illinois. Address: 3329 Noyes Street, Evanston, Illinois 60201.

Lenher, Iréné Kirkland

Artist, Homemaker. Personal: Born October 4, 1907; Married Samuel Lenher; Mother of John Kirkland, Ann L. Robinson, George Victor. Education: Attended Slade School of Art, London University and Grande Chaumiere, Paris, France; Honorary M.A., University of Delaware. Career: Staff Artist, *Cokesbury Courier;* Former Teacher, Tutor, Roedean School, Johannesburg, South Africa. Organizational Memberships; Studio Group (past president); Society of Mayflower Descendants, State of Delaware (past governor); National League of American Pen Women, State of Delaware (past president). Community Activities: Established and Operated Regional Art Exhibition, University of Delaware, Ten Years; Junior Board Delaware Division Wilmington Medical Center (associate); Delaware Art Museum (accessions committee); Philadelphia Museum of Art (women's committee); Rehoboth Art League, Rehoboth, Delaware (life member). Honors and Awards: Awarded Best in Show, Oil on Canvas, "Cocktail Party", 1955; Second Prize, Oil on Canvas, "Driftwood", 1962; Second Prize, National League of American Pen Women, "Mewensha Dock", 1962; Award of Merit, Watercolor, "Things of the Sea", 1961; "Sudden Squall in Rodney Square" Presented by Governor Carvel to Governor of Tokyo, 1963; Other Awards for Art. Address: 50 Cokesbury Village, Hockessin, Delaware 19707.

Leonard, Lawrence Le Roy Jr

Family Counselor. Personal: Born November 28, 1943; Son of Lawrence and Elizabeth Leonard. Education: B.A., Pacific College, 1972; Postgraduate Study at Columbia University, 1975; D.D. 1979, Ph.D. 1980, Ms.D. 1981, Universal Life Church. Military: Served in the United States Marine Corps, 1963-69, attaining the rank of Sergeant. Career: Family Counselor in Private Practice; President, Paper Talk; Chairman, Board of Trustees, Universal Life Church of St. Albans; President, Leonard Associates; Previously, Editor, *Axis* Magazine; Professional Photographer; Musician; Artist; Inventor. Organizational Memberships: International Platform Association, 1981. Community Activities: Southeast Queens Citizens Against Crime, 1978; Agency for Child Development (chairman, counselor's action committee, 1976); Community Liaison, Southeast Queens, New York, 1974-76; Amistad Child Care Center (supervisor, parents activity committee, 1974-76); Boy Scouts of America (scoutmaster, 1974); Creative Arts Festival, Amistad (producer, 1975); Fordham University Student Union (consultant, 1973-74); Community Music Festival, Neighborhood Services (producer, 1973); Camp Hayden Marks Fresh Air Fund (village leader, 1973); Bill Dave Club (counselor, baseball coach, 1972-73); San Diego City College (campus mediator, 1968); Civilian Volunteer Patrol Program, New York City (Marshall, 1974); Flippers Tumbling Team (coach, 1974); Recreational Park Director, Neighborhood Services, 1974; Neighborhood Services Economic Development Program (youth director, 1973-74). Religion: Minister, Universal Life Church, 1972 to present. Honors and Awards: Commendation, District Attorney, Queens County, New York, 1981; Commendation, Special Projects Coordinator, Day Care Council, New York, 1978; Commendation, Chance Program, Department of Social Services, New York City, 1975; Honorable Discharge, United States Marine Corps, 1969; Certificate of Appreciation, Disabled American Veterans, 1967; Recipient of Honors, French Consul, Marseilles, France, 1965; Tarawa Award for Excellence in Leadership, United States Marine Corps, 1964. Address:

179-71 Anderson Road, St. Albans, New York 11434.

Lessenberry, Robert Adams

Retail Executive. Personal: Born May 7, 1926, in Glasgow, Kentucky; Son of Robert Long and Hugh Barret Adams Lessenberry (both deceased); Married Mary Lloyd Howard, December 26, 1946; Father of Robert Howard, Hugh Barret Adams, Leigh Langford. Education: B.A., Centre College of Kentucky, 1950. Military: Served in the United States Army, 1944-46, rising through the ranks to Lieutenant Infantry; Captain Field Artillery, 1950-53. Career: Secretary-Treasurer, Vice-President, President, Director, Hardware Wholesalers Inc., 1973-79; President, Lessenberry Building Centre, Inc., 1953 to present; President 1965 to present, Treasurer, 1964, The Glasgow Railway Company, Inc.; President, Lessenberry Development Company, Inc., 1969 to present; President, Lessenberry Electric and Plumbing Center, Inc., 1973 to present; Vice President, Modern Manor Park, 1973-76; Partner 1959-80, Owner 1980 to present, Parkview Development Company; Partner, Lessenberry Enterprises, 1968 to present; Owner, Lessenberry Real Estate, 1972 to present. Organizational Memberships: Kentucky Retail Lumber and Building Material Dealers Association (director, 1977-80); Indiana-Kentucky Hardward Association (president, vice president, director, 1975 to present). Community Activities: Glasgow-Barren County Board of Realtors (director, 1979 to present); Glasgow Urban Renewal and Community Development Agency (chairman, 1979-81); Glasgow Electric Plant Board, 1978 to present; Barren River Area Development Council (director, 1969-72); Municipal Housing (board member, 1966-68); Glasgow Water Commission (chairman, 1966-68); Mayor, City of Glasgow, 1966-68; Finance Chairman, City of Glasgow, 1962-66; Glasgow City Council, 1962-66; Kentucky Independent College Foundation (trustee, 1972 to present); 32nd Degree Shriner, York and Scottish Rite; Parent Teacher Association (president, 1953-58); Glasgow Rotary Club (past president; director, 1954 to present); Glasgow Chamber of Commerce (director); Barren County Red Cross (director); Westminster Terrance Presbyterian Home for Senior Citizens and Health Care Centre, Louisville (president, board of trustees, 1968-79); Executive Council Louisville Presbytery (vice chairman, 1962-66). Religion: Presbyterian Elder, 1952 to present; Church School Teacher, 1963-67; Choir Director, 1953-68. Honors and Awards: Expert Infantry Badge, United States Army; Sigma Chi Balfour Award, Kentucky-Tennessee Province, 1949; Omicron Delta Kappa Honorary Leadership Fraternity, 1950; Honorary Citizen, Metro Nashville; Kentucky Colonel, 1967; Decorated Bronze Star with Cluster. Address: 913 South Green Street, Glasgow, Kentucky 42141.

Virginia L Lester

Lester, Virginia Laudano

Professor, Administrator. Personal: Born January 5, 1931 in Philadelphia, Pennsylvania; Daughter of Mr. and Mrs. Edmund F. Laudano; Mother of Pamela, Valerie. Education: B.A., The Pennsylvania State University, 1952; M.Ed., Temple University, 1955; Ph.D., Union Graduate School, Union for Experimenting Colleges and Universities, Cincinnati, 1972. Career: President, Professor of Interdisciplinary Studies, Mary Baldwin College, 1976 to present; Acting Dean, Statewide Programs, Empire State College, State University of New York, Saratoga Springs, 1976; Senior Associate Dean and Associate Professor, Statewide Programs, Empire State College, State University of New York, 1975-76; Consulting Core Faculty, Union Graduate School, 1975 to present; Associate Dean and Assistant Professor, Statewide Programs, Empire State College, 1973-75; Administrative Internship, Goddard College, Summer 1971; Skidmore College, Assistant to the President 1968-72, Director of Educational Research 1967-72, Part-Time Instructor Education Department 1962-64; Assistant Director, Capitol District Regional Supplemental Education Center, E.S.E.A., Title III, Albany, New York, 1966-67; First Grade Substitute Teacher, Greenfield Center, New York, 1956; Kindergarten Teacher, Abington Township Public Schools, Pennsylvania, 1954-55; Fifth Grade Teacher, Abington Township Public Schools, 1952-54; Consultant to Numerous Organizations including New York State Education Department, Bureau of College Evaluation and Bureau of Management and Planning Services, Vermont State College System, National Conference on Drug Abuse Training, Boston Visual Artists Union; Presenter for the American Association on Higher Education, Washington Dialogue on Social Policy, Council for the Advancement of Small Colleges, United Ministries in Higher Education, Others; Visiting Scholar Lecturer, Virginia Polytechnic Institute and State University 1979, University of Virginia 1981. Organizational Memberships: American Association of Higher Education; American Academy of Political and Social Sciences; The Conference Board (chairman, southeastern conference, winter 1981); American Council on Education (program design committee, 1981 annual meeting); Virginia Foundation for Independent Colleges (board member, 1976 to present); Council of Independent Colleges in Virginia (board member, 1976 to present); Association of Virginia Colleges (secretary/treasurer, 1978; vice-president, 1979; president, 1980); National Center for Higher Education Management Systems (board member, 1978-81; chairperson, implementation and evaluation committee, 1979; executive committee, 1979; fiscal affairs and operations committee, 1980 to present; executive committee, 1981; organization and memberships committee, 1981); Council for the Advancement of Small Colleges, Mid-Atlantic Region Representative (board member, 1978-81); National Association of Independent Colleges and Universities (board member, 1978-80; intrassociation president committee on accreditation); National Urban League (board member, 1979-82); Southern Bank (board member, 1980 to present; trust committee); New Virginia Review, Inc. (board member, 1981-81). Community Activities: Saratoga Springs Housing Board of Appeals, 1966-76; Saratoga Springs Chamber of Commerce (promotion committee, 1971; vice-president, 1957-59; secretary, 1962-64); Saratoga Springs Board of Education (citizen's advisory committee, 1964-70); Saratoga Springs Youth Employment Service (director, 1965); Saratoga Springs High School Selection Committee (chairperson, 1965); Virginia Governor's Advisory Committee Awards for the Arts, 1979; Community Arts Project (advisor, 1981). Published Works: Number of Professional Articles including "Adult Learning in the Context of Adult Development: Life Cycle Research and Empire State College Students", 1979; "Life Stages and Learning Interests", 1979 & 1981; "The Biggest Changes Must Come Within Ourselves", 1978. Honors and Awards: Freshman School of Education Award; Chimes, Junior Women's Honor Society; Pi Lambda Theta Education Honor Society; Pi Gamma Mu Social Science Honor Society; Pioneer of the Year, Distinguished High School Alumni Award, Frankford High School Alumni Association; Listed in *Who's Who in America, Personalities of the South, World Who's Who of Women, Dictionary of International Biography*. Address: 240 Kable Street, Staunton, Virginia 24401.

Harold A Levenson

Levenson, Harold Altman

Insurance Company Executive. Personal: Born May 2, 1919; Son of Samuel R. and Sadie D. Levenson (both deceased); Father of Lisa Lyn, Linda A. Randovan. Education: Life Underwriting Courses. Military: Served in the United States Army, 1941-44. Career: Insurance Agent, Occidental Life Insurance Company, Pasadena, California, 1950; General Agent, Guaranty Union Life Insurance Company, Beverly Hills, California, 1951-63; President, Harold Levenson Associates, 1963 to present; General Agent, United Life and Accident Insurance Company, 1958 to present. Community Activities: Million Dollar Round Table (life member); Greater Los Angeles Press Club; Academy of Magical Arts of Hollywood; Masquers Club (first vice president; chairman, finance committee); TWA Ambassadors, American Airlines Admirals Club; 1 Million Mile Club of United Airlines. Honors and Awards: Produced "The Pleasure of His Company" 1962, "Born Yesterday" 1963, "Abie's Irish Rose" 1963, "Flame Out", "Harvey", "Tom Jones", "There's a Girl in my Soup"; Testimonial Dinner and Award Presentation; Listed in *Who's Who in the West, Who's Who in Commerce and Industry, Who's Who in California, Who's Who in Life Insurance, Million Dollar Directory, Community Leaders and Noteworthy*

Americans, Notable Americans. Address: 7250 Franklin Avenue, Apt. 1104, Los Angeles, California 90046.

Levine, Suzanne

Managing Editor. Personal: Native New Yorker. Education: Graduate, cum laude, Radcliffe College, 1963. Career: Editor and Writer, *Seattle Magazine*, 1963; Reporter, Time/Life Books, 1965; Feature Editor, *Mademoiselle* Magazine, 1966; Associate Articles Editor, *McCall's*, 1969; Freelance Writer, Published in *Ladies Home Journal, Cosmopolitan, Today's Health*, 1970; Managing Editor, *Sexual Behavior Magazine*, 1971, Managing Editor, *Ms.* Magazine, 1972 to present. Organizational Memberships: American Society of Magazine Editors (member of the executive committee); Women in Communications (consultant for "A National Certificate Program"); Women's Media Group (board of directors); Women's Action Alliance (executive committee). Published Works: Co-Editor, *The Decade of Women: A Ms. History of the Seventies in Words and Pictures*, February 1980; Executive Producer, one-hour documentary "How to Be a Real Woman: American Women in the Twentieth Century". Honors and Awards: Listed in *Outstanding Women in Communications, Who's Who in America*. Address: 119 West 40th Street, New York, New York 10018.

Lew, Karen Leslie

Information Officer. Personal: Born February 19, 1942; Mother of Kent Charles, Danika Leslie, Mark Daren; Daughter of Lyman and Betsy Woodman. Education: Attended San Francisco State College 1960-61, El Camino Junior College 1966, University of California-Los Angeles 1967, University of Alaska-Anchorage 1971, 1975, 1977, Sheldon Jackson College 1979; Anchorage Community College 1980, 1981, 1982. Career: Information Officer, State of Alaska, Department of Natural Resources, 1979 to present; Advertising Representative/Writer, *Alaskafest* Magazine, 1979; Advertising Manager, *Alaska Advocate*, 1977-78; Copywriter/Continuity Director, KYAK/KGOT-FM, 1976-77; Media Specialist, Alaska Native Commission on Alcoholism and Drug Abuse, 1974-75; Classified Advertising Manager, *Anchorage Daily News*, 1973-74; Copywriter/Media Buyer, Graphix West, 1972-73; Copywriter/Continuity Director, KYAK Radio, 1971-72; Administrative Assistant, Mike Ellis Advertising, 1971; Information Specialist, ITT Arctic Services, Inc., 1969-71. Organizational Memberships: Alaska Press Women (member, 1971 to present; past vice president; current recording secretary); National Federation of Press Women (member, 1971 to present); Public Relations Society of America (member, 1979 to present). Community Activities: LaLeche League (instructor, 1962-68); Citizen's Advisory Educational Concerns Committee, 1980-82; Language Arts Curriculum Committee, 1980-82; Anchorage School District Community Resources Speaker, 1977-78; Anchorage Chess Club (publicity chairperson, 1976); United States Chess Federation, 1975-80; Anchorage Council on Alcoholism (2nd vice president, 1976); Anchorage Community Chorus; Theatre Guild, Inc; Volunteer Publicity Work for Anchorage Community Theatre, Anchorage Civic Opera, University of Alaska-Anchorage Theatre Department, Anchorage Arts Council, Sitka Summer Music Festival (donor), Southeast Alaska Regional Arts Council, Alaska Zoo (donor). Religion: Unitarian (Anchorage Liberal Religious Youth, Coordinator, 1976). Honors and Awards: Writing Awards from Alaska Press Women, Alaska Press Club, One of Top Ten Writers in National Federation of Women for 1972; Listed in *Who's Who in American Women, Who's Who in the West*. Address: 3120 West 79th Avenue, Anchorage, Alaska 99502.

Erv Lewis

Lewis, Barbara S

Personal Banker. Personal: Born December 23, 1944; Daughter of Rosa Belle Shannon; Mother of Youlanda A. Education: Graduate of Williston Senior High School, 1963; Studies in Secretarial Science, Durham Business College, 1966. Career: Personal Banker, Wachovia Bank and Trust Company; Past Secretary, National Association for the Advancement of Colored People. Organizatonal Memberships: American Business Women's Association. Community Activities: New Hanover County Hearing Board, 1981-82; Women's Auxiliary Community Boys Club (secretary, 1981-82); Williston Alumni Association. Religion: Mt. Nebo Baptist Church, Secretary, Usher Board #2. Address: 919 Ann Street, Wilmington, North Carolina 28401.

Lewis, Benjamin Pershing

Administrator. Personal: Born June 2, 1942; Son of Juanita Lewis Applewhite; Married Patricia Glover; Father of Laura Denise, Jason Matthew. Education: B.S. 1966, M.S. 1972, Auburn University. Military: Service with the United States Public Health Service, 1976 to present. Career: Health Scientist Administrator, Office of Orphan Products Development, F.D.A.; Head, Professional Labeling Bureau, Bureau of Drugs, Food and Drug Administration; Pharmacy Officer, University States Army, El Paso (Texas) and Fort Rucker (Alabama); Instructor, School of Pharmacy, Auburn University; Practicing Pharmacist, 1966-69. Organizational Memberships: American Pharmaceutical Association; Sigma Xi Research Society; Commissioned Officers Association of the United States Public Health Service; Phi Lambda Sigma Pharmacy Honorary, 1964-66. Community Activities: Adjunct Assistant Professor, Auburn University. Published Works: Author of 14 Scientific Papers and 1 Book (*Veterinary Drug Index*, 1982). Honors and Awards: Music Scholarship, 1960-62; Mr. Pharmacy Award, Auburn University, 1966; Listed in *Who's Who in the East, American Men and Women in Science*. Address: 9615 Marston Lane, Gaithersburg, Maryland 20879.

Lewis, Erv

Purchasing Manager. Personal: Born August 19, 1936; Son of Mr. and Mrs. Henry J. Lewis; Father of Hal, Pamela, Steven, Cynthia. Education: Attended The Citadel, Charleston, South Carolina; Certified Purchasing Manager. Military: Served with United States Naval Reserve, 1953-56; Served with United States Army National Guard, 1956-59; Served with United States Army Reserve, 1959-61. Career: Current Purchasing Manager; Former Photographer, Singer/Guitarist, Phono Record Producer. Organizational Memberships: Purchasing Management Association of Carolinas and Virginia (member of board of directors, chairman of professional development and scholarship committees). Community Activities: Parent-Teacher Association (president, 1961); Junior Chamber of Commerce, 1959-61; Boy Scout Leader, 1961; Coach of Golden Gloves Boxing Program, 1960-64; Director, Teen Crusade, Inc., 1975-78; Director, Jerry Arhelger Evangelistic Association, 1980 to present; Board of Advisors of Happenings, Inc., (christian outreach), 1978 to present; Organized and directed the Canadian-American Folk Music Festival, 1965-76; Local Director of Boy Scout fund raising, 1970-71; Local Director of United Fund, 1975; Member, Gospel Music Association; Fellowship of Christian Athletes; Fellowship of Contemporary Christian Ministries; Fellowship of Christians in Art, Media and Entertainment. Religion: Active Christian speaker, singer, songwriter and recording artist for Herald Records, in the U.S. and Europe (president, Erv Lewis Christian Outreach, Inc.). Honors and Awards: Citation from Mayor of Tampa, Florida for outstanding purpose in life; National Communications Award for promotion of basic human understanding through music; Key to the City of Florence, South Carolina, 1980; Listed in *Personalities of the South, International Who's Who of Intellectuals, Dictionary of International Biography, Men of Achievement, Personalities of America*. Address: P.O. Box 218, Wellman Heights, Johnsonville, South Carolina 29555.

Li, Choh-Luh

Clinical Professor. Personal: Born September 19, 1919, in Kwangchow, China; Married Julia Y. R. Li; Father of Claire-Ming, David-Yuan, Anne-Ling. Education: M.D., National Medical College of Shanghai, China, 1942; M.S. Neuroanatomy 1950, Ph.D. Neurophysiology 1954, McGill University, Canada. Career: Clinical Professor, Department of Neurosurgery, George Washington University School of Medicine, 1974 to present; Medical Officer, Neurosurgery, National Institute of Health, N.I.N.C.D.S., Department of Health, Education and Welfare, 1978 to present; Associate Neurosurgeon, National Institute of Health, N.I.N.C.D.S., 1955-78; Chief, Section of Experimental Neurosurgery, National Institute of Neurological Diseases and Blindness, N.I.H., Bethesda, Maryland, 1954-55; Research Fellow, Neuroanatomy, Senior Resident in Neurosurgery, Resident in Neurology, in Electroencephalography and Electromyography, Research Fellow in Neurophysiology and Instructor in Neuroanatomy, Montreal Neurological Institute, Canada, 1947-54; Assistant Resident in Medicine, Resident and Instructor in Surgery, National Medical College of Shanghai, 1942-47. Organizational Memberships: New York Academy of Sciences; American Academy of Neurology; Washington Academy of Neurosurgery; American Association for the Advancement of Science; American E.E.G. Society; American Society for Electromyography of Electrodiagnosis; American Society for Experimental Biology; American Society of Physiology; Chinese Medical Society in the United States; Society of Neuroscience; International Association for the Study of Pain; American Epilepsy Society; International Platform Association. Honors and Awards: Fellow, American Bureau of Medical Aid to China; Sigma Xi; Member, Editorial Board of *Journal E.E.G. and Clinical Neurophysiology*, 1959-70, 1979 to present; International Brain Research Organization, 1962 to present; Editorial Board of Life Sciences, 1963-64; Research Society of American Neurological Surgeons, 1963 to present; Editorial Board, *International Journal of Neuropharmacology*, 1963-64; Project Officer, Institute "Ruder Boskovic", Zagreb, Yugoslavia, 1970-73; Editorial Board, *American Journal of Chinese Medicine*, 1972 to present; Board Director, American Center of Chinese Medicine, 1977-79; Award for Distinguished Scientific Achievement, American-Chinese Medical and Health Association, 1978; National Board of Advisors, American Biographical Institute; Listed in *American Men of Science, World Who's Who in Science, American Men and Women of Science, Who's Who in the East, American Men and Women of Science, Book of Honor, Personalities of the South, Men of Achievement, International Who's Who of Intellectuals.* Address: 7001 Buxton Terrace, Bethesda, Maryland 20817.

Delmore Liggett

Liebson, Alice R

Special Assistant. Personal: Born October 2, 1950; Daughter of Sidney H. and Jeannette B. Liebson. Education: B.A. Journalism, Western Connecticut State College, 1973. Career: Special Assistant to Connecticut Commissioner of Housing; Former Positions include Chief Aide to Ella Grasso for Re-Election Committee; A.B.C. News Political Consultant. Organizational Memberships: Young Democrats of Stamford (president, 1976); Connecticut Women's Political Caucus (state board, 1980 to present); Common Cause (state board, 1980 to present); American Association of University Women (first vice-president, 1980 to present); United Way (allocations committee); Democratic National Party Conferences (delegate, 1978, 1982). Community Activities: Capitol Region Forum (mayor's appointee, 1979 to present); Red Cross Blood Drive (chairman, 1976); Youth Division, United Jewish Appeal (chairman, 1977); Women for Carter/Mondale (state chairman, 1980); Democratic Women's Federation (excutive committee, 1981); Justice of the Peace, 1977 to present. Honors and Awards: President Carter's Talent Bank of Women; Kentucky Colonel, 1976; Honored Twice by Connecticut General Assembly for Public Service; Special Community Service Award, G.E.C.C.; Listed in *Outstanding Young Women of America.* Address: 712 Farmington Avenue, West Hartford, Connecticut 06119.

Lieu, John

Physician. Personal: Born August 15, 1904; Son of Rev. and Mrs. F. H. Liu (both deceased); Married Dorothy A. Irwin; Father of Jon, Gladys. Education: M.D., St. John's University, Shanghai, China, 1926; D.T.M., Liverpool University, Liverpool, England, 1939. Career: Superintendent, Works and Mine Hospital, Hupeh, China, 1929-36; Assistant Medical Officer, Shanghai Municipal Council, Shanghai, China, 1929-36; Doctor-in-Charge, Municipal Hospital, Shanghai, 1936-45; Chief, Surgical Department, Municipal 6th Hospital, Shanghai, 1949-57; Assistant Port Health Officer, Hong Kong, 1957-59; Now Practicing in United States. Organizational Memberships: Academy of Medicine of Columbus; Ohio Medical Association; American Medical Association; American Association for the Advancement of Science; Ohio Academy of Science. Community Activities: Columbus Symphonic Orchestra (sponsor); Friend of the Ohio State University; Smithsonian Institute; Geographic Society; National Historical Society; Columbus Association for the Performing Arts. Religion: Broad Street Presbyterian Church, Columbus, Ohio, Deacon 1968. Honors and Awards: Citation from the Chairman of Municipal Council, Shanghai, 1937; Citation from the Superintendent of Municipal Hospital, Shanghai, 1939; Rockefeller Scholarship, Rockefeller Foundation, U.S.A., 1940; Citation from the Commissioner of Public Health Department, Shanghai, 1945; Fellow, Royal Society of Health of Great Britain, 1972; Listed in *Who's Who in the Midwest, Dictionary of International Biography, A.B.I. Directory, National Society Directory, International Who's Who of Intellectuals.* Address: 645 Neil Avenue, Apt. 1011, Columbus, Ohio 43215.

Elayne V Lindberg

Liggett, Delmore

Bible Scholar and Teacher (retired). Personal: Born May 19, 1906; Son of Harvey and Lydia Hannah Liggett (both deceased). Education: B.S., Indiana University, 1941; Ps.D., Ms.D., D.D.; Honorary F.I.B.A., F.W.A., F.A.B.I., D.F.A.B.I., L.H.D. Career: Bible Scholar and Teacher, Retired; Former Teacher, School Principal, School Psychologist, Farmer, Lecturer, Consultant. Organizational Memberships: Indiana State Teachers Association (consultant, 1966-75); National Education Association (consultant, 1966-75); Indiana R.E.M.C. (director, 1936-42); Century Club, Los Angeles, 1953 to present; United Nations Association, 1970-76; O.A.S., 1976; Museum of Natural History, 1970-76. Community Activities: National Historical Society (founding member); International Campine Society (life member); BonDurant Agape Ministry (trustee, 1970-76); New Rising Sun Cemetery (secretary, 1950-60); Retired Teachers Association (president, Ohio and Switzerland Counties); Postmaster, Rising Sun, Indiana, 1942-45. Religion: United Methodist Church, 1915 to present; Trustee, Treasurer, Sunday School Superintendent, Organist, Pianist, Violinist, Bible Teacher. Honors and Awards: Certificate of Appreciation, National Police Officers Association, 1972; Distinguished Service Award, Indiana State Teachers Association, 1968; Listed in *Who's Who in the Methodist Church, Dictionary of International Biography, Two Thousand Men of Achievement, Men of Achievement, Who's Who in the Midwest, Who's Who in America,* Others. Address: P.O. Box 35, Rural Delivery 1, Rising Sun, Indiana 47040.

Lindberg, Elayne Verna

Executive. Personal: Born April 27, in Browerville, Minnesota; Daughter of Leslie and Velma Breighhaupt Averill, (both deceased); Married Russell H. Lindberg on July 26; Mother of Gary Lindberg, Bonnie Lindberg-Carlson. Education: Degree in Social Sciences,

University of Minnesota. Career: Dayton's Department Store, Minneapolis, 1965-71; President, Elayne Galleries Inc., 1971 to present; Professional Restorer of Oil Paintings and Paper Art. Organizational Memberships: International Grapho Analysis Society; World Association Questioned Document Examiners (charter member); American Society of Appraisers (associate member). Community Activities: Calhoun Beach Club. Published Works: Co-Author and Composer of Verse and Sacred Music. Honors and Awards: Image Maker of the Year, National Home Fashions League, 1979; International Society of Appraisers, 1981; Listed in *Who's Who in the Midwest*. Address: 2950 Dean Parkway, Minneapolis, Minnesota 55416.

Linder, Robert J

University Dean, Orchestra Conductor. Personal: Born October 29, 1937; Son of Mr. and Mrs. Lonnie Linder; Married Diana Bland; Father of Christopher Robert, (Stepfather of:) Richard Woodruff Curran, Anne Elizabeth Curran. Education: B.M.E. 1959, M.M. 1962, University of Houston. Career: Dean, Professor, Orchestra Conductor, Houston Baptist University; Former Public School Teacher and Band Director. Organizational Memberships: College Band Directors National Association; American Symphonic Orchestra League; Texas Music Education Association; Kappa Kappa Psi; Phi Mu Alpha; Junior Chamber of Commerce. Community Activities: Young Audiences Inc. (advisory board, 1979 to present); Ima Hogg Houston Symphony Competition (advisory board, 1981); Houston Civic Symphony (orchestra conductor; conductor of Gilbert and Sullivan Opera and Theatre Under the Stars); Houston Municipal Band, Television Specials for N.B.C., C.B.S., P.B.S. and Movie "So Sad About Gloria". Religion: Baptist and Episcopalian. Honors and Awards: Listed in *International Who's Who in Music, Who's Who in Education, Outstanding Educators in America, Who's Who in the South and Southwest*. Address: 24 East Broad Oaks, Houston, Texas 77056.

Lindsay, Vaughnie J

Administrator. Personal: Born March 21, 1921; Daughter of Irvin Frank and Cora Kennedy Garrette; Married Joseph D. Lindsay III; Mother of Deborah Rogers, Sandra Doreson. Education: B.S.E., Central State University, Edmond, Oklahoma, 1940; M.B.E., University of Oklahoma, Norman, 1959; Ed.D., Indiana University, Bloomington, 1966. Career: Dean, Graduate School, Southern Illinois University-Edwardsville; Professor, Southern Illinois University; Associate Professor, University of Oklahoma-Norman; Assistant Professor, Southwestern State College, Weatherford, Oklahoma; Teacher, Guthrie High School and Mooreland High School, Oklahoma. Organizational Memberships: Council of Graduate Schools (member, 1973 to present; chairperson, task force on women in higher education, 1978, 1979; committee on women 1980, 1982); National Association for Business Teacher Education (member, 1969 to present; executive board, 1970-72, 1975-78; committee on professional organizational relationships, 1978-79; task force on organizational changes, 1971-72; committee on guidelines, 1969-70); National Business Education Association (member, 1970 to present; executive board, 1975-78; publications committee, 1972-73); Illinois Association of Graduate Schools (member, 1977 to present; president, 1981-82; president elect, 1980-81; program chairperson, annual conference, 1980; chairperson, ad hoc committee on resolution II, 1977-78; nominating committee, 1978); Illinois Business Education Association (executive board, 1972-73; chairperson, council of affiliated presidents, 1972, 1975); Illinois Business Teacher Educators Council (standards committee, 1971-72); Oklahoma Vocational Business Education Association (executive board, 1966-70); Midwestern Association of Graduate Schools (member, 1976 to present; graduate standards and graduate programs committee, 1979-81); American Association of Higher Education; American Council on Education; American Educational Research Association; American Management Association; National Council University Research Administrators; Delta Pi Epsilon Honorary Society (member 1958 to present; president, sigma chapter). Community Activities: Consultant to Associated Organizations for Teacher Education, 1973; United States Civil Service Commission, 1973; Oklahoma Department of Vocational-Technical Education, 1969; Job Corps Center, Guthrie, Oklahoma, 1967. Published Works: Co-Editor, *NABTE Review*, 1972; Editor, Special Interest Section, *National Business Education Forum*, May 1972; Associate Editor, Summer 1970, Editor, Summer 1971, *National Business Education Quarterly*. Honors and Awards: Outstanding Business Educator, Delta Pi Epsilon, Beta Beta Chapter, 1979; Teaching Excellence Award, Southern Illinois University-Edwardsville, School of Business, 1973; Ed.D. with Special Distinction, Indiana University-Bloomington, 1966; Danforth Fellowship, 1962-63, 1963-64. Address: 12773 Partridge Run Drive, Florissant, Missouri 63033.

Robert J Linder

Lindsey, Beverly Sue

Administrator. Personal: Born June 14, 1930; Daughter of Rollin William and Merkel Ruckman Lindsey. Education: Diploma, Methodist Hospital School of Nursing, 1952; B.S.N., University of Missouri, 1962; M.S.N., University of Colorado, 1972; Pre-Doctoral Studies at the University of Missouri-Kansas City, 1979 to present. Military: Served in the United States Air Force Nurse Corps, 1955-57; United States Air Force Reserves in the Position of Chief Nurse and Flight Nurse, 1960-78, attaining the rank of Lieutenant Colonel; Serves as Chief Nurse, 28 Medical Service Squadron (Rescue); Presently Mobilization Assistant to SAC Command Nurse, with the rank of Colonel. Career: Chairman, Department of Nursing, Avila College, 1980 to present; Other Positions at Avila College, Associate Chairperson of the Department of Nursing, 1978-79, Associate Professor in Nursing 1975 to present, Assistant Professor in Nursing Curriculum Coordinator, 1972-75; Assistant Instructor, University of Missouri School of Medicine at Kansas City, 1967-71; Programmed Cardiovascular Care Project, Education Coordinator, Missouri Regional Medical Program, Kansas City General Hospital and Medical Center, 1968-71; Nurse Instructor, Cardiology Department of Medicine, Kansas City General Hospital and Medical Center, 1965-66; Instructor, Practical Nurse Program, Kansas City Board of Education, 1965-66; Medical-Surgical Coordinator, Research Hospital and Medical Center School of Nursing, 1964-65; School Nurse Teacher, Kansas City Board of Education, 1964; Instructor, Medical-Surgical Nursing and Leadership, University of Missouri School of Nursing, Columbia, 1962-64; Head Nurse, Medical-Surgical Nursing and Thoracic Intensive Care Unit, Veterans Hospital, Kansas City, 1957-60; Staff Nurse, Medical-Surgical Intensive Care Unit, Veterans Hospital, Kansas City, 1953-55; General Duty Nurse, Psychiatry, University of Kansas Medical Center, Kansas City, 1952-53. Organizational Memberships: American Nurses Association (council of medical-surgical nursing, 1976 until terminated; member 1952 to present); Missouri Nurses Association (state planning committee, continuing education proposal, 1972-73; member, 1952 to present); District #2 Missouri Nurses Association (member, 1977-78; program committee; board member, 1978-79, 1979-80; representative for Academy of Health Professions, 1979-80); Reserve Officers Association; National League for Nursing; American Nurses Association. Community Activities: Eastern Star; Methodist Women Ruth Weslyan Service Guild; International Relations Council; St. Andrews Society; Kansas City Heart Association; American Heart Association; Scientific Council of the American Heart Association. Published Works: Authored and Prepared Telelectures on "The Nurses Role-Cardiac Arrest"; Co-Author with M. Deig, "Cardiac Arrest-Drug Therapy" and "Nursing Care of Patient Requiring a Pacemaker"; Other Articles and Training Manuals. Honors and Awards: Sigma Theta Tau; United States Air Force Reserve, Commendation Medal for Meritorious Service 1977, Meritorious Service Medal 1981; Listed in *Who's Who of American Women*. Address: 107 West Bannister Road, Kansas City, Missouri 64114.

Lindsey, Evelyn G

Staff Records Officer, Micrographics Specialist, T.V.A. Personal: Born October 2, 1934; Daughter of Mr. and Mrs. Charles L.

Gentry; Married William A. Lindsey; Mother of Yvonne Elizabeth Ownby, Thomas Lee Henderson (deceased). Education: B.S., Business Administration, Tennessee Technological University, 1968; Graduate Work in Industrial Education, University of Tennessee-Knoxville, 1970-72; M.S., Business Education, Middle Tennessee University, 1974. Career: United States Attorney's Office, Eastern District, Tennessee, 1962-65; Instructor, Walker County Technical Insitute, 1969-70; Instructor, State Area Vo-Tech School, 1970-72; Instructor, Edmondson College, 1972-75; 1975 to present, Co-Owner, Tennessee Valley Authority, North County Carpet Cleaning, Inc., and Lindsey Distributors, Inc. Organizational Memberships: Rock City Chapter, Association of Records Managers and Administrators (charter member; past membership chairman; past program chairman; past president); Tennessee Valley Chapter, (charter member; past program chairman; past membership chairman; president 1982-83), National Micrographic Association (board of directors); Eastern Tennessee Legal Assistants (charter member); Chattanooga Engineers Club. Community Activities: Daisy Junior Woman's Club (past president); American Vocational Association; Georgia Vocational Associaton; Tennessee Vocational Association; Workshop Instructor for Chattanooga Area Literacy Movement Teachers. Religion: Hixson First Baptist Church. Published Works: "Teaching All to Type", *American Vocational Journal*, 1971; "You, Too, Can Type", Tennessee Vocational Association, 1971. Honors and Awards: Broke Typing Record at Tennessee Technological University, 1967, Typing 102 Words per Minute with Two Errors; Received Outstanding Curriculum Award, American Vocational Association, 1969-70; Merit Award and Chapter Member of the Year, 1980, Rock City Chapter, Association of Records Managers and Administrators; Listed in *Who's Who in the South and Southwest, Personalities of the South, Directory of Distinguished Americans, World Who's Who of Women, Personalities of America, Book of Honor, International Who's Who of Intellectuals.* Address: 9022 Daisy Dallas Road, P.O. Box 215, Hixson, Tennessee 37343.

Lindsey, Mildred Rowe

Investor, Farmer, Poet, Songwriter. Personal: Born April 11, 1919; Mother of Susan L. Russell, Diane L. Perry. Education: Graduate of Middle Georgia College, 1937; Postgraduate Studies at the University of Georgia, 1938. Career: Investor, Farmer, Poet, Songwriter; Co-Founder, Dixie Oil Company, Inc. Community Activities: Quota Club (secretary, 1980); Friends of Battered Women, 1980-81; Lenox Medical Board, 1980-81; Women's Rights Project (advisory board, 1980-81); Lenox Garden Club (secretary); March of Dimes (Lenox chairman, 1957, 1958-59); Georgia Mental Health Association (chairman, Lenox chapter, 1977, 1978-79); Governor's Project Committee for City of Lenox, 1980. Religion: Adult Sunday School Teacher, Lenox Baptist Church; Women Missionary Union. Published Works: Poem Published in *Anthology of Verse*, New York's World's Fair 1939. Honors and Awards: Theme Songwriter for Quota Club of Valdosta, 1976; Abraham Baldwin College President's Club; Board of Directors, Lenox Enterprises; Board of Directors, Dixie Oil Distributing Company. Address: P.O. Box 317, Lenox, Georgia 31637.

Lipinsky de Orlov, Lino Sigismondo

Artist, Museum Curator. Personal: Born January 14, 1908, in Rome, Italy; Son of Sigismondo and Elinita K. Burgess Lipinsky De Orlov; Married Leah S. Penner, October 1, 1943; Father of Lino S., Lucian C. Education: Study in Rome and Munich, 1922-25; Graduate of Royal Academy of the Arts, Rome, 1937. Military: Served with Italian Army, 1936, United States Intelligance Division, 6th Service Command, O.S.S., World War II. Career: Painter; Etcher; Museum Curator; Historian; Head, Exhibits Design Department, Museum of the City of New York, 1959-67; Curator, History, John Jay Homestead, New York State Parks and Recreation Division for Historical Preservation, Katonah, 1967 to present; Member, Art Admissions Committee, Huntington Hartford Foundation , 1962-65; Director, Annual Winter Antiques Show, New York, 1957-60, Garibaldi-Meucci Memorial Museum, Staten Island, New York, 1956 to present; Art Consultant, Italian Embassy, Washington, D.C.; Consulate General, Italy, New York City; Works Exhibited in Foreign Countries, N.A.D., Art Institute of Chicago, Metropolitan Museum of Art, Albright Art Gallery, Cleveland Museum of Art, Detroit Museum of Art, Many Other Cities and Museums; One-Man Shows, including Palazzetto Venezia, Rome 1928, Boston Symphony Hall 1941, Junior League Gallery, Boston 1941, Knoedler Gallery, New York City 1945, Avery Hall, Columbia 1955, Cosmos Club, Washington, D.C. 1955, Smithsonian Institute, United States National Museum 1955, Galleria Costa, Palma de Mallorca, Spain 1955, Numerous Private Galleries; Represented in Permanent Collections, Museum of the City of New York, Library of Congress, Metropolitan Museum, New York Public Library, Columbia, Detroit Institute of the Arts, Gabinetto delle Stampe, Rome, Galleria Nazionale d'Arte Moderna, Rome, Numerous Other Museums and Private Collections; Executed Murals, Banquet Hall, Palace of Maharaja of Indore, 1947, Several Church Murals, 1942-48, Diorama: Verrazzano's Discovery of New York Bay in 1524, 1955, Circular Mural: View of New Amsterdam in 1660, Museum of the City of New York, 1965; Designed Museum Exhibit, New York World's Fair, 1964-65, Bedford Historical Society Museum, 1970; Member, Bedford, New York Tricentennial Commission, 1980. Organizational Memberships: Society of American Graphic Artists; Audobon Artists (chairman, exhibition committee, 1952); Chicago Society of Etchers; United Scenic Artists; American Association of Museums; Comitato Nazionale Per le Onoranze a Giovanni Da Verrazzano; Gruppo Romano Incisori Artisti; International Platform Association; National Society of Literature and Arts; Bedford Farmers' Club; New York State Association of Museums; Knights Mark Twain; New York State Employees Association; Bedford Historical Society. Published Works: *Pocket Anatomy in Color for Artists; Giovannia Verrazzano, The Discoverer of New York Bay, 1524;* Contributing Author, Numerous Art and History Books, Professional Journals. Honors and Awards: Silver Medal of Ministero dell'Educazione Nazionale, Rome, 1928, 1931; Diplome d'Honneur, Silver Medal Expn. de Budapest, 1936; Diplome de Grand Prix, Gold Medal, Diplome d'Honneur, Paris Exposition Internatonale, 1937; Chicago Society of Etchers, 1941, 1950; Society of American Etchers, 1942; Joseph Pennell Prize, Library of Congress, 1942; Detroit Institute of the Arts, 1943; Guild Hall, Easthampton, New York, 1946; Kosciuszko Foundation, New York, 1948; Decorated Officer of Merit, Rep. of Italy, 1958; Gold Medal, Certificate of Merit, Order of Sons of Italy in America, 1961; L.L. Huttleston Staff Award, New York State Council on Parks and Recreation, 1974; Historical Tomahawk Award, Westchester County Historical Society, 1979. Address: John Jay Homestead, Katonah, New York 10536; Via Margutta 33, 00187 Rome, Italy.

Littell, Norman Mather

Retired. Personal: Son of Reverend and Mrs. Joseph Littell (both deceased); Married Katherine Maher (deceased); Father of Katharine Mather, Norman Mather. Education: Graduate of Wabash College, Crawfordsville, Indiana, 1921; Attended Christ Church College, Oxford University, 1922-23; B.A., Oxford University. Military: Private, Student Army Training Corps, Wabash College. Career: Partner, Evans McClaren and Littell, South Washington; Appointed Assistant United States Attorney General, 1939-44; Private Practice, Washington, D.C., 1944-81; Consultant Drafting Foreign Investment Encouragement Law, with President Eisenhower; First Foreigner Invited to Speak before Legislation, Yuan; General Consultant and Claims Attorney for Navajo Tribe, Retiring in 1981. Organizational Memberships: International Bar Association (organizer and chairman, committee on foreign investment encouragement laws); American Bar Association. Religion: St. James Episcopal Church, Lothian, Maryland, 1962 to present. Published Works: *Trails of the Sea*, 1982. Honors and Awards: State, Interstate Intercollegiate Oratorical Contest, Indiana, 1920; Rhodes Scholarship to Attend Oxford University, 1922-23; Listed in *Community Leaders and Noteworthy Americans, Personalities of the South, Who's Who.* Address: 855 Mason Avenue, Deale, Maryland 20751.

Little, Florence E H

Educator. Personal: Born July 7, 1911; Daughter of Charles and Bertha Schlachter Herbert (both deceased); Widow; Mother of Alan Rush, Barbara Jean Little Votaw. Education: Graduate of Lincoln High School, Vicennes, Indiana, 1928; B.A., Michigan State University, 1932; M.S.E., Drake University, 1962; Undertook graduate studies at Western State College, Gunnison, Colorado and Denver University. Career: Tutor, Substitute Teacher; Former Positions include Teacher of Grades K-14, Accompanist, Private Teacher of Voice and Piano. Organizational Memberships: Mu Phi Epsilon National Professional Music Fraternity (50 years); Kappa Kappa Iota National Professional Music Teachers Sorority; Iowa State Education Association; Des Moines Education Association. Community Activities: Friends of the Cabildo (Louisiana State Museum); LaPlace Homeowners Association; Smithsonian Institution; River Parishes Family CB Club (corresponding secretary, vice president); St. John the Baptist Parish Civil Defense Unit; American Business Women's Association; Orchid Society of Jefferson, Inc. Religion: Sunday School Teacher, Choir Member. Honors and Awards: National Honor Society, 1928; N.S.F. Front, 1963-64. Address: 1093 A Belle Terre Drive, LaPlace, Louisiana 70068.

Liu, Shiao-Kung

Senior Scientist. Personal: Born August 27, 1940; Son of Chen and Betty Liu; Married to Emily T.; Father of John, Jeffrey, Joanne. Education: B.S., National Cheng-kung University, China; M.S., University of California at Berkeley; Ph.D., New York University. Career: Senior Scientist, the Rand Corporation, Santa Monica, California; Former Chief Hydraulic Engineer, Engineering-Science Inc., Berkeley; Former Professor of Hydraulic Engineering, National Cheng-kung University; Former Senior Consultant, The Netherlands Government; Former Visiting Lecturer, University of Southern California; Former Consultant, Taichung Harbor Bureau; Former Consultant, Virginia Institute of Marine Science and U.S. Department of Commerce. Organizational Memberships: American Society of Civil Engineers; International Association of Water Resource. Honors and Awards: Honorary Member, Society of Civil Engineers; Founder's Award for highest academic achievement, New York University; Elected to Phi Tau Phi; Listed in *American Men of Science, International Who's Who of Intellectuals, Who's Who in the West, American Men of Achievement*. Address: 3706 Oceanhill Way, Malibu, California 90265.

Lizut, Nona Moore Price

Administrative Secretary. Personal: Born August 8, 1923; Married William J. Lizut; Mother of Charles P. Price III (of a previous marriage). Education: Graduate, Tucumcari High School, Tucumcari, New Mexico, 1941; Undertook business administration courses, New Mexico State University, 1941-42. Career: Secretary, New Mexico State Health Department, 1942-44; Environmental Division, New Mexico State Health Department, 1951-68; Administrative Secretary, New Mexico Health and Social Services Department, 1968-74; Administrative Assistant to Deputy Director, New Mexico Health and Social Service Department, 1974-78; Administrative Assistant to Deputy Secretary, New Mexico Health and Environmental Department, 1978 to present. Organizational Memberships: National Secretaries Association (Santa Fe Chapter vice president, program chairman, recording secretary, corresponding secretary); New Mexico Water Pollution Control Association (honorary lifetime member, executive secretary); New Mexico Public Health Association (secretary-treasurer, president elect). Community Activities: Women's Division, Sante Fe Chamber of Commerce, 1977 to present; Capitol City Business and Professional Women (vice president, program chairman); New Mexico Round Dance Association (president with husband)). Honors and Awards: Ballroom Dancing Trophies for the Fox Trot, Waltz, Tango and Paso Doble; Listed in *Who's Who of American Women, Personalities of America, Personalities of the West and Midwest, Directory of Distinguished Americans, Who's Who in the West*. Address: 1408 Santa Rosa Dr., Santa Fe, New Mexico 87501.

Irene V F Locke

Lloyd, Corrine Avis

Microbiologist. Personal: Born May 15, 1943; Daughter of J. Howard and Pearl Lloyd. Education: B.S., Medical Technology, St. Louis University, 1965. Career: Microbiologist, St. Louis County Hospital: Former Medical Technologist, Chief of Microbiology, Infectious Disease Committee Member, Cardinal Glennon Memorial Hospital for Children; Assistant Instructor, Medical Technology, St. Louis University. Organizational Memberships: American Society for Microbiology; Missouri Society for Microbiology; American Society for Medical Technology; Missouri Society for Medical Technology; American Society of Clinical Pathologists (associate member). Community Activities: St. Louis University Nursing and Allied Health Professions Alumni Association (president, vice president, board member). Religion: Affton Presbyterian Church, Elder 1977, Deacon, Christian Educator. Honors and Awards: Presidential Sports Award for Swimming, 1975; Registered Microbiologist, American Academy of Microbiology, 1975; Registered Medical Technologist, American Society of Clinical Pathologists, 1966. Address: 6212 Bixby Avenue, Affton, Missouri 63123.

Locke, Irene Vivian Fisher

Civic Volunteer. Personal: Born April 5, 1909, in Birch Tree, Missouri; Daughter of Oliver David and Nellie Evelyn Hughes Fisher; Married John Loor Locke; Mother of Peggy Locke Newman, John Loor Locke Jr. (deceased), Evelyn Locke Dreitzler (deceased). Education: Guild and Evans Finishing School, Boston, Massachusetts; Continued Studies of the Prentice-Hall Federal Tax Codes, the Executive Tax Report Corporation, the Research Institute of America and the Institute of Business Planning. Career: Board of Directors, Treasurer, Assistant Secretary, O. D. Fisher Investment Company; Co-Chairman, Board of Directors, O. D. Fisher Charitable Foundation. Organizational Memberships: National Association of Female Executives; International Platform Association. Community Activities: Seattle Children's Home; Seattle Fruit and Flour Mission; Girl Scout Council of Seattle; United Good Neighbors of Seattle (formerly known as the Community Chest); Seattle Junior Programs; Seattle Visiting Nurse Service; Arboretum Foundation (Unit I); Early American Glass Club; Children's Orthopedic Hospital; Seattle Symphony Orchestra; Pacific Northwest Ballet; Seattle Art Museum; Historical Society of Seattle and King County; Seattle Repertory Theatre; Washington State Heart Association; Arranged Sponsorship of First Fellowship in Cardiology at the University of Washington School of Medicine; Selected to Founding Committee and Board to Form a National Citizen's Committee for Mental Health, National President of the American Medical Association, 1963; National Emergency Committee, National Council on Crime and Delinquency (founding member, 1967); National Board of the Intercollegiate Studies Institute (first and only woman elected); Applied to and Received Exemption from United States Internal Revenue Service for The John L. Locke Jr. Created Charitable Trust for the "Care, Treatment and Research of Heart Disease"; American Security Council (national advisory board, 1970 to present); United States Congressional Advisory Board (congressional advisor from the state of Washington, 1981). Honors and Awards: Two Citations from the Secretary of the Treasury Department; Honorary Ph.D., Hamilton State University, 1973; Invited to Membership in the American

Management Association, 1976; Citation of Merit, Disabled American Veterans, 1972; Inclusion in "Library of Human Resources of the United States of America", American Heritage Research Association, 1975; Fellowship, International Biographical Association, 1975; Fellowship, International Oceanographic Foundation, 1976; Certificate of Recognition, Washington Legal Foundation, 1981; Listed in *Community Leaders and Noteworthy Americans, Dictionary of International Biography, International Register of Profiles, International Who's Who of Intellectuals, Leaders of the English-Speaking World, National Register of Prominent Americans and International Notables, National Society of Literature and the Arts, Notable Americans of the Bicentennial Era, The Royal Blue Book, Who's Who of American Women, Who's Who in the West, World Who's Who of Women.* Address: 2148 Broadmoor Drive East, Seattle, Washington 98112.

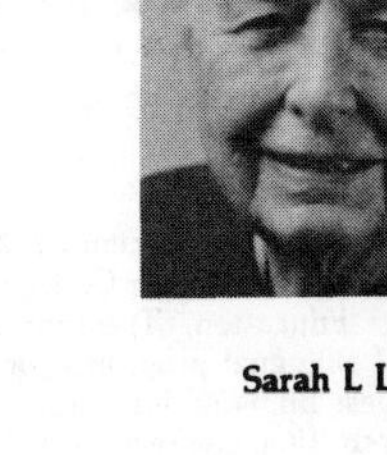
Sarah L Loening

Lodge, James Robert

Professor. Personal: Born July 1, 1925; Son of Ferrall Lodge, Margaret Funk; Married Jean Agnes Wessel; Father of Julie, James. Education: B.S. 1952, M.S. 1954, Iowa State University; Ph.D. Dairy Physiology, Michigan State University, 1957. Military: Served in the United States Army, 1944-46. Career: Research Assistant, Michigan State University, 1954-57; University of Illinois, Research Associate 1957-60, Assistant Professor 1960-63, Associate Professor 1963-69, Acting Assistant Dean Resident Instruction 1977, Professor of Physiology in Dairy Science. Organizational Memberships: American Physiological Society; American Association for the Advancement of Science; Society Study of Reproduction; American Dairy Science Association; Society for Cryobiology; New York Academy of Sciences; American Society of Animal Science. Community Activities: Phi Kappa Phi (scholarship committee, 1970-72); Undergraduate Instructional Award Committee, 1969; Faculty-Student Senate, 1969; College Courses and Curricula Committee, 1972-75; Search Committee for Associate Dean and Director of Resident Instruction, College of Agriculture, 1977; Student Agriculture Council (advisor, 3 years); Dairy Science Club (advisor, 8 years); Paul A. Funk Award Selection Committee, 1971; Number of Departmental Committees including the Graduate Student Committee and the Publicity Committee. Religion: First Methodist Church, Several Committees, Usher. Honors and Awards: Dairy Science Outstanding Instructor Award, 1969; Finalist, Campus Award for Excellence in Undergraduate Teaching, 4 Years; Nominated Several Times for Outstanding Instructor in College of Agriculture; Consistently Listed in Partial List of Excellent Instructors on Campus; Alpha Zeta Outstanding Instructor in University of Illinois College of Agriculture Award, 1981. Address: 1701 South Cottage Grove, Urbana, Illinois 61801.

Loening, Sarah Larkin

Author. Personal: Born December 9, 1896; Daughter of Adrian Hoffman and Katherine Bache Satterthwaite Larkin (both deceased); Widow; Mother of Albert Palmer Loening Jr. Education: Madame Marty's School, Paris, France, 1914; Miss Chapin's School, 1915. Career: Author of *Three Rivers, The Trevals: A Tale of Quebec, Radisson, Joan of Arc, Dimo* (in French and English), *Mountain in the Field, The Old Master and Other Tails, The Gift of Life.* Community Activities: Southampton Garden Club (president, 1938-40, 1942-44); St. John's First Monday Club (chairman); The Biblical Garden at the Cathedral of St. John the Divine, New York City (founder and chairman); Colony Club; National Society of Colonial Dames in the State of New York; Huguenot Society of America; Pen and Brush; Hroswithai Order of St. Luke the Physician; Meadow Club; Hampton Chapter of the American Red Cross (past chapter chairman). Religon: Trustee, St. John's Episcopal Church, Southampton. Honors and Awards: Dame Order of St. John of Jerusalem; Medaille de la Reconnaissance par le goverment Francais, 1920. Address: 119 First Neck Lane, Southampton, New York 11968.

George H Lokey

Lokey, George

Petroleum Executive. Personal: Born March 25, 1935, in Amarillo, Texas; Son of Ted Henry and Stella Alice Yeatts Lokey; Married Sheri Darlynn Mims, on November 2, 1968; Father of Alexander David. Education: B.A., Business Administration, University of Oklahoma, 1957. Military: Served in the United States Marine Corps Reserve, 1957-60, attaining the rank of First Lieutenant. Career: President, Texas Panhandle Heritage Foundation; President, Chief Executive Officer, Ted Lokey Oil Company, 1963 to present; Vice President, Ted Lokey Tire Company, Amarillo, 1963 to present; Director, Broadcasting Company, 1974 to present. Organizational Memberships: National Oil Jobbers Council; Texas Oil Marketers Association (president); Texas Tourist Council. Community Activities: Amarillo Bicentennial Commission (chairman); Amarillo Board of Conventions and Visitors Activities; Amarillo Zoological Society (president); Panhandle Heritage Foundation; Discover Texas Association (board of directors); Greater Southwest Music Festival; West Texas Chamber of Commerce; Chamber of Commerce (director); Les Amis du Vin (regional director); Confrerie des Vignerons de Saint Vincent de Macon; Confrerie de la Chaine des Rotisseus (Bailli de Amarillo); Amarillo Country Club; T Bar M Racquet Club; Taos Ski and Cricket Club; Angle Fire Country Club. Religion: Presbyterian. Honors and Awards: Outstanding Young Texan, Garland A. Smith Associates, 1976. Address: 2801 South Hughes Street, Amarillo, Texas 79109.

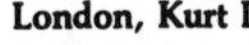
London, Kurt L

Retired. Personal: Born September 12, 1900; Married Jean Louise Fraser. Education: Ph.D., Political Science, University of Wuerzburg, 1928. Military: Served in the United States Air Force Reserves, attaining the rank of Lieutenant Colonel. Career: Director, Institute of Sino-Soviet Studies, George Washington University; Professor, Professor Emeritus, International Affairs. Organizational Memberships: American Association for the Advancement of Slavic Studies; American Political Science Association; International Studies Association; Cosmos Club, Washington D.C. Community Activities: Senior Regional Specialist, Office of War Information; Department of State, C.I.A., 1942-60. Published Works: Author of Twelve Books. Honors and Awards: Certificate of Merit with Distinction, United States Government, 1962. Address: 710 Christine Drive, Palo Alto, California 94303.

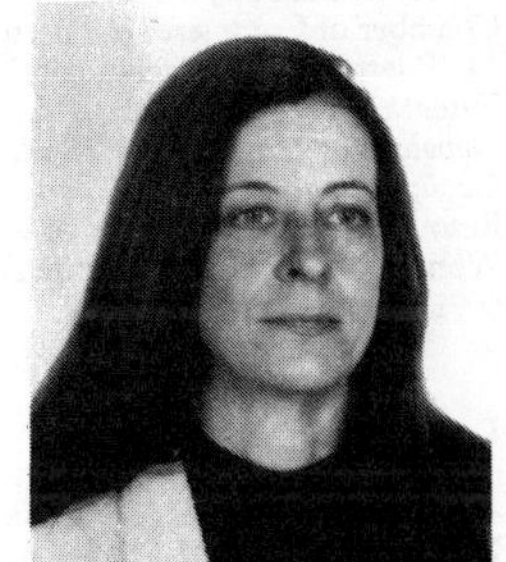
Shirley D Long

Long, Shirley D

General Contractor, Land Developer, Professional Speaker. Personal: Born in Guilford County, North Carolina; Daughter of Mrs. Louiva D. Davidson; Married Bruce E. Long (deceased) in 1966. Education: B.S.; Continued Study at the School of Design. Career: Founded Shirley D. Long Builders Inc., Radley Run Inc., Designs by Shirley Dee. Organizational Memberships: International Platform Association (life member); American Biographical Institute (life member); Smithsonian Institute (national life member). Community Activities: Oxford Orphanage, Oxford, North Carolina (donates all monies from speaking engagements). Published Works: *The Pen Robbers; The Pen Robbers, Part II.* Honors and Awards: Listed in *Who's Who in America, Personalities of America, Personalities of the South, Community Leaders & Noteworthy Americans, Library of Congress, Notable Americans, Book of Honor, The American Registry Series, International Register of Profiles, Men & Women of Distinction, Women of Distinction.* Address: P.O. Box 19183, Greensboro, North Carolina 27410.

Loper, Marilyn S

Executive. Personal: Born June 7, 1944; Daughter of Elmer C. and Thelma P. Haferkamp Loper. Education: Graduate of High School of Commerce, Detroit, Michigan, 1962; B.S., Eastern Michigan University, 1967; M.A., 1971; Attended Over 35 Workshops and Conferences since 1970. Career: President, Loper Construction, Inc., 1977 to present; Health and Rehabilitative Services, Office of Vocation Rehabilitation, Supervising Counselor 1978 to present, Counselor II 1973-78; Supervisor, 1975 to present; Salesperson, Henry Dingus Jr., Realtor, 1978 to present; Elementary School Teacher, Land O' Lakes, Florida 1970-73, Warren, Michigan 1969-70, Nankin Mills Public Schools, Michigan 1968-69, Annapolis, Maryland 1967-68. Organizational Memberships: National Association of Social Workers; Florida Association for Health and Social Services; National Rehabilitation Association; Florida Rehabilitation Association; National Rehabilitation Counselor Association; National Rehabilitation Administrator Association; Florida Rehabilitation Counselor Association; Florida Rehabilitation Administrator Association; Pasco Builders Association. Honors and Awards: Listed in *Who's Who of American Women*. Address: Post Office Box 64, Port Richey, Florida 33568.

Lopez, Anna Margaret

Educator. Personal: Born December 29, 1939; Daughter of Theodore (deceased) and Marie Gonzalez; Married to Antonio S. Education: B.A., Newark State College, 1961; M.Ed., Rutgers University, 1976. Career: Director of Bilingual Education, New Jersey Department of Education, Trenton; Former Teacher of mentally retarded, second grade and bilingual first grade; Former Coordinator of Bilingual programs for grades K-12. Organizational Memberships: New Jersey Teacher of English to Speakers of Other Languages; Bilingual Educators; National Association for Bilingual Education. Community Activities: Women's League for Medical Research (financial secretary, 1981 to present); Commissioner on Advisory Board on Status of Women, 1975-78; Girl Scout Leader, 1961-66. Religion: Teacher of catechism to deaf children, 1957-64. Honors and Awards: Member, International Platform Association and National Honor Society; Listed in *International Who's Who of Intellectuals, Book of Honor, World Who's Who of Women, Dictionary of International Biography, Hispanic Who's Who in America*. Address: 101-37 East Raritan Drive, Tuckerton, New Jersey 08087.

Lopez, Mary Gardner

Administrative Social Worker. Personal: Born April 30, 1930; Daughter of Mr. and Mrs. Kossi Gardner; Married George A. Lopez; Mother of Sharon Yolanda, Georgette Adrienne. Education: B.A., Fisk University; M.A., University of Michigan; Further Study at Columbia University. Career: Administrative Social Worker; Former Director of Education and Research. Community Activities: Elmoor Civic Association; Media Women's Association; National Business and Professional Women's Association; Urban League; Julias A. Thomas Society; EDGES Group Inc.; Alpha Kappa Alpha; Doll League Inc.; Reality House, Inc.; Operation Crossroads Africa, Inc. Address: 105-11 Ditmars Boulevard, East Elmhurst, New York 11369.

Marilyn S Loper

Lopez, Victoriano

Teacher. Personal: Born October 27, 1950; Son of Victoriano and Evelia Lopez; Married Maria Cristina Cossio. Education: Teacher, Miami Senior High School; Professional Musician, Composer, Arranger; Recent Performances with CBS Recording Artists, Miami Sound Machine. Organizational Memberships: Phi Mu Alpha; Kappa Kappa Psi; Florida Bandmasters Association. Religion: Catholic. Honors and Awards: Dade County Teacher of the Year, 1978; Florida State Teacher of the Year, 1979; Florida State Teacher of the Year Nominee, National Teacher of the Year Award. Address: 100 Fountainebleau Blvd. 202, Miami, Florida 33172.

Lopez-Roig, Lucy Enid

Clinical, Industrial Psychologist. Personal: Born November 23, 1936 in Rio Piedras, Puerto Rico; Daughter of Jose Antonio and Victoria Luisa Roig Lopez-Puig. Education: B.A., Seton Hill College, 1958; M.S., Caribbean Center for Advanced Studies, 1969; Ph.D., Purdue University, 1972. Career: Director of Training, Psychological Services, Puerto Rico Medical Center, Rio Piedras, 1966-67; Chief of Psychological Services, Puerto Rico Police Department, Hato Rey, 1961-66; Chief of Psychological Services, Chief Selection Program, Puerto Rico Water Resources Authority, Santurce, 1967-69; Chief Office of Motivation 1972-74, Chief Division Personnel 1974-75, Assistant Executive Director for Human Relations 1975-78; Consultant to President and Associate Professor, Interamerican University, Hato Rey, Puerto Rico, 1978 to present; Private Practice in Clinical Psychology, Hato Rey, 1972 to present; President, Lucy Lopez-Roig and Associates, 1978 to present; Professor, Caribbean Center for Advanced Studies, Santurce, 1975 to present; Director, Industrial-Organizational Psychology Program, Caribbean Center for Advanced Studies, 1978 to present; Consultant Puerto Rico Department of Education, 1967-68; Consultant, Colegio Puertorriqueno de Ninas, Puerto Rican Association of Private Schools, 1974-78; Board of Directors, Instituto Psicologico de Puerto Rico, 1975-76; President, Quality of Life Committee, Chamber of Commerce of Puerto Rico, 1982 to present. Organizational Memberships: American Psychological Association, Division 14; Puerto Rican Psychological Association; Asociación de Personal Público; Sigma Xi. Published Works: *An Approach to the Empathic Process*, 1972; *A Critical Review and Research Proposal for the Selection and Training of Paraprofessionals*, 1971; *Development of a Locus Scale for Managers*, 1972; Co-Author *Helping Supervisors to Cope*, 1977; *Sources of Stress in Six Occupational Groups in Puerto Rico*, 1982. Honors and Awards: Award for Contribution to Human Relations, Puerto Rico Water Resources Authority, 1976; Award for Contributions in Education, Puerto Rican Association of Private Schools, 1974; Outstanding Woman of the Year in Public Administration, Blue Cross of Puerto Rico, 1975. Address: 70 King's Court, Santurce, Puerto Rico 00911.

Lotterer, Wanda J

Artist, Piano Teacher. Personal: Born July 17, 1944; Daughter of Mr. and Mrs. A. W. Radford; Married John F. Lotterer III; Step-Mother of John F. IV, James B. Education: B.Mus., Northwestern State University, 1965; M.Mus., North Texas State University, 1974. Career: Artist, Teacher of Piano; Former Faculty Member, Central Missouri State University. Organizational Memberships: Music Teachers National Association (California state chairman of independent music teachers forum, 1979 to present); California Association of Professional Music Teachers (board member, 1979 to present); National Guild of Piano Teachers. Religion: United Methodist Church of Warsaw, Missouri, Church Organist, Youth Councilor, 1975-77. Honors and Awards: Graduate Teaching Fellowship 1969, Graduate Research Fellowship 1969, North Texas State University; Listed in *Personalities of the West and Midwest, Directory of Distinguished Americans*. Address: 23812 Via La Coruna, Mission Viejo, California 92691.

Loui, Beatrice Lan Que (deceased)

Consultant. Personal: Born June 18, 1907; Died July 14, 1982; Daughter of Heong Poo and Sui Shee Loui (both deceased). Education: B.A., University of Hawaii, 1930; M.A., Columbia University, 1948; Further Study at the University of California-Berkeley, University of Hawaii-Honolulu. Career: Consultant, Assessment and Evaluation of Educational Projects; Former Director/Specialist, Tests and Measurement in Hawaii State Department of Education; Counselor in High Schools, Hawaii; Teacher of Sciences and Mathematics in Secondary Schools, Hawaii; Employment Counselor, State Employment Service, Honolulu, Hawaii. Organizational Memberships: Pi Lambda Theta (president); Delta Kappa Gamma; American Educational Research Association; American Personnel and Guidance Association; National Council of Measurement in Education; Association of Measurement and Evaluation in Guidance; State Testing Program Group (director); Pi Gamma Mu; National Education Association (life member); Hawaii Educational Officers Association; Association of Chinese University Women; Hawaii Counselors Association. Community Activities: Honolulu Academy of Arts, Spalding East-West Center House (volunteer worker); Altrusa International. Religion: Charter Member, Community Church of Honolulu. Honors and Awards: Listed in *National Register of Prominent Americans and International Notables, National Social Directory, Who's Who of American Women, Who's Who in the West, World Who's Who of Women, Personalities of the West and Midwest, Two Thousand Women of Achievement, Dictionary of International Biography, Great and Successful Personalities of the World, Community Leaders and Noteworthy Americans.* Address: 1562 Kanalui Street, Honolulu, Hawaii 96816.

Therese S Love

Love, Richard H

Executive. Personal: Born December 27, 1939, in Schneider, Indiana; Married E. Geraldine Love; Father of Julie Renee, Jayce Christine. Education: Attended the University of Maryland, Bloom College, University of Illinois, Northwestern University, Villa Schifanoia (Florence, Italy); Independent Study undertaken in Europe. Career: President/Owner, R. H. Love Galleries, Inc., Chicago, Illinois; President, Haase-Mumm Publishing Company, Chicago; Professor of Art History, Prairie State College, Chicago Heights 1963-65; Former Art Critic, Star-Tribune Publishing Company; Art Commentator, WEFM, WBBM, WNIB (Chicago), WCIU-TV (Chicago) 1978-1983; Chairman, 19th Century Paintings, WTTW Art Auction, 1979; Advisory Board, Midwest Center, Archives of American Art; Former Contributing Editor, *Chicago Fortnightly, The Collector/Investor* Magazine. Community Activities: New England Historical Society; Yale Friends of American Art; United States Chamber of Commerce. Published Works: Books/*Cassatt: The Independent; John Barber: The Artist, the Man; Cyclopedia of American Impressionism;* Exhibition Catalogues: *Harriet Randall Lumis (1870-1953): An American Impressionist, William Chadwick (1879-1962): An American Impressionist, Walter and Eliot Clark: A Tradition in American Painting, A Century of American Impressionism (Co-Author).* Honors and Awards: Listed in *Who's Who in American Art, Who's Who in the Midwest, International Who's Who of Intellectuals, Men of Achievement, Dictionary of International Biography, Personalities of the West and Midwest, Community Leaders and Noteworthy Americans, Directory of Distinguished Americans.* Address: 100 East Ohio, Chicago, Illinois 60611.

Love, Therese Schuerman

Retired. Personal: Born October 16, 1914; Daughter of Theodore and Mary Schuerman (both deceased); Widow; Mother of Nancy Love Gordon. Education: Attended Columbia Basin College, 1967. Career: Retired Washington State Teaching Homemaker. Organizational Memberships: Benton-Franklin Department of Social and Health Services (staff librarian, 1974-79). Community Activities: Kennewick City Council (first woman member, 1972-76); Governor's Committee for Hiring the Handicapped; Kennewick Business and Professional Women's Club (president, 1976-77); R.S.V.P.; State Program for Voluntary Service, 1981. Religion: St. Joseph's Parish, 1934 to present. Honors and Awards: Goodwill, 1978; 4-H Leader, 13 years; American Association for Retarded Citizens, 27 Years; Catholic Golden Age. Address: 210 North Quincy Street, Kennewick, Washington 99336.

Lovelace, Dennis Joseph

Management Services Consultant. Personal: Born June 18, 1940; Son of Marcus and Joyce C. Lovelace; Married to Connie Lynn Han Soon Chung; Father of Deborah Ann, Darlene Ann. Education: A.A., 1976, B.A., 1977, University of Maryland; M.S., University of Southern California, 1979. Military: Served with United States Army with rank of Master Sergeant, 1958-78. Career: Management Services Consultant, Reno, Nevada; Former Personnel Manager. Organizational Memberships: Association for Systems Management (editor of newsletter, 1980); American Management Association; American Planning Association; International Platform Association; American Society of Professional Consultants. Community Activities: Fellow, American Biographical Association, 1981; Member, University of Southern California Alumni Association 1979; California Community College Lifetime Instructor in Business and Industrial Management, 1979. Honors and Awards: Received Meritorious Service Medal, 1978, Army Commendation Medal, 1965, Army Commendation Medal with first oak leaf cluster, 1968, and Army Commendation Medal with second oak leaf cluster, 1970. Address: P.O. Box 6475, Reno, Nevada 89503.

Dennis J Lovelace

Lovelady, Joe Render

Pastor. Personal: Born August 25, 1930; Son of Neely L. and Fronie Calloway Lovelady (both deceased); Married Betty Houston; Father of Joe Render Jr. Education: Attended the University of Mississippi, 1953; B.A. with distinction, Mississippi College, 1956; M.Div. 1959, Th.M. 1960, D.Min 1973, New Orleans Baptist Theological Seminary; Studies toward M.A. History, University of New Orleans; Continuing Education Course, Loyola University, 1979. Military: Served in the United States Air Force, 1948-53, attaining the rank of T/Sgt. Career: Pastor, Edgewater Baptist Church; Pastor, Mayersville Baptist Church, Mayersville, Mississippi, 1954-56; Pastor, Silver Springs Baptist Church, Osyka, Mississippi, 1956-60. Organizational Memberships: Baptist Association of Greater New Orleans (executive board, 1982; finance committee; trustee, *The Baptist Message;* administration committee); Louisiana Baptist Convention (public affairs committee); Louisiana Baptist Convention Church Site Corporation (president); Southern Baptist Convention (chairman, local arrangements committee, 1982); Consultant to Radio and Television Commission for Billy Graham Rally, 1982. Community Activities: Kiwanis Club of New Orleans (board of directors; editor, club bulletin, 1977; program chairman, 1974-1982; president, 1977-78); Kiwanis International (lieutenant governor, 1980-81); Chairman of Fund Drive for Housing for K Bar B Youth Ranch, 1975, 1976; Kiwanis/Sugarbowl Basketball Ticket Sales (general chairman, 1981-82). Religion: Baptist. Honors and Awards: Club Bulletin Award for Louisiana, Mississippi, Western Tennessee Kiwanis International, 1974; Clergyman of the Year, Kiwanis Club of New Orleans, 1971; Two Mayoralty Certificates of Merit, 1969, 1970; Honorary State Senator, 19782; Featured in *Times Picayune* Life Style Section as "Preacher Without a Gimmick", 1980; Listed in *Who's Who in Religion, Dictionary of International Biography.* Address: 6730 Manchester, New Orleans, Louisiana 70126.

Lower, Nellie Francena

Full-Gospel Minister and Administrator. Personal: Daughter of John and Favora Goddard Lower; Born-Again of Jesus Christ and Spirit-Baptized. Education: B.S. 1959, M.A. 1967, Ball State University; D.Min., Luther Rice Seminary, 1977. Career: Vice-President and Academic Dean, Zoe College; Associate Executive Director, Christian Joy Fellowship-Judy Fiorentino World Evangelism; Former High School Home Economics Instructor and Department Coordinator. Community Activities: Spiritual Life Teacher, Lecturer, and Noted Seminar Instructor on Nutrition for Spirit, Soul and Body; Local and Overseas Crusade Coordinator. Published Works: Author of Christian Books. Honors and Awards: Numerous 4-H Awards, Local and State Level, including Selection for National 4-H Club Congress, 1955; Phi Upsilon Omicron International Home Economics Honor Society; Outstanding Teacher of the Year, Vandalia, Ohio, 1967; Selection to Serve on Committee for Writing Evaluation Standards for Ohio Vocational Home Economics Programs 1971, Selected to Assist in Writing State Curriculum Guide for Boys' Home Economics Programs 1972, Ohio Department of Vocational Education; Called by God to Full-Time Christian Ministry, 1974; Team Member, Christian Joy Fellowship's Around-The-World Missionary Crusade, 1976; Listed in *Personalities of the South, Biographical Roll of Honor*. "To God be the glory for it is no longer I that liveth, but it is Christ in Me!" Address: P.O. Box 8448, Jacksonville, Florida 32239.

Lowry, Dolores Elizabeth-Anne Nunes

Real Estate Executive. Personal: Born March 29, 1922, in San Jose, California; Daugther of Manuel Silveira and Annie Silva-Duarte Nunes; Mother of Suzanne Monique Powell Burneikis. Education: Attended San Jose State University 1968-69, DeAnza College 1973-74. Career: Electrician, Moore-Drydock Company, 1941-45; Title Insurance Clerk, San Jose Abstract and Title Insurance Company, 1945-53; Title Examiner, Valley Title Company, 1953-60; Title Officer, Surety Title Company-City Title Insurance Company, 1960-62; Chief Executive, Title Officer, Trans-American Title Insurance Company, San Jose, 1962-68; Owner, Operator, Mt. Pleasant Homes, San Jose, 1980 to present. Organizational Memberships: Tri-County Apartment Association; National Apartment Association; National Association for Female Executives. Community Activities: American Red Cross (chairman of volunteers, 1973-76; executive committee, finance committee, disaster service committee, 1974 to present; board of directors, 1974 to present); O'Connor Hospital '89'ers (board of directors, executive secretary, 1974 to present); Alexian Brothers Hospital League, 1973; Alexian Brothers Foundation, 1980 to present; Luso American Education Foundation (board of directors, co-chairman fund raising, 1980 to present); Youth for Understanding; Homestay Foundation; San Jose Historical Museum Association; California Pioneers of Santa Clara County; Luso-America Fraternity Federation; Italian-American Heritage Foundation; KQOED Education Television; Smithsonian Institutes (national associate member); Democrat; Elks; San Jose Woman's Club; Rock Canyon Club; Portugal de Hoje Club; Statesman's Club. Religion: Roman Catholic. Honors and Awards: Outstanding Service Certificate, American Red Cross, 1980; Named to Clara Barton Honor Society, 1977; Listed in *Who's Who of American Women, Personalities of the West and Midwest, Personalities of America, Who's Who in the West, Directory of Distinguished Americans.* Address: 3552 Vista Del Valle, San Jose, California 95132.

Nellie Lower

Lozman, Jeffrey

Orthopaedic Surgeon. Personal: Born May 26, 1947, in Brooklyn, New York; Son of Teddy (deceased) and Laura Lozman; Married Nancy Lamora; Father of Joshua, Rebecca. Education: B.S., Fairleigh Dickinson University, 1968 M.D., Albany Medical College of Union University, 1972; Intern, Albany Medical Center Hospital; Resident, Albany Medical Center Hospital; Chief Resident, Orthopaedic Surgery, Albany Medical Center Hospital. Military: Served in the United States Navy Medical Corps, attaining the rank of Lieutenant Commander. Career: Assistant Instructor, Albany Medical Center Hospital, 1973-77; Chairman, Department of Orthopaedics, United States Naval Regional Medical Center, Okinawa, Japan, 1977-79; Assistant Clinical Professor, Albany Medical Center Hospital, 1979 to present; Orthopaedic Consultant, Active Protocol-Trauma and Shock Unit, Albany Medical Center Hospital. Organizational Memberships: American Thoracic Society; American Federation of Clinical Research; New York State Society of Medicine; American Academy of Orthopaedic Surgeons. Published Works: Co-Author in Trauma, Pulmonary Physiology and Orthopaedics. Address: 35 Axebridge, Delmar, New York 12054.

Lucas, Aubrey Keith

University President. Personal: Born July 12, 1934, in State Line, Mississippi; Son of Keith C. (deceased) and Audell Robertson Lucas; Married Ella F. Ginn; Father of Frances, Carol, Alan, Mark. Education: Graduate of State Line High School, 1952; B.S. with honors 1955, M.A. 1956, University of Southern Mississippi; Ph.D., Florida State University, 1966. Career: Assistant Director of Reading Clinic, University of Southern Mississippi, 1955-56; Instructor, Hinds Junior College, 1956-57; Director of Admissions and Associate Professor of Education, University of Southern Mississippi, 1957-61; Research Assistant, Computer Center and Office of Institutional Research and Service, Florida State University, 1961-63; University of Southern Mississippi, Registrar and Associate Professor of Education Administration 1963-70, Dean of Graduate School and Coordinator of Research/Professor of Higher Education 1970-71; President, Delta State University, 1971-75; President, University of Southern Mississippi, 1975 to present. Organizational Memberships: Consultant to Junior and Senior Colleges in Curriculum, Admissions and Records and Organization and Administration; State Commission on Post-Secondary Education; Mississippi Representative to Southern Regional Education Board; American Association of State Colleges and Universities (committee on federal relations; committee on policies and purposes); Mississippi Association of Colleges (past president); Southern Association of Colleges and Schools (team consultant); Commission on National Development in Post-Secondary Education, 1981, for the 97th Congress; College Football Association (faculty representatives committee, 1981); Omicron Delta Kappa Leadership Fraternity; Phi Kappa Phi Scholastic Society; Pi Kappa Pi Scholastic Society; Pi Gamma Mu Honor Society in Social Science; Pi Tau Chi Honor Society in Religion; Kappa Delta Pi Honor Society in Education; Phi Delta Kappa Men's Honor Society in Education; Red Red Rose, Honor Society of Administrators in Public Education; Kappa Pi Honor Society in Art; Mississipi Arts Commission; Mississippi Committee for the Humanities; Phi Theta Kappa (honorary member; national board, 1980 to present): Newcomen Society of North America. Community Activities: Hub City Kiwanis Club; Mississippi Forestry Association; Mississippi Economic Council (chairman-elect, 1981-82); Hattiesburg Chamber of Commerce (board of directors); Forrest-Lamar United Way (board of directors); Pine Burr Area Boy Scouts (board of directors); Mississippi Crusade, American Cancer Society (chairman, 1979); Forrest-Lamar United Way (chairman, 1980). Religion: Parkway Heights United Methodist Church, Council on Ministries; District Lay Leader, Hattiesburg District, United Methodist Church; Wesley Foundation, Board of Directors; Chairman, Mississippi Conference Efficiency Study Committee, United Methodist Church; Conference Lay Leader, United Methodist Church, 1980 to present. Published Works: *The Mississippi Legislature and Mississippi Public Higher Education: 1890-60; Higher Education Opportunities and Needs in the Meridian Area;* Contributing Author to *History of Mississippi;* Author of Consultative Studies and Reports. Honors and Awards: Listed in *Who's Who in America, Who's Who in the South and Southwest, Who's Who in American Colleges and Universities, Dictionary of International Biography, Leaders in Education.*

Lucas, Julia McDonald

Assistant Professor. Personal: Born September 21, 1946; Daughter of Mrs. Helen McDonald; Married Wallace Lucas; Mother of Robert Patrick. Education: B.S.Ed., Georgia Southern College, 1968; M.Ed. 1969, Ed.S. 1974, University of Georgia; Additional Graduate Studies undertaken at Auburn University, Oklahoma State University, Georgia College. Career: Assistant Professor, Home Economics, Middle Georgia College, 8 years; Director, Bleckley County Training Center for the Mentally Retarded, 3 years; High School Home Economics Teachers, Atlanta, 1 year. Organizational Memberships: American Home Economics Association (attended two conventions; voting delegate to 1981 convention); Georgia Home Economics Association (appointed to state executive board; chairman for continuing education); Georgia Student Home Economics Association (state vice president); Coalition of Home Economics Leaders in Georgia, 1981; Academic Committee on Home Economics (chairman, board of regents, 1981-82); Delta Kappa Gamma International Society for Women Educators, 1979. Community Activities: Pilot Club of Cochran (charter president, 1977-78; 2nd vice president, 1981-82); Cochran Chamber of Commerce (charter member, 1978 to present); Cochran Garden Club (2nd vice president, 1979-81); Hike-Bike for the Mentally Retarded (Bleckley County chairman, 1975-77); Bleckley County Association for Retarded Citizens (president, 1974-75); Mothers March for the March of Dimes (county chairman, 1975-77); American Cancer Society (county chairman, education/funds crusade, 1979); Bleckley County Unit, American Cancer Society (board of directors, 1980 to present; memorials chairman, 1981); Community Action Council, 1977-78; American Heart Association (trades chairman; residential chairman, 1979); Baker Academy (board of trustees, 1980 to present); Phi Mu Fraternity for Women; Georgia 4-H Clubs (state secretary-treasurer, 1962-63). Religion: Trinity Episcopal Church of Cochran, Altar Guild 2 years. Honors and Awards: Plaque for Outstanding Leadership, Pilot Club of Cochran, 1978; Woman of the Year, Cochran Garden Club, 1977; State Winner, 4-H, Attended National 4-H Congress in Chicago, 1964; High School Valedictorian, 1964; Listed in *Who's Who of American Women, Personalities of America, Community Leaders, Personalities of the South, World Who's Who of Women*. Address: Route 2 Box 332, Cochran, Georgia 31014.

Lucero, Marcela Christine

Associate Professor, Director of Chicano Studies. Personal: Daughter of Pete and Rose Lucero; Mother of Patricia Louise Trujillo-Garcia. Education: B.A., English Education, University of Denver, 1959; M.A., Spanish, Applied Linguistics, English as a Second Language; Ph.D., Latin American Literature and Linguistics. Career: Associate Professor, Director of Chicano Studies, Adams State College, 1981 to present; Assistant Professor, Minority Group Studies Center, Mankato State, 1980--81; Instructor, Chicano Studies, University of Minnesota, 1973-80. Organizational Memberships: A.A.T.S.P., 198-81; National Council of Teachers of English, 1970-73; T.E.S.O.L., 1968-72; Kappa Delta Pi, 1958-59; Phi Sigma Iota, 1958-59; Sigma Delta Pi, 1967-68; Modern Language Association, 1978-82; International Platform Association, 1981 to present. Community Activities: Centro Cultural Chicano, Minneapolis (board member, 1979-81); Young Women's Christian Association, Minneapolis (trustee, 1980-81); United Way (board of directors, 1979-81); Hispanic Advisory Committee to the Mayor, Minneapolis, 1978-80; H.R.A. Commissioner, Minneapolis, 1978-79; Governor's Appointments Committee, St. Paul, 1979-80; Co-Producer, "Feliz Navidad", KBTV, Channel 19, Denver, 1971. Honors and Awards: Estelle Hunter Scholarship, Denver University, 1957-59; *Denver Post* Gallery of Fame, 1971; Graduate Fellowship, Colorado University-Boulder, 1969-70; Teacher of the Year, Colorado University-Denver Center, 1971; Honorary Citizen, Pueblo, Colorado, 1976; *Denver Post* Student Editor, 1949; Leadership Award, University of Minnesota, Chicano Students, 1981; Selected Participant, Lake Itasca Seminar, Minnesota, 1976; Listed in Directory of American Poets and Writers, Several Editions of *Who's Who*. Address: 114 Richardson, Alamosa, Colorado 81102.

Luciano, Robert A

Consulting Engineer. Personal: Born July 15, 1934; Son of Mr. and Mrs. Anthony A. Luciano; Married Lorraine Chennette; Father of Susan, Robert Jr., Lawrence. Education: B.S.M.E. 1963, M.S. 1966, New Jersey Institute of Technology. Career: Consulting Engineer, President, Robert A. Luciano Associates; Consultant in Packaging and Automation; Fomer Manager, Packaging Engineering, Ortho Pharmaceutical; Project Engineer, Automatic Machinery, Colgate Palmolive Company; Mechanical Designer, Bell Telephone Laboratories. Organizational Memberships: Professional Engineer, New Jersey; New Jersey Young Engineers (former chairman); Packaging Institute (professional member); New York Metropolitan Chapter of Packaging Institute (past president). Community Activities: Lecturer, Seminar Leader, New York University; Instructor, Rutgers University; Former Machinery and Technical Editor, *Modern Packaging* Magazine; Number of Patents in Packaging Field; Republican Party; Warren Township Board of Health (past president); Planning Board; Boy Scouts of America (troop leader). Published Works: Author of Many Articles in the Packaging Field. Address: R.D. 2, Bissell Road, Lebanon, New Jersey 08833.

Luckey, Diane Virginia McKenney

Office and Financial Accounting Manager. Personal: Born July 16, 1946, in Meriden, Connecticut; Daughter of Warren Harold and Adriance Imogene Coosey McKenney; Married Richard Luckey, 1977; Mother of Three Stepdaughters, Tina Marie, Therasa Michell, Tonya Marcel. Education: Attended Ricker College (Houlton, Maine), Hillsborough Community College (Tampa, Florida); American Management Association Supervisory Management, Bureau of Business Practice, Woman Executives Workshop, 1978-79; Seminars in the Field; Graduate of Professional School of Horsemanship. Career: Stenographer, United States Government, 1964-65; Claims Development Clerk, United States Government, 1965-67; Assistant Bookkeeper, Guaranty Loan and Real Estate Company, West Memphis, Arkansas, 1967-71; Computer Specialist, Supervisor, Kandell Construction Company, Tequesta, Florida, 1971-75; Bookkeeper, Office Manager, Universal Coach, Hollywood, Florida, 1975-76; Office and Finance Accounting Manager, Hillsboro News Company, Tampa, Florida, 1977 to present; Owner, Horse Boarding Stables, "The Lucky Stables"; Notary Public, Florida, 1974 to present. Organizational Memberships: American Management Association; Junior Achievement (advisor); Women in Construction; Women in Management Association; American Society of Professional and Executive Women; National Defense Transportation Association (secretary, 1964-65); American Quarter Horse Association; American Horse Show Association; Florida Quarter Horse Association; Palomino Horse Breeders of America. Community Activities: Republican; Florida Comancheros; Eastern Star. Address: 209 Hayes Road, Lutz, Florida 33549.

Luk, King Sing

Professor, Executive. Personal: Born September 1, 1932; Son of Mr. and Mrs. Yau-king Kuk; Married Kit Ming; Father of Doris, Stephen, Eric, Marcus. Education: Teacher's Certificate, Northcote College, Hong Kong, 1953; B.S., Engineering, California State University, Los Angeles, 1957; M.S.C.E., University of Southern California, 1960; Ph.D. with distinction, Engineering, University of California-Los Angeles, 1970. Career: Professor of Engineering, California State University; President, King S. Luk and Associates,

Inc.; President, Cathay Pacific Inc.; Director, Several Other Corporations; Former Chairman and Professor, Civil Engineering Department, California State University, Los Angeles, 1968-73. Organizational Memberships: Structural Engineers Association of Southern California (chairman, education committee, 1967-68); American Society of Civil Engineers (fellow). Community Activities: California Seismic Safety Commission (commissioner, appointed by Governor Jerry Brown, 1980, and State Senate confirmed, 1981). Published Works: Numerous Articles on Engineering Education in National Journals and Conferences; Research and Publications in Concrete Structures and Earthquake Engineering. Honors and Awards: National Science Faculty Fellowship Award, 1967, 1970. Address: 1825 Alpha Avenue, South Pasadena, California 91030.

Lunn, Joseph Kenneth

Insurance Executive. Personal: Born April 16, 1946; Son of Joseph and Evelyn Lunn. Education: Graduate of Lane Technical High School, 1964; B.A. Psychology, North Park College, 1969; M.A., Roosevelt University, 1981; IIA General Insurance Program; CPCU, 1983; Individual Therapist Training, 1973-75; Group Therapy Training, 1973, 1972. Career: Insurance Executive, Agent, Computer Interface Task Force, Kemper Group; Other Positions in the Kemper Group include Personal Lines Underwriting Specialist 1976-81, Lines Supervisor 1974-76, Commercial Analyst 1973-74, Agency Analyst 1972-73, Personal Lines Underwriter 1969-72. Organizational Memberships: Chicago Association of Commerce and Industry (ex-officio director, 1977-78); World Trade Council, 1977-81; Chicago Psychological Association; Illinois Psychological Association; Midwest Psychological Association; American (Student) Psychological Association. Community Activities: School for the Treatment of Emotional Problems in Children (president, 1980-81); Joint Organization to Promote Equality (president, 1978-80); Chicago Junior Association of Commerce and Industry (president, 1977-78); Chicago Jaycee Foundation (president, 1977-78); Chicago Urban League Sickle Cell Education Committee (chairman, 1979-80); Business Impact Group (vice-chairman); Citywide Advisory Group on Desegregation, 1978-80; Cooperative Education Project, City Colleges of Chicago (chairman, events committee, 1975-77); Mental Health Association (chairman, mental health legislation committee, 1974); Urban League Computer Training Center Advisory Committee, 1978-80; Citizens School Committee, 1977-81; Citizen's Committee on Battered Children, 1973-75; Illinois Jaycees (chairman, government affairs committee, 1975); United Way Service Evaluation Committee, 1978-80; Chicago Jaycees (public relations manager, 1980-81). Honors and Awards: One of Chicago's Ten Outstanding Young Citizens of 1980; Beautiful People Award, Chicago Urban League, 1980; Outstanding Young Man of America, 1978; Jaycees International Senatorship, 1978; Community Service Award, S.T.E.P. Inc., 1978; Certificates of Merit, American Blind Skiing Foundation, 1976, 1978; Man of the Day, WAIT Radio, 1977; Distinguished Service Award, Chicago Jaycees, 1975; William Saltiel Award for Best New Community Project, 1974; Volunteer of the Year, Mental Health Association of Greater Chicago, 1974. Address: 4124 North Central Park Avenue, Chicago, Illinois 60618.

Joseph K Lunn

Luntz, Maurice Harold

Professor, Consultant. Personal: Born July 27, 1930; Son of Monte and Sarah Luntz; Married; Father of Melvyn Howard Benjamin, Caryn Susan, David Sean. Education: M.B.Ch.B., University of Capetown, 1952; M.D., University of Witwatersrand, 1974; F.R.C.S., Royal College of Surgeons, Edinburgh, 1958; F.A.C.S., American College of Surgeons, 1979. Career: Professor, Ophthalmology, Beth Israel Medical Center, New York, 1978 to present; Consultant, Manhattan Eye, Ear, and Throat Hospital, New York, 1978 to present; Consultant in Corneal Disease, H.I.P. Hospital Group, New York, 1978 to present; Consultant in Ophthalmology, University of Witwatersrand, Johannesburg, South Africa, 1964-78. Organizational Memberships: Medical Association of South Africa; Ophthalmological Society of the United Kingdom; Oxford Ophthalmological Society; Association for Eye Research; Ophthalmological Society of South Africa; College of Medicine of South Africa (associate founder, 1964); International Ophthalmic Microsurgery Study Group; Society of Eye Surgeons (honorary fellow); International Society of Geographic Ophthalmology (regional secretary); International Color Vision Research Group; Royal Society of Medicine, London (affiliate); International Glaucoma Congress (charter member); New York County Medical Society; Manhattan Ophthalmological Society; Beth Israel Medical Center (executive board committee; medical board committee; directors of service committee; committee on scientific activities; committee on utilizaton; committee on plan and scope; joint conference committee; committee on surgery). Published Works: Numerous Professional Articles including (most recently) "The Plasma Cell Response in Experimental Uveitis" 1979, "Rift Valley Fever and Rickettsial Retinitis Including Fluorescein Angiography" 1978, "Clinical Types of Cataracts" 1978. Honors and Awards: Lewis Memorial Scholarship for Anatomy and Physiology in 2nd M.B. Examination, 1948-52; Royal Society of Medicine, Most Original Research Published in the United Kingdom, 1963; International Council of Ophthalmology, 1974; Elected Charter Member, Academia Internationalis Ophthalmicus, 1975; Serving Officer, Order of St. John of Jerusalem, 1974; Listed in *Who's Who in the World.* Address: 180 East End Avenue, New York, New York 10028.

Lyells, Ruby E Stutts

Ruby E S Lyells

Federal Jury Commissioner. Personal: Born February 27, 1904, in Arding, Yazos County, Mississippi; Daughter of Tom and Rossie Cowan Stutts; Widow. Education: Graduate of Utica Institute High School; B.S., Alcorn State University; B.S. Library Science, Hampton Institute; M.A., University of Chicago. Career: Instructor, Alcorn State University, 1929; Acting Librarian, Auburn Branch, Atlanta Public Library, 1930; Librarian, Alcorn State University, 1930-45; Inspector, Julius Rosenwald School Libraries, Jackson State University, 1945-47; Director, Negro College Y.M.C.A.-Y.W.C.A.'s of Mississippi, 1947-50; Librarian, Carver and College Park Branches, Jackson Metropolitan Library, 1951-55; Executive Director, Mississippi State Council on Human Relations, 1955-59; Small Business Entrepreneur, MLS Service Company Drug Store, 1959-69; Federal Jury Commissioner, United States District Court, Southern District of Mississippi, 1980 to present. Organizational Memberships: Mississippi Library Association; American Library Association; Mississippi Negro Library Association (co-founder); Mississippi Teachers Association. Community Activities: Moderator League of Women Voters/Chanel 12 Radio Public Affairs Program "Learn with the League"; Mayor's Advisory Committee 1978-; Alpha Kappa Alpha Sorority, Past Basileus Beta Delta Omega chapter; Alcorn State University National Alumni Association (past president), Hampton Institute; University of Chicago National Alumni Association; American Association of University Women; Auxiliary to the Goodwill Industries; Blacks in Government; Boy Scouts of America, Andrew Jackson Council Century Club; Capitol Area Republican Club; Chamber of Commerce; Girl Scouts of America, Middle Mississippi Council; Hinds County Republican Woman's Club; Hinds County Chapter, American Red Cross (past board member); International Friends; Jackson Area Council on Human Relations (past president); Jacksonians for Public Education (president); League of Women Voters; Mary Church Terrell Literary Club (past president); Opera Guild; Opera-South Guild; Parent-Teacher Association; Symphony League; State Negro Library Association; Urban League; Young Women's Christian Association; Mississippi Association of Private Colleges (board of directors); Co-Blossom, Council of Black Leaders of State Organizations of Mississippi; Mississippi Common Cause; Mississippi Art Association; Mississippi Consumers Association (board member); Mississippi District Young Women's Christian Association (past board member); Mississippi Economic Council (state chamber of commerce); Mississippi Library Association; Mississippi State Federation of Colored Women's Clubs (past president); Mississippi Teachers Association-National

Education Association; Mississippi Wildlife Federation; Mississippians for Educational Television; Mississippi Women's Cabinet for Public Affairs; National Association of Landowners, Mississippi Chapter (president); State Institutions of Higher Education Special Committee of 60; National Association for the Advancement of Colored People (life member); National Council of Negro Women (life member); National Council of Women of the United States; National Negro Business and Professional Women's Clubs; Reading is Fundamental (state chairman); Smithsonian Institution Associates; Youth Argosy National Association of Colored Women's Club (life member; past chairman, board of directors); International Institute of Community Leaders (fellow); International Platform Association; Lady Sabena Club-Understanding Through Travel; Alcorn State University Foundation (charter member); Candidate for Nomination for Mississippi Senate, 1975; Precinct Chairman; Hinds County Republican Executive Committee, 1980 to present. Published Works: ". . . that which concerneth me", weekly column in *Jackson Advocate*, 1978 to present; Number of Articles in Professional Periodicals; Writings included in *Vital Speeches* of the Day, Professional Education and Library Journals and *New Voices in American Poetry*, Vantage Press. Honors and Awards: United Way Outstanding Volunteer Award 1982; World University Round Table Honorary Doctor of Literature, 1981; Julius Rosenwald Fellowship, Alcorn State University, 1929-30; Alcornite of the Year, Alcorn State University Alumni Association, 1957; Alpha Kappa Alpha Regional Outstanding Citizenship Award, 1959; *Pittsburg Courier* Best Dressed Women's List, 1959; Best Dressed Women's List 1968, Outstanding Citizen Award 1971, Sophisticated Lavorettes; National Association for the Advancement of Colored People Community Activist Citation with Life Membership, 1965; Prentiss Institute Named the Ruby E. Stutts Lyells Library and Awarded Doctor of Humanities Degree, 1968; Mississippi Black Leadership Conference Outstanding Leadership Award, 1974; Mary McLeod Bethune Centennial Certificate of Appreciation, National Endeavors, 1975; Concerned Citizens for Representative Government Bicentennial State for Outstanding Contribution, 1976; Fellow, International Institute of Community Service, 1976; Award for Distinguished Service and Outstanding Leadership, Hampton Institute, 1977; University of Chicago Alumni Association Citation for Public Service, 1977; Mississippi Independent Beauticians Association Community Service Award, 1978. Address: Jackson, Mississippi.

Lynch, Fauneil Mau

Government Auditor. Personal: Born November 29, 1922; Daughter of Carl and Emma Wieland Mau (both deceased); Brother, Anson (deceased); Married John B. Lynch (deceased). Education: B.A. 1967, M.S.E. 1970, Wayne State College; Advanced Courses, University of Nebraska-Lincoln, Summers 1973, 1974; Human Development Course, South Dakota State University, 1974; ABD, University of Northern Colorado, 1977. Career: Government Auditor; Former Tax Accountant and College Professor; Cooperative Education Coordinator, Secretarial Science, Eastern Oregon State College, 1976-77; Lecturer, University of Nebraska-Omaha, Financial Analysis 1976, Accounting 1975; Lecturer, Mid-Plains Community College, Principles of Management, 1981; Lecturer, Kearney State College, Managerial Finance, 1982. Organizational Memberships: German-American Club, North Platte, Nebraska (secretary); International Platform Association (speaker's bureau); Altrusa Club, International (North Platte chapter); South Dakota State Federation of National Business and Professional Women's Clubs (state treasurer, 1974); American Association of University Women; Midwest Business Management Association; Business and Professional Women's Club, Madison, South Dakota; National Business Teacher Education Association; Oregon State Education Association; Professional Secretaries International; Society of Data Educators (committee on prescreen texts and materials, 1970). Community Activities: Candidate for County Clerk, Wayne County, Nebraska, 1962; Alcohol and Drug Referral Center, Madison, (executive board, regular board); Daniel Carey Foundation Lecture Committee, Bellevue College, 1977; Nebraska Teachers Convention (chairperson, shorthand section, 1970). Religion: Trinity Lutheran Church Secretary, Madison, South Dakota, 1973-74; Current member of First Evangelical Lutheran Church, North Platte, Nebraska, transferring from Redeemer Lutheran Church, Wayne, Nebraska, 1982. Honors and Awards: Community Leader and Noteworthy Citizen Award, 1979-80; Listed in *International Book of Honor, International Who's Who of Intellectuals, Community Leaders of America.* Address: P.O. Box 776, North Platte, Nebraska 69101.

Fauneil M Lynch

Lynn, James Anthony

Manufacturers Representative. Personal: Born May 26, 1952, in Marin County, California; Son of James W. and Joy K. Lynn; Married Claudia Stafford; Father of Brandice Heather and Candice Holly, James Christian. Education: Graduate of Wagner High School, magna cum laude, Clark Air Base, Republic of the Philippines, 1970; A.A., McLennan Community College, Waco, Texas, 1972; B.B.A., Baylor University, Waco, 1975. Career: Territory Manager, Wyeth Laboratories Division, American Home Products. Organizational Memberships: Pharmaceutical Manufacturers Representative Association of Texas; Drug Travelers of Texas. Community Activities: P.M.R.A.T.; Sons of the Republic of Texas; Campus Lions Club (charter member; secretary-treasurer); Baylor Alumni Association (life member); Baylor Alumni Endowment Fund; Republican Party of Texas. Religion: Baptist. Published Works: Research in Teratogenisis in Chick Embryos, Behavior and Foraging Habits of the Solenopsis sp. Honors and Awards: National Honor Society; Award for Volunteer Work with the American Red Cross. Address: P.O. Box 7462, Waco, Texas 76714.

Lyons, Phillip Michael Sr

Administrator. Personal: Born November 22, 1941; Son of Joseph B. and Elder M. Lyons; Married Wynona Fay Meyers; Father of Phillip M. Jr., Wilton Joseph. Education: B.B.A, Accounting,, University of Houston, 1977; Attained Designation of Fellow, Life Office Management Institute, 1977. Career: Administrator, Insurance and Risk Management, Aramco Services Company; Former Positions include Insurance Executive, Accounting Manager Real Estate Broker, Insurance Consultant. Organizational Memberships: Risk Management and Insurance Society (national executive referral committee, 1981 to present); International Foundation of Employee Benefit Plans (member, 1981 to present). Community Activities: Chamber of Commerce, Galveston, Texas (member, 1960-77; streets and highways committee; housing committee; industrial development committee); Junior Chamber of Commerce, Galveston (director, 1970-72; board of directors, 1972-75); Alvin Masonic Lodge; Houston Scottish Rite Consistory; Houston Arabia Shrine Temple; Alvin Little League (coach, 1979 to present; president, minor's league, 1981); Alvin DeMolay Chapter (chapter advisor, 1980 to present). Honors and Awards: Annual Awards for Highest Individual Service and Participation, Galveston Jaycees, 1972, 1973; Listed in *Who's Who in the South and Southwest, Personalities of the South, Personalities of America.* Address: 223 West Sherwood Drive, Alvin, Texas 77511.

Ma, Pearl

Microbiologist. Personal: Born August 10, 1928; Daughter of Chiu-Ki and Yee Mui Lum Ma. Education: Graduate of St. Stephen's Girls College, Hong Kong, with Degree of London Matriculation, 1946; B.A., Biology, Rosemont College, Pennsylvania, 1950; M.S., Microbiology, University of Pennsylvania Graduate School of Liberal Arts and Sciences, Philadelphia, 1955; Ph.D., Microbiology, Jefferson University, Philadelphia, Pennsylvania, 1951. Career: Lecturer in Virology, Department of Public Health and Bacteriology, Wagner College, Staten Island, New York, 1972-73; Assistant Professor, Clinical Pathology, New York University School of Medicine, New York, New York, 1971 to present; Chief of Microbiology, St. Vincent's Hospital and Medical Center of New York, 1970 to present; Chief of Microbiology and Cytogenetics, Department of Clinical Pathology, Akron City Hospital, Akron, Ohio, 1965-69; Research Associate, Department of Pathology, Medical College of Virginia, Richmond, 1964-65; Associate in Medicine 1963-64, Adjunct Research Associate 1961-62, Research Associate in Public Health/Infectious Diseases 1961-62, Hehnemann Medical College and Hospital, Philadelphia, Pennsylvania; Chief of Microbiology, Woman's Hospital of Philadelphia, 1961-62; Consultant in Microbiology, Oncologic Hospital, Philadelphia, 1961-62; Consultant in Microbiology and Hematology, Toxicology Laboratory, Philadelphia, 1961; Consultant in Microbiology, Salem County Hospital, New Jersey, 1961; Instructor of Nursing Microbiology, School of Nursing, Jefferson Hospital, Philadelphia; Consultant in Mycology and Clinical Microbiology 1959-61, Chief of Mycology and Assistant Bacteriologist 1954-59, Jefferson University Hospital, Philadelphia. Organizational Memberships: Association for Women in Science; New York Academy of Sciences (advisory committee of microbiology section, 1976 to present); Public Health and Medical Laboratory Microbiology (registered specialist, 1973); Medical Mycology Society of New York, 1972; New York City Branch of the American Society for Microbiology; Mid-West Society for Electron Microscopists; American Association for the Advancement of Science; Women's American Medical Association; Eastern Pennsylvania Branch, American Society for Microbiology National-American Society for Microbiology; Association of Clinical Scientists. Published Works: Numerous Professional Articles including "A Case of Acanthamoeba Keratitis in New York City and a Review of Ten Cases" (with E. Willaert, K. B. Juechter and A. R. Stevens) 1982, "Three-Step Stool Examination for Cryptosporidiosis in Ten Homosexual Men with Protracted Watery Diarrhea" (with Rosemary Soave) 1982, "A Sudden Fall in Ampicillin Resistance in Salmonella Typhimurium" (with C. E. Cherubin, G. F. Timoney, M. F. Sierra and J. Marr) 1980, "The Microbiology Laboratory in Diagnosis and Therapy" 1980; Other Technical Publications and Professional Presentations, 1962 to present. Honors and Awards: Elected Member, Infectious Diseases Society of America, 1981; Coordinator of Inter-City Infectious Disease Rounds, St. Vincent's Hospital and Medical Center of New York, 1980 to present; Antimicrobial Tests of New Antibiotics on Clinical Isolates, 1978 to present; Biomedical Research Support Grant, St. Vincent's Hospital, 1977; Fellow, New York Academy of Sciences, 1977 to present; General Research Fund Award, United States National Institute of Health; Most Successful Alumnus of the Year, Rosemont College Alumni Association, 1965; Candidate, *Young Women of America*, 1965; Research Grant on Heat Shock Method of Phage Typing Non-Typable Staphylococcus Aureus, National Institute of Allergy and Infectious Diseases, National Institute of Health, 1965-68; Graduate with Distinction in Biology, Rosemont College, Pennsylvania; Kistler's Honor Society, Rosemont College; Listed in *Who's Who of American Women, Two Thousand Women of Achievement, Dictionary of International Biography, National Register of Prominent Americans, Who's Who in the Midwest, Who's Who in the East, International Who's Who in Community Service, World Who's Who of Women, Who's Who Directory, Who's Who in America, International Who's Who of Intellectuals, Notable Americans, Community Leaders of America, Men and Women of Distinction, Who's Who in Technology Today*. Address: 531 Main Street North, New York, New York 10044.

Macebuh, Sandy

Writer and Consultant. Personal: Parents Deceased. Education: Bachelor's Degree in Psychology and Theatre, University of Minnesota; Master's Degree in Communications, Theatre and Consumer Behavior, Wayne State University, Detroit, Michigan. Career: Consultant; Writer; Poet. Organizational Memberships: Dramatists Guild; Authors League of America; American Theatre Association; Women in Communications (associate member); American Management Association, 1981. Community Activities: Young Women's Christian Association; Volunteer during Political Campaigns of Betty Forness. Honors and Awards: Poet Laureate, University of Montana; Listed in *International Who's Who of Intellectuals, Directory of Distinguished Americans, Personalities of America, Notable Americans*. Address: 1520 First Street L-100, Coronado, California 92118.

Macfarlane, Alastair Iain R

Advertising Executive. Personal: Born March 7, 1940; Son of Alexander and Margaret Macfarlane; Married to Madge Anne; Father of Douglas, Dennis, Robert, Jeffrey. Education: B.Econ., with honors, University of Sydney, 1961; M.B.A., University of Hawaii, 1964; Special M.B.A., Columbia University, 1964; A.M.P., Harvard University, 1977; A.A.S.A., Australian Society of Accountants, 1962. Career: Group Senior Vice President for advertising agency; Former General Manager of food manufacturing; Former University Lecturer; Former Management Consultant; Former General Manager of advertising agency. Organizational Memberships: Australian Society of Accountants; Australian Institute of Management (fellow); Lecturer to government, business and social groups. Community Activities: Waverley District Cricket Club (vice president, 1975-77). Published Works: Contributions to professional journals. Honors and Awards: Australian Commonwealth Scholar, 1958-61; Australian Steel Industry Scholarship, 1958-61; U.S. Federal East-West Center Fellow, 1962-64. Address: 2 Whippoorwill Road, Chappaqua, New York 10514.

MacLellan, Helen M

Technical Information Specialist. Personal: Born May 15, 1950; Daughter of Mrs. Minnie B. MacLellan. Education: Graduate of Wyoming Seminary Preparatory School, Kingston, Pennsylvania, 1958; B.S. Biology 1972, M.S. Biology 1975, Wilkes College, Wilkes-Barre, Pennsylvania. Career: National Eye Institute, National Institutes of Health, Technical Information Specialist, Biologist in Glaucoma Research. Organizational Memberships: Sigma Xi; American Association for the Advancement of Science; Association for Women in Science; American Society of Zoologists; Marine Technology Society. Community Activities: United Nations Law of the Sea Treaty (nongovernmental observer for the World Council of Churches at conferences in New York, New York, and Geneva, Switzerland, 1980-81); Law of the Sea Treaty and Conference, Washington, D.C. Area (United Methodist Church project coordinator, 1980-81). Religion: Metropolitan Memorial National Methodist Church, Washington, D.C.; Chairperson, Christian Social Concerns Commission, 1980-83; Administrative Board, 1970-82; Nominating Commission, 1979-82; Director, Bread for the City Project, Washington, D.C., 1979 to present. Honors and Awards: Selected Equal Employment Opportunity Counselor, National Eye Institute, National Institutes of Health; Awarded Graduate Assistantship; 4-Year Undergraduate Scholarship; Listed in *Who's Who in the East*. Address: 8200 Wisconsin Avenue #1609, Bethesda, Maryland 20014.

Maesen, William August

President of Educational Institution. Personal: Born May 18, 1939; Son of August and Wilhelmina Maesen; Married Sherry Jaeger; Father of Ryan and Betsy, Steven. Education: B.A., B.S.B., Oklahoma City University; M.A., Indiana State University; Ph.D., University of Illinois-Chicago; Postdoctoral Studies, Michigan State University, University of Illinois-Chicago. Military: Served in the United States Air Force Reserves, rising through the grades to the rank of Staff Sergeant. Career: President, Chicago Institute for Advanced Studies; Former Positions include Associate Professor, School of Social Work, Grand Valley State College; Associate Professor of Behavioral Sciences, College of St. Francis, Joliet, Illinois. Organizational Memberships: American Sociological Association; National Association of Social Workers; Community Development Society. Community Activities: Retired Senior Volunteer Program, Joliet, Illinois (advisory board); Cathedral Shelter of Chicago (consultant); Religion: Christ Episcopal Church, Joliet, Illinois; Lay Reader; Vestryman; Senior Warden. Honors and Awards: Beta Gamma; Alpha Kappa Delta; Listed in Several Biographical References. Address: P.O. Box 4380, Chicago, Illinois 60680.

Magee, Albery Alphones

Real Estate Broker. Personal: Born January 13, 1930; Son of Albery and Sophia Magee (both deceased); Married Wilma Greenlee; Father of Clayton Michael, Eric Martin. Education: B.S., Southern University, 1953; Postgraduate Study, California State University, 1961-70. Military: Served in the United States Army. Career: Owner, Real Estate Broker, Magee's Realty, 1971 to present; District Counselor 1968-71, Teacher 1958-67, Union High School District, Compton, California; Teacher, Washington Parrish School Board, Franklinton, Louisiana, 1955-57. Organizational Memberships: Better Business Bureau; Long Beach District Board of Realtors; California Real Estate Association; National Association of Realtors; Long Beach Chamber of Commerce. Community Activities: Jesse L. Boyd Memorial Foundation; Century Club, Young Men's Christian Association; Optimist International; Southern University Alumni Association; Central Area Optimist Club; Head Start (parent policy council); New Hope Home (board of directors); Long Beach Branch, National Association for the Advancement of Colored People (board of directors); Senior Citizens Action Network (board of directors); Legal Aid Foundation (board of directors); United Way (regional planning commission). Religion: Christ Second Baptist Church. Honors and Awards: Humanitarian Award, California Youth Society, 1959; Certificate of Appreciation, Centennial High School, Compton, California, 1970; Certificate of Merit, Roosevelt Junior High School and Community, 1969; Community Service Award, Recreation Department of the City of Long Beach, 1975; Pearl Tillman Long Beach Central Area Community Award, 1977; Friend of Youth Award, 1977; Black Patriots of Freedom Bicentennial Award, 1975. Address: 1005 West Fernrest Drive, Harbor City, California 90710.

Americo Makk

Makk, Americo Imre

Artist (Painter). Personal: Born August 24, 1927 in Hungary; Son of Pal and Katalin Samoday Makk; Married Eva Holusa; Father of A. B. Education: Graduate of Saint Benedictin Gimnsaium, Gyor, Hungary; Hungarian National Academy of Fine Arts, Budapest; Academy of Fine Arts Scholarship Student, Rome, Italy. Career: Co-Chairman, Hawaii Heart Association Art for Heart Exhibition; Co-Chairman, Cerebral Palsey/Carnegie International Center Exhibition; Chairman, World Federation of Hungarian Artists, New York; Vice-President, American Hungarian Art Association, New York; Official Artist of the Brazilian Government; Professoro de Bela Artes de Associacao Paulista de Belas Artes; Professor of Fine Arts, Academia de Belas Artes, Sao Paulo, Brazil. Organizational Memberships: American Professional Art League, New York; The Fifty American Artists Association, New York; Associacao Paulista de Belas Artes, Sao Paulo, Brazil; Associacao Dos Professionais de Imprensa de Sao Paulo, Brazil; International Art Exchange, New York, Paris, Monaco; Two/Ten Association, U.S.A.; Metropolitan Museum of Art, New York; National Geographic Society, Washington, D.C.; Arpad Academy, U.S.A.; Accademia Italia delle Arti; Major Exhibitions with His Wife in Lafayette, Louisiana 1981, Vancouver, British Columbia, Canada 1980, Scottsdale, Arizona 1980, Wichita, Kansas 1979-80, San Francisco, California 1979-80, Chicago, Illinois 1979, Honolulu, Hawaii 1976-77, 1980, Caracas, Venezuela 1976-77, Sao Paulo, Brazil 1976, 1950-57, Beverly Hills, California 1975, Houston, Texas 1974-77, 1981, San Antonio, Texas 1972-78, 1981, El Paso, Texas 1971-80, Austin, Texas 1971-79, Los Angeles, California 1970-78, Amarillo, Texas 1969-76, Charleston, West Virginia 1972, 1975, Miami, Florida 1968-78, Washington, D.C. 1966, 1969, New Jersey 1963-65, Dayton, Ohio 1963, 1970, New York World's Fair 1963-64, New York 1963-67, Ponta Grossa 1962, Sao Carlos 1961, Rio de Janeiro, Sao Paulo, Joao Pessoa and Areia 1959, Manaus 1958, Sobral 1956-57, Victoria, Salvador, Recife, Natal and Fortaleza 1956 Rio de Janeiro 1956; Major Works, Individual and in Conjunction with Eva Makk, including Murals for Chapel of the Immaculate Conception, Cornwall, New York, "The Ascension" Mural for Memorial United Church of Christ, Dayton, Ohio, Portrait of Archbishop Scalabrini for Archdiocese of New York, Cupola and Murals for Basilica Nostra Senhora do Rosario, Ponta Grossa, Ceiling and Murals depicting the Life of St. Charles and Portrait of the Bishop, Palacio do Bispo, San Carlos, Murals depicting the Life of St. Sebastian, Igreja Matris, Taquaritinga, Sao Paulo, "La Via Sacra" Fourteen Stations of the Cross in large, modern compositions, Nostra Senhora do Carmo, Araraquara, Sao Paulo, Murals and Ceiling, Igreja Nostra Senhora dos Remedios, Sousa, Paraiba, and Many Others. Published Works: Works Published or Reviewed in Many Art Publications and Periodicals Internationally. Honors and Awards: Gold Medal World First Prize for Painting, Italian Academy of Art, 1980; Merit Award, *Notable Americans of the Bicentennial Era*, 1976; Merit Award, *International Who's Who in Art*, Cambridge, 1973; Diploma Award of Achievement, London, England, 1972; Certificates of Merit, London, England, 1970-72; Annual Masters of Contemporary Painters Salon Award, Miami, 1969; International Art Exchange Directors First Prize, New York-Paris, 1967; American Ecclesiastical Award of Achievement, New York, 1962; Merit Awards in Recognition of Outstanding Accomplishment, Rio de Janeiro, Sao Paulo, Manaus, Ceara, Paraiba, Bahia, Pernambuco, Parana, Joao Pessoa, Areia, Sao Carlos, Ponta Grossa, 1958-62; Metropolitan Honorable Mention, 1958; Special Merit Award, 1955; First Prize Eldorado (Gold Medal), Sao Paulo, Brazil, 1953; Vatican Portrait Award for Portrait of Cardinal Mindzhenty, 1948; Academy Italian Scholarship, Budapest, 1948; Centenarium Prize, Budapest, 1948. Address: 1515 Laukahi Street, Honolulu, Hawaii 96821.

Makk, Eva

Artist, Painter. Personal: Born December 1, 1933, in Hawas, Ethiopia, Africa; Daughter of Dr. Bert and Julia Ribenyi Holusa;

Married Americo Imre Makk; Mother of A. B. Education: Studied at the Academy of Fine Arts, Paris, France, and the Academy of Fine Arts, (summa cum laude), Rome, Italy. Career: Professor of Fine Arts, Academia de Belas Artes, Sao Paulo, Brazil; Professora de Belas Artes de Associacao Paulista de Belas Artes; Official Artist of the Brazilian Government; Director, American Hungarian Art Association; Director, World Federation of Hungarian Artists; Co-Chairman, Cerebral Palsy/Carnegie International Center Exhibition; Co-Chairman, Hawaii Heart Association Art for Heart Exhibition; Major Works include Igreja Sagrada Familia (tinted glass); Ingreja Santa Barbara (murals and ceiling); Ingreja San Jose (mural); Chapel of the Immaculate Conception, Cornwall, New York (murals); Memorial United Church of Christ, Dayton, Ohio (mural "The Ascension"); Others; Major Exhibitions include Lafayette, Louisiana, 1981; Vancouver, British Columbia, Canada, 1980; San Francisco, California, 1979-80; Many Others since 1950; Television Appearances: Annually since 1963 in conjunction with major exhibitions and major works in the United States. Organizational Memberships: American Professional Art League, New York; The Fifty American Artists Association, New York; Associacao Paulistas de Belas Artes, Sao Paulo, Brazil; Associacao Dos Professionais de Impresna de Sao Paulo, Brazil; International Art Exchange, New York, Paris, Monaco; Metropolitan Museum of Art, New York; National Geographic Society, Washington D.C.; Arpad Academy, U.S.A.; Accademia Italia delle Arti. Published Works: Works published or reviewed in National and International Periodicals and Newspapers. Honors and Awards: Silver Medal, Sao Paulo, 1953; First Prize, San Bernardo, 1954; Gold Medal, Sobral Museum, Sobral, Brazil, 1956; Academy First Prize, Sao Paulo, 1958; Metropolitan Honorable Mention, 1958; Merit Awards in Recognition of Outstanding Accomplishment, 1958-62; American Ecclesiastical Award of Achievement, New York, 1962; Mention of Merit, Carnegie Exhibition, 1966; Annual Masters and Contemporary Painters Salon Award, Miami, 1969; Certificates of Merit, London, England, 1970, 1971, 1972; Diploma Award of Achievement, London, 1972; Merit Award, Cambridge, 1973; Merit Award, Notable Americans of the Bicentennial Era, 1976; Gold Medal World First Prize for Painting, Italian Academy of Art, 1979. Address: 1515 Laukahi Street, Honolulu, Hawaii 96821.

Mallon, Thomas Francis Jr

Foreign Exchange Broker. Personal: Born January 2, 1944 in New York, New York; Son of Thomas Francis and Rose Marie McDonnell Mallon; Married Elizabeth Ann Kiely, June 4, 1966; Father of Eileen Elizabeth, Erin Cristin. Education: B.A., Manhattan College, 1966; Postgraduate Study, Hofstra University, 1966-71. Career: Secretary-Treasurer and Director, Mallon and Dorney Company, Limited, of Toronto, Canada, 1979 to 1981, Mallon & Dorney Company, Limited, 1975 to 1981; President and Director, Kirkland, Whittaker and Mallon, 1972-75; Owner and President, Thomas F. Mallon Associates, New York, 1971-72; Assistant Cashier, Foreign Exchange Dealer, Security Pacific International Bank, 1970-71; Chief Foreign Exchange Dealer, Banca Nazionale del Lavoro, New York, New York, 1969-70; Foreign Exchange Clerk and Dealer, Brown Brothers, Harriman and Company, New York, New York, 1966-69; Accounting Clerk, Exxon, New York, New York, 1965-66; Harlow Meyer Savage Inc., N.Y. 1981-82 (secretary-treasurer, director); Euro Brokers Harlow (Canada), Toronto 1981-82 (secretary-treasurer, director); Tullett and Riley Futures, Inc., N.Y. 1982 to present (director); Tullett and Riley, Inc. N.Y., Toronto, L.A. 1982 (S.V.P.); Thomas F. Mallon Assoc. Inc. N.Y. 1982 to present (president, owner). Organizational Memberships: Foreign Exchange Brokers Association of New York (past secretary); Association Cambiste International. Community Activities: American Institute of Banking, New York, New York (lecturer); Downtown Athletic Club. Religion: Roman Catholic. Address: 22 Bagatelle Road, Dix Hills, New York 11746.

Betty Manalatos

Malola, Mary E

English Teacher, Poet, Student of Arabic Language and Syrian History and Culture. Personal: Born May 25, 1923 in Evansville, Indiana; Daughter of John M. Work (deceased) and Irene Christine Marie Heinlin Work; Married Mousa A. Malola; Mother of Ann Tranbarger Phillips, Hane M. Education: A.B. English and Speech 1945, M.A. English 1959, 6th Year in English 1968, Indiana State University. Career: Vigo County School Corporation of Terre Haute, Teacher of English and Yearbook Sponsor, Terre Haute South Vigo High School, 1980-; Teacher of English and Journalism at Terre Haute North Vigo High School, 1972-80, Editor of School Corporation Newsletter and Public Relations Chairman 1961-65, Teacher of English and Journalism at Gerstmeyer High School 1959-72; Classified Advertising Supervisor, Tribune-Star Publishing Company, 1945-58. Organizational Memberships: National Council of Teachers of English; Indiana Council of Teachers of English (regional judge for writing competition, 1975 to present); National School Public Relations Association (convention delegate); National Association of Journalism Directors; Indian High School Press Association; Wabash Valley Press Association; National Education Association (life member); Indiana State Teachers Association (curriculum and instruction committee; curriculum and professional development committee; conference on instruction committees; district council); Vigo County Teachers Association (vice-president; public relations chairman; delegate to state representative assembly and leadership conference); American Association of University Women (past president; secretary; board of directors; Association of Teacher Educators (participant, national conference program, 1975, 1977). Community Activities: Terre Haute Quill and Scroll (founder, 1959); Delta Kappa Gamma (program and research committees); Republican Party (workshop newsletter editor); University Wives Club of Indiana State University. Religion: St. George Orthodox Church; President, Ladies Society; Secretary, Parish Council; Society of St. George; Teacher and Superintendent, Sunday School. Published Works: Contributor to *National Poetry Anthology*, 11 Years. Honors and Awards: Fellowship Grant Named in Her Honor, American Association of University Women; Listed in *Community Leaders and Noteworthy Americans, Notable Americans, Personalities of America, Book of Honor, Personalities of the West and Midwest, International Who's Who of Intellectuals, International Who's Who in Community Service, Dictionary of International Biography, World Who's Who of Women, Who's Who of American Women, Contemporary Personalities, Community Leaders of America, Directory of Distinguished Americans, Who's Who in the Middle West, Men and Women of Distinction, Who's Who of American Women, International Book of Honor, Contemporary Personalities (Italian Academy of Arts and Letters)*. Address: 4422 South 10th Street, Terre Haute, Indiana 47802.

Manalatos, Betty

Civic Worker. Personal: Born 1898 in Pennsylvania; Daughter of Charles and Joan Simpson Stein; Married Paul Manalatos (deceased); Mother of Paul. Education: Graduate of Saint Lukes High School, Scranton, Pennsylvania; Graduated as S.O.R., Westside Hospital, Scranton, Pennsylvania, 1926. Community Activities: Veterans Hospital (volunteer); Crippled Children's Hospital (volunteer); Retarded Children's Schools (volunteer); American Red Cross (blood donor of 7½ gallons); Senior Citizens Volunteer; Volunteer for the Blind; Order of the Rose Women's Advertising Club, Portland, Oregon; International Association of Turtles (life member); Mokattam Temple #12 of Daughters of the Nile, Los Angeles, California; Triangle Chapter #456 of Order of the Eastern Star, 25 Years; Order of the White Shrine of Jerusalem #23; Degree of Pocahontas of Triuma Council #273, Santa Monica, California, 25 Years; Ladies of the Grand Army of the Republic (Department of California, past president; past national president; life member; memorial home chairman, board of directors, 15 years); Sons of Civil War Veterans Auxiliary, Los Angeles, California (president); Steven Jackson Relief Corps #124 (president); Venice, California, Women's Club; International Platform Society (honored member). Honors and Awards: Keys to Cities of Boston (Massachustts), Scranton (Pennsylvania), Wilmington (Delaware), Oklahoma City (Oklahoma), San Francisco and Los Angeles (California), and New York (New York); Attendance of Commissioning

Ceremonies of *U.S.S. John F. Kennedy*, Newport News, Virginia, 1968; Numerous Awards and Citations. Address: 10731 Oregon Avenue, Culver City, California 90230.

Manders, Karl Lee

Neurological Surgeon. Personal: Born January 21, 1927; Son of Frances Edna Cohan; Married Ann Lorrain Laprell; Father of Darlanna, Maidena. Education: Cornell University, 1944-46; M.D., University of Buffalo School of Medicine, 1950; Resident in Neurological Surgery, University of Virginia Hospital 1950-52, Henry Ford Hospital 1954-56. Military: Served in the United States Navy as Lieutenant, 1952-54. Career: Coroner, Marion County, Indianapolis, Indiana, 1977 to present; Neurological Surgeon, 1956 to present; Medical Director, Community Hospital Rehabilitation Center for Pain; Chairman of Baromedical Department, Community Hospital. Community Activities: Crossroads Rehabilitation Center (medical board); Indiana Multiple Sclerosis Society (medical board). Religion: Guest Lecturer, Unitarian All Souls Church, 1979-80. Honors and Awards: Certificate of Achievement, United States Army, 1969; James Gibson Anatomical Society Award, 1946. Address: 5845 Highfall Road, Indianapolis, Indiana 46226.

Mann, Grace Carroll

Ballerina, Choreographer, Teacher and Director of Ballet. Personal: Born November 30; Daughter of Nell C. Mann. Education: B.A., University of California-Berkeley, 1941; Ballet Training, San Francisco Ballet; Ballet Training with Theodore Kosloff and Alexandra Baldina of the Imperial Russian Ballet, Hollywood, California. Career: Ballerina, Choreographer, Teacher and Director, The Ballet Center, Oakland, California; Former Teacher of Artists in Various Ballet Companies, including Alvin Alley, San Francisco Ballet, Mexico City Ballet, and the American Ballet Theatre; Founder, Ballet Valmann with her Brother, Artist Robert Vala; Founder, Studio of Dance Art, 1951; Ballerina, Summer Theatre, Oakland, California, 1945-46; Principal Dancer in the Original Ballet Russe of Colonel De Basil, 1947-48, including the Covent Garden Season; Original Ballet Russe, 1947-48; Ballerina, Kosloff Ballet, Hollywood, California, 1945-46; Dancer, Ben Hecht Film *Spectre of the Rose*, 1945; Ballerina, San Francisco Opera Auditions (judge, many years). Honors and Awards: Art Honor Society, University of California-Berkeley; Delta Epsilon; Listed in *World Who's Who of Women, Who's Who of American Women, Directory of Distinguished Americans.* Address: 5960 Margarido Drive, Oakland, California 94618.

Mann, James Darwin

Associate Professor of Mathematics. Personal: Born February 27, 1936; Son of Glinn W. Mann; Father of Terry Brian. Education: B.S., Morehead State University, 1962; Masters of Mathematics, University of South Carolina, 1965; Attended Indiana University, 1968-69; Attended Oberlin College, summer of 1968; Attended Vanderbilt University, summer 1967; Attended North Carolina State University, summer 1972. Career: Associate Professor of Mathematics, Morehead State University; High School teacher of mathematics, 1962-64; Instructor of mathematics, Presbyterian College, Clinton, South Carolina, 1965-66. Organizational Memberships: Mathematics Association of America, 1965 to present; National Council of Teacher of Mathematics, 1969 to present; Kentucky Section of Mathematics Association of America. Community Activities: Member, Morehead Jaycees, 1966-68; Fund raiser for United Way, 1977-78; Volunteer coach for Little League Baseball, 1973-76; Part-time coach of Babe Ruth Baseball, 1977; Served as Northeast Kentucky Science Fair Rules Chairman, 1969-76; Served as Judge at Northeast Kentucky Science Fair, 1967, 1968, 1977, 1979, 1980, 1981; Served as Counselor for Kentucky Zeta chapter of Sigma Phi Epsilon, 1970-76. Religion: Attends Baptist Church. Honors and Awards: National Science Foundation grants to attend University of South Carolina, 1964-65, Vanderbilt University, 1967, Oberlin College, 1968, and North Carolina State University, 1972; Received Outstanding Alumni Award, Kentucky Zeta chapter of Sigma Phi Epsilon, 1977; Listed in *Personalities of the South, Book of Honor, Notable Americans, Men and Women of Distinction, Directory of Distinguished Americans, International Book of Honor, Personalities of America.* Address: Box 234, Route 6, Morehead, Kentucky 40351.

Manor, Filomena Roberta

Dietician, Nutritionist. Personal: Born July 6, 1926; Daughter of Mrs. Mary C. Fusco. Education: B.S. with High Honors, Foods and Nutrition, Russell Sage College, Troy, New York, 1948; Dietetic Internship, Peter Bent Brigham Hospital, Boston, Massachusetts, 1949; M.S. Hospital Dietetics and Institution Management, Ohio State University, Columbus, 1960. Military: Served in the United States Air Force from 1950 to present; attaining ranks of 2nd Lieutenant 1950 through Colonel 1971 to present. Career: United States Air Force Senior Consultant to Surgeon General, Associate Chief for Dietetics and Nutrition, Biomedical Science Corps 1972-82, Representative to Foods and Nutrition Board, National Research Council 1973 to present, Chief, Medical Food Service Division and Director, Dietetic Internship, Malcolm Grow Medical Center 1970 to present; Staff Advisor for Women in the Biomedical Sciences Corps to the Defense Advisory Committee on Women in the Services 1972-79, Assistant for Dietetic Services, Strategic Air Command, 1963-65, and Military Airlift Command 1965-70, Command Consultant Dietitian for 15th Air Force 1960-62, in Europe 1958-69, and the Air Defense Command 1955-57. Organizational Memberships: Registered Dietitian; American Dietetic Association, 1949 to present; Dietetic Internship Board, 1972-75; Aerospace Medical Association, 1970 to present; Association of Military Surgeons of the United States (chairman, medical specialist section, 1972; member, 1962 to present); Air Force Association, 1973 to present. Honors and Awards: Meritorious Service Medal, Commendation Medal, United States Air Force; Omicron Nu Honorary Fraternity, 1960; McLester Award, Association of Military Surgeons of the United States, 1962; Distinguished Alumnus Award, Ohio State University, 1973; Listed in *Who's Who in the East, Who's Who of American Women, World Who's Who of Women.* Address: 307 Yoakum Parkway, Apartment 1104, Alexandria, Virginia 22304.

Manudhane, Krishna Shankar

Pharmaceutical Executive. Personal: Born August 20, 1927; Son of Shankar C. and Parvatibai Manudhane (both deceased); Married Shyama; Father of Meena M. Schaldenbrand, Pradeep. Education: B.S. Chemistry, University of Poona, 1949; B.S. Pharmacy 1951, M.S. Pharmacy 1954, University of Bombay; Ph.D. Pharmacy, University of Maryland, 1967. Career: I.C.N. Pharmaceuticals, Vice-President of Research and Development 1978 to present; Director of Product Development 1975-78; Director of Technical Services, Cord Laboratories, Detroit, Michigan, 1971-74; Scientist, Parke, Davis and Company, Detroit, Michigan, 1969-71; Head of Product Development Department, Smith, Miller and Patch, Inc., New Brunswick, New Jersey, 1967-69. Organizational Memberships: Academy of Pharmaceutical Sciences; American Pharmaceutical Association; Rho Chi Honorary Society. Community Activities: Bombay College of Pharmacy (Honorary Treasurer, 1960-62); Bombay State Pharmacy Council (Honorary Registrar, 1964);

American Biographical Institute (Editorial Advisory Board, 1980 to present); Honors and Awards: Notable Americans of the Bicentennial Era Award, 1976; Community Leaders and Noteworthy Americans Award, 1976; Bicentennial Biographical Plaque, Historical Preservations of America, 1976; Cultural Doctorate in Therapeutics, World University, 1981; Listed in *American Men and Women of Science, International Who's Who in Community Service, Dictionary of International Biography, Men of Achievement, Book of Honor, International Register of Profiles, International Who's Who of Intellectuals, Notable Americans, Who's Who in America, Dictionary of Distinguished Americans, Personalities of the West, Who's Who in Technology Today, Personalities of America, Community Leaders of America, American Registry, Community Leaders and Noteworthy Americans.* Address: 53 Mapledale Avenue, Succasunna, New Jersey 07876.

Marable, Simeon-David

Art Teacher. Personal: Born May 10, 1948; Son of Daniel Berry and Marsima Marable; Married Pamela Joyce Sorenson; Father of Simeon-David de Paul, Daniel-Dale, Christophere, Jason-Andrew Bartley. Education: B.A. English and Art, Lea College, Albert Lea, Minnesota, 1970; Postgraduate Study, Tyler School of Art, Philadelphia, Pennsylvania. Military: Served in the United States Army, 1970. Career: Art Teacher, Grades 6, 7 and 8, William Penn School, Pennsbury School System. Organizational Memberships: Bucks County Art Educators (president, 1973-74); Middletown Historical Association (resident artist, 1976-77); Three Arches Corporation (resident artist, 1975-81). Community Activities: Delta Sigma Phi Fraternity; Levittown Artists Association (teacher); Pennsbury Adulty Education; Neshaminy Adult Education; Middletown Athletic Associatoin (baseball and soccer coach). Religion: Roman Catholic. Honors and Awards: Artist of the Year, Albert Lea Lions Club, Painting in Chapel at Fort Dix, New Jersey, 1970; National Society of Arts and Literature, Nominated for Membership by Author James A. Michener; Creator and Copyrighter, Philadelphia City of Champs Logo; Listed in *Personalities of America, Who's Who in the East.* Address: 18 Spindle Tree Road, Levittown, Pennsylvania 19056.

Janice W Maran

Maran, Janice Wengerd

Senior Scientist, Project Manager. Personal: Born June 30, 1942, in Baltimore, Maryland; Daughter of Edgar A. (deceased) and Mildred I. Wengerd. Education: Graduate of Dundalk High School, Baltimore, Maryland, 1960; B.S., Juniata College, 1964; Ph.D. Physiology, Stanford University, 1974. Career: McNeil Pharmaceutical, Senior Scientist 1978 to present, Project Manager 1980 to present, Research Scientist 1977-78; N.I.H. Postdoctoral Fellow, Johns Hopkins Medical School, 1976-77; N.A.T.O. Postdoctoral Fellow, University of Bristol, England, 1974-75; Research Associate 1966-69, Research Assistant 1964-66, Stanford University. Organizational Memberships: American Physiological Society; Biomedical Engineering Society (chairman, finance committee, 1980-82); Society of Neuroscience; Sigma Xi; New York Academy of Sciences; American Association for the Advancement of Science; International Platform Association. Honors and Awards: N.S.F. Award for Summer Study, 1960; N.I.H. Predoctoral Fellowship, Stanford University, 1969-71; George D. and Grace H. Shafer Fellowship, Stanford University, 1971-74; N.A.T.O. Postdoctoral Fellowship in Science, University of Bristol, England, 1974-75; National Institutes of Health Postdoctoral Fellowship, Johns Hopkins Medical School, 1975-77; Listed in *Who's Who in the East, World Who's Who of Women, Men and Women of Science, Who's Who of American Women, Who's Who in Frontier Science and Technology, International Book of Honor, Personalities of America, Personalities of the East, Community Leaders of America, Directory of Distinguished Americans.* Address: 106 Anton Road, Wynnewood, Pennsylvania 19096.

Marcum, Gordon George II

Oil Company Executive. Personal: Born July 4, 1942; Son of Mr. and Mrs. Gordon Marcum; Married Margaret Marcum; Father of Michal Elizabeth, Gordon Matthew, Jeffrey Wallace. Education: B.B.A. Petroleum Land Management/Accounting Geology and Business Law 1974, J.D. 1967, University of Oklahoma. Military: Served as Captain and Senior Military Leadership Instructor, United States Army School of Administration and Finance, Fort Benjamin Harrison, Indiana. Career: Olix Energy and Olix Industries, Vice President-Exploration Manager, Marcum Drilling Company-Vice President-General Counsel; Director, Oil, Gas and Minerals, State Land Office, State of New Mexico; Landman, Continental Oil Company, Oklahoma City, Oklahoma; Trainee. Memberships: International Association of Drilling Contractors (president, 1979); American Association of Petroleum Landmen; Certified Petroleum Landmen, 1981. Community Activities: Oklahoma Bar Association; State Bar of Texas; Midland Chamber of Commerce; Planning and Zoning Commission; Permian Civic Ballet Association; Midland City Council; Midland Chapter March of Dimes (vice chairman); American Cancer Society; International Association of Drilling Contractors (vice president; board of directors); Midland Country Club (vice president; board of directors; Young Life (board of directors). Religion: First Presbyterian Church; Deacon; Church Treasurer; Elder. Honors and Awards: Outstanding Resident, University of Oklahoma, 1961; True Gentleman Award, Sigma Alpha Epsilon, 1962; J. C. Mayfield Award in R.O.T.C., 1963; American Association of Petroleum Landmen Award, 1963-64; Dean's Honor Roll, 1963-64; Distinguished Military Graduate, 1964; Julian Rothbaum Award for Outstanding Graduate, 1964; United States Army Commendation Medal, 1969. Address: 2607 Lockheed, Midland, Texas 79701.

Carol D Mardell-Czudnowski

Mardell-Czudnowski, Carol Dolores

Psychologist, Educator, Author. Personal: Born November 30, 1935; Daughter of Albert and Lee Goldstein; Married Moshe Czudnowski; Mother of Benjamin, Dina, Ruth. Education: B.S. Elemetary Education, University of Illinois, 1956; M.A. Educational Psychology, University of Chicago, 1958; Ph.D. Communicative Disorders, Northwestern University, 1972. Career: Associate Professor, Northern Illinois University, 1978 to present; Associate Professor, Northeastern Illinois University, 1974-78; Assistant Professor, Northwestern University, 1973-74; Research Project Director, Illinois Office of Education, Chicago, 1971-73; Learning Disabilities Consultant, 1970-71; Learning Disabilities Teacher, Highland Park, Illinois, 1969-70; Tutor, Skokie, Illinois, 1965-68; Private Practice Psychologist, Skokie, 1962-65; School Psychometrist, 1959-60; Classroom Teacher, 1956-59. Organizational Memberships: American Psychological Association; Council for Exceptional Children; Association for Children and Adults with Learning Disabilities; Midwestern Educational Research Association; Society for Learning Disabilities and Remedial Education; Foundation for Exceptional Children. Community Activities: Illinois Early Childhood Task Force, 1972-73; Fund for Perceptually Handicapped Children (board member, 1973-78); Illinois State Task Force for Child Care Training, 1973-75; *Journal of Learning Disabilities* (editorial board, 1976 to present); *Journal for Division for Early Childhood* (editorial board, 1981 to present); Kappa Delta Pi (faculty sponsor, 1980-82). Honors and Awards: Alpha Lambda Delta; Kappa Delta Pi; Pi Lambda Theta; Phi Kappa Phi; Phi Delta Kappa. Address: 6 Jennifer Lane, DeKalb, Illinois 60113.

Mardirosian, Florence

General Music Teacher (retired). Personal: Born in New York City, New York; Married Levon Mardirosian (deceased); Mother of Haig. Education: Graduate of Leonia High School, New Jersey, 1927; B.S. Music, School of Music Education of New York University, 1931; Extension and Graduate Courses, 1932-64. Career: General Music Teacher, Lewis F. Cole Middle School, Fort Lee, New Jersey, 1963-81; Music Supervisor, Park Ridge, New Jersey, 1962-63; General Music Teacher, Intermediate School, Fort Lee, New Jersey, 1962; Executive Secretary and Officer Manager, American Art Textile Printing Company, 1948-59; Secretary, City of New York Department of Welfare, 1935-46; Secretary and Programme Coordinator, C.B.S. Radio Culinary Commentator Ida Bailey Allen, 1934-35; Clerk, New York City, 1927-34; Private Teacher of Piano and Voice; Piano Soloist and Accompanist, Concert Appearances and Radio Performances. Organizational Memberships: Bergen County Music Educators; Music Educators National Conference; National Education Association; New Jersey Education Association. Community Activities: Metropolitan Opera Guild; Philharmonic Symphony Society of New York; Smithsonian Associates; Komitas Centennial Committee; Holy Cross and St. Illuminator's Armenian Apostolic Churches, New York City, and Sts. Vartanantz Armenian Apostolic Church, Ridgefield, New Jersey (choir director); St. Patrick's Cathedral, New York City (conductor of Armenian Mass, 4 times); Cosmopolitan Chorale (founder, 1950; director and conductor, 1950-65; performed at New York World's Fair 1939-40, Times Hall, Hunter College, New School of Social Research, Harvard University, Veterans Hospitals, folk festivals); Choristers of the City of New York Department of Welfare (organizer and director, 1941-49); Armenian National Chorus (past choral director). Honors and Awards: Testimonial for Contribution in Furthering the Musical Heritage and Culture of the Armenians, Armenian Communities of New York and New Jersey, 1962; Appointed Trustee, Bergen Youth Orchestra, 1979; Woman of the Year, Washington Heights Branch of Armenian Relief Society , 1980. Address: 200 Winston Drive, Unit 3015, Cliffside Park, New Jersey 07010.

Mariel

Executive. Personal: Born August 5, 1938, in Pasadena, California; Daughter of William N. Turner; Mother of Scott Craig Goodwin, William Cullen Coombes, Anna Maria Coombes, Joel Howard Coombes. Education: Self-Educated. Career: President, Majority Stockholder and Chief Executive Officer, Arizona Custom Manufacturing Inc. 1974 to present, Arizona Custom Steel 1976 to present, Arizona Custom Iron Inc., Eagle Erectors Inc. 1979 to present; Formerly, Corporate Officer & Chief Executive Officer, W.C.S. Construction Inc., Jack of All Trades Inc., Mineral Harvesters Inc. Organizational Memberships: Arizona Steel Fabricators Association (has held all offices 1976-80); American Subcontractors Association; Arizona Steel Field Erectors Association; American Society of Professional and Executive Women; National Association of Women Business Owners; National Association of Female Executives. Community Activities: Republican Party; Republican Early Birds; International Platform Association. Religion: Reorganized Church of Jesus Christ of Latter Day Saints. Honors and Awards: Listed in *Personalities of the West and Midwest, Community Leaders of America, Notable Americans, Personalities of America, Men and Women of Distinction, Dictionary of International Biography, International Who's Who of Intellectuals, World Who's Who of Women, Who's Who in Finance and Industry, Who's Who in the West, Who's Who in the World.* Address: P.O. Box 85, Paulden, Arizona 86334-0085

Alan Markworth

Marks, John D

Songwriter. Personal: Born November 10, 1909, in Mount Vernon, New York; Father of Three Children. Education: B.A., Colgate University, 1931; Music Courses, Columbia University; Further Study in Paris, France. Military: Served in the United States Army, 4 years, attaining the rank of Captain. Career: Songwriter, 1935 to present; Composer of Scores for Television Specials, including "Rudolph the Red-Nosed Reindeer", "Rudolph's Shiny New Year", "Rudolph and Frosty", "The Tiny Tree" and "The Ballad of Smokey the Bear"; Composer of Television Commercials for General Electric, 3 years; U.S.O. Songwriters Unit, American Society of Composers, Authors and Publishers, 1968; Music Publisher, St. Nicholas Music, Inc., since 1949. Organizational Memberships: American Society of Composers, Authors and Publishers (board of directors, 4 years; board of review; advisory committee). Published Works: Composer of Over 150 Published and 750 Unpublished Songs, including "Rudolph the Red-Nosed Reindeer" 1949, "I Heard the Bells on Christmas Day" 1956, "Rockin' Around the Christmas Tree" 1960, "Everything I've Always Wanted", "Anyone Can Move a Mountain", "Address Unknown", "Who Calls", "She'll Always Remember", "Don't Cross Your Fingers, Cross Your Heart"; Compiled and Edited, *Christmas Community Lyric Book*, 1956. Honors and Awards: Songwriters Hall of Fame; Gold Medal Award of the International Film and Television Festival for 1967 General Electric Commercial; Composer of Columbia Records All-Time Best-Selling Recording and Second Biggest Record of All Time, "Rudolph the Red-Nosed Reindeer"; First Award of International Society of Santa Claus in Recognition of Contribution to the Spirit of Christmas for "Rudolph the Red-Nosed Reindeer"; A.S.C.A.P. Country Music Awards for Four Christmas Recordings; Judge, Stephen Foster Memorial Singing Contest; Distinguished Alumni Award, Colgate University, 1979; Listed in *Who's Who in America, Who's Who in the World.* Address: Greenwich Village, New York City, New York.

Markworth, Alan John

Senior Research Scientist. Personal: Born July 13, 1937; Son of Mrs. Eleanore Markworth; Married Margaret G. Raines; Father (by Previous Marriage) of Sharon Marie, David John, Caroline Marie. Education: B.Sc. with honors Physics, Case Institute of Technology, 1959; M.Sc. Physics 1961, Ph.D. Physics 1969, The Ohio State University. Career: Senior Research Scientist, Physical Metallurgy Section, Battelle, Columbus (Ohio) Laboratories, employed at Battelle 1966 to present. Organizational Memberships: American Society for Metals; American Institute of Mining, Metallurgical and Petroleum Engineers; American Association of Physics Teachers, Ohio Section/American Physical Society. Community Activities: Big Brothers/Big Sisters of Columbus and Franklin County Inc. (1982 to present), Franklin County Children's Services (foster parent, 1967-70). Religion: First Community Church, Columbus, Ohio. Honors and Awards: Sigma Pi Sigma; Sigma Xi; American Society for Metals, "Computer Simulation in Materials Science" Technical Activity. Address: 1679 Cambridge Boulevard, Columbus, Ohio 43212.

Marler, John Robert

Corporate Executive. Personal: Born November 18, 1944; Son of Betty Canady; Married Sally Ann; Father of John Lee, James Gary, Joshua Robert. Education: A.B., Amarillo Junior College, 1964; M.B.A., West Virginia State University, 1966; Postgraduate Studies at the University of Nevada-Las Vegas. Military: Served in the United States Armed Forces, 502nd Batallion of the 5th Defense Group, attaining the rank of 2nd Lieutenant 1967, 1st Lieutenant 1968, Captain 1969. Career: President, Credicom Corporation; Executive Vice President, F.A.C. International; Regional Manager, California State Airlines; Regional Manager, Premiercol/Litton. Organizational Memberships: Commercial Law League of America (international relations committee). Community Activities: Special Olympics (Nevada state chairman); Retarded Children Association (board of directors); Key Club International

(international relations committee); B.F.A.E. International Animal Welfare Organization (board of directors); Oakland Ballet (board of directors); computers for Christ Christian Ministry (executive director). Religion: Los Gatos Christian Church, Member, 1977 to present, Chairman Data Committee 1980 to present, Chairman New Members Committee 1981 to present. Address: 6351 Almaden Road, San Jose, California 95123.

Marmouget, Ernestine Harris

Librarian (retired). Personal: Born September 7, 1908; Daughter of Urie Dallas and Mattie Woolsey Dickson Harris (both deceased); Married James Albert Marmouget (deceased). Education: Library Science, University of Oklahoma; B.A. 1935, Graduate Study, University of Arkansas; B.S. Library Science, University of Illinois, 1940. Career: Elementary School Librarian, Rogers, Arkansas, 1966-74; Chief Librarian, Veterans Administration Hospital, Oklahoma City, Oklahoma, 1946-53; Service Club Director, Camp Chaffee, Arkansas, 1945-46; Chief Librarian, Camp Howze, Gainsville, Texas, 1943-45; Librarian, Bacone College, Muskogee, Oklahoma, 1937-42; Librarian, Muskogee Public Library, 1930-37. Organizational Memberships: Oklahoma Library Association; American Library Association; Rogers Parent-Teacher Association (life member); Association of Childhood Education (treasurer); American Association of University Women (president; secretary). Community Activities: Delta Gamma Sorority, University of Arkansas; Rogers Panhellenic (president; historian); National Association of Retired Federal Employees (president; secretary); Arkansas Bicentennial Celebration Committee; National Society of the Daughters of the American Revolution (national vice president general; numerous committees); United Daughters of the Confederacy. Religion: Presbyterian Church; Elder, 1972 to present; Board Member; Librarian. Honors and Awards: Plaque for Outstanding Service, Governor David Pryor on Behalf of the Arkansas Bicentennial Celebration Committee, 1976; Listed in *Personalities of the South, Roster of Daughters of the American Revolution, Dickton-McEwan and Allied Families Genealogy* by Austin W. Smith. Address: 1314 West Oak, Rogers, Arkansas 72756.

Marth, Beatrice R

Elementary School Counselor. Personal: Born April 23, 1920; Daughter of Charles Henry and Sophie Louise Rangow (both deceased); Widow of Edward Albert Marth; Mother of 1 Stepdaughter. Education: Graduated cum laude, Victoria College, 1941; University of Texas, 1945-46; University of Houston, B. S. 1954, M. A. Special Education 1979, M. A. Psychology 1979, University of Houston; M. A. Counseling and Guidance, Texas A & I University, 1964. Career: Elementary Counselor, Victoria Independent School District; Lecturer, University of Houston-Victoria Campus; Elementary School Teacher, 1941-66. Organizational Memberships: Texas Personnel and Guidance Association (senator, 1979-82); Texas State Teachers Association; American Personnel and Guidance Association; Victoria Classroom Teachers (president, 1962-63); Texas Classroom Teachers; Local Texas State Teachers Association (secretary, 1964); Delta Kappa Gamma (local president, 1981; treasurer, 1963); Victoria Independent School District (many committees on research). Community Activities: Victoria Girl Scouts (board of directors; scout leader); Currier Belle Literary Club; Victoria Gem and Mineral Society (past president; past secretary); Freedom Foundation (school attendee on scholarship, 1973). Religion: First English Lutheran Church; Chairwoman, Board of Parish Education, 1974-78, 1980-82; Church Choir, 25 Years; Bible School and Sunday School Teacher; Church Council, 1974-78, 1980-82. Published Works; Unpublished Research on Teaching Reasoning Lessons to Elementary School Children. Honors and Awards: Cum Laude Graduate, Victoria College, 1941; Listed in *Who's Who in the Southwest, The World Who's Who of Women, The Directory of Distinguished Americans.* Address: 4904 Dahlia Lane, Victoria, Texas 77904.

Ernestine H Marmouget

Martin, Deborah Louise Morgan

Realtor Associate. Personal: Born October 21, 1917; Daughter of Jimmie Jubal and Callie Maude Wright Morgan (both deceased); Married John Dick Martin, Jr.; Mother of John Dick III. Education: Graduate of Stewartsville High School, Stewartsville, Virginia, 1935; Business Administration Graduate, National Business College, Roanoke, Virginia, 1937; Completed War Housing Management Classes 1944, War Housing Seminars 1944, 1945, Federal Public Housing Authority, Fort Worth, Texas; Training Conferences/Seminars, Paul D. Newton & Company, Peggy Newton Cosmetics, House of Hollywood Cosmetics, Camden Clothing Construction, Others; Various Courses, University of Virginia, 1955-63; Graduate, Dorothy Carnegie Course for Women in Personal Development, 1960; Real Estate Diploma, Newport News Adult Education Distributive Education Service, 1971; Real Estate Enrichment Seminars, Virginia Association of Realtors, 1974-76; Completed University of Virginia Realtor Institute Class A, 1976. Career: Realtor Associate, Powell and Morewitz Realty, Inc., Newport News, Virginia, 1980 to present; Marketing Consultant, University Equipment and Supply Company, Norfolk, Virginia, 1981; Realtor Associate, Eagle Properties, Ltd., Grafton, Virginia, 1977-79; Realtor, Chuck Klein Realty, Newport News, 1974-77; Realtor Associate, Landon Realty, Hampton, Virginia, 1973; Realtor Associate, Ward Realty and Insurance Company, Newport News, 1973; Sales Agent, Original Greeting Cards, Vinton, Virginia, 1961-70; Branch Sales Manager, House of Hollywood Cosmetics of California, Vinton, 1955-68; Beauty Advisor to Branch Sales Manager, Peggy Newton Cosmetics, Vinton, 1953-62; Civil Service Commission Appointments, United States Post Office, 1949-51; Housing Construction Office Manager, John D. Martin Company, Vinton, 1947-49; Owner, Martin Center Grocery, Roanoke, Virginia, 1947-52; Civil Service Commission Appointments, Assistant to Project Manager (Roanoke) 1946-47, Assistant Housing Manager (Bearden, Arkansas) 1945-46, Clerk-Stenographer to Housing Manager (Morgan City, Louisiana) 1943-45; Owner, Marlou Grocery, Bearden, Arkansas, 1945-46; Clerk-Secretary, Vicco Fuel Corporation, Roanoke, 1939-41; Receptionist-Secretary, Grace Hospital, Welch, West Virginia, 1937-39. Organizational Memberships: Newport News-Hampton Board of Realtors; Virginia Association of Realtors; National Association of Realtors; Women's Council of Realtors of the National Association of Realtors; Virginia Women's Council of Realtors of the Virginia Association of Realtors; Virginia Peninsula Women's Council of Realtors of the Newport News-Hampton Board of Realtors; Realtor-Salesman Association; Virginia Realtors Foundation. Community Activities: Boy Scouts of America (cub scout den mother, 1951-52); United Way (area manager, 1955, 1960); Order of the Eastern Star, Alice Chapter #5, 1946-61; Roanoke Broadway Theatre League, 1961-63; Community Theatre, Newport News, Virginia, 1967; Women's Club of Vinton (member, 1954 to present; delegate to several district meetings; delegate to state convention; club publicity chairman, 1962); Lady of Kazim Temple; Lady of Khedive Temple; Santa's Elf (while husband plays Santa) for Clubs, Groups, Parties; United States Historical Society (life member); Republican Party of Hampton; Newport News Republican Party. Religion: Parrish Chapel United Methodist Church, Vacation Bible School Teacher. Honors and Awards: Winner, Stewartsville Beauty Pageant, 1935; Blue Ribbon, First Prize, 4-H Club Group Song Contest, 1934; Trophy Peggy Newton's Garden of Achievement Award for Outstanding Recruiting Ability, 1957; Bronze Plaque, Peggy Newton Live Rose Garden of Achievement, Newark, New Jersey, 1957; Commended and Accorded Merit Citation, P. D. Newton Company, 1958; Fortuna Aves Novas Juvat in Honorable Recognition Certificate, Paul D. Newton Company, 1959; Competition Ribbons for Short Stories "One Enchanted Evening" 1962 and "Sweltering vs Comfortableness" 1963, Women's Clubs; Special Recognition Award for Participation in Presidential Campaign, Senator Howard Baker, Senate Minority Leader, 1980; American Biographical Institute Research Association, Life Patron Membership; Listed in

Who's Who of American Women, Personalities of the South, Directory of Distinguished Americans, Book of Honor, Personalities of America, Community Leaders of America, Who's Who in the South and Southwest. Address: 106 Booth Road, Hidenwood, Newport News, Virginia 23606.

Martin, Joseph John Baxter

Telecommunications Manager. Personal: Born August 19, 1943; Son of Joseph J. and Merrylin L. Baxter Martin; Married. Education: B.A. Political Science, DePauw University, 1965; M.A. Political Science, Monterey Institute of Foreign/International Studies, 1971; M.B.A. International Business 1980, M.B.A. Telecommunications Management 1980, Golden Gate University, San Francisco, California. Career: Lecturer, Golden Gate University, San Francisco, California, 1980 to present; Sales/Systems Engineer, Rolm Corporation, Santa Clara, California, 1982 to present; President, International Telecom Consultants, Oakland/San Francisco, California, 1982 to present; Telecommunications Manager, G.S.A./A.D.T.S. Region 9, 1978-82; Telecommunications Sales and Standard Life, Allstate Insurance Company Planned Estates Association, San Francisco, 1972-76; Teacher, Clay County Board of Education, Florida, 1967-69. Organizational Memberships: Telecommunications Association, 1978 to present; World Affairs Council of Northern California, 1981 to present. Community Activities: Monterey Institute Alumni Association (vice-president and secretary, 1979 to present); DePauw University Young Republicans (president, 1974-75); Beta Theta Pi (president, 1970-71); Student Body Association of Monterey Institute (vice-president, 1970); United Nations Association Council of International Relations (student body representative to northern California council chapter, 1970-71); United Nations Conference on Educational and Economic Problems, Elsinor, Denmark (delegate, 1971); National Congressional Club (national tax limit committee; National Conservative Political Acton Committee; Committee of Americans against Union Control of Government); Leadership Foundation, 1981 to present; National Advisory Committee to Restore School Prayer; TransWorld Radio Club. Religion: Valley Christian Center, Dublin, California, 1980 to present; Methodist Church, Ann Arbor, Michigan. Published Works: "FTS Federal Telecommunications for the Deaf", 1979; "Computer Conferencing", 1980; "Designing a Nationside Audio and Video Teleconferencing Network", 1981; Unpublished Master's Thesis, "The American Involvement in the Russian Revolution of 1917", 1971. Honors and Awards: Academic Scholarship, Monterey Institute of Foreign/International Studies, 1971; International Platform Association; Listed in *Who's Who in Finance and Industry, Who's Who in the West, Men of Achievement,* Other American Biographical Institute Listings. Address: 182 Caldecott Lane, Oakland, California 94618.

Martin, Philip J

Geophysicist. Personal: Born July 26, 1934; Son of Buford P. Martin (deceased) and Clarice V. Martin; Father of Michael B., Kimberly A., Susan Y. Education: B.S. Geological Engineering 1958, B.S. Physics 1958, University of Oklahoma. Military: Served in the United States Army, 1958, as PUT-E2. Career: Geophysicist, 1977 to present, 1959-68; Systems Analyst and Data Processing Consultant, 1968-77; Geologist, 1956-58. Organizational Memberships: Society of Exploration Geophysicists; Oklahoma City Geological Society; Geophysical Society of Oklahoma City. Community Activities: American Cancer Society (volunteer, 1982). Religion: Church of Christ. Honors and Awards: Listed in *Who's Who Among Students in American Universities and Colleges, Who's Who in the South and Southwest.* Address: P.O. Box 393, Oklahoma City, Oklahoma 73101.

Thomas H Martin

Martin, Thomas Howard

Pastor. Personal: Born August 22, 1952; Son of Mr. and Mrs. Howard V. Martin; Married to Vicki L.; Father of Tara Catherine, Aubrey Lynn. Education: Graduate, Clovis High School; Attended Baylor University; B.B.A., Eastern New Mexico University, 1974; M.Div., Southwestern Baptist Theological Seminary, 1978; Doctoral Student, New Orleans Baptist Theological Seminary. Career: Southern Baptist Pastor, Dallas, Texas; Licensed to Preach the Gospel, 1975; Ordained to the Gospel Ministry, 1977; Former Bank Teller, Real Estate Salesman, Office Manager of a car dealership, Owner of a retail gift and bridal store. Organizational Memberships: Call for Action Evangelism (president, 1980 to present); Evangelism Committee of Dallas; Baptist Association, 1979 to present; Tarrant Baptist Association (mission committee, 1976-78). Community Activities: Lions Club (treasurer, 1975-76, member 1974-76); Member, Nu Alpha Tau Epsilon, Baylor University, 1970-72 (pledge class president, 1970-71); International Order of De Molay (representative, master counsellor); Order of Knights of Templar; United Fund (executive committee, 1975); American Federation of Independent Businessmen, 1974-75; Clovis, New Mexico Association of Retail Merchants, 1974-75. Honors and Awards: Member, American Biographical Institute Research Association; Listed in *Outstanding Young Men of America, Personalities of the South, Personalities of America, Community Leaders of America.* Address: 6941 Hunnicut Road, Dallas, Texas 75227.

Mascardo, Angelina Gelera

Social Worker. Personal: Born October 3, 1937; Daughter of Benedicto and Oliva Mascardo, (both deceased); Mother of Richard, Grace, Maricel, Irene. Education: A.A., 1957, B.S., 1959, B.A., 1959, all from the University of Santo Tomas; M.A., M.L.Q. University, 1973, M.S.W., Wayne State University, 1972. Career: Psychologist; University Instructor; Public Relations Officer; Senior Social Worker; Director of Social Agency. Organizational Memberships: Social Planning Council of Metro Toronto (board member 1977-78); Kababayan Community Social Service Center (founding president of the board); National Association of Social Workers, 1972 to present. Community Activities: International Student Council (coordinator, 1971-72); Philippine National Red Cross (gray ladies 1961). Religion: Catholic. Honors and Awards: Graduate Professional Scholarship 1972-72; Henry Ford Foundation Fellowship; Episcopalian Church Grant; First Honorable Mention 1955; First Honorable Mention 1951. Address: 702 Grey Cedar Crescent, Mississauga, L4W 3J7, Ontario, Canada.

Masters, William H

Medical Doctor, Sex Therapist and Researcher, Author. Personal: Born December 27, 1915; Married Virginia Johnson; Father of Sarah W., William H. III. Education: Graduate of Lawrenceville School, New Jersey, 1934; B.S., Hamilton College, Clinton, New York, 1938; M.D., University of Rochester School of Medicine and Dentistry, New York, 1943; Obstetrics and Gynecology Internship, St. Louis Maternity and Barnes Hospitals, Washington University School of Medicine Department of Pathology, St. Louis, Missouri, 1944; Internship in Internal Medicine, Barnes Hospital, St. Louis, 1945; Assistant Resident, Obstetrics-Gynecology and Pathology, St. Louis Maternity and Barnes Hospitals, 1944; Assistant Resident, Gynecology, Barnes Hospital, 1944; Resident in Obstetrics, St. Louis Maternity Hospital, 1945-46; Resident in Gynecology, Barnes Hospital, 1946-47. Military: Served in the United States Naval Reserves, 1942-43, with the rank of Lieutenant (j.g.). Career: Chairman of the Board 1981 to present, Co-Director

1973-80, Director (under former name of Reproductive Biology Research Foundation) 1964-73, Masters and Johnson Institute, St. Louis, Missouri; Director, Division of Reproductive Biology, Washington University School of Medicine, St. Louis, 1960-63; Professor of Clinical Obstetrics-Gynecology 1969 to present, Associate Professor of Clinical Obstetrics-Gynecology 1964-69, Associate Professor of Obstetrics-Gynecology 1951-64, Assistant Professor 1949-51, Instructor 1947-49, Assistant 1944-47, Washington University School of Medicine; Consulting Gynecologist, St. Louis City Infirmary; Assistant Attending Obstetrician-Gynecologist, Jewish Hospital of St. Louis; Associate Obstetrician-Gynecologist, Washington University Clinics; Associate Gynecologist, St. Louis Children's Hospital; Associate Obstetrician-Gynecologist, Barnes Hospital, St. Louis; Associate Obstetrician-Gynecologist, St. Louis Maternity Hospital. Organizational Memberships: American Association for the Advancement of Science; American Association of Sex Educators, Counselors, and Therapists; American College of Obstetrics-Gynecology (founding fellow); American Fertility Society, Inc.; American Geriatrics Society, Inc.; American Medical Association; American Society of Andrology; American Society of Cytology; Eastern Association for Sex Therapy (life member); Endocrine Society; International Academy of Sex Research; Missouri State Medical Association; New York Academy of Sciences; Pan American Cancer Cytology Society; Pan American Medical Association; Sex Information and Education Council of the United States; St. Louis Gynecological Society; St. Louis Metropolitan Medical Society; Society for Scientific Study of Sex; Society for Study of Reproduction; Washington University Medical Center Alumni Association. Community Activities: *Contraceptive Technology Update Journal* (editorial board); Family and Children's Services (board of directors); Planned Parenthood Association (board of directors); Health and Welfare Council (board of directors); Social Planning Council (committee on adoptions); Alpha Delta Phi Fraternity; The St. Louis Club; The Racquet Club. Published Works: Over 130 Articles, Chapters, and Books Published, 1948 to present. Honors and Awards: Alpha Omega Alpha; Sigma Xi; Alpha Sigma Lambda; Honorary Sc.D., Hamilton College, 1973; Honorary Membership, Colombian Sexological Society, Eastern Missouri Psychiatric Society; Paul H. Hock Award, American Psychopathological Association, 1971; Citation Award, Sex Information and Education Council of the United States, 1972; Paul Harris Fellow Award, Rotary International, 1976; American Association of Marriage and Family Counselors Service Award, 1976; Modern Medicine Award for Distinguished Achievement, 1977; American Association of Sex Educators, Counselors and Therapists Award, 1978; World Association for Sexology Biomedical Research Award, 1979; Edward Henderson Lecture Award, American Geriatrics Society, 1981. Address: 4529 Pershing Place, St. Louis, Missouri 63108.

Masucci, Carmine

Engineering Executive. Personal: Born January 29, 1923; Son of Antonio Masucci (deceased) and Luigia Masucci; Married Carmela Marie Greco; Father of Marylou M. Rothfuss, Melinda. Education: B.E.E., College of the City of New York, 1944; M.E.E. Candidate, Polytechnic Institute of Brooklyn, 1955. Military: Served in the United States Naval Reserve as ETM 2/c, 1944-46. Career: Vice-President of Engineering, New Brunswick Scientific Company; Vice-President of Engineering, Izon Corporation, Stamford, Connecticut; General Manager of Government and Industrial Operation, C.B.S. Laboratories, Stamford, Connecticut; Consultant, C.M. Engineering Inc. and M.R.D., Inc. Organizational Memberships: Institute of Electrical and Electronic Engineers; Society of Photographic Instrumentation Engineers; Society of Instrumentation Display; Air Force Association; Society of Photographic Scientists and Engineers. Community Activities: Manhattan College Parents Council (president, 1979, 1980); Polytechnic Institute of New York Alumni Association (term director, 1980-85; associate director, 1973-80). Religion: Roman Catholic; Parish of Immaculate Conception Church, Tuckahoe, New York. Address: 64 Hickory Hill Road, Eastchester, New York 10709.

Matheny, Tom Harrell

Attorney. Personal: Born in Houston, Texas; Son of Whitman and Lorene Harrell Matheny. Education: B.A., Southeastern Louisiana University, 1954; J.D., Tulane University, 1957; Admitted to Louisiana Bar, 1957. Career: Partner, Pittman & Matheny Law Firm, Hammond, Louisiana, 1957 to present; General Counsel, First Guaranty Bank, Hammond, Louisiana; Vice-President, Southern Brick Supply, Inc.; Faculty Member, Holy Cross College, New Orleans, 3 Years; Faculty Member, Southeastern Louisiana University, 5 Years; Chairman, Board of Directors, First Guaranty Bank. Organizational Memberships: American Bar Association; Twenty-First Judicial District Bar Association (secretary-treasurer; vice-president); Louisiana State Bar Association (general chairman, committee on legal aid); World Peace Through Law Center (committee on conciliation and mediation of disputes); Louisiana Lawyer's Club; Association of National Colleges and Universities Attorney; American College of Mortgage Attorneys, Inc.; International Society of Barristers. Community Activities: Order of DeMolay (district governor to supreme council, 1964 to present); Masonic Youth Foundation of State of Louisiana (president, 1970-71); Baton Rouge Consistory; Jerusalem Temple of New Orleans; Tangipahoa Parish Shrine Club; Livingston Lodge #160 Free and Accepted Masons; Southeastern Alumni Association (president, 1961-62; board of directors, Tangipahoa parish chapter, 2 years); Boy Scouts of America (executive board, Istrouma council, 1966 to present; chairman, district advancement committee, 4 years; advisory committee to district area council); National Liberal Club of England (non-political); Tangipahoa Parish Mental Health Association (president, 1 year); Louisiana Mental Health Association (board of directors; president); American Academy of Religion and Mental Health; Louisiana Historical Association; Friends of Cabildo; Harry S. Truman Library Institute (honorary fellow); United Nations Association; International Platform Association; National Historical Society of Louisiana Annual Conference; Crime Control Committee-Goals for Louisiana (chairman, 1 year); Louisiana Commission on Law Enforcement and Administration of Criminal Justice (committee on community action and crime prevention, 2 years); Louisiana Moral and Civic Foundation (board of directors); Public Affairs Research Council; Louisiana Association of Business and Industry; Council for a Better Louisiana. Religion: First United Methodist Church, Hammond, Louisiana, Administrative Board, Commission of Stewardship and Finance, Committee on Pastor-Parish Relations; Lay Minister's License, Methodist Church; Baton Rouge District of the Methodist Church, District Lay Leader, 1960-64; Louisiana Interchurch Conference, Chairman of Finance Committee 2 Years, Board of Directors; Louisiana Area Conference, Board of Missions; Louisiana Annual Conference, Council on Ministries; Louisiana Area Council, Commission on Higher Education; United Methodist Church, Chairman of Budget Committee of Program Council, 1964-71; Jurisdictional Conference, Rules Committee, 1968; Centenary College, Shreveport, Louisiana, Board of Trustees; Academy of Religion and Mental Health; Gideons International; Japan International, Men's Committee; Christian University Foundation. Honors and Awards: Layman of the Year, Louisiana Annual Conference of the United Methodist Church, 1966, 1973; One of Three Outstanding Men of Louisiana, Jaycees, 1964; Distinguished Service Award, Hammond Junior Chamber of Commerce, 1960-64; Layman of the Year for Louisiana, Mississippi, West Tennessee, Kiwanis International, 1972; Honorary Doctor of Laws Degree, Centenary College of Louisiana and DePauw University; Distinguished Alumnus Award, Southeastern Louisiana University, 1981; Crackpot Club of Great Britain; Listed in *Who's Who in Education, Who's Who in Business, Who's Who in the South and Southwest, Dictionary of International Biography, Outstanding Young Men of America, Who's Who in Methodism, Personalities of the South, Outstanding Civic Leaders of America, Royal Blue Book, Community Leaders of America, Who's Who in the World.* Address: P.O. Box 221, Hammond, Louisiana 70404.

Matthews, Norma Rita

President, Washington Intelligence Bureau. Personal: Born January 31, 1920; Daughter of Helmer John and Helen Virginia Harriss

Kallio (both deceased); Mother of Shelley G. Neitzey, Pamela Harris, Glenn A., Bradford J. Education: Accounting Scholar, Southeastern University. Career: President, Washington Intelligence Bureau, Inc.; Budget Officer, Post Office Department, Washington, D.C. Organizational Memberships: Direct Mail Advertising Club; Small Business Association; Newsletter Association of America; Washington Metropolitan Postal Customers Council. Religion: Roman Catholic. Honors and Awards: National Honor Society, 1937; Scholarship, Southeastern University, 1937. Address: 2346 Hunter Mill Road, Vienna, Virginia 22180.

Mauch, Diane Farrell

Voice/Piano Teacher, Soloist, Director of Children's Choir. Personal: Born January 15, 1934; Daughter of Edward J. and Mary A. Farrell (both deceased); Married Robert K. Mauch; Mother of Anneliese Farrell Bernadette, Bronwen Adele. Education: Dominican Academy, 1947-51; Attended the Juilliard School of Music, 1948-51; B.A., Manhattanville College, 1955; Studies at the Aspen School of Music, 1961; Manhattan School of Music, 1962; Master's Program, Hunter College, 1964-65; M.Mus., University of Michigan, 1972; Further Studies at Indiana University, 1977; North Texas State University, 1979; Private Vocal Study under William P. Herman, Allen Rodgers, Marian Szekely-Freschl, Geri Chisolm, Jennie Tourel, Elizabeth Mannion, Paul Meyer, Eugene Bossart, John Moriarty. Career: Director of Children's Choir, Music Teacher, Epiphany Church School, Miami, Florida; Former Soloist and Director of Children's Choir, St. Henry Church; Private Studio for Voice and Piano Instruction; Former Positions include: Mary Louis Academy, Villa Maria Academy, New York; Kingswood School, Bloomfield Hills, Michigan; Trevecca College, Scarritt College, Tennessee State University, St. Bernard Academy, Cheekwook Fine Arts Center, Nashville; N.P.M. Instructor. Organizational Memberships: Music Teachers National Association (past vice president; scholarship chairman, Tennessee chapter); American Association of University Professors; National Association of Teachers of Singing (past secretary; president, Nashville chapter); National Association of Pastoral Musicians (instructor, national workshops); Choristers Guild. Community Activities: Citizens Advisory Commission (board of education); Community Concerts Association (board member; past membership chairman); Women's Symphony Association, Nashville. Religion: Roman Catholic. Published Works: Author "Music as a Ministry to Individual Creativity", "A Phenomenological Analysis of a Musical Listening Experience". Honors and Awards: Scholarship, Juilliard School of Music, 1949; Dean's List, 1951-55; Bronson Honor Society, 1954; Dean's List, University of Michigan, 1971. Grant, Tennessee Arts Commission, 1978; New York State Regents Scholar, 1951-55; Summa Cum Laude Latin Award, New York City, 1951; French, Dramatic, General Excellence Awards, Dominican Academy, 1951; Buddy Rogers Drama Award, Shakespeare, New York, 1950; Executive Leadership Award, N.P.M., 1979. Address: 653 Brook Hollow Road, Nashville, Tennessee 37205.

Mauldin, Jean Humphries

Aviation Company Executive. Personal: Born August 16, 1923 in Gordonville, Texas; Daughter of James Wiley and Lena Leota Noel-Crain Humphries; Married William Henry Mauldin, February 28, 1942; Mother of Bruce Patrick, William Timothy III. Education: B.S., Hardin Simmons University, 1943; M.S., University of Southern California, 1961; Postgraduate Studies, Westfield College, University of London 1977-78, Warnborough College, Oxford, England, 1977-78. Career: President, Stardust Aviation, Inc., Santa Ana, California, 1962 to present; President, Mauldin and Staff, Public Relations, Los Angeles, California, 1957-78; Psychological Counselor, 1st Baptist Church Social Services, 1953-57. Organizational Memberships: American Management Association; Experimental Aircraft and Pilots Association; National Women Pilots; Women for Experimental Aircraft and Pilots Association; International Platform Association. Community Activities: California Democratic Central Committee (executive board); Orange County Democratic Central Committee (executive board); California Democratic Council, 1953-70; California Democratic Central Committee, 1957 to present; Orange County Democratic Central Committee, 1960 to present; Democratic National Convention (delegate, 1974-78); United States Congressional Advisory Board; Santa Ana Friends of Public Library (president, 1973-76); McFadden Friends of the Library, Santa Ana, 1976-80; American Cancer Society (Orange County cancer crusade chairman, 1974); Historical Preservation Society (executive board member, 1970 to present); Business and Professional Women's Clubs of America; National Women's Political Caucus; Democratic Coalition Central Committees; California Friends of the Library (life member); L.W.V.; National Federation of Democratic Women; California Federation of County Central Committee Members; Jefferson Club; Democratic Alliance. Religion: Trinity Episcopal Church, Tustin, California; Protestant Episcopal Church of America (lay leader); Women's Missionary Society (chairman). Published Works: *Winters, The Pilot, The Man*, 1961; *The Consummate Barnstormer*, 1962; *The Daredevil Clown*, 1965; Advisory Producer of Television Film, "Attack on the Americas". Honors and Awards: Woman of the Year, Key Woman in Politics, California Democratic Party, 1960-80. Address: 1013 West Elliott Place, Santa Ana, California 92704.

Olivia L May

Maxwell, Edward Creighton

Rancher. Personal: Born March 25, 1904; Son of William K. and Eva Blossom Maxwell; Married Mary W. Maxwell; Father of Marie M. Thomas; Beverly M. Chambers; James P. McLoughlin, Thomas V. McLoughlin; Maureen M. Younkin. Education: LL.B., University of Illinois, 1926. Career: Rancher; Lawyer. Organizational Memberships: Ventura County Bar Association (president, 1937); California Bar Association, 1927-72; American Bar Association, 1927-72. Community Activities: 31st District Agriculture Association (director; past vice-president); Ventura County Planning Commission, 1937; Ventura County Sheriff's Possee (director and originator, 1942); Ventura County Rod and Gun Club (director, 1935-61; honorary life member); B.P.O.E. Elks (past exalted ruler, lodge 1443; honorary life member); Los Rancheros Visitadores International Equestrian Organization; Rancheros Adolfo (director). Honors and Awards: Honorary Life Member, Los Rancheros Visitadores, Campo Adolfo, B.P.O.E. Elks. Address: Post Office Box 5586, Oxnard, California 93031.

May, Olivia Lammert

Owner of Tax Service. Personal: Born December 20, 1912; Daughter of Frederick and Marie Lammer (both deceased); Married Vernon May (deceased); Mother of Curtis L. Education: Graduate of John H. Reagan High School, Houston, Texas, 1930; Houston Junior College, 1930-32; Night Classes, Draughan's Business College, 1930-31. Career: Owner, O.L.M. Business Service, Katy, Texas, 1949 to present; Senior Administrator, Exxon Company, U.S.A., Katy, Texas, 1944-77; Office Manager, Miller Motor Company, Katy, Texas, 1934-44. Organizational Memberships: Desk and Derrick Club, Houston, Texas (past treasurer); American Society of Women Accountants (corresponding secretary, 1966-67; recording secretary, 1967-68; 2nd vice-president, 1968-69; treasurer, 1969-70). Community Activities: City of Katy (accountant, 1944-49; auditor, 1949-61); Exxon Katy Federal Credit Union (chairman, auditing supervisory, 1948 to present). Religion: Sunday School Teacher, 1940-75; Organist, 1946-56. Honors and Awards: Listed in *Who's Who of American Women; Personalities of America.* Address: 1610 East Avenue, Katy, Texas 77449.

Mayes, Margie Ann Hammer

Mayor. Personal: Born July 29, 1940; Daughter of Jesse Edward and Rosa Dean Hammer (both deceased); Married Ronald Ray Mayes Sr.; Mother of Ronald Ray Jr., Valerie Dawn, Lorri Ann, Meneika Rae. Education: Graduate of Montevideo High School, 1959; Office Management Certificate, Office Machine Certificate, Secretarial Certificate, Blue Ridge Community College; Accounting Course, 1960; Local Government Course, James Madison University; Certificates in Real Estate Principles and Training. Career: Mayor, Town of Grottoes, Virginia, 1978 to present; Industrial Engineering Contractor, Industrial Engineering Stenographer, DuPont Company, Waynesboro, Virginia; Manager of Rental Property; Income Tax Preparer; Quality Control Clerk, General Electric, Waynesboro, Virginia; Relief Clerk, Celanese Corporation, Bridgewater, Virginia. Community Activities: Governor's Employment and Training Council (chairperson; Virginia Municipal League representative); High School Athletic Association (secretary-treasurer, 6 years); Rockingham Heart Association (board of directors, 6 years); Governor's Conference on Libraries (delegate, 1979); Reagan Task Force; Town Sections for the State of Virginia (co-chairman); Jury Commissioner (appointed by circuit court judge, 1976-78); Bridgewater College Centennial Committee; Intermediate/Junior High School Advisor, 5 years; Republican Party (member, 16 years; county committee; delegate to district and state conventions, 12 years); Multiple Sclerosis (chairman, Blue Ridge Chapter, Grottoes Area, 1980); V.M.L. (effective government policy committee). Religion: Port Republic United Methodist Church, Port Republic, Virginia; Sunday School Teacher; Secretary, Administrative Board; President, Young Adults; Choir. Honors and Awards: Republican President's Task Force; Mother of the Year, 1972. Address: Route 2 Box 164 E3, Grottoes, Virginia 24441.

Edward C Mazique

Mazique, Edward Craig

Physician. Personal: Born March 21, 1911; Father of Edward Houston, Jeffry Craig. Education: B.S., Morehouse College, 1933; M.A., Atlanta University, 1933; M.D., Howard University, 1941. Military: Served as United States Health Service Commander, 1950. Career: Practicing Physician of Internal Medicine, Washington, D.C. Organizational Memberships: National Medical Association (president, 1959); Howard University Medical Alumni Association (president, 1970); Howard University Alumni Federation (president, 1971); D.C. Political Action Committee District Medical Society (chairman, 1981). Community Activities: Citizens Advisory Council, Commissioners' District of Columbia Councilman, 1951; President of Medical Staff, Providence Hospital, Washington, D.C., 1981; Boys' Clubs of Greater Washington (president, 1980-81); Washington Community Broadcasting Company, Radio W.Y.C.B. (chairman, 1981); United National Bank (board of directors, 1980-81); Morehouse College (board of trustees, 1981); Morehouse Medical School (board of trustees, 1981). Religion: Member of St. Luke's Episcopal Church. Honors and Awards: Honorary D.Sc., Morehouse College, 1974; Community Service Award, District of Columbia Medical Society, 1979; Service to Youth Award, Y.M.C.A., 1952; Community Service Award, Bennett College Alumni, 1976; National Medical Association Distinguished Service Award, 1975. Address: 3201 Chestnut Street, Washington, D.C. 20015.

Don McAnally

McAnally, Don

Editor-Publisher. Personal: Born October 27, 1913 in Sewell, New Jersey; Son of James C. and Ina MacLeod McAnally; Married Edith P. McKinney, Dec. 11, 1934; Father of Shirley Ann English. Education: Grammar School, Sewell, N.J.; High School, Woodbury, N.J.; John Wanamaker Cadet Institute, Philadelphia; Sales Analysis Institute, Chicago. Career: Editor-Publisher, *California Senior Citizen News* 1977 to present, *The Automotive Booster of California* 1974 to present; Publisher, *California Businesswoman*, 1978; Owner, Hovercraft of Southern California, 1975-76; Editor, *Pacific Oil Marketer*, Los Angeles, 1960-66; Sales Promotion Manager and Product Sales Manager, LOF Glass Fibers Company, Toledo, 1953-59; Assistant Advertising Manager, Libbey-Owens-Ford Glass Company, Toledo, 1947-53; Editor, Owens-Illinois Company Publications, New Jersey and Ohio, 1945-47; Reporter and Editor, *Woodbury Daily Times*, New Jersey, 1932-45. Community Activities: Lions Club, Montrose, California; Elks Club, Burbank, California; Masquers, Hollywood, California; Silver Dollar Club, San Fernando Valley, California; Roorag, Los Angeles; Automotive Booster Club of Greater Los Angeles (executive secretary); OX 5 Aviation Pioneers, National and Southern California Wing; Greater Los Angeles Press Club. Honors and Awards: Man of the Year, Pacific Oil Conference, 1977; Appreciation Plaque, Douglas Oil Ex-Employees, 1980; Special Award, Western Oil Industry TBA Group, 1971; Award Winning Editor, Toledo Club of Printing House Craftsmen, 1950; Good Neighbor Award, Toledo, Ohio, 1948. Address: 4409 Indiana Avenue, La Canada, California 91011.

McBrayer, Odell Lavon

Attorney. Personal: Born August 16, 1930; Son of O. L. McBrayer (deceased) and Mrs. O. L. McBrayer; Married Nelda McBrayer; Father of Scott Alan, Stacy Arlene. Education: Graduate of Clarendon High School, 1948; Diploma, Clarendon Junior College, 1950; B.B.A., University of Texas, 1957; J.D., University of Texas Law School, 1958; Board Certification, Family Law Specialist, Texas Board of Legal Specialists, 1976 to present. Military: Served in the United States Air Force, 1951-55. Career: Self-Employed Attorney. Organizational Memberships: Texas State Bar Association; Tarrant County Bar Association; National Alliance for Family Life (professional member, 1974 to present); Association of Christian Marriage Counselors (professional member); National Christian Legal Society. Commmunity Activities: University of Texas School of Law (honor council, 1958-59); Chite Settlement, Fort Worth, Texas (city attorney, 1963); Dalhant Lions Club, Texas (treasurer, 1959); White Settlement Independent School Board, 1960-61; White Settlement Jaycees (president, 1961-62); Suicide Prevention of Tarrant County (district treasurer, 1967-68); District Judge Candidate, 1968; Republican Candidate, Governor of Texas, 1974; Republican Candidate, District Judge of Tarrant County, 1978; Republican Party (delegate, county and state conventions; precinct chairman, 1968-78); Downtown Civitan Club of Fort Worth (director, 1969); Tarrant County Republican Executive Committee (member, 1968-73, 1974-76; vice president, 1970); Town of Lakeside (city attorney, 1969-75; city municipal judge, 1975-78); Texas Alcohol Narcotics Education Agency (lecturer, 1969-76); Family Counseling Center of Fort Worth (professional advisor, 1969-80); Tarrant Chapter of parents Without Partners (professional advisor, 1973 to present); Downtown Fort Worth Kiwanis, International, 1974 to present; Teen Challenge, Fort Worth (chairman). Religion: Christ Church in Wedgewood, Elder 1980 to present; Reader, All Saints Episcopal Church, 1972-76; Treasurer, Normandale Baptist Church, 1961-62; Union Gospel Mission, Fort Worth, Director, President and Treasurer 1963-82; President and Founder, Northwest Chapter of Full Gospel Businessmen's Fellowship, International, 1972-76. Honors and Awards: United States Air Force Honorable Discharge, 1955; National Service Ribbon; Good Conduct Medal; Listed in *Who's Who in the South and Southwest, Who's Who in Texas, International Who's Who of Intellectuals, Creative and Successful Personalities.* Address: Route 5 Box 281A, Fort Worth, Texas 76116.

Stella M R McBride

McBride, Stella Maria Regina

Business Owner, Management Consultant, Public Speaker. Personal: Born May 17, 1936; Daughter of Edward August Demetrius and Lilla Alexander von Saher (both deceased). Education: Certified Manager, Institute of Certified Professional Managers, Dayton, Ohio, 1977. Career: Owner, Organization Plus, 1974 to present; Manager, Moffit Hospital, University of California Medical Center, San Francisco, California. Organizational Memberships: The National Management Association (Rocky Mountain Chapter, board of directors 1976 to 1982, treasurer 1977, executive vice-president 1978, executive vice-president 1979-80, president 1980-81, honorary chairman of the board 1981-82; Colorado Council, president, 1981-82); Colorado Women and Business Conference (executive committee, 1981, 1982); National Association of Parliamentarians, 1979 to present. Honors and Awards: Member of the Year, Rocky Mountain Chapter of the National Management Association. Address: 417 Meeker Road, Kerrville, Texas 78028.

McCallion, William John

Catholic Priest. Personal: Born July 8, 1923; Son of Edward J. and Rose Ann Smith McCallion. Education: Marist Seminary, 1939-41; St. Joseph's College, 1941-43; A.A., Notre Dame University, 1948; Postgraduate Study, Louisiana State University, 1963-64. Career: Pastor, St. Gertrude Des Allemands Catholic Church 1973 to present, Annunziata, Houma 1969-73, St. Agnes, New Orleans 1969, Morganza, Louisiana 1965-69; Chaplain, La St. Penetentiary, Angola, 1961-65; Assistant Pastor, St. Raphael, New Orleans 1956-61, Sacred Heart, Baton Rouge 1955-56, St. Henry's 1948-55; Ordained as Roman Catholic Priest, 1948. Community Activities: St. Charles Recreation Association (former chairman); Camp LeRoy Johnson, New Orleans (former assistant chaplain); Sacred Heart Athletic Association (life member); St. Raphael Athletic Association; Knights of Columbus; Catfish Festival (founder, president); Des Allemands Fire Department (chaplain). Religion: Roman Catholic; Archdiocesan Catholic Youth Advisory Board 1977-79. Honors and Awards: Ray Mock Award for Outstanding Service to Youth of New Orleans Area, United Givers Fund 1978, Executive Board 1980, Secretary-Treasurer 1981-82, St. Charles Industry and Development Board 1979 to present; Outstanding Citizen 1981, St. Charles Parish; Listed in *Who's Who in Religion, Community Leaders and Noteworthy Americans, Dictionary of International Biography, Personalities of the South, Two Thousand Notable Americans.* Address: Post Office Box G, Des Allemands, Louisiana 70030.

William J McCallion

McCarley, Carolyn Josephine Spence

Co-Owner of Shoe Store. Personal: Born October 16, 1919; Daughter of C. B. Spence (deceased) and Mrs. C. B. Spence; Married Clint Weldon McCarley; Mother of Clint Weldon Jr., Philip Allen, Charls Aubra, Kelvyn Joe. Education: Graduate of Amarillo High School, 1938; West Texas State University, 1938-40; B.A. Secondary Education and English, Texas A & I University, 1942; Graduate Study, University of Guadalajara, Mexico, 1944. Career: Co-Owner with Husband, Carolyn's Shoes; Teacher, Gay Junior High School, Harlingen 1952-53, Clarkwood 1948-49, Gregory 1944-45, Falfurrias 1943-44, Kingsville 1942-43. Organizational Memberships: Parent-Teacher Association (vice-president, Austin School, Harlingen, Texas, 1963-64; secretary, St. Paul's Lutheran School, 1966-68); American Association of University Women (social chairman, 1980-82). Community Activities: Family Emergency Assistance (board of directors, 1976 to present; secretary, 1980-81); Rio Grande Valley Museum (board of directors, 1977-82; secretary, 1978-82); Rio Grande Valley Museum Association (member, 1967 to present; president, 1973-75; secretary); Zonta (member, 1957-58, 1962 to present; president, 1968-70, finance, service, fellowship, public relations, and other committees); Texas Federation of Women's Clubs (scholarship fund committee, chairman 1975-77, secretary 1973-75; chairman, international hostess, gerontology, platform committees; secretary, 1980-82; 2nd vice president, 1982-84); South Texas District Federation (president, 1970-72; chairman, education, public affairs, community improvement committees); Rio Grande Valley Federation (president, 1979-81; chairman, hospitality, program, cultural affairs, and other committees); City Federation of Women's Clubs (president, 1965-67, 1972-74; second vice-president; secretary); Afflatus (president, 1970-72, 1979-80; other offices). Religion: Treasure Hills Presbyterian Church, Charter Member; Adult and Primary Sunday School Teacher, Christian Education committee; Founder and Editor, *The Treasure Chest* Newsletter; President, District and Regional Chairman, Women of the Church; Ruling Elder, 1977-81, 1982 to present. Honors and Awards: Citation, Texas Fine Arts Cultural Survey Committee, 1966-67; Outstanding Clubwoman, Rio Grande Valley Federation of Women's Clubs, 1973-74; Certificate of Community Service, City of Harlingen, 1981, 1982; Listed in *Who's Who in the South and Southwest, Who's Who in Finance, Personalities of the South, World Who's Who of Women, Dictionary of International Biography, 2000 Women of Achievement, World Who's Who of Community Service,* and others. Address: 102 Wildwood, Harlingen, Texas 78550.

McClung, David Charles

Lawyer. Personal: Born September 22, 1926; Son of Mr. and Mrs. John William McClung; Married Mildred Fong; Father of Sharon Kim Nyuk. Education: B.A. 1954, M.B.A. with distinction 1956, J.D. 1956, University of Michigan. Military: Served in the United States Navy, 1943-46. Career: Lawyer; Electronics Technician, Hawaiian Telephone Company (formerly Mutual Telephone Company). Organizational Memberships: Bar Association of Hawaii, 1957 to present; Central Labor Council (first executive secretary, 1958-59); International Platform Association; Honolulu Press Club. Community Activities: Democratic National Committee, 1976 to present; Democratic Party of Hawaii (chairman, 1968-73); Labor's International Hall of Fame (president, 1973-78; board chairman, 1968-73); State Senate (member, 1966-74; majority leader, 1966-68; president, 1968-74); State House of Representatives, 1959-64; Territorial House of Representatives, 1958-59; Variety Club Tent 50; Propeller Club; Navy League; Friendly Sons of St. Patrick; Hawaii Chinese History Center; I.B.E.W. Local 1357 (vice president, 1946; president, 1952; secretary). Honors and Awards: Alpha Kappa Psi, 1953; Beta Gamma Sigma, 1956; Phi Kappa Phi, 1956; Clarence Hicks Fellowship Award, 1956. Address: 3023 Pacific Heights Road, Honolulu, Hawaii 96813.

John McCoin

McCoin, John Mack

Social Worker. Personal: Born January 21, 1931, in Sparta, North Carolina; Son of Robert Avery and Ollie Osborne McCoin (both deceased). Education: A.A., Wingate Junior College, 1955; B.S., Appalachian State Teachers College (now Appalachian State University), 1957; M.S.S.W., Richmond Professional Institute School of Social Work, 1962; Ph.D., University of Minnesota School of Social Work, 1977; Attended University of North Carolina School of Social Work, 1959-69; Attended New York University School of Social Work, 1969; Attended Postgraduate Center for Mental Health in New York, 1970; Attended Academy of Health Sciences, U.S. Army, 1975-76 and 1977-78; Attended University of Chicago School of Social Service Administration, 1978. Military: Served with United States Marine Corps Air Station in Cherry Point, North Carolina holding rank of Staff Sergeant, 1948-52; Served with United States Marine Corps Reserves, 1957-72; Serving with United States Army Reserve with current rank of Major, 1972 to present. Career: Social Worker, Veterans Administration Medical Center, Battle Creek, Michigan, 1981 to present; Associate Professor, School of Social Work, Grand Valley State College, Allendale, Michigan, 1979-81; Assistant Professor, Department of Social Work, University of Wisconsin, Oshkosh, 1977-79; Social Worker, F.D.R. Veterans Administration Health Care Facility, Montrose, New York, 1975-77; Social Worker, Veterans Administration Hospital, Montrose, 1968-73; Senior Psychiatric Social

Worker, New York Hospital and Cornell University Medical Center, White Plains, New York, 1966-68; Psychiatric Social Worker, Toledo Mental Hygiene Clinic, Toledo, Ohio, 1964-66; Child Welfare Case Worker, Wake County Welfare Department, Raleigh, North Carolina, 1963-64; Clinical Social Worker, Dorothea Dix State Hospital, Raleigh, 1962-63; Social Service Worker, John Umstead State Hospital, Butner, North Carolina, 1960-61; Social Service Worker, Broughton State Hospital, Morganton, North Carolina, 1958-59; High School Teacher of general science and mathematics, Brevard County Board of Education, Titusville, Florida, 1956-57. Organizational Memberships: Academy of Certified Social Workers; Alpha Delta Mu social work honor society; American Society for Public Administration; Council on Social Work Education; National Association of Social Workers, Inc. Published Works: Has contributed articles to professional journals including *Clinical Social Work Journal, Social Work, Marine Corps Gazette*, various newspapers and local hospital publications; Author of unpublished manuscript, *Adult Foster Homes: An Empirial Study.* Honors and Awards: Outstanding Performance Award, F.D.R. Veterans Administration Hospital, 1971; Education Grant from National Institute of Mental Health, 1974; Education Grant from University of Wisconsin, 1978; Certified Social Worker in states of New York and Michigan; Listed in *Who's Who in the Midwest, Dictionary of International Biography, Book of Honor, Internatioal Who's Who of Intellectuals, Men of Achievement, Personalities of the West and Midwest, Register of Clinical Social Workers;* Member of International Biographical Centre and American Biographical Institute Research Association; Member, Reserve Officers Association of the United States. Address: 4231 West Dickman Road, #1-D, Springfield, Michigan 49015.

McCormack, Shirley Marie

Auditor. Personal: Born March 21, 1930; Daughter of Frank Lee Wheeler (deceased); Married Joseph McCormack (deceased); Mother of John, Joseph. Education: B.S. 1957, M.S. 1970, Pittsburg Kansas State University; Attended Washburn University (Topeka, Kansas) 1964-65, University of Oklahoma-Norman 1973-74; M.S., Central Michigan University, 1979. Career: Auditor, Office of Inspector General, Department of Housing and Urban Development, Kansas City, Missouri, 1975 to present; Instructor, Coffeyville Community Junior College 1974-75, Southwestern State College (Weatherford, Oklahoma) 1973-74, Dakota State College 1972-73; Teacher, Lakin High School (Kansas) 1966-72, Netawaka High School (Kansas) 1964-65, Williamsburg High School (Kansas) 1957-64; Clerk, Board of Education, Emporia, Kansas, 1965-66. Organizational Memberships: National Education Association, 1957-72, 1974-75; Franklin County Teachers Association, 1957-64; Jackson County Teachers Association, 1964-65; Kearny County Teachers Association, 1966-72; Higher Education Faculty Association, 1972-73; General Faculty Association (secretary, 1972-73); National Association of Female Executives, 1979-80; American Women's Society of Certified Public Accountants, 1978 to present; National Institute of Accounting, 1979 to present; International Platform Association, 1980 to present. Community Activities: American Federation of Women, 1966-72; Committee on Common Course Numbering in Higher Education, South Dakota, 1972-73. Religion: Women's Missionary Society, 1960-64, 1966-72; Sunday School Teacher of 3rd and 4th Graders, 1965-66. Honors and Awards: Graduate Fellowship, 1957; Special Award in Auditing, H.U.D. Disaster Field Office, 1979; Letter of Commendation, H.U.D., 1979; Certified Public Accountant, 1979; Certified Internal Auditor, 1981; Pi Omega Pi, 1957; Delta Pi Epsilon, 1975; Listed in *Who's Who of American Women, World Who's Who of Women, Personalities of America, Personalities of the West and Midwest, Directory of Distinguished Americans.* Address: 2910 South 51st Terrace, Kansas City, Kansas 66106

McCoy, Patricia Alice

Patricia A McCoy

Interpreter and Secretary. Personal: Born February 18, 1952; Daughter of Louise A. McCoy. Education: Attending Prince Georges Community College, 1973 to present, and Gallaudet College, 1973 to present. Career: Interpreter/Secretary for Admissions Office, Gallaudet College, Washington, D.C.; Former Secretary of Furniture Service; Former Secretary of Radio, T.V. and Appliance Service, George's Radio and T.V.; Former Cashier, G.C. Murphy Company. Organizational Memberships: Potomac Registry of Interpreters for the Deaf (board member-at-large); Deaf Media Council (co-chairperson, consultancy committee); National R.I.D.; W.M.D.A. (vice president); N.A.D.; F.E.S.N.A.D.; M.A.D.; T.D.I.; V.M.S.N.A.D.; Washington Metropolitan Association of the Deaf; International Platform Association; Deaf Awareness. Community Activities: Volunteer interpreter during Bicentennial, 1976; Interpreter for Very Special Arts Festival, 1974-77; Common Cause; Volunteer, Prince Georges County Hotline, 1973; Volunteer, Free Clinic; Volunteer interpreter, Second Mile; Volunteer interpreter, DEAFPRIDE, Inc., 1979 to present. Religion: New Life Ministry at D.C. Correctional Facility, Lorton, Virginia, 1979-80; Rock Gospel Sign/Singing Group, 1977; Church interpreter and synagogue interpreter. Honors and Awards: Certificate of Appreciation, National Red Cross, 1976; Certificate of Appreciation, National Committee of Arts for the Handicapped, 1979; Second runner-up, "Miss Prince Georges Plaza", 1972. Address: P.O. Box 26, Greenbelt, Maryland 20770-0026.

McCullough, Constance M

Writer, Lecturer, Consultant. Personal: Born January 15, 1912, in Indianapolis, Indiana; Daughter of John Simeon (deceased) and George Babette Mayer McCullough. Education: A.B., Vassar College, 1932; M.S., Butler University, 1933; Ph.D., University of Minnesota, 1938. Career: Emeritus Professor of Education, San Francisco State University, 1973 to present; Teaching Background includes positions at Western Reserve University, Hiram College, the University of Minnesota, Minneapolis Public Schools, the Institute for Education Leadership (Tokyo); Teachers College-Columbia University Team, India, 1963-65; Southern Illinois University Team, Nepal (1970); Visiting Professorships at Columbia University, the University of Chicago, the University of California, Brigham Young University, Harvard Graduate School of Education, University of Hawaii. Organizational Memberships: National Conference on Research in English (president 1961); International Reading Association (president 1974-75); Reading Hall of Fame (president 1976-78); National Council of Teachers of English; National Society for the Study of Education; American Educational Research Association; California Reading Association. Published Works: *McCullough Word Analysis Tests, Handbook for Teaching the Language Arts; Preparation of Textbooks in the Mother Tongue;* Contributor to *The National Society for the Study of Education Yearbooks,* 1961, 1968; *The Teaching of Reading (UNESCO),* 1973; Consultant for *Hindu Readers,* 1963-65; *Nepali Readers,* 1970. Honors and Awards: Pi Lambda Theta; Phi Kappa Phi; Delta Kappa Gamma; Delta Phi Upsilon; Citation for Distinguished Service in the Field of Reading, 1967, and International Citation in Reading, 1969, both from the International Reading Association; Distinguished Service Award, San Francisco State University; Marcus Foster Award, California Reading Association. Address: 1925 Cactus Court #4, Walnut Creek, California 94595.

McCune, Weston Edward

Accounts Executive. Personal: Born September 20, 1945; Son of Wesley Edwin McCune (deceased); Married Jan C.; Father of Christine Denise, Kyle Brandon, Maile Lauren; Education: B.A., Missouri State University. Military: Served with the United States Marine Corps, Graphics NCO - III MAFF Intelligence, 1969-70. Career: Senior Program Director, San Jose, California, Young Men's Christian Association (YMCA); Metropolitan Camp Director, Tucson, Arizona, YMCA; General Director, Baker, Oregon, YMCA;

General Director, Hilo, Hawaii, YMCA; Accounts Executive, Zales Insurance. Community Activities: Boy Scouts of America: Chairman Blue Mountain District, 1977-78; Chaplain Southwest Region, 1971-72; and Dean of Aquatics of Orange County, 1971-72; Awareness House, Hilo, Hawaii (board member 1979-80); Y S Men's Club, Hilo, Hawaii (secretary 1978-79); Oregon Cluster of YMCA's (executive committee, 1977-78); Interagency Task Force, Baker, Oregon, 1976-77; Metropolitan Youth Council, Tucson, Arizona, 1975-76. Religion: Church of Jesus Christ of Latter Day Saints. Honors and Awards: Developer of Hilo, Hawaii Joint Agency Co-op consisting of 20 Agency Executives, 1978-80; Appointed to Executive Board of Blue Mountain Council, Boy Scouts of America 1976-78; Appointed to Navajo Indian Social Worker, State of Arizona, 1974-76. Address: P.O. Box 2113, Kailua-Kona, Hawaii 96740.

McCurdy, (Betty) Martha Elizabeth

Mental Retardation Administrator. Personal: Born July 27, 1946; Daughter of Ruth and Gyp McCurdy. Education: B.A., Tift College, 1968; M.Ed., Auburn University, 1969; Ph.D., University of Georgia, 1975. Career: Owner, Lakewoods Trailer Park and Rental Property; Mental Retardation Administrator; Psychologist; Vocational Rehabilitation Counselor; Recreation Leader; Church Youth Director; Graduate Teaching Assistant, University of Georgia. Organizational Memberships: American Mental Health Counselor's Association, 1978; American Personnel and Guidance Association; National Rehabilitation Counseling Association (profesional member) 1979 to present; Center Director's Association, 1977 to present (regional vice president 1979, secretary 1980); Kappa Delta Pi, 1976; Friend of Preventive Medicine, 1981; Association for Retarded Citizens; Association for Specialists in Group Work, 1977; National Rehabilitation Association, 1976. Community Activities: Ruth Parker Jenkins Tift Alumni Association (charter member, past vice president, first vice president Tift Alumni chapter 1980). Religion: Georgia Lay Witness Mission Team, 1967-73; Conducted research on communication skills of church members, 1975; Youth Director, First Baptist Church, 1969. Honors and Awards: Plaque for Inspiring Leadership in Religious Activities, 1968; Listed in *Dictionary of International Biography, Who's Who in the South and Southwest, Outstanding Young Women of America, Personalities of the South, Personalities of America, World Who's Who of Women, Community Leaders of America, International Who's Who in Community Service.* Address: 303 Chalfont Drive, Athens, Georgia 30606.

Theresa B M McDonald

McDonald, Marianne Mori

Research Appointment, Instructor. Personal: Born January 2, 1937; Daughter of Inez McDonald; Married Torajiro Mori; Mother of Eugene, Conrad, Bryan, Bridget, Kirstie, Hiroshi. Education: B.A., magna cum laude, Bryn Mawr, 1958; M.A., University of Chicago, 1960; Ph.D., University of California-Irvine, 1975. Career: Research Appointment with Thesaurus Linguae Graecae, and Instructor, Classics Department, University of California-Irvine. Organizational Memberships: American Philological Association; American Association of University Professors; Hellenic Society; California Foreign Language Teacher's Association; American Classical League; Others. Community Activities: La Jolla Country Day (board member); American College of Greece (board member); Scripps Hospital (advisory board); American Biographical Institute (national board of advisors). Religion: Member Sts. Constantine and Helen Greek Orthodox Church. Honors and Awards: Many Publications, Books and Articles on Euripides and the General Field of Classics; Listed in *Directory of American Scholars, The World Who's Who of Women, International Who's Who of Intellectuals, Who's Who in American Education, International Who's Who in Education, Personalities of America, Community Leaders of America, International Register of Profiles.* Address: Box 929, Rancho Santa Fe, California 92067.

McDonald, Theresa Beatrice

Counselor, Supervisor, Teacher, Lecturer. Personal: Born April 11, 1929; Daughter of Leonard C. Pierce (deceased) and Ernestine Morris Pierce Templeton; Married Ollie McDonald. Education: Tougaloo College, 1946-47; Roosevelt University, 1954-56, 1959-62, 1964; University of Chicago, Industrial Relations Center, 1963-64. Career: Counselor; Supervisor; Teacher; Lecturer. Community Activities: Veterans Administration West Side Hospital, Chicago (volunteer representative of Liberty Baptist Church and the American Legion auxiliary, 1971-73); American Legion Auxiliary Unit 829 (president, 1975-76); White House Regional Conferences, Chicago (participant, 1961); Radio and Television Programs (guest speaker, 1972-81); Author of Poetry; Order of Eastern Star Venus Chapter #69 (Prince Hall affiliation member); Marschniel Club (vice-president, 1977; president, 1978; secretary, 1979 to present); Debonettes Matrons Club (vice-president, 1975-77; president, 1978-79; secretary, 1980-82; treasurer, 1982 to present). Religion: Liberty Baptist Church, Chicago (assistant superintendent, adult division, Sunday school, 1980 to present; vice-president, senior usher board, 1972, 1978, 1982 to present; president, Women's Guild, 1965; public relations staff, 1973-79); Guest Speaker at Churches and Other Organizations; Progressive National Baptist Convention, Inc., Washington, D.C. (chairman, committee on personnel 1982 to present; secretary of committee on planning and evaluations 1981 to present; vice-president at large of ushers department 1980-82; executive board 1980-82; executive committee 1981-82; constitution and by-law committee 1976; program committee consultant 1977; program committee 1980-82; ushers department, assistant national instructor 1972-73, national instructor 1973-75, national recording secretary 1975-76, national financial secretary 1976-78, national second vice-president 1978-80); Faculty Member of Congress of Christian Education, 1978 to present. Honors and Awards: Outstanding Service Awards, American Legion, 1972-73; 25-Year Service Award, United States Government, 1976; Performance Award, Veterans Administration Regional Office, Chicago, 1976; Merit Citation Award for Outstanding and Dedicated Service to Veterans and the Community, 379th Veterans Group, World War II, 1976; National Citation for Meritorious Service in Carrying Forward American Legion Auxiliary Programs and for Membership Increased, as President of American Legion Auxiliary Unit 829, 1976; Worthy Matron, Order of Eastern Star, 1974; Certificate of Appreciation for Services as a Volunteer Worker, Veterans Administration West Side Hospital, Chicago, 1973; Superior Accomplishment Award, Post Office Department, Chicago, 1964; Valedictorian, Bowman High School, Vicksburg, Mississippi, 1946; Annual Fellowship, International Biographical Institute; Fellow, American Biographical Institute Research Association; Listed in *Dictionary of International Biography, Who's Who in Religion, Community Leaders and Noteworthy Americans, Notable Americans, Personalities of the West and Midwest, Book of Honor, Personalities of America, International Register of Profiles, International Who's Who in Community Service, World Who's Who of Women, Biographical Roll of Honor, International Who's Who of Intellectuals.* Address: 9810 South Calumet Avenue, Chicago, Illinois 60628.

Marianne McDonald

McGee, Robert C Jr

Corporate Executive. Personal: Born May 24, 1936; Married Ann Peterson; Father of Marjorie Ann, Robert Matthew, Mary Katherine, Lauren Paige. Education: B.S. Aeronautical Engineering, University of Virginia, 1960. Military: Served in the United States Army as 1st Lieutenant, 1960-62. Career: President, Swan, Inc.; President, Forge Aerospace, Inc.; Vice-President, All American Industries; Director of Marketing, Fairchild Hiller Corporation; Washington Representative, Hiller Aircraft Corporation; Sales Engineer, Sikorsky Aircraft Company; Director of Spectrographic Analysis Laboratory, United States Army; Project Manager,

United States Army Light Observation Helicopter Project. Organizational Memberships: American Management Association; American Helicopter Society; National Security Industrial Association; United States Army Association; Aviation Association of America; National Aviation Club; Institute of Aeronautics and Astronautics. Community Activities: Young Men's Christian Association (director, 1978-79); Governors Small Business Advisory Council (member); State of Virginia, Member Taxation Committee; Virginia Manufacturer's Association (member); Legislative Sub-Committee, Small Business Steering Committee, Virginia State Chamber of Commerce. Honors and Awards: Meritorious Achievement Award, National Aviation Club; United States Army Commendation Award. Address: Route 2 Box 396 River Road, Richmond, Virginia 23233.

McGill, Betty Allen

Medical Social Work Consultant. Personal: Born July 28; Daughter of Carl and Johnnie Mae Allen (both deceased); Mother of Karen Denise. Education: Bachelor of Psychology and Sociology, Johnson C. Smith University; M.S.W., Atlanta University; Graduate Study, University of Southern California and University of California-Los Angeles. Career: Medical Social Work Consultant; Medical Social Worker; Supervising Medical Social Worker, Clinical Social Worker. Organizational Memberships: National Association of Social Workers; Child Welfare League of America; National Conference of Social Workers. Community Activities: Rosasharon Home for Battered Wives (vice president, board of directors); Delta Sigma Theta State Pre-School Head Start (board of directors); Angeles Mesa Young Women's Christian Association Board; League of Women Voters; American Association of University Women; Los Angeles Alumnae Chapter of Delta Sigma Theta (immediate past president); California State Museum of Science and Industry (volunteer); Venice Neighborhood Justice Center (volunteer mediator); National Projects Committee of Delta Sigma Theta. Religion: Park Hills Community Church, Steering Committee 1980 to present, Chairperson of Music and Worship Committees. Honors and Awards: Mayor's Commendation Certificate, City of Los Angeles, 1980; Los Angeles City Council Certificate of Commendation, 1980; Certificate of Commendation, California State Assembly, 1980; Certificates for Volunteering in Public Service Projects, Delta Sigma Theta, 1965-81; Listed in *Who's Who of American Women, Community Leaders and Noteworthy Americans, World Who's Who of Women.* Address: P.O. Box 43392, Los Angeles, California 90043.

Dan McIlrath

McIlhany, Sterling Fisher

Company President. Personal: Born April 12, 1930. Education: B.F.A., University of Texas, 1953; Graduate Studies, University of California-Los Angeles, 1953-56; Universita per Stranieri, Perugia, Italy, 1957; Accademia delle Belle Arti, Roma, Italy, 1957-58. Career: Editor, *Art Horizons* Magazine; President, I.F.O.T.A. Inc.; Senior Editor, *American Artist* Magazine 1969-71, Litton Educational Publishing 1969-70, Reinhold Book Corporation 1961-69, Watson-Guptill Publications 1959-61; Instructor, School of Visual Arts, 1961-69; Host, "Books and the Artist" WRVR Radio Series, 1960-61; Teaching Assistant, University of California-Los Angeles, 1953-56. Organizational Memberships: National Society of Literature and the Arts. Community Activities: St. Luke's in the Fields Outreach, New York City (community service chairman, 1979 to present); Christ College, Cambridge (fellow); Human Resources of the United States of America, Washington, D.C., 1976 to present; International Platform Association; International Biographical Centre; Rotary International (fellow); The Smithsonian Associates; American Museum of Natural History; Free Theatre (fellow; executive board). Religion: Roman Catholic. Honors and Awards: First Place National Award, Students International Travel Association Free Tour of European Art Centers, 1952; American Patriot of the Bicentennial, *Profiles of Freedom - A Cross Section of Proud Bicentennial Americans;* Listed in *The National Register of Prominent Americans and International Notables, Men and Women of Distinction, Book of Honor.* Address: 6376 Yucca Street, Los Angeles, California 90028.

McIlrath, Dan M

Plant Manager. Personal: Born May 18, 1928; Son of L. L. and Mable P. McIlrath; Married Marth A.; Father of Marie, David, Ellie, Jim, Beth, Rob, Becky. Education: B.S.P.E., Purdue University, 1952. Military: Served in the United States Navy as Quartermaster 3rd Class, 1946-48. Career: Keyston Group-Keyston Consolidated, Resident Plant Manager, Manager of Operations, Vice-President of Operations; Superintendent, Wire Division, Penn Dixie. Organizational Memberships: Wire Association International (board of directors, 1978); Indiana Manufacturers Association (board of directors, 1982); Chamber of Commerce. Community Activities: United Way (Muffy drive chairman, 1982); J.A. Fund (co-chairman, fund drives, 1980-81); Junior High Junior Achievement Courses (teacher, 1982); Cancer Drives, 1970's. Religion: Roman Catholic; Knights of Columbus; President, Parish Council, 1972; President, Parent-Teacher Organization, 1970. Honors and Awards: Wire Technology's First Wireman of the Year, 1975. Address: Rural Route 5, Crawfordsville, Indiana 47933.

Martha S McNabb

McKee, Dale

Promotions, Premiums and Incentives Company Executive. Personal: Born May 24, 1938, in Ironton, Ohio; Son of Frank and Eloise McKee; Married Barbara Jean Robinson, in June 15, 1957; Father of Dale, Jeffrey Scott. Education: B.S., University of Dayton, Ohio, 1966; Attended Sinclair Community College, 1975. Career: President, Del Diablo Recording, Miamisburg, 1978-79; President, Del Diablo Publishing Company, Miamisburg, 1978-79; Associate Realtor, Joe McNabb Realty, Miamisburg, 1978-79; Announcer, WCXL and WORP Radio-FM, 1978-79; Vice President and Director, Bar Del, Inc., Miamisburg, 1974 to present; President, McKee and McKee Building Contractors, Miamisburg, 1972-79; President, Treasurer, World Wide Crusade, Inc., Miamisburg, 1971-79; President, McKee and Parrish Building Contractors, Miamisburg, 1968-72; Supervisor, Frigidaire Division, General Motors Corporation, Dayton, 1956 to present. Organizational Memberships: Institute of Electrical and Electronic Engineers; Dayton Area Board of Realtors; Ohio Board of Realtors; Country Music Association; American Federation of Musicians. Community Activities: American Independent Party Central Committee, 1973-74; Democratic Party; Boy Scouts of America (scouts master, Sequoia Council, 1971-73); Foreman's Club of Dayton; Moose Lodge. Published Works: Composer of Songs "Ten Days I'll Be Getting Out of Prison" 1978, "The Bottle Almost Empty" 1978. Honors and Awards: International Platform Association; Listed in *Who's Who in the Midwest, Personalities of the West and Midwest, International Who's Who of Intellectuals, Men of Achievement.* Address: 1232 Holly Hill Drive, Miamisburg, Ohio 45342.

McNabb, Martha Sue Williams

Professional Writer and Restaurant Entrepreneur. Personal: Born March 18, 1936; Daughter of Cecil and Sue Forbes Williams; Mother of M. Ronald Marshall (deceased), Deborah Sue Marshall. Education: Attended Kirksville State Teachers College, 1953-54, and Northeast Missouri State Teachers College, 1962-64; B.S.E., University of California at Berkeley, 1965; D.Aetiol. with honors,

Fillmore Institute, 1966. Career: Distributor, Lord Jim's Parlour Restaurants, 1978 to present; Manpower Director, Missouri Community Action Agency (CETA), Kirksville, Missouri, 1978-80; Older Americans Supervisor, Missouri Green Thumb, Buffalo, 1974; Employment Specialist, Department of Labor, Washington, D.C., 1977; Teacher, Dudgeon School and rural schools, Fayette, Missouri. Organizational Memberships: National Association of Female Executives; National Retired Teachers Association; International Entrepreneurs Association; American Federation of Teachers; Missouri Division Extension Service; National Federation of Business and Professional Women (regional director, 1971); International Platform Association. Community Activities: Regional Manpower Advisory Council (advisory board); Assistant teacher, Dale Carnegie courses; National Organization for Women (task-master, National Action Center, 1975-76); Missouri Association for Community Action. Religion: Attends Adventist Church. Published Works: *The Basic Aspects and Concepts of Play Therapy* (1965), *Culture and Personality* (1966), *D.A.P. - a Catalogue for Interpretation* (1966), *The Pheromone Phenomenon* (1981), *Praimeri Kaer* (1981), *Testament of Seasons, Climbing the Crystal Stairs* (1981-82). Honors and Awards: Certificate of Appreciation and Commendation, Disadvantaged/Handicapped of Northeast Missouri, 1978; Invited to be Guest Speaker, International Congress on Arts and Communications, Queens' College, Cambridge, England; Listed in *The World Who's Who of Women.* Address: Road M, Route 3, Green City, Missouri 63545.

McNeely, E L

Chief Executive Officer. Personal: Born October 5, 1918; Son of Ralph H. and Viola Vogel; Married Alice Elaine Hall; Father of Gregory, Mark, Kevin, Sandra M. Gessl. Education: Bachelor's Degree in English and History, Northeast Missouri State University, Kirksville, Missouri, 1940; Postgraduate Courses, Northwestern University, Evanston, Illinois. Military: Served in the United States Navy, 1942-46, attaining the rank of Lieutenant (j.g.). Career: Chairman and Chief Executive Officer, Wickes Companies Inc.; Divisional Merchandise Manager, Montgomery Ward. Organizational Memberships: Dayco Corporation (director); Federal-Mogul Corporation (director); Pacific Telephone and Telegraph Company (director); Trans-American Corporation (director). Community Activities: Young Men's Christian Association, San Diego County (director); City of Hope (director); Scripps Clinic and Research Institution (trustee); University of Southern California Graduate School of Business Administration (board of councilors). Religion: Presbyterian. Honors and Awards: Golden Plate Award, American Academy of Achievement, 1973; National Jewish Hospital of Denver Honoree, 1978. Address: 1020 La Jolla Rancho Road, La Jolla, California 92037.

Meeks, Elsie M

Medical Record Administrator (Retired). Personal: Born June 8, 1917; Daughter of Downey Brown and Maude Goodwin; Married Leslie Cadillace Sr. (deceased); Mother of 2 Children. Education: A.A., East Los Angeles Junior College; National Certification, Registered Record Administrator. Career: Assistant Medical Records, Martin Luther King Hospital, Los Angeles, California; Teacher of Medical Records, Los Angeles City Unified School District. Community Activities: American Legion Auxiliary (Magellan C. Mars Unit 752); West Los Angeles Veterans Center (volunteer); Brentwood and Wadsworth Hospital (volunteer); Myasthenia Gravis Foundation; Center for Women's Studies, Inc.; Cub Scouts (den mother); Los Angeles Club of National Association of Negro Business and Professional Women's Clubs, Inc.; Anthurium Social and Charity Club; Women at Work Groups; Kairos Youth House (volunteer); Urban League (membership drive); National Association for the Advancement of Colored People (membership drive); Young Women's Christian Association (membership drive). Religion: Normandie Church of Christ; Bible School Teacher; Youth Committee; Visitation Team; Vacation Bible School Worker; Missionary Team, Georgetown, Guyana. Honors and Awards: Service Pin, Veterans Administration; Den Mother's Award and Instructor Training Certificate, Boy Scouts of America; Basic and Advanced Teacher Training Certificate, Bible Teachers of Normandie Church of Christ; Sojourner Truth Plaque, National Association of Negro Business and Professional Women's Clubs; 25-Year Pin, Myasthenia Gravis Foundation, California Chapter; Certificate and Plaque of Appreciation, Normandie Christian School; Award from Women at Work; Listed in Numerous Biographical References. Address: 3635 College Avenue, San Diego, California 92115.

Melgar, Julio

Mechanical Engineer. Personal: Born July 4, 1922; Son of Mrs. Maria Melgar. Education: Graduate of Brooklyn Technical High School, 1941; B.M.E., University of Detroit, 1952. Military: Served in the United States Marine Air Corps, 1943-45, rising through the ranks to Corporal. Career: Mechanical Engineer, Federal Aviation Administration; Draftsman, Tool Designer, Machinist. Organizational Memberships: American Society of Heating, Refrigerating and Air Conditioning Engineers (educational chairman); American Society of Mechanical Engineers; Texas Society of Professional Engineers; National Society of Professional Engineers. Community Activities: United States Marine Corps League (New York detachment, cadet chairman, 1945-46); University of Detroit Varsity Club (founder, 1947); Fort Worth Opera Association (board of directors, 1976 to present); Young Men's Christian Association (regional handball chairman, 1956-61); Fort Worth Handball (chairman, 1960-65); Forth Worth Opera Guild; Dallas Civic Opera Guild; Metroplex Recreation Council; Federal Business Association (bridge chairman); Federal Aviation Club (bridge chairman); Animal Protection Institute of America; Disabled American Veterans Organization; Tarrant City Humane Society; Dallas Society for the Prevention of Cruelty to Animals; American Museum of Natural History; American Association of Universities; Smithsonian Association; National Trust for Historic Preservation. Religion: Catholic. Honors and Awards: Gold Medal for High Score in Spanish, New York State Board of Regents, 1937; Outstanding Contribution to Handball, City of Fort Worth, 1965. Address: 6108 Menger Avenue, Dallas, Texas 75227.

Melton, Ira B

Business Owner and Executive. Personal: Born December 21, 1918 in Nashville, Tennessee; Son of Ira H. and Floy Dodgen Melton; Married Mildred Drumond; Father of Ira B. Jr., Donna Sue M. Benson, Timothy LaRue, Charles Alan, Kathleen Ruth M. Stephens. Military: Served in the United States Infantry During World War II; Received Two Bronze Battle Stars. Career: Vice-President and Director, Consolodated Consultants, Inc.; Vice-President and Director, C.C.I. Funds, Inc.; Vice-President and Director, C.C.I. Realty, Inc.; Owner, Ira B. Melton Enterprises; President, Melton-McKinney, Inc.; Vice-President, Mortgage Investments, Inc.; Vice-President and Director, Peachstone Development Corporation; Director, Shallowford Arms, Inc.; Member, Austin Realty Company; Partner, Warren 1-20 Association; Licensed Securities and Real Estate Representative. Organizational Memberships: Atlanta Metro Master Plumbers Association (past president); International Platform Association; DeKalb Grand Jury Association; Georgia Peace Officers Association; Board of Policy of Liberty Lobby, Washington, D.C.; American Society of Sanitary Engineers; Plumbing Inspectors Association (honorary member). Community Activities: Town of Pine Lake, Georgia (former judge of the municipal court; councilman; mayor); Civil Defense (Pine Lake commander); DeKalb Chamber of Commerce (director); DeKalb Young Men's Christian Association (director); American Legion (post commander); Loyal Order of Moose (past governor, Decatur lodge #902); Fulton County Voiture 217 40 and 8 Society (chef de gare); Elks; Dekalb County Zoning Appeals Board (chairman);

DeKalb Municipal Association; DeKalb County Board of Registrars; Boy Scouts of America (past scoutmaster of troop 202); Pine Lake Lions Club (president); Pine Lake Civic Club (past president); North Georgia Coon Hunters Association; Staff of Governors Marvin Griffin, Jimmy Carter and George Busbee. Religion: Pine Lake Baptist Church, Former Choir Director, Former Chairman of the Board of Trustees, Deacon; Baptist Witnessing Foundation, Jacksonville, Florida; Atlanta Baptist Association Property Committee. Honors and Awards: Fellow, Intercontinental Biographical Association, 1978; The Biographical Plaque of Honor, 1980; Honorary Fellowship, Anglo-American Academy, 1980; National Board of Advisors, American Biographical Institute, 1982; Listed in *Who's Who in Georgia, Who's Who in the National Council for Individual Excellence, Outstanding Americans in the South, Dictionary of International Biography, International Who's Who of Intellectuals, Personalities of the South, Men of Achievement, International Who's Who in Community Service, Book of Honor, Personalities of America, Notable Americans, Community Leaders and Noteworthy Americans, Men and Women of Distinction, American Registry, Anglo-American Who's Who, Directory of Distinguished Americans, Community Leaders of America, Contemporary Personalities Accademia Italia.* Address: 613 Dogwood Road, Pine Lake, Georgia 30072.

Mendelson, Sol

University Professor. Personal: Born October 10, 1926; Son of David and Frieda Mendelson (both deceased). Education: B.M.E. Mechanical Engineering cum laude, The City College of New York, 1955; M.S. 1957, Ph.D. 1961, Physical Metallurgy and Material Science, Columbia University. Career: Professor, The City University of New York; Visiting Professor of Physics, Williams College, Williamstown, Massachusetts, 1962-63; Professor of Engineering, City College of New York, 1955-59; Senior Scientist, Bendix Research Laboratories, Southfield, Michigan, 1967-68; Senior Scientist, Airborne Instruments Laboratories, Melville, New York, 1964-65; Senior Scientist, Sprague Electric Company, North Adams, Massachusetts, 1962-64. Organizational Memberships: American Physical Society; Materials Research Society; Metallurgical Society of American Institute of Metallurgical Engineers; American Society for Metals; New York Academy of Science; American Association of Advanced Sciences; American Association of Physics Teachers; Federation of American Sciences. Community Activities: Church of All Nations , 1945-62; The Fresh Air Fund, New York City, 1948-55; The City University of New York, 1955-59, 1972-81. Honors and Awards: Fellowship for Ph.D. Studies, Columbia University, 1958; Sigma Xi, Tau Beta Pi, Pi Tau Sigma (member, president 1954). Address: 446 West 25th Street, New York, New York 10001.

Méndez, Ana G

Education Administrator. Personal: Born January 17, 1908; Daughter of Francisco Gonzáles Monge and Ana Cofresi Sánchez; Married José Méndez Rivera; Mother of Dora M. Saar, Grecia M. Diaz Bonnet, José F. Méndez. Education: Graduate of Central High School, Santurce, Puerto Rico, 1935; B.S. Commercial Education, University of Puerto Rico, 1940; M.A. New York University, 1948; Honorary Degree, Catholic University. Career: President, Editorial Turabo, Inc., 1975 to present; Ana G. Méndez Education Foundation, Special Advisor to Board of Directors 1974 to present, President 1970-74; President, Puerto Rico Junior College Foundation, 1969-70; Puerto Rico Junior College, President 1952-69, Dean of Administration 1949-51, Co-Founder 1949, President of the Board 1952 to present; Founder, Puerto Rico Elementary School, 1950; Lecturing Professor, School of Business Administration, University of Puerto Rico Business Department; Co-Founder and Directress, Puerto Rico High School of Commerce, 1941-52. Organizational Memberships: Teachers Association of Puerto Rico, 1949 to present; National Education Association, 1950 to present; American Association of Junior Colleges Commission on Admissions, 1957-59; American Association of University Women, 1957 to present; Academia de Artes y Ciencias de Puerto Rico, 1965 to present; Grand Union of Puerto Rico (scholarship fund chairman, 1969 to present); Association of Colleges and Universities of Puerto Rico (president, 1969-70); Association of Community and Junior Colleges (board of directors, 1972-75); Puerto Rico Endowment for the Humanities Values in Community Affairs (founding member, 1975). Community Activities: Governor's Committee on Employment of the Physically Handicapped (chairman, 1961-75); State Commission on Higher Education, 1964; Government-Citizen Relations Committee, 1964; Consejo Asesor del Secretario del Trabajo, 1967; Governing Institutions of Higher Education (student participant, 1969); Estudio de las Matriculas en las Universidades de Puerto Rico, 1969; Junta Estatal de Salud, 1970; Comite de Planificacion de Recursos Humanos, 1972; Consejo Consultivo de Instruccion Vocacional (chairman, 1973); Small Business Advisory Board for Puerto Rico, 1964, 1976; Department of Health, Education and Welfare (national advisory board on nurse training, 1975; national advisory council on services and facilities for developmental disabilities, 1973); Puerto Rico State Federation of Business and Professional Women's Clubs (president, 1957-59); International Conference on Rehabilitation (social committee, 1959); Instituto del Hogar (board of directors, 1960; executive secretary, 1961; president, fund raising campaign, 1961); Educational Committee for the Prevention of Accidents in Puerto Rico (chairman, 1962-64); Council of Prevention of Accidents (president, 1964-75); American Red Cross (Puerto Rico chapter president, 1963-65); Asociacion de Maestros (comite para estudio de problemas educativos, 1967); College Board (comite de planificacion y evaluacion de los programas del board, 1969); Departmento de Instruccion (comite para el estudio de reglamento para certificaciones a maestros, 1968); Cuarto Congreso Interamericano de Prevencion de iesgos profesionales (presidente, comision local, 1972); United Fund of Puerto Rico (member, 1974; campaign chairman, 1975; chairman, board of governors, 1976); Ashford Community Hospital (board of trustees, 1980-82); American Red Cross (chairman, campaign, 1980-82); White House Conference on Children and Youth (committee for social welfare, 1960); Convencion de Orientacion Social (executive secretary, 1960; chairman, 1962; board of directors, 1962); Grand Union of Puerto Rico (advisory board, 1967); Eastern Airlines (board of directors, 1977); New York University (board of trustees chair). Published Works: Collaborator, Bookkeeping and Accounting Textbook; Contributor to Local Newspapers and Educational Magazines. Honors and Awards: Mother of Achievement for Bicentennial, U.S.A., 1976; Pontifical Medal, 1975; Outstanding Woman of the International Year, 1975; Top Management Award, Sales and Marketing Executives Association, 1972; Honored by Gurabo Club, 1972; Book of the Golden Deeds Award, Club Exchange of Puerto Rico, 1972; Medal of Merit, American Legion Department of Puerto Rico, 1970; Honored by Club Exchange of Puerto Rico, 1968; Woman of the Year, Gulf Petroleum, 1966; Honored by International Lions Club, District 51, 1965; Honored by Puerto Rico Federation of Business and Professional Women's Clubs, 1965; Outstanding Women of the World, Cazenovia College, New York, 1963; Honored by Hato Rey Lions Club, 1963; Phi Theta Kappa National Junior College Scholastic Fraternity, 1961; Semi-Finalist, Lane Bryant Award, 1960; Citizen of the Year, Division of Vocational Rehabilitation, Department of Education of Puerto Rico, 1959. Address: Parque de las Fuentes 2007, Hato Rey, Puerto Rico.

Merrill, Ambrose Pond Jr

Physician and Health Service Consultant. Personal: Born December 14, 1909, in Provo, Utah; Son of Ambrose Pond and Lydia Stephens Merrill; Married Elizabeth Call, April 7, 1931. Education: A.B. 1932, M.D. 1935, Stanford University; M.H.A. with distinction, Northwestern University, 1948. Career: President, A. P. Merrill, M.D., and Associates, Hospital and Health Services Consultants, Delmar, New York, 1968 to present; Assistant Director, Bureau of Hospital Certification, 1967-68; Assistant Clinical Professor of Physical Medicine and Rehabilitation, New York University, 1955-60; Lecturer in School of Hospital Administration

1948-53, Preceptor 1946-67, Columbia University; Executive Director, St. Barnabas Hospital, New York, New York, 1945-67; Medical Director 1942-45, Assistant Director 1940-42, St. Luke's Hospital, Chicago, Illinois; Assistant Superintendent 1938-40, Intern 1934-35, San Francisco County Hospital; Surgeon, San Francisco Emergency Hospital Service, Department of Public Health, 1936-38; General Practice of Medicine and Surgery, 1936-40; Surgeon House Officer, Assistant Resident, Stanford University Hospitals, 1935-36. Organizational Memberships: Middle Atlantic Hospital Assembly (president, 1958-59); Hospital Association of New York (president, 1956-57); Greater New York Hospital Association (president, 1953-54); New York Academy of Medicine (fellow); American College of Hospital Administrators (fellow); American College of Preventive Medicine; Alpha Kappa Kappa Medical Fraternity. Community Activities: New York City Mayor's Advisory Committee for the Aged, 1955-60; National Health Assembly (delegate, 1948); National Conference on Aging (delegate, 1950); International Gerontological Congress (delegate, 1951); National Conference on Care of the Long-Term Patient (delegate, 1954); White House Conference on Aging (delegate, 1961); Republican Party. Religion: Church of Jesus Christ of Latter-day Saints; High Council of New York Stake, 1961-67; Hudson River Stake, 1969-72. Published Works: Contributed Chapter to *Functional Planning of General Hospitals*, 1969; Contributor of Articles to Hospital and Medical Journals. Honors and Awards: Brotherhood Award, National Conference of Christians and Jews, 1967; Modern Hospital Award and Medal, 1945; Establishment of Dr. and Mrs. Ambrose P. Merrill Jr. Student Loan Fund for Medical Students, Stanford University, 1965. Address: 73 Greenock Road, Delmar, New York 12054.

Merrill, Maurice Hitchcock

Lawyer. Personal: Born October 3, 1897; Son of Mr. and Mrs. George Waite Merrill (both deceased); Married Orpha Roberts Merrill (deceased); Father of Jean M. Barnes. Education: B.A. 1919, LL.B. 1922, University of Oklahoma; S.J.D., Harvard University, 1925. Military: Served in the United States Army, 1918, with the rank of Private. Career: Lawyer; Acting Dean 1946-47, Law Teacher 1936-68, University of Oklahoma; Law Teacher, University of Nebraska 1926-36, University of Idaho 1925-26. Organizational Memberships: Cleveland County Bar Association (president); Oklahoma Bar Association (house of delegates); American Bar Association; National Conference of Commissioners on Uniform State Laws (life member, 1964; commissioner from Oklahoma, 1944 to present). Community Activities: Oklahoma Supreme Court (special justice, 1965-68). Religion: Methodist Church, 1920 to present; Board of Stewards; Administrative Board; Other Offices. Honors and Awards: Honorary Doctor of Humane Letters, Oklahoma Christian College, 1971; Hatton W. Wumners Award, Southwestern Legal Foundation, 1964; Distinguished Service Citation, University of Oklahoma, 1968; Oklahoma Hall of Fame, 1970; President's Award, Oklahoma Bar Association, 1972. Address: 800 Elm Avenue, Norman, Oklahoma 73069.

J Theodore Meyer

Meyer, J Theodore

Illinois General Assemblyman, Attorney. Personal: Born April 13, 1936; Son of Joseph T. (deceased) and Mary Meyer; Married Marilu Bartholomew; Father of Jean, Joseph. Education: Graduate of St. Ignatius High School; B.S., John Carroll University; Attended the University of Chicago; J.D., De Paul University College of Law. Career: Member, Illinois General Assembly, 1966-72, 1974 to present; Attorney at Law. Organizational Memberships: American Bar Association; Illinois Bar Association; Southwest Bar Association. Community Activities: Energy and Environment Committee (chairman); Natural Resource Committee, National Conference of State Legislature; Federal/State Task Force on Energy; Environment, Energy and Natural Resources Committee (past minority spokesman); Public Health Survey Study Commission; Lake Michigan and Adjoining Lands Commission; State Parks and Recreation Commission; House Environmental Study Committee (past chairman); Midwest Legislative Council on Environment (chairman; founder); Joint House/Senate Subcommittee to Review Statewide Air and Water Plans (chairman). Honors and Awards: Distinguished Legislator, Chicago Bar Association; Illinois Wildlife Federation; Illinois League of Conservative Voters; United States Environmental Protection Agency and Self-Help Center; Environmental Legislator of the Year Award, Committee on Courts and Justice; Legislator Appreciation Award, Veterans of Foreign Wars; Ten Years Outstanding Legislative Leadership Award, Chicago Lund Association. Address: 9007 South Leavitt, Chicago, Illinois 60620.

Middleton, Anthony Wayne Jr

Clinical Assistant Professor. Personal: Born May 6, 1939; Son of A. W. Middleton, Sr.; Married to Carol Samuelson; Father of Anthony W. III, Suzanne, Kathryn Ann, Jane. Education: B.S., University of Utah, 1963; M.D., Cornell University Medical College, 1966; General Surgery Resident, New York Hospital, 1967-68; Urology Resident, Massachusetts General Hospital, 1970-73. Military: Served with United States Air Force with rank of Captain, 1968-70. Career: Clinical Assistant Professor, Division of Urology, University of Utah; Clinical Faculty Member, Department of Family and Community Medicine, University of Utah. Organizational Memberships: American Medical Association, 1974; Utah State Medical Society; Salt Lake County Medical Society (treasurer, 1975-77); Utah State Urological Association (president, 1975-76); American Urological Association (board certified, 1976); American College of Surgeons (initiated, 1978); Pan-Pacific Surgical Association; Salt Lake Surgical Society (treasurer, 1977-78). Community Activities: Utah Medical Political Action Committee (vice chairman, 1978-81, chairman, 1981 to present); Board Member, Utah Division of American Cancer Society, 1977-80; President, Beta Theta Pi, 1960; Member of Board of Governors, Utah State Medical Insurance Association, 1979-81; President-elect, Primary Children's Medical Center, 1980-81; Chairman of Holy Cross Hospital Division of Urology, 1980 to present. Religion: Member of Church of Latter Day Saints (missionary to Great Britain, 1959-61, editor of *Millenial Star*, 1960-61, second counselor, Ward Bishopric, 1976-77, first counselor in Ward Bishopric, 1977-80). Published Works: Author of 19 scientific papers and book chapters. Honors and Awards: Elected to Phi Eta Sigma, University of Utah, 1959; Elected to Skull and Bones, University of Utah, 1963; Elected to Phi Beta Kappa, University of Utah, 1963; Elected to Alpha Omega Alpha, Cornell University Medical College, 1965; Named Outstanding Sophomore Citizen, University of Utah, 1959; Listed in *Who's Who Directory of Medical Specialists, Who's Who in the West, Men of Achievement, Personalities of the West and Midwest, Directory of Distinguished Americans, International Who's Who of Intellectuals.* Address: 2798 Chancellor Place, Salt Lake City, Utah 84108.

Anthony W Middleton Jr

Miethe, Terry Lee

Educator, Author, Minister. Personal: Born August 26, 1948 in Clinton, Indiana; Married Beverly Jo Deck; Father of John-Hayden. Education: A.B. cum laude 1970, M.A. 1973, Trinity Evangelical Divinity School; M.Div., McCormick Theological Seminary, 1973; Ph.D. Philosophy, Saint Louis University, 1976; M.A. Social Ethics 1981, Ph.D. Candidate 1983, University of Southern California. Career: Associate Minister, First Christian Church, Pomona, California 1979-83; Visiting Scholar, School of Theology at Claremont, California, 1979-80; Senior Engineering Project Analyst, Burroughs Corporation, 1978-79; Saint Louis University, Associate Professor in Department of Philosophy 1977-78, Assistant Professor in Department of Theological Studies 1976-77, Assistant Director of University Honors Program 1975-76, Professional Lecturer in Philosophy 1975-76; Minister, Woodburn, Illinois Congregational Church, 1973-74; Minister, Mellot, Indiana United Church of Christ, 1969-71. Organizational Memberships:

American Philosophical Association, 1975 to present; American Academy of Religion, 1976 to present; Evangelical Theological Society, 1973 to present; Society of Biblical Literature, 1976 to present; Evangelical Philosophical Society, 1976 to present. Community Service: Mountain View School, Claremont, California, Unified School District Board of Education (district advisory committee, 1978-79; vice-chairman, 1979-80); Family Service of Pomona Valley (board of directors, 1980 to present). Published Works: Contributor of 35 Articles in such Periodicals as *The Disciple, Christian Standard, The Modern Schoolman, Faith & Reason, Journal of the Evangelical Theological Society, The Presbyterian Journal, The New Scholasticism, Augustinian Studies; Friedrich Nietzsche & The Death of God: The Rejection of Absolutes*, 1973; *The Metaphysics of Leonard James Eslick: His Philosophy of God*, 1976; *Thomistic Bibliography: 1940-78*, co-authored with Dr. Vernon J. Bourke, 1980; *Reflections*, 1980; "Atheism: Nietzsche", in *Biblical Errancy: An Analysis of Its Philosophical Roots*, 1981; *Augustinian Bibliography and Thought: 1970-1980*, 1982; *Letters to New Christians*, 1982. Honors and Awards: Phi Beta Kappa, 1975 to present; Phi Alpha Theta, 1975 to present; Psi Chi, 1975 to present; Eta Sigma Phi, 1976 to present; Alpha Sigma Nu, 1976 to present; Phi Delta Gamma, 1980 to present; McCormick Theological Seminary Scholarship, 1973; Saint Louis University Fellowship, 1975; Finalist and Alternate, Fulbright Fellowship to the United Kingdom, United States Government, 1976; Babcock Fellow, University of Southern California, 1980-81; Miller Fellow, 1982-83; Listed in *Outstanding Young Men of America, Who's Who in Religion, Personalities of the West and Midwest, Dictionary of International Biography, Men of Achievement, Personalities of America, Men & Women of Distinction, Book of Honor, International Who's Who of Intellectuals, Who's Who in the West, Who's Who in California, Contemporary Authors.* Address: 3178 Florinda Street, Pomona, California 91767.

Miller, Earl Beauford

Artist. Personal: Born September 19, 1930; Married Marion Weinberg; Father of Joseph Dale, Hugh Stephen, Pringl Lee. Education: Attended Pratt Institute (Brooklyn, New York) 1954-56, Brooklyn Museum Art School 1956, Art Students League of New York 1957, Akademie der Bildenden Kunste (Munich, Germany) 1962-63. Career: Lettering Artist; Show Card Writer; Calligrapher; Theatrical Display Design Artist; Package-Carton Design Artist; Graphic Designer; Graphic Design Studio Board Artist. Organizational Memberships: American Association of University Professors. Community Activities: George Washington Carver Hi-Y Club (counselor); Wabash Young Men's Christian Association, Chicago, Illinois (counselor). Honors and Awards: Grand Concourse Award, The Art Students League of New York, 1958; First Prize Award, Jersey City Museum Association, 1959; Painting Award, National Institute of Arts and Letters, 1971; Academic Diploma and Gold Medal, Accademia Italia della Arti Aedel Lavoro, Parma, Italy, 1979; Prize Winnter, "Original Editions 1978", Orgeon Arts Commission, Sales, Oregon, 1979; University of Washington Graduate School Research Fund Committee Award, 1976-77; Second Prize, Seattle Arts Commission Wall Mural Competition, 1975; Nominee, Award in Painting, National Institute of Arts and Letters, New York, 1970; Tuition Scholarship, Brooklyn Museum Art School, 1956; First Prize, Tempera Painting, Jersey City Museum Annual, 1959; Tuition Scholarship, Akademie der Bildenden Kunste, 1963; Grant for Art Film on Topic of Collages, Bavarian Culture Ministry, 1963. Address: 5026 22nd Avenue N.E., Seattle, Washington 98105.

Miller, Laverne Gertrude Flueckiger

Laverne G Miller

Registered Professional Nurse. Personal: Born in Monroe, Wisconsin; Daughter of Fredrick Helmuth and Ida Marie Brand Flueckiger; Married Edward J. Miller Jr.; Mother of Gary E., Barbara J. Education: Graduate of Wilfred Academy for Girls, Chicago, Illinois; Attended Rush-Presbyterian-St. Luke Hospital School of Nursing; B.S. Health Arts, Master's Program in Health Service Administration, College of Saint Francis. Career: Clinical Specialist in Surgical Nursing; Registered Professional Nurse, West Suburban Hospital, Oak Park Hospital, Rush-Presbyterian-St. Luke Hospital; Teacher of Nurse's Aide Classes, Oak Park Hospital, 1974-76; Positions have included Head Nurse, Supervisor, Charge Nurse, Staff Nurse. Organizational Memberships: American Nurses Association; Chicago Archdiocese Council of Catholic Nurses (board of directors); National League of Nursing; International Platform Association. Community Activities: American Red Cross Blood Donor Drive; American Cancer Society (sponsor with Dr. John Tope, Seminar on Cancer); Fenwick Mothers Club (life member); Oak Park Hospital Women's Auxiliary; United Swiss Society; Swiss Benevolent Society; Swiss Ladies Benefit Society; Republican League of Voters. Religion: St. Vincent Ferrer Church; Guild of the Tabernacle. Published Works: "The Pre-Operative and Post-Operative Care of the Ostomy Patient". Honors and Awards: Outstanding Nursing Care Citation, Medical Staff of Rush-Presbyterian-St. Luke Hospital; Listed in *World Who's Who of Women, Book of Honor, International Who's Who of Intellectuals.* Address: 525 West Jackson Boulevard, Oak Park, Illinois 60304.

Miller, Robert J

Author. Personal: Born June 12, 1918 in Plainview, Arkansas; Son of Homer Cleo Miller and Matilda Alice Dalton (both deceased). Education: A.A., Hendrix College, B.S., State Teachers College (now University of Central Arkansas), 1941. Military: Served in the United States General Army. Career: Author; Resident Poet, McDowell Colony, Peterborough, New Hampshire, 1941. Organizational Memberships: American Poets Fellowship Society; Florida State Poetry Society Inc.; National Society of Poets, Inc. Community Activities: Cousteau Society; National Historical Society; Arkansas Sheriffs Association. Published Works: *To Span the Seasons*, 1977; *Freely Remembered*, 1972; *Weird Balk*, 1964; *Rustique*, 1947; Contributor to Anthologies such as *The Family Treasury of Great Poems* and *Our Twentieth Century's Greatest Poems* (both of which were published by World of Poetry Press); An Anthology, *Lyrical Treasures, Classic and Modern*, Fine Arts Press, 1983; *Lyrical Voices*, 1979; *Poetry Parade; Melody of the Muse; A Burst of Trumpets; Yearbooks of Modern Poetry; Versatility in Verse; Phytography* Sketch Manual; Contributor to Periodicals such as *United Poets, American Poet, Modern Images.* Honors and Awards: Distinguished Achievement Citation, International Biographical Center, Cambridge, England, 1976; Diploma di Merito, Terme, Italy, 1982; Listed in *Personalities of the South, Notable Americans, International Register of Profiles, International Who's Who in Poetry, Men of Achievement, Personalities of America.* Address: Highway 80 West, Box 17, Danville, Arkansas 72833.

Mills, Margie I

Educator (retired). Personal: Born September 17, 1908; Daughter of E. M. Ingram and Georgia Amner Dalton; Married T. M. Mills (deceased); Mother of Virginia Gay M. Narramore, James Dibrell (deceased). Education: B.S.E., Arkansas State Teachers College, 1933; M.S. Education, University of Arkansas, 1947; M.S. Library Science, University of Mississippi, 1960. Career: Educator, Librarian. Organizational Memberships: Phillips County Teachers Association (president, 1955-58); Arkansas Education Association, 1930-76; National Education Association, 1950-76; Retired Teachers Association, 1976 to present; Arkansas Library Association; Southwest Library Association. Community Activities: Parent-Teacher Association (member, 1932 to present; local president; county president; life member); Phillips County Historical Association (secretary, 1962 to present). Honors and Awards: Delta Kappa Gamma (member, 1945 to present; president, 1947); Mark Twain Society, 1952; International Platform Association,

1976; Listed in *Community Leaders and Noteworthy Americans, Personalities of the South, Dictionary of International Biography, Arkansas Lives, Women of Arkansas Delta.* Address: Box 343, Elaine, Arkansas 72333.

Mills, William A

Accounting Firm Partner (Retired). Personal: Born April 7, 1910, Washington County, Georgia; Son of Oscar Lee and Willie Mae Griffin Mills; Married Ruth H. Waters (deceased), August 31, 1940. Education: Graduate of Deepstep High School, 1928; B.S. Commerce/Accounting, University of Georgia-Athens, 1934; Passed Certified Public Accounting Examinations, 1934. Military: Served in the United States Armed Forces in the Fiscal Division of the Ordnance Department, Commissioned as 2nd Lieutenant and Serving to Rank of Captain, 1943-46. Career: Partner, Haskins and Sells Public Accountants, 1961-1973; Partner, Barnes, Askew, Mills and Company, C.P.A.'s, 1947-61; Accountant, M. H. Barnes and Company, C.P.A.'s, Savannah, Georgia, 1934-43. Organizational Memberships: Georgia Society of Certified Public Accountants (president, Savannah chapter, 1952-53); American Institute of Certified Public Accountants, Inc. (past president, estate planning council of the Savannah chapter); National Association of Accountants. Community Activities: Kiwanis Club; Chatham Club; Georgia Historical Society; Beta Gamma Sigma; Phi Kappa Phi; Beta Alpha Psi. Honors and Awards: Accounting Man of the Year, Savannah Chapter of the National Association of Accountants, 1973; Listed in *Who's Who in America, Who's Who in Commerce and Industry, Who's Who in the South and Southwest, Dictionary of International Biography, National Register of Prominent Americans, Royal Blue Book.* Address: 802 East 41st Street, Savannah, Georgia 31401.

William A Mills

Minyard, John Douglas

Associate Professor of Classical Civilization. Personal: Born September 16, 1943; Son of Mr. and Mrs. John H. Minyard; Father of Joshua Pruitt Anderson. Education: A.B. 1964, A.M. 1965, Brown University; Ph.D., University of Pennsylvania, 1970. Career: Associate Professor of Classical Civilization, University of North Carolina at Greensboro, 1977 to present; Visiting Lecturer in Classics, Haverford College, 1975; University of Pennsylvania, Assistant Professor of Classical Studies 1970-77, Instructor in Classical Studies 1969-70. Organizational Memberships: American Philological Association; Archaeological Institute of America; Classical Association of the Middle West and South; North Carolina Classical Association; The Petronian Society; The Vergilian Society; The Virgil Society of England; American Association of University Professors. Community Activities: Harbour Family Association (president, 1979 to present); The North Carolina Humanities Committee (lecturer and consultant for sponsored programs); United Chapters of Phi Beta Kappa; National Trust for Historic Preservation; Virginia Historical Society; South Carolina Historical Society; National Genealogical Society; Friends of the Jackson Library of University of North Carolina-Greensboro; Weatherspoon Gallery Association of University of North Carolina-Greensboro. Religion: First Baptist Church, Bronxville, New York. Published Works: *Mode and Value in the De Rerum Natura: A Study in Lucretius' Metrical Language,* 1978; Contributor of Articles and Reviews on Classical Subjects to Scholarly Journals; Presenter of Papers on Classics and on the Humanities at Professional Meetings and Public Lectures. Honors and Awards: Phi Beta Kappa, 1964; Magna Cum Laude Graduate with High Honors in Classics, 1964; Graduate Fellowships, Brown University and University of Pennsylvania, 1964-70; Fulbright Fellowship, University of Rome, 1968-69. Address: Department of Classical Civilization, University of North Carolina, Greensboro, North Carolina 27412.

Mitchell, C E

Minister. Personal: Born June 11, 1935; Son of Ida M. Mitchell; Married Racyne M. Rice; Father of Sherry D. Johnson, Ehila Y. Ford, Sonya L. Education: B.A., Bishop College, 1969; Leadership Certificate, University of Arkansas, 1977; B.Th., International Bible Institute and Seminary, 1981. Career: Minister, C.M.E. Church. Organizational Memberships: Texarkana Ministers Alliance (president, 1976-78); Los Angeles Ministers Alliance, 1981. Community Activities: Titus County Human Relations Council (president, 1968-72); Bowie County Welfare Board (vice president, 1975-78); Northeast Texas Health System Agency (board of directors, 1975-78); Young Men's Christian Association (board of directors, 1974-78); Texarkana Legal Service (board of directors, 1973-75); Bowie County Visiting Nurse Association (board of directors, 1975-78); Tulsa Metropolitan Ministry (board of directors, 1978-80). Religion: Pastor, Los Angeles 1981, Oklahoma 1978-81, Texas 1955-78; Dean, Leadership Training School of Oklahoma 1980, Oklahoma Conference on Christian Education 1979. Honors and Awards: Child Welfare Award, 1976; Senior Citizen Award, 1978; Community Service Award, 1978; Youth Service Award, 1977; Pastoral Award, 1980. Address: 1632 West 49th Street, Los Angeles, California 90062.

C E Mitchell

Mitchell, Peggy Riddle

Administrative Assistant. Personal: Born February 23, 1938 in Raleigh, North Carolina; Married Vernon Fuller Mitchell, December 15, 1978; Mother of Charles L. Hopson III, Helen Vaughn Hopson, Vaughn Lewis Hopson. Education: Graduate of Needham B. Broughton High School, 1956. Career: Administrative Assistant to Assistant Vice-Chancellor for Student Affairs, North Carolina State University, Raleigh, 1980 to present; Administrative Assistant to Secretary Howard M. Lee, Department of Natural Resources and Community Development, 1980; Office Manager, Medical-Educational Loans Branch, Division of Facility Services, North Carolina Department of Human Resources, 1979; State Department of Cultural Resources, Administrative Secretary to Chief of Archaeology Section of Division of Archives and History, 1974-78, Executive Secretary to Chief of Historic Sites and Museums Section of Division of Archives and History 1963-74; Secretary, State Insurance Department, 1962-63; Plant Manager's Secretary, Cornel Dubilier Electronics Plant, 1961; Secretary, Law Enforcement Division of State Board of Alcoholic Control, 1956-60. Community Activities: North Carolina Museums Council (member, 1963 to present; secretary-treasurer, 1968-73, 1978); North Carolina Archaeological Council (secretary, 1974-78); Southeastern Museum Conference (chairman, membership committee, 1969-78); Girl Scouts of America (bicentennial task force, 1974-78; leader, 1972-77; representative, North Carolina scouts, governor's committee on delinquency prevention, 1981 to present); Southeastern Underwater Conference and Film Festival (exhibits committee). Published Works: Editor, *The North Carolina Museum Council Newsletter, The Pines* Carolina Girl Scout Council Publication, *Tar Heel Diver* North Carolina Skin Diving Council Publication, *Cultural Resources* Publication of State Department of Cultural Resources, *Underwater News, Tar Heel Junior Historian* Quarterly, *N.A.C.U.F.S. Newsletter* of the National Association of College/University Food Services. Honors and Awards: Award for Promoting Public Awareness of the Need for Court Reform and Lobbying Activities in the Criminal Justice Area, Wake County Criminal Justice Council, 1978; Listed in *Who's Who of American Women, Who's Who in the South and Southwest, Community Leaders and Noteworthy Americans, Personalities of the South, Dictionary of International Biography, Book of Honor, Personalities of America.* Address: 3013 Wade Avenue, Raleigh, North Carolina 27607.

Moellering, Bernice

Instructor in English. Personal: Born June 18, 1917. Education: A.B. English, Quincy College, Illinois, 1952; M.A. English and Speech, Creighton, Omaha, Nebraska. Career: Instructor in English. Organizational Memberships: National Conference of Teachers of English; Missouri Association of Teachers of English. Community Activities: Missouri Correctional Institutes (teacher of literature, 4 years). Religion: Catholic. Honors and Awards: Great Teachers Award, 1971. Address: 204 North Main, O'Fallon, Missouri 63366.

Mohr, G Robert

Company President. Personal: Born February 15, 1922; Son of Adella I. Dye; Married Wilma Purdie; Father of Robert K., Deborah S. M. Foster, Loretta A. M. Reuss. Education: B.S. Accounting and Mathematics 1948, M.A. Statistics and Economics 1950, State University of Iowa, Iowa City; Graduate Studies, University of Tennessee, Michigan State University. Military: Served in the United States Coast Guard, 1941-45. Career: President, G. R. Mohr Enterprises; Associate Professor, Bethune-Courman College, Central State University, Central State University, Ferris State College, Mankato State College, Illinois Institute of Technology, Rockford College, Memphis State University, Northern Illinois University; Financial Analyst, Harris Trust and Savings Bank, Realtor Associate. Organizational Memberships: Jacksonville Society of Financial Analysts; Southern Financial Association; American Institute of Decision Sciences; American Economics Association; American Statistics Association; Econometric Society, American Veterans Committee, Chicago, Illinois (chairman, treasurer); Edmond Arts and Humanities Council (treasurer); Many Other Community Activities. Religion: Unitarian Church; Treasurer, Ormond Beach, Florida, Park Forest, Illinois, Mankato, Minnesota; Big Rapids, Michigan. Honors and Awards: Fellow Financial Analyst Federation; Economics-in-Action Fellowship, 1952; Alpha Iota Delta Honorary Fraternity. Address; 247 Brookline Avenue, Daytona Beach, Florida 32018.

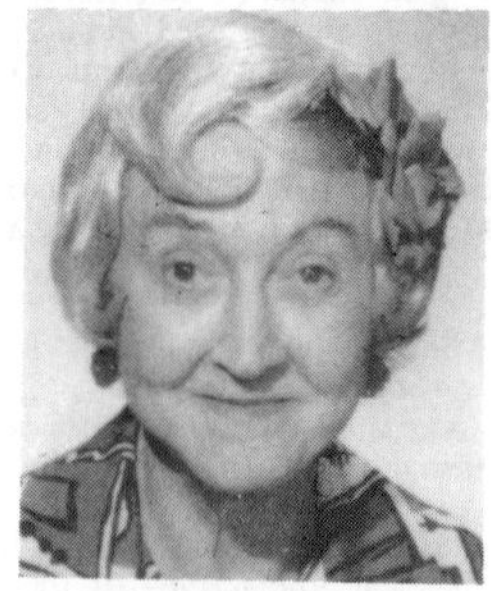

Gertrude M F Moir

Moir, Gertrude Mae Fisher

Educator (retired), Writer, Painter, Musician. Personal: Born February 15, 1896; Daughter of Henry Clay and Lillian Metz Fisher (both deceased); Married John T. Moir Jr.; Mother of John T. III, Mildred Mae Mason. Education: Attended the Philadelphia Academy of Fine Arts, Pennsylvania Academy of Music, Cornell University, Bates College; B.A., University of California, 1943; M.Ed., University of Hawaii, 1945. Career: Principal, Iao High School, Hawaii, 1961; One-Man Show Exhibiting 192 Paintings in Oil, Pastel and Watercolors, 1978. Community Activities: Kauai Music Club (charter member); Lahaina Art and Cultural Center (charter member); Hawaii Loa College (sponsor); American Red Cross (standardization and donation, first aid textbooks); Maui Women's Club (charter member; author of constitution); Hawaii Board of Award Records of the University of Hawaii (co-chairman); First Celebration of Independence of West Samoa (delegate); Sukarno's Cultural Asia-Africa Conference (guest of the embassy, 1965); White House Counseling Conference (delegate); O.E.S. Triennial (delegate, page, worthy matron). Published Works: *Hawaii's Flowers* Pictorial Book, 1978; "International Mail Bag" Radio Script; Contributor to *Sunset Magazine, Reader's Digest;* Social Editor, *Garden Island;* "Lahaina Part in World War II" for Hawaii Board of War Records, University of Hawaii"; "Report of the Evacuation Committee World War II", Hawaii Board of War Records of University of Hawaii; Collaborated with Porteus, *Blow Not the Trumpet,* World War II. Honors and Awards: Numerous Awards and Scholarships, National Honor Society, Phi Kappa Phi; Fellow, International Biographical Association; Academic of Italy with Gold Medal; Awards throughout Academic Career; Dancing Academy Gold Medal; Grand Prize for Paintings, Maui County Fair, West Maui Fair, Honolulu Academy of Arts; Letters of Commendation, Commanding General of the Pacific Area for Meritorious Service in Planning Observation Posts and Evacuation of Families, World War II; Letter of Commendation for Educational Help in Sending Over 100,000 Books to Start Libraries under President Kennedy's "People-to-People" Program, Prime Minister of West Samoa; Listed in *International Register of Profiles, Dictionary of International Biography, Cornell Alumni News, Blue Book of Hawaii, Social Directory of U.S.A., Social Directory of Hawaii, Community Leaders and Noteworthy Americans, Notable Americans, Personalities of America, Book of Honor, Personalities of the West and Midwest, World Who's Who of Women, Historical Homes of Hawaii, Men and Women of Distinction, Internatinal Who's Who of Intellectuals.* Address: 45090 Namoku Street, Kaneohe, Hawaii 96744.

Gail E Monaloy

Monaloy, Gail Elaine

Personal: Born May 16, 1943; Daughter of Florence and Morris Monaloy; Married Melvin Garbin. Education: B.S. cum laude, Pennsylvania State University, 1964; M.A., Stanford University, California, 1966. Career: Speech-Language Pathologist, Director of Private Practice, Lecturer; Speech-Language Pathologist, Hospital and School Environments as Salaried Employee. Organizational Memberships: American Speech-Language-Hearing Association; New Jersey Speech-Language-Hearing Association; New York State Speech-Language-Hearing Association. Community Activities: State of New Jersey Professional Standards Review Council (advisory committee nominee). Honors and Awards: V.R.A. Grant, Stanford University, 1964-66; Cum Laude Graduate, Pennsylvania State University, 1964; Listed in *Who's Who of American Women, World Who's Who of Women, Directory of Distinguished Americans, Personalities of America.* Address: 140 Hepburn Road, Clifton, New Jersey 07012.

Mondy, Nell I

Professor of Nutrition Science. Personal: Born October 27, 1921; Daughter of D. Daley and F. Ethel Carroll Mondy (both deceased). Education: B.A. summa cum laude 1943, B.S. summa cum laude 1943, Chemistry, Ouachita University; M.A., Biochemistry, Texas University, 1945; Ph.D., Biochemistry, Cornell University, 1953. Career: Professor of Nutritional Sciences (Department of Nutritional Sciences), Professor of Food Science (Institute of Food Sciences) 1981 to present, Associate Professor of Nutrition 1975-81, Associate Professor of Food and Nutrition 1957-75, Assistant Professor of Food and Nutrition 1953-57, Instructor of Food and Nutrition 1948-51, Sigma Xi Fellow 1951-53, Research Associate in Biochemistry and Nutrition 1945-46, Cornell University; Consultant, Environmental Protection Agency, Washington, D.C., 1979-80; Consultant, Ninon Kaken Company, Ltd., Tokyo, Japan, 1978-79; Consultant, S&B Shokuhin Company, Ltd., Tokyo, Japan, 1978-79; Food Consultant, Holmen Brenderi, Gjovik, Norway, 1972-73; Professor of Food and Nutrition, Florida State University, 1969-70; Food Consultant, R. T. French, 1966-67; Supervisory Food Specialist, Human Nutrition Research Division, Food Quality Laboratory, United States Department of Agriculture, Beltsville, Maryland, 1960-61; Associated Colleges in Upper New York, Assistant Professor of Chemistry 1947-48, Instructor in Chemistry 1946-47; Research Assistant, Biochemical Institute, Texas University, 1944-45; Assistant Professor of Chemistry, Ouachita University, 1943-44. Organizational Memberships: American Association of University Professors; American Chemical Society; Institute of Food Technologists; New York Academy of Sciences; American Home Economics Association; European Association for Potato Research; The Potato Association of America; Society for Cryobiology; American Institute of Chemists (elected fellow); American Association for the Advancement of Science (elected fellow); American Dietetics Association;

New York State Horticultural Society; Empire State Potato Association; The American Society of Plant Physiologists; The International Platform Association; Washington Women's Network. Community Activities: Cayuga Trails Club (executive board); Historic Ithaca; Graduate Women in Science, Cornell University (president; vice president; secretary; nominating committee); Agriculture Circle; Cornell Campus Club (hostess, international hospitality committee); United Way (fund raiser); Ouachita Baptist University Campaign (vice-chairman); Phi Kappa Phi (chairman, nomination committee); Sigma Xi (chairman, initiation committee); Cornell Tower Club; Phi Tau Sigma, Cornell Chapter (counselor; president; vice-president). Religion: First Baptist Church of Ithaca, Trustee and Board of Education Member; Cornell United Religious Work, Faculty Representative; New York Council of Churches. Published Works: Articles Published in *Journal of Biological Chemistry, Journal of the American Dietetic Association, Federal Processes, Architectural Biochemistry and Biophysics, Processes of Social Experimental Biology and Medicine, Food Technology, Food Research, American Potato Journal, Journal of Agriculture and Food Chemistry, Journal of Food Science, Potato News, Food and Life Sciences, Human Ecology Forum, HortScience*; Author, Book, *Experimental Food Chemistry*, 1980. Honors and Awards: Fellow, American Association for the Advancement of Science, 1982; Birkett-Williams Lecturer, Ouachita University, Arkadelphia, Arkansas, 1980 to present; Higher Education Act Award, Cornell University, 1967; Selected by Students as Special Faculty Member to be Featured in Cornell Yearbook *Cornellian*, 1966; N.A.T.O. Award to Participate in Recent Advances in Food Science Seminar, Royal College of Food Science and Technology, Glasgow, Scotland, 1960; Distinguished Alumna Award, Ouachita University, 1960; National Science Foundation Award for College and University Teachers of Chemistry, Bloomington, Indiana, 1959; Research Selected to be Featured in *Research at Cornell*, 1959; Danforth Award, Faculty Summer Seminar on Creative Teaching, University of California-Berkeley, 1958; Danforth Award, Seminar on Teaching of Natural Sciences, Pennsylvania State University, 1954; Cornell Sigma Xi Fellowship, 1952-53; Iota Sigma Pi; Sigma Delta Epsilon; Phi Kappa Phi; Omicron Nu; Pi Lambda Theta; Phi Tau Sigma; Sigma Xi; Listed in *Who's Who Among Students in American Universities and Colleges*. Address: 126 Honess Lane, Ithaca, New York 14850.

Monosson, Ira Howard

Consultant in Internal Medicine, Occupational Medicine and Medical Toxicology. Personal: Born March 23, 1937; Son of Myron and Yetta Malvin; Married Aviva Sokol; Father of Elana, Danielle, Ari. Education: University of Southern California, 1955-58; B.A. 1959, M.D. 1962, Stanford University; Internship in Medicine and Surgery, Montefiore Hospital, Bronx, New York, 1962-63; Residency in Internal Medicine, Los Angeles County General Hospital 1963-64, Cedars of Lebanon Hospital, Los Angeles 1964-65; Fellowship in Cardiopulmonary Diseases, National Institute of Health Training Grant, Scripps Clinic and Research Foundation, La Jolla, California 1965-66; Residency in Occupational Medicine, Department of Community and Environmental Medicine, University of California-Irvine College of Medicine, 1976-77; Licensed by National Board of Medical Examiners, 1963 to present; Licensed by California Board of Medical Examiners, 1963 to present. Career: Private Consulting Practice, 1982 to present; Division of Occupational Safety and Health of Department of Industrial Relations of State of California, Los Angeles, Chief Public Health Medical Officer 1980-82, Public Health Medical Officer 1976-80; Medical Examiner at Board of Education, Coordinator of Cardiac Stress Testing and Arteriosclerosis Prevention Clinic at Medical Services Division, City of Los Angeles, 1975; Private Practice of Internal Medicine, 1966-74; Staff Appointment, University of California-Los Angeles Medical Center, Cedars-Sinai Medical Center; Chief of Medicine, Doctors Hospital of Compton 1973, Mid-City Hospital of Los Angeles 1970-71; Chief of Staff, Mid-City Hospital, 1971-72; Clinical Instructor, Department of Family and Preventive Medicine, University of Southern California School of Medicine, 1980 to present; Assistant Clinical Professor of Medicine, University of California-Los Angeles School of Medicine, 1982 to present; Medical Clinic Instructor, Cedars of Lebanon Hospital 1971-74, 1977, San Diego County/University Hospital 1967-68; Research in Progress in Percutaneous Neurotoxicity of Hexane and in Inhalation Toxicology in Humans from Paraquat. Organizational Memberships: Society for Occupational and Environmental Health; San Diego County Medical Society, 1966-68; California Society of Internal Medicine, 1966-68; Los Angeles County Medical Association, 1974-76; American Occupational Medical Association; American Conference of Governmental Industrial Hygienists; American College of Cardiology, 1966-77; Royal Society of Health (fellow, 1972 to present); American College of Chest Physicians (associate fellow, 1974-78); American College of Angiology (fellow, 1974 to present); American Geriatric Society, Western Division (founding fellow, 1974 to present); American Industrial Hygiene Association (full member, 1977 to present); American Academy of Occupational Medicine, 1979 to present. Community Activities: Los Angeles 2000 Project of the California Tomorrow Project (steering committee); American Cancer Society (industrial branch advisory board, local chapter); Los Angeles City Attorney (consultant in toxicology); Los Angeles District Attorney (consultant in toxicology); Temple Isaiah, West Los Angeles (board of trustees, 1978-80); Southern California Federation of Scientists (board of directors); University of California Southern Occupational Health Center (continuing education advisory committee); Los Angeles City Hazardous Substances Task Force (advisory committee). Religion: Jewish; Temple Isaiah, West Los Angeles, California. Published Works: "Report of the Advisory Committee on Cutaneous Hazards", O.S.H.A., 1978; "Fatality from Occupational Inhalation Exposure to Paraquat: A Case Report"; "Two Deaths Possibly Due to Occupational Over-Exposure to 1,1,2-Trichloro-1,2,2,-Trifluoroethane", 1977. Honors and Awards: Listed in *Who's Who in Health Care, Who's Who in the West, Who's Who in California, Men of Achievement, Personalities of America, Directory of Distinguished Americans*. Address: 2310 Malcolm Avenue, Los Angeles, California 90064.

Ernest L Moody

Moody, Ernest L

Resource Conservationist. Personal: Born October 5, 1939; Son of Mr. and Mrs. Wilson P. Moody Sr. (both decased). Education: B.S. Agronomy, Virginia State University, 1959; Professional Training, Soil and Water Conservation, Michigan State University, 1964; Graduate Studies in Urban Planning, George Washington University, 1977, 1978. Military: Served in the United States Army to Specialist 4, 1961-63. Career: United States Department of Agriculture, Resource Conservationist for Washington, D.C. 1974 to present, District Conservationist for Washington County, Maryland 1966-74, Soil Conservationist for Carroll County, Maryland 1964-66. Organizational Memberships: Soil Conservation Society of America (Old Line chapter, member 1966 to present, conservation education committee chairman 1978-79, vice-president 1980, president 1981, chapter delegate 1980; Washington D.C. chapter, chairman of environmental education committee, 1977); Organization of Professional Employees of the United States Department of Agriculture, 1974 to present; American Society of Agronomy, 1968 to present; National Science Teachers Association, 1974 to present; American Associaton for the Advancement of Science, 1977; National Wildlife Federation, 1968; National Geographic Society, 1979; United States Capitol Historical Society, 1975. Community Activities: Boy Scouts of America (Mason-Dixon council, advisor and resource lecturer on soils and water resources and activities, 1981-82); Thomas L. Ayers Outdoor Classroom Awards Program (chairman, 1977 to present); George Washington University (resource lecturer on soils); University of District of Columbia (resource lecturer on soils); Garden Clubs and Community Groups (assistant, conservation education programs and activities, 1982). Religion: Apostolic; Young People's Choir Organizer, 1961; Church Organist and Pianist, 1951 to present; Choir Director and Minister of Music, 1968 to present; Trustee, 1978 to present. Honors and Awards: Maryland Wildlife Federation Soil Conservation Award, 1969; Letters of Commendation, Soil Conservation Service Administrator, 1973, 1974; Meritorious Service Award, United States Department of Agriculture, 1975; Letter of Appreciation, Vice-President Nelson Rockefeller, 1975; Superior Service Award, United States Department of Agriculture, 1976; Certificate of Appreciation, District of Columbia Public

Schools, 1977; Outstanding Service Award, Soil Conservation Society of America, 1978; 30 Years Service Award for Dedicated Leadership and Inspiration to the Church Senior Choir, 1981; Special Recognition and Appreciation for 20 Years Service and Inspiration to the Young Adult Choir, 1981; Ohaus Award for Innovative Science Teaching in Colleges and Universities, National Science Teachers Association, 1982. Address: 3309 - 25th Avenue, Temple Hills, Maryland 20748.

Mooney, John Allen

Company President and Chief Executive Officer. Personal: Born May 17, 1918; Son of Harry Edmon and Maybelle Mooney; Married Nettie Hayes; Father of John Allen Jr., Suzann, Jean, Nancy. Education: Pre-Medical Course, Fiver Falls College. Career: Western Dressing, Inc., Oak Park, Illinois, President, Chief Executive Officer and Director 1978 to present, National Sales Manager and Vice-President 1970-78; Monarch & Richelieu Sales Corporation, Oak Park, Illinois, President, Chief Executive Officer and Director 1978 to present, National Sales Manager and Vice-President 1969-78; Salesman, Consolidated Foods Corporation 1945-69, Reid Murdock and Company 1940-45. Organizational Memberships: La Crosse Elk's Club; La Crosse Plugs; La Crosse Country Club; The La Crosse Club. Community Activities: First National Bank of LaGrange, Illinois (director); Waunakee Alloy Casting Corporation, Waunakee, Wisconsin (director); Zor Shrine Temple, Madison, Wisconsin (potentate, 1962); Shrine Hospital for Crippled Children, Chicago, Illinois (board of governors); Shrine Hospital for Crippled Children, Minneapolis and St. Paul (board of governors 1952-69); Amery Fall Festival (parade marshal, 1962); Amery Masonic Lodge; LaGrange Memorial Hospital, Illinois (associate board of governors); LaCrosse Luthern Hospital, Wisconsin (hertitage club support committee); Board of Trustees and Vice President Gunderson Medical Foundation, La Crosse, Wisconsin; Board of Governors, National Fishing Hall of Fame, Hayward, Wisconsin; Boy Scouts of America Board (Gateway Council); Member, Rebild National Park Society, Aalborg, Denmark; Festmaster, Octoberfest U.S.A., La Crosse, Wisconsin 1982-83; Honorary Past Potentate, Medinah Shrine Temple, Chicago, 1983; Chairman, Shrine Hospital Day 1982 (Chicago Unit); Co-Chairman of Several Zor Shrine Temple Ceremonials, La Crosse, Wisconsin; Royal Court of Jesters No. 126, Madison, Wisconsin; Parade Marshal, River Falls, Wisconsin, Shrine Hospital Benefit Football Parade, 1962; Life Membership in American Biographical Institute Research Association. Religion: First Congregational Church, La Crosse, Wisconsin. Honors and Awards: Amery Masonic Lodge, Wisconsin Named in his Honor, 1979; Honorary Member, LaCrosse Boys Choir, Wisconsin; Kentucky Colonel, Appointed by Governor Burt Combs of Kentucky. Address: 1515 North Harlem Avenue, Oak Park, Illinois 60302.

Moore, Barbara L

Controller. Personal: Born June 25, 1940. Education: B.A., Queens College, 1961; M.A., Columbia University, 1972. Career: Controller. Organizational Memberships: National Association of Management Accountants; Audit Fraternity Association; Audit Financial Management Association; National Association of Female Executives. Community Activities: National Organization for Women. Address: 11 Possum Trail, Upper Saddle River, New Jersey 07458.

Jeanne M R Moore

Moore, Dan Tyler

Writer, Association Director. Personal: Born February 1, 1908; Son of Dan T. and Luvean Jones Butler (both deceased); Married Elizabeth Valley Oakes; Father of Luvean O. Owens, Elizabeth Oakes Thornton, Harriett Ballard, Dan Tyler Moore III. Education: B.S., Yale University, 1931. Military: Served with the United States Army, 1942-44, Chief of Counter Intelligence in the Middle East, Office of Strategic Services. Career: Director General and Chairman of the Board, International Platform Association; Contributor of Articles and Stories to Popular magazines in the United States, Great Britain, and aroung the world; Author of *The Terrible Game*, 1957; *Cloak and Cipher*, 1962; *Wolves, Widows and Orphans*, 1966; *Lecturing for Profit*, 1967; Former Positions with Middle East Company, and China Company; Assistant to the President of Intercontinental Hotels Corporation, Istanbul, Turkey, 1948-50. Community Activities: Board of Directors: Near East Rehabilitation Center, Near East College Association, Karamu Theatre of Cleveland, Cleveland Museum of Natural History; Greater Cleveland Muscular Dystrophy Association (president 1952-65); Cuyahoga County Democratic Party (executive committee 1951-70; state executive committee 1962-65); Ohio Federal Jury (commissioner 1961-68). Religion: Episcopalian. Honors and Awards: Artillery Medallion of the Order of St. Barbara; Award for "Best Adventure Speech Being Given in the United States", International Platform Association; Listed in *Book of Honor, Community Leaders and Noteworthy Americans*. Address: 2564 Berkshire Rd., Cleveland Heights, Ohio 44106.

Moore, Gibbs Berry

Company Vice-President. Personal: Born March 13, 1928; Son of J. B. and Beatrice Moore; Married Josephine T. Moore; Father of David Gibbs Moore, Susan M. Wamsley. Education: Graduate of East Fairmont High School, 1945; Fairmont State College, 1955-56; West Virginia University School of Mines, 1960-64. Military: Served in the United States Army, 1950-52. Career: Vice-President, Keystone Division, Eastern Associated Coal Corporation, Beckley, West Virginia, 1970 to present; Mine Superintendent and District Superintendent, Island Creek Coal Company, Craigsville, West Virginia, 1974-79; Mine Superintendent, Ranger Fuel, Beckley, West Virginia, 1973-74; General Belt Maintenance Foreman, Florence Mining Company, Seward, Pennsylvania, 1970-73; Consolidated Coal Company, Monongah, West Virginia, Mine Foreman, Section Foreman, Miner Operator, 1957-70. Organizational Memberships: A.I.M.E., 1975 to present; Mid-State Mining Institute (vice-president, 1977-79). Community Activities: Coal Age Advisory Panel, 1970 to present; Mid-Western Mining Firm (consultant); Family Planning Board, Indiana, Pennsylvania (board of directors, 1971-72); Nicholas County Ambulance Authority (board of directors, 1978-79); Appalachian Dance and Music Ensemble (board of directors, 1981 to present). Religion: Presbyterian; Elder, 1966 to present. Honors and Awards: Army Commendation Medal, United States Army, Korea, 1952. Address: Grandview Road, Route 9, Box 300, Beaver, West Virginia 25813.

Moore, Jeanne Marie

Psychotherapist; Lecturer and Workshop Leader; Writer; Language, Socialization and Speech Specialist; Educator. Personal: Born in Los Angeles, California; Daughter of Harold and Marie Redding; Mother of Lisa Jeanne, James Richard, Michelle Renee. Education: A.A., Los Angeles Harbor College; B.A. 1971, M.A. 1973, California State University-Los Angeles; Postgraduate Work, California State College; Courses in Specialized Training in Reality Therapy, Transactional Analysis, Sexual Dysfuntion and Behavioral Change, University of California-Santa Barbara. Career: Writer for *Bakersfield Life* Magazine, 1983; Column Writer of "Jeanne's Lantern", 1981-82; Language, Socialization and Speech Therapist, Easter Seal Society S.E.E.D. Program for Autistic Children, 1981-82; Lecturer on Behavioral Eating Change for Feminine Fitness, 1981; Guest Lecturer on Topics of Separation, Weight Control, "Fatproofing" Children, and Blending the Blended Family, Bakersfield Community College, 1979 to present; S.E.E. Sign Language

Class Developer and Instructor, Taft Community College, 1979; Freelance Writer of Articles on Coping Skills, Communication, Behavioral Change, Weight Control, Parenting, and Teaching Techniques, 1978 to present; Owner and Operator, Fashion Clothing Business, 1978-80; Psychotherapist, Mediator, Group Leader, and Lecturer; Developer of Materials for Working with Specific Groups; Workshop Titles include *Divorce is Not a Dirty Word, Fat: Love It or Lose It, Pleasurable Parenting, Fulfilling Your Inner Potential*; Leader of Groups including Parents of "Special" Children, Stepparents, Formerly-Marrieds, Uncouplers, Parents Without Partners, and Sexual Assault Victims; Private Practice, 1977 to present; Instructor of Child Growth and Development, Behavior Modification, Current Theories and History of Psychology, Training for Instructional Aides, Bakersfield Community College, 1974-76; Educator of Multi-Handicapped Deaf Children, Teacher of Deaf Pre-Schoolers, Created the Infant/Parent Program conducted both on the school site and in the children's homes, Unipac Writer, Master Teacher, Creator of "Three-Minute Movies" for Classroom and Home Instruction, Writer of Children's Books to Check Comprehension, Program Developer, Educator of Deaf Children, Physically Handicapped, Mentally Exceptional and Learning Disabled Ages Infant through Junior High, Kern County Superintendent of Schools, 1972 to present; Crisis Intervention and Referrals, Los Angeles Children's Hospital, 1970-72; Researcher on Behavioral Change, Hearing of Vietnam Veterans, Effects of Marijuana on Perception and Effects of Sound on Animal and Human Behaviors, 1969-72; Private Secretary to Professor, 1966-68; Helper and Teacher, Foundation for the Junior Blind, Los Angeles, 1962-63; Aide, Camp Easter Seal for Physically Handicapped Children, 1962; Earned Credentials, Life Restricted Deaf and Hard-of-Hearing, Life Standard Elementary, Life Community College, Ryan Specialist Learning Handicapped, State of California Department of Health School Audiometrist, Conference of Executives of American Schools for the Deaf, Inc., California State Marriage, Family, Child Counselor License. Organizational Memberships: Professionals Against Cancer (board of directors); Bakersfield Parents of the Gifted; International Transactional Analysis Association; Parent-Teacher Organization; National Educators Association; Stepparent Association of California; National Association of Family Therapists; Association of Parents of Special Children. Community Activities: Rape Hotline of Kern County (board member; counselor); Legislative Committee of Curren (chairperson); Girl Scouts of America; Support Group for Parents of the Deaf; Kern County Mental Health Association (board of directors); Parent-Teacher Association. Honors and Awards: Honors at Entrance, 1966; Award in Appreciation of Services as Legislative Chairperson; Listed in Many Publications. Address: 932 Baldwin Road, Bakersfield, California 93304.

Moore, Ola C

Regional Director of Civil Rights. Personal: Born January 19, 1939; Daughter of Mr. and Mrs. Luther Clark. Education: B.S. Home Economics/Elementary Education, Texas College, 1961; M.S. Studies in Aging/Public Personnel Administration, North Texas State University, Denton, Texas, 1971; Kansas State University, 1972. Career: Southwest Region Food and Nutrition Service, Regional Director of Civil Rights 1972 to present, Assistant Director of Nutrition and Technical Service 1971-72; Acting Equal Opportunity Director, Federal Women's Program in Agriculture, Washington, D.C., 1975; Agent Agriculture Extension Service, Paris, Texas, 1961-69. Organizational Memberships: Urban League; National Association for the Advancement of Colored People (life member); National American Welfare Association; National Human Rights; American Home Economics Association. Community Activities: National Security Bank, Tyler, Texas (advisory board); Federal Executive Board (former chair); Capitol Development Committee, Dallas, Texas; Young Women's Christian Association, Paris, Texas (former secretary). Religion: Baptist. Honors and Awards: Outstanding Government Service during International Women's Year, Federal Executive Board, Dallas and Fort Worth, Texas, 1975; Merit Service Award, Food and Nutrition Service, Dallas, Texas. Address: Post Office Box 222169, Dallas, Texas 75222.

Robert D Moreton

Moore, Sonia

Author, Teacher, Lecturer. Personal: Born December 4, 1902; Daughter of Evser and Sophie Shatzov; Married Leon Moore (deceased); Mother of Irene M. Jaglom. Education: Attended University of Kiev and University of Moscow, 1918-20; Drama Studio, Solovtzov Theatre, Kiev, 1919-20; Studio of Moscow Art Theatre, 1920-23; Diploma, Alliance Francaise, Paris, 1927; Instituto Interuniversitario Italiano, Rome, Italy, 1938; Degree, Reale Conservatorio di Musica Santa Cecilia, 1939; Degree, Reale Accademia Filarmonica, Rome, 1939. Career: Author; Teacher; Lecturer. Organizational Memberships: American Library Association; Authors Guild; Society of Stage Directors and Choreographers; American Theatre Association. Community Activities: International Biographical Association; Smithsonian Institution. Honors and Awards: American Heritage Award for Service to the Community; John Fitzgerald Kennedy Library for Minorities, 1972; Listed in *International Who's Who in Community Service*. Address: 485 Park Avenue 6A, New York, New York 10022.

Morahan, Daniel Michael Kevin

Writer, Manpower Economist. Personal: Born August 15, 1940; Son of John Joseph and Eileen Alice Morahan. Education: A.A., 1962; B.B.A., George Washington University, 1965; Strategic Management Studies, New York University; Attended the Computer Learning Center, Fairfax, Virginia, 1974. Military: Served in the United States Army as a Civilian Officer, 1973-74. Career: Management Consultant in Personnel and Industrial Relations; Chairman and President functioning as Management Consultant, Research Writer and Labor Economist (in matters of defense, personnel, politics, other areas), M-Metra Limited Enterprises, 1973 to present; Writer-Editor, Adjutant General's Office, 1972-73; Classifier, Army General Staff, Civilian Personnel Office, 1968-72; Economist, Bureau of Labor Statistics, United States Department of Labor, 1967-68; Manpower Advisor, Manpower Administrator, United States Department of Labor, 1965-67. Organizational Memberships: American Institute of Management (executive council); Association of M.B.A. Executives; International Platform Association. Published Works: *Academy Women: The Education of Tomorrow's Military Officers (Women in Leadership Roles)*. Honors and Awards: Listed in *American Registry Series*. Address: 4005-74th Place, Bellemead, Hyattsville, Maryland 20784.

Moreton, Robert Dulaney

Radiologist. Personal: Born September 24, 1913, in Brookhaven, Mississippi; Son of Robert D. and Lena Moreton (both deceased); Married Alma Williamson, September 21, 1945. Education: B.S., Millsaps College, 1935; Certificate in Medicine, University of Mississippi, 1936; M.D., University of Tennessee, 1938; Internship, Lloyd Noland Memorial Hospital, Fairfield, Alabama, 1938-39; Fellow, Radiology, Mayo Foundation, University of Minnesota, 1940-42; Licensed, Mississippi 1938, Minnesota 1940, Texas 1942; Board Certification, American Board of Radiology, 1943. Career: Instructor in Physiology, University of Mississippi School of Medicine, 1940; Staff Radiologist, Scott & White Hospital and Clinic, Temple, Texas 1942-50, Consultant Radiologist, United States Public Health Hospital, Fort Worth, Texas 1950-65, St. Joseph's Hospital, Fort Worth 1950-65, John Peter Smith Hospital, Fort Worth 1951-65, Santa Fe Railroad System, Fort Worth 1952-65, Texas and Pacific Railroad Company, Dallas, Texas 1954-62, T. & G.N. Division, Missouri Pacific Railroad Company, Houston, Texas 1955-61, Southwestern Bell Telephone Company, Dallas, 1956-65, Bell Helicopter Company, Hurst, Texas 1960-65; University of Texas, Lecturer in Radiology, Medical Branch, Galveston

1945-50, Instructor, Clinical Radiology, Southwestern Division, School of Medicine, Dallas 1951-57, Associate Professor of Clinical Radiology, Southwestern Medical School, Dallas 1957-65, M.D. Anderson Hospital and Tumor Institute, Houston, Assistant Director 1965-69, Professor of Radiology 1965 to present, Vice President for Professional and Public Affairs 1969-79, Vice President for Patient Cancer Center, 1979 to present, Cancer Coordinator for the Regional Medical Program 1969-70, Vice President for Professional and Developmental Affairs, Health Science Center at Houston 1972-76; Chairman and Partner, Bond Radiological Group, Fort Worth, 1950-65; Consultant Medical Staff, Hermann Hospital, Houston, 1965 to present; Professor, School of Public Health, Department of Administrative Sciences, 1977 to present. Organizational Memberships: American College of Radiology (numerous committee positions); American Medical Association (numerous committee positions); American Registry of Radiologic Technologists (several positions); American Roentgen Ray Society; Bell County Medical Society; Dallas-Fort Worth Radiological Society; Fort Worth Academy of Medicine; Geriatrics Society; Gulf Coast Committee on Heart Disease, Cancer and Stroke; Harris County Medical Society; Houston Academy of Medicine; Houston Radiological Society; Industrial Medical Association; Northwest Texas Medical Society; Rocky Mountain Radiological Society; Southern Medical Association (numerous committee positions); Texas Advisory Committee on Atomic Energy; Tarrant County Medical Society (several committee positions); Texas Medical Association (numerous committee positions); Texas Radiological Society (several positions); Texas State Board of Health; Texas State Board of Health Resources; United States Department of Health, Education, and Welfare; Radiological Society of North America, Inc. (numerous committee positions); Intercity Radiological Society; Mid-South Postgraduate Medical Assembly; New Orleans Medical Assembly; Sigma Chi; Pan Pacific Surgical Association; Texas Society of X-Ray Technicians. Community Activities: Mason Knight Templar; Boy Scouts of America (scoutmaster, Temple, Texas, 1945-46); Rotary Club (president, Temple, 1945-46; senior active member, Fort Worth); Carter Blood Bank, Fort Worth (founding member, board, 1946); Radiation and Research Foundation of the Southwest Fort Worth (founding board member, 1964); Life Member, Sigma Chi and Phi Chi fraternities; Medical Advisor, John S. Dunn Research Foundation; Executive Director, University Cancer Foundation; Member, Texas Health Foundation; Moncrief Radiation Center, Fort Worth (board, executive committee); Fort Worth Chamber of Commerce (chairman, health and hospital committee); Doctors' Club, Houston, 1965 to present; Community Welfare Planning Association of Greater Houston (board of directors, 1967-69). Religion: Member, Matthews Memorial Church, Fort Worth. Published Works: Author, Numerous Articles Published in Professional Publications, including "The Barium Enema in Checkups of Patients with Cancer of the Colon", "The Role of Pre-Placement Roentgen Examination of the Spine in Evaluation of Low Back Pain", "Breast Cancer: The Great New Concern". Honors and Awards: Gold Medal for Exhibits, American Medical Association, 1949; Gold Medal for Exhibit, Military Surgeons of the United States, 1949; Awards of Merit, American Roentgen Ray Society, Radiological Society of North America Inc., Chicago Medical Society, 1949; Brotherhood Citation Award, West Texas Region, National Conference of Christians and Jews, Inc., 1967; Distinguished Service Award, Southern Medical Association, 1967; Distinguished Citizen Award, Goodwill Industries, Inc., Houston, 1968; Gold Medal, Radiological Society of North America, 1973; Gold Medal Texas Radiological Society, 1974; Listed in *Who's Who in the World, Who's Who in America, Who's Who in the South and Southwest, World Who's Who in Science.* Address: 1600 Holcombe Boulevard, Houston, Texas 77030.

Morgan, Edmund Joseph Jr

Emergency Medicine Surgeon and Physician. Personal: Born January 30, 1923, in Boston, Massachusetts; Son of Edmund Joseph (deceased) and Frances Marie Clayton Morgan; Married Setsuko Fujiwara; Father of Norah Ann, Constance Marie, Edmund Joseph III, Charles William, Cecilia Ann, Thomas Clayton. Education: Harvard College, 1941-42; Yale University, 1943; M.D. cum laude, Tufts College Medical School, 1948; Intern and Resident in Surgery, Charity Hospital, New Orleans, Louisiana, 1948-50. Military: Served in the United States Army, 1943-46, attaining the rank of Captain. Career: Emergency Medicine Physician and Surgeon, Franklin County Public Hospital, Greenfield, Massachusetts, 1976 to present; Medical Surgery and Obstetrics Practice, Tokyo, Japan, 1959-76; Medical Advisor to American Embassy, Tokyo, Japan, 1959-76; Chief of Surgery and Obstetrics, Hospital of American Samoa, Pago Pago, 1956-59; Physician and Surgeon, Catholic Medical Center, Guam, 1956-57; Medicine and Surgery Practice, Boston, Massachusetts, 1954-56; Ship's Surgeon; United States Coast Guard Ship Explorer, Alaska, 1950. Organizational Memberships: Medical Society of Japan, 1963-81; American Board of Family Practice (diplomate, 1978-81); American College of Emergency Physicians, 1978-81; American Medical Association, 1976-81; Aerospace Medical Association, 1960-81; Massachusetts Medical Society; Alpha Omega Alpha National Medical Honors Society, 1948-81. Community Activities: State of Massachusetts Instructor of Emergency Medical Technicians and Paramedics, 1981; Advanced Cardiac Life Support Instructor, 1978-81; Franklin County Public Hospital (co-operator, 1978-81); Draft Board of Guam Island (medical director, 1956-57); American Embassy, Tokyo, Japan (medical advisor, 1964-76); American Club of Tokyo (board of governor's, 1970-75). Religion: Blessed Sacrament Church, Greenfield, Massachusetts. Honors and Awards: Letter of Commendation for Action (Medical) Performed in Alaska, United States Secretary of Commerce, 1950; United States Army Parachutist Badge for Combat; Medical Badge for Korean Campaign; 2 Battle Stars, Meritorious Unit Citation; Presidential Unit Citation; Recommended for Silver Star (refused on principle). Address: 1023 Bernardston Road, Greenfield, Massachusetts 01301.

Marianne M Mori

Morgan, Roy L

Consultant on International Trade. Personal: Born November 14, 1908; Son of Henry Clay Morgan (deceased); Married Rosamond W. Woodruff; Father of Richard W. Education: B.S. 1930, LL.B. 1933, J.D. 1971, University of Virginia. Military: Served in the Federal Bureau of Investigation, 1934-45. Career: Consultant on International Trade; Attorney, United States Department of Agriculture; Special Agent of Federal Bureau of Investigation; Private Practice Lawyer; Associate Prosecutor, International Tribunal for War Criminals, Japan; Member, 11-Nation Executive Committee for Selection of War Criminals; American Advisor to Prime Minister of Japan, 1955; Chief Justice, United States Civil Appellate Court in Far East; Special Assistant, United States Secretary of Commerce; Headed United States Trade Missions to Japan, 1962, 1968. Community Activities: Executives Club of Greensboro, North Carolina (president); Greensboro City Council, 1948-50; Greensboro Rotary Club, 1939-40; American Heart Association (North Carolina state chairman, 1949); American Cancer Society (Guildford County chairman, 1947-48); President's National Export Expansion Council (executive director, 1963-66). Religion: Baptist. Honors and Awards: Award and Plaque, Ex-F.B.I. Society Foundation, Washington, D.C., 1979; "This is Your Life", Washington, D.C., 1966; Plaques, United States and Japanese Cities. Address: Sugar Loaf Farms, Lambsburg, Virginia 24351.

Mori, Marianne McDonald

Researcher and Instructor in Classics. Personal: Born January 2, 1937; Daughter of Eugene and Inez McDonald; Married Torajiro Mori; Mother of Eugene, Conrad, Bryan, Bridget, Kristie, Hiroshi. Education: B.A. magna cum laude, Byrn Mawr, Pennsylvania, 1958; M.A., University of Chicago, Illinois, 1960; Ph.D., University of California-Irvine, 1975. Career: University of California-Irvine, Researcher with Thesaurus Linguae Graecae Project 1979 to present, Instructor in Department of Classics 1975-79, Teaching Assistant in Department of Classics 1972-74. Organizational Memberships: American Philological Association; American Classical

League; American Society of University Professors; Hellenic Society; Modern Language Association. Community Activities: La Jolla Country Day School (board member, 1974-75); American College of Greece (board member, 1981 to present) Hellenic University Club, 1982 to present; T.L.G. Advisory Board, 1982 to present. Published Works: *A Semilemmatized Concordance to Euripides' Alcestis*, 1977; *A Semilemmatized Concordance to Euripides' Cyclops*, 1978; *A Semilemmatized Concordance to Euripides' Adromache*, 1978; *A Semilemmatized Concordance to Euripides' Medea*, 1978; *A Semilemmatized Concordance to Euripides' Heraclidae*, 1979; *A Semilemmatized Concordance to Euripides' Hippolytus*, 1979; *A Semilemmatized Concordance to Euripides' Hecuba*, 1982; *Terms for Happiness in Euripides*, 1978; *Euripides in Cinema: The Heart Made Visible*, 1983;"Aeneas and Turnus: Labor vs. Amor", *Pacific Coast Philology*, 1972; "Acies: Virgil Georgics 1. 395", *Classical Philology*, 1973; "Sunt Lacrimae Rerum", *Classical Journal*, 1972-73; "Horace et Automedon" with Peter Colaclides, *Latomus*, 1974; "Bedtime Story", *Die Diagonale*, 1970; *"Terms for Life in Homer: An Examination of Early Concepts in Psychology"*, *Journal of the College of Physicians of Philadelphia*, 1981. Honors and Awards: Ellen Browning Scripps Humanitarian Award, 1975; Distinguished Service Award, University of California-Irvine, 1982; Listed in *Dictionary of American Scholars, World Who's Who of Women, International Who's Who of Intellectuals, Who's Who in American Education, International Who's Who in Education*. Address: Box 929 El Arco Iris, Rancho Santa Fe, California 92067.

Moriwaki, Sharon Yuriko

Program Administrator. Personal: Born December 29, 1945; Daughter of Mr. and Mrs. Yutaka Moriwaki. Education: B.A. 1967, M.A. 1969, Ph.D. 1972, University of Southern California. Career: Program Administrator, Department of Labor and Industrial Relations, State of Hawaii; Associate Director, Hawaii Gerontology Center; Evaluation Branch Chief/Training Director, California Department of Aging; University of Southern California, Research Project Director at Andrus Gerontology Center, Assistant Professor. Organizational Memberships: American Psychological Association; Gerontological Society; Western Gerontology Society; White House Conference on Aging (technical committee, 1981); Hawaii Senior Companion Advisory Council (vice-chair, 1978-81). Community Activities: Governor's Commission on the Status of Women (member, 1978 to present; secretary, 1979-82; statewide conference chair, 1979); Honolulu City and County Neighborhood Board, 1981 to present; Governor's White House Conference on Aging (delegate, technical issues chair, 1980 to present); State of Hawaii Policy Advisory Board for Elderly Affairs, 1980 to present; St. Louis Heights Community Association (secretary, 1978-80; president, 1981-82); Democratic Party of Hawaii (precinct secretary, 1978-81); Hawaii Public Broadcasting Authority Community Advisory Board, 1980 to present. Honors and Awards: National Retired Teachers Association Scholarship, 1971; Biomedical Support Grant, National Institute of Health, 1970-71; National Institute of Child Health and Human Development Fellowship, 1967-71; Phi Beta Kappa, 1967; Listed in *Who's Who of American Women, Who's Who in the West, World Who's Who of Women, Who's Who of Women*. Address: 1812 St. Louis Drive, Honolulu, Hawaii 96816.

Morris, Henry Allen Jr

Newspaper Journalist and General Manager. Personal: Born February 9, 1940; Son of Henry A. and Edith Wall Morris. Education: Palmer Junior College of Business, 1958; Dock Street Theatre School of Drama, 1959; Attended the University of South Carolina School of Journalism, 1967; B.A. cum laude, English, Belmont Abbey College, 1973; Studies at Universite d'Alliance Francais, Paris, France, 1972. Career: Journalist and General Manager, *The Berkeley Democrat* Newspaper; Headmaster, St. Stephen Academy; Editor, *Gateway to Charleston* Magazine; Cargo Coordinator, South Carolina State Port Authority; Public Relations, Belmont Abbey College. Organizational Memberships: South Carolina Press Association; South Carolina Independent School Association (board member); Low Country Headmasters Association (chairman). Community Activities: Moncks Corner Rotary Club (president); Moncks Corner Business Association (chairman); Berkeley County Arts Association (board member); Lower Episcopal Diocese of South Carolina (licensed lay reader); Berkeley County Chamber of Commerce (board member; past vice president); Berkeley County Heart Association (board member); Charleston Opera Company (co-founder; first president); Charleston Jaycees (vice president); Trident Multiple Sclerosis Society (board member); Footlight Players and Charleston Symphony (box office committee). Religion: Episcopal Church of the Holy Communion, Secretary to Vestry; Council Member, Church of the Holy Family; Licensed Lay Reader, Lower Episcopal Diocese of South Carolina. Honors and Awards: Palmetto Corps Award, South Carolina Jaycees, 1966; Special Presidential Award, Charleston Jaycees, 1971; First President Award, Charleston Opera Company, 1967; Delegate, Symposium on the American President, 1971; Alliance Francais, Scholarship for Study in France, 1972; Certificate of Merit, Distinguished Service to the Community, 1976; Listed in *Outstanding Young Men of America, Personalities of the South, Men of Achievement*. Address: 117 Merrimack Drive, Moncks Corner, South Carolina 29461.

Morris, LaRona J

Administrative Assistant. Personal: Born November 16, 1942; Daughter of Norma L. Walls; Married Oreido S. Morris; Mother of Bryant Keith, Ricci D'Andre, Crystal Ranee. Education: Diploma, Mildred Louise Business College, 1960; B.S. Business Education 1974, M.S. Counselor Education 1979, Southern Illinois University-Edwardsville. Career: Administrative Assistant to St. Clair County Regional Superintendent of Schools, 1979 to present; Adminstrative Assistant to the East St. Louis Aldermanic Council, 1975-79; Secretary, East St. Louis Aldermanic Commission, 1973-75; Public Relations Director, East St. Louis, 1972-74, East St. Louis Deputy City Clerk, 1974-75. Organizational Memberships: Phi Delta Kappa Professional Fraternity, 1981; Illinois Association of Women School Administrators, 1981; Illinois Basic Skills Advisory Committee, 1980; Illinois Young Authors Conference Program (regional coordinator, 1981); St. Clair County Most Difficult Child Committee, 1980. Community Activities: St. Clair County Bi-State Transportation Task Force, 1981 to present; St. Clair County A.D.D.C.O. (board of directors, 1980-81); St. Clair County Y.W.C.A. (board of directors, 1980 to present); National Youth Sports Program, Southern Illinois University-Edwardsville, 1978-79; National Association of Housing and Redevelopment Officials, 1978-80; East St. Louis Housing Authority (board of commissioners, 1978-80); Illinois Commission of the Status of Women (chair, committee on minority women, 1978-80); East-West Gateway Coordinating Council (regional forum, 1978-79); East St. Louis Political Women, Inc. (chair, 1977 to present); Illinois Women's Political Caucus, 1977 to present; Metro-East Lioness Club (charter member, 1977 to present); National Association for the Advancement of Colored People (life subscriber, 1977 to present); Metro-East Women's Political Caucus, 1975 to present); Illinois Black Caucus of Local Elected Officials (special appointment, 1975-77); Notaries Association of Illinois, 1974 to present; St. Clair County Urban League (board of directors, 1970-75); Sigma Gamma Rho Sorority, Inc. (chapter basileus, 1970 to present); Order of the Eastern Star, 1967 to present. Religion: Church of God in Christ Congregational Church. Honors and Awards: Invitation to the President's White House Forum on Inflation, 1975-78; Female Politician of the Year, HiPhiHi Social Club, 1975-77; Listed under "People" in *Jet* Magazine, 1974, 1978, 1981; Congressional Invitation for Tour of White House, 1975; Listed under "Woman Power" in Local Edition of *Metro-East Journal* Newspaper, 1972; Most Outstanding Civilian Award and Citation, Scott Air Force Base, Illinois, 1971; St. Clair County Big Brothers-Big Sisters (board of directors, 1982 to present); Illinois Association for the Advancement of Black Americans in Vocational Education, 1982 to present; Named "Community Leader", Southern Illinois Association of Club

Women, 1982; Named "Woman of the Year", East St. Louis Business and Professional Women, 1982; Named "Sigma-of-the-Year", Sigma Gamma Rho Sorority-Central Region, 1982; Listed in *Personalities of the West and Midwest, Outstanding Young Women of America, Community Leaders and Noteworthy Americans, Black Women Role Models of Greater St. Louis.* Address: 1610 North 45th Street, East St. Louis, Illinois 62204.

Morris, Richard

Psychotherapist and Hypno-Analyst. Personal: Born January 26; Son of Robert and Molly Morris; Married Dr. Margaret Morris. Education: B.A. Psychology, Dickinson College, (Penn. State), Carlisle, Pennsylvania; M.A. Social Sciences and Humanities/Counseling the Urban Disadvantaged 1969; Ph.D. Program in Clinical Psychology 1970-72, New York University; Trained and Certified as Director, Mount Vernon Crisis Hotline, Westchester County Narcotics Council; Permanent Certification as Counselor in New York State, Long Island University, 1977; M.A. Psychology, Clinical Mental Health Sciences and Psychotherapy, New School for Social Research, 1977; N.D., American College of Nutripathy; Ph.D. in Clinical Psychology Coursework Completed, School of Professional Psychology at F.I.T., 1981; R.H.D., American Association of Professional Hypnologists. Military: Officer in the United States Army Special Forces Division, 1966-67; Training at U.S.A.T.S.C.H., Fort Eustis, Virginia; Decorated as a Viet Nam Era Veteran. Career: (present) Founder, Director and Senior Staff Psychotherapist of Central Westchester Psychotherapy and Family Counseling Service; Lecturer, Adjunct Faculty in Psychology, Behavioral Sciences and Humanities Departments, Mercy College, Dobbs Ferry, New York; Psychological Sports Consultant for Several Professional and Collegiate Athletic Teams and Individual Athletes; (past) Guidance Counselor, Crisis Counselor, Recreation Counselor, Rehabilitation Counselor for United States Army, New York City Board of Education, Odessey House Group, Family Life Institute and Other Organizations; Teacher of All Levels and Subjects in Public Schools and Colleges; Karate Instructor for 16 years (3rd Degree Black Belt), Privately and in the United States Army. Organizational Memberships: American Association of Marriage and Family Therapists (full clinical member); Permanently Certified Counselor and Teacher, Secondary Level, Personnel Counseling, and Secondary Level Social Sciences Teacher, New York State and New York City; Certified Third Degree Black Belt Karate Master. Community Activities: Worked in Day Camps, Swimming Programs, Karate and Physical Fitness Training, in Summers; White Plains Young Men's Christian Association Weightlifting Teams (founder and captain); City of Yonkers Neighborhood Council (director, 1979); New York Metropolitan A.A.U. Powerlifting Committee (president, 1978-81); Psycho-nutritional Consultant to General Health Management Corp., Bloomfield, Connecticut to V.P.S. Health Corp., Middletown, New York; National Board of Advisors, American Biographical Institute (member); International Academy of Nutritional Consultants; (member); World Congress of Professional Hypnotists (advisory member). Honors and Awards: Powerlifting, Weightlifting and Wrestling Champion; Captain of Championship Teams, Eastern States Powerlifting Championships 1969, 1970, 1974, 1975; Winner of Over 300 Trophies and Titles, Holder of Numerous State, National, U.S. Army, and Regional Records for Football, Wrestling, Karate, and Weightlifing; Outstanding Teacher in Harrison, 1969; Several Military Meritorious Service During Viet Nam Era Medals, United States Army; Most Valuable Wrestling Coach Award, Westbester County, 1975; Athlete of the Year, New York Metropolitan American Association of Universities, 1977; Man of the Year Award, Yonkers City Youth Council, 1978; Athletic Scholarship to College; Recipient of 2 Presidential Sports Awards by Jimmy Carter (one in Karate, 1977; one in Jogging, 1978); Received Certificate of Participation-U.S. Olympic Committee; Received Certificate of Merit-U.S. Olympic Society; Football Centennial Certificate-awarded by the National Federation of State High School Athletic Association, 1962. Address: P.O. Box 75, Ardsley, New York 10502.

Morse, Samuel A

Hospital Administrator. Personal: Born February 24, 1943; Son of Samuel A. Morse; Married Jan Morse; Father of Joshua, Jeremy, Mary. Education: B.S., Abilene Christian University, 1966; M.S., Health Care Administration, Trinity University, 1971. Career: Administrator, Medical Center Hospital, Conroe, Texas; Executive Vice President, Brookhaven Medical Center; President, Hospital Resources Management, Inc.; Director of Management Systems, American Medicorp; Associate Hospital Director, Hermann Hospital; Assistant to the Vice President, American Medicorp. Organizational Memberships: American College of Hospital Administrators (fellow); American College of Nursing Home Administrators; Hospital Financial Management Association. Community Activities: Rotary Club; Kiwanis Club; Lions Club; Jaycees; Chamber of Commerce; Young Men's Christian Association (board member); American Cancer Society (board member); American Heart Association (board member); Boys Club of America (board member). Honors and Awards: Listed in *Outstanding Young Men of America, Who's Who in the South and Southwest, Personalities of the South, Men of Achievement, Men and Women of Distinction, International Who's Who of Community Leaders, Who's Who in Health Care.* Address: P.O. Box 1442, Conroe, Texas 77301.

Morton, Jean Sloat

Science Consultant and Writer. Personal: Born April 2, 1926; Daughter of Charles Victor and Cora Taylor Sloat (both deceased); Married Clyde D. Morton; Mother of Jennifer Sue. Education: B.S. District of Columbia Teachers College, Washington, D.C., 1958; M.S. Science Teacher 1962, M.S. 1964, American University; Master of Philosophy of Science 1969, Ph.D. 1970, George Washington University, Washington, D.C.; Postgraduate Study, University of Oslo, Norway and University Uppsala, Sweden, 1963. Career: Science Consultant and Writer, 1970 to present; Professional Lecturer, George Washington University, 1964-70; Researcher, Industrial Microbiology, 1964-70; Instructor of Biology, American University, 1961-64. Organizational Memberships: American Association for the Advancement of Science; Mississippi Academy of Science; New York Academy of Science; Phi Delta Gamma Women's Professional Society; International Platform Association. Community Activities: The Guild, 1978-79; Newcomer's Club, 1978-82. Religion: Assistant, Wabanna Christian Camp, 1966-76. Published Works: Instructional Manuals and Accompanying Teacher's Handbooks in *Chemical Structure and Change, Astronomy, Microbiology and Protozology, Motion and Its Measurement, Light and Sound, Physical Properties of Water, Our Sun and Other Stars, A Science Review*, 1978; Editor, *The Original McGuffey Series Primer* through 4th Grade, 1982; *Science in the Bible*, 1978; "Growth of Organs of Grass Seedling," Eleventh International Botanical Congress, 1969; "Effects of Sodium Chloride Concentration on Enzymatic Reactions of Brine Organisms," *Bacteriological Proceedings*, 1962. Honors and Awards: King Research Fellowship, 1965-69; National Science Foundation Research Fellowship, 1962; Smithsonian Research Fellowship, 1969-70; Sigma Xi Scientific Research Honor Society; Beta Beta Beta Biological Honor Society; Phi Epsilon Phi Botanical Honor Society; Kappa Delta Pi Educational Honor Society. Address: 2208 Millswood Road, Picayune, Mississippi 39466.

Morton, Jean W

Public Relations Consultant. Personal: Born March 21, 1927; Daughter of Curtis John and Jessie Garrison Wims (both deceased);

Mother of Melanie Ann. Education: University of Vermont-Burlington, 2 Years; American Institute of Banking Savings and Loan League Institute; Special Classes, University of California-Los Angeles. Career: Public Relations Consultant, 1977 to present; Public Relations Director, Meharry Medical College 1967-77, San Diego Teachers Association 1965-67; Assistant Executive Secretary for Public Relations and Communications, Metro-Nashville Education Association, 1967 to present; Loan Officer, Central Federal Savings and Loan Association, San Diego, 1958-65; Public Relations Officer, First National Trust and Savings Bank, San Diego, 1951-58. Organizational Memberships: Public Relations Society of America; American Women in Radio and Television; American Press Club; Tennessee Hospital Public Relations Council; Tennessee Society for Hospital Public Relations; American Hospital Association; American College Public Relations Association; American Schools Public Relations Association; Association of American Medical Colleges; International Platform Association. Community Activities: The Tennessee Commission on the Status of Women (commissioner); Davidson County Business and Professional Women's Club; Nashville Area Chamber of Commerce; Nashville University City Council; Cumberland Valley Girl Scout Council. Honors and Awards: The Governor's Outstanding Tennessean Award for Woman of the Year, 1976; Woman of the Year, Davidson County Business and Professional Women's Club, 1975; One of 15 Outstanding Americans, *Golden West* Magazine, 1975; First Annual Prism Citation for Outstanding Performance and Excellence in Hospital Public Relations, Tennessee Society of Hospital Public Relations, 1975; Certificate of Appreciation for Leadership as a Member of the 100 Sense Campaign Kidney Fund Drive, Meharry Medical College; Plaque for Outstanding and Dedicated Community Service through Outstanding Work for Meharry Medical College, Alpha Chi Omega Sorority; Selection as One of the Foremost Women in Communications, 1969-70; Listed in *Who's Who in Public Relations, Who's Who in the South, Who's Who of American Women, Biography of Prominent Americans, World Who's Who of Women, Personalities of the South;* Library of Human Resources of the American Bicentennial Research Institute, Inc. Address: 430 Summit Ridge Place, Nashville, Tennessee, 37216.

Mosely, Herbert Frederick

General and Orthopaedic Surgeon. Personal: Born January 28, 1906 in Sydney, Cape Breton Island, Nova Scotia, Canada; Married Helen MacArthur; Father of One Daughter. Education: B.A., McGill University, 1926; B.A., Oxford University, United Kingdom, 1930; St. Thomas Hospital, London, 1930; Merton College, Oxford University, 1927-30. Career: Surgeon and Director of Accident Service, Royal Vic. Hospital, Montreal, Canada, 1938-69; Associate Professor of Surgery, McGill University, 1938-70. Organizational Memberships: Royal Society of Medicine; Canadian Medical Association. Published Works: *Textbook of Surgery,* 1952, 3rd Edition, 1959; *Recurrent Dislocation of the Shoulder,* 1961; *Shoulder Lesions,* 3rd Edition, 1969. Honors and Awards: Hunterian Professor, Robert Jones Lecturer, Royal College of Surgeons, United Kingdom, 1950 and 1969; Cheselden, Meade and Bristowe Medals, St. Thomas Hospital, London. Address: 233 Via Linda, Palm Beach, Florida 33480.

Moses, James Anthony Jr

Clinical and Research Neuropsychologist. Personal: Born February 25, 1947; Son of James A. Sr. and Lucille M. Moses. Education: B.A. magna cum laude, San Francisco State University, 1968; M.S., San Jose State University, 1970; M.A. 1971, Ph.D. 1974, University of Colorado-Boulder. Career: Clinical and Research Neuropsychologist; School Psychologist, Group Counselor and Consultant, Campbell Union High School District. Organizational Memberships: American Psychological Association; Western Psychological Association; International Neuropsychological Society; National Academy of Neuropsychologists; Society for Personality Assessment; Stanford University Clinical Faculty Association. Community Activities; Islam Temple Shriners (clown unit, 1969-75); Stanford University (volunteer member, clinical faculty, 1975 to present; chief instructor, self-defense club, 1981 to present); Zen Budokai Self-Defense Academy (uncompensated instructor, 1968 to present); Order of DeMolay (past master councilor, Islam chaper, 1964-65; member, 1962-68). Honors and Awards: Outstanding Volunteer Service Award, Veterans Administration, 1974; Superior Performance Awards, Veterans Administration, 1978, 1980; Multiple Awards for Public Service, Order of DeMolay; Life Membership, California Scholarship Federation, 1964; Magna Cum Laude Graduate, San Francisco State University, 1968; Psi Chi National Psychology Honor Society, 1968; Karate Champion, Zen Budokai Society, 1968; George Hendry Memorial Scholarship, 1969-73; U.S.P.H.S. Intermediate Level Fellow in Clinical Psychology, 1970-71. Address: 177 Westlawn Avenue, Daly City, California 94015.

Maxine V Mosley

Mosley, Maxine V

Teacher. Personal: Born February 27, 1928; Daughter of Anna Ellsworth; Married Dr. Raymond J. Mosley (deceased); Mother of Linda K. Knight, Brenda J. Henry, Anita R. Skyles. Education: B.S., Northeast Missouri State University, 1957; M.A., University of Missouri, 1965. Career: Teacher of Business and English: Callao Public Schools, 1950-53; New Cambria High School, 1951-53; Shelby County R-1 School, 1953-56; Unionville, High School, 1961-63; St. Louis Community College at Meramec, 1964-78; D.C.T.A. Public Relations Committee Chairman, District Public Relations Coordinator and Communications Media Adviser, Dunkin School District R-5, Herculaneum, Missouri. Organizational Memberships: District Teachers of English (Northeast Missouri University secretary); Missouri State Teachers Association (English curriculum); College Composition and Communication (reservation chairman); National Council of English Teachers; Greater St. Louis Council of Teachers of English (executive council); National English Association; National, State, and District Junior College Associations; Others associations on the local, district, state, national and international levels. Community Activities: Girl Scouts of America (troop leader); Parent Teacher Association (secretary); Worked for passage of many school bond issues; United Way (chairman and member, 1966-78); Cancer Drive (chairman); Heart Fund Drive (chairman); 4-H Club (leader); Quill and Scroll (sponsor); Future Business Leaders of America (sponsor); International Platform Association, 1981; Teacher of needlepoint to senior citizens. Religion: United Methodist Church, 1951-53; O.E.S. 1948 to present. Published Works: *Developing Composition Skills,* 1967. Honors and Awards: Scholarship, Northeast Missouri State University, 1945; Selected to train teachers to teach composition using individualized instruction method in a community college in Saudi Arabia; Listed in *Dictionary of International Biography, Community Leaders and Noteworthy Americans, World Who's Who of Women in Education, International Who's Who in Education, Men and Women of Distinction, Book of Honor, Personalities of America, Dictionary of American Scholars, International Book of Intellectuals, World's Who's Who of Women, International Who's Who of Intellectuals, Personalities of the West and Midwest, Dictionary of Distinguished Americans, International Book of Honor.* Address: 907 Peggy Drive, Pevely, Missouri 63070.

Mosley, William F III

Certified Public Accountant. Personal: Born March 2, 1948; Son of Mr. and Mrs. William F. Mosley, Jr; Married to Pamela Jane; Father of Ryan Todd. Education: B.B.A., North Texas State University, 1970; Attended United States Air Force Academy, Colorado, 1966-67. Military: Served with U.S.A.F. Reserve as Sergeant, 1966-73. Career: Certified Public Accountant in Houston,

Texas. Organizational Memberships: American Institute of C.P.A.s; Texas Society of C.P.A.s; Houston Chapter of Texas Society of C.P.A.s (tax committee). Religion: Attends Episcopal Church. Honors and Awards: Institute of Internal Auditors, Dallas Essay Program, 1970; Listed in *Who's Who in the Southwest*. Address: 11323 Chevy Chase Avenue, Houston, Texas 77077.

Moss, Tommye Atkinson

Civic Worker. Personal: Born November 8, 1894; Daughter of Mr. and Mrs. Atkinson (deceased); Wife of William P. Moss (deceased); Mother of William P. Jr., Betty M. Dean. Education: B.A., Tift College, Forsyth, Georgia, 1917. Community Activities: Federation of Music Clubs (president, local chapter; officer, state and national levels; leadership training chairman, 1930). Religion: First Baptist Church, 1930 to present. Honors and Awards: First Lady of Odessa, 1955. Address: Post Office Box 3229, Odessa, Texas 79760.

Motter, Roberta L

Government Official. Personal: Born March 8, 1936, in Honolulu, Hawaii; Daughter of Donald D. and Florence B. Reed; Mother of Edwin, Lori, Lisa. Education: Completed numerous management courses; Attended Cornell University summer session in Hawaii for personnel management course, 1956. Career: Program Analyst, General Service Administration, Arlington, Virginia, 1980 to present; Executive Vice President and part owner of a consulting firm, Contacts Unlimited; Director of Administrative Services, New York State Insurance Department Liquidation Bureau, New York, 1975-80; Personnel Director and Office Manager, Summit Insurance Company of New York, Houston, Texas, 1974-75; Conversion Specialist, Accounts Payable, Medenco, Inc., Houston, 1973-74; Administrative Manager, P.R.C. Computer Center, 1972-73; Computer Specialist and Personnel Director, Alan M. Voorhees and Associates, McLean, Virginia, 1968-71; Accounts Receivable Supervisor, Mayflower Hotel, Washington, D.C., 1966-67; Paymaster Computer Specialist, Gate City Steel, Omaha, Nebraska, 1961-64; Office Manager, Fisher Construction Company, Honolulu, 1960-61; Director of Personnel, Hawaiian Village Hotel, Honolulu, 1956-59. Organizational Memberships: American Society of Personnel Administrators; Administrative Management Society of Washington, D.C. (board of directors, 1981-81); Washington, D.C. Purchasing Management Association; International Platform Association; Hawaii State Society; Beta Sigma Phi. Community Activites: Worked on 1981 Inaugural activities as a member of the Labor Committee; Member Board of Directors, Lincoln Community Center in New York, 1979; Honorary Member of Retarded Children Association of New York, 1979. Religion: Member of the Catholic Church (managed school carnival at Linton Hall Military School, Bristol, Virginia). Honors and Awards: Featured in *New York Metropolitan Magazine*, September, 1976; Named Girl of the Year, Delta Kappa Chapter of Beta Sigma Phi, 1979 and 1981; Listed in *Who's Who in the East, International Who's Who of Intellectuals, Community Leaders and Noteworthy Americans, Dictionary of International Biography, Book of Honor, Directory of Distinguished Americans*. Address: 6881 Brian Michael Court, Springfield, Virginia 22153.

Mouton, Jane Srygley

Research Company Executive. Born April 15, 1930; Daughter of T. Q. Srygley; Married Jackson C. Mouton Jr.; Mother of Janie, Jacqueline. Education: B.S.Ed. 1950, Ph.D. 1957, The University of Texas; M.S., Florida State University, 1951. Career: Vice President, Scientific Methods, Inc., 1961 to present; Assistant Professor in Department of Psychology 1959-64, Instructor in Department of Psychology 1957-59, Social Science Research Associate 1957-59, Research Scientist 1953-57, University of Texas. Organizational Memberships: American Board of Examiners of Psychologists (licensed and certified); Certified Consultants International (certification in internal organization development and community development); Institute of Business Administration and Management, Tokyo, Japan (honorary faculty of behavioral science); American Society for Training and Development; American Association for the Advancement of Science; American Psychological Association; American Academy of Political and Social Science; American Association of Group Psychotherapy and Psychodrama; Association for Humanistic Psychology; Institute of General Semantics (board of trustees). Community Activities: Junior League of Austin; Colonial Dames of Austin; Zeta Tau Alpha Alumnae. Published Works: *The Versatile Manager: A Grid Profile* (in press); *Social Dynamics for Productivity and Creativity* (in press); *The Academic Administrator Grid: A Guide to Developing Effective Management Teams* (in press); *Approaches for Managerial Leadership in Nursing* (with Mildred Tapper), 1981; *Grid Approaches to Managing Stress*, 1980; *Role Playing: A Practice Manual for Group Facilitators* (with Malcolm E. Shaw and Raymond J. Corsini), 1980; *The Real Estate Sales Grid: Dealing Effectively with the Human Side of Selling Real Estate* (with Jim and Wanell May), 1980; *The Grid for Sales Excellence*, 1980; *Social Worker Grid*, 1979; *The New Grid for Supervisory Effectiveness*, 1979; *The New Managerial Grid*, 1978; *Making Experience Work: The Grid Approach to Critique*, 1978; *Diary of an OD Man*, 1976; *Consultation*, 1976; *Instrumented Team Learning: A Behavioral Approach to Student-Centered Learning*, 1975; *The Marriage Grid*, 1972; *How to Assess the Strengths and Weaknesses of a Business Enterprise* 6 Volumes, 1972; *Building a Dynamic Corporation Through Grid Organization Development*, 1969; *Corporate Excellence Through Grid Organization Development*, 1968; *Corporate Darwinism: An Evolutionary Perspective on Organizing Work in the Corporation* (with Warren Avis), 1966; *Managing Intergroup Conflict in Industry* (with Herbert Shepard), 1964; *Group Dynamics: Key to Decision Making*, 1961; Other Books and Research, 400 Articles and Research Papers. Honors and Awards: Book Award for *The New Managerial Grid*, American College of Hospital Administrators, 1980; Best Writing Award, American Society for Training and Development, 1961-62; Listed in *Who's Who of American Women, World Who's Who of Women, National Register of Scientific and Technical Personnel*. Address: P.O. Box 195, Austin, Texas 78767.

Mowrey, Shirley M Davis

Associate Editor and Advertising Manager. Personal: Born October 29, 1925; Daughter of Mr. and Mrs. Trevor M. Davis; Widow; Mother of Ronald Montgomery Reed, Rachelle S. Reed, Renee C. Buck. Education: A.A., Cincinnati Conservatory of Music and Drama, University of Cincinnati, Ohio, 1944; Attended the Feagin School of Radio and Drama, New York City, 1946. Career: Associate Editor and Advertising Manager, *Coastal Guide* Magaizne, 1980 to present; Private Music Teacher, Santa Cruz, California, 1980 to present; Sales Representative, B. C. Cable Company, Juneau, Alaska; Sales Representative, Chinook Fireplace Manufacturing Company, Santa Cruz; Head of Sales Department, KJNO-TV; National Sales Coordinator, Traffic Manager, Head of Sales Department, KINY-TV; Cellist, Juneau Symphony; Sales Representative, KSCO; Teacher of Beginning Strings, Mt. View School; Staff, Hazard Advertising Agency, New York; Writer and Producer, Radio; Film Appearances in Film Series, Shorts, Commercial Film, Documentaries; Contractor of Women's String Group, The Twilighters; Staff, C.B.S. and WOR, New York; Various Roles, Dumont-TV and N.B.C.-TV. Organizational Memberships: National Press Women's Association; Alaska Press Women's Association; National League of American Pen Women; California Teachers Association. Community Activities: Volunteer, Los Angeles Community Project to Interest Students in Music. Address: 218 Oregon Street, Santa Cruz, California 95060.

Moxley, Thomas Irvin Sr

Research Chemist. Personal: Born July 11, 1922; Son of Wilford Irvin and Safronia Alma Sewell Moxley (both deceased); Married Winefred Georgette Wise Moxley; Father of Thomas Irvin Jr., Norman Alan. Education: B.S., University of Louisville, 1949. Military: Served in the United States Army, 1943-46, to the rank of Staff Sargeant. Career: Senior Research Chemist and Surgical Technologist, University of Louisville Health Sciences Center, Louisville, Kentucky, 1977 to present; Organ Transplant Technologist, 1976-77; Senior Research Assistant, 1968-76; Research Assistant, 1960-68; Senior Chemical Technician, 1955-60, Chemical Technician, 1951-55. Organizational Memberships: Sigma Xi (associate member); Beta Kappa Chi. Community Activities: Lecturer to Watterson College, 1976; Parkland Junior High School Mini-Board of Education (chairman); Male High School Advisory Committee (president); Louisville Philharmonic Chorus, 1960-65; National Geographic Society, 1981; Smithsonian Institute, 1981; United States School of Music (graduate, 1970); Boy Scouts of America (member, 1949-75; institutional representative, 1950-69); Kappa Alpha Psi. Religion: President of Council, Plymouth Congregational United Church of Christ, West Louisville United Church of Christ, President of Council of Presidents of 28 United Churches of Christ of Louisville, New Albany, Indiana and Jeffersonville, Indiana; Soloist, Chancel Choir; Director, Musical Clefs Youth Choir; Sunday School Teacher, High School Class. Published Works: Contributor to Scientific Journals on Nephrology, Physiology and Biophysics; Biomedical Technical Assistant and Consultant to 40 Medical Research Paper, University of Louisville. Honors and Awards: President's Award, Boy Scouts of America; Mayor's Award, City of Louisville, 1975; Kentucky Colonel; 25-Year Plaque, Service in Science, University of Louisville; Certificate of Award with Honor, United States School of Music, 1970; Service Award, Department of Microbiology and Immunology, University of Louisville, 1980-81; Listed in *Who's Who in America, Who's Who in Technology Today, Personalities of America.* Address: Post Office Box 11061, Louisville, Kentucky 40211.

Mühlanger, Erich Alois

Manufacturing General Supervisor. Personal: Born August 26, 1941; Son of Maria Mühlanger Liezen; Married Gilda Violeta Oliver; Father of Eric Jun. Education: Special Trade, Engineering, Berufsschule Murau, Austria, 1959; Foreign Language Studies in Italian 1960, Swiss German 1962, French 1963, Geneva, Switzerland; M.B.A., University of Connecticut, expected 1983. Military: Served to Corporal in the Austrian Air Force, 1959-60. Career: Manufacturing General Supervisor; Manufacturing Supervisor; Quality Control Inspector; Marketing and Sales; Custom Service and Manufacturing. Organizational Memberships: American Screenprinting Association. Religion: Roman Catholic. Address: 5H Drummond Drive, Rocky Hill, Connecticut 06067.

Mumford, Emily

Professor of Psychiatry and Preventive Medicine. Personal: Born December 19, 1920. Education: B.A., University of Tulsa, 1941; M.S. Sociology 1959, Ph.D. Sociology 1963, Columbia University. Career: Professor of Psychiatry and Preventive Medicine, University of Colorado Health Sciences Center; Professor of Psychiatry and Special Assistant to the Dean, Downstate Medical Center, State University of New York at Brooklyn; Professor of Sociology, Graduate Center and Lehman College, City University of New York; Associate Professor of Sociology in Psychiatry, Mount Sinai School of Medicine, New York. Organizational Memberships: Colorado Psychiatric Society (honorary member, 1980 to present); American Psychiatric Association (honorary fellow, 1979); American Sociological Association (medical sociology section, 1975); American Public Health Association (fellow, 1969). Community Activities: Health Care Financing Agency of National Institute of Health (study section, 1981); A.D.A.M.H.A. (national advisory mental health council, 1979-82); National Institute of Mental Health (consultant, psychiatry education branch, 1978-79). Honors and Awards: Principal Investigator, Evaluation and Outcome in Medical Education, 1979-82; National Institute of Mental Health Grant, 1979-86; Co-Investigator, Grant, "A Study of the Relationship between Mental Health Care Utilization through Computer Analysis of Blue Cross/Blue Shield F.E.P. Claims Data", 1978-79; Program Coordinator, "Teaching Behavioral Sciences in a Medical School", National Institute of Mental Health Grant, 1969-73; Support Grant-Commonwealth Fund Grant-in-Aid, 1968-70; Travel Grant, Medical Education and the Medical Care System of the U.S.S.R., 1969. Address: 6925 East Exposition Avenue, Denver, Colorado 80224.

Walter Mumm

Mumm, Walter John

Research Consultant. Personal: Born November 20, 1895; Son of Paul Henry and Minnie Grishow Mumm (both deceased); Married Marian Rideout (deceased); Father of Robert Franklin. Education: B.S. 1919, M.S. 1929, Ph.D. 1940, University of Illinois. Military: Served in the Coast Artillery Corps, 1918, with the rank of 2nd Lieutenant. Career: Research Consultant 1967 to present, Director of Research and Plant Breeding 1938-67, Crow's Hybrid Corn Company; Associate in Agronomy 1931-38, Instructor in Agronomy 1928-31, Assistant in Agronomy 1927-28, University of Illinois. Organizational Memberships: American Society of Agronomy; Crop Science Society; Illinois Academy of Science; Weed Science Society; American Farm Bureau; University of Illinois Alumni Association. Community Activities: Milford High School Board of Education (member, 1947-53); Salvation Army Fund (past treasurer); Milford Community Fund (past treasurer); Milford Lots for Veterans Committee (chairman). Religion: Milford Methodist Church; Teacher, Adult Men's Sunday School Class, Over 40 Years; Lay Speaker, 40 Years. Published Works: Bulletins on Soil Tilth, Corn Production and Performance. Honors and Awards: Discoverer, Two New Genes for Soft Starch in Dent Corn, including Floury-2, a Gene Associated with High Lysine; Creator, Multiple-Ear Hybrids by Crossing Corn with Teosinte; Producer, First Commerical Single Cross Corn Hybrids; Alpha Zeta Agriculture Honor Society; American Association for the Advancement of Science; Professional Crop Science Award; Honored for 50 Years in Corn Breeding and Research, 1977; Honored for 40 Years Service, Crow's Hybrid Corn Comapny, 1978. Address: 510 East Jones Street, Milford, Illinois 60953.

Murayama, Makio

Research Biochemist. Personal: Married to Sonoko Soga (now deceased); Father of Gibbs Soga, Alice Myra. Education: A.B., 1938, M.A., 1940, University of California at Berkeley; Ph.D., University of Michigan at Ann Arbor, 1953. Career: Research Biochemist, National Institutes of Health, Bethesda, Maryland; Former Special Research Fellow to Cavendish Laboratory, Cambridge University in England; Former Research Fellow in Chemistry with Professor Linus Pauling, Caltech, Pasadena, California; Former Research Biochemist, Harper Hosptial, Detroit, Michigan; Former Research Biochemist, Bellevue Hospital, New York City. Organizational Memberships: American Chemical Society; American Society of Biological Chemists; American Association for the Advancement of Science; Association of Clincial Chemists; Sigma Xi; New York Academy of Science. Community Activites: American Friends Service Committee in Chicago, 1942-43, in Detroit, 1943-48, and in Pasadena, 1954-56. Honors and Awards: Martin Luther King, Jr. Medical Achievement Award, 1972; Award in Research, Association for Sickle Cell Anemia, New York, 1969; Nisei of the Biennium Honoree, Japanese American Citizens League (national recognition award), 1971-72. Address: 5010 Benton Avenue, Bethesda,

Maryland 20014.

Murray, Karen Jane

Author. Personal: Born March 19, 1928. Education: B.A., St. Olaf College, Northfield, Minnesota, 1949; Coursework Completed for Ph.D. in American Studies, University of Minnesota, 1952; M.S.W., University of Minnesota, 1959. Career: Author; Director, Downtown Mental Health Center, San Jose, California; Director, Children's Services, Santa Clara County, San Jose, California; Director, Psychiatric Social Workers, Santa Clara County, San Jose, California; Lecturer in Administration, Graduate School of Social Work, San Jose State University. Organizational Memberships: National Association of Social Workers (chairman, Santa Clara chapter, 1964-67; delegate, delegate assembly, 6 years; national committee on inquiry, 1975-81); Clinical Society of Social Workers (charter founder, 1969). Community Activities: Mental Health Consultant to California State Legislature/Social Work, 1970; State of California Department of Mental Hygiene (staffing project, 1971); Mental Health Task Force (state committee, program chief, 1969); American Orthopsychiatric Association; Zonta Professional Women's Organization (vice president, 1969-70). Honors and Awards: Listed in *Who's Who in American Women, Who's Who in the Far West, Who's Who in World's Women, Who's Who in the West and Midwest*. Address: Route 6, Box 447 H, Fairview, North Carolina 28730.

Karen Murray

Music, Edward Cecil

Automobile Dealer, Commercial and Residential Builder. Personal: Born May 12, 1924; Son of Sam K. and Nora Davis Music (both deceased); Married Thelma Keath; Father of Peggy M. Carter, Judy M. Karaglanis. Career: President, Music-Carter-Hughes Chevrolet Buick, Inc.; President, C & M Leasing Company, Inc.; President, Natural Bridge Skylift, Inc.; President, Mountain Parkway Chairlift, Inc.; President, Music Motor Company, Inc.; President, Abbott Development, Inc.; President, Music Enterprises, Inc.; President, Archer Music Enterprises, Inc. Community Activities: Masons (thirty-second degree); Kiwanis Club (organizer, Martin club, 1953); Chamber of Commerce (board director, 9 years; organizer, Prestonsburg Floyd County chapter, 1951); Prestonsburg Industrial Foundation (chairman, 1967-81); Prestonsburg Housing Authority, 1960-74; Highlands Regional Medical Center (trustee, 14 years; chairman, 1973-75); Archer Park (chairman, 1964-76); Chevrolet Dealer Council (elected member, 1964-65, 1968-69, 1974-75); Buick Dealer Council (elected member, 1972-73). Honors and Awards: Outstanding Citizen Award, Prestonsburg Floyd County Chamber of Commerce, 1974; Faculty Assembly Service Award, Prestonsburg Community College, 1981; Listed in *Who's Who in Kentucky*. Address: 636 University Drive, Prestonsburg, Kentucky 41653.

Myers, John Philip

Social Work Educator. Personal: Born September 10, 1936; Son of Mr. and Mrs. L. H. Myers; Married Barbara Yohe; Father of Keith Alan, Mark Leslie. Education: B.M., University of Miami, Florida, 1959; M.S.W., University of Pittsburgh, 1964. Career: Assistant Professor of Social Work, New Mexico State University; Social Work Administrator; Social Work Practitioner. Organizational Memberships: National Association of Social Workers (board of directors, New Mexico state chapter, 1979 to present); Council on Social Work Education; Accreditation Site Visitor, 1978 to present; American Orthopsychiatric Association; American Public Health Association; National Conference on Social Welfare; American Correctional Association. Community Activities: New Mexico Health Systems Agency (governing board, 1981 to present); Mental Health Association in New Mexico (board member, 1980 to present); New Mexico Council on Crime and Delinquency (board member, 1981 to present); Las Cruces Emergency Medical Services Board, 1981 to present; Community Action Agency of Dona Ana County (secretary, board member, 1980 to present); Las Cruces Girls and Boys Club (vice-chairperson, board member, 1979 to present); Dona Ana County Human Services Consortium (chairperson, 1981 to present); Dona Ana County Mental Health Association (board member, president, 1982 to present). Religion: Unitarian/Universalist. Honors and Awards: Social Worker of the Year, Dona Ana Program Unit, New Mexico Chapter of National Association of Social Workers, 1982; Community Service Award, Breckinridge Chapter of National Association of Social Workers, 1973; U.A. Faust Award, District, 1973; Dean's Service Award, University of Kentucky College of Social Professions, 1973. Address: 1812 Ash, Las Cruces, New Mexico 88001.

Myers, Samuel L

President of Education Association. Personal: Born April 18, 1919, in Baltimore, Maryland; Married Marion Myers; Father of Samuel L., Jr., Yvette M. May, Tama M. Clark. Education: A.B. Social Science, Morgan State College, 1940; M.A. Economics, Boston University, 1942; M.A. Economics 1948, Ph.D. Economics 1949, Harvard University; Postdoctoral Study, Ford Foundation Faculty Fellow, University of Pennsylvania, 1960; Foreign Service Institute, United States Department of State, 1966. Military: Served in World War II, 1942-46, receiving the Pacific Theatre Ribbon and attaining the rank of Captain, United States Army. Career: National Association for Equal Opportunity in Higher Education, past Executive Director, President 1977 to present; President, Bowie State College, 1967-77; Advisor, Regional Integration and Trade, Bureau of Inter-American Affairs, United States Department of State, 1963-67; Associate Professor, Professor and Chairman of the Division of Social Services, Morgan State College, 1950-63; Economist, Bureau of Labor Statistics, United States Department of Labor, 1950; Research Associate, Harvard University, 1949. Organizational Memberships: American Association of State Colleges and Universities (member, board of directors, 1976-77; representative of National Advisory Council on International Teacher Exchange, 1972-77; chairman, committee on international programs, 1972-75); Task Force on International Study Centers, 1973; Maryland Association of Higher Education (president, 1971-72); Middle States Association of Colleges and Schools (Commission on Higher Education, 1976-77). Community Activities; Maryland Tax Commission, 1958; Governor's Commission on Prevailing Wage Law in Maryland, 1962; Morgan State College (leadership role in establishing Morgan State College Graduate School, 1962); Council on Consumer Information (national president, 1963); State Scholarship Board of Maryland, 1968-77; Governor's Commission to Study Aid to Non-Public Schools (vice chairman, 1969-70); Maryland Committee for the Humanities and Public Policy (vice chairman, 1974-76); Governor's Task Force on Desegregation of Higher Education, 1974; Committee on the Future of International Studies (steering committee, 1973); Technical Assistance Consortium to Improve College Services (vice chairman, 1974-77); National Education Advisory Committee of Consumers Union, 1976 to present; Delegation to College and University Presidents to India 1971, People's Republic of China 1975, Republic of China 1976; Chairperson, Delegation to India 1972, Delegation of Presidents to Pakistan 1973, Delegation of Educators to Nigeria 1973. Honors and Awards: Alpha Kappa Mu Honor Society; Graduate Assistant, Boston University; Research Fellow, Harvard University; Rosenwald Fellow, Harvard University; Outstanding Citizen of the Year, Bowie, Maryland, 1974; Alumnus of the Year, Morgan State University, 1976; Citation for Outstanding Community Service for Writing Series of Booklets Distributed by the Urban League to Help Low-Income Groups, Baltimore Urban League, 1964; President Emeritus, Bowie State College, 1977. Address: 2243 Wisconsin Avenue, Northwest, Washington, D.C. 20007.

Edward C Music

Naadimuthu, Govindasami

Associate Professor and Chairman. Personal: Born August 9, 1947; Son of G. Govindasami; Married Amirtha Doraiswamy; Father of Revathi. Education: B.E., Madras University, 1968; D.I.I.T., Indiana Institute of Technology, 1969; M.S. 1971, Ph.D. 1974, Kansas State University. Career: Chairman 1982 to present, Associate Professor 1978 to present, Assistant Professor 1974-78, Industrial Engineering and Management Science, Fairleigh Dickinson University; Assistant Professor, Industrial Engineering, California Polytechnic State University, San Luis Obispo, 1973-74. Organizational Memberships: American Institute of Industrial Engineers (senior member, 1980); Registered Professional Engineer, New Jersey, Pennsylvania. Community Activities: Unpaid Consultant to Many Past and Present Students on the Professional Problems of Various Industries and Business Concerns in Which They Work; Faculty Advisor for A.I.I.E., Fairleigh Dickinson University, Chapter #389; Faculty on the Courses on "Desalination", St. Croix, United States Virgin Islands, July and December 1977, December 1978, October 1982, and Singer Island, Florida, August 1978; Faculty on Continuing Education Programs in Industrial Engineering, Bendix Corporation, 1975, and GAF Corporation, 1976. Published Works: Co-Author "Stochastic Modeling and Optimization of Water Resource Systems", "Nonmetameric Color Matching", " Stochastic Maximum Principle in the Optimal Control of Water Resource Systems", " Water Resources Modeling and Optimization Based on Conservation and Flooding Pools", "Differential Quadrature and Partial Differential Equations: Some Numerical Results", "Application of Invariant Imbedding to the Estimation of Process Duration". Honors and Awards: Phi Kappa Phi; Alpha Pi Mu; Tau Beta Pi; 4.0 Grade Point Average for Ph.D. and M.S. Degrees; Awarded Medal for First Rank in the Graduating Class of D.I.I.T.; Listed in *Who's Who in Education, Directory of World Researchers.* Address: 631 Colonial Blvd., Washington Township, Westwood, New Jersey 07675.

Nacol, Barbara Leigh

Administrator. Personal: Born February 2, 1948; Daughter of E. B. Hunt. Education: B.A. 1973, M.Ed. 1975, Ph.D. 1982; University of Houston; Teacher Corps, 1973-75. Career: President and Executive Administrator, Hyperbaric Medical Center; Former Business Manager, Law Offices of Mae Nacol and Associates; Teacher, Houston Independent School District; Teacher Corps, Harris County, Texas. Organizational Memberships: Environmental Education Association (charter member); Under Sea Medical Society; American Judicature Society. Community Activities: Deputy Constable, Harris County, Texas; Certified Peace Officer, TECLOSE; HBO Medical Center of Houston (executive director). Honors and Awards: Outstanding Scholastic Achievement Award, Texas A & M University; Community Service Award, City of Houston. Address: 6012 Memorial Drive, Houston, Texas 77007.

Ouida Nance

Nakamura, Hiromu

Psychologist. Personal: Born November 6, 1926; Married Tamaye Yumiba; Father of Glenn V., Colleen P. Education: B.A., University of Redlands, 1948; M.A., University of California-Los Angeles, 1951; Ph.D., University of Southern California, 1973. Career: Clinical Psychology Intern, Massillon State Hospital, Massillon, Ohio, 1951-52; Staff Psychologist, Patton State Hospital, 1952-58; Staff Psychologist 1958 to present, Program Director 1971 to present, Lanterman State Hospital and Development Center. Organizational Memberships: California State Psychological Association; American Psychological Association; American Association of Mental Deficiency; American Public Health Association; Royal Society of Health (fellow). Community Activities: Town Hall of California; Los Angeles World Affairs Council; Fellows of the Menninger Foundation. Religion: Presbyterian. Honors and Awards: Fellow, World Wide Academy of Scholars; American Biographical Institute; International Personnel Research Creativity Award, 1972; Silver Medal, International Who's Who in Community Service; Listed in *Who's Who in California, Who's Who in the West, Community Leaders of America, Dictionary of International Biography, Royal Blue Book, Book of Honor.* Address: 3861 Shelter Grove Drive, Claremont, California 91711.

Nall, James Allen Sr

Professor of Mathematics. Personal: Born August 14, 1917; Father of James A. Jr., Joy Adronie. Education: B.S., Alabama State College, 1947; M.A., Columbia University, 1952; Studies in Mathematics, University of California-Los Angeles, 1958, 1962, New Mexico State University, 1964, 1965, 1966, University of Florida, Gainesville; Graduate Studies toward Ph.D. in Mathematics Education. Military: Served in the United States Army, 1943-46, attaining the rank of Technician 4th Grade. Career: Professor of Mathematics, Central Florida Community College; Dean of the College, Hampton Junior College, Ocala, Florida; Instructor in Mathematics and Science, Stevenson Junior High School, Los Angeles, 1958-60; Mathematics Instructor, Parker High School, Birmingham, Alabama, 1952-57; Coordinator of Guidance for all Ninth Grade Faculty, Mathematics Instructor and Assistant Principal, Training School, Jasper, Alabama. Organizational Memberships: Alpha Kappa Mu (charter member, Alabama State College, 1947); Phi Delta Kappa; national Council of Teachers of Mathematics. Community Activities: Community Development Block Grant Citizen Advisory Committee, 1978. Religion: Charter Member, Secretary of the Board of Directors, Twenty-Seventh Avenue Church of Christ, Inc., Ocala, 1979 to present. Honors and Awards: World War II Victory Medal: Bronze Star; Three Battle Stars; Listed in *Who's Who in American Education, International Who's Who in Education.* Address: P.O. Box 1047, Ocala, Florida 32678.

Nance, Ouida Frencho

College Counselor. Personal: Born June 19, 1926; Daughter of Huberto F. and Arjuna A. Petty (both deceaed); Married Allen A. Nancy Jr.; Mother of John T. Petty Sr., Rodger J. Earskins. Education: A.A., Central Y.M.C.A. Community College, Chicago, 1975; B.A., B.S., George Williams College, Downers Grove, Illinois, 1977; M.S.S.W., University of Louisville, Louisville, Kentucky, 1979. Career: Head Clinic Nurse, Mercy Hospital, 1956; Advisor, Community Health Workshop 1967, Community Youth Workshop

1975, Student Support Group Session 1978; College Counselor, 1977. Organizational Memberships: National Association of Social Workers; Illinois Council for Community Service; Omega Psi. Community Activities: Board of Election Commissioners, 1966-81; Edward J. Rosewell Committee for Cook County Treasurer, 1975; Spanish Immersion Weekend (hostess, 1976); National Association of Social Workers Convention Aid, 1976; Woman Day Discovery Workshop (hostess, 1977); Raymond A. Kent School of Social Work (graduation coordinator, 1979); Preschool Headstart Program, 1964; St. Mel Parish Ladies Social Committee, 1967; St. Mel Parish Fund Raising Chairperson, 1968; Christian Action Ministry Drug-Related Program (counselor, 1970). Honors and Awards: Phi Theta Kappa National Honor Fraternity, 1974; Seabury Upper Division Award, 1975, 1976; Central Young Men's Christian Association Community College, Outstanding and Dedicated Service Award 1975, Academic Honor Certificate 1975; Board of Election Commissioners Citation, 1977; Outstanding Award in Applied Behavioral Sciences Division, 1977; Dedicated Service Award for Campus Life Activities, 1977; Delta of Phi Theta Kapper Alumni Association Award, 1978; Listed in *Profiles of Accomplishment, Who's Who Among Students in American Universities and Colleges, World Who's Who of Women*. Address: 4248 West Monroe Street, Chicago, Illinois 60624.

Narciandi, Fernando M

Executive. Personal: Born May 30, 1947; Son of Mateo and Leonar Narciandi; Married Consuelo Narciandi; Father of Eric. Education: A.A., Spokane Junior College, 1966; B.S., Management-Finance, Woodburry University, 1971. Military: Served in the United States Marine Corps, 1966-69. Career: President, Fiesta Enterprises Inc.; President, YMC Corporation; Audit and Collection Manager, Penn Financial Corporation; General Manager and Controller; Employee Benefits Corporation, Division of Penn Financial; Audit Manager XXX Signal Insurance Companies. Organizational Memberships: Institute of Internal Auditors; Audit Managers Association; American Management Association. Community Activities: Disabled American Veterans; Republican Party Task Force; Zoological Society of Florida. Religion: Catholic. Honors and Awards: Decorated with the Purple Heart. Address: 14803 Southwest 140 Court, Miami, Florida 33186.

Hilel Nathan

Nathan, Hilel

Professor, Department Head. Personal: Born February 5, 1917; Son of Isaac and Sima Palchik Notkovick (both deceased); Married Madeleine Goldschmidt; Father of Malka, Sharona, Hanna, Nathalie, Sima. Education: M.D., Medical School of the University de Litoral, Rosario, Argentina, 1941; Attended Jefferson Medical College, Philadelphia, Pennsylvania, 1955-56. Military: Served in the Armed Forces in Argentina, 1937; Served in the Reserves in Israel, 1952-69. Career: Professor of Anatomy, Head of Department of Anatomy and Anthropology, Sackler School of Medicine, Tel-Aviv University, Ramat Aviv, Israel; Assistant to Associate Professor, Anatomy, Hebrew University, Hadassah School of Medicine, Jerusalem. Organizational Memberships: Israel Medical Association; American Association of Physical Anthropologists; Mexico Society of Anatomy; American Association of Anatomists; Israel Society of Anatomical Sciences (first president, 1974); International Symposium on Teaching of Morphological Sciences, Tel Aviv (president, chairman, 1977). Honors and Awards: Magnes Prize for Studies in United States Hebrew University, 1955; Dr. Federgreen Prize for Heart Research, Hebrew University, 1964; Maimonides Award of the Vth International Symposium on the Morphological Sciences, 1982, Rio de Janeiro, Brazil. Address: 10 Keren Hayesod Street, Herzlia, Israel.

Jose P Nazareno

Nazareno, Jose P

Pathologist. Personal: Born November 29, 1925, in Niac, Cavite, Philippines; Son of Maximino Nazareno Sr.; Married Charlene Boardman; Father of Christopher. Education: A.A., National University, 1948; M.D., Manila Central University, Manila, Philippines, 1953; Intern, Mt. St. Mary Hospital, Niagara Falls, New York, 1954-55; House Staff, Our Lady of Lourdes Hospital, Binghamton, New York, 1955-56; Pathology Residency, Kilmer Memorial Laboratory, Binghamton General Hospital 1956-57, Roswell Park Memorial Institute, Buffalo 1957-59, Deaconess Hospital, Buffalo, 1959-60. Career: Assistant Pathologist, Kilmer Memorial Laboratory, 1964-69; Director of Laboratories, Binghamton Psychiatric Center, 1969 to present; Owner, Director, Southern Tier Medical Laboratory, Inc., 1969 to present; Acupuncturist, Southern Tier Medical Laboratory, 1979 to present. Organizational Memberships: Associaton of Fil-American Pathologists (president, board of directors, 1969-71, 1977-79; secretary-treasurer, 1979 to present); Association of Philippine Practicing Physicians in America (board of governors, 1972, life member); Medical-Dental Staff, Binghamton Psychiatric Center (president, 1980 to present); Pan American Medical Association (diplomate); College of American Pathologists (fellow); American Society of Clinical Pathologists (fellow); New York State Society of Pathologists; Private Practitioners of Pathology Foundation, Inc.; Broome County Medical Society; American Medical Association; New York State Society of Acupuncture for Physicians and Dentists; Occidental Institute of Chinese Studies Alumni Association (supporting member). Community Activities: Manila Central University Alumni Association of United States and Canada (first president, 1976-77); American Civic Association, Binghamton, New York (board of directors, treasurer, 1962-70; board of directors, 1980 to present); Binghamton Sertoma Breakfast Club International (board of governors, 1965-68); Honorary Adviser, Cavite Association, U.S.A. (president, permanent). Published Works: "Lipoma of the Pleura", "The Cholangiogram: Postmortem Study", "Pathology of Acute Salt Poisoning in Infants". Honors and Awards: Award for Devoted Service, American Civic Association, 1970; Founding Father Award, Association of Philippine Practicing Physicians in America, 1979; Award for Most Outstanding Filipino Professional in America, Pathology and Acupuncture, United Filipino American Lawyer's Association in America, 1982; Listed in *Community Leaders and Noteworthy Americans, Men of Achievement, Who's Who in the East*. Address: 240 Riverside Drive, Johnson City, New York 13790.

Hazel M Neef

Neef, Hazel Mouton

Consultant Dietitian. Personal: Born July 4, 1926; Daughter of Mr. and Mrs. Rene F. Mouton; Married William G. Neef; Mother of Patricia Ann, Pamela Joan, Janette Lynn, Geralyn, William Stephen, Dorothy Marie, Thomas Michael. Education: B.S., Institutional Management, University of Southwest Louisiana, 1946; Dietetic Internship, Touro Infirmary, 1947; Management Credits, Nichols State University, 1966; Advanced Nutrition Studies, Louisiana State University, 1971. Career: Director of Dietary Department, Our Lady of Lourdes, 1969-780; Head, Dietary Department, St. Joseph Hospital, 1964-67; Dietary Consultant, Our Lady of Sea and St. Ann, 1965-67; Head Therapeutic Dietitian, Hermann Hospital, 1948-51; Formula Room and Pediatric Dietitian, Touro Infirmary, 1947-48. Organizational Memberships: Houston Dietetic Association; Texas Dietetic Association; Lafayette Dietetic Association (secretary, career guidance chairman, publicity chairman and legislative chairman, 1967 to present); Louisiana Dietetic Association (secretary, 1950; convention registration chairman, 1969; awards chairman, 1974-76; treasurer, 1977-79; food administration chairman, 1980; president, 1981); American Dietetic Association (preceptor of dietetic assistant program, 1974-77; coordinator of traineeship program, 1974-80; treasurer of state advisory committee for national meeting, 1975); U.S.L. Kappa Omicron Phi (charter member, 1976 to present); Nutrition Today Society (charter member, 1974 to present). Community Activities: Acadiana Health

Planning Council (board of directors, 1974-78); Mid-Louisiana Health Systems Agency, 1978 to present; U.S.L. Home Economics Alumni Club, 1969 to present; Area Agency on Aging, 1978-80; Council on Alcoholism, 1976-77; Lourdes Hospital Federal Credit Union (president, 1972). Religion: Catechism Instructor, 1970-75; Ladies Altar Society, 1969 to present. Honors and Awards: Mu Sigma, National Honor High School Fraternity; Salutatorian and Scholarship to University of Southwestern Louisiana, 1943; Lambda Omega, Honorary Freshman Fraternity, 1944; Sigma Theta, Honorary Home Economics Fraternity (President, 1945-46); Outstanding Dietitian, State of Louisiana, 1982; Home Economics Alumni Award, University of Southwestern Louisiana, 1981; Listed in *Who's Who in the South and Southwest, Personalities of America, World Who's Who of Women, Book of Honor, Directory of Distinguished Americans.* Address: Route 3 Box 35, Scott, Louisiana 70583.

Robert L Nelson

Nelson, Larry Dean

Executive. Personal: Born August 5, 1937; Son of Mr. and Mrs. C. Aaron Nelson; Married Linda Hawkins. Education: B.A., Mathematics, Physics, Phillips University, 1959; M.S., Mathematics, Kansas State University, 1962; Ph.D., Mathematics (Computer Science), Ohio State University, 1965. Career: Battelle Memorial Institute and Ohio State Research Foundation, 1962-65; Supervisor, M.T.S., Mathematics, and M.I.S., Bellcomm, Inc., 1965-72; Supervisor, Management Information Systems, Bell Telephone Laboratories, 1972-77; Supervisor, Rate and Tariff, Division of American Telephone and Telegraph Company, 1977-79; Deputy Administrator, Research and Special Programs Administration, United States Department of Transportation, 1979-81; President, MCS, Inc., 1981 to present. Organizational Memberships: Institute of Electrical and Electronic Engineering (secretary, 1982-83); Systems, Man and Cybernetics Society (vice president, 1982-83); Computer Society; A.C.M.; American Mathematical Society; New York Academy of Sciences; Mathematical Programming Society; Sigma Xi. Community Activities: Research and Special Programs Administration of the United States Department of Transportation (deputy administrator, 1979-81); Management Committee of the United States Transportation Test Center, 1979-81; American Delegation, Fifth Meeting of the U.S.-U.S.S.R. Joint Committee on Cooperation in the Field of Transportation and Head of American Delegation Working Group, Fifth Meeting of the United States-Soviet Working Group on "Transport of the Future", Moscow, U.S.S.R., June 1979; Odd Jobs Club (organizer and sponsor, 1967-72). Religion: Member National Executive Committee, Interdenominational Ecumenical Movement, 1961-62. Published Works: Several Articles in the Computer and Applied Mathematics Field. Honors and Awards: Sigma Xi; Phi Kappa Phi; Pi Mu Epsilon; Apollo Achievement Award, 1973; I.E.E.E. Washington Section Certificates of Appreciation, 1969 and 1971; Listed in *Outstanding Young Men of America.* Address: 440 New Jersey Avenue, S.E., Washington, D.C. 20003.

Melvin G Nembhard

Nelson, Robert L

Fine Artist, Painter. Personal: Born February 1, 1955; Son of Mrs. Irma Nelson. Education: Began Studies at Southern California Colleges at the Age of 13; Scholarship at Age of 14 to Mt. Sac. College; Studies and Copies of Renaissance Masters of Italy and Germany; Studied Durer and Contemporary Artists such as Wyeth, Rockwell, Parrish. Career: Fine Artist; Exhibitions with Major Corporate Collections; Number of Private Collections. Organizational Memberships: National Audubon Society; American Cetacean Society (board of directors); Pacific Whale Foundation (board of directors); Donation of Whale Painting to King Tupou IV of Tonga; Whale Graphic to Green Peace U.S.A. Honors and Awards: Features in *This Week, Decor, Hawaii Surf and Sea, Bunte* (German), *Pan, Oceans* (French), Others; Selected for Artists/U.S.A., 1981-82; One of Twelve American Artists Chosen to Represent Hawaii by the Hartford Insurance Company for 1980 Calendar. Address: 15P-5-6 Kapalua Golf Villas, Kapalua, Hawaii 96761.

Nembhard, Melvin G

Assistant Ministerial Secretary. Personal: Born January 26, 1916; Married to Hazel V.; Father of Leslie A., M.D., Linda V. Education: Theological Graduate of West Indies College of Mandeville, Jamaica, West Indies. Career: Assistant Ministerial Secretary, Coral Gables, Florida; Pastor-Evangelist, 1938-51; Former Secretary, West Indies Union of Seventh Day Adventists; Former President of East Caribbean Conference, S.D.A. Community Activities: Alumni Association of West Indies College (president, 1957-62); Editor of West Indies Union *Visitor*, 1960-75; Board Member, Andrews Memorial Hospital, 1960-75; Caribbean Union Committee, 1951-57; West Indies Union Committee, 1957-75; West Indies College Board, 1960-75; General Conference Inter-American Division Executive Committee, 1975-81. Honors and Awards: Certificate of Merit, Cambridge, England, 1978; Long Service Award, West Indies Union, 1957-75. Address: 6740 Southwest 48 Street, Miami, Florida 33155.

Phyllis S Nesbit

Nesbit, Phyllis Schneider

District Court Judge. Personal: Born September 21, 1919; Married Peter N. Nesbit; Children Deceased. Education: B.S. 1948, LL.B. 1958, University of Alabama; J.D. 1969. Career: Attorney at Law, 1958-76; Judge, Municipal Court of Daphne, Alabama, 1964-76; City Attorney, City of Loxley, Alabama, 1975-76; Judge, District Court, Baldwin County. Organizational Memberships: Baldwin County Bar Association (president, 1967-68); Alabama Women Lawyers Association (president, 1970-72); Alabama Council of Juvenile Court Judges (treasurer, 1979-81); American Judicature Society; Alabama Association of District Judges; National Association of Women Lawyers; National Association of Women Judges; American Bar Association. Community Activities: National Safety Council (southern Alabama chapter, vice president of women's activities 1978-79, 1980 to present); Joint Legislative Council of Alabama (auditor, 1971-72; treasurer, 1972-73); Baldwin County Mental Health Association (secretary, 1972-74); Baldwin Youth Services; Uncompensated Member of Selective Service System, 1961-75; Spanish Fort Business and Professional Women's Club (president, 1974-75). Religion: Eastern Shore Wesley Bible Church (secretary-treasurer, 1964 to present). Honors and Awards: Woman of Achievement, District I, Alabama Federation of Business and Professional Women, 1978, 1979, 1980, Second Place in State Competition, 1980. Address: 302 Creek Drive, Fairhope, Alabama 36532.

Eunice Neseth

Neseth, Eunice

Museum Curator. Personal: Born January 6, 1907; Daughter of Herman and Eulavia von Scheele. Education: Attended University of California-Berkeley, 1956; B.A., Education, Western Washington College of Education. Career: Curator, Baranof Museum, Kodiak, Alaska; Elementary School Teacher in Alaska for 23 Years. Organizational Memberships: Kodiak Education Association, 1944-67; Alaska Education Association (life member, 1942 to present); National Education Association (life member, 1952 to present); State Museum Advisory Committee, 1975 to 81; Kodiak Baranof Museum Board (various executive positions, 1956-81). Community Activities: Red Cross (Kodiak school representative, 1944-67); Baranof Museum Curator in Volunteer Capacity, 1956-76; Teacher of

Aleut Grass Basket Weaving, 1973 to present; Afognak Native Association (board member); Koniag Inc., Kodiak (board member). Published Works: Booklet on Aleut Weaving, 1981. Honors and Awards: Kodiak Woman of the Year, 1981, Beta Sigma Phi, Alaska Legislative Citation for Outstanding Contributions to the State, 1982. Address: Box 456, Kodiak, Alaska 99615.

NeSmith, Vera C

Administrative and Medical Secretary. Personal: Born October 24, 1917; Daughter of Ernest H. and Edith E. Cox (both deceased); Married to J. Vernon (now deceased); Mother of Patricia E., James E. and John S. (stepsons). Education: Graduate, Orlando, Florida Senior High School, 1936; Diploma, Orlando Secretarial School, 1937; Attended Orlando Junior College; Undertook courses sponsored by the University of Tennessee, Florida State University; Attended courses sponsored by the American Association of Medical Assistants. Career: Secretary, Department of Health and Rehabilitative Services, Orlando, Florida, 1976-80; Secretary, Vocational Rehabilitation, Orlando, 1938-76; Instructor and Secretary, Orlando Secretarial School, 1937-38; Retired, 1980; Currently working part-time with Kelly Services in Winter Park and Orlando; Instructor for training session at St. Petersburg, Florida under direction of University of Tennessee for special course, 1978; Former lecturer to secretarial groups in Department of Health and Rehabilitative Services through training section. Organizational Memberships: American Association of Medical Assistants (secretary-treasurer, program chairman for national convention); Florida State Society of American Association of Medical Assistants (president, president-elect, parliamentarian, membership chairman, board member, convention chairman); Orange County Chapter of American Association of Medical Assistants (president 2 terms, parliamentarian, chaplain); Florida Association of Rehabilitation Secretaries (president, installing officer); National Registry of Medical Secretaries (president, 1958-59); National Association of Rehabilitation Secretaries (member and committee member, 1974-80); Southeastern Regional Association of Rehabilitation Secretaries (chairman and committee member, 1974-80, wrote handbook and 5-year history); Orlando Association of Rehabilitation Secretaries (charter member, parliamentarian and committee member, 1974-80); Florida Association of Rehabilitation Secretaried (charter member, president-elect, parliamentarian); Orange County Chapter Florida Rehabilitation Association (charter member). Community Activities: Participated in American Cancer Society research study, 1966-81; Participant in projects to aid Cancer Society, Tumor Clinic, Orange County Convalescent Home, various nursing homes and hospitals, 1960 to present; Fund raiser for Cerebral Palsy, Heart Fund, Muscular Dystrophy; United Appeal Chairman, 1950-60; Collected and packaged artificial limbs, braces and orthopedic appliances for overseas handicapped, 1950-60; Chairman of Blood Bank Account for Vocational Rehabilitation, 1938-76. Religion: Member of Broadway United Methodist Church (kindergarten Sunday school teacher, 1932-62, choir member, 1932 to present, member of administrative board and council on ministries, 1970-80, chairman of evangelism commission, 1976-80, leader and member of sonshiners circle, 1979-82, member of women's society, 1979-82, chairman of publicity committee for women's society, 1980 and 1981, member of adult friendship Sunday school class, 1962 to present, member staff/pastor/parish comittee, 1982). Published Works: Wrote Handbooks for: Florida Association of Rehabilitation Secretaries, Florida State Society A.A.M.A., Orange County Chapter A.A.M.A. Honors and Awards: Citation, Florida Rehabilitation Association; Outstanding Member of the Year, Orange County Chapter of A.A.M.A., 1965; Medical Assistant of the Year, Florida State Society A.A.M.A., 1965; Plaque from State of Florida Vocational Rehabilition Services for 35 years service, 1973; Secretary of the Year, Florida Association of Rehabilitation Secretaries, 1976; Life Member, Orange County A.A.M.A. (first such award given); Plaque for outstanding service at state convention, Florida State Society A.A.M.A., 1980; Member of International Biographical Association, Cambridge, England; Plaque for Outstanding Service, Florida Association of Rehabilitation Secretaries, 1977; Secretary of the Week, Orlando, Florida, 1974; Engraved Silver Bowl, Department of Health and Rehabilitative Services, 1978; Listed in *Who's Who of American Women, Who's Who in the South and Southwest, Dictionary of International Biography, Community Leaders and Noteworthy Americans, Personalities of the South, Social Registry, World Who's Who of Women, Book of Honor, American Patriots of the 1980's, International Register of Profiles, The Directory of Distinguished Americans.* Address: 1912 Weber Street, Orlando, Florida 32803.

Vera C Nesmith

Ness, Howard L

Professor of Accounting. Personal: Born April 6, 1920; Married Joyce M.; Father of Carole S. Klein, Beverly J. Parke, Howard L. Jr., Kathryn J. Education: B.B.A., University of Toledo, 1942; M.B.A., Northwestern University, 1946; J.D., University of Toledo, 1949. Military: Served in the United States Naval Reserves, 1942-44; with the rank of Ensign. Career: Arizona State University, College of Business Administration, 1949-50; Practicing Attorney, 1950-52; General Counsel, Martin Brother Box Company, 1952-54; University of Toledo College of Business Administration, Accounting Department, Professor, 1946-49, 1954 to present. Organizational Memberships: Toledo Bar Association (taxation committee); Ohio Bar Association; American Bar Association (closely-held corporations, adjunct); Ohio Society of CPAs (education committee, Toledo chapter; continuing professional education); American Institute of CPAs; Beta Alpha Psi; Beta Gamma Sigma; Phi Kappa Phi. Community Activities: University of Toledo Alumni Association (president, 1961). Religion: Hope Lutheran Church, Immediate Past Financial Secretary; Board of Directors, Toledo Campus Ministry. Published Works: Editor and Writer for "The Employees Income Tax Guide" 1954 to present, "You and Your Congress" 1977 & 1979, "Social Security" 1960; Revising Editor, "Mertens Law of Federal Income Taxation" 1958. Honors and Awards: AICAP Elijah Watts Sells Award; Listed in *International Who's Who in Education.* Address: 2365 Goddard Road, Toledo, Ohio 43606.

Neumeyer, John Leopold

Professor. Personal: Born July 19, 1930; Married Evelyn Friedman; Father of Ann Martha, David A., Elizabeth J. Education: Graduate of Bronx High School of Science, 1948; B.S., Columbia University, 1952; Ph.D., University of Wisconsin, 1961. Military: Served in the United States Army, 1953-55, attaining the rank of Corporal. Career: Professor of Medicinal Chemistry and Chemistry, Northeastern University; Chemist. Organizational Memberships: American Chemical Society (chairman, medicinal chemistry division, 1982-83); Sigma Xi; Rho Chi; American Pharmaceutical Association; Northeastern Section, American Chemical Society (chairman, medicinal chemistry group, 1966); Phi Kappa Phi (president, N. J. chapter 1979-80); American Association for the Advancement of Science. Community Activities: Wayland, Massachusetts Board of Health (chairman, 1969-75); Massachusetts Pesticides Board, 1973-75; Wayland Pesticide Committee (chairman, 1980 to present). Honors and Awards: Pfeiffer Scholarship, American Foundation for Pharmaceutical Education Fellowship; N.I.H. Predoctoral Fellowship; First Prize, 1961 Lunsford Richardson Award; Fellow, Academy of Pharmaceutical Sciences, 1975; 1975 Gustavus A. Pfeifeer Memorial Research Fellowship; 1975-76 Senior Hays-Fulbright Fellow; Faculty Lecturer, Northeastern University, 1978; Distinguished University Professor, 1980 to present; 1982, Research Achievement Award in Pharmaceutical/Medicinal Chemistry, Academy Pharmaceutical Sciences, American; Pharmaceutical Association; 1983 Fellow American Association for the Advancement of Science. Address: 1 Holiday Road, Wayland, Massachusetts 01778.

Newby, John Melvin

College President. Personal: Born January 31, 1928; Son of James Edwin and Mary Augusta Williams Newby (both deceased); Married Rebecca Jean Hall; Father of Sharon Jean Page, Karen Jane White, Becky Lynette Holton, John Melvin Jr. Education: Diploma, Union Bible Seminary, 1948; Marion College, 1950; A.B., LaVerne College, 1952; M.S., Uiversity of Southern California, 1958; Ph.D., Michigan State University, 1972. Career: President, Central Wesleyan College, Central, South Carolina, 1979 to present; Formerly, Vice President for Administrative Affairs, Acting Dean of Academic Affairs, Director of Research and Planning, Registrar, Spring Arbor College, Spring Arbor, Michigan; Director of Business Affairs, Registrar and Instructor, Owosso College, Owosso, Michigan. Organizational Membership: American Association for Affirmative Action; Association for Institutional Research; American Association for Higher Education; Student Attrition Task Force and Student Learning Outcomes Task Force, Research and Management Projects (chairman); Undergraduate Assessment Program; Council Educational Testing Services; Small College Consulting Network; North Central Association (evaluator). Community Activities; Owosso Library Board (secretary); Owosso and Jackson, Michigan, and Clemson, South Carolina Rotary Clubs (board of Directors); Jackson Rotary Club (general program chairman); JHL Areawide Comprehensive Health Planning Association (council member); Michigan Heart Association (board member) Swim for Heart Fund-Raising Project (chairman). Religion: Ordained Minister of Pilgrim Holiness Church, 1951; Minister, Pilgrim Holiness Church, San Dimas and Pasadena, California, 1950-59; Instructor of Music, Upland California College, 1951-52; Manager of Schools, Pilgrim Holiness Church, Zambia, Africa, 1959-63; Acting Field Supervisor and Educational Secretary, 1963-64; 1970-1979, Ordained Elder of the Free Methodist Church; Currently, Ordained Elder of the Wesleyan Church, 1979. Honors and Awards: Phi Kappa Phi; Phi Delta Kappa; Listed in *Who's Who in the Midwest, Who's Who in America, Personalities of the South, American Registry Series, Men of Achievement, Publications of the International Biographical Centre and the American Biographical Institute*. Address: Box 408, Central Wesleyan College, Central, South Carolina 29630.

James H Nicholls

Newman, Annette Goerlich

Shopping Center Manager, Real Estate Developer, Registered Pharmacist. Personal: Born January 19, 1940; Daughter of David August and Mary Eloise Simpson Goerlich; Mother of Anne Kristen, Mark David, Gregory Hartley. Education: Doctor of Pharmacy, University of California School of Pharmacy, San Francisco, 1963. Career: Pharmacist, Village Drug, 1963-69; Pharmaceutical Consultant, 1962-72; Store Manager, The Drug Store of Fig Garden Village, 1972-77; Manager, Fig Garden Village Shopping Center, Fresno, 1977 to present. Organizational Memberships: Fig Garden Village Merchants Association (board of directors); R.B. Bailey Inc. (secretary); Sundown Inc. (secretary); Fig Garden Village Inc. (secretary). Community Activities: California Club Honorary Society, University of California-San Francisco; Blue Gold Club University of California School of Pharmacy; Fresno-Madera Pharmacy Association; Pharmacy Alumni Association, University of California; National Association of Female Executives; Junior League of Fresno; American Association of University Women; Women's Symphony League; Ladies Aide to Retarded Children. Honors and Awards: Honors at Entrance, University of California; Nominee, Rosalie M. Stern Award, 1971-72; Listed in *Who's Who in the West, Who's Who of American Women, World Who's Who of Women*. Address: 3909 West Fir, Fresno, California 93711.

Nguyen-Van-Huy, Pierre

Professor of French. Personal: Born September 25, 1929; Son of Paul and Maria Nguyen-Van-Hoanh (both deceased); Married Agnes Phan-Thi-Ngoc-Nga; Father of John, Bernadette. Education: M.A., French Literature, University of Fribourg, Switzerland, 1959; Ph.D., French Literature, University of Fribourg, 1962; Diploma in Curative Pedagogy, Institute of Orthopedagogy and Applied Psychology, University of Fribourg, 1964. Career: Professor of French, St. John's University; Visiting Assistant Professor of French, Louisiana State University, Baton Rouge; Assistant Professor of French, University of Mississippi, Oxford. Organizational Memberships: Modern Language Association; American Association of Teachers of French. Published Works: Books *La Metaphysique du Bonheur chez Albert Camus; La Chute de Camus;* Articles in the U.S.F. Language Quarterly; Lecturers with St. John's University Speakers Bureau. Honors and Awards: Listed in *International Who's Who in Education, International Book of Honor, International Who's Who of Intellectuals, Personalities of America, Directory of American Scholars, Directory of Distinguished Americans, The International Register of Profiles, The Biographical Roll of Honor, Community Leaders of America*. Address: 47-22 163 Street, Flushing, New York 11358.

Alice A Nickell

Nicholls, James Harold

Clergyman, Broadcast Consultant, Defender of Freedom. Personal: Born March 27, 1923, in Regina, Saskatchewan, Canada; Son of Mrs. Robert J. Nicholls; Married Merlyn; Father of Terrill James, Geoffrey Harold, Lauralee Louise. Career: Ordained Minister for over 40 Years; Former President and General Manager, Kaye Broadcasters Inc.; Host of "Party Line" for 8 Years; Pioneered Concept "The Public Has the Right to Know"; First to Broadcast Meetings of the Tacoma City Council, the Human Relations Commission, School Board, Budget Hearings, and Public Hearings; Gave Political Candidates, Government Officials, Supporters of Bonds and Levies, Petitions, Initiatives, Unlimitied Time to Meet and Acquaint the Public with Their Views. Organizational Memberships: American Association of Broadcasters (president); International Council of Christian Churches (chairman, radio and television commission). Community Activities: Democratic Candidate for Washington 6th District to the United States Congress, 1976; National Press Club; Puyallup Valley Chamber of Commerce (served on four committees including legislative and educational committees); Freedom Defense Council (executive director); Committee to Preserve Our Religious Minority Rights (secretary); Committee to Preserve Our Christian Heritage (director); Poverty Programme (vice president); Active in Programs for the Physically Disabled, Senior Citizens, Prison Rehabilitation, Drug Abuse, Alcoholics. Published Works: Numerous Articles on Biblical Themes; Editor, *Freedom Digest*. Honors and Awards: Distinguished Citizen of the State of Washington; Selected by 82 Clubs and Groups as Outstanding Citizen for Tacoma and Pierce County; Award of Merit, American Legion; Listed in *Who's Who in the West, Who's Who in America, Who's Who in Industry and Business, Dictionary of International Biography, Community Leaders and Noteworthy Americans, Honorary Society of America's Who's Who, International Who's Who of Intellectuals, Who's Who in the World, Working Press of America, Men of Achievement, Notable Americans, Personalities of the West and Midwest, Personalities of America, Men and Women of Distinction*. Address: Box 2106 National Press Building, Washington, D.C. 20045.

Nickell, Alice A

Educator (retired). Personal: Born February 27, 1904; Daughter of J. T. and Cordie Armstrong (both deceased); Married John O. Nickell; Mother of John T., Don P. Education: Attended John Tarleton Junior College, Stephenville, Texas, 1930; B.S., State Teacher College, Denton, Texas, 1938; M.A., Sam Houston College, Huntsville, Texas, 1940. Career: Retired Teacher, Texas Public

Schools, 43 Years; Retired Teacher, C. C. Cooke Development Center, 1921-69; Teacher, School and Training for Retarded Persons, 8½ Years; Supervisor, Mexia State School, 1971-80. Organizational Memberships: State and National Teacher Associations; State, National and Johnson County A.R.C.; Parent-Teacher Association of Texas (life member); Johnson County Teacher Association, Haskell County Teacher Association, 1921-69. Community Activities: Youth Camp Instructor, Camp Blue Haven, Los Angeles, New Mexico, 1955-71. Religion: Teacher, Primary or Junior Students, Central Church of Christ, Cleburne, Texas, Member 1916 to present, Teacher, Children's Classes 1920-68, Class for Angels (Retarded Children) 1967 to present, Teacher, Ladies Class 1980 to present. Honors and Awards: 1000-Hour Pin, for Volunteer Work with Retarded, Mexia State School; 10-Year Pin, Camp Blue Haven; Plaque for Work with Retarded Children from Johnson County Association of Retarded Citizens; Certificate, Pin for Teaching, Cleburne Schools. Address: 302 Pendell, Cleburne, Texas 76031.

Nicklin, Helen Isabel

Professor. Personal: Born July 9, 1923; Daughter of Percy A. and Isabel Maitland Gregg Nicklin (both deceased). Education: A.B. summa cum laude 1952, M.Ed. with highest honors 1958, Ed.D. with highest honors, 1964, University of California-Los Angeles; Post Graduate Studies at Stanford University's American Institute of History, University of Southern California, Kent State University, Duke University, San Diego State University. Career: Professor, School of Education Department of Educational Foundations, California State University-Los Angeles, 1963-82; Master Teacher, Life Credential, Los Angeles Senior High School (Social Studies, History, Psychology), 1953-64; Reader for Director of Teacher Training, University of California-Los Angeles, 1952-53; Bank Bookkeeper, Sundry in Personnel Department and Head Office Branches, 1941-43; Chief Pricer, U.S. Gypsum Company, 1943-46. Organizational Memberships: International Council of Psychologists (editor, Directory, 1980-81; Archivist, 1982; board member, 1979 to present; book review editor 1967-72, contributing editor 1972-82, Academic Therapy Journal); California State University, Los Angeles (Academic Senate, 1974, 1978, 1980; chair, International Study Programs; intern study; subcommittee member Instructional Affairs, Faculty Affairs; subcommittee-member, Instructional Affairs, Faculty Affairs); National Education Association (university member, 1978; School of Education chair, 1981-82, Faculty Affairs Committee); California College Faculty Association; American Association of University Professors (secretary, California State University-Los Angeles chapter; executive board, 1976-78); American Educational Research Association (historiography and curriculum sections); Far Western Philosophy of Education Society (executive board, 1973-74, 1975-76); History of Education Society, 1965-69; Comparative Education Society, 1973-76; National Council of Social Studies, 1952-72; California College and University Faculty Association (member, 1965-75; campus chapter secretary, 1965-68); Phi Beta Kappa (member, 1952 to present; Southern California alumni, 1952 to present; support International Scholarship Fellows; California State University Campus Alumni secretary-treasurer, 1965-67); Pi Lambda Theta (life member; University Faculty Advisor, 1966); Pacific Coast History of Education Society (Invitational Paper/Panelist-University of Hawaii, 1979); California Faculty Association; National Education Association; California Teachers Association (legislative chair, 1970); International Platform Association; California State Employees Association; American Association of University Women; International Council of Psychologists. Community Activities: California State University Speakers' Bureau, Invitational Speeches to International Kiwanis, Rotarian, Civitan Groups and Schools; Y.W.C.A. (sustaining member of board, 1973-81); Windsor Square/Hancock Park Historical Society; American Education Research Association; Los Angeles Heart Association; Crippled Children's Society; American Lung Association. Religion: Ordained Ruling Elder, Presbyterian Church, 1969; Member, American Bible Society, International Bible Society. Published Works: Editor, *Yearbook Directory* of the International Council of Psychologists, Book Review/Contributing Editor, *Academic Therapy Journal*; Co-Editor, *The Disabled Learner: Interdisciplinary Approach*, Others. Honors and Awards: Phi Beta Kappa; Pi Lambda Theta; Life Fellow, International Biographical Association; Coe Fellowship to Stanford University Institute of American History, 1954; Pi Lambda Theta/Kent State Fellowship, 1973, to Soviet Union Seminar/Travel; Sabbatical to 14 Countries in Western Europe, 1973; Listed in *World Who's Who of Women, World Who's Who of Intellectuals, Dictionary of International Biography, Leaders in Education, Who's Who in Education, Who's Who in the West.* Address: 360 South Kenmore Avenue, 106, Los Angeles, California 90020.

Helen I Nicklin

Nicolini, Claudio

Professor. Personal: Married; Father of Two Children. Career: Professor of Biophysics, Temple University Health Science Center; Former Associate Professor of Physics, University of Bari; Research Associate, Massachusetts Institute of Technology, Brown University, Brookhaven National Laboratory; Consultant to N.A.T.O., A.C.S., N.I.H., N.S.F., M.R.C. of Canada, C.N.R. of Italy. Organizational Memberships: New York Academy of Sciences; Biophysical Society; Analytical Cytology Society (founding member); Cell Kinetic Society (founding member; national program committee); University of Padua, Italy (president, student senate, 1964-66); University Students of Physics and Mathematics, Italy (national secretary, 1966); N.A.T.O.-A.S.I. (director, 1978, 1980, 1981, 1983); International School of Pure and Applied Biostructure (director, 1979 to present). Published Works: Contributor to Professional Periodicals; Editor, *Cell Biophysics*, An International Journal. Honors and Awards: Research Grants, National Institutes of Health, National Science Foundation. Address: Department of Biophysics, Temple University Health Science Center, Philadelphia, Pennsylvania 19140.

Niedzielski, Henry Zygmunt

Educator. Personal: Born March 30, 1931; Son of Sigismond Niedzielski; Married Krystyna; Father of Henry Jr., Daniel, Robert, Anna Pia. Education: Ph.B., Dijon, France, 1954; B.A. 1959, M.A. 1963, Ph.D. 1964, University of Connecticut. Military: Served in the French Armored Cavalry, 1951-53. Career: Instructor 1962-64, Assistant Professor 1965-66, University of Massachusetts; Freelance Interpreter 1960, Assistant Professor 1964-65, University of Hawaii; Chairman, Division of French 1968-70, Linguistics Specialist 1963-69, N.D.E.A., E.P.D.A.; Fulbright-Hays Lecturer, Krakow, Poland, 1972-74, Burundi, 1980-81. Organizational Memberships: American Council on the Teaching of French Language (director, 1971-72); Hawaiian Association of Language Teachers (president, 1968-69); Northeastern Conference on the Teaching of the French Language (delegate, 1966); Association of International Method (national representative, 1973 to present); Association of American Teachers of French, Hawaii (president, 1980 to present); Hawaii Association of Translators (founding president 1982). Community Activities: Family Education Centers of Hawaii (member, 1967 to present; president, 1968-70; chairman of the board, 1970-72); Alliance Francaise (director, 1969-70; president, 1978-79); Rotary International Waikiki (scholarship committee); Condominium Owners Association (director). Honors and Awards: National Defense Education Act Fellowship, 1959-62; Fulbright-Hays Lecturing Grants, 1972-74, 1980-81; Hawaii Community Service Award, 1971. Address: 419 Keoniana 904, Honolulu, Hawaii 96815.

Nikkel, Vernon Lloyd

Administrator/Executive. Personal: Born May 26, 1928; Son of Martha Nikkel; Married Lennea Oetinger; Father of Greta Ann,

Sanford Louis. Education: B.M.E., Bethany College, Lindsborg, Kansas, 1950; M.S., Kansas State College, Emporia, 1961. Career: Vice-President, Director of Industrial Relations, Excel Industries, Inc.; Chairman of the Board, Leasing U.S.A., Inc.; Former Positions include Public School Teacher, Farm Manager. Organizational Memberships: Wallace County Teacher Association (vice-president, 1952); Harvey County Teachers Association (president, 1960); American Society of Personnel Administration (member, 1965 to present; state director, 1970-77); Kansas Association of Commerce and Industry (member, 1968 to present; chairman of unemployment compensation sub-committee, 1975-81; vice-chairman 1970-81, chairman 1981 to present, employer-employee relations council); Newton Area Chamber of Commerce (board of directors, 1979 to present); Hesston Development, Inc. (president, 1972-76); Wichita Industrial Relations Council (president, 1975-76). Community Activities: Lions International (member, 1954 to present; numerous offices held including local president, lion tamer, board member; district offices of zone chairman, deputy district governor; delegate to Lions International convention, 1965); Elected to Hesston City Council, 1961-63; Elected Mayor of Hesston, 1967-69; Tri-County Mental Health Board, 1965-71; Harvey County Substance Abuse Board, 1976 to present; Harvey County Orchestra Association (secretary, 1973-79); Appointed by Governor Carlin to the Kansas Balance of State Private Industry Council, 1979 (chairman, 1979 to present); Appointed by Governor to the Balance of State Manpower Planning Council, 1979. Religion: United Methodist Church, 1954 to present; Sunday School Teacher; Delegate to Jurisdictional Conferences, 1980; Member Kansas West Conference Committees and Agencies, 1965 to present. Honors and Awards: Harvey County Mental Health Award, 1971; Alumni Award of Merit, Bethany College, 1980; Citation Award, Kansas Department of Employment Security, 1976. Address: 230 South Weaver, Hesston, Kansas 67062.

Nikolai, Lorraine C

Homemaker, Saleswoman, Writer. Personal: Born February 20, 1910, in Wausau, Wisconsin; Daughter of Theodore and Catherine Goeden; Married Jacob N. Nikolai; Mother of Two. Education: Dale Carnegie Course in Public Speaking. Career: Sold Products for Avon; Saleswoman for Industrial Aid for the Blind, Milwaukee, Wisconsin. Organizational Memberships: North Central Technical Institute Homemakers Club, Wausau (secretary); Wausau Writers Club; Wausau Regional Writers Auxiliary. Community Activities: Award Chairwoman for Cancer, Heart and Multiple Sclerosis Annual Fund Raising Drives, Wausau; World War I Veterans Auxiliary (junior vice commander, 1981); International Order of Volunteers for Peace; Girl Scouts of America; Veterans of Foreign Wars; Republican Women's Auxiliary. Religion: St. Michael's Catholic Parish, Chairwoman of Parish's Queen of Peace Group Seven; Treasurer, Wausau Key Project. Published Works: Author of Works in *Rib Mountain Echoes,* Volumes I and II, *Anthology,* Volume I; Contributor to *New World Poets, Bouquet of Roses, Quaderni Di Poesia, Times Review* Catholic Diocesan Paper, *Wausau Daily Herald, Masters of Modern Poetry.* Honors and Awards: Elected Founder-Fellow, International Academy of Poets, Cambridge, England; Certificate, Centro Studi E Scambi Internazionali; Certificate of Official Recognition, Bicentennial Committee of Marathon County, 1976; Listed in *Anthology on World Brotherhood and Peace;* Elected to Hall of Fame of American Poetry Society, Tampa, Florida, 1979; Elected Poet Laureate, Centro Studi E Scambi, Rome; Certificate of Recognition, National Society of Poets, Inc., 1979; Listed in *Men and Women of Distinction, International Who's Who in Poetry, International Authors and Writers Who's Who, International Register of Profiles, International Who's Who of Intellectuals, World Who's Who of Women, Book of Honor, Community Leaders and Noteworthy Americans, Personalities of the West and Midwest, American Registry Series.* Address: 701 Humboldt Avenue, Wausau, Wisconsin 54401.

Lorraine C Nikolai

Nilsson, Raymond

Opera and Concert Singer, Professor of Voice and Opera. Personal: Born May 26, 1920; Son of Leslie and Annie Arleen Nilsson (both deceased); Married Mildred Hartle Stockslager; Father of Michael John, Mary Anne, Diana Elizabeth. Education: Studies at Brighton College and the University of London (both in the United Kingdom); B.A., University of Sydney, Australia. Military: Served in Army Intelligence in the Australian 9th Division in New Guinea, 1941-44, attaining the rank of Lieutenant. Career: Teacher, Sydney Church of England Grammar School, Sydney, Australia; Principal Tenor, Royal Opera House, Covent Garden, London, San Francisco Opera Company and Opera Houses in Europe and Australia; Professor of Voice and Opera, Department of Music, San Jose State University. Community Activities: Organized Menlo Park Concert Series, 1972; Director, City of Menlo Park Concert Series, 1972, 1973; Conducted and Directed Opera "Street Scene" by Kurt Weill for Palo Alto, California, Musical Repertory Theater, 1971; Directed "Lucia di Lammermoor" for El Camino Opera Company, San Jose, 1979; Prepared the Principals in Gilbert and Sullivan's "Iolanthe" for San Jose Gilbert and Sullivan Society, 1979. Honors and Awards; Phi Kappa Phi (with special award); Layman Martin Harrison Scholarship, New South Wales State Conservatorium of Music, Australia; Licentiate of Royal Schools of Music; Winner of Both Opera and Oratorio Sections, City of Sydney Eisteddfod, 1939, 1945; Burke's Peerage, 1982. Address: 1285 Middle Avenue, Menlo Park, California 94025.

Niver, Pruella Cromartie

Choral Director, Educator. Personal: Born December 4, 1924; Daughter of Esten G. and Mary Lee Jones Cromartie (both deceased); Mother of Peddy Niver Hayhurst. Education: Graduate of High School; B.S., Georgia Southern College; Graduate Work and Workshops, Georgia Southern University, Alabama Polytechnic Institute, Auburn, Alabama, Florida State University, Tallahassee, University of Miami, Coral Gables, Florida, University of Florida in Gainesville, University of South Florida, Tampa, Florida Atlantic University, Boca Raton. Career: Soloist, Radio and Television, Georgia, Alabama, Florida, New York; Singer, Dance Band, One Year; Member, Singers Club of Long Island, Admitted by Audition Only; Appearances on Television and Radio Talk Shows Promoting the Arts; Guest Speaker, Panelist, Various Cultural Organizations, Florida, Other Southern States; Choral Director, Teacher of Business Career Mathematics, North Fort Myers High School, Seven Years to present; Teacher, Georgia, Alabama. Organizational Memberships: Music Educators National Conference; Florida Music Educators Association; American Choral Directors Association; Lee County Alliance of the Arts (charter member); Florida Vocal Association (past coordinator, state board); National Association of Teachers of Singing in America and Canada; Gallery Association, Eduson Community College; Lee County Dance Council; Fort Myers Community Concert Association; Southwest Florida Symphony and Chorus Association; Fort Myers Historical Museum; American Guild of Organists; Florida League of the Arts. Community Activities: Community Concerts Association (past board member); Ringling Museum (Lee chapter); Community Choirs (director); Symphony Chorus (guest director); Local Theater Groups (music consultant); Girl Scouts of America (volunteer service); Parent-Teacher Association (local officer); Beta Sigma Phi Sorority (vice president); Saba; Palms Garden Club (vice president). Religion: Soloist, Director, Church Choirs in Florida, Alabama, Georgia, New York. Honors and Awards: Appointed by Ralph Turlinton, State Commissioner on Education, to Serve as One of Nine Members on Florida State Secondary Music Instructional Materials Council; Appointed by Executive Board of Florida Vocal Music Teachers Association to Serve as Vocal Solo Literature Music Specialist for State of Florida; Served on Executive Board, Currently State President, Florida League of the Arts; Gannett Foundation Heart of Gold Humanitarian Award Nominee, 1981; Listed in *Who's Who Among Students in American Colleges and Universities, Personalities of the South, Directory of Distinguished Americans, Book of Honor, Heart of Community Leaders of America, World Who's Who of Women.* Address: 1271 Burtwood Drive, Fort Myers, Florida 33901.

Noble, Charles MacIntosh

Consulting Engineer. Personal: Born June 10, 1896; Son of Charles McIntosh Noble, Mary Jewell Taylor (both deceased); Married Kathryn Schubert; Father of Mrs. William M. Jamieson, Mrs. Robert Carter Henry, Mrs. Starling L. Hanford. Education: Diploma in Civil Engineering, International Correspondence Schools, 1929; Two Years Study in Higher Mathematics, Technical Mechanics and Mechanics of Materials, Columbia University. Military: Served in the United States Naval Reserve, 1917-21, 1942-58, retiring with the rank of Captain. Career: Consulting Engineer. Organizational Memberships: American Society of Civil Engineers (chairman, committee on classifications of existing street systems; member, committee on geometrics of highway design); H.R.B. Committee on Highway Capacity (chairman, committee on effect of controlled access expressways on urban areas); Civil Engineering Department, Princeton University (advisory council, 1947-51); E.C.P.D. Committee in Mid-Atlantic Area, Visiting Engineering Colleges and Reporting on Observations in Connection with Accrediting the College, 1950-56; Numerous Committee Memberships in Ohio in Connection with the Office of Highway Director. Community Activities: St. Johns County, Florida, Planning Agency; Ponte Vedra Beach, Florida, Zoning Board; Supporting Committees Dedicated to Balancing the National Budget and to the Reduction of the National Debt. Religion: Episcopalian. Honors and Awards: Registered Professional Engineer, Florida, Maryland, New Jersey, New York, Ohio, Pennsylvania; President, Jacksonville, Florida, Branch, English Speaking Union of the Year, 1979-80; Listed in *Who's Who in Engineering*. Address: P.O. Box 386, Ponte Vedra Beach, Florida 32082-0386.

Charles M Noble

Noell, Helen L

Executive. Personal: Born March 9, 1929; Daughter of Emory B. (deceased) and Cora Lee Smith; Married Jack D. Noell; Mother of Harold Wayne Stockdale, Charlotte Elizabeth Stockdale, Tommy W. McCollough. Education: B.A., South Western College, Willow Springs, Missouri, 1952. Career: Owner, President, Conroe Marine, Inc. Organizational Memberships: Marine Retailers Association of America; The Boating Trades Association of Texas; Boating Trades of Metropolitan Houston; American Society of Professional and Executive Women; American Society of Notaries. Community Activites: Notary Public, Montgomery County, Harris County, 1950 to present; Texas Parks and Wildlife Department (agent, 1974 to present); Coast Guard Auxiliary, Conroe, 1981. Religion: Mims Memorial Baptist Church, 43 years. Honors and Awards: In Recognition of Past Achievements, American Society of Notaries; Listed in *Who's Who in the South and Southwest, Who's Who in Finance and Industry, World Who's Who of Women, Book of Honor, Directory of Distinguished Americans, Personalities of the South.* Address: 413 Oak Hill Drive, Conroe, Texas 77304.

Nohe, B L'essor

Executive. Personal: Born December 1, 1943; Daughter of Roberta Steffen Newton; Married Richard E. Nohe; Mother of Louis William. Education: B.A., De Paul University, 1976; M.P.H., University of Illinois at the Medical Center, School of Public Health, 1977. Career: President, Qual Corporation Associates; Coordinator, J.C.A.H. and Planning Assistant, St. Anthony Hospital, 1970-71; Administrator, Research Service, West Side Veterans Administration Medical Center, 1971-74; Statistician, North Chicago Veterans Administration Medical Center, 1978; Program Analyst (Quality Assurance Coordinator), West Side Veterans Administration Medical Center; Instructor in Quality Assurance, School of Public Health, University of Illinois at the Medical Center, 1979; Program Analyst (Quality Assurance Specialist), West Roxbury Veterans Administration Medical Center, 1980; Administrative Officer to the Associate Chief of Staff for Research and Development, West Roxbury Veterans Administration Medical Center, 1980 to present; Quality Assurance Advisor, West Roxbury Veterans Administration, 1980 to present; President, Qual Corp Associates, Inc., 1979 to present. Organizational Memberships: American Academy of Medical Administrators; Independent Consultants of America; The American Sociological Association; The Inter-American Society; The American Public Health Association; The Illinois Public Health Association; American Academy of Health Administrators; American Association for the Advancement of Science; The Academy of Political Science; Pi Gamma Mu; National Historical Society; The Hastings Center; Smithsonian Institute; Milbank Memorial Fund. Community Activities: De Paul University Alumni Association; University of Illinois at the Medical Center School of Public Health Alumni Association (life member; newsletter committee, 1978-79; chairperson, public health issues committee, 1978-79; treasurer, 1978-79); Alumni Representative, Task Force on Accreditation, School of Public Health, University of Illinois at the Medical Center, 1978-79. Honors and Awards: Pi Gamma Mu National Social Science Honor Society, 1976; Outstanding Performance Award, Veterans Administration, 1979; Listed in *Who's Who in the East, Community Leaders of America, Directory of Distinguished Americans.* Address: 200 Springs Road, Bedford, Massachusetts 01730.

B L'essor Nohe

Nordby, Eugene Jorgen

Orthopaedic Surgeon. Personal: Born April 30, 1918; Son of Herman and Lucille Nordby (both deceased); Married Olive Marie Jensen; Father of Jon Jorgen. Education: B.A., Luther College, 1939; M.D., University of Wisconsin Medical School, 1943; Intern, Madison General Hospital, Wisconsin, 1943-44; Assistant in Orthopaedic Surgery, 1944-48. Military: Served in the United States Army Medical Corps, 1944-46, attaining the rank of Captain. Career: Consulting Orthopaedic Surgeon; Madison General Hospital, Orthopaedic Surgeon 1948-81, Chief of Staff 1957-63, Board of Directors 1957-76; Associate Clinical Professor, University of Wisconsin Medical School, 1961-81. Organizational Memberships: Wisconsin Medical Society (councilor, 1961-76; chairman, 1968-76; treasurer, 1976-82); American Academy of Orthopaedic Surgery (board of directors, 1972-73; chairman, board of councilors, 1973; chairman, committee on the spine, 1975-81); Association of Bone and Joint Surgeons (president, 1973); Clinical Orthopaedic Society; International Society for Study of Lumbar Spine. Community Activities: Wisconsin Physicians Service (board of directors, 1958-81; chairman, 1979-81); Wisconsin Regional Medical Program (director); Wisconsin Health Care Liability Plan; Norwegian American Museum (president of board, 1968-82); Sunset Village (board member, 1952-54); Sister City Committee, Madison-Oslo. Religion: Bethel Lutheran Church, 1934-82; President, Church Council, 1956-58; Chairman, Call Committee, 1959. Honors and Awards: Distinguished Service Award, Luther College, 1964; Council Award, State Medical Society of Wisconsin, 1976; Knights Cross, 1st Class, Royal Order of St. Olav, Norway, 1979; Eagle Scout, 1934. Address: 6234 South Highlands, Madison, Wisconsin 53705.

Eugene J Nordby

Norman, John Barstow

Associate Professor, Department Head. Personal: Born February 5, 1940; Son of John B. Sr. and Maxine Norman; Married Roberta Jeane Martin; Father of John B. III, Elizabeth J. Education: B.F.A. 1963, M.F.A. 1966, University of Kansas; Certificates in Supervisor Training (Hallmark Cards Inc.) 1967, Cost Accounting 1973, Front Line Management 1974, University of Denver School of Business. Career: Associate Professor of Art, Head of the Graphic Design Department, University of Denver School of Art, 1978 to present; Assistant Professor of Art, University of Denver School of Art, 1969-76; Art Director, Design Supervisor, Contemporary Department, Hallmark Cards Inc. 1966-69; Assistant Instructor of Design University of Kansas, 1963-66; Designer, Illustrator,

Advertising Design Inc., Kansas City Missouri, 1962-63. Organizational Memberships: Art Directions Club, Denver; American College Designers Association, National Wildlife Federation; Friends of Contemporary Art, Denver (honorary member). Community Activities: Colorado Celebration of the Arts, Design Exhibition (chairman, 1975, 1976); Career Educational Center, Denver Public School System (chairman, arts and sciences advisory board, 1975); Lectures, National Speech Communications Conference, University of Denver 1974, National Watercolor Society 1974, Denver Art Museum 1974, 1975. Honors and Awards: Grants from the National Endowment for the Arts and Humanities/Colorado Endowment for the Arts; Traveling Exhibition, Universities of Kansas, Nebraska, Oklahoma, Missouri, Iowa, Oklahoma State, Colorado, 1963; Exhibitions at the Hallmark Cards Museum of Contemporary Design 1967, Denver Art Museum 1973, University of Denver Annual Exhibition 1969-77, Denver Art Museum "Spaces and Structures" 1974-75; Participating Artist, New York Museum of Modern Art's Traveling Bicentennial Exhibition "Art Since 1945", Denver Art Museum, 1976; Filmmaker, Film Collection/New York Museum of Modern Art and the Denver Art Museum, 1977; Work Included in or Reviewed in *New York Times, Chicago Tribune, Denver Post, University of Denver News, Colorado Arts,* Other Publications; 3 Citations of Design Excellence, Denver Art Directors Club, 1970; 2 Citations of Design Excellence; 3 Citations of Design Excellence, National College of Designers, Association, 1973; Gold Medal Award for Design Excellence, Denver Art Directors Club, 1975; Gold Medal of Design Excellence, Denver Art Directors Club, 1976; Silver Medal Award (shared), New York International Film and Video Competition, 1975; National John Cottan Dana Award for Design Excellence, 1975; Honorable Mention Award (shared), 1976 Chicago International Film and Video Competition, 1977; Gold Medal, Art Directors Club of Denver, 1981; Distinguished Professor, University of Denver, 1979; Listed in *Who's Who in America, Who's Who in the West, Who's Who in Education.* Address: P.O. Box 302, Franktown, Colorado 80116.

Norman, Wallace Sr

Insurance Executive. Personal: Born February 5, 1926; Son of Leland Fleming (deceased) and Alma Lucile Brown Norman; Married Maurene Collums; Father of Wallace Jr., Karen Jean, Emily June, Lauren Beth, John Crocker. Education: Attended East Central Junior College 1942, University of Mississippi 1946, Millsaps College 1946; B.S., Oklahoma City University, 1948. Military: Served in the United States Naval Reserves, during World War II. Career: Owner, Operator, Wallace Norman Insurance Agency, 1949 to present; President, U.S. Plastics Inc., 1969 to present; President, Norman Oil Company; President, National Leasing Company, 1969 to present; President, Calhoun National Company, 1974 to present; President, Norman Trucking Company. Community Activities: Exchange Club; Gideons International; Boy Scouts of America (chairman, Running Bear district, 1971-73); Mississippi Association of Insurance Agents; Mississippi Manufacturing Association; American Water Works Association; D.A.V.; Veterans of Foreign Wars; American Legion. Religion: Methodist. Address: Highway 15 North, Houston, Mississippi 38851.

Northe, James Neill

Singer, Pianist, Lecturer, Composer, Educator, Poet, Dealer in Out of Print and Rare Books. Career: Editor, *Silhouettes, Warp and Woof* (first and only newspaper page of verse in the world); Editor, *Seven;* Sponsor, Jesse Stuart Contest; Editor of Anthologies *Threads and Shadows, Land of Gold;* Author *History of Ontario, Mata Hari, Though Sunsets Die, Gonfalon, Fire of a Tropic Moon, It Dawneth in the Easte* (first book ever published in analyzed rhyme, translated from the French); Work Tranlated into Italian, Spanish, Chinese, Japanese, French; Contributor to Numerous Periodicals including *Literary Digest, Christian Science Monitor, Wall Street Journal,* and *La Fiera Lettretaria* (Italy); Original Verse Forms included in *Poets Handbook and Rhyming Dictionary, Patterns for Poems, More Patterns for Poems, Still More Patterns, America Singing, Pioneering with Pegasus.* Organizational Memberships: Allied Arts Fine Arts Festival of Southern California (chairman); Speaker and Poet for League of Utah Writers, West Texas State, League of American Pen Women, Short Course for Professional Writers, Annual Midwest Chapparel, Kansas Authors Club, and Others. Honors and Awards: Listed in Various Who's Who Publications. Address: 3630 Northwest 22, Oklahoma City, Oklahoma 73107.

Northington, Chloe Cunningham

Farmer, Artist. Personal: Born May 24, 1909; Married W. Northington. Education: Two Years Study at Hollins College; Degree in Art, Austen Peay State University. Career: Farmer; Exhibits in Watercolors, Oils, Weaving, Stitchery; Handweaving Show, Cheekwood, Nashville, 1974. Community Activities: Montgomery County Grounds and Interiors Commission (chairman); Bicentennial Commission, Montgomery County, Tennessee; Daughters of the American Revolution (national society regent, treasurer, parliamentarian); Colonial Dames of America (chapter treasurer); Americans of Royal Descent, Order of the Crown; C.A.R. (senior president, Sevier Station Chapter); Farm Bureau, Hopkinsville, Kentucky; Art Guild. Honors and Awards: James Cross Award for Work and Conservation, Montgomery County, 1977; Award as Outstanding Senior Art Student, 1975; Best Craft, Two Rivers Art and Craft Show, 1981; Listed in *Dictionary of International Biography.* Address: 1650 Hopkinsville Highway, Clarksville, Tennessee 37040.

Northrup, William Carlton

Accountant, Statistician. Personal: Born December 1, 1930; Son of Mr. and Mrs. L. L. Northrup; Married Sharon Joan Carlson; Father of Richard Carlton, Karen Frances. Education: B.S. 1963, M.B.A. 1974, University of Missouri; Attended Middle Management Seminars, 1970-73; Studies in Hospital Budgeting, H.F.M.A., 1980. Career: Accountant V/Statistician, County of Cook/Cook County Hospital; Management Analyst III, Health and Hospital Governing Committee; Chief Accountant, National Congress of Parents and Teachers; Account Executive, London Commodity House; Supervisor, Research and Records, Missouri Crippled Childrens Service; Accountant II, Missouri Division of Health; Account Executive, Chief Estimator, Estimator, Cost Accountant, Assistant Product Manager, American Press Inc.; Production Planner, Production Scheduler/Merchandiser, Cut Editor, M.F.A. Publishing Division; Management Trainee, Thriftway Food Mart; Assistant Treasurer, M.F.A. Insurance; Research Associate, University of Missouri, Rural Sociology Department; Sales Representative, World Book International; Stock Broker. Organizational Memberships: H.F.M.A.; A.I.C.P.A.; American Statistial Association; Mathematics Association of America; American Management Association; Association of M.B.A. Executives; Delta Sigma Pi (life member; chancellor, 1953; historian, 1952; reporter, *Delta Sig Chatter,* 1951); Fifth Street Syndicate Investment Club. Community Activities: Chicago Council on Foreign Relations, 1982, APHA 1982; IPHA 1982; Presidential Task Force, 1982; National Conservative Political Action Committee, 1982; National Tax Limitation Committee and Better Government Association; Republican National Committee; Illinois Parent-Teacher Association, 1977; United States Senatorial Club, 1978 to present; American Secutiy Council (national advisory board); Twilight Optimist Club (president, 1st vice president, secretary-treasurer, board of directors, 1970-76); S.P.E.B.S.Q.S.A. (secretary-treasurer, board of directors, 1st vice president, 2nd vice president, 1972-76); Columbia Jaycees (secretary-treasurer, 1964); Teen Auto Club (steering committee, 1972); Camp Wannonoya (steering committee, 1976); Finance Study Commission, City of Columbia, 1974;

Mizzou Employees Federal Credit Union, 1972-74; Boone County Juvenile Court probation officer, 1971-72); A.B.I.R.A. (life member, 1979 to present); Republican Presidential Task Force, 1981; Cook Coutny Republicans (charter member, 1981); Columbia Town Meeting (steering committee, 1976; Stephens College Cultural Events Series house manager, 1976; Cub Scout Pack (committee chairman, 1965); Packyderm Club of Boone County, 1974-76; Advisory Council for Committee to Re-elect George Parker, 1974-76; American Mensa Selection Agency, 1970 to present; Columbia Little League (coach, 1976); International Platform Association; A.A.U.C.G., 1981; Missouri Public Health Association, 1974-76. Religion: Bethel Baptist Church, Columbia, Missouri, Youth Director, 1972, Sunday School Teacher, 1972, Nominating Committee 1972-74, Choir Director, 1974, Editor *Bethel Banner* 1972-76; Boone County Pastoral Alliance, Executive Committee, 1974; Student, Religious Council, University of Missouri, 1952. Honors and Awards: First Runner-up, Open Competition Exam, Candidate for M.B.A., Finance, University of Missouri, 1974; Special Advisory to the Governor of the State of Missouri for Printing and Publishing, 1965; Nominated to National Honor Society, 1946, 1947, 1948; Quiz Kids of Missouri, 1940; Highest Score Ever Recorded on Engineering Applicant Exam, Westinghouse, Kansas City, 1953. Address: 24 Williamsburg, Evanston, Illinois 60203.

Numano, Allen Stanislaus Motoyuki

Allen S M Numano

Writer and Industrial Designer. Personal: Born November 3, 1908, in Yokohama, Japan; Brought up in Chipstead, Surrey, England and Her Former Crown Colony, Ceylon, for 25 Years; Son of Mr. and Mrs. Hidekazu Numano (both deceased), Proprietors of Mikado & Company, Colombo, Ceylon 1908-1940. Education: Graduate of the primary school, Azabu, Tokyo, Japan, 1921; Graduate of St. Joseph's College, Colombo, Ceylon, 1929; Matriculated, 1930; Attended Worcester College in Oxford, England and the Royal College of Music in London, 1930-39. Career: Industrial Designer, Honolulu, Hawaii; Solo violinist, 1939-41; Senior Examiner and translator at the General Headquarters (Supreme Commander for Allied Powers), Tokyo, Japan, under General Douglas MacArthur, 1945-47; Buying agent for a Ceylonese firm, 1948-53; Consultant and chief technical translator for a U.S.-Japanese venture, Pfizer Taito Company, Ltd., in Tokyo, 1954-68; Lecturer in English composition, Sophia University, Tokyo, 1967-68; Established an independent Safilta Technical translation service, 1969; Compiling a technical report at the request of the F.A.A. in Washington on "Foolproof Runway Clearance and Siding Audiovisual Automatic Safety Airport System" and "a New, Crankshaftless Auto-Engine"; Currently serving as an overseas representative; Originator and pioneer in the field of "mentalogy", the study of variations and collective differences in human mentality with a view to finding some basic universal mentality, irrespective of physical and cultural differences. Organizational Memberships: Society of Authors, London, England (associate member); Institute of Linguists, London, England (fellow); Translators Association of London, England, 1963 to present. Community Activities: Performed violin recital at the Royal College Hall in Colombo, Ceylon to aid the British Red Cross (the Dukes of Gloucester Fund), 1940; Selected as a delegate for the Senior Citizens of Honolulu to attend the Governor's State Conference on Aging, 1980 (received the Governor's Certificate of Appreciation); Member of the Smithsonian Associates of Washington, D.C., 1979 to present. Published Works: Author under pseudonym of A.L.A. Corenanda, *Music and Reminiscences*, 1982-83; Translator into Japanese, L.P. Lochner's *Fritz Kreisler*, 1959, Maymie R. Krythe's *All About Christmas*, 1962, and Fairbanks-Morse' *Opposed Piston Engine Instructions 3800 D8/9*, 1964; Contributor to *The Times of Ceylon, The Japan Times, Organic Forum, Indian Labor Review*, on Music and Life, Music and Criticism, Management and Labour, Tribute to the Patriarch of Violinists. Honors and Awards: Received letters of congratulations on becoming a naturalized citizen of the United States from President Jimmy Carter, Senator Edward M. Kennedy, Lieutenant Governor Jean King of Hawaii, Mayor of Honolulu Frank F. Fasi, Congressman Daniel K. Akaka and Congressman Cecil Heftel (became naturalized on February 6, 1980); Exhibited pencil-sketchings at the 55th Annual Art Exhibition of the Ceylon Society of Art held in Colombo, 1952; One of approximately 12 people in the world specializing in the field of violin tonal adjustment; Received Letters of Appreciation from Senator Edward M. Kennedy, President Ronald Reagan, world-renowned violin maker Sergio Peresson, animal behaviorist Joy Adamson, author Pearl S. Buck; Poem "The Universe" included by personal invitation in anthology *Our Twentieth Century's Greatest Poems;* Listed in *Men of Achievement, Community Leaders and Noteworthy Americans, International Who's Who of Intellectuals, Book of Honor,* and many other biographical works. Address: P.O. Box 2442, Honolulu, Hawaii 96804-2442.

Nyabongo, Virginia Simmons

Virginia S Nyabongo

Author, Lecturer. Personal: Born March 20, 1913, in Baltimore, Maryland; Daughter of Vester and Mary Warren Simmons (both deceased). Education: B.A., French and History, Bennett College, 1934; M.A., French, University of Wisconsin, 1937; Ph.D., French, University of Wisconsin; M.A., Student Personnel Administration and Guidance, 1948; Professional Diploma, Dean of Students, Teachers College, Columbia University, 1962; Certificat d'Études Françaises, Certificat de Phonétique, Diplôme d'Études Avancées de Phonétique, University of Grenoble, France, 1939; Post-Doctoral Studies, Japan Program, Syracuse University. Career: Author/Lecturer; Professor of French, Research Professor, Director of Student Personnel and Guidance, 1944-58, Tennessee State University, 1944-78, Bennett College, 1934-36, 1941-42; Dean of Students, Acting Registrar, Instructor, Secretrary; Assistant Professor of French, Wilberforce University, 1937-41. Organizational Memberships: American Association of Teachers of French, Tennessee Chapter, (president, 1972-73); Tennessee Philological Association (president, 1967-68); Tennessee Foreign Language Teaching Association (board of directors, 1969, 1970; co-editor, newsletter, 1971); Modern Language Association (French VIII chairman); National Association of Dean's of Women Advisers Girls (president); National Association of Deans of Women, Administrators, Counselors (committee on international students). Community Activities: United Nations Association, U.S.A., Nashville Chapter (president, 1977); American Association of University Women (1st vice president, 1970-72; Tennessee division area representative, international relations, study topics chairman, redefining the goals of education; Nashville branch delegate to national conventions, Chicago, Albuquerque, and Centennial Convention in Boston, 1981); I.F.U.W., Tokyo and Kyoto, Japan (discussion group leader, interpreter in English and French, 1974); I.F.U.W. Karlsruhe, Philadelphia, Vancouver; National Education Association Delegate to World Confederation of Organizations of the Teaching Profession in Dublin, 1968, and Abidjan, Ivory Coast, 1969; Nashville Area Chamber of Commerce (committee on education, 1971; Metro Council committee); Citizens Coordinating Committee, Model Cities Program, 1972-75; Davidson County Democratic Women's Club (past vice-president); Tennessee Federation of Democratic Women (past corresponding secretary). Religion: First Baptist Church, Capital Hill, Nashville, Former Youth Committee, Chairman, Co-Chairman Centennial Committee 1965. Honors and Awards: Non-Resident Scholar, University Scholar, University of Wisconsin, 1936-37, 1942-44; Franco-American Fellow, Institute of International Education, Grenoble, France, 1938-39; Postdoctoral Research, Fulbright Program, Paris, 1952-53; Fellow, African Studies Association, International Institute of Arts and Letters, Postdoctoral Fellow, Society for Values in Higher Education; Tennessee State University Golden Anniversary Faculty Service Award, 1962; Tennessee State University Presidential Citation, 1978; Ministère de l'Éducation Nationale, République Française, Chevalier dans l'Ordre des Palmes Académiques, 1963, Officer 1968; Citations, N.A.W.D.A.C., A.A.U.W., 1981; Democratic National Committee, 1982. Address: 936 34th Avenue North, Nashville, Tennessee 37209.

Nye, William Preston

Research Entomologist (retired). Personal: Born January 10, 1917; Father of Pamela Quinnett (Mrs. Paul), James, Janet Anderson

(Mrs. Rodney), Ted W., David P. Education: B.S. 1940, M.S. 1947, Utah State University. Military: Served in the United States Marine Corps, 1940-45, and in the Marine Corps Reserve 1945-62, retiring with the rank of Lieutenant Colonel. Career: Retired Research Entomologist/Apiculturist USDA, ARS. Organizational Memberships: Entomology Society of America, 1947-77; International Bee Research Association, 1962-77; Organization of Professional Employees, U.S.D.A., 1960 to present; Western Apicultural Society of America, 1978 to present. Religion: Church of Jesus Christ of Latter-Day Saints, High Priest Leadership Group, Member Hyrum Fifth Ward. Honors and Awards: Numerous Photographic Awards from Entomological Society of America and International Groups; U.S.D.A. Merit Award, 1968. Address: 459 Valley View Drive, Hyrum, Utah 84319.

O'Banion, Marguerite E

Executive Secretary. Personal: Born February 18; Daughter of J. W. O'Banion, Mrs. J. W. O'Banion (deceased). Education: Graduate of Swifton High School, Arkansas, 1935; B.A., Harding University, 1942; Graduate of Dale Carnegie Program, 1954; LL.D., Alabama Christian College, 1979. Career Executive Secretary to Dr. George S. Benson, 38 years. Organizational Memberships: Business and Professional Women's Club (past present); American Association of University Women (past secretary, Searcy branch); Harding Business Women's Club (founding president; reporter); Associated Women for Harding (charter member; first life member; secretary, Searcy Chapter, one year); Arkansas Chapter, Freedoms Foundation of Valley Forge. Religion: Church of Christ. Honors and Awards: Distinguished Citizenship Award, National Education Program; LL.D., Alabama Christian College, 1979; First Woman Among Churches of Christ to Receive LL.D Degree. Address: Harding University, Box 751, Searcy, Arkansas 72143.

Oberman, Samuel Eugene

Management Consulting Executive. Personal: Born September 8, 1933; Son of Max and Betty Oberman; Married Judith Meshberg; Father of Scott Evan, Amy Lisa. Education: B.S., Economics, Wharton School of Finance and Commerce, University of Pennsylvania, 1955; M.B.A., University of Michigan, 1958. Military: Served in the United States Navy, 1955-57, with the rank of SK2. Career: President, Dan Rowe Associates, Management Consultants; Director of Personnel, Methodist Hospital of Brooklyn; Wage and Salary Administrator, New York Hospital; Wage and Salary Analyst, Columbia Broadcasting System. Organizational Memberships: American Institute of Management (Presidents Council); American Society of Professional Consultants; American Society for Personnel Administration; American Society of Business and Management Consultants (charter member). Community Activities: American Jewish Committee (President, Long Island chapter, 1977-79); Congressional Committee, 1980 to present; Greater Westbury Community Coalition (co-chairman, 1970-76); Young Men's Christian Association of Long Island (board of directors, 1976-80); Greater Westbury Arts Council (board of directors, 1976 to 1980); Community Conflict Resolution (mediator and arbitrator, 1972 to present). Religion: Community Reform Temple, Board of Directors, 1978-80. Honors and Awards: American Jewish Committee Human Relations Award, 1979; University of Wisconsin School of Banking Faculty, 1973-78; Listed in *Who's Who in Finance and Industry, Community Leaders of America, International Men of Achievement*. Address: 65 Chenango Drive, Jericho, New York 11753.

Marguerite E O'Banion

Obermayer, Herman J

Editor, Publisher. Personal: Born September 19, 1924, in Philadelphia, Pennsylvania; Son of Leon and Julia Obermayer; Married Betty Nan Levy, June 28, 1955; Father of Helen Julia, Veronica Levy, Adele Beatrice, Elizabeth Rose. Education: A.B. cum laude, Dartmouth College, Hanover, New Hampshire, 1948; Attended Universite de Geneve, Switzerland, 1946. Military: Served in the United States Army, 1943-46, attaining the rank of Staff Sergeant. Career: Editor, Publisher, *Northern Virginia Sun*, Arlington, Virginia, 1963 to present; Editor, Publisher, *Daily Record*, Long Branch, New Jersey, 1957-71; Assistant to Publisher, *New Bedford Standard Times*, Massachusetts, 1955-56; Classified Advertising Manager, *New Orleans Item*, 1953-55; Reporter, *Long Island Press*, Jamaica, New York, 1950-53; Contributor, "Editor's Viewpoint" Weekly Column in *Northern Virginia Sun*, 1971 to present, *Saturday Evening Post, This Week, Ebony, Darthmouth Alumni Magazine, Japan Economic Journal, American Society of Newspaper Editors Bulletin, Columbia Journalism Review*. Organizational Memberships: Southern Newspaper Publishers Association (director, 1981); American Society of Newspaper Editors (program committee); First Amendment Congress, 1980; White House Correspondents Association; American Newspaper Publishers Association. Community Activities: Arlington County Bicentennial Commission (trustee, 1971-77); Boy Scouts of America (Monmouth, New Jersey Council, executive board, 1958-71; National Capital Area executive board 1972-80; first vice president, 1975-77; national council, 1974-78); Monmouth Medical Center, Long Branch, New Jersey, 1958-71; Arlington Chapter, American Red Cross, 1973-77; Northern Virginia Chapter, American Heart Association, 1976 to present; Anti-Defamation League (regional advisory committee, 1962-71); Friends of Long Branch Libraries, 1958-72; Monmouth Art Museum, Red Bank, New Jersey, 1968-71; Twin Lights Historical Museum, Highlands, New Jersey, 1962-71; Appointed by Governor Linwood Holton to Virginia's Alcoholic Beverage Control Study Commission, 1972-74; Rotary Club; National Press Club, Washington, D.C.; Ocean Beach Club, Elberton, New Jersey; Washington Golf and Country Club, Arlington, Virginia; Dartmouth Club of New York; Sigma Chi; Sigma Delta Chi Society of Professional Journalists. Honors and Awards: Silver Beaver, Boy Scouts of America, 1977; Rhineland Campaign Star, United States Army. Address: 4114 North Ridgeview Road, Arlington, Virginia 22207.

O'Brian, Therese de Ste. Marthe McGinnis

Translator, Interpreter. Personal: Born December 30, 1942, in Philadelphia, Pennsylvania; Daughter of Maurice G. and Marie Antoinette de. Ste. Marthe McGinnis; Married Brian K. O'Brian, June 18, 1964 (deceased); Mother of Brian K. III (deceased), Maureen Karen (deceased). Education: A.B. summa cum laude, Catholic University of America; M.A., Columbia University Teachers College, Ed.D. summa cum laude; M.S., Journalism, Columbia University; Ph.D. summa cum laude, Psychology, Harvard University; Ph.D., summa cum laude, Psychology, Sorbonne, Paris; Further Studies (Rhodes Scholar), Oxford University. Career: Teacher, English Languages and Journalism; Editor for Magazines and Publishing Houses; Teacher, Spanish and Journalism, Columbia University College of Physicians and Surgeons; Translator, Interpreter, United Nations, to present; Teacher, Berlitz School of Languages; Consultant, New York State Department of Education. Organizational Memberships: American Society of Professional and Executive Women; American Association of University Women, New York State Teachers Union; National Organization of Women; National Education Association; American Association of Artist and Writers; Executive Women; United Federation of Teachers; Mensa; International Platform Association; Smithsonian Associates; Phi Beta Kappa; Kappa Tau Alpha; Delta Kappa Gamma. Community Activities: Democrat; Aspen Club; Lake Tahoe Club; Windham Mountain Club; Windham Country Club; Elmridge Bath and Tennis Club; Playboy Club; Lake Placid Club. Religion: Roman Catholic. Published Works:

Author of Articles for Magazines, Newspapers. Address: Box 894, Tannersville, New York 12485 and Riverdale, New York 10471.

O'Briant, Lois Poteet Hooks

Retired. Personal: Born October 29, 1905; Mother of James Poteet Hooks, Bentley Carroll Hooks Jr. Education: A.B., Southwest Texas State Teachers College, 1929; M.S., Education, Baylor University, 1956; Librarian Certificate, Baylor University, 1966. Career: Classroom Teacher, Fourth Grade, 25 years. Organizational Memberships: Texas Classroom Teachers Association, 1964-81; Texas State Teachers Association, 1960-81. Community Activities: Century Club, Southwest Texas State Teachers College, 1977-81. Religion: Protestant, Church Pianist 1921-24. Honors and Awards: Dean's List in Librarianship, Baylor University, Summer 1965; Daughters of the American Revolution; Order of Eastern Star. Address: Route 1 Box 138A, Lewisville, Texas 75067.

Odvarka, Robert Charles

R C Odvarka

Dentist. Personal: Born January 5, 1926; Son of V. L. and Helen Odvarka; Married Arlene Mae Fayman; Father of Sandra Faye Odvarka Weeder, Robert Scott, Scott Brian. Education: B.S., University of Nebraska, 1951; D.D.S., University of Nebraska, 1953. Military: Served in the United States Army, 1944-46, attaining the rank of Sargeant. Career: Dentist. Organizational Memberships: North District Dental Association; Nebraska Dental Association; American Dental Association; Xi Psi Phi Professional Fraternity; National Association of the 10th Mountain Division; Colfax County Dental Consultant, 1976 to present. Community Activities: Lion's Club International; Clarkson Board of Education (chairman; zone chairman); Boy Scouts of America (council and denmaster, Cub Scouts); Clarkson Commercial Club. Religion: Presbyterian. Address: 523 Pine Street, Drawer F, Clarkson, Nebraska 68629.

Ogg, Wilson Reid

Attorney, Real Estate Broker, Educator. Personal: Born February 26, 1928; Son of James and Mary Wilson Ogg (both deceased). Education: A.A. 1947, A.B. 1949, University of California-Berkeley; LL.B., J.D. 1952, Boalt Hall School of Law, University of California-Berkeley. Military: Served in the United States Army, 1952-54. Career: Director of Admissions, The International Society for Philosophical Enquiry; Member, State Board of California, 1955 to present; Licensed Real Estate Broker, 1974 to present; Credentials as California Community College Instructor, Law, Social Science, Real Estate, 1976 to present; Senior Editor, Continuing Education of the Bar, University of California, 1958-63; English Instructor, Taequ English Language Institute, Korea, 1954; Instructor, Psychology, 25th Station Hospital, Taequ, Korea, 1954. Organizational Memberships: National Panel of Arbitrators; American Arbitration Association; International Academy of Law and Science (fellow); Curator-in-Residence, Pinebrook, 1964 to present. Community Activities: Faculty Club, University of California-Berkeley; Commonwealth Club; Town Hall; The International Platform Association; Bar Association of San Francisco; Alameda County Bar Association; Berkeley-Albany Bar Association; Trustee, The World University, 1978-80; The Parapsychological Association; American Society of Psychical Research; American Mensa; Lawyers in Mensa; The Berkeley Architectural Heritage Society. Religion: First Unitarian Church of Berkeley, Secretary, Member Board of Trustees, 1957-58; Minister, Universal Church, 1969 to present. Honors and Awards: Commendation Ribbon with Medal Pendant, United States Army, 1954; Listed in *Two Thousand Men of Achievement, Notable Americans of the Bicentennial Era.* Address: 8 Bret Harte Way, Berkeley, California 94708.

Oglesby, Sarah Green

Television Hostess. Personal: Born March 8 1900; Married Walter E. Oglesby; Mother of Lori O. Reed. Education: Graduate of Avery Normal Institute, 1918; A.B., Fisk University, 1924; M.A., New York University, 1952. Career: Staff, WCSC-TV "Sadie Oglesby's Scrapbook"; Teacher of Latin, Avery Normal Institute, 2 years; Teacher of Latin and English, Allen University, 15 years; Teacher of Latin and English, Burke High School, Charleston, South Carolina, 27 years; Summer School Teacher, Extension School Teacher, Morris College, Sumter, South Carolina. Organizational Memberships: Gamma Xi Omega Chapter, Alpha Kappa Alpha Sorority (past basileus). Community Activities: Retired Teachers Association; Member Three Church Auxiliaries. Religion: Emanuel A.M.E Church, Senior Trustee. Honors and Awards: Inducted into Hall of Fame, Burke Alumni Association, 1980 Soror of the Year, 1977; Certificate from Governor Riley of South Carolina for Recognition of Interest for her People, 1980; Certificate of Appreciation, Mayor Riley, 1980; Two Scrolls of Honor, 1964, 1974 Plaque from School District 20, 1965; Plaque, Sorority, for 20 years Service. Address: 1107 Lango Avenue, Charleston, South Carolina 29407.

Sarah G Oglesby

Oien, Arthur Carlisle

Educator. Personal: Born April 10, 1930; Son of Alfred Carl Oien, Mable Margaret Martinson (both deceased). Education: B.A. summa cum laude, Concordia College, Moorhead, Minnesota, 1952; M.A., University of Minnesota, 1954; Further Studies at the University of Minnesota, 1957-60. Military: Served in the United States Army Security Agency, 1954-57. Career: Associate Professor of History, Bridgewater State College, 1963 to present; Instructor, Assistant Dean of Men, Luther College, Decorah, Iowa, 1960-62; Instructor, Bemidji State College, Bemidji, Minnesota, 1962-63. Organizational Memberships: Missouri Historical Society; National Education Association; Massachusetts Teachers Association; Bridgewater State College Association; American Association of University Professors; New England Historical Society; New England History Teachers Association; First Fellow of the Confederacy Historical Institute. Community Activities: Smithsonian Institution (associate); American Museum of Natural History (associate); National Audubon Society; University of Minnesota Alumni Associaton (life member); Concordia College Alumni Association (donations). Religion: Lutheran, Former Sunday School Teacher, Luther League. Honors and Awards: Alpha Society; Zeta Sigma Phi; Phi Alpha Theta; Regional Honors for Debate and Discussion; High School Valedictorian, 1948; International Platform Association; National Defense Ribbon; Good Conduct Medal; Sharpshooters Medal; Listed in *International Who's Who in Education, Who's Who in the East, Personalities of America, Directory of Distinguished Americans, Personalities of the East.* Address: Fox Run - 220 Bedford Street, Grayson Building #9, Bridgewater, Massachusetts 02324.

Olaeta, Julia O'Keefe McCurry

Elementary School Principal. Personal: Born January 26, 1923; Daughter of Con and Myrtle O'Keefe (both deceased); Married Thomas Olaeta; Mother of Mary Alice Barber, Ann Kathleen Lang, Patricia Louise Williams, Paul Michael McCurry. Education: Graduate of Silver Lake High School, Oregon, 1940; B.A., Oregon State University, Corvallis, 1944; M.A., Fresno State University, 1961; Further Studies at San Francisco State University, LaVerne University, Chapman College, University of California. Career:

Demonstration Nursery School at Oregon State University, 1946; Teacher, Portland, Oregon, 1945; Teacher, Atwater, California, 1956-66; Principal, Atwater Elementary School, 1966 to present; Director of Goals and Objectives, Director of Textbook Selection Atwater Elementary District, 1970 to present; Master Teacher, 1955-56. Organizational Memberships: American Association of School Administrators; Association of California School Administrators; Delta Kappa Gamma (president, 1981-82); American Association of University Women; Oregon State Alumni Association; Parent-Teacher Association. Community Activities: Beta Sigma Phi; Atwater Women's Club; Antique Study Club, 1981; Community Forum Advisory Committee; Friends of Battered Women. Religion: St. Anthony Rosary and Altar Society, 1960 to present. Honors and Awards: Danforth Foundation Leadership Certificate, 1940; Bernard Dally Scholarship Award, 1940-44; Kappa Delta Pi, 1944; Mu Beta Beta, 1943; Listed in *Who's Who of American Women, National Register of Prominent Americans, Personalities of the West and Midwest.* Address: 2115 Third Street, Atwater, California 95301.

Oliver, Clifton Jr

Professor. Personal: Born December 3, 1915; Son of Clifton and Laura Pearl Oliver. Education: B.A., M.A., Texas Tech University. Military: Served in the United States Army, attaining the rank of Second Lieutenant. Career: Associate Professor of Management, College of Business Administration, University of Florida; Consultant to a Number of Business Firms and Governmental Agencies. Organizational Memberships: American Arbitration Association; American Society of Training Directors; National Council of Small Business Management; A.S.P.A.; A.E.A.; A.A.A.; National Association of Purchasing Agents; National Football Foundation and Hall of Fame; Alpha Chi; Pi Sigma Alpha; Kappa Psi; Pi Gamma Mu; Alpha Kappa; Alpha Tau Omega. Community Activities: Florida Committee on Manpower; State of Florida Merit System (chairman, State Suggestion Committee); Industrial Communications Council (director); F Club Athletic Association, University of Florida; Elks; Kiwanis; American Legion; Florida Blue Key. Religion: Baptist. Honors and Awards: Recognized for Contributions to Alpha Kappa Psi, Florida Banking Association, Florida Purchasing Association; Listed in *International Who's Who of Community Service, American Men and Women of Science, Dictionary of International Biography, Royal Blue Book, National Social Directory, Directory of Educational Specialists, Personalities of the South.* Address: P.O. Box 14505, Gainesville, Florida 32604.

Werner O Oloffson

Oloffson, Werner Olaf

Advertising Consultant, Artist. Personal: Born June 21, 1905; Son of Walter and Margot Oloffson (both deceased). Education: Abiturium/Matura, Realgymnasium des Johanneums, Hamburg, Germany, 1923; Practical Aviation Certificate, New York University Guggenheim School of Aeronautics, 1933. Career: Salesman 1939-43, Professional Service Director and Export Manager, 1943-45, Wyeth Laboratories, Philadelphia; Copywriter and Member of Plans Board, Noyes and Sproul, New York Medical Advertising Agency, 1945-47; Sales Manager and Professional Service Director, Cheeseborough-Pond's New York City Professional Division, 1947-50; Advertising Manager, Ives Laboratories, New York City, 1950-54; Vice President and Copy and Scientific Director, Cortez F. Enloe, 1954-57; Director of the Medical Division, Ted Bates and Company, New York City, 1957-59; Technical Consultant on All Products, Ogilvy and Mather, New York City, 1959-62; Technical and Copy Consultant on Campaign Planning and Product Development, Medical Ghostwriter and Reporter on Technical Medical Meetings for Consumer and Medical Advertising Agencies, 1962 to present; Art Exhibited in Numerous Group and Juried Shows and One-Man Exhibitions in Hamburg (Germany), Monte Carlo, New York. Organizational Memberships: New York Academy of Sciences; American Association for the Advancement of Sleep; Pharmaceutical Advertising Club; American Watercolor Society; American Artists Professional League; Jersey Painters and Sculptors Society; National Society of Literature and the Arts; Accademia Italia delle Arti e del Lavoro; Salmgundi Club. Community Activities: Queens County Criminal Grand Jury. Honors and Awards: Many Prizes at Juried Art Shows. Address: 35-33 83rd Street, Jackson Heights, New York 11372.

Olsen, Carl Edwin (Pat)

Professional Engineer, Inventor. Personal: Born August 3, 1902; Son of Peter and Helen Olsen (both deceased); Married Elsie Duncan; Father of C. Edwin Jr. Education: B.S., Texas A.&M. University. Career: Registered Professional Engineer; Inventor; Former Professional Baseball Player; President, General Manager, Director, Geavench Manufacturing Company, 51 years. Community Activities: Nomad; Mason. Religion: Protestant. Honors and Awards: Baseball Field at Texas A.&M. University Named in His Honor; Yankee Alumni; Kentucky Colonel; Texas A.&M. Hall of Fame; Listed in *Who's Who in the South and Southwest; Personalities of the South and Southwest.* Address: 409 Dexter Drive, P.O. Box 10051-77840, College Station, Texas 77840.

Larry K Olsen

Olsen, Larry Kenith

Associate Professor. Personal: Born July 28, 1942; Son of Herman and Dorothy Olsen; Married Judith D. McKnight; Father of Larry Martin, Laura Elaine. Education: B.S. 1964, M.A.T. 1965, Lewis and Clark College; M.P.H., University of California-Berkeley, 1966; Dr.P.H., University of California-Los Angeles, 1970. Career: Associate Professor of Health Science, Department of Health and Physical Education, Arizona State University; Associate Professor, Health and Safety, University of Illinois-Urbana; Assistant Professor, Health and Safety, University of Illinois; Associate in Public Health, University of California-Los Angeles; Instructor, Health and Physical Education, Parkrose, Oregon; Consultant, United States Department of Health, Education and Welfare (Health and Human Services); Consultant, National Center for Health Education. Organizational Memberships: American School Health Association (coordinator of study committees, 1980-83; chairman, research council, 1976-77; research council member-at-large, 1972-75); American Public Health Association (school health education and services section, section counselor, 1979-81); Society for Public Health Education (board of directors, 1970-74; executive committee, 1974-75); Editorial Board, *Journal of School Health,* 1977-80; Associate Editor, *Journal Drug Education,* 1979 to present. Community Activities: Jane Wayland Mental Health Center (board of directors, 1978 to present; chairman, personnel committee, 1979 to present); American Heart Association (Dallas Heart Health in Youth committee 1975; Champaign County, Illinois, chairman, public education committee, 1969-77; board of directors, 1969-77); Maricopa County Heart Association (public health education committee, 1980 to present); American Heart Association, Arizona Affiliate (board of directors, 1980 to present; public education committee, 1980 to present); Mid-Eastern Lung Association (education committee, 1971-74); Mesa Young Men's Christian Association (soccer coach, 1977 to present); Southwest Little League (baseball coach, 1978 to present); American Cancer Society, Arizona Division (task force on smoking and health, 1978 to present). Honors and Awards: Distinguished Service Award, American School Health Association, 1981; Distinguished Service Award, American Cancer Society, 1979, 1980, 1981; Listed in *Outstanding Young Men of America, International Who's Who in Education, Directory of Distinguished Americans, Who's Who in the South and Southwest.* Address: 2300 East Balboa Drive, Tempe, Arizona 85282.

Olsen, M Eugene

Official Court Reporter. Personal: Born May 4, 1920, in Neol, Iowa; Son of Julius O. and Florence R. Olsen (both deceased). Education: Graduate of the American Institute of Business, Des Moines, Iowa, 1940; Graduate, Stenotype Institute of Washington, Washington, D.C., 1957; B.S., The Creighton University, Omaha, Nebraska, 1949; B.S. (honorary), Jones College, Jacksonville, Florida, 1965. Military: Served in the United States Air Force, 1942-45, attaining the rank of Master Sergeant. Career: Official Shorthand Reporter, Joint and Combined Chiefs of Staff, Washington, D.C., 1942-43; Reporter Assigned to Special Presidential Mission to South American Countries, 1943-44; United States Embassy, Ottawa, Canada, 1944-45; Official Court Reporter, International Military Tribunal for the Far East, Tokyo, 1945-47; Official Shorthand Reporter to Central Intelligance Agency Director Allen W. Dulles, Washington, D.C., 1952-57; Partner in Court Reporting Firm, 1957-72; Official Court Reporter, United States District Court, Washington, D.C., 1972 to present. Organizational Memberships: National Shorthand Reporters Association chairman, national seminar, Washington, D.C., 1976; board of academy of professional reporters, 1976-79; chairman or member of over 15 boards and committees; chairman, national speed contest, Atlanta 1980, San Francisco 1981); Associated Stenotypists of America (president, 1969-70); United States Court Reporters Association (chairman, ethics committee, 1974-75; board of directors, 1979-80); Pacific Northwest Court Reporters Association (chairman, examining committee, 1967-71; president-elect, 1971-72); Oregon Shorthand Reporters Association (secretary-treasurer, 1965-67; vice president, 1967-69; president, 1969-70; chairman, Oregon seminar, 1970; executive committee and chairman, examining committee, 1970-72); Maryland Shorthand Reporters Association (chairman, Maryland seminar, 1975; chairman, education committee, 1974-76); Virginia Shorthand Reporters Association (chairman, education committee, 1977 to present); Louisiana Shorthand Reporters Association (secretary-treasurer, 1963-64); Tennessee Court Reporters Association; Chartered Shorthand Reporters Association of Ontario, Canada (fellow, 1969); Oregon Shorthand Reporters Association (life member); North Dakota Shorthand Reporters Association (life member); West Virginia Shorthand Reporters Association (life member); Washington State Shorthand Reporters Association (life member); International Platform Association. Community Activities: Washington, D.C., Society for the Performing Arts; Washington, D.C., National Symphony Orchestra Association. Published Works: Author of Many Articles on Court Reporting. Honors and Awards: B.S. (honorary), Jones College, 1965; Certificate of Proficiency 1964, Certificate of Merit 1964, Top Recruiting Award 1969, Founding Fellow of Academy of Professional Reporters 1975, Distinguished Service Award 1977, National Shorthand Reporters Association; Bronze Medal at the 1965 National Shorthand Speed Contest (280 words per minute), Master Reporter Award 1965, Expert Reporter Award 1965, Associated Stenotypists of America; Award of Excellence 1966, Tiger Award 1967, Certificate of Achievement 1967, Spark Plug Award 1968, Distinguished Service Award 1978, Oregon Shorthand Reporters Association; Certificate of Achievement, Washington State Shorthand Reporters Association, 1968; Expert Reporter Certificate, Pacific Northwest Reporters Association, 1969; Army Commendation Medal, 1945; Certified Shorthand Reporter Certificate. Address: 800 Fourth Street, Southwest, Apartment N-801, Washington, D.C. 20024.

M Eugene Olsen

Olsen, Marian Sander

Personal: Born January 11, 1921; Daughter of Cornelius Hoving and Virginia Petterson Sander; Married Clair Boyd Olsen; Mother of Taunya Martin, Debra Berman, Chad, Terrell, Heidi. Education: Associate B.S., Weber Junior College, 1941; B.S., Utah State Agricultural College, 1943; Instructor's Certificate, Red Cross Aquatic and First Aid School, 1944. Career: Winter Assistant Director, Women's Recreation, Logan City, Utah, 1942-43; Student Assistant, Physical Education Department, Utah State Agricultural College, 1942-43; Summer Women's Recreation Supervisor, Hill Air Force Base, 1943; Weber High School Girls Physical Education, Dance, Health Instructor, 1943-44; Field Red Cross Swimming Instructor, 1944; Women's Recreational Director, Ogden City, Utah, 1944-45; Box Elder High School Girls Physical Education, Dance, Health Instructor, 1947-49; Writer, Sports Column for Campus Newspaper, Utah State Agricultural College, 1942-43; Composed and Directed Student Assembly to Climax Mother-Daughter Week, Utah State Agricultural College, 1943; 4 Original Creative Dances for Mid-Year Circus, Brigham City, Utah, 1949; Original Dance Interpretation of "Ferdinand the Bull", 1949; Directed and Composed Youth Theater Group, Dugway Proving Grounds, Utah, 1956; Co-Authored and Directed "Up the Attic Stairs", 1976; Researcher and Tableau Director of "Good Grief It's a Brass Band" or "Mama Why is Papa So Confused?", 1977; In Charge of Creative Writing Contest, Short Stories and Poetry for Elementary Children for Tooele County, 1979. Community Activities: Utah State Agricultural College (vice president of women's dorm 1943-44); College Women's Association (board of directors 1943-44); Dugaway Parent Teacher Association (secretary 1959-60); Fort Douglas Womens Club (program chairman 1961-62); American Association of University Women (Tooele Branch: second vice president 1977-78, first vice president 1978-79, president 1979-80; State of Utah: nominating committee 1980-81); Utah Girl Scouts of America (brownie leader: Dugway 1953-56, Tooele 1961-63; junior leader: Dugway 1956-58, Tooele 1963-65; cadet leader: Dugway 1958-60, Tooele 1965-69; neighborhood chairman, 1970-73; state board of directors, 1963-64; chairman for Tooele County drive for clothing for needy Indians, 1962; chairman for Tooele Toys for Tots Christmas party, 1966-68; director of pageant "Through the Years with Juliette Low" 1968; Director of day camp, 1973; chairman international day featuring Italy, 1971). Religion: Church of Jesus Christ of Latter Day Saints: Ogden Stake Board in Charge of Glenner Girls, 1943-45; Grantsville Stake Sunday School Board, 1958-60; North Tooele Stake Board Member in Charge of Leadership of Laurel Girls Teachers, 1960-65; North Tooele Stake Relief Society Board Member in Charge of Cultural Refinement Leadership, 1967-71; North Tooele Stake Relief Society Counselor in the Presidency, 1971-73; Counselor in the Second Ward Church Relief Society Presidency for Three Presidents, 1974-79. Honors and Awards: Silver Plate Engraved for Conducting the Youth Theater Group, 1956; Girl Scout Statuette, Dugway Proving Ground Troop, 1960; Girl Scout Statuette, Tooele Girls Scouts, 1973; Listed in *Personalities of the West and Midwest, The World Who's Who of Women; Dictionary of International Biography*. Address: 526 N. Nelson, Tooele, Utah 84074.

Olson, John Bennet Jr

Professor Emeritus. Personal: Born February 13, 1917; Son of John Bennet and Hedwig Christina Matthilda Munthe Olson (both deceased); Married Dorothy Daggett; Father of Christina Jane Loren Leslie, Mary Carol. Education: B.S. cum laude, Beloit College, 1938; M.S. 1941, Ph.D. 1950, University of California-Los Angeles. Military: Served in the United States Army, 1945-46. Career; Research Assistant, Scripps Institution of Oceanography; Research Engineer, Douglas Aircraft Company; Research Associate, Cardiology, Children's Hospital, Los Angeles; Senior Research Fellow, Chemistry, Tech.; Chairman, Natural Sciences, Shimer College; Professor Emeritus, Purdue University. Organizational Memberships: New York Academy of Sciences; Indiana Academy of Sciences; Association of Midwest College Biology Teachers (vice president, 1963; president, 1964); Indiana College Biology Teachers Association (president, 1975); National Association for Research in Science Teaching; National Association of Biology Teachers; Member, Number of Other Organizations. Community Activities: Mental Health Association, Carroll County, Illinois (vice president, 1961-64); Friends Service Committee (public speaker, 1957-58); Speakers Bureau, Indiana Academy of Science, 1965-70; National Science Foundation (panelist, 1963-72); National Institute for Campus Ministry (workshop leader, 1979); Thomas Jefferson Gallery, Santa Monica, California (director, 1943-45); Watson's Crick Gallery, Purdue University (director, 1974-80). Religion: Christian Science Church, 1920-38; Unitarian-Universalist, 1950 to present; Board Member, University Church of Purdue, 1972-78; Volunteer, Lafayette Urban Ministry, 1967 to present. Honors and Awards: Professor of the Year, 1972, Association of Midwest

College Biology Teachers; Distinguished Service Award, Beloit College Alumni Association, 1973; Best Painting in Show, First in Oils, First & Second in Enamels, Barnsdahl Park Gallery, Los Angeles, 1957. Address: 416 South Chauncey, West Lafayette, Indiana 47906.

O'Malley, William J

Administrator. Personal: Born October 27, 1915; Married Wini Shaw. Career: Owner, Lemon and Orange Grove, Pauma Valley, California; Treasurer, Hellinger Theater, New York City; Board Member, Secretary, Sceptre Travel International; Backer of Several Musical Shows. Organizational Memberships: Catholic Actors Guild of America (life member; chairman, board of directors); Actors Fund of America (life member); Ziegfeld Club (advisory board); The Institute of the American Musicals, Inc. (advisory board); The Thalians, California; The American Film Institute; George M. Cohan Awards (chairman, 4 times). Community Activities: Will Rogers Hospital Fund; St. Benedicts College Alumni (past president, New York chapter); Benedictine College Alumni (vice president, New York chapter); Benevolent Protective Order of Elks #1; Ancient Order of Hibernians; American Biographical Institute Research Association (life patron); Association for Help of Retarded Children; American Security Council (national advisory board); The Spirit of '76 Society; Pop Warner Little League (board of trustees); Friendly Sons of St. Patrick; United States Olympic Society; New York Athletic Club; Holy Name Society; International Alliance of Theatrical State Employers-Moving Picture Operators of the United States and Canada (sergeant-at-arms, local #751); Manhattan Repertory Company (board of directors); American Repertory Theatre, Inc. (board of directors). Honors and Awards: Award of Appreciation, St. Benedicts College; Knight of Malta; Irish American Institute of San Francisco, California. Address: 43-07 39th Place, Sunnyside, New York 11104.

Oman, LaFel Earl

District Judge Pro Tempore, Lawyer. Personal: Born May 7, 1912; Son of Mr. and Mrs. Earl A. Oman (both deceased); Married Arlie Giles; Father of Sharon O. Beck, Phyllis O. Bowman, Conrad LaFel, Kester LaFel. Education: J.D., University of Utah College of Law. Military: Served in the United States Navy, 1943-46, attaining the rank of Lieutenant. Career: District Judge Pro Tempore, Special Master, Lawyer; Former Positions include Justice and Chief Justice, New Mexico Supreme Court; Judge and Senior Judge, New Mexico Court of Appeals; Lawyer. Organizational Memberships: American Judicature Society (director, 1970-74); Continuing Legal Education of New Mexico; Conference of Chief Justices; American Bar Association; New Mexico Bar Association; Utah Bar Association; Dona Ana County Bar Association (president, 1952-53); First Judicial District Bar Association; Southwestern Legal Foundation (local representative); Law-Science Academy; Defense Research Institute; American Trial Lawyers Association; Phi Alpha Delta Fraternity; Institute of Judicial Administration; Section of Judicial Administration, American Bar Association (New Mexico membership chairman); Appellate Judges Conference; National Legal Aid and Defender Association; American Law Institute. Community Activities: Rotary Club of Las Cruces (member, 1948-66; president, 1952-53); Rotary Club of Santa Fe (member, 1966 to present; director, 1973-74; vice president, 1975-76; president, 1976-77); New Mexico Historical Society; Historical Society of Santa Fe; Santa Fe Opera Guild; Visiting Nurse Service, Inc. (director and vice president, 1980 to present); Assistant City Attorney, Las Cruces, 1958-59; City Attorney (T or C, 1959-61); New Mexico Board of Bar Examiners, 1964-66; New Mexico Judicial Standards Commission, 1968-70, 1971-72; New Mexico Judicial Council, 1972-76; New Mexico Court of Appeals, 1966-70; New Mexico Supreme Court, 1971-77; Chief Justice, New Mexico Supreme Court, 1976-77. Religion: St. John's United Methodist Church, Santa Fe, Chairman of Administrative Board 1972-74, Board of Trustees, Pastor Parish Relations, Finance Committee, Sunday School Teacher. Honors and Awards: Herbert Harley Award, American Judicature Society; Judicial Service Award, Outstanding Service Award, New Mexico State Bar Association; Senate Memorial 35, 33rd Legislature of the State of New Mexico, Commendation for Outstanding Work and Great Contributions to the People of the State of New Mexico and the Administration of Justice; Testimonial of Gratitude and Respect, New Mexico Judicial Council, 1977; Credential in Recognition and Appreciation of Active Service on the Supreme Court of New Mexico, Judicial Conference of New Mexico. Address: 510 Camino Pinones, Santa Fe, New Mexico 87501.

Yoshiaki Omura

Omura, Yoshiaki

Professor, Editor, Physician, Administrator. Personal: Born March 28, 1934; Son of Tsunejiro and Minako Omura. Education: Pre-Medical Studies undertaken at Nihon University, Department of Electrical Engineering, 1952-54; B.Sc., Department of Applied Physics, Waseda University, 1957; M.D., School of Medicine, Yokohama City University, 1958; Graduate Experimental Physics, Columbia University, 1960-63; Sc.D., Medicine, Departments of Pharmacology and Surgery, College of Physicians and Surgeons, Columbia University, 1965. Career; Rotating Intern, Tokyo University Hospital, 1958; Rotating Intern, Norwalk Hospital, Norwalk, Connecticut, 1959; Research Fellow, Cardiovascular Surgery, Columbia University, 1960; Resident Physician in Surgery, Francis Delafield Hospital, Cancer Institute of Columbia University, 1961-65; Research Consultant, Orthopedic Surgery, Columbia University, 1965-66; Research Consultant, Pharmacology Department, New York Down State Medical Center, State University of New York, 1966; Emergency Room Physician (part-time), Englewood Hospital, N.J., 1965-76; Assistant Professor of Pharmacology and Instructor in Surgery, New York Medical College, 1966-72; Consultant, Lincoln Hospital Drug De-Toxificaton Program, 1973-74; Visiting Professor, University of Paris, Summers 1973-77; Maitre de Recherche, Distinguished Foreign Scientist Program of INSERM of the French Government, 1977; Visiting Research Professor, Deparment of Electrical Engineering, Manhattan College, 1962 to present; Director of Medical Research, Heart Disease Research Foundation, 1972 to present; Adjunct Professor, Deparment of Pharmacology, Chicago Medical School, 1982 to present; Editor-in-Chief, *Acupuncture and Electro-Therapeutics Research, The International Journal*, 1974 to present; President, International College of Acupuncture and Electro-Therapeutics (Chartered College, New York State Department of Education), 1980 to present; Editorial Consultant, *Journal of Electrocardiology*, 1980 to present. Organizational Memberships: New York Cardiological Society (fellow); American College of Angiology (fellow); American College of Acupuncture (fellow); International College of Acupuncture and Electro-Therapeutics (fellow); New York Academy of Sciences; American Society for Artificial Internal Organs. Community Activities: Children's Art and Science Workshop, New York (chairman, science division, 1971 to present); Francis Delafield Hospital, (chairman, Columbia University affiliation and community medicine committee community board, 1974-75); New York Japanese Medical Society (president, 1963-75); Chairman, Electrical and Non-Electrical Acupuncture Seminar and Workshop, accredited by New York State Board of Medicine and Dentistry for acupuncture licensing, 1978 to present. Published Works: Author of over 100 original research articles in medical and scientific journals and educational publications, in addition to several books. Honors and Awards: Research Fellow, Cardiovascular Surgery, Columbia University, 1960; Research Grant, American Cancer Institute, 1961-63; Faculty Grant, John Polacek Foundation, 1966-72; National Institute of Health Research Grant, 1967-72; Research Grant, Heart Disease Research Foundation, 1972 to present; Maitre de Recherche, Distinguished Foreign Scientist Program of INSERM (National Institute of Health and Medical Research) of the French Government, Research Unit University of Paris, #95, Nancy, France, 1977; Listed in *American Men and Women of Science, Dictionary of International Biography, Men of Achievement, Notable Americans of 1976-77, International Medical Who's Who, Biographical Roll of Honor (first edition).* Address: 800 Riverside Drive (8-I), New York, New York 10032.

O'Neal, Robert Palmer

Aircraft Aeronautical Engineer. Personal: Born September 20, 1912, in Tonapah, Nevada; Son of Dr. Robert McWilliam and Aimee Ford O'Neal; Married Nancy Anne Monroe (deceased), Married Penelope Cuther, December 26, 1980; Father of Robert Monroe, Nancy Burke Arthur, Patricia McWilliam Colyer, Peggy Ford Perry. Education: A.B. 1935, M.A. Thermodynamics 1935, Occidental College; Advanced Extension Science Courses, 1949-51, University of North Carolina; Graduate, Aviation Ground Officers School, 10th Basic Class, November 1944. Military: Service in the United States Marine Corps, achieving the rank of Lieutenant Colonel. Career: Affiliated with Pratt and Whitney Aircraft Corporation and Monroe Chemical Company; Assigned to Marine Corps Air Station, Cherry Point, North Carolina, Which has been a Base of Operations for 33 years; Aircraft Maintenance Officer and Aircraft Maintenance Management Officer, A.W.S.S. Staff, F.M.F.L.A.N.T., Aviation Weapons Section, Norfolk, Virginia; Directed the Installation, Testing and Maintenance of Several Innovative Aircraft Engines and Developed F4B, A4 and F14 Aircraft; Officer and Instructor, has Served at Marine Corps Bases in Korea, South Vietnam, Japan and on Carriers *U.S.S. Forrestal*, *U.S.S. Saratoga*, *U.S.S. Ranger*, *U.S.S. Constellation*; Appointed Marine Liasion Officer, Commander Fleet Air Western Pacific, 1967-69; Fleet Marine Forces Atlantic Representative to Rewrite MAC/DAC Aircraft Maintenance Course and Four-Volume Naval Aviation Maintenance Program Manual, 1970. Organizational Memberships: American Institute of Aeronautics and Astronautics; American Chemical Society; American Association for the Advancement of Science; Society of American Military Engineers; American Ordinance Society; American Management Association; North Carolina Academy of Sciences; American Security Council; Engineers Joint Council Inc.; Institute of American Strategy. Community Activities: Fleet Reserve Association; Veterans of Foreign Wars; Marine Corps Aviation Association; Delta Upsilon; Optimists International; International Platform Association; Blue Key Association; Occidental College Alumni Association; Pine Knoll Shores Corporation, President; Director, Civil Defense, Pine Knoll Shores. Honors and Awards: Fellow, International Biographical Association; Life Member, American Biographical Society; Life Patron, American Biographical Society; Life Patron, American Biographical Institute; 19 Military Citations, including, Bronze Star with Combat V, Navy Letter of Commendation with Combat V, Navy Unit Citation; Listed in *Royal Blue Book*, *Who's Who of Leaders in American Science*, *Who's Who in the South*, *Dictionary of International Biography*, *Two Thousand Men of Achievement*, *International Register of Profiles*, *Notable Americans of the Bicentennial Era*, *International Who's Who of Intellectuals*, *Book of Honor*, *Community Leaders and Noteworthy Americans*. Address: Route 1, Pine Knoll Shores, Morehead City, North Carolina 28557.

O'Neil, Penelope Felton

University Treasurer. Personal: Born June 20, 1947; Daughter of Joseph P. Felton and Reva Bota; Married William J. O'Neil; Mother of Michael Sean. Education: B.S.B.A., Marketing, Ohio State University, 1971; M.B.A., Marketing, Xavier University, 1978. Career: Assistant Treasurer, Ohio State University, 1979 to present; Special Assignment as General Manager of Ohio State University Bookstores Retail Chain Operation, 1982 to present; Director of Administrative Services, Office of Registration Services, Ohio State University, 1977-79; Assistant Director of Systems and Administration, Registration Services, Ohio State University, 1976-77. Address: 7721 Riverside Drive, Dublin, Ohio 43017.

Margaret C Orlich

Oppelt, Kurt

Sports Psychologist/Consultant. Personal: Born March 18, 1932; Son of R. Oppelt; Married Cathleen Pavlis; Father of Kurt, Chris. Education: Studies in Sport Teaching 1953, Business 1960, Vienna, Austria; UBH, California, Ph.D., Education. Career: Private Practice in Sport Psychology, Management Consulting; Former Professor, Pennsylvania State University; Specialist, President John F. Kennedy Physical Fitness Program; Coach, Royal Dutch Figure Skating Team; Director, JKO Packaging Company; Founder of Ice Skating Therapy. Organizational Memberships: American College of Sports Medicine; American Public Health Association; National Recreational Park Society; National Recreational Therapy Association; American Society of Professional Consultants. Community Activities: Pennsylvania Association of Retired Citizens (vice president); Ice Skating Institute of America (chairman, committee on the handicapped); International Council on Therapeutic Ice Skating (executive vice president); Orlando Area Chamber of Commerce (education and hospitality committees; local school board advisory committee). Honors and Awards: Austrian, European, World Champion and Olympic Gold Medal Winner in Pair Skating, 1956; Olympic Hall of Fame; Ice Skating Hall of Fame; Sportsman of the Year; Ring of Republic; Key to City of Charlotte, North Carolina; Listed in *International Who's Who in Education*, *Men of Achievement*. Address: P. O. Box 4541, Winter Park, Florida 32793.

O'Reilly, Philip Francis

Financial Executive. Personal: Born February 27, 1941; Son of Edward F. and Therese A. Hoenninger O'Reilly (both deceased); Married Caryl Ann Maloy; Father of Philip F. Jr., Meegan E., Matthew C., Brooke A., Lindsay C. Education: B.S.B.A., Georgetown University, 1963; Attended Pace University Graduate School of Business, 1974-76. Career: Cable Television Financial Executive; Conference Faculty Member, Foundation for Accounting Education, 1981-82; Adjunct Instructor, New York University Graduate School of Business, 1974-76; Adjunct Instructor, Pace University, 1973-76; Certified Public Accountant, 1964-75. Organizational Memberships: American Institute of CPAs; New York State Society of CPAs; American Accounting Association; American Management Association. Community Activities: Martin Luther King Hertitage House, 1968-71); Cedar Grove Beach Club, Inc. (governor, 1972 to present; vice-president, 1976-77; president, 1978-79). Religion: Roman Catholic. Honors and Awards: Listed in *Who's Who in Finance and Industry*. Address: Eight Murray Place, Staten Island, New York 10304.

Orland, Henry

Composer, Conductor, Professor, Writer. Personal: Born April 23, 1918; Son of Theodore Orland, Hedwig Weill (both deceased). Education: B.Mus.; M.Mus.; Ph.D. Military: Served in the United States Army as Liaison Officer in the European Theatre during World War II. Career: Professor of Music and Department Chairman; Literary Critic; Conductor, Symphony Orchestras and Choruses. Honors and Awards: Pi Kappa Lambda; Purple Heart, 5 Campaign Stars, United States Army; Delius Prize, Composition; Chicago Music Critics Award, Composition; MacDowell Foundation Fellow; Fromm Foundation Fellow; Listed in *Personalities of America*. Address: 21 Bon Price, St. Louis-Olivette, Missouri 63132.

Orlich, Margaret Roberta Carlson

Administrator. Personal: Born February 27, 1917; Daughter of Mr. and Mrs. Henry J. Carlson (both deceased); Married Eli Orlich.

Education: B.S. 1939, M.A. 1955, University of Minnesota; Ed.D., California Western University, 1982. Career: Safety Education Program Director, University of Minnesota-Duluth; Former High School Teacher, Librarian, High School Principal, Superintendent of Schools, Supervising Teacher for University of Minnesota and Wisconsin, World Tour Director for College of St. Scholastica (Duluth). Organizational Memberships: Council of Presidents of National Organizations (national president, 1978-80); Alpha Delta Kappa (national and international president, 1971-73; international field representative; organized over 50 chapters in the United States, Canada, Thailand); National Association of Women Highway Safety Leaders (national board of directors, 1978-80); Minnesota Association of Women Highway Safety Leaders (first vice president, 1980-82; programming leader); National Safety Council; National Education Association (life member; served on curriculum committee; past local president); American Federation of Teachers (past local vice president); American Association of University Women (local international relations chairman, 1980-82); St. Louis County Historial Society; International Federation of Business and Professional Women's Clubs (past local president; various local and state committees); Campus Women Educators Association. Community Activities: 20th Century Club, General Federation of Women's Clubs (local president, 1980-82; 8th District president, 1982-84; county federation secretary, 1980-84); Head of the Lakes United Nations Association (founder, 1962; treasurer; membership chairman); Head of the Lakes World Affairs Council (co-founder, 1979; treasurer); Young Men's Christian Association (international committee, 1977 to present); Young Women's Christian Association (life member; various committees since 1970); League of Women Voters (unit leader, 8 years; number of local committees); Parent Teacher Student Association; Mayor's Committee on the United Nations; Assisted Nine Foreign Students to Graduate from the University of Minnesota and the University of Wisconsin; donations to Duluth's Depot, Duluth's Symphony, Friend of the Library, Duluth's Playhouse, St. Louis County Historical Society, Various Educational Television Stations, Various Funds. Honors and Awards: National Award on Membership American Association of the United Nations, 1965; Distinguished Service Awards from 3 Different Mayors of Duluth; Duluth's Hall of Fame Finalist, 1970; Feature in *Ladies Home Journal*, July 1970; National Federation of Business and Professional Women's United Nations Fellowship Award, 1970; State Business and Professional Women's Outstanding Service Award in International Relations, 1971; Y.M.C.A. Plaque for Service to Youth, 1974; Meritorious Service Plaque, Alpha Delta Kappa, 1975; United Nations Peace Award, 1975; Outstanding Sevice Plaque for Assisting the Handicapped, 1976. Address: 421 Anderson Road, Duluth, Minnesota 55811 and Department of Industrial and Technical Studies, University of Minnesota, Duluth, Minnesota 55812.

Ortiz, Araceli

Araceli Ortiz

Professor. Personal: Born January 15, 1937, in Culebra Island, Puerto Rico; Daughter of Jesus M. Ortiz (deceased) and Pura Martinez; Married Jesus Latimer; Mother of Paul. Education: Graduate of Colegio San Antonio (High School); B.S., University of Puerto Rico, 1958; D.D.M., University of Puerto Rico, 1962; Resident in General Pathology, University District Hospital, Puerto Rico, 1962-65; M.S.D., Specialty in Oral Pathology, Indiana University, 1967. Career: McGill University, Montreal, Canada, 1967-73; Professor, School of Dentistry, University of Puerto Rico, 1973 to present; Guest Lecturer, Forensic Odontology for the Interamerican University Law School, 1975 to present; Extensive Lecturer and Table Clinician in the United States, Canada, Puerto Rico and South America; Producer of 30 Minute Public Service Television Program, "Sonrie Puerto Rico". Organizational Memberships: American Academy of Oral Pathology (diplomate); American Board of Medicine (diplomate); American Board of Forensic Odontology (diplomate); American Dental Association; College of Dental Surgeons, Puerto Rico; American Academy of Oral Medicine; Canadian Academy of Oral Pathology; Canadian Academy of Oral Medicine; American Society of Forensic Sciences; Canadian Society of Forensic Odontology; Puerto Rico Society of Periodontology; Beta Beta Beta; Association of Women Dentists of Puerto Rico; Association for Educational Communications and Technology; American Cancer Society. Community Activities: Zonta International (area V director, district XI, 1980-82; president 1979-80); National Institute of Health, United States Department of Health, Education and Welfare (clinical care training committee, 1972-73); Producer and Moderator for Public Service Television Program on Dental Health. Religion: Roman Catholic. Honors and Awards: Public Service Program "Sonrie Puerto Rico" Chosen as Best Public Service Program of the Year (instructional), Tele Radial Institute of Ethics of Puerto Rico, 1978, 1980, 1981, Bronze Medal at the 25th International Film and Television Festival of New York, 1982; Distinguished Alumni, Colegio San Antonio, 1964; Distinguished Alumni, University of Puerto Rico School of Dentistry, 1965; Distinguished Alumni Association of Student Clinicians American Dental Association, 1966; Outstanding Lady of 1976, Chamber of Commerce, Puerto Rico; Distinguished Lady of the Year, 1977, Federation of Journalists and Press Writers of Puerto Rico; 1980 Faculty Advisor Award, Alumni Association of Student Clinicians of the American Dental Association; Distinguished Woman Dentist, American Association of Women Dentists, 1979; Consultant in Oral Pathology and Oral Medicine, Veterans Administration Hospital, Puerto Rico, 1973 to present. Address: Condominio Seqovia Apartment 410, Hato Rey, Puerto Rico 00918.

Oryshkevich, Roman Sviatoslav

Physician, Educator, Professor. Personal: Born August 5, 1928, in Olesko, Ukraine; Son of Simeon and Caroline Deneshchuk Oryshkevich; Married Oksana Lishchynsky, 1962; Father of Marta, Mark, Alexandra. Education: D.D.S. 1952, M.D. 1953, University of Heidelberg; West German Licensures to Practice Medicine and Surgery, 1953, Dentistry 1954; Post-Graduate Studies in Experimental Cancer Research Institute of Rupert-Charles University, earning Ph.D. cum laude 1955; Rotating Internship 1955-56, Coney Island Hospital, Brooklyn, New York; Resident-Fellowship, New York University Hospital-Bellevue Medical Center, New York City, and Western Reserve University affiliated Hospitals, Cleveland, Ohio. Career: Clinical Instructor 1962, Assistant Professor, Associate Clinical Professor 1975 to present, University of Illinois Affiliated Hospitals Integrated Residency Training Program in Physical Medicine and Rehabilitation; Assistant Chief 1961, Acting Chief 1974, Chief of Rehabilitation Medicine Service 1975 to present, Veterans Administration West Side Medical Center; Certified in Electromyography and Electrodiagnosis, 1964; Diplomate, American Board of Physical Medicine and Rehabilitation, 1966. Organizational Memberships: Ukrainian Medical Association of North America (secretary 1971-75, president-elect, 1975-77; president, 1977-79; Illinois Chapter); Illinois Society of Physical Medicine and Rehabilitation (secretary-treasurer, 1977-78; vice president and president-elect, 1978-79; president, 1979-80); World Federation of Ukrainian Medical Association (elected first executive secretary of science and research, 1977-79); Ukrainian World Medical Museum in Chicago (founder, 1977; elected first president, 1979); Chicago Society of Physical Medicine and Rehabilitation (elected first president, 1978); Ukrainian Academy of Medical Sciences (founder, 1979; elected first president, 1979-80); *Chicago Medicine Journal* (specialty consultant to editorial board in physical medicine and rehabilitation); American Museum of Physical Medicine and Rehabilitation (founder, 1980; first president 1978-); American Academy of Physical Medicine and Rehabilitation (fellow); Association of Academic Physiatrists; American Association of University Professors; American Congress of Rehabilitation Medicine; American Association of Electromyography and Electrodiagnosis; American Medical Writers Association; Association of Medical Rehabilitation Directors and Coordinators; Biofeedback Research Society of America; Illinois Society of Physical Medicine and Rehabilitation; Chicago Society of Physical Medicine and Rehabilitation; National Association of Veterans Administration Physicians; International Rehabilitation Medicine Association; International Society of Electrophysiological Kinesiology; International Association of University Professors and Lecturers; Federation of American Scientists. Religion: Ukrainian Catholic Church. Honors and Awards: Listed in *International Who's Who in Community Service, Notable Americans, International*

Who's Who of Intellectuals, Men of Achievement, Book of Honor, and many others. Address: 1819 North 78 Court, Elmwood Park, Illinois 60635.

Osborn, Prime F III

Executive. Personal: Born July 31, 1915; Son of Prime Francis and Anne Fowkes Osborn (both deceased); Married Grace Hambrick; Father of Prime F. IV, Mary Anne. Education: J.D. 1939, LL.D. (honorary) 1970, University of Alabama, Tuscaloosa. Military: Served in the United States Army, 1941-46, attaining the rank of Lieutenant Colonel of Artillery. Career: Assistant Attorney General, State of Alabama, 1939-41; Commerce Attorney, Gulf, Mobile and Ohio Railroad, Mobile, 1946-51; General Solicitor, Louisville and Nashville Railroad, Kentucky, 1951-57; Vice President and General Counsel, Atlantic Coast Line Railroad Company, Wilmington, North Carolina and Jacksonville, Florida, 1957-67; Vice President, Law, Seaboard Coastline Railroad Company, Jacksonville, Florida, 1967-69; President, Seaboard Coastline Railroad, 1970-72, 1974-78; President, Seaboard Coastline Industries, Inc., 1970-78; President and Chief Executive Officer, Louisville and Nashville Railroad Company, 1972-74; President and Chief Executive Officer, Seaboard Coast Line Industries, Inc., 1977-78; Chairman and Chief Executive Officer, Seaboard Coast Line Industries, Inc., Seaboard Coast Line Railroad, L & N Railroad, 1978-80; Chairman and Chief Executive Officer, Seaboard Coast Line Industries, Inc., 1980 to present; Chairman, Seaboard Coast Line Railroad, Louisville and Nashville Railroad, 1980 to present; Chairman, CSX Corporation, 1980 to 1982; Chairman (retired) CSX Corporation, 1982 to present; Alico Land Development Company, Seaboard Coast Line Industries, First National Bank of Louisville, Kentucky Trust Company, First Kentucky Corporation (1974-80), James Center Development Company, Ethyl Corporation, Atlantic National Bank (1960-72), State Planters Bank (1970-72), Florida Publishing Company. Community Activities: University of Alabama National Alumni Association (executive committee; national vice president, 1974-75); Boy Scouts of America (president, north Florida council, 1962-66; chairman, region six, 1965-69; regional executive committee, national executive board, national railroad committee on scouting, national exploring committee chairman, council executive board); Greater Jacksonville Area Chamber of Commerce (president, 1970-71); Greater Louisville Area Chamber of Commerce (director, 1972-74); United Fund of Louisville (director, 1972-74); United Fund of Jacksonville (director, 1962-70; senior vice president, 1971); Young Americans for Freedom (national advisory council); Protestant Episcopal Theological Seminary in Virginia (trustee, 1963-68); Sweet Briar College (board of overseers and director, 1968-77); Jacksonville Episcopal High School (director and trustee, 1969-72); Louisville Salvation Army (board of advisors, 1965-71); Jacksonville Salvation Army (board of advisors, 1965-71); National Advisory Council, Salvation Army, (chairman, 1978 to present); Southern States Industrial Council (executive committee; vice president); Spirit of '76 Foundation (advisory council); Berry College (board of visitors, 1972-77); Young Life Advisory Committee; Jacksonville University (board of trustees, 1963-77); State of Florida Governor's Advisory Council on Economic Development; Dean's Advisory Council, Purdue University; Florida Council of 100; Saint Vincent's Medical Center (lay advisory board); Public Charities; Freedoms Foundation at Valley Forge; Sigma Alpha Epsilon (president, Alabama Mu Chapter); Omicron Delta Kappa (vice president); Beta Gamma Sigma; Society of Colonial Wars; Sons of Confederate Veterans; Southern Society of New York; Rotary Club of Jacksonville; The Southern Academy of Letters, Arts and Sciences; Military Order of the World Wars; American Legion; Veterans of Foreign Wars; Sons of the American Revolution; Military Order of Stars and Bars. Religion: Episcopal. Honors and Awards: Man of the Year, Jacksonville, Florida, 1962; Silver Beaver Award 1965, Silver Antelope Award 1967, Boy Scouts of America; Management Award, Sales and Marketing Executive Association, 1970; Silver Buffalo Award, Boy Scouts of America, 1972; Religious Heritage of America Award, 1973; Bicentennial Brotherhood Award, National Conference of Christians and Jews, 1976; Award of Merit, Alabama State Bar, 1977; Man of the South, 1978; Executive of the Day, University of North Florida, 1978; Executive in Residence, Auburn University, 1979; Honorary President, Troy State University; William Booth Award, Salvation Army; Listed in *Who's Who in America, Who's Who in Railroading, Who's Who in Commerce and Industry, Who's Who in Religion, Who's Who in the Southeast, Who's Who in the South and Southwest, Dictionary of International Biography, National Register of Prominent Americans, Community Leaders of America, Men of Achievement, Book of Honor, Who's Who in the World,* Others. Address: 5005 Yacht Club Road, Jacksonville, Florida 32210.

Roy L Oswald

Osterholt, Walter B

Insurance Agent. Personal: Born December 5, 1918, in Fort Recovery, Ohio; Married Luella C. Hartings; Father of Mary Jane, Ruth Ann Proctor, Audrey Rose Woods, Nancy A. Hessler, Theresa M. Dirig, Karen Alice, Agnes C. Polston. Education: Graduate, Central High School, Fort Wayne, Indiana; Graduate, United States Army Infantry School, United States Army Command and General Staff College; American College-Charter Life Underwriter Degree; Certificates in Advanced Pension Planning, Advanced Estate Planning, Accounting and Business Valuation, Financial Counseling, Research Methods, American College. Military: Served in the United States Army, 1941-43, retiring with the rank of Lieutenant Colonel of the United States Army Reserves. Career: Joined New York Life Insurance Company, 1960, Agent's Advisory Council 1970-71. Organizational Memberships: National Association of Life Underwriters: Indiana Association of Life Underwriters; Fort Wayne Association of Life Underwriters (president, 1969-70; chairman, board of directors, 1970-71); Fort Wayne Estate Planning Council; American Society of Chartered Life Underwriters; Fort Wayne Chapter, Chartered Life Underwriters. Community Activities: Reserve Officers Association; Optimist International; Fort Wayne Rescue Mission; Downtown Optimist Club (president, 1967-68; attendance chairman, 1972; former member, board of directors); St. Vincent DePaul Society (past president, particular council of Fort Wayne); Board of Directors, Bishop Luers Catholic High School, Catholic Charities, St. Vincent Children's Services of Fort Wayne; St. Anne Homes (former member, board of directors); Knights of Columbus, 4th Degree; Children of the Resurrection Prayer Group (coordinator of leader team); Fort Wayne Rescue Mission (board of directors; vice president); Fort Wayne Chapter, The Full Gospel Businessman's Fellowship International. Religion: Ordained Deacon, Fort Wayne-South Bend Diocese, 1975; St. Hyacinth's Catholic Church, Member 1946 to present, Church Board, School Board, Trustees. Honors and Awards: National Quality Award, 18 years; National Sales Achievement Award, 12 years; NYLIC's Group Leader Award, 1969; Life Member, Indiana State Leaders Club; Fort Wayne Life Underwriter of the Year 1978, Life Underwriters Association; Man of the Year Award, New York Life Insurance Company, 1976; General Agent and Managers Association Agency Award, Man of the Year, 1976; Listed in *Who's Who in Finance and Industry, Men of Achievement.* Address: 3025 Reed Street, Fort Wayne, Indiana 46806

Oswald, Roy

Administrator. Personal: Born July 20, 1944; Son of Johnnie E. and Ruby C. Oswald. Education: B.S., Troy State University, 1969; Diploma in Graphic Arts, John Patterson Technical College, 1978. Military: Served in the United States Army, 1969-71, spending one year in Vietnam. Career: Owner and Manager, Rental Properties; Former Positions as Buyer, Sanitarian, Salesman, Social Worker. Organizational Memberships: International Academy of Poets; Academy of American Poets; American Biographical Institute; International Biographical Association; Western World Haiku Society; Society of Christian Poets. Honors and Awards: Bronze Star with "V" Device; Air Medal; Four Army Commendation Medals with Two "V" Devices; Other Service Awards; Numerous Prizes and Awards for Poetry. Address: 4396 Wares Ferry Road, Montgomery, Alabama 36109.

Otto, Mary Vincent

Counselor, Nun. Personal: Born August 5, 1932, in Scotland, Texas; Daughter of Edward H. and Margaret M. Meurer Otto. Education: B.A., 1965, and M.S., 1979, both from Our Lady of the Lake University, San Antonio, Texas. Career: Member Sisters of St. Mary of Namur, 1949-81; Joined Sisters for Christian Community, December 1981; Various Teaching and Administrative Positions in Parochial Elementary and Junior High Schools of Sisters of St. Mary, Texas and California, 1949-75; Resurrection School, Houston, Texas: Assistant Principal 1954-58, Principal 1958-59 and 1970-73; Field Director, Office of Camp Fire Girls, Wichita Falls, Texas, 1968-69; Guest Lecturer and Participant in Media Presentations on Mental Health Issues, 1976 to present; Private Practice in Family and Rahabilitation Counseling, Houston, 1979-81; Consultant to St. Thomas More Parish, Houston, 1979-81; Director of Family Life Services, St. Martin's Parish, Le Mesa, California, 1981 to present; Volunteer for the Southwest Unit, Bexar County (San Antonio, Texas) Mental Health-Mental Retardation Program, 1977-79; Board of Directors, Bexar County Mental Health Association, 1977-79; Board of Sponsors, Houston Holistic Health Association, 1979-81. Organizational Memberships: American Personnel and Guidance Association; Mental Health Association of San Diego County; National Rehabilitation Counseling Association; American Mental Health Counselors Association; Association for Religious and Value Issues in Counseling; National Alliance for Family Life, Inc.; National Assembly of Women Religious. Religion: Roman Catholic. Honors and Awards: Kenneth Donaldson Award; Listed in *Who's Who in the South and Southwest, Personalities of the South and Southwest, Personalities of America, Book of Honor, Community Leaders of America, Directory of Distinguished Americans, International Who's Who of Intellectuals, World's Who's Who of Women.* Address: 8633 La Mesa Blvd #80, La Mesa, California 92041.

Mary V Otto

Ovenfors, Carl-Olof Nils Sten

Professor of Radiology. Personal: Born September 26, 1923; Son of Carl (deceased) and Signe Olson; Married Aimee; Father of Claes Olof, Aimee. Education: Graduate of Nova Latin College, 1941; M.D. 1951, Ph.D. 1964, Docent 1964, Karolinska Institute Medical School, Stockholm, Sweden. Military: Served in the Swedish Navy as a Medical Officer, 1951-52, attaining the rank of Captain. Career: Chief of Department of Thoracic Radiology, Karalinska Institute, Stockholm, 1968-70; Chief of Radiology, Veterans Administration Center, San Francisco, 1970-77; Professor of Radiology, University of California Medical Center, San Francisco. Organizational Memberships: The Fleischmer Society (member, 1969 to present; chairman, rules committee, 1981 to present); North American Society for Cardiac Radiology; Radiology Society of North America; Society for Thoracic Radiology (founding member, 1982). Community Activities: University of California Medical Center, San Francisco (teaching and executive committees, 1970-77). Honors and Awards: Picker Research Fellow 1962-63, 1966-68, Picker Scholar 1961-62, The James Picker Foundation for Radiology Research. Address: 10 Fox Lane, San Anselmo, California 94960.

Overby, George Robert

University Chancellor. Personal: Born July 21, 1923, in Jacksonville, Florida; Son of T. E. Sr. and Virginia H. Overby (deceased). Education: B.A., Florida State University; M.Ed., Ed.S., University of Florida; Ph.D., Florida State University. Career: Chancellor, Freedom University, The University Without Walls; Former Positions include President, Christian Enterprises; Editor, *Christian Education;* Founder and President, The International Association for Christian Education. Organizational Memberships: American Association of Higher Education (life member); National Education Association of the United States (life member); American Association of School Administrators; National Association of Elementary School Principals; American Security Council; Citizens for Decency through Law; National Council for the Social Studies; Association of Supervision and Curriculum Development. Community Activities: American Biographical Institute Research Association (life patron); International Biographical Association (life patron); Intercontinental Biographical Association (life fellow); International Who's Who in Community Service (life fellow); United States Naval Association Museum (life member); Kappa Delta Pi (life member); Phi Delta Kappa (life member). Honors and Awards: Listed in *American Registry Series, International Who's Who of Intellectuals, International Register of Profiles, Book of Honor, Who's Who in the World, Who's Who in Community Service, Community Leaders and Noteworthy Americans, Who's Who in America, Who's Who in the East, Who's Who in the South and Southwest, Men and Women of Distinction, Directory of Distinguished Americans,* Others. Address: 5927 Windhover Drive, Orlando, Florida 32805.

Overby-Dean, Talulah Earle

Librarian. Personal: Born May 30, 1913, in Lumpkin, Georgia; Daughter of Taylor Earle Sr. and Jennie Hewett Overby. Education: B.A., University of Florida, 1950; M.A., Library Science, Appalachian State University, 1971; Doctoral Candidate, Freedom University, 1981. Career: Classroom Teacher, Elementary School, 1931-46; Visiting Teacher/School Case Worker, Public Schools, 1946-65; School Librarian, Elementary Schools, 1965-70; Head Librarian, Assistant Librarian, Christian School, 1974-75; Head Librarian, Miccoukee Community Library. Organizational Memberships: Duval County Teachers Association; Florida Education Association; National Education Association; Florida Education Association Section of Visiting Teachers; National Association of Visiting Teachers; National Association of Social Workers; Dade County Social Workers; Dade County School Librarians; Dade County Department of Audio-Visual Education; National Education Association Department of Aduio-Visual Education; Florida Library Association; Southwest Library Association; Delta Kappa Gamma Society International; Kappa Delta Pi. Community Activities: Federated Women's Club; Pilot Club International; National Congress of Parents and Teachers; Friends of the Library; International Association for Christian Education (charter member). Religion: Springfield Methodist Church, Sunday School Teacher, Member Board of Christian Education, Teacher/Speaker of Religious Education. Honors and Awards: Listed in *Dictionary of International Biography, World Who's Who of Women, Notable Americans, Personalities of the South, Who's Who in Library and Information Services, Who's Who in Florida, Contemporary Personalities.* Address: 2106 East Anderson Place, Orlando, Florida 32803.

Talulah E Overby-Dean

Overholser, J Homer Harold

Management and Investment Consultant, Executive. Personal: Born June 18, 1914; Son of Alden and Nora Overholser (both deceased); Married; Father of James Alan, Sharyl Ann. Education: Graduate of Springfield High School; Studies in Mechanical Engineering, Wittenberg College, 1935; 2 Years of Study in Aeronautical Engineering, University of California-Los Angeles, 1939-40. Career: Design Engineer, National Supply Company, 1935-36; Development Engineer, Chrysler Airtemp Division, 1936-38; Project Engineer, Vultee Aircraft Corp., 1938-39; Engineering Supervisor, Northrop Aircraft Corp., 1939-43; Chief Engineer 1943-46, Executive Vice President 1946-53, Hydro-Aire, Inc.; Vice President, Chairman of the Board, Skyline Caterine Corp., 1952-59; Vice President and Board Chairman, K & S Building Corp., 1952-56; Assistant General Manager, Pacific Division, Bendix Corp., 1953-58; Vice President, Director, Poly Industries Inc., 1959-60; Executive Vice President and Director, U.S. Systems Inc., 1961-62; President,

Chairman of the Board, Solar Systems, Inc., 1961-62; Vice President and Director, Buckingham Palace Corp., 1961-63; President and Chairman of the Board, Woodland Savings and Loan, 1961-63; Director, Casa Electronics Corp., 1961-62; President, Board Chairman, Corporation Service Inc., 1961-63; Vice President, Director, Woodlake Realty, Inc., 1982 to present; Vice President, Director, S.O.M. Corp., 1964 to present; Director, S.D.L. Optical Corp., 1968-70; President, The Overholser Foundation, 1968 to present; Secretary, Director, Chairman of Finance Committee, Varadyne Industries, Inc., 1969 to present; Chairman of the Board and President, Alphatec International Inc. 1977-79, National Golf Products Inc. 1977 to present, National Golf Media Inc. 1977 to present; Chairman of the Board and Executive Vice President, Franchise Associates, Inc., 1979 to present; Chairman of the Board, Secretary-Treasurer, Pusser's Inc., 1979 to present; Vice President and Chief Financial Officer, Vital Communications Inc., 1979 to present. Organizational Memberships: Institute of Aero Sciences; American Ordnance Association; American Society of Mechanical Engineers; American Institute of Management; American Helicopter Society; Air Force Association; Association of the United States Army; Registered California Professional Engineer; S.A.E. Fuel Valve Committee (chairman); American Society of Air Affairs. Community Activities: International Platform Association; Republican Party; North Hollywood Chamber of Commerce; Los Angeles Chamber of Commerce (aviation committee); Los Angeles County March of Dimes (industry chairman); Hollywood Chamber of Commerce; Lakeside Golf Club; Braemar Golf Club; Free and Accepted Masons; Lodge of Perfection 32nd Degree; Al Malaikah Shrine; Woodland Hills Shrine Club; Los Angeles County Museum of Art (patron member); San Fernando Wine and Food Society (chairman, board of governors); American Security Council (national voter advisory board); Los Angeles World Affairs Council; Sons of the American Revolution. Relgion: Church of God of Abrahamic Faith. Published Works: "Diversification in Business", *ASME Journal;* "Anti-Skid Braking System", *Aero Digest and Aviation Engineering;* Other Professional Articles. Honors and Awards: Certificate of Appreciation, National Foundation of Infantile Paralysis; Honorable Kentucky Colonel; Freedom Season Pioneer Award, Woodland Hills Chamber of Commerce; Certificate of Appreciation, Young Americans for Freedom; 2,000,000 Mile Club, United Airlines, 1957; Certificate of Merit for Distinguished Service in Business Development; Listed in *Who's Who in the World, Who's Who in America, Who's Who in California, Who's Who in the United States, Who's Who in Finance and Industry, Who's Who in the West, Who's Who in Business and Finance, Who's Who in Steel and Metals, Who's Who in California Business and Finance, World Who's Who in Commerce and Industry, Who's Who of Intellectuals, Directory of International Biography, Men of Achievement, Community Leaders of America, Directory of Distinguished Americans, Men and Women of Distinction, International Who's Who in Community Service, Businessman's Who's Who,* Many Others. Address: 4961 Palomar Drive, Tarzana, California 91356.

Oyler, Earl W

Vocal and Instrumental Supervisor. Personal: Son of Walter and Ethel Oyler (both deceased); Married Janet Marie; Father of Leiann. Education: B.M., James Millikin University, 1952; M.M., Illinois State University, 1956; Advanced Graduate Work, University of Illinois; Attending Lincoln Land Community College. Military: Served with the United States Army, Member and Vocalist of the United States Artillery Band in Japan and Korea. Career: Teacher of Vocal and Instrumental Music in Public Schools, 17 years; Band and Vocal Director, Tovey School, Tovey, Illinois; Formerly Vocal Director, Assumption Elementary and Junior High School, Assumption, Illinois; Vocal Supervisor, Elementary and High School Choral Director, Nokomis Community Unit School, Nokomis, Illinois; Vocal Director, Piper City School, Piper City, Illinois; Student of Computer Science, Electronic Data Processing and Business (Lincoln Land), Computer Languages of Cobol, Fortran, R.P.G. I and II, Basic, J.C.L. and Assembler. Organizational Memberships: Phi Theta Kappa; Alpha Beta Gamma; Decatur Area Music Teachers Association (president 1976-79); Nokomis Teachers Association (president, 1960-63); Illinois Education Association (representative of the general assembly, 3 years; vocalist, 2 years); Superintendents of the State of Illinois (vocalist); Illinois State Music Teachers Association, (member, former chairman, voice syllabus committee). Community Activities: Senior Olympics of the State of Illinois (vocalist); National Oratorical Society (vocalist); Taylorville Municipal Band (soloist); Springfield Municipal Band; Springfield Municipal Opera (vocal director, soloist, "1776"; vocalist, 1981 season, "Camelot"; vocal and dramatic lead, Mr. Bumble, "Oliver"); Oyler Family Historian (family farm manager). Religion: First Baptist Church of Taylorville, Deacon, Past Director of Music, Choir Director. Published Works: Words and Music for Bicentennial Song "1776 History"; Words and Music for Original Musical "The Tempo of the Times"; Official State Fair Song for State of Illinois; "Our Illinois, Our Land of Lincoln". Honors and Awards: Honorable Mention, American Song Festival, for "Off in the Distance" (a Christmas selection); Alpha Beta Gamma; Phi Theta Kappa; Music Scholarship to James Millikin University, 1948; State Certification in Organ and Piano; National Certification in Voice, Piano and Music Theory. Address: 620 Pauline Street, Taylorville, Illinois 62568.

Earl Oyler

Palmer, Arnold Daniel

Professional Golfer, Business Executive, Author. Personal: Born September 10, 1929, in Pennsylvania; Son of Milfred J. Deacon and Doris M. Palmer (both deceased); Married Winifred Walzer, 1954; Father of Margaret Anne Reintgen, Amy Lyn Saunders. Education: Attended Wake Forest University. Military: Served in the United States Coast Guard, 3 years. Career: Professional Golfer; President, Arnold Palmer Enterprises; President, Major Owner, Arnold Palmer Cadillac, Charlotte, North Carolina, and Arnold Palmer Motors, Latrobe, Pennsylvania; President, Sole Owner, Latrobe Country Club, 1971 to present; President, Principal Owner, Bay Hill Club and Lodge, Orlando, Florida, 1969 to present; Major Stockholder, Member of Board of Directors, ProGroup Inc., Sporting Good Manufacturer; Palmer Course Design; Arnold Palmer Aviation Charter Service. Organizational Memberships: Laurel Valley Golf Club; Arnold Palmer Enterprises (president, Division of National Broadcasting Company); Ironwood Country Club, Palm Desert, California (business associate); Westmoreland County, Pennsylvania, Airport Authority; United States Golf Association (national chairman, associates program; museum committee); Professional Golfers Association of America; Rolling Rock Club, Ligonier, Pennsylvania; Duquesne Club, Pittsburgh; Oakmont Country Club, Pennsylvania; Quail Hollow Country Club, Charlotte, North Carolina; Cherry Hills Country Club, Denver, Colorado; Lakeside Country Club, Hollywood, California; Wilshire Country Club, Los Angeles, California; Indian Wells Country Club, Palm Desert, California; Certified Business Jet Pilot. Community Activities: National Foundation of the March of Dimes (board of trustees; honorary national chairman, 1970); Latrobe Area Hospital, Pennsylvania (board of directors). Published Works: *Arnold Palmer Golf Book; Portrait of a Professional Golfer; My Game and Yours; Situation Golf; Go For Broke; Arnold Palmer's Best 54 Golf Holes.* Honors and Awards: Athlete of the Decade, 1960s, Association Press Poll; Winner, United States Amateur Championship, 1954; Hickok Athlete of the Year, 1960; Sportsman of the Year Trophy, *Sports Illustrated*, 1960; Charter Member, World Golf Hall of Fame, Pinehurst, North Carolina; American Golf Hall of Fame, Foxburg, Pennsylvania; Winner, Five West Penn Amateur Championships; Honorary Doctor of Laws Degree, Wake Forest University, National College of Education; Honorary Doctor of Humanities Degree, Thile College; Honorary Doctor of Humane Letters, Florida Southern College; Professional Golfers of America Hall of Fame; Bob Jones Award, United States Golf Association; William D. Richardson, Charles Bartlett Awards, Golf Writers Association of America; Herb Graffis Award, National Golf Foundation; Gold Tee Award, Metropolitan Golf Writers Association; Man of Silver Era, *Golf Digest*; Partner in Science Award, March of Dimes Birth Defects Foundation; P.G.A. Player of the Year, 1960, 1962; Vardon Trophy, 1961, 1962, 1964, 1967; United States Ryder Cup Team Member, 1961, 1963, 1965, 1967, 1971, 1973, and Team Captain 1963, 1975; Pennsylvania Sports Hall of Fame; Western Pennsylvania Sports Hall of Fame; Arthur J. Rooney Award, Catholic Youth Association, Pittsburgh; Lowman Humanitarian Award, Los Angeles; Theodore Roosevelt Award, National Collegiate Athletic Association; Old Tom Morris Award, Golf Course Superintendents of America; Distinguished Pennsylvanian, 1980; Winner, Canadian Open 1955, Panama Open 1956, Columbia Open 1956, Eastern Open 1956, Insurance City Open 1956, 1960, Houston Open 1957, Azalea Open 1957, Rubber City Open 1957, San Diego Open 1957, 1961, St. Petersburg Open 1958, Pepsi Open 1958, Masters Championship 1958, 1960, 1962, 1964, Oklahoma City Open 1959, 1964, United States Open Championship 1960, Mobile Open 1960, Baton Rouge Open 1960, 1961, Texas Open 1960, 1961, 1962, Canada Cup (with Partner Sam Snead) 1960, 1962, Pensacola Open 1960, 1963, Bob Hope Desert Classic 1960, 1962, 1968, 1971, 1973, Colonial National Invitational 1962, British Open Championship 1961, 1962, Tournament of Champions 1962, 1965, 1966, American Golf Classic 1962, 1967, Phoenix Open 1961, 1962, 1963, Cleveland Open 1963, Whitemarsh Open 1963, Australian Wills Masters 1963, Canada Cup (partner Jack Nicklaus) 1963, 1964, 1966, Los Angeles Open 1963, 1966, 1967, Thunderbird Classic 1963, 1967, World Cup (Partner, Jack Nicklaus) 1964, 1967, Australian Open 1966, Houston Champions International 1966, Professional Golfers Association Team Championship (Partner, Jack Nicklaus) 1966, 1970, 1971, Tucson Open 1967, World Cup International Trophy 1967, Kemper Open 19687, Heritage Classic 1969, Danny Thomas Diplomat Classic 1969, Citrus Open 1971, Westchester Classic 1971, Lancome Trophy (France) 1971, Spanish Open 1975, British Professional Golfers Association Championship 1975, Canadian Professional Golfers Association 1980, Professional Golfers Association Seniors 1980, United States Golf Association Senior Open 1981, Marlboro Classic 1981, Denver Post Champions of Golf 1982. Address: P.O. Box 52, Youngstown, Pennsylvania 15696-0052.

John D Palmer

Palmer, John David

Field Underwriter. Personal: Born January 25, 1936; Son of Cary D. Palmer; Married Robin West; Father of John David Jr., Elizabeth McMillan. Education: B.S., Business Administration, Northwestern University, Evanston, Illinois, 1958; Ph.D., American Government, University of Texas-Austin, 1965. Military: Served in the United States Navy, 1958-61, 1965-68, and in the United States Naval Reserve, 1980 to present, attaining the rank of Captain. Career: Field Underwriter, New York Life Insurance Company, 1980 to present; South Texas Coordinator, United States Naval Academy Information Program, 1981 to present; Professor of Political Science and Public Administration Program, Our Lady of the Lake University of San Antonio, Texas, 1978-82; Professor of Political Science, Coordinator of Public Administration Programs, East Texas State University, Texarkana, 1976-78; Associate Professor, Georgia State University-Atlanta 1968-76, School of Urban Life 1970-76, Institute of Health Administration 1975-76; Public Administration Fellow, Program Officer, United States Department of Housing and Urban Development Office of Personnel, Washington, D.C., 1971-72; Consultant, Resources Development Project, Southern Regional Education Board, Atlanta, 1968; Assistant Professor, Political Science and Research Associate, Bureau of Governmental Research, University of South Carolina-Columbia, 1965-68; Book Review Editor, *Health Administration Quarterly*, 1976-78; Associate Book Review Editor, *Appalachian Business Review*, 1980. Organizational Memberships: American Society for Public Administration (president, San Houston Chapter, 1979-80); International Personnel Management Association; American Management Association; American Society for Personnel Administration; Southwestern Political Science Association; Naval Reserve Association; National Municipal League. Community Activities: Planning Commission, Universal City, 1978 to present; City Manager, City of Hondo, Texas, 1982; Human Rights Commission, Bear County Mental Health and Mental Retardation Center, 1978-82; Olympia Homeowners Association (board of directors, 1979 to present); United Way of San Antonio and Bexar County (allocations panel, 1979 to present); Our Lady of the Lake University (chairman, university relations committee, 1978-80); United States Naval Academy Blue and Gold Information Officer, 1980-81; Greater San Antonio Chamber of Commerce (governmental affairs council, 1979 to present); Chief of Naval Operations Seapower Presentation Team, 1971 to present; Association of the Retarded Citizens of San Antonio (board of directors). Religion: Secretary, Board of Trustees, United Methodist Campus Ministry, San Antonio District, 1981 to present; Board of Directors, Wesley

Community Centers; Part-time Sunday School Teacher, University City United Methodist Church. Published Works: Co-Editor, *Natural Resources, Environment and Lifestyles;* Author, 20 Articles in Areas of Local Government, Personnel Administration; Six Reviews for Journals. Honors and Awards: Danforth Associate, Danforth Foundation, 1981-86; Title I, Higher Education Grant to Conduct Workshop on Optima Uses of Natural Resources; Commendation, Patriotic Service, United States Department of the Army; Special Certificate of Achievement, United States Department of Housing and Urban Development; Listed in *Who's Who in the South and Southwest, Personalities of America, International Who's Who in Community Service, Leadership Atlanta, Outstanding Young Men of America.* Address: 8310 Athenian, Universal City, Texas 78148.

Palmer, Spencer John

Educator, Director. Personal: Born October 4, 1927; Son of John Leroy Palmer (deceased) and Eliza E. Motes; Married Shirley Ann Hadley; Father of Dwight, Jennette, James. Education: Certificate, Eastern Arizona at Thatcher, 1947; B.A. Fine Arts, Brigham Young University, 1949; M.A. East Asiatic Studies 1958, Ph.D. Asian History 1964, University of California at Berkeley. Military: Served in the United States Army as Chaplain in Korea, Japan, Fort MacArthur, California, attaining the rank of First Lieutenant. Career: Brigham Young University, Professor 1969 to present, Associate Professor 1964-69, Assistant Professor 1962-64, Director, World Religions, Religious Studies Center present, Center for International and Area Studies, Director 1975-79, Associate Director president, Director, Jerusalem Study Abroad 1980; University of California, Institute of International Relations, Graduate Staff Assistant 1960-61, Department of History, Teaching Fellow 1959-60; Coordinator, Asian Studies, 1968-75. Organizational Memberships: Research Institute Korean Affairs (board of directors, 1973); Asian Education Resources (project director); Western Conference of the National Association of Asian Studies (organizer, first president); Royal Asiatic Society, Korea Branch (board of directors, publications chairman, 1966-68). Religion: Church of Jesus Christ of the Latter-Day Saints; Second Counselor, Edgemont South Stake, 1975-78; High Council, Brigham Young University 12th Stake, 1975-78; Melchizedek Priesthood Writing Committee, General Church Committee, 1971-73; Regional Representative, Mission Representative, 1972-74; High Priest Quorum Instructor, 8th Ward, Edgemont Stake, 1969-71; Mission President, Korea Mission, 1965-68; Bishop, Brigham Young University 8th Ward, 1965; High Council, Brigham Young University 1st Stake, 1964-65. Published Works: Author, Numerous Books including *The Expanding Church, Deity and Death, Education in Korea;* Editor, *Asian Perspectives: Korea, Japan, China, Pakistan;* Associate Editor, *Mormonism: A Faith for All Cultures;* Author, Numerous Articles, including "Where in the World Are We Going?", "Moments of Interview: Three Great Historians Speak", "What About Cremation?" Forthcoming Publication, *Confucian Rituals in Korea;* Manuscript in Process, Associate Editor of Encyclopedia Project for Greenwood Press, Entries on Non-Christian Religions in the United States. Honors and Awards: Karl G. Maeser Research Award, 1976. Address: 1159 East Mountain Ridge Road, Provo, Utah 84604.

Palmiter, Harry A

Publisher, Senior Editor. Personal: Born December 14, 1922; Son of Louis O. and Carrie T. Palmiter (both deceased); Married Marjory R.; Father of Lynn E., Steven J. Education: B.S., College of Agriculture, University of Wisconsin, 1950. Military: Served in the United States Army from 1943-46. Career: Olsen Publishing Company, Incorporated, Assistant Editor 1950-54, Manager, Merchandising Development Division 1954-58; Promotion Chief, Markets Division, Wisconsin Department of Agriculture, 1958-62; The Cheese Reporter Publishing Company, Editor 1962-78, Publisher/Senior Editor 1978 to present. Organizational Memberships: Alpha Gamma Rho; International Milk and Food Sanitarians; Wisconsin Marketing Advisory Council; International Cheese and Deli Seminar; Wisconsin Cheesemakers' Association (life member); North East Wisconsin Cheesemakers' and Buttermakers' Association (life member); Wisconsin Dairy Technology Society; Society of Dairy Technology, United Kingdom. Community Activities: Boy Scouts of America (scoutmaster, 1973-76; chairman, committee, 1976 to present; district committee, 1976 to present); Young Men's Christian Association (Metro Madison); Madison Lapidary & Mineral Club; Midwest Federation Minerology & Geological Society. Religion: United Presbyterian Church of United States, Elder, 1966 to present. Honors and Awards: Wisconsin Cheese Seminar Service Award, 1973; North East Wisconsin Cheesemakers' and Buttermakers' Association, Life Membership, Service Award, 1975; Wisconsin Cheesemaker's Association, Life Membership, Service Award, 1978; District Award of Merit, 1978, Leader of Distinction 1975, 1976, 1977, Order of the Arrow 1975, Brotherhood, 1976, Boy Scouts of America. Address: 917 Lorraine Drive, Madison, Wisconsin 53705.

Palumbo, Louis Alexander Jr

Clergyman, Scientist, Educator, Theologian, Humanitarian, Researcher. Personal: Born November 24, 1919, Johnston, Rhode Island; Son of Louis Albino and Michelina (Margaret) Albano Palumbo (both deceased). Education: B.D.; S.T.L.; Th.D.; D.D.; D. Rel. Sci.; L.L.D.; B.S.; M.S.; Sc.D.; A.B.; M.A.; Ph.D.; Ed.D.; Graduate of New England Institute of Anatomy, Sanitary Sciences and Embalming, Boston; Licensed Clinical Psychotherapist; Diplomate, P.B.P.T.C.; More and One Hundred Honorary Degrees, All maxima cum laude. Career: Registered Embalmer, 1946; President, Evangelical Bible Seminary and College, Italian Branch; Vice President, Academic Department, Fundamental Bible Seminary, Italian Branch, O.M.C.; Vice Dean, Thomas Alva Edison College, Palm Beach, Florida; Researcher, Various Fields of Science, Natural, Supernatural, Ecology, Nursing Education. Organizational Memberships: International Platform Association; National Society of Psychological Counsellors; Gamma Pi Epsilon; Ohio Christian College (international board of directors); Otay Mesa College, San Diego, California (president, all commissions, boards). Religion: Catholic. Published Works: Author, Numerous Publications, Fields of Theology, Philosophy, Supernatural and Natural Sciences. Honors and Awards: Cavalier of Justice, Delegate to Canada, Grand Official, Military Order of Sweden, Saint Bridget's; Knight of the Grand Cross, Order of Saint John of Jerusalem; Knight Commander, Thomas Alva Edison College; Honorary Pin for Free Humanitarian Service 1944-46, Rhode Island Hospital, Providence, Rhode Island; Honorary Right Reverend Title for Exceptional Moral, Spiritual Humanity, Theological/Divinity Achievement, Palumbo, Louis Alexander, Jr. Thomas Alva Edison College, Florida, 1976-77; Listed in *Book of Honor, Notable Americans, Directory of Distinguished Americans, Community Leaders and Noteworthy Americans, Community Leaders of America, American Registry, Personalities of America.* Address: c/o 5 Beckwith Street, Cranston, Rhode Island 02910.

Papageorgiou, John C

Educator. Personal: Born November 22, 1935; Son of Helen Papageorgiou; Married Thalia Christides; Father of Constantine, Elena, Demetrios, Antigone. Education: B.Sc., Athens School of Economics and Business Sciences, Greece, 1957; Dipl.Tech.Sc. 1963, Ph.D. 1965, University of Manchester, England. Military: Served in the Greek Armed Forces, 1958-60, attaining the rank of Second Lieutenant. Career: Professor of Management Science 1978 to present, Chairman of the Management Sciences Department 1976 to present, Associate Professor of Management Science 1976-78, University of Massachusetts at Boston; Associate Professor of

Operations Analysis 1974-76, University of Toledo; Visiting Professor of Operations Research 1972, Lecturer 1966-68, Athens School of Economics and Business Sciences, Athens, Greece; Associate Professor of Management Sciences, St. Louis University, 1971-72; Assistant Professor of Management Science, Wayne State University, 1969-71; Assistant Professor, York University, Toronto, Canada, 1968-69; Lecturer, Post-graduate Institute of Business Administration, Athens, Greece, 1966-68; Special Advisor in Operations Research, Center of Planning and Economic Research, Athens, Greece, 1972-73; Operations Research Analyst, ESSO-Pappas Industrial Company, Programming and Analysis Division, 1967-68; Operations Research Analyst 1966-67, Head 1966, Department of Economic Research, Agricultural Bank of Greece, Athens; Operations Research Trainee, Science in General Management Ltd., Croydon, England, 1965; Economist, Department of Foreign Exchange, Bank of Greece, 1961-62; Family Business, 1960-61, 1957; Seminars for Business, Industry and Government, 1965-81. Organizational Memberships: American Association for the Advancement of Science (fellow); Operations Research Society of America (full member); The Institute of Management Sciences; American Institute of Management Sciences; Sigma Xi (full member); Hellenic Operations Research Society; American Production and Inventory Control Society. Community Activities: Wayne State University School of Business Administration (research committee, 1969-71; ad-hoc committee on data processing 1970); University of Toledo College of Business Administration (graduate studies committee, 1973-74, 1975-76, research committee 1975-76); University of Massachusetts at Boston (faculty development committee, 1977-79; college personnel committee, College of Professional Studies, 1976-78; academic uses of the computer committee, 1976-78; dean search committee, College of Professional Studies, 1978-79; chairperson, college personnel committee, College of Management and Professional Studies, 1979-80). Published Works: Books and Monographs, *Data on the Greek Economy* (co-author) 1966, *Introduction to Operations Research* 1973, *Fundamentals of Operations Research* 1973, *Operations Research Applications to Health Care Problems* 1978, *Management Science and Environmental Problems* 1980; Numerous Papers, including (most recently) "Decision Making in the Year 2000" and "Some Operations Research Applications to Problems of Health Care"; Book Reviews and Research Reports. Honors and Awards: Faculty Development Grant, University of Massachusetts at Boston, 1978-79; Summer Faculty Research Program, Air Force Office of Scientific Research, 1980; Fellow, International Biographical Association, 1978; Editor, *The Boston TIMS Newsletter*, 1981 to present; Associate Editor, *Technos, A Journal of International Engineering*, 1971 to present, and *Operations Management Newsletter*, 1975 to present; Referee, *Operations Research Quarterly*, 1975 to present; Editor-at-Large, *Interfaces;* Book Reviewer, Wadsworth Publishing Company, Harper & Row Publishers; NATO Fellowship, 1965; Outstanding Teacher Award Nominee, University of Toledo, 1975; Chancellor's Award for Distinguished Scholarship Nominee, University of Massachusetts at Boston, 1977, 1981; Invited Participant, Production and Operations Management/Quantitative Methods Faculty Workshop, Harvard University Graduate School of Business, 1976; National Innovative Education Committee 1977-79, National Goals Development Committee 1978-79, American Institute for Decision Sciences; Subcommittee for the Development and Evaluation of Curricula for Greece, KRIKOS, Inc., 1976-80; Local Arrangement Chairman, 1981 National AIDS Conference; Listed in *Who's Who in the World, Who's Who in America, Who's Who in the East, Who's Who in the Midwest, American Men of Science, American Men and Women of Science, Men of Achievement, International Who's Who of Intellectuals, Dictionary of International Biography, International Who's Who in Education, Men and Women of Distinction, Who's Who in Community Service, Personalities of America, The Anglo-American Who's Who, American Registry Series, Hellenic America Who's Who in Business and the Professions, Directory of Distinguished Americans, Who's Who in Computer Education and Research,* Others. Address: 14 Putney Road, Wellesley Hills, Massachusetts 02181.

Pappas Hale, Linda Diana

Compensation Consultant, Management Consultant. Personal: Born February 5, 1942; Daughter of Mr. and Mrs. Joseph Soffranko; Married Thomas Morgan Hale; Stepmother of Rodney Hale, Kenneth Hale, Timothy Hale, Marilee Hale. Education: B.A. Sociology 1963, M.A. Sociology 1973, Graduate Study, Math 1966, Southern Illinois University. Career: Management Consultant, Principal, Hay Associates, 1974-77; Associate Director, President's Commission on Military Compensation, 1977-78; Director, Social Systems Research Department, General Research Corporation, 1977-80; Compensation Consultant, Management Consultant, present. Organizational Memberships: American Compensation Association; American Sociological Association. Community Activities: Offender Aid and Restoration Program (counselor, 1979-81); Red Cross CPR Instructor, 1978-80; Navy Relief Counselor (developed, implemented local casualty assistance program, 1967-69); Nuclear Regulatory Commission (speaker, federal women's program, 1977). Religion: Finance Committee, United Methodist Church, 1980, 1981; Administrative Board, 1981-83. Honor and Awards: Undergraduate Assistantship, 1961-63, Graduate Fellowship 1968, Graduate Assistantship 1969-70, Southern Illinois University; Letter of Commendation, Navy Relief Executive Secretary/Vice President, 1968. Address: 9804 Ward Court, Fairfax, Virginia 22032.

Papper, Emanuel Martin

Educator. Personal: Born July 12, 1915; Son of Lillian Weitzner Papper; Married Patricia Meyer; Father of Richard Nelson, Barbara Ellen Papper Lupatkin. Education: Graduate of Boys High School, 1931; A.B., Columbia University, 1935; M.D., New York University, 1938; Intern 1939, Resident 1940-42, Bellevue Hospital; Certification, American Board of Anesthesiology, 1943; F.F.A.R.C.S., England, 1964; F.A.C.P., 1968. Military: Served in the United States Army Medical Corps as Chief, Section of Anethesiology, Tourney Dibble and Walter Reed Hospitals, 1942-46, attaining the rank of Major. Career: Licensed in New York, California, Florida; Fellow in Medicine 1938, Fellow in Physiology 1940, Instructor in Anesthesiology 1942, Assistant Professor 1946-49, Associate Profesor 1949, New York University; Professor of Anesthesiology, Chairman of the Department of Anesthesiology, Columbia University, 1949-69; Director of Anesthesiology Service, Presbyterian Hospital, 1949-69; Director of Anesthesiology and Visiting Anesthesiologist, Francis Delafield Hospital, 1951-69; Vice President of Medical Affairs, Dean, University of Miami School of Medicine, 1969 to present; Professor of Anesthesiology 1969 to present, Professor of Pharmacology 1974 to present, University of Miami; Numerous Visiting Professorships and Named Lectures, including Rovenstine Lecture (New York State Society of Anesthesiologists, Inc.) and Shields Lecture (Toronto, Canada), 1955 to present; Number of Consulting Positions. Organizational Memberships: Alpha Omega Alpha; American Association for the Advancement of Science; American Association for Thoracic Surgery; American Board of Anesthesiology; American College of Anesthesiologists; American College of Physicians; American Heart Association; American Medical Association; American Pain Society; American Physicians Fellowship, Inc.; American Society of Anesthesiologists; American Society for Biographical Research; American Society for Clinical Investigation; American Society for Pharmacology and Experimental Therapeutics (life member); Division of Drug Metabolism; American Surgical Association; American Thoracic Society; American Trudeau Society; Association for Academic Health Centers; Association of American Medical Colleges; Association of Anaesthetics of Great Britain and Ireland; Association of University Anesthetists; Australian Society of Anesthesiologists; Cuban Medical Association in Exile; Eastern Pain Association; European Academy of Anesthesiology; California Society of Anesthesiologists; Finnish Society of Anesthesiologists; Florida Medical Association; Florida Society of Anesthesiologists; Florida Thoracic Society; German Society of Anesthesiologists; Halstead Society; Harvey Society; International Association for the Study of Pain; Israel Society of Anesthesiologists; Latin American Association of Toxicology; Maryland-District of Columbia Society of Anesthesiologists; Medical Society of the County of New York; United States-China Physicians Friendship Association; Venezulan Society of Anesthesiology; World Federation Societies of Anesthesiologists. Community Activities: Century Association; Cosmos Club; Grove Island Club; Miami Club; Palm Bay Club;

Rotary Club; Standard Club. Published Works: Author, 236 Scientific Papers Published in Various Medical and Scientific Journals; Author, 4 Books; Editor, 3 Books. Honors and Awards: Honorary President, French Society of Anesthesiology and Resuscitation; Wisdom Award, Wisdom Hall of Fame; Distinguished Service Award, American Society of Anesthesiologists; Medal of Honor, City of Paris; Honorary Professor, Silver Medal, Universidad Catolics de Santiago de Guayaquil, University of Madrid School of Medicine; Distinguished Alumnus Award in the Health Sciences, New York University School of Medicine; Several Honorary Alumnus and Professor Positions; Man of the Year, Boys High School; Outstanding Educator in America; Meritorious Service Award, A.A.M.C.M.; E. M. Papper Honorary Lectureships in Anesthesiology, Columbia University, University of California at Los Angeles; Honorary President V, European Congress of Anesthesiology; Honorary Member, European Academy of Anesthesiology; Honorary Professor, University of Santiago de Chile; Tel Aviv University's Board of Governors; Honorary Fellow, Faculty of Anaesthetics, Royal College of Surgeons; Honorary Member, Panamanian Society of Anesthesiologists, Latin American Society of Anesthesiologists; Listed in *Who's Who in America, Who's Who in the East, Who's Who in World Jewry, American Men of Science, American Men of Medicine, Modern Medicine Contemporaries, Blue Book, Dictionary of International Biography, Community Leaders of America, Directory of Educational Specialists, National Register of Prominent Americans and International Notables, Who's Who in Health Care, International Who's Who in Education*, Others. Address: 1 Grove Isle Drive, Apt. 1501, Miami, Florida 33133.

Parke, Margaret Bittner

Educator (retired). Personal: Born January 6, 1901; Daughter of Oscar and Laura Bittner (both deceased); Married Roger I. Parke (deceased). Education: Attended Bloomsburg State Teachers College, 1922-23; B.A., English, Pennsylvania State University, 1927; Teachers Certificates, Guidance and Personnel 1930, Curriculum and Teaching 1945, Columbia University. Career: Teacher, Rural School 1919-20, Grades 3 and 4 1920-22, Grades 7 and 8 1923-26, all in Pennsylvania; Mount Vernon Junior High School 1927-28, Guidance and Research, Eastchester 1928-37, both in New York; Evaluation and Curriculum in Language Arts, Bureau of Research, New York City Public Schools, 1937-51; Coordinator of Undergraduate and Graduate Programs, Brooklyn College, 1951-71. Organizational Memberships: International Reading Association; N.C.R.E. (childhood education); A.E.R.A.; National Council of Teachers of English (nationally elected member by elementary teachers, 1970-73); National Vocational Guidance; Administrative Women; New York State Teachers Association; T.E.P.S.; Retired Teachers Association; U.F.T.; National Education Association; Woman's Press Club of New York City (membership chairman, director, vice president, 1975-79); New York State College English Educators (executive board member, 1967-71); New York Teachers Pension Organization (committee member); National Conference on Research in English, 1952; New York Academy of Public Education (member, 1955 to present; board of directors, 1979). Community Activities: Brooklyn Woman's Club (program chairman, 1980-82); Daughters of the American Revolution (vice regent, Fort Greene Chapter, 1980-82); Alumni Associates of Teachers College, Columbia University (board of directors, 1979-82); New York Federation of Women (committee chairman, education priorities and scholarship, 1982-84). Religion: Riverside Church, New York City, 1940-80; Brooklyn Lutheran Church, 1981-82. Honors and Awards: Kappa Delta Pi, 1943; Pi Lambda Theta, 1943; Honorary Doctorate, Staley College, Massachusetts, 1959; Fulbright Award to University of Sydney, Australia, Philippines and Taiwan, 1960; Certificate of Merit for *Picture Dictionary of Most Used Works*, International Biography of London, 1969; Distinguished Alumnae Award, Pennsylvania State University, 1972; Distinguished Service Award, Bloomsburg State College, 1973; Valuable Human Resources, American Bicentennial Research Committee, 1974; Citations, Community Leaders, Brooklyn Reading Council of I.R.A., International Institute of Community Service, London, 1975. Address: 1655 Flatbush Avenue, Brooklyn, New York 11210.

Margaret B Parke

Parker, Donn Murray

Radio Station Owner. Personal: Born September 21, 1931; Son of Irving and Ida Wasserman Pressman (both deceased); Married Sally; Father of Linda, Elaine, Gerald, Barbara, Kenneth. Education: Communications Degree, Emerson College, 1950; Marketing Degree, University of New Hampshire, 1965; Business Degree, New Hampshire College, 1974. Career: Owner, WCMX, Leominster, Massachusetts; present, Station Manager, WFEA Radio, Manchester, New Hampshire, 1979-81; Air Personality, Program and News Director, Sales, WKBR RAdio, Boston, Massachusetts, 1958-62; Football and Baseball Official; Condominium Consultant; Writer, Newspaper Column, Ten Years. Organizational Memberships: Manchester, New Hampshire Association of Broadcasters (chairman); New Hampshire Ad Club (chairman); New Hampshire Association of Broadcasters (chairman); New Hampshire Football and Baseball Officials Association. Community Activities: Mountain Home Estates (president); Community Institute of America (national committee member); Manchester Little League Association (president); Manchester Parks and Recreation Commission, 1966-77; Guest Lecturer, New Hampshire College, Hesser Business College; Numerous State and City Committees. Religion: Ordained Minister, Universal Life Church. Honors and Awards: Citizen of the Year 1975; Manchester Chapter 1, Disabled American Veterans, 1975; Man of the Year, International Association of Fire Fighters, Local 856, 1972; Certificate of Recognition, United States Air Force Academy; Special Recognition, North Little League, Manchester. Address: 62 Coburn Woods, Nashua, New Hampshire 03063.

Parker, James

Roman Catholic Priest. Personal: Born October 22, 1930, in Charleston, South Carolina; Son of Luther W. and Bertha Wieters Parker (both deceased); Married Mary Alma Cole, 1953; Father of Margaret Elizabeth, Mary Clare. Education: A.B., University of South Carolina, 1953; M.Div., Virginia Theological Seminary, 1956; M.A.L.S., Rosary College, Illinois, 1968. Career: Roman Catholic Priest, 1981 to present; Episcopal Priest, until 1981. Religion: Ordained as First Married Catholic Priest in the United States. Honors and Awards: Royal Order of Saint Sava of Yugoslavia; Personally Knighted by His Majesty the Late King Peter II of Yugoslavia, 1969. Address: 936 South Craig Avenue, Springfield, Missouri 65802.

Parker, Lucy Thimann

Psychologist, Clinical Director. Personal: Born January 23, 1933, in Vienna, Austria; Daughter of Dr. and Mrs. Joseph Thimann (both deceased); Married Dr. Robert Alan Parker; Mother of Karen Sue, Janet Lee, Geoffrey Samuel, Linda Ann. Education: B.S. Elementary Education 1958, Ed.M. Counselor Education 1965, Ed.D. Education and Counseling 1974, Boston University; Ph.D. Clinical Psychology, Heed University, 1973; Leadership Training Institute, 1967; Newton Mental Health Center Teaching Conference, 1965-67. Career: Clincial Director, Senior Staff Psychologist, Chestnut Hill Psychotherapy Associates, Chestnut Hill Medical Center, Massachusetts, 1971 to present; Senior Consultant, Massachusetts Teachers Association, 1974-78; Senior Counseling Psychologist, Leslie B. Cutler Child Guidance Clinic, Masschusetts, 1967-70; Consulting Psychologist, Walker Home for Children, Massachusetts, 1968-72; School Adjustment Counselor, Needham Public Schools, Massachusetts, 1964-67; Psychological

Consultant, Camp Baird, Boston Children's Services Association Residential Camp, Massachusetts, 1966-68; Private Practice in Psychotherapy and Crisis Internvention, Massachusetts, 1965-72; Heed University, Professor in Psychology and Education 1972-78, Associate Professor in Psychology and Education, New England Coordinator 1972-74; Associate Professor in Education, Newton College, 1972-75; Research Associate in Behavorial Sciences, Massachusetts College of Optometry, 1973-75; Assistant Professor in Education, Lesley College, 1967-72; Northeastern University Graduate School of Education, Lecturer in Psychology 1966-67, Guest Lecturer 1966-72; Field Work Supervisor, Needham Public Schools, Boston University Graduate School of Education, 1965-67; Educational Therapist, Department of Special Education, Newton Public Schools 1960-65, Brocton Public Schools 1959-62; Junior High School Teacher, Temple Shalom, 1962-64; Elementary School Teacher, Bellingham Public Schools, 1958-59; Guest Lecturer, University of Massachusetts School of Education 1972-78, Framingham State College Psychology Department 1973-78, Bridgewater State College Psychology Department 1973-78, Boston University Graduate School of Education 1966-72, Northeastern University Graduate School of Education 1966-72, Rhode Island College Graduate School of Education 1966-72. Organizational Memberships: American Psychological Association, American Association of University Professors; American Society of Clinical Hypnosis; American Association of Sex Education and Counselors; America Group Psychotherapy Association; American Personnel and Guidance Association; American Association for Marriage and Family Counselors; International Association of Group Psychotherapy; International Society for Clinical and Experimental Hypnosis; Society for Clinical and Experimental Hypnosis; Massachusetts Psychological Association; American Orthopsychiatric Association; Massachusetts Association for Marriage and Family Counselors; Greater Boston Area Personnel and Guidance Association; Association for Humanistic Psychology; American Association of Marriage and Family Therapy (co-chairperson, regional screening board, 1981); Massachusetts Association of Marriage and Family Therapy (regional board, 1981-82); Psychologist License, Elementary Teacher's Certificate, Guidance Counselor's Certificate, School Adjustment Counselor's Certificate, State of Massachusetts. Community Activities: Sensitivity Group Trainer, Human Relations Consultant, National Training Laboratories, 1968 to present; Project Lighthouse, Title III, 1968-72; Crisis Intervention Work, Police Departments, Fire Departments, Community. Published Works: Numerous Articles in Professional Publications, including "The Management of Behavior in a Pediatric Clinical Setting", "Behavior: The Neglected Aspect of Eye Safety", "A Study of Vision Screening Programs in Massachusetts Public Schools"; Textbook Pending Publication, *Manual for Teachers Working with Problem Children in the Classroom.* Honors and Awards: Fellow, American Academy of Optometry 1974, International Council of Sex Education and Parenthood 1981, American Academy of Science, International Biographical Association; Diplomate, American Academy of Behavioral Medicine, 1982; Listed in *Who's Who of American Women, Who's Who in the East, Dictionary of International Biography, World Who's Who of Women, Community Leaders and Noteworthy Americans, International Register of Profiles, National Register of Health Service Providers in Psychology.* Address: Suite 108, 12 Boylston Street, Chestnut Hill, Massachusetts 02167.

Parks, Fred

Attorney-at-Law. Personal: Born July 9, 1906; Son of John and Nora Soden Parks (both deceased); Married Mabel Roberson; Father of Judith Stauffer. Education: Preparatory Education, Rice University; L.L.B., South Texas School of Law, 1937. Military: Served in the United States Army Air Corps; Honorable Discharge, 1945. Career: Instructor, South Texas School of Law, Houston, 1949, 1951-45; Attorney-at-Law. Organizational Memberships: Southeastern Legal Foundation (research fellow); Houston Junior Bar Association (president, 1940); Texas Junior Bar Association (president, 1942); Houston Bar Association (director, 1941-42, 1946-47); American Bar Association; International Bar Association; State Bar of Texas (grievance committee, 1941, 1947-49; director, 8th district, 1954-57; vice president, 1957-58); American Judicature Society; Maritime Law Association of the United States of America; Selden Society. Community Activities: Lecturer, "Some Practical Aspects of the Preparation and Trial of Damage Suits in Texas", University of Houston Law School, 1955, University of Texas School of Law 1956, South Texas School of Law, 1954, before State Bar of Texas Institute 1956, "Effective Utilization of Medical Evidence", Southwestern Legal Foundation, Southern Methodist University, 1957. Published Works: Author, "Legal Aspects of Medical Records", *Texas Association of Medical Records Librarians Bulletin,* 1958. Honors and Awards: Bronze Star, Numerous Battle Stars, Numerous Unit and Group Citations, United States Army Air Corps. Address: 3385 Del Monte Drive, Houston, Texas 77019.

Parris, George Nick

Prosecuting Attorney. Personal: Born May 14, 1921; Son of Mrs. Katherine Parris; Married Phyllis J. Bunker; Mother of Kathi, Nikki, Lorri, Sherri, Janni, Nickolas G., George Nick II. Education: Graduate of Pontiac High School, Michigan; Studied Business Administration, Business Institute, Pontiac, Michigan, 1940-42; Aviation Cadet Program, 1943; Bombadier Instructor School, 1945; A.B. Economics, University of Michigan, 1948; Juris Doctor with Honors, Wayne State University Law School, 1951. Military: Enlisted, Aviation Cadet, 1942; Commissioned 2nd Lieutenant, Bombadier's Wings, 1943; Served European Theatre Operations, World War II, 35 Combat Missions, B-24, D.F.C. Career: Law Instructor, Wayne State University Law School, 1950-51; Director of Celing Prices, N.P.A. & C.M.P., Udylite Corporation, Detroit, Michigan, 1951; Assistant Prosecuting Attorney, 1952; Public Administrator, Macomb County, Michigan, 1957-59; Private Law Practice; Prosecuting Attorney of Macomb County, Michigan, 1961 to date. Organizational Memberships: American Bar Association; Macomb County Bar Association; Michigan Prosecuting Attorney's Association (board of directors, 1961 to date; president, 1966-67); United County Officers (board of directors, president, 1970-71); National District Attorney's Association. Community Activities: Macomb County Chiefs of Police; Southeastern Michigan Association of Chiefs of Police; American Judicature Society; International Narcotic Enforcement Officers Association. Community Activities: Macomb County Community College Criminal Justice Center (advisory board); Macomb Traffic Safety Committee (board of directors); Macomb Drivers Safety School (board of directors); Harrison Community Hospital (secretary, board of directors, 1972 to present); Warren County Shrine Club; Macomb County Shrine Club; AmVets; Veterans of Foreign Wars; American Legion; Eagles, American Cancer Society; Michigan Cancer Foundation; March of Dimes; Wayne State University Law School Loan Fund, 1979. Religion: St. John Greek Orthodox Church, Fraser, Michigan, Founding Member, Legal Advisor, trustee, 1975-78. Honors and Awards: Father of the Year, Warren Jaycees, 1956; Outstanding Young Man of the Year 1953, 1956, Warren Jaycees; Michigan State Resolution of Tribute, 1967; Cited in the Congressional Record, 1964, 1966; Fraternal Order of Elks Reverence to Law, 1966; Macomb County Citizen of the Week Award 1967; Distinguished Contribution Award, United County Officers, 1978; Michigan Joint Senate-House Resolution of Tribute, 1980; Air Medal with 3 Clusters; 4 Battle Stars. Address: 39210 Gary Avenue, Mount Clemens, Michigan 48043.

Parrish, Joyce Ann Tucker

Secretary, Division of Science, Mathematics and Nursing. Personal: Born March 4, 1939; Daughter of Mr. and Mrs. William S. Tucker; Married Gerald Brannon Parrish, April 4, 1959. Education: Graduate of Frankfort High School, 1959; Honorable Graduate of Frankfort School of Business, Affiliated with Jefferson School of Commerce, 1958; Numerous Postgraduate Workshops, Secretarial Skills, Volunteering, Needs of Handicapped Children, Home Life, Education and the Arts, 1964-81. Career: Secretary,

Division of Science, Mathematics and Nursing, Kentucky State University, 1982 to present; Secretary, Allied Health Program, Division of Science, Mathematics and Nursing, Kentucky State University, 1980-82; Secretary, Legal Work, Office Management, Phyllis A. Sower, Attorney, 1978-80; Notary Public, 1978-86; Commonwealth of Kentucky, Department of Corrections, Division of Institutions, Senior Clerk Stenographer 1961-63, Professional Clerk Stenographer 1963-65, Department of Highways, Division of Public Relations, Clerk Typist 1957, Senior Clerk Stenographer 1957-61. Community Activities: Big Brothers/Big Sisters, Inc. (member, 1974-75; board of directors, 1981 to present); Frankfort Younger Woman's Club (member, 1971 to present; treasurer, Frankfort Junior Miss pageant, 1981-83; corresponding secretary, 1980-81; treasurer, 1979-80; home life chairman, 1978-79; volunteer services chairman, 1977-78; board of directors, 1977-81); Frankfort/Franklin County Community Council (member, 1978-81; board of directors, 1977-80); Frankfort Child Development Center (teacher aide, 1973-75); Girl Scouts of America (leader of cadet troop, 1971-72; liaison officer, leader of junior troop, 1970-71; liaison officer between new troops, Peaks Mill area and east Frankfort service unit 1969-70, Wilderness Road Council); Kentucky Heart Association (Heart Sunday chairman, Franklin County, 1978-80); Special Olympics State Basketball Tournament, Frankfort, 1978, 1979; Relief Work during and after Flood (clerical work, disaster center; cook for out-of-state volunteers, local church, 1978); March of Dimes, Franklin County Walkathon (publicity chairman, volunteer-recruiter, presentations area schools, 1977). Religion: Peaks Mill Christian Church, Frankfort, Kentucky; Teacher, Joy Class, 11 and 12 Year Olds, 1960-73; Sponsor, Mexican Orphans, Two Years; Teacher Vacation Bible School, 1960-72, 1982; Member 1959 to present. Honors and Awards: Heart Fund Leadership Award, Kentucky Heart Association, 1978, 1979; Volunteer Service Heart 1980; Outstanding Clubwoman for 1978/1979, 1979, Frankfort Young Woman's Club; Certificate of Appreciation, 1979, American Red Cross; Outstanding Volunteer 1978, Certificate of Appreciation 1978, Bureau of Volunteer Services; Appreciation Mug, Special Olympics State Basketball Tournament Committee, 1978; Boot Brigade Trophy, March of Dimes, 1977; Listed in *World Who's Who of Women.* Address: Route 6, Peaks Mill Road, Frankfort, Kentucky 40601.

R Patel

Patel, Ramesh Baldevbhai

Director of Architectural and Urban Design. Personal: Born September 24, 1937; Son of Baldevbhai and Chanchalben Patel; Married Ranjana Patel; Father of Neesha, Neeshad. Education: B.Arch., M.S., University of Baroda, India, 1961; M.Arch., Yale University, 1963; Participated in postgraduate programme in planning, Harvard University. Career: Chief Designer, John Portman and Associates. Formerly associated with leading architects and planners around the world, including Kenzo Tange, Paul Rudolph, Louis Kahn, John Portman. Organizational Memberships: American Institute of Architects; American Institute of Planners; Royal Institute of British Architects; Indian Institute of Architects; National Council of Architectural Registration Board. Community Activities: United Nations (recruitment member). Religion: Hindu. Honors and Awards: Runner-Up, National Competition, Berkeley Museum, 1964; Campus Planning Award, Washington University Competition, 1965; Tourist Center Award, State Architectural Competition, 1962; Painting Competition Award, India, 1954; International Publication on Various Designs, U.S. and Abroad. Address: 6420 Moore Dr., Los Angeles, California 90048.

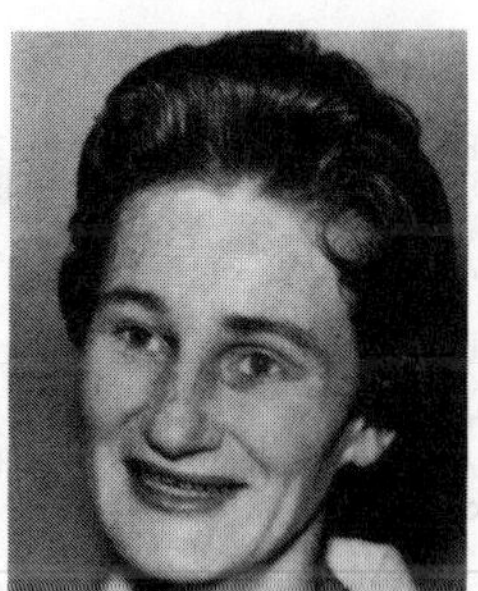

Jean Fraser Patrick

Patrick, Jean Fraser

Licensed Clinical Social Worker. Personal: Born September 11, 1934; Daughter of James A. and Jean Lynn Fraser; Married Paul A. Patrick; Mother of Jim, Rick, Bob, Scott, Mary Ann. Education: B.S. 1955, M.S.W. 1972, University of Kentucky. Career: Licensed Clinical Social Worker in Private Practice. Organizational Memberships: National Academy of Social Workers; I.T.A.A., 1971-81; Meninger Foundation, 1980-81; International Platform Association. Community Activities: Mother's March of Dimes (chairman, 1963, 1964); Parents Anonymous (organizer, Lexington chapter); Planning, Zoning Commission, 1973-80; Lexington Children's Theatre (board member, 1963, 1980); Lexington Campfire Girl Council (board member, 1980, 1981); Delta Zeta Sorority, 1951 to present; Tates Creek Band Boosters, 1978-81; Big Sisters of Lekington; Child Development Center; Kentucky Department of Human Resources. Religion: Faith Lutheran Church, Sunday School Teacher, 15 Years, Editor of Church Newsletter. Honors and Awards: Most Creative Woman, 1955; Editor, *Stylus* Magazine, 1953-54; Chi Delta Phi Literary Honorary Society, 1951-55; Phi Eta Sigma, 1951-55; Listed in *Who's Who in American Women.* Address: 516 Lakeshore Drive, Lexington, Kentucky 40502.

Patten, Bebe H

Minister and Educator. Personal: Born September 3, 1913, in Waverly, Tennessee; Daughter of Newton Felix Harrison and Mattie Priscilla Whitson (now deceased); Married to Carl Thomas (now deceased); Mother of Priscilla Carla and Bebe Rebecca (twins), Tom Jr. Education: D.D., McKinley-Roosevelt College, 1941; D.Litt., Temple Hall College and Seminary, 1943. Career: Founder and President, Christian Evangelical Churches of America, Inc., in Oakland, California, 1944 to present; Ordained to the ministry, Ministerial Association of Evangelism in Kansas City, Missouri, 1935; Founder of daily program and nightly nation-wide radio ministry, "The Shepherd Hour", 1934 to present; Held nation-wide evangelistic campaigns, 1935-50; Pastor, Christian Cathedral, Oakland, 1950 to present; Founder and President of Patten College, Oakland, 1945 to present; Founder and President of Academy of Christian Education (grades K-12), Oakland, 1944 to present; Editor-in-Chief of monthly paper, *The Trumpet Call,* 1953 to present; Composer of 20 published gospel songs; Has made 13 pilgrimages to Israel in the interest of Christian-Judaic relationships, 1962-81; Holds daily religious telecast (since 1976) and nationwide telecast (since 1979). Organizational Memberships: Zionist Organization of America; Religious Education Association; American Association for Higher Education; American Academy of Religion and Society of Biblical Literature; American Association of Presidents of Independent Colleges and Universities, 1980. Community Activities: Executive Board member, Bar-Ilan University Association of Israel; Member, American-Jewish Historical Society; Member of Oakland Museum Association, 1980. Published Works: *Give Me Back My Soul,* published in Japanese, Chinese, Spanish and English, 1973. Honors and Awards: Medallion presented by the Israeli Foreign Ministry for Religious Affairs, 1969; Medal from the Government Press Office in Jerusalem, 1971; Held private interview with David Ben-Gurion in 1972; Gentile Honoree of the Jewish National Fund, 1975; Hidden Heroine, San Francisco Bay Girl Scout Council, 1976; Held private interview with Prime Minister Menachim Begin in Tel Aviv, 1977; Presented Ben-Gurion Medallion, Sde Boker, Negev, Israel by the Ben-Gurion Research Institute, 1977; Received a resolution of commendation from the California Senate Rules Committee, 1978; Listed in *Who's Who in America, Directory of Contemporary Authors, Who's Who in Religion, Who's Who in the West, World Who's Who of Women, Dictionary of International Biography, Personalities of America,* and many other reference works. Address: 2433 Coolidge Avenue, Oakland, California 94601.

Bebe H Patten

Patten, Tom

Minister of Music. Personal: Born October 31, 1954; Son of Carl Thomas Patten (now deceased) and Bebe H. Patten. Education: B.A., summa cum laude, Patten Bible College, 1975; Attended California State University at Hayward, 1976; B.M., San Francisco Conservatory of Music, 1981. Career: Assistant Pastor of Christian Cathedral of the Christian Evangelical Churches of America,

Inc., Oakland, California, 1971 to present; Vice President, Christian Evangelical Churches of America, Inc., 1972 to present; Conductor of the 60-piece Patten Orchestra at Christian Cathedral, 1975 to present; Conductor of Community Ecumenical Choir and Orchestra, 1976; Produced movie for biographical Israeli film for college media and video, filmed in the Holy Land, 1976; Assisted in the production of a 30-minute film, *The Impossible Dream* (nominated for an Emmy Award in 1975). Community Activities: Member of Holy Names College Symphony, 1974 and 1976; Chairman of Boy Scouts of America; Participated in the planting of the David Ben-Gurion Forest in Negev, Israel and the Paula Ben-Gurion Forest, 1975 and 1977; Orchestral member of the San Francisco Conservatory of Music in 1979 and 1981, and the San Francisco Children's Opera, 1979-81. Honors and Awards: Received various awards from Patten Bible College including "Most Beloved Student" trophy, Gold "P" for 4.0 grade average and Heart Award; Listed in *Outstanding Young Men of America, Personalities of the West and Midwest, Personalities of America, Men of Achievement, Book of Honor, Who's Who in the West, Dictionary of International Biography, Men and Women of Distinction.* Address: 190 Alderwood Road, Walnut Creek, California 94596.

Tom Patten

Patterson, Lloyd Dale

International Business Consultant. Personal: Born May 23, 1934; Son of Ralph and Estelle Patterson; Married to Elizabeth; Father of Jeffrey Wynn. Education: Pre-med student, Kalamazoo College; B.S., Western Michigan University, 1956; D.M.D., McCarrie-Temple University, 1959; Post-graduate studies, University of Wisconsin, 1962; Special medical/dental studies, Brooke Medical Center, 1957. Military: Served with the United States Army Dental Corps; Received Honorable Discharge. Career: Consultant in private practice on new technology and licensing of new products; Assists in bringing new technology and product awareness to major developed countries; Lecturer on "New Business" involving government, universities and corporations; Former Prosthetic Dentist; Former Dental Materials Researcher; Former Anatomical and Physiological Researcher (product development); Former Vice President of an international licensing and acquisition firm. Organizational Memberships: The Scientific Research Society of America; Sigma Xi; Licensing Executives Society; Commercial Development Association; International Law-Licensing Association (honorary member); Management of University Technology Resources (honorary member). Community Activities: Member, Optimists International, 1967; Activities Chairman, Boy Scouts of America; Sports Coordinator, Young Men's Christian Association. Religion: Attends Protestant Church. Honors and Awards: Holds 2 honorary doctorates received in 1970 and 1971; Listed in *Who's Who in the South and Southwest, Directory of Distinguished Americans, Personalities of America.* Address: 608 John Anderson, Ormond Beach, Florida 32074.

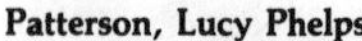

Patterson, Lucy Phelps

Educator. Personal: Born June 21, 1931; Daughter of John C. and Florence H. Phelps; Married to Albert S.; Mother of Albert Harllee. Education: A.B., Howard University, 1950; M.S.W., University of Denver, 1963; Post-master's study, University of Texas and University of Virginia. Career: Branham Professor and Director of Social Work Program, Bishop College, Dallas, Texas; Former Assistant Professor and Internship Coordinator for North Texas State University; Former Planning Director for Community Council of Greater Dallas; Former Social Agency Administrator and Executive Director, Dallas County Child Care Council and Inter-Agency Project; Former Social Worker and Supervisor, Dallas County Department of Public Welfare. Organizational Memberships: Texas Chapter of National Association of Social Workers (state-wide secretary, 1976-80, board member and executive committee member, 1976-80); Texas Council of National Association of Social Workers (board member, 1968-75); Dallas Chapter of National Association of Social Workers (board member, 1968-80, secretary, 1960-61); Council on Social Work Education; Texas Association of College Teachers; North Texas Association of Black Social Workers (founder and first president); National Association of Social Workers (charter member); Academy of Certified Social Workers (charter member). Community Activities: City Councilwoman for City of Dallas (first black woman elected), 1973-80; Region 13 of Texas Municipal League (first black president, 1975-76, vice president, 1974-75); Commissioner, Dallas Housing Authority; Board of Directors, Dallas/Ft. Worth Regional Airport Board; Chairwoman, Human Development Committee for City of Dallas; Member, National League of Cities (human resources committee, steering and policy committee, community development committee); President of John Neely Bryan Parent-Teacher Association, 1980-82; Black Adoption Advisory Board member of the Texas Department of Human Resources, 1979 to present; Honorary Chairwoman, Black Foster Family Recruitment Week, 1976; Regional Advisory Committee member, Early Periodic Screeing, Diagnosis and Treatment Project on Sickle Cell Anemia, 1976-80; White House Committee on Hospital Cost Containment (appointed by President Jimmy Carter, 1979-80). Religion: Member of St. Paul United Methodist Church (member of board of church and society, Northeast District United Methodist Church, 1974-81). Honors and Awards: "Black Women: Achievement Against the Odds", Women's Bureau, Department of Labor and East Oak Cliff District, 1980; Fair Housing Award, Greater Dallas Housing Opportunity; Galaxy of Stars Award for achievement in public service, D.I.S.D.; Award of Appreciation, National Association of Social Workers; Leadership Commendation, City of Dallas, 1979; Received Ethel Carter Branham Endowed Chair in Social Work, Bishop College; National Sojourner Truth Meritorious Service Award from Business and Professional Women; Women Helping Women Award from Women's Center of Dallas; State of Texas Legislative Commendation, 1975 and 1977; Mother of the Year, 1975-76, John Neely Bryan Elementary School; Outstanding Educator of America, 1975; Social Worker of the Year, National Association of Social Workers, 1976; Achievement Award from Henry W. Longfellow School, 1976; Citizen of the Year, 1975; Woman of the Year, Zeta Phi Beta, 1975; Higher Education Achievement Award, 1980-81; Listed in *The World Who's Who of Women.* Address: 2779 Almeda Drive, Dallas, Texas 75216.

Lloyd Patterson

Patterson, Zella Justina Black

Retired Home Economist, Researcher and Writer. Born May 20, 1909; Daughter of Thomas Sr., and Mary E. Horst Black (both deceased). Education: B.S., Langston University, Langston, Oklahoma; M.S., Colorado State University at Ft. Collins; Post-graduate studies, University of California at Berkeley and Oklahoma State University at Stillwater. Career: Teacher, Instructor, Associate Professor and Chairman of Department of Home Economics, Langston University, 1960-72; Former Family Living Specialist, Cooperative Extension Service in cooperation with Oklahoma State University and U.S. Department of Agriculture, 1972-74; Research team member on U.S.D.A. projects, Langston University, 1966-72. Religion: Member of New Hope Baptist Church (home missionary, 1920 to present, home missionary president and vice president, 1970-78, building fund secretary, 1972 to present, chairman of food committee); 1931 Class Reunion Activities, Langston University (coordinator 1981); Logan County Historical Society (board of directors). Published Works: Author Two Books: *Langston University: A History; A Garden of Poems.* Honors and Awards: Honor Alumnae Award, Colorado State University; Outstanding Oklahoma Education Award, Oklahoma Education Association; Alpha Kappa Alpha Regional Award; National Sorority of Phi Delta Kappa, Inc., Contemporary Black Heritage Award; Presidential Citation Award, National Association for Equal Opportunity in Higher Education; Listed in *Who's Who of American Women;* Appointed by Governor George Nigh of Oklahoma to the Diamond Jubilee Board of Commissioners. Address: P.O. Box 96, Langston, Oklahoma 73050.

Zella J B Patterson

Patton, Celestel Hightower

Educator. Personal: Born July 14, 1910. Education: D. H. Meharry Medical College, Nashville, Tennessee, 1947; B.S., Tennessee State University, 1952; M.A., Columbia University, New York, 1958; M.A. Spanish, La Universidad Interamericana, Coahuila, Mexico. Career: Dental Hygienist, Public School System, Texas, 1947-54; Dean of Women, Health Instructor, Bishop College, 1954-60; Director, Physical Education and Health, Wilberforce University, 1960-62; Assistant Professor, Associate Professor, Health Education, Southern University, 1962 to present. Organizational Memberships: Health, Physical Education and Recreation; Association of University Professors; American Association of University Women; A.D.H.A.; National Dental Hygienist Association (organizer); Texas Dental Hygienist Association; Texas Association of University Women. Community Activities: Medical College Alumni Association (national president, 1952-53); South Dallas Business and Professional Women's Club, 1956; Southwestern Sociological Society (secretary, 1965-76); Zeta Phi Beta Sorority (organizer, Bishop College campus, 1955); Annual Donations, Meharry Medical College, Teachers College, Bishop College, International House, New York. Religion: Warren Avenue Christian Church, Educational and Nominational committee, 1981 to present, Junior Choir, Senior Choir, 1940-48. Honors and Awards: First Negro Dental Hygienist in the Public School System in Texasm 1947; Alumni Award for Outstanding Achievement in the Area of Dental Hygiene 1972, President Award for 25 Years of Service to Mankind, 1972, Meharry Medical College; International House, New York. Address: 4934 Echo Avenue, Dallas, Texas 75215.

Celestel H Patton

Paul, Carol Ann

Administrator. Personal: Born December 17, 1936, in Brockton, Massachusetts; Daughter of Mr. and Mrs. J. W. Bjork; Married Dr. Robert D. Paul; Mother of Christine M., Dana J., Robert Rea. Education: B.S., Pre-Med, University of Massachusetts, Amherst, 1958; M.A.T., Rhode Island College, 1968; Brown University, 1970; Ed.D. Department of Systems, Development, an Adaptation, School of Education, Boston University, 1978. Career: Assistant Vice President of Academic Planning, Fairleigh Dickinson University, Rutherford, New Jersey, 1980 to present; Master Planner, Department of Higher Education, State of New Jersey, Trenton, 1978-80; North Shore Community College, Beverly, Massachusetts, Assistant Dean, Assistant Professor 1969-80, Assistant Dean of Faculty 1974-78, Assistant Professor of Biology 1969-74; Biology Teacher, Attleboro High School, Massachusetts, 1965-68; Substitute Teacher, K-12, Groton Public Schools, Connecticut, 1964-65; Mathematics Teacher, Fitch Senior High School, Groton, Connecticut, 1959-60; Research, Characteristics of College and University Administrators, Teaching "Planning and Budgeting in Higher Education", Institute for Leadership Studies, Ed.D. Program, Fairleigh Dickinson University; Professional Consultations, Presentations. Organizational Memberships: National Council of Administrative Women in Education, 1977 to present; Pi Lambda Theta, 1977 to present; Professional and Organizational Development Network in Higher Education (member, 1976 to present; national conference planning committee, 1977; professional relations and membership committee, 1978-79); National Council for Staff, Professional and Organizational Development (member, 1976 to present; national executive board, 1979-80; Northeast regional representative, 1979-80; charter member, Northeast region, 1976; Northeast conference planning committee, 1978 to present; chairperson, conference planning committee, 1980 to present); Phi Delta Kappa, 1976 to present; Association for Supervision and Curriculum Development, 1975-78; Massachusetts Administrators in Community Colleges, 1974-78; National Association of Biology Teachers, 1966 to present. Community Activities: League of Women Voters of the United States (member, 1958 to present; Groton, Connecticut chapter, 1959-65; Attleboro, Massachusetts chapter, 1965-69; Beverly, Massachusetts chapter, 1969-77; Cranford, New Jersey chapter, 1977 to present; board of directors, 1960-63, 1967-69, 1970-74, 1981 to present; vice president, 1971-73, 1981 to present); Brown University Alumni Representative, 1972 to present; College of Women's Club of Cranford, 1977-1981; City of Salem (college representative, 1976-77, advisory council for alternative education); Policy Committee for Mayorality Candidate, Beverly, 1975; Committee for Choice in the Beverly Schools (board of directors, 1974-75); Mayor's Task Force for Economic Development, City of Beverly, 1974. Religion: Teacher, Grades 9-12, Confraternity of Christian Doctrine, St. Mary's, Beverly, Massachusetts, 1976-77. Published Works: Author, Numerous Articles for Professional Publications, including "Personal, Educational, and Career Characteristics of Male and Female College Administrators in Massachusetts" with Phyllis R. Sweet, Nancy Brigham, "Are Women Obtaining Faculty and Administrative Positions in Higher Education?" with Nancy Brigham, "Women's Place in Academia"; Editor, *Northeastern Regional Newsletter*, National Council for Staff, Program, and Organizational Development; *Study Guide for Introductory Biology*, *Instructor's Manual for Introductory Biology*, both with Michele Balcomb; *Minicourses for Principles of Biological Science; Laboratory Experiments for Principles of Biological Science.* Honors and Awards: Pi Lambda Theta, 1977; Phi Delta Kappa, 1976; Academic Year Fellowship to Brown University 1968-69, In-Service Institute, Organic and Biochemistry 1967-68, Special Materials Workshop 1966, State College at Bridgewater, Intensive Training Workshop, Bowdoin College, Maine, 1966, National Science Foundation; State of Massachusetts Scholarship to attend the University of Massachusetts, 1954-58; National Honor Society; Listed in *International Who's Who of Women, Notable Americans, International Who's Who in Education, International Who's Who of Intellectuals.* Address: 18 Central Avenue, Cranford, New Jersey 07016.

Zlatko P Pavelic

Pavelic, Zlatko Paul

Physician, Specialist in Pathology. Personal: Born August 14, 1943, in Slavonski Brod, Croatia, Yugoslavia; Son of Mirko and Zlata Maria Godic Pavelic; Married Ljiljana Duic. Education: M.D. 1969, Postgraduate Course in Experimental Biology 1969-71, M.S. 1971, Residency 1971-74, Ph.D. 1974, Board Examination in Pathologic Anatomy 1974, Association Professor Thesis Study 1975, University of Zagreb, Croatia, Yugoslavia; Internship, Teaching Hospital, Zagreb, 1969-70, and General Hospital Surgical Department, Pakrac, Croatia, Yugoslavia, 1970-71. Career: Student Assistant, Department of Microbiology, Parasitology and Virology, University of Zagreb, 1966-69; Consultant, Department of Experimental Biology and Medicine, "Ruder Boskovic" Institute, University of Zagreb, 1970-75; Research Fellow, Medical School, Oxford, England, 1975; Medical Faculty, Assistant Professor in Pathologic Anatomy 1970-75, Associate Professor in Pathology 1975; Visiting Scientist 1975-77, Associate Cancer Research Scientist 1977 to present, Roswell Park Memorial Institute Department of Experimental Therapeutics; Clinical Assistant Professor, Department of Pathology, State University of New York at Buffalo Medical School, 1978 to present; Assistant Research Professor, Department of Pharmacology, Roswell Park Division Graduate School, 1978 to present. Organizational Memberships: Medical Association of Croatia; Yugoslavian Association of Immunology; Yugoslavian Association of Pathology; American Association for Cancer Research; American Society for Clinical Oncology; American Association for Pathology; Sigma Xi; New York Academy of Sciences; American Association for the Advancement of Science. Published Works: Numerous Articles for Professional Journals and Books, including "Insights on Biology of Human Solid Tumor Cloning *In Vitro*" (with H. K. Slocum, Y. M. Rustum, S. Polanskaya, C. Krakousis, H. Takita, A. Mittelman), "Is There Anatomical Segregation of Important Cell Population in Human Solid Tumors?" (with H. K. Slocum, Y. M. Rustum, W. R. Greco, C Karakousis, H. Takita, P. J. Creaven), "Correlation of Micrometastatic Involvement of Lungs and Some Biological Tumor Properties with Growth in Soft Agar". Honors and Awards: Grants and Contracts, National Institutes of Health, "Preclinical Toxicology and Pathology" 1977-82, "Comparative Study of the Effects of Surgery, Chemotherapy and Immunotherapy, Alone and In Combination, on Primary and Metastatic B16 Melanoma" 1978-82, "Colony Stem Cell Assay as Determination of Response in Solid Tumors" 1980-83, "Cloning Characterization and Drug Sensitivity of Murine Melanoma" (approved, not funded). Address: 58 Hiler Avenue, Kenmore, New York 14217.

Pavelka, Elaine Blanche

Educator. Personal: Daughter of Mrs. Mildred Pavelka. Education: B.A., M.S., Northwestern University; Ph.D., University of Illinois. Career: Mathematics Professor, Morton College, present; Mathematics Instructor, Leyden Community High School; Mathematician, Northwestern University Aerial Measurements Laboratory. Organizational Memberships: American Educational Research Association; American Mathematical Association of Two-Year Colleges (vice-president); American Mathematical Society; Association for Women in Mathematics; Canadian Society for the History and Philosophy of Mathematics; Mathematics Association of America; Mathematics Action Group; Illinois Council of Teachers of Mathematics; Illinois Mathematics Association of Community Colleges; National Council of Teachers of Mathematics; School Science and Mathematics Association; Society for Industrial and Applied Mathematics; Pi Mu Epsilon; Sigma Delta Epsilon. Community Activities: Northwestern University Alumni Association; University of Illinois Alumni Association. Honors and Awards: Member, American Mensa Limited; Member, Intertel; Only Community College Professor Asked to Present a Paper before the Third International Congress on Mathematics Education, Karlsruhe, Germany, 1976; Listed in *Who's Who of American Women, Who's Who in the Midwest, World Who's Who of Women, International Who's Who in Education, International Who's Who in Intellectuals, International Who's Who in Community Service, International Register of Profiles, Dictionary of International Biography, Men and Women of Distinction, Personalities of America, Personalities of the West and Midwest, Notable Americans, Directory of Distinguished Americans, Community Leaders and Noteworthy Americans, Who's Who in Technology Today, The Registry of American Achievement, Leading Consultants in Technology, Contemporary Personalities.* Address: 1900 Euclid Avenue, Berwyn, Illinois 60402.

Elaine Pavelka

Paxton, Juanita Willene

Director, Counseling Center. Personal: Daughter of Mr. and Mrs. Will Paxton (both deceased). Education: A.B., Psychology/Sociology, Birmingham Southern College, 1950; M.A., Counseling and Guidance, Michigan State University, 1951; Ed.D., Counseling and Guidance, Indiana University, 1971. Career: Director, Counseling Center; Dormitory Director, Texas Technological University; Assistant Dean of Students, Associate Dean of Students, State University Teachers College, Fredonia, New York; Assistant Dean of Women, University of New Mexico; Dean of Women, East Tennessee State University, Johnson City, Tennessee. Organizational Memberships: Tennessee Association of Women Deans and Counselors (vice president, 1964-66; president, 1966-68); East Tennessee Education Association (chairman, guidance division, 1967); Watauga Personnel and Guidance Association (secretary, 1966-67; president-elect, 1967-68); American Association of University Women (president, Johnson City Branch, 1966-68); Tennessee College Personnel Association (legislative committee; executive board; media board); Tennessee Personnel and Guidance Association; National Association of Women Deans, Administrators and Counselors; Association of Counselor Educators and Supervisors; American Association of Higher Education; American College Personnel Association (directorate, newsletter editor, media chairman, Commission XV); Southern College Personnel Association; Southern Association for Counselor Education and Supervision; Delta Kappa Gamma (chapter president, 1975-76; state secretary, 1977-79; state first vice president, 1979-81); Guidance Association of Educators and Supervisors; Pi Lambda Theta; Alpha Chi Omega; Psi Chi; Contact Teleministries (director of on-going training, 1978-80; director of training, 1980-81; vice chairperson, board of directors, 1980-81). Community Activities: Monday Club Auxiliary (secretary, 1978-79; president, 1980-81). Religion: Secretary, Administrative Board, Munsey Memorial Methodist Church, 1977-80; Adult Coordinator, Council on Ministries, 1980-81. Honors and Awards: N.D.E.A. Summer Institute, University of Texas, 1965; E.P.D.A. Year-Long Fellowship, Indiana University, 1968-69; Graduate Assistantships, Michigan State University 1950-51, Indiana University 1969-70; Junior League Scholarship, Birmingham Southern College, 1948-50. Address: 1203 Lester Harris Road, Johnson City, Tennessee 37601.

Paynter, Dorothy K

Director, Educator. Personal: Born July 1, 1935; Mother of Catherine Mary, Margaret Ellen, David Michael, Andrew Howard. Education: B.A./L.S. 1973, M.S. Ed. Counseling, State University of New York at Brockport; Ed.D. Adult Education, Syracuse University, 1982. Career: Assistant Professor, Business, 1975-77; Program Consultant, 1977-78; Acting Director, External Programs 1978-81; Director, Energy Education and Training Division, Associate Professor, Rochester Institute of Technology, 1981 to present. Organizational Memberships: Adult Education Association (national delegate, 1978); National University Continuing Education Association (chair, 1980-81, vice chair 1979-80, secretary 1978-79, region II); Associate Editor, Continuum, 1976-79. Community Activities: John Anderson Campaign (volunteer, 1980); American Red Cross (advisory committee, volunteer training, 1979); Women's Education Project (steering committee, 1975-78); Women's Career Center, Inc. (steering committee, board of directors, 1974-76); Junior League (speaker, 1974-75); Young Women's Christian Association. Honors and Awards: Listed in *Who's Who in the East, World Who's Who of Women.* Address: 423 Eastbrooke Lane, Rochester, New York 14618.

Norman Pearson

Pearman, Reginald A

Educator. Personal: Born August 8, 1918; Father of Jocelyn R., Reginald A. Jr. Education: B.S. Education 1942, Ed.M. 1949, Boston University; C.A.G.S., 1951; Advanced Study, Harvard University, Columbia University; Graduate, United States Athletic School, Chalons sur Marne, France. Military: Served in the United States Army Medical Branch, Grade T/5, in Europe, during World War II, 1943-46. Career: Junior High School Teacher, Inkster, Michigan; Director of Health and Physical Education, Leland College, Baker, Louisiana; Director of Health and Physical Education, Morristown College, Tennessee; Bowie State College, Maryland, Health Education Specialist 30 Years, Professor Emeritus. Organizational Memberships: American Physical Health Association; American Association of Health, Physical Education and Recreation; A.S.A.; National Recreation and Parks Society. Community Activities: Omega Pi Phi Fraternity (keeper of records and seals, keeper of finance, Gamma chapter, Boston, Massachusetts); St. Augustine's Camp, Foxboro, Massachustts (director, senior counselor); Leland College (health and physical education committee); Morristown College (health and physical education committee); Work with Democrat Club, Boston; Bel Air Boys Club, Bowie, Maryland. Religion: Shrine Catholic Immaculate Conception, Washington, D.C.; St. Augustine's Church, Boston, Massachusetts, Men's Club, Boys' Club. Honors and Awards: Maryland Meritorious Service Plaque, 1981; Fellow, American Physical Health Association; Fellow, American Association of Health, Physical Education and Recreation; Fellow, National Recreation and Parks Society. Address: P.O. Box 375, Bowie, Maryland 20715.

Pearson, Norman

Company President, Consultant Planner. Personal: Born October 24, 1928, in Staley, County Durham, United Kingdom; Married Gerda Maria Josefine Riedl, 1972. Education: Professional Degree, Bachelor of Arts with Honors, Town and Country Planning, University of Durham, 1951; Ph.D. Land Economics, International Institute for Advanced Studies, 1979; M.B.A., Pacific Western

University, 1980. Military: Served in the Royal Air Force-NATO-RCAF in the United Kingdom, Canada, Iceland and the United States from 1952-53 as Flying Officer, G.D./Nav (Aircrew); and in the same position in the Royal Air Force Volunteer Reserve from 1953-58. Career: Consultant to Stanley Urban District Council, United Kingdom, 1946-47; Planning Assistant, Accrington Town Plan and Bedford County Planning Survey, University of Durham Planning Team, United Kingdom, 1947-49; Planning Assistant, Messrs. Allen & Mattocks, Consulting Planners and Landscape Designers and Architects, United Kingdom, 1949-51; Administrative Assistant, Scottish Division, National Coal Board, Scotland, 1951-52; Planning Assistant, London City Council, 1953-54; Planner, Central Mortgage and Housing Corporation, Ottawa, 1954-55; Planning Analyst, City of Toronto Planning Board, Commissioner of Planning, Town of Burlington, Ontario, 1959-62; Planner, Professional Consulting Practice, 1962 to present; President, Norman Pearson Planning Associates Limited, 1976 to present; Many Achievements as Planner, including Official Plans, Township of Chingaua, Township of Chingauacousy 1964-70, Georgian Bay Regional Plan 1968-72, Official Plans, Welland Area Planning Board 1963-70, Research, Appraisal Institute of Canada, Land Banking Principles and Practice 1972-75; Study of Impact on Planning Bruce Nuclear Power Development, Kincardine and Several Related Municipalities 1974-75, Advisor, UDI London, Parks and Recreation Policies, Official Plan; Special Lecture in Planning, McMaster University 1956-64, Waterloo Lutheran University 1961-63; Assistant Professor, Geography, Chairman, Director, Center for Resources Development, University of Guelph, 1967-72; Professor of Political Science, University of Western Ontario, Urban/Regional Program, 1972-77; Adjunct Professor, International Institute for Advanced Studies, 1980 to present; Ontario Land Economist, 1963; Real Estate Professional Appraiser, Alpha Appraisal Association, 1976. Organizational Memberships: Royal Town Planning Institute, United Kingdom (associate member, 1955; fellow, 1972); International Society of City and Regional Planners, 1972; Canadian Institute of Planners (associate member, 1956; member, 1959); American Institute of Planners, 1973; American Institute of Certified Planners (charter member, 1978); Canadian Association of Certified Planning Technicians, 1979; Royal Economic Society (member, 1952; fellow, 1955; life fellow 1966); Intercontinental Biographical Association (fellow, 1975; life fellow, 1976); United States Committee for Monetary Research and Education (member, 1975; life member, 1976); American Geographical Society (life fellow, 1976); Atlantic Economic Association (life fellow, 1978); International Fraternity of Lambda Alpha (land economics), 1969; British Sociological Association (founder, member, 1953); International Joint Commission (Canadian universities representative, social sciences, economic and legal aspects standing committee, research advisory board, 1972-76); International Association of Great Lakes Research, Journal of Great Lakes Research (editorial board, 1973-80); Great Lakes Tomorrow (Canadian vice president, 1976-77); National Research Council, United States (committee A1BO3, economic and environmental factors of transportation, transportation research board, 1973-79; corresponding member, 1979); New Communities and Large-Scale Development Council, Urban Land Institute, United States, 1979 to present. Community Activities: Numerous Audio-Visual Presentations; Numerous, Public Lectures. Published Works: Editor, *The Ontario Land Economist,* 1978 to present; Co-Author or Co-Editor, Four Books, including Editing *Regional and Resource Planning in Canada;* Author, 68 Articles in Refereed Academic and Professional Journals or Chapters in Books; Author, 171 Articles in Non-Refereed Journals, Reports, Conference Papers or Abstracts; Author, 46 Newspaper Articles for Book Reviews. Honors and Awards: Knight of Malta (chavalier); President's Prize (Bronze Medal); Royal Town Planning Institute, United Kingdom, 1957; Honorary Member, Brue Pratt Association, 1960 to present; Listed in *Dictonary of International Biography, American Men and Women of Science; Who's Who in the Midwest; Men of Achievement; International Who's Who of Community Service, International Register of Profiles, World Edition, International Who's Who of Intellectuals, Men and Women of Distinction.* Address: P.O. Box 5362, Station A, London, Ontario, Canada N6A 4L6 Canada.

Peavoy, Sharon An

Continuing Education Counselor. Personal: Born March 11, 1951; Daughter of Edward E. (deceased) and Ann Peavoy. Education: B.A., Pfeiffer College, 1973; M.A., Education, East Carolina University, 1979. Career: Juvenile Court Counselor, 20th Judicial District, Wadesboro, North Carolina, 1973-76; Juvenile Intake Counselor, 12th Judicial District, Fayetteville, North Carolina, 1977-79; Continuing Education Counselor, 1980 to present. Organizational Memberships: North Carolina Juvenile Services Association, 1973 to present; American Personnel and Guidance Association, 1977-80; Public Offender Counselor Association, 1977-80. Community Activities: Children's Service Committee, Wadesboro, North Carolina (chairman, 1974-75); Anson County Youth Advisory Board, Wadesboro, North Carolina (chairman, 1975-76). Honors and Awards: Mental Health Appreciation Certificate, 1980. Address: 345 Letchworth Circle, Winterville, North Carolina 28590.

Peck, Dianne Kawecki

Architect. Personal: Born in 1945; Daughter of Thaddeus Walter and Harriet Ann Kawecki; Married Gerald Paul Peck; Mother of Samantha Gillian, Alexis Hilary. Education: Bachelor of Architecture, Carnegie-Mellon University, 1968; Certificate, Critical Path Construction; Three-Dimensional Vector Analysis, New York University. Organizational Memberships: Health Systems Agency of Northern Virginia; American Institute of Architects, 1970-78; Soroptimist International, 1977; Washington Professional Women's Cooperative, 1977; American Association of University Women, 1974-76. Community Activities: Vocational Education Foundation (vice president), 1976); Architect and Engineers United Way (chairwoman); Industrial Development Authority of Prince William (chairwoman, 1976; vice chair, 1977); Prince William Chamber of Commerce (director, 1977). Published Works: Inner-City Rehabilitation Study, 1973. Honors and Awards: Prince William Board of Supervisors Commendation, 1976; Health Systems Agency Commendation, 1977; Listed in *Who's Who in the Southeast, Who's Who of American Women, Who's Who-Personalities of the South, Who's Who-Women of the World.* Address: 11510 Wildflower Court, Woodbridge, Virginia 22192.

Peckham, Charles Wesley

Assistant Administrator, Educator, Community Leader. Personal: Born November 18, 1923; Son of Leo and Isabella Carmack Peckham; Married Arline Beasa; Father of Deborah, Charles, Jr., Mark, Elizabeth. Education: B.A., Indiana Central University, 1951; Master of Divinity 1954, Master of Sacred Theology 1962, United Theological Seminary; Ed.D., University of Cincinnati 1971. Military: Chaplain's Assistant, Korea, 1945. Career: Clergyman; Assistant Administrator for Program and Social Services, Otterbein Home, present; Adjunct Professor, Xavier University, United Theological Seminary, Methodist Theological Seminary, present. Organizational Memberships: National Association of Activity Professionals (chairperson, budget and finance); Resident Activity Personnel in Ohio (member, 1975 to present; executive secretary); National Health and Welfare Association (member, 1975 to present). Community Activities: Warren County Council on Aging (president); SCOPE-five County Community Action Board (member, 1975; president); Warren County Human Service Board (member, 1968, present, president); Warren County Health Planning Committee (vice chairperson); Otterbein Home (director, gerontology center); Warren County United Way Board (member, 1974 to present, president); Phi Delta Kappa; Common Cause. Religion: Wilmington District Council on Ministries, United Methodist Church; Christian Unity and Interreligious Affairs, West Ohio Conference, United Methodist Church; Served in Churches in California, Wisconsin, Ohio. Published Works: Co-Author with Arline Peckham, Three Books on Aging, *Thank You for Shaking My Hand, I Can Still Pray, Activities Keep Me Going.* Honors and Awards: Community Service Award, Ohio Commission on

Aging, 1976; Special Resolution Plaque, Ohio House of Representatives, Volunteer Service Award, Community Service Administration, 1980; Listed in *Who's Who in the Midwest, Community Leaders and Noteworthy Americans, Dictionary of International Biography, International Who's Who of Intellectuals.* Address: 689 North State Route 741, Lebanon, Ohio 45036.

Peery, James Brown

Physician. Personal: Born February 8, 1925; Son of Dr. and Mrs. John C. Peery; Married to Joan W; Father of Steven J. Peery and Brenda P. Collins. Education: Attended Newberry College, Newberry, South Carolina and University of Pennsylvania at Philadelphia; M.D., George Washington University School of Medicine. Military: Served with United States Army as Captain, Medical Corps, 1950-51. Career: Physician specializing in gynecology. Organizational Memberships: Fresno County Medical Society; California Medical Association; American Medical Association; Christian Medical Society; Fresno Community Hospital (board of trustees, 1977 to present). Religion: Member Hope Lutheran Church. Honors and Awards: Certified by American Board of Obstetrics-Gynecology, 1957, recertified, 1977. Address: 1464 West Morris Avenue, Fresno, California 93711.

Pehlke, Robert Donald

Educator. Personal: Born February 11, 1933; Son of Robert William Pehlke (deceased) and Mrs. O. H. Perry; Married Julie Anne Kehoe; Father of Robert Donald, Jr., Elizabeth Anne, David Richard. Education: B.S.E., University of Michigan, 1955; S.M. 1958, Sc.D. 1960, Massachusetts Institute of Technology; Attended Technological Institute, Aachen, Germany, 1956-57. Career: University of Michigan, Assistant Professor of Met. Engineering 1968 to present, Chairman, Department of Met. Engineering 1968 to present. Organizational Memberships: American Society for Metals (secretary, metals academy committee, 1977; technical divisions board, 1982 to present); A.I.M.E. Iron and Steel Society (director, 1976-77); A.I.M.E. Met. Society; American Foundrymen's Society; American Society of Engineering Education; German Iron and Steel Society; London Iron and Steel Society; Japan Iron and Steel Society; New York Academy of Science; Sigma Xi; Tau Beta Pi; Alpha Sima Mu (national president, 1977-78); Registered Professional Engineer, Michigan. Community Activities: Ann Arbor Amateur Hockey Association (president, 1977-79; board of directors, 1976-81). Honors and Awards: Fellow, American Society for Metals, 1977; Gold Medal Science of Extractive Met. 1976, Howe Memorial Lecturer 1980, Fellow, Met. Society 1983, Distinguished Life Member, Iron and Steel Society 1979, A.I.M.E.; National Science Foundation Fellow, 1955-56; Fulbright Scholar, 1956-57. Address: 9 Regent Drive, Ann Arbor, Michigan 48104.

Penland, Arnold Clifford Jr

Educator. Personal: Born October 8, 1933; Son of Mr. and Mrs. A. C. Penland; Married Joan Eudy; Father of Marcia Jean, Elizabeth Bailey. Education: B.S., Western Carolina University, 1956; M.A., George Peabody College, 1959; M.Ed., Duke University, 1966; Ph.D., Florida State University. Career: State Supervisor of Music, State of South Carolina; Supervisor of Music, Raleigh Public Schools, North Carolina; Teacher, Reidsville Public Schools, North Carolina; Music Director, Several Churches; Director, Raleigh Cultural Center, North Carolina; Professor of Music, Assistant Dean, College of Fine Arts, University of Florida, Gainesville. Organizational Memberships: North Carolina Music Educators Association (chairman, revision committee, state solo and ensemble contest lists; board of directors, 1963-64; chairman, selection committee for editor, 1962; chairman, promotional clinic for recruitment and training of singers, 1963); Music Educators National Conference (general conference planning committee, 1963, 1965, 1967, 1969, 1970, 1971, 1974, 1975; contemporary music project, composer-in-residence, 1964; philosophies and trends in music committee, 1967; contemporary music project, review of composers-in-residence, 1968; go-project, national commitee #14, 1969-70; media resources and technology committee, 1973-74; general music in high school committee, 1978-79); National Education Association; North Carolina Education Association; Association for Supervision and Curriculum Development; Tennessee Music Educators Association; American Choral Directors Association; South Carolina Music Educators Association (board of directors, 1970-71; program committee, 1969-70); Council of State Music Supervisors; Florida Music Educators Association (political action committee, 1973-74; chairman, North Florida building fund, 1973-74; competency committee on music teacher state certification, 1977-78; research committee, 1977-78; state advisor, Florida state chapters, 1978-80); Florida College Music Educators Association (secretary-treasurer, 1980-82); Florida Elementary School Music Educators Association; The College Music Society (life member); Association for Childhood Education International; Curriculum Guide for Choral Music in the Secondary Schools of North Carolina (chairman, revision committee, until 1967); National Association of Academic Affairs Administrators; American College Personnel Association; American Association for Higher Education. Community Activities: Raleigh Chamber Music Society (board of directors, 1963-66); Arts Council of Raleigh, Inc. (board of directors; charter member, 1964-67); Raleigh Cultural Center, Inc. (board of directors, charter member, 1962-67); North Carolina Symphony Society (board of directors, Raleigh Chapter, 1963-67); Raleigh Federated Music Club (board of directors, 1964-67; past vice president); Sir Walter Lions Club, Raleigh (board of directors, 1963-66; past vice president); Glen Forest Community Men's Club (vice president, North Carolina, 1962-63); Alachua County Arts Council, Inc., Florida (vice president, 1974-75); Gainesville Cultural Commission, Florida (appointed by mayor, 1975-76); Gainesville Civic Chorus, Florida (board of directors, 1977-79); Foundation for the Promotion of Music Inc., Gainesville (vice president, 1978-79); South Carolina State Arts Council (advisory committee, 1970); Music Education Advisory Committee, Florida State Fair, 1970-73. Religion: Grace Presbyterian Church, Gainesville, Florida, Elder 1972-79, Choir Soloist 1970-80; Choir Director and/or Soloist, Churches in North Carolina, South Carolina, Tennessee, Florida, 1956-80. Honors and Awards: Music Scholarship, Western Carolina University, 1952; Winner, Audition, Voice Scholarship, Private Study with Robert Malone, New York City, 1952; Winner, Audition, Drama Scholarship, Plymouth Drama School and Festival, Massachusetts, 1956; Full Tuition, Expense Scholarship for Master's Degree, Duke University, 1964-65; Full Tuition, Stipend, Faculty Development Institute in Higher Education, George Peabody College, Nashville, Tennessee, 1967-68; Phi Delta Kappa; Citation, Distinguished Service to the Cultural, Musical and Artistic Life of North Carolina, North Carolina Federation of Music Clubs, 1966; Grants, Arts and Humanities Program, U.S.E.O. 1964, Ford Foundation 1964-66, M.E.N.C. Contemporary Musicianship 1965-67, P.A.C.E., E.S.E.A., Title III 1967-69, National Endowment for the Arts 1970-71, Bureau of Research, College of Architecture and Fine Arts, University of Florida 1971, Graduate School O.C.O. Award, 1971, Fine Arts Council of Florida 1978-79, M.E.N.C. Co-Sponsored Regional Institute 1981; Listed in *Who's Who Among Students in American Universities and Colleges, Who's Who in Florida, International Who's Who of Music, Personalities of the South, Dictionary of International Biography, Notable Americans of the Bicentennial Era, Men of Achievement.* Address: 2809 Southwest 81st Street, Gainesville, Florida 32607.

Pennington, Dorthy Lee

Educator. Personal: Daughter of Walter and Susie Pennington. Education: B.A., University of Kansas. Career: Assistant Instructor; Lecturer; Consultant; Associate Professor, Researcher. Organizational Memberships: Speech Communication Association (chair, black caucus, 1974-76); International Communication Association; Society for Intercultural Education Training and Research.

Community Activities: Kansas Children's Service League (board of directors, black adoption program of Kansas City, 1977 to present); Kansas Committee for the Humanities (humanist, 1975 to present); National Association for the Advancement of Colored People (membership chair, Lawrence chapter, 1979-80); Zeta Phi Beta (Lawrence chapter sponsor); Organizer, Informal Support Group for Southern Graduate Students at University of Kansas; Speaker and Workshop Leader, Churches, Public Schools, Penal Institutions, Kansas; Rust College (alumni advisory board, 1976-78); Self-Culture Club of Lawrence (historian, treasurer, 1980-82); Editorial Boards, Various Journals. Religion: Director, Young People's Division, Steward, Choir Member, St. Luke A.M.E. Church, Lawrence. Honors and Awards: Presidential Citation as Distinguished Alumni of Historically Black Institutions, National Association for Equal Opportunity in Higher Education, 1981; Listed in *Who's Who Among American Women, Notable Americans, World Who's Who of Women, Outstanding Young Women of America.* Address: 1500 West 8th Terrace, Lawrence, Kansas 66044.

Charles H Percy

Percy, Charles Harting

United States Senator. Personal: Born September 27, 1919, in Pensacola, Florida; Married Jeanne Dickerson (deceased); Father of Valerie (deceased), Sharon, Roger; 2nd Wife, Loraine Guyer; Father of Gail, Mark. Education: Graduate of New Trier High School, Winnetka, Illinois; Bachelor's Degree Economics, University of Chicago, 1941. Military: Served in the United States Navy as apprentice seaman from 1943-45, attaining the rank of Lieutenant Senior Grade. Career: Bell & Howell, Director, 1942, Corporate Secretary 1945, President, Chief Executive Officer 1949, Chairman, Chief Executive Officer 1961-63, Chairman, 1961-66; United States Senator, 1966 to present. Organizational Memberships: Republican Precinct Worker, 1946; United Republican Fund of Illinois (president, 1955-58); Republican Finance Committee (vice chairman, 1955-59); Republican Committee on Program and Progress (chairman, 1959); Republican Platform Committee (chairman, 1960); Special Ambassador (personal representative of president Eisenhower, presidential inaugurations, Peru, Bolivia, 1956); Republican Candidate, Governor of Illinois, 1964; New Illinois Committee (chairman, 1965); Foreign Relations Committee (chairman; subcommittees, international economic policy, arms control, Near East); Governmental Affairs Committee (chairman, subcommittee on energy, nuclear proliferation and governmental processes); Special Committee on Aging; Republican Policy Committee. Community Activities: Principal Republican Sponsor, Civil Service Reform Act of 1978, Congressional Reform Act of 1974; Author, Major Legislation to Assist Elderly; Advocate, Legislation, Comprehensive National Energy Policy, Emphasis on Conservation; Chief Sponsor, Nuclear Non-Proliferation Act of 1978; Major Supporter, Broadcasts, Radio Free Europe, Radio Liberty, Voice of America; Alliance to Save Energy (founder; chairman); Kennedy Center for the Performing Arts (vice chairman, board of trustees); Ford Foundation (chairman of the board, fund for Adult Education); University of Chicago (trustee); California Institute of Technology (trustee); Chicago Boys Club (director); Business Council, 1974; Delegate, 29th United Nations General Assembly. Published Works: Author, Two Books, *Growing Old in the Country of the Young, I Want to Know About the United States Senate.* Honors and Awards: Admiral's Commendation for Administration and Supervision of Naval Ordnance, Training Units, Naval Air Station, Alameda, California, Rear Admiral V. H. Ragsdale, 1945; University Marshall to President Maynard Hutchins, Highest Honor Accorded Senior Student, University of Chicago, 1941; Honorary LL.D., Illinois College 1961, Roosevelt University 1961, Lake Forest College 1962, Bradley University 1963, Defiance College 1965, Northwestern University 1966; Honorary HH.D., Willamette University, 1962; Honorary D.H.L., National College of Education, 1964; Appointed Officer, French Legion of Honor, for Contributions to Freer International Trade, 1961; Businessman of the Year, *Saturday Review*, 1962; Statesmanship Award, Harvard Business School of Chicago; Abraham Lincoln Center Humanitarian Service Award; Top-Hat Award, National Federation of Business and Professional Woman's Clubs, 1965; Business Administration Award, Drexel Institute of Technology, 1965. Address: United States Senate, Washington, D.C. 20510.

A Ronald Perkins

Perkins, A Ronald

Mayor, City of Culver City, California. Personal: Born August 16, 1923; Son of Alfred Ward and Sue Glidden Perkins; Married to Barbara Joyce; Father of Ronald Edward, David Randall. Education: Attended Northwestern Traffic Institute; B.A., Hollywood Motion Picture Institute; Attended U.S.C. Delinquency Control Institute; Attended Woodbury Business College of University of Southern California. Military: Served with United States Army in counter-intelligence, 1945-46; Served with United States Air Force in the Air Police, 1951-52. Career: Current Juvenile Traffic Court Commissioner; Current Newspaper Columnist; Former Police Commander, Culver City Police Department; Instructor on criminal justice system; Consultant on computer systems and security. Organizational Memberships: American Management Association; Council of Traffic Judges and Educators; International Asssociation of Chiefs of Police; California State Peace Officers Association. Community Activities: Member, Masonic Lodge #602, 1970 to present; Charter member of Elks Lodge #1917; Member of Exchange Club for 15 years; President, Culver City Little League 4 years; President of Culver City Babe Ruth League 12 years. Honors and Awards: Citation for outstanding police and community service, Culver City Council, 1974; Award for saving a life, Culver City Council and Fire Department, 1979; Outstanding Community Service Award, Los Angeles County, 1979; Sustained Community Leadership Award, Culver City Police Department, 1981; Babe Ruth Outstanding Community Service Award, 1970-71; Received award as outstanding contributor to youth baseball, Helms Athletic Foundation, 1971; Outstanding Contributor to Youth, Culver City Little League, 1972-73; Outstanding Contributor to International Baseball, Confederation Deportive Mexicana, 1975; "Hands Across the Nation" award, Dover Township, New Jersey, 1973; Man of the Year, Coordinating Council, 1975; National Exchange Club "Book of Golden Deeds" award, 1980. Address: P.O. Box 2116, Culver City, California 90230.

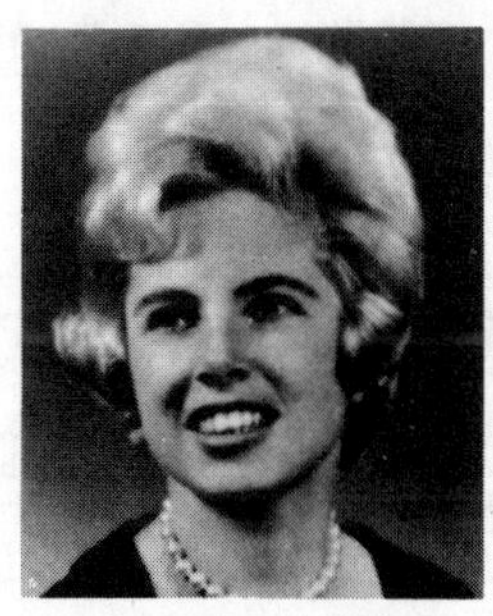

Barbara A Perks

Perks, Barbara Ann

Psychologist. Personal: Born July 1, 1937; Daughter of Alfred and Lillian Marcus; Married Anthony Perks. Education: B.S., Pennsylvania State University, 1959; M.A., Columbia University, 1963; Certificate in Educational Psychology, Oxford University, 1965; Graduate Studies, University of Oregon, 1973, 1974; Doctoral Studies, University of British Columbia, 1977 to present. Career: Educational Psychologist, Health Science Hospital, University of British Columbia, Child Psychiatry, 1979 to present; Supervisor, Student Teachers, Consultant, Research, 1976-79; School Psychologist, Vancouver, 1972-76; Reading Consultant, Littlemore, Oxfordshire, England, 1964-65; Teacher of Gifted, Hamden, Connecticut, 1959-62. Organizational Memberships: American Psychological Association; British Columbia Psychological Association; Association of Humanistic Psychology; National Association of School Psychology; American Educational Research Association; North American Adlerian Psychology; American Orthopsychiatric Association. Community Activities: National Figure Skating Association (volunteer skating teacher, skating judge, 1966-72). Published Works: Research Paper, Presented to National Association of School Psychologists, "Status and Training of School Psychologists in Canada", 1980; Paper: "The Role of the Canadian School Psychologist", *Journal of School Psychology*, Fall 1981, Volume 19, No. 3. Honors and Awards: Mortar Board, 1958-59; Pi Sigma Alpha, 1959; Pi Lambda Theta, 1963; Kappa Delta Pi, 1963; Dr. MacKenzie American Alumni Scholarship, 1979, 1980, 1981, 1982, 1983, University Fellowship 1982; Canadian Daughter's League Award, 1981; Council of British Columbia Award, 1981. Address: 4570 Glenwood Avenue, North Vancouver, British Columbia, Canada V7R 4G5.

Perlov, Dadie

Association Executive. Personal: Born June 8, 1929; Daughter of Aaron and Anna Heitman; Mother of Nancy, Jane, Amy. Education: B.A., New York University, 1950; Attended Vanderbilt University, 1973; Graduate Studies in Educational Psychology, Adelphi University, 1963; Courses in Management and Administration. Career: Executive Director 1981 to present, Director of Field Services 1968-74, National Council of Jewish Women, New York City; Executive Director, New York Library Association, 1974-81; Executive Director, Operation Open City, 1962-64. Organizational Memberships: A.S.A.E. (association evaluator, membership committee); Consultant on Association Administration, Conference Planning, Public Speaking; New York Society of Association Executives (board member); International Platform Association; Speaker on "Computerized Record Keeping", "Effective Grass Roots Lobbying", "Personnel Practices", "Not-for-Profit Association of the Future". Community Activities: Major Political Party (committeewoman); School Board Selection Panel; Audubon Society; New York Zoological Society; League of Women Voters (past president, Northeast Queens Chapter). Honors and Awards: Certified Association Executive, 1978; Association Executive of the Year, New York State, 1980; Recognition Award, New York Library Association, 1978. Address: 262 Central Park West, New York, New York 10024.

Peros, Alex George

Doctor of Chiropractic, Acupuncturist. Personal: Born January 17, 1934, in Pretoria, South Africa; Son of George and Irene Peros; Married Sharon Freitas; Father of Evangelina Anastasia, Andrew Graham, Trina Nanette, Brian Jay. Education: Graduate of Jeppe Preparatory School, Johannesburg, South Africa; Witerwatersrand Technical College, 1950-52; Britzuis Business College, 1952-53; Palmer College of Chiropractic, Glendale, California, 1960; Postgraduate Work, Gonstead Chiropractic Clinic, Mount Horeb, Wisconsin; First Acupuncture Residence Program to be Held in the United States, Denver, Colorado, 1974; Rocky Mountain Acupuncture Research Institute; Acupuncture Pressure Point Technique Seminars; Yennie Acupuncture Seminars; Bridges Acupuncture Seminars; Chines Medical College, Hong Kong; Studies in Drug and Alcohol Abuse and Treatment, Narcotic Enforcement, Ryodoraku Acupuncture, Auriculartherapy, Metabolic Nutrition, Polarity Balance-Nutritional Balance. Career: Company Doctor, United States Plywood Corporation, Eurake, California; President, Peros Acupuncture Teaching Institute, Denver, Colorado; President, Peros Acupuncture Chiropractic Clinic, Fairbury, Illinois; Chiropractic Practice, Northern California, Central Illinois; Licenses Held in Alberta, Canada, 1965, California 1961, Illinois 1967, Michigan Basic Science Medical Board 1966; Narcotic Undercover Police Officer, Iroqouis County Sheriff's Office, Watseka, Illinois. Organizational Memberships: International Chiropractic Association (past member, drug abuse committee); Prairie State Chiropractic Association of Illinois (past member, drug abuse committee); American Chiropractic Association; California Chiropractic Association; International Chiropractic-Physicians Acupuncture Association (board of directors, 1974-79); International Biographical Association (fellow); Rockley Research Academy (fellow member); Junior Chamber Internatinal Senate (senator); Academy of Chinese Medicine (charter member); Acupuncture Society of America; International Platform Association; New Breed of Doctor; Institute for Practicing Justice (national coordinator); Full Gospel Business Men's Fellowship International; Gideons International (vice president, Lake Country, California chapter); Nevada Acupuncture Association (honorary member). Community Activities: Eureka California Jaycees (vice president, 1963; Junior Chamber International (senator, 1964 to present); Gideons International (past secretary; president, Lake County chapter, 1981-82); Concerned Parents on Drug Abuse (past chairman, Livingston County, Illinois chapter, 1975-77; past chairman, Lake Mendocino Counties, California chapter, 1980-81); Lake County Abused Women and Children (chairman, 1982); Iroquois County Law Enforcement Association, Illinois (past program chairman); Lecturer, Various Groups, including Chamber of Commerce, Rotary Club, Kiwanis Club, Lions Club, Women's Clubs, Church Groups, Law Enforcement Associations, Schools International Platform Association, Various Professonal Associations, Medical, Nursing, Chiropractic, Central Illinois Rehabilitation Center, Joliet Junior College; Prison Counselor, Prayer, Prison and Praise, Squires of California, San Quinten's Utilization of Inmate Resources, Experiences and Studies; Numerous Radio and Television Appearances, Chicago, LaGrange, Champaign, Canton, Peoria, Watseka, Bloomington-Normal, Illinois, Lakeport, Ukiah, Modesto, California, Johannesburg, South Africa. Religion: Assemblies of God Church. Published Works: *Peros Acupuncture Training Manual*, 1975. Honors and Awards: Newspaper Write-Ups, *The Courier*, Champaign, Illinois, *The Daily Journal* Kankakee, Illinois, *The Herald*, Des Plaines, Illinois, *Watseka Daily Times* Illinois, *Daily Pantagraph* Bloomington, Illinois, *Penny Press* Peoria, Illinois, *The Daily Journal* Ukiah, California, *Sunday Express*, *The Citizen* Johannesburg, South Africa; Listed in *Who's Who of the Midwest, Who's Who of America, Community Leaders and Noteworthy Americans, Dictionary of International Biography, Who's Who of America, Book of Honor, International Who's Who of Intellectuals, Who's Who in Community Service, Personalities of America.* Address: 1090 Tunis Street, Lakeport, California 95453.

Perret, Roland Francis Jr

Receiving Clerk. Personal: Born February 18, 1946; Son of Roland and Anita D. Perret. Education: B.S. Chemistry, University of Southwestern Louisiana, 1968. Military: Served in the United States Army National Guard from 1968-73, attaining a rating of E-4. Career: Manager, Roland Perret Distribution, Inc., Jeanerette, Louisiana; Receiving Clerk, Voorhies Supply Company, present. Organizational Memberships: Louisiana Oil Marketers Association. Religion: Roman Catholic, 1946 to present. Address: 2810 West Main Street, Jeanerette, Louisiana 70544.

Perry, Curtis Lee

Administrator, Educator. Personal: Born January 6, 1944, in Tarboro, North Carolina; Married Annie Elizabeth Williams; Father of Nicole Denise. Education: Graduate of W. A. Pattillo High School, Tarboro, North Carolina; B.S., Sociology, Fayetteville State University, North Carolina; M.A., Educational Administration, East Carolina University, North Carolina. Career: Administrator, Tarboro City Schools, 1966 to present; Chairman of Social Studies Department, Teacher of United States History, Government, Economics, Civics and Sociology, Academic Planner, Developer of Social Studies Curriculum, Supervisor of Student Activities, Assistant Principal, Tarboro High School; Recruiter of Minority Teachers at 16 Universities; Part-time Teacher of Social Studies, United States History, State/Federal Government, Criminal Justice, North Carolina State and Local Government, Edgecombe Technical College, 1969, 1980; Assistant Manager, Daitch Shopwell Grocery Store, Monticello, New York, 1962; Concessions Supervisor, Monticello Raceway; Paint Contractor, Chinese-American Paint Company; Speaker, Educational Issues, Churches, Civic, Fraternal and Community Groups; Teacher and Administrator Certification, State of North Carolina. Organizational Memberships: North Carolina Congress of Parents and Teachers; National Education Association. Community Activities: North Carolina Young Democrats; United States Jaycees; Tarboro Student Aid Association (board member); Carol Caldwell Legal Scholarship Association; National Alumni Association; Edgecombe Credit Union (vice president); Kappa Alpha Psi Fraternity, Inc. (vice pole march); Fayetteville State University Alumni Association (president, Edgecombe County Chapter); Coker-Wimberly School Parent-Teacher Association (president); St Jude's Children's Bike-O-Thon (chairman); Edgecombe County United Fund (board member); Fayetteville State National Alumni Association (vice president); Tarboro High School (founder, monitors association; founder, North Carolina historical society); Precinct Captain, Lawrence Political Ward; Teacher, Law Enforcement, Drug Action Volunteer, Chapel Hill, North Carolina; Historical Book, Lawrence; Outlook Home for Girls, Tarboro-Edgecombe County (advisor); Coordinator, Battleboro Reading is Fundamental Project; Lawrence Water Commission (chairman); Fayetteville State University Centennial Committee; North Carolina Social Studies Conference (coordinator, Raleigh, 1980); Lawrence County Development Corporation (president); Phi Delta Kappa, East Carolina University Chapter (honorary member); Public Speaker for Churches and Civic Organizations. Religion: Trustee, Free Union Baptist Church. Honors and Awards: Educator of the Month; Distinguished Alumnus Award, Edgecombe County Chapter, Fayetteville State University; Monitors Founders Award, Woodman of the World Award; District 12 Parent-Teacher Association Executive Award; Edgecombe County Governor's Award; North Carolina Social Studies Award; Coker-Wimberly Parent-Teacher Association President's Award; Edgecombe County Volunteer Award; Listed in *Outstanding Young Men of America, Who's Who Among Personalities of the South.* Address: Route 2 Box 312, Tarboro, North Carolina 27886.

Perry, Reginald Carman

Retired Educator. Personal: Born August 15, 1903; Son of William Perry (deceased). Education: Diploma, Methodist College, 1921; Diploma, Memorial University College, 1927; B.A., Mt. Allison University, 1930; B.D., Victoria University, 1935; M.A. 1936, Ph.D. 1945, Toronto University; Post-Doctoral Studies, Harvard University, 1951-54. Career: Retired; Former School Principal, Newfoundland; Minister, United Church of Canada; Instructor, Syracuse University; Assistant Professor, Oklahoma A.&M. College (now Oklahoma State University); Associate Professor, A.M.&N. College (now University of Arkansas-Pine Bluff); Professor of Humanities and Philosophy, University of Arkansas-Pine Bluff. Organizational Memberships: American Philosophical Association; Arkansas Philosophy Association; Arkansas Retired Teachers Association (life member); National Retired Teachers Association; American Association of University Professors (former member); International Platform Association (former member); Arkansas Sheriff's Association (honorary charter member). Community Activities: Emmanuel College, Toronto (dean of one of men's residences 1932-33); Donations to United Fund, United Way, CARE, Arkansas Sheriff's Boys and Girls Ranches, Inc., National Foundation for Cancer Research, National Humane Education Society, Talking Bible for Nursing Homes-Pine Bluff, Asian-American Lions Relief Fund, Arkansas Lung Association, Easter Seals, Christian Blind Mission International, U.N.I.C.E.F., United Negro College Fund, African Enterprise. Religion: Active in Sunday Schools of Methodist and United Church; Professional Duties 1933-34, 1936-41; Taught Philosophy of Religion, Oklahoma A.&M. College and World Religions, A.M.&N., U.A.P.B. Published Works: "Some Observations Concerning the Philosophy of Charles S. Peirce", "Professor Ayer's 'Freedom and Necessity'", "Some Comments on Schlick's Ethical Theory", and Others. Honors and Awards: First in Physics and Honors Student, Methodist College; Honors Latin, Memorial University College; Bursary, Mt. Allison University; Plaque upon Retirement, International Club, U.A.P.B., 1976. Address: 110 S. Beech Street, Apt. 2, Pine Bluff, Arkansas 71601.

Reginald C Perry

Perry-Small, Vera Elizabeth

Educator. Personal: Born May 6, 1919; Daughter of John and Daisy Edmondson; Mother of Michele P. Coney, Rene A. Perry, Martel A. Perry. Education: B.S., Hampton Institute; M.A., Syracuse University; M.R. Certificate, University of Virginia; Professional Certificate L.D., Ph.D., Ohio State University; Certificate Public Education, Soprow, Hungary, 1974. Career: Teacher, Nutrition and Science, Head Teacher, Lanham Fund Nursery School; Director, Hampton Nursery, Kindergarten First Grade; Teacher, Fourth Grade, Director, Teacher, High School; Graduate Assistant, University of Virginia; Assistant Professor, Special Education, Director, University of Virginia Demonstration School; Research Assistant, Instructor, Ohio State University; Hampton Institute, Coordinator, Special Education Consultant Coordinator, Learning and Behavioral Disorders, Professor, Special Education, Coordinator, Graduate Program, Orthopedic and Multiple Handicapped Conditions; Professor, Special Education, Norfolk State University, Virginia, present. Organizational Memberships: American Association of University Women (member, 1959 to present; secretary, 1979-81); American Association of University Professors, 1974-82; Council for Exceptional Children, 1957 to present; Division of Children Learning Disorders, Disablilities, 1974 to present; Association of Children Behavioral Disorders, Coalition for Personnel Development; National Education Association; Virginia Education Association; Association of American Secondary Curriculum Development; State Educators of Colleges and Universities (state committee). Community Activities: Citizen Organization (founder, 1948); Girl Scouts of America (vice president; leader, 1950 to present); Tutoring Program 1979-82 Project Outreach, 1974; Teen Lift, 1980 to present; Voter Registration, 1960 to present; Volunteer, Heart Drive, Birth Defects, Multiple Sclerosis, Child Care Center; Special Work, Study Program, 1969; Volunteer Work, Patrick Henry Hosptial, 1975 to present; Volunteer, Veterans Hosptial, 1978; Woman's Day Speaker, 1978, 1979,); Missionary Anniversary Speaker, 1979; Phi Lambda Theta Honorary Sorority; Delta Sigman Theta; Phi Delta Kappa. Religon: First Baptist Church, Senior Chioir 1945 to present, Assistant Superintendent, Sunday School 1954-74, Assistant Men's Teacher, Bible Class 1979-82, Church Aid Club II 1968 to present; O.E.S., Past Matron, Past Deputy; Executive Member, Org. State Board, 1974-79; President, Christian Women United, 1979-82. Honors and Awards: Pioneer in Special Education Award, 1963; Outstanding Award in Special Education, 1965; Teaching Award, 1978; Outstanding Service Award, 1978; Listed in *International Who's Who in Education.* Address: 1101 Mary Peake Boulevard, Hampton, Virginia 23666.

Peters, Marsha

Social Worker. Personal: Born October 9, 1949; Daughter of Paul and Enid Peters. Education: B.S. 1973, M.S.W. 1975, University of Utah, Salt Lake City. Career: Social Worker, Ettie Lee Boys Homes, Inc., 1975; Social Worker, Utah States Division of Services for the Visually Handicapped, 1975 to present; Clinical Social Worker, 1978; A.C.S.W., 1977; Certified School Social Worker, 1976; Certified Social Worker, 1975. Organizational Memberships: National Association of Social Workers (national committee on nomination and leadership identification, 1979-82; national task force to develop standards for social work services in long-term care facilities, 1979-81); Utah Chapter, National Association of Social Workers (board of directors, 1976-80; chairperson, 1978-80; member, 1977-78; division of professional standards; ad hoc committee to study declassification, 1978; chairperson, research committee, 1977-78; chairperson, nominating committee, 1976; chairperson, community organization council, 1976; ad hoc committee to study third party vendor payments, 1976; ad hoc committee on nursing home personnel, 1976; program committee, 1975); Women's State Legislative Council of Utah (board of directors, 1979-81); American Society of Public Administration; Utah Public Employees Association (legislative committee, 1978-79; citizen action by public employees committee, 1977-78; representative, women's state legislative council of Utah, 1976-79); American Association of Workers for the Blind; National Retinitis Pigmentosa Foundation, Utah Chapter; Presentation, Teacher/Consultant, "Mental Health Continuing Education Institute", University of Utah Graduate School of Social Work, 1978-80; Presentation, "Relationships", University of Utah 1978 Women's Conference; Aging Seminar, The College of Southern Utah, Southeastern Association of Governments, 1976; Utah Health Care Association In-Service Training Program, 1976. Community Activities: Young Women's Christian Association (board of directors,

1975-80; chairperson, outreach program advisory committee, 1977-79; affirmative action committee, 1977-79; youth committee, 1977-79); University of Utah Graduate School of Social Work (board of directors, alumni association, 1978-80; clinical assistant professor, 1979 to present; dean's search committee, 1979-80; clinical instructor, 1976-79; continuing education committee, 1978 to present; practicum committee, 1977 to present; ad hoc committee for full-faculty workshops, 1977-78); Beta Sigma Phi Sorority; Junior League of Salt Lake City; Community Nursing Service (utilization review committee, 1981 to present); Utah State office of Education (Title XX project officer, division of services for the visually handicapped, 1979-80; Title IX committee, 1976); Project Reality (board of directors, 1980 to present); Utah Human Services Conference (chairperson, program committee, 1980); Utah International Women's Year Exhibit Committee (chairperson, 1977); Utah Council for the Blind (treasurer, 1975-78); Utah State Conference on Social Welfare Steering Committee, 1975; University of Utah Associated Students of Social Work (student body officer, 1974-75). Published Works: "The Blind Helping the Blind, Utah State Division of Services for the Visually Handicapped" *A.S.P.A. Buzz* (publication of the Utah Chapter of the American Society for Public Administration), January 1979; *Guidelines for the Delivery of Social Services in Nursing Care Facilities*, 1978; *Practicum Manual*, University of Utah Graduate School of Social Work Document, 1978. Honors and Awards: Internatonal Platform Association; Salt Lake's Outstanding Young Woman, Salt Lake Jaycees Women's Organization, 1981; Social Worker of the Year Award, Utah Chapter, National Association of Social Workers, 1979; Social Worker of the Month for Community Organization Award, Utah Chapter, National Association of Social Workers, October 1978; Name Submitted by Utah Chapter of National Association of Social Workers to National Association of Social Workers as an Expert in Areas of Community Organization and Work with Visually Handicapped Persons, 1976; Blanche Scowcroft Willey Memorial Award for Creativity and Promise in the Field of Social Work, University of Utah Graduate School of Social Work, 1975; Listed in *International Who's Who of Intellectuals, Who's Who of American Women, Outstanding Young Women of America.* Address: 826 16th Avenue, Salt Lake City, Utah 84103.

Petersen, Gary Michael

Executive. Personal: Born November 23, 1947; Son of S. E. and Kathleen Petersen; Married Alexandra; Father of Samantha Kate, Jesse Garett. Education: Attended College in Santa Monica. Career: Co-Owner, Vice President, Director of Sales, Disc Jockey, Radio Station KRCK-AM, Ridgecrest, California; Founder, President, Ecolo-Haul, Pacific Palisades, California, 1972 to present; National Science Foundation Consultant, Committee for National Recycling Policy; Advisor, United States Conference of Mayors, National Recycling Coalition; Consultant, Environmental Protection Agency. Organizational Memberships: State Solid Waste Management Board (steering committee); California Resource Recovery Association (founder; board of directors); California Industry Environment Council; Governor's Resource Utilization Task Force. Community Activities: Citizen's Solid Waste Environmental Advisory Committee, County of Los Angeles; Cousteau Society (founding member); Wilderness Society; World Wildlife Fund; Defenders of Wildlife; Los Angeles Beautiful (board of directors); Santa Monica Beautification and Recycling Program. Honors and Awards: Numerous Honors and Awards from City, County and State Government and Civic Organizations; Recycling Award, California Committee for Resource Recovery; Nominated Six Times for Tyler Ecology Award, Included in *The Peter Plan* by Laurence Peter (author of *The Peter Principle)*; Listed in *Who's Who in the World, Who's Who in Finance and Industry, Outstanding Young Men of America, Men of Achievement.* Address: P.O. Box 1263, Pacific Palisades, California 90272.

Leal Phelps

Petrich, Dean Gage

Professional Clown, Craftsman, Piano Technician, Portrait Photographer, Clivus Multrum Dealer, Public Speaker, Snow Ski Instructor. Personal: Born September 15, 1950; Son of Ray Petrich. Education: Graduate of Lakeside High School, 1968; B.S. English Literature, Willamette University, 1972; Attended University of Washington 1971, Belleme Community College 1973; Secondary Education Certificate; Studied Latin, French, Swedish, German, Russian, English. Organizational Memberships: Clowns of America; Seattle Magic Ring; Piano Technicians Guild; Pacific Northwest Ski Instructors Association. Community Activities: DeMolay; Unicycling Society of America; Cascade Bicycle Club; Whidbey Solar Association; Environmental Fair Organizer; Ski Patrol; Foreign Exchange Student to Sweden; Initiator, Seattle Children's Museum; Precinct Committeeman; Ecotopian Advocate, Spokesman, Exemplifier; Arcosanti Construction Promotion; Recycling Programs; Class Instructor, Fifteen Different Topics; Play Violin, Recorder, Guitar, Piano; Sing Tenor. Honors and Awards: College Yearbook Photographer and Editor; One of Top Ten College Seniors for Personality, Contributions, Activities, Attitude; Building A Totally Self-Sufficient House on Whidbey Island. Address: 1132 34th Street, Seattle, Washington 98122.

Petty, Elijah Edward

Chemical Engineer. Personal: Born June 12, 1920; Son of Mr. and Mrs. Curtis Petty (both deceased); Married Nelda Morris; Father of Montie Curtis, Vicki A. Education: B.S.Ch.E., University of Oklahoma, 1948; A.S.T.P., Mechanical Engineering, University of Arizona, 1944. Military: Served in the United States Army, attaining the rank of Technical Sergeant. Career: Chemical Engineer, Edible Oils/Protein Industry; Chemical Engineer, Chemical Agricultural Processes. Organizational Memberships: American Oil Chemists Society; American Institute of Chemical Engineers; Professional Engineer, State of Texas. Community Activities: Jacksonville, Illinois, School Board (advisory committee); Jacksonville Community Chest (chairman); São Paulo, Brazil, School Board (advisory engineer). Religion: Representative to C.O.D.A., 1980; Board of Directors, David Hulse Evangelistic Association, Inc., 1981; Outreach Chairman, Lost Coin Body of Christ, 1981. Honors and Awards: Recognition Certificate of Professional Achievement, American Institute of Chemical Engineers, 1979; Listed in *Community Leaders of America.* Address: #1 Curtis Court, Mount Zion, Illinois 62549.

Pfeiffer, John William

Publisher, Writer, Economist and Management Consultant. Personal: Born July 10, 1937; Son of Mr. and Mrs, J. W. Pfeiffer; Married to Judith; Father of Heidi, Wilson. Education: B.A., University of Maryland, 1962; Ph.D., University of Iowa, 1968. Military: Served with United States Army, 1958-62. Published Works: Author of *Instrumentation in Human Relations Training* (1973, 2nd edition in 1976), *Reference Guide to Handbooks and Annuals* (1975, 1977, 1981); Editor of *A Handbook of Structured Experiences for Human Relations Training* (8 volumes, 1969-80), *The Annual Handbook for Group Facilitators* (10 volumes, 1972-81), *The 1982 Annual for Facilitators, Trainers and Consultants, Group and Organization Studies: International Journal for Group Facilitators* (1976-80). Honors and Awards: Received honorary Doctor of Applied Behavioral Science, California American University, 1980. Address: 369 Mesa Way, La Jolla, California 92037.

Phelps, Leal

Piano Teacher. Personal: Born March 11, 1902; Daughter of Robert E. Lee and Martha Johnston R. (both deceased); Married James

Edward Phelps; Mother of Dr. Robert, Wilma Karayan. Education: Graduate of Kansas City Conservatory of Music, 1930; Piano Study, Sir Carl Busch, Composer/Teacher, John Thompson, Sergie Tarnowsky, Maurice Zam, Helen Poole. Career: Piano Teacher. Organizational Memberships: Piano Guild (member, over thirty years); Music Teacher's Association (member, over thirty years). Community Activities: Teacher to Bonnel Nunez, Author/Composer, William Pearson, Music Arranger/Composer; Maurice Kenton Phelps Ch. #1022, City of Hope (past president). Honors and Awards: Award, United States Veterans of Foreign Wars, Los Angeles City Hall Post 768, 19679. Address: 2585 Yardarm, Port Hueneme, California 93041.

Phillips, Jill Meta

Writer, Researcher, Critic, Historian. Personal: Born October 22, 1952; Daughter of Leyson K. and Leona Rasmussen Phillips. Education: Graduate of Royal Oak High School, Covina, California, 1970; Degrees of Nil. Autodidact. Career: Writer, Researcher, Critic, Historian; Ghostwriter; Literary Counselor. Organizational Memberships: London Club; Richard III Society; Ghost Club; Dracula Society of London; County Dracula Society; Titanic Society. Community Activities: Young Americans for Freedom. Published Works: *A Directory of American Film Scholars* (with Leona A. Phillips); *The Good Morning Cookbook; George Bernard Shaw: A Review of the Literature (An Annotated Bibliography); T. E. Lawrence: Portrait of the Artist as Hero (Controversy and Caricature in the Biographies of "Lawrence of Arabia"); The Occult: Hauntings, Witchcraft, Dreams and All Other Avenues of Paranormal Phenomena* (with Leona A. Phillips); *The Archeology of the Collective East; D. H. Lawrence: A Review of the Literature (An Annotated Bibliography; Film Appreciation: A College Guidebook* (with Leona A. Phillips); *Annus Mirabilis: Europe in the Dark and Middle Centuries; The Darkling Plain: The Great War in History, Biography, Diary, Poetry, Literature and Film; The Dark Frame: Occult Cinema* (with Leona A. Phillips); *The Sterile Promontory: The Second World War in History, Biography, Diary, Poetry, Literature and Film* (1982); Scheduled for Publications, 1983-85, *Misfit: The Films of Montgomery Clift, The Fatal Hickey: Vampyres in Legend, Literature and Cinema, The World's Sad Roses: Morbidity, Duplicity, and Obsessive Abnormality in the Writings of "Lawrence of Arabia"* (with Brian Carter), *Film Music: An Aesthete's View;* Current Research and Writing Projects include *The Clown with the Twisted Lip: Images of Nazis in English Speaking Films 1939-79* (with Leona A. Phillips), *Inside the Outsider: An Annotated Analysis of the Works of Colin Wilson, Butterflies in the Mind: A Precis of Dreams and Dreamers, Radiant Misery and the Man Who Would Be God: Napoleon Bonaparte and His Age, The Rose Bled White: A Novel of the War of the Roses, The Lord Byron Diet Book: How the "Beautiful People" Stayed Slim Through the Ages;* Contributor, *The Book of Lists #3;* Research for Scenario of Film *The Survivor* for Director David Hemmings, 1981. Honors and Awards: Listed in *Who's Who of American Women, Who's Who in the West, Contemporary Authors, Personalities of the West and Midwest, Book of Honor, World Who's Who of Women, International Register of Profiles.* Address: 851 North Garsden Avenue, Covina, California 91724.

Phillips, Leona Anna Rasmussen

Author, Researcher. Personal: Born November 11, 1925; Married Leyson K. Phillips, in 1948; Mother of Jill Meta, Glen Harry, Sally Clara, Donna Rose, Dorthy Ann. Education: Extension Courses, University of Michigan, 1947-53. Career: Author, Researcher, Gordon Press Publishers; Correspondent, *Tracks Magazine*, 1946-49; Production Assistant, Scriptwriter/Typist, Jam Handy Motion Picture Company, Detroit, Michigan, 1952-55. Religion: Teacher, Daily Vacation Bible School, Prince of Peace Lutheran Church, Covina, California, 1964-67. Published Works: *You Can Write, D. W. Griffith: Titan of the Film Art (A Critical Study), Colonial Days and the American Revolution: An Annotated Bibliography, Hitler and the Third Reich: An Annotated Bibliography, Chinese History, Edgar Allan Poe: An Annotated Bibliography, Christmas: An Annotated Bibliography, Silent Cinema: An Annotated Bibliography, Martin Luther and the Reformation, 'Twixt Wind and Water: A Novel of the Occult;* (With Jill M. Phillips) *A Directory of American Film Scholars, The Occult: Hauntings, Witchcraft, Dreams and All Other Avenues of Paranormal Phenomena, A Directory of American Film Scholars: Second Edition, Revised and Enlarged, Film Appreciation: A College Guidebook, The Dark Frame: Occult Cinema;* Current Projects include *Sea Disasters: An Annotated Bibliography, Liberty and Justice for Some: The Anatomy of Wealth, Power and Prestige within the Structure of America's Premiere Families-Past and Present, The Clown with the Twisted Lip: Images of Nazis in English Speaking Films 1939-79* (with Jill M. Phillips). Honors and Awards: Listed in *Who's Who of American Women, World Who's Who of Women, Contemporary Authors, Book of Honor, Who's Who in the West.* Address: 851 North Garsden Avenue, Covina, California 91724.

George B Pickett

Pickett, George Bibb Jr

Association Representative. Personal: Born March 20, 1918; Married Beryl Robinson (deceased), Second Wife Rachel Copeland; Father of James Miller, Kathleen Pickett Beale, Thomas Holmes. Education: B.S., United States Military Academy, West Point, New York, 1941; Armed Forces Staff College, 1956; National War College, 1960. Military: Served in the United States Army, 1941-73, attaining the rank of Major General. Career: Area Representative, National Rifle Association; Registered Land Surveyor, State of Alabama. Organizational Memberships: National Rifle Association (life member). Community Activities: Association of the United States Army; American Legion; Veterans of Foreign Wars; Military Order of World Wars; Kiwanis Club; Sons of the American Revolution (past chapter president); Old South Historical Society (past president); Sons of Confederate Veterans; English Speaking Union; River Bend Gun Club, Atlanta; Capital City Club, Montgomery. Religion: Layreader, St. Paul's Episcopal Church, Alexandria, Louisiana, 1967-69; St. John's Episcopal Church, Montgomery, Alabama. Honors and Awards: Medal of Highest Honor, Kyung Hee University, Seoul, Korea, 1967; Distinguished Service Medal (3); Silver Star; Legion of Merit (3); Bronze Star Medal (3); Army Commendation Medal (3); Purple Heart (2); Philippine Legion of Honor; Korean Order of Service Merit; Presidential Unit Citations, Korea, Philippines; Combat Infantry Badge. Address: 3525 Flowers Drive, Montgomery, Alabama 36109.

Pindera, Jerzy Tadeusz

Educator. Personal: Born 1914; Married Aleksandra Anna; Father of Marek-Jerzy, Maciej-Zenon. Education: Bachelor of Applied Science (equivalent), Warsaw Technical University, 1936; Master of Engineering in Aeronautical Engineering, Lodz Technical University, 1947; Doctor of Applied Sciences, Polish Academy of Sciences, 1959; Doctor hab., Technical University of Cracow, 1962. Military: Served in the Polish Army 1939 as an Officer of the Artillery; Wounded at Warsaw, 1939; Taken Prisoner by the German Army. Career: Professor of Engineering, University of Waterloo, 1965 to present; Visiting Professor, Michigan State University, 1963-65; Head of Experimental Mechanics Laboratory, Building Research Institute, Warsaw, 1959-62; Deputy Professor, Head of Experimental Mechanics Laboratory, Polish Academy of Sciences, 1954-59; Head of Laboratory, Aeronautical Institute, Warsaw, 1947-52; Assistant, Polish Airlines "Lot", 1947. Organizational Memberships: Mechanics Research Communications (editorial advisory board, 1974 to present); Society for Experimental Stress Analysis (member, various committees, reviewer, 1963 to present); *Applied Mechanics Review* (reviewer, 1965 to present); International Symposium on Experimental Mechanics, University of

Waterloo, Ontario, Canada (organizer, chairman, 1972); International Center for Mechanical Science, Udine, Italy (coordinator, session on "advanced topics of experimental mechanics" 1978); President, J. T. Pindera & Sons, Engineering Services, Inc. Community Activities: Resistance in the Concentration Camp Sachsenhausen in Oranienburg, 1940-45 (prisoner no. 28862). Published Works: About 100 Research Papers and Review Papers, 5 Books, 4 Patents, 2 Patents Applied for. Honors and Awards: M. M. Frocht Award, Outstanding Achievements in Education of Experimental Mechanics, Society for Experimental Stress Analysis, 1978; Price of the Polish Society for Theoretical and Applied Mechanics, for Paper "Investigations of Some Rheological Photoelastic Properties of Some Polyester Resins", 1960; Prize for Scientific and Organizational Achievement in the Field of Photoelasticity, Presidium of Polish Academy of Sciences, 1956; Award for Book *Outline of Photoelasticity*, Board of the State Technical Publishers, 1954. Address: 310 Grant Crescent, Waterloo, Ontario, N2K 3G1 Canada.

Piper, Kathryn T

Executive. Personal: Born November 26; Daughter of Thelma Thomas; Mother of James, Jerrold, Sue. Education: B.A. English, Speech, Journalism, Communications, Marketing, Radio/Television, Public Relations, Advertising, Loretto Heights College, Denver, Colorado; Attended University of Denver, University of Colorado. Career: President, Piper & Associates, Ltd., Public Relations and Advertising, 1965 to present; Radio, Television; Newspapers; Writer; Correspondent. Organizational Memberships: National Federation of Press Women; Colorado Press Women; Public Relations Society of America; National Association of Female Executives. Community Activities: Denver Civic Ballet; Denver Debutante Ball; New York Debutante Ball. Honors and Awards: First Place Awards, Various Categories of Writing and Advertising, National Federation of Press Women, 1967-80; Colorado Woman of Achievement, Colorado Press Women, 1976; National Woman of Achievement, National Federation of Press Women, 1978. Address: 120 South Marion Parkway, Denver, Colorado 80209.

Pirkle, Estus W

Pastor, Evangelist, Christian Film Producer. Personal: Born March 12, 1930; Son of Grover Washington Pirkle (deceased); Married Annie Catherine; Father of Letha Dianne, Gregory, Don. Education: Norman Junior College, Norman Park, Georgia, 1949; B.A., Mercer University, Macon, Georgia, 1951, Bachelor of Divinity, Master of Religious Education 1956, Master of Theology 1958, Southwestern Baptist Seminary, Fort Worth, Texas. Career: Pastor, Evangelist, present; Author of Christian Books; Producer, 60-Minute Color 16mm Full-Length Motion Pictures, "If Footmen Tire You, What Will Horses Do?" 1972, "The Burning Hell" 1974, " The Believer's Heaven" 1977; Preacher, 40 Revivals, Conferences, Camp Meetings, Each Year. Religion: Over 2,000,000 Have Professed Faith in Jesus Christ at the Showing of his Films. Published Works: *Preachers in Space*, 1969; *If Footmen Tire You, What Will Horses Do?*, 1969, *Book of Sermon Outlines*, 1973; *Who Will Build Your House?*, 1978. Honors and Awards: "The Burning Hell" has been Translated into Spanish and Portugese and have been Distributed All over the World; Valedictorian Norman Junior College, 1949; Cum Laude Graduate, Mercer University, 1957, Doctor of Divinity Degree by Covington Theological Seminary, Rossville, California, 1982.Address: P. O. Box 80, Myrtle, Mississippi 38650.

Estus W Pirkle

Pittman, James Eugene Jr

Vermiculturist; Executive. Personal: Born May 28, 1948 in Long Beach, California; Son of James E. Pittman and Lenora Fern Hunsake; Married Brenda June Petker on November 12, 1977; Father of Kerri Lynn, Michelle Nichole, Olivia Marie. Education: Graduate of Long Beach Polytechnic High School, 1966; Attended Long Beach City College, 1967-68; Los Angeles Trade Technical College, 1970; Extension Study, University of Iowa, Iowa State University; Additional Special Studies, University of Michigan, University of Missouri, 1977; Certification, Los Angeles County Health Department, Los Angeles City Department of Building and Safety, Long Beach City Department of Building and Safety, International Organic Growers Association, California Organic Growers Association. Career: Marketing Director, Jay-Fran, Inc., Iowa City 1977, Invivo, Inc., Iowa City 1977; Consultant, Consultant Services Associates, Inc.; P/C Enterprises, Indianapolis, Indiana; Marketing Consultant, Bio-Chemical Catalysts Inc., Grand Rapids, Iowa; Bio-Eco Systems, Inc., Franklin, Indiana, 1976; Owner, Templeton Worm Ranch, Templeton, California, 1974-79; Owner, American Eco-Systems, Oceanside, California, 1977 to present; Seminars, Lectures, "Earthworms in Agriculture Today", "Earthworms and Their Relation to Feeding Mankind", "Microflora - What is It?", "What Makes Things Grow?", "Earthworms and Crops", "Raising Earthworms for Profit", "Earthworms and Bacteria - Working Together". Organizational Memberships: California Farm Bureau; Western Organic Growers Association; Vermiculturists Trade Association; National Foundation of Independent Businesses. Community Activities: Rotary Club International (board of directors, 1977; chairman, local club; world community services, 1977-78); National S.B.A. Club; B.P.O. Elks Club; International Platform Association; Republican Presidential Task Force; National Rifle Association. Honors and Awards: Award of Appreciation, Rotary International 1977, Kiwanis Club 1977, Lions Club 1976, Chamber of Commerce, Atascadero, California 1976, California State University at Cal Poly, San Luis Obispo 1976, Madera Unified School District 1977, Fresno State University 1977; Outstanding Community Leaders, American Biographical Institute; Listed in *Who's Who in Finance and Industry*, *Who's Who in the West*, *Who's Who in California*, *International Who's Who of Intellectuals*, *Biographical Roll of Honor*. Address: 155 Madison Street, Oceanside, California 92054.

Pivirotto, Richard Roy

Corporate Director. Personal: Born May 26, 1930; Son of Arthur M. Pivirotto; Married Mary Burchfield; Father of Mary Pivirotto Murley, Richard R., Jr., Susan Pivirotto Kern, Nancy Patricia, David Horne, Jennifer Paton. Education: Graduate of Shady Side Academy, 1948; A.B. Princeton University, 1952; M.B.A., Harvard Business School, 1954. Military: Served in the United States Army, from 1955-56, attaining the rank of Private First Class. Career: President, Joseph Horne Company, 1961-70; Vice Chairman, Associtied Dry Goods Corporation, Vice Chairman 1970-72, President, 1972-75, Cahirman 1975-81; Corporate Director, Westinghouse Corporation, Gillette Corporation, New York Life Insurance Comapny, Chemical New York Corporation and Chemical Bank, Bowery Saving Bank, Associated Dry Goods, General American Investors Corporation. Organizational Memberships: National Retail Merchants Association (director, 1961-81; executive committee, 1970-81); American Retail Federation (director, 1970 to present; vice chairman, 1976 to present). Community Activities: National Savings Bond Committee (chairman, retail division, 1977-79); United Way of Tristate (retail division chairman, 1977); Princeton University (term trustee, 1972-76; charter trustee 1977-81; chairman, health and athletics committee, president of class of 1982, 1977-82; vice chairman, special gifts, a fund for Princeton, 1981. Religion: Christ Church, Episcopal, Investment Committee. Honors and Awards: Boys and Menswear National Green Thumb Award, 1977. Address: 111 Clapboard Ridge Road, Greenwich, Connecticut 06830.

Plyler, Bob Lee

Executive. Personal: Born December 20, 1936; Son of Lee Roy and Altha Cleo McSpadden Plyler; Married to Paulette Durso; Father of Vonda Lynn, Pamela Lee, Bobby Lee, Joseph Lane, Rick Todd. Education: A.A., Arlington State University, 1955; B.A., Texas A&M University, 1957; Honorary A.F.D., London Institute, 1972. Military: Served with United States Air Force, 1955-56. Career: Founder and President, Acme Ladders, Inc., Houston, Texas, 1966 to present; Plant Manager, Lone Star Ladder Company, 1957-66. Community Activities: Past President, Gulf Meadow Civic Association; Former Special Advisor and Master of Ceremonies, the Consular Ball of Houston; Former Master of Ceremonies, Noches Americas International Ball; Past Vice President, Greater Houston Civic Foundation; Former Protocol Representative to the office of the Mayor; Past member, Houston Jaycees; Chairman, Galveston County Drainage District; Board of Directors, Houston-Taipia Sister City Committee; Master Mason and Shriner. Religion: Attends Baptist Church. Honors and Awards: Fellow, American Biographical Institute; Listed in *Personalities of the South, Notable Americans of the Bicentennial Era, Who's Who in Texas, Who's Who in the South and Southwest, Book of Honor, International Who's Who in Community Service, Who's Who in Finance and Industry, Who's Who in Houston, Community Leaders of America.* Address: Box 26593, Houston, Texas 77207.

Poehner, Raymond Glenn

Retired Banker, Retired Naval Officer. Personal: Born October 1, 1923; Son of Raymond Frank Poehner (deceased), Winnifred McCracken; Married Ella Frances; Father of David R., Diane M., Leslie, Rebecca G., Jon A., (Stepfather of:) Bruce Gillespie, Tony Gillespie. Education: Attended Military Service School; Graduate of Dale Carnegie Course; Attended American Banking Institute. Military: Served in the United States Navy, 1941-65. Career: Security Pacific National Bank, 1966-78; Bank Speaking Group. Community Activities: March of Dimes Foundation; Optimist International (director); Veterans of Foreign Wars; Fleet Reserve Association; United States Naval Institute; Republican Senatorial Committee. Religion: Christian. Honors and Awards: Art Scholarship, Chicago Art Institute, 1937; Letters of Commendation, United States Navy, 1957, 1960, 1964; War Service Medal, World War II, Korean War, Vietnam; Letter of Appreciation, Security Pacific Bank; Listed in *Personalities of the West and Midwest.* Address: Gulf Breeze, Florida.

Frank A Pohole

Poellman, Sister Michaella

Teacher, Reading Resource. Personal: Born August 3, 1912. Education: Ph.B. 1946, M.A. 1959, Reading Specialist 1972, Cardinal Stritch College. Career: Teaching, Elementary, Secondary, College, Graduate Level; Workshops Leader; Diagnostic Evaluator; Adult Education in Communication; Work with Delinquent Boys. Organizational Memberships: International Reading Association, Ten Years; Wisconsin Area Reading Association; Milwaukee Area Reading Association, 1965 to present. Community Activities: Reading Services to Women's Group in Inner City; Coordinator for Students, Helping Group of Spanish-Americans, Tutoring Service; In-Service Workshops, Secondary Level; Archdiocesan Reading Committees; Lectures, Home, School Organizations; Part-Time Instructor, DeSales Preparatory School. Religion: Confraternity of Christian Doctrine, 1958-68; Volunteer Aid, High School Students, 1970 to present. Honors and Awards: Recognition for Service to Youth and Elderly, 1978; Literacy Award, International Reading Association, Milwaukee Area Reading Association, 1982; Listed in *Personalities of the West and Midwest, Community Leaders and Noteworthy Americans.* Address: 3221 South Lake Drive, Milwaukee, Wisconsin 53207.

Pohole, Frank Anthony

Artist and Restaurateur. Personal: Born September 8, 1920; Son of Franc Florian and Amalija Polonia Makovec Pohole; Married to Maria Filippa Falchi; Father of Francisco Mario. Education: Attended Trappist Monastery Seminary, Banja Luka, Yugoslavia, 1934-37; Comm.L., University of Ljubjana, 1940; Degree in International Sciences, University of Buenos Aires, Argentina, 1962. Military: Served with United States Army, 1943-46. Career: Painter with one-man shows at Asociacion Estimulo de Bellas Artes (Buenos Aires), 1954-62, Galeria Libertad (Buenos Aires), 1953-62, Galeria Renoir (Buenos Aires), 1953-62, Minerva Art Gallery (New York), 1977-79; Group shows at Buenos Aires, New York City and Brooklyn (New York); Special Investigator, State Education Department, State University of New York, 1965-68; Court Interpreter, Criminal Court of the City of New York, 1968-73. Organizational Memberships: New York Artists' Equity Association, Inc.; International Society of Artists; Society of North American Artists; World Art Services, Inc.; The Inter-American Society. Address: 753 39th Street, Brooklyn, New York 11232.

Polis, Harry John Sr

Chief of Police. Personal: Born August 16, 1947; Son of John and Lake Polis; Married Aimee Marie; Father of John, Robert, Laurene, Harry Jr. Education: A.A. Law Enforcement, Honors, P. G. College, 1978; 124th Session Graduate, Federal Bureau of Investigation National Academy, 1981; Attended Fourteen Specialized Law Enforcement Schools. Career: Chief of Police, Forest Heights Police; Certified Police Instructor, 1973 to present. Organizational Memberships: Maryland Chiefs of Police Association (president, 1980; vice-president, 1979; sergeant-at-arms, 1978). Community Activities: Maryland Police Training Commission, 1980. Religion: Catholic. Honors and Awards: Governor's Citation for Service, 1981; J. Edgar Hoover Memorial Award, 1974. Address: 112 Mohican Drive, Forest Heights, Maryland 20745.

Stephen J Pollack

Pollack, Robert H

Educator, Director. Personal: Born June 26, 1927; Son of Bertha Levy Pollack; Married Martha Katz; Father of Jonathan, Lance, Scott. Education: B.S. Psychology, City College of New York, 1948; M.A. Psychology, Ph.D. Psychology, Clark University, 1953. Military: Served in the United States Army from 1945-46, attaining the rank of Corporal. Career: Lecturer, Department of Psychology, University of Sidney, N.S.W., Australia, 1953-61; Deputy Director of Research, Department of Research, Institute for Juvenile Research, Chicago, Illinois, 1963-69; Professor of Psychology, Director, Graduate Training in Psychology, University of Georgia, Athens, 1969 to present. Organizational Memberships: American Association of Sex Educators, Counselors and Therapists; Gerontological Society; Society for the Scientific Study of Sex. Honors and Awards: Award for Significant Research Contributions, University of Georgia, 1978; N.I.M.H. Special Research Fellowship to Investigate Contour Interaction. Columbia University, 1961; N.I.C.H.D. Research Grant to Study "Intelligance and Perceptual Development in Childhood", 1965-66, 1967-71, 1972-75; National Institute of Health Research Grant to Study "Sensory and Perceptual Processes in the Aged", 1975-78. Address: 190 Gatewood Place, Athens, Georgia 30606.

Pollack, Stephen J

Executive, Stockbroker. Personal: Born August 25, 1937, in New York City; Son of Harold S. and Gladys H. Pollack. Education:

Graduate of the Hill School, Pottstown, Pennsylvania, 1956; B.S. Economics, Wharton School of Business and Finance, University of Pennsylvania, 1960. Military: Served in the United States Army, Honorably Discharged in 1966. Career: Vice President, Investments, Assistant Branch Manager, Dean Witter Reynolds Inc., 1977 to present. Organizational Memberships: International Association of Financial Planners; Association of Investment Brokers (board member). Community Activities: Yale Club; Town Club; Atrium Club; Young Men's Philanthropic Club; Schuykill Country Club; Wharton School Club of New York; University of Pennsylvania Club; Ionosphere Club of Eastern Airlines; Clipper Club of Pan American Airlines; Admirals Club of American Airlines; Ambassador Club of Trans World Airlines; Eastside Young Republican Club; Knickerbocker Republican Club. Religion: Sutton Place Synagogue; Temple Emanu-El, New York; Gotham B'Nai B'Rith. Address: 245 East 40th Street, Apartment 14 E, New York, New York 10016.

Pollitt, Gertrude S

Psychotherapist. Personal: Daughter of Julius and Sidonie Stein (both deceased); Married to Erwin P. (now deceased). Education: B.A., Roosevelt University, 1954; M.A., University of Chicago, 1956; Certificate, Chicago Institute for Psychoanalysis, 1963. Career: Psychotherapist and Clinical Social Worker; Former Psychiatric Social Worker; Former Director of Therapeutic Play Center; Principal Welfare Officer and Deputy Director with the United Nations Relief and Rehabilitation Administration, International Refugee Organization, U.S. Zone in Germany, 1945-49; Former Resident Social Worker with Anna Freud in Essex, England. Oganizational Memberships: National Association of Social Workers (member, 1955 to present, membership chairman, 1956-58, chairperson of psychiatric and mental health council, 1960-64, chairperson of private practice committee, 1969-72); World Federation of Mental Health, 1960 to present; American Orthopsychiatric Association, 1960 to present; Winnetka Organization of Rehabilitation and Training (program chairperson, 1978 to present); Academy of Certified Social Workers, 1981. Community Activities: Member, Menninger Foundation, 1960 to present; Member, Winnetka Women's Club, 1980 to present; Made donations to various social agencies. Honors and Awards: Licensed Clinical Social Worker, State of California, 1978 to present; Fellow, American Orthopsychiatric Association, 1967; Fellow, Illinois Society for Clinical Social Work, 1977; Case Record Exhibit, Child Welfare League of America, 1956 (record incorporated in permanent library of the league); Listed in *Registry of Health Care Providers in Clinical Social Work, Who's Who in the West and Midwest, Who's Who of American Women, The World Who's Who of Women, Personalities of the West and Midwest, Notable Americans.* Address: 481 Oakdale Avenue, Glencoe, Illinois 60022.

John W Pope

Polly, F Winston III

Attorney. Personal: Born August 23, 1945; Son of Felix and Thelma Polly (deceased); Marrried Linda M.; Father of Dannell Annette, Duywuna Auiyette. Education: B.A 1967, J.D. 1971, North Carolina Central University; Graduate Law Work, Georgetown Law Center, 1971-72. Career: Chief Assistant Prosecuting Attorney, 1978 to present; Private Law Practice, 1976-78; Senior Legal Counsel; State of West Virginia Workmen's Compensation Fund, 1975-76; E.E.O. Program Director, West Virginia Human Rights Commission, 1974-75; Attorney for Federal Trade Commission, Washington, D.C., 1971-73. Organizational Memberships: West Virginia State Bar; National Bar Association; American Bar Association; Raleigh County Bar Association, Beckley, West Virginia; Mountain State Bar (secretary); National Deputy Attorney, 1978 to present. Community Activities: City of Charleston (legal attache, committee to revise comprehensive plan) Raleigh County Planning and Zoning Commission (legal advisor); Raleigh County Young Men's Christian Association (board of directors, 1977 to present); City of Beckley Scholarship committee, 1978-79; Quad County Opportunities Industrialization Center (chairperson, 1977 to present); Raleigh County Civitan, 1980 to present; Greater West Virginia Cystic Fibrosis Foundation, Charleston, West Virginia (member, vice president, 1974-75); Boy Scouts of America (scoutmaster, assistant scoutmaster, troop 3, Buckskin Council, 1974-75); Omega Psi Phi Fraternity (member, district counsel, 4th district, 1978-80; basileus, vice basileus, Upsilon chapter 1976 to present); Opportunties Industrialization Center of America (national board of directors; chairperson, Quad County chapter, 1977 to present). Relgion: Central Street Baptist Church, Beckley, West Virginia, Board of Trustees 1980 to present, Men's Chorus, Central Baptist Church. Honors and Awards: Letter of Commendation, Workmen's Compensation Fund, State of West Virginia, 1975; Gold Pen Award for Service as Board Chairman to Quad County Industrialization Centers, Opportunties Industrialization Centers of America; Listed in *Who's Who in the South and Southwest, Directory of Distinguished Americans, Who's Who in Intellectuals.* Address: 127 Grant Street, Beckley, West Virginia 27801.

Pope, John Waring

Investment Accounts Manager (semi-retired). Personal: Born January 9, 1913; Son of Henry and Adele Prufrock Pope (both deceased); Married Elizabeth Louise; Father of John W., Jr., Henry DeWitt, Jane Pope Berger, Sabina Pope Sullivan, Roger Conant. Education: Graduate of Chicago High School, 1930; Ph.D., University of Wisconsin, 1935; Graduate School of Business Administration, Harvard, 1939. Military: Attended the University of Wisconsin Reserve Officer Training Corps Program from 1930-32, attaining the rank of Corporal of Infantry and Signal Corps. Career: Director and Vice President, Pope Brace Company Paramount Textile Machinery Company; Director, Bear Brand Hosiery Company; Owner, Farm, HcHenry County, Illinois, 1951-60, 1981, Operated with Tenant Farmer. Organizatonal Memberships: Chicago Farmers Club, 1952 to present; Investment Analyst Federation, 1955 to present; Investment Analysts Society of Chicago, 1955 to present; Pope Foundation, Inc. (director, member, vice president, treasurer, 1940's to present). Community Actvities: Sigma Phi (University of Wisconsin chapter, president, 1934-35). Religion: Hyde Park Baptist Church, Chicago, 1918-38; Winnetka Congregational Church, 1940 to present. Honors and Awards: Citations from and Biographical Inclusion in Various Publications of Marquis Who's Who, Inc., and International Biographical Centre, Cambridge, England. Address: 649 Locust Street, Winnetka, Illinois 60093.

Mary M Pope

Pope, Mary Maude

Bishop. Personal: Born January 27, 1916; Daughter of Delia Smith (now deceased); Married to Roy (now deceased). Education: Graduate, Riverdale High School; Attended North Carolina State University, University of North Carolina and American School of Chicago. Career: Bishop, Founder and Pastor of Mt. Sinai Churches worldwide with headquarters in Raleigh, North Carolina; Founder, Mt. Sinai Saints of God Holiness Churches of American, Inc., 1946; Established churches in London, England, Ghana, West Africa, Nigeria, West Afirca, Germany and other parts of the world; Founder, Mt. Sinai Training Center and Orphanage School in Nigeria, West Africa; Established 100 missions in Nigeria. Organizational Memberships: Raleigh Ministerial Alliance. Honors and Awards: Member, International Biographical Centre, Cambridge, England; Received award from Shaw University, 1978; Received award from Mayor J.J. Obot, Nto Akpan Village Council; Listed in *Who's Who in North Carolina, Who's Who Among Black Americans, Who's Who of American Women, Notable Americans, Dictionary of International Biography.* Address: 1220 Crosslink Road, Raleigh, North Carolina 27601.

Popovici, Petru

Minister, Writer, Radio Pastor. Personal: Born September 12, 1918; Son of Simion and Zana Popovici (both deceased); Father of Iedidia, Angela, Agnia. Education: Baptist Theological Seminary, Bucharest Romania. Military: Served in the Navy in Romania from 1941-45, attaining the rank of Sergeant. Career: Minister, Writer, Radio Pastor for Romania through T. W. R., present; Co-Editor, *Farul Crestin (The Christian Beacon)*, Arad, Romania, 1945-47; Editor, *Luminatorul (The Illuminator)*, 1981 Monthly Publication, Romanian Baptist Association of the United States and Canada. Organizational Memberships: Sunday School Association of Romania (president, 1946-49); Romanian Baptist Sunday of the United States of America (president, 1979-81); The Romanian Baptist Association of the United States of America and Canada (president, 1981 to present). Published Works: Author, *Biblia este totusi adevarata (The Bible is True), Promisiunile lui Dumnezeu (The Promises of God), Graiul Prooorociilor (The Voice of Prophesies), Graiul martirilor (The Voice of Martyrs), Intilnirea Cu Dumnezeu (The Meeting with God), Esti sigur? (Are You Sure?), Viata lui D. L. Moody (The Life of D. L. Moody), Lumini peste vaecuri (The Lights over the Ages), Pot sa cred in Isus? (Can I Believe in Jesus?)*; Translator, *Salvation of God* by Oswald Smith, *The Bible for Today's World, Did Man Just Happen?*, Both by W. A. Criswell, *All of Grace, Precious Sermons*, Both by C. H. Spurgeon. Address: 6902 Georgia Avenue, Bell, California 90201.

Porter, Michael LeRoy

Michael Porter

Security Officer. Personal: Born November 23, 1947; Son of Doretha B. Porter; Education: B.A., Virginia State University, 1969; M.A., Atlanta University, 1972; Ph.D., Emory University, 1974; Fulbright-Hays Postdoctoral Study, 1979; Postdoctoral Study, Christopher Newport College, 1979; Special Schooling, Thomas Nelson Community College, 1981. Military: Served in the United States Army from 1969-71 as Hospital Corpsman, attaining the rank of Private First Class. Career: Security Officer, present; Life Insurance Underwriter, North Carolina Mutual Insurance Company, 1980; Assitant Professor of History, Hampton Institute, 1977-80; Assistant Professor of History, Washington State University, 1974-75. Organizational Memberships: American Historical Society, 1978-80; Southern Historical Association, 1972-80; Association for the Study of Afro-American Life and History, 1972-75; Smithsonian Associates, 1980-81; National Trust for Historic Preservation in the United States, 1980-81. Community Activities: Peninsula Council of Clubs (secretary, 1980-81); Big Brothers/Big Sisters Organization (column writer, 1980 to present); Kecoughtan Veterans Administration Hospital (volunteer librarian, 1976); Girls Club of Hampton (board of directors); Citizens' Boys' Club (board of directors); King Street Community Center (board of directors); Catholic Home Bureau (board of directors); Peninsula Sickle Cell Anemia (board of directors); Peninsula Young Women's Christian Association (advisory board); Hampton Roads Jaycees (board of directors); Public Donation, 'Michael L. Porter Papers', Atlanta University Graduate School Archives, 1978. Religion: Church Pianist and Organist, 1960-65; 'Michael L. Porter Day', August 15, 1976, Shalom Baptist Church; Guest Speaker, Tidewater Baptist Convention, Williamsburg, Virginia, 1979. Honors and Awards: Citizenship Award, 1965; Marksmanship Award, 1969; Big Star Award for Education, 1978; Life Achiever Award, 1980; Man of the Hour Award, 1976; Man Achiever, 1981; International Author and Writer Award, 1981; Outstanding Graduate Student Award for History, 1972; Bachelor of the Year, 1981; Educational Celebrity Award, 1979; Voted One of 100 Most Influential Persons of Tidewater, 1980; Voted One of 50 Most Influential Blacks of Tidewater, 1980. Address: 3 Adrian Circle, Hampton, Virginia 23669.

Portnoi, Valery Alexandr

Physician, Internist, Geriatrician. Personal: Born May 10, 1939; Married Atalia Lazarevich; Father of Michel Michael, Dimitry Daniel. Education: Medical Doctor, Kuban Medical Institute, Union of Soviet Socialist Republics, 1962; Internship, Riga Municipal Hospital, 1962-63; Residency, Haadasah University Hospital, Jerusalem, Israel, 1971-75, Long Island-Hillside Jewish Institute for Geriatric Care, 1976-78. Career: Physician, Internist, Geriatrician, present. Organizational Memberships: D.C. Medical Society; American Geriatrics Society; American Geronological Society; Baltimore Washington Osychogeriatrics Society; D.C. Committee on Aging. Community Activities: George Washington University Hospital (patient advicacy committee, 1980 to present); D.C. Medical Society (committee on aging, 1979 to present); Local Nursing Home (various committees, medical director, present); Senate Subcommittee on Aging (gave expert opinion and medical care for the elderly); Extensive Lectures, Interviews and Publications, Team Approach to Care for Elderly, What is a Geriatrician, Drug Abuse and the Elderly. Honors and Awards: Physician's Recognition Award, 1980; Listed in *Who's Who in the East.* Address: 2032 17th Street Northwest, Washington, D.C. 20009.

Potente, Eugene Jr

Eugene Potente

Interior Designer. Personal: Son of Mr. and Mrs. Eugene Potente, Sr.; Married Joan C.; Father of Eugene J., Peter M., John, Suzanne M. Education: Ph.B., Marquette University, 1943; Military Government, Foreign Affairs, Stanford University, 1944; New York School of Interior Design, 1948. Military: Served in the U.S. Army Military Government as sergeant investigator. Career: President, Studios of Potente, Inc.; Architectural Services Associates, Inc.; Business Leasing Services of Wisconsin, Inc. Organizational Memberships: Interfaith Forum on Religion, Art and Architecture (president, 1982-83; American Society for Church Architecture (treasurer, 1976-78); American Society of Interior Designers (treasurer, Wisconsin Chapter, 1982-83); Institute of Business Designers; Interior Designer member Wisconsin State Capitol and Executive Mansion Board, 1981-87; Rotary International. Religion: Roman Catholic. Honors and Awards: member, Alpha Sigma Nu; member, Kappa Tau Alpha. Address: 6634 Third Avenue, Kenosha, Wisconsin 53140.

Powell, Diana Kearny

Writer, Poet, Researcher, Church Worker, Lawyer (retired). Personal: Born April 15, 1910; Daughter of Brigadier General, United States Marine Corps, Retired William G. and Alice Joline Van Voorhees Powell (both deceased). Education: LL.B. 1940, LL.M. 1942, Columbus University Law School; A.A. 1945, George Washington University; Graduate Courses, Labor, International Law 1956-78, Georgetown University Law School. Career: Writer, Poet, Researcher, Church Worker, present; Lawyer, retired; Admitted to Bar of District of Columbia 1940, Bar of Interstate Commerce Commission 1943, Bar of Supreme Court of the United States of America 1959; Law Practice, 1943-47, Foreign Trade Regulations 1959-66, General Practice, Criminal Trial. Organizational Memberships: The Circle, 1927-34; American Bar Association, 1965 to present; Women's Bar Association, 1940-54; National Association of Women Lawyers, 1940 to present; Pen and Palette Club (1929-34; president, 1932-34); National League of American Penwomen, 1930-45; International Platform Association, 1967 to present; Interstate Commerce Commission Practitioners Association, 1943-67; St. Thomas More Association 1960-67. Community Activities: C.A.R. until 1928; Daughters of the American Revolution, 1928-34; National Society of Colonial Dames of America, 1928-45; Republican Party (precinct chairman, 1965-68, ex officio member, D.C. committee, precinct co-chairman, 1973-75, precinct assembly, 1965-68, crime committee, 1968, *Precinct News,* transit rate hearings, 1963-71, Potomac Club, 1964 to present; Chin Lee campaign volunteer, 1968; William Phillips campaign committee, 1974;

pollwatcher, 1964 and subsequent elections; presidential task force, 1982); Anchor Mental Health Association, 1962-76 (house committee, 1974-76; visiting committee chairman, 1972-74; hostess, bazaar committee, flower booth, 1969-76). Religion: Sodality/Holy Name Society of St. Matthew's Cathedral, Workshop Committee chairman, 1974-81, Secretary 1979-81, President 1981 to present, By-Laws Committee 1979, 1982, St. Matthews Newsletter 1972-76, Prison Catechism 1965-66. Honors and Awards: Various Poetry Awards from 1939 to present, including League of American Penwomen, Pen and Palette Club, Circle; Anchor Mental Health Association Award of Appreciation, 1975; Republican Task Force Medal of Merit, 1982. Address: 1500 Massachusetts Avenue, Northwest, Washington, D.C. 20005.

Powell, Dwight E

Supervisor of Out-Patient Unit, Mental Health Center. Personal: Born February 16, 1948; Son of James C. and Lyvonne D. Powell; Married Marsandra M.; Father of Ryan Thomas. Education: Attended South City College 1966-69, University of Illinois, Chicago Circle Campus 1968; Graduate, Sociology, Roosevelt University, 1971; M.S.W., Jane Addams School of Social Work, University of Illinois, Chicago Circle Campus, 1975 Certificates, Cook County Adult Probation Department, University of Chicago-Summer Institute, 1976, 1977, 1978, 1980; Continuing Education in Conjuction with Mid-South Health Planning Alcoholic Treatment 1976, Live Supervision using Video Tapes and Audio Tapes, Special Training in Structural Family Therapy, Certified Social Worker with State of Illinois 1976, Adler Center for Behavior Modification and Psychotherapy 1976, South Beach Psychiatric Center, State of New York, 1977, John Marshall Law School, Law Program for Community Developers and Social Workers 1977, University of Illinois at Medical Center, College of Medicine 1979, Center for Family Studies, The Family Institute of Chicago, Institute of Psychiatry, Northwestern Memorial Hospital, Northwestern University Medical School, Family Services Association of America 1980, American Orthopsychiatric Association Institute 1981; Attended Several Workshops, Illinois Department of Mental Health; Work with Youth Organization, Avalon Park, 3 Years; Attended Week Seminar, Hyde Park, Neighborhood Club, 1969; Attended Seminar, Central State Committee of the American Society for Adolescent Psychiatry, 1976; Accreditation Certificate, Continuing Medical Education. Career: Assistant Specialist in Aging, Geriatrician, Mayor's Office for Senior Citizen's, Chicago, Two Years; Law Clerk, S. Ira Miller, Attorney-at-Law, Chicago, Three Years; Social Worker, Jane Addams School of Social Work, Miles Square Health Center, Chicago, One Year; Social Worker, Maywood Police Department, Maywood, Illinois, One year; Adult Probation Officer, Cook County Adult Probation Department, Chicago, 1½ Years; Part-time Social Worker, Methodist Youth Service, Inc., Chicago, One Year; Social Worker, United Charities of Chicago, Five Years; Course Implementer, Chicago State University, 1976 to present; Outside Lecturer, Malcolm College; Supervisor, Out-Patient Unit, Team Leader, Adult, Elderly and Family Service, ECHO Mental Health Center, Chicago, present; Consultant, Wentworth Nursing Center, present; Private Consultant, Morningside, Individual, Family, Group Work, present. Organizational Memberships: Illinois Probation Department (parole and correctional association); Association of Retired Persons; National Association of Social Workers National Registry of Health Care Providers; for Psychiatric Social Worker. Community Activities: Avalon Park-Chatham Community Youth Center (youth counselor, director/sponsor); The Substance Abuse Service, Chicago (advisory board member). Religion: Lutheran; Salem Lutheran Church. Published Works: "Crimes Against the Elderly", *Journal of Gerontological Social Work*, 1980; "Self-Acceptance" 1979, "Pluses and Minuses" 1979, *Mirror Newspaper*. Honors and Awards: Listed in *Who's Who in the Midwest, Personalities of the West and Midwest, Men of Achievement*. Address: 8231 South Jeffrey Boulevard, Chicago, Illinois 60617.

Vikram Prasad

Prasad, Vikram

Intern. Personal: Born July 1, 1941 at Ballia (V.P.), India; Son of Udai Narain (deceased) and Yashoda Devi; Married Indira; Father of Nilima Vikram, Ravi Vikram, Ravindra Vikram. Education: M.Sc., Bhagalpur University, India, 1963; M.S. University of Hawaii, Honolulu, 1966; Ph.D. Wayne State University, Detroit, Michigan, 1970; M.D., Escuela de Medecina, Juarez, Mexico, 1982. Career: Professor, Biology; Clinical Laboratory Director. Organizational Memberships: *International Journal of Acaraology*, A Journal of Mites and Ticks, (founder, managing editor, 1975 to present). Published Works: Author with D.R. Cook, Book, *Water Mite Larvae*, 1972; Author, *A Catalogue of Mites of India*, 1974; Editor, *History of Acarology*, 1982; Author, Over 30 Research Articles. Honors and Awards: Merit Scholarship, 1956; University Gold Medal, 1963; East West Center Scholarship. Address: 5828 Shillingham Drive, West Bloomfield, Michigan 48033.

Pratt, Harvey Arthur

Pharmacist, Small Business Representative. Personal: Born March 6, 1939; Son of James A. and L. Charlotte; Married Ann Louise; Father of Linda, Leann, Michelle, Jennine, Arriana. Education: B.S., University of Pittsburgh, 1960. Career: Pharmacist, Small Business Representative; Consultant; Teacher of Pharmacy, University of Colorado School of Pharmacy, 1977-80. Organizational Memberships: American Pharmaceutical Association; Colorado Pharmacal Association (grievance/peer review committee, 1979-80); Denver Area Pharmacy Association (board of directors, 1973-77); Twenty-Eighth Annual Western States Pharmacy Conference (general chairman, 1979); Colorado Foundation for Medical Care (board of directors, 1977-80; board secretary, 1978-80; chairman, P.S.R.O. advisory group nominating committee, 1979; co-chairman, drug criteria subcommittee, health care standards committee, 1976-77); National Association Retail Druggists (national legislation committee, 1978-79; third party insurance, 1979-80); National Association of Board of Pharmacy (appointed question writer; licensure examination, 1980); American Management Association. Community Activities: National Speakers Association; National Capital Speakers Association; Englewood/United Suburban Chamber of Commerce (president-elect, 1980; board of directors, 1976-80; chairman, compensation committee, 1978-80; chairman, business seminars task force, 1976-78; chairman, area retail task force, 1974-75); Englewood Holiday Parade (co-chairman, 1976-80); Englewood Board of Adjustment and Appeals (member, 1979-80; vice-chairman, 1980); Cheery Creek Breakfast Optimist Club (president, 1970; vice president, 1969; treasurer, 1968; secretary, 1967; board member, 1962-73). Honors and Awards: Pharmacist of Distinction Award, Lederle Laboratories; Elizabeth Taft Memorial Award, Colorado Pharmacal Association; Outstanding Service and Achievement Award, Englewood/United Suburban Chamber of Commerce; Listed in *Who's Who in Finance and Industry, Who's Who in the West, Personalities of America, Who's Who in the World*. Address: 237 Mallow Hill Road, Catonsville, Maryland 21229.

Prentice, Sartell Jr

Counselor on Incentive Employee Profit Participation Programs, Lecturer. Personal: Born December 28, 1903; Son of Rev. Sartell and Lydia Beekman Vanderpoel Prentice; Married Eleanor Hoyt (deceased), November 24, 1948; Father of Patricia Phelps, Adelaide Vanderpoel (both now deceased), Peter Sartell. Education: Taft School; Yale University; B.A., Stanford University, 1925; M.B.A., Harvard Business School, 1927; Attended Freedom School, Colorado, 1957; Courses at Free Enterprise Institute, Los Angeles, 1962 to present. Career: Security Salesman, National Cash Credit Association, New York, 1928-31; Training for Foreign Service, Socony

Vacuum Oil Company, New York, 1931; Executive Assistant to the President, Vacuum Oil Company, S.A.I., Genoa, Italy, 1931-35; Marketing Assistant, Foreign Department, Socony Vacuum Oil Company, New York, 1935; Research, Script Writer, March of Time Movie and Radio, New York, 1935-37; Actor, Summer Stock, Barter Theatre, Abingdon, Virginia, 1938; Salesman, Automatic Canteen Company, New York, 1940-41; Public Relations, Advertising Representative, *Time* Magazine, New York and Boston, 1941-46; Administrative Secretary, Commission of the Churches on International Affairs, 1947-48; Field Secretary, Northeastern Chapter, Council on Profit Sharing Industries (now Profit Sharing Council of America), 1950-54; On Lecture Circuit, Associated Clubs of America (addressed dinner clubs throughout country), 1956-58; New York State Chairman, National Committee for Economic Freedom, 1960; Counselor of Profit Sharing, 1954 to present. Organizational Memberships: American Waldemsian Aid Society (director, 1944-61); Society of Professional Management Consultants, Inc. (charter member); The Western Pension Conference; Town Hall of California; Toastmasters International; Yale, Stanford, Harvard and Harvard Business School Clubs of Southern California. Religion: Administrative Secretary, Commission of the Churches on International Affairs, 1947-48. Published Works: Articles have appeared in *Management Review, Stanford Review, The Freeman, Rampart Journal of Individualist Thought, Journal of Management*, as well as in many others. Honors and Awards: Liberty Award, Congress of Freedom Inc., 1967, 1973, 1974, 1975, 1976, 1977; Twice Recognized by Having His Talks Published in *Vital Speeches of The Day*; Listed in *Two Thousand Men of Achievement, Men of Achievement, Who's Who in Finance and Industry, Who's Who in the West, Royal Blue Book, Blue Book, Dictionary of International Biography, Personalities of the West and Midwest, Community Leaders and Noteworthy Americans, Notable Americans, Register of Prominent Americans.* Address: 1404 Chamberlain Road, Pasadena, California 91103.

Pressler, Larry

United States Senator. Personal: Born March 29, 1942; Son of Mr. and Mrs. Antone Pressler. Education: B.A., University of South Dakota, 1964; Rhodes Scholar, Oxford University, 1966; M.A., Kennedy School of Government, Harvard University; J.D., Harvard Law School, 1971. Military: Served with the United States Army, 1966-68, Vietnam Veteran. Career: Farmer; Lawyer; United States Representative from South Dakota; United States Senator from South Dakota. Organizational Memberships: American Association of Rhodes Scholars; Phi Betta Kappa; American Bar Association. Community Activities: Lions Club; Veterans of Foreign Wars; American Legion; South Dakota Historical Society; Committees in the United States Senate: Commerce, Science and Transportation Committee (chairman, business, trade and tourism subcommittee); Foreign Relations Committee (chairman, arms control, oceans, international operation and environment subcommittee); Special Committee on Aging (republican senatorial campaign committee). Honors and Awards: National and International 4-H Awards; Recipient of Rhodes Scholarship to Oxford University. Address: 700 New Hampshire Avenue, N.W., Washington, D.C. 20037.

Price, Betty M

Speech Pathologist. Personal: Born June 7, 1934; Daughter of Ruby Elizabeth Edwards; Mother of Katharine Ann, Ellen Elizabeth, Diane Christine. Education: A.A., West Valley College, B.A., M.A. San Jose State University. Career: Speech Pathologist. Organizational Memberships: American Speech/Language and Hearing Association; California Speech and Hearing Association; California Association of Post-Secondary Educators of the Disabled; Western Speech Association. Address: 1397 Sydney Drive, Sunnvale, California 94087.

Sartell Prentice

Price, Earl Lawrence

Chairman of the Board, Managing Partner. Personal: Born February 25, 1946; Son of Earl Raymond and Bella Williams Price; Married Elaine Duncan; Father of Julia Elizabeth. Education: Graduate of University Prep, Laramie, Wyoming, 1963; University of Wyoming, Laramie, 1963-67; General Motors Institute, Flint, Michigan, 1967-68. Career: President, Price Motors, Laramie, Wyoming, 1968-72; President, Real Estate Investment Corporation, Fort Collins, Colorado, 1970-72; International Financial Consulting, Europe, 1972-74; Managing Partner, Lawrence Price & Associates, Fort Collins, Colorado, 1974-76; Chairman of the Board, Newcomb Financial Group, 1978 to present; Managing Partner, Price & Company, 1976 to present; Managing Partner, Newcomb Government Securities, 1978 to present; Director, Imprint Editions, Publishing Company, 1980 to present; Director, The Light Company, Talent Agency, 1980 to present; Director, Newcomb Energy Corporation, 1981 to present. Organizational Memberships: International Associaton of Financial Planners; American Stock Exchange Committee for Development of Middle Range Companies; Chicago Association of Commerce and Industry Pacific Stock Exchange; Chicago Board of Options Exchange. Community Activities: Republican Leadership Council; Elephant Club, Colorado State Republican Party; Fort Collins Symphony Board; A Renaissance Trend Arts Funding Council (director); Open Stage Theatre Board. Religion: Episcopalian. Honors and Awards: Guest Artist with San Francisco Old First Orchestra; Listed in *Who's Who in the World, Who's Who in Finance and Industry, Personalities of America, Inventory of Distinguished Americans, Men of Achievement, Book of Honor, Fort Collins Symphony.* Address: 415 South Howes, #1104, Fort Collins, Colorado 80521.

Price, Richard Lee

Acting Justice of the Supreme Court, Civil Court Judge. Personal: Born September 19, 1940; Son of Saul and Claire Price; Married Carolyn; Father of Lisa, Howard. Education: B.A., Roanoke College, 1957; J.D., New York Law School, 1964. Career: Chief Law Assistant in Charge of Law Department, Civil Court; Law Secretary to Judge Harry Davis, Civil Court; Attorney, Harry L. Lipsig; Acting Justice of the Supreme Court, Bronx County, and Judge of Civil Court, Elected 1980. Organizational Memberships: American Bar Association; Association of the Bar of the City of New York; New York County Lawyers Association; New York State Bar Association; Association of Trial Lawyers of America; New York State Trial Lawyers Association, Inc.; Jewish Lawyers Guild (board of directors); New York City Criminal and Civil Courts Bar Association (vice president); Metropolitan Women's Bar Association (board of directors); American Judges Association (treasurer); American Judges Foundation (treasurer); Council of New York Law Associates. Community Activities: Claremore Lodge, Knights of Pythias; Community School Board District 1 (elected member, 1973-74, 1975-80; elected vice chairman, 1979-80); State Board of Certified Shorthand Reporting (appointed by New York State Board of Regents, 1978-82); Arbitrators Association of the Small Claims Court (president, 1979-80); Educational Alliance Alumni Association; Lawyers Lodge #2929, B'nai B'rith, 1976-78; Civil Court Law Secretaries Association (president, 1973-75); 7th Precinct, Auxiliary Police (executive officer/lieutenant, until 1980); Grand Street Consumers Society (board of directors); East River Housing Corporation (board member); East Side Chamber of Commerce; N.O.W.; Lower East Side Businessmen's Association (board of directors); New York Consumers Assembly (board of directors). Religion: East Side Torah Center (board of directors). Honors and Awards: Honorary Doctor of Laws, Shaw University, Raleigh, North Carolina, 1980. Address: 577 Grand Street, New York, New York 10002.

Prichard, John F

Periodontist. Personal: Born April 16, 1907; Son of Mr. and Mrs. J. A. Prichard (both deceased); Married Edna; Father of Catherine Prichard Kaplan. Education: Graduate, Baylor University College of Dentistry. Career: Practicing Periodontist Senior Consultant, Periodonia Department, University of Washington, Seattle; Visiting Lecturer, Periodontia Department, University of Pennsylvania, Graduate Periodontics Department, Baylor University; Former Consultant, Carswell and Lackland Air Force Bases, United States Public Health Service Hospital, Fort Worth; Postgraduate Lecturer, Courses given in the United States, Canada, Europe; Director, Dental Services Corporation, 1967-73. Organizational Memberships: American Society of Periodontists (president, 1964-65); Southwestern Society of Dental Medicine (past president); Texas Dental Association (vice president, 1943; good fellow, 1953); Fort Worth District Dental Society (president, 1942; major committees, 1930-50); American Board of Periodontology (diplomate, 1947; director, 1970-76; vice chairman, 1975-76); American Academy of Periodontology (membership committee, 1970; awards committee, 1976; chairman, 1980-81; history and necrology committee, 1968; chairman, research in periodontology committee, 1964; subcommittee on advanced education, 1975; advisory committee to commission on accreditation, 1975-78; chairman, committee on nomenclature, 1975-76); Fellow, American Medical Writers Association; Member, American Academy of Oral Roentgenology; International Association of Dental Research; District, State and American Dental Associations; Texas State Dental Association (chairman, insurance committee, 12 years). Community Activities: Delta Sigma Delta, Undergraduate Fraternity; Rivercrest Country Club; Century II Club; American Airlines (admiral of the fleet, 1964; life member); Established Scholarship Fund of $10,000, Texas Wesleyan College, Income of Which to be Used for Deserving and Interested PreDental Students at Texas Wesleyan College, 1969; Conducted Campaign to Raise Funds from Southwestern Society of Periodontists Members for Jewish Research Hospital, Denver, Colorado, 1975. Religion: Baptist; Retired Deacon. Published Works: Fifty Scientific Papers and Chapters for Textbooks; Textbook, *Advanced Periodontal Disease: Surgical and Prosthetic Management* and *The Diagnosis and Treatment of Periodontal Disease*, Editor, *Dental Clinics of North America;* Glossary of Terms, American Academy of Periodontology. Honors and Awards: William J. Gies Award for Achievement in Periodontology, 1977; Honorary Member, Texas Academy of General Dentistry, 1962; Omicron Kappa Upsilon, Honorary Society of Periodontists, American Academy of Periodontology 1938, American Medical Writers Association 1962, Academia Internationali Lex et Sceintiae 1964; Distinguished Service Award, Fort Worth District Dental Society, 1967; Life Member, American Dental Association, 1972; Outstanding Alumnus Award, Baylor University College of Dentistry, 1978; Testimonial Dinner, Southwestern Society of Periodontists, 1973, John Prichard Lectureship Foundation Established, American Academy of Periodontology Endowment, $10,000; Gold Medal Award, American Academy of Periodontology, 1974 (gold medal and $1000 which was contributed to University of Washington periodontal research fund); Honorary Member, Fifth District Dental Society, Atlanta, Georgia, 1975. Address: 3833 Camp Bowie Boulevard, Fort Worth, Texas 76107.

Prince, Gilbert Lee

Minister of Education. Personal: Born August 27, 1934; Son of Mr. and Mrs. Vernon L. Prince; Married Lorice Humphres; Father of Steven Paul. Education: B.S., University of North Alabama, 1970; M.R.E., New Orleans Baptist Theological Seminary, 1972. Military: Served with the United States Army, 1952-65, 1965-68; Served with the Alabama Army National Guard, achieving the rank of Sergeant First Class, 1973 to present; Recruiter, Alabama Army Reserve National Guard, 1978 to present. Career: Pastor: Waterloo Baptist Church, Waterloo, Alabama, 1965; Millilani Baptist Mission, Millilani, Hawaii, 1968; Big Coppitt First Baptist Church, Key West, Florida, 1972-73; Director, Howard Extension, Samford University, Sheffield, Alabama, 1976-81; Minister of Education, Southside Baptist Church, Sheffield, Alabama. Community Activities: Sheffield Little League (vice president, 1979). Religion: Baptist. Honors and Awards: Member 100 Club, Alabama Army Recruiters, 1979 and 1980; Recruiter of the Month, Alabama Army F.T.R.F., September 1980; Recruiter of the Month, Region One, January, March and September 1980. Address: P.O. Box 252, Sheffield, Alabama 35660.

Virginia Prochnow

Pringle, Kenneth G

Lawyer, Executive. Personal: Born May 13, 1914; Married Jean L. Herigstad; Father of Priscilla Wells, Roger K., Alice Heitlinger, Jane F. Hirst. Education: Attended Minot State Teachers College, 1932-34; B.S., North Dakota State University, 1934-36; Studied Law under a Supreme Court Clerkship, 1946-49. Military: Served with the United States Naval Reserve, 1944-46, rising through the ranks from Ensign to Lieutenant j.g. Career: High School Teacher, Harvey, North Dakota, 1936-37; Boy Scout Executive, Albert Lea, Minnesota, 1937-39; Boy Scout Executive, Sioux Falls, South Dakota, 1939-44; United States Naval Reserve, 1944-46; Lawyer; President, Pringle & Herigstad, P.C. Organizational Memberships: Ward County Bar Association (president, 1956); Fifth District Bar Association; State Bar Association of North Dakota (chairman, legislative economic committee, 1964-66); Defense of Indigents and Legal Aid Committee (chairman, 1966-67; president-elect, 1967-68; president, 1968-69); American Bar Association (advisory board, editors journal, 1964-67; house of delegates, 1971-76; chairman, special committee on legal assistants, 1974-75; chairman, standing committee on legal assistants, 1975-78; board of governors, 1974); American College of Probate Counsel (board of regents, 1971-77; executive committee, 1974); American Judicature Society; World Association of Lawyers (founding member); Association of the Bars of Northwestern Plains and Mountains (chancellor, 1970-71). Community Activities: Minot Chamber of Commerce (director); Kiwanis Club (president, 1951); Minot Metropolitan Dinner Club (past president and director); Boy Scouts of America: Great Plains Area Council (president, 1952-55, 1968); Northern Lights Council (president, 1973-75); National Council Member, 1955 to present; North Central Regional Committee Board, 1974 to present; National Law Exploring Committee (chairman, 1974-80); National Canoe Base Advisory Committee. Religion: Presbyterian. Honors and Awards: Outstanding Citizen Award, Minot Chamber of Commerce, 1975; Boy Scouts of America: Silver Beaver Award 1954, Silver Antelope Award, 1967, Distinguished Eagle Scout Award 1975. Address: 625 Third St. S. E., Minot, North Dakota 58701.

Prochnow, Virginia Wilma

Private Piano and Organ Instructor, Church Organist. Personal: Born March 30, 1935; Daughter of Leonard M. and Wilma L. Radsek Prochnow. Education: A.A. with honors, Yakima Valley College, 1955; B.A. cum laude, Pacific Lutheran University, 1957. Career: Private Piano and Organ Instructor; Organist, Handbell Choir Director, Central Lutheran Church, Yakima, Washington. Organizational Memberships: Music Teachers National Association (Yakima Chapter: president, 1961-63, 1971-73, 1979-81; vice president, 1959-61, 1969-71, 1966-67); Washington State Association (southeast president, 1966-67; state chairman, organ division, 1980 to present); Annual Yakima Chapter and Yakima Valley College Co-Sponsored Daniel Pollack Piano Workshop (chairman, 1977 to present); American Guild of Organists Association (dean, 1969-71, 1975-77; sub-dean, 1971-73); The American Guild of English Handbell Ringers Inc., 1980 to present. Community Activities: Yakima Community Concert Association (board of directors, 1965-66); Allied Arts Council (board of directors, 1968-71); College Concert Series (board member, 1969 to present; secretary-treasurer, 1975 to present); Patrons of Music, Yakima Symphony Board (trustee, 1962-65); Ladies Musical Club (president, 1974-75;

vice president, 1973-74). Religion: Lutheran; Lutheran Brotherhood, Board of Directors 1981 to present, Fraternal Communicator 1979-81, Area Branch; Organist, 1957 to present; Handbell Choir Director, 1980 to present; Chairman, Worship Committee, 1976-78, 1980 to present. Address: 1420 South 34th Avenue, Yakima, Washington 98902.

Promisel, Nathan E

Consulting Engineer. Personal: Born June 20, 1908; Father of David Mark, Larry Jay. Education: B.S. 1929, M.S. 1930, Massachusetts Institute of Technology; Doctoral Work, Yale University, 1932-33. Career: Assistant Laboratory Director, International Silver Company, 1930-40; Chief Materials Scientist and Engineer, Department of the United States Navy, Aeronautics and Weapons, 1940-66; Executive Director, National Materials Advisory Board, National Academy of Sciences, 1966-74; International Consultant, Materials and Policy, 1974 to present. Organizational Memberships: American Society of Metals (fellow; honorary member; president, 1972); Federation of Materials Societies (president, 1972-73); British Institute of Metallurgists (fellow); Society of Automotive Engineers (chairman, aerospace materials division, 1959-74); American Institute of Mining, Metallurgical and Petroleum Engineers (honorary member); American Society of Testing and Materials (honorary member); Alpha Sigma Mu Society (honorary member); Society for the Advancement of Materials and Process Engineering. Community Activities: North Atlantic Treaty Organization (chairman/member, aerospace panel, 1959-71); Organization for Economic Cooperation and Development (United States representative, materials, 1967-70); United States/U.S.S.R. Scientific Exchange Program (chairman, materials, 1973-77); National Materials Advisory Board; Advisory Committees, Oak Ridge National Laboratory, Lehigh University, University of Pennsylvania, United States Navy Laboratories, United States Congress Office of Technological Assessment. Published Works: Author of 50 Technical Articles; Contributor/Editor, Several Books. Honors and Awards: Honorary Doctor of Engineering, Michigan Technological Institute, 1978; Elected Member, National Academy of Engineering, 1978; National Capitol Engineer of the Year, Council of Engineering and Architectural Societies, 1974; Outstanding Accomplishment Awards, United States Navy, 1955-64; Carnegie Honorary Lecture, 1959; Gillett Distinguished Lecture, 1965; Burgess Award, 1961; Distinguished Lecture, Electrochemical Society, 1970; First Decennial Award, Federation of Materials Societies, 1982. Address: 12519 Davan Drive, Silver Spring, Maryland 20904.

Propst, E Allen

Pilot, Retired Educator. Personal: Born January 11, 1926, near Albany, Oregon; Son of Elmer E. and Eva Anna Propst; Father of Richard L. and Ronald D. Military: Served in Sensitive Security Area of the Military Police, 1945-46. Career: Aircraft Pilot; Flight and Ground Instructor; Teacher, Course in Airplanes and Their Instruments; Operator, Aerial Pesticide Applicator and Technical Field Advisory Service, 1951-69; Candidate for Governor of Oregon, Three Times. Community Activities: As Candidate for Office of Governor of Oregon, Called Attention to Alleged Secret United States Intelligence Agencies and Their Activities and/or Involvement on such Cases as the D. B. Cooper Airplane Hijacking; Has on File Pending Criminal Complaint on Alleged Secret Intelligence Agencies and has Pushed for a United States Senatorial Investigation on Involvement of These Agencies into American Politics. Religion: First Christian Church (co-founded by great-grandfather). Published Works: Author of Documents and Memoranda Pertaining to Internal and National Security. Honors and Awards: Listed in *Personalities of the West and Midwest, Dictionary of International Biography, Men of Achievement, International Who's Who of Intellectuals, International Register of Profiles of North America, Personalities of America, Community Leaders and Noteworthy Americans, Book of Honor, Men and Women of Distinction.* Address: 253 Southeast Scravel Hill Road, Albany, Oregon 97321.

H L Prosser

Prosser, H L

Writer. Personal: Born December 31, 1944; Married Grace Eileen; Father of Rachael Maranda, Rebecca Dawn. Education: A.A., English, Santa Monica College, 1968; Attended California State University-Northridge, 1968-69; B.S. Sociology 1974; B.S., Sociology 1974, Southwest Missouri State University and M.S.Ed., Social Sciences, 1982, Southwest Missouri State University. Career: Writer, Book Reviewer, Social Sciences Researcher, 1963 to present. Organizational Memberships: Society for Historians of the Early American Republic; Modern Language Association; American Academy of Poets. Community Activities: National Council for the Social Studies (ethics committee 1982-84). Religion: American Baptist; University Heights Baptist Church, Springfield, Missouri. Published Works: Most Recent Publication, *Summer Wine*, 1979; Most Recent Article, "American Fantasy Short Fiction", 1981; Pending, *A Gathering of Secret Places: Autobiographical Sketches.* Honors and Awards: Manuscripts and Papers on Permanent File, "The H. L. Prosser Collection", University of Wyoming, Archives and Contemporary History, Laramie, Wyoming. Address: 1313 South Jefferson Avenue, Springfield, Missouri 65807.

Pryor, Wallace Cyral

Oil Company Executive. Personal: Born September 16, 1922; Son of Harry Gwyn and Maude Johnson Pryor; Married to Jeanette Altman; Father of John Wallace (deceased), David Nelsen, Paul Richard, Mark Bernard, Peter Gwyn, Joel Phillip, Andrew George, (2 stepsons:) Charles Henry, Ronnie Dale Cheshire. Education: Graduate, Concord High School, Concord, Georgia, 1939; Attended St. Olaf College, Northfield, Minnesota, 1945. Military: Served with United States Navy during World War II, 1942-46. Career: President, Pryor Oil Company, Griffin, Georgia; Former President, Tara Oil Company. Organizational Memberships: Georgia Oilmen's Association; Southeastern Independent Oilmen's Association; Georgia Gasohol Association (founder and organizer; president, 1979-81; chairman emeritus, board of directors, lifetime appointment); Minority Contractors Association. Community Activities: Commander, American Legion Post #197 of Zebulon, Georgia, 1948-49; Worshipful Master, Masonic Lodge Montgomery #31, Zebulon, 1961-62; Worthy Patron, Order of Eastern Star, Griffin, 1961. Religion: Member of Friendship Presbyterian Church, Pedenville, Georgia (Sunday school teacher, 1957-62, Sunday school teacher for children at Devotie Baptist Church, 1970-73, adult training union teacher, 1975-79, assistant Sunday school teacher for adults, 1977 to present, board of directors of Full Gospel Businessmen Fellowship International, 1978-80, treasurer of the fellowship, 1981 to present, appointed liaison representative to Georgia state prison, 1981 to present). Honors and Awards: Good Conduct Medal, American Defense Campaign Medal and Atlantic Theatre Campaign Medal, U.S.N. Address: 715 West Poplar Street, Griffin, Georgia 30223.

Puckett, Ruby Parker

Director, Food and Nutrition Services Executive. Personal: Married Larry W. Puckett. Education: B.S. Food & Nutrition, Auburn University, 1954; Certificate, Dietetic Internship, Henry Ford Hospital, 1955; Certificate, Management by Objectives, Waterman Memorial Hospital, 1966; Vocational Education, Graduate School 1970-73, Postgraduate Work 1980, University of Florida; M.A.

Education-Health Care, Central Michigan University, 1976; Numerous Inservices Classes, Seminars and Workshops. Career: Staff Dietitian, Hospital, Houston, Texas, 1955-56; Only Dietitian, Hospital, Meridian, Mississippi, 1960-61; Director, Dietetics, Hospital, Knoxville, Tennessee 1961-63, Eustis, Florida 1963-68, Gainesville, Florida 1968-74; Director Food and Nutrition, J-325 Shands Hospital, University of Florida, Gainesville, 1974 to present; University of Florida, Education, CUPS Program 1974 to present; Instructor, Education, Community College, Gainesville, 1977-81; President, Square One, Inc. Consulting, Gainesville, 1979 to present; Numerous Postions in Education and Training, 1955 to present; Teacher of Dietetic Interns, Veterans Administration Hospital, Houston, 1955-56; Teacher of Nutrition and Diet Therapy, Meridian Junior College, Matty Hersee Hospital, 1957-58, Fort Sanders Presbyterian 1961-63; Preceptor, Coordinator, Food Service Correspondence Course, Waterman Memorial Hospital, 1963-68; Developer, One-Year Training Course for Food Service Supervisors, J Hillis Miller Health Center 1968 to present; Coordinator of Food Service Supervisor Course, Instructor, Division of Independent Study 1972; Clinical Instructor, Dietetic Students 1975 to present. Organizational Memberships: International Platform Association; American Dietetic Association (numerous committee positions); Florida Dietetic Association (numerous committee positions); Gainesville Dietetic Association (numerous committee positions); Field Agency Nutrition; Southeastern Hospital Conference for Dietitians; American Society of Hospital Food Service Administrator (several committee positions); Florida Council on Aging (nutrition section); University of Florida Clinical and Community Coordinated Undergraduate Dietetic Program; North Central Florida Planning Council; Florida Department of Education; North Florida Regional Vocational School; Nutrition Advisory Committee; National Research Council Advisory Board on Military Personnel Supplies; Hospital, Institution and Educational Food Service Society (competency committee; organized Florida chapter, advisor, 1965-78). Community Activities: Pilot Club's Marquis Library Society, Inc.; Gainesville Florida Campus Federal Credit Union Chairperson of Board; United Way, Stokes Report; Consultant to Nursing Homes 1965-67; Guest Speaker over 300 Times to Local, State, National Conventions or Annual Meetings 1965-78; Advisor, Several Junior Colleges, Developing Programs, 1968-69; Chosen one of Eight Administrative Dietitians in Nation to Develop Educational Tapes for American Dietetic Association; Assisted Development, Dietetic Internship, J. Hillis Miller Health Center, 1968-69; Part-time Instructor Santa Fe Community College, 1978 to present; Faculty of ADA-HEW Cost Containment Workshop, 1979-80. Religion: Church of Jesus Christ of the Latter-Day Saints; Stoke President, Young Women 1978-80, Junior Sunday School Coordinator 1975; Ward, President, Young Women, Adult Sunday School Teacher, Seminary Teacher, Primary Teacher, Counselor, Young Women, Bishop Committee for Youth. Published Works: Author, Numerous Books and Manuals, Contributing Editor, Numerous Trade Magazines; Letters to the Editor. Honors and Awards: Educational Leader in Florida Hospital, Institution, Educational Food Service Society Scholarship in Food Service Education, 1970; Representative of Florida Hospital Dietitians, White House Conference of Food, Nutrition and Health, 1969; Assisted with Organization Implementation, Florida Conference on Food, Nutrition and Health, 1970; Fellow, Royal Society of Health, 1971; Outstanding Dietitian in Florida, 1972; Outstanding Community Leader, Radio Station WRUF, 1972; Pi Lambda Theta Educational Honor Society, 1971; Kappa Delta Pi Educational Honor Society, 1971 to present; Florida Who is Who Advisory Board, 1974; National Nutritional Policy Study Hearings, Senate Select Committee on Nutrition and Human Needs, 1974; Who's Who Honorary Society of America, 1975; Scholarship Named in Honor, Given by Florida Hospital, Institution, Educational Food Service Society, 1975; One of 50 Women Who are Top Managers, 1977 Institutions and Volume Feeding; IFMA's Silver Plate Award, International Gold and Silver Plate Society, 1978; Ivy Award, Restauranteurs of Distinction, 1980; Hall of Fame 1982, Woodlawn High School; Listed in *Who's Who of Women, World Who's Who of Women, Dictionary of International Biography, Who's Who in the South and Southwest, Florida Who's Who, National Register of Prominent Americans and International Notables, Community Leaders and Noteworthy Americans, Contemporary Authors, Who's Who in America.* Address: Route 3, Box 108-B2, Gainesville, Florida 32606.

Pulitano, Concetta Norigenna

Learning Center Coordinator, Student Council Moderator, Director of Activities, Avon Group Sales Leader. Personal: Born June 16, 1941, in Sicily, Italy; Daughter of Mrs. Benedetta Norigenna; Married Francis Joseph; Mother of Maria Anne, Margaret Theresa, Angela Marie. Education: Graduate of High School; Secretarial Degree, 1959. Career: Secretary, Ka-Line Pool Products, Bookkeeper, Gena's Department Store, Hialeah, Florida, 1959-61; Secretary, Westinghouse, Baltimore, Maryland, 1961; Secretary, Bendix, Baltimore, Maryland, 1961-63; Cathedral School, Student Council Moderator, Learning Center Coordinator, Director of Activities, Part-Time Secretary, 1974 to present; Avon Group Sales Leader, 1982. Organizational Memberships: National Catholic Educational Association. Community Activities: Volunteer Work, Collecting Money for Organizations of United Fund; Brownie/Girl Scout Leader, 1974. Religion: Roman Catholic. Honors and Awards: Listed in *Who's Who of American Women.* Address: 1813 Landrake Road, Towson, Maryland 21204.

Concetta N Pulitano

Pulvari, Charles F

Educator. Personal: Born July 19, 1907, in Hunary. Education: Dipl.Ing., Royal Hungarian University of Technical Science, 1929. Career: Catholic University of America, Professor Emeritus, 1954 to present; President, Electrocristal Corporation, Inc., 1961 to present; Principal Investigator, United States Air Force and United States Navy, 1949-70; Owner, Pulvari Electrophysical Laboratory, 1943-49; Executive Director, Hungarian Radio and Communication Company, 1935-45; Lecturer, University of Technical Science, Budapest, 1943; Research Engineering Laboratory, Hungarian Tel. Manufacturing Company, Standard Company, Budapest, 1929-33; Director, Keilcrest Corporation, 1969 to present. Organizational Memberships: New York Academy of Sciences (life member; past chairman, crystal committee); Sigma Xi (past chairman, Catholic University chapter); Tau Beta Pi. Published Works: Author, 60 Papers, Reports, Articles; Contributing Editor, *Computer Handbook*, 1960. Honors and Awards: Fellow, New York Academy of Sciences 1978, American Ceramic Society 1978, Institute of Electrical and Electronic Engineering 1970; Americanism Medal, Daughters of the American Revolution, 1975; IR 100 Award, *Indus Research* Magazine, 1963; Patents Held, 75 in Ferroelectrics, Electrostatics, Television, Radio, Sound Reproduction, including Apparatus for Electrostatic Recording and Reproduction (ferroelectric memory) 1950, Force Sensor 1966, Polar Vapor Sensing Means 1971; Invented Method, Established Studio for Postsynchronizing Movies into Hungarian, 1935-45; Developed First Light Valve-Operated CRT, 1936; Developed First Noise Eliminator for Radio Receivers, 1935; Developed First Solid State Light Valve; Honorary Doctoral Degree, Golden Diploma, Royal Hungarian University of Technical Sciences, 1981. Address: 2014 Taylor Street, Northeast, Washington, D.C. 20018.

Purcell, George Richard

Retired Postal Worker. Personal: Born May 4, 1921; Married Mary Sutter. Education: B.S., Niagara University, 1947; Postgraduate Study, Syracuse University, 1952-53, 1955-56. Military: Served in the United States Army, Active Duty, Medical Corps, from 1943-46. Career: Eagan Real Estate, 1948-49; New York State Employment Interviewer, Unemployment Insurance Division, New York State Civil Service, 1949-50; United States Postal Service, 1957-81. Community Activities: Syracuse Catholic Medical Mission Board (founder, president, Syracuse chapter, 1973-76; representative, 1976 to present); Tutor in Philosophy, 1971 to present; African Book Program, Religious Books, 1977-78. Honors and Awards: New York State War Service Scholarship, 1955; Life Fellow,

International Biographical Association; Life Associate, American Biographical Institute Research Association; Listed in *Who's Who in Religion, Who's Who in the East.* Address: 1 Gregory Parkway, Syracuse, New York 13214.

Purvis, Dorothy LaRue

Administrator. Personal: Born September 20, 1934; Daughter of Alberta J. Simko; Mother of Dawn Patrice Jensen, Patricia LaRue Dumond, Wesley Jay LaRue, Mark H. LaRue, Diane Elizabeth LaRue. Education: Graduate, Thomas Carr Howe High School, 1952; Women in Management Certificate, College of St. Catherine, 1978; Attending College of St. Thomas, 1979 to present. Career: Indiana Bell Telephone: Traffic Engineer, 1965-70; Senior Clerk, Network Management Center, 1963-65; Long Distance Operator, 1951-63; Continental Telephone Company of Minnesota: Division Network Service Administrator, 1977 to present; Traffic Engineering Manager, 1973-77; Separations Manager, 1970-73. Organizational Memberships: National Association of Female Executives; All the Good Old Girls; American Management Association; Telephone Pioneers of America. Community Activities: Campfire Girls (leader 1961-62); Mother's March of Dimes. Address: 10650 Burnswick Road, Apt. 102, Bloomington, Minnesota 55438.

Queen, Sandra Jane

Community Health Consultant/Educator. Personal: Born January 25, 1946; Daughter of Ralph Bort, Nettie Mae Peeler Bort (deceased); Mother of David Brice, Lara Renee, Wendy Joy. Education: Attended the University of Maryland, 1964-65; Studies in Psychology and Health Sciences, Towson State University, 1973-76. Career: Director, Lifeworks, Health Consulting/Education Firm; Lifeworks Coordinator, Outreach Program, St. Joseph Hospital, Towson, Maryland, 1977-82; National Medical Consultants, Kansas City, Missouri, 1976-77; Research Aide and Office Manager, Marvin Ellin and Associates, 1975-76; Secretary, Social Service Department, Saint Joseph Hospital, Towson, 1973-75. Organizational Memberships: Organization of Wellness Networks (charter member, president elect 1982); Owner: "Paperworks" Craft Business; Marathon Runner. Community Activities: American Cancer Society (member, board of directors 1982-83; chairman, public health committee, 1982-83); American Heart Association (Run for Life committee, 1980; chairman, 1981-82; race director, 1983); Appointed by Governor to the 1982 State Commission on Physical Fitness for 4 Year Term. Published Works: *Wellness for Children: A Programming Guide* 1982. Honors and Awards: Founders Award, American Heart Association, 1980; Jaycee "Special Friend" Award 1982; Only Non-Nurse Certified by Several Large National Insurance Companies as Independent Medical Interviewer/Examiner; CPR-First Aid Certified Instructor; Listed in *Who's Who in the East, Who's Who in America, World Who's Who of Women.* Address: 9 Folly Farms, Reisterstown, Maryland 21136.

Rabon, Florence Graham

Semi-retired Tax Worker. Personal: Married to Wright Coswell, Jr. (deceased); Mother of Margaret Ritchie-Owens. Education: B.S. Career: Former management analyst-technician with the U.S. Government; Currently involved in part-time tax work. Community Activities: Alpha Omega chapter of Alpha Xi Delta; Beta Sigma Phi (charter member and founder of 4 chapters, past president of all chapters, held all offices, publicity director, 1951 to present); Key West Art and Historical Society (founder, board secretary, 1949-59, life member); Key West Alumnae Panhellenic Association (member, 1958 to present, public relations director, 1958 to present); Key West Lions Auxiliary (member, 1961 to present, publicity worker); Key West Council of the Navy League of the U.S. (member, 1964 to present, secretary and board member, 1974 to present); Key West Women's Club (associate member, 1969, regular member, 1970-79, honorary member, 1979 to present); Key West Garden Club (member, 1970-75, honorary member, 1975 to present, publicity chairman); Appointed by governor to Historic Key West Preservation Board, 1974 (secretary-treasurer, 1977-80); Appointed by city commission to Old Island Restoration Commission (secretary, 1977-79); Reporter, Key West Lions Club, 1958 to present; Publicity Director, Key West Heart Association, 1960-78; Served on all boards of Easter Seal Society, Cancer Society, and other civic organizations. Religion: Member of St. Paul's Episcopal Church (former Sunday school teacher). Honors and Awards: Outstanding Citizen Award, American Legion, 1958; Beta Sigma Phi Order of the Rose, honorary degree for 15 years of service, 1965; Key West Lions Club annual awards for meritorious service, 1959 and 1980; Key West Heart Association annual awards for meritorious service, 1961 and 1978; Listed in *2000 Women of Achievement, Dictionary of International Biography, Personalities of the South, Who's Who of American Women, Florida Women of Distinction, Americans of the Bicentennial Year, Writers' Directory, Who's Who in Florida Government, National Social Register*, and many other reference works. Address: 1622 Laird Street, P.O. Box 1243, Key West, Florida 33040.

Rainwater, Vivian Elaine

Secretary. Personal: Born November 3, 1913; Daughter of Julia Ann Mason; Married to Vincent C in 1940. Education: Attended Central Business College of Kansas City, Missouri, 1929-30. Community Activities: President, Women's Club; Dedication of trees for Tarzana Park Avenue; Volunteer worker at Veterans' Hospital; Member, Friends of the Library; Donation of books to the Veterans' Hospital and Tarzana Library; Served on election board, 1941-77; Involved in various civic projects to improve the community. Religion: Member of Christian Church of North Kansas City, Missouri (other church affiliations include Memorial Christian Church of Kansas City, Reseda Christian Church of California, Hermitage Christian Church). Honors and Awards: Named 2 junior high schools in Reseda, California and Tarzana; Received awards from Los Angeles City Councilmen, the Republican Club, Tarzana Chamber of Commerce, President Gerald R. Ford, President Ronald Reagan, President Richard M. Nixon and Senator Barry Goldwater Jr. Address: Cedar Crest Cove, Box 33H, Route 1, Hermitage, Missouri 65668.

John W Randell

Randall, Geoffrey Lance

Insurance Consultant and Executive. Personal: Born March 30, 1942, in Far Rockaway, New York; Son of Henry George and Henrietta Rose Gradinger Randall; Father of Adam Clinton. Education: B.A., University of Miami, 1964; Pension School Graduate, Purdue University, 1973. Career: South Florida Representative, Canada Life Assurance Company, 1967-71; President, Randall-Dade Underwriters Insurance Agency, Inc., North Miami, Florida, 1971 to present; Financial Insurance Consultant, Suave Shoe Corporation (Hialeah, Florida), Farm Stores Inc. (Miami). Organizational Memberships: Miami Association of Life Underwriters; National Association of Life Underwriters; Million Dollar Round Table (lifemember); Top of the Table (charter member, 1977); Travelers National Leaders Club, 1971; 125th Street Merchants Association (director). Community Activities: Democratic Advisory Committee, 1967-68; Greater Miami Jaycees. Honors and Awards: Key Man of the Year, Greater Miami Jaycees, 1969; Academic Scholarship, University of Miami; Debate Scholarship, University of Miami; Miami General Agent's and Manager's Association Man of the Year; Health Insurance Quality Award; Modern Security Life Insurance Company Man of the Year; Top Producer for Modern Security Life, 1972-73; Listed in *Men of Achievement, Directory of Distinguished Americans, Who's Who in Finance and Industry, Personalities of America.* Address: 13305 Biscayne Isle Terrace, Keystone Point, Miami, Florida 33181.

Randell, John Wildman

Director of Force Development and Management Engineering. Personal: Born December 16, 1928, in Holyoke, Massachusetts; Son of Heyward Davis and Emily Wildman O'Neil Randell; Widower; Father of Mark Steven, Leslie Alan, Marcia Sue. Education: Graduate, Holyoke Senior High School, 1946; Attended the Garey School of Drama, Springfield, Massachusetts, 1946-48; B.M.S., University of Maryland, 1963; M.B.A., Northwestern University, 1975; D.B.A., University of Tennessee, 1978; Graduate, U.S. Army Adjutant General Manpower-Management School, Indianapolis, Indiana, 1967; Graduate, Industrial College of the Armed Forces, Washington D.C., 1972. Military: Served with the United States Army in the Infantry, Airborne and Signal Corps, 1948-53, achieved permanent grade of Sergeant. Career: Communications Technician, United Nations Headquarters, Department of the Army, Tokyo, Japan, 1953-56; Civilian Personnel Representative, 71st Signal Battalion, Tokyo, 1956-58; Incentive Awards Director, U.S. Army, Japan at Camp Zama 1958-59; Communications Engineering Statistical Officer, 8235th Signal Communications Battalion, Camp Drake, Japan, 1959-65; Management Engineer with the Comptroller, U.S. Army, Japan, 1965-67; Editor *Koryu*, a monthly U.S. Forces psychological labor relations publication, 1967-72; Manpower-Management Engineer with G-3, U.S. Army, Japan, 1972-81; Teacher of English as a Second Language, Kyoritsu University, Kanda 1962-81, Athenee-Francais, Ochanomizu 1969-73, Japan Interpreter Training School, Meguro 1972-78, Fuji Xerox, Tokyo/Ebina 1974-81; Director of Force Development and Management Engineering, U.S. Army Communications Command, Japan, 1971 to present. Organizational Memberships: International Consultant's Institute (co-founder and vice president); Grollier International (management consultant advisor); East-West Cultural Exchange and Studies Association of Japan and Korea (life time chairman and special council 1981). Community Activities: Masonic Lodge (assists in programs for the blind, crippled children, orphans and education, scholarship and

Americanism); Tokyo Masonic Scottish Rite Education and Americanism Programs (chairman); Kentucky Colonel, 1976. Published Works: *Organizational Efficiency Techniques*, 1963; *The Bimbo Danao Biography*, 1972; *American Synonym and Slang Comparisons*, 1979; *English Language Procurement and Procedural Techniques*, 1978; *American Synonym and Anthonym Comparisons*, 1980; *Use of American Phrasal Verbs and their Idioms*, in progress. Honors and Awards: Silver Star; Bronze Star with V-device; Purple Heart with 3 Clusters; Korean and United Nations Service Medals; Good Conduct Medal (for action in Korea); Multiple Department of the Army Management Training and Outstanding Performance Awards (during 32 years combined military and civilian service); Honorary Doctor of Industrial Engineering, F.E.M.S.I., Tokyo, 1970. Address: Hqs. USACC Japan, Box 1182, A.P.O. San Francisco 96343.

Rangos, John G

Executive. Personal: Born July 27, 1929; Son of Mrs. Anna Rizakus; Married Patricia A. Concelman; Father of John Jr., Alexander, Jenica Anne. Education: Attended Houston Business College. Military: Served in the United States Army, 1951-54. Career: Chief Executive Officer, U.S. Services Corporation, Tri-Valley Municipal Supply, Ransales Inc., U.S. Utilities Services Corporation, Chambers Development Company Inc., Southern Alleghenies Disposal, William H. Martin Security Bureau Inc.; Individual Land Developer. Organizational Memberships: Craig House-Technoma (board of directors, 1974-75); United Nations Association (treasurer, 1975-76; national committee, 1977); United Nations International Children's Emergency Fund (chairman, fund raising, Pittsburgh, 1977; Western Pennsylvania committee chairman 1978-79); Greek Orthodox Church of Christ, Pittsburgh, (board of directors, 1968-70); Holy Cross Seminary, Boston (board of directors, 1962-63); United States Olympic National Committee, Colorado Springs, Colorado (delegate, 1980). Community Activities: Pioneer in Sewage Sludge Disposal Sites and Recovery Systems; Research of Bottom Ash for Anti-skid in State of Pennsylvania, Disposal of SO_2 Sludge for Power Plants, Construction and Design of Sanitary Landfills; Pioneer Major Technological and Operational in Enviromental Area. Religion: Church Laity Council, New York. Honors and Awards: Korean Medal; National Defense Medal; United States Army Unit Citations from Korean President and President of the United States. Address: 78 Locksley Drive, Pittsburgh, Pennsylvania 15235.

Rankine-Galloway, Honora M F

University Professor. Personal: Born July 9, 1947; Daughter of Catherine Feenan, Albany, N.Y.; Married Gerald P. F. Rankine-Galloway; Mother of Adrian J. T. Education: B.A., College of New Rochelle, 1969; M.A. 1970, Ph.D. 1973, University of Pennsylvania. Career: Assistant Professor, Department of English, Long Island University, C.W. Post Center, 1980-83; Lecturer in American Literature and Civilization, Institut d'etudes anglaises et nord-americaines, Universite de Caen, France, 1978-80; Fulbright Lecturer in American Literature, Universite de Caen, 1977-78; Assistant Professor, Department of English, Rutgers University, 1973-80; Instructor, University of Pennsylvania, College of General Studies, 1973; Instructor of English as a Foreign Language, Vacances Studieuses, Sutton, Serrey, England, Summer 1972; Lectrice, Universite de Provence, Departement d'Americain, Aix-en-Provence, France, 1971-72; Teaching Fellow, Department of English, University of Pennsylvania, 1970-71, 1972; Substitute Teacher, Philadelphia Public Schools, 1970; Reader, Department of English, University of Pennsylvania, 1969-70; Book Reviewer, United States International Communication Agency, Africa Regional Services, Paris, France, 1979-80; Faculty Advisor for Study in the United States, Universite de Caen, 1977-80. Organizational Memberships: American Association of University Professors, (treasurer, C.W. Post chapter); Modern Language Association; American Studies Association; Association francaise d-etudes americaines; International Biographical Association; American Federation of Teachers (executive committee, C.W. Post chapter). Community Activities: Fulbright Lecturer in American Literature, Universite de Caen, 1977-78; Lectures of U.S.I.C.A. in North and West Africa, 1979-80. Published Works: "*Mythologies* de Yeats: Les Cahiers du Poete" 1981, "Review of *The Life of John O'Hara* by Frank MacShane" 1983, "Nikki Giovanni" and "Daniel Hoffman" in *Critical Survey of Poetry* 1982, "John Barth's Short Fiction: The Key to the Treasure is the Treasurer" 1983. Honors and Awards: Major Research Grant, Long Island University, 1981-82; Fulbright Lecturer in American Literature, Universite de Caen, 1977-78; Faculty Academic Study Program Award 1977, Rutgers Research Council Grant 1977-78, Rutgers University; Readership 1969-70, Teaching Fellowship 1970-71, 1972-73, Secretary of Graduate English Club 1971, University of Pennsylvania; Honors at Entrance and Full Tuition Scholarship, Dean's Scholar 1966-67, 1967-69, First Honors 1965-66, 1968-69, Departmental Honors in English 1969, College of New Rochelle; New York State Beginning Teaching Fellowship, 1969-71; Elks National Most Valuable Student Award, 1965-66; New York State Regents Scholarship, 1965-69. Address: 123 West 93 Street, Apt. 7C, New York, New York 10025.

Ranson, Guy Harvey

Professor of Religion. Personal: Born November 26, 1916; Son of J. M. and Willie Ann Hardesty Ranson (both deceased); Married Rose Ellen Clark; Father of Kenneth Clark, Kelly Maurice, Diana Ranson Seklaoui. Education: B.A., Hardin-Simmons University, 1939; B.A., University of Kentucky, 1944; Ph.D., Yale University, 1956; Further Studies at the University of Cambridge, 1947-48. Career: Professor of Philosophy and Chairman of Department, William Jewell College, Missouri, 1948-52; Associate Professor of Christian Ethics, Southern Baptist Seminary, 1952-58; Research Scholar, Yale Divinity School, 1958-59; Associate Professor of Christian Ethics, Duke Divinity School, 1959-60; Associate Professor, Princeton Theological Seminary, 1960-61; Chairman of the Department of Religion 1961-77, Professor of Religion 1961 to present, Trinity University, San Antonio, Texas. Organizational Memberships: American Academy of Religion; American Society of Christian Ethics; American Association of University Professors; American Philosophical Society; American Society of Church History. Community Awards: Inman Christian Center, San Antonio (board of directors, 1966-69, chairman, 1968, 1969); San Antonio Council of Churches (chairman, social action committee, 1964-70); Social Welfare Council, San Antonio, 1979; Yale Club of San Antonio (board of directors, 1977 to present; president, 1978). Religion: Ordained Minister, United Presbyterian Church in the U.S.A.; Union Mission Presbytery; Ministerial Relations Committee, Ministerial Candidates Committee, Ecumenical Relations; Vice Moderator, 1972. Honors and Awards: Citation for Service to Yale Club, 1978; Research Grant to Undertake Archaeological Excavation at Hebron, 1966. Address: 115 Irvington Drive, San Antonio, Texas 78209.

Rapaport, Walter

Physician, Psychiatrist. Personal: Born August 8, 1895; Son of Charles and Reba Rapaport (both deceased); Married Leonie Mae Rannie; Father of Janet M. Einstoss, Robert J., Shirley Donovan, (Stepfather of) Gae Gravell, Judith Simonich, Steve Simonich. Education: B.S. 1917, M.D. 1919, Georgetown University; Honorary Doctor of Law, University of Santa Clara, 1970. Military: Served in the United States Navy during World War II, attaining the rank of Captain; Also Served in World War I with the rank of Private. Career: Physician, Psychiatrist; Intern Fellowship in Psychiatry, District of Columbia Hospital-Jail, 1917-20; United States

Public Health Service and Veterans Bureau, 1922-28; Staff Psychiatrist, Superintendent and Medical Director, California Mental Health, 1939-41, 1946-63; Director of Mental Hygiene, State of California, 1953-57. Organizational Memberships: Napa (California) Medical Association (president, 1939). Community Activities: Napa Kiwanis Club (president, 1939). Religion: Jewish. Honors and Awards: Military Ribbons, World War I and World War II; Citation from United States Navy, World War II. Address: 3325 Hunnicutt Lane, Sacramento, California 95821.

Raphael, Carl S

Executive, Administrator. Personal: Born April 23, 1943, in Kew Gardens, New York; Son of Harold and Ruth Raphael; Married Ellen Gibson Muller, on January 15, 1966; Father of Larissa, Heather. Education: B.S., Dalhousie University, 1965; M.A., Queens College, 1966; M.B.A., Fordham University, 1974. Career: Pharmaceutical Representative, Hoffmann-La Roche, Nutley, New Jersey, 1967-70; Medical Center Representative 1970-71, Marketing Research Assistant 1971-72, Marketing Research Analyst 1972-73, Senior Analyst, Coordinator of Health Economics 1973-75, Hoffman-La Roche; Marketing Manager, Health Application Systems Inc., Saddle Brook, New Jersey, 1975-76; Senior Marketing Analyst, Merck, Sharp and Dohme, West Point, Pennsylvania, 1976-78; Product Research Manager and Manager of Marketing Analysis, E. R. Squibb and Sons, Inc., Lawrenceville, New Jersey, 1978-79; Vice President, Research Director 1979-80, Senior Vice President 1980 to present, Danis Research, Inc., Fairfield, New Jersey; Consultant in Health Care Administration. Organizational Memberships: Group Health Association of America; Association of M.B.A. Executives; Pharmaceutical Manufacturers Association; American Marketing Association; Tau Epsilon Phi. Community Activities: Union County Consumer Affairs Advisory Committee, 1974 (vice chairman, 1975-76; chairman, 1976-77); Warrington Ambulance Corps (crew chief and president); R.E.M.T.A.; E.M.T.-P.; Bucks County Emergency Health Council. Address: 1705 LaRue Lane, Warrington, Pennsylvania 18976.

A Guinn Rasbury

Rasbury, Avery Guinn

Controller. Personal: Born December 18, 1923, in Fort Worth, Texas; Son of William Avery (deceased) and Annie Lee Lynn Rasbury; Married Linda Loo Baker; Father of Sandra Kay Cleveland. Education: Graduate of Decatur High School, Decatur, Texas, 1941; Attended Decatur Baptist College, 1947-48; B.B.A., Accounting, North Texas State University, 1948-50; Undertook Post-Graduate Work in Accounting at North Texas State University, 1950-51. Military: Served in the United States Marine Corps, 1941-47, as Assistant Navy Provost Marshall. Career: Assistant Accountant, McKesson & Robbins, Inc., Houston, Texas, 1951; Senior Accountant, Koshkin & Levingston, C.P.A.s, Houston, 1951-53; Executive Assistant, J. Robert Neal, 1953 to present; Building Manager, J. Robert Neal Building, Houston, 1953-60; Executive Vice President and General Manager, West-Jet Aviation, Houston, Texas, and Las Vegas, Nevada, 1969-74; President, General Manager, Multi-Fab, Inc., Houston, 1974-78; Executive Vice President and General Manager, Aerostar Nevada Corporation, Las Vegas, 1980 to present; Controller, Powertherm Company, Inc., Houston, 1980 to present. Community Activities: Optimist International (life member); Civitan International (life member); Houston Livestock Show and Rodeo (life member); Marine Corps League (member, 1955 to present; local club commandant, 1962-63); Second Marine Association (member, 1949 to present; national president, 1958-59; national tresurer, 1963-78; life member); North Texas State University Alumni Association (life member); International Platform Association; International Biographical Association (fellow, 1978 to present); Aviation Hall of Fame (charter member, 1978 to present). Religion: Member, Memorial Drive United Methodist Church, Houston, Texas. Honors and Awards: Presidential Unit Citation with One Star, Guadalcanal Gampaign; Good Conduct Medal with Two Stars; American Defense Medal; Asiatic-Pacific Campaign Medal; Victory Medal; Philippine Independence Medal; Outstanding Civic Leadership Award, 1967; Civitan of the Year, 1963; Outstanding Club President, Civitan International, 1966; Listed in *Who's Who in the South and Southwest, Who's Who in Finance and Industry, Who's Who in the World, Personalities of the South, Personalities of America, Book of Honor, Men of Achievement, Notable Americans, Dictionary of International Biography, International Register of Profiles, American Registry Series, Directory of Distinguished Americans.* Address: 1608 South Gessner, Houston, Texas 77063.

Ratliff, David Walter

Investor. Personal: Born July 3, 1949; Son of Arch Ratliff Sr.; Married Bonnie Jean; Father of David Jr., Tami. Education: B.B.A., McMurry College, 1971. Career: Investor; President, West Texas Marketing Corporation, 1978-81. Community Activities: Abilene Boys Ranch (board of Directors, 1982); Abilene Girls Home (board of directors, 1981-82); West Texas Rehabilitation Center (board of directors, 1980-82). Religion: University Church of Christ. Honors and Awards: Listed in *Outstanding Young Men of America.* Address: 1298 Kingsbury Road, Abilene, Texas 79602.

Gerald L Ratcliff

Ratliff, Gerald Lee

Associate Professor of Theatre. Personal: Born October 23, 1944; Son of Frank and Peggy Donisi. Education: B.A. magna cum laude, Georgetown University, 1967; M.A., University of Cincinnati, 1970; Ph.D., Bowling Green State University, 1975. Career: Feature Writer/Reporter, Lexington *Herald-Leader News*, 1967-68; Instructor, Glenville State College, 1970-72; Fellow, Bowling Green State University, 1972-75; Associate Professor, Deputy Chair/Graduate Advisor, Montclair State College, 1975 to present. Organizational Memberships; Theta Alpha Phi Honorary Drama Fraternity (national council); Speech Communications Association (national secretary, theatre interest area, 1978-80, 1980 to present); International Arts Association (vice president of research, 1975-78); Speech and Theatre Association of New Jersey (president, 1978-80); Speech Communication Association (national review board, "Educational Resources in Communication", 1976 to present); Popular Culture Association Center for the Study of Popular Culture, Bowling Green State University (national review panel, "The State of the Study of Popular Culture Studies in Four-Year Colleges and Universities", 1978-79); National Eastern Regional Research Seminar "A Homiletic on an Evaluation Assessment of Reader's Theatre in a 'Performance' Context" (director, 1982); Speech and Theatre Association of New Jersey State Convention (chairman, 1980); Eastern Communication Association National Convention (chairman, 1980); American Theatre Association National Convention (publicity chairman, 1979); Secondary School Theatre Association (chairman of publicity, region II, 1979-80); Speech Communication Association (states advisory council, 1975-77); Association Internationale du Theatre pour Lengance et la Jeunesse; American Studies Association; American Society for Theatre Research; College English Association; Edna St. Vincent Millay Society (charter member); International Platform Association: National Writers Club; New Jersey College English Association; Ibsen Society of America (charter member); National Council of Teachers of English; O'Neill Society (charter member); New York State Speech Association; Southeastern Theatre Conference. Published Works: Numerous Professional Papers and Presentations including (most recently) "Word Games": Verbal Gymnastics in Samuel Beckett's *Waiting for Godot* 1979, "To Be Young, Gifted and Black: The 'Poetic Vision' of Lorraine Hansberry's 'American Woman'" 1980, "The Theatrical Ingredient of 'Movement' in Readers Theatre" 1980, "The Performance Role of Reader's Theatre in the Secondary Classroom" 1981; Other Articles, Poems, Reviews and Critiques;

Editorial Board, *Communication Education*, 1981 to present; Referee, *Quarterly Journal of Speech*, 1981 to present; National Editor, *The Cue*, 1979 to present; Associate Editor, *Communication Quarterly*, 1978 to present; United States Poetry Editor, *Inscape*, 1976-78; Editor, "Reader's Theatre is Alive and Well", *Reader's Theatre News*, 1981 to present; Editorial Board, *Liberal and Fine Arts Review*, 1981 to present; Author of Several Textbooks, *Beginning Scene Study: Aristophanes to Albee, The Theatre Student: Speech and Drama Club Activities, Beginning Reader's Theatre: A Primer for Classroom Performance*. Honors and Awards: Fellow, International Academy of Poets; Fellow, American Film Institute; Poetry Congress Achievement Award, 1969; Listed in *Who's Who in Education, Dictionary of International Biography, International Who's Who of Poets, Directory of Distinguished Americans, Personalities of the East*. Address: 361 Crestmont Road, Cedar Grove, New Jersey 07043.

Sheila P Ratcliffe

Ratcliffe, Shelia Pannell

Manager, Instructor. Personal: Born July 23, 1953; Daughter of Mr. and Mrs. Craig D. Pannell; Married Carl R. Ratcliffe Jr. Education: B.A. 1973, M.A.Ed. 1977, Western Carolina University, Cullowhee, North Carolina; Further Studies undertaken at Centio Colombo Americano, Cali, Colombia, South America, 1973. Career: Industrial Relations Manager, Instructor in Personnel Management. Organizational Memberships: American Society for Training and Development (vice president, 1975-76); Altrusa Club of Asheville (extension chairman, 1979-80); Western Carolina Safety Council. Community Activities: Tri-County Community College, Murphy, North Carolina (chairman of adult basic education advisory committee, 1978); North Carolina Employment Security Commission (employer's advisory committee, 1979-80); Southeastern Planning Economic Development Commission (industrial representative, 1978-79); Cherokee County United Way (vice president, 1978-79). Honors and Awards: Young Career Woman of 1978, Cherokee County, North Carolina; Listed in *Who's Who in the South and Southwest, Personalities of the South, World Who's Who of Women, Who's Who in Finance and Industry*. Address: 556 Lost Tree Lane, Knoxville, Tennessee 37922.

Rau, John Edward

Bank Executive. Personal: Born June 19, 1948; Son of Edward and Grace Rau. Education: B.A., B.S., Boston College, 1970; M.B.A., Harvard, 1972. Military: Served in the United States Army, 1970-71. Career: Director of Corporate Development, First Chicago Corp., 1973-74; Corp. Officer Finance and Treasury, 1975; Manager, Planning and Administration, First National Bank of Chicago, 1976-77; Manager, Central Operation Group, 1977-78; General Manager, International Banking, 1979-80; Executive Vice President and Director, Exchange National Bank of Chicago, 1980 to present. Organizational Memberships: Keller Graduate School of Management (faculty). Community Activities: Henrotin Hospital (board of contributors, 1975); Child Care Association of Chicago (board of directors); Ada S. McKinley Foundation (board of directors, 1981); Election Judge Project LEAP, 1976; Chicago Council on Foreign Relations. Honors and Awards: Harvard-Goldman, Sachs Senior Finance Fellow, 1971-72; Finnegan Outstanding Graduate Grantee, 1969-70. Address: 1410 Asbury Avenue, Evanston, Illinois 60201.

John E Rau

Raymond, Gene

Actor, Producer and Director. Personal: Born August 13, 1908, in New York City; Son of Le Roy and Mary Smith Guion; Married Jeanette MacDonald (now deceased), on June 16, 1937; Married Nel Bentley Hees on September 8, 1974. Education: Attended Professional Children's School, New York City. Military: Served with United States Army Air Force during World War II, 1942-45; Served with United States Air Force Reserve Strategic Air Command and Military Airlift Command, 1945-68; Held ranks of Colonel, Command Pilot, C-141; Flew 9 missions in South Vietnam. Career: Made Broadway debut billed as Raymond Guion in *The Piper*, 1920; Made numerous other stage appearances under this name including *Eyvind of the Hills* 1921, *Why Not?* 1922, *The Potters* 1923, *Cradle Snatchers* 1925, *Take My Advice* 1927, *Mirrors* 1928, *Sherlock Holmes* 1928, *Say When* 1928, *The War Song* 1928, *Jonesy* 1929, *Young Sinners* 1929; Made numerous stage appearances using name of Gene Raymond, including *The Man in Possession* 1946, *The Guardsman* 1951, *The Voice of the Turtle* 1952, *Angel Street* 1952, *The Petrified Forest* 1952, *Call Me Madam* 1952, *Private Lives* 1953, *The Moon is Blue* 1953, *Be Quiet, My Love* 1953, *Detective Story* 1954, *The Devil's Disciple* 1954, *The Fifth Season* 1955, *Will Success Spoil Rock Hunter* 1956, *Romeo and Juliet* (Mercutio) 1956, *A Shadow of My Enemy* 1957, *The Seven Year Itch* 1958, *Holiday for Lovers* 1959, National Touring Company, *The Best Man* 1960, *Candida* 1961, *Majority of One* 1962, *Mr. Roberts* 1962, *Kiss Me Kate* 1962, *Write Me a Murder* 1962, *Madly in Love* 1963; Made film debut in *Personal Maid*, 1931; Appeared in numerous films including *Stolen Heaven* 1931, *Ladies of the Big House* 1932, *The Night of June 13th* 1932, *Forgotten Commandments* 1932, *If I Had a Million* 1932, *Red Dust* 1932, *Ex-Lady* 1933, *The House on 56th Street* 1933, *Zoo in Budapest* 1933, *Brief Moment* 1933, *Ann Carver's Profession* 1933, *Flying Down to Rio* 1933, *Sadie McKee* 1934, *I Am Suzanne* 1934, *Coming Out Party* 1934, *Trans-Atlantic Merry-Go-Round* 1934, *Behold My Wife* 1935, *The Woman in Red* 1935, *Seven Keys to Baldpate* 1935, *Hooray for Love* 1935, *Love on a Bet* 1936, *Walking on Air* 1936, *The Bride Walks Out* 1936, *The Smartest Girl in Town* 1936, *Transient Lady* 1936, *There Goes My Girl* 1937, *Life of the Party* 1937, *Cross Country Romance* 1940, *Mr. and Mrs. Smith* 1941, *Smilin' Through* 1942, *The Locket* 1946, *Assigned to Danger* 1948, *Million-Dollar Weekend* 1948, *Sofia* 1948, *Hit the Deck* 1955, *Plunder Road* 1957, *The Best Man* 1964, *I'd Rather be Rich* 1964; Appeared in popular television programs including Ed Sullivan's *Toast of the Town, The Ken Murray Show, Robert Montgomery Presents, Tales of Tomorrow, Lux Video Theater, Pulitzer Prize Theatre, Broadway T.V. Theatre, Schlitz Playhouse, Fireside Theater* (Host), *T.V.'s Readers' Digest* (Host), *Hollywood's Summer Theatre, The Barbara Stanwyck Show, Sam Benedict, U.S. Steel Hour, Adamsburg U.S.A., The Defenders, The Outer Limits, Channing, Ford Theatre, The Loretta Young Show, Matinee Theatre, Playhouse 90, Climax!, Johnny Ringo, Ethel Barrymore Theatre, The F.B.I., Ironside, Apple's Way, Judd for the Defense, The Bold Ones, The Interns, Name of the Game, Mannix*, Many Others; Was heard as "The Amazing Mr. Malone" on A.B.C. radio, 1950; Wrote the story and screenplay for *Prima Donna*, in which his wife, Jeanette MacDonald made her television debut; Composer of "Will You?" (published by Irving Berlin, Inc.), "Let Me Always Sing" and "Release" (both published by G. Schirmer, Inc.). Organizational Memberships: Screen Actors Guild (director); Academy of Television Arts and Sciences (trustee); Motion Picture and Television Fund (president, 1980). Community Activities: Arthritis Foundation of Southern California (past vice president, master of ceremonies for annual telethon); Past President, Los Angeles Chapter of Air Force Association; Member, The Players Club of New York; Member, New York Athletic Club and Bel-Air Country Club in Los Angeles; Member, Order of Daedalians, Army and Navy Club of Washington, D.C. Honors and Awards: Distinguished Service Award, Arthritis Foundation of Southern California; Humanitarian Award, Los Angeles Chapter of Air Force Association; Listed in *Who's Who of the American Theatre*. Address: 9570 Wilshire Boulevard, Beverly Hills, California 90212.

Gene Raymond

Reade, Charles Falkiner Jr

Manufacturing Executive. Personal: Born June 24, 1941 in Evanston, Illinois; Son of Charles Falkiner and Elizabeth Boomer Reade; Married Emily Schroeder, September 9, 1978; Father of Amanda Browning. Education: Graduate of the University of Miami, 1965; Harvard Business School, 1971; Continuing Courses at New York Graduate School of Business. Military: Served in the United States

Army, 1966-69, attaining the rank of Captain. Career: Salesman, Southern Bell Telephone and Telegraph Company, 1965-66; Institutional Salesman, Blyth Eastman Dillon and Company, 1973-77; Director of Metal Powder Division, General Manager of Chemical Division, General Manager of Reade Advertising Agency, Reade Manufacturing Company, Inc., Lakehurst, New Jersey, 1977 to present. Organizational Memberships: American Society for Testing Materials (committee for international standardization, voting member); American Institute of Mechanical Engineers; Air Force Association; American Defense Preparedness Association; American Foundrymen's Society; American Iron & Steel Institute; American Powder Metallurgy Institute; American Pyrotechnics Association; AMVETS (life member); Ductile Iron Society; International Pyrotechnics Society; NAM; Navy League (life member); American Chemical Society; Royal Society of Chemistry. Community Activities: Munson Geothermal Corporation (director); United States Army Special Warfare Museum (trustee); Boy Scouts of America (council executive board); Defender/Courageous 12-Meter Group (area finance chairman); Friends for Reagan Committee (national chairman, 1976); Businessmen for President Ford Committee (national chairman, 1976; New York City Urban Minority Consulting (volunteer consultant); Keep Rumson Safe Committee (chairman); M.C.O.S.S. Volunteer Nursing Service (finance committee); Republican National Finance Committee; Republican Party County Committeeman; Rumson Volunteer Fire Department; United Way (fund raising committee); Advertising Club of New York; Associate Clubs (life member); World Trade Club; Harvard Club of New York City and Philadelphia; Monmouth Boat Club; Navesink River Rod and Gun Club; New York Yacht Club; North Shrewsbury Ice Boat and Yacht Club. Religion: Episcopalian. Published Works: Founder, *R.E.I.T. Quarterly Journal*, Blyth Eastman Dillon & Company, Inc.; Contributor of Articles to Business and Leisure Publications. Honors and Awards: Bronze Stars (3); Air Medal; Army Commendation Medals (2); Thailand Ranger Badge; Scabbard and Blade, National Military Honorary Society, 1964; Distinguished Military Graduate, 1965; Outstanding Salesman Award, Southern Bell Telephone and Telegraph, 1966; Top Ten Salesman Award, Blyth Eastman Dillon & Company, Inc., 1972; Listed in *National Record of Prominent Americans and International Notables, Who's Who in Finance and Industry, Who's Who in the World, Directory of Distinguished Americans.* Address: 18 First Street, Rumson, New Jersey 07760.

Reagan, Joy Partney

Administrator. Personal: Born September 25, 1928; Daughter of Mr. and Mrs. Donald Partney; Married L. David Reagan; Mother of Cyndy R. Klinger, Bonnie, Eric. Education: Undergraduate Studies at Baylor University; B.A., Sociology, Lamar University; M.A., Criminal Justice, Sam Houston State University; Post-Graduate Studies undertaken at the University of Houston, University of Chicago, University of Texas; Research undertaken in London, England. Career: Administrator, Buckner Children's Village and Family Care Center, Beaumont, Texas (formerly Beaumont Children's Home), 1967 to present; Researched and Assisted in Design of Multi-Service Campus for Children and Family Services to Pine Woods Area of Southern Texas. Organizational Memberships: National Association of Homes for Children (peer review chairman); Southwestern Association of Child Care Executives (vice president); Texas Association of Licensed Children's Services (public relations chairman; legislative committee); Executives of Texas Homes for Children (secretary; legislative committee); American Association of Psychiatric Services for Children (paper at annual meeting). Community Activities: Beaumont Chamber of Commerce; Beaumont Executive Roundtable; State Center for Human Development (advisory board). Honors and Awards: Social Work Contribution of the Year, Southeast Texas Social Welfare Association, 1973. Address: 5565 Hooks, Beaumont, Texas 77706

L N Recktenwald

Reagan, Mary A

Academic Dean. Personal: Born August 24, 1929; Daughter of Daniel and Ellen M. Reagan (both deceased). Education: B.A. History, 1960; M.A. Art History, 1965; M.A. History, 1970; Ph.D. History, 1978. Career: Academic Dean, Holy Apostles College; Assistant Dean of Continuing Education, Professor of History and Art History, St. Joseph College, West Hartford, Connecticut; Assistant Professor of Art History, Catholic University, Washington, D.C.; Lecturer, American Studies, Fairfield University. Organizational Memberships: Catholic Fine Arts (vice president, 1968-70); Fulbright Alumni, 1970-82; National Historical Association; Consortium of Higher Education. Community Activities: Lecturer on History and Art History, Local and State Associations, 1975-82; Connecticut Arts Council; St. Joseph College Alumni Association; Writes and Produces Documentaries for Local Television Stations. Religion: Sister of Mercy, 1955 to present. Honors and Awards: N.D.C.A. Award for American Studies, 1965; Fulbright Grant for Study in Rome, 1970; Phi Alpha Theta; Penfield Scholarship for Research Abroad, 1974; Andrew Mellon Award from the University of California-Berkeley, 1977; Yale Visiting Professor Award, 1978; National Endowment for Humanities, Harvard University, 1980. Address: 1678 Asylum Avenue, West Hartford, Connecticut 06117.

Recht, Nadyne Marceille

Real Estate Broker. Personal: Born September 9, 1921; Daughter of Gladys Tierney; Married Ervin Recht; Mother of Diane Langin, Douglas, Mark, Michael, Jeannine Wells, Cynthia. Education: Graduate of Central Catholic High School, 1939; Real Estate Courses, Indiana University-Purdue University. Career: Real Estate Broker-Owner, Recht & Recht, Inc. Organizational Memberships: Multiple Listing Service (chairman, 1976; director, 1979-82); Fort Wayne Board of Realtors (chairman, grievance committee, 1981; director, 1976-79). Community Activities: Neighborhood Care Inc. (director); Maplewood Park Community Association (president, 1981-82, 1982-83); United Fund (worker and captain); Democratic Precinct Committeeman and Vice Chairman of 1st District. Religion: President, Rosary Sodality of St. Andrew's Church. Honors and Awards: Award from Multiple Listings Service of Fort Wayne Board of Realtors. Address: 6853 Woodcrest Drive, Fort Wayne, Indiana 46815.

Recktenwald, Lester Nicholas

Author. Personal: Son of Peter Wendel and Katherine Delsing Recktenwald (both deceased); Married to Hilda Gertrude Markert (now deceased); Father of John Francis. Education: Diploma, Minnesota State University at St. Cloud; B.S., with distinction; M.A.; Ph.D.; Further Study University of Minnesota, University of Wisconsin, Marquette University, Columbia University, University of New York and Sussex Tech. Career: Teacher and Administrator in Minnesota, North Dakota, Wisconsin, New York and Tennessee (conducted educational work on Manhattan Project); Organizer of Psychology Department and Professor, Villanova University, 1952-60; Professor and Chairman of Graduate Testing Programs, Pennsylvanian State College at West Chester, 1962-73; Counselor Educator, University of Scranton, 1960-61. Organizational Memberships: American Personnel and Guidance Association (president, 1939-40); Wisconsin Branch of American Personnel and guidance Association (program director); Association for Higher Education (president, West Chester State College branch, 1966-68, editor of journal); American, Eastern and Pennsylvania Psychological Associations (life member); Philadelphia Personnel and Guidance Association, 1952 to present); Involved in various other educational and counseling associations through the years. Community Activities: Held veterans counseling post during World War II at City College of New York, Marquette University, a private organization and Loyola University of New Orleans - last 2 years at Loyola as director of veterans counseling), 1945-51; Research work for the commission for the Investigation of History and the Social

Studies, University of Minnesota; Member of survey team from Columbia University Teachers College for the Newark, New Jersey school system, 1942; Lecturer on W.H.A.D. in Milwaukee, Wisconsin, 1937-39. Published Works: Author of 2 books, 7 monographs, 2 workbooks, numerous articles and other writings from 1934 to present. Honors and Awards: Honorary Citation in recognition of distinguished service to West Chester State College, Pennsylvania, 1973; Honorary member of International Mark Twain and Eugene Field Societies; Member, Phi Delta Kappa; Life Fellow, International Institute of Arts and Letters, 1960; Life Contributor to Archives of History of American Psychology, University of Akron, 1968; Life Member, International Council of Psychologists; Certified Counselor by Pennsylvania Professional Counselor Board, 1981; Listed in *International Authors and Writers Who's Who, Community Leaders of America, Men and Women of Distincton, International Who's Who of Intellectuals, Who's Who in Community Service; Leaders in American Science; Who's Who in Education.* Address: 480 Quigley Road, Wayne, Strafford, Pennsylvania 19087.

Reed, William Garrard

Retired. Personal: Born 1908; Son of Mark and Irene Simpson Reed (both deceased); Married Eleanor Henry, 1935; Father of Susan, Garrard, Mary. Education: Attended Culver Military Academy, 1922-25; A.B., University of Washington, 1929; Further Study at Harvard Business School, 1930-31. Military: Served in the United State Naval Reserve, 1942-45, attaining the rank of Lieutenant Commander. Career: Forest Products, 1931-70; Office Employee, Secretary, President, Chairman, Simpson Timber Company; Former President, Lumbermen's Mercantile Company, State Bank of Shelton, Olympia Oyster Company; Executive Vice President, Rayonier Inc., 1949-50; Managing Director, Malahat Logging Company, Chile. Organizational Memberships: Safeco Corporation (director, 1932-70); Seattle First National Bank (director, 1933-72); Boeing Company (director, 1946-80); Paccar Inc. (director, 1940-70); Burlington Northern Inc. (director, 1950-80). Community Activities: Seattle Foundation (president, 1951-53); Seattle Art Museum (director, 1935-78); Seattle Chamber of Commerce; Harvard Business School Alumni Association. Religion: Episcopal, Senior Warden 1960-62, Vestryman 1955-70, Ephiphany Parish of Seattle; Bishop's Committee of Diocese of Olympia, 1950-62. Honors and Awards: Bronze Star, United States Navy, 1945; Number of Service Awards from Corporations; Fellow, Columbia University 1975, Forest History Society, 1980. Address: 110 Holland Road, Box D, Sequim, Washington 98382.

Rees, Jane L

Professor, Department Chairman. Education: B.S., Syracuse University, 1945; M.S., Columbia University, 1947; Ph.D., Pennsylvania State University, 1959. Career: Visiting Professor and Curriculum Consultant, Ein Shams University, Cairo, 1963-64; Executive Director, American Home Economics Association, 1966-67; Professor, Chairman, Department of Home Economics and Consumer Sciences, Miami University (Ohio). Organizational Memberships: American Home Economics Association; Phi Upsilon Omicron (chairman, foundation board, 1970-73); National Council of Administrators in Home Economics (president and board chairman, 1970-71, 1973-74); Phi Kappa Phi, Miami University Chapter (president and chairman of the board, 1973-74). Community Activities: Family and Child Studies Director, Miami University, 1978 to present; Cincinnati Gas and Electric Company, (board of directors); Consumer Credit Advisory Council, Family Service (board of directors). Honors and Awards: Phi Sigma; Phi Kappa Phi; Pi Lambda Theta; Alpha Lambda Delta; Omicron Nu; Phi Upsilon Omicron; Syracuse Alumni Scholar, 1941-45; American Home Economics Association Doctoral Scholarship Award, 1957; Effie I. Rait Award; Fulbright Award for Postdoctoral Professorship, U.A.R. (Egypt), 1964; Listed in *Who's Who of American Women, Who's Who in the Midwest, Outstanding Educators of America.* Address: 940 Silvoor Lane, Oxford, Ohio 45056.

Reese, Wendell B

Development Executive. Personal: Born July 5, 1929; Son of Harry A. (deceased) and Dorothy R. Reese; Father of Byron E., Wendell A. Education: High School Graduate. Military: Served in the United States Army, 1951-53. Career: President, Reese Mobile Homes, Inc.; President, Reese Development, Inc.; Owner, Reese Trailer Sales, Empire, Ohio, 1950-67; Ohio Edison Company, Toronto, Ohio, 1947-69. Organizational Memberships: State of Ohio Commission to Motor Vehicle Dealers and Salesman's Licensing Board (board member, 1976 to 1982). Community Activities: Empire Village Council, 1959-61; Mayor, Village of Empire, 1961 to present; Jefferson County Democratic Executive Committee, 1966-67. Address; Harrison Street, Empire, Ohio 43926.

Reeve, Ronald Cropper Jr

Corporation Executive. Personal: Born January 29, 1943; Son of Ronald and Aldus Reeve; Married Deborah Crooks; Father of Heather Rene, Michael Scott, Thomas Adam. Education: B.S., Physics, Ohio State University, 1967; M.B.A., Xavier University, 1972. Military: Served in the United States Air Force, 1968-69, attaining the rank of Airman 1st Class; Served in the Ohio Air National Guard, 1965-68. Career: Chairman, President, Founder, Advanced Robotics Corporation; General Manager, Marketing Manager, Product Manager, Air Products and Chemicals Inc.; Product Planner, Product Engineer, Project Engineer, Development Engineer, The General Electric Company. Organizational Memberships: American Welding Society; American Society for Metals; Robotics International; Robot Institute of America. Community Activities: Thistle Fleet 126 (officer, 1978-80); Hoover Yacht Club; Annehurst Civic Association, 1970-75; Spring Grove Civic Association. Honors and Awards: SBA Small Business Person of the Year, 1981. Address: 1131 Hempstead Court, Westerville, Ohio 43081.

Reevy, William R

Clinical Psychologist. Personal: Born February 3, 1922; Son of Stefan Jan and Maria Soltis Revay (both deceased); Married; Father of Anthony William, Carolyn Upton, Gretchen Maria. Education: B.A. Economics and Psychology, Stanford University, 1946; Graduate Studies in Clinical Psychology, New York University Graduate School of Arts and Sciences 1946-48, Pennsylvania State University 1948-53; Ph.D., Clinical Psychology, Pennsylvania State University, 1954. Military: Served in the United States Army Air Force, attaining the rank of Corporal. Career: Associate Professor of Psychology, Richmond Professional Institute of the College of William and Mary, 1954-55; Instructor 1955, Assistant Professor 1956-57, DePaul University; Assistant Professor of Psychology, Counselor, Sacramento State College, 1957-60; Associate Professor of Psychology, Texas Tech College, 1960-61; Director of Clinical Studies, Northern Virginia Mental Health Project, 1961-62l Associate Chief Psychologist, District of Columbia General Hospital, and Assistant Professor of Psychiatry (psychology), Georgetown University Medical School, 1962-64; Associate Professor of Psychology, State University of New York-Cortland, Consultant, Department of Mental Hygiene, State of New York (Clinical Psychologist, Auburn State Prison), 1964-68; Associate Professor of Psychology and Head of the Department of Psychology and Education, N.M.I.M.T., 1968-69; New Mexico Institute of Mining and Technology, Professor of Psychology and Head, Department of

Psychology and Eduation 1969-71, Professor of Psychology 1971-73; Clinical Psychologist, Samaritan Hospital Unit, Rensselaer County Mental Health Center, Troy, New York, 1973-75; Staff Psychologist, Federal Reformatory, Petersburg, Virginia, 1975-76; Chief, Psychology Services, Unit Psychologist, Staff Psychologist, Mental Health Division, Federal Corrections Institution, Butner, North Carolina, 1976 to present. Organizational Memberships: Academy of Psychologists in Marital and Family Therapy (chairman, nominating committee, 1963; chairman, committee on training and standards, 1964; executive committee, 1964; president, 1967-70; chairman, constitution committee, 1970); American Association of Marriage and Family Therapy; American Psycholgocial Association; Institute of Rational Living (fellow); Academy of Political Science; American Society for Aesthetics; MacDowell Colony (associate fellow); New York Academy of Science (active member); Society for Applied Anthropology (fellow); Society for the Scientific Study of Sex (fellow); Society for the Psychological Study of Social Issues. Community Activities: Voluntary Community Visitation Service, Lubbock, Texas, Mental Health Association, 1964-68; Sacramento County, California, Mental Health Association (public education committee, 1960-61); Socorro, New Mexico, Mental Health Association (chairman, education committee, 1968-71); Extensive Donations of Books to North Carolina School of Science and Mathematics, 1980 to present. Published Works: Number of Professional Articles, including "Petting Experience and Marital Success: A Review and Statement" 1972, "Marriage Counseling, A Science" 1967, "Premarital Petting Behavior and Marital Happiness Prediction"1959. Honors and Awards: Phi Beta Kappa; Psi Chi; Sigma Xi; State of California License, Marriage and Family Counselors, 1966; Instructor's Certificate in Group Psychotherapy, New York State Department of Civil Service, 1967; Licensed Psychologist, States of California, New York, 1967; Certificate of Appreciation, Operation Sparrow, Las Vegas, New Mexico, Medical Center, 1970; Fellow, Intercontinental Biographical Association, 1970; Special Recognition Award, American Security Council Education Foundation, 1979; Listed in *Directory of Educational Specialists, American Men of Science, Community Leaders of America, The Blue Book, Dictionary of International Biography, International Scholars Directory, International Who's Who in Community Service, Leaders in American Science, Men of Achievement, National Register of Educational Researchers, Notable Americans of the Bicentennial Era, Personalities of the West and Midwest, Royal Blue Book, Two Thousand Men of Achievement, Who's Who Among Authors and Journalists, Who's Who in the South and Southwest, Who's Who in the East, Who's Who in the West.* Address: 730 Crestview Drive, Durham, North Carolina 27712.

Refior, Everett Lee

Labor Economist, Professor of Economics. Personal: Born January 23, 1919; Son of Fred C. and Daisy E. Refior; Married Marie E. Culp; Father of Gene Allan, Wendell Frederick, Paul Douglas, Donna Marie. Education: Graduate of Donnellson High School, Iowa, 1935; B.A. summa cum laude, Iowa Wesleyan College, 1942; Postgraduate Studies, University of Glasgow, Scotland, 1945; M.A., University of Chicago, 1955; Ph.D., University of Iowa, 1962. Military: Served in the Army of the United States, 1943-46, as a Medical Technician in the United States and England, with rank of Private First Class. Career: Instuctor, Iowa Wesleyan College, 1947-50; Associate Professor, Simpson College, 1952-54; Professor of Economics, University of Wisconsin-Whitewater. Organizational Memberships: Industrial Relations Research Association (academic vice president, Wisconsin chapter, 1978-82); American Economic Association; Midwest Economics Association; Wisconsin Federation of Teachers; Wisconsin Economics Association; Federation of American Scientists. Community Activities: Governor's Commission on the United Nations, 1971 to present; United Nations Association (president, Walworth County chapter, 1979-80); World Federalists Association (founder, Whitewater chapter, president 1960-68, 1976-78; president, Midwest Region, 1969-71, 1975 to present; national board, 1968-76, 1978 to present; United States delegate to World Congresses at Ottawa 1970, Brussels 1972, Paris 1977, Tokyo 1980); World Citizens Assembly (executive committee, 1980 to present); Democratic Party (precinct committeeman, 1966 to present; county chairman, 1968-72; district vice chairman, 1975-78; state platform committee, 1977 to present); Kiwanis; SANE; American Civil Liberties Union; Common Cause; Alcohol Problems Council of Wisconsin (board of directors, 1975 to present). Religion: Methodist Lay Speaker, 1959 to present; Janesville District Director of Christian Social Concerns, 1961-67; Wisconsin Conference Board of Church and Society, 1970-76; Board of Directors, Wisconsin Protestant Legislative Council, 1965-69. Honors and Awards: Order of Artus (now Omicron Delta Epsilon), 1951; Ford Foundation Summer Faculty Fellowship, 1959; Listed in *Wisconsin Men of Achievement, Who's Who in the Midwest, Who's Who in America, Who's Who in the World.* Address: 205 North Fremont, Whitewater, Wisconsin 53190.

Regnier, Claire N

Consulting Engineer. Personal: Born May 2, 1939. Education: B.S. cum laude, Journalism, Trinity University, 1961. Career: President, Metro Consultants; Established *Showboat*, a monthly newspaper, 1968, Editor 1968-80, Publisher's Representative; First Executive Director, San Antonio River Association, 1968-81. Organizational Memberships: Women in Communications, Inc.; Texas Public Relations Association; San Antonio Press Club; Texas Recreation and Parks Society; International Association of Business Communicators. Community Activities: Downtown Holiday River Festival (originator); Great Country River Festival (originator); St. Patrick's River Dyeing and Mariachi Festival (originator); Centro 21 Downtown Revitalization Task Force (chairman, 1977-83); Parks and Recreation Advisory Board, 1978 to present; Representative to San Antonio River Corridor Committee; San Antonio Council, Girl Scouts of America (board of directors; chairman); Fiesta San Antonio Commission (commissioner); University Roundtable; Council on International Relations; Altrusa Club of San Antonio; Trinity University Alumni Association. Religion: St. Luke's Episcopal Church. Honors and Awards: Awards of Excellence for Editing *Showboat*, 1970-74; Trinity University Alumni Council President's Citation for Outstanding Services, 1974-76; Communicator of the Year, 1977; Addressed Council on Urban Economic Development, 1980; Headliner Award for Public Endeavors, 1980; Southwest Region Banner Award, Excellence in Communication, 1981; Listed in *Outstanding Young Women of America, Notable Americans, Who's Who of American Women, World Who's Who of Women, Personalities of America, Who's Who of the South and Southwest.* Address: 772 Woodridge Street, San Antonio, Texas 78209.

Rehak, James R

Orthodontist. Personal: Married Joann Marie Tabbert, October 15, 1969; Father of Suzanne Therese. Education: B.S. 1960, D.D.S. cum laude 1962, M.S. 1967, Certificate of Orthodontists 1965, University of Illinois. Military: Served in the United States Army Reserves, 1963-68, attaining the rank of Captain. Career: Private Practice in Orthodontics, 1965 to present; Associate Professor, University of Illinois; Orthodontic Consultant, 1966-68. Organizational Memberships: American Association of Orthodontists; Illinois Association of Orthodontists; Southern Society of Orthodontists; American Dental Association; Illinois Dental Association; Chicago Dental Society; Florida Dental Association; West Coast Dental Society; Royal Society of Health (fellow); International Platform Association; Omicron Kappa Upsilon Honorary Dental Society; Federation Dentaire Internationale; International Biographical Association (life fellow). Published Works: Articles in Journal of Dental Research, Dental Clinics of North America, Journal of the American Medical Association. Honors and Awards: Listed in *Who's Who in the Midwest, Who's Who in the*

Southeast, Dictionary of International Biography, Men of Achievement, Notable Americans, Men of Distinction. Address: 4115 Del Prado Boulevard, Cape Coral, Florida 33904.

Reichle, Frederick A

Professor of Surgery, Department Chairman. Born April 20, 1935, Neshaminy, Pennsylvania. Education: B.A. 1957, M.D. 1961, M.S. Biochemistry 1961, M.S. Surgery 1966, Temple University; Intern, Abington Memorial Hospital, 1962; Resident, Temple University Hospital, 1966. Career: Professor of Surgery, Chairman of Department of Surgery, Presbyterian-University of Pennsylvania Medical Center; Surgeon, Presbyterian-University of Pennsylvania Medical Center; Associate Attending Surgeon, Epsicopal Hospital, St. Mary's Hospital, St. Christopher's Hospital for Children, Phoenixville Hospital; Consultant, Veterans Hospital, Wilkes-Barre, Pennsylvania; Consultant, The Germantown Dispensary and Hospital. Organizational Memberships: American Board of Surgery (diplomate, 1968); American Surgical Association; Society of University Surgeons; American Medical Association; Pennsylvania Medical Society; Phi Tho Sigma Medical Fraternity, 1959; Sigma Xi; Association for Academic Surgery; The New York Academy of Sciences; American Association for the Advancement of Science; American Biographical Institute (national board of advisors); Royal Society of Medicine; Delaware Valley Vascular Society; American College of Angiology; American Institute of Ultrasound in Medicine; American Physiological Society; The College of Physicians of Philadelphia (fellow); American Society for Pharmacology and Experimental Therapeutics, Inc.; Surgical Historical Society; Societe Internationale de Chirurgie; Collequim Internationale Chirurgie Digestive; Society for Vascular Surgery; Society for Surgery of the Alimentary Tract; National Kidney Foundation (professional member); International Society on Thrombosis and Haemostatis; Philadelphia Academy of Surgery; American College of Surgeons (fellow); American Gastroenterological Association; National Association of the Professions; American Federation for Clinical Research; Association of Program Directors in Surgery; Heart Association of Southeastern Pennsylvania; American Diabetes Association; American Association of Cancer Research; American Heart Association; American Society of Abdominal Surgeons; Surgical Biology Club; American Aging Association; American Geriatrics Society; American Society of Contemporary Medicine and Surgery; Board of Appeals in Accreditation Council for Graduate Medical Education. Community Activities: Site Visitor, Canadian Department of Health and Welfare, Programs Branch, 1977; Lectures and Forums Committee of the Medical Faculty Senate, 1976-79; Specialist Site Visitor, Residency Review Committee for Surgery, Liaison Committee on Graduate Medical Education, American Medical Association, 1979; Specialist Site Visitor, Inspection for Continuation of General Surgical Residency Training Program, 1980, the Society for Vascular Surgery. Honors and Awards: Temple University Full Tuition Competitive Scholarship, 1953; College of Liberal Arts Graduation Award, Temple University, 1957; Nathan Lane Award for the Highest Student Achievement in Chemistry, Temple University, 1957; Graduated summa cum laude, 1957; Fellowship in Nutrition, American Medical Association Summer of Medical School, 1961; Surgical Resident's Research Paper Award, Philadelphia Academy of Surgery, 1966, 1967; Gross Essay Prize of the Philadelphia Academy of Surgery; Recipient of Established Investigatorship Grant, American Heart Association, 1973; Omega Alpha; Honorary Member, Chilean Surgical Society; Listed in *Who's Who in the East, Who's Who in America, Who's Who in the World.* Address: 51 North 39th Street, Philadelphia, Pennsylvania 19104.

Reid, Harold Wilson

Entertainer. Personal: Born August 21, 1939; Son of Sidney Boxley and Mary Frances Craun Reid; Married Brenda Lee Armstrong; Father of Kimberley, Karmen, Kodia, Kasey, Harold Wilson II. Education: Graduate of Wilson Memorial High School. Career: Member Country-Western/Gospel Singing Group, The Statler Brothers. Organizational Memberships: Statler Brothers Productions, 1961 to present; American Cowboy Publishing Company, 1973 to present; Happy Birthday U.S.A. (board of directors, 1973). Religion: Olivet Presbyterian Church, Staunton, Virginia. Honors and Awards: Recipient of Several Grammy Awards, Several Country Music Association Awards, Music City News Awards; Broadcast Music Inc. Writer Award; Songs include " Bed of Roses", "Class of 57", "Whatever Happened to Randolph Scott". Address: P.O. Box 2703, Staunton, Virginia 24401.

Reifler, Henrietta

Librarian. Personal: Born July 29, 1917; Daughter of Mendel and Annie Brown (both deceased); Married Erwin Reifler (deceased); Mother of Victoria R. Bricker, Frank J. Reifler, Anna Irene Leepansen, Consuela Margaret Reifler, Michaela Thea Kaplowitz. Education: B.A., English Honors, University of London, 1941; B.A., 1950, M.A., 1959, M.L.S., 1969, all from the University of Washington-Seattle. Career: Teacher of English, Mary Farnham School for Girls, China, 1936-39; Teacher of English and Speech, St. Nicholas School, Seattle, 1954-58; Instructor, Department of English, Everett Community College, Washington, 1959-61; Instructor, Department of English, University of Washington-Seattle, 1961-68; Librarian, Washington State University-Pullman, 1969 to present. Organizational Memberships: National Council of Teachers of English (judge, achievement awards, 1961-65); Washington Library Association Women's Caucus (chairman and program chairman, 1976-80; continuing education committee, 1973-76); Washington State University Commission on the Status of Women (secretary, 1977-78); Pacific Northwest Library Association (indexer, 1973-76); Phi Beta Kappa (secretary, local chapter, 1973-76). Community Activities: Washington Women United, 1979 to present; Hadassah, 1971 to present; Donations to local and national charities such as United Way and Easter Seals, National Jewish and Israeli loan societies and orphanages, organizations for the blind, holocaust studies, Ethiopian Jews, tree planting, etc., Equal Rights Amendment, National Organization of Women; Political Contributions to the Democratic Party, 1971 to present; Committee of 100; Fortune Society; Klanwatch; National Association for the Advancement of Colored People. Religion: Member Herzl Conservation Congregation, Seattle, 1948 to present; Temple Beth Shalom, Spokane, 1970 to present. Honors and Awards: Phi Beta Kappa, 1950; The Cum Laude Society, 1956. Address: N.E. 435 Oak #2, Pullman, Washington 99163.

Reilly, Jeanette P

Consulting Clinical Psychologist. Personal: Born October 19, 1908; Daughter of George Lindsey and Marie Bloedorn Parker (both deceased); Married Peter C. Reilly Jr.; Mother of Marie R. Heed, Sara Jean R. Wilhelm, Patricia Ann R. Davis. Education: A.B., University of Colorado, 1929; M.A. 1951, Ed.D. 1959, Columbia University; Postdoctoral Studies in Clinical Psychology, Larue Carter Hospital, Indianapolis, 1960-61; Studies in Child Psychology, Riley Hospital, 1961. Career: Consulting Clinical Psychologist; Former Staff Member, St. Vincent's Hospital, Indianapolis; Lecturer, Butler Univeristy; Consultant, Christian Theological Seminary; Registrar, Veterans Administration Hospital, Indianapolis; Cerebral Palsy Clinic, University Medical Center; Teacher, Speech and Drama, Denver, Colorado. Organizational Memberships: American Psychological Association; National Register of Health Services Providers in Psychology; Indiana Psychology Association; Central Indiana Psychology Association; American Personnel and Guidance Association; American Vocational Guidance Association. Community Activities: Community Hospital Foundation Board, 1978 to present; Hanover College (board of trustees, 1975 to present); University of Notre Dame Women's Auxiliary Council, 1953 to present; Governor's Advisory Council on Division of Mental Retardation and Other Developmental Disabilities, 1975; Indiana State Board of Examiners in Psychology (chairman, 1969-70; board member, 1969-75); St. Richards School, Indianapolis (board member, 1967-73); Indianapolis Day Nursery Board, 1957-62; Indiana Mental Health Advisory Board, 1981 to present. Religion: Second Presbyterian Church, Indianapolis. Honors and Awards: Sagamore of the Wabash, 1980; Mayor's Citation, 1975; Governor's Citation, 1967, 1970; Mortar Board; Pi Lambda Theta; Kappa Delta Pi; Listed in *Who's Who of American Women, World Who's Who of Women, Who's Who in the Midwest.* Address: 1015 Stratford Hall, Indianapolis, Indiana 46260.

Reinker, Sherry M

Publisher. Personal: Born July 5, 1945; Daughter of Hugh T. Miller; Mother of Jeffrey Stephen. Education: Attended the University of California. Career: Chairman of the Board, Sherry Reinker Publications, Inc.; Publisher of the *International Good Life;* Former Editor, *The Bay Window* Magazine of the Balboa Bay Club, Newport Beach, California. Organizational Memberships: Public Relations Society of America; American Advertising Federation; International Writers Guild; Florida Magazine Association. Community Activities: Big Brothers/Big Sisters; Italian American Foundation; Other Charitable Organizations. Honors and Awards: Named to International Publishing Hall of Fame, International Biographical Centre of Contemporary Achievement, Cambridge, England; 1978 Award for Community Leadership; Listed in *Miami's Social Register, Who's Who in American Women.* Address: 1050 N.E. 203 Terrace, Miami, Florida 33179.

Sherry Reinker

Reinl, Harry Charles

Labor Economist. Personal: Born November 13, 1932; Son of Carl and Angela Plass Reinl (both deceased). Education: B.S., Fordham University, 1953; Certificate, United States Department of Agriculture Graduate School, 1966; A.M., The George Washington University, 1968; Student in Special Programs in Applied Urban Economics, Massachusetts Institute of Technology, 1972. Military: Served in the United States Army, 1953-55, attaining the rank of First Lieutenant. Career: Labor Economist, Office of Personal Management, Washington, D.C., 1968 to present; D.O.E. Program, Region III Labor Economist, Office Manpower Administrator, United States Labor Department, Washington, D.C., 1962-68; Junior Observer, Sperry Rand Corporation, New York City, 1958-62; Manager, New York Branch, Willmark Service System, 1971. Organizational Memberships: National Archives (associate, 1976 to present); Smithsonian Institution (resident associate, 1980 to present); American Police Academy (honorary trustee, 1979, Special Agent, to present); American Police Hall of Fame (ex officio board of trustees, 1981); American Security Council (national advisory board, 1972); The New York Academy of Science, 1982 to present; American Film Institute, 1979 to present. Community Activities: Participant in Eighth I.B.C. Congress, Beverly Hills, 1981 (I.B.C. Choir), Ninth I.B.C. Congress, Queens College, Cambridge, England 1982 (I.B.C. Choir); Special Letters, United States Senate; Republican National Committee (sustaining member, 1975; life member, 1979); National Republican Congressional Committee, 1978 to present; Center for International Security Studies (founder, 1977); American Police Conference (in-selected honor delegate, delegate-at-large, Miami, Florida, 1980 and 1982); Telethon Volunteer and Associate for Progress, The George Washington University, 1973, 1974, 1979; The Winterthur Guild, 1981; Contributor to the Colonial Williamsburg Fund, The Virginia State University Foundation, The New York Public Library (friends 1980), The Metropolitan Opera Guild 1981-82; The Memorial Sloane-Kettering Cancer Fund, The Linus Pauling Institute of Science and Medicine; Contributor and Participant, The President Ford Library and Museum; Charter Member, Republican National Committee Ambassador's Club 1981-82; Recognition from the U.S. President (Communication Dated November 29, 1982); Recognition from the State Advisor, Virginia U.S. Congressional Advisory Board, 1982. Religion: Roman Catholic. Honors and Awards: Citation for Participation in Formulating the Republican Legislative Agenda, 1981; Certificate of Service, Department of Labor, 1968; Certificate of Appreciation, American Police Academy, 1979; National Right to Work Legal Defense Foundation, 1979; Fellow A.B.I. (1978); International Biographical Association (1979); Fellow, Anglo-American Academy; Three Defense Medals, 1955; National Defense Service Medal; Korean Service Medal; United Nations Service Medal; Included in the Reel of Microfilm now being Processed, "The Story of My Life" Program, Memorial Data Services, Inc., on January 1983; Listed in *Book of Honor.* Address: 1111 Arlington Boulevard, M-521, Arlington, Virginia 22209.

Reisdorf, Edward Gary

Lawyer, Real Estate Investment Company Executive. Personal: Born March 8, 1941, in Milwaukee, Wisconsin; Son of Edward and Flora Reisdorf; Married Teresa Hermo on December 4, 1975; Father of Ted, Rachel, Greg, Christina. Education: B.S., United States Air Force Academy, 1963; J.D., Georgetown University, 1968. Military: Served in the United States Air Force, 1963-67, advancing through the grades to Captain. Career: With Firm of Kalb, Voorhis & Company, Stock Brokers, Washington, 1967-68; Admitted to New Jersey Bar, 1968; With Firm of Bourne & Noll, Attorneys, Summit, New Jersey, 1968-70; President, Reisdorf & Jaffe, P.A., Attorneys, Springfield, New Jersey, 1970 to present; President, E. G. Reisdorf, P.A., Attorneys, Springfield, 1980 to present; President, Equity Association, Inc., Investments, Springfield; President, 1980-81, New York Stars, Women's Professional Basketball Team. Organizational Memberships: American Bar Association; New Jersey Bar Association; Union County Bar Association. Community Activities: Independent. Religion: Roman Catholic. Address: 152 Fairmount Avenue, Chatham, New Jersey 07928.

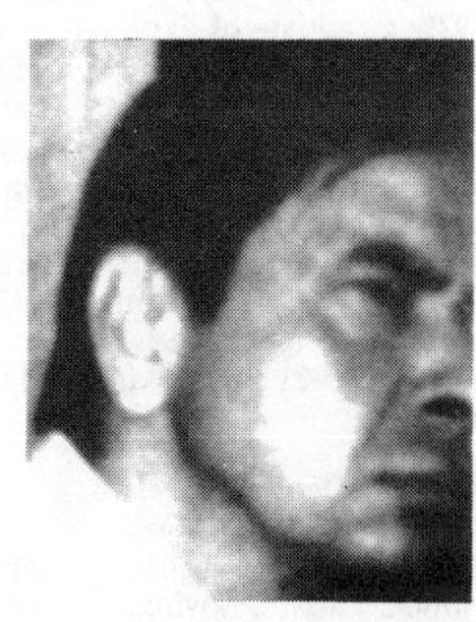
Harry C Reinl

Reisman, Arnold

Professor. Personal: Born August 2, 1934; Son of Rose Reisman; Married Ellen Kronheim. Education: B.S. Engineering 1955, M.S. Engineering 1957, Ph.D. Engineering 1963, University of California-Los Angeles. Career: Professor of Operations Research, Case Western Reserve University; Visiting Professor, Hebrew University of Jerusalem, 1975; Visiting Professor, Japan-American Institute of Management Science, Honolulu, Hawaii, 1975; Visiting Professor, Business Economics and Quantitative Methods, University of Hawaii, 1971; Visiting Professor of Engineering and Acting Chairman, Department of Industrial and Operations Science, University of Wisconsin-Milwaukee, 1966-68; Assistant to Associate Professor of Engineering, California State University at Los Angeles, 1957-66. Organizational Memberships: Greater Cleveland Coalition on Health Care Cost Effectiveness (board of directors, 1978 to present); Japan-American Institute of Management Science (institutional planning committee, board of trustees, 1975 to present); Operations Research Society of America (chairman, education sciences section, 1974, 1975); T.I.M.S.; American Institute of Industrial Engineers; American Association for the Advancement of Science; A.S.E.E.; A.S.U.P.; Omega Rho; Phi Delta Kappa. Community Activities: Jewish Community Federation (delegate assembly, 1973-78); Hillel Foundation (board of trustees, 1972-76); Shaker Heights Citizens Advisory Committee, 1972 to 1978; United Jewish Appeal and Israel Emergency Fund Drive, University Division (coordinator); Cleveland Coalition of Health Care Cost Effectiveness (founder and member, board of directors). Published Works: Author of 11 Professional (Text) Books, One Non-Fiction Book: "Welcome Tomorrow", Co-Authored with Ellen Reisman and Over 100 Articles in Professional Journals. Honors and Awards: Cleveland Engineer of the Year, 1973; Listed in *Who's Who in the World, Who's Who in America, Community Leaders and Noteworthy Americans, Who's Who in the Midwest, International Scholars Directory, Outstanding Educators in America, American Men and Women of Science.* Address: 18428 Parkland Drive, Shaker Heights, Ohio 44122.

Reker, Frances Farwell

Horsemanship Instructor. Personal: Born July 19, 1920; Daughter of Arthur and Rae Farwell; Married Robert Wayne Dahl; Mother of Donna R. Mohan, Frank "Chip". Education: Undertook studies at Ward-Belmont College, Nashville, Tennessee, 1938-40; University of Chicago, 1941; Nine Horsemanship Degrees after studying in Austria, Ireland, Mexico and the United States. Career: Horsemanship Instructor, College of St. Benedict; Previous Positions include Owner, Frances Reker School of Horsemanship (Tinley Park, Illinois), Happy Horse Stables (Rockford, Minnesota); Consultant to Eight Colleges; Owner, Reker Enterprises; Riding Director of Stables in Texas, Illinois, Florida and Wisconsin; National Horse Industry Clinician, Speaker, Teacher, Educator, Consultant. Organizational Memberships: Town and Country Equestrian Association (vice president, 1957); Horse Science National Schools (distinguished professor, 1965-70); Horses A to Z National Clinics (vice president, 1971-78); Minnesota Horse Owners and Breeders Association (secretary, 1968); Humane Society (director, 1974-76); Tri-State Horseman's Association (director, 1971); Minnesota Hunter and Jumper Association, 1971-81; Central State Dressage and Combined Training Association, 1971-81; Minnesota Horse Council (vice president, 1977-78). Community Activities: Chicago Girl Scout Drum and Bugle Corps (leader, 1950-54); Chicago Cook County Mounted Junior Rangers (founder, 1950); Minneapolis Humane Society County Fair (founder, 1975); Minneapolis Young Men's Christian Association, 1970-72; Minnesota Horse Council Approved Stables (founder, 1976). Honors and Awards: Ward-Belmont College All Around Athlete Award (winning five athletic letters in one season), 1940; Minneapolis Young Men's Christian Association Service to Youth Award, 1970, 1971, 1972; Dean of Riding Teachers Award, New York State College, 1974; Hennepin County, Minnesota, Vocational-Technical Schools Outstanding Service Award, 1978; Distinguished Professor of Horse Science Institute, 1970; Honorary Lifetime Member, Minnetonka Horsemen's Association, 1978; Minnesota Horseman of the Year, 1978 (first woman to receive state honor); Horseman's Hall of Fame, University of Minnesota, 1978 (first woman to receive honor). Address: Route 5, Box 201, Buffalo, Minnesota 55313.

JoAnn S Relf

Relf, Jo Ann Stepanek

Private Piano Teacher, Adjudicator. Personal: Born March 9, 1930; Daughter of Mr. and Mrs. Charles C. Stepanek; Married Dr. Kenneth Eldon Relf; Mother of Douglas Eldon, Murray Charles. Education: Attended Yankton College Conservatory 1944-48, the University of South Dakota-Vermillion 1948-50, Lamont School of Music (Denver University) summers 1949 & 1950; B.F.A., Carnegie Institute of Technology (now Carnegie-Mellon University); Private Study under Alexander Raab, Webster Aitken, Leonard Eisner. Career: Private Piano Teacher; Adjudicator; Formerly a Piano Instructor, Carnegie Institute of Technology; Private Teaching, Adjudication for the National Piano Guild, Florida Federation of Music Clubs and Florida State Music Teachers Association; Number of Performances in Recital and with Orchestras. Organizational Memberships: Music Teachers National Association (national certification); Florida State Music Teachers Association (state certification, district president 1979-81; local president 1977-79); Florida Federation of Music Clubs (state junior counselor 1977); National Guild of Piano Teachers (chairman of the Melbourne Audition Center 1974 to present, Adjudicator 1979 to present, member 1966 to present); American Matthay Association (workshop member 1976 to present); American Music Scholarship Association, 1979; Raab Club (member 1950-54, president 1952); Mu Phi Epsilon (college and alumnae chapter); Alpha Lambda Delta (South Dakota college chapter). Community Activities: Alpha Rho Chapter of Kappa Alpha Theta. Honors and Awards: First Medal in Piano, National Competition Festival, 1947; Scholarship Winner for First Place, Alexander Raab Audition, 1950 (on the basis of this honor, she was asked to reside and study with Alexander Raab and his wife); Founder's Scholar, Carnegie Institute of Technology, 1955; First Honors, Highest Honors Graduate, Carnegie Institute of Technology, 1956. Address: 966 Flotilla Club Drive, Indian Harbour Beach, Florida 32937.

Replogle, Rose Eleanor

Restorer. Personal: Born January 14, 1909; Widow; Mother of Ronald, Richard H., Charles M. Education: Graduate of Omaha Tech, 1927; Graduate of Faribault School of Christian Leadership, 1939. Career: Restorer of Oriental Carpets and Tapestries; Executive Secretary, Nebraska-Iowa Grain Company, Omaha, 1928-32. Organizational Memberships: Friends of Art, Nelson-Adkins Gallery, 1978-81. Community Activities: Women's Chamber of Commerce (attendance chairman; board of directors, 1980-81); Soroptimist International (hospitality chairman, 1979-80); Woman's City Club (hospital committee, 1980-81); King's Daughters and Sons International (cradle roll chairman, 1975-81); P.E.O. Sisterhood, Chapter J.I. (budget chairman, 1976-81); Red Mitten Writers Club (member, 20 years; president, 1977-79); Baptist Hospital Women's Auxiliary; Adult Friendship Club, Country Club Christian Church. Religion: Leader, Circle I, Country Club Christian Church, 1977-79; Bible Study Group, 13 years. Honors and Awards: Happiest Married Couple Citation, Minneapolis Aquatennial, 1948; State Winner National Chicken Cooking Competition, 1961, 1962, 1963, 1964, 1968; Chosen to Restore 18th Century Tapestries, University of Kansas Museum of Art, Lawrence, Kansas, 1977. Address: 6821 Brookside Road, Kansas City, Missouri 64113.

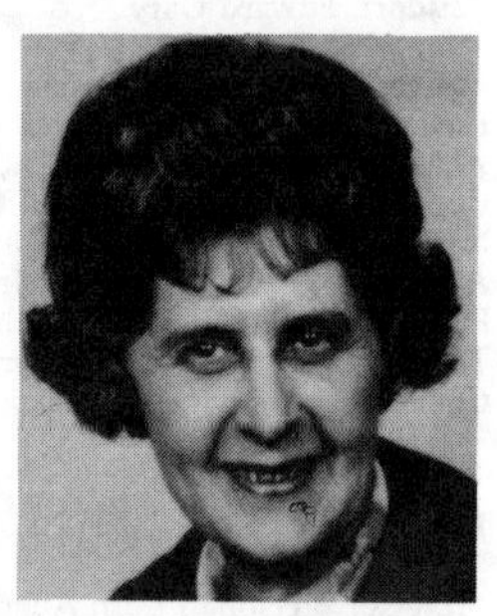

Rose E Replogle

Restout, Denise Therese

Administrator, Teacher, Writer. Personal: Born November 24, 1915, in Paris, France. Education: Certificat d'Etudes Primaires with Honor, Paris; Drawing, Geometry, History of Arts, Painting, Bazot Studi, Paris; Admitted to Ecole d'Arts Appliques, Paris, 1928; First Medal, Conservatoire National de Musique, Paris, 1930. Career: Numerous Appearances as Harpsichord Soloist, Landowska's Public Master Classes, France, Holland; Recitals in Paris, Strasbourg; Soloist with Chamber Orchestra, Paris, 1938; Accompanying Harpsichordist, Londowska's Concert, Carnegie Hall, 1945; Piano Teacher, 1930 to present; Conducted Classes in Ear Training, Solfege, Harmony, Music Appreciation, Paris and Saint-Leu-La-Foret, 1930-38; Director, Landowski Center; Member-at-Large of Faculties of Peabody Institute, Hartt College of Music, Hartford, Southern University of Mississippi, Purchase College; Lecturer, Sharon Creative Arts Foundation 1960, Hotchkiss School 1962, Hartford Conservatory 1962, Brooklyn Music School, Wykeham Rise School, Barlow School 1969, Noble Horizons, Georgetown University 1981 to present. Organizational Memberships: American Federation of Musicians, Local 514; French Musicological Society; American Musicological Society; French Guild of Organists; American Guild of Organists; Johann Sebastian Bach International Competition (honorary patron; jury member); Music Library Association. Religion: Roman Catholic, Member St. Mary's Church, Lakeville, Connecticut; Organist, Sacristin, Member Council of Catholic Women, Secretary of Parish Council. Published Works: Author *Landowska on Music* 1965; Numerous Concert Reviews; Feature Article in *Piano Quarterly, RCA Victor Review, High Fidelity Magazine, Harpsichord Magazine, Diapason, Revue Musicale de Suisse Romande.* Honors and Awards: Recipient, Amicus Poloniae with Citation; *Landowska on Music* Listed as One of Best Books of 1965 by American Library Association; Listed in *Who's Who in Music, Community Leaders and Noteworthy Americans,*

Women of Notes, Women Composers, Conductors and Musicians of the 20th Century, Poulenc's Songs. Address: Millerton Road, P.O. Box 313, Lakeville, Connecticut 06039.

Rex, Linda Kay

Administrative Assistant. Personal: Born January 24, 1949; Daughter of Richard Thomas Hall and Dorothy M. Hall (deceased); Married to James Wesley; Mother of Lissa Dawn. Education: Attended Indian Hills Community College and The Grantsmanship Center-Grant Tech. Career: Former Farmer, Clerk, Secretary, Floral Designer, Tax Preparer, Retail Business Owner, Corporation President, Professional Horse Trainer, Real Estate Salesperson. Organizational Memberships: Van Buren County Development Association (treasurer, tourist promotion director and member of budget and legislative committee, 1980-81); Grant Writer, The Grantmanship Center. Community Activities: Founder, Trot Right in 4-H Club (leader 1975-81); Van Buren Riding Club (board of directors, 1977, secretary-treasurer, 1978-79); Bonaparte Pony Express Riders for Easter Seals (chairman, 1977-78); Van Buren County Fair Board (director, 1980); Van Buren Fine Arts Council (assistant project director, 1981); National Family Opinion, 1966-81. Published Works: Published work in field. Honors and Awards: Listed in *The World Who's Who of Women, Personalities of America, Community Leaders of America, Who's Who of American Women, The Directory of Distinguished Americans, Personalities of the West and Midwest, Who's Who in the Midwest, Book of Honor.* Address: Rural Route 2, Bonaparte, Iowa 52620.

Rex, Lonnie Royce

Foundation Executive. Personal: Born May 11, 1928; Son of R. L. Rex; Married Betty Sorrells; Father of Royce DeWayne, Patricia R. Carnes, Debra K. Bowen. Education: B.M., Oklahoma City University, 1950. Career: President, David Livingstone Missionary Foundation, Inc.; David Livingstone Missionary Foundation of Canada, Inc. (president); David Livingstone Missionary Foundation of the Philippines (president); David Livingstone Missionary Foundation of India (president); David Livingstone Missionary Foundation of Mexico (president); David Livingstone Missionary Foundation of Korea (chairman); David Livingstone Missionary Foundation of Bangladesh (chairman); David Livingstone Missionary Foundation of Asia (chairman); Lepers of the World, Inc. (president); Medix International Inc. (president); Consultant to Nonprofit Organizations for 20 years; Community Bank and Trust Company, Tulsa (director; chairman of audit committee); David Livingstone Missionary Foundation of Germany (president); Director, World Missions Board; Business Management, Non-profit Organizations, 1955-1970. Honors and Awards: Citations and Meritorious Award, Korea, 1975; Presidential Award, Korea Order of Civil Merit, Moran Medal, 1981; Presidential Award-Korea Order of Civil Merit, Moran Medal; "Friend in Deed" Award, 1976; Listed in *Men of Achievement, Who's Who in Religion, International Who's Who in Community Service, International Register of Profiles, Notable Americans, Personalities of America, Personalities of the South, International Who's Who of Intellectuals, Directory of Distinguished Americans.* Address: 2300 Riverside Drive 11-E, Tulsa, Oklahoma 74114.

Rhiew, Francis C

Nuclear Radiologist. Personal: Born December 3, 1938; Son of Byung Kwon Rhiew; Father of Richard, Elizabeth. Education: B.S., Seoul National University, 1960; M.D., Seoul National University College of Medicine, 1964. Military: Served as a Medical Officer, 1964-67. Career: Nuclear Radiologist; Former Instructor, Radiology, West Virginia University School of Medicine. Organizational Memberships: A.C.R., S.N.M.; American Medical Association; Pennsylvania Medical Association; A.C.N.P.; A.I.U.S.M.; R.S.N.A. Community Activities: Elk Lodge of Scranton; Everhart Museum; Glenoak Country Club; Young Men's Christian Association. Religion: St. Gregory Church. Honors and Awards: Citations from Minister of Social Welfare and Health, Korea, 1963; Young Men's Christian Association Citations. Address: 101 Belmont Avenue, Clarks Summit, Pennsylvania 18411.

Frances Rhome

Rhim, Johng Sik

Medical Researcher. Personal: Born July 24, 1930; Son of Hak Yoon and Moo Duk Rhim; Married Mary Lytle; Father of Jonathan, Christopher, Peter, Andrew, Michael. Education: B.S. 1953, M.D. 1957, Seoul National University. Career: Medical Research (Cancer); Research Virologist at Various University Medical Schools (University of Cincinnati, Baylor University, University of Pittsburgh Graduate School of Public Health). Organizational Memberships: American Association for the Advancement of Science; American Association for Cancer Research; American Association for Immunologists; American Medical Association; American Society of Microbiologists; Society of Experimental Biology and Medicine; New York Academy of Sciences; International Association of Comparative Leukemia Research. Community Activities: Winchester School, Silver Spring, Maryland (board of directors). Religion: Protestant. Address: 8309 Melody Court, Bethesda, Maryland 20817.

Rhome, Frances Dodson

College Professor and Administrator. Personal: Born April 15, 1916; Daughter of May Howell Dodson; Married Lt. Colonel H. Stanton Rhome (deceased); Mother of Major Robert C. Education: A.A., Glendale College; B.A., University of California at Los Angeles; M.A., New Mexico State University; Ph.D., Indiana University. Career: Director, Affirmative Action Affairs, Indiana University System; Professor of English (tenured), Indiana University; Freelance Reader and Sub-Editor; Co-Publisher, *Montrose Herald-Tribune;* Executive Director, Chamber of Commerce; College Counselor and Student Personnel Administrator; Secondary School Teacher; Lecturer; Writer; Research Scholar; Contributor to Journals; Consultant. Honors and Awards: Distinguished Indiana Citizen, 1978; Scholarship, Indiana University, 1965; Fellowship, New Mexico Highlands University, 1965; National Award for Outstanding Dramatics Program in Secondary School, 1963; American Legion "Teacher of the Year" Award, 1962; Listed in *Dictionary of International Biography, Notable Americans of the Bicentennial Era.* Address: 9313 S. Pointe-LaSalle Drive, Bloomington, Indiana 47401.

Rhue, Beatrice Evans

Retired Teacher. Personal: Born August 10, 1905; Daughter of William Samuel and Fannie Margaret Johnson Evans (both deceased); Married Edward James Rhue; Mother of William Alonza. Education: A.B., Morris College, Sumter, South Carolina, 1928; B.S., Fayetteville State Teachers University, Fayetteville, North Carolina, 1946; Music Studies at Northwestern University, Evanston, Illinois, Summers 1925-28; Attended Hampton Institute for Library Science. Career: Retired Teacher; Teaches Private Piano Lessons;

Certified Librarian; 14 years as Principal; 27 years as Teacher, Guidance Counselor, Librarian. Organizational Memberships: Harnett County Retired School Personnel (treasurer). Community Activities: 4 H Club Leader twenty years; President of Deaconess Board; Board Member of Harnett County Senior Citizens Council; Board Member of Harnett County RSVP; Shawtown Senior Citizens Club (advisor); North Carolina Symphony. Religion: Missionary Baptist. Honors and Awards: Honored by Church, 1977, for many years of "Loyalty, Service and Devotion" (only organist for 40 years); Certificate of Appreciation, Department of Human Resources, 1981. Address: Route 1 Box 534, Lillington, North Carolina 27546.

Rice, Alice Marie

Executive Secretary, Office Manager. Personal: Born September 15, 1942; Daughter of Joseph C. and Opal H. Lane; Married Charles Aubrey Rice; Mother of David Timothy, Tammy Marie. Education: Graduate of Cullman High School, 1960; Attended Anderson Business College 1961-62, John C. Calhoun College 1962-63. Career: Executive Secretary, Office Manager, The Compton Company, 1962 to present; Corporate Secretary, Westmeade Inc.; PBX Operator, Baugh Wiley Smith Hospital, 1962. Organizational Memberships: The National Secretaries Association (international treasurer, 1968; corresponding secretary, 1969; vice president, 1970; president, 1971); Morgan County Board of Realtors. Community Activities: Alabama Heart Association (program chairman, 1973); Notary Public for State of Alabama, 1972 to present. Religion: Central Park Baptist Church. Honors and Awards: Secretary of the Year, Alabama Heart Fund Special Citation, 1973; Real Estate Broker's License, 1976; Certified Professional Secretary Award, 1971; Listed in *Who's Who of American Women, Personalities of the South, Personalities of America, World Who's Who of Women, Book of Honor.* Address: 2265 Westmeade Drive S.W., Decatur, Alabama 35603.

Alice M Rice

Rice, Frederick Anders Hudson

Professor. Personal: Born February 19, 1917; Son of Frederick L. and Karen B. Rice; Married Margaret M. Carson. Education: B.A., Dalhousie University, 1937; M.Sc., Dalhousie University, 1945; Ph.D., The Ohio State University, 1948. Career: Science Master, Kings College School, Windsor, Nova Scotia, Canada, 1938-41; Assistant Professor of Microbiology, The Johns Hopkins University, 1948-54; Chief High Polymer Sect., 1954-55; Associate Chief, Chemistry Division, 1955-57; Chief Fundamental Processes Division, Naval Propellant Plant, Indian Head, Maryland, 1957-59; Chief Research Branch, Office of the Quartermaster General, 1959-62; Scientist, Army Materiel Command, Arlington, Virginia, 1962-63; Professor of Chemistry, American University, 1963 to present. Honors and Awards: Demonstrator, Biochemistry, Dalhousie University Medical School, 1943-45; University Fellow, The Ohio State University, 1945-48; University Post Doctoral Fellow, The Ohio State University, 1948; Senior Fulbright Award, School of Hygiene and Tropical Medicine, University of London, 1952-53; N.I.H. Career Award, 1963-68; Hildebrand Award, 1972. Address: 8005 Carita Court, Bethesda, Maryland 20817.

Rice, Jerrie Morris

Bank Executive. Personal: Born May 27, 1908; Son of Morris and Jessie Rice (both deceased); Married Mildred Margaret; Father of Geneva Ruth Dodge. Education: Graduate, Strasburg High School, 1927. Career: First National Bank of Strasburg, Colorado, Assistant Cashier, Cashier, Vice President, President, Chairman of the Board, 1927 to present. Community Activities: Strasburg Volunteer Fire Department; Strasburg Water and Sanitation District; Strasburg School Board; Colorado 4-H Foundation (director). Religion: Member Masonic Lodge, 1939 to present. Honors and Awards: Presented Membership to Colorado Bankers Association 50 Year Club, 1977; Honorary Fellow, Harry S. Truman Library Institute. Address: 1836 Aspen Street, P.O. Box 434, Strasburg, Colorado 80136.

Rice, Patricia Brittingham

Executive. Personal: Born July 14, 1941; Daughter of Kenneth L. Brittingham, Faye McClelland Brittingham; Married Robert Leroy Rice; Mother of Philip Charles, Debora Faye, Jeffrey Allan. Education: Graduate of Chamblee High School, 1959; College Courses in Business Management and Accounting. Career: President, Property Management Firm; Former Accountant. Organizational Memberships: National Association of Female Executives; National Association of Women in Construction, 1973-78. Community Activities: Parent-Teacher Association (secretary). Honors and Awards: Listed in *Who's Who in American Women, Personalities of America.* Address: 155 Teepee Lane, Lavonia, Georgia 30553.

Rice, William David

Executive. Personal: Born January 30, 1920; Married JoAnne Twelves; Father of William E., Robert G., Taylor D., James A. Education: B.S. in Chemistry, University of Utah, 1942. Military: Served with the United States Navy, 1941-46; Commanding Officer, Minesweeper, 1945-46; Retired Commander, United States Naval Reserve, 1965. Career: President, Advertising Research Associates, Salt Lake City, 1946-47; Vice President, Cooper & Crowe Inc., 1947-53; President, Demiris, Rice & Associates, 1953 to present. Organizational Memberships: American Institute of Management (president's council 1971-72); Utah Association of Advertising Agencies; International Platform Association; Utah Advertising Federation. Community Activities: Utah Travelers Aide Society (president 1972-73, member of the board); Salt Lake Mental Health Association (president 1961-62); Utah Association of Mental Health (president 1964-66, member of the board); National Association of Mental Health (vice president of communications 1973-75); Utah Mental Health Advisory Council (chairman 1978-80, member of the council); Hospice of Salt Lake City (board of directors 1978 to present); Committee for the Severely Mentally Impaired in Utah (chairman 1979-81); American Mensa for Utah (proctor 1970 to present). Honors and Awards: Distinguished Service Award, Utah Medical Association, 1975; Honored by the National Association of Mental Health, 1975. Address: 1435 Military Way, Salt Lake City, Utah 84103.

William D Rice

Rice, William Yngve

Investor. Personal: Born June 22, 1930; Son of Mrs. J. H. Rice; Married Rachel Gallenkamp; Father of William Y. III, John Robin, Drew M. Education: B.B.A., Baylor University, 1951. Career: Investments. Organizational Memberships: Texas Oil Marketers Association; American Bankers Association; Texas Bankers Association. Community Activities: Town North National Bank (chairman of the board 1980 to present); Southland Savings Association (director and vice president 1973 to present); Mayor and City Councilman, 1969-80; Sabine River Authority of Texas (director and board secretary 1980 to present); East Texas Area Council of Governments (vice chairman 1971-72). Religion: Chairman, Deacon Board, First Baptist Church, 1974-77. Honors and Awards:

Citizen of the Year, 1974; Phillips Petroleum Company Community Service Award, 1976. Address: 1308 Inverness, Longview, Texas 75601.

Richard, Patricia Ingram

Director, Coordinator. Personal: Born in Honolulu, Hawaii; Daughter of Faye Knotts Ingram; Married James A. Richard. Education: B.S., Texas Woman's University, 1944; Graduate Studies in Theatre Arts University of Washington, 1948; Graduate Studies in Motion Picture Production, University of California-Los Angeles, 1950-51; MA. 1970, Ph.D. Candidate, University of Southern California; Further Studies undertaken at the University of Oklahoma 1980-81; Clinical Supervision, University of Idaho, 1981. Career: Head of Continuity at Radio Station KDKY Dallas, Head of Continuity and Relief Newscaster "Hollywood News Show" at WRR Dallas, 1944-47; Film Editor at KTLA Television Station, News Film Editor for American Broadcasting Corporation, 1951-54; Assistant Film Editor on Productions for Television including "Fury", "Mr. Ed", "Sea Hunt", "He and She", "Peyton Place" and "Gunsmoke", Assistant to Producer of CBS Special "Wonderful World of Wheels", 1954-68; Director, Cinema Arts and RA-TV Broadcasting Departments, Coordinator of Public Service Broadcasting, Executive Producer of NIC-TV Public Forum, North Idaho College, Coeur d'Alene, Idaho, 1971 to present. Organizational Memberships: Motion Picture Film Editors Guild (I.A.T.S.E. Local 776), 1953 to present; American Association of University Professors, 1974 to present; Spokane Public Radio KPBX-FM (board of directors, 1978); Spokane Cable System (board of directors, 1978). Community Activities: Pi Epsilon Delta; Beta Sigma Phi, Texas Alpha Epsilon; Hollywood Studio Club (twice president); Coeur d'Alene Community Theatre (sponsor, 1970). Honors and Awards: *Coeur d'Alene Press* Woman of the Year, 1973; Broadcasting Grant, The Association for the Humanities in Idaho, 1974-75; Listed in *World Who's Who of Women in Education, International Who's Who of Intellectuals, International Who's Who in Community Service*. Address: P.O. Box 84, Coeur d'Alene, Idaho 83814.

John Richmond

Richmond, John

Attorney at Law. Personal: Born December 10, 1907. Education: B.S. 1928, M.S. 1934, University of California-Berkeley; LL.B., Oakland College of Law, 1942; Honorary Ph.D., Hamilton State University, 1973. Military: Served in the United States Army Air Force, 1942-45, Career: President, Richmond Enterprises, 1928 to present; Attorney for Richmond Enterprises, 1946 to present; Attorney at Law in Private Practice, 1974 to present. Organizational Memberships: California State Bar Association; Alameda County Bar Association; Berkeley-Albany Bar Association; American Bar Association; Federal Bar Association; Supreme Court Historical Society; National Lawyers Club (founding member, 1952); American Association for the Advancement of Science; Intercontinental Biographical Association; International Platform Association; American Biographical Institute Research Association; Pan Xenia; National Historical Society. Community Activities: Henry Morse Stephens Lodge #541 Free and Accepted Masons (master, 1958); Ancient and Accepted Scottish Rite of Freemasonry Southern Jurisdiction of the United States; Aahmes Temple A.A.O.N.M.S.; Masters and Past Masters Association (Masons); University of California-Berkeley Alumni Association; Veterans of Foreign Wars, Berkeley Post #703 (commander, 1962); United Veterans Council of Berkeley (president, 1963); City of Berkeley Lincoln and Washington Patriotic Program (co-chairman, 1962); City of Berkeley Memorial Services (general chairman, 1963); City of Berkeley Marin-Point Aquatic Park Memorial Services (general chairman, 1963); Grand Lodge of Free and Accepted Masons of California Sojourners Committee, 1958-66; Veterans of Foreign Wars of the United States National Membership Committee of 1980, 1980-81; Supreme Court Historical Society (founder member, 1976); National Lawyers Club (founder member, 1952). Honors and Awards: Certificate, American Heritage Research Association, 1975; Listed in *National Register of Prominent Americans, Two Thousand Men of Achievement, Dictionary of International Biography, Who's Who of American Law, Who's Who Historical Society, Men of Achievement, International Who's Who of Community Service, International Register of Profiles, Community Leaders and Noteworthy Americans, Who's Who in the World, World Who's Who in Finance and Industry, Personalities of the West and Midwest, Notable Americans, Book of Honor, Personalities of America*. Address: 1611 Bonita Avenue, Berkeley, California 94709.

Richmond, Quinton B

Public Accountant. Personal: Born March 7, 1924, in New West, Virginia; Son of Calvin H. and Nora Ellen Garten Richmond; Married Patricia Lee; Father of Carolyn Sue Richmond Terry, Larry Dean, Ronald David. Education: Valedictorian, Richmond High School; B.A., Th.B., Southwestern Bible Institute, 1952. Career: Certified by the National Society of Public Accountants; Admitted to Practice before the Internal Revenue Service, 1977; Accountant, Corporate Officer, President, Chairman of the Board, South Ohio Professional Service and Sales Company, Inc.; Owner, Beauty World Salon, Dayton; Previous Positions as Accountant-Auditor, Internal Auditor, Contract Statistician, Office Manager, Supervisor and Cost Accountant, Price Analyst Contract Negotiator; Ordained to Ministry of the General Council of Assemblies of God; Pastored Churches in Kaufman and Dallas, Texas, and New Carlisle, Ohio; Composer Several Hymns Published in the Stamps-Baxter Song Book. Organizational Memberships: National Society of Public Accountants; Public Accountants Society of Ohio; International Platform Association. Community Activities: Secretary/Treasurer, Foundation-World Toys and Games for Education and Vocational Training. Honors and Awards: Certificate of Merit, Small Business Association, 1977; Letters of Commendation and Appreciation, Brigadier General Robert T. Marsh, U.S. Air Force, Wright-Patterson Air Force Base, Ohio; from Major General, U.S. Air Force, Andrews Air Force Base, Department of the Air Force, Washington, D.C., and from Brigadier General Theodore S. Coberly, U.S. Air Force, Washington, D.C., for his professional knowledge and competence which helped make possible the smooth launching of the development of vitally needed electronic warfare equipment; Listed in *Who's Who in the Midwest, Who's Who in America, Notable Americans, Community Leaders and Noteworthy Americans, Personalities of America, International Who's Who in Community Service, Personalities of the West and Midwest*. Address: 2860 Nacoma Place, Kettering, Ohio 45420.

Quinton B Richmond

Rickey, Martin Eugene

Professor of Physics. Personal: Born August 4, 1927; Son of Albert K. and Nell Ritnour Rickey (both deceased); Father of Ruth M., Albert E., Kirsten E. Education: B.S., Southwestern University, 1949; Attended Columbia University, 1949-50; Ph.D., University of Washington, 1958. Military: Served in the United States Naval Reserve, 1945-46. Career: Junior Physicist, Brookhaven National Laboratory, 1953-54; Assistant Professor 1958-61, Associate Professor 1961-65, University of Colorado; Associate Professor of Physics 1965-68, Professor of Physics 1968 to present, Cyclotron Facility 1965-73 (director 1972-73), Indiana University, Bloomington. Organizational Memberships: Sigma Xi; American Physical Society (fellow). Community Activities: National Research Council, 1968-73. Religion: Associate, Unitarian Church, 1968 to present. Honors and Awards: Sebastian Karrar Award, 1976; United States Senior Scientist Award; Alexander von Humboldt Foundation of West Germany, 1976. Address: 3171 Piccadilly, Bloomington, Indiana 47401.

Rickgarn, Ralph Lee Vurne

Senior Housing Administrator. Personal: Born June 1, 1934; Son of Mr. and Mrs. Henry W. Rickgarn; Married Glenys Agatha Neville; Father of MerLynne Ann. Education: B.A., cum laude, Political Science and Russian Language, University of Minnesota, 1960; M.A., Political Science, University of Minnesota, 1964; M.A., Psychoeducational Studies, University of Minnesota, 1981. Military: Served in the United States Army Military Intellegence, 1954-57. Career: Senior Housing Administrator, Centennial Hall, University of Minnesota, 1972 to present; Senior Residence Hall Director, Territorial Hall, University of Minnesota, 1971-72; Dean of Students, Ricker College, Houlton, Maine, 1968-71; Analyst, Department of Defense, Washington, D.C., 1965-68; Assistant to the Vice President of Development, University of Minnesota, 1964-65. Organizational Memberships: American Personnel and Guidance Association; American College Personnel Association; Minnesota Personel and Guidance Association; Minnesota College Personnel Association; Association of College and University Housing Officers. Community Activities: Neighborhood Involvement Project, Minneapolis (volunteer counselor, 1979-80); Various Committees within the University of Minnesota, 1971 to present. Religion: Junior and Senior Warden 1977-78, Worship Coordinator 1978 to present, Chairperson of Worship Commission 1976-77, Acolyte Master 1979 to present, St. Paul's Episcopal Church, Minneapolis, Minnesota. Published Works: Chapter "Manuals: Their Development and Use in Training", *New Directions for Student Services: Training Competent Staff*, 1978; Article "Immediacy Concept in Staff Training", *Acuho News*, 1978; *The Resident Assistant: Affective-Effective*, 1980; Article "Using the Theme Centered Interaction (TCI) Model in Residence Halls", In press, Volume 13, #1, June 1983, The Journal of College and University Student Housing; "Encounter: The Initiating Experience, A Training Workbook for RAs,", 1982; "The Issue is Suicide," (In press). Honors and Awards: Public Service Award, University of Minnesota Police Department, 1974; Regent's Scholarships, 1974-83; "U" Person of the Week, University of Minnesota, 1982; Pi Lambda Phi, Kappa Beta Chapter, fraternity; Omicron Delta Kappa; American College Personnel Association Award for Outstanding Residence Hall Program, 1981; Listed in *Who's Who in College and University Administration, Who's Who in the Midwest, Personalities of the West and Midwest, Men of Achievement, Personalities of America.* Address: 3536 Colfax Avenue South, Minneapolis, Minnesota 55408.

Ralph L Rickgarn

Riebe, Norman J

Executive. Personal: Born March 9, 1903; Son of William J. and Hattie Riebe; Married First Wife, Gwendolyn E. Main (deceased), in 1924; Married Second Wife, Eddie L. Growden, in 1978; Father of Norman W., Harriet M. Kircher. Education: Ph.D., Occidental University. Military: Served in the United States Army Corps of Engineer, retiring with the rank of Colonel, Chief Engineering and Construction, Carribean Defense Command and District Engineer, Buffalo Engineer District, 1938-46. Career: Draftsman and Die Designer, Pullman Division, Haskell and Barker Car Company; Steel Fabricating Corporation (later Stefco Steel Company), Chief Engineer, 1924-34; Private Consulting Engineering Practice 1934-38; Board of Directors, Cleveland Pneumatic Tool Company, 1946-47; Vice President, R. E. McKee, General Contractor, Los Alamos, New Mexico, 1947-52; Vice President, Zia Company, R. E. McKee's Los Alamos Management Firm, 1947-52; Vice President and General Manager, C.H. Leavell and Company General Contractors, El Paso, Texas, 1952-61; Founder, Chairman of the Board, N. J. Riebe Enterprises, Inc. General Contractors, 1961. Organizational Memberships: United States and Canada Water Resources Board (chairman, 1944-46); Society of American Military Engineers; Associated General Contractors, El Paso (president, 1960); American Ordinance Association (past president). Community Activities: Kiwanis Club, Michigan City, Indiana (first president, 1928-30); Mason; Shriner; Knight Templar (past commander, 1930-32); National Panel of Arbitrators, American Arbitration Association; Past Member, Lemon Administrative Committee. Religion: Episcopal, Past Vestryman. Honors and Awards: Boy's Club Community Service Award; Legion of Merit, 1946; Honorary Doctor of Science Degree, Occidental University. Address: 14141 South Avenue 4E, P.O. Box 4156, Yuma, Arizona 85364.

Ries, Herman E Jr

Research Associate, Department of Biology, University of Chicago. Personal: Born May 6, 1911, in Scranton, Pennsylvania; Son of Herman and Henrietta Ries; Married Elizabeth Hamburger (deceased), Second Wife Mildred Small Allen; Father of Walter E., Richard A. Education: B.S., University of Chicago, 1933; Ph.D., University of Chicago, 1936, Physical Chemistry. Career: Head of Physical Chemistry Section, Associate Director of Catalysis Division, Sinclair Research Laboratories, 1936-51; Research Associate, Standard Oil Company, 1951-72; Visiting Scientist, Cavendish Laboratory, University of Cambridge, England, 1964; Visiting Professor, Institute for Chemical Research, Kyoto University, Japan, 1972-74; Research Associate, Department of Biology, University of Chicago, 1974 to present; Consultant, Argonne National Laboratory, 1977 to present; Visiting Scientist, Summer 1978; Robert A. Welch Foundation Lecturer, University of Texas, 1978-79. Organizational Memberships: Gordon Research Conference on Chemistry at Interfaces (chairman, 1960); International Congresses on Surface Activity, London, 1957, Brussels 1964, Barcelona 1968, Zurich 1972, Moscow, 1976, Jerusalem 1981; A.C.S. Divisions of Colloid and Surface Chemistry, Petroleum Chemistry, Physical Chemistry, Polymer Chemistry, and Water, Air and Waste Chemistry; American Association for the Advancement of Science; A.S.D.E.; A.I.C.; Chemical Society, London; Chemical Society of Japan; Catalysis Club of Chicago; Coordinator of Critical Tables on Monolayers. Community Activities: University of Chicago String Quartette and Symphony. Honors and Awards: Phi Beta Kappa; Sigma Xi, Ipatieff Prize, American Chemical Society, 1950; Certificate of Merit Award, Division of Colloid and Surface Chemistry, American Chemical Society, 1975-76; Listed in *Who's Who in America, World Who's Who in Science, Who's Who in the World.* Address: 5660 Blackstone Avenue, Chicago, Illinois 60637.

Norman J Riebe

Rifkin, Sandra A

Interior Designer, Artist. Personal: Born May 22, 1938; Daughter of Mr. and Mrs. Ervin W. Anderson; Married Robert C. Rifkin; Mother of Terri Lin. Education: St. Mary's Hall, 1957; Bergman Art Institute, 1959. Career: Design Associates, Interior Design and Consulting Firm, 1971 to present; Established "Design Studios", 1968-70; Associate, Quiry's and Company, 1964-67. Organizational Memberships: Denver Public Library. Community Activities: Former Brownie Scout Leader; Former Scout Leader; Mile High Council (secretary). Address: 3864 South Quince Street, Denver, Colorado 80237.

Rigas, Anthony L

Professor, Administrator. Personal: Born May 3, 1931; Son of Mr. and Mrs. Leon A. Rigas; Married Harriett B. Rigas; Father of Marc L. Education: B.S.E.E. 1958, M.S.E.E. 1962, Ph.D. 1963, University of Kansas; Ph.D., Electrical Engineering, Stanford University, 1968; Diploma, Modern Systems Theory, Massachusetts Institute of Technology, 1968; Ph.D. Engineering, University of Beverly Hills, 1977-78. Military: Served in the United States Air Force, 1949-53, attaining the rank of Staff Sergeant. Career: Rigas Scientific Consultants, Inc., 1975 to present; Professor of Electrical Engineering 1967-73, Assistant Professor of Electrical Engineering

1966-67, University of Idaho; Assistant Professor of Electrical Engineering 1962-63, Teaching Assistant in Electrical Engineering 1961-62, University of Kansas; Energy Consultant, United States Senate, Washington, D.C., 1975-76; Senior Research Engineer, Aerospace Systems, Lockheed Missile and Space Company, 1963-65; Engineering Analyst, Computer Models and Simulation, Minneapolis Honeywell Company, 1962; Electrical Engineer, Guidance and Control, Naval Missile Center, 1958-61. Organizational Memberships: Institute of Electrical and Electronics Engineers (automatic control group; computers professional group; education society); National Cooperative Education Association; The Society for Computer Simulation; Computers in Education, Division of A.S.E.E.; National Society of Professional Engineers; American Association for the Advancement of Science. Published Works: Number of Professional Articles including (most recently) "The Role of the Engineer in Society" and "An Approach to the Development and Application of System Models for Alternate Energy Policy Strategies". Honors and Awards: American Society for Engineering Education Certificate of Merit, 1977; Elected Senior Member, Institute of Electrical and Electronic Engineers, 1976; Nominated to President's Science and Technology Advisory Committee, 1976; 1975-76 I.E.E.E. United States Congressional Fellowship; Associated Students of the University of Idaho 1975 Merit Citation; American Society for Engineering Education 1974 Outstanding Activities Coordinator Award; Associated Students of the University of Idaho 1974 Outstanding Service Award; University of Idaho Alumni Service Award, 1974; Recipient of Two N.S.F. Summer Fellowships, 1968; N.A.S.A.-Stanford Systems Engineering Fellowship, 1967; Lockheed Honors Graduate Fellowship Award to Pursue Ph.D. Degree in Electrical Engineering at Stanford University, 1963-65; Superior Service Award, American Institute of Electrical Engineers, 1961; Fellow, International Biographical Association, 1978; Sigma Xi; Sigma Tau; Tau Beta Pi (Eminent Engineer); Listed in *Who's Who in Greece, International Who's Who of Intellectuals, Community Leaders of America, International Scholars Directory, Who's Who in the West, American Men of Science*. Address: 457 Ridge Road, Moscow, Idaho 83843.

Anthony Rigas

Rigg, Carol Margaret Elizabeth Ruth

Calligrapher, Associate Professor of Visual Art. Personal: Born December 14, 1928; Daughter of Carl Hazelett and Ruth Standish Massey Rigg (both deceased); Mother of Barbara Russ-Cho. Education: Studies toward a B.F.A., Carnegie-Mellon University, Summers 1945-50; A.B., Painting and Graphics, Florida State University, 1951; M.A., Theology and English Bible, Presbyterian, 1955; Studies toward an M.F.A., Chicago Art Institute, 1963. Career: Associate Professor of Visual Art, Eckerd College, 1965 to present; Director, Elliott Teaching Gallery, Eckerd College, 1981; Art Editor, *motive* Magazine, Nashville, Tennessee, 1955-65; Art Director, Board of Publications, Florida State University, 1949-53. Community Activities: Southern Conference Educational Fund (board member, 1960-70); Women Calligraphers (president, 1969-73); St. Petersburg Society of Scribes (president, 1978-81); Bi-National Service, 1974 to present; Association of Religion, the Arts and Contemporary Culture, 1955 to present; Committee of Seventy-Five for Asian Women's Education, 1975 to present; Over 90 One-Person Visual Arts Exhibits, 1955 to present, 4 Rose Windows, Cathedral, Mexico City; Presbyterian Chapel, Chapel Hill, North Carolina. Religion: United Methodist Church. Honors and Awards: Two CBS-TV ½ Hour Programs of her Calligraphy, 1970 and 1972: "I Need to Hear From You" 1972 and 1973, "Keep in Touch"; Senior Research Grant in Chinese Calligraphy, Fulbright-Hays Grant in Korea, 1974; Lecturer, Stone Lecturer, Princeton Seminary, 1973; Director, Adult Literacy Team for Jamaican Literacy, 1967; Keynote Speaker, World Christian Student Conference, Finland, 1964. Address: 2960 58th Avenue South, St. Petersburg, Florida 33712.

Ringsdorf, Warren Marshall Jr

Professor, Dentist. Personal: Born May 2, 1930; Son of Dr. Warren M. and Mrs. Mary F. Ringsdorf; Married Doris Lemerle Carpenter; Father of Warren Marshall III, Valerie Ann. Education: B.A., Asbury College, 1951; M.S., University of Alabama Graduate School, 1956; D.M.D., University of Alabama School of Dentistry, 1956; Fellow in Oral Medicine, University of Alabama School of Dentistry, 1962. Military: Served in the United States Air Force, 1956-58, attaining the rank of Captain. Career: Dentist in the United States Air Force, 1956-58; Private Dental Practice, 1958-59; Assistant Professor in Dentistry, 1959-64, Associate Professor of Dentistry 1964-81, Professor of Dentistry 1982 to present, University of Alabama School of Dentistry; Private Practice in Nutritional Counseling. Organizational Memberships: Seventh District Dental Society; Alabama Dental Association; American Dental Association; American Academy of Oral Medicine; Academy of Orthomolecular Psychiatry; Nutrition Today Society. Community Activities: Teen Challenge of Birmingham (board of directors); Saint Anne's Home, Inc. (board of directors); Jefferson County Mental Health Society (committee on alcoholism; board of directors); Martha R. Jones Foundation for Health Education, Inc. (board of directors). Published Works: Author of 375 Articles in the Health Services, Five Books, most recently *Psychodietetics*. Honors and Awards: Research Award, Chicago Dental Society, 1966, 1968; Honors Achievement Award, Angiology Research Foundation, 1968; Scientific Fellow, Academy of Orthomolecular Psychiatry, 1981. Address: 728 Sussex Drive, Birmingham, Alabama 35226.

Warren Ringsdorf

Ripinsky, Michael

Administrator. Personal: Born March 23, 1944, in the U.S.S.R.; Father of Tariel Misha. Education: B.A. with distinguished honors, Anthropology, University of California-Berkeley; Ph.D., Archaeology and Art History, Pacific Western University; Research Assistant, Department of Anthropology, University of California-Berkeley, 1964-66. Career: Associate, University of California-Los Angeles, Conducting Research into the Applications of X-ray and Electron Analyses to Archaeological Materials for the Purposes of Dating and Characterization; Senior Research Anthropologist, Hebrew University, Hadassah Medical School, Jerusalem, Israel, University of California Extension, Berkeley; Faculty Member, Department of Anthropology-Geography, California State University, Hayward, Teaching Courses in Archaeology and Historico-Cultural Geography of the Near East; Curator, The Anthropos Gallery of Ancient Art, Beverly Hills, California, 1976-78; Chief Research Scientist, Archaeometric Data Laboratories, Beverly Hills, 1976-78; Director, Ancient Artworld Corporation, Beverly Hills; Executive Director, The Ripinsky Group Inc., Beverly Hills, Art Investment and Valuers. Organizational Memberships: Archaeological Institute of America; Society of American Archaeology; Israel Exploration Society; American Anthropological Association; Royal Anthropological Institute of Great Britain; American Oriental Society; American Geographical Society; American Ethnological Society; American Society of Metals; Metalluragical Society of the American Institute of Mechanical Engineers; History of Science Society; International Society of Appraisers; Association for the Advancement of Science; Ancient Art Council of Los Angeles County Museum of Art; Society for Archaeological Sciences; International Institute for Conservation of Historic and Artistic Works (associate); American Institute of Conservation (associate); Pepperdine University Associate; International Society of Fine Art Appraisers, Ltd. Honors and Awards: Ruth Benedict Institute Grant for Research Assistantship under Dr. Margaret Mead, American Museum of Natural History, 1964; Doris Duke Research Fellowship, University of New Mexico (declined); Grant-in-Aid, University of California-Berkeley, 1969; Teaching Assistantship, McGill University, Montreal, Canada (declined); Listed in *Who's Who in the Eastern United States and Canada, Dictionary of International Biography, Men of Achievement, Who's Who in California, Who's Who in the United States, Library of Human Resources*. Address: 9363 Wilshire Boulevard, Suite 216, Beverly Hills, California 90210.

Ritchie, John

Scholar-in-Residence. Personal: Born March 19, 1904; Married Sarah Wallace; Father of John Jr., Albert. Education: B.A. 1925, LL.B. 1927, University of Virginia; J.S.D., Yale University, 1931; LL.D. (honorary), College of William and Mary, 1979; Sterling Fellow, Yale University, 1930-31. Military: Served as the Judge Advocate 65th Infantry Division of the United States Army, 1942-46, attaining the rank of Colonel. Career: With Ritchie, Chase, Canady and Swenson, 1927-28; Assistant Professor, Furman University, 1928-30; Assistant Professor, University of Washington, 1931-36; Professor, University of Maryland, 1936-37; Professor, University of Virginia, 1937-52 and 1972-74; Dean of Law School and Kirby Professor, Washington University, 1952-53; Dean of Law School and Professor, University of Wisconsin, 1953-57; Dean of Law School and Wigmore Professor, Northwestern University, 1957-72; Dean and Wigmore Professor Emeritus, 1972 to present; Scholar-in-Residence, University of Virginia Law School since 1974. Organizational Memberships: Association of American Law Schools (president, 1964); Judge Advocates Association (president, 1952); Order of the Coif (national president, 1952-55); American Bar Association; Virginia Bar Association; Law Club of Chicago. Community Activities: American Council on Education (director, 1965-68); United Charities of Chicago (director, 1966-72); American Bar Foundation (life fellow, 1970 to present); Illinois Judicial Advisory Council, 1964-68; House of Delegates, American Bar Association, 1952-72; Editorial Board, Foundation Press, 1960 to present; Committee to Draft Code of Professional Responsibility, American Bar Association, 1964-69. Religion: Episcopalian. Honors and Awards: Phi Beta Kapa; Order of the Coif; Raven Society; Omicron Delta Kappa; Tucker Lecturer, Washington and Lee University, 1964; De Tocqueville Lecturer, Marquette University, 1967. Address: 1848 Westview Road, Charlottesville, Virginia 22903.

Rittenhouse, William Henry

Minister. Personal: Born April 6, 1922; Married Nell Crider; Father of Forshey (Mrs. Leo), JoAnn Crye (Mrs. Pete), Nancy Tully (Mrs. John). Education: B.S., Stetson University, 1942; M.A., University of North Carolina; Ph.D., Duke University School, 1949. Military: Served in the United States Army Air Corps, 1942-45, attaining the rank of Major. Career: Pastor, Southside Baptist Church (Miami, Florida) 1949-55, Sylvan Hills Baptist Church (Marietta, Georgia) 1962-64, Nassau Bay Baptist Church (Houston Texas) 1965-72; President, High Flight Foundation, Colorado Springs, Colorado, 1972-77; Pastor, First Baptist Church, Tupelo, Mississippi, 1977 to present. Organizational Memberships: Miami Air National Guard (chaplain, 1951-53); Miami Police Department (associate chaplain, 1952-54). Community Activities: Citizen's Advisory Committee for Atlanta City School, 1956-60; Chaplain of Georgia Senate, 1963; High Flight Foundation Bi-Racial Committee (board of directors); High Flight Mobile Space Museum and Bicentennial Program (director, 1975-76). Religion: National and State Committees of the Southern Baptist Convention, 1949 to present. Honors and Awards: Legion of Merit; D.F.C.; Bronze Star; Air Medal with Clusters; Presidential Citation; Purple Heart; Prisoner of War in Romania, 1944; N.B.C. "Crossroads" Award, 1959; Honorary Degrees from University of Tel Aviv (Israel) 1972, University of Cairo (Egypt) 1973, University of Quarter 1973, University of Jordan 1973. Published Works: Author of Book *Barbed Wire Preacher*. Address: 1400 Kennedy Street, Tupelo, Mississippi 38801.

Ritts, Roy Ellot Jr

Professor, Consultant. Personal: Born January 16, 1929, in St. Petersburg, Florida. Education: A.B., University Scholar, George Washington University, 1948; M.D., George Washington University School of Medicine, 1951; Intern, District of Columbia General Hospital, 1951-52; Fellow in Medicine (Infectious Diseases), George Washington University School of Medicine at the District of Columbia General Hospital, 1952-53; Resident in Medicine, Harvard Medical School, 1954-55; Certified by the National Board of Medical Examiners 1952, American Board of Medical Microbiology 1962; Licensed in District of Columbia and Minnesota. Military: Served in the United States Naval Reserve, Ensign 1948-51, Lieutenant (j.g.) 1951-56. Career: Assistant in Medicine, Peter Bent Brigham Hospital, 1954-55; Visiting Investigator, Rockefeller Institute, 1955-57; Research Associate, Rockefeller Institute, 1957-58; Associate Professor of Microbiology 1958-61, Chairman of the Department of Microbiology 1959-64, Professorial Lecturer in Medicine 1961-64, Professor of Microbiology 1961-64, Georgetown University School of Medicine; Professorial Lecturer in Immunology, University of Chicago School of Medicine, 1964-68; Director, A.M.A.-E.R.F. Institute for Biomedical Research, 1964-68; Director of Medical Research, American Medical Association, 1966-68; Chairman and Consultant, Department of Microbiology, Mayo Clinic, 1969-79; Professor of Microbiology, Mayo Graduate School of Medicine, University of Minnesota, 1968 to present; Professor of Microbiology, Mayo Medical School, 1972 to present; Head, Microbiology Research Laboratory, 1979 to present; Professor of Oncology, Mayo Medical School, 1979 to present; Consultant and Merit Grant Reviewer, Veterans Administration Central Office, Immunology of Cancer, 1972-78, 1980-82. Organizational Memberships: American Academy of Microbiology (fellow); American College of Physicians (fellow); American College of Chest Physicians (fellow); Association of Clinical Scientists (fellow); Infectious Disease Society of America (fellow); Royal Society of Health (fellow); Association of Clinical Scientists (fellow); American Association of Immunologists; American Association for Cancer Research; American Federation for Clinical Research; American Rheumatism Association; American Society for Clinical Oncology; American Society for Microbiology (vice president, Washington-Maryland branch, 1963; vice president, 1969; president, North Central branch, 1970); American Society of Surgical Oncology (Ewing Society); British Society of Immunologists; International Association for the Study of Lung Cancer (board of directors, 1974-76; secretary general, 1976-78); Reticuloendothelial Society; Society for Experimental Medicine and Biology; Society for General Microbiology (England); Gesellshaft fur Immunologie; Alpha Chi Simga; Phi Chi; Society of Sigma Xi; International Study Group on Cardiac Transplantation (registry committee, immunology committee, 1980 to present); American Board of Medical Laboratory Immunology (member, 1976-83; committee on oral examinations, 1978 to present; chairman, 1980-83); Committee on Allergy and Clinical Immunology, American College of Chest Physicians (member, 1976-78; executive committee, 1978-79); Federation of American Societies for Experimental Biology (national correspondent, 1974 to present); International Union of Immunology Societies (standards executive committee, chairman 1973 to present, council 1974 to present); WHO Expert Committee on Standardization, 1973 to present; Section Editor, *Journal of Immunology*, 1982 to present. Community Activities: Sigma Chi; Cosmos Club, Washington, D.C., 1964-78; University Club of Rochester (board of directors, 1971-75; president, 1975). Honors and Awards: Gate and Key; Alpha Theta Nu; William Beaumont Medical Society; Alpha Omega Alpha; Listed in *American Men and Women of Science, American Men of Medicine, Dictionary of International Biography, The Blue Book, Who's Who in the World, Who's Who in World Medicine, World Who's Who in Science*. Address: Microbiology Research Laboratory, Mayo Foundation, Rochester, Minnesota 55901.

Rivera, Nicolas Nogueras (deceased)

Labor Leader. Personal: Born September 10, 1902, in Cayey, Puerto Rico; Died March 25, 1982; Married Berta; Father of Nicolas Jr., Rosa Maria. Education: Elementary Teacher Certificate 1920, Elementary English Teacher Certificate 1926, University of Puerto Rico; Studied in the Labor Education Institute, 1935. Career: Organized and Became President of Labor Organization, Protective Labor Union, 1931; Musician, Composer of Two Waltzes; Secretary-Treasurer, Federal Labor Union, San Juan, 1936; Secretary-

Treasurer, Puerto Rico Free Federation of Labor, 1936-52 (Later President of Same); Alternate Vice President, I.C.F.T.U.; Member, Board of Appeals, United States Selective Service System, 30 years; President Emeritus for Life, Puerto Rico Free Federation of Labor; Consultant to Department of Labor and Human Relations, Commissioned to Write the History of Organized Labor Movement in Puerto Rico. Organizational Memberships: First Interamerican Labor Conference, Lima, Peru, 1948 (president, program and constitution committee), Leading to Foundation of Interamerican Regional Labor Organization and International Confederation of Free Trade Unions. Community Activities: Socialist Party, Served as Member of House of Representatives for Party, 1932-36; Founder and Organizer, First Statehood Convention and Convention for Plebiscitary Action; International Platform Association; American Security Council; United States Historical Society. Honors and Awards: Award for Distinguished Achievement, *International Register of Profiles*; Fellow, International Biographical Association; Life Member, American Biographical Institute Research Association; United States Selective Service Medal after World War II; Awards from Presidents Franklin D. Roosevelt, Harry S. Truman, Dwight D. Eisenhower, John F. Kennedy, Lyndon B. Johnson, Richard Nixon; Listed in *Who's Who in Community Service, North American Register of Profiles, International Register of Profiles, Personalities of the South, Who's Who in the World, Dictionary of International Biography, Notable Americans of the Bicentennial Era.*

Rizzo, Mary Joanna

Professor of Speech/Drama/Communications, Dominican Sister. Personal: Born December 5, 1910; Daughter of Joseph and Johanna Marsalisa Rizzo (both deceased). Education: Certificate, Nuss School of Dance, 1925; Certificate, Professor Specht School of Violin, 1927; Certificate, New Orleans College of Oratory, 1926; Graduate 1927, Teacher's Diploma 1931, New Orleans School of Speech and Dramatic Art; B.A., Loyola University of the South, 1935; B.A., St. Mary's Dominican College, 1931; M.A., Louisiana State University, Baton Rouge, 1945; Ph.D., University of Wisconsin, Madison, 1954. Career: Professor of Speech, Drama, Communication, St. Mary's Dominican College; Dominican Sister, Order of Saint Dominic, Congregation of St. Mary; Founder, Speech and Drama Department, Speech and Pathology Department, St. Mary's Dominican College; Founder Dominican College Players. Organizational Memberships: American Theatre Association; Speech Communication Association; Southern Speech Communication Association; Louisiana Communication Speech Association; Phi Beta, University of Wisconsin Chapter; Delta Epsilon Sigma, St. Mary's Dominican College; The Rosary Guild; The Legion of Mary; The Association of the Miraculous Medal; Salesian Missions; Our Lady of the Snows Mission; Seraphic Mass Association. Community Activities. The Right to Life Association of New Orleans. Religion: Catholic. Published Works: Editor, *Centennial Publication*, Dominican Sisters, Congregation of St. Mary; Religious Plays and Programs for Dominican; Carnival Balls. Honors and Awards: Best Director and Producer Awards, Best Speech Professor Awards, Dominican College, 1950 to present; Interpretative Reading Award, N.C. School of Speech and Dramatic Art; Phi Beta; Delta Epsilon Sigma; Listed in *Who's Who of American Women, Who's Who in the South and Southwest, Directory of American Scholars, World Who's Who of Women.* Address: 7214 St. Charles Avenue, New Orleans, Louisiana 70118.

Gertrud Roberts

Robbins, Wayne Lindsey

College Administrator. Personal: Born January 8, 1936, in Covington, Tennessee; Son of Mr. and Mrs. J. L. Robbins; Married Faye Elaine Wellborn; Father of Wayne Lindsey Jr. Education: B.S., English, Mississippi State University 1958; B.D. 1963, M.Div. 1966, Southwestern Baptist Theological Seminary; M.Ed. 1967, Ed.D. 1975, University of Arkansas; Further Study at the University of South Carolina. Military: Served in the United States Army Military Police Corps, 1958-59; Served in the United States Army Reserve, discharged in 1969 with the rank of Captain. Career: Professional Baseball Player, Baltimore Orioles, 1958; Special Agent, Pinkerton National Detective Agency, Summer 1959; Instructor of English, Head Baseball Coach, Riverside Military Academy, Gainesville, Georgia, 1959-60; Dean of Men, Bluefield College, Bluefield, Virginia, 1963-65; Assistant to the Dean of the College of Arts and Sciences, Head Baseball Coach, University of Arkansas, 1965-70; Press Secretary to United States Senator Strom Thurmond, 1970-73; Staff Assistant to United States Congressman John Paul Hammerschmidt, 1973; Press Assistant to United States Senator Bill Brock, 1973-74; Director of Federal Programs, Tennessee Department of Education, 1974-75; Dean of Students, Chattanooga State Community College, 1975-76; Vice President of Development, Belmont College, Nashville, Tennessee. Organizational Memberships: Military Police Association, 1959-67; United States Senate Staff Club, 1970-75; Phi Delta Kappa; American Association of University Administrators. Community Activities: Lions Club, 1963-73; Bellevue Chamber of Commerce, 1980; National Republican Association. Religion: Baptist; Deacon; Licensed Baptist Minister, 1959; Sunday School Teacher; Writer of Various Religious Articles for State Periodicals. Honors and Awards: Listed in *Community Leaders of America, Who's Who Among Students in American Colleges and Universities, Personalities of the South, Who's Who in the South and Southwest, Directory of Distinguished Americans, Men of Achievement.* Address: 500 Plantation Court V-2, Nashville, Tennessee 37221.

Roberts, Beverly Kay

Administrator. Personal: Born May 6, 1936; Daughter of Mr. and Mrs. H. S. Huber; Married Edward H. Roberts Jr.; Step-Mother of Mark D. Education: B.A., Sociology, Temple University, 1959; M.A. 1976, M.A. 1978, Central Michigan University. Military: Served in the United States Air Force, 1960-80, retiring with the rank of Major. Organizational Memberships: A.M.A.; S.A.M.; A.S.T.D.; A.B.W.A. Community Activities: Governor's Management Task Force, State of Nevada, 1980; Police Auxiliary Communications Team, Las Vegas. Religion: Founder, WIPE-OUT, 1973 to present; Member, Hoffmantown Baptist Church, Albuquerque, New Mexico. Honors and Awards: Boss of the Year, A.B.W.A., 1981; Bronze Star; Joint Service Commendation Medal; Meritorious Service Medal; Air Force Commendation Medal with One Oak Leaf Cluster; Air Force Outstanding Unit Award with One Oak Leaf Cluster and One "V" for Valor; National Defense Service Medal; Viet Nam Services Medal with Five Battle Stars; Air Force Longevity Ribbon with Three Oak Leaf Clusters; Armed Forces Reserve Medal; Small Arms Expert Marksmanship Ribbon; Republic of Viet Nam Campaign Ribbon with Palm. Address: 41 Penns Grove Road, Pedricktown, New Jersey 08067.

Roberts, Gertrud K

Concert Harpsichordist, Composer. Personal: Born August 23, 1906, in Hastings, Minnesota; Daughter of Adolph Gustav and Anna Marie Kloetzer Kuenzel (both deceased); Married Joyce O. Roberts, June 4, 1934; Mother of Michael Stefan, Marcia Roberts Morse. Education: B.A., University of Minnesota, 1928; Attended the Leipzig Conservatory of Music, 1930-31; Private Study with Madame Julia Elbogen, Vienna, Austria, 1935-36; Studied Art History under Dr. Gustav Ecke and Dr. Jean Charlot. Career: Recitals and Concerts in American and Europe since Age 12; Harpsichord Concerts throughout United States and Hawaii since 1936; First Public Performance on Harpsichord, including own compositions, Women's City Club, St. Paul, Minnesota, 1936; Traveled Coast to Coast and all Hawaiian Islands (except Molokai) with Harpsichords; Sponsored by State Foundation of Culture and the Arts to Introduce Harpsichord Concerts to Outer Islands of Kauai, Maui, Hawaii, 1968; Commissioned to Compose Music for Honolulu Community Theatre's Production of Jean Anouilh's "Thieves Carnival" and Shakespeare's "Tempest", Honolulu Youth Theatre's Production of

Eva Le Gallienne's "Alice in Wonderland", University of Hawaii's Theatre Development's Production of Lorca's "Yerma", Pineapple Companies of Hawaii Documentary Film Music for "Pineapple Country Hawaii"; Compositions include "Triptych" 1961, "Petite Suite" 1955, "Passacaille" 1956, "In a Secret Garden" 1954, "Elegy for John F. Kennedy" 1965, "Das Kleine Buch der Bilder", "Fantasy after Psalm 150", "Double Concerto"; Number of Short Compositions for Children. Organizational Memberships: National Society of Arts and Letters (president, 1971-74); Natonal Associatin of Composers and Conductors; American Music Center (composer member); National Guild of Piano Teachers (national judge; Hall of Fame); National League of American Pen Women (composer member; president Honolulu chapter, 1974-76); American Association of University Women; Sigma Alpha Iota; Alpha Gamma Delta. Community Activities: Honolulu Piano Teachers Association (president, 1970-72); Honolulu Chamber Music Society (founder, patron); Honolulu Morning Music Club; Honolulu Academy of Arts; Honolulu Museum (Polynesian artificats); Fritz Hart Foundation (founder, president); Jean Charlot Foundation (founder, president). Published Works: *Chaconne for Harpsichord; Rondo-Hommage to Couperin*; "Twelve Time-Gardens". Honors and Awards: Honorary Life Member, Honolulu Community Theatre; Honorary Citizen, Home-town of Hastings, Minnesota; Most Distinguished Citizen for 1975 in the Arts, Alpha Gamma Delta; Listed in *Men and Women of Hawaii, Personalities of the West and Midwest, Who's Who of American Women, Who's Who in the West, International Who's Who in Community Service, Two Thousand Women of Achievement, World Who's Who of Musicians, World Who's Who of Women, International Harpsichord Blue Book, National Register of Prominent Americans and International Notables, Dictionary of International Biography, Women Composers of America, International Who's Who in Music and Musicians Directory*. Address: 4723 Moa Street, Honolulu, Hawaii 96816.

Josephine F Roberts

Roberts, Josephine Frances

Retired. Personal: Born August 3, 1909; Daughter of Benjamin Rees (deceased), Cora Brammar Rees Brown (deceased); Mother of R. H., Cynthia, Taylor. Education: Advanced High School Studies in Language, Science, Art and Music; Participant in Seminars and Foundation and Charitable Workshops. Career: Retired; Former Owner/Operator, Commercial Fishing Lake and Real Estate Developer; Musician/Organist. Community Activities: Ohio Federation of Women's Clubs, 1937 to present; Chesapeake Women's Club (president, 1956-58, 1967-68); Committee to Establish First County Hospital, First Library, First County Health Department and Established Well Child Clinic, First Parent Teacher Association, Chesapeake; Member, First County Welfare Advisory Board; County Mental Health Association (past president); Ohio Mental Health Association (board member); United Way (chairman); Ohio Historical Society; National Historical Society; National Trust for Historical Preservation; Early American Society; International Platform Association; Smithsonian Institution (associate member); Order of Eastern Star (matron, 1951, 1952; organist, 17 years); Rainbow for Girls (instituting member; chairman of board; mother advisor; district choir "mom", 1970-74); Order of Amarantha Inc. (instituting member; past royal matron; grand musician, 1968, 1969, 1970); Order of White Shrine of Jerusalem (worthy high priestess, three times; deputy supreme to organize a White Shrine; supreme page; sup. obituary committee; supreme instructor, 1972-80); Job's Daughters, Bethel, (re-instituting member, 1948); Girl Scout Leader, 1948-54; Participant, First Cancer Drive; First Polio Drive in County; Daffodil Sale, 1981; Ohiana Library (district chairman); Community Improvement Committee (charter member; secretary); Easter Seal; County Bicentennial Commission (administrative secretary, 1975-76); County Chairwoman, 1955-62; Presiding Judge Precinct A, Chesapeake, 1962-78; Interim Clerk, Lawrence County Commission Officer, 1956, 1957, and 1958; Crew Leader, Agriculture Census, 1959; Crew Leader, Population Census, 1960; Conducted Title Surveys I through XX for County; First Neighborhood Youth Chairman, 1967-68; Township Republican Club (secretary-treasurer, 1977-79); Senior Citizens Program, 1979-80; Special Supporter, Ronald Reagan Campaign, 1976; Republican Party; National Republican Women's Club; Nominated by United States Senator John Connelly to United States Senatorial Club; United States Republican Congressional Committee. Religion: Bible School Teacher since Age 12; Vacation Bible School Director; Pianist and Organist, New Testament Christian Church, 60 years; Sunday School Superintendent *U.S.S. Freeman*, South Pacific, 1951; Chartered Two Christian Churches, 1962, 1975; Support of Warren Saunders, Missionary to Columbia, 1965-80; Charter Member, New Testament Christian Church, South Point, Ohio; Supported Operation Evangelize Team, 1976. Honors and Awards: Blue Book of Honor, Ohio Federation of Women's Clubs, 1968; Liberty Bell Award for Most New Members of Any Club Woman in United States, Gen. Federation of Women's Clubs, 1976; Life Fellow, International Biographical Association; Life Fellow, American Biographical Institute; Trail Blazer Award, Ohio Federation of Women's Clubs, 1968; Grand Cross of Color, International Rainbow, 1970; Diploma of Honor, Community Service, International Biographical Association, 1975; One of 4000 included in International Who's Who Hall of Fame, 1981; Selected to be Member of Advisory Board to Combined I.B.A. and A.B.I; Special Recognition Award as Co-Founder of Off-Campus College, Georgetown University; Founders Certificates as Co-Founder of Off-Campus College; Member, Coalition for Peace Through Strength; Honorable Kentucky Colonel, 1972; Charter Member, Postal Commemorative Society, First Day Covers and Gold Replicas of Stamps; Listed in *Book of Honor, World Who's Who of Women, Who's Who of Intellectuals, Men and Women of Distinction, International Who's Who in Music and Poetry, I.B.A. Yearbook and Biographical Directory, Directory of International Biography, Community Leaders and Noteworthy Americans, Notable Americans*. Address: Route 3, Box 491, Chesapeake, Ohio 45619.

Kathleen J D Roberts

Roberts, Kathleen

United States Army Officer. Personal: Born November 29, 1948; Daughter of Henry and Virginia Roberts. Education: A.A., College of Alameda, Alameda, California; B.A. Psychology, California State University at Northridge, Northridge, California. Military: Served in the United States Navy, 1967-75; Served in the United States Navy, 1975 to present. Career: First Lieutenant, United States Army, 1975 to present; Petty Officer 2nd Class (E-5), United States Navy, 1967-75. Organizational Memberships: Mental Health Association; M.A.C.A.D.; Association of Women Police; National Association for Female Executives, Inc.; Georgia Occupational Forum on Alcohol and Drugs. Community Activities: Peachtree/Parkwood Alcohol Advisory Council, 1979-81; Paces Ferry Hospital Council, 1979; Boy Scouts of America (cub master, pack #502, 1980); United States Army A.D.D.I.C. Council. Honors and Awards: Meritorious Service Medal, United States Navy, 1974; Listed in *Who's Who of American Women, Personalities of America*. Address: 750 Allgood Valley Court, Stone Mountain, Georgia 30083.

Merrill J Roberts

Roberts, Merrill Joseph

Educator. Personal: Born August 10, 1915; Son of Merrill and Inez Ludgate Roberts (both deceased); Married Janet Dion (now deceased); Father of David, Michael, James, Patricia. Education: B.A., University of Minnesota, 1938; M.B.A., 1939, Ph.D., 1951, University of Chicago. Military: Served with United States Navy through ranks of Ensign to Lieutenant, 1942-46; Served with U.S. Naval Reserve, 1946-58. Career: Professor of Transportation, University of Maryland at College Park, 1975 to present; Vice President and Director, Division of Economics, Wilbur Smith and Associates, 1972-75; Former Professor of Transportation and Economics, University of Pittsburgh and University of Florida; Former Professor of Economics, Michigan State University; Former Professor of Transportation at University of California at Los Angeles; Former Transportation Economist, Tennessee Valley Authority. Organizational Memberships: American Economics Association (transportation and public utilities group -

secretary/treasurer, 1956-62, vice chairman, 1963, chairman, 1964); Transportation Research Forum (vice president, 1966); Transportation Research Board (committee on applications of economics, 1975 to present); American Society of Traffic and Transportation; Transportation Association of American (research committee, 1968-72). Community Activities: Board of Directors, Port Authority of Allegheny County (Pittsburgh, Pennsylvania), 1962-69; Advisory Committee, U.S. Army Transport Command at Fort Eustis, 1958-62; Expert witness presenting testimony before a number of congressional committees, including the Senate Commerce and Judiciary committees, and House Committee on Interstate and Foreign Commerce; Consultant and advisor to numerous government agencies, including Department of Commerce, U.S. Agency for International Development, Interstate Commerce Commission. Religion: Member of Presbyterian Church. Address: 230 New Mark Esplanade, Rockville, Maryland 20850.

Roberts, Sammye Brown

Music Educator. Personal: Born November 21, 1940; Daughter of Mrs. Anne Ricks Scott; Married to William K. Education: A.A., Brewton Parker Junior College, Mt. Vernon, Georgia, 1960; B.A., University of Southern Mississippi, 1962; Candidate for Master's degree, University of Houston, 1978 to present. Career: Teacher of organ and piano; Administrative Assistant for the U.S. Astronaut Corps, N.A.S.A., at Johnson Space Center, Houston, Texas, 1973-75; Public Relations Executive with Chemco Photoproducts, Houston, 1972-73; Former librarian for elementary schools in Florida (Pennsacola), and Virginia (Norfolk); Voluntary school worker in Naples, Italy, 1965-69. Organizational Memberships: Music Teachers National Association; Gulf Coast Music Association (treasurer, 1978-80); Cultural Arts Council of Houston; Houston Symphony League; Houston Opera Guild; Young Women of the Arts. Community Activities: League of Women Voters, 1976 to present; National Organization for Women, 1973 to present; American Association of University Women; Bay Area Music Teachers representative to the Clear Lake Chamber of Commerce Cultural Arts Council, 1981-82. Honors and Awards: Superior Performance Award for work with Skylab/Apollo-Soyuz Test Project and for work with U.S. astronauts and U.S.S.R. cosmonauts during the first international space flight, N.A.S.A., Johnson Space Center, 1975; Listed in *Who's Who of American Women, International Who's Who of Women, Directory of Distinguished Americans, Who's Who in the South and Southwest*. Address: 18100 Nassau Bay Drive #29, Houston, Texas 77058.

Margaret E Robertson

Robertson, Margaret E

Retirement Community Counselor. Personal: Born Aberdeen, Mississippi; Married J. P. Robertson; Mother of Bonnie White. Education: Graduate of Ensley High School; Attended Massey Business College; Two Years of Study in Business Administration and Real Estate, University of Alabama. Career: Rice Realty Company, Mount Royal Towers, Development Assistant to Art Rice 1982 to present, Vice President, Resident Counselor, 1978-82; Property Manager, Southern Division, Hillmark Corporation, 1973-77; Vice President, Manager, Mountain Brook Realty Company, 1949-73; General Manager, Valley View Apartments, 1949-73; District Director, Counselor, Fairfield Manor Apartments, 1953-56; District Supervisor, La Sands Motel, 1953-56; Secretary/Treasurer, Bookkeeper, Transo Oil Company, 1953-56; B.B. Investments Corporation, Vice President and Manager, 1958-70; Resident Manager, Julius E. Marx Realtor, Snug Harbor Homes, 1944-48; Procurement, Cost Accounting, Brookly Field Air Force Base, 1942-44. Community Activities: Homewood City Council, 1976-84; Jefferson County Transportation Citizens Committee; Council Representative, Library Board, School Board; Citizens Committee, Regional Planning; Advisory Counselor, Retired Senior Volunteer Program of Jefferson County; American Cancer Board (member, 1983). Religion: Shades Mountain Baptist Church. Honors and Awards: Listed in *Who's Who of American Women*. Address: 1503 Valley Avenue, Birmingham, Alabama 35209.

Robinett-Weiss, Nancy Gay

Nutrition Coordinator. Personal: Born March 16, 1948; Daughter of Adam and Anne Robinett; Married Dayne M. Weiss. Education: B.S., Foods and Nutrition, West Virginia University, 1970; M.S., Nutrition Education, Drexel University, 1975. Career: Nutrition Consultant for Maternal and Child Health Bureau and Nutrition for Handicapped Children's Services, Utah State Department of Health, 1977-80; Chief, Nutrition Services, Woodhaven Center, Philadelphia, 1975-77; Nutrition Instructor, Camden County Vocational and Technical Schools, New Jersey, 1975-76; Nutritionist, Temple University Dental School, 1974-75; Therapeutic Dietitian, Temple University Hospital, 1971-74; Staff Therapeutic Dietitian, Our Lady of Lourdes Hospital, Camden, New Jersey, 1970-71; Nutrition Consultant for "What's Cooking" Educational Television Program, Channel 12, Philadelphia, Summer 1975. Organizational Memberships: American Dietetic Association, Registered Dietitian; American Dietetic Association Council on Practice, Public Health Nutritionists, Dietetics in Developmental and Mental Disorders; Utah Dietetic Association; American Public Health Association; Utah Public Health Association; American Association of Mental Deficiency. Honors and Awards: Listed in *Who's Who in the West*. Address: 5906 Sultan Circle, Salt Lake City, Utah 84107.

Arthur A Robinson

Robinson, Arthur Alexander Jr

Lecturer, Clergyman, Administrator, Poet. Personal: Born February 20, 1928, in Napoleonville, Louisiana; Son of Arthur Alexander Sr. and Odessa Sophronia Noel Robinson; Married Cynthia Parker; Father of Alaric Aurelius, Angel Alisa, Allison Alexander, (From Previous Marriages) Adrienne Antionette, Arthur Alexander III, Anthony Ambrose, Angelique Avis, Angela Antionette, Andre Alexis, Alicia Jean. Education: A.B., Dillard University, 1951; B.D., Gammon Theological Seminary, 1954; Undertook Graduate Studies at Atlanta University 1953, Xavier University 1950; Graduate of the United States Army Chaplain School, 1960; Completed United States Navy S.T.M. School, 1943. Military: Served in the United States Navy 1943-46; Served in the United States Army, 1949-52, Chaplain E.T.O. 1959-62; Delegate to the United States Army Chaplain Conference in Berchegaden, Germany, 1962. Career: Pastor of United Methodist Churches, Boynton Church Gretna (Louisiana) 1949-51, Forsyth Charge (Georgia) 1951-54, Hopewell Church (Georgia) 1951-54, Kynette Church 1951-54, Rocky Mount Church (Georgia) 1951-54, Camphor Memorial Church (Louisiana) 1954-56; Pastor, Builder of Sanctuary and Educational Building, Philips Memorial Church, New Orleans, 1959-60; St. James Church, Pine Bluff Arkansas, 1962-64; Duncan Chapel Church, Little Rock, 1965; Evergreen Baptist Church, Lake Charles, Louisiana, 1965-66; Pastor, Builder, Organizer, Mount Calvary Baptist Church, Indio, California, 1966-69; Committeeman, California Democratic State Central Committee, 1968-72; Pastor, St. Mark Church (Kingsport) 1969-70, Grace United Methodist Church (Chattanooga) 1970, Tennessee; Pastor, Thrikield Church and Harrys Chapel Church, Bogalusa, Louisiana, 1971-72; Teacher, Deser Sands Unified School District, Indio, California, 1966-69; Social and Community Worker, Indio, 1967-69; Blender, International Chemical and Starch Company, Inc., Indianapolis, 1951; District Manager, Negro Heritage Library Inc., Coachella Valley and Riverside County, California, 1967-69; Editor-in-Chief, Mt. Calvary Community News, Indio, 1967-69; Director of Bethlehem Community Center, Chattanooga, 1970; Pastor, Zion Temple A.M.E. Church (Madisonville, Kentucky) 1974-75, Ross Chapel A.M.E. Zion Church (Kentucky) 1974-75; Sales Representative, Metropolitan Life Insurance Company, 1975; Pastor, Peter A.M.E. Church (Mississippi) 1975-78; Program Director AJFC Community Services Agency, Community Service Program, Claiborne County Mississippi; Director of Social Action, A.M.E. Church, Natchez; Church Development Chairman, Mississippi

Annual Conference, A.M.E. Church; Other Ministerial Orders. Organizational Memberships: Interdominational Alliance, Kingsport, 1969-70; District Missionary, New Orleans, 1954-62; Evangelism Louisiana Conference (board member, 1954-62); National Baptist Convention U.S.A., 1965-69; International Platform Association, 1969-72; Louisiana State Baptist Convention, 1965-69; California Teachers Association, 1966-69; Delegate to Southern Christian Leadership Conference, 1957; Others. Community Activities: Scotlandville Branch, National Association for the Advancement of Colored People, Baton Rouge (president, 1954-56); Personnel Committee of Holston Homes, Greenville, Tennessee, 1970-71; Organizer, Chairman, Boycott and Citizens Committee, Pine Bluff, Arkansas, 1963; President of Pine Bluff Movement and Founder of Freedom House, Pine Bluff, 1963; Mexican -American Political Association, 1968-69; New Orleans Education Rehabilitation Civic Committee, New Orleans, 1956-60; Organizer, Martin Luther King Memorial March and Service, Indio, 1968; Delegate, California Democratic State Convention, 1968. Published Works: "Man's Responsiblity to His Community", 1960. Honors and Awards: Philippine Liberation Ribbon, World War II Navy Commendation Award, World War II; Honorable Warrant of Appointment, City of New Orleans Police Department, 1960; Special Scholarship Award to Attend National Clergy Economic Education Conference, University of Tennessee, 1970; Certificate of Ecclesiastical Endorsement, Commission of Chaplains, United Methodist Church, 1959; Listed in *Who's Who in American Politics, Personalities of the South, National Social Directory, Biographical Directory of Negro Ministers, International Speakers Network Inc., Who's Who Among Black Americans, Leaders of Black America, Outstanding Professionals of Human Services, Men of Achievement, International Who's Who in Community Service, Dictionary of International Biography, Two Thousand Men of Achievement, Who's Who Among Authors and Journalists, Community Leaders of America.* Address: 1122 Jane Sowers Road, Statesville, North Carolina 28677.

Robinson, Christine Hinckley

Author, Lecturer, Teacher, Interior Decorator. Personal: Born on May 11, 1908, in Salt Lake City, Utah; Married Dr. Oliver Preston Robinson in 1929; Mother of 1 son and 2 daughters. Education: Attended Brigham Young University, New York University, and Oxford University. Career: Owner, Christine H. Robinson Interiors, New York City, 1948-64; Head, Historical Interior Restorations, State of Utah, 1961-63, and Nauvoo, Illinois, 1963, 1967-69; Director, Church of Latter Day Saints Relief Society Organizations, Western Europe, 1964-67. Organizational Memberships: Institute of Relief Organization (board of directors); Utah Division of the International Traveller's Aid (president, vice president); Utah Community Welfare Services (board of directors and chairman, welfare division); International Crusade for Freedom (vice president, Utah division). Published Works: *Successful Retail Salesmanship*, 1942, 17th printing 1961, 4th edition 1963; *Living Truths*, 1964; *Inspirational Truths*, 1970; *Biblical Sites in the Holy Land*, 1963; *Israel's Bible Lands*, 1973; *Christ's Eternal Gospel*, 1976; Contributor to a number of magazines. Honors and Awards: Silver Bowl & Plaque, International Relief Society, 1962; Merit of Honor Plaque, Traveller's Aid, 1964; Joseph F. Smith Family Living Award, Brigham Young University, 1979; Listed in *The World Who's Who of Women*. Address: 670 East Three Fountains Dr. 3169, Murray, Utah 84107.

Robinson, James LeRoy

Architect, Planner, Developer. Personal: Born July 12, 1940; Son of Mr. and Mrs. Willie I. Robinson; Married Martha Narvaez; Father of Maria Teresa, Kerstin Gunilla. Education: B.Arch., Southern University, 1964; M.C.P., Pratt Institute, 1974. Military: Served in the United States Army, 1966. Career: Architect, Planner, Developer. Organizational Memberships York Council of Black Architects; New York State Society of Architects (past member); Arbitrator, American Arbitration Association. Religion: Protestant. Honors and Awards: A.I.A. Commendation, 1976; National Housing Awards (low rise housing), 1977; Bard Award, 1976, 1977; Listed in *Who's Who in the East, Who's Who in Black America*. Address: 67 Murray Street, New York, New York 10007.

Robinson, Mildred Blackwell

Mildred B Robinson

Administrator. Personal: Born February 20, 1917; Daughter of John and Frances Blackwell (both deceased); Mother of Edward DeWitt Riley Sr., Mamie Riley Clark. Education: B.S., Florida Memorial College, 1960; M.A., Fisk University, 1967; Ph.D., Florida State University, 1974. Career: Chairperson, Division of Education, E.W.C., 1977 to present; Secretary, Duval County Board of Public Instruction, 1953-60; Elementary School Teacher, Curriculum Assistant, 1960-75; Professor of Education, 1975 to present. Organizational Memberships: Florida Association for Teacher Education; Florida Association for Colleges of Teacher Education; Phi Delta Kappa; Kappa Delta Pi. Community Activities: Campfire Inc. (board of directors); National Association for the Advancement of Colored People; Young Men's Christian Association; Salom Chapter 106, Order of Eastern Star (matron, 1978 to present); Heroines of Jericho (senior matron, 1977 to present); Daughters of Isis, Rabia Court #25 (treasurer, 1968-72; high priestess, 1976-79). Religion: Central Baptist Church, President District #2, Trust Board, Former Sunday School Superintendent. Published Works: Author, "A Study of Socio-Economic Status on Pupil Progress", "The Development of an Awareness Scale Assessing Teacher Sensitivity to the Needs of Disadvantaged Children". Honors and Awards: Professional N.D.A. Grantee, 1965; Experienced Teacher Fellowship, 1966-67; Joint Economics Grantee, 1973; Outstanding Service Awards, Rabia Court #25, Daughters of Isis, 1975, 1977; Bethlehem Grand Chapter, Order of Eastern Star, 1979; Listed in *Who's Who in the South and Southwest, World Who's Who of Women*. Address: P.O. Box 40172, Jacksonville, Florida 32203.

Robinson, Ralph Rollin

Gynecologist-Obstetrician. Personal: Born July 7, 1913, in Nashville, Kansas; Son of Walter S. Sr. (deceased) and Mary Emma Inslee; Father of Mark Stuart, Kim Ella, Nancy Harriett, Ralph R. Jr., Rachel Catherine. Education: Engineering Degree, Oklahoma State University, 1935; Medical Degree, University of Washington School of Medicine, Seattle, 1951; Intern 1951-52, Resident in Obstetric-Gynecology 1952-55, University of Oklahoma; Certified by the American Board of Obstetrics-Gynecology, 1962; Postgraduate Course in Laparoscopy, Virginia Mason Medical Center, Washington, 1972. Career: Miners Memorial Hospital, Middlesboro, Kentucky, 1955-59; Swedish Hospital, Seattle, Washington, 1959-63; Middlesboro Community Hospital, Staff Member 1963 to present, Chief of Staff 1974-75; Clairborne County Hospital, Tazewell, Tennessee, 1963 to present; Pineville Community Hospital, 1963 to present; Holds Medical Licenses to Practice in West Virginia, Washington, Missouri, Mississippi, Ohio, Kentucky, Tennessee, Texas, North Carolina, South Carolina, Alabama, California, Virginia; Private Practice, Middlesboro, Kentucky; Medical Clinics - Birmingham Women's Medical Clinic, Mobile Women's Medical Clinic (both in Alabama), Volunteer Medical Clinic (Tennessee), Jackson Women's Medical Clinic (Mississippi); Consultant, Battelle Pacific Northwest Laboratories, Wyeth Laboratories, World Population Council, Abbott Laboratories, Julius Schmid Inc.; Number of Inventions, including Intra-Uterine Birth Control Device known as Saf-T-Coil, Currette Device, Intra-Uterine U Stem Pessary, Disposal Shoe Cover, Intrauterine Device Inserter, Rotating Wing Aircraft, Shielded Intrauterine Device. Organizational Memberships: American Board of Obstetrics-Gynecology (diplomate); American College of Surgeons; American College of Obstetrics-Gynecology; Washington State Obstetrical

Society; Seattle Professional Engineers Society; Southern Medical Association; Bell County Medical Society. Community Activities: World Population Council; Maternal and Infant Care Project, Bell County, Kentucky; M&I Clinics. Religion: First Presbyterian Church of Middlesboro, Deacon. Honors and Awards: Invitation to Scientific Sessions of Fifth National Congress of Iranian Gynecologists and Obstetricians in Tehran, Iran; Participant, Pan American Medical Association 42nd Annual Congress, Buenos Aires; Attended First International Congress of Gynecological Laparoscopy, November 1973; Listed in *Who's Who in the South, Men of Achievement, Royal Blue Book, Notable Americans, Marquis Who's Who, International Who's Who in Community Service,* Others. Address: 322 Englewood Road, Middlesboro, Kentucky 40965.

Robinson, Renault A

National Information Officer. Personal: Born September 8, 1942, in Chicago, Illinois. Education: B.A., M.A., Roosevelt College. Career: Patrolman, Chicago Police Department, 1964 to present; Executive Director, Afro-American Patrolmen's League, 1970 to present; National Information Officer, National Black Police Association, 1972 to present. Organizational Memberships: Chicago Forum; Meeting Planners International; American Society of Criminology; Committee on Foreign and Domestic Affairs; Concerned Committee on Police Reform. Community Activities: League to Improve the Community (secretary-treasurer, 1970 to present). Honors and Awards: Recognition Award, Catholic Interracial Council of Chicago, 1969; Civil Liberties Award, Illinois Division of American Civil Liberties Union, 1969; Named One of Top Ten Men of Year, Chicago Jaycees, 1970; Recognition Award, N.I.U. Black Arts Festival, 1971; Certificate of Brotherhood, Malcolm X College, 1972; Certificate of Merit, 1975, Malcolm X College; Humanitarian Award, Youth for Christ Choir, 1973; Award from Black Olympics, 1973; Certificate of Award, Search for Truth, 1973; Phi Beta Lambda; National Black Social Workers Award, 1974; Outstanding and Dedicated Service Award, Westside Christian Parish, 1974; Recognition of Community Service, League of Martin, Milwaukee, 1974; Black SPEAR for Serving the Masses, Farragut High School, 1974; Achievement Award, Charles Douglas and Company, 1974; Certificate of Appreciation for Outstanding and Dedicated Service, B.S.P.A., 1975; Award in Appreciation of Dedication to People, Paul J. Hall Boys Club, 1975; Third Annual Dr. Martin Luther King Jr. Award, S.C.L.C. Suburban Chapter, 1975; Award of Merit, Eternal Flames Production Inc., 1975; National Association of Black Social Workers Service Award for Outstanding Contribution to the Black Community, 1975; "I Am My Brother's Keeper" Award, Policemen for a Better Gary, Indiana, 1975; Award for Outstanding Achievement, Black Students Psychological Association, 1975; Appreciation Award, The Guardians, 1975; A.A.B.S. Award for Excellence, 1976; Service to the Community Award, Newspaper Guild, 1976; Humanitarian Service Award, Centers for New Horizons, Inc., 1976; Gratitude and Appreciation Award, Kiwanis Club of Roseland, 1976; Affirmative Action Award, Breadbasket Commercial Association, 1976; Public Service Award, Cook County Bar Association, 1976; John D. Rockefeller IV Youth Award, 1979; Listed in *Who's Who in the Midwest, Outstanding Young Men of America, International Who's Who in Community Service, Who's Who Among Black Americans, Contemporary Notables, Who's Who in America, Who's Who in the World, International Who's Who of Intellectuals.* Address: Lock Box 49122, Chicago, Illinois 60649.

Rodden, Donna Strickland

Mayor. Personal: Born August 10, 1926; Mother of Roberta Ann Tundermann (Mrs. Leonard), Ellen Christine Capurso (Mrs. Alphonse). Education: B.S., Syracuse University, 1946; M.S. State University of New York at Brockport, 1962; Further Studies at the University of Toronto, State University of New York at Geneseo, New York University (New York City). Career: Editor, Lyndonville, Enterprise, 1947-48; Editor, *Herald Tribune*, Middleport, New York, 1948-49; Television Director, Cayton, Inc., 1949-56; Library Media Specialist, Albion High School, 1963 to present; Owner, Teddy Bear Nursery School, 1956-58; Professional Writer, 1958 to present; Mayor, Village of Albion, 1973 to present. Organizational Memberships: National Education Association; New York State Teachers Association; Northwestern Frontier Association of Village Officials, 1973 to present (president, 1980-81). Community Activities: Staff Columnist for "Yankee Homesteader", 1981-82; Orleans County Mental Health Association (president, 1970-71); Orleans County Mental Hygiene Board Chairman (1975-77); NYS Program Director, Mental Health Association (1971-72); Orleans County Council on the Arts (president, 1975-77); Cobblestone Society (director, 1976-80); New York State Friendship Force, 1977 (by appointment of Governor); New York State Concerned Citizens for the Arts (co-chairman, 1978-81); Swan Library (director); National Business and Professional Women's Clubs (past president, past district director); International Platform Association; Order of the Eastern Star (past matron); A.B.E.E.L. Rebekkahs. Religion: Albion First Baptist Church, Sunday School Teacher. Published Works: Three Songs, "St. Mary's of the Snow", "You Are My Angel", "Top of the Tower"; Publisher of "The Bear House" (W.M.S. Publication) 1982; "Missouri Farm Boy" (McFadden) 1949. Honors and Awards: Commendation, President Nixon, 1970; Girl Scout U.S.A. Distinguished Sue Award, 1973; National Organization of Women, "Women Who Changed the World" Award, 1973; American Legion Citizenship Award, 1976; Kennedy Foundation Medal, 1975; League of Women Voters Woman in Government Award, 1975; Omega Alpha Junior Chamber of Commerce Presidential Award, 1975. Address: 327 West Bank Street, Albion, New York 14411.

Rodgers, Joseph J

College Professor. Personal: Born November 22, 1939; Son of Mrs. Mary H. Rodgers. Education: B.A., summa cum laude, Morehouse College, 1962; M.A., University of Wisconsin, 1965; Ph.D., University of Southern California, 1969. Career: Professor, Lincoln University; Professional Writer for Publication on Middle East/North Africa. Organizational Memberships: Black Conference on Higher Education (secretary, 1980 to present); Modern Language Association; American Association of University Professors; American Council on the Teaching of Foreign Languages. Community Activities: Caribbean-American Scholars Exchange Program, Special Assignment to the Dominican Republic, 1975; Host to Ambassador Andrew Young and Presenter of Honorary Degree to Him, 1977; Pennsylvania Advisory Group on Global Education, 1978; Appointed Danforth Associate, Danforth Foundation, 1981; Traveling Humanist Lecturer, Pennsylvania Humanities Council. Honors and Awards: Profiles in Feature Story in *The Philadelphia Bulletin*, 1981; Interviewed by United Press International Reporter Leslie Taylor; Interviewed by Joel A. Spivak of N.B.C.; Lindback Award for Distinguished Teaching, 1974; Merrill Travel-Study Fellow, Grenoble, France, 1959-60. Address: Oxhaven -38, Oxford, Pennsylvania 19363.

Rodine-Pederson, Gjerstru (Trudy) Maria

University Lecturer. Personal: Born April 24, 1929; Daughter of Nils and Alma Lansjoen; Married Floyd H. Rodine; Mother of Deborah Lee, Kristin Karin. Education: Attended Gustavus Adolphus College, St. Peter, Minnesota, 1946-48; B.A. 1966, M.A. 1970, Central Washington University, Ellensburg, Washington. Career: University Lecturer, Central Washington University; Former Elementary School Teacher; Owner/Manager, Pederson Press. Community Activities: Volunteer Teacher, West Kidlington, Oxfordshire, England, 1975; Summer Art Program Instructor, Community Gallery, Ellensburg, Washington; Contributor at Major

Conferences: International Congress on Arts and Communication, Queens College, Cambridge, England-July 1982; Washington Association for the Education of Young Children, May 1980 and May 1981. Religion: Presbyterian, Sunday School Superintendent 1955-61. Published Works: *Lessons from Britain; A Pioneer Experience.* Honors and Awards: Magna Cum Laude Graduate, Central Washington University, 1966; Teacher of the Year Award, 1971; Listed in *Who's Who in the West, Who's Who in Women of the World, International Register of Profiles, Who's Who of American Women, The Directory of Distinguished Americans for Contributions to Education, Personalities of the West and Midwest,* Phi Alpha Theta-International History Honorary. Address: Route 4, Box 133, Ellensburg, Washington 98926.

Rodkiewicz, Czeslaw M

Professor. Personal: Born in Poland. Education: Passed Special Entrance Examination to Technical University of Warsaw; Dip. Ing., Mechanical Engineering, Polish University College, London, England; M.Sc., University of Illinois; Ph.D., Cleveland Case Institute of Technology; Graduate, Artillery Academy, Zambrow, Poland. Military: Served in the Polish Home Army, after escaping from a German Prisoner of War Camp; Captured Again, Liberated in 1945; Joined Polish II Corps, Italy. Career: Research Engineer, English Electronic Company, working with a trans-sonic wind tunnel; Technical Assistant, Dowty Equipment, Canada; Staff, Ryerson Institute of Technology, 1955-58; Professor, Department of Mechanical Engineering, University of Alberta, Edmonton, Canada, 1958 to present; Survey of Manufacturing Processes of Major Industrial Plants in Ontario and Quebec, Summer 1956; Engine Laboratory of the National Research Council, Ottawa, Ontario, Summer 1959; Engineering Division, Atomic Engery of Canada Ltd., Chalk River, Ontario, Summer 1960. Organizational Memberships: New York Academy of Sciences; American Society of Mechanical Engineers (fellow); Polish Society of Theoretical and Applied Mechanics (honorary foreign member); Canadian Society of Mechanical Engineers; Sigma Xi; Canadian Medical and Biological Engineering Society; Professional Engineers of Ontario; First World Tribology Conference, Indian Institute of Technology, Madras, New Delhi, India (advisory council; chairman, 1972); National Canadian Congress of Applied Mechanics (sessional chairman, 1975, 1977); Engineering Students Society of the University of Canada, Edmonton (honorary president, 1962); Engineering Faculty Council Committee to Review the Executive and Administrative Structure of the Faculty of Engineering of the University of Alberta, 1977-78. Community Activities: Polish Canadian Congress in Alberta (president, 1969-71, 1971-73, 1973-75); Chairman of Committee for Building S.E.S.E.M. Day Care Centre, Edmonton, Alberta, 1976-77; Edmonton Flying Club, Holder of Private Pilot's License; E.E.E.S.S. (chairman, resolution committee, Banff, Alberta, 1977; research and academic advisory committee, 1976-77); Faculty of Engineering, University of Alberta (salaries and promotions committee, 1979-80) Invited by International Centre for Mechanical Sciences, Udine, Italy, to Organize International Seminar on Engineering Aspects of Arterial Blood Flow. Published Works: Author of Numerous Papers on Fluid Mechanics and Heat Transfer, Hypersonic Flight, Lubrication, Blood Flow land Ice Formations. Honors and Awards: Recipient of Grant from United States Air Force; Received Polish Canadian Congress Highest Honor, Gold Decoration for Outstanding Service to the Community, 1976; Invitation for Presentation at Physiologisches Institute der Universitat Graz, Graz, Austria, 1980; Presentation, 28th International Congress of Physiological Sciences, Budapest, Hungary, 1980; Seven Lectures at International Centre for Mechanical Sciences, Udine, Italy, 1980; Invited to International Congress of Scholars of Polish Origin Residing Outside Poland, 1979; Invited Lecturer at Technical University of Gdansk, 1979; Invited Presentation at Joint Session of Canadian Society of Mechanical Engineers and the Canadian National Research Council's Associate Committee on Tribology, University of Sherbrooke, Quebec, 1979; Invitation to Specialists Meeting of Twenty Scientists from Europe and North America on the Role of Fluid Mechanics in Atherogenesis, 1978; Keynote Speaker, 50th Anniversary Celebrations of Polish-Canadian Society, 1977, and 100th Anniversary of Canada Celebration, 1967; Listed in *Who's Who in the World, International Register of Profiles, Book of Honor, International Who's Who of Intellectuals, Community Leaders and Noteworthy Americans, Men of Achievement, Dictionary of International Biography, Notable Americans of the Bicentennial Era, Who's Who in the West, International Who's Who in Community Service, Men and Women of Distinction.* Address: Department of Mechanical Engineering, University of Alberta, Edmonton, Alberta, Canada.

Roemer, William Nicolas

Scientist. Personal: Born February 8, 1925; Married Rachel L. Hatton. Education: Attended Bowling Green Business University; Self-Education in Horticulture and Agricultural Chemicals, Plastics, Mechanical Engineering. Career: Self-Employed Scientist in Research and Development. Organizational Memberships: United States Chamber of Commerce; Weed Society, Oxford, England; Horticultural Society of America; Top Farmers of American Association. Community Activities: Kentucky Historical Society; Warren County Historical Society; Genealogical Society of Warren County; Kentucky Colonel; American Security Council; (national advisory board); Young Republican National Federation (sponsor); Liberty Lobby; Stockholders of America, Inc.; Kentucky Republican Party (1981 sustaining member); Lifetime Member of the G.O.P.; Capitol Hill Club, Washington D.C., Worked with P.O.W.'s in World War II, Korean War and Vietnam War by Being a Monitor of Their Messages on Short-Wave Radio; Conservation Caucus, Inc.; American Biographical Institute; International Biographical Institute (fellow); Knights of Columbus. Honors and Awards: Kentucky Colonel, 1969; 25 Year Award from Knights of Columbus. Address: 2150 Smallhouse Road, Bowling Green, Kentucky 42101.

Rogers, Gifford Eugene

Consulting Engineer. Personal: Born May 22, 1920; Son of Mr. and Mrs. George E. Monroe; Married E. Marjorie Mull; Father of Robert Dennis, Michael Edwin, Barry David, Gifford Eugene Jr. Education: B.S.C.E., University of Nebraska, 1943; M.S.C.E., Purdue University, 1948. Military: Served in the United States Army, 1942-46, attaining the rank of 1st Lieutenant in the Corps of Engineers. Career: Consulting Engineer; Former Positions of Chief Engineer and Military Engineer. Organizational Memberships: American Society of Civil Engineers (fellow); National Society of Professional Engineers; American Academy of Environmental Engineers (diplomate); Committee on Irrigation, Drainage and Flood Control (life member); American Water Works Association; Society for International Development (life member); American Society of Agricultural Engineers. Community Activities: Dominican-American Institute, Santo Domingo, Dominican Republic (board of directors, 1964); Union Church Troop, Boy Scouts of America Guatemala City (committee member, 1961-62). Honors and Awards: Diploma of Honor, Cartographic Institute of Guatemala, 1962; Diploma of Honor, Agrarian Institute of Guatemala, 1962; Explorers Club, Elected in Grade of Fellow, 1980. Address: c/o Monroe, 515 North Grace Street, Grand Island, Nebraska 68801.

Romain, Margaret Ann Kutcher

Public Accountant. Personal: Born January 1, 1940, in Mercer, Pennsylvania; Daughter of Peter Paul and Susie Anne Murcko Kutcher; Married Joseph Romain Jr.; Mother of Lucretia Ann, Kimberly Rose, Annette Marie. Education: Graduate of Mercer High

School, 1957; Attended Youngstown State University, 1957-58, 1968-69; LaSalle Extension University, Pennsylvania State University, Alliance College. Career: Secretary-Bookkeeper, Voytik Construction Company, 1957-58; Bookkeeper, Ernst, Inc., 1958-60; Bookkeeper, Mort-Bohn and Associates, CPAs, 1960-62; Bookkeeper, D. G. Reed and H. Hudson, P.A.s, 1962-64; Assistant Office Manager, J. V. McNicholas Transfer Company, 1965-66; Partner, Public Accounting, Reed-Romain and Associates, 1966-70; Self Employed Public Accountant, 1970-76, 1978 to present; Partner, Public Accounting, Romain-Pendel and Associates, 1976-78; Owner-Partner, R-P Computer Services, 1976-80; Owner-Partner, Romain Pendel Office Rental, 1976-80. Organizational Memberships: National Society of Public Accountants (associate state director, 1977 to present); National Association of Enrolled Agents (executive director of State of Pennsylvania, 1976 to present); Pennsylvania Society of Public Accountants (state board of directors, 1973 to present; executive committee, 1978 to present; state secretary, 1978 to present; editor, *Pennsylvania Accountant*, 1980 to present); Pennsylvania Society of Enrolled Agents (president, 1972, 1973, 1974; executive director, 1975 to present; received award for services as president); National Association of Enrolled Federal Tax Accountants (secretary, 1972, 1973); Pennsylvania Public Accountants Advisory Committee, 1977-79 (vice chairman, 1977-79). Community Activities: Saddlemates Saddle Club (treasurer, 1979); Sharpsville Centennial (chairperson for Children's Pet Parade; 1974 First Runner-Up in Queen's Contest); Baldwin Organ Club (president, 1969); 4-H Leader, Sharpsville Charmetters, 1978 to present. Religion: St. John's Episcopal Church, Assistant Treasurer 1974, 1975; executive board of Episcopal Churchwomen 1977-78. Honors and Awards: Dupont National Civic Endowment; Listed in *American Registry Series, Book of Honor, Community Leaders and Noteworthy Americans, Contemporary Personalities, Dictionary of International Biography, Directory of Distinguished Americans, International Book of Honor, International Who's Who in Community Service, International Who's Who of Intellectuals, Notable Americans, Personalities of the East, Personalities of America, Who's Who of American Women, Who's Who Among Women Civic Leaders, Who's Who in the East, Who's Who in Finance and Industry, World Who's Who of Women.* Address: 125 Koehler Drive, P.O. Box 27, Sharpsville, Pennsylvania 16150.

Romano, Geraldine M

Teacher, Counselor. Personal: Born July 7, 1937; Daughter of Mr. and Mrs. Daniel Romano. Education: B.A., M.A., Seton Hall University. Career: Teacher, Counselor, Hospice Worker; Former Elementary School Principal. Organizational Memberships: American Personnel and Guidance Association; American School Counselor, New York Personnel and Guidance Association. Community Activities: Hospice Volunteer Program in Schenectady, 1980 to present; Newark Archdiocesan Elementary School Program, 1979; Work with Terminally Ill Children, 1975 to present. Religion: Catholic, Member of Religious Teachers Filippini. Honors and Awards: Listed in *Who's Who in the East, Personalities of America, Community Leaders in America.* Address: 1383 Pleasant St., Schenectady, New York 12303.

Geraldine Romano

Romanoff, Marjorie Reinwald

Adjunct Professor. Personal: Born September 29, 1923; Daughter of David E. and Gertrude R. Reinwald; Married Milford M. Romanoff; Mother of Bennett S., Lawrence M., Janet Beth (deceased). Education: B.Ed. 1947, M.Ed. 1968, Ed.D. 1976, University of Toledo. Career: Teacher, Old Orchard Elementary School, Toledo, 1947-48; Substitute Teacher, Toledo Public Schools, 10 years; Tutored Children in Reading, 10 years; Teacher, McKinley School, Toledo, 1964-65; Conducted Seminars in New Math for Faculty at McKinley School, 1964-65; Consultant to Curriculum Revision in Language Arts, Toledo Public Schools, 1966; Conducted Workshops in Creative Writing for International Reading Association, 1972; Supervisor of Student Teachers, The University of Toledo, 1968-73; Chairperson, Long Range Planning Committee, National Pi Lambda Theta, 1979-84; Speaker, Toledo Association of Student Teachers, 1971; Speaker, Future Teachers of America, DeVilbiss High School, 1971; Demonstration, Beta Eta, Pi Lambda Theta, "Social Interaction Techniques", 1973; Consultant to Educational Planning Committee, Toledo Public Schools, for Curriculum Revisions in Reading Instruction, 1973; Consultant to Toledo Hebrew Academy Elementary School, 1969-75, 1976-79; Instructor, Mary Manse College, Toledo, 1974; Consultant, Toledo Hospital Nursing Educators, 1975; Consultant, Toledo Board of Education, Middle East Studies, 1975-76; Teacher, The Temple Religious School, 1947-73; Conducted Teacher Education Workshop, Ryder Elementary School, 1975; Teacher Education Workshops, Hebrew Academy Elementary School, 1975-76; Consultant, Toledo Public Schools, Ethnic Studies Program, 1976-77; Instructor, Adult Education, Children's Literature, Sylvania Public Schools, 1977; Workshop, Great Book Leaders, 1977; Attended National Conference, International Reading Association, 1977; Instructor, The University of Toledo Community and Technical College, 1977; Adjunct Assistant Professor, Bowling Green State University, Elementary Education, 1978 to present; Instructor, American Language Institute, The University of Toledo, 1978 to present; Assistant to the Director, American Language Institute, 1979; Speaker, Temple Shomer Emunim, Sylvania, 1979; Conducted Workshop, Hadassah, 1980; Ethnic Studies Committee, History Department, The University of Toledo, 1980. Organizational Memberships: American Educational Research Association; International Reading Association (national, state and local groups); American Association of Colleges of Teacher Education; National Society for the Study of Education; Association for Supervision and Curriculum Development; Toledo Association of Children's Literature; National Council of Teachers of English; Teachers of English to Speakers of Other Languages. Community Activities: Lucas County Children's Services Board (board of trustees, 1974-76); Cummings Treatment Center for Adolescents (board of trustees, 1976-79; president, liaison to community chest, 1978-80); Toledo Bureau of Jewish Education (board of trustees, 1976-79; vice president; president, 1982-84); Citizens Advisory Committee to Crosby Gardens, 1976-79 (board of trustees, 1979-82); Big Sisters (board of trustees, 1978-79); Big Brothers (board of trustees, 1980); Jewish Family Service (vice president, 1981-85; board of trustees, 1978-83); Jewish Welfare Federation (budget and planning committee, 1979-80); Juvenile Court, Citizens Review Board (board member, 1979-83); Community Planning Council (board member, 1980-83); Americans for Democratic Action (former board member); Common Cause; C.A.R.I.H. (asthma research); Council for Jewish Women; American Civil Liberties Union; Darlington House Home for the Aged; Great Books Group (founder of Toledo group); Hadassah (past president, Toledo chapter; former board member, Central States Region); Northwestern University Alumni Association; Planned Parenthood; Organization for Rehabilitation through Training; Toledo Museum of Art; Professor of Record, University of Toledo, College of Education; Course for Great Books Leaders, 1983; Toledo Symphony Orchestra Association; Toledo Modern Art Group; Toledo Zoological Society; The Temple Congregation Shomer Emunin (former Sisterhood board member); Jewish Welfare Federation Speakers Bureau (former executive board member, women's division); The University of Toledo Alumni Association; Women's International League for Peace and Freedom; Miami Children's Home Auxiliary; Board of Jewish Education; Cummings; Grosby Gardens. Honors and Awards: Phi Kappa Phi; Kappa Delta Pi; Pi Lambda Theta; Phi Delta Kappa; Fellow, International Biographical Association, 1979; Listed in *World Who's Who of Women, Community Leaders and Noteworthy Americans, International Register of Profiles, Who's Who in American Women, Who's Who in Midwest America.* Address: 2514 Bexford Place, Toledo, Ohio 43606.

Romanoff, Milford Martin

General Contractor, Architectural Designer. Personal: Born August 21, 1921; Son of Barney S. Romanoff (deceased); Edythe

Romanoff Bort; Married Marjorie R.; Father of Bennett S., Lawrence M., Janet Beth (deceased). Education: Attended the University of Michigan College of Architecture, 1939-42; B.B.A., University of Toledo, 1943. Military: Served in the United States Navy, 1943-45, attaining the rank of Lieutenant. Career: Designed and Built Innumerable Homes, Schools, Commerical and Industrial Buildings in Toledo and Surrounding Area, Columbus, Ohio, and Chicago, Illinois, 1946-81. Organizational Memberships: Neighborhood Improvement Foundation of Toledo, Inc. (charter member). Community Activities: Chamber of Commerce, 1946-50; B'nai B'rith Softball League (president, 1955-57); Toledo Lodge, B'nai B'rith (president, 1957-59); Ohio Association, B'nai B'rith (president, 1959-60); Anti-Defamation League (board of directors); Hillel Organization on Ohio Campuses (board of directors); National B'nai B'rith (district deputy, 1960-62); Masonic Lodge, Yondota, 25 years; Toledo Amateur Baseball and Softball Commission (chairman, 1979-80); Toledo Zoological Society; Lucas County Overall Economic Development Committee, 1979-81; University of Toledo Centennial Mall Committee, 1978-81; University of Toledo Beautification Committee, 1977-82; Citizens Advisory Recreation Commission of Toledo, 1973-81; Medical College of Ohio Campus Advisory Committee, 1980-81; Temple Shomer Emunim; Emunim Brotherhood (board of directors, 1956-58, 1979-81); Toledo Chapter of Hadassah (associate); Toledo Museum of Art; Toledo Symphony Orchestra Association; Crosby Gardens; University of Michigan Alumni Association; University of Toledo Tower Club; Zeta Beta Tau; Lucas County Children's Services (board of trustees, 1981-84); Cummings Treatment Center for Adolescents (board of trustees, 1981-84); Advisory Board of Mental Health and Retardation, 1982-84. Honors and Awards: Listed in *Personalities of the West and Midwest, Who's Who in Midwest America.* Address: 2514 Bexford Place, Toledo, Ohio 43606.

Romero-Barceló, Carlos Antonio

Governor of Puerto Rico. Personal: Born September 4, 1932; Son of Josefina Barceló de Romero, Antonio Romero-Moreno (both deceased); Married Kathleen Donnelly de Romero; Father of Carlos, Andrés, Juan Carlos, Melinda. Education: Graduate of Phillips Exeter Academy, Exeter, New Hampshire, 1949; B.A., Yale University, 1953; LL.B., University of Puerto Rico, 1956. Career: Attorney in Private Practice, San Juan, Puerto Rico, 1956-68; Mayor of San Juan, 1969-77; Governor of Puerto Rico, 1977 to present. Organizational Memberships: National League of Cities (former member; president, 1975); Southern Governors Association (chairman, 1980-81); National Governors Association; New Progressive Party of Puerto Rico (president, 1974 to present). Community Activities: National Advisory Council for Disadvantaged Children, 1976. Religion: Roman Catholic. Honors and Awards: Honorary LL.D., University of Bridgeport, 1977; Outstanding Young Man of the Year, Jaycees Award, 1968; James J. and Jane Hoey Award for Interracial Justice, Catholic Interracial Council of New York City, 1977; Special Gold Medal Award for Achievement in Bilingual Education, The Spanish Institute, New York City, 1979; Attorney General's Medal for Eminent Public Service, United States Department of Justice, 1981. Address: La Fortaleza, San Juan, Puerto Rico 00901.

Roper, William Edward

Milford M Romanoff

Federal Government Executive, Engineer. Personal: Born May 31, 1942, in Baraboo, Wisconsin; Son of William Laverne (deceased) and Gladys Rose Kingsley Roper; Education: B.S. 1965, M.S. 1966, University of Wisconsin, Ph.D., Michigan State University, 1969; Graduate, Federal Executive Institute, 1979; Graduate, Federal Executive Development Program, 1980. Military: Served in the United States Army Corps of Engineers, 1970-72, attaining the rank of Captain; Service in the United States Army Reserves, 1975 to present, with the rank of Major. Career: Farm Manager, Madison, Wisconsin, 1957-65; Faculty, University of Wisconsin-Madison, 1965-66; Faculty, Michigan State University. 1966-69; Faculty, North Carolina State University, 1969-70; Chief Industrial and Agricultural Waste Section, Office of Solid Waste Management, Environmental Protection Agency, Washington, D.C., 1972-73; Chief, Surface Transportation Regulatory Programs, Office of Noise Abatement and Control, 1973-74; Chief Engineer Advisor, Standards and Regulations Division, 1974-75; Chief, Surface Transportation Branch, 1975-80; Director, Plans and Programs Staff, 1980-81; Director, Research and Development for Civil Works Program, United States Army Corp of Engineers, Washington, D.C., 1981 to present. Organizational Memberships: Registered Professional Engineer, Wisconsin; American Association for the Advancement of Science; National Wildlife Federation; National Trust for Historic Preservation; National Academy of Science Transportation and Research Board; Smithsonian Institution Foundation (resident associate); A&P Corporation (board member, 1979 to present); B&K Associates (president, 1981 to present); Carl-Chris Corporation (board member, 1981 to present); Federal Executive Institute Alumni Association (policy issue committee, 1980 to present); Crystal Mall 2 (chairman, emergency preparedness committee, 1980-81); Interagency Task Force on Pesticide Container Disposal (deputy chairman, 1972-73); Presidential Committee on Forest Resources, 1972 to present; Secretary of Transportation Task Force on Automotive Designs for the 1980s, 1977-78. Community Activities: Sunny View Citizen Association (executive board, 1970-72). Religion: Aldergate Methodist Church, Administrative Board 1975-77. Published Works: Number of Professional Publications including "Ground Vehicle Noise Control", "Noise Control and Dieselization", "Evaluating Exhaust System Acoustical Performances". Honors and Awards: The Defense Service Award and Distinguished Military Service Award; Silver Medal for Superior Service, E.P.A., 1977; Distinguished Service, Monetary Award, 1978; Distinguished XX Quality Increase Award, 1979; Outstanding Performance Award, 1981. Address: 9339 Boothe Street, Alexandria, Virginia 22309.

Rorabaugh, Donald Thomas

Metallurgist, Project Engineer. Personal: Born September 8, 1944; Son of Mr. and Mrs. D. Rorabaugh; Married Joan Lorraine Hoff; Father of Dennis Allen. Education: B.S. 1967, M.S. Drexel University, Philadelphia, Pennyslvania; Postgraduate Studies in Business and Management, 1970; Number of Job-Related College and Government Short Courses, 1970 to present. Career: Metallurgist/Project Engineer, R&D Studies; Former Metallurgist/Project Associate and Quality Control Manager. Organizational Memberships: Research Society of North America; New York Academy of Sciences; American Society for Metals; American Institute of Metallurgical Mining and Petroleum Engineers; American Defense Preparedness Association. Community Activities: Young Men Christian Association (sports and building committee; judo instructor; self defense and exercise instructor); Amateur Athletic Union (sports committee; official; referee); Boy Scouts of America (Eagle Scout with Gold Palm; assistant scout master; assistant explorer leader). Religion: Usher, Holy Name Society. Honors and Awards: Number of Outstanding Performance Awards; Over 80 Suggestion Awards; Number of Letters of Commendation and Special Act Awards for Significant R&D Activities; Y.M.C.A. Award for Dedicated Service to the Community; Listed in Several Biographical Publications. Address: P.O. Box 477, Netcong, New Jersey 07857.

Rorschach, Martha Kay

Educator. Personal: Born July 14, 1938; Daughter of Mr. and Mrs. I. M. King, Jr.; Married to Richard G.; Step-Mother of Richard H., Reagan C., Andrew M. Education: Attended Baylor University, 1956-58; B.A., S.M.U., 1961; M.A., Stephen F. Austin State University, 1972. Career: Instructor of Fashion Merchandising, Kilgore College; Organizer and Director, City National Bank,

Kilgore, Texas (audit committee); Vice President and Director, Little River Drilling Company; Breeder of Arabian and half-Arabian horses, Shadowbrook Farm; Former Instructor of Art, Oxford Studio; Former Head Fashion Designer, Higginbotham-Bailey Manufacturing Company, Dallas, Texas; Former Freelance Fashion Designer, Miami, Florida, Dallas, and Los Angeles, California; Former Teacher, Groveton High School; Former Jr. High School Teacher. Organizational Memberships: Kappa Pi; East Texas Fine Arts Association (president, 1974, vice president, 1973); Texas Jr. College Teachers Association; Texas Jr. College Management Educators Association. Community Activities: American Cancer Society (director of benefit style show, 1979 and 1980); March of Dimes; Kilgore Community Concerts Association; Xi Pi Mu Chapter of Beta Sigma Phi (vice president, 1977); President of City Council, 1975; Kilgore Improvement and Beautification Association; Parent-Teacher Association; American Horse Show Association; Arabian Horse Club of Texas (vice president and director, 1979); Gulf Coast Arabian Horse Club; International Arabian Horse Association. Religion: Member of First Presbyterian Church, Kilgore, Texas (choir member, stewardship committee). Honors and Awards: Named "Miss Waco", 1957; First runner-up, "Miss Texas", 1957; Kappa Sigma Sweetheart, S.M.U., 1960; Outstanding Young Woman of America, 1972; Kentucky Colonel, 1978; Her horses have won many local, regional, national and international championships. Address: Shadowbrook Farm, Route 4, Box 210, Kilgore, Texas 75662.

Rosenberg, Leonard H

Insurance Executive. Personal: Born December 1, 1912, in Baltimore, Maryland; Son of Henry I and Laura Hollander Rosenberg (both deceased); Married Edna Mazer, on November 20, 1936; Father of Theodore, Victor, Laurie, Leonard Jr. Education: Graduate, Forest Park High School, 1930; B.S.M.S., Carnegie Institute of Technology, 1934; Graduate of the Air Force Navigation School,Central Instructors School; Courses in Philosophy, Loyola College; Life Insurance Marketing, S.M.U.; Courses in Insurance Management, University of Maryland; United States Air Force Command and General Staff School. Military: Served in the United States Air Force, Education Staff Specialty Rating, 1956 to present; Rank of Lieutenant Colonel, Retired. Career: The Chesapeake Life Insurance Company, President and Founder 1956-73, Chairman of the Board 1973 to present; Strasco Insurance Agency Inc., Insurance Salesman, Underwriter and General Manager 1935 to present, Vice President; Director, Bayshore Industries, 1949-61; The Chesapeake Fund, Inc., Vice President 1961-68, President 1968-74; The Chesapeake Investment Corp., Vice President 1963-68, President 1968-74; Columbus Mutual Life Insurance Company, State Agent 1939-55; Director, Green Associates, 1960-73; Mid-Atlantic Real Estate Investment Trust Board, Treasurer 1971-75; National City Bank of Maryland, Director, Chairman of the Finance Committee and Member of Executive Committee 1967-70; Preferred Equity Insurance Company, President, 1968-70, Chairman of the Board 1970-71; Reliance Life Insurance Company of Pittsburgh, District Manager 1935-39; Suburban Trust Company, Special Advisory Board 1970-73; Instructor, Civilian Pilot Training Program, The Johns Hopkins University and University of Baltimore, 1939-42; Instructor, Life Office Management Association Courses, 1957 to present; Math and Physics Instructor, Baltimore City College Night School, 1935-39. Organizational Memberships: Insurance Hall of Fame (board of governors, 1970 to present); International Insurance Seminars (board of directors and board of governors, 1970 to present; chairman, finance directorate, 1972 to present); Maryland Life and Health Insurance Guaranty Association (assistant secretary and treasurer, 1972-81; secretary/treasurer, 1981 to present); Maryland Public Broadcasting Commission (chairman, 1971 to present; commissioner, 1967-71); National Association of Life Companies (board of directors, 1965 to present; president, 1968-70); American Institute of Astronautics and Aeronautics. Community Activities: Center Stage (board of directors, 1977 to present); Community College of Baltimore (board of trustees, 1976 to present); The Humanities Institute, Inc. (board of advisors, 1979 to present); Baltimore Museum of Art; Baltimore Symphony Orchestra Association; Carnegie-Mellon University (Baltimore area advisory); Institute of Navigation; Walters Art Gallery. Published Works: *Development of Modern Merchandising in the Life Insurance Industry* 1972, *Pattern Selling* 1950, *Pointers* 1949-56; Number of Professional Articles, including "Adjusting Life Company Earnings: A Brief Survey of Alternatives", "Advancement Through Training", and "Average Income Families are our Average Sale." Honors and Awards: Career Development Award, B'nai B'rith Career and Counseling Services, 1975; Outstanding Contribution to the Field of Occupational Education, State University of New York at Buffalo; Executive Leadership in Training, American Society for Training and Development, 1970; Outstanding Alumni, Carnegie-Mellon University, 1967; Outstanding Alumni, Tau Delta Phi Fraternity, 1967; Outstanding Service to the Insurance Industry, William P. White Award, 1967; Listed in *Leading Men in the United States of America, Who's Who in Aviation, Who's Who in Commerce and Industry, Who's Who in Community Service, Who's Who in the East, Who's Who in Government, Who's Who in Insurance, Who's Who in World Jewry, Dictionary of International Biography, Men of Achievement, Men and Women of Distinction, Community Leaders and Noteworthy Americans, Personalities of the South, Personalities of America.* Address: 22 Bouton Green, Baltimore, Maryland 21210.

Leonard H Rosenberg

Rosenthal, Leonard Jason

Microbiologist, Virologist. Personal: Born June 23, 1942, in Boston, Massachusetts; Son of Louis and Dorothy Rosenthal; Married Nancy Jo Cox; Father of Rebecca Lee. Education: B.A., University of Vermont, 1964; M.A., Southern Illinois University, 1966; Ph.D., Kansas State University, 1969; Massachusetts General Hospital, 1969-73; University of Geneva, Switzerland, 1973-74; National Institute of Health, 1974-75. Career: N.I.H. Trainship, Southern Illinois University, 1964-66; Graduate Teaching Assistant 1966-69, N.S.F. Summer Trainee 1967-68, Kansas State University; Research Fellow 1969-71, Instructor 1972-73, Harvard Medical School; Research Fellow, Instructor, Massachusetts General Hospital, 1969-73; E.M.B.O. Fellow, L.S.A. Special Fellow, University of Geneva, 1973-74; Special Fellow, L.S.A. & N.I.H., National Institute of Health, 1974-75; Assistant Professor, Department of Microbiology and Member of Vincent T. Lombardi Cancer Center, Georgetown University Schools of Medicine and Dentistry, 1975 to present; Consultant, Bethesda Research Laboratories, 1976 to present. Organizational Memberships: American Society for Microbiology; Society of Sigma Xi (Georgetown Chapter, vice president 1978-79), president 1979-80); National Institute of Child Health and Human Development (contract reviewer, 1979 to present); National Science Foundation (reviewer, 1980 to present); Southeastern Organ Procurement Foundation (education committee, 1981 to present). Religion: Jewish. Honors and Awards: Leukemia Society of America Special Fellow, 1974-75; National Institutes of Health Special Fellow, 1975-76; United States Jaycees Outstanding Young Man of American National Award, 1977; Leukemia Society of America Scholar, 1980-85; Listed in *Who's Who in the East.* Address: 2 Marwood Court, Rockville, Maryland 20850.

Rosenzweig, Daphne Lange

Adjunct Associate Professor, Art Appraiser. Personal: Born July 7, 1941; Daughter of Col. and Mrs. W. W. Lange; Married Abraham Rosenzweig; Mother of Victoria Lange. Education: A.B., Mount Holyoke College, 1963; M.A. 1967, Ph.D. 1973, Columbia University. Career: Adjunct Associate Professor, Department of Art, University of South Florida; Exhibition Organizer for Museums; Art Appraiser; Former Teaching Positions at the University of New Mexico, Adelphi University, Oberlin College; Lectures Nationwide and Overseas. Organizational Memberships: College Art Association; Association for Asian Studies; Florida Japan Seminar; Japan Society; Asia Society; International House of Japan. Community Activities: Artists Alliance (board member; vice president, 1982-83); Consultant to Many American Museums and Collectors; Consultant to Morikami Museum, Norton Gallery, Museum of Fine Arts, in St. Petersburg, Society of Four Arts; Florida Japan Seminar (board member); Regional Conferences of Association of Asian Studies (former board member). Honors and Awards: Fulbright Fellowship, 1967-68, 1968-69, Republic of China; Other Travelling Fellowships, Columbia University, Oberlin College, Great Lakes Regional Association; Mary E. Woolley Fellowship, Mount Holyoke College. Address: 5212 Lawnwood Drive, Temple Terrace, Florida 33617.

Ross, Russell

Professor of Pathology. Personal: Born May 25, 1929; Married Jean Long Teller; Father of Valerie, Douglas. Education: Graduate of R. E. Lee High School, 1947; A.B., Chemistry, Cornell University, 1951; D.D.S., Columbia University, 1955; Ph.D, University of Washington, 1962. Career: Professor and Chairman of Pathology, Adjunct Professor of Biochemistry, University of Washington. Organizational Memberships: American Society for Cell Biology; Histochemical Society; Sigma Xi (secretary, University of Washington chapter); American Association for the Advancement of Science; Royal Microscopical Society (fellow); International Academy of Pathology; Electron Microscope Society of America; American Society for Experimental Pathology; American Association of University Professors; International Society for Cell Biology; American Association of Pathologists and Bacteriologists; American Heart Association (fellow, council on arteriosclerosis); Gerontological Society; The Tissue Culture Association, Foundation Cardiologique Princess Liliane, Brussels, Belgium (advisory board, 1977-82); Northwest-Rocky Mountain Regional Research Review and Advisory Committee, American Heart Association, 1979-83; American Longevity Association (scientific board, 1980 to present); National Diabetes Research Interchange (steering committee, 1980-82). Published Works: Editorial Board, Proceedings of the Society for Experimental Biology and Medicine 1971 to present, *Connective Tissue Research and International Journal* 1971 to present, *Blood Vessels* (Field Editor) 1973, *Experimental and Molecular Pathology* 1974 to present, *Cell Biology International Reports* 1976 to present, *Journal of Supramolecular Structure* 1980 to present, *American Journal of Pathology* 1980 to present; Associate Editor, *Arteriosclerosis: A Journal of Vascular Biology and Diseases*, 1980 to present; Associate Editor, *Journal of Cellular Physiology*, 1979 to present; Other Former Editorial Positions. Honors and Awards: Bausch and Lomb Science Award, 1947; Westinghouse Science Talent Search Award, Honorable Mention, 1947; Alpha Epsilon Delta; William Jarvie Society for Dental Research, 1953; Special Research Fellowship, National Institute of Dental Research, N.I.H., 1958; Career Development Research Award, National Institute Dental Research, 1962-67; Eleanor Roosevelt Fellowship, International Union Against Cancer (declined), 1966; John Simon Guggenheim Fellowship, 1966-67; Visiting Fellow, Clare Hall, Cambridge University, 1966-68; Visiting Scientist, Strangeways Research Laboratory, Cambridge, England, 1966-68; Birnberg Research Medal, Columbia University School of Dental and Oral Surgery, 1975; Tenth Geiger Memorial Lecturer, University of Southern California, 1976; Seventeenth Annual Herman Beerman Lecturer, Society for Investigative Dermatology, Washington, D.C., 1977; Sarnoff Professor of Cardiology, Duke University Medical Center, Durham, North Carolina, 1977; Organizer, Symposium to Celebrate 500th Anniversary, University of Uppsala, Sweden, 1977; Foreign Corresponding Member, Royal Belgium Academy of Sciences-Medicine, 1979 to present; George Lyman Duff Memorial Lecturer, American Heart Association Annual Scientific Sessions, Miami, Florida, 1980; Fourth International Postgraduate course on Myocardial Infraction and Angina Pectoris, Lecturer, Davos, Switzerland, 1981; Fourth I. H. Page Lecturer, Cleveland Clinic Foundation and Research Division, Cleveland, Ohio, 1981; Harvey Society, Harvey Lecture, 1982; Gordon Wilson Medal, American Clinical and Climatological Association, 1981. Address: 4811 NE 42nd St., Seattle, Washington 98105.

Rosvall, Charles William

Auctioneer. Personal: Born March 15, 1910, in Velits, Kansas; Married Opal Mae Jackson, in 1940; Father of One Son. Career: Founder, Chairman of the Board, Rosvall Auction Company, Inc., Denver, Colorado, 1940. Community Activities: Board of Counselors, Loma Linda University, California; Advisory Board, Porter Memorial Hospital, Denver. Address: 1238 South Broadway, Denver, Colorado 80210.

Roth, Frederic Hull

Certified Public Accountant. Personal: Born February 20, 1914, in Cleveland, Ohio; Son of Stanley E. and Myrtle Hull Roth (both deceased); Married Emmy Alice Braun; Father of Frederic Hull Jr., Robert Allan (deceased). Education: A.B., Wooster College, 1935; M.B.A., Harvard Graduate School of Business Administration, 1937. Career: Certified Public Accountant; Partner, Scovell, Wellington and Company, 1939; Partner, Lybrand, Ross Brothers and Montgomery; Lybrand became Coopers and Lybrand, 1973 (presently the largest international public accounting firm in the world). Organizational Memberships: National Association of Accountants; Tax Club of Cleveland; Institute of Internal Auditors; American Institute of Management; Ohio Society of C.P.A.s; American Institute of C.P.A.s; Newcomen Society of North America; International Platform Association. Community Activities: Chamber of Commerce; City Club; Rotary Club of Cleveland (director and treasurer, 1966-67); American Security Council (national advisory board); Honorary Knight of Royal Rosarians; Navy League of the United States; Cleveland Play House (director and treasurer, 1964-66; director, 1967-76; finance committee, 1968-72); U.S.S. Constitution Museum (charter member); Friends of Crawford Auto Museum (donor of classic 1957 Eldorado Brougham Cadillac); Lake Erie Lodge; Al Sirat Grotto; Lake Erie Consistory; Al Koran Shrine; Grotto Big Six; Museum of National Heritage; Ohio Historical Society Great Lakes Historical Society; Early Settlers Association; National Trust for Historic Preservation; International Society for British Genealogy and Family History; American Farmland Trust; Order of the Founders and Patriots of America; Sons of the Revolution; Sons of the American Revolution; Military Order of the Stars and Bars; Sons of Confederate Veterans; Sons of Union Veterans; Colonial Order of the Acorn; Order of Descendants of Colonial Physicians; Descendants of Colonial Clergy; Socity of the War of 1812; Sons and Daughters of Pilgrims; Center for International Security Studies. Religion: Methodist. Honors and Awards: Patriot's Award, George Washington Award, Museum of National Heritage; SIR Award 1976, Paul Harris Fellow 1979, Rotary Club of Cleveland; Listed in *Who's Who in America, Who's Who in Ohio, Who is Who in Ohio, Who's Who in the Midwest, Who's Who in Finance and Industry, Ohio Lives, National Register of Prominent Americans and International Notables; Community Leaders of America, International Yearbook and Statesmen's Who's Who, Two Thousand Men of Achievement, Dictionary of International Biography, National Cyclopedia of American Biography, International Who's Who in Community Service, Who's Who in the World, Men of Achievement, International Registry of Who's Who, Who's Who in the United States, Who's Who of Intellectuals, Personalities of the West and Midwest, Book of Honor, Personalities of America, Men and Women of Distinction, Directory of Distinguished Americans, American Registry Series.* Address: 20661 Avalon Drive, Rocky River, Ohio 44116.

Round, Bettye Hammons

Registered Real Estate Broker. Personal: Daughter of Della Ward Bishop Hammons (deceased); Mother of Alice Adair Brown (Mrs. D. D.). Education: Graduate of Forest Lake Academy; Degree in Recreation, University of Florida, 1954; Studies at the School of

Real Estate Law. Career: Real Estate Broker (Inactive as of 1980). Community Activities: Many Benefit Fashion Shows, Press Parties. Religion: Episcopalian. Honors and Awards: Women's Press Pin for Most Insurance Sold, Independent Life Insurance Company, 1951. Address: 722 Alameda Street, Orlando, Florida 32804.

Roush, Mildred Jessianna

Nutritionist. Personal: Born October 5, 1920; Daughter of Dr. and Mrs. L. L. Roush (deceased). Education: B.S., Ohio State University, 1942; M.A., Columbia University, 1947; Professional Diploma, Columbia University, 1950. Career: Research Assistant, Columbia University, New York City; Assistant Professor, Colorado State University, Fort Collins; Nutrition Consultant, The University of Peshawar, West Pakistan; Nutrition Officer, Food and Agriculture of the United Nations, Bangkok, Thailand, 1966-68; Nutritionist, Columbus Board of Education, Columbus, Ohio. Organizational Memberships: The American Dietetic Association; American Public Health Association; Society for Nutrition Education; Nutrition Today Society; Ohio Valley Food Technology Association. Community Activities: Nutrition Involving Columbus Elderly; Red Cross; Campfire Girls; Girl Scouts of America; Young Women's Christian Association; Clintonville Women's Club. Religion: Maple Grove United Methodist Church. Honors and Awards: Pi Lambda Theta; Kappa Delta Pi; Phi Tau Sigma; Listed in *Who's Who in the Midwest, World Who's Who of Women, International Who's Who of Intellectuals, Dictionary of International Biography, International Platform Association, International Register of Profiles, Personalities of America, Community Leaders of America, Personalities of the West and Midwest.* Address: 2889 Neil Avenue, Apt. 411B, Columbus, Ohio 43302.

Rousseau, Hamilton

Communications Generalist. Personal: Son of William Hamilton Rousseau Jr., Helen Hentz Rousseau (deceased). Education: Attended the University of South Carolina; Number of Apprenticeships. Career: Promotion Manager for Network Television Affiliate, Age 19 (nation's youngest); Editor of City Magazine, Age 20; Corporate Communications Director, Age 25; Communications Strategist, McCann-Erickson and Exxon, Age 30; Developed Two New Media, One Print, One Electronic, for the Purpose of Mass Communicating Data-Oriented Information, 1976; Founder, Chairman, Urban Information Networks Corporation, 1977 to present; Founder, Institute for the Development of Idiosyncratic Communications, 1981. Organizational Memberships: International Institute of Communications, London; World Future Society. Honors and Awards: Listed in *Personalities of America, Directory of Distinguished Americans, International Book of Honor, Men of Achievement, International Who's Who of Intellectuals.* Address: 74 Fifth Avenue, Suite 4A, New York, New York 10011.

Mildred Roush

Rowe, Herbert J

Association Executive. Personal: Born March 25, 1924; Married Ann Muter; Father of Edith L., Douglas H., Stephen F., James D. Education: Studies at the University of Texas, Purdue University, University of Illinois; Bachelor's Degree in Marketing and Management. Military: Served in the United States Marine Corps 1942-46, 1950-52, Captain in the United States Marine Corps Reserve. Career: Vice President 1978 to present, Board of Governors 1969-75, Electronic Industries Association; Former Associate Administrator, External Affairs, N.A.S.A. Headquarters, Washington, D.C.; Chairman of the Board, PEMCOR, Inc., Illinois; President, Chairman of the Board, The Muter Company. Organizational Memberships: American Loudspeaker Manufacturers Association; University of Illinois Foundation; Electronic Industries Foundation; Kappa Kappa Corporation of Sigma Chi Fraternity; Association of Electronic Manufacturers. Community Activities: Beta Gamma Sigma; Alpha Phi Omega; Sigma Chi; Ancient Free and Accepted Masons of Illinois; Ancient Accepted Scottish Rite; Medinah Temple; Ancient Arabic Order of Nobles of the Mystic Shrine; Flossmor Country Club; Field Museum of Natural History; Chicago Art Insitute; American Management Association; National Space Institute; National Association of Government Communicators; American Institute of Aeronautics and Astronautics; National Air and Space Museum of the Smithsonian Institute (advisory board); Boy Scouts of America (several national committees). Religion: Flossmoor Community Church. Honors and Awards: Boy Scouts of America, Distinguished Eagle Scout Award 1971, Silver Beaver, Silver Antelope. Address: 1451 Highwood Drive, McLean, Virginia 22101.

Royer, Charles

Mayor. Personal: Born August 22, 1939; Son of Russell and Mildred Royer (both deceased); Married Rosanne Gostovich; Father of Suzanne, Jordan. Education: B.A., Journalism, University of Oregon, 1966; Postgraduate Studies Undertaken at Harvard/Massachusetts Institute of Technology Joint Center for Urban Studies, 1969-70. Military: Served in the United States Army Intelligence, 1961-63. Career: Mayor, City of Seattle; Former Journalist. Organizational Memberships: National League of Cities (president, 1983); United States Conference of Mayors (advisory board); Center for Democratic Policy (board of directors); Democratic National Committee. Community Activities: National Council on Foreign Language and International Studies; Intergovernmental Science, Engineering and Technology Panel. Honors and Awards: Washington Journalism Center Fellow, 1968; American Political Science Association Fellow, 1969-70; Sigma Delta Chi Award, 1976; Edward R. Murrow Award, 1976. Address: 1200 Municipal Building, Seattle, Washington 98104.

Rubin, Lisa Ferris

Drama Teacher, Professional Fund Raiser, Social Worker. Personal: Daughter of Angelo and Katherine Paluzzi (both deceased); Married; Mother of One Son. Education: Attended Rockford College. Career: Drama Teacher; Social Worker; Youth Instructor; Lecturer. Address: 4129 Cushman Road, Rockford, Illinois 61111.

Rubin, Seymour Jeffrey

Executive Director, Professor. Personal: Born in Chicago, Illinios, in 1914; Married Janet B. Education: A.B., University of Michigan, 1936; LL.B., magna cum laude, 1938, and LL.M., 1939, both from Harvard Law School. Career: Law Clerk, Hon. A. N. Hand, 2nd Circuit, 1939-40; Various Government Positions, 1940-48; Assistant Legal Adviser, Department of State; Head of the United States Delegation on N.A.T.O. Tax Treaties, 1951-52; Deputy Administrator, Mutual Defense Assistance Administration, 1952-53; General Counsel Agency on International Development and United States Minister to Development Assistance Committee, 1962-64; Private Law Practice, 1964-73; Member, Inter-American Juridicial Committee, 1974 to present; U.S. Representative to the

United Nations Commission on Transnational Corporations, 1975 to present; Executive Director, American Society of International Law; Professor of Law, American Univeristy Law School. Organizational Memberships: American Society of International Law (executive vice president, 1975 to present). Community Activities: United Nations Commission on International Trade Law (U.S. representative, 1968-70); Special Expert Committee, United Nations Security Council (U.S. representative, 1964-65); Mutual Assistance Control Act (deputy administrator, 1951-53); Special Ambassador to Bolivia, 1962. Published Works: Author of numerous works in the field of international investment law and policy, expropriation, compensation and protection of private foreign investment and international procedures, including *Private Foreign Investment - Legal and Economic Realities,* 1956. Honors and Awards: Sesquicentennial Award, University of Michigan, 1966; Grand Cross of Austria, 1965. Address: 1675 35th Street N.W., Washington, D.C. 20007.

Rubly, Grant R

Retired Engineer. Personal: Born June 7, 1906, in Cleveland, Ohio; Son of Carl John and Louise F. Sump Rubly; Married Lucille A. Pickering, October 5, 1929; Father of John Charles, Grant Allen (deceased), Elizabeth Anne Sills, Carl Andrew, Sharon Eloise Tilley. Education: Graduate of East Technical High School, Cleveland, 1924; B.S. Mining Engineering 1928, Engineer of Mines 1939, Case School of Applied Science (now Case Western Reserve University). Career: Mining Engineer and Staff Assistant, Reynolds Mining Company; Chief Engineer, Miami Cooper Company; Resident Engineer, San Manuel Copper Corporation; Engineer, Oregon State Highway Department; Chief Engineer and Mine Superintendent, Magnet Cove Barium Corporation; Engineer of Defense Minerals, United States Bureau of Mines, Tuscon, Arizona. Organizational Memberships: American Institute of Mining Engineers; American Association for the Advancement of Science (fellow); American Institute of Mining, Metallurgical and Petroleum Engineers of Arizona (past chairman of district); Theta Tau; Sigma Xi. Community Activities: Grand Council of Royal and Select Masters of Arkansas (most illustrious grand master); Knights Templer of Arkansas (eminent grand junior warden of the grand commandry); Royal Arch Masons of Louisiana near the Grand Chapter of Arkansas (grand representative of the grand chapter); Grand Council of Royal and Select Masters of New Hampshire, near the Grand Council of Arkansas (grand representative); Rockport Lodge #58, Free and Accepted Masons (past master); Malvern Chapter #100, Royal Arch Masons (past high priest); Solomon Council #46, Royal and Select Masters (past thrice illustrious master); Knights Templar (past commander Trinity Commandry #33); Knights of the York (past prior, Albert Pike Priory #20); Order of the Sword and Trowel (past thrice illustrious master thrice illustrious council of Arkansas); Gilchrist Council #26, Allied Masonic Degrees (soverign master); Holy Grail Tabernacle #XI, Holy Royal Arch Knight Templar Priests; St. Giles Conclave, Red Cross of Constine and Appendant Orders; XX 32° Ancient and Accepted Scottish Rite of Freemasonry; Sahraa Temple, A.A.O.N.M.S.; Holy Order of High Priesthood; Order of the Eastern Star (past matron, Malvern Chapter #501); Order of Rainbow for Girls (grand cross of color); Philalethes Society; DeMolays (past assistant organizer). Honors and Awards: Founder Fellow, Medal, International Institute of Community Service; Fellow, Intercontinental Biographical Association; Fellow, Smithsonian Institution; Past President, Malvern Rotary International; International Platform Association; Listed in *Who Knows and What, Who's Who on Pacific Coast, Who's Who in the West, Who's Who in the South and Southwest, Men of Achievement, International Who's Who in Community Service, Notable Americans, International Biographical Association Yearbook and Biographical Directory, International Who's Who of Intellectuals, Who's Who in Arkansas, Personalities of the South, Community Leaders and Noteworthy Americans, Book of Honor.* Address: P.O. Box 154, Malcern, Arkansas 72104.

Rubly, Lucille A Pickering

Retired. Personal: Born November 23, 1903; Daughter of Ella A. Deggin and Arthur E. Pickering; Married Grant R. Rubly, October 5, 1929; Mother of John Charles, Grant Allen, Carl Andrew, Elizabeth Anne Sills (Mrs. Charles), Sharon Eloise Tillery (Mrs. William). Education: Attended the Y.W.C.A. Commercial School, Cleveland Preparatory School. Career: Stenographer, Garfield, McGregor and Baldwin; Secretary to Philip White, Attorney; Stenographer and Notary Public to Robert Johnson, Attorney; Stenographer to Edward R. Alexander Canfield Oil Company, Other Law Firms. Community Activities: Past Rainbow Mother; Interpreter, Displaced Polish People Sent to the Community; Band Mother; Circle Chairman, W.S.C.S.; International Social Order Beauceants (charter member; chaplain). Religion: First United Methodist Church. Honors and Awards: Grand Cross of Color, International Rainbow for Girls; Fellow Member, *Book of Honor;* American Biographical Institute Research Association; Listed in *World Who's Who of Women, Community Leaders and Noteworthy Americans.* Address: P.O. Box 154, Malcern, Arkansas 72104.

Rudnitzky, Sandra Rosenbloom

Social Worker. Personal: Daughter of Howard Rosenbloom (deceased) and Thelma Olitzky; Married Elliot M. Rudnitzky; Mother of Robyn Helene, Michelle Randi. Education: B.Mus., cum laude, Boston University; M.A., Columbia University, 1970; M.S.W., Hunter College School of Social Work, 1974. Career: Social Worker; Previous Positions include Music Teacher, Recreation Therapist. Organizational Memberships: Academy of Certified Social Workers; Mental Health Association of New Jersey; Association for Children of New Jersey. Community Activities: Middlesex County Child Placement Review Board (chairperson, 1979 to present); Parents Anonymous of New Jersey (board of directors, 1977 to present); Middlesex County Parents Anonymous (chapter sponsor, 1977 to present); Middlesex County Head Start Program (social service advisory board, 1979 to present); Middlesex County Human Service Council, 1980 to present; Perth Amboy Family Preservation Council, 1977 to present; Jewish Family Service of Northern Middlesex County (vice president, 1981 to present). Religion: Women's American ORT; National Council of Jewish Women. Honors and Awards: Phi Kappa Lambda; Listed in *Who's Who in the East.* Address: 98 James Street, Edison, New York 08837.

Rush, David H

Executive. Personal: Born April 18, 1921; Son of Joseph and Ida Rush (both deceased); Married Miriam Nelson; Father of Barbara Lanzar, Joel L. Education: Attended Rutgers University, 1939-40; B.S., New York University, 1942. Military: Served in the United States Army Air Force. Career: Chairman of the Board, Vexilar, Inc.; President, Chairman of the Board, ACR Electronics, Inc.; President, Chromalloy Electronics Division, 1948-60; Director, Group Vice President 1955-77, Vice President Electronics Group 1967-77, Chromalloy American Corporation; President, Rush Photo, 1945-48. Organizational Memberships: First Federal of Broward Savings and Loan Association (director, 1979 to present); Miami Branch, Federal Reserve Bank of Atlanta, (director, 1980 to present). Community Activities: United Way of Broward County (past president); Greater Hollywood Chamber of Commerce (past chairman); Easter Seal of Broward County (past president); National Multiple Sclerosis Society, New York City (director); Holy Cross Hospital, Fort Lauderdale (director). Honors and Awards: Silver Medallion, National Conference of Christians and Jews, 1979. Address: 4804 Banyan Lane, Tamarac, Florida 33319.

Russell, Carol Joanne

Banker. Personal: Born January 2, 1936; Daughter of Esthern Townzen; Married Ralph A. Russell; Mother of David A., Brent M., Sheri Dianne, Cary Jon, Scott T. Education: Graduate of El Dorado County High School, Career: Banker. Organizational Memberships: Business and Professional Club; National Association of Banking Women. Community Activities: Marshall Hospital Auxiliary; Highway 50 Association; Hangtown Women's Bowling Association (director); Placerville Emblem Club; Soroptimist Club; Hangtown Chamber of Commerce. Religion: Catholic. Honors and Awards: Listed in *Who's Who in Business and Finance, World Who's Who of Women.* Address: 2532 Sterling Drive, Rescue, California 95672.

Russell, Charles Roberts

Consulting Engineer, Chemist. Personal: Born July 13, 1914; Son of Dessie Russell; Married Dolores Marie; Father of Ann E. Jaep, John C., David F., Thomas R. Education: B.S.Ch.E., Washington State University, 1936; Ph.D., Chemical Engineering, Wisconsin University, 1941. Military: Served in the United States Naval Reserve, 1944-46, attaining the rank of Lieutenant. Career: Consulting Engineer and Chemist; Professor of Mechanical Engineering and Associate Dean, California Polytechnic State University, 1968-71; Engineer, General Motors, 1956-68; Engineer, United States Atomic Energy Commission, 1950-56. Organizational Memberships: American Chemical Society; Nuclear Standards Commission; American National Standards Association 1958-78. Community Activities: S.C.C. Advisory Committee on Rector Safeguard, 1950-56; Consultant to the United States Air Force Scientific Advisory Committee, 1956-59. Religion: Roman Catholic. Published Works: *Rector Safeguards*, 1962; *Elements of Energy Conversation*, 1967. Honors and Awards: Proctor and Gamble Fellow, University of Wisconsin, 1940, 1941; Address: 3071 Marilyn Way, Santa Barbara, California 93105.

Russell, Findlay Ewing

Research Professor of Pharmacology. Personal: Born September 1, 1919, in San Francisco, California; Son of William and Mary Jane Russell (both deceased); Married Marilyn R. Strickland; Father of Christa Ann, Sharon Jane, Robin Emile, Constance Susan, Mark Findlay. Education: B.A., Walla Walla College, 1941; Attended the University of Southern California, 1946; M.D., Loma Linda University, 1950. Military: Served in the United States Army, 1943-46. Career: Intern, White Memorial Hospital, Los Angeles, 1950-61; Research Fellow, California Institute of Technology, 1951-52; Giannini Honor Fellow, California Institute of Technology, 1952-53; Chief Physiologist, Institute of Medical Research, Huntington Memorial Hospital, 1953-55; Assistant Professor of Neurophysiology 1955-58, Associate Professor of Neurophysiology 1958-61, Professor of Neurophysiology 1961-66, Research Professor of Neurosurgery 1966 to present, Loma Linda University; Professor of Neurology, University of Southern California School of Medicine 1966-80; Professor of Biology, University of Southern California, 1968-80; Professor of Physiology, University of Southern California School of Medicine, 1969-80; Director of Laboratory of Neurological Research and Venom Poisoning Center, Los Angeles County/University of Southern California Medical Center, 1955-80; Adjunct Professor, Neurology, University of Southern California School of Medicine, 1980 to present; Research Professor, Pharmacology and Toxicology, University of Arizona College of Pharmacy, 1980 to present. Lecturer, University of California at Los Angeles School of Medicine, 1958 to present; Lecturer Loma Linda University School of Medicine, 1955 to present. Organizational Memberships: American College of Physicians (fellow); American College of Cardiology (fellow); Royal Society of Tropical Medicine (fellow); New York Academy of Science (fellow); American Association for the Advancement of Science (fellow); International Science (fellow); International Society on Toxinology (fellow); Herpetologist's League (fellow); Royal Society of Medicine (fellow); San Diego Zoological Society (fellow) Amercian Physiological Society; Sigma Xi; Society of Experimental Biology and Medicine; Society of Experimental Biology (England); American Association of University Professors; American Society of Ichthyologists and Herpetologists; Cambridge Philosophical Society; Western Pharmacology Society; International College of Surgeons. Published Works: Author of Over 200 Pages Related to Toxinology, Physiology, Pharmacology, Medicine and Literature; Five Books; 20 Chapters in Textbooks. Honors and Awards: President, International Society of Toxinology, 1961-66; President, Western Pharmacology Society, 1972-73; Chairman, Humanities Division, L.A.C./U.S.C. Medical Center, 1967-74; Chairman, Section Committee on Biographical Standardization, WHO, 1967; Chairman, Ad Hoc Committee on Marine Fish Poisoning, WHO, 1972; Consultant on Venoms and Venomous Animals, National Academy of Sciences, American Medical Association, American Association of Poison Control Centers, United States Armed Forces, International Red Cross, National Science Foundation, National Institutes of Health, Office of Naval Research, N.S.A., F.D.A.; Walter Reed Society; Awards from Ein Shams University 1954, Academia Nacional Medicina Buenos Aires 1966; F. Redi Award, 1967; Student-Faculty Award, 1968; Skylab Achievement Award, 1974; Loma Linda University Alumni Award, 1976; Institute Jozef Stefan Gold Award, 1977; Listed in *American Men of Medicine, American Men of Science, Dictionary of International Biography, Leaders in American Science, Notable Americans, Who's Who in the West, World Who's Who in Science.* Address P.O. Box 125, Portal, Arizona 85632.

Russell, Grace Jarrell Williams

Artist, Writer, Teacher. Personal: Born in Memphis, Tennessee; Daughter of Aubrey Hamilton Williams, Lill Senter Jarrell Williams (deceased); Married Henry Ewell Russell, 1945; Mother of Margaret Lill Rudolph (Mrs. Bill), Rose Ellen Weiner (Mrs. Bob), Henry E. III, Stephen A., Betty Grace Houser (Mrs. Phillip). Education: Honor Student, Humboldt; B.A., Southern Methodist University, 1946. Career: Teacher of Private Art Classes; Architectural and Interior Decoration Plans for Work on Churches and Parsonages; Teacher of High School English, Dyersburg, Tennessee, 1964-65; Magazine Cover Design, One-Man Art Shows; Speaker at Church and Civic Gatherings. Community Activities: Susanna Wesley Circle of Ministers Wives (district president, several districts); District Superintendents Wives (president of jurisdictional); Woman's Club; Tennessee American Mothers Committee; National League of American Penwomen (state president, 1980-82); Delegate to Christian Heritage in Government Conference, London, 1981; Delegate to World Methodist Conference, Honolulu, 1981. Honors and Awards; State and National Honors for Writing; Named Duchess of Paducah, 1972; Represented (with her husband) Memphis Conference of the United Methodist Church at Reopening of City Road Chapel in London, 1978; World Methodist Conference, Honolulu, 1981; Christian Heritage in Government Conference, London, 1981; Listed in *World Who's Who of Women, International Who's Who of Intellectuals, Dictionary of International Biography, Notable Americans, Book of Honor, Men and Women of Distinction, International Register of Profiles.* Published Works: Author of 3 Books, *How I See England, Rings and Things, Hope in my Heart;* Newspaper Column 'Gracelines'; Articles, Poetry and Study Materials. Address: 709 Wade Hampton Road, Dyersburg, Tennessee, 38024.

Russell, Henry Ewell

Clergyman. Personal: Born in Paducah, Kentucky; Son of H. Ewell Russell, Margaret Wurst Russell (deceased); Married Grace Jarrell

Williams, 1945; Father of Margaret Lill Rudolph, Rose Ellen Weiner, Henry E. III, Stephen A., Betty Grace Houser. Education: Attended Paducah Junior College; B.A., Lambuth College, Jackson, Tennessee, 1943; M.Th., Perkins School of Theology, Southern Methodist University, 1947; D.D., Lambuth College, 1972. Career: Pastor, United Methodist Church, Appointed to Wickliffe, Kentucky, 1946-49, and Reidland, Kentucky, 1949-50; Pastor, Ellendale, Tennessee 1950, Fulton, Kentucky 1955-58, Dyersburg First Church 1958-65; Preaching Mission in Cuba; World Methodist Council Ministerial Exchange, Serving The Albert Hall, Manchester England; Brownsville District Superintendent 1965-76, Broadway Paducah, Kentucky 1967-72, St. Luke's, Memphis 1972-78; District Superintendent, Dyersburg District; Built Wesley Homes of Dyersburg, Inc., 1981. Organizational Memberships: Memphis Annual Conference; World Methodist Conference, Honolulu (delegate, 1981); Christian Heritage in Government Conference, London (chairman delegate and discussion leader, 1981). Community Activities: Lambuth College (board of trustees); Methodist Hospital (cabinet representative, board of directors); Dyersburg Housing Authority; Mayor's Advisory Board, Paducah; Lions Club; Kiwanis; Rotary Club; Junaluska Associates, Lake Junaluska, North Carolina (board member, several years). Published Works: Wrote Newspaper Column "Vertical Horizons". Honors and Awards: Tennessee House of Representatives Passed Resolution Honoring Dr. Russell for Contribution to State, 1976; Named Duke of Paducah, 1972; Represented Memphis Conference at Reopening of City Road Chapel, London, 1978; Listed in *International Register of Profiles, Who's Who in Religion, Personalities of the South, Notable Americans, International Dictionary of Biography*, Number of Other Reference Volumes. Address: 709 Wade Hampton Road, Dyersburg, Tennessee 38024.

Russo, Jose

Pathologist. Personal: Born March 24, 1942, in Mendoza, Argentina; Son of Felipe and Teresa Russo; Married Irma Maydee; Father of Patricia Alexandra. Education: B.S., Agustin Alvarez National College, Mendoza, Argentina, 1959; Physicians Degree, School of Medicine, University of Cuyo, Mendoza, 1967; M.D., School of Medicine of Cuyo, 1968. Career: Chief, Experimental Pathology, Department of Biology, Michigan Cancer Foundation, 1973-74; Post-Doctoral Fellow, Institute of Molecular and Cellular Evolution, University of Miami, 1971-73; Assistant Professor in Biology, University of Miami, 1972-73; Chief of Instructors of the Embryology Section, Department of Morphology, Histology and Embryology Institute, School of Medicine, National University of Cuyo, 1969-71; Instructor in Histology and Embryology, Histology and Embryology Institute, National University of Cuyo, 1967-69; Research Assistant, Histology and Embryology Institute, National University of Cuyo, 1967-69; Research Assistant, Histology and Embryology Institute, School of Medicine, National University of Cuyo, 1966-67; Physician and Surgeon License in Argentina, 1967; Instructor of Histopathology in the Institute for General and Experimental Pathology, School of Medicine, National University of Cuyo, 1961-66. Organizational Memberships: International Academy of Pathology; American Society of Clinical Pathology; American Association for Cancer Research; Society for Experimental Biology and Medicine; American Society for Cell Biology; Society for the Study of Reproduction; Electron Microscopy Society of America; Tissue Culture Association; Sociedad Latinoamericana de Microscopia Electronica; Signma Xi; American Association for the Advancement of Science; Association Latinoamericana de Ciencias Fisiologicas; Wayne County Medical Society; New York Academy of Science; Michigan Pathology Society. Published Works: Over 100 Publications on Experimental Oncology, Immunology and Cancer in Human and Animals. Honors and Awards: Fellow, University Club of Buenos Aires, 1960-61; Fellow, Mendoza Club, 1960-61; Post-Doctoral Fellowship, National Council of Research, Argentina, 1967-69, 1969-71; Post-Doctoral Fellowship, Rockefeller Foundation, Institute for Molecular and Cellular Evolution, University of Miami, 1972-73; Listed in *Who's Who in the Midwest, American Men and Women of Science, Who's Who in Intellectuals.* Address: 1226 Audubon, Crosse Pointe Park, Michigan 48230.

Rustvold, Clarence Alfred

Clarence A Rustvold

Executive Director. Personal: Born February 13, 1930; Son of Al and Lilly Rustvold; Married to Donna J.; Father of Gordon, Jeralyn, Tamra, Linda, Alison, Karen. Education: A.A., Itasca Junior College, 1950; Attended University of Idaho, 1951; B.S.M.E., Texas A&M University, 1960; M.S., Rensselaer Polytechnic Institute, 1964; D.O.D., Computer Institute, 1970. Military: Served with United States Air Force with rank of Lieutenant Colonel, 1951-71; Served as Command Pilot and Missleman during the Korean Conflict and Vietnam War. Career: Executive Director, E.E.O. Services, Fountain Valley, California, 1974 to present; Vice President and officer, Boyden International Group, Inc., 1971-74; President, R & R Aeronautics, Inc., 1976-78; Director, Career Development Systems, Inc., 1978-80; Director, Execudex, Inc., 1975; Director, Boyden Australia Pty., 1972-74; Executive Officer to the Director of Operation and Administration of the Defense Nuclear Agency, 1970-71; Program Manager and Project Engineer for the Space and Missle Systems Organization of the U.S., 1967-70. Organizational Memberships: Air Force Association; Combat Pilots Association; Aircraft Owners and Pilots Association; Forward Air Controllers Association; International Platform Association. Community Activities: Newcomen Society; Town Hall; Lions Club International. Religion: Attends the Lutheran Church. Honors and Awards: Received numerous medals and awards from the U.S.A.F.; Listed in *Who's Who in the West, Who's Who in California Business and Finance.* Address: 18195 Santa Adela Circle, Fountain Valley, California, 92708.

Ruth, Marion (Babe) Weyant

Aviation Consultant, Instructor. Personal: Born February 7, 1918; Daughter of Lloyd J. and Marie E. Helmic Weyant (both deceased); Married Dale C. Ruth on September 7, 1946; Mother of Dale Lee Ruth Ross, Kim Carol Ruth Hite. Education: A.A.S. magna cum laude, Aviation Flight Technology, Lansing Community College, 1975; Flight Instructor Seminars, Mott Aviation Center 1964-65, Ohio State University 1966, Purdue University 1969-71; Lansing Eastern High School, 1936; Link Instructor Trainee, Link Aviation Devices, Binghamton, New York, 1942. Career: Operator, Lansing and Grand Rapids Airport Restaurants, 1934-44; Link Instructor, American Air Transport, Chicago, 1943-44; Link Instructor, Chicago and Southern Airlines, 1944; Link Instructor, Stewart Aviation, Parkersburg, West Virginia, 1945; Link and Flight Instructor, Hughes Flying Service, Lansing, 1945-46; Chief Flight Instructor, Hebert Aviation, Lansing, 1946; Flight Instructor, Capitol City Aviation, Lansing, 1947-50; Chief Flight Instructor, General Aviation, Lansing, 1959-63; Acting Chief Flight Instructor, Francis Aviation, Lansing, 1967-69; Flight Simulator Instructor, Lansing Community College, 1974-80; Aviation Consultant; Free-lance Flight and Simulator Instructor. Organizational Memberships: Michigan Aerospace History (steering committee, 1976); Michigan Aeronautic Commission (historical chairman, 50th anniversary association, 1979); OX-5 Aviation Pioneers, Michigan Wing (secretary, governor, 1st vice president, president 1983, chairperson); Silver Wings (chairman, national convention, 1977); Aircraft Owners and Pilots Association 1939 to present, #109. Community Activities: Zonta Club of Lansing, 1979 to present; F.A.A. Accident Prevention Counselor, 1972 to present; 99s (newsletter editor, 1943-44). Honors and Awards: Named #1 Pilot, Michigan Air Tour, 1938; 3rd Place, Bernard McFadden Trophy Race, 1939; Joyce Hartung Trophy, 1st Place, Michigan All Girls Air Show, 1941; W.T. Piper International Flying Farmer Women's Most Hours Award, 1964-65; 5th Place, Michigan Small Race, 1965; Diana Award, Community Service, 1980; Pioneer Women Pilot of the Year; OX-5 National Award; National Hall of Fame and National Awards Committee; Flew Repleca of "Spirit of St. Louis" with Captain Verne Jobst, United Airlines; Flew in All-Women's Transcontinental Races "Powder Puff Derby", 1955, 1972, 1973; Flew in All-Women's International Air Race (Angel Derby), 1976. Address: 14645 Airport Road, Lansing, Michigan 48906.

Rutherford, James William

Mayor. Personal: Born April 23, 1925; Married Betty J.; Father of Marcia Rutherford Alvord, Michelle Marie, Michael James, James Andrew. Education: A.A., Flint Community Jr. College, 1958; B.S. 1960, M.S. 1964, both from Michigan State University. Military: Served with the United States Navy, 1945-47. Career: Flint Police Department, 1948; Detective Lieutenant, 1953-56; Deputy City Manager, 1963; Inspector, 1965; Chief of Police, 1967; Mayor, City of Flint, Michigan, 1975, Re-elected, 1979. Organizational Memberships: Riverfront Advisory Committee; Tri-County Human Resources Committee (chairman); Downtown Development Authority (chairman); International Association Chiefs of Police (chairman membership committee); U.S. Conference of Mayors; Genesee County Police Chiefs (chairman); Governor's Crime Commission; Tourist & Convention Council (board of directors); Flint-Genesee Corporation (board of directors); Flint Renaissance, Inc. (board of directors); Forward Development Corporation. Community Activities: F&M Lodge 174; Bruin (Mott Community College) Boosters Executive Committee; Flint Area Conference Inc. (executive committee); Historic Flint AutoWorld Foundation (trustee). Honors and Awards: 1 of 10 Outstanding Officers in U.S., 1966; Michigan Fraternal Order of Eagles, "Reverence for the Law Award", 1968; Flint Exchange Club, "Golden Deeds Award", 1969; Gideon's Civic Award, 1971; J. Edgar Hoover Memorial Award, 1973. Address: 1713 Chelsea Circle, Flint, Michigan 48503.

Rutsch, Alexander

Artist. Personal: Born August 31, 1930; Son of Julius and Cinade Rutsch; Father of Alexandra, Vera-Nike, Nina. Education: Attended Academe Beaux Arts (received a grant from the French government). Organizational Memberships: International Beaux Arts Burr Artists. Honors and Awards: Received Silver Medal from City of Paris, France, 1958; Member, Academy of Arts, Sciences and Letters of Paris, 1958; "La monde de Rutsch", film award at Cannes Film Festival, 1966; "Inner Self of Alexander Rutsch", film, I.B.M. Address: 222 Highbrook Avenue, Pelham, New York 10803.

Ryan, James Walter

Research Physician. Personal: Born June 8, 1935, in Amarillo, Texas; Son of Lee W. and Emma Elizabeth Haddox Ryan; Married Una Harriett Scully; Father of James Patrict Andrew, Alexendra Lynette Elizabeth, Amy Jean Susan. Education: A.B., Political Science, Dartmouth College, 1957; M.D., Cornell University Medical College, 1961; D.Phil., Biochemistry, Oxford University, 1967. Military: Services with the United States Public Health Service, Lieutenant Commander. Career: Intern, Montreal General Hospital, McGill University 1962-63; Research Associate, National Institute of Mental Health, National Institutes of Health, 1963-65; Guest Investigator, Rockefeller University, New York, 1967-68; Assistant Professor of Biochemistry, Rockefeller University, 1968; Senior Scientist, Papanicolaou Cancer Research Institute, Miami, Florida, 1972-77; Associate Professor, Department of Medicine, University of Miami School of Medicine, Miami, Florida, 1968-70; Professor of Medicine (Research), Department of Medicine, University of Miami, 1979 to present. Organizational Memberships: American Association for the Advancement of Science; Biochemical Society; Southern Society for Clinical Investigation; New York Academy of Science; American Institute of Chemists (fellow); Sigmi Xi; American Society of Biological Chemists; American Chemical Society (Divisions of Biological Chemistry and Medicinal Chemistry); American Heart Association Council on Cardiopulmonary Diseases of the American Heart Association; Council for High Blood Pressure Research, American Heart Association (medical advisory board); Microcirculatory Society; European Microcirculation Society, 1979 to present. Religion: Baptist. Published Works: Number of Professional Journal Articles including (most recently) "Comparative Study of Three Parenteral Inhibitors of the Angiotensin Converting Enzyme" 1981, "Metabolic Functions of the Pulmonary Vascular Endothelium" 1981 (in press), and "Angiotensin-Converting Enzyme: II Pulmonary Endothelia Cells in Culture" 1980. Honors and Awards: Smith, Kline and French Travelling Fellowships, 1960; William Mecklenberg Polk Research Prize, Cornell University Medical College, 1960-61; Travel Award, Rockefeller Foundation, 1962; Research Prize, Montreal Clinical Society, 1963; Postdoctoral Fellow, U.S.P.H.S., 1965-67; Honorary Medical Officer to the Regius Professor of Medicine, Oxford, 1965-67; William Waldorf Astor Travelling Fellowship, 1966; Special Fellowship, U.S.P.H.S., 1967-68; Career Development Award, U.S.P.H.S., 1968; Investigator, Howard Hughes Medical Institute, 1968-71; Pfizer Travelling Fellow, University of Montreal, October 1972; Visiting Professor, Clinical Research Institute of Montreal, 1974; Visiting Faculty, Thoracic Disease Division, Department of Internal Medicine, Mayo Clinic, December 1974; Invited Speaker for 500th Anniversary of the University of Uppsalla, June 1977; Holds Several United States Patents and Has 42 Patent Applications Pending in 32 Countries. Address: 3420 Poinciana Avenue, Miami, Florida 33133.

Alexander Rutsch

Ryder, Sandra Smith

Communications Specialist. Personal: Born July 6, 1949; Daughter of Dennis M. and Olga Smith. Education: B.S., Northwestern University Medill School of Journalism, 1971. Career: Communications Specialist, Oxnard, California; Former Newspaper Reporter, Editor, Freelance Writer and Graphic Artist. Organizational Memberships: Association of California School Administrators; National School Public Relations Association; Southern California School Public Relations Association; Society of Professional Journalists, Los Padre Chapter (past president, held 2 terms); Women in Communications, Los Angeles Chapter, 1971-81; Greater Los Angeles Press Club. Community Activities: Member, Oxnard Chamber of Commerce (member, women's division), Camarillo Chamber of Commerce. Honors and Awards: Received John Swett Award for excellence in educational reporting, California Teachers Association, 1973; Listed in *Who's Who of American Women, Community Leaders and Noteworthy Americans, Dictionary of International Biography, World Who's Who of Women.* Address: 177 West Green Vale Drive, Camarillo, California 93010.

Saad, Nabil Nashed

Director of Pediatrics. Personal: Born December 3, 1925; Married Liliane Nabil; Father of Sam Nabil, Samia Nabil, Sally Nabil. Education: M.B., B.CH., Cairo University, 1950; Diploma, Pediatrics, Ain Shams University, 1959; Diploma, Public Health, 1964; Chief Resident in Pediatrics, French and Polytechnic Medical School, 1972; Fellow in Pediatrics, Hospital for Joint Diseases and Medical Center, New York, 1974; American Board of Pediatrics. Career: Director of Pediatrics, Joint Diseases North General Hospital; Chairman, Executive Committee, President of Medical Staff, Joint Disease North General Hospital; Assistant Attending Department of Pediatrics, Mt. Sinai Medical School. Organizational Memberships: American Academy of Pediatrics; American Medical Association; New York State Medical Association. Community Activities: Saad Foundation; Donation to Joint Diseases Orthopedic Institute. Published Works: Author of Manual on Well Child Care. Honors and Awards: American Medical Association Physicians Recognition Award, 1978-81; Recipient, Certificate of Appreciation, Friends of Centro de Estudious Universitarious Xochilcalco A.C., 1978; Federation Jewish Philanthropies Grantee, 1981; Listed in *Who's Who in the East*. Address: 3 Dale Carnegie, Great Neck, New York 11020.

Nabil N Saad

Saenz, Ray

Psychotherapist. Personal: Born May 6, 1948; Son of Felix C. and Carmen L. Saenz; Father of Kara Christine. Education: B.A., Texas A&I University, 1971; M.A., University of Chicago, 1975. Career: Psychotherapist in private practice, Corpus Christi, Texas; Assistant Professor of Psychology, Del Mar College (chairman of legislative committee, 1980, scholarship committee, 1978 to present, D.M.E.A. social action committee, administration evaluation committee, 1981); Former Director of Outreach and Mobilization Department, Mental Health/Mental Retardation Center. Organizational Memberships: National Association of Social Workers; Academy of Certified Social Workers; New York Academy of Science; American Group Psychotherapy Association; Texas Junior College Teachers Association; Group Psychotherapy Society (Corpus Christi group); Del Mar Educational Association; Coastal Bend Mental Health Association, 1971-73; American Association for the Advancement of Science. Community Activities: Coastal Bend Council of Governments, 1975-78; Voluntary Action Center Board of Directors (member, 1978-81, vice president, 1979, executive committee, 1979, nominations committee, 1979, executive director search committee, 1979, finance committee, 1981); Instituto de Cultura Hispanica de Corpus Christi (member, 1977 to present, board of directors, chairman of cultural program committee, 1978-81, scholarship committee, 1981, nominations committee, 1981); Chairman of Parental Advisory Committee, Crockett Elementary School, 1979; Lecturer and guest on local television progams, 1976 to present; Holds various workshops. Honors and Awards: Received a citation for outstanding contributions to public education, 1979. Address: 1718 Sante Fe, Corpus Christi, Texas 78404.

Sager, Robert J

Professor of Earth Sciences. Personal: Born December 26, 1942; Son of Mrs. Arlene H. Sager; Married Ingrid Davies. Education: B.S., Wisconsin State University, 1964; M.S., University of Wisconsin, 1966; J.D., Western State University School of Law, 1977. Career: Assistant Professor of Geography, California State University, 1967-71; Visiting Professor of Geography, Chapman College-World Campus Afloat, 1971-72; Professor of Earth Science, West Los Angeles College, 1974 to present. Organizational Memberships: Association of American Geographers; National Council for Geographic Education; National Marine Education Association; American Society of International Law. Community Activities: Oceanic Society, Los Angeles Chapter (board of directors, legislative chair, 1978-80); Local Coastal Plan Task Force, City of Laguna Beach, 1979-81; Conservation and Open Space Committee, City of Laguna Beach, 1978-80; Published Works: Co-Author, *Introduction to Physical Geography*, 1975; *Essentials of Physical Geography*, 1977; *Essentials of Physical Geography, Second Edition*, 1982; *Papua New Guinea*, 1976; *Coastal Morphology*, 1982. Honors and Awards: Thomas Olson Memorial Geology Award, 1964; Departmental Honors Graduate, 1964; National Science Foundation Scholarship, Summer 1969; Department of Energy Participantship, Summer 1978; Instructional Research Grant, 1980; Graduate Teaching Assistantships, 1964-67; Listed in *Directory of Distinguished Americans, Personalities of America*. Address: 840 Catalina, Laguna Beach, California 92651.

Ray Saenz

Sahai, Hardeo

Statistician, Educator. Personal: Born January 10, 1942; Son of Sukhdeo Prasad and Roopwati Srivastava; Married Lillian Sahai; Father of Amogh Sahai. Education: B.Sc., Mathematics, Statistics and Physics, First Division, Fourth in Class, Lucknow University, India, 1962; M.Sc., Mathematics, First Division, First in Class, Barnaras Hindu University, Varanasi, India, 1964; M.S., Statistics, University of Chicago, Illinois, 1968; Ph.D., Statistics, University of Kentucky, Lexington, 1971. Career: Professor, Department of Mathematics of the University of Puerto Rico-Rio Piedras, 1981 to present; University of Puerto Rico-Mayaguez, Associate Professor 1976-80, Research Investigator at Water Resources Research Institute 1975-76, Assistant Professor in Department of Mathematics 1972-76; Visiting Research Professor, Department of Statistics and Applied Mathematics, Federal University of Ceara, Fortaleza, Ceara, Brazil, 1978-79; Consultant, Puerto Rico University Consultant Corporation, Puerto Rico, 1977; Statistical Consultant, Puerto Rico Driving Safety Evaluation Project, San Juan, 1973; Management Scientist, Management Systems Development Department, Burrought Corporation, Detroit, Michigan, 1972; University of Kentucky-Lexington, Research Assistant in Department of Statistics 1969-71, Teaching Assistant in Department of Statistics 1968-69; Statistical Programmer for Chicago Health Research Foundation, Chicago Civic Center, Chicago, Illinois, 1968; Statistical Programmer for Cleft Palate Center, University of Illinois-Chicago, 1967; Statistician for Research and Planning Division, Blue Cross Association, Chicago, Illinois, 1966; Assistant Statistical Officer, Durgapur Steel Plant, Durgapur, West Bengal, India, 1965; Lecturer in Mathematics and Statistics, Banaras Hindu University, Varanasi, India, 1964-65; Organizational Memberships: Institute of Mathematical Statistics; Bernoulli Society for Mathematical Statistics and Probability; Biometrics Society, Eastern North American Region; Indian Statistical Association; American Statistical Association; Japan Statistical Society. Community Activities: Lecturer at Numerous National and Foreign

Universities such as Universidade Estadual de Campinas, Brazil, Universidade de Brasilia, Brazil, Universidade de Sao Paulo, Brazil, Universidad National de Trujilos, Peru, Universidade Nacional de Columbia. Published Works: *A Dictionary of Statistical Terms: English-Spanish and Spanish-English*, 1981; *Random Effects Analysis of Variance: Estimation of Various Components, Part I: Balanced Data, and Part II: Unbalanced Data*, 1982; *The Analysis of Variance: Fixed, Random and Mixed Models*, 1983; Contributor of Articles to a Variety of Professional and Educational Journals in the United States, United Kingdom, West Germany, Japan, India, Spain, Australia; Referee for *Biometrics* Candian Journal of Statistics; Reviewer, *Mathematical Reviews* and *International Statistical Review;* Editorial Board Member, *Lecturas en Matematicas*, Sociedad Colombiana de Matematicas. Honors and Awards: Fellow, Council of Scientific and Industrial Research, Government of India, 1964-65; Fellow University of Chicago, 1965-68; U.P. Board Merit Scholarship, 1957-59; Government of India Merit Scholarship, 1959-64; Banaras Hindu University Medal, 1964; New York Academy of Sciences; Listed in *American Men and Women of Science, Personalities of America, Book of Honor, Directory of Distinguished Americans, Men of Achievement, International Who's Who of Intellectuals.* Address: Calle I, D-25, Diudad Universitaria, San Juan, Puerto Rico 00760.

Sahni, Tiia Taks

Art Director, Creative Consultant. Personal: Born May 22, 1935; Daughter of Hilda Taks; Married Omesh Sahni; Mother of Sarita Lea, Tiina Anita. Education: A.A.S., Advertising Art, University of Buffalo, 1956; B.S., Art, Cleveland Institute of Art and Case Western Reserve University, 1968; Post Graduate Studies in Graphics, Paris, France, 1969. Career: Art Director, Avon Products Inc., 1980 to present; Helena Rubinstein, Inc., 1978-80; Doyle, Dane and Bernbach, Rapp & Collins, Inc., 1976-78; Fashion Creative Consultant, Alexander's Fur Vault, Inc., New York City; Reader's Digest Association, Inc., 1972-76; Agency Creative Director, Associate Communications Group, 1970-72; The Hall Brothers, Cleveland, Ohio, 1968-70; Marcus Advertising, Inc., Cleveland, 1962-68. Organizational Memberships: The Society of Illustrators; New York State Craftsmen. Community Activities: Organized Annual and Special Art and Craft Exhibitions in Cleveland, 1965-70; Committee for First Annual All Nations Fair in Albany, 1972; Number of Art Exhibitions, including, One Man Show in Enamels, College of St. Rose, Albany, New York, 1970; Three Artists Show of Graphics, College of St. Rose, 1970; One Man Show in Graphics, Rensselaer Polytechnic Institute, 1971. Honors and Awards: Art Directors Merit Award, Art Directors Club of Cleveland, 1963, 1964; Award of Excellence in Design, Art Director-Illustrators-Photographers of Cleveland, 1964; Outstanding New Citizen Award, The City of Cleveland, 1965; Baldwin Wallace Purchase Awards, Baldwin Wallace College, 1968, 1969; Mead Design Award, Mead Paper Company, 1970; Awards for Complete Campaign Poster and Print, Art Directors Club of Albany, 1972; Third Prize in Photography, Readers Digest Association, 1975, 1976; Part and Full Tuition Scholarships, Cleveland Institute of Art and Case Western Reserve University, 1965-67; Listed in *Who's Who in the East.* Address: R.F.D. Hanover Street, Box 47, Yorktown Heights, New York 10598.

David Saity

Saity, David

Executive. Personal: Born December 29, 1930; Son of Itzhak and Nina Saity; Married Chaya Polonsky 1965. Education: Attended New York University, 1966-68. Career: President, CDS Enterprises, Ltd. President, Saity Originals Inc. Organizational Memberships: Jewelers of America, Inc.; Chamber of Commerce of America. Honors and Awards: Listed in *Who's Who in Finance and Industry* and *Who's Who in the World.* Address: 240 West 73 Street, New York, New York 10023.

Saka, Stanley Masato

Supervisor. Personal: Born July 22, 1940; Son of Charles and Ayako Saka. Education: B.S., University of Hawaii, 1963. Military: Served with United States Army, Schofied Barracks, Hawaii, with the 25th Infantry Division's Photo Laboratory, 1963-65; Held rank of Specialist, 4th Class; Received Honorable Discharge, 1965. Career: Supervisor in charge of Maui County for Plant Quarantine Branch, Hawaii Department of Agriculture. Community Activities: Active member of Honolulu Japanese Jaycees, 1967-72 (vice president in charge of special area, 1968-69); Active member of Maui Jaycees (moved from Oahu to Maui, 1972, associate member, 1977 to present); Member, Maui Americans of Japanese Ancestry Veterans Club, 1974 to present; Member, Pacific chapter, National Foundation of March of Dimes, 1978-80. Religion: Buddhist. Honors and Awards: Shared "Officer of the Year" award due to work as vice president in charge of special area, Honolulu Japanese Jaycees, 1968-69; Jaycee of the Year, Maui Jaycees, 1976-77; Senatorship in Jaycees International, 1979; Listed in *Who's Who in the West*, 17th edition. Address: 2554 Main Street, Wailuku, Maui, Hawaii 96793.

Stanley M Saka

Salisbury, Frank Boyer

Professor. Personal: Born August 3, 1926, in Provo, Utah; Married L. Marilyn Olson, 1949; Father of Frank Clark, Steven S., Michael J., Cynthia K., Phillip B. (deceased), Rebecca L., Blake C. Education: B.S. Botany 1951, M.A. Botany and Biochemistry 1952, University of Utah; Ph.D., Plant Physiology and Geochemistry, California Institute of Technology, 1955; Atomic Energy Commission Predoctoral Fellow, 1951-53; McCallum Fellow, 1953-54. Military: Served in the United States Army Air Force, 1945. Career: Photographer, Boyart Studio, 1949-50; Part-time Portrait-Commercial Photography, 1950 to present; Assistant Professor of Botany, Pomona College, 1954-55; Assistant Professor of Plant Physiology, Colorado State University, 1955-61; Professor of Plant Physiology, Colorado State University, 1961-66; National Science Foundation Postdoctoral Fellow, Tubingen, Germany, and Innsbruck, Austria, 1962-63; Utah State University, Professor of Plant Physiology and Head of Plant Science 1966-70, Professor of Plant Physiology 1966 to present, Professor of Botany 1968 to present; Board of Trustees, Colorado State University Research Foundation, 1960-62; Technical Representative in Plant Physiology, United States Atomic Energy Commission, Germantown, Maryland (now Department of Energy), 1973-74. Organizational Memberships: American Society of Plant Physiologists; American Institute of Biological Sciences; American Association for the Advancement of Science (fellow); Aerial Phenomena Research Organization (former consultant); Botanical Society of America; Ecological Society of America; Phi Kappa Phi; Sigma Xi; Utah Academy of Arts, Letters and Science; Western Society of Naturalists; Editorial Board Member, *Plant Physiology* 1967 to present, *BioScience* 1972-78; Consultant to N.A.S.A.; Served on N.A.S.A./A.I.B.S. Space Biology Panel to Evaluate Research Proposals, 1974-79; A.I.B.S. Governing Board Member-at-Large, 1975-78. Religion: Church of Jesus Christ of Latter-Day Saints, Missionary to German-Speaking Switzerland 1946-49. Published Works: Author of Five Books, *The Flowering Process, Truth by Reason and by Revelation, The Biology of Flowering, The Utah UFO Display: A Biologist's Report, The Creation;* Co-Author, *Vascular Plants: Form and Function, Plant Physiology, Second Edition, Botany: An Ecological Approach;* Over 130 Technical Papers and Articles Concerning Flowering and Time Measurement in Plants, Physiological Ecology, Space Biology (plant responses to gravity, etc.), Unidentified Flying Objects, and Science and Religion. Honors and Awards: Award of Merit from the Botanical Society of America 1982. Address: 2020 North 1250 East, North Logan, Utah 84321.

Salzburg, Joseph Sheldon

Director of Administration. Personal: Born July 13, 1926; Son of Samuel and Anna Eber Salzburg (both deceased); Married Carmen Albaladejo. Education: Attended University of Southern California 1945-46, United States Armed Forces Institute 1947; B.A. Clinical Psychology and Graduate Studies, University of Miami, Florida, 1948-51; Government, University of Maryland, 1960; University of Pittsburgh School of Public and International Affairs, 1968; Ph.D. Candidate, Political Science, University of California Western, 1977-81. Military: Served in the United States Army, 1947-48. Career: Director of Administration, Agricultural Cooperative Development International, 1980 to present; Agency for International Development/United States Department of State, Foreign Service Reserve Officer, Project Manager, Senior Project Advisor, Rural Development Officer, 1967-80; Executive Director, Jersey City, New Jersey Chapter, American Red Cross, 1963-67; Field Director, Field Representative and Assistant Field Director, American National Red Cross, Worldwide, 1951-63. Organizational Memberships: American Foreign Service Association, 1971-80; International Platform Association, 1978-81; Society for International Development, 1980-81; Rotary Club International, 1963-67. Community Activities: Public Service with United States State Department, Mali, Afghanistan, Ethiopia, Cambodia, Nigeria, Vietnam, 1967-80; Public Service with American National Red Cross, Korea, Japan, Lebanon, Turkey, Germany, France, and Spain, 1951-56; Public Service with Agricultural Cooperative Development International, Washington, D.C. Published Works: *A Violation of Trust*, in Progress; *Reflections Through a Moving Lens*, Ready for Publication; *The Right Time, The Right Place*, 1978; *Vietnam,: Beyond the War*, 1975; *The Dream-Seeker*, 1972; *No Place of Her Own*, 1971; *A Thousand Delights*, 1970; *Evil Be My Good*, 1970; *Of Power and Faith*, 1967; *The Dividing Lines*, 1965; *The Joys of Living*, 1963; *Moments of Inspiration*, 1961; *Tales of Aragon*, 1960; *The Little Things*, 1956; *A Child of Unknown Parents*, 1954. Honors and Awards: Presidential Medal of Freedom, President Eisenhower, 1954; Vietnam Presidential Order of Merit First Class, President Nguyen Van Thieu, 1974; Purple Heart, Bronze Star, Korean Conflict, United States Army, 1953; Meritorious Honor Award, United States State Department, 1972; City Plaque for Outstanding Service, Jersey City, New Jersey, 1967; Letters of Commendation, Nigerian Government 1970, Cambodian Government 1973, Afghanistan Government 1976; Presidential Unit Citation, 31st Infantry Regiment, 1953; Regimental Citation, 31st Infantry Regiment; Three Official Commendations, 7th Infantry Division, 1953-54; Army Certificate of Achievement, Lebanon Crisis, 1958; Army Commendation, Berlin Crisis, 1959; Vietnam Honor Medal First Class, 1972; Vietnam Social Welfare Medal First Class, 1969; Vietnam Ethnic Minorities Medal First Class, 1974; Vietnam Rural Development Medal, 1971; Civilian Service Medal, Vietnam War, 1968; Assistantships in Experimental Psychology, University of Miami, 1950-51; Listed in *Who's Who in the East*, *Who's Who in Finance and Industry*, *International Men of Achievement*, *International Who's Who of Intellectuals*, *Personalities of America*. Address: 2272 Pimmit Run Lane, Falls Church, Virginia 22043.

Joseph S Salzburg

Salzman, Barnett Seymour

Psychiatrist. Personal: Born February 15, 1939; Married Dianna Olivia Toney; Father of Rachel Star, Sunshine Noel, Priscilla Magdalene, Star Barnett. Education: B.A., Hunter College, 1960; Postgraduate Teaching Fellowship, Northeastern University, 1960-61; M.D., University of Buffalo School of Medicine, 1965; Internship, Good Samaritan Hospital, Los Angeles, 1965-66; Southern California Psychoanalytic Institute, Beverly Hills, Chief Resident in Psychiatry, 1968-69, Clinical Associate 1968-74; Resident Psychiatrist, Cedars-Sinai Medical Center, Los Angeles, 1966-68; Diplomate National Board of Medical Examiners, 1966; American Board of Psychiatry and Neurology, 1982; Physicians and Surgeons License, Texas, Hawaii, California, Utah, Illinois; Specialist in Psychiatry, Board Certified. Career: Private Practice of Psychiatry-Bryan, Texas; Director of Psychiatry, Austin W. King Center, 1981-82, Beverly Hills 1980-81, 1968-74; Medical Advisor, Citizen's Commission on Human Rights, Los Angeles, 1980-81; Active Medical Staff, Protman Memorial Hospital, Culver City, California 1980-81, Woodview-Calabassas Hospital, California 1980-81; Private Practice of Psychiatry, Honolulu, Hawaii, 1978-80; Instructor of Marriage and Family Relations, Escondido Adult School, 1976-77; Radio Broadcaster, "Barnett and Salzman, M.D., Mind and Soul", KRIO-FM and XEMO-AM, San Diego, 1975-77; Private College, Santa Maria, 1975; Director of Mental Health Services, Santa Barbara County Medical Health Services, Santa Maria Division, 1975; Radio Commentator, KPFK Pacifica Radio of Los Angeles, 1973-74, KEYY Radio of Provo 1974-75; Guest Lecturer, Brigham Young University, Provo, 1974-75; Medical Director, Utah County Council on Drug Abuse Rehabilitation, Provo, 1974-75; Founder and Medical Director, Utah Valley Mental Health Clinic, Provo, 1974-75; Personal Physician to Grand Lama Sakya Trizin, Sakya Centre for Tibetan Buddhism, Dehra Dun, India, 1973; Medical Advisor, Advisory Board of Citizen's Commission on Human Rights, Hawaii Chapter 1979-80, Escondido Union School District 1975-76, International Academy of Biological Medicine, Phoenix 1975-78; Director and Founder, Laguna Beach Free Clinic, 1970-71; Staff Psychiatrist and Lieutenant Commander, United States Navy Medical Corps, 1969-71; Staff Psychiatrist, California Department of Corrections, Parole Outpatient Clinic, 1967-72. Organizational Memberships: American Psychiatric Association; Academy of Orthomolecular Psychiatry, American College of Forensic Psychiatry. Honors and Awards: Fellow, Royal Society of Health, Appointed by Queen Elizabeth II of Great Britain; Physician's Recognition Award, American Medical Association, 1970-81; Listed in *Dictionary of International Biography*, *International Who's Who in Community Service*, *International Men of Achievement*, *International Register of Profiles*, *Book of Honor*, *Notable Americans*, *American Patriots of the Eighties*, *Personalities of the West and Midwest*, *Distinguished Americans of 1981*, *Who's Who in the West*, *Who's Who in California*. Address: 1878-B Greenfield Plaza, Bryan, Texas 77801.

Barnett S Salzman

Sament, Sidney

Neurologist, Electroencephalographer. Personal: Born April 25, 1928, in Lithuania; Son of Bernard and Mina Liebe Sament (both deceased); Father of Hilary, David, Brian. Education: M.B., B.Ch., Witwatersrand University, Johannesburg, South Africa, 1952; Undertook Post Graduate Studies in England, 1960-64, in EEG, Neurology, Internal Medicine; Further Studies at Harvard Medical School, 1967-69. Career: Practice in Internal Medicine, South Africa, 1953-60; Intern, Baragwanath Hospital, Johannesburg, 1953-54; Resident in Neurology, Jersey City Medical Center, 1964-65; Resident, New England Medical Center, 1964-67; Fellow, Harvard Medical School, 1967-69; Assistant Professor in Neurology, Hahnemann Hospital, Philadelphia, 1970-73; Medical Practice Specializing in Neurology and Electroencephalography, Easton, Pennsylvania, 1973 to present. Organizational Memberships: American Medical Association; American EEG Society; American Epilepsy Society; American Academy of Neurology; Local Medical Society. Community Activities: Rotary Club of Easton. Honors and Awards: First to Describe Ketotic Coma in Diabetes, 1957; Papers on EEG and Neurology; Research on "Brain Death" at Massachusetts General Hospital, Boston, 1968-69; Special Award for Continuing Post-Graduate Education, American Medical Association, 1970-73. Address: 3515 Southwood Drive, Easton, Pennsylvania 18042.

Samford, William Jame Jr

Senior Legal Advisor to the Governor of Alabama. Personal: Born February 4, 1950; Son of Mr. and Mrs. William J. Samford. Education: B.A., Auburn University, 1972; J.D., University of Alabama School of Law, 1978; Attended Squadron Officers School,

1974. Military: Served with United States Air Force with rank of first Lieutenant, 1972-75. Career: Senior Legal Advisor to Governor Fob James of Alabama, Montgomery; Former Litigation Attorney for Federal Deposit Insurance Corporation, Washington, D.C.; Former President of the Alabama Public Service Commission; Former Squadron Section Commander, U.S.A.F. Organizational Memberships: American Bar Association; Alabama Bar Association; Alabama Trial Lawyers Association; National Association of Regulatory Utility Commissioners; Farrah Law Society. Community Activities: Chairman of State Employees division, United Way and Heart Association; Member, Alabama Boys and Girls Ranch; Appointed by Governor James as President of the Alabama Public Service Commission. Religion: Member of First United Methodist Church, Opelika, Alabama. Honors and Awards: Member of Bench and Bar Honor Society, 1977-78; Named an Outstanding Young Man of America, 1978 and 1979; Received a citation for outstanding service to national government in utility regulation; Listed in *Personalities of the South, Who's Who in the South and Southwest, Who's Who in Government.* Address: 575 Cloverdale Road, Montgomery, Alabama 36106.

Sams, Mary Ann

E.C.E. Administrator. Personal: Born September 14, 1933; Daughter of Carmen H. and Helen F. (Strauk) Pacella; Married Wendell Morris Sams; Mother of Derek John Thomas. Education: A.B. cum laude, Home Economics/Child Development, Mundelein College, Chicago, 1958; M.Ed., Elementary Counseling, University of Puget Sound, 1970; Certificate, Elementary Education, Chicago Teachers College, 1960; Certificate, Special Education, University of Kansas, 1964; Certificate, Montessori Certification for Early Childhood Education and Teacher Training, American Montessori Teacher Training Institute, 1966; Certificate, Gessell and ILG Developmental Placement Examiner, Central Washington State College, 1969; Certificate, Parent Effectiveness Trainer, Teacher Effectiveness Trainer, Effectiveness Training Associates, 1972; Certificate, School Administration, San Francisco State University, 1973; Ed.D. Candidate, University of San Francisco, 1977 to present. Career: Administrator, Piedmont Avenue Child Development Center, Oakland, California; Director, Children's Centers Department, Oakland Unified School District, 1979-80; Program Manager, Children's Centers Department, San Francisco Unified School District, 1975-78; Program Director, Western Region, Mini-Skools Ltd., Irvine, California, 1974-75; Coordinator, Reading and English as a Second Language, Department of Defense, Military Dependent Schools, Pacific Area, (Japan), 1973-74; Executive Director, Curriculum and Personnel, Sullivan Preschool Centers and Sullivan Schools, Irving, California, 1971-73; Director, Sullivan Preschool and Sullivan School, Redwood City, California, 1971; Project Manager, Project Learn, Behavioral Research Laboratories, Menlo Park, California, 1970-71; Early Childhood Specialist, Franklin Pierce Public School District, Tacoma, Washington, 1969-70; Instructor, University of Puget Sound, 1969-70; Teacher, Annie Wright Seminary, Tacoma, Washington, 1968-69; Master Teacher and Teacher Trainer, Park Ridge Montessori School, Park Ridge, Illinois, 1966-67; Master Teacher and Teacher Trainer, Spring Valley Montessori School, Federal Way, Washington, 1967-68; Teacher, Kindergarten-Primary Grades, Chicago, Illinois, 1964-66; Social and Personal Adjustment Teacher, Vocational Rehabilitation Division, Topeka, Kansas, 1962-64; Special Services Teacher, Kindergarten and Primary Grades, Chicago Public Schools, 1958 to present; Consultant to Huffman Educational Systems (Duarte, California) Behavioral Research Laboratories (Palo Alto), Sullivan Associates (Palo Alto), Photo and Sound (San Francisco), McGraw Hill and Company Webster Division (Chicago), Pscyhotechnics (Glenview, Illinois), Many Public School Systems and Others. Organizational Memberships: California Child Development Administrator's Association (state executive board, 1979-81; member-at-large, 1979-81); Phi Delta Kappa; United Administrators of Oakland Schools; National Association for Education of Young Children; Council for Exceptional Children; National Black Child Development Institute; American Association of School Personnel Administrators; American Society for Personnel Administrators; Bay Area School Personnel Association; American Montessori Society; Association Montessori Internationale; Association of California School Administrators; International Biographical Association (fellow). Community Activities: Children's Lobby of California, 1978 to present; Cenacle Convent of Chicago (retreat volunteer, 1951-60). Religion: Retreat-Promotion Speaker, Cenacle Convent of Chicago. Published Works: "A Very Good Year", 16mm Sound Film, 1974; "Sullivan Individualized Reading Program", 35mm Slide-Cassette Tape, 1972; "Safety the Montessori Way" 1967. Honors and Awards: Certificate of Appreciation, San Francisco Unified School District, 1978; Special Tribute, Board of Education, Oakland Unified School District, 1980; Resolution, Children's Center's Leadership Advisory Committee, 1980; Certificate of Excellence, California Child Development Administrator's Association, 1980, 1981; Keeper of the Dream Award, California Child Development Administrator's Association, 1981; Listed in *Who's Who in the West, World Who's Who of Women, Personalities of the West and Midwest, Directory of Distinguished Americans, International Who's Who of Intellectuals, Book of Honor.* Address: 76 Los Cerros Avenue, Walnut Creek, California 94598.

Paul E Sanford

Sanford, Paul Everett

University Professor, Nutritionist. Personal: Born January 14, 1919; Married Helen L. Crenshaw; Father of Paula Louise Schubert, Patricia Kathleen Banning, Carolyn Ruth Sanford-Elmore. Education: B.S., Agriculture, Kansas State University, 1941; M.S. Poultry Nutrition 1942, Ph.D. Poultry Nutrition 1949, Iowa State University. Military: Served in the United States Army, 1943-46, with the rank of Tech Sergeant in the Medical Corps. Career: Professor, Department of Animal Science and Industry, Kansas State University. Organizational Memberships: Poultry Science Association (general program chairperson, 1981 annual meeting); American Poultry Historical Society (secretary, 1967-70); NACTA (state coordinator for Kansas, 1976 to present); A.R.C.A.S.; Kansas Academy of Science; C.A.S.T.; A.N.R.C.; World's Poultry Science Association; American Association for the Advancement of Science (fellow, 1961); Sigma Xi (secretary, 1973-75; president-elect, 1975-76; president, 1976-77). Community Activities: Phi Kappa Phi (secretary, 1953-56; president, 1956-67); Gamma Sigma Delta (secretary, 1958-61; president, 1962-63); Alpha Zeta (faculty advisors committee, six years); Honorary Member, Broiler Society of Japan, 1963; Riley County Chapter, America Red Cross (chairman, 1966-69); Parent-Teacher Association (treasurer); Manhattan Senior High Parent-Teacher Association (president); City of Manhattan Environmental Board, 1971-74; City of Manhattan Citizens Involvement Committee (chairman, 1975-76). Religion: Presbyterian; Deacon, 1959-65; Elder, 1966-72. Honors and Awards: Fellow, American Association for the Advancement of Science, 1961; Gamma Sigma Delta Senior Faculty Award of Merit, 1973; E. Walter Morrison Award, 1976; Faculty Advisor of the Year, 1980-81; NACTA Distinguished Educator Award, 1982; National Poultry Science Association Outstanding Teaching Award, 1982. Address: 343 North 14th Street, Manhattan, Kansas 66503.

Issac J Sanger

Sanger, Isaac Jacob

Retired. Personal: Born January 8, 1899; Son of Samuel Abraham Sanger (deceased), Rebecca E. Bowman (deceased); Married Marjorie Graybill (deceased). Education: Attended Bridgewater College; B.S., Fine Arts Education, Columbia University Teachers College; Undertook Graduate Studies at The School of Painting and Sculpture, Columbia University and Art Students League, New York. Military: Served in the United States Army, 1942-43, attaining the rank of Private First Class. Career: Arts Illustrator, Military Air Transport Service, Department of Health, Education and Welfare, Washington, D.C. Organizational Memberships: Society of Washington Printmakers. Religion: Washington City Church of the Brethren. Published Works: Illustrations for *Land of the Free* by Walter Meigs, *Wood Engravings of the 1930's* by Clare Leighton, *Graphic Works of American 30's* and *American Prints from Wood* by Smithsonian Institution Press. Honors and Awards: Joint Prize, Philadelphia Print Club, 1929; Represented Four Times in 50 Prints of the Year; Included in Fine Prints of the Year, 1936, 1937; Honorable Mention, Philadelphia Print Club, Twice; Cited for Outstanding Achievement in Graphic Arts, Bridgewater College, Bridgewater, Virginia, 1977; Prints included in the Permanent Collections of National Museum of American Art, Library of Congress and in Other Public Collections; Certificate for Outstanding Contributions to the Art of Printmaking, National Museum of American Art; Included in Smithsonian Institution's Archives of American Art; Listed in *Personalities of America, Community Leaders and Noteworthy Americans, Notable Americans, A Directory of Washington Artists - Biographical Listings.* Address: 3610 Riviera Street, Temple Hills, Maryland 20748.

Sarafian, Armen

University President. Personal: Born March 5, 1920, in Van Nuys, California; Father of Winston, Norman, Joy. Education: Graduate of Bonita Union High School, California; A.B. magna cum laude, La Verne College; M.A., Claremont Graduate University; Ph.D., University of Southern California; LL.D., La Verne College. Career: President, University of La Verne, 1976 to present; President of Pasadena City College (now President Emeritus), Superintendent of Pasadena Area Community College District, 1965-76; Administrative Dean for Instruction, Pasadena City College, 1959-65; Adjunct Professor of Community College Administration, University of Southern California, 1968-78; Coordinator of Secondary and Junior College Education, Pasadena City Schools, 1951-59; Summer and Part-time Teaching at 12 Different Colleges and Universities, 30 years; History and Political Science Teacher, Pasadena Junior College District, 1947-51; Chairman, Banning High School English Department, 5 years. Organizational Memberships: California Junior College Association Legislation Committee, 1973-76; Adult and Continuing Education Committee for California Community Colleges, 1974-75; Select Committee on Restudy of California Master Plan on Higher Education, Coordinating Council on Higher Education, 1970-72; Southern California Community College Instructional Television Consortium (chairman, executive committee, 1965-76); La Verne College (board of trustees, 1969-76); Southern California Industry-Education Council (executive committee, 1967-71); Member of Steering Committee that Established "California Plan for Self-Appraisal and Accreditation of Secondary Schools", 1955-58; Pasadena Area School Trustees Association (founder; member); University of Southern California Educare. Community Activities: La Verne Chamber of Commerce (president, 1978-79); New Century Club of Pasadena (president, 1975-76); Pasadena Hall of Science Project (founder, member of executive committee, 1965-76); Native Sons of the Golden West; Pasadena Arts Council; South Pasadena Oneonta Club; Pasadena Chamber of Commerce (vice president, 1972); Pasadena Kiwanis Club (vice president, 1971); California Conservation Council (president, 1966-68); Pasadena Area Youth Council (founder, adult advisor, 1953-66); *Los Angeles Times* Scholarship Award Contest (judge); Arcadia Coordinating Council; Pasadena Historical Society; Pasadena Area Mexican-American Scholarship Committee (patron); Former Management Advisor to City of Pasadena Municipal Government. Honors and Awards: Life Membership Gold Seal Bearer, California Scholarship Federation; Full Tuition Scholarship, La Verne College, Claremont Graduate School; Honorary Life Member, Pasadena Council of Parents and Teachers; Honorary Life Member, Associated Student Body of Pasadena City College; Distinguished Community Service Award, Pasadena Education Association; Conservation Merit Award, California Conservation Council; Omicron Mu Delta Distinguished Service Award; Meritorious Service Award of Pasadena City College Faculty Senate; Citizen of the Day, Sierra Madre City Council; Phi Delta Kappa Special Recognition Award; Ralph Story Award for Outstanding Service to Education; University of Southern California Service Award; United States Public Health Service Recognition Award; Honorary Life Member, Pasadena Chamber of Commerce; Western Association of Student Financial Aid Administrators Award; Salvation Army "OTHERS" Award, 1975; Arthur Noble Award, Pasadena City Board of Directors as Most Distinguished Citizen of Pasadena, 1976; Recognition Award, Pasadena Arts Council, 1976; President-Emeritus, Pasadena City College; Delta Epsilon Distinguished Lecturer for 1973, University of Southern California; Listed in *Who's Who in American Education, Who's Who Among Students in American Colleges and Universities, Who's Who in California, Who's Who in the West, Who's Who Executive in California, Men of Achievement, Who's Who in America, Who's Who in the World.* Address: P.O. Box 1624, Glendora, California 91740.

Sarin, Vinod Kumar

Technical Staff Member. Personal: Born January 29, 1944; Married Rani Chandragupta; Father of Annika, Amit. Education: B.Sc., University of Wisconsin-Madison, 1965; M.Sc., University of Michigan-Ann Arbor, 1966; Sc.D., Massachusetts Institute of Technology, 1971. Career: Technical Staff, G.T.E. Laboratories; Senior Research Scientist, Adanas Carbide; Research Metallurgist; Sanduik AB, Sweden; Pool Officer, National Physical Laboratory, India; Lecturer, I.I.T., New Delhi, India. Organizational Memberships: Sigma Xi; American Powder Metallurgy Institute; American Society of Metals (machinability committee); American Society of Carbide and Tool Engineering. Religion: Hindu. Honors and Awards: Non-Resident Tuition Scholarship, University of Wisconsin, 1961-65; General Electric Fellow, University of Michigan, 1965-66; Incra Fellow, Massachusetts Institute of Technology, 1968-71; First Prize, International Metallographic Exhibition, 1975; Other Metallographic Prizes, 1974-78; Several Technical Papers and Patents; Listed in *Who's Who in the East.* Address: 7 Diamond Road, Lexington, Massachusetts 02173.

Sasso, Laurence J Jr

Administrator. Personal: Born December 28, 1942; Son of Mr. and Mrs. Laurence J. Sasso Sr.; Married Kathryn M. Gray; Father of Lauryn Ethne. Education: B.A. 1965, M.A. 1967, University of Rhode Island. Career: Director, Office of News and Information, Rhode Island College; Former Editorial Assistant, Observer Publications, Smithfield, Rhode Island; Free-Lance Writer, Poet; Poetry Editor, Providence, Rhode Island, *Journal-Bulletin*, 1970-77; Founder, Co-Publisher, Editor, *The Greyledge Review*, 1979; Author, *Harvesting the Inner Garden.* Organizational Memberships: Council for Advancement and Support of Education; Rhode Island Press Club. Community Activities: Historical Society of Smithfield (vice-president, 1981); Voting District 5, Smithfield, Rhode Island (district moderator, 1976-78, 1978-80, 1980 to present). Honors and Awards: *Sou'Wester* Magazine's Poetry Award, 1976; UNICO Foundation Literary Contest, 4th Place in Nation, 1978; Winner, Major Poetry Award, Worcester County Poetry Association, 1981; Listed in *Who's Who in the East.* Address: 142 Mann School Road, R.F.D. 3, Smithfield, Rhode Island 20917.

Satchidananda, Swami

Minister. Personal: Born December 22, 1914. Education: Studied Agriculture, Science and Technology, Coimbatore, India; Undertook Spiritual Study with Renowned Sages, including Sri Aurobindo, Ramana Maharshi, Swami Sivananda, all of India. Career: Minister; Founder/Director, Intergral Yoga Institutes and Satchidananda Ashrams, Center for Spiritual Studies. Organizational Memberships: Temple of Understanding (advisory board); California Yoga Teachers Association; Integral Health Services (board of directors); International Yoga Teachers Association (patron); European Yoga Union Federation. Community Activities: Light of Truth Universal Shrine Project (president); Satchidananda Charity Funds (president); Belgian Yoga Federation (patron). Religion: Founder, Yoga Ecumenical Retreats (Y.E.R.), and Yoga Ecumenical Services (Y.E.S.), 1970 to present. Honors and Awards: Martin Buber Award for Outstanding Service to Humanity, 1966; Awarded 1st U.S. Citizenship as "Minister of Divine Words", 1976; Private Audience with H.H. Pope Paul VI, 1968. Address: Rt. 1, Box 172, Buckingham, Virginia.

Sauer, James E Jr

Administrator. Personal: Born February 14, 1934; Married Sharon Ann; Father of Scott, Jeffrey, Steven. Education: B.S.B.A., University of North Dakota, 1956; M.H.A., University of Minnesota, 1964. Military: Served in the United States Air Force, 1956-62, attaining the rank of Captain. Career: Administrator, Saint Joseph Medical Center, Burbank, California, 1979 to present; President, Executive Director, California Hospital Medical Center, Los Angeles, 1973-79; Associate Administrator, Providence Hospital, Portland, Oregon, 1969-73; Assistant Administrator, Administrative Services, Providence Hospital, 1976-79; Assistant Administrator, Children's Orthopedic Hospital and Medical Center, Seattle, Washington, 1964-67; Administrative Resident, San Jose Hospitals and Health Center, 1963-64; Administrative Assistant, Methodist Hospital, Madison, Wisconsin, 1961-62. Organizational Memberships: American College of Hospital Administrators (fellow; college standards review committee, 1978-83); American Hospital Association (council on patient care services, 1978-83; chairman 1982-83); Oregon Conference of Catholic Hospitals Association (president, 1972-74); Portland Council of Hospitals (president, 1972-74); Hospital Council of Southern California (board of directors, 1975-81; executive committee, 1977-81; chairman and member many committees and task forces; treasurer, 1977-78; chairman-elect, 1978-79; chairman, 1979-80; nominating committee, 1981-83; program planning committee, 1981-82); California Hospital Association (board of trustees, 1979-80; treasurer, 1980-81; hospital management committee, 1976-78; cost containment committee, 1977-78; program planning committee, 1978; task force to study excess capacity, 1978; 1980 Walker Fellowship selection committee; CHA program planning committee, 1979; program planning committee, 1979-80; bylaws committee, 1981; executive committee, 1981; chairman of the board, 1982-83); Hollywood Academy of Medicine; California Hospitals-Political Action Committee (board of directors); California Association of Catholic Hospitals (board of trustees); American Arbitration Association (Los Angeles advisory council); Hospital Associated Supply Service Laundry Corporation (board of directors, 1973 to present; president, board of directors, 1976-77); Central Area Teaching Hospitals (board of directors, 1976-78; secretary, board of directors, 1978-79; chairman, management committee, 1977-78); Alcoholism Council of Greater Los Angeles (medical affairs committee); Blue Cross of Southern California (hospital advisory committee, 1976-79; chairman, hospital advisory committee, 1978-79; committee to study corporate membership structure, 1978-79); Salerni Collegium of the University of Southern California School of Medicine (regional coordinator). Published Works: Number of Professional Papers and Presentations including (most recently) "Competition in the Health Care Field; What Will it Mean for a Catholic Hospital?" 1981, "Innovative Plan Solves Nurse Shortage Problem" 1981, "Nursing Shortage: A Solution" 1980. Honors and Awards: University of North Dakota Outstanding Graduate, 1956; Listed in *Outstanding Young Men of America, Who's Who in the West, Who's Who in California.* Address: 1950 Oak Street, South Pasadena, California 91030.

Sauer, Mary L

Substitute Teacher. Personal: Born June 26, 1923; Daughter of Mr. and Mrs. George Barber; Married; Mother of Elisabeth Ruth, Gordon C. Jr., Margaret Louise, Amy Kietter Sauer Doyle. Education: Graduate of Cleveland Heights High School; B.M.E., Northwestern University; Post Graduate Studies at the University of Missouri-Kansas City. Career: Substitute Teacher for Kansas City Schools. Organizational Memberships: Mu Phi Epsilon; American Guild of Organists; Kansas City Musical Club (associate member, co-chairman). Community Activities: American Association of University Women; Philharmonic League (president, 1959-60); Women's Committee Council of the University of Missouri-Kansas City (board of directors, 1977-80); Conservatory of Music (trustee, 1980-82); Nettleton Retirement Home (board of directors, 1975-80); Research Hospital Junior Auxiliary, 1957-60; Shepherd Center Music Director, 1980; Daughters of the American Revolution, Westport Chapter; Lyric Opera Women's Guild, 1960. Religion: Presbyterian; Board of Women's Fellowship, 1960-76; Circle Leader, 1960-62, 1964-66; Pianist; Choir Member; Lay Pastor, 1981-82. Honors and Awards: Volunteer in Education, 1971-72, 1974-75; Listed in *Personalities of the West and Midwest, Book of Honor, Men and Women of Distinction, International Register of Profiles, Notable Americans, Community Leaders and Noteworthy Americans, Notable Americans of the Bicentennial Era.* Address: 830 West Fifty Eighth Terrace, Kansas City, Missouri 64113.

Lenwood O Saunders

Saunders, Lenwood O'Daniel

Minister. Personal: Born March 21, 1927 in Richlands, North Carolina; Married Lena Davis; Father of Alinda M. S. Gadson, Gwendolyn S. Flood, Louis O., Frank W., Wayman L. Education: Graduate of Georgetown High School, Jacksonville, North Carolina; Bachelor of Theology, Kittrell College; Attended Urban Training Center for Christian Mission, Chicago, Illinois; Studied Stewardship and Finance, Memphis, Tennessee African Methodist Episcopal Churches, Finance Departments; Certificate of Achievement and Attendance, Twelve-Week Course "The Christian Ministry", Shiloh Association Baptist Church, Warrenton, North Carolina; Master Barber Certificate, Modern Barber College, 1947. Military: Served in the United States Army, 1945-46. Career: Minister, African Methodist Episcopal Churches, Warrenton, Spring Hope, Enfield, Wilmington, Hickory, Durham and Rich Square, North Carolina; Minister, Gaston Chapter African Methodist Episcopal Church, Morganton, North Carolina; Lecturer in Black Studies, Lenoir Rhyne College, Hickory, North Carolina 1971-72, Caldwell Technical Institute, Lenoir, North Carolina, Lutheran Theological Seminary, Columbia, South Carolina, 1982; Carpenter and Painter, Warrenton, North Carolina, 1953-60; Master Barber, Kinston, North Carolina 1947-53, Warrenton, North Carolina, 1953-60, Wilmington, North Carolina 1960-66. Organizational Memberships: Western North Carolina Conference of the African Methodist Episcopal Church (board of examiners); Burke County Black Ministers Conference (vice-president). Community Activities: National Association for the Advancement of Colored People (chairman, religious affairs committee, North Carolina state branches; member, Burke County chapter); Burke County Chamber of Commerce (committee of governmental affairs); Democratic Party (executive committee, North Carolina, 1980 to present); Burke County Status of Women (board of directors); Burke County Arts Council (board of directors); Northampton County Human Relations Commission (former chairman, 1975-76); Catawba County Democrat Executive Committee (former first vice-chairman); Democratic Party (former precinct chairman, Wilmington, Hickory, and Rich Square, North Carolina); 10th Congressional District Executive Committee of the Democratic Party, 1970-72; North Carolina State Youth Advisory Council (appointed and reappointed by Governor James Hunt, 1978, 1980); Morganton's Interracial Inter-Denominational Ministerial Association (president, 1979-80); Prevention of Race Riot, Hickory, North Carolina, 1969-70; Blue Ridge Community Action (board of directors, 1979 to present; vice-chairman, 1980-82; chairman, 1982 to present). Honors and Awards: Outstanding Service Award for Outstanding Services to the Citizens of Hickory, North Carolina, as a Member of the Community Relations Council, 1971; Outstanding Minister of the Western North Carolina Conference of the African Methodist Episcopal Church in Recognition of Devotion to the Church, 1973; Minister of the Year for Outstanding Community Service, North Carolina Branches of the National Association for the Advancement of Colored People, 1975; Minister of the Year, President's Award, Burke County National Association for the Advancement of Colored People, 1978; Community Leadership Award for Outstanding Leadership in the Field of

Human Relations and Social Justice, North Carolina Human Relations Council, 1979; Invited to White House as a Black Leader of the South, President Carter, 1978; Key to the City, Mayor Andrew Kistler, 1979; Outstanding Minister of the Black Community for Outstanding Community Leadership, Hickory, North Carolina, 1973; Certificate of Appreciation for Interest and Involvement in Issues Affecting the Youth of North Carolina, Governor James B. Hunt, 1979. Address: 100 Bouchelle Street, Morganton, North Carolina 28655.

Savard, Lorena Berube

Office Manager. Personal: Daughter of J. Alfred and Florence H. Berube; Married Roger D. Savard; Mother of Dean R. Savard. Education; Postgraduate Cerfiticate of Achievement in General Business, 1962; Bookkeeping Certificate, Dudley Hall Business College, 1968; A.S. Accounting 1976, A.S. Management 1978, Quinebaug Valley Community College; Data Processing Course, Thames Valley Technical College, 1979; Computer Awareness Certificate, Northeast Connecticut Regional Adult Education Program, 1981. Career: Office Manager, Waters Bros. Oil Co., Inc., 1982 to present; Sales Representative, Southwest Telephone Company, 1981-82; Manager, DKH Credit Union, Inc., 1974-80; Teller, Citizens National Bank; Calculator Clerk, Phoenix Mutual Life Insurance Company; Invoice Records Clerk, Montgomery Ward. Organizational Memberships: National Association for Female Executives, Inc., 1978-79, 1981-82; International Platform Association; American Biographical Institute Research Association (life patron). Community Activities: Aspinock Historical Society; The Planetary Society; VW Club of Central New England (treasurer, 1972-76); Northeast Connecticut Association for Children with Learning Disabilities (treasurer, 1978 to present); Career Planning Support System for Local Students (steering committee, 1980-81); Putnam Elementary School (volunteer teacher aide, 1968); Quinebaug Valley Community College Business Office (volunteer, 1974); Teen Machine (volunteer, 1981); Quinebaug Valley Youth Services Bureau, Inc. (board of directors, 1981 to present); Day Kimbell Hospital Annual Giving Appeal (volunteer). Honors and Awards: Dean's List, Quinebaug Valley Community College, 1973-78; Listed in *Who's Who Among Students in American Junior Colleges, Who's Who of American Women, Personalities of America, Directory of Distinguished Americans, World Who's Who of Women, Community Leaders of America, Book of Honor.* Address: R.F.D. 1, Putnam, Connecticut 06260.

Savitz, Frieda Joyce

Artist, Teacher. Personal: Born December 3, 1931. Education: Cooper Union, New York City, 1953-54; Hans Hofmann School, Scholarship, 1954-55; B.S., M.A., Art Education, New York University, 1956-57; Master of Painting honoris causa Diploma, Universitai delle Arti, Accademia Italia, Parma, Italia, 1983. Career: Solo Art Exhibitions at Arizona State University-Tempe 1978, Hansen Galleries, New York City 1977-78, Southern Vermont Art Association, Manchester 1978, Rockland Community College, New York 1976, Hudson River Museum, New York 1973, St. Thomas Aquinas College, New York 1973; Group Exhibitions include Biennel Internationale de Gravure, Yugoslavia Summer 1983, Fourth Permanent Exhibiton at Palazzo delle Manites, Tazioni Accademia, Parma, Italia 1983-84, West/Art and the Law Exhibition 1982, Views by Women Artists 1982, Rutgers National Exhibition 1981-82, People '81, Hudson River Museum, New York 1981, Hampton International Expo, New York 1981, International Platform Association, Washington, D.C. 1981, Group Art Exposition 1981, World Tour, San Francisco Brigade Exhibit 1981, 6th International Independents Exhibition of Prints, Yokohama, Japan 1980, International Festival at Carlsberg Glystoteck Museum, World Women's United Nations Conference, Copenhagen, Denmark 1980, World Print Exhibition, New Orleans, Louisiana 1980's, Everson Museum, Syracuse, New York 1976-80, World Print Exhibition, San Francisco Museum of Modern Art 1977, International Ford Foundation Traveling Exhibition 1975-76, International XX Women's Pictures on Charletteborg, Copenhagen, Denmark 1975, Hudson River Museum, New York 1976, Brooklyn Museum, New York City 1975-76, Newark Museum, New Jersey, Smithsonian National Museum, Washington, D.C. 1957, Chrysler Museum, Massachusetts and Washington, D.C., Vermont Art Association, Manchester 1977-78, Guild Hall, East Hampton, New York 1979-82; Art in Private, Public and Corporate Collections such as Accademia Italia, Parma, Italia, Chrysler Museum, Washington, D.C., Smithsonian Institution Archives of American Art 1981, Sophia Smith Collection at Smith College in Women's History Archives, Northampton, Massachusetts 1980, Syracuse Print Collection, Syracuse, New York, Women's Archives of Carlsberg-Glystoteck Museum, Copenhagen, Denmark 1980, Southern Vermont Art Association of Manchester 1978 to present, San Francisco Museum of Modern Art Print Collection 1977, Bibliothque Nationale, Paris, France, Hudson River Museum, New York 1978, World Print Council, San Francisco, California 1978, A.T.&T. Collection, Minolta Collection, Philip Morris Collection, Guild Hall, East Hampton, New York 1979; Teacher of Painting, Drawing, Composition and Various Related Visual Areas, New York City and New Jersey, 1954-60, 1973-81. Organizational Memberships: Accademia of Italia Parma, Italy; International Platform Association, Washington, D.C.; C.A.A.; V.A.G.A.; A.E.A.; W.C.A.; N.Y.W.C.A.; W.W.A.C.; National Organization of Women; New York Ethical Society; World Print Council; International Artists Association; American Biographical Institute Research Association. Religion: American Ethical Society. Published Works: Poems, Fables and Articles, 1951-82. Honors and Awards: Master of Painting Honoris Causa, Accademia Italia, 1983; Golden Centaur Award, Accademia Italia, Parma, Italia, 1982; West/Art and the Law Exhibition Award, St. Paul, Minnesota, 1982; Honorary Diploma of Merit, Universitai delle Arti, Parma, Italia, 1981; Commemorative Award, American Biographical Institute Research Association, 1981; Gold Medal and Elected to Accademia Italia delle Arti del Lavoro, Parma, Italy 1980; Commemorative Award, International Biograpical Centre, Cambridge, England, 1979; Grant, New York Foundation for the Arts Artist in the School, National Endowments for the Arts Pilot Program, 1979; World Print Exhibition, San Francisco Museum of Modern Art, 1977; International Women's Award, Ford Foundation, 1975-76; Listed in *Who's Who in American Art, Who's Who in International Art, The World Who's Who of Women, Who's Who of American Women Artists, Dictionary of International Biography, Directory of Distinguished Americans, Personalities of America, Encyclopaedia of Contemporary Personalities, Book of Honor, Art Bibliographies Dictionary of Contemporary Artists, Two Thousand Notable Americans, Art Diary, The World's Art Guide, Tendenze & Testimonianze dell Arte Contemporanea, History of Interntional Art, Community Leaders of America, International Who's Who of Intellectuals, Catalog of the Golden Centaur Award, History of Contemporary Art.* Address: 109 West Clarkstown Road, New City, New York 10956.

Lorena B Savard

Sawyer, Valerie Estelle

Private Piano Teacher. Personal: Born July 14, 1936; Married John Edward Sawyer; Mother of John Edward Jr., Kyle David, James Matthew. Education: B.M.E., Baylor University, 1958; Two Years of Private Study at Huntingdon College. Career: Music Teacher in the Public Schools, 1958-61; Organist, Ridgecrest Baptist Church, Vincennes, Indiana, 1961-71; Private Piano Teacher. Organizational Memberships: Montgomery Piano Teacher Forum (program committee, 1981); Alabama Music Teachers Association; Music Teachers National Association (certified); Montgomery Symphony Orchestra Association; Montgomery Museum of Fine Arts; Parent-Teacher Association (executive board, Dannelly School, 1976-77); Cloverdale Community Council, 1979-81; Jeff David Parent-Teacher-Student Association; Montgomery Chamber Music Association. Religion: Pioneer Mission Work, Indiana, 1961-71; Children's Director, Vincenness Baptist Church, 1961-71; Pianist, Montgomery First Baptist Church, 1975-81. Honors and Awards: Listed in *Personalities of the South.* Address: 1829 Hill Hedge Drive, Montgomery, Alabama 36106.

Scanlin, Steven F

Medical Social Worker. Personal: Born September 25, 1945; Son of Donald and Millicent Scanlin. Education: B.S.Ed., Eastern Montana College, 1969; M.S.W., Portland State University, 1971. Military: Served in the United States Naval Reserve and United States Marine Corps, 1962-73, as a Hospital Corpsman First Class. Career: Medical Social Worker; Certified Urology Technician; Psychiatric Social Worker. Organizational Memberships: National Association of Social Workers (Central Idaho Branch chairman, 1976; Idaho Chapter treasurer, 1974-76). Community Activities: State Representative, Idaho House of Representative, 44th and 45th Legislatures, 1976-80; Chairman, Governor's Committee on the Handicapped, 1980 to present; Caldwell Meals on Wheels, Inc. (president, 1976); Idaho Arthritis Foundation (executive board); American Diabetes Association, Canyon County Unit (chairman). Religion: Mayflower Congregation Church, 1962 to present. Honors and Awards: Idaho Social Worker of the Year, 1980; Academy of Certified Social Workers, 1974 to present; Citation Award Winner, International Association of Personnel Employment Services, 1978. Address: 1019 LaCresta, Caldwell, Idaho 83605.

Steven F Scanlin

Scarcella, Vincent Anthony

Student. Personal: Born November 30, 1962; Son of Santi and Maria Scarcella. Education: Graduate of St. Peter's Boys High School, 1980; Candidate for Degree in Business Administration/Accounting, Wagner College. Community Activities: Songwriter, Composer, Music/Songs; Pianist in School Plays, School Assemblies, School Musicals; Actor in School Plays, School Musicals; Writer of School Plays; Band Member; Stage Crew; School Play Director; Number of Piano and Vocal Recitals, Wagner College; Number of Community Concerts; St. Peter's High School Tutor (mathematics, English, accounting); Newspaper Staff, St. Petersburg High School (reporter, writer, sports editor); Library/Office Aide; Volunteer in the Community; Intramural Sports (football, baseball, softball, basketball). Religion: Catholic; St. Joseph's Church, Altar Boy 1969-76, Church Organist, Church Commentator. Honors and Awards: Writer for the *Wagnerian* (The Wagner College Newspaper); Social Studies Award, 1976; Farewell Address Reader, 1976, St. Peter's High School; Academic Honor Roll, 1976-80; St. Peter's High School Honor Awards, Honor Certificates, Letters of Achievement and Commendation, 1976-80; National Honor Society, 1977-80; St. Peter's High School, Italian Honor Roll, 1978-79; Merit Achievement Award, 1978-79; First Prize in C.Y.O. Talent Show for Piano Performance, 1979; St. Peter's High School Italian Award, 1980; Wagner College Scholarship, 1980; Winner, Staten Island Advance Sports Letter Contest, Twice Winner for Best Letter, Other Sports Letters and Articles Published, 1981; Articles Published in Wagner College Newspaper, *Wagnerian*; Listed in *Who's Who Among American High School Students* (second year award, 1979-80), *International Youth in Achievement, Young Community Leaders of America*. Address: 14 Shaughnessy Lane, Staten Island, New York 10305.

Vincent Scarcella

Schaefer, Francis (Frank) Joseph

Teacher, Track Coach. Personal: Born September 18, 1947; Son of Mrs. James L. Sangster; Married Helen Marie Quick; Father of James Byron, Joy Christine, Jennifer Hope. Education: Graduate of Sam Houston High School, Houston, Texas; B.A., Political Science/Speech, Stephen F. Austin State University, 1970; M.Div., Southwestern Baptist Theological Seminary, 1974; Administrator and Supervisor Certification, Tarelton State University, 1981. Career: Oral Communication Teacher, Track Coach, Ellison High School, Killeen, Texas; Oral Communication Teacher, Part-time, Central Texas College; Pastor, First Baptist Church, Nolanville, Texas, 1977-78; Pastor, English and German Language, Trinity Baptist Church, Metterich, West Germany, 1974-77; Mission Pastor for Inner City, First Baptist Church, Dallas, Texas, 1970-74; Pastor, Old North Baptist Church, Nacogdoches, Texas, 1969-70. Organizational Memberships: Texas State Teachers Association (faculty representative, 1980-81); Texas Classroom Teachers Association; Texas High School Coaches Association. Community Activities: Boy Scouts of America (chaplain, Camp Pirtle, Carthage, Texas, 1969-70); Shelby-Doches Baptist Association (youth and resolutions committee, 1969-70); European Baptist Convention, West Germany (missions and continuing education committee, 1969-70); International Adoption Agency, Bitburg, West Germany (translator, 1974-77); Killeen Independent School District (citizenship curriculum committee, 1979-80); Author of Citizen Curriculum Activities for Middle Schools, Killeen Independent School District, 1980; Evening Lions Club (civic and crippled children's committee, 1980-81). Religion: Southern Baptist Minister, Full-time 1969-78, Part-time 1978 to present; Sunday School Teacher, First Baptist Church of Killeen, 1981. Honors and Awards: Finalist for Optimist Club Scholarship, 1966; Recipient, Kiwanis Club Scholarship, 1966; Eastern Star Religious Scholarship, 1970; Listed in *Outstanding Young Men of America, Personalities of the South, Personalities of America, Book of Honor, Community Leaders of America, Directory of Distinguished Americans.* Address: 803 Cedar Oak, Harker Heights, Texas 76541.

Schaefer, Henry Frederick III

Professor of Chemistry. Personal: Born June 8, 1944; Son of Mr. and Mrs. Henry F. Schaefer, Jr.; Married Karen Rasmussen; Father of Charlotte Ann, Pierre Edward, Theodore Christian. Education: B.S., Chemical Physics, Massachusetts Institute of Technology, 1966; Ph.D., Chemistry, Stanford University, 1969. Career: Professor of Chemistry, University of California-Berkeley; Wilfred T. Doherty, Professor of Chemistry, and Director, Institute of Theoretical Chemistry, University of Texas-Austin, 1979-80. Religion: Evangelism, Walnut Creek, California, Presbyterian Church, 1977 to present. Honors and Awards: Alfred P. Sloan Fellow, 1972-74; John S. Guggenheim Fellow, 1976-77; Fellow, American Physical Society, 1977; American Chemical Society Award in Pure Chemistry, 1979. Address: Department of Chemistry, University of California, Berkeley, California 94720.

Henry F Schaefer III

Schapiro, George A

Executive. Personal: Born March 21, 1946; Son of Irwin A. Schapiro; Married Jo Ann Katzman; Father of Rebecca Jeanne. Education: B.A., University of Virginia, 1967; M.S., Industrial Administration, Carnegie-Mellon University, 1969. Career: Financial Analyst, Data Processing Group, I.B.M., 1968; Product Marketing Manager, Data Systems Division, Hewlett-Packard, 1969-74; Product Marketing Manager, Medical Electronics Division, Hewlett-Packard, 1974-76; President and Chief Executive Officer, Andros Inc., 1976-80; President, Chief Executive Officer, Andros Analyzers Inc., 1979 to present; Director, Mercator Business Systems, Inc., 1982. Organizational Memberships: Association for Computer Machinery; Society for Computer Medicine. Community Activities: Guest Lecturer, Stanford Graduate School of Business, University of California-Berkeley College of Engineering, University of California-Berkeley Extension School, American Management Association Seminar Series. Honors and Awards: G.S.I.A. Fellowship, Carnegie-Mellon University, 1968-69; Listed in *Who's Who in the West, Who's Who in California Business and Finance, Who's Who in Technology Today, Men of Achievement, Who's Who in Finance and Industry.* Address: 1967 Pine Street, San Francisco, California 94109.

Schary, Susan

Artist. Personal: Born August 7, 1936; Mother of Jennifer Lynn, Karima Ann. Education: B.F.A. with honors, Tyler School of Fine Arts, Temple University; Graduate, Philadelphia High School for Girls. Career: Artist; Taught at Harcum Junior College, Fleisher Art Memorial, Private Lessons; National and International Art Exhibitions, including Saudi Arabia 1981 & 1982, Museum of Science and Industry (California) 1981, Louis Newman Galleries (Los Angeles) 1977, California Museum of Science and Industry 1976, McKenzie Gallery (Los Angeles), Hancock Park Arts Council (Los Angeles) 1972, Municipal Art Gallery (Los Angeles), Civic Center Museum (Philadelphia) 1968, 1971, 1974, Mascagni D'Italia Gallery (Los Angeles), 1971, Samuel S. Fleisher Art Memorial Faculty Exhibition (Philadelphia) 1968, 100 Distinguished Philadelphia Artists from 1840 to present (Philadelphia) 1967, Arno and Florence Art Galleries (Florence, Italy) 1965, Philadelphia Women in Fine Arts Annual Exhibitions at the Moore Institute of Art (Philadelphia) 1962-66, Many Others; Number of Distinguished Commissions and Collections. Organizational Memberships: Artists Equity Association (past board member); International Platform Association. Honors and Awards: B.W. Gottleib Memorial Prize, Samuel S. Fleisher Art Memorial Faculty Exhibition, 1968; Honorable Mention, Fidelity Arts Festival, Philadelphia, 1965; Listed in *Artist's U.S.A., Women Artists in America, Who's Who in American Art, Who's Who in American Women, International Directory of Arts, Dictionary of International Biography, World Who's Who of Women.* Address: 228 St. Albans Avenue, South Pasadena, California 91030.

Susan Schary

Schauss, Alexander George

Director of American Institute for Biosocial Research. Personal: Born July 20, 1948; Son of Frank and Anna Schauss; Married Sharon L. Education: B.A. 1970, M.A. 1972, University of New Mexico; Additional Post Graduate Studies at Several Universities. Career: Director, American Institute for Biosocial Research; Research Director, Graduate School, City Colleges of Washington State; Training Officer, Washington State Criminal Justice Training Commission, Olympia; Director for Adult Probation Services, Pierce County, Washington; State Assistant Administrator for Correctons, South Dakota; Federal Criminal Justice Planner, New Mexico. Organizational Memberships: American Public Health Association; American Association for the Advancement of Science; New York Academy of Sciences; American Orthopsychiatric Association (fellow); Academy of Criminal Justice Sciences; American Society of Criminology; International College of Applied Nutrition; German Academy of Color Sciences; American Correctional Association; American Association of Correctional Psychologists. Community Activities: New England Salem's Children's Trust (board member, 1980 to present); National Foundation for Nutrition Research (board member, 1982 to present); Price Pottinger Nutrition Foundation (board member, 1980 to present); Pierce County, Washington Law and Justice Committee (chairman, corrections sub-committee; executive committee, 1977-78); Washington State's First Conference on Domestic Violence (conference moderator, 1977); Washington State Criminal Justice Training Commission, 1977-78; Washington State House of Representatives Institutions Committee Advisory Task Force, 1979-81; AFL-CIO Community Service Program (instructor, 1977-82); South Dakota Committee on the Humanities (instructor, 1975-77); South Dakota Department of Social Services (advisory council member, 1975-77); Governor's Committee on Criminal Justice Standards and Goals of New Mexico, 1974-75; Middle Rio Grande Council of Governments (chairman, city county goals committee, 1973-75); Addictions Services Council of Albuquerque/Bernalillo County (chairman, 1972-74); Junor League Advisory Council of Albuquerque, 1971-74; Police Athletic League Women's Track and Cross Country Team (track coach, 1973-75); Albuquerque Public School's Education Advisory Committee, 1970-73. Honors and Awards: Mayor of New York Citation, 1966; National American Legion Award, 1966; Sid Morris Y.M.C.A. Scholarship Award, 1966-70; Albuquerque General Addiction Treatment Effort Award for Community Service, 1975; Southwest Valley Youth Program Award for Community Service, 1975; American Personnel and Guidance Association's Public Offender Counseling Association Award, 1978, Award of Appreciation, San Diego County Sheriff's Department, 1980; Speaker's Award, International College of Applied Nutrition, 1981; Visiting Scholar, Kansas Associaton of Colleges and Universities, 1982; Listed in *American Men and Women of Science, Personalities of America, Personalities of the West and Midwest, Who's Who in the West, International Who's Who in Community Service, Men of Achievement, International Who's Who of Intellectuals, Notable Americans, Men and Women of Distinction.* Address: P.O. Box 1174, Tacoma, Washington 98401.

Alexander Schaus

Schendel, Winfried George

Insurance Company Executive. Personal: Born June 19, 1931; Son of Mrs. Margarete Gassner; Married Joanne Wiiest; Father of Victor Winfried, Bruce Lawrence, Rachelle Laureen. Education: B.S., Electrical and Industrial Engineering, Hannover-Stadthagen University, Hannover, West Germany, 1952. Career: Electrical Draftsman, Houston Lighting and Power, 1954-57; Electrical Draftsman, Corrosion Technology, Transcontinental Gas Pipeline Company, Houston, 1957-59; Electrical Engineer, Ken R. White Consulting Engineers, Denver, Colorado, 1959-61; Sales Engineer, Weco Division Food Machinery and Chemical Corp., 1961-64; Insurance Field Underwriter, New York Life Insurance Company, Denver, 1964-66; Assistant Manager 1966-70, Management Assistant 1970-71, General Manager 1971-77, Manager 1979 to present, New York Life Insurance Company; Ind. General Agent, Denver, 1978-79; Lakewood Chamber of Commerce (membership chairman); Sales Manager for Denver General Office of New York Life, Denver, Colorado. Organizational Memberships: National Association of Life Underwriters; Colorado Association of Life Underwriters; General Agents and Managers Association; International Salesmen with a Purpose Club. Community Activities: Boy Scouts of America (institutional representative, advancement chairman, Denver Area Council, 1968-72); Republican Party (precinct chairman, Jefferson County, Colorado, 1976, 1978); Lakewood Chamber of Commerce (president, People-to-People); Lions Club; Edelweiss; International Order of Rocky Mountain Goats; Masons; Shriners. Religion: Presbyterian, Elder. Honors and Awards: General Agents and Managers Association, Recipient of Cof. National Management Award, 1975; Centurion Award, 1966; Northwestern Region Leader Manpower Development Award, New York Life Insurance Company, 1968; Jefferson County Salesman of the Year, 1981; Readers Digest Award for People-to-People Program; International Positive Mental Attitude Award, 1975. Address: 13802 West 20th Place, Golden, Colorado 80401.

Schilling, Frederick Augustus Jr

Geologist. Personal: Born April 12, 1931; Son of Frederick and Hope Schilling; Married Ardis I. Dovre; Father of Frederick Christopher, Jennifer Dovre. Education: B.S., Washington State College, 1953; Ph.D., Stanford University, 1962. Military: Served in the United States Army, 1953-55. Career: Geologist, Various Organizations in California, Oregon, Idaho, Alaska, 1956-61; United States Geological Survey, California 1961, Kentucky 1962-64, Colorado, 1964, Keradamex Inc., Anaconda Company, M.P. Grace, Reserve and Oil and Minerals and Ranchers Exploration & Development Corp., Grants and Albuquerque, New Mexico, 1968 to present; Engineer, Climax Molybdenum Corporation, Colorado, 1966-68. Organizational Memberships: Geological Society of America; American Association of Petroleum Geologists; Society of Mining Engineers of A.I.M.E.; Rocky Mountain Association of Geologists; Albuquerque Geological Society. Community Activities: Presbyterian, The Explorers Club (Fellow), International Platform Association, Masons, Albuquerque, 1977 to present. Honors and Awards: Sigma Gamma Epsilon, 1952-53; Sigma Xi, 1959 to present; Representative of Stanford University at Concordia College, Presidential Inauguration in 1975. Address: 11413 Biscayne, N.E., Albuquerque, New Mexico 87111.

Schimizzi, Ned Vincent

College Faculty Member. Personal: Born January 27, 1936 in Mishawaka, Indiana; Son of Anthony and Josephine Schimizzi (both deceased). Education: B.S. 1958, M.S. 1964, Ed.D. 1968, Indiana University-Bloomington. Military: Served in the United States Signal Corps, 1958-64 to the rank of Sergeant E-5; Honorably Discharged 1964 for successful completion of obligation. Career: Associate Professor of Education, Department of Curriculum and Instruction, State University of New York, Buffalo State College, 1968 to present; Coordinator of Elementary Student Teaching Program, Indianapolis Area for Indiana University, 1966-68; Classroom Teacher, Bloomington Metropolitan Schools 1964-66, LaPorte County Schools, Indiana 1961-63; Designer of Courses Teaching Metric System to Educators, Modules and Materials for Teaching Metric System on Any Level, Graduate Course in Futurism and Curriculum Development. Organizational Memberships: American Association of University Professors; Phi Delta Kappa; State University of New York; Association for Supervision and Curriculum Development; Indiana University Alumni Association; Indiana University Foundation; National Council of Teachers of Mathematics; New York State Teachers of Mathematics Association; World Future Society; Research Council for Diagnostic and Prescriptive Mathematics; Association for Computers in Mathematics and Science Education; Association for Supervision and Curriculum Development; Phi Delta Kappa. Community Activities: Harry F. Abate Urban Open Elementary School (major participant in two radio broadcasts concerning open education concept); Buffalo State College Program (major participant, 1972-73); Interstate Environmental Group, Galena, Kansas (consultant concerning lead pollution and its effect on the learning process); Kidwell, O'Keefe, Williamson and Moran, Attorneys at Law, Wichita, Kansas (consultant concerning the effects of lead on the human body, specifically the learning process of children); United States Senate Committee on Commerce Senator Warren G. Magnuson, Chairman (consultant concerning metric legislation, 1975); Buffalo State College (academic advisory committee on computer services; academic advisory committee on instructional resources; faculty senate committee for student admissions and standards; chairman, C.A.I. committee). Published Works: "An Analysis of the Opinions of Elementary Supervising Teachers Concerning the Improvement of Student Teaching Programs in Indiana", *Dissertation Abstracts XXIX*, 1968; "How Can Student Teaching Programs be Improved?", with Harold F. Brinegar, *Indiana Teacher*, 1969; "An Analysis of the Opinions of Elementary Supervising Teachers Concerning the Improvement of Student Teaching Programs in Indiana", *Studies in Education*, 1968; "Analysis of Supervising Teacher's Opinions Concerning Student Teaching Programs", *ERIC Clearinghouse on Teacher Education*, 1969; "How Could Educators Improve the Student Teaching Experience?", with Harold F. Brinegar, *Bulletin of the School of Education* 1969, *Psychological Abstracts* 1970; "Lead: A Hidden Factor in Urban Learning Disabilities?", *Phi Delta Kappan*, 1971; "Environmental Group Astonished by Professor's Research", *Galena Sentinal Times*, Kansas, 1972; "Renaissance U.S.A. 21st Century", *Improving College and University Teaching*, 1972; "Lactos Malabsorption and Milk Rejection in Negro Children - What Does this Mean to Educators?", *Phi Delta Kappan* 1972, Research Library of ERIC/ECE, University of Illinois-Champaign-Urbana Center; "Video-Tape Screen Tests for Teaching Applicants?", *Phi Delta Kappan*, 1973; *Mastering the Metric System*, 1975; "Is More Effective Preparation Needed for Teachers of Beginning Reading?", with Mary Atta, *Kappa Delta Pi Record*, 1975; Contributor of Biographies of John P. Gordy and of Leta Stetter Hollingworth, *Directory of Emminent Educators*; "Does Your State Have Free Lead Testing Program for Children?", *The Journal of School Health*, 1976. Honors and Awards: Holder of United States Patent Number 3,255,808, for Audio-Visual Classroom Equipment; Listed in *Leaders in Education, Who's Who in the East*. Address: 1978 Delaware Avenue #5, Buffalo, New York 14216.

Schirmer, Howard August Jr

Consulting Geotechnical Engineer/Engineering Manager. Personal: Born April 21, 1942, in Oakland, California; Son of Mr. and Mrs. H. A. Schirmer; Married Leslie Mecum; Father of Christine Nani, Amy Kiana, Patricia Leolani. Education: B.S.C.E. 1964, M.S.C.E. 1965, University of California-Berkeley; M.B.A. Program, University of Hawaii-Manoa, 1968-70; Continuing Education in Soil Dynamics, Hawaiian Geology, University of Hawaii, 1967. Career: Professional Engineer, Hawaii 1968, Guam 1972; Dames and Moore, Chief Operating Officer 1981 to present, Regional Manager/Partner (Pacific, Far East and Australia) 1978-1981, Partner and Managing Principal-in-Charge 1975-78, Associate 1972-75, Chief Engineer 1969-72, Acting Chief Engineer 1968-69, Staff Engineer 1967-68, Assistant Engineer 1965-67; Dames and Moore San Francisco, Assistant Engineer 1965, Engineering Analyst 1964-65; Engineer-in-Training, State of California, Division of Highways, Materials and Research Laboratory, Sacramento, 1960-64. Organizational Memberships: American Consulting Engineers Council (chairman, geotechnical engineering committee, 1976, 1977; member organization committee, 1975; A/E procurement committee, 1980-81; planning cabinet 1981 to present); American Society of Civil Engineers (member, committee on engineering management at the individual level, 1978 to present); American Society of Civil Engineers, Hawaii Section (president, 1974; 1st vice president; 2nd vice president; treasurer; chairman, auditing committee; employment practice committee; chairman, private practice subcommittee for employment practices; chairman, nominations committee; co-chairman, seminar on "Professionalism in the Practice of Engineering in the Pacific Basin", 1979); American Society of Civil Engineering, Pacific-Southwest Council (chairman, 1975 meeting); Consulting Engineers Council of Hawaii (national director, 1973; president, 1972; vice president, 1971; treasurer, 1970; chairman, past national directors committee; chairman, awards committee; chairman, education committee; chairman, engineering practices committee; chairman, constitution and by-law revision committee; chairman, program committee; co-chairman, professional practices committee; chairman, nominating committee); Engineering Association of Hawaii (2nd vice president, 1977-78; director, 1976-77; chairman, awards and special projects committee; member, program committee); International Society of Soil Mechanics and Foundation Engineering; American Public Works Association (director, 1979, 1980; secretary, 1977, 1978); 15th International Coastal Engineering Conference (chairman, committee on industrial participation, 1976); Consulting Engineers Association of California; Chi Epsilon Board of Trustees University of Hawaii Chapter, 1980; University of California Engineering Alumni (past Honolulu regional chairman); Honolulu Community College (chairman, advisory committee for engineering technology, 1975-79); University of Hawaii Engineering Liasion Committee (past member); Construction Industry Legislative Organization (past member, engineers committee); Structural Engineers Association of Hawaii (committee member, ladies activities, Western States Council of Structural Engineers Associations, 1979); Society of American Military Engineers. Community Activities: Aloha United Way (1974 engineer section chairman; budget committee, 1975-77); Mauna Kea Ski Patrol (founder and patrol leader, 1969-72); National Ski Patrol System (national status, 1975 appointment; certified ski proficiency instructor, 1971-79); American Red Cross First Aid Instructor, 1971-79; Outrigger Canoe Club (past member, sailing committee; instructor); Ski Association of Hawaii; La Canada/Flintridge Chamber of Commerce; Sigma Phi Epsilon. Religion: Episcopal. Honors and Awards: Chi Epsilon Chapter Honor Member, University of Hawaii, 1979; National A.S.C.E. Edmund Friedman Young Engineers Award for Professional Achievement; Listed in *Who's Who in America, Who's Who in the West, Who's Who in Engineering, Who's Who in Technology; Men of Achievement, Who's Who in the World, Leading Consultants in Technology*. Address: 827 Inverness Drive, Flintridge, California 91011.

Schlacks, William Frederick

College Professor, Conductor. Personal; Born April 5, 1948; Son of Mr. and Mrs. Clarence C. Schlacks; Married Mary M. Orth.

Education: B.S.Ed. 1970, M.Mus. 1973, Northern Illinois University; Ph.D., Music Education, University of Miami, Florida, 1981. Career: Assistant Professor of Music Education, Conducting, and Conductor of Wind Ensemble and Symphonic Band, Indiana University-Purdue University of Fort Wayne, 1978 to present; Graduate Assistant, University of Miami, 1976-78; Instrumental and Vocal Music Teacher, Kaneland C. U. School District, 1970-74. Organizational Memberships: M.E.N.C.; IM.E.A. (state board, 1981-83); C.B.D.N.A.; C.M.S.; Phi Mu Alpha Sinfonia. Community Activities: Fort Wayne Area Community Band Inc. (founder, conductor, 1979 to present); Director of Musicals in St. Charles and DeKalb, Illinois, Community Theatres, 1972-76; Music Contests and Festivals (judge/clinician, 1978 to present); Collegiate Fine Arts Expo, Fort Wayne (coordinator, 1981). Religion: North Christian Church, Fort Wayne, Choir Director 1979-81; St. John's United Church of Christ, Fort Wayne, Choir Director 1982-present. Honors and Awards: Conducting Participant, C.B.D.N.A. National Conducting Symposium, Greely, Colorado, 1981; Listed in *Personalities of the West and Midwest*. Address 2224 Otsego Drive, Fort Wayne, Indiana 46825.

Schlagenhauff, Reinhold E

Administrator. Personal: Born August 14, 1923; Married Erika Krimm; Father of Annette, Stephen. Education: M.D., 1951. Career: Director, Department of Neurology, Erie County Medical Center; Associate Professor of Neurology, State University of New York at Buffalo. Organizational Memberships: Academy of Neurology; American Medical Electroencephalographic Association; American Institute of Ultrasound in Medicine. Published Works: Author of 42 Papers on Neurology, Electroencephalography, Electromyography, Ultrasound. Address: 41 Chaumont Drive, Buffalo, New York 14221.

Schmall, Vicki Louise

Gerontology Specialist. Personal: Born March 14, 1947; Daughter of Grant and Iona Flagan; Married Rodney A. Schmall. Education: B.S., Montana State University, 1969; Ph.D., Oregon State University, 1977. Career: Gerontology Specialist, Oregon State University Extension Service; Director, Program on Gerontology, Oregon State University, 1975-78; Research Associate, Applied Systems Research and Development, 1977-78; Teaching Assistant, Family Life Department, Oregon State University, 1971-75; Field Instructor/Supervisor, Program on Gerontology, Oregon State University, 1973-74; Research Assistant/Trainer, National Nutrition Program for the Elderly, Oregon State University, 1972-73; Instructor, Wilsall Consolidated Schools, 1969-70. Organizational Memberships: American Gerontological Society; Western Gerontological Society (editorial board, 1980 to present); National Council on Family Relations (editorial board, 1981 to present); American Home Economics Association (publications advisory board, 1980 to present); National Council on Aging; Oregon Gerontological Association (board of director, 1981 to present); Oregon Council on Family Relations; Oregon Home Economics Association; Oregon Extension Association. Community Activities: Conducted Over 100 Workshops on a Volunteer Basis for Public Service Agencies and Volunteers Working in Programs Serving Older Adults; Community Nutrition Institute, Washington, D.C. (consultant, 1980 to present); Oregon White House Conference on Aging (delegate, 1981); Governor's Task Force, White House Conference on Families, 1980; Hospice Development Committee, Benton County, 1978-80; Task Force on Housing for the Elderly, 1978-80; Reviewer for KWIC/ASTRA Training Resources on Aging, Duke University, 1978-80; Area Agency on Aging Advisory Committee (chairman, budget and nutrition committees, 1977-80); Governors Technical Advisory Committee on Aging, 1976-77. Religion: Workshops on Various Subjects regarding Aging to Community Religious Leaders and Members of Congregations. Published Works: Over 20 Professional Articles, 2 Educational Games and two Media Productions. Honors and Awards: Superior Award, Agricultural Communicators in Education, for Educational Game "Sex and Aging: A Game of Awareness and Interaction", 1981; Phi Kappa Phi; Omicron Nu; Coach of the Year, 1970; Listed in *Outstanding Young Women of America, Outstanding Young Women of Oregon, Who's Who of International Women*. Address: 835 Marylhurst Circle South, West Inn, Oregon 97068.

Phyllis K Schmertz

Schmertz, Phyllis Kane

Executive. Personal: Born March 2, 1949; Daughter of Martin and Rhoda Kane; Married Robert J. Schmertz (deceased). Education: B.S., New York University, 1971. Career: Fund Raising Staff, State of Israel Bonds, 1971-72; Board of Directors, Women's Division, State of Israel Bonds, 1972-75; Speakers Bureau, State of Israel Bonds, 1972 to present; Director Volunteer Opportunities, Democratic National Convention, 1976; Deputy Campaign Manager, Mayor Abe Beame Re-Election Committee, 1977; Special Representative, Co-Founder, First Annual World Banking Congress, 1977; President, Embassy News Publications, 1977-81; Vice Chairman, Treasurer, Universal Video Enterprises, Ltd., 1982 to present. Organizational Memberships: Democratic House and Senate Council, 1978; International Platform Association, 1980 to present. Community Activities: Robert J. Schmertz Memorial Games (co-chairman, 1976 to present). Address: 1020 5th Ave., New York City, New York 10028.

Schmidt, Betty Jane

Accountant. Personal: Born September 3, 1938; Daughter of Mrs. Vivian Banks Day; Married to Don D.; Mother of LaVerne W., Dennis D., Linda L. Education: Attended University of Wyoming, 1980, and San Diego State University, 1981. Career: Former motel and ranch manager; Former Manager, Schmidt Limousin and Don Neit Limousin; Former restaurant and lounge manager. Organizational Memberships: National Association of Female Executives; Women in Management; National Association of Limousin Breeders; National Cattlemen's Association; Wyoming Limousin Breeders Association (vice president, 1974-76). Community Activities: Park County 4-H Leader, 1966-70; Member, High School Scholarship Committee, 1976-77; Donated steers to Future Farmers of America, 1975-78. Religion: Member of Missouri Synod Lutheran Church, 1956 and Wisconsin Synod Lutheran Church, 1979. Honors and Awards: Her entire family selected as total F.F.A. Family, 1976; Listed in *Who's Who Among American Women, Who's Who in the West, Personalities of America, Directory of Distinguished Americans, World Who's Who of Women*. Address: 8110 Stadler, La Mesa, California 92041.

Schmitt, Harrison Hagan

United States Senator. Personal: Born July 3, 1935, in Santa Rita, New Mexico; Son of Harrison A. and Ethel Hagan Schmitt. Education: B.S., California Institute of Technology, 1957; Undertook postgraduate studies (Fulbright Fellow), University of Oslo, 1957-58; Ph.D., (N.S.F. Fellow), Harvard University, 1964; D.Eng., (honors), Colorado School of Mines, 1973. Career: Geologist, United States Geological Survey, 1964-65; Astronaut, National Aeronautical and Space Administration, 1965-74; Lunar Module Pilot, Apollo 17, December 1972; Special Assistant to Administrator, 1974; Assistant Administrator, Office of Energy Programs, 1974-75; Member, U.S. Senate, New Mexico, 1977 to present. Organizational Memberships: Geological Society America (honorary fellow); New Mexico Geological Society (honorary life member); Norwegian Geological Society (honorary member); American

Geophysical Union; American Association for the Advancement of Science; American Association of Petroleum Geologists; A.I.A.A.; Navy League; Sigma Xi. Honors and Awards: M.S.C. Superior Achievement Award, 1970; Distinguished Service Medal, National Aeronautics and Space Administration, 1973; Arthur S. Fleming Award, 1973; National Order of Lion (Senegal), 1973; Others. Address: 5313 Dirksen Senate Office Bldg., Washington, D.C. 20510.

Schmueckle, Jean Zukowska

Advertising Agency Owner. Personal: Born October 10, 1913; Daughter of Mr. and Mrs. Ludwig Zukowski (both deceased); Married Richard A. Schmueckle. Education: Attended the University of Pennsylvania 1935-36, Charles Morris Price School of Advertising 1937-38, Columbia University 1941. Career: Director, Connelly Organization, Philadelphia, Pennsylvania, 1933-38; Assistant to the President, Allied Housing Associates, Langhorne, Pennsylvania and Washington, D.C., 1938-42; Owner, Jean Z. Schmueckle Advertising. Organizational Memberships: Philadelphia Club of Advertising Women; Women in Communications; American Society of Professional and Executive Women. Community Activities: Delaware Valley Music Club (president); Bucks County Pro Musica (board member); Bucks County Opera (committee member); Farm on the National Register of Historic Places (built 1768, researched and traced history to 1768); Bucks County Historical Society; America the Beautiful; New Hope Historical Society; American Farmland; Friends of Cliveden; The Philadelphia Art Alliance; Philadelphia Athenaeum; Elfreth's Alley Association; National Trust for Historic Preservation; Bucks County Conservancy; Work in Neuter-Spay Clinics, Bucks County Society for the Prevention of Cruelty to Animals; American Anti-Vivisection Society; New England Anti-Vivisection; Friends of Animals; Humane Society of U.S.; Others. Address: Overlook Valley Farm, Rushland, Bucks County, Pennsylvania 18956.

Jean Z Schmueckle

Scholl, Sharon Lynn

Professor of Humanities. Personal: Mother of Laura Ann, Lynn Carol. Education: B. Mus., Trinity University; M.M.E., Indiana University; Ph.D., Florida State University. Organizational Memberships: National Association for Humanities Education (board member); Florida Endowment for the Humanities; Society for Integrative Studies; American Association of University Professors. Community Activities: Jacksonville Historical and Cultural Commission; Preservation Association of Tree Hill (co-founder, 1970); Leadership Jacksonville (planning council); Governor's Conference on Public Leadership (delegate); Hospice of Northeast Florida; Educational Testing Service Teacher Certification Examination (revision committee, 1979); Jacksonville Campus Ministry (central committee member); Florida Community College Museum (board of directors). Religion: Assistant Choir Director/Organist, Arlington Presbyterian Church. Published Works: *Music and the Culture of Man*, 1970, *Death and the Humanities* 1983. Honors and Awards: Professor of the Year, Jacksonville University, 1974; Humanist of the Year, 1977; Four Year Service Award, Florida Endowment for the Humanities; Listed in *Outstanding Educators of America.* Address: 6854 Howalt Drive, Jacksonville, Florida 32211.

Schreiner, Robert Nicholas Jr

Deputy Assistant Project Director. Personal: Born January 12, 1935; Son of Robert Nicholas and Martha Louise (Picard) Schreiner, Sr.; Married Anne Louise Wendt, 1956; Father of Sue Anne, Wendy Louise, Robert Edward, Kurt Nicholas, Martha Elizabeth, David Paul. Education: B.S., Capital University, Columbus, Ohio, 1956; Graduate Studies, University of Southern California, Los Angeles, 1956-58. Career: Engineer, Northrop Corporation, Hawthorne, California, 1956-59; Staff Engineer, Engineering and Applied Mechanics 1959-65, Manager of Interactive Computer Graphics Advanced Technology 1965-68, Manager of Industrial/Educational Cooperative Research and Development 1968-72, Manager of Real Time Computer Application Design and Development 1972 to present, TRW Inc.; Lecturer in Mechanical Engineering and Advanced Computer Technology to Universities and Industrial Firms, 1965-72; Contributor of Articles to Professional Journals and Presentations to Professional Societies in Mechanical Engineering and Computer Technology, 1960-72. Community Activities: West Coast Regional Chairman during Centennial Anniversary of Capital University's Alumni Association, 1967; Regional Chairman, Lutheran Ingathering for Education, 1968. Religion: Lutheran Lay Assistant Pastor, St. Paul's Lutheran Church of Palos Verdes, California, 1972 to present; Lutheran Church Council, 1958-75. Honors and Awards: Listed in *Who's Who in Computers and Data Processing, Who's Who in the West, Dictionary of International Biography, Men of Achievement, Community Leaders and Noteworthy Americans, Who's Who Distinguished Citizens of North America, Personalities of the West and Midwest, International Who's Who in Community Service, Men and Women of Distinction, The American Scientific Registry, Community Leader of America, The Anglo-American Who's Who, Who's Who in Technology Today, The Directory of Distinguished Americans, Who's Who in California, Personalities of America, Contemporary Personalities, International Book of Honor.* Address: 30520 Via Rivera, Rancho Palos Verdes, California 90274.

Sharon L Scholl

Schuck, Marjorie Massey

Publisher, Editor. Personal: Born October 9, 1921, in Winchester, Virginia; Daughter of Carl Frederick and Margaret Harriet Parmele Massey; Married Earnest George Metcalfe, December 2, 1943; Married Franz Schuck (deceased), on November 11, 1953. Education: Attended the University of Minnesota 1941-43, New School (New York City) 1948, New York University 1952, 1954-55. Career: Editorial Board, St. Petersburg Poetry Association, 1967-68; Co-Editor 1968-69, Editor 1969-79, *Poetry Venture* Magazine, St. Petersburg; Editor, Poetry Anthologies, 1972 to present; Founder, Owner, President, Valkyrie Press Inc., 1972 to present (reorganized in 1981 as Valkyrie Publishing House, Inc.); Founder, Valkyrie Press Reference Library, 1975-80; Founder, Owner, Freedom Press, 1976-81; Consultant in Designs and Formats, Trade Publications, Annual Reports, Literature Books and Pamphlets, 1973 to present; Lecturer-in-Field, Publishing; Creative Writing, Politics, Founder, Owner, President, MS Records, Inc., 1974-79; Co-operative Publisher with Lorber Publishers, West Germany; Founder, Owner, President, Marjorie Schuck Publishing, Inc., 1974-79; Judge, Poetry and Speech Contests, 1970 to present; Administrative Board, Suncoast Management Institute, 1977-78; Chairman, Women and Management Seminars, 1977-78. Organizational Memberships: Academy of American Poets; Coordinating Council of Literary Magazines, 1967-81; American Society of Composers, Authors and Publishers, 1974-82; Committee of Small Magazine Editors and Publishers, 1967-81; Florida Suncoast Writers Conference (founder, co-director, lecturer, 1973 to present); National Federation of Press Women; Women in Management; Pi Beta Phi. Community Activities: Women's Auxiliary Hospital for Special Surgery, New York City (corresponding recording secretary, 1947-59); Pinellas County Arts Council (member, 1976-79; chairman, 1977-78); St. Petersburg Museum of Fine Arts (charter member); St. Petersburg Arts Center Association; Society for the Prevention of Cruelty to Animals (board of directors; public relations chairman, 1968-71); Pinellas Suncoast Chamber of Commerce, 1972-80; Committee of 100 of Pinellas County (member, 1976-80; executive board, 1977-78, 1978-79). Religion: Episcopal. Published Works: Speeches and Writings for the Cause of Freedom, 1973; Contributor of Poetry to Professional Journals; Publisher, Angel City by Patrick D. Smith, Produced as Feature Movie for CBS-TV 1980. Honors and Awards: Named One of 76 Florida Patriots, Florida Bicentennial Commission, 1976; Listed in *Who's Who in the South and Southwest.* Address: 8245 26th Avenue, North, St.

Petersburg, Florida 33710.

Schuetzenduebel, Wolfram Gerhard

Scientist/Engineer. Personal: Born February 17, 1932, in Alt-Landsberg, Germany; Son of G. E. and K. (deceased) Schuetzenduebel; Married Ingeborg Jutta Lesch, in 1960. Education: B.S.M.E., 1956; M.S.M.E., 1958; M.S., Power Engineering, 1958; Technical University Berlin, Berlin, Germany; D.Sc., Engineering, University of Beverly Hills, 1979. Career: Development Engineer, Manager of Boiler Engineering Department, Riley Stoker Corporation, Worcester, Massachusetts, 1958-61; Senior Research and Development Engineer, Boiler Design/Development, Supervisor of System Development, Combustion Engineering, Inc., Windsor, Connecticut, 1961-68; System Coordinator of Fort St. Vrain Steam Generators, Section Leader for Program Group of Heat Exchange Equipment Department, Manager of Technical Services in Steam Generator Program, Manager of Steam and Water Systems of Fort St. Vrain Project, Senior Staff Specialist of Fort St. Vrain Project, General Atomic Company, San Diego, California, 1969-79; Director of Utilities, Solvent Refined Coal Project, The Pittsburg and Midway Coal Mining Company, SRC-II Project, Denver, Colorado, 1979-80; Director of Utilities, Solvent Refined Coal International, Inc., Denver, 1980-81; Director of Utilities, Gulf Science and Technology Company, Engineering Division, Houston, Texas, 1981 to present; Registered Professional Engineer, Mechanical Engineering-Germany, Nuclear Engineering-California, Corrosion Engineering-California; Accredited Corrosion Specialist, National Association of Corrosion Engineers; United States Correspondent to Technical German Publications, *Energie* (Energy), *Waerme* (Heat), *Energy Developments;* 39 Patents in the United States, Australia, Belgium, Canada, France, Great Britain, Japan, Sweden, Switzerland. Organizational Memberships: VDI (Association of German Professional Engineers); National Association of Corrosion Engineers; DAFe.V. (German Atomic Forum); American Nuclear Society, San Diego Section, 1976-79; American Society of Mechanical Engineers; Sea Horse Institute, F.L. LaQue Corrosion Laboratory, 1965; American Society of Mechanical Engineers, Nuclear Engineering Division (nuclear heat exchanger committee vice chairman, 1975-76, chairman, 1976-78; nuclear codes and standards review committee, 1974-78; program committee, 1976-78; executive committee, 1976-78; liaison officer to heat transfer division, 1977-78). Published Works: 80+ Scientific and Engineering Papers in the United States, Germany, Great Britain, Canada, Switzerland; Co-Author of Book on Nuclear Steam Generators. Honors and Awards: Listed in *Who's Who in the West, Who's Who in America, Dictionary of International Biography, Men of Achievement, Community Leaders and Noteworthy Americans, Notable Americans in the Bicentennial Era, International Who's Who of Intellectuals, Personalities of the West and Midwest, Men and Women of Distinction, International Who's Who in Community Service, Personalities of America, Who's Who in California, Who's Who in Community Service, Book of Honor, American Scientific Registry, Who's Who in Technology Today.* Address: 6726 Ashmore Drive, Houston, Texas 77069.

Schut, Lawrence James

Physician, Clinical Professor, Neurological Coordinator. Personal: Born September 13, 1936; Son of Henry (deceased) and Hazel Schut; Married Loretta Fay Klemz; Father of Sherry, Maribeth, Ronald, David, James. Education: A.B., B.S., Hope College; M.D., University of Minnesota, 1962; Fellowship in Neurochemistry, 1966-67. Military: Served with the United States Army Reserve, 1963-69. Career: Resident in Neurology, University of Minnesota Medical School, 1963-66; Clinical Professor of Neurology, University of Minnesota Medical School; Neurological Coordinator, North Memorial Medical Center; Physician specializing in Neurology. Organizational Memberships: Minnesota Society of Neurological Sciences (secretary-treasurer, 1979 to present); Association of Neurologists of Minnesota (secretary-treasurer, 1979 to present); Minnesota Medical Association (vice chairman of interspecialty council); American Medical Association. Community Activities: National Ataxia Foundation (medical director, 1971 to present; board member, 1980 to present); Accessible Space Inc. (president, 1979 to present); Committee to Combat Huntington's Disease (medical advisor of north central chapter, 1973 to present). Religion: Northern Pines of Minnesota Christian Conference Center (board of directors, 1973-79; trustee, 1979 to present); Bryn Mawr Presbyterian Church, Minneapolis, Minnesota (elder, 12 years; trustee, 1979 to present). Honors and Awards: Graduated cum laude, 1958; Faculty Honors, 1958; Listed in *Who's Who in the Midwest.* Address: 434 Yosemite Avenue North, Minneapolis, Minnesota 55422.

Marvin A Schwam

Schwam, Marvin A

Executive. Personal: Born April 18, 1942; Son of Meyer and Fannie Lerman (both deceased); Married Jeanette Schwam; Father of Frederick Lawrence, Matthew Neal. Education: B.F.A., The Cooper Union for the Advancement of Science and Art, 1964. Career: President, American Christmas Decorating Service, Inc., 1978 to present; President, Marc Shaw Graphics and Florenco Graphic Systems, 1978 to present; Executive Vice-President, Chairman of the Board, Florenco Foliage Systems, Inc., 1978 to present; Executive Vice-President, Chairman of the Board, Display Arts, Incorporated, 1981 to present; Vice-President, Creative Animations, Inc.; President, M. Schwam Floralart, 1968-74; Manager, Flowerental Corporation, 1966-68; Artist, Doremus and Company, 1964-66). Organizational Memberships: Executive Association, New York City. Community Activities: The Young Adult Institute and Workshop, Inc.; Municipal Art Society, New York City; American Museum of Natural History; March of Dimes (industrial chairman, 1975-78); Happi Foundation for Autistic People (board of directors, 1980 to present); Alumni Association, Second Century Society Fellow, The Cooper Union; Jewish Genetic Disease Foundation (sponsor, 1982); Memorial Sloan Kettering Hospital Benefit, 1982. Honors and Awards: Award of Merit, General Motors, 1978; Award for Highlight of Christmas in New York, Citibank/Citicorp Center, 1978; Designer of Largest Artificial Christmas Tree in United States, Radio City Music Hall, New York City, 1979-80; Mayor's Committee to Decorate Pulitzer Fountain, Grand Army Plaza, New York City, 1981; Chief Designer, Town Square, New Orleans, Louisiana, 1982; Listed in *Who's Who of Finance and Industry, Who's Who in the World.* Address: 7 E 17th Street, New York City, New York 10003.

Schweitzer, Gertrude

Artist, Painter, Sculptor. Career: Solo Exhibitions at Montclair Art Museum, New Jersey, Washington Water Color Club, Cavuga Museum of History and Art, Auburn, New York; Potsdam Gallery of Art at State Normal School Currier Galley of Art, Manchester, New Hampshire, Bevier Gallery at Rochester Institute of Technology, Erie Public Museum, Pennsylvania, Cortland Library, New York, Norton Gallery and School of Art, West Palm Beach, Florida, Galerie Charpentier, Paris, France, Galleria Al Cavallineo, Venice, Italy, Gallerie 11 Naviglio, Milan, Italy, High Museum, Atlanta, Georgia (now Atlanta Art Association Galleries), Florida Southern College, Lakeland, Florida, Witte Memorial Museum, San Antonio, Texas, Hanover Gallery, London, England, Galleria L'Lobelisco, Rome, Italy, Worth Avenue Gallery, Palm Beach, Florida, The Philadelphia Art Alliance, Pennsylvania, Hokin Gallery, Palm Beach, Florida, Pratt Manhattan Center, New York City, The New Britain Museum of American Art, Connecticut, Lakeland College, Florida; Exhibited at Corcoran Gallery, Washington, D.C., Art Institute of Chicago, Illinois, Rhode Island School of

Design, Denver Society, New York City, Los Angeles County Fair, University of Minnesota, University of Fine Arts, Santa Fe, New Mexico, Museum of the Legion of Honor, San Francisco, California, Menina, Sicily at Exhibition "Viaggio Intorno al Mondo", Albi Museum Contemporary Collection, France (first American represented), Metropolitan Museum of Art's 200 Years of American Water Colors; Works Held in private collections in United States, England, France, Denmark, Italy, Milan, Venice, Italy; Works in Permanent Collections in the Brooklyn Museum, New York; Toledo Museum of Art, Ohio, Hackley Art Gallery, Muskegon, Michigan, Davenport Municipal Art Gallery, Iowa, Canajoharie Library and Art Gallery, New York, Norton Gallery and School of Art, West Palm Beach, Florida, Atlanta Art Association Galleries (formerly High Museum), Atlanta, Georgia, Witte Memorial Museum, San Antonio, Texas, The Montclair Art Museum, New Jersey, Museum of Modern Art, Paris, France, Albi Musieu, France, Walker Art Museum of Bowdin College, Brunswick, Maine, Rochester Memorial Art Gallery, Rochester, New York, Metropolitan Museum of Art, New York, New York, Whiteney Museum of American Art, New York, New York, Chicago Art Institute, Illinois, The New Britain Museum of American Art, Connecticut, The National Academy of Design, The Society of the Four Arts, Palm Beach, Florida, Museum of Fine Arts, Santa Fe, New Mexico. Organizational Memberships: National Academy of Design, 1951 to present. Community Activities: Arts and Skills Corps of American Red Cross, Fort Jay Regional Hospital, Governor's Island, New York (head during World War II). Published Works: *Peintures et Dessins*, 1965; *Outstanding Women Artists of America*, 1975. Honors and Awards: Bronzes, Stainless Steel Sculptures in Private College 10 foot S/S at Columbia University, New York City, 8 foot Sculputre, Permanence Coll. Museum of Fine Arts, New Mexico; Honorary Doctor of Fine Arts, Pratt Institute; The Youth Friends Awards, Highest Honor of the School Art League and Board of Education, New York; American Water Color Society Medal; Philadelphia Water Color Prize, Pennsylvania Academy of Fine Arts; American Artists Professional League Medal, State of New Jersey; First Prize, Norton Gallery and School of Art, West Palm Beach, Florida; Grand National Exhibition, Miami, Florida; First Prize, Best Woman Painter, New Jersey State Exhibition, Miami, Florida, Montclair Art Museum; American Artists Professional League, New York State Award for the Natonal Arts Club and Honor Roll Award; First Prize, Medal Award, Seton Hall University, Newark, New Jersey; Eleanor S. Higgings Award, 27th Annual New Jersey State Exhibition, Montclair Art Museum; First Grumbacher Purchase Award, Audubon 17th Annual Exhibition, New York City; Pauline Wick Award, American Artists Professional League, National Arts Club, New York, New York; Society of the Four Arts, Palm Beach, Florida, Listed in *Who's Who in America, Who's Who of American Women, Who's Who in the World, Who's Who in the South and Southwest, Who's Who in the East, World Who's Who in Art and Antiques, Dictionary of International Biography, Personalities of the South, Outstanding Women Artists of America, Men and Women of Distinction, National Register of Prominent Americans, Contemporary Personalities, International Directory of the Arts, Personalities of America, American Artists of Renown, World Who's Who of Women*. Address: Stone Hill Farm, Colts Neck, New Jersey 07722.

Fred J Schwertz

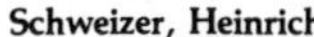

Schweizer, Heinrich

Conductor and Composer. Personal: Born September 5, 1943 in Switzerland; Son of Alfred Schweizer. Education: Studied under Paul Muller, Aurich, Switzerland; International Masters Course of Composition, Bonn, Germany; Diploma as Orchestra Musician 1967, Diploma as Teacher of Music Theoretical Themes 1973, Conservatory of Zurich. Career: Composer and Conductor, 1967 to present; Member, Cape Town Symphony Orchestra, 1970-71; Member, Zurich Tonhalle Orchestra under such conductors as Otto Klemperer, Rudolf Kempe, Karl Boehm and Jean Martinon. Organizational Memberships: Composers, Authors and Aritsts of America, New York Chapter. Community Activities: Lecturer on "Music in West Africa" at Many Schools and on the Radio. Religion: Protestant Church. Published Works: "Concerto for Piano and Orchestra", 1981; "Serenade for Harp and Woodwind-Quintet", 1980; "Carter String Serenade" for String Orchestra, 1978; "Serenade" for String Sextet, 1976; "Historical Symphony", 1975; "Concertino", for Xylophone and Orchestra, 1974; "Five Songs" for Soprano and Piano, 1972; "Ouverture for Orchestra", 1971; "King Drosselbart" Children's Musical, 1970; "September" Song for Soprano and Piano, 1967; "String Trio", 1967. Address: 35 West 67th Street, New York, New York 10023.

Schwertz, Frederick Joseph

Administrator, Representative. Personal: Born May 7, 1896; Son of Celestin and Anna Schwertz (both deceased). Education: B.A. 1916, M.A. 1920, Pontifical College Josephinum, Columbus, Ohio; Litt.D., School of Journalism, Denver, Colorado, 1956. Career: Superintendent, Mt. Calvary Cemetary, Wheeling, West Virginia; Secretary, Board of Directors, Welty Home for the Aged; Representative for Retired Clergy of Diocese on Senate of Priests; Former Positions include Professor, St. Edward College, Huntington, West Virginia; Editor, *Diocesan Weekly*; Chancellor, Diocese of Wheeling-Charleston; Diocesan Director, Catholic Relief Services; Secretary of Board of Directors, Wheeling Hospital; Secretary-Treasurer, Infirm Priests Association; Diocesan Director of Cemeteries; Examiner of Junior Clergy; Diocesan Director, Bureau of Publicity; Secretary, Diocesan Board of Education; Secretary, Board of Administration. Community Activities: United Nations Relief Association (chairman during World War II); Clothing Drive for City of Wheeling; Diocesan Director, Displaced Persons and Refugees of World War II. Religion: Represented Diocese of Wheeling-Charleston for Eucharistic Congresses, Manila, Philippines 1937, Rio de Janeiro, Brazil 1955, Barcelona, Spain 1952, Bombay, India 1964, Bogata, Colombia 1968, Melbourne, Australia 1973; Representative of Bishop of Fatima, Portugal, the International President of the Blue Army of Our Lady of Fatima, officiating at the American Embassy Chapel, Moscow, Russia, 1971, at Worldwide Anniversary Crowning of Statue of Our Lady, Queen of the Universe. Honors and Awards: Appointed Domestic Prelate with Title of Monsignor, 1949; Promoted to Highest Rank of Monsignor, Protonotary Apostolic, 1968; Honorary Citation, National Catholic Relief Services, 1975. Address: Mt. de Chantal Academy, Wheeling, West Virginia 26003.

Ted Schwinden

Schwinden, Ted

Governor of Montana. Personal: Born August 31, 1925, in Wolf Point, Montana; Married Jean Christianson, in 1946; Father of Mike, Chrys, Dore. Education: Graduate of Wolf Point High School, 1943; Attended the Montana School of Mines; B.A. 1949, M.A. 1950, University of Montana-Missoula; Undertook post-graduate studies at the University of Minnesota. Military: Served in the United States Army, 1943-46, attaining the rank of Staff Sergeant. Career: Owner, Operator of Grain Farm, Roosevelt County, 1954 to present; Elected to Montana House of Representatives, 1958; Named to Legislative Council, 1959-61; Served as Minority Whip, 1961 Session; Named as Commissioner of State Lands by Governor Forrest Anderson 1969, Reappointed 1973; Elected Lieutenant Governor of Montana, 1976; Inaugurated as Governor of Montana, 1981. Organizational Memberships: Montana Grain Growers Association (president, two years). Honors and Awards: Selected by United States Secretary of Agriculture Orville Freeman to Represent the United States on a Wheat Trade Mission to Asia, 1968. Address: Office of the Governor, State of Montana, Helena, Montana 59620.

Sclafani, Charles Carlo

Associate Professor of Languages. Personal: Born April 13, 1941; Son of Leonardo and Leonarda Sclafani; Married Emilia Simeone;

Father of Dina, Sandra. Education: B.A., City College of the City University of New York, 1964; M.A., Rutgers University, 1971. Career: Associate Professor of Languages, Westchester Community College, 1971 to present; Instructor of Languages, New York State University at Stony Brook, 1967-71. Organizational Memberships: Modern Language Association; American Association of Teachers of Italian (president, Long Island Chapter, 1972-73); New York State Association of Foreign Language Teachers; American Council on the Teaching of Foreign Language; American Italian Historical Association; Italian Historical Society. Community Activities: Societa Onoraria Italica-The Italian National Honor Society for High School Students, American Association of Teachers of Italian (president, 1974 to present); Italian Club, Westchester Community College (faculty advisory, 1971 to present); Antonio Meucci of the Order of Sons of Italy (assistant venerable, 1975-77). Honors and Awards: Nominated Twice for New York State Chancellor's Award for Excellence in Teaching, Westchester Community College; Man of the Year, Columbia Police Association of Westchester, 1979; Honored Several Times at Westchester Community College for Outstanding Services to the College and Community; Listed in *Who's Who in the East*. Address: 56 Atlantic Avenue, Hawthorne, New York 10532.

Scott, Joan Eleanor

Joan E Scott

Nursing and Hospital Administration. Personal: Born July 15; Daughter of Bessie Lee Scott. Education: Professional Registered Nurse, Jewish Hospital Medical Center of Brooklyn, 1954; B.A., magna cum laude, Jersey City State College, 1971; M.S., Hunter College City University of New York, 1972; Undertook postgraduate studies, Graduate School of Public Health Administration, New York University, 1978. Career: Nursing Administration Supervisor, Beth Israel Medical Center, 1964-70; Associate Director Nursing Service and Education, The Bronx Lebanon Hospital Center, 1971-79; Divisional Director Nursing Service and Administration (A.V.P.), The Bronx Lebanon Hospital Center, 1979 to present. Organizational Memberships: American Nurses Association; New York State Nurses Association (secretary, board of directors, executive committee, task force to study implications of 85 proposal, nominating committee, specialty group of directors, delegate to American Nurses Association); New York Counties Registered Nurses Association (treasurer, executive committee, board of directors, finance committee chairperson, bylaws committee, fund raising committee for 75th anniversary, public relations committee, chairman nominating committee); American Society of Nurse Administrators of the American Hospital Association (division of associates charter member, rules and regulations committee, executive committee at large, representative to society bylaws committee); National League for Nursing; Southern New York League for Nursing (secretary 1979-80); American Public Health Association; New York City Public Health Association (nominating committee 1978); Council Nursing Service Administrators of the American Nurses Association (charter member, nominating committee 1980-82). Community Activities: Health System Agency (South Bronx Board A, Bronx boroughwide board, project review committee, planning and development committee); Park West Tenant Association; Nursing Bureau of Manhattan and the Bronx, 1973-81; Goodwill People to People Leadership of Nurses Administration Tour to United Kingdom, Sweden, Poland and Hungary, 1980; International Platform Association; Contributor to: U.J.A., Wives of Congressional Black Caucus, Girls Town, United Negro College Fund, Oral Roberts Ministries, Federation fo Jewish Women. Religion: Baptist. Published Works: Articles, including "Nursing As a Career for the Black Woman", "Human Values in Nursing Care" and "A Fresh Look at the Nursing Services Administrator", published in *Essence Magazine, The Dallas Times, The Newark Community Alert.* Honors and Awards: Doctor of Humane Letters, New Haven Theological Seminary; Mabel K. Staupers Award for Leadership in Nursing Administration, Chi Eta Phi, Omicron Chapter, 1979; Recipient of Scholarships and Citations for Community Service and Achievement from Church and Community Groups; Listed in *Who's Who in the East, Directory of Distinguished Americans.* Address: 400 Central Park West, Apt. 8F, New York, New York 10025.

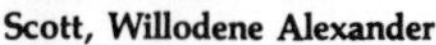

Scott, Willodene Alexander

Willodene A Scott

Educational Administrator. Personal: Born September 4, 1922; Daughter of Mr. and Mrs. J. C. Alexander; Married Ray Donald Scott; Mother of Pamela Dean. Education: B.A., George Peabody College for Teachers, 1946; B.S., Library Science, 1947; M.A., 1949; Ed.S., 1972; Ph.D. Candidate (currently). Career: Librarian, Sylvan Park Elementary School (Nashville) 1947-51, Waverly Belmont Junior High School (Nashville) 1951-54, Howard High School (Nashville) 1954-62, Peabody Demonstration School (Nashville) 1962-63, McCann Elementary School (Nashville) 1963-66; Supervisor, Instructional Materials Center, Metropolitan Nashville-Davidson County Schools, 1966-73; Director, Instructional Materials and Library Services, Metropolitan Nashville-Davidson County Schools, 1973 to present; Lecturer, Peabody College Library School, Nashville, Summers 1950-66, 1971-72, 1976; Lecturer, University of Tennessee, Nashville Center, 1970; Tennessee Representative, 1970 White House Conference; Chairman, National Alumni Fund-raising, George Peabody College for Teachers, 1975-76; George Peabody College for Teachers National Alumni (president and member of board of trustees, 1976-78); American Library Association; Southeastern Library Association (scholarship committee, 1968-70); Tennessee Library Association (membership committee; treasurer); Tennessee Education Association (library section president, 1954); Metropolitan Nashville Education Association; National Education Association (life member); American Association of University Women; Woman's National Book Association (charter member). Community Activities: Daughters of the American Revolution (organizing treasurer, Buffalo River chapter, 1967-69). Published Works: "Experiencing Literature with Children: A Thing of Joy" 1968; "Metropolitan Nashville-Davidson County Schools Instructional Materials Center" 1969. Address: 525 Clematis Drive, Nashville, Tennessee 37205.

Scruggs, Robert Gordon

Housing Officer. Personal: Born August 7, 1947; Son of R. W. Scruggs. Education: B.S., Business Administration, Mars Hill College, 1974; A.A.S., Business Administration, Asheville-Buncombe Technical College, 1972; Studies at the Air Force Management Analysis School and the Air Force N.C.O. Leadership School; Graduate Level Courses Taken at Western Carolina University, 1975-76; Additional Courses, Wake Technical College 1982. Military: Served in the United States Air Force, 1966-70, attaining the rank of Sergeant. Career: Housing Officer; Loan Assistant, F.M.H.A.; Veterans Outreach Representative, Employment Security Commission. Organizational Memberships: American Management Association; North Carolina State Employees Association; National Association of D.V.O.P.'s. Community Activities: American Legion (district commander, 1976-77; Post Level: first vice-commander, second vice-commander, executive committee, adjutant, publicity committee, chairman of entertainment committee, building and grounds committee, membership committee, go-getter, chairman of VAVS committee, club manager, American Legion extension course; District Level: commander, vice-commander, adjutant; Department Level: Vietnam era aide to 5th division commander, Viet-time Vets committee, All-Faith Chapel committee, new posts and development committee, publications commission, constitution and by-laws committee, employment committee, executive comittee); 40 and 8, 1977 to present; Veterans of Foreign Wars (Post Level: life member, post commander, senior vice-commander, quarter master, adjutant, hospital chairman, horseshoe tournament chairman, three year trustee; District Level: commander, senior vice-commander, junior vice-commander, service officer, three year trustee, two year trustee, one year trustee; Department Level: council of administration, employment committee, reports committee); Military Order of the Cooties; Pup Tent (life member Pup Tent 4); C.C.D.B.; Disabled American Veterans (Chapter Level: life member, service officer, judge advocate, executive committee, legislative officer, VAVS committee, chairman of constitution and by-laws committee; Department Level: 11th district commander, employment committee, chairman, resolution committee; executive committee, building fund committee, membership committee, nominations committee Department treasurer); National Order of Trench Rats (life member); AMVETS (life member); Air Force Association (life member; chairman, membership committee); Tri-County Veterans Council (commander; secretary); Wake County Veterans Council, President; Veterans Organization Representative on Region B, Regional Manpower Advisory Council, Buncombe, Henderson, Madison, Transylvania Counties; Trout Unlimited (life member, Pisgah Chapter; president, vice president, publicity committee, membership committee, fly fishing school committee); Phi Beta Lambda; Annual Member of American Hiking Society, American Management Association, AMRAN Shrine, National Historical Society, Raleigh Scottish Rite Bodies, Raleigh York Rite Bodies, Sons of Confederate Veterans, William G. Hill Lodge 218 AF & AM, Young Democrats of Wake County; Democratic Mens Club; Federation of Fly Fishermen (life member); National Geographic Society (life member); National Muzzleloaders Association (life member); National Rifle Association (life member); National Wildlife Federation (life member); North Carolina Rifle and Pistol Association (life member); North Carolina Geneological Society (life member). Religion: Baptist; Royal Ambassadors Advisor 1973; Cemetary and Grounds 1970-79. Honors and Awards: American Legion National Achievement Award; 3 Gallon Red Cross Donor Pin; 100 Hour VAVS Volunteer Pin and Certificate; 300 Hour VAVS Pin and Certificate; 150 + 300 Hour VAVS Volunteer Pin; Distinguished Service Pin, Veterans of Foreign Wars; Community Achievement Award, Asheville-Buncombe Technical College; American Legion Department Veterans Organization Representative Volunteer Certificate; American Legion Department Achievement Award; American Legion, D.A.V., Veterans of Foreign Wars Membership Recruitment Award; Disabled American Veterans Department Outstanding District Commander Award, North Carolina; Listed in *International Register of Profiles, International Who's Who of Intellectuals, Personalities of America, Book of Honor, Directory of Distinguished Americans, Men of Achievement, Personalities of the South, Who's Who in the South and Southwest, Who's Who in American Junior Colleges.* Address: P.O. Box 18626, Raleigh, North Carolina 27619.

Scullin, Dorothy Dodworth

Teacher of Painting, Freelance Writer and Illustrator, Children's Writer, Consultant/Tutor. Career: Consultant-Tutor on Writing and Illustrating Stories for Children, 1975-77; Instructor in Watercolor, North Adams State College, 1974; Consultant in Public Schools on Writing and Illustrating Books for Children and on Puppetry in Education, 1969-72; Teacher of Painting for Adults and Children, 1963 to present; Freelance Writer and Illustator for Magazines, Books, and Newspapers, 1952 to present; Assistant Children's Librarian, Arlington Town Library, Massachusetts 1955-57, Boston Public Library 1953-57. Address: 280 Stone Hill Road, Williamstown, Massachusetts 01267.

Robert G Scruggs

Selditch, Alan Daniel

Manager, Environmental Affairs Group. Personal: Born September 8, 1926, in Philadelphia, Pennsylvania; Son of Jacob and Sarah Molly Simons Selditch (both deceased); Divorced; Father of Gretchen, Edward, Michael, Ronald, Kimberly. Education: Engineering, Physics, Math, St. Lawrence University, Canton, New York, 1944-46; B.S. Engineering, Business, Public Administration, University of Southern California, 1948; Undertook Post Graduate Studies at Los Angeles City College, LaSalle University, California State Universities; M.S. Environmental Sciences, Heed University, 1982. Military: Served in the United States Naval Reserve, 1944-46, 1946-50. Career: Registered Professional Engineer, California; Certified in Material Management and Material Handling, International Material Management Society; Certified Instructor in MTM, University of Michigan and MTM Society; Certified in Methods Engineering, Maynard Research Institute; Certified in Flow Measurement, Open and Confined Channels, Los Angeles County Sanitation District; Chief of Projects and Engineering, President, Sigma Associates, Los Angeles, 1950-57; Chief Industrial and Project Engineering and Plant Maintainance, Rexall Drug and Chemical Company, 1962-65; Regional Consulting Manager, H. B. Maynard and Company, Sherman Oaks, California, 1965-69; Assistant to the President, P.O.P. Systems/I.S.I., Santa Ana, California, 1970-72; Manager, Facilities and Corporate Planning, Systems Resource Recovery/System Associates, Long Beach, California, 1972-75; General Manager, Flowtrace, Los Angeles, 1975-79; Manager, Corporate/Environmental Affairs Group, Signetics, Sunnyvale, California, 1977 to present; President, A.D. Selditch and Associates, Newark, California, 1977 to present. Organizational Memberships: American Association for the Advancement of Science; American Institute of Industrial Engineers; American Society of Management; American Society of Standards; Association of Energy Engineers; California Society of Professional Engineers; International Material Management Society; Methods, Time-Measurement Association for Standards and Research; National Association for Solid Waste; National Association of Professional Engineers; American Society of Mechanical Engineers; American Society of Standards; American Academy of Environmental Engineers; American Institute of Plant Engineers; American Public Works Association; American Society of Metals; Governmental Refuse, Collection and Disposal Association; International Platform Association; International Material Management Society; Institute of Electrical and Electronic Engineers; Institute of Solid Wastes; National Association of Professional Engineers; Signet Society. Community Activities: Republican. Religion: Jewish. Published Works: Number of Articles Contributed to Professional Journals, including (most recently) "Recovered Resources for Mixed Municipal Waste-A Sensitivity Analysis" 1975, "Proposal for the Design, Construction and Operation of Dade County, Florida, Solid Waste Resource Recovery System" 1973, and "Evaluation of Solid Waste as a Component of Cattle Feed" 1975. Honors and Awards: Listed in *Men of Achievement, Who's Who in California, Who's Who in the West, AEE Directory of Energy Engineering Pioneers;International Men of Achievement, Directory of Distinguished Americans, Personalities of America, International Book of Honor, Biographical Roll of Honor, Directory of International Biography, International Who's Who of Intellectuals, International Register of Profiles, Personalities of the West and Midwest, International Men of Science, National Council of Engineering Examiners, AEE Directory of Certified Energy Managers, Compendium of Environmental Engineers and Consultants, Directory of Environmental Consultants, Directory of Professional Engineers.* Address: 6267E Joaquin Murieta Avenue, Newark, California 94560.

Seneris, Plaridel Enerio

Case Worker. Personal: Born November 1, 1931; Married Ma. Asuncion T. Seneris. Education: Litt.B., University of Santo Tomas, Manila, Philippines, 1962. Career: Case Worker, Illinois State Department of Public Aid, 1976 to present; Special Agent, Board of Transportation, Department of Public Works and Communication, Republic of Philippines, 1972-74; Assistant Secretary and Liaison Officer, House of Representatives, Congress of the Philippines, 1968-72. Organizational Memberships: Fil-Am Lions Club (secretary, 1981-82); Kahirup Club of the Midwest (director, 1981-83); Merville Homeowner's Association, Dampalit, Malabon Rizal, Philippines (founder, 1972); Committee on attendance and Lion information (chairman, 1981-82); Permanent Delegate to Filipino American Council of Chicago; Lions International (cabinet, District I-A, 1981-82). Religion: Roman Catholic. Honors and Awards: Honorable Mention, Ibajay Elementary School, 1948-49; Class Historian, Ibajay Academy, Ibajay, Aklan, Philippines, 1953; First Prize Award, Oratorical and Debating Contest, Ibajay Academy, 1952. Address: 4807 North Belle Avenue, Apt. 2-B, Chicago, Illinois 60625.

Sengelaub, Mary Maurita

Provincial Councilor. Personal: Born June 28, 1918, in Reed City, Michigan. Education: Graduate of Mercy Central School of Nursing, Grand Rapids, Michigan, 1940; B.S.M.Ed., Mercy College of Detroit, 1949; M.H.A., St. Louis University, 1954. Career: Provincial Administrative Team Member, Chairman of Sisters of Mercy Health Corporation, 1977 to present; President, Catholic Hospital Association, 1970-77; Assistant to the Director, Department of Health Affairs, United States Catholic Conference, Washington, D.C., 1969-70; General Councilor, Sisters of Mercy Generalate, 1965-71; Assistant Mother Provincial and Coordinator of Hospitals, Homes and Health Care Facilities, Province of Detroit, 1961-65; Administrator, St. Mary's Hospital, Grand Rapids, Michigan, 1957-61; Administrator, Mercy Hospital, Bay City, Michigan, 1954-57; Supervisor-Medical Service, Mercy Hospital, Bay City, 1953-54; Director of Nursing Arts Department and Instructor, Mercy College of Detroit, 1948-51; Supervisor-Orthopedic Floor, St. Mary's Hospital, 1948; Assistant Director of Nursing Service and Clinical Instructor, Mercy Hospital, 1944-45; Clinical Instructor, Mercy Hospital, 1942-44; General Staff Nurse, Reed City Community Hospital, 1941-42; Assistant Head Nurse, St. Mary's Hospital, Grand Rapids, 1940-41. Organizational Memberships: American College of Hospital Administrators, F.A.C.H.A.; Michigan Hospital Association (life member); St. Louis University Alumni Association; Graduate Program in Hospital and Health Care Administration; The Catholic Hospital Association; National Migrant Worker Council. Community Activities: Sisters of Mercy Health Corporation (chairperson, member); Pope John XXIII Center for Medical-Moral Research and Education (director, chairman, board of directors); East Coast Migrant Health Project (project director, 1970 to present). Religion: Roman Catholic, Member of the Sisters of Mercy Provincialate. Published Works: Number of Professional Articles including "Supportive Management-Building Today for Tomorrow", "The Future of Catholic Hospitals", and "The Hospital Sister in Renewal". Honors and Awårds: 1965 Key Award for Meritorious Service, Michigan Hospital Association; 1974 Achievement Award, Health Industries Association; 1974 Achievement Award, Health Industries Association; 1975 Citation for Meritorious Service, American Hospital Association; The Newcomer Award-Medical Administrator of the Year, American Academy of Medical Administrators; Honorary Doctoral Degree in Humanities, St. Michael's College, Winooski, Vermont, 1979. Address: 29000 Eleven Mile Road, Farmington Hills, Michigan 48018.

Senne, Stephen Michael

Stephen A Senne

Financial Planner, Author. Personal: Born July 5, 1944, in Pasadena, California; Son of Delmar V. Senne, Penelope A. Senne; Married Ingrid Joy Larsen. Education: A.A., Riverside City College, 1972; Post Graduate Studies at the University of the Redlands, 1976-83, Charted Life Underwriters Degree, The American College of Life Underwriters, 1977; B.A., Business Management, University of Redlands, 1983. Career: Assistant Supervisor, SSP Products, Burbank, California, 1965-70; Life Field Underwriter, Supervisor, John Hancock Insurance, Whittier, California, 1970-76; Casualty Field Underwriter, Sentry Insurance, Ontario, California, 1976-79; President, Director, Stephen Michael Senne, A. Financial Planner, Inc., Ontario, 1977 to present; Director, Treasurer, Karate School of Oyama Inc., Leopard Karate School Inc.; Chairman, Nuclear Radiology Health and Safety Course, American Society of Non-Destructive Testings, 1970-83. Organizational Memberships: Southern California Association of the Amateur Athletic Union (re-established as amateur instead of professional, Karate, 1972); National Management Association; American Society for Non-Destructive Testing. Community Activities: National Detectives and Special Police Association; National Rifle Association of America (life member); International Police Hall of Fame Foundation; California Rifle and Pistol Assocation; American Sportsman Club; Glendale Elks Club. Religion: Lutheran. Published Works: Non-Ficton, *Your Financial Report Card* 1980; Fiction, *Jungle Detective* 1979. Honors and Awards: Full Chi Master, Awarded from China, 1980; Seventh Degree Black Belt, Leopard Karate School, 1979; Fifth Degree Black Belt, United States in Tiger Karate, 1974; Fourth Degree Black Belt, Japan in Kyokushinkai-kan Karate, 1974; Fourth Degree Black Belt, United States in Tiger Karate, 1971; Third Degree Black Belt, Japan in Kyokushinkai-kan Karate, 1967; Second Degree Black Belt, Japan in Krykushinkai-kan Karate, 1964; First Degree Black Belt, United States in A.K.A. Karate, 1964; First Degree Black Belt, United States in K.J.K.A. Karate, 1962; Received "Grand Slam" Award, for Successfully Completing Requirement of Sales Work in Real Estate, Business and Retirement Planning, 1974; Successful Qualification for National John Hancock All Star Team, 1973; Awarded Order of the Blue Vase for High Achievement in Successful Selling, 1970 (first and only time awarded on West Coast); Certificate of Achievement in Maintaining in Excess of 90% Persistency on $878,920 of Paid for Production, 1971; Sportsman of the Month, *Sportsman's Magazine*, November 1970; Winner, First Place Award in National Competition with Over 800 Companies as Editor of Stainless Steel Products Management Newspaper; Listed in *Who's Who in the West, Who's Who in Business and Finance, Who's Who in the World.* Address: P.O. Box 1655, Hesperia, California 92345.

Sevcik, John George

General Manager. Personal: Born May 15, 1909; Married Rose Vanek; Father of Joanne Shea, John. Education: J.D. 1939, LL.D. 1958, DePaul University; B.Sc., Central College, 1945; M.B.A., University of Chicago, 1947; M.P.L. 1950, LL.M. 1954, John Marshall Law School; LL.D., St. Mary's College, 1956; LL.D., St. Procopius College (now Illinois Benedictine College), 1960. Career: DePaul University, Board of Trustees 1954 to present, Chairman of Board of Trustees 1960-63, President of Alumni Association 1953-55, Chairman of 1952 Financial Campaign; Rosary College, Member Board of Trustees, Chairman 1966-69; Board of Trustees, St. Procopius College 1961-70, St. Mary's College 1957 to present; John Marshall Law School, Member of Board of Trustees, President of Alumni Association 1968-71; University of Chicago, Citizens Board 1965-71, Advisory Council of School of Business, President of the Executive Program Club, M.B.A. Graduates 1949-50; Member and Vice-Chairman, Board of Trustees, Illinois College of Podiatric Medicine; Lecturer, Numerous Colleges and Institutions; General Manager, McCormick Place, Chicago, 1971-81; President and Director, Burton-Dixie Corporation, 1949-71, Vice-President, Board of Directors 1971; Director, Brunswick Corporation; Director, Bus Captital Inc.; Director, Central National Bank; Director, Central Chicago Corporation; Director, Financial Marketing Sevices Company; Director, National Cotton Batting Insititute; 1982, Chief Executive Officer, Chicago Investment Corporation; American Furniture Mart, Member Board of Governors, Chairman 1968-69; Editorial Advisory Board, *Bedding;* Chairman of the Board, Financial Marketing Service Inc. Organizational Memberships: Wisdom Society; National Association of Bedding Manufacturers (president, 1959-60); Illinois Bar Association; American Bar Association; American Judicature Society; National Sales Executive Club; Chicago Association of Commerce and Industry (director and member, subscription investigating committee); National Association of Exposition Manufacturers; Illinois Manufacturers Association (committee member); Catholic Business Education Association, 1956-68; Institute of American Strategy (vice president). Community Activities: American Security Council (vice president); United Cerebral Palsy Association (past chairman of board of Greater Chicago; past president); Research and Educational Foundation, Inc. (board of directors); Boy Scouts of America; Chicago Crime Commission (board of directors); Public Building Commission of Chicago (commissioner, 1956 to present); Dialogue Association for the Blind (board of directors); Youth Welcome Commission of Chicago; National Conference of Christians and Jews (executive board, 1950-63); Illinois Brotherhood chairman, 1956; steering committee chairman, 1958); American Association of University Professors; Director of Catholic Charities; Citizens of Greater Chicago (board of governors, chairman, 1960-65; member board of governors and board of directors); Ivy Cancer Research Foundation (board of directors); Mayor's All Citizens Committee of Chicago; Fund Raiser for the American Cancer Society, Catholic Charities, National Foundation of Medical Education, Easter Seals; Kiwanis Club; Illinois Chamber of Commerce (membership committee); Illinois Manufacturers Association. Religion: Sponsor, B'nai B'rith Youth

Organization Scholarship Program. Honors and Awards: Selected as 1 of 100 of Chicago's Outstanding Citizens, Loyola University, 1957; Knighted by His Imperial Highness Franz Josef, Archduke of Austria, Order of Knight Templar, for Outstanding Work in Charity, 1965, Received Israel Prime Ministers Medical Study Israel Bonds, 1968; Mothers of World War II Certificate of Outstanding Achievement, 1959, Veterans Administration Certificate for Volunteer Service, 1959; Man of the Year, Furniture Industry, 1959; Phi Alpha Delta; Beta Gamma Sigma; Award from the University of Chicago, 1947; International Platform Association; Listed in *Who's Who in America, Who's Who in Commerce and Industry, 2000 Men of Achievement, National Society Directory*. Address: 2221 Ridgeland Ave., Berwyn, Illinois 60402.

Sensenig, David Martin

Surgeon. Personal: Born May 4, 1921, in Gladwyne, Pennsylvania; Married Bernice; Father of Philip, David Jr., Andrew, Thomas, (Stepfather of:) Judith, Diane, Deborah, Joanne. Education: Graduate of the Haverford School, 1938; B.S., Haverford College, Haverford, Pennsylvania, 1942; Attended the University of Pennsylvania School of Medicine, 1942-43; M.D., Harvard Medical School, Boston, Massachusetts, 1945; Rotating Internship, Allentown Hospital, Allentown, Pennsylvania, 1945-46; Surgical House Officer and Junior Assistant Resident, Peter Bent Brigham Hospital, Boston, 1948-50; Senior Assistant Resident and Resident Surgeon, New England Center Hospital, Boston, 1950-52; Surgical Resident, Westfield State Sanatorium, Westfield, Massachusetts, Cancer Section, 1952-53; Resident in Thoracic Surgery and Cardiac Surgery, University Hospital, State University of Iowa, 1957-59. Military: Served in the United States Army, 1943-48, rising through the ranks to Captain, Medical Corps. Career: Assistant Chief, Surgical Service, and Director, Surgical Research Laboratory, Veterans Administration Medical Teaching Group Hospital, Memphis, Tennessee, 1953-55; Assistant Chief, Surgical Service, Veterans Administration Hospital, Albany, New York, and Instructor in Surgery, Albany Medical College, 1955-57; Instructor in Surgery 1957-58, Associate in Surgery 1958-59, University Hospitals, State University of Iowa, Iowa City; Chief, Thoracic Surgery Section, Veterans Administration Hospital, Philadelphia, 1959-60; Assistant Professor and Associate Professor of Surgery, University Hospitals, State University of Iowa, 1960-62; Cardiothoracic Surgeon, Pennsylvania Hospital, and Assistant Professor of Surgery, University of Pennsylvania, 1962-63; Assistant Chief, Surgical Service, and Supervisor, Animal Research Laboratory, Veterans Administration Hospital, Philadelphia, Assistant Professor of Surgery, University of Pennsylvania, 1963-66; Private Surgical Practice, Bangor, Maine, 1966 to present; Staff Surgeon, Eastern Maine Medical Center, 1966 to present; Chief of Thoracic Surgery, St. Joseph Hospital, 1973-78; Surgical Consultant, Penobscot Valley Hospital, Lincoln, Maine. Organizational Memberships: Phi Beta Kappa; Society of Sigma Xi; American Medical Association; American College of Surgeons; Pennsylvania Association for Thoracic Surgery; Penobscot County Medical Society (president); Maine Thoracic Society; American Association for the Advancement of Science; International Cardiovascular Society; American Geriatrics Society; Iowa Academy of Surgery; American College of Chest Physicians; Philadelphia Academy of Surgery; Bangor Medical Club (president); American Thoracic Society; Maine Vascular Society (president); New England Surgical Society (executive committee); New York Academy of Sciences; New England Society for Vascular Surgery. Community Activities: Cub Scout Master, Gladwyn, Pennsylvania, Troop, 1964; Sebec Lake Association, Conservation Group (president, 1973). Religion: Protestant Episcopal Church. Honors and Awards: Phi Beta Kappa; Sigma Xi. Address: 436 State Street, Bangor, Maine 04401.

Richard N Severance

Severance, Richard N

Corporate Administrative Executive. Personal: Born January 16, 1933; Son of Arhcie William and Odena Gagnon Severance (both deceased); Married Judith Ellison; Father of Scott, Randy, Glenn, Mark, (Stepfather of:) Cheryl, Cindy Costello. Education: Graduate of Henniker High School, 1951; Studies in Higher Accountancy, LaSalle Extension University, 1953; LL.B., Blackstone School of Law, 1956. Career: Secretary/Treasurer, Keller Group of Companies, 1959 to present; Claims Clerk, New Hampshire Insurance Company, 1952-57; Accountant, B. F. Goodrich Retail Store, 1951-52. Organizational Memberships: National Association of Accountants. Community Activities: International Association of Y's Mens Club (charter secretary, 1953); Profile Club of New Hampshire Insurance Company (treasurer, 1956); Junior Chamber of Commerce (director, 1958-64); Manchester Winter Carnival (president, 1963); Parents Without Partners (president, 1966); Queen City Promenaders Square Dance Club (president, 1973, 1981); New England Square and Round Dance Convention (public relations and special events, 1979, 1980); Twirling T.N.T., Teen Square Dance Club (advisor, 1976-81); Square Dance Foundation of New England (public relations director, 1981-83); Square Dance Management Information Forum (speaker on public relations, 1982). Religion: Catholic. Published Works: Monthly Column for *Manchester Union Leader*, on N.H. Square Dancing, "The Square Beat", 1981. Honors and Awards: Jaycee Director of the Year, 1960; Jaycee of the Year, 1961; Listed in *Who's Who in the East*, *Personalities of America*. Address: 105 Oak Hill Avenue, Manchester, New Hampshire 03104.

John C Sevier

Sevier, John Charles

Educator. Personal: Born February 23, 1922, in Brooklyn, New York; Son of Charles E. and Lillian Owen Sevier; Married Grace Mary Rogers, on May 17, 1947. Education: Attended the City College of New York, 1936-42; B.S. cum laude, Temple University, 1952; M.A., University of Pennsylvania, 1954; Undertook Postgraduate Studies at the University of Pennsylvania, 1953-64; L.H.D., Combs College of Music, 1976; H.L.D., Widener University, 1979. Military: Served in the United States Army, 1942-48; U.S.A., Retired, W.D., Physical Disability. Career: Assistant Professor of Economics, Pennsylvania Military College, Chester, 1954-56; Assistant Professor of Management, Temple University School of Business Administration, Philadelphia, 1956-65; Assistant Professor of Economics and Management, Head of the Management Department PMC Colleges (now Widener College), Chester, Pennsylvania, after 1965; Associate Professor of Management Emeritus, Staff Statistician, Joint Center for Urban Affairs, Widener College, 1965 to present; Project Director, Research Bureau, Temple University, 1956-65. Organizational Memberships: International Institute for Community Service (fellow; founding member); American Institute of Property and Casualty Underwriters (board of examiners, 1957 to present). Community Activities: Boy Scouts of America (chairman, Northeast regional advisory committee on scouting for the handicapped, 1978 to present; national advisory committee on scouting for the handicapped, 1978 to present); Girl Scouts of America, Delaware County Council, 1968 to present; United Fund (staff member, annual drives, 1956 to present); Salvation Army Citadel, Chester (chairman, finance committee; advisory board); Concord Day Care Center, Chester (board of directors); Delaward County American Red Cross. Honors and Awards: Legion of Honor, Chapel of the Four Chaplains, 1973; Distinguished Service Award, Kiwanis, 1973; General E. E. MacMoreland Award for Civic Service, 1973; Outstanding Service Award, Valley Forge Council, Boy Scouts of America, 1973; Order of Merit, Explorer Division, 1975, 1978; Silver Beaver Award, 1978; Woods School Award for Service to the Handicapped, 1978; Scoutmaster's Explorer Advisor's Training Award, 1979; Distinguished Faculty Award, Widener College Alumni Association, 1973; Distinguished Service Award, Widener Society for the Advancement of Management, 1975; Distinguished Professor Award, 1979; Share Your Life Award, Pennsylvania District, Kiwanis International, 1974; Touch a Life Award, Kiwanis International, 1975; Bronze Medal, Chester Kiwanis Club, 1975; Distinguished Citizen Award, Delaware County Board of Realtors, 1977; Torch of Gold Award, Boy Scouts of America, for Outstanding Leadership in Scouting for the Handicapped, 1980; The Phoenix Award, Friendship Facilities, for Distinguished Service in the

Rehabilitation of the Handicapped, 1981; The Crown of Gold Award, Salvation Army, for Distinguished Community Service, 1980. Address: 401 Southcroft Road, Springfield, Pennsylvania 19064.

Sexauer, Arwin F B Garellick

Head Librarian (retired). Personal; Born August 18, 1921; Daughter of Linnie A. and Alson B. Fletcher (both deceased); Married Howard T. Sexauer; Mother of Dawn-Linnie Bashaw Mennucci, Alson C. Bashaw. Career: Head Librarian, Kellogg-Hubbard Library; Poet/Lyricist/Composer; Radio/Theatre Monologist; Editor; Co-Founder, Music Mission for World Peace, Inc. Organizational Memberships: Vermont Library Association; International Press Association; American Society of Composers, Authors and Publishers; Gospel Music Association; International Platform Association; Centro Studi e Scambi Internationali-Accademia Leonardo da Vinci (titular member); World Poetry Society Intercontinental; Dr. Stella Woodall Poetry Society International; New York Poetry Forum; American Academy of Poets (associate member); Eight Other Poetry Societies. Community Activities: 4-H Youth Leader, 21 Years. Published Works: Published Poet, Age 14; Radio/Theatre Monologist, Age 17; First Woman Editor, *Vermont Odd Fellow* Magazine; *Remembered Winds*, 1963; *Music Mission Songs from La Casa de Paz*, 1981; Published in Numerous American and European Poetry Journals; 14 Award-Winning Musical Pageants, including Gold Medal Pageant *From Sea to Shining Sea* 1957 and Second Gold Medal Pageant *I'm the Flag of All the People - Stand Up America* 1973; Premiered and Published Church, Fraternal and Civic Ceremonies; Music Award for Song *La Casa de Paz*, 1981; Song *The Poet's Peace Loom* Among Top Ten in International Competition, 1982; "A Better World Begins with Me", 1981; Worldwide Placement of Works in 20 Archival Deposits such as the Palace of Monaco, Sacred Institute of Music, Jerusalem, Marquette University People-to-People Archival Deposit. Honors and Awards: Four Medals, 2 Doctorates and Several Honorary Diplomas; Honorary D.Litt., Faculty of the World University; Honorary Diploma in Arts and Letters, Athens, Greece; Diploma de benemerenza, Accademia Leonardo da Vinci, Rome; Diploma of Life Fellowship, International Academy of Poets; Honorary Representative Appointment Diploma, Accademia Leonardo da Vinci; Honorary Life Membership Certificate, Hellenic Writer's Club, Athens, Greece; Honorary Life Fellow, Anglo-American Academy, Cambridge, England; Platform Association International Academy of Poets; Poet Laureate Certificate, Accademia Leonardo da Vincio; Poet Representative of Vermont, World Poetry Society Intercontinental, 1981; Distinguished Fellow and Honorary Advisor, American Biographical Institute; Global Portraits Hall of Fame; Awardee of Over 163 Honors from Prime Ministers of Israel and India, King of Thailand, Emir of Kuwait, Shah of Iran, Ministers of Cultural Affairs of Egypt, Ecuador, People's Republic of China, Sri Lanka, Afghanistan, Viet Nam, Ghana, Belgian Congo, Department of Music and Choir Directors of the United States; Music Award, Awards Jury of Fifth World Congress of Poets, San Francisco, California, 1981; Three George Washington Honor Medals, Freedoms Foundation, Valley Forge for Writing and Public Speaking in the American Way of Life, 1957, 1959, 1973; Among Top Ten Lyricists Selected, Virgilo-Mantegna Medal, International Competition, 1982; 14 American Society of Composers, Authors and Publishers Annual Popular Panel Awards for Lyrics, 1967-83; Richard Rodgers and Grand Ole Opry Music Awards; People-to-People Cultural Affairs Award; Two Gold Star Certificate of Merit Awards, National Federation of Music Clubs and American Society of Composers, Authors and Publishers, American Parade of Music Competition; American Federation of Musicians Award; Distinguished Service Citation for Poetry, World Board of Regents of the World Poetry Society, Intercontinental; First Prize for Illustrated Shell Art Poem, "Lady Collecting Shells", 46th Annual Competition of the Ozark Writers/Artists Guild; Sylvia Auxier Memorial Award for Lyrics; Prairie Poet Journal Award; Dr. Arthur Hewitt Memorial Award; Universal Friendship Poem Award; Poetry Society of Vermont Nature Poem Award; Distinguished American Poem Award; International Cloverleaf Anniversary Poem Award; World Peace Award; Robert Frost Chapter Award/Certificate; Two Viola Hayes Parsons Memorial Awards; Hoosier Challenger Honor/Award Certificate; Vermont Federation of Women's Clubs Honor Poem Award/Certificate; Special Citation for Poetry, International Congress of Poets, 1982; Exhibited Twice by Invitation, International Outdoor Poetry Show, New Orleans, Louisiana; Invitationals including Fourth and Fifth World Congress of Poets, International Biographical Centre Congress on Arts and Communications 1978-81, International Press Association and I.O.O.F. Annual Meets, Avalon International Poets and Editors Conference; Publication Salutes in Over 60 Fine Arts Magazines and Newspapers; Listed in *Who's Who of American Women, Who's Who in the East, International Who's Who of Intellectuals, World Who's Who of Women, Book of Honor* and Others. Address: Idle Tide Cottage, Box 303, Sanibel, Florida 33957 (December to May); Cherry Tree Hill, East Montpelier, Vermont 05651 (May to December).

Shadle, George Miller

Health Administrator. Personal: Born June 21, 1921, in Altoona, Pennsylvania; Son of Charlotta Shadle; Married to Dorothy McCall; Father of Graham, Gilbert, Mary Ellen, Paul Timothy. Education: Graduate, Crafton High School, Pittsburgh, Pennsylvania, 1939; B.S., Muskingum College, 1943; M.D., Temple University Medical School, 1947; Rotating Internship, University of Pittsburgh Medical Center, 1947-48; Resident in Pediatrics, Children's Hospital, Pittsburgh, 1948-50; Fellow in Pediatrics and M.S., 1948-51. Military: Served with United States Army, 1944-46; Received Honorable Discharge. Career: Chief, Office of Safety and Health, 1979 to present, Chief, Division of Occupational Health, 1975-79, Ohio Department of Health, Columbus, Ohio; Special Assistant to the Director of Health, 1974-75; Deputy Director and Chief, Maternal and Child Health Services, 1972-74; Pediatric Consultant to Ohio Department of Health, 1971; Medical Officer, Drug Regulatory Affairs, Roche Labs, Nutley, New Jersey, 1967-71; Private Practice in Pediatrics, Pittsburgh, 1958-67; Associate Clinical Researcher, Parke Davis and Company, Detroit, Michigan, 1952-55, Medical Coordinator, 1955-58, senior voting member on various committees; Clinical Assistant Professor, Department of Pediatrics, 1971 to present and Clinical Assistant Professor of Preventive Medicine, 1971 to present, Ohio State University; Assistant Professor of Pediatrics, University of Pittsburgh Medical School, 1958-67; Participated in the development and clinical testing of various experimental drugs for F.D.A. approval, including Chloromphenicol (an antibiotic), Povan (for treating pin worms), Milontin (for treating petit mal epilepsy), Elase (for burns and debridement of damaged tissue), and vaccines for Polio, Influenza and Adenovirus; Initiated and developed the Poison Control Center at Children's Hospital in Pittsburgh, 1960. Organizational Memberships: American Academy of Pediatrics; Ohio Public Health Association; Ohio chapter of American Academy of Pediatrics; Columbus and Franklin County Medical Society; American Public Health Association; Ohio State Medical Association; American Conferences of Governmental and Industrial Hygiene; Occupational Medicine Association; American Industrial Hygiene Association; Association of American Colleges and Universities; New York Academy of Sciences; American Medical Writers Association; American School Health Association; American Association for the Advancement of Sciences; World Health Organization; International Platform Association. Community Activities: Appointed to Governor's Occupational Health Task Force (member of executive committee, chairman of education and training committee, 1977 to present); Chairman of Public Employees' Safety and Health Program and Director of Health's Designee to the Governor, Ohio Department of Health, 1975 to present; Policy Advisory Committee member and Medical Advisory Committee member, Ohio Coalworkers' Respiratory Disease Program, 1975-77; Chairman of committee for Ob-Gyn and Nursery Regulations for Ohio Hospitals, 1972-74; Chairman of Sickle Cell Ad Hoc Committee, Ohio Department of Health, 1972-74; Chairman of Budget Committee, United Fund of Detroit, Michigan, 1955-57; Chairman of Cerebral Palsy Foundation of Children's Hospital, Pittsburgh, 1951-55; Member of Board of Directors, Cerebral Palsy of Pittsburgh, 1952-55; Member of Advisory Occupational Health Data Task Force, Health Services Foundation, 1975 to present; Chairman of School and Child Health Committee, Allegheny County Medical Society, 1959-65;

Worthington School Planning Committee, Worthington, Ohio, 1975-76; Member of International World Safety Congress. Religion: Member of United Presbyterian Church, 1940 to present. Published Works: "Complications of Contagious Childhood Diseases" with R. R. Macdonald, M.D. *Journal of the American Medical Association*, 1950. Honors and Awards: Fellow of the International Biographical Association; Member of the American Biographical Institute; Certified by the American Board of Pediatrics, American Occupational Medical Association, American Academy of Medical Directors and American Board of Preventive Medicine; Listed in *Who's Who in American Colleges and Universities, Community Leaders and Noteworthy Americans, International Who's Who in Community Service, Book of Honor, Dictionary of International Biography, International Who's Who of Intellectuals, Men of Achievement*. Address: 124 Glen Circle, Worthington, Ohio 43085.

Shah, Prakash A

Investment Banker. Personal: Born June 8, 1945; Son of Mr. and Mrs. Amritlal J. Shah; Married Rajul P. Jhaveri; Father of Kajal P. Education: B.S.M.E., Baroda University, India, 1967; M.S., Management Sciences, Stevens Institute of Technology, Hoboken, New Jersey, 1969; Ph.D., Management Sciences, New York University. Military: Served in the Air Force R.O.T.C., 1963-66. Career: General Partner, Bliss & Company, Investment Bankers, 1982 to present; Vice President, Strategic Planning and Development, American Express, and President and Chief Executive Officer, Amex-Birla Subsidiary, 1977-82; Director, Management Sciences and Consulting Services, Time Sharing Resources, Great Neck, New York, 1973-77; Senior Management Scientist, Avon Products, New York, 1970-73; Operations Research Analyst, Nabisco, New York, 1969; Systems Analyst, Foster Wheeler Corporation, Livingston, New Jersey, 1968. Organizational Memberships: National Association of Business Economists, 1977-81; The Institute of Manageent Sciences, 1977-81; The Future Society, 1978-82; INFO 197, INFO 1977, INFO 1979, Leading Information Industry Annual Exposition and Conference (program and steering committee). Community Activities: India Chamber of Commerce of America (executive director/secretary, 1979 to present); India-United States Joint Business Council (advisory member); National Council of Asian Indians in North America (vice president, 1980 to present); Federation of India Associations (board of directors, 1979 to present); India Development Service of New York (president, 1979 to present); Coalition of Asian Pacific American Association (steering committee, 1979-82); Sherwood Village Cooperation, New York (steering committee, 1979-82). Religion: Board of Directors, Jain Center of America, 1976-79. Honors and Awards: Second-Most Outstanding Student of India, 1967. Address: 124 Childs Road, Basking Ridge, New Jersey 07920.

Shaver, James P

Professor, Associate Dean. Personal: Born October 19, 1933; Son of G. C. Shaver; Married Bonnie R. Pehrson; Father of Kim, Jay, Guy. Education: B.A., University of Washington, 1955; A.M.T. 1957, Ed.D. 1961, Harvard University. Career: Professor and Associate Dean of Research, Utah State University; Research Associate and Instructor, Harvard Graduate School of Education; Visiting Professor, University of Washington, Harvard University; Director, Social Studies Curriculum Center, The Ohio State University; Teacher, Peter Bulkeley Junior High School, Concord, Massachusetts, Roy High School, Sky View High School, Utah. Organizational Memberships: American Educational Research Association; National Council for the Social Studies (president, 1976); American Association for the Advancement of Science; American Association of University Professors. Community Activities: National Commission on Educational Policy (advisor, 1965-67); Far West Laboratory for Educational Research and Development (executive panel, 1970-74); American Bar Association Advisory Committee on Youth Education for Citizenship, 1975-81; Utah Commission for Law and Citizenship, 1978 to present; Project '87 Education Committee, 1981 to present. Honors and Awards: Phi Beta Kappa; Faculty Honor Lecturer in the Humanities and Social Studies, Utah State University, 1972; Utah Council for Social Studies Outstanding University Service and Teaching Award, 1975, 1978; National Council for the Social Studies Citation for Exemplary Research in Social Studies Education, 1977. Address: P.O. Box 176, Hyrum, Utah 84319.

Prakash A Shah

Shaw, Andrew Jr

Dean of Management, Administrator. Personal: Born September 14, 1931; Son of Andrew (deceased) and Mary Shaw; Married Viola Mihalski; Father of Linda, Nancy, Robert. Education: Graduate of Plains (Pennsylvania) High School, 1949; B.S., Social Science, Wilkes College, 1958; M.S., Government Administration, Wharton Graduate School, University of Pennsylvania, 1960; M.P.A. 1976, D.P.A. 1978, Nova University. Military: Served in the United States Army, 1951-53. Career: Administrative Aide, City of Philadelphia, 1960; Transportation Researcher, Pennsylvania Economy League Inc., 1962-64; Executive Director, Economy League, Lehigh Valley Branch, 1964-67; Branch Coordinator, Central D Division, Pennsylvania Economy League, 1967-68; Director of Research 1968-72, Director of Institute of Regional Affairs 1972 to present, Wilkes College; Dean of Management, Wilkes College, 1972 to present; Director of Small Business Center, Professor of Political Science, Wilkes College. Organizational Memberships: Governmental Research Association, United States and Canada; American Society of Public Administration (president, N.E.P.A. Chapter); American Academy of Political and Social Science; Council on Basic Education; American Management Association; American Political Science Association; National Council of University Research Administrators. Community Activities: Susquehanna River Basin Association (president, 1976-77; treasurer, 1978 to present); Wilkes-Barre Chamber of Commerce (executive committee); Downtown Development Company (board member); Wilkes-Barre Industrial Development Authority (advisory board); Icarus Energy Research Institute (board member); United Health and Hospital Association (finance committee); Economic Development Council/N.E.P.A. (finance committee); Wyoming Valley United Way (health services committee); Rotary Club of Wilkes-Barre (chairman, vocational committee; education committee); Susquehanna S.E.S. Project Committee, Advisory Group to Nuclear Steam Electric Plant; Wilkes-Barre Young Men's Christian Association (board member, finance committee); Pennsylvania Mountains Council/Boy Scouts of America (financial vice president); Pennsylvania Institute of Municipal Management (chairman); Luzern County Chairman of Labor/Management Committee; Pennsylvania County Commissioners Advisory Committee. Honors and Awards: Distinguished Pennsylvanian, 1978, Ben Franklin Club, Philadelphia; Citation for Service, Civil Defense Preparedness Agency, 1973; Distinguished Service Award, University of Pennsylvania, Fels Institute of State and Local Governments; Honorary Member, Association of Pennsylvania Municipal Managers; Listed in *Community Leaders of America, Who's Who in the East*. Address: 30 Peartree Lane, Dallas, Pennsylvania 18612.

Shearer, Charles E Jr

Lawyer, Financial Planner. Personal: Born September 2, 1922; Son of Charles E. and Helen L. Shearer; Married Ruth Mae Nicholson; Father of Kay Ellen Shearer Gardiner, Beth Ann Shearer Gould. Education: A.S., Kokomo Junior College, 1943; A.B., Indiana University, 1947; J.D., Indiana University School of Law, 1953. Military: Served in the United States Army, 1943-46, attaining the rank of Sergeant; Served in the United States Army Reserve, 1946-55, attaining the rank of Lieutenant. Career: Lawyer, Financial Planner; Former Positions include Industrial Relations Consultant, International Harvester; Personnel Director, Indianapolis

Railways; Manager, Chamber of Commerce, Shelbyville, Indiana; Law Partnership, Supervisor, L. W. McDougal, Cleveland; Division Manager, Sales, College Life, Indianapolis; Senior Vice President, Export-Import, Bank of the United States. Organizational Memberships: District of Columbia Bar Association: Indiana Bar Association; Supreme Court of the United States; National Association of Life Underwriters; Chartered Life Underwriter. Community Activities: United States Jaycees (past state president, national vice president, president); United States Jaycee Foundation (chairman of the board, 1980-82); Metropolitan Washington Young Men's Christian Association (board member, vice-chairman 1982-83). Religion: Episcopalian. Honors and Awards: Y-Red Triangle Award, 1981; Named One of Three Outstanding Young Men in Indiana. Address: 4839 Yorktown Blvd., Arlington, Virginia 22207.

Shearer, Ruth Easter

College Professor. Personal: Born April 3, 1920; Daughter of Dr. and Mrs. A. R. Mansberger (both deceased); Married; Mother of Patricia Wilson, Suzanne Jones, Richard Judson. Education: B.A., Western Maryland College, 1941; M.Ed., University of Pittsburgh, 1943; Ed.D., Columbia University, 1963. Career: Professor of Education and Psychology, Alderson Broaddus College; Former High School Teacher of Latin, English, French. Organizational Memberships: Delta Kappa Gamma; Pi Lambda Theta; Kappa Delta Pi; Association of Teacher Educators. Religion: Executive Board, West Virginia Baptist Convention. Honors and Awards: West Virginia Mother of the Year, 1974; Mary Ward Lewis Prize, Awarded at the Undergraduate Level to the Outstanding Graduating Woman, 1941; Listed in *Who's Who of American Women, Who's Who in the East, Who's Who in the South and Southwest, Who's Who in American Education, World Who's Who of Women, Personalities of the South, Notable Americans, Outstanding Educators of America, Dictionary of International Biography, Leaders in Education*. Address: Alderson Broaddus College, Philippi, West Virginia 26416.

Sheeder, William B

University Administrator. Personal: Born January 21, 1938; Son of Fred T. and Amy F. Sheeder; Married D. Gayle Holden; Father of Lynn Suzanne, Traci JoAnn. Education: Graduate of Elmira Free Academy, Elmira, New York, 1956; A.B., Philosophy, Ottawa University, 1960; M.A., Human Relations, Ohio University, 1966. Career: Ottawa University, Ottawa, Kansas, Student Manager 1958-59, Student Council President, 1959-60, President of Kansas Conference Student Association 1959-60; Ohio University, Athens, Head Resident of Men's Residence Hall 1960-62, Part-time Instructor in Human Relations and Social Science 1961-65, Associate Director of Baker University Center 1962-64, Assistant to the Dean of the College of Arts and Sciences 1964-66; University of Miami, Coral Gables, Director of Whitten Memorial Student Union 1966-73, Director of Student Activities and Whitten Student Union 1968-73, Vice President and Secretary of University Rathskeller Inc. 1972 to present, Assistant Vice President for Student Affairs 1973 to present, Dean of Students, 1976 to present. Organizational Memberships: Association of College Unions International (member, 1967 to present; enrichment chairman, 1975 conference planning committee and co-host director); International Association of Auditorium Managers, 1971-74; Wesley Foundation, Dade County, Florida (board of directors; treasurer, 1971-73; chairman, 1973-77; member, 1971 to present); Centre for Experimental Learning and Living, Inc. (consultant, 1976); National Association of Student Personnel Administrators; National Orientation Directors Association; American Association for Higher Education; American Personnel and Guidance Association/American College Personnel Association. Religion: Work Area on Higher Education and Campus Ministry, Florida Conference Council on Ministries of the United Methodist Church, 1976-80, 1981-84. Published Works: "Role Playing as a Method of Selecting Dormitory Counselors", 1963; "A Framework for Student Development in Higher Education", 1974; Introduction to *Guide to the Best, Most Popular and Most Exciting Colleges*, 1982. Honors and Awards: Sigma Alpha Honor Society; Omicron Delta Kappa; Phi Delta Kappa; Orange Key, Leadership Recognition Society; Order of the Golden Leaf; Phi Kappa Epsilon, Outstanding Administrator Award and Honorary Member; Phi Mu Alpha; Faculty Honor Roll, Ohio University, 1965-66; Faculty Fellows Citation, Ohio University, 1965-66; Honorary Member, Federation of Cuban Students, University of Miami; Adjunct Brother, Zeta Beta Tau, 1971 to present; Listed in *Community Leaders of America, Community Leaders and Noteworthy Americans, Directory of Distinguished Americans, Dictionary of International Biography, International Who's Who in Community Service, International Who's Who of Intellectuals, Men of Achievement, Men of Distinction, Notable Americans, Outstanding Young Men of America, Personalities of America, Personalities of the South, Two Thousand Men of Achievement, Who's Who Among Students in American Colleges and Universities, Who's Who in the South and Southwest*. Address: 8315 Southwest 72 Avenue #301B, Miami, Florida 33143.

Ralph A Sheetz

Sheetz, Ralph Albert

Attorney. Personal: Born June 13, 1908, Halifax Township, Pennsylvania; Son of Harry Wesley and Manora Enders Sheetz; Married Ruth Lorraine Bender, May 19, 1938; Father of Ralph Bert. Education Graduated from East Pennsboro Township High School (with honors), 1926; Attended the University of California-Berkeley, Summer 1928; Ph.B., Dickinson College, Carlisle, Pennsylvania, 1930; Attended the University of Michigan School of Law, Summer 1932; LL.B., University of Alabama School of Law, 1933; J.D., University School of Law, 1969. Career: Admitted to Practice Law before the Supreme Court of Alabama 1933, Supreme Court of Pennsylvania 1934, Superior Court of Pennsylvania 1938, United States District Court for the Middle District of Pennsylvania 1944, Others; Solicitor, Peoples Bank of Enola (Pennsylvania), 40 years; Selective Service Official for Appeal, Area #4, Pennsylvania, 1941; Attorney from Employees Loan Society, 1966-76. Organizational Memberships: American Bar Association; Pennsylvania Bar Association; Dauphin County Bar Association; Cumberland County Bar Association; Farrah Law Society, University School of Law. Community Activities: Perry Lodge #458, Free and Accepted Masons of Pennsylvania (master mason, 1930; worshipful master, 1971; elected to represent Perry Lodge in Grand Lodge of Pennsylvania, 1972); Harrisburg Masonic School of Instructions (board of directors); General Alumni Association, Dickinson College (life member); Harrisburg Forest #43, Tall Cedars of Lebanon (drill team member, 1934-44; selected to play part of Prince Azariah in Pro-Logue and Royal Court at ceremonials, 1943; life membership for muscular dystrophy; historian, 1976 to present); Harrisburg Consistory, 32°, Ancient Accepted Scottish Rite; Zembo Temple, Ancient Arabic Order of Nobles of Mystic Shrine; Zembo Shrine Luncheon Club; York and Cumberland County Shrine Clubs; Harrisburg Council #499, Royal Arcanum (regent, 1952; presided over meeting of executive committee of supreme council of Royal Arcanum for U.S. and Canada, 1952; elected to represent Harrisburg Council at session of grand council of Royal Arcanum of Pennsylvania, 1952; committee on laws; chairman of grand council on laws; distinguished service member, elected to membership in Keystone Circle #3); East Pennsboro Township Republican Club; West Shore Twilight Baseball League (umpire); East Pennsboro Township (solicitor, 1937-53; assistant solicitor, 10 years; member of planning commission, 3 years; vice chairman, chairman, zoning commission; board of adjustments, chairman); Royal Arch Mason in Perseverance Royal Arch Chapter #21 (most excellent high priest; elected to serve in Grand Holy Royal Arch Chapter of Pennsylvania); Harrisburg Council #7 Royal and Select Masters (thrice illustrious master); Order of the Temple, Pilgrim Commandery #11, Knights Templar of Pennsylvania (commander); Enola Boys Club (incorporator, 1950; attorney, treasurer); Harrisburg Chamber of Commerce; East Pennsboro Township Parent-Teacher Association (president, 1951-53); Citizens Fire Company #1, Enola (incorporator, 1951; honorary member, attorney); Order of Penn

Priary #6, Knights of York Cross of Honour; East Pennsboro Township Senior Citizens Century Club (charter member, 1979). Religion: United Methodist Church. Honors and Awards: Represented the University of Alabama at the Inauguration of Walter Consuelo Langsam as 8th President of Gettysburg College, 1952; Fifty Year Masonic Service Emblem, Grand Lodge of Pennsylvania and Certificate of Congratulations, Perry Lodge #458, Free and Accepted Masons; Past High Priest's Certificate, Perseverance Chapter #21; Red Ribbon Certificate of Eminent Commander, Order of the Temple, Pilgrim Commandery; Speaker, Dedication of New Highway between Overview and Marysville, Pennsylvania, 1938; Resolution by Senator Edwin S. Bower, 1945; Pin, Medal and Badge, Headquarters for Selective Service, Commonwealth of Pennsylvania, 1946; Order of the Silver Trowel, Council of Anointed Kings of the Commonwealth of Pennsylvania, 1948; Numerous Certificates of Recognition and Appreciation; Listed in *Dictionary of International Biography, National Society Directory, Who's Who in American Law, International Who's Who of Intellectuals, Book of Honor*. Address: 798 Valley Street, Enola, Pennsylvania 17025.

Shell, Vicki

Training Director. Personal: Born July 4, 1947; Divorced; Mother of One Son. Education: B.S. cum laude 1968, M.A. 1969, M.A. + 30 Hours 1972, Murray State University; Ph.D., The Ohio State University 1979. Career: Training Director, Airco Carbide, Louisville, Kentucky, October 1982 to present; Safety and Training Manager, Airco Carbide, Calvert City, Kentucky, 1981-82; Coordinator of Special Activities, Department of Industrial Education, Murray State University, 1978-81; Research Associate, Interstate Distribution Education Curriculum Consortium, The Ohio State University, 1976-78; Distributive Education Coordinator and D.E.C.A. Advisor, Murray Area Vocational Education Center, 1972-76; Distributive Education Coordinator and D.E.C.A. Advisor, North Marshall High School, 1969-71; Teaching Assistant, Murray State University, 1968-69. Organizational Memberships: American Industrial Arts Association (convention exhibitor); American Council on Industrial Arts Teacher Education; Kentucky Industrial Education Association; Epsilon Pi Tau; National Association of Distributive Education Teachers (past national secretary-treasurer; past member, national public relations committee; past chairman, national nominating committee; past state membership chairman; life member); American Vocational Association (member of house of delegates; presenter for distributive education sessions; past member, advisory committee for member benefits; member and recorder for distributive education policy and planning committee, 1976-78); Kentucky Vocational Association (past vice president; past member of state nominating committee; past distributive education membership chairman; presenter at distributive education sessions); Distributive Education Clubs of America (central region conference consultant; Kentucky D.E.C.A. board of directors; Kentucky constitution committee; Kentucky summer camp instructor; chief advisor for national conference area of distribution event; Ohio fall delegates conference judge; Ohio state conference judge); Council for Distributive Teacher Educators; Kentucky Association of Distributive Education Teachers (past state president; regional secretary; vice president); Phi Delta Kappa; American Vocational Education Research Association; American Educational Research Association; Parent-Teacher Association (field day committee chairman; president, Murray, Kentucky). Community Activities: Murray Women's Club (Kappa department past treasurer and parliamentarian); Murray Swim Team (swim meet timer and line judge); Charity Ball, Murray, Kentucky (past decorations, publicity and food committees); Murray County Club (past social chairman); Children's Hospital Fund Drive (volunteer for Muirfield Golf Tournament); Murray-Calloway County Swim Team Board, 1981-84; Chairperson, First District Parent-Teacher Association Committee, 1981-82. Religion: First United Methodist Church, Hannah Circle, Past Treasurer, Bible School Teacher. Published Works: *Machine Shop State-of-the-Art Report*, 1981; Number of Reports and Articles. Honors and Awards: Outstanding Young Woman of Kentucky, 1980; Kentucky Board of Occupational Education Appointed Member of Advisory Committee to Area Vocational Education; Selected as Member of Advisory Committee on Eligibilty and Accreditation for United States Department of Health, Education and Welfare, 1975-78; Outstanding Distributive Education Teacher of Kentucky, 1975; Favorite Teacher of North Marshall High School, 1971; Listed in *Outstanding Young Women of America, Personalities of the South, Who's Who Among Students in American Colleges and Universities, Community Leaders of America*. Address: 1528 Oxford Drive, Murray, Kentucky 42071.

Bessie E Shelton

Shelton, Bessie Elizabeth

Educator. Personal: Daughter of Robert, (deceased), and Bessie P. Shelton. Education: B.A., West Virginia State College, 1958; M.S., State University of New York, 1960; Diploma, Universal Schools, 1971; Diploma, North American School of Travel, 1972; Diploma, Nashville School of Songwriting, 1975; Additional study at Northwestern University, University of Virginia, Virginia Western College. Military: Served with the United States Navy, Personnelman 1951-55; Member of Great Lakes and WAVE Choirs. Career: Young Adult Librarian, Brooklyn Public Library; Assistant Head Central Reference Division, Circulation Librarian, Art and Music Librarian, Queensborough Public Library, Jamaica, New York; Educator/Education Media Specialist, Lynchburg, Virginia, Public School System; Educator/Educational Media Associate, Board of Education of Allegany County. Organizational Memberships: National Education Association; Maryland State Teachers Association; Allegany County Teachers Association; American Association of Creative Artists; Intercontinental Biographical Association; International Entertainers Guild; Vocal Artists of America (lifetime member); Clover International Poetry Association (lifetime Danae member). Community Activities: Guest Vocal Artist in Community and School Musical Programs; Brooklyn Philharmonia Choral Society; Fine Arts Center Chorus, Lynchburg, Virginia; Community Chorus, Tri-State Community Concert Association; Young Women's Christian Association (ethnic studies committee); Research Specialist for Educational Projects; Judge for talent competitions. Religion: Church Soloist; Choir Member; Youth Counselor. Honors and Awards: Certificate of Merit for Service as Soloist, U.S.N.T.C., Great Lakes, Illinois, 1951; Scholarship Award, 1957; Pi Delta Phi, 1957 (president Beta Pi Chapter); Sigma Delta Pi, 1958; Certificate of Merit for Service to College Band as Majorette, West Virginia State College, 1958; B.A. with Honors; First Prize Talent Award, 1969; Sweetheart of the Day, Radio Station WLVA, September 13, 1973. Address: P.O. Box 187, Cumberland, Maryland 21502.

Shelton, Donald Wayne

Regional Representative. Personal: Born July 17, 1943, in Shawnee, Oklahoma; Son of Darrell W. and Vivian M. Shelton; Married JoAnn Dodd; Father of Donald Wayne II, JoAnna Lyn. Education: Attended Oklahoma University, Kansas University, Philanthropy Tax Institute. Military: Served in the Oklahoma National Guard, advancing through the grades to the rank of Staff Sergeant. Career: Mail Clerk to Manager of Solvents Sales Division, Apco Oil Corp., 1964-68; Director of Sales and Marketing, General Drug and Chemical Corporation, Kansas City, Missouri, 1968-70; Director of Stewardship and Trust Department, The General Council of the Assemblies of God, Springfield, Missouri, 1971-77; Broker/Partner, Red Carpet Realty, Professional School of Real Estate (Owner, Administrator, Teacher), Partner, Sims Kimball Music Center Inc., 1977-81; Regional Representative of the Secretary of the United States Department of Transportation, Region VI, Fort Worth, Texas, 1981 to present. Community Activities: Missouri State Board of Elementary and Secondary Education (board member); Springfield Green County Library (president, 5 years; board member); Republican Committeeman, Green County, Missouri; Reagan Alternate Delegate, Republican National Convention, 1976; 1980 Presidential Electoral College; City Councilman, Roeland Park, Kansas, 1969-71; Chairman, Roeland Park Republican Central

Committee, 1969-71; Republican Central Committee, Johnson City, Kansas (executive committee); Greater Ozarks Pachyderm Club (vice president); Southeast Rotary Club; Johnson County Cancer Society (past chairman); Old Mission Lodge #153; Scottish Rite 32; Abou Ben Adhem Temple Shrine (member of director's staff); Springfield Area Chamber of Commerce (action team; industrial development committee); Maranatha Retirement Center (past board member); Parent-Teacher Association; American Legion Post #676; Easter Seals Telethon (chairman, 1981); Southwest Missouri American Heart Association (board member). Religion: Central Assembly of God, Former Sunday School Teacher, Former Youth Director; Past Chairman, National Association of Evangelical Stewardship Commission. Honors and Awards: Jaycees Outstanding Young Man, 1973; Honorary Doctor Degree, Southwestern University; Million Dollar Sales Club, Real Estate; Honorary Mayor, San Antonio, Texas; Honorary Citizen, City of New Orleans (Louisiana), City of El Paso (Texas), City of Port Arthur (Texas), City of Corpus Christi (Texas), City of Fort Worth (Texas), State of Texas, State of Oklahoma, City of Lubbock (Texas); Honorary Citizen and Goodwill Ambassador, City of Houston; Colonel and Aide-de-Camp, Governor's Staff, State of Louisiana; Arkansas Traveler; Honorary Colonel and Aide-de-Camp, State of New Mexico; Commissioned Ambassador at Large, City of Oklahoma City; Honorary Ozark Hillbilly, Chamber of Commerce, Springfield, Missouri; Honorary Member, Christian Legal Society; Territorial Marshall, State of Oklahoma; Listed in *Outstanding Young Men of America, Who's Who in Religion, Who's Who in American Politics, Notable Americans, Who's Who in America, Who's Who in the Midwest*. Address: 5809 Silver Lake Court, Fort Worth, Texas 76117.

Shepard, Charles V

Vice President of Human Resources. Personal: Born November 14, 1940; Son of Mrs. Catherine E. Shepard; Married Judy A. Wells; Father of Cynthia Lynn. Education: B.A., Business Administration and Economics, Illinois College, 1962; M.B.A., University of Illinois, Sangamon State University, 1972. Career: Supervisor of Employee Benefits/Trainee Employee Relations, 1962-67, Administrative Assistant 1967-68, Manager of Personnel Services 1968-70, Manager of Organizational Planning and Development 1970-72, Manager of Industrial Relations/Manager of Personnel 1972-73, Allis-Chalmers Corporation; Director of Personnel 1973, Director of Industrial Relations of Dallas Region 1973-74, Group Director of Personnel for Collins Radio Group 1974-76, Vice President of Personnel in Electronics Operations 1976-77, Staff Vice President of Personnel in Electronics Operations 1977-78, Staff Vice President of Personnel in Aerospace and Electronics 1978, Staff Vice President of Employee Relations 1978-79, Vice President of Human Resources for General Industries Operations 1979 to present, Rockwell International. Organizational Memberships: Industrial Relations Committee, Aerspace Industries Association; International Business Council, Electronic Industries Association; Subcommittee on Multinational Labor Relations, National Association of Manufacturers. Community Activities: Pittsburgh Public Theatre (board of directors, 1979 to present); Junior Achievement Advisory Council, 1981. Honors and Awards: Listed in *Who's Who in Finance and Industry*. Address: 307 Butternut Court, Pittsburgh, Pennsylvania 15238.

Shepherd, Judy Carlile

Judy Shepherd

Social Science Analyst. Personal: Daughter of John Mercer and Mary Almeda Chapin Ellis (deceased); Married Joseph E. Shepherd; Mother of John Philip Carlile. Education: Attended Oklahoma State University; B.A., American University, 1960. Career: Social Science Analyst, Congressional Research Service, Library of Congress, Washington, D.C., 1976 to present; Director of Public Relations, National Association of Social Workers, Washington, D.C., 1973-74; O.E.O., Special Assistant to Department of Direct Operations 1970-73, Public Information Officer for Head Start, Elderly, Indian and Migrant Programs 1965-70; Congressional Liaison, Department of Agriculture, Washington, D.C., 1961-65; Government and Public Relations Official, National Counselors Association, Washington, D.C., 1959-61; Building Fund Campaign Manager, American Association of University Women, Washington, D.C., 1958-59; Real Estate Broker, United Farm Agency, 1952-58; Chief Probation Officer, Tulsa County Court, 1947-50. Organizational Memberships: National Press Club; Public Relations Society of America; National Association of Government Communicators; American Humanist Association; Association of Humanistic Psychology; American University Alumni Assocation; Oklahoma State Society Library of Congress Professional Association; Humanist Association (national Capital area president, 1977-78); National Congress of American Indians. Community Activities: Daughters of the American Revolution; Women's National Democratic Club, Washington, D.C.; America Discovers Indian Art Exhibit, Smithsonian Institution (arranger, 1967); Agricultural Symphony Orchestra (board of directors president, 1961-64); American Red Cross (board of directors, 1948-50); Boy Scouts of America (board of directors, 1948-50); Little Theater and Radio Shows (board of directors, 1956-57); Certified Humanist Counselor. Honors and Awards: First Place, Federal Editors Blue Pencil Award, 1967. Address: 2365 North Oakland Street, Arlington, Virginia 22207.

Sheppard, Ronald J

Administrator. Personal: Born April 13, 1939; Son of Mr. and Mrs. Lester Sheppard; Married Shirley C.; Father of Jeffrey Brandon, Mark Justin. Education: B.S., Physics, Rensselaer Polytechnic Institute, 1961; M.S. 1962, Ph.D. 1965, Howard University; M.B.A., Rochester Institute of Technology, 1974; Course Work Toward Juris Doctor. Career: Director, Strategy Analysis, Strategic Planning Department; Former Positions include Product Planning Manager, Ford Motor Company; Group Program Manager, Xerox Corporation; Director, Space Sciences Lab, Teledyne Brown Engineering; Principal Consultant, Booz Allen Hamilton Inc. Organizational Memberships: Engineering Society of Detroit; Detroit Economics Club; New Detroit, Inc. Community Activities: Rotary Club; Torch Club International; Rochester (New York) Montessori School (president, board of directors); Jaycees; Shriner; Accounting Aid Society (board of directors). Honors and Awards: K. B. Weisman Human Relations Award, 1955, 1957; Harry Diamond Labs Graduate Student Award, 1963; Lawrence Institute of Technology, Community Service Award, 1980. Address: 19521 Burlington Drive, Detroit, Michigan 48203.

Sheridan, Susan Jane

Consultant. Personal: Born December 6, 1941, in San Francisco, California; Daughter of Mr. and Mrs. W. J. Warner; Married Jack Michael Sheridan; Mother of Jane Margaret, Scott Michael, Lisl Warner. Education: Graduate of Menlo Atherton High School, Atherton, California, 1959; B.S.Ed. 1963, M.Ed. 1964, University of Oregon; Post-Masters Studies in Special Education, Psychology, Speech, Central Washington State University; Ed.D., University of Houston, 1974; Post-Doctoral Studies in Professional Education, Diagnosis and Administration, University of Houston at Clear Lake City. Career: Teacher of Trainable Mentally Retarded, Nursery Level, Teenage Level, Pearl Buck School, Eugene, Oregon, 1962-64; Teacher of Trainable Mentally Retarded, Nellie Burke School, Ellensburg, Washington, 1965-67; Instructor, Central Washington State College, Summers 1966-69; Teacher of Kindergarten, Non-graded Open Concept School, Ardmore Elementary School, Bellevue, Washington, 1967-68; Teacher of Mothers of Headstart Children, Preparation for High School Equivalency Exam, Ellensburg, Washington, 1968-69; Teacher of Trainable Mentally Retarded, Harris County Center for the Retarded, Inc., Houston, Texas, 1969-71; Demonstration Teaching Fellow, University of

Houston, 1971-73; Assistant to Director, Magnificat Half-way Houses, Houston, Summers 1971-73; Secondary Special Education Supervisor, Galena Park Independent School District, Texas, 1973-75; Part-time Lecturer, Faculty, University of Houston at Clear Lake City, 1975-76, 1978 to present; Supervisor, Harris County Center for the Retarded, Inc., Houston, 1975-76; Assistant Professor, Diagnostic Education, University of Houston at Clear Lake City, 1976-78; Part-time Faculty, University of Houston, 1981 to present; Consultant, Harris County Department of Education, Houston, 1978 to present; Organized, Founded and Staffed, Nellie Burke School, 1965-68; Organized Parent Study Group, Ardmore School, 1967-68; Organized and Staffed Language Development Program, Ellensburg, Washington, 1968; Test Coordinator, Project PRIME (Pupil Re-entry into the Mainstream of Education), Houston, 1971. Organizational Memberships: American Association on Mental Deficiency; Council for Exceptional Children (higher education representative to Gulf Coast Chapter #153); Phi Delta Kappa; Houston Metropolitan Chapter of Educational Diagnosticians; Hou-Met Texas Association of Educational Diagnosticians (advisor, 1979 to present). Community Activities: Magnificat Half-way Houses, Inc. (volunteer evaluator and counselor for residents, 1977-82; board of directors, 1974-82); Suzanna House for Battered Women (co-director, 1978); Spring Branch Academy School Board (a non-profit school for educational therapy). Published Works: *Decisions-Decisions, Aiming at Your Goal, Are You Listening?, To Question or Not To Question;* Number of Professional Articles, including "Who Says Kids Are Cruel?: Dina's Story" 1980, and "What Students Value and Think Their Teachers Value" 1978; Developed Teaching Material for Trainable Mentally Retarded Students: Right-Wrong Reading Signs; Pre-Vocational Game, "Employment: Where Does the Money Go?"; Using Functional Word Signs Program, 1981; Springboards to Learning, Kindergarten Curriculum, 1981. Honors and Awards: Special Recognition Award, Junior Chamber of Commerce, Ellensburg, Washington, 1966; Demonstration Teaching Fellow, University of Houston, 1971-73; Nominated for Piper Excellence in Teaching Award, University of Houston at Clear Lake City, 1976, 1981; Listed in *Outstanding Young Women of America, Who's Who in the South and Southwest, World Who's Who of Women, Personalities of the South.* Address: 2736 Quenby Avenue, Houston, Texas 77005.

Sheridan, Vincent George

Real Estate and Management Consultant, Securities Broker/Dealer. Personal: Born April 15, 1921; Son of Vincent Justus and Julie Martha Sheridan. Education: B.Sc. Business, B.S.C.E., University of Colorado, 1951; M.B.A., Fairleigh Dickinson University, 1979; Undergraduate Studies also undertaken at Stevens Institute of Technology, New York University, Mohawk College; Graduate Studies Undertaken at Cornell University School of Architecture, Russell Sage College School of Business, Union College School of Engineering, Cornell University School of Engineering, Institute of Real Estate Management, National Rural Development Leaders School, Cornell University Graduate School of Business and the Institute of Assessing Officers, University of Connecticut School of Business, American Society of Real Estate Counselors, Farm Income Tax School, University of Maryland School of Business, American Savings and Loan Institute, New York State Department of Public Works School of Appraising, Society of Industrial Realtors, Society of Real Estate Appraisers. Military: Served in the United States Naval Reserve, 1942-51. Career: Expediter, Western Electric Company, 1940-42; Industrial Engineer, DeLaval Separator Company, 1951-52; Assistant Project Engineer, Engineer, Assistant Superintendent, NYSDPW, Savin Construction Company, McDonald Engineering Company, Beacon Construction Company, 1952-55; Project Engineer, General Electric Company, 1955-57; Value Analyst, NYCBWS Bureau of Claims, 1957; Consultant, Engineer, Planner, Appraiser, Realtor, 1961 to present. Organizational Memberships: American Planning Association; American Arbitration Association; American Academy of Political and Social Sciences; American Planning and Civic Association; American Society of Planning Officials; American Accounting Association; American Society of Appraisers (senior member); American Judicature Society; American Institute of Professional Consultants; American Association of Cost Engineers (senior member); American Institute of Biological Sciences; American Defense Preparedness Association; American Society of Agricultural Engineers; American Real Estate and Urban Economics Association; American Society of Civil Engineers; American Right of Way Association (senior member); American Forestry Association; American Congress of Surveying and Mapping (fellow); American Academy of Religion; American Water Resources Association; American Society of Notaries; American College of Real Estate Consultants; American Water Works Association; American Society of Business and Management Consultants; American Society of Professional Consultants; American Association of Certified Appraisers (senior member); Associated Photographers International; Association of Federal Appraisers; Community Planning Association of Canada; Ecological Society of America; Financial Management Association; Federation of American Scientists; Independent Fee Appraisers Association (senior member); Institute of Real Estate Management (vice president, capital region area); Institute of Management Sciences; International Solar Energy Society; International College of Real Estate Consulting Appraisers; National Association of Financial Consultants; National Association of Fire Underwriters; New York State Society of Professional Engineers; New York State Association of Realtors; Society of Real Estate Appraisers; Member of Numerous Other Professional Organizations. Community Activities: Kiwanis International (president, director); Catskill Lodge 468 F&AM (master; trustee); Catskill Chapter 285 (high priest); Catskill Council 78, R&SM (illustrious master); Lafayette Commandry 7, KT (eminent commander); Knight, York Cross of Honor; Ancient Accepted Scottish Rite 32°; Ancient Arabic Order, Nobles of the Mystic Shrine; Greene County Shrine Club (president); Town Republican Club (president, secretary); Leeds Volunteer Fire Company (president, secretary); International Platform Association; The Explorers Club; Tau Beta Pi; Sigma Tau; Chi Epsilon; Others. Honors and Awards: Alpha Psi Omega; Wisdom Award of Honor; Listed in *Leaders in American Science, International Registry of Who's Who, Dictionary of International Biography, Who's Who in the United States, International Register of Profiles, International Who's Who in Community Service, National Register of Scientific and Technical Personnel, Men and Women of Distinction, International Who's Who of Intellectuals, Who's Who in Consulting, Who's Who in Engineering, Community Leaders of America, Who's Who in the East, Who's Who in North America, National Engineers Register, Wisdom Encyclopedia, Book of Honor, Men of Achievement, National Social Registry.* Address: R.D. 2, Box 500, Catskill, New York 12414.

A Robert Sherman

Sherman, A Robert

Professor of Psychology and Clinical Psychologist. Personal: Born November 18, 1942; Son of Mr. and Mrs. David R. Sherman; Married to Llana Helene; Father of Jonathan Colbert, Relissa Anne. Education: B.A., Columbia University, 1964; M.S., 1966, Ph.D., 1969, Yale University. Career: Professor of Psychology, University of California at Santa Barbara; Psychologist in private practice; Psychological Consultant; Author. Organizational Memberships: American Psychological Association; American Association of University Professors (chapter president for University of California at Santa Barbara, 1978-79); Association for the Advancement of Behavior Therapy; Phi Beta Kappa (chapter treasurer, 1972-74, chapter vice president, 1975-77, chapter president, 1977-78 for University of California at Santa Barbara); Behavior Therapy and Research Society; Santa Barbara Area Psychological Association; Psi Chi national honor society in psychology (chapter faculty advisor at University of California at Santa Barbara, 1979 to present). Community Activities: Santa Barbara Mental Health Association (board of directors, 1972-78 and 1981 to present, chairman of education committee, 1973-77, executive committee, 1974-78, first vice president, 1975-77, president, 1978); Mountain View School Site Council of Goleta Union School District (council member, 1978 to present, president, 1978 to present); Santa Barbara Continuing Education Advisory Council (member, 1979 to present, curriculum committee, 1979 to present). Honors and Awards: Elected to Phi Beta Kappa, Columbia University, 1963; National Institutes of Mental Health Predoctoral Research Fellow, Yale

University, 1964-69; Elected to Sigma Xi, Yale University, 1967; Received research grants, University of California at Santa Barbara, 1969-77; Received Faculty Fellowship, University of California at Santa Barbara, 1971; Received research grants from Exxon Education Foundation, 1973-76; Elected to Psi Chi, University of California at Santa Barbara, 1979; Listed in *Who's Who in the West*, *American Men and Women of Science*, *Contemporary Authors*, and many other reference works. Address: 961 Crown Avenue, Santa Barbara, California 93111.

Sherman, Eric

Filmmaker, Teacher, Author. Personal: Born June 29, 1947; Son of Vincent and Hedda Sherman; Married Eugenia Blackiston Dillard; Father of Cosimo and Daniel Rocky. Education: B.A. cum laude, Scholar of the House of Film, Yale University, 1968. Career: Head of Documentary Film Company, Film Transform; Documentaries: "Charles Lloyd-Journey Within", 1969; "Paul Weiss-A Philosopher in Process", 1972; "Inside Out", 1982; Instructor, Art Center College of Design, University of California-Los Angeles, California Institute of Technology, Pepperdine University; Guest Lecturer, Number of Colleges and Universities; Technical Advisor at Universal Pictures, 1980; Production Executive at Paramount, 1981. Organizational Memberships: Los Angeles International Film Exposition (FILMEX) (program selection committee); S.M.P.T.E.; I.F.P.A.; University Film Association; National Alliance of Media Arts Centers; Association of Independent Video and Filmmakers; A.F.I. Community Activities: Malibu Road Association. Published Works: College Texts *The Director's Event* 1970, *Directing the Film* 1976, Manual for Film Production 1983. Honors and Awards: New York Film Festival, 1969; San Sebastian Film Festival 1982; Melbourne Film Festival 1982; Montreal World Film Festival 1982; Columbus Film Festival 1982; Bilbao Film Festival 1982; Mellon Lecturer on the Arts, California Institute of Technology; Listed in *Who's Who in the West*, *Personalities of the West and Midwest*. Address: P.O. Box 845, Malibu, California 90265.

Eric Sherman

Sherrick, Anna Pearl

Retired Nurse Educator. Personal: Born November 26, 1899; Daughter of Mr. and Mrs. Joel Darrah Sherrick (deceased). Education: B.A., McMurray College, Jacksonville, Illinois, 1924; Nursing Diploma, University of Michigan, 1927; M.A., Colorado Teachers College, Greeley, Colorado, 1934; Ed.D., University of Washington, 1954; Honorary Doctor of Science, 1975. Career: Nurse Educator and Administrator, 1936-65, and Teacher, 1965-70, Montana State University School of Nursing; Work with the elderly, 1970 to present. Organizational Memberships: American Nurses Association; National League for Nursing; Teachers Organization; American Association of University Women; Retired Teachers of Bozeman Senior Center; A.A.R.P. Community Activities: Business and Professional Club. Religion: Sunday school teacher of 6th graders. Honors and Awards: Woman of the Year, Montana Association of Business and Professional Women, 1969; Distinguished Service Award, Western Interstate Commission for Nursing, 1965; Montana Retired Teachers Association Teacher of Montana, 1972. Address: 1106 South Willson, Bozeman, Montana 59715.

Shields, Robert Hazen

Business and Legal Consultant. Personal: Born April 1, 1905; Son of James and Anna Belle Shields (both deceased); Married Ruth Elizabeth Wood; Father of Jane Louise, Sarah Lowe, Robert Hazen II (deceased). Education: Graduate of Wymore, Nebraska, Public School, 1922; A.B., University of Nebraska, 1926; LL.B., J.D., Harvard Law School, 1929; Graduate Studies Undertaken at Georgetown Law School, 1935. Military: Service with the United States Citizens Military Training Corps, Fort Snelling, Minnesota, 1921; United States R.O.T.C., University of Nebraska, 1922-24. Career: Attorney, New York City, 1929-34; Attorney General Counsel Office AAA and Solicitors Office, United States Department of Agriculture, 1941-42; Solicitor, United States Department of Agriculture, 1942-45; Solicitor, War Food Administration 1943-45; President, Commodity Credity Corporation, Administrator of Product and Marketing, United States Department of Agriculture, 1946; President and General Counsel, United States Beet Sugar Association, Washington, D.C., 1947-72; Director, Viatech, Inc., Syosset, New York, 1967-75; Legal and Business Consultant, 1972 to present. Organizational Memberships: Sugar Association Inc, New York City (vice president and director, 1947-72); Sugar Research Foundation, New York City (vice president and director, 1949-68); International Sugar Research Foundation, Bethesda, Maryland (vice president and director, 1968-72); Sugar Information, New York City (vice president and director, 1947-72); United States Department of Agriculture Sugar Advisory Committee (chairman, 1947-49); Information and Standards Committee of the United States Sugar Industry (vice chairman, 1948); American Sugar Beet Industries Policy Committee (vice chairman, 1949-72); United States Delegations International Sugar Conferences (advisor, 1950-68); New York Sugar Club (president, 1960-61); New York Bar Association; District of Columbia Bar Association; American Bar Association (house of delegates, 1946-57); Interamerican Bar Association; Federal Bar Association (president, 1945-46; national council, 1942 to present); American Trade Association (executive director, 1952-53); Washington, D.C. Trade Association Exec. (president, 1952-53); American Society of Association Executives. Community Activities: Group Health Association, Washington, D.C. (trustee, 1940-46; president, 1944-46); Westmoreland Congregational Church, Washington, D.C. (trustee, 1942-48; board chairman, 1946-48); Leisure World Mutual 14 Condominium, Silver Spring, Maryland, Division, 1978-80. Honors and Awards: Cuban Government Order Carlos Manuel de Cespedes, 1950; Sugar Man of the Year, Dyer Memorial Award, 1967; Member, National Lawyers Club, Washington, D.C., and Congressional Country Club, Bethesda, Maryland. Address: 15119 Vantage Hill Road, Silver Spring, Maryland 20906.

Max Shiffman

Shiffman, Max

Professor Emeritus, Mathematician. Personal: Born October 30, 1914; Father of Bernard, David. Education: B.S., College of City of New York, 1935; M.S., New York University, 1936; Ph.D., New York University, 1938. Career: Instructor, College of City of New York and St. John's University; Consultant, United States Government; Mathematician and Associate Professor, New York University; Mathematician, George Washington University and Rand Corporation; Professor of Mathematics, California State University at Hayward and Stanford University; Professor Emeritus, California State University at Hayward; Mathematician and Owner, Mathematico. Organizational Memberships: American Mathematical Society; Society for Industrial and Applied Mathematics; Mathematical Association of America. Community Activities: Of Help to United States in Cuban Crisis of 1962, 1963; Helped Aid Israel and Obtain Truce in Egyptian-Israeli Conflict, 1969-73; Helped United States Withdraw and Make Truce in Vietnam, 1972; Helped Found the Peace and Freedom Party, 1966-68; California Republican League; Republican Party; Suggested Increasing Higher Educational and Economic Opportunities for Underprivileged Groups, 1966; Research in Mathematics, 1938 to present; In Favor of the Constitution of the United States of America and its Amendments, and of International Arms Control and Disarmament. Honors and Awards: Bulmenthal Fellow, New York University, 1935-38; Award of Merit, Highest Civilian Award to the United States Navy, End of World War II; Speaker at Problems of Mathematics Conference on 200th Anniversary of Founding of Princeton University, 1946, and at 100th Anniversary of Riemann's Doctoral Dissertation, 1951; Various Plaques and Certificates for Distinguished Achievement, 1976 to present; Number of Biographical Listings. Address: 16913 Meekland Avenue #7, Hayward, California 94541.

Shinn, Gerald Harris

Educator and Administrator. Personal: Born December 4, 1934, in Charlotte, North Carolina; Son of Rev. and Mrs. Fred H. Shinn; Married Louise Gorham Winstead on July 15, 1962; Father of Ruth Renette. Education: A.B., 1956, B.D., 1959, Ph.D., 1964, Duke University; Attended Methodistenseminar and Goethe Universitat, Frankfurt, Germany, 1959-60. Career: Assistant Professor of Philosophy and Religion, Louisburg College, North Carolina, 1963, Professor, 1964-67; Guest Professor of Church History, Southeastern Theological Seminary, Wake Forest, North Carolina, 1965; Assistant Professor of Philosophy, Religion and German, University of North Carolina at Wilmington, 1967-69, Director of Institutional Research, 1968-69, Associate Professor of Philosophy and Religion, 1970-79; Adjunct Professor of History of Experimental Science and Discovery, Institute for Marine Bio-Medical Research, Wrightsville Beach, North Carolina, 1974-79; Guest Professor for Department of Human Development and Learning, University of North Carolina at Charlotte, summer of 1972; Creator and Director of the Albert Schweitzer International Prizes, 1972-73, Director Emeritus, 1974 to present; Director of International Studies, 1974 to present, and Professor of Philosophy and Religion, 1979 to present, University of North Carolina at Wilmington; Director of the Bernard Boyd archaeological expeditions to Israel, 1976 and 1978; Director of the Institute for Human Potential, 1978 to present; Director of the North Carolina Institute of Biblical Archaeology, 1979 to present; Acting Director and Curator, World Culture Museum of the University of North Carolina at Wilmington, 1978 to present; Adjunct Professor of Epistemology, Institute for Marine Bio-Medical Research, Wrightsville Beach, 1980 to present; Director of the World Cultures Museum expedition to Egypt, Jordan and Israel, 1981; Chairman of the Harry S. Truman Scholarship Committee, 1981-82. Organizational Memberships: Society of Biblical Literature; American Schools of Oriental Research; Mediaeval Academy (contributing member); Danforth Foundation Associates; Benjamin Franklin Hall Philosophical and Theological Society; North Carolina Museum Society; North Carolina Educational, Historical and Scientific Foundation, Inc. (creator and member of the board of directors). Community Activities: Member, Smithsonian Associates. Published Works: Contributed translations to *History of Christianity*, (1962); Co-translator with Basil Blackwell of Ernst Haenchen's *The Acts of the Apostles*, (1971); Contributed to *Duke Divinity School Bulletin, The Journal of Creative Behavior, Educational Challenges of Creativity, the Ninth International Research Conference on Creativity, Manuscripta.* Honors and Awards: Gurney H. Kearns Graduate Fellowship, Duke University, 1963; Ford Foundation Fellow, Institute of Renaissance and Mediaeval Studies, 1964 and 1965; Outstanding Teacher of the Year, 1970; Outstanding Service Award, Alpha Phi Omega, 1971; Distinguished Achievement Award, International Biographical Association, 1973; Danforth Associate, 1974 to present; Albert Schweitzer International Prize for establishing the first international prize of its kind in the U.S., 1975 (other winners have included Mother Teresa of India, Dr. Theodor Binder of Austria, and Gian Carlo Menotti of Italy); Elected to Phi Eta Sigma, 1980; Teaching Excellence Award, University of North Carolina Board of Trustees, 1981; Listed in *Notable Americans, Community Leaders of America, Dictionary of International Biography, Personalities of the South.* Address: Zagyo-So, Route 5, Box 345-A, Wild Wood Lane, Wilmington, North Carolina 28403.

Shipman, Richard LaFayette

Richard L Shipman

Doctor of Chiropractic. Personal: Born May 20, 1919, in Hamilton, Texas; Son of Jesse Cleveland and Cora May Seymour Shipman (both deceased); Married Bettye Jones, on March 23, 1946; Father of Tona Jean. Education: Graduate of Abilene High School, Abilene, Texas, 1936; Attended Texas A&M College, 1940-41; United States Army Air Force Schools, 1943-44; Doctor of Chiropractic Degree, Carver Chiropractic College, Oklahoma City, 1949; Further Professional Studies in Chiropractic. Military: Served in the United States Army Air Force. Career: Doctor of Chiropracitc, Co-Owner and Director, Shipman Chiropractic Center, Sweetwater, Texas; Southwestern Chiropractic College, President, 1979-80, President Emeritus 1980; Carver Chiropractic College, Faculty Member 1949-52, Assistant Clinic Master 1949-52, Assistant to President 1951-52. Organizational Memberships: National Chiropractic Student Association, 1946-49; Oklahoma Chiropractic Association, 1949-52; Texas State Chiropractic Association (now Texas Chiropractic Association; board of directors, 1960-66; executive committee and convention committee, 1960-66; board of directors, 1975-79; chairman, first West Texas license renewal seminar, 1977; West Texas license renewal seminar committee, 1977-79; chaplain, board of directors, 1978-79; peer review committee, 1975-81; membership committee, 1975-79); American Chiropractic Association (charter member). Community Activities: Sweetwater Chamber of Commerce; Veterans of Foreign Wars, Post 2479, Sweetwater (post surgeon, one year); Kiwanis Club of Sweetwater (president, 1957; secretary, 1958, 1959; lieutenant governor, Division 12, Texas-Oklahoma District, Kiwanis International, 1960; secretary, 1962-80); West Texas Girl Scout Council (board of directors, 2 years). Religion: First Christian Church, Sweetwater, Member of Church Board, Deacon, Elder. Honors and Awards: Texas State Chiropractic Association Chiropractor of the Month, July 1956, June 1957; Commission as Special Assistant to the Governor of the State of Texas, 1977; Texas Chiropractic Association President's Award, 1977, 1979; Certificate of Outstanding Service, Texas Chiropractic Association, 1981; Kiwanis Club of Sweetwater, Kiwanian of the Year 1969, Outstanding and Devoted Service Award 1980, Honored with Dr. Ricky Shipman Day 1979; Certificate for Devoted Service 1968, Outstanding Service Certificate 1969-70, Leadership Citation 1967, Texas-Oklahoma District of Kiwanis International; Citation of Service, Kiwanis International, 1967; Air Medal; Philippine Liberation Ribbon with One Bronze Star; Asiatic Pacific Campaign Medal with Eight Bronze Stars; American Theater Campaign Medal; Victory Medal; Listed in *Outstanding Personalities of the South* (1967 edition and 12th edition), *Who's Who in Chiropractic International* (2nd edition), *Men of Achievement* (volume 9). Address: 209 Cedar Street, Sweetwater, Texas 79556.

Shircliff, Robert Thomas

Management Consultant. Personal: Born May 20, 1928; Son of Mr. and Mrs. T. M. Shircliff; Married Carol Reed; Father of Laura S. Howell, Elizabeth S. Education: Graduate of Culver Military Academy, 1946; B.S., Marketing, Indiana University, 1950. Military: Served in the United States Army Reserves, retiring with the rank of Captain in Military Intelligence. Career: President, Robert T. Shircliff and Associates, Inc.; President, Pepsi-Cola Allied Bottlers, Inc., 1963-73. Organizational Memberships: National Pepsi-Cola Bottlers Association (president, 1970-71). Community Activities: Jacksonville Chamber of Commerce (president, 1977); United Way of Jacksonville (president, 1975); Jacksonville University Council (president, 1972); Speech and Hearing Center (president, 1970); Rotary Club of West Jacksonville (president, 1969); Rotary International (district governor, 1976); Northeast Florida Red Cross (chairman, 1968); St. Vincents Medical Center Board (vice chairman, 1982 to present); Order of Malta. Honors and Awards: Chairman of the Board of Trustees, Jacksonville Community Foundation; Top Management Award, S.M.E.J., 1973; Brotherhood Award, National Conference of Christians and Jews, 1975. Address: 4918 Prince Edward Road, Jacksonville, Florida 32210.

Shirilla, Robert M

Vice President of Strategic Planning. Personal: Born March 21, 1949; Son of Michael and Jayne Shirilla. Education: B.A. magna cum laude, University of California-Los Angeles, 1971; M.B.A. with Honors, Harvard Business School, 1975; Graduate of the United States Army Infantry, Aiborne and Intelligence Schools. Military: Served as Chairman of the Junior Officers Council, 82nd Airborne

Division, United States Army; Rank of Major, Military Intelligence, Brigade Staff, United States Army Reserve, 1979 to present; Captain and Company Commander, United States Army Reserves, 1977-79; Captain, Senior Aide-de-Camp to Division Commander, United States Army Reserves, 1975-77. Career: Citicorp, Diners Club, Carte Blanche, Vice President of Strategic Planning 1982 to present, Director of Strategic Planning 1981; Norton Simon, Inc., Hunt-Wesson, Senior Marketing Manager of Wesson Oil Products 1980-81, Senior Marketing Manager of Hunt Tomato Products 1979-80, Marketing Manager of Hunt Convenience Products 1978-79, Product Manager of New Product Development 1977-78; Assistant Product Manager, General Foods Corporation, 1975-77; Consultant, Boston Consulting Group, Inc., Summer 1974. Organizational Memberships: International Platform Association; International Biographical Association; American Biographical Institute; World Affairs Council of Los Angeles; Academy of Political Science, New York City; Harvard Club of New York City and Southern California. Community Activities: Hugh O'Brien Youth Foundation (chairman); Los Angeles Business School (chairman); March of Dimes (chairman, advisory committee; board of directors; executive committee); Los Angeles Junior Chamber of Commerce (board of directors); Charity Foundation (board of directors); Golf Foundation (board of directors); American Management Association (board of directors). Honors and Awards: First on Commandant's List, United States Army Infantry School; Army Commendation Medal; Alpha Kappa Psi Scholarship Award; Army R.O.T.C. Scholarship Award; Member Nine National Honor Societies; Corning Fellowship; Outstanding Service Award, Workshop in Business Opportunities; Outstanding Junior Officer, United States Army Reserves; Outstanding Achievement Award, Reserve Officers Association, United States Army; Meritorious Service Medal; Listed in *Directory of Distinguished Americans, Personalities of America, Community Leaders of America, Who's Who in the West, International Book of Honor, International Who's Who, Personalities of the West and Midwest, International Men of Achievement, International Registry of Profiles, Who's Who in Finance and Industry*. Address: 300 High Point Drive #613, Hartsdale, New York 10530.

Shokeir, Mohamed H K

Professor and Department Head. Personal: Born July 2, 1938; Son of H. K. (deceased) and Lolia M. Kira Shokeir; Married Donna Jean Nugent; Father of Omar H. K., Vanessa May. Education: M.B.B.Ch., Faculty of Medicine, Cairo University; D.Ch., 1963, D.Ch. (Orth.), 1964, School of Post Graduate Studies, Cairo University; M.S., 1965, Ph.D., 1969, Horace H. Rackham School of Graduate Studies, University of Michigan. Career: Fulbright Research Scholar, University of Michigan; Queen Elizabeth II Scientist, University of Manitoba and Saskatchewan; Associate Professor of Pediatrics, Head, Section of Clinical Genetics, University of Manitoba; Professor of Pediatrics and Director, Division of Medical Genetiucs, University of Saskatchewan. Organizational Memberships: American Pediatric Society; Society of Pediatric Research; Canadian Society of Clinical Investigations (councillor, 1974-76); Canadian Pediatric Society (nominating committee, 1980 to present); American Society of Human Genetics; Western Pediatric Society; Midwestern Society for Pediatric Research; Canadian Society of Immunology; Genetics Society of America and of Canada; New York Academy of Science. Community Activities: Canadian Association of University Teachers (academic freedom and tenure committee, 1979 to prsent); Scouts Movement of Canada (vice-chairman, Saskatoon, 1975-78); Nuclear Energy Advisory Committee; University Review Committee, 1976-78. Honors and Awards: Fulbright Scholar, 1964-69; Queen Elizabeth II Scientist, 1969-75; Medical Research Council Grantee, 1970-76; Hamdy Award for Distinguished Contribution to Medicine (Gold Medal); John Phillips Award for Internal Medicine (Gold Medal), 1960; Solomon Award for Internal Medicine (Gold Medal), 1960; H.B. Day Award for Medicine (Gold Medal), 1960; Basic Sciences Award (Gold Medal), 1957. Address: 108 Riel Crescent, Saskatoon, Saskatchewan, Canada S7J 2W6.

James R Shrider

Shrider, James Russell

Executive. Personal: Born January 31, 1933; Son of George Fred (deceased) and Pearl Luticia Burkholder Shrider; Married Sharon Kay Shock; Father of Gary James, David Albert, (Stepfather of:) Kathleen Marie Corwin, Brian William Corwin. Education: Graduate of Lima Central High School, Lima, Ohio, 1951; Attended Tarleton State Teachers College, Stephenville, Texas, 1951-52; American Institute of Banking Classes, Lima, Ohio, 1959-63. Military: Served in the United States Air Force, 1951-55, attaining the rank of Staff Sergeant. Career: Secretary-Treasurer, General Manager, Sharon Utilities and Westwood Plaza Company; Assistant Cashier 1965-66, Branch Manager 1966-70, Assistant Vice President 1970-73, Tower National Bank of Lima; Head Teller and Assistant Branch Manager, First National Bank of Lima, 1955-65. Organizational Memberships: American Institute of Banking, 1959-63; Water Management Association of Ohio, 1974-83; Northwest District Pollution Control Council, 1976-83; Ohio School Board Association, 1980-83; American School Board Association, 1980-83. Community Activities: Breakfast Optimist Club of Lima (treasurer and board of directors, 1960-65); Boy Scouts of America (adult committeeman, 1967-69); Lima Chargers Hockey Club (president, 1968-69; secretary-treasurer, 1969-72; board of directors, 1968-72); Northland Neighborhood Society (president, 1968-69); Shawnee Elmwood Parent-Teacher Council (president, 1975-79); St. Gerards Band Boosters (president, 1968-69; board of trustees, 1969-70); Lima Area Chamber of Commerce (public affairs committee, 1974-81); Noon Optimist Club of Lima (member, 1975-83; new club building chairman, 1977-78; chairman, membership committee, 1978-79; chairman, home show committee, 1980-81; board of directors, 1978-81; second vice president, 1982-83); Lima City Council (chairman, utilities and sewers committee, finance committee; streets and transportation committee, 1969-73); Young Men's Christian Association Indian Guide Program (volunteer chairman, 1979 to present); Volunteer Coach, Baseball and Soccer, 1979 to present; Shawnee School Board of Education (member, 1980 to present; vice president, 1982; president, 1983); Apollo Joint Vocational School Board of Education, 1980-82. Religion: St. Gerards Parish Lay Councilman, Chairman of Public Relations Committee, 1968-71; Lector and Usher, 1968-73. Honors and Awards, United States Air Force Commendation, 1954; Good Conduct Medal with Clusters, United States Air Force, 1952-55; National Defense Medal, United States Air Force, 1955; Resolution of Recognition, City of Lima, 1974; Optimist International Keyman Award, 1977-78; Optimist International President's Golden Circle Award, 1978-79, 1979-80; Listed in *Who's Who in Ohio, Outstanding Americans, Personalities of the West and Midwest*. Address: 3292 Zurmehly Road, Lima, Ohio 45806.

Sicard, Raymond Edward

Assistant Professor of Biology. Personal: Born April 18, 1948; Son of Maurice and Jeannette Sicard; Married Mary Frances Lombard. Education: A.B., Merrimack College, North Andover, Massachusetts, 1969; M.S. 1972, Ph.D. 1975, University of Rhode Island, Kingston; Internship in Hematology, New England Deaconess Hospital, Boston, Massachusetts, 1970-73. Career: Assistant Professor, Department of Biology, Boston College, 1976 to present; Lecturer in Hematology, Division of Pharmacy and Allied Health, Northeastern University, Boston, 1975-76; Research Fellow, Department of Pediatrics, Shriners Burns Institute, Children's Service, Massachusetts General Hospital, and Department of Pediatrics, Harvard Medical School, Boston, 1975-76; Research Association, Department of Biology, Amherst College, 1974; Hematology Technologist, Department of Pathology, New England Deaconess Hospital, 1970-73; Junior Bacteriologist, Massachusetts Department of Public Health, Lawrence Experiment Station, Lawrence, Massachusetts, 1969. Organizational Memberships: American Association for the Advancement of Science; American Institute of Biological Sciences; American Society for Cell Biology; American Society of Clinical Pathologists; American Society of

Zoologists; International Federation for Cell Biology; International Society for Comparative and Developmental Immunology; International Society of Developmental Biologists; New York Academy of Sciences; Phi Sigma Society; Sigma Xi; Society for Developmental Biology. Community Activities: Massachusetts State Science Fair (judge, 1975 to present); American Institute of Biological Sciences (representative from Massachusetts for the Department of Government Relations, 1980 to present). Religion: Studies at Marist Preparatory Seminary, Bedford, Massachusetts, 1961-64. Honors and Awards: Phi Sigma Society, University of Rhode Island Chapter, 1972; Elected to Membership in Sigma Xi, University of Rhode Island Chapter, 1973; Listed in *Outstanding Young Men of America, Who's Who in the East*. Address: 290 Edgell Road, Framingham, Massachusetts 01701.

Siegel, Lester E

Writer. Personal: Born May 9, 1919, in Chicago, Illinois; Son of Emanuel and Bessie Bass Siegel (both deceased); Father of Paul, Steven. Education: Attended the University of Illinois, 1937-41, Northwestern University, 1945-57. Military: Served in the United States Army Air Force, 1943-45. Career: With Ruder and Finn, New York City, 1951-61; Director, Business Development, Martin E. Janis, Chicago, 1962-69; Freelands Business and Public Relations Consultant, Chicago, 1946-81; Consultant to Golda Meir, 1952, 1973-74. Organizational Memberships: Northern Illinois Industrial Association; Greater O'Hare Association; Sales-Marketing Executives Club; National Automatic Merchandising Association. Community Activities: Lake Point Tower Duplicate Bridge Club; B'nai B'rith. Address: 5225 North Kenmore, Chicago, Illinois 60640.

Silver, Barnard Stewart

Corporation Executive. Personal: Born March 9, 1933; Son of Harold F. and Madelyn S. Silver; Married Cherry B. Bushman; Father of Madelyn Stewart, Cannon Farnes. Education: B.S.M.E., Massachusetts Institute of Technology, 1957; M.S., Engineering Mechanics, Stanford University, 1958; Graduate of Advanced Management Program, Harvard University Graduate School of Business, 1977. Military: Member of R.O.T.C., Massachusetts Institute of Technology, 1951-57; Served in the United States Army Ordnance Corps, 1958-59, attaining the rank of Captain; Served in the United States Army Reserve, 1959-65. Career: Engineer, Aircraft Nuclear Propulsion Division, General Electric, Evendale, Ohio, 1957; Engineer, Silver Engineering Works, Denver, Colorado, 1959-66, Manager of Sales, 1966-71; Chief Engineer, Union Sugar Division, Consolidated Foods, Santa Maria, California, 1971-74; Directeur du Complexe SODESUCRE, Abidjan, Ivory Coast, 1974-76; Superintendent, Engineering and Maintenance, U & I Inc., Moses Lake, Washington, 1976-79; President, Silver Enterprises, 1979 to present; Instructor in Engineering, Big Bend Community College, 1980-81. Organizational Memberships: American Society of Mechanical Engineers; American Society of Sugar Beet Technologists; International Society of Sugar Cane Technologists; American Society of Sugar Cane Technologists, 1962-71; Sugar Industry Technicians, 1964-71; National Alcohol Fuel Producers Association. Community Activities: Junior Chamber of Commerce, 1961-63; City Advisory Finance Committee, Denver, Colorado, 1962-63; Boy Scouts of America (explorer advisor, Mauai, Hawaii, 1965-66); Cub Pack Committee (chairman, 1968-74); Scout Troop Commission (chairman, 1968-74); Educational Counselor, Massachusetts Institute of Technology, Santa Barbara County, 1971-74; Ivory Coast 1974-76, Grant County 1977 to present; Chief Moses Junior High School Parent-Teacher-Student Association (president, 1978-79); Silver Foundation (president, 1971 to present); Western History Association, 1967-82; Kiwanis, 1978-80. Religion: Church of Jesus Christ of Latter-Day Saints; Mission to Western Canada, 1953-55; District President, Peace River District, 1955; 2nd Counselor, Cambridge Branch Presidency, 1954-57; Sunday School Teacher, Counselor to Bishop, High Council, 1963-65, 1967-71, 1973-74; 2nd Counselor, Moses Lake Stake, 1980-81. Honors and Awards: Decorated Chevalier Ordre National by the President of the Republic of the Ivory Coast, 1976; Won Massachusetts Institute of Technology Freshman Competitive Scholarship, 1951; Sigma Xi, Life, 1955; Phi Tau Sigma; Sigma Chi, 1951-57; Alpha Phi Omega; University Archeological Society, Life, 1952; Utah State Historical Society, Life, 1962. Address: 1433 Skyline Drive, Moses Lake, Washington 98837.

Silver, Howard Finlay

Professor of Chemical Engineering, Consultant. Personal: Born September 16, 1930; Son of Marion M. Silver; Married Alice Graham; Father of Ronald Graham, James Howard, Carol Ann. Education: B.S., Petroleum Engineering, Colorado School of Mines, 1952; M.S.Ch.E. 1957, Ph.D. 1961, University of Michigan-Ann Arbor. Military: Served in the United States Army Chemical Corp, 1953-55, attaining the rank of Corporal. Career: Professor of Chemcial Engineering, University of Wyoming, Laramie; Former positions include Research Engineer, Chevron Research Corporation; Chemical Engineer, DuPont Company; Program Manager, Electric Power Research Institute. Organizational Memberships: American Institute of Chemical Engineers; American Chemical Society; Sigma Xi. Honors and Awards: Outstanding Engineering Faculty Award, 1966; International Scholars Directory, France, 1972; Tau Beta Pi; Sigma Gamma Epsilon; Phi Lambda Upsilon; Listed in *Who's Who in America, Who's Who in the West, Dictionary of International Biography, International Who's Who in Engineering, Men of Achievement, Directory of Distinguished Americans, Personalities of the West and Midwest, American Men and Women of Science, Who's Who in American Education, Who's Who in American Colleges and Universities*. Address: 607 South 27th, Laramie, Wyoming 82070.

Simko, Jan

Program Examiner. Personal: Born October 30, 1920; Son of Terezia Simko; Father of Jan, Vladimir. Education: Teacher's Diplomas in English, 1942, German, 1943, and Ph.D., 1944, University of Bratislava (Czechoslovakia); M.Ph., University of London, 1967. Career: Professor of English, University of Bratislava, 1945-67; Fellow, Folger Shakespeare Library, Washington D.C., 1967-68; Professor of English, Rio Grande College, Ohio, 1968-75; Instructor, Foreign Service Institute, Washington, D.C., 1974; Examiner, Critical Languages Program, Kent State University. Organizational Memberships: Modern Language Association of America, 1966 to present; Former Member: College English Association, The Medieval Academy of America, The Renaissance Society of America, Circle of Modern Philologists in Slovakia (president 1963-66). Community Activities: National Travel Club; Former Member International Platform Association; Organizer of College Students' Scholastic Creativity, 1955-65; Adviser to Publishing Houses on Shakespearean and Language Instruction Publications, 1950-67; Member of College Committee on Academic Policy; Donations to the Heart Fund, Columbia Lighthouse for the Blind, etc. Religion: Roman Catholic. Honors ans Awards: Listed in *Personalities of the South, Notable Americans, Book of Honor, The International Who's Who of Intellectuals*. Address: 1337 Pennsylvania Ave., S.E., Washington D.C. 20003.

Simonian, Simon John

Surgeon, Educator. Personal: Born April 20, 1932; Son of John and Marie Simonian; Married Arpi Ani Yeghiayan; Father of Leonard

Armen, Charles Haig, Andrew Hovig. Education: M.D., University of London, 1957; B.A. with honors, St. Edmund Hall, University of Oxford, England, 1964; M.A., University of Oxford, 1969; Sc.M. 1967, Sc.D. 1969, Harvard University. Career: Intern, University College Hospital, London, England, 1957; Edinburgh, Scotland, Royal Infirmary, 1957-58; Resident, Edinburgh Royal Infirmary, 1961-62; Resident, Edinburgh Western General Hospital, 1958-59; Resident, Birmingham Accident and Burns Hospital-University of Birmingham, England, 1959-60; Demonstrator, Department of Anatomy, Edinburgh University, 1960-61; Research Fellow, Pathology, Harvard University, 1965-68; Resident in Surgery, Boston City Hospital, 1970-74; Director of Surgical Immunology and Assistant in Surgery, Peter Bent Brigham Hospital, Boston, 1968-70; Attending Surgeon in Transplantation and General Surgery Services, University of Chicago Hospitals and Clinics, 1974-78; Instructor and Associate in Surgery, Harvard Medical School, Boston, 1968-70; Assistant Professor of Surgery, and member committee on immunology, University of Chicago, 1974-78; Head, Division of Renal Transplantation, Hahnemann University School of Medicine and Hospital, Hahnemann University, 1978 to present; Professor of Surgery, 1978 to present, Surgical Director, end stage renal disease program, 1980 to present; Lecturer in Field; Contributor in Field. Organizational Memberships: American Society of Transplant Surgeons (founding member, 1974; chairman, immuno-suppression study committee, 1974-77); Transplantation Society (membership committee, 1980-82); Academy of Sciences at Philadelphia (co-chairman, membership committee, 1980 to present); Greater Delaware Valley Society of Transplant Surgeons (Councillor, 1978-80; president-elect, 1980-82; president, 1982-84); End Stage Renal Disease Network 24 (medical review board, 1980-82); American Board of Surgery (diplomate); Royal College of Surgeons of Edinburgh (fellow); American College of Surgeons (fellow); Philadelphia Academy of Surgery (fellow); American Association for the Advancement of Science; Royal College of Surgeons of England; Association for Academic Surgery; American Federation for Clinical Research; New York Academy of Sciences; Philadelphia County Medical Society; Pennsylvania Medical Society; American Medical Association; International Cardiovascular Society; Sigma Xi; Visiting Professor, Vanderbilt University 1968, University of Cambridge 1977, Karolinska Instituet 1977, University of Stockholm 1977, Michigan State University 1977, University of California 1977, Medical College of Pennsylvania 1980, University of Pennsylvania 1981, Medical College of Pennsylvania 1981, University of Athens 1981, University of London 1981, Harvard University Medical School 1982, Tufts University 1982, Oxford University 1982, Edinburgh University 1982. Community Activities: Armenian Youth Society, London (founder, 1953; president, 1953-54); Friends School London (board of governors, 1964-65); Massachusetts Delegate to Armenian Assembly, Washington, D.C. 1970-74; Armenian American Medical Association (founder, 1972; treasurer, 1972-74); Armenian Studies Program Lecturer Series, University of Chicago (founder, 1975); Entry into Manhood and Womanhood Ceremony (founder, 1981); Armenian General Benevolent Union; National Association for Armenian Studies and Research; American Technion Society. Honors and Awards: Norman Nairn Scholor, 1949-52; Middlesex Scholar, 1952-57; Recipient, Suckling Prize, 1957; British Medical Research Council Award, 1962-64; Alt Prize, 1973; Thompson Award, 1974-77; Distinguished Citizen of Massachusetts, 1975; Johnson Award, 1975-77; Outstanding New Citizen of 1976-77, Washington, D.C.; Guest Lecturer, VIIIth International Congress of Nephrology, 1981; Filipino-American Lions Club Award, Philadelphia, 1982; Listed in *Who's Who in the East, Who's Who in America, Personalities of America, Community Leaders of America, Men of Achievement, The Biographical Roll of Honor, International Who's Who of Intellectuals, International Register of Profiles, Directory of Distinguished Americans, International Book of Honor, Who's Who in the World, Dictionary of International Biography, 5000 Notable Personalties of the World, Directory of Medical Specialists.* Address: 245 Cheswold Lane, Haverford, Pennsylvania 19041.

Simon Simonian

Simpson, Barbara Jean

Parole Officer. Personal: Born April 2, 1944; Daughter of Mrs. Margaret S. Simpson. Education: A.A., Chowan College, 1964; Attended Atlantic Christian College, Wilson, North Carolina, 1965; Other Courses Taken at Moody Bible Institute, North Carolina Criminal Justice Academy, 1979, 1980. Career: Adult Probation/Parole-Court Intake Officer; Claims Administrator, Carteret General Hospital, 1969-78; Department Manager, Carteret General Hospital, 1976-78; Office Clerk, Accounting Department, United States Civil Service, Cherry Point, North Carolina; Teacher of Sign Language at Carteret Technical College, Morehead City, North Carolina. Community Activities: Carteret County Prison Advisory Committee; Carteret County Historic Research Association; Miriam Rebekah Lodge; International Platform Association; Beaufort Junior Women's Club; National Association of Female Executives. Religion: First Baptist Church, Beaufort; Finance Committee, 1979-82; Director of Public Relations. Honors and Awards: Interpreter for the Deaf, 1975 to present; International Platform Association; Listed in *Who's Who of American Women, Personalities of America.* Address: 210 Belle Air Street, Beaufort, North Carolina 28516.

Simpson, Jack Benjamin

Investments. Personal: Born on October 30, 1937; Son of Benjamin Harrison and Verda Mae Woods Simpson; Married Clara Winona Walden; Father of Janet Lazann, Richard Benjamin, Randall Walden, Angela Elizabeth. Education: Studies in Medical Technology, Western Kentucky University. Career: Investor. Organizational Memberships: American Society of Medical Technologists; American Society of Clinical Pathologists; Indiana Society of Medical Technologists; Royal Society of Health, London, England; Indianapolis Society of Medical Technologists. Religion: Baptist. Honors and Awards: Kentucky Colonel; Royal Society of Health, London, U.K. (member); American Biographical Institute (life fellow); (Ernest Kay) Personal Hall of Fame; Registry of Medical Technologists; Listed in *Personalities of America, Who's Who in the South and Southwest, Notable Americans, Book of Honor, Personalities of America, Community Leaders and Noteworthy Americans, Personalities of the South, Dictionary of International Biography, International Register of Profiles, Men of Achievement, International Who's Who of Intellectuals, Men and Women of Distinction, The American Registry Series.* Address: 68 Isla Drive, Fort Lauderdale, Florida 33316.

Sincock, John Lloyd

Wildlife Research Biologist. Personal: Born January 29, 1928; Son of Edna Sincock Dean; Married Renae; Father of Cindy, Kelly, William, Jeanene. Education: B.S., M.S., Pennsylvania State University. Military: Served in the United States Navy, 1946-48, as Seaman First Class. Career: Wildlife Research Biologist, Endangered Species Program, United States Fish and Wildlife Service, 1967-82; Wildlife Research, Kentucky Department of Wildlife Resources, 1953-54; Waterfowl Biologist, Florida Department of Fish and Game, 1954-57; Wildlife Research, Biologist, United States Fish and Wildlife Service, 1957-62; Chief, Wetland Ecology, United States Fish and Wildlife Service, 1962-67. Organizational Memberships: United States Water Quality Control Commission, 1967; North America Waterfowl Research Commission, 1976; Mosquito Control Commission, 1962-67; Aquatic Plant Control Commission, 1962-67; Refuge Evaluation Commission, 1966; Lead Poisoning Commission, 1966; Committee to Evaluate Tripartite Studies, Haw. Leeward Islands, 1980. Community Activities: The Nature Conservatory (scientific advisory committee on endangered Hawaiian species, 1980 to present). Published Works: Author of *Waterfowl Tomorrow*, 1967; Number of Articles on Wildlife. Honors and Awards: United States Fish ad Wildlife Service Special Achievement Award, 1978. Address: R.R. 1, Box 197, Koloa, Hawaii 96756.

Singer, Jeanne Walsh

Composer, Pianist, Lecturer. Personal: Born August 4, 1924; Daughter of Professor and Mrs. Harold V. Walsh; Married Richard G. Singer; Mother of Richard V. Education: B.A., magna cum laude, Barnard College, 1944; Artist Diploma, National Guild of Piano Teachers, 1954. Career: Composer, Pianist, Lecturer, Private Teacher; Performed on Radio, Television, Lincoln Center; Performances in New York City, Canada, Europe, South America. Organizational Memberships: American Society of Composers, Authors and Publishers; National League of American Pen Women (national music chairman; vice president, New York City branch, 1979-81); Composers, Authors, and Artists of America (vice president, 1971-78; music editor of magazine); American Women Composers (board of directors, 1976-78); International Platform Association; International Biographical Association (life fellow). Community Activities: Great Neck Community Concerts Association (board of directors; executive vice president, 1978-81); North Shore Community Arts Center (music advisory board, 1978-81). Honors and Awards: Phi Beta Kappa; Special Award of Merit, National Federation of Music Clubs, 1976; Best Art Song Award, New York Poetry Forum, 1977; First Prize, Composers Guild, 1979; Hackleman Award, Natonal League of American Pen Women, 1980; First Prize, Composers, Authors and Artists of America, 1981; First Prize, National League of American Pen Women, 1982; American Society of Composers, Authors and Publishers Special Awards, 1978-82; 1982 Grand Prize, Composers Guild; Listed in *Who's Who in the East.* Address: 64 Stuart Place, Manhasset, New York 11030.

Singh, Vijay P

Associate Professor. Personal: Born July 15, 1946; Son of Mr. and Mrs. Gurdayal Singh; Married Anita; Father of Vinay, Arti. Education: Bachelor of Science and Technology, U.P. Agril. Univig., 1967; M.A., University of Guelph, 1970; Ph.S., Colorado State University, 1974. Career: Associate Professor of Civil Engineer Research and Teaching 1981 to present, Associate Professor of Civil Engineering 1978-81, Mississippi State University; Associate Research Professor of Civil Engineering, George Washington University, 1977-78; Assistant Professor of Hydrology, New Mexico Tech, 1974-77; Assistant Engineer, Rockefeller, Foundation, 1967-68. Organizational Memberships: American Society of Civil Engineers; A.W.R.A.; A.G.U.; I.AH.R.; I.A.H.; I.E.; I.A.S.E.; U.G.A.S.; C.S.U.A.S.; I.W.R.S.; Sigma Xi. Community Activities: Director, International Symposium on Rainfall-Runoff Modeling, 1981; Senior Judge, Science and Engineering Fairs, New Mexico, Maryland; Member of University Committee. Published Works: Editor, *Journal of Indian Association of Hydrologists.* Honors and Awards: College Merit, 1965-66, 1966-67; Scholarship Award for Scholastic Achievement, 1966-67; CBIP Certificate of Merit for Outstanding Paper; N.S.F. and O.W.R.T. Research Grants; United States-Indian Exchange Scientist; Listed in *Who's Who in the South and Southwest, Who's Who in Technology Today.* Address: 2360 Cardere Lane, Apt. B., Baton Rouge, Louisiana 70808.

Sarah Slavin

Singreen, Shirley Ann Basile

Attorney at Law. Personal: Born April 10, 1941; Daughter of Dominick J. and Rose O'Reilly Basile; Married Harry Voss Singreen; Mother of Michael Harry, Elizabeth Alexandra Singreen. Education: B.A., English Literature, 1962, Loyola University of the South; J.D., 1964, Loyola University of the South School of Law. Career: Attorney at Law. Organizational Memberships: Louisiana State Bar Association; New Orleans Notaries Association; Phi Alpha Delta International Legal Fraternity. Community Activities: First Woman Law Clerk of the Civil District Court of the Parish of New Orleans, Appointed by the Nine Judges of the Court, 1964-65; First Woman, Staff Counsel of the United States Fifth Circuit Court of Appeals, Appointed by the Judges of the Court, 1966-68; First Senior Law Clerk of 24th Judicial District Court, 1973-76. Honors and Awards: Listed in *Who's Who of American Women, World Who's Who of Women, Dictionary of International Biography, Book of Honor, Personalities of the South, Community Leaders and Noteworthy Americans, Men and Women of Distinction, Directory of Distiguished Americans.* Address: Suite 1110, First National Bank of Commerce Bldg., New Orleans, Louisiana 70112.

Skiff, Russell Alton

Executive. Personal: Born February 26, 1927; Son of Albert Alton (deceased) and Leah Gladys Allen Skiff; Married Dolores Theresa Molnar; Father of Russell James, Sandra Lee, Eric Alan, Rebecca Lynn. Education: B.S., Chemistry and Mathematics, University of Pittsburgh, 1950. Military: Served in the United States Army Air Force, 1944-46, attaining the rank of Staff Sergeant. Career: Metallurgical Chemist, Jones and Laughlin Steel Company, Aliquippa, Pennsylvania, 1950-51; Research and Development Chemist, General Electric Company, Erie, Pennsylvania, 1951-57; Manager, Tech. Sales and Plant Operation, Hysol Corporation of California, El Monte, California, 1957-60; Senior Research Engineer, Autonetics Division, North American Aviation, Downey, California, 1960-62; President, Delta Plastics Company, Visalia, California, 1962 to present. Organizational Memberships: National Federation of Independent Business; California Federation of Independent Business; Society of Plastics Engineers; American Chemical Society; American Society for Testing and Materials; United States Senatorial Business Advisory Board. Community Activities: Exchange Club of Visalia (president, 1981-82); Vasalia Breakfast Lions Club (vice president, 1981-82); Visalia Chamber of Commerce. Religion: Presbyterian. Honors and Awards: Member of First United States Manufacturer's People-to-People Goodwill Delegation to China, 1980; 9 United States Patents. Address: 26525 Mulanax Drive, Visalia, California 93277.

Slavin, Sarah

Political Scientist and Editor. Personal: Born March 26, 1942; Daughter of Ruth M. Slavin; Mother of Heidi R., Beth, Victor Hale. Education: B.A., University of Iowa, 1962; M.A.T., Webster College, 1973; Ph.D., George Washington University, 1981. Career: Managing Editor, *Women and Politics: A Quarterly Journal of Research and Policy Studies,* 1979 to present; Political Campaign Worker; Teacher, Kindergarten through 12th Grade. Organizational Memberships: American Political Science Association (committee on the status of women in the profession, 1978-81; task force on women and American government, 1981 to present); Women's Caucus for Political Science (president, 1979-80); Policy Studies Organization; Midwest and Southern Political Science Associations; National Women's Studies Association (charter member); Coalition of Women in Social Sciences and Humanities (steering committee member, 1978-80). Community Activities: National Organization of Women (chair, national committee to promote women's studies, 1972-76); Missouri Equal Rights Amendment Ratification Coalition (coordinator, 1972-73); Pittsburgh Board of Education (parent representative, 1974-76); Sweet Briar College president's parents council, 1977-83); National Women's Political Caucus; Pennsylvania Elected Women's Association (founding member, 1980); Emma the Buffalo Women's Bookstore (operating collective, 1981 to present). Religion: St. Louis Ethical Society, Member and Religious Education Director, 1972-73. Published Works: "On Reading *Woman and Nature*", *Room of One's Own,* 1983; *Plow Women Rather than Reapers: An Intellectual History of Feminism in the United States,* 1979; Editor, Volume 8 of *Female Studies Series,* 1975; Contributor of Articles to *Public Opinion Quarterly, Western Political Quarterly, University of Miami Law Review, Social Science Journal, Policy Studies Journal,*

American Political Science Review, and Several Edited Books. Honors and Awards: University of Iowa Honors Program; Phi Sigma Alpha National Political Science Honor Society; Doctoral Fellowships Awarded on Merit, George Washington University; Distinction on Doctoral Comprehensives; Editorial Internship, *American Political Science Review;* One of 700 Public Opinion Leaders called upon by President Carter to work in the S.A.L.T. II Ratification Campaign; Listed in *Who's Who of American Women, World Who's Who of Women*. Address: 41 Highland Avenue, Buffalo, New York 14222.

Sloan, Ronald James

Zoologist (Ecology). Personal: Born September 26, 1944; Son of Virgil and Ruth Sloan; Married Suzanne Ruth Field; Father of McIrvin George. Education: Graduate of Sheridan High School, Sheridan, Oregon, 1962; B.S., Wildlife Management, Oregon State University, Corvallis, Oregon, 1966; Ph.D., Zoology, State University of New York College of Environmental Science and Forestry, Syracuse, New York, 1973. Career: Senior Scientist, Coordinator of Toxic Substances Monitoring Program, Division of Fish and Wildlife, New York State Department of Environmental Conservation, 1977 to present; Research Associate, Gypsy Moth Population Dynamics, State University of New York Research Foundation and United States Forest Service, Hamden, Connecticut, 1975-77; Postdoctoral Research Association, Syracuse, New York, 1973-74; Consultant in Computer Programming/Wildlife Management, Syracuse, New York, 1969-73. Organizational Memberships: The Wildlife Society (member, 1965 to present; New York Chapter contaminants committee, chairman, 1980-83); New York Chapter, American Fisheries Society, 1981 to present; American Society of Mammalogists, 1967 to present; Animal Behavior Society, 1967 to present; New York Academy of Sciences, 1980 to present; Conservation Education Association, 1967 to present (life member); Society of Sigma Xi, 1971 to present; National Speleological Society (member, 1971 to present; Adirondack Grotto chairman, 1975; Helderberg Area Grotto secretary, 1981-83). Community Activities: Nature Conservancy (property steward, 1982-83); Northwestern Cave Rescue Network, 1975 to present; Benevolent Protective Order of Elks, 1979 to present. Religion: Protestant. Honors and Awards: Citation for Successful Cave Rescue Involvement, 1980; National Defense Education Act Title IV Fellowship, 1966-69; Invited Lecturer at Universities and Symposia, 1973 to present. Address: 26 Mildred Lane, Latham, New York 12110.

Ronald J Sloan

Smith, Albert Cromwell Jr

Investor, Real Estate. Personal: Born December 6, 1925; Married Laura Thaxton; Father of Albert III, Elizabeth, Laura. Education: B.S., Civil Engineering, Virginia Military Institute, 1949; M.S., George Washington University, 1965; M.B.A., Pepperdine University. Military: Served with the United States Marine Corps, 1944-74, achieving the rank of Colonel. Career: Retired from Marine Corps, 1974; Free-lance Writer; Real Estate Investor. Organizational Memberships: American Society of Civil Engineers; National and California Associations of Realtors, Coronado Board of Realtors; Friends of Salisbury Cathedral (life member). Religion: Epsicopal Church Vestry of St. Martin. Published Works: *The Individual Investor in Tomorrow's Stock Market; The Little Guy's Stock Market Survival Guide; Wake Up Detroit! The EV's Are Coming.* Honors and Awards: 2 Legions of Merit; Bronze Star; 3 Air Medals; Navy Commendation; Army Commendation; Purple Heart. Address: 6322 Via Maria, LaJolla, California 92087.

Smith, Beatrice Myrtle Warner

Senior Quality Engineer. Personal: Born October 4, in Danbury, Connecticut; Daughter of Llewellyn Steven and Minnie Edna Benham Warner; Married T. Leon Smith, on July 29, 1943; Mother of Patricia Ann Smith Johnson, Thomas Leon II. Education: B.S., Western Connecticut State College, 1943; M.B.A., Pepperdine University, 1976. Career: Advertising Manager, Sears Roebuck and Company, Danbury, 1953-57; Engineering Associate, Research, Rocketdyne Corp., Canoga Park, California, 1958-67; Quality Assurance Engineer, Xerox Corporation, 1967 to 1977, Transferred to Diablo Systems, 1977 to present, Hayward California; Board of Directors, Sabrina Creative Industries Inc., Office Furniture Restoring Inc. Organizational Memberships: American Society of Quality Control, American Management Association, Xerox Diablo Management Association (board of directors). Community Activities: Republican; Metropolitan Yacht Club, Jack London Square, Oakland, California. Religion: Roman Catholic. Honors and Awards: Suggestion Award, Rocketdyne, 1964; Listed in *Who's Who of American Women, Who's Who in Finance and Industry, Who's Who in the West and Midwest, World Who's Who of Women.* Address: 937 New England Village Drive, Hayward, California 94544.

Smith, Cornelia Marschall

Professor Emeritus. Personal: Born October 15, 1896; Daughter of Ernst and Lucy Meusebach Marschall (both deceased); Married Dr. Charles G. Smith. Education: B.A., Baylor University, 1918; M.A., University of Chicago, 1923; Ph.D., Johns Hopkins University, 1928. Career: Professor Emeritus, Professor of Biology 1940-67, Chairman of Biology Department 1943-67, Director of Strecker Museum 1943-67, Assistant Professor 1930-35, Instructor in Botany 1928-30, Baylor University; Professor of Biology and Chairman of Biology Department, J. B. Stetson University, 1935-40. Organizational Memberships: Texas State Board of Examiners of Basic Sciences (member, 1949-67; secretary-treasurer, 1959-67); American Society of Zoologists; Botanical Society of America; National Audubon Society; Texas Ornothological Society. Community Activities: American Association of University Women; American Association of University Professors; Modern Language Association; Sigma Xi; Beta Beta Beta; Alpha Epsilon Delta; Kappa Kappa Gamma. Religion: First Baptist Church of Waco, Texas, 1918 to present. Honors and Awards: Mortar Board, 1973 to present; Women's Day Outstanding Faculty Member, 1963; Minnie Piper Professor of the Year, 1965; Teacher of the Year, 1965-66; Outstanding Alumane Award, 1972; Baylor University Cornelia M. Smith Professorship in Biology, Initiated in 1980; Fellow, American Association for the Advancement of Science; Texas Academy of Science. Address: 801 James, Waco, Texas 76706.

David E Smith

Smith, David E

Educator, Physician. Personal: Born February 7, 1939, in Bakersfield, California; Son of Elvin and Dorthy Smith; Married Millicent Buxton; Father of Christopher Buxton-Smith, Julia, Suzanne. Education: Graduate of East Bakersfield High School, 1956; A.A., Bakersfield College, 1958; B.A., University of California-Berkeley, 1960; M.S. 1964, M.D. 1964, University of California-San Francisco; Intern, San Francisco General Hospital, 1965; Post-Doctoral Fellowship, Pharmacology and Toxicology, University of California-San Francisco, 1965-67; Ph.D. Program, Institute for Advanced Study of Human Sexuality, 1979 to present. Career: Founder and Medical Director, Haight Ashbury Free Medical Clinic, 1967 to preent; Consultant, Drug Abuse, Gladman Memorial Psychiatric Hospital, Oakland, California, 1978 to present; Consultant on Drug Abuse, Department of Psychiatry, San Francisco General Hospital, 1967-72; Director, Alcohol and Drug Abuse Screening Unit, San Francisco General Hospital, 1965-72; Physician, Contra Costa Alcoholic Clinic, 1965-67; Physician, Presbyterian Alcoholic Clinic, 1965-66; Assistant Clinical Professor of

Toxicology, Department of Pharmacology, University of California Medical Center, 1967-75; Lecturer in Criminology, University of California-Berkeley, 19658-69; Co-Director, National Training Center for Drug Education, San Francisco, 1970; Preceptor, Community Medicine Preceptorship Program, University of California-San Diego, 1972-73; Faculty, National College of Juvenile Justice, University of Nevada-Reno, 1971 to present; Honorary Lecturer, Department of Medicine, Addiction Research Foundation Clinical Institute, Toronto, Canada, 1975 to present; Associate Clinical Professor of Behavioral Pharmacology, University of Nevada Medical School, 1975 to present; Associate Clinical Professor of Toxicology, Department of Pharmacology, University of California Medical Center, San Francisco, 1975 to present; Consultant, Drug Abuse, Veteran's Administration Hospital, 1968 to present; Consultant, National Association of State Drug Abuse, 1972 to present; Advisory Board to PHARMCHEM Research Foundation, 1975 to present; Advisory Council on Narcotics and Drug Abuse, Sacramento; Advisory Committee on Controlled Substances, Food and Drug Administration, 1978 to present; Consultant, Committee on Alcoholism and Other Drug Dependencies, California Medical Association, 1978 to present; Consultant and Member, National and California NORML Advisory Committee, 1975 to present; Associate Principal Investigator, San Francisco Polydrug Project, 1974-77; Consultant, Department of Psychiatry, San Francisco General Hospital, 1966 to present; Consultant, Peralta Chemical Dependence Hospital, Marin A.C.T. Chemical Dependence Program 1979 to present. Organizational Memberships: San Francisco Medical Society; California Medical Association (chairman, research task force, California interagency council on drug abuse); American Medical Association (consultant on drug abuse); Phi Beta Kappa; Sigma Xi; F.A.S.E.B.; Youth Projects Inc. (president, 1967 to present); American Public Health Association, Mental Health Section, 1968 to present; American Academy of Clinical Toxicology (charter member); California Society for the Treatment of Alcoholism and Other Drug Dependencies (charter member, chairman, editor committee, 1973 to present; president, 1980-83); San Francisco Society Board of Medical Quality Assurance Committee, 1979; Western Pharmacology Society; California Medical Association. Community Activities: Health Advisor to Jimmy Carter, 1976; Democratic National Platform (alcoholism and drug abuse sub-committee, 1976); Governor's Advisory Panel on Narcotics and Drug Abuse, 1977; Consultant, F.D.A. Controlled Substances Advisory Committee, 1978 to present; Consultant, National Institute of Drug Abuse, 1976 to present. Published Works: Founder and Editor, *Journal of Psychoactive Drugs* (formerly *Journal of Psychedelic Drugs*), 1966 to present; Editorial Board, *The Journal*, Toronto Addiction Research Institute, 1974 to present; Editorial Board, *Clinical Toxicology*, 1975 to present; Author of Many Professional Articles, Books and Drug Abuse Films. Honors and Awards: Survey of Anesthesiology Research, 1964; Bordon Research Award, 1964; S.A.M.A. Research Award, 1966; California Junior College Alumnus of the Year, 1969; Chancellor's Award for Community Service, University of California-San Francisco, 1974; 16th Annual *San Francisco Examiner* "Ten Most Distinguished Award", 1974; American Medical Association Physician's Recognition Award in Continuing Education; Martin Luther King Humanitarian Award, Glide Church, San Francisco, 1980. Address: 82 Parnassus, San Francisco, California 94117.

Elizabeth M Smith

Smith, Elizabeth Mary

Assistant Professor. Personal: Born December 15, 1940. Education: B.A. 1960, M.S.W. 1962, University of Nebraska, Lincoln; Ph.D., Washington University, St. Louis, 1978. Career: Assistant Professor, Department of Psychiatry, Washington University School of Medicine; Chief Social Worker, Outpatient Psychiatric Clinic, Barnes Hospital, St. Louis, Missouri. Organizational Memberships: National Association of Social Workers (secretary, 1980-82); Missouri Chapter, National Association of Social Workers (president, 1979-81); Midwest Coalition, National Association of Social Workers (co-chairman, 1979-81); Council on Social Work Education; American Public Health Association; American Association of University Professors. Community Activities: Missouri Abortion Rights Alliance (board of directors, 1972-79; president, 1977-78); Reproductive Health Services, Inc. (board of directors and secretary, 1973 to present); Missouri Association for Social Welfare; American Civil Liberties Union. Honors and Awards: N.I.A.A.A. Grant for Research on Alcohol and Women, 1978-81; Academy of Certified Social Workers, 1981; Theta Sigma Phi, National Journalism Honorary; Various Publications in Professional Journals. Address: 8408 Winzenburg Drive, St. Louis, Missouri 63117.

Smith, James Montgomery Jr

Financial Consultant. Personal: Born May 23, 1918; Son of James M. Sr. and Mattie Glasgow Smith (both deceased); Married F. Harriet Harmon; Father of Martha Jean Smith Hampshire, James Montgomery III. Education: B.S., Business Administration, Newberry College, South Carolina, 1947; Certificates in Appraising, Management and Mortgage Lending, American Savings and Loan Institute. Military: Served in the United States Navy, 1942-75. Career: Financial Consultant, Newberry Federal Savings and Loan Association; Senior Vice President and Treasurer, Newberry Federal Savings and Loan Association. Organizational Memberships: Financial Managers Society for Savings Institutions (member, 1968 to present; panel speaker, 1969); South Carolina Savings and Loan League. Community Activities: Sertoma Club (past charter member; treasurer, 1967-75); Master Mason, 1950 to present; American Legion (member, 1947 to present); United Fund (past treasurer; board of directors); Aveleigh Kindergarten (past treasurer); Cub Scouts (past chairman, pack committee); Full Gospel Business Men's Fellowship International, 1976 to present; Chairman, Session's Witness Committee, 1970-73; Treasurer, Aveleigh Sunday School, 1950 to present; Sunday School Teacher, 1946-50; Committee Member, Annunities and Relief, 1968, 1969; Audits Committee, 1978, 1979; Former Deacon. Honors and Awards: 25 and 30 year Longevity Services Certificates, South Carolina League Savings and Loan League; 25-year Masonic Certificate, 1976; Sertoma Chapter Service Award, 1971; Confederate Cross, Calvin Crozier Chapter, U.D.C., 1959; Philippine Liberation Medal; Asiatic Pacific Medal with Bronze Star; American Theatre Campaign Medal; Good Conduct Medal; World War II Victory Medal; Listed in *Who's Who in Finance and Industry, Who's Who in the South and Southwest, Personalities of the South, Personalities of America.* Address: 1235 Calhoun Street, Newberry, South Carolina 29108.

James M Smith Jr

Smith, Judith Johns

Administrator. Personal: Born October 27, 1937; Daughter of Ruth Agar Johns. Education: B.A., cum laude, English, College of William and Mary, 1960; M.S.Ed., Special Education, Old Dominion University, 1970; Ph.D., Special Education, University of New Mexico, 1981. Career: Director of Dissemin/Action, National Significance Project Funded by United States Department of Education; Founder, Director of Atlantic Academy, Proprietary School for Disturbed Adolescents, Norfolk and Virginia Beach, Virginia; Chief Editor and Technical Writing Instructor, The Stanwick Corporation, Norfolk and Arlington, Virginia; Instructor, University of Virginia, Hampton Roads Center; Psychometrician and Adolescent Therapist, Psychiatric Associates of Tidewater, Inc., Norfolk; Teacher of English and Social Studies, Northside Junior High School, Norfolk. Organizational Memberships: International Council for Exceptional Children (member-at-large to the executive committee, teacher education division, 1980 to present); National Council for the Accreditation of Teacher Education (site visitation team, 1979 to present); Editorial Board Member, *Teacher Education and Special Education, Journal of Special Education, The Pointer, Education and Training the Mentally Retarded, Jash.* Community Activities: Muscular Dystrophy Association (area leader, telethon liaison, 1968-71); Committee for the Rights of the Handicapped, Albuquerque, New Mexico (public information chairman, 1975-76); United States Department of Education and Office of Developmental Disabilities of the former Rehabilitation Services Administration (field reader, panelist);

Dissemination Forum of the National Institute of Education and United States Office of Education (steering committee, 1978). Honors and Awards: Award for Significant Contribution to the Division of Mental Retardation of the International Council for Exceptional Children, 1977; Award, Edna St. Vincent Millay Memorial Poetry Contest, 1957; Listed in *World Who's Who of Women, Directory of Distinguished Americans, Who's Who in the South and Southwest.* Address: 3701 South George Mason Drive, #1613, Falls Church, Virginia 22041.

Smith, Marcia Jean

Tax Specialist, Investor. Personal: Born October 19, 1947; Daughter of Eugene Hubert (deceased) and Marcella Juanita Smith. Education: B.A., Jersey City State College, 1971; M.B.A., Taxation, 1976; M.S., Accounting, Pace University, 1982. Career: Tax Senior, Arthur Andersen and Company, New York City, 1979 to present; Corporate Executive, The Equitable Life Holding Company, 1977-79; Senior Tax Accountant, The Equtable Life Assurance Society of the United States, 1977; International Tax Accountant, Bechtel Corporation, 1974-77; Legislative Aide, United States Senator Harrison A. Williams, 1973. Organizational Memberships: American Business Association; American Management Association; Amerian Economics Association; International Tax Institute; American Society of Professional and Executive Women; American Association of Individual Investors. Community Activities: Republican National Committee (sustaining member, 1981); United States Senatorial Club; Postal Commemorative Society; Smithsonian Institution (associate member); American Museum of Natural History (associate member). Honors and Awards: Unicameral Award, State of Nebraska, 1967; Educational Opportunity Grantee, 1968-71; Mary McLeod Bethune Award, 1971; Certificate of Recognition, Central Missouri State College, 1965; St. Peter's College, 1971; Listed in *Men and Women of Distinction.* Address: 300 Mercer Street, 23C, New York, New York 10003.

Marcia J Smith

Smith, Margie Fine

Co-Owner and Manager of Credit Bureau (retired). Personal: Born August 16, 1904; Daughter of Mr. and Mrs. E. A. Fine, Sr. (both deceased); Married Herman H. Smith (deceased). Education: Graduate of Cleburne High School, 1922; Graduate of Cleburne Cullen School of Business, 1923; Attended Texas Christian University, Fort Worth, Texas and Hill Junior College, Cleburne, Texas; Certificate for the Proper Operation of a Credit Bureau, University of North Carolina-Chapel Hill, 1952. Career: Co-Owner and Manager, Retail Merchants Association, Credit Bureau of Cleburne, Texas, 1946-68; Assistant Cashier, First National Bank of Cleburne. Organizational Memberships: Credit Women International (international president, 1966-67; director, national board; first president, Cleburne club); National Association of Bank Women; Associated Credit Bureaus (R.C.D. committee, 1961-62; district 3 president, C.S.D. 1961, C.R.D. 1955; delegate, state and national conferences). Community Activities: Cleburne Altrusa Club (past president); Congress of Women, Washington, D.C. (delegate, 1966). Religion: Central Church of Christ, Cleburne. Published Works: Contributor of Articles to *Credit Bureau Management, The Credit World, C.W.I. International,* State Credit Bureau Organization Publications. Honors and Awards: International C.R.D. Award, Associated Credit Bureaus, 1967; Recognition as a Leader of the Credit Bureau Industry, 75th Anniversary Conference, New Orleans, Louisiana, 1981. Address: 815 Prairie Avenue, Cleburne, Texas 76031.

Smith, Mary Louise

Teacher, Consultant, Lecturer. Personal: Born October 6, 1914; Daughter of Frank and Louise Jager Epperson (both deceased); Married Elmer M. Smith (deceased); Mother of Robert C., Margaret L., James E. Education: B.A., University of Iowa, 1935. Career: Republican National Committee, Chairman 1974-77, Co-Chairman 1974, National Committeewoman for Iowa 1964 to present, Executive Committee Member; Republican National Convention, Delegate-at-Large 1968, 1972, 1976, Alternate Delegate 1964, Member and Special Advisor to Convention Arrangements Committee 1980, Iowa Delegate-at-Large, Chairman of the Site and Arrangements Committee, 1976, Vice-Chairman of Rule 29 Committee and Member of the Bipartisan Committee to Study Methods of Financing Quadrennial National Nominating Conventions 1972; Vice-Chairman, Midwest Region Republican Conference, 1969, 1971; Republican National Committee on Convention Reforms, 1966; State Vice-Chairman, Iowa Presidential Campaign, 1964; Case Worker, Iowa Employment Relief Administration, 1935-36. Organizational Memberships: Iowa Federation of Republican Women; Republican Party (volunteer campaign worker, early 1950's; precinct committeewoman; county vice-chairman); Reagan-Bush Committee (national women's policy board, 1980); American Political Foundation (member, bipartisan delegation to study European political party system, Lisbon, Madrid and Paris, 1980). Community Activities: Eagle Grove, Iowa, Community Activities, 1945-63; Board of Eduction, Eagle Grove, Iowa, 1945-63; Mental Health Center of North Iowa, Eagle Grove, Iowa, 1945-63; Iowa Commission for the Blind; Governor's Commission on Aging; United States Delegation to 15th Session of Population Commission of the Economic and Social Council of the United Nations, Geneva, Switzerland, 1969; President's Commission for the Observance of the 25th Anniversary of the United Nations, 1970-71; United States Delegation to the Third Extraordinary Session of the General Conference of the United Nations Educational, Scientific and Cultural Organization, Paris, France, 1973; Iowa Women's Political Caucus Convention (one of six co-convenors); National Commission on the Observance of International Women's Year, 1975-77; Governor Robert Ray's Successful Re-Election Campaign, Iowa (manager, 1978); Dial Corporation (board of directors, 1980-82); Robert A. Taft Institute of Government (trustee); Hoover Presidential Library Foundation (trustee); Woodrow Wilson National Fellowship Foundation (visiting fellow, 1979); National Women's Political Caucus (advisory board); College for Continuing Education of Drake University (faculty of Women/School); P.E.O. Sisterhood; Kappa Alpha Theta Social Sorority; American Medical Association Auxiliary; Duke University Forum on Presidential Nominations (panel member, 1981). Religion: Protestant. Honors and Awards: Honorary Doctor of Humane Letters, Drake University; Iowa Women's Hall of Fame, 1977. Address: 654 - 59th Street, Des Moines, Iowa 50312.

Margie F Smith

Smith, Sam

City Councilman. Personal: Born July 21, 1922; Son of Stephen K. and Berniece C. Smith (both deceased); Married Marion King; Father of Aldwin Carl, Anthony E., Donald C., Ronald C., Stephen K. II, Amelia I. Education: Bachelor of Social Science, Seattle University, 1951; B.A. Economics 1952, Graduate Work Political Science and Economics 1953, University of Washington. Military: Served in the United States Army as Enlisted Man 1942-43 and as Warrant Officer Junior Grade 1943-46. Career: City of Seattle, Washington, City Councilman 1967 to present, President of City Council 1974-78; State Capitol, Olympia, Washington, State Legislator, 1958-67; Expeditor, The Boeing Company, Seattle, Washington. Community Activities: National Association for the Advancement of Colored People (life member); Seattle Urban League; National Black Caucus of Local Elected Officials (area director); National Congress of Cities (communication and transportation committee). Religion: Brotherhood of the Mount Zion Baptist Church, President, 1961 to present; American Baptist Churches U.S.A., Board of Managers, 1970-73; Church School Teacher, 1957 to present. Honors and Awards: Commendation for Effective Leadership as President of the Seattle City Council,

Seattle King County Municipal League, 1978; Prince Hall Scottish Rite Gold Medal Achievement Award, 1979; Medal of Honor, Daughters of the American Revolution, 1980; Distinguished Alumnus Award, Seattle University, 1976; Distinguished Service Award, Central Area Jaycees, 1974; Exemplary Leadership Award, Mount Zion Baptist Church, 1973; Community Service Award, 1971; Seattle Urban League Annual Award, 1968; Legislator of the Year Award, State House of Representatives, 1967; Recognition, Kiwanis Club, Young Men's Christian Association and Other Civic Organizations. Address: 1814 - 31st Avenue, Seattle, Washington 98122.

Smith, Tom Eugene

Executive. Personal: Born May 2, 1941; Son of Mr. and Mrs. Ralph Smith; Married Catherine Wallace; Father of Leigh Anne, Nancy Thompson. Education: Graduate of China Grove High School, 1959; A.B., Business Administration, Catawba College, 1964. Military: Served in the United States Army Reserve, 1968-72. Career: President, Food Town Stores, Inc., 1981 to present; President, Save-Rite, Inc., 1973 to present; Food Town, Buyer 1970-74, Vice President of Distribution 1974-77, Executive Vice President 1977-81, Board of Directors 1977 to present; Del Monte, Director Account Manager 1967-78, Sales Supervisor 1969-70. Organizational Memberships: North Carolina National Bank (director, 1974 to present); National Association of Retail Grocers of the United States, 1979 to present; North Carolina Food Dealers Association (board of directors, 1981-83). Community Activities: United Way (board of directors, 1975-77); Salisbury Sales Executive Club (chairman of the board, 1981; president, 1980); Rotary Club (director, 1975-76); Chamber of Commerce (board of directors, 1975-77). Religion: Lutheran. Honors and Awards: Honorary Citizen of Prince George County, Virginia; Listed in *Who's Who in the Southeast, Who's Who in America, Who's Who in the World, Who's Who in Finance and Industry;* Catawba College Distinguished Alumnus Award 1982. Address: 620 Catawba Road, Salisbury, North Carolina 28144.

Smoot, Carolyn Elizabeth

Management Consultant. Personal: Born September 24, 1945; Daughter of Mrs. Mary Hickman; Married Douglas Bruce Smoot; Mother of Caroline Trucia. Education: B.S.Ed., West Virginia State College, 1967; M.P.A., West Virginia College of Graduate Studies, 1975. Career: Management Consultant; Former Commissioner of Employment Security for the State of West Virginia. Organizational Memberships: Charleston Political Caucus (co-chairman); Business and Professional Club (first vice president, 1982); National Women Political Caucus, 1980 to present; West Virginia Political Caucus, 1980 to present. Community Activities: Shawnee Community Center (board of directors, 1978 to present); West Virginia State Community College (advisory committee, 1978); Association for Community Education of West Virginia, 1980 to present; Co-Chairman of Governor's Committee of Employment of the Handicapped, 1977; West Virginia Manpower Services Council (advisory board, 1977); National Association for the Advancement of Colored People (Charleston board of directors, 1980 to present); The Multi-County Community Against Poverty, Inc. (board of directors, 1977). Honors and Awards: Participant in First White House Conference on Balanced National Growth and Economic Development; Listed in *Who's Who of American Women, Who's Who in Black America, Community Leaders of America, Personalities of America.* Address: Box 222, Institute, West Virginia 25112.

Tom E Smith

Snow, Edwina Feigenspan

Newspaper Publisher. Personal: Born July 14, 1927; Daughter of Edwin Christian and Flora Marie (Russ) Feigenspan (both deceased); Married; Mother of Dana Dodge Osborn de Tessan, Christopher Fairfield Osborn, Peter MacVicker, Eva-Marina, Christina Braggiotti, Mihajlo Milan Bradic. Education: Attended Barnard, Columbia, Julliard. Military: Service with U.S.O. during World War II. Career: Newspaper Publisher; Former Positions in Public Information/Relations, Commercial, Financial and International. Organizational Memberships: Overseas Press Club; A.S.C.A.P. Community Activities: Lioness; Honorary Kiwanian; Red Cross. Honors and Awards: U.S.O. Citation, World War II. Address: Centre Island, Oyster Bay, New York 11771.

Snyder, Don R

Artist, Educator, Author. Personal: Born June 14, 1934; Son of Evelyn Snyder; Married Michaelien Malter; Father of Degana O., Ariel Q. Education: B.F.A., Syracuse University, New York, 1956; Fine Arts and Photography, Cooper Union, New York, 1957-58; Photography with Brodovitch, New School for Social Research, New York, 1974-75; B.S., City College, New York, 1975; Photographics and Multimedia Video, School of Visual Art, New York, 1976-77. Military; Served in the United States Air Force, 1952-56, attaining the rank of First Lieutenant. Career: Teacher, School of Visual Arts, 1974-81, New School for Social Research/Parsons School of Design 1976, 1977, Germain School of Photography 1972, Syracuse University 1956; Consultant, Eastman Kodak, *McCalls* Magazine, Reinholt Publishing; Adivsor to New York State Council on the Arts, 1969-72; Works held in Permanent Collections in Museum of Modern Art, General Analine and Film Corporation, Rochester Institute of Technology; Motion Pictures and Videotapes including *Para 100* 1967, *Chroma, Nine O'Clock Dance Club* 1970, *A Fourth of July Parade, Song for Rent;* Director of Slide Projection, Lighting and Special Effects Photography, National Television Channels WNEW, NET, WABC, 1971-77; Magic Circle Exhibition, Bronx Museum of the Arts, 1977; Multimedia Light Show, St. Peter's Episcopal Church, New York, 1976; University of Minnesota Visual Communications Symposium, 1975; 8th, 9th and 10th Annual Avant Garde Festival, New York, 1972-74; Second Annual Film Fair, New York, 1974; Maimonides Hospital Visual Laboratory, Brooklyn, 1972-73; Multimedia Projection Photographic Slide Show, Cooper Union Alumni Fund Ball, 1972; Millenium Film Workshop Personal Cinema Series, New York, 1970-72; Underground Gallery for Photography, 1971; Eastman Kodak Exhibition of Chemically-Altered and Mediamix Photographs, Grand Central Station, New York, 1968-72; Harvard, Massachusetts, Institute of Technology, Cooper Union, Marymount College, New School for Social Research, Fordham University and Kent State University Exhibitions, 1971-73; Alwyn Nicholais Dance Company, 1970; Multimedia Light Show with Jimi Hendrix, Village Gate, New York, 1969; Group Westinghouse Television News, New York, 1968; Museum of Modern Art, New York, 1967; Doyle, Dane and Bernbach, 1965. Published Works: *Don Snyder's World of Photography*, 1965; *Aquarian Odyssey*, 1979; *The Ten Year Century*, forthcoming; *The Coney Island Inferno*, forthcoming; *Dance Disco Dance*, forthcoming; Feature Portfolio, "Portraiture of the Sixties", *Saturday Review of the Arts;* Feature Portfolio, "American Manners and Morals", *American Heritage;* Contributor to *Encyclopedia Britannica Yearbook of Science and the Future, Book of Knowledge Annual, Into the Unknown, Print* Magazine, *Look* Magazine, *Aspen, Psychedelic Art, Encyclopedia Americana,* United States Information Agency's *America Illustrated, The Book of Knowledge, Progressive Architecture* Magazine, Modern Photograph Magazine, *Eros Quarterly, Video Arts, Rolling Stone;* Book Covers for Ballantine Books, MacMillan Publishing Company, Pyramid Books, Random House; Record Jackets for Warner Brothers Records, Columbia Records, Mercury Philips Records, Cedda M.G.M., for Frank Sinatra, The Four Seasons and Others; Magazine Covers for *M.D.* Magazine, *Village Voice, Rolling Stone* and Others. Honors and Awards: Listed in *Directory of Distinguished Americans, Who's Who in the East, Men of Achievement.* Address: 348 West 23rd Street, New York, New York 10011.

Soder, Dee Ann

Insurance Executive. Personal: Daughter of Keats E. (deceased) and Dorothy Ann Soder. Education: B.A. with special distinction 1969, M.S. 1972, Ph.D. 1976, University of Oklahoma. Career: Vice-President, Human Resources Development, Prudential Insurance Company, Newark, New Jersey, 1981-82; Staff Psychologist, Equal Employment Opportunity Commission, 1981; Corporate Psychologist, Rohrer, Hibler and Replogle, 1980-81; Advisor to the District of Columbia Government, 1979-80; Chief, Policy, Research and Development Branch, Washington Metropolitan Police Department, 1978-79; Team Leader, President's Reorganization Project, Law Enforcement, Executive Office of the President of the United States, 1977-78; Personnel Research Psychologist, United States Civil Service Commission, 1974-78; Assistant Director, National Association of State Directors of Law Enforcement Training, 1973-74; University of Oklahoma, Director of Juvenile Personnel Training Program, Director of Evaluation, Psychometrist for Security Force Training and Post Office Programs, Personnel Research Assistant to the Medical Center, 1969-74. Organizational Memberships: American Management Association; Community Health Law Association (board of directors); American Psychological Association (awards committee, 1977-79); Personnel Testing Council (founder and former treasurer); International Personnel Management Association (former executive board member for Washington, D.C. area); Epilepsy Foundation of America (board of directors, New Jersey chapter). Community Activities: Considerable pro bono Service to the Handicapped, Women's Organizations and Law Enforcement. Honors and Awards: Advisor, President's Committee on Mental Retardation, 1974; Outstanding Pledge, Alpha Chi Omega, 1965; Outstanding Performance Rating Award, District of Columbia, 1979; Certificate of Appreciation, President of the United States, 1978; Listed in *Directory of Distinguished Americans, Who's Who of American Women, American Men and Women of Science, Personalities of the South, Community Leaders of America.* Address: 1200 Springfield Avenue, New Providence, New Jersey 07974.

Solberg, Ruell Floyd Jr

Research and Development Engineer. Personal: Born July 27, 1939; Son of Ruel and Ruby Rogstad Solberg; Married Laquetta Jane Massey; Father of Chandra Dawn, Marla Gaye. Education: B.S.M.E., 1962, M.S.M.E., 1967, University of Texas at Austin; M.B.A., Trinity University, 1977. Military: Served with the United States Army. Career: Research Engineer, Applied Research Laboratories, Austin, Texas, 1962-67; Assistant Supervisor, Mechanical Engineering Section, Austin, 1966-67; Southwest Research Institute, San Antonio, Texas: Research Engineer, Department of Applied Electromagnetics, 1967-79; Senior Research Engineer, 1970-74; Electromagnetics Division, 1974-75; Department of Electromagnetic Engineering, 1975 to present; Literature Reviewer, *Shock and Vibration Digest*, 1979 to present; Technical Assistant, *Applied Mechanics Reviews*, 1980 to present. Organizational Memberships: American Society of Mechanical Engineers; American Society for Metals; Robotics International; Society for Manufacturing Engineers; New York Academy of Sciences; National Society of Professional Engineers; Texas Society of Professional Engineers. Community Activities: Bosque Memorial Museum; Norwegian-American Historical Association; Vesterheim Genealogical Center; Norwegian Society of Texas (charter member); Nordland Heritage Foundation (charter member); Norwegian-American Museum; Friends of the Northwest Library; Leon Valley Crime Prevention Association; Explorer Post 853, Boy Scouts of America; Foundation of Christian Living; Oak Hills Terrace Elementary School (helping hand); Bronstad-Rogstad Family Reunion (president); Lutheran Marriage Encounter, San Antonio Community (census couple). Religion: Lutheran. Honors and Awards: Theta Pi Epsilon, 1959; Pi Tau Sigma, 1962; Tau Beta Pi, 1962; Sigma Xi, 1970; Sigma Iota Epsilon, 1977; American Society of Mechanical Engineers: Past Chairman Certificate, 1974; Charles E. Balleisen Award, San Antonio Section, 1976, 1978; Council Certificate, 1977, 1979, 1980, 1981,; Centennial Medallion, 1980; Centennial Award, Region X, 1980; Howell Instruments Scholarship, 1961; Listed in numerous biographical publications including *American Men and Women of Science, Men of Achievement, Who's Who in the South and Southwest, Dictionary of International Biography.* Address: 5906 Forest Cove, San Antonio, Texas 78240.

Ingeborg H Solbrig

Solbrig, Ingeborg Hildegard

Professor of German, Author. Personal: Born July 31, 1923; Daughter of Reinhold J. and Hildegard M. Adelheid Ferchland-Solbrig (both deceased). Education: Abitur and Diploma in Chemistry, Germany; B.A. summa cum laude, California State University-San Francisco, 1964; Undertook Graduate Studies at the University of California-Berkeley, 1964-65; M.A., Stanford University, 1966; Ph.D., Humanities, German Literature and Philosophy, Stanford University, 1969. Career: Chemical Engineer, Schoeller Company, Osnaburck, West Germany; Chemical Assistant, Stazione Zoologica, Naples, Italy; Assistant Professor of Modern Languages, University of Rhode Island-Kingston, and University of Tennessee-Chattanooga; Assistant Professor of German, University of Kentucky-Lexington; Associate Professor of German 1975-81, Professor of German 1981 to present, University of Iowa, Iowa City. Organizational Memberships: I.V.G. (International Association of Germanic Studies); Modern Language Association of America; American Association of Teachers of German; Goethe Society of North America (founding member); Goethe Society Weimar; Deutsche Schiller-Ges; American Council for Study of Austrian Literature; American Society of 18th Century Studies. Community Activities: Numerous Collegiate and Departmental Committees; Faculty Senate, University of Iowa, 1978-81; Judicial Commission of the University of Iowa, 1982; Organized Symposia and Exhibitions; Lectured at Congresses and Scholarly Conferences and at Civic Organizations. Published Works: Author of Three Books; Numerous Articles and Reviews. Honors and Awards: Stanford University Fellow, 1965-66; Tuition Grants, Stanford, 1965-68; Dissertation Fellow, Stanford, 1968-69; Fellow, Austrian Ministry of Education, 1968-69; Faculty Research Grant, University of Tennessee, 1971; Teaching Improvement Grant, University of Kentucky, 1972; Research Grant, Kentucky, 1973; Gold Medal, Austria, 1974; Old Gold Fellow, Iowa, 1977; Grant-in-Aid, American Council for Learned Societies, 1979; Developmental Leave, University of Iowa, Spring 1980; Financial Aid for Foreign Travel, Iowa, 1980; Grant from German Academic Exchange Service, 1980; Current Research for a Book on Islam in Western Literature; University of Iowa Senior Fellowship, 1983. Address: 1126 Pine Street, Iowa City, Iowa 52240.

Solk, Gerald

Law Professor. Personal: Born July 20, 1942; Son of Louis and Serene Solk. Education: B.A., Pepperdine University, 1964; J.D., University of California Law School, Berkeley, 1967; LL.M., New York University Law School, 1972; Ph.D., Sussex College (U.K.), 1981; M.L.A. Candidate, Harvard University. Career: Law Professor, Suffolk Law School, Harvard University; Former Positions include Law School Associate Dean, Attorney. Organizational Memberships: California State Bar; Hawaii State Bar; Ohio State Bar; New York State Bar; Massachusetts State Bar; District of Columbia Bar. Community Activities: Los Angeles Municipal Court (judge *pro tem*, 1978-80); American Arbitration Association (arbitrator); Business Law Arbitration Panel, Los Angeles County Superior Court (arbitrator, 1979-81). Honors and Awards: Outstanding Service Award, San Fernando Valley Bar Association, 1979; Law Teacher of the Year, 1978; Distinguished Service Award, American Civil Liberties Union, 1970. Address: 207 Commonwealth Avenue, Boston, Massachusetts 02116.

Sollitto, Andrea Lynn

Counseling Psychologist. Personal: Born January 9, 1948; Daughter of Mr. and Mrs. B. J. Sollitto; Married Harry J. Hawtin. Education: B.A., Georgian Court College, 1969; M.Ed., 1971, Ed.D. 1977, Boston University. Career: Counseling Psychologist, Private Practice; Psychologist, Private Practice, Boston, Massachusetts, 1980-81; Staff Psychologist, Regional Educational and Diagnostic Service, Lakeville, Massachusetts, 1977-79; Counsulting Psychologist to Program for the Hearing Impaired, Regional Educational and Diagnostic Service, Lakeville, 1979; Consulting Psychologist to Boston Public Schools, 1977; Visiting Lecturer on Developmental Psychology, Fitchburg State College, Massachusetts, 1976; Title I Coordinator, Westford Public Schools, Massachusetts, 1975-76; Title I Liaison Coordinator, Westford Public Schools, 1973-75; Psychologist Intern, Paul A. Dever State School, Tauton, Massachusetts, 1971-72; Research Assistant, Department of Counseling Psychology, Boston University, 1971-72; Psychology Intern, Framingham Public Schools, Framingham, Massachusetts, 1970-71; Sixth Grade Teacher, Mount Horeb School, Watchung, New Jersey, 1969-70. Organizational Memberships: American Psychological Association; New Jersey Psychological Association; Parent Counseling Association of New England (board member, 1975-78); Massachusetts Psychological Association; American Personnel and Guidance Association. Community Activities: Papers Presented, including "Profiles & Variables Associated with Women Who Achieve", Eastern Educational Research Association 1981, Hilton Hotel, Philadelphia, at the XVIII Interamerican Congress fo Psychology, 1981, Santa Domingo, Dominican Republic, at the New England Personnel and Guidance Association, 1981, Hartford, Connecticut, and at the New England Personnel and Guidance Association, 1981, Hartford, Connecticut, and at the International Interdisciplinary Congress on Women, 1981, Hafia, Israel; "An Educational Program for Disenfranchised Adolescents", New England Personnel and Guidance Association, 1981, Hartford, Connecticut; "Women and Stress", American Personnel and Guidance Association, 1982, Detroit, Michigan, and at the Women's Educational Institute, 1982, Boston, Massachusetts; Established Alternative High School with Federal Funding in 1974, Westford, Massachusetts, Public School System. Honors and Awards: Phi Delta Kappa; Pi Lambda Theta; Licensed Psychologist in Massachusetts and New Jersey; Listed in *Who's Who of American Women*, *International Who's Who of Intellectuals*. Address: Box 300, Wickatuck, New Jersey 07765.

Sommer, Patricia Ann

Associate Professor and Dean of School of Nursing. Personal: Born April 2, 1938; Daughter of Harold Alvin Sommer (deceased) and Mrs. Harold Alvin Sommer; Mother of Martha Ruth (adopted). Education: Nursing Diploma, Jackson Memorial Hospital School of Nursing, Miami, Florida, 1960; B.S.N. 1969, Ph.D. Studies in Sociology and Psychology 1973-76, Texas Christian University, Fort Worth, Texas; M.S., Maternal-Child Health/Education, Texas Woman's University, 1972; Ph.D., Nursing/Sociology, Texas Woman's University, Denton, Texas, 1979. Career: Associate Professor and Dean, Tennessee Technological University School of Nursing, 1980 to present; University of Texas-Arlington, Assistant Professor, Maternity Nursing 1973-79, Pediatric Nursing 1973-76; Nurse Consultant, Cookeville General Hospital, Tennessee, 1980-81; John Peter Smith Hospital, Obstetrics Labor and Delivery Nurse (Summers) 1977, 1978, Director of Special Projects in Clinical Nursing (Summers) 1975, 1976, Family Planning Nursing Supervisor 1970-73, Family Planning Assistant Nursing Director and Public Health Nurse 1968-69, Head Nurse in Newborn/Premature Nurseries 1967-68; Head Nurse, Surgical Floor, Variety Children's Hospital, Miami, Florida, 1959-60; Missionary Nurse, Victory Mission of the Americas, Colombia, South America, 1960-67. Organizational Memberships: American Nurses Association, 1960 to present; Texas Nurses Association, 1968 to present; State of Texas Nurses Association (professional services committee, 1979-80); District 3 (Texas) Nurses Association (chairperson, legislative committee; president-elect, 1976; president, 1977; board member, 1978-80); Nurses Association of the American College of Obstetrics-Gynecology (local vice-president, 1974 to present); National League for Nursing, 1975 to present; Sigma Theta Tau of University of Texas-Arlington, 1977 to present; Pi Lambda Theta of Tennessee Technological University, 1980 to present; Tennessee Nurses Association (member, 1980 to present; chairman, council on education, 1981-82); District 17 (Tennessee) Nurses Association (chairperson, Tennessee Nurses Association resolutions committee, convention delegate, 1980). Community Activities: Camp Fire Girls (leader, 1973-75; associate leader, 1976); Stephen F. Austin Elementary School Parent-Teacher Association (persident, 1974-75); American Red Cross (teacher of mother-baby care, 1967-80; disaster nursing course; baby-sitter course; junior life-saving course); Westside Young Men's Christian Association (board of directors, 1975-76); City Disaster Planning Committee, 1976-80; Ridglea Swimming Pool (secretary, board of directors, 1976-77); Auxiliary Multiple Sclerosis Association of Tarrant County, Texas (project director, 1980); Cookeville, Tennessee Chapter of American Red Cross (board member representing nursing, 1980 to present); Putnam County Board of Health, 1981 to present; Plateau Mental Health Center (board of directors, 1981 to present); Health Systems Agency (peri-natal committee, 1981 to present); United Way (volunteer). Religion: First Baptist Church, Cookeville, Tennessee, Member 1981 to present; Western Hills Baptist Church, Texas, Chairperson of Missions Committee. Honors and Awards: Educator of the Year Award, Pi Lambda Theta, Beta Psi Chapter; Alumni Award Certificate of Service, Tarrant County Multiple Sclerosis Association, Fort Worth, Texas, 1980; Health Systems Agency Service Award and Certificate of Service, 1980. Address: Route 5 Box 301A, Cookeville, Tennessee 38501.

Andrea L Sollitto

Sosnov, Amy W

Attorney-at-Law. Personal: Born August 9, 1943; Married Steven R. Sosnov; Mother of Jonathan Abraham, Elizabeth Hannah. Education: B.A., Temple University, 1970; J.D., Villanova University Law School, 1973. Career: Attorney-at-Law; Stockbroker; Real Estate Broker. Organizational Memberships: Montgomery County Bar Association; Pennsylvania Bar Association; American Bar Association. Community Activities: Consumer Education Project (founder and coordinator); Women's Legal Resource Group (founder and coordinator); "Ask Amy" Television Program (producer and anchorperson); Kadimah Group of Hadassah (president); Philadelphia Section of N.C.J.W. (president; committee member). Honors and Awards: Certificate of Appreciation, U.M. School District; Legion of Honor, Chapel of Four Chaplains. Address: 113 Yellowstone Road, Plymouth Meeting, Pennsylvania 19462.

Soto Ramos, Julio

Poet, Journalist, Essayist and Critic. Personal: Born April 20, 1903; Married; Father of Julio Soto Rivera, Venus Lidia Soto, Gloria Iris Soto. Education: Graduate of High School; Further Studies, Army Extension and Correspondence Courses. Military: Served in the United States Army; Enlisted in the 65th Regiment of Infantry, 1920, and Discharged as Corporal, 1927; Called to Active Duty, Serving from First Lieutenant to Captain, 1942-46. Career: Poet, Journalist, Essayist, and Critic; United States Customs Patrol Inspector; United States Treasury Department Alcohol and Tobacco Tax Division, Alcohol Tax Unit and Bureau of Industrial Alcohol, Prohibition Agent, Investigator, Storekeeper-Gauger and Inspector. Honors and Awards: United States Treasury, Gold Emblem with Ruby for 35 Years of Devoted Federal Service, United States Internal Revenue Service Retirement Button 1963, Diamond Emblem 1963, Albert Gallatin Award for Long and Honorable Service with the Treasury Department 1963; First Prize in Journalism, The Institute of Puerto Rican Literature, 1958; Winner of "Towards the Glory" Competition, Diploma of Merit, Gold Pen, and inclusion in *Artistic Literary Bilingual* and Illustrated Encyclopedia *Towards the Glory* for Three Sonnets, The International

Pontzen Academy, Naples, Italy, 1967; Member of Honor, Comite Cultural Argentine of Parna sillo Castellano, Madrid, Spain; Correspondent Academician, The International Pontzen Academy for Letters, Sciences and Arts, Naples, Italy. Address: 429 Salvador Brau, Floral Park, Hato Rey, Puerto Rico 00917.

Southward, B Morrison

Administrative Coordinator. Personal: Born November 24; Son of Mr. and Mrs. B. M. Southward Sr. Education: Attended Howard University, Washington, D.C., 1962-65; B.A., Augusta College, 1971; A.M., Columbia University Teachers College, 1972. Career: Administrative Coordinator, Pre-Release Center and Veterans' Self-Help Project, Green Haven Correctional Facility; Substitute Teacher; Correction Counselor; Senior Correction Counselor. Organizational Memberships: National Association of Blacks in Criminal Justice; National Association of Black Social Workers; American Personnel and Guidance Association; Public Offender Counselors Association. Community Activities: Think Tank Inc. (staff advisor, 1974 to present); Project Build (staff advisor, 1976 to present); Project New City (tutor/consultant, 1973-74); Dutchess County Chapter of International Key Women (consultant, 1975 to present). Honors and Awards: Listed in *Directory of Distinguished Americans, Who's Who in the East, Men of Achievement, Community Leaders and Noteworthy Americans, Personalities of America, International Who's Who of Intellectuals, International Who's Who in Community Service.* Address: P.O. Box 762, Beacon, New York 12508.

Wendell L Sowell

Sowell, Wendell Loraine

College Administrator. Personal: Born August 17, 1917; Son of Larkin A. (deceased) and Sallie Brewer Sowell; Married Alva Webb (deceased); Father of Bashaba S. Gibbons, Wendell L. Jr., Darrell B. Education: B.S. Chemistry 1947, M.S. Biological Sciences 1955, Auburn University; LL.B., Jones Law School, 1960; Ph.D., Preventive Medicine and Public Health/Toxicology, University of Oklahoma, 1967. Military: Served in the United States Army Military Police, 1941-42, with Medical Discharge in 1944. Career: Director, Patrick Henry State Junior College Division of Law Enforcement, 1977 to present; Associate Professor, Jacksonville State University School of Law Enforcement, 1971-77; Associate Professor of Biology, Livingston University, Alabama, 1968-71; State Toxicologist, State of Ohio, 1968; Assistant Superintendent, B.C.I.&I., London, Ohio, 1968; Director and Developer, Crime Laboratory, City of Fort Worth, Texas, 1960-65; Associate Toxicologist in Charge of Auburn Division, State of Alabama Department of Toxicology, 1947-60; Director, Sowell School of Realty, Anniston, Birmingham, Gadsden, Mobile, and Jacksonville, Alabama; Owner, Sowell Realty, 1971-78; Policeman, City of Mobile, Alabama, 1941-44. Organizational Memberships: American Academy of Forensic Sciences; Forensic Science Society; International Association of Forensic Toxicologists (charter member); Gamma Sigma Delta Honor Society of Agriculture, Auburn University; Southern Association of Criminal Justice; Academy of Criminal Justice Sciences; Sigma Delta Kappa Intercollegiate Law Fraternity. Religion: First Baptist Church, Monroeville, Alabama. Honors and Awards: Listed in *American Men and Women of Science, Who's Who in the South and Southwest, Notable Americans of the Bicentennial Era, Personalities of the South, Men of Challenge, Who's Who in Technology.* Address: Route 4, Box 669, Athens, Alabama 35611.

Spach, Jule Christian

Retirement Home Executive Director. Personal: Born December 21, 1923 in Winston-Salem, North Carolina; Son of Jule Christian and Margaret Stockton Coyner Spach (both deceased); Married Nancy Clendenin on September 18, 1948; Father of Nancy Lynn S. Lane, Margaret Elizabeth S. Creech, Dorothy Ann S. Thomerson, Cecilia Ruth S. Welborn, Robert Clendenin. Education: Attended Virginia Military Institute, 1942-43; B.S.C.E., Georgia Institute of Technology, 1949; Postgraduate Work, Union Theological Seminary, Richmond, Virginia, 1951-52, Duke University 1955-56; M.A. Educational Administration, University of North Carolina-Greensboro, 1976. Military: Served in the United States Air Force to First Lieutenant, 1943-45; Prisoner of War, Stalag Luft III, August 1944-February 1945; Stammlager VIIA, February 1945-May 1945. Career: Executive Director, Triad United Methodist Home, Inc., Winston-Salem, North Carolina, 1977 to present; Moderator, General Assembly of Presbyterian Churches in the United States, Atlanta, Georgia, 1976-77; Executive Secretary, Parliamentary Christian Leadership, Brasilia, Federal District, Brazil 1970-73, Presbyterian Mission in Brazil, Campinas, Sao Paulo 1973-75; Cruzada A.B.C.-Recife, Pernanbuco, President, 1969-70, Education Director 1965-70; Quinze de Novembro College, Garanhuns, Pernanbuco, Brazil, President 1956-64, Professor of Science and Athletic Director 1952-56; Salesman, Mengle Corporation, a Subsidiary of International Container Corporation, Winston-Salem, North Carolina, 1950-52. Community Activities: Republican Party; Lions International, Brazil; King College (board of directors, 1977-79); Montreat Anderson College (board of visitors); Lee's McRae College (board of visitors); Rotary Club, Winston-Salem, North Carolina (district chairman, international service and community service). Religion: First Presbyterian Church, Winston-Salem, North Carolina, Elder; Missionary, Presbyterian Church, 1951-76. Honors and Awards: Purple Heart, United States Air Force. Address: 444 Anita Drive, Winston-Salem, North Carolina 27104.

Eugene Spector

Spector, Eugene E

Podiatrist, Educator. Personal: Born January 19, 1945; Son of Irvin and Beatrice Spector; Father of Rachel, David. Education: B.A., Science, Pennsylvania State University, 1966; D.P.M., Pennsylvania College of Podiatric Medicine, 1970; First Year Residency, Parkview Hospital, Philadelphia, Pennsylvania, 1970-71; M.S. Surgery, Second Year Residency, California College of Podiatric Medicine, 1971-72; Diplomate, American Board of Podiatric Surgery, 1975; Further Podiatric Studies. Career: Instructor, Biomechanics Department, Pennsylvania College of Podiatric Medicine, 1970-71; California College of Podiatric Medicine, Chief of Hospital Surgical Education 1972-73, Assistant Professor in Surgery Department 1972-73, Liaison for University of California-California College of Podiatric Medicine Joint Program 1973-76, Assistant Chairman of Podiatric Surgery 1973-77, Associate Professor in Surgery Department 1973-78, Professor in Surgery Department 1978 to present; Senior Attending Podiatrist, Parkview Hospital, 1972 to present; Senior Attending Podiatrist, California Podiatry Hospital, 1972 to present; Senior Attending Staff, Levine Hospital, Hayward, California, 1977-80; Medical Staff, Vesper Memorial Hospital, San Leandro, California, 1977-78; Medical Staff, Laurel Grove Hospital, Castro Valley, California, 1977-78; Medical Staff, Childrens Hosptial, San Francisco, 1978 to present; Medical Staff and Chief Podiatric Surgical Service, Presbyterian Hosptial, San Francisco, 1978 to present; Medical Staff, Marshall Hale Memorial Hospital, San Francisco, 1980; Medical Staff, Mount Zion Hospital, San Francisco, 1979 to present; Private Practice, San Francisco, 1979 to present. Organizational Memberships: American Podiatry Association; California Podiatry Association; San Francisco-San Mateo Counties Podiatry Society (president, 1979 to 1980); American Public Health Association; American Association of Colleges of Podiatric Medicine (faculty representative, 1974-1977); Residents Alumni Association; American Medical Writers Association; American Academy of Podiatric Sports Medicine; National Board of Podiatry Examiners (diplomate); American College of Foot Surgeons (fellow); California Podiatry Hospital (interns and residents committee, 1972 to 1977; surgical audit committee, 1972-78; continuing education committee, 1972-77; patient care audit committee, 1973-78; surgery review committee, 1975-78); American Board of Podiatric Surgery (board of directors, 1978 to present; chairman, examination committee, 1978 to 1982); Alumni and Associates of the California College of Podiatric Medicine (secretary-treasurer, 1979 to present). Published Works: Number of Professional Articles including "Hallux Abducto-Valgus", "Syndactylis, Review Literature and Case Report", "Transfer to Tibialis Posterior" 1978, "A Discussion of the Rejection Phenomenon of Silastic Implants" 1976, and "Fundamental Skills in Surgery" 1976. Honors and Awards: Mead Johnson Scholarship, 1970; Golden Scalpel Award, 1971; Listed in *Outstanding Young Men of America, Who's Who Among Students in American Colleges and Universities.* Address: 2195 Beach #302, San Francisco, California 94123.

Richard E Spelts Jr

Spelts, Richard E Jr

Executive. Personal: Born January 1, 1919; Son of Mr. and Mrs. R. E. Spelts Sr.; Married Dorothy Tippon, in 1942; Father of Connie Brouillette (Mrs. Gary), Susan Richardson (Mrs. Richard). Education: B.S., University of Nebraska, 1941; A.B., Hastings College, Nebraska, 1948. Military: Served in the United States Navy, 1944-46, attaining the rank of Lieutenant (j.g.). Career: President and Chief Executive Officer, The First National Bank of Grand Island (Nebraska), Spelts of Nebraska Inc. (Grand Island), United Bank Services Company (Grand Island); Chairman, Bankshares of Nebraska Inc. (Grand Island), First Savings Company of Grand Island, First Savings Company of Hastings, First Savings Company of Kearney; Officer and Director, Spelts-Schultz Lumber Company of Grand Island, Mid-America Company (Grand Island), Spelts Lumber Company of Kearney, Spelts-Swanson Implement Company (Kearney); Director, M.E.I. Corporation, Minneapolis (third largest independent bottler of Pepsi-Cola in the United States), Northwestern Public Service Company (Huron, South Dakota), Business Development Corporation of Nebraska (Lincoln); Former Director/Officer, Alexander Hamilton Life Insurance Company (Detroit), Investors Life Insurance Company (Sioux Falls, South Dakota). Organizational Memberships: American Society of Agricultural Engineers. Community Activities: Masons; Shriner; Elk; American Legion; Rotary Club; Trustee, Hastings College, Grand Island Charitable Foundation, University of Nebraska Foundation; Chairman, 7.5 Million Dollar Platte River Maintenance Trust; Director, University of Nebraska Foundation, Nebraska Association of Commerce and Industry (president, 1962-63), St. Francis Medical Center Foundation, Grand Island Area Zoological Society (Children's Zoo), Stuhr Museum Foundation; Boy Scouts of America (national council); Nebraska Republican Party (chairman, 1955-59); Republican National Committee, 1955-59; Republican National Finance Committee, 1963-65; Republican National Conventions (delegate, 1960, 1980); Campaign Manager for Senator Carl T. Curtis, 1960, 1972; Republic National Convention (assistant floor leader, 1964); Republican National Committee "Truth Squad", 1964 Presidential Campaign (director); Nebraska Presidential Elector (elector). Religion: Presbyterian, Elder. Honors and Awards: United States Junior Chamber of Commerce Distinguished Service Award, 1952; Alumni Service Award, University of Nebraska, 1958; Distinguished Service Award, Nebraska Republican Party, 1959; Silver Beaver Award, Boy Scouts of America, 1962; Mr. Grand Island Award, 1963; American Cancer Society Award, 1965; KMMJ Radio Community Service Award, 1967; Wisdom Award of Honor, Wisdom Society, 1975; Golden Service Award, Hall County Housing Authority, 1979; Nebraska Outstanding Conservationist of the Year, 1980; Nebraskan of the Month, 1980 June; Recognition Award, The Nature Conservancy, 1980; Listed in *Who's Who in the United States, Who's Who in the Midwest, World Who's Who in Finance and Industry, International Who's Who in Community Service, Who's Who in Nebraska, Personalities of the West and Midwest, National Social Directory, Royal Blue Book, Dictionary of International Biography, National Register of Prominent Americans, Men of Achievement, Community Leaders and Noteworthy Americans, Personalities of America, Notable Americans, Book of Honor.* Address: 2203 West Charles, Grand Island, Nebraska 68801.

Henry L Spence

Spence, Henry Loston

Electronics Engineer. Personal: Born October 26, 1943; Son of Neahmiah E. and Laura A. Grimstead Spence; Married Justine Spencer; Father of Adrienne Reil, Laurietta Sharaga, Henry Loston Jr. Education: A.S., Norfolk State University, 1971; B.S.E.E. 1977, M.S.E.E. and M.S.Ed. 1979, Metropolitan Collegiate Institute; M.S. Candidate, Management, Columbia Pacific University, 1984; Honorary D.Div., Church of Gospel Ministry, 1976. Military: Served in the United States Air Force, 1965-69, attaining the rank of Sergeant. Career: Electronics Engineer; Former Position as Senior Systems Engineer, Communication ITT World Comm. Organizational Memberships: Institute of Electrical and Electronics Engineers; A.F.C.E.A.; American Notary Society of Washington, D.C.; State-wide Notary of Virginia; American Entrepreneurs Association; American Federation of Government Employees. Community Activities: National Technical Association; Freedom Jaycees (past president); Kawaida Jayees (past chairman of the board). Religion: Baptist. Honors and Awards: Honorary Doctor of Divinity, 1977; National Honor Society; Corporate Leadership Utilizing Business Award, 1979; Plank Honor Award, United States Navy *USS Virginia*, 1976; American Notary Society, 1979; State-wide Notary of Virginia, 1979-1987; Listed in *Marquis Who's Who of American East, Directory of Distinguished Americans, Community Leaders of America, Personalities of America, International Who's Who of Intellectuals.* Address: 1421 Palmetto Avenue, Virginia Beach, Virginia 23452.

Sperry, S Baxter

Educational Publisher. Personal: Born July 10, 1914; Daughter of John A. and Lillian M. Sperry (both deceased). Education: Graduate of Miss Burke's School, San Francisco, 1931; B.A., San Francisco College for Women, 1956; M.A., San Francisco State College, 1958; Further Studies at California School of Fine Arts, Saline Johnstone Business College, Washington State University-Pullman; Life Credential to Teach in California, 1962. Career: Women's Editor, *Utah Magazine*, Salt Lake City, 1937-38; Teacher, United States Army, I & E, Okinawa, 1951; Writer, United States Army, Okinawa, Staff I & E, 1952-53; Teacher, United States Navy, Subic Bay, Philippines, 1955-56; Editorial Writer and Assistant Director, Public Relations, California Redwood Association, San Francisco, 1963-64; Counselor, State Department of Rehabilitation, Los Angeles, 1966-67; Research and Writing, Inveraray, Scotland, 1967; Proprietor, Covenant and Laurel Hill Presses, Galt, California, 1968 to present. Organizational Memberships: National Trust for Historic Preservation; Dry Creek Antiquarian Society (secretary, 1969 to present); Psi Chi; American Biographical Institute Research Association; Anglo-American Academy (fellow). Community Activities: Galt Bicentennial Commission (director, 1974-77); Sacto. County Bicentennial Commission; Donor of Various Artifacts to San Joaquin County Museum, Micke Grove, Lodi, California; Sacramento County Museum, 1975 to present; University of California, 1978 to present; California State Library, 1973 to present; Washington State University, Pullman, 1970 to present; San Francisco State University, 1972. Honors and Awards: Prize, San Francisco Browning Society, 1968, for Dramatic Monologue; Literary Award, Sacramento Regional Arts Council, 1974; Plaque and Commendation, City of Galt, 1976; Gold Medal and Commendation, State of California, for Literature, 1976; Award, National Trust for Historic Preservation, 1978; Award for "Mexican Land Grants", National Endowment for Humanities, 1979. Address: P.O. Box 202, Galt, California 95632.

S Baxter Sperry

Spillers, James Parker (deceased)

Consultant, Executive. Personal: Born January 5, 1926; Died October 11, 1982; Son of Mrs. Chris Himel; Married Gwen Crawley;

Father of James Bernard, Elizabeth, Patricia, Annette, Jennifer. Education: B.S., University of North Carolina, 1948; M.S., Louisiana State University, 1952. Military: Served in the United States Marine Corps, 1941-45. Career: Consultant; Owner/President, Pacific-Atlantic Oil Company; Geologist, Gulf Oil Corporation, Aminoil, Humble; Chief Geologist, Louisiana State Mineral Board; Southeastern Regional Manager, Royal Resources Corporation. Organizational Memberships: New Orleans Geological Society (president, 1962-63; board of directors, 1963-64); Lafayette Geological Society; American Association of Petroleum Geologists. Community Activities: Gulf Coast Association of Geological Societies; Geological Society of America; American Institute of Professional Geologists (national secretary/treasurer, 1968); American Landman Association; Lafayette Landman Association. Address: 417 Shelly Drive, Lafayette, Louisiana 70503.

Spohn, Peggy Weeks

Banking Regulatory Agency Official. Personal: Born August 23, 1944, in Kingston, Pennsylvania; Daughter of Edwin Rice and Maudie Hewitt Weeks. Education: B.A., Le Moyne College, 1966; M.A., Sociology, Fordham University, 1967; Special Student in Sociology, Syracuse University, 1965-66; Special Student in Cross Cultural Community Development, Cornell University College of Agriculture, 1964. Career: Program Analyst, Concentrated Employment Program, Bronx, New York, 1967-68; Group Work Supervisor, Self Help Enterprises, Inc., Modesto, California, 1968-69; Research Analyst, Organization for Social and Technical Innovation, Cambridge, Massachusetts, 1969-70; Senior Analyst, ABT Associates, Cambridge, Massachusetts; Research Associate, The Urban Institute, Washington, D.C., 1970-74; Corporate Secretary and Deputy Director, The Housing Allowance Office, South Bend, Indiana, 1974-76; Manager, D.C. Office Contract Research Corporation, 1976-78; Co-Founder, Corporate Officer Network for Housing Research, Inc., Washington, D.C., 1968; Deputy Director Office of Community Investment, Federal Home Loan Bank Board, Washington, D.C., 1978; National Housing Conference, 1976; Volunteer Team Leader, Community Development Effort, International House, Le Moyne College, Mexico, 1962-66; Volunteer Developer of Hope Village, A Cooperative Community, Inc., 1968. Address: Federal Home Loan Bank Board, 1700 G Street, N.W., Washington, D.C. 20552.

Spragens, William Clark

Professor of Political Science. Personal: Born October 1, 1925; Son of T. Eugene and Edna Grace Clark Spragens; Married Elaine Jean Dunham. Education: Graduate of Lebanon High School, Kentucky, 1943; A.B., Journalism, University of Kentucky, 1947; M.A., University of Kentucky 1953; Ph.D., Michigan State University, 1966. Military: Served in the United States Army, 1943-45, with the rank of Private. Career: Professor of Political Science, Bowling Green State University; Former Newspaper Reporter and Editor. Organizational Memberships: American Political Science Association; Midwest Political Science Association; Center for the Study of the Presidency; Academy of Political Science. Community Activities: Bowling Green Kiwanis Club (former member; program chairman). Religion: First Presbyterian Church, Bowling Green, Adult Education Committee. Published Works: Author of Four Books; Numerous Articles in Professional Journals. Honors and Awards: Grant from Lyndon B. Johnson Foundation, 1978, 1979; National Endowment for Humanities Ethical Issues Seminar, A.P.S.A., 1980; Grants from National Science Foundation, 1972, and Bowling Green University Faculty Research Committee, 1969-81; Computer Science Trainee, N.S.F. Sponsored, 1974; Falk Fellow, Michigan State University, 1960-61; Ford Legislative Intern, 1961. Address: 607 Lafayette Blvd., Bowling Green, Ohio 43402.

Springborn, Robert Carl

Executive. Personal: Born October 19, 1929; Son of Carl and Mable Springborn; Married Carolyn Jean Kluesing; Father of Robert J., Deborah L. Education: B.S., Chemistry, University of Illinois, 1951; Ph.D., Organic Chemistry, Cornell University, 1954. Career: Chairman and President, Springborn Group, Inc., Research Laboratory in Field of Plastics and Bioresearch, 1972 to present; Chairman and President, General Economics Corporation, 1969-71; Vice President, Chemical Group, W. R. Grace and Company, 1967-69; General Manager, Ionics, Inc., 1965-67; Vice President and Technical Director, Ohio Rubber Company, 1963-65; Technical Director, Marbon Chemical Division, Borg-Warner Corporation, 1958-63; Chemist, Research, Monsanto, Chemical Company, 1954-58. Organizational Memberships: American Chemical Society; Chemical Society, London, England; American Institute of Chemical Engineers: American Management Association; Society for Paint and Varnish Technology; American Association of Advancement of Sciences; Plastics Institute of America (chairman, 1977-78); Society of Plastics Engineers; Society of Plastics Industry Inc.; Association of Research Directors; The International House of Japan, Inc.; National Association of Life Science Industries, Inc.; American Association of Textile Chemist and Colorist. Community Activities; Boy's Clubs of America; United Nations Day (chairman); White House Conference on Small Business; Committee for Small Business Innovation (national co-chairman). Address: P.O. Box 335, Somers, Connecticut 06071.

Spurlock, Jack

Director of College Office of Interdisciplinary Programs and Academic Research Administrator. Personal: Born August 16, 1930. Education: B.Ch.E.; M.S.Ch.E.; Ph.D. Military: Served in the United States Air Force to the rank of Captain to 1972. Career: Georgia Institute of Technology, Director of Office of Interdisciplinary Programs and Academic Research Administrator, Research Scientist. Organizational Memberships: American Institute of Chemists (fellow; member, Occupational Safety and Health National Committee); Royal Society of Health (fellow); American Institute of Aeronautics and Astronautics; American Institute of Chemical Engineers; American Chemical Society; Aerospace Medical Association (associate fellow). Community Activities: United States Department of Energy (biomass panel, advisory board). Religion: Presbyterian, Elder. Honor and Awards: Listed in *American Men and Women of Science, Who's Who in the South and Southwest, Personalities of the South, Dictionary of International Biography.* Address: 293 Indian Hills Trail, Marietta, Georgia 30067.

Stafford, Anita Faye

Child and Family Therapist, Professor. Personal: Born June 10, 1946; Daughter of Sidney Friend and Nina Eileen Johnson Rutherford; Married J. L. "Doc" Stafford; Mother of David Wayne, Steven Lee. Education: B.S., Central State University, 1970; M.Ed., Central State University, 1971; Ed.D., Oklahoma State University, 1975. Career: Child and Family Therapist; Vice President, Five Senses, Inc.; Former Position as Administrator, Department of Human Development. Organizational Memberships: Council for Exceptional Children; National Association of University Professors; Society for Child Development Research; National Association for Gifted Children; Association for the Gifted; Association for Special Education Technology. Community Activities: Altrusa International (public service committee). Religion: Baptist Sunday School Teacher. Published Works: *System I: Child and*

Adolescent Technology; System II: Techniques of Child and Adolescent Technology; Let's Sing Nature Songs; Let's Sing Family Songs; Let's Sing Funny Songs; Let's Sing Holiday Songs; Magic of Words; Magic of Eye Movement; Magic of Discipline; Magic of Understanding; Magic of Body Language; Magic of the Conscious and Unconscious Mind; Magic of Change; Magic of Motivation. Honors and Awards: Effective Teaching Award, 1975; Phi Delta Gamma; Phi Delta Kappa; Nominee for Osborn Award for Distinguished Service to Families, 1981; Listed in *World Who's Who of Women, Who's Who of American Women, Directory of Distinguished Americans, Personalities of the South, Personalities of America.* Address: 1228 Stanley, Denton, Texas 76201.

Staley, Kenneth Bernard

Professional Engineer, Minister. Personal: Born December 31, 1948; Son of Mr. and Mrs. Kinzy Staley; Married Sheila Keeys; Father of Tabbatha L. Education: B.S., Villanova University; Th.M., D.Div., Miller University. Career: Professional Engineer; Assistant Pastor, Christian Stronghold Baptist Church. Organizational Memberships: National Society of Professional Engineers; Ceramic Engineers Society. Religion: Baptist. Honors and Awards: Listed in *Outstanding Young Men of America, Who's Who in America.* Address: 1130 Lakeside, Philadelphia, Pennsylvania 19126.

Stamberger, Edwin H

Agricultural Specialist, Seed Corn and Machinery Development. Personal: Born February 16, 1916; Married Mabel Edith; Father of Larry Allan. Career: Former Director, Mendota Farmers Co-op and Supply Company; Volunteer Crop Reporter, 15 years; Goodwill Tours, Livestock to Central and South America 1966, Felco Grain to Russia, Hungary & N.A.T.O. Countries 1967, First People-to-People Africa Tour 1969, Farm Forum to Australia and New Zealand 1975, Prairie Farmer to India 1976, Tour to China 1977. Organizational Memberships: Mendota Watershed (steering committee); Agriculture/Stabilization and Conservation Committee, Soil Society of America; International Platform Association. Community Activities: Helped Develop Mendota Hospital, Mendota, Illinois; Subregional and Region III Comprehensive Health Planning Agency (review and comment committee, 1974 to present); Lions International; Civic Improvement Committee (chairman); Planning Agency. Religion: Lutheran. Honors and Awards: Recognition for Work in Community Development, Mendota Chamber of Commerce; Future Farmers of America State Farmer Degree; 4-H Awards; Listed in *The American Registry Series, Notable Americans, Illinois Lives, Who's Who in the Midwest.* Address: Route 1, Sabine Farm, Mendota, Illinois 61342.

Edwin H Stamberger

Stanat, Ruth E

Bank Executive. Personal: Born November 4, 1947; Daughter of Mr. and Mrs. James F. Corrigan; Mother of Scott. Education: B.S., Ohio University, 1969; M.A., 1973; M.B.A., 1977. Career: Vice President of Planning, Chase Manhattan Bank, New York, New York; Former Manager of Strategic Planning, International Paper Company; Former Product Manager of Special Markets and Reproduction Papers, International Paper Company; Former Senior Analyst of Corporate Planning, Springs Mills; Former Regulations Coordinator of Quality Control, United Airlines. Organizational Memberships: Financial Women's Association; Women's Economic Roundtable; National Business Forum; North American Society for Strategic Planning. Community Activities: Director of N.Y.U. School of Business M.B.A. Student Simulation Program, 1981; Involved with American Cancer Society, 1975, and Head Start Program, 1965. Honors and Awards: Graduated cum laude, Ohio University; Elected to Beta Gamma Sigma, New York University; Dean's List, Ohio University; Listed in *Who's Who in Finance and Industry, Personalities of America, Directory of Distinguished Americans, Book of Honor.* Address: 875 Fifth Avenue, 5-D, New York, New York 10021.

Standerwick, Donna M

Artist. Personal: Born July 4, 1937; Daughter of Mr. and Mrs. Henry Cony Chadbourne (both deceased); Married John T. Standerwick; Mother of John Tom Jr., Mary Ravana, David, Douglas, Jean. Education: Attended the University of Maine, 1955-57; Workshops with Ed Whitney, Zolton Szabo, Ed Betts. Career: Works Exhibited at Alexander's (Sitka, Alaska), Northwind Gallery (Juneau, Alaska), Scanlon Art Center (Ketchikan, Alaska and Sitka, Alaska); Work in Private Collections in the United States, Canada, Great Britain, Japan, Australia, New Zealand, Norway and Switzerland; Sitka Inter-cultural Art Center Booster Button Design; New Archangel Dancers Pin Design; Alaska State Jaycees Color Book Illustratons; Sheldon Jackson Bilingual Text Illustrations; Sitka Community College Decorative Panels on Building Exterior; Historical Sketch for National Society of Mural Painters, "Momentus Events in American History" Portfolio Phase I, II; Numerous Solo and Two-Person Shows. Organizational Memberships: International Platform Association; Alaska Watercolor Society; National League of American Pen Women (Sitka Branch president; Alaska State President 1980-82; Alaska State art chairman, 1978-79); Academia Italia delle Arti e de Lavoro; Associate, American Watercolor Society; Association Mid-west Watercolor Society; Baranof Arts and Crafts Association; Association National Society of Mural Painters. Community Activities: Sitka Cultural Facilities Development Committee, 1974-81. Religion: St. Peter's by the Sea, Altar Guild 1975 to present, Vestry 1981 to present, Sunday School Superintendent 1962-64. Honors and Awards: Best of Class, 1st, 2nd, 3rd Place Awards for Woodcarving, Print-making, Woodsculpture, Haines State Fair, 1977; All Alaska Women's Year Juried, 1975; All Alaska Juried Exhibit, 1976; BACA All Alaska Juried Exhibit, 1977, 1979, 1981, 1982; Resurrection Bay Juried Exhibit, 1978, 1981, 1982. NLAPW Biennial Juried, 1980; International Society of Artists Winter Snow Paintings Award, 1979; National League of American Pen Women Distinguished Service Award; Anchorage Audubon Society 2nd Annual Wildlife Juried Exhibit, 1980; Sitka Elks Club Commission, 1979; Scanlon Galleries Invitational, 1980; Rendezvous Gallery Invitational, 1981; Listed in *International Register of Profiles, American Artists of Renown, Personalities of America, Personalities of the West and Midwest, World Who's Who of Women, Dictionary of International Biography, Community Leaders and Noteworthy Americans, Book of Honor, Directory of Distinguished Americans, International Directory of Contemporary Aritsts.* Address: Box 1142, Sitka, Alaska 99835.

Stanford, Wiley W

Pension Consultant. Personal: Born July 20, 1926; Son of Lillian M. Sanford; Married Doran Wileford; Father of Susan S. Jemison, Charlotte S. Jackson. Education: B.S. Nautical Science, United States Merchant Marine Academy, 1946; B.S.B.A., Auburn University, 1948. Military: Served in the United States Naval Reserve, 1944-46, as Ensign. Career: President-Owner, Carlisle and Associates, Inc. Pension Consulting, Administrative and Actuarial, 1966 to present; Self-Employed, 1960-65; Vice-President, Southern Benefit Life Insurance Company, 1955-59; Employee, Elba Exchange Bank, 1948-54. Organizational Memberships: American Society of Pension Actuaries; International Association of Financial Planners; Southern Pension Conference; National

Association of Accountants. Community Activities: Boy Scouts of America Council; Lions Club (president). Address: 2483 Empire Forest Drive, Tucker, Georgia 30084.

Stanley, Charles Richard

Retired Proofreader. Personal: Born March 28, 1902 in Charleston, West Virginia; Son of Mr. and Mrs. Charles E. Stanley (both deceased). Education: Graduate of Charleston Junior High School. Career: Proofreader for Charleston Newspapers, 50 Years. Community Activities: Organizer and Leader of Children's Clubs, arranging camps and using his home for their daily recreation, 13 Years. Published Works: Edited Various Boys' and Girls' Magazine including *The Kanawha Chief* and *The Girl Friend.* Religion: Presbyterian Church, Deacon, Assistant Superintendent of Branch Mission; Central Methodist Church, Teacher, First Superintendent of Branch Mission; Baptist Church, Sunday School Church Business Worker; Producer of Christmas Plays for Sunday Schools. Address: 1408 Quarrier Street, Charleston, West Virginia 25301.

Charles R Stanley

Stanley, Kathleen Coold

Legislator. Personal: Born September 24, 1943; Married Patrick A. Stanley; Mother of Ryan Patrick. Education: Graduate of Bethlem Central High School, Delmar, New York, 1961 (New York State Regents Diploma, Regents Scholarship); B.A. History, Muskingum College, New Concord, Ohio, 1965; Master's in Social Studies Education, Syracuse University, 1967. Career: Hawaii State House of Representatives, Majority Floor Leader 1980 to present, Chairman of Committee on Public Empoyment and Government Operations 1977-80, Chairman of Committee on Public Assistance and Human Services 1975-76; Social Welfare Development and Research Center, University of Hawaii, Program Specialist 1969-74, Consultant 1969; Instructor, Field Training Officer, VISTA Training Program, University of Oregon, Eugene, 1969; Coordinator, OEO Community Action Program, Honolulu, 1968-69; VISTA Volunteer, 1967-68; Teacher, Liverpool Intermediate School, Liverpool, New York, 1966-67. Community Activities: Health and Community Services Council (2nd vice-president); Honolulu Theatre for Youth (board of trustees); Industrial Relations Research Association, Hawaii Chapter; League of Women Voters; National Association of Social Workers, Hawaii Chapter; Queen Liliuokalani Children's Center (advisory council); Waimanalo Council of Community Organizations; Young Women's Christian Association; 1980 Committee on Criminal Sexual Violence (chairman). Honors and Awards: One of Ten Outstanding Young Women of America, 1978; Outstanding Young Woman of America, 1977; One of Hawaii's Ten Most Effective Legislators, *Honolulu Star-Bulletin,* 1976. Address: 666 Prospect Street #301, Honolulu, Hawaii 96813.

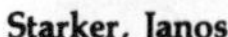

Starker, Janos

Concert Cellist and Distinguished Professor. Personal: Born July 5, 1924 in Budapest, Hungary; Married Rae Busch; Father of Gabrielle, Gwen. Education: Graduate of Franz Liszt Academy. Career: Concert Cellist and Distinguished Professor of Music, Indiana University-Bloomington, 1958 to present; Solo Cellist, Chicago Symphony 1953-58, Metropolitan Opera 1949-53, Dallas Symphony 1948-49, Budapest Opera 1945-46. Organizational Memberships: American Federation of Musicians. Published Works: Over 85 L.P.'s on Angel, Phillips, Mercury, Decca, Deutsche Grammophon, Victor Japan, Japan Columbia; Originator of Starker Bridge; Publications include *An Organized Method of String Playing, Bach Suite, Concerto Cadenzas, Schubert-Starker Sonatina, Bottermund-Starker Variations, Dvorak Concerto, Beethoven Sonatas and Variations* and Other Editions; Contributor of Many Articles and Essays to Various Magazines. Honors and Awards: Honorary Doctor of Music Degree, East West University 1982, Cornell College 1978, Chicago Conservatory 1961; Grand Prix du Disque, 1948; George Washington Award, 1972; Sanford Fellowship, Yale, 1974; Herzl Award, 1978; Honorary Member, Royal Academy, London, England, 1981. Address: Indiana University, Department of Music, Bloomington, Indiana 47401.

Staten, Marcea Bland

Legal Counsel. Personal: Born October 12, 1948; Daughter of Mr. and Mrs. Ralph Bland; Married Randolph W. Staten; Mother of Randy Jr., Shomari Bland. Education: B.A. Sociology/B.S. Psychology, Knox College, 1968; J.D., Northwestern University, 1971. Career: International Counsel, Medtronic Inc.; Senior Attorney, Montgomery Ward and Company, Chicago, Illinois; Attorney, The Pillsbury Company, Minneapolis, Minnesota; Staff Counsel, The Ghetto Project, American Civil Liberties Union. Organizational Memberships: National Bar Association; American Bar Association; Minnesota Bar Association; Minnesota Association of Black Lawyers. Community Activities: Minneapolis Young Women's Christian Association (board of trustees); Minneapolis Urban Coalition (vice-president, board of directors); The Links Incorporated; Iota Phi Lambda Professional Black Women's Group; Central Minnesota Legal Services Corporation (director); Minnesota Women's Political Caucus. Religion: Zion Baptist Church, Parliamentarian. Address: 2515 12th Avenue North, Minneapolis, Minnesota 55411.

Elcena Steinmann

Stauffer, R Gary

College Chairman and Chief Executive Officer. Personal: Born July 15, 1927, in Vestaburg, Michigan; Son of Clair C. and Mildred Tupper Stauffer, (both deceased); Married Willa M. Kirkendall on February 25, 1949; Father of Christine Lee, Robin Shelley, Jeffrey Todd, Jonathan Clair. Education: B.S., Central Michigan University, 1948; M.A., University of Michigan, 1954; Undertook further studies at Denison University in Ohio and Union College in New York. Military: Served in the United States Navy during World War II (Navy V-5 Program). Career: Vicksburg (Michigan) Community Schools, 1948-54: Teacher, Athletic Director, Head Basketball and Baseball Coach, Assistant Football Coach; Alma College, 1954-59: Assistant Professor in Physical Education, Head Basketball Coach, Footbal Backfield Coach, Associate Director of Admissions; Northwood Institute, 1959 to present: Co-Founder (with Dr. Arthur E. Turner, 1959), Exective Vice President, Vice Chairman of the College, President and Chief Executive Officer, Chairman of the College and Chief Executive Officer. Organizational Memberships: American Economic Association; Economists National Monetary Committee. Community Activities: Midland Chamber of Commerce; Detroit Athletic Club; Midland Country Club; Midland Art Council; Midland Symphony Orchestra; Midland Art Association; Midland Theatre Guild. Religion: Elder, Christian Church. Published Works: *Certified Automotive Merchandiser Library* (six volumes). Honors and Awards: Honorary Doctor of Humanities, Colegio Americano de Quito, Quito, Ecuador; Citations from Ecuadorian and Peruvian Governments for Contributions to Management Education; Listed in *Outstanding Educators of America, Who's Who in America.* Address: 4608 Arbor Dr., Midland, Michigan 48640.

Steinmann, Elcena Taggart

High School Department Head. Personal: Born May 15, 1915; Daughter of William John Taggart (deceased) and Margaret Louise

Shadle Taggart Ruff; Married Samuel Algot Steinmann; Mother of Elcena Olga Standish, Margaret Louise S. Irvine, Rae Christine S. Allen. Education: B.Ed. 1953, M.A. Education 1960, Superintendent's Credential 1962, Ed.D. 1968, University of Washington. Career: Seattle Public Schools, Department of Business Education in High School 1977 to present, Head Teacher in North Region Continuation School 1973-77; Teacher, Crittenton Home for Unwed Mothers, 1968-73; Advisor and Instructor, Office Management Division of School of Commerce and Finance, Seattle University, 1967-68; Professor, Everett Junior College, 1965-66; Instructor, Seattle Community College, 1962-65; Teacher, Seattle Public Schools, 1953 to present. Organizational Memberships: Delta Kappa Gamma; Kalm Brae Christian School, Redmond (trustee, 1977 to present); Washington Alliance Concerned with School-Age Parents (executive board, 1975 to present); National Education Association; Washington Education Association; Seattle Teachers Association (representative); A.V.A.; W.V.A.; N.B.E.A.; W.B.E.; W.W.B.E.A.; S.W.B.E.A.; American Association of University Professors; American Association of Higher Education; University of Washington Alumni; Seattle University Alumni. Community Activities: Seattle and King County Municipal League; Education Committee of Seattle; Mountaineers; Richmond Beach Community Club; Apple Tree Lane Utility District (local chairman). Religion: Protestant; Church Member, 1933 to present; Sunday School Worker. Honors and Awards: Standard General Teacher's Certificate for State of Washington, 1953 to present; Grand Cross of Colors for Initiating, Organizing and Editing First State Monthly Magazine, Rainbow Girls, 1935; Superintendent's Credential for Washington State, 1962; Listed in *World Who's Who of Women*, *International Register of Profiles*, *Men and Women of Distinction*, *Who's Who of American Women*. Address: 19623 - 27th Avenue N.W., Seattle, Washington 98177.

Steitz, Edward S

Director of Athletics, Professor of Physical Education. Personal: Born November 7, 1920, in Brooklyn, New York; Son of Charles and Madeline Steitz (both deceased); Married June Harrison; Father of Steve, Nancy, Robert. Education: R.S. 1943, M.Ed. 1948, Cornell University; Doctor of Physical Education, Springfield College, 1963. Military: Served in the United States Army, 1942-46. Career: Springfield College, Physical Education Instructor 1948, Assistant to Director of School of Physical Education 1950, Assistant Director of Athletics 1954, Athletic Director and Head Basketball Coach 1956; Editor, *Athletic Administration in Colleges and Universities*, *Official Basketball Rules*; Co-Editor, *Basketball Case Book*; National Editor and Interpreter of Basketball Rules in the United States and Canada; Panel of Experts on International Sports, United States State Department; Lecturer; Speaker; Consultant..Organizational Memberships: Executive Committees of United States Olympic Committee (board of directors), Special Olympics for the Mentally Retarded, National College Athletic Association (national volleyball tournament committee, chairman; national college division basketball tournament committee, chairman), National Basketball Committee for the United States and Canada, New England Conference of Athletics (president; chairman, basketball committe), New England Track and Field Association, New England Wrestling Association, National Summer Youth Sports Programs, New England Intercollegiate Amateur Athletic Association; Amateur Basketball Association (governing board for international playing); United States Olympic Basketball Committee, Tokyo 1964, Mexico 1968, Munich 1972 (vice chairman); United States Olympic Committee (drug abuse administration); Basketball Foundation of the United States (president; founder); National Collegiate Athletic Association (international relations committee; chairman, Olympic committee); Eastern Gymnastic League (president); Eastern College Athletic Basketball Association (president); New England Basketball Coaches Association (president); Eastern College Athletic Conference (chairman, holiday festival basketball tournament committee; principles and policies committee, chairman); New England Football Officials Association (chairman, executive committee); National Basketball Coaches Association (chairman, research committee); Basketball Rules Committee of the United States and Canada (chairman, research committee); Massachusetts Alliance of Health, Physical Education and Recreation; National Alliance of Health, Physical Education and Recreation; Council of Amateur Basketball Association of the United States; United States People-to-People Sports Committee; United States Representative to World Congress of Baskeball and Olympic Games, Rome, Mexico City, Munich, Montreal. Community Activities: Little League Baseball (national rules committee). Published Works: Contributor of 200 plus Articles for Magazines and Professional Journals. Honors and Awards: Number of Combat Ribbons; 6 Battle Stars; Presidential Unit Citation; Outstanding Servant of Public Award, TV Channel 22; Springfield College Distinguished Alumnus Award; Metro Award, National Basketball Coaches Association, United States State Department Medallion and Citation Award; Dr. E. S. Steitz Trophy Named in Honor for National Youth Basketball Championship, India Sports Foundation; Highest Award of Merit, International Association of Approved Basketball Officials; Walter Brown Award; Coach and Athlete Salutatorian Award; Honorary Life Member, College Basketball Officials Association, International Association of Approved Basketball Officials; Listed in *Distinguished International Leaders of Sports*, *International Who's Who in Community Service*, *Dictionary of International Biography*, *Community Leaders and Noteworthy Americans*. Address: 141 Elm Street, Longmeadow, Massachusetts 01028.

Edward S Steitz

Stenzler, William Mark

Educator, Systems Analyst, Computer Consultant. Personal: Born May 23, 1949; Son of George and Mildred Stenzler. Education: B.S. 1970, M.S. 1972, State University of New York at Albany; Completed Coursework for Ph.D., Hofsta University. Career: Adjunct Professor, Southampton College, 1981 to present; Assistant Educational Researcher, Commack Public Schools, 1975-76; Computer Consultant, B.O.C.E.S. III Gifted and Talented Institute, 1973 to present; Assisted Seven Ph.D. Candidates in Statistical Portions of Dissertations, 1972 to present; Adult Education Teacher, 1974 to present; Co-Director, Computer Accelerated Learning Project, 1977-78; Assistant Director, Project Stride, 1980 to present; Consultant, B.O.C.E.S. In-Service Teacher Training Courses on Computers, 1974 to present; Book/Film Reviewer for American Association for the Advancement of Science, 1976 to present; Vice-President, CompuCon Ltd., 1976-79; Vice-President, Star Computer Systems, 1979-80. Organizational Memberships: A.C.M.; N.C.T.M.; S.C.M.T.A. (membership chairman, 1977 to present; scheduling sessions for student symposium, 115 schools, 1979 to present; test-scoring S.C.M.T.A. contest, 120 schools, 1979 to present); N.Y.S.A.E.D.S.; A.E.R.A.; American Association for the Advancement of Science. Honors and Awards: B'nai B'rith Service Award, 1967; MENSA, 1970; Pi Mu Epsilon; S.C.M.T.A. Service Award, 1976; Listed in Numerous Biographical Works. Address: 8 Prospect Place, Plainview, New York 11803.

Stephen, John Erle

Attorney and Consultant. Personal: Born September 24, 1918; Son of John Earnest and Vida Klein Stephen; Married Gloria Yzaguirre; Father of Vida Leslie, John Lauro Kurt. Education: LL.B., J.D., University of Texas; Postgraduate Studies at the University of Mexico, Northwestern University, United States Naval Academy Postgraduate School, Naval War College. Military: Served to Commander in the United States Navy. Career: General Manager, Station KOPY, Houston, Texas, 1946; General Attorney, Executive Assistant to the President, Texas Star Corporation, Houston, 1947-50; Partner, Hofheinz and Stephen, Houston, 1950-57; Vice President and General Counsel, TV Broadcasting Company, Texas Radio Corporation, Gulf Coast Network, Houston, 1953-57; Special Counsel, Executive Assistant to Mayor, City of Houston, 1953-56; Vice President and General Counsel, Air Transport Association of America, Washington, D.C., 1958-70; Vice President and General Counsel, Amway Corporation, Ada, Michigan, 1971 to 1983. Organizational Memberships: American Bar Association (Council; former Chairman, Section of Public

Utility Law); Federal Bar Association Council; World Peace Through Law Center, Geneva (former Chairman, International Aviation Law Committee); District of Columbia Bar Association; Texas Bar Association; Michigan Bar Association; Federal Communications Bar Association; Association of Interstate Commerce Commission Practitioners; American Judicature Society. Religion: Baptist. Published Works: United States Editor, *Yearbook of International Aviation;* Associate Editor, *Air Laws and Treaties of the World;* Board of Advisors, *Journal of Air Law and Commerce;* articles published in numerous professional journals. Honors and Awards: Member and Advisor to the United States Delegations to Diplomatic Conferences: Warsaw Treaty and Hague Protocol, Bermuda Agreement, Tokyo Crimes Treaty, Montreal Liability; Visiting Lecturer, Harvard Graduate Business School, Washington Foreign Law Society, Pacific Agribusiness Conference; Chief of Protocol, City of Houston, 1953-56; Advisor, Consulates-General of Mexico in the United States, 1956-66; Advisor, United States Air Route Delegation to the United Kingdom, France, Belgium, Netherlands, South Korea, Japan, Spain, Australia, Brazil, Argentina; Honorary Member, Japanese Air Law Society, Venezuelan Society of Air and Space Law; Honorary Faculty Member, University of Miami School of Law; Accredited Correspondent, United Nations; Republican and Democratic Conventions; Navy Unit Citation with Bronze Star; Asiatic-Pacific Medal, 9 Battle Stars; Expert Marksman Medal; Expert Pistol Shot Medal; Listed in *Who's Who in the World, Who's Who in America, World Who's Who in Commerce and Industry, Who's Who in American Law, Who's Who in Finance and Industry, Who's Who in the South and Southwest, Who's Who in the Midwest, Who's Who in Aviation, Who's Who in World Aviation and Astronautics, Who's Who in American Universities and Colleges.* Address: 4118 Ridgeline Dr., Austin, Texas 78731.

Stern, Leslie Warren

Executive. Personal: Born July 3, 1938; Son of Mr. and Mrs. H. Stern; Married Madeline Carol Kuttner; Father of Derek Alexandre, Cory Jay. Education: B.S., Cornell University, 1960; M.B.A., Tulane, 1967. Career: President, L. W. Stern Associates, Inc. 1968 to present; Director, Management Services, Sonesta Hotels Corporation, 1961-68; Catering Manager, Irish International Airlines, 1960-61. Organizational Memberships: Cornell University Council (chairman, committee on career counseling and placement); Cornell University Alumni Association (president, 1980-82); Cornell Committee on Alumni Trustee Nomination (chairman, 1978); American Management Association; North American Society of Corporation Planners; National Association of Corporate and Professional Recruiters; Association for Corp. Growth; Tulane Alumni Association (director). Honors and Awards: Listed in *Who's Who in Finance and Industry.* Address: 75 East End Avenue, New York, New York 10028.

Stevens, Andrew

Actor, Singer. Personal: Born in Memphis, Tennessee. Education: Graduate of Messick High School, Memphis; Studies in Acting and Musical Theate Techniques, Immaculate Heart College, West Los Angeles College, Los Angeles Valley College. Career: Guest-Starred in Numerous Television Series, including "Police Story" and "The Quest"; Appeared in Many Television Movies including "The Werewolf of Woodstock", "The Last Survivors", "Secrets", Women at West Point", "Topper", "The Oregon Trail" and "Miracle on Ice"; Leading Roles in Television Dramas "The Bastard", "The Rebels", "Once an Eagle", "Beggarman Thief"; Motion Picture Credits include "Shampoo", "Vigilante Force", "Las Vegas Lady", "Deportee", "The Massacre at Central High", "Day of the Animals", "The Boys in Company C", "The Fury", "Death Hunt", and "The Seduction"; Leading Role in Television Series "Code Red"; Wrote and Recorded Song for "Code Red" entitled "750cc". Address: c/o Nancy Hamilton and Associates, Public Relations, 236½ South Robertson Boulevard, Beverly Hills, California 90211.

Andrew Stevens

Stewart, Fred

Farmer, Preacher (retired). Personal: Born October 31, 1895; Married Malda Ruth; Father of Freda (deceased), Estelle, Bobby, Horace, Ollie, Walter. Military: Served in the United States Army 1918-19. Career: Farmer; Preacher. Religion: Primitive Baptist. Published Works: *The Second Coming of Christ and the Thousand-Year Reign,* 1980. Address: 806 South Broad Street, Scottsboro, Alabama 35768.

Stewart, Meredith L

Supply Manager. Personal: Born August 20, 1940; Daughter of Norval and Dorothy Jones; Married Donald E. Stewart; Mother of Jamie, Jennifer, Jeffrey, Jean, Jason. Education: Registered Diagnostic Medical Somographer. Career: Bookkeeper 1970-71, Accounts Payable 1971-73, Echocardiographer and Cardiovascular Coordinator 1973-79, Deaconess Hospital; Part-time Instructor, Community College, 1977-79; Organizer and Speaker at Seminars in Field; Manager, Central Supply. Organizational Memberships: Cardiopulmonary and Echocardiography Program (advisory committee, 1977-79; president, echocardiography committee, 1979); American Echo Society; American Hospital Association; International Hospital Association of Hospital Management. Honors and Awards: Listed in *Who's Who of American Women, Who's Who in the West, Personalities of America.* Address: Route 1 Box 282A, Colbert, Washington 99005.

Stewart, Paul Alva

Consultant. Personal: Born June 24, 1909; Son of William O. and Achsah B. Stewart (both deceased); Married; Father of David Enos, Seth Michael. Education: B.S. 1952, M.S. 1953, Ph.D. 1957, Ohio State University. Career: Consultant, Blackbird-Starling Problems; Research Entomologist, United States Department of Agriculture, 1965-73; Research Biologist, United States Fish and Wildlife Service, 1959-65; Assistant to Director, Indiana Division of Fish and Game, 1958; Research Fellow, Ohio Cooperative Wildlife Research Unit, 1952-57. Organizational Memberships: American, British, South African Royal Australasian Ornithological Unions; Wilson and Cooper Ornithological Societies; American Society of Mammalogists; Donor, Paul A. Stewart Awards for Ornithological Research, Wilson Ornithological Society. Honors and Awards: Elective Member, American Ornithologists Union. Address: 203 Mooreland Drive, Oxford, North Carolina 27565.

Stiles, Sandra Jean

Marketing Research Analyst. Personal: Born July 2, 1950; Daughter of Genevieve Freeman; Married Richard Ladd Stiles. Education: B.A. Math and Economics, Immaculata College, 1972; Graduate Work in Statistics, Villanova University, 1972-73. Career: Marketing Research Analyst, Marketing Information Systems, Campbell Soup Company Headquarters, Camden, New Jersey, 1982 to present; Marketing Analyst, Certainteed Corporation Headquarters, Valley Forge, Pennsylvania, 1973-82; Statistical Marketing

Analyst; Statistician; Instructor, Immaculata College, 1976; Owner, Camelot Florist and Decorators, 1976 to present. Organizational Memberships: Producers Council; American Society of Professional and Executive Women; American Management Association. Community Activities: Republican National Committee (sustaining member). Honors and Awards: Economics Council of Forecasting Analysts, 1978; Sigma Zeta National Science Honor Society. Address: 1027 Valley Forge Road, Devon, Pennsylvania 19333.

Stokes, Jone Clifton

Retired. Personal: Born April 18, 1915, in Charlotte, North Carolina; Married Dorothy; Father of Kenneth. Education: Graduate Air War College, Air University; Studied Industrial Management, University of Southern California, 1956-57; Attended George Washington University, 1935-38. Military: Served in the United Sttes Air Force, retired as Lieutenant Colonel. Career: Retired in 1980; Previously President, Televisual Systems Corporation; Vice President, Teletrac Systems Corporation; Management President Consultant (Telecommunications). Organizational Memberships: A.I.A.-American Institute of Aeronautics and Astronautics, 1953-73; American Security Council (national advisory board, 1963-73); Federal Design Council (first honorary member; life member; president, 1971-72); Information Film Producers of America (national board of governors, 1970-75); Washington Film Council; Air Force Association; National Space Club. Community Activities: Center for the Study of the Presidency, 1978; Public Members Association of Foreign Service (vice president, 1978); Retired Officer's Association; American Cause. Published Works: Contibuting Editor, *Government Photography, Business Screen,* and *Technical Photography*, 1966-70; Supervised United States Air Force Senior Staff of Pentagon Speech Writers; Published Government Technical Manuals, Audio-Visual Staff Management Studies; Authored Public Affairs Brochures. Honors and Awards: Legion of Merit, Meritorious Service Medal, Armed Forces Commendation Medal with Three Oak Leaf Clusters; "Cindy" Award for Best Animated Film on Space; Silver Anvil Award for Outstanding Radio Science Report Series; Presidential Task Force for First Federal Design Assembly, 1972; D.O.D. Program Chairman, Armed Forces Audio-Visual Communications Conferences, 1967-69; Listed in *Who's Who in Aviation, Who's Who in Finance and Industry, Personalities of America.* Address: 7119 Westchester Drive, Temple Hills, Maryland 20748.

John T Stone Jr

Stone, Elaine Murray

Author, Realtor, Composer, Television Host and Producer. Personal: Born January 22, 1922; Daughter of Mrs. Catherine Murray-Jacoby; Married F. Courtney Stone; Mother of Catherine Rayburn (Mrs. Robert), Pamela Webb (Mrs. Don), Victoria Francis. Education: Graduate of Ashley Hall, Charleston, South Carolina, 1939; Attended Juilliard School of Music, New York City, 1939-41; Graduate in Piano, New York College of Music, 1943; Graduate in Organ with Licentiate Degree, Trinity College of Music, London, England, 1947; Further Studies at Florida Institute of Technology and the University of Miami. Career: Host of "Focus on History", a Television Show on WMDG-TV, Melbourne, Florida, 1982-83; Television Writer and Producer, 1978-80, KXTX-TV, Dallas, Texas; Radio Executive, WTAI, Melbourne, 1971-74; Editor, Cass Inc., Melbourne, 1970-71; Organist, New York, New Jersey, Florida, over 25 years; Accompanist for Strawbridge Ballet, 1944-45. Organizational Memberships: Warden, American Guild of Organists, Fort Lauderdale, 1953-54; Cape Canaveral Branch, National League of American Pen Women (president, 1979-80); Regent of Satellite Beach Chapter, Daughters of the American Revolution, 1981-82, 1983; Episcopal Diocese of Southern Florida (diocesan board of promotion, 1961-62). Community Activities: Melbourne Bicentennial Commission, 1975-76; Editor of the *Trumpet*, Publication of Brevard Symphony, 1965-75; Daughters of the American Revolution (librarian, Abigail Wright Chamberlin chapter, 1964-66); Florida Daughters of the American Revolution (chairman of music, 1964-66); Abe Lincoln Radio-Television National Awards, Southern Baptist Radio-Television Commission (judge, 1980); Brevard Poetry Club (judge, 1981). Religion: Vice President, Episcopal Churchwomen, Holy Trinity Episcopal Church, Melbourne, 1970; Third Order of St. Francis, 1955-65; Author of Articles in *The Living Church, Christian Life, Logos,* Others. Published Works: Author of 100 Articles; *The Taming of the Tongue* 1954, *Love One Another* 1957, *Pedro Menendez de Aviles* 1969, *Melbourne Bicentennial Book* 1976, *Uganda: Fire and Blood* 1977, *Tekla and The Lion* 1981. Honors and Awards: First Place, Piano, South Carolina State Music Contest, 1939; First Place in Journalism, Florida State Contest, National League of American Pen Women, 1964; First Place in Sales, Engle Realty, 1975, 1976, 1977, 1978; First Place in Books in Texas State Contest 1979, National League of American Pen Women, for *Uganda: Fire and Blood;* First Place in Short Story Contest, Texas State Contest, National League of American Pen Women, 1979. Address: 1945 Pineapple Avenue, Melbourne, Florida 32935.

Stone, John Timothy Jr

Author. Personal: Born July 13, 1933; Son of John Timothy and Marie Briggs Stone (both deceased); Married Judith Bosworth; Father of John Timothy III, George W.B. Education: Instituto Allende, San Miguel Allende, Guanajuato, Mexico, 1950; Attended Amherst College, Massachusetts, 1951-52; B.A., University of Miami, Coral Gables, 1955. Military: Served in the United States Army Counterintelligence Corps, 1956-58, as a Special Agent. Career: President, Continental Royal Services, 1973-74; President, Recreation International, 1972-74; President, Janeff Credit Corporation, 1971-74; Director, The Inn at Steamboat Inc., Steamboat Springs Holding and Development Company, The Compass Club Inc., Diamond J. Ranches Inc, Agricola Itzapan (Honduras), African Ponderosa (Kenya), Metcalf Farms Hawaii Inc., 1971-74. Organizational Memberships: Sigma Alpha Epsilon (president, Florida Alpha, 1954-55); Minarani Club, Kalifi, Kenya, 1972-74; Million Dollar Round Table, 1969-70. Community Activites: Wisconsin Lenders Exchange (founder, director, 1960-65); Madison Credit Bureau (board of directors, 1965-67); National Junior Chamber of Commerce, 1955-67; University of Miami Alumni Association, 1955 to present; Sigma Alpha Epsilon Alumni Association, 1955 to present; Wordsmiths Associates (to assist aspiring writers), 1979 to present; East African Wildlife Association, 1973 to present; Arizona Authors Association, 1982-83; Northern Michigan University Golden Wildcat Club, 1981-82; A.A.U., Wrestling Division, 1978-82; United States Wrestling Federation, 1978 to present; Olympic Contributor. Religion: Heritage Congregational Church, Pastor's Advisor 1977-81; Bible Voice Publishing, Author and Editorial Advisor, 1978-79. Published Works: *Going for Broke* 1956, *The Minnesota Connection* 1978, *Debby Boone-So Far* (ghostwriter) 1981, *He Calls Himself "An Ordinary Man"* (with John Dallas McPherson) 1982, *Fiercest of the Gentle People* 1983, *Tabasco* 1982-83, *Runaways* 1983, Assisted in the Publication of *The Court-Martial of George Armstrong Custer* (by Douglas C. Jones) 1977, *Blizzard* (by George Stone) 1977, 1978, *Raising Athletes-A Parents Guide* (by Conrad Adringa) 1983. Honors and Awards: Omicron Delta Kappa, 1954-55; Honor Graduate, United States Army Counterintelligence School, 1956; Honor Graduate, HFC Executive Training Program, 1960; Midland National Life Insurance Company Man of the Year, 1965; Government of the Republic of Kenya Citation for Foreign Business Development and Kenyan Ambassador's Award, 1973; Republic of Honduras Citation for Foreign Business Development, 1973; Warner Communications "Best of the Bestsellers", 1978; Listed in *Who's Who American Students in American Universities and Colleges, Who's Who in the Midwest, U.S. Directory of Speakers.* Address: 5508 Williamsburg Way, Madison, Wisconsin 53719.

J George Strachan

Strachan, John George

Retired Administrator, Lecturer, Program Consultant, Author. Personal: Born May 23, 1910, in Montreal, Quebec, Canada; Son of

Thomas Henry and Blanche Elizabeth Strauchan (both deceased); Married Jane Ragland; Father of Roger Thomas, John A. (deceased). Education: Attended the University of Dayton (Ohio), St. John's College (New York), Pace and Pace Institute (New York); Graduate, Yale School of Alcohol Studies, 1950. Military: Served in the United States Air Force, 1941-45. Career: Helped Organize the Wisconsin Council and State Bureau, the Milwaukee Information Referral Center, and Some of Earliest Treatment, Community and Industrial Programs on Alcoholism; Helped Establish Alcohol Study Sessions, University of Wisconsin (now Mid-West Institute), Marquette Labor College, Three Schools at University of Alberta (first in Canada); Founded and Directed Alberta's First Impared Drivers Program; Organized and Directed Alcoholism Foundation of Alberta, 1953-65, Milwaukee Information and Referral Center, 1947-53; Spearheaded Formation of Canadian Council on Alcoholism (now Canadian Addictions Foundation), 1954; Former Officer and Board Member, North American Association of Alcoholism Programs (now Alcohol and Drug Problems Association); Alcoholism Consultant, Department of the Attorney-General, Alberta, 1969-73; President, Gillain Foundation, 1972-80; President and Executive Director, Gillain Manor Ltd., Sidney, British Columbia, 1972-80. Organizational Memberships: North American Association of Alcoholism Program (chairman, 1960 annual conference); British Medical Association and International Council on Alcoholism Addictions Co-Sponsored to World Assembly, London, England, 1964; Royal Glenora Club; Canadian Authors Association; Association Litteraire et Artistique Internationale. Community Activities: E. M. Jellinek Memorial Fund (board member). Published Works: Author of Three Books, *Alcoholism: Treatable Illness, Practical Alcoholism Programming, Recovery from Alcoholism.* Honors and Awards: Life Membership, Alcohol and Drug Problems Association of North America; Fellow, Royal Society of Arts, London; Honorary Doctor of Laws, University of Alberta, 1973; Distinguished Service Award and Life Membership, Canadian Addictions Foundation, 1976; Queen Elizabeth Silver Jubilee Medal, 1977; Listed in *International Writers Biography, Dictionary of International Biography, Who's Who in the West, Men of Achievement, Community Leaders and Noteworthy Americans, International Who's Who in Community Service.* Address: 2035 Summergate Blvd. Sidney, British Columbia, Canada V8L 4K6.

Strandell, Marjatta

Engineer. Personal: Born April 17, 1933, in Finland. Education: B.A. Business Administration, B.S.M.E., 1964; M.S.M.E., 1966; Certified Cost Engineer, 1976. Career: Manager of Power, Plant Construction, Systems and Procedures, Central and South West Services, Inc., Dallas, Texas; Former Faculty Member, Portland State University, Department of Applied Science and Engineering; Other Former Positions include Technical Coordinator, Government Corporations in Europe; Cost Engineer, Southern California Edison Company, Rosemade; Engineer in Nuclear Construction, Northeast Utilities, Hartford, Connecticut; Senior Supervising Cost Engineer, Pacific Power and Light Company, Portland, Oregon; Director of Human Resource Planning and Development, Wisconsin Power and Light Company. Organizational Memberships: American Association of Cost Engineers (senior member); Society of Women Engineers; National Society of Professional Engineers,Oregon and Wisconsin State Chapters. Community Activities: Washington Park Zoo, Portland, Oregon (board member). Published Works: Author of Several Professional Publications and Papers Presented at National and International Meetings. Honors and Awards: Listed in *Who's Who in the West, International Who's Who in Community Service, International Who's Who in Public Affairs, Dictionary of International Biography, Personalities of the West and Midwest, American Men and Women of Science.* Address: 6611 Aberdeen Avenue, Dallas, Texas 75230.

Samuel Stroman

Stroman, Samuel David

Professor. Personal: Born December 18, 1924; Married, Father of Brenda D. Gumbs, Jamileh S.D., Sherolyn D., Synthia D., Samuel David II. Education: A.B., South Carolina State College, 1950; M.A., Howard University, 1964; M.S., University of Wisconsin-Milwaukee, 1972; Ph.D., The American University, 1976; Studies at the United States Army Command and General Staff College and Other Military Schools. Military: Served in the United States Army, 1941-45, rising through the ranks to First Sergeant; Regular Army Officer, 1950-76, 2nd Lieutenant to Full Colonel. Career: Assistant Professor, Department of Military Science, Howard University, 1959-63; Chairman, Department of Military Science, University of Wisconsin-Milwaukee, 1969-72; Chairman, Department of Military Science, Howard University, 1972-76; Army Officer, Platoon Leader, Company Commander, Battalion Commander, Inspector General, N.C.O. Academy Commandant, Senior Advisor, Vietnamese Infantry School; Department of the Army Branch Chief; Professor, South Carolina State College. Organizational Memberships: American Personnel and Guidance Association; South Carolina Personnel and Guidance Association; American Association for Counselor Education and Supervision; American Association for Non-White Concerns in Education; South Carolina Association for Non-White Concerns in Education; American Association of University Professors. Community Activities: Phi Delta Kappa (vice president for programs, Orangeburg chapter, 1980-81); National Association for the Advancement of Colored People (chairman, legal redress committee, Orangeburg chapter, 1977-79); Appointed to National Board of Advisors of American Biographical Institute, 1982; Chairman to Symposium on "Scientific Process of Decision Making", 81st Annual Convention of the American Psychological Association, Montreal, Canada, 1973; Board of Directors, Vasquez Association, Educational Research and Consulting Firm; Phi Kappa Phi; Kappa Delta Pi; Phi Delta Kappa. Published Works: Editorial Board, *Education* Magazine; Editorial Board, *Journal of Instructional Psychology.* Honors and Awards: Special Award from Students for Distinguished Teaching and Unselfish Devotion, 1977; Veterans of Foreign Wars Distinguished Service in Education Award, 1978; Veterans of Foreign Wars Award for Dedicated Service and Inspirational Leadership, 1981; Outstanding College Teacher of the Year, Orangeburg Chapter, Phi Delta Kappa, 1978-79; Inducted into South Carolina State College Army R.O.T.C. Hall of Fame, 1978; Award for Outstanding Service, Orangeburg Alumni Chapter, Kappa Alpha Psi, 1978; Southeastern Province Kappa Alpha Psi Achievement Award, 1978; Gold Medal Educator for the 1980's, 1980; Army Legion of Merit with Oak Leaf Cluster; Army Meritorious Service Medal with Oak Leaf Cluster; Army Commedation Medal with Oak Leaf Cluster; Army General Staff Badge; Bronze Star Medal; Listed in *Personalities of the South, Dictionary of International Biography, Who's Who in the South and Southwest, Book of Honor, American Biographical Directory, International Who's Who of Intellectuals, International Register of Profiles, Personalities of America, Men of Achievement, Men and Women of Distinction, Community Leaders of America, Biographical Role of Honor.* Address: P.O. Box 1601, South Carolina State College, Orangeburg, South Carolina 29117.

Strong, Leah Audrey

Professor. Personal: Born March 14, 1922; Daughter of Robert Leroy and Dorothy K. Strong. Education: A.B., Allegheny College, 1943; A.M., Cornell University, 1944; Ph.D., Syracuse University, 1953. Career: Professor, American Studies, and Chairman, Division of Humanities, Wesleyan College; Assistant Professor, English, Cedar Crest College, Allentown, Pennsylvania, 1953-61; Instructor, English Department, Syracuse University, 1947-52; Instructor, English Department, University of Bridgeport, 1946-47. Organizational Memberships: United States Coast Guard Auxiliary (flotilla staff officer, 1982 to present); Southeastern American Studies Association (president, 1981 to present); Southern Humanities Conference (executive secretary, 1980 to present); South Atlantic Modern Language Association; American Studies Association; Phi Kappa Phi; Pi Gamma Mu. Religion: Immanuel Congregational Church, Hartford, Connecticut, 1934 to present; Associate Minister, Longboat Island Chapel, Longboat Key,

Florida, Summers 1967-72. Published Works: *Joseph Hopkins Twichell: Mark Twain's Friend and Pastor*, 1966; Articles Published in Many Professional Journals. Address: 1173 Forest Hill Road, Macon, Georgia 31210.

Strother, Dora Jean Dougherty

Administrator. Personal: Born November 27, 1981; Married Lester James Strother. Education: A.A., Cottey College, 1941; Ph.B., Northwestern University, 1949; M.S., University of Illinois, 1953; Ph.D., New York University, 1955. Military: Served with the Women Air Force Service Pilots of the United States Army Air Corps, 1943-44; Retired with the Rank of Lieutenant Colonel from the United States Air Force Reserve. Career: Chief of Human Factors Engineering and Cockpit Arrangement Group, Bell Helicopter; Previous Position on Human Engineering Staff, The Martin Company, Baltimore. Organizational Memberships: Whirly Girls International (chairman, 1980-82); American Psychological Association (fellow); Human Factors Society of America (fellow); American Institute of Aeronautics and Astronautics (associate fellow); Association of Aviation Psychologists (international president, l971-72). Community Activities: Federal Aviation Administration (president's advisory committee on aviation, l966-68); International Science Fair (judge, 1966); Amelia Earhart Memorial Scholarship Fund of the 99s (chairman, board of trustees, 1967-70) vice chairman, 1975 to present); United Cerebral Palsy of Tarrant County, Texas (advisory board, 1972-75); National Aerospace Educational Advisory Committee, Civil Air Patrol, United States Air Force Auxiliary, 1976 to present; Council on Aerospace-Aviation Education, Texas Education Agency (chairman, 1978-79; chairman, advisory council). Religion: Episcopal. Honors and Awards: Certified and Licensed Psychologist, State of Texas; Achievement Award, New York University, 1955; Recognition Certificate, Fort Worth Chamber of Commerce, 1961; Aviation Woman of the Year Award, Women's International Association of Aero, 1961; Achievement Award, A.A.U.S., 1966; Merit Award, Northwestern University, 1968; F.A.A. Certificate of Commendation, 1968; Woman of Achievement Award, Toastmistress Clubs Council of Texas. Address: 3616 Landy Lane, Fort Worth, Texas 76118.

Hazel B Strother

Strother, Hazel Beall

Systems Accountant, Realtor. Personal: Born June 29, 1929; Daughter of Mrs. L. M. Beall. Education: A.A. 1951, B.A. Governmental Accounting 1952, George Washington University. Career: Systems Accountant; Part-time Realtor; Previous Positions as Accountant, Insurance Underwriter. Organizational Memberships: Association of Government Accountants (national chairwomen, public relations, 1971-73; coordinator for attendance in national symposium committee, 1980-81); Association for Systems Management (treasurer, patuxent chapter, 1981-82). Community Activities: Combined Federal Campaign (coordinator for office of finance, 1978, 1981). Religion: Mount Vernon Baptist Church (finance committee, 1979-80). Honors and Awards: Four Year Scholarship, West Virginia University, 1947; Daughters of the American Revolution Citizenship Award, 1947; One Year Scholarship, Davis and Elkins College, Elkins, West Virginia, 1947; High School Valedictorian; L. C. Oyster Scholaship, West Virginia Wesleyan College, 1947; Listed in *Two Thousand Women of Achievement, World Who's Who of Women*. Address: 2111 Jefferson Davis Highway, Arlington, Virginia 22202.

Sudbury, Herbert James

Real Estate Broker. Personal: Born February 25, 1895; Son of J. W. Sudbury (deceased); Married Mary Flora (deceased); Father of R. J., John D., Herbert Joe. Education: B.E., Freed-Hardeman College; B.A., University of Tennessee; M.A., School Administration, George Peabody College. Military: Civilian Instructor in Flight Navigation, United States Navy School. Career: Real Estate Broker; Former College Teacher of Psychology. Community Activities: Commission on Aging; A.A.R.R. (chairman); N.R.T.A. (chairman); Developed Three Subdivisions in Natchitoches Area; Donated Five Acre Playground to City of Natchitoches. Religion: Minister, Church of Christ, Brinkley, Arkansas, 1918; Donated Building Lot to Church of Christ, Natchitoches. Address: P.O. Box 325, Natchitoches, Louisiana 71457.

Suddith, Roberta Lucille

Registered Nurse, Cardiovascular Specialist. Personal: Born June 30, 1945; Daughter of Beaman and Effie L. Suddith (both deceased). Education: Diploma, Lutheran Hospital School of Nursing, Fort Wayne, Indiana; Student in Psychology, St. Francis College, Fort Wayne. Career: Staff Nurse, Lutheran Hospital, 1966-68; Assistant Head Nurse, Coronary Care Unit, Lutheran Hospital School of Nursing Alumni (secretary, 1969-70; various committees). Community Activities: American Heart Association, Northeast Indiana Chapter (board of directors); Cardiopulmonary Resuscitation Certified Instructor/Trainer, Chairperson Professional Education Committee. Honors and Awards: Good Heart Award 1973, Bronze Service Medallion 1974, Silver Service Medallion 1975, Gold Service Medallion 1977, American Heart Association; Listed in *Who's Who of American Women, World Who's Who of Women, Personalities of the West and Midwest*. Address: 9720 Hosler Road, Leo, Indiana 46765.

H J Sudbury

Sugarman, Betty A

Clinical Social Worker. Personal: Born April 8, 1945, in Fall River, Massachusetts; Daughter of Seymour and Gladys Sugarman. Education: B.A., Sociology, Connecticut College, New London, 1967; M.S., Columbia University School of Social Work, 1972; Field Work, Leake and Watts Children's Home 1970-71, Clifford Beers Child Guidance Center 1971-72; Certified Social Worker, New York, 1972; Academy of Certified Social Workers, National Association of Social Workers, 1974; Licensed Massage Therapist, State of Florida, 1981; Certified Marriage and Family Therapist, Florida, 1982; Certified Clinical Social Worker, Florida, 1982. Career: Investigator, Bronx Family Court, Support and Conciliation, Bronx, New York, 1967-68; Probation Officer Trainee, Bronx Family Court, Juvenile Team, 1968; Probation Officer Trainee, Bronx Criminal Court, 1968-70; Probation Officer, Bronx Criminal Court, 1970; Psychiatric Social Worker, Clifford Beers Child Guidance Center, New Haven, Connecticut, 1972-73; Instructor of Social Work in Psychiatry, Division of Child and Adolescent Psychiatry, Children's Mental Health Unit, Department of Psychiatry, University of Florida Medical School, Gainesville, 1973-79; Clinical Social Worker, Private Practice, 1979 to present. Organizational Memberships: National Association of Social Workers, National and Local Chapters (treasurer, Gainesville chapter, 1980 to present); Academy of Certified Social Workers; National Society for Autistic Children; Council on Social Work Education (voting member, 1978, 1979); American Orthopsychiatric Association; Arica Institute (certified apprentice instructor, 1978 to present); Florida Society for Clinical Social Workers; National Registry of Health Care Providers in Clincial Social Work; Health Resource Trainings and the School of T'ai Chi Chuan (advisory board, 1979 to present); Human Process Trainings (president, co-founder, 1980 to present); Mental Halth Association, Alachua County; American Association of Marriage and Family Therapists. Community Activities: City Commissioner Appointed Member, Crime Victim Relief Fund Review Committee, 1978 to present; Sophia's Creative Self

Development for Women (vice president and advisor, 1980-81). Academic Presentations: "Helping the Family: A Parent Speaks"; "The Changing Role of the Jewish Woman and Man", Others. Published Works: "Atypical Children: Perspectives on Parent-Professional Interaction". Honors and Awards: Listed in *Who's Who of American Women, Who's Who in the South and Southwest, World Who's Who of Women, Community Leaders and Noteworthy Americans.* Address: 6326 N.W. 18 Avenue, Gainesville, Florida 32605.

Suguitan, Carol Anne

Administrator. Personal: Born December 4, 1938; Daughter of Earl and Hazel Snoddy; Married Manuel G. Sugitan. Education: B.S., University of Arizona, 1960; Dietetic Internship, Massachusetts General Hospital, 1960-61; M.P.H., University of California-Berkeley, 1970. Career: Senior Research Dietitian, New York Hospital, New York City, 1961-64; Clinical Dietitian, Hammersmith Hospital, London, England, 1964-65; Nutritionist, New South Wales Department of Health, Sydney, Australia, 1966; Nutritionist, Maricopa County Health Department, Phoenix, Arizona, 1967-69; Dietetic Internship Director, Omaha, Nebraska; Regional Dietitian, Phoenix A.R.A. Services, 1971-74; Manager, National Health Care Accounts, Armour Food. Organizational Memberships: Omaha DT Association (president); Nebraska DT Association (president-elect); Mayors Task Force on Youth and Aging; Dietitians in Business and Industry (nominating committee); American Dietetic Association; Arizona Dietetic Association; American Home Economics Association; Arizona Home Economics Association; Society for Food Service Research; Home Economics in Business (nominating committee); American Society of Hospital Food Service Administration (nominating committee); American School Food Service Association; Society of Nutrition Education. Community Activities: Altrusa Club (vice president); Heard Museum Guild; Phoenix Art Museum; Maricopa County Hospital Auxiliary (public relations chairman, bylaws chairman, recording secretary). Honors and Awards: Alpha Lambda Delta; Omicron Nu; Listed in *Who's Who of American Women.* Address: 1036 East Orangewood, Phoenix, Arizona 85020.

Earl I Sullivan

Sullivan, Earl Iseman

Administrator. Personal: Born June 28, 1923; Son of Jesse Iseman and Birdie Melton Sullivan (both deceased). Education: B.A., English, Western Kentucky University, 1964; Graduate Study at Western Kentucky University, 1965. Military: Served in the United States Army, 1947-48. Career: Director, Army Education; Former Positions as Education Counselor and College Instructor. Organizational Memberships: Adult Education Association. Community Activities: Development of Military Career-Change Seminar for Pentagon, 1976-77; Metropolitan Organ Society of Washington, D.C. (vice president, 1976); Smithsonian Institution (volunteer information specialist, 1977-79); Little Colonel Theater, Louisville, Kentucky (assistant director, 1958-59); Junior Chamber of Commerce, Louisville (speaker's panel, 1957). Religion: Fourth Avenue Methodist Church, Louisville, Kentucky, 1957 to present. Honors and Awards: Meritorious Civilian Service Award for Outstanding Professional Contributions to the United States Army Education at the Pentagon, 1978; Outstanding Performance Awards, 1978-80; Awards for Poetry and Non-fiction, 1970-75; Listed in *Notable Americans, Men of Achievement, Personalities of the South, Dictionary of International Biography, Men and Women of Distinction, International Book of Honor, Personalities of America, Who's Who in the South and Southwest.* Address: 4 West Howell Avenue, Alexandria, Virginia 22301.

Edward J Sullivan

Sullivan, Edward Joseph

Electrotype Company Executive. Personal: Born May 17, 1915, in Concord, New Hampshire; Son of Edward J. and Ida Packard Sullivan; Married Dorothea M. Ash, September 30, 1944; Father of James Ash, Maureen Packard. Education: Attended St. Anslem's College, 1935-36. Military: Served in the United States Naval Reserve, 1942-46. Career: Treasurer 1950-55, President 1955 to present, Merrimack Electrotyping Corporation; Treasurer, Sheraton Properties Corporation, 1961 to present; Executive Vice President, Blanchard Press Corporation, 1968-69; President, Tridel Housing Developments, 1970 to present; President, Ho-Tei Corporation, St. Thomas, Virgin Islands; Director, Concord Federal Savings Bank; President, Allied Photo Engraving Corporation, 1964. Organizational Memberships: International Association of Electrotypers and Stereotypers Union; International Association of Electrotypers and Stereotypers Inc.; Aircraft Owners and Pilots Association; Printing Institute of America; One Hundred Club of New Hampshire. Community Activities: Concord Hospital Corporation; United States Commission on Civil Rights; Carmelite Monastery, Concord (chairman, building fund); Concord Housing Authority (citizens committee); Concord Urban Renewal Association (commissioner); Diocesan Bureau Housing Inc., Manchester (vice president, board of directors, 1975 to present); Carpenter Center, Inc., Manchester (board of directors); Concord Chapter, American Red Cross; Elks; Republican Party. Religion: Roman Catholic. Address: 99 Manor Road, Concord, New Hampshire 03301.

Swamy, Srikanta Mayasandra Nanjundiah

Professor of Electrical Engineering. Personal: Born April 7, 1935, in Bangalore, India; Son of M. K. Nanjudiah and M. N. Mahalakshamma; Married Leela Sitaramiah; Father of Saritha, Nikhilesh, Jagadish. Education: B.Sc. honors, University of Mysore, India, 1954; D.I.I.Sc., Indian Institute of Science, Bangalore, 1957; M.Sc. 1960, Ph.D. 1963, University of Saskatchewan, Canada. Career: Government of India Scientist, Indian Institute of Technology, Madras, 1963-65; Assistant Professor of Mathematics, University of Saskatchewan, 1964-65; Assistant, Associate and Professor of Electrical Engineering, Nova Scotia Technical College, Halifax, 1965-68; Professor of Electrical, Sir George Williams University, Montreal, 1968-69; Professor of Electrical Engineering, University of Calgary, 1969-70; Professor and Chairman of Electrical Engineering, Concordia University, Montreal, 1970-77; Dean of Engineering, Concordia University, 1977 to present. Organizational Memberships: Institute of Electrical and Electronics Engineers (fellow; vice president, circuits and systems society, 1976; program chairman, international symposium on circuit theory, Toronto, 1973); American Association of Engineering Education (director, mathematics sub-committee, 1973-75); Canadian Society for Electrical Engineering (chairman, publications council, 1981 to present); Engineering Institute of Canada (fellow); Institute of Electronics and Telecommunication Engineers, India (fellow); Institution of Engineers, India (fellow); American Biographical Institute Research Association (life fellow); International Biographical Association (life fellow); Eta Kappa Nu. Community Activities: International Student's Club, University of Saskatchewan (secretary, 1960; president, 1963); India-Canada Association, Saskatoon (general secretary, 1960; president, 1960); Bharatiya Sangeeta Sangam, Montreal (president, 1978-80). Published Works: Co-Author *Graphs, Networks and Algorithms,* 1981; Author/Co-Author over 100 Research Papers Published in Leading Technical Journals, including *I.E.E.E. Transactions on Circuit Theory, Proceedings of I.E.E.E., Journal of the Franklin Institute, Radio and Electronic Engineer; Alta Frequenza;* Editorial Board, *Fibonacci Quarterly;* Associate Editor, *Journal on Circuits, Systems and Signal Processing.* Honors and Awards: Listed in *Dictionary of International Biography, Two Thousand Men of Achievement, Who's Who in the West, I.B.A. Yearbook, International Register of Profiles, American Men and Woman of Science, International Who's Who of Intellectuals, Book of Honor, Registre Social du Canada.* Address: 275 Des Landes, St. Lambert, Ouebec, Canada J4S IV9.

Srikanta N S Swamy

Sween, Joyce Ann

Professor of Sociology. Personal: Born May 24, 1937; Daughter of Sigfried Ellmer (deceased); Mother of Terri Lynn, James Michael. Education: B.S., Mathematics, Antioch College, 1960; M.S. 1965, Ph.D. 1971, Northwestern University. Career: Professor of Sociology 1980 to present, Associate Professor of Sociology 1974-80, Assistant Professor 1971-74, DePaul University; Director of Computer Operations, Center for Metropolitan Studies, Northwestern University, 1965-69; Consultant and Evaluator for Bilingual Education Projects, Handicapped Effort, Reactions to Assassination, Employment Discrimination; Consulting Vice President, International Resource Development Corporation. Organizational Memberships: International Sociological Association; American Sociological Association; American Psychological Association; Scientific Research Society of North America, Sigma Xi; Sociologists for Women in Society; Southwestern Social Science Association; Midwest Society; Southern Sociological Society; American Association for the Advancement of Science. Community Activities: National Commission on the Causes and Prevention of Violence (consultant, 1968); National Science Foundation (peer review board, 1977); Response to Disaster (panelist, 1978); Evaluation of DePaul Communication Program, 1976. Published Works: Articles in Scientific Journals, 1969 to present. Honors and Awards: Research Grants, National Institute of Child Health and Development (to study childlessness and childbearing as they relate to careers of educated women) 1979 to present, National Science Foundation (evaluation of the science fellowship program) 1977 to present, National Institute of Health (co-investigator on familial lifestyles in urban Africa) 1971-75; University Fellowship, Northwestern University, 1960-63. Address: 1906 Holly Road, Highland Park, Illinois 60035.

Swerda, Patricia Fine

Teacher, Executive. Personal: Born August 10, 1916; Daughter of William (deceased) and Margaret Cull Fine; Married John Swerda; Mother of J. P. James, Susan A.S. Foss, Margaret R. S. Yovino. Education: Bachelor's Degree, cum laude, Texas Woman's University, 1941; Master's Ranking, Ikenobo University; (PhD Equivalent), Ikebana. Career: Teacher; President of Seattle N.W. Sakura Chapter, Ikenobo Ikebana Society. Organizational Memberships: Seattle Northwest Sakura Chapter of Ikenobo Ikebana Society (president 1965 to present); American Association of University Women; Seattle Chrysanthemum Society; Ikebana International; Seattle Rose Society; Bellevue-Yao Affiliation; Japan-America Society; Texas Woman's University Alumni Association; Texas Woman's University Regents Association (charter member). Community Activities: Represented Japanese People at Japan Pavilion, Expo 1970; Group Homes of Washington (secretary of board of directors, 1969-76); Grady Ladies, Base Hospital, Mildenhall, England, 1952-53; Assisted in War Relief, Vienna, Austria, 1946-47; Assisted Good Shepherd Movement, Kyoto, Japan, 1965-81. Religion: Roman Catholic; Worked with U.S. Catholic Charities in Vienna, England and Japan, 1941 to present. Honors and Awards: First Caucasian Woman Student at Ikenobo University, Tokyo, 1965; First Caucasian Woman Awarded Sokatoku Ranking of Highest Senior Professorship and Given the Golden Shears by Headmaster of Ikenobo, 1976. Address: 23025 N.E. 8th St, Redmond, Washington 98052.

Patricia Swerda

Swinger, Casimir Andrew

Ophthalmic Surgeon. Personal: Born December 3, 1940; Son of Mr. and Mrs. Swinger; Married Truyen; Father of Benjamin. Education: B.S.E.E., Illinois Institute of Technology, Chicago, 1962; M.D., University of California-San Diego, 1973. Career: Aerospace Engineer, 1962-66; Molecular Biologist, 1966-69; Ophthalmic Surgeon, Assistant Professor of Ophthalmology, Mt. Sinai School of Medicine, New York City. Organizational Memberships: International Society of Refractive Keratoplasty (scientific secretary, 1979 to present); American Medical Association; Pan American Society of Ophthalmology; Ophthalmologic Society of the United Kingdom; Association for Research in Vision and Ophthalmology; Contact Lens Association of Ophthalmologists; French Opthalmologic Society; Asia-Pacific Society of Ophthalmology; American College of Surgeons (fellow); American Academy of Ophthalmology (fellow). Community Activities: Project Orbis, 1982; Volunteer Ophthalmic Surgeon to India/Nepal, One Month Annually, 1976-82; Founder, Koregaon Park Eye Clinic, India, 1976; National Eye Institute Research Grant on Corneal Refractive Surgery, 1980-83. Honors and Awards: American Heart Association Fellow; A.A.M.C. Fellow to Israel, 1972; National Institutes of Health Fellow, 1969-73; Illinois State Scholar, 1958-62. Address: 10 Nathan D. Perlman Pl., New York, New York 10003.

Sywak, Zofia

Administrator. Personal: Born March 26, 1941. Education: B.A., Albertus Magnus College, 1964; M.A. 1966, Ph.D. 1975, St. John's University; Further Studies at Warsaw University (Warsaw, Poland) and American University (Washington, D.C.). Career: Assistant Registrar, Kean College of New Jersey; Director, Rhode Island Historical Records Survey; Archivist, Kelly Institute, St. Francis College; Archivist, New Haven, Colony Historical Society; Lecturer, Poznan University, Poznan, Poland; Lecturer, Warsaw University, Warsaw, Poland; Manager, New York Telephone Company; American Editor, *Paderewski*, 1980; Co-Author, *Poles in America: Bicentennial Essays*, 1978. Organizational Memberships: Society of American Archivists (status of women committee, 1980 to present); American Association for the Avancement of Slavic Studies; Association of Records Managers and Administrators (vice president, state chapter, 1981-82); New England Archivist; Polish Institute of Arts and Sciences in America. Community Activities: Rhode Island Ad Hoc Committee on Records, Gubernatorial Appointment, 1980 to 1982; New York Metropolitan Reference and Research Library Agency (archives task force, 1978-79); The Ukrainian Museum (board of trustees, 1979 to present); Rhode Island Historical Society (library committee, 1980 to 1982). Honors and Awards: International Research and Exchange Fellowship, Research Fellowship, Poland, 1977-78; Alfred Jurzykowski Grant, Hoover Institution, Stanford University, 1977; Kosciuszko Foundation Grant, Foreign Office, London, England, 1972; Polish Ministry of Higher Education Fellowship, Poland, 1968-70, 1972; Kosciuszko Foundation Travel Grant, 1968. Address: 888 Westfield Avenue, Elizabeth, New Jersey 07208.

Szegho, Emeric

Education: Attained a Licence at Law, University of Cernauti, Rumania, 1938; Doctor Juris Universi, University of Cluj, Rumania, 1947; Diploma as Attorney-at-Law, Rumanian Bar Association, Bucharest, 1941. Career: Founder, Center for International Security Studies of the American Security Council Education Foundation; Practicing Attorney-at-Law, 1941-60; Retired Professor, Alliance College, Cambridge Springs, Pennsylvania. Organizational Memberships: Emeritus Member, American Association of University Professors. Community Activities: National Advisory Board, American Security Council; Member, American Security Council Education Foundation (formerly the Institute for American Strategy); United States Senatorial Club (founding member); International Platform Association; International Biographical Association (fellow); American Biographical Institute (fellow); United States Congressional Advisory Board (state advisor); Member, Republican Presidential Task Force; United States Defense Committee. Religion: Member of the United Presbyterian Church, Cambridge Springs, Pennsylvania. Published Works: Author of Two Books, *Crime and Punishment, The Problem of Crime*, and *The Way of Life and the Crime*. Honors and Awards: Award of

Merit, United States Congressional Advisory Board; Honorary Appointment to the National Board of Advisors, American Biographical Institute; Special Recognition for the Cause of a Stronger America, American Security Council; Certificate of Leadership, Republican Party of Pennsylvania; Special Recognition Award, Center for International Security Studies; National Republican Victory Certificate; Certificate of Recognition, National Republican Congressional Committee; Special Recognition, National Security Educational Leadership, 1978; Award of Tenure, Alliance College, 1968; Listed in *International Who's Who of Community Service, International Who's Who of Intellectuals, International Register of Profiles, Men of Achievement, Dictionary of International Biography, Who's Who in North America, Notable Americans of the Bicentennial Era, Community Leaders of America, Notable Americans of 1978-79, Directory of Distinguished Americans, American Registry Series* (First Selected Edition), *Book of Honor, Hungarians in America, Personalities of America, Community Leaders and Noteworthy Americans, Men and Women of Distinction*. Address: 215 Ross Avenue, Cambridge Springs, Pennsylvania 19403.

Szekely, Deborah

Executive. Personal: Born May 3, 1922; Mother of Livia, Alex. Education: High School Graduate; Further Studies in New York, Tahiti, California. Career: Co-Founder, Rancho La Puerta; Founder/President, Golden Door, Inc. Organizational Memberships: President's Council on Physical Fitness and Sports, 1975-77; Fifth International Conference on Physical Fitness, Paris, France, 1977 (1 of 2 U.S. delegates). Community Activities: The Menninger Foundation (board of trustees, vice chairman for clinical services); Combined Arts and Education Council of San Diego County (founder, board of directors); Old Globe Theatre, San Diego (board of directors); University of California San Diego (board of overseers); San Diego Zoo Horticultural Committee; Travelers Aid Society (board of directors); Japanese Friendship Garden Association; California School of Professional Psychology (board of trustees). Honors and Awards: Honorary Doctor of Letters, California School of Professional Psychology, 1978; Volunteer of the Year, National Society of Fund-Raiser Executives, 1979; Charter 100/City Club Woman of the Year, 1979; 1 of 29 most influential people in San Diego, San Diego *Union*, 1 of 2 women included, 1977; Small Business Person of the Year, Small Business Administration, 1976. Address: 3232 Dove St., San Diego, California 92103.

T

Taffe, Betty Jo

State Legislator. Personal: Born November 19, 1942; Daughter of Elizabeth O. Miller; Married William J. Taffe; Mother of Daniel David, Michael Andrew. Education: B.A., Juniata College, 1964; M.A.T., University of Chicago, 1968. Career: State Legislator; High School Teacher; Dormitory Head Resident. Organizational Memberships: Education Commission of the States (New Hampshire commissioner, 1981 to present); National Council of State Legislatures (education committee, executive committee, 1981 to present). Community Activities: Lakes Region Mental Health Center (board member, 1979-81); Sceva Speare Hospital (board member, 1980 to present); New Hampshire School Boards Association (executive council, 1981 to present); Governor's Task Force on Handicapped Educational Services (appointed 1981); New Hampshire House of Representatives (member, 1976 to present; vice-chairman, house education committee, 1978 to present); Rumney School Board (member, 1974 to present; chairman, 1976-81, 1982-83); Grafton County Executive Committee (member, 1976 to present; clerk, 1978 to present). Address: Quincy Road, Rumney, New Hampshire 03266.

William F Taffee Jr

Taffee, William Frances Jr

Chemical and Environmental Engineer. Personal: Born May 22, 1922; Son of William Francis and Pearl Taffee (both deceased); Married Lois E. Luedders; Father of Kathleen, Patrick, Mary, Elizabeth. Education: Graduate of the Calhoun County Public Schools, Marshall, Michigan; B.S., M.S., Chemical Engineering, Michigan State University. Military: Served in the United States Army Air Corps in the China-Burma-India Theater, 1941-45, attaining the rank of Staff Sergeant. Career: Consulting Environmental Engineer; Chemical Engineer, Monsanto Company (Retired); Adjunct Assistant Professor in Chemical Engineering, Auburn University. Organizational Memberships: American Institute of Chemical Engineers. Community Activities: Boy Scouts and Cub Scouts of America (various posts, 1950-65); Girl Scouts of America (camp committee, 1972 to present); Civitan Club (board of directors 1952-57) 1970-75; Anniston Community Theater (board of directors, 1973 to 1982, stage band, technical director, actor); Jaycees; Registered Professional Engineer in Missouri and Alabama. Religion: Roman Catholic, Diocese of Birmingham, Permanent Ordained Deacon, 1975 to present; Knights of Columbus (state deputy, 1980 to 1982). Address: 1401 McCall Drive, Anniston, Alabama 36201.

Talley-Morris, Neva Bennett

Lawyer, Educator and Author. Personal: Born August 12, 1909; Daughter of John and Erma Bennett (both deceased); Widow. Education: Graduated Valedictorian of Judsonia High School, 1926; B.A. magna cum laude, Ouachita University, 1930; M.Ed., University of Texas, 1938; Postgraduate Education and Pre-Law, University of Texas, 1939-42. Military: Served in the United States Army Service Ordnance as Head Line Inspector, a Civil Service Wartime Appointment, 1942-46. Career: Lawyer, 1947 to present; Educator; Writer; Judge of Legal Essay Contests and Publications Organizational Memberships; World Association of Lawyers (founding member, 1973-82); American Bar Association (family law section chairman, 1969-70; house of delegates, 1970-74); National Association of Women Lawyers (president, 1956-57; life member; executive council); Arkansas Bar Association (house of delegates, 1974-78; desk book committee, chairman, 1981-82); American Academy of Matrimonial Lawyers (board of governors, 1974-80); Licensed Lawyer, All Arkansas Counties 1947 to present, United States Supreme Court 1950 to present, United States District Court of Eastern Arkansas 1947 to present. Community Activities: Arkansas Bar Foundation (hall of fellows, 1968 to present; founding fellow; board of directors, 1980-85; chairman, legal writers award committee, 1981-82); Special Committee for Arkansas Supreme Court (chairman, client security fund, 1980-82); North Little Rock Business and Professional Women (president, 1950-52; life member, Little Rock branch); American Association of University Women. Religion: Park Hill Baptist Church, Charter Member, 1946-50; Little Rock Second Baptist Church, 1950 to present. Honors and Awards: Delta Kappa Gamma, University of Texas Scholarship, 1938; Special Memberships Service Certificate 1979, Merit Award for Associate Judge of Writers Contest 1980-83, American Bar Association; Special Legal Service Award, Arkansas Bar Foundation, 1970; Annual Lawyer-Citizen Award, Arkansas Bar Association and Arkansas Bar Foundation, 1970; Special Service Award, National Association of Women Lawyers, 1961. Address: P.O. Box 67, Judsonia, Arkansas 72081.

Neva B Talley-Morris

Tan, Owen T

Professor of Electrical Engineering. Personal: Born August 30, 1931; Son of Mrs. Lan H. Tan; Married Martha G. Liem; Father of Joyce Yolanthe, Edward H., Cindy Liliane. Education: B.Sc. 1953, M.Sc. 1955, Electrical Engineering, Eindhoven University of Technology, The Netherlands; Full Professor, Associate Professor, and Assistant Professor of Electrical Engineering, Louisiana State Unviersity, Baton Rouge, Louisiana, 1966 to present; Senior Lecturer, Lecturer in Electrical Engineering, Bandung Institute of Technology, Idonesia, 1962-66; Research and Development Engineer, Smit-Slikkerveer, Rotterdam, The Netherlands, 1956-62. Organizational Memberships: Institute of Electrical and Electronic Engineers; Royal Institute of Engineers, Holland; Eta Kappa Nu. Honors and Awards: I.E.E.E.-I.A.S. Prize Paper Award, 1981; Research Fellowship, Eindhoven University of Technology, The Netherlands, 1977; Research Fellowship, Siemens Schuckert, West Germany, 1962. Address: 649 Rodney Dreive, Baton Rouge, Louisiana 70808.

Tang, Setwin

Acupuncturist, Herbologist. Personal: Born August 8, 1905; Married Yuet-Sim L. Tang; Father of Calvin K.S., Calmond. Education: Graduate of Traditional Chinese Medicine Institute, Kwungtung, China, 1920; Chinese Medical Institute, Hong Kong; Chinese Acupuncture Research Institute, Hong Kong; Ryodoraku Research Institute, Tokyo, Japan. Career: Proprietor and Manager, Tung Chun Tong Company, 1926 to present. Organizational Memberships: American Association of Acupuncture and Oriental Medicine, 1981 to present; Hawaii State Board of Acupuncture (appointed as member by Governor George R. Ariyoshi, 1974; first chairperson,

1974); Acupuncture Association of Hawaii (founder, president, 1974 to present); Center for Chinese Medicine, California; The Hong Kong Acupuncturists Federation; Japan Ryodoraku Autonomic Nerve Society; Cultural Center of Chinese Medicine, Hong Kong (honorary president); International General Chinese Herbalists and Medicine Professionals Associaton, Hong Kong (honorary president); Chinese Acupuncture Association, Taipei, Taiwan (advisor); Chinese Acupuncture Research Institute, Hong Kong (honorary member, board of directors). Community Activities: United Chinese Educational Association (president, 1960-64); Chinese Labor Association (president, 1960-64); United Chinese Society (trustee, 1960-63); Chamber of Commerce of Hawaii, 1940 to present. Religion: Founder and President, Hawaii Chinese Buddhist Society, 1955-64; President, See Yup Benevolent Society, 1956-62; President, Yee Yi Tong Benevolent Society, 1952-58. Honors and Awards: Certificate of Appreciation for Services as Chairman of the Board of Acupuncture, Governor of the State of Hawaii, 1978; Certificate of Inclusion, *International Who's Who of Intellectuals;* Outstanding Achievement Award, Marquis *Who's Who* Publication Board, 1976-77; Certificate of Appreciation, Ala Moana Lions Club, for Valuable Services and Cooperation Extended to the Lions Club, 1977; Certificate of Appreciation for Serving as Guest Speaker and for Other Courtesies Extended to the Lions Club, Honolulu Chinatown Lions Club, 1979; Aloha Award for Display of Instruments, Equipment and Techniques used in Acupuncture, Hawaii State Library System, 1975; Listed in *Who's Who in the West, International Who's Who of Intellectuals.* Address: 3030 Pacific Heights Road, Honolulu, Hawaii 96813.

Tannenbaum, Bernice Salpeter

Bernice Tannenbaum

Chairman of American Section of World Zionist Organization; National Chairman of Hadassah Medical Organization. Personal: Daughter of May and Isidore Franklin; Married Nathan Tannenbaum; Mother of Richard Salpeter. Education: B.A., Brooklyn College. Career: National Chairman, Hadassah Medical Organization, 1980 to present; Hadassah, National President 1976-80, National Vice-President 1968-72, National Secretary 1964-68, Chairman of Press/Radio/Television Department 1961-64, National Chairman of Junior Hadassah 1957-60, President of Long Island Region of Hadassah 1954-57, National Youth Aliyah Chairman 1968-72, National Membership Chairman 1964-68, Co-Chairman of Hadassah National Conventions 1961, 1962. Organizational Memberships: National Conference on Soviet Jewry (executive board, 1978 to present); American-Israel Public Affairs Committee (vice-president; member, 1978 to present); World Zionist Organization (chairman of American section, 1982 to present); World Jewish Congress (American section, executive board, 1971 to present; governing board, 1976); General Assembly of Jewish Agency (executive board, 1971 to present); World Confederation of United Zionists (co-president); First Mid-Winter Conference in Israel (chairman, 1963); Hadassah Medical Organization (chairman, fund raising, 1975-76); Hebrew University (governing board, 1976 to present); Long Island Women's Division of State of Israel Bonds (chairman, 1957-58); Queens Women's Division of United Jewish Appeal (chairman, 1959-60); United Israel Appeal Board, 1972 to present. Published Works: Co-Editor, *The Hadassah Idea;* Contributor of Monthly Articles to "President's Column", *Hadassah* Magazine. Honors and Awards: Henrietta Szold Award, Queens Region, 1981; Myrtle Wreath Award, New York Chapter 1980, Orange County and Long Beach Chapters 1980, Westchester Region 1979, Lower New York State Region 1979, Brooklyn Region 1979, Suffolk Region 1979, Southern New Jersey Region 1978, Nassau Region 1977, Eastern Pennsylvania Region 1976, Upper New York State Region 1975, Queens Region 1974; Negev Award, State of Israel Bonds, 1980; Citizen's Award, New England Region, 1979; Woman of the Year Award, Kew Gardens Chapter; Fellow of the Year, Hadassah Speakers Bureau. Address: Hadassah, 50 West 58th Street, New York, New York 10021.

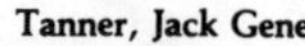

Tanner, Jack Gene

Company Executive. Personal: Born 1940; Son of Ira John and Arlene Harper Tanner; Married June Rita Tanner; Father of Craig Andrew, Vanessa Lundy. Education: LL.B. 1965, B.B.A. 1967, LaSalle University; National Law Enforcement Academy, 1973; International Academy of Criminology, 1976; B.S., Saint John's University; M.B.A., The College of Insurance, 1981. Military: Served in the United States Marine Corp and United States Naval Reserve. Career: Assistant Vice-President, Crum and Forster Insurance Companies; Claims Manager, Home Insurance Company; Vice-President, Intelligence Services, Inc.; Special Agent, INTERPOL. Organizational Memberships: American Bar Association; American Management Association; Excess Bond Reinsurance Association. Community Activities: New York City Auxiliary Police Force (sergeant, 1970-76). Religion: The Church of Jesus Christ of Latter-Day Saints. Address: 14 High Ridge Road, Long Valley, New Jersey 07853.

Jack G Tanner

Tanzmann, Virginia

Architectural Firm Proprietor. Education: B.A. School of Architecture 1968, B.Arch. Graduate School of Architecture 1969, Syracuse University. Career: Proprietor, The Tanzmann Associates, 1978 to present; Staff Architect, Southern California Rapid Transit District, 1975-78; Project Architect, SUA, Inc., 1974-75; Project Architect, Daniel L. Dworsky, F.A.I.A., 1972-74; Intern Architect, Burke Kober Nicolais Archuleta, 1969-72; Exhibits in Monterey Design Conference 1981, Los Angeles 1979, Seattle 1979, Paris, France 178, Los Angeles 1978, Ramsar, Iran 1976. Organizational Memberships: American Institute of Architects (chairman, National Task Force on Women in Architecture, 1978-80; board of directors, Los Angeles chapter, 1980-82); Association of Women in Architecture (Los Angeles chapter board of directors; past president); Architectural Guild (board of directors); L'Union Internationale des Femmes Architectes. Community Activities: Volunteer Center of Los Angeles (board of directors; vice-president); Young Women's Christian Association of Los Angeles (board of directors; chair, facilities committee); Mayor's Advisory Council on Voluntarism; United Way (building plans and sites committee); Frequent Speaker at Schools, Community Groups and Professional Groups. Honors and Awards: California Women in Government Certificate of Achievement Award; Achievement Award of the Soroptimist Club of Los Angeles; Architectural Award for Victory Park Recreation Center; Outstanding Young Women of America; Listed in Numerous Biographical Reference Publications. Address: The Tanzmann Associates, The Bradbury Building, 304 South Broadway, Los Angeles, California 90013.

Tautenhahn, Gunther

Composer. Personal: Born December 22, 1938. Education: Studied Composition, New York. Career: Composer; Author; Conductor; Inventor of Clockface Whereby a Child can Learn to Tell Note Values and Time. Organizational Memberships: American Society of Composers, Authors and Publishers; A.S.U.C.; N.A.C.U.S.A.; I.C.A.; A.M.C. Published Works: Author of *The Importance of One* 1972, *Controlled Expressionism* 1976, *Fiber Movements* 1978; Composer of *Numeric Serenade, Brass Quintet, Concerto for D-Brass and Orchestra, Double Concerto for French Horn and Trumpet with Orchestra,* Others. Honors and Awards: Listed in *Who's Who in Music, Who's Who in California, Who's Who in the West, Who's Who in America, Who's Who of Intellectuals, A.S.C.A.P. Directory and Symphony Catalog, A.M.C. Catalog, Chamber Music Catalog, Directory of New Music, Contemporary American Composers, Men of Achievement, International Register of Profiles, Dictionary of International Biography.* Address: 1534 3rd Street, Manhattan Beach, California 90266.

Taylor, Dolly Barron

Teacher Personal: Born July 21, 1941; Daughter of Mrs. and Mrs. Joseph Thomas Barron (deceased); Married John G. Taylor, Jr.; Mother of Kathryn McNell. Education: Graduate of Ralph L. Fike Senior High School, 1959; A.B. Spanish, Atlantic Christian College, 1962; A.B. English, East Carolina. Career: Teacher. Community Activities: Wilson Junior Women's Club (president, 1973-74; secretary, 1971-72); Wilson County Heart Association (city chairman, Heart Month, 1979); Wilson Evening Optimist Club Oratorical Contests (judge); Girl Scouts of America (volunteer, day camp activities and overnight camping outings); Crisis Center (volunteer). Religion: Methodist Church; Secretary, Administrative Board and Council on Ministries; Vacation Bible School Programs Volunteer. Honors and Awards: National Honor Society, Fike High School, 1959; Senior Spanish Award, Fike High School, 1959; President, Sigma Pi Alpha Honorary Language Fraternity, Atlantic Christian College, 1962; Wilson County Heart Association Founders Award, 1979. Address: 1407 Cherry Lane, Wilson, North Carolina 27893.

Taylor, Ernest Austin Jr

Electrical Engineer. Personal: Born January 18, 1918; Son of Ernest A. Taylor, Sr. (deceased) and Alma Robinson; Married Charleen Morgan; Father of Rachel Alma T. Clay, Charles Ernest. Education: B.S.E.E., Georgia Institute of Technology, Atlanta, Georgia. Military: Served in the United States Navy, 1943-45, as Chief Electrician's Mate, serving on repair ships in four invasions in the Pacific Theater. Career: Senior Specialist in Electrical Engineering, Monsanto Company, Decatur, Alabama, 1956-82; Electrical Engineer, Electrical Equipment Company, Augusta, Georgia, 1951-52; Electrical Engineer, Patchen and Zimmerman, Augusta, Georgia, 1952-56; Electrical Engineer, Phillips Petroleum Company, Bartlesville, Oklahoma, 1948-51. Organizational Memberships: National Society of Professional Engineers; Alabama Society of Professional Engineers; Fluid Power Society. Community Activities: International Bible College, Florence, Alabama (member and secretary, board of directors, 1972 to present); City of Decatur (secretary, bicycle committee, 1974). Religion: Hatton Church of Christ, Town Creek, Alabama, Education Director, 1974 to present; Beech Street Church of Christ, Education Director, 1972-74; Memorial Drive Church of Christ, Elder and Educational Director, 1964-72; Austinville Church of Christ, Decatur, Georgia, Education Director, 1958-64. Published Works: Numerous Proprietary Reports, Monsanto Company; "Thrusts of Free and Submerged Jets", Fluidic State-of-the-Art Symposium, Harry Diamond Laboratories, Washington, D.C., 1974. Honors and Awards: Norbett P. No-No Fellowship Award, 1972; Holder of 18 United States Patents and Numerous Foreign Patents. Address: 2202 Cleveland Avenue Southwest, Decatur, Alabama 35601.

Ernest A Taylor Jr

Taylor, Estelle Wormley

Professor and Chairman, Department of English. Personal: Born January 12, 1924; Daughter of Luther and Wilhelmina Wormley (both deceased); Married Ivan Earle Taylor. Education: B.S., Teachers College, 1945; M.A., Howard University, 1947; Ph.D., The Catholic University of America, 1969. Career: Howard University, Professor and Chairman, Department of English 1976 to present, Instructor in English and Humanities 1947-52; District of Columbia Teachers College, Acting Dean 1975-76, Instructor of English to Professor of English 1963-76; Associate Provost, Federal City College, 1974-76; Teacher of English, Eastern Senior High School, 1955-63; Teacher of English, Langley Junior High School, 1952-55. Organizational Memberships: College Language Association National Association of Teachers of English; Modern Language Association of America; Shakespeare Association of America; American Association for the Advancement of Humanities; Association of Governing Boards. Community Activities: University of the District of Columbia (board of trustees, 1979-83); District of Columbia Teachers College/Federal City College Board of Higher Education, 1974-75; Cromwell Academy (board of directors, 1973-75); Folger Shakespeare Library (felowships selection committee, member 1974-76, chairman 1976-77); Capital City Chapter of Links, Inc. (immediate past vice-president); National Endowment for the Humanities (panelist/evaluator); Middle States Evaluation Team (evaluator); Commission on Higher Education (reviewer/evaluator, 1982). Honors and Awards: Southern Fellowships Award, 1968-69; Outstanding Teacher of America Award, 1973; Rockefeller/Aspen Institute Fellow, 1978-79; Outstanding Teacher Award, College of Liberal Arts, Howard University, 1980; Outstanding Leadership, Service and Contribution to Excellence in Education, Kappa Delta Pi, Theta Alpha Chapter, Howard University Education Award, 1979; outstanding Service to College Community, District of Columbia Teachers College, 1976; Central Executive Committee, Folger Institute of Renaissance and Eighteenth-Century Studies, 1982-83. Address: 3221 - 20th Street N.E., Washington, D.C. 20018.

Taylor, John Calvin

Dentist, Evangelist, Author. Personal: Born July 22, 1914; Son of John Calvin V. and Elizabeth Siehl Taylor (both deceased); Married Adah B. Taylor; Father of Sarah Elizabeth, Margaret Louise, Virginia Alden, John Calvin VII, Frederick Christian, Adah Alison, Carla Susan. Education: B.S., Muskingum College, Ohio, 1937; B.D., Reformed Presbyterian Theological Seminary, Cedarville, Ohio, 1939; Certificate, Landour Language School, Mussoori, India, 1941; Certificate, Henry Martin School of Islamics, Mussoorie, India, 1941; Diploma, Northwestern School of Taxidermy, 1952; Diploma, Academy of General Dentistry, 1975; Medical College of Virginia School of Dentistry, Richmond, Virginia, 1945-46; D.D.S., University of Pittsburgh School of Dentistry, Pittsburgh, Pennsylvania, 1949. Career: Dentist, Evangelist, Author, and Member of 3 Foreign Mission Boards; Missionary, First Appointed under Denominational Salary then Pauline Type, Professionally Self-Supported; Ordained Minister of the Gospel; Pastored Several Congregations; Farmer; Carpenter; House Painter; Fence Builder; Big-Game Hunting Guide and Outfitter; Taxidermist; Photographer; Protector and Tamer of Wildlife for Parks; Missionary Dentist, Inc., Asian Representative since 1953. Organizational Memberships: Reformed Presbyterian Mission, India (missionary evangelist and superintendent, 1940-45); Reformed Presbyterian Denomination Home Mission Board (superintendent, 1947-52); Dental Clinic of Methodist Mission Hospital, Bariely, India (director, 1954-55); Dental Clinic of Landour Community Hospital (founder and director, 1955-59); American Dental Association, 1949 to present; Academy of General Dentistry, Johnsonburgh, Pennsylvania, 1964-69; Oral Clinic Center, Dera Dun, India (builder and founder, 1980). Community Activities: Rotary Club, Mount Union, Pennsylvania (president, 1960-64); Speaker to Civic and Religious Groups such as Rotarians, Lion's Clubs, Sportsmen and Dental Societies; Missionary Helper of Medical Missionary Parents and Registered Nurse Wife's Dispensary, 1940-45; Stated Supply Pastor, Fairview Church, Industry, Pennsylvania, 1946-47; Wildlife Preservation Society of India (organizing and life member, 1954 to present); Teacher of Emergency Dentistry at Vellore Medical College, 1958; E.L.W.A. Hospital Dental Clinic, Monrovia, Liberia, Africa (establisher, 1977); Worldwide Brotherhood Exchange Representative to Shanta Bhawan Hospital, Nepal; General Synod of the R.P.E.S. Denomination (active advisory member); Key Commissioner to Negotiate Indian Presbyteries to Form a Synod in India; Oral Clinic Center, Dera Dun, India (builder and founder, 1978-80); Overseas Training Seminars (teacher for missionary dentist, Inc.) Mexico, 1981; United States Congress and White House (advisor on crucial issues); Religion: Hindu, Moselem, and Christian Debate Participant, 1927-30, 1940-41; Student Volunteer Movement Activity, Muskingum College, 1933-37; Deputation Speaking to Many Churches, East to West Coasts, 1937-40; Preacher and Evangelist and Interpreter; Ordained in the Western Presbytery of Reformed Presbyterians 1939; Member, Monogalela Presbytery of United Presbyterian Denominations, Reordained, 1953. Published Works: *Wildlife in India's Tiger Kingdom*, 1981.

Honors and Awards: Athlete of the Year, Woodstock High School, 1931; 4-Letter Man, Muskingum College Sports, 1933-37; Several Medals, M Sweater and M Blanket; Winner, International Deck Tennis Tennis Singles Match with Prize, 1953; Past President Diamond-Studded Medallion, Mt. Union Rotary Club, 1965; Lecturer's Award for Serving 7th District Rotary Club International Biographical Association; Listed in *Who's Who in the East, Who's Who in North America, Dictionary of International Biography, Men of Achievement, Reformed Presbyterian Archives, International Who's Who of Intellectuals, Personalities of America, The American Registry Series, International Register of Profiles.* Address: 110 Highland Avenue, Herminie, Pennsylvania 15637.

Taylor, John Michael

Director of Public Utilities/City Engineer. Personal: Born August 25, 1950; Son of Mr. and Mrs. J. M. Taylor; Married Judy Ann Harless. Education: A.A.S., Civil Engineering, Guilford Technical Institute, Jamestown, North Carolina, 1971; B.S., Public Administration, 1981; Post-graduate Studies, North Carolina State University, University of North Carolina and U.G.C.C. Career: General Manager, Kerr Lake Regional Water System and Director of Public Utilities and Engineering, City of Henderson, North Carolina, 1980 to present; Civil Engineer 1978-80, Assistant to County Engineer, New Hanover City, Wilmington, North Carolina; Construction Superintendent, P. J. Coble Construction Company, Burlington, North Carolina, 1977; Construction Superintendent, Beamans Projects, Greensboro, North Carolina, 1976; Project Engineer, Davis, Martin and Powell Associates, 1972-76; Civil Engineering Technician, North Carolina Department of Transportation, 1970-72. Organizational Memberships: North Carolina Water Works Association; North Carolina Water Pollution Control Association; American Water Works Association; American Public Works Association; Solid Waste Management Association. Community Activities: North Carolina Beach Buggy Association; Boy Scouts of America (assistant leader, 1963-65). Religion: Protestant. Honors and Awards: Finalist, Rolex Awards for Enterprise, Work on Solid Waste Disposal, New Hanover County Commissioners, Newspapers and Radio Stations, 1980; Listed in *Personalities of the South, Book of Honor, Community Leaders of America, Who's Who in the South and Southwest, Directory of Distinguished Americans, Men of Achievement.* Address: 203 North College Street, Henderson, North Carolina 27536.

Taylor, Lisa

Museum Director. Personal: Born January 8, 1933; Daughter of Theo von Berger-Maier and Martina Weincerl (both deceased); Married Bertrand L. Taylor III; Mother of Lauren, Lindsay. Education: Attended Johns Hopkins University, 1956-58; Georgetown University, 1958-62; Corcoran School of Art, Washington, D.C., 1958-65; Private Studies in Painting, Pottery, Weaving, Photography, Film-Making. Career: Director, Cooper-Hewitt Museum, the Smithsonian Institution's National Museum of Design, New York, 1969 to present; Program Director, Smithsonian Institution, Washington, 1966-69; Membership Director, Corcoran Gallery, Washington, D.C., 1962-66; Administrative Assistant, President's Fine Arts Committee, Washington, D.C., 1958-62; Part-Time Program Advisor, Johns Hopkins University Young Men's Christian Association, Baltimore, Maryland, 1956-58. Organizational Memberships: National Council for Interior Design (member, qualifications board); Center for Holographic Arts (board member); Living Stage (board member); American Society of Interior Designers (honorary member); Smithsonian Institution (honorary life member). Community Activities: National Endowment for the Arts (museum panel, 1972-75); Bank Street College, New York (visiting committee); Fashion Institute of Technology, New York (visiting committee); University of Cincinnati (advisor); Friends of the Scottish Opera (board member); Municiapl Arts Society; Architectural League; I.C.P.; American Institute of Archtects (honorary member). Published Works: Editor, *Urban Open Spaces and Cities.* Honors and Awards: Trailblazer of the Year Award, Nominee 1977, Winner 1981; Nominee, Woman of the Year, 1977; Smithsonian Women's Council Award, 1979; Bronze Apple Award, 1977; Thomas Jefferson Award, 1976; Bronze Plaque, Johns Hopkins University Young Men's Christian Association, 1958; American Legion Medal of Honor, 1948; Smithsonian Institution Exceptional Service Award, 1969; Listed in *Who's Who in the World, International Who's Who of Intellectuals, Who's Who in America, Who's Who in Art, Who's Who in Government.* Address: 1115 Fifth Avenue, New York, New York 10028.

Taylor, Otrie Lee

Intake Counselor (Retired). Personal: Born May 22, 1907; Daughter of Alfred and Estella Edwards (both deceased); Married Theodore R. Taylor (deceased); Mother of Theodore R., Joane, E.T. Reasonover, Robert, Bettye T. Edwards. Education: Graduate of Waxahachie High School, Texas, 1924; B.S., Bishop College, Marshall, Dallas, Texas, 1928; Graduate Work, Los Angeles State College, 1949-50; Principles of Management, 1970. Career: Intake Counselor, State of California, 1966-74; Clerk and Consumer Aide, 1964-66; Co-Owner with Husband, Variety Store, 1940-64; Teacher, 1928-34. Community Activities: Parent-Teacher Association (president, 1942-44, 1948-50; honorary life member, 1950 to present); Adult Day Health Commission, Appointed by Kenneth Hahn, Supervisor of 2nd District of Los Angeles; Southern California Gas Company (advisory panel); United Way (agency relations committee); National Consumer Advisory Council (appointed by President Lyndon B. Johnson, 1967-69). Religion: Neighborhood Community Church, Member, 1944 to present; Assistant Superintendent of Sunday School, 12 years; Local and State Member, Church Women United. Honors and Awards: Bishop College Alumni Hall of Fame, 1981; Mayors Office, Councilman of 9th District, 1974; National Association of University Women, 1978; Gold Triangle Award, Young Women's Christian Association, 1973; Club 100, Young Women's Christian Association; Many Awards and Plaques Presented upon Retirement, 1974. Address: 211 West 51st Street, Los Angeles, California 90037.

Taylor, Stephen Lee

Attorney at Law. Personal: Born September 26, 1947; Son of Melfred E. and Margaret L. Taylor; Married Patricia Ann Smith; Father of Justin Patrick, Garrett Stephen. Education: B.A., Southeast Missouri University, 1969; J.D., Missouri University, 1972. Military: Served with the United States Army Reserve, 1972-80, achieving the rank of Captain. Career: Attorney at Law, Prosecuting Attorneys Office. Organizational Memberships: Missouri Bar Association; American Bar Association; Scott County Bar Association; Missouri Trial Lawyers Association. Community Activities: Scott County Young Democrats (president, 1974-75); Missouri Young Democrats (president, 1976-77); Missouri Democratic Executive Committee, 1976-77; Young Democrats of America (executive committee, 1975); Missouri Democratic Committee (state committeeman, 27th senatorial district, 1978-81); Jaycee Bootheel Rodeo Association (president); Scott County Cancer Drive (chairman). Honors and Awards: Outstanding Service Award, Young Democrats, 1976; Outstanding Jaycee, 1974; Jaycee of the Year, 1977; Distinguished Service Award, U.S. Jaycees, 1978; H. F. "Pat" Patterson Award, Missouri Young Democrats, 1978; Missouri Statesman, 1980; Order of Kentucky Colonel, 1977-81. Address: 801 Vernon, Sikeston, Missouri 63801.

Taylor, Timothy Davies

Psychologist. Personal: Born January 25, 1943; Son of Tom Taylor, Sr. Education: B.A. Education, Central University, 1968; M.Ed.,

University of Puget Sound, 1975; Ph.D. Psychology, United States International University, 1980. Military: Served in the United States Army to E-5, 1968-74. Career: Private Practice Psychologist; Counselor, Family Counseling Service; Insurance Broker, Tom Taylor Insurance Brokers. Community Activities: Pierce County March of Dimes (chairman, 1980-81); West Tacoma Optimist Club (president, 1976-77); Young Men's Christian Association (fund raising captain); United Way of Pierce County (associate chairman, 1981 and 1982). Honors and Awards: Optimist of the Year, 1977; Listed in *Outstanding Young Men of America, Who's Who in the West, Men of Achievement, Book of Honor.* Address: 4416 West 27th, Tacoma, Washington 98407.

Taymor, Betty

Director of College Program. Personal: Born March 22, 1921; Married; Mother of Michael, Laure, Julie. Education: B.A., Goucher College, 1942; M.A., Boston University, 1957. Career: Director, "Program for Women in Political and Governmental Careers," Boston College, 1973 to present; Instructor, Metropolitan College, "Master in Urban Affairs", Boston University, 1973-74; Consultant, Office of the President, University of Massachusetts, 1973-74; Instructor in Government, Northeastern University, 1969-71; Lecturer and Field Work Supervisor, "Program for Women in Political and Administrative Service", Simmons College, 1968-69. Organizational Memberships: Democratic National Committee, 1976-84; Democratic State Committee, 1956-84. Community Activities: John F. Kennedy Library Consortium, 1976; Democratic National Convention (delegate-at-large, 1976; Leader of minority peace plank report in delegation, 1968; secretary, Democratic rules committee, 1964; Massachusetts delegate-at-large, 1960, 1964); Governor's Commission on the Status of Women, 1975; Democratic National Charter Commission, 1973-74; Massachusetts Women's Political Caucus (steering committee, 1972); Americans for Democratic Action (vice-chairman, 1971; executive vice-chairman, 1954-56); Newton Coalition for New Politics (steering committee, 1970 to present); Massachusetts Democratic State Reform Committee on Party Organization (co-chairman, 1970-72); Newton Campaign Coordinator for Robert Drinan for Congress 1970, Senator Edward M. Kennedy 1962-64, Senator John F. Kennedy 1958, Stevenson for President Committee 1956; National Platform Committee, 1960-68; Massachusetts Dollars for Democrats Campaign (chairman, 1960); United States National Commission for United Nations Educational, Science and Cultural Organization, 1960-66; Massachusetts Democratic State Committee (vice-chairperson, 1956-68); Massachusetts State Democratic Convention (delegate, 1954-72). Honors and Awards: Elizabeth King Elliocott Fellow, Goucher College, 1959. Address: 14 Eliot Memorial Road, Newton, Massachusetts 02158.

Tazelaar, Edwin Joseph II

Sales Representative. Personal: Born June 16, 1947; Son of Edwin and Nancy Tazelaar Sr.; Married to Mary Anne Marnul on July 3, 1982; Father of Bradley James, Marcus Thomas, Edwin Joseph; Stepfather of Brian Thomas, Bradley Louis Siok. Education: Graduate of Palatine High School, 1965; Graduate, Northwest Police Academy, 1970; Harper College, Palatine, Illinois. Military: Served in the United States Army, 1966-68; Served with the 1st Infantry Division in Vietnam, 1967. Career: Sales Representative, A.L. Williams Company; Associate, American Family Life Assurance; Former Police Offier, Village of Hoffman Estates, Illinois; Former Manager, Robert Hall Clothes. Organizational Memberships: American Family Life Assurance's President's Club, 1977-82. Community Activities: International Platform Association; American Family Political Action Committee; Member of the American Legion. Religion: Roman Catholic. Honors and Awards: American Family Life Assurance Company, Fast Start and Fireball Awards 1977, Quarter Million Dollar Club, 1980; Numerous Other Sales Awards 1977-81; Listed in *Who's Who in the World, Who's Who in Finance and Industry, Who's Who in the Midwest, Personalities of America.* Address: 1345 Somerset, Deerfield, Illinois 60015.

Donald M Telford

Telford, Donald McCrea

College Mathematics Instructor. Personal: Born June 22, 1903 in Mt. Ida, Kansas; Married; Father of Diane T. Biscoglia, Dr. Janet Telford. Education: B.S., Kansas State University, Manhattan, 1930; M.S., East Tennessee State University, Johnson City, 1971. Military: Served in the United States Army as a Corporal 1918-19, reentered the Army as a Private in 1942 and rose to the rank of Lieutenant Colonel; Retired from the Army in 1961. Career: Retired Army Officer; College Mathematics Instructor; Football, Basketball, Track and Boxing Coach; Professional Baseball Umpire; Professional Boxer. Organizational Memberships: Retired Officers Association (life member, 1948 to present; chairman, resolution committee of European Department, 1954); Disabled American Veterans (life member, 1962 to present). Community Activities: Math Tutor, 1961 to present; Teenagers Club Manager, 1957-61; Volunteer Work with Teenagers, 1952-56. Religion: Roman Catholic. Published Works: "Correlation of Grades Made at Junior College vs. Senior Colleges"; "Why Some People are Alcoholics"; "The Effect of Tobacco Smoke on the Non-Smoker"; "A Teaching Guide to Chemical, Biological and Radiological Warfare" and Other Publications. Honors and Awards: Spotlight Teacher of the Year, Gordon Military College, 1964; Army Citations for Teenager Worker, 1961, 1953; United States Army Commendation Medal with Oak Leaf Clusters for Work as Researcher and Teacher of Chemical, Biological and Radiological Warfare, 1945, 1961; Outstanding Alumni Nominee, Kansas State University, 1977; Citation from President of Georgia Military College for Work as Math Teacher, 1977; Citation from Thomas County Community College, Thomasville, Georgia, for Work as a Math Teacher and Head of Math Department; Citation, University of Maryland as Teacher of Mathematics, 1954; Citation for Scoring in Upper 1% of All Chemical Corps Officers on Comprehensive Tests, Given by Research Organizations and the Chemical Corps United States Army, Research Organization. Address: 2952 Adrain Avenue, Largo, Florida 33540.

Temes, Clifford L

Head of Search Radar Branch, Naval Research Laboratory. Personal: Born February 4, 1930; Son of Dr. Julius H. Temes (deceased); Married Vivian L. Newman; Father of David, Lisa, Joel. Education: B.E.E., Cooper Union, 1951; M.S.E.E., Case Institute of Technology, 1954; E.E., Columbia, 1960; Ph.D., Polytechnic Institute of Brooklyn, 1965. Military: Served in the United States Army to SP-3, 1954-56. Career: Head, Search Radar Branch, Naval Research Laboratory, 1977 to present; Department Staff, Mitre Corporation, 1974-77; Technical Staff, General Research Corporation, 1965-74; Senior Project Engineer, Federal Scientific Corporation, 1960-65; Laboratory Supervisor, Columbia University Electronics Research Laboratory, 1956-60. Organizational Memberships: Institute of Electrical and Electronic Engineers (senior member; chairman, professional activities committee, 1977); Sigma Xi Honor Society. Community Activities: Cooper Union Student Council (president, 1951); Columbia University Electronics Research Laboratory (consultant, 1960-65); Institute of Electrical and Electronic Engineers (reviewer, 1960-74); Prentice-Hall (reviewer, 1968-69). Published Works: 10 Published Papers, 1954 to present. Honors and Awards; Sigma Xi Honor Society, 1954 to present; Quality Award, Naval Research Laboratory.

Tempero, Sue Ann

Employee Relations Director, *Des Moines Register.* Personal: Born May 11, 1939; Daughter of Chester and Helen Carkoski; Married

Richard M. Tempero; Mother of Catherine Marie, Howard Chester. Education: B.S., University of Nebraska, 1961; M.A., Northwestern University, Evanston, Illinois, 1965; 1-Year Grant to East-West Center, Honolulu, Hawaii, 1968-69; Many C.E.U.'s for Continuing Education Courses. Career: Assistant Personnel Manager and Instructor, Drake University College of Continuing Education, 1979 to present; Chief of Volunteers and Grants Coordination, Iowa Refugee Service, 1979; Staff, Committee for Re-Election of Governor Ray, Des Moines, Iowa, 1978; Education Specialist, United States Congressman Charles Thone, 1973-77; Instructor of Experimental College, Mankato State University, Minnesota; Program Specialist, Institute of International Education, Chicago, Illinois, 1967-68; Assistant Dean of Women, University of Chicago, 1965-67; Assistant to Dean of Women, Washington State University, 1962-64. Organizational Memberships: American Society of Personnel Administrators; American Society of Training and Development (program committee); Private Industry Council of Des Moines (vice-chairperson); Des Moines Merit Employers Council; Downtown Des Moines Corporation (steering committee); Chamber of Commerce (personnel committee). Community Activities: Iowa Children and Family Service (advisory board, 1979 to present; personnel committee, 1980 to present); Des Moines Council on Foreign Affairs; Friendship Force; Sister City Event Coordinator; Polk County Republican Central Committee (executive committee); Polk County Federation of Republican Women (executive committee); State Health Coordinating Council. Religion: Holy Trinity Church, Lector. Honors and Awards: Mortar Board, 1960; Ideal Nebraska Coed, 1960; Listed in *Outstanding Young Women of America, Who's Who of American Women, Who's Who in the Midwest, Community Leaders of America.* Address: 700 - 55th Street, Des Moines, Iowa 50312.

Tennant, Forest Searls Jr

Executive Director of Community Health Projects. Personal: Born January 23, 1941; Married Miriam Tennant. Education: A.A., Hutchinson Junior College, Kansas, 1960; B.A., University of Missouri, 1962; M.D., University of Kansas Medical School, 1967; Internship in Internal Medicine, University of Kentucky, 1967; Residency, University of Texas, 1968; M.P.H. 1973, Residency in Preventive Medicine 1974, D.P.H. 1974, University of California-Los Angeles. Military: Served in the United States Army to the Rank of Major, 1968-72. Career: Executive Director of Community Health Projects, Inc. and Associates; University of California-Los Angeles, Professor in Division of Epidemiology 1972-74, United States Public Health Service Postdoctoral Fellowship for School of Public Health; United States Army, Chief Physician for Special Action Office for Alcohol and Drug Abuse 1971-72, Major in Medical Corps 1970-71, Captain in Medical Corps 1968-70. Organizational Memberships: City of West Covina (city councilman, 1980-84); Southern California Association of Physicians in Drug Dependence (past president); American Association for the Advancement of Science; American Geriatrics Society; California Public Health Association; Association of Teachers of Preventive Medicine; American Medical Association; California Medical Association; Los Angeles County Medical Association; American College of Preventive Medicine (fellow). Community Activities: California State Department of Justice (consultant); California State Rehabilitation Center (consultant); West Covina Chamber of Commerce (past president); Rotary Club; Delhaven Community Center (fund raising chairman); We T.I.P. (advisory board); American Red Cross; American Cancer Society. Honors and Awards: United States Army Commendation Medal, 1971; Meritorious Service Medal, 1972; Student American Medical Association Research Award, 1973; Student American Medical Association Research Forum 1st Place in Neuropsychiatry, 1973; Small Business Award for Innovative System to Lower Health Care Costs, California State Chapter of Commerce, 1977; Citizen of the Year, West Covina, California, 1979; Director of the Year, West Covina Chamber of Commerce, 1979. Address: 1744 Aspen Village Way, West Covina, California 91791.

Terrell, Patricia

Assistant Professor of Elementary Education/Reading. Personal: Born September 17, 1945; Daughter of Albert L. Colby (deceased) and Mrs. Albert L. Colby; Mother of Wendi Loren Terrell. Education: B.S. 1968, M.Ed. 1972, Ph.D. 1974, University of Southern Mississippi. Career: Assistant Professor of Elementary Education/Reading, East Carolina University, Greenville, North Carolina; University Instructor at Undergraduate and Graduate Levels; Junior College Instructor; Director, Child Development Center; Teacher, Elementary School Physical Education, Kindergarten, First, Second and Fifth Grades. Organizational Memberships: International Reading Association; College Reading Association; Phi Delta Kappa (president); North Carolina College Professors of Reading (vice-president); Delta Kappa Gamma. Community Activities: Editorial Advisory Work for Publishing Companies; Evaluation of Effective Educational Programs; Researcher; Consultant to Educational Groups and School Districts; Campus-Related Organizations. Religion: Immanuel Baptist Church. Honors and Awards: An Outstanding Instructor, East Carolina University, 1977-78; Assistantship for Graduate Work, 1971-74; Listed in *Outstanding Young Women of America, Personalities of the South, Personalities of America, World Who's Who of Intellectuals, World Who's Who of Women, Dictionary of International Biography, Directory of Distinguished Americans, Book of Honor.* Address: 213 South Library Street, Greenville, North Carolina 27834.

Terzian, Shohig Sherry

Director of Mental Health Information Service. Personal: Daughter of Ardashes Garabed and Ebraxe Momjian Terzian (both deceased). Education: A.B. cum laude English Literature, Radcliffe College of Harvard University; M.S., Columbia University Graduate School of Library Services; Postgraduate Courses, New School for Social Research, Columbia University, University of Wisconsin. Career: University of California-Los Angeles, Director of Mental Health Information Service of the Neuropsychiatric Institute 1975 to present; Faculty Member/Dept. of Psychiatry and Biobehavioral Sciences in UCLA School of Medicine 1969 to present; Librarian of the Neuropsychiatric Institute in the UCLA Center for Health Science 1961-74; Librarian, Prudential Insurance Company of American Western Home Office, Los Angeles, California, 1948-61; Reserch Librarian, Time Inc., New York, New York, 1947-48; Picture Editor and Research Assistant, United States Department of State Office of International Information and Cultural Affairs, New York, New York, 1943-46; Assistant, Vassar College Library, Poughkeepsie, New York, 1942-43; First Librarian, Neurological Institute of Columbia-Presbyterian Medical Center, New York, New York, 1940-41. Organizational Memberships: Institute for the Study of Social Trauma of Shalvata Psychiatric Centre, Israel (literature consultant on genocide); Simon Wiesenthal Center for Holocaust Studies, Los Angeles (literature consultant of genocide); Association of Western Hospitals (founder and first chairman, hospital librarians section); Special Libraries Association (president, southern California chapter; chairman, employment and public relations committees; chairman, first behavioral sciences committee and other local and national committees; California Library Association (president, hospital and institutions roundtable). Community Activities: Association for Mental Health Affilitation with Israel (chairman, southern California library committee); Columbia University Alumni of Southern California (vice-president; editor, newsletter); Valley College Library/Media Technology Program (advisory committee); University of California Graduate School of Library Service (specialist advisor/consultant); Los Angeles Trade Technical College (advisory committee which initiated library technicians' program); California State Personnel Board (member of panels for oral interviews for the statewide positions of librarians) State Department of Mental Hygiene (chairman, workshop planning committee for first training workshop on modern psychiatric librarianship for librarians in California); Psychiatric Librarians Roundtable (pilot meeting at the Mental Hospitals Institute, American Psychiatric Association); Psychiatric Librarians of Los Angeles (founder, first chairman); Guest

Lecturer at University of California-Los Angeles Graduate School of Library Service, University of Southern California Graduate School of Library Science and Immaculate Heart College School of Library Science; Radcliffe Club of Southern California (vice-president; public relations director; director; Harvard affiliate); Harvard Club of Southern California (columnist, newsletter); Los Angeles County Commission on the Status of Women (committees on health, employment and senior women). Honors and Awards: Lifetime/Honorary Member, Association for Mental Health Affiliation with Israel; "George Santayana and the Genteel Tradition" Radcliffe Honors Thesis Citation for Distinction, Department of English of Harvard University and Personal Review by Philosopher George Santayana; Certificate, International Who's Who of Intellectuals; Listed in *American Registry, Anglo-Americn Who's Who, Book of Honor, Armenian Academic Personnel in the United States, Biographical Dictionary of Librarians in the United States and Canada, Biographical Directory of Librarians in the Field of Slavic and Central European Studies, Community Leaders and Noteworthy Americans, Dictionary of International Biography, Directory of Armenian Scholars, International Who's Who in Community Service, International Who's Who of Intellectuals, Men and Women of Distinction, Notable Americans, Personalities of America, Personalities of the West and Midwest, Who Knows-and What, Who's Who in California, Who's Who in Community Service, Who's Who in Library Service, Who's Who in the West, Who's Who of American Women, World Who's Who of Women, Who's Who in Library and Information Services.* Home Address: 11740 Wilshire Boulevard #2502, Los Angeles, California 90025. Office: Neuropsychiatric Institute, UCLA Medical Center, Los Angeles 90024, California.

Tharp, Lecile Confer

Real Estate Investment and Exchange Counselor. Personal: Born in Jay County, Indiana; Widow; Mother of Twanette T. Garvey, Stanley W. and Stanford V. Education: B.Mus.Ed., American Conservatory of Music, Chicago, Illinois; A.A., Accounting and Business Administration, San Bernardino Valley College, San Bernardino, California. Career: Real Estate Investment and Exchange Counselor; Owner/Instructor, Private Piano Studio; Automotive Accountant; Co-Owner, Manager, Drive-In Theater. Organizational Memberships: International Real Estate Federation; Institute of Certified Business Counselors; The Academy of Real Estate; National Council of Exchanges; Music Teachers Association of California (board of directors). Community Activities: Meals on Wheels (secretary, treasurer); Altrusa International (board of directors); Commerce Honor Society of San Bernardino Valley College (president). Religion: Society of Friends. Honors and Awards: Permanent State Member, Alpha Gamma Sigma Honorary Scholarship Society, President of San Bernardino Vally First Ladies of Finance in Railto; Listed in *Who's Who in California Business and Finance, Who's Who in Creative Real Estate, World Who's Who of Women, International Who's Who of Intellectuals, Men and Women of Distinction, Personalities of America, Who's Who in the Midwest.* Address: 130 West 8th Street, Claremont, California 91711.

Thimotheose, K G

Executive Director. Personal: Born February 11, 1938; Son of K. G. and Mariamma Varghese; Married Mariamma; Father of Geebee, Sonia. Education: M.A.; M.Ed.; M.A.; Ph.D.; C.S.W.; C.A.C.; Certified Psychologist; Diplomate-American Board of Psychotherapy; Certified Alcoholism Therapist. Career: Executive Director and Clinical Director, Alexandrine House Inc., Detroit, Michigan; Professor and Head of the Department of Educational Psychology, Teachers College, Kerala, India; Director, Ananndanilyam Orphanage and Widow Center, Kerala, India. Organizational Memberships: American Psychological Association (clinical member); Academy of Psychologists in Marital, Sex and Family Therapy; American Institute of Counseling and Psychotherapy (clinical member); Kerala University Forum of Educational Research and Studies (vice-president). Community Activities: University of Calicut, India (member, faculty of education, 1968-75); Advisory Board Member, Kerala Government Trivandrum Medical College Hospitals. Published Works: Former Editor, *Kerala Journal of Education;* Publisher of textbook in Educational Psychology for B. Ed. students. Honors and Awards: First Class and First Rank, University of Kerala for Master's Degree in Educational Psychology; Listed in Marquis' *Who's Who* and in International Biographical Centre and American Biographical Institute Publications. Address: 21701 Parklawn, Oak Park, Michigan 48237.

Thomas, Helen

White House Correspondent. Personal: Married Douglas B. Cornell. Education: B.A., Wayne State University. Career: United Press International, Chief White House Correspondent, Employee Since 1943. Organizational Memberships: White House Correspondents Association (president); Women's National Press Club (president); Sigma Delta Chi Hall of Fame. Honors and Awards: Newspaper Woman of the Year, 1968; Headline Award, Women in Communication. Address: 2501 Calvert Northwest, Washington, D.C. 20008.

Thomas, Larry Eugene

District Executive. Personal: Born April 8, 1945; Son of Orville G. and Wilma M. Wood Thomas; Married Phoeba Blanche Lee; Father of Brian Jay, Cheryl, Kari. Education: B.A., Calvary Bible College, Kansas City, Missouri, 1968; University of Evansville, Indiana; Indiana State University-Evansville; Bowling Green State University, Ohio. Career: Boy Scouts of America, Director of Program & Scouting for the Handicapped for Sagamore Council 1982 to present, District Executive, Bowling Green, Ohio. Community Activities: Bowling Green Bike Safety Commission, 1979 to present; Kiwanis Youth Services Committee, 1978 to present; Mental Health Association of Wood City, 1981 to present; Wood City Lodge #112-F&A.M. (junior deacon, 1980 to present); Crystal Chapter RAM #157; Bowling Green Council of R&SM #124; Findlay Commandery of Knights Templar #49; American Diabetes Association (state board of directors); Ancient Accepted Scottish Rite of Valley of Toledo (ambassador, 1981 to present); Superior Court of Posey County and Mt. Vernon, Indiana (probation officer, 1976-79). Honors and Awards: Pacemaker Award, Boy Scouts of America, 1979. Address: 810 Twyckingham Lane, Kokomo, Indiana 46901.

Thomas, Peggy Ruth

Manager of Supply and Procurement. Personal: Born December 19, 1933; Daughter of Mr. and Mrs. Sidney D. Coffman; Married Donald E. Thomas; Mother of Gene L. Gustafson, Richard L. Gustafson. Education: Graduate of Mangum High School; Oklahoma, 1951; University of Oklahoma-Norman, 1951-52; Southwestern State College, Weatherford, Oklahoma, 1952-53. Career: Manager, Supply and Procurement, The Alaska Railroad, 1979 to present; Purchasing Officer, Municipality of Anchorage, 1979; Federal Procurement and Contracting Official, 1953-78. Organizational Memberships: National Association of Female Executives; American Business Women's Association; National Federation of Business and Professional Women; Federal Executives Association (minority business opportunity committee); International Platform Association. Honors and Awards: Service Award, National Program for

Keeping America Beautiful, 1973; Distinguished Public Service Award, Governor of Idaho, 1974; Listed in *Who's Who of American Women, World Who's Who of Women, Directory of Distinguished Americans, Personalities of the West and Midwest, Who's Who in the West, Community Leaders of America, Personalities of America, International Who's Who of Intellectuals.* Address: S.R.A. Box 85T, Anchorage, Alaska 99507.

Thomas, Philip Robinson

Operational Management Consultant Executive. Personal: Born December 9, 1934; Son of Leslie R. and Margaret L. Thomas; Married Wayne Heirtzler; Father of Martin N. R., Stephen D. R. Education: B.Sc. Physics and Mathematics, M.Sc., Physics, Ph.D. Engineering, University of London. Military: Served in the British Royal Air Force, 1953-45. Career: President and Chief Executive Officer, Thomas Group Inc., Ethel, Louisiana, 1978 to present; Vice-President, Integrated Circuits Division of R.C.A., Somerville, New Jersey, 1975-78; General Manager, M.O.S. Product Division, Fairchild Camera and Instrument Corporation, Mountainview, California, 1973-75; Vice President and General Manager, M.O.S./L.S.I. Division, General Instrument Company, New York City, 1972-73; Texas Instruments Corporation, Operations Manager, Dallas, Texas 1963-72, Bedford, England 1961-63. Organizational Memberships: Institute of Electrical and Electronics Engineers; British Institute of Radio and Electronics Engineers. Address: Route 1 Box 181-D, Ethel, Louisiana 70730.

Andrew B Thompson

Thomason, Mary Diel

Teacher (Retired). Personal: Born December 21, 1908; Daughter of Friederich and Mary Busick Diel (both deceased); Married Joseph A. Thomason (deceased). Education: B.A., Fresno State University, 1931; M.A., University of the Pacific, 1958; Elementary California State Life Teaching Credential, 1930; Junior High California State Life Teaching Credential, 1931; Elementary Administrator's Credential, 1958. Career: Public School Teacher, California, 1931-70. Organizational Memberships: California Teachers Association (life member); California Retired Teachers Association (life member); National Retired Teachers Association (life member); American Association of University Women (life member, past president, local branch; bulletin editor, 5 years); University of the Pacific Alumni Association (life member); Zeta Rho Chapter of Delta Kappa Gamma Society International (corresponding secretary). Community Activities: Local Business and Professional Women's Club; Local Garden Clubs Inc. (scholarship chairman, 1979-81; awards chairman, 1981-82; donor of 8 Penny Pines plantations); Federated Women's Clubs (president, late 1950's); San Joaquin County Historical Museum Docent Council (librarian, 1971-82; secretary 1982); Museum Library (donor of historical artifacts and donor of funds for books); Free Evangelical Lutheran Cross Church of Fresno (donor of $1000); Joseph A. and Mary Diel Thomason Graduate Scholarship, University of the Pacific (founder, with husband); Two Local High School Scholarships (provider, 1981); Gerontology Center, Los Angeles Campus of University of Southern California (contributor of $1000 to building fund). Religion: Free Evangelical Lutheran Cross Church of Fresno, California, 1908-83. Honors and Awards: Freedoms Foundation Teacher Award; Teacher of the Year Award, 1958, Community Award and District X Award, California Federation of Women's Clubs; Merit Award, California Conservation Council; Parent-Teacher Association Award, California Congress of Parents and Teachers, George Washington School Association. Address: 536 York Street, Lodi, California 95240.

Thompson, Andrew Boyd Jr

Company President and Owner. Personal: Born March 30, 1930; Son of A. B. Thompson Sr.; Married June Guy; Father of Guy Bradley, Eric Kiepp. Education: Graduate of Sidney Lanier High School, Montgomery, Alabama, 1948; Studied Chemistry, Auburn University, Alabama, 1948-49; G.E.D. Tests for 1st and 2nd Year College Level, Passed 1952; Military Training Courses at Fort Jackson, South Carolina, Fort Riley, Kansas, Fort McClennan, Alabama, Ft. Benning, Georgia, Fort Levenworth, Kansas; National Security Management Course, 1974. Military: Served in the Alabama Army National Guard, 1949-51; Served in the United States Army as Second Lieutenant in the Chemical Corps and as Platoon Leader with the 388th Chemical Smoke Generator Company in Korea 1951-54; Served in the United States Army Reserve, 1954-80. Career: President, Owner, National Pricing Service, Inc., 1981 to present; Vice-President, General Manager and Editor, National Photo Pricing Service, Inc., 1966-81; Furniture Salesman, Sears, Roebuck and Company, 1966; Insurance Agent, The Prudential Insurance Company of America, 1956-58; Salesman and Store Manager, Mel's Photo Shop 21, Montgomery, Alabama, 1955-57, 1958-66; Laboratory Manager and Technician, Montgomery Branch of Southern Testing Laboratories, 1955; Materials Engineer Assistant, Alabama Highway Department, 1949-51, 1954-55. Organizational Memberships: Photo Marketing Association International Photographic Manufacturers and Distributors Association; Reserve Officers Association of the United States (life member); Military Order of the World Wars; Montgomery Area Chamber of Commerce; International Platform Association; Epilepsy Chapter of the Montgomery Area (co-founder; president; chairman of the board; past president; past vice-president; past secretary); 31st Infantry "Dixie" Division Club (president; past vice-president; past secretary); Mensa; American Legion; Veterans of Foreign Wars. Community Activities: Alabama Governor's Task Force on Epilepsy; Seth Johnson School Parent-Teacher Association; Boy Scouts of America (volunteer with cub scouts); Girl Scouts of America (teacher, photography merit badge course, late 1950's, early 1960's); American Biographical Institute (fellow member); American Biographical Institute Research Association (associate Member); International Biographical Association (life fellow member); Pi Kappa Alpha Social Fraternity. Religion: Normadale United Methodist Church. Honors and Awards: American Legion Medal for Outstanding Platoon Leader in High School Reserve Officers Training Corps, 1948; General Corgas Science Scholarship, 1948; Army Commendation Medal; Good Conduct Medal; National Defense Service Medal; Korean Service Medal with 2 Campaign Stars; Army Reserve Components Achievement Medal with 2 Oak Leaf Clusters; Armed Forces Reserve Medal with Ten-Year Device; United Nations Service Medal; Meritorious United Commendation with Oak Leaf Cluster; Two Republic of Korea Presidential Unit Citations; Expert Marksmanship Badge for Pistol; Sharpshooter Marksmanship Badges for Rifle and Carbine; American Red Cross 4-Gallon Blood Donor Award; Honorary Member of Editorial Advisory Board, American Biographical Institute; Certificates of Appreciation, Civic Groups for Talks on Photography; Listed in *Dictionary of International Biography, Men of Achievement, International Who's Who in Community Service, Men and Women of Distinction, International Register of Profiles, International Who's Who of Intellectuals, Who's Who in the South and Southwest, Personalities of the South, Notable Americans, Personalities of America, Community Leaders and Noteworthy Americans, Community Leaders of America, American Registry Series, Book of Honor, Directory of Distinguished Americans.* Address: 4353 Amherst Road, Montgomery, Alabama 36116.

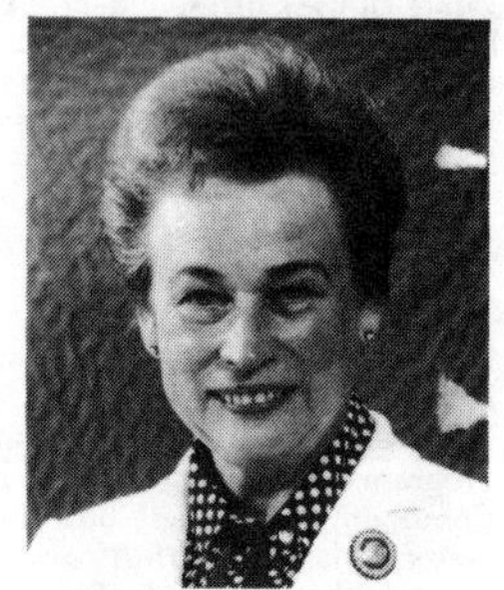

Barbara S Thompson

Thompson, Barbara Storck

Education Consultant. Personal: Born October 15, 1924; Daughter of John Storck; Married Glenn T. Thompson; Mother of David C., James T. Education: Ph.D., 1969, M.S., 1959, University of Wisconsin-Madison; B.S., 1956, University of Wisconsin-Platteville; Honorary Doctorate of Humane Letters, Carroll College, 1974; Further studies at the University of Iowa, Mt. Mary College, Edgewood College, University of Wisconsin-Milwaukee. Career: Education Consultant, Wisconsin Department of Public

Instruction, 1973 to present; Wisconsin State Superintendent of Public Instruction, 1973-81; Consultant, Wisconsin Department of Public Instruction, 1964-73; Administrator, Principal, School Supervisor, Reading Specialist, Instructor in College, Curriculum Coordinator, Classroom Teacher, 1944-64. Organizational Memberships: National Council of Administrative Women in Education; National Council of State Consultants in Elementary Education (president 1974-75); American Association of School Administrators; Wisconsin Association of School District Administrators; National, Wisconsin, Southwestern Wisconsin, and Southeastern Wisconsin Associations for Supervision and Curriculum Development; National and Wisconsin Elementary School Principals' Associations; Pi Lambda Theta; Alpha Beta; Parent Teachers Association; National Education Association; Wisconsin Education Association (life member); Southern Wisconsin Education Association; Wisconsin Educational Research Association; National Department of Elementary-Kindergarten-Nursery Education; National Association of Childhood Education International; Madison Branch, Association of Childhood Education; National Association for the Advancement of Colored People; Delta Kappa Gamma; Education Commission of the States. Honors and Awards: Outstanding Service to National Advisory Committee on Child Abuse, Education Commission of the States; Concerned Educator of the Arts Award, Wisconsin Arts Education Association; Degree of Honorary American Farmer, National Future Farmers of America; Honorary D.E.C.A. Member, Distributive Education Clubs of America, Wisconsin Vocational Student Organization, 1978; County 4-H Club Recognition Award, Dane County 4-H Club Organization, 1977; State 4-H Alumni Recognition Award, Cooperative Extension Service, 1977; Distinguished National Alumnus Recognition Award, National 4-H Clubs of America, 1977; Honorary Association Membership, Wisconsin Association of Agricultural Instructors, 1977; Distinguished Alumnus Award, University of Wisconsin Plattevile, 1977; Honorary State Farmer, Future Farmers of America, 1976; Certificate of Appreciation, Wisconsin Library Association, 1976; Certificate Awarded for Creation of Committee for Non-Sexist Textbooks, Wisconsin Women's Political Committee, 1976; Certificate of Membership, International Association of Lion's Club Lioness Club, 1976; Certificate of Appreciation, Wisconsin School Food Services A.S.F.S.A. and W.S.F.S.A., 1976; Certificate of Membership, Educare, University of Wisconsin-Oshkosh, 1976; Certificate of Distinguished Service, American Legion, Badger Boys State, 1975; Certificate of Appreciation, Wisconsin Secondary School Administrators; Outstanding Service Award, Wisconsin Association of Vocational Agricultural Instructors, 1974; Distinguished Service Award, Bloomer Chapter, Future Farmers of America, 1974; State Conservation Award, Madison Lions Club, 1974; Woman of the Year, National Council of Administrative Women in Education, 1974; Nominated to *Who's Who in America, Who's Who in Government, Leaders in Education;* Listed in *Dictionary of International Biography, Personalities of the West and Midwest;* Featured as "Your Madisonian", November 1, 1970; Waukesha Freeman Recipient to attend two-week workshop on use of newspaper in the classroom, University of Iowa. Address: 3591 Sabaka Trail, Verona, Wisconsin 53593.

Thompson, Jo Ann

District Manager. Personal: Born December 13, 1932; Daughter of Frank and Lorene Rutherford; Widow; Mother of Gregory Brian, Mark Stephen, Jeffrey Todd. Education: Graduate of Paris High School, 1949; A.A., Paris Junior College, 1951; B.S., Home Economics, East Texas State University, 1964. Career: Texas Power and Light Company, District Manager 1982 to present, Assistant District Manager 1980-82, Home Service Director 1972-80, Home Service Advisor 1967-72; Home Economist, Lone Star Gas Company, 1966-67; Manager, Mallory Studio, 1952-54; Claims Adjuster, Morneau Insurance, 1950-52. Organizational Memberships: National Home Economist in Business (national chairman, 1980-81); Texas Home Economics Association (president, 1980-82); Southwest Chapter, National Home Fashions League (president, 1978-80); Electrical Women's Roundtable (national director, 1977-80); American Home Economics Association (finance committee, 1981-82; professional section unit chairman). Community Activities: Camp Fire Inc. (board of directors, 1981-83); Altrusa Club of Sherman, 1980-82; Business and Professional Women of Sherman, 1981; North Texas Home Economists in Business (chairman, 1970-77); National Home Economics in Business Board (satellite chairman, 1977-78); El Centro College (advisory board); Texas Power and Light Company's Nuclear Speaker's Bureau, 1972 to present; University of Houston Executive Development Program, 1973. Religion: United Methodist Church; Finance Committee, First United Methodist, Sherman, Texas; Building Committee, First United Methodist, Plano, Texas; Church Women United, President 1970-72. Honors and Awards: Distinguished Alumni, East Texas University, 1981; First Outstanding Alumnus Award in Home Economics, East Texas State University, 1972; Honorary Member, Young Homemakers of Texas, 1976; Honorary Service Award, State Future Farmers of America, 1976; Outstanding Participant, Whirlpool Corporation Utility Marketing and Management Seminar, 1974. Address: 2812 Windy Drive, Commerce, Texas 75428.

Thompson, Vivian Opal

Registered Nurse. Personal: Born November 30, 1925; Daughter of Luther Smith and Cora Belle Baugh Thompson (both deceased). Education: Graduate of Richlands High School, Virginia, 1944; Diploma, Knoxville General Hospital School of Nursing, Knoxville, Tennessee, 1947; Classes and Seminars in Nursing, Southwest Community College, Richlands, Virginia, Supervisor and Obstetrics Charge Nurse, 1968-81, Supervisor 1957-61, General Duty Nurse 1948-52; Charge Nurse Rockingham Memorial Hospital, Harrisonburg, Virginia, 1956-68; Charge Nurse, Bluefield Sanitarium, Bluefield, West Virginia, 1961-65; Industrial Nurse, French Morocco, Africa, 1952-56; Obstetrics Supervisor, General Hospital, Knoxville, Tennessee, 1947-78. Organizational Memberships: Registered Nurse in Tennessee, Virginia and West Virginia; American Association of Industrial Nurses (former member); National League of Nurses; Virginia League of Nurses. Religion: Richlands Presbyterian Church. Honors and Awards: Certificate of Achievement, Clinch Valley Clinic Hospital, Richlands, Virginia, 1979; Listed in *Who's Who of American Women, Personalities of the South, Community Leaders of America, World's Book of Honor, World's Who's Who of Women, International Men and Women of Distinction, Dictionary of International Biography, Who's Who in the South and Southwest.* Address: 205 Penn Avenue, Richlands, Virginia 24641.

Thrailkill, Francis Marie

College President. Personal: Born September 21, 1937; Daughter of Frank Thrailkill (deceased) and Mrs. Frank Thrailkill. Education: B.A. cum laude History, College of New Rochelle, New York, 1961; M.A. Social Psychology, Marquette University, Milwaukee, Wisconsin, 1969; Ed.D. Curriculum Development, Nova University, Fort Lauderdale, Florida, 1975. Career: President, Springfield, College, Illinois, 1977 to present; Sabbatical Year Studying Educational Systems in Europe, 1977; Principal, Ursuline Academy High School, Dallas, Texas, 1970-77; Vice-Principal, Ursuline Academy High School, New Orleans, Louisiana, 1963-70; Teacher, Ursuline Academy, Dallas, Texas, 1961-63. Organizational Memberships: Illinois State Scholarship Commission (policy advisory committee, 1979-81); Central Illinois Consortium for Health Manpower Education (president, 1979-80); Springfield Community Music School (board, 1979-80); St. Teresa High School, Decatur, Illinois (board of trustees, 1978-81); College of New Rochelle, New York (board of trustees, 1978-81); Association of Supervision and Curriculum Development, 1972-81; Federation of Independent Illinois College and University, 1978-81. Community Activities: United Way of Springfield, Illinois (board, 1981); Pilot Programs in Region X of Texas Education Agency (accrediting team 1973-76); North Texas Secondary Principal's Association (president, 1972-74); Commission for Nonpublic Education (secretary, 1973-76); Educational Division of United Way Campaign (chairperson, 1980-81).

Address: 1622 North 5th, Springfield, Illinois 62702.

Thrash, Sara Arline

Educator. Personal: Born March 14, 1928, in Jefferson City, Tennessee; Daughter of Arlie Eugene and Leola McDonald Cate; Married Willard D. on January 1, 1952; Mother of Douglas, Diane, Mark, David. Education: B.A., Carson Newman College, 1949; M.A., University of South Florida, 1969; Ed.S., 1974; Ph.D., Brunnel University in England, 1977. Career: Teacher in public schools of Tennessee and Mississippi, 1949-52; Teacher of gifted children, Mid City School, New Orleans, Louisiana, 1961-63; Teacher in Florida public schools, 1966-71; Teacher of special education and educational director of Escambia Association for Retarded Children, Pensacola, Florida, 1971-73; Adjunct Teacher, University of West Florida in Pennsacola, 1971-73; Coordinator of learning disabilities, Western Carolina University, Cullowhee, North Carolina, 1975-78; Consultant to Polk County Child Development Center, University of North Carolina at Asheville, 1975-78, and Cherokee Reservation, 1975-78; Organizer of parent therapy groups in learning disabilities, 1975 to present; Visiting Professor in special education, St. Leo's College, Florida, 1979, Associate Professor of education, 1980 to present; Educational coordinator of Eckerd Wilderness Therapeutic Camping Program, 1980; Conducted workshop for First World Congress on Future of Special Education in Scotland, 1978; Conducted workshop for Tennessee A.C.L.D. convention, 1976 and 1979; Participant in or Keynote Speaker, Florida State Exceptional Child Convention, 1981, Carnegie Foundation Colloqium on Common Learning (Chicago, Illinois, 1981; Kiwanis, North Carolina 1979; Mobile, Alabama and Franklin, North Carolina 1978), International Medical Symposium (Exeter University in England), 1981, Illinois Home Economists State Convention, 1978, Kansas Home Economists State Convention, 1978, Nappa Valley Association of Children with Learning Disabilities, 1978; Business and Professional Womem's Banquet. Organizational Memberships: American Association of University Women; Council for Exceptional Children; Association for Children with Learning Disabilities; Association for Retarded Children; Florida Writers Guild; Association for Gifted and Talented Appalachian Writers; Phi Kappa Phi. Community Activities: Member of steering committee, Jackson County Family Life, 1977-78; Supporter of Special Olympics; Member of Parents are People. Religion: Attends Baptist Church (staff writer for Sunday school board, 1973-81, adult Sunday school teacher, 1973-81, guest lecturer in various churches). Published Works: *Little Things that Keep Families Together* (1976), *Professor Mom's Pilgrimage* (1982), *Gargantuans for the Gifted* (1982); Contributed to *International Perspectives on the Future of Special Education*, and various professional journals. Honors and Awards: Presidential Citation, Carson Newman College, 1977; First Baptist Church Family Life Recognition award, 1977; United States Florida Fellow, 1968-69; Listed in *Directory of Distinguished Americans, World Who's Who of Women, Dictionary of International Biography, Community Leaders and Noteworthy Americans, Personalities of the South, Who's Who of American Women, Eminent Men and Women of the World, International Who's Who of Intellectuals.* Address: 4200-14th Way Northeast, St. Petersburg, Florida 33703.

Sara A Thrash

Tiemeyer, Hope Elizabeth Johnson

Advertising Company Executive. Personal: Born May 20, 1908, in Fort Wayne, Indiana; Daughter of Edward Tibbens and Burton Meyers Johnson; Married Edwin H. Tiemeyer, October 30, 1929 (deceased); Mother of Ann Elizabeth T. Lewin, Edwin Houghton (deceased). Education: B.A., University of Cincinnati, 1932. Career: Owner, Mail-Way Advertising Company, Cincinnati, 1955 to present. Community Activities: Daughters of the American Revolution Cincinnati Chapter (regent, 1956-58; chairman, national school survey committee, 1961-62; national vice-chairman of Americanism Manual for Citizenship, 1962-65; Continental Congress program committee, 1962-65; Congress marshall committee, 1966-68; Congress hostess committee, 1969-75); Officers Club (president, 1974-77); National Chairmen's Association (recording secretary, 1969-71); Children of the American Revolution (senior national membership chairman, 1958-60; senior national recording secretary, 1960-62); Mountain School (national chairman, 1962-64; honorary senior national vice-president, 1963-64; senior national 1st vice-president, 1964-66; senior national president, 1966-68; honorary national life president, 1970 to present); National Officers Club (1st vice-president, 1965-69; president, 1970-73; honorary senior life president, Ohio Society); Ohio Congress of Parent-Teacher Associations (honorary life member; treasurer, 1957-62; vice-president and director of department of health, 1962-63); National Congress of Parent-Teacher Associations (honorary life member); Kappa Alpha Theta Mothers Club (life member; president, 1958-59); Cincinnati Symphony Orchestra (vice-president, women's committee, 1964-65); University of Cincinnati Parents Club (president, 1959-61; vice-president, 1963-64); State House Conference on Education (area chairman, 1953); American Association of University Women (director, 1963-64); Cincinnati Social Health Board (member, 1950-78; executive committee, 1965-70; vice-president, 1973-78; treasurer, 1975-78; life trustee, 1978); Singleton's of Cincinnati Club (president, 1969-71; travelers board president, 1973-74; art committee, 1971 to present; memberships committee, 1973-78; Newtown Garden Club (president, 1947-49); City Panhellenic Association (president, 1951-52); Ohio Hobby Club (president, 1958-59); Sigma Nu Mothers Club (president, 1963-65); Alumnae Chapter of Alpha Omicron Pi (president, 1930-32; national admissions committee, 1933-35); Craftshow for Handicapped (life member); Zonta Club of Cincinnati (chairman, Amelia Earhart Fellowship Committee, 1963-64; program chairman, 1964-65; orientation chairman, 1965-67; international relations chairman, 1967-68; director, 1969-74; executive committee, 1969-73; national nominating committee, 1970-73; vice-president, 1971-73); Cincinnati Women's Club (music committee; tearoom committee, 1969 to present); Queen City Chapter of National Association of Parliamentarians (treasurer, 1965-69); Cincinnati Chapter of Freedoms Foundation, Valley Forge (vice-president, 1974-76; president, 1978-80; secretary, 1980-83). Honors and Awards: Jonathon Moore Citation and Award, Sons of the American Revolution, 1967; Good Citizenship Medal, National Society, 1967; National Platform Association; English Speaking Union; Order of Kentucky Colonels; National Gavel Association. Address: 2786 Little Dry Run Road, Cincinnati, Ohio 45244.

Hope J Tiemeyer

Tilden, John (Jno) Leslie

Retired. Personal: Born June 19, 1897, on the "Oregon Trail"; Son of William Lincoln and Lisetta (Debo) Tilden, (both deceased); Married Marie Arnold; Father of John Leslie Jr., William Frederick. Education: Graduate St. Joseph (Missouri) High School; Graduate Junior College, 1918; Honorary Doctor Degree, San Francisco State College, 1940. Military: Served as a Sergeant in the Signal Corps, World War I; Fought in the final battle of Chateau Theirry (near Paris). Career: Assistant Boys Secretary, Young Men's Christian Association (YMCA), St. Joseph, Missouri, 1916; Boys Secretary and Physical Director, YMCA, Sedalia, Missouri; Credit Manager, Robison Heavy Hardware Company, St. Joseph, 1915; Boy Scout Executive, Boy Scout Administrative Council: St. Joseph, Missouri (1919-23), Wichita, Kansas (1923-32), Minneapolis, Minnesota (1932-38), San Francisco, California (1938-62); Retired 1962. Organizational Memberships: Rotary Clubs of St. Joseph, Wichita, Minneapolis, San Francisco (member or officer in "Boy's Committees", chairman of "June Division" in San Francisco). Community Activities: Organized the Air Scout Program with Mr. Cessna (manufacturer of Cessna Airplane); Albert Pike Lodge (Masonic); California Bodies Scottish Rite of San Francisco; War Defense Board (appointed by Mayor Rossi of San Francisco 1945); Birth of the United Nations (service board of San Francisco); Council of Social Agencies (appointed president by Community Chest of San Francisco). Religion: Organized Lakeside Presbyterian Church, San Francisco, 1940. Published Works: *Western Branch Tildens,* (in the Library of Congress); *Scouting in Action.* Honors and Awards: 50 Year Badge, Albert Pike Lodge; Many Scouting Awards including 60 year membership gold plaque, Boy Scouts of

America, 1971; "Distinguished Achievement" Plaque, England; Listed in *Who's Who in California, International Who's Who of Intellectuals, Personalities of the West and Midwest.* Address: 85 Vasquez Ave., San Francisco, California 94127.

Tillman, Celestine

Associate Professor. Personal: Born December 12, 1933; Daughter of Elbert Lee Sr. and Lillie Tillman (both deceased). Education: B.S. Liberal Arts and Sciences, Southern University, Baton Rouge, Louisiana, 1955; M.S. Inorganic and Analytical Chemistry, Howard University, Washington, D.C., 1957; Postgraduate Study, Penn State University, Louisiana State University, and Southern University; Research Fellow, Penn State University, Summers 1968, 1969, and 1971. Career: Associate Professor of Analytical and Inorganic Chemistry, Southern University, Baton Rouge, Louisiana, 1960 to present; Teaching Graduate Assistant, 1955-57. Organizational Memberships: American Chemistry Society; National Organizational for Professional Advancement of Black Chemists and Chemical Engineers; American Association for the Advancement of Science; Phi Delta Kappa International; Iota Sigma Pi; Sigma Delta Epsilon/Graduate Women in Science; Louisiana Academy of Science; Baton Rouge Analytical Instrument Discussion Group; Alpha Kappa Mu; Kappa Delta Pi; Beta Kappa Chi. Community Activities: Delta Sigma Theta Sorority; League of Women Voters; The International Platform Association; National Association for the Advancement of Colored People; Louisiana Council on Human Relations; Audubon Council of Girl Scouts of America U.S.A.; National Council of Negro Women; Eye Foundation of America (contributor); Community Association for the Welfare of School Children (contributor); North Shore Animals League (contributor); St. Jude Children Research Hospital (contributor); Easter Seals (contributor); North Baton Rouge Arthritis Guild (contributor); National Foundation for Cancer (contributor); United Way (contributor). Religion: King David Baptist Church, Baton Rouge, Louisiana; Young Women's Christian Association. Honors and Awards: Phi Delta Kappa Service Award, 1982; Chemistry Teacher of the Year, Southern University Award, 1979-80; Research Grant, Atlantic Richfield Hanford Company, 1976-77; NORCUS Research Fellow, Summers 1973, 1977; Listed in *Community Leaders of America; Personalities of America, World Who's Who of Women, Directory of Distinguished Americans, Book of Honor, Personalities of the South, International Who's Who of Intellectuals, Who's Who in the South and Southwest, Two Thousand Distinguished Southerners.* Address: 10761 South Gibbens Drive, Baton Rouge, Louisiana 70807.

Celestine Tillman

Tillman, Linda Ruth

Labor Relations Secretary. Personal: Born June 3, 1943; Daughter of Mr. and Mrs. Thomas J. Tillman. Education: Valencia Community College, Orlando, Florida, 1974; Florida Junior College, Jacksonville, Florida, 1976. Career: Labor Relations Secretary; Legal Secretary and Assistant. Organizational Memberships: National Association of Railway Business Women (public affairs and publicity chairman, 1981-82); National Secretaries Association (corresponding secretary, treasurer, 1975-79). Community Activities: United Way (volunteer worker and solicitor for community donations); Jacksonville Chamber of Commerce Constitutional Amendment Review Task Force, 1980; Women of the Jacksonville Art Museum (publicity chairman; fund raiser); Cumner Gallery; Women's Information Exchange; Jacksonville Wine and Food Society (secretary-treasurer, 1979-81). Religion: Jacksonville Church of Religious Science. Honors and Awards: Listed in Numerous Biographical Reference Publications.

Ting, Er Yi

Practicing Physician. Personal: Born June 3, 1919; Son of Yu Chuang and Mary Chang Ting; Married to Theresa; Father of Selene, Sandra, Selwyn. Education: M.D., National Defense Medical College, Shanghai, China, 1948, Resident, 1948-52; Resident, Bronx Municipal Hospital Center, Bronx, New York, 1954-56; Postdoctoral Fellow, University of Buffalo, 1956-57. Military: Served with Chinese Nationalist Army, 1940-44. Career: Physician of Internal Medicine in private practice, New York City, 1964 to present; Director of Pulmonary Function Research Laboratory, New York Medical College and Metropolitan Hospital Center, New York City, 1963-79; Attending Physician, Metropolitan Hospital Center, 1963-79 and Flower and Fifth Avenue Hospital, 1963-79; Attending Physician, National Defense Medical Center in Taipei, 1952-54; Instructor in medicine, National Defense Medical College, 1948-54, State University of New York, 1957-59, Albert Einstein College of Medicine, 1959-63; Assistant Professor of Medicine, New York Medical College, 1963-74, Clinical Associate Professor, 1974-79; Researcher in respiratory physiology (both basic and clinical) and respiratory mechanics. Organizational Memberships: American Association for the Advancement of Science; American Medical Association; American Physiological Society; American Thoracic Society; American College of Chest Physicians; Federation for Clinical Research; Medical Society of New York; New York Acupuncture Society for Physicians and Dentists. Community Activites: Member of Board of Directors of U.S.-China Foundation for Medical Science and Technology, Inc. Published Works: Contributor to *Journal of the American Medical Association, Journal of Applied Physiology, American Review of Respiratory Disease, Disease of the Chest, Bulletin of the New York Academy of Science, New York State Medical Journal, Journal of the Chinese Medical Association* (Taiwan edition), *The Physiologist*, and others. Address: 224 Highwood Avenue, Tenafly, New York 07670.

Tober, Barbara

Editor-in-Chief. Personal: Born August 19, 1934; Married Donald G. Tober. Education: Fashion Institute of Technology, New York, New York; Traphagen School of Fashion, New York, New York; New York School of Interior Design, New York, New York; Dwight-Morrow, Englewood, New Jersey; Kent Place, Summit, New Jersey. Career: Editor-in-Chief, *Bride's* Magazine, 1966 to present; Copy Editor, *Vogue Pattern Book;* Associate Beauty Editor, *Vogue;* Associate Food Editor, *Look;* Advertising and Promotion Department, Jack Braunstein Resident Buyers; Media Department, Hilton Ruggio Advertising, Geyer, Newell and Ganger Advertising. Organizational Memberships: The Fashion Group (lifestyle committee chairman, 1980; member, 1976-78); American Society of Magazine Editors; American Society of Interior Designers (press associate); National Academy of Television Arts and Sciences; Women in Communications, Inc.; Intercorporate Group. Community Activities: Wine and Food Society (chief of protocol, 1981; events committee); Dames d'Escoffier; Golden's Bridge Hounds; International Side-Saddle Organization; North Salem Bridle Trail Association; National Association of Underwater Instructors; American Ballet Theater (national council); Vivian Woodard Council of Fine Arts, 1964-65; Pan-Pacific Southeast Asia Women's Association, Inc. (communications director, 1982; national president, 1982; delegate, international conference, 1981); Asia Society; China Institute; Japan Society; Arlington House Publishers, Equestrian Book Club, Connecticut (advisory board); Traphagen School of Fashion, New York (advisory board); Tobe-Coburn School for Fashion Careers (advisory board); Sugar Foods Corporation (Sweet 'n' Low Marketing), New York (secretary, board of directors); Confrerie de la Chaine des Rotisseurs (member, board of directors and Charge de Presse, New York Baillage; Contributing Editor, *Gastronome*). Published Works: *China: A Cognizant Guide*, 1980; "Chaine Manners a Table", *Gastronome* Magazine, 1980; *The ABC's of Beauty*, 1963. Honors and Awards: *Bon Appetit* Great Cook Award, 1981; ALMA Award, 1968; Penney-Missouri Award, 1972; Traphagen Alumni Award, 1975; Tournament of Roses Rose Parade Judge, 1979; Listed in *Who's Who of America, Who's Who of American Women.* Address: 620 Park Avenue, New York, New York 10021.

Tollefson, Robert J

Professor of Philosophy and Religion. Personal: Born April 6, 1927; Married; Father of Becky, Beth T. Goudschaal, Priscilla, Jeff. Education: B.S.E.E. with honors, Michigan Technological University, 1950; B.D. 1954, Th.M. 1956, Princeton Theological Seminary; Ph.D., The University of Iowa, 1963. Military: Served in the United States Naval Reserve as ETl, 1945-46, 1950-51. Career: Professor of Philosophy and Religion, Buena Vista College, 1967 to present; Part-Time Community Resource Person, Midwest Center of the National Endowment for the Humanities, 1973; Pastor, 1955-58; Graduate Assistant in Electrical Engineering, Princeton University, 1951-55; Part-Time Instructor of Mathematics, Whitworth College, 1950-51. Organizational Memberships: American Society of Church History; American Academy of Religion; Society for the History of Technology; Institute of Society, Ethics and the Life Sciences. Community Activities: Storm Lake Area Arts Council (first president); Storm Lake Area Advisory Council on Environmental Concerns (chairperson); Citizens Advisory Council (curriculum committee); Kiwanis (local president, 1968; lieutenant governor of old division IX, 1970-71); Spiritual Aims (district chairman, 1981-82); Kiwanis International Foundation (district chairman, 1982-82). Religion: Pastor, 1955-58; Congregational, Presbytery, Synod and National Committees; Moderator, Synod of Lakes and Prairies, 1976-77. Honors and Awards: Faculty Study Grants, Buena Vista College, 1968, 1971; Outstanding Educator, 4 Times; National Endowment for the Humanities Summer Seminar, University of California-Los Angeles; Visiting Scholar, University of Cambridge, England, 1978-79; Listed in *Dictionary of American Scholars, Dictionary of International Biography, International Scholars Dictionary, International Who's Who of Intellectuals, Who's Who in American Education, Who's Who in Religion.* Address: 1305 Shoreway, Storm Lake, Iowa 50588.

John J Tolson III

Tolson, John Jarvis III

United States Army Officer (retired). Personal: Born October 22, 1915; Son of Mr. and Mrs. John J. Tolson Jr.; Married Margaret Young; Father of David C., John J. IV, Harriet B. Education: Attended University of North Carolina, 1932-33; B.S., United States Military Academy, 1933-37; United States Army Parachute School, 1941; Armed Forces Staff College (equivalent); Air Command and Staff College (equivalant), 1947; British Staff College, 1951; United States Army War College, 1953; United States Army Aviation School, 1957; Management, University of Pittsburgh, 1960; United States Military Assistance Institute, 1961. Military: Served in the United States Army from 2nd Lieutenant to Lieutenant General, 1937-73. Career: Officer, Regular United States Army, 1937-73; Secretary, North Carolina Department of Military and Veterans Affairs, 1973-77. Organizational Memberships: Association of the United States Army (vice-president, 1974-76, 1977-78; president, 1976-77); The Airborne Association (president, 1975-77); Army Aviation Association of America; American Helicopter Society; Order of Daedalians; Legion of Valor; Military Order of the Purple Heart; American Legion; Veterans of Foreign Wars; Disabled American Veterans; Retired Officers Association. Community Activities: The Army Aviation Museum Foundation, Inc. (president, 1977 to present) The Tammy Lynn Memorial Foundation Inc. (board of directors, 1980-82; vice-president, 1981-82); Budleigh Community Watch (chairman, 1979-82); Occoneechee Council of Boy Scouts of America (executive board, 1980 to present); Triangle Area Chapter, American Red Cross (board of directors, 1982 to present); Lees McRae College (board of advisors, 1978-82); North Carolina Governor's Blue Ribbon Study Commission on Transportation Needs and Financing (chairman, aviation committee, 1978-80). Religion: Kanuga Episcopal Center, Board of Visitors, 1979 to present; Christ Church, Raleigh, North Carolina, Vestry, 1977-79; Episcopal Faith Alive Weekends, Visitor Team Member and Witness, 1977 to present; Lay Reader, Diocese of Southern Alabama 1957-59, Episcopal Diocese of Atlanta 1955-56. Honors and Awards: Army Aviation Hall of Fame, 1975; Distinguished Service Cross; Distinguished Service Medal with 2 Oak Leaf Clusters; Silver Star; Legion of Merit with 2 Oak Leaf Clusters; Distinguished Flying Cross; Bronze Star Medal; Air Medal with 44 Oak Leaf Clusters; Army Commendation Medal; Purple Heart; Presidential Unit Citation; Combat Infantryman Badge; Master Parachutist Badge; Master Army Aviation Badge; National Guard Bureau Meritorious Service Award; Boy Scouts of American Silver Beaver Award; Distinguished Service Medal, State of North Carolina; Static Line Award, General of the Year, 1980. Address: 1610 Canterbury Road, Raleigh, North Carolina 27608.

Toms, Kathleen Moore

Director of Nursing Service. Personal: Born December 31, 1943; Daughter of Phyllis J. Stewart; Mother of Kathleen Marie, Kelly Terese. Education: R.N., A.A., City College of San Francisco, 1963; B.P.S., Elizabethtown College, Pennsylvania, 1973; M.S.Ed., Temple University, 1977. Military: Serving with United States Army Reserve Nurse Corps as Captain, 1973 to present. Career: Director of Nursing, Riverside Osteopathic Hospital, Wilmington, Delaware, 1980 to present; Medical Surgical Nurse, St. Joseph Hospital, Fairbanks, Alaska, 1963-65; Emergency Room Nurse, St. Joseph Hospital, Lancaster, Pennsylvania, 1965-69; Blood, Plasma and Components Nurse, 1969-71; President F. E. Barry Company, Lancaster, 1971 to present; Director of Inservice Education, Lancaster Osteopathic Hospital, 1971-75; Coordinator of Practical Nursing Program, vocational technical school, Coatesville, Pennsylvania, 1976-77; Director of Nursing, Pocopson Home, West Chester, Pennsylvania, 1978-80; Inventor of auto-infusor for blood or blood components, 1971. Organizational Memberships: Delaware Nurses Association; Pennsylvania Nurses Association (director, 1974-78); Temple University and Elizabethtown College Alumni Associations. Community Activities: Delaware Health Council; Medical-Surgical Task Force, 1980 to present; Member of Pennsylvania Governor's Council on Drug Abuse and Alcoholism, 1974-76; Nurses Advisory Committee of the American Cancer Society, 1971-75; Director and Founder, Lancaster Community Health Center, 1973-76; Lecturer for N.I.D.A.-H.E.W. through N.F.C.C., 1973-76; Sustaining member, Republican National Committee. Honors and Awards: Army Commendation Medal, 1978; Community Service Award, Citizens United for Better Public Relations (Pennsylvania), 1974; Outstanding Citizen Award, W.G.A.L.-T.V., 1975; Sertoma Award, Sertoma Club of Lancaster. Address: 400 Summitt House, 1450 West Chester Pke., West Chester, Pennsylvania 19380.

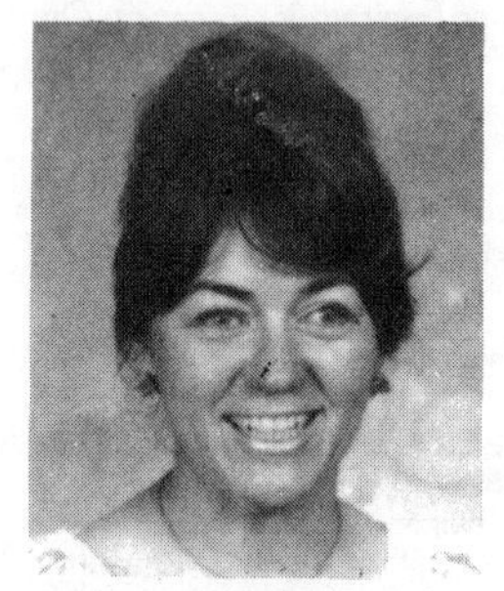

Kathleen M Toms

Torres-Aybar, Francisco G

Educator. Personal: Born July 12, 1934; Son of Francisco J. Torres; Married to Elga; Father of Elga, JoAnn Marie. Education: B.S., University of Puerto Rico, 1956; M.D., University of Barcelona, 1963. Career: Professor and Chairman of Department of Pediatrics, Ponce School of Medicine, Ponce, Puerto Rico; Pediatric Cardiologist and Pediatrician; Former Professor and Chairman of Department of Pediatrics, Catholic University of Puerto Rico School of Medicine; Director, Department of Pediatrics, Ponce District General Hospital. Address: A26 Jacaranda, Ponce, Puerto Rico 00731.

Torvend, Evelyn Sophia

Teacher (Retired). Personal: Born September 18, 1919; Daughter of Samuel and ReNettie Torvend (both deceased). Education: B.S., Mt. Angel Women's College, Oregon, 1950; M.S., Pacific University, Forest Grove, Oregon, 1960. Career: Teacher, Judson, Leslie and Parrish Junior High/Middle Schools, Salem, Oregon, 1960-81; Teachers, B.W. Barnes School, Hillsboro, Oregon, 1946-60;

Teacher, Marion County Elementary Schools, 1938-46. Organizational Memberships: National Education Association (life member, 1938 to present; northwest regional director, department of classroom teachers, 1956-59; secretary, Oregon department of classroom teachers, 1953-55); Oregon Education Association (teacher education and professional standards committee, 1952-55); Salem Education Association (parliamentarian and bulletin editor, 1962-66; numerous committees, 1967-81); National Council Accreditation of Teacher Education (team member 1974, 1976-78). Religion: American Lutheran Church; Senior High Consultant, 1965-70; World Mission Committee, 1972-76; Our Savior's Lutheran Church, Salem, Oregon, Parish Coordinator, 1975 to present. Honors and Awards: Delta Kappa Gamma, 1953 to present, Nu Chapter president, 1972-74; Listed in Numerous Biographical Reference Publications. Address: 225 Judson Street South, Salem, Oregon 97302.

Toutorsky, Basil P

Pianist, Composer, Professor and Director of Toutorsky Music Academy. Personal: Born January 10, 1896 in Novotcherkask, Russia; Son of Most Reverend Archpriest Peter V. and E. A. Samsonov Toutorsky; Married Maria I. Howard, 1936. Education: Musical Education Under Supervision of his Mother from Age 4; Studied Violin with Professor Stadji from Age 10; Graduate of Novotcherkask Gymnasya and Novotcherkask Musical College, 1913; Studied under Professors of Moscow Conservatory of Music; Law Degree, Moscow Imperial Lycee-University of Tsarevitch Nicholas and the University of Moscow, 1916. Military: Served during World War I in the Russian Naval as a Midshipman on the Staff of Commander-in-Chief of the Black Sea Fleet; Served on the "Empress Maria" which was blown up in 1916; Graduated from Naval Academy for Midshipmen of the Fleet in Petrograd and Commissioned as Naval Officer, 1917; Appointed to Legal Section of the staff of the White Army and Navy, serving until July 1920. Career: Teacher and Conductor, Istanbul, 1921-23; Founder and Director, Toutorsky Studio-Salon and Academy of Music, Los Angeles 1930-36, Washington, D.C. 1936 to present; Head of the Piano Department of Chevy Chase College in Maryland, 1943-50; Touring as Concert Pianist, United States, Mexico, Canada and Europe, Various Years. Organizational Memberships: The Washington Performing Arts Society (patron); National Symphony Orchestra (patron); International Platform Society; District of Columbia Chapter of National Association for American Composers and Conductors (vice-president, 1967-74); Military Order of World Wars (perpetual member, 1935 to present); English Speaking Union; Victorian Society; National Trust for Historic Preservation; Smithsonian Institution. Community Activities: Dupont Circle Citizens Association (sponsor of benefit tours to prevent the demolition of houses and mansions in Washington of great historical and artistic value; organizer of lectures, presenter of concert artists; adjudicator of contests; organizer of various benefit performances). Published Works: Author of Articles on Russian Music including "The Musical Development of Russia" and "Chords and Discords"; Many Musical Compositions including *Bicentennial Valse in A Minor, Mazurka in C Minor, Elegie in B Minor in Memory of S. V. Rachmanioff, Ballerinas Valse in C Major in Memory of Anna Pavlova, Poeme.* Honors and Awards: Honorary Doctor of Music Degree, American International Academy, 1937; Grand Prix Humanitaire de Belgique, Chevalier de Grand Croix, 1939; Diplôme de Medalle d'Or Compagnie Theatrale Philanthropique, France, 1947; Life Patron, American Biographical Institute; Life Patron, American Biographical Institute Research Association; Life Fellow, International Biographical Association, Cambridge, England; Listed in *Book of Honor.* Address: 1720 16th Street N.W., Washington, D.C. 20009.

June Traska

Tower, Catherine

Assistant Administrator, Nursing and Director of Nursing and Nursing Education. Personal: Born October 16, 1924; Daughter of Orlie and Hilda Anderson; Mother of Katheryn E., Mark S. Education: Nursing Diploma, Worcester City Hospital, 1947; B.S.N., Boston College, 1960; M.S.N. 1964, Postgraduate Study, Boston University. Career: Worcester Hahnemann Hospital, Assistant Administrator of Nursing 1974 to present, Project Director of Family Nurse Practitioner Program 1974-78, Director of Nursing Service 1961 to present, Instructor of the Fundamentals of Nursing, 1958-61, Staff Nurse 1957-58; Worcester City Hospital, Supervisor 1954-56, Staff Nurse 1956-57, Head Nurse 1948-49; Staff Nurse, Quincy City Hospital, 1949-50; Clinical Faculty, Graduate Program in Nursing Service Administration, Boston University and University of Massachusetts-Amherst; Consultant, Framingham Union Hospital Nursing Department; Continuing Education Faculty, Middlesex Community College. Organizational Memberships: American Nurses Association (certification, nursing administration advanced); American Society of Nursing Service Administrators (nominee, recognition program); American Nurses Association Council Nursing Administration; Massachusetts Nurses Association (past president, chairman, council on legal, ethical and professional practice; district II committee on practice; district II program committee; special interest group for directors, associates and assistants steering committee; district II, 2nd vice-president and program chairman; Task Force of Physicians Assistants); National League for Nursing/Massachusetts League for Nursing; Massachusetts Hospital Association/New England Hospital Association; Sigma Theta Tau Boston University Chapter; American Hospital Association; Massachusetts Society of Nursing Service Administrators; Worcester Area Directors of Nursing; Advisory Committees of Worcester State College Baccalaureate Degree Program in Nursing, Boston University Graduate Program in Nursing Administration, David H. Fanning School of Practical Nursing, Quinsigamond Community College Associate Degree Program in Nursing, Worcester State College Graduate Program for Nurse Practitioners, Anna Maria College Baccalaureate Degree Program in Nursing, A.H.E.C. Proposal for the University of Massachusetts-Worcester; H.S.A. II Task Force on Implementation of Ambulatory Care Plan; American Society of Law and Medicine; Central Massachusetts Family Planning Services (board of directors); Massachusetts Board of Registration in Nursing (vice-chairperson, 1977-81); Massachusetts Medical Society-Massachusetts Nurses Association Joint Practice Commission (co-chairman, 1973-75); Massachusetts Department of Public Health (advisory committee, standards nursing services); Comprehensive Health Planning (board of directors); Health Systems Agency Region II, Ambulatory Care Task Force; Worcester State College Search Committee on Nursing Studies (director); Great Brook Valley Professional Advisory Committee; Great Brook Valley Family Health Center (personnel committee); Massachusetts Board of Registration in Nursing-Board of Medicine Liaison Committee; Great Brook Valley Health Corporation (executive committee). Honors and Awards: American Nursing Administration Bicentennial Award, 1975; Massachusetts Nurses Association, Honorary Recognition Award 1975, Past President's Award 1980. Address: 7 Dartmoor Drive, Shrewsbury, Massachusetts 01545.

Traska, Irma June

Artist. Personal: Widow; Mother of 3 Children. Career: Watercolor and Oil Artist, Portrait Artist. Organizational Memberships: Oklahoma Art Guild; Oklahoma Watercolor Association; Oklahoma Art Center; Oklahoma Museum of Art; Midwest Art Society; Southwestern Watercolor Society; International Artists Society; Oklahoma Art League; American Association of Business Women; Oklahoma Historical Society; Oklahoma Heritage Association; Oklahoma County Medical Society (women's auxiliary); Richardson Civic Art Society, Richardson, Texas; National League of American Pen Women; International Platform Association; Kappa Pi National Honorary Art Fraternity. Community Activities: O.C.U. Alumni Association (board of directors); Women's Dinner Club (board of directors); American Association of University Women (board of directors); Arts Council (board of directors); Ladies Music Club (board of directors); MacDowell Club of Allied Arts (board of directors); Civic Music Association (board of directors). Community Activities: Painted Portrait of Astronaut General Tom Stafford, on Display in Oklahoma Hall of Fame, and Gave

Portrait Commission to Oklahoma Museum of Art, 1976; Donated Painting "Three Birds" to Zoological Society for Fund Drive; Teacher of Afternoon Art Demonstrations and Lessons to Students and Teachers, Banger School; Designer, Flyers and Miscellaneous Art Work to Nonprofit Organizations; Designer, Cover for Ladies Music Club Luncheon Program; Painter of Dual Portrait of Dr. Thomas Lynn, Dean, Oklahoma University Medical School and Dr. William Thurman, Provost, Oklahoma Health School Center, Reproduced on Cover of Oklahoma Unversity Medical School Bulletin and Permanently Placed in University of Oklahoma Health Sciences Center; Gave Watercolor Portrait Painting Demonstration, North Park Mall, Dallas, Texas, Painting now Displayed at Jan Maree Gallery, Oklahoma City; Designer, Cover of National Federation of Music Clubs Convention Program Prints Made for Awards for Students. Published Works: Author of Research Paper "Beginning of Art in Oklahoma". Honors and Awards: Artist Ambassador for Oklahoma to Ireland; Hostess, Oklahoma Hall of Fame Banquet; Honored at "Women in the News" Luncheon and Fashion Show, Oklahoma Hospitality Club, 1979; Nominated to Academia Italia belle Arte with Gold Medal; Listed in *Dictionary of Contemporary European Artists.* Address: Oklahoma City, Oklahoma.

Traugott, Fritz A

Consulting Mechanical Engineer. Personal: Born March 18, 1928; Son of Johann and Marie Traugott (both deceased); Married Frances Fortier. Education: B.S.M.E., Government Engineering School, Austria, 1957; Graduate Study, Syracuse University, 1953. Career: Robson and Woese, Inc., Vice-President and Senior Partner and Treasurer 1977 to present, Vice-President in Charge of HVAC Design 1970-77, Consultant and Head of HVAC Department 1968-70, Supervisor of Project Engineers 1958-68; Design and Specification Writer, Consulting Engineering Firm, 1955-57; Stefan Ammann & Son, District Engineer for Austria 1953-55, Design Engineer; Engineer-in-Training, Carried Corporation, 1948-52. Organizational Memberships: A.S.H.R.A.E. (chairman, nominating committee, 1982-83; chairman, honors and awards committee, 1982-83; finance committee, 1979-81; director and regional chairman, region I, 1976-79; TC9.1 "Large Building A/C Systems", member 1975 to present, chairman 1980 to present; nominating, standards, regional subcommittees, technical programs, workbook, 1970-78; central New York chapter, president, 1968-69, secretary 1966-67); American Consulting Engineers Council; Technology Club of Syracuse. Community Activities: Rotary Club of Syracuse (membership committee chairman, 1978-79, 1981-82; hospitality committee chairman, 1977-78; secretary, 1981-82); Century Club, 1977 to present; Cazenovia Ski Club, 1963 to present. Honors and Awards: United States Award of Achievement, 1952; Engineer of the Year, City of Syracuse, 1969; Distiguished Service Award, 1979; A.S.H.R.A.E., Fellow 1980, Region I Regional Award of Merit 1981; Paul Harris Fellow Award, 1982; Guest Lecturer, Syracuse University, 1972 to present. Address: 2996 Pompey Hollow Road, Cazenovia, New York 13035.

Tresmontan, Olympia Davis

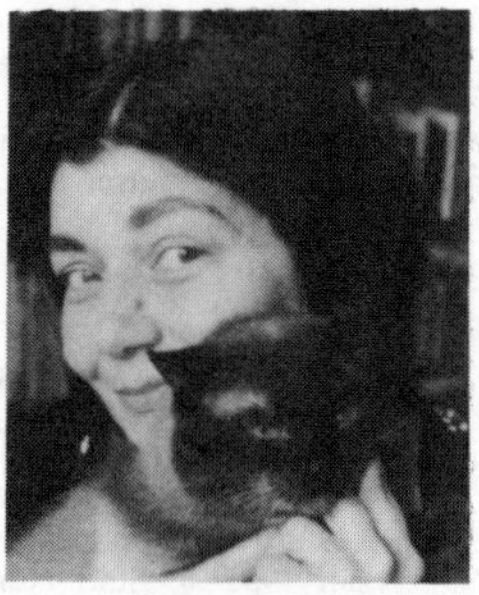
Olympia D Tresmontan

Psychotherapist, Counselor and Consultant. Personal: Born November 27, 1925; Daughter of Peter Konstantin and Mary Hazimanolis Davis (both deceased); Married Robert Baker Stitt, March 21, 1974. Education: B.S., Simmons College, Boston, Massachusetts, 1946; M.A., Wayne State University, Detroit, Michigan, 1960; Ph.D., University of California-Berkeley, 1971. Career: Private Practice Psychotherapist, Counselor and Consultant, 1970 to present; Director, Studio Ten Services, San Francisco, California, 1973 to present; Teacher, Chapman College Graduate Division 1971-74, University of California-San Francisco Extension Division 1971-73; Sensitivity Trainer, National Science Foundation Science Foundation Science Curriculum Improvement Project of University of California-Berkeley, 1967-68; Social Worker, San Francisco Child Welfare, 1964-66. Organizational Memberships: American Psychological Association, 1970 to present; American Orthopsychiatric Association, 1974 to present; American Association of Marriage Therapists, 1973 to present; California Association of Marriage and Family Therapists, 1973 to present. Community Activities: Childworth Learning Center, San Francisco (board of directors, 1976-80); Friends of the San Francisco Public Library, 1972 to present; International Hospitality Committee of the Bay Area, 1974 to present; National Association of Social Workers, 1947-79; Commonwealth Club of California, 1978 to present; American Association of University Women, 1980 to present. Honors and Awards: Wayne State University, Honors Convocation 1949-50, 1960; Schaefer Foundation Grantee, 1969-70; Pi Lambda Theta Honor Society for Women, University of California-Berkeley Chapter, 1967 to present; Honoring of Women, Thomas Starr King School of Religious Leadership, Berkeley, California, 1981. Address: 2611 Lake Street, San Francisco, California 94121.

Treuting, Edna Gannon

Director of Nursing Section. Personal: Born December 16, 1925; Daughter of Alphonse and Clara Gannon (both deceased); Married August Raymond Treuting, J.D.; Mother of Keith, Karen, Madeline, Jaime, Jay. Education: Diploma, Charity Hospital School of Nursing, 1946; B.S.N.Ed., Louisiana State University School of Nursing, 1953; M.P.H. 1972, F.N.P. 1973, D.P.H. 1978, Tulane University School of Public Health and Trop. Medicine. Career: Director of Nursing Section, Tulane School of Public Health and Tropical Medicine; Director, F.N.P. and P.N.P. Programs, 1972-81; Instructor of Public Health, 1972-74; Associate Professor of Public Health, 1977 to present; Director, O.H.N., 1977-80; Nursing Educator, Louisiana State University School of Nursing-Maternal Child Health and Pediatrics; Nursing Educator, Charity Hospital School of Nursing-Pediatrics; Industrial Nurse, Shell Oil and American Sugar Refinery; Head Nurse, Pediatrics and Pre-Mature Nursery, Charity Hospital; Private Duty Nurse. Organizational Memberships: American Nurses Association; National League of Nursing; Southern Region Education Board; Council on Primary Helath Care Nursing Programs. Community Activities: Lousiana State Health Department (consultant); Home Health Inc. (consultant); Teagle Foundation (consultant); Regional Medical Program and Tri-Way Hospital (consultant); City of Lafayette (consultant); Ross Laboratories (consultant); Lousiana Industrial Nurses Association (consultant); Medical Personnel Pool (consultant); Research Consultant to American Association of Critical Care; Editorial Consultant to *Nurse Practitioners Journal*; National, Regional and Local Groups, Speaker; Developed and Conducted Workshops for University of Hawaii, University f Southern Mississippi, L.N.L. Religion: Catholic; Holy Cross High School Board, 1966-72; Archdiocese Seminarian Physical Examinations, 1962-69; School Nurse, St. Frances Cobrini, 1960-69; Senior Trip Nurse, Dominion High School, 1974. Published Works: Contributor to Various Journals, O.H.N. Book; American Nursing Administration Book in Progress. Honors and Awards: Delta Omega (eta chapter, member 1976 to present, president 1981-82); Delta Omega Nominee Merit Award, 1978; School of Nursing Honor Society 1979, Mortar Board Outstanding Women's Day Speaker 1981, Louisiana State University; Sigma Theta Tau, 1982; International Citizen Ambassador to South America, 1979; University of Hawaii School of Public Health and School of Nursing Invitational Workshop, 1977. Address: 8040 Morrison Road, New Orleans, Louisiana 70126.

Trice, Dorothy Louise

Physician and Medical Director. Personal: Born January 12, 1924; Married James E. Willie (deceased). Education: R.N., Lincoln School for Nurses, New York, 1945; B.S.Ed., Hunter College, New York, 1947; M.D., Woman's Medical College of Pennsylvania,

Philadelphia, 1956; M.P.H., Columbia University School of Public Health and Administrative Medicine, New York, 1959. Career: Physician and Medical Director, Neponsit Home for the Aged, 1979 to present; Director of Ambulatory Care and Community Medicine, Queens General Hospital Affiliate of Long Island Jewish Medical Center, 1977-79; Physician, Health Officer, Borough Director, Deputy Commissioner and Regional Director, New York City Department of Health, 1957-77. Organizational Memberships: Medical Society of the County of Kings (past trustee; secretary); Provident Clinical Society of Brooklyn, Inc. (past president); Brooklyn Tuberculosis and Lung Association (community education committee); New York Diabetes Association (clinical society); Brooklyn Home for the Aged and Brooklyn Visiting Nurse Association (professional advisory committee); American Cancer Society (New York City and Queens chapters). Community Activities: Community Health Planning Boards of District 1, 3, 4, and 8 of Brooklyn, 1972-77; Willing Workers for Human Rights, 1963-70; Brooklyn Chapter of Soroptimist International of the Americas, 1976 to present; Kings County Hospital Community Board, 1970-77. Religion: St. George's Episcopal Church, Vestry 1972 to present; Diocesan Convention Delegate, 1972 to present; Diocesan Council Member, 1981 to present; Church Charity Foundation Member, 1973-78. Honors and Awards: St. George's Episcopal Church Scholarship Fund Award for Service, 1976; Susan Smith McKinney Stewart Medical Society Award, 1978. Address: 153-25 88th Street, Howard Beach, New York 11414.

Tropf, Cheryl G

Project Manager. Personal: Born October 15, 1946; Married William Jacob Tropf III; Mother of Andrew Zachary. Education: B.S. Physics, William and Mary University, 1968; M.A.M. 1972, Ph.D. 1973, Applied Mathematics, University of Virginia. Career: Project Manager, Operating Reactors, United States Nuclear Regulatory Commission, 1981 to present; Congressional Science Fellow, Senate Commerce, Science and Transportation Committee, 1980-81; Senior Physicist, Johns Hopkins University Applied Physics Laboratory, 1973-80. Organizational Memberships: S.I.A.M.; Washington Women's Network; National Association of Female Executives. Community Activities: Howard County (Maryland) Commission for Women (appointed by county executive). Honors and Awards: Phi Beta Kappa, 1968; Sigma Xi, 1972.

Trowbridge, Richard Stuart

Research Scientist. Personal: Born April 3, 1942; Son of Walter H. and Lamia A. Trowbridge; Married Sue Hitchcock; Father of John Richard. Education: B.S. 1964, M.S. 1966, Ph.D. 1971, University of Massachusetts-Amherst. Career: Research Scientist in Virology and Mammalian Cell Biology; Clinical Microbiologist; Public Health Bacteriologist; Public Health Inspector; Sanitarian. Organizational Memberships: American Society for Microbiology, 1964 to present; Tissue Culture Association, 1976 to present; The New York Academy of Sciences, 1981 to present. Community Activities: Staten Island Rotary Club, 1979 to present; Staten Island's Meals on Wheels (board of directors, 1979 to present; vice-president, 1981 to 1982; president, 1982 to present); Boy Scouts of America (district committee, member-at-large, 1978 to present; council executive committee, 1981 to present; scoutmaster, 1977 to present; troop committee chairman pro-tem, 1977-78; Webelos den leader, 1976-77; cub pack committee, 1977-78). Honors and Awards: N.D.E.A. Fellowship, 1968-70; Listed in *Who's Who in the East*. Address: 180 Woodward Avenue, Staten Island, New York 10314.

Truex, Duane Phillip III

Museum Director. Personal: Born August 30, 1947; Married Brenda; Father of Adriane Michelle. Education: B.A. Music, Ithaca College. Career: Museum Director; Executive Director, Arts and Humanities Council of Greater Baton Rouge, Inc.; Executive Director, Baton Rouge Symphony Association; Director of Public Relations, Kansas City Philharmonic; Assistant Director of Student Activities, Oklahoma State University. Organizational Memberships: Phi Mu Alpha National Professional Music Fraternity; Beta Gamma Sigma, Oklahoma State University Chapter, 1971. Community Activities: The Unknown Theater Company, Inc. (vice-chairman; board of directors, 1970-72); National Entertainment Conference (national board of directors, 1972); National Bureau of Discovery (board of directors, 1976-78); Binghamton Rotary Club (board of directors, 1981); New York State Association of Museums (secretary, 1981-83); Vice Chairman Commission on Architecture and Urban Design, 1978 to present. Honors and Awards: Listed in *Outstanding Young Men of America, Who's Who in the East, Who's Who in America*. Address: 5½ Haydn Street, Binghamton, New York 13905.

Tucker, Dorothy M

Professor of Psychology. Personal: Born August 22, 1942; Daughter of James Anderson and Cleo Christine Fant Tucker. Education: B.S., Bowling Green University, 1960; M.Ed., University of Toledo, 1968; Ph.D., The Ohio State University, 1972; Ph.D., California School of Professional Psychology, 1976. Career: Professor of Psychology; Associate Professor, Florida International University; Associate Professor, Charles R. Drew Postgraduate Medical School; Director of Clinical Training in Psychology, The Wright Institute Graduate School, Los Angeles; Special Assistant to the Speaker of the California State Assembly, Willie C. Brown, Jr. Organizational Memberships: Black Women in Psychology (founder/convenor, 1981 to present); United Negro College Fund of Southern California (chair, 1980-81); American Psychologists Association; Association of Black Psychologists; Swanza Foundation (board of directors); California State Psychological Association. Community Activities: California State Democratic Party Committee, 1979 to present; Alan Cranston for Senate Committee (field director, 1980); Judicial Nominees Evaluation Committee, 1980-81; Inglewood Housing Commission, 1980-81; Charter Review Commission of Inglewood, 1981 to present; National Women's Continuation Committee, 1977 to present. Honors and Awards: Ford Foundation Fellow; N.D.E.A. Fellow; Pi Lambda Theta; Citation, Outstanding Service, Florida Board of Regents; Listed in *Who's Who of Women in America, Who's Who of International Women*. Address: 107 South Broadway #8009, Los Angeles, California 90012.

Tung, Rosalie L

University Professor. Personal: Born December 2, 1948; Daughter of Andrew and Pauline Lam; Married Byron Tung; Mother of Michele Christine. Education: B.A., York University, 1972; M.B.A. 1974, Ph.D. Business Administration 1977, University of British Columbia. Career: University Professor, The Wharton School, University of Pennsylvania-Philadelphia. Organizational Memberships: Academy of International Business; Academy of Management; American Management Association; American Economic Association; American Institute of Decision Sciences; American Psychological Association; International Association of Applied Psychology. Honors and Awards: Listed in *The World Who's Who of Women, Who's Who of American Women, The Book of Honor, Directory of Distinguished Americans, Personalities of America*. Address: P.O. Box 8253, Philadelphia, Pennsylvania 19101.

Tureck, Rosalyn

Concert Artist, Author, Educator. Personal: Born December 14, 1914 in Chicago, Illinois; Daughter of Samuel and Monya Lipson Tureck. Education: Studied with Sophia Brilliant-Liven and Jan Chiapusso; Graduate cum laude, Juilliard School of Music, 1935. Career: Touring Concert Artist, United States 1937 to present, Europe 1947 to present, South Africa 1959, South America 1963, Israel 1963, Far East (Hong Kong, India, Australia) 1971; Conductor-Soloist, with London Philharmonic 1958, New York Philharmonic 1958, Collegium Musicum (Copenhagen), Tureck Bach Players (London) 1958 to present, San Antonio Symphony and Oklahoma Symphony 1962, Scottish National Symphony 1963, Israel Philharmonic 1963, Kol Israel Orchestra 1970, Nashville Symphony Orchestra 1977, Tureck Bach Players (London) 1980, Tureck Bach Players (United States) 1981; St. Louis Symphony Orchestra 1981; Television Appearances; Professor of Music, University of Maryland 1982 to present, University of California-San Diego 1967-72; Visiting Professor of Music, Washington University, St. Louis, 1963-64; Instructor, Columbia University 1953-55, Juilliard School of Music 1943-44, Mannes College of Music 1940-44, Philadelphia Conservatory of Music, 1935-42; Visiting Fellow, St. Hilda's College, Oxford University, 1974; Honorary Life Fellow, St. Hilda's College, 1974 to present; Visiting Fellow, Wolfson College, Oxford University, 1975 to present; Founder-Director, Composers of Today 1951-55, Tureck Bach Players (London) 1957 to present; International Bach Society, Inc. 1966, Institute for Bach Studies 1968, Tureck Bach Institute, Inc. 1981. Organizational Memberships: American Music Scholarship Association (honorary president); Music Library, Hebrew University, Jerusalem; Societe Johann Sebastian Bach de Belgique; The Bohemians, New York (honorary life member); American Musicological Society; New Bach Society; Royal Musical Association; Royal Philharmonic Society; Oxford Society. Published Works: *An Introduction to the Performance of Bach*, 3 Volumes, 1969-70, Japanese Translation 1966, Spanish Translation 1975; *Tureck Bach Urtext Series*, 1981; Transcriber of Music, 1960; Author of Numerous Periodical Articles for *Current Musicology, Making Music, Music and Letters, News Statesman, Saturday Review, Hi-Fi Magazine;* Recordings of *Goldberg Variations and Aria and Ten Variations in the Italian, Italian Concerto, Chromatic Fantasia and Fugue, Four Duets;* Film Perfomances in *Fantasy and Fugue: Rosalyn Tureck Plays Bach* 1972, *Rosalyn Tureck Plays on Harpsichord and Organ* 1977, *Joy of Bach* 1978, *Camera 3-Bach on the Frontier of the Future*, 1980. Honors and Awards: First Prize Award for Debut, Age 9, 1923; First Prize, Greater Chicago Piano Playing Tournament, 1928; Winner, Schubert Memorial Contest, 1935; National Federation of Music Clubs Competition, 1935; Phi Beta Award for Excellence; First Town Hall Endowment Award, 1938; Honorary Fellow, Guildhall School of Music and Drama, London, 1959; Honorary Mus.D. Degree, Colby College 1964; Roosevelt University, Chicago, 1968, Wilson College 1968, Oxford University, England 1977; Fellow, Macdowell Colony, 1978; Officers Cross of the Order of Merit of the Federal Republic of Germany, 1979; Nominee, Grammy Award, 1980. Address: Columbia Artists Management, 165 West 57th Street, New York, New York 10019.

Turner, Ellen Latheal H

Assistant Professor of English. Personal: Born November 18, 1911; Daughter of Mr. and Mrs. C. Otto Howard (both deceased); Married John E. Turner. Education: B.A., Simmons University, 1929; Postgraduate Study, Abilene Christian College, 1931, 1936; M.A., North Texas State Teachers College, 1948; Further Study, Hardin-Simmons University 1960, 1957, 1963, North Texas University 1968. Career: Assistant Professor of English, Hardin-Simmons University, 1967-79; Abilene High School, Teacher 1953-67, Chairman of the English Department 1961-67; Teacher, Woodrow Wilson Junior High School, 1943-53, Tuscola High School 1938-41, 1942-43, Dudley Elementary School, 1935-36, Nugent School 1934-35, Fairview High School 1931-34, Williams Elementary School 1930-31; Mankins Elementary School, Teacher 1936-38, Principal 1937-38. Organizational Memberships: T.J.C.T.E. (chairman, 1967); T.S.T.A.; National Education Association; C.C.E.; N.C.E.; T.C.T.A. (board of directors, 1964); Delta Kappa Gamma Society International, Zeta Psi Chapter (president, 1975-77; state convention coordinator, 1979-81; Alpha state personnel committee chairman, 1981-83); American Association of University Women (president, 1979-80). Community Activities: Abilene Cactus Lioness Club (charter member, 1976 to present; president, 1981-82); River Oaks Chapter of Order of the Eastern Star (member, 1947 to present; worthy matron, 1960-61); Community Service Committee, 1979-80; Abilene Shakespeare Club (member, 1960 to present; treasurer, 1965-67; president, 1969-71; secretary, 1980-82); Social Order of the Beauecent, Abilene Assembly (member, 1950 to present; president, 1965; supreme director of music, 1978-79). Religion: Belmont Baptist Church; Member, 1964 to present; Sunday School Teacher, 1964 to present; Director of Educational Training, 1980 to present; Member, Baptist Churches, 1921 to present; Teacher, 1924 to present; Organist in Various Churches, 1931-39; Esther Bible Club, Member 1977 to present, Tresurer 1980-81. Honors: Runner-Up, Best Teacher Award, 1952; Listed in *Outstanding Educators of American, Who's Who in Texas Education, World Who's Who of Women, Community Leaders, Who's Who of American Women.* Address: 1817 Jackson Street, Abilene, Texas 79602.

Herman N Turner Jr

Turner, Gladys Tressia

Social Work Administrator. Personal: Born September 16, 1935; Daughter of Willis and Mary Bluford Turner; Married Frederick Marshall Finney. Education: B.A., A.M.&N. College (now University of Arkansas-Pine Bluff), 1957; M.S.W., Atlanta University, 1959. Career: Social Work Administrator; Clinical Social Worker. Organizational Memberships; National Association of Social Workers (Miami Valley chapter, secretary 1961, 2nd vice-president, 1974, president 1975-76, delegate to delegate assembly, 1979; national nominating committee, member 1971-72, chairperson 1973). Community Activities: Montgomery County Children's Services (advisory board, 1969-75); Dayton Board of Education (advisory committee for special education, 1974); Montgomery County Combined General Health District Professional Advisory committee, 1974-77; Wright State University Medical School (medicine in society steering committee, 1975-76); Miami Valley Hospital Social Work Directors Organization (co-founder); Parents Association of Non-Ambulatory Retarded Children (co-founder). Religion: College Hill United Presbyterian Church, elder, 1976 to present; Nominating Committee Chairperson, 1981; Miami Presbytery Committee for the Self-Development of People, Chairperson, 1981 to present. Honors and Awards: Social Worker of the Year, Miami Valley Chapter of National Association of Social Workers. Address: 1107 Lexington Avenue, Dayton, Ohio 45407.

Turner, Herman Nathaniel Jr

Educator. Personal: Born November 6, 1925, in St. Louis, Missouri; Son of Herman Nathaniel, Sr., and Rosie Mae Williams Turner; Married Terrance Diane Parker on October 5, 1980, in St. Louis; Father of Anthony Cabot, Mark Courtney, Herman Nathaniel III, Erik Alexander (by previous marriage) and Marian Terese Simmons, Mariesta Marcella Simmons, Melita Diane Simmons (stepdaughters). Education: Graduate, Vashon High School, St. Louis, 1944; B.S., Bradley University, 1951; Undertook postgraduate work at Bradley University, 1951-52. Military: Served with United States Marine Corps during World War II in the South Pacific as Radar Operator, 1944-46. Career: Instructor of mathematics at Vaux Junior High School and Stoddart-Fleisher Junior High School (Philadelphia, Pennsylvania), 1956-59, Washington Senior High School (Caruthersville, Missouri), 1961-62, United Township High School (East Moline, Illinois), 1965-66, and Northwest High School (St. Louis), 1968 to present; Mathematician, White Sands Proving Ground, Flight Determination Laboratory, Data Reduction Branch, Optical Reduction

Section, Las Cruces, New Mexico, 1954-55; Cartographic Photogrammetric Aide, Aeronautical Chart and Information Center, Photogrammetry Division, Topography Branch, St. Louis, 1953-54. Organizational Memberships: Mathematical Association of America, 1962 to present; American Federation of Teachers, 1969 to present; American Mathematical Society, 1977 to present; Northwest High School Public Relations Committee, 1978 to present. Community Activities: Kiwanis Club of East Moline, Illinois (chairman of public relations committee, 1965-66). Religion: Presbyterian. Honors and Awards: Fellow, International Biographical Association, 1978 to present; Fellow, American Biographical Institute, 1979 to present; Honorary Fellow, Anglo-American Academy, 1980 to present; Certified Teacher in Missouri, Illinois, Pennsylvania, New Jersey and New York; Certificate of Appreciation, Kiwanis Club of East Moline, 1965; Scroll of the Anglo-American Academy, 1980; Received numerous awards of appreciation from students at Northwest High School, including Teacher of the Month (October-November, 1979) and Teacher of the Year, 1980; Listed in *Who's Who in the Midwest, International Who's Who of Intellectuals, Personalities of the West and Midwest, Community Leaders and Noteworthy Americans, Book of Honor, Personalities of America, Men of Achievement, International Who's Who in Community Service, Dictionary of International Biography*. Address: P.O. Box 1028, St. Louis, Missouri 63188.

Tyer, Travis Earl

Travis E Tyer

Librarian. Personal: Born October 23, 1930, in Lorenzo, Texas; Son of Mr. and Mrs. Charlie E. Tyer; Married Alma Lois Davis in 1951; Father of Alan Ross, Juanita Linn. Education: B.S., Abilene Christian University, 1952; B.S.L.S., North Texas State University, 1959; Ad.M., Florida State University, 1969; Undertook further courses at Midwestern University, Odessa College, Texas Technological University; Undertaking courses toward his Ph.D., Florida State University. Career: Teacher, Librarian, Audio-Visual Coordinator, Borden County Public Schools, Texas, 1952-54; Librarian, Carroll Thompson Junior High School, Lubbock, Texas, 1954-55; Librarian, Seminole Public Schools, Seminole, Texas, 1955-61; Vacation Relief Librarian, Lubbock Public Library, Summer 1957; Workshop Director, Texas Woman's University, Denton, Texas, Summers of 1960 and 1961; Dallas Public Library: Head, Y.A. Department, Central Library, July 1961-April 1962; Head, Oak Lawn Branch, May 1962-August 1962; Coordinator, Y.A. Services, September 1962-May 1966; Library Director, Lubbock Public Library, 1966; Library Director, Lubbock City-County Libraries, 1967-68; Summer Faculty, North Texas State University, 1970; Graduate Library School Faculty/State Coordinator, Personnel Development, Emporia State University, 1971-72; Senior Consultant, Professional Development, Illinois State Library, 1972-80; Executive Director, Great River Library System, Quincy, Illinois, 1980 to present. Organizational Memberships: American Library Association; Illinois Library Association; Continuing Library Education Network and Exchange; Adult Education Association; Midwest Federation of Library Associations (continuing library education committee, 1978-82); Association of Specialized and Cooperative Library Agencies (state library agency section, planning, organization and bylaws committee, 1979-80); Public Library Association (chairman, editorial board, *Public Libraries*, 1981-83; chairman, planning committee, 1980-83). Community Acitivies: Noon Kiwanis; Quincy Little Theatre (patron); Chamber of Commerce; Lincoln Club; City Colleges of Chicago (advisory committee, library technical assistant program, 1976 to present). Religion: Church of Christ. Honors and Awards: Listed in *Who's Who in America, International Who's Who of Intellectuals, Who's Who in the Midwest*. Address: 2 Aden Drive, Quincy, Illinois 62301.

Uchida, Tadao

Editor-in-Chief, United States Executive Vice-President. Personal: Born June 9, 1939; Son of Yoshiharu and Shique Uchida; Married Kazuko Hashimoto. Education: B.A. Economics, Keiko University, Tokyo, Japan, 1962. Career: *Japan Business News*, Executive Vice-President and Editor-in-Chief 1975 to present, Los Angeles Bureau Chief Correspondent 1966-75, Social Affair Writer 1964-65; *The Yomiuri Shimbun*, Sports Writer in Tokyo, 1962-64; Correspondent in Fukushima Office 1962. Organizational Memberships: International Correspondents Club; Japan National Press Club; Greater Los Angeles Press Club; The Society of Professional Journalists Sigma Delta Chi. Published Works: *Man and Environment*, Dai-ichi Shobo, 1972; "Japanese Mass-Media", "Hito to Nippon", Japanese Magazines, 1973-75. Honors and Awards: The Editorial Prizes of the Yomiuri Newspaper, 4 Times, 1968-75. Address: Plymouth Tower #22H, 340 East, New York, New York 10028.

Uehling, Barbara S

University Chancellor. Personal: Born June 12, 1932; Daughter of Mr. and Mrs. Roy W. Staner; Married Stanley Johnson; Mother of David, Jeff. Education: B.A., Psychology, Wichita State University, 1954; M.A. 1956, Ph.D. 1958, Experimental Psychology, Northwestern University. Career: Chancellor, University of Missouri-Columbia, 1978 to present; Provost, University of Oklahoma-Norman, 1976-78; Dean of Arts and Science, Illinois State University, 1974-76; Academic Dean, Roger Williams College, 1972-74; Psychology Professor, University of Rhode Island 1970-72, Emory University 1966-69; Faculty Member, Oglethorpe University, 1959-64. Organizational Memberships: American Association for Higher Education (board of directors); American Council on Education (board of directors); Carnegie Council on Educational Research (White House appointment); Meredith Corporation (board member); Mercantile Bancorporation (board member). Community Activities: North Central Association of Schools and Colleges (accreditation team); National Association of State Universities and Land Grant Colleges (policies and issues committee); N.C.A.A. Select Committee on Athletics; United Way (board of directors); American Cancer Society (Missouri chapter honorary educational chair). Honors and Awards: Distinguished Alumni Award, Wichita State University; Honorary Degree, Drury College; Honorary Doctor of Laws, Ohio State University; 100 Young Leaders of the Academy, *Change* Magazine; Missouri Institute of Public Administration Award for Outstanding Contributions to Public Administration; Listed in *Who's Who in America, Who's Who in the Midwest, Dictionary of International Biography, American Men and Women of Science, Men of Achievement.* Address: Chancellor's Residence, Columbia, Missouri 65201.

Howard A Unger

Uihlein, Henry Holt

Executive. Personal: Born August 17, 1921; Son of Claudia H. Uihlein; Married to Marion Strauss; Father of Henry Holt, James Christopher, Philip, Richard. Education: B.A., University of Virginia, 1943; Business Degree, Babson School of Business Administration, 1946. Military: Served with United States Marine Corps Reserve with rank of Corporal, 1944-46. Career: Refrigeration Company Executive; President, Jensen Service Corporation, 1962 to present; Various positions with U-Line Corporation (Milwaukee, Wisconsin), 1962 to present, Chairman of the Board, 1977 to present, Director, 1977 to present; Business Consultant, 1962-65; President and General Manager, Quic Frez, Inc., Fond du Lac, Wisconsin, 1955-60; President and General Manager, Ben Hur Manufacturing Company, Milwaukee, 1947-62. Community Activities: President, Herman A. Uihlein, Sr., Foundation, Inc. of Milwaukee, 1955 to present. Religion: Christian Scientist. Published Works: Contributor to professional journals. Honors and Awards: Named to Wisconsin Ice Hockey Hall of Fame, 1978. Address: 8500 North Green Bay Court, Milwaukee, Wisconsin 53209.

Unger, Howard Albert

College Professor, Artist-Photographer. Personal: Born October 13, 1944; Son of Howard and Florence Unger; Married Anrita Abelow; Father of Christopher Howard. Education: B.F.A. 1966, M.A. 1968, Kent State University, Ohio; M.Ed. 1972, Ed.D. 1975, Postdoctoral Studies in Educational Administration 1978, Teachers College, Columbia University, New York, New York; Art Students League, New York, New York, 1960-61; School of Visual Arts, New York, New York, 1975-76; New York Institute of Holography, New York, New York, 1976. Career: Professor, Ocean County College, Toms River, New Jersey; Artist-Photographer; Coordinator of Photography and Art, R.C.A. Records, New York, New York, 1969-70. Organizational Memberships: National Education Association, 1972 to present; New Jersey Education Association, 1972 to present; Society of Photography Educators, 1976 to present. Community Activities: Chinese Cultural Development Council, New York, New York (producer of documentary videotape on Chinese classical music, 1970); Dr. Martin Luther King Health Center, Bronx, New York (producer and director of television program on oral health education, 1972); Nutritional Education Program for Head Start in conjunction with the Urban League of Westchester County, New York (producer of photographic exhibition, 1973); Young Men's Christian Association Photography Club, Manhattan, New York, New York (judge of photography show, 1974); Westchester County Urban League, Port Chester, New York (graphic designer of brochures on health education with photographic illustration, 1975); United States Navy, Lakehurst, New Jersey (photography exhibition judge, 1976); New Jersey Equine Society of the State Department of Agriculture, New Jersey (art show judge, 1977). Religion: Lutheran; Director of Video Production, "Black Poets", Inter-Church Center, Union Theological Seminary, New York City, 1971. Honors and Awards: 1st Place, The American Greeting Card Competition, 1966; "Photographis Societas Photographis" Photography Show, Columbia University, New York, New York, 1971; Photography Exhibition, Ziegfeld Gallery, New York, New York, 1972; Honorarium, Department of Curriculum and Teaching, Teachers College, Columbia University, New York, New York, 1973; Annual Faculty Art Show, Ocean County College, Toms River, New Jersey, 1972-81; Listed in *Who's Who in the East.* Address: 437 East 76th Street, New York, New York 10021.

Upbin, Hal J

Chairman of the Board. Personal: Born January 15, 1939; Son of David Upbin (deceased) and Evelyn Stiefel; Married Shari Kiesler;

Father of Edward, Elyse, Danielle. Education: B.B.A., Accounting, Pace College, 1961; C.P.A., Certified Public Accounting Examination, 1965. Career: Chairman of the Board, Triton Group Ltd. (formerly Chase Manhattan Mortgage and Realty Trust, New York, New York), 1978 to present; Chase Manhattan Mortgage and Realty Trust, Chairman and President 1978 to present, Executive Vice-President and Chief Financial Officer 1975-78; President, Wheelabrator Financial Corporation, New York, New York, 1974-75; Treasurer, Wheelabrator Frye, Inc., New York, New York, 1972-75; Tax Manager, Price Waterhouse and Company, New York, New York, 1965-71; Tax Senior on Audit Staff, Peat, Marwick, Mitchell and Company, New York, New York, 1961-65. Organizational Memberships: New York State Society of Certified Public Accountants (guest speaker; municipal and local taxation committee); American Institute of Certified Public Accountants (guest speaker, various seminars). Community Activities: Isomedics Inc. (chairman of the board and director); Pace University (guest speaker at seminars; member, finance & facilities planning committee of the board of trustees and alumni advisory members); Interval Timeshare Association of New York, Inc. (vice-president); Temple Beth-El, Somerset, New Jersey (past president); Jaycees of Somerset County, New Jersey (past vice-president); Metropolitan Opera Guild; Metropolitan Museum of Art; Museum of Modern Art. Religion: Temple Beth-El. Published Works: Articles on Taxation, *The Journal of Accountancy*. Honors and Awards: Listed in *Who's Who in America*, *Who's Who in Finance and Industry*, *Notable Americans of 1978-79*, *The American Registry*, *Men of Achievement*, *Dictionary of International Biography*, *Directory of United States Banking Executives*, *Community Leaders of America*, *Men and Women of Distinction*, *The International Who's Who of Intellectuals*, *International Who's Who in Community Service*. Address: 45 East 89th Street, New York, New York 10028.

Urban, Walter J

Research Psychoanalyst. Personal: Born April 20, 1932. Education: B.A. cum laude Psychology 1953, M.A. Clinical School Psychology 1954, City College of New York; Ph.D., Clinical Psychology International College, Los Angeles, 1977; Certificate in Psychoanalysis, National Psychological Association for Psychoanalysis, New York, New York, 1958-65; Certficate in Mental Health Consultation, Postgraduate Center for Mental Health, New York, New York, Department of Community Education and Services, 1967-70; Family Therapy Training with Dr. Nathan Ackerman, Family Institute, New York, New York, 1966; Certificate in Hypnosis, Ethical Hypnosis Training Center, South Orange, New Jersey, 1976; Certificate of Attendance in Polarity Therapy, Orange, California, 1973; Gestalt Workshops with Elana Rubinfel, Dr. Julian Silverman, and Others, Esalen Massage, Esalen Institute, Big Sur, California, 1973; Basic Course in Jin Shin Jyutsu, Acupressure Workshop, Los Angeles, California, 1976. Career: Private Practice Research Psychoanalyst in Individual Group, Marital, Family and Integrative Therapy, 1962 to present; Tutor, International College, Los Angeles; Director, Theodor Reik Consultation Center, New York, 1976; Faculty, Humanistic Psychology Center of New York, 1976; Board of Directors, Education Committee and Faculty Member, National Psychological Association for Psychoanalysis, New York, 1976; Supervisor, Association for Psychotherapy, New York, 1976; Producer and Host, 1-Hour Weekly Television Program "Psychoanalysis", Manhattan Cable Television Channel D, 1976; Consultant, Matteawan State Hospital for Criminally Insane, Beacon, New York, Sponsored by National Institute of Mental Health, 1968-71; Supervisor and Faculty Member, Post-graduate Center for Mental Health, Department of Community Education and Services, 1968-71; Family Therapist, Jewish Family Service, Brooklyn, New York, 1967-69; Senior Therapist, Community Guidance Service, 1966-69; Administrative Director, Mental Health Consultation Center, Rockland County Division, Nanuet, New York, 1964-67; Psychotherapist, Mental Health Consultation Center, New York, New York, 1962-64; Attending Psychologist, Rockland County Clinic for Mental Health, Monsey, New York, 1961-67; School Psychologist, Putnam County Board of Cooperative Educational Services, Carmel, New York, 1961-62; Instructor, Department of Teacher Education, Brooklyn College, New York, 1960; Remedial Reading Therapist, Hoffman School, Riverdale, New York, 1959-60; Jewish Child Care Association, New York, 1959-60; Director of Remedial Education, Wiltwych School for Boys, New York, 1959-61; Teacher, Children's Village, Dobbs Ferry, New York, 1959; Special Teacher, Rockland County Center for Physically Handicapped, New City, New York, 1957-59; Teacher, Orangeburg Grammar School, New York, 1956; Speech Therapist, Monmouth Memorial Hospital, Long Branch, New Jersey, 1955-56; Fellow, Department of Speech, City College of New York, 1953-54; Teacher, Bernby Play Group, New York City, 1953-54. Organizational Memberships: California State Psychological Association; American Psychologicial Association; National Psychological Association for Psychoanalysis (training analyst; control analyst; clinical supervisor); New York Society of Clinical Psychologists (full member; former chairman, awards committee); American Society of Group Psychotherapy and Psychodrama; International Council of Psychologists; Psychoanalysis; Council of Psychoanalytic Psychotherapists (full member; former chairman, elections committee; memberships committee); The Association for the Integration of the Whole Person; New York Society of Freudian Psychologists (former member-at-large, board of director; training and control analyst; co-chairman, psychoanalytic consultation center); Psychologists Interested in the Advancement of Psychotherapy; Association for Applied Psychoanalysis (executive council and education chairman; delegate, board of affiliates of Council of Psychoanalytic Psychotherapists); Rockland County Psychological Society; Association for Humanistic Psychology; National Accreditation Association of American Examining Board of Psychoanalysts (certificate in psychoanalysis no. 122); Associaiton for Holistic Health. Published Works: *Integrative Therapy: The Foundation for Holistic and Self-Healing*, 1978; "Integrative Therapy", *Innovative Psychotherapies*, 1981. Honors and Awards: Listed in *Who's Who in the West*, *Community Leaders of America*. Address: 6320 Drexel Avenue, Los Angeles, California 90048.

Vacher, Carole Doughton

Clinical Psychologist. Personal: Born December 31, 1937; Daughter of Harold and Mamie Doughton; Married A. Ray Mayberry; Mother of Eizabeth M. Education: B.A., West Virginia Wesleyan, 1960; M.A., Ohio University, 1962; Ph.D., North Carolina State University, 1973; Clinical Internship in Psychology, Vanderbilt University School of Medicine, 1972-73. Career: Birth Defects Coordinator, West Virginia Medical School, 1962-63; Research Associate, University of North Carolina Medical School, 1965-70; Research Psychologist, North Carolina Department of Mental Health, 1973-75; Assistant Professor of Psychology, Family Practice Residency Program, East Tennessee University School of Medicine, 1975-77; Prevention Coordinator, Overlook Mental Health Center, Knoxville, Tennessee, 1977 to present; Private Practice in Clinical Psychology, Maryville Psychiatric Services, Maryville, Tennessee, 1974 to present. Organizational Memberships: American Psychological Association, 1975 to present: Division 29 (Psychotherapy), 1979 to present, and Division 27 (Community Psychology), 1979 to present; Tennessee Psychological Association, 1975 to present; Knoxville Area Psychological Association, 1977 to present; Knox County Child Abuse Review Team (consultant, 1977 to present); "Worry Clinic" on Pre-Teen and Teenage Alcohol and Drug Problems for Knox County and Surrounding Counties (organizer), 1981. Community Activities: Tennessee Medical Association Auxiliary (board member and state mental health chairman, 1981-82); Knoxville Medical Association Auxiliary (board member and mental health chairman, 1980 to present); Mental Health Association of Knox County (member of speakers bureau, 1979 to present); Orange County Mental Health Association, North Carolina, (board member, 1967-68). Religion: Volunteer mission work to rural areas near Les Cayes, Haiti, 1979; Helped to organize Contact Teleministries, Blount County, Tennessee; Organized and helped conduct training program for Contact Teleministries, 1981-82; Mental Health Training to Life Line Ministries, Australia, 1982. Published Works: Co-Author, Book, *Consultation Education: Development and Evaluation*, 1976; Author *Self Help Directory: Knox County and Surrounding Area;* Author and/or co-author several journal articles, including "Development of a Prevention Program at Overlook Mental Health Center", "Mental Health Report - A Few Minutes of Prevention Can Forestall a Lifetime of Illness" and "Comparison of the Slosson Intelligence Test with the Wechsler Adult Intelligence Scale on a Psychiatric Population"; "Stress Management", Chapter in *Wellness Manual;* Wrote and produced 4 mental health television programs "Preventing Problems by Finding Alternatives". Honors and Awards: Outstanding Volunteer Service to Tennessee Department of Human Services, 1978; Certified Licensed Ph.D. Clinical Psychologist, Tennessee, 1975 to present; Mental Health Scholarship Recipient, North Carolina Department of Mental Health, 1970-71; Phi Kappa Phi, 1971; Psi Chi, 1961; Haught Literary Society, 1959; Alpha Psi Omega, President, 1959-60; Wesleyan Key Award, 1960. Address: Route 23, Charlton Dr., Knoxville, Tennessee 37920.

Valakis, M Lois

Elementary Teacher. Personal: Born January 25, 1939; Daughter of John and Blanche Marquis Valakis. Education: Graduate of Milford High School, 1955; B.S. Education, Framingham State Teachers College, 1959. Career: Elementary Teacher, Juniper Hill School, Framingham, Massachusetts; Educational Consultant, Houghton Mifflin Publishing Company. Organizational Memberships: National Education Association, 1959 to present. Community Activities: Framingham Teachers Association (building representative, 1966-67, 1980-82; Title III Project-developer of instructional videotapes in economics and social studies, 1969-71); Development of Curriculum Material on Metric System 1974, Economics 1967-68, Humanities 1976, Maps and Globes 1977; Development of Elementary Level Tests for Minimal Competency Basic Skills in Writing, Listening and Language Arts, 1979-81. Religion: Non-Denominational Christian. Honors and Awards: Award for Curriculum Work on Trees, Chevron Chemical Company, 1973; Outstanding Leaders in Elementary and Secondary Education, 1976; Listed in *Notable Americans, Community Leaders and Noteworthy Americans, The International Who's Who of Intellectuals, The International Who's Who in Community Service, Dictionary of International Biography, Men and Women of Distinction, Book of Honor.* Address: 2 Concord Terrace, Framingham, Massachusetts 01701.

Valent, Henry

Attorney at Law. Personal: Born July 21, 1915; Son of Mr. and Mrs. Joseph Valent (both deceased); Married Joan Blanchard; Father of Nellie V. Hitchcock, Joseph A., Oscar B., Albert W., Henry W. Education: A.B. Arts 1936, L.L.B. 1938, Cornell University. Military: Served in the United States Army Infantry to the Rank of Lieutenant Colonel, 1941-46. Career: Attorney-at-Law. Organizational Memberships: Schuyler County Bar Association; New York State Bar Association; American Bar Association. Community Activities: American Legion (past post commander); Watkins-Montour Rotary Club (past president); Watkins Glen Youth Center (secretary; treasurer); Improved Order of Redmen (past national president); Schuyler Hospital Inc. (director); Glen Bank and Trust Company (director); Watkins Glen Grand Prix Corporation (president, 1953 to present); Schuyler County Chamber of Commerce. Religion: Roman Catholic; Holy Name Society. Honors and Awards: Paul Harris Fellowship, Rotary Club; Listed in *Who's Who in the East, Who's Who in Finance and Industry, Community Leaders and Noteworthy Americans, Book of Honor, Dictionary of Internatonal Biography, Two Thousand Men of Achievement, Men of Achievement, I.B.A. Yearbook, International Who's Who in Community Service, Wisdom Hall of Fame, International Who's Who of Intellectuals, Who's Who in American Law, Who's Who in the World.* Address: 2575 Old Corning Road, Watkins Glen, New York 14891.

Van Der Walt, Ruth Selby

Public School Music Teacher (retired). Personal: Born August 20, 1923; Daughter of Arthur L. and Amy W. Selby; Mother of Judith Amy. Education: B.Mus., West Virginia University, 1944; Certificate in Elementary Music, University of Florida, 1950. Career: Music Teacher, Fort Lauderdale (Florida) Public Schools, 1950 to present. Organizational Memberships: Music Educators National Conference; Broward Music Education Association (executive board); Broward County Elementary Music Educators Association (president, 1960-61); National Education Association; Florida Teachers Association; Classroom Teachers Association; Alpha Delta Kappa (chaplain, 1980-82). Community Activities: Beta Sigma Phi (president, 1962-63); Zonta International (Pompano Beach club, secretary, 1975-76; vice-president, 1980-81; president, 1981-82); Order of the Eastern Star (worthy matron, 1959-60). Religion: Methodist; Church Choir Soloist, 1950-67. Address: 3771 Northeast 17th Avenue, Pompano Beach, Florida 33064.

VanDuyn, Robert Gerald

Consultant in Education, Development and Management, Private Business Partner. Personal: Born February 12, 1913; Son of Robert Grover and Anna Gladys VanDuyn; Married Florence Noyer; Father of Elizabeth Ann V. Woods, Robert Mitchell. Education: B.A. 1934, M.A. 1939, Ball State University; Graduate Student, Harvard and Columbia Universities; Attended the Danish Folk School, Copenhagen, 1953; Ph.D., University of Chicago, 1953. Military: Served as Dean of Morgan Park Military Academy, 1943-44. Career: Consultant in Education, Development and Management; Private Business Partner; Special Assistant, United States Senate, 1977; Analyst, State Department/A.I.D.-T.A.E.H.R., Washington, D.C., 1976; Administrator and Consultant, UNESCO, 1972-75; Staff, Office of Regional Economic Development, United States Embassy, Bangkok, Thailand, 1969-71; Evaluation Specialist, Program Office, State Department/United States Operations Mission to Thailand, Bangkok, 1968; Deputy Director, Office of Institutional Development, Africa-Europe Bureau, State Department/A.I.D., Washington, D.C., 1962-67; Special Assignment to Assist in Creation and Establishment of the Peace Corps, on Detail from State Department/A.I.D., 1961; Chief Education Officer 1968-60, Deputy Chief Education Officer 1967, United States Operations Mission to Thailand, State Department/A.I.D.; Special Consultant to the Minister of Education, Philippine Islands and to the President of the University of the Philippines, 1955-57; Association Director, W. K. Kellogg Foundation, Battle Creek, Michigan, 1949-56; Faculty, University of Chicago, 1945-48; Dean and Teacher, Morgan Park Military Academy, 1943-44; Teacher, Public Schools, 1934-42. Organizational Memberships: National Association of Educational Broadcasters (International Committee, 5 years); National Committee to Study Rural Youth Organizations in the United States, 2 years; United States Committee for a National Project in Agriculture Communications, 6 years; Rangoon (Burma) Conference on Southeast Asian Problems in Higher Education; Established the Asian Institute of Technology, Bangkok (served as consultant to executive board, 6 years); Preparatory Commission on Southeast Asian University Problems (United States delegate); Conference of Heads of Southeast Asian Universities, Karachi, Pakistan (United States delegate); Peace Corps (member of creation, organization and establishment group); United Nations Educational, Scientific and Cultural Organization Conference on Development of Higher Education in Africa, Tananarive, Malagasy (United States delegate); Task Force on Technical Assistance, Agency for International Development, United States State Department; Committee to Study Indonesian Institutions of Higher Learning; Committee to Review the Indonesian Education System and Propose a Comprehensive Program for its Development. Religion: Protestant. Published Works: Many Proposals, Studies and Reports for Agencies and Institutions. Honors and Awards: Walgreen Fellow, University of Chicago, 1944-45; Two Distinguished Service Awards, Government of Thailand, 1959, 1961; Award from Government of Indonesia, 1975; Distinguished Service Awards, Ball State University Alumni Association, 1962; United States Government Foreign Service Award, 1976; Listed in *Who's Who in America, Who's Who in Government, International Who's Who in Community Service, Who's Who in the East, International Who's Who of Intellectuals.* Address: 21 West 88th Street, New York, New York 10024.

Van Vranken, Rose

Rose Van Vranken

Sculptor. Personal: Born May 15, 1919; Daughter of Dr. and Mrs. Gilbert Van Vranken (both deceased); Married Robert C. Hickey; Mother of Kathryn, Robert, Stephen, Dennis, Sarah. Education: B.A. cum laude, Pomona College, 1939; Student Sculpture with Robert Laurent and William Zorach, Art Students League, New York, New York, 1939-42; Studies in Art History, Graduate Institute of Fine Arts, New York University, 1941-42; M.A., Art, University of Iowa, Iowa City, 1943; Early Sculpture Training, California Art Schools. Career: Sculptor, Working Primarily in Direct Carving of Wood and Stone and Making Bronze Castings of the Carvings; Artist in Graphics, Intaglio Etchings and Other Media; Represented in Collections of Des Moines Art Center, Iowa (sculpture), Coventry Cathedral, England (sculpture), Laguna Gloria Museum, Austin, Texas (graphics), Texas Investment Bank, Houston (sculpture), Texas Commerce Bank, Houston (sculpture), Mitchell Energy Corporation, Houston (sculpture), St. Cyril of Alexandria Church, Houston (sculpture), Brand Library Art Gallery, Glendale, California (sculpture), Samuel Barker Collection, Birmingham, Alabama (sculpture), Houston Public Library (sculpture), Finial Investment Corporation, Houston (sculpture), Numerous Private Collections; Graphics and Water Colors in Collections of Pomona College Alumni Association, Smith College, Monona Public Library (Madison, Wisconsin), Mayland Publishing Company, Citizens National Bank (Baytown, Texas). Organizational Memberships: Artists Equity; National Association of Women Artists, New York; Salmagundi Club, New York; International Platform Association; Academic Artists Association, Springfield, Massachusetts; Pasadena Society of Artists; Texas Society of Sculptors (past president, Gulf Coast Chapter); Southern Association of Sculptors. Published Works: *Les Editions de la Review Moderne*, 1973; Featured on Cover and in Article, *The Texas Society of Sculptors Magazine*, 1973; Featured in Article "Garden Sculpture in Houston", *Houston Home and Garden Magazine*, 1978; "Profile on Rose Van Vranken", *Art Voices/South*, 1978; *Arte Contemporaneo Norteamericano en la residencia del Embajador de los Estados Unidos en Costa Rica*, 1978-79; *The North American Sculpture Exhibition Catalog*, The Foothills Art Center, Golden, Colorado, 1979. Honors and Awards: Honorable Mention for Sculpture, International Platform Association, Washington, D.C., 1981; Association Award for Sculpture, Academic Artists Association, Springfield, Massachusetts, 1980; Award for Sculpture, National Association of Women Artists, New York, 1980; 2nd Prize for Sculpture, 1980 Annual Award for Water Color and Sculpture, Salmagundi Club, New York, 1980; First Prize for Sculpture, Salmagundi Club Annual Exhibition, New York City, 1982; Academic Artists Council Award for Sculpture, Academic Artists Association, 1979; First Prize for Graphics, Museum of Fine Arts, Springfield, Massachusetts, 1968; Graphic Chosen for United States Touring Exhibition, National Association for Women Artists, 1953; Graphic Chosen for European Touring Exhibition, National Association of Women Artists, 1956; Sculpture Chosen for Art in Embassies Program, United States Department of States, Washington, D.C., 1977-80; Sculpture Chosen for Touring Exhibit to 6 Southeastern Museums, Southern Association of Sculptors, 1973; Award for Graphics, Walker Art Center, 1953; Award for Portrait Sculpture, Catharine Lorillard Wolf Art Exhibition, National Arts Club, New York, 1969; Two 1st Prizes for Sculpture and Two 2nd Prizes for Sculpture, Madison Art Center Museum, Wisconsin, 1965-67; 2nd Prize for Sculpture 1954, 3rd Prize for Sculpture 1955, Iowa Art Salon, Des Moines; 1st Prize for Graphics, Pasadena Society of Artists, Pasadena Museum, 1951; Award for Sculpture, Joslyn Museum, 1950; Award for Sculpture, Artists West of the Mississippi Exhibit, Denver Museum, 1952; Midwest Biennial Award for Sculpture, Walker Art Center, 1951; Medal of Honor for Graphics, National Association of Women Artists, National Academy, New York, 1952; 1st Prize for Sculpture, Des Moines Art Center, 1953; Two Bronze Medals for Sculpture, Oakland Museum, 1945-46; 1st Prize for Sculpture, Los Angeles County Museum Annual Award, 1944; Listed in *Who's Who in American Art, Who's Who of American Women, Smithsonian Institution's Archives of American Artists, International Who's Who in Art and Antiques, Dictionary of International Biography, International Who's Who of Women, Who's Who in Texas, California Artists.* Address: 435 Tallowood Drive, Houston, Texas 77024.

Varma, Man Mohan

Scientist, Professor. Personal: Son of Ishar Dass and Bhagirithi Oevi; Married Kiran; Father of Mohit, Umang. Education: B.S.C.E.,

Alabama Polytechnic Institute, Auburn, Alabama, 1957; M.S. Sanitary Engineering, Iowa State College, Ames, Iowa, 1958; M.S. Highway and Soils, Oklahoma State University-Stillwater, 1960; Ph.D. Engineering Sciences, University of Oklahoma-Norman, 1963. Career: Scientist and Professor. Organizational Memberships: American Water Works Association (glossary committee, 1975 to present; chairman, A.T.P. measurement, 1975 to present); Water Pollution Control Federation (glossary committee, 1975 to present; chairman, A.T.P. measurement, 1975 to present);American Society for Testing and Materials (water committee, 1977 to present; chairman, in-vitro mutagenicity testing procedures); National Environmental Health Association. Community Activities: American Public Health Association (glossary committee, 1975 to present; chairman, A.T.P. measurement, 1975 to present); Organization International de Normalization (United States Technical Advisory Group on Water Quality Measurement, 1975 to present); National Environmental Health (chairman, energy committee, 1975-79). Honors and Awards: Consultant, World Health Organization, 1972 to present; Consultant, Ministry of Public Health, Kuwait, 1976 to present; Visiting Professor, Harvard University, 1975-76; Diplomate, American Academy of Environmental Engineers; Reviewer of Technical Papers, *Journal of Water Pollution Control Federation, Environmental Health Journal,* and *Radiation Health Journal.* Address: 704 Chichester Lane, Silver Spring, Maryland 20904.

Varma, Rajendra

Director of Hospital Biochemistry Department. Personal: Born December 26, 1942; Married Ranbir S. Varma; Mother of Two Sons, Rajeev and Sunil. Education: B.S. 1958, M.S. 1960, University of Delhi, India; Ph.D. Biochemistry, University of New South Wales, Sydney, Australia, 1966. Career: Director, Biochemistry Department, Warren State Hospital, Warren, Pennsylvania, 1971 to present; Associate Professor, Edinboro State College, Pennsylvania, 1969-71; Assistant Professor, Alliance College, Cambridge Springs, Pennsylvania, 1968-69; Postdoctoral Fellow, Purdue University, Lafayette, Indiana 1968, Iowa State University-Ames 1967; Lecturer, Sydney Technical College, Sydney, Australia, 1963-66; Lecturer and Research Worker, University of Delhi, India, 1960-62. Organizational Memberships: American Institute of Chemists (fellow, 1976); American Chemical Society, 1967; Sigma Xi Society, 1968; New York Academy of Sciences, 1979. Published Works: About 50 Research Papers in International Journals; Two Medical Books. Honors and Awards: Medical Research Scientist Achievement Awards, Commonwealth of Pennsylvania, 1974-77, 1980; Presiding Officer, National Meetings of American Chemical Society, San Francisco, California 1976, Montreal, Canada 1977, Washington, D.C. 1979, Las Vegas, Nevada 1980, New York, New York 1981. Address: 305 Monroe Street, Warren, Pennsylvania 16365.

Rajendra Varma

Vaughan, Richard A

Chartered Life Underwriter. Personal: Born July 18, 1946; Married Terence T.; Father of Shannon, Elizabeth, Todd. Education: B.B.A. Finance, Management and Marketing, University of Texas-Austin, 1968. Military: Served in the United States Army-Texas National Guard-Airborne with an Honorable Discharge in 1973. Career: Chartered Life Underwriter. Organizational Memberships: Million Dollar Round Table (life and qualifying member); Life Underwriters Training Council, Washington, D.C. (instructor); State and National Tax and Estate Planning Seminars (featured speaker); Life Insurance Companies (product development consultant); National Association of Life Underwriters; Life Insurance Industry Organizations (director). Community Activities: Texoma Regional Planning Center Council of Government (director, 1977-79); Sherman (Texas) City Council, 1977-79; American Cancer Society (chairman, fund drive in Grayson County, Texas); University of Texas Ex-Students Association (past president). Honors and Awards: Agent of the Year, Indianapolis Life Insurance Company, 1975; Man of the Year, Mutual Benefit Life Insurance Company, 1981; Various Industry and Life Insurance Company Awards Recognizing Outstanding Performance, Sales Applications and Achievements; Listed in *Who's Who in Finance and Industry, Who's Who in the Southwest, Who's Who in the World; Mensa.* Address: 12 Timbercreek, Sherman, Texas 75090.

Veitel, Jenny Frieda

Company Partner. Personal: Born April 21, 1909 in Gornsdorf, Germany. Education: Graduate of Hornell Business School, 1926; Nurse's Training, Buffalo City Hospital, 1928-31; Registered Nurse, 1931. Career: Veitel Hosiery Company, Partner 1950 to present, Manager 1946 to present, Secretary 1942-46; Registered Nurse, 1931-42; Secretary to Dr. Carl Schwan, 1936-28. Community Activities: Diagnosed her own Toxic Poisoning due to a Malfunctioning Car she was driving; Offered Advice to Vice-Admiral Austin concerning the sinking of the submarine 'Thresher', 1963; Wrote to President of the United States concerning Gary Power's Airplane being shot down, showing that symptoms from hydraulic, anti-freeze and freon leakages could cause his misjudgment of his situation; Advised Houston that Solenoid Valve problems troubled 1971 space flight; Advised Houston concerning space flight, based on changes she had made in the air conditioning equipment at the hosiery mill to save fuel, enabling the space flight to be successful; Offered Advice enabling Houston engineers to bring Sky Lab down safely with no injuries; Offered Advice that Sky Lab's trouble was not electrical but rather an electric shutdown for safety due to a leak of liquid components, 1973; Responsible for Machine Voting on the Le Roy Central School Budget, 1976 to present; Environmental Agency, Le Roy (head); Trustee Candidate, 1977. Published Works: Book Alerting the Public to the Hazards Faced in Everyday Life Today (in progress). Honors and Awards: Recognition for Tenacity and Accuracy in Alerting the Public and Authorities about Hazardous Conditions; "Happy Birthday" Greeting from the Moon for Assistance with Space Flight. Address: 28 West Main Street, Le Roy, New York 14482.

Evelyn I Vernon

Vernon, Evelyn I

Professor (retired). Personal: Born June 1, 1911; Daughter of G. A. and Mary V. Elsen Iverson (both deceased); Married Clinton D. Vernon; Mother of Evelyn Marlene, Frances Yvonne (Bonnie) V. Lloyd. Education: B.A. English and Psychology, George Washington University, 1933; M.A. Speech Education, Columbia University Teachers College, 1936; Summer School, Sorbonne, Paris 1955, University of Hawaii 1958. Career: University of Utah, Assistant Professor of Educational Psychology 1975-77, Supervisor of Reading Classes for General Education 1971-75, Instructor in Educatonal Psychology Department 1963-71, Instructor in Speech Department 1960-63; Teacher, John Robert Powers Finishing School, Salt Lake City, Utah, 1955-60; Instructor in Speech and Drama Departments, 1936-40; Insurance Supervisor, United States Government Home Owners Loan Association, 1933-35. Organizational Memberships: International Reading Association, 1965-75; College Reading Association (member, 1967-77; director, 1975); National Association of Higher Education (Utah branch secretary, 1972); American Association of University Professors, 1970-77; University Faculty Women (president, 1969-70); International Platform Association, 1981-82. Community Activities: Maryland State Rural Women's Lectures, 1937-40; Utah State Society, Washington, D.C. (vice-president, president, 1933-34); Women's State Legislative Council of Utah (president, 1951-53); League of American Pen Women (local president, 1950-52; state president, 1952-54; state parliamentarian, 1977-82); Salt Lake Council of Women (chairman, 1979-82; first vice-president, 1982-83); Friendship Force (volunteer ambassador to 3 countries, Venezuela, Korea and West Berlin, Germany, 1978-82); Public Lectures and

Book Reviews, 1940-82; Assistance League of Salt Lake City (over 100 hours yearly volunteer service). Religion: Latter-Day Saints Church; President, Young Women's Mutual Association, Washington, D.C., 1933-35; President, Primary Children's Organization, Wastach Ward, 1958; Relief Society Teacher of Literature and Cultural Arts, 1950-60, 1968-78; Teacher Development Leader, Stake Sunday School, 1977-82; Teacher in Most Organizations. Honors and Awards: Twenty-Dollar Gold Piece for Being Most Outstanding Girl in Activities for 4 Years of College, George Washington University, 1933; Honor Roll, *Salt Lake Evening Telegram*, 1951; Graduate School of Education Plaque, 1977; Merit of Honor Award, Emeritus Club, University of Utah, 1982. Address: 1044 Oakhills Way, Salt Lake City, Utah 84108.

Vetlesen, Robert Vivian Arnbjorn

Piano Teacher. Personal: Born in September; Son of Vetle Arnbjorn and Hildar Walker Vetlesen (both deceased). Education: Juilliard School of Music, 1928-30; Columbia University, 1929-30; Studied with Artur Schnabel, Berlin 1930-32, Emil von Sauer, Vienna 1931, Bela Bartok 1931, Josef and Rosina Lhevinne, New York City and San Francisco 1927. Career: Piano Teacher; Concert Pianist; Teacher in Hawaii, California, Rio de Janeiro, Buenos Aires, Brussels, Berlin, Vienna, Budapest; Director of Music Camps for Boys and Girls, Sequoia National Park, Hawaii and Mexico. Organizational Memberships: National Guild of Piano Teachers (San Francisco chairman, member 1949 to present; Young Masters of the Piano (director, 1963-68); Pacific Musical Society (vice-president, 1963, 1965; president, 1965-67). Community Activities: Honolulu Music Academy (director, 1941-46); Academy of Music (director, 1949-53); Peninsula Conservatory (associate director, 1952-57); Honolulu Symphony Orchestra (board of directors, 1943-46); Honolulu Art Society (board of directors, 1943-46); San Francisco Children's Opera (president, 1959 to present); San Francisco Boys' Chorus (chairman, 1968; president, 1968); Ballet Celeste, San Francisco (advisory board, 1969); Artists Embassy (advisory board, 1970 to present). Honors and Awards: Honorary Doctor of Music Degree, Southwestern Conservatory of Fine Arts, Texas, 1976; Concert Appearances and Tours, Hawaii and the West Coast 1919, 1920, 1923, 1926, Europe, 1931, 1932, 1933, 1938, 1950, South America, 1949. Address: 2150 Lyon Street, San Francisco, California 94115.

Victor, Judi

Audio-Visual Production and Advertising Company President and Owner. Personal: Born April 12, 1949; Daughter of Mr. and Mrs. H. R. James; Married David Victor; Mother of David, Laurie, Andrew. Education: B.F.A. cum laude, University of Arizona, 1970. Career: President and Owner, The Producers, Inc.; President, Way Out West Productions, 1974 to present; Broadcast Production Manager, Mullen Advertising, 1973-74; Copy Director, Diamonds, 1971-73; Copywriter, Broadway-Hale, 1970-71; Columnist, Tucson Newspapers, Inc., 1970. Organizational Memberships: Women in Communications (president, 1978-79); I.A.B.C.; Charter 100 (publicity committee, 1981-82; secretary, 1982-83); Sigma Delta Chi; National Association of Television Arts and Sciences. Community Activities: Phoenix Park Foundation (board member, 1980 to present); Phoenix Environmental Quality Commission, 1979-80. Honors and Awards: Western Region Woman of Achievement Award, Women in Communications, 1979; National TELLY Award, 1st Place for Fritz Scholder Television Commercial, 1980; Listed in *World Who's Who of Women, Western Hemisphere Who's Who of Women, Who's Who of American Women*. Address: 3835 E. Sahuaro Boulevard, Phoenix, Arizona 85028.

Vincent, Bruce Havird

Investment Banking Executive. Personal: Born November 7, 1947; Son of Col. and Mrs. Dale L. Vincent; Married Pamela Jean Benson; Father of Jennifer Jean, Bryce Havird. Education: B.A. Business Administration, Duke University, 1969; M.B.A. Finance, University of Houston, 1976. Military: Served in the United States Navy to the rank of Lieutenant, 1969-73. Career: Owner/Partner, Johnson & Vincent, Inc. Investment Banking, 1982 to present; Executive Vice-President, Chief Operating Officer and Director, Peninsula Resources Corporation, 1980-82; Vice-President and Group Manager, First City National Bank of Houston, 1973-80; Lieutenant, United States Navy, 1969-73. Organizational Memberships: Independent Petroleum Association of America; Texas Mid-Continent Oil and Gas Association; International Association of Drilling Contractors; Corpus Christi Chamber of Commerce; South Texas Chamber of Commerce. Address: 200 Atlantic Street, Corpus Christi, Texas 78404.

Vinson, Clarence D Jr

Educator. Personal: Born June 23, 1933; Son of Clarence D. and Pearl P. Vinson (deceased); Married Frances H. Poole; Father of Two Stepchildren. Education: Graduate, Oxford High School, Oxford, Alabama, 1950; B.S., 1954, M.S., 1957, Jacksonville State University; Ph.D., University of Alabama, 1977; Additional graduate work at University of Northern Colorado at Greeley and University of Wyoming at Laramie. Military: Served with United States Army as 1st Lieutenant, Chemical Corps, 1955-57. Career: Associate Professor of Science, Jacksonvile State University, 1969 to present; Science Teacher and Coach, Saks High School, Anniston, Alabama, 1957-1965; Science Teacher and Coach, Munford High School, Munford, Alabama, 1965-69. Organizational Memberships: National Education Association; Alabama Education Association; Local Education Association; Northeast Alabama Regional Science Fair (assistant director); Northeast Region of the Alabama Junior Academy of Science (associate counselor). Community Activities: Numismatic Association; Calhoun County Coin Club; American Bowling Congress; Anniston Bowling Association (member board of directors, 1978 to present). Religion: Attends Baptist Church (teacher of bible study class, deacon, 1977). Honors and Awards: Balfour Medal for Academic Achievement in High School, 1950; Elected to Kappa Phi Kappa (1954), Scabbard and Blade (1954), and Phi Kappa Phi (1969); Listed in *Who's Who in the South and Southwest* (1980-81, 1981-82), and *Personalities of the South* (1981). Address: 435 Arnold Drive, Anniston, Alabama 36201.

Visco, Susan Josephine

Professor and Director of College Learning Program. Personal: Daughter of Rose M. Visco. Education: A.A. Liberal Arts, Massachusetts Bay Community College, 1965; B.S. Elementary Education/Psychology, Suffolk University, 1967; M.Ed. 1969, Ph.D. 1973, Special Education, Boston College; Internship, Boston Children's Hospital Medical Center, 1970-72. Career: Director, Psychoeducational and Evaluation Center, Saugus, Massachusetts; Professor and Director of College Learning Program, Developmental Evaluation Clinic, Bradford College, 1980; Director of Child Development Department and Special Needs, Stonehill College, 1971-76; Visiting Professor of Special Education, Lowell University, 1973-77; Director of Special Education, Suffolk University, 1976-78; Psychologist and Coordinator of Pre-School Evaluation, Medford School System, 1978-79. Organizational Memberships: Association of Children with Learning Disabilities; Massachusetts Association of Children with Learning Disabilities; Council on Exceptional Children (national and Massachusetts chapters, treasurer of division on children with learning disabilities, division of communcation disorders and teacher education division, 1973-74). Community Activities: Volunteer Preschool Child

Development Screening Programs in Several North Shore Community School Systems, Massachusetts (director, 1966-73); Speaker, Numerous Lectures, Addresses and Workshops, Massachusetts, Connecticut, Florida, New Hampshire, New York, Rhode Island. Honors and Awards: Listed in *Who's Who of American Women, Who's Who in America in the Child Development Profession, World Who's Who of Women.* Address: 438 Essex Street, Saugus, Massachusetts 01906.

Visos, Clara Lois Kandaris

Testifying for her Lord and Saviour. Personal: Born October 24, 1928; Daughter of Luois Emmanuel and Elizabeth Haniotis Kandaris; Married Charles Dennis Visos; Mother of John Dennis, Larry Carl, Dennis Charles. Education: Warwood High School, Wheeling, West Virginia, 1933-43; Straubemueller Textile High School, New York, New York, 1943-45. Career: Textifying for her Lord and Saviour after Recovery from Brain Surgery, 1979 and 1980 to present; Office Manager and Secretary, R.L. Polk and Company, St. Louis, Missouri, 1977-80; Consultant in Sales and Office Management, 1975-78; Branch Manager, Tradin' Times, Inc., St. Louis, Missouri, 1972-75; Office Manager and Executive Secretary, Grantwood Contracting Company, Realtors, 1959-62; One-Girl District Sales Office, Encyclopaedia Britannica, St. Louis, Missouri, 1955-59; Temporary and Part-Time Work, 1966-69, 1945-55. Organizational Memberships: Missouri Notary Association; National Association of Female Executives; The Smithsonian Associates; Den Mother; Room Mother; Daughters of Penelope, Cynthia Chapter No. 110; St. Nicholas Greek Folk Dancers (member, 1950-79). Religion: Hope Chapel Inter-Faith Fellowship, 1981 to present. Honors and Awards: Listed in *Who's Who of American Women, Who's Who in the Midwest, International Who's Who of Intellectuals.* Address: 817 Big Bend Woods Drive, Ballwin, Missouri 63011.

Visscher, Saralee Amy Neumann

Professor of Entomology. Personal: Born January 9, 1929; Daughter of Otto and Sarah Mershon Neumann; Married Paul Hummison Visscher; Mother of Kirby Alan Van Horn, Constance Van Horn, Amy Roena, Ernst Warren. Education: B.S. Biology, University of Montana-Missoula, 1949; M.S. Applied Science in Entomology 1958, Ph.D. Entomology 1963, Montana State University. Career: Montana State University, Professor of Entomology 1972 to present, Associate Professor of Entomology 1967-72, Assistant Professor of Entomology 1962-67; Postdoctoral Fellow, University of Virginia, 1965-66; Instructor in Biology, University of Kansas, 1958-59; Elementary Teacher, Denton, Montana, 1947-48. Organizational Memberships: American Society for Zoologists, 1965 to present; Entomological Society of America (member, 1963 to present; memberships chairman for Montana, 1980 to present); Society for Developmental Biology, 1965 to present; American Society for the Advancement of Science (fellow, 1967; member, 1966 to present); Pan American Acridological Society, 1979 to present; Society for the Sigma Xi (Montana State University chapter, president 1978-79, member 1963 to present); Montana Academy of Sciences (board of directors, 1976-79; president, 1979-80; member, 1962 to present). Community Activities: Mershon Past President Award for Outstanding Contribution to Science in Montana of the Montana Academy of Sciences (founder, 1981); Rocky Mountain Regional Conference for Developmental Biology, Yellowstone National Park (organizer, 1970); 1st International Symposium on Insect Embryology, XV International Congress of Entomology, Washington, D.C. (organizer, moderator, 1976); Symposium on Grylloblattoidea, XVI International Congress of Entomology, Kyoto (organizer, moderator, 1980); American Association of University Women (Lewistown member and officer); High School Commencement Speaker, Geyser, Montana 1976, Belt, Montana 1977, Fort Benton, Montana 1981. Religion: Episcopal Church; National Youth Commission, 1945-46; Organist, St. James, Lewistown and Churches in Bozeman, 1959-62. Honors and Awards: Honorable Guest Member, Japanese Society of Arthropodan Embryology, 1982; One of Eight Outstanding Women of Montana, *Montana* Magazine, 1979; Rockefeller Foundation Research Grant, 1980-81; National Science Foundation MONTS Grant, 1980-82; Dynamic American *Dynamic Years* Magazine; Dow Chemical U.S.A. Research Grant, 1980-81; AgRISTARS Grant, 1980-81; United States-Japan Cooperative Research Grant, 1977-80; National Institute of Health Research Grants, Co-Investigator, 1962-69; Fellow, American Association for the Advancement of Science, 1971; National Science Foundation Travel Grant to XIIth International Congress of Entomology, London, 1964; National Institute of Health Postdoctoral Fellowship, University of Virginia, 1965-66; National Science Foundation Predoctoral Fellowship, Montana State University, 1960-61; Honor Scholarship, University of Montana, 1945-46. Address: 516 South 6th Avenue, Bozeman, Montana 59715.

Clara Lois Visos

Vlachos, Estella Maria

Accountant and Controller. Personal: Born October 24, 1939; Daughter of Rudolph J. Carlson (deceased) and Estelle S. Carlson; Married Emanuel James Vlachos. Education: Graduate of Long Beach Polytechnic High School, 1957; A.A. Long Beach City College, 1959; Long Beach State College, 1959-60; Various Tax Courses for Professional Credits, Sponsored by Society of California Accountants, National Society of Public Accountants, American Society of Women Accountants, State of California Department of Human Resources. Career: Accountant and Controller. Organizational Memberships: Society of California Accountants; American Society of Women Accountants (president, 3 terms; treasurer and director); National Society of Public Accountants; National Notary Association; Tax Preparers Association (charter member); International Platform Association. Religion: Greek Orthodox; Parish Council; Church Treasurer, Choir Member and Treasurer. Honors and Awards: Mary E. Baker Memorial Scholarship, 1957; American Society of Women Accountants Award, 1959; Life Fellow, American Biographical Institute; Listed in *Who's Who of American Women, The World Who's Who of Women, Notable Americans, International Who's Who in Community Service, Personalities of the West and Midwest, Community Leaders and Noteworthy Americans, Book of Honor, Dictionary of International Biography, Who's Who in Finance and Industry, Personalities of America, International Register of Profiles, Men and Women of Distinction, Who's Who in the West, Who's Who in the World, Who's Who in California, Directory of Distinguished Americans, Community Leaders of America.* Address: Post Office Box 6094, Anaheim, California 92806.

Voge-Black, Victoria Mae

Aerospace Medicine Specialist. Personal: Born June 27, 1943; Daughter of Veryl Voge; Married Gerald Ralph Black; Mother of Robert, John, Catherine, Kimberly. Education: B.A., University of Minnesota, 1964; M.D., National Autonomous University of Mexico, 1971; M.P.H., Johns Hopkins School of Hygiene and Public Health, 1977. Military: Served in the United States Navy to rank of Commander, 1972 to present. Career: United States Navy, Naval Safety Center, Norfolk, Virginia, Aerospace, Medicine Specialist, Flight Surgeon. Organizational Memberships: American Medical Association; Aerospace Medical Association; S.A.F.E. Association; American Public Health Association; International Academy of Aviation and Space Medicine. Religion: Church of Jesus Christ of Latter-Day Saints, 1973 to present. Honors and Awards: Wiley Post Award for Operational Psychology, 1980. Address: P.O. Box 62, NAS Agane, Guam; F.P.O. San Francisco, California 96637.

Vogel, Irene Susan

Psychologist. Personal: Born January 12, 1939; Daughter of Alex and Nettie Kuzminsky; Married Leonard Vogel; Mother of Kenneth, Jay, Dianna. Education: B.A. 1956, M.A. 1971, Ph.D. 1972, American University. Career: Psychologist; Instructor, American University; Therapist and Researcher, School for Contemporary Education; Psychologist and Alcohol and Drug Abuse Program Coordinator, Walter Reed Hospital. Organizational Memberships: Prince George's Counties, Inc., of Association of Practicing Psychologists (president-elect, 1980-82); American Psychological Association; Maryland Psychological Association; District of Columbia Psychology Association; Association for the Advancement of Psychology; American Society for Psychologists in Private Practice; The Society for Psychologists in Private Practice; The Society for Clinical and Experimental Hypnosis, Inc.; American Society for Clinical Hypnosis; Morton Prince Center for Hypnotherapy (faculty); American Association of Sex Educators, Counselors and Therapists; American Holistic Medical Association. Community Activities: Montgomery County Chamber of Commerce; Head Start. Religion: Temple Beth-El; Hadassah; B'nai Brith. Honors and Awards: American University Honor Society; Psi Chi Honorary Psychological Fraternity; Assistantships and Fellowships, 1969-72; International Platform Association; Listed in *Who's Who in the East, Who's Who of American Women, International Directory of Distinuished Psychologists, Psychotherapists International Directory.* Address: 9624 Annlee Terrace, Bethesda, Maryland 20817.

Irene S Vogel

Vogt, Molly T

Associate Dean and Professor. Personal: Born April 15, 1939; Daughter of Gordon Thomas (deceased) and Evelyn Thomas; Mother of William Brian, Keith Thomas. Education: B.S. with honors, Biological Chemistry, Bristol University, England; Ph.D., University of Pittsburgh, 1967. Career: University of Pittsburgh School of Health-Related Professions, Pennsylvania, Associate Dean and Professor 1977 to present, Associate Professor and Chairman 1972-76, Assistant Professor of Biochemistry 1971-72. Organizational Memberships: *Journal of Allied Health* (associate editor and member, editorial board, 1972-79); American Society of Allied Health Professions (education committee chairman, 1979 to present; Task Force on Status of Women chairman, 1980 to present; planner-organizer, National Conference on Continuing Education, 1978-81). Community Activities: Presidential Task Force on Research, 1979-80; Council of Individual Members (elected member-at-large, 1977-79); University of Pittsburgh Chapter of Sigma Xi (president, 1979 to present); Pennsylvania State Department of Education (consultant, 1976); Executive Women's Council of Greater Pittsburgh Coordinating Committee, 1975-81; American Association for the Advancement of Science; Phi Delta Gamma; American Women in Science; American Association of Higher Education; National Association of Women Deans and Counselors. Honors and Awards: Certificate of Merit for Excellence in Writing and Outstanding Contribution to the Literature of Allied Health Professions, American Society of Allied Health Professions, 1978; Fellow, American Council on Education Academic Administration Internship Program, 1974-75. Address: 242 Race Street, Pittsburgh, Pennsylvania 15218.

Molly T Vogt

Volpe, Robert

Professor. Personal: Born March 6, 1926; Married Ruth Pullan; Father of Catherine Lillian, Elizabeth Anne, Peter George, Edward James, Rose Ellen. Education: M.D., University of Toronto, 1950; F.R.C.P. (C), 1956; F.A.C.P., 1965. Military: Royal Canadian Naval Volunteer Reserve, 1943-45. Career: Professor, Department of Medicine, University of Toronto; Physician-in-Chief, The Wellesley Hospital, Toronto, Ontario; Director, Endocrinology Research Laboratory, Wellesley Hospital. Organizational Memberships: American Thyroid Association (president, 1981-82); Canadian Society of Endocrinology and Metabolism (past president); Endocrine Society; Toronto Society for Clinical Research (past president); Royal Society of Medicine (London); Canadian Society for Clinical Investigation; Alpha Omega Alpha; American Federation of Clinical Research; American College of Physicians (governor for Ontario, 1977-82). Community Activities: Medical Research Council of Canada (endocrine committee 1975-78); National Institutes of Health, United States (task force for funding of endocrinology research 1978-79); Numerous University of Toronto Committees; Wellesley Hospital (chairman medical advisory committee 1981-83); Hospital Council for Metropolitan Toronto. Published Works: Author 140 articles or books dealing with immunology of the endocrine system. Honors and Awards: Goldie Prize for Medical Research, University of Toronto, 1972; State of the Art Lecturer, Endocrine Society, 1975; Jamieson Prize of the Canadian Society of Nuclear Medicine, 1980; Honorary Membership, Endocrine Society of Chile; State of the Art Lecturer, Department of Medicine, University of Toronto, 1981; Numerous Visiting Professorships. Address: 3 Daleberry Place, Don Mills, Ontario, M2B 2A5, Canada.

Voorthuyzen, Pieter

Freelance Teacher of Music and Science, Musical Performer, Speaker, Writer and Pastor. Personal: Born January 5, 1927 in the Netherlands. Education: Chemistry and Music Education in the Netherlands; Bible Studies and Sacred Music, Northeastern Collegiate Bible Institute, Essex Falls, New Jersey, 1964; M.Div., Gordon Conwell Theological Seminary, Massachusetts, 1968; Courses in Biochemistry, Genetics, Immunobiology and Sensory Physiology, Bates College, Maine, 1968-76. Career: Freelance Teacher of Music and Science, Performing Musician, Speaker and Writer, 1976 to present; Baptist Minister, United States and Abroad, 1964-76; Research Chemist, Marck, Sharp and Dohme, New Jersey, 1958-61; Analytical Chemist, Philips Dutch Pharmaceuticals, Weesp, Netherlands, 1951-58; Analytical Chemist, Several Industries, Netherlands, 1947-51. Organizational Memberships: American Chemical Society, 1959 to present; International Platform Association; Society of American Inventors. Community Activities: Community Orchestra (concert master); Rotary International, 1978 to present; Historical Society of Madison County. Published Works: *Chimes Without Response* (in progress); Patentee in Field of Chemistry and for "The Counterpressure System for Stringed Instruments". Honors and Awards: Certificate of Achievement in Professionalizing Programs, Meetings and Speakers Seminars, American Platform Association; Listed in *Who's Who in the East,* First Edition of the *American Registry Series, Men of Achievement, International Who's Who in Community Service, Dictionary of International Biography, International Who's Who of Intellectuals.* Address: 113 Ball Avenue, Canastota, New York 13032.

Robert Volpe

Votaw, Carmen Delgado

Information Executive. Personal: Married Gregory B. Votaw; Mother of Stephen Gregory, Michael Albert and Lisa Juliette. Education: The American University, School of Int. Service; DSS, School of Business Administration, University of Puerto Rico; Doctorate in the Humanities (honorary), Hood College, Maryland. Career: Vice President, Information and Services for Latin America; President, Inter American Commission of Women, 1978-80; Co-Chair, National Advisory Committee on Women; U.S. Foreign Service Promotion Board Review Panel (member, 1976); President, National Conference of Puerto Rican Women; Federal Programs Specialist, Office of the Commonwealth of Puerto Rico, Washington, D.C.; President, Inter American Commission of Women of the Organization of American States; Consultant to U.S. Department of State, United States Representative to the

Commission related to the U.S. OAS Mission and International Organization Affairs Bureau of the Department; Participant in World Conference on the United Nations Decade for Women, Copenhagen, Denmark and Numerous International Fora; Vice President, Overseas Education Fund, League of Women Voters of the United States (board member, 1968-81; executive board, executive committee, program development, Latin American and publications committees); Director, Caribbean Seminar on Women in Development; Co-Chair, National Advisory Committee for Women, Appointed by the President of the United States; Commissioner, U.S. Commission on the Observance of International Women's Year, 1977 (executive committee, chair of selection committee); Federal Programs Specialist, Federal Plans and Programs Section, Office of the Commonwealth of Puerto Rico, Washington, D.C.; Executive Assistant to the Administrator of the Office of the Commonwealth of Puerto Rico, Washington, D.C.; Short-term American Grantee, U.S. Department of State; Government Development Bank for Puerto Rico, San Juan, Puerto Rico (secretary to the President and to the General Counsel, Editor, *Ecos* Personnel Information Publication of the Bank, Editor, *Caribbean Highlights;* Teacher, Benedict Business School, San Juan, Puerto Rico. Organizational Memberships: Equity Policy Center (board member); Pan American Development Foundation; Americans for Democratic Action; Employment Task Force, National Urban Coalition (board of directors); Girl Scouts of America; Wonder Woman Foundation; Advisory Committees/Boards, Puerto Rican Family Institute, New York, Women's Educational Equity Action League, Washington, D.C., Aspira of America Fellowships Program, Ad Hoc Coalition for Women's Appointments, National Women's Political Caucus; National Puerto Rican Coalition, Coalition for International Development (board of directors); Foreign Service Selection Board, U.S. Department of State; Board, Public Members Association of the Foreign Service; National Conference of Puerto Rican Women (national president, president of D.C. Chapter, 1975; national board until 1980); Advisor and Participant in Series of Conferences on Cross Disciplinary Perspectives on Bilingual Education, Center for Applied Linguistics, 1976; Advisory Committee on Women of the Secretary of Labor of the United States; Committee on International Interdependence, U.S. National Commission on the Observance of International Women's Year (advisory committee); Hispanic Women's Center, Washington, D.C., (board of directors); Institute for Creative Leadership, Greensboro, North Carolina (trainee); White House Conference on Bilingual Education (participant); Political Participation of Women's Task Force, Women's Action Alliance; Overseas Education Fund (director, vice president, 1968-72); Steering Committee of Aspen Institute Project on Governance in the Western Hemisphere; World Bank Wives in Voluntary Service (founding member, executive committee member, 1969-72). Community Activites: Promoted and implemented plans for the creation of a Hispanic First Federal Credit Union to serve the Hispanic community in the District of Columbia Metropolitan Area; Collaborated in the program development and design of leadership seminars and activities to promote civic participation and action in community involvement to improve communities in Latin America and Domestically; Directed and guided the growth of a national organization functioning in ten states and improved its organizational development patterns to achieve effective, relevant national recognition to advance opportunities for Hispanics and Women; Establishment, direction and management of the National Advisory Committee for Women until 1979. Published Works: Writer and Editor of numerous studies and publications as well as articles and news features such as: *Foundations Support to Puerto Ricans, The Process of Self Determination During the Last Two Decades, A Study of Federal Public Assistance Payments to Puerto Rico, Puerto Rican Women: Some Biographical Profiles* (book), *Women in Development.* Honors and Awards: Listed in *Who's Who of American Women, Women's International Register.* Address: 6717 Loring Court, Bethesda, Maryland 20817.

Debra C Vuckovich

Vuckovich, Debra Carole

Geophysicist. Personal: Born September 9, 1952; Daughter of Dante and Virginia Giardini. Education: B.S. 1973, M.S. 1976, Mathematics, Wright State University, Dayton, Ohio; Studies in Mathematics, Indiana University, Bloomington; Studies in Engineering, University of Michigan, Dearborn. Career: Geophysicist, Shell Oil Company, 1981 to present; Product Design Engineer and Structural Analyst, Ford Motor Company, 1977-81; Administrative Officer, Engineering Department, Wright State University, 1975-77; Associate Instructor, Wright State University and University of Indiana. Community Activities: International Fund for Animal Welfare; Michigan Humane Society; East African Wildlife Society; Whale Protection Fund; Defenders of Wildlife; Ford Thunderbird Ski Club; United States Parachute Association; Balloon Federation of America; Southeastern Michigan Balloon Association. Honors and Awards: National Honor Society of Centerville High School, Ohio; Phi Eta Tau Honor Society of Wright State University; Listed in Numerous Biographical Reference Publications. Address: 19526 Coppervine, Houston, Texas 77084.

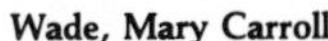

Waddington, Bette Hope

Violinist. Personal: Born July 27, 1921; Daughter of John and Marguerite Crowder Waddington (both deceased). Education: A.B. Music, University of California at Berkeley, 1945; M.A. Music and Art, San Francisco State University, 1953; Postgraduate Study, University of California; San Jose State University; Juilliard School of Music; General California Teaching Credentials, Kindergarten through 12th Grades, Junior High Librarianship; California Junior College Life Credentials, Music and Art. Career: Violinist (under stage name Elizabeth Crowder), St. Louis Symphony, 1958 to present; Former Positions include Librarian, National Aeronautics and Space Administration; Librarian, Children's Public Library, San Jose; Public School Teacher, Alameda & San Francisco Counties, California, and Erie, Pennsylvania; Dallas Symphony; Concert Mistress, Peninsula Symphony, Redwood City & San Mateo, California; Carmel Bach Festival, California; Conducted Fritz Mahler, Erie Symphony, Pennsylvania, 1951. Organizational Memberships: Alpha Beta Alpha; American String Teachers Association. Community Activities: Sierra Club; University of California Alumni Association; San Jose State University Alumni Association; United Services Organization and Red Cross (violin soloist, 1940-48); Camp Curry, Yosemite, California (soloist). Religion: Violin Soloist for Various Churches in the Bay Area and High Sierra, California, in Erie, Pennsylvania, and in New York City, New York. Honors and Awards: Scholarship as Student of Joseph Fuchs, Juilliard School of Music, 1950; Extensive Travel throughout United States, Europe, and Egypt Studying Art and Music. Address: 2800 Olive Street, St. Louis, Missouri 63103.

Bette H Waddington

Wade, Mary Carroll

Educator, Government Official, Psychologist. Personal: Born September 1, 1909; Daughter of Seaborn Rosa and Dollie Hill Carroll (both deceased); Married Richard Rudolph Ward (deceased). Education: B.A., Maryville College, 1931; Postgraduate Study, French School, University of the South, Summer 1938; M.A., George Washington University, 1948; Ed.D., American University, 1970. Career: High School Teacher and Drama Coach; Clerk Typist, War Department; Library Assistant, Library of Congress; Planner, Planner-in-Charge, Chief of Data Forms Section, United States Government Printing Office; Consultant Psychologist, Virginia Department of Rehabilitation; Chairman, Federal Women's Program, United States Government Printing Office; Lecturer, Montgomery College; Consultant. Organizational Memberships: American Psychological Association; Virginia Psychological Association; District of Columbia Psychological Association; Psi Chi (secretary, 1965); Kappa Delta Epsilon Business Forms Management Association (secretary, 1980-81); Washington Craftsmen's Club; Washington Litho Club; Franklin Technical Society. Community Activities: Washington Cerebral Palsy Association (member of the board, 1970-82); Northern Virginia Altrusa Club (member, 1977 to present; vice president, 1970-82; secretary, 1982-83); Scholarship Committee Board (secretary, 1982-83); Community Services (chairman, 1978); Business and Professional Women's Club of Fairfax (vice president, 1974-75; president, 1975-76; scholarship chairman, 1978); Phi Delta Gamma (chapter president, 1957-58; secretary, 1948-49; national council representative, 1968-72); Corporation of Alexandria Hospital; Alexandria Inter-Service Club Council (secretary, 1981); Northern Virginia Toastmistress Club (president, 1973; vice president, 1973; secretary, 1972; treasurer, 1972; delegate to national convention, 1974, 1982; club delegate to council, 1981); National Trust for Historic Preservation. Religion: Former Sunday School Teacher, Union Congregational Church, 1925-26; Member, Maryville Providence Presbyterian Church. Honors and Awards: Honorary Member of Staff of Tennessee Senator Anna Belle Clement O'Brien; Distinguished Service Medal, United Service Organization, 1946; Six Certificates of Merit 1962-65, Superior Service Awards, 1963, 1966-68, Special Achievement Awards 1971-72, United States Government Printing Office; Nominee for Federal Woman of the Year Award, 1975; Chairman, Government Printing Office Federal Women's Program, 1972-73; Equal Employment Opportunity Service Award, 1974-75; National Committee for Standardization of Optical Character Recognition Forms, 1973-74; Graduate of Maryville College Art Department, 1931. Address: 614 Bashford Lane, Apartment 103, Alexandria, Virginia 22314.

Wagner, Iwana B

Financial Coordinator, Officer, Home Rehabilitation Program, Energy Advisor and Chairman Sister Cities Activities. Personal: Born July 5, 1932; Daughter of Okley T. Lee; Mother of Kenneth C., Jr., Alana Lee. Education: Graduate of East High School, Akron, Ohio, 1950; Graduate of Comptometer Business School, Akron, 1950; Accounting Courses, North Central Technical College, Mansfield, Ohio. Career: Payroll Supervisor, National Seating Company; Owner, Iwana's Seamstress Business; Financial Officer, Home Rehabilitation Coordinator, Historic Coordinator, Energy Advisor, Sister City Coordinator, City of Mansfield, Ohio. Organizational Memberships: M.O.A.B.W.A. Charter Chapter, American Business Women's Association (president, 1973). Community Activities: Zonta of Mansfield (president, 1981); Area Secretary, Senator Robert Taft's Campaign Committee, 1969; Precinct Committeewoman, Republican Party, 1974-77; Jaycees Wives President, 1960. Religion: President, Women's Association, First United Presbyterian Church, Mansfield, Ohio, 1973. Honors and Awards: Woman of the Year, American Businesswomen's Association, M.O.A.B.W.A. Charter Chapter, 1973; Personality of the Week, *Mansfield News Journal*, 1976. Address: 576 Sherwood Drive, Mansfield, Ohio 44904.

Mary C Wade

Wahlberg, Eric C

Company President. Personal: Born in 1910; Son of Carl Victor and Anna Elizabeth Wahlberg (both deceased); Married Grace Alberta; Father of Nancy Edith Tabol, Carolyn Mae Ellingson. Education: B.S.E.E., Newark College of Engineering. Career: President, The Wahlred Company; Consulting Engineer, 1964-66; Program Manager, Engineer, AMF, 1956-64; Supervision of Research & Development, New Products, Government Contracts, Electrolux, 1941-56; Field Engineer, Asiatic Petroleum Company; Development of Electrolytic Condensers, Condenser Corporation. Organizational Memberships: Institute of Electrical and Electronic Engineering (senior member). Religion: First United Methodist Church of Stamford, Administrative Board. Honors and Awards: Distinguished Citizen of Connecticut, 1975; Honored for Research and Lab Performance during World War II by Colonel Holliday of Wright-Paterson Research Center; Honored at New York's World Fair for Technology. Address: The Wahlred Company, 32

Eighth Street, Stamford, Connecticut 06905.

Waite, Louis Edward

Vice President, Operations. Personal: Born February 11, 1926; Son of Clarence and Bessie Hoover Waite; Married Frances Clara Jackson; Father of Yvonne B. McClain, Louis, Jr., Duane D., John T. Education: Graduate of Camden School, Kipton, Ohio, 1944; Oberlin College, Ohio, 1950. Military: Served in the United States Army from 1944-45 in the 30th Infantry Regiment, 76th Infantry Division, European Theatre of Operations, France, Belgium, Luxembourg and German attaining a rank of Private First Class. Career: Vice President, Operations, TLI, Inc., 1976 to present; Manager, Truck Transportation, Inland Container Corporation, Indianapolis, Indiana, 1970-76; REA Express, Minneapolis/St. Paul Division Manager 1968-70, Various Supervisory Positions 1953-68; Diesel Engineer, City of Oberlin, Ohio, 1950-53. Organizational Memberships: Delta Nu Alpha Transportation Fraternity, 1969; Indiana Motor Truck Association (director, executive board, 1972-76; chairman, private carrier division, 1973-76); American Trucking Association (director, private carrier conference, 1975 to present); National Council of Physical Distribution; Missouri Truck and Bus Association. Community Activities: Volunteer Fireman, 1947-52; Boy Scouts of America (committeeman, Kipton, Ohio, 1947-52); Kiwanis International, Greenwood, Indiana, 1970-76; Parent-Teacher Association, Greenwood, Indiana (president, 1964-65); Toastmasters Club, Indianapolis, Indiana, 1973; Masonic Lodge, Greenwood, Indiana, 1962; Scottish Rite, 32°, Indianapolis, Indiana, 1971; Murat Shrine, Indianapolis, Indiana, 1971; SPEBSQSA, Florissant, Missouri, 1980. Religion: Sunday School Teacher, Various Times and Locations; Minister of Music, New Providence Baptist Church, Missouri, 1965-68; Choir President, First Baptist, Afton, Missouri, 1968-69. Honors and Awards: International Platform Association, 1982; Honorary Kentucky Colonel, State of Kentucky, 1973; Listed in *Who's Who in Business and Finance, Who's Who in the Midwest, Who's Who in America, Who's Who in the World, Personalities of America, The Directory of Distinguished Americans.* Address: 2265 Brook Drive, Florissant, Missouri 63033.

Wesley H Wakefield

Wakefield, Wesley H

Evangelist. Personal; Born August 22, 1929; Son of William James Elijah and Jane Mitchell Halpenny Wakefield (both deceased); Married Mildred June Shouldice on October 24, 1959. Education: Graduate of Vancouver Public Schools; Wesleyan Theological Studies to 1951; Special Studies in Constitutional Law and Addictions. Career: Evangelist and International Leader, Bishop-General, The Bible Holiness Movement, 1949 to present; Editor, *Truth on Fire!* 1949 to present, *Christian Social Vanguard* 1961-62; Manager, Liberty Press, 1966 to present; Manager, Evangelistic Book Services, 1951 to present; Director, Cumo Resources Limited, 1979 to present; Director, Seastar Resources Limited, 1981 to present; Administrator, Imperial Security Guard Service Limited, 1979 to present. Organizational Memberships: Christian Holiness Association; Evangelical Fellowship of Canada; National Black Evangelical Association; Anti-Slavery Society for the Protection of Human Rights; British Columbia Family Council; Concerned Christians for Racial Equality; Canadian Bible Society; Religious Information Centre (chairman, 1978 to present); Canadians for the Protection of Religious Liberty; Religious Freedom Conference of Christian Minorities (chairman, 1978). Community Activities: British Columbia Family Conference (delegate, 1974-75); Citizens' Committee, Penticton, British Columbia (chairman, 1956); Candians United For Separation of Church and State, 1977 to present; United Citizens for Integrity (research director, 1976 to present); Japan Evangelistic Band (board member, 1977 to present); National Association for the Advancement of Colored People; Canadian Bible Society. Religion: Conservative Wesleyan Evangelical. Published Works: *Bible Doctrine*, 1951; *Bible Basis of Christian Security*, 1957; *Jesus is Lord*, 1974; Editor, *Wesleyan Annotated Edition of the Bible* 1981, *Hallelujah Songbook* 1981, Others. Honors and Awards: Twice Awarded International Honour for Community Service; Opened First Legislature of New Democratic Party Government, British Columbia, 1972; Listed in *Who's Who in Religion, Who's Who in Canada, Dictionary of International Biography.* Address: #309 -319 West Pender, Vancouver, British Columbia, Canada V6B 1T4.

Edwin P Wald

Walchars, John S J

Educator. Personal: Born May 9, 1912. Education: Graduate of Teachers Academy, Vienna, Austria, 1932; M.A., University of Innsbruck Tyrol. Career: Lecturer; Writer; Priest; Teacher. Religion: Revivals Across the United States, England, Dublin, Canada. Published Works: Author, Four Books. Honors and Awards: Fellow, American Biographical Institute; Listed in *Contemporary Authors, International Who's Who of Authors, International Who's Who of Intellectuals, Book of Honor.* Address: 319 Concord Row, Weston, Massachusetts 02193.

Wald, Edwin Prescott

Civil Engineer. Personal: Born July 23, 1920 in Globe, Arizona; Son of George Gustav and Edith Percy Carpenter Wald; Father of Stephen, Suzanne Montgomery, Diane Larson, Kathleen Boyum. Education: B.S. Civil Engineering, California Institute of Technology, 1941. Career: Assayer, Arizona Magma Mining Company, Chloride, Arizona, Summers 1938-39; Assayer, Oro Plata Mining Company, Emerald Isle, Arizona, 1939; Loftsman Consolidated Aircraft Company, Lindbergh Field, San Diego, 1940; Draftsman, Designer, North American Aviation Company Inc., El Segundo, California, 1941-53; Designer, Cal Tech Jet Propulsion Lab, Pasadena, California, 1956-61; Assistant Civil Engineer, City of Alhambra, California, 1964 to present. Organizational Memberships: Leakey Foundation (fellow, 1970 to present); Lindbergh Foundation; American Society of Civil Engineers; Air Force Association; American Defense Preparedness Association; International Platform Association. Community Activities: Friends of Cal Tech Libraries; Cousteau Society; Nature Conservancy; Wildlife Preservation Federation; African Wildlife Leadership Foundation; American Film Institute; American Museum of Natural History; Smithsonian; Greater Los Angeles Zoo Association; American Forestry Association (life member); The Epigraphic Society; Republican Party. Religion: Episcopal. Published Works: *Properties of the Elements; Drainage Basin Planning; Water Conservation; Flood Control; Wilderness Planning; Highways Planning; Relating Game Preservations, Farms and Residencies; Habitat Planning, High Temperature Solar Energy; Solar-Powered Auto; Orbital Data; Tornado Control.* Address: 230 North Valencia, Alhambra, California 91801.

John Walchars

Walker, Glynda Marie

Director of Communications Department. Personal; Born May 31, 1940; Daughter of Mr. and Mrs. Robert Glenn Walker. Education: B.S., Southern Illinois University, 1962; M.A., Ohio State University, 1968; Ohio License in Speech Pathology, 1975. Career: Director of Communications Department and Speech/Language Pathologist, Wheeling Society for Crippled Children, West Virginia, Over 18 Years. Organizational Memberships: American Speech/Language and Hearing Association, 1962 to present; Council of Exceptional Children, 1968 to present; Zeta Alpha Eta; Zeta Phi Eta; Association for Retarded Citizens (board member,

1975 to present; treasurer, 1977-78; vice-president, 1979-80); Russell Nesbitt-Ohio County Council for Retarded Children (board member, 1981 to present; corresponding secretary, 1981-82); Headstart Agency (advisory board member, 1975 to present); Northern Panhandle Mental Health (developmental disabilities and mental retardation steering committee, 1977 to present); Handicapped United Organization, 1980 to present. Community Activities: Sunshine Friday Social Club for Retarded Teenagers and Young Adults (founder, volunteer coordinator, 1975 to present); Emoclew Handicapped Young Adult Club (sponsor, 1962 to present); Ohio Valley Stroke Club (volunteer coordinator, 1978 to present). Religion: Vance Memorial Presbyterian Church; Sunday School Teacher, Christ Methodist Church, 1962. Honors and Awards: Certificate of Clinical Competence in Speech Pathology, American Speech/Language and Hearing Association, 1961 to present; Jaycette State and Local Awards, Spokette First Place Local and Second Place State 1973-74, Spunkette First Place Local and First Place State 1974-75, Spunkette First Place Local and Second Place State 1975-76, Spunkette First Place Local and Second Place State 1976-77, Local Speak-Up Award and Hillhopper Visitation Awards 1973-77; Outstanding Young Women of America Award in Recognition of Personal and Professional Accomplishments, 1977; Outstanding Alumna Award for State of West Virginia, West Virginia Delta Zeta Sorority, 1977; February Citizen of the Month, Wheeling, West Virginia, Community Award presented by the Jaycees, 1978; Distinguished Service Award, Wheeling Jaycees, 1982; Member, American Biographical Institute Research Association, 1981; Listed in *Who's Who in the South and Southwest, World Who's Who of Women, Personalities of America.* Address: 200 B Betty Street, Wheeling, West Virginia 26003.

Glynda M Walker

Walker, Jesse Marshall

Director of Missions for Baptist Associations. Personal: Born July 21, 1917; Son of Jesse Makton and Marie C. Walker (both deceased); Married Anne Lashley; Father of Martha Martin, Frances Anne, Jesse M. Jr., William T. Education: A.B., Elon College, North Carolina, 1938; Th.M., D.Min., Southern Baptist Theological Seminary, Louisville, Kentucky. Career: Director of Missions, East River and Highlands Baptist Associations, Virginia; Pastor, Bethel & Dabney Baptist Churches, Holton, Indiana 1938-41, Stovall Baptist Field, Stovall, North Carolina 1941-46, Liberty Baptist Church, Appomattox, Virginia 1946-50, Braggtown Baptist Church, Durham, North Carolina 1950-56, Southside Baptist Church, Miami, Florida 1956-60, Bedford Baptist Church, Bedford, Virginia 1960-73. Address: Route 1 Number 3, Staff Village, Dublin, Virginia 24084.

Walker, Marilyn Muriel Hall

Writer-in-Residence. Personal: Born May 8, 1939; Daughter of Mrs. Harry A. Hall; Married Haywood A. Walker Jr.; Mother of Collin Harrison, Kent Graham. Education: B.A., University of Missouri-Columbia, 1961; M.A. 1965, Graduate Study 1966-67, University of Missouri-Kansas City; Institute for Advanced Professional Studies in Higher Education, 1976-79. Career: William Jewell College, Instructor of English 1965-69, Assistant Professor of English 1969-73, Associate Professor of English and Art History, 1973-80, Writer-in-Residence 1980 to present. Organizational Memberships: Modern Language Association; Southeastern Medieval Association; Delta Kappa Gamma. Community Activities: Annual Conference for College Writers (director, 1970 to present); Kansas City Regional Council for Higher Education Writer-in-Residence Program (director); Editor, *Pylons* 1970-78, *Perspectives* 1972-74; American Poetry Series (board of directors, 1968 to present); Martin & Central Printing Companies (board of directors); Fine Arts Guild of William Jewell College (vice-president, 1981 to present); Friends of Art, 1964 to present. Religion: Episcopalian. Published Works: Author, Book, *Visions and Revisions*, 1981; Author, Essays, Poems appearing in numerous small magazines. Honors and Awards: William Jewell College Faculty Award, 1970, 1978. Address: Box 432D Route 1, Liberty, Missouri 64068.

Marilyn H Walker

Walker, V Helen Brent

Retired Manager. Personal: Born May 19, 1910; Daughter of Julius H. and Elizabeth Kennedy Brent (both deceased); Married J. Marshall Walker (deceased); Mother of Joseph, Virginia Helen W. Burrows, Elizabeth W. Dunnaway. Education: B.A., William Carey College, 1932; AA, Whitworth College, 1944; MA, University of Southern Mississippi; Graduate Study, Mississippi State College. Career: Manager, Brent Interest; Former Elementary School Teacher and Principal; Founder (retired from), Brent's Specialty Shop. Community Activities: Mississippi United Daughters of the Confederacy; Daughters of the American Revolution; Colonial Dames; Magna Charter Dames; McComb Public Library (past board member). Religion: Baptist; Dorcas Society; Sunday School Teacher. Honors and Awards: American Security Council, United States Congressional Advisory Board; Mississippi Merit Board; World War II Citation for Sale of War Bonds; Listed in *Who's Who in Education, Who's Who in Mississippi Community Service, Who's Who in Biography, Who's Who in Mississippi*, Others. Address: Brentwood, Box 389, McComb, Mississippi 39648.

Walker-Piernas, Sherry Anne

Attorney. Personal: Born December 25, 1954; Daughter of Mr. and Mrs. Sherman Waler Walker; Married Lynch J. Piernas Jr. Educatio.ı: B.A., University of California-Los Angeles, 1976; J.D., Hastings College of Law, 1979. Career: Attorney for State Public Defenders; Former Attorney for Private Firm. Organizational Memberships: California State Bar; Charles Houston Bar Association; National Bar Association; American Bar Association; Black Women Lawyers Association. Community Activities: Lecturer, Corporate Law, Hastings College of Law, 1981; Tutor, Bar Preparation Program, 1981; San Francisco Rent Stabilization and Arbitration Board, 1980. Honors and Awards: Moot Court Oral Award, 1978; Deans Honor Roll, 1973-76; Honors Program in Psychology, 1974-76; Chairperson, Academic Affairs Committee, 1978; Tutoring Contracts and Torts, 1974; Outstanding Service Award, 1979; Certificate of Honor Award, Legal Defense, 1979. Address: 35645 Beeching Lane, Fremont, California 94536.

James D Walsh

Walsh, James David

Broadcasting Executive. Personal: Born December 17, 1947; Son of James A. Walsh and Dorothy S. Walsh (deceased); Married Mary Ellen Budge. Education: Northwestern College. Military: Served in the United States National Guard, 1967-73. Career: Announcer, WFLY-FM, Troy, New York, 1971-72; Account Executive and Announcer, WABY-AM, Albany, 1972-74; Account Executive, WPTR-AM, Albany, New York, 1974; Founder, General Manager, President, WWWD-AM Radio, Schenectady, New York, 1975 to present; President, Walvon Communications, Inc. Organizational Memberships: Platform Speakers of America, 1981. Community Activities: Deputy Sheriff, Schenectady County, 1980 to present; Young Men's Christian Association-Church League (basketball coach, 1966-68); Boys' Club (basketball coach, 1968-70); Rotterdam Men's Recreation League (basketball coach and official, 1971-76); Tri-City Comets Local Semi-Professional Basketball Team (founder, 1974; manager, coach, 1974-76). Religion: Church Sunday School Teacher, 1967-68. Published Works: Co-Author, *Greenburg's Guide to American Flyer Trains*, 1980. Honors and Awards: Three Platinum Albums, Fifteen Gold Records for Contributions to Success of Hit Phonograph Recordings; Nominated Music Director of the Year, Medium Market, 1976. Address: 142 Putnam Road, Schenectady, New York 12306.

Walter, Bert Mathew

Federal Mediation Commissioner. Personal: Born July 11, 1915 in Devils Lake, North Dakota; Son of Alois and Margaret Bauer Walter (both deceased); Married Phyllis Traynor, July 3, 1950. Education: A.A., University of Minnesota, 1936; B.B.A., University of Baltimore, 1938. Career: Shop Employee, General Electric Company, Pittsfield, Massachusetts, 1938-41; Director of Industrial Relations, Chesebrough Ponds, New York City, 1964-66; President, Leasing International Corporation, Madrid, Spain, 1966-68; Commissioner, Federal Mediation and Conciliation Services, Los Angeles, California, 1968 to present. Organizational Memberships: Society of Professionals in Dispute Resolution, Washington, D.C. (vice-president, 1977-78; national director); Conseil Internationale Organisation Scientifique (director, 1967); Council of International Progress Management (director, 1967); Buchanan, Michigan United Funds (president, 1956-57); National Metal Trades Association (president, 1962-63); American Society of Personnel Administration (founder, president, 1958-59); Industrial Relations Research Association. Community Activities: Rotary International (president, Niles, Michigan, 1959-60); Benevolent Protective Order of Elks (honorary life member, 1936 to present); Republican Party. Religion: Roman Catholic. Honors and Awards: Listed in *Who's Who in America, Who's Who in Government, New York Social Register, Blue Book of Europe, Who's Who in Labor*. Address: 1240 Via Pintada, Riverside, California 92507.

Bert M Walter

Walton, Frances Liz-Thompson

College Administrator and Reading Instructor. Personal: Daughter of James and Annie Thompson; Mother of Effie, Eva, Elizeria. Education: B.A., 1977, and M.A., 1978, both from Jersey City State College. Career: Academic Advisor; Tutorial Co-ordinator; Dormitory Counselor; Public School Reading Specialist; Reading Instructor; Assistant Registrar. Organizational Memberships: International Reading Association; New Jersey Reading Teacher Association; Hudson Reading Council; National Academic Council; National Academic Advising Association; Phi Delta Kappa; American Association of Collegiate Registrars. Community Activities: Action for Sickle Cell Anemia Inc. (president 1971 to present); Girl Scouts of America (co-ordinator 1973-80, leader 1968-73); National Association for the Advancement of Colored People (executive board 1970-74); Gray Lady 1968-70; Emergency Blood Bank Driver; Motor Service Corp; American Red Cross (board of directors); Cancer Care Task Force; Snyder High School Parents' Council (president 1974-76, board of trustees 1974-76); City Wide Parents' Council (4th vice president 1973); Ladies Aid Society (vice president 1969-70); Nurses' Unit, 1965 to present; Girl Scout Committee (chairlady 1974); Sewers Educational and Professional Organization, 1978 to present. Honors and Awards: Graduated magna cum laude; National Honor Society; Alpha Kappa Delta, President 1975-76; Kappa Delta Phi; Received the Middle Eastern International Scholarship, Jersey City State College; Listed in *Who's Who Among Students in American Universities and Colleges*. Address: 91 Oak Street, Jersey City, New Jersey 07304.

Wanbaugh, Rebecca Herrick

Professor of History. Personal: Born April 12, 1923; Daughter of Mrs. Chandler Bowden; Married Robert Clarence Wanbaugh Jr.; Step-Mother of Susan Jean. Education: B.A. Sociology 1945, M.A. History 1964, Ph.D. History 1980, University of Maine-Orono; Attended Andover-Newton Theological School, 1956-57. Career: Vocational Rehabilitation Counselor, New York State Department of Education, Division of Vocational Rehabilitation, Rochester, New York, 1958-59; Instructor of Sociology, University of Maine-Orono, 1959-62; University of Maine-Presque Isle, Dean of Women 1963-74, Assistant/Associate Professor of History 1963-82, Professor of History 1982 to present. Organizational Memberships: American Association of University Professors, 1961-76; American Historical Association, 1971 to present; American Sociological Association, 1961 to present; Maine Sociological Society (charter member); National Educational Association, 1963 to present; Maine Teachers Association, 1963 to present; National Association of Women Deans, Administrators and Counselors, 1963-74. Community Activities: University of Maine-Presque Isle Chapter, Presque Isle United Fund Drive (chairman, 1964-67); General Assembly of the Maine State Y.M.C.A., Northern District, Model United Nations (third committee - social, humanitarian, cultural - 1965); "Poverty in Affluence", Sponsored by Title I of High Education Act (consultant and lecturer in sociology, 1968); Presque Isle-University of Maine Presque Isle Drug Education Team, State of Maine Drug Education Workshop, 1971-73; Alcohol Information and Referral Services (advisory council, 1976-83); Maine Association for Retarded Citizens, 1965 to present; University of Maine-Presque Isle Faculty Representative to the University of Maine Board of Trustees, 1979-82; University of Maine Board of Trustees (academic planning committee on student life, 1979-80). Religion: College Forum of the Congregational Church, Presque Isle, Organized and Sponsored, 1963-67; Presque Isle Ministerial Conferences, Consultant in Sociology, 1968-70. Honors and Awards: Sigma Mu Sigma; Alpha Kappa Delta; Phi Alpha Theta; Listed in *Who's Who in American College and University Administration, Maine's Most Prominent People, World Who's Who of Women in Education, Who's Who in the East, Directory of Distinguished Americans, Dictionary of International Biography*. Address: P.O. Box 1311, Presque Isle, Maine 04769.

Rebecca Wanbaugh

Wang, Chia Ping

Research Physicist, Professor. Personal: Born September 1; Son of Guan Can and Tah Wang (both deceased). Education: B.Sc., University of London, 1950; M.Sc., University of Malaya, 1951; Ph.D., Universities of Malaya and Cambridge, 1953; D.Sc., Physics, University of Singapore, 1972. Career: Assistant Lecturer, University of Malaya, 1951-53; Associate Professor of Physics 1954-56, Professor of Physics 1956-58, Head of Electron Physics Division 1955-58, Steering Committee of Nuclear Physics Division 1956-58, Nankai Tientsin University; Head, Electron Physics Division, Lanchow Atomic Project, 1958; Senior Lecturer, Professor, Acting Head, Departments of Physics and Mathematics, Hong Kong University and Chinese University of Hong Kong, 1958-63; Research Associate, Laboratory of Nuclear Studies, Cornell University, Ithaca, New York, 1963-64; Associate Professor of Space Science and Applied Physics, Catholic University of America, Washington, D.C., 1964-68; Associate Professor of Physics, Case Institute of Technology, Case Western Reserve University, Cleveland, Ohio, 1966-70; Visiting Scientist, Visiting Professor, Universities of Cambridge (England), Leuven (Belgium), United States Naval Research Laboratory and University of Maryland (concurrently), Massachusetts Institute of Technology, 1970-75; Research Physicist, United States Army Natick Research and Development Laboratories, 1975 to present. Organizational Memberships: American Physical Society; Institute of Physics, London; Society of Sigma Xi; American Association for the Advancement of Science (life member); New York Academy of Sciences; Italian Physical Society; American Geophysical Union; American Association of University Professors. Community Activities: Guest of the British Council, London, 1962; Hong Kong Delegate, 1962 International Conference on High Energy Physics, CERN, Geneva, Switzerland; Delegate, United States, United Kingdom, 1967 International Conference on Cosmic Rays, Calgary, Canada; 1972 International Conference on High Energy Physics, Batavia, Illinois; 1978 International Symposium on Standardization of Radiation Dosimetry, Atlanta, Georgia; International Atomic Energy Agency, Vienna, Austria; 1969, 1971 International Conferences on Elementary Particles at Lund, Sweden and Amsterdam, The Netherlands. Honors and Awards: Converted for the First Time Picosecond Time Intervals into Pulse Heights, 1963; Deduced from Over 50 Experiments on Particle Multiplicity Distributions the Many-Subunits (now referred to as partons) Structures of the Nucleons and Other Hadrons, 1968; Obtained the Momentum Distribution Spectra in High Energy Collisions, including Electron-Nucleon and Neutrino-Nucleon Collission, 1971-72; First Observed with O. R. Frisch (at the Cavendish Laboratory, University of Cambridge) the Sinusoidal Light Waves with a Laser

Chia P Wang

Interferometer, 1970; Performed One of the First Experiments with the then 200 GeV Proton Accelerator at the Fermi National Laboratory, Batavia, Illinois, 1972; Formulated the General Integral Survival Fractions for Bacteria during Thermal Sterilization, 1978; Outstanding Performance Award 1980, Quality Increase Award 1980, Department of the Army; Citation, Consistently High Quality Performance in the Fields of Classical, Quantum, Mechanical and Experimental Physics, and Keen Ability to Use the Skills to Solve Practical Problems in Research and Development of the Food Irradiation Process. Address: 28 Hallett Hill Road, Weston, Massachusetts 02193.

Wang, Thomas Keliang

Social Services Administrator. Personal: Born June 26, 1920 in Yin-Chunn, Hu-Hsien, Shensi, China; Son of Chin Hsun and Yinn C. Wang Wang; Married En-Ming Chen, April 27, 1951; Father of George Hansen, John Linsen, Aveline Enming. Career: Private Secretary to President, Control Yuan, Chinese National Government, 1944-47; General Manager, Peking and Canton Restaurant, Brooklyn, New York, 1951-55; Office Manager, Trade Union Courier Publishing Corporation, New York City, 1955-56; Office Manager 1955-56, Comptroller 1956-61, Chief Executive Officer 1962-64, Director and Secretary-Treasurer, 1959-63; Comptroller, World Wide Press Syndicate, 1955-62; Department of Social Services, City of New York, Housing Advisor 1966-69, Special Assistant to Deputy Commissioner of Administration 1969-75; Chairman of the Board, Chinatown Service Center, Inc.; Chairman of the Board, New York Chinatown Senior Citizen Coalition Center, Inc., New York City, 1971 to present; Chinatown Daycare Center, Inc., New York City, Founder 1970, Chairman 1970 to present. Organizational Memberships: American Society of Public Administration; Asian-American Assembly for Policy Research. Community Activities: Committee for Formation of Siking College, 1972 to present; Chinese-American Republican Club of New York State (president, 1975 to present); Harry S Truman Library Institute; Smithsonian Association. Address: 34 Crooke Avenue, Brooklyn, New York 11226.

Warber, Esther M

Counseling Psychologist. Personal: Born March 21, 1923; Daughter of Alex and Helena Schippers (both deceased). Education: B.S., University of Michigan, 1951; Master of Psychology, Wayne State University, 1958; Graduate Work, Harvard University, Tufts University, Boston University, 1967-77; Doctoral Candidate Public Administration, Nova University. Military: Served in the United States WAVES, 1943-46, attaining the rank of Machinists Mate First Class. Career: Medical Technologist; Vocational Rehabilitation Counselor; Counseling Psychologist, Veterans Administration. Organizational Memberships: American Psychology Association, 1958; American Personnel and Guidance Association, 1958; American Society of Personnel Administrators, 1977; President's Committee on the Handicapped, 1967 to present; Licensed Psychologist, 1973 to present; National Vocational Rehabilitation Association, 1956 to present. Community Activities: Michigan State Constitutional Convention Planning, 1957-58; Civil Defense (volunteer, 1951-62; technology instructor, 1953-61); Red Cross (instructor, first aid, home nursing, 1951-67); Michigan Governor George Romney Human Resource Council, 1964-66; Vice-President Hubert Humphrey Human Resource Council, 1964; Peace Corps in Ecuador (national public health instructor, community action worker, 1962-64); Head Start Community Action Volunteer, 1964-67; United Nations Student Advisory (six television segments, 1967); Detroit Mayor's Committee on Skid Row Problems, 1958-62; Massachusetts Health Council; New Hampshire Occupational Education Planning Council. Honors and Awards: Pi Lambda Theta National Honor Society, 1958; Graduate Scholarship in Rehabilitation, Department of Health, Education and Welfare; Dean's Scholarship, President's Scholarship, Wayne State University; Papers Accepted, University of Michigan Graduate Library; Listed in *Who's Who of American Women, Creative Personalities, International Who's Who of Women*. Address: 410 Faxon Commons, 1047 South Artery, Quincy, Massachusetts 02169.

Eleanor B Warner

Ward, William Theophilus Thomas Sr

Historian, Anthropologist. Personal: Born March 9, 1919; Son of John Wilmer Sr. and Nancy Ward (both deceased); Married Isabel Salvador; Father of Nancy Lee, John Wilmer II, Catherine Lavinia, William Theophilus Thomas Jr. Education: A.B.; B.S.; M.A.; Ph.D. Career: Historian, 13th Air Force, 1951-79; Director, Community Relations, Clark Air Base, Philippines, 1964; Chief Information Officer, 1962-63; Assistant Information Officer, 1959-62; Lecturer, University of Philippines, 1954-55; Anthropologist, Trust Territory of Micronesia, 1950-51; Teacher, Pago Pago, American Samoa, 1949-50; Teacher, Marietta, Georgia, 1948-49. Organizational Memberships: Numerous Professional Associations. Religion: St. John's Episcopal Church, Florence, South Carolina. Published Works: Author, Numerous Historical and Anthropological Publications, including *The Death of President Roxas* 1960, *The Taiwan Straits Difficulty* 1958, 208 Volumes of 13th Air Force, 6th Air Division, 6200th Air Base Wing and 405th Fighter Wing Histories, 1951-79. Honors and Awards: Certificate of Appreciation, University of Philippines, 1959; Delegate, 8th Pacific Science Congress, Bangkok, Thailand, 1957; Member, Numerous Scholastic Honorary Societies. Address: 500 South Warley Street, Florence, South Carolina 29501.

Warner, Eleanore Burtis

Educator. Personal: Born January 14, 1923, in Allentown, New Jersey; Married Dr. L. Richard Warner; Mother of Five. Education: B.S.Ed., Trenton State College, 1947; M.Ed. 1958, Ed.D. 1965, Rutgers Graduate School of Education, Rutgers University. Career: Classroom Teacher, Grades 2, 4, 5, 8, New Jersey Schools, 1946-58; Curriculum Supervisor, Grades K-8, Two Schools, Little Silver, New Jersey, 1958-64; Director, Escola Americana De Santos, Santos, Brazil, 1965-67; Demonstration Teacher, Grade 6, Antheil School, Laboratory School for Trenton State College, 1967-69; Associate Professor, Department of Elementary/Early Childhood Education and Reading, Trenton State College, 1969 to present; Trenton State College Exchange Professor to Worcester College of Higher Education, Worcester, England, 1980-81. Organizational Memberships: National Education Association, 1947 to present; New Jersey Education Association (member, 1947 to present; Delegate Assembly, 1958-64); New Jersey Association of Teacher Educators (co-editor, *Bulletin*, 1976-78); Association for Supervision and Curriculum Development (active member, 1958-65; member, 1980-81); Tri-County Reading Association, 1976-78; Graduate School of Education Alumni Association, Rutgers State University (vice president, 1977-78; president, 1978-79); New Jersey State College Faculty Association; Mercer County Education Association, 1967 to present; Monmouth County Education Association, 1950-65; Bergen County Education Association, 1946-50. Community Activities: People-to-People International (homestay coordinator, 1978-80; host family, 1973, 1975, 1978, 1979; Trenton Chapter representative to Harrogate, England 1980, Grangemouth, Scotland 1980); Capital Squares Square Dance Club, Trenton, New Jersey; Princeton Masqueraders Square Dance Club, Princeton, New Jersey; Co-Ordin-8's Square Dance Club, Blakedown, England; Stourbridge Square Dance Club, Step-A-Round Dance Club, Stourbridge, England; Trenton State College (Faculty Dames; Gourmet Club; Travel Club; Teacher Corps Program, Wilson School; Competency Based Teacher Education Program; Department of Elementary Early Chidhood Education and Reading Language Arts Conference, 1977-80; Committee on Promotions, Reappointments and Tenure, Social Committee, Curriculum Revision Committee; Traffic Appeals Board; Teacher Education Advisory Board; Academic Calendar Committee; Academic Policies Committee; Academic Progress Committee, secretary, chairperson; College and Community Relations Committee, secretary, chairperson; Committee on Travel and Exchange; Faculty Senate, elected 1981; Graduate School of Education, Rutgers University, Dean's Search Committee 1978-79, Dean's Invitational Conference 1973 to present, Phonothon 1977-83; School of Education Professional Enrichment Conference, 1971, 1972; Faculty Colloquium, "British Education", 1982); Featured Speaker, Bi-National Schools of South American Conference, Buenos Aires, Argentina, 1967; Language Arts Workshops, Escola Americana de Campinas, Brazil (coordinator, speaker, 1967); American Schools Association (language arts coordinator, Eastern Brazil Conference, 1966); Sao Paulo University (doctoral committee for doctoral candidate, 1966); Kappa Delta Pi, Delta Xi Chapter (scholarship committee, editor/historian, 1970-75; vice president, 1975-76; president, 1976-78; lecture-slide presentations); National Foreign Policy Conference for Leaders in Teacher Education, Invitational Conference Department of State, 1972; Multi-Media Presentations; Radio Interviews, Soviet Culture and Education; Trenton Chapter Representative, Lord Mayor of Stoke-on-Trent, England, 1981; Mercer County Association for Gifted and Talented Children, Saturday Morning Program, Science Activities Teacher, 1981-82. Religion: West Trenton United Presbyterian Church, 1970 to present; Allentown, New Jersey, Presbyterian Church, 1923-50; Asbury Park, New Jersey, Presbyterian Church, 1950-70. Honors and Awards: Citation, Bi-National Schools of South American Conference, Buenos Aires, Argentina, 1967; Certificate of Merit, Escola Americana De Santos, Santos, Brazil, 1967; Compatriot in Education, National Kappa Delta Pi Award, 1976; Delta Xi Chapter, Kappa Delta Pi, 1956 to present; Phi Delta Kappa, Greater Trenton Area Chapter, 1972 to present; Certificate of Appreciation, Graduate School of Education Alumni Association, 1979; Distinguished Service Award, Rutgers University Graduate School of Education, 1982; Listed in *World Who's Who of Women in Education, Dictionary of International Biography, International Who's Who of Intellectuals, Notable Americans.* Address: 2060 Pennington Road, Trenton, New Jersey 08618.

Warnes, Deanna Suzanne

District Sales Manager, Insurance. Personal: Born January 29, 1945; Daughter of Ralph and Violet Wood. Education: J.D., University of London. Career: Claims Manager; Attorney; District Sales Manager Allstate Insurance Company. Organizational Memberships: National Association of Insurance Women (regional director, 1976-77); American Business Women's Association (vice-president, 1980); Claim Managers Association (chairman, 1981). Community Activities: San Mateo City Housing Commission (vice-chairman, 1972-78); San Jose City Housing Commission, 1980 to present; American Arbitration Association, 1972-81; Peninsula Symphony Guild, 1972-80; American Society of Training Directors, 1980; Insurance Company Education Directors, 1980 to present. Honors and Awards: Insurance Woman of the Year, 1976; Woman of the Year, Pacific Telephone, 1974; Listed in *Who's Who of American Women.* Address: 3155 Payne Avenue #17, San Jose, California 95117.

Warnick, Edward Eugene

Manager. Personal: Born January 3, 1927; Son of Michael Warnick; Married Angela Marie Stanziola; Father of Pamela Lee Moyer, Mark Geoffrey, Phillip Tyler, (Stepfather of:) Michele Renee Kirstein, Joseph Biagio Mistretta, Chrystie Ann Mistretta. Education: Attended Clemson A&M College, 1944; B.S.E.E., Duke University, 1950; Graduate Work, Johns Hopkins University 1952, University of Rochester 1964-67. Military: Served in the United States Army Air Corps, 1944-46. Career: Electronics Design Engineer, Westinghouse Electric Company, 1950-53; Eastman Kodak Company, 1953 to present, Senior Design Engineer, Project Engineer, Supervising Engineer, Divisional Research Laboratory Manager, Program Manager, Assembly Superintendent, Assistant Manager of Consumer Products Engineering, Assistant Manager, Director of Program Development, Copy Products. Organizational Memberships: American Management Association; Society of Photographic Scientists & Engineers; International Photographic Society. Community Activities: Chamber of Commerce; Boy Scouts of America, 1967-69; Regional Scouting Council; Monroe County Regional Planning Council, 1964-68; Town of Sweden Planning Board (chairman, 1964-68); Rochester Eye Bank and Research Society, 1963 to present; United States Power Squadrons (boating education, 1968 to present). Honors and Awards: Pi Mu Epsilon, 1949; Omicron Delta Kappa, 1949; Order of Red Friars, 1950; Order of St. Patrick, 1949; Tau Beta Pi, 1949; Citation, Boy Scouts of America; Listed in *Who's Who Among Students in American Universities and Colleges, Who's Who in the East.* Address: 198 Penfield Road, Rochester, New York 14610.

Gene E Washington

Warren, Jeffry C

Clinical Psychologist. Personal: Born November 1, 1949; Son of Florence S. Warren; Married April Yarbrough; Father of Adam B. Education: B.A., University of California-Santa Barbara, 1971; M.A. 1974, Ph.D. 1976, California School of Professional Psychology, San Diego. Career: Edwards Institute of Advanced Study, Director of Professional and Academic Training, Consultant, Director 1981 to present; Clinical Psychologist. Organizational Memberships: National Registrar, 1979 to present; American Psychological Association, 1976 to present; American Association of Psychologists, 1976 to present; San Diego Psychology & Law Society, 1979 to present. Community Activities: Tri-Community Services Systems (director of education and training, 1981 to present); Julie-Eliese Memorial Foundation (executive board, 1981 to present); Center for the Study and Application of Personal Construct Theory (executive board, 1981 to present). Honors and Awards: Listed in *Who's Who in the West, Who's Who in California.* Address: 7511 High Avenue, La Jolla, California 92037.

Washington, Gene Edward

Executive. Personal: Born August 12, 1931; Son of Horace Webster Washington; Married Jacqualin Ann Kaiser; Father of Robert Todd, James Allen, Steven Lee, Darren Scott. Education: B.S., Oklahoma State University, 1951; M.B.A., University of Chicago, 1970. Military: Served in the United States Air Force, 1952-56, to the rank of Captain, Instructor Pilot, Base Adjutant. Career: Systems Assurance & Financial Corporation, Chairman, President, Director; Environmental Chemic Systems, Inc., Past Director, Former Chairman, Former President; Boothe Computer Corporation, San Francisco, California, Senior Vice-President and Group Executive, 1971-73; Greyhound Computer Corporation, Director, Vice-President 1968-70; International Business Machines, Senior Marketing Representative 1956-63, Marketing Manager 1963-67; Director, Greyhound Time-Sharing Corporation, Greyhound Computer of Canada Ltd., Computer Personnel Consultants Inc., Boothe Computer of Canada Ltd., Boothe Management Systems Inc., Boothe Computer Marketing Inc., Boothe A. G. (Zurich), CLS of South Africa. Organizational Memberships: Alpha Kappa Psi; Arnold Air Society (treasurer, 1951-52); Blue Key; Computer Lessors Association; Data Processing Management Association; Gamma Theta Psi; Mu Kappa Tau; Scabbard and Blade; Sigma Chi (treasurer, 1951-52). Community Activities: H.O.P.E. (founder, director, 1961-62); Republican Party (precinct treasurer, 1965-66); Junior Achievement (director, 1958-59); Common Wealth Club, 1970-71. Religion: Deacon, First Presbyterian Church, Bloomfield Hills, Michigan, 1964-65. Honors and Awards: Manager of the Year 1966, Industry Leader 1962, Sales Training Number One Graduate 1957, Golden Circle 1958, Regional Managers Award 1960, 1962, 1963, Quota Club 1957-66, International Business Machines; Listed in *Who's Who in America, Who's Who in Finance and*

Industry, Who's Who in the West, Men of Achievement, Community Leaders of America, Who's Who in California, Directory of Distinguished Americans, Personalities of America. Address: 1427 Buchanan Street, Novato, California 94947.

Waterman, Thelma Marie

Executive. Personal: Born June 10, 1937; Daughter of Lucille Hosendove; Mother of Steven Nile, Kevin Bruce. Education: A.A., Liberal Arts, Hartford College for Women, 1969; B.A., Trinity College, Hartford, Connecticut, 1971; M.Div., Yale University, New Haven, Connecticut, 1978. Career: Executive Director, Greater Hartford Criminal Justice Coalition, 1980 to present; Director, Office of Community Affairs, Connecticut College, New London, 1971-80; Head Teacher, Hartford Headstart Program, 1971. Organizational Memberships: State of Connecticut Commission for Higher Education (review accreditation committee, 1977; five-year master plan, resource group VIII, finance, 1972-73); State of Connecticut Commission on Aid to Higher Education (advisory committee, 1973). Community Activities: Opportunities Industrialization Center, New London, 1972 to present; Trinity College, Hartford (board of fellows, 1976 to present); Tames Science Center, New London, 1978-80; Eastern Connecticut Health Systems Agency, Norwich, 1976-80; Young Parents Program, New London, 1974-80; Social Planning Council, United Way, Gales Perry, 1972-80; Noank Group Homes for Girls, 1979-80; Connecticut College Representative, Connecticut Talent Assistance Cooperative, 1973-76; Hartford College for Women Representative, 1969-70; Yale Black Seminarians, Yale University Divinity School, 1973-77; Information and Referral Agency, 1974-77; Southeastern Connecticut Youth Services, United States Submarine Base, 1973-74; Comprehensive Youth Services, 1972-74; Catholic Charities, 1971-74; New London-Groton Volunteers, Inc., 1971-73; Trinity College (board of fellows, 1976 to present; student representative, urban and environmental studies committee, 1970-71); Inner City Summer School, 1971; Catholic Family Services, 1971; Parents of Warm Energetic Rascals, 1970-71; Dwight School Parent-Teacher Association, 1970-71; American Friends Association, 1967-69; Drop Outs Anonymous, 1967-69; Organizer, First Public Housing Project Preschool in Connecticut History 1962, Playtime for Tots School, First Headstart Center in Hartford 1965; Producer, Hostess, "Perspective", Eastern Connecticut Cable Television, 1973-74. Religion: Ordained American Baptist Minister, 1979. Honors and Awards: Martin Luther King Jr. Community Service Award, Club Cosmos, New London, 1980; Community Service Recognition, Norwich Branch, National Association for the Advancement of Colored People, 1980; Samuel S. Fishzoln Award for Community Service, 1971; Rudolph Haffner Award for Community Service, 1965; Listed in *Who's Who in the East, Who's Who Among Black Americans, Who's Who of American Women, Community Leaders of America, Men and Women of Distinction, Directory of International Biography, World Who's Who of Women, International Who's Who in Community Service, Notable Americans of 1978-79, Community Leaders and Noteworthy Americans.* Address: 48 Godfrey Street, Gorton, Connecticut 06340.

Waters, Thomas Lyle

Thomas Waters

Educator, Consulting Engineer. Personal: Born March 11, 1929; Son of Theodore E. (deceased) and Lucile Taylor Waters; Married E. Yvonne Miller; Father of Wendy, Timothy Alan. Education: B.E.E.E., Youngstown State University, 1953; M.S. Systems Management, Florida Institute of Technology, 1973; M.S. Education, University of Southern California, 1975; Ph.D., Higher Education, American University, 1981. Military; Served in the United States Army, 1953-76, attaining the rank of Lieutenant Colonel, Retired. Career: College Teacher; Consulting Engineer; Former Positions include Military Officer; Military Research and Development; College Administrator, Two Colleges. Organizational Memberships: S.O.L.E.; S.A.M.E.; U.S.A.; A.A.H.E.; N.A.C.A.D.A.; American Society of Engineering Education. Community Activities: Boy Scouts of America (commissioner; S.M.E. chairman; scouting program chairman; scoutmaster; camp director). Religion: Lutheran Church L.C.A., Usher 1978 to present; Lutheran Church, Korea, Usher 1973-75; Lutheran Church Missouri Synod, Killeen, Texas, Member 1970-73, Elder, Usher. Honors and Awards: Legion of Merit, 1970; Two Bronze Star Medals, 1966, 1967; Meritorious Service Medal, 1972-73; Three Army Commendation Medals, 1959-60, 1960-64, 1966; Boy Scouts of Korea Medal of Appreciation, 1975; Boy Scouts of America Award of Merit, 1975. Address: P.O. Box 459 West Sand Lake, New York 12196.

Watson, Beulah Beatrice

Homemaker. Personal: Born August 27, 1892; Daughter of Mr. and Mrs. Elmer E. Beggs (both deceased); Married Leroy Hugh Watson (deceased); Mother of Antoinette Besin Sanderson. Career: Homemaker; Retired Concert Pianist. Organizational Memberships: American Institute of Fine Arts (fellow). Community Activities: National Society of the Daughters of the American Revolution (numerous positions; regent, 1960-63); American History Essay Contest (past chairman). Religion: All Saints Episcopal Church. Honors and Awards: Award for Dedicated Service to French School in National Contest, Lycee Francaise de Los Angeles. Address: 701 North Elm Drive, Beverly Hills, California 90210.

Wayne, David Michael

Psychiatrist, Administrator. Personal: Born December 7, 1906; Father of Robert Andrew. Education: A.B., Syracuse University, 1929; M.D., University of Vienna Medical School, 1934. Military: Served in the United States Marine Corps, 1941-44, attaining the rank of Captain. Career: Psychiatrist; Director, Bluefield Mental Health Center, Bluefield, West Virginia. Organizational Memberships: American Medical Association; American Psychiatric Association; American College of Psychiatrists (fellow). Honors and Awards: Grant, Southern Regional Education Board. Address: 3612 Bridge Road, Cooper City, Florida 33026.

Weatherholtz, Joan H

Chief. Personal: Born November 10, 1933; Daughter of Mr. and Mrs. A. G. Hulter, Jr.; Married Clyde M. Weatherholtz. Education: A.A., Potomac State College, 1954; B.S., West Virginia University, 1956; M.Ed., University of Maryland, 1966. Career: Teacher, Howard County, Maryland; Supervisor, Howard County Board of Education; Supervisor, School Lunch and Home Economics; Chief, Food and Nutrition Branch, Mary State Department of Education. Organizational Memberships: Maryland-D.C. A.S.B.O. Association; Delta Kappa Gamma; American School Food Service Association; Maryland School Food Service Association (advisor 1974 to present); American Home Economics Association (nominations committee 1974); Maryland Home Economics Association (president, secretary); American Vocational Association; Maryland Vocational Association (section leader); Home Economics Education Association of National Education Association. Religion: Presbyterian. Address: 10184 Owen Brown Road, Columbia, Maryland 20144.

Weaton, George Frederic

Retired Educator, Mining Executive. Personal: Born August 19, 1911; Son of George F. and Gertrude L. Weaton (both deceased);

Married Lois Irene Nordin Landis; Father of Brenda Whittaker, Janet Johnson. Education: B.S. Mining Engineering 1936, E.M. Mining Engineering 1940, Carnegie Institute of Technology; Graduate Study in Management Training, University of Wisconsin, 1953. Military: Served in the United States Navy, 1943-53, attaining the rank of Lieutenant. Career: Retired Professor of Mining Engineering, University of Minnesota, 1976-82; Vice President, Mining, Colorado Consolidated Metals Corporation, 1978 to present; Mining Consultant, Commissioner of Revenue, Minnesota, 1958-75; Mining Consultant, Department of Revenue, Arizona, 1964-75; Mine Superintendent 1955-58, Shift Foreman to Mine Captain 1947-55, St. Joe Minerals Corporation; General Administrator and General Mine Foreman, Cerro de Pasco Copper Corporation, Yauricocha and Casapalca, Peru, 1937-47. Organizational Memberships: Society of Mining Engineers of the American Institute of Mining Engineers (numerous offices, both local and national, 1936 to present; director, Twin City subsection, 1981 to present; GEM chairman, memberships chairman, Minnesota section, 1981). Religion: Lay Reader, Chalice Bearer, St. George's Episcopal Church, St. Louis Park, Minnesota, 1977 to present. Honors and Awards: Public Service Award, Citizens for the Taconite Amendment Committee, 1962; Service and Achievement Award, Minnesota Section A.I.M.E., 1971; 46-Year Honor Member Award 1979, National Membership Awards 1975, 1979, 1980, American Institute of Mining Engineers. Address: 2925 Toledo Avenue South, Minneapolis, Minnesota 55416.

Weaver, Katherine Grey Dunlap (Kitty)

Writer. Personal: Born September 24, 1910, in Frankfort, Kentucky; Daughter of Arch Robertson Dunlap (deceased) and Rebecca Johnson (deceased); Married Henry B. Weaver. Education: Summer School, Sorbonne University, Paris, France, 1929; A.B., College of William and Mary, Williamsburg, Virginia, 1932; Study with Dr. Alfred Adler, Vienna, Austria, Summer 1932; M.A., George Washington University, Washington, D.C., 1933; B.S. Agriculture, University of Maryland, College Park, 1947; Graduate Work, Russian Area Studies, Georgetown University, Washington, D.C., 1964-67; Attended Graduate School of Education, University of Pennsylvania, Philadelphia, 1967-68. Career: Teacher, Reading and English, St. Petersburg Junior High Schools; Poultry Farmer, Aldie, Virginia, 1947-55; Author. Organizational Memberships: International Platform Association; American Committee for Early Childhood Education. Community Activities: Piedmont Fox Hounds (past field secretary); Middleburg Hunt (past member); Fauquier-Loudoun Garden Club (horticulture chairman); Aldie Horticulture Society (past president); Garden Club of Virginia (accredited flower show judge); Certificate, Ikebana, Japanese Flower Arranging; Fauquier-Loudoun Day Care Center, Upperville, Virginia (co-founder; board member, present); Loudoun Hospital (ladies board); Manhattan Eye, Ear, Nose and Throat Hospital, New York (ladies board); Delegate, White House Conference on Children; Volunteer Work, Cancer, Community Chest; Irish Wolfhound Club of America (hostess, two annual specialty shows); Virginia Museum of Fine Arts (hostess, benefit art show); Sulgrave Club, Washington, D.C.; Acorn Club, Philadelphia (past member); River Club, New York; Middleburg Tennis Club, Virginia. Published Works: Author, *Lenin's Grandchildren*, Simon and Schuster, 1971; *Russia's Future*, Praeger, 1981. Address: "Glengyle", Aldie, Virginia 22001.

Webb, Mabel Lucile

Educator (retired). Personal: Born October 13, 1907; Daughter of Mr. and Mrs. George Death Webb (both deceased). Education: B.A., North Texas State University, 1930. Career: School Teacher; Chemical Laboratory Technician; Social Worker. Organizational Memberships: American Association of University Women (member, 1944-67; financial secretary, Long Beach, California, Chapter, 2 years); Fannin Retired Teachers Association, 1975 to present. Community Activities: Daughters of the American Revolution (Susan B. Anthony Chapter, registrar, corresponding secretary, librarian, historian; George Blakey Chapter, member 1973 to present, regent 1975-77, 1978-79); Bonham Woman's Club; United Daughters of the Confederacy, 1976 to present; Fannin County Historical Commission, 1975 to present; Friends of Sam Rayburn, 1975 to present. Religion: Missionary Society, Congregational Methodist Church, 1983. Honors and Awards: Gold Award, 1976, 1977, 1979, George Blakey Chapter, Daughters of the American Revolution. Address: 1021 Park Avenue, Bonham, Texas 75418.

Lucile Webb

Webb, William Yates

Retired. Personal: Born October 12, 1910, in Shelby, North Carolina; Married Laura Mae Brown, on October 12, 1941; Father of Shirley Webb McCall. Education: Graduate of Shelby High School; Attended Wake Forest University; B.A. 1932, M.A. 1933, Columbia University; Graduate Fellowships, Duke University 1933-34, New York University 1934-35 and 1936-37, Brookings Institution 1935-36. Military: Served in the Materials Division, Executive Office of the Navy Secretary, 1941-46, with promotions from Lieutenant (j.g.) to Commander; Retired 1970. Career: Industrial Economist (retired); Office of the Secretary of Defense, 1965, 1969; Vulnerability Analyst, Office of Civil Defense, 1961-65; Industrial Specialist, Office of the Secretary of Defense, 1954-61; Industrial Specialist, Munitions Board, 1951-53; Industrial Engineer, Office of Naval Material, 1946-51; Economist, WPB, 1942; Chief Oil and Gas Section, Mines and Quarries Division, Census Bureau, 1940-42; Economist, Bituminous Coal Consumers Council, 1937-40; Economist, Tin Investigating Committee, 1934. Organizational Memberships: A.E.A.; American Defense Preparedness Association; A.A.R.P.; American Security Council. Community Activities: American Legion; Metro Police Boys and Girls Club; National Symphony Orchestra Fund; National Economists Club; National Conference of St. Soc.; North Carolina Democratic Club of Washington, D.C.; North Carolina Society of Washington; Navy League; Reserve Officers Association; Roanoke Island Historical Association; Cleveland County Historical Association; Kappa Alpha; Pi Gamma Mu; Alto Clarinetist, Palisades Community Orchestra and American University Symphonic Wind Ensemble; Kenwood Golf and Country Club; Women's National Democratic Club; Columbia University Alumni Association. Religion: Methodist, Men's Club of Memorial United Methodist Church; Played Clarinet in Church's Former "Metrotones". Honors and Awards: Graduate Fellowships, Duke University, New York University, Brookings Institution; Commendations, Secretaries of the Army, Navy, Defense; Kenwood Golf and Country Club Champion Bowling Teams, 1976-77, 1979-80. Address: 3614 Warren Street, N.W., Washington, D.C. 20008.

Weber, Darrell Jack

Educator. Personal: Born November 16, 1933; Son of John and Norma Weber; Married Carolyn Foremaster; Father of Brad, Becky, Todd, Kelly, Jason, Brian, Trent. Education: B.S. 1958, M.S. 1959, Biochemistry, University of Idaho; Ph.D., Plant Pathology, University of California-Davis, 1963; Postdoctoral Work in Biochemistry undertaken at the University of Wisconsin 1965, and Michigan State University 1976. Military: Served in the United States Air Force Reserve Officer Training Corps for two years. Career: Professor of Botany, Brigham Young University; Associate Professor, University of Houston, 1965-69; Research Association of Biochemistry, University of Wisconsin, 1963-65; Research Assistant, University of California-Davis, 1959-63; Research Assistant, University of Idaho-Moscow, 1958-59. Organizational Memberships: Alpha Zeta; American Society of Microbiologists; Sigma Xi; American Institute of Biological Scientists; American Mycological Society (editor); American Botanical Society (editor); American Phytopathological Society; Phytochemical Society. Religion: Bishopric 1957-59 & 1983, High Councilman 1967-82, Church of Jesus

Christ of Latter-day Saints (Mormon). Published Works: Author, Over 70 Scientific Articles and Three Books; Research on Physiology of Fungi, Plant Diseases, Allergy of Plants, Salt Tolerance of Plants, Medical Value of Plant Products. Honors and Awards: Recipient of 17 Research Grants Worth $500,000; Elected Fellow, Utah Academy of Sciences, 1972; Karl G. Maeser Research Award of $3000, 1974. Address: 560 East Robin, Orem, Utah 84057.

Weber, Gertrude Christina

Private Music Teacher, Soloist, Organist. Personal: Born December 23, 1934; Daughter of William and Lillian Hill (both deceased); Married Eldon N. Weber; Mother of Karen, Brenda, Brian, Kevin. Education: A.R.C.T. Solo Performer and Teacher, Royal Conservatory of Music, Toronto, Ontario, Canada; L.T.C.L. Teacher Licentiate of Trinity College of Music, London, England. Career: Private Music Teacher; Soloist, Organist, Accompanist, Two-Piano Ensembles. Organizational Memberships: Ontario Registered Music Teachers Association (treasurer, vice-president, 1972-81); Canadian Music Educators Association, 1978; International Society of Music Educators, 1977; Alumni Association of the Royal Conservatory of Music. Community Activities: Kinette Club of Walkerton (secretary, 1974-75; director, 1975-76); Grey-Bruce Arts Council Representative, 1974-77; Grey County Music Festival (director, 1970-72); Performing Arts Organization, Walkerton, 1981. Religion: Church Organist, 1953 to present; Convenor, Lutheran Church Women, 1957-80; Carilloneur, 1956-65. Address: 11 Park Street, Box 94, Walkerton, Ontario, Canada N0G 2U0.

Burnice H Webster

Webster, Burnice Hoyle

Internist, Educator. Personal: Born March 3, 1910, in Leeville, Tennessee; Son of Thomas Jefferson Webster and Martha Ann Melton; Married Georgia Kathryn Hoyle. Education: B.A. 1936, M.D. 1940, Vanderbilt University; Commonwealth Fellow, 1936-45; Internship, Assistant Residency, Residency, St. Thomas and Vanderbilt Hospitals, 1940-45; Th.B. 1968, S.T.D. 1969, D.Sc. 1971, Holy Trinity College; D.D., Ph.D., Florida Research Institute, 1972; Doctor of Humanities, St. Geneva College, 1980. Career: Assistant in Medicine, Vanderbilt University, 1943 to present; Private Practice, Internal Medicine, 1945 to present; Medical Director, Nashville Health Care Center, University Health Care Center; Professor of Allied Sciences, Trevelco College; Chairman, Tennessee Selective Medical Service, 1971; President, Holy Trinity College, 1965 to present. Organizational Memberships: Arthritis Foundation (president); Muscular Dystrophy Society (president); American Medical Association (fellow); Royal Society of Health (fellow); American College of Chest Physicians (fellow); Nashville Academy of Medicine. Community Activities: Sons of the American Revolution (president, Andrew Jackson Chapter; president, Tennessee Chapter; national trustee); Sons of the War of 1812 (vice president general); Sons of Confederate Veterans (commander-in-chief); Sons of Colonial Wars (deputy president general); Order of Stars and Bars (honorary commander general); Baptist and Protestant Hospitals (president). Religion: Prelate, Southern Episcopal Church. Published Works: Author, Over Fifty Scientific Articles. Honors and Awards: Patriot Award; Southern Heritage Award; Silver Stethoscope Award; Various Honorary Titles, including Kentucky Colonel, Tennessee Colonel, Arkansas Traveller. Address: 2315 Valley Brook Road, Nashville, Tennessee 37215.

Weed, Mary T

Assistant Professor, Clinical Psychologist. Personal: Born November 11, 1928; Daughter of Mr. and Mrs. John George Theophilos (both deceased); Mother of Heather. Education: B.A., University of Miami, 1953; M.A., University of Chicago, 1960. Career: School Psychologist, Chicago Board of Education, 1960-62; Assistant Professor of Psychology, Chicago City College, 1962 to present; Part Time Private Practice in Clinical Psychology. Organizational Memberships: American Psychological Association; Illinois Psychological Association. Community Activities: Laboratory Schools, University of Chicago (middle school chairperson 1980-81). Honors and Awards: Registered Psychologist in Illinois; Listed in *National Register of Health Service Providers in Psychology*. Address: 5534 S. Harper, Chicago, Illinois 60637.

Diana Y Wei

Wei, Diana Yun-dee

Educator. Personal: Born June 8, 1930; Daughter of Shou-Kang Fan; Married Benjamin M. Wei; Mother of Victor Mark. Education: B.S., Taiwan Normal University, 1953; M.A., University of Nebraska-Lincoln, 1960; Post-Graduate Study, University of Washington-Seattle, 1960-62; Ph.D., McGill University, Montreal, Quebec, Canada, 1967. Career: Professor, Department of Mathematics, Norfolk State University, Virginia, 1975 to present; Professor, Baldwin School Commission, Pointe-Claire, Quebec, Canada, 1972-75; Assistant Professor, Sir George Williams University, Quebec, Canada, 1965-68; Lecturer, McGill University, 1964-65; Lecturer, Taipei Institute of Technology, Taiwan, 1953-58. Organizational Memberships: American Mathematical Society; Canadian Mathematical Society; New York Academy of Sciences, 1970. Community Activities: Norfolk State University (research committee; curriculum committee, 1975 to present). Religion: Protestant. Published Works: Author, "On the Concept of Torsion & Divisibility for General Rings", *Illinois Journal of Mathematics*, 1969; Co-Author, *Modern Algebra*, in Chinese, Northwest University, Xian, Shangsi, China. Honors and Awards: National Research Council of Canada Grant, 1969-72; Listed in *Book of Honor, International Who's Who of Intellectuals, International Register of Profiles, Personalities of America, Personalities of the South, Notable Americans of the Bicentennial Era, National Register of Prominent Americans, Community Leaders and Noteworthy Americans, Who's Who of American Women*. Address: 1152 Janaf Place, Norfolk, Virginia 23502.

Weiden, Paul Lincoln

Physician. Personal: Born August 21, 1941 in Portland, Oregon; Married; Father of Two Children. Education: Graduate of Menlo-Atherton High School, California; B.A. summa cum laude, Harvard College, Cambridge, Massachusetts, 1963; M.D. cum laude, Harvard Medical School, 1967; Licensure, Washington, California, Ohio; Diplomate, National Medical Board of Examiners 1968, American Board of Internal Medicine 1972, Subspecialty of Medical Oncology, American Board of Internal Medicine 1973. Career: Clinical Associate, Immunophysiology Section, Metabolism Branch, National Cancer Institute, National Institute of Health, Bethesda, Maryland, 1969-71; University of Washington School of Medicine, Seattle, Oncology and Hematology Fellow 1971-73, Instructor in Division of Oncology 1973-74; Assistant Professor 1974-78, Associate Professor 1978-80, Clinical Associate Professor of Medicine 1981 to present; Fred Hutchinson Cancer Research Center, Seattle, Washington, Assistant Member 1973-78, Associate Member 1978-80, Affiliate Investigator in Medical Oncology 1981 to present; Physician, Section of Hematology-Oncology, The Mason Clinic, Seattle, Washington, 1981 to present. Organizational Memberships: American College of Physicians (fellow); American Society of Hematology; International Society of Experimental Hematology; American Society of Clinical Oncology; *Experimental Hematology* (editorial board, 1981-83); Honors and Awards: Detur Prize, Harvard College, 1960; Phi Beta Kappa,

1963; Alpha Omega Alpha, 1966; Dean's Prize for Performance in Pre-Clinical Years, Harvard Medical School, 1967; Junior Faculty Clinical Fellowship, American Cancer Society, 1974-77; Listed in *Who's Who in the West, Personalities of the West and Midwest, Men of Achievement.* Address: The Mason Clinic, 1100 Ninth Avenue, P.O. Box 900, Seattle, Washington 98111.

Wei-ming, Tu

Historian and Philosopher. Personal: Born February 26, 1940 in Kunming, China; Son of Shou-tsin and Shu-li Tu; Father of Eugene Lung-sun Tu. Education: B.A. Chinese Studies, Tunghai University, Taichung, Taiwan, 1961; M.A. East Asian Regional Studies 1963, Ph.D. Joint Degree in History and Far Eastern Languages 1968, Harvard University. Military: Served in the Reserve Officer Training Corps, Tunghai University, Taiwan, 1958-61; Served as 2nd Lieutenant, Platoon Leader, 1961-62. Career: Visiting Lecturer in the Humanities, Tunghai University, Princeton University, 1966-67; Visiting Lecturer in Oriental Studies 1967-68, Assistant Professor in East Asian Studies 1968-71; University of California-Berkeley, Assistant Professor of History 1971-73, Associate Professor of History 1973-77, Professor of History 1977-81; Professor of Chinese History and Philosophy, Harvard University; Research, Confucian Thought, Chinese Intellectual History, Religious Philosophy of East Asia. Organizational Memberships: Association for Asian Studies (board of directors, 1972-75); American Historical Society; Society for Asian and Comparative Philosophy (founding member); American Academy of Religion; China Society of Japan; American Association for the Advancement of Sciences; Phi Tau Phi. Community Activities: Consultant, National Endowment for the Humanities; Chinese Cultural Foundation of San Francisco (board of directors); Ministry of Education, Singapore (consultant). Religion: Residential Fellow, Center for the Study of World Religions, Harvard University, 1970-71; Member, Committee on the Study of Religion, Harvard University; Chairperson Group Major in Religious Studies, University of California-Berkeley, 1979-80. Honors and Awards: Harvard-Yenching Fellow 1962-64, Graduate Fellowship 1964-67, Harvard University; Princeton Humanities Fellowship, 1968-69; American Council of Learned Societies Fellowship, 1970-71; Mellon Fellow, Aspen Institute for Humanistic Studies, 1974; Humanities Fellowship, University of California-Berkeley, 1974-75; Senior Scholar Award, Committee on Scholarly Communication with the People's Republic of China of the National Academy of Sciences, 1979-80. Published Works: Co-Author with James T. C. Liu, *Traditional China; Neo-Confucian Thought in Action--Wang-ming's Youth; Centrality and Commonality: An Essay on Chung-yung; Humanity and Self-Cultivation: Essays in Confucian Thought;* Numerous Articles and Reviews in Various Professional Journals. Address: Department of East Asian Languages and Civilizations, Harvard University, Cambridge, Massachusetts 02138.

Weisler, Sherry Jacobs

School Psychologist. Personal: Born May 18, 1951; Daughter of Barnet Jacobs (deceased) and Eve Jacobs; Married Jeffrey Mark Weisler; Mother of Stacey Melissa, Robert Allen. Education: B.S. cum laude Psychology, Brooklyn College, 1972; M.S. and Certificate in School Psychology Brooklyn College, 1974. Career: Brooklyn College, Adjunct Lecturer in Psychology 1972, Adjunct Lecturer in Counseling in the School of Education 1972-74, College Assistant in Testing and Research 1973-75; School Psychologist in Training, Bureau of Child Guidance, New York City Board of Education, 1974-75; School Psychologist, Kennedy Learning Center, Brooklyn, New York, 1974-76; Assistant Research Scientist, Child Psychiatric Education and Research Unit, New York Department of Mental Hygiene, Brooklyn, New York, 1976; Psychologist, Comprehensive Mental Health Services, Inc., Clearwater, Florida, 1978-80; Social Sciences Instructor, St. Petersburg Junior College, St. Petersburg, Florida, 1977-80; Psychologist and Consultant, Pinellas County Head Start. Organizational Memberships: American Psychological Association; Association of School Psychologists of Brooklyn College. Community Activities: Women's American ORT, 1976 to present; B'nai B'rith, 1976 to present; Health Advisory Board of Pinellas County Head Start, 1979 to present. Honors and Awards: Listed in *Who's Who of American Women.* Address: 2868 Meadow Oak Drive East, Clearwater, Florida 33519.

Donald Wells

Wells, Donald T

Financial Executive. Personal: Born December 26, 1931, in Henderson, Kentucky; Son of Mr. and Mrs. Melvin J. Wells; Married Josephine G., 1954; Father of Renetta G., Kathy L. Education: Graduate of Barret High School, Henderson, Kentucky; B.S., Marketing/Finance, University of Kentucky, 1957; Attended the University of Indiana, 1957-59. Military: Served in the United States Armed Forces, 1951-53, as Instructor for the Counter Intelligence Section. Career: Lecturer; Financial and Tax Consultant; Assistant Secretary-Treasurer, Von Hoffman Press, Inc., St. Louis, Missouri, 1963-68; President, Treasurer, American Mortgage Equipment Leasing Corporation, St. Louis, Missouri, 1968-71; Group Controller, Interlake Steel Corporation, Dallas, Texas, 1971-73; Corporate Controller, Fiscal Officer, Multi-Amp Corporation, Dallas, Texas, 1973 to present; Director, Prairie Creek Bootery, Inc. Organizational Memberships: National Association of Accountants; American Management Association. Community Activities: Masons; Kiwanis; Chamber of Commerce. Religion: Baptist; Deacon; Past Officer, Deacon Council; Chairman of Budget and Finance Committees; Sunday School Superintendent; Lay Speaker; Pioneer Mission Developmemt Activities. Honors and Awards: Listed in *Who's Who in the South and Southwest, Who's Who in Finance and Industry, Personalities of the South, Personalities of America, Men of Achievement.* Address: Multi-Amp Corporation, Subsidiary of Indian Head, Inc., 4271 Bronze Way, Dallas, Texas 75237.

Wells, Dorothy Burton

Part-time Candy Manufacturer. Personal: Born December 26, 1911; Daughter of Elias Burton and Jan Betsy Holmes Wells (both deceased). Education: A.B., Hood College, 1935; M.S., University of Pennsylvania at Philadelphia, 1943. Career: Former Research Assistant in Virus Research and Teacher, University of Pennsylvania. Organizational Memberships: American Leather Chemists Association; Retain Confectioners International. Honors and Awards: Woman of the Year, Business and Professional Club of Johnstown, New York, 1979. Address: R.D. 1, Norboro Road, P.O. Box 1321, Gloversville, New York 12078.

Wells, Ernest Hatton

Engineer and Scientist. Personal: Born August 1, 1921, in Crossville, Tennessee; Son of Noah and Chloe Burgess Wells (both deceased); Married Signa Faye Stinnett, 1954; Father of David Allen (deceased), William Ernest, Ronald Eston, Lawrence Robert. Education: Graduate with Distinction of Cumberland County High School, 1940; Attended Georgia Tech, Alanta, North Carolina State University, Raleigh, Bendix, Philco Schools for Electronics, No. 5 Radio School, Clinton, Ontario, Boea Raton, Florida, Radar Training, Air Force Radar and Electronics School; B.S.E.E. Tennessee Technological University, 1951; D.Sc. 1973, Ph.D. 1974, Sussex College of Technology, England; Over 33 Postgraduate Courses, Ten Colleges and Universities; First Class and Amateur Federal Communications Commission Radio Licenses. Military: Served in the United States Signal Corps from 1942-43, and in the

United States Air Force from 1943-46 in the Position of Radar Chief in Guam and Iwo Jima; Honorable Discharge, 1946. Career: Operator, Wells Radio Service, until 1941; Engineer, Station WHUB; Electronic Project Engineer, Airplane Marine Instruments Inc., Clearfield, Pennsylvania until 1953; Washington National Airport; Research and Development Project Engineer, ERDL Fort Belvoir, Virginia, Leader, Expeditions to Greenland Ice Cap for Research on Guidance Systems; Radar Engineer, Navy Department; Telemetry Engineer for Cape Kennedy (Canaveral) Redstone Firings, Project Engineer for White Sands, New Mexico Firings, ABMA Wernher Von Braun Rocket Team, Redstone Arsenal, Huntsville, Alabama, from 1957; Supervisor, Electronics and Optics, Four Laboratories; National Aeronautics and Space Administration, MSFC, AST Space Scientist on Geophysical Satellites 1962, Assigned to Lunar Surface Studies, Optics and Planetology, Discovered Water on Mars, Designed SSL Solar Observatory, Pursued Research in Solar Phenomena, Raman Spectroscopy, Remote Sensing of Natural Resources, Water and Air Contamination, Space Instruments, Design of Solar Stimulators and Space Telescopes, Comets and Meteors, Manager, Study for Rocket-Borne Manned Telescope for Lunar Use, Staff of the Optics and RF Systems Division EC31, Marshall Space Flight Center, Alabama; Electronics Instructor, Tennessee Technological University, 1947-48; Instructor, Courses in Religion and UFOs and World Mysteries, Mountain Gap School and University of Alabama, 1978; Research, Phenomena, Genealogy, Galactic Dynamics, Solar System Origin, Properties and Origin of the Moon, Solar H-Alpha, Solar Wind, Arctic Ice Radar and Electromagnetic Properties, Optical Radar Telescoptic Optics, Atmospheric Pollution, Antennas, UFOs, Artificial Gravity; Founder, Director, The Order of Magnitude, Correspondence School for Inspiration and High Attainment, present. Organizational Memberships: American Rocket Society (past member); American Astronomical Association (past member); Rocket City Astronomical Association (past member); Institute of Radio Engineers (past senior member and memberships chairman); Society of Professional Engineers (Tennessee chapter); Broadcast Music Institute; International Biographical Center (fellow); Optical Society of America (Huntsville chapter); Mutual UFO Network; Huntsville Radio Club. Community Activities: Boy Scouts of America (committee chairman, troop 17; assistant scoutmaster, troop 382); Designed Telescope and Donated Dome, Madison Academy Wells Observatory. Religion: Past Teacher, Genesis, Central Church of Christ; Teacher, Fanning Heights Church of Christ. Published Works: Author, 54 Papers and Reports (many Published in Professional Journals); Author, Books, *Astronomy Finds the Days of Creation, Search for Life in Space;* and Other Manuscripts; Writer, Two Songs, "Impeachment Blues", "America Stand Up and Sing". Honors and Awards: 30-Year Service Award, Many Participation Awards, including Apollo-Soyuz Award and Medal 1969, Award of Achievement 1969, Space Shuttle Certificates of Recognition, National Aeronautics and Space Administration, Consultant to Teledyne Brown Engineering, Radar. Address: 712 Kilkenny Street, Northwest, Huntsville, Alabama 35801.

Wells, Patricia A Bennett

Educator, Management/Organizational Behavior. Born March 25, 1935; Daughter of Benjamin Beekman Bennett (deceased) and Catherine Bennett Breckinridge; Mother of Bruce Bennett, Barbara Lee. Education: A.A. Business, Allen Hancock College, Santa Maria, California, 1964; B.S. magna cum laude, Business, College of Great Falls, Montana, 1966; M.S. Business Education, University of North Dakota, 1967; Ph.D. Business and Vocational Education 1971, University of North Dakota; Certified Administrative Manager, 1979; New York State Permanent Certification in Business Subjects and Social Studies, Grades 7-12; California Community College Instructor Credential, Valid for Life. Career: Professor of Business Administration, Oregon State University, 1974 to present; Associate Professor, Chairman, Department of Business Education, Virginia State University, 1973-74; Visiting Professor, University of Southern California, 1972; Visiting Professor, Chapman College, 1971-72; Summer Visiting Professor, University of Montana, 1972; Instructor, Western New England College, 1967-69; President, Chairman of the Board, Administrative Organizational Services, Inc., 1967 to present; Civilian Medical Services Accounts Officer, United States Air Force, 1962-64. Organizational Memberships: American Management Association; Administrative Management Society (member, 1974 to present; Eugene chapter, chairman, education committee 1976, certified administrative manager committee 1977, chapter achievement program committee 1978, committee of 500 1978, education committee 1979, cam of 1979); American Association of University Professors (member, 1973 to present; chapter secretary 1968, chapter board members 1982-83); American Business Women's Association (member, 1973 to present; secretary, 1974-75; program director, 1975-76; special events chairman, 1977-78; vice president, 1977-78; president, 1978-79; education chairman, 1979-80); American Vocational Association (member, 1967 to present; nominating committee, 1976); American Business Communication Association (member, 1975 to present; regional chairman, business liasion committee, 1976; methodology committee, 1976; 1979 international program chairman, proceeding committee chairman, 1979-80; international board of directors, 1980-83; vice president, northwest, 1981-82; 2nd vice president, 1982-83); Corvallis Word Processing Management Group (founder, charter member, 1975 to present); Data Processing Management Association, 1979 to present; Delta Pi Epsilon, Graduate Honorary Society (member, Alpha Nu chapter, 1967 to present; program director, registration chairman, 1978-81); International Word Processing Association (member, 1974 to present; chairman, task force on professional certification, 1978-79; steering committee, educators advisory council, 1978-81; Willamette Valley chapter, member 1974 to present, charter member, chairman-nomination committee, 1974, board of directors 1974-80, new chapter committee, president, 1977-78, 1978-79, nominated to international board of directors 1979, joint data processing management, international word processing association show and symposium co-chairman 1980); Oregon Associated Faculties, 1978 to present; Oregon State Employee Association (member, 1974-80; president, OSU chapter 47, professional certification, 1978-79; steering committee, educators advisory council, 1978-81); National Business Education Association, 1965 to present; National Association of Teacher Education for Business Office Education (member, 1970 to present; program chairman, 1973 convention; vice president, 1975-76; president, 1976-77; chairman, public relations committee, 1978-81; life member, 1976 to present); Sigma Kappa Sorority; Western Business Education Association, 1974-1980. Community Activities: Numerous Positions in University Service, Oregon State University, 1975-82; Numerous Continuing Education Short Courses and Conferences, 1970-81; Human Relations Committee, 1968; Higher Education Representative, Oregon Business Education Association Council, 1977-79; Newman Foundation (board member, 1977-80; president, 1978-79); Rosewood Estates Road District (budget committee, 1978); Linn Benton Tax Relief Steering Committee, 1978; Lane Community College (business advisory board, 1978-79); Judge, Philomath Frolic Queen Contest, 1979; American Council on Education (state panel member, Oregon identification program for women in administration, 1979); Consultant, Numerous State, Local, Professional, Academic, Research, Civic Organizations; Benton County Association for Retarded Citizens (board of directors, 1981-84). Published Works: *Office Systems; Word Processing: A Management View;* Numerous Papers and Journal Articles, including "Word Processing in the Typewriting Classroom", "Alcoholism Drug Abuse in the Workforce", "Evaluating Seminars". Honors and Awards: Phi Kappa Phi; Delta Epsilon Sigma National Undergraduate Honorary Society; Delta Kappa Gamma Women's Educational Honorary Society; Inscribed Plaque, for Outstanding Contributions to the National Association of Teacher Educators in Business and Office Education, 1976; Listed in *Who's Who in the West, Who's Who Among American Women.* Address: 2145 Primrose Loop, Philomath, Oregon 97376.

Welsh, Carol June

Educator. Personal: Born October 31, 1931; Daughter of Clyde William and Redith K. Summerlot; Married Robert Walter Welsh; Mother of Phillip Paul, Robin Walter. Education: Graduate of Honey Creek High School, Terre Haute, Indiana; B.S., Indiana State University, Terre Haute, Indiana. Career: Personal Manager, Secretary-Treasurer, X-Tra Quality Laundry and Dry Cleaners; Former

Positions include Physical Education Teacher, Science Teacher, Drivers Education Teacher, Kindergarten Teacher. Community Activities: Marshall Illinois Home Extension Council; Parent-Teacher Association, Marshall, Illinois (council; 2nd vice-president); Wabash Extension Unit; Numerous Committees; Alpha Sigma Alpha Sorority, Terre Haute, Indiana; Athenaeum Club, Indiana State University. Religion: Armstrong Methodist Church, Marshall, Illinois (women's society of Christian service); Philosophy Instructor, Concept Therapy Institute, San Antonio, Texas. Honors and Awards: Sportsman Award 1949, Attendant to Queen 1949, Honey Creek High School Girls Athletic Association; Class and Sorority Volleyball and Basketball Teams, Indiana State University. Address: P.O. Box 377, Cedar Crest, New Mexico 87008.

West, Dorothy Anne

Speech and Hearing Therapist. Personal: Born March 21, 1936; Daughter of Dr. Philip W. West; Mother of Jeffrey West Freeman. Education: B.S. Education 1958, M.Ed. 1973, 35 Hours above Master's Degree, Louisiana State University. Career: Speech and Hearing Therapist; Assistant to Dean of Women, Louisiana State University. Organizational Memberships: American Speech-Language-Hearing Association; Louisiana Speech and Hearing Association; Association of Teacher Educators; Phi Delta Kappa. Community Activities: Diamondhead Community Association (board of directors, 1981); Lakeside Villa Condominium Association (board of directors, 1978 to present; secretary-treasurer, 1978, 1979; president, 1980, 1981); Baton Rouge Mortar Board Alumnae Chapter (president, 1960-62); Delta Gamma Fraternity (international positions; membership study committee, 1962-64; fraternity scholarship chairman, 1965-69; nominating committee, 1968-70; province collegiate chairman, 1970-75; fraternity awards chairman, 1975-79; Louisiana State University, advisory board chairman 1960-61, 1979-82, pledge advisor 1959-60, scholarship advisor 1978-79; rush consultant at Louisiana State University, University of Alabama, Tulsa University, Morehead University, Memphis State University, University of Arkansas, William Woods College, Baylor University, University of Southern Mississippi). Religion: Sunday School Teacher, Choir Member, Building Committee, 1959-61. Honors and Awards: Silver Anchor 1968, Gold Anchor 1978, Cable Award 1980, Delta Gamma. Address: 976 Baird Drive, Baton Rouge, Louisiana 70808.

Westpheling, Robert Paul Jr

Newspaper Publisher. Personal: Born January 2, 1942; Son of R. P. Westpheling (deceased) and Martha T. Westpheling; Married Johanna M.; Father of Mary Johanna Butts, Robert Paul, III. Education: B.J., University of Missouri, 1936. Military: Served in the United States Army from 1942-46; Two Years Overseas in ETO and PTO; Served in the Army Reserve from 1946-72, retiring with the rank of Major. Career: Advertising Staff, *St. Joseph News-Press*, Missouri; Advertising Manager, *Effingham Daily Record*, Illinois; Advertising Manager, *Gallatin Examiner*, Tennessee; Advertising Staff, *Racine DAY*, Wisconsin; Advertising Manager, *Clarksdale Daily Press*, Mississippi; Advertising Staff, *Washington Post;* Publisher, *Fulton County News*, Kentucy; President, Ken-Tenn Broadcasting Corporation, Fulton, Kentucky (all the previous, 1936-72). Organizational Memberships: Kentucky Press Association (president, 1960; executive board, 1957-61). Community Activities: Kentucky Development Commission, 1963-70; International Banana Festival (activity, 1964-68); Hickman-Fulton County Riverport Authority (chairman, 1975-80); Fulton Rotary Club (member, 1947-68; president, 1960; honorary rotarian); Boy Scouts of America (area council, 1962-74); Fulton Chamber of Commerce (board of directors, 1948-52); Kentucky Colonel, Commodore of Kentucky Lake, Kentucky Mounted Rifleman, Governor's Council on Higher Education, 1960-80; Hickman Chamber of Commerce (board of directors, 1976-80; special activity chairman, 1981). Religion: Parish Council, St. Edward's Catholic Church, Fulton, 1976-80; Member, Knights of Columbus, 1960-81. Honors and Awards: Philippine Liberation Medal, 1945; Air Force Commendation Medal, 1960; Recipient, 57 Excellence Awards in Newspaper Publishing, Kentucky Press Association, 1948-76; American Federation of Musicians, 1934-83. Address: P.O. Box 598, Fulton, Kentucky 42041.

Wettach, George Edward

Medical Director. Personal: Born June 11, 1940 in San Jose, California; Son of George and Glodine Wettach; Married Rose Ann; Father of George Randolphe, Shannon Elizabeth, Robin Scott. Education: M.D., St. Louis University School of Medicine, Missouri, 1966; Internship, St. Louis City Hospital, 1966-67; Medical Residency, Highland General Hospital, Oakland, California, 1970-71; Cardiac Fellow, Huntington Memorial Hospital, Pasadena, California, 1971-72; Cardiac Fellow, Stanford University, Stanford, California, 1972-73; Chief Medical Resident, St. Louis University, 1973-74. Military: Served in the United States Naval Reserve, 1968 to present, attaining the rank of Commander. Career: Instructor, Department of Surgery, Washington University, St. Louis, Missouri; Medical Director, St. Louis Emergency Service. Organizational Memberships: Aerospace Medical Association (associate fellow); New York Academy of Sciences; American College of Emergency Physicians. Community Activities: Upgrading of City of St. Louis Emergency Medical Service, 1977-78; Prehospital Cooling of Heat Stroke Victims during Heat Wave of 1980 in St. Louis; First Heat Stroke Prevention Program in the United States, Summer of 1981; St. Louis Hypothermia Prevention Program, Winter 1981-82. Honors and Awards: Physicians Recognition Award for Continuing Medical Education, American Medical Association, 1972-75; Tau Delta Phi, Men's Honorary Scholastic Fraternity, San Jose College, California, 1960; Most Improved Stock Car Driver 1979, Sportsman of the Year 1981, Humanitarian Award, Allied Auto Racing Association, St. Louis, Missouri, Address: 1553 Meadowside Drive, Creve Coeur, Missouri 63141.

Weyer, Frank Elmer

Educator (retired). Personal: Born January 14, 1890; Son of John and Elizabeth Weyer (both deceased); Married Mabelle Carey (deceased); Father of Mary Elizabeth Nutting, Dorothy Creigh (deceased), Phyllis Lucille Garriss. Education: A.B., Hastings College, 1911; M.A. 1916, Ph.D. 1940, University of Nebraska-Lincoln; Attended Columbia University, 1916-17, Summers 1917, 1932; Attended Stanford University, Summer 1924. Career: Principal, Newport (Nebraska) Public School, 1911-13; Superintendent of Schools, Atkinson (Nebraska) Public Schools, 1913-16; Professor of Education and Psychology, Kendall College, Tulsa, Oklahoma, 1917-18; Professor of Education 1918-60, Retired Dean Emeritus and Historian, Hastings College; Member of Faculty, United States Army University, Biarritz, France; Fulbright Lecturer, Minister of Education, Pakistan, 1960-61; Visiting Professor of Education, Head of Education Department 1961-71, Professor Emeritus, Campbell University, Buies Creek, North Carolina. Organizational Memberships: Nebraska Education Association (president, District 4, 1943); National Education Association (vice president, 1944); Nebraska Schoolmasters Club (president, 1959); Phi Delta Kappa; North Central Association of Academic Deans (president); American Association of University Professors; Nebraska Council on Teacher Education (past president). Community Activities: Adams County Selective Service Draft Board, 1943-60; Hastings Kiwanis Club (vice president). Religion: Presbyterian Elder, Atkinson (Nebraska) 1915, Tulsa (Oklahoma) 1917, Hastings (Nebraska) 1919-59. Honors and Awards: LL.D. 1950, New Men's Dormitory Named Weyer Hall 1950, Alumni Citation 1975, Citation of Appreciation 1960, Hastings College; Paul Harris Award, Rotary Club, 1982. Address: 503 East 6th Street, Hastings, Nebraska 68901.

Wheelbarger, J J

Educator, Pastor. Personal: Born February 15, 1937, in Ottobine, Virginia; Son of Mr. and Mrs. Charles W. Wheelbarger (both deceased); Married Bonnie M. Propst. Education: A.B., Religion, Bethany Nazarene College, Bethany, Oklahoma, 1963; M.Ed. (Elementary Education) 1967, Ed.D. (Curriculum and Instruction with Specialization in Audiovisual Education) 1971, University of Virginia-Charlottesville; M.L.S. (with Specialization in Academic Libraries) 1975, Ph.D. (Educational Administration) 1977, George Peabody College for Teachers, Nashville, Tennessee. Career: Pastor, Virginia District Church of the Nazarene, 1963-67; Teacher of Sixth Grade, Virginia Public Schools, Manassas Park Elementary 1964-66, Parkside Junior High School 1966-68; Instructor, University of Virginia Extension Division, 1969-70; Assistant Professor, Education and Media Director, Eastern Nazarene College, Quincy, Massachusetts, 1970-71; Trevecca Nazarene College, (Nashville, Tennessee), Associate Professor of Education 1971-75, Professor of Education 1975 to present, Director of Learning Resources 1972 to present; Pastor, Santa Fe Circuit of Churches of the Nazarene, Maury County, Tennessee, 1973 to present; Southeast Educational Zone Federal Credit Union, Vice President 1978-79, President 1979 to present. Organizational Memberships: National Education Association; Tennessee Education Association; Association for Educational Communications and Technology; American Library Association; Tennessee Library Association; Tennessee Audiovisual Association; Mid-State Library Associaton; Nashville Library Club; Association of Teacher Educators; Phi Delta Kappa. Published Works: Monographs, "An Investigation of the Role of Pictorial Complexity in Visual Perception", "The Effectiveness of a Computerized Library Network in Meeting the Performance Expectation of the Members in the Administration of Academic Libraries"; Articles, "Legal Ramifications of Computerized Library Networks and Their Implications for the Library Director", "Network Effectiveness Information for Tennessee Libraries", "Metrication Materials: A Nonprint Bibliography", "The Learning Resource Center at the Four-Year College Level". Honors and Awards: Kappa Delta Pi Honor Society in Education; Beta Phi Mu International Library Science Honor Society; Phi Delta Lambda National Nazarene Honor Society; Listed in *Outstanding Educators of America, Dictionary of International Biography, Who's Who Biographical Record of Child Development Professionals, Who's Who in the South and Southwest*. Address: Route 2 Box 294 A-4, Goodlettsville, Tennessee 37072.

Whetle, Margaret Maie

Educator, Lecturer. Personal: Born October 19, 1934; Daughter of Albert F. Sr. and Ruth Morse Wheltle (both deceased). Education: Attended Cathedral School, Baltimore, Maryland; Graduate of Notre Dame of Maryland Preparatory School, Baltimore; B.A., Commerce, Mount Saint Agnes College, Baltimore, 1956; J.D., University of Maryland School of Law, Baltimore, 1959; Study toward a C.P.A. Degree, Loyola Evening College, Baltimore, 1960-61; Attended Catholic University of America School of Theology, Washington, D.C., 1967-69; S.T.M., St. Mary's Seminary and University, Baltimore, 1972. Career: Swimming Instructor, American Red Cross, Summer 1955; Typist, Freeman & Requardt Insurance Company, Baltimore, Summers 1957, 1958; Student Assistant Director, Graduate Students Resident Hall Development Office, Catholic University, 1968, 1969; Department Instructor, Theology, Business Law, Harmony Hill High School, Watertown, South Dakota, 1969-70; Associate, Harley, Wheltle, Victor & Rosser, Law Firm, 1959-64; Assistant to the President, Director of Development, Television Production Coordinator, Mount Saint Agnes College, 1964-67; Coordinator of Religious Education for Adults and Public School Students, St. Agnes Roman Catholic Congregation, Inc., 1971-74; Theology Instructor 1978 to present, Religion Department Chairperson 1979 to present, Mount de Sales Academy; Lecturer, Theology and Law with Related Fields. Community Activities: Mount Saint Agnes College (national alumnae president, 1961-65; president's council, 7 years); International Federation of Catholic Alumnae (Maryland Chapter, vice governor, 1964-66); Papal Volunteers for Latin America (board of directors, fund raising project, one year); Catholic University of America (student records committee observer, one year); Saint William of York, Baltimore (sodality prefect, 2 years; confraternity of Christian doctrine, six years; teaching certificate, 1968; parish planning team for total Christian education, 1971; total parish education committee, 1975-76; adult education instructor, 1976; national catechism directory committee, steering committee 1975, member 1977); St. Agnes Church (parish planning team for total Christian education, 1971); Speaker's Bureau, Howard County Right to Life 1974 to present, Archdiocese of Baltimore, Adult Education 1976 to present; Birthright of Maryland Inc. (speakers bureau, 1975-78; vice chairman, 1975-76); St. Martin's Home for the Aged (lecturer, 1975; ladies auxiliary, co-founder and first board chairperson 1973-76, board member 1976 to present; advisor, 1977 to present); Little Sisters of the Poor (advisor, 1977 to present); Archdiocese Pastoral Council (Archdiocese of Baltimore, public relations committee, 1975-76); Mount de Sales Academy (board of trustees, 1979-82). Honors and Awards: 20 Year Appreciation Certificate for Service to Catholic Education, Archdiocese of Baltimore, 1981; Mount de Sales Academy Cetificate of Appreciation, 1982; Listed in *Outstanding Young Women of America, Who's Who of American Women, Who's Who in the East, Directory of International Biography, Two Thousand Women of Achievement, Personalities of the South, International Who's Who in Community Service, Bicentennial Edition of Personalities of the South, Notable Americans of the Bicentennial Era, Community Leaders and Noteworthy Americans, Notable Americans of 1976-77, Personalities of America, World Who's Who of Women, Who's Who in American Law, Virginia, Maryland, Delaware and D.C. Legal Directory, People Who Matter, International Who's Who of Intellectuals, Men and Women of Distinction, Anglo-American Who's Who, Directory of Distinguished Americans*. Address: 515 Stamford Road, Baltimore, Maryland 21229.

J J Wheelbarger

Whipple, Walter L

Design Specialist, Professional Electrical Engineer. Personal: Born June 23, 1940; Son of Rear Admiral and Mrs. Jones Whipple; Married Jean Anne Ewer; Father of Sara Marie, Kathryn Ann. Education: B.S., Engineering Science, Harvey Mudd College, 1962; M.S.E. Computer Information and Control Engineering 1974, Ph.D. Candidate 1976, University of Michigan. Career: Senior Electrical Engineer, Professional Services Division, Control Data Corporation, Waltham, Massachusetts, 1969-78; Engineer, Space and Information Systems Division, Raytheon Company, Sudbury, Massachusetts, 1967-69; Field Service Representative, Ordnance Department, General Electric Company, Pittsfield, Massachusetts, 1962-65; Engineering Aide, Vidya Division, Itak Corporation, Palo Alto, California, 1961; Chairman, Technical Advisory Committee for Software, General Dynamics, Pomona, California; Visiting Professor in Computer Science, Harvey Mudd College. Organizational Memberships: Association for Computing Machinery (chairman, Arrowhead AdaTec); Institute of Electrical and Electronic Engineers (senior member); American Institute for Aeronautics and Astronautics (associate fellow); Society for Computer Simulation; National Society of Professional Engineers; Armed Forces Communication and Electronics Association; American Association of University Professors; Pascal Users Group; National Management Association. Community Activities: University of Michigan Alumni Association; Harvey Mudd College Alumni Association (board of governors, 1981-85); A.C.M. Annual Conference, Boston (simulation session chairman, 1970); Winter Cmputer Simulation Conference, Sacramento (financial and econometric session chairman, 1972); Harvey Mudd College Galileo Society, 1980-82. Honors and Awards: Quartermaster Award, Boy Scouts of America, 1957; Registered Professional Electrical Engineer, California, Massachusetts, Michigan; Registered Business Programmer, D.P.M.A.; Eta Kappa Nu, Honorary Fraternity for Electrical Engineering; Listed in *Who's Who in Engineering, Who's Who in the Midwest, Who's Who in California, International Who's Who in Engineering, Notable Americans*. Address: 1678 Spruce View Drive, Pomona, California 91766.

Whitacre, Walter Emmett

Aerospace Engineer. Personal: Born September 28, 1931, in Detroit, Michigan; Son of Arthur James (deceased) and Reba Adeline

England Whitacre; Married Donna Lee Longstreet, on November 26, 1950; Father of Donn Arthur, Kirk Alexander, Chris Martin. Education: Graduate of Central High School, Muncie, Indiana, 1949; B.S. Aeronautical Engineering 1959, M.S. Industrial Administration 1968, Purdue University; Graduate Study in Research and Technology Management, Southeastern Institute, 1980 to present. Career: Aerodynamics Engineer, Lockheed Missiles and Space Company, Sunnyvale, California, 1959-63, and Huntsville, Alabama, 1963-64; Aerospace Engineer, National Aeronautics and Space Administration, Marshall Space Flight Center, Huntsville, Alabama, 1964 to present. Organizational Memberships: American Society for Public Administration. Community Activities: Benevolent and Protective Order of the Elks, 1979 to present; Huntsville Power Squadron (assisted in teaching safe boating; taught seamanship course, 1970-80); Young Men's Christian Association (board of management, Southeast Branch, 1965-67); Boy Scouts of America (San Jose, California, cub pack 360 committee chairman 1961-62, cubmaster 1962-63, committeeman 1963-64; Huntsville, Alabama, cubmaster, pack 314, 1963-64, helped form cub pack 364 1966; formation of boy scout troop 314 1964, scoutmater 1964-66, formation of troop 364 1966, scoutmaster 1966-67, 1968 to present; sea explorers, ship 364, formation 1968, skipper 1968-70; ship 666, formation 1970, skipper 1970 to present; Order of the Arrow, chapter advisor, Caddo Chapter, 1976-80; associate advisor, Kaskanampo Lodge 310, 1979 to present; district committee, 1968 to present; district training staff, 1969-73; chairman, several district camporees; chief event judge, Baden-Powell Jamboree, 1972; chairman, Heart-of-Dixie sea explorer rendezvous, 1973; scoutmaster, council contingent to Philmont, 1974; von Braun chapter, National Eagle Scout Association, organized 1975, advisor 1975-76; staff, area wood badge course, 1978; director, area wood badge course, 1979, 1981, 1983; scoutmaster, council troop to national jamboree, 1981; chairman, King Neptune sea explorer rendezvous, 1975, 1977-83; chairman, area IV sailing championship, 1976, 1978-81; chairman, area IV sea exploring, 1978-81; committee member, Southeast Region, 1978 to present; director, regional sea badge conference, 1981, 1982; classroom events coordinator, T. J. Keane rendezvous, 1979-81; chairman, sea exploring for Southeast Region, 1981 to present). Religion: Sunday School Teacher, Trinity Presbyterian Church, San Jose, California, 1962-63; Latham United Methodist Church, Hunstville, Alabama, Member 1963 to present, President of the Men's Club 1966-67, Scouting Coordinator, Chairman Scouting/Exploring Committee 1968 to present, Board of Trustees 1972-78, Grounds and Maintenance Committee 1972 to present, Administrative Board 1981 to preent. Honors and Awards: Scouter's Key, Cub Scouts, 1964; Scouter's Training Award 1965, Scouter's Key 1967, Wood Badge 1970, Valley Scouter Award (District Award of Merit) 1971, Scouter's Key 1975, William H. Spurgeon III Award 1977, Sea Badge 1978, Sea Exploring; Thanks to You Award, Huntsville Metropolitan Kiwanis Club, 1973; Liberty Bell Award, Madison County Bar Association, 1979; Youth Group Conservation Award, Alabama Environmental Quality Association, 1981; Service to Mankind Award, Huntsville Sertoma Club, 1981. Address: 301 Belvidere Drive, S.E., Huntsville, Alabama 35803.

White, Ella Elizabeth

Administrator. Personal: Born October 20, 1948; Daughter of Mr. and Mrs. Herschel S. White, Sr. Education: B.S., Southern University, 1970; M.Mus., Miami University, 1971; Ph.D., Kansas State University, 1976. Career: Associate Director of the Department of Federal Affairs, Senior Research Associate in the Department of Governmental Relations, Director of Department of Governmental Relations, Howard University; Coordinator, Resource Department, ACCtion Consortium; Choral Director and Instructor, Music Department, Alcorn State University. Organizational Memberships: Council for the Advancement and Support of Education (national governmental relations committee); National Council for Research Administrators; American Association of University Women; American Educational Research Association; Society for Research Administrators; Association for Supervision and Curriculum Development. Community Activities: Young Women's Christian Association (national capital area board of directors, vice president); International Student House (board of directors); Hannah Harrison Career School (board of directors); Delta Sigma Theta Public Service Sorority; Phi Delta Kappa; Kappa Delta Pi; Phi Delta Gamma; Mu Phi Epsilon Music Fraternity; Prince George County Links, Inc. Religion: Methodist. Honors and Awards: Mu Phi Epsilon Senior Achievement Award, 1970; Southern University Music Scholarship, 1966-70; Miami University Research Grant, 1970, 1971; Kansas State University Fellowship, 1974, 1975, 1976; Listed in *Outstanding Young Women in America*. Address: 3003 Van Ness Street, N.W., Washington, D.C. 20008.

Nelson H White

White, Nelson H

Bishop, Corporate Director, Author. Personal: Born October 29, 1938; Son of Dr. T. Robert White, Edith Eyre White (deceased); Married Anne. Education: A.A., Electronics, San Bernardino Valley College, 1961; B.A. 1968, Graduate Studies 1968, University of the Redlands; Teaching Credentials, University of California-Los Angeles, 1969-70; D.Div., Light of Truth Church, 1973. Military: Served in the United States Navy, 1956-58, as Hospital Corpsman. Career: Electronics Instructor, 1969-70; Customs Officer, 1970; Co-Founder, Vice President, Church of Hermetic Science, 1970-73; Inspector General, Ordo Templi Astarte, 1970-73; Bishop, Corporate Director, Light of Truth Church; Author. Organizational Memberships: Southern California Representative, Aquarian Anti-Defamation League, 1972-78; Grand Master, Temple of Truth, 1972 to present. Published Works: Author, *Introduction to Magick, What and Why of Magick, Magic and the Law Volumes 1-5;* Co-Author with Anne White, *Success in Candle Burning, Secret Magick Revealed, Lemegeton: Clavicula Salomonis, Index and Reference Volume to the Lemegeton of Solomon, Working High Magick, Selected Conjurations from the Lemegeton,* Others; Editor, *The White Light*, 1973 to present. Honors and Awards: Listed in *Personalities of America, Personalities of the West and Midwest, International Book of Honor, Community Leaders of America, Directory of Distinguished Americans, Men of Achievement, Dictionary of International Biography, Who's Who in the West, Who's Who in California.* Address: P.O. Box 93124, Pasadena, California 91109.

White, Norman Douglas

Unit Director. Personal: Born May 17, 1943; Son of Donald L. and Rhoda S. White; Married P. Kaye Williams; Father of Kirstin Elena, William Simon. Education: B.S., Wisconsin State University, Eau Claire; M.S.W., Columbia University School of Social Work. Career: Unit Director, Hawthorne Cedar Knolls School; Clinical Director, Search for Change, Inc.; Clinical/Administrative Director, Harlem Outpatient Service; Director, Christian Herald Youth Program; Director, Long House Camp; Mathematics Teacher, New Rochelle High School, New York; Field Instructor, Columbia University School of Social Work, 1977-80; Part-time Instructor, 1977-80; Adjunct Professor, Hunter College School of Social Work, 1977-80. Organizational Memberships: National Association of Social Workers, 1970 to present. Community Activities: New York City Department of Mental Health (Harlem Catchment area planning board, chairman, adult subcommittee, 1976-78); District 10 Community Planning Board, New York City (health and hospital sub-committee, 1980); Abbott House Neighborhood Advisory Board White Plains, New York (chairman, 1979-81); Fisher Hill Association, White Plains, New York, 1976 to present; Post Road School Parent-Teacher Association, 1978 to present. Religion: Councilman 1974-78, Member 1966-77, St. Peters Lutheran Church, New York City; Trinity Lutheran Church, White Plains, 1981 to prsent. Honors and Awards: Outstanding Senate Service, Wisconsin State University, 1965; Dean's Award for Leadership, Columbia University School of Social Work, 1972; Listed in *Who's Who Among Students in American Universities and College, Who's Who in the East, Community Leaders of America.* Address: 94 Quinby Avenue, White Plains, New York 10606.

White, Robert Joseph

Professor and Co-Chairman of Neurosurgery. Personal: Born January 21, 1926 in Duluth, Minnesota; Married Patricia R. Murray; Father of Robert T., Christopher E., Patricia E., Michael J., Daniel J., Pamela M., James W., Richard P., Marguerite L., Ruth A. Education: B.S., University of Minnesota, 1951; M.D. with honors, Harvard University, 1953; Ph.D. Neurosurgery and Physiology, University of Minnesota, 1962. Military: Served in the United States Army in the South Pacific, 1944-45. Career: Professor and Co-Chairman of Neurosurgery, Case Western Reserve University School of Medicine; Director of the Department of Neurosurgery and the Brain Research Laboratory, Cleveland Metropolitan General Hospital; Mayo Clinic, Rochester, Minnesota, Assistant Professor to Associate Professor 1961-66, Research Associate to Neurophysiologist 1959-61, Assistant to Staff Member 1958-59; Resident, Boston Children's Hospital and Peter Bent Brigham Hospital, Boston, Massachusetts, 1954-55; Surgical Intern, Peter Bent Brigham Hospital, Boston, Massachusetts, 1953-54; First to Isolate the Brain in the Experimental Animal and Keep it Alive Outside the Body; First to Successfully Transplant and Hypothermically Store the Brain of an Experimental Animal; Introduced New Technique Employing Low Temperature Phenomena to Treat Acute Spinal Cord Trauma and Protect the Brain during Operation and Following Injury. Organizational Memberships: Cleveland Academy of Medicine (board of directors; president, 1978-79); Society of University Neurosurgeons (past president); American College of Surgeons (officer, committee on trauma); Member of the Foremost Research and Surgical Societies, United States and Europe; Officer in Numerous National Organizations. Community Activities: University Hospitals (associate neurosurgeon); Veterans Administration Hospital (visiting staff); Lakewood Hospital of Greater Cleveland (visiting staff); *Surgical Neurology* (editor); *Resuscitation* (editor); *The Journal of Trauma* (editor); *Neurological Research* (editor); Extensive Lectures in the United States, China, Europe and the Soviet Union. Religion: Recipient of Private Papal Audiences with Pope Paul VI 1972-77 and John Paul II to discuss his clinical and experimental work, 1980 & 1981. Published Works: Author of Over 300 Publications on Clinical Neurosurgery, Brain Research, Medical Ethics, and Health Care Delivery; Writings Translated into Many Languages including Russian and Chinese. Honors and Awards: Papal Knighthood; Svien Lectureship of the Mayo Clinic, 1978; L.W. Freeman Award, National Paraplegia Foundation, 1977; Alumni Research Award, Mayo Clinic; Medical Mutual Honor Award of Northeast Ohio; Honorary Doctor of Science Degrees, John Carroll University 1979, Cleveland State University; Listed in *Who's Who in the World, Who's Who in America, Who's Who in the Midwest, American Men of Science, National Registry of Prominent Americans, Royal Blue Book, Dictionary of International Biography.* Address: 2895 Lee Road, Shaker Heights, Ohio 44120.

White, Ruby Blackmore

Director of Overseas Projects. Personal: Born December 16, 1919; Daughter of Mr. and Mrs. J. E. Blackmore (both deceased); Married Loftin E. White Jr. (deceased); Mother of Loftin E. White III (deceased), James Christopher. Education: A.A., Christian College, Columbia, Missouri, 1938; B.A., University of Missouri, Columbia, Missouri, 1941. Career: Director of Overseas Projects, including Orphanages, Hospitals, Disaster Shipments, Food and Medicines, David Livingstone Missionary Foundation. Community Activities: Children's Home (secretary-treasurer, junior board, 1950-56); Tulsa Boys Home (vice-president, junior board, 1951-52); Boy Scouts of America (Cub Scout leader, 1951-56). Honors and Awards: Phi Theta Kappa, 1939; Alpha Kappa Delta, 1940. Address: Tulsa, Oklahoma 74136.

Sally White

White, Ruth

Psychiatric Social Worker (retired). Personal: Born October 2, 1899; Daughter of William H. and Cecilia Bigler Romig (both deceased); Married Richard M. White (deceased); Mother of Walter F., Lois E., William W. Education: B.S., University of Wisconsin, 1922; Advanced Work at University of Wisconsin, University of California, Fordham University, New York School of Social Research. Career: Psychiatric Social Worker. Community Activities: Senior Citizens Check Line (volunteer, 1979-81); Prosser Memorial Hospital (volunteer receptionist, 1980-81); Board of Common Ministry, 1976-81; Jail Committee (chairman, 1976-81); Lower Valley Art Association (president, 1960-64); Governor's Comprehensive Health Committee; National League of American Pen Women, 1976-81; Planned Parenthood (board member); Lower Valley Art Exhibit (chairman, 1960-64). Religion: Episcopal Church; CPC National Church Organization, National Board, Provincial President, Diocesan Director, 1964-78; Episcopal Church Women, President; Organist, 1964-78; Diocesan Council, 1978. Honors and Awards: Presiding Bishop's Citation 1981, Vicar's Cross 1968, Bishop's Committee 1964-78, Episcopal Church. Address: 938 Memorial, Presser, Washington 99350.

White, Sally Fox

Public Relations Manager. Personal: Daughter of Mr. and Mrs. J. Gilbert Fox (both deceased); Married Joseph Andrew White; Mother of Clair Fox. Education: Bachelor of Journalism with honors, University of Texas, 1946; Economics Studies, University of Mexico, 1945; Graduate of Allied Stores Executive Training, 1947; Scheil School of Art, Chicago, 1954; Dallas School of Commercial Art, 1956; Virginia Commonwealth University Graduate School, 1967-68. Career: Public Relations Manager, Neiman-Marcus, Atlanta, Georgia; Fiber Consultant and Publicist, DuPont Textile Fiber Division, U.S.A.; Retail Promotion Account Manager, The Merchandising Group, Inc., New York, New York; Freelance Fashion Commentator, Publicist, Retail Sales Training, Chicago, Dallas and New Orleans; Merchandising Representative, Curtis Publications, Assistant to Merchandising Editor, *Ladies' Home Journal;* Advertising Manager, Meacham's, Fort Worth, Texas; Commentator and Continuity Writer, Radio KGKL, San Antonio, Texas; Copywriter, Layout Artist, Assistant to the Advertising Manager, Joske's, San Antonio, Texas; *Daily Texan*, Feature Writer, Advertising Manager; Admissions Counselor, William Woods College, Fulton, Missouri; Publicity Chairman, United Fund, Richmond, Virginia; Research and Design for Home Sewing, DuPont Textile Fibers; Textile Fiber Training, DuPont Textile Fibers, Wilmington; Amateur Radio Operator's License, General Class. Organizational Memberships: Atlanta Press Club (charter member); The Fashion Group (regional director; treasurer; project chairman, 1975 to present); Atlanta Communications Club; Women in Communications Club (chapter president; creator of "Day on the Job" project; chairman, publicity clinics and handbook projects); Leaderships Atlanta Inc., 1980-81; Atlanta Historic Preservation Association (docent, 1982-83); Atlanta Professional Women (Image Maker listing, 1982). Community Activities: Young Women's Christian Association of Atlanta (board member, 1980); Atlanta Chamber of Commerce (council member); High Museum of Art; League of Women Voters; American Association of University Women; Business and Professional Women's Association; Alumnae Council of Women's Colleges; Atlanta Metro United Way (solicitation committee); Atlanta Art Association; North Springs High School Parent-Teacher Association; Atlanta Zoological Society; Atlanta Women's Chamber of Commerce (Dogwood Festival tour committee; creative committee); Atlanta Historical Society (Tullis Smith House restoration costume project chairman); Rabun-Gap-Nacoochee Club; Atlanta Visitors and Convention Bureau (international visitor's committee); Atlanta Botanical Garden (gift committee). Religion: Presbyterian. Honors and Awards: Georgia Chamber of Commerce Awards, Historical Society Project 1974-76, Neiman-Marcus Advertising/Business 1976; Leading Ladies of Atlanta, 1974; Service Awards, The Fashion Group, Inc., 1967, 1976; Dogwood Festival Award, Women's Chamber of Commerce, 1975; Parade Honor 1976, Exhibit Honor 1982, WSB-TV; Listed in *Who's Who of American Women, World Who's Who of Women, Community Leaders of America, Who's Who in the South and Southwest, Dictionary of International Biography, Who's Who in Georgia.* Address: 6410 Colewood Court Northwest, Atlanta, Georgia 30328.

Whitescarver, Edward Augustus

Retired Educator. Personal: Born May 31, 1914, in Pruntytown, West Virginia; Married Anne Benda, February 12, 1944; Father of John Edward. Education: Graduate of Grafton High School, 1931; Attended Alderson-Broaddus College; B.A., West Virginia Wesleyan, 1935; M.A., West Virginia University. Military: Served in the United States Army, 1942-45. Career: Teacher of English, French and World History, Flemington High School, 1937-59; Assistant Principal 1959-66, Principal 1966-74, Retired 1974, Grafton Senior High School. Organizational Memberships: Retired School Personnel (vice president, legislative chairman). Community Activities: Kiwanis International (past lieutenant governor; State Chairman of Membership Growth and Education); Grafton Kiwanis Club (director; past president); Grafton Lodge #15, A.F.&A.M.; Naomi Chapter #12, Order of the Eastern Star; American Legion Post #12 (Americanism officer for 15 years; district chairman of Legion Oratorical Contest, 7 years); City-County Planning Commission, 1961 to present; Tygart Valley Development Association (director); Taylor County Sheltered Workshop Inc. (director); West Virginia Industrial School for Boys (advisory committee); Alderson-Broaddus College Alumni (council member; past president); Taylor County Historical and Genealogical Society (charter member); Boy Scouts of America (past official); M.D.T.A. Coordinator for Taylor County; Citizens Advisory Committee, Comprehensive Education Plan; Region VI Comprehensive Advisory Committee; Educators Investors Insurance Company (board of governors). Religion: Beulah Baptist Church, Church School Superintendent 1948 to present, Chairman of Board of Deacons; Past President, Union Baptist Association of Young People; Past President, Interdenominational Sunday School Convention; Two Terms as Moderator, Union Baptist Convention. Honors and Awards: West Virginia University Chapter of Kappa Delta Pi, 1936; Veterans of Foreign Wars Patriotism Award, 1968; Chosen to Deliver National Cemetery Veteran's Day Address, 1970, 1974; Future Farmers of America Outstanding Service Award, 1974; Outstanding Service in Education Award, 1974; Kiwanis International President's Award, 1977; Distinguished Lieutenant Governor Award, 1977; United States Jaycees Distinguished Service Award, 1978; International Platform Association; Listed in *Personalities of the South, Dictionary of International Biography, Men of Achievement, International Who's Who in Community Service, International Register of Profiles, International Who's Who of Intellectuals, Book of Honor.* Address: Route 2, Box 171, Grafton, West Virginia 26354.

Whittlesey, Eunice Baird

Legislative Liaison. Personal: Daughter of Stuart J. Baird (deceased), Mrs. Stuart J. Baird; Married Joseph Insull Whittlesey; Mother of Anne B. Donlan. Education: B.A. cum laude, State University of New York-Albany. Career: Executive Director, New York Statue of Liberty Celebration Foundation, 1982 to present; Legislative Liaison, New York State Committee on Commerce and Economic Development, 1979-82; Organizer and Executive Director, New York State Environmental Council Program, "Keep New York State Clean"; Consultant and Program Associate, New York State Environmental Health Services Unit, Pure Waters Division, 2 Years; Supervisor, Classified Document Library, Knolls Atomic Power Laboratory, 5 Years; Statistical Assistant, Animal Genetics Department, Cornell University; Teacher of English, Speech and Drama, New Hartford High School and Springfield Central School. Community Activities: State University of New York-Albany (national chairman, fund drive; member of the foundation); New York State Legislative Forum; State University of New York-Albany Foundation (board member); Schenectady County Republican Women's Club; Schenectady County Historical Society; State University of New York Agricultural and Technical College (past council member, 16 years); Schenectady County Volunteer Bureau (past board member, advisory committee); Family and Child Service of Schenectady County (past board member); Schenectady County Department of Social Services (past member and secretary, advisory committee); Tuberculosis and Respiratory Disease Association (past board member, clean air committee); Volunteers Tie-Line (past organizer and chair at request of Governor Rockefeller); President Ford Campaign (New York vice-chairman); "People for Ford" (state co-chairman); Nixon Lodge Volunteers (Schenectady County chairman); "Housewives for Rockefeller" (state co-chairman). Religion: Union Presbyterian Church. Honors and Awards: Distinguished Alumni Award 1979, Excellence in Service Awards 1978, State University of New York-Albany; Grant Honoree, Gift in Her Name Contributed to National Research Fund, American Association of University Women; Creator of Environmental Circle, Symbol of First Earth Day, New York State; Listed in *Who's Who in the East, Directory of Distinguished Americans.* Address: 118 Acorn Drive, Scotia, New York 12302.

Edward A Whitescarver

Whyte, Edna Gardner

Airport Owner and Operator. Personal: Born November 3, 1902; Daughter of Walter Carl and Myrtle Brush Gardner (both deceased); Married George Murphy Whyte (deceased); Stepmother of Georgana Ann. Education: Graduate of High School, 1920; Registered Nurse, 1924; Pre-Medicine, 1 Year; Commercial Single-Engine Land and Seaplane, Multi-Engine Land Plane, Flight Instructor, Airplane, Instrument, Multi-Engine Rotorcraft, Glider, Link, All Ground Ratings, Federal Aviation Agency. Military: Served in the United States Navy Nurse Corps 1929-35; Served as War Training Flight Instructor during World War II and received Commission in Army Nurse Corps at end of World War II, serving on duty in Phillipings on Luzon at Camp Stasaberg and Clark Field. Career: Owner and Operator, Aero Valley Airport; Registered Nurse. Organizational Memberships: Ninety-Nines, Inc., International Organization of Licensed Women Pilots (president, 1966-67); Airplane and Pilots Association; OX-5 Pioneer Pilots of America; Silver Wings. Community Activities: American Red Cross (polio nurse, 1949-50). Honors and Awards: Over 30,102 Hours Flying in 57 Years, Now 80 Years Old and Still Flight Training Instructor, Built Large Private Airport after 70 Years of Age; Name Placed in Bronze in Concrete in Memory Lane International Forest of Friendship for Outstanding Dedication to Aviation, Atchison, Kansas, 1978; Flying Eagle, Fun in Sun, Winter Haven, Florida, 1976; Aviation Great, Experimental Aircraft Association, Oshkosh (Wisconsin) International Fly-In, 1975; OX-5 Aviation Hall of Fame, OX-5 Club of America, New York, 1975; Outstanding Contestant for Best Sportsmanship on Pylon Racing, National Air Races, Cleveland, Ohio, 1967; Tiney Broadwick Award for Activities in the Promotion and Development of Aviation, OX-5 Pioneer Pilots of America, Birmingham, Alabama, 1967; Woman of the Year in Aviation, Women's National Aeronautical Association, 1966; Second Place, Air Race Classic 2400-Mile Air Race in Commanche 400-Horsepower, 1982. Address: Route 4 Box 16D, Roanoke, Texas 76262.

Wilcox, Jeanne Burden

Publishing Executive. Personal: Born January 23, 1948; Daughter of Lewis A. Burden, Roma M. Burden; Married Peter Wilcox. Education: B.A., California State University, Long Beach, 1971. Career: President, Jeanne Wilcox Associates, Publications Specialists; Former Positions include Manager, Editorial Services/Editor, *Connections* Magazine, Boys Clubs of America, New York; Publications Specialist, New York Association for the Blind; Editor, Marcel Dekker, Inc., New York; Public Relations Director,

Direct Mail Fundraisers Association; Writer/Editor, *Motorcycle Woman* (free-lance). Organizational Memberships: Women in Communications; Women in Production; International Association of Business Communicators; Business and Professional Women's Clubs. Community Activities: Volunteer, Citizens for a Cleaner New York Recycling Project, Brooklyn, New York, 1973-76; Proposal Writer/Member, Women in Prison (ad hoc committee of National Organization of Women), 1974-75; Board Member, The 15th Street School and the Chelsea Day School, 1981 to present. Address: 130 West 26th Street, New York, New York 10001.

Wilkinson, Nana Miriam

Realtor. Personal: Born June 8, 1912; Daughter of Mrs. John R. Slaten; Married Wesley O. Wilkinson (deceased). Education: Graduate of Eldorado High School, Illinois, 1929; Attended Carthage College, Illinois, 1930-32. Career: Secretary, President's Office, DePauw University, 1935-37; Executive Secretary to Vice President, Beach and Arthur Paper Company, Indianapolis and New York City, 1937-45; Realtor, Henry B. Trachy Real Estate Agency, 1970-83. Organizational Memberships: Lakes Region Board of Realtors (board of trustees, 1965-70); Arthur S. Brown Foundation, Tilton (trustee, 1974-76); Tilton Town Budget Committee, 1976-79; Representative to New Hampshire Legislature, 1970-72; Resources, Recreation and Development Committee, 1970-72; Appointed 1 of 9 Member Interim Flood Plains Commission by Governor, 1971-72; Appointed Member, Interim Housing Committee, House of Representatives, 1971-72; National Republican Congressional Committee (certificate of recognition, 1981); Tilton-Northfield Woman's Club (president, 1953-55); Tilton-Northfield Garden Club (president, 1959-61); Ladies Circle of Tilton Congregational Church (president, 1961-62, 1970-71); New Hampshire Federation of Garden Clubs, Inc. (parliamentarian to federation, 1961-67; District Director of Lakes District West, 1963-64; first vice president, 1966-67; State President, 1967-69; Editor, state publication, *Lilac Letter*, 1969-71; legislation chairman, 1972-73; chairman, inter-club and inter-district relations, 1973-75; legislative chairman, 1975-77; Parliamentarian to Federation, 1979-83); National Council of State Garden Clubs, Inc. (Parliamentarian, New England region, 1965-67; Board of Directors, 1967-69, 1971-73, 1975-77; treasurer, New England regional symposium, 1969-71; chairman, New England youth activities, 1969-71; national nominating committee, 1971-73; vice-chairman, 1974 Boston convention of National Council of State Garden Clubs Inc.; National Council organizational study committee, 1975-79; Parliamentarian, New England region of National Council, 1975-79; National Council Corresponding Secretary, 1979-81; National Council chairman of policy and procedure, 1981 to present); National Wildlife Federation; Smithsonian Institute Association; Audubon Society of New Hampshire; Natural Resources Council of New Hampshire; Society for the Protection of New Hampshire Forests; National Association of Parliamentarians; National Association of Women Legislators. Honors and Awards: Presidential Citation, New Hampshire Federation of Garden Clubs, 1981; Life Member, National Council of State Garden Clubs; Life Member, Tilton-Northfield Garden Club; Life Member, New Hampshire Federation of Garden Clubs; Order of the Purple Finch, New Hampshire Federation of Garden Clubs, Presented to Outstanding Woman of the Year, 1970; Presidential Citation, New Hampshire Federation of Garden Clubs, 1970, 1974; Presidential Citation, National Council of State Garden Clubs, Inc., 1981; Listed in *Who's Who in Politics, Two Thousand Women of Achievement, World Who's Who of Women, Who's Who of American Women, Dictionary of International Biography, Who's Who in the East.* Address: 90 Andora Drive, Fox Chase Manor, Elkton, Maryland 21921.

Anne O Willard

Willard, Anne O

Physical Therapist. Personal: Born August 4, 1916, in Cleveland, Ohio; Daughter of Rt. Reverend John Lorraine and Olga Carolina Wellington Oldham. Education: B.A., Rollins College, 1940; Attended the University of Wisconsin, School of Physical Therapy, 1942-45; Undertook postgraduate studies, University of Pennsylvania, 1959; Ph.D., Hamilton State University, 1974; Continuing Education Programs to date. Military: Served as 1st Lieutenant, United States Army, 1940-46; Retired Captain of the Reserves. Career: Chief Physical Therapist, Rex Hospital, Raleigh, North Carolina, 1949-51; Chief Physical Therapist, Lawton Memorial, Lawton, Oklahoma, 1951-53; Chief Physical Therapist, National Polio Foundation, Buffalo, New York, 1953-54; Head Physical Therapist, 17 Counties, State Crippled Childrens Service, State of Alabama, 1954-57; Therapist for Special Services, Cerebral Palsy Society, Fort Worth, Texas, 1957-60; Organized and Directed Physical Therapy Department, Crippled Childrens Society, Mineral Wells, Texas, 1960-61; Organized and Directed Physical Therapy Department, Flow Memorial Hospital, 1961-71; Organized and Directed Physical Therapy Department, Collin Memorial Hospital, McKinney, Texas, 1971 to present; Private Practice, 1957 to present; Relief Chief Therapist, St. Joseph's Hospital, Paris, Texas. Organizational Memberships: American Physical Therapy Association; Lancaster-Pittard Professional Association (advisor-consultant); Business and Professional Women's Club (finance chairman 1977, president elect 1978-79, president 1979-80); International Platform Association. Community Activities: Alpha Phi; National Wildlife Federation; Order of Eastern Star (officer 7 years); Soroptimist (Denton chapter, vice president, president, chief delegate, chairman of ways and means committee); St. Monica's Episcopal Church Guild (past president); Rainbow Girls (board of directors); Tarrant and Collin Counties Humane Societies (past president, Collin County Humane Society). Religion: Episcopalian. Honors and Awards: Listed in *World Who's Who of Women, Who's Who of American Women, Who's Who of Women, Who's Who of South and Southwest, International Who's Who of Intellectuals, Who's Who in the United States, Personalities of the South, Royal Blue Book, Notable Americans, International Register of Profiles, Directory of International Biography, National Social Directory, Two Thousand Women of Achievement, I.B.A. Yearbook and Biographical Directory* (1979-80). Address: P. O. Box 703, McKinney, Texas 75069.

Sue S Willbanks

Willbanks, Sue Sutton

Department Chairperson. Personal: Born September 24, 1935; Daughter of William Herbert (deceased) and Melba Ward Sutton; Married Charles Walter Willbanks (deceased); Mother of Jill Ann, Brenda Kay. Education: Attended Sul Ross University; B.S., Home Economics Education, Texas Tech University, 1955; M.A.Ed., Counseling with State Certification, University of Texas, Permian Basin, 1980. Career: Chairperson, Homemaking Department, Big Spring High School, Big Spring, Texas, 1980 to present; Psychology Intern, Outpatient Clinic and Psychiatric Unit, Big Spring State Hospital, 1979 (Summer); Homemaking Teacher, Big Spring High School, 1972-79. Organizational Memberships: Big Spring Classroom Teachers Association (president, 1980-81); District 17 Texas Classroom Teachers Association Coordinating Council (vice president, 1980-81); Vocational Homemaking Teachers of Texas; Texas State Teachers Association. Community Activities: Permian Basin Regional Planned Parenthood Association (board of directors, 1980-82; chairman, information and education committee, 1982); Volunteer, Big Spring State Hospital, 1979; Speaker to Various City/Area Groups; Judge for Numerous City/Area Contests. Religion: Big Spring First Methodist Church Chancel Choir, 1955-81, and Handbell Ringers, 1969-72; Church Organist, Big Spring Immaculate Heart of Mary Church, 1975-78. Honors and Awards: Phi Upsilon Omicron; High School Salutatorian; National Honor Society; Listed in *Who's Who in Texas Education, Personalities of the South.* Address: 1290-D Maunakea Street, Suite 131, Honolulu, Hawaii 96817.

Willcox, Larry Austin

Agricultural Consultant (retired). Personal: Born May 13, 1904; Son of Edward Kellogg and Ella Jane Austin Willcox (both deceased);

Married Virginia Burroughs (deceased); Father of Burr L. (deceased), Guy James. Education: B.S., College of Agriculture, University of Illinois. Career: Agricultural Consultant; Farm and Ranch Loan Officer, Mutual Life Insurance Company of New York. Organizational Memberships: Oklahoma City Farm Club (president); Oklahoma City Chamber of Commerce (chairman, livestock committee); Oklahoma Partners of the Americas (president). Community Activities: Oklahoma Farm Service Organization (president). Address: 1726 Coventry Lane, Oklahoma City, Oklahoma 73120.

Williams, C Michael

Political Consulting and Public Relations. Personal: Born February 23, 1952; Son of John and Roberta Williams. Education: Graduate, Woodward High School, 1970; Undertook studies at the University of Oklahoma, 1970-73. Career: Television News; Radio News; Governor's Staff; Advertising; Public Relations; Political Consulting. Organizational Memberships: Oklahoma Director of Volunteerism, 1975-76; O.K.C. Press Club (president, 1978, 1981; board of directors, 1976 to present); Sigma Delta Chi, 1975-80; Community Activities: Oklahoma League for the Blind (board of directors, 1979 to present); United Way (advertising committee); O.K.C. Chamber of Commerce. Honors and Awards: Outstanding News Report, United Press International, 1975; Outstanding News Report, Associated Press, 1975-76; Listed in *Outstanding Young Men of America, Personalities of the South, Community Leaders of America.* Address: 4847 N. Blackwelder, Apt. 125, Oklahoma City, Oklahoma 73118.

E Alita T J Williams

Williams, Clyde Ezra

Real Estate Appraiser and Land Developer. Personal: Born January 22, 1920; Son of John Ezra and Harriet Rhoda Miller; Married Geraldine "Jeri" Hadley; Father of Deborah Lynn W. Nordgan, Jon Timothy. Education: Graduate of Wever State College; Postgraduate Studies at Brigham Young University, University of Utah, University of Purdue, University of San Francisco, Eastern Washington State College. Military; Served in the United States Army Air Force during World War II as Captain and Pilot. Career: Real Estate Appraiser and Land Developer; Contractor. Organizational Memberships: South Davis Home Builders Association (president, 1957, 1958); Society of Real Estate Appraisers (president, Salt Lake chapter, 1978-79). Community Activities: Bountiful City Planning Commission (member, 1957-64; chairman, 1958-65); Bountiful Capital Improvements Commission, 1958-61; Sertoma International; Kiwanis Club (past vice-president). Religion: Church of Jesus Christ of Latter-Day Saints, Member and High Priest. Honors and Awards: Air Medal and Distinguished Flying Cross, World War II, United States Army Air Force; Senior Real Property Appraiser, Society of Real Estate Appraisers. Address: 868 East 1050 North, Bountiful, Utah 84010.

Williams, Edna Aleta Theadora Johnston

Journalist and Family Editor. Personal: Born September 19, 1923; Daughter of Clarence and Edna Lewis Johnston (both deceased); Married Albert Murray (deceased); Mother of Murleta, Norma, Martin, Charla, Kerrick, Renwick, Julia. Education: Graduate of Bloomfield High School, Halifax, Nova Scotia, Canada; Attended Maritime Business College, Halifax, Nova Scotia, Canada, 1943-44. Career: Journalist, Family Editor, *New Glasgow Evening News;* Typist, Halifax Dockyard (Treasury Department), Naval Armament Depot, Bedford, Nova Scotia; Presbyterian Office, New Glasgow; Thompson and Sutherland, New Glasgow. Organizational Memberships: Canadian Press. Community Activities: Pictou County Council of Churches (Baptist representative; secretary, 1978-82); African Baptist Women's Institute (vice-president; representative, 1980-82); Pictou County Young Men's and Young Women's Christian Association (founding member, 1966; board of directors, 1967-77, corresponding secretary and vice-president, 1975-77, 1974-75); Home and School (past president; provincial board of directos); New Glasgow Interracial Council (past officer); United Way (board of directors, 1980 to present). Religion: Second Baptist Church, New Glasgow, President of Ladies' Auxiliary 1979-82, Assistant Organist 1960 to present, Co-Director of Youth Work, Organist-Director of Brotherhood Choir; Cornwallis St. Baptist Church, Halifax, Organist 1944-46, Sunday School Teacher. Honors and Awards: Honored by Black United Front 1976, Pictou County Young Men's and Young Women's Christian Association 1969, Town of Stellarton Committee 1981, East Pictou Rural High School 1979. Address: 230 Reservoir Street, New Glasgow, Nova Scotia, Canada B2H 4K4.

Williams, Melva Jean

Company Executive Vice-President and Director. Personal: Born June 11, 1935; Daughter of Wayne and Mildred Graham Mulholland; Married J. B. Williams; Mother of Mark Proctor, Doris, Robin, Jeannie. Education: Graduate of Roberta's Finishing School, Miami, Florida, 1950; Graduate of Charron-Williams Commercial College, Miami, Florida, 1954. Career: Executive Vice-President and Director, Southeastern Resources Corporation, a Texas Corporation; President and Director, SERPCO, Inc.; Vice-President and Director, J. J. & L. Drilling Company, Inc.; Secretary-Treasurer and Director, Brownwood Pipeline Corporation; Secretary-Treasurer, Rising Star Processing Corporation; Partner, Tenabo Venture, Gold Mining; Partner, Laser Drilling Company, Inc.; Partner, MAGNAFRAC; President, MJW Enterprises, Inc.; Partner, B. & W. Real Estate Investments; Partner F. & W. Real Estate Investments; Former Vice-President and Director, Delta Gas Company, Inc.; Former Registered Securities Broker, Officer and Director, J. B. Williams and Company, Inc. Honors and Awards: Listed in *Who's Who of American Women, Directory of Distinguished Americans, Personalities of the South, World Who's Who of Women, Book of Honor.* Address: 6150 Indigo Court, Fort Worth, Texas 76112.

Melva J Williams

Williams, Randall Alan

Orthopaedic Surgeon. Personal: Born April 7, 1936; Married; Father of Laura W. Bergeron, Ethelyn Kelley. Education: Attended University of Chattanooga; M.D., Tulane Medical School, 1960. Military: Served in the United States Air Force to the rank of Captain, 1961-63. Career: Orthopaedic Surgeon. Organizational Memberships: American Academy of Orthopaedic Surgeons (fellow); American College of Surgeons (fellow); American Board of Orthopaedic Surgery (certification); Southern Medical Association; Louisiana State Medical Society. Community Activities: Jefferson Parish Sheriff's Office (emergency medical advisor); City of Kenner Police Department (emergency medical advisor); Southeast Louisiana Emergency Medical Services (board of directors). Religion: Episcopal. Honors and Awards: Assistant Clinical Professor of Orthopaedic Surgery, Tulane Medical School; Listed in *Who's Who of Medical Specialties, Who's Who in the South and Southwest.* Address: 3939 Houma Boulevard, Metairie, Louisiana 70002.

Williams, W R

Accounting Executive. Personal: Born March 15, 1930; Son of Eddie S. and Edna Rashall Williams (both deceased); Father of Julie

Marie, Janet Lynn. Education: B.S. with high honors, University of Arkansas, 1956. Military: Served in the United States Air Force, 1948-52. Career: Peat, Marwick, Mitchell & Co., Personnel Committee, Petroleum Committee; Managing Partner, Tulsa Office, Peat, Marwick, Mitchell & Co., 1970-74; Partner, 1968 to present; Continental Europe Firm's Operating Committee; Senior Partner, German Practice, 1974-78; Board of Directors, Operating Committee, Vice Chairman, Peat, Marwick, Mitchell & Co. Organizational Memberships: Oklahoma State Board of Public Accountancy (past chairman; past secretary); American Institute of Certified Public Accountants, 1959 to present; Oklahoma Society of Certified Public Accountants (past member, board of directors; past president, member 1958-74, Tulsa Chapter); National Association of Accountants, 1973 to present; American Accounting Association, 1973 to present; National Association of State Boards of Accountancy, 1969-74; Downtown Optimist Club of Tulsa (past first vice president; member, 1970-74); Tulsa University Accounting Conference (past general chairman; member, 1970-74); Petroleum Society of Accountants, 1969-74. Community Activities: University of Arkansas Alumni Association (life member); Frankfurt International School, Germany (chairman); United States Chamber of Commerce (past member); American Chamber of Commerce in West Germany, 1974-78; Tulsa Chamber of Commerce, 1970-74; Houston Grand Opera Association (past governing board; member, 1979 to present); Forum Club of Houston, 1981 to present; Tulsa Press Club, 1970-74; Southern Hills Country Club, 1970-74; Tulsa Club, 1970-74; Summit Club, 1969-74; Frankfurt Golf Club, 1973-74; Houston Club, 1978 to present; Houston Athletic Club, 1978 to present; Houston Racquet Club, 1979 to present; The Houstonian, 1980 to present; Brae Burn Country Club, 1980 to present; Lakeside Country Club,, 1982 to present; Toastmasters International; Magic Empire Toastmasters Club, Tulsa, Oklahoma; Oklahoma State University Development Council of Tulsa County, Oklahoma (charter member, 1973-74). Honors and Awards: Accountant of the Year, Alpha Iota Chapter, Beta Alpha Psi, University of Arkansas, 1978, 1980; Frankfurt International School became First Institution in the World to be Jointly Accredited by Both European Council of International Schools and Middle State Association in the United States while under Chairmanship of Mr. Williams; Beta Gamma Sigma; Beta Alpha Psi; Alpha Kappa Psi. Address: 5555 Del Monte Drive #305, Houston, Texas 77056.

Charles W Wilson

Wilson, Charles William

Medical Doctor. Personal: Born August 12, 1916; Son of Jacob Resor and Estella Cherrie Wilson (both deceased); Married Frances Preshia Stephenson; Father of Charles William II, Walter Stephen, Cherrie, James Robin. Education: B.A., University of Wichita, 1938; M.D., University of Kansas School of Medicine, 1942; Intern, Harper Hospital, Detroit, Michigan, 1942-43; Resident Physician in Neurology, University Hospitals, Iowa City, Iowa, 1946-47; Resident Physician in Psychiatry, Central State Hospital, Norman, Oklahoma, 1964-67. Military: Served in the United States Navy Reserves on Active Duty, 1943-46, as Lieutenant, Medical Corps. Career: Medical Doctor specializing in Psychiatry, Medical Hypnosis, Research, Development and Use of Rapid Psychotherapies, Santa Maria, California, 1971 to present; Staff Psychiatrist in Community Mental Health Centers, Atascadero State Hospital, California 1975-79, San Luis Obispo, California 1973-75, Ponca City, Oklahoma 1967-71; Director, Mental Health Clinic for Students, Oklahoma State University-Stillwater, Oklahoma 1968-71; Private Practice, Psychiatry and Medical Hypnosis, Ponca City, Oklahoma, 1967-81; General Practice, St. Francis, Kansas, 1947-62, and Lacrosse, Kansas, 1962-64. Organizational Memberships: American Medical Association; American Psychiatric Association; Southern California Psychiatric Society; Academy of Parapsychology and Medicine; Society for Clinical and Experimental Hypnosis; International Society of Hypnosis; American Society of Hypnosis (charter member); American Academy of General Practice; American Association for the Advancement of Science; Northwest Kansas Medical Society (president, 1951). Community Activities: Parent-Teacher Association; American Legion; Mason; Eastern Star; Phi Lambda Phi; Men of Webster; Phi Beta Pi; Delta Upsilon; Rotary International (member, St. Francis, Kansas and Ponca City, Oklahoma, 19 years; president, St. Francis, Kansas, 1955); Boy Scouts of America (scout, scoutmaster, explorer leader, neighborhood commissioner, council trainer of scouters, 23 years); International Platform Association; Elementary School Board, St. Francis, Kansas. Religion: Methodist Church, Lacrosse, Kansas; Sunday School Teacher; Church Committee Member; Lay Leader, 1963. Honors and Awards: Letter of Citation, National Parent-Teacher Association; Eagle Scout, Silver Award, Scoutmasters Key, Wood Badge, Boy Scouts of America; Listed in *Who's Who in the West, Who's Who in America, Who's Who in the World, Book of Honor, Notable Americans, Personalities of America, Personalities of the West and Midwest, Men of Achievement, Dictionary of International Biography, International Who's Who of Intellectuals, International Who's Who of Community Service, Men and Women of Distinction, National Social Registry*, and Others. Address: 4655 Basque Drive, Santa Maria, California 93455.

John W Wilson Jr

Wilson, John William Jr

Research Chemist (retired). Personal: Born April 1, 1916 in Albany, New York; Son of John William and Lena May Gardner Wilson; Married Margaret Shaw Marshall Cunningham on October 5, 1940 in Hartford, Connecticut; Father of John William III, Elizabeth Anne. Education: Graduate of Albany Academy, Albany, New York, 1934; A.B. cum laude Chemistry, Amherst College, Massachusetts, 1938; Studied Organic Chemistry, Massachusetts Institute of Technology, 1938-39. Career: Mobil Research and Development Corporation (formerly Research Department, Mobil Oil Corporation), Supervising Chemist in Advanced Lubrication Technology 1972-81, Supervising Chemist for Water-Base Lubricants 1970-72, Manager of Industrial Lubricants Division of Research and Technical Service Department in London 1968-70, Supervising Chemist for Metal Processing Fluids 1968, Senior Research Chemist 1948-68, Research Chemist assigned to Grease Group 1942-48, Analytical Chemist 1940-42, Summer Experience as Analytical Chemist 1936-39. Organizational Memberships: Electron Microscopy Society of America; Philadelphia Electron Microscope Society (former member; chairman, 1962-63); Philadelphia Organic Chemists Club (former member); 5th International Congress for Electron Microscopy (local chairman, 1962); Sigma Xi; New York Academy of Sciences; Institute of Petroleum (fellow); American Institute of Chemists (fellow). Community Activities: Board of Education, Redding, Connecticut (member, 8 years); Redding Volunteer Fire Company No. 1 (member, 1946-60); National Model Railroad Association (former chairman of inspection committee); Danbury Camera Club, Connecticut (former president); Delaware Valley Ornithological Society (former member); Wildfowl Trust (former member); Royal Society for the Protection of Birds (former member); National Audubon Society; Philadelphia Museum of Art; The Smithsonian Associates; Friends of Independence National Park; Pennsylvania Horticultural Society; Legion of Honor of the Chapel of the Four Chaplains; United Way (campaigns, 5 years); Barclay Farm Civic Association, Cherry Hill, New Jersey (executive board); East African Wildlife Society; Pennsylvania Academy of Fine Arts; American Museum of Natural History; Advisory Committee on Education, Cherry Hill, New Jersey (former member); American Red Cross (11-gallon blood donor); Anglo-American Academy (honorary fellow); Boy Scouts of America (scoutmaster, 1951-56; explorer advisor, 1953-58; wood badge training, assistant course director 1956-70, course director 1971 to present staff advisor 1976 to present; training committee, district chairman, council chairman; chairman, council organizational and extension committee; council executive board, 1956-60, 1961 to present; council commissioner, 1962-79; council president 1979 to 1982; New Jersey Area Scout Committee, vice-president, 1977 to 1982; Northeast Region committee and executive board; National Council; vice-chairman, national volunteer training committee; national committee on insignia and uniform; international committee; United States Foundation for International Scouting, corporate member, chairman of committee for community developemht; inter-American training committee; world community development committee, 1976-79; world training committee, 1979 to present; delegate to many national and international conferences, seminars, training sessions and jamborees). Religion: Christ Church, Redding Connecticut, Vestryman 6 years, Sunday School Superintendent 3 years, Diocesan Convention Delegate 4 years; St. Bartholomew's Church, Cherry Hill, New Jersey, Vesteryman 1 year, Stewardship Chairman 2 years, Sunday School Superintendent 4 years. Published Works: Holder of United States Patent 3,010,898, for Barium C_{20}-C_{22} Soap-Barium Carbonate Grease Composition and Process for Forming Same, 1961; "Synthesized Hydrocarbon Fluids-Next Generation Lubricants", with D. S. Taber, L. E. Tedrow and H. Raich, *Assessment of Lubricant Technology*, 1972; "3-D Viewing, A New Way to Evaluate Greases", *Research/Development 14*, 1963; "Electron Microscope Examination of Thin Sections of Lubricating Grease Thickeners"; *N.L.G.I. Spokesman*, 1961; "Shadowcasting Lubricating Greases for Electron Microscope Examination", with Gerard S. Mapes, Annual Meeting of the Electron Microscope Society of America, 1954; Other Articles Published in Professional Journals. Honors and Awards: Boy Scouts of America, District Award of Merit, Silver Beaver Award for Distinguished Service to Boyhood from Camden County Council 1966, Silver Antelope Award for Distinguished Service to Boyhood from Northeast Region 1973, Scouter's Key, Arrowhead Award, Eagle Scout, Explorer Silver Award; St. George Award, Episcopal, 1980; Listed in *International Who's Who in Community Service, Community Leaders of America, American Men of Science, Who's Who in the East, Chemical Who's Who, Dictionary of International Biography, Royal Blue Book, 2000 Men of Achievement, Notable Americans of the Bicentennial Era, Community Leaders and Noteworthy Americans, Men and Women of Distinction, International Who's Who of Intellectuals.* Address: 117 Saw Mill Court, Barclay Farm, Cherry Hill, New Jersey 08034.

Wilson, Katherine Ann

Teacher. Personal: Born July 26, 1946; Daughter of Steve and Hedwig Oros; Married Mark Joseph Wilson. Education: B.A., University of Detroit, 1968. Career: Teacher, Third Grade 1982 to present, 1970-74, Fourth Grade 1980-81, Kindergarten 1979-80, 1977-78, Special Education 1969-70, First Grade 1968-69. Community Activities: Beta Sigma Phi (Delta Lambda chapter, Goldsboro, North Carolina, 1974; Beta chapter, Adana, Turkey, founder 1975, president 1975-76; Theta Chi chapter, Rantoul, Illinois, member 1976-81, vice-president 1977-78, president 1978-79, extension officer 1979-81, chairman of convention 1980). Honors and Awards: Girl of the Year, Beta Sigma Phi, Beta Chapter 1975, Theta Chi Chapter 1980; Outstanding Elementary Teacher, 1974; Listed in *Who's Who of American Women, World Who's Who of Women, International Who's Who of Intellectuals.* Address: 4 G Maria Drive, Poquoson, Virginia 23662.

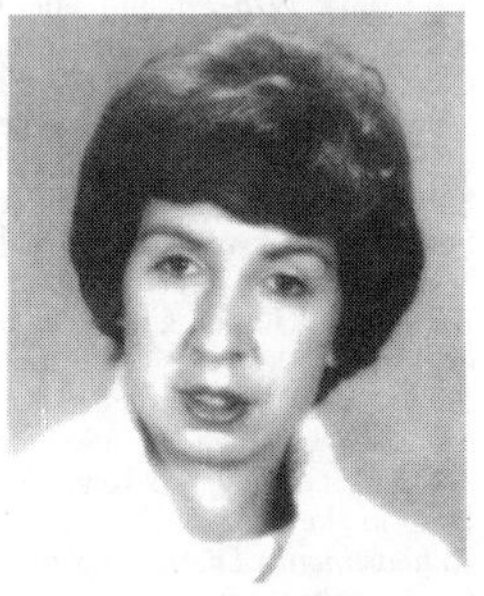
Katherine A Wilson

Wilson, William Feathergail

Chief Geologist. Personal: Born December 25, 1934; Married Elizabeth Gail Wilson; Father of Clayton, Douglas, Wendy. Education: B.A. English 1957, B.S. Geology 1960, M.S. Geology 1962, University of Texas-Austin. Career: Placid Oil Company, Chief Geologist 1981 to present, Texas Exploration Manager 1977-81; Senior Exploration Geologist to Exploration Manager of the Eastern Hemisphere, Tesoro Petroleum Corporation, 1974-77; Account Executive, Merrill Lynch, 1970-74; Environmental Geologist, Alamo Area Council of Government, 1970; Independent Petroleum Geologist, 1966-70; Senior Exploration Geologist, El Paso Natural Gas Company, 1965-66; Developmental Geology, Texaco, Inc., 1961-65. Address: 7918 Briaridge, Dallas, Texas 75248.

Wimmer, Glen Elbert

Engineer. Personal: Born February 16, 1903, in Creston, Iowa; Married Mildred G. McCullough; Father of Frank Thomas. Education: B.S.M.E., 1925, and M.S.M.E., 1933, both from Iowa State University; M.B.A., Northwestern University, 1936. Military: Served with the United States Army Reserve Corps, 1925-38 (active duty, 1925-28). Career: Engineer, Engineering Department, General Electric Company, Fort Wayne, Indiana, 1925-29; Assistant Engineer, Western Electric Company, Chicago, Illinois, 1929-36; Engineering Staff, Michigan Technological University in Houghton, 1936-37; Firestone Tire and Rubber Company, 1937-38; Engineer in Charge of Design, Ditto Inc., 1938-39; Assistant to the Chief Engineer, Victograph Corporation, 1939-41; Designer of Industrial Machinery, Pioneer Engineering and Manufacturing Company; Designer and Checker, Engineering Service Corporation, 1941-42; Checker and Assistant Superintendent of Design, Norman E. Miller and Associates, 1942; Engineering Checker, Lee Engineering Company, 1942-43; Head, Design and Development Department, Cummins Perforator Company, 1943-45; Staff Engineer, Tammen and Denison Inc., in Charge of Design and Development Projects, 1945-58; Instructor of Cost Accounting, Evening Division Classes, Illinois Institute of Technology, 1946-47; Staff Engineer, Barnes and Reinecke Inc., 1958-69; Engineer, Alpha Services Inc., 1969-70; Retired, 1971; Part-Time Consulting Professional Engineer and Management Consultant. Organizational Memberships: Illinois Engineering Council, 1958-66; Illinois Society of Professional Engineers; National Society of Professional Engineers; Ameican Defense Preparedness Association; Society of Automotive Engineers; Society of Manufacturing Engineers; Delta Chi; International Platform Association; Intercontinental Biographical Association; International Biographical Association (fellow). Honors and Awards: Holder of U.S. and Canadian Patents; Listed in *Who's Who in Engineering, Leaders in American Science, International Blue Book of World Notables, Dictionary of International Biography, Community Leaders and Noteworthy Americans, Dictionary of International Biography, Community Leaders and Noteworthy Americans, Personalities of the West and Midwest, International Register of Profiles, Two Thousand Men of Achievement, Notable Americans of the Bicentennial Era, National Social Directory, The Blue Book, Men of Achievement, International Who's Who of Intellectuals, Who's Who in the West, International Who's Who in Community Service, Illinois Lives, Social Directory of the United States, Who's Who in the Midwest, Profiles of Freedom - The Impressions of the American Historical Society, Men and Women of Distinction, Personalities of America, Book of Honor, Who's Who in California, American Patriots of the 1980's, The American Registry Series, California Who's Who in Business and Finance, Who's Who in Technology Today.* Address: 3839-48 Vista Campana S., Oceanside, California 92056.

Windham, Revish

Social Worker. Personal: Born May 31, 1940; Son of Ike and Lille Windham; Married Joanna Windham; Father of Veronica. Education: B.A., Morris Brown College; Studies at Paine College, Old Dominion College, Hunter College, New York City College, G.R.O.W., The New York State Division for Youth. Military: Served in the United States Navy to rank of Radioman 3rd Class, 1964-68. Career: Youth Counselor, Social Worker. Organizational Memberships: New York State Division for Youth (regional chairperson, educational council for human relations); The Black Caucus of Division for Youth Employees, Inc. (secretary, board of directors). Community Activities: *Black Forum* Magazine (editor-in-chief, 1977, 1980-81); Martin Luther King Junior Center for Social Change New York Support Group (charter member); Zeta Chapter of Phi Beta Sigma Fraternity (president, 1961-62); New York Chapter of The Association of Black Social Workers, 1978; Harlem Writers Guild; Morris Brown College Alumni Association of New York (president, 1978 to present). Religion: Convent Avenue Baptist Church. Honors and Awards: Poet of the Year, J. Mark Publishers, 1970; Professional Citation, Morris Brown College National Alumni Association, 1978; Letter of Recognition, The Association for the Study of Negro Life and History Inc., 1971; Award of Appreciation, *Black Forum* Magazine, 1981; Listed in

Who's Who in Black America, Community Leaders of America. Address: 111 Wadsworth Avenue, Apartment 6F, New York, New York 10033.

Princess Red Wing of Seven Crescents

Musuem Curator. Personal: Born March 21, 1896; Married High Chief White Oak (Mohegan) (deceased); Mother of Metacomet, Fairflower. Education: Graduate, Burrillville High School, 1914; Teachers Training School, 1916; Doctor of Human Affairs, University of Rhode Island, 1975; New York School of Art, attended one year. Career: Curator, Tomquag Indian Memorial Museum; Taught Indian Arts and Crafts, Nature in Summer Camps, 28 years; Made Video Tape of Lecturer at University of Montreal to be used in Schools in Canada, 1979; Column in *South County News,* Rhode Island, "Peace Pipes and Calumets", 1950's. Organizational Memberships: International Speakers Platform; Charlestown Historical Society (historian); Speakers Research Committee for United Nations, 1947-70. Community Activities: President Reagan's Task Force; International Biographical Association, Cambridge, England; Wrote School Song for Mohawk Indian, St. Regis, New York, 1948 (still in use). Religion: Berean Baptist Church, Harrisville, Rhode Island. Published Works: Phamphlet "Indians of Southern New England". Honors and Awards: President Reagan's Proclamation of Thanksgiving; Honorary Doctor of Human Affairs, University of Rhode Island, 1975; Nine Bicentennial and Covered Wagon Scrolls; Rhode Island Hall of Fame, 1978; Woman of the Year, Business and Professional Women of Rhode Island; Testimonial Dinner, 1978; Scroll from Rhode Island Governor for 50 years of Achievement of Keeping Indian Culture Alive in Rhode Island; Listed in *Who's Who Among Women of the World, Distinguished Men and Women of the World, American Indians Encyclopedia of America.* Address: Dovercrest, Summit Road, Exeter, Rhode Island 02822.

Princess Red Wing

Winston, S Colleen

Director of Catholic Diocese Office of Communication. Personal: Born August 29, 1937; Daughter of Wright and Marian Bacon Winston. Education: A.B., English/Secondary Education, Thomas More College, Edgewood, Kentucky, 1955; M.S., Biology, St. Mary College, Winona, Minnesota, 1972; M.A., Communications/Theology, University of Dayton, Ohio, 1977; Studies at Marquette University (Milwaukee, Wisconsin), Edgewood College (Cincinnati, Ohio) and University of Cincinnati (Ohio). Career: Director, Office of Communication, Catholic Diocese of Covington, Kentucky, 1981 to present; Former Positions include Consultant and Writer for Various Groups and Audiences; Archdiocese of Cincinnati, Media Consultant to Religious Education Office, Newsletter Editor of Office of Purchasing; Freelance Producer, Writer, Photographer, Slide/Filmstrip Programs for Religious Education; Lecturer, Teacher, Writer, Consultant in Media, Local, Regional and National Levels; High School Teacher of English, Sciences, Media, Religion and History. Organizational Memberships: Unda-U.S.A. (regional representative, 1982 to present); Catholic Committee of Appalachia; American Benedictine Academy; Benedictine Musicians of America; Salesian Guild. Community Activities: Villa Madonna Academy (board of directors, 1976-80; secretary, 1977-78); Campbell County Cable Citizens Advisory Board, 1982 to present; Kentucky Council of Churches (delegate and member of media commission, 1982 to present; chairperson of commission, 1983 to present). Religion: Roman Catholic, Member of Community of Benedictine Sisters of Covington, 1959 to present; Co-Founder and Present Coordinator, Mannafold Time and Space House, 1974 to present; Planner, Coordinator, Writer and Musician, Innumerable Prayer or Reflection Experiences. Honors and Awards: *Wall Street Journal* Fellowship, 1962; National Science Foundation Fellowship, 1964-68; Catholic Communications Foundation Scholarship, 1981; Listed in *Who's Who of American Women, Men and Women of Distinction, Personalities of the West and Midwest, Community Leaders.* Address: 2500 Amsterdam Road, Covington, Kentucky 41016.

Wirtschafter, Irene N

Tax Consultant, Real Estate Agent and Amway Distributor. Personal: Born August 5 in Elgin, Illinois; Daughter of David A. and Ethel G. Nerove; Widow. Education: B.C.S., Columbus University. Military: Served in the United States Navy in Supply Corps, Retiring at rank of Captain; Sea Duty, 1956; Treasurer and member of the board of HTR, Inc., Internal Revenue Agent, United States Treasury Office of International Operations; Commercial Instrument Pilot SEL SES; 17 Air Races. Organizational Memberships: Association of Enrolled Agents; National Aviation Club; AAVW. Community Activities: International Platform Association; The Retired Officers Association; Reserve Officers Association (chapter vice president for the Navy); Association of Naval Aviators (charter member); Naval Order of the United States, National Commandry (charter member); Naval Reserve Association (national treasurer, 1977-79; national advisory committee, 1979 to present); Retiree Council, Patrick Air Force Base; The 99s (international section and chapter offices); Senate Senior Intern Program, 1981; Brevard Symphony Guild; Girl Scouts of America (past troop leader); Civil Air Patrol (lieutenant colonel; mission pilot); Co-Chairman, Washington, D.C. International Women's Year Takeoff Dinner; Johnny Horizon Clean-Up Campaign (chairman, College Park Day, 1975); International Forest of Friendship (national committee, 1976 to present); Founder of Senior Action Committee, 1981. Honors and Awards: Honorary Citizen, Vancouver, Canada, Winnipeg, Atchison, Kansas; Kentucky Colonel; Louisiana Colonel; Air Race Trophies; Golf Trophies; Ninety Nines Achievement Award, 1965. Address: (home) 1825 Minutemen Causeway, Cocoa Beach, Florida 32931; (business) 2500 Q St. N.W., Washington, D.C. 10007.

Irene N Wirtschafter

Witt, Louise Schaub

Business Woman, Writer, Lecturer, Consultant. Personal: Born February 14, 1914; Daughter of Russell and Stella Turner Schaub (both deceased); Married Keith L. Witt; Mother of Marjorie W. Stevens, Thomas K., Philip K., Mary Catherine W. Russell, Susan. Education: Attended Independence Junior College, Kansas, and Kansas University. Career: Owner and Operator, The Gallery Gifts and Graphic Arts, Prairie Village, Kansas; Internationally-Recognized Author on Collector Plates; Conductor of Wonderful World of Plates Tour to European Factories; Special Consultant to Erik Ehrmann, Author of *Hummel Book;* Editorial Board Member, *Plate World* Magazine; Lecturer on Collectors Items from London, England, to California. Organizational Memberships: International Platform Association; Registered Bridal Consultant; National League of Pen Women. Community Activities: Daughters of the American Revolution. Published Works: *Wonderful World of Plates,* First Book on This Topic. Honors and Awards: Guest of Honor and Recipient of Winnie Watson Award, 3rd International Plate Collectors Convention, 1979; Listed in *World Who's Who of Women, Who's Who of American Women, Personalities of America, Personalities of the Midwest.* Address: 4324 West 70 Terrace, Prairie Village, Kansas 66208.

Witt, Neil Orand

Educator, Management Consultant. Personal: Born October 30, 1941; Son of Mr. and Mrs. Orand Witt. Education: Certificate, Southern Nevada University, 1965; A.S., Clark County Community College, 1974; B.S., University of Nevada-Las Vegas, 1976;

M.B.A., Golden Gate University, 1980. Military: Served in the United States Navy to E3, 1959-65, with Honorable Discharge. Career: Public Relations, KFM/KUEG Radio, 1980-82; Coordinator of Business Laboratory, Educator and Management Consultant, M.C.S. Associates; Instructor, Business, Nevada State Prison, 1981 to present; Technical Consultant, Lincoln County Hospital, 1974; Instructor, C.E.T.A. Program, 1979-80; Registered Radiologic Technologist, 1965-79; Senior Corpsman, United States Naval Hospital, Balboa. Organizational Memberships: American Management Association; National Business Education Association; American Association of University Professors; American Registry of Radiologic Technologists; American Society of Radiologic Technologists. Community Activities: Muscular Dystrophy Association (volunteer, 1981). Honors and Awards: Listed in *Who's Who in Finance and Industry, Who's Who in the West, Who's Who in the World.* Address: 5809 Granada Avenue, Las Vegas, Nevada 89107.

Wittcoff, Constance Cynthia

Researcher, Social Psychologist. Personal: Born November 12, 1931; Daughter of Noman Ward and Therese Budwig Clein; Mother of Mark, Caroline. Education: B.A., Stanford University, 1952; M.A., Washington University, 1977; Ph.D. in progress, Washington University, 1979 to present. Career: Television Producer; Educational Broadcaster; Counselor for Women, University of Missouri-St. Louis; Researcher, Washington University Medical School, Department of Psychology in Psychiatry. Organizational Memberships: National Association of Professional Broadcasters; American Association of University Professors; American Association of Higher Education; Missouri Psychology Association; American Association of Educational Researchers; American Association of Behaviour Therapy; American Personnel and Guidance Association. Community Activities: Child Guidance Clinic (board of directors, 1981 to present); Adult Education Council (board of directors, 1978 to present); Women's Association, St. Louis Symphony Society, Jr. Division, 1960-68; Friends Committee, St. Louis Certified Museum, Contemporary Art Council, 1968-75; Stanford University Alumni of St Louis (director, 1979 to present); Dance Concert Society (director, 1972-78); Danforth Foundation Family Project (consultant, 1979); Honors and Awards: Numerous Civic and Community Awards. Address: 50 Randelay Dr., St. Louis, Missouri 63124.

Wolf, Seymour L

Business Executive. Personal: Born May 12, 1921; Son of Charles and Mae Lando Wolf (both deceased); Married Ellie Schreiber; Father of Susan Coval, Steve, Charles. Education: Northwestern University, Evanstown, Illinois, 1941; LL.B., College Pacific, Stockton, California, 1943. Military: Served in the United States Army Security and Intelligence Division 1952, Provost Marshall's Office 1943-45, and Military Police 1944-45. Career: President, Ceramic World; Vice-President, Selected Brands, Limited. Community Activities: Justice of the Peace, Niles Township, Cook County, Illinois. Religion: Jewish. Honors and Awards: Services to the Community and Industry; City of Hope Appreciation Award; World Golf Hall of Fame, 1977; Roger Sullivan Recognition Award; All-City Football, All-State, 1940; Parichy Football Conference; 49'ers Football Conference; Canadian Football Conference; Listed in *Who's Who in the Midwest, Personalities of the West and Midwest.* Address: 2245 Vista Court, Northbrook, Illinois 60062.

Wolfe, Deborah Cannon Partridge

Professor of Education, Associate Minister. Personal: Born December 22; Daughter of Rev. Dr. and Mrs. David Wadsworth Cannon; Mother of H. Roy Partridge Jr. Education: B.S. Jersey City State College; M.A., Ed.D., Columbia University; Advanced Study at Vassar College, University of Pennsylvania, Union Theological Seminary. Career: Professor of Education, Queens College of City University of New York, Flushing, New York; Professor, Head of the Department of Elementary Education and Director of Graduate Work, Tuskegee Institute; Visiting Professor, Grambling College, New York University, Fordham University, University of Michigan, Texas College, Columbia University, University of Illinois, Wayne State University; Associate Minister, First Baptist Church, Cranford, New Jersey, 1975 to present. Organizational Memberships: National Education Association (life member); American Association of University Women (national education chairman); American Association of University Professors; International Reading Association; National Society for the Study of Education; Association of Childhood Education; Association of Supervision and Curriculum Development (chairman, review committee); American Association for the Advancement of Science (chairman, teacher education; vice-chairman, commission of science education; trustee, Science Service); Church Women United (permanent representative to the United Nations); National Alliance of Black School Educators (past national president); Zeta Phi Beta Sorority, Inc. (international grand basileus). Community Activities: Council of National Organizations for Children and Youth (secretary); Lisle Fellowship (board of directors); National Council of Negro Women (vice-president); National Conference on Christians and Jews (education committee); National Association of Business and Professional Women (chairman, speakers bureau); Board of Education, Cranford, New Jersey (citizens advisory committee); New Jersey State Board of Higher Education; New Jersey State Board of Education. Honors and Awards: National Honor Society, Cranford High School, New Jersey; Honor Society, New Jersey State Teachers College, Jersey City; Kappa Delta Pi Honor Society in Education, Columbia University; Pi Lambda Theta Honor Society, Columbia University; Fellowship, General Education Board; Invitation to White House Conference on Children and Youth, Presidents Truman, Eisenhower, and Johnson; Citation for Outstanding Contribution to the Religious and Civic Welfare of America, National Baptist Convention; Invitation to White House Conference on Education, President Eisenhower; Honorary Member, National Society for the Prevention of Juvenile Delinquency, Inc.; Citizens Advisory Committee on Youth Fitness, Appointed by President Eisenhower; Invitation to Inaugurations of President John F. Kennedy and President Lyndon B. Johnson; High School Named in Her Honor, Macon County, Alabama; Dormitory Named in Her Honor, Trenton State College, New Jersey; National Achievement Award, National Association of Negro Business and Professional Women's Clubs, Inc., 1958; Woman of the Year, Delta Beta Zeta Chapter of Zeta Phi Beta Sorority, 1959; Woman of the Year, Women of Morgan State College, Baltimore, Maryland, 1959; Outstanding Black Woman, Radcliffe College, 1980; Delta Kappa Gamma Honor Society, Queens, New York, 1972; Phi Delta Kappa Fraternity, Rutgers University Chapter, First Woman Initiated in This Chapter; *Amsterdam News* Honoree, 1959. Address: P.O. Box 370, Cranford, New Jersey 07016.

Wolfe, Jane Elisabeth

Management Consultant. Personal: Born June 2, 1922; Daughter of George J. and Elisabeth Brumm Wolf; Married Arthur V. Wolfe; Mother of Brett, Kent, Grant. Education: B.S., Indiana University, 1943; Graduate Study, Texas A.&M. University, 1970. Career: Management Consultant and President, Local Government Management Consulting Company, Pittsburg, Texas; Vice-President and Partner, Arthur Wolfe and Associates, Management Consultants. Organizational Memberships: Mountain States Management Association (presentation of paper at conference, Estes Park, Colorado, 1978); Management Department of Texas A.&M. University (guest lecturer). Community Activities: Texas Commission on the Arts (appointment to its community arts review panel, 1980); Texas Assembly of Arts Councils (appointment to Texas liaison committee for the Arts, 1978; state president, 1975-77; state treasurer, 1974; co-organizer, 1973); Arts Council of Brazos Valley (president, 1974-75; incorporating officer, 1970); Citizens for Historic Preservation, Brazos County, Texas (organizer, 1974); Youth Symphony Concerts, Brazos County, Texas (treasurer, 1970-73); American Association of University Women (Bryan-College Station Branch, treasurer, 1970-72; organizer of sponsorship of Cleveland, Ohio Ballet performances for children, 1966; state treasurer of Alabama state division, 1964-66; state mass media chairman of Alabama state division, 1963; organizer of sponsorship of Mobile Ballet performances for children, 1960-62; treasurer, Mobile branch, 1958-60); Reynolds Parent-Teacher Association (president, 1956); League of Women Voters; Young Women's Christian Association; Symphony Society; Federated Women's Club. Religion: Presbyterian Church; Officer and Board Member of Women's Organizations, Several Cities. Honors and Awards: Outstanding Woman of Brazos Valley, Selected by the Bryan-College Station Chamber of Commerce and Other Local Organizations, 1978; Outstanding Person for the Arts, Brazos Valley, 1976; Honorary Member, Association of Students from Mexico at Texas A.&M. University, 1976; Co-Sponsor, Organization of Students from India, Texas A.&M. University, 1971; Recognition for efforts to bring E.T.V. to Mobile, Governor of Alabama, 1964; Listed in Seven National and International Biographical Publications. Address: 18 Meadowlake Estates, Texas 75686.

Wolfe, Margaret Ripley

Professor of History. Personal: Born February 3, 1947; Daughter of Clarence E. and Gertrude B. Ripley; Married David E. Wolfe; Mother of Stephanie Ripley. Education: B.S. 1967, M.A. 1969, East Tennessee State University; Ph.D., University of Kentucky, 1974. Career: Professor of History, East Tennessee State University; Classroom Teacher, Hawkins County Public Schools, Rogersville, Tennessee. Organizational Memberships: Tennessee Historical Society; Southern Historical Association; Southern Association of Women Historians (president-elect, 1982-83); Organization of American Historians (Tennessee Representative to membership committee, 1977 to present). Community Activities: Sullivan County American Revolution Bicentennial Committee (advisor, 1975-76); East Tennessee State University Foundation (contributor; Crawford-Williams Fund executive committee member); Title IA Project, Hawkins County, Tennessee (consultant, summer 1979); *Glamour* Magazine (working women's panel); Conference on Status of Women in Higher Education in Tennessee (representative, 1977); National Endowment for the Humanities (public project grant proposals reviewer). Religion: Independent. Honors and Awards: Magna Cum Laude Graduate, 1967; Graduate Assistantship, East Tennessee State University, 1968; Outstanding Graduate Student in History, East Tennessee State University, 1968; Haggin Fellow, University of Kentucky, 1972-73; Distinguished Faculty Member, East Tennessee State University, 1977; East Tennessee State University Foundation Research Award, 1979; Listed in *Who's Who of American Women, World Who's Who of Women*. Address: Route 9 Box 6, Church Hill, Tennessee 27642.

Leo Wollman

Wollman, Leo

Physician, Psychiatrist. Personal: Born March 14, 1914; Son of Joseph and Sarah Wollman; Married Eleanor Rakow Wollman; Father of Arthur Lee, Bryant Lee. Education: B.S., Columbia University, 1934; M.S., New York University, 1938; M.D., Edinburgh Medical School, 1942. Career: Physician; Psychiatrist. Organizational Memberships: American Society of Psychosomatic Dentistry and Medicine (president, 1968-72; journal editor, 1968 to present; executive director, 1974 to present); Society for Scientific Study of Sex (immediate past president, 1979-81); Royal Medical Society (president, 1940); American Society of Clinical Hypnosis (life fellow); American Medical Writers Association (life fellow); New York Academy of Science (life fellow); American Society of Psychical Research (life fellow); National Association on Standard Medical Vocabulary (secretary, 1964 to present); Academy of Psychosomatic Medicine (secretary, 1965-66). Published Works: *Write Yourself Slim*, 1966; *Eating Your Way to a Better Sex Life*, 1982; Films, including *I Am Not This Body* 1970, *Strange Her* 1971, *Let Me Die A Woman* 1978. Honors and Awards: Elected to Royal Medico-Psychological Association of England, 1970; Certificates of Award, American Society of Psychosomatic Dentistry and Medicine, 1966, 1968; Pioneer in Hypnosis Award, Jules Weinstein Annual Award, 1964; Certificate of Award for Significant Contribution to the Advancement of Hypnosis in the Therapeutic Arts, American Society of Clinical Hypnosis, 1968; Certificate of Award, Academy of Psychosomatic Medicine, 1962. Address: 4505 Beach 45 Street, Brooklyn, New York 11224.

Womack, Sharon Genelle

Director of Department of Library, Archives and Public Records. Personal: Born June 13, 1940; Daughter of Mary Martin; Widow. Education: B.S.B.A. 1972, Master of Library Science 1976, University of Arizona; Attended Phoenix College, 1961-67. Career: Department of Library, Archives and Public Records, State Capitol, Phoenix, Arizona, Director, Deputy Director; Director, Maricopa County Library; Director, Miami Memorial-Gila County Library; Reference Librarian, University of Arizona Social Sciences Department; Library Assistant, University of Arizona Government Documents Section. Organizational Memberships: Arizona State Library Association (president, 1977-78); Southwest Library Association (executive board, 1977-78); American Library Association (advisory committee, 1976 to present). Address: 6810 N. 29th Lane, Phoenix, Arizona 85017.

Sharon Womack

Wood, Arletta Renee

Booking Agency President and Founder. Personal: Born April 19, 1945; Daughter of Clem and Sarah Hairston (both deceased); Education: Graduate of East High School, Columbus, Ohio, 1963; Business Administration/English, Howard University, 1964-66. Career: Founder and President, Affiliated Enterprises, Inc., Booking Agency, 1967 to present; Beauty Instructor, 1971-79; President of Better Informed to Counsel His/Her Eclat Success, a Subsidiary Corporation of A.E.I.; Executive and Administrative Positions with Howard University's Botany Department, American Federation of Teachers, Americans United for Separation of Church and State, Air Transport Association of America, Ohio State Department of Education. Organizational Memberships: International Platform Association; International Toastmistress Association; International Toastmasters Association; American Society of Professional and Executive Women; American Management Association; American Film Institute; American Federation of Musicians; Employees Association of Air Transport Association (president). Community Activities: Notary Public, State of Maryland, Montgomery County, 1978-80. Honors and Awards: Arletta Renee Day Proclamation by Mayor Marion Barry Jr., Washington, D.C., January 8, 1982; Listed in *Who's Who in Finance and Industry, Who's Who in the South*. Address: 2418 Homestead Drive, Silver Spring, Maryland 20902.

Wood, Lucille

Educator and Coach. Personal: Born January 9, 1931; Daughter of George S. and Edna Myres Wood (mother now deceased). Education: Graduate, Louisville High School, 1949; A.A., East Central Junior College, 1951; B.S., 1953, M.A., 1955, University of Southern Mississippi. Career: Physical Education Instructor and Women's Basketball Coach, East Central Junior College, Decatur,

Mississippi, 1955 to present; Physical Education Instructor and Tennis/Basketball Coach, Copial-Lincoln Junior College, Wesson, Mississippi, 1953-55. Organizational Memberships: National Education Association; Mississippi Association of Educators; Delta Kappa Gamma; Mississippi Junior College Faculty Association; National Junior College Coaches Association; Mississippi Junior College Coaches Association. Religion: Member of Calvary Baptist Church, Louisville, Mississippi (B.S.U. board of directors, East Central Junior College, 1974-78). Honors and Awards: East Central Junior College Alumna of the Year, 1964; Mississippi Junior College Women's Basketball All-Star Coach, 1978 and 1981; Mississippi Association of Coaches "Coach of the Year", 1979; Mississippi Junior College Association "Coach of the Year", 1979; National Junior College "Coach of the Year" Top 20, 1979; Member of Stayfree National Coach of the Year Selection Committee, 1980 and 1981; Coached championship basketball teams in 1968, 1970, 1973, 1976, 1979 (division champions in 1976 and 1979); Coached teams in regional tournaments in 1973, 1977, 1978, 1979, 1980. Address: Route 2, Box 303, Louisville, Mississippi, 39339.

Wood, Marylaird (Larry)

Journalist. Personal: Born in Sandpoint, Idaho; Daughter of Edward Hayes and Alice McNeel Small; Married W. Byron Wood on January 30, 1942 (divorced May 1975); Mother of Mary, Marcia, Barry. Education: B.A., magna cum laude, University of Washington, 1938; M.A., 1940; Undertook postgraduate studies at Stanford University, 1941-42, University of California-Berkeley, 1943-44; Certificate in Photography, 1971; Postgraduate studies in journalism, University of Wisconsin, 1971-72, University of Minnesota, 1971-72, University of Georgia, 1972-73. Career: By-Line Columnist, Oakland (California) *Tribune*, *San Francisco Chronicle*, 1946 to present; Feature Writer, *Odyssey*, *Checron U.S.A.*, *California Today*, *Motorland*, Western Region *Christian Science Monitor*, C.S.M. Radio Syndicate and International News, 1973 to present; Stringer, *Travelday* magazine, 1976 to present; Regional Correspondent, *Spokane* magazine; California Correspondent, *Seattle Times Sunday* magazine; Freelance Writer for a number of magazines including: *Parents'*, *Sports Illustrated*, *Mechanix Illustrated*, *Oceans*, *Sea Frontiers*, *House Beautiful*, *American Home*, *Off-Duty*, and other national magazines, 1946 to present; Contributing Editor, *Fodor's California*, *Fodor's San Francisco*, *Science '83*; Director of Public Relations, Northern California Association of Phi Beta Kappa, 1969 to present; Assistant Professor of Journalism, San Diego State University, 1975 to present; Professor of Journalism, San Jose State University, Spring 1976; Assistant Professor of Journalism, California State University, Hayward; Director of Public Relations/Consultant in the Field of Science, Environmental Affairs and Recreation to numerous firms, institutions and associations. Organizational Memberships: Public Relations Society of America; National School Public Relations Association; Environmental Consultants of North America; International Environmental Consultants; Oceanic Society; International Oceanographic Society; American Association of Education in Journalism; University of Washington Ocean Sciences Alumni Association (charter member); Investigative Reporters and Editors; Society of Travel Writers of America; Society of Professional Journalists; Women in Communications; California Academy of Environmental News Writers; National Press Photographers Association; San Francisco Press Club; Eastbay Women's Press Club; California Writers Club; Sigma Delta Chi; Theta Sigma Phi; Association for Education in Journalism (executive board, magazine division/newspaper division, 1976-82); National Association of Education in Journalism and Society of American Travel Writers Joint Contest (chairman); American Book Awards (judge). Community Activities: Public Relations Director: Young Women's Christian Association (Y.W.C.A.); YM-YW USO Seattle 1942-46; Y.W.C.A., Oakland, California, 1946-56; Children's Home Society, California, 1946-56; Children's Medical Center, Northern California, 1946-70; Eastbay Regional Park District, 1946-58; California Spring Garden Shows, 1946-58; Girl Scouts of U.S.A., Oakland, 1948-56; Speaker for Educational Institutions and Professional Groups, 1946 to present; Junior Center of Arts, Oakland (secretary 1952 to present); Volunteer Public Relations Director: American Cancer Society, Young Men's Christian Association (Y.M.C.A.), 1946-52; American Red Cross (public relations writer 1946-56); Consultant: Oakland Park Department; Y.M.C.A., Seattle, Oakland; Camp Fire Girls, Oakland (board of directors); Joaquin Miller Parent Teacher Association, Oakland; California State Parks Foundation (trustee 1976). Honors and Awards: Received Citations from U.S. Forest Service 1975 and the National Park Service 1976; Winner of Special Award, Discover America Travel Organization; Award for Architectural Coverage and Art Coverage, Oakland Museum; Citation for Features on Nation's First National Historical Reserve, Ebey's Landing on Whidbey Island and for Work on Bald Eagles in Klamath National Wildlife Refuge with U.S. Fish and Wildlife Service; Chosen to Join Selected Press in Covering the U.S. Navy's New Patrol Hydrofoil Missileship Squadron; Representing Press at First International Hydrofoil Conference, Nova Scotia, July 1981; Listed in Professional Journalistic and Photographic Rosters and in *Who's Who in America*, *Who's Who of American Women*, *Who's Who in the West*, *Who's Who in Finance and Industry*, *Who's Who in the World*. Address: 6161 Castle Dr., Oakland, California 94611.

Stella Woodall

Wood, Sumner Sr

Lawyer. Personal: Born in 1902; Married Mary Rawlings (deceased), Second Wife Peggy Angel; Father of Sumner Jr., David Eliab, Judson Rawlings, Brooks C. B., Octavia Wood Cooper, Wriley C. A. Education: S.B., Harvard University, 1925; LL.B., George Washington University; J.D. with honors, George Washington University School of Law, 1968. Career: Lawyer in District of Columbia, 1933 to present; Co-Trustee with Two Banks. Organizational Memberships: Harvard Club of the District of Columbia. Community Activities: Mason, 1922 to present; Rotary Club of Rockville, Maryland; District of Columbia Society of Mayflower Descendants. Religion: Vestry Christ Episcopal Church. Published Works: *Malta*, 1935; *The Virginia Bishop*, 1961; *Laws Everyone Should Know*, 1941; *The Wood Family Index*, 1966; *Cupid's Path in Ancient Plymouth*, 1957; *The Horseshoe of the Potomac*, 1973. Honors and Awards: J.D. with honors, 1968. Address: 19430 Beallsville Road, Beallsville, Maryland 20839.

Woodall, Stella

Biographer, Poet, Editor, Publisher. Personal: Born January 15, 1899; Widow; Mother of Orena Ruth Proctor James, Anna Warren Proctor Frost, Clara Elizabeth Woodall Urban. Education: Doctor of Literature, Institute de Artes y Humanidades, Andora; Doctor of Letters and Humanities. Career: President-Director and Editor-Publisher, *Adventures in Poetry* Magazine; United States Air Force Historian-Writer, with One Air Force History Selected as Model History for All Flying/Training Air Force Bases Worldwide. Organizational Memberships: Stella Woodall Poetry Society International (president); Patriotic Poetry Seminar (president-director of international seminar); American Poetry League (national president); National League of American Pen Women (charter president, San Antonio branch); La Junta Study Club (president); *International Who's Who of Poetry* (editorial advisory board); International Academy of Poets (vice-chancellor); United Poets Laureate International (public relations chairman); World Poetry Society (national liaison officer); The New York Poetry Forum (life member); World Poets Resource Center, New York City (honorary member); Armed Forces Writers' League (past president). Community Activities: *Community Leaders and Noteworthy Americans* (judge, editorial and advisory board; honorary member); Texas Senate Advisory Council on Legislative Affairs; Beautify San Antonio Association (director); Centro Studi e Scambi International, Rome, Italy; Texas Commission on the Arts and Humanities; National Association of Retired Federal Employees. Religion: Methodist Church, San Antonio; Chairman, Stella Woodall Circle, 8½ Years. Honors and Awards: Editorial Advisory Board, American Biographical Institute; Churchmanship Award for Chairing Stella Woodall Circle; Two Citations in International Hall of Fame for Women of Distinction, World Poetry Society;

Freedoms Foundation Award; Two Gold Laurel Leaf Crowns, United Poets Laureate International; Silver Bowl for Services as Chairman of Strategy Board Round Table, San Antonio Women's Club; Gold Plaque, Stella Woodall Poetry Society International Members; Gold Plaque, Third World Congress of Poets, Baltimore, Maryland; Named Mrs. Uncle Sam, Bicentennial Representative, 1976; Gold Plaque in Appreciation of Cooperation in the Celebration of the United States of America's Bicentennial; Silver Hand-Carved Praying Hands Locket for Published Prayers; Hundreds of Poems Dedicated to Her; Dr. Stella Poetry Pattern Named for Her by its Inventor, James Gray of California; Listed in *Community Leaders and Noteworthy Americans, American Society of Distinguished Citizens, National Social Register, Who's Who in Texas, Personalities of the South, International Who's Who in Poetry, Book of Honor, The Writer's Directory, International Who's Who in Community Service, The World Who's Who of Women, International Authors and Writers Who's Who, Dictionary of International Biography, Who's Who of American Women, International Biographical Association Yearbooks, Notable Americans, Notable Americans of the Bicentennial Era, Women of Distinction*. Address: 206 Patricia Drive, Junction, Texas 76849.

Woodard, Dorothy Marie

Industrial Developer. Personal: Born February 7, 1932; Daughter of Gerald E. and Bessie Katherine Floeck (both deceased); Married Jack W. Woodard (deceased). Education: Studies at New Mexico State University, 1950, 1980, 1981; Thomas Hill Insurance Course Degree, United Nations Insurance Company, 1968. Career: United Nations Insurance Company, Broker, Agent, District Manager, 1968-74; Western National Life Insurance Company, Broker, Agent, 1976-81; Industrial Development, Executive Director for City of Tucumcari, New Mexico, 1979 to present; Owner, Manager, Western Oil Company, 1950 to present. Organizational Memberships: Regional Eastern Plains Council of Governments (board of directors); Bravo Dome CO_2 (board of directors); Resource Conservation and Development Area Council (board of directors); Railroad Planning Conference Panel, State of New Mexico. Community Activities: New Mexico Industrial Development Executive Association; Chamber of Commerce; National Association for Female Executives, Inc., International Travelers Association; Mesa Country Club. Honors and Awards: Top Agent, United Nations Insurance Company, 1968, 1969. Address: P.O. Box 823, Tucumcari, New Mexico 88401-0823.

Woodruff, Georgia Delores Wilbur

Inservice Director. Personal: Born March 31, 1926; Daughter of Clarence Nelson (deceased) and Gertrude Alice Sewell Wilbur; Married James Calvin (deceased); Mother of James Calvin Jr., Barbara Jean, Jesse J. Education: Nursing Diploma; A.A., Lamar College. Career: Registered Nurse and Inservice Director, Mary Dickerson Memorial Hospital. Organizational Memberships: American Nurses Association; National League of Nurses. Community Activities: Democratic Party; President's Committee. Religion: Pentecostal. Honors and Awards: Listed in *Who's Who of American Women*. Address: 511 Mays Street, Jasper, Texas 75951.

Dorothy M Woodard

Woodruff, Jean Leigh

Assistant Professor and Department Chairman. Personal: Born September 19, 1950; Daughter of Mrs. Jean Tulli. Education: B.S., History, University of North Carolina-Greensboro, 1972; M.B.A., Marketing, Emory University, 1974; Study at Clemson University, 1975-80; Certificate in Norwegian, University of Oslo, Norway, Summer 1979; Work Toward Ph.D., Marketing and Management Science, University of Georgia, 1977-80; Certificates in Norwegian and Economics Policy, University of Oslo, Summer 1982. Career: Clemson University, Chairperson of Marketing and Management Seminars of the Office of Professional Development 1975-81, Instructor 1974-81; Editor, *Textile Marketing Newsletter*, 1981; Assistant Editor, *Textile Marketing Letter*, 1975-80; Assistant Professor, Department Chairperson 1982-83, Western New England College. Organizational Memberships: American Marketing Association; Southern Marketing Association; Mid-Atlantic Marketing Association (1980 proceedings editor); Western Massachusetts International Trade Association; Phi Gamma Nu; The Institute of Management Science. Community Activities: Western New England College Women; Western New England College Student Chapter of Advertising and Marketing Club (faculty associate, 1981); Clemson Collegiate Civitan (faculty advisor, 1975-81); Phi Gamma Nu (faculty advisor, 1975-81); Girl Scouts of America (troop leader, 1974-81); University Women's Club, 1974-81; American Association of University Women, 1974-81; League of Women Voters, 1974-76; Helping Hands, 1979-81; Volunteer, Quadrangle Association, 1981. Religion: New Life Baptist Church; Women's Bible Conference, 1981; Bill Gothard Conferences, 1978. Honors and Awards: Young Careerist of the Month, Anderson, South Carolina, September 1977, Business and Professional Women's Club; Certificate of Outstanding Service, South Carolina Civitan, 1981; Certificate of Recognition, South Carolina Department of Social Services, 1981; Listed in *Outstanding Young Women of America, Who's Who in the South and Southwest, Personalities of the South, World Who's Who of Women, International Who's Who of Intellectuals, Personalities of America, International Youth in Achievement*. Address: 108 Breckwood Circle, Springfield, Massachusetts 01119.

Woodruff, Joseph Franklin

Research Manager (retired). Personal: Born August 8, 1913; Son of Frank and Carolina Parks Woodruff (both deceased); Married Marie M. Miller on June 17, 1938; Father of Joanne Marie W. Wedder, Carolyn Jeanette W. Vail. Education: B.S., Capital University, Columbus, Ohio, 1935; Attended Ohio State University, Columbus, Ohio, 1935-36. Career: Armco, Inc., Manager 1968-77, Supervising Spectrochemist 1958-68, Senior Spectrochemist 1951-58, Spectrochemist 1946-51, Junior Research Engineer 1945-46, Spectroanalyst 1943-45, Chem-Analyst 1941-43; Instructor of Chemistry and Head of Science Department, McClain High School, Greenfield, Ohio, 1939-41; Instructor of Math, Greenhills High School, Cincinnati, Ohio, 1938-39; Instructor of Math, Physics and Chemistry, Kings Mills High School, Ohio, 1936-38. Organizational Memberships: National Education Association (life member); Ohio School Board Association; Society of Applied Spectroscopy; Canadian Society of Applied Spectroscopy; Miami Valley Spectrographic Society; American Institute of Physics; Optical Society of America; American Management Association; Cleveland Society of Spectroscopy; American Society of Testing and Materials (committees E-2, E-4, S-17); CORVA Northern Sub-Area Council; Ohio Valley Spectrographic Society. Community Activities: Free and Accepted Masons 760; R.A.M. #87; Middletown Council #136; Middletown Commandery #71; Middletown Safety Council; Middletown Area United Way; Middletown Chamber of Commerce; Forest Hills Country Club; Lions Club of Middletown; Butler County Mental Hygiene Association; Butler County Heart Association; Middletown High School Boosters Club; F.A.M.A. of Fenwick High School; Lemon-Monroe and Middletown Band Association (life member); Moose Lodge; Middletown Area Young Republicans; Ohio Historical Society; Butler County Council on Aging; Middletown Board of Education (president, 7 years; member, 1955-63, 1971, 1973); 5-County Science Awards Competition (chairman, 1955-56); Red Cross Drive, Middletown (co-chairman, 1943); Ohio School Board Association (chairman, hospitality committee, convention, 1956; finance committee chairman, 1959-63; executive board, 1957-63); Southwestern Ohio School Boards Association (executive board, 1951-63); Middletown Heart Association Drive (chairman, 1955); Capital University Alumni

Association Board, 1953-56; Citizens Advisory Committee of the Special Service Bureau, Miami University, 1956-63; Franklin, Ohio, Air Raid Warden, 1942; District War Bond Salesman, Franklin, Ohio, 1942; Boy Scouts of America (Pokey district, organizatonal and extension committee, 1949-52); Initiated Establishment of Miami University Extension Campus, Middletown, Ohio, 1962; Research Bureau of Miami University (advisory committee, 1961-65); Community-Wide Appreciation Night for Howard Cromwell, Retiring Superintendent of Schools (chairman, 1966); Middletown School District (administrative council, 1967-69); Initiated Parent-Teacher Organizations and Parent-Teacher Associations, Middletown City School District; Armco Research Employee Representatives (chairman, 1945); Research Benefit Association (chairman, 1946). Religion: First Baptist Church, Middletown, Ohio, Board of Christian Education, Building Committee, Remote Control Engineer for Radio Broadcasts 1955-59; Sunday School Teacher for Elementary, Junior High, Senior High, and Young Married Classes, First Baptist Churches in Greenfield and Kings Mills, Ohio. Published Works: "Application of Vacuum Optical Emission Spectroscopy in the Steel Industry", *Industrial Heating*, 1967; "The Use of Briquetted Samples in the Spectrochemical Analysis of Carbon and Alloy Steels and Other Metals", *Journal of the Optical Society of America*, 1950; "Quality Control of Steel Using Clock-and-Chart Recording Photoelectric Spectrometers", *Developments in Applied Spectroscopy, I*, 1962; "Introduction", *Sampling, Standards and Homogenenity;* "Rapid Spectrochemical Analysis for Control of Basic Oxygen and Open Hearth Shops", *Open Heart Proceedings*, 1964; Numerous Other Articles and Contributions to Books. Honors and Awards: Outstanding Layman Award, Ohio Association of Elementary School Principles, 1976; All-Southwest Honorary School Board, 1973; Middletown Jaycees Good Government Award, 1958; Annual Lay Award, Middletown Classroom Teachers Association and Ohio Education Association, 1966; Distinguished Service Award, Middletown Elementary Principals Association, 1975; Jaycees Man of the Year Award, 1960; Distinguished Service Award, Jaycees, 1964; American Society for Testing and Materials, H. V. Churchill Award, 1974, Joseph F. Woodruff Steel Ingot Award 1973, Award of Merit 1978, Honorary Life Member 1975, Fellow 1970; Honorary Doctor of Science, Capital University, 1981; Listed in *The International Yearbook and Statesmen's Who's Who, World Who's Who, Who's Who in Commerce and Industry, International Who's Who in Commerce and Industry, Who's Who in the Midwest, Who Knows-And What, American Men of Science, Notable Americans of the Bicentennial Era, Men of Achievement, Men and Women of Distinction, Dictionary of International Biography, Directory of Distinguished Americans.* Address: 3457 Central Avenue, Middletown, Ohio 45043.

Woods, Larry David

Lawyer/Teacher. Personal: Born September 10, 1944; Son of Mrs. Loyce Woods: Married Jinx Schwenke; Father of Rachel, Allen, Sarah. Education: B.A., Emory University, 1966; J.D., Northwestern University, 1969. Career: Lawyer/Teacher. Organizational Memberships: Tennessee Advisory Committee on Legal Services (chairman); Tennessee Bar Association; Nashville Bar Association; Continuing Legal Education (education committee). Community Activities: Committee to Re-Elect Congressman Allen (chairman, 1976, 1978); Blanton for Governor Campaign Committee, 1974; Tennesseans for McGovern, 1972; Middle Tennessee Civil Liberties Union (board of directors, 1972-79); Barkley Forum Foundation (chairman, 1972-73, 1977); Tennessee Democratic Telethon (director, 1972); National Alliance of Handgun Control Organizations, Inc. (director and general counsel). Honors and Awards: United States Law Week Award; Ford Foundation Grant for Legal Research, Northwestern National Moot Court Team; First Place, Midwestern United States Moot Court Competition; Award for Best Brief, Midwestern United States Moot Court Competition; American Jurisprudence Award in Federal Courts. Address: 121 - 17th Avenue South, Nashville, Tennessee 37203.

Willie G Woods

Woods, Margaret Staeger

Educational Consultant. Personal: Born August 21, 1911; Daughter of Mr. and Mrs. Carl Staeger (both deceased); Widow; Mother of Pamela Fay Fyman, Frederick Waring. Education: B.A. Education, Washington State University, 1932; M.Ed., University of Washington, 1954. Career: Lecturer, Creative Dramatics, University of Washington, 1949-58; High School Teacher, Seattle, 1932-37; Kindergarten Teacher, 1956, 1957; Professor of Education, Seattle Pacific University, 1958-76; Professor Emeritus, Part-Time Instructor in Creative Education, Seattle Pacific University, 1976-81. Organizational Memberships: Elementary Kindergarten Nursery Educators (president, 1964, 1969); Education Leadership Council of America (board of directors, 1979-82); A.C.E.I. (teacher education committee, 1980-82; chairman, Pacific Coast Regional Conference, 1977); National Educational Arts Association (chairman, 1974); N.A.E.Y.S. Pre-Session "Play as Education" (chairman, 1973); Director of Workshops on Early Childhood Education in Newfoundland, Puerto Rico, Australia, 1971-74. Community Activities: Your Community Program in Seattle Public Schools (director, creative dramatics, 1949-58); Founder and Director of Community-Sponsored Pre-School Creative Dramatics Program "Let's Pretend with the Fours and Fives", 1953-76; Director of Children's World of New York World's Fair, 1964; Seattle Parent-Teacher Association (first creative arts chairman, 1949-58); Washington Congress of Parents and Teachers (first creative arts chairman, 1958-62); Recorded for Speak Out on TV for Children for the Educational Broadcasting Company, 1972; Moderator, Television Series, "Creativity", KCTS, Seattle, 1944. Religion: Lecturer, Lenten Series, Congregational Church, 1954; Director, Children's World, Council of Churches, Seattle World's Fair, 1962; Director of Workshops for Baptist, Presbyterian, Lutheran Churches; Presenter, International Conference on Christian Education, Newport Beach, California, 1976; Board of Deaconesses, Fauntleroy Congregational Church, 1954-57. Published Works: *Thinking, Feeling, Experiencing: Toward Realization of Full Potential*, 1964; *Creativity: Process and Product*, 1976; "Storied Ventures", 1977; "Model for Staff Development", 1977; "Fusion of Emotion and Intellect: Right...Left, Right...Left", 1982. Honors and Awards: Life Membership, Washington Congress of Parents and Teachers, 1962; Norman Borgerson Award for Outstanding Article on Safety Education, 1964; Personality of the Day, New York World's Fair, 1964; Distinguished Service Award, Zeta Phi Eta, 1966; National Woman of the Year, Delta Zeta, 1977. Address: 1206 West Leisure, Coupeville, Washington 98239.

Woods, Willie G

Educational Administrator. Personal: Daughter of John and Jessie Woods. Education: B.A. Shaw University, Raleigh, North Carolina, 1965; M.Ed., Duke University, Durham, North Carolina, 1968; Postgraduate Study, Pennsylvania State University, Temple University, University of New Hampshire, New York University. Career: Teacher, Raleigh School District, North Carolina, 1965-67; Teacher, Caroline County School System, Preston, Maryland, 1967-69; Harrisburg Area Community College, Pennsylvania, Tutorial Coordinator 1972-78, Supervisor of The Writing Center 1975-78, Instructor, Assistant Professor, Associate Professor of English and Education 1969-81, Director of Act 101/Basic Studies Program 1981 to present. Organizational Memberships: Pennsylvania Association of Developmental Educators (board of directors, 1979 to present; conference chair, 1980, 1981; secretary, 1981-82; charter member); Western Region Act 101 Directors Council (executive committee, 1978 to present; council chair, 1981-82; subregion representative, 1980-81); Pennsylvania Black Conference on Higher Education (representative council, 1972 to present; secretary, 1977-79; conference committee, 1978-80, 1981-82); National Council of Teachers of English; National Education Association; American Association of University Professors. Community Activities: Harrisburg Area Community College Faculty Organization (faculty council, 1975-77; co-founder, professional growth committee, 1975; curriculum, instruction, library committee, 1976 to present; chairperson, community services committee for middle states self-study); Alternative Rehabilitation

Committee, Inc. (board of directors, 1978 to present); Youth Urban League; Harrisburg Area Young Men's Christian Association (board of managers, youth urban services, 1981 to present; board of managers, camp curtin branch, 1971-79); People for Progress (secretary, executive board, 1971-73); National Association for the Advancement of Colored People; Alpha Kappa Alpha Sorority, Inc.; Conductor, Many Workshops for Community and Professional Organizations. Religion: Harmony Mission Baptist Church, Maryland, Member; Church Choir, 12 Years; Speaker for Several Events & Activities. Honors and Awards: Alpha Kappa Mu National Honor Society; Certificate of Merit for Community Service, Harrisburg, Pennsylvania, 1971; Meritorious Contributor to College, Harrisburg, 1977; Outstanding Service Award, Pennsylvania Black Conference on Higher Education, 1980; Listed in *Who's Who Among Students in American Universities and Colleges, Who's Who in the East.* Address: 610 Humphrey Court Apartment 302, Harrisburg, Pennsylvania 17109.

Worker, George F Jr

Agronomist, Superintendent of Field Station. Personal: Born June 1, 1923; Son of George F. Worker Sr.; Married Donna Rae; Father of Debbie (deceased), Kent, Stephanie Shoup, Cathy, Melinda. Education: Graduate of Del Nort High School, Colorado, 1941; Attended Adams State College, Colorado, 1941-43, 1946; B.S., Colorado State University, 1949; M.S., Nebraska University, 1953. Military: Served in the United States Army Air Corps, 1943-47. Career: Assistant in Agronomy (Lincoln), Assistant County Agent (Holdridge), University of Nebraska; Agronomist and Superintendent of Imperial Valley Field Station, University of California, El Centro; Consultant, Agronomist, Dr. Tamayo, Venezuela; Manager, Field Trials, Kufra Agricultural Project, Libya; Agronomist, Hawaiian Agronomics, Iran; Agronomist, IRI, North Yemen. Organizational Memberships: Agronomy Society of America (member, western section, crop science; member, California Chapter); Gamma Sigma Delta. Community Activities: Rotary Club, 1955 to present; Meadows Union School Board, El Centro, California; Holtville Unified School Board. Published Works: Author, Chapter 8, *Agriculture in Semi-Arid Environment*; Numerous Research Papers in *Journal of Agricultural Sciences, Agronomy Journal, Crop Science Journal, California Agriculture.* Honors and Awards: Developed and Released Meloland Grain Sorghum and UC Signal Barley. Address: 1004 East Holton Road, El Centro, California 92243.

George F Worker Jr

Worley, Nancy L

Educator. Personal: Born November 7, 1951; Daughter of Lillian S. Worley. Education: B.A., University of Montevallo, 1973; M.A., Jacksonville State University, 1974; Postgraduate Study, Birkbeck College, University of London, University of Edinburgh, University of Alabama. Career: Teacher of Latin, Speech, English. Organizational Memberships: National Junior Classical League (southeast membership chairman; dramatic reading chairman); Alabama Junior Classical League (state chairman, 1979 to present); American Classical League (promotion committee); Classical Association of the Middle West and South (membership committee; vice president, 1981 to present); Decatur Education Association (president, 1979-80; vice president, 1978-79; board of directors, 1980-83; secretary, 1977-78; legislative chairman, A-vote chairman, faculty representative to state assembly, 8 years); U.T.P. Uniserv Council 5 (president, 1979-80); Alabama Education Association (president, 1983-84; president-elect, 1982-83; board of directors, 1979-82; legislative commission, public relations commission, negotiations team, IPD commission); National Education Association (resolutions committee alternate, delegate to representative assembly, 5 years); Alabama Classroom Teachers Association (president, 1982-83; vice president, 1980-81; president-elect, 1981-82); Decatur Classroom Teachers Association (president, 1980-81; board of directors, 1977-80; secretary, 1978); Virgilian Society of England and the United States; Alabama Foreign Language Teachers Association (president, 1982-83; vice president, 1981-82); National Alabama Council of Teachers of English; Alabama Speech and Theatre Association; Huntsville Literary Association; International Association for Human Relations Literary Training. Community Activities: Opportunity Toastmistress Club (vice president, secretary, parliamentarian, speech contest chairman, southeast regional audit committee); Delta Kappa Gamma, Gamma Beta Chapter (vice president); Kappa Delta Pi; American Association of University Women (president, 1981-83; division community area representative; division parliamentarian; Decatur first vice president; Decatur secretary/treasurer; scholarshp committee, creative writing committee, art fair committee); Morgan County League of Women Voters; American Field Service (student sponsor); Alabama/Madison County Young Democrats; Alabama Women's Campaign Organization; Phi Mu Alumnae of Northeast Alabama (secretary); Huntsville Broadway Theatre League (faculty sponsor); Huntsville Little Theatre Alabama Shakespeare Festival (patron); University of Montevallo Alumni Association (scholarship committee); Town and Gown Theatre of Birmingham; Alabama Cystic Fibrosis Foundation (Morgan County chairman, two years); Wheeler Basin Library Reading for the Blind; Morgan County Mental Health Association (education committee); Decatur Concert Association (membership worker); International Bus Stop (publicity chairman); Donations to St. Jude's Research Hospital, Chamber of Commerce Education Committee, Project HOPE, Girl Scouts of America, Junior Achievement, Alabama Sheriff's Boy's and Girl's Ranches. Religion: Youth Choir Pianist. Honors and Awards: Alabama's Outstanding Young Educator, 1980; Morgan County Outstanding Young Educator, 1979; Latin Scholarship Award, 1970, 1971; Phi Mu Scholarship Award, 1970, 1971, 1972; Academic Honors Scholarship, 1969; Highest Honors Scholarships, 1970, 1971, 1972; Sigma Tau Delta English Honorary Society; Kappa Delta Pi Education Honorary Society; Eta Sigma Phi Scholarship Honorary Society; Dean's List, 1969; President's List, 1970, 1971, 1972; Cum Laude Graduate, 1973; Two Young Leaders of Decatur, 1980; Listed in *Who's Who Among Students in American Universities and Colleges, Personalities of the South, Book of Honor, Personalities of America, Directory of Distinguished Americans, Community Leaders of America, Outstanding Young Women of America.* Address: 622 Seventh Avenue, Southwest, Decatur, Alabama 35601.

Nancy L Worley

Wray, John Lawrence

Vice-President of Engineering. Personal: Born June 17, 1935; Son of Lawrence P. Wray; Married Sally Gerdes; Father of Mary, Nancy, Carolyn. Education: B.S., Mechanical Engineering, University of Missouri, 1957; M.S. Mechanical Engineering, Stanford University, 1958; M.B.A., University of Santa Clara, California, 1966. Military: Served in the United States Air Force, 1958-62. Career: Quadrex Corporation, Vice-President of Computer Systems and Operations 1982 to present, Vice-President of Engineering 1980-82, Director of Engineering Services at M.S.C. 1978-80, Manager of Mechanical Engineering at M.S.C. 1978; General Electric Company, San Jose, California, Manager of Market Research and Planning 1976-78, Manager of Product Planning 1972-76, Area Sales Manager 1970-72, Manager of Licensing and Safety Engineering 1968-70, Manager of Mechanical, Electrical and Chemical System Engineering 1967-68, Manager of Core Proposal Engineering 1965-67, Proposal Engineer 1963-65, Program Engineer 1962-63; University of Virginia Instructor, George Mason College, Arlington, Virginia, 1961-62. Organizational Memberships: American Society of Mechanical Engineers; American Nuclear Society (professional divisions committee, 1980-83); Registered Professional Engineer, States of California, Illinois, New York, North Carolina, Ohio, Oregon, Michigan, Minnesota, Texas, Missouri, Oklahoma, Pennsylvania. Community Activities: Elementary School District, Saratoga, California (financial committee, 1974-75). Honors and Awards: United States Air Force Commendation Medal. Address: 14961 Haun Court, Saratoga, California 95070.

Wretlind, Arvid Karl Johannes

Visiting Professor. Personal: Born January 28, 1919; Son of Johannes and Agnes Wretlind; Married Astrid Wretlind; Father of Bengt, Sophie W. Ekman. Education: M.D., Medical School, Karolinska Institutet, Stockholm, Sweden, 1949. Career: Visiting Professor, Department of Human Nutrition College of Physicians and Surgeons, Columbia University, New York, 1980 to present; Head of Vitrum and Cutter-Vitrum Institute of Human Nutrition, Stockholm, Sweden and Berkeley, California, 1975-80; Professor and Head, Department of Human Nutrition, Karolinska Institutet, Stockholm, Sweden, 1970-75; Professor and Head, Department of Nutrition and Food Hygiene, Swedish National Institutes of Health, 1962-70; Assistant Professor of Pharmacology, 1949-62. Organizational Memberships: New York Academy of Science; Swedish Society of Physicians; Swedish Royal Academy of Engineering Sciences; Rotary International. Community Activities: Swedish Food Law Committee (chairman of committee that proposed the new Swedish Food Administration, 1964-70); Fourth W. H. Sebrell Junior International Lecturer on Nutrition, 1979. Honors and Awards: Honorary Degree of Doctor of Science, Rutgers, The State Universioty of New Jersey, 1980; Swedish Royal Order of Polar Star, 1965; Commander of Swedish Royal Order of Vasa, 1972; Annual Golden Medal Prize, Swedish Royal Academy of Engineering Sciences, 1979. Address: Apartment 10J - 45 West 60th Street, New York, New York 10023.

Wright, Bessie Margaret Shrontz Roberts

Co-Owner, Secretary and Treasurer of Nursery. Personal: Born May 23, 1905; Daughter of Sarah E. Shrontz Roberts; Widow; Mother of John (Jack) Robert. Education: Graduate of Rupert High School, 1923; Diploma, American School of Landscape Architecture and Gardening, Newark, New York, 1965; Foreign Language, College of Southern Idaho, 1965, 1981. Career: Co-Owner, Secretary, Treasurer, Kimberly Nurseries, Inc., Twin Falls Idaho, 57 Years. Organizational Memberships: National Federation of Independent Business; Twin Falls Chamber of Commerce; American Nurseryman; Idaho Nursery Association; National Watch and Clock Collectors; B.A.R. and B.A.S. Biblical Archeology. Community Activities: Hagerman Valley Historical Society; Renobia Club #2, Twin Falls, Idaho (past president); Daughters of the Nile; Republican Party. Religion: Methodist Church; Sunday School Teacher, 1946-56. Honors and Awards: Listed in *Who's Who of American Women, Who's Who Women of the World, Who's Who in the West.* Address: P.O. Box L, Kimberly, Idaho 83341.

Wright, Carolyn Jean

Director of Nurses. Personal: Born August 30, 1945; Daughter of D. L. and Betty Davison; Married Dellis Wright; Mother of Angela Kay, (Stepmother of:) Robert Carloss, Edwin Andrew, Anna Marie W. Robertson. Education: A.D. Nursing, Boise Junior College, 1965. Career: Madison Memorial Hospital, Rexburg, Idaho, Director of Nurses, Obstetrics Supervisor, Staff Nurse; St. Luke's Hospital, Boise, Idaho, Assistant Head Nurse, Staff Nurse. Organizational Memberships: N.L.N.; Idaho Society for Nursing Service Administrators; Idaho Heart Association. Community Activities: American Red Cross Blood Drive (organizer of staffing of volunteers). Honors and Awards: Employee of the Month, August, 1979. Address: Route 1 Box 280, Rexburg, Idaho 83440.

Jeanette T Wright

Wright, Eugene Box

Lawyer, Energy Corporation Executive. Personal: Born February 21, 1943 in Fulton, Kentucky; Son of Hugh French and Madeline Box Wright; Married Linda Gatlin; Father of Laura Elizabeth, Alan Fulton, Julia Anne. Education: B.A., Southern Methodist University, 1965; J.D., University of Houston, 1968. Career: Private Practice of Law, Cleveland, Texas; President, Wright Energy Corporation; Approved Attorney, United States Life Title Insurance Company, Dallas, Southwest Title Insurance Company, Title Insurance Company of Minnesota, Pioneer National Title Insurance Company, Lawyers Title Insurance Corporation, Chicago Title Insurance Company, Stewart Title Guaranty Company; Former Positions include Secretary, Director, Olympic, Inc.; Secretary, Director, Cleveland Publishing Company, Inc.; Director, Secretary, Triangle Press, Inc.; Director, Secretary, Splendora Lumber Company; City Attorney, City of Cleveland, Texas, 1969-72. Organizational Memberships: Chambers-Liberty Bar Association (president); West Liberty Industrial Foundation (director); Texas Bar Association; United States Supreme Court Bar; United States Court of Appeals; 5th Circuit Court; United States District Court; Eastern District Court of Texas; American Judicature Society; American Trial Lawyers Association. Community Activities: City of Cleveland, Texas (bicentennial committee chairman; United Nations Day chairman, 1977, 1978); Cleveland Rotary Club (president); Greater Cleveland Chamber of Commerce (director); Cleveland Country Club (secretary); Phi Mu Alpha Sinfonis; Delta Sigma Pi. Honors and Awards: Honorary Kentucky Colonel, 1971; Listed in *Who's Who in Texas, Outstanding Young Men of America, Who's Who in American Law, Dictionary of International Biography, Personalities of the South, Personalities of America, International Who's Who of Intellectuals.* Address: Route 1 Box 313A, Liberty, Texas 77575.

Wright, Jeannette T

Junior College President. Personal: Born September 8, 1927; Daughter of Julius and Ida Tornow (both deceased); Married Wilfred D. Wright. Education: B.A. 1956, M.A. 1959, George Washington University; Ed.D., Boston University, 1967. Career: Teacher of Emotionally Disturbed Children, Arlington County Public Schools, Arlington, Virginia; Bay Path Junior College, President, Former Vice President, Dean of College, Dean of Students, Chairman of Department of Behavioral Sciences, Instructor in Psychology. Organizational Memberships: American Psychological Association; Massachusetts Psychological Association (fellow); National Council of Independent Junior Colleges (president, executive committee; board of directors); New England Junior College Council (board member). Community Activities: Governor's Commission on the Status of Women (commissioner, 1973-74); Baystate Medical Center (corporator, 1980 to present); Community Savings Bank (trustee, 1982 to present); Springfield Adult Education Council (board member); Auto Club of Springfield, American Automobile Association (director); Carew Girls' Club (chairman of the board, 1967-70); Girls' Club of America (New England regional chairman, national board member, 1970-71); Women's Symphony League; Joint Civic Agencies (women's division); Springfield Boys Club (board member, 1969-80); Springfield Mental Health Association (vice president, 1968-69); Longmeadow Professional Council; Springfield Women's Club; Springfield Young Women's Christian Association (past trustee). Honors and Awards: Golden Boy Award, Boys Club of America, 1974; Meritorious Achievement Award for Significant Accomplishment in Educational Administration, *Outstanding Educators of America,* 1971. Address: 130 Arlington Road, Longmeadow, Massachusetts 01106.

Wu, Jimmy Ching

Medical Radiologist. Personal: Born May 12, 1905; Son of W. P. and Loo-shih Wu (both deceased); Married to Tang Shiu-jen; Father of Chun lin, Chun-yen, 3 other children in China. Education: M.D., National Peking University of China, 1926; M.S., University of Chicago, 1932. Career: Retired Researcher and Instructor in Radiology; Intern, Peking American Medical College, China, 1926-27; Resident in Radiology, 1927-30; Instructor, Assistant and Associate Professor, 1934-40; Professor and Chairman of Department of Radiology, National Defense Medical Center, Taiwan, 1948-59; Fellow, Los Angeles Tumor Institute, California, 1955-56; Research Radioloist, New England Deaconess Hospital, Boston, Massachusetts, 1956-57; Resident in Radiology, Newark Beth Israel Hospital, 1959-61 and Newton Lower Falls Hospital (Massachusetts), 1961; Research Radiologist, Hospital for Joint Diseases, 1961-67; Associate Professor of Radiology, New York Universtiy, 1968-72; Emeritus Professor, 1972; Visiting Professor, Tokyo University, 1952-54 and University of Southern California, 1959; Chairman of Delegation to International Radiology Congress, 1953 and 1956; Chairman of Delegation to International Military Medicine and Documentations Conferences, 1958 and 1959; Exhibited new method of bronchography without anesthesia at the 1972 annual meeting of the American Roentgen Ray Society in Boston; Chairman of delegation to World Medical Congress, 1957. Organizational Memberships: American Roentgen Ray Society, 1925-81; American Association of University Professors, 1969-81; Chinese Roentgen Ray Society (president, 1948-59); Chinese Medical Association (president, 1956-57); American Medical Association; New York University Medical School Library Club. Community Activities: Member of Republican Capital Hill Club (Washington, D.C.); Advisory Board member of American Security Council; Senior Advisory Council of Young Americans for Freedom; Member of Metropolitan Republican Club; Honorary Founding Member of U.S. Senatorial Club of the U.S. Senate. Religion: Member of Christian Church. Published Works: Author of various works on chest disease and modern medicine in English and Chinese; Contributor to *World Medical Journal, American Journal of Radiology, American Journal of Roentgenology, International Congress of Radiology.* Honors and Awards: Diplomate in Radiology, Pan American Medical Association, 1971; Governor and Honored Professor, American College of Medical Imaging, 1978; Honored by Optimist Club of America, 1975; Member, International Biographical Association of Cambridge, England; Gold Medal from the Republic of China, 1952; Received various awards from the American Medical Association; Member of the Fifty Year Club of American Medicine; Received National Institute of Health grants for research in tomography, 1965; Honored by Republican Party for efforts in the election of President Ronald Reagan, 1981; Listed in *Book of Honor.* Address: 2 Birdseye Circle, Stony Brook, New York 11790.

Jimmy C Wu

Wu, William Lung-Shen

Retired Medical Doctor. Personal: Born September 1, 1921 in Hangchow, Chekiang Province, China. Education: A.S. 1943, M.D. 1946, Stanford University; M.S. Chemistry, Tulane Medical School, 1955; Diploma, United States Naval School of Aviation Medicine, 1956; Diploma, United States Air Force School of Aviation Medicine, 1961; Certificate of Training in Aviation Medicine, University of California, 1962, 1964. Military: Served in the United States Naval Reserve as Commander in the Medical Corps and received Lifetime Grade of Naval Flight Surgeon #1115, 1954-57. Career: Staff Physician, Laguna Honda Hospital, San Francisco, 1968-74; Aerospace Medical and Bioastonautical Specialist, Lovelace Foundation for Medical Education and Research, Albuquerque, New Mexico, 1965; Aerospace Medical Specialist and Medical Monitor for All Manned Tests Performed by the Life Scientist Section, 1961-65; Staff Physician for the Aviation, Space and Radiation Medical Group, General Dynamics/Convair, 1958-61; Fellow and Instructor, Tulane Medical School; Assistant Visiting Physician and Visiting Physician, Charity Hospital and Hutchinson Memorial Teaching and Diagnostic Clinics, 1948-54. Organizational Memberships: San Diego Biomedical Research Institute (fellow; board of directors, 1961-65; secretary of fellows, 1961-62; chairman of fellows, 1963); American Institute of Aeronautics and Astronautics (nominating committee, San Diego section; plant representative, life science section, 1963-65); Institute of Electrical and Electronic Engineers (vice-chairman, San Diego chapter); Professional Technical Group on Biomedical Electronics, 1962-65; Sigma Xi; New York Academy of Sciences; San Diego Biomedical Research Institute (fellow); Institute of Environmental Sciences; International Platform Association. Community Activities: Emeritus Institute, Little House, Menlo Park (board of directors); Planning, Research and Development Commission, Redwood, California. Published Works: "Applicability of Metal Coordination Principles to Metal Enzymes"; "Project Apollo Spacecraft Proposal"; *Medical Procedures Textbook for Nuclear Operations.* Honors and Awards: Listed in a Number of National and International Reference Publications. Address: Corinthian House No.219, 250 Budd Avenue, Campbell, California 95008.

Wyand, Martin Judd

Educator. Personal: Born May 28, 1931 in Greenwich, Connecticut; Married Margaret A. Knox. Education: B.A. Social Science 1953, M.A. Economics 1954, Pennsylvania State University; Ph.D. Economics, University of Illinois, Urbana, 1964; J.D., University of Denver, 1969; Graduate, Professional Military Education, Air War College, Command and Staff College, Industrial College of the Armed Forces. Military: Served in the United States Air Force, Active Duty at Andrews Air Force Base, Washington, D.C., 1954-56, attaining the rank of Lieutenant; Serves in the United States Air Force Reserves at Lowry Air Force Base, Denver, Colorado, 1956 to present, attaining the rank of Colonel. Career: Lowry Air Force Base, Denver, Colorado, Chairman of Air War College Seminar Division 1974, Academic Instructor in Armed Forces Intelligence Training Center 1978; Instructor of Economics, Pennsylvania State University, 1956-57; Administrative Assistant, Bell Telephone Company of Pennsylvania, 1957-60; Graduate Teaching Assistant in Economics, University of Illinois; Assistant, Associate and Full Professor of Economics, University of Denver, 1964 to present; Accreditation Examiner, North Central Association of Colleges and Universities. Organizational Memberships: American Economics Association; Association for Evolutionary Economics; Rocky Mountain Social Sciences Associaton; Air Force Association; Reserve Officers Association (commander, Geddes chapter); North Central Association of Colleges and Universities; American Collegiate Schools of Business. Community Activities: Colorado Right-to-Work Association (board of directors); University of Denver (faculty marshall, commencement exercises). Religion: Park Methodist Church, Denver, Colorado, Administrative Board of Directors, Bass Singer in Chancel Choir. Published Works: Author, Various Articles Published in Professional Journals; Author, Book Review on Roger Sherman's *Economics of Industry;* Author, Textbook, *The Economics and Law of Antitrust Policy,* in Progress. Honors and Awards: Shell Oil Company Research Grant, 1966; University of Denver Faculty Research Grant, 1976; Listed in *Who's Who in the West, Who's Who in American Law, Who's Who in Community Service, Royal Blue Book, Dictionary of International Biography, Men of Achievement, Outstanding Educators of America, Community Leaders and Noteworthy Americans, American Men and Women of Social Science, Personalities of America, Personalities of the West and Midwest, People Who Matter, Noteworthy Americans of 1978.* Address: 15740 East Greenwood Drive, Aurora, Colorado 80013.

Martin J Wyand

Wyatt, Jeanine M

Hotel Administrator. Personal: Born September 27, 1948; Daughter of Kenneth W. and Betty Elaine Moesser; Married to Joseph S.; Mother of Quincy Shay, Jessica Leigh. Education: A.A., Brigham Young University, 1971. Career: Assistant General Manager, Ramada Inn, Salt Lake City, Utah, 1979 to present; Director of Operations, Salt Lake Valley Convention and Visitors Bureau, 1972-79; Secretary and Bookkeeper, Shurtleff and Andrews Construction Company, 1970-72; Secretary, Brigham Young University, 1968-70; Secretary, Hercules Powder Company, 1968; Secretary, Dugway Proving Ground, 1966. Organizational Memberships: Salt

Lake Valley Hotel/Motel Association (vice president of board of trustees, 1980-81, secretary, 1979-80); American Management Association, 1977-80; National Tour Brokers Association; Discover America Travel Organization; H.S.M.A., 1979 to present; Executive Women International, 1976-79. Community Activities: President, Springhill Condominiums, 1976-80; Western Baseball Boys Association, 1980-81. Address: 631 Springhill Drive, Salt Lake City, Utah 84107.

Wyndewicke, Kionne Annette

Educator. Personal: Daughter of Clifton Thomas and Missouria Johnson. Education: B.S. Social Science, Illinois State Normal University, 1960; Graduate Study, National College of Education, 1972-81; Attended Williams College, Innovative Teacher Training Institute. Career: Teacher, Chicago Board of Education; Former Positions include Case Worker, Cook County Department of Public Aid, Chicago, Illinois. Organizational Memberships: Illinois Speech and Theatre Association (past member); Speech Communications Association of America; C.A.R.A. Community Activities: Professional Women's Auxiliary of Provident Hospital (charter member; corresponding secretary, 1965; installation committee, 1963; yearbook committee, 1963, 1965, 1967; constitution committee, 1969; dinner dance committee, 1969; publicity committee, member 1969, 1976, co-chairman 1975, chairman 1974; volunteer service committee, 1967; hospitality committee, 1967; benefit committee, 1973; numerous other committees, 1960 to present). Religion: Christ the Mediator Lutheran Church; Member; Church Council, 1978-81; Altar Guild, 1960, 1961, 1962. Honors and Awards: One of 25 Black Women Selected in Chicago to Receive Kizzy Award, 1978; Community Service Award from South Central Community Committee, Honored 1982, The Beatrice Caffrey Youth Service, Inc.; M.Ed., National College of Education. Address: 533 East 33rd Place Apt. 1100, Chicago, Illinois 60616.

Kionne A Wyndewicke

Wynn, Daniel Webster

Writer and Consultant. Personal: Born in Wewoka, Oklahoma; Married Father of Marian Danita, Patricia Ann. Education: Ph.D., Boston University, Boston, Massachusetts, 1954. Career: Writer and Consultant; Associate Director, Department of Educational Institutions, Board of Higher Education and Ministry, The United Methodist Church, Nashville, Tennessee, 1965-76; Chaplain and Professor, Tuskegee Institute, Alabama, 1953-54; Dean, School of Religion, Bishop College, Marshall (now Dallas), Texas, 1946-53. Organizational Memberships: American Association of Higher Education: United Methodist Association of Colleges and Universities, 1966, 1976; Central Alabama Conference of The United Methodist Church (secretary, conference board of education, 1957-68). Community Activities: American Association of Higher Education, 1965-76; National Association of College and University Chaplains (newsletter editor, 1962-64); National Association for the Advancement of Colored People (life member); Kappa Alpha Psi Fraternity (life member); Tuskegee Civic Association (life member); Hydes Ferry Park Civic Association (secretary, 1967-68); Claflin College, Orangeburg, South Carolina (board of trustees, 1966 to present); Religion: Methodist; College Chaplain; Pastor, Calvary-Longview United Methodist Church, Memphis, Tennessee, 1980-81. Honors and Awards: Distinguished Alumnus Award, Langston University, Oklahoma, 1963; Man of the Year Award for Oklahoma, The Muskogee Service League, 1964; Rust College Shield for Leadership in Religion and Social Development, Rust College, Holly Springs, Mississippi, 1974; Service Plaque, Wiley College, Marshall, Texas, 1973; Special Service in Education Certificate, Phi Delta Kappa Fraternity, Jackson, Mississippi, 1979. Address: 3926 Drakes Branch Road, Nashville, Tennessee 37218.

Daniel W Wynn

Wysong, Earl M Jr

Professor/Consultant. Personal: Born June 3, 1925; Son of Mary E. Wysong; Married Lois A. Wysong; Father of Joyce W. Gordy, Cheryl W. Dankulich. Education: B.A., Eastern Washington University, Washington, D.C. Military: Served in the United States Air Force to the rank of Major, 1943-46, 1949-62. Career: Professor/Consultant; Accountant/Auditor; Electronic Data Processing Systems Evaluator and Consultant; Aircraft Pilot. Organizational Memberships: Association for Systems Management (international director, 1981-84); Association of Government Accountants (chairman of automated data processing committee, 1975-78); American Institute of Certified Public Accountants; Institute of Internal Auditors. Community Activities: Calverton Citizens Association (assistant treasurer, 1970-73; auditor, 1974-81). Honors and Awards: Certified Public Accountant; Certified Information Systems Auditor; Certified Manager; Career Development Award 1968, Literary Award 1967, 1973, United States General Accounting Office; Distinguished Service Award, Association for Systems Management, 1978; Achievement of the Year Award, Association of Government Accountants, 1975. Address: 213 Farmgate Lane, Silver Spring, Maryland 20904.

Yanker, Mary Margaret

Executive, Management Training and Consulting Specialist. Personal: Born March 3, 1936; Daughter of Mary Frances Crawley; Married Robert Henry; Mother of Mary Anne, Robert, Jr., Rodney, Randall, Holly. Education: Attended Vanderbilt University, Nashville, Tennessee, 1953-55; A.B. Anthropology 1960, Doctoral Program, Sociology 1962, 1963, 1966, University of Pittsburgh, Pennsylvania; M.S.Ed. 1969, Ed.D. 1973, Northern Illinois University, Dekalb. Career: Instructor, Northern Illinois University, Illinois Waubonsee Community College, Illinois West High School, District 129, University of Pittsburgh, Pennsylvania, Management, Sociology, Anthropology, Education, Behavioral Science, 1962-72; Aurora College, Illinois, Chairperson, Social and Behavioral Science Division 1973-79, Associate Professor, Behavioral Science 1973-81, Dean of Graduate Studies, 1979-81; Director, Officer, Chicago Consulting Group, 1975-77; President, Owner, Yanker Associates, Management Training and Consulting Specialists, 1978 to present. Organizational Memberships: Chicago Association of Women Business Owners (board of directors). Community Activities: Young Women's Christian Association (board of directors); Drug Abuse Council (board of directors); Family Support Center (board of directors); United Way (board of directors; executive committee); Mercy Center (institutional review committee); Illinois Commission on the Status of Women (education, employment and pensions committees); City Alderwoman; National Humanistic Education Center (value trainer, value trainer network); Inservice Workshops, over 10,000 Teachers and Administrators in Illinois, Indiana, Michigan, Florida; Workshops, Consulting, School-Related Groups, Businesses and Business Organizations, Police Departments and Other Governmental Agencies, Private Social and Community Agencies and Organizations, Health-Related Groups; Core Staff Member, Four-Person Team, Three-Year Grant for Values Education Development, Aurora Schools; Numerous Speaking and Consulting, Management, Values, Decision-Making, Leadership, Motivation, Communication, Stress and Time Management, Team-Building, Women and Consumer Issues. Published Works: Numerous Publications, including "Management Skills for Women in Engineering and Science", "Consumer Complaints for Product and Service Industries", "Humanizing Through Value Clarification". Honors and Awards: Kellogg Fellow, for Faculty Development, 1977; Danforth Associate for Innovative Teaching and Interest in Values, 1976, Continuous for Education Career, Woman of the Year, Aurora, Illinois, 1979; Listed in *Who's Who of Women in Illinois Education, Who's Who of American Women.* Address: 7143 Springdale Drive, Northeast, Brookfield, Ohio 44403.

Freda E K Yeager

Yarbro, Claude Lee Jr

Life Scientist. Personal: Born September 26, 1922; Son of Claude Lee Sr. and Laura Belle Yarbro (both deceased); Married Mary Clare Frazier; Father of Laura Anne, Elizabeth Mary, David Lee. Education: B.A. magna cum laude, Chemistry, Lambuth College, 1943; Graduate Studies in Biochemistry undertaken at Vanderbilt University, 1949-51; Ph.D., Biochemistry, University of North Carolina-Chapel Hill, 1954. Military: Served in the United States Naval Reserve, Active Duty 1943-46, Inactive Duty 1947-70, attaining the rank of Commander (retired). Career: Acting Professor, Mathematics and Physics, Lambuth College, 1946-47; Instructor, Physics, Union University, 1948; Instructor, Biochemistry, Vanderbilt University, 1949-51; Instructor, Research Associate, University of North Carolina-Chapel Hill, 1954-60; Biologist, United States Atomic Energy Commission, Oak Ridge, Tennessee; Biological Scientist, United States Energy Research and Development Administration, 1975-78; Life Scientist, United States Department of Energy, Oak Ridge. Organizational Memberships: Society of Sigma Xi, 1954 to present; Elisha Mitchell Scientific Society, 1954-60; American Association for the Advancement of Science, 1953 to present; New York Academy of Sciences, 1954 to present; American Institute of Chemists (fellow, 1968 to present); Ecological Society of America, 1975 to present; American Forestry Association, 1975 to present. Community Activities: Oak Ridge Parent-Teacher Association, 1960-78; Oak Ridge Band Parents, 1968-78; St. Andrews Society (member, 1977 to present; president, East Tennessee Chapter, 1980-81). Religion: Protestant. Honors and Awards: Coker Award, Elisha Mitchell Scientific Society, 1954; Sustained Superior Performance Award, United States Atomic Energy Commission, 1966; Superior Job Performance Award, United States Department of Energy; Military Decorations, American Theatre, Asiatic Pacific Theatre, World War II, Victory Medal, Naval Reserve Medal, Armed Forces Medal, Philippines Liberation Medal. Address: 147 Alger Road, Oak Ridge, Tennessee 37830.

Yarbrough, Joyce L

Executive. Personal: Born October 7, 1948; Daughter of Dr. William S. Yarbrough (deceased) and Mrs. Hortense Jackson. Education: B.A., Political Science, Fisk University, 1970; M.B.A., Management, Golden Gate University, 1977. Career: Administrative Operations Supervisor, Department of Commerce, Bureau of the Census, 1980 Census; Sales/Statistician, Macy's of California, 1971 to present; Special Projects Coordinator, Economic Opportunity Council of San Francisco, 1971-79; President, Le Nore Company, 1978 to present. Community Activities: Scott-Wada Youth Fund (treasurer, 1977 to present); Westside Community Mental Health (board of directors, 1971-79; treasurer, 1976-78); Bay Area Urban League (board of directors, 1973-79); United Way of the Bay Area (panelist, 1971-76); San Francisco Mental Health Association (board of directors, 1972-78); Catholic Youth Organization (secretary, 1977 to present). Honors and Awards: National Mortar Board Scholastic Society, 1970 to present; Listed in *Who's Who of American Women.* Address: P.O. Box 15117, San Francisco, California 94115.

Yeager, Freda E Knoblett

Educator. Personal: Born February 23, 1928; Daughter of Fred and Julia Knoblett (both deceased); Mother of Debra Alayne. Education: B.A., Franklin College, Indiana, 1965; M.A., Sam Houston State University, 1970; Ph.D., Texas A & M University, 1977. Career: Homemaker and Mother until Return to College, 1962; Teacher, Columbus Senior High School, Indiana, Three Years; Part-Time Instructor, Texas A & M University, One Year; Sam Houston State University, Fellowship 1968, Instructor while pursuing Ph.D. 1971, Associate Professor present. Organizational Memberships: Kappa Delta Pi, 1963; Phi Alpha Theta (president, Beta Sigma chapter, 1965); C.C.T.E., 1981; S.C. Modern Language Association, 1982. Community Activities: Huntsville Planned Parenthood, (board advocacy council; chairman, finance committee, 1981, 1982); Huntsville National Organization for Women (treasurer, 1981, 1982); Sam Houston State University (business manager, *Texas Review*, 1980, 1981, 1982). Religion: St. Stephens Episcopal Church, Huntsville, Texas. Honors and Awards: Knobe Prize Awards for Creative Writing, 1964, 1965; Alpha Honor Society, 1965; Magna Cum Laude Graduate, Franklin College, 1965; Listed in *World Who's Who of Women in Education, World Who's Who of Women, International Who's Who of Intellectuals, Personalities of America, Dictionary of International Biography*. Address: 508 Hickory Drive, Huntsville, Texas 77340.

Yiantsou, Chris G

Physician. Personal: Born October 23, 1947; Son of Athanasios Moutzakas and Pinelopi Trigoni; Married Barbara Tibbets. Education: A.A. Frank Phillips Junior College, 1969; B.S., Pharmacy, University of Houston, 1972; M.D., Texas Tech University School of Medicine, 1975; Internship 1975-76, Residency in Gastroenterology 1976-78, Fellow in Gastroenterology 1978-79, St. Paul Hospital, Dallas, Texas; Resident in Gastroenterology and Hepatology, Veterans Administration Hospital, Dallas, 1979. Career: Physician. Organizational Memberships: American Medical Association; American College of Physicians; American Society of Internal Medicine. Community Activities: Rotary International HEB Chamber of Commerce; Young Men's Christian Youth Association; Donated Building in Borger, Texas to be Converted into Museum for Hutchinson County Sheriffs' Association of Texas (associate member). Religion: Greek Orthodox Church of the Mid-Cities. Honors and Awards: Phi Theta Kappa Honor Society, 1969; Rho Chi Pharmaceutical Honor Society, 1971; Phi Kappa Phi Honor Society, 1971; Bristol Award for Academic Excellence in Pharmacy School, 1972.

Chris G Yiantsou

Yip, Jethro Sutherland

Entomologist, Agricultural Chemist. Personal: Born on July 28, 1895, in Victoria, British Columbia, Canada; Naturalized United States Citizen, April 20, 1959, in Fresno, California; Married Mabel Leo (deceased) on July 6, 1936 in Reno, Nevada. Education: B.S., M.S., both from the University of California, Berkeley. Career: Control Chemist, F. A. Frazier Company, Richmond, California, 1924-25; Research Entomologist, California Spray Chemical Company, Watsonville, 1925-29; Standard Oil Company of California, San Francisco, 1930-31; Growers Chemical Company, San Francisco, 1932; Entomological Bureau of Plant Industry, Department of Agriculture, Washington D.C., 1934-36; Research Associate, Division of Plant Nutrition, University of California, Berkeley, 1936-41; Chemist and Entomologist, Twining Laboratory, Fresno, California, 1941-65; Chemist, Coast Laboratory, Fresno, 1966-67; Retired, 1968. Published Works: Contributed to *Pyrethrum Culture, Pennsylvania Farmer, Journal of Economic Entomology, Industrial Engineering Soap and Chemicals*. Honors: Has received 32 awards to date, including a Distinguished Service Entomologist Award, *Dictionary of International Biography*, 1969; Award, *Two Thousand Men of Achievement*, 1971; Commemorative Award with Plaque, *Men of Achievement*, 1978; *Community Leaders and Noteworthy Americans* Annual Awards, 1974-77; *Book of Honor* Award, 1978; "American Bicentennial Recognition" Award, Chinese Consolidated Benevolent Association of Fresno, 1976. Address: 3901 East Dakota, Fresno, California 93727.

You, Richard W

Physician, Surgeon. Personal: Born December 23, 1916, in Honolulu, Hawaii; Married Eleanor; Father of Pamela, Aleta. Education: B.A., University of Hawaii, 1939; M.D., Creighton Medical School, 1943; Post-graduate Medical Work in North and South America, Europe, Asia, Africa, 1952 to present; Participant in Number of Sports Medicine Clinics. Military: Served in the Hawaii National Guard, 1932-39, attaining the rank of Sergeant. Career: Olympic Staff Physician and Associate Chief, Medical and Training Staff, United States Olympic Teams, 1952, 1956; Physician and Trainer, United States Pan-Am Teams 1955, International Track and Field Meet 1956; Physician, World Championship United States Olympic Teams 1952, United States and Russian International Weightlifting Meets 1958, United States vs. Poland International Track and Field Meet 1962, United States vs. U.S.S.R. International Track and Field Meet 1962; Official, United States Track and Field Team 1970, United States Swimming Team 1970; Ring Physician, 1952, 1956 Olympic Games; Hawaiian A.A.U. Ring Physician, 1950-81; Hawaiian A.A.U. Martial Arts Physician, 1970-81; Staff, Queen's Hospital, St. Francis Hospital, Kapiolani Hospital, Kuakini Hospital, Children's Hospital; Coach, Trainer, Developer of Many National and World Weightlifting, Boxing, Track, Baseball, Swimming Champions. Organizational Memberships: United States Delegate and Member, International Weightlifting Federation Congress Olympic Games (Helsinki, Finland) 1952, (Melbourne, Australia) 1956, International Sports Medicine Congress (Vienna, Austria) 1960, Olympic Medicine Congress (Rome, Italy) 1960, International Sports Medicine Congress (Mexico City, Mexico) 1968; Participant in International Biographical Centre Royal Jubilee Conference on Arts and Communications, 1977; World Tae Kwon Do Championship (appointed member of medical committee, 1977); Pan Pacific International Sports Council, 1961; First Korean American Brotherhood Friendship Mission to Korea, 1961; International Section, National Weightlifting Committee, 1963-73; International A.A.U. Boxing Committee, 1972-75; United States Olympic Weightlifting Committee (member, 1973-81; secretary, 1957-72); United States Olympic Weightlifting Medical Committee (chairman, 1973-77); Olympian International (vice president, 1964-81); National A.A.U. (life member; long distance running committee, 1951-76; board of governors, 1953-81; weightlifting medical and coaching committee, 1976-81; gymnastic committee, 1953-55, 1976-79; foreign relations and executive committee, 1959-76); Western A.A.U. Association of the United States, 1959-81; United States Olympians, Hawaii Chapter, (president, 1958-81); American Medical Association. Community Activities: Honolulu Quarterback Club; University of Hawaii Alumni Association; University of Hawaii East-West Center (life member); Ancient Order of the Chammori of Guam, 1963-77; Mr. and Miss Baby Hawaii Contests (founder, organizer, advisor, judge, 1951-59). Honors and Awards: Asiatic-Pacific Service Medal; World War II Victory Medal; Participant in an Official Capacity in 9 Olympic Games; One of Youngest Individuals Listed in *International World's Who's Who*, 1948-49; Featured Speaker, International Medical and Scientific Congress, 1977; Awarded 4th Dan Black Belt, Un Yong Kum, President of World Tae Kwon Do Federation, 1975; Finalist, One of Two for Managership of United States Olympic Weightlifting Team, 1968, 1972, 1976; Elected to International Helms Hall of Fame for Weightlifting 1968, Helms International Hall Lifetime Membership 1968; Certificate of Merit, International Federation of Bodybuilders 1972, Olympians International 1972; Gold Medal, International Federation of Weightlifting, 1972; South Korea's Order of Civil Merit, 1973; South Korea's Presidential Citation, 1973; Fellow, International Biographical Association, 1973-81; International Sports Medicine and Coaching Diploma in Hungary, International Olympic Weightlifting Federation and Hungarian Olympic Committee, 1981; Hawaii's Sportman of the Year, 1951, 1955, 1962, 1965; Hawaii's Father of the Year Sports Award, Honolulu Chamber of Commerce; Listed in *Royal Blue Book, Two Thousand Men of Achievement, International Who's Who of Intellectuals, International Register of Profiles, Men and Women in Hawaii*. Address: 1104 Alewa Drive, Honolulu, Hawaii 96817.

Richard W You

Young, Patti K

Realty Corporation Executive. Personal: Born December 9, 1944; Daughter of Edmund and Mary B. King Nuss. Education: Attended the University of Oklahoma 1963-65, West Texas State University 1965, Amarillo College 1965-67. Career: President, Real Realty

Inc.; Past President, International Condominium Enterprises, Inc.; Co-Owner, Real Condominiums, Inc.; Traffic Director, Continuity Writer, KIXZ, Amarillo, Texas; Continuity Writer, WFAI Radio, Fayetteville, North Carolina; Production Scheduler, Bell Helicopter, Amarillo; Swearington Aircraft, San Antonio; Executive Vice President, Kirkland Mortgage Corporation, Dallas; Vice President, Hibbard, O'Connor and Weeks, Inc., Houston. Organizational Memberships: National Association of Realtors; Texas Savings and Loan League; Texas Real Estate Political Action Committee (life member); Greater Dallas Board of Realtors; El Paso Board of Realtors; Brownsville Board of Realtors; Texas Apartment Association. Community Activities: Active in Texas Legislature on Uniform Condominiums, 1981 to present; Dallas Chamber of Commerce; Volunteer Speaker on Condominium Conversions; M.P.F. Research, Investors Mortgage Insurance Corporation, Lou Smith Realtors. Religion: First Baptist Church, Dallas, Texas, 1976 to present. Honors and Awards: Life Member, Texas Real Estate Political Action Group, 1981; Listed in *Who's Who of American Women, Who's Who in Dallas/Fort Worth.* Address: 3420 Douglas, Dallas, Texas 75219.

Young, James Hilliard

Education Management Specialist. Personal: Born January 29, 1946, in Rocky Mount, North Carolina; Son of J.W. Young, Jr.; Married Rebecca Barrow; Father of Laura, Lisa. Education: Graduate of Ahoskie High School, North Carolina, 1964; B.S. 1968, M.A.Ed. 1973, East Carolina University; Ed.D., North Carolina State University, 1977. Career: Executive Director, James H. Young and Associates, Education Management Specialists; Director of Institutional Development, Pitt Community College, Greenville, North Carolina, 1977 to present; Assistant to the President 1972-75, Director of Farmville Branch 1969-71, Pitt Technical Institute, Greenviille, North Carolina; Director of Sports Information 1971-72, Acting Assistant Dean of Men 1968-69, East Carolina University; Adjunct Graduate Professor of Adult and Community College Education, North Carolina State University; Adjunct Graduate Professor of Higher and Adult Education, George Washington University. Organizational Memberships: North Carolina Community College Adult Education Association; North Carolina Association for Research in Education; National Council for Resource Development; American Association of Community and Junior Colleges (member; board of directors; national chairman, committee on state councils; Region IV coordinator, eight southeastern states); National Council for Staff, Program and Organizational Development; Council of Officers for Resource Development (member, past president); *The Community College Review* (editorial assistant). Community Activities: *Buccaneer*, University Newspaper (editor-in-chief, business manager, classes editor); *East Carolinian*, Student Newspaper (editor-in-chief, managing editor); *The Key*, Official Student Handbook (associate editor); Student Government Association (student legislature, parliamentarian, budget committee); East Carolina University Board of Publications, 3 years; Dean's Advisory Council, 4 years; East Carolina University Race Relations Board (chairman); East Carolina University Law Society; Phi Kappa Tau Social Fraternity; Delegate to North Carolina State Student Legislature; Mid-South Model United Nations (vice president; chairman, economic council). Religion: First Presbyterian Church, Greenville, North Carolina. Published Works: Numerous Articles and Papers Published in Professional Journals and Presented at Professional Meetings, including "Resource Development in the Community College: A Time to Re-Think Priorities", "Vocational Education Data Reporting and Accounting System (VEDS) Problems and Alternatives", and "Shotgunning for Dollars"; Book *The Complete Guide to Administration of Title III Grants.* Honors and Awards: East Carolina University Publications Board Award, 1967; Most Outstanding Student Legislator, 1968; Listed in *Who's Who Among Students in American Universities and Colleges, Who's Who in the South and Southwest, Personalities of the South, Men of Achievement, Directory of Distinguished Americans, International Who's Who of Intellectuals.* Address: 1900 East Sixth Street, Greenville, North Carolina 27834.

Daniel D Yun

Youssef, Kamal A

Physician and Scientist. Personal: Born September 15, 1933. Education: M.D., 1957, and D.M.Sc., 1964, both from Cairo University; Ph.D., New York University, 1976. Career: Physician; Scientist. Organizational Memberships: American Society for Microbiology; Medical Mycological Society of New York; Medical Mycological Society of the Americas; American Medical Association; International Society for Human and Animal Mycology. Community Activities: World Nutrition Islamic Foundation (founder and president); Avicenna Institute for Cancer and Medical Research, 1981; Saudi-American Institute for Arid Lands and Energy Development, 1981. Honors and Awards: Recognition Award, United Scientists and Inventors of the United States, 1976; Listed in *Who's Who in Finance and Industry, Who's Who in the World.* Address: P. O. Box 6548, W. Palm Beach, Florida 33405.

Yun, Daniel Duwhan

Physician, Administrator. Personal: Born January 20, 1932; Son of Kap Ryong Yun; Married Rebecca Sungja Choi; Father of Samuel, Lois, Caroline, Judith. Education: Pre-Medical Graduate College of Science and Engineering, 1954 Graduate, College of Medicine 1958, Yon Sei University, Seoul, Korea; Graduate Study, Trudeau School of Tuberculosis and Other Pulmonary Diseases, Saranec Lake, New York, 1962, University of Pennsylvania Graduate School of Medicine 1963; Internship, Quincy City Hospital, Massachusetts, 1960; Residency, Internal Medicine, Presbyterian-University of Pennsylvania, Philadelphia, 1961-63; Fellowship, Cardiology, Presbyterian-University of Pennsylvania, Philadelphia, 1964-65. Career: Philip Jaisohn Memorial Foundation, Inc., Founder, President: Medical Director, Philip Jaisohn Memorial Medical Center, 1975 to present; Rolling Hill Hospital, Elkins Park, Pennsylvania, Director of Special Care Unit, 1966-79, Medical Staff 1966 to present; Medical Director, Paddon Memorial Hospital, Happy Valley, Labrador, Canada, Medical Missionary among Deep-Sea Fishers, Northern Labrador, International Grenfell Association, 1965-66; Clinical Professor of Medicine, University of Xochichalo, Guernavaca, Mexico, 1978. Organizational Memberships: American Association of Internal Medicine; American College of Cardiology; American Heart Association (council on clinical cardiology); Philadelphia County Medical Society; Pennsylvania Medical Society; American Medical Association; Royal Society of Health (fellow); American College of International Physicians (fellow); American College of Contemporary Medicine & Surgery; Montgomery/Bucks Professional Standards Review Organization; World Medical Association; Federation of State Medical Boards of the United States; United States Senatorial Business Advisory Board; United States Congressional Advisory Board; Co-founder, Republican Presidential Task Force; Advisory Council on Peaceful Unification Policy of Korea (Honorary Member). Community Activities: International Cultural Society of Korea (honorary member); Advisor to Korean and American Friendship Society; American Law Enforcement Officers Association; Director of Bank of World. Published Works: Author, Several Professional Articles, Nurses' Manual for Intensive Care Nursing. Honors and Awards: Human Rights Awards, City of Philadelphia, 1981; Distinguished Community Service Award, Korean American Association, 1971, 1979. Address: 3903 Somers Drive, Huntingdon Valley, Pennsylvania 19006.

Yuthas, Ladessa Johnson

Educator, Specialist in Remedial and Developmental Reading. Personal: Married; Mother of Four Children. Education: B.S., Sociology, Colorado State University, 1949; M.S.Ed., Purdue University, 1954; Ph.D., Reading, University of Colorado-Boulder,

1969. Career: Professor of Reading, Department Chairman, Metropolitan State College, Denver, Colorado, 1966 to present; Consultant, Right-to-Read College Technical Assistant, Colorado Department of Education, 1973-79; Second Grade Teacher, Fort Collins, Colorado, 1955-56; Remedial Reading Supervisor, West Lafayette Public Schools, Indiana, 1952-55; First Grade Teacher, Aurora, Colorado, 1951-52; Graduate Assistant, Office of Dean of Students, Washington State University, Pullman, 1949-51; Summer Workshop Consultant, Purdue University, 1953, 1954; Graduate Assistant in Reading Center 1968-69, Director of E.P.D.A. Institute 1970, 1971, Graduate Extension Course 1970, University of Colorado; Visiting Professor, Fort Lewis College, Durango, Colorado, 1969; Consultant, E.S.E.A. Migrant Education, Colorado State Department of Education 1968-71, Bureau of Indian Affairs, State of New Mexico 1969-70, Division of Youth Services, State of Colorado 1969-71, Adams County SJ/29 J. Bennett Right-to-Read Program 1975-76. Organizational Memberships: International Reading Association (nominating committee, 1975-76; Colorado Council board of directors 1969-75, president 1972-73); Colorado Optometric Association (advisory board Annual Forum on Vision and Learning); Children's Hospital Conference on Learning Disabilities (advisory board). Published Works: Author, Articles Contributed to Various Professional Journals, including *Journal of Rocky Mountain Reading Specialists, Journal of Reading, Colorado Read*. Honors and Awards: Listed in *World Who's Who of Women, World Who's Who of Women in Education, Who's Who in Colorado, Who's Who Biographical Record of Child Development Professionals, Outstanding Educators of America*. Address: Reading Department, Metropolitan State College, 1006 Eleventh Street, Box 17, Denver, Colorado 80204.

Z

Zaborowski, Robert Ronald John Maria

Archbishop. Personal: Born March 14, 1946; Son of Mr. and Mrs. Richard Kuhlman. Education: Graduate of Holy Cross Old Catholic Seminary; St. Ignatius B.M., Old Catholic Seminary, 1968; D.D., S.T.D., J.C.D., Ph.D., D.S.S., D.D.M., D.Th.D., 1974, 1976, 1977. Career: Archbishop of Mariavite Old Catholic Church, Province of North America; Church Organist and Choirmaster; Lecturer, Para-professional Counselor. Religion: Ordained to Priesthood, 1968; Elected Bishop, 1971; Consecrated Bishop Cum Jure Successionis, 1972; Succeeded to Rank of Archiepiscopate and Office of Prime Bishop, 1972. Published Works: Author, Numerous Articles on Mariaviate Old Catholic Church. Honors and Awards: Honorary Member, St. Irenaeus Institute, France; Knight of the Grand Cross of Sovereign Order of St. John of Jerusalem Knights of Malta, Rome; Knight of Justice of Sovereign Order of St. John of Jerusalem Knights Hospitaller, Malta; Prelate of Sovereign Teutonic Order of the Levant, England; Count of the City of Santo Stefano Alberto I. Policastro, Prince of Manche-Normandia, Sovereign Titular of Crete, Italy. Address: Mariavite Old Catholic Church Administrative Center, 2803 Tenth Street, Wyandotte, Michigan 48192-4994.

Linda L Zange

Zange, Linda Lee

Chiropractic Physician, Educator. Personal: Born July 10, 1948; Daughter of Robert C. and Florence N. Zange. Education: Doctor of Chiropractic, National College of Chiropractic, 1970; B.A., Lewis University, Lockport, Illinois, 1978; DABCO Diplomate, American Board of Chiropractic Orthopedists, 1977; Diplomate, National Board of Chiropractic Examiners, 1970. Career: Chiropractic Physician, present; Physiologic Therapeutics, Meridian Therapy, Acupuncture, Instructor, National College of Chiropractic; Post-graduate Instructor, Orthopedics and Acupuncture. Organizational Memberships: American Chiropractic Association (councils of women chiropractors, liaison officer to NCC 1974-78, vice president, 1977-78; council on orthopedics and nutrition); Illinois Chiropractic Society (vice chairman, continuing medical education committee; committee on peer review); Chicago Chiropratic Society (secretary, 1982 to present); NCC Research Committee on Acupuncture; Foundation for Chiropractic Education and Research; National College Alumni Association; Society of Electro-Acupuncture. Published Works: Author, "Sesamoiditis: A Sesamometarsal Lesion", 1981, Diplomate Congress V, 1982 *Journal of the American Chiropractic Association.* Honors and Awards: Certificate of Appreciation, American Chiropractic Association, 1969; Service Award, National College of Chiropractic, 1970; Citation, Chicago Board of Election Commission, 1974. Address: 6240 West Newport, Chicago, Illinois 60634.

Zastoupil, Mark Alan

Corporate Engineering Manager. Personal: Born August 29, 1951; Son of Mr. and Mrs. Arthur Zastoupil; Married Margaret H. Holtz; Father of Jeanna Kay. Education: B.S.I.E., University of Wisconsin, 1973; Business Management Diploma, LaSalle Extension University, 1976. Career: Various Engineering Management Positions, Green Giant Company, 1973-78; Corporate Engineering Manager, Doric Foods Corporation, Division of Associated Coca Cola Bottling Company, Inc., 1978 to present. Organizational Memberships: American Institute of Industrial Engineers (senior member); American Association of Cost Engineers. Community Activities: Mt. Dora High School Business Department (advisory board committee, 1980-81); Governor's Industrial Task Force on Energy, 1981; Wisconsin Alumni Organization; Rotary Club of Mt. Dora, 1979 to present (director 1980-82); Mt. Dora Chamber of Commerce. Religion: Member, First United Methodist Church of Mt. Dora. Honors and Awards: Listed in *Who's Who in the South and Southwest, Personalities of the South, Directory of Distinguished Americans, Book of Honor, Community Leaders of America.* Address: P.O. Box 1184, Mt. Dora, Florida 32757.

Zehel, Wendell Evans

General Surgeon. Personal: Born March 6, 1934; Son of Emma Zehel; Married Joan; Father of Lori Ann, Wendell, Jr. Education: B.A., Washington and Jefferson College, 1956; M.D., University of Pittsburgh, 1960. Military: Served in the United States Air Force from 1961-63, attaining the rank of Captain. Career: General Surgeon. Organizational Memberships: American College of Surgeons: American Medical Association. Address: 553 Harrogate Drive, Pittsburgh, Pennsylvania 15241.

Lev Zetlin

Zetlin, Lev

Consulting Engineer. Personal: Born July 14, 1918; Son of Mark and Alexandra Zetlin (both deceased); Married to Eve; Father of Alexandra, Thalia, Michael Steven. Education: Engineering Diploma, London, England, 1939; M.C.E., 1951, Ph.D., 1953, Cornell University. Military: Served with rank of Captain, 1948-59. Career: Professor of Engineering, New York, New York. Community Activities: Member, Advisory Board of U.S. General Services Administration; Member of New York Council of the Arts; Board of Trustees, Manhattan College; Board of Advisors, Montreal Olympics. Honors and Awards: St. John of Jerusalem Gold Medal, Knights of Malta; Received award from Academy of Arts, Sciences and Letters, France; Received engineering awards from Concrete Institute, American Institute of Steel Construction and Pre-stressed Construction Institute. Address: 6 Fairway Drive, Manhassett, New York 11030.

Zimmerman, Shirley Lee

Educator. Personal: Born November 23, 1925; Daughter of Harry and Rose Schwartz (both deceased); Married Peter David Zimmerman; Mother of Michael Reed, Daniel Stephen, Kevin Charles, Julie Deborah. Education: B.A. 1947, M.S.W. 1967, Ph.D. 1977, University of Minnesota. Career: Assistant Professor, Family Social Science; Assistant Director/Educator, Family Policy and Continuing Education in Social Work; Social Planner; Child Welfare Consultant, Case Worker. Organizational Memberships:

National Association of Social Workers (board member, 1969-72; elected delegate, national delegate assembly, Minnesota Chapter, 1975; cabinet member, Elan, 1971-74); Minnesota Alumni Association (secretary, social work section, 1971-74); Minnesota Council on Family Relations (board member, 1973-75, 1982-83); Minnesota Mental Health Planning Council (steering committee, 1960-64); Minnesota Human Genetics League (board member, 1981-83); American Public Welfare Association; National Conference on Social Welfare; Council on Social Work Education; National Council on Family Relations; Policy Studies Organization; Minnesota Social Services Association. Community Activities: Conference on Income Maintenance Alternatives (chairperson, organizer, 1969); Minnesota Women's Committee on Civil Rights (steering committee, 1963-64); Brookside Elementary School Parent-Teacher Association (secretary, 1961-62); Minneapolis Charter Reform (steering committee, 1962-63); National Council of Jewish Women (president, Minneapolis section, 1961-63; state chairman, legislative affairs, 1963-65; vice president, education and public affairs, 1959-61); Midwest Parent-Child Resource Center (advisory committee, 1977-78); Pennsylvania Economy League (consultant, 1978); Hennepin County Welfare Department (consultant on I&R); National Association of Social Workers (corresponding member, Futures Commission, 1978-79); University Senate Sub-Committee on Social Concerns, 1979 to present; Student Legal Services Project Committee, 1981; Minnesota Interreligious Bio-Medical Ethics Committee (advisory committee, 1980 to present); Governor's Task Force on Work and Families (consultant, 1981). Honors and Awards: Post-doctoral Fellow, Family Impact Analysis Training Program, Family Study Center, University of Minnesota, 1978-79; Phi Kappa Phi Honorary Society, 1977. Address: 3843 Glenhurst, Minneapolis, Minnesota 55416.

Shirley L Zimmerman

Zinn, Elias Paul

Entrepreneur. Personal: Born November 7, 1954; Son of Mr. and Mrs. Julius Zinn; Married Janis Ann. Education: University of Texas, 1972-74. Organizational Memberships: APRO. Community Activities: Houston Chamber of Commerce; Houston Better Business Bureau; Dallas Better Business Bureau. Religion: Member, United Jewish Appeal. Honors and Awards: Listed in *Who's Who in the Southwest*, *Personalities of America*. Address: 1480 Sugar Creek Boulevard, Sugarland, Texas 77478.

Zitko, Howard John

Minister, Educational Administrator. Personal: Born October 26, 1911, in Milwaukee, Wisconsin; Father of Lenodene Muriel, Terrel Thomas, Beth Ellen Peters. Education: Graduate of Waunatosa High School, Wisconsin, 1929; Attended University of Wisconsin at Milwaukee 1929-31, University of California-Los Angeles 1946-48, D.Div., Golden State University, Los Angeles, California, 1949; Participator, Conferences, Seminars, United States Commission for UNESCO 1957, 1959, 1961, 1963, Yoga World Brotherhood Convention 1969, World University Tri-Continental Conference 1970. Career: Lemurian Fellowship, Co-Founder, Vice President in Charge of Cooperative Development, Minister, Fellowship Chapel, Milwaukee 1939-41, National Lecturer, Religious Philosophy, Prehistory 1936-46 Temple of the Jewelled Cross, Los Angeles, California, Executive Coordinator, Departments of Education, Commerce, Agriculture, Health, Family, Industry, Supervisor, Experimental Ranch, 1942-46; World University, Roundtable, Founder, Chief Executive 1946 to present, President, Chairman of the Board 1947 to present, Office Head, Los Angeles 1947-48, Burbank 1949-54, Hollywood 1954-55, Huntington Park 1955-64, Tucson 1964 to present, Promotion, Publicity, Public Relations, Counseling, Lecturing, Publishing, Executive Secretarial Coordination, World-Wide Memberships Organization, Founder, President, Board of Trustees, Tucson, Chief Architect, Constitution, 1967 to present; Minister, Church of the Abundant Life, Huntington Park, California, Supervisor, Building of Church Edifice 1957, Minister 1955-59. Organizational Memberships: World University Roundtable (life member); World University (charter member); American Ministerial Association (ordained minister); Huntington Park Ministerial Association, California (past member). Community Activities: American Civil Liberties Union; American Association of Retired Persons; American Association for the United Nations; Honorable Order of Kentucky Colonels; National Register of Prominent Americans; Tucson Chamber of Commerce (past member, education committee). Religion: Minister, Temple of the Jewelled Cross, 1942-46; Minister, Church of the Abundant Life, 1955-59. Published Works: *The Lemurian Theo-Christic Conception*, Basic Text of Religious Philosophy for the Lemurian Fellowship; *Be It Resolved; Democracy in Economics; Streamers of Light from the New World;* Editor, *An Earth Dwellers Return;* Annual Keynote Addresses, World University Conferences, Published for Distribution; Editor, Publisher, "International Newsletter of the World University"; Various Articles, Catalogs, Bulletins; *New Age Tantra Yoga*, Five Editions; *World University Insights with Your Future in Mind.* Honors and Awards: Honorary Degrees, Doctor of Letters, China Academy, Taiwan, Doctor of Humane Letters, American World Patriarchates 1972, Doctor of Modern Humanities, L'Universite Libre Asia 1970, Doctor of American Ethical Heritage, Universidad De Los Pueblos De Las Americas 1973, Doctor of Indian Philosophy, The Indian Association of America 1946, Doctor of Literature, The Ministerial Training College 1960; Institut Nord-Africain D'Etudes Metaphysiques, Algeria; Honorary Member, L'Association Francaise pour l'Avancement des Sciences de l'Homme 1965, Columbus Association, International Institution of Culture and Assistance 1970, Universala Ordeno de Antares 1960, World Jhana Sadhuk Society 1973 (honorary life member), Federationa Internationale Des Societes Scientifiques 1960, Sancta Maria Gloriosa Sereenissumus Militaris Ordo 1960, Physical Naturapathic Medical Herbalist Society 1959 (honorary fellow), Arbeitsgemeinschaft Der Esateriker 1959 (engineer of the spirit), Gran Fraternidad Universal 1960 (diploma of honor), Order of Eternal Light and Sages 1959 (hierophant of the grand cross); Malayan Kris, Homeopaths of Malaya, 1959; Bronze Medal, St. Olaf's Academy, London, England, 1969; Silver Chalice World University Roundtable, 1972; Listed in *Two Thousand Men of Achievement*. Address: 711 East Blacklidge Drive, Tucson, Arizona 83719.

Howard J Zitko

Zsigmond, Elemer K

Educator. Personal: Born May 16, 1930; Son of Elemer Zsigmond, J.D., Ph.D. (deceased); Married Kathryn; Father of William Zoltan. Education: M.D., University of Budapest Medical School, 1955; Resident in Anesthesiology, Allegheny General Hospital, Pittsburgh, Pennsylvania, 1961-63. Career: Clinical Anesthesiologist, Director, Anesthesiology Research Laboratory, Allegheny General Hospital, 1963-68; Professor, Department of Anesthesiology, University of Michigan, 1968-79; Professor, Department of Anesthesiology, University of Illinois, 1979 to present. Organizational Memberships: American Society of Anesthesiology; Michigan Society of Anesthesiology; Cook County Medical Society; Illinois State Medical Society; American Medical Association; American Society of Regional Anesthesiology; International Anesthesiology Research Society; Society of Anesthesiology. Community Activities: Intergrated Curriculum Committee, 1969-71; Pharmacy and Therapeutics Committee, 1971-72, 1979-81; Civil Liberties Board, 1978-79. Honors and Awards: Recipient, Numerous Professional Awards. Address: 6609 North LeRoy Avenue, Lincolnwood, Illinois 60646.

Zuckerman, Jerold Jay

Educator. Personal: Born February 29, 1936, in Philadelphia, Pennsylvania; Son of Harry Earl (deceased) and Evlyn Weisman Zuckerman; Married Rose Elizabeth Stinson, on June 4, 1959; Father of Lesley Jeanne, Thomas Abraham, Amanda Joy, Kathryn

Jane, Amy Jo Allyn. Education: B.S., University of Pennsylvania, Philadelphia, 1957; A.M. 1959, Ph.D. 1960, Harvard University; Ph.D. 1962, Sc.D. 1976, University of Cambridge, England. Career: Chemist, Smith Kline and French Laboratories, Philadelphia, Summer 1956; Chemist, Houdry Process Corporation, Marcus Hook, Pennsylvania, Summer 1957; Teaching Fellow, Harvard University, 1957-60; Chemist, Massachusetts Institute of Technology, Lincoln Laboratories, Lexington, Massachusetts, Summer 1958; Supervisor of Students in Chemistry, Sidney Sussex College, University of Cambridge, 1961-62; Assistant Professor, Cornell University, 1962-68; Assistant Professor, Harvard University Summer School, 1967; State University of New York at Albany, Associate Professor 1968-72, Professor of Chemistry 1972-76, Director of Research 1972-73; Associate Professor, Harvard University Medical School, 1970; Visiting Professor, Technical University of Berlin, Germany, 1973; Chairman of the Department of Chemistry 1976-80, Professor 1976 to present, University of Oklahoma-Norman; Professeur Associé, Universitié d'Aix, Marseille III, France, 1979, 1982. Organizational Memberships: Alpha Chi Sigma Professional Chemical Fraternity; American Association for the Advancement of Science; American Association of University Professors; American Institute of Chemists (fellow); American Society for Testing Materials; Association of Harvard Chemists; Association of University of Pennsylvania Chemists; The Cambridge Society; Phi Lambda Upsilon Honorary Chemical Fraternity; The Royal Society of Chemistry of London; The Society of the Sigma Xi; *Inorganic Reactions and Methods, Verlag Chemie* (managing editor); *Review of Si, Ge, Sn, Pb Compounds* (editorial advisory board); American Chemical Society (inorganic chemistry subcommittee, examinations committee, division of chemical education; past chairman, committee on nominations and symposia planning; past program chairman, division of inorganic chemistry); NRC-NAS (past chairman, ad hoc panel on Mossbauer data evaluation, numerical data advisory board); Pergamon Press (past regional editor, inorganic nuclear chemistry letters); Academic Press (past editor, Determination of Organic Structures by Physical Methods); National Science Foundation (panelist). Community Activities: Consultant, National Institute of Occupational Safety and Health (Bethesda, Maryland), Walter de Gruyter Company (Berlin), Midwest Research Institute (Kansas City), Life Systems Inc., ICAIR Systems Division (Cleveland); Brunswick Common School District (president, board of trustees, 1972-76). Published Works: Author, Over 120 Scientific Papers, Over 90 Communications at Scientific Meetings; Editor of Nine Books; Article on "Molecular Structure", 15th Edition, *Encyclopedia Britannica.* Honors and Awards: Philadelphia Board of Education Scholarship, 1953-57; Edgar Fahs Smith Scholarship, 1956-57, University of Pennsylvania; Summer Fellowship 1959, Research Grant 1964 to present, National Science Foundation; National Institutes of Health Fellowship, 1958-60, 1960-62; National Institutes of Health/National Cancer Research Grant, 1963-68; Research Corporation Grant, 1968-70; American Chemical Society, Petroleum Research Fund Research Grant, 1968-71; North Atlantic Treaty Organization Grant, 1977-79; Office of Naval Research Grantee, 1977 to present; Alexander von Humboldt Senior Fellowship Award; Docteur honoris causa, Universitie d'Aix Marseille III, Marseille, France, 1981; Listed in *Who's Who in the South and Southwest, Men of Achievement, Community Leaders of America, Outstanding Educators of America, Registry of American Achievement, Who's Who in America.* Address: 1608 Chestnut Lane, Norman, Oklahoma 73069.

Zuhdi, Nazih

Nazih Zuhdi

Cardiovascular and Thoracic Surgeon. Personal: Born May 19, 1925, in Beirut, Lebanon; Son of Mrs. Lutfiye Zuhdi; Married Annette; Father of Bill, Omar, Adam, Nazette, Zachariah. Education: B.A. 1946, M.D. 1950, American University, Beirut, Lebanon; Rotating Internship, St. Vincent's Hospital, New York, 1950-51; Surgical Internship, Columbia-Presbyterian Medical Center, New York City, 1951-52; Resident in General Surgery 1952-53, Fellow in Cardiovascular Research 1953-54, Resident, Senior Resident in Surgery 1954-56, State University of New York; Resident in Cardiac Surgery, University Hospital, Minneapolis, 1956; Chief Resident, Thoracic Surgery, University Hospital, Oklahoma City, Oklahoma, 1957-58. Career: Private Practice, Cardiovascular and Thoracic Surgery, Creer, Carey, Zuhdi, Inc., Oklahoma City, 1958 to present; Research Work, Internal Hypothermia, Oxygenators, Extracorporal Pumps, Hemodilution, Assisted Circulation, Implanted Devices to Replace Portion or All of Heart, 1958 to present; Visiting Faculty, Heart Association of Greater Miami, 1966; Speaker, Alverno Heights Hospital 1966, Scientific Sessions Committee, Oklahoma County Heart Unit 1966; Task Force, Cardiovascular Services, Baptist Hospital, 1968; Oklahoma Clinical Society Annual Fall Conference, Presiding, 1968; Discussant, Presenting Author's Series on Valvular Porcine Heterografts 1971, American College of Chest Physicians Meeting of Cardiovascular Committee 1972, Meeting for Society of Thoracic Surgeons 1973, Society of Thoracic Surgeons 1974; Presentation, Meeting of 11th International Cardiovascular Society 1975, Meeting of American College of Chest Physicians 1973. Organizational Memberships: American Medical Association; Oklahoma State Medical Association; Oklahoma County Medical Society; Oklahoma City Clinical Society; Oklahoma City Surgical Society; Oklahoma Surgical Association; Southwestern Surgical Congress; American Thoracic Society; Oklahoma State Heart Association; Osler Society, Oklahoma International College of Angiology; American College of Angiology; American College of Chest Physicians; American College of Cardiology; American College of Surgeons; American College of Chest Physicians (fireside conference, 1964, 1965; committee on cardiovascular surgery, 1964-65, present; speaker, implanted mechanical hearts, Honduras chapter, 1964; visiting faculty, cardiopulmonary function and physiology, 1966); American Society for Artificial Internal Organs; Society of Thoracic Surgeons (founding member); International Cardiovascular Society; American Association for Thoracic Surgery (associate member); Guest Speaker, American University of Beirut 1962, Association of Cardiology 1962, University of Maryland Medical School 1962, Columbian College of Cardiology 1963, Brazilian College of Surgeons 1963, University of Sao Paulo 1963; International Committee on Cardiovascular Surgery, VIII International Congress of Diseases of the Chest, 1964; Fireside Conference, Speaker, Joint Meeting of American College of Chest Physicians and Southern Medical Association 1965. Community Activities: Oklahoma Science and Arts Foundation (science committee, 1972-73); Speaker, Midwest Health Congress, 1974, Region VIII of AmSect 1976; Oklahoma Symphony (board of directors); Oklahoma Chamber of Commerce; Lakeshore Bank (board of directors); Cardiovascular Institute of St. Anthony Hospital, Oklahoma City, Oklahoma (chairman of the board). Religion: Moslem; Islamic Medical Association of America. Published Works: Numerous Articles in Professional Journals, including "The Echocardiogram and Aortic Porcine Prosthesis Insufficiency", "The Porcine Aortic Valve Bioprosthesis: A Significant Alternative", "Six-Year Follow-Up of Glutaraldehyde Preserved in Heterografts". Honors and Awards: Honorary Member, Association des Medicins et Chirurgiens Cardiologues du Liban, 1962; Correspondiente, La Sociedad Columbiana de Cardiologia, 1963; Certificat of Honor, International College of Angiology, 1963; Diploma Instituto Barazileiro de Investigacoes Cardio-Vasculares, 1963; Honorary Citizen of Brazil; Listed in *Who's Who in the South and Southwest, Personalities of the South, Who's Who in Science, Who's Who of America, Dictionary of International Biography.* Address: 7528 Northwest 150th, Oklahoma City, Oklahoma 73142.

The Governing Board of Editors, Board of Directors and Staff of *THE AMERICAN BIOGRAPHICAL INSTITUTE* wish to congratulate the preceding biographees on their

leadership, dedication and achievements.

Appendix I

Honorary Editorial Advisory Board
The American Biographical Institute

THE EDITORIAL ADVISORY BOARD advises *Institute* officials on the broadening and strengthening of editorial and productional scopes. This select group of less than 75 members is reviewed, evaluated and appointed annually. Contributions are aimed toward overall publishing policies, functions and purpose of the *Institute.*

Arnold Brekke, Ph.D., F.A.B.I.
1085 Montreal Avenue, No. 1804, St. Paul, Minnesota 55116
Consultant and Proprietor, Brekke Knowledge-Resources Creation-Production Enterprises
Researcher, Scientist, Educator, Lecturer, Consultant, Inventor

Juanita Sumner Brightwell, F.A.B.I.
1037 Hancock Drive, Americus, Georgia 31709
Retired Director of Library Services, Lake Blackshear Regional Library, Americus
Researcher, Administrator, Librarian

Sylvia Leigh Bryant, F.I.B.A., A.M.A.B.I.
Route 5, Box 498A, Madison Heights, Virginia 24572
Editor-Publisher, *The Anthology Society*
Poet, Free-Lance Writer, Editor

Frederick D. Byington, Ed.D., F.A.B.I.
1420 Locust Street, No. 14I, Philadelphia, Pennsylvania 19102
Director, Byton Private School, Philadelphia
Administrator, Educator, Consultant

Juan B. Calatayud, M.D., F.A.C.A.
1712 Eye Street, NW, Suite 1004, Washington, D.C. 20006
Professor, George Washington University School of Medicine; Private Physician

Joseph Peter Cangemi, Ed.D., F.A.C.A.
Psychology Department, Western Kentucky University, Bowling Green, Kentucky 42101
Professor of Psychology, Western Kentucky University
Management Consultant, Researcher, Educator

Avery G. Church, F.A.A.A., F.A.B.I., F.I.A.P.
351 Azalea Road, Apartment B-28, Mobile, Alabama 36609
Research Staff and Board of Directors, The Sociological and Anthropological Services Institute, Inc.; Lecturer in Anthropology, University of South Alabama
Educator, Scientist, Poet

C. Eugene Coke, Ph.D.
F.R.S.C., F.A.B.I., F.S.D.C., F.T.I., F.C.I.C.
26 Aqua Vista Drive, Ormond Beach, Florida 32074
Chairman, Coke and Associate Consultants
Scientist, Author, Educator, International Authority on Man-Made Fibers

Vera Estelle Sellars Colyer
1001 West 1st Street, Grandfield, Oklahoma 73546
President-Agent, Colyer Insurance Agency, Inc.

TWO THOUSAND NOTABLE AMERICANS

James F. L. Connell, Ph.D., C.P.G.
Box 144, Montevallo, Alabama 35115

Professor of Geology and Geography, University of Montevallo;
Independent Consulting Geologist

Grover F. Daussman, P.E., Ph.D.
1910 Colice Road, SE, Huntsville, Alabama 35801

Engineering Consultant; Former United States Government Engineer

Elias D. Dekazos, Ph.D.
408 Sandstone Drive, Athens, Georgia 30605

Plant Physiologist, R. Russell Agriculture Research Center

Veena B. Desai, M.D.
M.R.C.O.G., F.A.C.O.G., F.A.C.S., F.I.C.S.
110 Court Street, Portsmouth, New Hampshire 03801

Private Practice of Obstetrics and Gynecology

James Don Edwards, Ph.D., C.P.A.
J. M. Tull School of Accounting, College of Business Administration, University of Georgia, Athens, Georgia 30602

J. M. Tull Professor of Accounting, University of Georgia
Researcher, Educator

Henri C. Flesher, D.D. (Ret.), B.L.D., Ph.D., F.I.B.C., F.A.B.I.
Route 1, Box 218-11 West Scorpio, Silverbell Estates, Eloy, Arizona 85231

Retired Publisher and Journalist

Sandra Fowler, F.A.B.I., L.A.A.B.I.
West Columbia, West Virginia 25287

Associate Editor, *Ocarina* and *The Album*
Editor, Publisher

Lorraine S. Gall, Ph.D., F.A.B.I.
6812 Academy, Apartment 605, Houston, Texas 77025

President, Bacti-Consult Associates; Senior Microbiological Consultant, Private Business
Researcher, Space Scientist, Educator

Carrie Leigh George, Ph.D., M.Div., Ed.S., M.A., D.Rel.
1652 Detroit Avenue, NW, Atlanta, Georgia 30314

Research Associate and Assistant Professor of Curriculum and Instruction, Georgia State University
Ordained Clergywoman, Consultant, Researcher, Educator

Vivian W. Giles
Post Office Box 31, Danville, Virginia 24541
Owner-Manager, Vivian Giles Business Services

Antonio Giraudier, F.A.B.I., L.P.A.B.I.
215 East 68th Street, New York City, New York 10021
Writer, Author, Poet, Artist, Musician

Admiral A. B. J. Hammett
2500 East Las Olas Boulevard, Apt. 705, Fort Lauderdale, Florida 33302
Retired, United States Naval Reserve

Lewis Daniel Houck, Jr., Ph.D., L.F.I.B.A., F.A.B.I.
11111 Woodson Avenue, Kensington, Maryland 20795
Project Leader for Economic Research Service,
United States Department of Agriculture
Management Consultant, Author, Educator, Businessman

Geraldine Grosvenor Hunnewell, D.L.
F.I.B.A., F.A.B.I., A.F.S, F.T.L.A., F.I.P.A.
10799 Sherman Grove Avenue, No. 39, Sunland, California 91040
Researcher, Naturalist, Author, Scholar

Anna M. Jackson, Ph.D., A.B.P.P., F.A.B.I.
4200 East Ninth Avenue, Box C258, Denver, Colorado 80262
Associate Professor of Psychiatry, University of Colorado; Clinical Psychologist
Researcher, Educator

Catherine Earl Bailey Kerr, L.P.A.B.I.
14-12 West Hendricks, Roswell, New Mexico 88201
Owner-Manager, Kerr International School of Art
International Professional Handicapped Artist

Mozelle Bigelow Kraus, Ed.D., L.A.A.B.I.
The Seasons, 4710 Bethesda Avenue, Suite 614, Bethesda, Maryland 20814
Private Psychology Practice

Enrique Roberto Larde, M.G.A., F.A.B.I.
PO Box 2992, Old San Juan, Puerto Rico 00903
Director, South Continental Insurance Agency, Inc.; Director and President,
Corporacion Insular de Seguros
Researcher, Business Executive

TWO THOUSAND NOTABLE AMERICANS

Shu-Tien Li, P.E., Ph.D., Eng.D.
F.A.S.C.E., F.A.A.A.S., F.A.C.I.
Post Office Drawer 5505, Orange, California 92667

Founder, Chairman and President, Li Institution of Science and Technology and President of its World Open University, A Graduate School
Researcher, Engineer, Educator, Administrator, Consultant

Florence E. H. Little, F.I.B.A., F.A.B.I., L.F.A.B.I.
333 Lee Drive, Apt. 327, Baton Rouge, Louisiana 70808

Genealogist, Educator, Musician

Ruby E. Stutts Lyells, L.H.D.
1116 Isiah Montgomery Street, Jackson, Mississippi 39203

Federal Jury Commissioner, United States District Court, Southern District of Mississippi; Trustee, Prentiss Institute
Researcher, Writer, Librarian

Krishna Shankar Manudhane, Ph.D., F.A.B.I.
53 Mapledale Avenue, Succasunna, New Jersey 07876

Pharmaceutical Technology Associate Manager, Warner-Lambert Company
Researcher

Robert C. McGee, Jr., F.A.B.I.
Route 2, Box 396, River Road, Richmond, Virginia 23233

President, Swan, Inc.
Business Executive, Aeronautical Engineer, Consultant, Administrator

Rod McKuen
Post Office Box G, Beverly Hills, California 90213

Poet, Composer-Lyricist, Author, Performer
President: Stanyan Records, Discus New Gramophone Society, Mr. Kelly Productions, Montcalm Productions, Stanyan Books, Cheval Books, Biplane Books, Rod McKuen Enterprises

Herbert B. Mobley
Ph.D., D.D., S.T.D., L.P.A.B.I.
Post Office Box 165, Summit Station, Pennsylvania 17979

Pastor Emeritus, St. Mark's (Brown's) United Church of Christ, Summit Station; Acting Pastor, St. Peter's United Church of Christ, Frackville, Pennsylvania

Irving Morris, M.L.S., F.A.B.I.
21-15 34th Avenue, Apt. 2D, Long Island City, New York 11106

Educator and Librarian in Charge, L. D. Brandeis High School, New York City

Makio Murayama, Ph.D.
5010 Benton Avenue, Bethesda, Maryland 20814

Research Biochemist, National Institute of Health

Virginia Simmons Nyabongo, Ph.D.
936 34th Avenue North, Nashville, Tennessee 37209
Professor Emeritus of French, Research, Tennessee State University
Researcher, Author, Educator

George Robert Overby, Ph.D., F.A.B.I., L.P.A.B.I.
5927 Windhover Drive, Orlando, Florida 32805
Chancellor and President of the Board of Directors, Freedom University;
Founder, President, The International Association of Christian Education
Author, Lecturer, Consultant, Educator

Dr. D. C. Parks, F.A.B.I.
2639 Belle Terrace, Bakersfield, California 93304
Founder, President, Addictive Drugs Educational Foundation
Consultant, Counselor, Analyst

Sartell Prentice, Jr.
1404 Chamberlain Road, Pasadena, California 91103
Counselor on Incentive Profit Sharing; Lecturer

Roland B. Scott, M.D.
1723 Shepherd Street, NW, Washington, D.C. 20011
Distinguished Professor of Pediatrics and Child Health and Director Sickle Cell Disease Center, Howard University
Educator, Administrator

Herbert H. Tarson, Ph.D., F.A.B.I.
4611 Denwood Road, La Mesa, California 92041
Senior Vice President, National University, San Diego
Researcher, Educator

Andrew B. Thompson, Jr., F.A.B.I., L.P.A.B.I., L.F.I.B.A.
Post Office Box 3008, Montgomery, Alabama 36109
President, National Pricing Service, Inc.

Basil P. Toutorsky, D.Mus., L.P.A.B.I., F.A.B.I., L.F.I.B.A.
1720 16th Street, NW, Washington, D.C. 20009
Director, Toutorsky Academy of Music
Professor, Composer, Pianist

Aliyah W. M. von Nussbaumer, Ph.D., D.Th.
11110 Hazen Road, Houston, Texas 77072
Research Librarian, Published Author, Educator

Marian Williams, C.M.A.B.I.
1289 Mathews Avenue, Lakewood, Ohio 44107
Free-Lance Writer and Poet, Researcher

TWO THOUSAND NOTABLE AMERICANS

Roger Lodge Wolcott
4796 Waterloo Road, Atwater, Ohio 44201

Former Specialist in Aeromechanical Research and Development, Engineering Department, Goodyear Aerospace Corporation, Akron; Secretary, The Lighter Than Air Society
Aviation Pioneer, Inventor, Association Executive

Stella Woodall, D.Lit., F.A.B.I.
206 Patricia Drive, Junction, Texas 76849

President-Director, Stella Woodall Poetry Society International; Editor-Publisher, *Adventures in Poetry Magazine*
Author, Editor, Publisher, Poet

Howard John Zitko, D.D., D.L.
Post Office Box 40638, Tuscon, Arizona 85717

President and Chairman of the Board, World University

Appendix II

Roster of Fellow Members
The American Biographical Institute

THE ROSTER OF FELLOW MEMBERS constitutes a learned society of internationally acclaimed advisors and distinguished associates devoted to the principles of educational and professional advancement, public service and cultural enrichment of humanity. These individuals' careers, signal honors and accomplishments have been recognized and published in the Collector Editions of THE BOOK OF HONOR and through this review and selection have been elected unanimously to the Fellowship of The American Biographical Institute. This is an honorary and permanent seating.

John Gregory Abernethy
Christian Campbell Abrahamsen
Bergljot Abrahamson
Diane M. Abrahamson
Anthony (Tony) Salvatore Accurso
Louise Ida Acker
Cecile Neomi Walker Adams
Rev. Leroy Adams
Harold V. Addison
Steven V. Agid
Hugh Stephen Ahern
John Madison Airy
Ralph Hardie Akin, Jr.
Esther Ann Teel Albright
Signe Henreitte Johnson Aldeborgh
Larry J. Alexander, Ed.D.
Byron Paul Allen
Edgard Yan Allen
John Eldridge Allen
Rev. Thomas G. Allen
Frank E. Allison, Sr.
Mujahid Al-Sawwaf, Ph.D.
Peter C. Altner, M.D.
Thelma L. Alvarez
Ali Reza Amir-Moez, Ph.D.
Doris Ehlinger Anderson, J.D.
Gloria Long Anderson, Ph.D.
Harriet Idell Anderson
Herbert Frederick Anderson, M.D.
Rozena Hammond Anderson
Ursula M. Anderson, M.D., D.P.H., M.R.C.S., L.R.C.P., D.C.H., F.A.A.P.
George Fredrick Andreasen, D.D.S.
Hyrum Leslie Andrus, Ph.D.
Walter Thomas Applegate, Ph.D., D.D.
Mahmoud Zaky Arafat, Ph.D.
Pedro Alfonzo Araya
Wendell Sherwood Arbuckle, Ph.D.
Violet Balestreri Archer, D.Mus.
Sylvia Argow
Floro Fernando Arive, M.D.
Edward James Arlinghaus
Claris Marie Armstrong
Naomi Young Armstrong, D.H.L.
William Harrison Armstrong, Jr.
Kenneth D. Arn, M.D.
James Edward Arnett, Ph.D.
Dwight Lester Arnold, Ph.D.
Florence M. Arnold
Edward Lee Arrington, Jr.
Albert J. Arsenault, Jr.
Franzi Ascher-Nash
Dell Shepherd Ashworth
Chuck Aston
Katharine Oline Aston
Grace Marie Smith Auer
Aurelia Marie Richard Augustus
Beryl David Averbook, M.D.
William Marvin Avery, Jr.
Florence M. Gotthelf Axton, Ph.D.
Roderick Honeyman Aya
Anne Louise Ayers
James Wilbur Ayers
Catherine Beatrice Aymar
Edith Annette Aynes

Peter J. Babris, Ph.D.
Rosalie Wride Bacher
Manson Harvey Bailey, Jr.
Daljit S. Bais
Judge Anna Dorthea Baker
Elsworth Fredrick Baker
John A. Baker
Justine Clara Baker
Roberta Rymer Balfe
Howard Balin, M.D.
Iris Georgia Ball
Louis Alvin Ball
Joseph G. Ballard, Sr.
Susan Lee Ballew
Betsy Ross Anne Ballinger
Lloyd Kenneth Balthrop, Th.D.
Barbara A. Bancroft
Helen Virginia Bangs
Candace Dean Bankhead
Jean Bare
Vivian Miller Barfield
Alexander John Barket
Herman Zulch Barlow, Jr., Ed.D.
George Hugh Barnard, J.D.
Frances Ramona Barnes
Marylou Riddleberger Barnes, Ed.D.
Melver Raymond Barnes
Charlotte A. Barr
Nona Lee Barr
Kathleen Corlelia Parker Barriss
Margaret Bentley Hamilton Barrows
Mihaly Bartalos, M.D.
Arline Ruth Barthlein
Larry H. Barton
Florence S. Bartova
G. Robert Bartron, M.D.
Nina M. Barwick
Henrietta Elizabeth (Beth) Bassett
Harold Ronald Eric Battersby
R. Ray Battin, Ph.D.
Ethel Hines Battle
Carl Edward Baum, Ph.D.
Donald Otto Baumbach, Ph.D.
Magdalena Charlotte Bay ('Magdalena')
Everett Minot Beale
Gary Floyd Beard
Donald Ray Beason
Roberta Ann Beaton
Mary Dawn Thomas Beavers
Adeline C. Becht
Harriet Perry Beckstrom, D.O.
Rexine Ellen Beecher
Phyllis Tenney Belcher
Lenore Breetwor Belisle, Ed.D.
George Wilbur Bell
James Milton Bell, M.D., F.A.P.A., F.A.C.P.
Harold James Bender
John A. Benedict
Christopher Aaron Bennett
Margarita Orelia Benskina
Betty Jones Benson
Dailey J. Berard
Julia Irene Berg
Muriel Mallin Berman
Harmon Gordon Berns
Leonard Bernstein
Frank Weldon Berry, Sr.
Irving Aaron Berstein
Norman M. Better, Ed.D.
Clifford Allen Betts
Laura Elizabeth Beverly
Brian William Louis Bex
Awinash P. Bhatkar, Ph.D.
Henrietta DeWitte Bigelow
Annette C. Billie
Novella Stafford Billions
Carol H. Bird
Donald Raymond Black
Harold Stephen Black
Willa Brown Black
Joe Ronald Blackston
Frank Blair
Ilene Mills Blake
Terri Blake (AKA-Theresa Blalack)
William H. Blakely, Jr.
Roger Neal Blakeney, Ph.D.
B. Everard Blanchard, D.Div.
Ronald Gail Blankenbaker, M.D.
Maija Sibilla Blaubergs
Gustav Henry Bliesner
Edna J. Gossage Blue
Wendell Norman Bodden
Carmen Page Bogan
Johnita Schuessler Bohmfalk
Gerald L. Boland
Oran Edward Bollinger, Ph.D.
Robert Howard Boltz
Suzanne Poljacik Bolwell
Loraine Mary Bomkamp
Dr. Floyd A. Bond
Drew Adrian Bondy
Tal D. Bonham, Th.D.
Ophelia Calloway Bonner
Earl James Eugene Books
Emily Clark Kidwell Linder Boone
Myron Vernon Boor
Mary Elizabeth Borst
Metodij Boretsky, Ph.D.

TWO THOUSAND NOTABLE AMERICANS

Raymond Paul Botch
Shirley Marie Oakes Bothwell
Harvey John Bott
Wilhelmina Wotkyns Botticher
Badi Mansour Boulous, M.D., Ph.D.
Mary Bancroft Boulton
Jean A. H. Bourget
Geoffrey Howard Bourne, D.Sc., D.Phil.
Gloria Diane Parrish Bousley, Ph.D.
Mildred Hazel Bowen
Theodore Stanley Boyer
Frances L. Boykin
Mervell Winzer Bracewell, R.N., DR.P.H.
Margaret Anowell Brame, Jr. II
Sister M. Teresa Bramsiepe
Wayne Keith Brattain
Helen Raymond Braunschweiger
Pius Brazauskas
Ruby Blanche Franklin Breads
Virginia Huffman Break
Arnold Brekke, Ph.D.
George Matthew Brembos
Lynn D. Brenneman
Charlotte Mae Brett
Anne A. Brevetti
Virginia Rose Alexander Brewer
Ethel Craig Brewster
A. Morgan Brian, Jr.
Joan Briggs
Juanita Sumner Brightwell
Angie R. Brinkley
Willis R. Brinkmeyer
Bobby Leroy Brisbon, Ed.D.
Jan Leeman Brooks
June Brooks Brooks
Margaret Alyce Page Brooks
Edith Petrie Brown, M.D.
Edward Kinard Brown, Ed.D.
Gwendolyn Ruth Brown
Hazel Claire MacCalla Brown
Jerry Joseph Brown
Joseph Leandrew Brown
Louis Daniel Brown, J.D.
Luther Daniel Brown, Ph.D.
Thomas Cartwright Brown
Thomas Lewis Brown
May L. Brumfield
Nancy Louise Bruner
Lillian Sholtis Brunner
Jacob Franklin Bryan, III
Elizabeth Ann Bryant
Kathryn Henriette Bryant
Richard John Brzustowicz
Wesley F. Buchele
Henry L. Buckardt
Bronius Budriunas
Richard S. Budzik
Vera Mildred Buening
Elizabeth Whitney Buffim
Ethel Munday Bullard
Claire R. Cohen Burch
Jewel Calvin Burchfield
Patricia Ann Burdette
Suanna Jeanette Burnau
Alta Hazel Burnett
William Earl Burney, D.R.E.
Grover Preston Burns, D.Sc.
Billie Burrow
Barbara J. Burton
Elizabeth Allene Burtt
Anna Gardner Butler
Broadus Nathaniel Butler, Ph.D.
Elaine Ruth Marjorie Mallory Butler, Ph.D.
Joseph Buttinger
Mercy Lynne Buttorff
Frederick D. Byington
Joseph Keys Byrd

Edward Joseph Cabbell
John F. Cahlan
Joseph Alexander Cain
Ardith Faulkner Caldwell
Gladys Lillian Caldwell
Stratton Franklin Caldwell
John Calhoun, LL.D., Ph.D.
Carey S. Callaway
Alfonso De Guzman Calub, Ph.D.
Victor Joseph Camardo
George B. Camboni
Agnes Knight Campbell
Bruce Alexander Campbell
Clay Reese Campbell
Jean Chidester Campbell
Robert Craig Campbell, III, J.D.
Winnie B. Campbell
Louis J. Camuti, D.V.M.
Julia Elizabeth Cane
Joseph Peter Cangemi
Nixon Louis Cannady
Antonio Capone, M.D.
Wayne Caraway, Ph.D.
Patricia Jean Carey
Darol Wayne Carlson
Erma Wood Carlson
Martha Lu Carlson
William Howard Carlson
Arthur Commons Carmichael, Jr.
Rebecca L. Carner, Ed.D.
Dario Carnevale
Charles Whitney Carpenter, II, Ph.D.
Beatrice Johnson Carroll
Elizabeth Boyd Carroll
Mitchell Benedict Carroll, J.D., LL.D.
William Edwards Carson
Anna Curry Carter
Charlotte Radsliff Carter, Ph.D.
Joyce Elaine Arndt Carter
Marion Elizabeth Carter, Ph.D.
Nettie Mae Carter
Grace W. Cartwright
Emily Roxana Carus
Dorothy Lee Eskew Carver
George William Casarett, Ph.D.
Paul Conway Case
Francis W. Cash
Francois Cassagnol, Ph.D.
Dianne Marie Cassidy
Patricia Anne Cassner
Robert Woods Castle
Alan Cathcart
Deloris Vaughan Cauthen
Marguerite E. Cavanagh
Mary Magdalene Cavasina
Vernal G. Cave, M.D.
Joseph Douglas Cawley, Ph.D.
Billie Jean Cawood
Augusta Cecconi-Bates
Jose David Lujan Cepeda
Mary Ellen Cerney, Ph.D
Robert A. Chahine, M.D.
Bobby Lee Chain
Hwa Ying Chang
Carlton J. Chapman
Wai Sinn Char, D.D.S.
Susan Charnley
E. Charles Chatfield
Tapan Kumar Chaudhuri, M.D.
John L. Childs
Howard Goodner Chilton
John Camillo Chinelly, Sr.
Andrew J. Chishom
Stanley Matthew Chittenden
Jerry Melvin Christensen, P.E.
Louis Washington Christensen
Ruth Ellen Christensen, M.D.
Odis Dwain Christian
Kenneth E. Christoff
A. John Christoforidis, M.D., M.MSc., Ph.D.
Sister Mildred Christoph, A.S.C.
Kyung-Cho Chung, LL.D., Litt.D.
Young Sup Chung, Ph.D.
Avery Grenfell Church
Lloyd Eugene Church, D.D.S., Ph.D.
Lillian Cicio
Robert Henry Cilke
John Henry Cissik, Ph.D.
Eugen Ciuca
John (Jack) P. Clancy, Ph.D.
Vance Curtis Clapp, Ed.D.
Stewart Clare, Ph.D.
Tema Shults Clare
Ann Nolan Clark
Bill P. Clark, Ph.D.
Lillie Rebecca Clark
Marie Tramontana Clark
Marion Jo Clark
Elsie Catoe Clarke
John G. P. Cleland
Emma Walker Cleveland
Hattye Mae Johnson Cleveland
Patrick Denton Closser
LaVerne Carole Clouden
John Daniel Clouse, J.D.
Robert Clunie
Patricia Ann Clunn
Charles E. Coatie
Annetta P. Cobb
McKendree Thomas Cochran, Jr.
Richard Earle Cochran
Claude O'Flynn Cockrell, Jr.
Gail Debbie Cohen, F.I.B.A.
Irwin Cohen
Chauncey Eugene Coke, Ph.D.
Mary Catherine Coleman
Zelia S. Coleman
Dr. Johnnie Colemon
Barbara W. Colle
Louis Malcolm Collier
Evelyn Padgett Collins
Zelma Mitchell Collins
Bundy Colwell, J.D.
Allen J. Comeaux
Archimedes Abad Concon, M.D.
Jo W. Conibear
James Frederick Louis Connell, Ph.D.
James H. Conrod, D.Min.
Patricia Cochran Cook
J. F. Cooley, D.C.L., D.D.
Robert Tytus Coolidge
Mariel Coombes
George Augustin Cooney, J.D.
Eldo J. Coons, Jr., Ph.D.
Herbert Press Cooper, Ph.D.
Jimmy Lee Cooper
Patricia Evelyn Pennington Cooper
Gretchen J. Corbitt
George Bronnie Corder
Erlinda Balancio Corpuz-Ambrosio
Leota Rae Cornett
Ernest S. Corso
Lyn Cortlandt
Evelyn M. Costello
Robert W. Costley, Sr.
Constantinos Haralampos Coulianos
Naomi Miller Coval, D.D.S.
Mary E. Cox
Yvonne Peery Cox
Ella Hobbs Craig
Vernon Eugene Craig
Marlene Rae Cram
Ira Carlton Crandall, Ph.D., D.S.Sc., D.Litt., Ed.D.
Josephine Lackey Crawford
Ioan Crihan
Adrian Loreto Cristobal
Charles Harrison Criswell
Tillie Victoria Swanson Croft
Charles Marion Cromer
Rev. Irvie Keil Cross
Joe George Crowell, D.D.S.
Carolyn Ann Crutchfield, Ed.D.
Randall Edward Culberson
Alfred Samuel Cummin, Ph.D.
Sylvia E. Cummin
Anne Bernice Smith Cunningham
David S. Cunningham, Jr.
Frank Earl Curran
Alton Kenneth Curtis, Ph.D.
Dorothy Massie Custer
Patsy Smith Czvik

Rev. Lawrence C. Dade
Bradford Ivan Daggett
Leola Lenora Dahlberg
Abdulhusein S. Dalal, Ph.D.
Charlotte Owens Dalo
Ruth C. Dameron

TWO THOUSAND NOTABLE AMERICANS

Frances Mueller Danforth
Huddie Dansby
Wayne Martel Daubenspeck
Ethel Hinton Daughtridge
Mabel Elizabeth Davidson
Alexander Schenck Davis
Beatrice Grace Davis, J.D.
Chaplain Rev. Dr. Clarence Davis, Jr.
Claudine Davis
Ernest Davis, Jr.
Evelyn Marguerite Bailey Davis
Father Francis R. Davis
Col. Gordon William Davis
Irma Blanche Davis
Lowell Livingston Davis
Mable Wilson Davis
Robert Wilson Davis
William Ackelson Davis
William Claude Davis
Kenneth Arthur Davison
Mary McCoy Deal
Michael Thomas Dealy
Robert Gayle Dean, Jr.
Walter John Deane
Patricia Ann de Champlain
David Michael DeDonato
Thelma B. DeGraff, Ph.D.
Dolores Tejeda de Hamilton
Michael Dei-Anang, Litt.D.
Jose C. Roman de Jesus
Elias Demetrios Dekazos, Ph.D.
Curtis Martin Delahoussaye
Violette de Mazia
Eugene F P C de Mesne
Aryola Marieanne Demos
Judianne Densen-Gerber
Sarah Lee Creech Denton
Mary Jane Denton-Learn, Ed.D.
Adelaida Batista De Rodriquez
Lawrence Aloysius DeRosa
Veena Balvantrai DeSai
Kenneth Noel Derucher
Ruth S. de Treville
Robert Marshall DeuPree
Adele K. Devera
Julia Anne Bonjour DeVere
Albert Kenneth De Vito, Ph.D., Mus.D.
Inez Stephens Dewberry
Franklin Roosevelt DeWitt, J.D.
Muriel Herrick DeYoung
Tejpal Singh Dhillon, M.D.
G. Di Antonio
Darrell Thomas Dibona
June M. Dickinson
Joan T. Diedolf
Russell E. Diethrick, Jr.
H. Brent Dietsche, Ph.D.
Rudolph Gerard Di Girolamo
Anne Holden Dill
William G. Dilley
Otis B. Dillon
Priya Chitta Dimantha
Evelyn Lois Dittmann
Loy Henderson Dobbins, Ph.D.
Sofia Hilario Doctor
Jeannette Betts Dodd
Elizabeth C. Doherty, Ph.D.
Henry Dolezal
Sylvia Maida Dominiguez, Ph.D.
Norbert Frank Dompke
Richard Francis Domurat
Mary H. O'Neill Dooley
Susan Sherley Dorsey
Robert F. Doster
Richard Bary Douglass
Helen Jeannette Dow, Ph.D.
Marguerite Ruth Dow
Charyl Wayne Kennedy Dragoo
Josephine Eleanor Drake
Zelphia Pollard Drake
Claude Evans Driskell, D.D.S.
Eugene Ardent Drown
Satya Deva Dubey, Ph.D.
Diana D. DuBroff
George William Dudley
Anne Marie Marcelle Dumouchel

Deidra Renee Duncan
Dyna Duncan
William Archibald Duncan
Helen Faye Kindle Dungee
Lawrence Dunkel, Ph.D.
Estelle Cecilia Diggs Dunlap
Elsie Hyder Dunn
Mildred Elaine Dunn
Clydrow John Durbney
Lewis M. Durden, D.D., Ph.D.
Nancy E. Dworkin, Ph.D.
Robert Francis Dyer, Jr., M.D.
Edith Wuergler Dylan

Thomas Capper Eakin
John Benjamin Ebinger (d. 1979)
Bertha Elizabeth Eckman
Elly Helen Economou, Ph.D.
Alan Michael Eddington
Harold W. Edmonson
Adrian Rose Edwards
Louis Mavis Way Eggleston, D.Litt. (d. 1979)
Gordon Frederick Ehret, P.E.
Lois Eleanor Eisenmann
Alfred Eisenstein
Monday U. Ekpo
Oscar Reed Elam, Jr.
Norman Orville Eldred
Mohamed Tawfik El Ghamry, Ph.D.
Sami El Hage, Ph.D.
Johnnie Carl Eli, Jr., D.D.S.
Rosemary Taylor Elias
Afton Yeates Eliason
Donald J. Ely
Bessie Miriam Embree
Raymond Terry Emrick, Ph.D.
Elizabeth Lois English, Ph.D.
Charles Thomas Epps, Ph.D., Ped.D.
Rev. William Saxe Epps
Eugenia Eres
Ellsworth Burch Erickson
Anita Bonilla Ernouf, Ph.D.
Dorothy W. Erskine
Jean Hocking Erwin, Ph.D.
Billie Lee Eskut
Oskar M. Essenwanger, Ph.D.
Gene Gordon Essert, M.D.
Ann H. M. Estill
Eddie Estrada
L. Ken Evans, D.D.S.
Louise Evans, Ph.D

Tuula Jokinen Fabrizio, D.M.S.
Mary Waring Falconer
Sally Basiga Famarin
Sadie Patton Fant
Francisco Cabreros Farinas
Dr. Dorothy Anne Farley
George Leonard Farmakis, Ph.D.
Helen Horne Farr, Ed.D.
Margaret Marion Farrar, Ph.D.
George E. Farrell, M.D.
Darlene Faucher
George D. Fawcett
Marie Ann Formanek Fawcett
Blair Fearon, M.D.
Eugene W. Fedorenko, Ph.D.
Shirley Feinstein
Gary Spencer Felton, Ph.D.
Tse-Yun Feng, Ph.D.
Nicholas Vasilievich Feodoroff
Patricia Marguerita Fergus
Anthony Ralph Fernicola, M.D.
Elizabeth Ashlock Field
Donald George Finch
Donnie Wayne Finch
Alice Elizabeth Fine
Richard I. Fine, Ph.D.
Aaron Fink, Ph.D.
Joan Lockwood Finn
William Francis Finn, M.D.
Carmine Fiorentino
O. Y. Firestone, J.D.
Charles Frederick Fisher, D.Ed.

Mary Hannah Fisher
H. William Fister, M.D.
Leonard Donald Fitts, Ph.D.
Stanton T. Fitts
Admiral Gerald Joseph FitzGerald
Harold Alvin Fitzgerald
Paul Leo Flicker, M.D.
Edward Francis Flint, Jr.
William Mathew Floto
Donald Ray Flowers, Sr.
Henry Bascom Floyd, III
Lyman John Floyd
Luella Lancaster Floyd, D.Min.
Claude Lee Fly, Ph.D.
Frank Foglio
Elinor R. Ford, L.H.D., LL.D.
Prof. Dr. Gordon Buell Ford, Jr.
Judith Anne Ford
Lee Ellen Ford, J.D.
Ruth VanSickle Ford
Gary Walton Fordham
Willmon Albert Fordham
Luella Helen Formanek
Virginia Ransom Forrest
Jane L. Forsyth, Ph.D.
Caroline Robinson Foster,
Marietta Allen Foster
Inez Garey Fourcard
Clara M. Fouse
Abraham Harvey Fox
Lauretta Ewing Fox, Ph.D.
Arthur Norman Foxe, M.D.
Charles Leonard Foxworth, Ph.D.
Florence Gerald Foxworth
Dr. Irving A. Fradkin
Dorothy Killian Franchino
Donald Ely Frank
Elaine Koenigsdorf Frank
Richard Symons Frazer, Ph.D.
Danny Lee Fread, Ph.D.
Annie Belle Hamilton Freas
Eldine A. Frederick
Leonard Harland Frederick
Elizabeth Hicks Freeman
Elizabeth Bouldin Freeze
Ruth Evelyn French
Joyce Chlarson Frisby
Mary Elizabeth Louise Froustet
Louise Scott Fry
Wilhelmine E. Fuhrer
Fred Franklin Fulton
Gary Sudberry Funderburk
Mrs. Courtney H. Funn
Quint E. Furr

Diana Ruth Gabhart
Ruby Jackson Gainer, Ph.D.
Dorothy L. W. Gaither
John J. Gajec
Lilyan King Galbraith, Ed.D.
Lorraine S. Gall, Ph.D.
Joan Mildred Gallipeau
Mario R. Garcia-Palmieri, M.D.
Arwin F. B. Garellick
Lawrence Garrison
Ricardo F. Garzia
Sharon Lee Gates
Alexander V. J. Gaudieri
Charles Gottliev Geltz
Meta Wade George
Sonya Ziporkin Gershowitz
Mary Frances Gibson
Milton Eugene Gibson, M.D.
Weldon B. Gibson, Ph.D.
Katherine Jefferson Strait Giffin
Margaret Gill
Edna Avery Gillette
Rev. Perry Eugene Gillum
Antonio Giraudier
Perry Aaron Glick
Alberic O. Girod
Emilio R. Giuliani, M.D.
Arthur G. Glass
Joseph William Givens Godbey, Ph.D.
Joseph Gold

TWO THOUSAND NOTABLE AMERICANS

Patricia Anne Goler, Ph.D.
Nelida Gomez
William Raymond Gommel
E. Larry Gomoll
Carlos La Costa Gonzalez
Rafael A. Gonzalez-Torres, Ph.D.
Pamela J. Gonzlik
Hope K. Goodale, Ph.D.
Robert Thomas Gordon, M.D.
Mimi Gospodaric
Edna Jenkins Gossage
William B. Graham
Queenette Faye Grandison
Peter Hendricks Grant, Ph.D.
Edwin Milton Grayson
Frank Joseph Greenberg, Ed.D., Ph.D., L.F.I.B.A.
Janelle Garlow Greene
Edna Jensen Gregerson
Walter Greig, Sci.D., D.C.S.
Charles Allen Griffith, M.D.
Ione Quinby Griggs
Wilbur Wallace Griggs, Jr.
James Dehnert Gross, M.D.
Clarence Edward Grothaus, Ph.D.
Ivan H. Grove
Raymond Louis Guarnieri
Halldor Viktor Gudnason, M.D., Ph.D.
Laura Guggenbuhl, Ph.D.
Sr. St. Michael Guinan, Ph.D.
Rev. Jon Crawford Gulnac
Howard L. Gunn
Evelyn Coleman Gunter
Nina Nadine Gutierrez
Mildred Dorothy Guy

Merrill W. Haas
Maj. William David Hackett
Howard Smith Hackney
Lorena Grace Hahn
Major Arnold Wayne Hale
Dr. Tenny Hale
Gladys Murphy Haley
Karen Louise Haley
David Gunther Hall
Mildred Verzola Hall
Wilbur A. Hall
Jean-Pierre Hallet
Gerald Halpin, Ed.D.
Glennelle Halpin, Ph.D.
Earle Hartwell Hamilton
Madrid Turner Hamilton
Lillian Hammer
Eugene Kirby Hammett, Jr.
Frances LaCoste Hampson
Charles Robert Hamrick
Dr. Joyce McCleskey Hamrick
Laura Alice Green Hamrick
Franklin Jesse Hannah
Alberta Pierson Hannum
Kathryn G. Hansen
Freddie Phelps Hanson, Ph.D.
Vera Doris Hanson
Maria Harasevych
Jakob Harich, Ph.D.
Bobbye Roberts Harkins
Ethel Harper
V. Aileene Harpster, D.D., Th.D.
Hardy Matthew Harrell
Florence H. Harrill
Paul R. Harrington, M.D.
Louise Harris
Mary Imogene Harris, Ed.D.
Thomas Lee Harris
Virgil William Harris, III, Ph.D.
Daniel D. Harrison, Ph.D.
Shirley M. Harrison
Winnie M. Harrison
Newman Wendell Harter, D.D.S.
William O. Hartsaw, Ph.D.
Eleanor T. M. Harvey
Frances Marie Kirkland Harz
Nora Mae Rucker Hashbarger
James S. Haskins
Beatrice Giroux Jones Hasty
Col. Benjamin Frank Hatfield

Robert S. Hatrak
Jacob Hauser
Orressa Harris Hauser
Joseph Key Hawkins
Robert A. Hawkins, Ed.D.
Willard Hayden Hawley
Mildred Fleming Haworth
George Austin Hay
Arthur C. Hayes
Charles Patrick Hayes
D. Virginia Pate Hayes
Mary Katherine Jackson Hays
Mattie Sue Martin Hays
H. Lynn Hazlett, D.B.A.
William Hugh Headlee, Ph.D.
Gladys Levonia Moyers Heath
Robert Hezron Heckart, D.D.
Henrietta Irene Henderson
Morris Henderson
Graham Fisher Hendley
Donald Wayne Hendon, Ph.D.
Phyllis Jean Hendrickson
Robert Lee Henney, Ph.D.
Martha Alice Grebe Henning
Beverly Jean Smith Henschel, Ed.D.
Kirby James Hensley
Peter Hans Herren
Howard Duane Herrick, M.D.
Lettie Marie Herrman
Irene Rose Hess
Ah Kewn Hew
Carl Andreas Hiaasen, J.D.
Elizabeth Blake Hiebert
Doris Ross Higginbotham
Claudette D. Hill
George B. Hill
William Harwood Hinton, Ph.D.
Aurora Tagala Hipolito, M.D.
Charles Norwood Hitchens
Lore Hirsch, M.D.
Jane Richter Hoade, J.D.
Sidney LaRue Hodgin
Loren H. Hoeltke
Elise Hoffman, Ph.D.
Judy Hogan
Edward Lionel Holbrook
Dorothy Turner Holcomb
Gene 'Scotty' Grigsby Holland
Ray G. L. Holland, M.D.
Ruby Love Holland
Shelby W. Hollin, J.D.
Lawrence Milton Holloway, M.D.
Helen Marie Holzum
Daisy Bishop Honor
Burrell S. Hood, III, Ed.D.
Thomas Richard Hood
Marjorie Seaton Hooper
Alice Elizabeth Hoopes
Albert Bartow Hope
Annie Pearl Cooke Horne
J. Marie Hornsby
J. Russell Hornsby
Louis A. Horwitz
Franziska Porges Hosken
Lewis Daniel Houck, Jr., Ph.D.
Reuben Arthur Houseal, Th.D., Ph.D., LL.D.
Ruth Arnold Houseal, D.R.E., L.H.D.
Edmund L. Housel, M.D.
Edna Gertrude Houser
Thelma L. Howard, M.D.
Lyman H. Howe, III, Ph.D.
John S. Hoyt, Jr., Ph.D.
Jean Ayr Wallace Hrinko
Joseph Jen-Yuan Hsu, Ph.D.
Wen-ying Hsu
Yao Tsai Huang
Elizabeth Desmond Hudson
Norman Nelson Huff
Phyllis Huffman
Edwin McCulloc Hughes, Ed.D.
Janice Baxter Hull
S. Loraine Boos Hull, Ph.D.
Hazel Lucia Humphrey
Lugene G. Hungerford
Geraldine Grosvenor Hunnewell
John DuBois Hunt, J.D.

Lula Mai Hunt
Cannie Mae Hunter
Miriam Eileen Hunter
Priscilla Payne Hurd, D.D.
Abdo Ahmed Husseiny, Ph.D.
Edward Lee Husting, Ph.D.
Janet Lois Hutchinson
Colonel John K. Hyun, J.D.

Francis Joseph Ibranyi, Ph.D., D.S.T.
Celina Sua Lin Ing
Thomas Peter Ipes, D.Min.
Linda Jean Garver Iungerich

Anna Mitchell Jackson, Ph.D.
Carolyn Jane Jackson
Harvey L. Jackson, Jr.
Ruby L. Jackson
Thomas William Jackson
Gordon Waldemar Jacobs, M.D.
Benjamin William Henry Jacobs
Michael Harold Jacobson
Edward Louis John, Sr.
Paula Hermine Sophie Jahn
Advergus Dell James, Jr.
Robert Bleakley James, Jr.
Isabel Jansen
Nana Belle Clay Jarrell
Diane M. Jasek
Ina J. Javellas
Maria Bustos Jefferson
Woodie Rauschers Jenkins, Jr.
Ronald Paul Jensh, Ph.D.
Sue Allen Jent
Lester Earl Jeremiah, Ph.D.
Ann Elizabeth Jewett, Ed.D.
Hugh Judge Jewett, M.D.
Mary Alice Jezyk
Herta Helena Jogland, Ph.D.
Rev. Charlie James Johnson
Dorothy P. Johnson
Esta D. Johnson
James Andrew Johnson, Sr.
Patricia Lee Johnson
Colonel Rufus Winfield Johnson
Scott Edwin Johnson
Rev. William R. Johnson, Sr.
Agueda Iglesias Johnston, D.H.L.
Lillian B. Spinner Johnston
George Jones
Faye C. Jones
Mallory Millett Jones
Myrtis Idelle Jones
Patricia Jones, Ed.D.
Professor Vernon A. Jones
Gary Blake Jordan, Ph.D.
Lan Jordan, Ph.D.
Carmen A. Jordan-Cox
Kathleen Doris Jorgenson
Leslie James Judd
John Louis Juliano
Felix Joseph Jumonville, Jr., Ed.D.
Willa Dee June
Msgr. Francis M. Juras
Ioliene Justus

Woodland Kahler
Faith Hope Kahn, R.N., O.R.N., R.M.S.
Julian Kahn
Krishan K. Kaistha, Ph.D.
Nora Evelyn Kalbhin
Robert Gray Kales
Shirley M. Kales
Ted Reimann Kalua
Robert Kiyoshi Kanagawa
Joseph Kapacinskas
Anne Kaplan
Dorothy Theresa Karl
Marian Joan Karpen
Nikolai Kasak
Michael Kasberg
Nicolai Nicolaevich Kashin
Robert Stephen Kaszynski

TWO THOUSAND NOTABLE AMERICANS

Hilda Katz
Alvina Nye Kaulili
Rita Davidson Kaunitz
Lawrence Kayton, M.D.
Anita M. Kearin
Helen Revenda Kearney, Ph.D.
Jean Clarke Keating
Rosalie Ausmus Keever
Shirley Yvonne Kellam, M.D.
Paul Dudley Keller, M.D., F.A.C.S.
Louise Salter Kelley
Doris Lillian Kelly
Margaret McLaurin Ricaud Kelly
Greta Kempton
Charles William Kenn
D. James Kennedy, D.D., Ph.D.
Bettie Ilene Cruts 'Bik' Kenny
Donald Keith Kenny
Ethel Marie Kerchner
Minuetta Shumiatcher Kessler
Maj. Frank Howard Kiesewetter
Joseph Eungchan Kim
Keith Kim
Mary Lee Evans Kimball
Dr. Clifton W. King
Ethel Marguerite King, Ph.D.
Helen Blanche King
J. B. King, Jr.
Joseph Jerone King
Louise Willis King
Sarah Nell King
Mattie Armstrong Kinsey
Ellen Irene Groves Kirby
Henry Vance Kirby, M.D.
Mayme Clark Kirby
Nellie Woll Kirkpatrick
Sister Joan Kister, F.M.M.
Dorothea M. Klajbor
Dr. Edgar Albert Klein
I. Maxine Klein
Martin John Herman Klein
Jean Ross Kline
Tex R. Kline
Kurt L. Klippstatter
Paul E. Klopsteg, Ph.D., Sc.D.
Arthur Alexander Knapp, D.Opth.
Gloria Ann Mackey Knight
William Albert Koch
Dr. Boris Kochanowsky
Dr. Constantin Neophytos Kockinos
Dorothy June Koelbl
Lawrence Compton Kolawole
Adam Anthony Komosa, Ph.D.
Jin Au Kong, Ph.D.
Elaine Ferris Decker ('Sunny') Korn
D. G. Kousoulas
Father William Armstrong Kraft
Father Ljubo Krasic
Mozelle De Witte Bigelow Kraus
Pansy Daegling Kraus
Dr. Rev. Violet Joan Krech-Cisowski
Adrian Henry Kreig
James Morrison Kress
Adrian Henry Krieg
Albertine Krohn, Ph.D.
Yu Hsiu Ku, Sc.D., LL.D.
Ruth Peyton Kube
Isaac Newton Kugelmass, M.D.
Ida Carolyn Kugler, Ph.D.
William John Kugler
Stanley A. Kulpinski, Th.D.
Ina West Kurzhals
Leigh Elena Kutchinsky, Ph.D., M.D.
Lubomyr Ihor Kuzmak, M.D., D.Sc.
Christine Irene Kwik-Kostek, M.D.

V. Duane Lacey
Lloyd Hamilton Lacy
Shue-Lock Lam, Ph.D.
Lawrence Webster Lamb
Eleanor Lambert
E. Henry Lamkin, Jr., M.D.
Selma H. Lamkin
Labelle David Lance
Edward Clark Lander
Newlin J. Landers
Vernette Trosper Landers, Ed.D.
Georgina Barbara Landman
Mary Frances Kernell Lane
Audrey Pearl Knight Laney
Enrique Roberto Larde
Lena Schultz Larsen
Agnes D. Lattimer, M.D.
Elaine Marie Laucks
Frances Louise Peacock Lauer
Ralph Aregood Law, Jr.
Betty N. Lawson
Verna Rebecca Lawson
Obert M. Lay, M.D.
Harry Christopher Layton, D.D., Ph.D., D.F.A., H.H.D.
Lillian Frances Warren Lazanberry
Albert Lazarus Leaf, Ph.D.
Miriam Leahy
Walden Albert Leecing
Sylvia Leeds
Dwight Adrian Leedy
Helen Ames Leete-Spaulding
Frank Edward LeGrand, Ph.D.
Silvia Weiner Leiferman
Ellen A. Leinonen, Ph.D.
Yoko Ono Lennon
Professor William Robert Lennox
John Anthony Lent, Ph.D.
Mae Grace Leone, Ph.D.
Barbara C. LeRoy
William M. Lester
Lois May Letch
Elmer A. Letchworth, Ed.D.
Harold A. Levenson
Philip Levine, M.D.
Keith Kerton Lewin
Eldwyn Ernest Lewis, Ph.D.
Leon Starks Lewis
Loraine Ruth Lewis
Shirley Jeane Lewis
William Howard Lewis, D.D.
Carol Ann Liaros
Eugene Aaron Lichtman
Ruth Dorothy Liebe
Morris B. Lieberman, Ph.D.
Luan Eng Lie-Injo, M.D.
Janis Lielmezs
Carol Asnin Liff
Rosalind Caribelle Lifquist
David Arthur Liggett
Dr. Delmore Liggett
Harriett Anna Grimm Lightfoot
Ping-Wha Lin, Ph.D., P.E.
Dorothy Insley Linker
Ivan L. Lindahl
Helge W. Lindholm
Mary Frances Lindsley, D.H.L., D.L.A.
Timothy Young Ling, Ph.D.
Elizabeth Charlotte Lippitt
Peggy Elaine Lipscomb
Darin V. Liska, P.E.
Robert Barry Litman, M.D.
Bertha Felder Littell
Florence Elizabeth Herbert Little
Terril D. Littrell, Ph.D., D.D.
Si-kwang Liu, Ph.D.
Richard W. Livesay, M.D.
Von Edward Livingston, J.D.
Addie Mae Curbo Lloyd
Dame Jean Loach, D.C.M.S.A., D.C.T., C.C.A., F.M.L., F.I.B.A.
Floyd Otto Lochner, Ed.D.
L. W. Locke
David M. Lockwood, Ph.D.
Louisa Loeb
Sarah Elizabeth Larkin Loening
Hazel Anderson Loewenstein
Leslie Celeste Logan
Dr. Jennifer Mary Hildreth Loggie
Pauline Teresa Di Bitose Longo
ArLeen Patterson Lonneker
Rita A. Lopes
Anna M. Gonzalez Lopez
Maria Trinidad Lopez
Evelyn June Lorenzen, Ph.D., M.D.
Ann Louise Lotko
Joann Love
Dallas Landon Lovejoy, L.L.S.
Thelma Spessard Loyd
Judith Bagwell Luahiwa
Lilibel Pazoureck Lucy
Ruby Ballard Ludwig
Archie William Luper
Edythe Lutzker
Adelheid Wilhelmine Luhr
Ruby Elizabeth Stutts Lyells
Angela Yaw-Guo Lyie
Jerry Lee Lyons, P.E.

Vera Sonja Maass, Ph.D.
Roy Walter Machen, Th.D., D.D., D.R.E., D.Min.
Ruth Jean Maddigan
Eugenie Cassatt Madeina
Visweswara Laxminarayana Madhyastha, Ph.D.
William August Maesen, D.S.W.
Larry Elliot Magargal, M.D.
Albert A. Magee, Jr.
Thomas Harold Mahan
Francis Elizabeth Dougherty Maierhauser
James I. Maish, Ph.D.
Americo Bartholomew Makk
Raymond Howard Malik, Ph.D.
Wilfred Michael Mallon, S.J.
Mary E. Tranbarger Malola
June Culler Malone
Dr. Lucinda Johnson Malone
Joyce Morgan Maloof
Rt. Rev. Lucien Malouf, B.S.O.
James Darwin Mann
Santa Singh Mann
Colonel Filomena Roberta Manor
Krishna Shankar Manudhane, Ph.D.
Mamie Jane Jimerson Marbley
Paula Dee Thompson Markham
John D. Marks
V. Steven Markstrom
Don Welch Marsh
Milton Marsh
Otis 'Dock' Marston
James Larence Martin, D.D.S.
Melvin D. Martin
Paul J. Martin, Ph.D.
Peggy Smith Martin
Ernesto Pedregon Martinez
John S. Martinez, Ph.D.
Ellen Marxer
Aretha H. Mason
Dean T. Mason
Frank Henry Mason
Madeline Mason
Joseph F. Masopust
Elinor Tripato Massoglia, Ed.D.
John Ross Matheson, C.D., U.E.
Helen K. Mathews
Hugh Spalding Mathewson, M.D.
Bill G. Matson
Jean Foster Matthew, Ph.D.
Alvin Leon Matthews
Elsie Catherine Spears Matthews
Norma Jean Humphries Mauldin
Rev. Charles Alexander Maxell
Katherine Gant Maxwell, Ph.D.
Wythel Louween Killen Mayborn
Cynthia Francis May-Cole
Frederick J. Mayer
Edythe Beam Mayes
James Thomas Mayne
Lawrence Clayton McAlister
Bernice Jacklyn Lyons McAllister
Van A. McAuley
Honorable Rita Cloutier McAvoy
William V. McBride
Judge Daniel Thompson McCall, Jr.
Robert John McCandliss, M.D.
William Harroll McCarroll, M.D.
Mildred M. McCleave
Dr Sherwin D. C. McCombs
Grace McCormack
Irene McCrystal, Ph.D.
Constance M. McCullough, Ph.D.

TWO THOUSAND NOTABLE AMERICANS

John Phillip McCullough, Ph.D.
(Betty) Martha Elizabeth McCurdy, Ph.D.
Henry Arwood McDaniel, Jr.
Khlar Elwood McDonald, M.D.
Theresa Beatrice Pierce McDonald
Barbara Ann McFarlin
Ambassador Gale W. McGee
Robert C. McGee, Jr.
William A. McGee, III
Helen McGinty
Marjorie Frances McGowan
Sterling Fisher McIlhany
Donald D. McKee
Marion Elizabeth McKell
Malcolm F. McKesson
Harry J. McKinnon, Jr., M.D.
Mary Cannon McLean, Ed.D.
Robert George McLendon
Gwen Edith McMillan
Ambrose M. McNamara
Thomas Parnell McNamara, Sr.
Esther M. Mealing
Dr. M. S. Megahed
Ira B. Melton, Sr.
Sol Mendelson, Ph.D.
Carlos Mendez-Santos
Samuel D. Menin
Vasant V. Merchant, Ph.D.
Addie Hylton Merrimee
Ruth Evelyn Parks Mertz
Juozas Meskauskas, Ph.D., M.D.
Dorothy Taylor Mesney
Maqbul A. Mian, M.D.
Cyril Michael
Barbara Falgout Michaelis
Hubert Sheldon Mickel, M.D.
Capt. Alfred Alexander Mickalow, Jr.
Mildred M. Milazzo
Charles E. Miles
Robert Wiliam Miles
Vivian Turner Millard
C. Edward Miller
Carol Miller Miller
Dolphus O. Miller
Dorothea Welsh Miller
Earl Beauford Miller
Maj. Gen. Frank Dickson Miller
J. Malcolm Miller
Jeanne-Marie A. Miller, Ph.D.
L. T. Miller, Jr., Ph.D.
Mary Frances Miller
Robert J. Miller
William A. Mills
Jewel Brooks Milner
John Herbert Milnes
Frank Kuipong Min
Giulio Romano Antonio Minchella, M.D., D.S.
Horst Minkofski-Garrigues
Barry Leonard Steffan Mirenburg
George Miskovsky, J.D.
Kegham Aram Mississyan, Ph.D.
Barbara Jean Mitchell
George E. Mixon, M.D.
Marjorie Frances Griner Mixon
Dr. Herbert Brooks Mobley
Edward Francis Mohler, Jr.
Gertrude M. F. Moir
John Troup Moir, Jr.
Eleanor Moore Montgomery
Lt. Gen. Richard M. Montgomery
Dan Tyler Moore
Frank E. Moore
Hershell Edward Moore
Paul Richard Moore
Phyllis Clark Moore, Ph.D.
Dr. George Alexander Moorehead
Daniel M. Morahan
Kenneth Carol Morgan
Felix Cleveland Moring
Alvin E. Morris, Ed.D.
Eugene Morris
Florence Eden Morris
Irving Morris
Ruth Morris
Sue Hannah Morris
Francine Reese Morrison, D.S.M., D.D.

Leger R. Morrison, Ed.D.
Samuel Alton Morse, D.B.A.
Hans Birger Mortensen
Helen Luella Morton, M.D.
Walter Graydon Morton
Wilbur Young Morton
Dr. Herbert Frederick Moseley
Dr. James Anthony Moses, Jr.
James P. Mosley
Tommye Atkinson Moss
Beatrice Carroll Mullen
J. B. Mumford
Walter John Mumm, Ph.D.
Makio Murayama, Ph.D.
Walter John Mumm, Ph.D.
Wanda M. Penrod Munson, M.A.
Noveree Murdaugh
Percy Murdock
Mary Kathleen Connors Murphy, Ph.D.
William Joseph Murphy, Jr.
Joan Murray
Edward Cecil Music
Tofigh Varcaneh Mussivand, Ph.D.
Fred L. Myrick, Jr., Ph.D.

Toyozo W. Nakarai, Ph.D.
Hiromu Nakamura, Ph.D.
John B. Nanny
Sunil Baran Nath, Ph.D.
Pleas C. Naylor, Jr.
William Arthur Nebel, M.D.
Lucien Needham
Clarence E. Neff
America Elizabeth Nelson, M.D.
Lorraine Lavington Nelson
Robert Lee Nelson, Ph.D., D.D.
Thomas Harry Nelson
Elsie Paschal Nespor
Lois H. Neuman
Sister Laurine Neville, O.P.
Joyce Nevitt
Capitola Dent Newbern, Ed.D.
Martha R. Newby, Ed.D.
Virginia Shaw Newell
Emma Read Newton
Annette Evelyn Nezelek
Rev. James Harold Nicholls
Thomas S. Nichols
William Roger Niehaus
Mary Martin Niepold
Masami 'Sparky' Niimi
Lorraine C. Nikolai
George Washington Noble
Mark Gerard Noel
Patricia Joyce Brownson Norman
William Carlton Northup
Joachim Robert Nortmann
Marie A. Norton
Allen Stanislaus Motoyuki Numano
Walenty Nowacki
Crosby Llewelle Grant Nurse

Gene S. Obert
Paul M. Obert, M.D.
Robert Paul O'Block
D. Susan J. O'Brien
James P. O'Flarity
Wilson Reid Ogg
Clifton Oliver, Jr.
Hester Grey Ollis
Jaime Alberto Olmo, M.D.
Carl Edwin Olsen
M. Eugene Olsen
Benedict Bernard O'Malley, Ph.D.
William Joseph O'Malley
Col. Robert Palmer O'Neal
Paul de Verez Onffroy, Ph.D.
Helen Marie Opsahl
William Dabney O'Riordan, M.D.
Henry Orland, Ph.D.
Margaret Roberta Carlson Orlich
Robert Louis Ory, Ph.D.
Roman Sviatoslav Oryshkevich, D.D.S., M.D.
Prime F. Osborn, III

Cyrus Warren Ostrom
Marshall Voigt Otis
Edward Thomas O'Toole, Ph.D.
Marie Louise Molera O'Toole
George Robert Overby, Ph.D.
J. Homer Harold Overholser
Ronald Overholser
Edwin Dean Overton
Esen Sever Ozgener, Ed.D.

Margaret Ann Pace
Edward Thurston Pagat, M.D.
Marcelo Pagat, Jr.
Matthew John Page, M.D.
Thomas J. Pallasch, D.D.S.
Kayton R. Palmer
Rt. Rev. Dr. Louis Alexander Palumbo, Jr.
Robert Boisseau Pamplin, Jr.
Marciano Vega Pangilinan
John Pao
Spyros Demitrios Papalexiou
Leah Ann Pape
Margaret Pardee
Ruby Inex Myers McCollum Parham
Margaret Bittner Parke, Ed.D.
Boots Farthing Parker
Charles W. Parker, Jr.
Earl Melvin Parker, Sr.
Jacquelyn Susan Parker
Loislee M. Parker
Marilyn Morris Parker
William Dale Parker, Ph.D., Sc.D.
Belvidera Ashleigh Dry Parkinson, Ph.D.
D. C. Parks
Olivia Maxine Parks
Sandra Lou Parks
George N. Parris, J.D.
Andrew Mentlow Parsley, Ph.D.
Eugenia Pasternak
Lucille E. Pastor
Jonh R. Pate
Bebe Rebecca Patten, Ph.D.
Priscilla Carla Patten, Ph.D.
Tom Patten
Celestel Patton
James Edward Payne
Virginia Alice Thompson Paysinger
Ralph Reed Payton
Reginald A. Pearman, Sr.
Betsy DeCelle Pearson
Norman Pearson
Judge John Wesley Peavy, Jr.
William Henry Peckham, III
Mary Ann Pellerin
Eugene Falero Pereda
Francisco Arriola Perez
Lynn Perkins Perez, J.D.
Anna Rebecca Perkins
Iris Francis Perkins
Robert Ronald Perkinson, Ph.D.
Alex G. Peros, D.C.
Robert J. Perry
Ruth Lucille Persch
Martin Ross Petersen
Norvell Louis Peterson, M.D.
Nan Dee Phelps
Helen Cecelia Phillips, LL.D.
Jacqueline Anne Mary Phillips
Karen Phillips
Michael Joseph Phillips, Ph.D.
Alyre Joseph Picard, M.D.
Patricia Jobe Pierce
Mary Isabelle Plum, M.A.
Alan L. Plummer, M.D.
Bob Lee Plyler
Marianna Cicilia Pisano
William M. (Bill) Pitchford
James Harvey Platt, Ph.D.
Father Joseph Kieran Pollard
Elizabeth Marie Polley
Gertrude Pollitt
Lauren Lester Pond, Jr.
Nelda Lee Pool
Finis Winston Poole
Bishop Mary Maude Pope

TWO THOUSAND NOTABLE AMERICANS

Darwin Fred Porter
Milton C. Porter, H.H.D.
Roy E. Posner
Roy Wilson Potter
Nancy D. Potts
Russell Francis Powell
Ruth Hollowell Powell
Sartell Prentice, Jr.
James Travis Price
John Michael Price
Richard Lee Price
Ruby J. Timms Price
E. Allen Propst
Lois M. Provda
Ava Fay Pugh
George R. Purcell
William F. Purkiss
Walter lee Pursell
Mary Belle Purvis

Seaborn Bryant Timmons Ragan
Karen Louise Ragle
Shahbudin Hooseinally Rahimtoola, M.D.
Robert Anton Rajander
Rawleigh H. Ralls, D.B.A.
Edward Ramov
Gerald Robert Randall
Helen Marietta Rasmussen
Maye Mitchell Ratliff
Ajit Kumar Ray, D.Sc.
Ollie Mae Ray, Ph.D.
Robert Benjamin Read, P.E.
Donald David Reber, Ed.D.
Judge Thomas J. Reddick, Jr.
Paschal E. Redding, Jr.
Pannala Jagan Mohan Reddy, M.D., D.P.M., F.R.C.P., A.B.P.N.
Maxwell Scott Redfearn, Ph.D., D.V.M.
Princess Red Wing
Minerva Tabitha Smith Reeve
William R. Reevy, Ph.D.
Frederick A. Reichle, M.D.
Lota Spence Reid
Siegfried Gerhard Reinhardt
Harry Charles Reinl
Regina F. Relford
Friedrich Otto Rest, A.B., B.D., D.D.
Benjamin Joseph Reynolds
Michael Eugene Reynolds, D.Min.
Randall Oscar Reynolds, D.D.S.
Movelda Earlean Rhine
O. W. Richard
Christine-Louise Richards
Frederick Douglass Richardson, A.A., C.S.R.
James M. Richcreek, Ed.D.
John Richmond, Ph.D.
Mossie J. Richmond, Jr., Ed.D.
Quinton Blaine Richmond
Jarnagin Bernard Ricks
Norman J. Riebe, D.Sc.
Jose M. Rigau-Marques, M.D.
Professor Margaret R. Rigg
Karl A. Riggs, Ph.D.
Elias R. Rigsby
Edna E. Riley
Warren Marshall Ringsdorf, Jr., D.M.D.
Florence L. Rippel
Mabel Amelia Rippel
Nicolas Nogueras Rivera
Arliss Lloyd Roaden, Ed.D.
Maj. Beverly Kay Roberts
Lt. Col. Edward Hartwell Roberts, Jr.
Evelyn Hoard Roberts, Ed.D.
Gertrud Hermine Kuenzel Roberts
Gertrude Brill Roberts
Josephine Frances Rees Roberts
Mark George Roberts
Lillyan Rose Robeson
Phyllis Isabel Robichaud
Erwin Robin, M.D.
Miriam B. Robins, Ph.D.
James D. C. Robinson, Ed.D.
Colonel James Hill Robinson
Ralph Rollin Robinson, M.D.
John D. (Jay) Rockefeller, IV

Donna Strickland Rodden
Carl E. Rodenburg, D.D.S.
William Harry Rodgers, Sr.
Czeslaw Mateusz Rodkiewicz, Ph.D.
Juan Francisco Rodriguez-Rivera, D.D.
Gifford Eugene Rogers
Rolf Ernst Rogers, Ph.D.
Thomas H. Rogers
David T. Rollins, Ph.D.
Fred G. Rollins, Sr., D.D.S.
Margaret Ann Romain
Clare Rose, Ed.D.
Wesley H. Rose
DeAnne Rosenberg
Julius L. Rothman, Ph.D.
Frederick Hull Roth
Agnes Brown Rowbotham
Iris Guider Rowe
Grant Russell Rubly
Lucille Alyce Pickering Rubly
Aldelmo Ruiz
Philip Reed Rulon, Ed.D.
Bob R. Rundell
Mary Russell
Phebe Gale Russell
Robert Rowland Russell, Jr.
Mary Anne Petrich Rust, Ph.D.
Katharine Phillips Rutgers
James William Rutherford
Varian Palmer Rutledge

Mike Sablatash, Ph.D.
E. 'Steve' M. Sadang, M.D.V., Ph.D.
Stanley Cecil Winston Salvary, Ph.D.
Dorothy Vermelle Sampson, J.D.
Archbishop Mar Athanasius Yeshue Samuel
Carol Lee Sanchez
James Julian Sanchez, M.D.
Betty M. Sandella
Sylvia Ann Santos
Mary Louise Steinhilber Sauer
Robert Leonard Sawyer, Sr., Th.D.
Frank John Scallon
Helen Carol Schabbel
Lucrezia C. Schiavone
William Michael Schimmel, D.M.A.
Dolores F. Schjaastad
Minnie Anne Schmidt
Carl E. Schmollinger
George Ferdinand Schnack, M.D.
Mary E. Schwappach, M.D.
Wilhlem Schwarzotto
James L. Scott
Marie M. Scott
Col. Wilton C. Scott
Clara Kalhoefer Searles
Lorraine E. King Seay
Margielea Stonestreet See
JoAnn Semones
Doris Shay Serstock
John George Sevcik, J.D.
Dr. John Charles Sevier
Flossie Tate Sewell
George Miller Shadle, M.D.
Erwin E. Shalowitz
Lucille M. Hogue Shealy
Ernest Shell
Vincent George Sheridan
Roy Allen Shive, Ph.D.
Mary F. Barnie Shuhi
Carrie Spivey Shumate
James McBride Shumway
C. Leroy Shuping, Jr., J.D.
Myrtis Irene Siddon
Howard M. Siegler, M.D.
Jan Simko, Ph.D.
Alyne Johnson Simpkins
Marion Carlyn Simpson
Eric John Sing, Ph.D.
Bhagwant Singh, Ph.D.
Kathern Ivous Sisk
James Dudley Sistrunk
Lydia Arlene Sitler, Ed.D.
Florence K. Slack
James Merritt Small, D.D.

Mary Ann U. Small
Ada Mae Blanton Smith, Ph.D.
Bettye L. Sebree Smith
Dock G. Smith, Jr.
Jessie Addie Smith
Norvel Emory Smith
Robert J. Smith
Wayne Delarmie Smith, D.V.M.
John Joseph Snyder, O.D.
Birger Kristoffer Soby
Walter W. Sohl
Ruell Floyd Solberg, Jr.
Donald Wayne Solomon, M.D., Ph.D.
Donald Henry Soucek, D.D.S.
Hattie T. Spain
Ellen Wilkerson Spears
James Parker Spillers
William Herschel Spinks
Ruth Evans Stadel
Edwin Henry Stamberger
Jacqueline J. Stanley
Linnie Marie Stearman
Lt. David Eric Stein
Andre Louis Steiner, D.Sc.
William Mark Stenzler
Dorothy Elizabeth Shay Stickman
Barbara Marshall Stockton
Willard Stone, D.H.A.
Jeremy Averill Stowell, M.D.
Dr. John George Strachan
Peter MacDonald Strang
Nellie Cora Straub
C. Clarke Straughan
Gustav Stueber
Glory Sturiale
Lakshminarayana Subramaniam
Eugene Y. C. Sung
M. N. Srikanta Swamy, Ph.D.
Arleen Wiley Swanson
Bonnie Ethel Wolfe Swickard
Maria Swiecicka-Ziemianek, Ph.D.
Ruby B. Sykes, D.D.S.
Emeric Szegho, J.D.

Neva Bennett Talley-Morris, M.Ed.
Peter J. Talso, M.D.
Noboru Tashiro, L.L.B.
Gunther Tautenhahn
Bertrand Leroy Taylor III
Grier Corbin Taylor
Rev. Horace Melvin Taylor, Th.M.
Lisa Taylor
Wesley Daniel Taylor, M.D.
Neal Gary Tepper
Esther Irene Test
Harry Pemberton Thatcher
Joseph Theodore, Jr.
Kadakampallil G. Thimotheose, Ph.D.
Alan Thomas, Ph.D.
J. C. Thomas, Jr.
Lowell Thomas
Minna Lee Thomas
Mary Diel Thomason
Henry George Thompson
William LaMont Thompson
Jean Kaye Tinsley
Betty Ann Tinsley-Brown
George John Tiss, M.D.
Vivian Edmiston Todd, Ph.D.
Hugh Pat Tomlinson
Francisco G. Torres-Aybar, M.D.
Basil P. Toutorsky, L.L.M.
Dennis Takeshi Toyomura
June Traska
Evelyn Ladene Trennt
Harvey W. Trimmer, Jr.
Laura McCleese G. Trusedell
Wanda Hall Tucker
Dr. Arthur E. Turner
Herman Nathaniel Turner, Jr.
Helen Flynn Tyson

Robert Takeo Uda
Friedrich Karl Urschler, M.D.

TWO THOUSAND NOTABLE AMERICANS

M. Lois Valakis
Henry Valent
Verne Leroy van Breemen, M.D., Ph.D.
Barbara Jane Dixon VanGilder
Richard C. Van Vrooman
Henry Varner, Jr.
Larry Ivan Vass, D.D.S.
Mary Vaughn
Prudence Melvina Veatch
June J. Veckerelli
Marion G. Vedder
James Joseph Venditto
Josefina Vera
Sister Mary Vernice (Makovic), S.N.D.
Santos Luis Villar, Ph.D.
Anthony Joseph Viscido, D.D.S.
Estella Maria Vlachos
John J. Vollmann, Ph.D.
Robert Volpe, M.D., F.R.C.P.
Arthur Voobus, Th.D.

Greta Evona Wade
Gerald Richard Wagner, Ph.D.
Betty Joanne Wahl
Mary Lee Sellers Wainwright
Edwin Prescott Wald
Kathryn Law Carroll Walden
Roy Willard Walholm, Jr.
Claudius R. Walker, Jr.
Iris Walker
Westbrook Arthur Walker, Ph.D.
William David Waller
James Arthur Waln
Doris E. Walsh
Bert Mathew Walter
Robert Ancil Walters
Rosie Reella Graham Ward
Marie Haley Warren
Lillian Frances Warren-Lazenberry
John Edward Warthen
Sharon Margaret Washburn
Lidia Cherie Wasowicz
Sydney Earle Watt
George Frederic Weaton, Jr.
Henry Weaver
Dr. Bernice Larson Webb
Ernest Packard Webb
Rozana Webb
Earl C. Weber
Gertrude Christian Weber
Sheila K. Weber, Ph.D.
Burnice Hoyle Webster, S.T.D., D.Sc., D.D., Ph.D.
Ernest Wesley Webster
Ruth S. Wedgworth
George C. Wee, M.D.
Milo Pershing Weeren
Diana Yun-Dee Wei, Ph.D.
Charles Kenneth Weidner

Norman Sidney Weiser
James Athanasius Weisheipl, Ph.D., D.Phil.
John W. Welch
Fay Gillis Wells
Josephine Mildred Wenck
L. Birdell Eliason Wendt
William W. Wendtland, Mus.D.
Wasyl Weresh, Ph.D.
Julian Ralph West
Lee Roy West, L.L.M.
Robert Warren Whalin, Ph.D.
William Polk Wharton, Jr., Ph.D.
Arline Z. Wheeler
James Edwin Wheeler
Charles Safford White
Ethyle Herman White
Frances R. Marjorie White
John Dudley White, Jr.
Mary Geraldine White
Saundra Sue White
Thurman James White, Ph.D.
Anna Whitefield
Alice McLemore Jones Whitehead
Edward Augustus Whitescarver
Vallie Jo Fox Whitfield
Cuthbert Randolph Whiting
Edward G. Whittaker
Grace Evelyn McKee Whittenburg
Carol Ann Wick
Jetie Boston Wilds, Jr.
William Garfield Wilkerson, M.D.
Harold Lloyd Wilkes, D.D.
Anne Oldham Willard
Carol Jane Petzold Willard, M.Ed.
Jack A. Willard
Albert J. Williams, Jr.
Anita T. J. L. Williams
Annie John Williams
Ather Williams, Jr.
Charlotte Evelyn Forrester Williams
Clarence Leon Williams, Ph.D.
Donald Jacob Williams
Dorothy Parmley Williams
Harvey Williams, Ph.D., D.Div.
Jean Taylor Williams
Leola K. Williams
William Harvey Williamson, Ph.D.
Francena Willingham
Mary Jane Willingham
James H. Willis
William Clarence Willmot
David Roger Willour, N.G.T.S.
Parker O. Willson
Charles William Wilson, M.D.
Cora Morgan Wilson
E. C. Wilson, Jr.
Hugh Edward Wilson
James Walter Wilson, Ph.D.

Leigh R. Wilson
Nevada Pearl Brown Wilson
Dorr Norman Wiltse, Sr.
Glen Elbert Wimmer
Lt. Gregory Lynn Winters
Nora Edna Wittman
Sophie Mae Wolanin, Ph.D.
Seymour "Sy" Wolf
Bradley Allen Wolfe
Deborah Cannon Partridge Wolfe, Ed.D.
Rev. Francis Wolle
Muriel Sibell Wolle
Colin Chockson Wong, D.D.S., F.R.S.H.
F.A.G.D., F.A.D.I., F.I.C.D., F.A.C.D.
Marylaird (Larry) Wood
Stella Woodall, D.Lit., D.H.L.
Geraldine Pittman Woods, Ph.D., D.Sc.
Margaret Herbert Ratrie Woods
Margaret S. Woods
Clifton Ward Woolley, M.D., F.A.A.P.
Darrell Wayne Woolwine
Bertrand Ray Worsham, M.D.
Elizabeth Wrancher
John Lawrence Wray
Eugene Box Wright, J.D.
Inez Meta Maria Wright
Kenneth Kun-Yu Wu, M.D.
William Lung-Shen Wu, M.D.
Doris Stork Wukasch
Angela Jane Wyatt
Rev. Claude S. Wyatt, Jr.
Kionne Annette Wyndewicke
Darlene Fry Wyatt

Alex Peralta Yadao, M.D.
Elizabeth Juanita Yanosko
Claude Lee Yarbro, Jr., Ph.D.
James Edgar Yarbrough
Fowler Redford Yett, Ph.D.
Jethro Sutherland Yip
Luella May Nafzinger Yoder
Ronald Eugene Yokely
James N. Young
Patrick J. H. Young
Adele Linda Younis, Ph.D.

Lawrence Thomas Zagar, Ph.D.
Edward Francis Zampella
Estelle M. Zelner
Dr. Melvin Eddie Zichek
Gladys Avery Zinn
Howard John Zitko, D.D.
Herman David Zweiban

Appendix III

National Board of Advisors
The American Biographical Institute

THE NATIONAL BOARD OF ADVISORS encompasses an extensive body of individuals who advise the *Institute* in the area of editorial nominations. Quarterly Nomination Campaigns are conducted annually. Appointment to this Board enables the member to influence the content of *ABI* publications, promote permanent biographical documentation and bring selective biographical credentials to light.

Dr. Betty Webber Abercrombie
Miss Louise I. Acker
Reverend Toby W. Adair, Jr.
Mrs. Odessa C. Adams
Mrs. Gerard James Aitken, III
Miss Minnis Amelia Alderman
Mrs. Jeanne Merchant Alexander
Ms. Jody R. Alexis
Mr. Julius O. Allen
Mr. William Thomas Allen
Ms. Martha Kinzer Allman
Dr. Amy L. Altenhaus
Mr. Ali R. Amir-Moez
Mrs. Leigh Perry Amos
Dr. Rajen S. Anand
Suresh C. Anand, M.D., F.A.C.P.
Ms. Ann Anderson
Mrs. Claire Anderson
Mrs. Frances Swem Anderson
Gordon Wood Anderson, Ph.D.
Ms. Vergie L. Anderson
Ms. Virginia S. Anderson, MS, CCC-A
Dr. Nancy Leah Ansevics
Juan M. Aranda, M.D., F.A.C.C.
Steven L. Arnold, M.D., F.A.A.F.P.
Mr. Leo Arsen
Ms. Marcia Patricia Ascher
Mr. Dell Shepherd Ashworth
Mrs. Bobbie J. Atchley
Reverend Thomas Lee Atkins
Arthur W. Avery, Ph.D.
Dr. Florence M. G. Axton
Mr. James W. Ayers

Dr. Roger Lee Bacon
Dr. Marie Ann Badalamente
Mr. Joseph R. Bagby
Mrs. Anita W. Bain
Mrs. Mary Helen Bair
Dr. Constance M. Baker, R.N.
Dr. Frank H. Baker
Dr. Helen Vaughan B. Baker
Mrs. Lillian Baker
Mr. Louis A. Ball
Ms. Charlotte A. Ballance
Mrs. Joan Ballantyne
Ms. Susie L. Ballew
Mrs. Howard V. Ballinger
Mr. Endre Balogh
Rev. Carroll A. Baltimore, Sr., Th.D., D.D.
Professor Sandra Powell Barber
Mrs. Doris D. Barberena
The Very Rev. L. Barcynski, OSV, LPABI, FIBA
Mrs. Virginia G. Barfield
Dr. Vivian M. Barfield
Mr. Melver R. Barnes
Dr. Camille Cates Barnett
Nona Lee Barr, Ph.D.
Mr. Samuel L. Barres
Mr. Bobby C. Barron
Margaret R. Bartok, Ph.D.
B. Bassim, M.D.
Mr. Frank Battle, Jr.
Dr. Ruth Howell Baxter
Mrs. Magdalena Bay
Professor Barbara S. Bayne
Mr. Everett M. Beale
Mrs. Margarine G. Beaman
Mr. Mark J. Beaudry
Mrs. S. Phyllis Tenney Belcher
Professor Jeanette Lobach Bely, Ph.D.
Jesse L. Bemley, Ph.D.
Dr. George S. Benson
Ms. Suzanne Benton
Mr. Dailey J. Berard
Dr. Violet E. Bergquist
Mr. Jesus (Jesse) R. Bernal
Ms. Dorothy D. Bettis
Ms. Theria M. Beverly
Annette C. Billie, Ph.D.
Mr. Robert M. Billig, A.C.S.W.
Mr. J. Larry Bishop
Dr. Larry K. Black
Mr. W. Thomas Blackall
Mr. Floyd F. Blackmon, Jr.
Ms. Martha Blakely
Dr. Roger N. Blakeney
Dr. Danny E. Blanchard
Laurel L. Bland-Schricker, Ph.D.
Dr. Douglas P. Blankenship
Dr. Dallas R. Blevins
Mrs. Edna Gossage Blue
Professor James F. Blumstein
Dr. Gail Parsons Boger
Dr. William H. Bolen
Ms. Karen L. Bolesky
Audrey S. Bomberger, R.N., M.S.Ed.
Donald J. Boon, M.D.
Ms. Emily Clark Boone
Ms. Jean Young Booth
Mr. Oru Bose
Mr. Raymond P. Botch
Harisios Boudoulas, M.D.
Mrs. Janette L. Bowers
Dr. Ronald Reed Boyce
Mrs. Alta E. Boyer
Dr. Mervell Winzer Bracewell
Mrs. Rosanne B. Bradbury
Major Ernest C. Bradley
Mrs. Ramona K. Bradley
Professor James P. Bradshaw
Assoc. Prof. Lawrence James Bradshaw
Mrs. Sylvia Woingust Branchcomb
Mrs. Emma C. Brannon
Mr. James H. Bratt
Professor A. T. Bratton
Mrs. Ruby Franklin Breads
Mr. A. Morgan Brian, Jr.
Mrs. Kay A. Brick
Mr. Perry L. Bridges, Sr.
Dr. Nancy E. Briggs
Mrs. Juanita Sumner Brightwell
Ms. Angie Brinkley
Chaplain (Lt.) Michael Linn Britton
Judge John G. Brosky
Sister Eileen Marie Brost
Mrs. Brenda A. Brothers
Mrs. Bette Dawn Brown
Mrs. Betty Ann Brown
Dr. Grainger Browning
Miss Beverly Olive Bruff
Mr. Jacob F. Bryan, III
Mr. Joe P. Bryant
Dr. Henry L. Buckardt
Mr. Alvah Buckmore, Jr.
Mr. Angelito T. Buhisan, Jr., J.D.
Mrs. Ethel M. Bullard
Mrs. Jessie B. Payne Bullock
John J. Bunting, M.D.
Ms. Caroline R. Burgess
Ms. Ceara Sue Burman
Miss Maretta Jo Burns
Dr. William J. Burton
Mrs. Irene H. Byrne

Ms. Joann C. Cadovich
Dr. Stratton F. Caldwell
Mr. James R. Callan
Mrs. Caroline Krause Campbell
Mr. David G. Campbell
Ms. Davita Louise Cannon
Ms. Kizzie Cantrell
Mr. Truett Vaughn Cantrell
Mrs. Catherine E. Capers
Dr. Anthony A. Cardoso
Ms. Mary Carilli
Charles Whitney Carpenter, II, Ph.D.
Mrs. Luz M. Carpio
Mr. William E. Carson
Miss Deloris Juanita Carter
Ms. Gladys Stone Carter
Mrs. Lillie Mae Bland Carter
Dr. Marion Elizabeth Carter

Mr. Jack W. Case
Dr. Isabel Chaly Caserta
Dr. Paul W. Cates
Mrs. Augusta Cecconi-Bates
Mr. Dominic N. Certo
Pyoung R. Peter Chang, M.D., F.A.C.S.
Mrs. Phyllis W. Chapman
Dr. Wai Sinn Char
Mrs. Janey Chen
Dr. Franklin Y. Cheng
Ms. Mary R. Childres
Shirle M. Childs, Ph.D.
Mr. Howard Goodner Chilton
Dr. Sue S. Chin
Sylvia C. Chism, R.N., Ph.D.
Mr. Louis J. Chmielowiec
San Yon Cho, M.D., F.C.A.P.
Dr. Pritindra Chowdhuri
Mr. Don Edward Christensen
Mr. L. R. Chudomelka
Sae-il Chun, M.D.
Hyung Doo Chung, M.D.
Ms. Irene Zaboly Church
Mrs. Emma V. Cintron
John H. Cissik, Ph.D.
Mrs. Evelyn Smith Clarke
Miss Mary Sue Clausell
Dr. Charles E. Clay
Rev. Robert L. Clayton
Mr. Vincent Burton Clemmons
Mrs. Hattye M. Cleveland, O.T.R., F.A.B.I.
Miss Annie Sue Clift
Mr. Patrick Denton Closser, L.F.I.B.A.
Reverend Charles E. Coatie
Mr. Claude Cockrell, Jr.
Mr. Norman Girard Cohen
Dr. C. Eugene Coke
Mrs. Annie Josephine Smith Colbert
Mr. Eugene Roger Cole
Mr. Louis Malcolm Collier
Rev. Dr. Clarence C. Collins
Professor Patrick J. Collins
Mrs. Wilma McIntyre Collins
Ms. Elizabeth Combier
Miss Janet Constance Combs
Mrs. Willie Bernice Combs
Miss Christine O. Comfort
Mr. Donald S. Condon
Ms. Eunice Eileen Conner
Mr. Jerome Charles Conrad
Mr. Joseph A. Consigli
Mr. David Hall Cook
Mrs. Carolyn A. Cooley
Dr. J. F. Cooley
Mr. John T. Cooney
Mrs. Imelda Calcote Cooper
Dr. Ray B. Copple
Mrs. Carolyn W. Parsons Core
Ms. Lily J. Corsello
Miss Camille Cote-Beaupre
Mr. M. Douglass Couch
Dr. Naomi Miller Coval
Dr. Theron Michael Covin
Dr. Alan Cowlishaw
Clark B. Cox, D.D.S.
Ms. R. Jean Cranshaw
Mr. Harold R. Crews
Ms. Helen L. Crofford
Mr. Kenneth Andrew Crownover
Mr. Thomas C. Croxton, Jr.
Mrs. Irma R. Cruse
Mr. David C. Culbertson
John D. Culbertson, Ph.D.
Dr. Charles L. Culpepper, Sr.
Dr. Ernest B. Cunningham, Sr.
Mrs. Eva Ireta Cushing, B.A., M.A.
Dr. Dorothy Massie Custer

Mrs. Eunice B. Daniel
Dr. Evangeline R. Darity
Mrs. Mabel Elizabeth Davidson
Mr. Alexander Schenck Davis
Judge Beatrice Grace Davis
Ms. Dorothy L. Davis
Mrs. Evelyn Marguerite Bailey Davis
Colonel Gordon William Davis
Dr. Kenneth P. Davis
Ms. Lottie Givens Davis
Dr. Rosie L. Davis
Mr. Kenneth Arthur Davison, F.A.B.I.
Professor Stacey B. Day, M.D., Ph.D., D.Sc.
Mr. Bennett Wayne Dean, Sr.
Mr. Lloyd Dean
Mr. Tibor Louis De Dobeau
Dr. Carlo J. De Luca
Dr. Aryola M. Demos
Dr. Adelaida Batista de Rodriguez
Mr. Homer Derrick
Ms. Aileen A. DeSomogyi
Mr. David H. Deters
Ms. Jessie M. DeVane
Dr. Albert Kenneth DeVito
Mr. Darrell T. Di Bona
Ms. Denise G. Dijak, A.C.S.W.
Mrs. Donna Dilsaver
Ms. Bonnie J. Dobson
Dr. Elizabeth C. Doherty
Clay Dorminey, M.D.
Miss Virginia Ann Dorough
Mrs. Pauline P. Douglas
Prof. Marguerite R. Dow, M.A., L.F.A.B.I.
Ms. Josephine E. Drake
Mrs. Line Bloom Draper
Miss Nancy J. Driscoll
Ms. Barbara L. Drisko
Dr. Eugene A. Drown
Professor Meyer Drucker
Satya D. Dubey, Ph.D.
Mrs. Joyce P. Dudley
Ms. Joanne C. Dula
Captain Dyna Duncan
Ms. Anneliese Antonie Dunetz, C.P.P.
Dr. Lawrence Dunkel
Mrs. Estelle Dunlap, MS, FIBA, LAABI
Mrs. Helen Elizabeth Joos Dunn
Mrs. Lucy Ann Duplechain
Kathryn Joyce Dupree, Cpt., AUS (Ret.)
Mrs. DeLores Lance Dupuis
Dr. Laurice Kafrouni Durrant

Ms. Joie Hill Earley
Mrs. Angela L. Edwards, F.R.C., L.F.A.B.I.
Mr. Del M. Edwards
Dr. H. Randall Edwards
Mr. Leif Eie
Mr. Alfred Eisenstein
Albert F. Eiss, Ph.D.
Mr. Oscar R. Elam, Jr.
Mrs. Gloria Jordan Elder
Dr. Gita Elguin-Body
Ms. Sondra R. Elliot
Mr. Joe Y. Eng
Dr. Jean H. Erwin
Dr. Ralph Escandon
Thomas Esparza, Sr., Ph.D.
Dr. Oskar Essenwanger
Mrs. Mary Ellen Ester
Mrs. Jo Burt Evans
Mr. Peter K. Evans
Mr. E. Kyle Everett

Mr. Zoltan J. Farkas
Dr. Dorothy A. Farley
Mrs. Betty Farquhar
Mr. Charles L. Farr, Jr.
Margaret Marian Farrar, Ph.D.
Mrs. Roscoe Kent Fawcett
Mrs. Mary M. Featherston
Ms. Estelle Fedelle, F.R.S.A.
Ms. Leslie Feher, M.A.
Mrs. Virginia Fenske
Dr. Harry Ferguson
Ms. Bernadette Feist-Fite, R.D., M.S., C.F.E.
Professor Nicholas V. Feodoroff
Dr. David M. Fetterman
Mr. Thomas W. Finch
Mr. Aaron Fink
Mr. Carmine Fiorentino
Robert Jay Fish, B.S., D.D.S.
Mr. Stanton T. Fitts
Dr. Claude L. Fly
Lee Ellen Ford, Ph.D., J.D.
Mrs. Ruth Love Forman
Mrs. Caroline R. Foster
Miss Cheryl A. Foster
Professor Dudley E. Foster, Jr.
Mr. Harold E. Foster, R.H.U.
Mr. Abraham Harvey Fox
Miss Laurette E. Fox
Miss Mary Elizabeth Fox
Mrs. Vivian S. Fox
Ms. Marzetta Frazier
Dr. Danny L. Fread
Dr. Harland Frederick
Lanny R. Freeman, Ph.D.
Mrs. Elizabeth B. Freeze
Mrs. E. Frances Freund
Mr. William John Freyler
Mrs. Althia Marie Johnson Fuller
James Walker Fuller, M.D.

Dr. Marguerite H. Gailey
Dr. Ruby Jackson Gainer
Professor Lowell E. Gallaway
Mr. Sabino Galvan
Mrs. Juanita F. Gardine
Dr. Martin Garkinkle
Miss Carol A. Garrett
Mrs. Gayle H. M. Gary
Ms. Mariellen Gasser
Mr. Thomas R. Gauthier
Mr. Robert D. Gebo
Mr. Francis J. Geck
Mr. Robert C. Geizer, M.A., M.F.C.T.
Mrs. Marlene A. Gentry
Mr. Michael W. Gerjovich
Mr. Finley LaFayette German
Ms. Sonya Ziporkin Gershowitz
Dr. Weldon B. Gibson
Mrs. Dee L. Gilchrist
Ms. Avery Gillette
Reverend Perry E. Gillum
Mrs. Wendy D. Glass
Mr. Lonnie Delano Glenn
Mr. Perry A. Glick
Mrs. Donna Sue Gloe
Ms. Debi Glogower
Mrs. Peggy Grace Gober
Mrs. Constance J. Golden
Annie Lucille Golightly, Ph.D.
Professor Nelida Gomez
William Raymond Gommel, Ph.D.

TWO THOUSAND NOTABLE AMERICANS

Dr. Barbara Gonzalez
Mrs. Lucille Contreras Gonzales
Rafael A. Gonzalez Torres, Ph.D., F.I.B.A.
Mr. Wade C. Goode
Mr. Sanford R. Goodkin
Mr. David Michael Goodman
Mr. Jess Thompson Goodman
James Tait Goodrich, M.D., Ph.D.
Miss Mimi Gospodaric
Ms. Darlene Geer Gould
Mrs. Geraldine H. Grant
Mr. Robert M. Gravina
Ms. Dora E. Clyburn Gray
Mr. Nolan K. Gray
Reverend Albert W. Green
Mrs. Virginia Mae H. Green
Mrs. Millicent C. Dickenson Greenaway
Professor Lewis M. Greenberg
Miss Sharon Elizabeth Greene
Adam Greenspan, M.D., Med.Sc.D
Mrs. Sheila Esther Holman Gregory
Mr. William Robert Grier
Mr. Edwin L. Griffin, Jr.
Ms. Patricia M. Griffin
Mrs. Ione Quinby Griggs
Dr. Mildred A. Grigory, H.A.S.
Dr. Dorothy R. Griffin
Ms. Kathleen Gulli
Howard J. Guterman, M.D.

Mr. Arthur Phillip Haas
Charles D. Haas, D.M.D.
Major William D. Hackett, USA (Ret.)
Mr. Howard S. Hackney
Professor J. Russell Hale
Ms. Linda Pappas Hale
Ms. Diane H. Halferty
Captain Charles Worth Leo Hall
Ms. Sarah Hall
Dr. Gail Ghigna Hallas
Ms. Patricia A. Halpern
Miss Linda G. Hamilton
Dr. Madrid Turner Hamilton
Dr. Lillian Hammer
Dr. William E. Hanford
Mr. Christian A. Hanns
Mr. George Hantgan
Dr. Shelia C. Harbet
Patricia K. Hardman, Ph.D.
Lt. Col. Mary P. Hardy
Mrs. Kathryn Amy Haren
Ms. Patricia Ann Haring
Mrs. Arlene Mitchell Harnden
Mr. James A. Harrell
Ms. Sherrie Minton Harrell
Dr. David Harris, Jr., BS, BD, MRE, LHD
Mrs. Louise Harris
Ms. Marian Sabrina Harris
Mrs. Patricia Ann Harris
Mr. Paul A. Harris
Mr. Troy J. Harris
Mr. Vander E. Harris
Ms. Rose HarrisCross, M.S.W., C.S.W.
Dr. Winnie M. Harrison
Mrs. Laurian S. Harshman
Dr. Linda J. Hartwell
Reverend J. Patrick Hash
Ms. Anne L. Haulsee
Mr. Jack Hauser
Vaschahar Havar
Ms. Dourniese R. Hawkins
June D. Hayes, Ph.D.
Ms. Marcie Hayes
Mr. William I. Head, Sr.

Mrs. Tee Heald
Dr. Robert H. Heckart
John Paul Heggers, Ph.D.
Mr. Robert A. O. Hegstrom
Mrs. Marilyn M. Heilman
Dr. Sylvester John Hemleben
Dr. Orval F. Hempler
Dr. Jean Smith Henschel
Mr. Edward F. Herbert
Mr. Peter H. Herren
Ms. Kathleen Magara Herrick
Mr. William R. Hertzer, F.I.B.A.
Miss Ah Kewn Hew
Mrs. Anna B. Hicks
Mr. William F. Hicks
Mr. William E. Hignite
Dr. James L. Hill
Mr. Jerome Jay Hipscher
Mr. Charles Norwood Hitchens
Mrs. Frances L. Hobdy
Mr. David Carroll Hodge
Mr. Edward L. Holbrook, P.E., F.I.B.A.
Dr. Doyle Holder
Shelby W. Hollin, J.D.
Dr. Paul M. Hollingsworth
Dr. Robert E. Hollmann
Dr. Ernest L. Holloway
B. Leonard Holman, M.D.
Mrs. Megan Victoria Hopkins
Mr. Marion Horn, Jr.
Mrs. J. Marie Hornsby
Mrs. Margaret Horswell-Chambers
Mr. Louis Aaron Horwitz
Rev. Reuben Arthur Houseal, ThD, PhD, LLD
Mrs. Ruth Arnold Houseal, DRE, LHD
Mrs. Edna Dellinger Houser
Dr. Joseph J. Hsu
Miss Joan M. Huber
Miss Elizabeth Desmond Hudson
Mr. James Alvin Hugghins
Ms. Cannie Mae Huggins
Dr. Edwin McCulloc Hughes
Mr. Larry W. Hulvey
Mrs. Ann Bernice S. Hunley
Mr. John B. Hunter, III
Mr. Ira K. Hutchinson, FACS&M, FASA, CRA
Mrs. Evangeline Sheibley Hyett
Mr. Jack L. Hymer

Professor Francis J. Ibranyi
Dr. Martha Strawn Iley
Mrs. Norma C. Imbody
Mrs. Arbutus B. Ingram
Mr. Benny G. Ingram
Dr. Thomas Peter Ipes
Dr. M. Ali Issari
Mrs. Virginia R. Iverson
Professor R. N. Iyer

Mr. Ernest M. Jackson
Mr. Graham Washingham Jackson, Sr.
Colonel Eugene C. Jacobs
Mr. William D. Jacobsen
Dr. Elizabeth O. Jarvis
Kirpal Singh Jassal, M.D.
Ms. Ina J. Javellas, A.C.S.W.
Dr. Robert Mitchell Jaye
Mr. Will M. Jenkins, Jr.
Mr. Atiq A. Jilani
Mrs. Dorothy Purnell Johnson
Kenneth L. Johnson, Sr., Col. (R)
Ms. Leanne Johnson
Mr. Rufus W. Johnson

Dr. George Yovicic Jones
Mrs. Myrtle J. Jones
Dr. Patricia Jones
Mrs. Ruthanne Jones
Mr. Virgil Carrington Jones
Mrs. Delores Joyner

Mr. Roland J. Kalb
Captain Robert G. Kales
Ms. Flora Kane
Professor Robert M. Kane
Mrs. Margaret McCaffrey Kappa
Mr. George Kappes, Jr.
Alisa R. Kasachkoff, Ph.D., S.M. in Hyg.
Professor Judith B. Kase
Professor James C. Kasperbauer
Ms. Margaret F. Hampton Kauffman
Dr. Stanley R. Kay
Professor Keith Keating
Professor P. Ray Kedia
Mrs. Sally Jane Mettee Keeler
Dr. Edmund D. Keiser
Mrs. Margaret Ricaud Kelly
Mr. Russell T. Kelley
Mrs. Frances Troxler Keogh
Dr. Anne P. Kernaleguen
Mrs. Grace C. Keroher
Mrs. Beulah Frances Kershaw
Dr. Darrel J. Kesler
Professor Allie Callaway Kilpatrick
Mrs. Ellen Groves Kirby
Mr. Phillip H. Kirkpatrick
Ms. El Wanda Jo Shields Kirkwood
Mr. Tex R. Kline
Mrs. Gloria Ann Mackey Knight
Dr. Yih-Song Ko, M.D., F.A.A.F.P.
Ms. Chris Kobayashi
Mrs. Frances Taylor Koch
Mrs. Isabel Winifred Koehler
Ms. Wanda Koehler, M.S.W.
Dr. George K. Korey-Krzeczowski
Miss Anna Josephine Kraus
Mr. Bernard A. Kuttner
Pavlos Kymissis, M.D.

Mr. V. Duane Lacey
Mr. Wilson Alexander Lacy
Mrs. Barbara Maria Reynolds Ladson
Dr. Helen Lair
Dr. Charles M. Lamb
Miss Sylvia M. Lamoutte
Vernette Landers, Ed.D.
Professor Mary Frances Kernell Lane
Mrs. Audrey Laney
Ms. Gloria Helen Lang
Dr. Aimee Langlois
Dr. Jeffrey L. Lant
Mrs. Gertie Mae Larkin
Mrs. DeRette Sartain LaRue
Dr. Vera Laska
Mrs. Wanda Lee Laudenslager
Mrs. Frances P. Lauer
Mrs. Eula Mae Taylor Lavender
Dr. Kenneth R. Lawson
Mrs. Lillian Warren Lazenberry
Mr. John L. Leake
Ms. Betty Jean Leasure
Dr. Charles L. Leavitt
Rhoda P. LeCocq, Ph.D.
Dr. P. J. Ledbetter
Dr. Min Shiu Lee
Miss Virginia Fern Lee
Mr. William Johnson Lee, J.D.

TWO THOUSAND NOTABLE AMERICANS

Professor Walden A. Leecing
Margaret Clark Lefevre, Ph.D.
Dr. A. Alane LeGrand
Dr. Lawrence L. Leonard, Jr.
Dr. Nels Leonard, Jr.
Mr. Robert A. Lessenberry
Mrs. Bernice A. Lettenmaier
Mr. Michael Levin
Mrs. Barbara H. Levine
Mr. Erv Lewis
Colonel John C. Lewis
Choh-Luh Li, M.D., M.Sc., Ph.D.
Mr. Robert J. Linder
Mr. Lyman G. Li
Mrs. Ruth Dorothy Liebe
Delmore Liggett, Ps.D., Ms.D., D.D.
Dr. Ping-Wha Lin
Mrs. Elayne D. Lindberg
Reverend Angelus Lingenfelser
Peggy E. Lipscomb, Ph.D.
The Rev. Dr. Terril D. Littrell
Mrs. Nona M. Lizut
Dr. J. Robert Lodge
Dr. Jennifer Loggie
Mrs. Mary Ellen Lewis London
Miss Marian Lorenz
Mrs. Joann Love
Mr. Dallas L. Lovejoy, L.L.S.
Mr. Dennis J. Lovelace
Mrs. Mary F. Loving
Mr. Joseph L. Loviza, Ed.S.
Dr. Pat Lowman, O.S.U.
Dr. Marcela Lucero
King S. Luk, Ph.D.
Mr. Joseph K. Lunn
Maurice H. Luntz, M.D.
Dr. R. W. Lutz
Mr. James A. Lynn
Mr. Phillip M. Lyons, Sr.

Ms. Sandy Macebuh
Dr. Roy W. Machen
Beryce W. MacLennan, Ph.D.
Miss Sandra Macnair
Rear Admiral D. L. Madeira, US Navy, Ret.
Larry E. Magargal, M.D., F.A.C.S.
Dr. David Lee Mahrer
Mr. Thomas F. Mallon, Jr.
Mrs. Mary E. Tranbarger Malola
Mr. Manny Celestino Manahan
Ms. M. Melanie Mansir
Ms. Carolyn J. Maples
Mr. Reed Markham
Mrs. Ruby Mae Marrero
Dr. Ann Bodenhamer Martin
Dr. Carolann Martin
Mr. Wayne Mallott Martin
Dean T. Mason, M.D.
Mrs. Diane Farrell Mauch
Colonel Jean Humphries Mauldin
Dr. Cynthia R. Mayo
Edward C. Mazique, M.D.
Mr. David M. McBride
Dr. Donald Lee McCabe
Mrs. Jean McCasland
Mrs. Mildred M. McCleave
Sister Mary Matthew McCloskey, R.S.M.
John M. McCoin, Ph.D.
Professor Grace McCormack, FAIC, FRSH
Ms. Patricia A. McCoy
Dr. Constance M. McCullough
Mr. Weston E. McCune
Dr. Betty M. E. McCurdy
Dr. Richard W. McDuffie, Jr.

Dr. M. Ann McFarland
Commander Stephen Alderman McLean
Ms. Sue Williams McNabb
Mrs. JoAnn Wyrick McNabney
Mr. Glen A. McNurlan
Ms. M. E. McQuiddy
Mrs. Janice R. McRee
Mrs. Lucie Anne Mellert
Dr. Michael V. Mellinger
Mr. Ira B. Melton, Sr.
Dr. Jay Stanley Mendell
Mrs. Mary Dotterweich Michaels
Miss Marienka (Mary) Michna
Ms. Arlene Louise Geibe Miller
Ronald L. Miller, Ph.D.
Mrs. Virginia F. Miller
Mrs. Margie I. Mills
Mrs. Peggy R. Mitchell
Dr. Gopal C. Mitra
Mrs. Gertrude M. F. Moir
Mr. Bernhard Mollenhauer
Mrs. Alice Poston Montgomery
Ms. Elaine Moore
Mrs. Jan L. Moore
Ms. Julia S. Moore
Ms. Lynn Moore
Ms. Ola C. Moore
Dr. Marianne McDonald Mori
Mrs. Neva Bennett Talley Morris
Richard Morris, R.D.H.
Mrs. Esther E. Franks Morrison, CCSM, MIBA
Mrs. Francine Reese Morrison, DD, DSM
Ms. Patricia Gayle Vawter Morrison
Dr. Jean S. Morton
Professor James P. Mosley, II
Ms. Maxine Ellsworth Mosley
Ms. Roberta L. Motter
Dr. Julian Movchan, M.D.
Mr. Thomas I. Moxley, Sr.
Mrs. Margaret J. Mozingo
Mrs. Helen Kiyoko Mukoyama
Dr. Makio Murayama
Mr. Avery Murray
Mrs. Karen J. Murray
Miss Bertha G. Myrick

Mrs. Elfriede K. Naglee
Dr. Pleas C. Naylor, Jr.
Mrs. Hazel M. Neef, R.D.
Mr. Ralph Arnold Neeper
Mr. Raymond J. Neetzel
Dr. Clary Nelson-Cole
Pastor M. G. Nembhard
Mrs. Vera C. NeSmith
Rev. Dr. Captolia Dent Newbern
Professor Henry Niedzielski
Mr. Robert E. Nisbet
Mrs. B. L'essor Nohe, M.P.H.
Dr. M. Wayne Nolen
Mr. William C. Northup, M.B.A., A.B.I.R.A.
Annamaria Nucei, M.D., Ph.D.
Prof. Peter U. Nwangwu, Pharm.D., Ph.D.

Dr. Marguerite E. O'Banion
Mr. Samuel E. Oberman
Mrs. Lois Poteet Hooks O'Briant
Dr. Katsuhiko Ogata
Reverend David Lawrence Ogletree
Mrs. Sara Buckner O'Meara
Ms. Gloria Orsi, F.A.B.I., F.I.B.A.
Mr. Prime F. Osborn, III
Sister Mary Vincent Otto, SFCC, MS

Mrs. Jane B. Page
Mrs. Wanda T. Pantle
Dr. Margaret B. Parke
Ms. Maria Parker-Jackson, M.A.
Mrs. Olivia Maxine Parks
Mrs. Maria L. Parr
Dr. Dev S. Pathak
Dr. Lloyd Patterson
Mrs. Zella J. Black Patterson
Celestel H. Patton, R.D.H.
Prof. Dr. Zlatko P. Pavelic
Dr. Elaine B. Pavelka
Mrs. Juanita Brinkley Payne
Ms. Margaret A. Payne
Professor Dorothy K. Paynter
Mr. Rayno W. Penttila
Ms. Alice L. F. Pearson
Norman Pearson, PhD, FRTPI, AICP, MCIP
Miss Sharon Ann Peavoy
Ms. Gjerstru Maria Rodine Pederson
Dr. Mary Ann Pellerin
Dr. R. C. Perry
Ms. Marguerite H. Peters
Ms. Symiria Peters-Barnes
Mrs. Patricia E. Peterson
Mrs. Vickie D. McBride Petonic
Mr. Herbert F. Petracek
Sylvia R. Petterson, M.D.
Mrs. Fanny Piemontese
Prof. Jerzy T. Pindera, Dr.Sc.
Reverend Estus W. Pirkle
Miss Mary Isabelle Plum
Ms. Edna S. Plummer
Mr. Bob L. Plyler
Mr. Raymond G. Poehner
Mrs. Elizabeth Marie Polley
Mr. F. Winston Polly, III
Dr. Edgar C. Polome
Mr. Otis D. Ponds, Jr., A.C.S.W.
Reverend Petru Popovici
Dr. Michael Leroy Porter
Marlin S. Potash, Ed.D.
Mr. Russell F. Powell
Dr. Lawrence M. Prescott
Mrs. Ruby J. Timms Price
Mrs. Thora Boone Prichard
Ms. Edna S. Pringle
Dr. James C. Prodan
Mr. E. Allen Propst, L.F.I.B.A.
Mrs. Lois Maharam Provda
Professor Robert J. Pugel
Mrs. Concetta N. Pulitano
Mr. George R. Purcell
Dr. N. Diane Purdy
Ms. Dorothy LaRue Purvis
Miss Mary Belle Purvis

Mrs. Kathryn T. Rabenold
Mrs. Florence Graham Rabon
Mr. S. Bryant T. Ragan
Reverend Eugene Randall, D.Min.
Dr. John Wildman Randell
Guy H. Ranson, Ph.D.
Mrs. Alice Louise Holly Ray
Donald D. Reber, Ed.D.
Lester Nicholas Recktenwald, Ph.D., F.I.A.L.
Ms. Vivian C. Redd
Dr. John Plume Reed
Mrs. Angela N. Reemelin
William R. Reevy, Ph.D.
Ms. Claire N. Regnier
Frederick A. Reichle, M.D.
Mrs. Henrietta Reifler
Mrs. Dorothy L. Reihel

Dr. Jeanette P. Reilly
Mrs. Eleanor Replogle
Dr. Lucy J. Reuben
Veula J. Rhodes, Ph.D.
Mrs. Alice Marie Rice
Ms. Joyce H. Richardson
Mr. Quinton B. Richmond
Mr. Ralph L. Rickgarn
Mrs. Josephine Jones Ridgely
Col. Norman J. Riebe, D.S.C.
Professor Margaret R. Rigg
Dr. Karl A. Riggs
Dr. W. Marshall Ringsdorf, Jr.
Mrs. Ruby Lucille Coy Robbins, R.N.
Mrs. Viola Mae Robbins
Dr. Wayne L. Robbins
Mrs. Josephine F. Roberts, F.I.B.A.
Ms. Kathleen Roberts
Ms. Roy Lenin Roberts
Mrs. Sammye Scott Roberts
Bessie M. Shrontz Roberts-Wright, L.F.I.B.A.
Mrs. Phyllis Isabel Robichaud
Reverend Arthur Alexander Robinson, Jr.
Ms. B. Lynn Robinson
Mrs. Dorris R. Brown Robinson
Mildred Blackwell Robinson, Ph.D.
Mrs. Donna S. Rodden
Carl E. Rodenburg, D.D.S., A.B.A.S., A.A.S.
Dr. Czeslaw M. Rodkiewicz
Colonel William N. Roemer
Ms. Irma Rogell
Mr. Gifford E. Rogers
David T. Rollins, Ph.D., F.I.B.A.
Mrs. Margaret A. Romain
Mrs. Alice Mann Roney
Johanna Roode, Ph.D., L.F.I.B.A.
Mrs. Martha K. Rorschach
Mr. Delbert Eugene Rose
Ms. Marian June Rose
Dr. Leonard J. Rosenthal
Mr. Monte Ross
Mr. Frederic Hull Roth
Mr. Barry Kenneth Rothman
Ms. Mildred J. Roush
Mr. Richard James Ruane
Mr. Grant Russell Rubly
Mrs. Lucille A. Pickering Rubly
Dr. Ralph Ruby, Jr.
Mr. Jaime Zavala Ruiz
Ms. Carol Joanne Russell
Jose Russo, M.D.
Mr. Clarence (Al) Rustvold
Mr. Alexander Rutsch
Professor James Walter Ryan
Mrs. Emma Navajas Rytting
Mr. Peter J. Rzeminski

Mr. Ray Saenz-Larrasquitu, M.A., A.C.S.W.
Mr. Stanley M. Saka
Ms. Rosalie M. Salazar
Mrs. Mary Ann Sams
Dr. Paul E. Sanford
Ms. Sharon Marie Sarver-Schultz
Mrs. Valerie Estelle Sawyer
Dr. Alexander G. Schauss
Ms. Susan Schary
Mrs. Jean Z. Schmueckle
Mrs. Vicki L. Schoedel
Professor Evelyn Schroth
Dr. Roy A. Schultz
Peggy H. Schulze, Ph.D.
Professor Wilhelm Schwarzott
Ms. Patricia Anne Scott
Rev. Patrick J. Sena, C.PP.S.
Mr. P. Larry E. Seneris
Sister Mary Maurita Sengelaub, R.S.M.
Dr. Arwin F. B. Garellick Sexauer
George M. Shadle, M.D.
Mr. Erwin E. Shalowitz
Dr. Ernest Shaw
Miss Pearl Shecter
Ms. Bessie Elizabeth Shelton
Mr. Charles V. Shepard
Mrs. Judy Carlile Shepherd
Dr. A. Robert Sherman
Mr. Eric Sherman
Mrs. Aloise Tracy Shoenight
Mr. James R. Shrider
Dr. W. F. Sigler
Dr. Clyde Frederick Simeck
Miss Barbara Jean Simpson
Ms. Carole J. Simpson, M.S.W.
Mr. Jack B. Simpson
Mr. John Lloyd Sincock
Dr. Vijay P. Singh
Mr. Russell A. Skiff
Ms. Janice R. Sletager, M.A., F.A.B.I.
Ms. Rosemary Small
Mrs. Candace Maurine Smith
Ms. Diane L. Smith
Mrs. Donna Mae Squire Smith
Dr. John Julius Smith
Mr. Joseph M. Smith, P.E., C.P.E., C.E.M.
Mrs. Ruth A. Smith
Mr. Sam Smith
Miss Valentine Joy Smith, P.A.A.
Mrs. June Buendgen Snell
Dr. Patricia A. Sommer
Mr. B. Morrison Southward, Jr., L.F.A.B.I.
Mr. Richard E. Spelts, Jr.
Ms. S. Baxter Sperry
Ms. Dorothy Spethmann
Mr. James P. Spillers
Lt.Col. John L. Spinks, P.E., D.A.A.E.E.
Mr. Lee W. Spitler
Dr. Garry L. Spriggs
Ms. Frances B. Spruce
The Most Rev. Alan S. Stanford
Mr. Billy P. Stanford
Mr. Randall L. Stertmeyer
Mr. Herbert Erech Stockman
Mrs. Patsy Ann Stodghill
Jeremy A. Stowell, M.D.
Ms. Marjatta Strandell
Mrs. Julia Montgomery Street
Mrs. Johnnie Ruth Ervin Stripling
Samuel D. Stroman, Ph.D., Col. AUS (Ret.)
Dr. Leah A. Strong
Ms. Hazel Beall Strother
Ms. Roberta L. Suddith, R.N.
Sheila M. Suliin, Ed.D.
Mrs. Teresa Chi-Ching Sun
Dr. M. N. S. Swamy
Mr. Walter E. Swarthout
Mr. Jay L. Sweet
Mr. John W. Sweezy
Dr. Harry P. Sweitzer
Mr. Lawrence C. Switaj
Emeric Szegho, JD, LFIBA, FABI

Doris Dee Tabor, Ed.D.
Mr. Gunther Tautenhahn
Mrs. Cora Hodge Taylor
Mrs. Otrie Lee Edwards Taylor
Timothy D. Taylor, Ph.D.
Mrs. Dora Holladay Tennyson
Ms. Virginia Terpening
Mrs. Sara Yarbrough Thagard
Mr. Joseph Theodore, Jr.
Mr. Leslie G. Thomas
Mr. William Victor Thomas
Mr. William L. Thompson
Dr. Sara Arline Thrash
Mrs. Hope Johnson Tiemeyer
Ms. Celestine Tillman
Mr. Gary Lee Tipton
Mr. Rains Lamarr Tipton
Elizabeth L. Torre, Ph.D.
Francisco G. Torres-Aybar, M.D.
Mr. Milt Trosper, Jr.
Mrs. Geneva R. Trotta, R.N.
Mr. Raymond L. Tune
Miss Phyllis Tunick
Mr. Herman Nathaniel Turner, Jr.
Miss Katherine M. Tynes

Surrogate-Judge Walter E. Ulrich

Mrs. Agatha Fang Min-Chun Vaeth
Dr. Rima Gretel Rothe de Vallbona
Mr. Jon R. Vandagriff
Mr. Richard Clyde Van Vrooman
Dr. M. M. Varma
Mrs. Barbara Pace Varner
Mrs. Barbara H. Vassar
Mr. Howard B. Vaughn
Mrs. Pearl Henderson Vaughn
Ms. Betty Faye Veach
Mr. James Joseph Venditto
Mrs. Evelyn Iverson Vernon
Dr. Robert Vetlesen
Mrs. Estella M. Vlachos
Dr. Lloyd B. Volkmar
Professor Robert Volpe
Mr. Don W. Volpert
Mr. Gopal Vyas

Ms. Bette Hope Waddington
Dr. Thomas E. Wade
Mrs. Mary Lee Wainwright
Reverend John Walchars, S.J.
Mrs. Kathryn C. Walden
Dr. J. Marshall Walker
Joel K. Wallace, D.Min., F.I.B.A.
Richard G. Wanderman, M.D., F.A.A.P.
Dr. Shirley Ward
Dr. Allan D. Waren
Miss Sharon Margaret Washburn
David Michael Wayne, M.D., F.A.C.P.
Mrs. Gertrude Weber
B. H. Webster, M.D.. Ph.D.
Mrs. Maudie Hewitt Weeks, C.S.W.
Mr. Norman S. Weiser
Mrs. Gail Wellman
Mrs. Josephine Mildred Wenck
Mr. Paul Westpheling, Jr.
Mr. Walter E. Whitacre
Mrs. Loraine P. White
Ms. Vallie Jo Fox Whitfield
Ms. Ann T. Wienstroer
Ms. Colleen Bridget Wilcox
Mr. Jetie B. Wilds, Jr.
Miss Anita T. J. L. Williams
Miss Annie John Williams
Mr. Clyde Ezra Williams
Mr. Felton Carl Williams
Mrs. Leola Kathryn Williams
Mr. Patrick N. Williams
Mr. Willie LeThait Williams
Ms. Ginny C. Wilson
Mrs. Wanda M. Ragster Wilson, L.C.S.W.

Mr. Paul Windheim
Mrs. LaNelle B. Winn
Captain Irene N. Wirtschafter, USNR (Ret.)
Ms. Janet Rumpf Wolfe
Ms. Dorothy M. Woodard
Margaret S. Woods, Professor Emeritus
Ms. Willie G. Woods
Mrs. Virginia W. Workman
Professor Elizabeth A. Wrancher
Mrs. Dana Lawrence Wright
Ms. Kionne A. Wyndewicke

Mrs. Elizabeth Juanita Yanosko
Mrs. Ella G. Yates-Edwards
Mrs. Rena Mercedes Henderson Yazzie
Mr. Ronald E. Yokely, P.E.
Ms. Natalie Ann C. Yopconka
Mrs. Faye Yost
Mr. Francis B. Young, Jr.
Mr. James N. Young
Ms. Sonia J. Young

Mr. Mark A. Zastoupil
Wendell E. Zehel, M.D.
Mr. Elias (Ez) Zinn
Professor J. J. Zuckerman

Appendix IV

Roster of Life and Annual Members
The American Biographical Institute
Research Association

THE AMERICAN BIOGRAPHICAL INSTITUTE RESEARCH ASSOCIATION (ABIRA) was established in 1979. Functional aims of this organization are channeled to further extend the biographical research begun by *The American Biographical Institute* in 1967 when it published its first biographical reference volume and thus expand the objectives of the *Institute*, to provide a framework for individuals of diverse backgrounds and environments to join together to share knowledge and interests, and ultimately to offer incentive for dedication and stimulation. All members of the *ABIRA* are chosen by the Executive Council based on individual merit and these individuals comprise an alliance in excess of six hundred members. They are drawn from all regions of the North American Continent and are involved in a search for social, intellectual, and cultural enrichment in general. Backgrounds are varied with wide-ranging educations, outstanding professional careers, and extensive involvement in public affairs on community, state, regional and/or national levels. Benefits of the organization include group assemblies, media coverage, biographical research, consultation, advertising, association magazines/publications *(ABIRA DIGEST, ABIRA MEMBERSHIP ROSTER)*, discounts and awards.

PROFESSIONAL/ADMINISTRATIVE STAFF

CHAIRMAN.......................JANET MILLS EVANS
Vice Chairman.......................J. S. Thomson
Registrar.......................Andrew R. Holland
Communications Assistant.......................Sandra J. Brown

Reference: *Gale Encyclopedia of Associations*
I.S.S.N.: *0196-0652*

Forward all communications or membership inquiries to:

Chairman, ABIRA
205 West Martin Street
Post Office Box 226
Raleigh, North Carolina 27602 U.S.A.

Abrams, Rosalie
Abrell, Ronald L.
Acker, Louise
Allen, Edgar Y.
Allison, Frank E., Sr.
Allison, William L.
Ames, John D.
Amir-Moez, Ali Reza
Anderson, Gordon Wood
Anderson, Thelma Bills
Anderson, Ursula
Anderson, Vivian M.
Aragona, Ronald J.
Arrington, Abner Atman
Ashiofu, Anthony I.
Aston, Katherine O.
Averell, Lois Hathaway
Averhart, Lula
Ayers, Anne L.
Bacher, Rosalie Wride
Baily, Doris
Bair, Mary Helen
Baker, Elsworth F.
Balogh, Endre
Banik, Sambhu N.
Barbour, Judy
Barcynski, Leon
Bardis, Panos D.
Bare, Jean
Barnes, Melver Raymond
Barr, Nona Lee
Baum, Carl E.
Baxter, Ruth H.
Bay, Magdalena
Beardmore, Glenn E.
Belisle, Lenore
Bell, Deanne
Benner, Richard B.
Benskina, Margarita Orelia
Benton, Suzanne
Berg, Julia I.
Berkey, Maurice E., Jr.
Besche-Wadish, Pamela Patricia
Binford, Linwood Thomas
Black, Harold S.
Black, Larry K.
Blakely, Martha
Blakeney, Roger N.
Bohmfalk, Johnita Schuessier
Bomkamp, Loraine Mary
Booth, Jean Y.
Bothwell, Shirley M.
Bourne, Geoffrey
Boyer, Theodore S.
Boykin, Frances Lewis
Bradley, Ramona K.
Brame, Arden H.
Break, Virginia Huffman
Breazeale, Morris H.
Brett, Charlotte Mae
Briggs, Nancy E.
Britton, Michael L.
Brodersen, Gordon M.
Brost, Eileen Marie
Brott, Alexander
Brown, Earle Porter
Brown, Edward K.
Brown, F. W. 'Bill'
Brownell, Daphne
Brumagim, Duane T.
Bryan, Jacob F., III
Bryant, Sylvia Leigh
Buhisan, Angelito T., Jr.
Bullard, Ethel M.
Burgess, Caroline R.
Burley-Allen, Madelyn F.

TWO THOUSAND NOTABLE AMERICANS

Burns, Maretta Jo

Callahan, Wilma Jean
Campazzi, Betty C.
Campbell, Caroline Krause
Campbell, Maxine Elizabeth
Capitol, Viola W.
Cardinale, Kathleen
Carnevale, Dario
Carpenter, Charles Whitney
Carson, William E.
Carter, Lillie Mae Bland
Carter, Marion Elizabeth
Carver, George Bryan
Carver, J. A.
Cates, Paul W.
Cauthen, Deloris Vaughan
Cecconi-Bates, Augusta
Cellini, William Q., Jr.
Chapman, Colin R.
Chilton, Howard Goodner
Chin, Sue S.
Christensen, Don E.
Christensen, R. M.
Chun, Sae-il
Ciancone, Lucy
Cintron, Emma V.
Clark, Fred
Clark, Richard L.
Cleveland, Hattye M.
Clift, Annie Sue
Cohen, Irwin
Cole, Eddie-Lou
Colston, Freddie C.
Cook, David H.
Cook, J. Sue
Corey, Margaret J.
Coriaty, George M.
Corsello, Lily Joann
Couch, M. Douglass
Cox, Donald J.
Crafton-Masterson, Adrienne
Craig, Robert John
Crihan, Ioan G.
Croxton, Thomas C., Jr.
Cucin, Robert L.

D'Agostino, Ralph B.
Dansby, Huddie
Davidson, Mabel E.
Davis, Alexander Schenck
Davis, Evelyn Marguerite
Davis, Gordon W.
Davis, Robert H.
De Dobeau, Tibor Louis
Dennison, Jerry L.
Denton, Thomas S.
DeRosa, Lawrence A.
Deyton, Camilla Hill
Di Ponio, Concetta Celia
Dillon, Robert W.
Doherty, Elizabeth C.
Dolezal, Henry
Dow, Marguerite R.
Downing, Everett R.
Drake, Josephine E.
Drummond, Malcolm
Dubard, Walter Highgate
DuBroff, Diana D.
Dumouchel, Anne Marcelle
Dunbar, Gertrude
Duncan, Dyna
Duncan, Gertrude B.
Dunlap, Estelle Cecilia
Dunn, Helen Elizabeth
Durbney, Clydrow J.

Edwards, Angela L.
Edwards, Ray C.
El Ghamry, Mohamed T.
Ellerbee, Estelle
Emrick, Raymond T.
Engle, Patricia A. Pendleton
Erwin, Jean
Essenwanger, Oskar M.
Ester, Mary Ellen
Evans, Raymond

Fales, DeCoursey, Jr.
Farley, Dorothy A.
Farmakis, George Leonard
Farrar, Margaret M.
Fawcett, James D.
Fehrman, Cherie
Fenske, Virginia
Fergus, Patricia M.
Ferguson, Harry
Field, Elizabeth Ashlock
Fink, Aaron
Fisher, Mary
Foley, Kevin M.
Follingstad, Henry G.
Ford, Gordon B., Jr.
Forman, Ruth Love
Fowler, Sandra
Fox, Pauline
Fox, Portland P.
Fox, Vivian Estelle Scrutchin
Franks, Dorothy S.
Freeze, Elizabeth
French, Ruth E.
Freund, E. Frances
Fuchs, Helmuth Hans
Fuertes, Abelardo
Fuller, James W.

Gaither, Dorothy L. W.
Galamaga, Donald Peter
Gale, James E.
Galvan, Sabino
Gambrell, Mildred Katherine
Gardine, Juanita F.
Garrett, Samuel J.
Garrison, Patricia Ann Medley
Gary, Gayle Harriet
Gausman, Harold W.
Gauthier, Thomas R.
Gebo, Robert D.
German, Fin L.
Gershowitz, Sonya
Gerstman, Judith R.
Ghattas, Sonia R.
Gibson, Curtis A.
Gibson, Weldon B.
Giraudier, Antonio
Glaze, Diana Lisowski
Gomez, Nelida
Goodman, Jess Thompson
Gospodaric, Mimi
Gray, Dora E. Clyburn
Green, Ruth G.
Greene, Sharon Elizabeth
Grigory, Mildred A.
Groeber, Richard Francis

Haas, Arthur P.
Hackett, William D.
Hackney, Howard S.
Hale, Arnold W.
Hall, Wilfred McGregor
Hamilton, Ethel M.
Hamilton, Madrid
Hanf, James A.
Hanns, Christian Alexander
Hansen, Kathryn G.
Hanson, Freddie P.
Harding, Jeanne C.
Haritun, Rosalie Ann
Harpster, V. Aileen
Harrell, Hardy M.
Harris, Jane Maddox
Harris, Louise
Harris, Thomas Lee
Harris, Vander E.
Harrison, Winnie M.
Harz, Frances M.
Havelos, Sam George
Havilland, Ben
Headlee, William Hugh
Hearn, Charles V.
Hendricks, Robert Michael
Henney, R. Lee
Herren, Peter H.
Hobdy, Frances L.
Holland, Ray G. L.
Holland, Ruby Love
Hooper, Marjorie S.
Horan, Linda M.
Horn, Marion, Jr.
Hornsby, J. Russell
Houseal, Reuben Arthur
Houseal, Ruth Arnold
Hsu, Wen-ying
Hubbard, L. Ron
Huff, Cherry Irby
Huff, Norman N.
Hunnewell, Geraldine Grosvenor
Hunt, Edward H.
Hunter, Cannie Mae
Huraj, Helen Icea
Husseiny, A. A.

Ibranyi, Francis
Igals, Dagmara
Inglima, June King

Jackson, Linda D.
Jacobsen, William D.
James, Shaylor Lorenza
Johnson, Iris M.
Johnson, Peggy McKinney
Johnson, Rufus W.
Johnson-Branch, Flora
Johnston, Ruth LeRoy
Jones, Myrtle Jones
Jordan, Lan
Jordan, W. A.

Kagey, F. Eileen
Kales, Robert G.
Kalvinskas, John J.
Kanagawa, Robert K.
Kane, Flora
Kar, Anil Krishna
Karl, Dorothy T.
Karr, Don John
Kaufman, Irene Mathias
Kemp, Dorothy E.
Keroher, Grace Cable
Kerr, Catherine Earl Bailey
Kiehm, Tae Gee
King, Helen B.
King, Joseph Jerone
Kitada, Shinichi
Kline, Tex R.
Knaebel, Jeff
Knauf, Janine B.
Knelson, Nelda Rife
Knepper, Eugene A.
Ko, Yih-Song
Kobayshi, Chris
Koch, Frances T.
Koehler, Isabel W.
Kokenzie, Henry
Kolman, Laurence
Kraus, Mozelle Bigelow
Kraus, Pansy D.
Kristjanson, Harold G.
Ksiazek, Marilyn C.
Kurjakovic, Mira B.

LaClaustra, Vera Derrick
Lair, Helen
Landers, Newlin J.
Landers, Vernette
Larde, Enrique Roberto
Larkin, Gertie Mae
Laudenslager, Wanda Lee
Lauer, Frances L. P.
Leahy, Miriam K.
Leavitt, Charles L.
Leba, Samuel
Lee, Gerald Francisco
Leeds, Sylvia
Lennox, William R.
Lester, William M.
Lettenmaier, Bernice Anne
Levandowski, Barbara S.
Lewis, Loraine R.
Lindberg, Elayne V.
Little, Florence
Loening, Sarah
Lonneker, ArLeen Patterson
Loper, Marilyn S.
Lowry, Dolores E.
Luahiwa, Judith Bagwell
LaClaustra, Vera Derrick
Lair, Helen
Landers, Newlin J.
Landers, Vernette
Larde, Enrique Roberto
Larkin, Gertie Mae
Laudenslager, Wanda Lee
Lauer, Frances L. P.
Leahy, Miriam K.
Leavitt, Charles L.
Leba, Samuel
Lee, Gerald Francisco
Leeds, Sylvia
Lennox, William R.
Lester, William M.
Lettenmaier, Bernice Anne
Levandowski, Barbara S.
Lewis, Loraine R.
Lindberg, Elayne V.
Little, Florence
Loening, Sarah
Lonneker, ArLeen Patterson
Loper, Marilyn S.
Lowry, Dolores E.
Luahiwa, Judith Bagwell
Lundell, Frederick W.

Maass, Vera S.
Mabe, Ruth A.
MacLellan, Helen M.
MacLennan, Beryce W.
Mader, Eileen Lloyd
Magargal, Larry E.
Malin, Howard G.
Mallon, Thomas F., Jr.
Malone, June C.
Manahan, Manny Celestino
Manogura, Ben J.
Marchetti, Jean Woolley
Marrett, Michael M.
Martin, Deborah Louise Morgan
Martin, James L.
Mason, Aretha H.
Mason, Madeline
Mathewson, Hugh S.
Matthews, Elsie S. Spears
Mauldin, Jean
Mavros, Constantin A.
McAnally-Miller, Virginia F.
McCabe, Donald Lee
McCoin, John M.
McCormack, Grace
McCoy, Patricia Alice
McCullough, Constance M.
McCune, Weston E.
McDowell, Margaret Frances G.
McKee, John W.
McNabb, Sue W.
Meeks, Elsie M.
Mellichamp, Josephine
Mello, Henry Goulart
Mendelson, Sol
Mestnik, Irmtraut M.
Michna, Marienka
Miles, Donald M.
Miller, C. Edward
Miller, Laverne G.

TWO THOUSAND NOTABLE AMERICANS

Miller, Robert J.
Mills, George H., III
Mills, William A.
Min, Frank K.
Mitchell, Arlene L.
Mitra, Gopal C.
Mobley, Herbert B.
Mollenhauer, Bernhard
Mooney, John Allen
Moore, Dalton, Jr.
Morahan, Daniel M.
Morgan, Branch, Jr.
Mori, Marianne McDonald
Morler, Edward E.
Morris, Richard
Morrison, Francine Reese
Mott, Bob
Mowrey, Shirley Davis
Mozingo, Margaret J.
Mscichowski, Lois I.
Muhlanger, Erich
Murray, Avery
Music, Edward C.

Naidu, Shrinivas H.
Naylor, Pleas C., Jr.
Nazareno, Jose P.
Nelson, Lorraine L.
Nelson, Robert L.
Nelson, Thomas H.
NeSmith, Vera C.
Nevel, Eva Mary
Newbern, Captolia D.
Newell, Virginia Shaw
Nicholls, James H.
Nichols, Thomas S.
Nikolai, Lorraine C.
Nohe, B. L'essor
Norby, Alice Simons
Northup, William C.
Nzegwu, Ifeanyi Louis

Oberman, Samuel E.
Oien, Arthur C.
O'Malley, William J.
O'Neal, Robert P.
Opalka, Joyce A.
Orphanos, Richard Peter
Osborn, Prime F., III
Oswald, Roy
Overby, George Robert
Overby-Dean, Talulah Earle
Overton, Dean

Pace, Jon A.
Pasternak, Eugenia
Patten, Clara Lucille
Patterson, E. Terry
Pearson, Norman
Pedersen, William D.
Perks, Barbara A.
Persch, Ruth Lucille Kelly
Peterson, Constance Lou Bostwick
Peterson, Daniel Loren
Phillips, Karen A.
Phillips, Virginia G.
Philpott, Emalee Isola
Pirkle, Estus W.
Plewinski, Gustaw L.
Plewinski, Teresa S.
Poehner, Raymond G.
Pollack, Stephen J.
Pollard, Joseph
Polley, Elizabeth M.
Pollitt, Gertrude
Pope, Mary Maude
Porter, Michael Leroy
Powell, Russell
Prentice, Sartell, Jr.
Prichard, Thora
Puh, Chiung
Pulliam, Paul Edison
Purcell, George R.
Purvis, Mary Belle
Puskarich, Michael

Radovich, Zorine Zagorka
Ragan, Bryant Timmons
Rahimtoola, S. H.
Ramov, Edward S.
Rasmussen, Helen Giese
Ray, Alice Louise
Ray, Robert W.
Redd, Vivian C.
Reifler, Henrietta
Reinhardt, Siegfried Gerhard
Reinl, Harry C.
Rex, Lonnie R.
Reyman, Maria L.
Rhemann, Eugene E.
Richards, Novelle Hamilton
Richmond, John
Riemann, Wilhelmina Goettlich
Rifkind, Lawrence J.
Ringsdorf, W. M.
Ripa, Karol
Ritter, Olive Mai
Rivera, Nicolas N.
Roberts, Josephine R.
Roberts, Roy L.
Robeson, Lillyan R.
Robichaud, Phyllis Isabel
Robinson, Ralph R.
Rockwell, Stanley B., Jr.
Rodenburg, Carl E.
Rodkiewicz, Czeslaw Mateusz
Rodriguez, Beatriz M.
Rogell, Irma
Rogers, Gayle
Rogers, Gifford E.
Rolston, Margaret Elizabeth
Roney, Alice Mann
Roode, Johanna
Roth, Frederic Hull
Rowe, Iris Guider
Rubins, Jack L.
Rubly, Grant R.
Rubly, Lucille A.
Rulon, Philip Reed
Rutledge, Varian Palmer

Sakhadeo, Shrihari S.
Salter, Margaret M.
Sanders, Frances B.
Sanford, Paul E.
Savard, Lorena B.
Sawyer, Joseph C., Jr.
Schabbel, Helen C.
Schirripa, Dennis J.
Schwarzott, Wilhelm
Scott, Wilton C.
Seale, Ruth L.
Sealy, Vernol St. Clair
Sebastianelli, Mario J.
Shaw, Imara
Shelton, Bessie Elizabeth
Shiffman, Max
Shirilla, Robert M.
Silvers, Morgan D.
Simeck, Clyde Frederick
Simpson, Jack B.
Singer, Jeanne Walsh
Slack, Florence K.
Sliwinski, M. S.
Small, Fay
Smith, Norvel E.
Snookal, Donald Greg
Snyder, John J.
Southward, B. Morrison, Jr.
Speir, Kenneth G.
Sperry, S. Baxter
Stallworth, Charles D.
Stanat, Ruth
Stein, David E.
Steiner, A. Louis
Stevens, Ben D.
Stevens, Myrtle Chandler
Stewart, Roberta D.
Stockton, Barbara M.
Stodghill, Patsy A.
Stottsberry, Teresa L.
Straton, Andrew C.
Straub, Nellie Cora Perry
Stueber, Gustav
Sun, Teresa Chi-Ching
Sutton, Doris G.
Swamy, M. N. Srikanta
Swarthout, Walter E.
Sweeney, James E.
Switaj, Lawrence C.
Szegho, Emeric

Talley-Morris, Neva B.
Tashiro, Noboru
Terpening, Virginia
Tew, E. James, Jr.
Thomas, William Victor
Thomasson, Raymond F.
Thompson, Andrew B., Jr.
Tipton, Rains L.
Todd, Vivian E.
Todres, Bernice
Torres, Rafael A. Gonzalez
Torres-Aybar, Francisco G.
Toutorsky, Basil P.
Toyomura, Dennis T.
Tung, Rosalie L.
Tunick, Phyllis
Turk, Oscar
Turner, Terrance Diane

Ulrich, Walter E.
Varner, Barbara Pace
Vaughn, Pearl Henderson
Vlachos, Estella M.
Volpert, Don

Waddington, Bette Hope
Wainwright, Mary Lee
Walden, Kathryn C.
Walker, Annita C.
Walker, Glynda Marie
Walters, Helen Hamer
Wanderman, Richard G.
Waters, Raymond Woolsey
Waters, Rowena Kimzey-Cohan
Weaton, George F.
Webb, Rozana
Webb, William Yates
Weber, Gertrude C.
Webster, Burnice H.
Welsh, Carol June Summerlot
Westerfield, Hilda Odle
Whisenant, Mary Sue
Whitfield, Vallie Jo Fox
Wiemann, Marion R., Jr.
Wilhelm, Willa Metta
Williams, Annie John
Williams, Harvey
Williams, I. Joseph
Williams, Marian
Williams, Melva Jean
Williams, Patrick
Williams, Yvonne G. H.
Wolanin, Sophie M.
Wolfe, Janet Rumpf
Woods, Willie G.
Workman, Virginia W.
Wray, John Lawrence
Wright, Dana Lawrence

Yanosko, Elizabeth J.
Yett, Fowler Redford
Yopconka, Natalie C.
Young, James N.
Yanosko, Elizabeth J.
Yett, Fowler Redford
Yopconka, Natalie C.
Young, James N.

Zibrun, S. Michael